D1370699

Department of Economic and Social Affairs
Statistics Division

Département des affaires économiques et sociales
Division de statistique

Statistical Yearbook
Forty-eighth issue

2001
Data available as of
15 December 2003

Annuaire statistique
Quarante-huitième édition

Données disponibles
au 15 décembre 2003

United Nations/Nations Unies • New York, 2004

The Department of Economic and Social Affairs of the United Nations Secretariat is a vital interface between global policies in the economic, social and environmental spheres and national action. The Department works in three main interlinked areas: (i) it compiles, generates and analyses a wide range of economic, social and environmental data and information on which States Members of the United Nations draw to review common problems and to take stock of policy options; (ii) it facilitates the negotiations of Member States in many intergovernmental bodies on joint courses of action to address ongoing or emerging global challenges; and (iii) it advises interested Governments on the ways and means of translating policy frameworks developed in United Nations conferences and summits into programmes at the country level and, through technical assistance, helps build national capacities.

Le Département des affaires économiques et sociales du Secrétariat de l'Organisation des Nations Unies sert de relais entre les orientations arrêtées au niveau international dans les domaines économiques, sociaux et environnementaux et les politiques exécutées à l'échelon national. Il intervient dans trois grands domaines liés les uns aux autres : i) il compile, produit et analyse une vaste gamme de données et d'éléments d'information sur des questions économiques, sociales et environnementales dont les Etats Membres de l'Organisation se servent pour examiner des problèmes communs et évaluer les options qui s'offrent à eux; ii) il facilite les négociations entre les Etats Membres dans de nombreux organes intergouvernementaux sur les orientations à suivre de façon collective afin de faire face aux problèmes mondiaux existants ou en voie d'apparition; iii) il conseille les gouvernements intéressés sur la façon de transposer les orientations politiques arrêtées à l'occasion des conférences et sommets des Nations Unies en programmes exécutables au niveau national et aide à renforcer les capacités nationales au moyen de programmes d'assistance technique.

Note

The designations employed and the presentation of material in this publication do not imply the expression of any opinion whatsoever on the part of the Secretariat of the United Nations concerning the legal status of any country, territory, city or area or of its authorities, or concerning the delimitation of its frontiers or boundaries.

In general, statistics contained in the present publication are those available to the United Nations Secretariat up to December 2003 and refer to 2001/2002 or earlier. They therefore reflect country nomenclature currently in use.

The term "country" as used in this publication also refers, as appropriate, to territories or areas.

The designations "developed" and "developing" are intended for statistical convenience and do not necessarily express a judgement about the stage reached by a particular country or area in the development process.

Symbols of United Nations documents are composed of capital letters combined with figures.

Note

Les appellations employées dans la présente publication et la présentation des données qui y figurent n'impliquent, de la part du Secrétariat de l'Organisation des Nations Unies, aucune prise de position quant au statut juridique des pays, territoires, villes ou zones, ou de leurs autorités, ni quant au tracé de leurs frontières ou limites.

En règle générale, les statistiques contenues dans la présente publication sont celles dont disposait le Secrétariat de l'Organisation des Nations Unies jusqu'à décembre 2003 et portent sur la période finissant en 2002. Elles reflètent donc la nomenclature des pays en vigueur à l'époque.

Le terme "pays", tel qu'il est utilisé ci-après, peut également désigner des territoires ou des zones.

Les appellations "développées" et "en développement" sont employées à des fins exclusivement statistiques et n'expriment pas nécessairement un jugement quant au niveau de développement atteint par tel pays ou telle région.

Les cotes des documents de l'Organisation des Nations Unies se composent de lettres majuscules et de chiffres.

ST/ESA/STAT/SER.S/24

UNITED NATIONS PUBLICATION
Sales No. E/F.04.XVII.1

PUBLICATION DES NATIONS UNIES
Numéro de vente : E/F.04.XVII.1

ISBN 92-1-061208-6
ISSN 0082-8459

Enquiries should be directed to:

Sales and Marketing Section
Outreach Division
Department of Public Information
United Nations
New York 10017
USA

Adresser toutes demandes de renseignements à la :

Section des ventes et de la commercialisation
des publications des Nations Unies
Division de l'action
Département de l'information
Nations Unies
New York 10017
Etats-Unis d'Amérique

E-mail: publications@un.org
Internet: http://www.un.org/Pubs

Preface

The present United Nations *Statistical Yearbook* is the forty-eighth issue in a series initiated in 1948. It has been prepared by the Statistics Division of the Department of Economic and Social Affairs, and generally contains series covering the years between 1992 and 2002. For the most part the statistics presented are those which were available to the Statistics Division as of mid-December 2003.

The 84 tables of the *Yearbook* are based on data compiled by the Statistics Division from over 35 international and national sources. These sources include the United Nations Statistics Division in the fields of national accounts, industry, energy, transport and international trade, the United Nations Statistics Division and Population Division in the field of demographic statistics, and over 20 offices of the United Nations system and international organizations in other specialized fields.

The United Nations agencies and other international, national and specialized organizations which furnished data are listed under "Statistical sources and references" at the end of the *Yearbook*. Acknowledgement is gratefully made for their generous cooperation in continually providing data.

The *Yearbook* has also been published on CD-ROM since the thirty-eighth issue. The CD-ROM contains time series data from 1980 to the most recent year available, and includes the historical data of those series not shown in the present print version due to space limitations.

The *Yearbook* is organized in four parts. The first part, World and Region Summary, presents key world and regional aggregates and totals. In the other three parts, the subject matter is generally presented by countries or areas, with world and regional aggregates shown in some cases only. Parts two, three and four cover, respectively, population and social topics, national economic activity, and international economic relations. Each chapter ends with brief technical notes on statistical sources and methods for the tables it includes. References to sources and related methodological publications are provided at the end of the *Yearbook* in the section "Statistical sources and references".

Annex I provides complete information on country and area nomenclature, and regional and other groupings used in the *Yearbook*. Annex II lists conversion coefficients and factors used in various tables. A list of tables added to or omitted from the last issue of the *Yearbook* is given in annex III. Symbols and conventions used in the *Yearbook* are shown in the section "Explanatory notes", preceding the Introduction

As described more fully in the Introduction below, every attempt has been made to ensure that the series contained in the *Yearbook* are sufficiently comparable to provide a reliable general description of economic and social topics throughout the world. Nevertheless, the

Préface

La présente édition de l'*Annuaire statistique* des Nations Unies est la quarante-huitième d'une série instaurée en 1948. Elle a été préparée par la Division de statistique du Département des affaires économiques et sociales et contient des séries qui portent d'une manière générale sur la période 1992 à 2002 et pour lesquelles ont été utilisées les informations dont disposait la Division de statistique au milieu de décembre 2003.

Les 84 tableaux de l'*Annuaire* sont établis à partir des données que la Division de statistique a recueillies auprès de plus de 35 sources, internationales et nationales. Ces sources sont: la Division de statistique du Secrétariat de l'Organisation des Nations Unies pour ce qui concerne les comptabilités nationales, les industries manufacturières, l'énergie, les transports et le commerce international, la Division de statistique et la Division de la population du Secrétariat de l'Organisation des Nations Unies pour les statistiques démographiques; et plus de 20 bureaux du système des Nations Unies et d'organisations internationales pour les autres domaines spécialisés.

Les institutions spécialisées des Nations Unies et les autres organisations internationales, nationales et spécialisées qui ont fourni des données sont énumérées dans la section "Sources statistiques et références" figurant à la fin de l'ouvrage. Les auteurs de l'*Annuaire statistique* les remercient de leur généreuse coopération.

L'*Annuaire* a été publiée sur disque compact (CD-ROM) depuis la publication de la trente-huitième édition. Le CD-ROM contient des séries chronologiques allant de 1980 à la dernière année pour laquelle on dispose de statistiques, y compris les données historiques qui, faute d'espace suffisant, n'apparaissent pas dans la présente version imprimée de l'*Annuaire*.

Le plan de l'*Annuaire* comprend quatre parties. La première partie, "Aperçu mondial et régional", se compose des principaux agrégats et totaux aux niveaux mondial et régional. Les trois autres sont consacrées à la population et aux questions sociales (deuxième partie), à l'activité économique nationale (troisième partie) et aux relations économiques internationales (quatrième partie). Chaque chapitre termine avec une brève note technique sur les sources et méthodes statistiques utilisées pour les tableaux du chapitre. On trouvera à la fin de l'*Annuaire*, dans la section "Sources statistiques et références", des références aux sources et publications méthodologiques connexes.

L'annexe I donne des renseignements complets sur la nomenclature des pays et des zones et sur la façon dont ceux-ci ont été regroupés pour former les régions et autres entités géographiques utilisées dans l'*Annuaire*; l'annexe II fournit des renseignements sur les coefficients et facteurs de conversion employés dans les différents tableaux. Une liste des tableaux ajoutés et supprimés depuis la dernière édition de l'*Annuaire* figure à l'annexe III. Les divers symboles et conventions utilisés dans

reader should carefully consult the footnotes and technical notes for each table for explanations of general limitations of the series presented and specific limitations affecting particular data items. The section "comparability of statistics" should also be consulted. Readers interested in more detailed figures than those shown in the present publication, and in further information on the full range of internationally assembled statistics in specialized fields, should also consult the specialized publications listed in the "Statistical sources and references" at the end of the *Yearbook*.

The Statistics Division also publishes the *Monthly Bulletin of Statistics* [26]*, which provides a valuable complement to the *Yearbook* by covering current international economic statistics for most countries and areas of the world and quarterly world and regional aggregates. Subscribers to the print version of the *Monthly Bulletin of Statistics* are provided full on-line access to the Internet version. The *MBS On-Line* allows time-sensitive statistics to reach users much faster than the traditional print publication. For further information see <http://unstats.un.org/unsd/>.

Ad hoc or standing orders for the *Yearbook* in print and/or on CD-ROM may be placed with United Nations Publications sales offices in New York and Geneva.

Needless to say, much more can be done to improve the *Yearbook*'s scope, coverage, timeliness, design, and technical notes. The process is inevitably an evolutionary one. Comments on the present *Yearbook* and its future evolution are welcome and should be addressed to the Director, United Nations Statistics Division, New York 10017 USA, or via e-mail to statistics@un.org.

l'*Annuaire* sont présentés dans la section "Notes explicatives" qui précède l'introduction.

Comme il est précisé ci-après dans l'introduction, aucun effort n'a été épargné afin que les séries figurant dans l'*Annuaire* soient suffisamment comparables pour fournir une description générale fiable de la situation économique et sociale dans le monde entier. Néanmoins, le lecteur devra consulter avec soins les renvois individuels et les notes techniques de chaque tableau pour y trouver l'explication des limites générales imposées aux séries présentées et des limites particulières propres à certains types de données; aussi le lecteur devra consulter la section "comparabilité des statistiques". Les lecteurs qui souhaitent avoir des chiffres plus détaillés que ceux figurant dans le présent volume ou qui désirent se procurer des renseignements sur la gamme complète des statistiques qui ont été compilées à l'échelon international dans tel ou tel domaine particulier devraient consulter les publications énumérées dans la section "Sources statistiques et références".

La Division de Statistique publie également le *Bulletin Mensuel de Statistiques* [26]*, qui est un complément intéressant à l'*Annuaire Statistique* qui couvre les statistiques économiques courantes sur la plupart des pays et zones du monde et des aggrégats trimestriels, au niveau du monde et des grandes régions. Les abonnés à l'édition imprimée du *Bulletin Mensuel de Statistiques* ont aussi à leur disposition le *Bulletin* en ligne, accessible sur Internet. Grâce à "BMS en ligne" les utilisateurs disposent plus rapidement des données conjonctuelles que par la voie traditionnelle de la publication imprimée. Pour des informations supplémentaires, voir <http://unstats.un.org/unsd/>.

Les commandes individuelles et les abonnements à l'*Annuaire statistique* (édition imprimée ou sur CD-ROM) peuvent être adressées aux bureaux de vente des publications des Nations Unies à New York et à Genève.

Inutile de dire qu'il reste beaucoup à faire pour mettre l'*Annuaire* pleinement à jour en ce qui concerne son champ, sa couverture, sa mise à jour, sa conception générale, et ses notes techniques. Il s'agit là inévitablement d'un processus évolutif. Les observations sur la présente édition de l'*Annuaire* et les modifications suggérées pour l'avenir seront reçues avec intérêt et doivent être adressées au Directeur de la Division de statistique de l'ONU, New York, N.Y. 10017 (États-Unis d'Amérique), ou e-mail à statistics@un.org.

---

*   Numbers in square brackets in the text refer to numbered entries in the section "Statistical sources and references ".

*   Les chiffres entre crochets dans le texte se réfèrent aux entrées numérotées dans la section «Sources statistiques et références».

Contents

Preface v
Explanatory notes xi
Introduction 1

Part One, World and Region Summary

I. *World and region summary*
1. Selected series of world statistics 9
2. Population, rate of increase, birth and death rates, surface area and density 12
3. Index numbers of total agricultural and food production 14
4. Index numbers of per capita total agricultural and food production 15
5. Index numbers of industrial production: world and regions 16
6. Production, trade and consumption of commercial energy 24
7. Total exports and imports: index numbers 26
   Technical notes, tables 1-7 28

Part Two, Population and Social Statistics

II. *Population and human settlements*
8. Population by sex, rate of population increase, surface area and density 33
** Population in urban and rural areas, rates of growth and largest urban agglomeration population Technical notes, table 8 46
III. *Education and literacy*
9. Education at the primary, secondary and tertiary levels 47
** Illiterate population by sex
** Public expenditure on education: total and current Technical notes, table 9 60
IV. *Health, nutrition and childbearing*
10. Food supply 63
11. Selected indicators of life expectancy, childbearing and mortality 70
** HIV/AIDS epidemic Technical notes, tables 10 and 11 78
V. *Culture and communication*
12. Book production: number of titles by UDC classes 81
13. Daily newspapers 87
14. Non-daily newspapers and periodicals 90
15. Cinemas: number, seating capacity and annual attendance 96
16. Cellular mobile telephone subscribers 101

Table des matières

Préface v
Notes explicatives xi
Introduction 1

Première partie, Aperçu mondial et régional

I. *Aperçu mondial et régional*
1. Séries principales de statistiques mondiales 9
2. Population, taux d'accroissement, taux de natalité et taux de mortalité, superficie et densité 12
3. Indices de la production agricole totale et de la production alimentaire 14
4. Indices de la production agricole totale et de la production alimentaire par habitant 15
5. Indices de la production industrielle: monde et régions 16
6. Production, commerce et consommation d'énergie commerciale 24
7. Exportations et importations totales: indices... 26
   Notes techniques, tableaux 1 à 7 28

Deuxième partie, Population et statistiques sociales

II. *Population et établissements humains*
8. Population selon le sexe, taux d'accroissement de la population, superficie et densité 33
** Population urbaine, population rurale, taux d'accroissement et population de l'agglomération urbaine la plus peuplée Notes techniques, tableau 8 46
III. *Instruction et alphabétisation*
9. Enseignement primaire, secondaire et supérieur 47
** Population analphabète, selon le sexe
** Dépenses publiques afférentes à l'éducation: totales et ordinaires Notes techniques, tableau 9 60
IV. *Santé, nutrition et maternité*
10. Disponibilités alimentaires 63
11. Choix d'indicateurs de l'espérance de vie, de la maternité et de la mortalité 70
** L'épidémie de VIH/SIDA Notes techniques, tableaux 10 et 11 78
V. *Culture et communication*
12. Production de livres: nombre de titres classés d'après la CDU 81
13. Journaux quotidiens 87
14. Journaux non quotidiens et périodiques 90
15. Cinémas: nombre d'établissements, nombre de sièges et fréquentation annuelle 96
16. Abonnés au téléphone mobile 101

17. Telephones 110
18. Internet users 120
** Television and radio receivers in use
   Technical notes, tables 12-18 129

17. Téléphones 110
18. Usagers d'Internet 120
** Récepteurs de télévision et de radiodiffusion
   sonore en circulation
   Notes techniques, tableaux 12 à 18 129

Part Three, Economic Activity

VI.   *National accounts and industrial production*
   19. Gross domestic product and gross domestic
      product per capita 133
   20. Expenditure on gross domestic product
      in current prices 151
   21. Value added by industries in current
      prices 163
   22. Relationships among the principal national
      accounting aggregates 176
   23. Government final consumption expenditure
      by function in current prices 188
   24. Household consumption expenditure by
      purpose in current prices 194
   25. Index numbers of industrial production 199
      Technical notes, tables 19-25 228
VII. *Financial statistics*
   26. Rates of discount of central banks 233
   27. Short-term interest rates 238
      Technical notes, tables 26 and 27 247
VIII. *Labour force*
   28. Employment by industry 248
      A. ISIC Rev. 2 248
      B. ISIC Rev. 3 254
   29. Unemployment 271
      Technical notes, tables 28 and 29 292
IX.   *Wages and prices*
   30. Wages in manufacturing 295
   31. Producers' prices or wholesale prices 305
   32. Consumer price index numbers 312
      Technical notes, tables 30-32 330
X.   *Agriculture, forestry and fishing*
   33. Agricultural production (index numbers) 333
   34. Cereals 341
   35. Oil crops 348
   36. Livestock 356
   37. Roundwood 379
   38. Fish production 385
   39. Fertilizers (production and consumption) 394
      Technical notes, tables 33-39 415
XI.   *Manufacturing*
      A. Food, beverages and tobacco
   40. Sugar (production and consumption) 419
   41. Meat 430
   42. Beer 447
   43. Cigarettes 452

Troisième partie, Activité économique

VI.   *Comptabilités nationales et production industrielle*
   19. Produit intérieur brut et produit intérieur
      brut par habitant 133
   20. Dépenses imputées au produit intérieur
      brut aux prix courants 151
   21. Valeur ajoutée par branche d'activité
      aux prix courants 163
   22. Relations entre les principaux agrégats de
      comptabilité nationale 176
   23. Consommation finale des administrations
      publiques par fonction aux prix courants 188
   24. Dépenses de consommation des ménages
      par fonction aux prix courants 194
   25. Indices de la production industrielle 199
      Notes techniques, tableaux 19 à 25 228
VII. *Statistiques financières*
   26. Taux d'escompte des banques centrales 233
   27. Taux d'intérêt à court terme 238
      Notes techniques, tableaux 26 et 27 247
VIII. *Main-d'oeuvre*
   28. Emploi par industrie 248
      A. CITI Rév. 2 248
      B. CITI Rév. 3 254
   29. Chômage 271
      Notes techniques, tableaux 28 et 29 292
IX.   *Salaires et prix*
   30. Salaires dans les industries manufacturières . 295
   31. Prix à la production ou prix de gros 305
   32. Indices des prix à la consommation 312
      Notes techniques, tableaux 30 à 32 330
X.   *Agriculture, forêts et pêche*
   33. Production agricole (indices) 333
   34. Céréales 341
   35. Cultures d'huile 348
   36. Cheptel 356
   37. Bois rond 379
   38. Production halieutique 385
   39. Engrais (production et consommation) 394
      Notes techniques, tableaux 33 à 39 415
XI.   *Industries manufacturières*
      A. Alimentation, boissons et tabac
   40. Sucre (production et consommation) 419
   41. Viande 430
   42. Bière 447
   43. Cigarettes 452

B.   Textiles and leather products
44. Fabrics (cotton, wool, cellulosic
    and non-cellulosic fibres) 458
45. Leather footwear 463
    C.   Wood and wood products;
    paper and paper products
46. Sawnwood 468
47. Paper and paperboard 474
    D.   Chemicals and related products
48. Cement 479
49. Sulphuric acid 485
    E.   Basic metal industries
50. Pig-iron and crude steel 488
51. Aluminium 494
    F.   Fabricated metal products,
    machinery and equipment
52. Radio and television receivers 497
53. Passenger cars 500
54. Refrigerators for household use 502
55. Washing machines for household use 505
56. Machine tools 507
57. Lorries (trucks) 512
    Technical notes, tables 40-57 516
XII.   *Transport*
58. Railways: traffic 521
59. Motor vehicles in use 531
60. Merchant shipping: fleets 548
61. International maritime transport 558
62. Civil aviation 566
    Technical notes, tables 58-62 581
XIII.   *Energy*
63. Production, trade and consumption
    of commercial energy 584
64. Production of selected energy
    commodities 614
    Technical notes, tables 63 and 64 630
XIV.   *Environment*
65. Land 633
66. CO_2 emissions estimates 643
67. Ozone-depleting chlorofluorocarbons 652
68. Water supply and sanitation coverage 658
69. Threatened species 664
    Technical notes, tables 65-69 673

XV.   *Science and technology, intellectual property*
70. Researchers, technicians and other
    supporting staff engaged in research
    and development 679
71. Gross domestic expenditure on research and
    development by source of funds 687
72. Patents 692
    Technical notes, tables 70-72 698

B.   Textiles et articles en cuir
44. Tissus (coton, laines, fibres cellulosiques
    et non cellulosiques) 458
45. Chaussures de cuir 463
    C.   Bois et produits dérivés; papier
    et produits dérivés
46. Sciages 468
47. Papiers et cartons 474
    D.   Produits chimiques et apparentés
48. Ciment 479
49. Acide sulfurique 485
    E.   Industries métallurgiques de base
50. Fonte et acier brut 488
51. Aluminium 494
    F.   Fabrications métallurgiques, machines
    et équipements
52. Récepteurs radio et télévision 497
53. Voitures de tourisme 500
54. Réfrigérateurs à usage domestique 502
55. Machines à laver à usage domestique 505
56. Machines-outils 507
57. Camions 512
    Notes techniques, tableaux 40 à 57 516
XII.   *Transports*
58. Chemins de fer: trafic 521
59. Véhicules automobiles en circulation 531
60. Transports maritimes: flotte marchande 548
61. Transports maritimes internationaux 558
62. Aviation civile 566
    Notes techniques, tableaux 58 à 62 581
XIII.   *Energie*
63. Production, commerce et consommation
    d'énergie commerciale 584
64. Production des principaux biens de
    l'énergie 614
    Notes techniques, tableaux 63 et 64 630
XIV.   *Environnement*
65. Terres 633
66. Estimations des émissions de CO_2 643
67. Chlorofluorocarbones qui appauvrissent la
    couche d'ozone 652
68. Accès à l'eau et à l'assainissement 658
69 Espèces menacées 664
    Notes techniques, tableaux 65 à 69 673

XV.   *Science et technologie, propriété intellectuelle*
70. Chercheurs, techniciens et autre personnel
    de soutien employés à des travaux
    de recherche et de développement 679
71 Dépenses intérieures brutes de recherche et
    développement par source de fonds 687
72. Brevets 692
    Notes techniques, tableaux 70 à 72 698

Part Four, International Economic Relations

XVI. *International merchandise trade*
   73. Total imports and exports............................. 703
   74. Total imports and exports:
       index numbers.................................... 720
   75. Manufactured goods exports..................... 726
       Technical notes, tables 73-75..................... 732
XVII. *International tourism*
   76. Tourist/visitor arrivals by region
       of origin.. 737
   77. Tourist/visitor arrivals and tourism
       expenditure.................................... 766
   78. Tourism expenditure in other countries......... 775
       Technical notes, tables 76-78..................... 783
XVIII. *Balance of payments*
   79. Summary of balance of payments................. 785
       Technical notes, table 79 818
XIX. *International finance*
   80. Exchange rates................................. 821
   81. Total external and public/publicly
       guaranteed long-term debt of developing
       countries...................................... 837
       A. Total external debt 837
       B. Public and publicly guaranteed
       long-term debt 839
       Technical notes, tables 80 and 81................. 845
XX. *Development assistance*
   82. Disbursements of bilateral and
       multilateral official development assistance
       and official aid to individual recipients......... 847
   83. Net official development assistance
       from DAC countries to developing
       countries and multilateral organizations........ 858
   84. Socio-economic development assistance
       through the United Nations
       system–Development grant expenditures...... 859
       Technical notes, tables 82-84..................... 867

     Annexes
I.   Country and area nomenclature,
     regional and other groupings.................. 868
II. Conversion coefficients and factors.............. 878
III. Tables added and omitted...................... 880

Statistical sources and references 881
Index (English only) 885

Quatrième partie
Relations économiques internationales

XVI. *Commerce international des marchandises*
   73. Importations et exportations totales............. 703
   74. Importations et exportations totales: indices. 720
   75. Exportations des produits manufacturés 726
       Notes techniques, tableaux 73 à 75 732
XVII. *Tourisme international*
   76. Arrivées de touristes/visiteurs par
       régions de provenance 737
   77. Arrivées de touristes/visiteurs et
       dépenses touristiques 766
   78. Dépenses touristiques dans d'autres pays 775
       Notes techniques, tableaux 76 à 78 783
XVIII. *Balance des paiements*
   79. Résumé des balances des paiements............. 785
       Notes techniques, tableau 79 818
XIX. *Finances internationales*
   80. Cours des changes 821
   81. Total de la dette extérieure et dette publique
       extérieure à long terme garantie par l'Etat
       des pays en développement 837
       A. Total de la dette extérieure.................. 837
       B. Dette publique extérieure à long
       terme garantie par l'Etat 839
       Notes techniques, tableaux 80 et 81 845
XX. *Aide au développement*
   82. Versements d'aide publique au développement
       et d'aide publique bilatérales et
       multilatérales aux bénéficiaires................... 847
   83. Aide publique au développement nette de
       pays du CAD aux pays en développement
       et aux organisations multilatérales................ 858
   84. Assistance en matière de développement
       socioéconomique fournie par le système
       des Nations Unies–Aide au développement .. 859
       Notes techniques, tableaux 82 à 84 867

     Annexes
I.   Nomenclature des pays et des zones, groupe-
     ments régionaux et autres groupements......... 868
II. Coefficients et facteurs de conversion 878
III. Tableaux ajoutés et supprimés.................. 880

Sources statistiques et références 881

Explanatory notes

In general, the statistics presented in the present publication are based on information available to the Statistics Division of the United Nations Secretariat as of mid-December 2003.

Units of measurement

The metric system of weights and measures has been employed throughout the *Statistical Yearbook*. For conversion coefficients and factors, see annex II.

Country notes and nomenclature

As a general rule, the data presented in the *Yearbook* relate to a given country or area within its present de facto boundaries. A complete list of countries and territories is presented in Annex I.

Changes in country names are reflected in Annex I. The most recent name changes that the reader should be aware of are: Serbia and Montenegro, previously listed as Yugoslavia; and Timor-Leste, formerly listed as East Timor.

It should also be noted that unless otherwise indicated, for statistical purposes the data for China exclude those for Hong Kong Special Administrative Region of China, Macao Special Administrative Region of China and Taiwan province of China.

Symbols and conventions used in the tables

A point (.) is used to indicate decimals.

A hyphen (-) between years, e.g., 1994-1995, indicates the full period involved, including the beginning and end years; a slash (/) indicates a financial year, school year or crop year, e.g., 1994/95.

Data not available or not applicable	...
Less than half of unit employed	0 or 0.0
Provisional or estimated figure	*
Marked break in series	#

Details and percentages in the tables do not necessarily add to totals because of rounding.

Numbers in square brackets ([ ]) in the text refer to the numbered entries in the section "Statistical sources and references" at the end of the *Yearbook*.

Notes explicatives

En général, les statistiques qui figurent dans la présente publication sont fondées sur les informations dont disposait la Division de statistique du Secrétariat de l'ONU au milieu de décembre 2003.

Unités de mesure

Le système métrique de poids et mesures a été utilisé dans tout l'*Annuaire statistique*. On trouvera à l'annexe II les coefficients et facteurs de conversion.

Notes sur les pays et nomenclature

En règle générale, les données renvoient au pays ou zone en question dans ses frontières actuelles effectives. Une liste complete des pays et territoires figure à l'annexe I.

Le lecteur est renvoyé à l'annexe I où il trouvera une liste des changements de désignation. Les changements de nom de pays survenus récemment sont: Serbie-et-Monténégro, apparaissait antérieurement sous le nom de Yougoslavie; et Timor-Leste, apparaissait antérieurement sous le nom de Timor Oriental.

Il convient de noter aussi que sauf indication contraire, les données statistiques relatives à la Chine ne comprennent pas celles qui concernent la région administrative spéciale de Hong Kong, la région administrative spéciale de Macao et la province chinoise de Taiwan.

Signes et conventions employés dans les tableaux:

Les décimales sont précédées d'un point (.).

Un tiret (-) entre des années, par exemple "1994-1995", indique que la période est embrassée dans sa totalité, y compris la première et la dernière année; une barre oblique (/) renvoie à un exercice financier, à une année scolaire ou à une campagne agricole, par exemple "1994/95".

Données non disponibles ou non applicables	...
Valeur inférieure à la moitié de la dernière unité retenue	0 ou 0.0
Chiffre provisoire ou estimatif	*
Discontinuité notable dans la série	#

Les chiffres étant arrondis, les totaux ne correspondent pas toujours à la somme exacte des éléments ou pourcentages figurant dans les tableaux.

Les chiffres figurant entre crochets ([ ]) se réfèrent aux entrées numérotées dans la liste des sources et références statistiques à la fin de l'ouvrage.

Introduction

This is the forty-eighth issue of the United Nations *Statistical Yearbook*, prepared by the Statistics Division, Department of Economic and Social Affairs, of the United Nations Secretariat. The tables include series covering from two to ten years, depending upon data availability and space constraints. The ten-year tables generally cover the years 1992 to 2001 or 1993 to 2002. For the most part, the statistics presented are those which were available to the Statistics Division as of 15 December 2003.

The main purpose of the *Statistical Yearbook* is to provide in a single volume a comprehensive compilation of internationally available statistics on social and economic conditions and activities, at world, regional and national levels, covering, whenever possible, a ten-year period.

Most of the statistics presented in the *Yearbook* are extracted from more detailed, specialized databases prepared by the Statistics Division and by many other international statistical services. Thus, while the specialized publications concentrate on monitoring topics and trends in particular social and economic fields, the *Statistical Yearbook* tables provide data for a more comprehensive, overall description of social and economic structures, conditions, changes and activities. The objective has been to collect, systematize and coordinate the most essential components of comparable statistical information which can give a broad picture of social and economic processes.

The contents of the *Statistical Yearbook* are planned to serve a general readership. The *Yearbook* endeavours to provide information for various bodies of the United Nations system as well as for other international organizations, for governments and non-governmental organizations, for national statistical, economic and social policy bodies, for scientific and educational institutions, for libraries and for the public. Data published in the *Statistical Yearbook* are also of interest to companies and enterprises and to agencies engaged in marketing research. The *Statistical Yearbook* thus provides systematic information on a wide range of social and economic issues which are of concern in the United Nations system and among the governments and peoples of the world. A particular value of the *Yearbook* is that it facilitates meaningful analysis of these issues by systematizing and coordinating the data across many fields. These interrelated issues include:

    – General economic growth and related economic conditions;

    – The economic situation in developing countries and progress towards the objectives adopted for the United Nations development decades;

    – Population and urbanization, and their growth and impact;

    – Employment, inflation and wages;

    – Energy production and consumption and the

Introduction

La présente édition est la quarante-huitième de *l'Annuaire statistique* des Nations Unies, établi par la Division de statistique du Département des affaires économiques et sociales du Secrétariat de l'Organisation des Nations Unies. Les tableaux présentent des séries qui couvrent de deux à dix ans, en fonction de la disponibilité des données et des contraintes d'espace. Les tableaux décennaux couvrent généralement les années 1992 à 2001 ou 1993 à 2002. La majeure partie des statistiques présentées ici sont celles dont disposait la Division de Statistique au 15 décembre 2003.

L'*Annuaire statistique* a principalement pour objet de présenter en un seul volume un inventaire complet de statistiques disponibles sur le plan international et concernant la situation et les activités sociales et économiques aux échelons mondial, régional et national, pour une période d'environ dix ans.

Une bonne partie des données qui figurent dans l'*Annuaire* existent sous une forme plus détaillée dans les bases de données spécialisées établies par la Division de statistique et par bien d'autres services statistiques internationaux. Alors que les publications spécialisées suivent essentiellement l'évolution dans certains domaines socio-économiques précis, l'*Annuaire statistique* présente les données de manière à fournir une description plus globale et exhaustive des structures, conditions, transformations et activités socio-économiques. On a cherché à recueillir, systématiser et coordonner les principaux éléments de renseignements statistiques comparables, de manière à dresser un tableau général des processus socio-économiques.

Le contenu de l'*Annuaire statistique* a été préparé à l'intention de tous les lecteurs intéressés. Les renseignements fournis devraient pouvoir être utilisés par les divers organismes du système des Nations Unies ainsi que par d'autres organisations internationales, par les gouvernements et les organisations non gouvernementales, par les organismes nationaux de statistique et de politique économique et sociale, par les institutions scientifiques et les établissements d'enseignement, les bibliothèques et les particuliers. Les données publiées dans l'*Annuaire statistique* peuvent également intéresser les sociétés et entreprises, et les organismes spécialisés dans les études de marché. L'*Annuaire statistique* a pour objet de présenter des renseignements systématiques sur toutes sortes de questions socio-économiques qui sont liées aux préoccupations actuelles du système des Nations Unies ainsi que des gouvernements et des peuples du monde. L'*Annuaire* vise tout particulièrement à faciliter une analyse approfondie de ces questions en systématisant et en harmonisant les données d'un domaine/secteur à l'autre. Ces questions apparentées comprennent:

    – La croissance économique générale et les aspects connexes de l'économie;

    – La situation économique dans les pays en développement et les progrès accomplis vers la

development of new energy sources;
- Expansion of trade;
- Supply of food and alleviation of hunger;
- The financial situation of countries and external payments and receipts;
- Education, training and eradication of illiteracy;
- Improvement in general living conditions;
- Pollution and protection of the environment;
- Assistance provided to developing countries for social and economic development purposes.

Organization of the *Yearbook*

The 84 tables of the *Yearbook* are grouped into four broad parts:
- Part One: World and Region Summary (chapter I, tables 1-7);
- Part Two: Population and Social Statistics (chapters II-V: tables 8-18);
- Part Three: Economic Activity (chapters VI-XV: tables 19-72);
- Part Four: International Economic Relations (chapters XVI-XX: tables 73-84).

The more aggregated information shown in part one provides an overall picture of development at the world and region levels. More specific and detailed information for analysis concerning individual countries or areas is presented in the other three parts. Each of these parts is divided into chapters, by topic, and each chapter ends with a section on "Technical notes", which provides brief descriptions of major statistical concepts, definitions and classifications required for interpretation and analysis of the data. Information on the methodology used for the computation of the figures can be found in the publications on methodology of the United Nations and its agencies, listed in the section "Statistical sources and references" at the end of the *Yearbook*. Additional general information on statistical methodology is provided in the section below on "Comparability of statistics" and in the explanatory notes preceding the Introduction.

Part One, World and Region Summary, comprises seven tables highlighting the principal trends in the world as well as in each of the regions and in the major economic and social sectors. It contains global totals of important aggregate statistics needed for the analysis of economic growth, the structure of the world economy, major changes in world population and expansion of external merchandise trade. The global totals are, as a rule, subdivided into major geographical areas.

Part Two, Population and Social Statistics, comprises 11 tables which contain more detailed statistical series on population, as well as education, nutrition, life expectancy, childbearing and mortality, and culture and communication. The organization of the population and social topics generally follows the arrangement of subject matter in the United Nations *Handbook on Social Indicators* [48].

Of the 54 tables in Part Three, Economic Activity, 29 provide data on national accounts, index numbers of

réalisation des objectifs des décennies des Nations Unies pour le développement;
- La population et l'urbanisation, leur croissance et leur impact;
- L'emploi, l'inflation et les salaires;
- La production et la consommation d'énergie et la mise en valeur des énergies nouvelles;
- L'expansion des échanges;
- Les approvisionnements alimentaires et la lutte contre la faim;
- La situation financière, les paiements extérieurs et les recettes extérieures;
- L'éducation, la formation et l'élimination de l'analphabétisme;
- L'amélioration des conditions de vie;
- La pollution et la protection de l'environnement;
- L'assistance fournie aux pays en développement à des fins socio-économiques.

Présentation de l'*Annuaire*

Les 84 tableaux de l'*Annuaire* sont groupés en quatre parties:
- La première partie: Aperçu mondial et régional (chapitre I, tableaux 1 à 7);
- La deuxième partie: Statistiques démographiques et sociales (chapitres II à V, tableaux 8 à 18);
- La troisième partie: Activité économique (chapitres VI à XV, tableaux 19 à 72);
- La quatrième partie: Relations économiques internationales (chapitres XVI à XX, tableaux 73 à 84).

Les valeurs les plus agrégées qui figurent dans la première partie donnent un tableau global du développement à l'échelon mondial et régional, tandis que les trois autres parties contiennent des renseignements plus précis et détaillés qui se prêtent mieux à une analyse par pays ou par zones. Chacune de ces trois parties est divisée en chapitres portant sur des sujets donnés, et chaque chapitre comprend une section intitulée "Notes techniques" où l'on trouve une brève description des principales notions, définitions et classifications statistiques nécessaires pour interpréter et analyser les données. Les méthodes de calcul utilisées sont décrites dans les publications se référant à la méthodologie des Nations Unies et de leurs organismes, énumérées à la fin de l'*Annuaire* dans la section "Sources et références statistiques". Le lecteur trouvera un complément d'informations générales ci-après dans la section intitulée "Comparabilité des statistiques", ainsi que dans les notes explicatives qui précedent l'introduction.

La première partie, intitulée "Aperçu mondial et régional", comprend sept tableaux présentant les principales tendances dans le monde et dans les régions ainsi que dans les principaux secteurs économiques et sociaux. Elle fournit des chiffres mondiaux pour les principaux agrégats statistiques nécessaires pour analyser la croissance économique, la structure de

industrial production, interest rates, labour force, wages and prices, transport, energy, environment, science and technology and intellectual property; 25 tables provide data on production in the major branches of the economy (using, in general, the International Standard Industrial Classification, ISIC), namely agriculture, hunting, forestry and fishing, and manufacturing. Consumption data are combined with the production data in tables on specific commodities, where feasible.

Part Four, International Economic Relations, comprises 12 tables on international merchandise trade, balance of payments, international tourism, international finance and development assistance.

An index (in English only) is provided at the end of the *Yearbook*.

Annexes and regional groupings of countries or areas

The annexes to the *Statistical Yearbook* and the section "Explanatory notes" preceding the Introduction, provide additional essential information on the *Yearbook*'s contents and presentation of data.

Annex I provides information on countries or areas covered in the *Yearbook* tables and on their arrangement in geographical regions and economic or other groupings. The geographical groupings shown in the *Yearbook* are generally based on continental regions unless otherwise indicated. However, strict consistency in this regard is impossible. A wide range of classifications is used for different purposes in the various international agencies and other sources of statistics for the *Yearbook*. These classifications vary in response to administrative and analytical requirements.

Similarly, there is no common agreement in the United Nations system concerning the terms "developed" and "developing" when referring to the stage of development reached by any given country or area, and its corresponding classification in one or the other grouping. The *Yearbook* thus refers more generally to "developed" or "developing" regions on the basis of conventional practice. Following this practice, "developed regions" comprises Northern America, Europe and the former USSR, Australia, Japan and New Zealand, while all of Africa and the remainder of the Americas, Asia and Oceania comprise the "developing regions". These designations are intended for statistical convenience and do not necessarily express a judgement about the stage reached by a particular country or area in the development process.

Annex II provides detailed information on conversion coefficients and factors used in various tables, and annex III provides listings of tables added and omitted in the present edition of the *Yearbook*. Tables for which a sufficient amount of new data is not available are not being published in this *Yearbook*. Their titles nevertheless are still listed in the table of contents since it is planned that they will be published in a later issue as new data are compiled by the collecting agency. However, the complete set of tables is retained in the

l'économie mondiale, les principaux changements dans la population mondiale et l'expansion du commerce extérieur de marchandises. En règle générale, les chiffres mondiaux sont ventilés par grandes régions géographiques.

La deuxième partie, intitulée "Statistiques démographiques et sociales", comporte 11 tableaux où figurent des séries plus détaillées concernant la population, l'éducation, la nutrition, l'espérance de vie, la maternité, la mortalité, et la culture et la communication. L'organisation de la deuxième partie, "Population et questions sociales", suit généralement le plan adopté par l'ONU "*Manuel des indicateurs sociaux*" [48].

La troisième partie, intitulée "Activité économique", comporte 54 tableaux, 29 qui présentent des statistiques concernant les comptes nationaux, les nombres indices relatifs à la production industrielle, les taux d'intérêt, la population active, les prix et les salaires, le transport, l'énergie, l'environnement, la science et technologie, et la propriété intellectuelle; et 25 qui présentent des données sur la production des principales branches d'activité économique (en utilisant en général la *Classification internationale type, par industrie, de toutes les branches d'activité économique*): agriculture, chasse, sylviculture et pêche, et industries manufacturières. Les tableaux traitant de certains produits de base associent autant que possible les données relatives à la consommation aux valeurs concernant la production.

La quatrième partie, intitulée "Relations économiques internationales", comprend 12 tableaux relatifs au commerce international de marchandises, aux balances des paiements, au tourisme international, aux finances internationales, et à l'aide au développement.

Un index (en anglais seulement) figure à la fin de l'*Annuaire*.

Annexes et groupements régionaux des pays et zones

Les annexes à l'*Annuaire statistique* et la section intitulée "Notes explicatives" qui précède l'introduction, offrent d'importantes informations complémentaires quant à la teneur et à la présentation des données figurant dans le présent ouvrage.

L'annexe I donne des renseignements sur les pays ou zones couverts par les tableaux de l'*Annuaire* et sur leur regroupement en régions géographiques et groupements économiques ou autres. Sauf indication contraire, les groupements géographiques figurant dans l'*Annuaire* sont généralement fondés sur les régions continentales, mais une présentation absolument systématique est impossible à cet égard car les diverses institutions internationales et autres sources de statistiques employées pour la confection de l'*Annuaire* emploient, selon l'objet de l'exercice, des classifications fort différentes en réponse à diverses exigences d'ordre administratif ou analytique.

Il n'existe pas non plus dans le système des

CD-ROM version of the *Yearbook*.

Comparability of statistics

One major aim of the *Statistical Yearbook* is to present series which are as nearly comparable across countries as the available statistics permit. Considerable efforts are also made among the international suppliers of data and by the staff of the *Yearbook* to ensure the compatibility of various series by coordinating time periods, base years, prices chosen for valuation and so on. This is indispensable in relating various bodies of data to each other and to facilitate analysis across different sectors. Thus, for example, relating data on economic output to those on employment makes it possible to derive some trends in the field of productivity; relating data on exports and imports to those on national product allows an evaluation of the relative importance of external trade in different countries and reveals changes in the role of trade over time.

In general, the data presented reflect the methodological recommendations of the United Nations Statistical Commission issued in various United Nations publications, and of other international bodies concerned with statistics. Publications containing these recommendations and guidelines are listed in the section "Statistical sources and references" at the end of the *Yearbook*. Use of international recommendations not only promotes international comparability of the data but also ensures a degree of compatibility regarding the underlying concepts, definitions and classifications relating to different series. However, much work remains to be done in this area and, for this reason, some tables can serve only as a first source of data, which require further adjustment before being used for more in-depth analytical studies. While on the whole, a significant degree of comparability has been achieved in international statistics, there are many limitations, for a variety of reasons.

One common cause of non-comparability of economic data is different valuations of statistical aggregates such as national income, wages and salaries, output of industries and so forth. Conversion of these and similar series originally expressed in national prices into a common currency, for example into United States dollars, through the use of exchange rates, is not always satisfactory owing to frequent wide fluctuations in market rates and differences between official rates and rates which would be indicated by unofficial markets or purchasing power parities. For this reason, data on national income in United States dollars which are published in the *Yearbook* are subject to certain distortions and can be used as only a rough approximation of the relative magnitudes involved.

The use of different kinds of sources for obtaining data is another cause of incomparability. This is true, for example, in the case of employment and unemployment, where data are collected from such non-comparable

Nations Unies de définition commune des termes "développé" et "en développement" pour décrire le niveau atteint en la matière par un pays ou une zone donnés ni pour les classifier dans l'un ou l'autre de ces groupes. Ainsi, dans l'*Annuaire*, on s'en remet à l'usage pour qualifier les régions de "développées" ou "en développement". Selon cet usage, les régions développées sont l'Amérique septentrionale, l'Europe et l'ancienne URSS, l'Australie, le Japon et la Nouvelle-Zélande, alors que toute l'Afrique et le reste des Amériques, l'Asie et l'Océanie constituent les régions en développement. Ces appellations sont utilisées pour plus de commodité dans la présentation des statistiques et n'impliquent pas nécessairement un jugement quant au stade de développement auquel est parvenu tel pays ou telle zone.

L'annexe II fournit des renseignements sur les coefficients et facteurs de conversion employés dans les différents tableaux, et l'annexe III contient les listes de tableaux qui ont été ajoutés ou omis dans la présente édition de l'*Annuaire*. Les tableaux pour lesquels on ne dispose pas d'une quantité suffisante des données nouvelles, n'ont pas été publiés dans cet *Annuaire*. Comme ils seront repris dans une prochaine édition à mesure que des données nouvelles seront dépouillées par l'office statistique d'origine, ses titres figurent toujours dans la table des matières. Tous les tableaux sont cependant repris dans l'édition publiée sur CD-ROM.

Comparabilité des statistiques

L'*Annuaire statistique* a principalement pour objet de présenter des statistiques aussi comparables d'un pays à l'autre que les données le permettent. Les sources internationales de données et les auteurs de l'*Annuaire* ont réalisés des efforts considérables pour faire en sorte que les diverses séries soient compatibles en harmonisant les périodes de référence, les années de base, les prix utilisés pour les évaluations, etc. Cette démarche est indispensable si l'on veut rapprocher divers ensembles de données pour faciliter l'analyse intersectorielle de l'économie. Ainsi, en liant les données concernant la production à celles de l'emploi, on parvient à dégager certaines tendances dans le domaine de la productivité; de même, en associant les données concernant les exportations et importations aux valeurs du produit national, on obtient une évaluation de l'importance relative des échanges extérieurs dans différents pays et de l'évolution du rôle joué par le commerce.

De façon générale, les données sont présentées selon les recommandations méthodologiques formulées par la Commission de statistique de l'ONU et par les autres organisations internationales qui s'intéressent aux statistiques. Les titres des publications contenant ces recommandations et lignes directrices figurent à la fin de l'ouvrage dans la section intitulée "Sources et références statistiques". Le respect des recommandations internationales tend non seulement à promouvoir la

sources as sample surveys, social insurance statistics and establishment surveys. Non-comparability of data may also result from differences in the institutional patterns of countries. Certain variations in social and economic organization and institutions may have an impact on the comparability of the data even if the underlying concepts and definitions are identical.

These and other causes of non-comparability of the data are briefly explained in the technical notes to each chapter.

Statistical sources and reliability and timeliness of data

Statistics and indicators have been compiled mainly from official national and international sources, as these are more authoritative and comprehensive, more generally available as time series and more comparable among countries than other sources. In a few cases, official sources are supplemented by other sources and estimates, where these have been subjected to professional scrutiny and debate and are consistent with other independent sources. The comprehensive international data sources used for most of the tables are presented in the list of "Statistical sources and references" at the end of the *Yearbook*.

Users of international statistics are often concerned about the apparent lack of timeliness in the available data. Unfortunately, most international data are only available in print with a delay of sometimes one to three years after the latest year to which they refer. The reasons for the delay are that the data must first be processed by the national statistical services at the country level, then forwarded to the international statistical services and processed again to ensure as much consistency across countries and over time as possible.

* * *

The *Statistical Yearbook* is prepared by the General Statistics Section, Statistical Services Branch of the Statistics Division, Department of Economic and Social Affairs of the United Nations Secretariat. The programme manager is Gloria Cuaycong and the chief editor is Mary Jane Holupka. Bogdan Dragovic is the software developer. They are assisted by Anna Marie Scherning, David Carter and Maria Jakosalem. Thomas Hotz, Juni Sairin, Paul Narain and Pansy Benjamin also contribute to the production of the *Yearbook*.

comparabilité des données à l'échelon international, mais elle assure également une certaine comparabilité entre les concepts, les définitions et classifications utilisés. Mais comme il reste encore beaucoup à faire dans ce domaine, les données présentées dans certains tableaux n'ont qu'une valeur indicative et nécessiteront des ajustements plus poussés avant de pouvoir servir à des analyses approfondies. Bien que l'on soit parvenu, dans l'ensemble, à un degré de comparabilité appréciable en matière de statistiques internationales, diverses raisons expliquent que subsistent encore de nombreuses limitations.

Une cause commune de non-comparabilité des données réside dans la diversité des méthodes d'évaluation employées pour comptabiliser des agrégats tels que le revenu national, les salaires et traitements, la production des différentes branches d'activité industrielle, etc. Il n'est pas toujours satisfaisant de ramener la valeur des séries de ce type—exprimée à l'origine en prix nationaux—à une monnaie commune (par exemple le dollar des États-Unis) car les taux de change du marché connaissent fréquemment de fortes fluctuations tandis que les taux officiels ne coïncident pas avec ceux des marchés officieux ni avec les parités réelles de pouvoir d'achat. C'est pourquoi les données relatives au revenu national, qui sont publiées dans l'*Annuaire* en dollars des États-Unis, souffrent de certaines distorsions et ne peuvent servir qu'à donner une idée approximative des ordres de grandeur relatifs.

Le recours à des sources diverses pour la collecte des données est une autre facteur qui limite la comparabilité, en particulier dans les secteurs de l'emploi et du chômage où les statistiques sont obtenues par des moyens aussi peu comparables que les sondages, le dépouillement des registres d'assurances sociales et les enquêtes auprès des entreprises. Dans certains cas, les données ne sont pas comparables en raison de différences entre les structures institutionnelles des pays. Certaines variations dans l'organisation et les institutions économiques et sociales peuvent affecter la comparabilité des données même si les concepts et définitions sont fondamentalement identiques.

Ces causes de non-comparabilité des données sont parmi celles qui sont brièvement expliquées dans les notes techniques de chaque chapitre.

Origine, fiabilité et actualité des données

Les statistiques et les indicateurs sont fondés essentiellement sur des données provenant de sources officielles nationales et internationales; c'est en effet la meilleure source si l'on veut des données fiables, complètes et comparables et si l'on a besoin de séries chronologiques. Dans quelques cas, les données officielles sont complétées par des informations et des estimations provenant d'autres sources qui ont été examinées par des spécialistes et confirmées par des sources indépendantes. On trouvera à la fin de l'*Annuaire* la liste des "Sources statistiques et

références", qui récapitule les sources des données internationales utilisées pour la plupart des tableaux.

Les utilisateurs des statistiques internationales se plaignent souvent du fait que les données disponibles ne sont pas actualisées. Malheureusement, la plupart des données internationales ne sont disponibles qu'avec un délai de deux ou trois ans après la dernière année à laquelle elles se rapportent. S'il en est ainsi, c'est parce que les données sont d'abord traitées par les services statistiques nationaux avant d'être transmises aux services statistiques internationaux, qui les traitent à nouveau pour assurer la plus grande comparabilité possible entre les pays et entre les périodes.

* * *

L'*Annuaire statistique* est établi par la Section des statistiques générales, Service des statistiques de services de la Division de statistique, Département des affaires économiques et sociales du Secrétariat de l'Organisation des Nations Unies. La responsable du programme est Gloria Cuaycong et la rédactrice en chef est Mary Jane Holupka. Bogdan Dragovic est chargé des logiciels. Ils sont secondés par Anna Marie Scherning, David Carter and Maria Jakosalem. Thomas Hotz, Juni Sairin, Paul Narain and Pansy Benjamin contribuent également à la publication de l'*Annuaire*.

Part One
World and Region Summary

Chapter I   World and region summary (tables 1-7)

This part of the *Statistical Yearbook* presents selected aggregate series on principal economic and social topics for the world as a whole and for the major regions. The topics include population and surface area, agricultural and industrial production, motor vehicles in use, external trade, government financial reserves, and energy production and consumption. More detailed data on individual countries and areas are provided in the subsequent parts of the present *Yearbook*. These comprise Part Two: Population and Social Statistics; Part Three: Economic Activity; and Part Four: International Economic Relations.

Regional totals may contain incomparabilities between series owing to differences in definitions of regions and lack of data for particular regional components. General information on regional groupings is provided in annex I of the *Yearbook*. Supplementary information on regional groupings used in specific series is provided, as necessary, in table footnotes and in the technical notes at the end of chapter I.

Première partie
Aperçu mondial et régional

Chapitre I   Aperçu mondial et régional (tableaux 1 à 7)

Cette partie de l'*Annuaire statistique* présente, pour le monde entier et ses principales subdivisions, un choix d'agrégats ayant trait à des questions économiques et sociales essentielles: population et superficie, production agricole et industrielle, véhicules automobiles en circulation, commerce extérieur, réserves financières publiques, et la production et la consommation d'énergie. Des statistiques plus détaillées pour divers pays ou zones figurent dans les parties ultérieures de l'*Annuaire*, c'est-à-dire dans les deuxième, troisième et quatrième parties intitulées respectivement: population et statistiques sociales, activités économiques et relations économiques internationales.

Les totaux régionaux peuvent présenter des incomparabilités entre les séries en raison de différences dans la définition des régions et de l'absence de données sur tel ou tel élément régional. A l'annexe I de l'*Annuaire*, on trouvera des renseignements généraux sur les groupements régionaux. Des informations complémentaires sur les groupements régionaux pour certaines séries bien précises sont fournies, lorsqu'il y a lieu, dans les notes figurant au bas des tableaux et dans les notes techniques à la fin du chapitre I.

1
Selected series of world statistics
Population, production, transport, external trade and finance
Séries principales de statistiques mondiales
Population, production, transports, commerce extérieur et finances

Series / Séries	Unit or base / Unité ou base	1993	1994	1995	1996	1997	1998	1999	2000	2001	2002
World population [1] / **Population mondial [1]**	million	**5513**	**5594**	**5674**	**5735**	**5834**	**5914**	**5978**	**6057**	**6134**	**6225**

Agriculture, forestry and fishing production • Production agricole, forestière et de la pêche
Index numbers · Indices

Series / Séries	Unit or base / Unité ou base	1993	1994	1995	1996	1997	1998	1999	2000	2001	2002
All commodities / Tous produits	1989-91 = 100	104	107	109	114	117	119	123	125	126	127
Food / Produits alimentaires	1989-91 = 100	105	108	110	115	118	120	124	127	128	129
Crops / Cultures	1989-91 = 100	104	107	109	115	117	118	122	124	126	126
Cereals / Céréales	1989-91 = 100	100	103	100	109	111	110	111	110	112	108
Livestock products / Produits de l'élevage	1989-91 = 100	103	106	109	111	113	117	119	122	123	127

Quantities · Quantités

Series / Séries	Unit or base / Unité ou base	1993	1994	1995	1996	1997	1998	1999	2000	2001	2002
Oil crops / Cultures d'huile	million t.	80	88	92	93	98	103	110	110	112	115
Meat / Viande	million t.	140	144	146	146	151	157	161	161	162	167
Roundwood / Bois rond	million m³	3188	3193	3244	3238	3308	3224	3327	3400	3345	3381
Fish production / Production halieutique	million t.	104.8	112.9	116.7	120.4	122.9	118.1	127.1	130.9	130.2	…

Industrial production • Production industrielle
Index numbers [2] · Indices [2]

Series / Séries	Unit or base / Unité ou base	1993	1994	1995	1996	1997	1998	1999	2000	2001	2002
All commodities / Tous produits	1995 = 100	90	95	100	105	111	110	113	122	121	126
Mining / Mines	1995 = 100	96	98	100	103	107	108	106	113	111	111
Manufacturing / Manufactures	1995 = 100	89	95	100	106	111	108	114	124	123	128

Quantities · Quantités

Series / Séries	Unit or base / Unité ou base	1993	1994	1995	1996	1997	1998	1999	2000	2001	2002
Coal / Houille	million t.	3453	3580	3730	3794	3825	3703	3470	3439	3724	…
Lignite and brown coal / Lignite et charbon brun	million t.	993	962	937	943	925	915	878	900	909	…
Crude petroleum / Pétrole brut	million t.	3036	3063	3097	3151	3252	3288	3202	3355	3354	…
Natural gas / Gaz naturel	petajoules / pétajoules	63839	64014	68074	73163	73946	75258	78197	80667	81926	…
Pig-iron and ferro-alloys / Fonte et ferro-alliages	million t.	512	523	540	528	552	544	548	584	626	…
Fabrics · Tissus											
Cellulosic and non-cell. fibres / Cellulosiques et non cell.	million m²	17181	12848	13525	13348	13579	13302	13145	12877	12729	…
Cotton and wool / Coton et laines	million m²	67309	65175	70307	65021	70958	68737	68322	72648	74624	…
Leather footwear / Chaussures de cuir	million pairs	4226	3978	3893	3868	3789	3753	3669	3553	3627	…
Sulphuric acid / Acide sulfurique	million t.	80	81	87	88	92	95	98	97	98	…
Refrigerators / Réfrigérateurs	million	57	62	65	63	69	67	69	73	74	…
Washing machines / Machines à laver	million	48	50	47	49	54	54	57	60	60	…

1

Selected series of world statistics

Population, production, transport, external trade and finance *[cont.]*

Séries principales de statistiques mondiales

Population, production, transports, commerce, extérieur et finances *[suite]*

Series Séries	Unit or base Unité ou base	1993	1994	1995	1996	1997	1998	1999	2000	2001	2002
Machine tools · Machines outils											
Drilling and boring machines	thousands										
Perceuses	milliers	88	71	76	66	65	53	48	51	44	...
Lathes	thousands										
Tours	milliers	7016	6801	6347	4751	4944	6962	12487	21638	20541	...
Lorries · Camions											
Assembled	thousands										
Assemblés	milliers	685	684	691	729	762	670	697	754	715	...
Produced	thousands										
Fabriqués	milliers	10889	10858	10421	10624	10791	10923	10733	11019	10818	...
Aluminum	thousands t.										
Aluminum	milliers t.	25065	25158	25570	27056	28180	28913	30570	31294	30490	...
Cement	thousands										
Ciment	milliers	1308	1384	1455	1506	1547	1555	1654	1717	1797	...
Electricity [3]	billion kWh										
Electricité [3]	milliard kWh	12615	12928	13376	13805	14111	14296	14783	15340	15533	...
Fertilizers [4]											
Engrais [4]	million t.	132.1	135.0	142.7	146.9	146.2	147.3	147.6	144.4	145.8	...
Sugar, raw											
Sucre, brut	million t.	109.3	108.0	118.6	125.0	125.0	125.9	135.0	130.0	130.6	142.2
Woodpulp											
Pâte de bois	million t.	151.3	162.0	161.7	156.6	162.7	159.9	163.6	171.5	165.7	167.6
Sawnwood											
Sciages	million m³	431	434	425	424	431	375	384	388	377	389
Motor vehicles · Véhicules automobiles											
Passenger cars											
Voitures de tourisme	million	32.08	33.76	33.35	34.74	35.75	35.22	36.67	38.30	36.25	...
Commercial vehicles											
Véhicules utilitaires	million	12.23	12.19	11.85	11.95	12.17	12.37	12.45	12.55	12.41	...

Transport   •   Transports

Motor vehicles in use [5] · Véhicules automobiles en circulation [5]

	Unit or base	1993	1994	1995	1996	1997	1998	1999	2000	2001	2002
Passenger cars	thousands										
Voitures de tourisme	milliers	449990	469303	457763	470587	452101	475450	489982	495759	521466	...
Commercial vehicles	thousands										
Véhicules utilitaires	milliers	141023	149548	165368	186867	176943	184862	191891	197496	210791	...

External trade   •   Commerce extérieur

Value · Valeur

	Unit or base	1993	1994	1995	1996	1997	1998	1999	2000	2001	2002
Import, c.i.f.	billion US$										
Importations c.a.f.	milliard $E.-U.	3644.1	4140.3	4937.5	5178.4	5351.3	5293.1	5507.0	6234.2	5990.1	6192.5
Exports, f.o.b.	billion US$										
Exportations f.o.b.	milliard $E.-U.	3605.4	4108.5	4908.6	5110.4	5298.1	5230.6	5412.6	6062.7	5816.2	6070.7
Volume: index of exports · Volume : indice des exportations											
All commodities											
Tous produits	1990 = 100	112	122	135	142	157	167	177	199	199	209
Manufactures											
Produits manufacturés	1990 = 100	115	130	141	152	171	176	191	215	217	...
Unit value: index of exports [6] · Valeur unitaure : indice des exportations [4]											
All commodities											
Tous produits	1990 = 100	97	101	109	108	101	94	91	91	87	86
Manufactures											
Produits manufacturés	1990 = 100	99	101	110	106	99	97	92	90	87	...
Primary commodities: price indexes [6][7] · Produits de base : indices des prix [6][7]											
All commodities											
Tous produits	1990 = 100	85	66	72	76	71	56	63	81	73	...
Food											
Produits alimentaires	1990 = 100	82	87	92	90	87	80	74	69	69	...

1

Selected series of world statistics
Population, production, transport, external trade and finance *[cont.]*
Séries principales de statistiques mondiales
Population, production, transports, commerce, extérieur et finances *[suite]*

Series Séries	Unit or base Unité ou base	1993	1994	1995	1996	1997	1998	1999	2000	2001	2002
Non-food: of agricultural origin											
Non alim. : d'origine agricole	1990 = 100	84	95	106	98	90	81	73	72	66	...
Minerals											
Minéraux	1990 = 100	55	53	58	67	62	43	57	87	76	...

Finance   •   Finances

Internatonal reserves minus gold, billion SDR [8]   ·   Réserves internationals moins l'or, milliard de DTS [8]

	Unit	1993	1994	1995	1996	1997	1998	1999	2000	2001	2002
All countries	billion SDR										
Tous les pays	milliard DTS	797.8	858.3	988.4	1142.2	1261.3	1244.0	1371.0	1551.3	1704.3	1848.9
Position in IMF	billion SDR										
Disponibilité au FMI	milliard DTS	32.8	31.7	36.7	38.0	47.1	60.6	54.8	47.4	56.9	66.1
Foreign exchange	billion SDR										
Devises	milliard DTS	750.4	811.8	932.0	1085.7	1193.7	1163.1	1297.8	1485.5	1627.8	1763.2
SDR (special drawing rights)	billion SDR										
DTS (droits de triage spéc.)	milliard DTS	14.6	15.8	19.8	18.5	20.5	20.4	18.5	18.5	19.6	19.7

Source:
Databases of the Food and Agriculture Organization of the United Nations (FAO), Rome; the International Monetary Fund (IMF), Washington, D.C.; and the United Nations Statistics Division, New York.

Source:
Les bases de données de l'Organisation des Nations Unies pour l'alimentation et l'agriculture (FAO), Rome ; du Fonds Monétaire International (FMI), Washington, D.C. ; et de la Division de statistique de l'Organisation de Nations Unies, New York.

1	Annual data: mid-year estimates.
2	Excluding China and the countries of the former USSR (except Russian Federation and Ukraine).
3	Electricity generated by establishments for public or private use.
4	Year beginning 1 July.
5	Source: World Automotive market Report, Auto and Truck International (Illinois).
6	Indices computed in US dollars.
7	Export price indices.
8	End of period.

1	Données annuelles : estimations au milieu de l'année.
2	Non compris la Chine et les pays de l'ancienne URSS (sauf la Fédération de Russie et Ukraine).
3	L'électricité produite par des enterprises d'utilisation publique ou privée.
4	L'année commençant le 1er juillet.
5	Source : "World Automotive Market Report, Auto and Truck Internationl: (Illinois).
6	Indice calculé en dollars des Etats-Unis.
7	Indices des prix à l'exportation.
8	Fin de la période.

2
Population, rate of increase, birth and death rates, surface area and density
Population, taux d'accroissement, taux de natalité et taux de mortalité superficie et densité

Major areas and region Grandes régions	Mid-year population estimates (millions) Estimations de population au milieu de l'année (millions)							Annual rate of increase Taux d'accrois sement annuel %	Birth rate Taux de natalité (0/00)	Death rate Taux de mortalité (0/00)	Surface area (km²) Superficie (km²) (000)	Density[1] Densité[1]
	1950	1960	1970	1980	1990	2000	2001	2000 - 2005			2001	2001
World **Monde**	**2 519**	**3 021**	**3 692**	**4 345**	**5 264**	**6 071**	**6 148**	**1.2**	**21**	**9**	**136 056**	**45**
Africa **Afrique**	**221**	**277**	**357**	**470**	**622**	**796**	**814**	**2.2**	**37**	**15**	**30 250**	**27**
Eastern Africa Afrique orientale	66	83	108	144	195	253	259	2.2	41	19	6 300	41
Middle Africa Afrique centrale	26	32	40	53	71	93	95	2.7	47	20	6 613	14
Northern Africa Afrique du Nord	53	67	86	111	143	174	177	1.9	26	7	8 525	21
Southern Africa Afrique australe	16	20	26	33	42	50	51	0.6	24	18	2 675	19
Western Africa Afrique occidentale	60	75	97	128	172	226	232	2.6	41	15	6 138	38
Northern America[2] **Amérique septentrion.[2]**	**172**	**204**	**232**	**256**	**284**	**316**	**319**	**1.0**	**14**	**8**	**21 776**	**15**
Latin America and the Caribbean **Amérique latine et Caraïbes**	**167**	**218**	**285**	**361**	**442**	**520**	**528**	**1.4**	**22**	**6**	**20 546**	**26**
Caribbean Caraïbes	17	20	25	29	34	38	38	0.9	20	9	234	162
Central America Amérique centrale	37	49	68	90	111	135	138	1.7	24	5	2 480	56
South America Amérique du sud	112	148	192	242	296	347	352	1.4	21	7	17 832	20
Asia[3] **Asie[3]**	**1 398**	**1 701**	**2 143**	**2 632**	**3 168**	**3 680**	**3 728**	**1.3**	**20**	**8**	**31 870**	**117**
Eastern Asia Asie orientale	671	792	987	1 178	1 350	1 481	1 492	0.7	14	7	11 763	127
South-central Asia Asie centrale et du Sud	499	620	783	981	1 225	1 486	1 512	1.7	26	9	10 791	140
South-eastern Asia Asie du Sud-Est	178	223	286	358	440	520	528	1.4	22	7	4 495	117
Western Asia[3] Asie occidentale[3]	51	67	87	115	153	192	196	2.1	27	6	4 822	41
Europe[3] **Europe[3]**	**547**	**604**	**656**	**692**	**721**	**728**	**728**	**-0.1**	**10**	**12**	**22 050**	**33**
Eastern Europe Europe orientale	220	253	276	295	311	305	303	-0.5	11	13	18 814	16
Northern Europe Europe septentrionale	77	81	87	89	92	94	94	0.2	11	10	1 748	54
Southern Europe Europe méridionale	109	118	127	138	143	146	146	0.1	10	10	1 317	111
Western Europe Europe occidentale	141	152	166	170	176	184	184	0.2	10	10	1 108	166
Oceania[2] **Océanie[2]**	**12.8**	**15.9**	**19.4**	**22.8**	**26.7**	**31.0**	**31.0**	**1.2**	**17**	**8**	**8 564**	**4**
Australia and New Zealand Australie et Nouvelle-Zélande	10.1	12.6	15.4	17.7	20.2	22.9	23.1	0.9	13	7	8 012	3
Melanesia Mélanésie	2.3	2.8	3.4	4.4	5.5	7.0	7.1	2.1	30	8	541	13

2

Population, rate of increase, birth and death rates, surface area and density *[cont.]*
Population, taux d'accroissement, taux de natalité et taux de
mortalité, superficie et densité *[suite]*

Major areas and region Grandes régions	Mid-year population estimates (millions) Estimations de population au milieu de l'année (millions)							Annual rate of increase Taux d'accrois sement annuel %	Birth rate Taux de natalité (0/00)	Death rate Taux de mortalité (0/00)	Surface area (km²) Superficie (km²) (000)	Density[1] Densité[1]
	1950	1960	1970	1980	1990	2000	2001	2000 - 2005			2001	2001
Micronesia Micronésie	0.2	0.2	0.2	0.3	0.4	0.5	0.5	1.7	25	5	3	167
Polynesia Polynésie	0.2	0.3	0.4	0.5	0.5	0.6	0.6	1.3	24	6	8	75

Source:
United Nations Statistics Division, New York, "Demographic Yearbook 2001" and the demographic statistics database.

Source:
Organisation des Nations Unies, Division de statistique, New York, "Annuaire démographique 2001" et la base de données pour les statistiques démographiques.

1   Population per square kilometre of surface area. Figures are merely the quotients of population divided by surface area and are not to be considered either as reflecting density in the urban sense or as indicating the supporting power of a territory's land and resources.

2   Hawaii, a state of the United States of America, is included in Northern America than Oceania.

3   The European portion of Turkey is included in Western Asia rather than Europe.

1   Nombre d'habitants au kilomètre carré. Il s'agit simplement du quotient du chiffre de la population divisé par celui de la superficie: il ne faut pas y voir d'indication de la densité au sens urbain du terme ni de l'effectif de population que les terres et les ressources du territoire sont capables de nourrir.

2   Hawaii, un Etat des Etats-Unis d'Amérique, est compris en Amérique septentrionale plutôt qu'en Océanie.

3   La partie européenne de la Turquie est comprise en Asie Occidentale plutôt qu'en Europe.

3

Index numbers of total agricultural and food production
Indices de la production agricole totale et de la production alimentaire

1989 – 1991 = 100

Country or area Pays ou zone	1993	1994	1995	1996	1997	1998	1999	2000	2001	2002
World Monde										
Total agricultural production										
Production agricole totale	**104**	**107**	**109**	**114**	**117**	**119**	**123**	**125**	**126**	**127**
Food production										
Production alimentaire	**105**	**108**	**110**	**115**	**118**	**120**	**124**	**127**	**128**	**129**
Africa Afrique										
Total agricultural production										
Production agricole totale	106	108	110	121	120	125	129	130	132	133
Food production										
Production alimentaire	106	109	110	122	120	125	130	132	134	134
America, North Amérique du Nord										
Total agricultural production										
Production agricole totale	101	114	110	114	118	119	121	124	122	121
Food production										
Production alimentaire	101	114	110	114	118	120	122	125	122	122
America, South Amérique du Sud										
Total agricultural production										
Production agricole totale	106	113	119	121	125	128	136	138	142	149
Food production										
Production alimentaire	107	115	122	124	129	131	140	142	146	153
Asia Asie										
Total agricultural production										
Production agricole totale	118	122	127	133	137	142	147	151	154	157
Food production										
Production alimentaire	118	123	128	134	138	144	150	154	157	160
Europe Europe										
Total agricultural production										
Production agricole totale	91	86	86	88	89	87	88	87	88	88
Food production										
Production alimentaire	92	86	86	88	89	87	88	88	88	88
Oceania Océanie										
Total agricultural production										
Production agricole totale	107	102	109	117	119	124	128	127	130	115
Food production										
Production alimentaire	112	107	118	128	128	134	139	137	144	129

Source:
Food and Agriculture Organization of the United Nations (FAO),
Rome, "FAO Production Yearbook 2002" and the FAOSTAT
database.

Source:
Organisation des Nations Unies pour l'alimentation et l'agriculture
(FAO), Rome, ''Annuaire FAO de la production 2002'' et la base de
données FAOSTAT.

4

Index numbers of per capita total agricultural and food production
Indices de la production agricole totale et de la
production alimentaire par habitant

1989 – 1991 = 100

Country or area Pays ou zone	1993	1994	1995	1996	1997	1998	1999	2000	2001	2002
World Monde										
Per capita agricultural prod.										
Prod. agricole par habitant	100	101	102	104	105	106	108	108	108	108
Per capita food production										
Prod. alimentaire par habitant	100	102	102	105	106	107	109	110	110	109
Africa Afrique										
Per capita agricultural prod.										
Prod. agricole par habitant	98	98	96	104	100	102	103	102	101	99
Per capita food production										
Prod. alimentaire par habitant	98	99	97	105	100	103	104	103	102	100
America, North Amérique du Nord										
Per capita agricultural prod.										
Prod. agricole par habitant	97	108	103	106	107	107	108	109	106	104
Per capita food production										
Prod. alimentaire par habitant	97	108	103	105	107	108	109	110	106	105
America, South Amérique du Sud										
Per capita agricultural prod.										
Prod. agricole par habitant	101	105	110	110	112	112	118	118	119	123
Per capita food production										
Prod. alimentaire par habitant	102	107	113	113	115	115	121	121	123	127
Asia Asie										
Per capita agricultural prod.										
Prod. agricole par habitant	110	112	115	118	121	123	126	127	128	129
Per capita food production										
Prod. alimentaire par habitant	110	113	116	119	122	125	128	130	130	131
Europe Europe										
Per capita agricultural prod.										
Prod. agricole par habitant	91	85	85	87	88	86	87	87	87	87
Per capita food production										
Prod. alimentaire par habitant	91	85	85	88	88	86	87	87	87	87
Oceania Océanie										
Per capita agricultural prod.										
Prod. agricole par habitant	102	96	101	106	107	110	112	109	111	97
Per capita food production										
Prod. alimentaire par habitant	107	100	109	116	115	119	122	119	122	108

Source:
Food and Agriculture Organization of the United Nations (FAO),
Rome, "FAO Production Yearbook 2002" and the FAOSTAT
database.

Source:
Organisation des Nations Unies pour l'alimentation et l'agriculture
(FAO), Rome, ''Annuaire FAO de la production 2002'' et la base de
données FAOSTAT.

5
# Index numbers of industrial production: world and regions
# Indices de la production industrielle : monde et régions
1995 = 100

Region and industry [ISIC Rev. 3] Régions et industrie [CITI Rév. 3]	Weight(%) Pond.(%)	1996	1997	1998	1999	2000	2001	2002
World • Monde								
Total industry [CDE]								
Total, industrie [CDE]	**100.0**	**103.1**	**108.3**	**110.2**	**114.7**	**123.0**	**120.7**	**120.7**
Total mining [C]								
Total, industries extractives [C]	**7.4**	**102.9**	**104.8**	**105.4**	**103.9**	**107.2**	**106.3**	**106.5**
Coal								
Houille	0.7	100.3	100.9	99.0	99.8	100.5	103.0	103.9
Crude petroleum and natural gas								
Pétrole brut et gaz naturel	5.0	102.6	104.3	104.2	101.6	105.4	104.0	104.0
Metal ores								
Minerais métalliques	0.7	106.5	109.3	115.7	116.7	122.6	122.1	122.1
Total manufacturing [D]								
Total, industries manufacturières [D]	**82.6**	**103.0**	**108.9**	**110.9**	**116.1**	**125.4**	**122.7**	**122.3**
Food, beverages, tobacco								
Industries alimentaires, boissons, tabac	10.3	101.4	103.1	103.5	104.5	105.9	106.2	107.2
Textiles								
Textiles	2.4	98.6	101.9	97.7	96.2	97.2	91.8	88.7
Wearing apparel, leather and footwear								
Articles d'habillement, cuir et chaussures	2.7	97.3	95.2	90.8	86.4	84.3	78.6	73.1
Wood and wood products								
Bois et articles en bois	1.9	100.7	103.1	102.8	104.4	106.1	100.4	95.6
Paper, printing, publishing and recorded media								
Papier, imprimerie, édition et supports enregistré	7.1	100.1	102.9	103.6	105.3	106.7	103.5	103.4
Chemicals and related products								
Produits chimiques et alliés	14.0	103.1	108.6	109.6	113.5	117.0	117.1	119.5
Non-metallic mineral products								
Produits minéraux non métalliques	3.4	101.6	104.5	102.0	103.4	105.9	104.9	104.4
Basic metals								
Métallurgie de base	4.7	101.1	106.6	102.9	103.4	108.6	105.5	106.5
Fabricated metal products								
Fabrications d'ouvrages en métaux	11.7	102.0	105.6	104.7	104.1	111.4	107.6	104.2
Office and related electrical products								
Machines de bureau et autres appareils élect.	12.7	111.2	127.7	142.8	170.2	214.7	208.1	206.4
Transport equipment								
Equipement de transports	8.0	103.2	111.8	114.5	119.5	123.7	122.9	125.7
Electricity, gas, water [E]								
Electricité, gaz et eau [E]	**10.0**	**103.8**	**105.7**	**107.5**	**110.6**	**114.2**	**115.4**	**118.0**
Developed regions [1] • Régions développées [1]								
Total industry [CDE]								
Total, industrie [CDE]	**100.0**	**102.5**	**107.7**	**110.5**	**115.0**	**123.2**	**120.5**	**119.4**
Total mining [C]								
Total, industries extractives [C]	**4.6**	**102.5**	**102.7**	**102.6**	**101.7**	**101.9**	**102.0**	**101.4**
Coal								
Houille	0.6	98.7	98.1	94.6	93.5	91.7	91.1	89.5
Crude petroleum and natural gas								
Pétrole brut et gaz naturel	2.7	103.5	103.7	103.0	101.7	102.3	102.8	102.3
Metal ores								
Minerais métalliques	0.4	102.4	104.1	105.2	100.4	102.2	100.1	96.2
Total manufacturing [D]								
Total, industries manufacturières [D]	**84.9**	**102.5**	**108.4**	**111.5**	**116.5**	**125.8**	**122.6**	**121.0**
Food, beverages, tobacco								
Industries alimentaires, boissons, tabac	9.5	100.4	102.0	102.8	103.4	104.5	104.7	104.7
Textiles								
Textiles	1.8	96.8	100.7	97.7	94.7	94.0	87.9	82.7
Wearing apparel, leather and footwear								
Articles d'habillement, cuir et chaussures	2.4	96.2	93.6	88.1	82.6	78.5	72.4	65.9
Wood and wood products								
Bois et articles en bois	2.0	100.3	102.8	104.5	106.9	108.7	102.6	96.8
Paper, printing, publishing and recorded media								
Papier, imprimerie, édition et supports enregistré	8.1	99.9	102.6	103.7	105.3	106.5	103.3	102.9

5

Index numbers of industrial production: world and regions *[cont.]*

Indices de la production industrielle : monde et régions *[suite]*

1995 = 100

Region and industry [ISIC Rev. 3] Régions et industrie [CITI Rév. 3]	Weight(%) Pond.(%)	1996	1997	1998	1999	2000	2001	2002
Chemicals and related products								
Produits chimiques et alliés	13.7	102.0	106.7	108.0	111.5	114.7	114.8	116.8
Non-metallic mineral products								
Produits minéraux non métalliques	3.2	100.1	102.1	101.2	101.8	104.2	102.6	100.3
Basic metals								
Métallurgie de base	4.7	99.7	104.9	101.6	100.7	106.0	102.0	101.9
Fabricated metal products								
Fabrications d'ouvrages en métaux	12.7	101.7	105.2	105.9	104.7	110.9	106.8	102.7
Office and related electrical products								
Machines de bureau et autres appareils élect.	14.0	111.3	128.3	144.4	171.3	215.9	208.8	204.0
Transport equipment								
Equipement de transports	8.7	102.4	110.5	115.3	119.5	122.2	120.7	123.1
Electricity, gas, water [E]								
Electricité, gaz et eau [E]	**10.5**	**103.3**	**104.2**	**105.6**	**108.1**	**111.2**	**111.7**	**113.9**

Developing countries [2]   •   Pays en développement [2]

Total industry [CDE]								
Total, industrie [CDE]	**100.0**	**105.3**	**110.8**	**109.0**	**113.6**	**122.3**	**121.7**	**125.9**
Total mining [C]								
Total, industries extractives [C]	**18.3**	**103.3**	**106.9**	**108.3**	**106.1**	**112.5**	**110.6**	**111.7**
Coal								
Houille	1.2	103.3	106.1	107.2	111.5	116.8	125.0	130.7
Crude petroleum and natural gas								
Pétrole brut et gaz naturel	14.3	102.0	104.8	105.1	101.5	107.8	104.9	105.2
Metal ores								
Minerais métalliques	1.7	110.7	114.5	126.4	133.3	143.2	144.5	148.3
Total manufacturing [D]								
Total, industries manufacturières [D]	**73.7**	**105.6**	**111.5**	**108.2**	**114.3**	**123.9**	**123.1**	**128.0**
Food, beverages, tobacco								
Industries alimentaires, boissons, tabac	13.3	104.3	106.3	105.5	107.6	110.1	110.7	114.4
Textiles								
Textiles	4.8	101.4	103.8	97.8	98.5	102.0	97.8	98.0
Wearing apparel, leather and footwear								
Articles d'habillement, cuir et chaussures	3.6	100.3	99.6	98.0	96.6	100.1	95.6	92.4
Wood and wood products								
Bois et articles en bois	1.5	103.0	104.4	93.8	90.4	91.5	88.2	88.6
Paper, printing, publishing and recorded media								
Papier, imprimerie, édition et supports enregistré	3.2	102.3	105.4	103.3	105.8	108.7	105.4	108.3
Chemicals and related products								
Produits chimiques et alliés	15.0	107.3	115.7	115.5	120.5	125.3	125.6	129.4
Non-metallic mineral products								
Produits minéraux non métalliques	4.2	106.1	111.8	104.7	108.3	111.0	111.9	117.1
Basic metals								
Métallurgie de base	4.7	106.4	113.2	108.1	114.0	119.1	119.1	124.7
Fabricated metal products								
Fabrications d'ouvrages en métaux	7.9	103.9	108.4	96.6	100.4	114.7	112.6	113.8
Office and related electrical products								
Machines de bureau et autres appareils élect.	7.3	109.8	122.7	130.5	161.8	205.9	202.1	224.4
Transport equipment								
Equipement de transports	5.2	108.4	120.4	109.2	119.4	133.8	138.0	143.1
Electricity, gas, water [E]								
Electricité, gaz et eau [E]	**8.0**	**106.5**	**113.8**	**117.7**	**123.9**	**130.1**	**134.7**	**139.8**

Northern America [3]   •   Amérique septentrionale [3]

Total industry [CDE]								
Total, industrie [CDE]	**100.0**	**104.6**	**113.1**	**121.3**	**131.7**	**145.8**	**142.5**	**141.6**
Total mining [C]								
Total, industries extractives [C]	**6.6**	**100.7**	**102.3**	**102.2**	**100.4**	**100.3**	**101.1**	**99.6**
Coal								
Houille	0.6	102.5	106.0	106.9	105.0	104.4	107.1	101.7
Crude petroleum and natural gas								
Pétrole brut et gaz naturel	4.8	100.3	101.2	100.3	98.4	98.1	99.3	98.8

5

Index numbers of industrial production: world and regions *[cont.]*

Indices de la production industrielle : monde et régions [suite]
1995 = 100

Region and industry [ISIC Rev. 3] Régions et industrie [CITI Rév. 3]	Weight(%) Pond.(%)	1996	1997	1998	1999	2000	2001	2002
Metal ores								
Minerais métalliques	0.6	102.7	104.6	105.7	98.6	100.6	95.7	88.2
Total manufacturing [D]								
Total, industries manufacturières [D]	**81.6**	**105.1**	**115.3**	**125.3**	**137.8**	**154.8**	**150.8**	**149.3**
Food, beverages, tobacco								
Industries alimentaires, boissons, tabac	8.1	99.2	101.3	104.8	103.9	105.3	104.4	105.0
Textiles								
Textiles	1.6	97.9	104.6	104.0	104.2	103.2	91.9	88.2
Wearing apparel, leather and footwear								
Articles d'habillement, cuir et chaussures	2.1	97.8	97.3	92.2	88.3	86.7	77.7	72.4
Wood and wood products								
Bois et articles en bois	2.9	103.4	108.1	113.3	118.0	118.5	110.9	113.2
Paper, printing, publishing and recorded media								
Papier, imprimerie, édition et supports enregistré	9.1	99.2	101.5	102.1	103.6	104.1	99.3	99.0
Chemicals and related products								
Produits chimiques et alliés	14.2	102.4	107.5	109.2	112.7	115.2	113.7	114.5
Non-metallic mineral products								
Produits minéraux non métalliques	2.0	106.9	111.7	117.5	119.1	120.4	121.1	122.9
Basic metals								
Métallurgie de base	3.5	102.3	106.8	110.0	109.9	108.1	97.9	96.0
Fabricated metal products								
Fabrications d'ouvrages en métaux	12.1	103.3	108.6	111.3	110.6	118.0	107.8	103.4
Office and related electrical products								
Machines de bureau et autres appareils élect.	13.7	122.0	159.6	202.5	266.3	359.1	362.6	355.0
Transport equipment								
Equipement de transports	9.5	101.8	110.5	119.7	127.6	124.0	117.1	120.3
Electricity, gas, water [E]								
Electricité, gaz et eau [E]	**11.8**	**103.2**	**103.4**	**104.5**	**106.9**	**109.1**	**108.0**	**112.5**

Latin America and the Caribbean   •   Amérique latine et Caraïbes

	Weight(%) Pond.(%)	1996	1997	1998	1999	2000	2001	2002
Total industry [CDE]								
Total, industrie [CDE]	**100.0**	**104.7**	**111.2**	**112.2**	**112.3**	**117.9**	**117.4**	**118.9**
Total mining [C]								
Total, industries extractives [C]	**10.2**	**108.9**	**119.9**	**124.2**	**126.3**	**131.7**	**133.0**	**133.9**
Coal								
Houille	0.3	107.6	111.9	97.8	98.6	109.4	119.8	121.2
Crude petroleum and natural gas								
Pétrole brut et gaz naturel	5.6	107.4	114.5	118.7	116.5	120.5	121.3	123.1
Metal ores								
Minerais métalliques	2.7	113.6	121.5	124.6	139.2	145.9	146.7	144.9
Total manufacturing [D]								
Total, industries manufacturières [D]	**81.2**	**104.1**	**110.0**	**110.4**	**109.7**	**115.5**	**114.4**	**115.7**
Food, beverages, tobacco								
Industries alimentaires, boissons, tabac	18.4	103.0	105.8	107.7	110.6	111.7	113.3	117.7
Textiles								
Textiles	3.3	101.4	102.2	95.6	90.8	96.5	89.7	85.0
Wearing apparel, leather and footwear								
Articles d'habillement, cuir et chaussures	3.4	101.4	102.1	99.7	92.1	97.4	90.1	86.2
Wood and wood products								
Bois et articles en bois	2.0	105.1	115.0	115.6	115.5	118.5	114.5	123.3
Paper, printing, publishing and recorded media								
Papier, imprimerie, édition et supports enregistré	3.7	101.7	105.7	108.4	107.9	113.0	109.1	111.1
Chemicals and related products								
Produits chimiques et alliés	19.5	105.5	111.4	114.5	115.6	118.7	116.8	118.1
Non-metallic mineral products								
Produits minéraux non métalliques	4.0	105.6	112.8	114.8	110.8	114.0	113.0	114.3
Basic metals								
Métallurgie de base	4.1	106.2	115.3	116.1	114.9	117.4	115.6	118.2
Fabricated metal products								
Fabrications d'ouvrages en métaux	8.8	100.5	108.1	104.8	102.2	113.4	113.9	117.9
Office and related electrical products								
Machines de bureau et autres appareils élect.	4.9	109.0	115.7	113.2	107.7	119.9	120.1	110.4

5
Index numbers of industrial production: world and regions *[cont.]*
Indices de la production industrielle : monde et régions *[suite]*
1995 = 100

Region and industry [ISIC Rev. 3] Régions et industrie [CITI Rév. 3]	Weight(%) Pond.(%)	1996	1997	1998	1999	2000	2001	2002
Transport equipment								
Equipement de transports	5.5	107.0	123.0	119.2	117.0	135.9	133.8	132.9
Electricity, gas, water [E]								
Electricité, gaz et eau [E]	**8.6**	**105.6**	**111.5**	**115.9**	**120.5**	**124.3**	**127.6**	**130.8**

Asia • Asie

Region and industry [ISIC Rev. 3] Régions et industrie [CITI Rév. 3]	Weight(%) Pond.(%)	1996	1997	1998	1999	2000	2001	2002
Total industry [CDE]								
Total, industrie [CDE]	**100.0**	**103.4**	**107.2**	**102.0**	**105.0**	**112.0**	**107.2**	**108.6**
Total mining [C]								
Total, industries extractives [C]	**7.9**	**102.2**	**103.0**	**104.4**	**101.4**	**107.5**	**105.0**	**106.4**
Coal								
Houille	0.7	102.8	102.6	105.3	110.4	113.6	121.0	124.6
Crude petroleum and natural gas								
Pétrole brut et gaz naturel	5.8	100.8	102.1	102.7	98.8	105.7	101.9	101.7
Metal ores								
Minerais métalliques	0.3	113.4	111.7	141.2	142.4	159.3	159.3	182.4
Total manufacturing [D]								
Total, industries manufacturières [D]	**82.8**	**103.4**	**107.4**	**100.8**	**104.2**	**111.5**	**105.8**	**106.9**
Food, beverages, tobacco								
Industries alimentaires, boissons, tabac	10.3	102.6	102.6	99.1	100.0	101.6	101.2	100.2
Textiles								
Textiles	2.8	100.0	101.9	93.5	93.5	94.0	90.0	89.1
Wearing apparel, leather and footwear								
Articles d'habillement, cuir et chaussures	2.9	96.8	91.5	84.3	81.5	77.0	70.3	64.3
Wood and wood products								
Bois et articles en bois	1.2	99.8	95.5	81.1	76.9	75.1	69.1	64.7
Paper, printing, publishing and recorded media								
Papier, imprimerie, édition et supports enregistré	5.7	101.8	103.4	100.2	100.6	100.1	97.9	97.3
Chemicals and related products								
Produits chimiques et alliés	13.1	103.3	108.6	105.5	109.8	112.6	112.5	114.0
Non-metallic mineral products								
Produits minéraux non métalliques	3.7	102.0	103.8	91.3	91.6	93.3	89.9	89.2
Basic metals								
Métallurgie de base	5.9	100.6	105.4	94.2	95.8	104.0	101.8	104.4
Fabricated metal products								
Fabrications d'ouvrages en métaux	9.0	103.5	104.2	91.6	91.5	99.0	91.5	86.5
Office and related electrical products								
Machines de bureau et autres appareils élect.	16.4	108.3	115.8	113.9	127.9	154.3	135.4	143.1
Transport equipment								
Equipement de transports	7.3	104.3	112.9	102.0	106.0	111.2	113.0	120.5
Electricity, gas, water [E]								
Electricité, gaz et eau [E]	**9.3**	**104.7**	**109.2**	**111.2**	**114.9**	**120.2**	**122.2**	**124.9**

Asia excluding Israel and Japan • Asie à l'exception de l'Israël et du Japon

Region and industry [ISIC Rev. 3] Régions et industrie [CITI Rév. 3]	Weight(%) Pond.(%)	1996	1997	1998	1999	2000	2001	2002
Total industry [CDE]								
Total, industrie [CDE]	**100.0**	**105.8**	**110.9**	**106.7**	**114.9**	**126.4**	**125.8**	**132.1**
Total mining [C]								
Total, industries extractives [C]	**19.1**	**101.8**	**103.0**	**104.2**	**101.0**	**107.9**	**105.0**	**105.9**
Coal								
Houille	1.8	102.8	105.5	109.3	114.4	119.0	126.9	133.3
Crude petroleum and natural gas								
Pétrole brut et gaz naturel	15.7	100.8	102.0	102.7	98.8	105.6	101.9	101.7
Metal ores								
Minerais métalliques	0.7	114.2	112.5	143.3	144.3	162.4	162.6	186.4
Total manufacturing [D]								
Total, industries manufacturières [D]	**73.2**	**106.6**	**112.5**	**106.0**	**117.3**	**130.3**	**129.7**	**137.4**
Food, beverages, tobacco								
Industries alimentaires, boissons, tabac	11.0	105.9	106.9	101.5	102.6	106.7	107.0	110.6
Textiles								
Textiles	5.6	101.8	104.6	98.2	101.4	104.3	101.1	103.7
Wearing apparel, leather and footwear								
Articles d'habillement, cuir et chaussures	3.7	98.8	94.5	92.3	95.9	98.0	94.3	91.7

5

Index numbers of industrial production: world and regions [cont.]

Indices de la production industrielle : monde et régions [suite]

1995 = 100

Region and industry [ISIC Rev. 3] Régions et industrie [CITI Rév. 3]	Weight(%) Pond.(%)	1996	1997	1998	1999	2000	2001	2002
Wood and wood products Bois et articles en bois	1.2	102.8	102.2	86.3	81.7	82.3	78.3	76.5
Paper, printing, publishing and recorded media Papier, imprimerie, édition et supports enregistré	3.1	102.6	104.9	98.3	102.7	103.5	100.2	103.5
Chemicals and related products Produits chimiques et alliés	13.6	108.3	119.2	116.6	125.0	131.9	133.2	139.0
Non-metallic mineral products Produits minéraux non métalliques	4.3	105.6	110.9	95.9	103.9	108.0	110.0	118.2
Basic metals Métallurgie de base	5.4	106.5	112.3	102.8	112.5	119.2	120.6	127.9
Fabricated metal products Fabrications d'ouvrages en métaux	7.9	106.1	107.4	88.4	97.4	114.9	110.9	110.1
Office and related electrical products Machines de bureau et autres appareils élect.	9.0	110.1	124.9	136.1	179.8	234.9	229.7	262.7
Transport equipment Equipement de transports	5.4	109.7	119.1	102.0	121.4	133.2	142.3	152.1
Electricity, gas, water [E] **Electricité, gaz et eau [E]**	**7.7**	**107.5**	**115.9**	**119.4**	**126.9**	**135.4**	**140.6**	**146.9**
Europe • Europe								
Total industry [CDE] **Total, industrie [CDE]**	**100.0**	**100.7**	**104.2**	**107.9**	**110.0**	**115.9**	**116.4**	**115.2**
Total mining [C] **Total, industries extractives [C]**	**5.1**	**103.2**	**101.9**	**100.5**	**101.3**	**102.1**	**101.5**	**101.5**
Coal Houille	1.1	96.8	93.2	83.3	79.9	76.6	73.6	72.9
Crude petroleum and natural gas Pétrole brut et gaz naturel	3.1	107.1	106.3	105.2	106.1	107.5	108.2	109.4
Metal ores Minerais métalliques	0.2	102.0	96.2	125.8	124.4	129.7	126.2	130.5
Total manufacturing [D] **Total, industries manufacturières [D]**	**85.0**	**100.3**	**104.4**	**108.6**	**110.8**	**117.3**	**117.6**	**116.1**
Food, beverages, tobacco Industries alimentaires, boissons, tabac	10.4	100.6	102.4	103.4	104.9	106.6	108.3	110.7
Textiles Textiles	2.5	96.0	99.5	97.8	93.8	95.1	91.5	86.5
Wearing apparel, leather and footwear Articles d'habillement, cuir et chaussures	2.7	96.1	94.0	90.6	84.1	81.2	78.7	72.6
Wood and wood products Bois et articles en bois	1.9	97.1	100.4	104.2	107.1	113.0	109.0	93.5
Paper, printing, publishing and recorded media Papier, imprimerie, édition et supports enregistré	7.4	99.5	103.7	108.1	111.6	115.2	113.0	113.2
Chemicals and related products Produits chimiques et alliés	13.9	102.0	107.6	111.2	115.4	121.1	123.0	127.8
Non-metallic mineral products Produits minéraux non métalliques	4.2	97.4	98.5	100.8	103.4	107.8	107.6	105.6
Basic metals Métallurgie de base	4.6	98.2	104.4	104.4	102.3	110.2	109.1	108.6
Fabricated metal products Fabrications d'ouvrages en métaux	15.5	99.2	102.5	106.7	106.0	112.7	114.3	111.8
Office and related electrical products Machines de bureau et autres appareils élect.	9.7	103.2	109.6	119.0	127.2	145.6	143.6	134.5
Transport equipment Equipement de transports	8.1	102.7	110.2	120.8	124.7	133.1	135.3	134.0
Electricity, gas, water [E] **Electricité, gaz et eau [E]**	**9.8**	**102.8**	**103.4**	**105.1**	**107.6**	**111.3**	**113.5**	**114.2**
European Union [4] • Union européenne [4]								
Total industry [CDE] **Total, industrie [CDE]**	**100.0**	**100.8**	**104.5**	**108.5**	**110.5**	**115.9**	**115.9**	**114.2**
Total mining [C] **Total, industries extractives [C]**	**3.6**	**102.3**	**100.0**	**99.3**	**100.4**	**97.9**	**94.6**	**94.0**

5

Index numbers of industrial production: world and regions *[cont.]*

Indices de la production industrielle : monde et régions *[suite]*

1995 = 100

Region and industry [ISIC Rev. 3] Régions et industrie [CITI Rév. 3]	Weight(%) Pond.(%)	1996	1997	1998	1999	2000	2001	2002
Coal Houille	0.8	94.3	91.1	81.3	77.9	72.0	66.7	65.5
Crude petroleum and natural gas Pétrole brut et gaz naturel	2.0	107.1	104.3	105.2	106.2	103.1	100.5	101.0
Metal ores Minerais métalliques	0.1	95.7	90.4	85.7	77.7	73.8	70.2	66.3
Total manufacturing [D] **Total, industries manufacturières [D]**	**86.8**	**100.4**	**104.7**	**109.1**	**111.1**	**117.0**	**117.0**	**114.8**
Food, beverages, tobacco Industries alimentaires, boissons, tabac	10.2	100.8	103.5	104.4	106.0	107.2	108.7	110.4
Textiles Textiles	2.6	96.2	100.1	98.7	94.7	95.5	91.9	86.3
Wearing apparel, leather and footwear Articles d'habillement, cuir et chaussures	2.8	95.3	93.0	89.7	82.7	78.8	75.7	69.0
Wood and wood products Bois et articles en bois	1.7	97.0	100.5	104.1	107.1	112.1	108.0	87.2
Paper, printing, publishing and recorded media Papier, imprimerie, édition et supports enregistré	7.8	99.4	103.6	107.7	110.8	113.7	111.4	111.6
Chemicals and related products Produits chimiques et alliés	14.1	101.6	107.1	111.0	114.9	120.2	121.4	125.8
Non-metallic mineral products Produits minéraux non métalliques	4.2	97.2	99.3	101.7	103.9	106.9	105.7	103.1
Basic metals Métallurgie de base	4.2	97.7	103.8	104.8	102.2	108.5	106.3	106.2
Fabricated metal products Fabrications d'ouvrages en métaux	16.9	100.1	103.5	107.9	107.2	113.2	114.5	111.7
Office and related electrical products Machines de bureau et autres appareils élect.	10.3	103.3	109.2	118.6	125.8	143.6	141.5	131.4
Transport equipment Equipement de transports	8.7	102.5	110.2	121.5	125.0	133.3	135.5	133.5
Electricity, gas, water [E] **Electricité, gaz et eau [E]**	**9.6**	**103.9**	**104.3**	**106.3**	**109.0**	**112.4**	**114.8**	**115.5**

Oceania • Océanie

Total industry [CDE] **Total, industrie [CDE]**	**100.0**	**102.5**	**104.3**	**108.3**	**108.4**	**111.5**	**114.8**	**117.9**
Total mining [C] **Total, industries extractives [C]**	**18.3**	**102.6**	**103.4**	**112.3**	**108.9**	**120.9**	**124.8**	**126.4**
Coal Houille	4.2	103.1	103.4	108.5	116.6	126.5	134.3	142.5
Crude petroleum and natural gas Pétrole brut et gaz naturel	6.0	98.9	100.1	107.9	94.9	116.4	119.4	114.3
Metal ores Minerais métalliques	6.7	106.4	109.9	121.0	121.1	131.4	137.5	137.4
Total manufacturing [D] **Total, industries manufacturières [D]**	**69.4**	**102.4**	**104.3**	**107.3**	**108.5**	**109.7**	**112.6**	**116.3**
Food, beverages, tobacco Industries alimentaires, boissons, tabac	15.0	103.7	104.9	112.6	115.2	116.8	119.3	119.4
Textiles Textiles	1.9	95.2	95.9	96.5	96.4	94.7	90.8	81.6
Wearing apparel, leather and footwear Articles d'habillement, cuir et chaussures	2.2	95.2	95.9	96.4	96.2	94.6	90.6	81.4
Wood and wood products Bois et articles en bois	2.8	101.4	99.3	99.2	97.7	107.4	104.7	114.6
Paper, printing, publishing and recorded media Papier, imprimerie, édition et supports enregistré	7.3	102.2	104.8	104.0	104.3	105.9	108.9	113.8
Chemicals and related products Produits chimiques et alliés	10.0	105.1	107.3	109.0	110.3	113.9	118.2	122.1
Non-metallic mineral products Produits minéraux non métalliques	3.7	94.0	95.3	98.4	104.0	109.3	111.1	107.2
Basic metals Métallurgie de base	8.5	102.7	105.0	105.8	107.9	104.0	103.7	116.0

5

Index numbers of industrial production: world and regions *[cont.]*

Indices de la production industrielle : monde et régions *[suite]*

1995 = 100

Region and industry [ISIC Rev. 3] Régions et industrie [CITI Rév. 3]	Weight(%) Pond.(%)	1996	1997	1998	1999	2000	2001	2002
Fabricated metal products Fabrications d'ouvrages en métaux	5.6	103.3	105.8	107.9	107.9	107.7	111.9	118.3
Office and related electrical products Machines de bureau et autres appareils élect.	4.8	103.8	107.1	110.7	110.0	109.7	119.2	121.5
Transport equipment Equipement de transports	5.8	103.9	107.1	110.9	110.3	109.9	119.6	121.9
Electricity, gas, water [E] **Electricité, gaz et eau [E]**	**12.3**	**103.3**	**105.5**	**107.8**	**106.6**	**108.1**	**112.2**	**114.3**

Source:
United Nations Statistics Division, New York, the index numbers of industrial production database.

Source:
Organisation des Nations Unies, Division de statistique, New York, la base de données pour les indices de la production industrielle.

1   Northern America (Canada and the United States), Europe, Australia, Israel, Japan, New Zealand and South Africa.

2   Latin America and the Caribbean, Africa (excluding South Africa), Asia (excluding Israel and Japan), Oceania (excluding Australia and New Zealand).

3   Canada and the United States.

4   Austria, Belgium, Denmark, Finland, France, Germany, Greece, Ireland, Italy, Luxembourg, Netherlands, Portugal, Spain, Sweden and the United Kingdom.

1   Amérique septentrionale (le Canada et les Etats-Unis), Europe, l'Australie, l'Israël, la Nouvelle-Zélande et l'Afrique du Sud.

2   Amérique latine et Caraïbes, Afrique (non compris l'Afrique du Sud), Asie (non compris l'Israël et le Japon), Océanie (non compris l'Australie et la Nouvelle-Zélande).

3   Le Canada et les Etats-Unis.

4   L'Autriche, la Belgique, le Danemark, la Finlande, la France, l'Allemagne, la Grèce, l'Irlande, l'Italie, le Luxembourg, les Pays-Bas, le Portugal, l'Espagne, la Suède et le Royaume-Uni.

Table 6 follows overleaf
Le tableau 6 est présenté au verso

6

Production, trade and consumption of commercial energy
Thousand metric tons of oil equivalent and kilograms per capita

Production, commerce et consommation d'énergie commerciale
Milliers de tonnes d'équivalent pétrole et kilogrammes par habitant

| Region, country or area | Year Année | Primary energy production – Production d'énergie primaire | | | | | Changes in stock Variations des stocks | Imports Importations | Exports Exportations |
		Total Totale	Solids Solides	Liquids Liquides	Gas Gaz	Electricity Electricité			
World	1995	8 661 357	2 320 854	3 435 081	2 048 773	856 649	16 317	3 036 001	3 008 824
	1996	8 883 305	2 360 959	3 475 589	2 162 317	884 439	3 137	3 217 041	3 148 701
	1997	8 993 876	2 380 437	3 585 271	2 145 485	882 684	25 784	3 346 240	3 297 774
	1998	9 053 195	2 309 588	3 639 961	2 203 359	900 286	53 352	3 387 879	3 395 942
	1999	8 912 519	2 185 005	3 571 702	2 226 337	929 475	-87 150	3 418 572	3 385 363
	2000	9 118 671	2 173 001	3 714 154	2 282 656	948 860	-49 947	3 647 430	3 598 831
	2001	9 397 483	2 328 232	3 715 066	2 365 660	988 525	46 498	3 706 945	3 650 734
Africa	1995	596 978	149 260	354 054	85 259	8 405	7 529	58 321	356 976
	1996	621 078	148 924	371 823	91 407	8 924	7 115	61 848	373 246
	1997	655 482	158 144	386 849	101 148	9 341	8 537	68 812	401 941
	1998	654 906	160 372	381 032	103 797	9 704	16 837	71 337	395 751
	1999	659 624	160 920	374 979	113 358	10 367	8 452	78 095	409 904
	2000	680 840	161 392	387 501	121 704	10 242	976	76 356	432 272
	2001	686 784	162 260	393 725	120 688	10 111	4 133	76 250	429 113
America, North	1995	2 270 748	573 356	730 916	679 505	286 971	-10 736	648 278	350 164
	1996	2 288 141	589 982	706 521	700 065	291 572	-6 767	684 055	364 506
	1997	2 305 939	605 486	725 251	700 448	274 754	-7 199	734 997	380 112
	1998	2 326 111	613 242	713 673	720 392	278 804	18 079	774 038	390 417
	1999	2 296 152	600 079	689 404	708 452	298 217	-28 172	794 937	377 553
	2000	2 279 173	586 670	700 459	691 933	300 112	-54 318	844 027	395 890
	2001	2 381 064	617 134	699 291	739 927	324 712	52 281	879 445	399 684
America, South	1995	421 310	22 976	290 887	65 925	41 522	-460	71 295	202 063
	1996	463 661	24 847	322 774	73 061	42 979	6 393	78 117	221 947
	1997	492 405	28 191	340 616	78 085	45 513	-17	81 850	247 144
	1998	503 439	30 206	345 493	81 150	46 590	1 231	84 742	249 841
	1999	500 202	29 239	342 760	81 750	46 454	-4 010	76 738	238 444
	2000	519 954	33 753	349 886	86 882	49 434	1 811	76 628	245 979
	2001	514 691	36 584	343 948	84 904	49 255	4 696	77 265	247 611
Asia	1995	2 957 647	1 003 346	1 396 714	390 517	167 070	10 856	992 021	1 139 312
	1996	3 036 055	1 038 398	1 399 673	423 473	174 510	2 350	1 068 203	1 172 418
	1997	3 088 221	1 030 855	1 449 254	426 603	181 509	22 314	1 133 027	1 228 146
	1998	3 126 018	970 276	1 519 991	443 245	192 507	13 345	1 097 763	1 297 792
	1999	3 006 366	862 563	1 484 060	466 553	193 190	-46 640	1 125 669	1 287 039
	2000	3 144 211	856 323	1 566 199	522 333	199 356	-5 573	1 241 972	1 388 750
	2001	3 264 306	955 968	1 548 664	556 650	203 024	-11 990	1 235 121	1 406 210
Europe	1995	2 208 279	438 397	627 412	795 438	347 031	6 909	1 237 411	846 615
	1996	2 265 162	423 010	640 447	840 879	360 826	-5 128	1 292 951	900 837
	1997	2 232 857	412 660	648 693	805 557	365 947	155	1 294 723	917 988
	1998	2 209 673	379 650	642 504	820 614	366 905	3 455	1 327 258	928 038
	1999	2 219 509	374 244	649 307	820 786	375 172	-12 655	1 303 506	934 467
	2000	2 242 745	367 049	669 631	822 503	383 562	6 304	1 373 025	987 788
	2001	2 281 291	373 167	687 770	825 212	395 141	-2 270	1 402 298	1 006 117
Oceania	1995	206 395	133 519	35 097	32 129	5 650	2 219	28 675	113 693
	1996	209 208	135 798	34 351	33 432	5 626	-826	31 867	115 747
	1997	218 973	145 102	34 608	33 644	5 619	1 993	32 832	122 442
	1998	233 048	155 842	37 269	34 161	5 776	405	32 740	134 103
	1999	230 666	157 961	31 192	35 438	6 075	-4 125	39 626	137 955
	2000	251 747	167 815	40 477	37 300	6 155	853	35 422	148 152
	2001	269 346	183 118	41 667	38 279	6 282	-351	36 565	161 999

Source:
United Nations Statistics Division, New York, "Energy Statistics Yearbook 2001" and the energy statistics database.

Source:
Organisation des Nations Unies, Division de statistique, New York, "Annuaire des statistiques de l'énergie 2001" et la base de données pour les statistiques énergétiques.

| Bunkers - Soutes | | | Consumption - Consommation | | | | | | |
Air Avion	Sea Maritime	Unallocated Nondistribué	Per capita Par habitant	Total Totale	Solids Solides	Liquids Liquides	Gas Gaz	Electricity Electricité	Year Année Région, pays ou zone
81 946	**124 785**	**399 291**	**1 368**	**8 066 195**	**2 328 133**	**2 838 659**	**2 042 754**	**856 649**	**1995 Monde**
86 423	**131 783**	**367 287**	**1 397**	**8 363 014**	**2 407 818**	**2 910 050**	**2 160 707**	**884 439**	**1996**
90 310	**134 781**	**412 106**	**1 382**	**8 379 361**	**2 395 765**	**2 943 049**	**2 157 864**	**882 684**	**1997**
92 026	**140 496**	**382 456**	**1 364**	**8 376 802**	**2 331 373**	**2 967 130**	**2 178 012**	**900 286**	**1998**
96 605	**143 405**	**401 391**	**1 348**	**8 391 478**	**2 237 034**	**2 985 115**	**2 239 855**	**929 475**	**1999**
97 593	**148 977**	**449 512**	**1 351**	**8 521 133**	**2 256 353**	**3 014 846**	**2 301 074**	**948 860**	**2000**
99 117	**140 144**	**442 398**	**1 362**	**8 725 535**	**2 338 627**	**3 048 231**	**2 350 152**	**988 525**	**2001**
2 595	7 748	21 632	346	258 819	110 549	89 458	50 407	8 405	1995 Afrique
2 730	8 222	20 791	352	270 821	112 422	95 820	53 655	8 924	1996
2 652	7 433	28 366	348	275 364	115 164	95 651	55 207	9 341	1997
2 583	7 290	23 192	348	280 590	113 475	102 601	54 810	9 704	1998
3 023	8 399	14 695	354	293 245	117 627	108 543	56 709	10 367	1999
2 853	7 683	23 772	341	289 639	116 396	105 210	57 790	10 242	2000
3 325	7 545	23 044	340	295 875	116 725	108 893	60 147	10 111	2001
18 774	33 141	104 776	5 378	2 422 906	510 613	933 381	691 940	286 971	1995 Amérique du Nord
19 431	31 406	91 737	5 413	2 471 883	534 261	946 165	699 885	291 572	1996
20 947	27 730	108 553	5 430	2 510 794	566 845	968 656	700 538	274 754	1997
21 513	27 908	102 826	5 426	2 539 406	575 254	983 227	702 121	278 804	1998
22 984	31 143	95 082	5 468	2 592 499	574 772	999 337	720 173	298 217	1999
22 318	38 286	97 713	5 408	2 623 310	581 934	1 017 203	724 062	300 112	2000
21 250	24 608	101 671	5 400	2 661 015	588 938	1 031 532	715 833	324 712	2001
1 775	3 145	22 837	831	263 244	19 591	136 395	65 736	41 522	1995 Amérique du Sud
2 161	3 430	28 551	868	279 296	20 734	142 785	72 798	42 979	1996
2 271	3 640	28 488	897	292 728	21 908	147 453	77 855	45 513	1997
2 356	3 394	30 382	908	300 978	21 188	152 051	81 149	46 590	1998
2 225	4 384	37 554	882	298 343	21 166	150 006	80 718	46 454	1999
1 984	4 988	38 085	885	303 736	20 101	147 314	86 887	49 434	2000
2 173	5 262	29 344	863	302 870	19 531	149 402	84 683	49 255	2001
17 333	41 406	191 476	739	2 549 285	1 104 811	887 497	389 906	167 070	1995 Asie
20 024	46 584	165 447	770	2 697 434	1 158 765	935 435	428 723	174 510	1996
20 807	50 173	180 962	766	2 718 845	1 139 129	953 005	445 201	181 509	1997
20 272	54 574	160 305	744	2 677 494	1 085 976	944 005	455 006	192 507	1998
19 250	53 763	180 519	723	2 638 104	1 003 689	956 878	484 347	193 190	1999
20 046	49 861	220 341	734	2 712 758	1 009 880	987 032	516 491	199 356	2000
20 499	53 085	217 262	749	2 814 363	1 073 692	986 469	551 177	203 024	2001
38 560	37 864	59 578	2 870	2 456 166	537 869	749 450	821 816	347 031	1995 Europe
38 992	40 663	60 660	2 945	2 522 088	533 289	745 919	882 053	360 826	1996
40 449	44 380	63 606	2 875	2 461 001	502 531	737 514	855 009	365 947	1997
41 903	46 044	63 150	2 869	2 454 340	482 536	744 288	860 612	366 905	1998
45 635	44 357	70 145	2 854	2 441 065	465 663	727 910	872 321	375 172	1999
47 236	46 740	66 709	2 883	2 460 994	473 829	714 829	888 774	383 562	2000
48 124	48 317	69 874	2 943	2 513 426	477 972	730 489	909 824	395 141	2001
2 910	1 481	-1 008	4 113	115 776	44 699	42 477	22 951	5 650	1995 Océanie
3 084	1 477	101	4 223	121 492	48 347	43 926	23 593	5 626	1996
3 183	1 426	2 131	4 175	120 630	50 188	40 769	24 053	5 619	1997
3 398	1 286	2 601	4 194	123 994	52 944	40 959	24 315	5 776	1998
3 488	1 359	3 395	4 284	128 221	54 117	42 442	25 587	6 075	1999
3 157	1 418	2 893	4 310	130 696	54 213	43 259	27 070	6 155	2000
3 746	1 327	1 204	4 415	137 987	61 769	41 447	28 489	6 282	2001

7
Total imports and exports : index numbers
Volume and unit value indices and terms of trade (1990 = 100)

Importations et exportations : indices
Indices du volume et de la valeur unitaire et termes de l'échange (1990 = 100)

Region [&]	1995	1996	1997	1998	1999	2000	2001	2002	Région [&]
Total									**Total**
Exports : Volume [1]	135	142	157	167	177	199	199	209	Exp.: Volume [1]
Exports : Unit value indices US $ [2]	109	108	101	94	91	91	87	86	Exp.: Indices de la val. unit. en $ E.-U. [2]
Imports : Volume [1]	136	144	156	165	176	197	197	203	Imp.: Volume [1]
Imports: Unit value indices US $ [2]	105	104	99	93	91	92	88	88	Imp: Indices de la val. unit en $ E.-U. [2]
Developed economies [3]									**Economies développées [3]**
Exports : Volume [1]	129	136	150	157	164	182	182	184	Exp.: Volume [1]
Exports : Unit value indices US $ [2]	109	107	99	95	92	88	86	87	Exp.: Indices de la val. unit. en $ E.-U. [2]
Imports : Volume [1]	129	136	148	160	173	191	188	191	Imp.: Volume [1]
Imports: Unit value indices US $ [2]	103	102	95	90	88	87	85	86	Imp: Indices de la val. unit. en $ E.-U. [2]
Terms of trade [4]	106	105	104	105	105	101	101	102	Termes de l'echange [4]
Africa [5]									**Afrique [5]**
Exports : Volume [1]	103	116	126	115	122	138	141	...	Exp.: Volume [1]
Exports : Unit value indices US $ [2]	114	106	105	97	93	93	89	...	Exp.: Indices de la val. unit. en $ E.-U. [2]
Imports : Volume [1]	150	160	177	169	155	171	171	...	Imp.: Volume [1]
Imports: Unit value indices US $ [2]	112	103	102	95	94	96	91	...	Imp: Indices de la val. unit en $ E.-U. [2]
Terms of trade [4]	102	103	102	102	98	97	98	...	Termes de l'echange [4]
North America									**Amérique du Nord**
Exports : Volume [1]	137	145	160	166	175	189	179	172	Exp.: Volume [1]
Exports : Unit value indices US $ [2]	107	108	106	102	101	104	102	101	Exp.: Indices de la val. unit. en $ E.-U. [2]
Imports : Volume [1]	137	144	163	180	199	220	214	221	Imp.: Volume [1]
Imports: Unit value indices US $ [2]	106	106	104	98	99	105	101	99	Imp: Indices de la val. unit en $ E.-U. [2]
Terms of trade [4]	101	101	102	103	102	99	101	102	Termes de l'echange [4]
Asia									**Asie**
Exports : Volume [1]	108	109	121	120	122	136	121	130	Exp.: Volume [1]
Exports : Unit value indices US $ [2]	143	131	121	113	119	124	116	111	Exp.: Indices de la val. unit. en $ E.-U. [2]
Imports : Volume [1]	138	145	146	138	152	167	166	166	Imp.: Volume [1]
Imports: Unit value indices US $ [2]	105	103	99	87	87	96	90	86	Imp: Indices de la val. unit en $ E.-U. [2]
Terms of trade [4]	136	127	122	130	136	129	130	130	Termes de l'echange [4]
Europe									**Europe**
Exports : Volume [1]	130	138	152	162	170	191	195	200	Exp.: Volume [1]
Exports : Unit value indices US $ [2]	105	103	93	90	86	79	77	80	Exp.: Indices de la val. unit. en $ E.-U. [2]
Imports : Volume [1]	125	131	143	157	166	186	184	185	Imp.: Volume [1]
Imports: Unit value indices US $ [2]	101	99	90	87	82	77	77	79	Imp: Indices de la val. unit en $ E.-U. [2]
Terms of trade [4]	104	104	103	104	104	101	101	101	Termes de l'echange [4]
EU - 15									**UE - 15**
Exports : Volume [1]	131	139	154	164	172	194	198	203	Exp.: Volume [1]
Exports : Unit value indices US $ [2]	105	103	93	91	86	78	77	79	Exp.: Indices de la val. unit. en $ E.-U. [2]
Imports : Volume [1]	126	132	145	158	168	188	186	188	Imp.: Volume [1]
Imports: Unit value indices US $ [2]	101	99	90	87	82	78	77	79	Imp: Indices de la val. unit en $ E.-U. [2]
Terms of trade [4]	104	104	103	104	104	100	100	100	Termes de l'echange [4]
EFTA+									**AELE+**
Exports : Volume [1]	118	124	133	136	141	148	153	154	Exp.: Volume [1]
Exports : Unit value indices US $ [2]	104	103	93	87	88	93	91	95	Exp.: Indices de la val. unit. en $ E.-U. [2]
Imports : Volume [1]	108	113	122	134	140	151	149	148	Imp.: Volume [1]
Imports: Unit value indices US $ [2]	105	101	91	86	81	76	76	80	Imp: Indices de la val. unit en $ E.-U. [2]
Terms of trade [4]	99	102	103	101	109	123	120	120	Termes de l'echange [4]
Oceania									**Océanie**
Exports : Volume [1]	139	155	167	166	174	190	191	192	Exp.: Volume [1]
Exports : Unit value indices US $ [2]	97	98	94	82	79	82	81	82	Exp.: Indices de la val. unit. en $ E.-U. [2]
Imports : Volume [1]	132	140	148	157	169	176	167	187	Imp.: Volume [1]
Imports: Unit value indices US $ [2]	110	111	105	95	95	93	88	89	Imp: Indices de la val. unit en $ E.-U. [2]
Terms of trade [4]	88	88	89	87	83	87	92	92	Termes de l'echange [4]
Developing economies [3]									**Econ. en dévelop. [3]**
Exports : Volume [1]	153	160	179	197	219	250	254	289	Exp.: Volume [1]
Exports : Unit value indices US $ [2]	108	111	106	91	89	96	89	83	Exp.: Indices de la val. unit. en $ E.-U. [2]
Imports : Volume [1]	159	171	181	178	183	213	221	241	Imp.: Volume [1]
Imports: Unit value indices US $ [2,6]	113	112	111	102	103	108	99	96	Imp: Indices de la val. unit en $ E.-U. [2,6]
Terms of trade [4,6]	96	99	95	89	86	89	89	87	Termes de l'echange [4,6]
Africa									**Afrique**
Exports : Volume [1]	100	120	129	152	152	164	165	229	Exp.: Volume [1]
Exports : Unit value indices US $ [2]	100	91	84	64	75	86	76	57	Exp.: Indices de la val. unit. en $ E.-U. [2]

7
Total imports and exports : index numbers
Volume and unit value indices and terms of trade (1990 = 100)
Importations et exportations : indices
Indices du volume et de la valeur unitaire et termes de l'échange (1990 = 100)

Region [&]	1995	1996	1997	1998	1999	2000	2001	2002	Région [&]
Imports : Volume [1]	102	111	118	146	...	...	...	...	Imp.: Volume [1]
Imports: Unit value indices US $ [2]	108	101	96	88	...	...	...	...	Imp: Indices de la val. unit en $ E.-U. [2]
Terms of trade [4]	92	90	87	73	...	...	...	...	Termes de l'echange [4]
Americas									**Amériques**
Exports : Volume [1]	159	148	158	172	181	202	217	237	Exp.: Volume [1]
Exports : Unit value indices US $ [2]	98	118	122	112	113	121	108	101	Exp.: Indices de la val. unit. en $ E.-U. [2]
Imports : Volume [1]	152	170	164	185	187	211	225	229	Imp.: Volume [1]
Imports: Unit value indices US $ [2]	126	125	152	141	134	137	126	116	Imp: Indices de la val. unit. en $ E.-U. [2]
Terms of trade [4]	78	94	80	79	84	88	86	86	Termes de l'echange [4]
Asia									**Asia**
Exports : Volume [1]	161	171	194	212	241	279	281	318	Exp.: Volume [1]
Exports : Unit value indices US $ [2]	111	111	104	89	86	93	86	82	Exp.: Indices de la val. unit. en $ E.-U. [2]
Imports : Volume [1]	171	182	194	180	188	225	232	258	Imp.: Volume [1]
Imports: Unit value indices US $ [2]	111	111	106	95	99	104	95	93	Imp: Indices de la val. unit. en $ E.-U. [2]
Terms of trade [4]	100	100	99	93	87	89	90	89	Termes de l'echange [4]
Asia Middle East									**Moyen-Orient d'Asie**
Exports : Volume [1]	117	123	139	160	146	151	154	169	Exp.: Volume [1]
Exports : Unit value indices US $ [2]	97	106	100	74	101	136	126	116	Exp.: Indices de la val. unit. en $ E.-U. [2]
Imports : Volume [1]	124	138	154	160	159	196	187	...	Imp.: Volume [1]
Imports: Unit value indices US $ [2]	103	104	99	92	90	92	93	...	Imp: Indices de la val. unit. en $ E.-U. [2]
Terms of trade [4]	94	102	101	80	112	148	135	...	Termes de l'echange [4]
Other Asia									**Autre Asie**
Exports : Volume [1]	172	183	208	226	269	319	320	365	Exp.: Volume [1]
Exports : Unit value indices US $ [2]	114	112	105	93	83	85	79	76	Exp.: Indices de la val. unit. en $ E.-U. [2]
Imports : Volume [1]	180	190	202	182	192	229	239	267	Imp.: Volume [1]
Imports: Unit value indices US $ [2]	112	112	107	96	101	107	95	92	Imp: Indices de la val. unit. en $ E.-U. [2]
Terms of trade [4]	102	100	98	96	83	80	83	83	Termes de l'echange [4]

Source:
United Nations Statistics Division, New York, trade statistics database.

Source:
Organisation des Nations Unies, Division de statistique, New York, la base de données pour les statistiques du commerce extérieur.

[&] The regional analysis in this table is in accordance with the groupings of countries or areas specified in Table 74.

[&] L'analyse régionale dans ce tableau est conforme aux groupes des pays ou zones paraissant dans tableau 74.

[+] For Member States of this grouping, see Annex I – Other groupings.

[+] Pour les Etats membres de ce groupement, voir annexe I – Autres groupements

[1] Volume indices are derived from value data and unit value indices. They are base period weighted.

[1] Les indices du quantum sont calculés à partir des chiffres de la valeur et des indices de valeur unitaire. Ils sont àcoéfficients de pondération correspondant à la périod en base.

[2] Regional aggregates are current period weighted.

[2] Les totaux régionaux sont à coéfficients de pondération correspondant à la période en cours.

[3] This classification is intended for statistical convenience and does not, necessarily, express a judgement about the stage reached by a particular country in the development process.

[3] Cette classification est utilisée pour plus de commodité dans la presentation des statistique et n'implique pas nécessairement un jugement quant au stage de développement auquel est parvenu un pays donné.

[4] Unit value index of exports divided by unit value index of imports.

[4] Indices de la valeur unitaire des exportations divisé par l'indice de la valeur unitaire des importations.

[5] Beginning January 1998, data refer to South Africa only. Prior to January 1998, data refer to Southern African Common Customs Area.

[5] A compter de janvier 1998, les données se rapportent qu'à l'Afrique du Sud. Avant janvier 1998, le données se rapportent à l'Union Douanière de l'Afrique.

[6] Indices, except those for Europe, are based on estimates prepared by the International Monetary Fund.

[6] Le calcul des indices, sauf ceux pour l'Europe, sont basés sur les estimations préparées par le Fonds monétaire.

Technical notes, tables 1-7

Table 1: The series of world aggregates on population, production, transport, external trade and finance have been compiled from statistical publications and databases of the United Nations and the specialized agencies and other institutions [1, 6, 7, 8, 9, 15, 22, 23, 24, 25]. The sources should be consulted for details on compilation and coverage.

Table 2 presents estimates of population size, rates of population increase, crude birth and death rates, surface area and population density for the world and regions. Unless otherwise specified, all figures are estimates of the order of magnitude and are subject to a substantial margin of error.

The population estimates and rates presented in this table were prepared by the Population Division of the United Nations Secretariat and published in *World Population Prospects: 2002 Revision* [29].

The average annual percentage rates of population growth were calculated by the Population Division of the United Nations Secretariat, using an exponential rate of increase formula.

Crude birth and crude death rates are expressed in terms of the average annual number of births and deaths respectively, per 1,000 mid-year population. These rates are estimated.

Surface area totals were obtained by summing the figures for the individual countries or areas.

Density is the number of persons in the 2000 total population per square kilometre of total surface area.

The scheme of regionalization used for the purpose of making these estimates is presented in annex I. Although some continental totals are given, and all can be derived, the basic scheme presents eight macro regions that are so drawn as to obtain greater homogeneity in sizes of population, types of demographic circumstances and accuracy of demographic statistics.

Tables 3-4: The index numbers in table 3 refer to agricultural production, which is defined to include both crop and livestock products. Seeds and feed are excluded. The index numbers of food refer to commodities which are considered edible and contain nutrients. Coffee, tea and other inedible commodities are excluded.

The index numbers of total agricultural and food production in table 3 are calculated by the Laspeyres formula with the base year period 1989-1991. The latter is provided in order to diminish the impact of annual fluctuations in agricultural output during base years on the indices for the period. Production quantities of each commodity are weighted by 1989-1991 average national producer prices and summed for each year. The index numbers are based on production data for a calendar year.

Notes techniques, tableaux 1 à 7

Tableau 1: Les séries d'agrégats mondiaux sur la population, la production, les transports, le commerce extérieur et les finances ont été établies à partir de publications statistiques et bases de données des Nations Unies et les institutions spécialisées et autres organismes [1, 6, 7, 8, 9, 15, 22, 23, 24, 25]. On doit se référer aux sources pour tous renseignements détaillés sur les méthodes de calcul et la portée des statistiques.

Le *Tableau 2* présente les estimations mondiales et régionales de la population, des taux d'accroissement de la population, des taux bruts de natalité et de mortalité, de la superficie et de la densité de population. Sauf indication contraire, tous les chiffres sont des estimations de l'ordre de grandeur et comportent une assez grande marge d'erreur.

Les estimations de la population et tous les taux présentés dans ce tableau ont été établis par la Division de la population du Secrétariat des Nations Unies et publiés dans "*World Population Prospects: 2002 Revision*" [29].

Les pourcentages annuels moyens de l'accroissement de la population ont été calculés par la Division de la population du Secrétariat des Nations Unies, sur la base d'une formule de taux d'accroissement exponentiel.

Les taux bruts de natalité et de mortalité sont exprimés, respectivement, sur la base du nombre annuel moyen de naissances et de décès par tranche de 1.000 habitants au milieu de l'année. Ces taux sont estimatifs.

On a déterminé les superficies totales en additionnant les chiffres correspondant aux différents pays ou régions.

La densité est le nombre de personnes de la population totale de 2000 par kilomètre carré de la superficie totale.

Le schéma de régionalisation utilisé aux fins de l'établissement de ces estimations est présenté dans l'annexe I. Bien que les totaux de certains continents soient donnés et que tous puissent être déterminés, le schéma de base présente huit grandes régions qui sont établies de manière à obtenir une plus grande homogénéité en ce qui concerne l'ampleur des populations, les types de conditions démographiques et la précision des statistiques démographiques.

Tableaux 3-4: Les indices du tableau 3 se rapportent à la production agricole, qui est définie comme comprenant à la fois les produits de l'agriculture et de l'élevage. Les semences et les aliments pour les animaux sont exclus de cette définition. Les indices de la production alimentaire se rapportent aux produits considérés comme comes-

As in the past, the series include a large number of estimates made by FAO in cases where figures are not available from official country sources.

Index numbers for the world and regions are computed in a similar way to the country index numbers except that instead of using different commodity prices for each country group, "international commodity prices" derived from the Gheary-Khamis formula are used for all country groupings. This method assigns a single "price" to each commodity.

The indexes in table 4 are calculated as a ratio between the index numbers of total agricultural and food production in table 3 described above and the corresponding index numbers of population.

For further information on the series presented in these tables, see the FAO *Production Yearbook* [6] and <http://faostat.fao.org>.

Table 5: The index numbers of industrial production are classified according to tabulation categories, divisions and combinations of divisions of the International Standard Industrial Classification of All Economic Activities, Revision 3, (ISIC Rev. 3) [50] for mining (category C), manufacturing (category D), and electricity, gas and water (category E).

The indices indicate trends in value added in constant US dollars. The measure of value added used is the national accounts concept, which is defined as gross output less the cost of materials, supplies, fuel and electricity consumed and services received.

Each series is compiled using the Laspeyres formula, that is, the indices are base-weighted arithmetic means. The weight base year is 1995 and value added, generally at factor values, is used in weighting.

For most countries the estimates of value added used as weights are derived from the results of national industrial censuses or similar inquiries relating to 1995. These data, in national currency, are adjusted to the ISIC where necessary and are subsequently converted into US dollars.

Within each of the ISIC categories (tabulation categories, divisions and combinations of divisions) shown in the tables, the indices for the country aggregations (regions or economic groupings) are calculated directly from the country data. The indices for the World, however, are calculated from the aggregated indices for the groupings of developed and developing countries.

China and the countries of the former USSR (except Russian Federation and Ukraine) are excluded from their respective regions.

Table 6: For a description of the series in table 6, see the technical notes to chapter XIII.

tibles et contenant des éléments nutritifs. Le café, le thé et les produits non comestibles sont exclus.

Les indices de la production agricole et de la production alimentaire présentés au tableau 3 sont calculés selon la formule de Laspeyres avec les années 1989-1991 comme période de référence, cela afin de limiter l'incidence, sur les indices correspondant à la période considérée, des fluctuations annuelles de la production agricole enregistrée pendant les années de référence. Les chiffres de production de chaque produit sont pondérés par les prix nationaux moyens à la production pour la période 1989-1991 et additionnés pour chaque année. Les indices sont fondés sur les données de production de l'année civile. Comme dans le passé, les séries comprennent un grand nombre d'estimations établies par la FAO lorsqu'elle n'avait pu obtenir de chiffres de sources officielles dans les pays eux-mêmes.

Les indices pour le monde et les régions sont calculés de la même façon que les indices par pays, mais au lieu d'appliquer des prix différents aux produits de base pour chaque groupe de pays, on a utilisé des "prix internationaux" établis d'après la formule de Gheary-Khamis pour tous les groupes de pays. Cette méthode attribue un seul "prix" à chaque produit de base.

Les indices du tableau 4 sont calculés comme ratio entre les indices de la production alimentaire et de la production agricole totale du tableau 3 décrits ci-dessus et les indices de population correspondants.

Pour tout renseignement complémentaire sur les séries présentées dans ces tableaux, voir l'*Annuaire FAO de la production* [6] et <http://faostat.fao.org>.

Tableau 5: Les indices de la production industrielle sont classés selon les catégories de classement, les divisions ou des combinaisons des divisions de la Classification Internationale type, par industrie, de toutes les branches d'activité économique, Révision 3 (CITI Rev. 3) [50] qui concernent les industries extractives (la catégorie C) et les industries manufacturières (la catégorie D), ainsi que l'électricité, le gaz et l'eau (la catégorie E).

Ces indices représentent les tendances de la valeur ajoutée en dollars constants des Etats-Unis. La mesure utilisée pour la valeur ajoutée correspond à celle qui est appliquée aux fins de la comptabilité nationale, c'est-à-dire égale à la valeur de la production brute diminuée des coûts des matériaux, des fournitures, de la consommation de carburant et d'électricité ainsi que des services reçus.

Chaque série a été établie au moyen de la formule de Laspeyres, ce qui signifie que les indices sont des moyennes arithmétiques affectées de coefficients de pondération. L'année de base de pondération est l'année 1995 et on utilise généralement pour la pondération la valeur ajoutée aux coûts des facteurs.

Table 7: For a description of the series in table 7, see the technical notes to chapter XVI. The composition of the regions is presented in table 74.

Pour la plupart des pays, les estimations de la valeur ajoutée qui sont utilisées comme coefficients de pondération sont tirées des résultats des recensements industriels nationaux ou enquêtes analogues concernant l'année 1995. Ces données, en monnaie nationale, sont ajustées s'il y a lieu aux normes de la CITI et ultérieurement converties en dollars des Etats-Unis.

A l'intérieur de chacune des subdivisions de la CITI (catégories de classement, divisions et combinaisons des divisions) indiquées dans les tableaux, les indices relatifs aux assemblages de pays (régions géographiques ou groupements économiques) sont calculés directement à partir des données des pays. Toutefois, les indices concernant le *Monde* sont calculés à partir des indices agrégés applicables aux groupements de pays développés et de pays en développement.

La Chine et les pays de l'ancienne URSS (sauf la Fédération de Russie et Ukraine) sont exclus de leurs régions respectives.

Tableau 6: On trouvera une description de la série de statistiques du tableau 6 dans les notes techniques du chapitre XIII.

Tableau 7: On trouvera une description de la série de statistiques du tableau 7 dans les notes techniques du chapitre XVI. La composition des régions est présentée au tableau 74.

Part Two
Population and Social Statistics

Chapter II	Population (table 8)
Chapter III	Education (table 9)
Chapter IV	Nutrition and childbearing (tables 10 and 11)
Chapter V	Culture and communication (tables 12-18)

Part Two of the *Yearbook* presents statistical series on a wide range of population and social topics for all countries or areas of the world for which data have been made available. The topics include population and population growth, surface area and density; education: life expectancy, childbearing and mortality; food supply; book production; newspapers and periodicals; cinemas; telephones; and Internet users.

Deuxième partie
Population et statistiques sociales

Chapitre II	Population (tableau 8)
Chapitre III	Instruction (tableau 9)
Chapitre IV	Nutrition et maternité (tableaux 10 et 11)
Chapitre V	Culture et communication (tableaux 12 à 18)

La deuxième partie de l'*Annuaire* présente, pour tous les pays ou zones du monde pour lesquels des données sont disponibles, des séries statistiques intéressant une large gamme de questions démographiques et sociales: population et croissance démographique, superficie et densité; l'instruction l'espérance de vie, la maternité et la mortalité; disponibilités alimentaires; production de livres; journaux et périodiques; cinémas; téléphones; et usagers d'Internet.

8

Population by sex, rate of population increase, surface area and density
Population selon le sexe, taux d'accroissement de la population, superficie et densité

Country or area Pays ou zone	Latest census Dernier recensement Date	Both sexes Les deux sexes	Men Hommes	Women Femmes	Mid-year estimates (thousands) Estimations au milieu de l'année (milliers) 1995	2001	Annual rate of increase Taux d'accrois-sement annuel % 1995-01	Surface area (km²) Superficie (km²) 2001	Density Densité 2001+
Africa · Afrique									
Algeria [1] Algérie [1]	25 VI 1998	29 100 867	14 698 589	14 402 278	28 060	*30 836	1.6	2 381 741	13
Angola [2] Angola [2]	15 XII 1970	5 646 166	2 943 974	2 702 192	...	...	...	1 246 700	...
Benin [3] Bénin [3]	11 II 2002	*6 752 569	...	...	5 412	*6 417	2.8	112 622	57
Botswana Botswana	17 VIII 2001	*1 680 863	*813 488	*867 375			...	581 730	...
Burkina Faso Burkina Faso	10 XII 1996	10 312 609	4 970 882	5 341 727	...	...	...	274 000	...
Burundi Burundi	16 VIII 1990	5 139 073	2 473 599	2 665 474	...	...	...	27 834	...
Cameroon Cameroun	10 IV 1987	10 493 655	...	...	...	...	...	475 442	...
Cape Verde Cap-Vert	11 VI 2000	*434 812	...	...	386	*442	2.3	4 033	110
Central African Rep. Rép. centrafricaine	8 XII 1988	2 463 616	1 210 734	1 252 882	...	...	...	622 984	...
Chad [4] Tchad [4]	8 IV 1993	6 279 931	...	...	...	...	...	1 284 000	...
Comoros [5] Comores [5]	15 IX 1991	446 817	221 152	225 665	...	...	...	2 235	...
Congo Congo	22 XII 1984	1 843 421	...	...	...	...	...	342 000	...
Côte d'Ivoire Côte d'Ivoire	1 III 1988	10 815 694	5 527 343	5 288 351	14 230	*16 939	2.9	322 463	53
Dem. Rep. of the Congo Rép. dém. du Congo	1 VII 1984	29 916 800	14 543 800	15 373 000	...	...	...	2 344 858	...
Djibouti Djibouti	11 XII 1960	81 200	...	...	...	...	...	23 200	...
Egypt Egypte	19 XI 1996	59 312 914	30 351 390	28 961 524	57 510	*67 886	2.8	1 001 449	68
Equatorial Guinea [6] Guinée équatoriale [6]	4 VII 1983	300 000	144 760	155 240	...	...	...	28 051	...
Eritrea Erythrée	9 V 1984	2 748 304	1 374 452	1 373 852	...	...	...	117 600	...
Ethiopia Ethiopie	11 X 1994	53 477 265	26 910 698	26 566 567	54 649	*65 374	3.0	1 104 300	59
Gabon Gabon	31 VII 1993	1 014 976	501 784	513 192	1 066	*1 237	2.5	267 668	5
Gambia Gambie	13 IV 1993	1 025 867	514 530	511 337	...	...	...	11 295	...
Ghana Ghana	26 III 2000	18 912 079	9 357 382	9 554 697	...	...	...	238 533	...
Guinea [7] Guinée [7]	4 II 1983	4 533 240	...	...	...	...	...	245 857	...
Guinea-Bissau Guinée-Bissau	1 XII 1991	983 367	476 210	507 157	...	...	...	36 125	...

8

Population by sex, rate of population increase, surface area and density *[cont.]*
Population selon le sexe, taux d'accroissement de la population, superficie et densité *[suite]*

Country or area Pays ou zone	Latest census Dernier recensement Date	Both sexes Les deux sexes	Men Hommes	Women Femmes	Mid-year estimates (thousands) Estimations au milieu de l'année (milliers) 1995	2001	Annual rate of increase Taux d'accrois- sement annuel % 1995-01	Surface area (km²) Superficie (km²) 2001	Density Densité 2001+
Kenya Kenya	24 VIII 1999	28 686 607	14 205 589	14 481 018	...	...	...	580 367	...
Lesotho Lesotho	14 IV 1996	1 862 275	312 444	1 549 831	...	...	...	30 355	...
Liberia Libéria	1 II 1984	2 101 628	1 063 127	1 038 501	...	...	...	111 369	...
Libyan Arab Jamah. [8] Jamah. arabe libyenne [8]	11 VIII 1995	4 404 986	2 236 943	2 168 043	4 395	*5 299	3.1	1 759 540	3
Madagascar Madagascar	1 VIII 1993	12 092 157	5 991 171	6 100 986	...	...	...	587 041	...
Malawi Malawi	1 IX 1998	9 933 868	4 867 563	5 066 305	9 788	*11 140	2.2	118 484	94
Mali [3] Mali [3]	17 IV 1998	9 790 492	4 847 436	4 943 056	...	...	...	1 240 192	...
Mauritania Mauritanie	1 XI 2000	2 548 157	1 240 414	1 307 743	2 284	*2 724	2.9	1 025 520	3
Mauritius [1] Maurice [1]	2 VII 2000	1 178 848	583 756	595 092	1 122	*1 200	1.1	2 040	588
Morocco Maroc	2 IX 1994	26 019 280	12 944 517	13 074 763	26 386	29 170	1.7	446 550	65
Mozambique Mozambique	1 VIII 1997	15 521 090	7 442 135	8 078 955	15 820[9]	*17 656[9]	1.8[9]	801 590	22
Namibia Namibie	27 VIII 2001	1 826 854	936 718	890 136	...	...	...	824 292	...
Niger Niger	20 V 1988	7 248 100	3 590 070	3 658 030	...	...	...	1 267 000	...
Nigeria Nigéria	26 XI 1991	88 992 220	44 529 608	44 462 612	...	...	...	923 768	...
Réunion [3] Réunion [3]	08 III 1999	706 180	347 076	359 104	...	...	...	2 510	...
Rwanda Rwanda	15 VIII 1991	7 142 755	...	...	...	...	...	26 338	...
Saint Helena ex. dep. Sainte-Hélène sans dép.	8 III 1998	5 157	2 612	2 545	...	...	...	122	...
Ascension Ascension	31 XII 1978	849	608	241	...	...	...	88	...
Tristan da Cunha Tristan da Cunha	31 XII 1988	296	139	157	...	...	...	...	...
Sao Tome and Principe Sao Tomé-et-Principe	4 VIII 1991	116 998	57 837	59 161	...	...	...	964	...
Senegal Sénégal	27 V 1988	6 896 808	3 353 599	3 543 209	8 347	*9 803	2.7	196 722	50
Seychelles Seychelles	29 VIII 1997	75 876	37 589	38 287	75	81	1.3	455	178
Sierra Leone [10] Sierra Leone [10]	15 XII 1985	3 515 812	1 746 055	1 769 757	...	...	...	71 740	...
Somalia Somalie	15 II 1987	7 114 431	3 741 664	3 372 767	...	...	...	637 657	...
South Africa [11] Afrique du Sud [11]	10 X 1996	40 583 573	19 520 887	21 062 686	39 477[9]	*44 328[9]	1.9[9]	1 221 037	36
Sudan Soudan	15 IV 1993	24 940 683	12 518 638	12 422 045	27 008	*31 627	2.6	2 505 813	13

8
Population by sex, rate of population increase, surface area and density [cont.]
Population selon le sexe, taux d'accroissement de la population, superficie et densité [suite]

Country or area Pays ou zone	Latest census Dernier recensement Date	Both sexes Les deux sexes	Men Hommes	Women Femmes	Mid-year estimates (thousands) Estimations au milieu de l'année (milliers) 1995	2001	Annual rate of increase Taux d'accrois- sement annuel % 1995-01	Surface area (km^2) Superficie (km^2) 2001	Density Densité 2001+
Swaziland Swaziland	11 V 1997	929 718	440 154	489 564	...	...	...	17 364	...
Togo Togo	22 XI 1981	2 703 250	...	...	...	...	...	56 785	...
Tunisia Tunisie	20 IV 1994	8 785 711	4 439 289	4 346 422	8 958	*9 674	1.3	163 610	59
Uganda Ouganda	12 IX 2002	*24 748 977	*12 124 761	*12 624 216	19 263	*22 788	2.8	241 038	95
United Rep. of Tanzania Rép.-Unie de Tanzanie	24 VIII 2002	*34 569 232	*16 910 321	*17 658 911	...	...	...	883 749	...
Western Sahara [12] Sahara occidental [12]	31 XII 1970	76 425	43 981	32 444	...	...	...	266 000	...
Zambia Zambie	25 X 2000	10 285 631	5 070 891	5 214 740	...	...	...	752 618	...
Zimbabwe Zimbabwe	2 VIII 2002	*11 634 663	...	...	11 526	*12 960	2.0	390 757	33
America, North · Amérique du Nord									
Anguilla Anguilla	9 V 2001	11 430	5 628	5 802	10	*12	2.7	96	120
Antigua and Barbuda Antigua-et-Barbuda	28 V 2001	77 426	37 002	40 424	...	...	...	442	...
Aruba [1] Aruba [1]	6 X 1991	66 687	32 821	33 866	82	*92	2.0	193	476
Bahamas Bahamas	1 V 2000	303 611	147 715	155 896	...	...	...	13 878	...
Barbados Barbade	1 V 2000	250 010	119 926	130 084	...	...	...	430	...
Belize Belize	12 V 2000	240 204	121 278	118 926	216	*257	2.9	22 966	11
Bermuda [1,13] Bermudes [1,13]	20 V 1991	58 460	...	...	60	*62	0.6	53	...
British Virgin Islands Iles Vierges britanniques	12 V 1991	17 809	...	...	...	...	...	151	...
Canada [1] Canada [1]	15 V 2001	*30 007 090	*14 706 850	*15 300 240	29 354[9]	*31 111[9]	1.0[9]	9 970 610	3
Cayman Islands [1] Iles Caïmanes [1]	11 XII 1999	39 410	...	...	33	*41	3.9	264	157
Costa Rica [1] Costa Rica [1]	26 VI 2000	3 810 179	1 902 614	1 907 565	3 333	*3 873	2.5	51 100	76
Cuba Cuba	11 IX 1981	9 723 605	4 914 873	4 808 732	10 978	*11 230	0.4	110 861	101
Dominica Dominique	12 V 2001	*71 239	*36 313	*34 926	...	...	...	751	...
Dominican Republic Rép. dominicaine	24 IX 1993	7 293 390	3 550 797	3 742 593	7 705	*8 528	1.7	48 511	176
El Salvador El Salvador	27 IX 1992	5 118 599	2 485 613	2 632 986	5 669	6 397	2.0	21 041	304
Greenland [1] Groenland [1]	26 X 1976	49 630	26 856	22 774	...	...	...	2 175 600	...
Grenada [14] Grenade [14]	25 V 2001	102 632	50 798	51 834	98	101	0.4	344	293

8

Population by sex, rate of population increase, surface area and density *[cont.]*
Population selon le sexe, taux d'accroissement de la population, superficie et densité *[suite]*

Country or area Pays ou zone	Latest census Dernier recensement Date	Both sexes Les deux sexes	Men Hommes	Women Femmes	Mid-year estimates (thousands) Estimations au milieu de l'année (milliers) 1995	2001	Annual rate of increase Taux d'accrois-sement annuel % 1995-01	Surface area (km²) Superficie (km²) 2001	Density Densité 2001+
Guadeloupe [1,15] Guadeloupe [1,15]	08 III 1999	422 222	203 146	219 076	...	...	...	1 705	...
Guatemala [3] Guatemala [3]	24 XI 2002	*11 237 196	...	...	9 976[9]	*11 683[9]	2.6[9]	108 889	107
Haiti [1] Haïti [1]	30 VIII 1982	5 053 792	2 448 370	2 605 422	7 180	*8 132	2.1	27 750	293
Honduras Honduras	29 V 1988	4 248 561	2 110 106	2 138 455	...	...	...	112 088	...
Jamaica Jamaïque	7 IV 1991	2 314 479	1 134 386	1 180 093	2 503	*2 621	0.8	10 991	238
Martinique [1] Martinique [1]	08 III 1999	381 325	180 910	200 415	...	...	...	1 102	...
Mexico [1] Mexique [1]	14 II 2000	97 483 412	47 592 253	49 891 159	91 992	101 754	1.7	1 958 201	52
Montserrat Montserrat	12 V 1991	10 639	5 290	5 349	...	...	...	102	...
Netherlands Antilles [16] Antilles néerlandaises [16]	29 I 2001	175 653	82 521	93 132	...	...	...	800	...
Nicaragua [1] Nicaragua [1]	25 IV 1995	4 357 099	2 147 105	2 209 994	4 427	*5 205	2.7	130 000	40
Panama Panama	14 V 2000	2 839 177	1 432 566	1 406 611	2 631	*2 897	1.6	75 517	38
Puerto Rico [1,17] Porto Rico [1,17]	1 IV 2000	3 808 610	1 833 577	1 975 033	3 655	3 840	0.8	8 875	433
Saint Kitts and Nevis Saint-Kitts-et-Nevis	14 V 2001	45 841	22 784	23 057	...	...	...	261	...
Saint Lucia Sainte-Lucie	22 V 2001	158 147	77 264	80 883	145	*158	1.4	539	293
Saint Pierre and Miquelon Saint-Pierre-et-Miquelon	08 III 1999	6 316	3 147	3 169	...	...	...	242	...
St. Vincent-Grenadines [18] St. Vincent-Grenadines [18]	14 V 2001	109 202	...	...	111	*109	-0.3	388	281
Trinidad and Tobago Trinité-et-Tobago	15 V 2000	1 262 366	633 051	629 315	...	...	...	5 130	...
Turks and Caicos Islands Iles Turques et Caïques	31 V 1990	12 350	6 289	6 061	...	...	...	430	...
United States [1,19] Etats-Unis [1,19]	1 IV 2000	281 421 906	138 053 563	143 368 343	263 044	284 797	1.3	9 629 091	30
United States Virgin Is. [1,17] Iles Vierges américaines [1,17]	1 IV 2000	108 612	51 864	56 748	...	...	...	347	...
America, South · Amérique du Sud									
Argentina Argentine	18 XI 2001	*36 223 947	*17 667 874	*18 556 073	34 768	37 487	1.3	2 780 400	13
Bolivia Bolivie	5 IX 2001	*8 274 325	*4 123 850	*4 150 475	...	...	...	1 098 581	...
Brazil [3,20] Brésil [3,20]	1 VIII 2000	169 799 170	*83 576 015	*86 223 155	155 822	172 386	1.7	8 514 047	20
Chile Chili	22 IV 1992	13 348 401	6 553 254	6 795 147	14 210	*15 402	1.3	756 626	20
Colombia Colombie	24 X 1993	33 109 840	16 296 539	16 813 301	38 542	43 071	1.9	1 138 914	38

8

Population by sex, rate of population increase, surface area and density *[cont.]*
Population selon le sexe, taux d'accroissement de la population, superficie et densité *[suite]*

Country or area Pays ou zone	Latest census Dernier recensement Date	Both sexes Les deux sexes	Men Hommes	Women Femmes	Mid-year estimates (thousands) Estimations au milieu de l'année (milliers) 1995	2001	Annual rate of increase Taux d'accrois- sement annuel % 1995-01	Surface area (km²) Superficie (km²) 2001	Density Densité 2001+
Ecuador [21] Equateur [21]	25 XI 2001	12 156 608	6 018 353	6 138 255	11 460[9]	12 879[9]	1.9[9]	283 561	45
Falkland Is. (Malvinas) [22,23] Iles Falkland (Malvinas) [22,23]	8 IV 2001	2 913	1 598	1 315	...	...	...	12 173	...
French Guiana [1] Guyane française [1]	08 III 1999	156 790	78 963	77 827	...	...	...	90 000	...
Guyana Guyana	12 V 1991	701 704	344 928	356 776	...	...	...	214 969	...
Paraguay Paraguay	28 VIII 2002	*5 206 101	*2 640 068	*2 566 033	...	...	...	406 752	...
Peru [24] Pérou [24]	11 VII 1993	22 048 356	10 956 375	11 091 981	23 532[9]	*26 347[9]	1.9[9]	1 285 216	20
Suriname Suriname	1 VII 1980	355 240	...	...	...	...	...	163 820	...
Uruguay Uruguay	22 V 1996	3 163 763	1 532 288	1 631 475	3 218[9]	3 361[9]	0.7[9]	175 016	19
Venezuela [24] Venezuela [24]	20 X 1990	18 105 265	9 019 757	9 085 508	21 844[9]	24 632[9]	2.0[9]	912 050	27
Asia · Asie									
Afghanistan [25] Afghanistan [25]	23 VI 1979	13 051 358	6 712 377	6 338 981	...	...	...	652 090	...
Armenia [3] Arménie [3]	10 X 2001	*3 458 303	...	...	3 760	*3 802	0.2	29 800	128
Azerbaijan [3] Azerbaïdjan [3]	27 I 1999	7 953 438	3 883 155	4 070 283	7 685	8 111	0.9	86 600	94
Bahrain Bahreïn	6 IV 2001	650 604	373 649	276 955	578	655	2.1	694	943
Bangladesh Bangladesh	22 I 2001	123 151 246	*62 735 988	*60 415 258	...	...	...	143 998	...
Bhutan Bhoutan	11 XI 1969	1 034 774	...	...	582	699	3.1	47 000	15
Brunei Darussalam Brunéi Darussalam	7 VIII 1991	260 482	137 616	122 866	296	344	2.5	5 765	60
Cambodia [26] Cambodge [26]	3 III 1998	11 437 656	5 511 408	5 926 248	10 200	13 311	4.4	181 035	74
China [27,28] Chine [27,28]	1 XI 2000	1 242 612 226	640 275 969	602 336 257	...	...	...	9 596 961	...
China, Hong Kong SAR [29,30] Chine, Hong Kong RAS [29,30]	14 III 2001	6 708 389	3 285 344	3 423 045	6 156	6 725	...	1 099	6 119
China, Macao SAR Chine, Macao RAS	23 VIII 2001	435 235	208 865	226 370	409	434	1.0	26	16 825
Cyprus [31] Chypre [31]	1 X 2001	689 471	...	...	733	*759	0.6	9 251	82
Georgia [3] Géorgie [3]	12 I 1989	5 400 841	2 562 040	2 838 801	5 417	*4 946	-1.5	69 700	71
India [32] Inde [32]	01 III 2001	1 027 015 247	531 277 078	495 738 169	921 989	1 017 544	1.6	3 287 263	310
Indonesia [33] Indonésie [33]	30 VI 2000	206 264 595	103 417 180	102 847 415	...	...	...	1 904 569	...
Iran (Islamic Rep. of) [1] Iran (Rép. islamique d') [1]	1 X 1996	60 055 488	30 515 159	29 540 329	59 187	*64 530	1.4	1 648 195	39

8

Population by sex, rate of population increase, surface area and density [cont.]
Population selon le sexe, taux d'accroissement de la population, superficie et densité [suite]

Country or area Pays ou zone	Latest census Dernier recensement				Mid-year estimates (thousands) Estimations au milieu de l'année (milliers)		Annual rate of increase Taux d'accrois- sement annuel %	Surface area (km²) Superficie (km²)	Density Densité
	Date	Both sexes Les deux sexes	Men Hommes	Women Femmes	1995	2001	1995-01	2001	2001+
Iraq [34] Iraq [34]	16 X 1997	19 184 543	9 536 570	9 647 973	20 536	24 813	3.2	438 317	57
Israel [1,35] Israël [1,35]	4 XI 1995	5 548 523	2 738 175	2 810 348	5 545[9]	6 439[9]	2.5[9]	22 145	291
Japan Japon	1 X 2000	126 925 843	62 110 764	64 815 079	125 472	127 130	0.2	377 873	336
Jordan [36,37] Jordanie [36,37]	10 XII 1994	4 139 458	2 160 725	1 978 733	...	...		89 342	...
Kazakhstan [3] Kazakhstan [3]	26 II 1999	14 953 126	7 201 785	7 751 341	16 066	*14 831	-1.3	2 724 900	5
Korea, Dem. P. R. Corée, R. p. dém. de	31 XII 1993	21 213 378	10 329 699	10 883 679	...	...		120 538	...
Korea, Republic of [38] Corée, République de [38]	1 XI 2000	46 136 101	23 158 582	22 977 519	45 093	47 343	0.8	99 538	476
Kuwait Koweït	20 IV 1995	1 575 570	913 402	662 168	1 802	2 275	3.9	17 818	128
Kyrgyzstan [3] Kirghizistan [3]	24 III 1999	4 822 938	2 380 465	2 442 473	4 555	4 955	1.4	199 900	25
Lao People's Dem. Rep. Rép. dém. pop. lao	1 III 1985	3 584 803	1 757 115	1 827 688	...	...		236 800	...
Lebanon [39,40] Liban [39,40]	15 X 1989	2 126 325	1 080 015	1 046 310	...	...		10 400	...
Malaysia [41,42] Malaisie [41,42]	5 VII 2000	23 274 690	11 853 432	11 421 258	...	...		329 847	...
Maldives Maldives	31 III 2000	270 101	137 200	132 901	...	...		298	...
Mongolia Mongolie	5 I 2000	2 373 493	1 177 981	1 195 512	2 299	*2 442	1.0	1 566 500	2
Myanmar [3] Myanmar [3]	31 III 1983	35 307 913	17 518 255	17 789 658	...	...		676 578	...
Nepal [1,43] Népal [1,43]	22 VI 2001	23 151 423	11 563 921	11 587 502	...	...		147 181	...
Occupied Palestinian Terr. [44] Terr. palestinien occupé [44]	9 XII 1997	2 601 669	1 322 264	1 279 405	2 483	3 299	4.7	6 020	548
Oman Oman	1 XII 1993	2 018 074	1 178 005	840 069	2 131	*2 478	2.5	309 500	8
Pakistan [45] Pakistan [45]	2 III 1998	130 579 571	67 840 137	62 739 434	122 360	*142 280	2.5	796 095	179
Philippines [1] Philippines [1]	1 V 2000	*76 500 000	...	...	...	...		300 000	...
Qatar Qatar	1 III 1997	522 023	342 459	179 564	...	...		11 000	...
Saudi Arabia Arabie saoudite	27 IX 1992	16 948 388	9 479 973	7 468 415	...	...		2 149 690	...
Singapore [46] Singapour [46]	30 VI 2000	4 017 700	2 061 800	1 955 900	3 526	4 131	2.6	683	6 049
Sri Lanka [47] Sri Lanka [47]	17 VII 2001	*16 864 544	*8 343 964	*8 520 580	18 136	*18 700	0.5	65 610	285
Syrian Arab Republic [48] Rép. arabe syrienne [48]	3 IX 1994	13 782 315	7 048 906	6 733 409	14 153	16 720	2.8	185 180	90
Tajikistan Tadjikistan	20 I 2000	*6 127 000	*3 082 000	*3 045 000	5 836	*6 293	1.3	143 100	44

8

Population by sex, rate of population increase, surface area and density *[cont.]*

Population selon le sexe, taux d'accroissement de la population, superficie et densité *[suite]*

Country or area Pays ou zone	Latest census Dernier recensement Date	Both sexes Les deux sexes	Men Hommes	Women Femmes	Mid-year estimates (thousands) Estimations au milieu de l'année (milliers) 1995	2001	Annual rate of increase Taux d'accrois-sement annuel % 1995-01	Surface area (km²) Superficie (km²) 2001	Density Densité 2001+
Thailand [1] Thaïlande [1]	1 IV 2000	60 617 200	29 850 100	30 767 100	...	...	...	513 115	...
Timor-Leste Timor-Leste	31 X 1990	747 750	386 939	360 811	...	...	...	14 874	...
Turkey Turquie	21 X 1990	56 473 035	28 607 047	27 865 988	61 706	68 610	1.8	774 815	89
Turkmenistan Turkménistan	10 I 1995	4 483 251	2 225 331	2 257 920	...	...	...	488 100	...
United Arab Emirates [49] Emirats arabes unis [49]	11 XII 1995	2 377 453	1 579 743	797 710	...	...	...	83 600	...
Uzbekistan [3] Ouzbékistan [3]	12 I 1989	19 810 077	9 784 156	10 025 921	22 690	*25 068	1.7	447 400	56
Viet Nam Viet Nam	01 IV 1999	76 324 753	37 519 754	38 804 999	...	...	...	331 689	...
Yemen Yémen	16 XII 1994	14 587 807	7 473 540	7 114 267	15 369	*18 863	3.4	527 968	36
Europe · Europe									
Albania Albanie	12 IV 1989	3 182 400	1 638 900	1 543 500	...	...	...	28 748	...
Andorra Andorre	11 XI 1954	5 664	...	...	...	...	...	468	...
Austria [1] Autriche [1]	15 V 2001	8 065 465	3 907 244	4 158 221	8 047	8 130	0.2	83 858	97
Belarus [3] Bélarus [3]	16 II 1999	10 045 237	4 717 621	5 327 616	10 281	*9 973	-0.5	207 600	48
Belgium [1] Belgique [1]	1 III 1991	9 978 681	4 875 982	5 102 699	10 137	*10 287	0.2	30 528	337
Bosnia and Herzegovina [1] Bosnie-Herzégovine [1]	31 III 1991	4 377 033	2 183 795	2 193 238	...	...	...	51 197	...
Bulgaria Bulgarie	11 III 2001	*7 928 901	*3 862 465	*4 066 436	8 406	7 913	-1.0	110 912	71
Channel Islands [3] Iles Anglo-Normandes [3]	29 IV 2001	146 993	71 623	75 370	...	...	...	195	...
Croatia [1] Croatie [1]	31 III 2001	4 437 460	...	...	4 669	*4 437	-0.8	56 538	78
Czech Republic [1] République tchèque [1]	01 III 2001	10 292 933	5 019 381	5 273 552	10 331	10 224	-0.2	78 866	130
Denmark [1,50] Danemark [1,50]	1 I 1998	5 294 860	2 615 669	2 679 191	5 228	*5 359	0.4	43 094	124
Estonia Estonie	31 III 2000	*1 370 500	*631 900	*738 600	1 484	*1 361	-1.4	45 100	30
Faeroe Islands [1] Iles Féroé [1]	22 IX 1977	41 969	21 997	19 972	...	...	...	1 399	...
Finland [1] Finlande [1]	31 XII 2000	5 181 115	2 529 341	2 651 774	5 108	5 188	0.3	338 145	15
France [51] France [51]	08 III 1999	58 520 688	28 419 419	30 101 269	57 844	59 191	0.4	551 500	107
Germany [1,52] Allemagne [1,52]		...	...	...	81 661	*82 348	0.1	357 022	231
F. R. Germany [1] R. f. Allemagne [1]	25 V 1987	61 077 042	29 322 923	31 754 119	...	...	...	248 647	...

8

Population by sex, rate of population increase, surface area and density *[cont.]*

Population selon le sexe, taux d'accroissement de la population, superficie et densité *[suite]*

Country or area Pays ou zone	Latest census Dernier recensement Date	Both sexes Les deux sexes	Men Hommes	Women Femmes	Mid-year estimates (thousands) Estimations au milieu de l'année (milliers) 1995	2001	Annual rate of increase Taux d'accrois-sement annuel % 1995-01	Surface area (km²) Superficie (km²) 2001	Density Densité 2001+
German D. R.(former)[1] R. d. allemande (anc.)[1]	31 XII 1981	16 705 635	7 849 112	8 856 523	...	...	...	108 333	...
Gibraltar[53] Gibraltar[53]	14 X 1991	26 703	13 628	13 075	27	28	0.6	6	4 707
Greece[54,55] Grèce[54,55]	17 III 1991	10 259 900	5 055 408	5 204 492	10 454	*10 020	-0.7	131 957	76
Holy See[56] Saint-Siège[56]	30 IV 1948	890	548	342	...	...	...	...	...
Hungary Hongrie	1 II 2001	10 198 315	4 850 650	5 347 665	10 229	10 188	-0.1	93 032	110
Iceland[1] Islande[1]	1 XII 1970	204 930	103 621	101 309	267	*285	1.1	103 000	3
Ireland Irlande	28 IV 2002	*3 917 336	*1 945 187	*1 972 149	3 601	*3 854	1.1	70 273	55
Isle of Man Ile de Man	29 IV 2001	76 315	37 372	38 943	...	...	...	572	...
Italy[1] Italie[1]	21 X 2001	*56 305 568	*27 260 953	*29 044 615	57 301	*57 948	0.2	301 318	192
Latvia[3] Lettonie[3]	31 III 2000	2 377 383	1 094 964	1 282 419	2 485	2 355	-0.9	64 600	36
Liechtenstein Liechtenstein	2 XII 1980	25 215	...	...	31	*33	1.2	160	207
Lithuania[3] Lituanie[3]	6 IV 2001	3 483 972	1 629 148	1 854 824	3 629	3 481	-0.7	65 300	53
Luxembourg[1] Luxembourg[1]	15 II 2001	*439 539	*216 540	*222 999	410	442	1.3	2 586	171
Malta[57,58,59] Malte[57,58,59]	26 XI 1995	378 132	186 836	191 296	378	395	0.7	316	1 249
Monaco[1] Monaco[1]	23 VII 1990	29 972	14 237	15 735	...	...	...	1	...
Netherlands[1,60] Pays-Bas[1,60]	1 I 1991	15 010 445	7 419 501	7 590 944	15 459	*16 046	0.6	41 526	386
Norway[1] Norvège[1]	3 XI 1990	4 247 546	2 099 881	2 147 665	4 359	4 514	0.6	323 877	14
Poland[61] Pologne[61]	6 XII 1988	37 878 641	18 464 373	19 414 268	38 588	*38 638	...	323 250	120
Portugal[62] Portugal[62]	12 III 2001	*10 355 824	*4 999 964	*5 355 860	9 916	*10 299	0.6	91 982	112
Republic of Moldova[63,64] République de Moldova[63,64]	12 I 1989	4 337 592	2 058 160	2 279 432	4 348	3 631	-3.0	33 851	107
Romania Roumanie	7 I 1992	22 810 035	11 213 763	11 596 272	22 681	22 408	...	238 391	94
Russian Federation Fédération de Russie	9 X 2002	145 537 200	*67 805 700	*77 731 500	147 774	143 954	-0.4	17 075 400	8
San Marino Saint-Marin	30 XI 1976	19 149	9 654	9 495	...	...	...	61	...
Serbia and Montenegro[1,65] Serbie-et-Monténégro[1,65]	31 III 1991	10 394 026	5 157 120	5 236 906	10 547	10 651	0.2	102 173	104
Slovakia[1] Slovaquie[1]	26 V 2001	5 379 455	2 612 515	2 766 940	5 364	5 380	...	49 012	110
Slovenia[1] Slovénie[1]	31 III 2002	*1 948 250	*943 994	*1 004 256	1 988	1 992	...	20 256	98

8

Population by sex, rate of population increase, surface area and density *[cont.]*

Population selon le sexe, taux d'accroissement de la population, superficie et densité *[suite]*

Country or area Pays ou zone	Latest census Dernier recensement				Mid-year estimates (thousands) Estimations au milieu de l'année (milliers)		Annual rate of increase Taux d'accrois-sement annuel %	Surface area (km²) Superficie (km²)	Density Densité
	Date	Both sexes Les deux sexes	Men Hommes	Women Femmes	1995	2001	1995-01	2001	2001+
Spain [64,66] Espagne [64,66]	1 XI 2001	*40 847 371	...	...	39 223	40 266	0.4	505 992	80
Svalbard and Jan Mayen Is [67] Svalbard et îles Jan Mayen [67]	1 XI 1960	3 431	2 545	886	...	...	...	62 422	...
Sweden [1] Suède [1]	1 XI 1990	8 587 353	4 242 351	4 345 002	8 827	8 896	0.1	449 964	20
Switzerland [1] Suisse [1]	5 XII 2000	7 204 055	3 519 698	3 684 357	7 041	7 233	0.4	41 284	175
TFYR of Macedonia [68] L'ex-R.y. Macédoine [68]	20 VI 1994	1 945 932	974 255	971 677	1 963	2 026	...	25 713	79
Ukraine [3] Ukraine [3]	5 XII 2001	48 457 102	22 441 344	26 015 758	51 728	*49 037	-0.9	603 700	81
United Kingdom [69] Royaume-Uni [69]	29 IV 2001	*58 789 194	...	...	58 612	*59 756	0.3	242 900	246
Oceania · Océanie									
American Samoa [1,17] Samoa américaines [1,17]	1 IV 2000	57 291	29 264	28 027	...	...	...	199	...
Australia [1] Australie [1]	30 VI 1996	17 892 423	8 849 224	9 043 199	18 072[9]	19 387[9]	1.2[9]	7 741 220	3
Cook Islands [70] Iles Cook [70]	31 XII 2000	18 027	...	...	19	*18	-1.1	236	77
Fiji Fidji	25 VIII 1996	775 077	393 931	381 146	...	...	...	18 274	...
French Polynesia [71] Polynésie française [71]	3 IX 1996	219 521	113 830	105 691	...	...	...	4 000	...
Guam [1,17] Guam [1,17]	1 IV 2000	154 805	79 181	75 624	...	...	...	549	...
Kiribati [72] Kiribati [72]	7 XI 1995	*77 658	*38 478	*39 180	...	...	...	726	...
Marshall Islands Iles Marshall	15 IX 1999	50 848	26 034	24 814	56	55	-0.3	181	302
Micronesia (Fed. States) [1] Micronésie (Etats féd. de) [1]	18 IX 1994	105 506	53 923	51 583	107	117	1.5	702	167
Nauru Nauru	17 IV 1992	9 919	...	...	...	...	...	21	...
New Caledonia [73] Nouvelle-Calédonie [73]	16 IV 1996	196 836	100 762	96 074	194	*214	1.7	18 575	12
New Zealand [1,74] Nouvelle-Zélande [1,74]	5 III 1996	3 618 303	1 777 464	1 840 839	3 656	*3 850	0.9	270 534	14
Niue Nioué	17 VIII 1997	*2 088	*1 053	*1 035	...	...	...	260	...
Norfolk Island Ile Norfolk	30 VI 1986	2 367	1 170	1 197	...	...	...	36	...
Northern Mariana Islands Iles Mariannes du Nord	1 IV 2000	69 221	31 984	37 237	...	...	...	464	...
Palau Palaos	15 IV 2000	19 129	...	...	17	20	2.2	459	43
Papua New Guinea [75] Papouasie-Nvl-Guinée [75]	9 VII 2000	5 190 786	2 691 744	2 499 042	...	...	...	462 840	...
Pitcairn Pitcairn	31 XII 1991	66	...	...	...	...	...	5	...

8

Population by sex, rate of population increase, surface area and density *[cont.]*

Population selon le sexe, taux d'accroissement de la population, superficie et densité *[suite]*

Country or area Pays ou zone	Latest census Dernier recensement				Mid-year estimates (thousands) Estimations au milieu de l'année (milliers)		Annual rate of increase Taux d'accrois-sement annuel %	Surface area (km²) Superficie (km²)	Density Densité
	Date	Both sexes Les deux sexes	Men Hommes	Women Femmes	1995	2001	1995-01	2001	2001+
Samoa Samoa	5 XI 1991	161 298	...	...	...	...	...	2 831	...
Solomon Islands [76] Iles Salomon [76]	21 XI 1999	409 042	211 381	197 661	...	...	...	28 896	...
Tokelau Tokélaou	11 XII 1991	1 577	...	...	...	...	...	12	...
Tonga Tonga	30 XI 1996	97 784	49 615	48 169	98	101	0.5	650	155
Tuvalu Tuvalu	17 XI 1991	9 043	4 376	4 667	...	...	...	26	...
Vanuatu Vanuatu	16 XI 1999	193 219	95 682	90 996	...	...	...	12 189	...
Wallis and Futuna Islands Iles Wallis et Futuna	3 X 1996	14 166	6 984	7 182	...	...	...	200	...

Source:
United Nations Statistics Division, New York, "Demographic Yearbook 2001" and the demographic statistics database.

Source:
Organisation des Nations Unies, Division de statistique, New York, "Annuaire démographique 2001" et la base de données pour les statistiques démographiques.

+ Population per square kilometre of surface area in 2001. Figures are merely the quotients of population divided by surface area and are not to be considered either as reflecting density in the urban sense or as indicating the supporting power of a territory's land and resources.

+ Nombre d'habitants au kilomètre carré en 2001. Il s'agit simplement du quotient du chiffre de la population divisé par celui de la superficie: il ne faut pas y voir d'indication de la densité au sens urbain du terme ni de l'effectif de population que les terres et les ressources du territoire sont capables de nourrir.

1	De jure population.
2	Including the enclave of Cabinda.
3	Census results for de jure population.
4	Census results have been adjusted for under-enumeration, estimated at 1.4 per cent.
5	Census results, excluding Mayotte.
6	Comprising Bioko (which includes Pagalu) and Rio Muni (which includes Corisco and Elobeys).
7	Census data exclude adjustment for under-enumeration.
8	For Libyan nationals only.
9	Data have been adjusted for under-enumeration, at latest census.
10	Census results have been adjusted for under-enumeration, estimated at 9 per cent.
11	Census results have been adjusted for under-enumeration, estimated at 68 per cent.
12	Comprising the Northern Region (former Saguia el Hamra) and Southern Region (former Rio de Oro).
13	Excluding institutional population.
14	Including Carriacou and other dependencies in the Grenadines.
15	Including dependencies: Marie-Galante, la Désirade, les Saintes, Petite-Terre, St. Barthélemy and French part of St. Martin.
16	De jure population, comprising Bonaire, Curaçao, Saba, St. Eustatius and Dutch part of St. Martin.
17	Including armed forces stationed in the area.
18	Including Bequia and other islands in the Grenadines.
19	Excluding armed forces overseas and civilian citizens absent from

1	Population de droit.
2	Y compris l'enclave de Cabinda.
3	Les résultats du recensement, population de droit.
4	Les résultats du recensement ont été ajustées pour compenser les lacunes du dénombrement, estimées à 1,4 p. 100.
5	Les résultats du recensement, non compris Mayotte.
6	Comprend Bioko (qui comprend Pagalu) et Rio Muni (qui comprend Corisco et Elobeys).
7	Les données de recensement n'ont pas été ajustées pour compenser les lacunes du dénombrement.
8	Pour les nationaux libyens seulement.
9	Les données ont été ajustées pour compenser les lacunes du dénombrement lors du dernier recensement.
10	Les résultats du recensement ont été ajustées pour compenser les lacunes du dénombrement, estimées à 9 p 100.
11	Les résultats du recensement ont été ajustées pour compenser les lacunes du dénombrement, estimées à 6,8 p 100.
12	Comprend la région septentrionale (ancien Saguia-el-Hamra) et la région méridionale (ancien Rio de Oro).
13	Non compris la population dans les institutions.
14	Y compris Carriacou et les autres dépendances du groupe des îles Grenadines.
15	Y compris les dépendances: Marie-Galante, la Désirade, les Saintes, Petite-Terre, Saint-Barthélemy et la partie française de Saint-Martin.
16	Population de droit, comprend Bonaire, Curaçao, Saba, Saint-Eustache et la partie néederlandaise de Saint-Martin.
17	Y compris les militaires en garnison sur le territoire.
18	Y compris Bequia et des autres îles dans les Grenadines.
19	Non compris les militaires à l'étranger, et les civils hors du pays

8

Population by sex, rate of population increase, surface area and density *[cont.]*

Population selon le sexe, taux d'accroissement de la population, superficie et densité *[suite]*

	country for an extended period of time.
20	Data refer to de facto estimates, including persons in remote areas, military personnel outside the country, merchant seamen at sea, civilian seasonal workers outside the country, and other civilians outside the country, and excluding nomads, foreign military, civilian aliens temporarily in the country, transients on ships and Indian jungle population.
21	Excluding nomadic Indian tribes.
22	A dispute exists between the governments of Argentina and the United Kingdom of Great Britain and Northern Ireland concerning sovereignty over the Falkland Islands (Malvinas).
23	Excluding dependencies, of which South Georgia (area 3 755 km2) had an estimated population of 499 in 1964 (494 males, 5 females). The other dependencies namely, the South Sandwich group (surface area 337 km2) and a number of smaller islands, are presumed to be uninhabited.
24	Excluding Indian jungle population.
25	Census results, excluding nomad population.
26	Excluding foreign diplomatic personnel and their dependants.
27	For statistical purposes, the data for China do not include those for the Hong Kong Special Administrative Region (Hong Kong SAR), Macao Special Administrative Region (Macao SAR) and Taiwan province of China.
28	For the civilian population of 31 provinces, municipalities and autonomous regions.
29	Data refer to Hong Kong resident population at the census moment, which covers usual residents and mobile residents Usual residents refer to two categories of people: (1) Hong Kong permanent residents who had stayed in Hong Kong for at least three months during the six months before or for at least three months during the six months after the census moment, regardless of whether they were in Hong Kong or not at the census moment; and (2) Hong Kong non-permanent residents who were in Hong Kong at the census moment Mobile Residents, they are Hong Kong permanent residents who had stayed in Hong Kong for at least one month but less than three months during the six months before or for at least one month but less than three months during the six months after the census moment, regardless of whether they were in Hong Kong or not at the census moment.
30	After 1996, population is de jure.
31	For government controlled areas.
32	Including data for the Indian-held part of Jammu and Kashmir, the final status of which has not yet been determined.
33	For the 2000 census, including estimated population of 459 557 persons in urban and 1 857 659 persons in rural areas, and of non-response of 566 403 persons in urban and 1 717 578 persons in rural areas. Also including 421 399 non permanent residence (the homeless, the crew of ships carrying national flag, boat/floating house people, remote located tribesmen and refugees).
34	For the 1997 population census, data exclude population in three autonomous provinces in the north of the country.
35	Including data for East Jerusalem and Israeli residents in certain other territories under occupation by Israeli military forces since June 1967.
36	Including military and diplomatic personnel and their families abroad, numbering 933 at 1961 census, but excluding foreign military and diplomatic personnel and their families in the country, numbering 389 at 1961 census. Also including registered Palestinian refugees numbering 722 687 at 31 May 1967.
37	Census results, excluding data for Jordanian territory under

	pendant une période prolongée.
20	Les données se rapportent aux évaluations de fait, y compris des personnes dans des régions éloignées, au personel militaire en dehors du pays, aux marins marchands aux ouvriers saisonniers civils de couture en dehors du pays, et à d'autres civils en dehors du pays, et non compris les nomades, les militaires étrangers, les étrangers civils temporairement dans le pays, les transiteurs sur des bateaux et les Indiens de la jungle.
21	Non compris les tribus d'Indiens nomades.
22	La sourveraineté sur les îles Falkland (Malvinas) fait l'objet d'un différend entre le Gouvernement argentin et le Gouvernement du Royaume-Uni de Grande-Bretagne et d'Irlande du Nord.
23	Non compris les dépendances, parmi lesquelles figure la Georgie du Sug (3 755 km2) avec une population estimée à 499 personnes en 1964 (494 du sexe masculin et 5 du sexe féminin). Les autres dépendances, c'est-à-dire le groupe des Sandwich de Sud (superficie: 337 km2) et certaines petites-îles, sont présumées inhabitées.
24	Non compris les Indiens de la jungle.
25	Les résultats du recensement, non compris les nomades.
26	Non compris le personnel diplomatique étranger et les membres de leur famille les accompagnant.
27	Pour la présentation des statistiques, les données pour Chine ne comprennent pas la Région Administrative Spéciale de Hong Kong (Hong Kong RAS), la Région Administrative Spéciale de Macao (Macao RAS), et la province chinoise de Taiwan.
28	Pour la population civile seulement de 31 provinces, municipalités et régions autonomes.
29	Les données se rapportent à la population résidente à Hong Kong au moment du recensement Cette population est composée des résidants habituels et des résidants mobiles La population résidente est partagée en deux catégories: (1) les résidents permanents qui ont habité à Hong Kong au moins trois mois pendant les six mois précédents ou les six mois suivants le recensement; (2) les habitants non-permanents de Hong Kong qui étaient à Hong Kong au moment du recensement La population mobile se rapporte aux résidents permanents de Hong Kong qui ont habité à Hong Kong pendant les six mois après le recensement pour une période comprise entre un mois et trois mois, indépendamment du fait qu'ils étaient à Hong Kong au moment du recensement au pays.
30	Après 1996, la population est de droit.
31	Pour les zones contrôlées par le Gouvernement.
32	Y compris les données pour la partie du Jammu et du Cachemire occupée par l'Inde dont le statut définitif n'a pas encore été déterminé.
33	Pour le recensement de l'année 2000, y compris l'estimation de 459 557 personnes dans les zones urbaines et de 1 857 659 personnes dans les zones rurales, aussi que l'estimation de 566 403 personnes qui non pas répondu dans les zones urbaines et de 1 717 578 personnes dans les zones rurales. Y compris 421 399 résidants non permanents (les sans abri, l'équipage des bateaux portant le drapeau national, les habitants des embarcations ou des maisons flottantes, les habitants des tribus isolées et les réfugiés).
34	Pour le recensement de 1997, la population des trois provinces autonomes dans le nord du pays est exclue.
35	Y compris les données pour Jérusalem-Est et les résidents israéliens dans certains autres territoires occupés depuis 1967 par les forces armées israéliennes.
36	Y compris les militaires et le personnel diplomatique à l'étranger et les membres de leur famille les accompagnant au nombre de 933 au recensement de 1961, mais non compris les militaires et le personnel diplomatique étranger en poste dans le pays et les membres de leur famille les accompagnant au nombre de 389 au recensement de 1961. Y compris également les réfugiés de Palestine immatriculés, au nombre de 722 687 au 31 mai 1967.
37	Les résultats du recensement, non compris les données pour le

8

Population by sex, rate of population increase, surface area and density *[cont.]*

Population selon le sexe, taux d'accroissement de la population, superficie et densité *[suite]*

	occupation since June 1967 by Israeli military forces.	territoire jordanien occupé depuis juin 1967 par les forces armées israéliennes.
38	Including diplomats and their families abroad, but excluding foreign diplomats, foreign military personnal, and their families in the country.	38	Y compris le personnel diplomatique et les membres de leurs familles à l'étranger, mais sans tenir compte du personnel diplomatique et militaire étranger et des membres de leurs familles.
39	Based on results of a sample survey.	39	D'après les résultats d'une enquête par sondage.
40	Excluding Palestinian refugees in camps.	40	Non compris les réfugiés de Palestine dans les camps.
41	Excluding Malaysian citizens arriving by land.	41	Non compris les arrivées de malaysiens par voie terrestre.
42	Data have been adjusted for under-enumeration, at 2000 census.	42	Les données ont été ajustées pour compenser les lacunes du dénombrement lors du recensement de 2000.
43	Data including estimated population from household listing from Village Development Committees and Wards which could not be enumerated at the time of census.	43	Les données incluent la population estimée par les listes des ménages des comités de développement des villages et des circonscriptions qui n'ont pas pu être énumérée au moment du recensement.
44	Total population does not include palestinian population living in those parts of Jerusalem governorate which were annexed by Israel in 1967, amounting to 210,209 persons. Likewise, the result does not include the estimates of not enumerated population based on the findings of the post enumeration study, i.e. 83,805 persons.	44	Les données relatives à la population totale ne comprennent pas la population palestinienne -équivalent à 210 209 personnes - habitant dans les territoires du gouvernorat de Jérusalem qui ont été annexés par Israël en 1967 Egalement, les données ne tiennent pas compte des estimations de la population calculée sur la base des résultats de l'enquête postcensitaire, équivalent à 83 805 personnes.
45	Excluding data for Jammu and Kashmir, the final status of which has not yet been determined, Junagardh, Manavadar, Gilgit and Baltistan.	45	Non compris les données pour le Jammu et Cachemire dont le statut définitif n'a pas encore été déterminé, le Junagardh, le Manavadar, le Gilgit et le Baltistan.
46	Census results, excluding transients afloat and non-locally domiciled military and civilian services personnel and their dependants and visitors.	46	Les résultats du recensment, non compris les personnes de passage à bord de navires ni les militaires et agents civils non-résidents et les membres de leur famille les accompagnant et visiteurs.
47	The Population and Housing Census 2001 did not cover the whole area of the country due to the security problems; the Census was complete in 18 districts only; in three districts it was not possible to conduct it; and in four districts it was partially conducted.	47	Le recensement de la population et de l'habitat en 2001 n' pas couvert la totalité du pays pour les problèmes de sécurité ; le recensement à été complété seulement en 18 districts ; dans 3 districts ça n'a pas été possible de conduire le recensement et dans 4 districts il a été partialement conduit.
48	Including Palestinian refugees.	48	Y compris les réfugiés de Palestine.
49	Comprising 7 sheikdoms of Abu Dhabi, Dubai, Sharjah, Ajaman, Umm al Qaiwain, Ras al Khaimah and Fujairah, and the area lying within the modified Riyadh line as announced in October 1955.	49	Comprend les sept cheikhats de Abou Dhabi, Dabai, Ghârdja, Adjmân, Oumm-al-Quiwaïn, Ras al Khaïma et Foudjaïra, ainsi que la zone délimitée par la ligne de Riad modifiée comme il a été annoncé en octobre 1955.
50	Excluding the Faeroe Islands and Greenland.	50	Non compris les îles Féroé et Groenland.
51	Excluding Overseas Departments, namely French Guiana, Guadeloupe, Martinique and Reunion, shown separately. De jure population but excluding diplomatic personnel outside country and including members of alien armed forces not living in military camps and foreign diplomatic personnel not living in embassies or consulates.	51	Non compris les départements d'outre-mer, c'est-à-dire la Guyane française, la Guadeloupe, la Martinique et la Réunion, qui font l'objet de rubriques distinctes. Population de droit, non compris le personnel diplomatique hors du pays et y compris les militaires étrangers ne vivant pas dans des comps militaires et le personnel diplomatique étranger ne vivant pas dans les ambassades ou les consulats.
52	All data shown pertaining to Germany prior to 3 October 1990 are indicated separately for the Federal Republic of Germany and the former German Democratic Republic based on their respective territories at the time indicated.	52	Toutes les données se rapportant à l'Allemagne avant le 3 octobre 1990 figurent dans deux rubriques séparées basées sur les territoires respectifs de la République fédérale de l'Allemagne et l'ancienne République démocratique allemande selon la période.
53	Excluding armed forces.	53	Non compris les militaires.
54	Mid-year population excludes armed forces stationed outside the country, but includes alien armed forces stationed in the area.	54	Les estimations au millieu de l'année non compris les militaires en garnison hors du pays, mais y compris les militaires étrangers en garnison sur le territoire.
55	Census data including armed forces stationed outside the country, but excluding alien armed forces stationed in the area.	55	Les données de recensement y compris les militaires hors du pays, mais non compris les militaires étrangers en garnison sur le territoire.
56	Data refer to the Vatican City State.	56	Les données se réfèrent à la Cité du Vatican.
57	Maltese population only.	57	Population Maltaise seulement.
58	Including work and resident permit holders and foreigners residing in Malta.	58	Y compris les personnes qui ont un permis de travail ou de résidence et les étrangers habitant à Malte.
59	Including Gozo and Comino Islands.	59	Y compris les îles de Gozo et de Comino.
60	Census results, based on compilation of continuous accounting and sample surveys.	60	Les résultats du recensement, d'aprés les résultats des dénombrements et enquêtes par sondage continue.
61	Excluding civilian aliens within country, but including civilian nationals temporarily outside country.	61	Non compris les civils étrangers dans le pays, mais y compris les civils nationaux temporairement hors du pays.
62	Including the Azores and Madeira Islands.	62	Y compris les Açores et Madère.
63	Data do not include information for Transnistria and the municipality of Bender.	63	Les données ne tiennent pas compte de l'information sur la Transnistria et la municipalité de Bender.
64	Mid-year estimates for de jure population.	64	Les estimations sont établies au milieu de l'année et se rapportent à la population de droit.

8

Population by sex, rate of population increase, surface area and density *[cont.]*

Population selon le sexe, taux d'accroissement de la population, superficie et densité *[suite]*

65	Beginning with 1998, estimates of Kosovo and Metohia computed on the basis of natural increases from year 1997.	65	A partir du 1998, les estimations pour le Kosovo et la Metohia ont été calculées sur la base des incréments naturelles depuis 1997.
66	Including the Balearic and Canary Islands, and Alhucemas, Ceuta, Chafarinas, Melilla and Penon de Vélez de la Gomera.	66	Y compris les Baléares et les Canaries, Al Hoceima, Ceuta, les îles Zaffarines, Melilla et Penon de Vélez de la Gomera.
67	Inhabited only during the winter season. Census data are for total population while estimates refer to Norwegian population only. Included also in the de jure population of Norway.	67	N'est habitée pendant la saison d"hiver. Les données de recensement se rapportent à la population totale, mais les estimations ne concernent que la population norvégienne, comprise également dans la population de droit de la Norvège.
68	For 2001, de jure population.	68	Pour 2001, population de droit.
69	Excluding Channel Islands and Isle of Man, shown separately.	69	Non compris les îles Anglo-Normandes et l'île de Man, qui font l'objet de rubriques distinctes.
70	Excluding Niue, shown separately, which is part of Cook Islands, but because of remoteness is administered separately.	70	Non compris Nioué, qui fait l'objet d'une rubrique distincte et qui fait partie des îles Cook, mais qui, en raison de son éloignement, est administrée séparément.
71	Comprising Austral, Gambier, Marquesas, Rapa, Society and Tuamotu Islands.	71	Comprend les îles Australes, Gambier, Marquises, Rapa, de la Societé et Tuamotou.
72	Including Christmas, Fanning, Ocean and Washington Islands.	72	Y compris les îles Christmas, Fanning, Océan et Washington.
73	Including the islands of Huon, Chesterfield, Loyalty, Walpole and Belep Archipelago.	73	Y compris les îles Huon, Chesterfield, Loyauté et Walpole, et l'archipel Belep.
74	Including Campbell and Kermadec Islands (population 20 in 1961, surface area 148 km2) as well as Antipodes, Auckland, Bounty, Snares, Solander and Three Kings island, all of which are uninhabited.	74	Y compris les îles Campbell et Kermadec (20 habitants en 1961, superficie: 148 km2) ainsi que les îles Antipodes, Auckland, Bounty, Snares, Solander et Three Kings, qui sont toutes inhabitées.
75	Comprising eastern part of New Guinea, the Bismarck Archipelago, Bougainville and Buka of Solomon Islands group and about 600 smaller islands.	75	Comprend l'est de la Nouvelle-Guinée, l'archipel Bismarck, Bougainville et Buka (ces deux dernières du groupe des Salomon) et environ 600 îlots.
76	Comprising the Solomon Islands group (except Bougainville and Buka which are included with Papua New Guinea shown separately), Ontong, Java, Rennel and Santa Cruz Islands.	76	Comprend les îles Salomon (à l'exception de Bougainville et de Buka dont la population est comprise dans celle de Papouasie-Nouvelle Guinée qui font l'objet d'une rubrique distincte), ainsi que les îles Ontong, Java, Rennel et Santa Cruz.

Technical notes, table 8

Table 8 is based on detailed data on population and its growth and distribution published in the United Nations *Demographic Yearbook* [22], which also provides a comprehensive description of methods of evaluation and limitations of the data.

Unless otherwise indicated, figures refer to de facto (present-in-area) population for the present territory; surface area estimates include inland waters.

Notes techniques, tableau 8

Le *tableau 8* est fondé sur des données détaillées sur la population, sa croissance et sa distribution, publiées dans l'*Annuaire démographique* des Nations Unies [22], qui offre également une description complète des méthodes d'évaluation et une indication des limites des données.

Sauf indication contraire, les chiffres se rapportent à la population effectivement présente sur le territoire tel qu'il est actuellement défini; les estimations de superficie comprennent les étendues d'eau intérieures.

9

Education at the primary, secondary and tertiary levels
Number of students enrolled and percentage female
Enseignement primaire, secondaire et supérieur
Nombre d'étudiants inscrits et étudiantes feminines en pourcentage

Country or area Pays ou zone	Year Année	Primary education Enseignement primaire		Secondary education Enseignement secondaire		Tertiary education Enseignement supérieur	
		Total	% F	Total	% F	Total	% F
Africa · Afrique							
Algeria	1998	4 778 870	46.65	2 808 675	49.69	456 358[1]	...
Algérie	1999	4 843 313	46.76	2 817 710	50.58	...	...
	2000	4 720 950	46.82	2 991 232	50.70	...	...
	2001	4 691 870	46.98	3 157 134	50.74	...	...
Angola	1998	1 342 116	45.58	291 708	...	8 337	41.08
Angola	1999	1 057 182[1]	46.38[1]	300 480	45.53[1]	7 845	39.01
	2000	...	...	354 984	45.34	...	...
	2001	...	...	413 695	44.18	...	...
Benin	1998	872 217	39.28	213 474	31.36	16 284	20.55
Bénin	1999	932 424	40.18	229 228	31.17	18 753	19.83
	2000	1 054 936	40.56	256 744[1]	31.81[1]	...	...
	2001	1 152 798	41.26	287 288[1]	31.80[1]	...	...
Botswana	1998	321 271	49.62	147 525	52.13	5 532	44.03
Botswana	1999	322 478	49.72	153 635	51.76	6 332	42.39
	2000	324 283	49.68	156 289	51.39	7 651	47.01
	2001	329 451	49.63	157 021	51.22	8 372	44.84
Burkina Faso	1998	816 393	40.43	173 205	37.54	...	...
Burkina Faso	1999	852 160	40.82	189 689	38.95	...	...
	2000	901 321	41.28	199 278	39.15	...	...
	2001	927 283[1]	41.28[1]	204 847[1]	39.15	15 535	25.40
Burundi	1998	561 756[1]	44.94[1]	73 115[1]	45.80[1]	5 037	29.54
Burundi	1999	710 364[2]	44.47[2]	87 110[1]	44.92[1]	6 132	26.79
	2000	750 589	44.40	113 427[1]	43.80[1]	6 289	27.22
	2001	817 223	43.98	122 469[1]	42.27[1]	10 546	30.45
Cameroon	1998	2 133 707	44.87	626 053[1]	45.00[1]	66 902	...
Cameroun	1999	2 237 083	45.74	...	...	65 697[1]	...
	2000[3]	2 689 052	46.16	...	...	68 495	...
	2001	2 741 627[2]	45.93[2]	835 791[1]	44.77[1]	77 707	38.78
Cape Verde	1998	92 023	48.71	40 486[1]	...	...	...
Cap-Vert	1999	91 636	49.01	...	...	...	...
	2000	90 640	48.99	45 545[1]	...	...	...
	2001	89 809	48.94	46 119	50.96	1 698	46.82
Central African Rep.	1998	...	...	...	...	6 229	16.09
Rép. centrafricaine	1999	...	...	...	...	6 323	16.24
	2000[2]	458 585	40.91	...	...	...	...
	2001[2]	410 562	40.41	...	...	...	...
Chad	1998	839 932	36.74	123 408	20.69	...	...
Tchad	1999	913 547	37.79	137 269	22.10	5 901	15.00
	2000	984 224	38.72	137 269[1]	22.10[1]	...	...
	2001[1]	1 016 267	38.71	...	...	...	...
Comoros	1998	82 789	45.34	28 718	44.33	649	42.68
Comores	1999	93 421	45.00[1]	28 122[1]	44.50[1]	714	41.88
	2000[1]	97 706	44.60	...	...	...	...
	2001	104 274	44.33	33 874	45.28	...	...
Congo	1998	276 451	48.76	...	...	...	...
Congo	1999	418 707	47.77	...	...	15 629	23.78
	2000	500 921	48.24	197 184[1]	38.88[1]	13 403	11.93
	2001	525 093	48.30	182 699[1]	41.66[1]	12 164	15.81
Côte d'Ivoire	1998	1 910 820	42.57	591 549[1]	34.92	96 681	26.27
Côte d'Ivoire	1999	1 943 501	42.70	619 969[1]	35.08	...	...
	2000	2 046 861	43.22	...	...	...	...
	2001	2 116 223	42.34	...	...	...	...
Dem. Rep. of the Congo Rép. dém. du Congo	1998	4 022 411	47.38	...	...	60 341[1]	...

9

Education at the primary, secondary and tertiary levels
Number of students enrolled and percentage female *[cont.]*
Enseignement primaire, secondaire et supérieur
Nombre d'étudiants inscrits et étudiantes feminines en pourcentage *[suite]*

Country or area Pays ou zone	Year Année	Primary education Enseignement primaire		Secondary education Enseignement secondaire		Tertiary education Enseignement supérieur	
		Total	% F	Total	% F	Total	% F
Djibouti	1998	38 194	41.17	15 511	41.56	175	50.86
Djibouti	1999	38 106	42.00	15 812	39.29	190[1]	46.84
	2000	42 692	42.77	18 808	38.06	496	41.73
	2001	44 321	42.91	20 516	37.92	728	44.51
Egypt[1]	1998	8 086 230	46.69	7 671 031	46.75	2 447 088	...
Egypte[1]	1999	7 947 488	46.91	8 028 170	47.05	...	...
	2000	7 856 340	47.16	8 323 597	47.27	...	...
	2001[4]	7 855 433	47.37	8 644 567	47.08	...	...
Equatorial Guinea	1998	74 940	47.60[1]	...	...	...	...
Guinée équatoriale	1999	73 307	48.80[1]	20 679[1]	37.57[1]	1 003	30.31
	2000	78 477	48.82	19 809[1]	...	...	...
	2001	78 390	47.57	21 173[1]	36.41[1]	...	...
Eritrea	1998	261 963	45.19	115 393	40.89	3 994	13.52
Erythrée	1999	295 941	44.92	135 209	41.14	4 135	14.32
	2000	298 691	44.98	142 124	41.55	5 505	13.41
	2001	330 278	44.27	152 727	39.33	5 507	13.40
Ethiopia	1998	5 167 582	37.61	1 059 753	40.25	52 305	18.68
Ethiopie	1999	5 847 259	39.20	1 194 792	39.99	67 732	21.68
	2000	6 650 841	40.57	1 495 445	39.75	87 431	21.40
	2001	7 213 043	41.37	1 734 131	38.32	101 829	26.41
Gabon	1998	265 244	49.66	86 543	46.33	7 473	35.69
Gabon	1999	270 549[1]	49.66[1]	89 572[1]	46.33	...	...
	2000	265 714	49.58	100 718[1]	...	...	...
	2001	281 871	49.45	105 191[1]	...	...	...
Gambia	1998	150 399	45.91	47 106	39.80	...	...
Gambie	1999	154 664	45.90	53 048	39.75	...	...
	2000	156 839	47.60	56 582	41.40	...	...
	2001	160 949[1]	47.62[1]	58 549[1]	41.42	...	...
Ghana	1998	2 377 444	46.95	1 024 135	43.64	...	...
Ghana	1999	2 560 886	47.17	1 056 351[1]	44.05	54 658	24.97
	2000	2 477 990	47.43	1 029 104	44.69	64 098	28.52
	2001	2 586 434	47.45	1 107 461[1]	44.90	68 389	27.77
Guinea	1998	726 561	38.08	171 934[1]	26.02	...	...
Guinée	1999	790 497	39.82	...	...	...	...
	2000	853 623	41.05	...	...	...	...
	2001	997 645	42.05	...	...	...	...
Guinea-Bissau Guinée-Bissau	1999	150 041	40.25	25 736	35.44	463	15.55
Kenya	1998	5 480 689	49.44	1 156 289[1]	47.26	...	...
Kenya	1999	5 415 840	49.25	1 195 593	47.43	89 016	35.12
	2000	5 699 956	49.49	1 251 205[1]	47.61	95 104	34.67
	2001	5 828 463	49.35	1 331 068	47.32	98 607[1]	34.67
Lesotho	1998	369 515	51.79	72 235	58.38	4 046	63.74
Lesotho	1999	365 251	51.63	73 620	57.43	4 470[1]	61.83
	2000[3]	410 745	50.64	74 133	54.10	4 976	63.46
	2001	415 007	50.20	79 536	55.78	5 005	58.04
Liberia	1998	395 611	42.38	113 878	38.95	...	...
Libéria	1999	496 253	41.92	136 590	40.43	44 107	42.78
Libyan Arab Jamah.	1998	821 775	48.50	...	...	308 474	48.62
Jamah. arabe libyenne	1999	794 293[1]	48.47[1]	...	...	290 060	48.62
	2000	766 087	49.23	...	...	287 172[1]	48.27
	2001	750 204	48.81	824 538	50.51	359 146	51.41
Madagascar	1998	2 012 416	49.10	346 941[1]	48.90	31 013	45.75
Madagascar	1999	2 208 321	49.00	...	...	32 156	46.21
	2000	2 307 500	49.03	...	...	31 386	45.46
	2001	2 407 644	49.03	...	...	32 593	45.36

9

Education at the primary, secondary and tertiary levels
Number of students enrolled and percentage female *[cont.]*
Enseignement primaire, secondaire et supérieur
Nombre d'étudiants inscrits et étudiantes feminines en pourcentage *[suite]*

Country or area Pays ou zone	Year Année	Primary education Enseignement primaire		Secondary education Enseignement secondaire		Tertiary education Enseignement supérieur	
		Total	% F	Total	% F	Total	% F
Malawi	1998	2 525 323	48.83[1]	519 388	41.07	3 179	27.56
Malawi	1999	2 581 698	48.73	556 322	41.23	...	...
	2000	2 694 645	48.86	597 276	41.17	...	...
	2001	2 845 836	48.90	518 251	43.60	...	...
Mali	1998	958 935	41.00	217 700	34.18	18 662	...
Mali	1999	1 016 575	42.02	...	...	...	...
	2000	1 127 360	41.66	...	...	...	...
	2001	1 227 267	42.34	...	...	27 464	...
Mauritania	1998	346 222	48.39	63 482[1]	42.03	12 912	...
Mauritanie	1999	355 822	48.39	65 606	41.66	...	...
	2000	360 677	48.18	76 658	42.85	9 033	16.79
	2001	375 695	48.77	78 730	43.12	8 173	21.25
Mauritius	1998	130 505	49.40	101 517	49.63	7 559	46.14
Maurice	1999	133 489	49.39	104 070	48.92	8 256	44.99
	2000	135 237	49.19	105 432	47.80	12 481	56.95
	2001	134 085	49.28	108 792	48.43	12 602	55.82
Morocco	1998	3 461 940	43.97	1 469 794	43.36	273 183	41.79
Maroc	1999	3 669 605	44.81	1 541 100	43.67	276 375	42.30
	2000	3 842 000	45.63	1 608 279[1]	43.83	310 258	43.72
	2001	4 029 112	46.15	...	...	315 343[1]	43.74
Mozambique	1998	1 968 234[1]	42.34[1]	270 121[1]	40.40	...	...
Mozambique	1999	2 108 790	42.77	303 323	39.63	9 303[1]	44.18
	2000	2 315 547	43.35	352 083	39.23	...	...
	2001	2 555 975	43.97	402 499	39.28	...	...
Namibia	1998	386 647	50.04	110 076	53.48	11 209	53.27
Namibie	1999	383 267	50.10	116 131	52.74	...	...
	2000	389 434	50.02	124 196	52.84	...	...
	2001	398 381	49.97	130 577	53.15	13 339	45.63
Niger	1998	529 806	39.18	104 933	37.97	...	...
Niger	1999	579 486	39.35	106 182[1]	38.69	...	...
	2000	656 589	39.56	108 033[1]	38.87	13 400	24.81
	2001	760 987	39.76	112 033	38.46	13 854[1]	24.82
Nigeria [1]	1998	16 045 567	42.46	...	...	...	...
Nigéria [1]	1999	17 907 010	43.83	...	...	...	...
	2000	19 158 439	43.91	...	...	...	...
	2001	19 385 177	43.60	...	...	...	...
Rwanda	1998	1 288 669	49.96	91 219	49.63	5 678	...
Rwanda	1999	1 431 657	49.58	129 620[1]	49.11	...	...
	2000	1 475 572	50.00	161 086	49.90	12 802	33.66
	2001	1 534 510	50.26	166 784[1]	49.90	13 562[1]	33.66
Sao Tome and Principe	1998	23 769	48.65	...	...	...	...
Sao Tomé-et-Principe	2000	27 795[1]	47.94[1]	...	...	181	35.91
	2001	28 780[1]	48.29[1]	7 367[1]	45.41	183[1]	36.07
Senegal	1998	1 034 065	45.90[1]	239 223[1]	38.94	29 303	...
Sénégal	1999	1 107 712	46.00	251 456[1]	39.29	...	...
	2000	1 159 721	46.55	262 738[1]	39.56	...	...
	2001	1 197 081	47.08	291 318[1]	39.96	...	...
Seychelles	1998	9 738	49.20	8 027	48.97	...	...
Seychelles	1999	9 931	49.32	7 788	50.14	...	...
	2000	10 026	49.27	7 742	50.56	...	...
	2001	9 782	49.01	7 514	50.75	...	...
Sierra Leone	1999	442 915	...	...	...	...	...
Sierra Leone	2000	554 308	41.56	155 567	41.60	8 795	28.78
	2001	...	...	...	...	9 041[1]	28.78
South Africa	1998	7 997 945[2]	49.19[2]	4 244 415[2]	53.05	633 918	53.77
Afrique du Sud	1999	7 935 221	49.10	4 239 197	52.88	632 911	53.86
	2000	7 444 802	48.57	4 141 946	52.41	644 763	55.31
	2001	7 413 414	48.88	4 229 209[1]	52.24	658 588	53.47

9
Education at the primary, secondary and tertiary levels
Number of students enrolled and percentage female *[cont.]*
Enseignement primaire, secondaire et supérieur
Nombre d'étudiants inscrits et étudiantes feminines en pourcentage *[suite]*

Country or area Pays ou zone	Year Année	Primary education Enseignement primaire		Secondary education Enseignement secondaire		Tertiary education Enseignement supérieur	
		Total	% F	Total	% F	Total	% F
Sudan	1998	2 512 824[1]	45.16[1]	964 518[1]	...	200 538	47.20
Soudan	1999	2 566 503	45.14	979 514	...	...	...
	2000	2 799 783	45.04	1 113 062	46.35	...	...
	2001	2 889 062	45.09	1 141 199	...	...	...
Swaziland	1998	212 052	48.66	60 830	50.30	4 880	47.89
Swaziland	1999	213 041	48.65	61 551	50.08	4 738	48.52
	2000	213 986	48.39	60 253	50.20	4 761[1]	46.90
	2001	212 064	48.61	61 277	50.22	5 193	54.59
Togo	1998	953 886	43.08	231 948	28.62	15 028	17.40
Togo	1999	914 919	43.82	260 877[1]	30.52	15 171	16.90
	2000	945 103	44.28	...	...	...	...
	2001	977 534	44.89	...	...	...	...
Tunisia	1998	1 442 904	47.38	1 058 877	49.26	157 479[1]	48.31
Tunisie	1999	1 413 795	47.43	1 087 818	49.94	180 044	...
	2000	1 373 904	47.60	1 143 082	50.19	207 388[1]	48.15
	2001[4]	1 325 707	47.62	1 169 368	49.86	226 102[1]	...
Uganda	1998	6 591 429	47.40	465 605[1]	39.16	40 591	34.50
Ouganda	1999	6 288 239	47.49	...	...	55 767	33.85
	2000	6 559 013	48.23	546 974	43.38	62 586	34.47
	2001	6 900 916	48.88	570 520[1]	43.35	71 544[1]	34.47
United Rep. of Tanzania	1998	4 042 568	49.70	249 784[1]	45.11	18 867	21.04
Rép.-Unie de Tanzanie	1999	4 189 816	49.89	271 146[1]	44.82	...	...
	2000	4 328 410	50.13	...	...	21 960	23.92
	2001	4 845 185	49.30	...	...	...	...
Zambia	1998	1 557 257	47.93	225 777	43.25	22 701	31.63
Zambie	1999	1 555 707	47.79	237 307	43.40	23 155[1]	31.63
	2000	1 589 544	48.08	276 301	44.52	24 553[1]	31.63
	2001	1 625 647	48.18	297 165	44.32	...	...
Zimbabwe	1999	2 460 323	49.13	834 880	46.93	42 775[1]	...
Zimbabwe	2000	2 460 669	49.12	844 183	46.81	48 894[1]	37.42
	2001[4]	2 534 796	49.21	866 171	47.01	59 582[1]	36.69
America, North · Amérique du Nord							
Anguilla	1998	1 569	50.22	1 012	52.67	...	...
Anguilla	1999	1 539	50.29	1 130	50.80	...	...
	2000	1 489	48.89	1 096	51.00	...	...
	2001	1 427	48.98	1 098	50.64	...	...
Antigua and Barbuda Antigua-et-Barbuda	1999	13 025	62.03	5 276	71.66	...	...
Aruba	1998	9 096	48.86	6 159	50.72	1 446	53.94
Aruba	1999	9 263	48.60	6 178	50.50	1 578	60.65
	2000	9 436	48.64	6 428	51.06	1 628	60.57
	2001	9 840	48.24	6 757	51.49	1 592	60.43
Bahamas Bahamas	2001	34 153	49.52	31 703	50.12	...	...
Barbados	1998	28 383	49.08	21 841[1]	50.64[1]	6 915	69.21
Barbade	1999	24 476	48.90	21 016	50.26	8 078[1]	72.05[1]
	2000	24 225	49.12	20 866	49.42	7 539	71.36
	2001	23 394	49.22	20 872	49.43	...	...
Belize	1998	44 180	48.47	21 659	51.24	...	...
Belize	1999	44 788	48.25	23 235	50.87	...	...
	2000	45 246	48.48	24 331	51.23	...	...
Bermuda	2000	4 959	49.65	4 566	51.12	1 942	...
Bermudes	2001	4 910	50.26	4 565	51.48	1 960	55.10
British Virgin Islands	1998	2 757	48.97	1 511	46.79	...	...
Iles Vierges britanniques	1999	2 783[1]	50.31[1]	1 556	49.61	...	...
	2000	2 775	49.66[1]	1 519	50.76	...	...
	2001	2 831	48.39	1 593	50.47	758	69.00

9

Education at the primary, secondary and tertiary levels
Number of students enrolled and percentage female *[cont.]*
Enseignement primaire, secondaire et supérieur
Nombre d'étudiants inscrits et étudiantes feminines en pourcentage *[suite]*

Country or area Pays ou zone	Year Année	Primary education Enseignement primaire		Secondary education Enseignement secondaire		Tertiary education Enseignement supérieur	
		Total	% F	Total	% F	Total	% F
Canada Canada	1998	2 403 709	48.76	2 564 963	48.51	1 192 570	55.65
	1999	2 428 620	48.83	...	...	1 220 651	55.98
	2000	2 456 436	48.83	2 621 457	48.56	1 212 161	56.01
Cayman Islands Iles Caïmanes	1998	3 231	46.83	2 151	48.40	373[1]	73.73
	1999	3 435	49.87	2 342	49.23	380[1]	73.68
	2000	3 549	49.03	2 336	48.46	390	74.62
	2001	3 579	49.37	2 341	50.45	...	...
Costa Rica Costa Rica	1998	...	...	...	...	57 580[1]	52.94
	1999	552 280	48.11	212 945	51.55	58 761	52.78
	2000	551 465	48.13	255 643	50.81	61 654	53.40
	2001	552 302	48.50	287 309	49.28	79 182	52.69
Cuba Cuba	1998	1 074 097	47.82	739 980	50.33	156 224[2]	...
	1999	1 045 578	47.74	789 927	49.92	158 810	53.46
	2000	1 006 888	47.74	836 642	50.01	173 904[2]	52.53
	2001	971 542	47.76	895 742	48.55	191 262	54.39
Dominica Dominique	1998	12 044	48.29	7 126	53.16	...	...
	1999	11 774	48.31	7 429	52.83	...	...
	2000	11 430	48.31	7 456	52.17	...	...
	2001	10 984	48.02	7 500	52.15	...	...
Dominican Republic Rép. dominicaine	1998[1]	1 315 342	48.62	610 275	54.88	...	...
	1999[1]	1 363 609	48.38	653 558	54.75	...	...
	2000[1]	1 385 972	48.38	664 277	54.75	...	...
	2001	1 399 844	49.36	756 240	54.35	...	...
El Salvador El Salvador	1998	925 511	48.45	401 545	49.14	117 991[1]	55.01
	1999	939 877	48.17	405 998	48.79	118 491	55.11
	2000	949 077	47.97	420 959	49.18	114 675	54.26
	2001	967 748	48.14	435 571	49.51	109 946	54.16
Grenada Grenade	2000	15 974	48.38	8 312	31.95	...	...
	2001	17 378	48.35	6 224	48.52	...	...
Guatemala Guatemala	1998	1 685 411[2]	46.05[2]	399 652[2]	47.00	...	...
	1999	1 823 989	46.09	434 912	45.49	...	...
	2000	1 909 389	46.80	503 884	46.85	...	...
	2001	1 971 539	46.99	547 913	47.13	...	...
Honduras Honduras	1998	...	...	...	...	77 768	55.38
	1999	...	...	...	...	85 000[1]	55.73
	2000	1 094 792	49.62	...	...	90 620	56.11
	2001	1 115 579[1]	49.61[1]	...	...	90 388[1]	56.12
Jamaica Jamaïque	1998	316 290[1]	49.27[1]	231 177[1]	50.26	...	...
	1999	326 847	49.18	228 764	50.56	35 995	65.03
	2000	328 496	48.88	227 703	50.53	42 502	65.02
	2001[4]	329 762	48.88	228 305	50.40	44 878	68.83
Mexico Mexique	1998	14 697 915	48.64	8 721 726	49.95	1 837 884	48.30
	1999	14 765 603	48.73	9 094 103	50.22	1 962 763	48.72
	2000	14 792 528	48.78	9 357 144	50.51	2 047 895	49.05
	2001[4]	14 843 381	48.81	9 692 976	50.89	2 147 075	49.33
Montserrat Montserrat	1998	392	43.88	272	47.06	...	...
	1999	330	44.24	284	48.59	...	...
	2000	413	44.79	297	47.47	...	...
	2001	456	45.18	301	48.17	...	...
Netherlands Antilles Antilles néerlandaises	1998	25 398	48.20	15 426	53.66	2 320	53.19
	1999	24 911	48.40	14 418	52.40	2 561	55.53
	2000	23 650	45.92	14 640	52.62	2 433	57.75
	2001	22 924	49.25	15 426	52.37	2 285	59.69
Nicaragua Nicaragua	1998	783 090	49.86	287 217[1]	53.66	...	...
	1999	830 206	49.36	321 493[1]	53.74	...	...
	2000	838 437	49.44	333 210	53.42	...	...
	2001	868 070	49.35	353 724	53.49	...	...

9

Education at the primary, secondary and tertiary levels
Number of students enrolled and percentage female *[cont.]*
Enseignement primaire, secondaire et supérieur
Nombre d'étudiants inscrits et étudiantes feminines en pourcentage *[suite]*

Country or area Pays ou zone	Year Année	Primary education Enseignement primaire		Secondary education Enseignement secondaire		Tertiary education Enseignement supérieur	
		Total	% F	Total	% F	Total	% F
Panama	1998	391 415[1]	48.17[1]	229 000[1]	50.96	...	...
Panama	1999	393 030	48.16	230 034	50.78	89 352[1]	61.86
	2000	400 408	48.19	234 153	50.55	...	...
	2001	408 249	48.19	244 097	50.75	...	...
Saint Kitts and Nevis	1999	6 922	48.63	4 768	50.46	...	...
Saint-Kitts-et-Nevis	2000	6 717	49.86	5 134[1]	56.78	...	...
	2001	6 440[1]	49.35[1]	4 492[1]	50.87	...	...
Saint Lucia	1998	25 581	48.96	11 784	56.86	3 881	46.38
Sainte-Lucie	1999	24 999	49.73	13 049	56.76	...	...
	2000	25 481	48.73	12 738	56.48	...	...
	2001	24 954	48.93	12 743	56.93	...	...
St. Vincent-Grenadines	1999	19 183	48.19	9 753	53.36	...	...
St. Vincent-Grenadines	2000	19 052	48.34	9 915[1]	53.77	...	...
	2001	18 130	48.39	9 606	54.10	...	...
Trinidad and Tobago	1998	172 204	49.12	117 011[1]	51.57	7 572	57.41
Trinité-et-Tobago	1999	168 532	49.06	113 128[1]	51.72	7 737	59.30
	2000	155 360	48.85	114 567[1]	51.26	8 614	59.98
	2001	154 947[1]	49.03[1]	96 225[1]	50.66	9 866	60.16
Turks and Caicos Islands	1998	1 822	48.57	1 114	51.08	27	100.00
Iles Turques et Caïques	1999	2 018	47.72	1 089	52.53	30[1]	50.00
	2000	2 176	49.22	1 201	53.12	...	...
	2001	2 137	48.95	1 266	50.00	...	...
United States	1998	24 937 931	49.47	...	...	...	...
Etats-Unis	1999	24 973 176	48.39	22 593 562	49.00	13 202 880	55.76
	2000	25 297 600	48.74	23 087 042	49.03	13 595 580	55.87
	2001[4]	24 855 480	49.01	23 196 310	48.46	15 927 987	56.30
America, South · Amérique du Sud							
Argentina	1998	4 821 090	49.25	3 555 848	51.20	1 526 515	...
Argentine	1999	4 820 908	49.24	3 722 449	50.96	1 600 882	61.66
	2000	4 898 224	49.09	3 832 258	50.90	1 766 933[1]	60.35[1]
	2001[4]	4 900 225	49.12	3 953 677	50.79	1 918 708	59.22
Bolivia	1998	1 400 205	48.57	756 213	47.19	228 168	35.24
Bolivie	1999	1 444 879	48.69	823 432	47.58	252 706	...
	2000	1 492 023	48.73	876 841	48.24	278 763	...
	2001	1 501 040	48.76	949 029	48.31	301 984	...
Brazil	1998	...	...	...	...	2 203 599	54.96
Brésil	1999	20 939 076	47.73	24 982 899	51.81	2 456 961	55.56
	2000	20 211 506	47.70	26 096 870	51.64	2 781 328	56.17
	2001[4]	19 727 684	47.75	26 441 248	51.60	3 125 745	56.10
Chile	1998	1 777 257	48.41	1 245 787	50.20	406 553	46.08
Chili	1999	1 804 612	48.42	1 304 679	50.13	450 952	47.11
	2000	1 798 515	48.51	1 391 283	49.72	452 177	47.16
Colombia	1998	5 062 284	49.05	3 549 368	51.85	822 500[1]	51.38
Colombie	1999	5 162 260	49.01	3 589 425	51.72	877 944	52.12
	2000	5 221 018	48.91	3 568 889	51.52	934 085	51.60
	2001	5 131 463	48.76	3 377 954	51.58	977 243	51.81
Ecuador	1998	1 899 466	49.11	903 569	49.91	...	...
Equateur	1999	1 925 420	49.01	917 245	49.65	...	...
	2000	1 955 060	49.12	936 406	49.73	...	...
	2001	1 982 636	49.08	966 362	49.39	...	...
Guyana	1998	107 207	48.98	66 495	49.86	...	...
Guyana	1999	108 909	48.61	69 189	50.33	...	...
Paraguay	1998	909 394[1]	48.78[1]	367 567	50.45	...	...
Paraguay	1999	951 481[1]	48.22[1]	425 214	50.18	66 065	57.21
	2000	966 476[1]	48.21[1]	459 260	50.06	83 088	56.93
	2001[4]	966 548[1]	48.23[1]	497 935	49.78	96 598	57.22

9

Education at the primary, secondary and tertiary levels
Number of students enrolled and percentage female *[cont.]*
Enseignement primaire, secondaire et supérieur
Nombre d'étudiants inscrits et étudiantes feminines en pourcentage *[suite]*

Country or area Pays ou zone	Year Année	Primary education Enseignement primaire		Secondary education Enseignement secondaire		Tertiary education Enseignement supérieur	
		Total	% F	Total	% F	Total	% F
Peru	1998	4 299 407	48.88	2 212 033	47.89	...	...
Pérou	1999	4 349 594	49.01	...	...	...	...
	2000	4 338 080	49.03	2 375 796[1]	47.49	...	...
	2001[4]	4 317 368	49.10	2 486 451[1]	47.53	823 995[1]	48.78
Suriname	2000	64 852	48.95	41 875	53.09	...	...
Suriname	2001	64 023	48.67	42 253	57.23	5 186	61.96
Uruguay	1998	365 297	48.63	...	...	94 219	64.01
Uruguay	1999	366 461	48.59	...	...	91 175	62.99
	2000	360 834	48.52	303 883	52.21	97 541	63.99
	2001[4]	359 557	48.41	315 968	52.21	99 301	63.73
Venezuela	1998	3 261 343	48.52	1 439 122	54.13	...	...
Venezuela	1999	3 327 797	48.53	1 543 425	53.57	668 109	58.62
	2000	3 331 441[1]	48.47[1]	1 720 571[1]	52.77	660 000[1]	56.06
	2001	3 506 780	48.47	1 811 127	52.77	650 000[1]	56.92
Asia · Asie							
Afghanistan	1998	1 046 338	6.70[1]	...	...	...	...
Afghanistan	1999	957 403	6.70	...	...	...	...
	2000	500 068	...	...	...	...	...
	2001	773 623	...	362 415	...	...	...
Armenia	1999[1]	...	...	...	...	67 193	54.45
Arménie	2000	155 423	48.74	384 165	50.78	68 704	54.62
	2001	143 815	48.50	377 716	50.78	75 474	53.68
Azerbaijan	1998	691 259	48.68	929 065	48.87	146 099[1]	45.69[1]
Azerbaïdjan	1999	696 823	48.89	945 393	48.89	156 832	47.16
	2000	693 760	48.19	1 020 131	48.04	163 305	48.96
	2001	668 902	48.14	1 040 175	48.08	170 678	51.75
Bahrain	1998	76 302	48.72	58 804	50.85	11 048	60.01[1]
Bahreïn	1999	77 720	48.90	61 058	50.64	...	...
	2000	79 407	48.85	62 221	50.96	...	...
	2001	81 057	48.69	64 439	50.70	...	...
Bangladesh	1998	17 627 000[1]	47.84[1]	9 133 579	47.44	709 224	32.27
Bangladesh	1999	17 621 731	48.56	9 912 318	48.73	726 701	32.31
	2000	17 667 985	48.88	10 329 065	49.68	878 537	33.84
	2001	17 659 220	49.09	10 690 742	50.92	855 339	32.01
Bhutan	1998	78 007	45.15	17 374	43.57	1 337[1]	32.46
Bhoutan	1999	81 156	45.66	20 123	44.15	1 479[1]	36.44
	2000	85 092	46.13	23 301	44.73	1 837[1]	33.75
	2001	88 204	46.76	26 258	45.42	1 893[1]	33.76
Brunei Darussalam	1998	45 369	47.13	32 663	50.94	2 917	64.55
Brunéi Darussalam	1999	45 822	47.00	34 426	50.75	3 705	65.91
	2000	44 981	47.48	36 077	49.74	3 984	64.76
	2001	44 487	47.63	36 986	49.60	4 479	63.18
Cambodia	1998	2 127 428	45.72	318 101[1]	34.35	...	...
Cambodge	1999	2 248 109	45.85	351 357	34.90	22 108	25.09
	2000	2 431 142	46.27	396 876	35.65	25 416	27.34
	2001	2 728 698	46.52	475 637	36.97	32 010	28.83
China	1998	135 479 642	47.64	81 487 960	...	7 364 111	...
Chine	1999	130 132 548	47.60	86 516 712	45.63[1]	9 398 581	...
	2000	125 756 891	47.34	90 722 795	...	12 143 723	...
China, Hong Kong SAR	2000	498 175[1]	48.18[1]	482 631[1]	48.20	128 052	50.25
Chine, Hong Kong RAS	2001	497 376	48.18[1]	480 216[1]	48.18	134 038	50.34
China, Macao SAR	1998	46 893	47.29	31 859	51.35	7 458	46.26
Chine, Macao RAS	1999	47 262	47.31	35 367	50.48	7 471	51.97
	2000	45 663	47.24	38 943	50.21	13 996	44.56
	2001	44 368	47.04	42 017	50.16	20 420	36.89

9

Education at the primary, secondary and tertiary levels
Number of students enrolled and percentage female *[cont.]*
Enseignement primaire, secondaire et supérieur
Nombre d'étudiants inscrits et étudiantes feminines en pourcentage *[suite]*

Country or area Pays ou zone	Year Année	Primary education Enseignement primaire		Secondary education Enseignement secondaire		Tertiary education Enseignement supérieur	
		Total	% F	Total	% F	Total	% F
Cyprus	1998	64 248	48.40	63 050	49.49	10 842	56.03
Chypre	1999	63 952	48.50	63 677	49.38	10 414	57.09
	2000	63 637	48.55	64 065	49.11	11 934	58.01
Georgia	1998	302 488	48.73	448 737	49.73	130 164	51.98
Géorgie	1999	298 352	48.72	450 589	49.42	137 046	49.19
	2000	276 389	48.82	433 156	49.68	140 627	48.95
	2001	254 030	48.68	456 470	50.68	149 142	49.83
India	1998	126 026 221	43.24	52 049 548	38.75	...	...
Inde	1999	113 612 541	43.58	71 030 515	39.58	9 404 460	37.77
	2000	113 826 978	43.77	72 392 727	39.79	9 834 046	38.66
Indonesia	1999	28 201 934[1]	48.33[1]	14 263 912[1]	48.07	...	...
Indonésie	2000	28 690 131	48.62	14 828 085	48.78	3 017 887	42.85
	2001[4]	28 926 377	48.62	15 140 713	48.98	3 175 833	45.92
Iran (Islamic Rep. of)	1998	8 667 147	47.38	9 726 948	46.97	1 308 150	43.43
Iran (Rép. islamique d')	1999	8 287 537	47.53	9 954 767	47.25	1 404 880	45.27
	2000	7 968 437	47.60	9 933 471	47.34	1 569 776	47.39
	2001	7 513 015	47.76	9 916 372	47.52	1 566 509	49.05
Iraq	1998	3 603 864	43.97	1 105 028	37.59	271 508	34.21
Iraq	1999	3 639 362	43.99	1 224 453	37.02	288 670	34.05
	2001	...	...	...	...	317 993[1]	34.04
Israel	1998	722 293	48.54	569 408	48.52	246 806	57.61
Israël	1999	738 610	48.54	587 663	48.76	255 891	57.30
	2000	748 580	48.66	594 210	48.60	270 979	56.70
	2001[4]	760 346	48.66	606 141	48.48	299 716	56.50
Japan	1998	7 691 872	48.77	8 958 699	49.12	3 940 756	44.67
Japon	1999	7 528 907	48.76	8 782 114	49.09	3 982 069	44.88
	2000	7 394 582	48.78	8 605 812	49.05	3 972 468	44.86
	2001[4]	7 325 866	48.78	8 394 050	49.00	3 966 667	45.12
Jordan	1998	706 198	48.84	579 445	49.43	...	...
Jordanie	1999	723 508	48.84	583 535	49.55	142 190	51.41
	2001[4]	765 788	48.80	605 228	49.45	162 688	48.92
Kazakhstan	1998	1 248 900	49.18	1 966 471	49.21	323 949	53.38
Kazakhstan	1999	1 208 320	49.26	2 002 880	49.58	370 321	54.03
	2000	1 190 069	48.85	2 031 675	48.64	445 651[1]	54.24
	2001	1 158 299	48.82	2 019 821	48.69	519 815	55.24
Korea, Republic of	1999	3 945 977	47.21	4 176 780	47.92	2 837 880	35.18
Corée, République de	2000	4 030 413	47.00	3 958 702	47.85	3 003 498	35.63
	2001[4]	4 099 649	46.88	3 768 040	47.72	3 129 899	36.02
Kuwait	1998	139 691	48.77	235 106[1]	49.13	32 320[1]	67.66
Koweït	1999	140 182	48.94	239 997	49.52	...	...
	2000	141 419	48.87	243 757[1]	49.97	...	...
	2001	148 712	48.60	243 517[1]	49.75	...	...
Kyrgyzstan	1998	470 746	48.97	633 356	50.10	131 222	50.77
Kirghizistan	1999	466 250	48.83	660 404	50.24	134 096[1]	50.70
	2000	459 721	48.63	683 832	49.50	190 508	50.80
	2001	454 692	48.70	689 036	49.55	209 245	52.99
Lao People's Dem. Rep.	1998	827 664	45.11	240 267	40.30	12 076	32.13
Rép. dém. pop. lao	1999	831 521	45.18	264 586	40.54	14 074	34.02
	2000	828 113	45.37	288 443	40.98	16 621	36.66
	2001	852 857	45.48	320 275	41.41	23 018	35.63
Lebanon	1998	394 505	47.97	372 365	51.55	113 022	50.30
Liban	1999	384 539	47.94	383 217	51.43	116 014	51.72
	2000[5]	453 986	48.16	322 136	51.71	134 018	51.90
	2001	452 050	48.10	336 170	51.49	142 951	52.95
Malaysia	1998	2 876 919	48.60	2 153 537	51.22	442 625	51.14
Malaisie	1999	3 032 987	48.17	2 176 863	51.00	473 357	49.99
	2000	3 017 902	48.74	2 205 426	51.16	549 205	51.00
	2001[4]	3 024 959	48.71	2 246 874	51.06	557 118	...

9

Education at the primary, secondary and tertiary levels
Number of students enrolled and percentage female *[cont.]*
Enseignement primaire, secondaire et supérieur
Nombre d'étudiants inscrits et étudiantes feminines en pourcentage *[suite]*

Country or area Pays ou zone	Year Année	Primary education Enseignement primaire		Secondary education Enseignement secondaire		Tertiary education Enseignement supérieur	
		Total	% F	Total	% F	Total	% F
Maldives	1998	73 519	49.10	12 281	50.64	...	...
Maldives	1999	74 050	48.89	14 988	51.13	...	...
	2000	73 522	48.64	20 046	51.16	...	...
	2001	71 054	48.39	24 607	50.98	...	...
Mongolia	1998	251 476	50.21	207 295	55.53	65 272	64.93
Mongolie	1999	253 441	50.20	235 099	54.58	74 025	63.83
	2000	250 436	50.11	259 928[1]	54.36	84 970	63.19
	2001	241 258	49.97	282 089	53.91	90 275	63.25
Myanmar	1998	4 732 947	49.12	2 059 007	49.56	...	...
Myanmar	1999	4 857 955	49.28	2 268 402	51.19	...	...
	2000	4 781 543	49.35	2 301 919	48.42	553 456	63.44
	2001	4 788 851	49.52	2 372 593	48.09	555 060[1]	...
Nepal	1998	3 349 202[1]	42.00[1]	1 265 458	39.61	...	...
Népal	1999	3 529 046[1]	42.71[1]	1 348 212	40.06	94 401	27.54
	2000	3 623 150	44.09	1 501 503	40.21	103 290	20.65
	2001	3 853 618	44.80	1 690 198	40.98	119 670	20.59
Occupied Palestinian Terr.	1998	368 321	49.04	444 401	49.56	66 282	45.56
Terr. palestinien occupé	1999	388 163	48.91	477 378	50.12	71 207	46.52
	2000	398 978	49.05	510 214	50.57	80 543	47.42
	2001	402 370	49.02	544 935	50.29	88 930	47.92
Oman	1998	315 557	47.91	229 031	49.14	...	...
Oman	1999	315 976	47.97	242 533	49.10	...	...
	2000	316 889	48.21	254 496	48.92	19 297	57.94
	2001	316 633	48.35	266 923	48.62	19 864[1]	57.93
Pakistan	1999	13 987 198[2]	41.03[1]	...	...	...	...
Pakistan	2000	14 561 580[2]	41.02[2]	5 790 146[2]	38.31	...	...
Philippines	1998	12 502 524	48.91	5 117 459	51.28	2 208 635	54.94
Philippines	2000	12 759 918	48.91	5 386 434	51.33	2 432 002	...
	2001[4]	12 826 218	48.67	5 816 699	51.45	2 467 267	55.57
Qatar	1998	60 989	47.81	44 403	50.48	8 880[1]	71.85
Qatar	1999	61 067	48.20	47 413	49.11	...	...
	2000	62 465	48.77	46 931	50.09	7 808	73.23
	2001	64 255	47.94	49 042	49.71	7 831	72.51
Saudi Arabia	1998	2 259 707	47.98	1 773 725	45.94	349 599	56.98
Arabie saoudite	1999	2 285 328	47.96	1 861 755	46.25	404 094	55.93
	2000	2 308 460	47.99	1 914 465	46.28	432 348[1]	54.89
	2001	2 316 166	48.13	1 995 522	46.19	444 800[1]	58.75
Sri Lanka	1998	1 801 933	48.50	2 135 075[1]	50.83	...	...
Sri Lanka	2001[4]	1 763 208	48.97	2 228 926	...	...	...
Syrian Arab Republic	1998	2 738 083	46.84	1 029 769	46.84	94 110[1]	...
Rép. arabe syrienne	1999	2 774 922	47.00	1 069 040	46.89	...	...
	2000	2 835 023	47.20	1 124 752	46.42	...	...
	2001	2 904 569	47.24	1 182 424	46.57	...	...
Tajikistan	1998	690 306	47.95	772 633	45.60	76 293	25.43
Tadjikistan	1999	691 891	47.44	798 701	45.55	79 978	25.16
	2000	680 100	47.40	847 445	44.81	78 540	23.86
	2001	684 542	48.08	899 236	44.55	85 171	24.48
Thailand	1998	6 120 400	48.26	...	...	1 814 096	53.39
Thaïlande	1999	6 100 647	48.29	...	...	1 900 272	54.11
	2000	6 179 325	48.36	5 577 364	48.35	2 095 694	52.63
	2001[4]	6 228 095	48.45	...	...	2 155 334	52.07
Timor-Leste	2000	188 900	...	40 350[1]	...	5 412[1]	52.88
Timor-Leste	2001	183 626	...	46 680	...	6 349[2]	52.87
Turkey	1999[1]	7 850 103	46.74	...	...	...	...
Turquie	2000	8 014 733[1]	47.00[1]	5 271 056[1]	42.04	1 607 388	40.81
	2001[4]	8 210 961[1]	47.20[1]	5 500 246[1]	42.48	1 677 936	41.38

9

Education at the primary, secondary and tertiary levels
Number of students enrolled and percentage female *[cont.]*
Enseignement primaire, secondaire et supérieur
Nombre d'étudiants inscrits et étudiantes feminines en pourcentage *[suite]*

Country or area Pays ou zone	Year Année	Primary education Enseignement primaire		Secondary education Enseignement secondaire		Tertiary education Enseignement supérieur	
		Total	% F	Total	% F	Total	% F
United Arab Emirates	1998	270 486	48.03	201 522	50.11	21 000[1]	...
Emirats arabes unis	1999	273 144	47.86	210 002	50.00	...	...
	2000	280 248	47.98	220 134	49.59	...	...
	2001	285 744	48.06	226 407	49.86	...	...
Uzbekistan							
Ouzbékistan	2001	2 559 151[1]	48.97[1]	4 236 741[1]	48.57	227 490[1]	...
Viet Nam	1998	10 250 214	47.24	7 400 872	46.77	810 072	42.91
Viet Nam	1999	10 063 025	47.71	7 926 126	47.02	732 187	41.64
	2000	9 751 434	47.65	8 318 193	47.11	749 914	42.04
	2001	9 336 913	47.52	8 783 340	47.38	784 675	42.80
Yemen	1998	2 302 787	34.95	1 041 816	26.04	164 166	20.75
Yémen	1999	2 463 540[1]	37.59[1]	1 150 869[1]	28.26	173 130[1]	20.77
	2000	2 643 579	37.59	1 249 016[1]	28.29	...	...
	2001	2 783 371	38.79	...	...	...	...
Europe · Europe							
Albania	1998[1]	286 646	48.15	363 273	48.73	...	...
Albanie	1999	283 249	48.27	363 689	48.74	40 125	59.86
	2000	274 233	48.58	377 198	48.75	40 859	61.35
Austria	1998	388 777	48.47	747 681	47.59	252 893	50.03
Autriche	1999	392 407	48.45	748 659	47.71	261 229	50.96
	2000	392 339	48.46	749 135	47.71	264 669	51.85
Belarus	1998	632 127	47.69	1 002 621	49.84	353 108	56.14
Bélarus	1999	599 732	48.36	1 002 334	49.84	377 167	56.10
	2000	560 437	48.36	992 293	49.88	437 995	56.18
	2001	511 863	48.26	982 230	49.72	463 544	56.80
Belgium	1998	762 734	48.55	1 033 484	50.63	351 788	...
Belgique	1999	773 742	48.64	1 057 536	51.23	355 748	52.26
	2000	771 889	48.65	1 125 256	51.43	359 265	52.83
Bulgaria	1998	411 726	48.13	699 957	48.22	270 077	59.47
Bulgarie	1999	392 876	48.12	696 073	48.14	261 321	57.27
	2000	374 361	48.08	695 474	48.17	247 006	56.31
Croatia	1998	202 999	48.52	426 915	49.64	95 889	52.90
Croatie	1999	199 084	48.55	420 689	49.75	96 798	52.71
	2000	195 638	48.55	415 522	49.73	104 168	52.45
	2001	193 179	48.58	401 921	49.39	112 537	52.45
Czech Republic	1998	654 511	48.50	928 467	49.87	231 224	49.73
République tchèque	1999	644 956	48.56	957 763	49.27	253 695	49.78
	2000	630 680	48.44	1 004 130	49.58	260 044	50.11
	2001[4]	603 843	48.35	998 608	49.51	284 485	51.23
Denmark	1998	371 694	48.65	422 399	50.32	189 970	56.30
Danemark	1999	384 197	48.63	426 149	50.06	189 162	56.91
	2000	395 870	48.68	...	...	191 645[1]	56.39
Estonia	1998	126 671	47.92	115 885	50.08	48 684	57.77
Estonie	1999	123 406	47.90	116 886	49.93	53 613	58.47
	2000	117 289	47.69	118 980	49.53	57 778	60.09
Finland	1998	382 746	48.81	479 882	51.02	262 890	53.97
Finlande	1999	388 063	48.78	490 454	51.10	270 185	53.70
	2000	392 150	48.84	493 187	51.40	279 628	53.85
France	1998	3 944 227	48.55	5 955 495	48.87	2 012 193	54.43
France	1999	3 884 560	48.58	5 928 745	48.93	2 015 344	54.21
	2000	3 837 902	48.57	5 876 047	49.01	2 031 743	54.12
Germany	1998	3 767 460	48.51	8 185 146	48.24	2 087 044	47.40
Allemagne	1999	3 655 859	48.53	8 307 277	48.35	...	...
	2000	3 519 051	48.54	8 387 525	48.37	...	...
	2001[4]	3 373 176	48.54	8 465 149	48.35	2 159 708	49.03

9

Education at the primary, secondary and tertiary levels
Number of students enrolled and percentage female *[cont.]*
Enseignement primaire, secondaire et supérieur
Nombre d'étudiants inscrits et étudiantes feminines en pourcentage *[suite]*

Country or area Pays ou zone	Year Année	Primary education Enseignement primaire		Secondary education Enseignement secondaire		Tertiary education Enseignement supérieur	
		Total	% F	Total	% F	Total	% F
Gibraltar	1998	2 607	40.58	1 370	47.45	...	...
Gibraltar	1999	2 366[1]	47.97	1 483	48.42	...	...
	2000	2 377	47.96	1 550	49.10	...	...
Greece	1998	645 534	48.44	770 883	48.93	...	...
Grèce	1999	645 313	48.42	738 744	49.38	422 317	49.98
	2000	636 460	48.42	743 462	49.11	478 205	51.11
Holy See Saint-Siège	1998	...	...	...	...	9 389	30.08
Hungary	1998	503 302	48.40	1 006 546	49.28	279 397	54.21
Hongrie	1999	500 946	48.44	1 001 855	49.11	307 071	53.87
	2000	489 768	48.44	...	...	330 549	54.78
	2001[4]	477 865	48.45	1 013 471	49.11	354 386	55.27
Iceland	1998	30 355	48.17	32 480	50.39	...	...
Islande	1999	31 282	48.31	32 133	50.68	9 667	61.91
	2000	31 786	48.52	32 186	50.40	10 184	62.68
Ireland	1998	456 564	48.53	346 316	50.21	151 137	53.53
Irlande	1999	449 638	48.49	338 247	50.64	160 611	54.11
	2000	443 617	48.50	328 424	50.77	166 600	54.72
Italy	1998	2 875 852	48.47	4 450 012	48.61	1 797 241	55.17
Italie	1999	2 836 333	48.62	4 404 331	...	1 770 002	55.52
	2000	2 810 337	48.47	4 473 362	48.14	1 812 325	56.00
Latvia	1998	141 408	48.33	255 381	49.95	82 042	61.60
Lettonie	1999	134 919	48.45	266 498	49.65	91 237	63.41
	2000	125 634	48.56	274 193	49.32	102 783	61.80
Lithuania	1998	219 661	48.45	406 951	49.24	107 419	60.00
Lituanie	1999	218 181	48.68	421 120	48.91	121 904	59.96
	2000	211 650	48.55	433 054	48.81	135 923	59.84
Luxembourg	1998	31 492	49.23	...	...	2 717	51.67
Luxembourg	1999	32 458	49.16	32 996	50.19	2 437	54.21
	2000	33 266	48.73	33 606	50.39	2 533	53.14
Malta	1998	34 914	48.63	36 946	45.90	5 768	51.47
Malte	1999	34 261	48.62	36 081	48.69	6 315	53.30
	2000	33 530	48.38	36 243	47.94	7 422	54.81
Monaco	1998	2 022	49.90	2 883	50.92	...	...
Monaco	1999	2 008	48.46	2 929	50.73	...	...
	2000	1 985	48.92	2 971	48.37	...	...
Netherlands	1998	1 268 093	48.32	1 364 806	47.78	469 885	49.29
Pays-Bas	1999	1 278 581	48.33	1 379 253	47.88	487 649	49.96
	2000	1 282 041	48.32	1 402 928	48.13	504 042	50.50
Norway	1998	411 878	48.66	377 640	49.36	187 482	57.40
Norvège	1999	419 805	48.74	371 659	49.37	190 943	58.42
	2000	426 475	48.69	369 943	49.30	189 947	59.26
Poland	1998	...	...	...	...	1 399 090	57.02
Pologne	1999	3 398 868[1]	48.05[1]	3 916 560[1]	48.78	1 579 571	57.53
	2000	3 221 253	48.50	3 973 962	48.27	1 774 985	58.02
	2001[4]	3 105 262	48.54	3 949 993	48.10	1 906 268	57.90
Portugal	1998	815 231	47.73	847 516	50.92	356 790	55.90
Portugal	1999	810 996	47.73	831 193	50.55	373 745	...
	2000	801 545	48.40	813 172	50.29	387 703	57.01
Republic of Moldova	1998	262 137	49.08	418 243	49.44	105 493	55.46
République de Moldova	1999	252 193	48.71	413 910	49.84	106 053[1]	55.76
	2000	238 713	48.89	413 418	49.86	102 825	55.70
	2001	227 470	48.70	413 916	49.88	107 731	56.64
Romania	1998	1 284 507	48.51	2 218 025	49.34	407 720	51.03
Roumanie	1999	1 189 058	48.46	2 225 691	49.37	452 621	51.83
	2000	1 090 172	48.35	2 248 802	49.34	533 152	53.51
Russian Federation	1999	6 138 300	48.59	...	...	...	...
Fédération de Russie	2000	5 702 348	48.59	...	...	7 224 014	55.82
	2001[4]	5 554 607	48.62	14 769 021	49.18	8 030 034	56.70

9

Education at the primary, secondary and tertiary levels
Number of students enrolled and percentage female [cont.]
Enseignement primaire, secondaire et supérieur
Nombre d'étudiants inscrits et étudiantes feminines en pourcentage [suite]

Country or area Pays ou zone	Year Année	Primary education Enseignement primaire		Secondary education Enseignement secondaire		Tertiary education Enseignement supérieur	
		Total	% F	Total	% F	Total	% F
San Marino Saint-Marin	1999	1 249	48.04	988	47.98	942	57.86
Serbia and Montenegro	1998	417 830	48.56	813 956	49.23	197 410	53.51
Serbie-et-Monténégro	1999	389 314	48.70	784 526	49.38	233 043	53.01
	2000	381 439	48.74	761 255	49.32	208 689	53.70
Slovakia	1998	316 601	48.51	674 405	49.51	122 886	51.70
Slovaquie	1999	309 399	48.53	671 670	49.41	135 914	50.39
	2000	300 189	48.66	663 555	49.27	143 909	51.29
	2001[4]	284 312	48.69	666 238	49.19	152 182	52.08
Slovenia	1998	91 536	48.47	220 033	49.46	79 126	56.04
Slovénie	1999	86 850	49.21	218 251	49.63	83 816	56.09
	2000	86 388	48.55	224 747	49.32	91 494	56.09
Spain	1998	2 579 908	48.31	...	...	1 786 778	53.04
Espagne	1999	2 539 995	48.36	3 245 950	50.19	1 828 987	52.94
	2000	2 505 203	48.35	3 183 282	50.04	1 833 527	52.47
	2001[4]	2 490 744	48.35	3 106 777	50.22	1 832 760	53.15
Sweden	1998	763 028	49.43	963 918	54.78	335 124	57.58
Suède	1999	775 706	49.33	933 669	54.60	346 878	58.22
	2000	786 027	49.33	928 424	54.43	358 020	59.07
	2001[4]	785 774	49.39	934 608	53.48	382 851	59.47
Switzerland	1998	529 610	48.57	544 433	46.80	156 390	41.71
Suisse	1999	538 372	48.62	549 369	46.96	156 879	42.64
	2000	537 744	48.61	553 618	47.21	163 373	42.69
TFYR of Macedonia	1998	129 633	48.12	218 666	48.03	35 141	55.09
L'ex-R.y. Macédoine	1999	126 606	48.36	221 961	47.84	36 922	55.05
	2000	123 661	48.50	222 081	47.90	40 246	55.81
Ukraine	1998	2 200 098	48.59	...	...	1 583 354	52.58
Ukraine	1999	2 080 883[1]	48.69[1]	5 204 506[1]	48.60	1 954 817[1]	52.95
	2000	2 065 348	48.73	5 123 602	48.59	1 950 755	53.05
	2001	2 047 085	48.69	4 982 947	48.92	2 134 676	53.38
United Kingdom	1998	4 661 234	48.83	8 092 272	52.01	2 080 960	53.20
Royaume-Uni	1999	4 631 623	48.80	8 298 776	52.43	2 024 138	53.94
	2000	4 596 110	48.78	8 374 404	52.66	2 067 349	54.54
Oceania · Océanie							
Australia	1999	1 885 341	48.68	2 491 404	48.80	845 636	54.12
Australie	2000	1 905 951	48.63	2 589 474	48.89	845 132	54.26
	2001[4]	1 914 395	48.64	2 499 676	48.39	868 689	54.18
Cook Islands	1998	2 711	47.58	1 779	50.48	...	...
Iles Cook	1999	2 594	46.38	1 751	50.03	...	...
	2000[1]	2 596	46.38	1 750	49.71	...	...
Fiji	1998[1]	116 410	48.26	...	...	...	...
Fidji	1999[1]	114 589	48.04	...	...	...	...
	2000	114 709[1]	48.05[1]	96 837[1]	50.68	...	...
	2001	115 014[1]	48.40[1]	96 429[1]	50.27	...	...
Kiribati Kiribati	1998	17 557	49.00	...	...		
Marshall Islands	1998	8 209	48.24	5 957	50.46	...	...
Iles Marshall	1999[1]	8 300	47.59	...	...	...	...
	2000[1]	8 530	47.13	...	...	...	...
	2001	8 777	46.93	6 353	49.54	903	56.48
Micronesia (Fed. States) Micronésie (Etats féd. de)	1998	...	...	18 686	...	1 510	...
Nauru Nauru	1998	1 598[1]	50.56[1]	738[1]	51.22	...	...
New Zealand	1998	...	...	...	...	167 308	59.01
Nouvelle-Zélande	1999	360 621	48.56	436 901	50.14	167 308	59.01
	2000	359 555	48.56	443 882	50.32	171 962	58.78
	2001[4]	355 532	48.36	456 155	50.88	177 634	58.63

9

Education at the primary, secondary and tertiary levels
Number of students enrolled and percentage female *[cont.]*
Enseignement primaire, secondaire et supérieur
Nombre d'étudiants inscrits et étudiantes feminines en pourcentage *[suite]*

Country or area Pays ou zone	Year Année	Primary education Enseignement primaire		Secondary education Enseignement secondaire		Tertiary education Enseignement supérieur	
		Total	% F	Total	% F	Total	% F
Niue	1998	282	43.26	282	46.81	...	...
Nioué	1999	268	46.27	268	54.10	...	...
	2000	250[1]	48.00[1]	260[1]	51.92	...	...
	2001	234	45.73	242	49.59	...	...
Palau	1998	1 901	46.55	2 177	48.69	...	...
Palaos	1999	1 942	47.73	1 901	47.92	480[1]	63.54
	2000	1 943[1]	47.97[1]	1 898[1]	48.21[1]	480	63.54
	2001	...	...	...	...	484[1]	63.43
Papua New Guinea	1998	580 623	45.16	132 635	40.09	9 859	35.53
Papouasie-Nvl-Guinée	1999	622 828	45.43	143 158	40.44	...	...
	2000	647 804	47.91	156 144	40.87	...	...
	2001	663 170[1]	47.91[1]	159 846[1]	40.87	...	...
Samoa	1998	27 439	48.70	21 522	50.01	1 482	45.07
Samoa	1999	27 297	47.65	21 748	49.51	1 871	47.46
	2000	28 026	48.09	21 681	50.37	1 182	44.33
	2001	29 203	48.12	22 185	50.41	1 179[1]	44.36
Tonga	1998	16 460	46.19	13 661	50.73	...	...
Tonga	1999	16 783	46.43	14 710	50.02	364	54.95
	2000	16 666	46.73	14 954[1]	48.86	370[1]	56.76
	2001	17 026	47.23	14 127	49.25	380[1]	57.89
Tuvalu	1998	1 419[1]	45.95[1]	830[1]	44.82	...	...
Tuvalu	2001	1 427	50.25	912	46.16	...	...
Vanuatu	1998	34 000[1]	47.06[1]	9 950[1]	43.52	...	...
Vanuatu	1999	34 333	47.63	10 023	43.46	...	...
	2000	35 674	47.58	9 753	52.66	...	...
	2001	36 482	47.86	9 635	48.65	675	...

Source:
United Nations Educational, Scientific and Cultural Organization, (UNESCO), Institute for Statistics, Montreal, the UNESCO Institute for Statistics database March 2004.

Source :
L'Institut de statistique de l'Organisation des Nations Unies pour l'éducation, la science et la culture (UNESCO), Montréal, la base de données de l'Institut de Statistiques de l'UNESCO, Mars 2004.

1 UIS estimate.
2 National estimate.
3 Policy change: Introduction of free universal education in 2000.
4 All 2001 data for OECD and World Education Indicators programme countries are provisional.
5 Policy change: Increase due to duration of primary being extended by one year in 2000.

1 Estimation de l'Institut de statistique de l'UNESCO.
2 Estimation nationale.
3 Changement de politique: L'introduction de l'éducation universelle gratuite en 2000.
4 Toutes les données pour 2001 pour les pays de l'OCDE et pour les pays participant au programme sur les indicateurs de l'éducation dans le monde sont provisoires.
5 Changement de politique: augmentation dûe à l'extension de la durée de l'éducation primaire par une année.

Technical notes, table 9

Detailed data and explanatory notes on education can be found on the UNESCO Institute for Statistics website <www.uis.unesco.org> and in the *UNESCO Statistical Yearbook* [31]. Brief notes which pertain to the statistical information shown in table 9 are given below.

Table 9: The definitions and classifications applied by UNESCO are those set out in the *Revised Recommendation concerning the International Standardization of Education Statistics* (1978) and the 1976 and 1997 versions of the *International Standard Classification of Education* (ISCED). Data are presented in Table 9 according to the revised terminology of the ISCED-97.

According to the ISCED, these educational levels are defined as follows:

Primary education (ISCED level 1), of which the main function is to provide the basic elements of education at such establishments as elementary schools or primary schools.

Secondary education (ISCED levels 2 and 3), providing general and/or specialized instruction at middle schools, secondary schools, high schools, teaching training schools and schools of a vocational or technical nature.

Tertiary education (ISCED levels 5, 6 and 7) provided at universities, teachers' colleges, and higher professional schools, which requires, as a minimum condition of admission, the successful completion of secondary education or evidence of the attainment of an equivalent level of knowledge.

The ISCED-97 also introduces a new category or level between upper secondary and tertiary education called post-secondary non-tertiary education (ISCED level 4). Beginning 1997, this level is included in secondary education in Table 9 for those countries footnoted accordingly. It is assumed that the programmes which countries now report separately to UNESCO as post-secondary non-tertiary have also been reported in the past, in either secondary or tertiary education depending on the country. These programmes typically fall into two categories: (a) second cycle programmes at upper secondary and (b) access or foundation programmes for entry to tertiary programmes. Countries with type (a) programmes will typically have reported them in the past as secondary programmes whilst countries with type (b) programmes will more often have reported them as tertiary in the past. Some countries will have both types of programmes.

In general, the statistics shown in table 9 refer to both public and private education. Since 1994, special needs education is, in principle, included in the statistics reported.

Notes techniques, tableau 9

On trouvera des données détaillées et des notes explicatives sur l'instruction sur le site Web de l'Institut de statistique de l'UNESCO <www.uis.unesco.org> et dans l'*Annuaire statistique de l'UNESCO* [31]. Ci-après figurent des notes sommaires, relatives aux principaux éléments d'information statistique figurant dans le tableau 9.

Tableau 9: Les définitions et classifications appliquées par l'UNESCO sont tirées de la *Recommandation révisée concernant la normalisation internationale des statistiques de l'éducation* (1978) et des versions de 1976 et de 1997 de la *Classification internationale type de l'éducation* (CITE). La terminologie utilisée dans le tableau 9 est celle de la CITE-1997.

Dans la CITE, les niveaux d'enseignement sont définis comme suit:

Enseignement primaire (niveau 1 de la CITE), dispensé par exemple dans les écoles élémentaires ou les écoles primaires, et dont la fonction principale est de fournir un enseignement de base.

Enseignement secondaire (niveaux 2 et 3 de la CITE), dispensé par exemple dans les écoles moyennes, les écoles secondaires, les lycées, les collèges, les écoles de formation des maîtres et les écoles professionnelles ou techniques.

Enseignement supérieur (niveaux 5, 6 et 7 de la CITE), dispensé par exemple dans les universités, les établissements d'enseignement pédagogique et d'enseignement spécialisé, exigeant comme condition minimale d'admission d'avoir achevé avec succès des études secondaires ou de faire preuve de connaissances équivalentes.

La CITE de 1997 introduit également une catégorie nouvelle, à savoir un niveau intermédiaire entre le deuxième cycle de l'enseignement secondaire et l'enseignement supérieur, appelé "enseignement post secondaire qui n'est pas du supérieur" (niveau 4 de la CITE). À compter de 1997, dans le tableau 9, pour les pays marqués d'une note à cet effet, ce niveau est inclus dans l'enseignement secondaire. On suppose que les programmes que les pays signalent désormais à l'UNESCO comme programmes d'enseignement post secondaire qui n'est pas du supérieur l'étaient par le passé comme programmes d'enseignement soit secondaire soit supérieur selon le pays. Ils relèvent généralement de l'une ou l'autre des deux catégories suivantes: (a) programmes de deuxième cycle du secondaire, et (b) cours de base ou de transition préparant à l'enseignement supérieur. Les pays où ces programmes relèvent du type (a) les auront normalement inclus dans l'enseignement secondaire avant 1997, les pays où ils

relèvent du type (b) les auront souvent inclus dans l'enseignement supérieur. Dans certains pays, il y a des programmes de niveau 4 relevant de l'un et de l'autre type.

En règle générale, les statistiques du tableau 9 portent sur l'enseignement public et privé. Depuis 1994, l'éducation répondant à des besoins spéciaux est en principe incluse dans les statistiques communiquées par les pays.

10
Food supply
Calories, protein and fat: average supply per capita per day
Disponibilités alimentaires
Calories, protéine et lipides: disponibilités moyennes par habitant, par jour

Country or area	Calories (number) Calories (nombre)			Protein (grams) Protéine (grammes)			Fat (grams) Lipides (grammes)		
Pays ou zone	1987-89	1989-91	1999-01	1987-89	1989-91	1999-01	1987-89	1989-91	1999-01
World **Monde**	**2 692.5**	**2 706.7**	**2 802.8**	**71.3**	**71.6**	**75.8**	**66.6**	**67.8**	**75.9**
Africa · Afrique									
Algeria Algérie	2 831.9	2 898.8	2 965.2	76.6	77.9	80.8	65.3	71.3	69.1
Angola Angola	1 747.8	1 729.1	1 902.6	43.8	40.5	40.4	44.4	45.0	38.2
Benin Bénin	2 104.2	2 326.0	2 480.8	51.2	54.9	59.6	40.3	42.8	45.3
Botswana Botswana	2 341.3	2 345.9	2 270.3	71.1	73.4	71.0	55.9	62.3	55.4
Burkina Faso Burkina Faso	2 182.4	2 267.5	2 463.7	65.1	66.0	70.8	45.2	46.1	54.7
Burundi Burundi	1 890.4	1 850.2	1 609.3	57.5	56.7	44.7	14.3	13.8	10.5
Cameroon Cameroun	2 087.6	2 094.1	2 240.0	50.6	50.4	56.4	44.1	43.8	47.6
Cape Verde Cap-Vert	2 998.6	3 001.7	3 294.9	76.8	72.6	75.5	71.7	69.9	97.9
Central African Rep. Rép. centrafricaine	1 860.3	1 869.6	1 955.2	37.8	38.8	43.6	63.1	61.5	60.3
Chad Tchad	1 685.8	1 736.5	2 143.1	49.3	50.6	65.6	40.3	43.8	67.7
Comoros Comores	1 839.8	1 897.1	1 752.8	40.8	44.3	42.3	36.5	42.9	40.6
Congo Congo	2 265.4	2 120.2	2 213.5	46.0	45.1	41.9	53.2	49.6	52.1
Côte d'Ivoire Côte d'Ivoire	2 506.5	2 454.3	2 585.5	52.7	51.1	51.5	47.5	49.3	55.5
Dem. Rep. of the Congo Rép. dém. du Congo	2 224.9	2 197.6	1 566.1	33.9	33.3	24.2	33.1	33.3	23.6
Djibouti Djibouti	1 917.9	1 885.4	2 161.1	50.3	45.3	47.7	43.5	41.5	66.0
Egypt Egypte	3 117.7	3 152.7	3 365.6	82.1	83.2	95.5	60.8	57.9	61.0
Eritrea Erythrée	...	...	1 667.4	...	...	52.0	...	...	28.5
Ethiopia Ethiopie	...	...	1 908.3	...	...	55.4	...	...	19.6
Ethiopia incl. Eritrea Ethiopie y comp. Erythrée	1 713.6	1 685.8	...	49.4	49.6	...	24.2	24.5	...
Gabon Gabon	2 499.1	2 459.6	2 580.1	73.7	70.1	73.5	48.8	49.9	63.1
Gambia Gambie	2 419.8	2 396.4	2 282.3	52.6	52.6	50.0	49.8	52.7	75.4
Ghana Ghana	2 008.1	2 024.1	2 621.3	44.7	44.6	54.3	38.9	36.6	38.5
Guinea Guinée	1 926.8	2 021.4	2 327.4	45.0	46.9	50.4	39.2	42.1	54.5
Guinea-Bissau Guinée-Bissau	2 406.3	2 429.0	2 440.0	48.9	48.9	48.0	58.3	59.5	58.2
Kenya Kenya	2 035.8	1 962.0	2 043.9	54.4	52.2	53.2	42.5	45.0	48.1

10

Food supply
Calories, protein and fat: average supply per capita per day *[cont.]*
Disponibilités alimentaires
Calories, protéine et lipides: disponibilités moyennes par habitant, par jour *[suite]*

Country or area Pays ou zone	Calories (number) Calories (nombre)			Protein (grams) Protéine (grammes)			Fat (grams) Lipides (grammes)		
	1987-89	1989-91	1999-01	1987-89	1989-91	1999-01	1987-89	1989-91	1999-01
Lesotho Lesotho	2 226.9	2 255.2	2 306.9	63.5	63.5	63.8	35.7	34.4	32.4
Liberia Libéria	2 524.6	2 326.4	2 080.0	48.1	42.0	37.0	43.9	46.6	55.7
Libyan Arab Jamah. Jamah. arabe libyenne	3 302.5	3 274.6	3 316.4	82.6	83.6	89.6	106.0	107.6	103.8
Madagascar Madagascar	2 159.2	2 106.1	2 069.2	51.6	50.1	47.8	31.2	31.1	30.7
Malawi Malawi	1 985.6	1 937.1	2 164.4	56.3	53.0	54.1	28.5	26.8	28.5
Mali Mali	2 301.7	2 308.0	2 370.6	64.3	64.2	68.1	48.0	50.9	48.3
Mauritania Mauritanie	2 558.9	2 588.1	2 732.7	80.4	81.1	75.3	64.3	62.7	67.8
Mauritius Maurice	2 762.1	2 846.8	2 982.3	65.3	69.3	78.0	69.5	72.1	85.1
Morocco Maroc	3 016.8	3 048.0	3 001.5	82.9	85.0	81.3	59.4	58.7	59.3
Mozambique Mozambique	1 789.1	1 755.8	1 945.3	32.7	31.5	37.7	38.8	37.9	32.6
Namibia Namibie	2 216.9	2 225.5	2 698.0	62.5	62.1	74.9	36.9	35.1	52.9
Niger Niger	2 064.0	2 047.7	2 127.8	57.2	54.4	59.2	30.4	30.7	36.5
Nigeria Nigéria	2 228.6	2 429.8	2 768.0	53.0	56.2	63.4	53.6	59.4	64.1
Rwanda Rwanda	2 026.8	1 961.3	1 992.2	48.5	47.1	45.7	15.9	16.5	17.0
Sao Tome and Principe Sao Tomé-et-Principe	2 102.3	2 312.6	2 463.8	46.8	52.1	48.0	83.2	83.1	75.4
Senegal Sénégal	2 159.0	2 269.2	2 274.8	68.8	67.8	62.8	48.7	53.1	67.7
Seychelles Seychelles	2 325.0	2 352.8	2 433.6	66.0	69.3	77.9	49.8	53.7	79.3
Sierra Leone Sierra Leone	1 973.4	1 986.3	1 928.4	41.4	42.2	43.6	58.6	56.3	45.2
South Africa Afrique du Sud	2 857.8	2 873.8	2 893.7	74.8	75.6	75.4	69.7	69.0	74.8
Sudan Soudan	2 165.0	2 162.1	2 290.0	64.8	66.7	72.3	61.7	58.9	72.9
Swaziland Swaziland	2 575.0	2 594.2	2 564.6	64.9	63.4	65.5	48.8	50.4	51.6
Togo Togo	2 067.4	2 184.6	2 315.4	50.9	51.6	53.3	40.9	44.5	47.1
Tunisia Tunisie	3 109.0	3 145.5	3 343.6	84.6	84.9	91.8	83.3	84.3	99.7
Uganda Ouganda	2 251.2	2 329.8	2 371.1	51.3	55.0	56.6	26.2	29.3	31.8
United Rep. of Tanzania Rép.-Unie de Tanzanie	2 182.2	2 148.0	1 969.9	55.1	53.4	47.7	31.9	31.1	29.5
Zambia Zambie	2 027.9	1 997.3	1 900.3	52.1	50.2	47.1	29.0	30.3	32.8
Zimbabwe Zimbabwe	2 143.1	2 102.2	2 095.3	53.9	52.9	49.5	49.9	50.3	56.2

10
Food supply
Calories, protein and fat: average supply per capita per day *[cont.]*
Disponibilités alimentaires
Calories, protéine et lipides: disponibilités moyennes par habitant, par jour *[suite]*

Country or area Pays ou zone	Calories (number) Calories (nombre)			Protein (grams) Protéine (grammes)			Fat (grams) Lipides (grammes)		
	1987-89	1989-91	1999-01	1987-89	1989-91	1999-01	1987-89	1989-91	1999-01
America, North · Amérique du Nord									
Antigua and Barbuda Antigua-et-Barbuda	2 372.2	2 473.4	2 366.8	83.5	82.1	79.7	96.0	101.5	88.0
Bahamas Bahamas	2 786.2	2 716.4	2 724.7	82.5	81.3	87.1	95.2	91.2	96.0
Barbados Barbade	3 137.5	3 134.5	2 959.1	96.3	96.7	87.4	104.2	108.8	96.8
Belize Belize	2 566.9	2 593.6	2 863.2	66.9	65.3	72.3	70.3	64.5	69.3
Bermuda Bermudes	2 988.3	2 899.7	2 945.8	105.1	101.8	89.2	126.3	123.1	120.1
Canada Canada	3 036.1	3 004.8	3 176.5	95.7	95.2	103.3	129.4	128.8	127.0
Costa Rica Costa Rica	2 718.2	2 687.2	2 757.6	66.2	67.1	70.3	66.9	69.4	74.1
Cuba Cuba	3 019.1	2 880.4	2 607.0	72.3	67.6	60.4	81.9	80.1	52.3
Dominica Dominique	2 952.0	2 987.5	2 981.0	74.0	76.2	87.2	81.4	84.1	82.9
Dominican Republic Rép. dominicaine	2 304.8	2 272.9	2 322.9	50.9	50.4	50.0	59.9	65.0	81.1
El Salvador El Salvador	2 361.0	2 453.4	2 459.5	56.1	60.0	61.0	53.6	53.9	54.8
Grenada Grenade	2 610.6	2 658.6	2 742.3	70.4	71.9	71.6	90.9	88.1	98.4
Guatemala Guatemala	2 348.5	2 336.6	2 160.3	61.1	59.3	54.7	41.6	43.7	46.8
Haiti Haïti	1 788.6	1 770.9	2 040.6	46.8	43.9	45.1	28.8	28.7	42.7
Honduras Honduras	2 259.1	2 306.7	2 397.8	53.4	55.1	60.3	57.9	56.7	66.2
Jamaica Jamaïque	2 589.6	2 531.5	2 690.2	66.6	63.4	68.9	66.5	64.1	78.1
Mexico Mexique	3 074.4	3 091.2	3 151.6	80.6	80.9	88.9	82.7	80.8	86.6
Netherlands Antilles Antilles néerlandaises	2 575.0	2 518.5	2 581.4	83.3	80.8	80.9	88.2	82.4	90.7
Nicaragua Nicaragua	2 291.9	2 231.9	2 246.6	55.8	55.3	59.3	43.5	44.6	47.8
Panama Panama	2 281.0	2 285.5	2 252.4	58.7	59.7	62.2	63.1	65.8	72.5
Saint Kitts and Nevis Saint-Kitts-et-Nevis	2 601.3	2 591.8	2 976.8	69.1	70.0	89.1	87.1	84.6	92.8
Saint Lucia Sainte-Lucie	2 596.7	2 690.6	2 920.8	77.7	82.8	92.9	59.4	64.4	78.3
St. Vincent-Grenadines St. Vincent-Grenadines	2 432.8	2 378.4	2 637.6	60.6	60.4	68.4	66.2	70.9	76.5
Trinidad and Tobago Trinité-et-Tobago	2 805.2	2 680.5	2 713.6	67.8	63.2	62.1	75.6	72.0	77.2
United States Etats-Unis	3 435.4	3 474.7	3 768.7	106.6	107.7	114.8	139.3	138.8	151.6

10

Food supply
Calories, protein and fat: average supply per capita per day *[cont.]*
Disponibilités alimentaires
Calories, protéine et lipides: disponibilités moyennes par habitant, par jour *[suite]*

Country or area Pays ou zone	Calories (number) Calories (nombre)			Protein (grams) Protéine (grammes)			Fat (grams) Lipides (grammes)		
	1987-89	1989-91	1999-01	1987-89	1989-91	1999-01	1987-89	1989-91	1999-01
America, South · Amérique du Sud									
Argentina Argentine	3 028.7	2 957.8	3 177.6	98.0	94.2	103.6	107.2	102.7	111.4
Bolivia Bolivie	2 150.4	2 151.4	2 236.4	55.5	55.0	58.8	49.3	50.1	49.6
Brazil Brésil	2 772.4	2 801.4	3 001.7	66.7	68.1	79.8	76.9	80.7	87.9
Chile Chili	2 487.8	2 537.1	2 851.0	67.2	69.8	77.7	56.5	62.9	84.5
Colombia Colombie	2 344.4	2 409.8	2 572.3	51.5	53.6	59.2	53.6	55.5	64.8
Ecuador Equateur	2 499.3	2 492.3	2 734.6	50.8	49.9	56.7	77.9	87.3	90.2
Guyana Guyana	2 450.9	2 361.3	2 536.2	56.6	58.0	73.3	29.9	30.7	49.2
Paraguay Paraguay	2 546.3	2 453.7	2 560.2	69.6	68.6	72.4	67.7	69.1	92.5
Peru Pérou	2 252.8	2 027.8	2 601.9	55.6	50.1	63.9	48.3	41.6	50.4
Suriname Suriname	2 420.7	2 484.0	2 630.3	60.6	63.6	61.5	46.1	46.9	67.4
Uruguay Uruguay	2 569.9	2 577.6	2 841.2	80.2	79.5	90.8	90.8	89.7	97.0
Venezuela Venezuela	2 580.0	2 390.3	2 331.0	63.7	58.0	61.7	76.9	68.9	60.6
Asia · Asie									
Armenia Arménie	...	...	2 000.5	...	...	58.2	...	...	40.1
Azerbaijan Azerbaïdjan	...	...	2 381.5	...	...	70.4	...	...	37.9
Bangladesh Bangladesh	2 060.2	2 064.8	2 155.6	44.2	44.4	45.9	19.7	17.9	26.3
Brunei Darussalam Brunéi Darussalam	2 817.8	2 765.5	2 771.0	83.4	81.4	82.1	75.0	71.6	77.6
Cambodia Cambodge	1 814.8	1 834.2	1 972.8	43.3	43.7	47.7	20.1	21.3	28.8
China Chine	2 625.1	2 675.2	2 971.6	63.2	64.5	84.5	46.5	51.5	81.6
China, Hong Kong SAR Chine, Hong Kong RAS	3 260.8	3 275.1	3 099.3	93.3	93.1	97.9	131.3	141.4	136.8
China, Macao SAR Chine, Macao RAS	2 591.7	2 706.3	2 509.0	71.5	75.8	69.4	100.4	108.2	112.4
Cyprus Chypre	2 989.7	3 070.4	3 256.8	92.8	94.9	103.9	123.6	126.5	131.4
Georgia Géorgie	...	...	2 288.6	...	...	66.4	...	...	45.0
India Inde	2 303.4	2 365.1	2 492.0	56.5	57.4	58.5	39.6	41.3	52.8
Indonesia Indonésie	2 561.5	2 641.6	2 902.9	55.6	58.6	65.2	48.5	51.3	59.2
Iran (Islamic Rep. of) Iran (Rép. islamique d')	2 797.2	2 844.6	2 933.3	73.6	74.9	79.0	58.8	60.8	59.7

10
Food supply
Calories, protein and fat: average supply per capita per day *[cont.]*
Disponibilités alimentaires
Calories, protéine et lipides: disponibilités moyennes par habitant, par jour *[suite]*

Country or area Pays ou zone	Calories (number) Calories (nombre)			Protein (grams) Protéine (grammes)			Fat (grams) Lipides (grammes)		
	1987-89	1989-91	1999-01	1987-89	1989-91	1999-01	1987-89	1989-91	1999-01
Israel Israël	3 419.6	3 379.5	3 517.8	111.1	111.4	114.4	121.9	120.6	126.0
Japan Japon	2 829.5	2 821.1	2 752.6	94.4	94.2	90.7	78.5	79.5	82.4
Jordan Jordanie	2 754.2	2 799.7	2 736.2	74.4	74.3	73.3	70.2	70.6	80.9
Kazakhstan Kazakhstan	...	...	2 361.9	...	...	75.9	...	...	68.8
Korea, Dem. P. R. Corée, R. p. dém. de	2 207.5	2 438.8	2 176.0	76.0	79.7	61.3	44.8	47.4	33.8
Korea, Republic of Corée, République de	3 080.7	3 027.2	3 073.6	84.5	82.2	89.3	52.5	57.2	75.1
Kuwait Koweït	3 052.3	2 434.7	3 151.5	90.4	72.8	96.8	100.8	84.1	100.3
Kyrgyzstan Kirghizistan	...	...	2 857.2	...	...	94.3	...	...	52.8
Lao People's Dem. Rep. Rép. dém. pop. lao	2 057.0	2 107.2	2 281.6	49.6	50.7	59.0	21.8	22.8	28.9
Lebanon Liban	3 066.0	3 137.6	3 166.4	76.9	77.5	83.1	93.5	101.7	111.7
Malaysia Malaisie	2 635.6	2 720.7	2 915.6	59.7	64.0	76.3	90.6	95.0	82.6
Maldives Maldives	2 289.9	2 366.0	2 561.3	84.2	77.1	113.3	44.5	47.1	61.8
Mongolia Mongolie	2 249.9	2 205.1	2 068.4	73.6	74.6	77.2	75.1	79.8	80.8
Myanmar Myanmar	2 681.6	2 619.5	2 812.6	68.2	65.0	73.1	44.5	41.7	46.8
Nepal Népal	2 337.8	2 457.3	2 442.4	60.5	63.4	62.1	30.7	32.5	37.7
Pakistan Pakistan	2 277.6	2 295.6	2 457.9	55.1	57.4	62.6	54.1	55.5	69.1
Philippines Philippines	2 244.5	2 324.6	2 373.5	52.5	55.5	55.2	37.2	41.0	48.5
Saudi Arabia Arabie saoudite	2 687.5	2 769.1	2 836.6	75.4	76.6	77.4	80.8	83.7	78.9
Sri Lanka Sri Lanka	2 274.4	2 222.3	2 328.4	48.5	47.6	53.2	43.3	43.9	44.9
Syrian Arab Republic Rép. arabe syrienne	2 871.9	2 805.6	3 042.7	75.8	71.4	74.4	80.7	82.5	103.1
Tajikistan Tadjikistan	...	...	1 716.4	...	...	44.5	...	...	34.2
Thailand Thaïlande	2 270.6	2 219.2	2 465.6	50.4	50.5	55.5	42.3	45.4	49.3
Turkey Turquie	3 511.3	3 526.7	3 356.9	100.9	101.5	96.4	92.3	91.9	89.1
Turkmenistan Turkménistan	...	...	2 756.2	...	...	77.9	...	...	72.2
United Arab Emirates Emirats arabes unis	2 988.2	2 974.7	3 331.8	95.3	93.8	104.5	104.7	107.8	107.2
Uzbekistan Ouzbékistan	...	...	2 272.8	...	...	65.9	...	...	59.4
Viet Nam Viet Nam	2 208.3	2 216.9	2 501.5	50.2	50.5	60.1	26.8	27.6	39.6

10

Food supply
Calories, protein and fat: average supply per capita per day *[cont.]*
Disponibilités alimentaires
Calories, protéine et lipides: disponibilités moyennes par habitant, par jour *[suite]*

Country or area Pays ou zone	Calories (number) Calories (nombre)			Protein (grams) Protéine (grammes)			Fat (grams) Lipides (grammes)		
	1987-89	1989-91	1999-01	1987-89	1989-91	1999-01	1987-89	1989-91	1999-01
Yemen Yémen	2 165.9	2 062.0	2 045.8	60.3	57.9	57.4	37.4	35.7	37.1
Europe · Europe									
Albania Albanie	2 616.8	2 565.5	2 942.7	77.9	78.9	98.7	61.7	66.0	86.0
Austria Autriche	3 426.2	3 497.2	3 788.2	98.8	101.7	111.1	152.8	156.2	163.3
Belarus Bélarus	...	...	2 963.7	...	...	89.2	...	...	96.8
Belgium-Luxembourg Belgique-Luxembourg	3 502.7	3 537.3	3 673.6	102.5	103.5	104.6	156.4	156.6	160.1
Bosnia and Herzegovina Bosnie-Herzégovine	...	...	2 730.6	...	...	70.7	...	...	65.0
Bulgaria Bulgarie	3 696.5	3 460.8	2 626.1	111.3	106.6	82.0	122.8	115.8	94.5
Croatia Croatie	...	...	2 619.1	...	...	68.7	...	...	87.5
Czechoslovakia-former Tchécoslovaquie (anc.)	3 564.9	3 519.4	...	106.1	102.1	...	135.9	130.7	...
Czech Republic République tchèque	...	...	3 081.6	...	...	90.2	...	...	113.7
Denmark Danemark	3 222.2	3 191.1	3 437.4	102.8	102.1	109.5	133.2	131.9	139.4
Estonia Estonie	...	...	3 020.5	...	...	93.0	...	...	95.1
Finland Finlande	3 090.9	3 160.1	3 182.7	98.1	99.2	103.0	126.7	126.7	123.9
France France	3 555.9	3 539.0	3 602.8	116.0	116.6	117.3	162.4	163.0	166.7
Germany Allemagne	3 482.0	3 391.9	3 498.7	101.4	98.6	96.9	141.7	142.4	152.1
Greece Grèce	3 559.6	3 563.6	3 730.2	110.5	112.5	119.2	140.1	140.4	151.8
Hungary Hongrie	3 733.5	3 668.9	3 497.8	106.2	101.6	92.8	153.0	151.1	142.3
Iceland Islande	3 156.1	3 107.4	3 205.6	118.0	114.4	120.8	125.9	122.9	129.1
Ireland Irlande	3 616.4	3 619.7	3 690.7	116.9	116.0	115.4	141.9	136.3	135.6
Italy Italie	3 543.7	3 597.8	3 664.9	108.3	110.6	113.1	148.2	150.7	155.5
Latvia Lettonie	...	...	2 785.8	...	...	75.6	...	...	99.1
Lithuania Lituanie	...	...	3 261.6	...	...	96.7	...	...	92.4
Malta Malte	3 232.2	3 259.4	3 511.0	99.1	101.5	113.5	114.3	113.7	111.1
Netherlands Pays-Bas	3 164.9	3 276.0	3 293.6	94.7	96.0	107.0	135.2	138.5	142.5
Norway Norvège	3 203.5	3 170.7	3 366.3	99.4	97.7	104.6	132.9	129.6	135.0
Poland Pologne	3 484.6	3 375.9	3 385.4	105.2	102.8	99.6	117.7	113.3	114.0

10
Food supply
Calories, protein and fat: average supply per capita per day *[cont.]*
Disponibilités alimentaires
Calories, protéine et lipides: disponibilités moyennes par habitant, par jour *[suite]*

Country or area Pays ou zone	Calories (number) Calories (nombre)			Protein (grams) Protéine (grammes)			Fat (grams) Lipides (grammes)		
	1987-89	1989-91	1999-01	1987-89	1989-91	1999-01	1987-89	1989-91	1999-01
Portugal Portugal	3 297.2	3 399.0	3 748.5	97.5	101.6	119.7	107.4	118.2	137.4
Republic of Moldova République de Moldova	...	...	2 681.8	...	...	63.1	...	...	50.3
Romania Roumanie	2 943.1	3 016.4	3 339.8	91.1	90.9	102.6	86.7	92.0	89.9
Russian Federation Fédération de Russie	...	...	2 943.8	...	...	87.2	...	...	78.1
Serbia and Montenegro Serbie-et-Monténégro	...	...	2 717.4	...	...	79.2	...	...	114.1
Slovakia Slovaquie	...	...	2 905.1	...	...	74.5	...	...	107.6
Slovenia Slovénie	...	...	3 056.7	...	...	104.1	...	...	110.0
Spain Espagne	3 191.2	3 266.9	3 405.3	102.2	104.4	112.2	133.0	139.6	152.6
Sweden Suède	2 944.8	2 963.2	3 137.2	95.2	95.4	102.6	123.1	122.7	126.1
Switzerland Suisse	3 345.6	3 309.7	3 381.6	94.7	94.7	93.0	152.6	150.6	149.9
TFYR of Macedonia L'ex-R.y. Macédoine	...	...	2 661.9	...	...	67.6	...	...	88.9
Ukraine Ukraine	...	...	2 898.8	...	...	80.4	...	...	74.3
United Kingdom Royaume-Uni	3 216.3	3 203.5	3 343.1	92.6	92.4	99.0	136.3	135.4	140.8
Yugoslavia, SFR Yougoslavie, Rfs	3 644.0	3 587.4	...	102.3	102.6	...	117.2	111.8	...
USSR - former URSS (anc.)	3 378.7	3 246.4	...	106.5	104.4	...	104.9	100.1	...
Oceania · Océanie									
Australia Australie	3 178.8	3 195.6	3 109.5	109.5	108.6	106.0	128.2	130.3	133.9
Fiji Fidji	2 596.4	2 602.0	2 782.2	64.6	68.4	72.5	92.0	97.0	100.7
French Polynesia Polynésie française	2 822.1	2 845.2	2 880.1	82.4	87.0	95.0	102.1	101.5	115.0
Kiribati Kiribati	2 502.4	2 585.6	2 917.5	63.0	63.9	71.2	90.5	91.5	105.7
New Caledonia Nouvelle-Calédonie	2 834.1	2 829.4	2 769.0	77.2	77.7	80.2	101.9	103.5	107.5
New Zealand Nouvelle-Zélande	3 149.4	3 192.2	3 210.8	96.5	96.7	101.2	126.3	130.8	117.3
Papua New Guinea Papouasie-Nvl-Guinée	2 215.1	2 211.1	2 176.0	47.8	47.2	44.7	42.4	41.8	46.3
Solomon Islands Iles Salomon	2 176.9	2 055.4	2 235.9	54.9	51.9	51.9	46.6	44.7	42.8
Vanuatu Vanuatu	2 634.1	2 526.8	2 575.0	59.4	58.0	60.2	100.7	100.6	90.7

Source:
Food and Agriculture Organization of the United Nations (FAO), Rome, FAOSTAT Nutrition database.

Source :
Organisation des Nations Unies pour l'alimentation et l'agriculture (FAO), Rome, les données alimentaires de FAOSTAT.

11
Selected indicators of life expectancy, childbearing and mortality
Choix d'indicateurs de l'espérance de vie, de la maternité et de la mortalité

		Life expectancy at birth (years) Espérance de vie à la naissance (en années)		Total fertility rate	Infant Infantile p. 1,000	Mortality rates – Taux de mortalité	Child – Juvenile p. 1,000		Maternal Maternale p.100,000
Country or area Pays ou zone	Year Année	Males Hommes	Females Femmes	Taux de fecondité	M+F	Year Année	Males Hommes	Females Femmes	1995
Africa · Afrique									
Algeria	1995-00	66.6	69.3	3.2	53.5	1982[1,2]	12.5	12.8	...
Algérie	2000-05	68.1	71.3	2.8	43.9	1998[1,2,3,4]	8.8	7.3	150
Angola	1995-00	38.7	41.8	7.2	150.5	...	...	...	...
Angola	2000-05	38.8	41.5	7.2	140.3		...	...	1 300
Benin	1995-00	49.1	53.8	6.1	96.4	...	...	...	...
Bénin	2000-05	48.4	53.0	5.7	92.7		...	...	880
Botswana	1995-00	53.6	58.8	4.0	56.6	...	...	...	...
Botswana	2000-05	38.9	40.5	3.7	56.6		...	...	480
Burkina Faso	1995-00	44.6	47.0	6.9	102.2	...	...	...	...
Burkina Faso	2000-05	45.2	46.2	6.7	93.2		...	...	1 400
Burundi	1995-00	38.7	39.9	6.8	116.7	...	...	...	...
Burundi	2000-05	40.4	41.4	6.8	107.4		...	...	1 900
Cameroon	1995-00	50.1	53.9	5.1	85.6	...	...	...	...
Cameroun	2000-05	45.1	47.4	4.6	88.1		...	...	720
Cape Verde	1995-00	65.5	71.3	3.8	35.5	1985[3]	21.1	19.3	...
Cap-Vert	2000-05	67.0	72.8	3.3	29.7	1990	3.4	3.4	190
Central African Rep.	1995-00	40.5	44.7	5.3	102.5	...	...	...	...
Rép. centrafricaine	2000-05	38.5	40.6	4.9	100.4	1988[5]	14.9	12.8	1 200
Chad	1995-00	43.0	45.8	6.7	123.2	...	...	...	...
Tchad	2000-05	43.7	45.7	6.7	115.3		...	...	1 500
Comoros	1995-00	57.4	60.2	5.4	76.3	...	...	...	...
Comores	2000-05	59.4	62.2	4.9	67.0		...	...	570
Congo	1995-00	46.8	51.8	6.3	84.1	...	...	...	...
Congo	2000-05	46.6	49.7	6.3	84.0		...	...	1 100
Côte d'Ivoire	1995-00	42.2	44.3	5.3	101.9	...	...	...	...
Côte d'Ivoire	2000-05	40.8	41.2	4.7	101.3		...	...	1 200
Dem. Rep. of the Congo	1995-00	36.8	39.1	6.7	157.2	...	...	...	...
Rép. dém. du Congo	2000-05	40.8	42.8	6.7	119.6		...	...	940
Djibouti	1995-00	45.5	48.5	6.1	109.8	...	...	...	...
Djibouti	2000-05	44.7	46.8	5.7	102.4		...	...	520
Egypt	1995-00	65.2	69.0	3.5	49.0	1996	2.5	2.7	...
Egypte	2000-05	66.7	71.0	3.3	40.6	1999	2.4	2.4	170
Equatorial Guinea	1995-00	47.0	50.1	5.9	109.0	...	...	...	...
Guinée équatoriale	2000-05	47.8	50.5	5.9	100.9		...	...	1 400
Eritrea	1995-00	50.3	53.7	5.9	79.6	...	...	...	...
Erythrée	2000-05	51.2	54.2	5.4	73.0		...	...	1 100
Ethiopia	1995-00	44.7	47.5	6.5	108.9	...	...	...	...
Ethiopie	2000-05	44.6	46.3	6.1	100.4		...	...	1 800
Gabon	1995-00	55.2	58.0	4.5	64.3	...	...	...	...
Gabon	2000-05	55.8	57.5	4.0	56.8		...	...	620
Gambia	1995-00	51.1	54.4	5.2	88.9	...	...	...	...
Gambie	2000-05	52.7	55.5	4.7	80.5		...	...	1 100
Ghana	1995-00	55.4	59.2	4.6	65.3	...	...	...	...
Ghana	2000-05	56.5	59.3	4.1	57.8		...	...	590
Guinea	1995-00	46.5	47.6	6.3	115.3	...	...	...	...
Guinée	2000-05	48.8	49.5	5.8	101.7		...	...	1 200
Guinea-Bissau	1995-00	42.8	46.1	7.1	130.0	...	...	...	...
Guinée-Bissau	2000-05	43.8	46.9	7.1	120.0		...	...	910
Kenya	1995-00	48.2	53.4	4.6	68.3	...	...	...	...
Kenya	2000-05	43.5	45.6	4.0	69.3		...	...	1 300
Lesotho	1995-00	42.5	50.9	4.3	98.0	...	...	...	...
Lesotho	2000-05	32.3	37.7	3.8	92.1		...	...	530
Liberia	1995-00	40.7	42.9	6.8	152.5	...	...	...	...
Libéria	2000-05	40.7	42.2	6.8	147.4		...	...	1 000

11
Selected indicators of life expectancy, childbearing and mortality [cont.]
Choix d'indicateurs de l'espérance de vie, de la maternité et de la mortalité [suite]

Country or area Pays ou zone	Year Année	Life expectancy at birth (years) Espérance de vie à la naissance (en années)		Total fertility rate Taux de fecondité	Mortality rates – Taux de mortalité					Maternal Maternale p.100,000
		Males Hommes	Females Femmes		Infant Infantile p. 1,000 M+F	Child – Juvenile p. 1,000				
						Year Année	Males Hommes	Females Femmes		1995
Libyan Arab Jamah.	1995-00	69.6	74.2	3.4	23.6	...	...	...		...
Jamah. arabe libyenne	2000-05	70.8	75.4	3.0	20.7		...	...		120
Madagascar	1995-00	50.5	52.8	6.1	100.2	...	...	...		...
Madagascar	2000-05	52.5	54.8	5.7	91.5		...	...		580
Malawi	1995-00	39.3	42.2	6.5	125.4	...	...	...		...
Malawi	2000-05	37.3	37.7	6.1	115.4	1998[5]	51.2	41.6		580
Mali	1995-00	47.2	48.5	7.0	125.7	...	...	...		...
Mali	2000-05	48.0	49.1	7.0	118.7	1987[3,5]	41.5	35.7		630
Mauritania	1995-00	48.9	52.1	6.0	105.6	...	...	...		...
Mauritanie	2000-05	50.9	54.1	5.8	96.7		...	...		870
Mauritius	1995-00	66.9[6]	74.8[6]	2.1[6]	18.5[6]	1997[7]	0.5	0.5		...
Maurice	2000-05	68.4[6]	75.8[6]	2.0[6]	16.0[6]	2000[4,7]	0.6	0.6		45
Morocco	1995-00	64.8	68.5	3.0	52.2	1996[3]	4.6	4.2		...
Maroc	2000-05	66.8	70.5	2.8	42.1	1999[3,8]	4.6	4.3		390
Mozambique	1995-00	39.2	43.8	5.9	130.3	...	...	...		...
Mozambique	2000-05	36.6	39.6	5.6	122.0	1997[3,9]	81.5	66.5		980
Namibia	1995-00	51.6	57.5	5.2	62.3	...	...	...		...
Namibie	2000-05	42.9	45.6	4.6	59.8	...	...	...		370
Niger	1995-00	43.9	44.5	8.0	136.1	...	...	...		...
Niger	2000-05	45.9	46.5	8.0	125.7	...	...	...		920
Nigeria	1995-00	51.8	53.3	5.9	85.9	...	...	...		...
Nigéria	2000-05	51.1	51.8	5.4	78.8	...	...	...		1 100
Réunion	1995-00	70.4	78.8	2.3	8.4	1986[1,10]	0.7	0.8		...
Réunion	2000-05	71.2	79.3	2.3	7.9	1987[1,10]	0.6	0.6		39
Rwanda	1995-00	34.7	36.4	6.2	121.1	...	...	...		...
Rwanda	2000-05	38.8	39.7	5.7	111.5	...	...	...		2 300
Sao Tome and Principe	1995-00	65.5	71.3	4.5	36.4	...	...	...		...
Sao Tomé-et-Principe	2000-05	67.0	72.8	4.0	31.6	...	...	...		...
Senegal	1995-00	48.8	53.1	5.4	66.4	...	...	...		...
Sénégal	2000-05	50.8	55.1	5.0	60.7	...	...	...		1 200
Sierra Leone	1995-00	33.5	36.4	6.5	182.3	...	...	...		...
Sierra Leone	2000-05	33.1	35.5	6.5	177.2	...	...	...		2 100
Somalia	1995-00	43.3	46.3	7.3	133.4	...	...	...		...
Somalie	2000-05	46.4	49.5	7.3	117.7	...	...	...		1 600
South Africa	1995-00	53.7	63.1	2.9	48.0	...	...	...		...
Afrique du Sud	2000-05	45.1	50.7	2.6	47.9	1996	2.4	2.1		340
Sudan	1995-00	53.6	56.4	4.9	84.1	...	...	...		...
Soudan	2000-05	54.1	57.1	4.4	77.0	...	...	...		1 500
Swaziland	1995-00	43.9	50.4	5.1	81.0	...	...	...		...
Swaziland	2000-05	33.3	35.4	4.5	78.3	1997[3,9]	15.8	14.2		370
Togo	1995-00	49.6	54.0	5.8	85.2	...	...	...		...
Togo	2000-05	48.2	51.1	5.3	81.5	...	...	...		980
Tunisia	1995-00	69.8	73.7	2.3	27.6	1995[3]	5.9	4.8		...
Tunisie	2000-05	70.8	74.9	2.0	23.3	1998[3]	5.9	4.7		70
Uganda	1995-00	40.3	42.0	7.1	96.0	...	...	...		...
Ouganda	2000-05	45.4	46.9	7.1	86.1	...	...	...		1 100
United Rep. of Tanzania	1995-00	44.0	47.1	5.7	100.3	...	...	...		...
Rép.-Unie de Tanzanie	2000-05	42.5	44.1	5.1	99.8	...	...	...		1 100
Western Sahara	1995-00	59.8	63.1	4.4	64.5	...	...	...		...
Sahara occidental	2000-05	62.3	65.6	3.9	53.6	...	...	...		850
Zambia	1995-00	34.8	36.5	6.1	109.6	...	...	...		...
Zambie	2000-05	32.7	32.1	5.6	104.8	...	...	...		870
Zimbabwe	1995-00	39.7	42.0	4.5	61.7	...	...	...		...
Zimbabwe	2000-05	33.7	32.6	3.9	58.4	...	...	...		610
America, North · Amérique du Nord										
Bahamas	1995-00	63.4	71.4	2.4	19.1	...	...	...		...
Bahamas	2000-05	63.9	70.3	2.3	17.7	1994[7]	1.4	0.9		10
Barbados	1995-00	73.7	78.7	1.5	12.4	1987[4]	0.8	0.2		...
Barbade	2000-05	74.5	79.5	1.5	10.9	1988[4]	0.5	0.5		33

11
Selected indicators of life expectancy, childbearing and mortality *[cont.]*
Choix d'indicateurs de l'espérance de vie, de la maternité et de la mortalité *[suite]*

Country or area Pays ou zone	Year Année	Life expectancy at birth (years) Espérance de vie à la naissance (en années) Males Hommes	Females Femmes	Total fertility rate Taux de fecondité	Infant Infantile p. 1,000 M+F	Child – Juvenile p. 1,000 Year Année	Males Hommes	Females Femmes	Maternal Maternale p.100,000 1995
Belize Belize	1995-00	71.0	74.2	3.6	33.3	1997[3]	6.7	6.0	...
	2000-05	69.9	73.0	3.2	31.1	1998[3]	4.8	5.3	140
Canada Canada	1995-00	75.9	81.4	1.6	5.5	1995[11]	0.3	0.2	...
	2000-05	76.7	81.9	1.5	5.3	1998[11]	0.3	0.2	6
Costa Rica Costa Rica	1995-00	75.0	79.7	2.6	11.8	1996[3]	3.5	3.0	...
	2000-05	75.8	80.6	2.3	10.5	1997[3]	4.3	3.4	35
Cuba Cuba	1995-00	74.2	78.0	1.6	7.5	1995	0.8	0.6	...
	2000-05	74.8	78.7	1.6	7.3	1999[8]	0.5	0.4	24
Dominican Republic Rép. dominicaine	1995-00	64.5	69.5	2.9	40.9	...	...	...	...
	2000-05	64.4	69.2	2.7	35.7	...	...	...	110
El Salvador El Salvador	1995-00	66.5	72.5	3.2	32.0	1992	1.4	1.3	...
	2000-05	67.7	73.7	2.9	26.4	2000	0.9	0.8	180
Guadeloupe Guadeloupe	1995-00	73.6	80.9	2.1	8.3	...	...	...	...
	2000-05	74.8	81.7	2.1	7.4	1985[1,3]	4.8	4.2	5
Guatemala Guatemala	1995-00	61.4	67.2	4.9	46.0	1985[3]	22.2	20.1	...
	2000-05	63.0	68.9	4.4	41.2	1999	3.6	3.5	270
Haiti Haïti	1995-00	47.2	49.2	4.4	70.5	...	...	...	...
	2000-05	49.0	50.0	4.0	63.2	...	...	...	1 100
Honduras Honduras	1995-00	66.2	71.2	4.3	35.6	...	...	...	...
	2000-05	66.5	71.4	3.7	32.1	1981[4]	4.6	4.3	220
Jamaica Jamaïque	1995-00	72.9	76.8	2.5	21.9	1989[4]	1.4	1.1	...
	2000-05	73.7	77.8	2.4	19.9	1991[4]	1.3	1.0	120
Martinique Martinique	1995-00	75.5	82.0	1.9	7.0	1990[1,3]	2.1	2.5	...
	2000-05	75.8	82.3	1.9	6.8	1992[1,3,7]	1.8	1.4	4
Mexico Mexique	1995-00	69.5	75.5	2.8	31.0	1995[3]	5.8	4.7	...
	2000-05	70.4	76.4	2.5	28.2	2000[8,12]	0.9	0.8	65
Netherlands Antilles Antilles néerlandaises	1995-00	72.5	78.4	2.1	14.2	...	...	...	...
	2000-05	73.3	79.2	2.1	12.6	1992[7]	0.9	0.6	20
Nicaragua Nicaragua	1995-00	65.7	70.4	4.3	39.5	...	...	...	...
	2000-05	67.2	71.9	3.8	35.7	...	...	...	250
Panama Panama	1995-00	71.3	76.4	2.8	23.7	1996[3]	4.7	4.1	...
	2000-05	72.3	77.4	2.7	20.6	1999[3]	4.7	3.9	100
Puerto Rico Porto Rico	1995-00	70.4	79.6	2.0	11.0	1997	0.4	0.3	...
	2000-05	71.2	80.1	1.9	10.3	2000	0.4	0.3	30
Saint Lucia Sainte-Lucie	1995-00	69.8	73.1	2.4	16.9	...	...	...	...
	2000-05	70.8	74.1	2.3	14.8	...	...	...	...
St. Vincent-Grenadines St. Vincent-Grenadines	1995-00	71.8	74.6	2.4	18.1	...	...	...	...
	2000-05	72.6	75.6	2.2	15.7	...	...	...	...
Trinidad and Tobago Trinité-et-Tobago	1995-00	69.2	75.2	1.7	15.1	1995[7]	0.7	0.6	...
	2000-05	68.4	74.4	1.6	14.1	1997	0.8	0.7[7]	65
United States Etats-Unis	1995-00	73.2	79.1	2.1	7.2	1995	0.4	0.4	...
	2000-05	74.3	79.9	2.1	6.7	2000[3]	1.9	1.6	12
United States Virgin Is. Iles Vierges américaines	1995-00	73.4	81.5	2.3	11.4	...	...	...	...
	2000-05	74.2	82.0	2.2	10.1	1990[7]	1.1	...	...

America, South · Amérique du Sud

Country or area Pays ou zone	Year Année	Males Hommes	Females Femmes	Total fertility	Infant M+F	Year Année	Males Hommes	Females Femmes	Maternal 1995
Argentina Argentine	1995-00	69.7	76.8	2.6	21.8	1993[3]	5.6	4.5	...
	2000-05	70.6	77.7	2.4	20.0	1995[3,12]	5.5	4.5	85
Bolivia Bolivie	1995-00	60.1	64.0	4.3	66.7	...	...	...	...
	2000-05	61.8	66.0	3.8	55.6	...	...	...	550
Brazil Brésil	1995-00	63.0	71.5	2.3	42.4	1995[13]	1.2	1.0	...
	2000-05	64.0	72.6	2.2	38.4	1998[13]	1.0	0.9	260
Chile Chili	1995-00	72.3	78.3	2.4	12.8	1998	0.6	0.4	...
	2000-05	73.0	79.0	2.4	11.6	1999	0.4	0.4	33
Colombia Colombie	1995-00	67.3	74.3	2.8	30.0	1993[4,8,12,14]	4.3[3]	3.5[3]	...
	2000-05	69.2	75.3	2.6	25.6	2000[4,8,12,14]	0.9	0.8	120
Ecuador Equateur	1995-00	67.3	72.5	3.1	45.6	1992[15]	3.1	3.0	...
	2000-05	68.3	73.5	2.8	41.5	1997[15]	2.3	2.1	210
French Guiana Guyane française	1995-00	71.5	77.5	3.8	16.4	...	...	...	...
	2000-05	72.5	78.3	3.3	14.3	...	...	...	...

11

Selected indicators of life expectancy, childbearing and mortality *[cont.]*
Choix d'indicateurs de l'espérance de vie, de la maternité et de la mortalité *[suite]*

		Life expectancy at birth (years) Espérance de vie à la naissance (en années)		Total fertility rate	Infant Infantile p. 1,000	Mortality rates – Taux de mortalité			Maternal Maternelle p.100,000
						Child – Juvenile p. 1,000			
Country or area Pays ou zone	Year Année	Males Hommes	Females Femmes	Taux de fecondité	M+F	Year Année	Males Hommes	Females Femmes	1995
Guyana	1995-00	60.2	67.1	2.5	55.6	...	...	...	
Guyana	2000-05	60.1	66.3	2.3	51.2				...
Paraguay	1995-00	67.5	72.0	4.2	39.2	1985[3]	5.4	4.8	150
Paraguay	2000-05	68.6	73.1	3.8	37.0	1992	0.7	0.6	...
Peru	1995-00	65.9	70.9	3.2	42.1	1984[13]	4.7	4.6	170
Pérou	2000-05	67.3	72.4	2.9	33.4	1985[3,13]	10.8	9.9	...
Suriname	1995-00	67.5	72.7	2.6	29.1	1995[3]	6.2	4.7	240
Suriname	2000-05	68.5	73.7	2.5	25.7	2000[3]	4.2	4.5	...
Uruguay	1995-00	70.5	78.0	2.4	17.5	1990[13]	5.6	4.5	230
Uruguay	2000-05	71.6	78.9	2.3	13.1	2000[12]	0.7	0.5	...
Venezuela	1995-00	70.0	75.7	3.0	20.9	1990[3,13]	7.0	5.7	50
Venezuela	2000-05	70.9	76.7	2.7	18.9	2000[3,13]	4.2	3.3	43
Asia · Asie									
Afghanistan	1995-00	41.9	42.3	6.9	166.6	...	...	...	
Afghanistan	2000-05	43.0	43.3	6.8	161.7				...
Armenia	1995-00	68.0	74.6	1.4	21.5	1996[16]	0.8	0.7	820
Arménie	2000-05	69.0	75.6	1.2	17.3	2000[16]	0.9	0.8	29
Azerbaijan	1995-00	67.2	74.5	2.3	32.5	1996[16]	3.7	3.3	...
Azerbaïdjan	2000-05	68.7	75.5	2.1	29.3	2001[4,16]	2.4	2.2	37
Bahrain	1995-00	71.3	75.1	3.0	16.3	1995[3]	4.4	4.1	...
Bahreïn	2000-05	72.5	75.9	2.7	14.2	1998[3]	2.1	1.8	38
Bangladesh	1995-00	58.1	58.8	4.0	77.5	1981	14.1	15.8	...
Bangladesh	2000-05	61.0	61.8	3.5	64.0	1986[3]	43.1	41.1	600
Bhutan	1995-00	59.5	62.0	5.5	62.9	...	...	...	...
Bhoutan	2000-05	62.0	64.5	5.0	53.6	...	...	...	500
Brunei Darussalam	1995-00	73.4	78.1	2.7	6.7	...	...	...	...
Brunéi Darussalam	2000-05	74.2	78.9	2.5	6.1	...	...	...	22
Cambodia	1995-00	55.1	59.0	5.3	82.0	...	...	...	...
Cambodge	2000-05	55.2	59.5	4.8	73.2	...	...	...	590
China	1995-00	67.8	71.9	1.8	41.5	...	...	...	...
Chine	2000-05	68.9	73.3	1.8	36.6	1999[3]	6.1	7.3	60
China, Hong Kong SAR	1995-00	76.5	82.0	1.1	4.2	1997	0.3	0.2	...
Chine, Hong Kong RAS	2000-05	77.3	82.8	1.0	4.1	2000[7,12]	0.2	0.2	0
China, Macao SAR	1995-00	75.7	80.4	1.2	9.3	1997[3,7]	1.2	1.2	...
Chine, Macao RAS	2000-05	76.5	81.2	1.1	8.6	2000[3,7]	0.8	0.6	20
Cyprus	1995-00	75.2	80.1	2.0	8.2	1997[3,7,17]	0.3	0.1	...
Chypre	2000-05	76.0	80.5	1.9	7.7	1999[3,17]	1.2	1.2[7]	0
Timor-Leste	1995-00	46.7	48.4	4.4	135.0	...	...	...	...
Timor-Leste	2000-05	48.7	50.4	3.9	123.7	...	...	...	850
Georgia	1995-00	68.5	76.8	1.6	19.4	...	...	...	...
Géorgie	2000-05	69.5	77.6	1.4	17.6	2000[16]	0.4	0.3[7]	22
India	1995-00	61.7	62.5	3.5	72.3	...	...	...	...
Inde	2000-05	63.2	64.6	3.0	64.5	...	...	...	440
Indonesia	1995-00	63.0	66.8	2.6	49.5	...	...	...	...
Indonésie	2000-05	64.8	68.8	2.4	41.6	...	...	...	470
Iran (Islamic Rep. of)	1995-00	67.4	69.9	2.5	41.1	1986	3.9	1.4	...
Iran (Rép. islamique d')	2000-05	68.9	71.9	2.3	33.3	1991	5.1	3.9	130
Iraq	1995-00	57.2	60.3	5.3	94.8	1987[3]	5.7	4.4	...
Iraq	2000-05	59.2	62.3	4.8	83.3	1988[3]	5.7	4.4	370
Israel	1995-00	76.3	80.2	2.9	6.3	1996[18]	0.4	0.4	...
Israël	2000-05	77.1	81.0	2.7	5.9	1998[8,18]	0.5	0.3	8
Japan	1995-00	77.1	83.8	1.4	3.8	1997[19]	0.4	0.3	...
Japon	2000-05	77.9	85.1	1.3	3.2	2000[20]	0.3	0.3	12
Jordan	1995-00	68.5	71.0	4.1	28.3	...	...	...	...
Jordanie	2000-05	69.7	72.5	3.6	23.9	...	...	...	41
Kazakhstan	1995-00	58.9	70.7	2.1	58.5	1997[16]	2.1	1.7	...
Kazakhstan	2000-05	60.9	71.9	2.0	51.7	1999[16]	1.7	1.5	80
Korea, Dem. P. R.	1995-00	60.5	66.0	2.1	45.1	...	...	...	...
Corée, R. p. dém. de	2000-05	60.5	66.0	2.0	45.1	1993[3]	5.6	5.1	35

11

Selected indicators of life expectancy, childbearing and mortality *[cont.]*
Choix d'indicateurs de l'espérance de vie, de la maternité et de la mortalité *[suite]*

Country or area Pays ou zone	Year Année	Life expectancy at birth (years) Espérance de vie à la naissance (en années)		Total fertility rate Taux de fecondité	Infant Infantile p. 1,000 M+F	Mortality rates – Taux de mortalité			Maternal Maternale p.100,000
		Males Hommes	Females Femmes			Child – Juvenile p. 1,000			
						Year Année	Males Hommes	Females Femmes	1995
Korea, Republic of	1995-00	70.6	78.3	1.5	7.8	1995[21,22]	0.7	0.7	...
Corée, République de	2000-05	71.8	79.3	1.4	5.0	2000[21]	0.5	0.4	20
Kuwait	1995-00	74.1	78.2	2.9	12.3	1996[3]	3.4	3.1	...
Koweït	2000-05	74.9	79.0	2.7	10.8	1998	0.6	0.5	25
Kyrgyzstan	1995-00	62.8	71.1	2.9	43.2	1996[16]	2.8	2.5	...
Kirghizistan	2000-05	64.8	72.3	2.6	37.0	2000[16]	2.8	2.4	80
Lao People's Dem. Rep.	1995-00	51.3	53.8	5.3	96.6	...	...	...	...
Rép. dém. pop. lao	2000-05	53.3	55.8	4.8	88.0	...			650
Lebanon	1995-00	71.1	74.1	2.3	20.0	...			...
Liban	2000-05	71.9	75.1	2.2	17.2	...	...	...	130
Malaysia	1995-00	69.6	74.5	3.3	11.6	1997	0.8	0.7	...
Malaisie	2000-05	70.8	75.7	2.9	10.1	1998	0.7	0.7	39
Maldives	1995-00	66.3	64.5	5.8	46.4	1990	3.8	4.3	...
Maldives	2000-05	67.8	67.0	5.3	38.3	1996[3]	6.6	6.1	390
Mongolia	1995-00	59.9	63.9	2.7	65.8	1998	4.1	3.7	...
Mongolie	2000-05	61.9	65.9	2.4	58.2	2000	3.6	2.8	65
Myanmar	1995-00	54.0	58.9	3.3	90.8	...	...	...	...
Myanmar	2000-05	54.6	60.2	2.9	83.5	...			170
Nepal	1995-00	57.6	57.1	4.7	82.6	...	...	...	...
Népal	2000-05	60.1	59.6	4.3	70.9	...			830
Occupied Palestinian Terr.	1995-00	69.8	73.0	6.0	24.0	...	...	...	...
Terr. palestinien occupé	2000-05	70.8	74.0	5.6	20.7	...			120
Oman	1995-00	70.2	73.4	5.4	22.6	...	...	...	...
Oman	2000-05	71.0	74.4	5.0	19.7	...			120
Pakistan	1995-00	59.2	58.9	5.5	95.3	...			...
Pakistan	2000-05	61.2	60.9	5.1	86.5	1997[3,23]	28.0	25.8	200
Philippines	1995-00	66.5	70.7	3.6	34.4	1990	3.8	3.3	...
Philippines	2000-05	68.0	72.0	3.2	29.0	1991	2.8	2.5	240
Qatar	1995-00	69.3	74.2	3.7	15.8	...	...	...	...
Qatar	2000-05	70.5	75.4	3.2	12.3	...	...	...	41
Saudi Arabia	1995-00	69.9	72.2	5.1	25.0	...	...	...	...
Arabie saoudite	2000-05	71.1	73.7	4.5	20.6	...			23
Singapore	1995-00	75.1	79.3	1.6	3.5	1998[3,4,24]	1.1	1.0	...
Singapour	2000-05	75.9	80.3	1.4	2.9	2000[3,24]	1.0	0.8	9
Sri Lanka	1995-00	69.0	74.7	2.1	22.9	1995[3,4]	3.2	2.8	...
Sri Lanka	2000-05	69.9	75.9	2.0	20.1	1996[3,4]	3.4	2.8	60
Syrian Arab Republic	1995-00	69.4	71.6	3.8	26.9	...	...	...	...
Rép. arabe syrienne	2000-05	70.6	73.1	3.3	22.3	1984[25]	2.8	2.9	200
Tajikistan	1995-00	64.2	70.2	3.7	56.6	1991[16]	5.1	4.8	...
Tadjikistan	2000-05	66.2	71.4	3.1	50.0	1993[16]	9.0	8.5	120
Thailand	1995-00	64.0	72.5	2.0	23.4	1990[3]	2.3	1.6	...
Thaïlande	2000-05	65.3	73.5	1.9	19.8	1999[3]	2.2	1.9	44
Turkey	1995-00	66.5	71.7	2.7	47.0	...	...	...	...
Turquie	2000-05	68.0	73.2	2.4	39.5	...	...	...	55
Turkmenistan	1995-00	61.9	68.9	3.0	54.8	...	...	...	...
Turkménistan	2000-05	63.9	70.4	2.7	48.6	...			65
United Arab Emirates	1995-00	72.3	76.4	3.2	15.7	...	...	...	...
Emirats arabes unis	2000-05	73.3	77.4	2.8	13.6	...			30
Uzbekistan	1995-00	65.3	71.3	2.9	41.0	1997[16]	3.6	3.3	...
Ouzbékistan	2000-05	66.8	72.5	2.4	36.7	2000[16]	2.4	2.2	60
Viet Nam	1995-00	64.9	69.6	2.5	40.1	...	...	...	...
Viet Nam	2000-05	66.9	71.6	2.3	33.6	...	...	...	95
Yemen	1995-00	56.9	59.1	7.3	80.0	...	...	...	...
Yémen	2000-05	58.9	61.1	7.0	70.6	...	...	...	850
Europe · Europe									
Albania	1995-00	69.9	75.9	2.4	28.3	...	...	...	...
Albanie	2000-05	70.9	76.7	2.3	25.0	...	...	...	31
Austria	1995-00	74.4	80.7	1.4	5.4	1991	0.4	0.3	...
Autriche	2000-05	75.4	81.5	1.3	4.7	2001[3]	1.3	0.9	11

11
Selected indicators of life expectancy, childbearing and mortality *[cont.]*
Choix d'indicateurs de l'espérance de vie, de la maternité et de la mortalité *[suite]*

		Life expectancy at birth (years) Espérance de vie à la naissance (en années)		Total fertility rate Taux de fecondité	Infant Infantile p. 1,000	Mortality rates – Taux de mortalité			Maternal Maternale p.100,000
							Child – Juvenile p. 1,000		
Country or area Pays ou zone	Year Année	Males Hommes	Females Femmes	Taux de fecondité	M+F	Year Année	Males Hommes	Females Femmes	1995
Belarus	1995-00	62.9	74.3	1.3	12.5	1997[16]	0.8	0.6	...
Bélarus	2000-05	64.9	75.3	1.2	11.3	1999[16]	1.0	0.7	33
Belgium	1995-00	74.7	81.1	1.6	4.4	1987[26]	0.4	0.4	...
Belgique	2000-05	75.7	81.9	1.7	4.2	2001[3,26]	1.3	1.0	8
Bosnia and Herzegovina	1995-00	70.5	75.9	1.4	15.0	...	...	...	...
Bosnie-Herzégovine	2000-05	71.3	76.7	1.3	13.5	...	...	...	15
Bulgaria	1995-00	67.4	74.6	1.1	15.2	1997	1.2	1.2	...
Bulgarie	2000-05	67.4	74.6	1.1	15.2	2001	0.7	0.7	23
Channel Islands	1995-00	75.2	79.9	1.5	5.8	...	...	...	...
Iles Anglo-Normandes	2000-05	75.7	80.7	1.5	5.5	...	...	...	...
Croatia	1995-00	69.3	77.3	1.6	10.1	1991	0.4	0.3	...
Croatie	2000-05	70.3	78.1	1.7	8.1	2001	0.4	0.2[7]	18
Czech Republic	1995-00	70.8	77.7	1.2	6.9	2000	0.3	0.3	...
République tchèque	2000-05	72.1	78.7	1.2	5.6	2001[3]	1.1	0.9	14
Denmark	1995-00	73.4	78.3	1.8	5.9	1997	0.3	0.2[7]	...
Danemark	2000-05	74.2	79.1	1.8	5.0	2001[3]	1.1	1.2	15
Estonia	1995-00	64.5	75.8	1.3	10.7	1995[16]	1.3	0.8	...
Estonie	2000-05	66.5	76.8	1.2	9.4	2000[7,16,27]	0.7	0.5	80
Finland	1995-00	73.4	80.7	1.7	4.4	1998[7,28]	0.2	0.1	...
Finlande	2000-05	74.4	81.5	1.7	4.0	2001[3,28]	0.9	0.6	6
France	1995-00	74.2	82.0	1.8	5.5	1990[3,29,30]	2.5	1.8	...
France	2000-05	75.2	82.8	1.9	5.0	1999[29,30]	0.3	0.2	20
Germany	1995-00	74.2	80.4	1.3	4.9	1996	0.3	0.3	...
Allemagne	2000-05	75.2	81.2	1.4	4.5	1999[3]	1.2	1.0	12
Greece	1995-00	75.2	80.4	1.3	6.8	1991	0.3	0.2	...
Grèce	2000-05	75.7	80.9	1.3	6.4	1998	0.3	0.3	2
Hungary	1995-00	66.2	75.0	1.4	9.7	1997[31]	0.5	0.4	...
Hongrie	2000-05	67.7	76.0	1.2	8.8	2001[31]	0.4	0.2	23
Iceland	1995-00	77.1	81.4	2.1	3.5	2000[7]	0.1	0.4	...
Islande	2000-05	77.6	81.9	2.0	3.4	2001[3,7]	0.7	...	16
Ireland	1995-00	73.5	78.8	1.9	6.3	1996[4,32]	0.3	0.3	...
Irlande	2000-05	74.4	79.6	1.9	5.8	2001[3,4,32]	1.7	1.3	9
Italy	1995-00	75.0	81.4	1.2	5.6	1994	0.3	0.3	...
Italie	2000-05	75.5	81.9	1.2	5.4	1995	0.3	0.3	11
Latvia	1995-00	63.6	75.0	1.2	16.0	1997[16]	0.8	0.4[7]	...
Lettonie	2000-05	65.6	76.2	1.1	14.2	2001[16]	0.8	0.5[7]	70
Lithuania	1995-00	66.0	76.6	1.4	10.7	1997[16]	0.7	0.5	...
Lituanie	2000-05	67.5	77.6	1.3	8.7	2001[16]	0.7	0.5	27
Luxembourg	1995-00	74.1	80.6	1.7	5.9	1996[7]	0.4	0.6	...
Luxembourg	2000-05	75.1	81.4	1.7	5.4	2001[3,7]	1.7	1.3	0
Malta	1995-00	74.9	79.7	1.9	7.9	1996[3,33]	2.1	2.7	...
Malte	2000-05	75.9	80.7	1.8	7.1	2001[3,7,33]	1.5	0.8	0
Netherlands	1995-00	75.1	80.5	1.6	4.6	1996[34,35]	0.3	0.3	...
Pays-Bas	2000-05	75.6	81.0	1.7	4.5	2001[34]	0.5	0.3	10
Norway	1995-00	75.2	81.1	1.9	4.8	1997[36]	0.3	0.3	...
Norvège	2000-05	76.0	81.9	1.8	4.5	2001[3,36]	1.1	0.8	9
Poland	1995-00	68.6	77.2	1.5	10.0	1999	0.4	0.3	...
Pologne	2000-05	69.8	78.0	1.3	9.1	2001[3]	1.9	1.5	12
Portugal	1995-00	71.6	78.8	1.5	6.6	1991[8]	0.9	0.7	...
Portugal	2000-05	72.6	79.6	1.5	6.1	2001[3,8]	1.5	1.1	12
Republic of Moldova	1995-00	63.5	71.0	1.6	19.6	1992[16]	1.6	0.9	...
République de Moldova	2000-05	65.5	72.2	1.4	18.1	2001[16]	1.1	0.7	65
Romania	1995-00	67.0	74.2	1.3	20.0	1997	1.2	1.0	...
Roumanie	2000-05	67.0	74.2	1.3	20.0	2001	0.9	0.8	60
Russian Federation	1995-00	60.2	72.5	1.3	16.8	1995[16]	1.2	0.9	...
Fédération de Russie	2000-05	60.8	73.1	1.1	15.9	1999[16]	1.1	0.9	75
Serbia and Montenegro	1995-00	69.9	74.6	1.8	14.8	1997	0.6	0.4	...
Serbie-et-Monténégro	2000-05	70.9	75.6	1.7	13.0	2000	0.6	0.6	15
Slovakia	1995-00	68.1	76.4	1.4	10.0	1991	0.6	0.5	...
Slovaquie	2000-05	69.8	77.6	1.3	8.0	2001	0.4	0.3	14

11
Selected indicators of life expectancy, childbearing and mortality *[cont.]*
Choix d'indicateurs de l'espérance de vie, de la maternité et de la mortalité *[suite]*

Country or area Pays ou zone	Year Année	Life expectancy at birth (years) Espérance de vie à la naissance (en années) Males Hommes	Females Femmes	Total fertility rate Taux de fecondité	Infant Infantile p. 1,000 M+F	Mortality rates – Taux de mortalité Child – Juvenile p. 1,000 Year Année	Males Hommes	Females Femmes	Maternal Maternale p.100,000 1995
Slovenia	1995-00	71.4	78.8	1.3	6.0	1994[7]	0.5	0.3	...
Slovénie	2000-05	72.6	79.8	1.1	5.5	2001[3]	1.0	0.8	17
Spain	1995-00	74.9	82.0	1.2	5.5	1996	0.4	0.3	...
Espagne	2000-05	75.9	82.8	1.2	5.1	2000	0.3	0.2	8
Sweden	1995-00	76.8	81.8	1.6	3.5	1996	0.2	0.2	...
Suède	2000-05	77.6	82.6	1.6	3.4	2001[3]	1.0	0.8	8
Switzerland	1995-00	75.4	81.8	1.5	5.1	1990	0.5	0.3	...
Suisse	2000-05	75.9	82.3	1.4	4.8	2001[3]	1.3	1.0	8
TFYR of Macedonia	1995-00	70.6	74.8	1.9	18.2	1997	0.7	0.7	...
L'ex-R.y. Macédoine	2000-05	71.4	75.8	1.9	16.0	2001[7]	0.4	0.4	17
Ukraine	1995-00	62.7	73.7	1.3	15.3	1998[16]	1.0	0.8	...
Ukraine	2000-05	64.7	74.7	1.2	13.8	2001[16]	1.0	0.7	45
United Kingdom	1995-00	74.7	79.7	1.7	5.9	1997[37]	0.3	0.2	...
Royaume-Uni	2000-05	75.7	80.7	1.6	5.4	1999[3]	1.5	1.2	10
Oceania · Océanie									
Australia	1995-00	75.9[38]	81.5[38]	1.8[38]	6.3[38]	1995[4]	0.4	0.3	...
Australie	2000-05	76.4[38]	82.0[38]	1.7[38]	5.5[38]	2000[4]	0.3	0.2	6
Fiji	1995-00	66.6	70.3	3.2	20.1	1986[4]	1.2	1.3	...
Fidji	2000-05	68.1	71.5	2.9	17.8	1987[4]	1.1	0.8	20
French Polynesia	1995-00	69.4	74.4	2.6	9.7	...	...	...	...
Polynésie française	2000-05	70.7	75.8	2.4	8.7	...	...	...	20
Guam	1995-00	71.4	76.0	3.2	11.0	...	...	...	...
Guam	2000-05	72.4	77.0	2.9	9.8	...	...	...	12
Micronesia (Fed. States)	1995-00	66.5	67.6	4.3	40.0	...	...	...	...
Micronésie (Etats féd. de)	2000-05	68.0	69.1	3.8	33.9	...	...	...	...
New Caledonia	1995-00	71.5	76.7	2.6	7.2	...	...	...	...
Nouvelle-Calédonie	2000-05	72.5	77.7	2.5	6.6	1994[7]	1.3	1.4	10
New Zealand	1995-00	75.0	80.2	2.0	6.9	1996[4,8]	0.5	0.4	...
Nouvelle-Zélande	2000-05	75.8	80.7	2.0	5.8	2000[4,8]	0.4	0.3	15
Papua New Guinea	1995-00	54.8	56.7	4.6	69.0	...	...	...	...
Papouasie-Nvl-Guinée	2000-05	56.8	58.7	4.1	62.1	...	...	...	390
Samoa	1995-00	65.4	71.9	4.5	29.9	...	...	...	...
Samoa	2000-05	66.9	73.4	4.1	26.1	...	...	...	15
Solomon Islands	1995-00	66.4	68.7	5.0	24.0	...	...	...	...
Iles Salomon	2000-05	67.9	70.7	4.4	20.7	...	...	...	60
Tonga	1995-00	66.5	67.6	4.2	40.0	...	...	...	...
Tonga	2000-05	68.0	69.1	3.7	33.9	...	...	...	...
Vanuatu	1995-00	66.0	69.0	4.6	32.5	...	...	...	...
Vanuatu	2000-05	67.5	70.5	4.1	28.5	...	...	...	32

Source:
United Nations, "World Population Prospects: The 2002 Revision" and "Demographic Yearbook, 2001"; World Health Organization, the United Nations Children's Fund and the United Nations Population Fund, "Maternal Mortality in 1995: Estimates developed by WHO, UNICEF, UNFPA".

Source :
Organisation des Nations Unies, "World Population Prospects: The 2000 Revision" et "Annuair démographique 1999"; Organisation mondiale de la la santé, Fonds des Nations Unies pour l'enfance et Fonds des Nations Unies pour la population, "Maternal Mortality in 1995 : Estimates developed by WHO, UNICEF, UNFPA".

1   Excluding live-born infants dying before registration of birth.
2   For Algerian population only.
3   0-4 years old.
4   Data tabulated by date of registration rather than occurrence.
5   Based on the results of the population census.
6   Including Agalega, Rodrigues and Saint Brandon.
7   Rates based on 30 or fewer deaths.
8   Urban/rural figures, excluding deaths of unknown residence.

1   Non compris les enfants nés vivants décédés avant l'enregistrement de leur naissance.
2   Pour la population algérienne seulement.
3   De 0 à 4 ans.
4   Données exploitées selon l'année de l'enregistrement et non l'année de l'événement.
5   D'après les résultats du recensement de la population.
6   Y compris Agalega, Rodrigues et Saint Brandon.
7   Taux basés sur 30 décès ou moins.
8   Les données selon la résidence urbaine/rurale, non compris les décès dont on ignore la résidence.

11
Selected indicators of life expectancy, childbearing and mortality *[cont.]*
Choix d'indicateurs de l'espérance de vie, de la maternité et de la mortalité *[suite]*

9	Data refer to last twelve months preceding census of 1997.	9	Les données se réfèrent aux 12 mois précédant le recensement de 1997.
10	Domicile population only.	10	Pour la population dans les domiciles seulement.
11	Including Canadian residents temporarily in the United States, but excluding United States residents temporarily in Canada.	11	Y compris les résidents canadiens se trouvant temporairement aux Etats-Unis, mais ne comprennent pas les résidents des Etats-Unis se trouvant temporairement au Canada.
12	Data for males/females, excluding deaths of unknown sex.	12	Les données pour le sexe masculin et féminin, non compris les décès dont on ignore le sexe.
13	Excluding Indian jungle population.	13	Non compris les Indiens de la jungle.
14	Deaths based on burial permits.	14	Décès d'après les permis d'inhumer délivrés.
15	Excluding nomadic Indian tribes.	15	Non compris les tribus d'Indiens nomades.
16	Excluding infants born alive after less than 28 weeks' gestation, of less than 1 000 grams in weight and 35 centimeters in length, who die within seven days of birth.	16	Non compris les enfants nés vivants après moins de 28 semaines de gestation, pesant moins de 1 000 grammes, mesurant moins de 35 centimètres et décédés dans les sept jours qui ont suivi leur naissance.
17	Beginning 1986, for government controlled areas.	17	De compter à l'année 1986, pour les zones contrôlées par le Gouvernement.
18	Including data for East Jerusalem and Israeli residents in certain other territories under occupation by Israeli military forces since June 1967.	18	Y compris les données pour Jérusalem-Est et les résidents israéliens dans certains autres territoires occupés depuis 1967 par les forces armées israéliennes.
19	For Japanese nationals in Japan only.	19	Pour les nationaux japonais au Japon seulement.
20	For Japanese nationals in Japan only; however, rates computed on population including foreigners except foreign military and civilian personnel and their dependants stationed in the area.	20	Pour les nationaux japonais au Japon seulement; toutefois, les taux sont calculés sur la base d'une population comprenant les étrangers, mais ne comprenant ni les militaires et agents civils étrangers en poste sur la territoire ni les membres de leur famille les accompangnant.
21	Excluding alien armed forces, civilian aliens employed by armed forces, foreign diplomatic personnel and their dependants and Korean diplomatic personnel and their dependants outside the country.	21	Non compris les militaires étrangers, les civils étrangers employés par les forces armées, le personnel diplomatique étranger et les membres de leur famille les accompagnant et le personnel diplomatique coréen hors du pays et les membres de leurs familles les accompagnant.
22	Based on the results of the Continuous Demographic Sample Survey.	22	D'après les résultats d'une enquête démographique par sondage.
23	Based on the results of the Population Growth Survey.	23	D'après les résultats de la 'Population Growth Survey'.
24	Excluding transients afloat and non-locally domiciled military and civilian services personnel and their dependants.	24	Non compris les personnes de passage þ bord de navires, ni les militaires et agents civils domiciliés hors du territoire et les membres de leur famille les accompagnant.
25	Excluding deaths for which cause is unknown.	25	Non compris les décès dont on ignore la cause.
26	Including armed forces stationed outside the country, but excluding alien armed forces stationed in the area.	26	Y compris les militaires nationaux hors du pays, mais non compris les militaires étrangers en garnison sur le territoire.
27	Excluding deaths of unknown residence.	27	Non compris les décès dont on ignore la résidence.
28	Including nationals temporarily outside the country.	28	Y compris les nationaux se trouvant temporairement hors du pays.
29	Including armed forces stationed outside the country.	29	Y compris les militaires nationaux hors du pays.
30	Excluding nationals outside the country.	30	Non compris les nationaux se trouvant hors du pays.
31	Data for urban/rural residence, for the de jure population.	31	Les données selon la résidence urbaine/rurale, pour la population de droit.
32	Events registered within one year of occurrence.	32	Evénements enregistrés dans l'année qui suit l'événement.
33	Rates computed on population including civilian nationals temporarily outside the country.	33	Les taux sont calculés sur la base d'un chiffre de population qui comprend les civils nationaux temporairement hors du pays.
34	Total including residents outside the country if listed in a Netherlands population register.	34	Y compris les résidents hors du pays, s'ils sont inscrits sur un registre de population néerlandais.
35	Urban and rural residence, excluding persons on the Central Register of Population (containing persons belonging in the Netherlands population but having no fixed municipality of residence).	35	Résidence urbaine et rurale, non compris les personnes inscrites sur le Registre Central de la population (personnes appartenant à la population néerlandaise mais sans résidence fixe dans l'une des municipalités).
36	Including residents temporarily outside the country.	36	Y compris les nationaux se trouvant temporairement hors du pays.
37	Data tabulated by date of occurrence for England and Wales, and by date of registration for Northern Ireland and Scotland.	37	Données exploitées selon l'année de l'événement pour l'Angleterre et pays de Galles et selon l'année de l'enregistrement pour Irlande du Nord et l'Ecosse.
38	Including Christmas Island, Cocos (Keeling) Islands and Norfolk Island.	38	Y compris les îles Christmas, Cocos (Keeling) et Norfolk.

Technical notes, tables 10 and 11

Table 10: Estimates on food supply are published by the Food and Agriculture Organization of the United Nations in *Food Balance Sheets* [5] and on its Web site <http://faostat.fao.org>, in which the data give estimates of total and per caput food supplies per day available for human consumption during the reference period in terms of quantity and, by applying appropriate food composition factors for all primary and processed products, also in terms of caloric value and protein and fat content. Calorie supplies are reported in kilocalories. The traditional unit of calories is being retained for the time being until the proposed kilojoule gains wider acceptance and understanding (1 calorie = 4.19 kilojoules). Per caput supplies in terms of product weight are derived from the total supplies available for human consumption (i.e. Food) by dividing the quantities of Food by the total population actually partaking of the food supplies during the reference period, i.e. the present in-area (de facto) population within the present geographical boundaries of the country. In other words, nationals living abroad during the reference period are excluded, but foreigners living in the country are included. Adjustments are made wherever possible for part-time presence or absence, such as temporary migrants, tourists and refugees supported by special schemes (if it has not been possible to allow for the amounts provided by such schemes under imports). In almost all cases, the population figures used are the mid-year estimates published by the United Nations Population Division.

Per caput supply figures shown in the commodity balances therefore represent only the average supply available for the population as a whole and do not necessarily indicate what is actually consumed by individuals. Even if they are taken as an approximation of per caput consumption, it is important to bear in mind that there could be considerable variation in consumption between individuals.

Table 11: "Life expectancy at birth", "Infant mortality rate" and "Total fertility rate" are taken from the estimates and projections prepared by the Population Division of the United Nations Secretariat, published in *World Population Prospects: The 2002 Revision* [29].

"Life expectancy at birth" is an overall estimate of the expected average number of years to be lived by a female or male newborn. Many developing countries lack complete and reliable statistics of births and deaths based on civil registration, so various estimation techniques are used to calculate life expectancy using other sources of data, mainly population censuses and demographic surveys. Life expectancy at birth by sex gives a statistical summary of current differences in male and female mortality across all ages. However, trends and differentials in infant and child mortality rates are the predominant influence on trends and differentials in life

Notes techniques, tableaux 10 et 11

Tableau 10: Les estimations sur les disponibilités alimentaires sont publiées par l'Organisation des Nations Unies pour l'alimentation et l'agriculture dans les *Bilans alimentaires* [5] et sur le site Web <www.fao.org> où les données donnent des estimations des disponibilités alimentaires totales et par habitant par jour pour la consommation humaine durant la période de référence, en quantité, en calories, en protéines et en lipides. Les calories sont exprimées en kilocalories. L'unité traditionnelle pour les calories n'est pas utilisée pour l'instant jusqu'à ce que le kilojoule soit plus largement accepté (1 calorie = 4,19 kilojoules). Les disponibilités par habitant exprimées en poids du produit sont calculées à partir des disponibilités totales pour la consommation humaine (c'est-à-dire "Alimentation humaine") en divisant ce chiffre par la population totale qui a effectivement eu accès aux approvisionnements alimentaires durant la période de référence, c'est-à-dire par la population présente (de facto) dans les limites géographiques actuelles du pays. En d'autres termes, les ressortissants du pays vivant à l'étranger durant la période de référence sont exclus, mais les étrangers vivant dans le pays sont inclus. Des ajustements ont été opérés chaque fois que possible pour tenir compte des présences ou des absences de durée limitée, comme dans le cas des imigrants/émigrants temporaires, des touristes et des réfugiés bénéficiant de programmes alimentaires spéciaux (s'il n'a pas été possible de tenir compte des vivres fournis à ce titre à travers les importations). Dans la plupart des cas, les données démographiques utilisés sont les estimations au milieu de l'année publiées par la Division de la population des Nations Unies.

Les disponibilités alimentaires par habitant figurant dans les bilans ne représentent donc que les disponibilités moyennes pour l'ensemble de la population et n'indiquent pas nécessairement la consommation effective des individus. Même si elles sont considérées comme une estimation approximative de la consommation par habitant, il importe de ne pas oublier que la consommation peut varier beaucoup selon les individus.

Tableau 11: L'"espérance de vie à la naissance", le "taux de mortalité infantile" et le "taux de fécondité" sont proviennent des estimations et projections de la Division de la population du Secrétariat de l'ONU, qui ont publiées dans *World Population Prospects: The 2002 Revision* [29].

L'"espérance de vie à la naissance" est une estimation globale du nombre d'années qu'un nouveau-né de sexe masculin ou féminin vivant, peut s'attendre à vivre. Comme dans beaucoup de pays en développement, les registres d'état civil ne permettent pas d'établir des statistiques fiables et complètes des naissances et des décès, diverses techniques d'estimation ont été utilisées pour calculer l'espérance de vie à partir d'autres sources et notamment des recensements et enquêtes démographi-

expectancy at birth in most developing countries. Thus, life expectancy at birth is of limited usefulness in these countries in assessing levels and differentials in male and female mortality at other ages.

"Infant mortality rate" is the total number of deaths in a given year of children less than one year old divided by the total number of live births in the same year, multiplied by 1,000. It is an approximation of the number of deaths per 1,000 children born alive who die within one year of birth. In most developing countries where civil registration data are deficient, the most reliable sources are demographic surveys of households. Where these are not available, other sources and general estimates are made which are necessarily of limited reliability. Where countries lack comprehensive and accurate systems of civil registration, infant mortality statistics by sex are difficult to collect or to estimate with any degree of reliability because of reporting biases, and thus are not shown here.

"Total fertility rate" is the average number of children that would be born alive to a hypothetical cohort of women if, throughout their reproductive years, the age-specific fertility rates for the specified year remained unchanged.

"Child mortality rate" is defined as the annual number of deaths among children aged 1-4 years per 1,000 population of the same age. These series have been compiled by the Statistics Division of the United Nations Secretariat for the *Demographic Yearbook* [22] and are subject to the limitations of national reporting in this field.

Data on maternal mortality are estimates developed by the World Health Organization, UNICEF and the United Nations Population fund and published in *Maternal Mortality in 1995* [36].

ques. Sur la base des statistiques de l'espérance de vie par sexe, on peut calculer la différence entre la longévité des hommes et celle des femmes à tous les âges. Cependant, ce sont les tendances et les écarts des taux de mortalité infantile et juvénile qui influent de façon prépondérante sur les tendances et les écarts de l'espérance de vie à la naissance dans la plupart des pays en développement. Ainsi, l'espérance de vie à la naissance ne revêt qu'une utilité limitée dans ce pays pour évaluer les niveaux et les écarts de la mortalité des femmes et des hommes à des âges plus avancés.

Le "taux de mortalité infantile" correspond au nombre total de décès au cours d'une année donnée des enfants de moins de 5 ans divisé par le nombre total de naissances vivantes au cours de la même année, multiplié par 1 000. Il s'agit d'une approximation du nombre de décès pour 1 000 enfants nés vivants qui meurent la première année. Dans la plupart des pays en développement, où les données d'état civil sont déficientes, les sources les plus fiables sont les enquêtes démographiques auprès des ménages. Lorsque de telles enquêtes ne sont pas réalisées, d'autres sources sont utilisées et des estimations générales sont réalisées qui sont nécessairement d'une fiabilité limitée. Lorsqu'il n'a pas dans les pays de systèmes complets et exacts d'enregistrement des faits d'état civil, les statistiques de la mortalité infantile par sexe sont difficiles à rassembler ou à estimer avec quelque fiabilité que ce soit en raison des distorsions de la notification; elles ne sont donc pas indiquées ici.

Le "taux de fécondité" est le nombre moyen d'enfants que mettrait au monde une cohorte hypothétique de femmes si, pendant toutes leurs années d'âge reproductif, les taux de fécondité par âge de l'année en question restaient inchangés.

Le "taux de mortalité juvénile" est par définition le nombre de décès d'enfants âgés de 1 à 4 ans pour 1 000 enfants de cet âge. Cette série a été compilée par la Division de statistique du Secrétariat de l'ONU pour l'*Annuaire démographique* [22] et les données qui sont incluses sont présentées sous réserve de mises en garde formulées à leur sujet.

Les données concernant la mortalité maternelle sont des estimations de l'Organisation mondiale de la santé, de l'UNICEF, et du Fonds des Nations Unies pour la population publiées dans "*Maternal Mortality in 1995*" [36].

12

Book production: number of titles by the Universal Decimal Classification (UDC)
Production de livres: nombre de titres classés d'après la Classification Décimale Universelle (CDU)

Country or area Pays ou zone	Year Année	Total	General- ities Général- ités	Philoso- phy/ Psychol- ogy Philoso- phie/ Psychol- ogie	Religion /Theo- ogy Religion /Théol- ogie	Social sciences Sciences sociales	Philol- ogy Philol- ogie	Pure sciences Sciences pures	Applied sciences Sciences appli- qués	Arts and recrea- tion Beaux- arts et loisirs	Litera- ture Littér- ature	Geogra- phy/ History Géogra- phie/ Histoire
Africa · Afrique												
Algeria	1996	670[1]	39	21	112	96	34	71	157	30	77	33
Algérie	1999	133	...	4	2	57	1	11	46	2	10	...
Angola												
Angola	1995	22	0	0	0	0	0	0	0	0	22	0
Benin												
Bénin	1998	9	...	...	2	...	...	...	1	...	5	1
Burkina Faso	1995	17[2]	1	0	0	3	0	0	0	1	11	1
Burkina Faso	1996	12[1,2]	1	0	0	1	0	0	1	0	9	0
	1997	5	...	...	...	...	...	...	...	1	4	...
Cameroon[3]												
Cameroun[3]	1999	52	...	...	...	52			...	...	...	...
Dem. Rep. of the Congo												
Rép. dém. du Congo	1996	112	...	...	40	46	...	1	10	1	12	2
Egypt	1996	1 917	85	53	205	186	315	180	282	63	442	106
Egypte	1997	2 507	246	79	481	285	260	224	203	128	460	141
	1998	1 410	96	18	200	126	215	219	150	44	256	86
Ethiopia												
Ethiopie	1999	444	40	...	63	203	8	6	77	8	18	21
Gambia	1996	14[4]	0	0	0	10	0	0	2	0	0	2
Gambie	1998	10	...	...	...	6	...	1	1	1	1	...
Ghana												
Ghana	1998	7	0	0	0	3	2	1	1	0	0	0
Madagascar	1995	131	3	3	32	44	2	2	13	4	19	9
Madagascar	1996	119	1	3	25	22	2	4	36	6	18	2
	1997	108	7	0	26	36	0	2	21	5	8	3
Malawi	1995	182	10	0	44	81	5	5	18	5	14	0
Malawi	1996	120[2,5]	0	0	1	76	14	10	5	3	0	8
Mali	1995	14[1,2]	1	0	0	1	0	0	1	0	11	0
Mali	1998	33	23	...	...	...	...	...	5	...	5	...
Mauritius	1995	64	4	1	3	20	6	1	4	2	18	5
Maurice	1996	80	1	4	4	14	4	1	6	6	32	8
	1998	55	10	0	5	12	6	0	2	2	5	13
Morocco	1997	1 339	37	28	82	549	15	67	175	142	141	103
Maroc	1998	894	41	9	90	377	21	16	75	21	150	94
	1999	386	25	3	34	151	5	1	33	12	75	47
Nigeria												
Nigéria	1995	1 314	18	36	203	530	91	80	116	52	133	55
South Africa												
Afrique du Sud	1995	5 418	136	33	516	1 262	566	330	1 002	156	1 227	190
Togo												
Togo	1998	5	...	...	1	1	1	...	1	...	...	1
Tunisia	1995	563[1]	8	25	7	132	23	9	19	24	166	150
Tunisie	1996	720[6]	24	18	14	138	6	4	38	23	338	111
	1999	1 260	13	13	41	200	...	119	103	39	656	76
Uganda												
Ouganda	1996	288[1,6,7]	0	0	7	0	45	41	7	0	4	9
America, North · Amérique du Nord												
Belize												
Belize	1996	107	0	0	7	39	4	16	15	14	5	7

12

Book production: number of titles by the Universal Decimal Classification (UDC) *[cont.]*
Production de livres: nombre de titres classés d'après la Classification Décimale Universelle (CDU) *[suite]*

Country or area Pays ou zone	Year Année	Total	General-ities Général-ités	Philoso-phy/ Psychol-ogy Philoso-phie/ Psychol-ogie	Religion /Theol-ogy Religion /Théol-ogie	Social sciences Sciences sociales	Philol-ogy Philol-ogie	Pure sciences Sciences pures	Applied sciences Sciences appli-qués	Arts and recrea-tion Beaux-arts et loisirs	Litera-ture Littér-ature	Geogra-phy/ History Géogra-phie/ Histoire
Canada	1997	21 669	654	533	648	8 386	683	1 040	3 429	1 207	3 491	1 598
Canada	1998	20 848	553	527	660	7 756	646	1 041	3 266	1 199	3 616	1 584
	1999	22 941	594	516	740	8 182	620	1 101	3 634	1 402	4 248	1 904
Costa Rica	1995	1 034[1,6,7]	36	22	26	307	25	51	150	14	186	58
Costa Rica	1997	949	23	8	46	495	14	39	88	27	166	43
	1998	1 464	60	23	49	656	20	66	253	40	221	76
Cuba	1997	785	44	16	13	170	35	30	96	35	279	67
Cuba	1998	796	59	32	10	209	15	24	61	38	306	42
	1999	952	75	11	6	253	15	43	73	34	380	62
El Salvador	1996	103	0	0	0	27	0	6	0	42	25	3
El Salvador	1998	663	...	...	5	125	1	4	458	5	59	6
Haiti Haïti	1995	340	...	...	...	...	...	...	...	...	...	...
Mexico	1996	6 183[1]	423	690	425	1 894	291	172	1 093	374	419	402
Mexique	1998	6 952	473	725	475	2 059	341	256	1 241	478	468	436
United States [1,6,8]	1995	62 039	2 751	2 068	3 324	12 840	732	3 323	9 891	4 238	11 537	5 657
Etats-Unis [1,6,8]	1996	68 175	3 027	2 333	3 803	14 225	898	3 725	10 762	4 245	13 221	6 583
America, South · Amérique du Sud												
Argentina	1996	9 850[1,7]	339	818	541	2 529	111	111	900	490	2 520	525
Argentine	1997	10 590	419	846	634	3 021	124	194	1 049	638	3 044	621
	1998	11 991	357	953	656	3 428	138	271	1 409	821	3 210	748
Brazil	1996	18 883	1 566	1 739	2 192	4 964	1 138	360	2 064	922	3 158	780
Brésil	1997	22 071	2 097	1 997	3 738	5 780	1 702	328	2 195	919	2 582	733
	1998	21 689	1 113	2 162	4 003	5 562	649	644	2 264	636	3 524	1 132
Chile	1995	2 469	18	59	158	707	33	71	261	80	860	222
Chili	1999	1 443	3	44	112	394	31	30	125	43	538	123
Colombia Colombie	1997	5 302	616	261	236	1 830	132	230	717	212	884	184
Ecuador	1997	735	...	...	...	...	...	...	...	...	...	...
Equateur	1998	904	...	...	...	...	...	...	...	...	...	...
	1999	996	...	...	...	...	...	...	...	...	...	...
Guyana	1996	42[2]	3	0	2	23	0	1	1	3	4	5
Guyana	1997	25	3	0	2	13	0	2	1	1	1	2
Peru	1996	612	44	24	25	266	13	27	66	11	97	39
Pérou	1997	1 416	30	26	92	702	25	47	134	42	224	94
	1998	1 942	42	26	85	862	200	173	107	63	273	111
Suriname Suriname	1996	47[2]	18	1	16	6	2	0	2	0	1	1
Uruguay	1996	934	22	33	33	264	9	29	201	77	193	73
Uruguay	1997	1 191	26	42	40	311	9	42	250	95	281	95
	1999	674	16	19	7	194	6	5	153	28	181	65
Venezuela	1995	4 225[2]	229	217	186	1 106	85	187	1 032	243	636	304
Venezuela	1996	3 468[2]	87	210	188	955	81	136	608	274	682	247
	1997	3 851[2]	166	155	203	1 082	57	230	719	294	701	244
Asia · Asie												
Armenia	1997	387	3	9	25	134	17	7	26	17	113	36
Arménie	1998	535	15	18	6	167	16	17	56	20	182	38
	1999	516	20	23	25	131	12	21	32	27	188	37
Azerbaijan	1996	542	12	10	25	167	21	17	44	9	209	28
Azerbaïdjan	1997	496	4	7	13	112	13	15	24	17	235	56
	1998	444	9	6	7	107	8	20	26	15	196	50
Bahrain	1996	40[2]	6	0	0	7	0	0	1	0	14	12
Bahreïn	1998	92	3	0	10	15	1	0	8	4	39	12
Brunei Darussalam Brunéi Darussalam	1998	38	0	1	10	7	6	6	6	0	0	2

12

Book production: number of titles by the Universal Decimal Classification (UDC) *[cont.]*
Production de livres: nombre de titres classés d'après la Classification Décimale Universelle (CDU) *[suite]*

Country or area Pays ou zone	Year Année	Total	Generalities Généralités	Philosophy/ Psychology Philosophie/ Psychologie	Religion /Theology Religion /Théologie	Social sciences Sciences sociales	Philology Philologie	Pure sciences Sciences pures	Applied sciences Sciences appliqués	Arts and recreation Beaux-arts et loisirs	Literature Littérature	Geography/ History Géographie/ Histoire
China, Macao SAR	1996	67	2	0	0	44	3	0	2	13	2	1
Chine, Macao RAS	1999	340	5	1	11	93	...	6	31	53	91	49
Cyprus	1997	918	15	8	40	370	85	20	165	96	72	47
Chypre	1998	927	19	7	43	362	97	17	168	97	71	46
	1999	931	21	10	32	381	87	20	154	94	80	52
Georgia	1995	1 104	574	17	17	81	23	36	67	10	216	63
Géorgie	1996	581[2]	4	17	18	124	38	49	74	16	190	51
	1999	697	476	14	17	84	14	16	7	4	65	0
India	1996	11 903	505	354	764	2 504	256	593	1 314	298	4 423	892
Inde	1997	12 006	359	411	927	2 474	220	465	876	252	4 979	1 043
	1998	14 085	406	408	1 150	3 350	275	570	760	573	5 294	1 299
Indonesia	1997	1 902	78	42	226	523	141	170	402	56	176	88
Indonésie	1998	537	13	9	17	117	12	145	69	72	5	78
	1999	121	17	...	...	88	...	...	16	...	...	...
Iran (Islamic Rep. of)	1997	10 410	392	541	3 112	953	944	1 388	1 499	531	431	619
Iran (Rép. islamique d')	1998	12 020	299	565	3 617	1 325	1 307	1 437	1 790	566	291	823
	1999	14 783	612	706	4 504	1 319	1 486	1 844	2 426	733	247	906
Israel Israël	1998	1 969	43	71	130	439	59	221	181	30	630	165
Japan Japon	1996	56 221[1,2]	1 149	1 791	1 078	12 770	1 402	1 363	12 155	10 046	11 924	2 543
Jordan	1995	465	15	9	74	106	10	19	26	22	128	56
Jordanie	1996	511	25	8	60	122	16	39	45	21	116	59
Kazakhstan	1995	1 115	65	12	17	339	50	44	197	31	291	69
Kazakhstan	1996	1 226	53	22	23	464	44	58	202	39	253	68
	1999	1 223	52	13	21	579	40	89	173	18	166	72
Korea, Republic of	1995	35 864	1 854	947	2 146	4 300	4 421	2 692	4 422	6 614	6 958	1 510
Corée, République de	1996	30 487[1,2,7]	303	678	1 605	3 201	1 384	359	3 513	6 543	4 164	716
Kuwait	1997	460	11	16	61	169	32	55	33	28	21	34
Koweït	1998	295	36	6	45	74	8	8	36	6	38	38
	1999	219[3]	36	13	31	71	1	8	9	5	19	26
Kyrgyzstan	1995	407	16	3	6	177	17	15	58	4	97	14
Kirghizistan	1996	351	11	5	3	176	16	19	25	8	73	15
	1998	420	0	2	15	157	26	13	92	9	93	13
Lao People's Dem. Rep. Rép. dém. pop. lao	1995	88[2]	0	0	2	41	6	6	9	2	15	7
Lebanon	1997	516	54	10	256	131	...	...	12	1	47	5
Liban	1998	289	183	5	0	41	5	2	19	1	26	7
Malaysia	1996	5 843	73	36	606	1 088	1 043	685	538	221	1 259	294
Malaisie	1998	5 816	100	55	721	751	803	467	443	133	2 160	183
	1999	5 084	157	59	547	1 058	662	526	614	222	998	241
Myanmar Myanmar	1999	227	106	...	1	76	20	16	1	1	4	2
Occupied Palestinian Terr. Terr. palestinien occupé	1996	114[2]	3	2	8	47	3	12	21	0	10	8
Oman	1996	7[2]	0	0	4	0	0	0	1	0	1	1
Oman	1998	136	18	2	24	15	3	27	...	4	34	9
	1999	12	0	1	5	0	0	0	1	5	0	0
Philippines	1997	546	26	11	36	212	18	38	63	15	103	24
Philippines	1998	958	88	22	40	329	41	37	130	17	208	46
	1999	1 380	63	15	41	631	79	53	117	79	227	75
Qatar	1995	419[1]	21	5	70	84	36	120	40	5	16	22
Qatar	1996	209[1,4]	9	3	26	88	7	19	27	6	12	12
Saudi Arabia	1996	3 900[2]	209	154	1 042	620	250	404	363	128	421	309
Arabie saoudite	1997	3 780	300	60	850	310	180	270	440	132	710	528
Sri Lanka	1996	4 115	338	29	28	2 505	139	55	390	33	483	115
Sri Lanka	1998	2 822	328	71	312	639	127	76	192	124	809	144
	1999	4 655	426	368	533	1 384	169	68	347	103	1 110	147

12

Book production: number of titles by the Universal Decimal Classification (UDC) *[cont.]*
Production de livres: nombre de titres classés d'après la Classification Décimale Universelle (CDU) *[suite]*

Country or area Pays ou zone	Year Année	Total	General- ities Général- ités	Philoso- phy/ Psychol- ogy Philoso- phie/ Psychol- ogie	Religion /Theol- ogy Religion /Théol- ogie	Social sciences Sciences sociales	Philol- ogy Philol- ogie	Pure sciences Sciences pures	Applied sciences Sciences appli- qués	Arts and recrea- tion Beaux- arts et loisirs	Litera- ture Littér- ature	Geogra- phy/ History Géogra- phie/ Histoire
Tajikistan	1995	226[9]	0	6	2	58	17	22	42	3	33	10
Tadjikistan	1996	132[2,9]	0	5	0	18	11	14	19	9	27	12
	1997	150	0	0	0	61	9	9	21	8	42	0
Thailand Thaïlande	1996	8 142	464	202	275	2 456	259	617	2 371	407	644	447
Turkey	1997	5 109	109	126	513	1 557	141	110	1 003	190	927	433
Turquie	1998	9 313	182	369	669	2 585	205	255	938	255	3 014	841
	1999	2 920	45	139	255	649	82	68	285	91	1 096	210
Uzbekistan	1995	1 200	18	20	20	414	60	60	213	11	316	68
Ouzbékistan	1996	1 003	8	7	22	367	44	42	158	10	277	68
Europe · Europe												
Andorra	1998	104	19	0	0	39	6	5	4	11	12	8
Andorre	1999	173	5	0	1	45	4	0	17	47	27	27
Austria	1995	8 222[10]	406	255	239	2 948	239	657	738	929	1 208	603
Autriche	1996	8 056[6,10]	243	289	289	2 851	209[11]	651	682	963	1 188	691
Belarus	1996	3 809	214	84	153	930	146	182	776	100	1 127	97
Bélarus	1997	5 331	206	167	199	1 304	189	265	1 092	118	1 640	151
	1998	6 073	206	193	139	1 970	235	316	1 380	188	1 236	210
Bulgaria	1997	3 773	132	224	116	777	118	145	478	113	1 520	150
Bulgarie	1998	4 863	183	208	152	1 039	161	159	722	176	1 819	244
	1999	4 971	170	235	205	1 029	159	211	715	178	1 803	266
Croatia	1997	3 015	63	108	235	773	70	98	421	153	936	158
Croatie	1998	3 265	75	126	262	858	73	116	639	170	818	128
	1999	2 309	78	83	209	655	5	106	398	110	554	111
Czech Republic	1997	11 519	187	443	425	1 972	367	1 138	1 413	788	3 807	979
République tchèque	1998	11 738	263	383	406	2 223	359	1 081	1 655	719	3 581	1 068
	1999	12 551	358	387	363	2 440	396	1 277	1 771	781	3 708	1 070
Denmark	1997	13 450	356	595	307	2 642	356	916	3 216	923	2 850	1 289
Danemark	1998	13 175	264	485	306	2 757	366	959	2 987	756	3 055	1 240
	1999	14 455	306	642	381	2 914	338	1 090	3 228	864	3 369	1 323
Estonia	1997	3 317	229	108	109	820	0	273	416	236	990	136
Estonie	1998	3 090	226	99	90	774	...	285	362	177	925	152
	1999	3 265	122	86	99	718	0	274	519	186	1 082	179
Finland	1997	12 717	316	248	313	3 176	316	1 183	3 554	792	1 851	968
Finlande	1998	12 887	253	221	319	2 986	355	1 148	3 188	746	1 945	1 726
	1999	13 173	294	238	318	3 068	364	1 169	3 252	760	2 144	1 566
France	1997	45 453	1 068	2 051	1 514	7 738	1 033	1 889	5 822	4 132	14 663	5 543
France	1998	47 916	1 765	2 138	1 562	7 031	1 082	2 052	6 178	4 399	15 695	6 014
	1999	39 083	5 226	...	1 214	8 810	313	...	2 791	1 316	12 013	7 400
Germany	1996	71 515	6 287	3 580	3 718	16 210	0[12]	2 756	10 550	5 921	12 798	9 695
Allemagne	1997	77 889	...	...	...	...	...	...	...	...	...	...
	1998	78 042	...	...	...	...	...	...	...	...	...	...
Greece	1995	4 134[1]	152	98	204	613	190	254	287	284	1 598	454
Grèce	1996	4 225[1]	166	83	242	659	131	363	300	282	1 595	404
	1997	4 067	139	119	208	596	156	239	318	296	1 568	428
Holy See [13]	1995	298	0	48	198	42	1	0	0	2	0	7
Saint-Siège [13]	1996	228	0	38	105	78	2	0	0	0	5	0
Hungary	1997	9 343	320	393	361	1 395	684	614	1 390	482	2 663	1 041
Hongrie	1998	11 306	196	454	615	1 456	541	787	1 832	670	3 642	1 113
	1999	10 352	290	378	593	1 121	602	854	1 609	565	3 338	1 002
Iceland	1996	1 527	29	30	43	354	124	114	168	107	414	144
Islande	1997	1 652	23	26	49	435	149	121	192	105	403	149
	1998	1 796	44	27	46	476	150	140	192	138	444	139
Italy	1997	36 217	700	2 175	2 444	6 893	772	1 036	4 271	4 258	8 644	5 024
Italie	1998	30 835	1 030	1 804	2 346	5 577	628	909	3 433	3 518	7 457	4 133
	1999	32 365	603	2 075	2 338	6 446	608	1 110	3 537	3 353	7 826	4 469

12

Book production: number of titles by the Universal Decimal Classification (UDC) *[cont.]*
Production de livres: nombre de titres classés d'après la Classification Décimale Universelle (CDU) *[suite]*

Country or area Pays ou zone	Year Année	Total	General- ities Général- ités	Philoso- phy/ Psychol- ogy Philoso- phie/ Psychol- ogie	Religion /Theol- ogy Religion /Théol- ogie	Social sciences Sciences sociales	Philol- ogy Philol- ogie	Pure sciences Sciences pures	Applied sciences Sciences appli- qués	Arts and recrea- tion Beaux- arts et loisirs	Litera- ture Littér- ature	Geogra- phy/ History Géogra- phie/ Histoire
Latvia	1996	1 965[9]	91	63	87	414	67	54	166	87	364	65
Lettonie	1998	2 093	102	114	113	740	86	81	282	81	381	113
	1999	2 178	104	131	104	627	158	102	343	87	385	137
Lithuania	1997	3 827	303	104	168	768	217	282	566	180	1 064	175
Lituanie	1998	4 109	335	123	138	783	258	346	546	218	1 172	190
	1999	4 097	301	126	153	794	309	320	509	215	1 151	219
Malta	1995	404	4	6	78	159	8	4	13	28	47	57
Malte	1998	237	5	3	40	65	10	0	6	11	46	51
Monaco	1997	52	13	1	3	9	...	3	2	13	2	6
Monaco	1998	29	4	1	3	8	...	1	...	10	1	1
	1999	72	14	1	10	14	...	11	1	18	1	2
Norway	1997	6 220[10,14]	141	172	192	1 084	120	266	613	322	2 656	654
Norvège	1998	5 068	152	141	221	858	96	170	597	355	2 146	332
	1999	4 985	162	141	242	814	69	143	556	315	2 130	413
Poland	1997	15 996	231	417	1 078	3 147	623	1 371	2 951	844	3 798	1 536
Pologne	1998	16 462	621	496	944	3 081	621	1 319	2 670	803	4 311	1 596
	1999	19 192	676	589	1 274	3 829	823	1 545	3 304	1 045	4 176	1 931
Portugal	1996	7 868	312	178	233	1 207	17	190	506	260	4 554	411
Portugal	1997	8 331	324	160	295	2 255	23	157	852	268	3 503	494
	1998	2 186	...	...	...	...	...	...	...	145	2 041	...
Republic of Moldova	1997	1 097	53	12	23	281	75	103	242	21	224	63
République de Moldova	1998	1 196	67	27	38	267	21	94	250	45	313	74
	1999	1 166	181	23	22	320	44	76	215	25	177	83
Romania	1997	6 471	728	246	386	886	383	867	1 617	96	931	331
Roumanie	1998	6 231	1 398	149	233	902	352	759	1 907	125	57	349
	1999	7 874[6]	925	207	357	943	24	761	1 629	134	2 466[15]	428
Russian Federation	1995	33 623	2 968	1 038	854	7 719	988	2 790	6 783	685	7 704	2 094
Fédération de Russie	1996	36 237	3 362	1 275	984	8 801	1 171	2 869	7 003	664	8 493	1 615
Serbia and Montenegro	1995	3 531	121	54	75	1 023	3	151	624	225	975	280
Serbie-et-Monténégro	1996	5 367	206	102	136	1 515	6	234	791	302	1 613	462
Slovakia	1997	2 064	39	64	111	515	61	188	439	84	428	135
Slovaquie	1998	4 386	107	177	291	1 045	204	418	852	175	901	216
	1999	3 153	69	123	264	681	97	254	684	117	711	153
Slovenia	1997	3 647	83	135	124	706	115	333	624	460	761	306
Slovénie	1998	3 722	85	159	147	672	121	320	654	521	770	273
	1999	3 450	78	163	157	740	...	242	671	137	929	333
Spain	1997	48 713	1 409	1 807	1 807	9 147	2 119	3 196	7 561	4 063	13 004	4 600
Espagne	1998	55 774	1 381	2 314	2 032	9 884	2 164	3 318	8 352	4 717	16 455	5 157
	1999	59 174	1 446	2 455	1 962	10 899	2 064	3 245	8 800	5 032	18 145	5 126
Sweden	1996	13 496	396	328	502	2 685	464	900	3 285	850	2 876	1 210
Suède	1997	13 220	367	351	498	2 562	474	975	3 222	794	2 901	1 076
	1998	12 547	323	364	373	2 480	400	826	2 986	821	2 974	1 000
Switzerland	1997	16 241	315	803	835	4 165	269	1 656	3 564	1 695	2 077	862
Suisse	1998	13 816	212	620	748	3 516	203	1 491	3 138	1 442	1 730	716
	1999	18 273	336	825	1 101	4 885	306	1 761	3 862	1 881	2 379	937
TFYR of Macedonia	1997	791	36	10	25	347	15	29	25	47	197	60
L'ex-R.y. de Macédoine	1998	738	39	17	9	325	19	26	36	40	197	30
	1999	733	29	7	8	345	25	27	46	47	174	25
Ukraine	1997	7 362	260	213	364	2 455	398	382	1 669	164	1 166	291
Ukraine	1998	7 065	298	173	218	3 231	187	241	1 225	114	1 034	344
	1999	6 282	198	121	186	2 960	137	213	1 086	100	1 011	270
United Kingdom	1996	107 263	2 082	3 548	5 003	23 889	3 563	9 417	16 616	9 431	21 686	12 028
Royaume-Uni	1997	106 444	2 047	3 357	4 968	24 009	3 213	8 973	16 761	9 898	21 222	11 996
	1998	110 965	2 143	3 570	5 199	24 714	4 274	8 902	17 106	10 520	22 104	12 433

12

Book production: number of titles by the Universal Decimal Classification (UDC) *[cont.]*
Production de livres: nombre de titres classés d'après la Classification Décimale Universelle (CDU) *[suite]*

Country or area Pays ou zone	Year Année	Total	General- ities Général- ités	Philoso- phy/ Psychol- ogy Philoso- phie/ Psychol- ogie	Religion /Theol- ogy Religion /Théol- ogie	Social sciences Sciences sociales	Philol- ogy Philol- ogie	Pure sciences Sciences pures	Applied sciences Sciences appli- qués	Arts and recrea- tion Beaux- arts et loisirs	Litera- ture Littér- ature	Geogra- phy/ History Géogra- phie/ Histoire
Oceania · Océanie												
New Zealand	1997	5 088	173	64	104	1 989	429	381	830	380	433	305
Nouvelle-Zélande	1998	5 204	132	58	140	2 034	382	362	771	380	540	405
	1999	5 405	182	50	119	2 173	401	400	798	357	535	390

Source:
United Nations Educational, Scientific and Cultural Organization (UNESCO) Institute for Statistics, Montreal, the UNESCO Institute for Statistics database.

Source:
L'Institut de statistique de l'Organisation des Nations Unies pour l'éducation, la science et la culture (UNESCO), Montréal, la base de données de l'Institut de statistique de l'UNESCO.

1   Not including pamphlets.
2   First editions only.
3   National estimate.
4   Data refer to school textbooks and government publications only.

5   Books for children are included in the total but are not distributed among the other categories.
6   The difference between the total and the sum of the different categories is the result of data not being reported in the category breakdown.
7   The category "Philology" includes titles on history of literature and literary criticism.
8   Not including school textbooks, government publications and university theses.
9   School textbooks, children's books and government publications are included in the total but are not distributed among the other categories.
10   Not including school textbooks or yearbooks.
11   Subject group on philology, languages and linguistics includes titles on history of literature and literary criticism.

12   Data on philology are included with those on literature.

13   Data refer to the Vatican City State.
14   Not including government publications.
15   Data include books for children.

1   Non compris les brochures.
2   Premières éditions seulement.
3   Estimation nationale.
4   Les données se réfèrent aux manuels scolaires et aux publications officielles seulement.
5   Les livres pour enfants sont inclus dans le total mais ne sont pas répartis à travers les autres catégories.
6   La différence entre le total et la somme des différentes catégories résulte des données qui n'ont pas été reportées dans la ventilation par catégorie.
7   La catégorie « Philologie » comprend les ouvrages d'histoire de la littérature et de critique littéraire.
8   Non compris les manuels scolaires, les publications officielles et les thèses universitaires.
9   Les manuels scolaires, les livres pour enfants et les publications officielles sont inclus dans le total mais ne sont pas répartis à travers les autres catégories.
10   Non compris les manuels scolaires ou les annuaires.
11   Le groupe thématique de la philologie, des langues et de la linguistique comprend les ouvrages d'histoire de la littérature et de critique littéraire.
12   Les données relatives à la philologie sont comprises avec celles de la littérature.
13   Les données se réfèrent à la Cité du Vatican.
14   Non compris les publications officielles.
15   Y compris les livres pour enfants.

13
Daily newspapers
Journaux quotidiens

Country or area Pays ou zone	Number of titles Nombre de titres				Total average daily circulation or copies printed (thousands) Diffusion moyenne ou nombre imprimé (en milliers)				Circulation or copies printed per 1000 inhabitants Diffusion ou nombre imprimé pour 1000 habitants			
	1997	1998	1999	2000	1997	1998	1999	2000	1997	1998	1999	2000
Africa · Afrique												
Algeria Algérie	18	24	...	...	761	796	...	...	25.9	27.3	...	...
Benin Bénin	...	...	13	...	...	...	33	...	...	...	5.3	...
Burundi Burundi	1	1	...	...	...	...	...	...	...	...	...	...
Chad Tchad	2	2	...	...	2[1]	2[1]	...	...	0.2	0.2	...	...
Egypt Egypte	14	15	16	...	2 100	2 332	2 080	...	32.4	35.6	31.2	...
Ethiopia Ethiopie	2	2	...	...	23	23	...	...	0.4	0.4	...	...
Mauritius Maurice	8	6	6	5	88	82	116	138	77.7	71.7	100.7	118.8
Morocco Maroc	21	22	22	23	657	715	728	846	24.4	24.8	24.8	28.3
Mozambique Mozambique	12	12	...	...	43	43	...	...	2.3	2.5	...	...
Senegal Sénégal	4	5	...	...	...	...	...	...	...	...	...	...
Togo Togo	...	...	1	1	...	...	10	10	...	...	2.3	2.2
Tunisia Tunisie	...	...	...	7	...	...	...	180	...	...	...	19.0
Zambia Zambie	...	...	...	...	...	...	...	228	...	...	...	21.9
America, North · Amérique du Nord												
Bermuda Bermudes	...	...	1	1	...	...	15	15	...	...	...	...
Costa Rica Costa Rica	8	8	8	8	...	...	...	...	...	...	...	...
Cuba Cuba	...	...	2	2	...	...	565	600	...	...	50.7	53.6
Dominican Republic Rép. dominicaine	10	10	10	9	...	...	230	230	...	...	27.9	27.5
El Salvador El Salvador	4	4	...	...	219	171	...	...	37.1	28.3	...	...
Mexico Mexique	...	...	300	311	...	...	9 332	9 251	...	...	95.9	93.6
America, South · Amérique du Sud												
Bolivia Bolivie	27	29	...	...	...	...	...	...	...	...	...	...
Brazil Brésil	400	372	...	...	6 892	7 163	...	...	42.1	43.1	...	...
Ecuador Equateur	11	11	36	36	569	529	1 220	1 220	47.7	43.5	98.3	96.5
Guyana Guyana	...	...	2	2	...	...	57	57	...	...	74.9	74.6
Suriname Suriname	2	2	...	...	29	28	...	...	69.2	67.7	...	...

13

Daily newspapers *[cont.]*
Journaux quotidiens *[suite]*

Country or area Pays ou zone	Number of titles Nombre de titres				Total average daily circulation or copies printed (thousands) Diffusion moyenne ou nombre imprimé (en milliers)				Circulation or copies printed per 1000 inhabitants Diffusion ou nombre imprimé pour 1000 habitants			
	1997	1998	1999	2000	1997	1998	1999	2000	1997	1998	1999	2000
Asia · Asie												
Armenia Arménie	8	7	7	8	...	...	31	19	...	...	8.2	5.0
China, Macao SAR Chine, Macao RAS	...	...	10	10	...	...	158	167	...	...	358.2	376.5
Cyprus Chypre	8	7	8	8	76	79	86	87	99.6	115.7	124.6	124.7
Georgia Géorgie	...	...	30	35	...	...	43	26	...	...	8.2	4.9
India Inde	5 044	5 221	...	...	46 452[2]	59 023[2]	...	...	48.1	60.5	...	...
Indonesia Indonésie	81	172	...	...	4 975	4 713	...	...	24.5	22.8	...	...
Jordan Jordanie	8	8	5	5	350	352	...	...	57.1	75.5	...	...
Kyrgyzstan Kirghizistan	...	...	3	3	...	...	...	...	...	...	...	...
Lebanon Liban	...	...	...	10	...	...	...	...	...	...	...	...
Mongolia Mongolie	...	3	5	5	...	...	...	...	...	...	...	...
Myanmar Myanmar	4	4	...	...	420	400	...	...	9.6	8.6	...	...
Occupied Palestinian Terr. Terr. palestinien occupé	...	...	3	3	...	...	...	...	...	...	...	...
Oman Oman	5	5	...	...	...	...	...	...	...	...	...	...
Pakistan Pakistan	359	...	352	...	3 915	...	5 559	...	27.2	...	40.4	...
Turkey Turquie	980	960	560	542	...	...	...	...	...	...	...	...
Turkmenistan Turkménistan	...	...	2	2	...	...	26	32	...	...	5.7	6.7
Europe · Europe												
Andorra Andorre	...	...	2	2	...	...	...	...	...	...	...	...
Austria Autriche	17	17	...	...	...	...	...	...	...	...	...	...
Belarus Bélarus	19	20	...	...	1 437	1 559	...	...	138.8	152.0	...	...
Bulgaria Bulgarie	...	...	52	...	...	...	936	...	...	...	116.4	...
Croatia Croatie	...	...	14	14	...	...	...	...	...	...	...	...
Czech Republic République tchèque	99	103	104	103	...	...	...	...	...	...	...	...
Denmark Danemark	37	36	33	33	1 615	1 613	1 558	1 507	307.3	305.1	293.7	283.3
Estonia Estonie	15	16	17	16	...	...	...	...	...	...	...	...
Finland Finlande	56	56	56[3]	55[3]	2 336	2 343	2 331	2 304	454.4	454.6	451.4	445.5
Germany Allemagne	402	398	...	...	25 200	25 000	...	...	307.1	304.8	...	...

13

Daily newspapers *[cont.]*
Journaux quotidiens *[suite]*

Country or area Pays ou zone	Number of titles Nombre de titres				Total average daily circulation or copies printed (thousands) Diffusion moyenne ou nombre imprimé (en milliers)				Circulation or copies printed per 1000 inhabitants Diffusion ou nombre imprimé pour 1000 habitants			
	1997	1998	1999	2000	1997	1998	1999	2000	1997	1998	1999	2000
Gibraltar Gibraltar	1	1	...	...	6	6	...	...	234.2	...	...	...
Greece Grèce	...	207	...	...	...	...	...	...	...	...	...	...
Hungary Hongrie	33	33	...	...	4 660	4 688	...	...	458.9	465.5	...	...
Iceland Islande	4	3	3	...	100	...	93	...	365.6	...	335.7	...
Latvia Lettonie	...	...	27	26	...	...	354	327	...	...	145.4	135.1
Lithuania Lituanie	23	23	29	22	113	123	126	108	30.6	33.2	33.9	29.3
Malta Malte	5	4	...	...	...	...	...	...	...	...	...	...
Norway Norvège	82	81	82[4]	81[4]	2 598	2 592	2 591	2 545	591.0	585.4	582.4	569.5
Poland Pologne	55	52	46	42	4 194	4 168	3 870	3 928	108.4	107.9	100.2	101.8
Portugal Portugal	31	...	...	...	316	...	...	...	32.0	...	...	...
Republic of Moldova République de Moldova	5	6	6	6	480	660	...	...	109.7	153.0	...	...
Romania Roumanie	74	95	139	145[1]	...	...	...	...	...	...	...	...
San Marino Saint-Marin	3	3	...	...	2	2	...	...	70.4	...	...	...
Slovakia Slovaquie	21	19	24	16	1 324	939	851	705	246.5	174.2	157.8	130.6
Slovenia Slovénie	5	5	5	5	343	340	341	335	171.9	170.5	171.3	168.5
Spain Espagne	...	...	84	87	...	...	4 191	4 003	...	...	105.1	100.3
Sweden Suède	94	94	94	90	3 881	3 820	3 750	3 627	438.2	431.3	423.7	410.2
Switzerland Suisse	78	74	81	...	2 680	2 620	2 676	...	369.6	365.5	373.2	...
TFYR of Macedonia L'ex-R.y. Macédoine	4	4	5	6	88	106	109	108	44.2	52.7	53.9	53.3
Ukraine Ukraine	53	41	67	61	3 495	5 059	6 107	8 683	68.4	100.3	122.1	175.2
Oceania · Océanie												
New Zealand Nouvelle-Zélande	28	28	28	28	821	786	774	765	218.4	211.5	206.5	202.5

Source:
United Nations Educational, Scientific and Cultural Organization (UNESCO) Institute for Statistics, Montreal, the UNESCO Institute for Statistics database.

Source :
L'Institut de statistique de l'Organisation des Nations Unies pour l'éducation, la science et la culture (UNESCO), Montréal, la base de données de l'Institut de statistique de l'UNESCO.

1 National estimate.
2 Includes tri-weeklies and bi-weeklies.
3 Data do not include non-members of the Finnish Newspaper Association.
4 Data do not include Sunday issues.

1 Estimation nationale.
2 Y compris les journaux paraissant deux ou trois fois par semaine.
3 Les données n'incluent pas les non membres de l'Association finnoise de journaux.
4 Les données n'incluent pas les parutions du dimanche.

14
Non-daily newspapers and periodicals
Journaux non quotidiens et périodiques

Country or area Pays ou zone	Non-daily newspapers Journaux non quotidiens				Periodicals Périodiques		
	Year Année	Number of titles Nombre de titres	Circulation Diffusion		Number of titles Nombre de titres	Circulation Diffusion	
			Total average or copies printed (000) Totale moyenne ou copies imprimées (000)	Per 1000 inhabitants Pour 1000 habitants		Total average or copies printed (000) Totale moyenne ou copies imprimées (000)	Per 1000 inhabitants Pour 1000 habitants
Africa · Afrique							
Algeria	1997	64	1 266	43	...	...	...
Algérie	1998	82	909	31	106	...	...
Benin							
Bénin	1999	2	44	7	62	110	18
Burundi	1997	5	8	1	...	...	...
Burundi	1998	5	8	1	...	...	...
Chad	1997	14	...	...	35	...	...
Tchad	1998	10	...	...	32	...	...
Egypt	1997	46	1 470	23	259	2 332	36
Egypte	1998	47	1 448	22	237	2 223	34
	1999	45	1 371	21	235	2 773	42
Ethiopia	1997	85	338	6	7	598	10
Ethiopie	1998	78	402	7	10	688	11
	1999	...	...	...	15	...	...
	2000	...	...	...	15	...	...
Mauritius	1997	36	18	16	...	...	...
Maurice	1998	33	...	...	...	...	...
	1999	31	125	108	43	43	37
	2000	33	150	129	64	65	55
Morocco	1997	807	3 390	126	828	4 684	169
Maroc	1998	693	4 064	141	715	4 422	157
	1999	581	3 724	127	586	4 329	151
	2000	507[1]	4 108	137	364	4 956	170
Mozambique	1997	40	206	11	32	83	5
Mozambique	1998	40	206	12	32	83	5
Rwanda	1999	13	11	2	*10	...	...
Rwanda	2000	8	13	2	*10	...	...
Senegal							
Sénégal	1997	139	...	...	...	...	...
South Africa							
Afrique du Sud	1997	48	1 287	33	...	...	...
Sudan	1997	11	5 644	204	54	68	2
Soudan	1998	11	5 644	189	54	68	2
Togo	1999	41	4 032	919	23	2 256	510
Togo	2000	52	5 184	1 145	24	2 496	547
Tunisia							
Tunisie	2000	29	940	99	182	525	55
America, North · Amérique du Nord							
Bermuda	1999	3	29	...	...	...	...
Bermudes	2000	3	29	...	...	...	...
Costa Rica	1997	22	...	...	235	...	...
Costa Rica	1998	25	...	...	206	...	...
	1999	24	...	...	142	...	...
	2000	27	...	...	306	...	...
Cuba	1999	31	912	82	...	...	...
Cuba	2000	31	923	82	...	...	...
Dominican Republic	1997	6	183	23	132	5 966	750
Rép. dominicaine	1998	6	183	23	132	6 274	776
	1999	8	215	26	180	...	...
	2000	8	215	26	188	...	...

14
Non-daily newspapers and periodicals *[cont.]*
Journaux non quotidiens et périodiques *[suite]*

Country or area Pays ou zone	Year Année	Non-daily newspapers Journaux non quotidiens			Periodicals Périodiques		
		Number of titles Nombre de titres	Circulation Diffusion Total average or copies printed (000) Totale moyenne ou copies imprimées (000)	Per 1000 inhabitants Pour 1000 habitants	Number of titles Nombre de titres	Circulation Diffusion Total average or copies printed (000) Totale moyenne ou copies imprimées (000)	Per 1000 inhabitants Pour 1000 habitants
Mexico	1999	27	805	8	296	19 592	201
Mexique	2000	26	614	6	278	20 362	206
Montserrat	1997	1	1	93	...	...	...
Montserrat	1998	1	1	...	...	...	...
America, South · Amérique du Sud							
Argentina	1997	...	2 041	57	...	...	...
Argentine	1998	...	1 933	54	...	...	...
	1999	...	...	...	119	5 748	157
	2000	...	...	...	113	4 936	133
Bolivia	1997	10	8 626	1 110	...	...	...
Bolivie	1998	10	7 884	991	...	...	...
Brazil	1997	892	...	...	...	...	...
Brésil	1998	1 251	...	...	...	...	...
Colombia							
Colombie	1997	5[2]	71[2]	2	...	...	...
Ecuador	1997	34	150	13	133	820	69
Equateur	1998	45	175	14	146	1 615	134
	1999	40	...	...	27	1 086	89
	2000	40	...	...	27	1 086	87
Guyana	1999	4	48	63	24	131	173
Guyana	2000	4	48	63	24	131	173
Peru							
Pérou	1998	...	...	...	43	...	...
Suriname	1997	9	65	157	4	4	8
Suriname	1998	9	63	153	8	8	20
Asia · Asie							
Armenia	1997	100	116	33	45	...	...
Arménie	1998	119	...	...	75	220	69
	1999	95	168	44	...	...	...
	2000	83	283	75	41	114	36
Azerbaijan	1997	...	...	...	34	57	7
Azerbaïdjan	1998	...	...	...	38	50	6
Bangladesh							
Bangladesh	1997	...	...	...	274	30 216	234
China, Macao SAR	1999	8	24	54	169	...	...
Chine, Macao RAS	2000	7	20	44	188	...	...
Cyprus	1997	7	33	43	30	310	407
Chypre	1998	31	185	271	29	290	377
	1999	33	188	272	45	360	464
	2000	38	200	287	50	372	475
Georgia	1999	122	...	...	122	...	...
Géorgie	2000	...	...	...	149	...	...
India	1997	36 661	59 256	61	...	...	...
Inde	1998	38 607	67 826	69	...	...	...
Indonesia	1997	90	4 711[3]	23	114	4 390	22
Indonésie	1998	433	7 838	38	266	4 156	20
Iran (Islamic Rep. of)							
Iran (Rép. islamique d')	1999	843	152 534	2 203	...	...	...
Japan							
Japon	1997	6	...	...	...	...	...

14

Non-daily newspapers and periodicals *[cont.]*
Journaux non quotidiens et périodiques *[suite]*

| | | Non-daily newspapers Journaux non quotidiens | | | Periodicals Périodiques | | |
| | | | Circulation Diffusion | | | Circulation Diffusion | |
Country or area Pays ou zone	Year Année	Number of titles Nombre de titres	Total average or copies printed (000) Totale moyenne ou copies imprimées (000)	Per 1000 inhabitants Pour 1000 habitants	Number of titles Nombre de titres	Total average or copies printed (000) Totale moyenne ou copies imprimées (000)	Per 1000 inhabitants Pour 1000 habitants
Jordan	1997	13	154	25	256	144	31
Jordanie	1998	13	155	33	270	148	31
	1999	17	...	...	...	...	...
	2000	20	...	...	...	...	...
Kyrgyzstan	1999	164	...	...	33	95	20
Kirghizistan	2000	181	...	...	36	170	35
Lebanon Liban	2000	7	9 340	2 671	49	7 038	2 024
Malaysia Malaisie	1997	3	312	15	...	...	...
Mongolia	1997	16	64	25	...	...	...
Mongolie	1998	26	...	...	...	...	...
	1999	23	...	...	27	177	71
	2000	27	...	...	38	85	34
Myanmar	1997	...	...	...	54	4 483	99
Myanmar	1998	...	...	...	38	3 397	74
Nepal	1997	2 144	...	...	...	...	...
Népal	1998	2 288	...	...	...	...	...
Occupied Palestinian Terr.	1999	10	1 617	526	57	2 244	730
Terr. palestinien occupé	2000	13	2 058	645	62	1 854	581
Oman	1997	...	...	...	29	...	...
Oman	1998	...	...	...	29	...	...
Pakistan	1997	681	...	...	...	...	...
Pakistan	1999	560	1 782	13	559	1 713	12
Philippines Philippines	1997	47	199	3	...	...	...
Singapore Singapour	1997	2	68	20	...	...	...
Sri Lanka Sri Lanka	1997	29	1 320	72	...	...	...
Thailand Thaïlande	1997	...	85	1	...	...	...
Turkey	1997	400	...	...	1 590	...	...
Turquie	1998	425	...	...	1 670	...	...
	1999	610	...	...	1 572	...	...
	2000	688	...	...	1 635	...	...
Turkmenistan	1999	23	294	63	20	36	8
Turkménistan	2000	22	338	71	20	47	10
Europe · Europe							
Austria	1997	125	...	...	2 637	...	...
Autriche	1998	155	...	...	2 685	...	...
Belarus	1997	539	7 823	756	302	1 647	162
Bélarus	1998	560	8 973	875	318	1 687	167
Bulgaria	1997	...	3 070	366	...	1 016	123
Bulgarie	1998	...	3 259	401	...	1 426	173
	1999	527	2 649	330	619	1 247	153
Croatia	1997	220	575	128	...	...	...
Croatie	1999	234	...	...	1 827	...	...
	2000	229	...	...	2 003	...	...
Czech Republic	1997	1 169	...	...	3 814	...	...
République tchèque	1998	1 169	...	...	3 936	...	...
	1999	675	...	...	2 277	...	...
	2000	712	...	...	2 437	...	...

14

Non-daily newspapers and periodicals *[cont.]*
Journaux non quotidiens et périodiques *[suite]*

| | | Non-daily newspapers Journaux non quotidiens | | | Periodicals Périodiques | | |
| | | | Circulation Diffusion | | | Circulation Diffusion | |
Country or area Pays ou zone	Year Année	Number of titles Nombre de titres	Total average or copies printed (000) Totale moyenne ou copies imprimées (000)	Per 1000 inhabitants Pour 1000 habitants	Number of titles Nombre de titres	Total average or copies printed (000) Totale moyenne ou copies imprimées (000)	Per 1000 inhabitants Pour 1000 habitants
Denmark	1997	...	...	...	140	6 263	1 189
Danemark	1998	11	1 509	285	...	...	...
	1999	10	1 482	279	127	...	...
	2000	10	1 415	266	117	...	...
Estonia	1997	56	501	346	572	2 044	1 453
Estonie	1998	93	...	...	578	1 830	1 313
	1999	88	...	...	930	1 972	1 428
	2000	93	...	...	956	2 144	1 569
Finland	1997	158	1 000	195	5 612	...	...
Finlande	1998	155	965	187	5 712	...	...
	1999	151[4]	942	182	5 777	...	...
	2000	149[4]	924	179	5 711	...	...
Germany	1997	26	2 043	25	...	...	...
Allemagne	1998	33	6 500	79	...	...	...
Gibraltar	1997	3	4	156	...	...	...
Gibraltar	1998	3	4	...	...	...	...
	1999	2	3	...	...	...	...
Hungary Hongrie	1997	121	5 209	513	...	...	...
Iceland	1997	75	...	...	1 021	...	...
Islande	1998	68	...	...	880	...	...
	1999	22	57[5]	206	*938	...	...
Ireland Irlande	1997	61	916	250	...	...	...
Latvia	1997	117	509	207	...	...	...
Lettonie	1999	208	1 751	719	262	1 391	581
	2000	201	1 754	725	325	1 856	782
Lithuania	1997	425	1 367	369	750	...	...
Lituanie	1998	399	1 283	346	757	...	...
	1999	354	956	258	720	...	...
	2000	339	949	257	753	...	...
Luxembourg Luxembourg	1997	1	10	24	...	...	...
Malta	1997	11	...	...	502	...	...
Malte	1998	11	...	...	523	...	...
Netherlands Pays-Bas	1997	58[2]	564[2]	36			
Norway	1997	71[2]	359[2]	82	...	...	...
Norvège	1998	74	383	87	...	...	...
	1999	74[6]	374	84	...	...	...
	2000	70	367	82	...	...	...
Poland	1997	141[3]	...	...	4 718	67 739	1 752
Pologne	1998	29	870	23	5 297	72 336	1 870
	1999	28	722	19	5 518	65 997	1 706
	2000	24	583	15	5 468	67 820	1 754
Portugal	1997	248	1 473	149	702	...	...
Portugal	1999	557	3 282	328	1 065	15 762	1 577
Republic of Moldova	1997	208	598	137	81	182	42
République de Moldova	1998	239	801	186	86	210	49
	1999	177	933	217	88	238	55
	2000	170	915	213	99	258	60

14
Non-daily newspapers and periodicals *[cont.]*
Journaux non quotidiens et périodiques *[suite]*

Country or area Pays ou zone	Year Année	Non-daily newspapers Journaux non quotidiens			Periodicals Périodiques		
		Number of titles Nombre de titres	Circulation Diffusion		Number of titles Nombre de titres	Circulation Diffusion	
			Total average or copies printed (000) Totale moyenne ou copies imprimées (000)	Per 1000 inhabitants Pour 1000 habitants		Total average or copies printed (000) Totale moyenne ou copies imprimées (000)	Per 1000 inhabitants Pour 1000 habitants
Romania	1997	...	...	...	1 781	...	...
Roumanie	1998	...	...	...	1 455	...	...
	1999	315	...	...	1 589	...	...
	2000[7]	320	...	...	1 608	...	...
San Marino	1997	8	12	470	...	...	...
Saint-Marin	1998	8	12	...	...	...	...
Slovakia	1997	...	...	...	734	10 107	1 878
Slovaquie	1998	374	3 752	696	876	11 210	2 082
	1999	445	4 201	779	821	10 196	1 892
	2000	435	2 651	491	1 014	13 823	2 564
Slovenia	1997	196	...	...	1 109	...	...
Slovénie	1998	242	...	...	1 161	...	...
	1999	221	...	...	1 304	...	...
	2000	200	...	...	1 278	...	...
Spain	1997	10[8]	4 971[8]	125	...	...	...
Espagne	1999	11	5 371	135	...	...	...
Sweden	1997	68	360	41	393	22 063	2 491
Suède	1998	70	376	42	381	21 832	2 464
	1999	70	370	42	374	21 632	2 443
	2000	71	382	43	389	22 112	2 497
Switzerland	1997	131	707	98	...	...	...
Suisse	1998	119	1 144	160	...	...	...
	1999	120	1 190	166	...	...	...
TFYR of Macedonia	1997	33	96	48	104	286	144
L'ex-R.y. Macédoine	1998	26	93	46	93	244	122
	1999	29	102	50	109	231	115
	2000	33	121	59	116	235	116
Ukraine	1997	2 275	25 361	497	817	3 096	61
Ukraine	1998	2 351	33 894	672	1 009	5 215	103
	1999	2 572	36 106	722	1 374	5 090	102
	2000	2 606	38 985	786	1 245	3 988	80
United Kingdom Royaume-Uni	1997	462[2]	5 840[2]	100	...	...	...

Oceania · Océanie

Country or area Pays ou zone	Year Année	Number of titles	Total average	Per 1000	Number of titles	Total average	Per 1000
Australia Australie	1997	96	370	20	...	...	...
New Zealand	1997	...	...	...	164	4 524	1 228
Nouvelle-Zélande	1998	...	...	...	188	5 500	1 479
	1999	126	3 077	821	...	...	...
	2000	123	3 076	814	...	...	...

Source:
United Nations Educational, Scientific and Cultural Organization (UNESCO) Institute for Statistics, Montreal, the UNESCO Institute for Statistics database.

Source :
L'Institut de statistique de l'Organisation des Nations Unies pour l'éducation, la science et la culture (UNESCO), Montréal, la base de données de l'Institut de statistique de l'UNESCO.

1   Data do not include non-dailies issued 2 or 3 times a week.

2   Data refer to regional/local non-dailies only.

3   Including Sunday issues.

4   Data do not include non-members of the Finnish Newspaper

1   Les données n'incluent pas les parutions non quotidiennes publiées 2 à 3 fois par semaine.

2   Les données se réfèrent aux journaux non quotidiens régionaux/locaux seulement.

3   Inclut les parutions du dimanche.

4   Les données n'incluent pas les non membres de l'Association finnoise

14
Non-daily newspapers and periodicals *[cont.]*
Journaux non quotidiens et périodiques *[suite]*

Association (non-members: 13 non-dailies in 1999 and 9 in 2000).

5   Data refer to titles published 1 to 3 times a week.
6   Data do not include Sunday issues.
7   National estimate.
8   Data refer to weekly newspapers only.

de journaux (Non membres : 13 parutions non quotidiennes en 1999 et 9 en 2000).

5   Les données concernent les titres paraissant 1 à 3 fois par semaine.
6   Les données n'incluent pas les parutions du dimanche.
7   Estimation nationale.
8   Les données ne concernent que les journaux hebdomadaires.

15
Cinemas: number, seating capacity and annual attendance
Cinémas : nombre d'établissements, nombre de sièges, et fréquentation annuelle

Country or area Pays ou zone	Year Année	Number Nombre	Seating capacity Sièges		Annual attendance Fréquentation annuelle	
			Thousands Milliers	Per 1000 Pour 1000	Millions	Per capita Par habitant
Africa · Afrique						
Algeria	1996	136	...	...	0.6	0.02
Algérie	1997	136	...	...	0.6	0.02
Benin	1996	3	2.5	0.5	0.3	0.06
Bénin	1997	3	2.5	0.4	0.3	0.05
Burkina Faso	1996	35	55.0	5.1	4.7	0.44
Burkina Faso	1997	35	55.0	5.0	4.9	0.45
Congo						
Congo	1995	30[1]	4.4	1.7	...	...
Egypt						
Egypte	1996	122	96.1	1.5	10.6	0.17
Kenya	1998	20	6.6	0.2	0.6	0.02
Kenya	1999	20	6.6	0.2	0.9	0.03
Libyan Arab Jamah.	1998	27	14.4	2.8	2.5	0.50
Jamah. arabe libyenne	1999	27	14.4	2.8	2.9	0.56
Mauritius	1998	25	13.0	11.4	1.3	1.09
Maurice	1999	32	16.0	13.9	1.3	1.15
Morocco	1995	185	131.0	5.1	17.3	0.67
Maroc	1996	183	130.0	4.9	16.3	0.62
	1997	175	124.0	4.6	14.3	0.53
Zimbabwe	1998	22	...	...	1.5[2]	0.12
Zimbabwe	1999	22	...	...	1.2[2]	0.10
America, North · Amérique du Nord						
Bermuda	1998	4	1.0	...	0.3	...
Bermudes	1999	4	1.0	...	0.3	...
Canada	1996	...	...	...	92.0	3.07
Canada	1997	685	588.9	19.5	99.1	3.27
	1998	692	646.7	21.4	112.8	3.73
Costa Rica						
Costa Rica	1995	39	...	...	1.7	0.48
Cuba	1996	944	193.3	17.5	10.8	0.98
Cuba	1997	782	172.5	15.6	9.2	0.84
El Salvador						
El Salvador	1995	33	...	...	...	...
Mexico	1997	1 842	...	...	95.0	1.01
Mexique	1998	2 313	627.3	6.6	112.6	1.18
	1999	2 320	624.1	6.4	120.0	1.23
Nicaragua	1998	6	1.8	0.4	0.7	0.15
Nicaragua	1999	10	2.7	0.6	1.2	0.24
United States	1997	31 640	...	...	1 320.5	4.86
Etats-Unis	1998	...	...	...	1 390.0	5.01
	1999	...	...	...	1 465.0	5.22
America, South · Amérique du Sud						
Argentina	1996	523	...	...	21.5	0.61
Argentine	1997	635	...	...	26.6	0.74
	1998	780	...	...	32.5	0.90
Bolivia	1997	72	...	...	1.2	0.15
Bolivie	1998	27	...	...	1.6	0.20
	1999	27	...	...	1.4	0.18
Brazil	1997	1 400	...	...	52.5	0.32
Brésil	1998	1 300	...	...	70.0	0.42
	1999	1 400	...	...	70.0	0.42
Chile						
Chili	1998	198	...	...	6.8	0.46

15

Cinemas: number, seating capacity and annual attendance *[cont.]*
Cinémas : nombre d'établissements, nombre de sièges, et fréquentation annuelle *[suite]*

Country or area Pays ou zone	Year Année	Number Nombre	Seating capacity Sièges		Annual attendance Fréquentation annuelle	
			Thousands Milliers	Per 1000 Pour 1000	Millions	Per capita Par habitant
Colombia	1998	258	...	...	18.4	0.45
Colombie	1999	277	43.0	1.0	...	...
Peru	1996	124	...	...	...	...
Pérou	1997	116	...	...	...	...
	1998	148	...	...	6.5	0.26
Suriname	1996	1	0.8	1.9	0.2	0.37
Suriname	1997	1	0.8	1.9	0.1	0.25
Venezuela	1996	220	...	...	6.2	0.28
Venezuela	1997	241	...	...	6.4	0.28
	1998	284	...	...	14.2	0.61
Asia · Asie						
Armenia						
Arménie	1995	599[1]	124.9	35.0	...	...
Azerbaijan	1997	234	37.6	4.9	0.2	0.03
Azerbaïdjan	1998	225	37.1	4.7	0.2	0.02
	1999	222	34.8	4.4	0.2	0.02
China	1995	...	...	...	130.0	0.11
Chine	1996	...	...	...	140.0	0.11
China, Hong Kong SAR						
Chine, Hong Kong RAS	1995	184	94.8	15.2	28.0	4.50
China, Macao SAR	1998	...	5.0	11.5	0.2	0.41
Chine, Macao RAS	1999	...	5.0	11.4	0.2	0.35
Cyprus	1997	29	8.0	10.5	0.9	1.22
Chypre	1998	26	9.3	13.6	1.0	1.48
	1999	28	9.6	13.9	0.8	1.22
Georgia	1996	97	22.8	4.4	20.5	3.95
Géorgie	1997	97	22.8	4.5	18.7	3.65
India	1996	21 848	...	...	3 380.0	3.56
Inde	1997	21 801	...	...	3 580.0	3.71
	1998	...	...	...	2 860.0	2.93
Indonesia	1995	...	...	...	170.0	0.86
Indonésie	1996	1 009	674.4	3.4	180.0	0.90
	1997	1 009	674.4	3.3	190.0	0.93
Iran (Islamic Rep. of)						
Iran (Rép. islamique d')	1995	287	173.0	2.8	26.0	0.42
Iraq	1996	144	...	...	...	...
Iraq	1997	144	...	...	...	...
Japan	1997	1 884	...	...	140.7	1.12
Japon	1998	1 993	...	...	153.1	1.21
	1999	2 221	...	...	145.0	1.14
Kazakhstan	1995	1 580	346.7	21.0	6.2	0.38
Kazakhstan	1996	1 720	...	...	3.4	0.21
	1997	1 129	...	...	1.0	0.06
Korea, Republic of	1997	241	...	...	47.5	1.04
Corée, République de	1998	507	182.0	4.0	50.2	1.09
	1999	588	195.0	4.2	54.7	1.18
Kyrgyzstan	1997	305	80.8	17.5	0.4	0.09
Kirghizistan	1998	296	...	...	0.4	0.09
	1999	293	...	...	0.3	0.07
Lebanon	1997	25	35.6	11.3	...	...
Liban	1998	...	38.9	11.5	10.9	3.22
	1999	...	38.9	11.3	10.9	3.16
Malaysia	1997	106	37.6	1.8	16.1	0.77
Malaisie	1998	162	...	...	0.3	0.01
	1999	...	...	...	0.3	0.02

15
Cinemas: number, seating capacity and annual attendance *[cont.]*
Cinémas : nombre d'établissements, nombre de sièges, et fréquentation annuelle *[suite]*

Country or area Pays ou zone	Year Année	Number Nombre	Seating capacity Sièges		Annual attendance Fréquentation annuelle	
			Thousands Milliers	Per 1000 Pour 1000	Millions	Per capita Par habitant
Oman	1996	2	0.9	0.4	0.3	0.11
Oman	1997	2	0.9	0.4	0.3	0.11
	1998	17	4.7	2.0	...	...
Pakistan	1997	652	...	...	9.7	0.07
Pakistan	1998	574	...	...	...	...
	1999	574	...	...	...	...
Singapore	1995	80	...	...	18.1	5.46
Singapour	1996	...	...	...	17.0	5.04
	1997	...	...	...	17.0	4.96
Tajikistan Tadjikistan	1995	172	39.0	6.8	0.4	0.07
Turkey	1996	300	115.0	1.8	9.5	0.15
Turquie	1997	344	118.0	1.9	11.3	0.18
	1998	...	...	...	31.5	0.49
Europe · Europe						
Austria	1997	441	73.2	9.0	13.7	1.69
Autriche	1998	...	...	...	15.2	1.88
	1999	...	...	...	15.0	1.86
Belgium	1997	438	...	...	22.1	2.18
Belgique	1998	463	...	...	25.4	2.49
	1999	463	...	...	21.9	2.14
Bulgaria	1997	216	98.0	11.7	3.2	0.38
Bulgarie	1998	205	94.0	11.6	3.2	0.39
	1999	191	83.0	10.3	1.9	0.24
Croatia	1997	146	53.0	11.8	3.2	0.72
Croatie	1998	147	52.0	11.2	2.7	0.59
	1999	141	52.0	11.2	2.3	0.49
Czech Republic	1997	851	300.0	29.1	9.8	0.95
République tchèque	1998	832	290.0	28.2	9.2	0.90
	1999	823	292.0	28.4	8.4	0.81
Denmark	1997	321	51.0	9.7	10.8	2.06
Danemark	1998	167	50.6	9.6	11.0	2.08
	1999	169	52.0	9.8	10.9	2.06
Estonia	1997	200	...	...	1.0	0.66
Estonie	1998	...	...	...	1.1	0.74
	1999	...	...	...	0.9	0.62
Finland	1997	321	55.5	10.8	5.9	1.15
Finlande	1998	232	55.8	10.8	6.4	1.24
	1999	...	...	...	7.0	1.36
France	1997	3 331	942.0	16.1	148.1	2.53
France	1998	2 150	990.0	16.8	170.1	2.89
	1999	...	...	...	155.4	2.63
Germany	1997	4 182	772.0	9.4	143.1	1.74
Allemagne	1998	4 491	801.0	9.8	148.9	1.81
	1999	4 712	835.0	10.2	149.0	1.82
Greece	1997	...	...	...	11.6	1.10
Grèce	1998	...	...	...	12.4	1.17
	1999	...	...	...	13.0	1.23
Hungary	1997	652	121.0	11.9	16.6	1.63
Hongrie	1998	628	121.0	12.0	14.6	1.45
	1999	...	...	...	13.4	1.34
Iceland	1997	32	10.0	36.6	1.5	5.41
Islande	1998	45	9.0	32.8	1.5	5.51
	1999	46	9.0	32.5	1.5	5.53
Ireland	1997	...	...	...	11.5	3.14
Irlande	1998	...	...	...	12.4	3.33
	1999	...	...	...	12.4	3.30

15

Cinemas: number, seating capacity and annual attendance *[cont.]*
Cinémas : nombre d'établissements, nombre de sièges, et fréquentation annuelle *[suite]*

Country or area Pays ou zone	Year Année	Number Nombre	Seating capacity Sièges		Annual attendance Fréquentation annuelle	
			Thousands Milliers	Per 1000 Pour 1000	Millions	Per capita Par habitant
Italy	1997	...	...	...	102.8	1.79
Italie	1998	4 603	...	...	119.6	2.08
	1999	...	...	...	104.9	1.82
Latvia	1997	118	23.0	9.4	1.3	0.52
Lettonie	1998	117	24.1	9.8	1.4	0.58
	1999	115	26.1	10.7	1.4	0.56
Lithuania	1997	124	28.2	7.6	0.5	0.14
Lituanie	1998	113	26.8	7.2	1.6	0.42
	1999	105	26.1	7.1	1.8	0.48
Luxembourg	1997	26	5.3	12.7	1.2	2.84
Luxembourg	1998	21	4.5	10.5	1.4	3.32
	1999	21	4.5	10.4	1.3	3.05
Netherlands	1997	444	88.8	5.7	18.9	1.21
Pays-Bas	1998	461	...	...	20.1	1.28
	1999	465	...	...	18.6	1.18
Norway	1997	631	90.1	20.5	10.9	2.49
Norvège	1998	604	88.0	19.9	11.5	2.60
	1999	605	89.0	20.0	11.4	2.55
Poland	1997	686	200.0	5.2	24.3	0.63
Pologne	1998	686	201.0	5.2	20.3	0.53
	1999	695	211.0	5.5	27.5	0.71
Portugal	1997	595	97.1	9.9	13.5	1.37
Portugal	1998	516	180.0	18.1	14.8	1.49
	1999	537	143.0	14.3	15.2[2]	1.52
Republic of Moldova	1997	50	23.0	5.3	0.2	0.05
République de Moldova	1998	48	28.8	6.7	0.2	0.04
	1999	48	28.8	6.7	0.1	0.02
Romania	1997	469	149.0	6.6	9.5	0.42
Roumanie	1998	330	110.0	4.9	6.8	0.30
	1999	331	129.0	5.7	4.2	0.19
Russian Federation	1997	1 746	778.9	5.3	16.2	0.11
Fédération de Russie	1998	1 568	691.0	4.7	20.2	0.14
	1999	1 416	613.0	4.2	19.1	0.13
San Marino	1995	2	1.8	72.3	0.1	2.05
Saint-Marin	1996	3	1.8	70.6	0.1	2.69
	1997	3	1.9	74.4	0.1	2.97
Serbia and Montenegro	1997	195	80.0	7.5	5.4	0.50
Serbie-et-Monténégro	1998	164	70.0	6.6	5.3	0.50
	1999	165	70.5	6.7	3.9	0.37
Slovakia	1997	296	83.6	15.6	4.0	0.75
Slovaquie	1998	296	83.5	15.5	4.1	0.76
	1999	335	95.3	17.7	3.0	0.56
Slovenia	1997	91	27.0	13.5	2.5	1.25
Slovénie	1998	90	26.0	13.0	2.6	1.29
	1999	85	24.0	12.1	2.0	0.99
Spain	1997	2 530	...	...	101.4	2.56
Espagne	1998	3 025	...	...	112.1	2.81
	1999	3 354	...	...	131.3	3.29
Sweden	1997	1 164	435.0	49.1	15.2	1.72
Suède	1998	839	198.9	22.5	15.8	1.79
	1999	1 167	...	...	15.8	1.79
Switzerland	1997	502	110.9	15.3	15.6	2.14
Suisse	1998	499	191.0	26.6	15.9	2.22
	1999	384	230.8	32.2	15.4	2.15
TFYR of Macedonia	1997	37	10.0	5.0	0.5	0.23
L'ex-R.y. de Macédoine	1998	23	9.0	4.5	0.6	0.28
	1999	30	12.0	5.9	0.5	0.24

15
Cinemas: number, seating capacity and annual attendance *[cont.]*
Cinémas : nombre d'établissements, nombre de sièges, et fréquentation annuelle *[suite]*

Country or area Pays ou zone	Year Année	Number Nombre	Seating capacity Sièges		Annual attendance Fréquentation annuelle	
			Thousands Milliers	Per 1000 Pour 1000	Millions	Per capita Par habitant
United Kingdom	1997	...	...	...	139.3	2.38
Royaume-Uni	1998	...	...	...	135.4	2.29
	1999	...	...	...	139.5	2.35
Oceania · Océanie						
Australia	1996	1 251	356.0	19.6	74.0	4.08
Australie	1997	1 422	387.0	21.1	76.0	4.15
	1998	...	...	...	80.0	4.27
New Zealand	1997	285	...	...	16.5	4.40
Nouvelle-Zélande	1998	290	...	...	16.3	4.38
	1999	315	...	...	16.8	4.47

Source:
United Nations Educational, Scientific and Cultural Organization
(UNESCO) Institute for Statistics, Montreal, the UNESCO Institute for
Statistics database.

Source:
L'Institut de statistique de l'Organisation des Nations Unies pour
l'éducation, la science et la culture (UNESCO), Montréal, la base de
données de l'Institut de statistique de l'UNESCO.

1   Including non-commercial units.
2   National estimate.

1   Y compris des établissements non commerciaux.
2   Estimation nationale.

16

Cellular mobile telephone subscribers
Number

Abonnés au téléphone mobile
Nombre

Country or area Pays ou zone	1995	1996	1997	1998	1999	2000	2001	2002
Afghanistan Afghanistan	0	0	0	0	0	0	0	12 000
Albania Albanie	0	2 300	3 300	5 600	11 008	29 791	392 650	851 000
Algeria Algérie	4 691	11 700	17 400	18 000	72 000	86 000	100 000	400 000
American Samoa Samoa américaines	2 000	2 500	2 550	2 650	2 377	...	...	...
Andorra Andorre	2 825	5 488	8 618	14 117	20 600	23 543	...	...
Angola Angola	1 994	3 298	7 052	9 820	24 000	25 806	86 500	130 000
Anguilla Anguilla	160	359	707	787	*1 475	2 163	1 773	...
Antigua and Barbuda Antigua-et-Barbuda	...	1 300	*1 400	*1 500	8 500	22 000	25 000[1]	38 205
Argentina Argentine	340 743	568 000	1 588 000	2 530 000	4 434 000	6 049 963	6 974 939	6 500 000[2]
Armenia Arménie	0	300	5 000	7 831	8 161	17 486	25 504	71 949
Aruba Aruba	1 718	3 000	3 402	5 380	12 000	15 000	53 000	...
Australia Australie	2 242 000	3 990 000	4 578 000	4 918 000	6 315 000	8 562 000	11 132 000	12 579 000
Austria Autriche	383 535	598 708	1 159 700	2 292 900	4 250 393	6 117 000	6 541 000	6 415 000
Azerbaijan Azerbaïdjan	6 000	17 000	40 000	65 000	370 000	420 400	730 000	870 000
Bahamas Bahamas	4 100	4 948	6 152	8 072	15 911	31 524	60 555	121 759
Bahrain Bahreïn	27 600	40 080	58 543	92 063	133 468	205 727	300 829	388 990
Bangladesh Bangladesh	2 500	4 000[2]	26 000[2]	75 000	149 000	279 000	520 000[2]	1 075 000
Barbados Barbade	4 614	6 283	8 013	12 000	20 309	28 467	53 111	...
Belarus Bélarus	5 897	6 548	8 167	12 155	23 457	49 353	138 329	462 630
Belgium Belgique	235 258	478 172	974 494	1 756 287	3 186 602	5 629 000	7 697 000	8 135 512[2]
Belize Belize	1 547	2 184	2 544	3 535	6 591	16 812	39 155	51 729
Benin Bénin	1 050	2 707	4 295	6 286	7 269	55 476	125 000	218 770[2]
Bermuda Bermudes	6 324	7 980	*10 276	12 572	...	...	13 333[1]	*30 000
Bolivia Bolivie	7 229	33 400	118 433	239 272	420 344	582 620	779 917	872 676
Bosnia and Herzegovina Bosnie-Herzégovine	0	1 500	9 000	25 181	52 607	93 386	444 711	748 780
Botswana [3] Botswana [3]	0	0	0	15 190	92 000	200 000	316 000	415 000
Brazil Brésil	1 285 533	2 498 154	4 550 000	7 368 218	15 032 698	23 188 171	28 745 769	34 881 000

16

Cellular mobile telephone subscribers
Number *[cont.]*
Abonnés au téléphone mobile
Nombre *[suite]*

Country or area Pays ou zone	1995	1996	1997	1998	1999	2000	2001	2002
British Virgin Islands Iles Vierges britanniques	...	1 200	...	...	...	...	...	8 000
Brunei Darussalam Brunéi Darussalam	35 881	43 524	45 000	49 129	66 000	95 000	137 000	...
Bulgaria Bulgarie	20 920	26 588	70 000	127 000	350 000	738 000	1 550 000	2 597 548
Burkina Faso Burkina Faso	0	525	1 503	2 730	5 036	25 245	45 000[4]	89 900[4]
Burundi Burundi	564	561	619	620	800	16 320	30 687[2]	52 000
Cambodia Cambodge	14 100	23 098	33 556	61 345	89 117	130 547	223 458	380 000
Cameroon Cameroun	2 800	3 500	4 200	5 000	6 000	148 000	310 000[5]	675 668
Canada Canada	2 589 780	3 497 779	4 265 778	5 365 459	6 911 038	8 726 636	10 861 563	11 849 020
Cape Verde Cap-Vert	0	0	20	1 020	8 068	19 729	31 507	42 949
Cayman Islands Iles Caïmanes	2 534	...	4 109	5 170	8 410	10 700	17 000	...
Central African Rep. Rép. centrafricaine	44	1 071	1 370	1 633	4 162	4 967	11 000	12 600
Chad Tchad	0	0	0	0	0	5 500	22 000	34 200[5]
Chile Chili	197 314	319 474	409 740	964 248	2 260 687	3 401 525	5 271 565	6 445 698[2]
China Chine	3 629 000	6 853 000	13 233 000	23 863 000	43 296 000	85 260 000	144 820 000	206 620 000
China, Hong Kong SAR Chine, Hong Kong RAS	798 373	1 361 861	2 229 862	3 174 369	4 275 048	5 447 346	5 776 360	6 395 725
China, Macao SAR Chine, Macao RAS	35 881	44 788	50 624	82 114	118 101	141 052	194 475	276 138
Colombia Colombie	274 590	522 857	1 264 763	1 800 229	1 966 535	2 256 801	3 265 261	4 596 594
Congo Congo	0	1 000	...	3 390	5 000	70 000	150 000	221 800[5]
Cook Islands Iles Cook	0	182[6]	196	285	506	552	942[1]	1 499
Costa Rica Costa Rica	18 750	46 531	64 387	108 770	138 178	205 275	311 329	459 757
Côte d'Ivoire Côte d'Ivoire	0	13 549	36 000	91 212	257 134	472 952	728 545	1 027 058
Croatia Croatie	33 688	64 943	120 420	182 500	295 000	1 033 000	*1 755 000	2 340 000
Cuba Cuba	1 939	2 427	2 994	4 056	5 136	6 536	8 579	17 851
Cyprus Chypre	44 453	70 781	91 968	116 429	151 649	218 324	314 355	417 933
Czech Republic République tchèque	48 900	200 315	526 339	965 476	1 944 553	4 346 009	6 947 151	8 610 177
Dem. Rep. of the Congo Rép. dém. du Congo	8 500[2]	7 200	8 900	10 000	12 000	15 000	150 000	560 000
Denmark Danemark	822 264	1 316 592	1 444 016	1 931 101	2 628 585	3 363 552	3 960 165	4 477 752

16

Cellular mobile telephone subscribers
Number [cont.]
      Abonnés au téléphone mobile
      Nombre [suite]

Country or area Pays ou zone	1995	1996	1997	1998	1999	2000	2001	2002
Djibouti Djibouti	0	110	203	220	280	230	3 000	15 000
Dominica Dominique	0	461	*556	650	*800	*1 200	7 710	9 358
Dominican Republic Rép. dominicaine	55 979	82 547	141 592	209 384	424 434	705 431	1 270 082	1 700 609
Ecuador Equateur	54 380	59 779	126 505	242 812	383 185	482 213	859 152	1 560 861
Egypt Egypte	7 368	7 369	65 378	90 786	480 974	1 359 900	2 793 800	4 494 700[3]
El Salvador El Salvador	13 475	23 270	40 163	137 114	511 365	743 628	857 782	888 818
Equatorial Guinea Guinée équatoriale	0	61	300	297	600	5 000	15 000	32 000
Estonia Estonie	30 452	69 500	144 200	247 000	387 000	557 000	651 200	881 000
Ethiopia Ethiopie	0	0	0	0	6 740[7]	17 757[7]	27 500[7]	50 369[7]
Faeroe Islands Iles Féroé	2 558	3 265	4 701	6 516	10 761	16 971	24 487	30 709[2]
Fiji Fidji	2 200	3 700	5 200	8 000	23 380	55 057	80 933	89 900
Finland Finlande	1 039 126	1 502 003	2 162 574	2 845 985	3 273 433	3 728 625	4 175 587	4 516 772[2]
France France	1 302 496	2 462 700	5 817 300	11 210 100	21 433 500	29 052 360	35 922 270	38 585 300
French Guiana Guyane française	0	0	0	4 000	18 000	39 830	75 320	138 200
French Polynesia Polynésie française	1 150	2 719	5 427	11 060	21 929	39 900	67 300	90 000
Gabon Gabon	4 000	6 800	9 500	9 694	8 891	120 000	258 087	279 289
Gambia Gambie	1 442	3 096	4 734	5 048	5 307	*5 600	55 085	100 000
Georgia Géorgie	150	2 300	30 000	60 000	133 243	194 741	301 327	503 619
Germany Allemagne	3 725 000	5 512 000	8 276 000	13 913 000	23 446 000	48 202 000	56 245 000	60 043 000
Ghana Ghana	6 200	12 766	21 866	41 753	70 026	130 045	193 773	449 435
Gibraltar Gibraltar	660	1 002	1 620	2 445	3 648	5 558	9 797	...
Greece Grèce	273 000	532 000	937 700	2 047 000	3 904 000	5 932 403	7 963 742	9 314 260
Greenland Groenland	2 052	4 122	6 481	8 899	13 521	15 977	16 747	19 924
Grenada Grenade	400	570	976	1 410	2 012	4 300	6 414	7 553
Guadeloupe Guadeloupe	0	0	0	14 227	88 080	169 840	292 520	323 500
Guam Guam	4 965	5 803	5 673	12 837[2]	20 000	27 200	32 600	...
Guatemala Guatemala	29 999	43 421	64 194	111 445	337 800	856 831	1 146 441	1 577 085

16

Cellular mobile telephone subscribers
Number *[cont.]*
Abonnés au téléphone mobile
Nombre *[suite]*

Country or area Pays ou zone	1995	1996	1997	1998	1999	2000	2001	2002
Guinea Guinée	950	950	2 868	21 567	25 182	42 112	55 670	90 772
Guyana Guyana	1 243	1 200	1 400	1 454	2 815	39 830	75 320	87 300
Haiti Haïti	0	0	0	10 000	25 000	55 000	91 500	140 000
Honduras Honduras	0	2 311	14 427	34 896	78 588	155 271	237 629	326 508
Hungary Hongrie	265 000	473 100	705 786	1 070 154	1 628 153	3 076 279	4 967 430	6 862 766
Iceland Islande	30 883	46 805	65 368	104 280	172 614	214 896	248 131	260 938[2]
India Inde	76 680	327 967	881 839	1 195 400	1 884 311	3 577 095	6 431 520	12 687 637
Indonesia Indonésie	210 643	562 517	916 173	1 065 820	2 220 969	3 669 327	6 520 947	11 700 000
Iran (Islamic Rep. of) Iran (Rép. islamique d')	15 902	59 967	238 942	389 974	490 478	962 595	2 087 353	2 186 958
Iraq Iraq	0	0	0	0	0	0	0	20 000
Ireland Irlande	158 000	288 600	545 000	946 000	1 677 000	2 461 000	2 970 000	3 000 000[3]
Israel Israël	445 456	1 047 582	1 672 442	2 147 000	2 880 000	4 400 000	5 900 000	6 334 000
Italy Italie	3 923 000	6 422 000	11 737 904	20 489 000	30 296 000	42 246 000	51 246 000	53 003 000[5]
Jamaica Jamaïque	45 138	54 640	65 995	78 624	144 388	366 952	*635 000	1 400 000
Japan[8] Japon[8]	11 712 137	26 906 511	38 253 893	47 307 592	56 845 594	66 784 374	74 819 158	81 118 400
Jordan Jordanie	12 400	16 100	45 037[2]	82 429	118 417	388 949	866 000	1 219 597
Kazakhstan Kazakhstan	4 600	9 798	11 202	29 700	49 500	197 300	582 000	1 027 000
Kenya Kenya	2 279	2 826	6 767	10 756	23 757	127 404[1]	600 000	1 325 222
Kiribati Kiribati	0	0	0	22	200	395	498	545
Korea, Republic of Corée, République de	1 641 293	3 180 989	6 878 786	14 018 612	23 442 724	26 816 398	29 045 596	32 342 000
Kuwait Koweït	117 609	151 063	210 000	250 000	300 000	476 000	877 920	1 227 000
Kyrgyzstan Kirghizistan	0	0	0	1 350	2 574	9 000	27 000	53 084
Lao People's Dem. Rep. Rép. dém. pop. lao	1 539	3 790	4 915	6 453	12 078	12 681	29 545	55 160
Latvia Lettonie	15 003	28 500	77 100	167 460	274 344	401 272	656 835	917 196
Lebanon Liban	120 000	198 000	373 900	505 300	627 000	743 000	766 754	775 104
Lesotho Lesotho	0	1 262	3 500	9 831	12 000	21 600	57 000	92 000[5]
Liberia Libéria	0	0	0	0	0	1 500	2 000	...

16

Cellular mobile telephone subscribers
Number *[cont.]*
      Abonnés au téléphone mobile
      Nombre *[suite]*

Country or area Pays ou zone	1995	1996	1997	1998	1999	2000	2001	2002
Libyan Arab Jamah. Jamah. arabe libyenne	0	0	10 000[2]	20 000	30 000	40 000	50 000	70 000
Liechtenstein * Liechtenstein *	...	...	...	7 500	9 000	10 000	11 000	11 402
Lithuania Lituanie	14 795	50 973	165 337	267 615	332 000	524 000	1 017 999	1 645 568
Luxembourg Luxembourg	26 838	45 000	67 208	130 500	209 190	303 274	409 064	473 000[2]
Madagascar Madagascar	1 300	2 300	4 100	12 784	35 752	63 094	147 500	163 010
Malawi Malawi	382	3 700	7 000	10 500	22 500	49 000	55 730	86 047
Malaysia Malaisie	1 005 066	1 520 320	2 000 000	2 200 000	2 990 000	5 121 748	7 477 642	9 241 387
Maldives Maldives	0	20	1 290	1 606	2 926	7 638	18 894	41 899
Mali Mali	0	1 187	2 842	4 473	6 387	10 398	45 340	52 639
Malta Malte	10 791	12 500	17 691	22 531	37 541	114 444	239 416	276 859
Marshall Islands Iles Marshall	264	365	466	345	443	447	489	552
Martinique Martinique	0	0	15 000	55 000	102 000	162 080	286 120	319 900
Mauritania Mauritanie	0	0	0	0	0	15 300	110 463	247 238
Mauritius Maurice	11 735	20 843	42 515	60 448	102 119	180 000	272 416	350 000
Mayotte Mayotte	0	0	0	0	0	0	0	21 700
Mexico Mexique	688 513	1 021 900	1 740 814	3 349 475	7 731 635	14 077 880	21 757 559	25 928 263
Micronesia (Fed. States) Micronésie (Etats féd. de)	0	0	0	0	0	0	0	1 750
Monaco Monaco	3 005	5 400	7 200	11 474	16 000	17 003	17 894	19 307
Mongolia Mongolie	0	900	2 000	9 032	34 562	154 600	195 000	216 000
Montserrat Montserrat	84	250	325	250	300	489	...	...
Morocco Maroc	29 511	42 942	74 472	116 645	369 174	2 342 000	4 771 739	6 198 670
Mozambique Mozambique	0	0	2 500	6 725	12 243	51 065	152 652	254 759
Myanmar Myanmar	2 766	7 260	8 492	8 516	11 389	13 397	22 671	47 982
Namibia Namibie	3 500	6 644	12 500	19 500	30 000	82 000	100 000	*150 000
Nauru[2] Nauru[2]	500	600	750	850	1 000	1 200	1 500	...
Nepal Népal	0	0	0	0	5 500	10 226	17 286[1]	21 881
Netherlands Pays-Bas	539 000	1 016 000	1 717 000	3 351 000	6 745 460	10 755 000	12 352 000	12 060 000

16

Cellular mobile telephone subscribers
Number *[cont.]*
Abonnés au téléphone mobile
Nombre *[suite]*

Country or area Pays ou zone	1995	1996	1997	1998	1999	2000	2001	2002
Netherlands Antilles Antilles néerlandaises	11 698	13 977	*14 500	16 000	...	...	...	...
New Caledonia Nouvelle-Calédonie	825	2 060	5 198	13 040	25 450	49 948	67 917	80 000
New Zealand Nouvelle-Zélande	365 000	492 800	566 200	790 000	1 395 000	1 542 000	2 288 000	2 449 000
Nicaragua Nicaragua	4 400	5 100	7 560	18 310	44 229	90 294	154 526	202 799
Niger Niger	0	0	98	1 349	2 192	2 056	2 126	16 648
Nigeria Nigéria	13 000	14 000	15 000	20 000	25 000	30 000	*400 000	1 607 931
Niue Nioué	0	0	...	...	380	410	400	...
Northern Mariana Islands Iles Mariannes du Nord	1 200	...	...	...	2 905[9]	3 000	...	...
Norway Norvège	981 305	1 261 445	1 676 763	2 106 414	2 744 793	3 367 763	3 759 862	3 840 377[2]
Occup. Palestinian Terr. [10] Terr. palestinien occupé [10]	20 000	25 000	40 000	100 000	117 000	175 941	300 000	320 000
Oman Oman	8 052	12 934	59 822	103 032	124 119	164 348	324 540	464 896
Pakistan Pakistan	40 964	68 038	135 027	206 908	278 830	349 460	812 000	1 238 602
Panama Panama	0	7 000	18 542	85 883	232 888	410 401	475 354	569 650
Papua New Guinea Papouasie-Nvl-Guinée	0	2 285	3 857	5 558	7 059	8 560	10 700	15 000
Paraguay Paraguay	15 807	32 860	84 240	231 520	435 611	820 810	1 150 000	1 667 018
Peru Pérou	73 543	200 972	421 814	742 642	1 013 314	1 273 857	1 545 000	2 306 944
Philippines Philippines	493 862	959 024	1 343 620	1 733 652	2 849 980	6 454 359	12 159 163	15 201 000
Poland Pologne	75 000	216 900	812 200	1 928 042	3 956 500	6 747 000	10 004 661	*14 000 000
Portugal Portugal	340 845	663 651	1 506 958	3 074 633	4 671 458	6 664 951	7 977 537	8 528 900[5]
Puerto Rico [11] Porto Rico [11]	287 000	329 000	367 000	580 000	813 800	926 448	1 211 111	...
Qatar Qatar	18 469	28 772	43 476	65 756	84 365	120 856	178 789	267 201
Republic of Moldova République de Moldova	14	920	2 200	7 000	18 000	139 000	225 000	338 225
Réunion Réunion	5 500	14 000	26 700	50 300	111 000	276 100	421 100	489 800
Romania Roumanie	9 068	17 000	201 000	643 000	1 355 500	2 499 000	3 845 116	5 110 591
Russian Federation Fédération de Russie	88 526	223 002	484 883	747 160	1 370 630	3 263 200	7 750 499	17 608 756
Rwanda Rwanda	0	0	0	5 000	11 000	39 000	65 000	110 762[5]
Saint Kitts and Nevis Saint-Kitts-et-Nevis	...	300	205	440	700	1 200	*2 100	5 000

16

Cellular mobile telephone subscribers
Number *[cont.]*
Abonnés au téléphone mobile
Nombre *[suite]*

Country or area Pays ou zone	1995	1996	1997	1998	1999	2000	2001	2002
Saint Lucia * Sainte-Lucie *	1 000	1 400	1 600	1 900	2 300	2 500	2 700	14 313
St. Vincent-Grenadines St. Vincent-Grenadines	*215	*280	346	750	1 420	2 361	7 492	9 982
Samoa Samoa	0	0	766[12]	1 480	2 432	2 500	2 500	2 700
San Marino Saint-Marin	2 340	2 279	2 350	4 980	9 580	14 503	15 854	16 759
Sao Tome and Principe Sao Tomé-et-Principe	0	0	0	0	0	0	0	1 980
Saudi Arabia Arabie saoudite	16 008	190 736	332 068	627 321	836 628	1 375 881	2 528 640	5 007 965
Senegal Sénégal	122	1 412	6 942	27 487	87 879	250 251	301 811	553 427
Serbia and Montenegro * Serbie-et-Monténégro *	0	14 800	87 000	240 000	605 697	1 303 609	1 997 809	2 750 397
Seychelles Seychelles	50	1 043	2 247	5 190	16 316	25 961	36 683	44 731
Sierra Leone Sierra Leone	0	0	0	0	0	11 940	26 895	66 250
Singapore Singapour	306 000	431 010	848 600	1 094 700	1 630 800	2 747 400	2 991 600	3 312 600
Slovakia Slovaquie	12 315	28 658	200 140	473 173	664 072	1 109 888	2 147 331	2 923 383
Slovenia Slovénie	27 301	41 205	93 611	161 606	631 411	1 215 601	1 470 085	1 667 234
Solomon Islands Iles Salomon	230	337	658	702	1 093	1 151	967	999
Somalia Somalie	0	0	0	0	0	...	...	35 000
South Africa Afrique du Sud	535 000	953 000	1 836 000	3 337 000	5 188 000	8 339 000	10 789 000	13 814 035[5]
Spain Espagne	944 955	2 997 645	4 337 696	6 437 444	15 003 708	24 265 059	29 655 729	33 530 997[2]
Sri Lanka Sri Lanka	51 316	71 029	114 888	174 202	256 655	430 202	667 662	931 580
Sudan Soudan	0	2 200	3 800	8 600	13 000	23 000	103 846	190 778[13]
Suriname Suriname	1 687	2 416	2 258	6 007	17 500	41 048	87 000	108 363
Swaziland Swaziland	0	0	0	4 700	14 000	33 000	55 000	63 000[5]
Sweden Suède	2 008 000	2 492 000	3 169 000	4 109 000	5 165 000	6 372 300	7 177 000	7 949 000
Switzerland Suisse	447 167	662 713	1 044 379	1 698 565	3 057 509	4 638 519	5 275 791	5 747 000
Syrian Arab Republic Rép. arabe syrienne	0	0	0	0	4 000	30 000	200 000	400 000
Tajikistan Tadjikistan	0	102	320	420	625	1 160	1 630	13 200
Thailand Thaïlande	1 297 826	1 844 627	2 203 905	1 976 957	2 339 401	3 056 000	7 550 000	16 117 000
TFYR of Macedonia L'ex-R.y. Macédoine	0	1 058	12 362	30 087	48 733	115 748	223 275	365 346

16

Cellular mobile telephone subscribers
Number *[cont.]*
Abonnés au téléphone mobile
Nombre *[suite]*

Country or area Pays ou zone	1995	1996	1997	1998	1999	2000	2001	2002
Togo Togo	0	0	2 995	7 500	17 000	50 000	95 000	170 000
Tonga [2] Tonga [2]	300	302	120	130	140	180	236	3 354
Trinidad and Tobago Trinité-et-Tobago	6 353	9 534	17 140	26 307	38 659	161 860	256 106	361 911
Tunisia Tunisie	3 185	5 439	7 656	38 973	55 258	119 075	389 208	503 911
Turkey Turquie	437 130	806 339	1 609 809	3 506 127	8 121 517	16 133 405	19 572 897	23 374 364 [2]
Turkmenistan Turkménistan	0	0	2 500	3 000	4 000	7 500	8 173	8 173
Uganda Ouganda	1 747	4 000	5 000	30 000	56 358	188 568	276 034	393 310
Ukraine Ukraine	14 000	30 000	57 200	115 500	216 567	818 524	2 224 600	4 200 000
United Arab Emirates Emirats arabes unis	128 968	193 834	309 373	493 278	832 267	1 428 115	1 909 303	2 428 071
United Kingdom Royaume-Uni	5 735 785	7 248 355	8 841 000	14 878 000	27 185 000	43 452 000	46 283 000	49 677 000
United Rep. of Tanzania Rép.-Unie de Tanzanie	3 500	9 038	20 200	37 940	50 950	180 200	426 964	670 000
United States Etats-Unis	33 785 661	44 042 992	55 312 293	69 209 321	86 047 003	109 478 031	128 374 512	140 766 842
United States Virgin Is. * Iles Vierges américaines *	...	...	16 000	25 000	30 000	35 000	41 000	...
Uruguay Uruguay	39 904	78 601	99 235	151 341	319 131	410 787	519 991	652 000
Uzbekistan Ouzbékistan	3 731	9 510	17 232	26 826	40 389	53 128	128 012	186 900
Vanuatu Vanuatu	121	154	207	220	300	365	350	4 900
Venezuela Venezuela	403 800	581 700	1 071 900	2 009 757	3 784 735	5 447 172	6 472 584	6 463 561
Viet Nam Viet Nam	23 500	68 910	160 457	222 700	328 671	788 559	1 251 195	1 902 388
Yemen Yémen	8 250	8 810	12 245	16 146	27 677	32 000	152 000	411 083
Zambia Zambie	1 547 [14]	2 721 [14]	4 550 [14]	8 260	28 190	98 853	121 200	139 092
Zimbabwe Zimbabwe	0	0	5 734	19 000	174 000	309 000	328 669	353 000

Source:
International Telecommunication Union (ITU), Geneva, the ITU database.

+ Note: The data shown generally relate to the fiscal year used in each country, unless indicated otherwise. Countries whose reference periods coincide with the calendar year ending 31 December are not listed.
Year beginning 22 March: Iran (Islamic Republic).
Year beginning 1 April: Antigua and Barbuda, Barbados, Belize, Bermuda, British Virgin Islands, Cayman Islands, China - Hong Kong, Cocos Islands, Cook Islands, Dominica, Gambia, India, Ireland, Israel (prior to 1986), Jamaica, Japan, Lesotho, Seychelles, Singapore (beginning 1983), Solomon Islands, South Africa, St. Helena, St. Kitts and Nevis, St. Lucia, St. Vincent,

Source:
Union internationale des télécommunications (UIT), Genève, la base de données de l'UIT.

+ Note: sauf indication contraire, les données indiquées concernent généralement l'exercice budgétaire utilisé dans chaque pays. Les pays ou territoires dont la période de référence coïncide avec l'année civile se terminant le 31 décembre ne sont pas répertoriés ci-dessous.
Exercice commençant le 22 mars : Iran (République islamique d').
Exercice commençant le 1er avril : Afrique du Sud, Antigua-et-Barbuda, Barbade, Belize, Bermudes, Chine - Hong Kong, Dominique, Gambie, Îles Caïmanes, Îles des Cocos, Îles Cook, Îles Salomon, Îles Vierges britanniques, Inde, Irlande, Israël (antérieur à 1986), Jamaïque, Japon, Lesotho, Royaume-

16

Cellular mobile telephone subscribers
Number *[cont.]*
Abonnés au téléphone mobile
Nombre *[suite]*

Swaziland, Trinidad and Tobago, United Kingdom, and Zambia.
Year ending 30 June: Australia, Bangladesh, Egypt, Ethiopia, Iraq, Kenya, New Zealand (beginning 2000; prior to 2000, year ending 1 April), Pakistan, Uganda, and Zimbabwe.
Year ending 15 July: Nepal.
Year ending 30 September: Argentina, Namibia (beginning 1993), and Thailand.

Uni, Saint-Kitts-et-Nevis, Saint-Vincent-et-les Grenadines, Sainte-Hélène, Sainte-Lucie, Seychelles, Singapour (à partir de 1983), Swaziland, Trinité-et-Tobago et Zambie.
Exercice se terminant le 30 juin : Australie, Bangladesh, Égypte, Éthiopie, Iraq, Kenya, Nouvelle-Zélande (à partir de 2000; avant 2000, exercice se terminant le 1er avril), Ouganda, Pakistan et Zimbabwe.
Exercice se terminant le 15 juillet : Népal.
Exercice se terminant le 30 septembre : Argentine, Namibie (à partir de 1993), et Thaïlande.

1	As of 31 December.
2	ITU estimate.
3	December.
4	Including Celtel subscribers.
5	September.
6	As of May 1997.
7	Excluding Eritrea.
8	Including PHS.
9	As of 31 March 2000.
10	Users use Israel cellular network.
11	Data refer to the Puerto Rico Telephone Authority.
12	As of 10 February 1998.
13	August.
14	Zamtel (Zambian Telecommunications Company Limited) only.

1	Dès le 31 décembre.
2	Estimation de l'UIT.
3	Décembre.
4	Y compris les abonnés au Celtel.
5	Septembre.
6	Dès mai 1997.
7	Non compris Erythrée.
8	Y compris "PHS"
9	Dès le 31 mars 2000.
10	Les abonnés utilisent le réseau israélien de téléphonie mobile.
11	Les données se réfèrent à "Puerto Rico Telephone Authority".
12	Dès le 10 février 1998.
13	Août.
14	Zamtel seulement.

17
Telephones
Main telephone lines in operation and per 100 inhabitants
Téléphones
Nombre de lignes téléphoniques en service et pour 100 habitants

Country or area Pays ou zone	Number (thousands) Nombre (en milliers)					Per 100 inhabitants Pour 100 habitants				
	1998	1999	2000	2001	2002	1998	1999	2000	2001	2002
Afghanistan Afghanistan	*29	*29	*29	29	*33	0.1	0.1	0.1	0.1	0.1
Albania Albanie	116	140	153	197	220	3.7	4.5	4.9	6.4	7.1
Algeria Algérie	1 477	1 600	1 761	1 880	1 908	5.0	5.3	5.8	6.1	6.1
American Samoa Samoa américaines	14	14	*14	*15	...	24.6	24.8	25.0	25.2	...
Andorra Andorre	33	34	34	*35	...	43.9	44.7	43.9	43.8	...
Angola Angola	65[1]	67[1]	70[1]	80[1]	85[1]	0.5	0.5	0.5	0.6	0.6
Anguilla Anguilla	6	6[2]	6	6	...	68.9	71.1	74.5	53.6	...
Antigua and Barbuda + Antigua-et-Barbuda +	34	37	38	37[3]	38	46.8	48.9	50.0	48.1	48.8
Argentina + Argentine +	7 323	7 357	7 894	8 108	8 009	20.9	20.7	22.0	22.4	21.9
Armenia Arménie	557	544	533	531	543	14.7	14.3	14.0	14.0	14.3
Aruba Aruba	35	37	*38	37	...	37.3	37.2	37.2	35.0	...
Australia + Australie +	9 540	9 760	10 350	10 485	10 590	50.9	51.5	54.0	54.1	53.9
Austria Autriche	3 997[4]	3 862[4]	3 995[4]	3 997[4,5]	3 988[4]	49.1	47.2	49.2	49.1	48.9
Azerbaijan Azerbaïdjan	680	730	801	865	924	8.9	9.5	10.2	10.8	11.4
Bahamas Bahamas	106	111	114	123	127	35.8	36.9	37.5	40.2	40.6
Bahrain Bahreïn	158	165	171	174	175	26.1	26.7	26.9	26.7	26.3
Bangladesh + Bangladesh +	413	433	472	565	682	0.3	0.3	0.4	0.4	0.5
Barbados + Barbade +	113	115	*124	129	133	42.4	43.0	46.3	48.1	49.4
Belarus Bélarus	2 490	2 638	2 752	2 862	2 967	24.8	26.3	27.6	28.8	29.9
Belgium Belgique	5 056[4]	5 215[4]	5 302[4]	5 132[4]	5 120[4]	49.5	50.9	51.7	49.8	49.4
Belize + Belize +	32	36	36	35	31	14.3	15.4	14.9	14.3	12.4
Benin Bénin	38	44	52	59	63	0.6	0.7	0.8	0.9	0.9
Bermuda + Bermudes +	*54	*55	*56	*56	*56	84.0	85.7	87.0	86.9	86.2
Bhutan Bhoutan	10	12	14	18	20	1.6	1.8	2.2	2.6	2.8
Bolivia Bolivie	452	503	511	524	564	5.7	6.2	6.2	6.3	6.8
Bosnia and Herzegovina Bosnie-Herzégovine	333	368	780[4]	847	903	9.1	9.6	20.6	22.3	23.7
Botswana + Botswana +	102	124	136	143	*150	6.5	7.7	8.3	8.5	8.7

17

Telephones
Main telephone lines in operation and per 100 inhabitants *[cont.]*

Téléphones
Nombre de lignes téléphoniques en service et pour 100 habitants *[suite]*

Country or area Pays ou zone	Number (thousands) Nombre (en milliers)					Per 100 inhabitants Pour 100 habitants				
	1998	1999	2000	2001	2002	1998	1999	2000	2001	2002
Brazil Brésil	19 987[2]	24 985[2]	30 926[2]	37 431[2]	38 810[2]	12.1	14.9	18.2	21.8	22.3
British Virgin Islands + Iles Vierges britan. +	*10	*10	*10	*11	12	52.9	52.9	52.8	50.9	53.2
Brunei Darussalam Brunéi Darussalam	78	79	*81	*88	90	24.7	24.6	24.3	25.9	25.6
Bulgaria Bulgarie	2 758	2 833	2 882	2 914	2 868	33.1	34.2	35.4	35.9	36.8
Burkina Faso Burkina Faso	41	47	53	58	64	0.4	0.4	0.5	0.5	0.5
Burundi Burundi	18	19	*20	*20	22	0.3	0.3	0.3	0.3	0.3
Cambodia Cambodge	24[6]	28[6]	31[6]	33[6]	35[6]	0.2	0.2	0.2	0.3	0.3
Cameroon Cameroun	94	95	*95	*106	111	0.7	0.6	0.6	0.7	0.7
Canada Canada	19 294	20 051	20 347	20 336	19 962	65.8	67.9	66.1	65.4	63.6
Cape Verde Cap-Vert	40	47	55	62	70	9.6	10.9	12.6	14.3	16.0
Cayman Islands + Iles Caïmanes +	28	32	35	38	...	72.1	78.8	82.1	84.9	...
Central African Rep. Rép. centrafricaine	10	10	9	9	9	0.3	0.3	0.3	0.2	0.2
Chad Tchad	9	10	10[2]	11[2]	12	0.1	0.1	0.1	0.1	0.2
Chile Chili	3 047	3 109	3 303	3 478	3 467	20.6	20.7	21.7	22.6	23.0
China Chine	87 421	108 716	144 829	180 368	214 420	7.0	8.6	11.2	13.7	16.7
China, Hong Kong SAR + Chine, Hong Kong RAS +	3 729	3 869	3 926	3 898	3 832	57.0	58.6	58.9	58.0	56.5
China, Macao SAR Chine, Macao RAS	174	178	177	176	176	40.4	40.8	40.2	40.4	39.9
Colombia Colombie	6 367	6 665	7 193	*7 372	7 766	15.6	16.0	17.0	17.2	17.9
Comoros Comores	6	7	7	9	10	1.0	1.0	1.0	1.2	1.4
Congo Congo	22[2]	22[2]	22[2]	22	22	0.8	0.8	0.8	0.7	0.7
Cook Islands + Iles Cook +	5	5	6	6[3]	6	28.1	29.4	31.0	32.8[3]	34.3
Costa Rica Costa Rica	742	803	899	945	1 038	19.3	20.4	22.3	23.0	25.1
Côte d'Ivoire Côte d'Ivoire	170	219	264	294	336	1.2	1.5	1.8	1.8	2.0
Croatia Croatie	1 558	1 634	1 721	*1 781	1 825	34.8	36.5	38.5	40.7	41.7
Cuba Cuba	388	434	489	574	...	3.5	3.9	4.4	5.1	...
Cyprus Chypre	405	424	440	435	492	61.4[7]	63.4[7]	64.8[7]	63.1[7]	68.8[7]
Czech Republic République tchèque	3 741	3 806	3 872	3 861	3 675	36.3	37.0	37.7	37.8	36.2

17

Telephones
Main telephone lines in operation and per 100 inhabitants *[cont.]*

Téléphones
Nombre de lignes téléphoniques en service et pour 100 habitants *[suite]*

Country or area Pays ou zone	Number (thousands) Nombre (en milliers)					Per 100 inhabitants Pour 100 habitants				
	1998	1999	2000	2001	2002	1998	1999	2000	2001	2002
Dem. Rep. of the Congo Rép. dém. du Congo	*9	*10	*10	*10	*10	0.0	0.0	0.0	0.0	0.0
Denmark Danemark	3 496[4]	3 638[4]	3 809[4]	3 865[4]	3 701[4]	66.0	68.5	71.5	72.2	68.9
Djibouti Djibouti	8	9	10	10	10	1.3	1.4	1.5	1.5	1.5
Dominica + Dominique +	20	21	*23	23[8]	24	26.5	27.9	29.4	29.9	30.4
Dominican Republic Rép. dominicaine	772	827	894	955	909	9.5	9.9	10.5	11.0	11.0
Ecuador Equateur	991	1 130	1 224	1 336	1 426	8.1	9.1	9.7	10.4	11.0
Egypt + Egypte +	3 972	4 686	5 484	6 688	7 430[8]	6.5	7.5	8.6	10.4	11.0
El Salvador El Salvador	387	495	625	650	668	6.4	8.1	10.0	10.2	10.3
Equatorial Guinea Guinée équatoriale	*6	*6	*6	*7	*9	1.3	1.3	1.4	1.5	1.7
Eritrea Erythrée	24	27	31	31	36	0.7	0.8	0.8	0.8	0.9
Estonia Estonie	499	515	523	506	475	34.4	35.7	36.3	35.4	35.1
Ethiopia +[9] Ethiopie +[9]	164	194	232	284	354	0.3	0.3	0.4	0.4	0.5
Faeroe Islands Iles Féroé	24	25	25	23	23	54.4	55.7	55.5	51.4	48.2
Falkland Is. (Malvinas) Iles Falkland (Malvinas)	2	2	2	2	2	93.2	96.1	98.6	99.0	98.5
Fiji Fidji	77	82	86[2]	92	98	9.7	10.1	10.7	11.3	11.9
Finland Finlande	2 841[10]	2 850[10]	2 849[10]	2 806[10]	*2 726[10]	55.1	55.2	55.0	54.0	52.4
France France	34 099[4]	33 888[4]	33 987[4]	34 033[4]	33 929[4]	58.4	57.8	57.7	57.4	56.9
French Guiana Guyane française	46	49	50[2]	51[2]	...	27.7	28.3	27.6	26.8	...
French Polynesia Polynésie française	53	52	54[2]	53	53	23.5	22.8	23.0	22.3	21.4
Gabon Gabon	39	38	39	37	32	3.3	3.2	3.2	3.0	2.5
Gambia + Gambie +	*26	*29	*33	*35	*38	2.1	2.3	2.6	2.6	2.8
Georgia Géorgie	629	672	509[11]	569[11]	648[11]	12.2	13.0	10.1	11.4	13.1
Germany Allemagne	46 530[4]	48 210[4]	50 220[4]	52 280[4]	53 720[4]	56.7	58.7	61.1	63.4	65.1
Ghana Ghana	133	159	237	242	274	0.7	0.8	1.2	1.2	1.3
Gibraltar Gibraltar	20	22	24	25	...	74.8	80.2	85.9	89.2	...
Greece Grèce	5 536	5 611	5 659	5 608[12]	5 413	52.2	52.8	53.6	52.9	49.1
Greenland Groenland	25	26	26	26	25	44.6	45.7	46.8	46.7	44.7

17

Telephones
Main telephone lines in operation and per 100 inhabitants [cont.]
Téléphones
Nombre de lignes téléphoniques en service et pour 100 habitants [suite]

Country or area Pays ou zone	Number (thousands) Nombre (en milliers)					Per 100 inhabitants Pour 100 habitants				
	1998	1999	2000	2001	2002	1998	1999	2000	2001	2002
Grenada Grenade	27	29	31	33	34	29.8	31.5	33.2	32.8	31.7
Guadeloupe Guadeloupe	197	201	205	210[2]	...	44.5	47.6	44.9	45.7	...
Guam Guam	75	78	74	80	...	50.0	50.9	48.0	50.9	...
Guatemala Guatemala	517	611	677	756	846	4.8	5.5	5.9	6.5	7.1
Guinea Guinée	15	21	24	25	26	0.2	0.3	0.3	0.3	0.3
Guinea-Bissau Guinée-Bissau	8	6	11	10	11	0.7	0.5	0.9	0.8	0.9
Guyana Guyana	60	64	*68	80	80	7.1	7.5	7.9	9.2	9.2
Haiti Haïti	65[2]	70[2]	73[2]	80[2]	130[2]	0.8	0.9	0.9	1.0	1.6
Honduras Honduras	249	279	299	310	322	4.0	4.4	4.8	4.7	4.8
Hungary Hongrie	3 423	3 726	3 798	3 742	3 666	33.6	37.1	38.0	37.5	36.1
Iceland Islande	178[4]	189[4]	192[4]	191[4]	188[4]	64.8	67.7	68.3	66.4	65.3
India + Inde +	21 594	26 511	32 436	38 536	41 420[13]	2.2	2.7	3.2	3.8	4.0
Indonesia Indonésie	5 572	6 080	6 663	7 219	7 750[14]	2.7	3.0	3.2	3.5	3.7
Iran (Islamic Rep. of) + Iran (Rép. islamique d') +	7 355	8 371	9 486	10 897	12 200	11.9	13.3	14.9	16.9	18.7
Iraq + Iraq +	650	*675	*675	675	675	3.0	3.0	2.9	2.9	2.8
Ireland +[4] Irlande +[4]	1 633	1 737	1 832	1 860	1 975	44.1	46.4	48.4	48.5	50.2
Israel Israël	2 807	2 878	2 974	3 033	3 100	46.9	47.2	47.4	46.6	46.7
Italy[4] Italie[4]	25 986	26 502	27 153	27 353[5]	27 142	45.3	46.2	47.4	47.2	48.1
Jamaica Jamaïque	463	487	512	*500	444	18.3	19.1	19.8	19.2	17.0
Japan + Japon +	67 488[15]	70 530[15]	74 344[15]	73 325[15]	71 149[15]	53.4	55.7	58.6	57.6	55.8
Jordan Jordanie	511	565	614	668	675	10.7	11.5	12.2	12.9	12.7
Kazakhstan Kazakhstan	1 775	1 760	1 834	1 940	2 082	10.9	10.8	11.3	12.1	13.0
Kenya + Kenya +	288	305	321	326[16]	328	1.0	1.1	1.1	1.0	1.0
Kiribati Kiribati	3	3	3[2]	4	4	3.4	3.7	4.0	4.2	5.1
Korea, Dem. P. R.[10] Corée, R. p. dém. de[10]	*500	*500	*500	*500	*500	2.2	2.2	2.2	2.1	2.1
Korea, Republic of Corée, République de	20 089	20 518	21 932	22 725	23 257	44.2	44.9	47.7	48.6	48.9
Kuwait Koweït	427	456	467	472	482	21.1	21.6	21.3	20.8	20.4

17

Telephones
Main telephone lines in operation and per 100 inhabitants *[cont.]*

Téléphones
Nombre de lignes téléphoniques en service et pour 100 habitants *[suite]*

Country or area Pays ou zone	Number (thousands) Nombre (en milliers)					Per 100 inhabitants Pour 100 habitants				
	1998	1999	2000	2001	2002	1998	1999	2000	2001	2002
Kyrgyzstan Kirghizistan	368	371	376	388	395	7.8	7.6	7.7	7.8	7.8
Lao People's Dem. Rep. Rép. dém. pop. lao	28	35	41	53	62	0.6	0.7	0.8	1.0	1.1
Latvia Lettonie	742	732[17]	735[17]	722	701	30.2	30.0	30.3	30.7	30.1
Lebanon Liban	566[2]	571[2]	576	626	679	17.7	17.7	17.5	18.7	19.9
Lesotho + Lesotho +	21	*22	*22	21[8]	29[8]	1.0	1.0	1.0	1.0	1.3
Liberia Libéria	*7	*7	*7	7	...	0.2	0.2	0.2	0.2	...
Libyan Arab Jamah. Jamah. arabe libyenne	500	*550	*605	660	...	9.1	10.1	10.8	11.8	...
Liechtenstein Liechtenstein	20	20	20	20	20	61.7	61.0	61.1	60.0	58.3
Lithuania Lituanie	1 113[18]	1 153[18]	1 188[18]	1 152[18]	936[18]	30.1	31.2	32.2	31.3	27.0
Luxembourg Luxembourg	293[19]	311[19]	331[19]	347[19]	355[19]	68.7	71.9	75.5	78.9	79.7
Madagascar Madagascar	47	50	55	58	59	0.3	0.3	0.4	0.4	0.4
Malawi Malawi	37	41	45	54	73	0.4	0.4	0.4	0.5	0.7
Malaysia Malaisie	4 384	4 431	4 634	4 710	4 670	20.2	20.3	19.9	19.7	19.0
Maldives Maldives	20	22	24	27	29	7.7	8.4	9.1	9.9	10.2
Mali Mali	27	34	39	51	57	0.3	0.3	0.4	0.5	0.5
Malta Malte	192	198	204	208	207	49.9	51.2	52.4	53.0	52.3
Marshall Islands Iles Marshall	4	4	4	4	4	7.5	7.6	7.6	7.7	7.7
Martinique Martinique	172	172	172[2]	172[2]	...	44.3	45.1	43.4	43.0	...
Mauritania Mauritanie	15	17	19	25	32	0.6	0.7	0.7	1.0	1.2
Mauritius Maurice	245	257	281	307	327	21.2	21.9	23.5	25.6	27.0
Mayotte Mayotte	12	10	10	*10	...	9.5	7.3	7.2	7.0	...
Mexico Mexique	9 927[20]	10 927[20]	12 332[20]	13 774[20]	14 942[20]	10.4	11.2	12.5	13.7	14.7
Micronesia (Fed. States) Micronésie (Etats féd. de)	9	10[2]	10[2]	10	...	8.2	8.7	8.4	8.7	...
Monaco Monaco	30	30	34	34	34	95.9	94.0	106.9	106.5	104.0
Mongolia Mongolie	103	103	118	124	128	4.5	4.4	5.0	5.2	5.3
Montserrat Montserrat	*3	*3	3	...	...	95.7	74.3	70.3	...	...
Morocco Maroc	1 393	1 471	1 425	1 191	1 127	5.0	5.3	5.0	4.1	3.8

17

Telephones
Main telephone lines in operation and per 100 inhabitants *[cont.]*

Téléphones
Nombre de lignes téléphoniques en service et pour 100 habitants *[suite]*

Country or area Pays ou zone	Number (thousands) Nombre (en milliers)					Per 100 inhabitants Pour 100 habitants				
	1998	1999	2000	2001	2002	1998	1999	2000	2001	2002
Mozambique Mozambique	75	78	86	89	84	0.5	0.5	0.5	0.5	0.5
Myanmar Myanmar	229	249	271	295	342	0.5	0.6	0.6	0.6	0.7
Namibia + Namibie +	106	108	110	117	121	6.3	6.2	6.2	6.4	6.5
Nauru Nauru	2	2[2]	2[2]	2	...	15.0	15.5	15.7	16.0	...
Nepal + Népal +	208	253	267	298[3]	328	1.0	1.2	1.2	1.3	1.4
Netherlands Pays-Bas	9 337[4]	9 613[4]	9 889[4]	10 003[4]	10 004[2,4]	59.2	60.6	61.9	62.1	61.8
Netherlands Antilles Antilles néerlandaises	*78	*79	*80	*81	...	36.7	36.8	37.2	37.2	...
New Caledonia Nouvelle-Calédonie	49	51	51	51	52	24.0	24.1	23.8	23.1	23.2
New Zealand + Nouvelle-Zélande +	1 809	1 833	1 831	1 823	1 765	48.5	48.9	48.5	47.7	44.8
Nicaragua Nicaragua	141	150	164	158	172	3.0	3.0	3.2	3.0	3.2
Niger Niger	18	19[2]	20	22	22	0.2	0.2	0.2	0.2	0.2
Nigeria Nigéria	407	450	497	541	702	0.4	0.4	0.4	0.5	0.6
Niue Nioué	1[2]	1[2]	1[2]	1	1	42.0	49.7	56.5	58.7	61.8
Northern Mariana Islands Iles Mariannes du Nord	21	21	21	...	...	40.4	39.5	39.6	...	...
Norway Norvège	2 935	3 176	3 302	3 314	3 343	66.0	70.9	73.3	73.3	73.4
Occupied Palestinian Terr. Terr. palestinien occupé	167	222	272	292	302	5.8	7.4	8.6	8.9	8.7
Oman Oman	220	220	222	231	*228	9.2	9.0	8.7	8.8	8.4
Pakistan + Pakistan +	2 756	2 986	3 053	3 252	3 655	2.1	2.2	2.2	2.3	2.5
Panama Panama	419	462	429	376	367	15.1	16.4	15.1	13.0	12.2
Papua New Guinea Papouasie-Nvl-Guinée	57	60	65	62	64	1.2	1.2	1.3	1.2	1.2
Paraguay Paraguay	261	268	283	289[21]	273	5.0	5.0	5.2	5.1	4.7
Peru Pérou	1 555	1 688	1 717	2 022	1 766	6.3	6.7	6.7	7.8	6.6
Philippines Philippines	2 492[10]	2 892[10]	3 061	3 315	3 311	3.4	3.9	4.0	4.2	4.2
Poland Pologne	8 812[4]	10 175[4]	10 946[4]	11 400[4]	...	22.8	26.3	28.3	29.5	...
Portugal Portugal	4 117[4]	4 230[4]	4 314[4]	4 383[4]	4 355[4]	41.3	42.3	43.0	42.4	42.1
Puerto Rico Porto Rico	1 262[22,23]	1 295[22,23]	1 332[22,23]	1 330[22,23]	...	33.7	34.3	35.0	34.6	...
Qatar Qatar	151	155	160	167	177	26.0	26.3	26.8	27.5	28.9

17

Telephones
Main telephone lines in operation and per 100 inhabitants *[cont.]*

Téléphones
Nombre de lignes téléphoniques en service et pour 100 habitants *[suite]*

Country or area Pays ou zone	Number (thousands) Nombre (en milliers)					Per 100 inhabitants Pour 100 habitants				
	1998	1999	2000	2001	2002	1998	1999	2000	2001	2002
Republic of Moldova République de Moldova	657	555	584	639	707	15.0	12.7	13.3	14.6	16.1
Réunion Réunion	243	268	280²	300²	...	35.6	38.0	40.1	41.0	...
Romania Roumanie	3 599	3 740	3 899	4 116	4 215	16.0	16.7	17.4	18.4	19.4
Russian Federation Fédération de Russie	29 246	30 949	32 070	33 278	35 500	19.9	21.0	21.8	22.7	24.2
Rwanda Rwanda	11	13	18	22	23	0.2	0.2	0.2	0.3	0.3
Saint Helena + Sainte-Hélène +	2	2	2	2³	2	31.9	32.4	32.9	33.7	35.9
Saint Kitts and Nevis + Saint-Kitts-et-Nevis +	18	20	*22	*23	24	41.7	45.0	48.6	48.8	50.0
Saint Lucia + Sainte-Lucie +	40	44	*49	50	51	26.9	29.2	31.5	31.7	32.0
Saint Pierre and Miquelon Saint-Pierre-et-Miquelon	4	5	*5	...	...	65.8	69.1	72.7	...	...
St. Vincent-Grenadines + St. Vincent-Grenadines +	21	24	25	26	27	18.8	20.9	22.0	22.7	23.4
Samoa Samoa	8	9²	9²	10	10	4.9	4.9	4.8	5.4	5.7
San Marino Saint-Marin	19	20	20	21	21	77.3	76.0	75.2	75.9	76.3
Sao Tome and Principe Sao Tomé-et-Principe	4	5	5	5	6	3.1	3.2	3.1	3.6	4.1
Saudi Arabia Arabie saoudite	2 167	2 706	2 965	3 233	3 318	10.7	13.0	13.7	14.5	14.4
Senegal Sénégal	140	166	206	237	225	1.6	1.8	2.2	2.4	2.2
Serbia and Montenegro Serbie-et-Monténégro	2 319	2 281	2 406	2 444	2 493	21.8	21.4	22.6	22.9	23.3
Seychelles + Seychelles +	19	20	19	21	22	23.8	24.4	23.5	25.5	26.9
Sierra Leone Sierra Leone	17	18	19	23	24	0.4	0.4	0.4	0.5	0.5
Singapore + Singapour +	1 778	1 877	1 947	1 948	1 927	45.3	47.5	48.5	47.1	46.3
Slovakia Slovaquie	1 539	1 655	1 698	1 556	1 443	28.5	30.7	31.4	28.9	26.8
Slovenia Slovénie	723	758	785	802	1 010	36.3	38.1	39.5	40.2	50.6
Solomon Islands + Iles Salomon +	8²⁴	8²⁴	8²⁴	7²⁴	7²⁴	2.0	2.0	1.8	1.7	1.5
Somalia Somalie	*20	*35	*35	*35	*100	0.2	0.4	0.4	0.4	1.0
South Africa + Afrique du Sud +	5 075	5 493	4 962	4 924	4 844⁵	12.1	12.8	11.4	11.1	10.7
Spain Espagne	16 289	16 480	17 104	17 531	20 595	41.4	41.0	42.6	43.4	50.6
Sri Lanka Sri Lanka	524	672	767	829	883	2.9	3.7	4.2	4.4	4.7
Sudan Soudan	162	251	387	453	672	0.6	0.9	1.2	1.4	2.1

17

Telephones
Main telephone lines in operation and per 100 inhabitants *[cont.]*

Téléphones
Nombre de lignes téléphoniques en service et pour 100 habitants *[suite]*

Country or area Pays ou zone	Number (thousands) Nombre (en milliers)					Per 100 inhabitants Pour 100 habitants				
	1998	1999	2000	2001	2002	1998	1999	2000	2001	2002
Suriname Suriname	67	71	75	77	79	15.8	16.5	17.4	17.6	16.4
Swaziland + Swaziland +	29	31	32	*32	35	3.1	3.2	3.2	3.1	3.4
Sweden Suède	6 389[4]	6 519[4]	6 728[4]	6 717[4]	6 579[4]	72.2	73.6	75.8	75.4	73.6
Switzerland Suisse	4 884[4]	5 066[4]	5 236[4]	5 383[4,5]	5 419[4]	68.4	70.6	72.6	74.3	74.4
Syrian Arab Republic Rép. arabe syrienne	1 477	1 600	1 675	1 817	2 099	9.5	9.9	10.4	10.9	12.3
Tajikistan Tadjikistan	221	213	219	227	238	3.7	3.5	3.6	3.7	3.7
Thailand + Thaïlande +	5 038	5 216	5 591	6 049	6 500	8.5	8.7	9.2	9.9	10.5
TFYR of Macedonia L'ex-R.y. Macédoine	439	471	507	539	560	21.9	23.4	25.1	26.4	27.1
Togo Togo	31	38	43	48	51	0.7	0.9	0.9	1.0	1.1
Tokelau Tokélaou	0	*0	0	0	...	13.0	12.3	11.5	15.0	...
Tonga Tonga	9	9	10[2]	11	11	8.7	9.3	9.8	10.9	11.3
Trinidad and Tobago + Trinité-et-Tobago +	264	279	317	312	325	20.6	21.6	24.5	24.0	25.0
Tunisia Tunisie	752	850	955	1 058	1 148	8.1	9.0	10.0	10.9	11.7
Turkey Turquie	16 960	18 054	18 395	18 904	18 915	26.7	28.1	28.2	28.5	28.1
Turkmenistan Turkménistan	354	359	364	388	374	8.2	8.2	8.2	8.0	7.7
Turks and Caicos Islands Iles Turques et Caïques	*5	*5	*6	...	...	30.5	32.5	34.3	...	...
Tuvalu Tuvalu	1	1	*1	1	...	5.5	5.5	5.6	6.5	...
Uganda + Ouganda +	57	57[25]	62	56	55	0.3	0.3	0.3	0.2	0.2
Ukraine Ukraine	9 698	10 074	10 417	10 670	10 833	19.1	19.9	20.7	21.2	21.6
United Arab Emirates Emirats arabes unis	915	975	1 020	1 053	1 094	38.9	40.7	34.7	34.0	31.4
United Kingdom + Royaume-Uni +	32 829[4]	34 021[4]	35 228[4]	35 660[4,8]	34 898[4]	55.4	57.2	58.9	59.4	59.1
United Rep. of Tanzania Rép.-Unie de Tanzanie	122	150	174	148	162	0.4	0.5	0.5	0.4	0.5
United States Etats-Unis	179 822	183 521	187 002	*190 994	186 232	65.5	66.0	66.5	67.1	64.6
United States Virgin Is. Iles Vierges américaines	65	67	68	*69	...	60.3	62.3	62.9	63.5	...
Uruguay Uruguay	824	897	929	951	947	25.0	27.1	27.8	28.3	28.0
Uzbekistan Ouzbékistan	1 537	1 599	1 655	1 663	1 681	6.4	6.6	6.7	6.7	6.7
Vanuatu Vanuatu	5	*6	7	7	7	2.9	3.0	3.5	3.4	3.3

17

Telephones
Main telephone lines in operation and per 100 inhabitants *[cont.]*

Téléphones
Nombre de lignes téléphoniques en service et pour 100 habitants *[suite]*

Country or area Pays ou zone	Number (thousands) Nombre (en milliers)					Per 100 inhabitants Pour 100 habitants				
	1998	1999	2000	2001	2002	1998	1999	2000	2001	2002
Venezuela Venezuela	2 592	2 551	2 536	2 705	2 842	11.2	10.8	10.5	10.9	11.3
Viet Nam Viet Nam	1 744	2 106	2 543	3 050	3 929	2.3	2.7	3.2	3.8	4.8
Wallis and Futuna Islands Iles Wallis et Futuna	1	2	2	2	...	9.8	10.6	11.8	13.0	...
Yemen Yémen	250	284	347	423	542	1.5	1.6	1.9	2.2	2.8
Zambia + Zambie +	78	83	83	86	88[8]	0.8	0.8	0.8	0.8	0.8
Zimbabwe + Zimbabwe +	237	239	*249	254	288	2.1	2.1	2.2	2.2	2.5

Source:
International Telecommunication Union (ITU), Geneva, the ITU database.

+ Note: The data shown generally relate to the fiscal year used in each country, unless indicated otherwise. Countries whose reference periods coincide with the calendar year ending 31 December are not listed.
Year beginning 22 March: Iran (Islamic Republic).
Year beginning 1 April: Antigua and Barbuda, Barbados, Belize, Bermuda, Botswana, British Virgin Islands, Cayman Islands, China - Hong Kong, Cocos Islands, Cook Islands, Dominica, Gambia, India, Ireland, Israel (prior to 1986), Jamaica, Japan, Lesotho, Seychelles, Singapore (beginning 1983), Solomon Islands, South Africa, St. Helena, St. Kitts and Nevis, St. Lucia, St. Vincent, Swaziland, Trinidad and Tobago, United Kingdom, and Zambia.
Year ending 30 June: Australia, Bangladesh, Egypt, Ethiopia, Iraq, Kenya, New Zealand (beginning 2000; prior to 2000, year ending 1 April), Pakistan, Uganda, and Zimbabwe.
Year ending 15 July: Nepal.
Year ending 30 September: Argentina, Namibia (beginning 1993), and Thailand.

Source:
Union internationale des télécommunications (UIT), Genève, la base de données de l'UIT.

+ Note: Sauf indication contraire, les données indiquées concernent généralement l'exercice budgétaire utilisé dans chaque pays. Les pays ou territoires dont la période de référence coïncide avec l'année civile se terminant le 31 décembre ne sont pas répertoriés ci-dessous.
Exercice commençant le 22 mars : Iran (République islamique d').
Exercice commençant le 1er avril : Afrique du Sud, Antigua-et-Barbuda, Barbade, Belize, Bermudes, Botswana, Chine-Hong Kong, Dominique, Gambie, Îles Caïmanes, Îles des Cocos, Îles Cook, Îles Salomon, Îles Vierges britanniques, Inde, Irlande, Israël (antérieur à 1986), Jamaïque, Japon, Lesotho, Royaume-Uni, Saint-Kitts-et-Nevis, Saint-Vincent-et-les Grenadines, Sainte-Hélène, Sainte-Lucie, Seychelles, Singapour (à partir de 1983), Swaziland, Trinité-et-Tobago et Zambie.
Exercice se terminant le 30 juin : Australie, Bangladesh, Égypte, Éthiopie, Iraq, Kenya, Nouvelle-Zélande (à partir de 2000; avant 2000, exercice se terminant le 1er avril), Ouganda, Pakistan et Zimbabwe.
Exercice se terminant le 15 juillet : Népal.
Exercice se terminant le 30 septembre : Argentine, Namibie (à partir de 1993), et Thaïlande.

1	Data refer to Angola Telecom.
2	ITU estimate.
3	As of 31 December.
4	Including ISDN channels.
5	September.
6	WLL lines included.
7	Excluding 8,960 main lines in the occupied areas.
8	December.
9	Excluding Eritrea.
10	Telephone subscribers (Finland: from 1996 the basis for the compilation of the statistics changed).
11	Data provided by the Commission based on counts made by technical experts.
12	Decrease was due to switching of users to ISDN and mobile services.
13	Subscriber lines.

1	Les données se réfèrent à "Angola Telecom".
2	Estimation de l'UIT.
3	Dès le 31 décembre.
4	RNIS inclu.
5	Septembre.
6	Y compris les lignes "WLL".
7	Non compris 8 960 lignes principales dans les territoires occupés.
8	Décembre.
9	Non compris Erythrée.
10	Abonnés au téléphone. (Finland : à compter de 1996, la base de calcul des statistiques à changé).
11	Données fournies par la Commission fondées sur un dénombrement effectué par des experts techniques.
12	La diminution tient au fait que les usagers sont passés au RNIS et aux téléphones portables.
13	Lignes d'abonnés au téléphone.

17

Telephones
Main telephone lines in operation and per 100 inhabitants *[cont.]*

Téléphones
Nombre de lignes téléphoniques en service et pour 100 habitants *[suite]*

14	September. Telkom.		14	Septembre. Telkom.
15	Main lines with ISDN channels.		15	Lignes principales inclu RNIS.
16	November.		16	Novembre.
17	Lattelekom.		17	Lattelekom.
18	Excluding public call offices.		18	Cabines publiques exclues.
19	Including digital lines.		19	Y compris lignes digitales.
20	Lines in service.		20	Lignes en service.
21	Decrease in lines available in the public sector.		21	Diminution des lignes disponibles dans la secteur publique.
22	Data refer to the Puerto Rico Telephone Authority.		22	Les données se réfèrent à "Puerto Rico Telephone Authority".
23	Switched access lines.		23	Lignes d'accès déviées.
24	Billable lines.		24	Lignes payables.
25	Including data from MTN.		25	Y compris les données du "MTN".

18

Internet users
Estimated number

Usagers d'Internet
Nombre estimatif

Country or area Pays ou zone	1995	1996	1997	1998	1999	2000	2001	2002
Afghanistan Afghanistan	...	...	...	...	...	...	...	1 000
Albania Albanie	350	1 000	1 500	2 000	2 500	3 500	10 000	12 000
Algeria Algérie	500	500	3 000	6 000	60 000	150 000	200 000	500 000
Andorra Andorre	...	1 000	2 000	4 500	5 000	7 000	...	...
Angola Angola	...	100	750	2 500	10 000	15 000	20 000	41 000
Anguilla Anguilla	80	...	...	...	...	2 500	3 000	...
Antigua and Barbuda Antigua-et-Barbuda	1 500	2 000	2 500	3 000	4 000	5 000	7 000	10 000
Argentina [1] Argentine [1]	30 000	50 000	100 000	300 000	1 200 000	2 600 000	3 650 000	4 100 000
Armenia Arménie	1 700	3 000	3 500	4 000	30 000	40 000	50 000	60 000
Aruba Aruba	...	2 300	...	...	4 000	14 000	24 000	...
Ascension Ascension	...	...	150	300	380	450	500 [2]	...
Australia Australie	500 000	600 000	1 600 000	4 200 000	5 600 000	6 600 000	7 200 000	9 472 000
Austria Autriche	150 000 [3]	550 000 [4]	760 000 [4]	1 230 000 [4]	1 840 000 [4]	2 700 000 [4]	3 150 000 [4]	3 340 000 [4]
Azerbaijan Azerbaïdjan	160	500	2 000	3 000	8 000	12 000	25 000	300 000
Bahamas Bahamas	2 700	5 000	3 967	6 908	11 307	13 130	16 923	60 000 [5]
Bahrain Bahreïn	2 000	5 000	10 000	20 000	30 000	40 000	132 330	165 035
Bangladesh Bangladesh	...	...	1 000	5 000	50 000	100 000	186 000	204 000
Barbados Barbade	20	1 000	2 000	5 000	6 000	10 000	15 000	30 000 [3]
Belarus Bélarus	300	3 000	5 000	7 500	50 000	187 036	430 263	808 663
Belgium Belgique	100 000	300 000	500 000	800 000	1 400 000	3 000 000	3 200 000	3 400 000
Belize Belize	100	2 000	3 000	5 000	10 000	15 000	18 000	30 000 [3]
Benin Bénin	...	100	1 500	3 000	10 000	15 000	25 000	50 000
Bermuda Bermudes	4 200	10 000	15 000	20 000	25 000	27 000	30 000	...
Bhutan Bhoutan	...	...	...	...	750	2 250	5 000	10 000
Bolivia Bolivie	5 000	15 000	35 000	50 000	80 000	120 000	180 000	270 000
Bosnia and Herzegovina Bosnie-Herzégovine	...	500	2 000	5 000	7 000	40 000	45 000	100 000
Botswana Botswana	1 000	2 500	5 000	10 000	19 000	25 000	50 000	...

18

Internet users
Estimated number *[cont.]*
Usagers d'Internet
Nombre estimatif *[suite]*

Country or area Pays ou zone	1995	1996	1997	1998	1999	2000	2001	2002
Brazil [3] Brésil [3]	170 000	740 000	1 310 000	2 500 000	3 500 000	5 000 000	8 000 000	14 300 000
British Virgin Islands Iles Vierges britanniques	...	...	...	...	...	...	...	4 000
Brunei Darussalam Brunéi Darussalam	3 000	10 000	15 000	20 000	25 000	30 000	35 000	...
Bulgaria Bulgarie	10 000	60 000	100 000	150 000	234 600	430 000	605 000	630 000
Burkina Faso Burkina Faso	...	100	2 000	5 000	7 000	9 000	19 000	25 000
Burundi Burundi	0	50	500	1 000	2 500	5 000	6 000	8 400
Cambodia Cambodge	...	...	700	2 000	4 000	6 000	10 000	30 000
Cameroon Cameroun	...	...	1 000	2 000	20 000	40 000	45 000	60 000
Canada Canada	1 220 000	2 000 000	4 500 000	7 500 000	11 000 000	12 971 000 [6]	14 000 000 [7]	16 110 000 [3]
Cape Verde Cap-Vert	...	...	1 000	2 000	5 000	8 000	12 000	16 000 [3]
Cayman Islands Iles Caïmanes	1 300	...	...	...	...	...	...	...
Central African Rep. Rép. centrafricaine	...	200	500	1 000	1 500	2 000	3 000	5 000
Chad Tchad	...	...	50	335	1 000	3 000	4 000	15 000
Chile Chili	50 000	100 000	156 875	250 000	625 000	2 537 308	3 102 200	3 575 000
China Chine	60 000	160 000	400 000	2 100 000	8 900 000	22 500 000	33 700 000	59 100 000
China, Hong Kong SAR Chine, Hong Kong RAS	200 000 [3]	300 000 [3]	675 000 [3]	947 000 [3]	1 400 000 [3]	1 855 200 [8]	2 601 300 [8]	2 918 800 [8]
China, Macao SAR Chine, Macao RAS	1 153	3 037	10 000	30 000	40 000	60 000	101 000	115 000
Colombia Colombie	68 560	122 500	208 000	433 000	664 000	878 000	*1 154 000	2 000 000
Comoros Comores	...	...	0	200	800	1 500	2 500	3 200
Congo Congo	...	100	100	100	500	800	1 000	5 000
Cook Islands Iles Cook	220	1 000 [9]	1 200	...	2 300	2 750	3 200	3 600
Costa Rica Costa Rica	14 500	30 000	60 000	100 000	150 000	228 000	384 000	800 000
Côte d'Ivoire Côte d'Ivoire	30	1 300	3 000	10 000	20 000	40 000	70 000	90 000
Croatia Croatie	24 000	40 000	80 000	150 000	200 000	299 380	518 000	789 000
Cuba Cuba	10	3 500	7 500	25 000	34 800	60 000	120 000	...
Cyprus Chypre	3 000	5 000	33 000	68 000	88 000	120 000	150 000	210 000
Czech Republic République tchèque	150 000	200 000	300 000	400 000	700 000	1 000 000	1 500 000	2 600 000

18

Internet users
Estimated number *[cont.]*
Usagers d'Internet
Nombre estimatif *[suite]*

Country or area Pays ou zone	1995	1996	1997	1998	1999	2000	2001	2002
Dem. Rep. of the Congo Rép. dém. du Congo	...	50	100	200	500	3 000	6 000	50 000
Denmark Danemark	200 000[3]	300 000[3]	600 000[3]	1 200 000[3]	1 626 000[10]	2 090 000[10]	2 300 000[3]	2 756 000[11]
Djibouti Djibouti	100	200	550	650	750	1 400	3 300	4 500
Dominica Dominique	377	800	...	2 000	2 000	6 000	9 000	12 500
Dominican Republic Rép. dominicaine	1 400	6 200	12 000	20 000	96 000	159 000	186 000[12]	300 000
Ecuador Equateur	5 000	10 000	13 000	15 000	100 000	180 000	333 000	537 881
Egypt Egypte	20 000	40 000	60 000	100 000	200 000	450 000	600 000	1 900 000[13]
El Salvador El Salvador	...	5 000	15 000	25 000	50 000	70 000	150 000	300 000
Equatorial Guinea Guinée équatoriale	...	...	200	470	500	700	900	1 800
Eritrea Erythrée	0	0	300	300	900	5 000	6 000	9 000
Estonia Estonie	40 000	50 000	80 000	150 000	200 000	391 600	429 656	444 000
Ethiopia Ethiopie	10	1 000	3 000	6 000	8 000	10 000	25 000	50 000
Faeroe Islands Iles Féroé	0	1 000	2 000	5 000	10 000	15 000	20 000	25 000
Falkland Is. (Malvinas) Iles Falkland (Malvinas)	0	...	100	...	1 600	1 700	1 900	1 900
Fiji Fidji	70	500	1 750	5 000	7 500	12 000	15 000	50 000
Finland [14,15] Finlande [14,15]	710 000	860 000	1 000 000	1 311 000	1 667 000	1 927 000	2 235 320[16]	2 650 000
France France	950 000[3]	1 504 000[17]	2 485 000[17]	3 704 000[17]	5 370 000[6]	8 460 000[6]	15 653 000[17]	18 716 000[17]
French Guiana Guyane française	...	500	1 000	1 500	2 000	2 700	3 200	...
French Polynesia Polynésie française	...	200	480	3 000	8 000	15 000	20 000	35 000
Gabon Gabon	...	0	550	2 000	3 000	15 000	17 000	25 000
Gambia Gambie	100	400	600	2 500	9 000	12 000	18 000	25 000
Georgia Géorgie	600	2 000	3 000	5 000	20 000	23 000	46 500	73 500
Germany Allemagne	1 500 000	2 500 000	5 500 000	8 100 000	17 100 000	24 800 000	30 800 000	34 000 000
Ghana Ghana	60	1 000	5 000	6 000	20 000	30 000	*40 000	170 000
Gibraltar Gibraltar	...	...	765	1 201	1 707	5 530	6 179	...
Greece Grèce	80 000	150 000	200 000	350 000	750 000	1 000 000	1 400 000	1 704 936
Greenland Groenland	30	1 000	4 434	8 187	12 102	17 841	20 000	25 000

18

Internet users
Estimated number *[cont.]*
Usagers d'Internet
Nombre estimatif *[suite]*

Country or area Pays ou zone	1995	1996	1997	1998	1999	2000	2001	2002
Grenada Grenade	0	300	1 000	1 500	2 500	4 113	5 200	15 000
Guadeloupe Guadeloupe	...	100	1 000	2 000	7 000	14 000	20 000	...
Guam Guam	960	1 842	3 536	6 787	13 028	25 007	40 000	50 000
Guatemala Guatemala	300	2 000	10 000	50 000	65 000	80 000	200 000	400 000
Guinea Guinée	50	150	300	500	5 000	8 000	15 000	35 000
Guinea-Bissau Guinée-Bissau	...	...	200	300	1 500	3 000	4 000	5 000
Guyana Guyana	...	500	1 000	2 000	30 000	50 000	100 000	125 000
Haiti Haïti	...	600	...	2 000	6 000	20 000	30 000	80 000
Honduras Honduras	2 055	2 500	10 000	18 000	35 000	55 000	90 000	168 560
Hungary Hongrie	70 000	100 000	200 000	400 000	600 000	715 000	1 480 000	1 600 000
Iceland Islande	30 000	40 000	75 000	100 000	150 000	168 000	172 000	186 600
India Inde	250 000	450 000	700 000	1 400 000	2 800 000	5 500 000	7 000 000	16 580 000
Indonesia Indonésie	50 000	110 000	384 000	510 000	900 000	2 000 000	4 000 000	8 000 000
Iran (Islamic Rep. of) Iran (Rép. islamique d')	2 600	10 000	30 000	65 000	250 000	625 000	1 005 000	3 168 000
Iraq Iraq	...	...	...	...	...	...	12 500	25 000
Ireland Irlande	40 000[3]	80 000[3]	150 000[3]	300 000[3]	410 000[15]	679 000[15]	895 000[15]	1 065 000[15]
Israel Israël	50 000	120 000	250 000	600 000	800 000	1 270 000	1 800 000	2 000 000
Italy Italie	300 000	585 000	1 300 000	2 600 000	8 200 000	13 200 000	15 600 000	19 900 000
Jamaica Jamaïque	2 700	14 700	20 000	50 000	60 000	80 000	100 000	600 000
Japan Japon	2 000 000	5 500 000	11 550 000	16 940 000	27 060 000	38 000 000	48 900 000	57 200 000
Jordan Jordanie	1 000	2 000	27 354	60 816	120 000	127 317	234 000	307 469
Kazakhstan Kazakhstan	1 800	5 000	10 000	20 000	70 000	100 000	150 000	250 000
Kenya Kenya	200	2 500	10 000	15 000	35 000	100 000	200 000	400 000
Kiribati Kiribati	...	...	...	500	1 000	1 500	2 000	2 000
Korea, Republic of Corée, République de	366 000	731 000	1 634 000	3 103 000	10 860 000	19 040 000	24 380 000	26 270 000
Kuwait Koweït	3 500	15 000	40 000	60 000	100 000	150 000	200 000	250 000
Kyrgyzstan Kirghizistan	...	...	...	3 500	10 000	51 600	150 600	152 000

18

Internet users
Estimated number *[cont.]*
Usagers d'Internet
Nombre estimatif *[suite]*

Country or area Pays ou zone	1995	1996	1997	1998	1999	2000	2001	2002
Lao People's Dem. Rep. Rép. dém. pop. lao	...	...	...	500	2 000	6 000	10 000	15 000
Latvia Lettonie	...	20 000	50 000	80 000	105 000	150 000	170 000	310 000
Lebanon Liban	2 500	5 000	45 000	100 000	200 000	300 000	260 000	400 000
Lesotho Lesotho	...	50	100	200	1 000	4 000	5 000	21 000
Liberia Libéria	...	...	100	100	300	500	1 000	...
Libyan Arab Jamah. Jamah. arabe libyenne	...	...	...	...	7 000	10 000	20 000	125 000
Liechtenstein Liechtenstein	...	...	...	...	...	12 000	15 000	20 000
Lithuania Lituanie	...	10 000	35 000	70 000	103 000	225 000	250 000	500 000
Luxembourg Luxembourg	6 500[3]	23 000[3]	30 000[3]	50 000[3]	75 000[3]	100 000[3]	160 000[18]	165 000[15]
Madagascar Madagascar	...	500	2 000	9 000	25 000	30 000	35 000	55 000
Malawi Malawi	...	...	500	2 000	10 000	15 000	20 000	27 000
Malaysia Malaisie	30 000	180 000	500 000	1 500 000	2 800 000	4 977 000	6 338 000	7 841 000
Maldives Maldives	0	575	800	1 500	3 000	6 000	10 000	15 000
Mali Mali	...	200	1 000	2 000	6 277	15 000	20 000	25 000
Malta Malte	850	4 000	15 000	25 000	30 000	51 000	99 000	82 880
Marshall Islands Iles Marshall	0	19	...	...	500	800	900	1 250
Martinique Martinique	...	...	...	2 000	5 000	30 000	40 000	...
Mauritania Mauritanie	...	...	100	1 000	3 000	5 000	7 000	10 000
Mauritius Maurice	...	2 100	5 500	30 000	55 000	87 000	158 000	120 000
Mexico Mexique	94 000	187 000	595 700	1 222 379	1 822 198	2 712 375	3 635 600	10 033 000
Micronesia (Fed. States) Micronésie (Etats féd. de)	...	300	616	2 000	3 000	4 000	5 000	6 000
Monaco Monaco	...	...	...	...	...	13 500	15 000	16 000
Mongolia Mongolie	200	415	2 600	3 400	12 000	30 000	40 000	50 000
Morocco Maroc	1 000	1 552	6 000	40 000	50 000	200 000	400 000	700 000
Mozambique Mozambique	...	500	2 000	3 500	10 000	20 000	30 000	...
Myanmar Myanmar	...	...	...	...	500	7 000	10 000	25 000
Namibia Namibie	100	150	1 000	5 000	6 000	30 000	45 000	50 000

18

Internet users
Estimated number *[cont.]*
Usagers d'Internet
Nombre estimatif *[suite]*

Country or area Pays ou zone	1995	1996	1997	1998	1999	2000	2001	2002
Nauru Nauru	...	...	...	...	...	...	300	...
Nepal Népal	200	1 000	5 000	15 000	35 000	50 000	60 000[2]	80 000
Netherlands Pays-Bas	1 000 000	1 500 000	2 200 000	3 500 000	6 200 000	7 000 000	7 900 000	8 200 000
Netherlands Antilles Antilles néerlandaises	...	500	...	...	2 000	...		...
New Caledonia Nouvelle-Calédonie	10	500	2 000	4 000	12 000	20 000	24 900	30 000
New Zealand Nouvelle-Zélande	180 000	300 000	550 000	750 000	1 113 000	1 515 000	1 762 000	1 908 000
Nicaragua Nicaragua	1 400	4 000	10 000	15 000	25 000	50 000	75 000	90 000
Niger Niger	...	100	200	300	3 000	4 000	12 000	15 000
Nigeria Nigéria	...	10 000	20 000	30 000	50 000	80 000	115 000	420 000
Niue Nioué	...	...	...	...	300	500	600	900
Norway Norvège	280 000[3]	800 000[3]	1 300 000[3]	1 600 000[3]	1 800 000	1 950 000	2 100 000	2 288 000
Occupied Palestinian Terr. Terr. palestinien occupé	...	...	...	...	...	35 000	60 000	105 000
Oman Oman	...	0	10 000	20 000	50 000	90 000	120 000	180 000
Pakistan Pakistan	160	4 000	37 800	61 900	80 000	300 000	500 000	1 500 000
Palau Palaos	...	...	...	...	...	...	...	4 000
Panama Panama	1 500	6 000	15 000	30 000	45 000	90 000	120 000	...
Papua New Guinea Papouasie-Nvl-Guinée	...	100	5 000	12 000	35 000	45 000	50 000	75 000
Paraguay Paraguay	...	1 000	5 000	10 000	20 000	40 000	60 000	100 000
Peru Pérou	8 000	60 000	100 000	300 000	500 000	800 000	2 029 000	2 500 000
Philippines Philippines	20 000	40 000	100 000	823 000	1 090 000	1 540 000	2 000 000	3 500 000
Poland Pologne	250 000	500 000	800 000	1 581 000	2 100 000	2 800 000	3 800 000	8 880 000
Portugal Portugal	150 000[3]	300 000[3]	500 000[3]	1 000 000[3]	1 500 000[3]	2 500 000	2 900 000	2 000 000
Puerto Rico [19] Porto Rico [19]	5 000	10 000	50 000	100 000	200 000	400 000	600 000	...
Qatar Qatar	1 000	5 000	17 000	20 000	24 000	30 000	40 000	70 000
Republic of Moldova République de Moldova	150	200	1 200	11 000	25 000	52 600	60 000	150 000
Réunion [20] Réunion [20]	...	...	...	9 000	10 000	130 000	150 000	...
Romania Roumanie	17 000	50 000	100 000	500 000	600 000	800 000	1 000 000	1 800 000

18

Internet users
Estimated number *[cont.]*
Usagers d'Internet
Nombre estimatif *[suite]*

Country or area Pays ou zone	1995	1996	1997	1998	1999	2000	2001	2002
Russian Federation Fédération de Russie	220 000	400 000	700 000	1 200 000	1 500 000	2 900 000	4 300 000	6 000 000
Rwanda Rwanda	...	50	100	800	5 000	5 000	20 000	25 000
Saint Helena Sainte-Hélène	...	...	...	79	300	300	400[2]	500
Saint Kitts and Nevis Saint-Kitts-et-Nevis	...	850	1 000	1 500	2 000	2 700	3 600	10 000
Saint Lucia Sainte-Lucie	450	1 000	1 500	2 000	3 000	8 000	13 000	...
St. Vincent-Grenadines St. Vincent-Grenadines	139	522	1 000	2 000	3 000	3 500	5 500	7 000
Samoa Samoa	...	...	300	400	500	1 000	3 000	4 000
San Marino Saint-Marin	350	370	370	370	11 360	13 150	13 850	14 340
Sao Tome and Principe Sao Tomé-et-Principe	...	...	...	400	500	6 500	9 000	11 000
Saudi Arabia Arabie saoudite	2 000	5 000	10 000	20 000	100 000	460 000	1 016 208	1 418 880
Senegal Sénégal	60	1 000	2 500	7 500	30 000	40 000	100 000	105 000
Serbia and Montenegro Serbie-et-Monténégro	...	20 000	50 000	65 000	80 000	400 000	600 000	640 000
Seychelles Seychelles	...	500	1 000	2 000	5 000	6 000[3]	9 000[2]	11 736
Sierra Leone Sierra Leone	0	100	200	600	2 000	5 000	7 000	8 000
Singapore Singapour	100 000	300 000	500 000	750 000	950 000	1 300 000	1 700 000	2 100 000
Slovakia Slovaquie	28 000	50 000[3]	100 000[3]	144 539	292 359	507 029	674 039	862 833
Slovenia Slovénie	57 000	100 000	150 000	200 000	250 000	300 000	600 000	750 000
Solomon Islands Iles Salomon	90	1 000	1 500	2 000	2 000	2 000	2 000	2 200
Somalia Somalie	0	0	0	100	200	500	1 000	89 000
South Africa Afrique du Sud	280 000	355 000	700 000	1 266 000	1 820 000	2 400 000	2 890 000	3 100 000
Spain [21,22] Espagne [21,22]	150 000	526 000	1 110 000	1 733 000	2 830 000	5 486 000	7 388 000	6 358 800
Sri Lanka Sri Lanka	1 000	10 000	30 000	55 000	65 000	121 500	150 000	200 000
Sudan Soudan	0	0	700	2 000	5 000	30 000	56 000	84 000
Suriname Suriname	500	1 000	4 494	7 587	8 715	11 709	14 520	20 000
Swaziland Swaziland	10	500	900	1 000	5 000	10 000	14 000	20 000
Sweden Suède	450 000	800 000	2 100 000	2 961 000	3 666 000	4 048 000	4 600 000	5 125 000
Switzerland Suisse	250 000	322 000	548 000	939 000	1 473 000	2 096 000	2 224 000	2 556 000

18

Internet users
Estimated number *[cont.]*
    Usagers d'Internet
    Nombre estimatif *[suite]*

Country or area Pays ou zone	1995	1996	1997	1998	1999	2000	2001	2002
Syrian Arab Republic Rép. arabe syrienne	0	0	5 000	10 000	20 000	30 000	60 000	220 000
Tajikistan Tadjikistan	...	...	...	...	2 000	3 000	3 200	3 500
Thailand Thaïlande	55 000	135 000	375 000	500 000	1 300 000	2 300 000	3 536 019	4 800 000
TFYR of Macedonia L'ex-R.y. Macédoine	800	1 500	10 000	20 000	30 000	50 000	70 000	100 000
Togo Togo	0	500	10 000	15 000	30 000	100 000	150 000	200 000
Tonga Tonga	120	160	500	750	1 000	2 400	2 800	2 900
Trinidad and Tobago Trinité-et-Tobago	2 000	5 000	15 000	35 000	75 000	100 000	120 000[13]	138 000[13]
Tunisia Tunisie	1 000	2 500	4 000	10 000	150 000	250 000	400 000	505 500
Turkey Turquie	50 000	120 000	300 000	450 000	1 500 000	2 000 000	4 000 000	4 900 000
Turkmenistan Turkménistan	...	...	...	...	2 000	6 000	8 000	...
Tuvalu Tuvalu	...	...	...	...	...	500	1 000	1 250
Uganda Ouganda	600	1 000	2 300	15 000	25 000	40 000	60 000	100 000
Ukraine Ukraine	22 000	50 000	100 000	150 000	200 000	350 000	600 000	900 000
United Arab Emirates Emirats arabes unis	2 503[23]	9 669	90 000	200 000	458 000	765 000	976 000	1 175 615
United Kingdom Royaume-Uni	1 100 000[3]	2 400 000[3]	4 310 000[3]	8 000 000[3]	12 500 000[3]	15 800 000[24]	19 800 000[24]	25 000 000[24]
United Rep. of Tanzania Rép.-Unie de Tanzanie	...	500	2 500	3 000	25 000	40 000	60 000	80 000
United States Etats-Unis	25 000 000	45 000 000	60 000 000	84 587 000	102 000 000	124 000 000	142 823 000	159 000 000
United States Virgin Is. Iles Vierges américaines	3 000	5 000	7 500	10 000	12 000	15 000	20 000	30 000
Uruguay Uruguay	10 000	60 000	110 000	230 000	330 000	370 000	400 000	...
Uzbekistan Ouzbékistan	350	1 000	2 500	5 000	7 500	120 000	150 000	275 000
Vanuatu Vanuatu	...	100	250	500	1 000	4 000	5 500	7 000
Venezuela Venezuela	27 000	56 000	90 000	322 244	680 000	820 022	1 152 502	1 274 429
Viet Nam Viet Nam	...	100	3 000	10 000	100 000	200 000	1 009 544	1 500 000
Wallis and Futuna Islands Iles Wallis et Futuna	...	...	...	...	350	800	900	...
Yemen Yémen	...	100	2 500	4 000	10 000	15 000	17 000	100 000
Zambia Zambie	800	850	900	3 000	15 000	20 000	25 000	52 420[13]
Zimbabwe [3] Zimbabwe [3]	900	2 000	4 000	10 000	20 000	50 000	100 000	500 000

18

Internet users
Estimated number *[cont.]*

Usagers d'Internet
Nombre estimatif *[suite]*

Source:
International Telecommunication Union (ITU), Geneva, the ITU database.

Source:
Union internationale des télécommunications (UIT), Genève, la base de données de l'UIT.

+ Note: The data shown generally relate to the fiscal year used in each country, unless indicated otherwise. Countries whose reference periods coincide with the calendar year ending 31 December are not listed.
Year beginning 22 March: Iran (Islamic Republic).
Year beginning 1 April - Antigua and Barbuda, Barbados, Belize, Bermuda, Botswana, British Virgin Islands, Cayman Islands, China - Hong Kong, Cocos Islands, Cook Islands, Dominica, Gambia, India, Ireland, Israel (prior to 1986), Jamaica, Japan, Lesotho, Seychelles, Singapore (beginning 1983), Solomon Islands, South Africa, St. Helena, St. Kitts and Nevis, St. Lucia, St. Vincent, Swaziland, Trinidad and Tobago, United Kingdom, Zambia.
Year ending 30 June: Australia, Bangladesh, Egypt, Ethiopia, Iraq, Kenya, New Zealand (beginning 2000; year ending 1 April prior to 2000), Pakistan, Uganda, Zimbabwe.
Year ending 15 July: Nepal.
Year ending 30 September: Argentina, Namibia (beginning 1993), Thailand.

+ Note: Sauf indication contraire, les données indiquées concernent généralement l'exercice budgétaire utilisé dans chaque pays. Les pays ou territoires dont la période de référence coïncide avec l'année civile se terminant le 31 décembre ne sont pas répertoriés ci-dessous.
Exercice commençant le 22 mars : Iran (République islamique d').
Exercice commençant le 1er avril : Afrique du Sud, Antigua-et-Barbuda, Barbade, Belize, Bermudes, Botswana, Chine - Hong Kong, Dominique, Gambie, Îles Caïmanes, Îles des Cocos, Îles Cook, Îles Salomon, Îles Vierges britanniques, Inde, Irlande, Israël (antérieur à 1986), Jamaïque, Japon, Lesotho, Royaume-Uni, Saint-Kitts-et-Nevis, Saint-Vincent-et-les Grenadines, Sainte-Hélène, Sainte-Lucie, Seychelles, Singapour (à partir de 1983), Swaziland, Trinité-et-Tobago et Zambie.
Exercice se terminant le 30 juin : Australie, Bangladesh, Égypte, Éthiopie, Iraq, Kenya, Nouvelle-Zélande (à partir de 2000; avant 2000, exercice se terminant le 1er avril), Ouganda, Pakistan et Zimbabwe.
Exercice se terminant le 15 juillet : Népal.
Exercice se terminant le 30 septembre : Argentine, Namibie (à partir de 1993), et Thaïlande.

1	Year ending November.	Année s'achevant en novembre.
2	Data refer to 31 December.	Les données se réfèrent au 31 décembre.
3	ITU estimate.	Estimation de l'UIT.
4	Regular users of the Internet, age 14+.	Utilisateurs réguliers de l'Internet âgés de plus de 14 ans.
5	ITU estimate based on 3 times the number of subscribers.	Estimation de l'UIT basée sur le nombre d'abonnés multiplié par 3.
6	Population 15+ using in last year.	Population âgée de plus de 15 ans utilisant l'Internet au cours de l'année écoulée.
7	Population 18+ using in last week.	Population âgée de plus de 18 ans utilisant l'Internet au cours de la dernière semaine.
8	Population age 10+ who accessed Internet in previous year.	Population âgée de plus de 10 ans s'étant branchée sur l'Internet au cours de l'année écoulée.
9	Year ending November 1997.	Année s'achevant en novembre 1997.
10	E-mail users.	Utilisateurs du courrier électronique
11	Age 15-74 using at least once in last 3 months.	Population d'âge compris entre 15 et 74 ans ayant utilisé l'Internet une fois au moins au cours des trois derniers mois.
12	As of 30 September.	Dès le 30 septembre.
13	December.	Décembre.
14	Has used at least one other Internet application besides e-mail in last 3 months. Age 15+.	A utilisé au moins une application Internet autre que le courrier électronique au cours des trois derniers mois. Population âgée de plus de 15 ans.
15	Age 15+.	Population âgée de plus de 15 ans.
16	June.	Juin.
17	1996-98, 18+; from 2001, 11+, using in the last month.	1996 à 1998, population âgée de plus de 18 ans; à partir de 2001, population âgée de plus de 11 ans ayant utilisé l'Internet au cours du dernier mois.
18	Age 12+.	Population âgée de plus de 12 ans.
19	Data refer to the Puerto Rico Telephone Authority.	Les données se réfèrent à "Puerto Rico Telephone Authority".
20	France Télécom only.	France Télécom seulement.
21	November.	Novembre.
22	Age 14+.	Population âgée de plus de 14 ans.
23	Internet dial-up customers.	Clients accédant à l'Internet par numérotation.
24	Adult (age 16+) population using in the last month.	Population adulte (âgée de plus de 16 ans) ayant utilisé l'Internet au cours du dernier mois.

Technical notes, tables 12-18

Tables 12-15: The data on books, newspapers, periodicals and cinemas have been compiled from the UNESCO Institute for Statistics database (see <www.uis.unesco.org>).

Table 12: Data on books by subject groups cover printed books and pamphlets and, unless otherwise stated, refer to both first editions and re-editions. The grouping by subject follows the Universal Decimal Classification (UDC).

Table 13: For the purposes of this table, a daily general interest newspaper is defined as a publication devoted primarily to recording general news. It is considered to be "daily" if it appears at least four times a week.

Table 14: For the purposes of this table, a non-daily general interest newspaper is defined as a publication which is devoted primarily to recording general news and which is published three times a week or less. Under the category of periodicals are included publications of periodical issue, other than newspapers, containing information of a general or of a specialized nature.

Table 15: The data refer to fixed cinemas and mobile units regularly used for the commercial exhibition of long films. The term fixed cinema used in this table refers to establishments possessing their own equipment and includes indoor cinemas (those with a permanent fixed roof over most of the seating accommodation), outdoor cinemas and drive-ins (establishments designed to enable the audience to watch a film while seated in their automobile). Mobile units are defined as projection units equipped and used to serve more than one site.

The seating capacity of fixed cinemas is the sum of the number of seats in indoor and outdoor cinemas plus the number of places for automobiles, multiplied by a factor of 4 in the case of drive-ins.

Cinema attendance is calculated from the number of tickets sold during a given year.

As a rule, figures refer only to commercial establishments but in the case of mobile units, it is possible that the figures for some countries may also include non-commercial units.

The statistics included in *Tables 16-18* were obtained from the statistics database (see <www.itu.int>) and the *Yearbook of Statistics, Telecommunication Services* [18] of the International Telecommunication Union.

Table 16: The number of mobile cellular telephone subscribers refers to users of portable telephones subscribing to an automatic public mobile telephone service using cellular technology which provides access to the Public Switched Telephone Network (PSTN).

Notes techniques, tableaux 12 à 18

Tableaux 12 à 15: Les données concernant les livres, les journaux, les périodiques et les cinémas proviennent de la base de données de l'Institut de statistique de l'UNESCO (voir <www.uis.unesco.org>).

Tableau 12: Les données concernant la production de livres par groupes de sujets se rapportent aux livres et brochures imprimés, sauf indication contraire, aux premières éditions et aux rééditions. Les sujets sont groupés selon la Classification décimale universelle (CDU).

Tableau 13: Dans ce tableau, par "journal quotidien d'information générale", on entend une publication qui a essentiellement pour objet de rendre compte des événements courants. Il est considéré comme "quotidien" s'il paraît au moins quatre fois par semaine.

Tableau 14: Aux fins de ce tableau, par "journal non quotidien d'information générale", on entend une publication qui a essentiellement pour objet de rendre compte des événements courants et qui est publié trois fois par semaine ou moins. La catégorie périodique comprend les publications périodiques autres que les journaux, contenant des informations de caractère général ou spécialisé.

Tableau 15: Les données concernent les établissements fixes et les cinémas itinérants d'exploitation commerciale de films longs. Le terme établissement fixe désigne tout établissement doté de son propre équipement; il englobe les salles fermées (c'est-à-dire celles où un toit fixe recouvre la plupart des places assises), les cinémas de plein air et les cinémas pour automobilistes ou drive-ins (conçus pour permettre aux spectateurs d'assister à la projection sans quitter leur voiture). Les cinémas itinérants sont définis comme groupes mobiles de projection équipés de manière à pouvoir être utilisés dans des lieux différents.

La capacité d'allocation des places de cinémas fixes est la somme du nombre de sièges dans les salles fermées et les cinémas de plein air, plus le nombre de places d'automobiles multiplié par le facteur 4 dans le cas des drive-ins.

La fréquentation des cinémas est calculée sur la base du nombre de billets vendus au cours d'une année donnée.

En général, les statistiques présentées ne concernent que les établissements commerciaux: toutefois, dans le cas des cinémas itinérants, il se peut que les données relatives à certains pays tiennent compte aussi des établissements non-commerciaux.

Les données présentées dans les *Tableaux 16 à 18* proviennent de la base de données (voir <www.itu.int>) et *l'Annuaire statistique, Services de télécommunications* [18] de l'Union internationale des télécommunica-

Table 17: This table shows the number of main lines in operation and the main lines in operation per 100 inhabitants for the years indicated. Main telephone lines refer to the telephone lines connecting a customer's equipment to the Public Switched Telephone Network (PSTN) and which have a dedicated port on a telephone exchange. Note that in most countries, main lines also include public telephones. Main telephone lines per 100 inhabitants is calculated by dividing the number of main lines by the population and multiplying by 100.

Table 18: Internet user data is based on reported estimates, derivations based on reported Internet Access Provider subscriber counts, or calculated by multiplying the number of hosts by an estimated multiplier. However, comparisons of user data are misleading because there is no standard definition of frequency (e.g., daily, weekly, monthly) or services used (e.g., e-mail, World Wide Web).

tions.

Tableau 16: Les abonnés mobiles désignent les utilisateurs de téléphones portatifs abonnés à un service automatique public de téléphones mobiles ayant accès au Réseau de téléphone public connecté (RTPC).

Tableau 17: Ce tableau indique le nombre de lignes principales en service et les lignes principales en service pour 100 habitants pour les années indiquées. Les lignes principales sont des lignes téléphoniques qui relient l'équipement terminal de l'abonné au Réseau de téléphone public connecté (RTPC) et qui possèdent un accès individualisé aux équipements d'un central téléphonique. Pour la plupart des pays, le nombre de lignes principales en service indiqué comprend également les lignes publiques. Le nombre de lignes principales pour 100 habitants se calcule en divisant le nombre de lignes principales par la population et en multipliant par 100.

Tableau 18: Les chiffres relatifs aux usagers d'Internet sont basés sur les estimations communiquées, calculés à partir des chiffres issus de dénombrements d'abonnés aux services de fournisseurs d'accès, ou obtenus en multipliant le nombre d'hôtes par un facteur estimatif. Mais les comparaisons de chiffres relatifs aux usagers prêtent à confusion, car il n'existe pas de définition normalisée de la fréquence (quotidienne, hebdomadaire, mensuelle) ni des services utilisés (courrier électronique, Web).

Part Three
Economic Activity

Chapter VI	National accounts and industrial production (tables 19-25)
Chapter VII	Financial statistics (tables 26 and 27)
Chapter VIII	Labour force (tables 28 and 29)
Chapter IX	Wages and prices (tables 30-32)
Chapter X	Agriculture, forestry and fishing (tables 33-39)
Chapter XI	Manufacturing (tables 40-57)
Chapter XII	Transport (tables 58-62)
Chapter XIII	Energy (tables 63 and 64)
Chapter XIV	Environment (tables 65-69)
Chapter XV	Science and technology, intellectual property (tables 70-72)

Part Three of the *Yearbook* presents statistical series on production and consumption for a wide range of economic activities, and other basic series on major economic topics, for all countries or areas of the world for which data are available. Included are basic tables on national accounts, finance, labour force, wages and prices, a wide range of agricultural, mined and manufactured commodities, transport, energy, environment, research and development personnel and expenditure, and intellectual property.

International economic topics such as external trade are covered in Part Four.

Troisième partie
Activité économique

Chapitre VI	Comptabilités nationales et production industrielle (tableaux 19 à 25)
Chapitre VII	Statistiques financières (tableaux 26 et 27)
Chapitre VIII	Main-d'oeuvre (tableaux 28 et 29)
Chapitre IX	Salaires et prix (tableaux 30 à 32)
Chapitre X	Agriculture, forêts et pêche (tableaux 33 à 39)
Chapitre XI	Industries manufacturières (tableaux 40 à 57)
Chapitre XII	Transports (tableaux 58 à 62)
Chapitre XIII	Energie (tableaux 63 et 64)
Chapitre XIV	Environnement (tableaux 65 à 69)
Chapitre XV	Science et technologie, propriété intellectuelle (tableaux 70 à 72)

La troisième partie de l'*Annuaire* présente, pour une large gamme d'activités économiques, des séries statistiques sur la production et la consommation, et, pour tous les pays ou zones du monde pour lesquels des données sont disponibles, d'autres séries fondamentales ayant trait à des questions économiques importantes. Y figurent des tableaux de base consacrés à la comptabilité nationale, aux finances, à la main-d'oeuvre, aux salaires et aux prix, à un large éventail de produits agricoles, miniers et manufacturés, aux transports, à l'énergie, à l'environnement, au personnel employé à des travaux de recherche et développement, et dépenses de recherche et développement, et à la propriété intellectuelle.

Les questions économiques internationales comme le commerce extérieur sont traitées dans la quatrième partie.

19

Gross domestic product and gross domestic product per capita

In millions of US dollars[+] at current and constant 1990 prices; per capita US dollars; real rates of growth

Produit intérieur brut et produit intérieur brut par habitant

En millions de dollars E.-U.[+] aux prix courants et constants de 1990 ; par habitant en dollars E.-U. ; taux de l'accroissement réels

Country or area	1995	1996	1997	1998	1999	2000	2001	Pays ou zone
World								**Monde**
At current prices	29 367 968	30 048 478	29 915 099	29 712 482	30 696 132	31 375 763	31 041 311	Aux prix courants
Per capita	5 180	5 230	5 130	5 030	5 130	5 170	5 050	Par habitant
At constant prices	24 947 247	25 735 606	26 663 931	27 317 318	28 164 053	29 301 901	29 752 345	Aux prix constants
Growth rates	2.7	3.2	3.6	2.4	3.1	4.0	1.5	Taux de l'accroissement
Afghanistan								**Afghanistan**
At current prices	3 460	3 687	4 175	4 394	3 851	2 169	2 169	Aux prix courants
Per capita	180	186	206	214	184	101	98	Par habitant
At constant prices	3 723	3 967	4 492	4 728	4 144	2 333	2 333	Aux prix constants
Growth rates	-4.7	6.6	13.3	5.2	-12.4	-43.7	0.0	Taux de l'accroissement
Albania								**Albanie**
At current prices	2 479	2 689	2 294	3 058	3 676	3 752	4 114	Aux prix courants
Per capita	778	851	731	980	1 181	1 205	1 317	Par habitant
At constant prices	1 950	2 128	1 978	2 136	2 291	2 469	2 605	Aux prix constants
Growth rates	13.3	9.1	-7.0	8.0	7.3	7.8	5.5	Taux de l'accroissement
Algeria								**Algérie**
At current prices	42 066	46 942	48 177	47 841	48 791	54 462	54 855	Aux prix courants
Per capita	1 509	1 654	1 670	1 633	1 639	1 801	1 784	Par habitant
At constant prices	62 635	64 496	65 736	68 837	71 317	72 557	75 658	Aux prix constants
Growth rates	4.3	3.0	1.9	4.7	3.6	1.7	4.3	Taux de l'accroissement
Andorra								**Andorre**
At current prices	1 003	1 098	1 059	1 160	1 242	1 208	1 309	Aux prix courants
Per capita	15 647	16 892	16 209	17 743	18 943	18 236	19 397	Par habitant
At constant prices	943	1 014	1 104	1 205	1 312	1 426	1 531	Aux prix constants
Growth rates	8.0	7.5	9.0	9.1	8.8	8.7	7.3	Taux de l'accroissement
Angola								**Angola**
At current prices	5 040	5 595	7 649	6 507	6 153	9 130	8 936	Aux prix courants
Per capita	464	501	668	555	511	737	700	Par habitant
At constant prices	8 306	9 249	9 959	10 508	10 789	11 177	11 759	Aux prix constants
Growth rates	10.7	11.4	7.7	5.5	2.7	3.6	5.2	Taux de l'accroissement
Anguilla								**Anguilla**
At current prices	75	79	89	94	105	108	110	Aux prix courants
Per capita	7 315	7 568	8 320	8 691	9 493	9 613	9 643	Par habitant
At constant prices	53	55	60	63	69	69	70	Aux prix constants
Growth rates	-4.1	3.5	9.2	5.2	8.7	-0.1	1.6	Taux de l'accroissement
Antigua and Barbuda								**Antigua-et-Barbuda**
At current prices	436	477	513	547	575	594	611	Aux prix courants
Per capita	6 458	6 969	7 392	7 790	8 091	8 282	8 461	Par habitant
At constant prices	421	389	411	431	452	456	466	Aux prix constants
Growth rates	9.1	-7.6	5.6	4.9	4.9	0.8	2.3	Taux de l'accroissement
Argentina								**Argentine**
At current prices	258 097	272 242	293 006	299 098	283 664	206 791	197 674	Aux prix courants
Per capita	7 423	7 728	8 210	8 273	7 747	5 578	5 267	Par habitant
At constant prices	188 226	198 629	214 739	223 007	215 458	213 758	204 334	Aux prix constants
Growth rates	-2.8	5.5	8.1	3.9	-3.4	-0.8	-4.4	Taux de l'accroissement
Armenia								**Arménie**
At current prices	1 287	1 597	1 639	1 892	1 845	1 912	2 118	Aux prix courants
Per capita	387	488	508	595	587	614	686	Par habitant
At constant prices	7 978	8 446	8 727	9 367	9 672	10 243	11 224	Aux prix constants
Growth rates	6.9	5.9	3.3	7.3	3.3	5.9	9.6	Taux de l'accroissement
Aruba								**Aruba**
At current prices	1 321	1 380	1 532	1 665	1 725	1 858	1 889	Aux prix courants
Per capita	16 746	16 853	18 041	18 950	19 017	19 922	19 762	Par habitant
At constant prices	1 365	1 447	1 533	1 624	1 721	1 823	1 932	Aux prix constants
Growth rates	6.0	6.0	6.0	6.0	6.0	6.0	6.0	Taux de l'accroissement
Australia								**Australie**
At current prices	372 732	414 666	416 534	371 847	405 575	388 043	368 762	Aux prix courants
Per capita	20 625	22 662	22 491	19 846	21 404	20 260	19 056	Par habitant
At constant prices	364 321	378 123	394 958	415 935	432 562	440 148	457 480	Aux prix constants
Growth rates	4.2	3.8	4.5	5.3	4.0	1.8	3.9	Taux de l'accroissement

19

Gross domestic product and gross domestic product per capita
In millions of US dollars[+] at current and constant 1990 prices; per capita US dollars; real rates of growth *[cont.]*
Produit intérieur brut et produit intérieur brut par habitant
En millions de dollars E.-U.[+] aux prix courants et constants de 1990 ; par habitant en dollars E.-U. ;
taux de l'accroissement réels *[suite]*

Country or area	1995	1996	1997	1998	1999	2000	2001	Pays ou zone
Austria								**Autriche**
At current prices	235 156	231 421	205 753	211 898	210 045	190 747	189 580	Aux prix courants
Per capita	29 224	28 647	25 420	26 163	25 932	23 545	23 388	Par habitant
At constant prices	178 956	182 538	185 447	192 719	197 995	204 991	206 364	Aux prix constants
Growth rates	1.6	2.0	1.6	3.9	2.7	3.5	0.7	Taux de l'accroissement
Azerbaijan								**Azerbaïdjan**
At current prices	2 417	3 177	3 962	4 446	4 581	5 273	5 657	Aux prix courants
Per capita	310	403	498	554	566	646	688	Par habitant
At constant prices	9 218	9 333	9 875	10 859	11 663	12 957	14 240	Aux prix constants
Growth rates	-11.8	1.3	5.8	10.0	7.4	11.1	9.9	Taux de l'accroissement
Bahamas								**Bahamas**
At current prices	3 069	3 093	3 116	3 140	3 164	3 189	3 213	Aux prix courants
Per capita	10 836	10 743	10 671	10 615	10 566	10 520	10 476	Par habitant
At constant prices	2 751	2 867	2 962	3 050	3 212	3 356	3 493	Aux prix constants
Growth rates	-1.1	4.2	3.3	3.0	5.3	4.5	4.1	Taux de l'accroissement
Bahrain								**Bahreïn**
At current prices	5 850	6 102	6 349	6 184	6 620	7 969	8 328	Aux prix courants
Per capita	9 972	10 075	10 171	9 627	10 032	11 773	12 012	Par habitant
At constant prices	5 661	5 895	6 078	6 369	6 643	6 996	7 241	Aux prix constants
Growth rates	3.9	4.1	3.1	4.8	4.3	5.3	3.5	Taux de l'accroissement
Bangladesh								**Bangladesh**
At current prices	41 294	43 236	45 607	46 838	48 301	48 626	48 635	Aux prix courants
Per capita	335	342	353	355	358	352	345	Par habitant
At constant prices	39 640	41 776	43 960	46 100	48 841	51 416	53 884	Aux prix constants
Growth rates	4.6	5.4	5.2	4.9	5.9	5.3	4.8	Taux de l'accroissement
Barbados								**Barbade**
At current prices	1 871	1 997	2 206	2 374	2 483	2 592	2 547	Aux prix courants
Per capita	7 126	7 577	8 338	8 937	9 314	9 688	9 486	Par habitant
At constant prices	1 650	1 691	1 738	1 810	1 863	1 919	1 869	Aux prix constants
Growth rates	2.3	2.5	2.8	4.2	2.9	3.0	-2.6	Taux de l'accroissement
Belarus								**Bélarus**
At current prices	10 538	14 500	14 098	15 222	12 163	10 418	12 355	Aux prix courants
Per capita	1 028	1 419	1 385	1 502	1 206	1 038	1 237	Par habitant
At constant prices	42 353	43 529	48 501	52 596	54 410	57 559	60 279	Aux prix constants
Growth rates	-10.4	2.8	11.4	8.4	3.4	5.8	4.7	Taux de l'accroissement
Belgium								**Belgique**
At current prices	276 651	269 687	244 892	250 321	251 039	227 998	227 543	Aux prix courants
Per capita	27 292	26 533	24 038	24 520	24 541	22 242	22 150	Par habitant
At constant prices	213 289	215 871	223 613	228 120	235 391	244 157	246 038	Aux prix constants
Growth rates	2.4	1.2	3.6	2.0	3.2	3.7	0.8	Taux de l'accroissement
Belize								**Belize**
At current prices	587	604	616	629	689	757	766	Aux prix courants
Per capita	2 748	2 757	2 744	2 740	2 932	3 152	3 123	Par habitant
At constant prices	501	509	525	533	568	627	658	Aux prix constants
Growth rates	4.1	1.6	3.2	1.5	6.5	10.4	5.0	Taux de l'accroissement
Benin								**Bénin**
At current prices	2 009	2 208	2 141	2 306	2 360	2 255	2 371	Aux prix courants
Per capita	367	393	371	390	389	362	371	Par habitant
At constant prices	2 281	2 395	2 491	2 590	2 719	2 876	3 020	Aux prix constants
Growth rates	6.3	5.0	4.0	4.0	5.0	5.8	5.0	Taux de l'accroissement
Bermuda								**Bermudes**
At current prices	2 544	2 680	2 889	3 053	3 272	3 397	3 599	Aux prix courants
Per capita	32 951	34 465	36 904	38 743	41 247	42 533	44 753	Par habitant
At constant prices	2 191	2 255	2 329	2 409	2 495	2 543	2 532	Aux prix constants
Growth rates	7.0	2.9	3.3	3.4	3.6	2.0	-0.5	Taux de l'accroissement
Bhutan								**Bhoutan**
At current prices	310	333	394	396	444	483	511	Aux prix courants
Per capita	171	180	208	203	222	234	241	Par habitant
At constant prices	373	393	422	450	483	510	540	Aux prix constants
Growth rates	7.4	5.2	7.6	6.4	7.4	5.7	5.9	Taux de l'accroissement

19

Gross domestic product and gross domestic product per capita
In millions of US dollars[+] at current and constant 1990 prices; per capita US dollars; real rates of growth *[cont.]*

Produit intérieur brut et produit intérieur brut par habitant
En millions de dollars E.-U.[+] aux prix courants et constants de 1990 ; par habitant en dollars E.-U. ;
taux de l'accroissement réels *[suite]*

Country or area	1995	1996	1997	1998	1999	2000	2001	Pays ou zone
Bolivia								**Bolivie**
At current prices	6 715	7 397	7 926	8 497	8 285	8 356	7 969	Aux prix courants
Per capita	898	967	1 014	1 064	1 017	1 005	940	Par habitant
At constant prices	5 950	6 210	6 517	6 845	6 874	7 037	7 123	Aux prix constants
Growth rates	4.7	4.4	5.0	5.0	0.4	2.4	1.2	Taux de l'accroissement
Bosnia and Herzegovina								**Bosnie-Herzégovine**
At current prices	2 043	2 750	3 639	4 169	4 683	4 440	4 685	Aux prix courants
Per capita	597	802	1 032	1 132	1 218	1 117	1 152	Par habitant
At constant prices	8 802	13 203	16 874	20 770	24 297	26 909	28 892	Aux prix constants
Growth rates	33.0	50.0	27.8	23.1	17.0	10.7	7.4	Taux de l'accroissement
Botswana								**Botswana**
At current prices	4 423	4 273	4 859	4 771	4 654	4 971	5 025	Aux prix courants
Per capita	2 854	2 689	2 987	2 868	2 743	2 881	2 872	Par habitant
At constant prices	4 359	4 601	4 859	5 250	5 467	5 909	6 450	Aux prix constants
Growth rates	3.2	5.5	5.6	8.1	4.1	8.1	9.2	Taux de l'accroissement
Brazil								**Brésil**
At current prices	704 169	774 935	807 746	787 742	536 633	601 732	508 994	Aux prix courants
Per capita	4 386	4 760	4 893	4 708	3 165	3 503	2 925	Par habitant
At constant prices	511 426	525 030	542 198	543 391	547 684	572 330	580 921	Aux prix constants
Growth rates	4.2	2.7	3.3	0.2	0.8	4.5	1.5	Taux de l'accroissement
British Virgin Islands								**Iles Vierges britanniques**
At current prices	385	442	512	593	662	691	777	Aux prix courants
Per capita	20 752	23 541	26 933	30 789	33 891	34 849	38 530	Par habitant
At constant prices	289	317	348	387	423	465	512	Aux prix constants
Growth rates	5.0	9.6	9.7	11.4	9.1	10.1	10.1	Taux de l'accroissement
Brunei Darussalam								**Brunéi Darussalam**
At current prices	5 217	5 450	5 422	4 846	4 215	4 316	4 252	Aux prix courants
Per capita	17 667	17 986	17 451	15 220	12 923	12 922	12 435	Par habitant
At constant prices	3 895	4 034	4 198	4 240	4 349	4 472	4 537	Aux prix constants
Growth rates	3.0	3.6	4.1	1.0	2.6	2.8	1.5	Taux de l'accroissement
Bulgaria								**Bulgarie**
At current prices	13 106	9 900	10 365	12 737	12 955	12 600	13 557	Aux prix courants
Per capita	1 559	1 187	1 251	1 549	1 587	1 556	1 688	Par habitant
At constant prices	17 781	16 110	15 212	15 821	16 185	17 058	17 746	Aux prix constants
Growth rates	2.9	-9.4	-5.6	4.0	2.3	5.4	4.0	Taux de l'accroissement
Burkina Faso								**Burkina Faso**
At current prices	2 216	2 367	2 327	2 508	2 466	2 192	2 329	Aux prix courants
Per capita	215	223	213	223	213	184	190	Par habitant
At constant prices	3 636	3 872	4 094	4 320	4 596	4 705	4 978	Aux prix constants
Growth rates	5.9	6.5	5.7	5.5	6.4	2.4	5.8	Taux de l'accroissement
Burundi								**Burundi**
At current prices	1 000	877	973	894	808	710	661	Aux prix courants
Per capita	166	145	160	146	131	113	103	Par habitant
At constant prices	1 032	943	946	989	980	971	1 002	Aux prix constants
Growth rates	-7.1	-8.6	0.3	4.6	-1.0	-0.9	3.2	Taux de l'accroissement
Cambodia								**Cambodge**
At current prices	3 309	3 386	3 319	3 035	3 306	3 367	3 413	Aux prix courants
Per capita	288	286	273	243	258	256	253	Par habitant
At constant prices	2 365	2 474	2 580	2 636	2 816	3 032	3 224	Aux prix constants
Growth rates	5.9	4.6	4.3	2.1	6.9	7.7	6.3	Taux de l'accroissement
Cameroon								**Cameroun**
At current prices	8 945	9 370	9 201	9 736	9 759	9 273	8 973	Aux prix courants
Per capita	667	681	652	673	660	613	582	Par habitant
At constant prices	13 122	13 774	14 476	15 200	15 838	16 678	17 445	Aux prix constants
Growth rates	3.1	5.0	5.1	5.0	4.2	5.3	4.6	Taux de l'accroissement
Canada								**Canada**
At current prices	581 664	604 371	627 595	606 924	649 808	706 648	694 478	Aux prix courants
Per capita	19 816	20 379	20 956	20 076	21 302	22 966	22 385	Par habitant
At constant prices	624 996	635 059	662 016	689 033	726 678	759 804	770 829	Aux prix constants
Growth rates	2.8	1.6	4.2	4.1	5.5	4.6	1.5	Taux de l'accroissement

19

Gross domestic product and gross domestic product per capita
In millions of US dollars[+] at current and constant 1990 prices; per capita US dollars; real rates of growth *[cont.]*

Produit intérieur brut et produit intérieur brut par habitant
En millions de dollars E.-U.[+] aux prix courants et constants de 1990 ; par habitant en dollars E.-U. ;
taux de l'accroissement réels *[suite]*

Country or area	1995	1996	1997	1998	1999	2000	2001	Pays ou zone
Cape Verde								**Cap-Vert**
At current prices	491	502	506	539	588	558	560	Aux prix courants
Per capita	1 254	1 255	1 238	1 289	1 378	1 282	1 259	Par habitant
At constant prices	397	413	435	467	508	542	558	Aux prix constants
Growth rates	7.5	4.0	5.4	7.4	8.6	6.8	3.0	Taux de l'accroissement
Cayman Islands								**Iles Caïmanes**
At current prices	1 019	1 075	1 173	1 237	1 280	1 357	1 438	Aux prix courants
Per capita	32 914	33 515	35 288	35 952	35 990	36 912	37 891	Par habitant
At constant prices	720	721	724	735	747	755	764	Aux prix constants
Growth rates	-0.5	0.2	0.5	1.5	1.5	1.2	1.2	Taux de l'accroissement
Central African Rep.								**Rép. centrafricaine**
At current prices	1 065	1 000	929	979	988	907	914	Aux prix courants
Per capita	318	291	265	273	270	244	242	Par habitant
At constant prices	1 346	1 303	1 377	1 444	1 496	1 523	1 523	Aux prix constants
Growth rates	6.0	-3.2	5.7	4.8	3.6	1.8	0.0	Taux de l'accroissement
Chad								**Tchad**
At current prices	1 442	1 589	1 540	1 702	1 486	1 303	1 484	Aux prix courants
Per capita	214	229	215	230	195	166	183	Par habitant
At constant prices	1 896	1 928	2 044	2 152	2 149	2 141	2 328	Aux prix constants
Growth rates	1.3	1.7	6.0	5.3	-0.1	-0.4	8.7	Taux de l'accroissement
Chile								**Chili**
At current prices	72 065	75 770	82 812	79 374	73 047	75 516	66 450	Aux prix courants
Per capita	5 071	5 254	5 661	5 353	4 861	4 960	4 310	Par habitant
At constant prices	50 820	54 588	58 194	60 074	59 487	62 096	63 842	Aux prix constants
Growth rates	10.6	7.4	6.6	3.2	-1.0	4.4	2.8	Taux de l'accroissement
China								**Chine**
At current prices	700 253	816 510	898 222	946 312	991 393	1 080 350	1 159 035	Aux prix courants
Per capita	584	675	736	768	798	862	918	Par habitant
At constant prices	685 087	750 711	817 058	880 792	942 919	1 017 828	1 092 129	Aux prix constants
Growth rates	10.5	9.6	8.8	7.8	7.1	7.9	7.3	Taux de l'accroissement
China, Hong Kong SAR								**Chine, Hong Kong RAS**
At current prices	141 709	156 572	173 669	165 249	160 626	165 362	163 995	Aux prix courants
Per capita	22 821	24 700	26 820	24 989	23 821	24 106	23 499	Par habitant
At constant prices	98 787	103 041	108 267	102 888	106 403	117 218	117 961	Aux prix constants
Growth rates	3.9	4.3	5.1	-5.0	3.4	10.2	0.6	Taux de l'accroissement
China, Macao SAR								**Chine, Macao RAS**
At current prices	6 946	6 941	7 009	6 505	6 134	6 198	6 199	Aux prix courants
Per capita	16 970	16 721	16 796	15 404	14 351	14 394	14 281	Par habitant
At constant prices	4 340	4 322	4 310	4 113	3 988	4 173	4 262	Aux prix constants
Growth rates	3.3	-0.4	-0.3	-4.6	-3.0	4.6	2.1	Taux de l'accroissement
Colombia								**Colombie**
At current prices	92 503	97 147	106 671	98 513	86 301	83 208	82 415	Aux prix courants
Per capita	2 400	2 474	2 668	2 421	2 084	1 975	1 924	Par habitant
At constant prices	59 249	60 467	62 541	62 898	60 253	61 903	62 769	Aux prix constants
Growth rates	5.2	2.1	3.4	0.6	-4.2	2.7	1.4	Taux de l'accroissement
Comoros								**Comores**
At current prices	215	213	194	197	204	185	201	Aux prix courants
Per capita	352	340	300	296	298	262	278	Par habitant
At constant prices	243	247	245	242	246	244	248	Aux prix constants
Growth rates	-2.3	1.7	-1.1	-1.1	1.9	-1.1	2.0	Taux de l'accroissement
Congo								**Congo**
At current prices	2 116	2 541	2 323	1 949	2 217	2 998	2 758	Aux prix courants
Per capita	721	837	740	601	662	870	779	Par habitant
At constant prices	2 788	2 907	2 894	3 002	2 905	3 139	3 230	Aux prix constants
Growth rates	2.1	4.3	-0.5	3.8	-3.2	8.1	2.9	Taux de l'accroissement
Cook Islands								**Iles Cook**
At current prices	102	102	95	78	82	78	80	Aux prix courants
Per capita	5 366	5 420	5 082	4 212	4 469	4 254	4 388	Par habitant
At constant prices	75	75	73	70	74	81	83	Aux prix constants
Growth rates	-4.4	-0.2	-2.8	-4.2	5.8	9.8	3.0	Taux de l'accroissement

19

Gross domestic product and gross domestic product per capita
In millions of US dollars[+] at current and constant 1990 prices; per capita US dollars; real rates of growth *[cont.]*
Produit intérieur brut et produit intérieur brut par habitant
En millions de dollars E.-U.[+] aux prix courants et constants de 1990 ; par habitant en dollars E.-U. ;
taux de l'accroissement réels *[suite]*

Country or area	1995	1996	1997	1998	1999	2000	2001	Pays ou zone
Costa Rica								**Costa Rica**
At current prices	11 716	11 844	12 829	14 094	15 796	15 957	16 382	Aux prix courants
Per capita	3 372	3 324	3 510	3 760	4 113	4 062	4 082	Par habitant
At constant prices	9 466	9 550	10 083	10 929	11 828	12 040	12 171	Aux prix constants
Growth rates	3.9	0.9	5.6	8.4	8.2	1.8	1.1	Taux de l'accroissement
Côte d'Ivoire								**Côte d'Ivoire**
At current prices	11 105	12 139	11 722	12 641	12 561	10 682	10 501	Aux prix courants
Per capita	773	827	782	828	808	675	652	Par habitant
At constant prices	12 879	13 748	14 529	15 274	15 571	15 156	15 019	Aux prix constants
Growth rates	7.1	6.7	5.7	5.1	1.9	-2.7	-0.9	Taux de l'accroissement
Croatia								**Croatie**
At current prices	18 811	19 872	20 294	21 628	19 906	18 428	19 534	Aux prix courants
Per capita	4 225	4 499	4 602	4 891	4 486	4 145	4 394	Par habitant
At constant prices	17 958	19 016	20 309	20 817	20 630	21 228	22 033	Aux prix constants
Growth rates	6.8	5.9	6.8	2.5	-0.9	2.9	3.8	Taux de l'accroissement
Cuba								**Cuba**
At current prices	21 737	22 815	22 952	23 901	25 504	27 635	28 589	Aux prix courants
Per capita	1 983	2 071	2 073	2 150	2 285	2 467	2 544	Par habitant
At constant prices	13 626	14 694	15 060	15 248	16 199	17 111	17 624	Aux prix constants
Growth rates	2.5	7.8	2.5	1.2	6.2	5.6	3.0	Taux de l'accroissement
Cyprus								**Chypre**
At current prices	8 856	8 923	8 505	9 064	9 243	8 816	9 120	Aux prix courants
Per capita	11 907	11 838	11 157	11 777	11 906	11 259	11 552	Par habitant
At constant prices	6 947	7 079	7 256	7 609	7 958	8 364	8 699	Aux prix constants
Growth rates	6.1	1.9	2.5	4.9	4.6	5.1	4.0	Taux de l'accroissement
Czech Republic								**République tchèque**
At current prices	52 035	57 726	52 997	56 971	55 028	51 423	57 190	Aux prix courants
Per capita	5 037	5 591	5 139	5 532	5 351	5 008	5 576	Par habitant
At constant prices	33 240	34 668	34 403	34 044	34 203	35 316	36 407	Aux prix constants
Growth rates	5.9	4.3	-0.8	-1.0	0.5	3.3	3.1	Taux de l'accroissement
Dem. Rep. of the Congo								**Rép. dém. du Congo**
At current prices	5 637	5 771	5 942	6 218	5 089[1]	5 061[1]	4 526[1]	Aux prix courants
Per capita	127	127	129	133	107[1]	104[1]	91[1]	Par habitant
At constant prices	6 417	6 359	5 994	5 898	5 284[1]	5 057[1]	4 835[1]	Aux prix constants
Growth rates	0.7	-0.9	-5.8	-1.6	-10.4[1]	-4.3[1]	-4.4[1]	Taux de l'accroissement
Denmark								**Danemark**
At current prices	180 238	182 954	169 025	172 428	173 123	158 451	159 233	Aux prix courants
Per capita	34 476	34 863	32 088	32 615	32 633	29 772	29 833	Par habitant
At constant prices	147 024	150 727	155 203	159 033	163 224	167 950	170 348	Aux prix constants
Growth rates	2.8	2.5	3.0	2.5	2.6	2.9	1.4	Taux de l'accroissement
Djibouti								**Djibouti**
At current prices	510	496	491	498	536	553	574	Aux prix courants
Per capita	897	850	813	795	828	830	842	Par habitant
At constant prices	506	480	502	502	513	516	526	Aux prix constants
Growth rates	5.6	-5.1	4.6	-0.2	2.2	0.7	1.9	Taux de l'accroissement
Dominica								**Dominique**
At current prices	219	236	245	259	268	270	263	Aux prix courants
Per capita	2 919	3 119	3 210	3 374	3 459	3 465	3 367	Par habitant
At constant prices	181	187	192	198	199	199	191	Aux prix constants
Growth rates	2.0	3.5	2.5	3.2	0.6	0.1	-4.3	Taux de l'accroissement
Dominican Republic								**Rép. dominicaine**
At current prices	15 418	16 915	15 062	15 850	17 361	19 603	21 329	Aux prix courants
Per capita	2 006	2 164	1 894	1 960	2 112	2 347	2 514	Par habitant
At constant prices	11 647	12 613	13 647	14 657	15 830	16 985	17 529	Aux prix constants
Growth rates	4.6	8.3	8.2	7.4	8.0	7.3	3.2	Taux de l'accroissement
Ecuador								**Equateur**
At current prices	20 196	21 268	23 636	23 255	16 674	15 934	21 024	Aux prix courants
Per capita	1 771	1 831	1 999	1 934	1 364	1 283	1 666	Par habitant
At constant prices	13 298	13 617	14 169	14 469	13 557	13 937	14 651	Aux prix constants
Growth rates	1.7	2.4	4.1	2.1	-6.3	2.8	5.1	Taux de l'accroissement

19

Gross domestic product and gross domestic product per capita
In millions of US dollars[+] at current and constant 1990 prices; per capita US dollars; real rates of growth *[cont.]*

Produit intérieur brut et produit intérieur brut par habitant
En millions de dollars E.-U.[+] aux prix courants et constants de 1990 ; par habitant en dollars E.-U. ;
taux de l'accroissement réels *[suite]*

Country or area	1995	1996	1997	1998	1999	2000	2001	Pays ou zone
Egypt								**Egypte**
At current prices	67 626	78 402	84 810	90 791	100 169	103 311	96 073	Aux prix courants
Per capita	1 097	1 248	1 325	1 392	1 507	1 524	1 390	Par habitant
At constant prices	81 831	86 019	89 480	94 947	100 059	103 585	106 884	Aux prix constants
Growth rates	4.6	5.1	4.0	6.1	5.4	3.5	3.2	Taux de l'accroissement
El Salvador								**El Salvador**
At current prices	9 496	10 310	11 127	12 002	12 458	13 132	13 739	Aux prix courants
Per capita	1 675	1 783	1 889	2 001	2 041	2 115	2 176	Par habitant
At constant prices	7 190	7 312	7 623	7 909	8 182	8 360	8 513	Aux prix constants
Growth rates	6.4	1.7	4.2	3.8	3.4	2.2	1.8	Taux de l'accroissement
Equatorial Guinea								**Guinée équatoriale**
At current prices	163	278	553	449	758	1 253	1 724	Aux prix courants
Per capita	408	676	1 310	1 037	1 707	2 746	3 680	Par habitant
At constant prices	261	379	649	792	1 120	1 309	2 008	Aux prix constants
Growth rates	16.1	45.3	71.2	22.0	41.4	16.9	53.4	Taux de l'accroissement
Eritrea								**Erythrée**
At current prices	574	631	655	681	648	608	681	Aux prix courants
Per capita	179	193	195	197	181	164	177	Par habitant
At constant prices	526	561	605	629	634	582	605	Aux prix constants
Growth rates	2.9	6.8	7.9	3.9	0.8	-8.2	4.0	Taux de l'accroissement
Estonia								**Estonie**
At current prices	3 567	4 356	4 614	5 225	5 200	5 141	5 498	Aux prix courants
Per capita	2 467	3 060	3 280	3 751	3 767	3 760	4 065	Par habitant
At constant prices	8 146	8 471	9 355	9 827	9 759	10 430	10 993	Aux prix constants
Growth rates	4.6	4.0	10.4	5.0	-0.7	6.9	5.4	Taux de l'accroissement
Ethiopia								**Ethiopie**
At current prices	5 502	5 973	6 180	6 309	6 163	6 019	6 051	Aux prix courants
Per capita	96	101	102	101	96	92	90	Par habitant
At constant prices	9 056	10 017	10 535	10 478	11 140	11 746	12 668	Aux prix constants
Growth rates	6.2	10.6	5.2	-0.5	6.3	5.4	7.9	Taux de l'accroissement
Fiji								**Fidji**
At current prices	1 990	2 114	2 119	1 587	1 861	1 653	1 683	Aux prix courants
Per capita	2 592	2 719	2 693	1 995	2 312	2 031	2 046	Par habitant
At constant prices	1 526	1 573	1 559	1 581	1 735	1 686	1 729	Aux prix constants
Growth rates	2.5	3.1	-0.9	1.4	9.7	-2.8	2.6	Taux de l'accroissement
Finland								**Finlande**
At current prices	129 695	127 765	122 665	129 499	127 805	119 987	121 512	Aux prix courants
Per capita	25 392	24 924	23 857	25 124	24 739	23 177	23 424	Par habitant
At constant prices	132 667	137 898	146 696	153 815	159 050	167 850	168 939	Aux prix constants
Growth rates	3.8	3.9	6.4	4.9	3.4	5.5	0.6	Taux de l'accroissement
France								**France**
At current prices	1 553 131	1 554 363	1 406 117	1 451 952	1 443 704	1 308 401	1 320 418	Aux prix courants
Per capita	26 714	26 625	23 993	24 683	24 449	22 066	22 168	Par habitant
At constant prices	1 281 851	1 295 989	1 320 670	1 365 589	1 409 468	1 462 929	1 493 587	Aux prix constants
Growth rates	1.7	1.1	1.9	3.4	3.2	3.8	2.1	Taux de l'accroissement
French Guiana								**Guyane française**
At current prices	1 675	1 672	1 500	1 518	1 488	1 316	1 308	Aux prix courants
Per capita	12 091	11 656	10 086	9 854	9 341	8 011	7 737	Par habitant
At constant prices	1 516	1 540	1 565	1 590	1 616	1 642	1 668	Aux prix constants
Growth rates	1.6	1.6	1.6	1.6	1.6	1.6	1.6	Taux de l'accroissement
French Polynesia								**Polynésie française**
At current prices	4 111	4 123	3 703	3 753	3 703	3 297	3 292	Aux prix courants
Per capita	19 150	18 877	16 668	16 617	16 129	14 131	13 891	Par habitant
At constant prices	3 597	3 656	3 698	3 737	3 836	3 938	4 022	Aux prix constants
Growth rates	-2.3	1.6	1.1	1.1	2.7	2.7	2.1	Taux de l'accroissement
Gabon								**Gabon**
At current prices	4 959	5 630	5 341	4 666	4 612	5 024	4 334	Aux prix courants
Per capita	4 470	4 937	4 559	3 883	3 748	3 995	3 379	Par habitant
At constant prices	6 304	6 556	6 851	6 995	6 561	6 693	6 860	Aux prix constants
Growth rates	5.0	4.0	4.5	2.1	-6.2	2.0	2.5	Taux de l'accroissement

19

Gross domestic product and gross domestic product per capita
In millions of US dollars[+] at current and constant 1990 prices; per capita US dollars; real rates of growth [cont.]
Produit intérieur brut et produit intérieur brut par habitant
En millions de dollars E.-U.[+] aux prix courants et constants de 1990 ; par habitant en dollars E.-U. ;
taux de l'accroissement réels [suite]

Country or area	1995	1996	1997	1998	1999	2000	2001	Pays ou zone
Gambia								**Gambie**
At current prices	367	390	394	418	432	434	405	Aux prix courants
Per capita	330	338	330	339	339	331	300	Par habitant
At constant prices	377	397	400	440	468	494	523	Aux prix constants
Growth rates	-3.4	5.3	0.8	9.9	6.4	5.6	5.7	Taux de l'accroissement
Georgia								**Géorgie**
At current prices	2 841	3 046	3 575	3 627	2 799	3 044	3 192	Aux prix courants
Per capita	531	571	672	683	529	579	611	Par habitant
At constant prices	6 348	7 059	7 805	8 029	8 267	8 426	8 820	Aux prix constants
Growth rates	2.6	11.2	10.6	2.9	3.0	1.9	4.7	Taux de l'accroissement
Germany								**Allemagne**
At current prices	2 458 277	2 383 351	2 110 965	2 144 484	2 107 972	1 870 277	1 853 406	Aux prix courants
Per capita	30 103	29 097	25 722	26 102	25 638	22 730	22 507	Par habitant
At constant prices	1 849 398	1 863 567	1 889 542	1 926 504	1 965 929	2 022 090	2 033 691	Aux prix constants
Growth rates	1.7	0.8	1.4	2.0	2.0	2.9	0.6	Taux de l'accroissement
Ghana								**Ghana**
At current prices	6 458	6 926	6 884	7 474	7 493	4 978	5 301	Aux prix courants
Per capita	369	386	375	398	391	254	265	Par habitant
At constant prices	7 679	8 032	8 369	8 762	9 150	9 491	9 888	Aux prix constants
Growth rates	4.0	4.6	4.2	4.7	4.4	3.7	4.2	Taux de l'accroissement
Greece								**Grèce**
At current prices	117 563	124 360	121 339	121 957	125 844	113 422	117 160	Aux prix courants
Per capita	11 246	11 795	11 400	11 350	11 615	10 403	10 702	Par habitant
At constant prices	89 448	91 557	94 888	98 079	101 615	105 854	110 194	Aux prix constants
Growth rates	2.1	2.4	3.6	3.4	3.6	4.2	4.1	Taux de l'accroissement
Grenada								**Grenade**
At current prices	240	257	274	297	329	357	378	Aux prix courants
Per capita	2 883	3 099	3 329	3 625	4 041	4 410	4 682	Par habitant
At constant prices	220	226	235	253	271	289	299	Aux prix constants
Growth rates	3.1	3.0	4.1	7.3	7.4	6.5	3.5	Taux de l'accroissement
Guadeloupe								**Guadeloupe**
At current prices	4 439	4 575	4 453	4 697	4 645	4 295	4 460	Aux prix courants
Per capita	10 850	11 085	10 693	11 172	10 947	10 030	10 323	Par habitant
At constant prices	2 711	2 828	3 089	3 217	3 237	3 387	3 543	Aux prix constants
Growth rates	-4.3	4.3	9.2	4.1	0.6	4.6	4.6	Taux de l'accroissement
Guatemala								**Guatemala**
At current prices	14 656	15 783	17 797	19 008	17 952	18 741	20 131	Aux prix courants
Per capita	1 469	1 540	1 690	1 756	1 614	1 641	1 717	Par habitant
At constant prices	9 432	9 712	10 129	10 612	11 020	11 416	11 678	Aux prix constants
Growth rates	4.9	3.0	4.3	4.8	3.8	3.6	2.3	Taux de l'accroissement
Guinea								**Guinée**
At current prices	3 729	3 959	3 895	3 782	3 635	3 155	3 092	Aux prix courants
Per capita	509	527	506	482	455	389	375	Par habitant
At constant prices	3 386	3 542	3 712	3 879	4 023	4 224	4 351	Aux prix constants
Growth rates	4.4	4.6	4.8	4.5	3.7	5.0	3.0	Taux de l'accroissement
Guinea-Bissau								**Guinée-Bissau**
At current prices	245	265	279	206	230	219	244	Aux prix courants
Per capita	206	217	221	160	173	160	174	Par habitant
At constant prices	283	297	316	228	245	263	284	Aux prix constants
Growth rates	4.4	5.0	6.3	-28.0	7.6	7.5	7.8	Taux de l'accroissement
Guyana								**Guyana**
At current prices	622	706	749	718	695	713	713	Aux prix courants
Per capita	839	947	1 001	954	919	939	936	Par habitant
At constant prices	558	598	635	624	648	639	651	Aux prix constants
Growth rates	5.1	7.0	6.2	-1.7	3.8	-1.3	1.9	Taux de l'accroissement
Haiti								**Haïti**
At current prices	2 458	2 863	3 209	3 632	4 040	3 644	3 623	Aux prix courants
Per capita	328	377	417	466	511	455	447	Par habitant
At constant prices	2 140	2 191	2 231	2 295	2 339	2 344	2 304	Aux prix constants
Growth rates	4.0	2.4	1.8	2.9	1.9	0.2	-1.7	Taux de l'accroissement

19

Gross domestic product and gross domestic product per capita
In millions of US dollars[+] at current and constant 1990 prices; per capita US dollars; real rates of growth *[cont.]*

Produit intérieur brut et produit intérieur brut par habitant
En millions de dollars E.-U.[+] aux prix courants et constants de 1990 ; par habitant en dollars E.-U. ;
taux de l'accroissement réels *[suite]*

Country or area	1995	1996	1997	1998	1999	2000	2001	Pays ou zone
								Saint-Siège[2]
Holy See[2]								
At current prices	15	17	16	16	16	15	15	Aux prix courants
Per capita	19 148	21 483	20 307	20 810	20 528	18 651	18 928	Par habitant
At constant prices	16	16	16	17	17	18	18	Aux prix constants
Growth rates	2.9	1.1	2.2	1.8	1.7	3.0	1.8	Taux de l'accroissement
Honduras								**Honduras**
At current prices	3 960	4 080	4 716	5 262	5 424	5 898	6 358	Aux prix courants
Per capita	703	704	791	859	862	914	960	Par habitant
At constant prices	3 628	3 758	3 946	4 060	3 984	4 182	4 308	Aux prix constants
Growth rates	4.1	3.6	5.0	2.9	-1.9	5.0	3.0	Taux de l'accroissement
Hungary								**Hongrie**
At current prices	44 669	45 163	45 724	47 049	48 044	46 681	51 833	Aux prix courants
Per capita	4 373	4 437	4 509	4 659	4 778	4 662	5 200	Par habitant
At constant prices	32 038	32 467	33 952	35 601	37 086	39 012	40 513	Aux prix constants
Growth rates	1.5	1.3	4.6	4.9	4.2	5.2	3.8	Taux de l'accroissement
Iceland								**Islande**
At current prices	6 836	7 137	7 231	7 999	8 385	8 373	7 603	Aux prix courants
Per capita	25 568	26 405	26 453	28 934	30 005	29 659	26 686	Par habitant
At constant prices	6 337	6 663	6 971	7 356	7 645	8 066	8 303	Aux prix constants
Growth rates	0.1	5.1	4.6	5.5	3.9	5.5	2.9	Taux de l'accroissement
India								**Inde**
At current prices	366 364	386 138	419 281	421 949	448 176	464 600	482 765	Aux prix courants
Per capita	393	407	434	429	448	457	467	Par habitant
At constant prices	416 774	447 593	467 555	495 521	530 685	551 480	581 260	Aux prix constants
Growth rates	7.5	7.4	4.5	6.0	7.1	3.9	5.4	Taux de l'accroissement
Indonesia								**Indonésie**
At current prices	202 131	227 370	215 749	95 445	140 001	152 227	145 307	Aux prix courants
Per capita	1 025	1 136	1 063	464	671	720	678	Par habitant
At constant prices	166 814	179 856	188 308	163 590	164 884	172 960	178 697	Aux prix constants
Growth rates	8.2	7.8	4.7	-13.1	0.8	4.9	3.3	Taux de l'accroissement
Iran (Islamic Rep. of)								**Iran (Rép. islamique d')**
At current prices	101 810	109 670	102 720	101 476	103 305	99 250	108 008	Aux prix courants
Per capita	1 632	1 733	1 602	1 564	1 573	1 494	1 606	Par habitant
At constant prices	227 695	242 931	255 964	265 689	270 293	284 233	298 488	Aux prix constants
Growth rates	3.3	6.7	5.4	3.8	1.7	5.2	5.0	Taux de l'accroissement
Iraq[1]								**Iraq**[1]
At current prices	10 395	10 613	13 266	15 256	16 476	18 289	21 032	Aux prix courants
Per capita	514	510	620	694	729	787	881	Par habitant
At constant prices	10 395	10 613	13 266	15 256	16 476	18 289	21 032	Aux prix constants
Growth rates	-4.0	2.1	25.0	15.0	8.0	11.0	15.0	Taux de l'accroissement
Ireland								**Irlande**
At current prices	66 468	73 183	80 110	86 989	95 640	94 813	102 441	Aux prix courants
Per capita	18 418	20 083	21 745	23 335	25 345	24 824	26 503	Par habitant
At constant prices	59 450	64 250	71 269	77 569	86 213	94 795	100 185	Aux prix constants
Growth rates	9.9	8.1	10.9	8.8	11.1	10.0	5.7	Taux de l'accroissement
Israel								**Israël**
At current prices	95 108	104 074	107 901	107 504	107 920	119 444	116 866	Aux prix courants
Per capita	17 779	18 910	19 110	18 598	18 258	19 770	18 930	Par habitant
At constant prices	78 541	82 480	84 996	87 473	89 884	97 050	96 185	Aux prix constants
Growth rates	6.9	5.0	3.1	2.9	2.8	8.0	-0.9	Taux de l'accroissement
Italy								**Italie**
At current prices	1 097 208	1 232 884	1 166 801	1 196 664	1 180 980	1 073 124	1 088 751	Aux prix courants
Per capita	19 148	21 483	20 307	20 810	20 528	18 651	18 928	Par habitant
At constant prices	1 174 313	1 187 150	1 211 205	1 232 934	1 252 573	1 288 494	1 311 368	Aux prix constants
Growth rates	2.9	1.1	2.0	1.8	1.6	2.9	1.8	Taux de l'accroissement
Jamaica								**Jamaïque**
At current prices	5 692	6 395	7 288	7 481	7 532	7 709	7 784	Aux prix courants
Per capita	2 303	2 565	2 899	2 950	2 945	2 988	2 990	Par habitant
At constant prices	4 924	4 872	4 788	4 772	4 751	4 783	4 865	Aux prix constants
Growth rates	1.0	-1.1	-1.7	-0.3	-0.4	0.7	1.7	Taux de l'accroissement

19

Gross domestic product and gross domestic product per capita
In millions of US dollars[+] at current and constant 1990 prices; per capita US dollars; real rates of growth [cont.]
Produit intérieur brut et produit intérieur brut par habitant
En millions de dollars E.-U.[+] aux prix courants et constants de 1990 ; par habitant en dollars E.-U. ;
taux de l'accroissement réels [suite]

Country or area	1995	1996	1997	1998	1999	2000	2001	Pays ou zone
Japan								**Japon**
At current prices	5 303 790	4 706 299	4 323 063	3 946 205	4 469 583	4 763 833	4 175 594	Aux prix courants
Per capita	42 271	37 406	34 269	31 203	35 258	37 500	32 809	Par habitant
At constant prices	3 288 120	3 400 795	3 463 152	3 424 119	3 427 492	3 523 597	3 538 110	Aux prix constants
Growth rates	1.9	3.4	1.8	-1.1	0.1	2.8	0.4	Taux de l'accroissement
Jordan								**Jordanie**
At current prices	6 815	7 028	7 324	7 963	8 131	8 480	8 947	Aux prix courants
Per capita	1 604	1 587	1 595	1 679	1 663	1 684	1 726	Par habitant
At constant prices	5 553	5 670	5 843	6 015	6 105	6 270	6 489	Aux prix constants
Growth rates	6.4	2.1	3.1	2.9	1.5	2.7	3.5	Taux de l'accroissement
Kazakhstan								**Kazakhstan**
At current prices	16 640	21 035	22 166	22 135	16 871	18 292	22 153	Aux prix courants
Per capita	1 005	1 284	1 369	1 385	1 068	1 170	1 426	Par habitant
At constant prices	43 959	44 179	44 930	44 076	45 266	49 702	56 412	Aux prix constants
Growth rates	-8.2	0.5	1.7	-1.9	2.7	9.8	13.5	Taux de l'accroissement
Kenya								**Kenya**
At current prices	9 047	9 257	10 614	11 465	10 553	10 449	11 396	Aux prix courants
Per capita	330	330	369	390	352	342	367	Par habitant
At constant prices	9 234	9 616	9 817	9 975	10 104	10 087	10 198	Aux prix constants
Growth rates	4.4	4.1	2.1	1.6	1.3	-0.2	1.1	Taux de l'accroissement
Kiribati								**Kiribati**
At current prices	46	50	49	46	52	45	40	Aux prix courants
Per capita	592	631	613	565	626	539	468	Par habitant
At constant prices	35	36	38	40	42	42	43	Aux prix constants
Growth rates	5.4	3.0	5.7	5.0	6.2	0.2	1.8	Taux de l'accroissement
Korea, Dem. P. R.								**Corée, R. p. dém. de**
At current prices	5 244	10 588	10 323	10 273	10 280	10 608	11 022	Aux prix courants
Per capita	245	490	474	468	465	476	492	Par habitant
At constant prices	13 333	12 853	12 043	11 910	12 649	12 813	13 287	Aux prix constants
Growth rates	-4.2	-3.6	-6.3	-1.1	6.2	1.3	3.7	Taux de l'accroissement
Korea, Republic of								**Corée, République de**
At current prices	489 256	520 203	476 486	317 080	406 071	461 520	427 235	Aux prix courants
Per capita	10 862	11 449	10 400	6 867	8 730	9 854	9 063	Par habitant
At constant prices	361 868	386 294	405 651	378 516	419 751	458 900	473 138	Aux prix constants
Growth rates	8.9	6.8	5.0	-6.7	10.9	9.3	3.1	Taux de l'accroissement
Kuwait								**Koweït**
At current prices	26 554	31 070	29 866	25 122	29 190	35 830	32 793	Aux prix courants
Per capita	15 660	17 957	16 332	12 759	13 791	15 947	13 935	Par habitant
At constant prices	31 030	30 191	30 550	31 515	29 968	26 943	26 642	Aux prix constants
Growth rates	1.4	-2.7	1.2	3.2	-4.9	-10.1	-1.1	Taux de l'accroissement
Kyrgyzstan								**Kirghizistan**
At current prices	1 492	1 827	1 767	1 640	1 250	1 370	1 527	Aux prix courants
Per capita	327	396	377	344	258	278	306	Par habitant
At constant prices	6 514	6 975	7 667	7 830	8 116	8 558	9 014	Aux prix constants
Growth rates	-5.4	7.1	9.9	2.1	3.7	5.4	5.3	Taux de l'accroissement
Lao People's Dem. Rep.								**Rép. dém. pop. lao**
At current prices	1 764	1 874	1 747	1 286	1 451	1 733	1 750	Aux prix courants
Per capita	376	390	355	255	281	328	324	Par habitant
At constant prices	1 181	1 262	1 349	1 403	1 505	1 593	1 683	Aux prix constants
Growth rates	7.0	6.9	6.9	4.0	7.3	5.8	5.7	Taux de l'accroissement
Latvia								**Lettonie**
At current prices	4 415	5 097	5 628	6 090	6 647	7 169	7 578	Aux prix courants
Per capita	1 768	2 071	2 312	2 524	2 778	3 022	3 224	Par habitant
At constant prices	9 300	9 642	10 450	10 947	11 258	12 028	12 952	Aux prix constants
Growth rates	-0.8	3.7	8.4	4.8	2.8	6.8	7.7	Taux de l'accroissement
Lebanon								**Liban**
At current prices	10 965	12 819	14 289	15 525	16 796	17 220	17 995	Aux prix courants
Per capita	3 481	3 970	4 333	4 620	4 913	4 951	5 087	Par habitant
At constant prices	5 001	5 201	5 383	5 544	5 766	5 881	6 058	Aux prix constants
Growth rates	6.5	4.0	3.5	3.0	4.0	2.0	3.0	Taux de l'accroissement

19

Gross domestic product and gross domestic product per capita
In millions of US dollars[+] at current and constant 1990 prices; per capita US dollars; real rates of growth *[cont.]*

Produit intérieur brut et produit intérieur brut par habitant
En millions de dollars E.-U.[+] aux prix courants et constants de 1990 ; par habitant en dollars E.-U. ;
taux de l'accroissement réels *[suite]*

Country or area	1995	1996	1997	1998	1999	2000	2001	Pays ou zone
Lesotho								**Lesotho**
At current prices	933	943	1 024	890	911	863	752	Aux prix courants
Per capita	554	553	592	508	515	483	419	Par habitant
At constant prices	752	826	894	852	854	867	896	Aux prix constants
Growth rates	4.4	10.0	8.1	-4.6	0.2	1.5	3.4	Taux de l'accroissement
Liberia								**Libéria**
At current prices	135	159	289	360	442	526	523	Aux prix courants
Per capita	63	71	121	139	160	179	169	Par habitant
At constant prices	107	120	243	315	387	466	490	Aux prix constants
Growth rates	-4.3	12.1	101.5	29.7	22.9	20.3	5.3	Taux de l'accroissement
Libyan Arab Jamah.								**Jamah. arabe libyenne**
At current prices	30 847	33 679	37 082	32 375	28 313	34 136	29 120	Aux prix courants
Per capita	6 493	6 954	7 508	6 428	5 512	6 518	5 453	Par habitant
At constant prices	24 712	25 681	26 021	26 135	26 163	27 003	27 897	Aux prix constants
Growth rates	0.9	3.9	1.3	0.4	0.1	3.2	3.3	Taux de l'accroissement
Liechtenstein								**Liechtenstein**
At current prices	1 326	1 288	1 126	1 167	1 165	1 090	1 136	Aux prix courants
Per capita	43 164	41 416	35 725	36 556	36 067	33 384	34 449	Par habitant
At constant prices	982	994	1 022	1 058	1 088	1 133	1 159	Aux prix constants
Growth rates	1.2	1.2	2.8	3.6	2.8	4.1	2.3	Taux de l'accroissement
Lithuania								**Lituanie**
At current prices	6 026	7 892	9 585	10 748	10 664	11 287	11 990	Aux prix courants
Per capita	1 691	2 230	2 718	3 054	3 036	3 224	3 441	Par habitant
At constant prices	11 676	12 227	13 116	13 787	13 250	13 752	14 570	Aux prix constants
Growth rates	3.3	4.7	7.3	5.1	-3.9	3.8	5.9	Taux de l'accroissement
Luxembourg								**Luxembourg**
At current prices	18 082	18 146	17 467	18 900	20 104	19 636	19 760	Aux prix courants
Per capita	44 638	44 137	41 871	44 662	46 842	45 117	44 783	Par habitant
At constant prices	13 451	13 900	15 056	16 093	17 495	19 049	19 283	Aux prix constants
Growth rates	1.4	3.3	8.3	6.9	8.7	8.9	1.2	Taux de l'accroissement
Madagascar								**Madagascar**
At current prices	3 155	3 987	3 546	3 741	3 721	3 878	4 569	Aux prix courants
Per capita	229	281	242	248	240	243	278	Par habitant
At constant prices	3 030	3 095	3 209	3 336	3 492	3 660	3 880	Aux prix constants
Growth rates	1.7	2.1	3.7	3.9	4.7	4.8	6.0	Taux de l'accroissement
Malawi								**Malawi**
At current prices	1 399	2 310	2 593	1 748	1 793	1 743	1 963	Aux prix courants
Per capita	139	225	247	162	162	153	169	Par habitant
At constant prices	2 271	2 215	2 363	2 399	2 473	2 555	2 516	Aux prix constants
Growth rates	4.6	-2.5	6.7	1.5	3.1	3.3	-1.5	Taux de l'accroissement
Malaysia								**Malaisie**
At current prices	88 833	100 850	100 169	72 175	79 148	90 041	88 050	Aux prix courants
Per capita	4 362	4 827	4 674	3 286	3 519	3 915	3 748	Par habitant
At constant prices	69 219	76 143	81 718	75 704	80 351	87 046	87 437	Aux prix constants
Growth rates	9.8	10.0	7.3	-7.4	6.1	8.3	0.4	Taux de l'accroissement
Maldives								**Maldives**
At current prices	401	460	512	540	569	598	584	Aux prix courants
Per capita	1 600	1 786	1 926	1 972	2 014	2 054	1 947	Par habitant
At constant prices	299	325	362	354	380	397	406	Aux prix constants
Growth rates	7.1	8.8	11.2	-2.2	7.4	4.6	2.1	Taux de l'accroissement
Mali								**Mali**
At current prices	2 310	2 669	2 437	2 699	2 714	2 544	2 453	Aux prix courants
Per capita	223	251	223	240	235	214	200	Par habitant
At constant prices	2 903	3 196	3 412	3 614	3 861	4 004	4 061	Aux prix constants
Growth rates	6.0	10.1	6.8	5.9	6.8	3.7	1.4	Taux de l'accroissement
Malta								**Malte**
At current prices	3 245	3 333	3 338	3 507	3 650	3 555	3 626	Aux prix courants
Per capita	8 588	8 757	8 713	9 103	9 426	9 136	9 274	Par habitant
At constant prices	3 019	3 133	3 283	3 397	3 529	3 696	3 840	Aux prix constants
Growth rates	6.3	3.8	4.8	3.5	3.9	4.8	3.9	Taux de l'accroissement

19

Gross domestic product and gross domestic product per capita
In millions of US dollars[+] at current and constant 1990 prices; per capita US dollars; real rates of growth *[cont.]*
Produit intérieur brut et produit intérieur brut par habitant
En millions de dollars E.-U.[+] aux prix courants et constants de 1990 ; par habitant en dollars E.-U. ;
taux de l'accroissement réels *[suite]*

Country or area	1995	1996	1997	1998	1999	2000	2001	Pays ou zone
Marshall Islands								**Iles Marshall**
At current prices	105	97	92	95	97	98	100	Aux prix courants
Per capita	2 202	2 004	1 878	1 914	1 921	1 910	1 938	Par habitant
At constant prices	76	64	58	59	59	58	59	Aux prix constants
Growth rates	9.8	-15.9	-9.4	1.1	0.1	-0.9	1.7	Taux de l'accroissement
Martinique								**Martinique**
At current prices	4 838	4 863	4 377	4 617	4 566	4 113	4 161	Aux prix courants
Per capita	12 961	12 942	11 573	12 125	11 914	10 664	10 723	Par habitant
At constant prices	3 635	3 695	3 755	3 910	3 935	4 019	4 105	Aux prix constants
Growth rates	1.6	1.6	1.6	4.1	0.6	2.1	2.1	Taux de l'accroissement
Mauritania								**Mauritanie**
At current prices	1 058	1 081	1 071	983	964	900	961	Aux prix courants
Per capita	460	457	441	394	375	340	353	Par habitant
At constant prices	1 294	1 329	1 395	1 447	1 506	1 581	1 654	Aux prix constants
Growth rates	5.7	2.7	5.0	3.7	4.1	5.0	4.6	Taux de l'accroissement
Mauritius								**Maurice**
At current prices	4 042	4 406	4 184	4 150	4 266	4 554	4 526	Aux prix courants
Per capita	3 594	3 873	3 638	3 571	3 634	3 840	3 779	Par habitant
At constant prices	3 272	3 453	3 652	3 872	3 985	4 350	4 587	Aux prix constants
Growth rates	4.4	5.6	5.8	6.0	2.9	9.2	5.5	Taux de l'accroissement
Mexico								**Mexique**
At current prices	286 166	332 337	400 871	421 008	480 492	580 121	617 181	Aux prix courants
Per capita	3 140	3 584	4 252	4 393	4 933	5 864	6 144	Par habitant
At constant prices	283 417	298 023	318 205	334 212	346 319	369 306	368 285	Aux prix constants
Growth rates	-6.2	5.2	6.8	5.0	3.6	6.6	-0.3	Taux de l'accroissement
Micronesia (Fed. States)								**Micronésie (Etats féd. de)**
At current prices	215	218	211	210	217	229	238	Aux prix courants
Per capita	2 009	2 020	1 958	1 952	2 029	2 138	2 215	Par habitant
At constant prices	187	183	174	170	172	175	178	Aux prix constants
Growth rates	3.0	-1.8	-5.1	-2.1	0.9	2.1	1.5	Taux de l'accroissement
Monaco								**Monaco**
At current prices	848	855	778	809	810	736	743	Aux prix courants
Per capita	26 715	26 623	23 989	24 677	24 446	22 019	22 015	Par habitant
At constant prices	700	713	731	761	790	825	846	Aux prix constants
Growth rates	2.4	1.8	2.6	4.1	3.9	4.4	2.5	Taux de l'accroissement
Mongolia								**Mongolie**
At current prices	1 235	1 203	1 071	992	906	970	1 055	Aux prix courants
Per capita	516	498	440	404	366	388	417	Par habitant
At constant prices	2 717	2 783	2 893	2 994	3 068	3 100	3 134	Aux prix constants
Growth rates	6.3	2.4	4.0	3.5	2.5	1.1	1.1	Taux de l'accroissement
Montserrat								**Montserrat**
At current prices	60	49	41	37	35	35	35	Aux prix courants
Per capita	5 894	5 300	5 216	5 982	7 201	8 916	10 184	Par habitant
At constant prices	52	41	33	29	26	25	23	Aux prix constants
Growth rates	-7.6	-21.4	-20.0	-10.1	-12.6	-2.7	-7.8	Taux de l'accroissement
Morocco								**Maroc**
At current prices	32 985	36 639	33 414	35 817	35 249	33 322	33 876	Aux prix courants
Per capita	1 229	1 343	1 205	1 271	1 231	1 145	1 145	Par habitant
At constant prices	27 049	30 354	29 678	31 955	31 930	32 242	34 326	Aux prix constants
Growth rates	-6.6	12.2	-2.2	7.7	-0.1	1.0	6.5	Taux de l'accroissement
Mozambique								**Mozambique**
At current prices	2 247	2 841	3 382	3 874	3 985	3 685	3 436	Aux prix courants
Per capita	141	173	201	226	227	206	189	Par habitant
At constant prices	2 919	3 117	3 462	3 899	4 193	4 257	4 809	Aux prix constants
Growth rates	3.3	6.8	11.1	12.6	7.5	1.5	13.0	Taux de l'accroissement
Myanmar [1]								**Myanmar** [1]
At current prices	25 066	26 681	28 189	29 586	31 281	32 988	34 572	Aux prix courants
Per capita	568	596	620	640	667	694	717	Par habitant
At constant prices	25 066	26 681	28 189	29 586	31 281	32 988	34 572	Aux prix constants
Growth rates	6.9	6.4	5.7	5.0	5.7	5.5	4.8	Taux de l'accroissement

19

Gross domestic product and gross domestic product per capita
In millions of US dollars[+] at current and constant 1990 prices; per capita US dollars; real rates of growth *[cont.]*

Produit intérieur brut et produit intérieur brut par habitant
En millions de dollars E.-U.[+] aux prix courants et constants de 1990 ; par habitant en dollars E.-U. ;
taux de l'accroissement réels *[suite]*

Country or area	1995	1996	1997	1998	1999	2000	2001	Pays ou zone
Namibia								**Namibie**
At current prices	3 503	3 491	3 636	3 399	3 385	3 458	3 163	Aux prix courants
Per capita	2 128	2 057	2 078	1 886	1 829	1 826	1 639	Par habitant
At constant prices	2 979	3 074	3 213	3 320	3 463	3 597	3 619	Aux prix constants
Growth rates	4.1	3.2	4.5	3.3	4.3	3.9	0.6	Taux de l'accroissement
Nauru								**Nauru**
At current prices	41	41	37	32	34	33	31	Aux prix courants
Per capita	3 772	3 716	3 290	2 773	2 837	2 698	2 500	Par habitant
At constant prices	36	34	31	31	30	30	29	Aux prix constants
Growth rates	-7.3	-7.3	-7.3	-1.9	-1.9	-1.0	-0.8	Taux de l'accroissement
Nepal								**Népal**
At current prices	4 224	4 391	4 836	4 560	5 012	5 317	5 447	Aux prix courants
Per capita	202	205	220	203	218	226	226	Par habitant
At constant prices	4 534	4 776	5 017	5 134	5 347	5 693	5 973	Aux prix constants
Growth rates	3.5	5.3	5.0	2.3	4.1	6.5	4.9	Taux de l'accroissement
Netherlands								**Pays-Bas**
At current prices	414 800	411 828	376 900	393 471	398 529	370 922	384 043	Aux prix courants
Per capita	26 832	26 480	24 096	25 017	25 203	23 332	24 029	Par habitant
At constant prices	326 973	336 911	349 843	365 060	379 646	392 229	397 180	Aux prix constants
Growth rates	3.0	3.0	3.8	4.3	4.0	3.3	1.3	Taux de l'accroissement
Netherlands Antilles								**Antilles néerlandaises**
At current prices	2 360	2 470	2 535	2 446	2 427	2 491	2 546	Aux prix courants
Per capita	11 518	11 900	12 080	11 555	11 370	11 569	11 725	Par habitant
At constant prices	2 115	2 142	2 130	2 086	2 046	1 999	1 999	Aux prix constants
Growth rates	0.3	1.3	-0.6	-2.1	-1.9	-2.3	0.0	Taux de l'accroissement
New Caledonia								**Nouvelle-Calédonie**
At current prices	3 628	3 607	3 176	3 425	3 817	3 350	3 460	Aux prix courants
Per capita	18 792	18 254	15 719	16 589	18 100	15 560	15 750	Par habitant
At constant prices	2 905	2 919	2 978	2 882	2 908	2 969	2 946	Aux prix constants
Growth rates	5.9	0.5	2.0	-3.2	0.9	2.1	-0.8	Taux de l'accroissement
New Zealand								**Nouvelle-Zélande**
At current prices	60 818	66 838	66 608	54 575	56 661	51 690	51 389	Aux prix courants
Per capita	16 874	18 328	18 077	14 674	15 104	13 662	13 470	Par habitant
At constant prices	50 792	52 569	53 333	53 568	56 220	57 721	59 732	Aux prix constants
Growth rates	4.1	3.5	1.5	0.4	5.0	2.7	3.5	Taux de l'accroissement
Nicaragua								**Nicaragua**
At current prices	1 836	1 921	1 969	2 068	2 213	2 433	2 561	Aux prix courants
Per capita	415	422	420	430	448	480	492	Par habitant
At constant prices	2 316	2 427	2 551	2 655	2 850	3 006	3 098	Aux prix constants
Growth rates	4.3	4.8	5.1	4.1	7.4	5.5	3.1	Taux de l'accroissement
Niger								**Niger**
At current prices	1 672	2 020	1 856	2 076	2 018	1 798	1 909	Aux prix courants
Per capita	185	216	192	207	195	167	171	Par habitant
At constant prices	2 703	2 809	2 876	3 160	3 109	3 101	3 285	Aux prix constants
Growth rates	1.9	3.9	2.4	9.9	-1.6	-0.3	5.9	Taux de l'accroissement
Nigeria								**Nigéria**
At current prices	90 327	73 321[1]	75 667[1]	77 407[1]	35 955	48 979	51 218	Aux prix courants
Per capita	906	714[1]	716[1]	713[1]	322	427	435	Par habitant
At constant prices	37 161	38 610[1]	39 845[1]	40 762[1]	41 903	43 495	45 322	Aux prix constants
Growth rates	2.6	3.9[1]	3.2[1]	2.3[1]	2.8	3.8	4.2	Taux de l'accroissement
Norway								**Norvège**
At current prices	147 975	159 217	157 117	150 048	158 099	166 906	169 780	Aux prix courants
Per capita	33 946	36 327	35 659	33 879	35 519	37 317	37 783	Par habitant
At constant prices	140 228	147 596	155 254	159 336	162 736	167 353	170 579	Aux prix constants
Growth rates	4.4	5.3	5.2	2.6	2.1	2.8	1.9	Taux de l'accroissement
Oman								**Oman**
At current prices	13 802	15 277	15 839	14 086	15 713	19 868	19 944	Aux prix courants
Per capita	6 165	6 601	6 634	5 726	6 202	7 615	7 421	Par habitant
At constant prices	15 533	15 984	16 971	17 429	17 390	18 343	20 050	Aux prix constants
Growth rates	4.8	2.9	6.2	2.7	-0.2	5.5	9.3	Taux de l'accroissement

19

Gross domestic product and gross domestic product per capita
In millions of US dollars[+] at current and constant 1990 prices; per capita US dollars; real rates of growth *[cont.]*
Produit intérieur brut et produit intérieur brut par habitant
En millions de dollars E.-U.[+] aux prix courants et constants de 1990 ; par habitant en dollars E.-U. ;
taux de l'accroissement réels *[suite]*

Country or area	1995	1996	1997	1998	1999	2000	2001	Pays ou zone
Pakistan								**Pakistan**
At current prices	67 321	67 624	65 440	65 380	64 073	63 679	60 177	Aux prix courants
Per capita	538	527	496	483	461	446	411	Par habitant
At constant prices	58 886	59 483	61 000	63 233	65 926	67 719	70 706	Aux prix constants
Growth rates	4.8	1.0	2.6	3.7	4.3	2.7	4.4	Taux de l'accroissement
Palau								**Palaos**
At current prices	128	138	152	187	176	204	237	Aux prix courants
Per capita	7 493	7 872	8 469	10 161	9 357	10 609	12 051	Par habitant
At constant prices	94	104	115	119	123	118	117	Aux prix constants
Growth rates	7.3	10.9	10.4	3.9	2.8	-3.9	-0.7	Taux de l'accroissement
Panama								**Panama**
At current prices	7 906	8 151	8 658	9 345	9 637	10 019	10 195	Aux prix courants
Per capita	2 961	2 991	3 114	3 294	3 331	3 396	3 391	Par habitant
At constant prices	6 942	7 137	7 457	7 781	8 031	8 228	8 306	Aux prix constants
Growth rates	1.8	2.8	4.5	4.4	3.2	2.5	0.9	Taux de l'accroissement
Papua New Guinea								**Papouasie-Nvl-Guinée**
At current prices	4 601	5 217	4 912	3 792	3 416	3 469	2 974	Aux prix courants
Per capita	978	1 081	992	747	656	650	545	Par habitant
At constant prices	4 871	5 248	5 043	5 265	5 220	5 156	5 059	Aux prix constants
Growth rates	-3.3	7.7	-3.9	4.4	-0.8	-1.2	-1.9	Taux de l'accroissement
Paraguay								**Paraguay**
At current prices	9 016	9 629	9 612	8 596	7 741	7 722	6 848	Aux prix courants
Per capita	1 867	1 944	1 892	1 650	1 450	1 412	1 222	Par habitant
At constant prices	6 171	6 251	6 413	6 387	6 417	6 395	6 569	Aux prix constants
Growth rates	4.7	1.3	2.6	-0.4	0.5	-0.4	2.7	Taux de l'accroissement
Peru								**Pérou**
At current prices	53 636	55 813	59 033	56 830	51 641	53 512	54 114	Aux prix courants
Per capita	2 250	2 301	2 392	2 263	2 022	2 062	2 053	Par habitant
At constant prices	40 496	41 506	44 306	44 070	44 488	45 879	45 925	Aux prix constants
Growth rates	8.6	2.5	6.7	-0.5	0.9	3.1	0.1	Taux de l'accroissement
Philippines								**Philippines**
At current prices	74 120	82 847	82 344	65 171	76 157	74 862	71 382	Aux prix courants
Per capita	1 084	1 186	1 154	895	1 026	989	925	Par habitant
At constant prices	49 325	52 208	54 915	54 599	56 453	58 928	60 824	Aux prix constants
Growth rates	4.7	5.8	5.2	-0.6	3.4	4.4	3.2	Taux de l'accroissement
Poland								**Pologne**
At current prices	127 054	143 847	144 040	159 280	155 054	163 900	183 031	Aux prix courants
Per capita	3 292	3 723	3 725	4 118	4 008	4 238	4 735	Par habitant
At constant prices	65 675	69 634	74 388	77 991	81 149	84 380	85 244	Aux prix constants
Growth rates	7.0	6.0	6.8	4.8	4.1	4.0	1.0	Taux de l'accroissement
Portugal								**Portugal**
At current prices	107 238	112 080	106 368	112 386	115 094	106 455	110 046	Aux prix courants
Per capita	10 814	11 284	10 687	11 268	11 514	10 629	10 968	Par habitant
At constant prices	77 766	80 522	83 712	87 547	90 874	94 225	95 772	Aux prix constants
Growth rates	4.3	3.5	4.0	4.6	3.8	3.7	1.6	Taux de l'accroissement
Puerto Rico								**Porto Rico**
At current prices	45 341	48 187	54 086	57 841	61 045	67 897	73 244	Aux prix courants
Per capita	12 309	12 980	14 461	15 356	16 099	17 794	19 083	Par habitant
At constant prices	39 374	41 296	43 580	45 927	47 033	49 656	51 864	Aux prix constants
Growth rates	2.3	4.9	5.5	5.4	2.4	5.6	4.4	Taux de l'accroissement
Qatar								**Qatar**
At current prices	8 138	9 059	11 298	10 255	12 393	17 760	17 127	Aux prix courants
Per capita	15 562	16 962	20 693	18 373	21 739	30 558	28 959	Par habitant
At constant prices	8 391	8 795	10 909	11 827	12 204	13 425	14 257	Aux prix constants
Growth rates	2.9	4.8	24.0	8.4	3.2	10.0	6.2	Taux de l'accroissement
Republic of Moldova								**République de Moldova**
At current prices	1 441	1 693	1 929	1 698	1 172	1 288	1 478	Aux prix courants
Per capita	332	391	447	395	273	301	346	Par habitant
At constant prices	7 415	6 979	7 094	6 630	6 407	6 542	6 939	Aux prix constants
Growth rates	-1.4	-5.9	1.6	-6.5	-3.4	2.1	6.1	Taux de l'accroissement

19

Gross domestic product and gross domestic product per capita
In millions of US dollars[+] at current and constant 1990 prices; per capita US dollars; real rates of growth *[cont.]*

Produit intérieur brut et produit intérieur brut par habitant
En millions de dollars E.-U.[+] aux prix courants et constants de 1990 ; par habitant en dollars E.-U. ;
taux de l'accroissement réels *[suite]*

Country or area	1995	1996	1997	1998	1999	2000	2001	Pays ou zone
Réunion								**Réunion**
At current prices	7 420	7 564	6 929	7 172	7 184	6 514	6 744	Aux prix courants
Per capita	11 177	11 191	10 075	10 253	10 102	9 014	9 188	Par habitant
At constant prices	5 998	6 169	6 360	6 553	6 750	6 952	7 119	Aux prix constants
Growth rates	2.7	2.9	3.1	3.0	3.0	3.0	2.4	Taux de l'accroissement
Romania								**Roumanie**
At current prices	35 478	35 315	35 286	42 115	35 592	36 866	39 714	Aux prix courants
Per capita	1 564	1 562	1 564	1 869	1 581	1 640	1 770	Par habitant
At constant prices	34 348	35 704	33 543	31 927	31 560	32 119	33 807	Aux prix constants
Growth rates	7.1	3.9	-6.1	-4.8	-1.2	1.8	5.3	Taux de l'accroissement
Russian Federation								**Fédération de Russie**
At current prices	337 890	419 005	428 464	282 435	193 617	259 721	309 947	Aux prix courants
Per capita	2 281	2 835	2 908	1 923	1 324	1 784	2 139	Par habitant
At constant prices	600 537	580 417	585 641	556 944	587 019	639 851	671 844	Aux prix constants
Growth rates	-4.1	-3.4	0.9	-4.9	5.4	9.0	5.0	Taux de l'accroissement
Rwanda								**Rwanda**
At current prices	1 283	1 389	1 869	2 009	1 896	1 749	1 653	Aux prix courants
Per capita	250	258	317	306	263	226	205	Par habitant
At constant prices	1 499	1 722	1 968	2 150	2 289	2 432	2 592	Aux prix constants
Growth rates	33.5	14.9	14.3	9.2	6.5	6.3	6.6	Taux de l'accroissement
Saint Kitts and Nevis								**Saint-Kitts-et-Nevis**
At current prices	231	246	275	287	305	330	344	Aux prix courants
Per capita	5 301	5 639	6 343	6 684	7 168	7 821	8 187	Par habitant
At constant prices	229	244	260	263	273	282	288	Aux prix constants
Growth rates	3.6	6.6	6.7	1.2	3.5	3.4	2.2	Taux de l'accroissement
Saint Lucia								**Sainte-Lucie**
At current prices	554	571	578	628	684	709	733	Aux prix courants
Per capita	3 955	4 042	4 057	4 370	4 730	4 863	4 994	Par habitant
At constant prices	461	475	471	493	510	513	516	Aux prix constants
Growth rates	1.1	2.9	-0.8	4.6	3.5	0.7	0.5	Taux de l'accroissement
St. Vincent-Grenadines								**St. Vincent-Grenadines**
At current prices	264	279	294	318	330	335	348	Aux prix courants
Per capita	2 308	2 423	2 539	2 731	2 816	2 847	2 940	Par habitant
At constant prices	230	232	239	253	264	268	268	Aux prix constants
Growth rates	8.5	1.1	3.0	5.8	4.1	1.5	0.2	Taux de l'accroissement
Samoa								**Samoa**
At current prices	200	226	244	223	232	236	245	Aux prix courants
Per capita	1 210	1 351	1 451	1 316	1 353	1 363	1 402	Par habitant
At constant prices	201	216	218	224	229	245	261	Aux prix constants
Growth rates	6.4	7.3	1.2	2.4	2.6	6.9	6.5	Taux de l'accroissement
San Marino								**Saint-Marin**
At current prices	707	794	751	807	853	775	787	Aux prix courants
Per capita	28 280	31 298	29 194	30 917	32 282	28 982	29 078	Par habitant
At constant prices	756	765	780	839	914	940	957	Aux prix constants
Growth rates	2.9	1.1	2.0	7.5	9.0	2.9	1.8	Taux de l'accroissement
Sao Tome and Principe								**Sao Tomé-et-Principe**
At current prices	45	45	44	41	47	46	48	Aux prix courants
Per capita	347	334	318	288	323	311	312	Par habitant
At constant prices	62	63	63	65	67	69	71	Aux prix constants
Growth rates	2.0	1.5	1.0	2.5	2.5	3.0	4.0	Taux de l'accroissement
Saudi Arabia								**Arabie saoudite**
At current prices	127 811	157 743	164 994	145 967	161 172	188 693	186 489	Aux prix courants
Per capita	6 738	8 077	8 191	7 019	7 507	8 520	8 169	Par habitant
At constant prices	118 515	120 167	123 304	126 786	125 761	131 870	133 434	Aux prix constants
Growth rates	0.5	1.4	2.6	2.8	-0.8	4.9	1.2	Taux de l'accroissement
Senegal								**Sénégal**
At current prices	4 476	4 653	4 376	4 655	4 751	4 374	4 611	Aux prix courants
Per capita	537	545	500	520	518	466	479	Par habitant
At constant prices	6 111	6 430	6 780	7 167	7 525	7 943	8 388	Aux prix constants
Growth rates	4.7	5.2	5.4	5.7	5.0	5.6	5.6	Taux de l'accroissement

19

Gross domestic product and gross domestic product per capita
In millions of US dollars[+] at current and constant 1990 prices; per capita US dollars; real rates of growth *[cont.]*
Produit intérieur brut et produit intérieur brut par habitant
En millions de dollars E.-U.[+] aux prix courants et constants de 1990 ; par habitant en dollars E.-U. ;
taux de l'accroissement réels *[suite]*

Country or area	1995	1996	1997	1998	1999	2000	2001	Pays ou zone
Serbia and Montenegro								**Serbie-et-Monténégro**
At current prices	25 772	16 064	19 309	15 552	17 842	11 278	10 630	Aux prix courants
Per capita	2 443	1 519	1 824	1 470	1 688	1 068	1 008	Par habitant
At constant prices	14 495	15 346	16 477	16 888	13 189	14 033	13 261	Aux prix constants
Growth rates	6.1	5.9	7.4	2.5	-21.9	6.4	-5.5	Taux de l'accroissement
Seychelles								**Seychelles**
At current prices	508	503	563	608	623	599	584	Aux prix courants
Per capita	6 778	6 640	7 354	7 868	7 983	7 603	7 335	Par habitant
At constant prices	424	445	497	534	545	553	558	Aux prix constants
Growth rates	-0.8	4.9	11.7	7.4	2.0	1.4	1.0	Taux de l'accroissement
Sierra Leone								**Sierra Leone**
At current prices	941	950	832	662	703	636	748	Aux prix courants
Per capita	230	231	201	157	164	144	164	Par habitant
At constant prices	492	522	431	427	392	407	429	Aux prix constants
Growth rates	-1.6	6.1	-17.6	-0.8	-8.1	3.8	5.4	Taux de l'accroissement
Singapore								**Singapour**
At current prices	83 089	90 951	94 476	82 229	82 639	92 744	85 647	Aux prix courants
Per capita	23 893	25 362	25 545	21 578	21 093	23 091	20 865	Par habitant
At constant prices	56 749	61 091	66 311	66 250	70 843	78 107	76 513	Aux prix constants
Growth rates	8.0	7.7	8.5	-0.1	6.9	10.3	-2.0	Taux de l'accroissement
Slovakia								**Slovaquie**
At current prices	19 147	20 506	21 080	21 996	20 205	19 741	20 459	Aux prix courants
Per capita	3 570	3 815	3 917	4 085	3 750	3 662	3 793	Par habitant
At constant prices	14 685	15 543	16 419	17 069	17 295	17 675	18 258	Aux prix constants
Growth rates	6.5	5.8	5.6	4.0	1.3	2.2	3.3	Taux de l'accroissement
Slovenia								**Slovénie**
At current prices	18 744	18 878	18 206	19 585	20 072	18 124	18 810	Aux prix courants
Per capita	9 419	9 460	9 117	9 816	10 075	9 109	9 463	Par habitant
At constant prices	16 881	17 478	18 274	18 967	19 955	20 875	21 494	Aux prix constants
Growth rates	4.1	3.5	4.6	3.8	5.2	4.6	3.0	Taux de l'accroissement
Solomon Islands								**Iles Salomon**
At current prices	365	403	409	358	380	338	342	Aux prix courants
Per capita	975	1 044	1 026	872	897	774	760	Par habitant
At constant prices	301	312	305	308	304	261	248	Aux prix constants
Growth rates	6.7	3.5	-2.3	1.1	-1.3	-14.0	-5.0	Taux de l'accroissement
Somalia								**Somalie**
At current prices	1 122	1 260	1 482	1 926	2 013	1 841	995	Aux prix courants
Per capita	153	167	191	239	240	211	110	Par habitant
At constant prices	684	711	692	709	724	746	768	Aux prix constants
Growth rates	0.0	3.9	-2.7	2.5	2.1	3.0	3.0	Taux de l'accroissement
South Africa								**Afrique du Sud**
At current prices	151 113	143 732	148 814	133 767	131 409	127 928	113 274	Aux prix courants
Per capita	3 692	3 450	3 515	3 114	3 020	2 907	2 550	Par habitant
At constant prices	116 928	121 964	125 192	126 146	128 819	133 147	136 109	Aux prix constants
Growth rates	3.1	4.3	2.6	0.8	2.1	3.4	2.2	Taux de l'accroissement
Spain								**Espagne**
At current prices	584 186	609 852	561 546	588 021	602 155	561 377	583 119	Aux prix courants
Per capita	14 628	15 211	13 947	14 541	14 829	13 775	14 266	Par habitant
At constant prices	549 563	562 957	585 623	611 071	636 723	663 360	681 098	Aux prix constants
Growth rates	2.8	2.4	4.0	4.3	4.2	4.2	2.7	Taux de l'accroissement
Sri Lanka								**Sri Lanka**
At current prices	13 013	14 053	15 208	15 800	15 698	16 280	15 634	Aux prix courants
Per capita	732	783	840	864	851	876	834	Par habitant
At constant prices	10 420	10 812	11 509	12 055	12 580	13 329	13 144	Aux prix constants
Growth rates	5.5	3.8	6.4	4.7	4.3	6.0	-1.4	Taux de l'accroissement
Sudan								**Soudan**
At current prices	13 950	8 259	10 642	9 918	9 697	11 549	12 099	Aux prix courants
Per capita	497	287	362	330	315	367	376	Par habitant
At constant prices	42 478	43 739	46 670	49 003	52 385	55 999	58 967	Aux prix constants
Growth rates	5.3	3.0	6.7	5.0	6.9	6.9	5.3	Taux de l'accroissement

19

Gross domestic product and gross domestic product per capita
In millions of US dollars[+] at current and constant 1990 prices; per capita US dollars; real rates of growth *[cont.]*

Produit intérieur brut et produit intérieur brut par habitant
En millions de dollars E.-U.[+] aux prix courants et constants de 1990 ; par habitant en dollars E.-U. ;
taux de l'accroissement réels *[suite]*

Country or area	1995	1996	1997	1998	1999	2000	2001	Pays ou zone
Suriname								**Suriname**
At current prices	519	758	848	1 015	883	886	842	Aux prix courants
Per capita	1 268	1 840	2 046	2 429	2 095	2 085	1 965	Par habitant
At constant prices	1 182	1 206	1 286	1 319	1 302	1 288	1 351	Aux prix constants
Growth rates	0.4	2.1	6.6	2.6	-1.3	-1.0	4.9	Taux de l'accroissement
Swaziland								**Swaziland**
At current prices	1 364	1 323	1 435	1 347	1 376	1 389	1 274	Aux prix courants
Per capita	1 453	1 378	1 460	1 340	1 341	1 330	1 204	Par habitant
At constant prices	1 007	1 046	1 087	1 121	1 161	1 185	1 206	Aux prix constants
Growth rates	3.8	3.9	3.8	3.2	3.5	2.1	1.8	Taux de l'accroissement
Sweden								**Suède**
At current prices	248 416	270 976	247 573	248 287	251 566	239 762	219 439	Aux prix courants
Per capita	28 143	30 620	27 947	28 027	28 406	27 072	24 766	Par habitant
At constant prices	254 263	257 575	263 842	273 451	285 960	298 422	301 786	Aux prix constants
Growth rates	4.0	1.3	2.4	3.6	4.6	4.4	1.1	Taux de l'accroissement
Switzerland								**Suisse**
At current prices	307 263	295 979	255 887	262 095	258 640	240 123	245 839	Aux prix courants
Per capita	43 165	41 416	35 725	36 556	36 063	33 478	34 274	Par habitant
At constant prices	227 551	228 276	232 207	237 674	241 311	248 933	251 126	Aux prix constants
Growth rates	0.5	0.3	1.7	2.4	1.5	3.2	0.9	Taux de l'accroissement
Syrian Arab Republic [1]								**Rép. arabe syrienne** [1]
At current prices	21 184	23 265	24 434	26 092	25 165	25 316	26 176	Aux prix courants
Per capita	1 451	1 553	1 590	1 656	1 558	1 529	1 543	Par habitant
At constant prices	21 184	23 265	24 434	26 092	25 165	25 316	26 176	Aux prix constants
Growth rates	7.0	9.8	5.0	6.8	-3.6	0.6	3.4	Taux de l'accroissement
Tajikistan								**Tadjikistan**
At current prices	568	1 044	922	1 320	1 087	870	1 059	Aux prix courants
Per capita	99	180	157	221	180	143	172	Par habitant
At constant prices	3 919	3 264	3 320	3 496	3 625	3 926	4 326	Aux prix constants
Growth rates	-12.4	-16.7	1.7	5.3	3.7	8.3	10.2	Taux de l'accroissement
Thailand								**Thaïlande**
At current prices	168 019	181 948	150 891	111 860	122 499	122 276	114 774	Aux prix courants
Per capita	2 905	3 112	2 554	1 874	2 031	2 007	1 865	Par habitant
At constant prices	129 105	136 724	134 849	120 676	126 024	131 867	134 255	Aux prix constants
Growth rates	9.2	5.9	-1.4	-10.5	4.4	4.6	1.8	Taux de l'accroissement
TFYR of Macedonia								**L'ex-R.y. Macédoine**
At current prices	4 475	4 413	3 699	3 504	3 432	3 290	3 227	Aux prix courants
Per capita	2 279	2 235	1 862	1 752	1 706	1 626	1 586	Par habitant
At constant prices	3 530	3 571	3 623	3 729	3 829	4 024	3 863	Aux prix constants
Growth rates	-1.1	1.2	1.4	2.9	2.7	5.1	-4.0	Taux de l'accroissement
Timor-Leste								**Timor-Leste**
At current prices	315	368	384	375	228	263	312	Aux prix courants
Per capita	375	448	487	502	319	374	438	Par habitant
At constant prices	312	345	360	352	355	372	428	Aux prix constants
Growth rates	9.4	10.8	4.1	-2.1	0.8	4.8	15.0	Taux de l'accroissement
Togo								**Togo**
At current prices	1 307	1 450	1 497	1 415	1 413	1 244	1 280	Aux prix courants
Per capita	338	363	363	331	319	273	273	Par habitant
At constant prices	1 666	1 733	1 808	1 768	1 819	1 785	1 835	Aux prix constants
Growth rates	8.8	4.0	4.3	-2.2	2.9	-1.9	2.8	Taux de l'accroissement
Tonga								**Tonga**
At current prices	156	170	164	147	148	148	130	Aux prix courants
Per capita	1 573	1 708	1 652	1 470	1 481	1 473	1 284	Par habitant
At constant prices	137	137	137	140	144	154	159	Aux prix constants
Growth rates	2.7	-0.4	0.1	2.4	3.1	6.7	3.0	Taux de l'accroissement
Trinidad and Tobago								**Trinité-et-Tobago**
At current prices	5 329	5 760	5 738	6 044	6 809	8 172	9 096	Aux prix courants
Per capita	4 227	4 543	4 504	4 725	5 302	6 340	7 031	Par habitant
At constant prices	5 430	5 710	6 103	6 571	7 271	8 090	8 301	Aux prix constants
Growth rates	4.0	5.2	6.9	7.7	10.6	11.3	2.6	Taux de l'accroissement

19

Gross domestic product and gross domestic product per capita
In millions of US dollars[+] at current and constant 1990 prices; per capita US dollars; real rates of growth *[cont.]*
Produit intérieur brut et produit intérieur brut par habitant
En millions de dollars E.-U.[+] aux prix courants et constants de 1990 ; par habitant en dollars E.-U. ;
taux de l'accroissement réels *[suite]*

Country or area	1995	1996	1997	1998	1999	2000	2001	Pays ou zone
Tunisia								**Tunisie**
At current prices	18 030	19 587	18 897	19 813	20 799	19 468	19 989	Aux prix courants
Per capita	2 015	2 158	2 056	2 129	2 210	2 045	2 077	Par habitant
At constant prices	14 885	15 950	16 817	17 621	18 689	19 566	20 516	Aux prix constants
Growth rates	2.3	7.2	5.4	4.8	6.1	4.7	4.9	Taux de l'accroissement
Turkey								**Turquie**
At current prices	169 319	181 465	189 879	200 307	184 858	199 263	148 018	Aux prix courants
Per capita	2 685	2 830	2 913	3 025	2 749	2 918	2 136	Par habitant
At constant prices	176 473	188 836	203 053	209 331	199 474	214 154	198 333	Aux prix constants
Growth rates	7.2	7.0	7.5	3.1	-4.7	7.4	-7.4	Taux de l'accroissement
Turkmenistan								**Turkménistan**
At current prices	5 879	2 380	2 681	2 862	3 857	4 932	6 512	Aux prix courants
Per capita	1 396	552	610	638	845	1 062	1 380	Par habitant
At constant prices	7 201	7 683	6 807	7 148	8 291	9 750	11 749	Aux prix constants
Growth rates	-7.2	6.7	-11.4	5.0	16.0	17.6	20.5	Taux de l'accroissement
Tuvalu								**Tuvalu**
At current prices	12	13	14	14	15	14	14	Aux prix courants
Per capita	1 234	1 376	1 414	1 394	1 469	1 409	1 342	Par habitant
At constant prices	11	12	13	15	15	15	16	Aux prix constants
Growth rates	-5.0	10.3	3.5	14.9	3.0	3.0	3.0	Taux de l'accroissement
Uganda								**Ouganda**
At current prices	6 184	6 267	6 676	6 691	6 277	5 699	5 779	Aux prix courants
Per capita	305	300	311	302	275	243	239	Par habitant
At constant prices	5 364	5 662	5 965	6 394	6 712	7 248	7 709	Aux prix constants
Growth rates	9.6	5.6	5.3	7.2	5.0	8.0	6.4	Taux de l'accroissement
Ukraine								**Ukraine**
At current prices	37 009	44 559	50 152	41 883	31 581	31 262	38 009	Aux prix courants
Per capita	718	869	985	829	630	629	771	Par habitant
At constant prices	120 018	107 964	104 738	102 702	102 536	108 577	118 602	Aux prix constants
Growth rates	-12.2	-10.0	-3.0	-1.9	-0.2	5.9	9.2	Taux de l'accroissement
United Arab Emirates								**Emirats arabes unis**
At current prices	42 280	47 403	48 745	45 899	49 775	53 309	57 041	Aux prix courants
Per capita	16 932	18 432	18 469	16 991	18 029	18 906	19 816	Par habitant
At constant prices	37 760	41 688	42 500	39 513	40 501	42 688	44 822	Aux prix constants
Growth rates	7.1	10.4	1.9	-7.0	2.5	5.4	5.0	Taux de l'accroissement
United Kingdom								**Royaume-Uni**
At current prices	1 134 941	1 189 179	1 327 798	1 423 237	1 460 155	1 437 995	1 429 665	Aux prix courants
Per capita	19 670	20 540	22 855	24 414	24 962	24 502	24 281	Par habitant
At constant prices	1 079 645	1 107 973	1 146 124	1 179 628	1 208 056	1 245 292	1 271 571	Aux prix constants
Growth rates	2.9	2.6	3.4	2.9	2.4	3.1	2.1	Taux de l'accroissement
United Rep. of Tanzania								**Rép.-Unie de Tanzanie**
At current prices	5 255	6 496	7 684	8 383	8 638	9 028	9 341	Aux prix courants
Per capita	170	205	236	251	253	259	263	Par habitant
At constant prices	4 592	4 785	4 943	5 190	5 467	5 604	5 935	Aux prix constants
Growth rates	3.6	4.2	3.3	5.0	5.3	2.5	5.9	Taux de l'accroissement
United States								**Etats-Unis**
At current prices	7 338 400	7 751 100	8 256 500	8 720 200	9 212 800	9 762 100	10 019 700	Aux prix courants
Per capita	27 185	28 400	29 923	31 261	32 672	34 253	34 788	Par habitant
At constant prices	6 472 153	6 705 518	7 005 384	7 307 807	7 610 494	7 898 012	7 918 033	Aux prix constants
Growth rates	2.7	3.6	4.5	4.3	4.1	3.8	0.3	Taux de l'accroissement
Uruguay								**Uruguay**
At current prices	19 298	20 515	21 704	22 371	13 798[1]	13 599[1]	13 144[1]	Aux prix courants
Per capita	5 996	6 327	6 644	6 796	4 160[1]	4 070[1]	3 905[1]	Par habitant
At constant prices	10 217	10 786	11 317	11 792	11 507[1]	11 341[1]	10 961[1]	Aux prix constants
Growth rates	-1.5	5.6	4.9	4.2	-2.4[1]	-1.4[1]	-3.3[1]	Taux de l'accroissement
Uzbekistan								**Ouzbékistan**
At current prices	10 169	13 954	15 526	14 987	17 081	13 759	10 577	Aux prix courants
Per capita	446	601	656	622	697	552	418	Par habitant
At constant prices	39 534	40 206	42 297	44 158	46 101	47 853	50 006	Aux prix constants
Growth rates	-0.9	1.7	5.2	4.4	4.4	3.8	4.5	Taux de l'accroissement

19

Gross domestic product and gross domestic product per capita
In millions of US dollars[+] at current and constant 1990 prices; per capita US dollars; real rates of growth *[cont.]*

Produit intérieur brut et produit intérieur brut par habitant
En millions de dollars E.-U.[+] aux prix courants et constants de 1990 ; par habitant en dollars E.-U. ;
taux de l'accroissement réels *[suite]*

Country or area	1995	1996	1997	1998	1999	2000	2001	Pays ou zone
Vanuatu								**Vanuatu**
At current prices	228	239	238	230	226	226	219	Aux prix courants
Per capita	1 323	1 350	1 308	1 229	1 180	1 148	1 085	Par habitant
At constant prices	208	213	216	221	215	224	222	Aux prix constants
Growth rates	0.0	2.5	1.5	2.2	-2.5	3.7	-0.5	Taux de l'accroissement
Venezuela								**Venezuela**
At current prices	77 389	73 063[1]	77 718[1]	77 850[1]	73 113[1]	75 478[1]	77 583[1]	Aux prix courants
Per capita	3 536	3 267[1]	3 402[1]	3 338[1]	3 072[1]	3 109[1]	3 134[1]	Par habitant
At constant prices	57 570	57 456[1]	61 117[1]	61 221[1]	57 495[1]	59 355[1]	61 010[1]	Aux prix constants
Growth rates	4.0	-0.2[1]	6.4[1]	0.2[1]	-6.1[1]	3.2[1]	2.8[1]	Taux de l'accroissement
Viet Nam								**Viet Nam**
At current prices	20 736	24 657	27 609	27 458	28 684	31 349	32 944	Aux prix courants
Per capita	285	333	368	361	372	401	416	Par habitant
At constant prices	9 600	10 496	11 352	12 006	12 579	13 429	14 348	Aux prix constants
Growth rates	9.5	9.3	8.2	5.8	4.8	6.8	6.8	Taux de l'accroissement
Yemen								**Yémen**
At current prices	12 514	7 821	6 875	6 250	7 274	8 532	8 030	Aux prix courants
Per capita	827	497	422	371	418	474	431	Par habitant
At constant prices	16 447	17 416	18 824	19 747	20 476	21 524	22 518	Aux prix constants
Growth rates	10.9	5.9	8.1	4.9	3.7	5.1	4.6	Taux de l'accroissement
Zambia								**Zambie**
At current prices	3 470	3 312	3 956	3 384	3 518	3 504	3 647	Aux prix courants
Per capita	370	345	403	337	343	336	345	Par habitant
At constant prices	3 687	3 931	4 060	3 985	4 073	4 219	4 437	Aux prix constants
Growth rates	-2.3	6.6	3.3	-1.9	2.2	3.6	5.2	Taux de l'accroissement
Zimbabwe								**Zimbabwe**
At current prices	7 127	8 553	8 503	6 054	5 494	7 437	8 970	Aux prix courants
Per capita	608	716	700	490	439	588	703	Par habitant
At constant prices	9 306	10 271	10 546	10 850	10 774	9 929	9 204	Aux prix constants
Growth rates	0.2	10.4	2.7	2.9	-0.7	-7.8	-7.3	Taux de l'accroissement

Source:
United Nations Statistics Division, New York, the national accounts database.

Source:
Organisation des Nations Unies, Division de statistique, New York, la base de données sur les comptes nationaux.

+ In converting estimates expressed in national currency units into United States dollars, the prevailing annual average of market exchange rates as reported by the IMF has been used. For countries that are non-members of the IMF, the conversion rate used is usually the annual average of United Nations operational rates of exchange.

+ Les taux de conversion utilisés pour exprimer les chiffres nationaux en dollars des États-Unis correspondent à la moyenne annuelle des taux de change du marché donnés par le FMI. Pour les pays qui ne sont pas membres du FMI, on utilise généralement la moyenne annuelle des taux de change pratiqués pour les opérations de l'ONU.

It should be noted that the international comparability of data expressed in United States dollars between countries may not be entirely scientific because the exchange rates applied may, in practice, only be used for the conversion of a limited number of external transactions and may not be relevant for the much larger portion of GDP covering domestic transactions.

Il est à noter que la comparabilité internationale des données exprimées en dollars des États-Unis peut ne pas être strictement scientifique car les taux de change appliqués peuvent, dans la pratique, n'être utilisés que pour convertir un nombre restreint de transactions avec l'étranger et ne pas être pertinents pour la partie plus importante du PIB qui concerne les transactions nationales.

1   Price-adjusted rates of exchange (PARE) were used due to large distortions in the levels of per capita GDP with the use of IMF market exchange rates.
2   Data refer to the Vatican City State.

1   On a utilisé des taux de change corrigés des prix, car importantes dans les montants du produit intérieur brut par habitant.
2   Les données se réfèrent à la Cité du Vatican.

20

Expenditure on gross domestic product in current prices
Percentage distribution
Dépenses imputées au produit intérieur brut aux prix courants
Répartition en pourcentage

			% of GDP – en % du PIB					
Region, country or area Région, pays ou zone	Year Année	GDP in current prices (Mil. nat.cur.) PIB aux prix courants (Millions monnaie nat.)	Govt. final consumption expenditure Consom. finale des admin. publiques	Household final consumption expenditure Consom. finale des ménages	Changes in inventories Variation des stocks	Gross fixed capital formation Formation brute de capital fixe	Exports of goods and services Exportations de biens et services	Imports of goods and services Importations de biens et services
Albania	1988	17 001	9.5	63.3	-2.6	31.9	-2.0[1]	...
Albanie	1989	18 674	8.8	61.0	0.4	31.3	-1.5[1]	...
	1990	16 812	10.2	72.7	-10.1	34.6	-7.4[1]	...
Algeria	1999	3 248 198	16.7	51.4	2.2	24.3	28.1	22.7
Algérie	2000	4 098 817	13.7	41.8	1.6	20.8	42.3	20.2
	2001	4 235 620	14.7	43.6	4.9	22.7	36.7	22.7
Angola	1988	239 640	32.9	45.5	0.0	14.6	32.8	25.8
Angola	1989	278 866	28.9	48.2	0.9	11.2	33.8	23.1
	1990	308 062	28.5	44.7	0.6	11.1	38.9	23.8
Anguilla	1999	283	15.0	86.5	...	43.8	68.5	113.5
Anguilla	2000	292	20.2	86.6	...	43.5	64.4	114.7
	2001	298	21.5	71.5	...	30.9	67.4	91.3
Antigua and Barbuda	1984	468	18.5	69.8	0.0	23.6	73.7	85.6
Antigua-et-Barbuda	1985	541	18.3	71.5	0.0	28.0	75.7	93.5
	1986	642	18.9	69.7	0.0	36.1	75.2	99.9
Argentina[2]	1999	283 522[3]	13.7	70.1	...	18.0[4]	9.8	11.5
Argentine[2]	2000	284 204[3]	13.8	69.3	...	16.2[4]	10.9	11.5
	2001	268 697[3]	14.2	68.9	...	14.2[4]	11.4	10.2
Armenia[2]	1999	987 444[3]	11.9	96.4[5]	1.9[6]	16.4	20.8	49.8
Arménie[2]	2000	1 031 338[3]	11.8	97.1[5]	0.2[6]	18.4	23.4	50.5
	2001	1 175 487[3]	10.7	94.2[5]	1.7[6]	17.0	25.6	45.9
Aruba[2]	1999	3 087	22.4	52.4	2.0	26.8	80.9	84.4
Aruba[2]	2000	3 326	19.9	49.9	1.1	24.1	74.8	69.8
	2001	3 381	22.7	52.7	1.1	20.0	72.1	68.6
Australia +[2]	1999	628 621	18.2	59.6	0.4	24.0	20.0	22.3
Australie +[2]	2000	669 307	18.1	60.3	0.0	21.5	22.9	22.8
	2001	712 980[3]	17.9	60.1	0.1	22.2	21.4	21.6
Austria[2]	2000	207 037[3]	19.2	56.7[5]	0.4[6]	23.9	50.2	50.8
Autriche[2]	2001	211 857[3]	19.1	57.4[5]	0.0[6]	23.2	52.5	52.5
	2002	216 831[3]	19.1	57.6[5]	0.0[6]	21.7	52.1	50.9
Azerbaijan[2]	2000	23 590 500[3]	15.2	64.4[5]	-2.5[6]	23.1	40.2	38.4
Azerbaïdjan[2]	2001	26 578 000	13.6	61.5[5]	-2.2[6]	22.9	41.5	37.3
	2002	29 602 000[3]	12.8	60.6[5]	-2.0[6]	34.8	43.8	51.2
Bahamas[2]	1993	2 854[3]	14.3	69.6	1.2	18.4	53.2	51.6
Bahamas[2]	1994	3 053[3]	16.7	67.3	1.0	20.1	51.4	53.5
	1995	3 069[3]	15.8	67.7	0.5	22.7	54.7	59.3
Bahrain	1998	2 325	20.8	57.1	7.4	14.0	64.6	63.9
Bahreïn	1999	2 489	20.8	55.4	-4.8	13.6	77.2	62.2
	2000	2 996	17.6	47.1	-2.6	13.5	88.1	63.7
Bangladesh +[2]	1999	2 370 856[3]	4.6	77.5	...	23.0	14.0	19.2
Bangladesh +[2]	2000	2 535 464[3]	4.5	77.5	...	23.0	15.4	21.5
	2001	2 714 142[3]	4.4	77.6	...	23.2	16.9	22.8
Barbados	1999	4 965	20.7	65.5	0.6	18.8	51.3	56.9
Barbade	2000	5 183	20.9	67.3	0.1	18.1	49.8	56.3
	2001	5 093	22.2	64.5	-0.3	16.5	50.9	53.7
Belarus[2]	1999	3026060000[3,7]	19.5	58.6[5]	-2.6[6]	26.3	59.2	61.6
Bélarus[2]	#2000	9 133 800[3,8]	19.5	56.9[5]	0.2[6]	25.2	69.2	72.4
	2001	17 173 200[3,8]	21.6	57.6[5]	1.1[6]	22.7	66.7	70.3
Belgium[2]	2000	247 469	21.2	54.1[5]	0.4	21.2	85.5	82.3
Belgique[2]	2001	254 282	21.7	54.5[5]	-0.4	20.8	85.4	81.8
	2002	260 744	21.4	55.2[5]	-0.2	19.6	82.3	78.3

20

Expenditure on gross domestic product in current prices
Percentage distribution [cont.]

Dépenses imputées au produit intérieur brut aux prix courants

Répartition en pourcentage *[suite]*

			% of GDP – en % du PIB					
Region, country or area Région, pays ou zone	Year Année	GDP in current prices (Mil. nat.cur.) PIB aux prix courants (Millions monnaie nat.)	Govt. final consumption expenditure Consom. finale des admin. publiques	Household final consumption expenditure Consom. finale des ménages	Changes in inventories Variation des stocks	Gross fixed capital formation Formation brute de capital fixe	Exports of goods and services Exportations de biens et services	Imports of goods and services Importations de biens et services
Belize [2] Belize [2]	1998	1 258	17.4	67.3	3.1	21.3	52.9	62.1
	1999	1 377	17.1	65.1	3.0	26.5	51.3	63.2
	2000	1 514	15.3	68.4	3.2	31.0	48.8	66.7
Benin Bénin	1989	479 200	13.0	81.4	-0.6	12.5	18.3	24.5
	1990	502 300	13.2	80.4	0.8	13.4	20.4	28.2
	1991	535 500	12.0	82.6	0.9	13.6	22.0	31.1
Bermuda + [2] Bermudes + [2]	1998	3 053	10.6	60.8[5]	0.6[6]	19.3	47.4	38.7
	1999	3 272	10.8	61.2[5]	0.6[6]	19.4	47.0	39.0
	2000	3 397	10.8	61.2[5]	0.6[6]	19.4	47.0	39.0
Bhutan Bhoutan	1998	16 337	20.2	57.1	0.3	37.9	31.5	47.0
	1999	19 123	22.3	52.6	0.6	42.5	29.9	47.9
	2000	21 698	20.4	52.2	0.2	43.5	29.8	46.1
Bolivia Bolivie	1999	48 156	14.8	76.8	-0.3	19.1	16.9	27.3
	2000	51 667	14.3	77.4	-0.4	17.6	17.8	26.7
	2001	52 652	14.8	78.4	-1.1	14.1	18.3	24.5
Botswana + [2] Botswana + [2]	1999	21 524	30.6	32.2[5]	7.7	29.1	46.7	46.3
	2000	25 363	29.7	30.9[5]	-8.1	26.6	60.4	39.4
	2001	29 353	31.6	29.6[5]	-7.1	22.8	56.2	33.2
Brazil [2] Brésil [2]	1999	973 846	19.1	62.3	1.3	18.9	10.3	11.8
	2000	1 101 255	19.1	60.9	2.3	19.3	10.7	12.2
	2001	1 200 060	19.2	60.6	1.7	19.4	13.2	14.2
British Virgin Islands [2] Iles Vierges britanniques [2]	1997	512	12.3	43.2	0.4	25.2	102.9	84.0
	1998	593	12.0	41.0	-2.0	26.3	102.7	79.8
	1999	662	11.0	40.6	-0.8	24.6	104.4	80.1
Brunei Darussalam Brunéi Darussalam	1982	9 126	10.0	5.5	0.0	12.4	89.3	17.2
	1983	8 124	11.4	9.5	0.0	9.9	88.3	19.0
	1984	8 069	31.1	-5.6	0.0	6.5	84.5	16.5
Bulgaria Bulgarie	#1999	23 790	16.6	71.3[5]	2.8	15.1	44.6	50.3
	2000	26 753	17.9	69.2[5]	2.6	15.7	55.7	61.1
	2001	29 618[3]	17.6	69.6[5]	2.6	17.8	55.7	63.2
Burkina Faso Burkina Faso	1991	811 676	14.7	76.2	1.4	21.8	11.4	25.4
	1992	812 590	14.4	76.2	-0.2	21.3	9.7	21.4
	1993	832 349	14.4	77.2	0.8	20.4	9.7	22.5
Burundi Burundi	1990	196 656	19.5	83.0	-0.6	16.4	8.0	26.2
	1991	211 898	17.0	83.9	-0.5	18.1	10.0	28.5
	1992	226 384	15.6	82.9	0.4	21.1	9.0	29.0
Cambodia [2] Cambodge [2]	1999	12 587 090[3]	5.3	88.0[5]	1.4	14.4	38.0	46.1
	2000	12 931 530[3]	5.7	84.5[5]	-1.7	15.1	49.3	51.4
	2001	13 364 930[3]	6.0	82.5[5]	2.0	15.9	50.6	53.5
Cameroon + [2] Cameroun + [2]	1996	4 793 080	79.8[9]	...	-0.2	13.1	24.7	17.4
	1997	5 370 580	82.0[9]	...	0.1	12.8	24.0	19.0
	1998	5 744 000	82.9[9]	...	-0.1	13.5	24.0	20.4
Canada [2] Canada [2]	1999	965 440[3]	19.1	56.7[5]	0.5	20.2	43.5	40.1
	2000	1 049 448[3]	18.6	55.3[5]	0.8	20.0	46.0	40.8
	2001	1 075 576	18.9	56.3[5]	-0.6	20.1	43.8	38.6
Cape Verde Cap-Vert	1993	29 078	23.3	83.5	-1.0	40.0	18.0	63.8
	1994	33 497	21.6	83.0	0.7	43.7	18.4	67.3
	1995	37 705	22.8	86.3	2.0	38.8	16.6	66.5
Cayman Islands Iles Caïmanes	1989	474[3]	14.1	65.0	...	23.2	60.1	68.8
	1990	590[3]	14.2	62.5	...	21.4	64.1	58.5
	1991	616[3]	15.1	62.5	...	21.8	58.9	52.8

20

Expenditure on gross domestic product in current prices
Percentage distribution [cont.]
Dépenses imputées au produit intérieur brut aux prix courants
Répartition en pourcentage [suite]

			% of GDP – en % du PIB					
Region, country or area Région, pays ou zone	Year Année	GDP in current prices (Mil. nat.cur.) PIB aux prix courants (Millions monnaie nat.)	Govt. final consumption expenditure Consom. finale des admin. publiques	Household final consumption expenditure Consom. finale des ménages	Changes in inventories Variation des stocks	Gross fixed capital formation Formation brute de capital fixe	Exports of goods and services Exportations de biens et services	Imports of goods and services Importations de biens et services
Central African Rep. Rép. centrafricaine	1986	388 647	15.6	82.1	-0.1	12.9	18.2	28.6
	1987	360 942	17.5	80.6	-0.2	12.9	17.8	28.6
	1988	376 748	16.1	80.7	0.7	9.8	17.7	25.1
Chad Tchad	1999	915 000[10]	16.8	28.5	-2.6	14.0	18.1	40.7
	2000	928 000[10]	17.6	24.6	2.2	15.5	18.1	44.9
	2001	1 088 000[10]	17.3	24.5	2.1	38.7	16.9	62.0
Chile[2] Chili[2]	1999	37 164 386	12.3	64.4[5]	0.3	21.1	29.3	27.4
	2000	40 436 215	12.3	63.8	1.5	21.0	31.7	30.3
	2001	42 191 778	12.7	64.5	-0.7	21.4	34.7	32.7
China[2] Chine[2]	1999	8 206 750[3]	12.7	47.9	1.5	35.9	22.0	19.3
	2000	8 944 220[3]	13.1	48.0	-0.1	36.5	25.9	23.4
	2001	9 593 330[3.10]	13.6	47.9	0.7	38.4	25.8	23.5
China, Hong Kong SAR[2] Chine, Hong Kong RAS[2]	1999	1 246 134	9.6	59.4[5]	-0.9	26.1	130.7	125.0
	2000	1 288 338	9.3	57.8[5]	1.1	27.0	146.7	141.9
	2001	1 278 995	10.1	58.3[5]	-0.2	26.7	141.1	136.0
China, Macao SAR[2] Chine, Macao RAS[2]	1999	49 021	13.8	41.6[5]	0.2	17.7	80.0	53.3
	2000	49 742	11.9	41.0[5]	0.1	11.9	93.9	58.8
	2001	49 802	12.2	41.4[5]	0.1	10.4	97.7	61.9
Colombia[2] Colombie[2]	1999	151 565 005	22.2	64.4[5]	-0.4[6]	13.2	18.3	17.8
	2000	173 729 806	21.8	64.6[5]	0.6[6]	12.7	19.9	19.6
	2001	189 525 312	87.4[9]	...	...	14.5[4]	18.9	20.8
Comoros Comores	1989	63 397	27.6	77.8	4.6	14.4	14.9	39.3
	1990	66 370	25.7	79.7	8.0	12.2	11.7	37.3
	1991	69 248	25.3	80.9	4.0	12.3	15.5	38.0
Congo Congo	1987	690 523	20.6	56.6[5]	-1.1	20.9	41.7	38.6
	1988	658 964	21.1	60.1[5]	-1.0	19.6	40.6	40.4
	1989	773 524	18.7	52.8	-0.5	16.4	47.6	35.0
Costa Rica[2] Costa Rica[2]	1999	4 512 763	12.5	64.6	-0.8	18.0	51.6	45.9
	2000	4 917 764	13.3	66.9	-0.7	17.8	48.5	45.7
	2001	5 387 526	14.3	68.5	2.0	18.1	41.6	44.5
Côte d'Ivoire Côte d'Ivoire	1998	7 457 508	13.7	65.1[5]	0.6	14.3	41.3	34.9
	1999	7 734 000	14.6	63.2[5]	-1.3	14.5	39.7	30.8
	2000	7 605 000	15.5	67.2[5]	-1.0	12.3	39.8	33.8
Croatia[2] Croatie[2]	1999	141 579	26.5	58.9[5]	-0.3	23.3	40.9	49.3
	2000	152 519	24.8	60.1[5]	-1.6	21.8	47.1	52.3
	2001	162 909	22.4	61.2[5]	-1.0	22.9	49.1	54.7
Cuba Cuba	1998	23 901[3]	23.6	71.6	-2.3	10.2	15.2	18.0
	1999	25 504[3]	23.5	70.9	-1.6	10.4	16.0	18.7
	2000	27 635[3]	23.1	68.9	-1.0	10.8	15.7	18.2
Cyprus Chypre	1999	5 019[3]	17.1	66.3	1.2	18.1	44.6	47.6
	2000	5 487[3]	16.5	68.6	1.4	17.7	46.5	52.3
	2001	5 865[3]	17.3	68.7	1.2	17.3	46.9	51.8
Czech Republic[2] République tchèque[2]	2000	1 984 833	19.6	54.1[5]	1.4	28.3	69.8	73.2
	2001	2 175 238	20.0	53.1[5]	1.8	27.7	70.8	73.5
	2002	2 275 609	21.4	52.8[5]	1.8	26.3	65.2	67.5
Dem. Rep. of the Congo Rép. dém. du Congo	1985	147 263	11.6	47.8	7.7	21.7	72.2	61.1
	1986	203 416	19.0	48.1	8.3	23.0	61.4	59.6
	1987	326 946	22.4	77.1	5.3	20.3	63.2	88.2
Denmark[2] Danemark[2]	2000	1 280 784	25.3	47.5[5]	0.6[6]	20.6	44.3	38.3
	2001	1 325 272	25.9	47.3[5]	0.3[6]	20.1	45.1	38.6
	2002	1 358 297	26.1	48.2[5]	0.3[6]	19.5	44.2	38.3

20

Expenditure on gross domestic product in current prices

Percentage distribution [cont.]

Dépenses imputées au produit intérieur brut aux prix courants

Répartition en pourcentage *[suite]*

Region, country or area Région, pays ou zone	Year Année	GDP in current prices (Mil. nat.cur.) PIB aux prix courants (Millions monnaie nat.)	Govt. final consumption expenditure Consom. finale des admin. publiques	Household final consumption expenditure Consom. finale des ménages	Changes in inventories Variation des stocks	Gross fixed capital formation Formation brute de capital fixe	Exports of goods and services Exportations de biens et services	Imports of goods and services Importations de biens et services
Djibouti	1996	88 233	33.6	64.6	-0.9	19.3	40.3	56.8
Djibouti	1997	87 289	34.7	59.3	0.2	21.4	42.2	57.8
	1998	88 461	29.0	67.3	0.2	23.2	43.4	63.0
Dominica	1999	723	22.0	60.6	0.0	27.7	57.9	68.2
Dominique	2000	728	22.6	63.0	0.0	27.6	54.6	67.8
	2001	711	22.6	64.9	0.0	25.2	51.1	63.8
Dominican Republic[2]	1994	179 130	4.6	76.8	3.4	17.9	37.4	40.2
Rép. dominicaine[2]	1995	209 646	4.3	78.6	3.3	16.1	34.5	36.7
	1996	232 993	4.7	81.4	3.6	17.3	18.1	25.1
Ecuador[2]	1999	16 674[11]	12.5	66.2	-2.2	17.0	31.5	25.0
Equateur[2]	2000	15 934[11]	9.8	64.0	-0.4	20.5	37.1	31.0
	2001	21 024[11]	10.1	68.9	4.1	21.6	26.7	31.4
Egypt +	1999	340 100	...	88.4[5]	0.6	17.6	16.2	22.8
Egypte +	2000	358 700	...	87.8[5]	0.5	16.5	17.5	22.3
	2001	381 700	...	88.6[5]	0.4	15.7	17.8	22.6
El Salvador	1999	109 066	10.0	85.9	0.4	16.1	24.9	37.3
El Salvador	2000	114 967	9.9	88.3	0.0	16.9	27.3	42.5
	2001	120 215	10.0	87.9	-0.5	16.5	28.9	42.9
Equatorial Guinea	1989	42 256	22.2	54.3	0.0	19.6	40.4	36.6
Guinée équatoriale	1990	44 349	15.3	53.2	-3.1	34.6	59.7	59.7
	1991	46 429	14.4	75.9	-2.3	18.4	28.4	34.7
Estonia[2]	1999	76 327[3]	23.4	58.2[5]	-0.4[6]	24.9	77.2	82.1
Estonie[2]	2000	87 236[3]	20.8	56.4[5]	2.4[6]	25.4	93.8	97.9
	2001	96 571[3]	20.3	56.4[5]	1.6[6]	26.1	90.6	94.4
Ethiopia +	1997	41 465	10.9	79.2	...	19.1	16.2	23.3
Ethiopie +	1998	44 896	14.2	78.4	...	19.0	16.2	26.4
	1999	48 949	16.0	81.4	...	20.8	14.5	30.2
Fiji	1998	3 154[3]	18.0	67.3	1.3	12.7	58.2	60.8
Fidji	1999	3 665[3]	16.5	58.5	1.1	12.7	60.3	63.7
	2000	3 518[3]	17.8	62.4	1.1	9.9	60.2	64.5
Finland[2]	2000	130 234[3]	20.7	49.5[5]	0.7	19.9	43.0	33.7
Finlande[2]	2001	135 791[3]	20.8	49.9[5]	0.4	20.4	39.8	31.6
	2002	139 734[3]	21.6	50.3[5]	-0.3	19.9	38.1	30.2
France[2]	2000	1 420 138	23.2	54.4[5]	0.8[6]	20.1	28.5	27.3
France[2]	2001	1 475 584	23.2	54.7[5]	-0.1[6]	20.0	27.9	26.3
	2002	1 520 804	23.9	54.8[5]	...	19.3[4]	27.1	25.0
French Guiana	1990	6 526	35.0	64.4	-0.2	47.8	67.3	114.3
Guyane française	1991	7 404	34.4	60.1	1.5	40.5	81.1	117.6
	1992	7 976	34.2	58.9	1.5	30.8	65.4	90.8
French Polynesia	1991	305 211	39.3	63.9	-0.2	18.4	9.3	30.7
Polynésie française	1992	314 265[10]	47.8	63.9	0.0	16.7	8.3	27.4
	1993	329 266	38.3	61.5	-0.2	16.2	10.5	26.4
Gabon	1987	1 020 600	23.7	48.6	...	26.7[4]	41.3	40.3
Gabon	1988	1 013 600	21.8	48.1	...	36.2[4]	37.3	43.4
	1989	1 168 066	18.4	48.4	...	23.3[4]	50.3	40.3
Gambia +	1991	2 920	13.0	83.7	...	18.2	45.3	60.1
Gambie +	1992	3 078	13.2	81.2	...	22.4	45.2	61.9
	1993	3 243	15.1	78.1	...	27.1	36.6	56.9
Georgia[2]	1999	5 666[3]	10.3	84.0[5]	1.2	18.1	19.1	38.1
Géorgie[2]	2000	6 016[3]	8.4	89.5[5]	1.3	16.9	23.1	39.8
	2001	6 617[3]	9.3	84.6[5]	1.2	17.4	23.0	38.9

20

Expenditure on gross domestic product in current prices
Percentage distribution [cont.]
Dépenses imputées au produit intérieur brut aux prix courants
Répartition en pourcentage *[suite]*

Region, country or area Région, pays ou zone	Year Année	GDP in current prices (Mil. nat.cur.) PIB aux prix courants (Millions monnaie nat.)	Govt. final consumption expenditure Consom. finale des admin. publiques	Household final consumption expenditure Consom. finale des ménages	Changes in inventories Variation des stocks	Gross fixed capital formation Formation brute de capital fixe	Exports of goods and services Exportations de biens et services	Imports of goods and services Importations de biens et services
				% of GDP – en % du PIB				
Germany [2] Allemagne [2]	2000	2 030 000	19.1	58.7[5]	0.3[6]	21.6	33.8	33.4
	2001	2 071 200	19.0	59.5[5]	-0.5[6]	20.1	35.1	33.2
	2002	2 108 200	19.1	58.9[5]	-0.3[6]	18.4	35.5	31.6
Ghana Ghana	1994	5 205 200	13.7	73.7	1.4	22.6	22.5	33.9
	1995	7 752 600	12.1	76.2	-1.1	21.1	24.5	32.8
	1996	11 339 200	12.0	76.1	0.9	20.6	24.9	34.5
Greece [2] Grèce [2]	2000	121 628	15.7	69.5[5]	-0.1	22.6	24.1	31.8
	2001	130 927	15.3	68.4[5]	0.1	22.8	22.7	29.3
	2002	141 132	15.8	67.3[5]	0.1	23.1	20.5	26.8
Grenada Grenade	1990	541	20.5	64.9	3.1	38.9	44.4	71.8
	1991	567	18.8	69.2	3.7	40.0	45.4	77.1
	1992	578	19.9	66.5	2.1	32.4	38.6	59.4
Guadeloupe Guadeloupe	1990	15 201	30.8	92.8	1.1	33.9	4.9	63.5
	1991	16 415	31.0	87.3	1.0	33.0	6.1	58.4
	1992	17 972	29.3	84.1	1.3	27.8	4.5	47.0
Guatemala Guatemala	1996	95 479	5.1	87.0	-0.6	13.3	17.8	22.6
	1997	107 943	4.9	86.9	-1.0	14.8	17.9	23.6
	1998	121 548	6.2	86.6	-0.2	15.7	17.9	26.2
Guinea-Bissau Guinée-Bissau	1990	510 094	11.4	100.9	0.9	13.8	12.0	39.0
	1991	854 985	12.6	100.6	0.9	10.4	13.4	38.0
	1992	1 530 010	10.7	111.1	...	26.5[4]	8.2	56.5
Guyana Guyana	1999	123 665[10]	24.2	43.8	...	38.5[4]	-10.1[1]	...
	2000	130 013	27.5	49.9	...	38.5[4]	...	...
	2001	133 403	22.9	55.5	...	38.5[4]	...	...
Haiti + Haïti +	1997	51 578	103.1[9]	...	...	12.5	11.5	27.1
	1998	59 055	102.5[9]	...	...	12.9	13.2	28.6
	1999	66 425	101.8[9]	...	...	13.1	13.3	28.2
Honduras Honduras	1998	70 438	10.1	67.0	2.7	28.2	46.1	54.1
	1999	77 095	11.3	68.8	4.8	29.8	41.3	56.0
	2000	87 523	12.0	70.0	4.6	27.2	42.3	56.1
Hungary [2] Hongrie [2]	2000	13 172 293	20.8	52.2[5]	6.7	24.1	74.9	78.7
	2001	14 849 622	21.4	53.0[5]	3.5	23.6	74.4	75.9
	2002	16 980 065	24.7	53.5[5]	1.7	22.3	64.5	66.7
Iceland [2] Islande [2]	2000	658 247	23.8	59.2[5]	0.4	23.8	35.2	42.3
	2001	740 747	23.6	55.1[5]	-0.3	22.0	41.0	41.5
	2002	774 418	25.1	54.2[5]	0.0	18.9	39.7	37.9
India + Inde +	1998	17 409 350[3]	12.3	65.1	-0.1	21.5	11.2	12.9
	1999	19 296 410[3]	12.9	65.4	1.7	21.6	11.8	13.8
	2000	20 879 880[3]	13.2	64.2	1.0	21.9	13.9	14.7
Indonesia Indonésie	1999	1099732000	6.6	73.9[5]	-8.8	20.1	35.5	27.4
	2000	1282018000	7.1	67.7[5]	-6.3	21.0	42.4	31.7
	2001	1490974000	7.4	67.4[5]	-3.9	20.5	41.1	32.6
Iran (Islamic Rep. of) + [2] Iran (Rép. islamique d') + [2]	1999	430 990 500[3]	14.2	51.2[5]	-2.4	30.5	21.7	14.8
	2000	568 799 400[3]	14.0	46.1[5]	1.5	30.2	23.2	17.1
	2001	665 656 300[3]	14.6	45.8[5]	2.5	31.1	20.0	18.4
Iraq Iraq	1998	4 570 100	7.9	79.0	...	3.8[4]	...	...
	1999	6 809 790	6.4	61.0	...	3.9[4]	...	...
	2000	7 398 604	6.2	59.7	...	7.3[4]	...	...
Ireland [2] Irlande [2]	1999	89 770[3]	13.9	48.1[5]	0.5[6]	23.7	88.0	74.2
	2000	102 910[3]	13.8	47.6[5]	0.6[6]	24.1	98.0	84.4
	2001	114 479[3]	14.7	46.8[5]	0.3[6]	23.3	98.2	83.4

20

Expenditure on gross domestic product in current prices
Percentage distribution [cont.]

Dépenses imputées au produit intérieur brut aux prix courants

Répartition en pourcentage *[suite]*

Region, country or area Région, pays ou zone	Year Année	GDP in current prices (Mil. nat.cur.) PIB aux prix courants (Millions monnaie nat.)	Govt. final consumption expenditure Consom. finale des admin. publiques	Household final consumption expenditure Consom. finale des ménages	Changes in inventories Variation des stocks	Gross fixed capital formation Formation brute de capital fixe	Exports of goods and services Exportations de biens et services	Imports of goods and services Importations de biens et services
				% of GDP – en % du PIB				
Israel [2] Israël [2]	1999 2000 2001	446 760 487 013 491 499	27.2 26.5 27.9	53.9[5] 53.6[5] 55.3[5]	1.7 1.2 2.2	20.6 19.0 17.8	34.3 38.6 33.9	37.8 39.0 37.2
Italy [2] Italie [2]	2000 2001 2002	1 166 548 1 220 147 1 258 349	18.3 18.8 18.8	60.5[5] 60.0[5] 60.2[5]	0.4[6] -0.1[6] 0.2[6]	19.8 19.8 19.7	28.3 28.4 26.9	27.3 26.9 25.8
Jamaica Jamaïque	1996 1997 1998	221 763 242 762 257 392	14.4 16.4 17.8	66.5 65.7 64.8	0.2 0.2 0.2	31.6 31.5 28.2	47.8 42.6 44.3	60.4 56.5 55.3
Japan [2] Japon [2]	2000 2001 2002	513 376 800 507 455 500 500 728 600	16.8 17.4 17.8	55.7[5] 56.4[5] 57.2[5]	-0.1 0.0 ...	26.2 25.6 23.7[4]	10.8 10.4 11.1	9.3 9.7 9.9
Jordan Jordanie	1999 2000 2001	5 767 5 989 6 310	24.1 23.7 23.1	72.2[5] 80.9[5] 81.3[5]	-1.9 1.1 1.3	23.5 21.1 19.6	43.4 41.9 42.4	61.3 68.6 67.7
Kazakhstan [2] Kazakhstan [2]	1999 2000 2001	2 016 456[3] 2 599 902[3] 3 250 593[3]	11.5 12.1 13.4	72.4[5] 61.4[5] 57.7[5]	1.6 0.8 3.1	16.2 17.3 23.7	42.5 57.0 46.5	40.1 48.4 48.1
Kenya Kenya	1999 2000 2001	37 107 39 799 44 764	17.0 17.5 16.8	72.6 76.6 77.7	1.0 0.8 0.6	15.2 14.6 13.9	25.5 26.6 26.2	31.3 36.1 35.1
Kiribati Kiribati	1980	21	36.4	92.8	...	44.0[4]	22.5	95.7
Korea, Republic of [2] Corée, République de [2]	2000 2001 2002	521 959 212[3] 551 557 522[3] 596 381 161[3]	10.1 10.4 10.6	57.3[5] 59.1[5] 60.2[5]	-0.2[6] -0.1[6] -0.7[6]	28.4 27.0 26.7	44.8 42.2 40.0	41.7 40.0 38.6
Kuwait Koweït	1999 2000 2001	8 886 10 991 10 057	27.7 22.6 26.3	50.6 42.2 47.7	0.4	14.6 7.5 8.6	47.4 59.4 54.7	40.7 31.7 37.4
Kyrgyzstan [2] Kirghizistan [2]	1999 2000 2001	48 744 65 358 73 883	19.1 20.0 17.5	77.6[5] 65.7[5] 64.8[5]	2.3[6] 2.0[6] 1.2[6]	15.7 18.0 16.8	42.2 41.8 36.7	57.0 47.6 37.0
Latvia [2] Lettonie [2]	1999 2000 2001	3 890 4 348 4 759	20.6 19.7 18.7	62.9[5] 61.9[5] 62.3[5]	1.7[6] 0.5[6] 3.2[6]	25.2 26.5 27.3	43.9 45.6 44.8	54.2 54.3 56.2
Lebanon Liban	1982 1994 1995	12 599 14 992 000 17 779 000	38.5 10.6 9.9	125.7 110.8 107.7	... ...	9.4[4] 36.4 36.3	41.7 8.4 11.0	115.3 66.3 64.9
Lesotho [2] Lesotho [2]	1999 2000 2001	5 565 5 986 6 478	21.3 19.1 18.2	102.8[5] 101.1[5] 101.7[5]	1.0 -2.3 -2.6	47.6 44.4 43.1	24.4 29.7 39.3	94.8 92.1 99.6
Liberia Libéria	1987 1988 1989	1 090[3] 1 158[3] 1 194[3]	13.2 11.8 11.9	65.5 63.3 55.0	0.6 0.3 0.3	11.1 10.0 8.1	40.2 39.0 43.7	32.7 27.8 23.1
Libyan Arab Jamah. Jamah. arabe libyenne	1983 1984 1985	8 805 8 013 8 277	32.7 33.6 31.7	39.2 38.6 37.6	-1.1 0.5 0.4	25.1 25.3 19.7	42.1 41.4 37.4	38.0 39.4 26.7
Lithuania [2] Lituanie [2]	1999 2000 2001	42 655 45 148 47 958	22.2 21.4 20.1	65.5[5] 64.5[5] 63.6[5]	0.6[6] 2.0[6] 2.5[6]	22.1 18.5 19.2	39.7 45.3 50.4	50.1 51.7 55.9
Luxembourg [2] Luxembourg [2]	2000 2001 2002	21 313 22 082 22 340	15.7 16.8 18.3	39.7[5] 41.4[5] 43.1[5]	1.6[6] 0.8[6] -0.8[6]	20.8 21.7 21.2	151.9 152.4 145.3	129.7 133.1 127.1

20
Expenditure on gross domestic product in current prices
Percentage distribution [cont.]
Dépenses imputées au produit intérieur brut aux prix courants
Répartition en pourcentage *[suite]*

Region, country or area Région, pays ou zone	Year Année	GDP in current prices (Mil. nat.cur.) PIB aux prix courants (Millions monnaie nat.)	% of GDP – en % du PIB					
			Govt. final consumption expenditure Consom. finale des admin. publiques	Household final consumption expenditure Consom. finale des ménages	Changes in inventories Variation des stocks	Gross fixed capital formation Formation brute de capital fixe	Exports of goods and services Exportations de biens et services	Imports of goods and services Importations de biens et services
Madagascar	1990	4 601 600	8.0	86.0	...	17.0	15.9	26.9
Madagascar	1991	4 906 400	8.6	92.2	...	8.2	17.3	26.2
	1992	5 584 500	8.2	90.0	...	11.6	15.6	25.3
Malawi	1994	10 319[10]	28.3	74.4[12]	...	12.0	31.8	40.7
Malawi	1995	20 923[10]	21.9	30.4[12]	...	11.9	32.2	38.2
	1996	33 918[10]	17.5	56.1[12]	...	11.2	15.5	27.1
Malaysia	1999	300 764	11.0	41.6[5]	0.5	21.9	121.3	96.3
Malaisie	2000	342 157	10.6	42.3[5]	1.5	25.6	124.8	104.8
	2001	334 589	12.8	45.0[5]	-1.1	24.9	116.3	98.0
Maldives	1982	454	14.3	80.8	0.4	22.7	-18.3[1]	...
Maldives	1983	466	16.3	82.6	2.6	35.6	-37.1[1]	...
	1984	537	17.7	77.5	1.5	39.5	-36.1[1]	...
Mali	1990	683 300	15.2	79.0	2.2	20.0	17.3	33.7
Mali	1991	691 400	15.3	85.1	-2.4	20.0	17.5	35.5
	1992	737 400	14.2	82.2	2.7	17.6	17.8	34.6
Malta	1999	1 456	18.7	62.8	0.6[3]	23.3	90.7	96.3
Malte	2000	1 558	18.7	64.1	1.7[3]	26.3	103.0	113.8
	2001	1 632	20.1	64.1	-2.9[3]	23.1	87.5	92.0
Martinique	1990	19 320	29.7	83.6	1.9	26.7	8.4	50.3
Martinique	1991	20 787	28.8	84.0	1.4	25.6	7.4	47.1
	1992	22 093	28.7	84.3	-0.9	23.6	6.8	42.5
Mauritania	1986	59 715	14.3	85.4	1.5	22.7	55.4	79.4
Mauritanie	1987	67 216	13.6	82.6	1.7	20.8	48.3	67.0
	1988	72 635	14.2	79.6	1.4	17.0	49.1	61.3
Mauritius [2]	1999	107 444	13.2	64.0	-1.3	27.6	64.3	67.8
Maurice [2]	2000	119 529	13.0	61.9	2.2	23.5	61.8	62.3
	2001	131 835	12.6	60.8	-1.4	22.3	68.6	62.9
Mexico [2]	1999	4 593 685	11.0	67.1[5]	2.3	21.2	30.8	32.4
Mexique [2]	2000	5 485 372	11.1	67.4[5]	2.2	21.3	31.1	33.0
	2001	5 765 922	11.6	70.2[5]	1.0	19.6	27.6	30.0
Mongolia	1998	833 727[3]	17.3	66.7[5]	1.6[6]	33.5	54.3	67.5
Mongolie	1999	925 801[3]	17.2	68.4[5]	2.0[6]	34.9	58.5	72.5
	2000	1 018 886[3]	17.7	71.9[5]	4.6[6]	31.6	66.0	83.0
Montserrat	1984	94	20.6	96.4	2.7	23.7	13.6	56.9
Montserrat	1985	100	20.3	96.3	1.5	24.7	11.7	54.4
	1986	114	18.7	89.5	2.8	33.0	10.1	53.9
Morocco	1999	345 593	19.1	62.0	-0.6	23.7	24.5	28.8
Maroc	2000	354 068	19.1	63.5	-0.5	24.1	26.4	32.7
	2001	382 897	19.5	61.4	0.6	22.3	27.5	31.2
Mozambique [2]	2000	56 917 388	13.6	78.5	-16.6	50.5	12.9	38.9
Mozambique [2]	2001	71 134 761	14.5	72.7	4.1	22.4	21.8	35.4
	2002	82 747 356	19.6	74.2	...	21.4[4]	24.2	39.4
Myanmar +	1996	791 980	88.5[9]	...	-2.7	14.9	0.7	1.5
Myanmar +	1997	1 109 554	88.1[9]	...	-0.9	13.5	0.6	1.3
	1998	1 559 996	89.4[9]	...	-0.7	11.8	0.5	1.0
Namibia [2]	1999	20 681[3]	30.3	59.2[5]	0.3	23.0	46.2	56.9
Namibie [2]	2000	23 995[3]	28.4	59.1[5]	0.7	18.6	45.1	50.5
	2001	27 231[3]	27.8	60.6[5]	1.5	22.2	44.3	54.3
Nepal +	1999	342 036	8.9	77.5	1.4	19.1	22.8	29.7
Népal +	2000	379 488	9.0	75.9	5.0	19.3	23.3	32.4
	2001	410 287	9.8	75.3	4.9	19.0	22.4	31.5

20

Expenditure on gross domestic product in current prices
Percentage distribution [cont.]
Dépenses imputées au produit intérieur brut aux prix courants
Répartition en pourcentage *[suite]*

Region, country or area Région, pays ou zone	Year Année	GDP in current prices (Mil. nat.cur.) PIB aux prix courants (Millions monnaie nat.)	Govt. final consumption expenditure Consom. finale des admin. publiques	Household final consumption expenditure Consom. finale des ménages	Changes in inventories Variation des stocks	Gross fixed capital formation Formation brute de capital fixe	Exports of goods and services Exportations de biens et services	Imports of goods and services Importations de biens et services
Netherlands [2]	2000	402 599	22.6	49.9[5]	-0.2[6]	22.5	67.3	62.3
Pays-Bas [2]	2001	429 172	23.2	49.6[5]	0.0[6]	21.9	65.3	60.0
	2002	444 050	24.2	50.0[5]	-0.6[6]	21.0	61.7	56.4
Netherlands Antilles	1995	4 224	27.2	67.2	-0.1	20.8	72.0	87.1
Antilles néerlandaises	1996	4 422	27.0	63.1	0.8	24.5	70.1	85.6
	1997	4 537	24.8	60.0	1.0	19.8	70.9	76.5
New Caledonia	1990	250 427[3]	32.6	57.3	-1.1	24.4	22.0	35.4
Nouvelle-Calédonie	1991	272 235[3]	32.8	53.8	1.3	23.9	20.1	32.2
	1992	281 427[3]	33.7	56.7	0.1	23.7	16.8	31.4
New Zealand + [2]	1999	107 068[3]	18.9	61.3[5]	1.5	19.7	31.3	32.2
Nouvelle-Zélande + [2]	2000	113 778[3]	18.0	60.2[5]	1.3	18.9	36.3	34.5
	2001	122 241[3]	17.9	58.7[5]	1.6	18.9	35.7	32.5
Nicaragua	1999	26 130	18.9	95.2	0.2	43.1	34.5	91.9
Nicaragua	2000	30 858	18.6	92.3	-0.2	35.2	35.9	81.8
	2001	34 242	20.1	92.3	0.1	32.9	32.4	77.8
Niger	1988	678 200	15.5	65.9	7.9	11.9	20.7	21.9
Niger	1989	692 600	18.0	73.0	-0.1	12.3	18.6	21.8
	1990	682 300	17.2	74.1	1.1	11.7	16.8	20.9
Nigeria +	1999	3 320 311	7.6	59.3	0.0	5.3	49.7	21.9
Nigéria +	2000	4 980 943	5.2	49.1	0.0	5.4	58.9	18.6
	2001	5 639 863	4.9	60.3	0.0	7.0	55.4	27.5
Norway [2]	2000	1 469 075	19.1	42.6[5]	2.4[6]	18.6	46.7	29.4
Norvège [2]	2001	1 526 601	20.3	43.0[5]	1.8[6]	17.7	45.7	28.5
	2002	1 520 728	66.9[9]	...	1.9[6]	17.0	41.5	27.3
Oman [2]	1999	6 041	23.8	49.7	0.1	14.7	48.6	37.0
Oman [2]	2000	7 639	20.7	39.3	0.0	11.9	59.1	31.0
	2001	7 668	23.8	41.4	0.0	12.6	57.3	35.0
Pakistan +	1999	3 147 167	11.2	74.4	1.6	14.4	16.3	18.0
Pakistan +	2000	3 416 252	10.3	75.2	1.6	14.3	18.0	19.4
	2001	3 726 611	11.4	75.0	1.6	12.3	17.7	18.0
Panama	1998	9 345	16.1	56.5	4.0	28.1	89.9	94.6
Panama	1999	9 637	15.6	55.3	2.9	30.2	76.7	80.6
	2000	10 019	16.0	56.6	2.4	26.3	79.3	80.6
Papua New Guinea [2]	1997	7 064	19.3	58.3	5.8	15.3	46.9	45.5
Papouasie-Nvl-Guinée [2]	1998	7 863	17.9	59.7	3.9	13.8	50.1	45.5
	1999	8 781	16.9	69.7	4.3	12.1	47.3	50.4
Paraguay	1993	11 991 719	6.7	81.3	0.9	22.0	36.9	47.9
Paraguay	1994	14 960 131	6.8	88.4	0.9	22.5	34.2	52.8
	1995	17 699 000	7.2	85.3	0.9	23.1	35.0	51.2
Peru [2]	1999	174 221	10.8	70.3	-0.6	21.7	14.8	17.2
Pérou [2]	2000	185 143	10.9	70.7	-0.1	20.3	16.1	18.0
	2001	187 251	11.1	71.9	0.0	18.6	16.0	17.6
Philippines	1999	2 976 904[3]	13.1	72.6	-0.3	19.1	51.5	51.3
Philippines	2000	3 308 318[3]	13.3	70.6	-0.2	18.6	56.2	50.1
	2001	3 639 980[3]	12.8	70.5	0.3	17.3	48.5	47.0
Poland [2]	#2000	712 322	17.8	63.8[5]	1.1	23.9	28.3	34.9
Pologne [2]	2001	749 311	17.8	64.9[5]	0.1	21.0	28.1	31.8
	2002	772 248	18.0	66.2[5]	0.0	19.1	30.0	33.3
Portugal [2]	1999	108 030	19.7	62.4[5]	1.0[6]	27.3	29.7	40.1
Portugal [2]	2000	115 546	20.5	61.5[5]	0.9[6]	28.3	31.6	42.8
	2001	122 978	20.7	61.0[5]	0.9[6]	27.2	31.0	40.7

20

Expenditure on gross domestic product in current prices
Percentage distribution [cont.]
Dépenses imputées au produit intérieur brut aux prix courants
Répartition en pourcentage *[suite]*

			% of GDP – en % du PIB					
Region, country or area Région, pays ou zone	Year Année	GDP in current prices (Mil. nat.cur.) PIB aux prix courants (Millions monnaie nat.)	Govt. final consumption expenditure Consom. finale des admin. publiques	Household final consumption expenditure Consom. finale des ménages	Changes in inventories Variation des stocks	Gross fixed capital formation Formation brute de capital fixe	Exports of goods and services Exportations de biens et services	Imports of goods and services Importations de biens et services
Puerto Rico + Porto Rico +	1998	57 841	13.0	58.8[5]	0.9	19.8	69.7	62.1
	1999	61 045	11.8	58.9[5]	0.5	19.4	72.5	63.2
	2000	67 897	11.4	55.4[5]	0.7	17.2	78.3	63.1
Qatar[2] Qatar[2]	1999	45 111	25.7	21.1	0.5	18.3	60.0	25.7
	2000	64 646	19.7	15.2	0.7	19.5	67.3	22.3
	2001	62 341	20.7	16.3	0.9	22.6	65.6	26.1
Republic of Moldova[2] République de Moldova[2]	2000	16 020	14.7	88.4[5]	8.5	15.4	49.6	76.6
	2001	19 052	14.4	86.7[5]	6.5	16.7	50.1	74.4
	2002	22 040	17.3	85.3[5]	6.1	16.6	55.5	80.9
Réunion Réunion	1992	33 787	28.4	76.1	2.1	28.6	3.4	38.6
	1993	33 711[10]	28.6	76.4	-0.4	25.7	3.1	36.2
	1994	35 266	28.9	78.0	0.1	28.1	2.9	38.0
Romania[2] Roumanie[2]	1999	545 730 127	14.5	74.3[5]	-1.6[6]	17.7	28.0	32.9
	2000	800 308 100	15.6	70.3[5]	0.8[6]	18.9	33.0	38.7
	2001	1154126400	14.9	71.3[5]	2.9[6]	19.0	33.5	41.6
Russian Federation[2] Fédération de Russie[2]	2000	7 305 742[13]	15.1	46.2[5]	1.8	16.9	44.1	24.0
	2001	9 040 690[13]	16.3	48.9[5]	3.4	18.6	36.2	23.5
	2002	10 863 362[3,13]	16.9	51.2[5]	3.1	17.9	34.3	23.8
Rwanda Rwanda	2000	681 455	8.9	90.2	...	18.0	6.3	23.4
	2001	732 276	9.5	90.4	...	17.4	8.7	26.1
	2002	794 998	9.4	90.3	...	17.7	7.0	24.3
Saint Kitts and Nevis Saint-Kitts-et-Nevis	1999	823	21.3	68.0	...	35.6[4]	47.4	72.3
	2000	891	21.1	58.7	...	49.5[4]	45.6	75.0
	2001	928	19.8	49.2	...	57.0[4]	45.0	71.1
Saint Lucia Sainte-Lucie	1996	1 543	16.9	64.4	...	24.7	61.8	67.9
	1997	1 562	18.2	65.5	...	26.8	62.0	72.4
	1998	1 695	18.5	65.5	...	24.7	60.7	69.4
St. Vincent-Grenadines St. Vincent-Grenadines	1999	890	18.8	69.8	...	32.5	52.9	73.8
	2000	905	19.4	61.5	...	27.3	53.1	61.4
	2001	940	19.8	64.7	...	29.6	50.7	64.8
San Marino Saint-Marin	1997	1 279 857	62.6[9]	...	3.2	38.4	234.2	238.3
	1998	1 400 841	59.9[9]	...	4.9	37.0	202.0	203.8
	1999	1 551 010	56.2[9]	...	5.3	41.4	197.1	200.0
Sao Tome and Principe Sao Tomé-et-Principe	1986	2 478[3]	30.3	76.1	0.9	13.6	...	50.8
	1987	3 003[3]	24.8	63.1	1.1	15.4	...	43.1
	1988	4 221[3]	21.2	71.8	0.0	15.7	...	66.8
Saudi Arabia + Arabie saoudite +	1999	603 589	25.5	41.8	1.6	19.6	34.8	23.3
	2000	706 657	26.0	36.5	1.3	17.5	43.7	24.9
	2001	698 403	27.0	36.6	0.7	18.1	41.9	24.4
Senegal Sénégal	1998	2 746 000	11.8	75.5	2.1	17.7	29.9	37.0
	1999	2 925 000	12.7	74.3	1.1	19.6	30.4	38.0
	2000	3 114 000	14.0	72.9	5.6	17.3	29.7	39.6
Serbia and Montenegro Serbie-et-Monténégro	1998	148 370[3]	28.6	98.9[5]	-1.1[6]	11.6	23.4	32.8
	1999	191 099[3]	28.3	96.9[5]	-0.5[6]	12.6	11.2	20.3
	2000	381 661[3]	28.6	99.0[5]	-6.6[6]	15.4	9.0	16.8
Seychelles Seychelles	1998	3 201	31.2	50.0	0.6	34.0	-15.8[1]	...
	1999	3 330	27.8	45.3	1.8	41.5	-16.4[1]	...
	2000	3 424	27.1	39.4	0.5	35.7	-2.6[1]	...
Sierra Leone + Sierra Leone +	1988	43 947	7.5	86.7	0.8	12.7	14.5	22.3
	1989	82 837	6.6	84.7	0.5	13.5	19.7	25.1
	1990	150 175	10.4	77.9	1.8	10.1	25.4	25.7

20

Expenditure on gross domestic product in current prices
Percentage distribution [cont.]
Dépenses imputées au produit intérieur brut aux prix courants
Répartition en pourcentage *[suite]*

% of GDP – en % du PIB

Region, country or area Région, pays ou zone	Year Année	GDP in current prices (Mil. nat.cur.) PIB aux prix courants (Millions monnaie nat.)	Govt. final consumption expenditure Consom. finale des admin. publiques	Household final consumption expenditure Consom. finale des ménages	Changes in inventories Variation des stocks	Gross fixed capital formation Formation brute de capital fixe	Exports of goods and services Exportations de biens et services	Imports of goods and services Importations de biens et services
Singapore Singapour	1999	140 070[3]	10.1	41.1	-1.8	33.7	19.0[1]	...
	2000	159 888[3]	10.5	40.1	2.1	29.5	17.9[1]	...
	2001	153 455[3]	11.9	42.2	-4.9	29.2	21.7[1]	...
Slovakia[2] Slovaquie[2]	2000	908 801[3]	19.8	56.2[5]	-2.4[6]	29.5	71.8	74.2
	2001	989 297[3]	20.0	56.6[5]	0.7[6]	31.3	74.0	82.5
	2002	1 073 613[3]	19.9	56.2[5]	1.4[6]	29.8	72.8	79.9
Slovenia[2] Slovénie[2]	1999	3 648 401	20.2	55.8[5]	1.0[6]	27.4	52.5	56.9
	2000	4 035 518	20.8	54.9[5]	1.1[6]	26.7	59.1	62.7
	2001	4 566 191	21.3	53.6[5]	0.5[6]	24.9	60.1	60.5
Solomon Islands Iles Salomon	1986	253	33.3	63.1	1.0	25.2	52.6	75.2
	1987	293	36.3	63.1	2.7	20.4	55.9	78.4
	1988	367	31.4	68.6	2.7	30.0	52.4	85.0
Somalia Somalie	1985	87 290	10.6	90.5	2.9	8.9	4.2	17.0
	1986	118 781	9.7	89.1	1.0	16.8	5.8	22.4
	1987	169 608	11.1	88.8	4.8	16.8	5.9	27.2
South Africa[2] Afrique du Sud[2]	1999	800 696[3]	18.6	63.0	0.5	15.4	25.7	23.1
	2000	888 057[3]	18.7	62.7	0.7	14.8	28.6	25.8
	2001	982 944[3]	18.9	61.9	0.4	14.7	30.7	26.9
Spain[2] Espagne[2]	2000	609 319	17.6	59.0[5]	0.4	25.3	30.1	32.4
	2001	651 641	17.5	58.4[5]	0.3	25.4	29.9	31.6
	2002	693 925	17.6	57.9[5]	0.6	25.4	28.5	30.0
Sri Lanka[2] Sri Lanka[2]	1999	1 108 845[3]	13.8	67.6	0.5	25.7	35.5	43.3
	2000	1 253 622[3]	14.1	70.1	0.7	25.4	39.3	49.7
	2001	1 397 453[3]	13.5	69.4	2.1	21.1	38.9	45.5
Sudan + Soudan +	1994	5 522 838	4.6	84.1	6.8	9.4	4.6	9.5
	#1996	10 330 678	7.5	81.9	9.6	12.3	8.0	19.2
	1997	16 769 372	5.4	85.6	5.7	12.2	10.2	19.2
Suriname Suriname	1996	303 970	14.7	58.9	6.2	29.1	65.5	74.4
	1997	340 220	17.7	60.2	5.9	24.0	57.4	65.1
	1998	407 130	18.7	71.5	...	23.2[4]	42.3	55.7
Swaziland +[2] Swaziland +[2]	1999	8 408	22.2	73.9	...	18.8	72.7	87.6
	2000	9 639	20.0	75.5	...	19.9	63.7	79.1
	2001	10 971	18.2	76.8	...	18.1	70.2	83.3
Sweden[2] Suède[2]	2000	2 196 764	26.8	49.1[5]	0.7[6]	17.7	45.8	40.2
	2001	2 266 619	27.2	48.6[5]	0.3[6]	17.8	45.3	39.3
	2002	2 339 949	28.0	48.7[5]	0.2[6]	17.1	44.3	37.2
Switzerland Suisse	2000	405 530	13.7	60.6[5]	0.1	20.7	46.2	41.4
	2001	414 881	14.0	61.0[5]	1.4	19.5	45.1	41.0
	2002	416 840	76.1[9]	...	-0.7	18.2	44.2	37.7
Syrian Arab Republic Rép. arabe syrienne	1999	819 092	10.6	70.3	...	18.8	32.3	32.0
	2000	903 944	12.4	63.4	...	17.3	36.1	29.2
	2001	947 808	14.6	60.9	...	18.3	37.7	31.4
Tajikistan[2] Tadjikistan[2]	1997	518 400[3]	10.6	60.0[5]	2.0	17.7	81.8	85.4
	1998	1 025 200[3]	7.8	68.9[5]	2.0	13.4	49.7	57.5
	1999	1 344 900[3]	8.6	70.0[5]	1.9	17.2	67.9	66.4
Thailand Thaïlande	1998	4 626 447[3]	11.1	54.2	-1.9	22.4	58.9	43.0
	1999	4 632 132[3]	11.5	55.9	-0.4	20.9	58.4	45.8
	2000	4 904 725[3]	11.4	56.1	0.6	22.1	67.1	58.4
TFYR of Macedonia[2] L'ex-R.y. Macédoine[2]	1998	194 979	20.3	72.4[5]	4.8	17.4	41.2	56.1
	1999	209 010	20.6	69.7[5]	3.1	16.6	42.2	52.2
	2000	236 389	18.2	74.4[5]	5.2	16.2	48.3	62.4

20

Expenditure on gross domestic product in current prices
Percentage distribution [cont.]
Dépenses imputées au produit intérieur brut aux prix courants
Répartition en pourcentage *[suite]*

			% of GDP – en % du PIB					
Region, country or area Région, pays ou zone	Year Année	GDP in current prices (Mil. nat.cur.) PIB aux prix courants (Millions monnaie nat.)	Govt. final consumption expenditure Consom. finale des admin. publiques	Household final consumption expenditure Consom. finale des ménages	Changes in inventories Variation des stocks	Gross fixed capital formation Formation brute de capital fixe	Exports of goods and services Exportations de biens et services	Imports of goods and services Importations de biens et services
Togo Togo	1984	304 800	14.0	66.0	-1.5	21.2	51.9	51.6
	1985	332 500	14.2	66.0	5.2	22.9	48.3	56.7
	1986	363 600	14.4	69.0	5.3	23.8	35.6	48.2
Tonga + Tonga +	1999	238	22.3	97.5[5]	1.3	19.7	13.4	54.2
	2000	252	21.4	96.8[5]	0.8	20.6	16.3	56.0
	2001	274	23.4	101.8[5]	1.1	20.1	12.8	59.1
Trinidad and Tobago[2] Trinité-et-Tobago[2]	1999	42 889	14.7	58.5	0.4	20.6	50.0	44.2
	2000	51 485	12.0	54.1	0.3	19.6	59.1	45.2
	2001	56 700	13.0	54.4	0.3	22.0	53.3	43.0
Tunisia[2] Tunisie[2]	1999	24 672	15.5	60.4	0.9	25.4	42.5	44.8
	2000	26 651	15.6	60.7	1.4	26.0	44.5	48.2
	2001	28 793	15.6	60.9	1.7	26.4	47.7	52.2
Turkey Turquie	2000	124 583458275[3]	14.1	71.5	2.2	22.4	24.0	31.5
	2001	178 412438500[3]	14.2	72.0	-1.4	18.2	33.7	31.3
	2002	276 002987851[3]	14.0	66.7	4.7	16.7	28.8	30.5
Turkmenistan[2] Turkménistan[2]	1995	652 044	8.4	60.6[5]	10.4[6]	23.1	142.5	145.0
	1996	7 751 754[3]	7.1	49.2[5]	8.7[6]	41.3	105.8	107.0
	1997	11 108 783[3]	13.3	68.4[5]	7.7[6]	40.9	51.3	82.4
Uganda Ouganda	1997	7 230 521[3]	9.6	92.3	-0.1	16.9	11.5	25.5
	1998	8 298 977[3]	9.2	90.6	...	17.3	10.4	28.2
	1999	9 132 410[3]	9.2	91.0	...	20.1	10.3	28.5
Ukraine[2] Ukraine[2]	1999	130 442	19.8	57.2[5]	-1.8[6]	19.3	54.3	48.8
	2000	170 070	18.6	56.6[5]	0.1[6]	19.7	62.4	57.4
	2001	204 190	19.6	56.9[5]	2.1[6]	19.7	55.5	53.8
United Arab Emirates Emirats arabes unis	1990	124 008	16.3	38.6	1.0	19.4	65.4	40.8
	1991	124 500	16.9	41.4	1.1	20.7	67.6	47.7
	1992	128 400	17.8	45.5	1.2	23.2	69.1	56.8
United Kingdom[2] Royaume-Uni[2]	2000	950 415	18.7	65.9[5]	0.6[6]	16.7	27.9	29.8
	2001	993 124	19.3	66.3[5]	0.2[6]	16.5	27.0	29.2
	2002	1 043 301	20.0	66.0[5]	0.0[6]	15.8	25.8	27.6
United Rep. of Tanzania Rép.-Unie de Tanzanie	2000	7 277 800[3]	6.6	83.4	0.2	17.4	14.6	23.0
	2001	8 284 685[3]	6.2	83.5	0.2	16.8	15.5	23.7
	2002	9 374 559[3]	6.4	80.0	0.2	19.1	16.7	22.4
United States[2] Etats-Unis[2]	2000	9 762 100	14.6	68.5[5]	0.7	20.1	11.3	15.0
	2001	10 019 700	15.1	69.7[5]	-0.6	19.2	10.3	13.8
	2002	10 383 100	15.6	70.3[5]	0.0	18.1	9.8	13.9
Uruguay Uruguay	2000	243 027	13.2	74.5[5]	0.8	13.2	19.3	21.0
	2001	247 211	13.7	74.4[5]	1.3	12.5	18.3	20.2
	2002	261 987	12.8	72.8[5]	2.1	10.2	21.6	19.5
Uzbekistan[2] Ouzbékistan[2]	1999	2 128 660	20.6	62.1[5]	-10.1	27.2	0.1[1]	...
	2000	3 255 600	18.7	61.9[5]	-4.4	24.0	-0.2[1]	...
	2001	4 868 400	18.4	61.6[5]	-5.5	25.7	-0.3[1]	...
Vanuatu Vanuatu	1993	23 779[3]	28.4	49.2	2.3	25.5	45.3	53.8
	1994	24 961[3]	27.7	49.2	2.3	26.5	47.3	57.2
	1995	27 255[3]	25.4	46.9	2.1	29.8	44.2	53.6
Venezuela Venezuela	1999	62 577 039	7.5	69.1[5]	2.4	15.7	21.6	16.4
	2000	82 450 674	7.2	63.4[5]	3.0	14.2	28.4	16.3
	2001	91 324 773	8.6	66.9[5]	3.3	16.4	22.3	17.5
Viet Nam[2] Viet Nam[2]	1998	361 017 000[3]	7.6	70.9	2.0	27.0	-7.3[1]	...
	1999	399 942 000[3]	6.8	68.6	1.9	25.7	-2.9[1]	...
	2000	444 139 000[3]	6.4	66.6	2.0	27.4	-2.3[1]	...

20
Expenditure on gross domestic product in current prices
Percentage distribution [cont.]
Dépenses imputées au produit intérieur brut aux prix courants
Répartition en pourcentage *[suite]*

Region, country or area / Région, pays ou zone	Year / Année	GDP in current prices (Mil. nat.cur.) PIB aux prix courants (Millions monnaie nat.)	Govt. final consumption expenditure Consom. finale des admin. publiques	Household final consumption expenditure Consom. finale des ménages	Changes in inventories Variation des stocks	Gross fixed capital formation Formation brute de capital fixe	Exports of goods and services Exportations de biens et services	Imports of goods and services Importations de biens et services
Yemen [2] / Yémen [2]	1998	849 321	14.7	67.8	1.0	31.5	27.6	42.6
	1999	1 132 619	13.8	68.0	1.2	23.4	36.3	42.7
	2000	1 379 812	14.1	57.8	0.9	18.2	50.5	41.5
Yugoslavia, SFR / Yougoslavie, Rfs	1988	15 833 [3]	14.2	50.1	19.9	17.2	29.5	30.4
	1989	235 395 [3]	14.4	47.4	28.0	14.5	25.3	29.2
	1990	1 147 787 [3]	17.6	66.1	7.3	14.7	23.7	29.4
Zambia / Zambie	1998	6 028 600	15.8	80.3	1.6	14.8	26.7	39.2
	1999	7 479 500	12.9	88.2	1.6	16.0	22.4	41.1
	2000	10 074 600	9.5	82.2	1.4	17.2	21.1	31.4
Zimbabwe / Zimbabwe	1997	102 982	16.2	71.8 [5]	1.1	17.9	37.3	44.2
	1998	143 364	16.6	63.7 [5]	0.1	21.3	43.5	45.2
	1999	210 409	15.2	69.1 [5]	1.2	14.9	46.2	46.6

Source:
United Nations Statistics Division, New York, national accounts database.

+ Note: The national accounts data generally relate to the fiscal year used in each country, unless indicated otherwise. Countries whose reference periods coincide with the calendar year ending 31 December are not listed below.
Year beginning 21 March: Afghanistan, Iran (Islamic Republic).
Year beginning 1 April: Bermuda, India, Myanmar, New Zealand, Nigeria (beginning 1982).
Year beginning 1 July: Australia, Bangladesh, Cameroon, Egypt, Gambia, Pakistan, Puerto Rico, Saudi Arabia, Sierra Leone, Sudan.
Year ending 30 June: Botswana, Swaziland, Tonga.
Year ending 7 July: Ethiopia.
Year ending 15 July: Nepal.
Year ending 30 September: Haiti.

Source:
Organisation des Nations Unies, Division de statistique, New York, la base de données sur les comptes nationaux.

+ Note : Sauf indication contraire, les données sur les comptes nationaux concernent généralement l'exercice budgétaire utilisé dans chaque pays. Les pays ou territoires dont la période de référence coïncide avec l'année civile se terminant le 31 décembre ne sont pas répertoriés ci-dessous.
Exercice commençant le 21 mars: Afghanistan, Iran (République islamique d').
Exercice commençant le 1er avril: Bermudes, Inde, Myanmar, Nigéria (à partir de 1982), Nouvelle-Zélande.
Exercice commençant le 1er juillet: Arabie saoudite, Australie, Bangladesh, Cameroun, Égypte, Gambie, Pakistan, Porto Rico, Sierra Leone, Soudan.
Exercice se terminant le 30 juin: Botswana, Swaziland, Tonga.
Exercice se terminant le 7 juillet: Éthiopie.
Exercice se terminant le 15 juillet: Népal.
Exercice se terminant le 30 septembre: Haïti.

1   Net exports.
2   Data are classified according to the 1993 SNA.
3   Including statistical discrepancy.
4   Gross capital formation.
5   Including "Non-profit institutions serving households" (NPISHs) final consumption expenditure.
6   Including acquisition less disposals of valuables.
7   Data in Russian roubles.
8   Re-denomination of Belarussian rubles at 1 to 1000.
9   Including household final consumption expenditure.
10 Discrepancy between components and total.
11 Data in US dollars.
12 Including changes in inventories.
13 Re-denomination of Russian rubles at 1 to 1000.

1   Exportations nettes.
2   Les données sont classifiées selon le SCN 1993.
3   Y compris une divergence statistique.
4   Formation brute de capital.
5   Y compris la consommation finale des institutions sans but lucratif au service des ménages.
6   Y compris les acquisitions moins cessions d'objets de valeur.
7   Les données sont exprimées en roubles russiens.
8   Instauration du nouveau rouble bélarussien par division par 1000 du rouble bélarussien ancien.
9   Y compris la consommation finale des ménages.
10 Ecart entre les rubriques et le total.
11 Les données sont exprimées en dollars des États-Unis.
12 Y compris les variations des stocks.
13 Instauration du nouveau rouble par division par 1000 du rouble ancien.

21
Value added by industries in current prices
Percentage distribution
Valeur ajoutée par branche d'activité aux prix courants
Répartition en pourcentage

% of Value added – % de la valeur ajoutée

Region, country or area / Région, pays ou zone	Year / Année	Value added, gross (Mil. nat.cur.) / Valeur ajoutée, brute (Mil. mon. nat.)	Agriculture, hunting, forestry and fishing / Agriculture, chasse, sylviculture et pêche	Mining and quarrying / Activités extractives	Manufacturing / Activités de fabrication	Electricity, gas and water supply / Electricité, gaz et eau	Construction / Construction	Wholesale, retail trade, restaurants and hotels / Commerce, restaurants, hôtels	Transport, storage & communication / Transports, entrepôts, communications	Other activities / Autres activités
Albania [1] / Albanie [1]	1998	460 631	54.4	11.9[2,3]	...	...	12.6	18.0[4]	3.0	...
	1999	506 205	52.6	11.9[2,3]	...	...	13.5	18.8[4]	3.3	...
	2000	539 210	51.0	11.5[2,3]	...	...	14.8	19.2[4]	3.5	...
Algeria / Algérie	1999	3 100 918	11.6	30.1	7.6	1.3	8.7	14.7	7.7	18.3
	2000	3 934 942	8.8	42.3	6.2	1.1	7.4	12.1	6.9	15.1
	2001	4 048 169	10.5	36.7	6.4	1.2	7.4	13.1	8.4	16.3
Angola / Angola	1988	236 682	16.0	27.1	8.3	0.2	4.1	11.7	3.5	29.1
	1989	276 075	19.3	29.7	6.2	0.2	3.3	11.4	3.0	27.1
	1990	305 831	18.0	32.9	5.0	0.1	2.9	10.7	3.2	27.0
Anguilla / Anguilla	1999	259[5]	2.7	0.9	1.2	3.8	15.2	34.4	13.1	28.9
	2000	265[5]	2.5	0.9	1.2	2.9	13.6	32.4	13.8	32.5
	2001	273[5]	2.6	0.7	1.1	3.3	11.0	33.7	13.9	34.1
Antigua and Barbuda / Antigua-et-Barbuda	1986	567[5]	4.3	1.7	3.8	3.5	8.9	23.6	15.6	38.5
	1987	649[5]	4.5	2.2	3.5	3.5	11.3	24.1	15.6	35.3
	1988	776[5]	4.1	2.2	3.1	4.0	12.7	23.7	14.3	35.9
Argentina [1] / Argentine [1]	1999	254 769[5]	5.0	1.8	16.7	2.3	6.0	17.9	9.2	43.3
	2000	255 552[5]	5.2	2.8	16.2	2.5	5.2	17.2	9.4	43.9
	2001	244 705[5]	5.0	2.7	15.5	2.5	4.7	16.4	9.3	45.7
Armenia [1] / Arménie [1]	1999	921 400	28.9[3,6]	...	23.5	...	8.9	9.7	8.1	20.9
	2000	951 800	25.1[3,6]	...	24.9	...	11.1	10.0	7.8	21.0
	2001	1 079 277	27.3[3,6]	...	22.8	...	11.7	10.7	8.1	19.5
Aruba [1] / Aruba [1]	1998	2 904	0.4[6]	...	2.9[7]	6.5[7]	8.6	24.8	8.2	48.7
	1999	2 987	0.4[6]	...	3.0[7]	7.1[7]	6.1	24.1	8.7	50.6
	2000	3 234	0.4[6]	...	2.8[7]	6.6[7]	6.2	24.6	8.9	50.5
Australia + [1] / Australie + [1]	1999	577 705[8]	3.5	4.6	12.4	2.5	6.7	13.8	8.5	48.0
	2000	610 159[8]	3.5	5.6	12.0	2.5	5.7	13.3	8.4	48.9
	2001	648 964[8]	3.8	5.3	11.7	2.5	6.2	13.5	8.2	48.9
Austria [1] / Autriche [1]	1999	184 018	2.3	0.3	20.4	2.6	8.1	16.7	7.0	42.6
	2000	194 842	2.2	0.4	20.7	2.3	7.8	16.9	6.9	42.9
	2001	200 394	2.3	0.4	20.6	2.1	7.4	16.8	6.9	43.5
Azerbaijan [1] / Azerbaïdjan [1]	2000	22 271 400	17.0	29.3	5.6	3.3	6.9	7.1	12.7	18.1
	2001	24 658 300	16.0	32.0	7.0	1.6	6.3	8.4	10.9	17.8
	2002	27 475 600	15.3	29.6	6.6	1.4	11.6	8.6	10.6	16.4
Bahamas [1] / Bahamas [1]	1993	2 404	3.3	0.7	3.7	4.0[9]	3.6	27.0	10.9	46.8
	1994	2 608	3.8	0.7	3.4	4.6[9]	3.1	26.0	11.9	46.4
	1995	2 656	3.8	1.0	3.0	4.4[9]	2.7	26.5	11.1	47.6
Bahrain / Bahreïn	1998	2 575	0.8	12.3	11.5	1.7	3.7	11.2	7.5	51.3
	1999	2 745	0.8	16.5	11.2	1.6	3.8	9.6	7.1	49.3
	2000	3 336	0.7	25.2	10.3	1.3	3.2	9.0	6.3	44.0
Bangladesh + [1] / Bangladesh + [1]	1999	2 287 605	25.5	1.0	15.2	1.3	7.7	13.4	8.6	27.2
	2000	2 449 992	24.1	1.1	15.6	1.4	7.9	13.9	9.0	27.0
	2001	2 622 197	23.3	1.1	15.7	1.4	8.0	14.2	9.2	27.0
Barbados / Barbade	1999	4 139[5]	4.9	0.7	6.3	3.1	5.8	29.1	10.4	39.7
	2000	4 291[5]	4.4	0.7	6.3	3.3	5.8	29.0	10.3	40.1
	2001	4 223[5]	4.7	0.7	6.1	3.5	5.8	26.4	11.1	41.8
Belarus [1] / Bélarus [1]	1999	2 687 694 200	14.3[3,6]	...	33.6	...	6.5	10.8	12.9	21.9
	2000	7 970 800	13.9[3,6]	...	32.7	...	7.4	10.9	12.7	22.5
	2001	15 202 100	11.7[3,6]	...	31.5	...	6.6	11.3	13.0	25.9
Belgium [1] / Belgique [1]	1999	218 608	1.3	0.2	19.0	2.7	4.9	13.3	6.9	51.8
	2000	228 320	1.4	0.2	19.0	2.6	5.0	13.1	6.8	51.8
	2001	235 817	1.4	0.1	18.3	2.5	5.0	13.4	6.9	52.3

21

Value added by industries in current prices
Percentage distribution *[cont.]*
Valeur ajoutée par branche d'activité aux prix courants
Répartition en pourcentage *[suite]*

Region, country or area Région, pays ou zone	Year Année	Value added, gross (Mil. nat.cur) Valeur ajoutée, brute (Mil. mon. nat.)	Agriculture, hunting, forestry and fishing Agriculture, chasse, sylviculture et pêche	Mining and quarrying Activités extractives	Manu-facturing Activités de fabri-cation	Electricity, gas and water supply Electricité, gaz et eau	Cons-truc-tion Con-struc-tion	Wholesale, retail trade, restaurants and hotels Commerce, restaurants, hôtels	Transport, storage & commu-nication Transports, entépôts, communi-cations	Other activi-ties Autres activités
Belize [1] Belize [1]	1998	1 051[10]	19.1	0.6	13.2	3.4	5.7	18.9	10.4	37.9
	1999	1 154[10]	19.7	0.6	13.0	3.4	6.5	20.8	11.0	36.1
	2000	1 311[10]	17.2	0.7	13.1	3.3	7.1	21.6	9.9	29.8
Benin Bénin	1987	430 800	36.3	1.2	7.8	0.9	3.5	17.0	8.5	24.7
	1988	451 080	37.2	0.9	8.9	1.0	3.3	18.7	8.1	21.9
	1989	465 735	38.0	0.9	9.2	0.9	3.3	17.6	7.8	22.2
Bermuda + [1] Bermudes + [1]	1999	3 270[11]	0.8	0.2	2.5	2.3	5.9	17.3	7.2	63.9
	2000	3 387[11]	0.7	0.2	2.5	2.3	6.1	16.9	7.2	64.0
	2001	3 574[11]	0.7	0.1	2.5	2.3	6.8	16.0	7.1	64.3
Bhutan Bhoutan	1998	16 537[5]	36.6	1.6	9.8	11.7	10.2	7.0	8.3	14.8
	1999	18 957[5]	35.0	1.7	9.3	12.2	11.1	6.8	8.6	15.2
	2000	21 654[5]	35.9	1.6	8.0	11.6	12.5	6.8	8.6	15.0
Bolivia Bolivie	1999	44 603	14.3	5.9	14.7	3.1	3.5	11.5	12.8	34.3
	2000	47 311	14.3	7.0	15.0	3.2	2.9	11.5	12.3	33.8
	2001	48 529	14.9	6.8	14.5	3.2	2.7	11.7	13.0	33.2
Bosnia and Herzegovina [1] Bosnie-Herzégovine [1]	1999	7 230	15.8	2.1	13.0	7.9	6.3	12.8	9.8	32.3
	2000	7 816	13.3	2.3	12.6	8.0	5.9	12.0	10.3	35.6
	2001	8 392	13.0	2.1	12.6	8.2	5.2	13.7	11.0	34.2
Botswana + [1] Botswana + [1]	1999	20 477	3.2	32.7	5.5	2.2	6.6	11.4	4.0	34.3
	2000	23 815	2.8	35.2	5.2	2.4	6.0	11.5	3.9	33.0
	2001	27 815	2.6	37.0	4.9	2.5	5.6	11.5	3.9	32.0
Brazil [1] Brésil [1]	1999	870 459[12]	8.3	1.5	20.5	3.3	9.4	7.1[13]	5.2	48.6[13]
	2000	981 861[12]	8.0	2.6	22.1	3.5	9.1	7.4[13]	5.4	45.7[13]
	2001	1 065 093[12]	8.4	2.9	22.6	3.6	8.5	7.5[13]	5.7	46.0[13]
British Virgin Islands [1] Iles Vierges britanniques [1]	1997	523	1.6	0.1	4.8	2.0	6.1	30.2	11.1	44.1
	1998	606	1.5	0.1	4.6	1.8	7.3	29.2	11.2	44.4
	1999	674	1.4	0.1	4.0	1.7	7.3	28.0	11.7	46.0
Brunei Darussalam Brunéi Darussalam	1996	7 886	2.5	34.7[2]	...	1.0	5.8	11.9	4.8	39.3
	1997	8 268	2.6	33.6[2]	...	1.0	6.2	12.1	4.9	39.6
	1998	8 331	2.8	31.6[2]	...	1.1	6.5	12.6	5.1	40.4
Bulgaria [1] Bulgarie [1]	#1999	21 205	16.3	1.9	16.9	4.3	5.0	10.1	10.0	35.4
	2000	23 697	13.9	1.6	17.8	5.1	4.6	10.3	11.5	35.1
	2001	26 204	13.7	1.5	17.5	5.1	4.4	10.6	12.9	34.4
Burkina Faso Burkina Faso	1991	780 492	33.8	0.9	14.2	0.9	5.7	1.7	4.1	...
	1992	782 551	32.7	0.9	19.5	1.1	5.7	1.6	4.2	...
	1993	808 487	33.9	0.8	14.7	1.3	5.6	1.7	4.4	...
Burundi Burundi	1988	149 067	48.9	1.0[3]	16.5	...	2.9	12.9	2.6	15.2
	1989	175 627	47.0	1.2[3]	18.5	...	3.3	10.8	3.3	16.0
	1990	192 050	52.4	0.8[3]	16.8	...	3.4	4.9	3.1	18.5
Cambodia [1] Cambodge [1]	1999	11 879 240	45.3	0.1	12.5	0.4	5.1	15.1	6.6	14.9
	2000	12 216 080	40.4	0.2	16.3	0.4	5.2	14.8	7.2	15.6
	2001	12 573 010	39.2	0.2	16.7	0.5	5.9	14.8	7.5	15.2
Cameroon + [1] Cameroun + [1]	1996	4 467 110	22.0	5.5	21.3	0.9	3.2	21.0	5.2	20.9
	1997	5 013 530	23.6	5.6	21.3	0.8	2.1	19.9	5.8	20.8
	1998	5 362 130	23.6	5.6	21.3	0.8	2.1	19.9	5.8	20.8
Canada [1] Canada [1]	1997	816 756	2.5	4.2	18.0	3.4	5.3	13.6	7.4	45.7
	1998	846 535	2.6	3.2	18.3	3.3	5.2	13.9	7.4	46.1
	1999	907 578	2.5	3.8	19.2	3.1	5.2	13.8	7.2	45.3
Cape Verde Cap-Vert	1993	27 264	14.7	1.0	7.5	1.4	11.6	17.8	18.9	27.0
	1994	31 175	13.8	0.9	7.5	1.4	11.2	18.9	20.2	26.2
	1995	35 256	14.6	1.1	7.3	1.9	10.1	18.6	18.0	28.5

21
Value added by industries in current prices
Percentage distribution *[cont.]*
Valeur ajoutée par branche d'activité aux prix courants
Répartition en pourcentage *[suite]*

Region, country or area Région, pays ou zone	Year Année	Value added, gross (Mil. nat.cur) Valeur ajoutée, brute (Mil. mon. nat.)	Agriculture, hunting, forestry and fishing Agriculture, chasse, sylviculture et pêche	Mining and quarrying Activités extractives	Manu-facturing Activités de fabri-cation	Electricity, gas and water supply Electricité, gaz et eau	Cons-truc-tion Cons-truc-tion	Wholesale, retail trade, restaurants and hotels Commerce, restaurants, hôtels	Transport, storage & commu-nication Transports, entrepôts, communi-cations	Other activi-ties Autres activités
Cayman Islands	1989	473	0.4	0.6	1.9	3.2	11.0	24.5	11.0	47.6
Iles Caïmanes	1990	580	0.3	0.3	1.6	3.1	9.7	24.5	10.9	49.8
	1991	605	0.3	0.3	1.5	3.1	9.1	22.8	10.7	52.1
Central African Rep.	1983	243 350	40.8	2.5	7.8	0.5	2.1	21.2	4.2	20.8
Rép. centrafricaine	1984	268 725	40.7	2.8	8.1	0.9	2.7	21.7	4.3	18.8
	1985	308 549	42.4	2.5	7.5	0.8	2.6	22.0	4.2	17.9
Chad	1999	875 000[5]	39.9	...	12.9	0.7[9]	1.7	22.4	3.3	...
Tchad	2000	889 000[5]	40.2	...	11.8	0.7[9]	1.7	22.3	3.4	...
	2001	1 045 000[5]	38.2	...	13.7	0.7[9]	1.6	23.0	3.4	...
Chile [1]	1998	34 294 698[11]	5.9	4.9	18.2	2.9	10.0	12.0	7.6	38.5
Chili [1]	1999	34 992 167[11]	6.0	6.2	18.4	3.0	8.5	11.5	7.4	39.2
	2000	38 029 455[11]	6.0	7.8	18.5	3.1	7.8	11.4	7.2	38.3
China	1995	5 847 810	20.5	42.3[2,3]	...	...	6.5	8.4	5.2	17.0
Chine	1996	6 788 460	20.4	42.8[2,3]	...	...	6.7	8.2	5.1	16.8
	1997	7 477 240	18.7	42.5[2,3]	...	...	6.7	8.4	6.1	17.7
China, Hong Kong SAR [1]	1999	1 272 376	0.1[14]	0.0	5.3	2.9	5.3	23.3	8.9	54.2
Chine, Hong Kong RAS [1]	2000	1 324 842	0.1[14]	0.0	5.4	2.9	4.8	24.5	9.5	52.7
	2001	1 305 131	0.1[14]	0.0	4.7	3.1	4.6	24.2	9.8	53.5
China, Macao SAR [1]	1998	43 961[12]	...	0.0	9.2	3.1	3.6	9.8	6.7	73.8
Chine, Macao RAS [1]	1999	41 461[12]	...	0.0	9.4	3.3	3.6	9.8	7.2	72.2
	2000	42 737[12]	...	0.0	9.7	2.8	2.5	10.7	7.6	72.4
Colombia [1]	1999	148 452 480	13.3	5.4	14.1	3.5	4.3	11.2	7.4	40.8
Colombie [1]	2000	168 527 223	12.8	6.0	15.3	3.9	3.7	11.3	7.5	39.6
	2001	182 045 787	12.4	5.1	15.7	4.5	3.4	11.5	8.0	39.4
Comoros	1989	64 731	40.0	...	3.9	0.8	3.4	25.1	3.9	22.8
Comores	1990	67 992	40.4	...	4.1	0.9	3.1	25.1	4.1	22.3
	1991	71 113	40.8	...	4.2	0.9	2.7	25.1	4.2	22.1
Congo	1987	678 106	12.2	22.9	8.8	1.6	3.2	15.1	10.5	25.8
Congo	1988	643 830	14.2	17.1	8.8	2.0	2.7	16.7	11.3	27.2
	1989	757 088	13.3	28.6	7.2	1.9	1.8	14.7	9.3	23.3
Cook Islands	1999	161	13.7	...	3.0	2.4	2.4	30.0	16.8	31.7
Iles Cook	2000	177	16.1	...	2.7	2.0	2.8	30.2	16.3	29.9
	2001	189	12.0	...	2.8	1.6	2.9	32.0	17.0	31.5
Costa Rica [1]	1999	4 265 973	10.2	0.1	28.1	2.2	3.6	18.1	7.4	30.3
Costa Rica [1]	2000	4 635 619	9.1	0.2	24.4	2.5	3.9	18.6	8.1	33.2
	2001	5 051 320	8.3	0.2	21.2	2.8	4.5	19.0	8.1	35.9
Côte d'Ivoire	1998	6 744 000[12]	26.5	0.7	22.7	1.7	2.4	21.1	6.2	22.1
Côte d'Ivoire	1999	7 186 000[12]	24.0	0.3	23.0	2.0	3.7	22.7	5.9	21.8
	2000	7 054 000[12]	25.7	0.3	23.3	1.7	3.1	19.7	5.7	24.1
Croatia [1]	1999	119 216	9.6	0.5	20.5	3.5	5.3	13.0	8.7	38.8
Croatie [1]	2000	127 661	8.8	0.7	21.0	3.0	4.6	13.6	9.7	38.5
	2001	136 892	8.5	24.7[2,3]	...	...	4.6	14.7	10.9	36.6
Cuba	1998	23 515[11]	6.3	1.5	37.9	2.0	5.5	21.4	4.5	20.9
Cuba	1999	25 094[11]	6.5	1.5	39.3	1.9	5.5	20.1	4.5	20.6
	2000	27 240[11]	6.8	1.8	37.7	2.0	5.7	21.2	4.7	20.3
Cyprus	1999	4 829	4.2	0.3	10.9	2.0	7.7	22.1	9.2	43.5
Chypre	2000	5 259	3.7	0.3	10.7	2.1	7.1	22.5	9.4	44.1
	2001	5 603	3.9	0.3	10.0	2.1	7.1	22.6	10.0	44.0
Czech Republic [1]	2000	1 840 174	4.3	1.4	26.9	3.9	7.1	16.5	8.1	31.7
République tchèque [1]	2001	2 001 217	4.3	1.4	27.4	4.0	6.7	16.9	8.4	...
	2002	2 108 798	3.7	1.2	26.7	3.9	6.6	16.8	9.0	...

21

Value added by industries in current prices
Percentage distribution *[cont.]*
Valeur ajoutée par branche d'activité aux prix courants
Répartition en pourcentage *[suite]*

Region, country or area Région, pays ou zone	Year Année	Value added, gross (Mil. nat.cur) Valeur ajoutée, brute (Mil. mon. nat.)	Agriculture, hunting, forestry and fishing Agriculture, chasse, sylviculture et pêche	Mining and quarrying Activités extractives	Manu-facturing Activités de fabri-cation	Electricity, gas and water supply Electricité, gaz et eau	Cons-truc-tion Con-struc-tion	Wholesale, retail trade, restaurants and hotels Commerce, restaurants, hôtels	Transport, storage & commu-nication Transports, entépôts, communi-cations	Other activi-ties Autres activités
Denmark [1] Danemark [1]	1999	1 066 468	2.6	1.5	16.4	2.3	4.8	14.8	8.1	49.5
	2000	1 150 415	2.5	3.1	16.3	2.2	4.9	14.2	8.6	48.3
	2001	1 195 309	2.7	2.2	16.5	2.1	4.5	14.1	9.1	48.7
Djibouti Djibouti	1996	76 435	3.5[15]	0.2	2.8	6.8[9]	5.7	15.9	21.7	43.4
	1997	75 964	3.6[15]	0.2	2.8	6.6[9]	6.0	16.1	23.1	41.6
	1998	78 263	3.6[15]	0.2	2.7	5.3[9]	6.4	16.4	26.0	39.4
Dominica Dominique	1999	662[5]	17.2	0.7	7.4	5.1	7.4	10.6	16.6	...
	2000	671[5]	16.8	0.7	8.1	5.2	7.5	10.8	15.6	...
	2001	657[5]	15.7	0.7	7.2	5.5	7.5	10.9	14.9	...
Dominican Republic [1] Rép. dominicaine [1]	1994	165 808	10.8	1.1	20.2	1.4	7.7	16.4	9.8	32.6
	1995	193 436	10.1	1.3	19.6	1.7	7.7	17.3	9.0	33.3
	1996	228 022	8.9	1.0	19.3	1.8	7.3	20.4	8.8	32.5
Ecuador [1] Equateur [1]	1999	15 154[11,12]	12.9	13.6[16]	10.6	1.5	5.9	16.8	12.0	28.9
	2000	14 326[11,12]	11.8	23.9[16]	5.7	1.2	7.9	18.7	12.0	21.5
	2001	18 815[11,12]	10.0	13.8[16]	9.2	1.9	8.0	17.6	17.9	25.3
Egypt + Egypte +	1999	315 667[5]	16.7	7.4	19.4[17]	1.6[18]	4.8	17.4	8.8	23.9[18]
	2000	332 437[5]	16.6	7.2	19.6[17]	1.6[18]	4.7	16.9	9.1	24.4[18]
	2001	354 519[5]	16.5	7.6	19.6[17]	1.6[18]	4.7	16.1	9.2	24.7[18]
El Salvador El Salvador	1999	106 354[11]	10.7	0.4	23.2	2.0	4.4	19.5[13]	8.6	31.1[13]
	2000	111 978[11]	10.0	0.4	23.7	1.7	4.5	19.9[13]	8.7	31.1[13]
	2001	116 678[11]	9.8	0.5	23.7	1.6	4.8	20.1[13]	8.7	30.8[13]
Equatorial Guinea Guinée équatoriale	1989	40 948	56.1	...	1.3	3.1	3.7	8.8	2.0	25.0
	1990	42 765	53.6	...	1.3	3.4	3.8	7.6	2.2	28.0
	1991	43 932	53.1	...	1.4	3.1	3.0	7.6	1.9	30.0
Estonia [1] Estonie [1]	1999	69 011	6.7	1.1	16.5	3.6	6.0	15.8	15.2	35.2
	2000	78 002	6.1	1.0	18.1	3.3	6.1	15.3	16.3	33.8
	2001	86 329	5.8	1.0	18.4	3.3	5.9	15.6	16.4	33.4
Ethiopia incl. Eritrea + Ethiopie y comp. Erythrée +	1990	11 436[5]	41.1	0.2	11.1	1.5	3.6	9.6	7.2	25.7
	1991	12 295[5]	41.0	0.3	10.3	1.5	3.2	9.4	7.1	27.3
	1992	12 544[5]	50.3	0.3	9.1	1.3	2.8	10.2	5.4	20.6
Fiji Fidji	1987	1 399[5]	21.9	2.2	11.2	3.1	3.6	14.9	9.5	33.5
	1988	1 518[5]	18.4	4.1	9.0	3.4	4.0	18.6	10.7	31.8
	1989	1 759[5]	18.5	3.2	9.9	3.1	3.8	21.5	9.6	30.3
Finland [1] Finlande [1]	1999	106 182	3.5	0.3	24.8	2.1	5.6	12.0	10.3	41.3
	2000	116 352	3.7	0.2	25.9	1.7	5.7	11.2	10.4	41.2
	2001	121 577	3.4	0.2	25.0	1.8	5.7	11.3	10.6	42.0
France [1] France [1]	1999	1 241 789	3.0	0.2	18.0	2.2	4.4	12.9	6.4	53.0
	2000	1 305 678	2.7	0.2	17.9	2.0	4.6	12.8	6.3	53.4
	2001	1 358 915	2.7	0.2	17.9	1.9	4.8	12.9	6.5	53.1
French Guiana Guyane française	1990	6 454	10.1	7.6	...	0.7	12.8	13.5	7.7	47.5
	1991	7 385	7.4	7.6	...	0.5	12.1	13.1	12.3	47.0
	1992	8 052	7.2	9.0	...	0.6	10.8	11.9	11.4	49.1
French Polynesia Polynésie française	1991	305 211	4.1	...	7.5	1.8	5.7	...	...	...
	1992	314 265	3.8	...	7.5	2.1	5.9	...	...	...
	1993	329 266	3.9	...	6.7	2.1	5.7	...	...	...
Gabon Gabon	1987	986 000	10.9	28.4	7.1	2.7	7.2	9.2	8.1	26.5
	1988	965 700	11.2	22.6	7.3	3.0	5.2	14.4	9.1	27.3
	1989	1 128 400	10.4	32.3	5.7	2.5	5.5	12.4	8.2	23.1
Gambia + Gambie +	1991	2 962	22.3	0.0	5.5	0.9	4.4	39.1	10.9	17.0
	1992	3 100	18.4	0.0	5.7	1.0	4.7	41.7	11.2	17.4
	1993	3 296	20.2	0.0	5.1	1.0	4.5	38.3	12.5	18.4

21
Value added by industries in current prices
Percentage distribution *[cont.]*
Valeur ajoutée par branche d'activité aux prix courants
Répartition en pourcentage *[suite]*

% of Value added – % de la valeur ajoutée

Region, country or area / Région, pays ou zone	Year / Année	Value added, gross (Mil. nat.cur) / Valeur ajoutée, brute (Mil. mon. nat.)	Agriculture, hunting, forestry and fishing / Agriculture, chasse, sylviculture et pêche	Mining and quarrying / Activités extractives	Manu-facturing / Activités de fabri-cation	Electricity, gas and water supply / Electricité, gaz et eau	Cons-truc-tion / Con-struc-tion	Wholesale, retail trade, restaurants and hotels / Commerce, restaurants, hôtels	Transport, storage & commu-nication / Transports, entêpots, communi-cations	Other activi-ties / Autres activités
Georgia [1] / Géorgie [1]	2000	5 702	21.3	...	18.3[3,6]	...	3.9	15.8	15.1	25.5
	2001	6 249	21.9	...	17.7[3,6]	...	4.0	16.5	14.6	25.3
	2002	6 848	19.5	...	18.2[3,6]	...	4.8	16.6	15.7	25.3
Germany [1] / Allemagne [1]	2000	1 889 410	1.2	0.3	22.2	1.8	5.1	12.6	5.9	51.0
	2001	1 929 130	1.2	0.3	22.2	1.9	4.7	12.7	6.0	51.0
	2002	1 963 580	...		22.0	...	4.4	12.5	6.1	...
Ghana / Ghana	1994	4 686 000	42.0	6.3	10.1	3.0	8.3	6.4	4.8	18.2
	1995	7 040 200	42.7	5.3	10.3	2.9	8.3	6.5	4.3	18.8
	1996	10 067 000	43.9	5.3	9.7	3.0	8.5	6.5	4.2	17.9
Greece [1] / Grèce [1]	1999	102 277	7.9	0.6	11.4	2.1	7.3	21.2	7.1	42.5
	2000	110 173	7.3	0.6	11.3	1.9	7.2	21.4	7.9	42.4
	2001	119 111	7.0	0.6	11.2	1.9	7.8	21.7	8.2	42.0
Grenada / Grenade	1989	393	18.7	0.4	5.3	2.9	10.3	18.8	13.9	34.4
	1990	440	16.2	0.4	5.1	3.0	10.1	18.7	13.7	32.8
	1991	463	14.9	0.4	5.3	3.1	10.4	19.5	14.3	32.1
Guadeloupe / Guadeloupe	1990	15 036	6.7	5.4[2]	...	1.0	7.4	18.3	5.9	55.2
	1991	16 278	7.3	6.1[2]	...	1.4	7.0	16.5	6.0	55.5
	1992	17 968	6.7	6.9[2]	...	1.7	6.5	16.2	7.9	54.1
Guinea-Bissau / Guinée-Bissau	1989	358 875	44.6	7.9[2,3]	...	...	9.7	25.7	3.6	8.5
	1990	510 094	44.6	8.2[2,3]	...	...	10.0	25.7	3.7	7.8
	1991	854 985	44.7	8.5[2,3]	...	...	8.4	25.8	3.9	8.7
Guyana / Guyana	1999	105 095[5]	41.2	15.4	3.5[3]	...	4.5[19]	4.1[13]	6.8	24.5[13]
	2000	108 087[5]	36.1	15.9	3.2[3]	...	4.9[19]	4.4[13]	7.8	27.7[13]
	2001	112 218[5]	35.4	15.7	3.2[3]	...	5.0[19]	4.4[13]	8.6	27.8[13]
Honduras / Honduras	1998	60 068[5]	19.1	1.8	18.6	5.1	5.1	12.3	5.0	33.0
	1999	65 881[5]	15.9	2.0	19.6	4.9	5.9	12.7	5.2	33.8
	2000	75 924[5]	15.0	2.0	19.8	4.8	5.7	12.8	5.2	34.7
Hungary [1] / Hongrie [1]	1999	9 973 026	4.8	0.3	23.5	3.9	4.7	12.8	10.2	39.8
	2000	11 482 673	4.3	0.3	24.0	3.6	5.2	12.5	8.5	41.7
	2001	13 090 637	4.3	0.2	22.7	3.2	5.1	13.2	8.4	42.8
Iceland [1] / Islande [1]	#1997	453 513	10.1	0.2	15.5	3.8	7.8	14.1	8.1	40.5
	1998	495 429	10.0	0.1	14.6	3.6	8.5	14.4	8.2	40.5
	1999	526 762	9.5	0.1	13.2	3.4	8.2	14.7	7.7	43.3
India + / Inde +	1998	15 980 770[5]	27.7	2.2	15.8	2.7	5.8	13.8	7.0	24.9
	1999	17 556 380[5]	26.2	2.3	15.2	2.5	6.0	13.8	7.1	26.9
	2000	18 958 430[5]	24.9	2.4	15.8	2.6	6.1	13.8	7.3	27.1
Indonesia / Indonésie	1999	1 099 732 000[11]	19.6	10.0	26.0	1.2	6.1	16.0[13]	5.0	16.0[13]
	2000	1 282 018 000[11]	17.0	13.8	26.2	1.2	5.9	15.2[13]	5.0	15.7[13]
	2001	1 490 974 000[11]	16.4	13.6	26.1	1.2	5.6	16.1[13]	5.4	15.7[13]
Iran (Islamic Rep. of) + [1] / Iran (Rép. islamique d') + [1]	1999	430 549 500[12]	14.6	15.0	13.1	0.9	3.8	15.5	7.4	29.7
	2000	568 192 900[12]	13.2	18.1	12.9	1.2	3.5	14.5	8.3	28.2
	2001	663 390 800[12]	13.0	15.5	13.8	1.3	3.6	14.2	9.0	29.7
Iraq / Iraq	1998	4 653 524[5]	36.6	0.3	3.0	...	0.8	21.4[20]	26.7	...
	1999	6 301 285[5]	34.6	0.5	3.9	...	0.7	21.0[20]	28.5	...
	2000	7 377 758[5]	31.3	0.5	4.7	...	1.2	19.3[20]	28.8	...
Ireland [1] / Irlande [1]	1999	79 969	4.0	0.6	33.7	1.3	6.6	12.2	5.5	36.1
	2000	91 606	3.8	0.7	33.3	1.2	7.3	12.6	5.1	36.0
	2001	102 911	3.4	0.6	32.9	1.3	7.3	12.7	5.5	36.2
Israel [1] / Israël [1]	1999	394 671	1.8	...	17.8[6]	1.9	5.9	10.1	7.9	55.0
	2000	432 267	1.6	...	17.6[6]	1.9	5.3	10.1	7.8	56.1
	2001	437 086	1.7	...	16.6[6]	1.9	4.9	9.8	7.7	57.6

21

Value added by industries in current prices
Percentage distribution *[cont.]*
　　Valeur ajoutée par branche d'activité aux prix courants
　　　Répartition en pourcentage *[suite]*

			% of Value added – % de la valeur ajoutée							
Region, country or area Région, pays ou zone	Year Année	Value added, gross (Mil. nat.cur) Valeur ajoutée, brute (Mil. mon. nat.)	Agriculture, hunting, forestry and fishing Agriculture, chasse, sylviculture et pêche	Mining and quarrying Activités extractives	Manu- facturing Activités de fabri- cation	Electricity, gas and water supply Électricité, gaz et eau	Cons- truc- tion Con- struc- tion	Wholesale, retail trade, restaurants and hotels Commerce, restaurants, hôtels	Transport, storage & commu- nication Transports, entépôts, communi- cations	Other activi- ties Autres activités
Italy [1] Italie [1]	2000	1 082 138	2.8	0.5	20.4	2.2	4.8	16.6	7.4	45.3
	2001	1 140 830	2.7	0.4	20.1	2.3	4.9	16.6	7.4	45.5
	2002	1 176 803	2.6	0.4	19.7	2.2	4.9	16.5	7.1	46.4
Jamaica [1] Jamaïque [1]	1999	294 808[11]	7.0	4.1	13.2	3.5	9.4	20.2	10.0	32.6
	2000	327 874[11]	6.5	4.2	13.2	3.9	9.4	20.4	9.8	32.5
	2001	351 948[11]	6.5	4.2	13.2	4.0	9.9	20.3	10.7	31.1
Japan [1] Japon [1]	1999	530 109 600	1.4	0.1	20.9	2.7	7.3	13.8[21]	6.2	48.1
	2000	531 836 500	1.3	0.1	21.1	2.7	7.1	13.4[21]	6.1	48.7
	2001	527 029 800	1.3	0.1	19.8	2.8	6.8	13.4[21]	6.1	...
Jordan Jordanie	1999	4 949	2.3	3.3	14.5	2.6	4.2	11.7	15.4	46.0
	2000	5 255	2.3	3.3	14.6	2.6	3.9	11.8	15.6	46.0
	2001	5 538	2.2	3.2	14.3	2.5	4.2	12.0	15.9	45.7
Kazakhstan [1] Kazakhstan [1]	2000	2 466 199	8.6	13.7	18.1	3.2	5.5	13.7	12.1	25.1
	2001	3 059 400	9.3	12.1	17.4	3.0	5.8	12.8	11.9	27.6
	2002	3 530 500	8.4	31.1[2,3]	...	...	6.5	12.7	12.2	29.0
Kenya Kenya	1999	34 062[5,10]	21.9	0.1	11.6	1.1	4.0	20.3	6.7	30.2
	2000	35 846[5,10]	18.9	0.2	12.4	1.1	4.1	22.7	7.0	29.3
	2001	40 066[5,10]	18.3	0.2	12.1	1.1	4.1	24.3	6.6	28.8
Korea, Republic of [1] Corée, République de [1]	2000	521 669 039[11]	4.7	0.3	31.3	2.8	8.0	12.1	6.7	34.1
	2001	554 630 919[11]	4.3	0.3	30.3	2.8	8.3	12.2	6.6	35.1
	2002	605 294 647[11]	3.9	0.3	28.8	2.9	8.3	11.8	6.5	37.5
Kuwait Koweït	1999	9 247[11]	0.4	36.0	11.0	-0.5	2.6	7.5	5.3	37.8
	2000	11 399[11]	0.4	48.6	7.0	-0.9	2.1	5.9	4.4	42.2
	2001	10 467[11]	0.4	43.8	6.4	-1.0	2.3	6.6	4.9	36.6
Kyrgyzstan [1] Kirghizistan [1]	1999	45 201	37.6	...	23.9[3,6]	...	3.3	13.9	5.2	16.2
	2000	61 018	36.7	...	25.6[3,6]	...	4.1	12.9	4.1	16.7
	2001	69 044	37.0	...	24.8[3,6]	...	4.0	13.2	4.7	16.3
Lao People's Dem. Rep. Rép. dém. pop. lao	1999	10 253 626	53.7	0.5	17.0	2.4	2.7	11.8	5.8	6.1
	2000	13 565 564	52.5	0.5	17.0	3.1	2.3	11.7	5.9	7.0
	2001	15 563 971	51.2	0.5	17.9	2.9	2.4	11.8	6.0	7.3
Latvia [1] Lettonie [1]	1999	3 411	4.5	0.1	15.3	4.4	7.1	18.9	15.3	34.3
	2000	3 823	4.6	0.1	14.7	3.9	6.7	19.2	15.5	35.3
	2001	4 204	4.5	0.1	14.9	3.8	6.2	20.1	15.4	35.1
Lebanon Liban	1982	12 600	8.5	...	13.0	5.4	3.4	28.3	3.7	37.5
	1994	14 992 000[22]	12.1	...	17.7	...	9.5	28.8	2.8	29.5
	1995	17 779 000[22]	12.6	...	17.5	...	9.4	30.4	2.9	28.4
Lesotho [1] Lesotho [1]	1999	5 182[5]	16.9	0.1	15.9	6.2	17.9	9.5	3.5	29.8
	2000	5 210[5,10]	19.3	0.2	17.4	6.1	18.9	10.9	3.7	31.7
	2001	5 636[5,10]	19.4	0.2	18.1	6.2	18.6	11.2	3.8	30.5
Liberia Libéria	1987	1 009	37.8	10.4	7.2	1.9	3.2	6.0	7.5	26.0
	1988	1 080	38.2	10.7	7.4	1.7	2.7	5.9	7.3	26.1
	1989	1 119	36.7	10.9	7.3	1.7	2.4	5.7	7.1	28.3
Libyan Arab Jamah. Jamah. arabe libyenne	1983	8 482[5]	3.0	48.8	3.2	0.9	10.4	6.1	4.6	23.0
	1984	7 681[5]	3.4	40.9	3.9	1.2	11.1	7.9	5.3	26.4
	1985	8 050[5]	3.5	41.6	4.5	1.3	11.4	7.0	5.0	25.8
Lithuania [1] Lituanie [1]	1999	38 054	8.4	0.7	17.6	4.5	7.9	16.9	11.4	32.4
	2000	40 788	7.7	0.9	20.9	4.0	6.1	17.1	12.2	31.0
	2001	43 454	7.1	1.1	22.5	4.3	6.1	17.0	12.5	29.6
Luxembourg [1] Luxembourg [1]	1998	17 470	0.7	0.1	12.1	1.2	6.0	12.4	9.8	54.6
	1999	19 754	0.7	0.1	10.8	1.1	5.6	11.4	8.8	53.1
	2000	21 237	0.6	0.1	10.9	1.0	5.8	11.6	9.4	52.6

21
Value added by industries in current prices
Percentage distribution [cont.]
Valeur ajoutée par branche d'activité aux prix courants
Répartition en pourcentage [suite]

% of Value added – % de la valeur ajoutée

Region, country or area / Région, pays ou zone	Year / Année	Value added, gross (Mil. nat.cur) / Valeur ajoutée, brute (Mil. mon. nat.)	Agriculture, hunting, forestry and fishing / Agriculture, chasse, sylviculture et pêche	Mining and quarrying / Activités extractives	Manufacturing / Activités de fabrication	Electricity, gas and water supply / Electricité, gaz et eau	Construction / Construction	Wholesale, retail trade, restaurants and hotels / Commerce, restaurants, hôtels	Transport, storage & communication / Transports, entépôts, communications	Other activities / Autres activités
Madagascar	1983	1 187 400	44.2	15.6	...	...	...	30.4	...	9.7
Madagascar	1984	1 323 100	43.9	16.2	...	...	...	30.3	...	9.7
	1985	1 500 600	43.5	16.9	...	...	...	30.1	...	9.5
Malawi	1987	2 505[22]	28.1	...	17.7	1.1	2.4	17.0	3.9	23.9
Malawi	1988	3 200[22]	29.5	...	17.4	1.2	1.8	17.2	3.7	22.2
	1989	3 961[22]	31.2	...	16.5	1.8	2.2	15.2	4.3	23.1
Malaysia	1999	316 357	10.3	7.3	29.4	3.0	4.4	14.0	6.4	25.1
Malaisie	2000	358 337	8.3	10.4	31.5	3.0	3.9	13.1	6.4	23.3
	2001	350 895	8.1	10.3	29.1	3.4	4.1	13.7	6.9	24.5
Mali	1990	655 600	47.8	1.6	8.1[23]	3.8[24]	...	18.8	4.9	15.1
Mali	1991	662 500	46.1	1.7	6.9[23]	4.3[24]	...	20.2	5.0	15.9
	1992	707 000	47.2	1.5	7.0[23]	4.4[24]	...	19.3	5.0	15.6
Malta	1995	989[5]	2.8	3.5[24]	24.4	6.2	...	13.3	6.7	43.1
Malte	1996	1 053[5]	2.9	3.4[24]	23.6	5.6	...	12.6	6.5	45.4
	1997	1 111[5]	3.0	3.4[24]	22.7	6.7	...	12.2	6.2	46.1
Marshall Islands	1995	105	14.9	0.3	2.6	2.0	10.2	17.0	6.2	46.8
Iles Marshall	1996	95	14.3	0.3	1.6	2.7	7.0	18.7	7.3	48.2
	1997	90	14.3	0.4	1.7	3.1	7.0	17.9	7.9	47.7
Martinique	1990	18 835	5.7	7.9[2]	...	2.5	4.9	18.9	6.2	53.9
Martinique	1991	20 377	5.7	7.8[2]	...	2.4	5.3	18.9	6.3	53.6
	1992	21 869	5.1	8.1[2]	...	2.2	5.2	18.4	6.5	54.5
Mauritania	1987	60 302[5]	32.3	8.3	12.1	...	6.3	13.0	5.1	22.8
Mauritanie	1988	65 069[5]	32.4	7.7	13.0	...	6.3	13.2	5.1	22.3
	1989	75 486[5]	34.2	10.4	10.3	...	6.4	...	4.9	14.5
Mauritius[1]	1999	97 684	5.7	0.1	23.0	1.4	5.8	18.4	11.6	34.0
Maurice[1]	2000	110 224	6.5	0.1	22.4	1.7	5.6	17.1	12.3	34.2
	2001	123 242	6.9	0.1	21.9	2.1	5.3	17.3	12.4	34.0
Mexico[1]	1998	3 553 149	5.2	1.4	21.1	1.2	4.6	19.7	10.7	36.0
Mexique[1]	1999	4 262 714	4.5	1.4	20.7	1.3	4.9	19.7	11.0	36.4
	2000	5 035 548	4.0	1.4	20.1	1.1	5.0	21.2	11.0	36.1
Mongolia	1999	929 984	36.8	8.6	5.9	3.6	2.5	20.6	9.1	12.9
Mongolie	2000	1 030 144	28.8	11.4	6.1	2.4	1.9	23.7	10.9	14.9
	2001	1 136 506	24.4	8.9	7.9	2.9	1.9	26.2	12.8	15.0
Montserrat	1985	90[5]	4.8	1.3	5.7	3.7	7.9	18.0	11.5	47.2
Montserrat	1986	103[5]	4.3	1.4	5.6	3.7	11.3	18.7	11.6	43.4
	1987	118[5]	4.1	1.3	5.7	3.2	11.5	22.1	11.1	41.0
Morocco	1999	334 593	15.8	2.2	17.8	8.1	4.9	25.3	6.5	19.4
Maroc	2000	343 121	14.4	2.1	18.1	7.4	5.3	25.7	7.2	19.7
	2001	372 719	16.2	2.0	17.4	7.1	5.2	24.5	7.1	20.4
Mozambique[1]	2000	56 585 088	24.3	0.4	12.1	2.3	9.4	23.2	9.4	19.1
Mozambique[1]	2001	71 011 848	24.2	0.4	13.9	2.1	8.7	22.4	9.6	18.9
	2002	82 410 040	24.3	0.3	13.2	2.2	9.5	22.4	9.4	18.7
Myanmar +	1996	791 980	60.1	0.6	7.1	0.3[18]	2.4	22.6[13]	3.5	3.4[13,25]
Myanmar +	1997	1 109 554	59.4	0.6	7.1	0.1[18]	2.4	23.2[13]	3.9	3.1[13,25]
	1998	1 559 996	59.1	0.5	7.2	0.1[18]	2.4	23.9[13]	4.0	2.7[13,25]
Namibia[1]	1999	18 487	11.2	10.5	11.2	2.9	2.6	11.9	6.6	43.0
Namibie[1]	2000	21 616	10.8	12.1	11.0	2.8	2.2	14.3	6.3	40.6
	2001	24 729	9.8	14.1	10.7	2.6	3.1	14.1	5.8	39.8
Nepal +	1999	330 018[5]	40.1	0.5	9.2	1.4	10.1	11.9	7.5	19.3
Népal +	2000	366 251[5]	39.6	0.5	9.2	1.6	10.2	11.7	8.0	19.2
	2001	393 566[5]	38.4	0.5	9.0	1.8	10.1	11.3	8.5	20.5

21
Value added by industries in current prices
Percentage distribution *[cont.]*
Valeur ajoutée par branche d'activité aux prix courants
Répartition en pourcentage *[suite]*

% of Value added – % de la valeur ajoutée

Region, country or area Région, pays ou zone	Year Année	Value added, gross (Mil. nat.cur) Valeur ajoutée, brute (Mil. mon. nat.)	Agriculture, hunting, forestry and fishing Agriculture, chasse, sylviculture et pêche	Mining and quarrying Activités extractives	Manu- facturing Activités de fabri- cation	Electricity, gas and water supply Électricité, gaz et eau	Cons- truc- tion Con- struc- tion	Wholesale, retail trade, restaurants and hotels Commerce, restaurants, hôtels	Transport, storage & commu- nication Transports, entepôts, communi- cations	Other activi- ties Autres activités
Netherlands [1] Pays-Bas [1]	1999	344 022	2.8	1.9	16.3	1.7	5.6	15.5	7.3	49.0
	2000	370 972	2.7	2.6	16.3	1.5	5.7	15.2	7.1	48.9
	2001	393 843	2.7	3.0	15.6	1.5	5.9	14.9	7.0	49.4
Netherlands Antilles Antilles néerlandaises	1995	4 443	0.7[6]	...	6.3	3.7	6.5	24.0	12.4	46.3
	1996	4 644	0.6[6]	...	6.5	3.6	6.8	23.6	10.1	48.6
	1997	4 759	0.6[6]	...	5.7	4.1	7.0	22.9	10.5	49.3
New Caledonia Nouvelle-Calédonie	1994	306 748	1.9	7.4	6.6	1.5	6.0	23.0[13]	6.3	47.4[13]
	1995	329 296	1.8	8.7	6.0	1.5	5.7	22.2[13]	6.3	47.7[13]
	1996	335 482	1.7	8.5	5.7	1.6	5.0	22.8[13]	6.7	47.8[13]
New Zealand + [1] Nouvelle-Zélande + [1]	1996	92 906	7.3	1.4	17.3	2.7	4.4	15.1	8.1	43.8
	1997	96 285	6.9	1.3	17.0	2.8	4.5	15.1	7.9	44.4
	1998	97 809	6.7	1.2	16.2	2.7	4.3	15.4	7.7	45.8
Nicaragua Nicaragua	1999	26 130	31.6	1.0	14.8	1.1	6.0	23.0	3.4	19.1
	2000	30 858	33.0	0.7	14.3	1.1	6.2	22.4	3.3	18.9
	2001	34 242	32.9	0.7	14.1	1.1	6.3	22.3	3.3	19.2
Niger Niger	1985	627 027	37.9	8.3	7.4	2.3	3.6	16.3	4.4	19.9
	1986	622 426	37.3	7.6	7.9	2.6	4.6	14.6	4.2	21.1
	1987	632 248	34.6	7.8	9.0	2.8	5.3	14.1	4.3	22.2
Nigeria + Nigéria +	1992	549 809	26.5	46.6	5.7	0.3	1.1	11.5[26]	1.7	6.7
	1993	701 473	33.1	35.9	6.2	0.2	1.1	14.6[26]	2.2	6.8
	1994	914 334	38.2	25.0	7.1	0.2	1.1	17.5[26]	3.5	7.3
Norway [1] Norvège [1]	1995	835 001	2.8	13.4	13.3	2.9	4.0	12.6	10.6	40.0
	1996	913 191	2.4	17.1	12.2	2.6	4.0	12.1	10.2	38.8
	1997	987 454	2.2	17.5	12.2	2.6	4.2	11.9	10.2	38.1
Oman [1] Oman [1]	1999	6 156[11]	2.6	38.7	4.3	1.2	2.3	13.4	7.1	30.5
	2000	7 797[11]	1.9	47.9	5.3	1.0	1.9	11.2	5.8	25.1
	2001	7 817[11]	2.0	42.0	8.2	1.0	2.1	12.1	6.3	26.3
Pakistan + Pakistan +	1999	2 921 988[5]	26.7	0.6	15.3	3.9	3.3	15.2[13]	10.7	24.3[13]
	2000	3 161 923[5]	25.0	0.7	15.8	3.3	3.2	15.5[13]	11.3	25.3[13]
	2001	3 428 318[5]	24.2	0.7	15.7	3.1	3.0	14.9[13]	11.5	26.9[13]
Panama Panama	1998	9 391[11]	7.0	0.4	8.0	3.4	4.6	19.4	14.8	42.4
	1999	9 733[11]	6.9	0.5	7.5	3.6	4.9	17.7	15.8	43.1
	2000	10 194[11]	6.7	0.4	7.0	3.9	4.8	17.3	17.0	42.9
Papua New Guinea [1] Papouasie-Nvl- Guinée [1]	1997	7 064[22]	31.3	18.5	9.2	1.1	5.3	9.5[27]	5.0	...
	1998	7 863[22]	30.9	20.8	9.2	1.1	4.7	9.0[27]	4.9	...
	1999	8 781[22]	28.7	23.8	9.1	1.1	4.1	9.5[27]	4.9	...
Paraguay Paraguay	1993	11 991 719	24.5	0.4	16.5	3.4	5.9	30.4[13]	3.9	15.0[13]
	1994	14 960 131	23.7	0.4	15.7	3.9	6.0	30.5[13]	3.9	15.9[13]
	1995	17 699 000	24.8	0.3	15.7	4.3	6.0	29.5[13]	3.7	15.8[13]
Peru [1] Pérou [1]	1999	158 526	9.0	5.4	15.4	2.4	6.4	19.6	8.6	33.1
	2000	168 949	8.7	5.8	16.0	2.5	5.8	19.5	8.9	32.7
	2001	171 350	8.5	5.8	15.9	2.6	5.5	19.4	9.0	33.3
Philippines Philippines	1999	2 976 904	17.1	0.6	21.6	2.9	5.5	16.0	5.4	30.8
	2000	3 308 318	15.9	0.6	22.5	2.9	5.3	16.2	6.0	30.5
	2001	3 639 980	15.1	0.6	22.8	3.2	5.0	16.1	6.8	30.4
Poland [1] Pologne [1]	#2000	622 840[8]	3.6	2.6	20.0	3.1	8.2	21.6	6.9	33.9
	2001	656 048[8]	3.8	2.3	18.1	3.7	7.3	21.7	7.3	35.7
	2002	674 501[8]	3.1	2.4	17.4	4.0	6.5	22.2	7.9	36.5
Portugal [1] Portugal [1]	1997	85 102	4.2	0.4	19.4	3.0	7.2	17.3	6.4	42.1
	1998	91 721	3.9	0.4	18.7	3.0	7.4	17.5	6.6	42.5
	1999	97 489	3.7	0.4	18.2	2.9	7.5	17.1	6.5	43.8

21

Value added by industries in current prices
Percentage distribution [cont.]
Valeur ajoutée par branche d'activité aux prix courants
Répartition en pourcentage [suite]

% of Value added – % de la valeur ajoutée

Region, country or area Région, pays ou zone	Year Année	Value added, gross (Mil. nat.cur) Valeur ajoutée, brute (Mil. mon. nat.)	Agriculture, hunting, forestry and fishing Agriculture, chasse, sylviculture et pêche	Mining and quarrying Activités extractives	Manu-facturing Activités de fabri-cation	Electricity, gas and water supply Electricité, gaz et eau	Cons-truc-tion Cons-truc-tion	Wholesale, retail trade, restaurants and hotels Commerce, restaurants, hôtels	Transport, storage & commu-nication Transports, entépôts, communi-cations	Other activi-ties Autres activités
Puerto Rico +	1998	57 312	0.6	0.1	40.7	2.3	2.8[28]	15.3	4.8	33.5
Porto Rico +	1999	60 340	0.9	0.1	38.7	2.5	3.0[28]	15.0	4.6	35.2
	2000	67 062	0.7	0.1	40.4	2.3	2.9[28]	13.9	4.7	35.0
Qatar [1]	1998	38 356	0.7	33.9	7.7	1.6	7.1	8.2	4.9	36.0
Qatar [1]	1999	46 170	0.6	44.7	6.2	1.6	5.2	7.2	4.1	30.3
	2000	60 948	0.4	64.1	5.8	1.3	3.8	6.2	3.3	23.0
Republic of Moldova [1]	2000	14 402	28.3	0.2	15.8	2.1	3.0	14.7	10.6	25.3
République de	2001	17 206	24.8	0.2	17.5	3.0	3.4	14.3	11.5	25.3
Moldova [1]	2002	19 653	23.6	0.2	17.0	3.6	3.3	13.8	11.5	27.0
Réunion	1990	27 417	4.0	9.1[2]	...	4.7	5.9	20.5	4.0	51.7
Réunion	1991	30 371	3.7	9.1[2]	...	4.1	7.1	19.9	4.6	51.5
	1992	32 832[10]	3.5	9.0[2]	...	4.1	6.8	20.0	4.5	50.1
Romania [1]	1999	488 881 658	14.9	2.4	21.2	4.1	5.6	15.3	11.1	25.5
Roumanie [1]	2000	717 421 200	12.3	28.1[2,3]	...	...	5.6	16.1	11.7	26.2
	2001	1 044 982 300	14.8	28.4[2,3]	...	...	5.5	15.3	11.0	25.0
Russian Federation [1]	1999	4 282 941[29]	7.7	...	31.6[3,6]	...	6.1	23.1	9.7	21.8
Fédération de Russie [1]	2000	6 527 328[29]	6.7	...	32.7[3,6]	...	7.2	23.4	9.1	20.9
	2001	8 059 962[29]	7.0	...	29.7[3,6]	...	8.2	22.9	10.1	22.1
Rwanda	2000	680 822	40.7	0.3	10.0	0.6	8.9	10.4	7.3	22.0
Rwanda	2001	731 919	41.4	0.5	9.9	0.5	8.5	10.2	7.5	21.5
	2002	794 978	43.1	0.5	9.5	0.4	8.1	10.0	7.5	20.9
Saint Kitts and Nevis	1999	740[5]	3.1	0.3	9.7	1.8	12.7	21.9	13.2	37.4
Saint-Kitts-et-Nevis	2000	815[5]	2.6	0.4	9.8	2.1	15.1	18.2	12.6	39.1
	2001	843[5]	2.7	0.4	8.5	2.1	16.6	18.4	12.6	38.7
Saint Lucia	1996	1 409	8.2	0.4	6.2	3.6	7.1	24.7	17.4	32.4
Sainte-Lucie	1997	1 454	7.0	0.4	5.8	3.7	7.0	25.4	17.7	32.9
	1998	1 544	7.5	0.4	5.3	4.1	7.2	25.6	17.3	32.6
St. Vincent-Grenadines	1999	792[5]	10.0	0.3	5.9	5.6	12.2	18.3	19.7	28.0
St. Vincent-Grenadines	2000	812[5]	10.1	0.2	5.7	6.2	10.6	19.2	19.1	28.9
	2001	836[5]	9.8	0.2	5.4	6.6	11.0	19.5	17.8	29.7
Sao Tome and Principe	1986	2 259	29.2[6]	...	2.3	0.3	3.4	19.4	5.3	40.1
Sao Tomé-et-Principe	1987	2 797	31.5[6]	...	1.3	1.4	3.8	17.1	5.6	39.2
	1988	3 800	32.1[6]	...	1.7	1.0	4.2	18.8	4.1	38.1
Saudi Arabia +	1999	601 020	5.7	29.2	10.4	0.5	6.6	7.7	4.6	35.3
Arabie saoudite +	2000	704 765	5.0	37.2	9.7	0.4	5.9	6.8	4.1	30.9
	2001	698 302	5.1	34.5	10.0	0.5	6.2	7.1	4.4	32.2
Senegal	1998	2 746 000	17.9	1.0	12.3	2.3	4.0	27.5	11.1	23.1
Sénégal	1999	2 925 000	18.6	1.1	12.1	2.2	4.4	27.0	11.3	22.6
	2000	3 114 000	19.4	1.1	12.0	2.2	4.3	25.7	11.9	22.4
Serbia and Montenegro [1]	1998	134 968	18.4	5.0	22.3	4.2	5.3	10.1	10.2	24.6
Serbie-et-Monténégro [1]	1999	176 542	20.6	3.9	21.9	4.5	4.2	10.4	9.4	25.1
	2000	358 750	21.1	3.6	22.1	2.5	3.9	11.9	7.1	27.8
Seychelles	1999	3 179	3.2	...	15.8[6,23]	2.4	10.2	8.3	32.8	27.2
Seychelles	2000	3 274	3.1	...	15.0[6,23]	1.9	10.4	9.0	33.8	26.8
	2001	3 278	3.1	...	14.6[6,23]	2.5	9.4	9.2	33.0	28.1
Sierra Leone +	1988	42 364	39.3	6.3	7.7	0.3	2.6	20.9	10.5	12.3
Sierra Leone +	1989	81 921	37.3	7.0	7.1	0.2	1.9	25.0	10.8	10.6
	1990	148 652	35.3	9.5	8.7	0.1	1.3	20.3	8.9	15.9
Singapore	1999	149 121	...	...	23.2[6,30]	1.6	7.5	17.2	11.1	39.3
Singapour	2000	168 290	...	...	25.6[6,30]	1.5	5.9	18.3	10.6	38.1
	2001	163 067	...	...	22.2[6,30]	1.9	5.8	18.2	10.6	41.4

21
Value added by industries in current prices
Percentage distribution *[cont.]*
Valeur ajoutée par branche d'activité aux prix courants
Répartition en pourcentage *[suite]*

% of Value added – % de la valeur ajoutée

Region, country or area Région, pays ou zone	Year Année	Value added, gross (Mil. nat.cur) Valeur ajoutée, brute (Mil. mon. nat.)	Agriculture, hunting, forestry and fishing Agriculture, chasse, sylviculture et pêche	Mining and quarrying Activités extractives	Manu-facturing Activités de fabri-cation	Electricity, gas and water supply Electricité, gaz et eau	Cons-truc-tion Cons-truc-tion	Wholesale, retail trade, restaurants and hotels Commerce, restaurants, hôtels	Transport, storage & commu-nication Transports, entépôts, communi-cations	Other activi-ties Autres activités
Slovakia [1] Slovaquie [1]	2000	827 319	4.7	0.9	22.8	4.0	5.4	16.7	10.9	34.8
	2001	903 505	4.5	0.8	23.3	2.6	5.0	16.7	12.3	34.8
	2002	984 314	4.5	0.7	22.4	3.4	5.4	15.7	11.1	36.8
Slovenia [1] Slovénie [1]	1999	3 179 760	3.6	1.2	27.0	3.1	6.2	14.5	8.1	36.3
	2000	3 562 382	3.2	1.0	27.2	3.2	6.0	14.5	7.9	36.9
	2001	4 043 150	3.1	0.9	26.8	3.3	5.8	14.6	7.7	37.7
Solomon Islands Iles Salomon	1984	199	53.5	-0.2	3.6	0.9	3.8	10.6	5.2	22.6
	1985	213	50.4	-0.7	3.8	1.0	4.2	10.4	5.1	25.8
	1986	224	48.3	-1.2	4.5	1.2	5.1	8.4	5.8	27.9
Somalia Somalie	1985	84 050[5]	66.1	0.3	4.9	0.1	2.2	10.1	6.7	9.5
	1986	112 584[5]	62.5	0.4	5.5	0.2	2.7	10.3	7.3	11.1
	1987	163 175[5]	64.9	0.3	5.1	-0.5	2.9	10.7	6.8	9.8
South Africa [1] Afrique du Sud [1]	1999	728 758	3.4	6.3	18.7	3.0	3.1	13.1	9.7	42.7
	2000	808 241	3.2	6.8	18.6	2.8	3.0	13.3	10.0	42.4
	2001	894 901	3.5	7.5	18.6	2.5	2.9	13.3	9.9	41.9
Spain [1] Espagne [1]	1999	529 880	3.8	0.4	18.2	2.4	7.9	19.4	8.2	39.7
	2000	571 392	3.5	0.4	18.1	2.2	8.4	19.4	8.1	39.9
	2001	615 642	3.4	0.4	17.3	2.1	8.7	18.9	8.6	40.3
Sri Lanka [1] Sri Lanka [1]	1999	987 176	19.5	1.3	19.5	2.0	7.4	20.8	12.2	17.3
	2000	1 116 455	18.1	1.5	20.1	1.9	7.3	21.9	12.1	17.1
	2001	1 243 978	17.4	1.4	20.3	2.3	7.2	21.5	12.6	17.2
Sudan + Soudan +	1994	4 440 648	40.5	6.5[2]	...	0.7	3.8	46.6[31]	...	1.9[32]
	1996	9 015 824	37.1	9.6[2]	...	0.9	5.0	44.4[31]	...	3.0[32]
	1997	15 865 432	40.5	9.1[2]	...	0.8	6.9	39.8[31]	...	2.8[32]
Suriname Suriname	1999	694 625	9.3	8.1	8.4	3.6	3.5	15.1	6.5	29.4
	2000	1 102 550	10.8	9.5	8.3	3.1	3.1	14.4	8.0	29.8
	2001	1 651 322	10.0	18.1	5.4	3.3	3.1	11.6	7.5	26.6
Swaziland + [1] Swaziland + [1]	1999	6 069[5]	17.0	1.0	35.8	1.9	5.4	9.1	4.7	25.0
	2000	6 670[5]	15.6	0.6	36.0	1.6	6.7	9.3	5.4	24.8
	2001	7 260[5]	14.5	0.3	38.0	1.5	6.2	9.5	5.4	24.5
Sweden [1] Suède [1]	1998	1 762 347	2.2	0.3	22.2	2.8	4.1	12.3	8.5	47.6
	1999	1 855 625	2.1	0.3	22.0	2.5	4.1	12.5	8.6	48.0
	2000	1 969 670	1.9	0.2	22.2	2.4	4.0	12.1	8.3	49.0
Switzerland Suisse	1985	234 650	3.5	...	25.1	2.1	7.4	17.8	6.2	37.9
	1990	324 289	3.0	...	23.7	1.9	8.1	18.7	5.7	39.0
	1991	343 983	2.9	...	22.6	1.9	7.8	16.6	5.8	42.4
Syrian Arab Republic Rép. arabe syrienne	1999	819 092	24.3	19.9	5.6	1.1	3.4	18.7	12.7	14.3
	2000	903 944	24.7	27.5	1.5	1.1	3.2	14.9	12.6	14.4
	2001	947 808	25.9	20.3	5.6	1.0	3.2	15.6	12.7	15.7
Tajikistan [1] Tadjikistan [1]	1998	950 700	27.1	...	23.2[3,6]	...	4.2	24.2	4.5	16.9
	1999	1 251 600	27.3	...	24.5[3,6]	...	5.8	21.2	7.9	13.3
	2000	1 661 800	29.4	...	26.8[3,6]	...	3.7	19.9	5.3	15.0
Thailand Thaïlande	1998	4 150 240	13.6	1.7	27.4	3.2	4.0	14.3	8.7	27.1
	1999	4 160 550	11.9	1.8	29.2	2.9	3.8	14.3	9.0	27.0
	2000	4 420 474	11.4	2.3	30.5	3.1	3.2	14.0	8.9	26.6
TFYR of Macedonia [1] L'ex-R.y. Macédoine [1]	1998	169 094	11.8	...	27.0[6]	2.9	6.4	14.3	7.2	30.4
	1999	171 948	11.0	...	25.8[6]	2.8	7.2	15.0	8.2	30.0
	2000	191 066	9.4	...	26.1[6]	2.8	6.7	18.2	8.6	28.2
Togo Togo	1980	223 479	28.5	9.8	7.4	1.8	6.2	20.6	6.9	...
	1981	242 311	28.6	9.3	6.7	1.7	4.5	21.8	7.1	...

21
Value added by industries in current prices
Percentage distribution *[cont.]*
Valeur ajoutée par branche d'activité aux prix courants
Répartition en pourcentage *[suite]*

% of Value added – % de la valeur ajoutée

Region, country or area Région, pays ou zone	Year Année	Value added, gross (Mil. nat.cur) Valeur ajoutée, brute (Mil. mon. nat.)	Agriculture, hunting, forestry and fishing Agriculture, chasse, sylviculture et pêche	Mining and quarrying Activités extractives	Manu-facturing Activités de fabri-cation	Electricity, gas and water supply Electricité, gaz et eau	Cons-truc-tion Con-struc-tion	Wholesale, retail trade, restaurants and hotels Commerce, restaurants, hôtels	Transport, storage & commu-nication Transports, entépôts, communi-cations	Other activi-ties Autres activités
Tonga + Tonga +	1999	213[5]	29.1	0.5	5.2	1.9	6.1	12.2	8.5	37.1
	2000	223[5]	26.5	0.4	5.4	1.8	6.3	14.3	8.1	37.7
	2001	244[5]	26.2	0.4	4.9	2.0	6.1	14.3	7.8	38.1
Trinidad and Tobago[1] Trinité-et-Tobago[1]	1998	37 682[10,11]	1.5	9.1	17.5	2.3	12.4	18.4	10.4	31.4
	1999	41 140[10,11]	1.6	10.4	23.0	2.2	11.7	18.5	10.1	30.8
	2000	49 654[10,11]	1.3	11.7	19.8	1.9	10.5	18.3	9.2	27.2
Tunisia[1] Tunisie[1]	1999	22 093[5]	14.5	4.1	20.2	2.1[9]	5.1	16.9[13]	8.6	28.5[13]
	2000	23 858[5]	13.8	4.3	20.4	2.0[9]	5.3	16.6[13]	8.9	28.8[13]
	2001	25 725[5]	13.0	4.0	20.7	2.0[9]	5.4	16.2[13]	9.3	29.3[13]
Turkey Turquie	1995	7 748 669 629	15.7	1.3	22.6	2.5	5.5	20.5	12.7	19.3
	1996	15 022 756536	16.6	1.2	20.8	2.7	5.7	20.1	12.9	19.9
	1997	29 235 581842	15.0	1.2	21.3	2.5	5.9	20.7	13.8	20.9
Turkmenistan[1] Turkménistan[1]	1999	20 056 000	24.8	...	31.4[3,6]	...	12.2	4.1	6.7	20.8
	2000	25 648 000	22.9	...	35.0[3,6]	...	6.8	3.5	6.6	25.1
	2001	33 863 000	24.7	...	36.6[3,6]	...	5.7	4.2	5.4	23.5
Uganda Ouganda	1997	6 565 455[5]	42.4	0.6	8.7	1.4	7.5	13.9	4.5	20.9
	1998	7 568 986[5]	43.5	0.6	8.8	1.3	7.6	13.7	4.5	20.0
	1999	8 356 013[5]	42.5	0.6	9.2	1.3	8.2	13.7	5.0	19.6
Ukraine[1] Ukraine[1]	1998	88 000	14.1	...	31.4[3,6]	...	5.6	8.6	14.3	25.9
	1999	109 600	14.1	...	34.4[3,6]	...	4.9	8.5	14.1	24.2
	2000	146 000	16.8	...	32.7[3,6]	...	4.2	10.4	13.6	22.3
United Arab Emirates Emirats arabes unis	1988	90 137	1.8	33.2	9.1	2.3	9.8	11.3	5.6	26.8
	1989	104 730	1.8	37.3	8.3	2.1	9.1	10.2	5.4	25.7
	1990	127 737	1.6	45.4	7.2	1.8	7.8	8.8	4.6	22.7
United Kingdom[1] Royaume-Uni[1]	1999	826 395	1.1	2.1	18.4	1.9	5.0	15.2	7.9	48.3
	2000	876 014	1.0	2.9	17.5	1.8	5.0	14.9	7.9	49.0
	2001	921 915	0.9	2.8	16.6	1.7	5.1	14.8	7.6	49.6
United Rep. of Tanzania Rép.-Unie de Tanzanie	2000	6 867 161	44.0	1.6	7.3[23]	1.6	5.0	12.0	4.8	23.7
	2001	7 792 480	43.7	1.7	7.2[23]	1.6	5.2	11.9	4.6	24.0
	2002	8 805 683	43.2	2.0	7.3[23]	1.7	5.3	11.8	4.6	24.2
United States[1] Etats-Unis[1]	1999	8 627 800[5,33]	1.5	1.2	17.2	2.4	4.9	19.4	7.2	53.4
	2000	9 236 200[5,33]	1.5	1.4	16.5	2.3	5.0	19.4	7.1	53.8
	2001	9 477 300[5,33]	1.5	1.5	15.0	2.3	5.1	19.3	7.0	55.3
Uruguay Uruguay	2000	254 778[11]	5.9	0.3	16.1	3.9	5.6	12.7	8.6	46.8
	2001	261 593[11]	5.8	0.3	15.4	4.2	5.1	12.3	8.6	48.4
	2002	277 551[11]	8.9	0.2	16.4	4.5	4.0	11.5	8.6	45.8
Uzbekistan[1] Ouzbékistan[1]	1998	1 212 700	31.3	...	17.4[3,6]	...	8.8	9.9	7.9	24.7
	1999	1 842 900	33.5	...	16.5[3,6]	...	7.8	10.4	8.0	23.7
	2000	2 788 100	34.9	...	15.8[3,6]	...	7.0	10.9	9.3	22.2
Vanuatu Vanuatu	1996	28 227	24.9	...	5.0	1.7	5.6	32.0	7.3	23.5
	1997	29 477	25.2	...	4.9	1.7	5.5	32.4	7.3	23.1
	1998	29 545	23.1	...	4.9	1.8	4.6	34.3	7.4	23.9
Venezuela Venezuela	1999	60 336 461	4.8	13.8[34]	13.6[16]	1.5[9]	5.6	16.2	9.5	34.9
	2000	79 740 289	4.1	20.0[34]	13.3[16]	1.4[9]	4.8	14.7	8.7	33.1
	2001	88 043 190	4.4	15.0[34]	12.4[16]	1.5[9]	5.7	15.3	9.2	36.4
Viet Nam[1] Viet Nam[1]	1998	361 017 000	25.8	6.7	17.1	2.9	5.8	18.9	3.9	18.9
	1999	399 942 000	25.4	8.4	17.7	2.9	5.4	18.2	3.9	18.0
	2000	444 140 000	24.3	9.5	18.7	2.9	5.5	17.7	4.0	17.4
Yemen[1] Yémen[1]	1998	847 533	19.4	16.4	10.2	0.9	5.3	11.2	14.4	22.2
	1999	1 132 153	16.1	29.2	8.2	0.7	4.7	9.0	11.6	20.8
	2000	1 380 603	15.3	33.8	7.5	0.7	4.2	8.6	10.3	19.4

21

Value added by industries in current prices
Percentage distribution *[cont.]*
Valeur ajoutée par branche d'activité aux prix courants
Répartition en pourcentage *[suite]*

% of Value added – % de la valeur ajoutée

Region, country or area Région, pays ou zone	Year Année	Value added, gross (Mil. nat.cur) Valeur ajoutée, brute (Mil. mon. nat.)	Agriculture, hunting, forestry and fishing Agriculture, chasse, sylviculture et pêche	Mining and quarrying Activités extractives	Manu-facturing Activités de fabri-cation	Electricity, gas and water supply Électricité, gaz et eau	Cons-truc-tion Cons-truc-tion	Wholesale, retail trade, restaurants and hotels Commerce, restaurants, hôtels	Transport, storage & communication Transports, entrepôts, communi-cations	Other activi-ties Autres activités
Yugoslavia, SFR	1988	14 645	11.2	2.7	40.3	2.2	6.2	7.6	11.1	18.6
Yougoslavie, Rfs	1989	224 684	11.3	2.4	41.4	1.7	6.4	6.6	10.5	19.7
	1990	966 420	12.9	2.5	31.2	1.7	7.9	8.5	12.3	23.1
Zambia	1998	5 650 600	20.0	6.7	12.3	3.9	4.7	20.9	6.0	25.5
Zambie	1999	7 066 100	22.8	4.0	11.4	3.5	4.5	21.6	6.1	26.0
	2000	9 541 300	21.0	4.4	10.8	3.4	5.2	21.9	6.7	26.7
Zimbabwe	1997	91 155[5]	18.7	1.5	17.8	3.1[9]	2.8	18.8	5.7	31.5
Zimbabwe	1998	125 787[5]	21.6	1.9	16.5	2.5[9]	2.9	18.0	5.3	31.3
	1999	185 766[5]	19.3	1.8	16.4	2.8[9]	2.8	19.5	6.1	31.3

Source:
United Nations Statistics Division, New York, national accounts database.

+ Note: The national accounts data generally relate to the fiscal year used in each country, unless indicated otherwise. Countries whose reference periods coincide with the calendar year ending 31 December are not listed below.
Year beginning 21 March: Afghanistan, Iran (Islamic Republic).
Year beginning 1 April: Bermuda, India, Myanmar, New Zealand, Nigeria (beginning 1982).
Year beginning 1 July: Australia, Bangladesh, Cameroon, Egypt, Gambia, Pakistan, Puerto Rico, Saudi Arabia, Sierra Leone, Sudan.
Year ending 30 June: Botswana, Swaziland, Tonga.
Year ending 7 July: Ethiopia.
Year ending 15 July: Nepal.
Year ending 30 September: Haiti.

Source:
Organisation des Nations Unies, Division de statistique, New York, la base de données sur les comptes nationaux.

+ Note : Sauf indication contraire, les données sur les comptes nationaux concernent généralement l'exercice budgétaire utilisé dans chaque pays. Les pays ou territoires dont la période de référence coïncide avec l'année civile se terminant le 31 décembre ne sont pas répertoriés ci-dessous.
Exercice commençant le 21 mars: Afghanistan, Iran (République islamique d').
Exercice commençant le 1er avril: Bermudes, Inde, Myanmar, Nigéria (à partir de 1982), Nouvelle-Zélande.
Exercice commençant le 1er juillet: Arabie saoudite, Australie, Bangladesh, Cameroun, Égypte, Gambie, Pakistan, Porto Rico, Sierra Leone, Soudan.
Exercice se terminant le 30 juin: Botswana, Swaziland, Tonga.
Exercice se terminant le 7 juillet: Éthiopie.
Exercice se terminant le 15 juillet: Népal.
Exercice se terminant le 30 septembre: Haïti.

1	Data are classified according to the 1993 SNA.
2	Including "manufacturing".
3	Including electricity, gas and water.
4	Including "other activities".
5	Value added at factor cost.
6	Including mining and quarrying.
7	Oil refining included in "Electricity, gas and water".
8	Financial intermediation services indirectly measured (FISIM) is distributed to uses.
9	Excluding gas.
10	Including statistical discrepancy.
11	Value added at producer's prices.
12	Excluding Financial intermediation services indirectly measured (FISIM).
13	Restaurants and hotels are included in "other activities".
14	Agriculture and fishing only.
15	Excluding hunting.
16	Including petroleum refining.
17	Including non-petroleum mining.
18	Electricity only. Gas and water are included in "other activities".

1	Les données sont classifiées selon le SCN 1993.
2	Y compris les industries manufacturières.
3	Y compris l'électricité, le gaz et l'eau.
4	Y compris "autres activitiés".
5	Valeur ajoutée au coût des facteurs.
6	Y compris les industries extractives.
7	Le raffinage du pétrole y compris dans l'électricité, le gaz et l'eau.
8	Services d'intermédiation financière mesurés indirectment (SIFMI) est distribué à ses utilizations.
9	Non compris le gaz.
10	Y compris une divergence statistique.
11	Valeur ajoutée aux prix à la production.
12	Non compris les Services d'intermédiation financière mesurés indirectment (SIFMI).
13	Restaurants et hôtels sont incluses dans "autres activités".
14	Agriculture et la pêche seulement.
15	Non compris le chasse.
16	Y compris le raffinage du pétrole.
17	Y compris l'extraction du non-pétrole.
18	Seulement électricité. Le gaz et l'eau sont incluses dans les "autres

21
Value added by industries in current prices
Percentage distribution *[cont.]*
Valeur ajoutée par branche d'activité aux prix courants
Répartition en pourcentage *[suite]*

19	Including engineering and sewage services.
20	Distribution of petroleum products and gas is included in wholesale and retail trade.
21	Wholesale and retail trade only.
22	Gross domestic product.
23	Including handicrafts.
24	Including construction.
25	Including gas and water supply.
26	Including import duties.
27	Excluding restaurants and hotels.
28	Contract construction only.
29	Re-denomination of Russian rubles at 1 to 1000.
30	Including agriculture, hunting, forestry and fishing.
31	Including "Transport, storage and communication".
32	Other activities refer only to public administration and defence; compulsory social security; all other services and activities are included in wholesale and retail trade.
33	Taxes less subsidies are included in the industry data.
34	Including crude petroleum and natural gas production.

	activités".
19	Y compris génie civil et services d'égouts.
20	La distribution des produits pétroliers et du gaz est comprise dans le commerce de gros et de détail.
21	Commerce de gros et de détail seulement.
22	Produit intérieur brut.
23	Y compris l'artisanat.
24	Y compris la construction.
25	Y compris le gaz et l'eau.
26	Droits d'importation compris.
27	Non compris les restaurants et hôtels.
28	Construction sous contrat seulement.
29	Instauration du nouveau rouble par division par 1000 du rouble ancien.
30	Y compris l'agriculture, la chasse, la sylviculture et la pêche.
31	Y compris transports, entrepôts et communications.
32	Les "autres activités" ne comprennent que l'administration publique et la défense, et la sécurité sociale obligatoire. Tous les autres services et activités sont compris dans le commerce de gros et de détail.
33	Les impôts, moins les subventions, sont inclus dans les données sur les industries.
34	Y compris la production de pétrole brut et de gas naturel.

22

Relationships among the principal national accounting aggregates
As a percentage of GDP
Relations entre les principaux agrégats de comptabilité nationale
En pourcentage du PIB

As a percentage of GDP – En pourcentage du PIB

Region, country or area Région, pays ou zone	Year Année	GDP in current prices (Mil.nat.cur.) PIB aux prix courants (Millions Monnaie nat.)	Plus: Compensation of employees and property income from/to the rest of the world, net Plus : Rémuneration des salariés et revenus de la propriété – du et au reste du monde, net	Equals: Gross national income Égale : Revenu national brut	Plus: Net current transfers from/to the rest of the world Plus : Transferts courants du/au reste du monde, net	Equals: Gross national disposable income Égale : Revenu national disponible brut	Less: Final consumption expenditure Moins : Dépense de consommation de finale	Equals: Gross savings Égale : Épargne brut	Less: Consumption of fixed capital Moins : Consommation de capital fixe
Algeria Algérie	1999 2000 2001	3 248 198 4 098 816 4 235 620	-4.5[1] -4.3[1] -2.9[1]	95.5 95.7 97.1	2.9 1.8 2.5	98.4 97.5 99.6	68.2 55.5 58.4	30.2 42.0 41.2	8.2 6.4 7.1
Angola Angola	1988 1989 1990	239 640 278 866 308 062	-11.1 -10.5 -12.4	88.9 89.5 87.6	-1.9 -1.6 -4.2	87.0 87.9 83.4	78.4 77.1 73.2	8.6 10.8 10.2	... ...
Anguilla Anguilla	1999 2000 2001	283 292 298	-3.1 -2.7 -0.7	96.9 97.3 99.0	-0.3 1.4 -0.7	96.6 98.6 98.3	101.3 106.8 93.3	-4.6 -8.2 5.4	... ...
Argentina[2] Argentine[2]	1999 2000 2001	283 523 284 204 268 697	-2.6 -2.6 -3.0	97.4 97.4 97.0	0.1 0.1 0.1	97.5 97.5 97.0	83.9 83.1 83.1	13.6 14.4 14.0	... ...
Armenia[2] Arménie[2]	1999 2000 2001	987 400 1 031 300 1 175 900	-0.9[1] -1.2[1] -0.1[1]	99.1 98.8 99.9	9.2 9.5 8.3	108.3 108.3 108.2	108.3 108.9 104.8	0.0 -0.6 3.4	14.1 14.6 14.3
Aruba[2] Aruba[2]	1998 1999 2000	2 981 3 087 3 326	-4.6 -5.4 -5.5	95.4 94.6 94.5	-0.2 -0.6 -2.7	95.2 94.0 91.8	72.3 74.7 69.8	22.9 19.2 22.0	11.1 10.7 10.2
Australia +[2] Australie +[2]	1999 2000 2001	628 621 669 307 712 980	-2.9 -2.9 -2.8	97.1 97.1 97.1	0.0 0.0 0.0	97.1 97.2 97.1	77.9 78.4 78.0	19.3 18.7 19.1	15.6 15.7 15.8
Austria[2] Autriche[2]	2000 2001 2002	207 037 211 857 216 831	-1.6 -1.9 -1.1	98.4 98.1 98.9	-0.4 -0.3 -0.6	98.0 97.8 98.4	76.0 76.5 76.7	22.0 21.3 21.6	14.3 14.7 14.9
Azerbaijan[2] Azerbaïdjan[2]	1999 2000 2001	18 875 400 23 590 500 26 578 000	-0.1 -5.4 -5.9	99.9 94.6 94.1	17.6 15.2 13.1	117.5 109.8 107.2	91.4 79.6 75.1	26.1 30.2 32.1	15.6 12.5 12.3
Bahamas[2] Bahamas[2]	1993 1994 1995	2 854 3 053 3 069	-2.6 -2.9 -3.2	97.4 97.1 96.8	0.5 0.5 0.2	97.9 97.6 97.0	83.9 84.0 83.4	14.0 13.6 13.6	6.0 5.9 4.9
Bahrain Bahreïn	1998 1999 2000	2 325 2 489 2 997	-2.6[1] -4.1[1] -2.8[1]	97.4 95.9 97.2	-10.7 -12.4 -12.4	86.7 83.5 84.8	77.9 76.2 64.7	... ...	14.7 14.2 12.1
Bangladesh +[2] Bangladesh +[2]	1999 2000 2001	2 370 856 2 535 464 2 714 142	3.7 3.5 3.7	103.7 103.5 103.7	1.5 0.9 0.8	105.2 104.4 104.5	82.1 82.0 82.0	23.1 22.4 22.5	7.9 8.0 8.0
Belarus[2] Bélarus[2]	1999 #2000 2001	3 026 060 000 9 133 800[3] 17 173 200[3]	0.1 0.1 0.2	100.1 100.1 100.2	1.0 1.3 1.3	101.1 101.4 101.4	78.1 76.4 79.2	23.0 25.0 22.3	... ...
Belgium[2] Belgique[2]	2000 2001 2002	247 469 254 282 260 744	2.1 1.8 2.1	102.1 101.8 102.1	-0.9 -0.9 -0.6	101.2 101.0 101.4	75.2 76.1 76.6	25.9 24.8 24.9	14.5 15.0 15.2

22

Relationships among the principal national accounting aggregates
As a percentage of GDP [cont.]
Relations entre les principaux agrégats de comptabilité nationale
En pourcentage du PIB *[suite]*

Region, country or area Région, pays ou zone	Year Année	GDP in current prices (Mil.nat.cur.) PIB aux prix courants (Millions Monnaie nat.)	Plus: Compensation of employees and property income from/to the rest of the world, net Plus : Rémuneration des salariés et revenus de la propriété – du et au reste du monde, net	Equals: Gross national income Égale : Revenu national brut	Plus: Net current transfers from/to the rest of the world Plus : Transfers courants du/au reste du monde, net	Equals: Gross national disposable income Égale : Revenu national disponible brut	Less: Final consumption expenditure Moins : Dépense de consommation de finale	Equals: Gross savings Égale : Épargne brut	Less: Consumption of fixed capital Moins : Consommation de capital fixe
Belize [2]	1997	1 231	...	96.1	...	100.2	83.5	...	4.9
Belize [2]	1998	1 258	...	94.9	...	100.2	84.8	...	4.7
	1999	1 377	...	95.1	...	...	82.3	...	5.9
Benin	1987	469 554	...	98.2	8.7	106.9	96.5	10.4	...
Bénin	1988	482 434	...	97.9	9.3	107.2	95.3	11.9	...
	1989	479 200	...	99.2	11.1	110.2	94.4	12.6	...
Bermuda + [2]	1998	3 053	4.2	104.2	...	...	71.4	...	...
Bermudes + [2]	1999	3 272	4.6	104.6	...	...	72.0	...	...
	2000	3 397	4.9	104.9	...	...	72.0	...	...
Bhutan	1998	16 337	-14.2	94.1	4.2	99.0	77.3	36.6	8.1
Bhoutan	1999	19 123	-16.1	83.9	4.5	88.4	75.0	...	8.2
	2000	21 698	-15.9	84.1	5.8	89.8	72.6	...	8.1
Bolivia	1997	41 644	-2.5	97.5	3.7	101.2	88.6	12.6	...
Bolivie	1998	46 822	-1.9	98.1	3.9	102.0	89.3	12.7	...
	1999	48 156	-2.4	97.6	3.9	101.5	91.6	9.8	...
Botswana + [2]	1999	21 524	-1.6	98.4	-0.1	98.2	62.8	35.4	12.3
Botswana + [2]	2000	25 363	-5.2	94.1	-0.1	93.9	60.6	34.1	12.1
	2001	29 353	...	94.2	...	93.9	61.4	...	...
Brazil [2]	1999	973 846	-3.5	96.5	0.3	96.8	81.4	15.4	...
Brésil [2]	2000	1 101 255	-3.0	97.0	0.3	97.3	80.0	17.3	...
	2001	1 200 060	-3.9	96.1	0.3	96.5	79.8	16.6	...
British Virgin Islands [2]	1997	512	-9.4	90.6	1.5	92.2	55.5	36.7	...
Iles Vierges	1998	593	-8.1	92.1	2.6	94.6	53.0	41.7	...
britanniques [2]	1999	662	-7.3	92.9	3.1	95.9	51.7	44.1	...
Bulgaria [2]	1995	880 322 [4]	-3.3 [1]	96.7	0.1	96.8	85.9	...	8.7
Bulgarie [2]	1996	1 748 701 [4]	-4.0 [1]	96.0	1.0	97.0	88.5	...	8.2
	1997	17 055 205 [4]	-3.5 [1]	96.5	2.3	98.9	83.1	...	6.8
Burkina Faso	1991	811 676	0.3	100.3	1.5	...	90.9	...	...
Burkina Faso	1992	812 590	0.2	100.2	1.9	...	90.6	...	...
	1993	832 349	-0.1	99.9	1.9	...	91.6	...	...
Burundi	1990	196 656	...	98.0	...	...	102.5	...	4.2
Burundi	1991	211 898	...	99.0	...	...	100.9	...	...
	1992	226 384	...	98.7	...	...	98.5	...	...
Cambodia	1994	6 201 001	...	92.1	...	...	104.7	...	...
Cambodge	1995	7 542 711	...	95.1	...	...	95.6	...	...
	1996	8 324 792	...	93.6	...	...	95.5	...	...
Cameroon + [2]	1994	3 754 530	...	94.6	0.0	94.7	84.4	10.2	...
Cameroun + [2]	1995	4 465 080	...	95.2	0.5	95.8	80.3	15.5	...
	1996	4 793 080	...	95.7	0.3	95.9	79.8	16.1	...
Canada [2]	1999	965 440	-3.0	97.0	0.1	97.1	75.8	21.3	13.3
Canada [2]	2000	1 049 448	-2.1	97.9	0.1	98.1	73.9	24.2	12.9
	2001	1 075 576	-2.2	97.8	0.2	98.0	75.3	22.7	13.4
Cape Verde	1993	29 078	...	166.4	...	...	106.8	...	...
Cap-Vert	1994	33 497	...	161.3	...	...	104.5	...	...
	1995	37 705	...	163.5	...	...	109.1	...	...

22
Relationships among the principal national accounting aggregates
As a percentage of GDP [cont.]
Relations entre les principaux agrégats de comptabilité nationale
En pourcentage du PIB *[suite]*

			As a percentage of GDP – En pourcentage du PIB						
Region, country or area Région, pays ou zone	Year Année	GDP in current prices (Mil.nat.cur.) PIB aux prix courants (Millions Monnaie nat.)	Plus: Compensa- tion of employees and property income from/to the rest of the world, net Plus : Rémuneration des salariés et revenus de la propriété – du et au reste du monde, net	Equals: Gross national income Égale : Revenu national brut	Plus: Net current transfers from/to the rest of the world Plus : Transfers courants du/au reste du monde, net	Equals: Gross national disposable income Égale : Revenu national disponible brut	Less: Final con- sumption expenditure Moins : Dépense de consom- mation de finale	Equals: Gross savings Égale : Épargne brut	Less: Consump- tion of fixed capital Moins : Consom- mation de capital fixe
Cayman Islands	1989	474	-10.8	89.2	...	92.0	79.3	12.7	8.0
Iles Caïmanes	1990	590	-10.3	89.7	...	92.2	76.8	15.4	7.1
	1991	616	-9.4	90.6	...	93.0	77.6	15.4	7.6
Chile [2]	1999	37 164 386	-2.7[5]	97.3	0.6	98.0	76.8	21.2	13.6
Chili [2]	2000	40 436 215	-3.8[5]	96.2	0.7	96.8	76.1	20.7	12.8
	2001	42 191 778	-3.8[5]	96.2	0.7	96.8	77.3	19.6	...
China [2]	1999	8 206 750	-1.8	98.2	...	...	...	...	...
Chine [2]	2000	8 944 220	-1.4	98.7	...	...	...	...	...
	2001	9 593 330	-1.7	98.3	...	...	...	...	...
China, Hong Kong SAR [2]	1999	1 246 134	2.8	102.8	-1.0	101.8	69.1	32.8	...
Chine, Hong Kong	2000	1 288 338	1.7	101.7	-1.0	100.7	67.1	33.6	...
RAS [2]	2001	1 278 995	2.8	102.8	-1.0	101.8	68.4	33.4	...
Colombia [2]	1998	140 953 206	-2.4	97.6	3.2	100.8	86.2	14.6	...
Colombie [2]	1999	151 565 005	-1.8	98.2	1.9	100.1	86.6	13.6	...
	2000	173 729 806	-3.0	97.0	2.1	99.1	86.3	12.7	...
Comoros	1989	63 397	...	100.7	...	...	...	...	...
Comores	1990	66 370	...	99.8	12.3	112.1	105.5	6.7	...
	1991	69 248	...	99.6	...	...	...	...	...
Congo	1986	640 407	-6.5	93.5	-1.3	92.2	84.4	7.8	24.4
Congo	1987	690 523	-11.1	88.9	-1.6	87.3	77.2	10.2	23.8
	1988	658 964	-13.7	86.3	-1.8	84.5	81.2	3.3	22.0
Costa Rica [2]	1999	4 512 763	-11.5	88.5	0.6	89.1	77.2	12.0	5.9
Costa Rica [2]	2000	4 917 764	-7.8	92.2	0.6	92.7	80.2	12.6	6.0
	2001	5 387 526	-4.9	95.1	0.9	96.0	82.8	13.2	6.2
Côte d'Ivoire	1998	7 457 508	-5.7	94.3	-3.1	91.2	78.7	12.4	4.3
Côte d'Ivoire	1999	7 734 000	-6.9	92.1	-2.7	89.1	77.8	11.3	4.4
	2000	7 605 000	-5.7	94.3	-3.5	90.8	82.7	8.1	4.9
Cuba	1998	23 901	-1.9	98.1	3.4	101.5	95.2	6.3	...
Cuba	1999	25 504	-2.0	98.0	3.1	101.1	94.4	6.7	...
	2000	27 635	-2.5	97.5	3.0	100.5	92.1	8.5	...
Cyprus	1999	5 019	0.4	100.4	...	100.5	83.4	...	10.5
Chypre	2000	5 487	0.4	100.4	...	...	...	...	...
	2001	5 865	0.3	100.3	...	...	...	...	...
Czech Republic [2]	2000	1 984 833	-2.7	97.3	0.7	98.1	73.7	24.4	20.3
République tchèque [2]	2001	2 175 238	-3.8	96.2	...	...	73.2	...	...
	2002	2 275 609	-4.3	95.7	...	...	74.2	...	...
Dem. Rep. of the Congo	1983	59 134	...	95.7	...	...	76.9	...	2.9
Rép. dém. du Congo	1984	99 723	...	88.5	...	...	49.5	...	2.5
	1985	147 263	...	97.2	...	...	59.4	...	2.9
Denmark [2]	2000	1 280 784	-2.0	98.0	-2.4	95.6	72.8	22.8	15.8
Danemark [2]	2001	1 325 272	-1.4	98.6	-2.0	96.6	73.2	23.5	15.9
	2002	1 358 297	-1.1	98.9	-2.0	97.0	74.3	22.7	15.8
Djibouti	1982	59 383	...	91.5	...	...	...	...	...
Djibouti	1983	59 997	...	90.2	...	...	...	...	...
	1984	60 234	...	89.0	...	...	...	...	...

24
Household consumption expenditure by purpose in current prices
Percentage distribution
Dépenses de consommation des ménages par fonction
aux prix courants
Répartition en pourcentage

Region, country or area Région, pays ou zone	Year Année	Household final consumption expenditure (M.nat.curr.) Dépenses de consommation finale des ménages (M.monn. nationale)	Food, beverages, tobacco, narcotics Alimentation, boissons, tabac et stupéfiants (%)	Clothing and footwear Articles d'habillement et chaussures (%)	Housing, water, electricity, gas and other fuels Logement, eau, gaz, électricité et autres combustibles (%)	Furnishings, household equipment, routine home maintenance Meubles, articles de ménage et entretien courant de l'habitation (%)	Health Santé (%)	Transport and communication Transport et communication (%)	Recreation, culture, education, restaurants, hotels Loisirs, culture, enseignement, restaurants et hôtels (%)	Others Autres (%)
Australia [1] Australie [1]	1998	354 420	14.7	4.1	20.8	5.4	4.1	14.6	22.1	14.3
	1999	374 922	14.6	4.1	20.9	5.6	4.2	14.3	22.2	14.0
	2000	403 875	14.7	3.8	20.7	5.3	4.6	14.6	22.1	13.8
Austria [1] Autriche [1]	1999	111 992[2]	15.8	6.8	19.2	8.7	3.3	15.3	23.7	7.2
	2000	117 445[2]	15.6	6.6	19.0	8.5	3.3	15.6	24.3	7.0
	2001	121 580[2]	15.5	6.7	19.4	8.4	3.4	15.4	24.5	6.8
Azerbaijan [1] Azerbaïdjan [1]	2000	15 194 800[2]	76.9	5.7	1.3	1.7	1.8	6.1	3.9	2.8
	2001	16 343 800[2]	76.9	5.7	1.3	1.7	1.8	6.1	3.9	2.7
	2002	17 950 600[2]	77.1	5.7	1.3	1.7	1.8	6.1	3.9	2.5
Belarus [1] Bélarus [1]	1999	1 774 583300[2,3]	61.6	9.8	4.8	3.8	1.4	6.9	5.5	6.3
	2000	5 198 100[2,4]	63.1	8.2	5.4	3.1	1.5	7.2	4.9	6.5
	2001	9 895 900[2,4]	57.4	9.0	6.9	3.8	2.1	8.0	5.5	7.2
Belgium [1] Belgique [1]	1999	126 609[2]	16.1	5.4	22.3	5.7	3.6	16.5	14.8	15.6
	2000	133 834[2]	15.7	4.8	22.2	5.8	3.7	17.1	15.3	15.3
	2001	138 457[2]	15.6	4.7	22.4	5.8	3.8	16.9	15.5	13.4
Bolivia Bolivie	1994	21 444	34.7	6.7	...	...	...	...	9.2	...
	1995	24 440	34.4	6.5	...	...	...	...	9.5	...
	1996	28 200	35.7	6.5	...	...	...	...	9.8	...
Botswana [1] Botswana [1]	1999	6 937[2]	41.3	5.1	11.7	3.9	2.2	7.5	7.5	4.6[5]
	2000	7 841[2]	40.8	4.9	12.8	3.5	2.3	6.9	7.6	4.7[5]
	2001	8 281[2]	43.3	3.8	14.0	...	2.8	7.4	9.6	...
British Virgin Islands [1] Îles Vierges britanniques [1]	1997	221[6]	17.2	10.9	21.3	7.2	1.8	12.7	6.8	22.2
	1998	243[6]	16.9	9.9	22.2	7.0	2.1	12.3	6.6	23.0
	1999	269[6]	16.4	10.4	22.3	6.7	2.6	11.5	5.9	23.8
Canada [1] Canada [1]	1999	547 105[2]	13.6	5.4	23.5	6.4	4.2	16.9	19.0	11.1
	2000	579 903[2]	13.4	5.3	23.2	6.4	4.2	17.2	19.2	11.1
	2001	605 806[2]	13.5	5.3	23.1	6.4	4.3	16.9	19.4	11.1
China, Hong Kong SAR [1] Chine, Hong Kong RAS [1]	1999	740 819[2]	12.7	14.9	20.5	10.1	4.2	8.9	8.0	20.8[7]
	2000	744 401[2]	12.6	14.1	19.6	11.3	4.2	9.6	8.3	20.4[7]
	2001	745 537[2]	12.9	13.7	20.0	11.4	4.1	9.9	8.1	20.0[7]
China, Macao SAR [1] Chine, Macao RAS [1]	1999	20 403[2]	11.7	3.9	22.6	2.4	1.7	9.4	31.2	17.1
	2000	20 377[2]	11.6	2.8	21.9	2.2	1.7	9.9	32.8	17.1
	2001	20 626[2]	10.7	2.5	21.0	2.0	1.8	9.9	33.6	18.5
Colombia [1] Colombie [1]	1997	79 193 752[2]	33.3	5.5	17.5	5.7	3.6	12.8	15.4	6.2
	1998	92 521 201[2]	33.3	5.6	17.5	5.4	3.8	12.7	15.7	6.0
	1999	95 931 531[2]	32.8	5.3	16.5	5.6	4.2	13.6	16.0	6.1
Côte d'Ivoire Côte d'Ivoire	1996	4 046 064	51.1	5.3	7.2	3.8	0.4	9.9	4.7	16.8
	1997	4 329 400	49.8	5.3	7.2	4.0	0.5	10.0	4.6	17.4
	1998	4 836 550	49.9	5.4	7.2	4.0	0.5	9.3	3.9	18.3
Cyprus Chypre	1994	2 104[2]	35.7	10.9	10.1	14.9	5.3	...	32.6	...
	1995	2 592[2]	30.9	10.3	8.9	13.0	4.9	...	27.2	...
	1996	2 750[2]	30.3	9.9	9.1	12.8	5.6	...	26.5	...
Czech Republic [1] République tchèque [1]	1997	899 910[2]	32.8	6.7	16.7	6.1	1.0	12.6	13.6	10.5
	1998	966 113[2]	32.5	6.3	19.4	5.3	1.1	11.9	13.5	9.9
	1999	1 019 196[2]	31.4	5.6	19.7	5.6	1.1	12.6	14.0	9.9

22
Relationships among the principal national accounting aggregates
As a percentage of GDP [cont.]
Relations entre les principaux agrégats de comptabilité nationale
En pourcentage du PIB *[suite]*

Region, country or area Région, pays ou zone	Year Année	GDP in current prices (Mil.nat.cur.) PIB aux prix courants (Millions Monnaie nat.)	Plus: Compensation of employees and property income from/to the rest of the world, net Plus : Rémuneration des salariés et revenus de la propriété – du et au reste du monde, net	Equals: Gross national income Égale : Revenu national brut	Plus: Net current transfers from/to the rest of the world Plus : Transferts courants du/au reste du monde, net	Equals: Gross national disposable income Égale : Revenu national disponible brut	Less: Final consumption expenditure Moins : Dépense de consommation de finale	Equals: Gross savings Égale : Épargne brut	Less: Consumption of fixed capital Moins : Consommation de capital fixe
Dominica Dominique	1989	423	...	101.0	...	...	92.0	...	...
	1990	452	...	101.1	...	...	84.4	...	...
	1991	479	...	101.0	...	...	91.4	...	...
Dominican Republic [2] Rép. dominicaine [2]	1994	179 130	-2.2	97.8	6.7	104.5	81.4	23.1	3.6
	1995	209 646	-2.3	97.7	6.2	103.9	82.9	21.0	4.0
	1996	243 973	-5.4	94.6	6.1	100.7	82.2	18.5	3.8
Ecuador Equateur	1998	107 421 048	-8.2	91.8	3.9	95.7	82.0	13.7	...
	1999	161 350 379	-12.7	87.3	8.1	95.3	75.8	19.5	...
	2000	340 021 704	-12.8	87.2	9.9	97.2	71.6	25.6	...
Egypt + Egypte +	1980	17 149	4.3[1]	104.3	1.5	...	81.6	...	...
	1981	20 222	1.3[1]	101.3	1.3		81.7	...	...
El Salvador El Salvador	1999	109 066	-2.3	97.7	12.7	110.4	95.9	14.5	...
	2000	114 968	-1.9	98.1	13.7	111.8	98.2	13.5	...
	2001	120 215	-1.9	98.1	14.6	112.7	98.0	14.7	...
Estonia [2] Estonie [2]	1996	52 446	0.0	100.0	2.3	102.4	84.8	17.6	10.8
	1997	64 324	-3.1	96.9	2.5	99.4	81.2	18.2	11.5
	1998	73 325	-1.6	98.4	2.8	101.3	81.3	19.9	13.7
Ethiopia + Ethiopie +	1997	41 465	-0.5[5]	99.5	7.0	106.5	...	7.0	...
	1998	44 896	-0.4[5]	99.6	8.3	107.9	...	8.3	...
	1999	48 949	-0.4[5]	99.6	7.6	107.2	...	7.6	...
Fiji Fidji	1991	2 042	-1.4	105.1	-1.6	103.6	92.1	11.5	8.2
	1992	2 302	-1.7	101.5	-0.9	100.7	88.1	12.5	7.9
	1993	2 522	-0.6	100.2	-0.5	99.7	87.4	12.3	7.3
Finland [2] Finlande [2]	2000	130 234	-1.3	98.7	-0.7	98.0	70.3	27.7	16.2
	2001	135 791	-0.7	99.3	-0.7	98.6	70.7	27.9	16.4
	2002	139 734	-0.1	99.9	-0.8	99.2	71.9	27.2	16.3
France [2] France [2]	2000	1 420 138	0.8	100.8	-0.8	100.0	77.7	22.4	13.8
	2001	1 475 584	0.8	100.8	-0.8	100.0	78.0	22.0	13.9
	2002	1 520 804	0.5	100.5	-0.9	99.5	78.7	20.9	14.1
French Guiana Guyane française	1990	6 526	-1.9[1]	98.1	36.3	134.4	99.4	35.0	...
	1991	7 404	-5.8[1]	94.2	35.9	130.1	94.5	35.6	...
	1992	7 976	-6.9[1]	93.1	36.4	129.6	93.1	36.4	...
Gabon Gabon	1987	1 020 600	-6.2[1]	93.8	-4.2	89.7	72.4	17.3	19.2
	1988	1 013 600	-7.4[1]	92.6	-7.6	85.0	69.9	15.1	12.0
	1989	1 168 066	-8.6[1]	91.4	-6.1	85.3	66.8	18.5	14.5
Gambia + Gambie +	1991	2 920	...	98.3	...	115.7	96.7	19.0	11.7
	1992	3 078	...	98.7	...	114.1	94.4	19.7	12.3
	1993	3 243	...	98.5	...	114.4	93.3	21.1	12.9
Georgia [2] Géorgie [2]	#1995	3 694	-2.1	97.9	4.0	101.9	91.2	10.7	11.2
	1996	5 300	1.7	101.7	2.0	103.7	93.2	10.5	11.6
	1997	6 431	2.6	102.6	3.9	106.5	100.0	6.5	11.7
Germany [2] Allemagne [2]	2000	2 030 000	-0.5	99.5	-1.0	98.6	77.7	20.8	14.9
	2001	2 071 200	-0.7	99.3	-1.0	98.3	78.5	19.8	15.1
	2002	2 108 200	-0.4	99.6	-1.1	98.5	78.0	20.5	15.1

22

Relationships among the principal national accounting aggregates
As a percentage of GDP [cont.]
Relations entre les principaux agrégats de comptabilité nationale
En pourcentage du PIB *[suite]*

As a percentage of GDP – En pourcentage du PIB

Region, country or area / Région, pays ou zone	Year / Année	GDP in current prices (Mil.nat.cur.) / PIB aux prix courants (Millions Monnaie nat.)	Plus: Compensation of employees and property income from/to the rest of the world, net / Plus : Rémuneration des salariés et revenus de la propriété – du et au reste du monde, net	Equals: Gross national income / Égale : Revenu national brut	Plus: Net current transfers from/to the rest of the world / Plus : Transferts courants du/au reste du monde, net	Equals: Gross national disposable income / Égale : Revenu national disponible brut	Less: Final consumption expenditure / Moins : Dépense de consommation de finale	Equals: Gross savings / Égale : Épargne brut	Less: Consumption of fixed capital / Moins : Consommation de capital fixe
Ghana	1994	5 205 200	...	98.0	...	...	...	...	7.9
Ghana	1995	7 752 600	...	98.0	...	...	...	...	6.6
	1996	11 339 200	...	98.1	...	...	...	...	7.1
Greece [2]	2000	121 628	1.2	101.2	2.5	103.7	85.2	18.6	9.0
Grèce [2]	2001	130 927	0.6	100.6	1.6	102.3	83.7	18.6	9.0
	2002	141 132	0.3	100.3	1.3	101.6	83.1	18.5	8.8
Grenada	1984	275	...	98.9	...	...	99.1	...	...
Grenade	1985	311	...	98.9	...	...	99.0	...	...
	1986	350	...	99.2	...	...	97.7	...	...
Guadeloupe	1990	15 201	-2.5	97.5	37.3	134.8	123.6	11.2	...
Guadeloupe	1991	16 415	-3.4	96.6	35.4	132.0	118.3	13.7	...
	1992	17 972	-3.0	97.0	36.6	133.6	113.4	20.2	...
Guatemala	1996	95 479	-1.5[1]	98.5	3.4	101.9	92.1	10.2	...
Guatemala	1997	107 943	-1.3[1]	98.7	3.4	102.1	91.8	10.8	...
	1998	121 548	-0.8[1]	99.2	3.8	103.0	92.8	10.6	...
Guinea-Bissau	1986	46 973	-1.7	98.3	2.9	101.3	102.8	-1.5	...
Guinée-Bissau	1987	92 375	-0.5	99.5	4.1	103.6	100.8	2.8	...
Guyana	1999	123 665	...	90.1	...	...	68.0	...	...
Guyana	2000	130 013	...	93.8	...	...	77.4	...	...
	2001	133 403	...	92.8	...	...	78.3	...	...
Haiti +	1995	35 207	...	98.7	22.8	121.5	108.1	13.4	2.2
Haïti +	1996	43 234	...	99.6	17.1	116.7	104.9	11.8	2.3
	1997	51 789	...	99.6	14.1	113.7	103.7	10.0	2.0
Honduras	1998	70 438	...	95.9	9.3	105.2	77.1	28.1	5.8
Honduras	1999	77 095	...	96.9	13.6	110.5	80.1	30.4	6.0
	2000	87 523	...	97.0	12.5	109.6	82.0	27.6	6.0
Hungary [2]	1999	11 393 500	-7.8	92.2	...	...	74.0	...	...
Hongrie [2]	2000	13 172 293	-7.8	92.0	...	...	73.0	...	...
	2001	14 849 622	-7.8	92.0	...	...	74.4	...	...
Iceland [2]	2000	658 247	-2.9	97.1	-0.1	96.9	83.0	13.9	13.2
Islande [2]	2001	740 747	-3.3	96.7	-0.1	96.6	78.8	17.8	13.8
	2002	774 418	-1.7	98.3	0.1	98.4	79.3	19.1	14.5
India +	1998	17 409 350	-0.9	99.1	2.5	101.6	77.4	21.7[6]	9.7
Inde +	1999	19 296 410	-0.8	99.2	2.8	102.0	78.2	23.2[6]	9.5
	2000	20 879 880	-0.8	99.2	2.8	102.0	77.4	23.4[6]	9.5
Indonesia	1999	1 099 732 000	...	92.4	...	...	80.5	...	5.0
Indonésie	2000	1 282 018 000	...	92.8	...	...	74.8	...	5.0
	2001	1 490 974 000	...	96.1	...	...	...	...	5.0
Iran (Islamic Rep. of) + [2]	1999	430 990 500	-0.1	99.9	...	99.9	65.5	34.9[6]	17.7
Iran (Rép. islamique d') + [2]	2000	568 799 400	-0.1	99.9	...	99.9	60.1	37.8[6]	16.6
	2001	665 656 300	-0.5	99.5	...	99.5	60.4	34.7[6]	16.0
Iraq	1989	21 026	...	96.7	...	95.9	81.9	14.0	8.7
Iraq	1990	23 297	...	96.7	...	96.5	76.8	19.6	8.8
	1991	19 940	...	96.7	...	97.4	83.5	13.9	9.6

22

Relationships among the principal national accounting aggregates
As a percentage of GDP [cont.]
Relations entre les principaux agrégats de comptabilité nationale
En pourcentage du PIB *[suite]*

As a percentage of GDP – En pourcentage du PIB

Region, country or area Région, pays ou zone	Year Année	GDP in current prices (Mil.nat.cur.) PIB aux prix courants (Millions Monnaie nat.)	Plus: Compensation of employees and property income from/to the rest of the world, net Plus : Rémuneration des salariés et revenus de la propriété – du et au reste du monde, net	Equals: Gross national income Égale : Revenu national brut	Plus: Net current transfers from/to the rest of the world Plus : Transfers courants du/au reste du monde, net	Equals: Gross national disposable income Égale : Revenu national disponible brut	Less: Final consumption expenditure Moins : Dépense de consommation de finale	Equals: Gross savings Égale : Épargne brut	Less: Consumption of fixed capital Moins : Consommation de capital fixe
Ireland [2]	1999	89 770	-13.6	86.4	0.3	86.6	62.1	24.6	9.8
Irlande [2]	2000	102 910	-13.7	86.3	0.1	86.4	61.4	25.0	10.0
	2001	114 479	-14.6	85.4	-0.4	85.0	61.5	23.4	10.0
Israel [2]	1999	446 760	-4.3	95.7	5.9	101.6	81.1	20.5	14.0
Israël [2]	2000	487 013	-5.9	94.1	5.4	99.5	80.1	19.3	13.4
	2001	491 499	-4.1	95.9	5.5	101.4	83.2	18.2	14.2
Italy [2]	2000	1 166 548	-0.8	99.2	-0.3	98.8	78.8	20.0	13.1
Italie [2]	2001	1 220 147	-0.7	99.3	-0.4	98.8	78.9	20.0	13.1
	2002	1 258 349	-1.0	99.0	-0.4	98.6	79.0	19.7	13.2
Jamaica	1987	16 640	-11.4	84.8	3.7	88.4	73.5	14.9	7.9
Jamaïque	1988	19 458	-10.1	86.2	12.2	98.4	74.4	24.0	7.0
	1989	23 400	-10.5	84.5	7.5	92.0	72.6	19.3	7.5
Japan [2]	2000	513 376 800	1.3	101.3[6]	-0.2	101.1[6]	72.4	27.7[6]	19.1
Japon [2]	2001	507 455 500	1.6	101.6[6]	-0.2	101.5[6]	73.8	26.4[6]	19.5
	2002	500 728 600	1.6	101.6			75.0	...	...
Jordan	1999	5 767	-0.2	99.9	23.0	122.9	96.3	26.6	11.7
Jordanie	2000	5 989	1.6	101.6	25.9	127.5	104.6	22.9	11.2
	2001	6 310	2.1	102.1	23.1	125.2	104.4	20.8	11.0
Kazakhstan [2]	1999	2 016 456	-3.1	96.9	0.9	97.8	84.0	13.8	14.2
Kazakhstan [2]	2000	2 599 902	-6.2	93.8	1.4	95.1	73.4	21.7	16.2
	2001	3 250 593	-5.0	95.0	1.0	96.0	71.1	24.9	15.3
Kenya	1999	37 107	...	98.4	6.4	...	89.6	...	...
Kenya	2000	39 799	...	98.7	8.8	...	94.1	...	...
	2001	44 764	...	98.7	7.5	...	94.4	...	...
Korea, Republic of [2]	2000	521 959 212	-0.5	99.5	0.1	99.6	67.4	32.2	11.8
Corée, République de [2]	2001	551 557 522	-0.3	99.7	-0.1	99.6	69.5	30.1	11.9
	2002	596 381 161	0.1	100.1	-0.3	99.8	70.7	29.1	11.3
Kuwait	1999	8 886	17.5	117.5	-6.9	110.6	78.3	32.4	6.9
Koweït	2000	10 991	18.7	118.7	-5.5	113.2	64.8	48.5	4.0
	2001	10 057	15.1	115.1	-6.3	108.8	74.0	34.7	4.7
Kyrgyzstan [2]	1999	48 744	-6.0	94.0	4.0	98.0	96.8	1.2	13.0
Kirghizistan [2]	2000	65 358	-5.9	94.1	6.0	100.1	85.7	14.4	13.2
	2001	73 883	-4.2	95.8	3.4	99.1	82.3	16.8	12.1
Latvia [2]	1994	2 043	-0.2	99.8	3.6	103.4	78.8	24.6	12.5
Lettonie [2]	1995	2 349	0.5	100.5	1.5	102.0	84.8	17.2	12.2
	1996	2 829	0.8	100.8	1.8	102.6	89.3	13.4	10.7
Lesotho [2]	1999	5 565	25.0	126.8	17.9	144.8	122.4	22.4	...
Lesotho [2]	2000	5 980	25.5	125.5	17.5	142.9	120.4	22.5	...
	2001	6 478	23.4	123.4	20.3	143.7	119.8	23.8	...
Liberia	1987	1 090	...	83.2	...	...	...	...	8.6
Libéria	1988	1 158	...	84.2	...	...	...	...	8.3
	1989	1 194	...	84.9	...	...	...	...	8.5
Libyan Arab Jamah.	1983	8 805	...	91.0	-0.2	90.9	72.0	18.9	5.0
Jamah. arabe libyenne	1984	8 013	...	92.7	-0.3	92.4	72.2	20.2	5.7
	1985	8 277	...	96.7	-0.2	96.5	69.2	27.3	5.8

22

Relationships among the principal national accounting aggregates
As a percentage of GDP [cont.]

Relations entre les principaux agrégats de comptabilité nationale
En pourcentage du PIB *[suite]*

Region, country or area Région, pays ou zone	Year Année	GDP in current prices (Mil.nat.cur.) PIB aux prix courants (Millions Monnaie nat.)	Plus: Compensation of employees and property income from/to the rest of the world, net Plus : Rémuneration des salariés et revenus de la propriété – du et au reste du monde, net	Equals: Gross national income Égale : Revenu national brut	Plus: Net current transfers from/to the rest of the world Plus : Transfers courants du/au reste du monde, net	Equals: Gross national disposable income Égale : Revenu national disponible brut	Less: Final consumption expenditure Moins : Dépense de consommation de finale	Equals: Gross savings Égale : Épargne brut	Less: Consumption of fixed capital Moins : Consommation de capital fixe
Lithuania[2] Lituanie[2]	1995	24 103	-0.2	99.8	1.8	101.6	87.1	14.5	8.7
	1996	31 569	-1.2	98.8	1.8	100.7	85.3	15.3	9.7
	1997	38 340	-2.1	97.6	2.4	100.0	84.0	13.5	10.0
Luxembourg[2] Luxembourg[2]	1999	18 870	-2.7	97.3	...	...	58.4	...	12.9
	2000	21 313	-9.5	90.5	...	...	55.4	...	12.2
	2001	22 082	-10.6	89.4	...	...	58.2	...	12.9
Madagascar Madagascar	1980	689 800	...	99.9	...	...	...	...	...
Malawi Malawi	1994	10 319	...	104.7	...	...	...	...	11.8
	1995	20 923	...	93.7	...	...	...	...	7.6
	1996	33 918	...	69.5	...	...	...	...	5.4
Malaysia Malaisie	1999	300 764	-6.9[1]	93.1	-2.2	90.9	52.6	38.3	...
	2000	342 157	-8.4[1]	91.6	-2.1	89.4	52.9	36.5	...
	2001	334 589	-7.7[1]	92.3	-2.4	89.9	57.8	32.1	...
Mali Mali	1990	683 300	-1.2[1]	98.8	11.5	110.3	94.3	16.1	3.9
	1991	691 400	-1.3[1]	98.7	13.0	111.9	100.4	11.5	4.0
	1992	737 400	-1.2[1]	98.8	11.4	110.2	96.4	13.8	3.5
Malta Malte	1999	1 456	0.9[1]	100.9	...	...	...	...	...
	2000	1 558	-3.5[1]	96.5	...	...	...	...	...
	2001	1 632	-0.1[1]	99.9	...	...	...	...	...
Martinique Martinique	1990	19 320	-4.2	95.8	33.7	...	113.3	...	...
	1991	20 787	-4.4	95.6	30.7	...	112.8	...	...
	1992	22 093	-3.9	96.1	33.4	...	113.1	...	...
Mauritania Mauritanie	1987	67 216	-5.1	94.9	8.1	103.0	96.2	6.7	...
	1988	72 635	-5.6	94.4	7.9	102.3	93.7	8.5	...
	1989	83 520	-3.6	96.4	9.0	105.4	...	...	...
Mauritius[2] Maurice[2]	1999	107 444	-0.4	99.6	3.4	102.9	77.2	25.8	...
	2000	119 529	-0.7	99.3	1.4	100.7	74.9	25.8	...
	2001	131 835	0.3	100.3	1.5	101.8	73.4	28.4	...
Mexico[2] Mexique[2]	1998	3 846 350	-3.1	96.9	1.4	98.3	77.8	20.5	10.3
	1999	4 593 685	-2.7	97.3	1.3	98.6	78.2	20.5	10.1
	2000	5 485 372	-2.3	97.7	1.2	98.9	78.5	20.4	9.5
Mongolia Mongolie	1996	659 698	...	98.8	...	...	...	...	6.0
	1997	846 344	...	95.0	...	...	...	...	8.4
	1998	833 727	...	99.3	...	...	...	...	10.5
Morocco Maroc	1999	345 594	-2.3	...	6.1	103.8	...	22.6	...
	2000	354 068	-2.3	...	7.3	104.8	...	22.2	...
	2001	382 897	-2.2	...	10.5	108.6	...	27.7	...
Mozambique[2] Mozambique[2]	1999	51 913 228	-2.7	97.3	1.4	98.7	91.0	7.7	9.8
	2000	56 917 388	0.8	100.8	-0.1	100.7	92.1	17.7	11.6
	2001	71 134 761	-0.3	106.0	-0.1	105.9	87.2	39.5	15.2
Myanmar + Myanmar +	1996	791 980	0.0[1]	100.0	...	100.0	88.5	11.4	2.3
	1997	1 109 554	0.0[1]	100.0	...	100.0	88.1	11.9	1.9
	1998	1 559 996	0.0[1]	100.0	...	100.0	89.4	10.6	1.7

22

Relationships among the principal national accounting aggregates
As a percentage of GDP [cont.]

Relations entre les principaux agrégats de comptabilité nationale
En pourcentage du PIB *[suite]*

			As a percentage of GDP – En pourcentage du PIB						
Region, country or area Région, pays ou zone	Year Année	GDP in current prices (Mil.nat.cur.) PIB aux prix courants (Millions Monnaie nat.)	Plus: Compensation of employees and property income from/to the rest of the world, net Plus: Rémunération des salariés et revenus de la propriété – du et au reste du monde, net	Equals: Gross national income Égale: Revenu national brut	Plus: Net current transfers from/to the rest of the world Plus: Transfers courants du/au reste du monde, net	Equals: Gross national disposable income Égale: Revenu national disponible brut	Less: Final consumption expenditure Moins: Dépense de consommation de finale	Equals: Gross savings Égale: Épargne brut	Less: Consumption of fixed capital Moins: Consommation de capital fixe
Namibia [2] Namibie [2]	1999	20 681	-0.5	99.5	12.3	111.8	89.5	22.3	13.8
	2000	23 995	1.0	101.0	12.5	113.5	87.6	25.9	12.9
	2001	27 231	1.0	101.0	11.0	112.0	88.4	23.6	13.1
Nepal + Népal +	1999	342 036	3.2	103.2	0.4	...	86.4	16.8	...
	2000	379 488	3.5	103.5	0.3	...	84.8	18.6	...
	2001	410 287	3.9	103.9	0.4	...	85.1	18.8	...
Netherlands [2] Pays-Bas [2]	2000	402 599	1.0	101.0	-0.8	100.2	72.6	27.6	15.2
	2001	429 172	-1.2	98.8	-0.8	98.0	72.8	25.3	15.4
	2002	444 050	-2.6	97.4	-0.7	96.7	74.3	...	16.1
Netherlands Antilles Antilles néerlandaises	1995	4 224	4.1	104.1	10.5	114.7	94.4	20.3	12.8
	1996	4 422	4.5	104.5	2.6	107.0	90.1	16.9	12.9
	1997	4 537	2.9	102.9	2.5	105.4	84.8	20.7	12.7
New Zealand + [2] Nouvelle-Zélande + [2]	1999	107 068	-6.2	93.8	0.4	94.2	80.3	14.0	13.4
	2000	113 778	-6.9	93.1	0.4	93.5	78.1	15.4	13.4
	2001	122 241	-5.5	94.5	0.2	94.7	76.6	18.2	13.4
Nicaragua Nicaragua	1999	26 130	-3.1	96.9	13.6	110.5	114.1	-3.6	...
	2000	30 858	-2.9	97.1	13.2	110.3	110.9	-0.6	...
	2001	34 242	...	100.0	13.2	100.0	112.4	-12.4	...
Niger Niger	1982	663 022	-3.1	96.9	1.5	98.4	85.1	13.3	8.7
	1983	687 142	-3.1	96.9	1.1	98.0	88.8	9.2	9.3
	1984	638 406	...	96.2	1.6	97.8	88.2	9.6	10.4
Nigeria Nigéria	1992	549 809	-11.7	88.3	2.3	90.6	77.2	13.4	3.0
	1993	701 043	-10.5	89.5	2.5	92.0	80.6	11.5	2.5
	1994	914 334	-7.2	92.8	1.2	94.0	85.5	8.5	2.0
Norway [2] Norvège [2]	2000	1 469 075	-1.0	99.0	-0.8	98.2	61.7	36.5	13.9
	2001	1 526 601	-0.6	99.4	-1.0	98.4	63.3	35.1	14.2
	2002	1 520 728	0.3	100.3	-1.2	99.0	66.9	32.1	14.1
Oman [2] Oman [2]	1999	6 041	-4.6	95.4	-8.9	86.5	73.5	13.0	11.2
	2000	7 639	-3.8	96.2	-7.1	89.1	60.0	29.2	9.1
	2001	7 668	-3.1	96.9	-7.5	89.4	65.2	24.2	9.5
Pakistan + Pakistan +	1999	3 147 167	...	98.6	...	...	85.6	...	5.5
	2000	3 416 252	...	98.5	...	...	85.4	...	6.7
	2001	3 726 611	...	100.7	...	...	86.4	...	6.4
Panama Panama	1998	9 345	-6.5	93.5	1.7	95.2	72.7	23.1	7.1
	1999	9 637	-8.2	91.8	1.8	93.6	70.9	22.7	7.5
	2000	10 019	-7.0	93.0	1.8	94.8	72.6	22.1	7.5
Papua New Guinea [2] Papouasie-Nvl-Guinée [2]	1997	7 064	-4.4	88.0[7]	1.5	89.6[7]	77.6	12.0[7]	...
	1998	7 863	-4.4	88.8[7]	0.7	89.5[7]	77.6	11.9[7]	...
	1999	8 781	-4.1	89.9[7]	0.9	90.8[7]	86.7	4.1[7]	...
Paraguay Paraguay	1993	11 991 719	...	100.4	...	100.4	88.0	12.4	7.8
	1994	14 960 131	...	100.5	...	100.5	95.2	5.3	7.8
	1995	17 699 000	...	100.9	...	100.9	92.5	8.4	7.8
Peru Pérou	1996	148 278	...	97.3	...	...	80.6	...	...
	1997	172 389	...	97.5	...	...	78.7	...	...
	1998	183 179	...	97.7	...	...	80.9	...	...

22

Relationships among the principal national accounting aggregates
As a percentage of GDP [cont.]
   Relations entre les principaux agrégats de comptabilité nationale
En pourcentage du PIB *[suite]*

Region, country or area Région, pays ou zone	Year Année	GDP in current prices (Mil.nat.cur.) PIB aux prix courants (Millions Monnaie nat.)	Plus: Compensation of employees and property income from/to the rest of the world, net Plus : Rémuneration des salariés et revenus de la propriété – du et au reste du monde, net	Equals: Gross national income Égale : Revenu national brut	Plus: Net current transfers from/to the rest of the world Plus : Transfers courants du/au reste du monde, net	Equals: Gross national disposable income Égale : Revenu national disponible brut	Less: Final consumption expenditure Moins : Dépense de consommation de finale	Equals: Gross savings Égale : Épargne brut	Less: Consumption of fixed capital Moins : Consommation de capital fixe
Philippines	1999	2 976 904	5.4	105.4	2.0	107.4	85.7	21.7	8.5
Philippines	2000	3 308 318	5.7	105.7	0.1	105.8	83.9	22.0	8.8
	2001	3 639 980	5.9	105.9	0.6	106.5	83.2	23.2	9.2
Poland [2]	#2000	712 322	...	99.1	...	...	81.6	...	...
Pologne [2]	2001	749 311	...	99.2	...	...	82.7	...	...
	2002	772 248	...	...	...	...	84.2	...	...
Portugal [2]	1999	108 030	-1.6	98.4	3.2	101.6	82.1	19.6	16.4
Portugal [2]	2000	115 546	-2.2	97.8	3.0	100.8	82.1	18.8	17.3
	2001	122 978	-2.7	97.3	2.7	100.0	81.6	18.4	17.4
Puerto Rico +	1998	57 841	-34.3	65.7	15.2	80.9	71.8	6.0	7.5
Porto Rico +	1999	61 045	-32.6	67.4	13.5	81.6	70.8	5.2	7.6
	2000	67 897	-35.5	64.5	13.2	77.6	66.9	3.3	7.1
Republic of Moldova [2]	1999	12 322	2.9	102.9	6.5	109.4	90.0	19.4	...
République de	2000	16 020	5.0	105.0	11.2	116.2	103.0	13.1	...
Moldova [2]	2001	19 052	7.5	107.5	10.5	118.0	101.1	16.9	...
Réunion	1990	28 374	...	97.5	44.3	141.7	108.1	33.6	...
Réunion	1991	31 339	...	100.7	42.7	143.4	103.5	39.9	...
	1992	33 787	...	98.4	43.6	142.1	104.5	37.6	...
Romania [2]	1994	49 773 200	...	100.0	2.2	102.2	77.3	24.9	...
Roumanie [2]	1995	72 135 500	...	100.0	1.2	101.2	81.3	19.9	...
	1996	108 390 900	...	100.0	...	101.2	83.0	18.3	...
Russian Federation [2]	2000	7 302 233[8]	-2.6	97.4	0.0	97.4	61.6	35.8	...
Fédération de Russie [2]	2001	9 039 441[8]	-1.3	98.7	-0.2	98.5	65.2	33.2	8.0
	2002	10 863 362[8]	-1.2	98.8	0.0	98.8	68.1	30.7	7.6
Rwanda	1987	171 430	-1.6	98.4	2.5	100.9	93.5	7.4	6.5
Rwanda	1988	177 920	-2.0	98.0	2.9	100.9	93.6	7.3	6.9
	1989	190 220	-1.2	98.8	2.4	101.3	95.4	5.9	7.6
Saint Kitts and Nevis	1999	823	...	91.0	6.7	97.7	89.3	8.4	...
Saint-Kitts-et-Nevis	2000	891	...	91.1	19.0	110.1	79.7	30.4	...
	2001	928	...	90.2	5.8	95.9	69.1	26.8	...
Saint Lucia	1996	1 543	...	92.6	3.6	96.2	81.4	14.8	...
Sainte-Lucie	1997	1 562	...	92.3	3.6	95.9	83.7	12.3	...
	1998	1 695	...	92.8	3.4	96.2	84.0	12.2	...
St. Vincent-Grenadines	1999	890	-6.6	95.6	4.4	100.0	85.8	14.2	...
St. Vincent-Grenadines	2000	905	-6.0	94.0	5.6	99.7	81.0	18.7	...
	2001	940	-5.6	94.4	4.6	98.9	84.5	14.5	...
San Marino	1997	1 279 857	...	92.2	...	76.4	...	...	...
Saint-Marin	1998	1 400 841	...	90.9	...	74.2	...	...	...
	1999	1 551 010	...	89.3	...	73.7	...	...	...
Saudi Arabia +	1996	529 250	-2.8	97.2	-13.2	84.0	65.5	18.5	10.0
Arabie saoudite +	1997	548 620	-2.6	97.4	-12.3	85.1	65.2	19.9	10.0
	1998	480 773	-1.6	98.4	-13.4	84.9	73.9	11.1	10.0
Senegal	1996	2 380 000	...	108.1	...	...	91.0	...	...
Sénégal	1997	2 554 300	...	104.1	...	...	88.8	...	...
	1998	2 746 000	...	104.5	...	...	87.3	...	...

22

Relationships among the principal national accounting aggregates
As a percentage of GDP [cont.]

Relations entre les principaux agrégats de comptabilité nationale
En pourcentage du PIB *[suite]*

As a percentage of GDP – En pourcentage du PIB

Region, country or area / Région, pays ou zone	Year / Année	GDP in current prices (Mil.nat.cur.) / PIB aux prix courants (Millions Monnaie nat.)	Plus: Compensation of employees and property income from/to the rest of the world, net / Plus: Rémunération des salariés et revenus de la propriété – du et au reste du monde, net	Equals: Gross national income / Égale: Revenu national brut	Plus: Net current transfers from/to the rest of the world / Plus: Transfers courants du/au reste du monde, net	Equals: Gross national disposable income / Égale: Revenu national disponible brut	Less: Final consumption expenditure / Moins: Dépense de consommation finale	Equals: Gross savings / Égale: Épargne brut	Less: Consumption of fixed capital / Moins: Consommation de capital fixe
Seychelles	1998	3 201	...	97.2		...	81.2	...	...
Seychelles	1999	3 330	...	97.3	...	...	73.1	...	
	2000	3 424		96.3			66.4		
Sierra Leone +	1988	43 947	-0.9[1]	100.9	0.6	101.5	94.3	7.3	5.8
Sierra Leone +	1989	82 837	-0.8[1]	100.8	0.5	101.3	91.3	10.0	5.9
	1990	150 175	-5.0[1]	95.0	0.7	95.7	88.4	7.3	5.6
Singapore	1999	140 070	2.5	102.5	-1.4	101.0	51.2	51.9	14.5
Singapour	2000	159 888	0.6	100.6	-1.4	99.2	50.7	48.8	13.1
	2001	153 455	0.8	100.8	-1.6	99.2	54.2	45.2	14.2
Slovakia [2]	1996	628 588	-0.2	99.8	1.0	100.8	75.6	25.2	18.5
Slovaquie [2]	1997	708 617	-0.6	99.4	0.8	100.3	74.3	25.9	19.5
	1998	775 002	-0.7	99.3	1.7	101.0	75.9	25.1	20.1
Slovenia [2] / Slovénie [2]	1993	1 435 095	-0.4	...	...	...	...	...	...
Solomon Islands	1984	222	...	94.2	...	100.8	78.2	22.6	5.9
Iles Salomon	1985	237	...	95.0	...	101.0	91.6	9.4	6.7
	1986	253	...	92.6	...	115.7	94.8	20.9	7.6
Somalia	1985	87 290	...	97.8	10.1	107.9	101.1	6.8	...
Somalie	1986	118 781	...	96.3	14.2	110.5	98.8	11.7	...
	1987	169 608	...	96.8	21.3	118.0	99.9	18.2	...
South Africa [2]	1999	800 696	-2.4[1]	97.6	-0.7	96.9	81.6	15.4[6]	13.5
Afrique du Sud [2]	2000	888 057	-2.4[1]	97.6	-0.7	96.8	81.4	15.2[6]	13.4
	2001	982 944	-3.3[1]	96.7	-0.6	96.0	80.8	14.9[6]	13.1
Spain [2]	2000	609 319	-1.0	99.0	0.0	99.0	76.6	22.4	13.7
Espagne [2]	2001	651 641	-1.4	98.6	0.0	98.6	75.9	22.7	13.9
	2002	693 925	-1.1	98.9	0.0	98.9	75.5	...	...
Sri Lanka [2]	1999	1 108 845	-1.6	98.4	5.6	104.0	81.4	22.5[6]	5.1
Sri Lanka [2]	2000	1 253 622	-1.8	98.2	5.9	104.0	84.2	19.7[6]	5.1
	2001	1 397 453	-1.8	98.2	6.0	104.2	82.9	20.8[6]	4.2
Sudan +	1991	421 819	...	85.5	...	104.0	86.0	18.0	7.0
Soudan +	1992	948 448	...	99.7	...	102.2	88.2	14.0	6.4
	1993	1 881 289	...	99.8	...	100.6	88.3	12.3	7.1
Suriname	1998	358 114	-0.1	99.9	-0.2	99.7	105.3	-5.6	10.8
Suriname	1999	603 483	0.0	100.0	-0.2	99.7	...	...	...
	2000	873 865	1.3	101.3	-0.3	101.0	...	...	...
Swaziland + [2]	1999	8 408	...	106.4	9.5	115.9	96.1	19.8	...
Swaziland + [2]	2000	9 639	...	104.8	8.9	113.6	95.5	18.2	...
	2001	10 971	...	102.7	6.2	109.0	95.0	14.0	...
Sweden [2]	2000	2 196 764	-0.7	99.3	-0.9	98.4	75.9	22.5	13.9
Suède [2]	2001	2 266 619	-0.9	99.1	-0.9	98.2	75.9	22.3	14.7
	2002	2 339 949	-0.9	99.1	-1.0	98.1	76.7	21.4	14.9
Switzerland	1999	388 518	7.9	107.9	-1.4	106.5	75.2	31.4	16.0
Suisse	2000	405 530	9.9	109.9	-1.4	108.5	74.3	34.2	16.4
	2001	414 882	6.1	106.1	...	...	75.0	...	...

22

Relationships among the principal national accounting aggregates
As a percentage of GDP [cont.]
Relations entre les principaux agrégats de comptabilité nationale
En pourcentage du PIB *[suite]*

Region, country or area Région, pays ou zone	Year Année	GDP in current prices (Mil.nat.cur.) PIB aux prix courants (Millions Monnaie nat.)	Plus: Compensation of employees and property income from/to the rest of the world, net Plus : Rémuneration des salariés et revenus de la propriété – du et au reste du monde, net	Equals: Gross national income Égale : Revenu national brut	Plus: Net current transfers from/to the rest of the world Plus : Transferts courants du/au reste du monde, net	Equals: Gross national disposable income Égale : Revenu national disponible brut	Less: Final consumption expenditure Moins : Dépense de consommation de finale	Equals: Gross savings Égale : Épargne brut	Less: Consumption of fixed capital Moins : Consommation de capital fixe
Thailand	1998	4 626 447	-3.5	96.5	0.4	97.0	65.2	31.8	14.7
Thaïlande	1999	4 632 132	-2.7	97.3	0.3	97.6	67.5	30.1	15.2
	2000	4 904 725	-1.6	98.4	0.5	98.9	67.5	31.4	14.8
TFYR of Macedonia [2]	1991	935	...	99.4	-0.4	99.0	85.5	13.5	12.0
L'ex-R.y. Macédoine [2]	1992	12 006	...	96.9	-0.4	96.6	83.8	12.8	27.1
	1993	58 145	...	97.7	0.7	98.4	88.9	9.5	22.2
Togo	1980	238 872	-1.8	98.2	6.3	104.4	80.3	24.1	7.5
Togo	1981	54	6.3	106.3	23.7	130.0	136.9	15.1	4.6
Tonga +	1982	64	6.9	106.9	35.8	142.7	137.9	29.0	4.5
Tonga +	1983	73	4.4	104.4	27.1	130.5	140.0	10.2	4.0
Trinidad and Tobago [2]	1999	42 889	-5.9	94.1	0.6	94.7	73.2	21.5	12.2
Trinité-et-Tobago [2]	2000	51 485	-7.7	92.3	0.5	92.8	66.2	26.6	10.7
	2001	56 700	-5.2	94.8	0.4	95.2	67.4	27.8	10.3
Tunisia [2]	1999	24 672	-4.1	95.9	4.2	100.1	75.9	24.2	9.6
Tunisie [2]	2000	26 651	-4.7	95.3	4.1	99.4	76.3	23.1	9.3
	2001	28 793	-4.6	95.4	4.8	100.3	76.5	23.8	9.3
Turkey	2000	124583458275	0.8	100.8	0.0	100.8	85.6	15.2	6.6
Turquie	2001	178412438500	-1.1	98.9	0.0	98.9	86.3	12.6	8.3
	2002	276002987851	-0.9	99.1	...	...	80.7	...	...
Ukraine [2]	1999	130 442[9]	-2.7	97.3	2.2	99.5	77.0	22.5	17.8
Ukraine [2]	2000	170 070[9]	-3.0	97.0	2.9	99.9	75.3	24.6	17.8
	2001	204 190[9]	-1.8	98.2	3.9	102.2	76.6	25.6	16.8
United Arab Emirates	1988	87 106	0.3	100.3	-1.2	99.1	65.8	33.3	16.5
Emirats arabes unis	1989	100 976	0.4	100.4	-0.7	99.7	61.7	38.0	15.0
	1990	124 008	-1.0	99.0	-8.9	90.1	54.9	35.1	13.0
United Kingdom [2]	2000	950 415	0.6	100.6	-0.7	99.9	84.6	15.3	11.2
Royaume-Uni [2]	2001	993 124	1.3	101.3	-0.3	101.0	85.6	15.4	11.2
	2002	1 043 301	1.6	101.6	-0.7	101.0	86.1	14.9	11.0
United Rep. of Tanzania	2000	7 277 800	-0.9[1]	91.2	4.6	101.0	90.0	11.0	...
Rép.-Unie de Tanzanie	2001	8 284 685	-0.9[1]	91.2	4.2	100.9	89.7	11.2	...
	2002	9 374 559	-0.9[1]	91.1	4.3	100.3	86.4	13.9	...
United States [2]	2000	9 762 100	0.2	101.6	-0.6	101.0	83.0	18.0	11.9
Etats-Unis [2]	2001	10 019 700	0.2	101.4	-0.5	100.9	84.8	16.1	12.6
	2002	10 383 100	-0.1	101.0	-0.5	100.5	85.9	14.6	12.8
Uruguay	2000	243 027	-1.4[1]	98.6	0.3	98.9	87.7	11.1	...
Uruguay	2001	247 211	-2.1[1]	97.9	0.3	98.2	88.1	10.1	...
	2002	261 987	-1.5[1]	98.5	0.7	99.1	85.7	13.4	...
Vanuatu	1996	28 227	...	91.1	...	...	...	...	...
Vanuatu	1997	29 477	...	91.7	...	...	...	...	...
	1998	29 545	...	93.5	...	...	...	...	...
Venezuela	1999	62 577 039	-1.5	98.5	0.1	98.6	76.6	22.0	7.6
Venezuela	2000	82 450 674	-1.0	99.0	-0.2	98.8	70.7	28.2	7.2
	2001	91 324 773	-1.2	98.8	-0.5	98.3	75.5	22.8	7.5

22

Relationships among the principal national accounting aggregates
As a percentage of GDP [cont.]
Relations entre les principaux agrégats de comptabilité nationale
En pourcentage du PIB [suite]

Region, country or area Région, pays ou zone	Year Année	GDP in current prices (Mil.nat.cur.) PIB aux prix courants (Millions Monnaie nat.)	Plus: Compensation of employees and property income from/to the rest of the world, net Plus : Rémuneration des salariés et revenus de la propriété – du et au reste du monde, net	Equals: Gross national income Égale : Revenu national brut	Plus: Net current transfers from/to the rest of the world Plus : Transfers courants du/au reste du monde, net	Equals: Gross national disposable income Égale : Revenu national disponible brut	Less: Final consumption expenditure Moins : Dépense de consommation de finale	Equals: Gross savings Égale : Épargne brut	Less: Consumption of fixed capital Moins : Consommation de capital fixe
Yemen [2]	1998	849 321	-5.6	94.4	19.1	113.5	82.5	31.0	9.3
Yémen [2]	1999	1 132 619	-9.3	90.7	17.2	107.9	81.8	24.7	8.6
	2000	1 379 812	-13.4	86.6	17.6	104.1	71.8	37.3	8.2
Yugoslavia, SFR	1988	15 833	...	105.0	...	...	64.3	...	12.2
Yougoslavie, Rfs	1989	235 395	...	106.9	...	...	61.9	...	12.1
	1990	1 147 787	...	108.7	...	...	83.7	...	11.2
Zambia	1986	12 963	-18.1	81.9	-1.2	80.7	77.4	3.3	17.2
Zambie	1987	19 778	-11.4	88.6	0.5	89.1	82.0	7.1	17.3
	1988	27 725	-14.2	85.8	1.0	86.9	79.8	7.1	14.5
Zimbabwe	1997	102 982	-4.8	95.2	2.8	97.1	88.0	9.0	...
Zimbabwe	1998	143 364	-6.4	93.6	3.8	92.1	80.2	11.9	...
	1999	210 409	-6.3	93.7	4.6	...	84.3	...	...

Source:
United Nations Statistics Division, New York, national accounts
database.

+ Note: The national accounts data generally relate to the fiscal year
used in each country, unless indicated otherwise. Countries whose
reference periods coincide with the calendar year ending 31
December are not listed below.
Year beginning 21 March: Afghanistan, Iran (Islamic Republic).
Year beginning 1 April: Bermuda, India, Myanmar, New Zealand,
Nigeria (beginning 1982).
Year beginning 1 July: Australia, Bangladesh, Cameroon, Egypt,
Gambia, Pakistan, Puerto Rico, Saudi Arabia, Sierra Leone, Sudan.
Year ending 30 June: Botswana, Swaziland, Tonga.
Year ending 7 July: Ethiopia.
Year ending 15 July: Nepal.
Year ending 30 September: Haiti.

Source:
Organisation des Nations Unies, Division de statistique, New York, la
base de données sur les comptes nationaux.

+ Note : Sauf indication contraire, les données sur les comptes
nationaux concernent généralement l'exercice budgétaire utilisé dans
chaque pays. Les pays ou territoires dont la période de référence
coïncide avec l'année civile se terminant le 31 décembre ne sont pas
répertoriés ci-dessous.
Exercice commençant le 21 mars: Afghanistan, Iran (République
islamique d').
Exercice commençant le 1er avril: Bermudes, Inde, Myanmar, Nigéria
(à partir de 1982), Nouvelle-Zélande.
Exercice commençant le 1er juillet: Arabie saoudite, Australie,
Bangladesh, Cameroun, Égypte, Gambie, Pakistan, Porto Rico, Sierra
Leone, Soudan.
Exercice se terminant le 30 juin: Botswana, Swaziland, Tonga.
Exercice se terminant le 7 juillet: Éthiopie.
Exercice se terminant le 15 juillet: Népal.
Exercice se terminant le 30 septembre: Haïti.

1	Property income - from and to the rest of the world, net.
2	Data are classified according to the 1993 SNA.
3	Re-denomination of Belarussian rubles at 1 to 1000.
4	Data in levs.
5	Compensation of employees - from and to the rest of the world, net.
6	Including statistical discrepancy.
7	Net.
8	Re-denomination of Russian rubles at 1 to 1000.
9	Data in karbovanets.

1   Revenus de la propriété - du et reste du monde, net.
2   Les données sont classifiées selon le SCN 1993.
3   Instauration du nouveau rouble bélarussien par division par 1000 du
rouble bélarussien ancien.
4   Les données sont exprimées en lev.
5   Rémunération des salariés - du et au reste du monde, net.
6   Y compris une divergence statistique.
7   Net
8   Instauration du nouveau rouble par division par 1000 du rouble
ancien.
9   Les données sont exprimées en karbovanets.

23
Government final consumption expenditure by function in current prices
Percentage distribution
Dépenses de consommation finale des administrations publiques, par fonction, aux prix courants
Répartition en pourcentage

Region, country or area / Région, pays ou zone	Year / Année	General govt. final cons. exp. (M.nat.curr.) Dépenses de consommation finale des administrations publiques (M.monn.nat.)	General public services Services généraux des adminis-trations publiques (%)	Defence Défense (%)	Public order and safety Ordre et securité publics (%)	Environ-ment protection Protection de l'envir-onnement (%)	Health Santé (%)	Education Enseigne-ment (%)	Social protection Protection sociale (%)	Others Autres (%)
Anguilla	1999	64	42.2	...	9.4	...	15.6	17.2	1.6	15.6
Anguilla	2000	58	41.4	...	10.3	...	15.5	19.0	3.4	10.3
	2001	62	38.7	...	11.3	...	16.1	19.4	3.2	9.7
Argentina	1996	43 617	10.8	4.5	3.2	0.2	8.4	5.9[1]	43.2	...
Argentine	1997	45 156	9.4	4.4	3.1	0.2	7.1	6.0[1]	42.0	...
	1998	46 463	9.5	4.2	3.0	0.2	6.6	6.0[1]	41.0	...
Australia +	1994	79 341	15.1	11.6	7.3	...	17.6	20.7	5.6	21.9
Australie +	1995	83 437	15.0	10.9	7.6	...	18.2	20.3	5.8	22.2
	1996	86 419	15.4	10.1	7.8	...	18.5	21.0	5.8	21.5
Austria[2]	1999	39 042	15.0	4.7	7.3	1.0	25.3	27.0	6.6	13.1
Autriche[2]	2000	39 800	14.6	4.7	7.3	0.9	24.5	27.3	7.7	12.9
	2001	40 544	15.0	4.6	7.3	0.9	24.4	27.4	7.5	13.0
Azerbaijan[2]	2000	3 573 977	14.4	13.6	0.0	...	18.2[3]	3.4	...	50.3[4]
Azerbaïdjan[2]	2001	3 627 000	20.6	14.7	0.0	...	18.4[3]	3.4	...	42.8[4]
	2002	3 789 100	20.6	14.7	0.1	...	18.4[3]	3.4	...	42.8[4]
Bahamas[2]	1993	408	17.4	4.2	14.5	...	18.6	24.0	4.2	17.4
Bahamas[2]	1994	511	20.2	3.7	13.3	...	18.0	23.1	3.5	18.8
	1995	484	18.4	3.9	14.5	...	18.0	22.1	3.9	19.4
Bangladesh +[2]	1998	88 546	15.3	24.3	13.0	...	10.3	17.1	1.0	19.0
Bangladesh +[2]	1999	92 450	12.9	24.0	13.4	...	12.3	16.6	1.4	19.2
	2000	105 351	12.9	22.0	12.9	...	12.0	16.5	1.4	22.3
Belgium[2]	1999	49 957	12.4	6.0	6.6	1.1	28.3	28.3	6.2	11.2
Belgique[2]	2000	52 362	11.9	5.8	6.7	1.3	28.8	28.0	6.2	11.2
	2001	55 103	11.8	5.8	6.7	1.3	29.1	27.9	6.4	11.0
Belize	1990	279	12.7	3.4	7.9	...	6.8	15.3	3.3	50.7
Belize	1991	321	16.6	3.4	7.0	...	6.6	16.8	4.0	45.7
Bolivia	1991	2 310	74.7	0.0	...	...	0.0	7.7	1.9	15.6
Bolivie	1992	2 833	76.2	...	...	...	0.0	8.1	1.9	13.7
	1993	3 270	75.9	...	...	...	0.0	9.0	2.4	12.7
Botswana[2]	1999	6 579	45.4[5]	...	...	...	6.2	25.0	2.9	20.6
Botswana[2]	2000	7 525	44.0[5]	...	...	...	6.5	26.4	3.4	19.7
	2001	9 268	43.2[5]	...	...	...	7.0	27.5	3.5	18.7
Brazil[2]	1999	185 828	71.2	...	...	...	12.2	16.6	...	...
Brésil[2]	2000	209 953	73.1	...	...	...	11.3	15.6	...	...
	2001	230 741	73.3	...	...	...	11.2	15.5	...	...
Cayman Islands	1990	94[6]	26.6	...	14.9	...	16.0	14.9	4.3	23.4
Iles Caïmanes	1991	103[6]	27.2	...	14.6	...	14.6	14.6	5.8	23.3
Chad	1996	42 080	1.5	24.6	4.6	5.3	5.7	22.8	27.0	8.3
Tchad	1997	40 078	1.0	26.6	9.5	5.2	6.9	23.6	20.7	7.7
	2001	60 157	...	20.2	8.4	5.2	6.3	25.0	28.0	6.9
China, Macao SAR[2]	1998	6 029	16.4	...	29.0	0.1	17.3	13.4	8.6	15.1
Chine, Macao RAS[2]	1999	6 772	22.0	...	25.7	0.1	15.8	10.7	8.6	17.2
	2000	5 901	17.9	...	28.9	0.1	17.0	10.2	9.1	16.8
Colombia	1992	3 965 104	29.5	10.8	...	...	7.7	24.8	8.9	18.2
Colombie	1993	5 108 076	28.5	10.2	...	...	11.0	24.0	8.2	18.0
	1994	7 652 736	36.2	9.8	...	...	14.3	21.0	8.6	10.1
Cook Islands	1999	54	23.6	...	6.4	...	9.0	15.1	...	45.9
Iles Cook	2000	63	14.8	...	6.1	...	9.9	10.4	...	58.8
	2001	75	21.2	...	5.9	...	13.0	12.4	...	47.5

23
Government final consumption expenditure by function in current prices
Percentage distribution [*cont.*]

Dépenses de consommation finale des administrations publiques, par fonction, aux prix courants

Répartition en pourcentage *[suite]*

Region, country or area / Région, pays ou zone	Year / Année	General govt. final cons. exp. (M.nat.curr.) / Dépenses de consommation finale des administrations publiques (M.monn.nat.)	General public services / Services généraux des administrations publiques (%)	Defence / Défense (%)	Public order and safety / Ordre et securité publics (%)	Environment protection / Protection de l'environnement (%)	Health / Santé (%)	Education / Enseignement (%)	Social protection / Protection sociale (%)	Others / Autres (%)
Costa Rica [2] / Costa Rica [2]	1999	565 207	34.9	...	...	...	33.1	31.9	...	...
	2000	652 509	34.4	...	...	...	32.8	32.8	...	...
	2001	770 806	34.1	...	...	...	32.6	33.3	...	...
Côte d'Ivoire / Côte d'Ivoire	1996	983 370	73.5	...	...	...	6.2	20.3	...	...
	1997	1 029 358	69.3	...	...	...	19.7	11.0	...	...
	1998	1 018 653	68.3	...	...	...	19.9	11.8	...	...
Croatia [2] / Croatie [2]	1996	30 973	6.2	25.1	12.0	...	0.5	11.6	14.2	30.4
	1997	34 395	6.3	20.3	12.1	...	0.5	11.8	18.8	30.1
	1998	41 390	8.2	17.8	10.3	...	2.0	11.3	19.4	31.1
Cyprus / Chypre	1992	591	10.3	32.3	8.7	...	9.5	16.3	11.6	11.2
	1993	553	13.0	16.3	10.2	...	11.7	19.7	15.0	14.1
	1994	608	11.8	16.2	9.4	...	11.6	20.4	16.1	14.5
Denmark [2] / Danemark [2]	2000	323 812	7.9	6.1	3.4	...	19.7	22.9	26.6	13.5
	2001	342 920	7.5	6.1	3.4	...	19.9	22.6	27.5	13.1
	2002	354 983	7.9	6.1	3.4	...	20.4	22.9	26.5	12.8
Dominican Republic [2] / Rép. dominicaine [2]	1994	8 265	66.3	...	2.7	...	12.8	18.1	...	...
	1995	9 115	61.2	...	2.7	...	12.6	23.4	...	...
	1996	10 843	61.1	...	2.3	...	12.5	24.1	...	...
Ecuador / Equateur	1990	777 131	13.0	14.5	7.0	...	4.8	27.5	6.1	27.0[7]
	1991	1 009 000	13.0	15.0	7.1	...	4.6	27.8	6.2	26.4[7]
	1992	1 498 000	12.8	15.9	7.3	...	3.9	26.8	7.8	25.4[7]
Estonia [2] / Estonie [2]	1994	6 790	12.9	4.3	12.5	...	16.5	29.2	4.3	20.3
	1995	10 350	11.2	4.5	11.2	...	17.7	27.8	3.9	23.8
	1996	12 632	11.0	4.6	11.7	...	17.3	27.8	4.1	23.4
Fiji / Fidji	1993	467	28.1	9.9	...	...	11.6	24.8	0.2	25.5
	1994	441	25.6	10.2	...	...	13.2	25.4	0.2	25.2
	1995	451	26.8	10.0	...	...	12.9	24.8	0.2	25.3
Finland [2] / Finlande [2]	1999	25 940	9.4	6.8	5.4	1.0	23.6	22.6	15.8	15.5
	2000	27 005	9.6	6.6	5.3	0.9	24.0	22.6	16.1	14.8
	2001	28 263	9.7	5.1	5.5	0.9	24.8	22.7	16.6	14.7
France [2] / France [2]	1999	315 725	16.5	9.4	3.8	2.7	12.4	21.1	24.8	9.3
	2000	329 854	16.3	9.5	3.7	2.8	12.3	20.7	25.3	9.2
	2001	342 781	16.3	9.0	3.8	2.5	12.4	20.5	25.8	9.7
Gambia + / Gambie +	1990	819	22.0	...	...	...	6.4	12.9	0.1	58.7
	1991	804	22.2	...	...	...	5.7	12.6	0.1	59.5
Georgia [2] / Géorgie [2]	#1993	1 213[8]	...	1.9	8.2	...	0.6	5.7	0.5	83.2
	1994	119 012[8]	...	5.4	10.1	...	3.2	4.8	9.0	67.5
	#1995	295	...	12.9	45.8	...	6.1	10.2	12.5	12.5
Germany [2] / Allemagne [2]	1999	378 800	11.9	6.8	8.4	0.4	32.0	18.7	16.0	5.9
	2000	387 240	11.7	6.7	8.4	0.4	32.5	18.4	16.1	5.9
	2001	393 520	11.7	6.6	8.3	0.4	32.6	18.3	16.1	5.9
Greece / Grèce	1990	2 220 840	41.4	25.3	...	...	11.9	15.7	1.5	4.3
	1991	2 548 186	42.6	24.7	...	...	11.7	15.6	1.3	4.1
Honduras / Honduras	1995	3 495	27.8	9.5	...	...	20.5	39.1	...	3.1
	1996	4 556	26.0	8.2	...	...	27.6	36.7	...	1.6
	1997	5 377	31.0	7.3	...	...	24.9	35.2	...	1.5
Hungary / Hongrie	1992	780 638	15.0	6.3	7.5	...	16.3	22.2	9.4	23.3
	1993	1 013 524	15.1	12.8	7.3	...	14.4	20.4	8.7	21.3
	1994	1 145 444	17.1	6.2	8.0	...	15.7	21.4	9.3	22.3
Iceland [2] / Islande [2]	1998	127 722	7.4	...	5.5	...	30.4	20.9	8.2	16.5
	1999	142 088	7.7	...	5.6	...	32.0	20.5	8.3	15.9
	2000	156 740	8.0	...	5.4	...	31.7	20.3	8.7	16.3

23

Government final consumption expenditure by function in current prices
Percentage distribution [*cont.*]
Dépenses de consommation finale des administrations publiques, par fonction, aux prix courants
Répartition en pourcentage [*suite*]

Region, country or area Région, pays ou zone	Year Année	General govt. final cons. exp. (M.nat.curr.) Dépenses de consommation finale des administrations publiques (M.monn.nat.)	General public services Services généraux des adminis- trations publiques (%)	Defence Défense (%)	Public order and safety Ordre et securité publics (%)	Environ- ment protection Protection de l'envir- onnement (%)	Health Santé (%)	Education Enseigne- ment (%)	Social protection Protection sociale (%)	Others Autres (%)
India + Inde +	1997	1 335 550	23.1[9]	31.2	...	...	6.3	16.1	3.5	19.8
	1998	1 679 310	23.3[9]	29.4	...	...	6.3	16.1	3.5	21.4
	1999	1 968 680	23.3[9]	28.5	...	...	6.5	16.7	3.5	21.5
Iran (Islamic Rep. of) +[2] Iran (Rép. islamique d')+[2]	1999	61 384 900	4.1	20.1	5.5	...	4.6	23.6	12.3	29.8
	2000	79 801 400	4.4	19.4	7.4	...	5.2	25.6	13.0	24.9
	2001	97 219 200	4.4	19.6	7.4	...	5.2	25.5	12.9	25.0
Ireland[2] Irlande[2]	1998	11 207	10.5	5.2	9.9	...	34.7	17.5	3.3	19.0
	1999	12 464	11.5	4.7	9.1	...	36.9	17.2	3.1	17.5
	2000	13 880	11.5	4.7	9.1	...	36.9	17.2	3.1	17.5
Israel[2] Israël[2]	1999	121 517	7.4	31.7	5.5	3.0	16.3	24.2	4.2	7.6
	2000	128 951	7.3	30.9	5.6	3.0	16.6	24.5	4.3	7.7
	2001	137 237	7.4	30.7	5.7	3.0	16.7	24.5	4.3	7.6
Italy[2] Italie[2]	1999	199 692	12.1	5.9	10.9	1.2	30.0	25.3	3.7	10.8
	2000	212 187	12.3	5.7	10.4	1.3	31.2	24.9	3.9	10.3
	2001	224 663	12.3	5.5	9.9	1.3	31.9	24.7	4.0	10.3
Japan[2,10] Japon[2,10]	1999	83 365 500	10.0	5.1	7.1	6.2	31.5	21.3	5.0	13.8
	2000	86 946 400	9.3	4.9	6.9	6.1	34.1	20.8	4.2	13.7
	2001	88 645 100	9.2	4.9	6.7	6.2	34.8	20.2	4.2	13.8
Jordan Jordanie	1993	939	53.6[5]	...	...	...	10.2	21.9	1.0	13.4
	1994	986	59.3[5]	...	...	...	8.2	20.4	1.0	11.1
	1995	1 111	60.0[5]	...	...	...	8.3	21.3	0.9	9.5
Kazakhstan[2] Kazakhstan[2]	1999	232 713	14.3	7.7	12.5	...	17.4	30.6	5.6	11.8
	2000	313 985	12.0	6.1	14.7	...	16.3	24.1	3.9	23.0
	2001	436 036	14.2	7.1	15.1	...	13.0	21.6	2.9	26.1
Kenya Kenya	1999	6 297	29.8	10.4	...	...	10.0	35.2	...	...
	2000	6 958	27.7	9.6	...	...	9.4	36.8	...	...
	2001	7 522	28.1	10.9	...	...	9.9	37.8	...	...
Korea, Republic of[2] Corée, République de[2]	1999	50 089 364	18.6	27.2	11.6	...	1.7	24.8	5.5	10.6
	2000	52 479 749	18.8	27.1	12.3	...	1.6	24.4	5.1	10.9
	2001	57 179 686	18.1	24.8	13.1	...	1.5	26.1	6.2	10.3
Kuwait Koweït	1997	2 452	...	55.1	...	...	10.0	19.8	3.4	11.7
	1998	2 411	...	52.2	...	...	10.4	21.3	3.7	12.4
	1999	2 463	...	51.9	...	...	10.2	22.0	3.8	12.0
Kyrgyzstan[2] Kirghizistan[2]	1999	9 320	32.0	12.3	2.4	...	13.8	20.0	4.1	15.4
	2000	13 099	38.7	11.8	3.2	...	13.0	17.4	4.6	11.4
	2001	12 912	39.3	7.3	2.8	...	12.6	20.9	6.2	10.9
Lesotho[2] Lesotho[2]	1999	1 188	25.6	...	19.1	...	13.1	6.1	...	15.4
	2000	1 144	27.7	...	20.2	...	13.2	8.1	...	17.1
	2001	1 176	27.4	...	20.6	...	14.0	7.7	...	18.5
Luxembourg[2] Luxembourg[2]	1999	3 145	15.6	1.4	5.5	3.8	23.8	24.4	7.8	17.8
	2000	3 292	15.4	1.5	5.4	4.0	23.5	24.6	7.0	18.8
	2001	3 722	15.4	1.4	5.3	3.9	23.4	24.1	8.8	17.7
Malaysia Malaisie	1997	30 341	13.0	19.4	8.7	...	10.7	31.5	5.3[11]	11.4
	1998	28 454	15.4	16.2	8.4	...	12.4	31.0	6.4[11]	10.1
	1999	33 467	14.7	19.1	7.8	...	11.9	28.8	5.9[11]	11.8
Malta Malte	1994	210	17.6	12.4	...	...	24.3	27.6	2.4	15.2
	1995	235	19.6	11.9	...	...	23.4	28.1	2.6	14.5
	1996	260	18.8	12.3	...	...	23.1	27.7	2.3	15.8
Mauritius[2] Maurice[2]	1999	14 193	26.4	1.6	14.2	...	16.1	19.0	2.5	20.4
	2000	15 582	26.2	1.6	13.6	...	16.9	19.2	2.2	20.3
	2001	16 673	25.9	1.6	13.8	...	17.7	18.4	2.2	20.4

23

Government final consumption expenditure by function in current prices
Percentage distribution [cont.]

Dépenses de consommation finale des administrations publiques, par fonction, aux prix courants
Répartition en pourcentage [suite]

Region, country or area Région, pays ou zone	Year Année	General govt. final cons. exp. (M.nat.curr.) Dépenses de consommation finale des administrations publiques (M.monn.nat.)	General public services Services généraux des adminis- trations publiques (%)	Defence Défense (%)	Public order and safety Ordre et sécurité publics (%)	Environ- ment protection Protection de l'envir- onnement (%)	Health Santé (%)	Education Enseigne- ment (%)	Social protection Protection sociale (%)	Others Autres (%)
Mexico [2] Mexique [2]	1998	399 956	11.7	...	14.8	...	21.1	37.9	1.6	13.0
	1999	506 459	12.7	...	14.5	...	21.8	36.9	1.6	12.6
	2000	607 479	13.3	...	14.9	...	21.6	36.0	1.6	12.6
Mozambique [2] Mozambique [2]	1997	9 113	...	9.2	...	...	...	...	3.9	33.7
	1998	10 042	...	10.1	...	...	...	...	4.1	37.5
Netherlands [2] Pays-Bas [2]	1999	85 526	7.8	7.1	5.7	1.3	17.2	18.4	21.3	21.1
	2000	91 188	7.7	7.2	5.4	1.2	17.6	18.3	21.6	21.0
	2001	99 461	8.3	6.7	5.7	1.2	17.7	18.1	21.6	20.7
Netherlands Antilles Antilles néerlandaises	1995	1 147	14.9	0.5	11.7	...	8.4	22.8	24.3	17.4
	1996	1 193	18.6	0.6	11.3	...	6.0	21.5	23.2	18.6
	1997	1 126	16.9	0.9	12.0	...	7.0	23.4	21.7	18.2
New Zealand + Nouvelle-Zélande +	1992	12 658	22.5	8.0	9.7	...	20.1	26.3	7.7	5.8
	1993	12 692	22.3	8.2	10.2	...	19.9	26.3	7.4	5.6
	1994	12 682	22.9	7.3	10.3	...	20.1	26.1	7.5	5.9
Norway Norvège	1990	139 115	7.9	15.9	4.2	...	22.4	25.7	10.0	13.9
	1991	147 478	8.1	15.1	4.3	...	22.6	25.7	10.5	13.7
Oman [2] Oman [2]	1998	1 402	10.7	31.9[12]	11.9	...	9.8	19.6	1.2	15.0
	1999	1 440	10.5	30.6[12]	11.4	...	9.9	20.8	1.2	15.7
	2000	1 580	10.5	29.3[12]	11.6	...	10.1	21.4	1.2	...
Pakistan + [10] Pakistan + [10]	1999	351 302	55.1	...	7.0	...	3.9	18.6	0.5	14.9
	2000	352 471	41.0	...	5.2	...	4.0	15.4	11.8	22.7
	2001	425 903	43.2	...	5.5	...	3.6	13.4	12.6	21.7
Panama Panama	1998	1 508	14.7	...	14.1	...	12.1	27.9	20.8	10.5
	1999	1 500	14.5	...	13.7	...	11.5	28.0	21.2	10.1
	2000	1 605	21.6	...	13.6	...	9.8	25.9	21.6	7.6
Portugal [2] Portugal [2]	1999	21 254	7.6	7.1	8.6	2.1	26.9	30.6	4.1	13.0
	2000	23 697	8.5	7.5	8.4	2.0	27.2	29.5	3.9	12.9
	2001	25 413	9.0	7.2	8.2	2.0	27.2	29.4	4.1	13.0
Republic of Moldova [2] République de Moldova [2]	2000	2 348	26.3[13]	...	...	...	18.8	32.2	1.2	21.5
	2001	2 736	26.6[13]	...	...	...	18.5	34.6	1.5	18.8
	2002	3 823	31.8[13]	...	...	...	18.2	31.6	1.5	16.9
Romania [2] Roumanie [2]	1993	2 473 200	36.5[5]	...	...	...	22.3	22.6	2.1	16.4
	1994	6 851 800	39.0[5]	...	...	...	28.6	19.4	2.2	13.0
	1995	9 877 000	37.3[5]	...	...	...	19.0	21.4	2.3	20.0
Russian Federation [2] Fédération de Russie [2]	2000	1 102 497[14]	57.7[13]	...	...	...	20.2	16.6	...	5.6
	2001	1 475 837[14]	56.8[13]	...	...	...	20.8	16.7	...	5.7
	2002	1 836 835[14]	50.4[13]	...	...	...	24.1	19.0	...	6.6
St. Vincent-Grenadines St. Vincent-Grenadines	1999	167	8.4	...	12.0	...	19.8	27.5	7.2	25.1
	2000	178	12.4	...	11.8	...	19.7	26.4	8.4	21.3
	2001	186	12.4	...	11.8	...	19.4	26.3	8.6	21.5
San Marino Saint-Marin	1997	354 322	18.9	0.3	4.8	...	19.5	17.4	16.2	22.9
	1998	377 657	19.6	0.3	5.1	...	17.3	17.6	16.1	23.9
	1999	423 728	17.0	0.3	5.0	...	20.7	16.8	17.4	22.7
Saudi Arabia + Arabie saoudite +	1998	156 650	20.5	35.9	...	...	6.9	19.8	0.5	16.4
	1999	154 094	19.8	27.4	...	...	11.0	29.4	0.4	11.9
	2000	183 803	19.7	29.1	...	...	11.9	26.1	0.4	12.8
Senegal Sénégal	1994	258 400	8.8	14.6	8.1	...	5.8	31.4	...	5.4
	1995	278 500	8.8	14.6	7.3	...	5.7	30.2	...	5.0
	1996	289 100	9.0	15.4	8.0	...	5.6	30.1	...	5.2
Seychelles Seychelles	1990	544	9.5	10.2	5.1	...	12.8	29.2	3.5	29.8
	1991	558	10.3	11.0	5.7	...	13.7	26.4	5.2	27.7

23

Government final consumption expenditure by function in current prices
Percentage distribution [*cont.*]
Dépenses de consommation finale des administrations publiques, par fonction, aux prix courants
Répartition en pourcentage *[suite]*

Region, country or area Région, pays ou zone	Year Année	General govt. final cons. exp. (M.nat.curr.) Dépenses de consommation finale des administrations publiques (M.monn.nat.)	General public services Services généraux des adminis- trations publiques (%)	Defence Défense (%)	Public order and safety Ordre et sécurité publics (%)	Environ- ment protection Protection de l'envir- onnement (%)	Health Santé (%)	Education Enseigne- ment (%)	Social protection Protection sociale (%)	Others Autres (%)
Sierra Leone + Sierra Leone +	1990	32 337	11.9	5.6	0.0	...	2.1	6.2	0.6	73.5
Slovenia [2] Slovénie [2]	1991	65 845	35.5	7.6	0.0	...	25.6	21.0	7.3	3.0
	1992	213 669	34.1	7.6	0.0	...	28.6	19.8	7.0	2.9
	1993	297 449	40.5[13]	...	0.0	...	28.8	24.3	2.0	4.4
Spain Espagne	1993	10 700 500	8.4	9.6	11.8	...	24.7	22.2	5.3	18.1
	1994	10 963 200	8.0	8.7	11.9	...	25.8	22.3	4.9	18.3
	1995	11 647 100	8.3	9.0	12.5	...	24.1	22.9	4.8	18.4
Sri Lanka Sri Lanka	1998	143 298	18.9	31.6	...	...	8.0	14.4	16.4	10.7
	1999	152 958	17.4	31.9	...	...	9.1	14.3	15.3	11.9
	2000	176 856	16.6	34.9	...	...	9.9	13.2	14.3	11.1
Sweden [2] Suède [2]	1999	571 393	8.6	8.7	4.6	0.2	22.3	23.2	20.8	11.6
	2000	589 620	10.2	8.1	4.7	0.2	22.7	22.7	21.8	9.6
	2001	617 538	8.3	7.4	4.9	0.2	23.6	24.3	21.5	9.8
Thailand Thaïlande	1998	511 691	20.1	28.1[15]	...	...	11.7	35.3	0.7	4.2
	1999	533 507	25.8	24.2[15]	...	...	11.4	33.3	0.9	4.4
	2000	560 767	25.2	24.0[15]	...	...	11.4	34.6	0.8	4.0
TFYR of Macedonia [2] L'ex-R.y. Macédoine [2]	1991	199	37.6	...	...	...	21.8	27.1	6.7	6.9
	1992	2 302	38.3	...	...	...	28.9	23.4	4.7	4.7
	1993	12 472	42.6	...	...	...	24.3	23.5	5.5	4.2
Trinidad and Tobago [2] Trinité-et-Tobago [2]	1999	6 301	27.0	...	17.4	...	10.3	18.0	0.5	26.9
	2000	6 201	21.5	...	18.8	...	11.8	19.0	0.5	28.4
	2001	7 374	23.4	...	18.3	...	11.0	20.0	0.7	26.6
Ukraine [2] Ukraine [2]	1998	22 120	32.8[13]	...	...	...	25.2	23.0	...	19.0[4]
	1999	25 866	39.2[13]	-10.9[16]	...	...	20.5	25.2	...	25.9[4]
	2000	31 667	32.2[13]	-4.7[16]	...	...	24.4	27.3	...	20.9[4]
United Kingdom [2] Royaume-Uni [2]	1999	166 614	5.7	14.3	10.0	2.2	30.1	17.8	10.3	9.6
	2000	177 801	5.4	15.0	9.4	2.0	30.3	17.9	10.2	9.8
	2001	190 663	5.7	13.5	9.3	2.1	31.2	18.6	9.9	9.8
United Rep. of Tanzania [17] Rép.-Unie de Tanzanie [17]	1992	225 639[18]	17.5	8.5	8.5	...	5.9	7.7	0.7	51.2
	1993	336 855[18]	21.5	6.8	6.8	...	5.7	7.5	0.2	51.6
	1994	408 440[18]	21.1	4.9	7.5	...	7.2	7.6	0.2	51.6
Vanuatu Vanuatu	1991	4 693	20.5	8.4	...	...	10.3	19.8	...	41.0[19]
	1992	5 112	22.6	8.7	...	...	10.1	21.2	...	37.4[19]
	1993	5 194	27.1	9.2	...	...	9.7	20.0	...	34.0[19]
Zimbabwe Zimbabwe	1990	7 425	28.1	13.1	4.9	...	6.5	19.9	3.1	24.3
	1991	7 788	16.7	14.3	6.1	...	7.4	26.7	4.1	27.5

Source:
United Nations Statistics Division, New York, national accounts
database.

Source:
Organisation des Nations Unies, Division de statistique, New York, la
base de données sur les comptes nationaux.

+ Note: The national accounts data generally relate to the fiscal year
used in each country, unless indicated otherwise. Countries whose
reference periods coincide with the calendar year ending 31
December are not listed below.
Year beginning 21 March: Afghanistan, Iran (Islamic Republic).
Year beginning 1 April: Bermuda, India, Myanmar, New Zealand,
Nigeria (beginning 1982).
Year beginning 1 July: Australia, Bangladesh, Cameroon, Egypt,
Gambia, Pakistan, Puerto Rico, Saudi Arabia, Sierra Leone, Sudan.
Year ending 30 June: Botswana, Swaziland, Tonga.

+ Note : Sauf indication contraire, les données sur les comptes
nationaux concernent généralement l'exercice budgétaire utilisé dans
chaque pays. Les pays ou territoires dont la période de référence
coïncide avec l'année civile se terminant le 31 décembre ne sont pas
répertoriés ci-dessous.
Exercice commençant le 21 mars: Afghanistan, Iran (République
islamique d').
Exercice commençant le 1er avril: Bermudes, Inde, Myanmar, Nigéria
(à partir de 1982), Nouvelle-Zélande.
Exercice commençant le 1er juillet: Arabie saoudite, Australie,

23

Government final consumption expenditure by function in current prices
Percentage distribution [*cont.*]
Dépenses de consommation finale des administrations publiques, par fonction, aux prix courants
Répartition en pourcentage [*suite*]

Year ending 7 July: Ethiopia.
Year ending 15 July: Nepal.
Year ending 30 September: Haiti.

Bangladesh, Cameroun, Égypte, Gambie, Pakistan, Porto Rico, Sierra Leone, Soudan.
Exercice se terminant le 30 juin: Botswana, Swaziland, Tonga.
Exercice se terminant le 7 juillet: Éthiopie.
Exercice se terminant le 15 juillet: Népal.
Exercice se terminant le 30 septembre: Haïti.

1	Including expenditure on culture.
2	Data are classified according to the 1993 SNA.
3	Including social security.
4	Including science and related services.
5	Including defence and public order and safety.
6	Total government current expenditure only.
7	Including transport and communication.
8	Data in Georgian coupons.
9	Including "Public order and safety".
10	General government expenditure data refer to fiscal year 1 April.
11	Including housing and community amenities and recreation, culture and religion.
12	Data refer to defense affairs and services.
13	Including "Defence".
14	Re-denomination of Russian rubles at 1 to 1000.
15	Including justice and police.
16	Data refer to transactions in military equipment.
17	General government expenditure data refer to fiscal year beginning 1 July.
18	Central government estimates only.
19	Including "Social protection".

1	Y compris dépenses de culture.
2	Les données sont classifiées selon le SCN 1993.
3	Y compris sécurité sociale.
4	Y compris services scientifiques et services connexes.
5	Y compris défence et sureté publique.
6	Dépenses publiques courants seulement.
7	Y compris transports et communications.
8	Les données sont exprimées en coupons géorgiens.
9	Y compris "Ordre et securité publics".
10	Les données relatives aux dépenses générales de l'État portent sur l'année budgétaire commençant le 1e avril.
11	Y compris logement et équipements collectifs et loisirs, culture et religieuses
12	Les données se réfèrent aux affaires et services de la défense.
13	Y compris "Défense".
14	Instauration du nouveau rouble par division par 1000 du rouble ancien.
15	Y compris justice et police.
16	Ces données portent sur des transactions concernant du matériel militaire.
17	Les données relatives aux dépenses générales de l'État portent sur l'année budgétaire commençant le 1e juillet.
18	Administration centrale seulement.
19	Y compris "protection sociale".

24

Household consumption expenditure by purpose in current prices
Percentage distribution [*cont.*]
Dépenses de consommation des ménages par fonction aux prix courants
Répartition en pourcentage [*suite*]

Region, country or area Région, pays ou zone	Year Année	Household final consump- tion expenditure (M.nat.curr.) Dépenses de consomma- tion finale des ménages (M.monn. nationale)	Food, beve- rages, tobacco, narcotics Alimen- tation, boissons, tabac et stupé- fiants (%)	Clothing and footwear Articles d'habille- ment et chaus- sures (%)	Housing, water, electricity, gas and other fuels Logement, eau, gaz, électricité et autres combus- tibles (%)	Furnishings, household equipment, routine home maintenance Meubles, articles de ménage et entretien courant de l'habitation (%)	Health Santé (%)	Trans- port and commu- nication Trans- port et commu- nication (%)	Recreation, culture, education, restaurants, hotels Loisirs, culture, enseigne- ment, restaurants et hôtels (%)	Others Autres (%)
Denmark [1] Danemark [1]	1999	599 497[2]	16.9	5.0	26.8	5.8	2.5	15.1	16.5	11.5
	2000	608 672[2]	17.0	4.8	27.6	5.8	2.5	13.9	16.5	11.8
	2001	626 519[2]	17.1	4.7	27.9	5.8	2.6	13.3	16.7	11.8
Dominican Republic [1] Rép. dominicaine [1]	1994	137 616	33.3	4.1	20.6	6.4	5.2	14.2	10.2	5.9
	1995	164 689	34.1	4.0	20.3	6.2	5.2	13.5	11.1	5.6
	1996	189 675	32.0	3.4	20.1	6.5	5.0	14.1	14.1	4.8
Ecuador Equateur	1991	8 432 000	38.9	9.9	5.3[8]	7.4	4.2	...	4.2[9]	17.5
	1992	13 147 000	38.7	9.5	5.1[8]	7.2	4.5	...	4.4[9]	18.3
	1993	19 374 000	37.8	9.2	5.2[8]	6.6	4.6	...	4.4[9]	18.6
Fiji Fidji	1990	1 292[2]	31.2	8.1	12.9	7.7	2.0	...	...	1.2[5]
	1991	1 421[2]	30.9	7.8	13.1	7.8	2.0	...	...	1.1[5]
Finland [1] Finlande [1]	1999	60 214[2]	18.2	4.7	24.5	4.6	3.3	16.1	18.1	10.5
	2000	64 486[2]	17.6	4.4	24.1	4.6	3.5	16.6	18.0	11.2
	2001	67 792[2]	17.8	4.3	24.2	4.8	3.7	15.7	18.1	11.5
France [1] France [1]	2000	773 238[2]	17.7	5.0	23.7	6.4	3.6	17.6	17.2	8.8
	2001	807 494[2]	18.0	4.8	23.6	6.3	3.6	17.6	17.2	9.0
	2002	833 261[2]	18.1	4.7	23.6	6.1	3.7	17.4	17.5	9.1
Germany [1] Allemagne [1]	1999	1 156 500[2]	15.0	6.2	22.7	6.9	3.7	16.2	14.5	14.9
	2000	1 190 910[2]	14.9	6.1	22.9	6.9	3.8	15.7	14.6	15.2
	2001	1 232 150[2]	15.2	6.1	23.1	6.7	3.8	15.5	14.4	15.0
Greece [1] Grèce [1]	1999	79 772[2]	22.5	11.5	18.3	6.8	5.8	11.3	23.9	-0.1
	2000	84 493[2]	22.8	11.6	18.1	6.9	5.3	11.6	24.1	-0.3
	2001	89 601[2]	22.8	11.5	18.1	6.8	5.5	11.6	24.5	-0.6
Hungary [1] Hongrie [1]	1999	5 976 045[2]	30.0	5.1	20.8	7.2	3.5	19.7	14.3	-0.4
	2000	6 879 138[2]	29.4	4.9	20.3	7.2	3.6	20.9	14.6	-0.8
	2001	7 866 460[2]	29.5	4.9	19.6	7.1	3.9	21.0	14.7	-0.7
Iceland [1] Islande [1]	2000	389 574[2]	21.2	6.1	16.7	6.6	2.5	14.2	19.0	13.8
	2001	408 413[2]	22.1	5.9	17.1	6.6	2.8	12.3	20.5	12.5
	2002	419 474[2]	22.9	5.5	17.7	6.3	2.9	12.3	20.7	11.8
India Inde	1998	11 394 110	52.6	4.6	9.9	2.9	5.7	12.6	4.6	7.1
	1999	12 653 490	50.2	4.9	10.1	2.8	6.6	12.6	4.9	8.0
	2000	13 409 620	46.7	4.9	11.3	3.0	7.3	13.3	5.0	8.3
Iran (Islamic Rep. of) [1] Iran (Rép. islamique d') [1]	1999	220 883 000[2]	35.2	7.0	29.8	6.7	5.3	8.6	3.1	4.3
	2000	262 021 500[2]	33.2	8.8	28.9	6.5	5.7	9.2	3.2	4.6
	2001	304 570 400[2]	33.0	8.8	29.1	6.5	5.7	9.3	3.2	4.6
Ireland [1] Irlande [1]	1999	43 207[2]	17.0	6.7	18.1	7.3	2.6	12.9	22.7	12.8
	2000	48 987[2]	16.6	6.8	18.8	7.1	2.6	14.0	22.4	11.8
	2001	53 611[2]	16.0	6.5	19.9	7.1	2.6	12.5	22.3	13.0
Israel [1] Israël [1]	1999	240 957[2]	22.1	3.7	26.5	11.0	4.8	12.6	13.7	5.7
	2000	261 268[2]	21.0	3.9	25.9	11.1	4.7	13.0	14.0	6.5
	2001	271 737[2]	21.1	3.8	26.1	10.3	4.5	12.6	13.2	8.5
Italy [1] Italie [1]	2000	706 182[2]	17.0	9.5	19.6	9.4	3.2	15.8	18.1	7.3
	2001	732 679[2]	17.0	9.6	19.7	9.3	3.0	15.4	18.4	7.7
	2002	757 796[2]	17.0	9.4	19.9	9.0	3.0	15.0	18.3	8.3
Japan [1] Japon [1]	1999	286 582 900[2]	18.1	5.9	24.2	4.6	3.3	11.9	19.1	12.8
	2000	285 807 800[2]	17.3	5.6	24.7	4.4	3.5	12.5	19.1	12.9
	2001	286 240 100[2]	17.4	5.2	25.1	4.3	3.6	12.8	18.7	12.8
Korea, Republic of [1] Corée, République de [1]	2000	299 121 846[2]	17.2	4.0	17.1	4.5	7.0	16.5	19.3	14.3
	2001	326 209 873[2]	16.5	3.8	17.2	4.3	7.5	16.4	19.7	14.5
	2002	358 834 527[2]	15.7	4.0	16.7	4.2	7.4	16.1	19.8	16.1

24

Household consumption expenditure by purpose in current prices
Percentage distribution [cont.]
Dépenses de consommation des ménages par fonction aux prix courants
Répartition en pourcentage [suite]

Region, country or area Région, pays ou zone	Year Année	Household final consumption expenditure (M.nat.curr.) Dépenses de consommation finale des ménages (M.monn. nationale)	Food, beverages, tobacco, narcotics Alimentation, boissons, tabac et stupéfiants (%)	Clothing and footwear Articles d'habillement et chaussures (%)	Housing, water, electricity, gas and other fuels Logement, eau, gaz, électricité et autres combustibles (%)	Furnishings, household equipment, routine home maintenance Meubles, articles de ménage et entretien courant de l'habitation (%)	Health Santé (%)	Transport and communication Transport et communication (%)	Recreation, culture, education, restaurants, hotels Loisirs, culture, enseignement, restaurants et hôtels (%)	Others Autres (%)
Malta	1994	608	37.5	8.7	7.2	11.2	4.3	...	30.6	...
Malte	1995	700	36.0	8.3	6.6	10.9	3.9	...	27.7	...
	1996	765	34.5	8.6	6.3	10.7	3.9	...	26.7	...
Mexico[1]	1998	2 593 350[2]	27.3	4.0	14.2	8.8	4.1	18.5	14.0	9.9
Mexique[1]	1999	3 084 138[2]	27.3	3.8	13.5	8.6	4.2	18.7	14.0	10.9
	2000	3 696 140[2]	26.5	3.7	13.3	8.5	4.2	19.7	14.3	10.8
Namibia[1]	1999	12 241[2]	43.3	5.0	15.1	...	...	...	...	-5.6
Namibie[1]	2000	14 192[2]	37.8	4.3	14.6	...	...	...	...	-2.6
	2001	16 500[2]	38.3	4.0	13.8	...	...	...	...	-2.9
Netherlands[1]	1999	187 593[2]	14.3	6.2	20.2	7.1	3.9	15.2	17.3	15.8
Pays-Bas[1]	2000	201 088[2]	13.8	6.0	20.1	7.2	3.7	15.6	17.1	16.5
	2001	212 905[2]	13.9	6.0	20.3	7.2	3.8	15.1	16.9	16.9
New Zealand[1]	1999	65 667[2]	16.6	4.6	20.9	10.6	3.0	14.1	19.0	10.2
Nouvelle-Zélande[1]	2000	68 439[2]	16.1	4.7	20.4	10.4	3.1	14.1	20.1	10.2
	2001	71 744[2]	16.6	4.8	19.6	10.4	3.3	14.6	20.3	9.2
Norway[1]	1995	462 262[2]	19.8	5.8	21.5	6.1	2.4	14.9	16.2	12.1
Norvège[1]	1996	498 965[2]	19.1	5.7	21.0	5.8	2.5	15.5	16.1	12.0
	1997	527 135[2]	19.2	5.7	20.6	5.9	2.5	15.8	16.4	12.1
Philippines	1999	2 161 645	53.4	2.9	4.3	14.4	...	4.5[10]	...	20.6
Philippines	2000	2 335 535	51.7	2.8	4.6	14.2	...	5.3[10]	...	21.4
	2001	2 565 022	50.4	2.7	4.8	14.0	...	6.1[10]	...	22.0
Poland[1]	1999	396 361[2]	29.0	5.0	23.1	4.9	4.1	14.0	10.7	9.2
Pologne[1]	#2000	454 206[2]	28.0	4.6	24.4	4.6	4.2	14.4	10.9	9.0
	2001	486 375[2]	27.6	4.3	25.2	4.4	4.4	14.4	10.8	8.9
Portugal[1]	1999	67 394[2]	23.0	7.7	10.7	7.4	4.5	21.0	18.0	7.7
Portugal[1]	2000	71 115[2]	22.7	7.9	11.0	7.2	4.6	20.9	18.2	7.5
	2001	74 961[2]	23.4	8.0	11.1	7.2	4.7	19.9	18.4	12.7
Puerto Rico	1998	34 008[2]	18.7	7.5	14.6	7.1	13.6	15.7	10.9	...
Porto Rico	1999	35 976[2]	17.7	7.7	15.5	6.3	14.0	15.7	11.2	...
	2000	37 639[2]	18.8	6.9	16.5	6.3	13.8	15.0	11.2	...
Republic of Moldova[1]	1993	735[2]	48.9	6.4	5.9	5.6	8.5	4.2	17.5	2.8
République de Moldova[1]	1996	5 331[2]	42.2	6.5	4.9	2.9	9.7	9.1	15.9	8.7
Saudi Arabia	1996	206 336	34.6	7.8	14.7	9.2	0.9	17.9[10]	2.1	7.2
Arabie saoudite	1997	206 185	34.7	7.7	14.7	9.1	0.9	17.8[10]	2.1	7.0
	1998	198 574	37.3	8.2	15.7	9.7	1.0	18.9[10]	2.2	7.2
Singapore	1995	50 020	15.6	5.9	13.7	8.3	4.9	21.1	23.9	6.5
Singapour	1996	53 920	15.4	5.5	13.7	8.4	5.0	19.4	23.0	9.6
	1997	58 067	14.7	5.2	13.6	8.3	4.9	18.1	21.9	13.2
Slovakia[1]	1999	470 582[2]	32.2	6.8	21.8	4.7	1.1	11.7	13.6	8.1
Slovaquie[1]	2000	510 676[2]	31.0	6.3	23.2	4.4	1.2	11.8	14.1	7.9
	2001	560 237[2]	29.6	6.2	22.9	4.3	1.2	13.8	13.9	8.1
South Africa[1]	1999	504 289	30.7	5.2	12.2	8.9	7.3	14.1[11]	9.5	12.1
Afrique du Sud[1]	2000	556 652	30.1	5.0	12.1	8.8	7.5	15.1[11]	9.4	12.0
	2001	608 646	29.7	4.9	12.0	8.8	7.9	15.7[11]	9.4	11.6
Spain[1]	1999	335 246[2]	19.6	7.0	15.2	6.5	3.5	16.5	30.9	0.8
Espagne[1]	2000	359 491[2]	19.7	6.9	15.1	6.5	3.5	16.4	31.3	0.6
	2001	380 690[2]	20.0	6.8	15.2	6.3	3.6	16.3	31.1	0.6
Sri Lanka	1997	596 917	55.1	7.9	3.9	5.5	1.6	14.9	3.9	7.3
Sri Lanka	1998	668 901	54.6	8.0	3.6	5.0	1.8	15.0	4.3	7.7
	1999	749 533	54.3	8.1	3.4	5.1	1.8	15.3	4.1	8.0

24

Household consumption expenditure by purpose in current prices
Percentage distribution [*cont.*]
Dépenses de consommation des ménages par fonction aux prix courants
Répartition en pourcentage [*suite*]

Region, country or area Région, pays ou zone	Year Année	Household final consumption expenditure (M.nat.curr.) Dépenses de consommation finale des ménages (M.monn. nationale)	Food, beverages, tobacco, narcotics Alimentation, boissons, tabac et stupéfiants (%)	Clothing and footwear Articles d'habillement et chaussures (%)	Housing, water, electricity, gas and other fuels Logement, eau, gaz, électricité et autres combustibles (%)	Furnishings, household equipment, routine home maintenance Meubles, articles de ménage et entretien courant de l'habitation (%)	Health Santé (%)	Transport and communication Transport et communication (%)	Recreation, culture, education, restaurants, hotels Loisirs, culture, enseignement, restaurants et hôtels (%)	Others Autres (%)
Sweden [1] Suède [1]	1999	1 015 743[2]	16.0	5.2	29.2	4.6	2.3	15.4	15.6	10.4
	2000	1 078 034[2]	15.6	5.2	27.7	4.7	2.3	14.9	15.6	12.0
	2001	1 102 627[2]	16.0	5.3	27.9	4.8	2.3	14.3	15.9	11.0
Switzerland Suisse	1994	214 091[2]	23.7	5.0	23.0	5.0	12.0	...	...	2.9
	1995	219 087[2]	23.5	4.6	23.3	4.7	12.2	...	...	3.2
	1996	223 061[2]	...	4.4	23.7	4.6	12.5	...	...	3.7
Thailand Thaïlande	1998	2 505 312	34.9	12.1	9.8	7.4	6.7	13.3	17.7	-1.9
	1999	2 491 129	34.7	12.7	9.7	7.6	7.2	14.6	14.3	-1.0
	2000	2 751 901	31.5	11.9	9.2	7.5	7.1	15.5	18.1	-0.8
Ukraine [1] Ukraine [1]	1997	53 869[2]	...	...	6.9	...	1.0	4.6	1.0	6.0
	1998	61 449[2]	...	...	7.6	...	0.9	5.0	1.4	5.1
	1999	74 615[2]	...	...	6.9	...	0.7	5.7	1.5	4.4
United Kingdom [1] Royaume-Uni [1]	1999	591 631[2]	13.7	5.6	17.2	5.5	1.4	16.2	24.1	16.2
	2000	626 584[2]	13.2	5.6	17.1	5.6	1.4	16.2	24.3	16.6
	2001	658 125[2]	13.0	5.7	17.1	5.7	1.4	16.1	23.9	16.7
United States [1] Etats-Unis [1]	2000	6 683 700	9.4	5.2	17.0	5.1	16.5	13.3	17.8	15.7
	2001	6 987 000	9.3	5.1	17.2	5.0	17.1	13.2	17.8	15.4
	2002	7 303 700	9.1	5.0	17.1	4.9	17.6	12.8	17.9	15.5
Venezuela Venezuela	1999	43 236 872[2]	34.1	2.4	11.6	2.4	3.8	9.0	18.4	18.3
	2000	52 295 053[2]	32.0	2.4	11.7	2.6	3.9	9.8	18.2	19.4
	2001	61 107 870[2]	31.6	2.0	11.7	2.5	3.9	11.2	17.1	19.8

Source:
United Nations Statistics Division, New York, national accounts database.

+ Note: The national accounts data generally relate to the fiscal year used in each country, unless indicated otherwise. Countries whose reference periods coincide with the calendar year ending 31 December are not listed below.
Year beginning 21 March: Afghanistan, Iran (Islamic Republic).
Year beginning 1 April: Bermuda, India, Myanmar, New Zealand, Nigeria (beginning 1982).
Year beginning 1 July: Australia, Bangladesh, Cameroon, Egypt, Gambia, Pakistan, Puerto Rico, Saudi Arabia, Sierra Leone, Sudan.
Year ending 30 June: Botswana, Swaziland, Tonga.
Year ending 7 July: Ethiopia.
Year ending 15 July: Nepal.
Year ending 30 September: Haiti.

Source:
Organisation des Nations Unies, Division de statistique, New York, la base de données sur les comptes nationaux.

+ Note : Sauf indication contraire, les données sur les comptes nationaux concernent généralement l'exercice budgétaire utilisé dans chaque pays. Les pays ou territoires dont la période de référence coïncide avec l'année civile se terminant le 31 décembre ne sont pas répertoriés ci-dessous.
Exercice commençant le 21 mars: Afghanistan, Iran (République islamique d').
Exercice commençant le 1er avril: Bermudes, Inde, Myanmar, Nigéria (à partir de 1982), Nouvelle-Zélande.
Exercice commençant le 1er juillet: Arabie saoudite, Australie, Bangladesh, Cameroun, Égypte, Gambie, Pakistan, Porto Rico, Sierra Leone, Soudan.
Exercice se terminant le 30 juin: Botswana, Swaziland, Tonga.
Exercice se terminant le 7 juillet: Éthiopie.
Exercice se terminant le 15 juillet: Népal.
Exercice se terminant le 30 septembre: Haïti.

1	Data are classified according to the 1993 SNA.
2	Including "Non-profit institutions serving households" (NPISHs).
3	Data in Russian roubles.
4	Re-denomination of Belarussian rubles at 1 to 1000.

1	Les données sont classifiées selon le SCN 1993.
2	Y compris les institutions sans but lucratif au service des ménages.
3	Les données sont exprimées en roubles russiens.
4	Instauration du nouveau rouble bélarussien par division par 1000 du rouble bélarussien ancien.

24

Household consumption expenditure by purpose in current prices
Percentage distribution [*cont.*]

Dépenses de consommation des ménages par fonction aux prix courants
Répartition en pourcentage [*suite*]

5	Data refer to non-profit institutions serving households (NPISHs) only.	
6	Household final consumption expenditure in domestic market.	
7	Including restaurant expenditure.	
8	Including transport and communication.	
9	Restaurants and hotels only.	
10	Transport only.	
11	Excluding communication, which is included in "Others".	

5   Les données sont la consommation finale des institutions sans but lucratif au service des ménages seulement.

6   Dépenses de consommation finale des ménages sur le marché intérieur.

7   Y compris les dépenses de restauration.

8   Y compris transports et communications.

9   Les restaurants et hôtels seulement.

10 Les transports seulement.

11 Non compris les communications, déjà inclues dans la rubrique "autres".

25

# Index numbers of industrial production
# Indices de la production industrielle
1995 = 100

Country or area and industry [ISIC Rev. 3] Pays ou zone et industrie [CITI Rév. 3]	1995	1996	1997	1998	1999	2000	2001	2002
Africa · Afrique								
Algeria Algérie								
Total industry [CDE]								
Total, industrie [CDE]	**100.0**	**92.6**	**89.6**	**95.7**	**96.0**	**97.3**	**97.0**	**98.3**
Total manufacturing [D]								
Total, industries manufacturières [D]	**100.0**	**88.7**	**82.3**	**89.7**	**88.3**	**86.8**	**86.0**	**85.1**
Total mining [C]								
Total, industries extractives [C]	**100.0**	**95.7**	**84.1**	**87.3**	**93.0**	**98.2**	**95.3**	**101.1**
Food, beverages and tobacco								
Aliments, boissons et tabac	100.0	95.5	93.4	107.1	105.5	96.1	84.0	68.0
Textiles, wearing apparel, leather, footwear								
Textiles, habillement, cuir et chaussures	100.0	70.8	63.7	69.5	51.0	45.7	41.3	43.4
Chemicals, petroleum, rubber and plastic products								
Prod. chimiques, pétroliers, caoutch. et plast.	100.0	94.1	100.9	99.7	103.8	104.8	108.8	106.0
Basic metals								
Métaux de base	100.0	66.5	53.9	62.9	75.1	72.2	77.9	86.1
Metal products								
Produits métalliques	100.0	76.5	60.7	64.7	72.0	74.5	85.5	84.1
Electricity [E]								
Electricité [E]	**100.0**	**104.5**	**108.5**	**118.0**	**126.4**	**129.4**	**135.9**	**141.8**
Burkina Faso Burkina Faso								
Total industry [CDE]								
Total, industrie [CDE]	**100.0**	**95.9**	**117.8**	**136.7**	**116.8**	**127.0**	**128.4**	**135.0**
Cameroon [1] Cameroun [1]								
Total industry [DE]								
Total, industrie [DE]	**100.0**	**118.9**	**117.1**	**121.1**	**128.5**	**130.1**	**128.3**	**...**
Total manufacturing [D]								
Total, industries manufacturières [D]	**100.0**	**120.3**	**117.5**	**121.1**	**120.4**	**113.3**	**124.6**	
Electricity, gas and water [E]								
Electricité, gaz et eau [E]	**100.0**	**108.4**	**113.7**	**121.0**	**127.1**	**128.3**	**118.2**	
Central African Rep. Rép. centrafricaine								
Total industry [CDE]								
Total, industrie [CDE]	**100.0**	**100.9**	**...**	**...**	**...**	**...**	**...**	**...**
Total manufacturing [D]								
Total, industries manufacturières [D]	**100.0**	**81.7**	**...**	**...**	**...**	**...**	**...**	**...**
Total mining [C]								
Total, industries extractives [C]	**100.0**	**93.8**	**...**	**...**	**...**	**...**	**...**	**...**
Electricity, gas and water [E]								
Electricité, gaz et eau [E]	**100.0**	**96.5**	**...**	**...**	**...**	**...**	**...**	**...**
Côte d'Ivoire Côte d'Ivoire								
Total industry [CDE]								
Total, industrie [CDE]	**100.0**	**112.1**	**125.0**	**138.8**	**143.2**	**132.0**	**126.5**	**...**
Total manufacturing [D]								
Total, industries manufacturières [D]	**100.0**	**106.6**	**119.2**	**139.5**	**139.6**	**126.9**	**121.5**	**...**
Total mining [C]								
Total, industries extractives [C]	**100.0**	**238.5**	**220.0**	**165.5**	**169.5**	**146.5**	**99.1**	**...**
Food, beverages and tobacco								
Aliments, boissons et tabac	100.0	108.3	116.8	127.1	139.5	133.0	130.2	...
Textiles and wearing apparel								
Textiles et habillement	100.0	100.8	117.6	164.0	157.6	106.4	92.8	...
Chemicals, petroleum, rubber and plastic products								
Prod. chimiques, pétroliers, caoutch. et plast.	100.0	107.6	124.6	137.8	129.0	121.9	120.9	...
Metal products								
Produits métalliques	100.0	107.9	108.2	112.8	106.5	89.5	76.2	...
Electricity and water [E]								
Electricité et eau [E]	**100.0**	**110.3**	**132.8**	**134.7**	**157.0**	**156.5**	**159.7**	**...**
Egypt [2] Egypte [2]								
Total industry [CDE]								
Total, industrie [CDE]	**100.0**	**111.0**	**124.5**	**127.2**	**134.6**	**132.8**	**138.2**	**...**

25

Index numbers of industrial production *[cont.]*

Indices de la production industrielle

1995 = 100 *[suite]*

Country or area and industry [ISIC Rev. 3] Pays ou zone et industrie [CITI Rév. 3]	1995	1996	1997	1998	1999	2000	2001	2002
Total manufacturing [D]								
Total, industries manufacturières [D]	**100.0**	**120.4**	**134.0**	**144.7**	**133.8**	**127.3**	**125.2**	**...**
Total mining [C]								
Total, industries extractives [C]	**100.0**	**98.2**	**113.8**	**99.3**	**143.8**	**148.7**	**168.1**	**...**
Food, beverages and tobacco								
Aliments, boissons et tabac	100.0	112.8	118.0	147.1	153.1	170.5	127.1	...
Textiles and wearing apparel								
Textiles et habillement	100.0	87.7	117.5	113.8	111.8	100.1	92.8	...
Chemicals, petroleum, rubber and plastic products								
Prod. chimiques, pétroliers, caoutch. et plast.	100.0	135.5	129.5	97.8	121.2	106.6	125.6	...
Basic metals								
Métaux de base	100.0	120.7	110.0	139.0	156.3	164.2	146.5	...
Metal products								
Produits métalliques	100.0	136.0	182.7	236.8	173.3	163.0	143.7	...
Electricity, gas and water [E]								
Electricité, gaz et eau [E]	**100.0**	**105.6**	**110.6**	**117.3**	**127.1**	**137.4**	**151.6**	**...**
Ethiopia [2] Ethiopie [2]								
Total industry [CDE]								
Total, industrie [CDE]	**100.0**	**104.8**	**111.3**	**119.3**	**129.4**	**...**	**...**	**...**
Total manufacturing [D]								
Total, industries manufacturières [D]	**100.0**	**107.6**	**113.9**	**122.5**	**129.6**	**...**	**...**	**...**
Total mining [C]								
Total, industries extractives [C]	**100.0**	**113.1**	**127.8**	**143.7**	**161.0**	**...**	**...**	**...**
Electricity and water [E]								
Electricité et eau [E]	**100.0**	**92.7**	**98.1**	**101.7**	**121.5**	**...**	**...**	**...**
Gabon Gabon								
Total industry [DE]								
Total, industrie [DE]	**100.0**	**108.8**	**110.0**	**118.4**	**121.8**	**114.1**	**127.5**	**132.9**
Total manufacturing [D]								
Total, industries manufacturières [D]	**100.0**	**111.6**	**112.4**	**115.8**	**121.7**	**110.5**	**125.3**	**128.8**
Food, beverages and tobacco								
Aliments, boissons et tabac	100.0	103.5	105.0	111.0	105.1	114.1	128.3	119.7
Chemicals and petroleum products								
Produits chimiques et pétroliers	100.0	117.1	126.3	131.8	141.0	110.7	119.6	150.5
Electricity and water [E]								
Electricité et eau [E]	**100.0**	**105.3**	**107.0**	**121.8**	**121.8**	**118.5**	**130.3**	**138.2**
Ghana Ghana								
Total industry [CDE] [3]								
Total, industrie [CDE] [3]	**100.0**	**104.4**	**96.6**	**103.3**	**109.3**	**110.9**	**...**	**...**
Total manufacturing [D]								
Total, industries manufacturières [D]	**100.0**	**104.6**	**91.9**	**94.3**	**98.4**	**101.7**	**...**	**...**
Total mining [C]								
Total, industries extractives [C]	**100.0**	**100.3**	**109.3**	**140.8**	**158.8**	**153.8**	**...**	**...**
Food, beverages and tobacco								
Aliments, boissons et tabac	100.0	103.5	106.9	107.6	101.4	102.0	...	...
Textiles, wearing apparel, leather, footwear								
Textiles, habillement, cuir et chaussures	100.0	102.4	101.3	102.0	102.2	102.6	...	...
Chemicals, petroleum, rubber and plastic products								
Prod. chimiques, pétroliers, caoutch. et plast.	100.0	104.3	110.7	90.3	97.5	106.0	...	...
Basic metals								
Métaux de base	100.0	104.7	124.5	114.1	133.1	133.2	...	...
Metal products								
Produits métalliques	100.0	116.6	125.3	121.8	119.7	119.8	...	...
Electricity [E]								
Electricité [E]	**100.0**	**108.0**	**112.2**	**115.9**	**119.6**	**117.8**	**...**	**...**
Kenya Kenya								
Total industry [CD] [3]								
Total, industrie [CD] [3]	**100.0**	**104.5**	**111.2**	**120.9**	**108.5**	**106.7**	**108.2**	**...**
Total manufacturing [D]								
Total, industries manufacturières [D]	**100.0**	**104.5**	**111.2**	**121.2**	**108.2**	**106.6**	**107.5**	**...**

25

Index numbers of industrial production *[cont.]*

Indices de la production industrielle
1995 = 100 *[suite]*

Country or area and industry [ISIC Rev. 3] Pays ou zone et industrie [CITI Rév. 3]	1995	1996	1997	1998	1999	2000	2001	2002
Total mining [C]								
Total, industries extractives [C]	**100.0**	**103.4**	**111.6**	**110.6**	**122.3**	**110.6**	**138.2**	...
Food, beverages and tobacco								
Aliments, boissons et tabac	100.0	97.7	97.7	99.6	97.2	95.5	95.3	...
Textiles, wearing apparel, leather, footwear								
Textiles, habillement, cuir et chaussures	100.0	96.1	90.0	89.4	87.7	89.9	91.8	...
Chemicals, petroleum, rubber and plastic products								
Prod. chimiques, pétroliers, caoutch. et plast.	100.0	104.3	115.3	121.5	125.8	133.2	144.2	...
Metal products								
Produits métalliques	100.0	118.9	114.0	100.1	95.1	84.5	83.8	...
Madagascar Madagascar								
Total industry [CDE]								
Total, industrie [CDE]	**100.0**	**99.9**	**120.8**	**124.3**	**129.3**	**147.6**	**159.3**	...
Total manufacturing [D]								
Total, industries manufacturières [D]	**100.0**	**99.0**	**122.1**	**124.5**	**131.0**	**148.3**	**160.9**	...
Total mining [C]								
Total, industries extractives [C]	**100.0**	**119.7**	**106.8**	**124.8**	**75.2**	**109.2**	**108.6**	...
Food, beverages and tobacco								
Aliments, boissons et tabac	100.0	103.0	97.6	107.6	131.8	139.1	150.6	...
Textiles, wearing apparel, leather, footwear								
Textiles, habillement, cuir et chaussures	100.0	92.8	91.5	106.1	119.7	152.1	172.2	...
Chemicals and petroleum products								
Produits chimiques et pétroliers	100.0	95.0	157.8	146.7	145.9	163.8	184.2	...
Basic metals								
Métaux de base	100.0	142.6	151.1	162.3	167.8	121.3	165.8	...
Metal products								
Produits métalliques	100.0	107.9	100.3	107.4	111.1	99.9	92.3	...
Electricity [E]								
Electricité [E]	**100.0**	**102.7**	**112.3**	**121.1**	**129.7**	**152.4**	**159.0**	...
Malawi Malawi								
Total industry [DE]								
Total, industrie [DE]	**100.0**	**103.5**	**102.7**	**99.4**	**90.4**	**91.2**	**81.8**	**81.9**
Total manufacturing [D]								
Total, industries manufacturières [D]	**100.0**	**103.5**	**100.2**	**94.4**	**81.2**	**80.2**	**68.1**	**68.2**
Food, beverages and tobacco								
Aliments, boissons et tabac	100.0	101.9	103.1	65.1	50.0	48.5	43.4	41.4
Textiles, wearing apparel, leather, footwear								
Textiles, habillement, cuir et chaussures	100.0	90.3	146.2	181.8	222.5	137.3	111.9	60.7
Electricity and water [E]								
Electricité et eau [E]	**100.0**	**103.5**	**112.8**	**120.3**	**118.7**	**128.1**	**131.6**	**137.7**
Mali Mali								
Total industry [DE]								
Total, industrie [DE]	**100.0**	**106.2**	**121.5**	**140.2**	**133.4**	...	...	...
Food, beverages and tobacco								
Aliments, boissons et tabac	100.0	104.3	110.1	104.3	98.7	...	...	...
Wearing apparel								
Habillement	100.0	108.3	138.4	141.4	121.8	...	...	...
Chemicals and chemical products								
Produits chimiques	100.0	112.6	106.5	101.2	91.3	...	...	...
Mauritius Maurice								
Total industry [CDE]								
Total, industrie [CDE]	**100.0**	**106.5**	**111.6**	**118.6**	**121.8**	**132.9**	**140.0**	...
Total manufacturing [D]								
Total, industries manufacturières [D]	**100.0**	**106.4**	**112.9**	**119.7**	**122.4**	**132.4**	**138.6**	...
Total mining [C]								
Total, industries extractives [C]	**100.0**	**106.0**	**110.2**	**113.5**	**116.9**	**120.4**	**124.1**	...
Food, beverages and tobacco								
Aliments, boissons et tabac	100.0	104.1	110.4	113.7	108.5	121.3	127.7	...
Textiles, wearing apparel, leather, footwear								
Textiles, habillement, cuir et chaussures	100.0	108.7	114.9	121.9	129.3	137.1	142.8	...

25

Index numbers of industrial production *[cont.]*

Indices de la production industrielle

1995 = 100 *[suite]*

Country or area and industry [ISIC Rev. 3] Pays ou zone et industrie [CITI Rév. 3]	1995	1996	1997	1998	1999	2000	2001	2002
Chemicals, petroleum, rubber and plastic products Prod. chimiques, pétroliers, caoutch. et plast.	100.0	99.7	105.0	114.0	120.9	130.3	130.8	...
Basic metals Métaux de base	100.0	104.4	107.4	118.2	124.1	130.3	137.4	...
Metal products Produits métalliques	100.0	101.0	108.4	119.1	124.8	130.2	129.8	...
Electricity, gas and water [E] **Electricité, gaz et eau [E]**	**100.0**	**107.5**	**116.4**	**128.5**	**139.5**	**171.9**	**192.8**	**...**
Morocco Maroc								
Total industry [CDE] [3] **Total, industrie [CDE]** [3]	**100.0**	**103.3**	**108.3**	**110.6**	**111.8**	**114.6**	**119.7**	**123.8**
Total manufacturing [D] [4] **Total, industries manufacturières [D]** [4]	**100.0**	**103.2**	**107.5**	**110.2**	**112.7**	**116.6**	**120.4**	**124.0**
Total mining [C] [5] **Total, industries extractives [C]** [5]	**100.0**	**102.5**	**111.6**	**109.8**	**107.5**	**103.8**	**106.3**	**109.0**
Food, beverages and tobacco Aliments, boissons et tabac	100.0	102.8	101.8	112.4	114.6	120.6	130.0	131.6
Textiles, wearing apparel, leather, footwear Textiles, habillement, cuir et chaussures	100.0	103.2	108.9	110.7	109.2	110.5	109.1	108.9
Chemicals, petroleum, rubber and plastic products Prod. chimiques, pétroliers, caoutch. et plast.	100.0	101.3	108.6	109.5	116.5	118.1	123.3	127.8
Basic metals Métaux de base	100.0	98.1	110.5	109.3	122.0	122.2	130.8	152.1
Metal products Produits métalliques	100.0	98.9	102.5	103.0	109.6	114.9	120.1	123.3
Electricity [E] **Electricité [E]**	**100.0**	**104.4**	**111.2**	**112.6**	**109.7**	**111.1**	**126.6**	**135.8**
Nigeria Nigéria								
Total industry [CDE] **Total, industrie [CDE]**	**100.0**	**102.8**	**109.2**	**104.0**	**...**	**...**	**...**	**...**
Total manufacturing [D] **Total, industries manufacturières [D]**	**100.0**	**101.2**	**101.6**	**97.7**	**...**	**...**	**...**	**...**
Total mining [C] **Total, industries extractives [C]**	**100.0**	**103.7**	**113.7**	**107.8**	**...**	**...**	**...**	**...**
Electricity [E] **Electricité [E]**	**100.0**	**97.6**	**95.7**	**92.2**	**...**	**...**	**...**	**...**
Senegal Sénégal								
Total industry [CDE] **Total, industrie [CDE]**	**100.0**	**96.1**	**98.0**	**102.9**	**104.4**	**99.7**	**100.5**	**124.9**
Total manufacturing [D] [3] **Total, industries manufacturières [D]** [3]	**100.0**	**94.4**	**94.5**	**100.1**	**99.6**	**91.7**	**90.0**	**123.1**
Total mining [C] **Total, industries extractives [C]**	**100.0**	**96.3**	**105.6**	**104.5**	**122.4**	**123.7**	**107.8**	**120.0**
Food, beverages and tobacco Aliments, boissons et tabac	100.0	89.3	84.9	95.2	96.5	93.7	77.4	94.6
Textiles Textiles	100.0	104.4	106.1	101.0	82.2	79.2	98.9	50.2
Chemicals, petroleum, rubber and plastic products Prod. chimiques, pétroliers, caoutch. et plast.	100.0	95.8	111.7	108.5	79.5	101.3	84.6	124.0
Metal products Produits métalliques	100.0	92.0	89.9	92.2	89.7	91.4	43.8	75.1
Electricity and water [E] **Electricité et eau [E]**	**100.0**	**102.7**	**108.7**	**113.0**	**116.1**	**121.3**	**137.2**	**133.4**
South Africa Afrique du Sud								
Total industry [CDE] [3] **Total, industrie [CDE]** [3]	**100.0**	**102.8**	**105.7**	**102.8**	**101.8**	**104.5**	**106.7**	**111.1**
Total manufacturing [D] **Total, industries manufacturières [D]**	**100.0**	**103.6**	**106.4**	**102.8**	**102.2**	**106.0**	**109.0**	**114.7**
Total mining [C] **Total, industries extractives [C]**	**100.0**	**98.3**	**100.3**	**99.2**	**97.2**	**95.8**	**97.1**	**98.3**

25

Index numbers of industrial production *[cont.]*

Indices de la production industrielle
1995 = 100 *[suite]*

Country or area and industry [ISIC Rev. 3] Pays ou zone et industrie [CITI Rév. 3]	1995	1996	1997	1998	1999	2000	2001	2002
Food and beverages Aliments et boissons	100.0	101.4	102.5	101.0	99.7	96.9	102.4	101.7
Textiles, wearing apparel, leather, footwear Textiles, habillement, cuir et chaussures	100.0	93.6	96.7	89.2	88.7	86.4	83.9	89.3
Chemicals, petroleum, rubber and plastic products Prod. chimiques, pétroliers, caoutch. et plast.	100.0	100.8	103.6	103.3	106.6	107.9	112.1	121.7
Basic metals Métaux de base	100.0	110.4	114.7	111.8	114.4	134.6	133.5	139.9
Metal products Produits métalliques	100.0	105.6	108.0	102.8	100.9	107.9	114.7	121.9
Electricity [E] Electricité [E]	100.0	107.2	112.6	110.0	108.8	112.8	112.5	116.6
Swaziland Swaziland								
Total industry [CDE] [3] Total, industrie [CDE] [3]	100.0	100.1	112.0	114.1	109.7	109.6	110.7	126.3
Total manufacturing [D] Total, industries manufacturières [D]	100.0	99.3	112.6	114.0	109.0	110.1	111.1	128.0
Total mining [C] Total, industries extractives [C]	100.0	96.5	78.4	99.6	85.6	65.9	52.8	59.0
Electricity, gas and water [E] Electricité, gaz et eau [E]	100.0	112.7	115.1	120.4	126.4	117.9	124.4	126.0
Tunisia Tunisie								
Total industry [CDE] Total, industrie [CDE]	100.0	102.7	107.2	114.6	120.7	128.3	136.0	135.8
Total manufacturing [D] Total, industries manufacturières [D]	100.0	101.9	108.2	115.9	122.5	133.2	144.1	143.0
Total mining [C] Total, industries extractives [C]	100.0	105.4	102.6	109.8	112.9	109.6	106.1	106.9
Food, beverages and tobacco Aliments, boissons et tabac	100.0	102.3	113.4	117.9	132.7	143.4	144.1	152.2
Textiles, wearing apparel, leather, footwear Textiles, habillement, cuir et chaussures	100.0	100.9	106.0	114.6	117.8	133.0	147.7	144.1
Chemicals, petroleum, rubber and plastic products Prod. chimiques, pétroliers, caoutch. et plast.	100.0	101.3	105.7	108.1	108.3	112.1	113.0	116.1
Basic metals Métaux de base	100.0	100.7	105.0	100.3	119.6	124.5	118.5	96.2
Metal products Produits métalliques	100.0	105.1	111.7	129.9	141.3	153.7	169.9	172.1
Electricity and water [E] Electricité et eau [E]	100.0	102.1	108.4	114.5	124.7	131.7	140.3	146.7
Uganda Ouganda								
Total manufacturing [D] Total, industries manufacturières [D]	100.0	119.1	137.9	153.5	165.1	164.4	168.1	196.8
Food, beverages and tobacco Aliments, boissons et tabac	100.0	122.4	125.9	138.8	148.5	82.2	147.1	159.6
Textiles, wearing apparel, leather, footwear Textiles, habillement, cuir et chaussures	100.0	85.3	168.3	148.2	155.9	121.1	87.6	110.5
Chemicals, rubber and plastic prod. Prod. chimiques, caoutchouc et plastiques	100.0	101.0	146.9	174.8	192.1	199.1	227.0	203.4
Basic metals Métaux de base	100.0	98.0	255.6	280.7	319.3	286.8	307.3	523.8
Metal products Produits métalliques	100.0	128.0	106.4	81.9	73.1	65.6	58.3	103.9
United Rep. of Tanzania Rép.-Unie de Tanzanie								
Total manufacturing [D] Total, industries manufacturières [D]	100.0	101.0	106.7	115.4	119.2	137.0	142.6	162.0
Food, beverages and tobacco Aliments, boissons et tabac	100.0	117.9	133.7	139.8	130.5	156.4	167.2	175.7
Textiles, leather and footwear Textiles, cuir et chaussures	100.0	97.8	91.2	104.6	106.0	185.4	241.9	341.4

25

Index numbers of industrial production *[cont.]*

Indices de la production industrielle
1995 = 100 *[suite]*

Country or area and industry [ISIC Rev. 3] Pays ou zone et industrie [CITI Rév. 3]	1995	1996	1997	1998	1999	2000	2001	2002
Chemicals, rubber and plastic prod. Prod. chimiques, caoutchouc et plastiques	100.0	104.1	82.8	80.0	86.6	138.1	127.6	113.4
Basic metals Métaux de base	100.0	31.3	29.2	81.3	16.7	127.0	134.9	182.5
Metal products Produits métalliques	100.0	117.5	119.9	122.3	132.1	120.3	113.5	104.0
Zambia Zambie								
Total industry [CDE] [3] **Total, industrie [CDE]** [3]	**100.0**	**103.5**	**105.9**	**108.6**	**93.4**	**95.8**	...	...
Total manufacturing [D] **Total, industries manufacturières [D]**	**100.0**	**91.6**	**94.8**	**82.0**	**87.5**	**95.4**	...	...
Total mining [C] **Total, industries extractives [C]**	**100.0**	**114.3**	**114.5**	**129.5**	**92.8**	**96.1**	...	...
Food, beverages and tobacco Aliments, boissons et tabac	100.0	72.0	54.7	52.2	57.1	57.6	...	...
Textiles and wearing apparel Textiles et habillement	100.0	128.2	218.3	165.1	179.5	187.3	...	...
Chemicals, petroleum, rubber and plastic products Prod. chimiques, pétroliers, caoutch. et plast.	100.0	138.9	115.4	112.7	96.3	169.4	...	...
Basic metals Métaux de base	100.0	80.0	68.1	74.4	76.4	78.1	...	...
Metal products Produits métalliques	100.0	68.0	65.3	70.2	58.3	65.0	...	...
Electricity and water [E] **Electricité et eau [E]**	**100.0**	**86.4**	**100.1**	**92.0**	**93.0**	**94.5**	...	...
Zimbabwe Zimbabwe								
Total industry [CDE] [3] **Total, industrie [CDE]** [3]	**100.0**	**108.9**	**106.8**	**109.9**	**103.2**	**96.6**	**87.8**	**79.5**
Total manufacturing [D] **Total, industries manufacturières [D]**	**100.0**	**113.0**	**112.9**	**112.0**	**103.7**	**97.4**	**88.6**	**75.7**
Total mining [C] **Total, industries extractives [C]**	**100.0**	**99.0**	**90.9**	**108.6**	**103.4**	**95.0**	**81.7**	**83.6**
Food, beverages and tobacco Aliments, boissons et tabac	100.0	102.0	105.7	111.8	101.6	108.8	90.2	71.5
Textiles, wearing apparel, leather, footwear Textiles, habillement, cuir et chaussures	100.0	123.6	125.4	137.7	148.3	132.2	130.0	103.3
Chemicals, petroleum, rubber and plastic products Prod. chimiques, pétroliers, caoutch. et plast.	100.0	106.2	126.8	120.0	107.0	75.5	75.4	78.6
Basic metals and metal products Métaux de base et produits métalliques	100.0	107.0	96.2	81.1	78.7	76.7	68.4	59.5
Electricity [E] **Electricité [E]**	**100.0**	**96.3**	**94.1**	**87.3**	**94.6**	**93.2**	**104.5**	**112.7**

America, North · Amérique du Nord

	1995	1996	1997	1998	1999	2000	2001	2002
Barbados Barbade								
Total industry [CDE] **Total, industrie [CDE]**	**100.0**	**100.2**	**104.3**	**112.1**	**112.9**	**111.1**	**104.3**	**104.8**
Total manufacturing [D] **Total, industries manufacturières [D]**	**100.0**	**100.1**	**104.3**	**109.1**	**107.2**	**106.5**	**98.3**	**98.8**
Total mining [C] **Total, industries extractives [C]**	**100.0**	**89.5**	**92.9**	**141.4**	**164.8**	**140.4**	**121.9**	**115.1**
Food, beverages and tobacco Aliments, boissons et tabac	100.0	100.5	106.2	114.5	112.7	109.8	106.7	109.0
Wearing apparel Habillement	100.0	90.9	94.4	69.2	65.0	69.9	44.1	32.9
Chemicals and petroleum products Produits chimiques et pétroliers	100.0	101.1	118.6	105.3	104.7	83.8	78.7	75.5
Metal products Produits métalliques	100.0	106.5	103.3	87.5	80.8	78.9	54.9	53.5
Electricity and gas [E] **Electricité et gaz [E]**	**100.0**	**103.8**	**107.8**	**117.3**	**123.6**	**123.5**	**128.0**	**130.2**

25

Index numbers of industrial production *[cont.]*

Indices de la production industrielle
1995 = 100 *[suite]*

Country or area and industry [ISIC Rev. 3] Pays ou zone et industrie [CITI Rév. 3]	1995	1996	1997	1998	1999	2000	2001	2002
Belize Belize								
Total industry [DE]								
Total, industrie [DE]	100.0	100.6	106.0	105.0	105.0	120.0	120.2	115.7
Total manufacturing [D]								
Total, industries manufacturières [D]	100.0	100.2	105.2	101.8	107.2	125.4	125.2	119.6
Food, beverages and tobacco								
Aliments, boissons et tabac	100.0	99.0	105.2	102.4	107.0	124.8	125.3	119.6
Wearing apparel								
Habillement	100.0	100.7	100.9	108.6	108.4	89.1	76.3	59.9
Chemicals and chemical products								
Produits chimiques	100.0	93.0	80.9	80.1	94.8	87.5	89.2	102.2
Metal products								
Produits métalliques	100.0	80.6	66.1	54.6	46.3	40.2	31.0	29.4
Electricity and water [E]								
Electricité et eau [E]	100.0	102.7	111.0	122.3	93.1	91.4	93.3	94.6
Canada Canada								
Total industry [CDE]								
Total, industrie [CDE]	100.0	101.2	106.2	109.9	116.1	125.6	122.1	124.6
Total manufacturing [D]								
Total, industries manufacturières [D]	100.0	101.1	107.7	113.0	121.8	135.4	130.4	133.9
Total mining [C]								
Total, industries extractives [C]	100.0	101.1	104.1	105.7	105.2	104.6	106.3	104.5
Food, beverages and tobacco								
Aliments, boissons et tabac	100.0	99.1	100.0	105.2	104.8	108.9	114.0	115.8
Textiles, wearing apparel, leather, footwear								
Textiles, habillement, cuir et chaussures	100.0	97.0	102.8	106.2	104.1	120.5	110.5	109.1
Chemicals, petroleum, rubber and plastic products								
Prod. chimiques, pétroliers, caoutch. et plast.	100.0	102.9	99.8	101.8	106.4	117.6	120.3	130.0
Basic metals								
Métaux de base	100.0	101.6	107.2	116.3	120.6	129.4	127.8	132.5
Metal products								
Produits métalliques	100.0	100.5	109.3	116.5	134.4	155.6	141.8	141.1
Electricity, gas and water [E]								
Electricité, gaz et eau [E]	100.0	102.0	101.4	99.6	100.9	101.5	99.7	102.3
Costa Rica Costa Rica								
Total industry [DE] [3]								
Total, industrie [DE] [3]	100.0	100.8	108.2	120.1	146.3	143.9	134.4	134.9
Total manufacturing [D]								
Total, industries manufacturières [D]	100.0	100.5	108.2	120.5	150.3	145.9	133.7	132.9
Food, beverages and tobacco								
Aliments, boissons et tabac	100.0	101.9	109.3	115.9	118.7	117.3	118.6	113.9
Textiles, wearing apparel, leather, footwear								
Textiles, habillement, cuir et chaussures	100.0	91.2	87.5	91.5	83.1	74.1	71.9	70.7
Chemicals, petroleum, rubber and plastic products								
Prod. chimiques, pétroliers, caoutch. et plast.	100.0	97.2	101.7	100.1	100.6	103.4	105.6	114.5
Metal products								
Produits métalliques	100.0	100.1	109.7	113.8	112.1	108.4	98.9	104.3
Electricity and water [E]								
Electricité et eau [E]	100.0	102.6	108.2	117.7	125.0	133.0	138.5	145.8
Cuba Cuba								
Total industry [CDE]								
Total, industrie [CDE]	100.0	113.8	117.0	111.4	118.7	128.2	...	...
Total manufacturing [D]								
Total, industries manufacturières [D]	100.0	109.3	114.2	113.4	116.7	126.8	...	...
Total mining [C]								
Total, industries extractives [C]	100.0	106.4	108.1	121.8	163.7	201.9	...	...
Food, beverages and tobacco								
Aliments, boissons et tabac	100.0	105.7	111.3	116.8	127.1	124.2	...	...
Textiles, wearing apparel, leather, footwear								
Textiles, habillement, cuir et chaussures	100.0	110.5	118.2	122.5	132.8	126.0	...	...

25
Index numbers of industrial production *[cont.]*
Indices de la production industrielle
1995 = 100 *[suite]*

Country or area and industry [ISIC Rev. 3] Pays ou zone et industrie [CITI Rév. 3]	1995	1996	1997	1998	1999	2000	2001	2002
Chemicals, petroleum, rubber and plastic products Prod. chimiques, pétroliers, caoutch. et plast.	100.0	108.9	114.0	94.6	94.4	122.7	...	...
Basic metals Métaux de base	100.0	122.7	141.4	149.9	147.8	158.0	...	...
Metal products Produits métalliques	100.0	166.2	165.4	110.1	136.8	121.9	...	...
Electricity and water [E] Electricité et eau [E]	100.0	106.2	113.4	113.4	116.3	120.5	...	...
Dominican Republic Rép. dominicaine								
Total industry [CDE] Total, industrie [CDE]	100.0	103.6	111.1	115.5	121.9	131.6	130.9	...
Total manufacturing [D] Total, industries manufacturières [D]	100.0	103.1	110.8	117.1	124.2	133.6	131.9	...
Total mining [C] Total, industries extractives [C]	100.0	102.4	105.6	88.8	87.4	99.0	84.0	...
Electricity [E] Electricité [E]	100.0	120.2	131.7	139.0	162.4	170.3	189.2	...
El Salvador El Salvador								
Total industry [CDE] Total, industrie [CDE]	100.0	102.1	110.2	117.5	121.7	126.4	131.8	...
Total manufacturing [D] Total, industries manufacturières [D]	100.0	101.7	109.9	117.2	121.5	126.5	131.8	...
Total mining [C] Total, industries extractives [C]	100.0	101.1	107.5	113.2	113.7	108.4	121.3	...
Food, beverages and tobacco Aliments, boissons et tabac	100.0	101.6	106.2	111.4	114.3	118.0	120.8	...
Textiles, wearing apparel, leather, footwear Textiles, habillement, cuir et chaussures	100.0	99.1	102.2	108.4	111.7	113.6	107.6	...
Chemicals, petroleum, rubber and plastic products Prod. chimiques, pétroliers, caoutch. et plast.	100.0	101.1	106.9	114.4	124.2	121.6	128.6	...
Basic metals and metal products Métaux de base et produits métalliques	100.0	107.3	117.4	129.9	132.3	135.3	145.1	...
Electricity [E] Electricité [E]	100.0	139.1	142.0	156.8	160.2	146.0	150.4	...
Haiti [6] Haïti [6]								
Total industry [DE] [3] Total, industrie [DE] [3]	100.0	101.5	108.1	112.2	115.2	120.8	114.8	116.1
Total manufacturing [D] Total, industries manufacturières [D]	100.0	99.2	102.0	107.4	110.9	118.2	120.9	122.3
Food, beverages and tobacco Aliments, boissons et tabac	100.0	105.2	112.6	112.0	149.8	173.4	179.8	182.0
Chemicals and chemical products Produits chimiques	100.0	96.1	94.2	101.7	101.9	104.7	108.3	110.9
Electricity [E] Electricité [E]	100.0	110.4	131.6	130.7	132.0	130.8	91.0	92.1
Honduras Honduras								
Total industry [CDE] Total, industrie [CDE]	100.0	106.3	113.0	117.1	120.3	127.5	132.0	136.5
Total manufacturing [D] Total, industries manufacturières [D]	100.0	104.6	111.0	114.8	117.8	124.3	130.8	134.4
Total mining [C] Total, industries extractives [C]	100.0	107.3	112.5	116.7	122.9	125.0	124.0	127.1
Food, beverages and tobacco Aliments, boissons et tabac	100.0	121.2	149.0	162.9	180.0	195.9	214.3	229.1
Textiles, wearing apparel, leather, footwear Textiles, habillement, cuir et chaussures	100.0	133.5	166.0	193.6	221.4	246.3	274.6	295.6
Chemicals, petroleum, rubber and plastic products Prod. chimiques, pétroliers, caoutch. et plast.	100.0	106.3	124.1	140.1	157.0	172.3	185.6	196.9
Basic metals Métaux de base	100.0	115.5	136.6	143.7	155.9	174.8	189.1	204.6

25

Index numbers of industrial production *[cont.]*

Indices de la production industrielle

1995 = 100 *[suite]*

Country or area and industry [ISIC Rev. 3] Pays ou zone et industrie [CITI Rév. 3]	1995	1996	1997	1998	1999	2000	2001	2002
Metal products								
Produits métalliques	100.0	116.8	134.0	153.4	174.4	193.1	204.7	219.5
Electricity, gas and water [E]								
Electricité, gaz et eau [E]	100.0	115.4	121.8	127.2	133.9	147.7	144.5	152.0
Mexico Mexique								
Total industry [CDE] [7]								
Total, industrie [CDE] [7]	100.0	110.1	120.3	128.0	133.3	141.3	136.4	136.3
Total manufacturing [D]								
Total, industries manufacturières [D]	100.0	110.8	121.8	130.8	136.4	145.8	140.3	139.5
Total mining [C]								
Total, industries extractives [C]	100.0	108.1	112.9	116.0	113.6	117.9	118.9	118.5
Food, beverages and tobacco								
Aliments, boissons et tabac	100.0	103.4	106.7	113.7	118.3	122.9	126.1	127.6
Textiles and wearing apparel								
Textiles et habillement	100.0	115.6	127.8	132.6	136.9	144.2	132.5	124.3
Chemicals, petroleum, rubber and plastic products								
Prod. chimiques, pétroliers, caoutch. et plast.	100.0	106.5	113.8	120.7	123.5	127.6	122.7	122.0
Basic metals								
Métaux de base	100.0	118.7	131.9	137.3	137.8	141.9	131.8	132.7
Metal products								
Produits métalliques	100.0	122.4	145.7	162.4	173.6	197.2	183.6	180.6
Electricity [E]								
Electricité [E]	100.0	104.6	110.1	112.1	120.9	122.1	123.7	128.4
Panama Panama								
Total industry [CDE] [3]								
Total, industrie [CDE] [3]	100.0	102.6	110.2	115.6	112.2	110.3	106.8	...
Total manufacturing [D]								
Total, industries manufacturières [D]	100.0	99.9	105.6	109.9	105.3	100.0	93.4	90.0
Total mining [C]								
Total, industries extractives [C]	100.0	79.9	160.5	202.2	230.5	228.6	137.1	...
Food, beverages and tobacco								
Aliments, boissons et tabac	100.0	102.3	110.7	119.7	111.8	108.3	106.9	108.4
Textiles, wearing apparel, leather, footwear								
Textiles, habillement, cuir et chaussures	100.0	90.4	85.2	80.4	68.9	62.1	56.1	39.5
Chemicals, petroleum, rubber and plastic products								
Prod. chimiques, pétroliers, caoutch. et plast.	100.0	117.7	121.5	126.5	125.8	116.9	117.3	83.0
Basic metals								
Métaux de base	100.0	112.1	148.9	124.3	177.1	135.6	55.1	24.1
Metal products								
Produits métalliques	100.0	104.7	111.0	116.3	112.3	120.3	111.0	111.8
Electricity and water [E]								
Electricité et eau [E]	100.0	109.2	120.3	127.6	126.3	132.7	137.8	...
Trinidad and Tobago Trinité-et-Tobago								
Total industry [DE]								
Total, industrie [DE]	100.0	105.7	112.4	125.0	139.0	146.4	157.6	...
Total manufacturing [D] [3]								
Total, industries manufacturières [D] [3]	100.0	106.0	113.0	125.4	140.1	148.7	162.2	...
Food, beverages and tobacco								
Aliments, boissons et tabac	100.0	106.4	122.3	174.0	183.4	234.2	266.7	
Textiles, leather and footwear								
Textiles, cuir et chaussures	100.0	101.3	135.6	180.8	364.1	458.0	434.1	...
Chemicals and petroleum products								
Produits chimiques et pétroliers	100.0	116.5	134.5	175.6	236.6	270.6	264.1	
Metal products								
Produits métalliques	100.0	121.8	110.6	154.3	154.4	155.4	172.2	...
Electricity [E]								
Electricité [E]	100.0	102.6	106.3	120.1	127.1	121.5	106.4	...
United States Etats-Unis								
Total industry [CDE]								
Total, industrie [CDE]	100.0	104.4	112.1	118.4	123.4	129.3	124.7	123.9

25

Index numbers of industrial production *[cont.]*

Indices de la production industrielle
1995 = 100 *[suite]*

Country or area and industry [ISIC Rev. 3] Pays ou zone et industrie [CITI Rév. 3]	1995	1996	1997	1998	1999	2000	2001	2002
Total manufacturing [D]								
Total, industries manufacturières [D]	**100.0**	**104.7**	**113.6**	**121.0**	**127.0**	**133.4**	**128.0**	**126.6**
Total mining [C]								
Total, industries extractives [C]	**100.0**	**101.8**	**103.7**	**101.9**	**97.5**	**99.6**	**100.2**	**97.3**
Food, beverages and tobacco								
Aliments, boissons et tabac	100.0	99.2	101.4	104.7	103.8	104.9	103.3	103.7
Textiles, wearing apparel, leather, footwear								
Textiles, habillement, cuir et chaussures	100.0	97.9	100.2	96.6	94.4	91.8	81.7	76.9
Chemicals, petroleum, rubber and plastic products								
Prod. chimiques, pétroliers, caoutch. et plast.	100.0	102.4	108.0	109.7	113.1	115.0	113.3	113.5
Basic metals								
Métaux de base	100.0	102.3	106.7	109.2	108.5	105.4	94.1	91.4
Metal products								
Produits métalliques	100.0	110.7	130.1	150.9	178.0	216.6	213.2	209.4
Electricity and gas [E]								
Electricité et gaz [E]	**100.0**	**103.4**	**103.7**	**105.3**	**107.9**	**110.4**	**109.4**	**114.2**

America, South · Amérique du Sud

	1995	1996	1997	1998	1999	2000	2001	2002
Argentina Argentine								
Total manufacturing [D]								
Total, industries manufacturières [D]	**100.0**	**106.4**	**116.3**	**115.9**	**103.8**	**101.8**	**90.4**	**87.5**
Food, beverages and tobacco								
Aliments, boissons et tabac	100.0	100.4	105.1	107.3	107.2	103.5	94.5	89.9
Textiles, wearing apparel, leather, footwear								
Textiles, habillement, cuir et chaussures	100.0	111.8	111.0	98.7	78.2	78.2	67.1	56.5
Chemicals, petroleum, rubber and plastic products								
Prod. chimiques, pétroliers, caoutch. et plast.	100.0	107.1	116.4	117.1	111.4	112.2	102.8	96.7
Basic metals								
Métaux de base	100.0	111.6	124.2	129.5	99.7	103.4	97.5	104.9
Metal products								
Produits métalliques	100.0	108.5	124.5	120.0	91.6	88.4	73.2	61.2
Bolivia Bolivie								
Total industry [CDE] [3]								
Total, industrie [CDE] [3]	**100.0**	**101.4**	**104.8**	**109.8**	**104.6**	**104.1**	**102.2**	**102.6**
Total manufacturing [D]								
Total, industries manufacturières [D]	**100.0**	**104.1**	**108.4**	**112.0**	**113.4**	**113.8**	**113.0**	**113.3**
Total mining [C]								
Total, industries extractives [C]	**100.0**	**98.5**	**100.6**	**106.7**	**95.1**	**93.6**	**90.5**	**90.7**
Food, beverages and tobacco								
Aliments, boissons et tabac	100.0	105.8	106.3	111.8	114.9	119.7	122.5	126.1
Textiles, wearing apparel, leather, footwear								
Textiles, habillement, cuir et chaussures	100.0	99.5	105.1	103.5	92.9	95.7	81.9	77.5
Chemicals, petroleum, rubber and plastic products								
Prod. chimiques, pétroliers, caoutch. et plast.	100.0	111.6	121.5	123.5	122.0	113.3	110.8	111.5
Basic metals								
Métaux de base	100.0	93.4	108.4	84.7	87.1	90.5	79.1	82.4
Metal products								
Produits métalliques	100.0	92.0	92.9	95.0	88.2	75.6	70.2	60.4
Electricity, gas and water [E]								
Electricité, gaz et eau [E]	**100.0**	**109.3**	**118.5**	**126.2**	**131.6**	**135.6**	**136.5**	**141.8**
Brazil Brésil								
Total industry [CD]								
Total, industrie [CD]	**100.0**	**101.8**	**105.7**	**103.5**	**102.9**	**109.7**	**111.5**	**114.1**
Total manufacturing [D]								
Total, industries manufacturières [D]	**100.0**	**101.1**	**104.7**	**101.4**	**99.7**	**105.8**	**107.2**	**108.8**
Total mining [C]								
Total, industries extractives [C]	**100.0**	**109.8**	**117.7**	**132.4**	**144.4**	**161.6**	**167.2**	**185.1**
Food, beverages and tobacco								
Aliments, boissons et tabac	100.0	104.7	107.1	106.0	108.3	106.4	110.5	116.3
Textiles, wearing apparel, leather, footwear								
Textiles, habillement, cuir et chaussures	100.0	95.9	89.6	84.5	83.9	89.2	83.6	82.9

25

Index numbers of industrial production [cont.]
Indices de la production industrielle
1995 = 100 [suite]

Country or area and industry [ISIC Rev. 3] Pays ou zone et industrie [CITI Rév. 3]	1995	1996	1997	1998	1999	2000	2001	2002
Chemicals, petroleum, rubber and plastic products Prod. chimiques, pétroliers, caoutch. et plast.	100.0	105.3	110.3	113.3	113.8	115.9	114.6	116.0
Basic metals and metal products Métaux de base et produits métalliques	100.0	98.2	103.8	95.9	90.6	102.8	107.2	108.5
Chile Chili								
Total industry [CDE] [3] **Total, industrie [CDE]** [3]	100.0	108.3	115.6	118.8	124.8	130.1	132.2	132.9
Total manufacturing [D] **Total, industries manufacturières [D]**	100.0	102.7	108.0	109.0	108.7	112.3	113.6	116.5
Total mining [C] **Total, industries extractives [C]**	100.0	122.3	134.8	142.5	164.6	173.7	176.4	170.0
Food, beverages and tobacco Aliments, boissons et tabac	100.0	101.5	102.6	100.2	101.6	104.5	108.3	111.4
Textiles, wearing apparel, leather, footwear Textiles, habillement, cuir et chaussures	100.0	97.8	90.2	77.6	68.7	67.2	59.3	56.2
Chemicals, petroleum, rubber and plastic products Prod. chimiques, pétroliers, caoutch. et plast.	100.0	106.9	116.5	123.2	128.3	140.6	148.1	153.1
Basic metals Métaux de base	100.0	102.8	111.3	119.9	123.5	92.3	96.5	95.6
Metal products Produits métalliques	100.0	101.4	114.0	106.8	97.6	105.6	104.7	99.4
Electricity [E] **Electricité [E]**	100.0	112.7	121.2	129.9	139.6	147.4	153.7	157.7
Colombia Colombie								
Total manufacturing [D] **Total, industries manufacturières [D]**	100.0	97.3	99.6	98.2	85.0	93.2	94.3	95.4
Food, beverages and tobacco Aliments, boissons et tabac	100.0	101.1	101.5	102.2	93.2	92.7	94.3	99.8
Textiles, wearing apparel, leather, footwear Textiles, habillement, cuir et chaussures	100.0	96.2	101.3	119.0	102.7	120.6	117.0	109.9
Chemicals, petroleum, rubber and plastic products Prod. chimiques, pétroliers, caoutch. et plast.	100.0	98.1	98.3	94.6	86.0	93.1	89.7	92.5
Basic metals Métaux de base	100.0	94.6	107.0	97.9	93.3	123.7	118.0	123.6
Metal products Produits métalliques	100.0	92.8	100.0	91.4	66.6	75.1	83.7	85.0
Ecuador Equateur								
Total manufacturing [D] **Total, industries manufacturières [D]**	100.0	102.3	104.4	105.2	100.0	114.9	127.6	130.9
Food, beverages and tobacco Aliments, boissons et tabac	100.0	102.0	103.3	105.9	104.5	107.7	119.6	123.4
Textiles, leather and footwear Textiles, cuir et chaussures	100.0	101.9	104.0	101.3	95.8	114.7	118.0	119.5
Chemicals, petroleum, rubber and plastic products Prod. chimiques, pétroliers, caoutch. et plast.	100.0	102.3	104.7	106.8	97.0	107.4	112.5	116.4
Basic metals Métaux de base	100.0	101.4	102.4	102.7	95.5	127.1	129.6	132.8
Metal products Produits métalliques	100.0	99.4	100.8	101.6	67.1	97.0	151.8	153.6
Paraguay Paraguay								
Total manufacturing [D] **Total, industries manufacturières [D]**	100.0	97.8	97.6	98.6	98.6	99.6	101.0	97.8
Food, beverages and tobacco Aliments, boissons et tabac	100.0	101.2	105.0	106.6	110.0	112.5	114.2	117.9
Textiles, wearing apparel, leather, footwear Textiles, habillement, cuir et chaussures	100.0	97.7	81.2	88.3	84.9	92.3	99.1	82.4
Chemicals, petroleum, rubber and plastic products Prod. chimiques, pétroliers, caoutch. et plast.	100.0	85.6	76.9	72.0	68.6	64.2	67.3	63.3
Basic metals Métaux de base	100.0	96.0	90.7	86.3	82.5	83.2	79.9	84.2

25

Index numbers of industrial production *[cont.]*

Indices de la production industrielle

1995 = 100 *[suite]*

Country or area and industry [ISIC Rev. 3] Pays ou zone et industrie [CITI Rév. 3]	1995	1996	1997	1998	1999	2000	2001	2002
Metal products Produits métalliques	100.0	99.6	99.1	99.1	99.1	99.1	99.1	99.1
Peru Pérou								
Total industry [CDE] **Total, industrie [CDE]**	**100.0**	**102.5**	**109.4**	**108.8**	**109.9**	**113.3**	**113.9**	**119.8**
Total manufacturing [D] **Total, industries manufacturières [D]**	**100.0**	**101.5**	**106.9**	**103.4**	**102.9**	**109.8**	**108.9**	**113.5**
Total mining [C] **Total, industries extractives [C]**	**100.0**	**105.1**	**114.6**	**118.9**	**134.3**	**137.5**	**153.9**	**171.3**
Food, beverages and tobacco Aliments, boissons et tabac	100.0	100.3	103.8	99.0	112.4	122.0	118.1	122.3
Textiles, wearing apparel, leather, footwear Textiles, habillement, cuir et chaussures	100.0	102.6	107.2	99.9	97.2	110.1	105.6	108.8
Chemicals, petroleum, rubber and plastic products Prod. chimiques, pétroliers, caoutch. et plast.	100.0	106.3	118.3	114.1	114.3	118.6	122.9	127.7
Basic metals Métaux de base	100.0	108.6	115.6	121.4	121.9	128.1	132.7	128.9
Metal products Produits métalliques	100.0	90.9	98.3	91.7	75.6	83.4	82.1	78.2
Electricity [E] **Electricité [E]**	**100.0**	**105.9**	**119.4**	**129.2**	**132.5**	**138.6**	**144.0**	**151.7**
Suriname Suriname								
Total industry [CDE] **Total, industrie [CDE]**	**100.0**	**103.8**	**107.6**	**106.7**	**99.0**	...	...	...
Total manufacturing [D] **Total, industries manufacturières [D]**	**100.0**	**101.8**	**104.5**	**86.5**	**79.3**	...	...	...
Total mining [C] **Total, industries extractives [C]**	**100.0**	**103.9**	**168.9**	**194.2**	...	...	...	...
Food, beverages and tobacco Aliments, boissons et tabac	100.0	120.3	118.4	125.8	142.2	...	...	...
Electricity, gas and water [E] **Electricité, gaz et eau [E]**	**100.0**	**121.3**	**140.4**	**159.6**	**86.2**	**62.8**	...	...
Uruguay Uruguay								
Total manufacturing [D] **Total, industries manufacturières [D]**	**100.0**	**104.1**	**110.0**	**116.1**	**106.1**	**108.2**	**102.3**	**84.9**
Food, beverages and tobacco Aliments, boissons et tabac	100.0	106.3	115.7	118.6	120.1	114.3	107.6	99.2
Textiles, wearing apparel, leather, footwear Textiles, habillement, cuir et chaussures	100.0	100.6	108.5	89.0	64.0	64.5	52.6	40.9
Chemicals, petroleum, rubber and plastic products Prod. chimiques, pétroliers, caoutch. et plast.	100.0	106.4	100.4	114.8	103.1	112.6	102.8	98.6
Basic metals Métaux de base	100.0	98.1	107.0	111.5	105.2	101.0	99.7	99.7
Metal products Produits métalliques	100.0	70.5	83.8	115.8	92.5	111.9	85.5	41.1
Venezuela Venezuela								
Total industry [CDE] **Total, industrie [CDE]**	**100.0**	**95.7**	**100.1**	**95.2**	**87.3**	**90.8**	**93.4**	**85.0**
Total manufacturing [D] **Total, industries manufacturières [D]**	**100.0**	**94.8**	**99.0**	**99.6**	**86.7**	**92.2**	**95.8**	**79.7**
Total mining [C] **Total, industries extractives [C]**	**100.0**	**102.6**	**109.5**	**104.6**	**93.7**	**101.3**	**102.5**	**102.9**
Electricity and water [E] **Electricité et eau [E]**	**100.0**	**101.2**	**106.0**	**110.3**	**109.8**	**114.8**	**120.7**	**123.7**

Asia · Asie

Armenia Arménie								
Total industry [CDE] **Total, industrie [CDE]**	**100.0**	**101.4**	**102.4**	**100.2**	**105.5**	**112.3**	**118.3**	**135.1**
Total manufacturing [D] **Total, industries manufacturières [D]**	**100.0**	**99.0**	**101.9**	**97.1**	**107.3**	**114.7**	**125.7**	**157.1**

25

Index numbers of industrial production *[cont.]*
Indices de la production industrielle
1995 = 100 *[suite]*

Country or area and industry [ISIC Rev. 3] Pays ou zone et industrie [CITI Rév. 3]	1995	1996	1997	1998	1999	2000	2001	2002
Total mining [C]								
Total, industries extractives [C]	100.0	116.1	110.2	143.1	166.3	207.4	248.3	290.0
Food, beverages and tobacco								
Aliments, boissons et tabac	100.0	101.5	113.5	101.4	112.1	117.0	123.7	137.6
Textiles, wearing apparel, leather, footwear								
Textiles, habillement, cuir et chaussures	100.0	104.9	133.0	117.5	75.1	73.0	84.4	84.5
Chemicals, petroleum, rubber and plastic products								
Prod. chimiques, pétroliers, caoutch. et plast.	100.0	107.5	78.1	93.0	101.5	115.3	97.9	81.4
Basic metals								
Métaux de base	100.0	76.9	44.5	184.7	151.3	318.0	460.1	568.2
Metal products								
Produits métalliques	100.0	93.9	81.0	68.2	74.4	88.1	120.2	96.9
Electricity and gas [E]								
Electricité et gaz [E]	100.0	108.3	105.2	105.7	100.0	102.6	95.1	81.4
Azerbaijan Azerbaïdjan								
Total industry [CDE]								
Total, industrie [CDE]	100.0	93.3	93.6	95.6	99.1	105.9	111.3	115.3
Total manufacturing [D]								
Total, industries manufacturières [D]	100.0	90.0	90.7	80.1	72.8	84.0	86.3	91.1
Total mining [C]								
Total, industries extractives [C]	100.0	97.9	97.3	121.2	145.3	146.9	155.5	159.4
Electricity, gas and water [E]								
Electricité, gaz et eau [E]	100.0	105.8	98.6	103.6	104.7	108.6	109.3	114.4
Bangladesh [2] Bangladesh [2]								
Total industry [CDE]								
Total, industrie [CDE]	100.0	106.2	110.3	112.5	121.4	131.5	140.9	146.0
Total manufacturing [D]								
Total, industries manufacturières [D]	100.0	106.2	109.8	120.0	123.8	132.8	139.9	144.6
Total mining [C]								
Total, industries extractives [C]	100.0	107.3	106.4	113.5	114.6	134.5	150.8	156.4
Food, beverages and tobacco								
Aliments, boissons et tabac	100.0	96.1	94.4	99.4	98.0	105.2	108.3	121.7
Textiles, wearing apparel, leather, footwear								
Textiles, habillement, cuir et chaussures	100.0	106.6	111.8	122.8	127.7	132.3	141.9	153.4
Chemicals, petroleum, rubber and plastic products								
Prod. chimiques, pétroliers, caoutch. et plast.	100.0	106.8	99.1	104.4	98.2	103.5	112.7	109.3
Basic metals								
Métaux de base	100.0	87.0	94.3	105.1	89.3	93.0	103.0	107.8
Metal products								
Produits métalliques	100.0	93.6	108.5	151.9	116.6	117.5	117.3	111.1
Electricity [E]								
Electricité [E]	100.0	105.8	109.3	118.8	127.3	135.8	149.8	159.3
China, Hong Kong SAR Chine, Hong Kong RAS								
Total industry [DE] [3]								
Total, industrie [DE] [3]	100.0	97.0	96.6	90.2	84.7	85.1	82.4	76.4
Total manufacturing [D]								
Total, industries manufacturières [D]	100.0	96.3	95.6	87.2	81.7	81.2	77.7	70.1
Food, beverages and tobacco								
Aliments, boissons et tabac	100.0	99.1	98.6	89.7	88.2	85.5	84.0	90.9
Textiles and wearing apparel								
Textiles et habillement	100.0	94.8	93.9	86.2	84.1	86.9	86.7	80.8
Chemicals and other non-metallic mineral products								
Prod. chimiques et minéraux non-métalliques	100.0	100.2	101.4	88.1	74.9	64.1	59.1	48.9
Basic metals and metal products								
Métaux de base et produits métalliques	100.0	94.1	91.3	84.0	80.0	79.2	72.5	56.0
Electricity and gas [E]								
Electricité et gaz [E]	100.0	102.3	104.6	111.9	106.8	113.4	117.0	122.7
China, Macao SAR [8] Chine, Macao RAS [8]								
Total industry [CDE]								
Total, industrie [CDE]	...	99.9	100.0	100.9	101.2	112.6	106.2	...

25

Index numbers of industrial production *[cont.]*

Indices de la production industrielle
1995 = 100 *[suite]*

Country or area and industry [ISIC Rev. 3] Pays ou zone et industrie [CITI Rév. 3]	1995	1996	1997	1998	1999	2000	2001	2002
Total manufacturing [D] Total, industries manufacturières [D]	...	100.8	100.0	97.9	98.8	113.2	103.6	...
Total mining [C] Total, industries extractives [C]	...	95.0	100.0	99.3	75.0	36.0	71.9	...
Electricity and gas [E] Electricité et gaz [E]	...	97.2	100.0	110.1	109.1	112.6	115.1	...
Cyprus Chypre								
Total industry [CDE] Total, industrie [CDE]	100.0	96.8	96.7	99.4	100.9	105.4	105.1	105.2
Total manufacturing [D] Total, industries manufacturières [D]	100.0	94.9	94.3	95.4	96.3	100.1	98.2	95.8
Total mining [C] Total, industries extractives [C]	100.0	97.6	101.4	121.1	130.2	135.3	129.0	143.6
Food, beverages and tobacco Aliments, boissons et tabac	100.0	95.1	93.9	94.5	98.1	102.0	100.8	96.9
Textiles, wearing apparel, leather, footwear Textiles, habillement, cuir et chaussures	100.0	83.9	80.2	81.7	76.0	70.1	67.2	55.3
Chemicals, petroleum, rubber and plastic products Prod. chimiques, pétroliers, caoutch. et plast.	100.0	98.1	102.9	101.7	101.8	102.6	105.7	107.0
Metal products Produits métalliques	100.0	98.6	100.0	103.2	109.2	117.4	120.6	132.2
Electricity, gas and water [E] Electricité, gaz et eau [E]	100.0	105.6	107.8	116.0	123.5	131.7	141.6	153.6
India[9] Inde[9]								
Total industry [CDE] Total, industrie [CDE]	100.0	106.1	113.1	117.8	125.6	131.9	135.4	143.2
Total manufacturing [D] Total, industries manufacturières [D]	100.0	107.3	114.5	119.5	128.0	134.9	138.7	147.1
Total mining [C] Total, industries extractives [C]	100.0	98.0	104.9	104.1	105.1	108.1	109.5	115.9
Food, beverages and tobacco Aliments, boissons et tabac	100.0	105.5	110.9	113.3	118.9	125.8	124.6	140.8
Textiles, wearing apparel, leather, footwear Textiles, habillement, cuir et chaussures	100.0	109.5	112.9	109.7	117.0	123.9	124.0	126.0
Chemicals, petroleum, rubber and plastic products Prod. chimiques, pétroliers, caoutch. et plast.	100.0	104.1	116.4	125.2	134.8	146.4	154.3	160.4
Basic metals Métaux de base	100.0	106.7	109.5	106.8	112.1	114.2	119.0	130.1
Metal products Produits métalliques	100.0	108.4	113.2	125.2	137.7	145.2	145.1	156.2
Electricity [E] Electricité [E]	100.0	104.0	110.8	118.0	126.6	131.7	135.7	140.1
Indonesia Indonésie								
Total industry [CDE][3] Total, industrie [CDE][3]	100.0	101.6	105.2	97.6	95.1	108.2	111.5	116.6
Total manufacturing [D] Total, industries manufacturières [D]	100.0	100.6	106.0	86.7	88.3	91.5	90.5	84.1
Total mining [C] Total, industries extractives [C]	100.0	101.8	103.3	103.8	96.9	117.7	124.6	139.0
Food, beverages and tobacco Aliments, boissons et tabac	100.0	103.9	100.8	93.5	87.3	85.4	83.7	80.3
Textiles, wearing apparel, leather, footwear Textiles, habillement, cuir et chaussures	100.0	98.4	100.0	99.1	107.1	100.7	92.8	90.8
Chemicals, petroleum, rubber and plastic products Prod. chimiques, pétroliers, caoutch. et plast.	100.0	107.0	113.8	104.3	109.6	106.7	102.3	91.7
Basic metals Métaux de base	100.0	99.2	104.1	81.1	89.3	109.3	111.6	98.2
Metal products Produits métalliques	100.0	98.2	106.2	50.6	59.4	95.2	109.7	78.8
Electricity [E] Electricité [E]	100.0	114.4	130.1	147.6	167.5	185.2	187.2	190.3

25
Index numbers of industrial production [cont.]
Indices de la production industrielle
1995 = 100 [suite]

Country or area and industry [ISIC Rev. 3] Pays ou zone et industrie [CITI Rév. 3]	1995	1996	1997	1998	1999	2000	2001	2002
Iran (Islamic Rep. of) Iran (Rép. islamique d')								
Total manufacturing [D]								
Total, industries manufacturières [D]	100.0	105.8	108.6	130.3	135.8	141.2	146.6	...
Food and beverages								
Aliments et boissons	100.0	109.2	119.2	123.5	131.7	139.3	133.8	...
Textiles, wearing apparel, leather, footwear								
Textiles, habillement, cuir et chaussures	100.0	107.0	109.5	104.9	102.0	97.7	98.9	...
Chemicals, rubber and plastic prod.								
Prod. chimiques, caoutchouc et plastiques	100.0	110.7	117.7	115.2	124.4	129.6	137.6	...
Metal products								
Produits métalliques	100.0	110.7	146.4	154.2	173.3	187.1	212.2	...
Israel Israël								
Total industry [CD]								
Total, industrie [CD]	100.0	105.4	107.2	110.2	111.8	123.1	116.4	113.6
Total manufacturing [D]								
Total, industries manufacturières [D]	100.0	105.4	107.3	110.3	112.0	123.6	116.7	113.6
Total mining [C]								
Total, industries extractives [C]	100.0	107.8	104.9	109.2	108.2	105.6	107.8	116.1
Food, beverages and tobacco								
Aliments, boissons et tabac	100.0	100.1	103.1	103.9	105.3	105.5	104.3	102.8
Textiles								
Textiles	100.0	94.6	94.6	97.7	102.3	96.6	88.4	85.4
Chemicals, petroleum, rubber and plastic products								
Prod. chimiques, pétroliers, caoutch. et plast.	100.0	108.2	108.8	119.1	118.1	122.1	124.4	136.4
Basic metals								
Métaux de base	100.0	105.9	107.4	101.1	100.6	102.5	95.2	86.6
Metal products								
Produits métalliques	100.0	104.9	107.5	106.6	104.4	114.4	108.7	106.0
Japan Japon								
Total industry [CDE]								
Total, industrie [CDE]	100.0	102.4	106.0	99.0	99.3	104.9	98.2	96.9
Total manufacturing [D]								
Total, industries manufacturières [D]	100.0	102.3	106.0	98.5	98.8	104.5	97.4	96.0
Total mining [C]								
Total, industries extractives [C]	100.0	101.4	92.8	86.4	85.6	86.3	86.0	80.8
Food, beverages and tobacco								
Aliments, boissons et tabac	100.0	100.9	100.4	97.8	98.6	99.0	98.2	94.8
Textiles, wearing apparel, leather, footwear								
Textiles, habillement, cuir et chaussures	100.0	96.4	92.6	82.4	77.1	70.9	63.9	56.7
Chemicals, petroleum, rubber and plastic products								
Prod. chimiques, pétroliers, caoutch. et plast.	100.0	101.0	104.0	100.5	103.1	104.2	103.4	102.9
Basic metals								
Métaux de base	100.0	99.1	103.7	92.0	91.5	100.1	97.0	98.5
Metal products								
Produits métalliques	100.0	105.2	110.3	102.7	105.7	117.5	104.7	105.8
Electricity and gas [E]								
Electricité et gaz [E]	100.0	103.2	105.6	106.8	108.6	112.2	112.4	113.3
Jordan Jordanie								
Total industry [CDE]								
Total, industrie [CDE]	100.0	94.8	99.6	102.1	102.5	106.5	117.2	129.7
Total manufacturing [D]								
Total, industries manufacturières [D]	100.0	95.2	100.9	104.1	102.0	107.3	120.7	134.9
Total mining [C]								
Total, industries extractives [C]	100.0	101.4	104.0	99.4	106.6	108.0	111.4	120.5
Food, beverages and tobacco								
Aliments, boissons et tabac	100.0	92.1	83.4	107.7	119.0	140.5	166.4	199.4
Textiles, wearing apparel, leather, footwear								
Textiles, habillement, cuir et chaussures	100.0	108.7	100.6	100.5	82.9	74.9	55.8	60.2
Chemicals, petroleum, rubber and plastic products								
Prod. chimiques, pétroliers, caoutch. et plast.	100.0	90.8	109.2	103.0	94.7	97.1	107.8	106.8

25

Index numbers of industrial production *[cont.]*

Indices de la production industrielle
1995 = 100 *[suite]*

Country or area and industry [ISIC Rev. 3] Pays ou zone et industrie [CITI Rév. 3]	1995	1996	1997	1998	1999	2000	2001	2002
Basic metals Métaux de base	100.0	108.7	78.1	64.4	75.3	70.7	88.1	84.2
Electricity [E] **Electricité [E]**	**100.0**	**107.2**	**112.1**	**123.9**	**130.1**	**131.2**	**134.6**	**142.3**
Korea, Republic of Corée, République de								
Total industry [CDE] **Total, industrie [CDE]**	**100.0**	**108.5**	**113.6**	**106.2**	**131.9**	**154.1**	**155.0**	**167.6**
Total manufacturing [D] **Total, industries manufacturières [D]**	**100.0**	**108.2**	**113.1**	**105.6**	**132.0**	**154.6**	**154.9**	**167.7**
Total mining [C] **Total, industries extractives [C]**	**100.0**	**98.1**	**94.0**	**72.7**	**78.6**	**77.5**	**77.4**	**80.4**
Food, beverages and tobacco Aliments, boissons et tabac	100.0	105.0	104.0	95.2	103.1	106.0	111.5	114.3
Textiles, wearing apparel, leather, footwear Textiles, habillement, cuir et chaussures	100.0	93.5	82.9	69.7	74.0	75.1	68.3	65.8
Chemicals, petroleum, rubber and plastic products Prod. chimiques, pétroliers, caoutch. et plast.	100.0	111.7	125.4	115.1	128.0	134.6	136.6	141.5
Basic metals Métaux de base	100.0	106.1	112.2	98.7	112.7	122.2	124.0	129.7
Metal products Produits métalliques	100.0	112.7	120.5	119.0	163.2	204.1	211.1	241.0
Electricity and gas [E] **Electricité et gaz [E]**	**100.0**	**112.3**	**123.2**	**119.0**	**133.7**	**149.9**	**160.3**	**172.4**
Malaysia Malaisie								
Total industry [CDE] **Total, industrie [CDE]**	**100.0**	**111.0**	**122.8**	**114.0**	**124.3**	**148.1**	**142.0**	**147.8**
Total manufacturing [D] **Total, industries manufacturières [D]**	**100.0**	**112.3**	**126.2**	**113.3**	**127.7**	**159.8**	**149.2**	**156.0**
Total mining [C] **Total, industries extractives [C]**	**100.0**	**105.9**	**108.4**	**109.6**	**106.1**	**105.9**	**108.8**	**110.7**
Food, beverages and tobacco Aliments, boissons et tabac	100.0	108.8	117.8	113.1	127.1	150.9	158.8	166.0
Textiles, wearing apparel, leather, footwear Textiles, habillement, cuir et chaussures	100.0	99.9	103.9	97.8	101.4	112.0	103.9	97.7
Chemicals, petroleum, rubber and plastic products Prod. chimiques, pétroliers, caoutch. et plast.	100.0	115.8	136.6	134.8	152.7	174.4	169.0	171.7
Basic metals Métaux de base	100.0	117.2	132.5	93.7	134.6	141.6	140.8	144.1
Metal products Produits métalliques	100.0	110.8	125.4	111.1	128.2	179.4	155.9	167.9
Electricity [E] **Electricité [E]**	**100.0**	**112.8**	**128.8**	**133.2**	**138.3**	**146.8**	**160.6**	**166.1**
Mongolia Mongolie								
Total industry [CDE] **Total, industrie [CDE]**	**100.0**	**97.5**	**101.9**	**186.2**	**106.7**	**108.9**	**121.9**	**122.7**
Total manufacturing [D] **Total, industries manufacturières [D]**	**100.0**	**89.5**	**82.1**	**73.3**	**71.1**	**65.9**	**81.1**	**97.8**
Total mining [C] **Total, industries extractives [C]**	**100.0**	**107.3**	**125.5**	**116.5**	**121.0**	**128.1**	**141.1**	**128.0**
Food and beverages Aliments et boissons	100.0	75.5	70.8	69.6	60.7	59.5	70.4	66.1
Textiles, wearing apparel, leather, footwear Textiles, habillement, cuir et chaussures	100.0	92.1	80.8	80.6	88.4	83.0	121.6	149.5
Chemicals and chemical products Produits chimiques	100.0	97.4	96.1	103.0	108.0	108.4	117.3	135.4
Basic metals Métaux de base	100.0	92.9	167.3	143.1	145.1	133.3	158.9	254.3
Electricity and gas [E] **Electricité et gaz [E]**	**100.0**	**96.2**	**93.7**	**98.1**	**101.1**	**103.6**	**108.4**	**103.0**

25

Index numbers of industrial production *[cont.]*

Indices de la production industrielle
1995 = 100 *[suite]*

Country or area and industry [ISIC Rev. 3] Pays ou zone et industrie [CITI Rév. 3]	1995	1996	1997	1998	1999	2000	2001	2002
Pakistan[1] Pakistan[1]								
Total industry [CDE]								
Total, industrie [CDE]	100.0	97.9	104.7	107.4	108.0	115.2	122.9	...
Total manufacturing [D]								
Total, industries manufacturières [D]	100.0	97.9	105.3	109.1	109.1	118.4	124.6	...
Total mining [C]								
Total, industries extractives [C]	100.0	102.1	96.1	101.0	104.1	113.1	112.2	...
Electricity [E]								
Electricité [E]	100.0	96.7	105.1	100.5	103.9	98.2	117.5	...
Singapore Singapour								
Total manufacturing [D]								
Total, industries manufacturières [D]	100.0	103.3	108.1	107.6	122.5	141.3	125.0	135.5
Food, beverages and tobacco								
Aliments, boissons et tabac	100.0	101.8	98.9	87.8	92.0	93.5	97.5	94.7
Textiles, wearing apparel, leather, footwear								
Textiles, habillement, cuir et chaussures	100.0	81.1	79.1	84.4	88.1	101.0	86.3	72.6
Chemicals, petroleum, rubber and plastic products								
Prod. chimiques, pétroliers, caoutch. et plast.	100.0	104.2	119.7	136.0	159.9	168.7	174.4	230.8
Basic metals								
Métaux de base	100.0	100.1	105.2	87.3	92.7	98.4	99.4	102.7
Metal products								
Produits métalliques	100.0	98.8	102.3	100.0	114.5	138.2	115.7	120.7
Sri Lanka Sri Lanka								
Total manufacturing [D]								
Total, industries manufacturières [D]	100.0	93.5	91.0	85.9	92.0	...	...	...
Food, beverages and tobacco								
Aliments, boissons et tabac	100.0	89.3	89.4	83.0	93.3	...	...	...
Textiles, wearing apparel, leather, footwear								
Textiles, habillement, cuir et chaussures	100.0	98.1	106.4	106.3	116.4	...	...	...
Chemicals, petroleum, rubber and plastic products								
Prod. chimiques, pétroliers, caoutch. et plast.	100.0	120.0	95.1	93.3	100.2	...	...	...
Basic metals								
Métaux de base	100.0	95.8	90.7	71.0	66.4	...	...	...
Metal products								
Produits métalliques	100.0	95.6	120.1	115.7	116.2	...	...	...
Syrian Arab Republic Rép. arabe syrienne								
Total industry [CDE]								
Total, industrie [CDE]	100.0	101.0	107.0	109.0	109.0	109.0	112.3	118.8
Total manufacturing [D]								
Total, industries manufacturières [D]	100.0	101.0	109.0	110.0	110.0	109.0	105.7	110.1
Total mining [C]								
Total, industries extractives [C]	100.0	100.0	101.0	102.0	101.0	97.0	93.1	95.1
Food, beverages and tobacco								
Aliments, boissons et tabac	100.0	101.3	108.0	102.1	108.3	107.6	112.4	123.9
Textiles, wearing apparel, leather, footwear								
Textiles, habillement, cuir et chaussures	100.0	98.7	106.9	108.3	113.7	126.3	134.9	140.5
Chemicals, petroleum, rubber and plastic products								
Prod. chimiques, pétroliers, caoutch. et plast.	100.0	95.4	109.6	109.3	95.1	95.1	112.9	109.0
Basic metals								
Métaux de base	100.0	146.0	163.0	159.0	147.0	138.0	150.4	131.1
Metal products								
Produits métalliques	100.0	96.3	88.9	85.4	93.2	60.6	107.4	90.4
Electricity and water [E]								
Electricité et eau [E]	100.0	108.0	115.0	129.0	142.0	155.0	164.3	176.5
Tajikistan Tadjikistan								
Total industry [CDE]								
Total, industrie [CDE]	100.0	76.7	74.4	81.4	86.0	95.3	109.3	...
Total manufacturing [D]								
Total, industries manufacturières [D]	100.0	73.2	65.9	68.3	78.0	85.4	100.0	...
Total mining [C]								
Total, industries extractives [C]	100.0	96.9	118.8	131.3	131.3	125.0	129.7	...

25

Index numbers of industrial production *[cont.]*

Indices de la production industrielle
1995 = 100 *[suite]*

Country or area and industry [ISIC Rev. 3] Pays ou zone et industrie [CITI Rév. 3]	1995	1996	1997	1998	1999	2000	2001	2002
Electricity, gas and water [E] Electricité, gaz et eau [E]	100.0	97.9	109.5	112.6	126.3	112.6	116.8	...
Thailand Thaïlande								
Total manufacturing [D] Total, industries manufacturières [D]	100.0	108.3	107.8	96.5	108.6	111.9	113.5	123.2
Turkey Turquie								
Total industry [CDE] Total, industrie [CDE]	100.0	105.9	117.2	118.3	112.3	118.4	107.9	117.7
Total manufacturing [D] Total, industries manufacturières [D]	100.0	106.5	118.8	118.4	111.6	118.1	106.5	117.8
Total mining [C] Total, industries extractives [C]	100.0	103.3	109.4	120.2	110.0	105.1	96.8	87.6
Food, beverages and tobacco Aliments, boissons et tabac	100.0	109.4	118.1	120.4	119.2	124.3	122.3	126.2
Textiles, wearing apparel, leather, footwear Textiles, habillement, cuir et chaussures	100.0	108.3	115.1	111.6	105.0	114.2	108.4	118.8
Chemicals, petroleum, rubber and plastic products Prod. chimiques, pétroliers, caoutch. et plast.	100.0	105.0	118.5	120.4	118.3	123.1	116.2	130.4
Basic metals Métaux de base	100.0	107.7	118.1	118.7	116.5	120.9	114.9	126.4
Metal products Produits métalliques	100.0	115.1	140.4	138.5	127.6	148.2	115.0	143.9
Electricity, gas and water [E] Electricité, gaz et eau [E]	100.0	110.5	119.6	128.7	135.0	144.9	142.3	150.0

Europe · Europe

Country or area and industry	1995	1996	1997	1998	1999	2000	2001	2002
Albania Albanie								
Total industry [CDE] Total, industrie [CDE]	100.0	82.8	53.6	82.5	59.7	121.3	91.3	...
Total manufacturing [D] Total, industries manufacturières [D]	100.0	81.1	74.8	68.5	77.7	116.0	77.6	...
Total mining [C] Total, industries extractives [C]	100.0	87.7	54.5	56.2	41.4	36.4	32.1	...
Electricity, gas and water [E] Electricité, gaz et eau [E]	100.0	131.1	116.0	114.6	121.5	104.5	81.5	...
Austria Autriche								
Total industry [CDE] Total, industrie [CDE]	100.0	101.0	107.4	116.2	123.2	134.1	138.0	138.1
Total manufacturing [D] Total, industries manufacturières [D]	100.0	100.7	108.0	117.8	124.9	137.3	139.8	139.9
Total mining [C] Total, industries extractives [C]	100.0	100.2	96.7	103.9	107.4	112.3	109.4	112.9
Food, beverages and tobacco Aliments, boissons et tabac	100.0	100.0	108.4	113.2	117.1	121.2	122.7	126.4
Textiles, wearing apparel, leather, footwear Textiles, habillement, cuir et chaussures	100.0	94.3	95.3	97.5	90.8	88.9	86.8	86.0
Chemicals, petroleum, rubber and plastic products Prod. chimiques, pétroliers, caoutch. et plast.	100.0	101.0	103.7	112.1	116.8	126.6	131.5	127.2
Basic metals Métaux de base	100.0	96.3	111.2	114.6	113.9	126.5	134.0	135.5
Metal products Produits métalliques	100.0	102.6	111.5	128.4	142.3	162.2	164.3	166.5
Electricity, gas and water [E] Electricité, gaz et eau [E]	100.0	102.9	104.8	106.6	112.9	114.6	129.0	137.3
Belarus Bélarus								
Total industry [CDE] Total, industrie [CDE]	100.0	103.5	123.0	138.3	152.5	164.4	173.3	181.9
Total manufacturing [D] Total, industries manufacturières [D]	100.0	104.3	125.6	143.9	159.8	174.3	184.4	194.0
Total mining [C] Total, industries extractives [C]	100.0	99.0	111.7	118.6	123.9	117.5	131.6	134.8

25

Index numbers of industrial production *[cont.]*
Indices de la production industrielle
1995 = 100 *[suite]*

Country or area and industry [ISIC Rev. 3] Pays ou zone et industrie [CITI Rév. 3]	1995	1996	1997	1998	1999	2000	2001	2002
Electricity [E]								
Electricité [E]	100.0	98.4	103.9	96.2	101.4	98.6	97.4	100.6
Belgium Belgique								
Total industry [CDE]								
Total, industrie [CDE]	100.0	100.8	105.4	108.9	110.1	115.5	115.0	116.7
Total manufacturing [D]								
Total, industries manufacturières [D]	100.0	100.5	105.4	108.4	109.7	116.2	116.1	117.1
Total mining [C]								
Total, industries extractives [C]	100.0	106.7	113.4	116.6	125.2	138.1	139.5	182.2
Food, beverages and tobacco								
Aliments, boissons et tabac	100.0	100.4	105.0	107.3	103.0	107.3	111.3	117.3
Textiles, wearing apparel, leather, footwear								
Textiles, habillement, cuir et chaussures	100.0	91.3	93.9	91.0	85.2	87.0	83.2	80.4
Chemicals, petroleum, rubber and plastic products								
Prod. chimiques, pétroliers, caoutch. et plast.	100.0	103.3	113.7	115.1	122.5	134.9	131.8	140.3
Basic metals								
Métaux de base	100.0	97.8	98.2	101.2	101.5	106.9	94.7	95.5
Metal products								
Produits métalliques	100.0	101.2	105.3	111.8	112.3	119.2	122.1	116.8
Electricity, gas and water [E]								
Electricité, gaz et eau [E]	100.0	103.6	105.6	112.7	112.8	109.8	106.9	109.6
Bulgaria Bulgarie								
Total industry [CDE]								
Total, industrie [CDE]	100.0	105.1	85.8	78.5	72.2	78.2	79.9	83.6
Total manufacturing [D]								
Total, industries manufacturières [D]	100.0	104.8	84.2	74.8	69.7	74.7	75.7	81.3
Total mining [C]								
Total, industries extractives [C]	100.0	115.5	93.3	90.9	78.6	80.7	73.7	73.3
Food, beverages and tobacco								
Aliments, boissons et tabac	100.0	102.0	75.5	78.2	73.8	73.3	71.1	71.9
Textiles, wearing apparel, leather, footwear								
Textiles, habillement, cuir et chaussures	100.0	114.0	91.8	87.9	75.2	85.5	94.1	115.7
Chemicals, petroleum, rubber and plastic products								
Prod. chimiques, pétroliers, caoutch. et plast.	100.0	113.4	84.4	61.9	61.7	69.7	70.7	67.7
Basic metals								
Métaux de base	100.0	102.8	100.7	82.7	69.6	80.9	67.7	72.9
Metal products								
Produits métalliques	100.0	96.6	87.2	84.0	71.4	72.3	76.5	87.9
Electricity, gas and water [E]								
Electricité, gaz et eau [E]	100.0	101.6	98.6	109.2	95.0	112.3	121.7	120.0
Croatia Croatie								
Total industry [CDE]								
Total, industrie [CDE]	100.0	103.0	110.0	114.2	112.5	114.4	121.3	127.9
Total manufacturing [D]								
Total, industries manufacturières [D]	100.0	101.2	105.2	108.6	105.4	108.5	115.4	120.5
Total mining [C]								
Total, industries extractives [C]	100.0	97.0	96.6	94.2	96.0	97.8	99.7	116.7
Food, beverages and tobacco								
Aliments, boissons et tabac	100.0	102.9	95.8	99.1	94.1	94.3	100.5	106.1
Textiles, wearing apparel, leather, footwear								
Textiles, habillement, cuir et chaussures	100.0	87.8	89.1	88.3	79.4	78.4	82.1	74.4
Chemicals, petroleum, rubber and plastic products								
Prod. chimiques, pétroliers, caoutch. et plast.	100.0	96.6	91.6	88.8	91.5	96.7	92.4	96.8
Basic metals								
Métaux de base	100.0	91.0	114.1	133.3	115.6	120.6	125.7	113.3
Metal products								
Produits métalliques	100.0	101.0	111.4	118.4	120.4	121.1	137.0	143.6
Electricity, gas and water [E]								
Electricité, gaz et eau [E]	100.0	125.3	155.7	169.3	181.0	172.4	180.7	183.8

25

Index numbers of industrial production *[cont.]*

Indices de la production industrielle

1995 = 100 *[suite]*

Country or area and industry [ISIC Rev. 3] Pays ou zone et industrie [CITI Rév. 3]	1995	1996	1997	1998	1999	2000	2001	2002
Czech Republic République tchèque								
Total industry [CDE] **Total, industrie [CDE]**	**100.0**	**102.0**	**106.5**	**108.2**	**104.7**	**105.7**	**117.6**	**123.2**
Total manufacturing [D] **Total, industries manufacturières [D]**	**100.0**	**101.6**	**108.1**	**110.9**	**107.9**	**108.2**	**121.8**	**128.4**
Total mining [C] **Total, industries extractives [C]**	**100.0**	**101.4**	**98.5**	**92.8**	**81.6**	**88.2**	**89.4**	**89.7**
Food, beverages and tobacco Aliments, boissons et tabac	100.0	103.8	108.0	107.8	107.2	103.4	104.9	108.4
Textiles, wearing apparel, leather, footwear Textiles, habillement, cuir et chaussures	100.0	94.0	95.4	92.0	81.1	90.4	92.7	89.9
Chemicals, petroleum, rubber and plastic products Prod. chimiques, pétroliers, caoutch. et plast.	100.0	104.6	108.0	107.1	105.1	101.5	117.8	125.1
Basic metals Métaux de base	100.0	88.8	92.6	86.2	69.0	58.7	60.5	59.5
Metal products Produits métalliques	100.0	110.4	125.2	139.9	145.9	157.1	191.1	201.3
Electricity, gas and water [E] **Électricité, gaz et eau [E]**	**100.0**	**103.7**	**100.9**	**99.4**	**95.9**	**102.1**	**103.8**	**103.9**
Denmark Danemark								
Total industry [CD] **Total, industrie [CD]**	**100.0**	**101.4**	**106.2**	**109.4**	**109.6**	**115.5**	**117.2**	**119.2**
Total manufacturing [D] **Total, industries manufacturières [D]**	**100.0**	**101.3**	**106.4**	**109.5**	**109.7**	**115.6**	**117.9**	**119.1**
Total mining [C] **Total, industries extractives [C]**	**100.0**	**100.8**	**87.8**	**93.0**	**93.5**	**93.8**	**92.3**	**97.6**
Food, beverages and tobacco Aliments, boissons et tabac	100.0	98.6	103.1	98.3	101.6	103.3	103.3	111.0
Textiles, wearing apparel, leather, footwear Textiles, habillement, cuir et chaussures	100.0	103.6	102.8	105.1	101.1	103.2	93.4	88.2
Chemicals, petroleum, rubber and plastic products Prod. chimiques, pétroliers, caoutch. et plast.	100.0	105.9	111.6	116.1	130.7	141.7	152.3	155.4
Basic metals Métaux de base	100.0	95.3	103.4	107.0	98.0	120.3	109.1	82.6
Metal products Produits métalliques	100.0	101.7	106.7	112.8	109.3	116.1	121.4	123.3
Estonia Estonie								
Total industry [CDE] **Total, industrie [CDE]**	**100.0**	**102.9**	**117.9**	**122.8**	**118.6**	**135.9**	**148.0**	**156.8**
Total manufacturing [D] **Total, industries manufacturières [D]**	**100.0**	**102.2**	**121.1**	**127.9**	**124.7**	**145.4**	**159.9**	**169.8**
Total mining [C] **Total, industries extractives [C]**	**100.0**	**105.7**	**105.3**	**100.8**	**86.9**	**91.3**	**94.8**	**109.8**
Food, beverages and tobacco Aliments, boissons et tabac	100.0	92.9	108.7	103.4	83.1	89.0	97.7	97.2
Textiles, wearing apparel, leather, footwear Textiles, habillement, cuir et chaussures	100.0	115.0	127.5	134.0	135.6	160.7	179.5	194.6
Chemicals, rubber and plastic prod. Prod. chimiques, caoutchouc et plastiques	100.0	105.8	126.1	123.7	115.7	133.8	161.6	173.2
Basic metals Métaux de base	100.0	75.5	111.3	167.3	162.6	181.3	277.9	400.6
Metal products Produits métalliques	100.0	102.9	122.0	141.2	149.4	188.3	203.5	231.6
Electricity and gas [E] **Électricité et gaz [E]**	**100.0**	**106.3**	**103.0**	**99.3**	**93.8**	**94.3**	**95.4**	**96.6**
Finland Finlande								
Total industry [CDE] **Total, industrie [CDE]**	**100.0**	**102.9**	**111.8**	**122.1**	**129.0**	**144.3**	**144.4**	**146.9**
Total manufacturing [D] **Total, industries manufacturières [D]**	**100.0**	**102.5**	**111.8**	**123.5**	**130.9**	**147.9**	**147.2**	**149.7**

25

Index numbers of industrial production *[cont.]*

Indices de la production industrielle
1995 = 100 *[suite]*

Country or area and industry [ISIC Rev. 3] Pays ou zone et industrie [CITI Rév. 3]	1995	1996	1997	1998	1999	2000	2001	2002
Total mining [C]								
Total, industries extractives [C]	**100.0**	**100.6**	**127.0**	**92.7**	**128.1**	**99.4**	**120.0**	**129.4**
Food, beverages and tobacco								
Aliments, boissons et tabac	100.0	103.2	106.3	106.8	110.7	109.3	113.4	114.5
Textiles, wearing apparel, leather, footwear								
Textiles, habillement, cuir et chaussures	100.0	100.8	101.4	100.5	100.4	98.3	100.2	93.8
Chemicals, petroleum, rubber and plastic products								
Prod. chimiques, pétroliers, caoutch. et plast.	100.0	103.0	108.2	114.5	117.2	127.7	127.1	124.7
Basic metals								
Métaux de base	100.0	105.7	112.0	118.2	122.5	129.4	129.0	128.5
Metal products								
Produits métalliques	100.0	106.7	118.1	140.1	154.2	191.3	194.0	199.9
Electricity, gas and water [E]								
Electricité, gaz et eau [E]	**100.0**	**108.9**	**108.7**	**110.2**	**109.9**	**110.7**	**116.9**	**118.7**
France France								
Total industry [CDE]								
Total, industrie [CDE]	**100.0**	**100.9**	**104.7**	**110.2**	**112.3**	**116.3**	**117.6**	**116.4**
Total manufacturing [D]								
Total, industries manufacturières [D]	**100.0**	**100.6**	**105.4**	**111.6**	**113.7**	**117.8**	**118.8**	**117.5**
Total mining [C]								
Total, industries extractives [C]	**100.0**	**91.7**	**89.5**	**88.8**	**89.8**	**91.3**	**89.5**	**84.5**
Food, beverages and tobacco								
Aliments, boissons et tabac	100.0	102.0	104.8	105.9	107.7	107.1	107.9	109.5
Textiles, wearing apparel, leather, footwear								
Textiles, habillement, cuir et chaussures	100.0	88.2	86.0	83.4	75.3	69.0	64.4	57.3
Chemicals, petroleum, rubber and plastic products								
Prod. chimiques, pétroliers, caoutch. et plast.	100.0	102.0	106.9	112.4	114.4	120.1	122.6	122.1
Basic metals								
Métaux de base	100.0	97.4	105.1	108.1	105.9	112.8	109.3	107.8
Metal products								
Produits métalliques	100.0	102.3	108.9	118.9	123.6	128.8	131.0	129.6
Electricity, gas and water [E]								
Electricité, gaz et eau [E]	**100.0**	**103.7**	**101.8**	**102.8**	**105.2**	**108.6**	**112.2**	**112.1**
Germany Allemagne								
Total industry [CDE]								
Total, industrie [CDE]	**100.0**	**100.7**	**104.4**	**108.7**	**110.4**	**117.2**	**117.8**	**116.2**
Total manufacturing [D]								
Total, industries manufacturières [D]	**100.0**	**100.5**	**104.8**	**109.7**	**111.5**	**119.2**	**120.0**	**118.2**
Total mining [C]								
Total, industries extractives [C]	**100.0**	**94.4**	**91.3**	**85.0**	**84.1**	**78.7**	**73.3**	**72.4**
Food, beverages and tobacco								
Aliments, boissons et tabac	100.0	101.3	102.4	101.9	104.7	107.5	106.5	106.8
Textiles, wearing apparel, leather, footwear								
Textiles, habillement, cuir et chaussures	100.0	93.0	90.6	89.0	82.1	81.2	77.8	71.4
Chemicals, petroleum, rubber and plastic products								
Prod. chimiques, pétroliers, caoutch. et plast.	100.0	103.1	108.6	110.4	114.1	118.2	116.0	121.2
Basic metals								
Métaux de base	100.0	94.7	103.8	104.7	101.2	108.7	108.8	111.2
Metal products								
Produits métalliques	100.0	100.9	106.1	114.7	116.7	129.7	132.8	128.0
Electricity and gas [E]								
Electricité et gaz [E]	**100.0**	**105.5**	**104.7**	**104.8**	**105.2**	**106.4**	**106.0**	**106.4**
Greece Grèce								
Total industry [CDE]								
Total, industrie [CDE]	**100.0**	**100.9**	**102.8**	**112.0**	**114.2**	**122.5**	**123.8**	**125.9**
Total manufacturing [D]								
Total, industries manufacturières [D]	**100.0**	**99.6**	**101.9**	**110.2**	**109.2**	**114.8**	**117.0**	**118.2**
Total mining [C]								
Total, industries extractives [C]	**100.0**	**103.6**	**103.9**	**102.6**	**96.4**	**109.3**	**107.7**	**117.5**
Food, beverages and tobacco								
Aliments, boissons et tabac	100.0	97.9	102.4	111.8	111.6	113.5	116.0	117.4

25

Index numbers of industrial production *[cont.]*

Indices de la production industrielle
1995 = 100 *[suite]*

Country or area and industry [ISIC Rev. 3] Pays ou zone et industrie [CITI Rév. 3]	1995	1996	1997	1998	1999	2000	2001	2002
Textiles, wearing apparel, leather, footwear Textiles, habillement, cuir et chaussures	100.0	94.3	92.7	91.4	85.9	86.6	83.2	79.5
Chemicals, petroleum, rubber and plastic products Prod. chimiques, pétroliers, caoutch. et plast.	100.0	108.1	110.7	124.8	121.6	130.9	137.4	145.2
Basic metals Métaux de base	100.0	97.8	106.2	98.3	109.7	125.5	127.4	135.1
Metal products Produits métalliques	100.0	97.8	97.5	108.0	110.4	119.1	122.5	118.0
Electricity and gas [E] Electricité et gaz [E]	100.0	103.8	104.5	120.0	135.1	151.0	149.9	152.8
Hungary Hongrie								
Total industry [CDE] Total, industrie [CDE]	100.0	103.4	114.8	129.0	142.7	168.7	175.2	181.0
Total manufacturing [D] Total, industries manufacturières [D]	100.0	103.4	118.5	137.7	154.6	186.5	194.4	201.3
Total mining [C] Total, industries extractives [C]	100.0	102.5	93.9	74.7	75.1	68.2	79.4	71.9
Food, beverages and tobacco Aliments, boissons et tabac	100.0	99.6	92.4	93.1	95.3	101.6	100.8	102.7
Textiles, wearing apparel, leather, footwear Textiles, habillement, cuir et chaussures	100.0	97.3	98.9	112.4	121.6	133.8	136.7	130.0
Chemicals, petroleum, rubber and plastic products Prod. chimiques, pétroliers, caoutch. et plast.	100.0	97.3	101.7	105.9	100.2	107.6	109.8	114.4
Basic metals Métaux de base	100.0	109.4	122.4	118.8	113.5	132.2	127.8	133.2
Metal products Produits métalliques	100.0	111.2	158.7	216.4	297.8	402.2	407.5	421.9
Electricity and gas [E] Electricité et gaz [E]	100.0	105.0	106.0	105.9	104.4	101.6	102.1	106.0
Ireland Irlande								
Total industry [CDE] Total, industrie [CDE]	100.0	107.6	127.0	152.1	174.6	201.5	222.2	239.5
Total manufacturing [D] Total, industries manufacturières [D]	100.0	108.0	129.5	157.0	180.6	209.1	231.3	250.4
Total mining [C] Total, industries extractives [C]	100.0	98.4	84.2	77.6	92.3	113.6	108.3	94.2
Food, beverages and tobacco Aliments, boissons et tabac	100.0	101.6	103.8	109.1	114.4	120.5	126.1	130.9
Textiles, wearing apparel, leather, footwear Textiles, habillement, cuir et chaussures	100.0	100.5	100.3	102.1	90.0	73.6	75.6	54.1
Chemicals, rubber and plastic prod. Prod. chimiques, caoutchouc et plastiques	100.0	115.9	157.3	218.9	273.1	310.3	376.2	463.6
Basic metals Métaux de base	100.0	98.5	95.0	93.6	92.0	94.2	85.6	87.1
Metal products Produits métalliques	100.0	108.8	126.0	143.9	161.6	213.5	220.7	200.4
Electricity, gas and water [E] Electricité, gaz et eau [E]	100.0	105.7	110.2	113.3	122.9	129.3	137.8	142.5
Italy Italie								
Total industry [CDE] Total, industrie [CDE]	100.0	99.1	102.4	104.3	104.4	107.7	106.8	105.3
Total manufacturing [D] Total, industries manufacturières [D]	100.0	98.9	102.2	103.9	103.6	106.7	105.8	104.4
Total mining [C] Total, industries extractives [C]	100.0	102.4	108.5	107.9	107.8	98.4	90.8	104.4
Food, beverages and tobacco Aliments, boissons et tabac	100.0	99.7	102.2	104.4	107.6	109.9	114.1	115.0
Textiles, wearing apparel, leather, footwear Textiles, habillement, cuir et chaussures	100.0	98.8	102.1	99.9	95.2	95.6	95.3	88.5
Chemicals, petroleum, rubber and plastic products Prod. chimiques, pétroliers, caoutch. et plast.	100.0	99.6	105.2	106.8	106.3	108.4	106.4	107.0

25

Index numbers of industrial production *[cont.]*
Indices de la production industrielle
1995 = 100 *[suite]*

Country or area and industry [ISIC Rev. 3] Pays ou zone et industrie [CITI Rév. 3]	1995	1996	1997	1998	1999	2000	2001	2002
Basic metals								
Métaux de base	100.0	99.9	102.0	101.8	94.1	100.8	97.3	96.2
Metal products								
Produits métalliques	100.0	99.4	102.2	104.0	102.5	106.5	104.4	101.6
Electricity and gas [E]								
Electricité et gaz [E]	100.0	100.6	103.4	107.3	111.4	118.3	117.2	120.8
Latvia Lettonie								
Total industry [CDE]								
Total, industrie [CDE]	100.0	105.5	120.1	123.8	101.7	104.9	112.1	118.6
Total manufacturing [D]								
Total, industries manufacturières [D]	100.0	107.3	125.6	130.2	103.6	108.4	116.5	123.8
Total mining [C]								
Total, industries extractives [C]	100.0	102.4	110.4	117.2	123.9	134.9	141.4	154.2
Food, beverages and tobacco								
Aliments, boissons et tabac	100.0	111.6	127.7	124.0	102.0	100.6	107.0	113.9
Textiles, wearing apparel, leather, footwear								
Textiles, habillement, cuir et chaussures	100.0	126.5	138.9	140.8	121.3	133.1	137.9	136.8
Chemicals, rubber and plastic prod.								
Prod. chimiques, caoutchouc et plastiques	100.0	98.1	115.6	105.5	56.5	48.7	54.7	63.2
Basic metals								
Métaux de base	100.0	99.7	139.7	237.6	325.9	325.8	379.9	373.4
Metal products								
Produits métalliques	100.0	92.8	103.2	91.7	72.9	91.3	94.5	102.7
Electricity, gas and water [E]								
Electricité, gaz et eau [E]	100.0	98.1	97.4	98.5	92.5	89.8	94.6	98.8
Lithuania Lituanie								
Total industry [CDE]								
Total, industrie [CDE]	100.0	104.1	108.9	117.8	104.6	110.1	127.7	131.6
Total manufacturing [D]								
Total, industries manufacturières [D]	100.0	100.9	106.6	115.4	102.8	111.9	129.6	133.3
Total mining [C]								
Total, industries extractives [C]	100.0	122.0	136.3	185.7	177.1	198.1	263.1	250.8
Food, beverages and tobacco								
Aliments, boissons et tabac	100.0	100.0	102.9	107.1	97.6	103.6	106.1	103.9
Textiles, wearing apparel, leather, footwear								
Textiles, habillement, cuir et chaussures	100.0	108.3	111.6	109.9	111.9	121.3	132.1	131.0
Chemicals, petroleum, rubber and plastic products								
Prod. chimiques, pétroliers, caoutch. et plast.	100.0	111.9	120.7	137.5	134.2	143.0	143.6	169.2
Basic metals								
Métaux de base	100.0	75.4	69.2	79.3	172.2	255.8	265.3	211.0
Metal products								
Produits métalliques	100.0	100.1	103.2	114.4	117.3	134.5	153.2	180.9
Electricity, gas and water [E]								
Electricité, gaz et eau [E]	100.0	106.7	96.8	99.9	80.7	68.7	79.1	83.3
Luxembourg Luxembourg								
Total industry [CDE]								
Total, industrie [CDE]	100.0	100.1	105.3	114.5	116.3	122.1	126.1	126.3
Total manufacturing [D]								
Total, industries manufacturières [D]	100.0	100.3	106.1	115.7	117.7	123.6	127.8	127.5
Total mining [C]								
Total, industries extractives [C]	100.0	89.9	89.4	100.2	107.8	108.8	111.0	101.2
Food and beverages								
Aliments et boissons	100.0	99.5	99.6	101.2	105.6	106.6	115.1	118.5
Textiles, wearing apparel, leather, footwear								
Textiles, habillement, cuir et chaussures	100.0	81.4	93.2	98.8	91.6	98.4	100.5	102.9
Chemicals, rubber and plastic prod.								
Prod. chimiques, caoutchouc et plastiques	100.0	104.5	109.9	129.6	119.5	128.3	139.0	145.6
Basic metals								
Métaux de base	100.0	93.7	102.9	90.1	114.2	120.6	118.4	109.6
Metal products								
Produits métalliques	100.0	106.4	106.9	121.6	122.0	122.5	125.9	123.3

25

Index numbers of industrial production *[cont.]*

Indices de la production industrielle
1995 = 100 *[suite]*

Country or area and industry [ISIC Rev. 3] Pays ou zone et industrie [CITI Rév. 3]	1995	1996	1997	1998	1999	2000	2001	2002
Electricity and gas [E] Electricité et gaz [E]	100.0	99.2	98.2	102.0	99.8	106.9	107.2	116.2
Malta Malte								
Total industry [CDE] Total, industrie [CDE]	100.0	95.3	...	...	...	...	...	...
Total manufacturing [D] Total, industries manufacturières [D]	100.0	93.8	...	...	...	...	...	...
Total mining [C] Total, industries extractives [C]	100.0	111.1	...	...	...	...	...	...
Food, beverages and tobacco Aliments, boissons et tabac	100.0	104.5	...	...	...	...	...	...
Textiles, wearing apparel, leather, footwear Textiles, habillement, cuir et chaussures	100.0	107.7	...	...	...	...	...	...
Chemicals, petroleum, rubber and plastic products Prod. chimiques, pétroliers, caoutch. et plast.	100.0	101.8	...	...	...	...	...	...
Metal products Produits métalliques	100.0	90.6	...	...	...	...	...	...
Electricity and water [E] Electricité et eau [E]	100.0	103.7	...	...	...	...	...	...
Netherlands Pays-Bas								
Total industry [CDE] Total, industrie [CDE]	100.0	102.4	102.6	104.9	106.3	110.6	112.1	109.8
Total manufacturing [D] Total, industries manufacturières [D]	100.0	100.6	103.1	106.2	108.8	114.2	114.4	111.3
Total mining [C] Total, industries extractives [C]	100.0	113.5	104.2	103.3	100.0	97.5	103.4	103.8
Food, beverages and tobacco Aliments, boissons et tabac	100.0	101.7	102.1	102.1	103.8	105.4	107.3	106.9
Textiles, wearing apparel, leather, footwear Textiles, habillement, cuir et chaussures	100.0	99.5	99.8	103.9	105.0	108.1	101.7	98.9
Chemicals, petroleum, rubber and plastic products Prod. chimiques, pétroliers, caoutch. et plast.	100.0	97.5	99.3	100.2	105.1	112.3	115.8	119.4
Basic metals Métaux de base	100.0	97.7	105.5	107.6	108.0	110.4	108.2	106.2
Metal products Produits métalliques	100.0	102.1	105.7	110.1	111.8	121.8	120.0	111.5
Electricity, gas and water [E] Electricité, gaz et eau [E]	100.0	104.9	97.6	97.9	96.0	97.4	103.3	103.0
Norway Norvège								
Total industry [CDE] Total, industrie [CDE]	100.0	105.4	109.0	108.3	108.1	111.2	110.9	110.8
Total manufacturing [D] Total, industries manufacturières [D]	100.0	102.8	106.2	109.4	107.0	104.1	103.1	102.4
Total mining [C] [10] Total, industries extractives [C] [10]	100.0	99.5	103.3	99.4	98.3	101.7	107.1	102.4
Food, beverages and tobacco Aliments, boissons et tabac	100.0	101.9	102.9	102.1	98.8	97.1	96.3	95.0
Textiles, wearing apparel, leather, footwear Textiles, habillement, cuir et chaussures	100.0	101.3	99.9	95.1	83.1	76.4	72.5	66.4
Chemicals, petroleum, rubber and plastic products Prod. chimiques, pétroliers, caoutch. et plast.	100.0	101.9	103.3	105.7	105.9	104.3	104.2	103.7
Basic metals Métaux de base	100.0	102.8	106.6	112.0	115.5	116.7	111.7	110.3
Metal products Produits métalliques	100.0	103.9	108.1	117.3	115.2	109.6	109.9	112.3
Electricity and gas [E] Electricité et gaz [E]	100.0	85.1	90.8	95.1	99.8	116.0	99.0	106.4
Poland Pologne								
Total industry [CDE] Total, industrie [CDE]	100.0	109.4	121.7	127.4	133.5	143.5	144.1	146.1

25

Index numbers of industrial production *[cont.]*

Indices de la production industrielle
1995 = 100 *[suite]*

Country or area and industry [ISIC Rev. 3] Pays ou zone et industrie [CITI Rév. 3]	1995	1996	1997	1998	1999	2000	2001	2002
Total manufacturing [D] Total, industries manufacturières [D]	100.0	111.5	126.6	134.9	142.4	153.7	153.5	156.4
Total mining [C] Total, industries extractives [C]	100.0	101.3	99.7	86.6	83.2	82.1	77.9	75.5
Food, beverages and tobacco Aliments, boissons et tabac	100.0	111.9	118.3	127.0	129.0	130.1	133.9	138.5
Textiles, wearing apparel, leather, footwear Textiles, habillement, cuir et chaussures	100.0	108.5	118.1	120.0	115.9	114.5	110.3	109.4
Chemicals, petroleum, rubber and plastic products Prod. chimiques, pétroliers, caoutch. et plast.	100.0	108.3	121.3	124.9	132.8	147.1	153.2	163.0
Basic metals Métaux de base	100.0	100.3	112.9	107.2	97.2	106.5	89.8	85.8
Metal products Produits métalliques	100.0	116.6	136.6	152.3	163.8	180.1	181.1	187.2
Electricity, gas and water [E] Electricité, gaz et eau [E]	100.0	100.4	102.8	104.7	107.1	116.9	126.3	126.2
Portugal Portugal								
Total industry [CDE] Total, industrie [CDE]	100.0	107.0	109.6	114.0	117.6	118.1	121.8	121.4
Total manufacturing [D] Total, industries manufacturières [D]	100.0	105.3	110.0	112.8	114.4	114.8	117.4	118.1
Total mining [C] Total, industries extractives [C]	100.0	103.3	103.3	105.2	102.2	103.8	105.7	100.2
Food, beverages and tobacco Aliments, boissons et tabac	100.0	102.5	105.4	109.3	113.5	116.8	119.4	122.9
Textiles, wearing apparel, leather, footwear Textiles, habillement, cuir et chaussures	100.0	96.4	95.1	91.4	86.2	80.4	81.0	77.2
Chemicals, petroleum, rubber and plastic products Prod. chimiques, pétroliers, caoutch. et plast.	100.0	101.8	107.7	110.3	115.0	114.2	113.5	120.0
Basic metals Métaux de base	100.0	96.6	109.9	112.5	126.3	124.1	114.6	115.5
Metal products Produits métalliques	100.0	112.6	121.9	130.7	134.8	136.2	158.2	143.4
Electricity and gas [E] Electricité et gaz [E]	100.0	117.9	113.1	124.3	144.3	145.6	158.7	150.4
Romania Roumanie								
Total industry [CDE] Total, industrie [CDE]	100.0	105.7	98.7	81.9	77.7	83.2	90.3	95.7
Total manufacturing [D] Total, industries manufacturières [D]	100.0	107.2	100.8	82.5	78.5	85.1	93.6	100.9
Total mining [C] Total, industries extractives [C]	100.0	100.7	95.0	81.6	76.1	79.8	84.0	80.7
Food, beverages and tobacco Aliments, boissons et tabac	100.0	101.3	86.2	85.0	85.9	97.2	114.2	128.2
Textiles, wearing apparel, leather, footwear Textiles, habillement, cuir et chaussures	100.0	109.4	111.1	71.8	73.8	82.5	90.7	96.6
Chemicals, petroleum, rubber and plastic products Prod. chimiques, pétroliers, caoutch. et plast.	100.0	91.0	75.3	64.7	59.1	66.9	73.3	78.2
Basic metals Métaux de base	100.0	91.7	93.0	92.4	63.9	79.9	93.3	121.0
Metal products Produits métalliques	100.0	117.8	119.5	97.0	92.2	84.2	88.5	91.3
Electricity, gas and water [E] Electricité, gaz et eau [E]	100.0	100.6	88.8	77.8	72.9	72.7	72.0	70.8
Russian Federation Fédération de Russie								
Total industry [CDE] Total, industrie [CDE]	100.0	95.5	97.4	92.3	102.5	114.7	120.3	...
Total manufacturing [D] Total, industries manufacturières [D]	100.0	85.5	78.8	73.0	84.0	96.1	99.6	...
Total mining [C] Total, industries extractives [C]	100.0	98.4	97.5	105.9	111.4	121.4	127.2	...

25
Index numbers of industrial production *[cont.]*
Indices de la production industrielle
1995 = 100 *[suite]*

Country or area and industry [ISIC Rev. 3] Pays ou zone et industrie [CITI Rév. 3]	1995	1996	1997	1998	1999	2000	2001	2002
Food, beverages and tobacco Aliments, boissons et tabac	100.0	89.6	87.1	87.5	95.5	105.4	113.1	...
Textiles, wearing apparel, leather, footwear Textiles, habillement, cuir et chaussures	100.0	77.7	69.2	55.5	67.3	76.8	79.7	...
Chemicals, petroleum, rubber and plastic products Prod. chimiques, pétroliers, caoutch. et plast.	100.0	93.5	92.0	86.6	101.6	114.7	120.1	...
Basic metals Métaux de base	100.0	98.4	100.1	95.0	107.3	121.9	123.2	...
Metal products Produits métalliques	100.0	77.4	65.8	54.9	64.1	79.6	81.3	...
Electricity and gas [E] **Electricité et gaz [E]**	**100.0**	**96.8**	**95.1**	**93.5**	**92.8**	**95.6**	**98.0**	**...**
Serbia and Montenegro Serbie-et-Monténégro								
Total industry [CDE] **Total, industrie [CDE]**	**100.0**	**107.3**	**117.2**	**121.2**	**91.7**	**102.1**	**102.2**	**103.9**
Total manufacturing [D] **Total, industries manufacturières [D]**	**100.0**	**111.1**	**127.8**	**133.4**	**94.7**	**108.4**	**109.3**	**111.4**
Total mining [C] **Total, industries extractives [C]**	**100.0**	**99.2**	**106.0**	**105.4**	**86.0**	**93.8**	**81.9**	**95.8**
Food, beverages and tobacco Aliments, boissons et tabac	100.0	102.0	98.2	113.5	109.5	110.5	107.5	119.4
Textiles, wearing apparel, leather, footwear Textiles, habillement, cuir et chaussures	100.0	106.2	112.3	127.2	90.3	106.4	108.0	85.0
Chemicals, petroleum, rubber and plastic products Prod. chimiques, pétroliers, caoutch. et plast.	100.0	136.0	194.1	226.0	124.6	141.3	164.2	147.0
Basic metals Métaux de base	100.0	143.3	177.4	192.6	105.2	142.2	138.3	151.0
Metal products Produits métalliques	100.0	101.8	120.3	134.4	94.7	114.8	101.5	119.8
Electricity, gas and water [E] **Electricité, gaz et eau [E]**	**100.0**	**102.5**	**108.4**	**109.3**	**103.1**	**104.6**	**105.3**	**102.4**
Slovakia Slovaquie								
Total industry [CDE] **Total, industrie [CDE]**	**100.0**	**102.5**	**103.8**	**108.6**	**106.4**	**115.7**	**124.2**	**132.6**
Total manufacturing [D] **Total, industries manufacturières [D]**	**100.0**	**102.3**	**104.0**	**110.4**	**106.8**	**117.2**	**129.5**	**140.9**
Total mining [C] **Total, industries extractives [C]**	**100.0**	**105.6**	**118.0**	**104.9**	**103.9**	**101.4**	**88.5**	**113.8**
Electricity, gas and water [E] **Electricité, gaz et eau [E]**	**100.0**	**104.8**	**101.5**	**95.6**	**98.6**	**105.3**	**103.3**	**97.3**
Slovenia Slovénie								
Total industry [CDE] **Total, industrie [CDE]**	**100.0**	**101.0**	**102.0**	**105.8**	**105.3**	**111.9**	**115.1**	**117.9**
Total manufacturing [D] **Total, industries manufacturières [D]**	**100.0**	**101.2**	**101.4**	**105.4**	**105.4**	**112.9**	**116.0**	**118.3**
Total mining [C] **Total, industries extractives [C]**	**100.0**	**100.5**	**102.3**	**102.0**	**97.8**	**95.5**	**87.7**	**94.6**
Food, beverages and tobacco Aliments, boissons et tabac	100.0	105.1	101.5	101.8	101.6	110.2	113.9	109.4
Textiles, wearing apparel, leather, footwear Textiles, habillement, cuir et chaussures	100.0	94.8	96.8	94.8	85.9	89.2	83.2	71.2
Chemicals, petroleum, rubber and plastic products Prod. chimiques, pétroliers, caoutch. et plast.	100.0	101.4	107.2	109.4	110.1	122.8	130.1	135.4
Basic metals Métaux de base	100.0	92.7	80.6	81.6	88.9	100.4	105.4	107.7
Metal products Produits métalliques	100.0	101.1	90.9	102.2	104.7	111.8	119.5	126.1
Electricity [E] **Electricité [E]**	**100.0**	**100.7**	**109.0**	**112.7**	**107.5**	**109.1**	**118.1**	**126.2**

25

Index numbers of industrial production *[cont.]*

Indices de la production industrielle

1995 = 100 *[suite]*

Country or area and industry [ISIC Rev. 3] Pays ou zone et industrie [CITI Rév. 3]	1995	1996	1997	1998	1999	2000	2001	2002
Spain Espagne								
Total industry [CDE]								
Total, industrie [CDE]	100.0	99.3	106.1	111.9	114.8	119.3	117.9	118.0
Total manufacturing [D]								
Total, industries manufacturières [D]	100.0	99.3	106.6	113.2	115.8	119.7	117.3	117.7
Total mining [C]								
Total, industries extractives [C]	100.0	94.4	92.0	92.1	90.2	91.2	88.3	87.8
Food, beverages and tobacco								
Aliments, boissons et tabac	100.0	96.9	104.6	109.1	109.3	108.3	110.2	114.1
Textiles, wearing apparel, leather, footwear								
Textiles, habillement, cuir et chaussures	100.0	95.4	99.5	101.5	99.4	97.6	91.3	81.3
Chemicals, petroleum, rubber and plastic products								
Prod. chimiques, pétroliers, caoutch. et plast.	100.0	100.3	107.0	112.6	118.7	119.7	119.7	125.1
Basic metals								
Métaux de base	100.0	97.2	103.8	108.5	109.5	124.7	120.2	127.9
Metal products								
Produits métalliques	100.0	102.4	111.5	121.0	122.7	128.8	123.8	119.5
Electricity and gas [E]								
Electricité et gaz [E]	100.0	100.6	107.0	108.4	115.1	124.9	130.3	130.3
Sweden Suède								
Total industry [CDE]								
Total, industrie [CDE]	100.0	100.9	107.0	111.5	114.5	123.5	119.3	117.8
Total manufacturing [D]								
Total, industries manufacturières [D]	100.0	101.0	107.8	112.4	116.0	125.8	121.4	120.6
Total mining [C]								
Total, industries extractives [C]	100.0	98.3	94.4	94.2	91.7	93.4	90.4	89.7
Food, beverages and tobacco								
Aliments, boissons et tabac	100.0	104.5	103.1	103.8	103.9	103.0	105.8	103.8
Textiles, wearing apparel, leather, footwear								
Textiles, habillement, cuir et chaussures	100.0	97.6	97.7	94.6	86.6	87.8	87.0	81.6
Chemicals, petroleum, rubber and plastic products								
Prod. chimiques, pétroliers, caoutch. et plast.	100.0	103.9	109.6	112.2	116.0	125.6	129.8	133.9
Basic metals								
Métaux de base	100.0	101.5	105.6	105.4	105.0	110.4	119.1	124.4
Metal products								
Produits métalliques	100.0	101.6	111.7	119.7	126.0	142.1	131.3	126.9
Electricity, gas and water [E]								
Electricité, gaz et eau [E]	100.0	100.6	101.9	106.2	105.2	106.1	104.5	94.9
Switzerland Suisse								
Total industry [CDE]								
Total, industrie [CDE]	100.0	100.0	104.6	108.4	112.2	121.7	121.5	115.0
Total manufacturing [D]								
Total, industries manufacturières [D]	100.0	100.3	104.9	109.1	112.7	123.2	121.8	115.4
Total mining [C]								
Total, industries extractives [C]	100.0	98.3	100.5	87.9	93.4	94.2	94.7	93.3
Food, beverages and tobacco								
Aliments, boissons et tabac	100.0	101.2	92.2	88.2	86.8	88.5	85.8	90.6
Textiles and wearing apparel								
Textiles et habillement	100.0	99.0	99.0	93.1	87.5	87.7	79.7	74.4
Chemicals and chemical products								
Produits chimiques	100.0	110.2	125.7	135.8	152.0	163.0	172.0	181.7
Basic metals and metal products								
Métaux de base et produits métalliques	100.0	99.1	106.3	108.6	108.8	123.9	123.5	108.6
Electricity, gas and water [E]								
Electricité, gaz et eau [E]	100.0	97.5	101.5	102.4	108.1	107.6	112.2	107.6
TFYR of Macedonia L'ex-R.y. Macédoine								
Total industry [CDE]								
Total, industrie [CDE]	100.0	103.2	104.7	109.5	106.7	110.4	99.2	94.0
Ukraine Ukraine								
Total industry [CDE]								
Total, industrie [CDE]	100.0	94.9	93.1	91.6	95.9	109.0	123.1	131.2

25
Index numbers of industrial production *[cont.]*
Indices de la production industrielle
1995 = 100 *[suite]*

Country or area and industry [ISIC Rev. 3] Pays ou zone et industrie [CITI Rév. 3]	1995	1996	1997	1998	1999	2000	2001	2002
Total manufacturing [D] Total, industries manufacturières [D]	100.0	94.9	94.5	93.7	97.1	113.2	132.7	144.5
Total mining [C] Total, industries extractives [C]	100.0	94.8	97.9	95.3	98.3	104.6	108.1	110.6
Electricity, gas and water [E] Electricité, gaz et eau [E]	100.0	93.2	90.8	90.6	88.3	89.2	91.2	92.5
United Kingdom Royaume-Uni								
Total industry [CDE] Total, industrie [CDE]	100.0	101.3	102.4	103.3	104.1	105.9	103.6	99.9
Total manufacturing [D] Total, industries manufacturières [D]	100.0	100.6	102.0	102.8	103.1	105.2	102.6	98.5
Total mining [C] Total, industries extractives [C]	100.0	103.2	102.1	104.2	108.1	106.8	101.5	99.6
Food, beverages and tobacco Aliments, boissons et tabac	100.0	101.4	103.6	101.8	101.2	99.9	101.2	102.7
Textiles, wearing apparel, leather, footwear Textiles, habillement, cuir et chaussures	100.0	98.3	96.8	89.1	82.5	78.4	68.7	63.6
Chemicals, petroleum, rubber and plastic products Prod. chimiques, pétroliers, caoutch. et plast.	100.0	99.1	100.4	101.6	102.4	105.3	106.0	106.2
Basic metals Métaux de base	100.0	101.1	102.3	99.1	94.2	89.8	85.3	76.0
Metal products Produits métalliques	100.0	102.5	104.6	108.0	110.2	115.9	111.0	101.2
Electricity, gas and water [E] Electricité, gaz et eau [E]	100.0	105.2	105.7	107.5	109.4	111.4	113.8	113.0
Oceania · Océanie								
Australia [2] Australie [2]								
Total industry [CDE] Total, industrie [CDE]	100.0	103.3	105.0	108.5	109.9	112.3	116.5	119.0
Total manufacturing [D] Total, industries manufacturières [D]	100.0	102.3	104.4	107.7	109.8	110.9	114.0	118.5
Total mining [C] Total, industries extractives [C]	100.0	107.8	109.0	112.5	113.3	121.7	129.5	129.2
Food, beverages and tobacco Aliments, boissons et tabac	100.0	103.6	105.1	113.6	117.6	119.3	121.5	121.4
Textiles, wearing apparel, leather, footwear Textiles, habillement, cuir et chaussures	100.0	94.9	94.0	95.9	96.0	93.5	88.2	76.3
Chemicals, petroleum, rubber and plastic products Prod. chimiques, pétroliers, caoutch. et plast.	100.0	105.8	108.1	110.8	112.4	116.0	119.5	124.2
Basic metals and metal products Métaux de base et produits métalliques	100.0	103.3	106.2	108.9	109.9	107.3	112.6	119.7
Electricity, gas and water [E] Electricité, gaz et eau [E]	100.0	101.4	101.1	104.7	106.4	108.7	110.1	109.6
Fiji Fidji								
Total industry [CDE] Total, industrie [CDE]	100.0	86.8	90.9	92.5	98.7	91.8	97.3	...
Total manufacturing [D] Total, industries manufacturières [D]	100.0	73.8	78.5	81.1	84.3	76.5	81.2	...
Total mining [C] Total, industries extractives [C]	100.0	127.4	133.7	106.6	126.8	108.6	110.6	...
Food, beverages and tobacco Aliments, boissons et tabac	100.0	99.0	86.1	89.1	96.7	88.6	97.5	...
Textiles and wearing apparel Textiles et habillement	100.0	132.0	169.3	220.9	240.6	227.3	297.6	...
Chemicals and chemical products Produits chimiques	100.0	93.2	113.5	124.7	109.2	95.0	92.3	...
Electricity and water [E] Electricité et eau [E]	100.0	107.5	110.1	113.9	124.8	121.8	129.3	...

25

Index numbers of industrial production *[cont.]*

Indices de la production industrielle
1995 = 100 *[suite]*

Country or area and industry [ISIC Rev. 3] Pays ou zone et industrie [CITI Rév. 3]	1995	1996	1997	1998	1999	2000	2001	2002
New Zealand [11] Nouvelle-Zélande [11]								
Total industry [CDE]								
Total, industrie [CDE]	100.0	102.3	104.0	103.6	100.9	104.2	106.7	107.2
Total manufacturing [D]								
Total, industries manufacturières [D]	100.0	101.9	103.5	102.9	99.0	103.3	105.3	106.7
Total mining [C] [12]								
Total, industries extractives [C] [12]	100.0	102.0	112.6	113.9	112.7	116.3	119.0	120.8
Food, beverages and tobacco								
Aliments, boissons et tabac	100.0	104.2	104.3	108.6	104.3	106.2	109.9	110.7
Textiles, wearing apparel, leather, footwear								
Textiles, habillement, cuir et chaussures	100.0	95.6	103.2	95.3	92.9	96.3	96.7	100.7
Chemicals, petroleum, rubber and plastic products								
Prod. chimiques, pétroliers, caoutch. et plast.	100.0	99.7	102.0	95.8	95.2	98.5	108.7	106.8
Basic metals and metal products								
Métaux de base et produits métalliques	100.0	103.1	105.3	104.7	100.7	107.5	109.6	113.2
Electricity, gas and water [E]								
Electricité, gaz et eau [E]	100.0	105.2	97.3	97.3	100.8	97.3	102.4	95.5

Source:
United Nations Statistics Division, New York, the index numbers of industrial production database.

Source:
Organisation des Nations Unies, Division de statistique, New York, la base de données pour les indices de la production industrielle.

1	Twelve months beginning 1 July of the year stated.
2	Twelve months ending 30 June of the year stated.
3	Calculated by the Statistics Division of the United Nations from component national indices.
4	Excluding petroleum refineries.
5	Excluding coal mining and crude petroleum.
6	Twelve months ending 30 September of the year stated.
7	Including construction.
8	Base: 1997=100.
9	Figures relate to 12 months beginning 1 April of the year stated.
10	Excluding gas and oil extraction.
11	Figures relate to 12 months ending 31 March of the year stated.
12	Including forestry and fishing.

1	Période de 12 mois commençant le 1er juillet de l'année indiquée.
2	Période de 12 mois finissant le 30 juin de l'année indiquée.
3	Calculé par la Division de Statistiques de l'Organisation des Nations Unies à partir d'indices nationaux plus détaillés.
4	Non compris les raffineries de pétrole.
5	Non compris l'extraction du charbon et de pétrole brut.
6	Période de 12 mois finissant le 30 septembre de l'année indiquée.
7	Y compris la construction.
8	Base: 1997=100.
9	Les chiffres se rapportent à 12 mois commençant le 1er avril de l'année indiquée.
10	Non compris l'extraction de gaz et de pétrole brut.
11	Les chiffres se rapportent à 12 mois finissant le 31 mars de l'année indiquée.
12	Y compris l'exploitation forestière et la pêche.

Technical notes, tables 19-25

Detailed internationally comparable data on national accounts are compiled and published annually by the Statistics Division, Department of Economic and Social Affairs of the United Nations Secretariat. Data for national accounts aggregates for countries or areas are based on the concepts and definitions contained in *A System of National Accounts* (1968 SNA) [58] and in *System of National Accounts 1993* (1993 SNA) [59]. A summary of the conceptual framework, classifications and definitions of transactions is found in the annual United Nations publication, *National Accounts Statistics: Main Aggregates and Detailed Tables* [27].

The national accounts data shown in this publication offer, in the form of analytical tables, a summary of selected principal national accounts aggregates based on official detailed national accounts data of some 180 countries and areas. Every effort has been made to present the estimates of the various countries or areas in a form designed to facilitate international comparability. The data for the majority of countries or areas has been compiled according to the 1968 SNA. Data for those countries or areas which have started to follow the concepts and definitions of the 1993 SNA is indicated with a footnote. To the extent possible, any other differences in concept, scope, coverage and classification are footnoted as well. Detailed footnotes identifying these differences are also available in the annual national accounts publication mentioned above. Such differences should be taken into account in order to avoid misleading comparisons among countries or areas.

Table 19 shows gross domestic product (GDP) and GDP per capita in US dollars in current prices, and GDP in constant 1990 prices and the corresponding rates of growth. The table is designed to facilitate international comparisons of levels of income generated in production. In order to present comparable coverage for as many countries as possible, the official GDP national currency data are supplemented by estimates prepared by the Statistics Division, based on a variety of data derived from national and international sources. The conversion rates used to translate national currency data into US dollars are the period averages of market exchange rates (MERs) for members of the International Monetary Fund (IMF). These rates, which are published in the *International Financial Statistics* [15], are communicated to the IMF by national central banks and consist of three types: (a) market rates, determined largely by market forces; (b) official rates, determined by government authorities; and (c) principal rates for countries maintaining multiple exchange rate arrangements. Market rates always take priority and official rates are used only when a free market rate is not available.

Notes techniques, tableaux 19 à 25

La Division de statistique du Département des affaires économiques et sociales du Secrétariat de l'Organisation des Nations Unies établit et publie chaque année des données détaillées, comparables au plan international, sur les comptes nationaux. Les données relatives aux agrégats des différents pays et territoires sont établies en fonction des concepts et des définitions du *Système de comptabilité nationale* (SCN de 1968) [58] et du *Système de comptabilité nationale* (SCN de 1993) [59]. On trouvera un résumé de l'appareil conceptuel, des classifications et des définitions des opérations dans *National Accounts Statistics: Main Aggregates and Detailed Tables* [27], publication annuelle des Nations Unies.

Les chiffres de comptabilité nationale présentés ici récapitulent sous forme de tableaux analytiques un choix d'agrégats essentiels de comptabilité nationale, issus des comptes nationaux détaillés de quelque 180 pays et territoires. On n'a rien négligé pour présenter les chiffres des différents pays et territoires sous une forme facilitant les comparaisons internationales. Pour la plupart des pays, les chiffres ont été établis selon le SCN de 1968. Les données des pays et territoires qui ont commencé à appliquer les concepts et les définitions du SCN de 1993 sont signalées par une note. Dans toute la mesure possible, on signale également au moyen de notes les cas où les concepts, la portée, la couverture et la classification ne seraient pas les mêmes. Il y a en outre des notes détaillées explicitant ces différences dans la publication annuelle mentionnée plus haut. Il y a lieu de tenir compte de ces différences pour éviter de tenter des comparaisons qui donneraient matière à confusion.

Le *tableau 19* fait apparaître le produit intérieur brut (PIB) total et par habitant, exprimé en dollars des États-Unis aux prix courants et à prix constants (base 1990), ainsi que les taux de croissance correspondants. Le tableau est conçu pour faciliter les comparaisons internationales du revenu issu de la production. Afin que la couverture soit comparable pour le plus grand nombre possible de pays, la Division de statistique s'appuie non seulement sur les chiffres officiels du PIB exprimé dans la monnaie nationale, mais aussi sur diverses données provenant de sources nationales et internationales. Les taux de conversion utilisés pour exprimer les données nationales en dollars des États-Unis sont, pour les membres du Fonds monétaire international (FMI), les moyennes pour la période considérée des taux de change du marché. Ces derniers, publiés dans *Statistiques financières internationales* [15], sont communiqués au FMI par les banques centrales des pays et reposent sur trois types de taux : a) taux du marché, déterminés dans une large mesure par les facteurs du marché; b) taux officiels, déterminés par les pouvoirs publics; c) taux principaux, pour les pays pratiquant diffé-

For non-members of the IMF, averages of the United Nations operational rates, used for accounting purposes in United Nations transactions with member countries, are applied. These are based on official, commercial and/or tourist rates of exchange.

It should be noted that there are practical constraints in the use of MERs for conversion purposes. Their use may result in excessive fluctuations or distortions in the dollar income levels of a number of countries particularly in those with multiple exchange rates, those coping with inordinate levels of inflation or countries experiencing misalignments caused by market fluctuations. Caution is therefore urged when making intercountry comparisons of incomes as expressed in US dollars.

The GDP constant price series, based primarily on data officially provided by countries or areas and partly on estimates made by the Statistics Division, are transformed into index numbers and rebased to 1990=100. The resulting data are then converted into US dollars at the rate prevailing in the base year 1990. The growth rates are based on the estimates of GDP at constant 1990 prices. The growth rate of the year in question is obtained by dividing the GDP of that year by the GDP of the preceding year.

Table 20 features the percentage distribution of GDP in current prices by expenditure breakdown. It shows the portions of GDP spent on consumption by the government and the household (including the non-profit institutions serving households) sector, the portions spent on gross fixed capital formation, on changes in inventories, and on exports of goods and services, deducting imports of goods and services. The percentages are derived from official data reported to the United Nations by the countries and published in the annual national accounts publication.

Table 21 shows the percentage distribution of value added originating from the various industry components of the *International Standard Industrial Classification of All Economic Activities, Revision 3* (ISIC Rev. 3) [50]. This table reflects the economic structure of production in the different countries or areas. The percentages are based on official gross value added at basic current prices broken down by the kind of economic activity: agriculture, hunting, forestry and fishing (categories A+B); mining and quarrying (C); manufacturing (D); electricity, gas and water supply (E); construction (F); wholesale and retail trade, repair of motor vehicles, motorcycles and personal and household goods, restaurants and hotels (G+H); transport, storage and communication (I) and other activities comprised of financial intermediation (J), real estate, renting and business activities (K), public administration and defence, compulsory social security (L), education (M),

rents arrangements en matière de taux de change. On donne toujours la priorité aux taux du marché, n'utilisant les taux officiels que lorsqu'on n'a pas de taux du marché libre.

Pour les pays qui ne sont pas membres du FMI, on utilise les moyennes des taux de change opérationnels de l'ONU (qui servent à des fins comptables pour les opérations de l'ONU avec les pays qui en sont membres). Ces taux reposent sur les taux de change officiels, les taux du commerce et/ou les taux touristiques.

Il est à noter que l'utilisation des taux de change du marché pour la conversion des données se heurte à des obstacles pratiques. On risque, ce faisant, d'aboutir à des fluctuations excessives ou à des distorsions du revenu en dollars de certains pays, surtout dans le cas des pays qui pratiquent plusieurs taux de change et de ceux qui connaissent des taux d'inflation exceptionnels ou des décalages provenant des fluctuations du marché. Les comparaisons de revenu entre pays sont donc sujettes à caution lorsqu'on se fonde sur le revenu exprimé en dollars des États-Unis.

La série de statistiques du PIB à prix constants est fondée principalement sur des données officiellement communiquées par les pays, et en partie sur des estimations de la Division de statistique; les données permettent de calculer des indices, la base 100 correspondant à 1990. Les chiffres ainsi obtenus sont alors convertis en dollars des États-Unis au taux de change de l'année de base (1990). Les taux de croissance sont calculés à partir des estimations du PIB aux prix constants de 1990. Le taux de croissance de l'année considérée est obtenu en divisant le PIB de l'année par celui de l'année précédente.

Le *tableau 20* montre la répartition (en pourcentage) du PIB aux prix courants par catégorie de dépense. Il indique la part du PIB consacrée aux dépenses de consommation des administrations publiques et du secteur des ménages (y compris les institutions sans but lucratif au service des ménages), celle qui est consacrée à la formation brute de capital fixe, celle qui correspond aux variations de stocks et celle qui correspond aux exportations de biens et services, déduction faite des importations de biens et services. Ces pourcentages sont calculés à partir des chiffres officiels communiqués à l'ONU par les pays, publiés dans l'ouvrage annuel.

Le *tableau 21* montre la répartition (en pourcentage) de la valeur ajoutée par branche d'activité, selon le classement retenu dans la *Classification internationale type, par industrie, de toutes les branches d'activité économique, Révision 3* (CITI Rev. 3) [50]. Il rend donc compte de la structure économique de la production dans chaque pays. Les pourcentages sont établis à partir des chiffres officiels de valeur ajoutée brute aux prix de base courants, ventilés selon les différentes catégories d'activité économique: agriculture, chasse, sylviculture et pêche (catégo-

health and social work (N), other community, social and personal service activities (O) and private households with employed persons (P).

Table 22 presents the relationships among the principal national accounting aggregates, namely: gross domestic product (GDP), gross national income (GNI), gross national disposable income (GNDI) and gross saving. GNI is the term used in the 1993 SNA instead of the term Gross National Product (GNP) which was used in the 1968 SNA. The ratio of each aggregate to GDP is derived cumulatively by adding net primary income (or net factor income) from the rest of the world, (GNI); adding net current transfers from the rest of the world, (GNDI) and deducting final consumption to arrive at gross saving. Net national income, net national disposable income and net saving can be derived by deducting consumption of fixed capital from the corresponding gross values mentioned above.

Table 23 presents the distribution of government final consumption expenditure by function in current prices. The breakdown by function includes: general public services; defence; public order and safety; environment protection; health; education; social protection; and other functions which include housing, community amenities, recreational, cultural, religious affairs and other functions not specified. The government expenditure is equal to the service produced by general government for its own use. These services are not sold; they are valued in the GDP at their cost to the government.

Table 24 shows the distribution of total household consumption expenditure by purpose in current prices. Household consumption expenditure measures the expenditure of all resident non-government units which includes all households and private non-profit institutions serving households. The percentage shares include: food, beverages, tobacco and narcotics; clothing and footwear; housing, water, electricity, gas and other fuels; furnishings, household equipment, routine maintenance of the house; health; transport and communication; recreation, culture, education, restaurants, hotels; and other functions which include miscellaneous goods and services, purchases abroad by resident households deducting the expenditure of non-resident in the domestic market and, if available, the expenditure of private non-profit institutions serving households.

Table 25: The national indices in this table are shown for the categories "Mining and Quarrying", "Manufacturing" and "Electricity, gas and water". These categories are classified according to Tabulation Categories C, D and E of the ISIC Revision 3 [50]. Major deviations from ISIC in the scope of the indices for the above categories are indicated by footnotes to the table.

The category "Total industry" covers Mining, Manufacturing and Electricity, gas and water. The indices for "Total industry", however, are the combination

ries A + B); activités extractives (C); activités de fabrication (D); production et distribution d'électricité, de gaz et d'eau (E); construction (F); commerce de gros et de détail, réparation de véhicules automobiles, de motocycles et de biens personnels et domestiques, hôtels et restaurants (G + H); transports, entreposage et communications (I) et intermédiation financière (J); immobilier, locations et activités de services aux entreprises (K); administration publique et défense, sécurité sociale obligatoire (L); éducation (M); santé et action sociale (N); autres activités de services collectifs, sociaux et personnels (O); et ménages privés employant du personnel domestique (P).

Le *tableau 22* montre les rapports entre les principaux agrégats de la comptabilité nationale, à savoir le produit intérieur brut (PIB), le revenu national brut (RNB), le revenu national brut disponible et l'épargne brute. Le revenu national brut est l'agrégat qui remplace dans le SCN de 1993 le produit national brut, utilisé dans le SCN de 1968. Chacun d'entre eux est obtenu par rapport au PIB, en ajoutant les revenus primaires nets (ou revenus nets de facteurs) engendrés dans le reste du monde, pour obtenir le revenu national brut; en ajoutant les transferts courants nets reçus de non-résidents, pour obtenir le revenu national disponible; en soustrayant la consommation finale pour obtenir l'épargne brute. Le revenu national net, le revenu national disponible net et l'épargne nette s'obtiennent en déduisant de la valeur brute correspondante la consommation de capital fixe.

Le *tableau 23* donne la répartition des dépenses de consommation finale des administrations publiques, par fonction, aux prix courants. La répartition par fonction est la suivante: services généraux des administrations publiques; protection de l'environnement; santé; éducation; protection sociale; défense; ordre et sécurité publics; et autres fonctions incluant le logement, les aménagements collectifs, les équipements de loisir, les activités culturelles et religieuses, et autres fonctions non spécifiés. Les dépenses des administrations sont considérées comme égales aux services produits par l'administration pour son propre usage. Ces services ne sont pas vendus et ils sont évalués, dans le PIB, à leur coût pour l'administration.

Le *tableau 24* donne la répartition des dépenses de consommation finale des ménages par fonction aux prix courants. Les dépenses de consommation des ménages mesurent donc les dépenses de toutes les entités résidentes autres que les administrations, y compris tous les ménages et les entités privées à but non lucratif fournissant des services aux ménages. La répartition en pourcentage distingue les rubriques suivantes: alimentation, boissons, tabac et stupéfiants; articles d'habillement et chaussures; logement, eau, gaz, électricité et autres combustibles; meubles, articles de ménage et entretien courant de l'habitation; santé; transports et communication; loisirs, culture; enseignement, restaurants et hôtels; et autres fonctions, y compris les biens et services divers, achats à

of the components shown and share all deviations from ISIC as footnoted for the component series.

For the purpose of presentation, the national indices have been rebased to 1995=100, where necessary.

l'étranger effectués par les ménages résidents, moins les dépenses des non-résidents sur le marché intérieur, et si disponible, dépenses des institutions privées à but non lucratif fournissant des services aux ménages.

Tableau 25: Les définitions des catégories "Industries extractives", "Industries manufacturières" et "Electricité, gaz et eau", pour lesquelles des indices nationaux sont donnés dans ce tableau correspondent aux catégories C, D et E des tableaux de la CITI Révision 3 [50]. Toutes différences importantes par rapport à la CITI dans la portée des indices de ces catégories sont indiquées dans les notes du tableau.

La catégorie "Total, industrie" couvre Industries extractives, Industries manufacturières et Electricité, gaz et eau. Toutefois, les indices de cette catégorie "Total, industrie" ne portent que sur la combinaison des indices partiels indiqués, et partagent toutes les différences par rapport à la CITI notées dans le cas des indices partiels.

Pour les besoins de la présentation, les indices nationaux ont été dans certains cas recalculés en prenant 1995=100 comme base de référence.

26
Rates of discount of central banks
Per cent per annum, end of period
Taux d'escompte des banques centrales
Pour cent par année, fin de la période

Country or area Pays ou zone	1993	1994	1995	1996	1997	1998	1999	2000	2001	2002
Albania Albanie	34.00	25.00	20.50	24.00	32.00	23.44	18.00	10.82	7.00	8.50
Algeria Algérie	11.50	21.00	#14.00	13.00	11.00	9.50	8.50	6.00	6.00	5.50
Angola Angola	...	...	160.00	2.00	48.00	58.00	120.00	150.00	150.00	150.00
Anguilla Anguilla	...	9.00	9.00	9.00	8.00	8.00	8.00	8.00	7.00	7.00
Antigua and Barbuda Antigua-et-Barbuda	...	9.00	9.00	9.00	8.00	8.00	8.00	8.00	7.00	7.00
Armenia Arménie	210.00	210.00	77.80	26.00	65.10	...	...	...	...	...
Aruba Aruba	9.50	9.50	9.50	9.50	9.50	9.50	6.50	6.50	6.50	6.50
Australia Australie	5.83	5.75	5.75	...	...	...	...	...	...	...
Austria [1] Autriche [1]	5.25	4.50	3.00	2.50	2.50	2.50	...	...	...	...
Azerbaijan Azerbaïdjan	100.00	200.00	80.00	20.00	12.00	14.00	10.00	10.00	10.00	7.00
Bahamas Bahamas	7.00	6.50	6.50	6.50	6.50	6.50	5.75	5.75	5.75	5.75
Bangladesh Bangladesh	6.00	5.50	6.00	7.00	8.00	8.00	7.00	7.00	6.00	6.00
Barbados Barbade	8.00	9.50	12.50	12.50	9.00	9.00	10.00	10.00	7.50	7.50
Belarus Bélarus	210.00	480.00	66.00	8.30	8.90	9.60	23.40	#80.00	48.00	38.00
Belgium [1] Belgique [1]	5.25	4.50	3.00	2.50	2.75	2.75	...	...	...	...
Belize Belize	12.00	12.00	12.00	12.00	12.00	12.00	12.00	12.00	12.00	12.00
Benin Bénin	#6.00	6.00	6.00	6.00	6.00	6.00	6.00	6.00	6.00	6.00
Bolivia Bolivie	...	...	...	16.50	13.25	14.10	12.50	10.00	8.50	12.50
Botswana Botswana	14.25	13.50	13.00	13.00	12.50	12.50	13.25	14.25	14.25	15.25
Brazil Brésil	...	...	...	25.34	45.09	39.41	21.37	#18.52	21.43	25.50
Bulgaria Bulgarie	52.00	#72.00	34.00	180.00	6.65	5.08	4.46	4.63	4.65	3.31
Burkina Faso Burkina Faso	#6.00	6.00	6.00	6.00	6.00	6.00	6.00	6.00	6.00	6.00
Burundi Burundi	10.00	10.00	10.00	10.00	12.00	12.00	12.00	14.00	14.00	15.50
Cameroon Cameroun	11.50	#7.75	8.60	7.75	7.50	7.00	7.30	7.00	6.50	6.30
Canada Canada	4.11	7.43	5.79	3.25	4.50	5.25	5.00	6.00	2.50	3.00
Central African Rep. Rép. centrafricaine	11.50	#7.75	8.60	7.75	7.50	7.00	7.60	7.00	6.50	6.30
Chad Tchad	11.50	#7.75	8.60	7.75	7.50	7.00	7.60	7.00	6.50	6.30
Chile Chili	7.96	13.89	7.96	11.75	7.96	9.12	7.44	8.73	6.50	3.00

26
Rates of discount of central banks
Per cent per annum, end of period [cont.]

Taux d'escompte des banques centrales
Pour cent par année, fin de la période [suite]

Country or area Pays ou zone	1993	1994	1995	1996	1997	1998	1999	2000	2001	2002
China Chine	10.08	10.08	10.44	9.00	8.55	4.59	3.24	3.24	3.24	2.70
China, Hong Kong SAR Chine, Hong Kong RAS	4.00	5.75	6.25	6.00	7.00	6.25	7.00	8.00	3.25	2.75
Colombia Colombie	33.49	44.90	40.42	35.05	31.32	42.28	23.05	18.28	16.40	12.73
Congo Congo	11.50	#7.75	8.60	7.75	7.50	7.00	7.60	7.00	6.50	6.30
Costa Rica Costa Rica	35.00	37.75	38.50	35.00	31.00	37.00	34.00	31.50	28.75	31.25
Côte d'Ivoire Côte d'Ivoire	#6.00	6.00	6.00	6.00	6.00	6.00	6.00	6.00	6.00	6.00
Croatia Croatie	34.49	8.50	8.50	6.50	5.90	5.90	7.90	5.90	5.90	4.50
Cyprus Chypre	6.50	6.50	6.50	#7.50	7.00	7.00	7.00	7.00	5.50	5.00
Czech Republic République tchèque	8.00	8.50	11.30	12.40	14.75	9.50	5.25	5.25	4.50	2.75
Dem. Rep. of the Congo Rép. dém. du Congo	95.00	145.00	125.00	238.00	13.00	22.00	120.00	120.00	140.00	24.00
Denmark Danemark	6.25	5.00	4.25	3.25	3.50	3.50	3.00	4.75	3.25	2.86
Dominica Dominique	...	9.00	9.00	9.00	8.00	8.00	8.00	8.00	7.00	7.00
Ecuador Equateur	33.57	44.88	59.41	46.38	37.46	61.84	64.40	#13.16	16.44	14.55
Egypt Egypte	16.50	14.00	13.50	13.00	12.25	12.00	12.00	12.00	11.00	10.00
Equatorial Guinea Guinée équatoriale	11.50	#7.75	8.60	7.75	7.50	7.00	7.60	7.00	6.50	6.30
Euro Area [2] Zone euro [2]	...	...	...	...	...	...	4.00	5.75	4.25	3.75
Fiji Fidji	6.00	6.00	6.00	6.00	1.88	2.50	2.50	8.00	1.75	1.75
Finland [1] Finlande [1]	5.50	5.25	4.88	4.00	4.00	3.50	...	...	...	...
Gabon Gabon	11.50	#7.75	8.60	7.75	7.50	7.00	7.60	7.00	6.50	6.30
Gambia Gambie	13.50	13.50	14.00	14.00	14.00	12.00	10.50	10.00	13.00	18.00
Germany [1] Allemagne [1]	5.75	4.50	3.00	2.50	2.50	2.50	...	...	...	...
Ghana Ghana	35.00	33.00	45.00	45.00	45.00	37.00	27.00	27.00	27.00	24.50
Greece [1] Grèce [1]	21.50	20.50	18.00	16.50	14.50	...	#11.81	8.10	...	...
Grenada Grenade	...	9.00	9.00	9.00	8.00	8.00	8.00	8.00	7.00	7.00
Guinea Guinée	17.00	17.00	18.00	18.00	15.00	...	...	11.50	16.25	16.25
Guinea-Bissau Guinée-Bissau	#6.00	6.00	6.00	6.00	6.00	6.00	6.00	6.00	6.00	6.00
Guyana Guyana	17.00	20.25	17.25	12.00	11.00	11.25	13.25	11.75	8.75	6.25
Hungary Hongrie	22.00	25.00	28.00	23.00	20.50	17.00	14.50	11.00	9.75	8.50

26
Rates of discount of central banks
Per cent per annum, end of period [cont.]
Taux d'escompte des banques centrales
Pour cent par année, fin de la période [suite]

Country or area Pays ou zone	1993	1994	1995	1996	1997	1998	1999	2000	2001	2002
Iceland Islande	...	4.70	5.93	5.70	6.55	#8.50	10.00	12.40	12.00	8.20
India Inde	12.00	12.00	12.00	12.00	9.00	9.00	8.00	8.00	6.50	6.25
Indonesia Indonésie	8.82	12.44	13.99	12.80	20.00	38.44	12.51	14.53	17.62	12.93
Ireland [1] Irlande [1]	7.00	6.25	6.50	6.25	6.75	4.06	...	...	...	...
Israel Israël	9.78	17.01	14.19	15.30	13.72	13.47	11.20	8.21	5.67	9.18
Italy [1] Italie [1]	8.00	7.50	9.00	7.50	5.50	3.00	...	...	...	...
Japan Japon	1.75	1.75	0.50	0.50	0.50	0.50	0.50	0.50	0.10	0.10
Jordan Jordanie	8.50	8.50	8.50	8.50	7.75	9.00	8.00	6.50	5.00	4.50
Kazakhstan Kazakhstan	170.00	230.00	#52.50	35.00	18.50	25.00	18.00	14.00	9.00	7.50
Kenya Kenya	45.50	21.50	24.50	26.88	32.27	17.07	26.46	...	...	...
Korea, Republic of Corée, République de	5.00	5.00	5.00	5.00	5.00	3.00	3.00	3.00	2.50	2.50
Kuwait Koweït	5.75	7.00	7.25	7.25	7.50	7.00	6.75	7.25	4.25	3.25
Lao People's Dem. Rep. Rép. dém. pop. lao	25.00	30.00	32.08	35.00	...	35.00	34.89	35.17	35.00	20.00
Latvia Lettonie	27.00	25.00	24.00	9.50	4.00	4.00	4.00	3.50	3.50	3.00
Lebanon Liban	20.22	16.49	19.01	25.00	30.00	30.00	25.00	20.00	20.00	20.00
Lesotho Lesotho	13.50	13.50	15.50	17.00	15.60	19.50	19.00	15.00	13.00	16.19
Libyan Arab Jamah. Jamah. arabe libyenne	5.00	...	...	...	...	3.00	5.00	5.00	5.00	5.00
Malawi Malawi	25.00	40.00	50.00	27.00	23.00	43.00	47.00	50.23	46.80	40.00
Malaysia Malaisie	5.24	4.51	6.47	7.28	...	...	...	...	...	...
Mali Mali	#6.00	6.00	6.00	6.00	6.00	6.00	6.00	6.00	6.00	6.00
Malta Malte	5.50	5.50	5.50	5.50	5.50	5.50	4.75	4.75	4.25	3.75
Mauritius Maurice	8.30	13.80	11.40	11.82	10.46	17.19	...	...	...	...
Mongolia Mongolie	628.80	180.00	150.00	109.00	45.50	23.30	11.40	8.65	8.60	9.90
Montserrat Montserrat	...	9.00	9.00	9.00	8.00	8.00	8.00	8.00	7.00	7.00
Morocco Maroc	...	7.17	...	...	...	6.04	5.42	5.00	4.71	3.79
Mozambique Mozambique	...	69.70	57.75	32.00	12.95	9.95	9.95	9.95	9.95	9.95
Myanmar Myanmar	11.00	11.00	12.50	15.00	15.00	15.00	12.00	10.00	10.00	10.00
Namibia Namibie	14.50	15.50	17.50	17.75	16.00	18.75	11.50	11.25	9.25	12.75

26
Rates of discount of central banks
Per cent per annum, end of period *[cont.]*
Taux d'escompte des banques centrales
Pour cent par année, fin de la période *[suite]*

Country or area Pays ou zone	1993	1994	1995	1996	1997	1998	1999	2000	2001	2002
Nepal Népal	11.00	11.00	11.00	11.00	9.00	9.00	9.00	7.50	6.50	5.50
Netherlands [1] Pays-Bas [1]	5.00	...	...	...	...	...	...	...	...	...
Netherlands Antilles Antilles néerlandaises	5.00	5.00	6.00	6.00	6.00	6.00	6.00	6.00	6.00	6.00
New Zealand Nouvelle-Zélande	5.70	9.75	9.80	8.80	9.70	5.60	5.00	6.50	4.75	5.75
Niger Niger	#6.00	6.00	6.00	6.00	6.00	6.00	6.00	6.00	6.00	6.00
Nigeria Nigéria	26.00	13.50	13.50	13.50	13.50	13.50	18.00	14.00	20.50	16.50
Norway Norvège	7.00	6.75	6.75	6.00	5.50	10.00	7.50	9.00	8.50	8.50
Pakistan Pakistan	10.00	#15.00	17.00	20.00	18.00	16.50	13.00	13.00	10.00	7.50
Papua New Guinea Papouasie-Nvl-Guinée	#6.30	6.55	18.00	10.30	10.20	18.15	12.80	4.41	11.25	13.25
Paraguay Paraguay	27.17	19.15	20.50	15.00	20.00	20.00	20.00	20.00	20.00	20.00
Peru Pérou	28.63	16.08	18.44	18.16	15.94	18.72	17.80	14.00	14.00	4.75
Philippines Philippines	9.40	8.30	10.83	11.70	14.64	12.40	7.89	13.81	8.30	4.19
Poland Pologne	29.00	28.00	25.00	22.00	24.50	18.25	19.00	21.50	14.00	7.75
Portugal [1] Portugal [1]	11.00	8.88	8.50	6.70	5.31	3.00	...	...	...	...
Russian Federation Fédération de Russie	...	...	160.00	48.00	28.00	60.00	55.00	25.00	25.00	21.00
Rwanda Rwanda	11.00	11.00	16.00	16.00	10.75	11.38	11.19	11.69	13.00	13.00
Saint Kitts and Nevis Saint-Kitts-et-Nevis	...	9.00	9.00	9.00	8.00	8.00	8.00	8.00	7.00	7.00
Saint Lucia Sainte-Lucie	...	9.00	9.00	9.00	8.00	8.00	8.00	8.00	7.00	7.00
St. Vincent-Grenadines St. Vincent-Grenadines	...	9.00	9.00	9.00	8.00	8.00	8.00	8.00	7.00	7.00
San Marino Saint-Marin	10.00	9.50	9.00	7.60	5.93	4.28	2.55	3.93	3.98	...
Sao Tome and Principe Sao Tomé-et-Principe	30.00	32.00	50.00	35.00	55.00	29.50	17.00	17.00	15.50	15.50
Senegal Sénégal	#6.00	6.00	6.00	6.00	6.00	6.00	6.00	6.00	6.00	6.00
Seychelles Seychelles	1.00	1.00	1.00	1.00	1.00	1.00	1.00	1.00	1.00	1.00
Slovakia Slovaquie	12.00	12.00	9.75	8.80	8.80	8.80	8.80	8.80	#7.75	6.50
Slovenia Slovénie	19.00	17.00	11.00	11.00	11.00	11.00	9.00	11.00	12.00	10.50
South Africa Afrique du Sud	12.00	13.00	15.00	17.00	16.00	#19.32	12.00	12.00	9.50	13.50
Spain [1] Espagne [1]	9.00	7.38	9.00	6.25	4.75	3.00	...	...	...	...
Sri Lanka Sri Lanka	17.00	17.00	17.00	17.00	17.00	17.00	16.00	25.00	...	18.00

26

Rates of discount of central banks
Per cent per annum, end of period *[cont.]*

Taux d'escompte des banques centrales
Pour cent par année, fin de la période *[suite]*

Country or area Pays ou zone	1993	1994	1995	1996	1997	1998	1999	2000	2001	2002
Swaziland Swaziland	11.00	12.00	15.00	16.75	15.75	18.00	12.00	11.00	9.50	13.50
Sweden Suède	5.00	7.00	7.00	3.50	2.50	2.00	1.50	2.00	2.00	2.00
Switzerland Suisse	4.00	3.50	1.50	1.00	1.00	1.00	0.50	#3.20	1.59	0.50
Syrian Arab Republic Rép. arabe syrienne	5.00	5.00	5.00	5.00	5.00	5.00	5.00	5.00	5.00	5.00
Tajikistan Tadjikistan	...	...	...	...	76.00	36.40	20.10	20.60	20.00	#24.75
Thailand Thaïlande	9.00	9.50	10.50	10.50	12.50	12.50	4.00	4.00	3.75	3.25
TFYR of Macedonia L'ex-R.y. Macédoine	295.00	33.00	15.00	9.20	8.90	8.90	8.90	7.90	10.70	10.70
Togo Togo	#6.00	6.00	6.00	6.00	6.00	6.00	6.00	6.00	6.00	6.00
Trinidad and Tobago Trinité-et-Tobago	13.00	13.00	13.00	13.00	13.00	13.00	13.00	13.00	13.00	7.25
Tunisia Tunisie	8.88	8.88	8.88	7.88	...	...	...	...	...	...
Turkey Turquie	48.00	55.00	50.00	50.00	67.00	67.00	60.00	60.00	60.00	55.00
Uganda Ouganda	24.00	15.00	13.30	15.85	14.08	9.10	15.75	18.86	8.88	13.08
Ukraine Ukraine	240.00	252.00	110.00	40.00	35.00	60.00	45.00	27.00	12.50	7.00
United Rep. of Tanzania Rép.-Unie de Tanzanie	14.50	67.50	47.90	19.00	16.20	17.60	20.20	10.70	8.70	9.18
United States Etats-Unis	3.00	4.75	5.25	5.00	5.00	4.50	5.00	6.00	1.25	0.75
Uruguay Uruguay	164.30	182.30	178.70	160.30	95.50	73.70	66.39	57.26	71.66	316.01
Vanuatu Vanuatu	...	...	...	...	...	7.00	7.00	7.00	6.50	6.50
Venezuela Venezuela	71.25	48.00	49.00	45.00	45.00	60.00	38.00	38.00	37.00	40.00
Viet Nam Viet Nam	...	...	...	18.90	10.80	12.00	6.00	6.00	4.80	4.80
Yemen Yémen	...	...	27.40	28.51	15.00	19.95	18.53	15.89	15.16	13.13
Zambia Zambie	72.50	20.50	40.20	47.00	17.70	...	32.93	25.67	40.10	27.87
Zimbabwe Zimbabwe	28.50	29.50	29.50	27.00	31.50	#39.50	74.41	57.84	57.20	29.65

Source:
International Monetary Fund (IMF), Washington, D.C., "International Financial Statistics," January 2004 and the IMF database.

Source:
Fonds monétaire international (FMI), Washington, D.C.,"Statistiques Financières Internationales," janvier 2004 et la base de données du FMI.

1   Beginning 1999, see Euro Area. Greece, beginning 2001.
2   "Euro Area" is an official descriptor for the European Economic and Monetary Union (EMU). The participating member states of the EMU are Austria, Belgium, Finland, France, Germany, Greece (beginning 2001), Ireland, Italy, Luxembourg, Netherlands, Portugal, and Spain.

1   A partir de 1999, voir la Zone euro. Grèce, à partir de 2001.
2   L'expression "zone euro" est un intitulé officiel pour l'Union économique et monétaire (UEM) européene. L'UEM est composée des pays membres suivants : Allemagne, Autriche, Belgique, Espagne, Finlande, France, Grèce (à partir de 2001), Irlande, Italie, Luxembourg, Pays-Bas et Portugal.

27
Short-term interest rates
Treasury bill and money market rates: per cent per annum
Taux d'intérêt à court terme
Taux des bons du Trésor et du marché monétaire : pour cent par année

Country or area Pays ou zone	1993	1994	1995	1996	1997	1998	1999	2000	2001	2002
Albania Albanie										
Treasury bill Bons du trésor	...	...	13.84	17.81	32.59	27.49	17.54	10.80	7.72	9.49
Algeria Algérie										
Money market Marché monétaire	...	19.80	#21.05	18.47	11.80	10.40	10.43	6.77	3.35	4.20
Treasury bill Bons du trésor	9.50	16.50	...	...	...	#9.96	10.05	7.95	5.69	1.80
Anguilla Anguilla										
Money market Marché monétaire	5.25	5.25	5.25	5.25	5.25	5.25	5.25	5.25	#5.64	6.32
Antigua and Barbuda Antigua-et-Barbuda										
Money market Marché monétaire	5.25	5.25	5.25	5.25	5.25	5.25	5.25	5.25	#5.64	6.32
Treasury bill Bons du trésor	7.00	7.00	7.00	7.00	7.00	7.00	7.00	7.00	7.00	7.00
Argentina Argentine										
Money market Marché monétaire	6.31	7.66	9.46	6.23	6.63	6.81	6.99	8.15	24.90	41.35
Armenia Arménie										
Money market Marché monétaire	...	...	...	48.56	36.41	27.84	23.65	18.63	19.40	12.29
Treasury bill Bons du trésor	...	...	37.81	#43.95	57.54	46.99	55.10	24.40	#20.59	14.75
Australia Australie										
Money market Marché monétaire	5.11	5.18	#7.50	7.20	5.50	4.99	#4.78	5.90	5.06	4.55
Treasury bill Bons du trésor	5.00	5.69	#7.64	7.02	5.29	4.84	4.76	5.98	4.80	...
Austria[1] Autriche[1]										
Money market Marché monétaire	7.22	5.03	4.36	3.19	3.27	3.36	...	...	...	...
Azerbaijan Azerbaïdjan										
Treasury bill Bons du trésor	...	...	...	...	12.23	14.10	18.31	16.73	16.51	14.12
Bahamas Bahamas										
Treasury bill Bons du trésor	3.96	1.88	3.01	4.45	4.35	3.84	1.97	1.03	1.94	2.50
Bahrain Bahreïn										
Money market Marché monétaire	3.53	5.18	6.24	5.69	...	5.69	5.58	6.89	3.85	2.02
Treasury bill Bons du trésor	3.33	4.81	6.07	5.49	5.68	5.53	5.46	6.56	3.78	1.75
Barbados Barbade										
Treasury bill Bons du trésor	5.44	7.26	8.01	6.85	3.61	5.61	5.83	5.29	3.14	2.10
Belgium Belgique										
Money market[1] Marché monétaire[1]	8.21	5.72	4.80	3.24	3.46	3.58	...	...	...	...
Treasury bill Bons du trésor	8.52	5.57	4.67	3.19	3.38	3.51	2.72	4.02	4.16	3.17
Belize Belize										
Treasury bill Bons du trésor	4.59	4.27	4.10	3.78	3.51	3.83	5.91	5.91	5.91	4.59
Benin Bénin										
Money market Marché monétaire	...	...	...	...	...	4.81	4.95	4.95	4.95	4.95

27

Short-term interest rates
Treasury bill and money market rates: per cent per annum *[cont.]*

Taux d'intérêt à court terme
Taux des bons du Trésor et du marché monétaire : pour cent par année *[suite]*

Country or area Pays ou zone	1993	1994	1995	1996	1997	1998	1999	2000	2001	2002
Bolivia Bolivie										
Money market										
Marché monétaire	...	...	22.42	20.27	13.97	12.57	13.49	7.40	6.99	8.41
Treasury bill										
Bons du trésor	...	17.89	24.51	19.93	13.65	12.33	14.07	10.99	11.48	12.41
Brazil Brésil										
Money market										
Marché monétaire	3 284.44	4 820.64	53.37	27.45	25.00	29.50	26.26	17.59	17.47	19.11
Treasury bill										
Bons du trésor	...	...	49.93	25.73	24.79	28.57	26.39	18.51	20.06	19.43
Bulgaria Bulgarie										
Money market										
Marché monétaire	48.07	66.43	53.09	119.88	66.43	2.48	2.93	3.02	3.74	2.47
Treasury bill										
Bons du trésor	45.45	57.72	48.27	114.31	78.35	6.02	5.43	4.21	4.57	...
Burkina Faso Burkina Faso										
Money market										
Marché monétaire	...	...	...	...	...	4.81	4.95	4.95	4.95	4.95
Canada Canada										
Money market										
Marché monétaire	4.63	5.05	6.92	4.33	3.26	4.87	4.74	5.52	4.11	2.45
Treasury bill										
Bons du trésor	4.84	5.54	6.89	4.21	3.26	4.73	4.72	5.49	3.77	2.59
Chile Chili										
Money market										
Marché monétaire	...	...	...	...	...	...	...	10.09	6.81	4.08
China, Hong Kong SAR Chine, Hong Kong RAS										
Money market										
Marché monétaire	4.00	5.44	6.00	5.13	4.50	5.50	5.75	7.13	2.69	1.50
Treasury bill										
Bons du trésor	3.17	5.66	5.55	4.45	7.50	5.04	4.94	5.69	1.69	1.35
China, Macao SAR Chine, Macao RAS										
Money market										
Marché monétaire	3.79	5.91	6.01	5.60	7.54	5.41	5.70	6.29	2.11	1.48
Colombia Colombie										
Money market										
Marché monétaire	...	...	22.40	28.37	23.83	35.00	18.81	10.87	10.43	6.06
Côte d'Ivoire Côte d'Ivoire										
Money market										
Marché monétaire	...	...	...	...	...	4.81	4.95	4.95	4.95	4.95
Croatia Croatie										
Money market										
Marché monétaire	1 370.50	26.93	21.13	17.60	9.71	11.16	10.21	6.78	3.42	1.75
Cyprus Chypre										
Money market										
Marché monétaire	...	...	...	6.85	4.82	4.80	5.15	5.96	4.93	3.42
Treasury bill										
Bons du trésor	6.00	6.00	6.00	6.05	5.38	5.59	5.59	6.01	...	...
Czech Republic République tchèque										
Money market										
Marché monétaire	8.00	12.65	10.93	12.67	17.50	10.08	5.58	5.42	4.69	2.63
Treasury bill										
Bons du trésor	6.62	6.98	8.99	11.91	11.21	10.51	5.71	5.37	5.06	2.72
Denmark Danemark										
Money market										
Marché monétaire	#11.49	6.30	6.19	3.98	3.71	4.27	3.37	4.98	...	3.56
Dominica Dominique										
Money market										
Marché monétaire	5.25	5.25	5.25	5.25	5.25	5.25	5.25	5.25	#5.64	6.32
Treasury bill										
Bons du trésor	6.40	6.40	6.40	6.40	6.40	6.40	6.40	6.40	6.40	6.40

27

Short-term interest rates
Treasury bill and money market rates: per cent per annum *[cont.]*

Taux d'intérêt à court terme
Taux des bons du Trésor et du marché monétaire : pour cent par année *[suite]*

Country or area Pays ou zone	1993	1994	1995	1996	1997	1998	1999	2000	2001	2002
Dominican Republic Rép. dominicaine										
Money market Marché monétaire	...	...	...	14.70	13.01	16.68	15.30	18.28	13.47	14.50
Egypt Egypte										
Treasury bill Bons du trésor	...	...	...	...	8.80	8.80	9.00	9.10	7.20	5.50
El Salvador El Salvador										
Money market Marché monétaire	...	...	...	...	10.43	9.43	10.68	6.93	5.28	4.40
Estonia Estonie										
Money market Marché monétaire	...	5.67	4.94	3.53	6.45	11.66	5.39	#5.68	5.31	3.88
Ethiopia Ethiopie										
Treasury bill Bons du trésor	12.00	12.00	12.00	7.22	3.97	3.48	3.65	2.74	3.06	1.30
Euro Area [2] Zone euro [2]										
Money market Marché monétaire	...	...	...	...	...	...	2.97	4.39	4.26	3.32
Fiji Fidji										
Money market Marché monétaire	2.91	4.10	3.95	2.43	1.91	1.27	1.27	2.58	0.79	0.92
Treasury bill Bons du trésor	2.91	2.69	3.15	2.98	2.60	2.00	2.00	3.63	1.51	1.66
Finland Finlande										
Money market Marché monétaire	7.77	5.35	5.75	3.63	3.23	3.57	2.96	4.39	4.26	3.32
France France										
Money market [1] Marché monétaire [1]	8.75	5.69	6.35	3.73	3.24	3.39	...	...	...	...
Treasury bill Bons du trésor	8.41	5.79	6.58	3.84	3.35	3.45	2.72	4.23	4.26	...
Georgia Géorgie										
Money market Marché monétaire	...	...	...	43.39	26.58	43.26	34.61	18.17	#17.52	27.69
Treasury bill Bons du trésor	...	...	...	...	...	...	...	...	29.93	43.42
Germany Allemagne										
Money market Marché monétaire	7.49	5.35	4.50	3.27	3.18	3.41	2.73	4.11	4.37	3.28
Treasury bill Bons du trésor	6.22	5.05	4.40	3.30	3.32	3.42	2.88	4.32	3.66	2.97
Ghana Ghana										
Treasury bill Bons du trésor	30.95	27.72	35.38	41.64	42.77	34.33	26.37	36.28	40.96	25.11
Greece Grèce										
Money market [1] Marché monétaire [1]	...	24.60	16.40	13.80	12.80	13.99	...	...	...	...
Treasury bill Bons du trésor	20.25	17.50	14.20	11.20	11.38	10.30	8.30	#6.22	4.08	3.50
Grenada Grenade										
Money market Marché monétaire	5.25	5.25	5.25	5.25	5.25	5.25	5.25	5.25	#5.64	6.32
Treasury bill Bons du trésor	6.50	6.50	6.50	6.50	6.50	6.50	6.50	6.50	#7.00	7.00
Guatemala Guatemala										
Money market Marché monétaire	...	...	...	...	7.77	6.62	9.23	9.33	10.58	9.11
Guinea-Bissau Guinée-Bissau										
Money market Marché monétaire	...	...	...	...	...	4.81	4.95	4.95	4.95	4.95

27

Short-term interest rates
Treasury bill and money market rates: per cent per annum [cont.]
Taux d'intérêt à court terme
Taux des bons du Trésor et du marché monétaire : pour cent par année [suite]

Country or area Pays ou zone	1993	1994	1995	1996	1997	1998	1999	2000	2001	2002
Guyana Guyana										
Treasury bill										
Bons du trésor	16.83	17.66	17.51	11.35	8.91	8.33	11.31	9.88	7.78	4.94
Haïti Haïti										
Treasury bill										
Bons du trésor	...	...	...	...	14.13	16.21	7.71	12.33	13.53	7.56
Hungary Hongrie										
Treasury bill										
Bons du trésor	17.22	26.93	32.04	23.96	20.13	17.83	14.68	11.03	10.79	8.91
Iceland Islande										
Money market										
Marché monétaire	8.61	4.96	6.58	6.96	7.38	8.12	9.24	11.61	14.51	11.21
Treasury bill										
Bons du trésor	8.35	4.95	7.22	6.97	7.04	7.40	8.61	11.12	11.03	7.99
India Inde										
Money market										
Marché monétaire	8.64	7.14	15.57	11.04	5.29	...	...	...	...	...
Indonesia Indonésie										
Money market										
Marché monétaire	8.66	9.74	13.64	13.96	27.82	62.79	23.58	10.32	15.03	13.54
Ireland Irlande										
Money market										
Marché monétaire	10.49	#5.75	5.45	5.74	6.43	3.23	3.14	4.84	3.31	2.88
Treasury bill										
Bons du trésor	#9.06	5.87	6.19	5.36	6.03	5.37	...	...	...	...
Israel Israël										
Treasury bill										
Bons du trésor	10.54	11.77	14.37	15.34	13.39	11.33	11.41	8.81	6.50	7.38
Italy Italie										
Money market										
Marché monétaire	10.20	8.51	10.46	8.82	6.88	4.99	2.95	4.39	4.26	3.32
Treasury bill										
Bons du trésor	10.58	9.17	10.85	8.46	6.33	4.59	3.01	4.53	4.05	3.26
Jamaica Jamaïque										
Treasury bill										
Bons du trésor	28.85	42.98	27.65	37.95	21.14	25.65	20.75	18.24	16.71	15.54
Japan Japon										
Money market										
Marché monétaire	#3.06	2.20	1.21	0.47	0.48	0.37	0.06	0.11	0.06	0.01
Kazakhstan Kazakhstan										
Treasury bill										
Bons du trésor	...	214.34	48.98	28.91	15.15	23.59	15.63	6.59	5.28	5.20
Kenya Kenya										
Treasury bill										
Bons du trésor	49.80	23.32	18.29	22.25	22.87	22.83	13.87	12.05	12.60	8.95
Korea, Republic of Corée, République de										
Money market										
Marché monétaire	12.12	12.45	12.57	12.44	13.24	14.98	5.01	5.16	4.69	4.21
Kuwait Koweït										
Money market										
Marché monétaire	7.43	6.31	7.43	6.98	7.05	7.24	6.32	6.82	4.62	2.99
Treasury bill										
Bons du trésor	...	6.32	7.35	6.93	6.98	...	...	...	...	...
Kyrgyzstan Kirghizistan										
Money market										
Marché monétaire	...	...	...	...	...	43.98	43.71	24.26	11.92	...
Treasury bill										
Bons du trésor	...	143.13	34.90	40.10	35.83	43.67	47.19	32.26	19.08	10.15
Lao People's Dem. Rep. Rép. dém. pop. lao										
Treasury bill										
Bons du trésor	...	...	20.46	...	...	23.66	30.00	29.94	22.70	21.41

27

Short-term interest rates
Treasury bill and money market rates: per cent per annum *[cont.]*

Taux d'intérêt à court terme
Taux des bons du Trésor et du marché monétaire : pour cent par année *[suite]*

Country or area Pays ou zone	1993	1994	1995	1996	1997	1998	1999	2000	2001	2002
Latvia Lettonie										
Money market										
Marché monétaire	...	37.18	22.39	13.08	3.76	4.42	4.72	2.97	5.23	3.01
Treasury bill										
Bons du trésor	...	...	28.24	16.27	4.73	5.27	6.23	#4.85	5.63	3.52
Lebanon Liban										
Treasury bill										
Bons du trésor	18.27	15.09	19.40	15.19	13.42	12.70	11.57	11.18	11.18	10.90
Lesotho Lesotho										
Treasury bill										
Bons du trésor	#10.01	9.44	12.40	13.89	14.83	15.47	12.45	9.06	9.49	11.34
Libyan Arab Jamah. Jamah. arabe libyenne										
Money market										
Marché monétaire	4.00	...	...	...	...	4.00	4.00	4.00	4.00	4.00
Lithuania Lituanie										
Money market										
Marché monétaire	...	69.48	26.73	20.26	9.55	#6.12	6.26	3.60	3.37	2.21
Treasury bill										
Bons du trésor	...	...	26.82	20.95	8.64	10.69	11.14	#9.27	5.68	3.72
Luxembourg [1] Luxembourg [1]										
Money market										
Marché monétaire	8.09	5.16	4.26	3.29	3.36	3.48	...	...	...	...
Madagascar Madagascar										
Money market										
Marché monétaire	...	0.00	29.00	10.00	...	11.24	...	16.00	...	...
Treasury bill										
Bons du trésor	...	...	...	...	...	...	...	...	10.28	...
Malawi Malawi										
Treasury bill										
Bons du trésor	23.54	27.68	46.30	30.83	18.31	32.98	42.85	39.52	42.41	41.75
Malaysia Malaisie										
Money market										
Marché monétaire	6.53	4.65	5.78	#6.98	7.61	8.46	3.38	2.66	2.79	2.73
Treasury bill										
Bons du trésor	6.48	3.68	5.50	6.41	6.41	6.86	3.53	2.86	2.79	2.73
Maldives Maldives										
Money market										
Marché monétaire	5.00	5.00	6.80	6.80	6.80	6.80	6.80	6.80	...	...
Mali Mali										
Money market										
Marché monétaire	...	...	...	...	...	4.81	4.95	4.95	4.95	4.95
Malta Malte										
Treasury bill										
Bons du trésor	4.60	4.29	4.65	4.99	5.08	5.41	5.15	4.89	4.93	4.03
Mauritius Maurice										
Money market										
Marché monétaire	7.73	10.23	10.35	9.96	9.43	8.99	10.01	7.66	7.25	6.20
Mexico Mexique										
Money market										
Marché monétaire	17.39	16.47	#60.92	33.61	21.91	26.89	24.10	16.96	12.89	8.17
Treasury bill										
Bons du trésor	14.99	14.10	48.44	31.39	19.80	24.76	21.41	15.24	11.31	7.09
Montserrat Montserrat										
Money market										
Marché monétaire	5.25	5.25	5.25	5.25	5.25	5.25	5.25	5.25	#5.64	6.32
Morocco Maroc										
Money market										
Marché monétaire	...	12.29	10.06	8.42	7.89	6.30	5.64	5.41	4.44	2.99

27

Short-term interest rates
Treasury bill and money market rates: per cent per annum *[cont.]*

Taux d'intérêt à court terme
Taux des bons du Trésor et du marché monétaire : pour cent par année *[suite]*

Country or area Pays ou zone	1993	1994	1995	1996	1997	1998	1999	2000	2001	2002
Mozambique Mozambique										
Money market										
Marché monétaire	...	...	...	...	...	...	9.92	16.12	#25.00	20.40
Treasury bill										
Bons du trésor	...	...	...	...	...	...	...	16.97	24.77	...
Namibia Namibie										
Treasury bill										
Bons du trésor	12.16	11.35	13.91	15.25	15.69	17.24	13.28	10.26	9.29	11.00
Nepal Népal										
Treasury bill										
Bons du trésor	4.50	6.50	9.90	11.51	2.52	3.70	4.30	5.30	5.00	3.80
Netherlands [1] Pays-Bas [1]										
Money market										
Marché monétaire	7.10	5.14	4.22	2.89	3.07	3.21	...	...	...	...
Netherlands Antilles Antilles néerlandaises										
Treasury bill										
Bons du trésor	4.83	4.48	5.46	5.66	5.77	5.82	6.15	6.15	6.15	4.96
New Zealand Nouvelle-Zélande										
Money market										
Marché monétaire	6.25	6.13	8.91	9.38	7.38	6.86	4.33	6.12	5.76	5.40
Treasury bill										
Bons du trésor	6.21	6.69	8.82	9.09	7.53	7.10	4.58	6.39	5.56	5.52
Niger Niger										
Money market										
Marché monétaire	...	...	...	...	...	4.81	4.95	4.95	4.95	4.95
Nigeria Nigéria										
Treasury bill										
Bons du trésor	24.50	12.87	12.50	12.25	12.00	12.26	17.82	15.50	17.50	19.03
Norway Norvège										
Money market										
Marché monétaire	7.64	5.70	5.54	4.97	3.77	6.03	6.87	6.72	7.38	7.05
Pakistan Pakistan										
Money market										
Marché monétaire	11.00	8.36	11.52	11.40	12.10	10.76	9.04	8.57	8.49	5.53
Treasury bill										
Bons du trésor	13.03	11.26	12.49	13.61	#15.74	...	...	8.38	10.71	6.08
Papua New Guinea Papouasie-Nvl-Guinée										
Treasury bill										
Bons du trésor	6.25	6.85	17.40	14.44	9.94	21.18	22.70	17.00	12.36	10.93
Paraguay Paraguay										
Money market										
Marché monétaire	22.55	18.64	20.18	16.35	12.48	20.74	17.26	10.70	13.45	13.19
Philippines Philippines										
Money market										
Marché monétaire	13.77	13.99	11.93	12.77	16.16	13.90	10.16	10.84	9.75	7.15
Treasury bill										
Bons du trésor	12.45	12.71	11.76	12.34	12.89	15.00	10.00	9.91	9.73	5.49
Poland Pologne										
Money market										
Marché monétaire	24.51	23.32	25.82	20.63	22.43	20.59	13.58	18.16	16.23	9.39
Treasury bill										
Bons du trésor	33.16	28.81	25.62	20.32	21.58	19.09	13.14	16.62	...	...
Portugal Portugal										
Money market [1]										
Marché monétaire [1]	13.25	10.62	8.91	7.38	5.78	4.34	2.71	...	...	...
Treasury bill										
Bons du trésor	...	...	7.75	5.75	4.43	...	...	...	...	...

27

Short-term interest rates
Treasury bill and money market rates: per cent per annum *[cont.]*

Taux d'intérêt à court terme
Taux des bons du Trésor et du marché monétaire : pour cent par année *[suite]*

Country or area Pays ou zone	1993	1994	1995	1996	1997	1998	1999	2000	2001	2002
Republic of Moldova **République de Moldova**										
Money market										
Marché monétaire	...	...	...	...	28.10	30.91	32.60	20.77	11.04	5.13
Treasury bill										
Bons du trésor	...	...	52.90	39.01	23.63	30.54	28.49	22.20	14.24	5.89
Romania **Roumanie**										
Treasury bill										
Bons du trésor	...	...	...	51.09	85.72	63.99	74.21	51.86	42.18	27.03
Russian Federation **Fédération de Russie**										
Money market										
Marché monétaire	...	...	190.43	47.65	20.97	50.56	14.79	7.14	10.10	8.19
Treasury bill										
Bons du trésor	...	...	168.04	86.07	23.43	...	...	12.12	12.45	12.72
Saint Kitts and Nevis **Saint-Kitts-et-Nevis**										
Money market										
Marché monétaire	5.25	5.25	5.25	5.25	5.25	5.25	5.25	5.25	#5.64	6.32
Treasury bill										
Bons du trésor	6.50	6.50	6.50	6.50	6.50	6.50	6.50	6.50	7.50	7.50
Saint Lucia **Sainte-Lucie**										
Money market										
Marché monétaire	5.25	5.25	5.25	5.25	5.25	5.25	5.25	5.25	#5.64	6.32
Treasury bill										
Bons du trésor	7.00	7.00	7.00	7.00	7.00	7.00	7.00	7.00	6.80	6.80
St. Vincent-Grenadines **St. Vincent-Grenadines**										
Money market										
Marché monétaire	5.25	5.25	5.25	5.25	5.25	5.25	5.25	5.25	#5.64	6.32
Treasury bill										
Bons du trésor	6.50	6.50	6.50	6.50	6.50	6.50	6.50	6.50	7.00	7.00
Senegal **Sénégal**										
Money market										
Marché monétaire	...	...	...	...	...	4.81	4.95	4.95	4.95	4.95
Seychelles **Seychelles**										
Treasury bill										
Bons du trésor	12.91	12.36	12.15	11.47	10.50	7.96	4.50	4.50	4.50	4.50
Sierra Leone **Sierra Leone**										
Treasury bill										
Bons du trésor	28.64	12.19	14.73	29.25	12.71	22.10	32.42	26.22	13.74	15.15
Singapore **Singapour**										
Money market										
Marché monétaire	2.50	3.68	2.56	2.93	4.35	5.00	2.04	2.57	1.99	0.96
Treasury bill										
Bons du trésor	0.92	1.94	1.05	1.38	2.32	2.12	1.12	2.18	1.69	0.81
Slovakia **Slovaquie**										
Money market										
Marché monétaire	...	...	...	...	...	...	...	8.08	7.76	6.33
Slovenia **Slovénie**										
Money market										
Marché monétaire	39.15	29.08	12.18	13.98	9.71	7.45	6.87	6.95	6.90	4.93
Treasury bill										
Bons du trésor	...	...	...	...	...	...	8.63	10.94	10.88	8.73
Solomon Islands **Îles Salomon**										
Treasury bill										
Bons du trésor	12.15	11.25	12.50	12.75	12.88	6.00	6.00	7.05	8.23	6.87
South Africa **Afrique du Sud**										
Money market										
Marché monétaire	10.83	10.24	13.07	15.54	15.59	17.11	13.06	9.54	#8.49	#11.11
Treasury bill										
Bons du trésor	11.31	10.93	13.53	15.04	15.26	16.53	12.85	10.11	9.68	11.16

27

Short-term interest rates
Treasury bill and money market rates: per cent per annum *[cont.]*
Taux d'intérêt à court terme
Taux des bons du Trésor et du marché monétaire : pour cent par année *[suite]*

Country or area Pays ou zone	1993	1994	1995	1996	1997	1998	1999	2000	2001	2002
Spain Espagne										
Money market										
Marché monétaire	12.33	7.81	8.98	7.65	5.49	4.34	2.72	4.11	4.36	3.28
Treasury bill										
Bons du trésor	10.53	8.11	9.79	7.23	5.02	3.79	3.01	4.61	3.92	3.34
Sri Lanka Sri Lanka										
Money market										
Marché monétaire	25.65	18.54	41.87	24.33	18.42	15.74	16.69	17.30	21.24	12.33
Treasury bill										
Bons du trésor	16.52	12.68	16.81	#17.40	...	12.59	12.51	14.02	17.57	12.47
Swaziland Swaziland										
Money market										
Marché monétaire	9.73	7.01	8.52	9.77	10.35	10.63	8.86	5.54	5.06	7.31
Treasury bill										
Bons du trésor	8.25	8.35	10.87	13.68	14.37	13.09	11.19	8.30	7.16	8.59
Sweden Suède										
Money market										
Marché monétaire	9.08	7.36	8.54	6.28	4.21	4.24	3.14	3.81	4.08	...
Treasury bill										
Bons du trésor	8.35	7.40	8.75	5.79	4.11	4.19	3.12	3.95	...	...
Switzerland Suisse										
Money market										
Marché monétaire	4.94	3.85	2.89	1.78	1.35	1.22	0.93	#3.50	1.65	0.44
Treasury bill										
Bons du trésor	4.75	3.97	2.78	1.72	1.45	1.32	1.17	2.93	2.68	0.94
Thailand Thaïlande										
Money market										
Marché monétaire	6.54	7.25	10.96	9.23	14.59	13.02	1.77	1.95	2.00	1.76
Togo Togo										
Money market										
Marché monétaire	...	...	...	...	...	4.81	4.95	4.95	4.95	4.95
Trinidad and Tobago Trinité-et-Tobago										
Treasury bill										
Bons du trésor	9.45	10.00	8.41	10.44	9.83	11.93	10.40	10.56	8.55	4.83
Tunisia Tunisie										
Money market										
Marché monétaire	10.48	8.81	8.81	8.64	6.88	6.89	5.99	5.88	6.04	5.93
Turkey Turquie										
Money market										
Marché monétaire	62.83	136.47	72.30	76.24	70.32	74.60	73.53	56.72	91.95	49.51
Treasury bill										
Bons du trésor	...	...	...	...	...	...	...	25.18	85.33	59.50
Uganda Ouganda										
Treasury bill										
Bons du trésor	#21.30	12.52	8.75	11.71	10.59	7.77	7.43	13.19	11.00	5.85
Ukraine Ukraine										
Money market										
Marché monétaire	...	...	...	...	22.05	40.41	44.98	18.34	16.57	5.50
United Kingdom Royaume-Uni										
Money market										
Marché monétaire	5.91	4.88	6.08	5.96	6.61	7.21	5.20	5.77	5.08	3.89
Treasury bill										
Bons du trésor	5.21	5.15	6.33	5.78	6.48	6.82	5.04	5.80	4.77	3.86
United Rep. of Tanzania Rép.-Unie de Tanzanie										
Treasury bill										
Bons du trésor	34.00	35.09	40.33	15.30	9.59	11.83	10.05	9.78	4.14	3.55
United States États-Unis										
Money market [3]										
Marché monétaire [3]	3.02	4.20	5.84	5.30	5.46	5.35	4.97	6.24	3.89	1.67
Treasury bill										
Bons du trésor	3.02	4.27	5.51	5.02	5.07	4.82	4.66	5.84	3.45	1.61

27

Short-term interest rates
Treasury bill and money market rates: per cent per annum *[cont.]*

Taux d'intérêt à court terme
Taux des bons du Trésor et du marché monétaire : pour cent par année *[suite]*

Country or area Pays ou zone	1993	1994	1995	1996	1997	1998	1999	2000	2001	2002
Uruguay Uruguay										
Money market										
Marché monétaire	...	39.82	36.81	28.47	23.43	20.48	13.96	14.82	22.10	89.37
Treasury bill										
Bons du trésor	...	44.60	39.40	29.20	23.18	...	...	...	...	...
Vanuatu Vanuatu										
Money market										
Marché monétaire	6.00	6.00	6.00	6.00	6.00	8.65	6.99	5.58	5.50	5.50
Venezuela Venezuela										
Money market										
Marché monétaire	...	...	...	16.70	12.47	18.58	7.48	8.14	13.33	28.87
Viet Nam Viet Nam										
Treasury bill										
Bons du trésor	26.40	...	...	...	...	...	...	5.42	5.49	5.92
Yemen Yémen										
Treasury bill										
Bons du trésor	...	...	...	25.20	15.97	12.53	20.57	14.16	13.25	11.55
Zambia Zambie										
Treasury bill										
Bons du trésor	124.03	74.21	39.81	52.78	29.48	24.94	36.19	31.37	44.28	34.54
Zimbabwe Zimbabwe										
Money market										
Marché monétaire	34.18	30.90	29.64	26.18	25.15	37.22	53.13	64.98	21.52	32.35
Treasury bill										
Bons du trésor	33.04	29.22	27.98	24.53	22.07	32.78	50.48	64.78	17.60	28.51

Source:
International Monetary Fund (IMF), Washington, D.C., "International Financial Statistics," January 2004 and the IMF database.

Source:
Fonds monétaire international (FMI), Washington, D.C.,"Statistiques Financières Internationales," janvier 2004 et la base de données du FMI.

1   Beginning 1999, see Euro Area. Greece, beginning 2001.
2   Interbank rate (3 month maturity).
3   Federal funds rate.

1   A partir de 1999, voir la Zone euro. Grèce, à partir de 2001.
2   Taux interbancaire (3 mois).
3   Taux des fonds du système fédérale.

Technical notes, tables 26 and 27

Detailed information and current figures relating to tables 26 and 27 are contained in *International Financial Statistics*, published by the International Monetary Fund [15] (see also <www.imf.org>) and in the United Nations *Monthly Bulletin of Statistics* [26].

Table 26: The discount rates shown represent the rates at which the central bank lends or discounts eligible paper for deposit money banks, typically shown on an end-of-period basis.

Table 27: The rates shown represent short-term treasury bill rates and money market rates. The treasury bill rate is the rate at which short-term securities are issued or traded in the market. The money market rate is the rate on short-term lending between financial institutions.

Notes techniques, tableaux 26 et 27

Les informations détaillées et les chiffres courants concernant les tableaux 26 et 27 figurent dans les *Statistiques financières internationales* publiées par le Fonds monétaire international [15] (voir aussi <www.imf.org>) et dans le *Bulletin mensuel de statistique* des Nations Unies [26].

Tableau 26: Les taux d'escomptes indiqués représentent les taux que la banque centrale applique à ses prêts ou auquel elle réescompte les effets escomptables des banques créatrices de monnaie (généralement, taux de fin de période).

Tableau 27: Les taux indiqués représentent le taux des bons du Trésor et le taux du marché monétaire à court terme. Le taux des bons du Trésor est le taux auquel les effets à court terme sont émis ou négociés sur le marché. Le taux du marché monétaire est le taux prêteur à court terme entre institutions financières.

28A
Employment by industry, ISIC Rev. 2
Total employment and persons employed by branch of economic activity (thousands)
Emploi par industrie, CITI Rév.2
Emploi total et personnes employées par branches d'activité économique (milliers)

Country or area / Pays ou zone	Year / Année	Total employment / Emploi total M	F	Major division 1 / Branche 1 M	F	Major division 2 / Branche 2 M	F	Major division 3 / Branche 3 M	F	Major division 4 / Branche 4 M	
Bangladesh[6]	1990	30 443.0	19 716.0	16 560.0	16 743.0	15.0	...	4 240.0	1 685.0	39.0	
Bangladesh[6]	1996[7]	33 765.0	20 832.0	18 382.0	16 148.0	22.0	1.0	2 586.0	1 499.0	90.0	1.
	2000	32 369.0[1]	19 395.0[1]	17 256.0[1]	14 914.0[1]	107.0[1]	188.0[1]	2 346.0[1]	1 436.0[1]	116.0[1]	1
Barbados[1,2]	1999	65.5	56.9	3.4	1.8	...	...	5.4	4.9	1.4	
Barbade[1,2]	2000	66.6	59.8	...	...	...	...	...	...	...	
	2001	67.8	60.9	3.2	2.2	...	...	4.8	4.4	1.3	
Belarus[5]	2000	4 441.0	...	...	...	...	...	...	...	...	
Bélarus[5]	2001	4 417.4	...	...	...	...	...	...	...	...	
	2002	4 380.8	...	...	...	...	...	...	...	...	
Brazil[7,11,12]	1998	42 312.0	27 650.0	10 996.0	5 342.0	712.0[13]	150.0[13]	5 910.0	2 320.0	...	
Brésil[7,11,12]	1999	42 813.0	28 864.0	11 470.0	5 902.0	657.0[13]	126.0[13]	5 849.0	2 430.0	...	
	2001	44 748.0	30 711.0	10 577.0	4 957.0	712.0[13]	132.0[13]	6 516.0	2 784.0	...	
Chile[1,2,24]	2000	3 600.5	1 781.0	695.3	81.6	68.4	1.9	552.2	201.9	23.3	
Chili[1,2,24]	2001	3 663.7	1 815.8	661.3	84.2	69.3	2.3	567.2	214.6	27.9	
	2002	3 697.0	1 834.3	660.1	86.5	66.1	3.7	581.0	199.4	26.1	
China[5,25,26,27]	2000	720 850.0	...	333 550.0	...	5 970.0	...	80 430.0	...	2 840.0	
Chine[5,25,26,27]	2001	730 250.0	...	329 740.0	...	5 610.0	...	80 830.0	...	2 880.0	
	2002	737 400.0	...	...	...	...	...	...	...	...	
China, Hong Kong SAR[1,2,29]	2000	1 854.5	1 352.8	6.3	3.0	0.3	...	213.3	120.4	14.7	
Chine, Hong Kong RAS[1,2,29]	2001	1 846.9	1 405.4	5.1	2.1	0.2	...	210.1	116.2	13.5	
	2002	1 799.8	1 432.5	6.6	3.2	0.3	0.1	181.7	107.8	13.0	
Colombia[32,33]	2000	3 237.3	2 672.4	51.7	13.5	10.9	1.5	684.8	509.5	29.2	
Colombie[32,33]	2001	9 950.1	6 547.5	3 231.4	429.7	95.1	96.3	1 133.3	985.1	65.6	2
	2002	9 935.0	6 685.0	3 021.6	470.3	135.5	45.4	1 154.0	1 046.4	61.1	1
Cuba[1,5]	1998	3 753.6	...	921.6	...	53.7	...	577.0	...	57.9	
Cuba[1,5]	1999	3 821.3	...	912.6	...	42.3	...	637.1	...	65.5	
	2000	3 843.0	...	937.9	...	50.5	...	615.0	...	53.2	
Honduras[2,7]	1997[44]	1 374.5	714.0	722.0	50.7	2.9	0.1	170.6	191.1	5.6	
Honduras[2,7]	1998[45]	1 400.8	734.2	680.9	57.6	4.4	0.1	177.1	191.3	5.8	
	1999[45]	1 472.1	826.9	732.5	73.6	2.3	1.5	180.2	196.6	6.6	
Indonesia[1,46]	1997	53 971.0	33 079.0	21 960.0	13 889.0	710.0	186.0	6 189.0	5 026.0	214.0	1
Indonésie[1,46]	1998	53 900.5	33 773.1	23 871.3	15 543.5	573.9	100.7	5 482.4	4 451.2	131.1	1
	1999	54 908.0	33 908.3	23 764.0	14 613.8	621.0	104.6	6 481.0	5 034.7	178.0	1
Jamaica[2,30]	2000	552.5	383.1	159.1	35.4	4.1	0.6	47.6	18.2	3.8	
Jamaïque[2,30]	2001	556.6	385.7	158.2	37.0	4.7	0.5	50.0	19.1	4.9	
	2002	546.3	396.0	145.0	37.4	3.3	0.6	45.1	19.5	5.0	
Japan[1,51]	2000	38 180.0	26 300.0	1 910.0	1 450.0	50.0	10.0	8 600.0	4 610.0	300.0	5
Japon[1,51]	2001	37 830.0	26 290.0	1 750.0	1 380.0	50.0	10.0	8 420.0	4 430.0	300.0	4
	2002	37 360.0	25 940.0	1 680.0	1 270.0	40.0	10.0	8 110.0	4 110.0	290.0	5
Malaysia[2,40]	1998	5 718.9	2 880.7	1 185.0	431.5	25.3	3.1	1 146.9	761.0	44.2	
Malaisie[2,40]	1999	5 851.2	2 986.6	1 222.3	401.4	33.9	3.9	1 187.9	802.9	43.5	
	2000	6 096.2	3 235.5	1 257.3	454.4	23.8	3.5	1 248.1	877.7	43.0	
Myanmar[2,5]	1994	16 817.0	...	11 551.0	...	87.0	...	1 250.0	...	17.0	
Myanmar[2,5]	1997	17 964.0	...	11 381.0	...	132.0	...	1 573.0	...	21.0	
	1998	18 359.0	...	11 507.0	...	121.0	...	1 666.0	...	48.0	
Nicaragua[5]	1999	1 544.2	...	655.3	...	11.7	...	125.3	...	5.8	
Nicaragua[5]	2000	1 637.1	...	711.8	...	9.4	...	127.8	...	5.9	
	2001	1 701.7	...	739.0	...	9.6	...	131.6	...	6.1	
Pakistan[2,7,59]	1998	31 344.0	5 075.0	13 682.0	3 527.0	64.0	6.0	3 181.0	446.0	247.0	
Pakistan[2,7,59]	1999	32 099.0	5 197.0	14 011.0	3 612.0	66.0	6.0	3 257.0	457.0	253.0	
	2000	31 688.0	5 159.0	14 080.0	3 761.0	24.0	1.0	3 797.0	433.0	255.0	
Paraguay[2,7,10]	1994	616.0	433.6	36.9	3.5	1.8	...	126.7	53.1	10.1	
Paraguay[2,7,10]	1995	644.8	505.6	...	...	...	...	...	...	...	
	1996	684.8	505.6	48.1	14.1	0.1	...	121.3	49.2	6.3	

Major division 5 Branche 5		Major division 6 Branche 6		Major division 7 Branche 7		Major division 8 Branche 8		Major division 9 Branche 9	
M	F	M	F	M	F	M	F	M	F
485.0	41.0	4 262.0	123.0	1 600.0	11.0	284.0	12.0	1 647.0	262.0
936.0	80.0	5 573.0	488.0	2 263.0	45.0	197.0	16.0	3 343.0	1 748.0
999.0[1]	100.0[1]	5 769.0[1]	506.0[1]	2 432.0[1]	77.0[1]	357.0[1]	46.0	1 243.0[1]	1 726.0[1]
13.2	0.8	12.5	17.0	3.3	1.2	13.6	16.7	12.7	13.7
...	...	...	...	...	...	...	...	...	...
13.2	1.0	14.3	18.5	3.9	1.8	3.9	6.5	11.1	11.8
...	...	...	...	...	...	...	...	...	...
...	...	...	...	...	...	...	...	...	...
4 787.0	193.0	5 639.0[14]	3 778.0[14]	2 501.0[15]	285.0[15]	842.0[16]	467.0[16]	10 925.0[17]	15 115.0[17]
4 558.0	185.0	5 731.0[14]	3 887.0[14]	2 542.0[15]	274.0[15]	844.0[16]	500.0[16]	11 162.0[17]	15 560.0[17]
4 791.0	131.0	6 299.0[14]	4 486.0[14]	2 877.0[15]	291.0[15]	817.0[16]	524.0[16]	12 159.0[17]	17 406.0[17]
397.2	8.9	550.4	445.1	371.0	59.2	270.0	155.8	672.7	821.5
412.2	12.0	571.3	457.6	379.2	59.8	250.9	163.3	724.9	816.6
426.1	13.7	592.0	481.1	384.8	60.0	261.7	169.2	699.1	817.1
35 520.0	...	46 860.0	...	20 290.0	...	4 270.0[28]	...	20 250.0	...
36 690.0	...	47 370.0	...	20 370.0	...	4 430.0[28]	...	20 770.0	...
...	...	...	...	...	...	...	...	...	...
282.7	19.1	503.5	478.1	284.0	72.6	270.6	182.0	279.0	475.7
270.8	20.6	499.6	481.5	280.8	72.6	281.8	196.3	284.9	513.9
265.0	21.7	493.2	490.4	273.2	72.8	283.1	191.6	283.6	542.0
253.9	11.7	814.4	720.4	342.9	59.2	276.8	204.7	770.7	1 140.3
616.6	25.8	2 278.1	1 956.4	937.5	130.9	512.6	330.7	1 077.1	2 568.1
727.0	32.7	2 277.9	1 914.7	941.9	127.8	515.7	372.7	1 089.2	2 655.8
224.9	...	446.5	...	199.6	...	59.8	...	1 212.6	...
208.1	...	482.0	...	181.1	...	69.7	...	1 222.9	...
204.5	...	473.6	...	194.9	...	55.0	...	1 258.4	...
86.7	1.6	157.3	236.5	43.0	3.8	26.8	14.6	159.6	214.5
108.8	1.8	183.5	256.4	48.9	5.7	36.5	15.9	154.8	204.3
114.3	3.5	182.3	306.8	51.8	4.2	31.2	18.7	170.8	220.3
4 050.0	150.0	8 404.0	8 817.0	4 023.0	115.0	447.0	209.0	7 972.0	4 666.0
3 385.9	135.8	8 245.0	8 570.2	4 023.6	130.2	412.0	205.8	7 775.3	4 618.9
3 295.0	120.0	8 456.0	9 073.4	4 083.0	123.5	445.0	188.9	7 585.0	4 639.3
79.2	3.2	82.0	122.8	46.2	11.4	25.9	30.0	103.5	157.9
78.0	2.5	83.3	131.4	47.2	13.4	21.8	24.6	106.7	155.2
86.1	4.3	80.3	128.7	51.1	11.8	27.0	33.4	102.1	157.0
5 550.0	980.0	7 170.0[52]	7 570.0[52]	3 370.0	780.0	3 460.0	2 700.0	7 630.0[53]	8 000.0[53]
5 360.0	960.0	7 160.0[52]	7 570.0[52]	3 290.0	780.0	3 520.0	2 770.0	7 740.0[53]	8 190.0[53]
5 260.0	920.0	6 970.0[52]	7 410.0[52]	3 250.0	770.0	3 610.0	2 780.0	7 820.0[53]	8 400.0[53]
700.4	45.5	982.6	633.3	364.7	57.0	247.4	178.4	1 022.6	764.9
677.6	45.2	1 006.2	654.5	361.8	58.5	274.2	192.0	1 043.8	821.6
750.0	48.9	1 073.8	716.2	368.7	54.0	271.9	190.1	1 049.7	885.5
292.0	...	1 450.0	...	420.0	...	486.0	...	1 264.0[54]	...
378.0	...	1 746.0	...	470.0	...	577.0	...	1 686.0[54]	...
400.0	...	1 781.0	...	495.0	...	597.0	...	1 744.0[54]	...
88.1	...	259.2	...	49.7	...	20.1	...	261.5	...
97.3	...	268.3	...	51.2	...	21.8	...	278.8	...
102.3	...	279.8	...	52.9	...	22.6	...	294.3	...
2 250.0	31.0	4 961.0	90.0	1 967.0	30.0	303.0	13.0	4 672.0	925.0
2 304.0	32.0	5 081.0	92.0	2 014.0	31.0	311.0	13.0	4 785.0	947.0
2 105.0	25.0	4 844.0	132.0	1 841.0	12.0	291.0	10.0	4 450.0	781.0
89.2	...	151.1	159.0	48.7	6.2	30.5	16.8	121.0	193.4
...	...	...	...	...	...	...	...	...	...
82.5	...	198.9	199.7	56.5	5.2	41.0	15.9	130.0	219.5

28A

Employment by industry, ISIC Rev. 2 *[cont]*

Total employment and persons employed by branch of economic activity (thousands)

Emploi par industrie, CITI Rév. 2 *[suite]*

Emploi total et personnes employées par branches d'activité économique (milliers)

Country or area Pays ou zone	Year Année	Total employment Emploi total		ISIC Rev. 2 Major divisions + CITI Rév. 2 Branches +						
				Major division 1 Branche 1		Major division 2 Branche 2		Major division 3 Branche 3		Major division 4 Branche 4
		M	F	M	F	M	F	M	F	M
Puerto Rico [2,65] Porto Rico [2,65]	2000	677.0	497.0	21.0	1.0	1.0	...	96.0	67.0	11.0
	2001	661.0	489.0	22.0	1.0	2.0	...	86.0	61.0	12.0
	2002	676.0	514.0	22.0	1.0	1.0	...	82.0	54.0	11.0
Sri Lanka [7,71,72] Sri Lanka [7,71,72]	1995	3 661.0	1 655.0	1 298.5	686.9	49.3	7.2	415.7	448.4	23.9
	1996	3 797.4	1 789.5	1 244.2	718.5	58.4	10.3	429.9	408.2	20.8
	1998	3 855.3	2 090.8	1 451.6	1 020.7	68.3	9.8	479.5	435.1	30.2
Suriname [1] Suriname [1]	1997	55.2	27.6	3.5	0.8	3.5	0.1	5.2	1.0	1.2
	1998	59.8	28.5	4.0	0.9	3.3	0.1	5.2	1.9	1.6
	1999[73]	47.8	25.1	4.0	0.5	1.7	...	2.9	...	1.0
Syrian Arab Republic [1] Rép. arabe syrienne [1]	2001	4 001.6	842.5	...	...	...	...	...	...	...
	2002	3 933.4	888.4	946.0	515.8	609.7[76]	51.7	...	...	...
Thailand [2,77,78] Thaïlande [2,77,78]	1999	17 721.2	14 365.9	8 826.0	6 737.3	40.6	11.2	2 224.8[79]	2 169.6[79]	124.6[80]
	2000	18 164.9	14 836.1	9 049.2	7 046.3	31.6	7.3	2 454.7[79]	2 330.1[79]	134.0[80]
	2001	18 471.1	15 012.7	8 862.4	6 546.5	30.5	9.2	2 203.6[79]	2 546.7[79]	89.1[80]
Trinidad and Tobago [1] Trinité-et-Tobago [1]	1999	310.1	179.3	34.6	5.1	13.2	2.4	37.3	15.7	5.3
	2000	316.9	186.2	30.9	5.4	13.9	2.6	39.0	15.9	5.6
	2001	326.0	188.1	34.4	5.9	14.5	2.1	38.0	14.7	6.4
United Rep. of Tanzania [5,7,85] Rép.-Unie de Tanzanie [5,7,85]	2001	16 914.8	...	13 890.1		29.2	...	245.4	...	14.7
United States [2,65] Etats-Unis [2,65]	2000	72 293.0	62 915.0	2 552.0	905.0	450.0	71.0	13 458.0	6 482.0	1 146.0[80]
	2001	72 080.0	62 992.0	2 377.0	900.0	484.0	83.0	12 937.0	6 033.0	1 102.0[80]
	2002	72 903.0	63 582.0	2 585.0	894.0	453.0	63.0	12 571.0	5 576.0	1 143.0[80]
Uzbekistan [5] Ouzbékistan [5]	1997	8 680.0	...	3 515.0	...	1 109.0[76]	...	...	...	...
	1998	8 800.0	...	3 467.0	...	1 114.0[76]	...	...	...	...
	1999	8 885.0	...	3 421.0	...	1 142.0[76]	...	...	...	...
Venezuela [1,2] Venezuela [1,2]	2000	5 621.5	3 200.3	851.6	47.9	47.8	6.8	802.9	344.1	49.8
	2001	5 852.2	3 552.3	838.3	53.8	43.9	5.8	825.6	381.5	46.7
	2002	5 972.8	3 726.1	881.1	67.9	38.7	8.6	767.5	382.9	39.5
Viet Nam [5] Viet Nam [5]	1995	...	...	...	...	...	...	3 227.2	...	...
	1996	...	...	...	...	...	...	3 288.8	...	...
	1997	...	...	...	...	...	...	3 292.5	...	...

Source:
International Labour Office (ILO), Geneva, "Yearbook of Labour Statistics 2003" and the ILO labour statistics database.

Countries using the latest version of the International Standard Industrial Classification of all Economic Activities, Revision 3 (ISIC Revision 3), are presented in Part B. Countries using the former classification, ISIC Revision 2 are presented in Part A.

+ Major divisions of ISIC Rev. 2 :
1. Agriculture, hunting, forestry and fishing.
2. Mining and quarrying.
3. Manufacturing.
4. Electricity, gas and water.
5. Construction.
6. Wholesale and retail trade and restaurants and hotels.
7. Transport, storage and communications.
8. Financing, insurance, real estate and business services.
9. Community, social and personal service.

1 Persons aged 15 years and over.
2 Civilian labour force employed.

Source:
Bureau international du travail (BIT), Genève, "Annuaire des statistiques du travail 2003" et la base de données du BIT.

On trouvera dans la partie B les chiffres relatifs aux pays que appliquent la version la plus récente de la Classification internationa type, par industrie, de toutes les branches d'activité économique, Révision 3 (CITI Rév. 3). Les pays qui utilisent encore la classificatio dans sa version précédente (Révision 2) figurent à la partie A.

+ Branches de la CITI Rév. 2
1. Agriculture, chasse, sylviculture et pêche.
2. Industries extractives.
3. Industries manufacturières.
4. Electricité, gaz et eau.
5. Bàtiment et travaux publics.
6. Commerce de gros et de détail ; hôtels et restaurants.
7. Transports, entrepôts et communications.
8. Banques, assurances, affaires immobilières et services fournis aux enterprises.
9. Services fournis à la collectivité, services sociaux et services personnels.

1 Personnes âgées de 15 ans et plus.
2 Main-d'oeuvre civile occupée.

Major division 5 Branche 5		Major division 6 Branche 6		Major division 7 Branche 7		Major division 8 Branche 8		Major division 9 Branche 9	
M	F	M	F	M	F	M	F	M	F
79.0	4.0	145.0[52]	101.0[52]	31.0	10.0	16.0	25.0	275.0[53]	286.0[53]
80.0	4.0	135.0[52]	103.0[52]	34.0	10.0	16.0	24.0	272.0[53]	283.0[53]
81.0	4.0	138.0[52]	112.0[52]	33.0	11.0	17.0	25.0	290.0[53]	304.0[53]
281.7	18.7	469.4	87.7	230.0	14.7	57.2	34.3	573.0	320.5
309.2	11.7	552.6	152.5	234.2	25.3	78.8	39.2	691.1	392.0
295.2	14.0	469.5	124.2	251.5	16.5	85.5	31.6	607.7	398.9
7.0	0.3	9.4	6.9	4.9	0.6	2.2	2.1	15.0	15.3
9.2	0.7	10.0	6.4	5.0	0.8	2.2	1.5	16.4	15.6
4.8	0.1	9.9	7.4	4.2	1.6	2.7	1.9	13.9	13.4
...	...	...	...	...	...	...	...	...	...
625.4	8.9	702.6	21.9	258.9	6.0	52.5	8.6	738.3	275.5
1 064.4	220.9	2 229.0[81]	2 506.9[81]	873.3	115.8	...	...	2 331.0[82]	2 561.4[82]
1 089.5	190.5	2 258.8[81]	2 542.7[81]	836.6	114.6	...	...	2 304.6[82]	2 560.2[82]
1 213.3	196.0	3 156.2[81]	3 439.4[81]	844.6	132.8	...	...	2 061.1[82]	2 121.9[82]
56.6	4.2	39.5	49.3	29.5	6.2	18.6	19.0	75.2	76.3
57.8	5.0	43.8	51.4	31.8	7.4	20.4	18.8	73.2	78.2
65.4	5.8	39.9	50.0	31.2	7.7	21.2	19.8	74.4	80.2
151.7	...	1 263.0	...	111.6	...	26.5	...	1 182.7	...
8 520.0	913.0	14 705.0[52]	13 127.0[52]	5 800.0	2 494.0	8 039.0	8 477.0	17 625.0[86]	30 144.0[86]
8 647.0	934.0	14 661.0[52]	13 011.0[52]	5 796.0	2 534.0	8 150.0	8 519.0	17 925.0[86]	30 674.0[86]
8 772.0	897.0	14 971.0[52]	13 125.0[52]	5 768.0	2 444.0	8 225.0	8 454.0	18 416.0[86]	31 802.0[86]
550.0	...	715.0	...	360.0	...	48.0	...	1 910.0	...
573.0	...	717.0	...	362.0	...	49.0	...	1 920.0	...
583.0	...	734.0	...	372.0	...	50.0	...	1 968.0	...
679.3	28.1	1 219.7	1 072.9	560.2	51.9	279.7	175.9	1 125.0	1 458.6
746.2	28.1	1 251.2	1 204.1	600.8	53.5	294.8	187.4	1 199.7	1 621.0
745.1	30.7	1 300.8	1 284.5	645.9	57.6	301.5	180.4	1 239.8	1 692.9
995.6	...	...	...	781.0	...	...	...	...	...
975.1	...	...	...	855.6	...	...	...	...	...
976.5	...	...	...	856.0	...	...	...	...	...

	Beginning 1989: estimates based on the 1991 Census of Population and Housing.	3
	Including armed forces, except conscripts not employed before their military service.	4
	Both sexes.	5
	Year ending in June of the year indicated.	6
	Persons aged 10 years and over.	7
	Including professional army; excluding compulsory military service.	8
	April of each year.	9
0	Urban areas.	10
1	Excluding rural population of Rondônia, Acre, Amazonas, Roraima, Pará and Amapá.	11
2	September of each year.	12
3	Including electricity, gas, water and sanitary services.	13
4	Excluding restaurants and hotels.	14
5	Excluding storage.	15
6	Including international and other extra-territorial bodies and activities not adequately defined.	16
7	Including restaurants, hotels and storage; excluding sanitary services and international bodies.	17
8	Excluding armed forces.	18
	Including veterinary services.	19
	Including major divisions 2 and 4.	20
	Excluding veterinary services, radio and TV broadcasting, repair and installation services.	21

3 A partir de 1989: estimations basées sur le recensement de la population et de l'habitat de 1991.
4 Y compris les forces armées, sauf les conscrits n'ayant pas travaillé avant leur service militaire.
5 Les deux sexes.
6 Année se terminant en juin de l'année indiquée.
7 Personnes âgées de 10 ans et plus.
8 Y compris les militaires de carrière; non compris les militaires du contingent.
9 Avril de chaque année.
10 Régions urbaines.
11 Non compris la population rurale de Rondônia, Acre, Amazonas, Roraima, Pará et Amapá.
12 Septembre de chaque année.
13 Y compris l'électricité, le gaz, l'eau et les services sanitaires.
14 Non compris les restaurants et hôtels.
15 Non compris les entrepôts.
16 Y compris les organisations internationales et autres organismes extra-territoriaux et les activités mal désignées.
17 Y compris les restaurants, hôtels et entrepôts; non compris les services sanitaires et les organismes internationaux.
18 Non compris les militaires.
19 Y compris les services vétérinaires.
20 Y compris les branches 2 et 4.
21 Non compris les services vétérinaires, la radiodiffusion et télévision, et les services de réparation et d'installation.

28A

Employment by industry, ISIC Rev. 2 *[cont]*

Total employment and persons employed by branch of economic activity (thousands)

Emploi par industrie, CITI Rév. 2 *[suite]*

Emploi total et personnes employées par branches d'activité économique (milliers)

22	Excluding full-time members of the armed forces.	22	Non compris les membres à temps complet des forces armées.
23	Sample design revised.	23	Plan d'échantillonnage révisé.
24	Fourth quarter of each year.	24	Quatrième trimestre de chaque année.
25	December of each year.	25	Décembre de chaque année.
26	Excluding armed forces and reemployed retired persons.	26	Non compris les forces armées et les retraités réemployés.
27	Whole national economy.	27	Ensemble de l'économie nationale.
28	Excluding business services.	28	Non compris les services aux entreprises.
29	Including unpaid family workers who worked for one hour or more.	29	Y compris les travailleurs familiaux non rémunérés ayant travaillé une heure ou plus.
30	Persons aged 14 years and over.	30	Personnes âgées de 14 ans et plus.
31	Estimates based on the 2001 Population Census results.	31	Estimations basées sur les résultats du Recensement de la population de 2001.
32	Persons ages 12 years and over.	32	Personnes âgées de 12 ans et plus.
33	Prior to 2001: seven main cities; Sep. of each year.	33	Avant 2001: Sept villes principales; septembre de chaque année.
34	July of each year.	34	Juillet de chaque année.
35	Beginning 1987: methodology revised. Data not strictly comparable.	35	A partir de 1987: méthodologie révisée. Les données ne sont pas strictement comparables.
36	Second quarter of each year.	36	Deuxième trimestre de chaque année.
37	Persons aged 15 to 74 years.	37	Personnes âgées de 15 à 74 ans.
38	November of each year.	38	Novembre de chaque année.
39	May and November of each year.	39	Mai et novembre de chaque année.
40	Persons aged 15 to 64 years.	40	Personnes âgées de 15 à 64 ans.
41	Including the armed forces.	41	Y compris les forces armées.
42	May.	42	Mai.
43	Including repairs.	43	Y compris les réparations.
44	September.	44	Septembre.
45	March of each year.	45	Mars de chaque année.
46	May of each year.	46	Mai de chaque année.
47	Including mining and quarrying.	47	Y compris les industries extractives.
48	Including permanent members of institutional households.	48	Y compris les membres permanents des ménages collectifs.
49	Including conscripts.	49	Y compris les conscrits.
50	Including electricity, gas and water.	50	Y compris l'électricité, le gaz et l'eau.
51	Including self-defence forces.	51	Y compris les forces d'autodéfense.
52	Excluding hotels.	52	Non compris les hôtels.
53	Including hotels.	53	Y compris les hôtels.
54	Including activities not adequately defined.	54	Y compris les activités mal désignées.
55	Beginning 1992, questionnaire revised.	55	A partir de 1992, questionnaire revisée.
56	Curaçao.	56	Curaçao.
57	Persons aged 16 to 74 years.	57	Personnes âgées de 16 à 74 ans.

58	Beginning 2nd quarter 1988, methodology revised.
59	July of preceding year to June of current year.
60	August of each year.
61	Asunción metropolitan area and persons aged 12 years and over, except for 1993: 10 years and over.
62	Including members of the armed forces living in private households.
63	Including restaurants and hotels.
64	Persons aged 12 years and over; including the Azores and Madeira.
65	Persons aged 16 years and over.
66	31 December of each year.
67	Prior to 1992: state and cooperative sector.
68	June of each year.
69	Excludes compulsory military service.
70	Data classified according to ISIC, Rev. 3.
71	Excluding Northern and Eastern provinces.
72	First quarter of each year.
73	First semester.
74	Persons aged 16 to 64 years.
75	Methodology revised; data not strictly comparable.
76	Including major divisions 2 to 4.
77	Third round (August) of each year.
78	Persons aged 13 years and over.
79	Including repair and installation services.
80	Including sanitary services.
81	Including financing, insurance and real estate; excluding restaurants and hotels.
82	Including restaurants and hotels; excluding repair and installation services and sanitary services.
83	Persons aged 15-70 years.
84	Excluding unpaid family workers and employees in private domestic services.
85	Year ending in March of the year indicated.
86	Including hotels; excluding sanitary services.

58	A partir de 2e trimestre de 1988, méthodologie revisée.
59	Juillet de l'année précédente à juin de l'année en cours.
60	Août de chaque année.
61	Région métropolitaine d'Asunción; personnes âgées de 12 ans et plus, mais ne comprenant pour 1993: personnes âgées de 10 ans et plus.
62	Y compris les membres des forces armées vivant en ménages privés.
63	Y compris les restaurants et les hôtels.
64	Personnes âgées de 12 ans et plus; y compris les Açores et Madère.
65	Personnes âgées de 16 ans et plus.
66	31 décembre de chaque année.
67	Avant 1992: secteur d'Etat et coopératif.
68	Juin de chaque année.
69	Non compris les militaires du contingent.
70	Données classifiées selon la CITI, Rév. 3.
71	Non compris les provinces du Nord et de l'Est.
72	Le primer trimestre de chaque année.
73	Premier trimestre.
74	Personnes âgées de 16 à 64 ans.
75	Méthodologie révisée; les données ne sont pas strictement comparables.
76	Y compris les branches 2 à 4.
77	Troisième enquête (août) de chaque année.
78	Personnes âgées de 13 ans et plus.
79	Y compris les services de réparation et d'installation.
80	Y compris les services sanitaires.
81	Y compris les banques, les assurances et affaires immobilières; non compris les restaurants et les hôtels.
82	Y compris les restaurants et hôtels; non compris les services de réparation et d'installation, et les services sanitaires.
83	Personnes âgées de 15 à 70 ans.
84	Non compris les travailleurs familiaux non rémunérés et les personnes occupées à des services domestiques privés.
85	Année se terminant en mars de l'année indiquée.
86	Y compris les hôtels; non compris les services sanitaires.

28B
Employment by industry, ISIC Rev. 3
Total employment and persons employed by branch of economic industry (thousands)
Emploi par industrie, CITI Rév. 3
Emploi total et personnes employées, par branches d'activité économique (milliers)

Country or area Pays ou zone	Year Année	Sex	Total employment Emploi total	Categ. A Catég. A	Categ. B Catég. B	Categ. C Catég. C	Categ. D Catég. D	Categ. E Catég. E	Categ. Catég.
Algeria [1,2] Algérie [1,2]	1997	MF	5 708.0	884.0[3]	...	584.0[4]	...	...	58
	2000	MF	5 725.9	898.0[3]	...	720.9[4]	...	...	66
	2001	MF	6 228.8	1 312.1[3]	...	861.1[4]	...	...	65
Anguilla [1,8] Anguilla [1,8]	1999[9]	M	3.3	0.1[12]	...	...	0.2	0.1	
	1999[9]	F	2.9	0.0[12]	...	...	0.1	0.1	
	2001[10]	M	3.0	0.0	0.1	0.0	0.1	0.1	
	2001[10]	F	2.6	0.0	0.0	0.0	0.1	0.0	
	2002[11]	M	3.0	...	...	...	...	...	
	2002[11]	F	2.5	...	...	...	...	...	
Argentina [15,16,17] Argentine [15,16,17]	2000	M	4 942.0	42.0	5.6	14.9	846.8	40.7	634
	2000	F	3 319.8	7.7	0.0	0.6	308.6	7.7	19
	2001	M	4 832.4	51.1	7.1	18.7	817.6	40.9	570
	2001	F	3 310.9	9.4	0.0	1.0	314.4	11.2	12
	2002	M	4 653.6	55.1	7.2	18.2	760.3	34.7	486
	2002	F	3 362.5	15.5	0.5	2.7	295.3	7.7	10
Australia [1,8,18] Australie [1,8,18]	2000	M	5 062.3	289.7	14.2	60.9	832.5	53.7	613
	2000	F	3 947.1	131.5	3.3	7.5	308.6	11.1	87
	2001	M	5 093.1	280.2	15.4	60.9	817.9	53.8	593
	2001	F	4 030.9	134.7	3.2	7.4	291.2	13.6	85
	2002	M	5 191.9	266.1	14.6	63.0	829.3	51.9	621
	2002	F	4 119.5	121.2	2.8	7.9	290.7	15.0	89
Austria [1] Autriche [1]	2000	M	2 145.6	118.1	0.1	8.7	566.3	25.3	313
	2000	F	1 631.0	99.6	0.2	0.9	197.6	4.7	25
	2001	M	2 142.5	113.8	0.1	8.6	553.9	26.9	308
	2001	F	1 657.1	101.4	0.1	0.9	192.4	4.6	30
	2002	M	2 139.0	113.8	0.4	7.5	558.3	30.6	309
	2002	F	1 696.7	100.8	0.3	0.8	188.8	4.7	28
Azerbaijan Azerbaïdjan	2000	M	1 937.5	703.0	2.0	29.7	76.5	29.4	124
	2000	F	1 767.0	814.2	...	9.9	92.8	11.1	19
	2001	M	1 945.0	725.1	2.3	31.9	77.3	28.6	136
	2001	F	1 770.0	756.9	...	10.2	86.6	12.4	18
	2002	M	1 948.0	795.0	2.3	33.6	74.2	28.5	160
	2002	F	1 778.5	700.0	0.2	8.6	95.3	11.4	17
Bahamas [19,20] Bahamas [19,20]	1996	M	70.4	5.7[3]	...	1.3[21]	2.8	...	11
	1996	F	59.4	0.7[3]	...	0.4[21]	2.6	...	0
	1997	M	71.3	4.3[3]	...	1.4[21]	2.7	...	11
	1997	F	63.9	1.4[3]	...	0.5[21]	2.7	...	0
	1998	M	74.6	4.4[3]	...	1.2[21]	2.9	...	14
	1998	F	69.8	0.9[3]	...	0.3[21]	2.5	...	1
Belgium [1,23,24] Belgique [1,23,24]	2000	M	2 367.6	53.2[3]	...	7.0	588.9	30.0	243
	2000	F	1 724.5	19.2[3]	...	0.7	183.7	4.6	17
	2001	M	2 346.3	47.2	0.8	6.0	576.5	25.6	243
	2001	F	1 704.9	18.2	...	0.7	179.7	5.3	16
	2002	M	2 339.2	48.2	0.5	6.4	557.5	25.8	242
	2002	F	1 730.7	20.5	0.2	0.4	179.7	4.6	17
Belize [8,19,27] Belize [8,19,27]	1997	M	49.3	19.8[3]	...	0.1	5.1	0.8	3
	1997	F	21.4	1.3[3]	...	...	3.9	0.2	0
	1998	M	50.1	17.1[3]	...	0.3	5.3	1.0	4
	1998	F	23.3	1.2[3]	...	...	2.3	0.2	0
	1999	M	53.7	19.8[3]	...	0.3	4.7	0.9	4
	1999	F	24.1	1.5[3]	...	0.0	2.6	0.1	0
Bolivia [29,30] Bolivie [29,30]	1997	M	1 065.6	74.0	0.1	43.9	214.8	9.7	153
	1997	F	812.0	32.9	...	4.9	124.0	1.3	4
	1999	M	1 130.2	55.6	1.0	16.3	224.9	4.8	174
	1999	F	886.8	20.9	...	0.0	145.6	0.8	1
	2000	M	1 171.1	71.7	...	30.1	203.9	14.5	210
	2000	F	924.9	31.0	...	5.3	116.2	1.4	8

Categ. G / Catég. G	Categ. H / Catég. H	Categ. I / Catég. I	Categ. J / Catég. J	Categ. K / Catég. K	Categ. L / Catég. L	Categ. M / Catég. M	Categ. N / Catég. N	Categ. O / Catég. O	Categ. P / Catég. P	Categ. Q / Catég. Q
838.0[5]	...	...	...	...	1 317.0	1 496.0[6]	...	...	...	...
669.8[5]	...	...	...	...	1 773.2	932.6[6]	...	...	...	...
...	...	...	...	...	...	...	...	...	...	3 405.6[7]
0.2	0.6	0.4	0.1[13]	...	0.3	0.1[14]	...	...	...	...
0.3	0.8	0.1	0.3[13]	...	0.3	0.4[14]	...	0.0	0.1	...
0.3	0.6	0.3	0.1	0.2	0.3	0.1	0.0	0.1	0.2	...
0.3	1.0	0.1	0.1	0.1	0.4	0.2	0.1	0.1	0.0	...
...	...	...	...	...	...	...	...	0.8	0.1	...
1 074.7	142.2	589.4	128.8	381.8	389.2	138.0	153.9	294.7	40.7	...
608.6	112.7	85.0	78.3	218.7	244.3	487.8	320.6	190.1	614.5	1.2
1 051.2	158.5	574.1	116.6	348.3	400.4	150.4	150.4	321.3	44.3	1.3
606.8	116.3	81.8	81.7	221.3	259.1	496.0	292.7	193.4	594.8	0.2
989.2	131.6	524.2	108.4	342.9	457.2	167.9	156.4	346.2	55.8	1.2
554.7	102.3	78.1	77.9	213.1	322.7	555.4	340.0	234.7	536.2	0.1
949.3	205.4	436.7	148.1	596.8	269.9	197.9	184.0	208.0	1.6	2.6
830.1	251.8	155.4	187.4	470.7	186.9	414.4	665.3	229.5	5.0	0.5
961.0	205.7	445.3	151.4	597.8	280.0	207.7	201.1	219.7	1.2	0.9
831.4	256.1	155.6	196.5	487.6	200.4	426.2	697.3	239.8	3.8	0.9
996.8	199.4	432.3	160.2	613.9	306.9	205.6	206.8	221.6	0.9	0.9
860.1	261.3	142.0	186.1	489.9	216.4	449.2	725.7	255.7	5.1	0.5
270.7	76.2	185.2	71.4	132.1	160.3	70.8	75.0	69.5	0.2	2.3
323.0	137.8	60.5	67.1	137.2	92.7	154.8	224.9	89.9	11.6	2.7
269.5	74.9	193.8	66.3	144.5	163.9	70.9	74.7	69.6	0.8	1.7
333.2	132.9	61.0	66.1	148.7	94.4	153.6	235.9	86.4	11.8	2.9
265.0	80.2	190.2	65.3	147.1	155.4	67.4	76.0	71.0	0.2	1.6
336.2	137.6	61.6	67.5	156.3	93.0	162.7	251.3	91.2	13.2	1.9
318.9	6.4	127.5	8.1	58.0	162.4	132.4	73.6	75.3	0.2	...
307.2	3.4	39.5	5.4	40.0	95.3	185.5	95.3	47.9	...	...
297.5	6.7	126.0	8.3	58.7	168.4	125.7	73.9	78.2	0.3	...
362.0	4.3	41.5	4.7	38.3	98.9	192.3	96.1	46.8	0.1	...
232.6	6.9	128.1	8.6	58.7	170.1	100.9	68.3	79.7	0.4	...
379.3	4.4	41.7	4.6	38.5	95.2	229.0	105.3	47.0	0.1	...
8.0	8.7	7.7	4.9[13]	...	19.2[22]	...	...	...	...	...
10.4	11.7	3.7	6.2[13]	...	23.0[22]	...	...	...	...	...
8.0	9.2	7.9	5.0[13]	...	20.7[22]	...	...	...	...	...
9.6	12.2	4.0	7.4[13]	...	25.9[22]	...	...	...	...	...
8.7	9.3	7.5	5.9[13]	...	20.3[22]	...	...	...	...	...
11.4	12.8	4.3	8.1[13]	...	28.4[22]	...	...	...	...	...
297.2	64.6	250.0	297.6[13]	...	522.0[25]	...	...	...	13.6[26]	...
275.2	68.2	67.6	214.9[13]	...	849.3[25]	...	...	...	23.6[26]	...
290.6	66.0	252.0	87.3	207.2	226.7	107.6	118.2	80.0	2.3	8.9
263.8	63.6	73.6	74.0	151.3	165.8	240.9	352.0	80.1	9.1	10.2
305.8	69.6	248.8	84.4	217.4	218.1	109.0	126.3	71.4	2.4	5.2
277.1	69.4	64.7	72.6	152.3	177.0	230.1	367.8	82.4	8.2	6.0
6.8	1.5	3.2	0.7	0.7	3.0	1.9[14]	...	1.3	0.6	0.2[28]
4.5	2.4	0.5	0.6	0.3	1.2	3.7[14]	...	1.2	2.4	0.1[28]
7.8	2.3	3.3	0.6	1.0	3.4	1.9[14]	...	1.3	0.4	0.2[28]
5.1	3.0	0.5	0.6	0.4	1.5	4.6[14]	...	1.4	2.3	0.1[28]
7.4	2.5	3.7	0.8	1.2	3.4	2.3[14]	...	1.7	0.5	0.1[28]
4.9	3.3	0.5	0.7	0.3	1.6	4.7[14]	...	1.5	2.4	0.1[28]
179.7	21.8	141.4	12.2	36.5	58.9	46.5	22.3	37.4	11.0	1.6
271.4	88.9	10.2	7.3	20.7	14.8	74.1	35.6	28.3	91.4	0.4
206.0	34.6	164.0	9.1	43.7	59.9	63.3	20.1	41.8	3.1	1.2
336.5	92.2	9.0	8.5	28.0	18.8	66.3	43.1	34.9	80.0	...
209.0	29.9	131.0	13.5	71.4	54.6	56.6	21.1	47.2	5.2	1.0
327.1	94.5	13.4	6.4	24.5	18.1	76.2	27.7	51.6	121.6	1.8

28B

Employment by industry, ISIC Rev. 3
Total employment and persons employed by branch of economic industry (thousands)
Emploi par industrie, CITI Rév. 3
Emploi total et personnes employées, par branches d'activité économique (milliers)

Country or area Pays ou zone	Year Année	Sex	Total employment Emploi total	ISIC Rev. 3 Tabulation categories + CITI Rév. 3 Catégories de classement + Categ. A Catég. A	Categ. B Catég. B	Categ. C Catég. C	Categ. D Catég. D	Categ. E Catég. E	Categ. Catég.
Botswana [8,31]	1995[32]	M	189.3	37.1[3]	...	12.8	14.2	2.6	28
Botswana [8,31]	1995[32]	F	156.1	16.7[3]	...	2.4	15.4	0.2	12
	1998	M	248.9	65.1[3]	...	11.6	22.5	2.7	26
	1998	F	192.2	24.8[3]	...	1.4	24.6	0.3	3
	2000	M	269.4	58.9[3]	...	10.0	19.8	2.0	39
	2000	F	214.0	36.4[3]	...	1.2	22.8	0.2	5
Bulgaria [2,20]	1999	MF	3 087.8	795.2	0.4	48.6	651.9	58.5	132
Bulgarie [2,20]	2000	MF	2 980.1	781.2	0.4	40.7	615.7	59.7	127
	2001	MF	2 968.1	766.4	0.4	37.3	609.5	59.6	125
Canada [1,33,34]	2000	M	8 049.3	334.8	28.5	135.0	1 644.5	90.2	723
Canada [1,33,34]	2000	F	6 860.4	122.6	6.4	28.3	635.7	26.1	84
	2001	M	8 109.7	298.0	26.3	156.1	1 635.3	91.6	751
	2001	F	6 967.1	104.5	5.8	31.0	639.2	31.4	88
	2002	M	8 262.0	294.4	26.4	140.9	1 657.8	99.0	790
	2002	F	7 149.8	107.8	4.3	28.3	668.4	32.5	85
China, Macao SAR [8,27]	2000	M	103.2	...	0.2	...	11.9	0.7	14
Chine, Macao RAS [8,27]	2000	F	92.1	...	0.1	...	26.1	0.1	1
	2001	M	106.7	...	0.1	...	13.0	0.9	15
	2001	F	96.1	...	0.1	...	31.1	0.2	1
	2002	M	104.1	0.1	0.1	...	12.6	1.0	13
	2002	F	96.5	0.1	0.1	...	28.3	0.2	1
Costa Rica [8,31,35]	1999	M	879.6	230.5	6.2	1.9	133.4	11.8	81
Costa Rica [8,31,35]	1999	F	420.5	19.7	0.1	0.2	70.6	1.4	1
	2000	M	902.5	239.7	7.0	2.4	125.6	9.3	87
	2000	F	416.1	22.4	0.2	0.2	64.7	1.6	2
	2001	M	1 013.0	214.3	7.3	1.6	148.2	15.8	104
	2001	F	539.9	20.0	0.3	0.2	84.7	3.8	3
Croatia [1]	2000	M	848.7	113.2	4.5	6.7	188.9	23.7	88
Croatie [1]	2000	F	704.3	107.0	0.5	0.5	122.0	6.0	11
	2001	M	818.9	125.2	3.8	7.5	183.3	23.5	87
	2001	F	650.6	99.3	...	1.6	122.3	5.6	9
	2002	M	842.5	124.6	5.3	8.2	190.9	21.5	95
	2002	F	684.7	102.5	0.4	0.8	121.7	5.3	9
Cyprus [1,37,38]	2000	M	176.1	9.4	0.4	0.7	23.3	2.2	26
Chypre [1,37,38]	2000	F	112.5	5.4	...	...	12.7	0.5	1
	2001	M	176.2	9.1	0.6	0.5	25.3	2.5	28
	2001	F	133.3	5.3	...	...	14.2	0.6	1
	2002	M	176.8	10.1	0.5	0.5	24.2	2.6	29
	2002	F	138.6	5.9	...	...	14.3	0.4	2
Czech Republic [1]	2000	M	2 676.0	164.0[3]	...	60.0	781.0	60.0	402
République tchèque [1]	2000	F	2 056.0	76.0[3]	...	10.0	501.0	17.0	37
	2001	M	2 674.0	158.0[3]	...	54.0	806.0	65.0	386
	2001	F	2 054.0	68.0[3]	...	13.0	504.0	22.0	41
	2002	M	2 700.0	157.0[3]	...	52.0	816.0	63.0	388
	2002	F	2 065.0	71.0[3]	...	9.0	502.0	21.0	37
Denmark [39]	2000	M	1 458.1	64.2	3.1	2.6	347.5	12.3	169
Danemark [39]	2000	F	1 263.9	22.6	0.1	...	162.5	2.3	14
	2001	M	1 456.3	64.5	4.0	2.6	335.2	10.4	167
	2001	F	1 268.9	20.4	...	0.0	153.2	3.0	14
	2002	M	1 449.3	60.4	5.2	3.8	313.5	12.0	165
	2002	F	1 265.9	19.9	...	0.6	145.7	2.9	15
Dominican Republic	1997	M	1 891.4	502.5	...	7.5	332.7	13.7	150
Rép. dominicaine	1997	F	760.6	16.5	...	0.9	150.7	6.6	3
Ecuador [17,30,40]	2000	M	2 078.2	186.4	45.1	18.1	347.1	17.2	230
Equateur [17,30,40]	2000	F	1 297.9	51.2	5.7	2.0	179.7	3.4	8
	2001[11]	M	2 211.7	186.7	38.9	16.6	388.0	22.6	227
	2001[11]	F	1 461.6	53.1	3.4	1.7	222.6	5.2	7
	2002	M	2 131.7	204.8	30.3	20.0	331.2	12.3	226
	2002	F	1 327.7	56.4	5.4	2.3	170.3	1.6	14

| Categ. G | Categ. H | Categ. I | Categ. J | Categ. K | Categ. L | Categ. M | Categ. N | Categ. O | Categ. P | Categ. Q |
Catég. G	Catég. H	Catég. I	Catég. J	Catég. K	Catég.L	Catég. M	Catég. N	Catég. O	Catég. P	Catég. Q
19.5	2.5	5.8	1.8	5.8	37.9	12.4	2.1	4.3	2.0	0.2
24.6	7.5	1.9	2.3	1.9	22.0	20.9	7.3	3.0	17.0	0.0
21.2	3.0	8.4	1.9	7.9	43.5	16.4	4.3	1.8	4.9	0.3
27.5	8.2	2.3	2.3	3.2	26.3	28.8	9.1	1.7	24.2	0.3
25.3	2.4	10.8	2.0	11.7	47.6	18.3	4.4	11.0	2.8	0.2
38.3	7.4	3.0	2.3	6.1	25.7	24.3	7.8	11.0	18.4	0.1
354.6	79.9	233.1	34.5	114.1	90.0	230.9	164.1	99.8	...	...
352.4	85.1	219.5	32.8	121.0	91.7	218.3	148.3	85.9	...	...
360.0	86.0	223.6	35.9	132.8	98.1	204.9	144.8	83.4	...	...
1 412.1	390.5	795.0	220.1	955.9	404.5	343.2	288.7	277.3	4.5	0.3
1 165.5	570.1	350.0	394.6	788.0	354.6	631.6	1 237.7	387.4	75.0	1.9
1 459.4	395.3	796.4	225.4	971.0	406.1	334.2	276.0	282.6	3.8	...
1 190.2	580.7	366.1	410.0	805.7	357.9	631.9	1 266.1	395.6	61.0	1.6
1 464.0	398.9	780.0	244.7	1 007.4	413.0	348.4	286.3	304.1	4.7	1.1
1 227.9	605.0	338.1	408.6	812.0	362.7	667.4	1 320.7	411.6	68.5	1.0
16.9	10.2	11.0	3.3	6.9	11.8	2.5	1.7	10.9	0.4	...
13.2	10.9	3.7	3.6	3.6	4.6	5.5	3.5	10.6	4.9	...
16.9	11.6	10.5	2.7	7.3	11.4	2.4	1.8	12.1	0.3	0.1
13.3	10.8	4.1	3.3	3.4	4.5	5.7	3.3	10.1	4.5	0.1
16.9	11.1	9.3	2.8	7.3	11.9	3.1	1.4	12.2	0.3	...
13.9	12.0	3.5	3.4	3.5	5.0	6.9	2.8	10.8	4.5	0.1
126.1	30.4	66.9	12.9	3.8	115.1[36]	21.2	24.7	...	6.9	1.4
77.7	34.4	7.7	7.5	1.6	43.7[36]	44.2	31.1	...	76.6	0.8
128.8	29.6	69.9	15.2	3.0	121.9[36]	23.3	23.6	...	8.3	1.3
75.5	33.0	8.9	8.7	2.4	40.7[36]	51.4	28.2	...	73.1	0.2
193.2	40.9	76.1	18.5	58.3	46.4	25.1	20.7	31.6	5.7	1.5
99.6	45.1	9.9	10.8	34.5	26.9	59.0	38.7	29.3	69.9	0.6
107.3	40.1	80.6	11.5	33.3	74.4	24.1	21.2	28.4	2.3	...
112.5	39.6	27.5	25.7	34.9	49.3	63.9	70.1	29.8	1.5	...
101.8	35.8	80.3	7.0	30.8	67.0	19.8	18.2	25.8	0.7	...
109.5	41.2	22.9	21.5	29.0	38.5	56.6	64.6	23.1	3.2	...
102.4	39.8	81.4	9.4	33.2	66.9	19.6	16.8	25.7	1.4	0.3
110.4	46.2	24.8	28.0	28.0	43.7	67.9	66.2	25.4	4.7	0.7
31.3	13.9	11.2	7.2	7.5	17.0	4.6	3.2	7.1	0.1	1.6
19.9	13.0	5.1	8.4	8.7	7.7	11.2	7.2	5.4	5.0	0.7
32.1	13.9	12.1	8.4	8.3	15.9	5.3	4.0	8.1	0.1	1.6
24.6	14.5	6.3	11.0	8.3	8.3	14.0	8.4	6.7	8.3	0.8
33.7	13.4	10.7	7.8	8.3	14.9	6.4	3.9	8.5	0.1	2.0
25.6	14.6	5.5	10.4	9.7	8.9	13.8	8.9	7.5	10.1	0.8
285.0	66.0	256.0	34.0	147.0	206.0	70.0	59.0	83.0	...	1.0
328.0	90.0	117.0	66.0	119.0	137.0	229.0	232.0	93.0	2.0	1.0
277.0	70.0	251.0	42.0	147.0	200.0	74.0	63.0	79.0	...	0.0
328.0	89.0	112.0	60.0	109.0	139.0	226.0	241.0	99.0	1.0	...
289.0	76.0	258.0	39.0	147.0	186.0	77.0	64.0	83.0	...	1.0
331.0	94.0	110.0	56.0	122.0	140.0	232.0	240.0	96.0	3.0	...
212.9	27.6	126.3	43.3	152.5	82.3	86.4	69.9	52.5	0.5	0.6
163.7	38.9	49.9	41.8	97.0	78.0	110.6	404.7	69.6	3.6	0.8
218.5	27.2	128.4	41.1	149.4	81.0	85.5	76.2	61.4	0.3	0.5
160.4	36.1	54.5	43.3	108.0	80.8	116.9	406.8	66.9	1.2	0.2
223.5	29.6	133.1	45.4	146.3	79.8	85.1	77.9	64.9	0.1	...
166.5	37.9	52.4	40.2	106.1	81.1	123.5	403.9	63.4	2.6	1.1
356.1	59.5	190.0	17.3	...	99.5	...	...	152.2	...	...
176.1	55.8	12.9	16.8	...	25.9	...	...	295.3	...	...
515.8	61.5	188.8	20.2	90.3	109.5	83.4	35.8	110.9	16.9	0.5
382.8	83.8	22.6	23.3	44.5	29.0	138.4	70.0	55.9	197.1	0.1
583.1	57.0	216.5	16.4	108.2	117.2	81.4	35.3	86.0	22.5	0.3
443.6	101.2	28.2	17.1	50.1	42.6	130.1	64.5	68.1	209.7	1.0
547.9	65.6	196.8	24.1	125.2	109.5	104.1	43.3	72.1	18.2	0.4
423.6	81.8	25.5	22.2	29.8	36.7	134.7	75.2	48.9	198.8	...

28B

Employment by industry, ISIC Rev. 3
Total employment and persons employed by branch of economic industry (thousands)
Emploi par industrie, CITI Rév. 3
Emploi total et personnes employées, par branches d'activité économique (milliers)

Country or area Pays ou zone	Year Année	Sex	Total employment Emploi total	ISIC Rev. 3 Tabulation categories + CITI Rév. 3 Catégories de classement + Categ. A Catég. A	Categ. B Catég. B	Categ. C Catég. C	Categ. D Catég. D	Categ. E Catég. E	Categ. Catég.
Egypt [8,41,42] Egypte [8,41,42]	1999	M	13 611.0	3 688.1	117.1	46.4	1 897.8	188.3	1 29
	1999	F	3 139.2	996.3	5.5	1.0	309.8	18.7	2(
	2000	M	13 958.5	3 722.5	96.7	45.7	1 870.2	191.3	1 33:
	2000	F	3 244.8	1 278.0	...	1.7	178.0	17.9	2(
	2001	M	14 361.1	3 883.6	108.8	58.1	1 835.6	194.8	1 32:
	2001	F	3 195.6	1 017.9	0.3	1.4	279.4	15.4	2!
El Salvador [17] El Salvador [17]	2000	M	1 374.4	450.6	15.6	1.5	204.8	8.5	117
	2000	F	948.3	34.3	1.3	...	228.7	0.3	1
	2001	M	1 459.1	481.8	12.0	3.0	215.7	10.5	12!
	2001	F	992.2	39.1	1.4	...	215.9	0.4	:
	2002	M	1 404.4	432.7	14.7	3.4	203.4	9.2	131
	2002	F	1 008.4	25.7	1.2	0.1	230.7	1.5	!
Estonia [45] Estonie [45]	2000	M	291.1	25.4	2.8	5.7	71.4	10.6	3!
	2000	F	281.4	12.9	0.1	1.5	57.8	4.1	:
	2001	M	293.9	26.5	2.5	4.4	74.8	9.1	3(
	2001	F	283.8	10.8	0.2	1.4	59.3	2.3	2
	2002	M	297.5	26.8	1.7	5.0	72.2	8.6	3!
	2002	F	288.1	11.9	0.2	0.7	56.0	2.0	:
Finland [45] Finlande [45]	2000	M	1 248.0	97.0	2.0	3.0	329.0	17.0	13!
	2000	F	1 108.0	43.0	...	1.0	138.0	5.0	1(
	2001	M	1 261.0	91.0	2.0	3.0	331.0	17.0	136
	2001	F	1 127.0	42.0	1.0	...	141.0	5.0	!
	2002	M	1 249.0	84.0	1.0	5.0	328.0	16.0	137
	2002	F	1 144.0	41.0	1.0	...	138.0	5.0	11
Georgia [1] Géorgie [1]	2000	M	934.8	442.3	0.8	5.5	77.8	25.7	29
	2000	F	814.0	468.1	...	0.8	26.1	3.4	2
	2001	M	966.6	509.2	0.4	5.6	68.2	25.0	21
	2001	F	911.0	480.7	0.1	1.7	34.2	4.2	1:
	2002	M	954.1	499.0	0.5	4.1	62.2	20.9	33
	2002	F	885.1	489.4	0.1	1.1	23.1	5.7	1
Germany [1,19] Allemagne [1,19]	2000[46]	M	20 680.0	635.0	4.0	139.0	6 128.0	235.0	2 729
	2000[46]	F	15 924.0	347.0	2.0	13.0	2 414.0	55.0	389
	2001	M	20 629.0	604.0	4.0	127.0	6 170.0	221.0	2 522
	2001	F	16 187.0	333.0	1.0	12.0	2 439.0	61.0	382
	2002	M	20 336.0	597.0	4.0	123.0	6 104.0	224.0	2 391
	2002	F	16 200.0	321.0	2.0	12.0	2 379.0	64.0	359
Greece [1,24,37] Grèce [1,24,37]	2000	M	2 457.3	374.1	9.7	15.5	387.1	29.9	271
	2000	F	1 489.0	285.4	1.4	1.0	169.9	8.2	5
	2001	M	2 431.4	353.2	10.4	16.7	392.7	29.2	279
	2001	F	1 486.1	262.5	0.9	1.1	164.7	5.2	5
	2002	M	2 442.5	342.7	12.1	18.0	383.5	28.8	288
	2002	F	1 506.4	267.6	1.4	0.9	157.2	4.9	5
Hungary [45,47] Hongrie [45,47]	2000	M	2 122.4	190.3[3]	...	15.4	542.6	60.5	247
	2000	F	1 726.7	61.4[3]	...	3.8	388.7	19.6	20
	2001	M	2 130.6	179.3[3]	...	11.4	557.5	60.3	251
	2001	F	1 728.9	60.1[3]	...	1.6	398.3	19.2	21
	2002[48]	M	2 112.5	176.9[3]	...	13.4	564.3	55.6	250
	2002	F	1 758.1[48]	64.0[3,48]	...	1.4[48]	395.6[48]	18.6[48]	20
Iceland [8,49,50] Islande [8,49,50]	2000	M	83.6	4.5	5.3	0.2	16.6	1.0	1(
	2000	F	72.8	2.4	0.8	...	7.3	0.3	0
	2001	M	85.0	4.3	5.5	0.2	15.9	1.1	1(
	2001	F	74.0	2.1	0.5	...	7.0	0.3	0
	2002	M	83.0	4.0	4.8	0.2	15.1	1.0	11
	2002	F	73.8	2.1	0.5	0.1	7.1	0.5	0
Iran (Islamic Rep. of) Iran (Rép. islamique d')	1996	M	12 806.2	3 024.4	38.4	115.2	1 968.8	145.2	1 634
	1996	F	1 765.4	294.2	0.3	4.7	583.2	5.4	15

Categ. G	Categ. H	Categ. I	Categ. J	Categ. K	Categ. L	Categ. M	Categ. N	Categ. O	Categ. P	Categ. Q
Catég. G	Catég. H	Catég. I	Catég. J	Catég. K	Catég.L	Catég. M	Catég. N	Catég. O	Catég. P	Catég. Q
1 741.8	257.2	1 019.6	143.6	239.0	1 292.2	1 061.7	255.2	333.5	28.8	...
278.4	42.4	40.6	41.6	34.0	339.5	702.8	275.9	23.0	9.2	...
1 803.2	257.4	1 066.3	142.0	268.9	1 444.1	1 064.6	296.5	314.0	41.7	...
203.7	11.6	59.7	43.6	44.5	381.0	725.8	235.7	28.7	7.6	...
1 903.2	271.4	1 078.7	152.6	299.5	1 495.6	1 107.5	297.2	315.8	33.2	...
222.4	53.3	63.5	46.8	38.4	391.2	712.3	269.3	38.1	19.6	...
246.0[43]	...	101.0	59.8[13]	...	86.4	25.8	49.7[44]	...	6.7	...
364.9[43]	...	8.5	28.0[13]	...	37.4	44.1	105.2[44]	...	93.7	...
264.3[43]	...	100.7	62.9[13]	...	70.7	32.0	65.0[44]	...	9.5	...
403.0[43]	...	12.7	37.6[13]	...	26.7	56.0	90.3[44]	...	105.5	...
267.4[43]	...	94.3	62.6[13]	...	71.9	36.5	58.0[44]	...	9.6	...
421.1[43]	...	9.1	35.4[13]	...	28.7	58.0	97.4[44]	...	93.6	...
34.2	4.4	39.0	3.4	20.5	16.3	7.5	3.3	11.0	...	...
45.1	15.5	17.9	4.3	19.5	17.8	37.1	25.2	18.6	...	...
34.2	3.1	37.3	2.6	19.9	18.2	9.6	5.0	10.5	...	...
49.4	14.3	16.4	4.5	18.4	16.7	41.4	25.9	19.8	...	...
35.8	4.5	36.1	2.4	25.5	17.0	10.8	5.1	10.3	...	...
50.5	13.4	18.4	5.5	18.8	16.2	44.8	26.4	19.8	...	...
144.0	22.0	125.0	15.0	138.0	74.0	54.0	37.0	48.0	...	...
134.0	54.0	46.0	34.0	100.0	60.0	110.0	289.0	75.0	4.0	...
144.0	23.0	128.0	16.0	144.0	74.0	54.0	39.0	54.0	1.0	...
133.0	57.0	46.0	34.0	108.0	59.0	110.0	303.0	72.0	3.0	...
143.0	23.0	122.0	14.0	148.0	75.0	54.0	40.0	53.0	...	...
138.0	59.0	47.0	33.0	114.0	61.0	109.0	306.0	76.0	3.0	...
91.1	7.6	59.9	3.3	29.2	83.5	21.6	26.5	27.2	2.0	1.5
83.7	7.4	12.0	5.7	8.5	22.3	92.6	58.7	18.1	1.2	0.4
113.1	4.5	68.2	3.1	14.6	74.0	26.3	12.2	19.4	0.1	1.0
68.4	11.5	14.9	7.1	24.1	31.6	112.4	73.1	27.1	4.0	1.0
115.0	5.2	63.5	2.6	10.1	75.8	24.2	11.6	25.1	1.1	0.2
100.4	9.9	14.8	5.1	10.3	32.7	105.5	51.8	26.9	7.1	0.1
2 393.0	507.0	1 426.0	648.0	1 530.0	1 804.0	669.0	939.0	868.0	7.0	19.0
2 797.0	712.0	582.0	685.0	1 393.0	1 299.0	1 259.0	2 757.0	1 076.0	130.0	14.0
2 416.0	519.0	1 465.0	651.0	1 573.0	1 771.0	698.0	956.0	905.0	7.0	20.0
2 832.0	709.0	590.0	695.0	1 432.0	1 294.0	1 298.0	2 841.0	1 123.0	135.0	10.0
2 327.0	532.0	1 438.0	646.0	1 634.0	1 705.0	687.0	990.0	906.0	9.0	19.0
2 758.0	708.0	592.0	696.0	1 487.0	1 281.0	1 333.0	2 936.0	1 132.0	129.0	11.0
422.1	143.7	208.4	56.2	108.5	196.1	94.7	63.9	72.6	3.1	0.2
255.8	109.0	43.0	51.5	87.1	97.0	147.4	119.8	55.8	51.5	...
408.0	136.7	209.0	56.1	115.2	191.3	97.9	61.4	71.4	2.5	...
265.2	118.3	41.0	51.9	97.7	99.0	153.2	116.3	55.5	48.6	...
406.7	146.7	204.8	47.7	124.6	194.1	91.9	65.1	82.3	4.5	0.3
267.9	126.0	38.7	45.2	106.8	100.0	156.5	114.4	65.3	47.9	0.4
262.8	63.3	225.8	28.2	111.0	164.9	70.5	59.7	78.7	0.5	1.2
278.1	70.0	86.0	55.5	93.6	134.1	247.3	182.0	84.1	1.4	0.3
269.4	72.9	225.4	24.3	121.6	157.0	69.7	55.0	74.7	0.5	0.4
279.0	70.1	85.5	54.6	98.0	132.6	240.1	179.9	85.6	2.0	0.8
263.8	62.5	227.3	23.2	128.4	147.8	69.4	56.6	72.4	0.3	0.3
288.3[48]	74.8[48]	82.4[48]	52.1[48]	104.4[48]	134.3[48]	248.6[48]	184.1[48]	86.1[48]	1.9[48]	0.8[48]
11.5	3.1	6.2	2.6	7.9	3.8	2.7	2.7	4.5	...	0.6
10.4	3.4	4.3	4.0	5.1	3.2	7.1	17.9	5.9	...	0.2
12.6	2.8	6.0	2.1	8.4	3.2	3.4	3.0	4.6	...	0.7
10.6	3.4	4.1	4.4	5.1	3.0	8.3	19.1	5.0	...	0.2
11.2	2.6	6.1	2.1	7.6	4.1	3.6	3.4	4.8	...	0.5
10.2	2.8	3.6	4.0	5.7	3.6	9.0	18.2	5.3	...	0.3
1 804.1	82.3	955.3	139.3	137.0	1 519.4	581.6	184.2	183.2	57.0	0.7
38.1	2.5	17.5	13.6	12.1	98.7	459.5	118.9	41.2	4.9	0.2

28B
Employment by industry, ISIC Rev. 3
Total employment and persons employed by branch of economic industry (thousands)
Emploi par industrie, CITI Rév. 3
Emploi total et personnes employées, par branches d'activité économique (milliers)

Country or area / Pays ou zone	Year / Année	Sex	Total employment Emploi total	ISIC Rev. 3 Tabulation categories + / CITI Rév. 3 Catégories de classement +					
				Categ. A / Catég. A	Categ. B / Catég. B	Categ. C / Catég. C	Categ. D / Catég. D	Categ. E / Catég. E	Categ. / Catég.
Ireland[1,51]	2000	M	989.9	113.5	2.9	5.9	198.0	9.1	159
Irlande[1,51]	2000	F	680.8	14.4	0.2	0.4	94.1	2.3	7
	2001	M	1 013.9	104.4	2.8	6.7	205.9	9.7	172
	2001	F	702.5	12.6	0.3	0.6	92.0	2.2	8
	2002	M	1 017.2	104.7	3.6	7.4	195.8	9.9	172
	2002	F	732.7	12.1	0.3	0.4	87.3	2.0	8
Isle of Man[1]	1991	M	18.3	...	...	...	...	...	
Ile de Man[1]	1991	F	13.6	...	...	...	...	...	
	1996	M	18.7	...	...	...	...	...	
	1996	F	14.9	...	...	...	...	...	
	2001	M	21.3	0.4	0.0	0.1	2.4	0.4	2
	2001	F	17.7	0.1	0.0		0.7	0.1	0
Israel[1,8,52]	2000	M	1 211.7	39.2[3]	...	286.3[53]	...	16.0	107
Israël[1,8,52]	2000	F	1 009.5	8.7[3]	...	110.3[53]	...	3.3	8
	2001	M	1 236.1	38.8[3]	...	284.0[53]	...	15.2	108
	2001	F	1 028.6	6.3[3]	...	108.7[53]	...	3.6	9
	2002	M	1 238.0	37.4[3]	...	272.9[53]	...	15.4	109
	2002	F	1 046.4	7.4[3]	...	104.6[53]	...	3.6	9
Italy[1,54,55]	2000	M	13 461.0	723.0	46.0	55.0	3 417.0	146.0	1 516
Italie[1,54,55]	2000	F	7 764.0	348.0	3.0	9.0	1 501.0	21.0	102
	2001	M	13 574.0	724.0	40.0	51.0	3 399.0	141.0	1 603
	2001	F	8 060.0	360.0	3.0	13.0	1 508.0	21.0	104
	2002	M	13 685.0	710.0	36.0	51.0	3 453.0	139.0	1 634
	2002	F	8 236.0	347.0	2.0	12.0	1 509.0	20.0	113
Kazakhstan	2000[2]	MF	6 201.0	...	...	...	...	...	
Kazakhstan	2001	M	3 470.2	1 264.8	10.7	125.2	334.1	107.1	213
	2001	F	3 228.6	1 101.5	2.4	41.3	179.7	42.9	50
	2002	M	3 486.4	1 250.9	12.1	131.0	322.9	107.3	218
	2002	F	3 222.5	1 115.8	1.4	36.3	180.8	45.7	50
Korea, Republic of[1,8]	1998	M	11 910.0	1 241.0	58.0	21.0	2 553.0	52.0	1 435
Corée, République de[1,8]	1998	F	8 084.0	1 158.0	24.0	...	1 345.0	9.0	143
	1999	M	11 978.0	1 189.0	59.0	19.0	2 563.0	52.0	1 354
	1999	F	8 303.0	1 075.0	26.0	1.0	1 443.0	9.0	122
	2000	M	12 353.0	1 140.0	59.0	18.0	2 713.0	52.0	1 449
	2000	F	8 707.0	1 063.0	26.0	...	1 530.0	11.0	132
Kyrgyzstan	1997	M	907.9	435.1	...	6.9	82.4	14.3	46
Kirghizistan	1997	F	781.4	380.5	...	2.0	61.3	4.7	10
	1998	M	918.7	450.4	...	6.3	78.7	15.3	41
	1998	F	786.2	385.0	...	1.9	64.6	5.0	9
	1999	M	971.6	501.9	0.5	7.7	74.1	16.6	38
	1999	F	792.7	421.9	0.1	1.8	52.9	5.5	6
Latvia[23,56]	2000[1]	M	479.7	77.5	1.3	1.6	97.3	15.0	51
Lettonie[23,56]	2000[1]	F	461.4	56.4	0.8	0.2	72.9	6.1	5
	2001[1]	M	486.4	87.7	1.9	1.1	88.9	15.8	62
	2001[1]	F	475.7	55.1	0.5	0.3	76.7	3.4	5
	2002[45]	M	504.6	92.4	3.5	2.9	96.7	17.9	53
	2002[45]	F	484.3	54.5	2.0	0.5	70.4	4.6	6
Lithuania[1]	2000	M	686.5	151.2	2.9	1.5	128.9	23.2	76
Lituanie[1]	2000	F	711.3	106.9	0.6	1.6	125.0	10.6	7
	2001	M	664.5	142.8	2.5	2.2	115.5	28.9	77
	2001	F	687.3	88.4	0.1	0.6	127.7	6.2	7
	2002	M	707.8	150.9	0.8	3.0	129.9	24.0	84
	2002	F	698.1	98.9	...	1.4	130.6	4.4	9
Luxembourg[2,57]	2000	MF	262.3	4.0[3]	...	0.3	33.3	1.5	25
Luxembourg[2,57]	2001	MF	277.0	3.6[3]	...	0.3	34.2	1.6	27
	2002	MF	285.7	3.6[3]	...	0.3	34.0	1.6	28
Maldives	1995	M	48.9	0.9	12.3	0.4	4.5	0.7	2
Maldives	1995	F	18.1	1.4	0.2	0.0	7.6	0.1	0
	2000	M	57.4	1.1	9.2	0.4	4.3	1.0	3
	2000	F	28.9	1.4	0.1	0.0	6.8	0.1	0

| Categ. G | Categ. H | Categ. I | Categ. J | Categ. K | Categ. L | Categ. M | Categ. N | Categ. O | Categ. P | Categ. Q |
Catég. G	Catég. H	Catég. I	Catég. J	Catég. K	Catég.L	Catég. M	Catég. N	Catég. O	Catég. P	Catég. Q
125.7	44.0	75.5	29.4	77.7	45.8	33.4	27.2	35.8	0.6	0.3
110.1	65.0	25.2	39.1	65.9	32.0	68.9	105.2	38.0	6.8	0.3
130.7	43.1	80.9	29.4	81.1	45.4	32.3	27.4	37.3	0.9	0.2
117.1	61.6	29.5	39.2	68.6	35.0	70.4	115.1	38.9	6.4	0.4
125.0	44.7	81.4	29.0	85.0	48.2	33.8	31.2	39.0	0.6	0.3
120.8	60.1	28.8	41.7	73.4	41.0	76.2	125.8	43.3	5.6	0.2
...	...	...	...	...	...	...	...	...	...	...
...	...	...	...	...	...	...	...	...	...	...
...	...	...	...	...	...	...	...	...	...	...
2.4	1.0	2.0	3.3	1.6	1.7	0.9	0.7	2.0	0.0	...
2.3	1.0	0.9	4.1	1.4	1.1	1.8	2.5	1.5	0.1	...
175.5	57.3	102.8	30.5	147.2	66.9	61.3	51.1	52.5	4.1	0.6
120.1	44.4	42.1	42.7	111.5	53.0	211.1	162.5	53.9	30.6	0.7
176.4	57.4	108.1	30.5	155.6	73.5	65.3	54.9	54.4	2.6	0.8
122.7	38.5	41.8	44.7	122.2	55.5	214.2	170.1	52.8	32.3	0.8
181.3	52.7	106.1	33.3	159.7	75.0	68.4	54.1	54.9	3.3	1.4
130.6	40.2	40.8	42.9	115.5	59.2	219.0	179.6	55.4	31.5	0.6
2 110.0	434.0	954.0	419.0	854.0	1 327.0	421.0	518.0	467.0	46.0	11.0
1 267.0	380.0	236.0	243.0	624.0	615.0	1 046.0	770.0	438.0	150.0	9.0
2 108.0	463.0	938.0	405.0	880.0	1 327.0	430.0	526.0	485.0	42.0	10.0
1 308.0	417.0	242.0	254.0	669.0	660.0	1 090.0	795.0	453.0	151.0	10.0
2 119.0	480.0	919.0	410.0	942.0	1 316.0	424.0	516.0	490.0	37.0	9.0
1 336.0	427.0	248.0	254.0	733.0	666.0	1 107.0	812.0	480.0	162.0	7.0
...	...	...	...	...	...	...	...	...	...	...
397.0	14.3	369.5	15.4	129.2	171.6	146.8	55.0	90.4	25.5	0.1
609.4	40.1	136.8	30.5	84.4	108.9	429.5	232.1	92.7	45.9	...
415.4	15.9	364.2	19.5	131.4	158.7	160.1	61.8	90.0	26.5	0.3
591.8	40.6	139.5	30.6	72.0	121.7	428.9	230.8	96.3	40.3	...
2 151.0	563.0	1 045.0	357.0	771.0	571.0	488.0	113.0	467.0	5.0	18.0
1 667.0	1 190.0	124.0	404.0	323.0	174.0	656.0	247.0	421.0	197.0	1.0
2 172.0	586.0	1 080.0	351.0	855.0	610.0	463.0	120.0	483.0	4.0	17.0
1 732.0	1 234.0	122.0	372.0	347.0	260.0	659.0	261.0	442.0	197.0	...
2 040.0	608.0	1 121.0	337.0	942.0	538.0	466.0	123.0	725.0	4.0	18.0
1 786.0	1 317.0	144.0	392.0	414.0	215.0	697.0	289.0	520.0	191.0	1.0
86.2	6.0	65.4	3.1	21.7	44.6	46.6	23.0	26.5	...	...
88.5	6.1	13.9	4.1	19.6	15.8	92.8	65.6	15.6	...	...
82.9	6.9	61.9	4.4	23.5	47.2	47.7	23.2	28.9	...	...
97.3	7.0	13.4	3.7	15.4	15.8	91.6	61.3	15.0	...	...
102.5	5.7	52.6	3.3	17.4	50.0	46.4	22.3	28.4	3.5	...
81.2	5.8	13.2	3.8	11.3	15.7	94.3	62.9	14.6	1.3	
60.6	5.6	55.2	4.7	23.5	39.6	18.5	6.7	20.6	0.9	...
84.7	16.5	23.5	7.6	21.3	31.4	68.2	41.3	23.7	1.6	...
61.2	5.1	54.1	4.8	22.0	38.0	16.0	8.0	18.7	0.5	...
89.6	17.1	24.1	8.9	18.9	29.5	72.3	41.8	30.4	1.2	...
59.5	4.1	58.9	5.0	21.8	36.5	18.7	9.7	21.7	1.6	...
88.2	20.4	27.3	7.7	16.7	31.3	69.0	50.8	31.5	2.9	...
90.4	7.3	62.7	6.2	23.0	40.4	34.6	13.6	23.9	0.1	...
109.9	19.8	27.7	8.3	20.2	33.3	126.4	82.9	29.7	1.3	...
100.6	5.9	59.9	5.3	21.1	39.3	31.8	12.3	16.4	2.5	...
105.1	19.9	26.1	5.6	20.0	32.6	123.2	87.3	35.5	1.7	...
103.7	6.3	63.4	5.5	26.8	40.9	29.7	14.1	22.4	2.4	...
107.4	21.8	24.0	8.5	28.1	40.4	109.2	80.5	31.4	2.3	0.1
37.5	12.5	20.9	29.4	· 40.3	13.9	11.6	15.7	9.7	5.8	...
38.9	12.6	22.7	32.7	43.6	14.4	12.4	16.7	10.2	6.3	...
39.8	13.1	23.6	33.1	46.3	14.9	12.8	17.5	10.5	6.6	...
4.5	6.9	5.8	1.4[13]	...	7.2[58]	...	...	...	...	...
0.8	0.3	0.6	0.7[13]	...	5.7[58]	...	...	...	...	...
4.8	9.2	7.2	1.1[13]	...	9.7[58]	...	...	...	...	...
1.0	0.5	0.7	0.6[13]	...	8.4[58]	...	...	...	...	...

28B

Employment by industry, ISIC Rev. 3
Total employment and persons employed by branch of economic industry (thousands)
Emploi par industrie, CITI Rév. 3
Emploi total et personnes employées, par branches d'activité économique (milliers)

Country or area Pays ou zone	Year Année	Sex	Total employment Emploi total	ISIC Rev. 3 Tabulation categories + CITI Rév. 3 Catégories de classement +					
				Categ. A Catég. A	Categ. B Catég. B	Categ. C Catég. C	Categ. D Catég. D	Categ. E Catég. E	Categ. F Catég. F
Malta [1,59] Malte [1,59]	2000	M	101.4	2.2	0.3	0.8	24.1	3.1	9.7
	2000	F	43.8	0.1	...	...	9.6	0.3	0.4
	2001	M	103.6	2.2	0.7	0.5	23.0	3.0	11.1
	2001	F	42.0	0.2	0.0	...	8.4	0.1	0.2
	2002	M	102.1	2.4	...	...	19.0	3.3	11.6
	2002	F	46.3	0.2	...	...	9.3	0.4	0.5
Mauritius Maurice	2000	M	318.7	41.6[3]	...	1.2	70.5	2.8	42.0
	2000	F	164.9	14.2[3]	...	0.1	71.5	0.1	0.8
	2001	M	321.6	40.5[3]	...	1.2	71.0	2.8	42.7
	2001	F	169.2	13.8[3]	...	0.1	72.5	0.2	0.8
	2002	M	324.0	36.2[3]	...	1.2	70.9	2.9	43.3
	2002	F	166.1	10.7[3]	...	0.1	68.6	0.2	0.8
Mexico [31,37] Mexique [31,37]	1999	M	26 049.7	6 855.8	153.3	122.5	4 675.5	168.7	2 116.4
	1999	F	13 019.4	1 192.8	6.7	10.8	2 669.3	24.5	41.6
	2000	M	25 672.6	5 949.2	150.2	137.6	4 715.5	157.2	2 461.7
	2000	F	13 311.2	952.6	8.8	18.0	2 831.2	31.3	66.0
	2001	M	25 747.9	6 099.2	141.5	114.6	4 560.7	164.4	2 331.3
	2001	F	13 256.4	821.5	12.2	12.6	2 812.3	30.5	65.6
Mongolia [60,61] Mongolie [60,61]	2000	M	416.9	211.0[3]	...	13.1	32.3	11.0	13.7
	2000	F	392.1	182.5[3]	...	5.5	22.3	6.8	9.7
	2001	M	424.6	212.8[3]	...	14.1	30.3	12.2	12.8
	2001	F	407.7	189.6[3]	...	5.8	25.3	5.6	7.6
	2002	M	440.5	208.8[3]	...	17.0	25.2	12.1	13.7
	2002	F	430.3	182.6[3]	...	6.8	30.4	7.7	11.8
Morocco [1] Maroc [1]	2001	M	6 914.1	...	...	...	...	...	...
	2001	F	2 415.7	...	...	...	...	...	...
	2002	M	7 100.6	2 845.9[3]	...	49.1	730.8	33.7	640.7
	2002	F	2 387.0	1 363.4[3]	...	1.8	440.5	3.6	6.9
Namibia [63] Namibie [63]	2000	M	226.8	69.8	4.7	3.2	11.4	3.7	20.7
	2000	F	205.0	56.7	3.1	0.7	11.5	0.5	1.0
Netherlands [41] Pays-Bas [41]	1999	M	4 361.0	158.0	3.0	8.0	855.0	31.0	437.0
	1999	F	3 241.0	69.0	...	2.0	256.0	6.0	34.0
	2000	M	4 420.0	167.0	4.0	10.0	866.0	27.0	424.0
	2000	F	3 311.0	76.0	...	2.0	255.0	8.0	41.0
	2001	M	4 460.0	148.0	3.0	8.0	860.0	27.0	468.0
	2001	F	3 405.0	73.0	...	1.0	256.0	7.0	40.0
Netherlands Antilles [1,64] Antilles néerlandaises [1,64]	1997	M	30.5	0.5[3]	...	0.0	4.3	0.8	4.3
	1997	F	25.8	0.1[3]	...	0.0	1.0	0.1	0.3
	1998	M	29.5	0.5[3]	...	0.0	4.0	0.8	3.9
	1998	F	24.7	0.0[3]	...	0.0	0.9	0.1	0.3
	2000	M	27.3	0.5[3]	...	0.1	3.6	0.8	3.4
	2000	F	24.9	0.0[3]	...	0.0	1.0	0.1	0.3
New Caledonia Nouvelle-Calédonie	1996	M	39.6	3.6[3]	...	1.8	4.1	0.6	6.4
	1996	F	24.8	1.0[3]	...	0.1	1.4	0.1	0.5
New Zealand [1,8] Nouvelle-Zélande [1,8]	2000	M	972.7	103.4	3.6	3.3	197.1	6.3	107.1
	2000	F	806.3	46.6	0.5	0.5	84.4	2.3	11.2
	2001	M	993.9	112.6	3.1	3.0	205.7	7.1	100.7
	2001	F	829.5	48.8	0.8	0.5	83.4	3.0	11.4
	2002	M	1 025.1	113.6	2.9	3.1	210.2	7.3	106.1
	2002	F	851.7	47.7	0.7	0.7	80.5	2.5	14.7
Norway [50] Norvège [50]	2000	M	1 212.0	55.0	14.0	28.0	214.0	16.0	135.0
	2000	F	1 057.0	22.0	2.0	6.0	76.0	4.0	12.0
	2001	M	1 214.0	52.0	15.0	29.0	211.0	14.0	140.0
	2001	F	1 064.0	20.0	2.0	7.0	74.0	3.0	12.0
	2002	M	1 210.0	50.0	15.0	30.0	214.0	12.0	144.0
	2002	F	1 076.0	19.0	2.0	6.0	75.0	3.0	13.0

Categ. G	Categ. H	Categ. I	Categ. J	Categ. K	Categ. L	Categ. M	Categ. N	Categ. O	Categ. P	Categ. Q
13.6	6.7	10.1	2.9	4.1	9.5	5.6	4.6	3.9	0.1	0.1
7.0	3.9	1.1	2.4	1.8	2.9	6.2	5.8	2.0	0.3	0.1
14.1	8.6	11.0	2.7	3.9	8.5	4.5	6.0	3.6	0.1	0.1
6.5	3.9	2.0	2.8	1.9	2.4	6.5	4.7	1.8	0.4	0.1
15.0	9.0	10.0	2.9	5.4	9.3	4.6	5.1	3.5	...	...
5.8	4.1	2.8	2.9	1.9	3.2	7.1	5.6	2.1	...	...
43.2	16.5	27.4	4.4	10.2	28.3	11.3	6.7	12.6	...	...
20.5	6.2	3.4	2.9	3.9	6.8	11.4	5.9	17.2	...	...
43.9	17.6	27.7	4.5	10.3	28.8	11.2	6.6	12.8	...	...
21.2	6.6	3.9	3.0	4.0	7.4	12.1	5.7	17.9	...	...
45.3	18.5	29.4	4.5	10.1	30.2	11.4	6.8	13.3	...	...
22.1	6.9	4.0	3.0	4.2	8.0	12.9	5.9	18.7	...	...
3 502.0	827.2	1 548.2	178.7	732.8	1 186.7	731.4	365.1	2 573.0	179.0	124.5
3 080.4	980.2	190.3	124.0	423.9	541.6	991.5	659.6	521.5	1 528.4	26.5
5 239.9	842.7	1 571.2	150.8	773.7	1 171.8	768.2	362.8	890.5	206.2	0.4
3 284.6	1 001.7	159.4	142.2	404.2	567.6	1 109.3	699.8	432.1	1 564.7	1.3
5 448.4	891.2	1 581.6	170.9	823.4	1 140.6	802.2	362.0	795.1	206.0	0.8
3 390.8	1 091.0	195.1	109.3	401.0	541.5	1 169.3	677.1	431.2	1 467.1	0.1
38.8	3.7	19.2	2.5	3.4	19.2	20.7	10.8	15.1	2.4	...
45.1	9.6	14.9	4.3	3.8	15.5	33.7	22.7	13.9	1.8	...
39.2	6.4	22.1	2.8	2.9	23.7	19.6	9.5	13.8	2.4	...
51.1	10.1	13.0	4.5	3.9	17.3	35.6	23.5	13.1	1.7	...
46.1	8.7	21.1	4.2	6.2	26.7	21.8	11.6	14.6	2.5	...
58.4	12.2	17.7	5.2	4.7	17.2	37.5	22.9	12.9	2.5	...
...	...	...	...	...	...	...	...	...	...	...
...	...	...	...	...	...	...	...	...	...	...
1 282.4	152.0	312.5	77.7[13]	...	414.8	558.2[62]	...	...	...	...
88.9	22.9	19.4	37.6[13]	...	87.9	312.9[62]	...	...	...	...
17.2	3.0	12.2	2.5	17.9	15.4	11.7	...	...	...	...
21.7	4.7	2.1	2.4	21.4	9.0	18.8	3.0	24.3	4.8	0.2
672.0	128.0	339.0	156.0	532.0	353.0	218.0	10.1	22.0	17.5	0.2
566.0	153.0	125.0	132.0	359.0	165.0	263.0	227.0	146.0	1.0	2.0
705.0	138.0	349.0	156.0	568.0	320.0	202.0	821.0	164.0	16.0	...
586.0	151.0	123.0	120.0	377.0	168.0	256.0	230.0	159.0	1.0	2.0
685.0	143.0	358.0	169.0	567.0	340.0	213.0	841.0	197.0	4.0	...
569.0	148.0	129.0	138.0	377.0	201.0	266.0	222.0	152.0	2.0	1.0
							912.0	194.0		
5.3	1.6	2.9	1.4	2.4	3.6	0.9	0.9	1.3	0.1	0.1
5.4	2.4	1.3	2.3	1.4	2.2	1.9	3.4	2.0	2.0	0.1
5.1	1.7	2.7	1.4	2.5	3.4	1.0	0.9	1.4	0.1	0.1
5.1	2.1	1.4	2.3	1.5	2.0	1.9	3.4	1.9	1.7	0.1
4.7	1.7	2.5	1.3	2.4	3.0	1.0	0.8	1.3	0.1	0.1
5.2	1.9	1.5	2.2	1.6	1.9	1.9	3.5	2.0	1.7	0.1
5.0	1.2	2.7	0.6	2.1	6.3	2.8	1.1	0.5	0.3	0.5
3.4	1.7	1.0	0.9	1.2	3.3	3.8	2.3	0.4	3.1	0.4
171.6	35.7	77.4	23.6	94.4	46.0	34.8	25.2	37.8	0.9	0.5
139.4	57.2	33.5	31.8	81.1	45.3	94.9	117.2	48.5	7.7	0.4
170.6	37.0	78.6	19.9	100.4	44.3	38.9	28.6	40.4	0.6	0.3
143.5	57.4	33.8	32.3	80.2	49.1	98.5	129.4	48.3	6.6	0.6
173.3	43.2	77.8	22.6	104.9	42.0	44.0	29.5	42.4	0.5	0.6
143.5	63.7	35.6	31.1	85.4	42.5	102.7	143.3	49.8	6.1	0.4
189.0	26.0	117.0	24.0	126.0	90.0	65.0	68.0	41.0	...	...
157.0	47.0	51.0	25.0	80.0	67.0	119.0	335.0	48.0	4.0	...
174.0	24.0	118.0	26.0	139.0	85.0	70.0	71.0	42.0	...	...
156.0	43.0	51.0	23.0	84.0	66.0	120.0	346.0	52.0	2.0	...
174.0	24.0	116.0	26.0	137.0	78.0	68.0	77.0	43.0	...	...
159.0	45.0	45.0	25.0	84.0	67.0	120.0	363.0	49.0	2.0	...

28B

Employment by industry, ISIC Rev. 3
Total employment and persons employed by branch of economic industry (thousands)
Emploi par industrie, CITI Rév. 3
Emploi total et personnes employées, par branches d'activité économique (milliers)

Country or area / Pays ou zone	Year / Année	Sex	Total employment / Emploi total	ISIC Rev. 3 Tabulation categories + / CITI Rév. 3 Catégories de classement +					
				Categ. A / Catég. A	Categ. B / Catég. B	Categ. C / Catég. C	Categ. D / Catég. D	Categ. E / Catég. E	Categ. F / Catég. F
Occupied Palestinian Terr. [1]	2000	M	504.2	49.2	0.3	1.7	73.8	1.4	117.9
Terr. palestinien occupé [1]	2000	F	93.2	32.3	...	0.0	10.2	...	0.3
	2001	M	429.7	40.0	0.3	1.4	61.8	1.2	73.3
	2001	F	78.2	20.6	...	...	7.7	0.1	0.6
	2002	M	406.8	48.0	0.3	1.7	54.6	0.9	52.9
	2002	F	79.4	23.8	...	...	6.4	0.1	0.2
Panama [1,65]	2000	M	625.0	144.8	9.3	0.7	61.8	5.3	66.8
Panama [1,65]	2000	F	315.1	5.0	0.4	0.0	25.1	1.2	2.4
	2001	M	659.2	157.7	10.3	1.6	64.2	7.4	67.5
	2001	F	325.1	8.9	0.8	0.2	24.2	2.3	3.0
	2002	M	687.6	161.3	10.0	1.6	66.7	7.2	68.9
	2002	F	362.0	10.2	0.6	0.0	29.6	1.5	2.9
Peru [27,30,66]	1999	M	3 980.4	250.9	63.1	28.3	555.7	35.1	370.0
Pérou [27,30,66]	1999	F	3 230.8	104.1	2.2	3.0	341.9	6.3	8.2
	2000	M	4 067.6	339.3	24.4	48.7	631.1	24.4	287.4
	2000	F	3 060.7	117.0	1.4	3.8	332.4	3.7	12.1
	2001	M	4 232.6	414.9	46.8	43.4	625.5	17.3	333.9
	2001	F	3 387.3	205.8	0.3	2.5	330.9	3.1	7.4
Philippines [1,8]	2001	M	18 334.0	7 252.0	1 078.0	96.0	1 535.0	96.0	1 540.0
Philippines [1,8]	2001	F	11 751.0	2 850.0	73.0	7.0	1 357.0	19.0	31.0
Poland [1,67]	2000	M	8 004.0	1 521.0	10.0	250.0	1 847.0	210.0	936.0
Pologne [1,67]	2000	F	6 522.0	1 195.0	1.0	43.0	1 054.0	53.0	89.0
	2001	M	7 797.0	1 491.0	7.0	236.0	1 815.0	210.0	888.0
	2001	F	6 410.0	1 220.0	1.0	38.0	1 015.0	59.0	70.0
	2002	M	7 529.0	1 483.0	8.0	228.0	1 661.0	204.0	779.0
	2002	F	6 253.0	1 169.0	4.0	29.0	914.0	59.0	73.0
Portugal [1]	2000	M	2 707.3	284.2	18.1	15.0	594.2	25.4	570.7
Portugal [1]	2000	F	2 213.8	312.9	1.1	1.0	487.0	3.5	22.8
	2001	M	2 744.9	291.7	18.0	15.2	596.0	31.1	558.0
	2001	F	2 254.9	317.5	1.5	0.9	485.8	5.0	23.8
	2002	M	2 804.8	295.6	19.6	16.1	580.7	33.7	595.9
	2002	F	2 310.3	314.6	1.1	1.1	468.9	5.7	26.4
Republic of Moldova [1]	2000	M	747.4	387.3	1.3	1.6	70.0	22.8	37.6
République de Moldova [1]	2000	F	767.2	381.7	0.1	0.2	65.8	5.7	6.7
	2001	M	736.5	379.8	1.4	1.6	70.8	21.2	37.0
	2001	F	762.5	383.6	...	0.3	66.0	5.2	6.3
	2002	M	730.9	368.6	1.9	1.9	71.9	21.1	39.2
	2002	F	774.2	376.6	...	0.7	70.4	5.5	6.8
Romania [1,23]	2000	M	5 772.2	2 325.7	7.0	141.8	1 118.5	151.4	352.6
Roumanie [1,23]	2000	F	4 991.6	2 273.1	0.9	21.4	935.3	44.4	50.9
	2001	M	5 719.4	2 280.7	3.0	131.3	1 066.2	150.6	378.3
	2001	F	4 977.6	2 242.4	0.8	18.7	958.5	48.3	51.7
	2002	M	5 031.5	1 737.2	4.6	125.9	1 049.1	150.8	371.6
	2002	F	4 202.6	1 619.5	0.1	18.4	922.6	44.0	41.1
Russian Federation [23,68,69]	1997	M	31 554.0	4 874.0	180.0	878.0	6 511.0	1 082.0	2 928.0
Fédération de Russie [23,68,69]	1997	F	28 467.0	2 214.0	28.0	250.0	5 065.0	425.0	873.0
	1998	M	30 486.0	4 540.0	135.0	802.0	6 146.0	1 173.0	2 634.0
	1998	F	27 374.0	1 962.0	19.0	247.0	4 743.0	459.0	785.0
	1999	M	31 524.0	4 659.0	133.0	925.0	6 513.0	1 126.0	2 627.0
	1999	F	28 884.0	2 328.0	25.0	285.0	5 002.0	451.0	818.0
Saint Helena	1998	M	1.1	0.2	0.0	...	0.1	0.0	0.3
Sainte-Hélène	1998	F	0.9	0.0	...	...	0.0	0.0	0.0
San Marino [27,60]	1999	M	11.3	0.1	...	...	4.2	...	1.5
Saint-Marin [27,60]	1999	F	7.3	0.1	...	...	1.7	...	0.1
	2001	M	11.4	0.1	...	...	4.5	...	1.5
	2001	F	7.7	0.0	...	...	1.8	...	0.1
	2002	M	11.5	0.1	...	...	4.5	...	1.5
	2002	F	7.8	0.0	...	...	1.7	...	0.1

Categ. G Catég. G	Categ. H Catég. H	Categ. I Catég. I	Categ. J Catég. J	Categ. K Catég. K	Categ. L Catég.L	Categ. M Catég. M	Categ. N Catég. N	Categ. O Catég. O	Categ. P Catég. P	Categ. Q Catég. Q
84.5	12.9	29.0	3.7	5.8	66.5	30.2	12.3	13.1	0.1	1.7
6.5	0.7	0.7	1.4	1.3	5.0	23.9	7.0	2.9	0.3	0.7
82.2	9.6	27.6	3.4	5.9	66.9	29.2	12.7	10.9	0.1	3.0
6.1	0.5	0.3	1.6	1.6	4.8	24.4	6.5	2.1	0.5	0.6
82.9	8.9	26.7	3.4	6.9	62.5	28.1	13.1	11.5	0.1	3.8
5.6	0.1	0.3	1.1	1.2	5.4	24.4	7.4	1.9	0.3	1.1
113.0	17.1	60.1	11.6	24.2	41.8	18.9	11.1	30.5	7.6	0.5
67.0	17.4	11.6	14.8	13.3	28.6	36.9	21.1	24.3	45.6	0.3
117.3	19.2	67.3	9.5	23.6	41.7	18.3	14.3	33.3	5.7	0.2
64.5	23.1	10.8	13.2	10.8	27.7	39.3	22.2	23.7	50.2	0.2
119.8	20.8	70.6	9.4	28.3	41.9	18.8	14.1	40.4	7.5	0.2
73.4	27.0	11.1	13.1	13.6	27.6	42.6	24.5	29.7	54.4	...
956.6	111.0	568.9	42.6	270.4	258.2	225.3	63.4	169.8	11.3	...
1 120.4	359.6	49.3	33.7	137.1	90.7	326.2	101.7	203.2	342.4	...
952.5	109.7	591.0	42.0	283.7	255.3	213.2	57.1	196.4	11.3	...
1 108.0	322.2	48.0	24.6	129.7	91.4	266.5	112.6	171.8	315.5	...
998.0	155.4	601.2	33.5	233.6	212.1	227.5	75.5	189.0	23.1	...
1 126.5	438.5	39.9	14.4	109.1	86.0	324.6	138.1	217.2	343.1	...
2 090.0	296.0	2 073.0	128.0	339.0	858.0	248.0	95.0	416.0	193.0	2.0
3 436.0	405.0	98.0	185.0	194.0	528.0	707.0	244.0	474.0	1 141.0	2.0
969.0	75.0	669.0	120.0	303.0	416.0	258.0	166.0	254.0	1.0	...
1 074.0	165.0	225.0	260.0	228.0	348.0	755.0	773.0	253.0	7.0	...
939.0	83.0	631.0	103.0	370.0	398.0	237.0	150.0	237.0	1.0	...
1 068.0	170.0	220.0	237.0	257.0	351.0	718.0	753.0	222.0	10.0	...
925.0	77.0	616.0	102.0	401.0	415.0	222.0	167.0	238.0	2.0	...
1 030.0	175.0	216.0	212.0	274.0	386.0	711.0	774.0	217.0	9.0	1.0
404.8	98.9	143.2	54.7	103.8	206.6	63.2	49.9	71.4	1.9	1.2
318.3	154.7	37.2	33.4	101.7	112.7	208.0	193.1	80.4	144.9	1.1
423.6	101.0	152.2	53.9	117.8	207.1	64.3	49.1	63.1	1.4	1.1
328.6	154.0	41.9	32.8	106.7	114.4	216.3	202.8	82.7	139.5	0.6
438.2	103.4	160.6	45.1	121.1	218.8	60.1	45.7	67.2	2.1	1.2
330.9	162.0	40.9	37.5	117.9	122.0	224.0	209.0	94.7	153.4	0.2
65.3	4.2	48.0	3.4	10.7	42.8	21.7	14.2	13.1	3.3	...
82.0	13.8	15.8	4.6	8.8	21.7	79.8	60.0	15.1	5.3	...
63.9	4.2	48.8	3.2	11.1	42.9	22.2	14.9	12.2	1.4	0.1
80.6	15.1	15.5	6.0	8.5	22.9	78.7	55.9	16.1	1.7	...
67.8	4.6	46.1	3.1	12.8	42.4	23.6	14.5	10.4	0.9	0.1
87.3	15.1	15.6	6.2	7.4	23.4	81.6	57.7	17.3	2.6	...
407.2	47.1	388.9	27.9	74.5	422.0	117.7	65.6	124.4	...	...
521.2	75.8	122.4	64.6	57.8	141.1	297.3	280.1	105.2	...	...
423.3	45.6	397.3	24.4	77.1	426.5	116.4	73.1	125.5	...	...
528.6	85.4	122.1	51.6	47.0	154.9	292.9	277.4	97.4	...	...
392.8	37.6	345.6	26.3	79.7	396.4	118.6	82.1	113.1	...	...
466.5	74.4	112.2	49.2	55.5	152.4	292.1	268.3	86.5	...	...
2 961.0	124.0	3 805.0	260.0	939.0	2 714.0	1 104.0	760.0	2 434.0	...	...
4 178.0	561.0	1 711.0	626.0	921.0	1 515.0	4 583.0	3 416.0	2 100.0	...	...
2 914.0	130.0	3 743.0	243.0	988.0	2 723.0	1 145.0	767.0	2 404.0	...	...
4 113.0	559.0	1 590.0	569.0	889.0	1 534.0	4 476.0	3 368.0	2 064.0	...	...
2 933.0	177.0	3 772.0	264.0	938.0	3 082.0	1 186.0	778.0	2 411.0	...	...
4 275.0	661.0	1 715.0	540.0	852.0	1 507.0	4 697.0	3 555.0	2 173.0	...	...
0.1	0.0	0.1	0.0	0.0	0.1	0.0	0.0	0.0	0.0	0.0
0.2	0.0	0.1	0.0	0.0	0.2	0.1	0.1	0.1	0.0	0.0
1.2	0.3	0.3	0.3	0.6	1.5	0.2	0.3	0.4	0.0	...
1.3	0.3	0.1	0.2	0.5	0.8	0.8	0.7	0.5	0.1	0.0
1.2	0.3	0.3	0.3	...	0.8	0.0	0.3	2.0	...	...
1.4	0.4	0.2	0.3	...	1.5	0.0	0.8	1.3	...	...
1.5	0.1	0.3	0.4	...	0.8	0.0	0.3	2.1	...	...
1.6	0.2	0.2	0.3	...	1.4	0.0	0.8	1.5	...	...

28B

Employment by industry, ISIC Rev. 3
Total employment and persons employed by branch of economic industry (thousands)
Emploi par industrie, CITI Rév. 3
Emploi total et personnes employées, par branches d'activité économique (milliers)

Country or area / Pays ou zone	Year / Année	Sex	Total employment Emploi total	ISIC Rev. 3 Tabulation categories + / CITI Rév. 3 Catégories de classement +					
				Categ. A / Catég. A	Categ. B / Catég. B	Categ. C / Catég. C	Categ. D / Catég. D	Categ. E / Catég. E	Categ. F / Catég. F
Saudi Arabia [1]	1999	M	4 800.6	331.4	11.0	86.0	432.0	74.1	566.7
Arabie saoudite [1]	1999	F	792.2	7.8	...	3.0	9.8	0.9	515.5
	2000	M	4 943.5	323.7	7.9	98.1	434.0	75.5	0.4
	2000	F	769.8	17.8	...	3.8	6.6	0.5	585.0
	2001	M	5 027.7	334.2	9.1	87.1	460.3	77.3	0.3
	2001	F	780.9	6.1	...	0.8	7.5	...	
Singapore [1,70]	2000	M	1 270.8[10]	4.3[10]	...	0.5[10]	279.3[10]	5.8[10]	257.5[10]
Singapour [1,70]	2000	F	824.0[10]	0.8[10]	...	0.1[10]	155.6[10]	1.3[10]	16.5[10]
	2001	M	1 148.7	4.8[3]	...	0.4	240.9	8.1	105.1
	2001	F	898.0	1.5[3]	...	0.2	143.1	2.3	19.9
	2002	M	1 137.1	5.1[3]	...	1.0	229.7	7.0	102.1
	2002	F	880.3	0.9[3]	...	...	137.9	1.9	17.0
Slovakia [1,47,72]	2000	M	1 137.3	101.3[3]	...	21.7	320.3	41.2	153.9
Slovaquie [1,47,72]	2000	F	964.4	38.4[3]	...	3.1	220.1	8.8	13.8
	2001	M	1 145.8	94.0[3]	...	19.4	329.5	44.0	155.8
	2001	F	977.9	36.5[3]	...	2.8	224.1	9.2	13.7
	2002	M	1 156.8	92.0[3]	...	19.9	339.9	38.5	163.9
	2002	F	970.2	39.4[3]	...	1.5	233.7	7.7	12.2
Slovenia [1,37]	2000	M	481.0	45.0	...	6.0	160.0	8.0	43.0
Slovénie [1,37]	2000	F	413.0	40.0	...	1.0	109.0	2.0	5.0
	2001	M	497.0	50.0	...	5.0	166.0	10.0	49.0
	2001	F	417.0	40.0	...	...	112.0	1.0	6.0
	2002	M	500.0	48.0	...	3.0	173.0	9.0	49.0
	2002	F	423.0	41.0	...	...	114.0	1.0	5.0
Spain [56,61]	2000	M	9 736.8	689.9	56.4	61.3	2 184.2	84.4	1 632.5
Espagne [56,61]	2000	F	5 632.9	256.8	9.0	4.8	724.3	14.2	83.2
	2001	M	10 029.1	696.6	55.8	58.6	2 250.7	84.2	1 761.9
	2001	F	5 916.4	257.9	8.9	4.6	754.8	14.6	88.3
	2002	M	10 146.6	663.0	47.2	59.2	2 230.1	74.4	1 813.9
	2002	F	6 111.0	242.6	8.5	4.0	769.1	17.1	99.3
Sweden [73]	2000	M	2 167.0	73.0	3.0	8.0	557.0	21.0	208.0
Suède [73]	2000	F	1 992.0	23.0	...	1.0	200.0	8.0	18.0
	2001	M	2 203.0	71.0	3.0	6.0	551.0	20.0	214.0
	2001	F	2 036.0	23.0	...	1.0	197.0	8.0	18.0
	2002	M	2 197.0	67.0	3.0	6.0	528.0	19.0	217.0
	2002	F	2 047.0	21.0	...	1.0	186.0	7.0	18.0
Switzerland [1,23,37,75]	2000	M	2 172.0	115.0[3]	...	515.0[4]	...	...	234.0
Suisse [1,23,37,75]	2000	F	1 707.0	66.0[3]	...	178.0[4]	...	...	33.0
	2001	M	2 190.0	112.0[3]	...	527.0[4]	...	...	226.0
	2001	F	1 748.0	59.0[3]	...	184.0[4]	...	...	34.0
	2002	M	2 169.0	108.0[3]	...	510.0[4]	...	...	222.0
	2002	F	1 790.0	59.0[3]	...	187.0[4]	...	...	31.0
Tajikistan	1995	M	1 038.0	1 095.0[2]	...	...	183.0[2]	24.0[2]	81.0[2]
Tadjikistan	1995	F	815.0	...	...	...	...	...	...
	1996	M	927.0	1 026.0[2]	...	...	181.0[2]	21.0[2]	68.0[2]
	1996	F	804.0	...	...	...	...	...	...
	1997[2]	M	...	527.6[2]	...	...	136.5[2]	18.0[2]	44.3[2]
TFYR of Macedonia [1,19]	2001	M	357.3	...	...	...	...	...	...
L'ex-R.y. Macédoine [1,19]	2001	F	242.0	...	...	...	...	...	...
	2002	M	342.8	79.7	0.7	6.5	73.1	12.7	29.9
	2002	F	218.6	53.9	0.1	0.5	59.3	2.0	2.9
Turkey [1,8]	2000	M	15 177.0	3 898.0	22.0	74.0	2 866.0	83.0	1 282.0
Turquie [1,8]	2000	F	5 403.0	3 182.0	1.0	4.0	704.0	6.0	31.0
	2001	M	14 903.0	3 847.0	32.0	90.0	2 868.0	86.0	1 052.0
	2001	F	5 463.0	3 337.0	1.0	3.0	681.0	7.0	21.0
	2002	M	14 614.0	3 436.0	18.0	109.0	2 879.0	95.0	909.0
	2002	F	5 671.0	3 290.0	1.0	5.0	796.0	4.0	22.0

Categ. G / Catég. G	Categ. H / Catég. H	Categ. I / Catég. I	Categ. J / Catég. J	Categ. K / Catég. K	Categ. L / Catég. L	Categ. M / Catég. M	Categ. N / Catég. N	Categ. O / Catég. O	Categ. P / Catég. P	Categ. Q / Catég. Q
843.4	140.5	230.6	48.0	143.8	1 053.0	386.6	161.5	123.3	160.3	5.3
4.0	...	5.4	1.3	3.3	19.8	316.6	67.5	4.1	348.5	1.0
896.4	163.7	242.3	41.5	138.8	1 098.7	399.7	168.6	130.6	201.6	5.3
5.1	0.9	...	1.0	0.6	17.5	313.2	49.0	2.8	349.4	...
832.6	154.2	242.1	56.8	144.3	1 139.0	411.1	187.9	100.2	191.7	5.8
4.6	0.4	5.8	1.7	...	18.6	308.9	90.2	1.7	329.6	1.0
171.2[10]	58.9[10]	147.5[10]	41.9[10]	136.2[10]	82.3[10]	39.5[10,14]	...	44.8[10,71]	...	1.1[28]
115.6[10]	55.6[10]	49.0[10]	54.4[10]	90.0[10]	23.6[10]	87.9[10,14]	...	172.5[10,71]	...	0.9[28]
173.7	61.1	168.7	46.1	133.2	105.9	47.1[14]	...	52.2[71]	...	1.5[28]
129.9	67.2	59.5	62.6	110.0	28.0	112.7[14]	...	160.3[71]	...	1.0[28]
173.8	62.6	165.3	44.7	132.7	108.6	50.1[14]	...	53.3[71]	...	1.2[28]
130.6	62.7	53.5	63.2	104.7	26.8	116.1[14]	...	163.9[71]	...	1.1[28]
106.6	25.3	115.8	11.7	55.1	76.9	35.0	26.3	45.5	...	0.1
153.0	39.9	51.4	25.4	35.7	81.5	126.6	121.5	41.1	0.2	0.1
109.4	28.6	111.8	10.2	62.2	77.5	34.5	25.4	42.8	3.7	0.3
146.3	43.0	50.3	28.2	42.1	80.2	134.4	118.3	44.2	0.1	0.3
118.7	26.8	109.3	13.2	61.4	71.1	35.8	27.7	38.6	4.6	0.2
152.8	41.7	45.1	26.6	41.9	78.7	126.9	113.8	40.5	0.2	0.1
57.0	14.0	46.0	7.0	25.0	26.0	12.0	9.0	17.0	7.7	0.3
62.0	20.0	14.0	15.0	18.0	26.0	45.0	37.0	17.0	...	...
57.0	13.0	43.0	8.0	25.0	23.0	15.0	10.0	17.0	...	...
57.0	22.0	14.0	15.0	20.0	25.0	47.0	36.0	17.0	...	...
57.0	14.0	42.0	8.0	25.0	25.0	14.0	12.0	16.0	...	...
62.0	23.0	13.0	14.0	20.0	25.0	47.0	39.0	17.0	...	...
1 394.6	519.1	744.8	261.9	586.5	606.8	324.7	243.4	297.9	...	...
1 107.5	448.2	178.2	149.3	534.5	369.4	512.2	586.4	296.2	47.1	1.3
1 393.9	510.1	772.0	239.6	636.7	644.7	333.9	234.1	308.2	358.1	0.4
1 162.1	461.0	193.2	152.4	601.6	363.4	554.9	618.6	307.4	45.8	2.2
1 399.9	522.9	789.6	241.1	665.1	668.8	348.1	241.3	332.7	372.1	0.6
1 152.4	496.0	204.1	159.5	628.2	377.4	595.0	671.8	316.8	48.6	0.7
290.0	51.0	200.0	38.0	287.0	111.0[74]	107.0	100.0	93.0[71]	368.1	1.2
230.0	66.0	79.0	48.0	194.0	112.0[74]	222.0	670.0	118.0[71]	...	...
292.0	52.0	200.0	39.0	339.0	111.0[74]	110.0	101.0	97.0[71]	...	...
229.0	66.0	84.0	50.0	210.0	121.0[74]	233.0	677.0	117.0[71]	...	...
287.0	51.0	200.0	39.0	344.0	113.0[74]	111.0	105.0	102.0[71]	...	...
228.0	62.0	84.0	51.0	220.0	129.0[74]	237.0	687.0	116.0[71]	...	...
312.0	44.0	149.0	115.0	239.0	122.0[74]	105.0	114.0	103.0[71]	...	...
279.0	74.0	75.0	81.0	151.0	97.0[74]	164.0	331.0	174.0[71]	...	...
302.0	48.0	152.0	123.0	248.0	126.0[74]	119.0	115.0	90.0[71]	...	...
298.0	86.0	79.0	83.0	156.0	81.0[74]	179.0	338.0	167.0[71]	...	...
296.0	56.0	159.0	122.0	250.0	127.0[74]	108.0	104.0	97.0[71]	...	...
309.0	87.0	75.0	94.0	159.0	87.0[74]	171.0	345.0	175.0[71]	...	...
87.0[2]	...	58.0[2]	...	...	...	168.0[2]	88.0[2]	...	...	...
69.0[2]	...	58.0[2]	...	...	...	161.0[2]	84.0[2]	...	...	...
40.2[2]	...	50.9[2]	...	...	...	160.0[2]	82.3[2]	...	...	...
39.4	7.3	26.2	3.3	7.1	24.1	13.6	7.7	11.1	...	0.3
24.8	4.0	6.3	5.1	4.9	8.9	20.1	18.5	6.4	...	0.6
2 673.0	697.0	973.0	168.0	311.0	977.0	439.0	242.0	410.0	59.0	3.0
316.0	63.0	65.0	105.0	108.0	156.0	285.0	222.0	76.0	78.0	1.0
2 575.0	718.0	949.0	165.0	328.0	984.0	480.0	235.0	433.0	58.0	3.0
308.0	64.0	60.0	87.0	100.0	133.0	287.0	215.0	70.0	88.0	...
2 733.0	728.0	912.0	153.0	341.0	961.0	508.0	247.0	522.0	62.0	1.0
360.0	77.0	60.0	76.0	109.0	135.0	301.0	243.0	83.0	109.0	...

28B

Employment by industry, ISIC Rev. 3
Total employment and persons employed by branch of economic industry (thousands)
Emploi par industrie, CITI Rév. 3
Emploi total et personnes employées, par branches d'activité économique (milliers)

Country or area / Pays ou zone	Year / Année	Sex	Total employment / Emploi total	ISIC Rev. 3 Tabulation categories + / CITI Rév. 3 Catégories de classement +					
				Categ. A / Catég. A	Categ. B / Catég. B	Categ. C / Catég. C	Categ. D / Catég. D	Categ. E / Catég. E	Categ. F / Catég. F
Ukraine [76]	2000	M	10 504.4	2 380.9	24.6	645.9	2 133.3	422.0	825.
Ukraine [76]	2000	F	9 915.4	1 766.4	5.4	206.2	1 704.8	237.6	239.
	2001	M	10 374.7	2 250.1	22.1	637.7	2 147.6	442.2	793.
	2001	F	9 863.4	1 714.9	6.1	177.2	1 592.2	236.4	198.
	2002	M	10 416.5	2 268.7	25.2	606.4	2 196.6	470.4	789.
	2002	F	9 984.2	1 750.8	4.6	191.2	1 586.1	270.7	176.
United Arab Emirates	1995 [10]	M	1 159.7	96.7	8.1	29.4	125.2	13.0	252.
Emirats arabes unis	1995 [10]	F	152.1	0.1	0.0	0.9	18.4	0.1	1.
	2000	M	1 553.0	129.5	10.8	39.4	167.7	17.4	337.
	2000	F	226.0	0.1	0.0	1.3	27.3	0.1	2.
United Kingdom [51,61]	2000	M	15 335.9	315.8	13.7	87.2	3 511.3	145.2	1 807.
Royaume-Uni [51,61]	2000	F	12 456.6	95.6	0.7	13.6	1 228.3	55.1	188.
	2001	M	15 562.5	290.8	14.2	103.7	3 445.4	150.5	1 857.
	2001	F	12 662.9	84.0	2.2	10.9	1 173.3	52.4	199.
	2002	M	15 604.5	287.8	17.3	97.5	3 317.5	162.6	1 880.
	2002	F	12 810.1	85.1	2.4	12.4	1 115.6	54.2	193.
Uruguay [24,27,30]	2000	M	613.4	38.1 [3]	...	1.9	112.1 [77]	...	88.
Uruguay [24,27,30]	2000	F	454.2	5.2 [3]	...	0.1	58.9 [77]	...	1.
	2001	M	617.7	37.7 [3]	...	1.2	107.5 [77]	...	85.
	2001	F	458.5	7.7 [3]	...	0.1	59.6 [77]	...	2.
Yemen [1]	1999	M	2 731.6	1 146.4	31.4	16.7	112.5	11.0	236.
Yémen [1]	1999	F	890.1	781.3	...	1.0	23.0	0.8	1.

Source:
International Labour Office (ILO), Geneva, "Yearbook of Labour Statistics 2003" and the ILO labour statistics database.

Source:
Bureau international du travail (BIT), Genève, "Annuaire des statistiques du travail 2003" et la base de données du BIT.

Countries using the latest version of the International Standard Industrial Classification of all Economic Activities, Revision 3 (ISIC Revision 3), are presented in this table. Countries using the former classification, ISIC Revision 2 are presented in Part A.

On trouvera dans la partie B les chiffres relatifs aux pays que appliquent la version la plus récente de la Classification internation type, par industrie, de toutes les branches d'activité économique, Révision 3 (CITI Rév. 3). Les pays qui utilisent encore la classifica dans sa version précédente (Révision 2) figurent à la partie A.

+   Tabulation categories of ISIC Rev. 3 :
A.   Agriculture, hunting and forestry.
B.   Fishing.
C.   Mining and quarrying.
D.   Manufacturing.
E.   Electricity, gas and water supply.
F.   Construction.
G.   Wholesale and retail trade, repair of motor vehicles, motor cycles and personal and household goods.
H.   Hotels and restaurants.
I.   Transport, storage and communications.
J.   Financial intermediation.
K.   Real estate, renting and business activities.
L.   Public administration and defence ; compulsory social security.
M.   Education.
N.   Health and social work.
O.   Other community, social and personal service activities.
P.   Private households with employed persons.
Q.   Extra-territorial organizations and bodies.

+   Catégories de classement de la CITI Rév. 3
A.   Agriculture, chasse et sylvculture.
B.   Pêche.
C.   Activitiés extractives.
D.   Activitiés du fabrication.
E.   Production et distribution d'électricité, de gaz et d'eau.
F.   Construction.
G.   Commerce de gros et de détail ; réparation de véhicules automobiles , de motorcycles et de biens personneles et domestiques.
H.   Hôtels et restaurants.
I.   Transports, entreposage et communications.
J.   Intermédiation financière.
K.   Immobilier, locations et activitiés de services aux enterprises.
L.   Administration publique et défense ; sécurité sociale obligatoi
M.   Education.
N.   Santé et action sociale.
O.   Autres activités de services collectifs, sociaux et personnels.
P.   Ménages privés employant du personnel domestique.
Q.   Organisations et organismes extraterritoriaux.

1   Persons aged 15 years and over.
2   Both sexes.
3   Tabulation categories A-B.
4   Tabulation categories C-E.
5   Tabulation categories G-K.
6   Tabulation categories M and O.

1   Personnes âgées de 15 ans et plus.
2   Les deux sexes.
3   Catégories de classement A à B.
4   Catégories de classement C à E.
5   Catégories de classement G à K.
6   Catégories de classement M et O.

Categ. G / Catég. G	Categ. H / Catég. H	Categ. I / Catég. I	Categ. J / Catég. J	Categ. K / Catég. K	Categ. L / Catég.L	Categ. M / Catég. M	Categ. N / Catég. N	Categ. O / Catég. O	Categ. P / Catég. P	Categ. Q / Catég. Q
1 045.2	62.4	1 016.0	64.6	244.3	705.6	396.1	301.8	233.9	2.4	...
1 267.9	197.3	477.4	165.9	258.8	461.0	1 356.6	1 262.2	302.4	6.3	...
1 093.2	79.0	965.9	62.3	268.3	653.0	433.1	298.1	227.9	0.4	...
1 355.0	251.0	461.8	149.4	287.1	486.9	1 364.4	1 247.7	329.4	5.7	...
1 099.2	79.8	960.9	72.7	305.2	640.3	391.9	299.8	208.0	1.8	...
1 417.0	263.4	467.6	143.9	306.2	473.2	1 317.6	1 267.3	338.2	9.6	...
173.1	42.2	89.6	13.8	30.6	168.3	24.2	12.7	38.1	40.7	1.0
10.0	3.6	4.2	3.0	3.0	6.7	25.0	10.9	1.8	62.5	0.2
231.9	56.5	119.9	18.4	40.9	225.4	32.4	17.0	51.1	54.5	1.3
14.8	5.4	6.3	4.4	4.4	10.0	37.2	16.2	2.7	92.8	0.4
2 160.7	476.1	1 428.3	577.5	1 814.6	943.0	631.1	566.6	755.2	41.2	18.1
2 138.7	672.8	476.8	622.8	1 257.0	773.5	1 579.4	2 435.4	788.9	93.2	6.7
2 142.0	505.8	1 511.6	595.7	1 888.3	979.8	627.7	630.3	714.6	35.8	12.7
2 111.6	678.7	494.7	634.8	1 322.5	892.0	1 621.8	2 492.4	778.4	80.5	6.8
2 148.2	544.8	1 527.9	647.9	1 925.5	959.7	668.3	610.6	720.0	38.9	9.7
2 112.4	749.2	488.0	650.3	1 332.0	933.5	1 653.3	2 526.6	790.2	80.3	8.6
145.6[43]	...	52.3	47.7[13]	...	56.2	13.2	19.2	28.5[78]	9.9	...
93.7[43]	...	9.5	39.4[13]	...	26.4	50.6	51.8	25.3[78]	91.4	...
145.7[43]	...	56.2	59.7[13]	...	57.6	13.6	17.9	28.5[78]	6.1	...
95.1[43]	...	10.6	37.7[13]	...	27.5	43.7	54.6	27.6[78]	92.4	...
382.3	42.0	121.0	9.3	18.0	347.7	171.0	31.8	49.1	3.4	...
11.9	0.9	1.5	1.7	0.9	10.3	38.2	10.6	4.0	2.2	0.3

7 Tabulation categories G-Q.
8 Civilian labour force employed.
9 September.
10 Population census.
11 July.
12 Tabulation categories A-C.
13 Tabulation categories J-K.
14 Tabulation categories M and N.
15 May and October of each year.
16 28 urban agglomerations.
17 Persons aged 10 years and over.
18 Estimates based on 1996 census of population benchmarks.
19 April of each year (Belgium, prior to 1999; Ireland, prior to 1998).
20 Excluding armed forces.
21 Tabulation categories C and E.
22 Tabulation categories L-P.
23 Labour force sample survey data are presented. Official estimates provided by national authorities are also available, but not shown in the table.
24 Including professional army; excluding compulsory military service.
25 Tabulation categories L-O.
26 Tabulation categories P-Q.
27 Prior to 1981, persons aged 14 years and over.
28 Tabulation categories Q and X. (Additional category X, not shown separately in the table, comprises activities which are not classifiable by economic activity).
29 Persons aged 10 years and over; civilian labour force employed.
30 Urban areas.
31 Prior to 1982, persons aged 12 years and over.
32 Year beginning in August of year indicated.
33 Beginning 1999, methodology revised; data not strictly comparable.
34 Excluding full-time members of the armed forces.
35 July of each year.
36 Tabulation categories L and O.

7 Catégories de classement G à Q.
8 Main-d'oeuvre civile occupée.
9 Septembre.
10 Recensement de population.
11 Juillet.
12 Catégories de classement A à C.
13 Catégories de classement J à K.
14 Catégories de classement M et N.
15 Mai et octobre de chaque année.
16 28 agglomérations urbaines.
17 Personnes âgées de 10 ans et plus.
18 Estimations basées sur les données de calage du recensement de population de 1996.
19 Avril de chaque année (Belgique, avant 1999; Irlande, avant 1998).
20 Non compris les militaires.
21 Catégories de classement C et E.
22 Catégories de classement L à P.
23 Les données présentées proviennent des enquêtes par sondage sur la main d'oeuvre. Des évaluations officielles fournies par les autorités nationales sont également disponibles, mais elles ne figurent pas dans le tableau.
24 Y compris les militaires de carrière; non compris les militaires du contingent.
25 Catégories de classement L à O.
26 Catégories de classement P à Q.
27 Avant 1981, personnes âgées de 14 ans et plus.
28 Catégories de classement Q et X. (Catégorie supplémentaire X comprend les activités ne pouvant être classés selon l'activité économique).
29 Personnes âgées de 10 ans et plus; main-d'oeuvre civile occupée.
30 Régions urbaines.
31 Avant 1982, personnes âgées de 12 ans et plus.
32 Année commençant en août de l'année indiquée.
33 A partir de 1999, méthodologie révisée; les données ne sont pas strictement comparables.
34 Non compris les membres à temps complet des forces armées.
35 Juillet de chaque année.
36 Catégories de classement L et O.

28B

Employment by industry, ISIC Rev. 3
Total employment and persons employed by branch of economic industry (thousands)
Emploi par industrie, CITI Rév. 3
Emploi total et personnes employées, par branches d'activité économique (milliers)

37	Second quarter of each year.	37	Deuxième trimestre de chaque année.
38	Government-controlled area.	38	Région sous contrôle gouvernemental.
39	Persons aged 15 to 66 years.	39	Personnes âgées de 15 à 66 ans.
40	November of each year.	40	Novembre de chaque année.
41	Persons aged 15 to 64 years.	41	Personnes âgées de 15 à 64 ans.
42	May and November of each year.	42	Mai et novembre de chaque année.
43	Tabulation categories G-H.	43	Catégories de classement G à H.
44	Tabulation categories N and O.	44	Catégories de classement N et O.
45	Persons aged 15 to 74 years.	45	Personnes âgées de 15 à 74 ans.
46	May.	46	Mai.
47	Excluding conscripts.	47	Non compris les conscrits.
48	Estimates based on the 2001 Population Census results.	48	Estimations basées sur les résultats du Recensement de la population de 2001.
49	April and November of each year.	49	Avril et novembre de chaque année.
50	Persons aged 16 to 74 years.	50	Personnes âgées de 16 à 74 ans.
51	March to May of each year.	51	Mars-mai de chaque année.
52	Beginning 1998: methodology revised.	52	A partir de 1998: méthodologie révisée.
53	Tabulation categories C-D.	53	Catégories de classement C à D.
54	Including permanent members of institutional households.	54	Y compris les membres permanents des ménages collectifs.
55	Including conscripts.	55	Y compris les conscrits.
56	Excluding compulsory military service.	56	Non compris les militaires du contingent.
57	Including armed forces.	57	Y compris les forces armées.
58	Tabulation categories L-Q.	58	Catégories de classement L à Q.
59	December of each year.	59	Décembre de chaque année.
60	31 December of each year.	60	31 décembre de chaque année.
61	Persons aged 16 years and over.	61	Personnes âgées de 16 ans et plus.
62	Tabulation categories M-Q.	62	Catégories de classement M à Q.
63	Persons aged 15 to 69 years.	63	Personnes âgées de 15 à 69 ans.
64	Curaçao.	64	Curaçao.
65	August of each year.	65	Août de chaque année.
66	Third quarter.	66	Troisième trimestre.
67	Excluding regular military living in barracks and conscripts.	67	Non compris les militaires de carrière vivant dans des casernes et les conscrits.
68	October of each year.	68	Octobre de chaque année.
69	Persons aged 15 to 72 years.	69	Personnes âgées de 15 à 72 ans.
70	June of each year.	70	Juin de chaque année.
71	Tabulation categories O-P.	71	Catégories de classement O à P.
72	Excluding persons on child-care leave.	72	Non compris les personnes en congé parental.
73	Persons aged 16 to 64 years.	73	Personnes âgées de 16 à 64 ans.
74	Tabulation categories L and Q.	74	Catégories de classement L et Q.
75	Civilian labour force employed; excluding seasonal/border workers.	75	Main-d'oeuvre civile occupée; non compris les travailleurs saisonniers et frontaliers.
76	Persons aged 15-70 years.	76	Personnes âgées de 15 à 70 ans.
77	Tabulation categories D-E.	77	Catégories de classement D à E.
78	Tabulation categories O and Q.	78	Catégories de classement O et Q.

29

Unemployment
Number (thousands) and percentage unemployed, by sex

Chômage
Nombre (milliers) et pourcentage des chômeurs, par sexe

Country or area, source § Pays ou zone, source §	1995	1996	1997	1998	1999	2000	2001	2002
Albania Albanie								
MF [A]	...	...	...	...	...	...	305.5	...
M [A]	...	...	...	...	...	...	150.1	
F [A]	...	...	...	...	...	...	155.4	
MF [FB]	171.0	158.0	194.0	235.0	240.0	215.0	181.0	172.0
M [FB]	91.0	88.0	110.0	127.0	130.0	113.0	96.0	91.0
F [FB]	80.0	70.0	84.0	108.0	110.0	102.0	85.0	81.0
%MF [FB]	12.9	12.3	14.9	17.7	18.4	16.8	16.4	15.8
%M [FB]	11.6	11.4	13.8	15.8	16.4	14.9	14.2	13.6
%F [FB]	14.8	13.6	16.6	20.9	21.4	19.3	19.9	19.1
Algeria [1] Algérie [1]								
MF [E]	2 105.0	...	2 049.0	...	...	2 427.7	2 339.4	...
M [E]	1 626.0	...	1 769.0	...	...	2 132.7	1 934.9	...
F [E]	478.0	...	280.0	...	...	295.0	404.5	...
%MF [E]	27.9	...	26.4	...	...	29.8	27.3	...
%M [E]	26.0	...	26.9	...	...	33.9	...	...
%F [E]	38.4	...	24.0	...	...	29.7	...	...
Angola [2] Angola [2]								
MF [FB]	...	19.0	...	...	...	...	...	...
M [FB]	...	15.5	...	...	...	...	...	...
F [FB]	...	3.5	...	...	...	...	...	...
Anguilla [3] Anguilla [3]								
MF [BA]	...	...	...	...	0.6[4]	...	0.4[5]	0.5[6]
M [BA]	...	...	...	...	0.2[4]	...	0.2[5]	0.2[6]
F [BA]	...	...	...	...	0.4[4]	...	0.2[5]	0.3[6]
%MF [BA]	...	...	...	...	8.3[4]	...	6.7[5]	7.8[6]
%M [BA]	...	...	...	...	4.6[4]	...	6.5[5]	6.3[6]
%F [BA]	...	...	...	...	12.1[4]	...	7.0[5]	9.5[6]
Argentina [7,8] Argentine [7,8]								
MF [BA]	963.6[9]	1 531.4[10]	1 375.1[10]	1 218.7[10]	1 359.6[10]	1 460.9[10]	1 709.8[10]	1 955.8[10]
M [BA]	508.1[9]	866.1[10]	731.4[10]	680.0[10]	764.9[10]	809.9[10]	1 021.9[10]	1 175.2[10]
F [BA]	455.6[9]	665.3[10]	643.7[10]	538.7[10]	594.7[10]	651.0[10]	688.4[10]	780.6[10]
%MF [BA]	18.8[9]	17.2[10]	14.9[10]	12.8[10]	14.1[10]	15.0[10]	17.4[10]	19.6[10]
%M [BA]	16.5[9]	15.8[10]	13.0[10]	11.9[10]	13.3[10]	14.1[10]	17.4[10]	20.2[10]
%F [BA]	22.3[9]	19.4[10]	17.9[10]	14.3[10]	15.2[10]	16.4[10]	17.2[10]	18.8[10]
Armenia Arménie								
MF [BA] [3,11]	...	...	423.7	...	...	...	...	...
M [BA] [3,11]	...	...	247.0	...	...	...	...	...
F [BA] [3,11]	...	...	176.7	...	...	...	...	...
%MF [BA] [3,11]	...	...	36.4	...	...	...	...	...
%M [BA] [3,11]	...	...	38.0	...	...	...	...	...
%F [BA] [3,11]	...	...	34.4	...	...	...	...	...
MF [FB] [12]	131.7	159.3	174.4	133.8	175.0	153.9	138.4	127.3
M [FB] [12]	39.9	43.5	49.7	40.9	62.3	54.4	47.1	85.7
F [FB] [12]	91.8	115.8	124.7	92.8	112.7	99.5	91.3	41.6
%MF [FB] [12]	6.7	9.3	10.8	9.4	11.2	11.7	10.4	9.4
%M [FB] [12]	3.8	4.7	6.3	5.6	7.6	8.0	6.9	6.1
%F [FB] [12]	10.4	15.2	15.1	13.3	15.0	15.7	14.1	13.1
Australia [3,13] Australie [3,13]								
MF [BA]	751.0	750.6	769.1	728.1	660.7	615.6	666.7	631.3
M [BA]	445.3	442.2	449.4	428.1	383.2	353.4	385.4	362.1
F [BA]	305.8	308.4	319.7	300.0	277.6	262.2	281.2	269.2
%MF [BA]	8.4	8.3	8.4	7.8	7.0	6.4	6.8	6.3
%M [BA]	8.7	8.5	8.6	8.1	7.2	6.5	7.0	6.5
%F [BA]	7.9	7.9	8.1	7.5	6.8	6.2	6.5	6.1
Austria [3] Autriche [3]								
MF [BA]	143.7	160.4	164.8	165.0	146.7	138.8	142.5	116.0
M [BA]	71.4	86.5	87.3	88.4	81.7	73.8	77.0	91.7
F [BA]	72.3	73.9	77.5	76.6	65.0	65.0	65.5	69.3
%MF [BA]	3.7	4.1	4.2	4.2	3.8	3.6	3.6	4.0
%M [BA]	3.2	3.9	3.9	4.0	3.7	3.3	3.5	4.1

29

Unemployment
Number (thousands) and percentage unemployed, by sex *[cont.]*

Chômage
Nombre (milliers) et pourcentage des chômeurs, par sexe *[suite]*

Country or area, source § Pays ou zone, source §	1995	1996	1997	1998	1999	2000	2001	2002
%F [BA]	4.3	4.5	4.6	4.6	3.9	3.8	3.8	3.9
MF [FB]	215.7	230.5	233.3	237.8	221.7	194.3	203.9	232.4
M [FB]	120.0	128.0	128.6	129.4	121.5	107.5	115.3	134.4
F [FB]	95.7	102.5	104.8	108.4	100.2	86.2	88.6	98.0
%MF [FB]	6.6	7.0	7.1	7.2	6.7	5.8	6.1	6.9
%M [FB]	6.4	6.9	6.9	6.9	6.5	5.8	6.2	7.2
%F [FB]	6.8	7.3	7.4	7.5	6.9	5.9	5.9	6.4
Azerbaijan[14] Azerbaïdjan[14]								
MF [FB]	28.3	31.9	38.3	42.3	45.2	43.7	48.4	51.0
M [FB]	11.4	13.1	16.2	18.2	19.6	19.3	21.8	23.1
F [FB]	16.9	18.8	22.1	24.1	25.6	24.5	26.6	27.9
%MF [FB]	0.8	0.9	1.0	1.1	1.2	1.2	1.3	1.3
%M [FB]	0.6	0.7	0.8	0.9	1.0	1.0	1.1	1.2
%F [FB]	1.0	1.1	1.2	1.4	1.4	1.4	1.5	1.5
Bahamas[3,15] Bahamas[3,15]								
MF [BA]	15.6	16.9	14.7	12.1	...	...	...	...
M [BA]	7.5	6.6	6.5	4.7	...	...	...	...
F [BA]	8.1	10.3	8.2	7.4	...	...	...	...
%MF [BA]	10.9	11.5	9.8	7.7	...	...	...	...
%M [BA]	10.1	8.6	8.3	5.9	...	...	...	...
%F [BA]	11.8	14.7	11.3	9.6	...	...	...	...
Bahrain Bahreïn								
MF [A]	...	...	...	...	...	...	16.1	...
M [A]	...	...	...	...	...	...	9.4	...
F [A]	...	...	...	...	...	...	6.7	...
MF [FB][16]	5.1	...	6.1	4.1	3.8	6.2	...	...
M [FB][16]	3.4	...	4.1	2.7	2.6	4.2	...	...
F [FB][16]	1.7	...	2.0	1.4	1.1	2.0	...	...
Bangladesh[17] Bangladesh[17]								
MF [BA]	...	1 417.0[7]	...	...	...	1 750.0[3]	...	...
M [BA]	...	933.0[7]	...	...	...	1 083.0[3]	...	...
F [BA]	...	484.0[7]	...	...	...	666.0[3]	...	...
%MF [BA]	...	2.5[7]	...	...	...	3.3[3]	...	...
%M [BA]	...	2.7[7]	...	...	...	3.2[3]	...	...
%F [BA]	...	2.3[7]	...	...	...	3.3[3]	...	...
Barbados[3] Barbade[3]								
MF [BA]	26.9	21.1	19.6	16.7	14.3	13.1	14.1	...
M [BA]	11.4	8.6	7.9	5.9	5.5	5.4	5.9	...
F [BA]	15.5	12.6	11.7	10.8	8.7	7.8	8.2	...
%MF [BA]	19.7	15.8	14.5	12.3	10.5	9.4	9.9	...
%M [BA]	16.5	12.4	11.3	8.4	7.7	7.5	8.0	...
%F [BA]	22.9	18.9	17.8	16.4	13.3	11.5	11.9	...
Belarus[18] Bélarus[18]								
MF [FB]	131.0	182.5	126.2	105.9	95.4	95.8	102.9	130.5
M [FB]	46.7	66.1	42.1	35.3	34.2	37.6	40.9	47.8
F [FB]	84.3	116.4	84.1	70.6	61.2	58.2	62.0	82.7
%MF [FB]	2.9	4.0	2.8	2.3	2.1	2.1	2.3	3.0
%M [FB]	2.2	3.0	1.9	1.6	1.6	1.7	1.9	2.3
%F [FB]	3.5	5.0	3.6	3.0	2.6	2.4	2.6	3.5
Belgium Belgique								
MF [BA][3]	390.1[15]	404.0[15]	375.1[15]	384.0[15]	375.2	308.5	286.4	332.1
M [BA][3]	178.9[15]	181.7[15]	173.2[15]	179.3[15]	179.4	144.6	147.9	168.1
F [BA][3]	211.2[15]	222.3[15]	201.9[15]	204.7[15]	195.8	163.9	138.4	164.0
%MF [BA][3]	9.3[15]	9.6[15]	8.9[15]	9.1[15]	8.6	7.0	6.6	7.5
%M [BA][3]	7.3[15]	7.5[15]	7.1[15]	7.3[15]	7.2	5.8	6.0	6.7
%F [BA][3]	12.2[15]	12.8[15]	11.5[15]	11.4[15]	10.4	8.7	7.5	8.7
MF [FB][19]	596.9	588.2	570.0	541.0	507.5	474.4	469.7	491.5
M [FB][19]	259.6	255.5	249.6	237.4	224.7	208.7	210.9	228.0
F [FB][19]	337.3	332.7	320.5	303.6	282.9	265.8	258.9	263.4

29

Unemployment

Number (thousands) and percentage unemployed, by sex [cont.]

Chômage

Nombre (milliers) et pourcentage des chômeurs, par sexe [suite]

Country or area, source § Pays ou zone, source §	1995	1996	1997	1998	1999	2000	2001	2002
%MF [FB][19]	13.9	13.7	13.1	12.4	11.6	10.9	10.8	11.2
%M [FB][19]	10.7	10.5	10.2	9.7	9.2	8.6	8.7	9.4
%F [FB][19]	18.1	17.7	16.8	15.9	14.7	13.8	13.4	13.6
Belize[2,15] Belize[2,15]								
MF [BA]	8.9	10.4	10.3	12.3	11.5	...	...	...
M [BA]	4.8	6.1	4.8	5.9	5.3	...	...	...
F [BA]	4.1	4.3	5.5	6.3	6.1	...	...	...
%MF [BA]	12.5	13.8	12.7	14.3	12.8	...	...	...
%M [BA]	9.9	11.7	8.9	10.6	9.0	...	...	...
%F [BA]	17.9	18.6	20.3	21.3	20.3	...	...	...
Bolivia[7] Bolivie[7]								
MF [BA]	47.5[20]	73.6[11]	71.2[11]	...	156.7[11]	167.5[11]	...	...
M [BA]	24.3[20]	37.6[11]	40.8[11]	...	74.4[11]	77.0[11]	...	...
F [BA]	23.1[20]	36.0[11]	30.4[11]	...	82.3[11]	90.5[11]	...	...
%MF [BA]	3.6[20]	3.8[11]	3.7[11]	...	7.2[11]	7.4[11]	...	...
%M [BA]	3.3[20]	3.6[11]	3.7[11]	...	6.2[11]	6.2[11]	...	...
%F [BA]	4.0[20]	4.1[11]	3.6[11]	...	8.5[11]	8.9[11]	...	...
Botswana[21] Botswana[21]								
MF [BA]	94.5[22]	...	...	115.7	...	90.7	...	...
M [BA]	45.5[22]	...	...	56.7	...	46.3	...	...
F [BA]	49.1[22]	...	...	59.0	...	44.5	...	...
%MF [BA]	21.5[22]	...	...	20.8	...	15.8	...	...
%M [BA]	19.4[22]	...	...	18.6	...	14.7	...	...
%F [BA]	23.9[22]	...	...	23.6	...	17.2	...	...
Brazil[7,23,24] Brésil[7,23,24]								
MF [BA]	4 509.8	5 076.2	5 881.8	6 922.6	7 639.1	...	7 785.1	...
M [BA]	2 327.9	2 498.3	2 854.9	3 301.1	3 667.9	...	3 643.0	...
F [BA]	2 181.9	2 577.9	3 026.9	3 621.5	3 971.2	...	4 142.0	...
%MF [BA]	6.1	7.0	7.8	9.0	9.6	...	9.4	...
%M [BA]	5.3	5.7	6.4	7.2	7.9	...	7.5	...
%F [BA]	7.3	8.8	10.0	11.6	12.1	...	11.9	...
Bulgaria Bulgarie								
MF [BA][3,25]	564.6	488.7	491.4	438.8	486.7	559.0	661.1	599.2
M [BA][3,25]	295.2	259.5	265.0	240.8	258.6	306.3	363.2	328.7
F [BA][3,25]	269.4	229.1	226.4	198.0	228.1	252.6	297.8	270.4
%MF [BA][3,25]	15.7	13.5	13.7	12.2	14.1	16.3	19.4	17.6
%M [BA][3,25]	15.5	13.5	13.9	12.6	14.0	16.7	20.2	18.3
%F [BA][3,25]	15.8	13.4	13.5	11.8	14.1	15.9	18.4	16.9
MF [FB][18,26]	423.8	478.8	523.5	465.2	610.6	682.8	662.3	602.5
M [FB][18,26]	188.0	215.4	236.5	211.1	284.5	323.4	321.1	281.1
F [FB][18,26]	235.8	263.4	287.1	254.1	326.1	359.4	341.2	321.5
%MF [FB][18,26]	11.1	12.5	13.7	12.2	16.0	17.9	17.3	16.3
Burkina Faso[27] Burkina Faso[27]								
MF [FB]	13.9	13.5	9.2	9.4	7.5	6.6	...	...
M [FB]	11.8	11.0	7.6	7.8	6.2	5.4	...	...
F [FB]	2.1	2.5	1.6	1.6	1.4	1.2	...	...
Burundi[28] Burundi[28]								
MF [FB]	1.3	0.5	1.6	2.8	0.7	...	...	...
%MF [FB]	...	...	...	...	14.0	...	...	...
%M [FB]	...	...	...	...	15.0	...	...	...
%F [FB]	...	...	...	...	13.2	...	...	...
Cambodia[7,29] Cambodge[7,29]								
MF [BA]	...	...	...	...	...	133.6	115.8	...
M [BA]	...	...	...	...	...	55.0	44.9	...
F [BA]	...	...	...	...	...	78.6	71.0	...
%MF [BA]	...	...	...	...	...	2.5	1.8	...
%M [BA]	...	...	...	...	...	2.1	1.5	...
%F [BA]	...	...	...	...	...	2.8	2.2	...
Canada[3,30,31] Canada[3,30,31]								
MF [BA]	1 422.1	1 469.2	1 413.5	1 305.1	1 190.1[32]	1 089.6[32]	1 169.5[32]	1 277.6[32]
M [BA]	801.1	822.5	779.1	727.4	668.2[32]	600.0[32]	659.5[32]	727.8[32]

29

Unemployment
Number (thousands) and percentage unemployed, by sex *[cont.]*

Chômage
Nombre (milliers) et pourcentage des chômeurs, par sexe *[suite]*

Country or area, source § Pays ou zone, source §	1995	1996	1997	1998	1999	2000	2001	2002
F [BA]	621.0	646.7	634.3	577.7	521.9[32]	489.6[32]	510.0[32]	549.8[32]
%MF [BA]	9.5	9.7	9.2	8.3	7.6[32]	6.8[32]	7.2[32]	7.7[32]
%M [BA]	9.8	9.9	9.2	8.5	7.8[32]	6.9[32]	7.5[32]	8.1[32]
%F [BA]	9.2	9.4	9.2	8.1	7.3[32]	6.7[32]	6.8[32]	7.1[32]
Cape Verde Cap-Vert								
MF [FB]	0.6	...	...	...	...	...	...	...
Central African Rep.[33] Rép. centrafricaine[33]								
MF [FB]	7.6	...	...	...	...	...	...	...
M [FB]	6.7	...	...	...	...	...	...	...
F [FB]	0.9	...	...	...	...	...	...	...
Chile[3,34] Chili[3,34]								
MF [BA]	248.1[35]	302.0[36]	303.6[36]	419.2[36]	529.1[36]	489.4[36]	469.4[36]	468.7[36]
M [BA]	158.4[35]	180.9[36]	180.8[36]	271.1[36]	322.9[36]	312.5[36]	302.6[36]	298.5[36]
F [BA]	89.8[35]	121.1[36]	122.8[36]	148.1[36]	206.2[36]	176.9[36]	166.9[36]	170.2[36]
%MF [BA]	4.7[35]	5.4[36]	5.3[36]	7.2[36]	8.9[36]	8.3[36]	7.9[36]	7.8[36]
%M [BA]	4.4[35]	4.8[36]	4.7[36]	7.0[36]	8.2[36]	8.0[36]	7.6[36]	7.5[36]
%F [BA]	5.3[35]	6.7[36]	6.6[36]	7.6[36]	10.3[36]	9.0[36]	8.4[36]	8.5[36]
China[18,37] Chine[18,37]								
MF [E]	5 196.0	5 528.0	5 768.0	5 710.0	5 750.0	5 950.0	6 810.0	7 700.0
M [E][38]	...	2 637.0	2 737.0	2 705.0	...	...	...	...
F [E][38]	...	2 891.0	3 031.0	3 005.0	...	...	...	...
%MF [E]	2.9	3.0	3.0	3.1	3.1	3.1	3.6	4.0
China, Hong Kong SAR[3,39] Chine, Hong Kong RAS[3,39]								
MF [BA]	95.6	87.4	71.2	154.1	207.5	166.9	174.8	255.5
M [BA]	62.3	58.7	45.2	101.2	140.6	109.6	118.3	164.8
F [BA]	33.3	28.7	26.0	52.9	66.9	57.3	56.5	90.7
%MF [BA]	3.2	2.8	2.2	4.7	6.2	4.9	5.1	7.3
%M [BA]	3.4	3.1	2.3	5.2	7.2	5.6	6.0	8.4
%F [BA]	2.9	2.3	2.0	4.0	4.9	4.1	3.9	6.0
China, Macao SAR[2,40] Chine, Macao RAS[2,40]								
MF [BA]	6.7	8.6	6.5	9.5	13.2	14.2	13.9	13.4
M [BA]	4.3	5.3	4.1	6.4	9.1	9.8	9.4	8.9
F [BA]	2.4	3.3	2.4	3.1	4.2	4.4	4.4	4.4
%MF [BA]	3.6	4.3	3.2	4.6	6.3	6.8	6.4	6.3
%M [BA]	4.1	4.7	3.7	5.7	8.0	8.6	8.1	7.9
%F [BA]	3.0	3.6	2.6	3.3	4.4	4.6	4.4	4.5
Colombia[21] Colombie[21]								
MF [BA]	521.9[41]	735.2[41]	782.1[41]	998.3[41]	1 415.4[41]	1 526.0[41]	2 846.0	3 084.4
M [BA]	230.2[41]	336.3[41]	353.5[41]	457.2[41]	649.8[41]	660.2[41]	1 303.5	1 440.7
F [BA]	291.7[41]	398.9[41]	428.6[41]	541.1[41]	765.6[41]	865.8[41]	1 542.5	1 643.8
%MF [BA]	8.7[41]	12.0[41]	12.1[41]	15.0[41]	20.1[41]	20.5[41]	14.7	15.7
%M [BA]	6.8[41]	9.6[41]	9.8[41]	12.5[41]	17.2[41]	16.9[41]	11.6	7.3
%F [BA]	11.3[41]	15.1[41]	15.1[41]	18.0[41]	23.3[41]	24.5[41]	19.1	8.4
Costa Rica[21,42] Costa Rica[21,42]								
MF [BA]	63.5[32]	75.9[32]	74.3[32]	76.5	83.3	71.9	100.4	...
M [BA]	39.1[32]	45.3[32]	43.5[32]	40.6	45.6	41.2	55.8	...
F [BA]	24.4[32]	30.6[32]	30.8[32]	36.0	37.7	30.8	44.6	...
%MF [BA]	5.2[32]	6.2[32]	5.7[32]	5.6	6.0	5.2	6.1	...
%M [BA]	4.6[32]	5.3[32]	4.9[32]	4.4	4.9	4.4	5.2	...
%F [BA]	6.5[32]	8.3[32]	7.5[32]	8.0	8.2	6.9	7.6	...
Croatia Croatie								
MF [BA][3]	...	170.2[43]	175.2[44]	198.5	234.0	297.2	276.2	265.8
M [BA][3]	...	88.3[43]	90.7[44]	100.9	117.4	149.8	134.8	129.7
F [BA][3]	...	82.0[43]	84.5[44]	97.5	116.6	147.4	141.4	136.0
%MF [BA][3]	...	10.0[43]	9.9[44]	11.4	13.5	16.1	15.8	14.8
%M [BA][3]	...	9.5[43]	9.5[44]	11.9	12.8	15.0	14.2	13.4
%F [BA][3]	...	10.5[43]	10.4[44]	12.1	14.5	17.3	17.9	16.6
MF [FB]	241.0	261.0	278.0	288.0	322.0	358.0	380.0	390.0
M [FB]	117.0	131.0	141.0	139.0	153.0	169.0	177.0	177.0
F [FB]	124.0	130.0	137.0	149.0	169.0	189.0	203.0	213.0

29

Unemployment
Number (thousands) and percentage unemployed, by sex *[cont.]*
Chômage
Nombre (milliers) et pourcentage des chômeurs, par sexe *[suite]*

Country or area, source § Pays ou zone, source §	1995	1996	1997	1998	1999	2000	2001	2002
%MF [FB]	14.5	16.4	17.5	17.2	19.1	21.1	22.0	22.3
%M [FB]	...	...	...	15.6	17.2	19.0	19.5	19.3
%F [FB]	...	...	...	19.0	21.2	23.4	24.7	25.6
Cyprus [3,45] Chypre [3,45]								
MF [BA] [46]	...	...	...	...	16.9	14.5	13.0	10.8
M [BA] [46]	...	...	...	...	7.7	5.5	4.9	4.7
F [BA] [46]	...	...	...	...	9.1	8.9	8.1	6.0
%MF [BA] [46]	...	...	...	...	5.7	4.9	4.0	3.3
%M [BA] [46]	...	...	...	...	4.3	3.2	2.7	2.6
%F [BA] [46]	...	...	...	...	7.9	7.4	5.7	4.2
MF [FB]	7.9	9.4	10.4	10.4	11.4	10.9	9.5	10.6
M [FB]	3.6	4.3	5.0	5.4	5.6	5.3	4.5	4.7
F [FB]	4.3	5.1	5.4	5.0	5.8	5.7	5.0	5.9
%MF [FB]	2.6	3.1	3.4	3.3	3.6	3.4	2.9	3.1
%M [FB]	1.9	2.3	2.7	2.8	2.9	2.7	2.3	2.3
%F [FB]	3.7	4.3	4.5	4.2	4.8	4.4	3.8	4.3
Czech Republic République tchèque								
MF [BA] [3]	208.0[47]	201.0[47]	248.0[47]	336.0	454.0	455.0	418.0	374.0
M [BA] [3]	98.0[47]	95.0[47]	113.0[47]	146.0	211.0	212.0	193.0	169.0
F [BA] [3]	110.0[47]	106.0[47]	136.0[47]	190.0	243.0	243.0	225.0	205.0
%MF [BA] [3]	4.0[47]	3.9[47]	4.8[47]	6.5	8.7	8.8	8.1	7.3
%M [BA] [3]	3.4[47]	3.3[47]	3.9[47]	5.0	7.3	7.3	6.8	5.9
%F [BA] [3]	4.8[47]	4.7[47]	6.0[47]	8.3	10.5	10.6	9.9	9.0
MF [FB] [18]	153.0	186.0	269.0	387.0	488.0	457.0	462.0	514.0
M [FB] [18]	65.0	81.0	117.0	182.0	240.0	227.0	230.0	257.0
F [FB] [18]	88.0	105.0	152.0	205.0	248.0	230.0	232.0	257.0
%MF [FB] [18]	2.9	3.5	5.2	7.5	9.4	8.8	8.9	9.8
%M [FB] [18]	2.3	2.8	4.1	6.3	8.2	7.8	7.9	8.7
%F [FB] [18]	3.6	4.3	6.7	9.0	10.8	10.0	10.1	11.2
Denmark Danemark								
MF [BA] [48]	195.5	194.5	174.2	155.3	...	131.1	137.0	134.0
M [BA] [48]	85.6	87.6	74.8	68.5	...	61.2	66.0	66.0
F [BA] [48]	109.9	107.0	99.5	86.9	...	69.8	71.0	68.0
%MF [BA] [48]	7.0	6.9	6.1	5.5	...	4.6	4.8	4.7
%M [BA] [48]	5.6	5.7	4.9	4.5	...	4.0	4.4	4.4
%F [BA] [48]	8.6	8.3	7.6	6.6	...	5.2	5.3	5.1
MF [FB] [49]	288.4	245.6	220.2	182.7	158.2	150.5	145.1	144.7
M [FB] [49]	134.1	115.8	99.4	81.0	72.8	68.5	66.5	68.8
F [FB] [49]	154.3	129.8	120.8	101.8	85.4	82.0	78.6	75.9
%MF [FB] [49]	10.3	8.8	7.9	6.6	5.7	5.4	5.2	5.1
%M [FB] [49]	9.0	7.8	6.7	5.5	4.9	4.6	4.5	4.5
%F [FB] [49]	12.0	10.1	9.4	7.8	6.5	6.2	6.0	5.7
Dominican Republic Rép. dominicaine								
MF [E]	452.1[2]	505.7[7]	503.7[2]	...	...	...	...	...
M [E]	187.3[2]	218.6[7]	199.0[2]	...	...	...	...	...
F [E]	264.8[2]	287.2[7]	304.7[2]	...	...	...	...	...
%MF [E]	15.8[2]	16.6[7]	15.9[2]	...	...	...	...	...
%M [E]	10.2[2]	10.6[7]	9.5[2]	...	...	...	...	...
%F [E]	26.2[2]	28.4[7]	28.6[2]	...	...	...	...	...
Ecuador [7] Equateur [7]								
MF [BA]	212.7[29]	334.6[29]	311.6[29]	409.3[29]	543.5[29]	333.1[29]	450.9[6]	352.9[29]
M [BA]	104.2[29]	156.1[29]	143.4[29]	175.5[29]	239.5[29]	138.3[29]	169.0[6]	136.2[29]
F [BA]	108.4[29]	178.5[29]	168.3[29]	233.8[29]	304.0[29]	194.8[29]	282.0[6]	216.7[29]
%MF [BA]	6.9[29]	10.4[29]	9.2[29]	11.5[29]	14.0[29]	9.0[29]	11.0[6]	9.3[29]
%M [BA]	5.5[29]	8.0[29]	7.0[29]	8.4[29]	10.8[29]	6.2[29]	7.1[6]	6.0[29]
%F [BA]	8.8[29]	14.0[29]	12.7[29]	16.0[29]	19.6[29]	13.1[29]	16.2[6]	14.0[29]
Egypt [50] Egypte [50]								
MF [BA]	1 916.9[51]	...	1 446.4[52]	1 447.5[52]	1 480.5[52]	1 698.0[52]	1 783.0[52]	...
M [BA]	997.2[51]	...	701.5[52]	703.0[52]	726.2[52]	743.5[52]	851.8[52]	...
F [BA]	919.7[51]	...	744.9[52]	744.5[52]	754.3[52]	954.5[52]	931.2[52]	...

29

Unemployment
Number (thousands) and percentage unemployed, by sex *[cont.]*

Chômage
Nombre (milliers) et pourcentage des chômeurs, par sexe *[suite]*

Country or area, source § Pays ou zone, source §	1995	1996	1997	1998	1999	2000	2001	2002
%MF [BA]	11.3[51]	...	8.4[52]	8.2[52]	8.1[52]	9.0[52]	9.2[52]	...
%M [BA]	7.6[51]	...	5.2[52]	5.1[52]	5.1[52]	5.1[52]	5.6[52]	...
%F [BA]	24.1[51]	...	19.8[52]	19.9[52]	19.4[52]	22.7[52]	22.6[52]	...
El Salvador [7] El Salvador [7]								
MF [BA]	163.4	171.0	180.0	175.7	170.2	173.7	183.5	160.2
M [BA]	116.8	117.5	136.0	119.9	125.2	136.8	128.8	123.6
F [BA]	46.6	53.4	44.0	55.8	45.0	36.9	54.7	36.6
%MF [BA]	7.7	7.7	8.0	7.3	7.0	7.0	7.0	6.2
%M [BA]	8.7	8.4	9.5	8.2	8.5	9.1	8.1	8.1
%F [BA]	5.9	6.5	5.3	6.0	4.6	3.6	5.2	3.5
Estonia Estonie								
MF [BA]	68.1[54]	68.4[54]	65.8[55]	66.1[55]	80.5[55]	89.9[55]	83.1[55]	67.2[55]
M [BA]	38.3[54]	37.8[54]	35.6[55]	37.4[55]	45.7[55]	49.5[55]	43.7[55]	36.1[55]
F [BA]	29.7[54]	30.6[54]	30.2[55]	28.7[55]	34.8[55]	40.5[55]	39.3[55]	31.0[55]
%MF [BA]	9.7[54]	9.9[54]	9.6[55]	9.8[55]	12.2[55]	13.6[55]	12.6[55]	10.3[55]
%M [BA]	10.5[54]	10.6[54]	10.1[55]	10.8[55]	13.4[55]	14.5[55]	12.9[55]	10.8[55]
%F [BA]	8.9[54]	9.2[54]	9.2[55]	8.8[55]	10.9[55]	12.6[55]	12.2[55]	9.7[55]
MF [FB] [53]	15.6	17.3	...	18.8	44.0	46.3	54.1	48.2
M [FB] [53]	5.1	5.2	...	...	...	...	...	...
F [FB] [53]	10.5	12.1	...	...	...	...	...	...
%MF [FB] [53]	...	...	...	2.2	5.1	5.3	6.5	5.9
Ethiopia [17] Ethiopie [17]								
MF [FB]	23.5	28.3	34.6	29.5	25.7	...	...	...
M [FB]	14.0	16.6	19.1	16.6	14.3	...	...	...
F [FB]	9.4	12.4	15.4	12.9	11.4	...	...	...
Fiji [3] Fidji [3]								
MF [E]	15.4	...	...	...	...	...	...	...
%MF [E]	5.4	...	...	...	...	...	...	...
Finland Finlande								
MF [BA] [55]	382.0	363.0	314.0	285.0	261.0	253.0	238.0	237.0
M [BA] [55]	204.0	186.0	160.0	143.0	130.0	122.0	117.0	123.0
F [BA] [55]	178.0	176.0	154.0	142.0	131.0	131.0	121.0	114.0
%MF [BA] [55]	15.2	14.4	12.5	11.3	10.1	9.7	9.1	9.1
%M [BA] [55]	15.3	14.0	12.1	10.7	9.6	8.9	8.6	9.1
%F [BA] [55]	15.1	14.8	13.0	11.9	10.7	10.6	9.7	9.1
MF [FB] [3,19,56]	451.0	434.0	398.0	362.0	337.0	321.0	302.0	294.0
M [FB] [3,19,56]	244.0	231.0	207.0	183.0	169.0	162.0	153.0	154.0
F [FB] [3,19,56]	207.0	203.0	191.0	179.0	168.0	159.0	149.0	140.0
France France								
MF [BA] [3]	2 899.2[57]	3 059.3[57]	3 104.9[57]	3 006.6[57]	3 014.3[59]	2 590.2[57]	2 285.0[57]	2 341.0[57]
M [BA] [3]	1 339.3[57]	1 438.0[57]	1 495.7[57]	1 411.0[57]	1 424.6[59]	1 185.0[57]	1 004.0[57]	1 122.5[57]
F [BA] [3]	1 559.9[57]	1 621.3[57]	1 609.2[57]	1 595.6[57]	1 589.7[59]	1 405.1[57]	1 281.0[57]	1 218.5[57]
%MF [BA] [3]	11.6[57]	12.1[57]	12.3[57]	11.8[57]	11.7[59]	10.0[57]	8.8[57]	8.9[57]
%M [BA] [3]	9.7[57]	10.3[57]	10.8[57]	10.2[57]	10.2[59]	8.5[57]	7.1[57]	7.9[57]
%F [BA] [3]	13.8[57]	14.2[57]	14.1[57]	13.8[57]	13.6[59]	11.9[57]	10.7[57]	10.1[57]
MF [FB] [53]	2 976.2[58]	3 063.0	3 102.4	2 976.8	2 772.1	2 338.2	2 152.2	2 258.9
M [FB] [53]	1 457.7[58]	1 519.8	1 545.7	1 464.1	1 357.5	1 129.5	1 070.4	1 158.0
F [FB] [53]	1 518.5[58]	1 543.2	1 556.7	1 512.6	1 414.2	1 208.7	1 082.8	1 101.0
MF [E] [3]	2 886.9	3 075.0	3 109.3	2 993.4	2 845.0	2 517.8	2 321.4	2 437.2
M [E] [3]	1 342.1	1 456.3	1 488.7	1 403.9	1 329.2	1 141.1	1 048.1	1 161.7
F [E] [3]	1 544.8	1 618.7	1 620.6	1 589.5	1 515.8	1 376.7	1 273.2	1 275.5
%MF [E] [3]	11.4	12.0	12.1	11.5	10.8	9.5	8.7	9.0
%M [E] [3]	9.7	10.4	10.6	9.9	9.3	7.9	7.3	8.0
%F [E] [3]	13.6	14.0	13.9	13.5	12.7	11.4	10.4	10.2
French Polynesia [2] Polynésie française [2]								
MF [FB]	...	...	...	3.8	...	...	...	...
Georgia [3] Géorgie [3]								
MF [BA]	...	...	...	294.7	277.5	212.2	235.6	265.0
M [BA]	...	...	...	161.8	160.1	116.7	126.9	155.5
F [BA]	...	...	...	132.9	117.4	95.5	108.7	109.5

29

Unemployment
Number (thousands) and percentage unemployed, by sex [cont.]
Chômage
Nombre (milliers) et pourcentage des chômeurs, par sexe [suite]

Country or area, source § Pays ou zone, source §	1995	1996	1997	1998	1999	2000	2001	2002
%MF [BA]	...	...	...	14.5	13.8	10.8	11.0	12.3
%M [BA]	...	...	...	15.4	15.3	11.1	11.6	13.7
%F [BA]	...	...	...	13.9	12.2	10.5	10.7	10.7
Germany Allemagne								
MF [BA] [3,15]	4 035.0	3 473.0	3 890.0	3 849.0	3 503.0	3 127.0[60]	3 150.0	3 486.0
M [BA] [3,15]	1 991.0	1 858.0	2 083.0	2 074.0	1 905.0	1 691.0[60]	1 754.0	1 982.0
F [BA] [3,15]	2 044.0	1 614.0	1 806.0	1 775.0	1 598.0	1 436.0[60]	1 396.0	1 504.0
%MF [BA] [3,15]	10.1	8.8	9.8	9.7	8.8	7.9[60]	7.9	8.7
%M [BA] [3,15]	8.7	8.2	9.2	9.2	8.4	7.6[60]	7.8	8.9
%F [BA] [3,15]	11.9	9.6	10.6	10.4	9.2	8.3[60]	7.9	8.5
MF [FB] [23,52]	3 521.0	3 848.4	4 308.1	3 965.4	3 943.0	3 685.0	3 743.0	3 942.0
M [FB] [23,52]	1 764.9	1 996.1	2 220.5	2 046.8	2 013.0	1 899.0	1 961.0	2 133.0
F [FB] [23,52]	1 756.1	1 852.3	2 087.6	1 918.6	1 930.0	1 786.0	1 782.0	1 809.0
%MF [FB] [23,52]	10.2	11.2	12.5	11.4	11.2	10.0	10.0	10.9
%M [FB] [23,52]	9.2	10.4	11.6	10.7	10.5	9.6	9.9	11.4
%F [FB] [23,52]	11.4	12.1	13.5	12.2	12.0	10.4	10.1	10.3
Ghana [61] Ghana [61]								
MF [FB]	40.5	...	...	...	...	...	...	...
Gibraltar [48] Gibraltar [48]								
MF [FB]	2.1	1.9	1.7	0.5	0.4	0.4	0.4	0.5
M [FB]	1.3	1.2	1.1	0.3	0.3	0.3	0.4	0.3
F [FB]	0.8	0.7	0.6	0.2	0.1	0.1	0.2	0.2
Greece [46] Grèce [46]								
MF [BA]	424.7[2]	446.4[2]	440.4[2]	478.5[3]	523.4[3]	491.1[3]	444.7[3]	420.1[3]
M [BA]	176.1[2]	167.1[2]	173.0[2]	188.8[3]	201.8[3]	193.4[3]	175.2[3]	161.7[3]
F [BA]	248.6[2]	279.3[2]	267.3[2]	289.8[3]	321.6[3]	297.7[3]	269.5[3]	258.4[3]
%MF [BA]	10.0[2]	10.3[2]	10.3[2]	10.8[3]	11.7[3]	11.1[3]	10.2[3]	9.6[3]
%M [BA]	6.7[2]	6.3[2]	6.6[2]	7.0[3]	7.6[3]	7.3[3]	6.7[3]	6.2[3]
%F [BA]	15.4[2]	16.6[2]	15.9[2]	16.5[3]	17.9[3]	16.7[3]	15.4[3]	14.6[3]
Greenland Groenland								
MF [FB]	2.0	2.0	1.9	...	...	...	...	...
Guatemala [7] Guatemala [7]								
MF [BA]	...	...	...	...	...	...	...	...
M [BA]	...	...	...	...	...	64.9	...	90.6
F [BA]	...	...	...	...	...	40.3	...	50.0
%MF [BA]	...	...	...	...	...	24.6	...	40.6
%M [BA]	...	...	...	...	...	1.4	...	1.8
%F [BA]	...	...	...	...	...	1.4	...	1.6
MF [FB] [62]	1.4	...	...	...	...	1.5	...	2.3
M [FB] [62]	0.9	...	...	...	...	...	...	...
F [FB] [62]	0.5	...	...	...	...	...	...	...
Honduras [7] Honduras [7]								
MF [BA]	59.1[60]	89.4[4]	69.4[4]	87.7[57]	89.3[57]	...	103.4[4]	...
M [BA]	40.3[60]	58.9[4]	45.4[4]	55.5[57]	56.7[57]	...	62.0[4]	...
F [BA]	18.8[60]	30.4[4]	23.9[4]	32.2[57]	32.6[57]	...	41.4[4]	...
%MF [BA]	3.2[60]	4.3[4]	3.2[4]	3.9[57]	3.7[57]	...	4.2[4]	...
%M [BA]	3.1[60]	4.2[4]	3.2[4]	3.8[57]	3.7[57]	...	4.0[4]	...
%F [BA]	3.4[60]	4.4[4]	3.2[4]	4.2[57]	3.8[57]	...	4.8[4]	...
Hungary Hongrie								
MF [BA] [55]	416.5	400.1	348.8	313.0	284.7	262.5	232.9	238.8[64]
M [BA] [55]	261.5	243.7	214.1	189.2	170.7	159.5	142.7	138.0[64]
F [BA] [55]	155.0	156.4	134.7	123.8	114.0	103.0	90.2	100.8[64]
%MF [BA] [55]	10.2	9.9	8.7	7.8	7.0	6.4	5.7	5.8[64]
%M [BA] [55]	10.7	10.7	9.5	8.5	7.5	7.0	6.3	6.1[64]
%F [BA] [55]	8.7	8.8	7.8	7.0	6.3	5.6	5.0	5.4[64]
MF [FB] [18]	495.9[63]	477.5	464.0	404.1	404.5	372.4	342.8	344.9
M [FB] [18]	285.3[63]	275.4	261.4	222.7	220.1	202.2	188.7	186.9
F [FB] [18]	210.6[63]	202.1	202.6	181.3	184.4	170.2	154.1	158.1
%MF [FB] [18]	12.0[63]	10.7	10.4	9.6	9.6	...	...	...

29

Unemployment
Number (thousands) and percentage unemployed, by sex *[cont.]*

Chômage
Nombre (milliers) et pourcentage des chômeurs, par sexe *[suite]*

Country or area, source § Pays ou zone, source §	1995	1996	1997	1998	1999	2000	2001	2002
Iceland Islande								
MF [BA] [65,66]	7.2	5.5	5.7	4.2	3.1	3.7	3.7	5.3
M [BA] [65,66]	3.8	2.7	2.6	1.8	1.2	1.5	1.8	3.1
F [BA] [65,66]	3.4	2.8	3.1	2.3	1.9	2.2	1.9	2.2
%MF [BA] [65,66]	4.9	3.7	3.9	2.7	2.0	2.3	2.3	3.3
%M [BA] [65,66]	4.8	3.4	3.3	2.3	1.5	1.8	2.0	3.6
%F [BA] [65,66]	4.9	4.1	4.5	3.3	2.6	2.9	2.5	2.9
MF [FB] [53]	6.5	5.8	5.2	3.8	2.6	1.9	2.0	3.6
M [FB] [53]	3.1	2.5	2.0	1.4	1.0	0.7	0.8	1.8
F [FB] [53]	3.5	3.3	3.2	2.4	1.6	1.1	1.2	1.8
%MF [FB] [53]	5.0	4.3	3.9	2.8	1.9	1.3	1.4	2.5
%M [FB] [53]	4.1	3.2	2.6	1.8	1.2	0.9	1.0	2.1
%F [FB] [53]	6.2	5.8	5.5	4.0	2.7	1.9	1.9	3.0
India [2,18] Inde [2,18]								
MF [FB]	36 742.3	37 430.0	39 140.0	40 090.0	40 371.0	41 344.0	41 996.0	41 171.0
M [FB]	28 722.0	29 050.0	30 107.0	30 563.0	30 438.0	30 887.0	31 111.0	30 521.0
F [FB]	8 020.0	8 380.0	9 033.0	9 526.0	9 933.0	10 457.0	10 885.0	10 650.0
Indonesia [3] Indonésie [3]								
MF [BA] [67]	...	3 624.8	4 197.3	5 062.5	6 030.3	5 813.2	8 005.0	9 132.1
M [BA] [67]	...	1 851.8	...	2 862.2	...	...	...	...
F [BA] [67]	...	1 773.0	...	2 200.3	...	...	...	...
%MF [BA] [67]	...	4.0	4.7	5.5	6.4	6.1	8.1	9.1
%M [BA] [67]	...	3.3	...	...	...	...	...	...
%F [BA] [67]	...	5.1	...	...	...	...	...	...
MF [FB]	953.2	1 041.8	1 542.2		1 191.8			
Iran (Islamic Rep. of) Iran (Rép. islamique d')								
MF [A]	...	1 455.7	...	...	...	...	...	...
M [A]	...	1 184.1	...	...	...	...	...	...
F [A]	...	271.6	...	...	...	...	...	...
%MF [A]	...	9.1	...	...	...	...	...	...
%M [A]	...	8.5	...	...	...	...	...	...
%F [A]	...	13.3	...	...	...	...	...	...
MF [E]	...	...	...	...	...	1 598.3	1 633.7	1 687.4
M [E]	...	...	...	...	...	1 005.4	1 318.8	1 117.6
F [E]	...	...	...	...	...	592.9	314.9	569.8
%MF [E]	...	...	...	...	...	12.6	12.4	12.3
%M [E]	...	...	...	...	...	8.1	8.4	8.2
%F [E]	...	...	...	...	...	4.5	4.0	4.1
Ireland Irlande								
MF [BA] [3]	177.4 [15]	179.0 [15]	159.0 [15]	126.6 [68]	96.9 [68]	74.9 [68]	65.4 [68]	77.2 [68]
M [BA] [3]	110.4 [15]	109.8 [15]	97.1 [15]	78.8 [68]	59.4 [68]	44.9 [68]	39.8 [68]	48.8 [68]
F [BA] [3]	67.1 [15]	69.1 [15]	62.0 [15]	47.8 [68]	37.5 [68]	30.0 [68]	25.6 [68]	28.3 [68]
%MF [BA] [3]	12.2 [15]	11.9 [15]	10.3 [15]	7.8 [68]	5.7 [68]	4.3 [68]	3.7 [68]	4.6 [68]
%M [BA] [3]	12.1 [15]	11.9 [15]	10.4 [15]	8.1 [68]	5.9 [68]	4.3 [68]	3.8 [68]	3.7 [68]
%F [BA] [3]	12.2 [15]	11.9 [15]	10.3 [15]	7.4 [68]	5.5 [68]	4.2 [68]	3.5 [68]	4.2 [68]
MF [FB] [53]	276.9	279.2	254.4	227.1	193.2	155.4	142.3	162.5
M [FB] [53]	178.5	175.6	155.8	135.7	111.6	88.7	83.0	96.3
F [FB] [53]	99.3	103.6	98.5	91.4	81.6	66.7	59.3	66.2
%MF [FB] [53]	14.1	11.8	10.1	7.4	5.5	4.1	3.8	4.3
Isle of Man Ile de Man								
MF [A] [3]	...	1.2	...	...	...	...	0.6 [69]	...
M [A] [3]	...	0.8	...	...	...	...	0.4 [69]	...
F [A] [3]	...	0.4	...	...	...	...	0.3 [69]	...
%MF [A] [3]	...	3.5	...	...	...	...	1.6 [69]	...
%M [A] [3]	...	4.3	...	...	...	...	1.7 [69]	...
%F [A] [3]	...	2.6	...	...	...	...	1.5 [69]	...
MF [FB]	1.5	1.2	0.7	0.4	0.3	0.2	0.2	0.2
M [FB]	1.1	0.9	0.5	0.3	0.2	0.2	0.1	0.1
F [FB]	0.4	0.3	0.2	0.1	0.1	0.1	0.1	0.1

29

Unemployment
Number (thousands) and percentage unemployed, by sex *[cont.]*
Chômage
Nombre (milliers) et pourcentage des chômeurs, par sexe *[suite]*

Country or area, source § Pays ou zone, source §	1995	1996	1997	1998	1999	2000	2001	2002
%MF [FB]	4.4	3.4	...	...	0.8	0.6	0.5	0.5
%M [FB]	...	4.4	...	...	1.0	0.8	0.6	0.7
%F [FB]	...	2.1	...	...	0.5	0.4	0.3	0.4
Israel[3] Israël[3]								
MF [BA]	145.0[70]	144.1	169.8	193.4[71]	208.5[71]	213.8[71]	233.9[71]	262.4[71]
M [BA]	66.6[70]	70.8	84.6	100.4[71]	108.8[71]	111.7[71]	120.9[71]	138.4[71]
F [BA]	78.4[70]	73.3	85.2	93.0[71]	99.7[71]	102.1[71]	113.0[71]	124.0[71]
%MF [BA]	6.9[70]	6.7	7.7	8.5[71]	8.9[71]	8.8[71]	9.4[71]	10.3[71]
%M [BA]	5.6[70]	5.8	6.8	8.0[71]	8.5[71]	8.4[71]	8.9[71]	10.1[71]
%F [BA]	8.6[70]	7.8	8.8	9.2[71]	9.4[71]	9.2[71]	9.9[71]	10.6[71]
Italy[3] Italie[3]								
MF [BA]	2 638.0	2 653.0	2 688.0	2 745.0	2 669.0	2 495.0	2 267.0	2 163.0
M [BA]	1 280.0	1 286.0	1 294.0	1 313.0	1 266.0	1 179.0	1 066.0	1 016.0
F [BA]	1 358.0	1 367.0	1 394.0	1 431.0	1 404.0	1 316.0	1 201.0	1 147.0
%MF [BA]	11.3	11.4	11.5	11.7	11.4	10.5	9.5	9.0
%M [BA]	8.9	8.9	9.0	9.1	8.8	8.1	7.3	6.9
%F [BA]	15.2	15.3	15.6	16.0	15.7	14.5	13.0	12.2
Jamaica[2] Jamaïque[2]								
MF [BA]	186.7	183.0	186.9	175.0				
M [BA]	66.9	61.3	64.8	61.4	...	...	...	...
F [BA]	119.8	121.7	122.1	113.5	...	...	...	...
%MF [BA]	16.2	16.0	...	...	...	...	...	...
%M [BA]	10.8	9.9	...	...	...	...	...	...
%F [BA]	22.5	23.0	...	...	...	...	...	...
Japan[3] Japon[3]								
MF [BA]	2 100.0	2 250.0	2 300.0	2 790.0	3 170.0	3 200.0	3 400.0	3 590.0
M [BA]	1 230.0	1 340.0	1 350.0	1 680.0	1 940.0	1 960.0	2 090.0	2 190.0
F [BA]	870.0	910.0	950.0	1 110.0	1 230.0	1 230.0	1 310.0	1 400.0
%MF [BA]	3.2	3.4	3.4	4.1	4.7	4.7	5.0	5.4
%M [BA]	3.1	3.4	3.4	4.2	4.8	4.9	5.2	5.5
%F [BA]	3.2	3.3	3.4	4.0	4.5	4.5	4.7	5.1
Kazakhstan Kazakhstan								
MF [FB][14]	139.6	282.4	257.5	251.9	251.4	231.4	216.1	193.7
M [FB][14]	55.7	104.0	86.0	95.5	102.0	...	...	...
F [FB][14]	83.9	178.4	171.5	156.4	149.4			
%MF [FB][14]	2.1	4.2	3.8	3.7	3.9	3.7	2.9	2.6
%M [FB][14]	1.6	2.9	2.4	2.6	...	...	...	...
%F [FB][14]	2.7	5.6	5.5	5.0	...	...	...	...
MF [E]	203.2	391.7	382.8	382.0	264.0	...	...	...
M [E]	88.5	156.6	139.5	161.9	117.0	...	...	...
F [E]	114.7	235.1	243.3	220.1	147.0	...	...	...
%MF [E]	11.0	13.0	13.0	13.7	...	...	...	...
Korea, Republic of[3] Corée, République de[3]								
MF [BA]	420.0	426.0	556.0	1 461.0	1 353.0	913.0[72]	845.0	708.0
M [BA]	280.0	291.0	352.0	983.0	911.0	613.0[72]	561.0	467.0
F [BA]	140.0	135.0	204.0	478.0	442.0	300.0[72]	284.0	241.0
%MF [BA]	2.0	2.0	2.6	6.8	6.3	4.2[72]	3.8	3.1
%M [BA]	2.3	2.3	2.8	7.6	7.1	4.7[72]	4.3	3.5
%F [BA]	1.7	1.6	2.3	5.6	5.1	3.3[72]	3.1	2.5
Kuwait Koweït								
MF [A][52]	15.9	...	...	...	...	...	...	...
M [A][52]	13.2	...	...	...	...	...	...	...
F [A][52]	2.7	...	...	...	...	...	...	...
%MF [A][52]	2.1	...	...	...	...	...	...	...
%M [A][52]	2.3	...	...	...	...	...	...	...
%F [A][52]	1.4	...	...	...	...	...	...	...
MF [FD][14]	...	7.9	8.4	8.7	8.9	9.3	9.5	...
M [FD][14]	...	6.8	7.0	7.1	7.3	7.5	7.6	...
F [FD][14]	...	1.1	1.3	1.5	1.7	1.8	1.9	...

29

Unemployment
Number (thousands) and percentage unemployed, by sex *[cont.]*

Chômage
Nombre (milliers) et pourcentage des chômeurs, par sexe *[suite]*

Country or area, source § Pays ou zone, source §	1995	1996	1997	1998	1999	2000	2001	2002
%MF [FD] [14]	...	0.7	0.7	0.7	0.7	0.8	0.8	...
%M [FD] [14]	...	0.8	0.8	0.8	0.8	0.8	0.8	...
%F [FD] [14]	...	0.5	0.5	0.5	0.6	0.7	0.6	...
Kyrgyzstan Kirghizistan								
MF [FB]	50.4	77.2	54.6	55.9	54.7	...	...	...
M [FB]	20.5	32.5	22.7	22.6	24.2	...	...	...
F [FB]	29.9	44.7	31.9	33.3	30.6	...	...	...
Latvia Lettonie								
MF [BA]	...	247.4^3	176.7^3	162.4^3	161.4^3	158.7^3	144.7^3	134.5^{55}
M [BA]	...	131.4^3	92.3^3	86.4^3	88.7^3	87.0^3	81.9^3	74.9^{55}
F [BA]	...	116.0^3	84.4^3	76.0^3	72.7^3	71.7^3	62.7^3	59.6^{55}
%MF [BA]	...	20.6^3	15.1^3	14.1^3	14.3^3	14.4^3	13.1^3	12.0^{55}
%M [BA]	...	21.0^3	15.4^3	14.4^3	15.0^3	15.4^3	14.4^3	12.9^{55}
%F [BA]	...	20.3^3	14.9^3	13.8^3	13.5^3	13.5^3	11.7^3	11.0^{55}
MF [FB] [14,73]	83.2	90.8	84.9	111.4	109.5	93.3	91.6	89.7
M [FB] [14,73]	39.7	41.1	34.5	46.2	46.7	39.5	39.1	37.1
F [FB] [14,73]	43.5	49.7	50.4	65.2	62.8	53.8	52.6	52.7
%MF [FB] [14,73]	6.6	7.2	7.0	9.2	9.1	7.8	7.7	8.5
%M [FB] [14,73]	6.1	6.4	5.6	7.5	7.6	6.5	6.4	6.7
%F [FB] [14,73]	7.0	8.1	8.5	11.0	10.7	9.2	9.0	10.5
Lebanon Liban								
MF [E]	...	...	116.1	...	...	...	...	...
Lithuania Lituanie								
MF [BA]	347.1^2	317.4^2	257.2^2	244.9^2	263.3^2	273.7^3	284.0^3	224.4^3
M [BA]	...	155.4^2	137.1^2	137.2^2	150.3^2	158.5^3	165.6^3	121.1^3
F [BA]	...	162.0^2	120.1^2	107.7^2	113.0^2	115.2^3	118.4^3	103.3^3
%MF [BA]	17.1^2	16.4^2	14.1^2	13.3^2	14.1^2	16.4^3	17.4^3	13.8^3
%M [BA]	...	...	14.2^2	14.3^2	15.6^2	18.8^3	19.9^3	14.6^3
%F [BA]	...	...	13.9^2	12.2^2	12.6^2	13.9^3	14.7^3	12.9^3
MF [FB] [14,74]	127.7	109.4	120.2	122.8	177.4	225.9	224.0	191.2
M [FB] [14,74]	57.4	49.8	58.3	61.7	94.6	123.1	117.7	95.1
F [FB] [14,74]	70.3	59.6	61.9	61.1	82.8	102.8	106.3	96.1
%MF [FB] [14,74]	7.3	6.2	6.7	6.5	10.0	12.6	12.9	10.9
%M [FB] [14,74]	6.6	5.7	6.6	6.5	10.6	13.5	13.5	10.8
%F [FB] [14,74]	8.1	6.7	6.9	7.0	9.3	11.6	12.2	11.0
Luxembourg [75] Luxembourg [75]								
MF [FB]	5.1	5.7	6.4^{76}	5.5	5.4	5.0	4.9	5.8
M [FB]	2.9	3.2	3.6^{76}	2.9	2.8	2.6	2.6	3.2
F [FB]	2.2	2.5	2.8^{76}	2.6	2.5	2.3	2.3	2.7
%MF [FB]	3.0	3.3	3.3^{76}	3.1	2.9	2.7	2.7	3.0
Madagascar [18,77] Madagascar [18,77]								
MF [FB]	3.3	...	...	...	...	...	...	...
Malaysia Malaisie								
MF [BA] [52]	248.1	216.8	214.9	284.0	313.7	294.4	357.1	381.0
%MF [BA] [52]	2.8	2.5	2.5	3.2	3.4	3.1	3.6	3.8
MF [FB] [3,78]	24.0	23.3	23.1	33.4	31.8	27.8	34.2	32.3
Maldives [21] Maldives [21]								
MF [A]	0.5	...	...	...	...	1.7	...	...
M [A]	0.3	...	...	...	...	0.9	...	...
F [A]	0.2	...	...	...	...	0.8	...	...
Malta [18] Malte [18]								
MF [BA] [3]	...	...	...	...	...	10.2	10.2	10.9
M [BA] [3]	...	...	...	...	...	7.6	6.6	6.7
F [BA] [3]	...	...	...	...	...	2.5	3.5	4.2
%MF [BA] [3]	...	...	...	...	...	6.5	6.5	6.8
%M [BA] [3]	...	...	...	...	...	7.0	6.0	6.2
%F [BA] [3]	...	...	...	...	...	5.4	7.8	8.2
MF [FB] [79]	5.2	6.2	7.1	7.4	7.7	6.6	6.8	6.8
M [FB] [79]	4.4	5.2	6.0	6.4	6.6	5.7	5.6	5.6
F [FB] [79]	0.8	1.1	1.1	1.0	1.1	0.9	1.1	1.2

29

Unemployment

Number (thousands) and percentage unemployed, by sex *[cont.]*

Chômage

Nombre (milliers) et pourcentage des chômeurs, par sexe *[suite]*

Country or area, source § Pays ou zone, source §	1995	1996	1997	1998	1999	2000	2001	2002
%MF [FB][79]	3.7	4.4	5.0	5.1	5.3	4.5	...	...
%M [FB][79]	4.3	5.0	5.8	6.1	6.3	5.4	...	...
%F [FB][79]	2.3	2.9	2.8	2.5	2.6	2.2	...	...
Mauritius Maurice								
MF [FB][3,80]	8.5	10.4	10.7	10.7	12.1	18.0	21.6	22.0
M [FB][3,80]	3.4	4.5	4.6	4.6	5.3	8.6	10.5	10.1
F [FB][3,80]	5.0	5.9	6.0	6.1	6.8	9.5	11.1	11.9
MF [E]	24.3	27.9	32.2	34.4	39.0	45.0	47.7	50.8
M [E]	13.1	15.0	18.5	20.4	23.8	28.5	30.5	29.6
F [E]	11.2	12.9	13.7	14.0	15.2	16.5	17.2	21.2
%MF [E]	5.1	5.8	6.6	6.9	7.7	8.8	9.1	9.7
%M [E]	4.1	4.6	5.6	6.1	7.0	8.3	8.8	8.5
%F [E]	7.3	8.2	8.5	8.5	9.0	9.6	9.8	12.0
Mexico [21,46] Mexique [21,46]								
MF [BA]	1 677.4	1 354.7	984.9	903.6	695.0	659.4	687.4	783.7
M [BA]	1 100.2	860.7	544.7	526.2	395.4	407.1	422.8	505.0
F [BA]	577.2	494.0	440.2	377.5	299.6	252.3	264.6	278.8
%MF [BA]	4.7	3.7	2.6	2.3	1.8	1.6	1.7	1.9
%M [BA]	4.6	3.5	2.1	2.0	1.5	1.5	1.6	1.9
%F [BA]	5.0	4.1	3.4	2.8	2.2	1.8	1.9	2.0
Mongolia [14] Mongolie [14]								
MF [FB]	45.1	55.4	63.7	49.8	39.8	38.6	40.3	30.9
M [FB]	21.6	27.3	31.1	23.8	18.2	17.8	18.4	14.1
F [FB]	23.6	28.1	32.6	26.0	21.6	20.8	21.9	16.8
%MF [FB]	5.5	6.7	7.7	5.9	4.7	4.6	4.6	3.4
%M [FB]	5.0	6.3	7.3	5.4	4.1	4.1	4.2	...
%F [FB]	6.7	7.2	8.1	6.4	5.3	5.0	5.1	...
Morocco [3] Maroc [3]								
MF [BA]	1 111.7[11]	871.2[11]	844.7[11]	969.2[11]	1 432.2	1 394.3	1 275.0	1 202.7
M [BA]	631.5[11]	568.1[11]	574.8[11]	676.1[11]	1 044.8	1 035.5	952.0	878.4
F [BA]	480.2[11]	303.1[11]	269.9[11]	293.0[11]	387.9	358.7	323.0	324.3
%MF [BA]	22.9[11]	18.1[11]	16.9[11]	19.1[11]	13.9	13.6	12.5	11.6
%M [BA]	18.7[11]	16.1[11]	15.3[11]	17.5[11]	14.2	13.8	12.5	11.6
%F [BA]	32.2[11]	23.6[11]	21.8[11]	24.4[11]	13.3	13.0	12.5	12.5
Myanmar [81] Myanmar [81]								
MF [FB]	...	...	535.3	451.5	425.3	382.1	398.4	433.7
Namibia [54] Namibie [54]								
MF [BA]	...	...	211.4	...	...	220.6	...	...
M [BA]	...	...	88.0	...	...	89.4	...	...
F [BA]	...	...	123.4	...	...	131.3	...	...
%MF [BA]	...	...	35.0	...	...	33.8	...	...
%M [BA]	...	...	29.0	...	...	28.3	...	...
%F [BA]	...	...	40.0	...	...	39.0	...	...
Netherlands Pays-Bas								
MF [BA][52]	523.0	489.0	422.0	337.0	277.0	262.0	220.0	...
M [BA][52]	255.0	228.0	196.0	155.0	124.0	118.0	101.0	...
F [BA][52]	268.0	262.0	227.0	181.0	153.0	144.0	119.0	...
%MF [BA][52]	7.1	6.6	5.5	4.4	3.5	3.3	2.7	...
%M [BA][52]	5.9	5.3	4.5	3.5	2.8	2.6	2.2	...
%F [BA][52]	8.8	8.4	7.0	5.5	4.5	4.2	3.4	...
MF [FB][75]	464.0	440.0	375.0	286.0	221.5	187.0	146.0	170.0
M [FB][75]	260.0	240.0	199.0	156.0	115.0	98.0	77.0	91.0
F [FB][75]	204.0	201.0	176.0	132.0	106.0	90.0	69.0	79.0
%MF [FB][75]	7.0	6.6	5.5	4.1	3.2	2.6	2.0	2.3
%M [FB][75]	6.4	5.9	4.8	3.7	2.7	2.3	1.8	2.1
%F [FB][75]	8.1	7.8	6.5	4.8	3.7	3.1	2.4	2.6
Netherlands Antilles [3,82] Antilles néerlandaises [3,82]								
MF [BA]	8.2	9.3	10.1	10.5	...	8.5	...	...
M [BA]	3.3	3.7	4.3	4.7	...	3.7	...	...
F [BA]	4.9	5.6	5.8	5.8	...	4.8	...	...

29

Unemployment
Number (thousands) and percentage unemployed, by sex *[cont.]*

Chômage
Nombre (milliers) et pourcentage des chômeurs, par sexe *[suite]*

Country or area, source § Pays ou zone, source §	1995	1996	1997	1998	1999	2000	2001	2002
%MF [BA]	13.1	14.0	15.3	16.6	...	14.0	...	...
%M [BA]	9.9	10.5	12.4	13.7	...	12.0	...	...
%F [BA]	17.0	10.1	10.4	19.2	...	16.2	...	...
New Caledonia Nouvelle-Calédonie								
MF [A] [2]	...	15.0	...	...	...	...	...	...
M [A] [2]	...	7.8	...	...	...	...	...	...
F [A] [2]	...	7.2	...	...	...	...	...	...
%MF [A] [2]	...	18.6	...	...	...	...	...	...
%M [A] [2]	...	9.7	...	...	...	...	...	...
%F [A] [2]	...	8.9	...	...	...	...	...	...
MF [FB] [53]	7.4	7.7	7.9	8.3	8.8	9.4	9.9	10.5
M [FB] [53]	...	...	...	...	3.9	4.2	4.4	4.8
F [FB] [53]	...	...	...	...	4.9	5.2	5.4	3.7
New Zealand Nouvelle-Zélande								
MF [BA] [3]	111.5	112.3	123.3	139.1	127.8	113.4	102.3	102.5
M [BA] [3]	61.8	61.9	67.9	77.4	72.4	63.4	56.2	54.6
F [BA] [3]	49.7	50.4	55.5	61.8	55.4	50.0	46.1	47.9
%MF [BA] [3]	6.3	6.1	6.6	7.5	6.8	6.0	5.3	5.2
%M [BA] [3]	6.2	6.1	6.6	7.6	7.0	6.1	5.4	5.1
%F [BA] [3]	6.3	6.1	6.7	7.4	6.5	5.8	5.3	5.3
MF [FB] [61,83]	157.7	154.0	168.9	193.9	221.4	226.9	192.2	168.3
M [FB] [61,83]	103.1	100.0	107.3	121.8	127.2	120.3	103.5	89.1
F [FB] [61,83]	54.6	54.0	61.6	68.0	94.1	106.6	88.7	79.2
Nicaragua [7] Nicaragua [7]								
MF [E]	244.7	225.1	208.4	215.5	185.1	178.0	122.5	135.3
M [E]	162.3	149.2	138.2	142.9	122.8	118.0	77.3	84.0
F [E]	82.4	75.9	70.2	72.6	62.3	60.0	45.2	51.3
%MF [E]	16.9	14.9	13.3	13.3	10.9	9.8	11.3	12.2
%M [E]	15.9	14.0	12.6	8.8	...	...	...	...
%F [E]	19.3	17.1	14.8	14.5	...	...	...	...
Norway Norvège								
MF [BA] [65]	107.0	108.0	92.0	74.0	75.0	81.0	84.0	94.0
M [BA] [65]	61.0	58.0	49.0	40.0	42.0	46.0	46.0	52.0
F [BA] [65]	46.0	50.0	44.0	35.0	33.0	35.0	38.0	41.0
%MF [BA] [65]	4.9	4.8	4.0	3.2	3.2	3.4	3.6	3.9
%M [BA] [65]	5.2	4.8	3.9	3.2	3.4	3.6	3.7	4.1
%F [BA] [65]	4.6	4.9	4.2	3.3	3.0	3.2	3.4	3.6
MF [FB] [53]	102.2	90.9	73.5	56.0	59.6[71]	62.6	62.7	75.2
M [FB] [53]	57.7	50.4	39.9	29.8	33.5[71]	36.3	35.7	42.6
F [FB] [53]	44.5	40.6	33.6	26.2	26.0[71]	26.4	27.0	32.6
%MF [FB] [53]	4.7	4.2	3.3	2.4	2.6[71]	2.7	2.7	...
%M [FB] [53]	4.9	4.1	...	...	...	...	...	...
%F [FB] [53]	4.5	3.9	...	...	...	...	...	...
Occupied Palestinian Terr. [3] Terr. palestinien occupé [3]								
MF [BA]	...	132.0	121.0	92.0	79.0	98.8	174.1	221.3
M [BA]	...	117.1	104.1	79.2	66.1	85.4	161.3	204.9
F [BA]	...	14.9	16.9	12.8	12.9	13.4	12.9	16.4
%MF [BA]	...	23.8	20.1	14.4	11.8	14.2	25.5	31.3
%M [BA]	...	24.2	20.1	14.3	11.6	14.5	27.3	33.5
%F [BA]	...	19.1	19.9	15.0	13.0	12.6	14.1	17.1
Pakistan Pakistan								
MF [BA] [7,84]	1 783.0	1 845.0	2 254.0	2 279.0	2 334.0	3 127.0	...	...
M [BA] [7,84]	1 179.0	1 220.0	1 317.0	1 386.0	1 419.0	2 046.0	...	...
F [BA] [7,84]	604.0	625.0	937.0	893.0	915.0	1 081.0	...	...
%MF [BA] [7,84]	5.4	5.4	6.1	5.9	5.9	7.8	...	...
%M [BA] [7,84]	4.1	4.1	4.2	4.2	4.2	6.1	...	...
%F [BA] [7,84]	13.7	13.7	16.8	15.0	15.0	17.3	...	...
MF [FB] [85]	...	180.0	262.0	212.0	217.0	469.0	...	...
Panama [3,86] Panama [3,86]								
MF [BA]	141.2	144.9	140.3	147.1	128.0	147.0	169.7	172.4
M [BA]	70.7	74.8	72.5	69.5	62.1	77.7	92.0	86.5

29

Unemployment
Number (thousands) and percentage unemployed, by sex *[cont.]*
Chômage
Nombre (milliers) et pourcentage des chômeurs, par sexe *[suite]*

Country or area, source § Pays ou zone, source §	1995	1996	1997	1998	1999	2000	2001	2002
F [BA]	70.5	70.1	67.8	77.6	65.9	69.3	77.8	85.9
%MF [BA]	14.0	14.3	13.4	13.6	11.8	13.5	14.7	14.1
%M [BA]	10.8	11.3	10.7	10.0	8.9	11.1	12.2	11.2
%F [BA]	20.1	20.0	18.1	19.9	16.9	18.0	19.3	19.2
Paraguay[7,11]　Paraguay[7,11]								
MF [BA]	...	105.7	...	...	...	...	...	...
M [BA]	...	58.1	...	...	...	...	...	...
F [BA]	...	47.5	...	...	...	...	...	...
%MF [BA]	...	8.2	...	...	...	...	...	...
%M [BA]	...	7.8	...	...	...	...	...	...
%F [BA]	...	8.6	...	...	...	...	...	...
Peru[2,11,87]　Pérou[2,11,87]								
MF [BA]	...	461.6	565.0	582.5	624.9	566.5	651.5	...
M [BA]	...	247.4	279.9	274.4	322.8	318.8	327.5	...
F [BA]	...	214.2	285.1	308.1	302.2	247.7	324.0	...
%MF [BA]	...	7.0	7.7	7.8	8.0	7.4	7.9	...
%M [BA]	...	6.4	6.8	6.5	7.5	7.3	7.2	...
%F [BA]	...	7.9	8.9	9.3	8.6	7.5	8.7	...
Philippines[3,88]　Philippines[3,88]								
MF [BA]	2 342.0	2 195.0	2 377.0	3 016.0	2 931.0	3 133.0	3 269.0	...
M [BA]	1 354.0	1 293.0	1 411.0	1 857.0	1 835.0	1 978.0	1 912.0	...
F [BA]	988.0	902.0	966.0	1 159.0	1 096.0	1 156.0	1 356.0	...
%MF [BA]	8.4	7.4	7.9	9.6	9.6	10.1	9.8	...
%M [BA]	7.7	7.0	7.5	9.5	9.7	10.3	9.4	...
%F [BA]	9.4	8.2	8.5	9.8	9.3	9.9	10.3	...
Poland[3]　Pologne[3]								
MF [BA]	2 277.0	2 108.0	1 923.0	1 808.0	2 391.0[89]	2 785.0	3 170.0	3 431.0
M [BA]	1 119.0	1 015.0	889.0	843.0	1 147.0[89]	1 344.0	1 583.0	1 779.0
F [BA]	1 157.0	1 093.0	1 035.0	965.0	1 244.0[89]	1 440.0	1 587.0	1 652.0
%MF [BA]	13.3	12.3	11.2	10.5	13.9[89]	16.1	18.2	19.9
%M [BA]	12.1	11.0	9.6	9.1	12.4[89]	14.4	16.9	19.1
%F [BA]	14.7	13.9	13.2	12.3	15.8[89]	18.1	19.8	20.9
MF [FB][14]	2 628.8	2 359.5	1 826.4	1 831.4	2 349.8	2 702.6	3 115.1	3 217.0
M [FB][14]	1 180.2	983.9	723.2	760.1	1 042.5	1 211.0	1 473.0	1 571.2
F [FB][14]	1 448.6	1 375.6	1 103.2	1 071.3	1 307.3	1 491.6	1 642.1	1 645.8
%MF [FB][14]	14.9	13.2	10.3	10.4	13.1	15.1	17.5	18.1
Portugal　Portugal								
MF [BA]	338.4[2]	343.9[2]	324.1[2]	247.9[2,3]	221.6[3]	204.6[3]	211.5[3]	272.3[3]
M [BA]	165.8[2]	167.0[2]	158.5[2]	107.6[2,3]	105.9[3]	87.9[3]	90.9[3]	122.0[3]
F [BA]	172.6[2]	177.0[2]	165.6[2]	140.4[2,3]	115.7[3]	116.7[3]	120.6[3]	150.3[3]
%MF [BA]	7.1[2]	7.2[2]	6.7[2]	5.0[2,3]	4.4[3]	4.0[3]	4.1[3]	5.1[3]
%M [BA]	6.3[2]	6.4[2]	6.0[2]	3.9[2,3]	3.8[3]	3.2[3]	3.2[3]	4.2[3]
%F [BA]	8.1[2]	8.2[2]	7.5[2]	6.2[2,3]	5.1[3]	5.0[3]	5.1[3]	6.1[3]
MF [FB]	429.9	467.7	442.9	400.6	356.8	327.4	324.7	344.6
M [FB]	190.3	204.1	187.0	165.3	144.9	128.7	127.0	139.6
F [FB]	240.0	263.6	255.8	235.4	211.9	198.8	197.7	205.3
Puerto Rico[53,56]　Porto Rico[53,56]								
MF [BA]	170.0	172.0	176.0	175.0	153.0	132.0	147.0	166.0
M [BA]	117.0	114.0	112.0	112.0	102.0	91.0	98.0	103.0
F [BA]	53.0	58.0	64.0	63.0	51.0	42.0	49.0	63.0
%MF [BA]	13.7	13.4	13.5	13.3	11.8	10.1	11.4	12.3
%M [BA]	15.6	14.9	14.4	14.4	13.2	11.8	13.0	13.2
%F [BA]	10.8	11.2	12.1	11.8	9.6	7.7	9.1	10.9
Republic of Moldova　République de Moldova								
MF [BA][3]	...	...	...	...	187.2	140.1	117.7	110.0
M [BA][3]	...	...	...	...	113.6	80.6	70.1	64.0
F [BA][3]	...	...	...	...	73.6	59.5	47.6	45.0
%MF [BA][3]	...	...	...	...	11.1	8.5	7.3	6.8
%M [BA][3]	...	...	...	...	13.3	9.7	8.7	8.1
%F [BA][3]	...	...	...	...	8.9	7.2	5.9	5.5

29

Unemployment
Number (thousands) and percentage unemployed, by sex [cont.]

Chômage
Nombre (milliers) et pourcentage des chômeurs, par sexe [suite]

Country or area, source § Pays ou zone, source §	1995	1996	1997	1998	1999	2000	2001	2002
MF [FB][18]	24.5	23.4	28.0	32.0	34.9	28.9	27.6	24.0
M [FB][18]	8.4	7.5	10.3	13.0	13.3	11.9	13.6	11.7
F [FB][18]	16.1	15.9	17.7	19.0	21.6	17.0	14.0	12.3
%MF [FB][18]	1.0	1.5	1.5	1.9	2.1	2.1	2.0	1.9
Romania Roumanie								
MF [BA]	967.9[90]	790.9[3]	706.5[3]	732.4[3]	789.9[3]	821.2[3]	750.0[3]	845.3[3]
M [BA]	487.6[90]	399.1[3]	364.2[3]	410.3[3]	462.5[3]	481.6[3]	436.1[3]	494.1[3]
F [BA]	480.3[90]	391.7[3]	342.2[3]	322.1[3]	327.4[3]	339.6[3]	313.9[3]	351.2[3]
%MF [BA]	8.0[90]	6.7[3]	6.0[3]	6.3[3]	6.8[3]	7.1[3]	6.6[3]	8.4[3]
%M [BA]	7.5[90]	6.3[3]	5.7[3]	6.5[3]	7.4[3]	7.7[3]	7.1[3]	8.9[3]
%F [BA]	8.6[90]	7.3[3]	6.4[3]	6.1[3]	6.2[3]	6.4[3]	5.9[3]	7.7[3]
MF [FB][18]	998.4	657.6	881.4	1 025.1	1 130.3	1 007.1	826.9	760.6
M [FB][18]	446.9	302.2	452.8	539.9	600.2	535.5	445.8	421.1
F [FB][18]	551.5	355.4	428.6	485.2	530.1	471.6	381.1	339.5
%MF [FB][18]	9.5	6.6	8.9	10.4	11.8	10.5	8.8	8.1
%M [FB][18]	7.9	5.7	8.5	10.4	12.1	10.8	9.2	8.7
%F [FB][18]	11.4	7.5	9.3	10.4	11.6	10.1	8.4	7.5
Russian Federation Fédération de Russie								
MF [BA][91]	6 712.0	6 732.0[92]	8 058.0	8 876.0	9 094.0	6 999.0	6 303.0	...
M [BA][91]	3 616.0	3 662.0[92]	4 371.0	4 787.0	4 801.0	3 781.0	3 411.0	...
F [BA][91]	3 096.0	3 070.0[92]	3 687.0	4 090.0	4 293.0	3 219.0	2 793.0	...
%MF [BA][91]	9.5	9.7[92]	11.8	13.3	12.6	9.8	8.9	...
%M [BA][91]	9.7	10.0[92]	12.2	13.6	12.8	10.2	9.3	...
%F [BA][91]	9.2	9.3[92]	11.5	13.0	12.3	9.4	8.5	...
MF [FB][18]	2 327.0	2 506.0	1 998.7	1 929.0	1 263.4	1 037.0	1 122.7	1 309.4
M [FB][18]	872.0	930.0	721.0	682.0	383.0	322.2	359.5	412.8
F [FB][18]	1 455.0	1 576.0	1 278.0	1 247.0	880.0	714.8	763.2	896.6
%MF [FB][18]	8.9	9.9	11.3	13.3	...	...	...	...
Rwanda[93] Rwanda[93]								
MF [B]	...	16.3	...	...	...	...	...	...
M [B]	...	10.7	...	...	...	...	...	...
F [B]	...	5.5	...	...	...	...	...	...
%MF [B]	...	0.6	...	...	...	...	...	...
%M [B]	...	0.8	...	...	...	...	...	...
%F [B]	...	0.3	...	...	...	...	...	...
Saint Helena Sainte-Hélène								
MF [A][54]	...	...	...	0.4	...	...	...	...
M [A][54]	...	...	...	0.3	...	...	...	...
F [A][54]	...	...	...	0.2	...	...	...	...
MF [FB]	0.3	0.4	0.4	0.5	0.4	0.3	...	...
M [FB]	0.2	0.2	0.3	0.3	0.3	0.2	...	...
F [FB]	0.1	0.1	0.1	0.1	0.1	0.1	...	...
San Marino[14] Saint-Marin[14]								
MF [E]	0.5[2]	0.6[3]	0.5	0.6	0.4	0.4	0.5	0.7
M [E]	0.1[2]	0.1[3]	0.1	0.1	0.1	0.1	0.2	0.2
F [E]	0.4[2]	0.5[3]	0.4	0.4	0.3	0.3	0.4	0.5
%MF [E]	3.9[2]	5.1[3]	4.4	4.1	3.0	2.8	2.6	3.6
%M [E]	1.5[2]	2.0[3]	1.9	1.8	1.6	1.7	1.4	1.6
%F [E]	7.0[2]	8.8[3]	7.3	6.9	4.6	4.1	4.3	6.3
Saudi Arabia[3] Arabie saoudite[3]								
MF [BA]	...	...	...	...	254.1	273.6	281.2	...
M [BA]	...	...	...	...	183.8	194.3	202.6	...
F [BA]	...	...	...	...	70.3	79.3	78.6	...
%MF [BA]	...	...	...	...	4.3	4.6	4.6	...
%M [BA]	...	...	...	...	3.7	3.8	3.9	...
%F [BA]	...	...	...	...	8.1	9.3	9.1	...
Serbia and Montenegro Serbie-et-Monténégro								
MF [BA][3]	609.3[94]	598.6[60]	613.1	617.0	528.0[96]	480.5[96]	490.2[96]	517.3[96]
M [BA][3]	288.0[94]	294.5[60]	310.8	303.4	248.9[96]	223.6[96]	242.5[96]	261.5[96]
F [BA][3]	321.3[94]	304.1[60]	302.3	313.6	279.0[96]	257.0[96]	247.7[96]	255.8[96]

29

Unemployment
Number (thousands) and percentage unemployed, by sex *[cont.]*
Chômage
Nombre (milliers) et pourcentage des chômeurs, par sexe *[suite]*

Country or area, source § / Pays ou zone, source §	1995	1996	1997	1998	1999	2000	2001	2002
%MF [BA][3]	13.4[94]	13.2[60]	13.8	13.7	13.7[96]	12.6[96]	12.8[96]	13.8[96]
%M [BA][3]	11.3[94]	11.3[60]	12.2	11.8	11.7[96]	10.6[96]	11.1[96]	12.4[96]
%F [BA][3]	16.1[94]	15.6[60]	16.1	16.1	16.2[96]	15.2[96]	15.0[96]	15.8[96]
MF [FB]	...	...	814.1[95]	837.6[95]	811.1[96]	805.8[96]	850.0[96]	...
M [FB]	...	...	...	364.5[95]	349.3[96]	346.0[96]	369.6[96]	...
F [FB]	...	...	...	473.1[95]	461.8[96]	459.8[96]	480.4[96]	...
%MF [FB]	...	...	...	18.6[95]	21.1[96]	21.2[96]	22.3[96]	...
%M [FB]	...	...	...	14.2[95]	16.4[96]	20.5[96]	22.6[96]	...
%F [FB]	...	...	...	24.3[95]	26.8[96]	21.8[96]	22.1[96]	...
Singapore Singapour								
MF [BA][3,25]	47.2	53.8	45.5	62.1	90.1	97.5[5]	72.9	111.2
M [BA][3,25]	28.4	31.0	26.8	35.5	51.4	53.5[5]	41.7	65.0
F [BA][3,25]	18.8	22.8	18.7	26.6	38.7	44.0[5]	31.2	46.2
%MF [BA][3,25]	2.7	3.0	2.4	3.2	4.6	4.4[5]	3.4	5.2
%M [BA][3,25]	2.7	2.9	2.4	3.2	4.5	4.0[5]	3.5	5.4
%F [BA][3,25]	2.8	3.1	2.4	3.3	4.6	5.1[5]	3.4	5.0
MF [FB][2]	1.1	1.5	2.6	4.4	5.9	4.2	6.4	11.6
M [FB][2]	0.7	0.8	1.2	2.3	3.2	2.3	3.2	5.6
F [FB][2]	0.4	0.7	1.4	2.1	2.7	1.8	3.2	6.0
Slovakia Slovaquie								
MF [BA][3,47]	323.7	284.2	297.5	317.1	416.8	485.2	508.0	486.9
M [BA][3,47]	171.4	140.7	151.8	167.5	226.6	265.5	282.5	263.9
F [BA][3,47]	152.4	143.5	145.6	149.6	190.3	219.7	225.4	223.0
%MF [BA][3,47]	13.1	11.3	11.8	12.5	16.2	18.6	19.2	18.5
%M [BA][3,47]	12.6	10.2	10.9	11.9	16.0	18.6	19.5	18.4
%F [BA][3,47]	13.8	12.7	12.8	13.2	16.4	18.6	18.8	18.7
MF [FB]	349.8	324.3	336.7	379.5	485.2	519.1	520.6	513.2
M [FB]	174.8	155.1	162.9	193.0	265.8	294.6	284.7	280.8
F [FB]	175.0	169.2	173.8	186.5	219.4	224.5	235.9	232.4
%MF [FB]	13.8	12.6	12.9	13.7	17.3	18.3	18.3	17.8
%M [FB]	12.8	11.3	11.7	13.3	17.9	19.7	18.9	19.0
%F [FB]	14.8	14.1	14.3	14.1	16.6	16.9	17.5	16.5
Slovenia[3] Slovénie[3]								
MF [BA]	70.0[60]	69.0[60]	69.0[46]	75.0[46]	71.0[46]	69.0[46]	57.0[46]	58.0[46]
M [BA]	39.0[60]	38.0[60]	36.0[46]	40.0[46]	37.0[46]	36.0[46]	29.0[46]	30.0[46]
F [BA]	31.0[60]	31.0[60]	32.0[46]	35.0[46]	34.0[46]	33.0[46]	28.0[46]	28.0[46]
%MF [BA]	7.4[60]	7.3[60]	7.1[46]	7.7[46]	7.4[46]	7.2[46]	5.9[46]	5.9[46]
%M [BA]	7.7[60]	7.5[60]	7.0[46]	7.6[46]	7.2[46]	7.0[46]	5.6[46]	5.7[46]
%F [BA]	7.0[60]	7.0[60]	7.3[46]	7.7[46]	7.6[46]	7.4[46]	6.3[46]	6.3[46]
MF [FB]	...	...	125.2	126.1	119.0	106.6	101.9	102.6
M [FB]	...	...	64.1	63.2	58.8	52.5	50.2	50.1
F [FB]	...	...	61.1	62.9	60.2	54.1	51.7	52.1
South Africa Afrique du Sud								
MF [BA][48]	...	...	...	...	3 158.0[88]	4 208.0[99]	4 383.0[99]	4 788.0[99]
M [BA][48]	...	...	...	...	1 480.0[88]	2 015.0[99]	2 114.0[99]	2 252.0[99]
F [BA][48]	...	...	...	...	1 677.0[88]	2 194.0[99]	2 268.0[99]	2 535.0[99]
%MF [BA][48]	...	...	...	...	23.3[88]	26.3[99]	28.0[99]	30.0[99]
%M [BA][48]	...	...	...	...	19.8[88]	24.1[99]	25.5[99]	26.7[99]
%F [BA][48]	...	...	...	...	27.8[88]	28.7[99]	30.7[99]	33.6[99]
MF [FB][3,97,98]	273.0	295.7	309.6	...	...	...	...	...
M [FB][3,97,98]	186.7	197.4	207.8	...	...	...	...	...
F [FB][3,97,98]	86.2	98.3	101.8	...	...	...	...	...
%MF [FB]	4.5	5.1	5.4	...	...	...	...	...
Spain Espagne								
MF [BA][53]	3 715.6	3 657.2	3 471.9	3 177.2	2 722.4	2 486.9	1 869.1	2 082.9
M [BA][53]	1 813.7	1 778.8	1 633.5	1 420.8	1 159.7	1 032.9	808.0	887.9
F [BA][53]	1 901.9	1 878.4	1 838.4	1 756.4	1 562.7	1 454.0	1 061.1	1 195.0
%MF [BA][53]	22.9	22.2	20.8	18.7	15.7	13.9	10.5	11.4
%M [BA][53]	18.0	17.5	16.0	13.7	11.0	9.6	7.5	8.1
%F [BA][53]	30.8	29.7	28.3	26.6	23.1	20.5	15.2	16.4

29

Unemployment
Number (thousands) and percentage unemployed, by sex *[cont.]*

Chômage
Nombre (milliers) et pourcentage des chômeurs, par sexe *[suite]*

Country or area, source § Pays ou zone, source §	1995	1996	1997	1998	1999	2000	2001	2002
MF [FB][75]	2 449.0	2 275.4	2 118.7	1 889.5	1 651.6	1 557.5	1 529.9	1 621.5
M [FB][75]	1 156.0	1 064.9	968.4	818.2	682.2	615.9	601.5	656.4
F [FB][75]	1 292.9	1 210.4	1 150.3	1 071.3	969.4	941.6	928.4	965.1
Sri Lanka[7,100] Sri Lanka[7,100]								
MF [BA][101]	759.1[101]	710.3[101]	...	701.0[101]	612.7[87]	546.1[101]	518.3[101]	632.8[101]
M [BA][101]	352.9[101]	328.2[101]	...	296.2[101]	330.7[87]	290.3[101]	261.8[101]	305.8[101]
F [BA][101]	406.2[101]	382.0[101]	...	404.8[101]	282.0[87]	255.8[101]	256.5[101]	327.0[101]
%MF [BA][101]	12.5[101]	11.3[101]	10.7[101]	10.6[101]	9.1[87]	8.0[101]	7.7[101]	8.7[101]
%M [BA][101]	8.8[101]	8.0[101]	8.0[101]	7.1[101]	7.4[87]	6.4[101]	5.8[101]	8.7[101]
%F [BA][101]	19.7[101]	17.6[101]	16.2[101]	16.2[101]	12.6[87]	11.1[101]	11.7[101]	12.8[101]
Suriname Suriname								
MF [BA][3]	7.6	10.7	9.7	10.5	11.8[102]	...	...	...
M [BA][3]	4.1	4.9	4.4	4.6	5.4[102]	...	...	...
F [BA][3]	3.4	5.8	5.3	5.8	6.5[102]	...	...	...
%MF [BA][3]	8.4	10.9	10.5	10.6	14.0[102]	...	...	...
%M [BA][3]	7.0	7.9	7.4	7.2	10.0[102]	...	...	...
%F [BA][3]	10.9	16.4	16.0	17.0	20.0[102]	...	...	...
MF [FB]	0.9	0.9	...	...	...	...	...	...
M [FB]	0.3	0.3	...	...	...	...	...	...
F [FB]	0.6	0.6	...	...	...	...	...	...
Sweden Suède								
MF [BA][75]	333.0	347.0	342.0	276.0	241.0	203.0	175.0	176.0
M [BA][75]	190.0	192.0	188.0	154.0	133.0	114.0	99.0	101.0
F [BA][75]	142.0	155.0	154.0	122.0	107.0	89.0	76.0	76.0
%MF [BA][75]	7.7	8.0	8.0	6.5	5.6	4.7	4.0	4.0
%M [BA][75]	8.5	8.5	8.4	6.9	5.9	5.0	4.3	4.4
%F [BA][75]	6.9	7.5	7.5	6.0	5.2	4.3	3.6	3.6
MF [FB][3]	436.2	407.6	367.0	285.6	276.7	231.2	193.0	185.8
M [FB][3]	238.2	220.2	199.5	156.3	151.7	126.9	107.2	105.4
F [FB][3]	198.0	187.3	167.4	129.3	125.0	104.3	85.8	80.4
%MF [FB][3]	10.1	9.5	8.6	6.7	6.4	5.3	4.4	4.2
%M [FB][3]	10.6	9.8	8.9	7.0	6.7	5.6	4.7	4.6
%F [FB][3]	9.6	9.1	8.2	6.4	6.1	5.0	4.1	3.8
Switzerland[3] Suisse[3]								
MF [BA][46]	129.0	144.6	162.1	141.8	121.6	105.9	100.6	120.0
M [BA][46]	63.6	74.7	94.7	70.0	59.2	51.0	37.9	63.0
F [BA][46]	65.4	69.9	67.4	71.8	62.4	54.9	62.6	57.0
%MF [BA][46]	3.3	3.7	4.1	3.6	3.1	2.7	2.5	2.9
%M [BA][46]	2.9	3.4	4.3	3.2	2.7	2.3	1.7	2.8
%F [BA][46]	3.9	4.1	3.9	4.1	3.5	3.1	3.5	3.1
MF [FB]	153.3	168.6	188.3	139.7	98.6	72.0	67.2	100.5
M [FB]	85.5	96.8	108.7	77.1	52.6	37.8	35.4	55.9
F [FB]	67.8	71.8	79.6	62.6	46.0	34.2	31.8	44.6
%MF [FB]	4.2	4.7	5.2	3.9	2.7	1.8	1.7	2.5
%M [FB]	3.9	4.4	4.9	3.5	2.4	1.7	1.6	2.5
%F [FB]	4.8	5.1	5.7	4.4	3.3	2.0	1.8	2.6
Syrian Arab Republic[3] Rép. arabe syrienne[3]								
MF [BA]	...	...	...	...	...	...	613.4	637.8
M [BA]	...	...	...	...	...	...	348.4	355.8
F [BA]	...	...	...	...	...	...	265.0	282.0
%MF [BA]	...	...	...	...	...	...	11.2	11.7
%M [BA]	...	...	...	...	...	...	8.0	8.3
%F [BA]	...	...	...	...	...	...	23.9	24.1
Tajikistan Tadjikistan								
MF [FB]	37.5	45.7	51.1	...	...	...	...	...
M [FB]	20.2	22.8	24.1	...	...	...	...	...
F [FB]	17.3	22.9	27.0	...	...	...	...	...
%MF [FB]	2.0	2.6	2.7	...	...	...	...	...
%M [FB]	1.9	2.4	2.4	...	...	...	...	...
%F [FB]	2.1	2.8	2.9	...	...	...	...	...

29

Unemployment
Number (thousands) and percentage unemployed, by sex *[cont.]*

Chômage
Nombre (milliers) et pourcentage des chômeurs, par sexe *[suite]*

Country or area, source § Pays ou zone, source §	1995	1996	1997	1998	1999	2000	2001	2002
Thailand [103,104] **Thaïlande** [103,104]								
MF [BA]	375.0	353.9	292.5	1 137.9	985.7	812.6	896.3	...
M [BA]	167.1	186.5	154.4	625.2	546.4	454.5	511.2	...
F [BA]	207.9	167.4	138.1	512.7	439.3	358.0	385.1	...
%MF [BA]	1.1	1.1	0.9	3.4	3.0	2.4	2.6	...
%M [BA]	0.9	1.0	0.8	3.4	3.0	2.4	2.7	...
%F [BA]	1.4	1.1	0.9	3.4	3.0	2.3	2.5	...
TFYR of Macedonia **L'ex-R.y. Macédoine**								
MF [BA] [3,15]	...	...	...	...	...	...	263.2	263.5
M [BA] [3,15]	...	...	...	...	...	...	149.4	159.1
F [BA] [3,15]	...	...	...	...	...	...	113.8	104.3
%MF [BA] [3,15]	...	...	...	...	...	...	30.5	31.9
%M [BA] [3,15]	...	...	...	...	...	...	29.5	31.7
%F [BA] [3,15]	...	...	...	...	...	...	32.0	32.3
MF [FB]	216.2	238.0	253.0	...	...	...	354.4	363.4
M [FB]	101.0	110.0	138.0	...	...	...	...	208.1
F [FB]	115.0	128.0	115.0	...	...	...	...	163.7
%MF [FB]	35.6	38.8	40.6	46.6	51.5	53.7	...	...
%M [FB]	31.9	35.0	...	...	...	...	...	...
%F [FB]	41.7	44.5	...	...	...	...	...	...
Trinidad and Tobago [3,105] **Trinité-et-Tobago** [3,105]								
MF [BA]	89.4	86.1	81.2	79.4	74.0	69.6	62.4	...
M [BA]	49.5	43.1	41.3	39.0	37.9	36.1	30.7	...
F [BA]	39.9	43.0	39.9	40.4	36.1	33.5	31.7	...
%MF [BA]	17.2	16.2	15.0	14.2	13.1	12.2	10.8	...
%M [BA]	15.1	13.2	12.3	11.3	10.9	10.2	8.6	...
%F [BA]	20.6	21.0	19.4	18.9	16.8	15.2	14.4	...
Tunisia **Tunisie**								
MF [BA] [3]	...	...	474.7	...	509.9	510.8	...	...
%MF [BA] [3]	...	...	15.7	...	15.8	15.6	...	...
MF [FB] [81]	189.7	180.9	225.3	278.3	277.8	334.8	347.6	...
M [FB] [81]	160.4	115.9	136.8	165.9	156.9	196.6	207.6	...
F [FB] [81]	29.3	64.9	88.4	112.4	120.9	138.3	142.0	...
Turkey **Turquie**								
MF [BA]	1 608.0 [106]	1 417.0 [106]	1 463.0 [106]	1 528.0 [106]	1 774.0 [106]	1 453.0 [3]	1 901.0 [3]	2 412.0 [3]
M [BA]	1 165.0 [106]	1 054.0 [106]	1 007.0 [106]	1 107.0 [106]	1 275.0 [106]	1 077.0 [3]	1 435.0 [3]	1 787.0 [3]
F [BA]	443.0 [106]	363.0 [106]	456.0 [106]	421.0 [106]	499.0 [106]	376.0 [3]	466.0 [3]	625.0 [3]
%MF [BA]	7.5 [106]	6.5 [106]	6.7 [106]	6.8 [106]	7.7 [106]	6.6 [3]	8.5 [3]	10.6 [3]
%M [BA]	7.6 [106]	6.8 [106]	6.3 [106]	6.8 [106]	7.7 [106]	6.6 [3]	8.8 [3]	10.9 [3]
%F [BA]	7.3 [106]	5.9 [106]	7.8 [106]	6.9 [106]	7.5 [106]	6.5 [3]	7.9 [3]	9.9 [3]
MF [FB] [2,18]	401.3	416.8	463.0	465.2	487.5	730.5	718.7	464.3
M [FB] [2,18]	324.7	341.8	382.1	386.0	413.8	591.9	582.9	379.8
F [FB] [2,18]	76.6	75.0	81.2	79.2	73.7	138.6	135.8	84.5
Ukraine **Ukraine**								
MF [BA] [107]	1 437.0 [88]	1 997.5 [88]	2 330.1 [88]	2 937.1 [88]	2 698.8	2 707.6	2 516.9	2 301.0
M [BA] [107]	805.7 [88]	1 057.2 [88]	1 216.9 [88]	1 515.1 [88]	1 435.5	1 392.2	1 303.8	1 196.4
F [BA] [107]	631.3 [88]	940.3 [88]	1 113.2 [88]	1 422.0 [88]	1 263.3	1 315.4	1 213.1	1 104.6
%MF [BA] [107]	5.6 [88]	7.6 [88]	8.9 [88]	11.3 [88]	11.9	11.7	11.1	10.1
%M [BA] [107]	6.3 [88]	8.0 [88]	9.5 [88]	11.9 [88]	12.3	11.7	11.2	10.3
%F [BA] [107]	4.9 [88]	7.3 [88]	8.4 [88]	10.8 [88]	11.5	11.7	11.0	10.0
MF [FB] [14,108]	126.9	351.1	637.1	1 003.2	1 174.5	1 155.2	1 008.1	...
M [FB] [14,108]	34.7	115.3	220.6	382.8	444.9	424.8	362.5	...
F [FB] [14,108]	92.2	235.8	416.5	620.4	729.6	730.4	645.6	...
%MF [FB] [14,108]	0.6	1.5	2.7	4.3	5.5	5.4	4.8	...
%M [FB] [14,108]	0.3	0.9	1.8	3.2	4.0	3.8	3.4	...
%F [FB] [14,108]	0.8	2.1	3.7	5.5	7.3	7.3	6.3	...
United Arab Emirates **Emirats arabes unis**								
MF [E]	24.1 [5]	...	...	...	...	41.0	...	...
M [E]	20.4 [5]	...	...	...	...	34.7	...	...
F [E]	3.7 [5]	...	...	...	...	6.3	...	...

29

Unemployment
Number (thousands) and percentage unemployed, by sex *[cont.]*

Chômage
Nombre (milliers) et pourcentage des chômeurs, par sexe *[suite]*

Country or area, source § Pays ou zone, source §	1995	1996	1997	1998	1999	2000	2001	2002
%MF [E]	1.8[5]	...	...	...	...	2.3	...	...
%M [E]	1.7[5]	...	...	...	...	2.2	...	...
%F [E]	2.4[5]	...	...	...	...	2.6	...	...
United Kingdom Royaume-Uni								
MF [BA][53,109]	2 460.4	2 340.1	2 037.3	1 776.4	1 751.7	1 619.1	1 412.9	1 519.4
M [BA][53,109]	1 611.8	1 549.0	1 305.8	1 097.8	1 095.2	991.5	864.1	933.5
F [BA][53,109]	848.6	791.0	731.5	678.6	656.5	627.6	548.8	585.9
%MF [BA][53,109]	8.6	8.2	7.1	6.1	6.0	5.5	4.8	5.1
%M [BA][53,109]	10.1	9.6	8.1	6.8	6.7	6.1	5.3	5.6
%F [BA][53,109]	6.8	6.3	5.7	5.3	5.1	4.8	4.2	4.4
MF [FA][56,110]	2 325.7	2 122.2	1 602.4	1 362.4	1 263.1	1 102.3	983.0	...
M [FA][56,110]	1 770.0	1 610.3	1 225.5	1 037.7	963.5	839.6	746.8	...
F [FA][56,110]	555.6	511.9	377.3	324.7	299.5	262.6	236.2	...
%MF [FA][56,110]	8.3	7.6	5.7	4.7	4.3	3.8	3.3	...
%M [FA][56,110]	11.3	10.3	7.7	6.5	6.0	5.2	4.6	...
%F [FA][56,110]	4.5	4.2	2.9	2.5	2.3	2.0	1.7	...
United Rep. of Tanzania[7,111] Rép.-Unie de Tanzanie[7,111]								
MF [BA]	...	...	...	...	...	...	912.8	
M [BA]	...	...	...	...	...	...	388.4	
F [BA]	...	...	...	...	...	...	524.4	
%MF [BA]	...	...	...	...	...	...	5.1	
%M [BA]	...	...	...	...	...	...	4.4	
%F [BA]	...	...	...	...	...	...	5.8	
United States[53] Etats-Unis[53]								
MF [BA]	7 404.0	7 236.0	6 739.0	6 210.0	5 880.0	5 655.0	6 742.0	8 378.0
M [BA]	3 983.0	3 880.0	3 577.0	3 266.0	3 066.0	2 954.0	3 663.0	4 597.0
F [BA]	3 421.0	3 356.0	3 162.0	2 944.0	2 814.0	2 701.0	3 079.0	3 781.0
%MF [BA]	5.6	5.4	4.9	4.5	4.2	4.0	4.8	5.8
%M [BA]	5.6	5.4	4.9	4.4	4.1	3.9	4.8	5.9
%F [BA]	5.6	5.4	5.0	4.6	4.3	4.1	4.7	5.6
United States Virgin Is.[112] Iles Vierges américaines[112]								
MF [FB]	2.7	2.4	2.7	...	...	...	...	...
%MF [FB]	5.7	5.2	5.9	...	...	...	...	...
Uruguay[2,11] Uruguay[2,11]								
MF [BA]	137.5	...	...	123.8	137.7	167.7	193.2	
M [BA]	61.5	...	...	53.7	59.4	74.7	80.4	...
F [BA]	76.0	...	...	70.1	78.3	93.0	112.8	...
%MF [BA]	10.2	...	...	10.1	11.3	13.6	15.3	...
%M [BA]	8.0	...	...	7.8	8.7	10.9	11.5	...
%F [BA]	13.2	...	...	13.0	14.6	17.0	19.7	...
Uzbekistan Ouzbékistan								
MF [FB]	31.0	...	...	...	...	...	...	...
M [FB]	12.1	...	...	...	...	...	...	...
F [FB]	18.9	...	...	...	...	...	...	...
%MF [FB]	0.4	...	...	...	...	...	...	...
%M [FB]	0.3	...	...	...	...	...	...	...
%F [FB]	0.5	...	...	...	...	...	...	...
Venezuela[3] Venezuela[3]								
MF [BA]	874.7	1 042.9	1 060.7	1 092.6	1 525.5	1 423.5	1 435.8	1 822.6
M [BA]	509.4	605.0	592.4	616.4	877.8	867.7	827.1	998.0
F [BA]	366.3	437.9	468.3	476.2	647.8	555.8	608.7	824.1
%MF [BA]	10.3	11.8	11.4	11.2	14.9	13.9	13.2	15.8
%M [BA]	9.1	10.4	9.8	9.9	13.6	13.4	12.4	14.3
%F [BA]	12.9	14.5	14.2	13.4	17.1	14.8	14.6	18.1
Yemen[3] Yémen[3]								
MF [BA]	...	...	...	...	469.0	...	...	...
M [BA]	...	...	...	...	389.6	...	...	...
F [BA]	...	...	...	...	79.4	...	...	...
%MF [BA]	...	...	...	...	11.5	...	...	...
%M [BA]	...	...	...	...	12.5	...	...	...
%F [BA]	...	...	...	...	8.2	...	...	...

29

Unemployment
Number (thousands) and percentage unemployed, by sex *[cont.]*
Chômage
Nombre (milliers) et pourcentage des chômeurs, par sexe *[suite]*

Country or area, source § Pays ou zone, source §		1995	1996	1997	1998	1999	2000	2001	2002
Zimbabwe[3]	Zimbabwe[3]								
MF [BA]		...	...	341.1	...	297.8	...	...	...
M [BA]		...	...	219.4	...	187.1	...	...	...
F [BA]		...	...	121.8	...	110.7	...	...	...
%MF [BA]		...	...	6.9	...	6.0	...	...	...
%M [BA]		...	...	8.7	...	7.3	...	...	...
%F [BA]		...	...	5.1	...	4.6	...	...	...

Source:
International Labour Office (ILO), Geneva, the ILO labour statistics database and the "Yearbook of Labour Statistics 2003".

§   Data sources:
   A: Population census.
   B: Household surveys.
   BA: Labour force sample surveys.
   E: Official estimates.
   FA: Insurance records.
   FB: Employment office records.
   FD: Administration reports.

Source:
Bureau international du Travail (BIT), Genève, la base de données du BIT et "l'Annuaire des statistiques du travail 2003".

§   Sources de données :
   A: Recensement de la population.
   B: Enquêtes auprès des ménages.
   BA: Enquêtes par sondage sur la main-d'œuvre.
   E: Evaluations officielles.
   FA: Fichiers des assurances.
   FB: Fichiers des bureaux de placement.
   FD: Rapports administratifs.

1	Persons aged 16 to 60 years.	Personnes âgées de 16 à 60 ans.
2	Persons aged 14 years and over.	Personnes âgées de 14 ans et plus.
3	Persons aged 15 years and over.	Personnes âgées de 15 ans et plus.
4	September.	Septembre.
5	Population census.	Recensement de population.
6	July.	Juillet.
7	Persons aged 10 years and over.	Personnes âgées de 10 ans et plus.
8	May and October of each year.	Mai et octobre de chaque année.
9	Prior to 1996, Gran Buenos Aires.	Avant 1996, Gran Buenos Aires.
10	28 urban agglomerations.	28 agglomérations urbaines.
11	Urban areas.	Régions urbaines.
12	Persons aged 16 to 63 years.	Personnes âgées de 16 à 63 ans.
13	Estimates based on 1996 census of population benchmarks.	Estimations basées sur les données de calage du recensement de population de 1996.
14	31 December of each year.	31 décembre de chaque année.
15	April of each year (Belgium, prior to 1999; Ireland, prior to 1998).	Avril de chaque année (Belgique, avant 1999; Irlande, avant 1998).
16	Private sector.	Secteur privé.
17	Year ending in June of the year indicated.	Année se terminant en juin de l'année indiquée.
18	December of each year.	Décembre de chaque année.
19	Excluding elderly unemployment pensioners no longer seeking work.	Non compris chômeurs âgés devenus non demandeurs d'emploi.
20	Prior to 1996, main towns.	Avant 1996, villes principales.
21	Persons ages 12 years and over.	
22	Year beginning in August of year indicated.	Année commençant en août de l'année indiquée.
23	September of each year.	Septembre de chaque année.
24	Excluding rural population of Rondônia, Acre, Amazonas, Roraima, Pará and Amapá.	Non compris la population rurale de Rondônia, Acre, Amazonas, Roraima, Pará et Amapá.
25	June of each year.	Juin de chaque année.
26	Men aged 16 to 60 years; women aged 16 to 55 years. After 1999, age limits vary according to the year.	Hommes âgés de 16 à 60 ans; femmes âgées de 16 à 55 ans. Après 1999, les limites d'âge varient selon l'année.
27	Four employment offices.	Quatre bureaux de placement.
28	Bujumbura.	Bujumbura.
29	November of each year.	Novembre de chaque année.
30	Excluding residents of the Territories and indigenous persons living on reserves.	Non compris les habitants des Territoires et les populations indigènes vivant dans les réserves.
31	Excluding full-time members of the armed forces.	Non compris les membres à temps complet des forces armées.
32	Methodology revised; data not strictly comparable.	Méthodologie révisée; les données ne sont pas strictement comparables.
33	Bangui.	Bangui.

29

Unemployment
Number (thousands) and percentage unemployed, by sex *[cont.]*

Chômage
Nombre (milliers) et pourcentage des chômeurs, par sexe *[suite]*

34	Fourth quarter of each year.	34	Quatrième trimestre de chaque année.
35	Beginning fourth quarter 1985, sample design revised. 1985: quarter November 1985 - January 1986.	35	A partir du quatrième trimestre de 1985 : plan d'échantillonnage révisé. 1985 : trimestre novembre 1985-Janvier 1986.
36	Sample design revised.	36	Plan d'échantillonnage révisé.
37	Unemployed in urban areas.	37	Chômeurs dans les régions urbaines.
38	Young people aged 16 to 25 years.	38	Jeunes gens de 16 à 25 ans.
39	Excluding unpaid family workers who worked for one hour or more.	39	Non compris les travailleurs familiaux non rémunérés ayant travaillé une heure ou plus.
40	February, May, August and November.	40	Février, mai, août et novembre.
41	Prior to 2001: seven main cities; Sep. of each year.	41	Avant 2001: Sept villes principales; septembre de chaque année.
42	July of each year.	42	Juillet de chaque année.
43	November.	43	Novembre.
44	June.	44	Juin.
45	The data relate to the government-controlled areas.	45	Les données se réfèrent aux régions sous contrôle gouvernemental.
46	Second quarter of each year.	46	Deuxième trimestre de chaque année.
47	Excluding persons on child care leave actively seeking a job.	47	Non compris les personnes en congé parental cherchant activement un travail.
48	Persons aged 15 to 66 years.	48	Personnes âgées de 15 à 66 ans.
49	Persons aged 16 to 66 years.	49	Personnes âgées de 16 à 66 ans.
50	May and November of each year.	50	Mai et novembre de chaque année.
51	Persons aged 12 to 64.	51	Personnes âgées de 12 à 64 ans.
52	Persons aged 15 to 64 years.	52	Personnes âgées de 15 à 64 ans.
53	Persons aged 16 years and over.	53	Personnes âgées de 16 ans et plus.
54	Persons aged 15 to 69 years.	54	Personnes âgées de 15 à 69 ans.
55	Persons aged 15 to 74 years.	55	Personnes âgées de 15 à 74 ans.
56	Excluding persons temporarily laid off.	56	Non compris les personnes temporairement mises à pied.
57	March of each year.	57	Mars de chaque année.
58	Excluding registered applicants for work who worked more than 78 hours during the month.	58	Non compris les demandeurs d'emploi inscrits ayant travaillé plus de 78 heures dans le mois.
59	January.	59	Janvier.
60	May.	60	Mai.
61	Persons aged 15 to 60 years.	61	Personnes âgées de 15 à 60 ans.
62	Guatemala city.	62	Ville de Guatemala.
63	Including unemployed temporarily unable to undertake work (child-care allowance, military service, etc.).	63	Y compris chômeurs qui temporairement ne peuvent pas travailler (allocation congé parental, service militaire, etc.).
64	Estimates based on the 2001 Population Census results.	64	Estimations basées sur les résultats du Recensement de la population de 2001.
65	Persons aged 16 to 74 years.	65	Personnes âgées de 16 à 74 ans.
66	April and November of each year.	66	Avril et novembre de chaque année.
67	May of each year.	67	Mai de chaque année.
68	March to May of each year.	68	Mars-mai de chaque année.
69	April.	69	Avril.
70	Revised definitions of labour force characteristics.	70	Révision des définitions des caractéristiques de la main-d'oeuvre.
71	Methodology revised.	71	Méthodologie révisée.
72	Estimates based on the 2000 Population Census results.	72	Estimations basées sur les résultats du recensement de la population de 2000.
73	Age limits vary according to the year.	73	Les limites d'âge varient selon l'année.
74	Men aged 16 to 61 years; women aged 16-57 years.	74	Hommes âgés de 16 à 61 ans; femmes âgées de 16 à 57 ans.
75	Persons aged 16 to 64 years.	75	Personnes âgées de 16 à 64 ans.
76	Revised series.	76	Série révisée.
77	6 provincial capitals.	77	6 chefs-lieux de province.
78	Annual averages.	78	Moyens annuels.
79	Persons aged 16 to 61 years.	79	Personnes âgées de 16 à 61 ans.
80	Excluding Rodrigues.	80	Non compris Rodrigues.
81	Persons aged 18 years and over.	81	Personnes âgées de 18 ans et plus.
82	Curaçao.	82	Curaçao.
83	Including students seeking vacation work.	83	Y compris les étudiants qui cherchent un emploi pendant les vacances.
84	July of preceding year to June of current year.	84	Juillet de l'année précédente à juin de l'année en cours.
85	Persons aged 18 to 60 years.	85	Personnes âgées de 18 à 60 ans.
86	August of each year.	86	Août de chaque année.
87	Third quarter.	87	Troisième trimestre.
88	October.	88	Octobre.
89	First and fourth quarters.	89	Première et quatrième trimestres.

29

Unemployment
Number (thousands) and percentage unemployed, by sex *[cont.]*

Chômage
Nombre (milliers) et pourcentage des chômeurs, par sexe *[suite]*

90	March: persons aged 14 years and over.
91	Persons aged 15 to 72 years.
92	March.
93	Socio-demographic survey. Persons aged 10 to 65 years.
94	March and September.
95	Including Kosovo and Metohia.
96	Excluding Kosovo and Metohia.
97	Whites, Coloureds and Asians; eligibility rules for registration not specified.
98	Excluding Transkei, Bophuthatswana, Venda, Ciskei; elsewhere persons enumerated at de facto dwelling place.
99	February and September of each year.
100	Excluding Northern and Eastern provinces.
101	First quarter of each year.
102	First semester.
103	Third round (August) of each year.
104	Persons aged 13 years and over.
105	Excluding the unemployed not previously employed.
106	Persons aged 12 years and over; April and October of each year.
107	Persons aged 15-70 years.
108	Men aged 16 to 59 years; women aged 16 to 54 years.
109	March - May of each year.
110	Claimants at unemployment benefits offices.
111	Year ending in March of the year indicated.
112	Persons aged 16 to 65 years.

90	Mars: Personnes âgées de 14 ans et plus.
91	Personnes âgées de 15 à 72 ans.
92	Mars.
93	Enquête socio-démographique. Personnes âgées de 10 à 65 ans.
94	Mars et septembre.
95	Y compris Kosovo et Metohia.
96	Non compris Kosovo et Metohia.
97	Blancs, personnes de couleur et asiatiques; conditions d'éligibilité pour l'enregistrement non spécifiées.
98	Non compris Transkei, Bophuthatswana, Venda, Ciskei; ailleurs personnes énumérées aux logis de facto.
99	Février et septembre de chaque année.
100	Non compris les provinces du Nord et de l'Est.
101	Premier trimestre de chaque année.
102	Premier trimestre.
103	Troisième enquête (août) de chaque année.
104	Personnes âgées de 13 ans et plus.
105	Non compris les chômeurs n'ayant jamais travaillé.
106	Personnes âgées de 12 ans et plus. Avril et octobre de chaque année.
107	Personnes âgées de 15 à 70 ans.
108	Hommes âgés de 16 à 59 ans; femmes âgées de 16 à 54 ans.
109	Mars - mai de chaque année.
110	Demandeurs auprès des bureaux de prestations de chômage.
111	Année se terminant en mars de l'année indiquée.
112	Personnes âgées de 16 à 65 ans.

Technical notes, tables 28 and 29

Detailed data on labour force and related topics are published in the ILO *Yearbook of Labour Statistics* [13] and on the ILO Web site <http://laborsta.ilo.org>. The series shown in the *Statistical Yearbook* give an overall picture of the availability and disposition of labour resources and, in conjunction with other macro-economic indicators, can be useful for an overall assessment of economic performance. The ILO *Yearbook of Labour Statistics* provides a comprehensive description of the methodology underlying the labour series. Brief definitions of the major categories of labour statistics are given below.

"Employment" is defined to include persons above a specified age who, during a specified period of time, were in one of the following categories:

(a)   "Paid employment", comprising persons who perform some work for pay or profit during the reference period or persons with a job but not at work due to temporary absence, such as vacation, strike, education leave;

(b)   "Self-employment", comprising employers, own-account workers, members of producers' cooperatives, persons engaged in production of goods and services for own consumption and unpaid family workers;

(c)   Members of the armed forces, students, homemakers and others mainly engaged in non-economic activities during the reference period who, at the same time, were in paid employment or self-employment are considered as employed on the same basis as other categories.

"Unemployment" is defined to include persons above a certain age and who, during a specified period of time were:

(a)   "Without work", i.e. were not in paid employment or self-employment;

(b)   "Currently available for work", i.e. were available for paid employment or self-employment during the reference period; and

(c)   "Seeking work", i.e. had taken specific steps in a specified period to find paid employment or self-employment.

Persons not considered to be unemployed include:

(a)   Persons intending to establish their own business or farm, but who had not yet arranged to do so and who were not seeking work for pay or profit;

(b)   Former unpaid family workers not at work and not seeking work for pay or profit.

For various reasons, national definitions of employment and unemployment often differ from the recommended international standard definitions and thereby limit international comparability. Intercountry comparisons are also complicated by a variety of types of data

Notes techniques, tableaux 28 et 29

Des données détaillées sur la main-d'oeuvre et des sujets connexes sont publiées dans l'*Annuaire des Statistiques du Travail* du BIT [13] et sur le site Web du BIT <http://laborsta.ilo.org>. Les séries indiquées dans l'*Annuaire des Statistiques* donnent un tableau d'ensemble des disponibilités de main-d'œuvre et de l'emploi de ces ressources et, combinées à d'autres indicateurs économiques, elles peuvent être utiles pour une évaluation générale de la performance économique. L'*Annuaire des statistiques du Travail* du BIT donne une description complète de la méthodologie employée pour établir les séries sur la main-d'œuvre. On trouvera ci-dessous quelques brèves définitions des grandes catégories de statistiques du travail.

Le terme "Emploi" désigne les personnes dépassant un âge déterminé qui, au cours d'une période donnée, se trouvaient dans l'une des catégories suivantes:

(a)   La catégorie "emploi rémunéré", composée des personnes faisant un certain travail en échange d'une rémunération ou d'un profit pendant la période de référence, ou les personnes ayant un emploi, mais qui ne travaillaient pas en raison d'une absence temporaire (vacances, grève, congé d'études);

(b)   La catégorie "emploi indépendant" regroupe les employeurs, les travailleurs indépendants, les membres de coopératives de producteurs et les personnes s'adonnant à la production de biens et de services pour leur propre consommation et la main-d'œuvre familiale non rémunérée;

(c)   Les membres des forces armées, les étudiants, les aides familiales et autres personnes qui s'adonnaient essentiellement à des activités non économiques pendant la période de référence et qui, en même temps, avaient un emploi rémunéré ou indépendant, sont considérés comme employés au même titre que les personnes des autres catégories.

Par "chômeurs", on entend les personnes dépassant un âge déterminé et qui, pendant une période donnée, étaient:

(a)   "sans emploi", c'est-à-dire sans emploi rémunéré ou indépendant;

(b)   "disponibles", c'est-à-dire qui pouvaient être engagées pour un emploi rémunéré ou pouvaient s'adonner à un emploi indépendant au cours de la période de référence; et

(c)   "à la recherche d'un emploi", c'est-à-dire qui avaient pris des mesures précises à un certain moment pour trouver un emploi rémunéré ou un emploi indépendant.

Ne sont pas considérés comme chômeurs:

(a)   Les personnes qui, pendant la période de ré-

collection systems used to obtain information on employed and unemployed persons.

Table 28 presents absolute figures on the distribution of employed persons by economic activity. In part A the figures are according to Revision 2 (ISIC 2) of the *International Standard Industrial Classification* [50], and in part B according to ISIC 3. In part A, the column for total employment includes economic activities not adequately defined and that are not accounted for in the other categories. Data are arranged as far as possible according to the major divisions of economic activity of the *International Standard Industrial Classification of All Economic Activities* [50].

Table 29: Figures are presented in absolute numbers and in percentages. Data are normally annual averages of monthly, quarterly or semi-annual data.

The series generally represent the total number of persons wholly unemployed or temporarily laid off. Percentage figures, where given, are calculated by comparing the number of unemployed to the total members of that group of the labour force on which the unemployment data are based.

férence, avaient l'intention de créer leur propre entreprise ou exploitation agricole, mais n'avaient pas encore pris les dispositions nécessaires à cet effet et qui n'étaient pas à la recherche d'un emploi en vue d'une rémunération ou d'un profit;

(b)   Les anciens travailleurs familiaux non rémunérés qui n'avaient pas d'emploi et n'étaient pas à la recherche d'un emploi en vue d'une rémunération ou d'un profit.

Pour diverses raisons, les définitions nationales de l'emploi et du chômage diffèrent souvent des définitions internationales types recommandées, limitant ainsi les possibilités de comparaison entre pays. Ces comparaisons se trouvent en outre compliquées par la diversité des systèmes de collecte de données utilisés pour recueillir des informations sur les personnes employées et les chômeurs.

Le *tableau 28* présente les effectifs de personnes employées par activité économique. Dans la partie A, les chiffres sont classés en fonction de la Révision 2 de la *Classification internationale type, par Industrie, de toutes les branches d'activité économique* [50] et dans la partie B en fonction de la Révision 3. Dans la partie A, l'emploi total inclut les personnes employées à des activités économiques mal définies et qui ne sont pas classées ailleurs. Les données sont ventilées autant que possible selon les branches d'activité économique de la *Classification internationale type, par industrie, de toutes les activités économiques* [50].

Tableau 29: Les chiffres sont présentés en valeur absolue et en pourcentage. Les données sont normalement des moyennes annuelles des données mensuelles, trimestrielles ou semestrielles.

Les séries représentent généralement le nombre total des chômeurs complets ou des personnes temporairement mises à pied. Les données en pourcentage, lorsqu'elles figurent au tableau, sont calculées par comparaison du nombre de chômeurs au nombre total des personnes du groupe de main-d'œuvre sur lequel sont basées les données relatives au chômage.

30
Wages in manufacturing
By hour, day, week or month
Salaires dans les industries manufacturières
Par heure, jour, semaine ou mois

Country or area § Pays ou zone §	1995	1996	1997	1998	1999	2000	2001	2002
Albania[1] (lek) Albanie[1] (lek)								
MF(I) - month mois	...	...	9 121.0	9 674.0	10 734.0	11 708.0	...	...
Algeria[1] (Algerian dinar) Algérie[1] (dinar algérien)								
MF(I) - month mois	10 462.0	12 323.0						
Anguilla (EC dollar) Anguilla (dollar des Carraïbes orientales)								
MF(I) - month mois	1 358.9		...	...	...	1 494.7[1]	...	
Argentina[1,2,3] (Argentine peso) Argentine[1,2,3] (peso argentin)								
MF(II) - hour heure	3.9	4.0	4.1	4.1	4.2	4.2	4.3	...
Armenia[1] (dram) Arménie[1] (dram)								
MF(I) - month mois	7 680.0	12 464.0	17 656.0	21 278.0	24 515.0	29 307.0	35 848.0	
Australia[4,5] (Australian dollar) Australie[4,5] (dollar australien)								
MF(I) - hour heure	15.6	16.4[1]	...	17.4[1]	...	18.2[1]	...	20.5[1]
M(I) - hour heure	16.1	16.9[1]	...	18.0[1]	...	19.1[1]	...	20.8[1]
F(I)- hour heure	13.7	14.3[1]	...	15.2[1]	...	16.8[1]	...	18.5[1]
Austria[1] (Austrian schilling, euro) Autriche[1] (schilling autrichien, euro)								
MF(I) - month mois	26 020.0	27 239.0	27 776.0	28 455.0	29 136.0	2 417.0[6]	2 501.0	...
M(I) - month mois	28 815.0	30 084.0	30 667.0	31 471.0	32 195.0	2 738.0[6]	2 837.0	...
F(I) - month mois	19 903.0	20 667.0	21 051.0	21 480.0	22 009.0	1 662.0[6]	1 716.0	...
MF(II) - month mois	23 374.0	24 496.0	24 878.0	25 471.0	26 104.0	1 973.0[6]	2 046.0	...
Azerbaijan (manat) Azerbaïdjan (manat)								
MF(I) - month mois	95 556.7	146 174.7	200 030.1	202 082.6[1]	244 087.1[1]	284 272.3[1]	303 164.0[1]	348 815.6[1]
Bahrain[7,8] (Bahrain dinar) Bahreïn[7,8] (dinar de Bahreïn)								
MF(I) - month mois	...	...	...	257.0	227.0	231.0	215.0	228.0
M(I) - month mois	...	...	...	276.0	250.0	255.0	241.0	252.0
F(I) - month mois	...	...	...	125.0	109.0	107.0	100.0	111.0
Bangladesh[9,10] (taka) Bangladesh[9,10] (taka)								
MF(III) - day jour		61.9			...	...	...	
Belgium[1] (Belgian franc, euro) Belgique[1] (franc belge, euro)								
MF(II) - hour heure	388.2	398.2	406.8	417.6	11.0[11]	...	...	...
M(II) - hour heure	405.5	416.2	425.2	436.1	12.0[11]	...	...	...
F(II) - hour heure	320.9	331.0	335.8	345.5	9.0[11]	...	...	...
MF(V) - month mois	104 773.0	106 983.0	109 980.0	112 682.0	2 864.0[11]	...	...	...
M(V) - month mois	113 618.0	116 279.0	119 233.0	122 031.0	3 095.0[11]	...	...	...
F(V) - month mois	80 118.0	82 096.0	85 194.0	87 869.0	2 193.0[11]	...	...	...
Bolivia[12] (boliviano) Bolivie[12] (boliviano)								
MF(I) - month mois	959.0[13,14,15]	749.0[1,16]	873.0[1,16]	972.0[1,16]	1 055.0[1,16]	1 120.0[1,16,17]		
Botswana[15,18] (pula) Botswana[15,18] (pula)								
MF(I) - month mois	582.0	607.0[19]	598.0	695.0[1]	785.0[1]	783.0[1]	891.0[1]	...
M(I) - month mois[1]	...	...	...	821.0	1 004.0	1 067.0	...	
F(I) - month mois[1]	...	...	...	447.0	588.0	555.0	681.0	
Brazil[1,20] (real) Brésil[1,20] (real)								
MF(I) - month mois	631.0	698.9	738.0	717.6	730.3	762.6	844.6	...
M(I) - month mois	712.0	786.2	826.8	800.8	816.0	854.7	946.9	...
F(I) - month mois	405.0	458.1	487.2	487.5	503.2	524.0	576.5	...
Bulgaria (lev) Bulgarie (lev)								
MF(I) - month mois	8 448.0[22,23]	15 276.0[1,21]	148 460.0[1,21]	194 612.0[1,21]	203.0[1,21,24]	219.0[1,21]	227.0[1,21]	244.0[1,21]
M(I) - month mois[1,21]	...	17 794.0	172 043.0	224 492.0	232.0[24]	257.0	271.0	...
F(I) - month mois[1,21]	...	12 658.0	123 423.0	163 045.0	172.0[24]	181.0	185.0	...
Cambodia[1,8,12] (riel) Cambodge[1,8,12] (riel)								
MF(I) - month mois		243 000.0	...	243 000.0	...	...	243 000.0	
Canada[1,25] (Canadian dollar) Canada[1,25] (dollar canadien)								
MF(I) - week semaine	712.8	733.8	752.4	770.9	782.4	796.9	808.1	830.1
MF(II) - hour heure[26]	16.6	17.1	17.2	17.6	17.8	18.3	18.6	19.1
Chile[27,28,29] (Chilean peso) Chili[27,28,29] (peso chilien)								
MF(I) - month mois	159 085.0	176 480.0	189 753.0	200 773.0	203 540.0	208 257.0	213 394.0	218 740.0
China[1,30] (yuan) Chine[1,30] (yuan)								
MF(I) - month mois	430.8	470.2	494.4	588.7	649.5	729.2	814.5	916.8
China, Hong Kong SAR (Hong Kong dollar) Chine, Hong Kong RAS (dollar de Hong Kong)								
MF(II) - day jour[9]	278.0	296.9	322.6	335.3	334.7	335.4	342.6	326.1
M(II) - day jour[9]	357.7	386.3	423.8	430.6	422.6	428.8	428.5	419.2

30

Wages in manufacturing
By hour, day, week or month *[cont.]*

Salaires dans les industries manufacturières
Par heure, jour, semaine ou mois *[suite]*

Country or area § Pays ou zone §	1995	1996	1997	1998	1999	2000	2001	2002
F(II) - day jour [9]	233.5	245.3	258.8	262.9	268.9	278.1	280.6	268.2
MF(V) - month mois [12]	9 508.3	10 323.8	11 331.2	11 711.6	11 853.0	11 869.7	12 133.1	11 950.7
M(V) - month mois [12]	10 421.4	11 260.0	12 165.2	12 555.7	12 893.2	12 697.1	12 929.7	12 810.2
F(V) - month mois [12]	8 684.2	9 390.4	10 467.0	10 915.9	10 846.7	11 101.4	11 395.0	11 123.2
China, Macao SAR [31] (Macao pataca) Chine, Macao RAS [31] (pataca de Macao)								
MF(VI) - month mois	3 210.0	3 082.0	3 260.0	3 080.0[1]	2 921.0[1]	2 960.0[1]	2 760.0[1]	2 766.0[1]
M(VI) - month mois	4 388.0	4 511.0	4 981.0	4 762.0[1]	4 738.0[1]	4 690.0[1]	4 525.0[1]	4 479.0[1]
F(VI) - month mois	2 682.0	2 658.0	2 808.0	2 656.0[1]	2 510.0[1]	2 613.0[1]	2 431.0[1]	2 435.0[1]
Colombia [15,32] (Colombian peso) Colombie [15,32] (peso colombien)								
MF(I) - month mois	225 995.0	275 905.0	322 695.0	441 965.0	455 252.0	420 734.0	...	...
Costa Rica [33] (Costa Rican colón) Costa Rica [33] (colón costa-ricien)								
MF(I) - month mois	54 365.0[34]	63 894.0[34]	75 672.0[34]	85 899.0[1]	97 774.5[1]	108 777.0[1]	128 207.0[1]	...
M(I) - month mois	60 273.0[34]	69 627.0[34]	78 917.0[34]	91 493.0[1]	106 594.0[1]	115 642.0[1]	135 707.0[1]	...
F(I) - month mois	42 739.0[34]	50 028.0[34]	67 531.0[34]	73 122.0[1]	77 969.3[1]	93 773.0[1]	112 596.0[1]	...
Croatia (kuna) Croatie (kuna)								
MF(I) - month mois	1 672.0	3 034.0[1]	3 358.0[1]	3 681.0[1]	3 869.0[1]	4 100.0[1]	4 465.0[1]	4 794.0[1]
Cuba [35] (Cuban peso) Cuba [35] (peso cubain)								
MF(I) - month mois	211.0	210.0	212.0	214.0	225.0	234.0		
Cyprus [29,36] (Cyprus pound) Chypre [29,36] (livre chypriote)								
MF(II) - week semaine	113.4	130.1	117.5	166.5[1]	185.9[1]	...	...	
M(II) - week semaine	143.4	170.8	145.0	96.4[1]	100.8[1]	...	...	
F(II) - week semaine	86.1	90.1	92.4	96.4[1]	100.8[1]	...		
MF(V) - month mois	710.0	758.0	762.0	741.0[1]	776.0[1]	806.0[1]		
M(V) - month mois	822.0	864.0	871.0	884.0[1]	919.0[1]	954.0[1]		
F(V) - month mois	476.0	504.0	530.0	509.0[1]	545.0[1]	556.0[1]		
Czech Republic [1] (Czech koruna) République tchèque [1] (couronne tchèque)								
MF(I) - month mois	7 854.0[37]	9 259.0[37]	10 411.0[38]	11 513.0[38]	12 271.0[38]	13 188.0[38]	14 130.0[38]	14 883.0[38]
Denmark [1,8] (Danish krone) Danemark [1,8] (couronne danoise)								
MF(I) - hour heure	152.8	163.5	167.3	174.6	182.3	188.6	199.1	...
M(I) - hour heure	160.2	172.9	176.5	183.3	192.2	197.6	207.7	...
F(I)- hour heure	135.5	143.1	147.4	154.8	160.3	166.7	178.8	
Dominican Republic (Dominican peso) Rép. dominicaine (peso dominicain)								
MF(I) - month mois [12]	2 010.0	...	...	...	...	...	...	...
MF(VI) - hour heure [39]	16.6	18.0	21.6					
Ecuador [1] (sucre, US dollar) Equateur [1] (sucre, dollar des Etats-Unis)								
MF(I) - month mois [40]	1 302.7[41]	1 726.4[41]	2 179.7[41]	3 252.0[41]	4 158.3[41]	346.7[41]	203.7	...
MF(II) - hour heure [41]	2 469.3	3 226.7	4 380.4	6 119.0	8 556.2	0.8	1.3	
Egypt [7] (Egyptian pound) Egypte [7] (livre égyptienne)								
MF(II) - week semaine	84.0	93.0[1]	103.0[1]	107.0[1]	121.0[1]	125.0[1]	136.0[1]	
M(II) - week semaine	87.0	97.0[1]	107.0[1]	112.0[1]	125.0[1]	131.0[1]	142.0[1]	
F(II) - week semaine	64.0	87.0[1]	80.0[1]	77.0[1]	94.0[1]	87.0[1]	97.0[1]	
El Salvador (El Salvadoran colón) El Salvador (cólon salvadorien)								
MF(I) - month mois [1]	...	...	...	1 993.4	1 746.6	...		
M(I) - month mois [1]	...	...	...	2 348.5	2 157.8	...		
F(I) - month mois [1]	...	...	...	1 646.0	1 337.1	...		
MF(II) - hour heure	6.9	7.5	...	10.3	10.7	10.1		
M(II) - hour heure	7.0	7.7	...	12.0	12.1	11.4		
F(II) - hour heure	6.8	7.3	...	9.0	9.2	9.0		
Eritrea [1,12] (Nakfa) Erythrée [1,12] (Nakfa)								
MF(I) - month mois	...	478.5	...	...	...	...		
M(I) - month mois	...	522.0	...	...	...	...		
F(I) - month mois	...	346.5	...	...	...	...		
Estonia [1] (Estonian kroon) Estonie [1] (couronne estonienne)								
MF(I) - month mois	2 421.0	2 991.0	3 578.0	4 081.0	4 117.0	4 772.0	5 149.0	5 665.0
Fiji [9,42] (Fiji dollar) Fidji [9,42] (dollar des Fidji)								
MF(II) - day jour		16.3	15.1	14.5	15.1	...	...	
Finland (Finnish markka, euro) Finlande (markka finlandais, euro)								
MF(I) - month mois [1,43]	11 004.0	11 434.0	11 677.0	12 054.0	12 510.0	13 124.0[45]	...	...
M(I) - month mois [1,43]	11 810.0	12 240.0	12 523.0	12 880.0	13 305.0	13 939.0[45]	...	
F(I) - month mois [1,43]	9 232.0	9 674.0	9 842.0	10 237.0	10 683.0	11 239.0[45]	...	

30
Wages in manufacturing
By hour, day, week or month *[cont.]*

Salaires dans les industries manufacturières
Par heure, jour, semaine ou mois *[suite]*

Country or area § Pays ou zone §	1995	1996	1997	1998	1999	2000	2001	2002
MF(II) - hour heure [44]	60.1	...	...	...	...	...	...	...
M(II) - hour heure [44]	63.4	...	...	...	...	...	...	...
F(II) - hour heure [44]	50.3	...	...	...	...	...	...	...
France (French franc, euro) France (franc français, euro)								
MF(I) - month mois [1]	...	...	13 600.0	13 860.0	1 459.4[47]	1 477.0	1 506.9	1 562.7
M(I) - month mois [1]	...	...	14 520.0	14 770.0	1 573.8[47]	1 591.0	1 618.5	1 668.8
F(I) - month mois [1]	...	...	11 210.0	11 490.0	1 191.8[47]	1 205.9	1 241.7	1 307.9
MF(II) - hour heure	52.8	54.2	55.4[46]	...	...	...	...	...
M(II) - hour heure	55.8	57.2	58.5[46]	...	...	...	...	...
F(II) - hour heure	44.3	45.4	46.3[46]	...	...	...	...	...
Gambia [1,48,49] (dalasi) Gambie [1,48,49] (dalasi)								
MF(I) - month mois	...	...	...	969.7				
Georgia [1] (lari) Géorgie [1] (lari)								
MF(I) - month mois	...	...	51.2	68.9	87.4	99.3	120.8	143.4
M(I) - month mois	...	...	...	...	101.1	111.2	141.5	165.1
F(I) - month mois	...	...	...	...	63.3	69.3	82.7	143.0
Germany [1] (deutsche mark, euro) Allemagne [1] (deutsche mark, euro)								
MF(II) - hour heure	...	25.7	26.2	26.8	27.5	27.8	14.4[50]	14.7
M(II) - hour heure	...	27.0	27.4	28.0	28.8	29.1	15.1[50]	15.4
F(II) - hour heure	...	20.0	20.3	20.8	21.4	21.4	11.1[50]	11.4
F. R. Germany (deutsche mark, euro) R. f. Allemagne (deutsche mark, euro)								
MF(II) - hour heure [1]	25.5	26.4	26.8	27.4	...	28.8	15.0[50]	15.3
M(II) - hour heure [1]	26.8	27.7	28.0	28.6	...	30.1	15.6[50]	15.9
F(II) - hour heure [1]	19.7	20.5	20.8	21.3	...	22.4	11.6[50]	11.9
MF(II) - week semaine [51]	975.0	...	...	...	...	...	...	...
M(II) - week semaine [51]	1 031.0	...	...	...	...	...	...	...
F(II) - week semaine [51]	733.0	...	...	...	...	...	...	...
German D. R.(former) (deutsche mark, euro) R. d. allemande (anc.) (deutsche mark, euro)								
MF(II) - hour heure [1]	17.0	18.0	18.6	19.2	...	19.6	10.2[50]	10.6
M(II) - hour heure [1]	17.8	18.8	19.5	20.1	...	20.8	10.8[50]	11.2
F(II) - hour heure [1]	14.1	15.0	15.4	15.9	...	15.9	8.3[50]	8.6
MF(II) - week semaine	685.0	...	...	...	...	...	...	...
M(II) - week semaine	719.0	...	...	...	...	...	...	...
F(II) - week semaine	557.0	...	...	...	...	...	...	...
Gibraltar [52] (Gibraltar pound) Gibraltar [52] (livre de Gibraltar)								
MF(II) - hour heure [1]	...	...	...	6.6	6.8	6.4	6.6	7.0
M(II) - hour heure [1]	...	...	...	6.8	7.0	6.6	6.7	7.2
F(II) - hour heure [1]	...	...	...	4.9	5.3	5.3	5.7	5.7
MF(II) - week semaine	279.3	307.3	226.3	339.3	320.0	291.6	299.5	311.3
M(II) - week semaine	295.3	345.0	243.3	358.9	332.6	299.8	306.4	339.5
F(II) - week semaine	193.8	192.5	172.5	192.9	210.4	213.8	233.9	237.1
Greece [7] (drachma) Grèce [7] (drachme)								
MF(II) - hour heure	1 243.3	1 349.9	1 470.5	1 539.8	...	...	...	...
M(II) - hour heure	1 353.3	1 459.8	1 585.9	1 653.0	...	...	...	...
F(II) - hour heure	1 088.6	1 183.4	1 287.8	1 355.8	...	...	...	...
MF(V) - month mois	332 568.0	363 857.0	399 599.0	423 142.0	...	...	...	...
M(V) - month mois	358 318.0	391 700.0	430 889.0	456 488.0	...	...	...	...
F(V) - month mois	244 904.0	278 996.0	303 900.0	323 153.0	...	...	...	...
Guam [8,20] (US dollar) Guam [8,20] (dollar des Etats-Unis)								
MF(II) - hour heure	10.6		...	...	...	...	...	...
Guatemala (quetzal) Guatemala (quetzal)								
MF(I) - month mois	1 138.0	1 368.9	1 430.0	1 541.0	1 602.3	1 655.3		
Guinea [12] (Guinean franc) Guinée [12] (franc guinéen)								
MF(I) - month mois	130 000.0	153 000.0	...	...	...	...		
Hungary [1,43] (forint) Hongrie [1,43] (forint)								
MF(I) - month mois [48]	39 554.0[38]	48 195.0[38]	58 915.0[38]	68 872.0[38]	76 099.0	88 551.0	101 700.0	113 817.0
M(I) - month mois [48]	45 466.0[38]	55 437.0[38]	68 396.0[38]	79 892.0[38]	86 866.0	100 351.0	115 830.0	...
F(I) - month mois	31 853.0[38]	38 897.0[38]	46 897.0[38]	54 985.0[38]	61 898.0[38,48]	72 962.0[48]	82 761.0[48]	...
Iceland (Icelandic króna) Islande (couronne islandaise)								
MF(I) - hour heure [53]	...	...	...	828.0	864.0[1]	945.0[1]	1 049.0[1]	1 108.0[1]
M(I) - hour heure [1,53]	...	...	...	902.0	957.0	1 044.0	1 153.0	1 216.0

30

Wages in manufacturing
By hour, day, week or month *[cont.]*
Salaires dans les industries manufacturières
Par heure, jour, semaine ou mois *[suite]*

Country or area § Pays ou zone §	1995	1996	1997	1998	1999	2000	2001	2002
F(I)- hour heure [1,53]	...	...	...	730.0	760.0	814.0	905.0	968.0
MF(I) - month mois [1,54]	...	...	...	...	119 800.0	129 800.0	140 700.0	...
India (Indian rupee) Inde (roupie indienne)								
MF(II) - month mois	1 211.0	1 188.8	1 137.3	1 211.1	1 548.5	1 280.8		
Indonesia [20,40,55,56] (Indonesian rupiah) Indonésie [20,40,55,56] (roupie indonésien)								
MF(II) - week semaine	39.3	45.1	52.4	64.2	75.3	98.0	129.2	
Ireland [15,57] (Irish pound) Irlande [15,57] (livre irlandaise)								
MF(II) - hour heure	6.5	6.6	6.9	7.2	...	...	...	...
M(II) - hour heure	7.1	7.3	7.5	7.9	...	...	...	...
F(II) - hour heure	5.3	5.4	5.6	5.9	...	...	...	...
Isle of Man [1,42] (pound sterling) Ile de Man [1,42] (livre sterling)								
MF(I) - hour heure	6.9	6.6	7.1	7.8	9.1	8.5	9.0	10.3
M(I) - hour heure	6.9	7.0	7.6	9.0	9.5	9.2	9.2	10.9
F(I)- hour heure	6.7	5.0	5.7	5.7	7.5	6.8	8.5	7.7
M(I) - week semaine	288.6	294.6	320.5	366.0	408.9	407.3	381.5	417.3
Israel [1,58] (new sheqel) Israël [1,58] (nouveau sheqel)								
MF(I) - month mois	5 061.0	5 757.0	6 676.0	7 418.0	8 227.0	8 665.0	4 051.0	...
Italy [1] (Italian lira, euro) Italie [1] (lire italienne, euro)								
MF(I) - month mois [40]	2 614.0	...	...	...	110.9	113.1	101.4[61]	104.2
MF(II) - hour heure [59,60]	128.7	101.8	105.7	108.6	110.9	113.1	101.6[61]	104.5
MF(V) - hour heure [59,60]	131.3	102.2	106.4	109.6	112.1	114.4	101.6[61]	104.5
Japan [62,63] (yen) Japon [62,63] (yen)								
MF(I) - month mois	278 800.0	283 700.0	287 200.0	289 600.0	291 100.0	293 100.0	297 500.0	296 400.0
M(I) - month mois	318 200.0	322 500.0	325 600.0	327 900.0	327 700.0	328 100.0	331 400.0	328 300.0
F(I) - month mois	177 900.0	181 800.0	184 500.0	187 300.0	189 000.0	190 700.0	195 000.0	195 600.0
Jordan (Jordan dinar) Jordanie (dinar jordanien)								
MF(I) - day jour	5.3[48]	5.6[48]	5.7[48]	5.9[48]	5.5	...	...	...
M(I) - day jour	5.5[48]	5.8[48]	6.0[48]	6.2[48]	5.8	...	...	...
F(I) - day jour	3.4[48]	3.6[48]	3.6[48]	3.7[48]	4.0	...	...	...
MF(I) - month mois [1,48]	176.4	188.2	192.9	198.5	...	...	...	...
M(I) - month mois [1,48]	184.0	197.8	203.5	210.6	...	...	...	...
F(I) - month mois [1,48]	113.7	117.9	119.1	122.2	...	...	...	...
Kazakhstan [1] (tenge) Kazakhstan [1] (tenge)								
MF(I) - month mois	7 274.0	9 288.0	11 092.0	11 357.0	13 821.0	17 717.0	19 982.0	22 130.0
M(I) - month mois	...	...	...	12 246.0	14 991.0	19 510.0	22 184.0	24 479.0
F(I) - month mois	...	...	...	9 641.0	11 433.0	13 981.0	15 597.0	17 433.0
Kenya [42,64] (Kenya shilling) Kenya [42,64] (shilling du Kenya)								
MF(I) - month mois	6 228.7	4 998.6	5 510.8	...	...	...	...	...
M(I) - month mois	6 867.7	...	5 294.3	...	...	...	...	...
F(I) - month mois	3 314.4	...	6 509.5	...	...	...	...	...
Korea, Republic of [1,7,29,40] (Korean won) Corée, République de [1,7,29,40] (won coréen)								
MF(I) - month mois	1 123.9	1 261.2	1 326.2	1 284.5	1 475.5	1 601.5	1 702.4	1 907.0
M(I) - month mois	1 314.7	1 463.4	1 527.2	1 467.3	1 686.3	1 826.4	1 936.4	2 177.0
F(I) - month mois	711.1	795.6	852.0	820.1	933.1	1 055.8	1 121.3	1 211.0
Kyrgyzstan [1] (Kyrgyz som) Kirghizistan [1] (som kirghize)								
MF(I) - month mois	377.1	652.1	844.7	988.8	1 280.8			
Latvia [1] (lats) Lettonie [1] (lats)								
MF(I) - month mois	86.5	95.2	114.7	128.3	129.0	135.1	140.3	145.5
M(I) - month mois	94.6	101.4	121.5	136.1	137.5	146.0	150.9	157.3
F(I) - month mois	77.8	88.3	107.9	119.2	118.5	122.9	127.1	131.1
Lithuania [1] (litas) Lituanie [1] (litas)								
MF(I) - hour heure [65,66]	3.4	4.0	4.9[67]	5.9[67]	6.2[67]	6.2	6.3	6.5
M(I) - hour heure [65,66]	...	...	5.4[67]	6.6[67]	6.9[67]	6.9	7.1	7.2
F(I)- hour heure [65,66]	...	...	4.4[67]	5.1[67]	5.4[67]	5.5	5.5	5.7
MF(I) - month mois [65,66]	486.0	656.0	809.0	911.0	963.0	955.0	963.0	991.0
M(I) - month mois [43,67]	...	...	909.0	1 089.0	1 135.0	...	...	...
F(I) - month mois [43,67]	...	...	733.0	847.0	875.0	...	...	...
Luxembourg [1] (Luxembourg franc, euro) Luxembourg [1] (franc luxembourgeois, euro)								
MF(II) - hour heure	459.0	456.0	465.0	470.0	12.2[68]	12.5	12.6	13.1
M(II) - hour heure	479.0	476.0	485.0	490.0	12.7[68]	13.1	13.1	13.6
F(II) - hour heure	322.0	319.0	335.0	337.0	8.7[68]	9.4	9.5	9.8

30

Wages in manufacturing
By hour, day, week or month [cont.]

Salaires dans les industries manufacturières
Par heure, jour, semaine ou mois [suite]

Country or area § Pays ou zone §	1995	1996	1997	1998	1999	2000	2001	2002
MF(V) - month mois	140 424.0	145 876.0	145 433.0	144 697.0	3 680.0[68]	3 995.0	3 816.0	3 941.0
M(V) - month mois	151 095.0	157 238.0	156 574.0	155 036.0	3 944.0[68]	3 995.0	4 104.0	4 251.0
F(V) - month mois	92 033.0	94 413.0	97 209.0	98 614.0	2 535.0[68]	2 621.0	2 710.0	2 782.0
Malawi (Malawi kwacha) Malawi (kwacha malawien)								
MF(I) - month mois	195.8	...	...	...	...	...	...	...
Malaysia (ringgit) Malaisie (ringgit)								
MF(I) - month mois	1 002.0	1 115.0	1 210.0	...	...	1 387.8	1 530.7	...
M(I) - month mois	1 242.0	1 343.0	1 449.0	...	...	...	...	...
F(I) - month mois	719.0	842.0	912.0	...	...	...	...	...
Malta[1] (Maltese lira) Malte[1] (lire maltaise)								
MF(VI) - hour heure	...	...	...	...	...	2.1	2.2	2.3
M(VI) - hour heure	...	...	...	...	...	2.2	2.3	2.4
F(VI) - hour heure	...	...	...	...	...	1.8	1.9	2.1
Mauritius[69] (Mauritian rupee) Maurice[69] (roupie mauricienne)								
MF(I) - month mois[1]	...	...	...	...	5 142.0	5 544.0	5 856.0	6 155.0
MF(II) - day jour[70]	132.0	138.0	148.7	161.4	166.0	174.3	...	...
MF(V) - month mois	5 659.0	5 972.0	6 282.0	6 912.0	7 034.0	7 638.0	...	...
Mexico (Mexican peso) Mexique (peso mexicain)								
MF(I) - day jour	55.2	66.1	78.0	92.0	108.7	125.6	143.6	...
MF(I) - month mois[1]	1 220.6	1 404.2	1 651.8	2 077.2	2 377.7	2 909.6	3 363.5	...
M(I) - month mois[1]	1 338.3	1 526.3	1 816.7	2 286.0	2 632.9	3 253.4	3 737.5	...
F(I) - month mois[1]	919.9	1 104.1	1 281.7	1 622.4	1 835.9	2 240.4	2 630.0	...
MF(II) - hour heure[1]	8.3	10.2	12.4	14.8	17.8	20.8	23.5	...
MF(II) - month mois	1 605.0	1 963.0	...	...	...	...	...	25.1
Mongolia[1] (togrog) Mongolie[1] (togrog)								
MF(I) - month mois	...	...	...	...	...	66.0	73.6	73.3
F(I) - month mois	...	...	...	...	...	70.0	63.2	73.3
Myanmar[71,72] (kyat) Myanmar[71,72] (kyat)								
M(I) - hour heure[60]	...	...	...	...	...	13.5	19.0	20.8
F(I) - hour heure[60]	...	...	...	...	...	20.8	17.5	19.6
M(I) - month mois	...	...	1 043.3	1 054.3	1 066.0	...	...	...
F(I) - month mois	...	...	998.9	1 010.6	1 190.9	...	...	...
Netherlands[1,20,73] (Netherlands guilder, euro) Pays-Bas[1,20,73] (florin néerlandais, euro)								
MF(I) - hour heure	28.9	30.2	31.1	32.0	33.3	34.4	...	...
M(I) - hour heure	30.1	31.4	32.3	33.4	34.7	35.8	...	...
F(I) - hour heure	22.6	24.0	24.8	25.7	26.9	28.0	...	...
MF(I) - month mois[43]	4 184.0	4 369.0	4 472.0	4 614.0	4 797.0	4 958.0	...	...
M(I) - month mois[43]	4 318.0	4 497.0	4 601.0	4 750.0	4 932.0	5 099.0	...	...
F(I) - month mois[43]	3 270.0	3 474.0	3 567.0	3 684.0	3 870.0	4 001.0	...	...
Netherlands Antilles[1,74] (Netherlands Antillean guilder) Antilles néerlandaises[1,74] (florin des Antilles néerlandaises)								
MF(I) - month mois	2 364.0	2 475.0	2 591.0	2 462.0	...	2 565.0	...	...
New Zealand[1,75,76,77] (New Zealand dollar) Nouvelle-Zélande[1,75,76,77] (dollar néo-zélandais)								
MF(I) - hour heure	14.6	15.1	15.6	16.0	16.5	17.0	17.4	18.0
M(I) - hour heure	15.5	16.1	16.5	16.9	17.4	17.9	18.3	18.9
F(I) - hour heure	12.0	12.5	12.9	13.4	13.9	14.5	14.8	15.3
Nicaragua (córdoba) Nicaragua (córdoba)								
MF(I) - hour heure	10.0	11.0	11.2	12.0	12.0	13.2	13.5	13.5
MF(I) - month mois	2 443.6	2 672.0	2 724.0	2 846.0	3 097.7	3 221.9	3 272.9	3 276.0
Norway (Norwegian krone) Norvège (couronne norvégienne)								
MF(I) - month mois[1,43,73]	...	...	20 005.0	21 417.0	22 441.0	23 388.0	24 426.0	25 991.0
M(I) - month mois[1,43,73]	...	...	20 571.0	22 017.0	23 039.0	23 964.0	25 006.0	26 623.0
F(I) - month mois[1,43,73]	...	...	17 839.0	19 109.0	20 017.0	21 091.0	22 051.0	23 483.0
MF(II) - hour heure[36,64]	109.8	114.4	118.9	125.5[46]	...	...	...	...
M(II) - hour heure[36,64]	112.3	117.0	121.6	128.3[46]	...	...	...	...
F(II) - hour heure[36,64]	97.9	102.2	106.1	112.4[46]	...	...	...	...
Occupied Palestinian Terr.[1,78,79] (new sheqel) Terr. palestinien occupé[1,78,79] (nouveau sheqel)								
MF(I) - day jour	...	38.5	49.9	57.3	65.4	68.8	68.0	70.1
M(I) - day jour	...	41.3	53.2	61.1	69.3	73.2	73.0	74.4
F(I) - day jour	...	23.2	27.5	32.6	32.4	36.0	35.2	36.8
Pakistan (Pakistan rupee) Pakistan (roupie pakistanaise)								
MF(I) - month mois	2 970.0	2 878.0	3 211.5	3 706.0	2 865.8	2 981.0	...	...

30

Wages in manufacturing
By hour, day, week or month *[cont.]*

Salaires dans les industries manufacturières
Par heure, jour, semaine ou mois *[suite]*

Country or area § Pays ou zone §	1995	1996	1997	1998	1999	2000	2001	2002
Panama (balboa) Panama (balboa)								
MF(I) - hour heure	...	2.5	...	...	...	...	...	...
MF(I) - month mois [1]	...	597.0[81]	...	247.0[31,69]	250.9[31,69]	...	...	...
M(I) - month mois [1,31,69]	...	...	...	249.8	259.0	...	...	...
F(I) - month mois [1,31,69]	...	...	...	238.5	241.3	...	...	1.8
MF(VI) - hour heure [1,31,80]	...	...	...	...	...	...	...	1.8
M(VI)- hour heure [1,31,80]	...	...	...	...	...	...	...	1.9
F(VI) - hour heure [1,31,80]	...	...	...	...	...	...	...	
Paraguay (guaraní) Paraguay (guaraní)								
MF(I) - month mois	610 414.0	686 436.0	761 675.0	898 598.0	741 416.0	...	...	
M(I) - month mois	645 759.0	721 289.0	800 340.0	947 853.0	923 124.0	...	...	
F(I) - month mois	485 113.0	563 271.0	628 963.0	729 160.0	404 458.0	...	...	
Peru [1] (new sol) Pérou [1] (nouveau sol)								
MF(II) - day jour [9,82]	24.0	22.6	24.5	24.9	25.6	27.2	27.1[85]	28.1[86]
M(II) - week semaine [56,83]	29.0	...	...	...	...	...	...	
F(II) - week semaine [56,83]	15.9	...	...	...	...	...	...	
MF(V) - month mois [12,82,84]		1 624.6	1 875.2	2 067.0	2 155.6	2 315.7	2 286.8[85]	2 430.2[86]
Philippines [87] (Philippine peso) Philippines [87] (peso philippin)								
MF(I) - month mois [7]	6 654.0[7]	6 817.0[1,7]	7 283.0[1,7]	6 400.0[88]	6 900.0[88]	7 300.0[88]	...	
M(I) - month mois [7]	7 529.0	7 605.0[1]	8 065.0[1]	8 522.0[1]	...	...	...	
F(I) - month mois [7]	5 592.0	5 814.0[1]	6 310.0[1]	6 810.0[1]	...	...	...	
Poland [1,64] (new zloty) Pologne [1,64] (nouveau zloty)								
MF(I) - month mois	656.7	832.8	1 014.9	1 164.4	1 598.9	1 756.4	1 866.5	1 970.1
Portugal (Portuguese escudo) Portugal (escudo portugais)								
MF(I) - month mois	100 700.0	107 800.0	116 100.0	120 803.0[1]	122 327.0[1]	...	...	
M(I) - month mois	118 900.0	127 200.0	136 900.0	140 720.0[1]	146 138.0[1]	...	...	
F(I) - month mois	78 100.0	83 900.0	88 900.0	94 837.0[1]	94 057.0[1]	...	...	
MF(II) - hour heure	470.0	498.0	539.0	...	...	...	...	
M(II) - hour heure	551.0	586.0	626.0	...	...	...	...	
F(II) - hour heure	378.0	402.0	434.0	...	...	...	...	
Puerto Rico (US dollar) Porto Rico (dollar des Etats-Unis)								
MF(II) - hour heure	7.4	7.7	8.0	8.4	8.9	9.4	9.8	10.3
Republic of Moldova (Moldovan leu) République de Moldova (leu moldove)								
MF(I) - month mois	209.5	282.2[1,38]	352.0[1,38]	399.0[1,38]	492.6[1,38]	677.7[1,38]	813.1[1,38]	971.8[1,38]
Romania [1] (Romanian leu) Roumanie [1] (leu roumain)								
MF(I) - month mois	268 436.0	424 587.0	826 902.0	1 198560.0	1 712748.0	2 535223.0	3 734701.0	4 632583.0
Russian Federation [1] (ruble) Fédération de Russie [1] (ruble)								
MF(I) - month mois	464 792.0	748 189.0	919.0[89]	1 026.0	...	...	...	...
Saint Helena [1,90] (pound sterling) Sainte-Hélène [1,90] (livre sterling)								
MF(I) - month mois	184.7	238.4	236.3	246.8	237.5	263.1	263.4	...
M(I) - month mois	272.2	243.9	242.2	276.1	251.8	272.5	272.9	
F(I) - month mois	84.8	223.6	215.7	129.9	195.3	222.4	229.0	
St. Vincent-Grenadines [1,9] (EC dollar) St. Vincent-Grenadines [1,9] (dollar des Caraïbes orientales)								
MF(I) - day jour	25.0	25.0	25.0	25.0	25.8	25.8	26.5	26.5
San Marino (Italian lira) Saint-Marin (lire italienne)								
MF(I) - day jour	127 347.0	135 278.0	142 712.0	149 357.0	157 158.0	...	3 289 004.0	...
MF(I) - month mois [1]	...				...			1 868.2[91]
Saudi Arabia [1] (Saudi Arabian riyal) Arabie saoudite [1] (riyal saoudien)								
MF(I) - week semaine	...		657.0					
Serbia and Montenegro [1,79,92] (Yugoslav dinar) Serbie-et-Monténégro [1,79,92] (dinar yougoslave)								
MF(I) - month mois			647.0[17]	823.0	1 053.0[93]	2 230.0	4 786.0	
Seychelles [1,94] (Seychelles rupee) Seychelles [1,94] (roupie seychelloises)								
MF(I) - month mois	2 513.0	2 646.0	2 727.0	2 853.0	2 962.0	3 067.0	3 235.0	...
Singapore (Singapore dollar) Singapour (dollar singapourien)								
MF(I) - month mois	2 157.3	2 319.5	2 486.7	2 716.0[1,95]	2 803.0[1]	3 036.0[1]	3 117.0[1]	3 154.0[1]
M(I) - month mois	2 644.0	2 815.2	2 999.7	3 311.0[1,95]	3 384.0[1]	3 653.0[1]	3 752.0[1]	3 762.0[1]
F(I) - month mois	1 541.2	1 674.4	1 811.0	1 916.0[1,95]	2 007.0[1]	2 181.0[1]	2 226.0[1]	2 283.0[1]
Slovakia [1,96] (Slovak koruna) Slovaquie [1,96] (couronne slovaque)								
MF(I) - month mois	7 194.0[97]	8 230.0[97]	9 197.0[97]	9 980.0	10 758.0	11 722.0	12 908.0	13 837.0

30

Wages in manufacturing
By hour, day, week or month *[cont.]*

Salaires dans les industries manufacturières
Par heure, jour, semaine ou mois *[suite]*

Country or area § Pays ou zone §	1995	1996	1997	1998	1999	2000	2001	2002
Slovenia[1] (tolar) Slovénie[1] (tolar)								
MF(I) - month mois	92 877.0	106 144.0	118 960.0	132 080.0	144 110.0	161 296.0	178 596.0	196 220.0
Solomon Islands[42,98] (Solomon Islands dollar) Iles Salomon[42,98] (dollar des Iles Salomon)								
MF(I) - month mois	632.0	987.0	...	...				
South Africa (rand) Afrique du Sud (rand)								
MF(I) - month mois	...	...	...	3 802.0	4 017.0	4 323.0	4 695.0	...
Spain (peseta, euro) Espagne (peseta, euro)								
MF(I) - hour heure	1 263.0	1 311.0[1,99]	1 372.0[1,99]	1 429.0[1,99]	8.5[1,100]	8.7[1,100]	9.0[1,100]	9.5[1,100]
Sri Lanka[72] (Sri Lanka rupee) Sri Lanka[72] (roupie sri-lankaise)								
MF(II) - day jour	145.4	151.2	166.3	174.2	199.2	222.5	230.7	273.1
M(II) - day jour	151.7	151.6	167.8	175.6	203.9	222.6	233.1	278.1
F(II) - day jour	136.2	138.7	142.5	145.7	165.8	185.6	201.3	235.1
MF(II) - hour heure	16.5	17.9	18.2	20.3	22.0	24.9	27.1	31.9
M(II) - hour heure	17.1	17.9	18.4	20.8	22.3	25.3	27.5	32.1
F(II) - hour heure	16.2	17.6	16.3	16.4	18.1	20.4	22.6	28.0
Swaziland[8,42] (lilangeni) Swaziland[8,42] (lilangeni)								
M(III) - month mois	2 134.0	2 388.0	2 948.0	...	...	...	...	...
F(III) - month mois	1 507.0	1 530.0	1 850.0	...	...	...	...	...
Sweden[1,101] (Swedish krona) Suède[1,101] (couronne suédoise)								
MF(II) - hour heure	107.0[102]	115.0[102]	101.2[102,103]	105.1[102]	106.9[102]	111.3[102]	114.9[104]	118.2[104]
M(II) - hour heure	109.1[102,103]	117.4[102,103]	103.3[102,103]	107.0[102]	108.7[102]	113.3[102]	116.9[104]	120.2[104]
F(II) - hour heure	98.2[102]	105.7[102]	93.4[102,103]	97.6[102]	99.6[102]	103.4[102]	106.6[104]	109.4[104]
Switzerland[1,105] (Swiss franc) Suisse[1,105] (franc suisse)								
MF(I) - month mois	...	5 565.0	...	5 717.0	...	5 862.0	...	...
M(I) - month mois	...	5 970.0	...	6 128.0	...	6 296.0	...	...
F(I) - month mois	...	4 280.0	...	4 413.0	...	4 550.0	...	...
Tajikistan[23] (somoni) Tadjikistan[23] (somoni)								
MF(I) - month mois	1 559.0[106]	8 080.0	14 977.0	...	...	...	...	...
Thailand[12] (baht) Thaïlande[12] (baht)								
MF(I) - month mois	4 994.0[107]	5 502.0[107]	5 935.0[107]	6 389.0[107]	5 907.0[107]	5 839.0	6 064.6[1]	...
M(I) - month mois	6 234.0[107]	...	...	...	...	6 612.0	7 112.7[1]	...
F(I) - month mois	4 250.0[107]	...	...	...	...	5 052.0	5 122.4[1]	...
TFYR of Macedonia[1,79] (TFYR Macedonian denar) L'ex-R.y. Macédoine[1,79] (denar de l'ex-R.Y. Macédoine)								
MF(I) - month mois	...	...	...	...	...	...	9 577.0	9 944.0
Trinidad and Tobago[1] (Trinidad and Tobago dollar) Trinité-et-Tobago[1] (dollar de la Trinité-et-Tobago)								
MF(I) - week semaine	790.6	810.1	865.4	908.7	938.8	1 170.1	1 161.2	...
Turkey (Turkish lira) Turquie (livre turque)								
MF(I) - day jour[1,7,40]	958.4	1 671.0	3 215.5	5 861.8	10 477.2	16 221.1	...	...
M(I) - day jour[15]	...	758 475.1	1 661886.0	...	...	...	...	...
F(I) - day jour[15]	...	747 788.8	1 611526.0	...	...	...	...	...
MF(I) - hour heure[1,7,108,109]	127.8	222.8	428.7	781.6	1 397.0	2 162.8	...	...
MF(I) - month mois[1,7,109,110]	23 001.6	40 104.5	77 171.2	140 683.6	251 453.0	389 307.4	...	...
Ukraine[1] (hryvnia) Ukraine[1] (hryvnia)								
MF(I) - month mois	76.9	131.1	148.8	159.7	191.3	270.7	368.3	441.3
M(I) - month mois	...	...	...	...	...	...	...	509.0
F(I) - month mois	...	...	...	...	...	...	...	358.9
United Kingdom[1,73,111,112] (pound sterling) Royaume-Uni[1,73,111,112] (livre sterling)								
MF(I) - hour heure	7.9	8.2	8.5	9.1	9.5	9.9	10.5	11.1
M(I) - hour heure	8.4	8.8	9.1	9.7	10.1	10.4	11.0	11.6
F(I)- hour heure	6.0	6.2	6.6	7.0	7.5	7.9	8.5	9.1
United States (US dollar) Etats-Unis (dollar des Etats-Unis)								
MF(II) - hour heure[113]	12.4	12.8	13.2	13.5	13.9	14.4	14.8	15.3
MF(II) - week semaine[114]	514.6	531.2	553.1	562.5	579.6	567.8	603.6	625.8
United States Virgin Is. (US dollar) Iles Vierges américaines (dollar des Etats-Unis)								
MF(II) - hour heure	15.8	17.0	18.1	...	...	...	...	...
Venezuela[17] (bolívar) Venezuela[17] (bolívar)								
MF(I) - month mois	...	...	141 122.0	...	...	...	...	...
Zimbabwe (Zimbabwe dollar) Zimbabwe (dollar zimbabwéen)								
MF(I) - hour heure	10.6	12.9	16.4	20.5	29.4	45.9	80.2	...
MF(I) - month mois	1 702.5	2 056.7	2 619.8	3 276.8	4 700.4	7 351.1	12 823.7	...

30

Wages in manufacturing
By hour, day, week or month [cont.]

Salaires dans les industries manufacturières
Par heure, jour, semaine ou mois [suite]

Source:
International Labour Office (ILO), Geneva, the ILO labour statistics database and the "Yearbook of Labour Statistics 2003".

§   I.   Employees.
    II.   Wage earners.
    III.   Skilled wage earners.
    IV.   Unskilled wage earners.
    V.   Salaried employees.
    VI.   Total employment.

1	Data classified according to ISIC, Rev. 3.
2	Production and related workers.
3	Local units with 10 or more workers.
4	May of each year.
5	Full-time adult non-managerial employees.
6	Prior to 2000: ATS;1 Euro = 13.7603 ATS.
7	Establishments with 10 or more persons employed.
8	Private sector.
9	Daily wage rates.
10	Managerial, administrative, technical, and production workers.
11	Euros; 1 Euro=40.3399 BEF.
12	Monthly wage rates.
13	Private sector establishments with 5 or more employees.
14	La Paz and El Alto.
15	September of each year.
16	Main cities, except Pando.
17	September.
18	Citizens only.
19	March.
20	December of each year.
21	Employees under labour contract.
22	State and cooperative sector.
23	Including major divisions 2 and 4.
24	New denomination: 1 new lev = 1,000 old leva.
25	Including overtime payments.
26	Employees paid by the hour.
27	Beginning April: sample design and methodology revised.
28	April of each year (Belgium, prior to 1999; Ireland, prior to 1998).
29	Including family allowances and the value of payments in kind.
30	State-owned units, urban collective-owned units and other ownership units.
31	Median.
32	Seven main cities.
33	July of each year.
34	Beginning 1987: methodology revised.
35	State sector (civilian).
36	Adults.
37	Enterprises with 100 or more employees.
38	Enterprises with 20 or more employees.
39	Estimations based on National Accounts.
40	Figures in thousands.
41	Prior to March 2000: sucres; 25,000 sucres =1 US dollar.
42	June of each year.
43	Full-time employees.
44	Including mining, quarrying and electricity.
45	Until 2000: FIM; 1 Euro = 5.94573 FIM.
46	Series discontinued.
47	Euros; 1 Euro=6.55957 FRF; net earnings.

Source:
Bureau international du Travail (BIT), Genève, la base de données du BIT et " Annuaire des statistiques du travail 2003".

§   I.   Salariés.
    II.   Ouvriers.
    III.   Ouvriers qualifiés.
    IV.   Ouvriers non qualifiés.
    V.   Employés.
    VI.   Emploi total.

1	Données classifiées selon la CITI, Rév. 3.
2	Ouvriers à la production et assimilés.
3	Unités locales occupant 10 ouvriers et plus.
4	Mai de chaque année.
5	Salariés adultes à plein temps, non compris les cadres dirigeants.
6	Avant 2000: ATS;1 Euro = 13.7603 ATS.
7	Entreprises occupant 10 salariés et plus.
8	Secteur privé.
9	Les taux de salaires journaliers.
10	Directeurs, cadres administratifs supérieurs, personnel technique et travailleurs à la production.
11	Euros; 1 Euro=40,3399 BEF.
12	Les taux de salaires mensuels.
13	Etablissements du secteur privé occupant 5 salariés ou plus.
14	La Paz et El Alto.
15	Septembre de chaque année.
16	Villes prinipales, sauf Pando.
17	Septembre.
18	Nationaux seulement.
19	Mars.
20	Décembre de chaque année.
21	Salariés sous contrat de travail.
22	Secteur d'Etat et coopératif.
23	Y compris les branches 2 et 4.
24	Nouvelle dénomination: 1 nouveau lev = 1,000 anciens leva.
25	Y compris la rémunération des heures supplémentaires.
26	Salariés rémunérés à l'heure.
27	A partir d'avril : plan d'échantillonnage et méthodologie révisés.
28	Avril de chaque année (Belgique, avant 1999; Irlande, avant 1998).
29	Y compris les allocations familiales et la valeur des paiements en nature.
30	Unités d'Etat, unités collectives urbaines et autres.
31	Médiane.
32	Sept villes principales.
33	Juillet de chaque année.
34	A partir de 1987: méthodologie révisée.
35	Secteur d'Etat (civils).
36	Adultes.
37	Entreprises occupant 100 salariés et plus.
38	Entreprises occupant 20 salariés et plus.
39	Estimations basées sur la Comptabilité nationale.
40	Données en milliers.
41	Avant mars 2000: sucres; 25 000 sucres = 1 dollar EU.
42	Juin de chaque année.
43	Salariés à plein temps.
44	Y compris les industries extractives et l'électricité.
45	Jusqu'en 2000: FIM; 1 Euro = 5.94573 FIM.
46	Série arrêtée.
47	Euros; 1 Euro=6,55957 FRF; gains nets.

30
Wages in manufacturing
By hour, day, week or month *[cont.]*
Salaires dans les industries manufacturières
Par heure, jour, semaine ou mois *[suite]*

48	Enterprises with 5 or more employees.
49	Survey results influenced by a low response rate.
50	Euros; 1 Euro = 1.95583 DEM.
51	Including family allowances paid directly by the employers.
52	Excluding part-time workers and juveniles.
53	Adult employees; excluding irregular bonuses and the value of payments in kind.
54	Adult employees; excluding overtime payments and payments in kind.
55	Production workers.
56	Weekly wage rates.
57	Including juveniles.
58	Including payments subject to income tax.
59	Index of hourly wage rates (Dec. 1995 = 100); prior to 1996: 1990 = 100.
60	Hourly wage rates.
61	Index of hourly wage rates (Dec.2000=100).
62	Private sector; establishments with 10 or more regular employees; June of each year .
63	Regular scheduled cash earnings.
64	Including the value of payments in kind.
65	All employees converted into full-time units.
66	Excluding individual unincorporated enterprises.
67	April.
68	Euros; 1 Euro = 40.3399 LUF.
69	March of each year.
70	Wage-earners on daily rates of pay.
71	Regular employees.
72	March and Sep. of each year
73	Excluding overtime payments.
74	Curaçao.
75	Establishments with the equivalent of more than 0.5 full-time paid employees.
76	February of each year.
77	Full-time equivalent employees.
78	Persons aged 15 years and over.
79	Net earnings.
80	August.
81	Prior to 1995: establishments with 5 or more persons engaged; 1996: incorporated entreprises.
82	Prior to 1996, Lima; June. Beginning 1996, urban areas; annual averages.
83	Lima.
84	Urban areas.
85	Average of the first three quarters.
86	Metropolitan Lima.
87	Computed on the basis of annual wages.
88	Data classified according to ISIC Rev. 3. Establishments with 20 or more persons employed. Excl. bonuses and gratuities.
89	New denomination: 1 new rouble = 1,000 old roubles.
90	Year ending in March of the year indicated.
91	Euros; 1 Euro=1936.27 ITL.
92	Excluding private sector.
93	Excluding Kosovo and Metohia.
94	Earnings are exempted from income tax.
95	Methodology revised; data not strictly comparable.
96	Excluding enterprises with less than 20 employees.
97	Excluding enterprises with less than 25 employees.
98	Including mining and quarrying.
99	Prior to 1999: Pesetas; 1 Euro = 166.386 Pesetas.
100	Excluding irregular gratuities.
101	Excluding holidays, sick-leave and overtime payments.

48	Entreprises occupant 5 salariés et plus.
49	Résultats de l'enquête influencés par un taux de réponse faible.
50	Euros; 1 Euro = 1,95583 DEM.
51	Y compris les allocations familiales payées directement par l'employeur.
52	Non compris les travailleurs à temps partiel et les jeunes.
53	Salariés adultes; non compris les prestations versées irrégulièrement et la valeur des paiements en nature.
54	Salariés adultes; non compris la rémunération des heures supplémentaires et la valeur des paiements en nature.
55	Travailleurs à la production.
56	Taux de salaire hebdomadaires.
57	Y compris les jeunes gens.
58	Y compris les versements soumis à l'impôt sur le revenu.
59	Indice des taux de salaires horaires (déc. 1995 = 100); avant 1996: 1990 = 100.
60	Taux de salaires horaires.
61	Indice des taux de salaire horaire (déc.2000=100).
62	Secteur privé; établissements occupant 10 salariés stables ou plus; juin de chaque années.
63	Gains en espèce tarifés réguliers.
64	Y compris la valeur des paiements en nature.
65	Ensemble des salariés convertis en unités à plein temps.
66	Non compris les entreprises individuelles non constituées en société.
67	Avril.
68	Euros; 1 Euro = 40,3399 LUF.
69	Mars de chaque année.
70	Ouvriers rémunérés sur la base de taux de salaire journaliers.
71	Salariés stables.
72	Mars et sept. de chaque année.
73	Non compris la rémunération des heures supplémentaires.
74	Curaçao.
75	Etablissements occupant plus de l'équivalent de 0.5 salarié à plein temps.
76	Février de chaque année.
77	Salariés en équivalents à plein temps.
78	Personnes âgées de 15 ans et plus.
79	Gains nets.
80	Août.
81	Avant 1995: établissements occupant 5 personnes ou plus; 1996: entreprises constituées en sociétés.
82	Avant 1996, Lima; juin. A partir de 1996, zones urbaines; moyennes annuelles.
83	Lima.
84	Régions urbaines.
85	Moyenne des trois premiers trimestres.
86	Lima métropolitaine.
87	Calculés sur la base de salaires annuels.
88	Données classifiées selon la CITI, Rév. 3. Entreprises occupant 20 salariés et plus. Non compris les primes et gratifications.
89	Nouvelle dénomination: 1 nouveau rouble = 1,000 anciens roubles.
90	Année se terminant en mars de l'année indiquée.
91	Euros; 1 Euro=1936,27 ITL.
92	Non compris le secteur privé.
93	Non compris Kosovo et Metohia.
94	Les gains sont exempts de l'impôts sur le revenu.
95	Méthodologie révisée; les données ne sont pas strictement comparables.
96	Non compris les entreprises occupant moins de 20 salariés.
97	Non compris les entreprises occupant moins de 25 salariés.
98	Y compris les industries extractives.
99	Avant 1999: Pesetas; 1 Euro = 166.386 Pesetas.
100	Non compris les gratifications versées irrégulièrement.
101	Non compris les versements pour les vacances, congés maladie ainsi

30

Wages in manufacturing
By hour, day, week or month *[cont.]*

Salaires dans les industries manufacturières
Par heure, jour, semaine ou mois *[suite]*

102	Adults; prior to 1998: 2nd quarter of each year; 1998-2000: Sept-Oct. of each year.	102	Adultes; avant 1998: 2ème trimestre de chaque année; 1998-2000: sept.-oct. de chaque année.
103	Including holidays and sick-leave payments and the value of payments in kind.	103	Y compris les versements pour les vacances et congés de maladie et la valeur des paiements en nature.
104	Private sector; Sep. of each year.	104	Secteur privé; sept. de chaque année.
105	Standardised monthly earnings (40 hours x 4 1/3 weeks).	105	Gains mensuels standardisés (40 heures x 4 1/3 semaines).
106	Prior to 1995: roubles; 1 Tajik rouble = 100 roubles.	106	Avant 1995: roubles; 1 rouble Tajik = 100 roubles.
107	March of each year. Average wage rates for normal/usual hours of work. Excl. public enterprises.	107	Mars de chaque année. Taux de salaire moyens pour la durée normale/usuelle du travail. Non compris les entreprises publiques.
108	Excluding overtime payments and irregular bonuses and allowances.	108	Non compris la rémunération des heures supplémentaires et les prestations versées irrégulièrement.
109	Figures in thousands; Jan - June.	109	Chiffres en milliers; jan - juin.
110	Including overtime payments and irregular bonuses and allowances.	110	Y compris la rémunération des heures supplémentaires et les prestations versées irrégulièrement.
111	April; excl. Northern Ireland.	111	Avril; non compris l'Irlande du Nord.
112	Full-time employees on adult rates of pay.	112	Salariés à plein temps rémunérés sur la base de taux de salaire pour adultes.
113	Private sector; production workers.	113	Secteur privé. Travailleurs à la production.
114	Private sector: production and construction workers and non-supervisory employees.	114	Secteur privé: ouvriers à la production, travailleurs à la construction et salariés sans activité de surveillance.

que la rémunération des heures supplémentaires.

31
Producers' prices or wholesale prices
Index numbers: 1990 = 100
Prix à la production ou prix de gros
Indices : 1990 = 100

Country or area	1996	1997	1998	1999	2000	2001	2002	Pays ou zone
Argentina								**Argentine**
Domestic supply [1,2]	248	249	241	232	241	235	417	Offre intérieure [1,2]
Domestic production	252	253	245	236	246	241	413	Production intérieure
Agricultural products [2]	283	254	237	189	184	180	427	Produits agricoles [2]
Industrial products [2,3]	248	252	249	241	244	233	386	Produits industriels [2,3]
Imported goods [3]	204	196	187	177	177	172	444	Produits importés [3]
Australia [4,5]								**Australie** [4,5]
Domestic supply [6]	...	...	100	104	108	110	110	Offre intérieure [6]
Domestic production [6]	...	...	100	104	108	110	...	Production intérieure [6]
Agricultural products [6]	...	106	100	110	114	135	141	Produits agricoles [6]
Industrial products [2,3,7]	111	112	109	114	118	122	...	Produits industriels [2,3,7]
Imported goods [6]	92	92	100	98	107	...	...	Produits importés [6]
Raw materials	102	105	102	106	110	117	115	Matières premières
Intermediate products [6]	...	...	100	104	110	112	112	Produits intermédiaires [6]
Consumers' goods [6]	...	...	100	102	107	109	112	Biens de consommation [6]
Capital goods [6]	...	...	100	103	107	109	112	Biens d'équipement [6]
Austria								**Autriche**
Domestic supply [2,8]	102	102	102	101	105	106	106	Offre intérieure [2,8]
Agricultural products	76	74	77	75	77	80	79	Produits agricoles
Consumers' goods [2]	106	106	107	106	110	113	113	Biens de consommation [2]
Capital goods [2]	101	101	100	98	96	96	96	Biens d'équipement [2]
Bangladesh [5]								**Bangladesh** [5]
Domestic supply [2,8]	127	128	135	144	141	141	144	Offre intérieure [2,8]
Agricultural products [2,9]	126	126	133	146	142	141	145	Produits agricoles [2,9]
Industrial products [2,3,9]	131	132	137	128	138	140	...	Produits industriels [2,3,9]
Raw materials	120	123	...	134	131	132	136	Matières premières
Belgium								**Belgique**
Domestic supply	102	104	103	...	...	...	...	Offre intérieure
Domestic production [10]	...	...	...	...	100	...	102	Production intérieure [10]
Agricultural products [2]	107	111	109	107	111	116	...	Produits agricoles [2]
Industrial products	102	104	103	102	111	113	...	Produits industriels
Intermediate products	98	99	97	97	111	113	113	Produits intermédiaires
Consumers' goods	108	111	110	109	112	110	111	Biens de consommation
Capital goods	109	109	109	108	108	109	108	Biens d'équipement
Bolivia								**Bolivie**
Industrial products	174	179	187	190	200	202	207	Produits industriels
Raw materials	197	204	204	192	181	176	195	Matières premières
Consumers' goods	170	175	185	190	204	208	209	Biens de consommation
Capital goods	150	157	159	161	164	146	178	Biens d'équipement
Brazil [11]								**Brésil** [11]
Domestic supply [12]	169	181	189	220	261	293	339	Offre intérieure [12]
Agricultural products [12]	172	200	215	252	306	358	435	Produits agricoles [12]
Industrial products [12]	165	172	175	203	237	262	301	Produits industriels [12]
Raw materials [12]	162	179	179	212	251	284	333	Matières premières [12]
Consumers' goods [12]	177	192	212	243	288	314	375	Biens de consommation [12]
Capital goods	172	176	178	198	220	239	266	Biens d'équipement
Bulgaria [13]								**Bulgarie** [13]
Domestic supply	233	2 500	2 914	3 010	3 521	3 674	...	Offre intérieure
Canada [14]								**Canada** [14]
Raw materials	122	120	103	111	136	134	...	Matières premières
Chile								**Chili**
Domestic supply	181	184	188	198	220	237	254	Offre intérieure
Domestic production	190	195	197	205	229	243	258	Production intérieure
Agricultural products	193	197	204	200	216	214	244	Produits agricoles
Industrial products [8]	190	193	200	210	235	251	262	Produits industriels [8]
Imported goods	147	145	152	165	182	207	226	Produits importés
China, Hong Kong SAR								**Chine, Hong Kong RAS**
Industrial products	111	111	109	107	107	106	99	Produits industriels
Colombia [15]								**Colombie** [15]
Domestic supply [2]	67	84	95	100[16]	119	128	139	Offre intérieure [2]
Domestic production	71	84	95	100[16]	118	127	136	Production intérieure
Agricultural products	73	88	97	100[16]	114	123	...	Produits agricoles

31

Producers' prices or wholesale prices
Index numbers: 1990 = 100 [cont.]

Prix à la production ou prix de gros
Indices : 1990 = 100 [suite]

Country or area	1996	1997	1998	1999	2000	2001	2002	Pays ou zone
Industrial products	71	83	95	100[16]	120	...	134	Produits industriels
Imported goods	73	85	96	100[16]	125	131	...	Produits importés
Raw materials	71	83	93	100[16]	...	...	...	Matières premières
Intermediate products	73	86	96	100[16]	120	127	...	Produits intermédiaires
Croatia[17]								**Croatie**[17]
Industrial products	94	96	#86	88	97	100	91	Produits industriels
Consumers' goods	99	101	#99	99	100	100	101	Biens de consommation
Capital goods	99	97	#93	96	102	100	97	Biens d'équipement
Cyprus								**Chypre**
Industrial products	122	122	124	126	135	...		Produits industriels
Czech Republic								**République tchèque**
Agricultural products	140	144	147	130	142	153	139	Produits agricoles
Denmark								**Danemark**
Domestic supply[2,12]	104	106	105	106	112	115	115	Offre intérieure[2,12]
Domestic production[2,12]	105	107	106	107	113	116	117	Production intérieure[2,12]
Imported goods[12]	103	105	104	104	111	112	111	Produits importés[12]
Raw materials	94	100	90	89	113	112	106	Matières premières
Consumers' goods	104	106	106	106	109	112	113	Biens de consommation
Ecuador								**Equateur**
Agricultural products	...	...	...	...	110	128	...	Produits agricoles
Egypt[5]								**Egypte**[5]
Domestic supply[8]	176	183	186	188	185	181	...	Offre intérieure[8]
Raw materials	133	140	133	132	129	126	...	Matières premières
Intermediate products	162	165	169	163	162	159	...	Produits intermédiaires
Capital goods	158	163	165	159	158	157	...	Biens d'équipement
El Salvador								**El Salvador**
Domestic supply[18]	145	147	138	136	140	...	...	Offre intérieure[18]
Domestic production	147	148	142	147	148	...	...	Production intérieure
Imported goods	130	126	119	119	123	...	...	Produits importés
Finland								**Finlande**
Domestic supply	106	108	106	106	115	115	113	Offre intérieure
Domestic production	102	104	105	104	111	113	111	Production intérieure
Imported goods	120	121	115	115	130	126	123	Produits importés
Raw materials	105	107	100	98	109	107	108	Matières premières
Consumers' goods[19]	108	109	112	113	114	116	106	Biens de consommation[19]
Capital goods	105	108	109	109	113	114	105	Biens d'équipement
France								**France**
Agricultural products	89	90	90	86	88	91	...	Produits agricoles
Intermediate products	99	98	97	96	100	102	102	Produits intermédiaires
Germany[20]								**Allemagne**[20]
Domestic supply	104	105	103	102	106	110	110	Offre intérieure
Domestic production	100	101	100	...	...	...	...	Production intérieure
Agricultural products	91	93	88	84	89	92	88	Produits agricoles
Imported goods	96	97	97	97	108	109	...	Produits importés
Intermediate products	100	101	100	...	...	111	111	Produits intermédiaires
Greece[21]								**Grèce**[21]
Domestic supply[22]	176	182	189	193	205	210	215	Offre intérieure[22]
Domestic production[22]	176	182	190	194	204	209	215	Production intérieure[22]
Agricultural products[23]	174	189	200	204	207	228	254	Produits agricoles[23]
Industrial products[22]	180	186	193	198	208	214	219	Produits industriels[22]
Imported goods[22]	171	175	184	185	197	201	202	Produits importés[22]
Guatemala								**Guatemala**
Domestic supply	202	222	228	236	260	274	...	Offre intérieure
Domestic production	205	221	231	238	263	281	...	Production intérieure
Agricultural products	200	213	235	246	272	294	...	Produits agricoles
Industrial products	209	226	229	233	258	273	...	Produits industriels
Imported goods	197	223	222	234	256	264	...	Produits importés
India[24]								**Inde**[24]
Domestic supply	174	184	197	203	210	220	225	Offre intérieure
Agricultural products	189	201	225	237	249	240	254	Produits agricoles
Industrial products[3]	169	176	184	188	188	192	208	Produits industriels[3]
Raw materials[25]	181	189	210	219	223	224	216	Matières premières[25]

31

Producers' prices or wholesale prices
Index numbers: 1990 = 100 *[cont.]*

Prix à la production ou prix de gros
Indices : 1990 = 100 *[suite]*

Country or area	1996	1997	1998	1999	2000	2001	2002	Pays ou zone
Indonesia								**Indonésie**
Domestic supply [22]	145	158	319	355	404	462	474	Offre intérieure [22]
Domestic production	168	179	296	326	406	469	512	Production intérieure
Agricultural products	209	233	393	533	604	746	807	Produits agricoles
Industrial products [3]	151	156	258	325	344	383	420	Produits industriels [3]
Imported goods [22]	127	136	313	325	349	393	389	Produits importés [22]
Raw materials	141	161	357	352	452	496	499	Matières premières
Intermediate products	141	148	317	342	376	430	446	Produits intermédiaires
Consumers' goods	151	164	299	395	440	522	...	Biens de consommation
Capital goods	132	139	248	291	296	320	316	Biens d'équipement
Iran (Islamic Rep. of) [2,9]								**Iran (Rép. islamique d')** [2,9]
Domestic supply	582	644	740	860	1 013	1 111	1 202	Offre intérieure
Domestic production	573	619	749	868	1 015	...	...	Production intérieure
Agricultural products	505	541	690	822	943	1 021	1 150	Produits agricoles
Industrial products	493	486	536	663	882	820	853	Produits industriels
Imported goods	668	731	798	910	1 067	1 587	...	Produits importés
Raw materials	572	598	608	691	832	934	985	Matières premières
Ireland								**Irlande**
Domestic supply [2,26]	111	110	112	112	119	119	123	Offre intérieure [2,26]
Agricultural products [2,26]	103	96	96	91	98	103	98	Produits agricoles [2,26]
Industrial products [2,3,26]	112	111	112	113	120	...	...	Produits industriels [2,3,26]
Capital goods [9]	115	117	120	123	128	...	...	Biens d'équipement [9]
Israel [22]								**Israël** [22]
Industrial products	180	192	201	214	218	219	...	Produits industriels
Italy								**Italie**
Domestic supply [2,22]	132	134	135	134	142	145	145	Offre intérieure [2,22]
Intermediate products	124	126	125	123	135	138	135	Produits intermédiaires
Consumers' goods	133	134	136	137	139	143	145	Biens de consommation
Capital goods	133	137	139	141	142	144	145	Biens d'équipement
Japan								**Japon**
Domestic supply [2]	93	95	93	91	91	91	90	Offre intérieure [2]
Domestic production	95	94	94	92	93	92	91	Production intérieure
Agricultural products [9]	90	90	85	88	86	86	85	Produits agricoles [9]
Industrial products [9]	95	95	94	92	93	92	91	Produits industriels [9]
Imported goods	103	102	92	93	102	98	96	Produits importés
Raw materials	88	93	83	78	89	92	92	Matières premières
Intermediate products	92	94	92	90	91	91	90	Produits intermédiaires
Consumers' goods	96	97	96	95	94	94	93	Biens de consommation
Capital goods	93	93	93	90	88	87	86	Biens d'équipement
Jordan [2]								**Jordanie** [2]
Domestic supply	119	121	122	119	114	113	111	Offre intérieure
Korea, Republic of								**Corée, République de**
Domestic supply	121	125	141	138	140	140	139	Offre intérieure
Agricultural products [9,27]	134	136	142	157	151	157	160	Produits agricoles [9,27]
Industrial products	117	121	139	134	137	134	132	Produits industriels
Raw materials	126	140	104	96	118	120	122	Matières premières
Intermediate products	117	123	123	111	116	116	111	Produits intermédiaires
Consumers' goods	126	131	144	147	147	149	147	Biens de consommation
Capital goods	112	114	139	132	128	127	122	Biens d'équipement
Kuwait								**Koweït**
Domestic supply	115	114	112	111	111	113	117	Offre intérieure
Agricultural products	111	112	115	112	115	111	118	Produits agricoles
Raw materials	110	115	114	116	117	123	127	Matières premières
Intermediate products	119	123	121	116	114	114	118	Produits intermédiaires
Consumers' goods	126	128	128	127	127	128	131	Biens de consommation
Capital goods	98	89	84	81	82	86	94	Biens d'équipement
Latvia [28]								**Lettonie** [28]
Domestic supply	323	336	343	329	331	...	...	Offre intérieure
Lithuania								**Lituanie**
Domestic supply	42 796	44 611	41 636	42 912	51 238	50 358	47 549	Offre intérieure

31

Producers' prices or wholesale prices
Index numbers: 1990 = 100 *[cont.]*

Prix à la production ou prix de gros
Indices : 1990 = 100 *[suite]*

Country or area	1996	1997	1998	1999	2000	2001	2002	Pays ou zone
Luxembourg								**Luxembourg**
Industrial products	94	95	97	93	97	98	97	Produits industriels
Imported goods	106	109	112	110	116	119	121	Produits importés
Intermediate products	86	88	90	84	90	88	87	Produits intermédiaires
Consumers' goods [19]	104	104	104	104	105	115	117	Biens de consommation [19]
Capital goods	111	112	114	113	117	120	121	Biens d'équipement
Malaysia								**Malaisie**
Domestic supply	115	118	131	127	131	124	130	Offre intérieure
Domestic production	118	121	135	130	134	126	133	Production intérieure
Imported goods	104	107	117	116	118	117	117	Produits importés
Mexico								**Mexique**
Domestic supply [8,29]	278	327	379	438	474	500	520	Offre intérieure [8,29]
Agricultural products	287	333	349	434	514	496	491	Produits agricoles
Raw materials	287	325	358	400	447	...	462	Matières premières
Consumers' goods [9,29]	288	349	404	455	503	536	555	Biens de consommation [9,29]
Capital goods [8,9,29]	266	312	363	418	457	479	494	Biens d'équipement [8,9,29]
Morocco								**Maroc**
Domestic supply	130	128	132	134	...	...	...	Offre intérieure
Agricultural products	140	134	138	136	141	141	144	Produits agricoles
Industrial products	124	126	129	130	135	132	131	Produits industriels
Netherlands								**Pays-Bas**
Industrial products	101	104	102	102	110	113	113	Produits industriels
Imported goods	104	109	102	106	132	128	126	Produits importés
Raw materials	97	100	95	97	115	115	113	Matières premières
Intermediate products	104	107	104	103	114	118	116	Produits intermédiaires
Consumers' goods	108	110	109	110	121	114	122	Biens de consommation
Capital goods	108	109	111	113	114	115	118	Biens d'équipement
New Zealand [30]								**Nouvelle-Zélande** [30]
Agricultural products [2]	99	100	99	99	110	137	136	Produits agricoles [2]
Industrial products [2,31]	101	100	101	102	109	114	115	Produits industriels [2,31]
Intermediate products [32]	100	100	101	102	108	116	116	Produits intermédiaires [32]
Norway								**Norvège**
Domestic supply	108	110	110	112	117	122	123	Offre intérieure
Industrial products [10]	91	93	94	96	100	102	101	Produits industriels [10]
Imported goods	98	97	98	96	101	108	...	Produits importés
Raw materials	97	101	100	101	109	108	96	Matières premières
Intermediate products	110	111	113	113	116	...	115	Produits intermédiaires
Consumers' goods	111	113	114	116	119	...	123	Biens de consommation
Capital goods	112	113	114	115	116	119	122	Biens d'équipement
Pakistan [5]								**Pakistan** [5]
Domestic supply [2,8]	199	237	227	229	238	250	...	Offre intérieure [2,8]
Agricultural products	206	221	236	237	241	249	...	Produits agricoles
Industrial products	185	189	195	201	204	211	...	Produits industriels
Raw materials	216	233	256	245	236	247	...	Matières premières
Panama								**Panama**
Domestic supply	113	111	106	109	119	...	...	Offre intérieure
Peru								**Pérou**
Domestic supply	1 344	1 443	1 548	1 624	1 694	1 708	1 700	Offre intérieure
Domestic production	1 341	...	1 545	1 606	1 673	1 698	1 680	Production intérieure
Agricultural products [33]	1 592	1 763	2 061	1 891	1 793	1 863	1 730	Produits agricoles [33]
Industrial products [3,9]	1 264	1 355	1 437	1 525	1 616	1 642	1 631	Produits industriels [3,9]
Imported goods	1 230	1 295	1 376	1 513	1 608	1 623	1 608	Produits importés
Philippines [34]								**Philippines** [34]
Domestic supply	145	145	162	172	175	179	185	Offre intérieure
Portugal								**Portugal**
Domestic supply	121	124	119	121	140	141	...	Offre intérieure
Intermediate products	114	115	115	114	120	121	...	Produits intermédiaires
Capital goods [10]	...	...	...	...	100	102	102	Biens d'équipement [10]
Romania								**Roumanie**
Industrial products	11 236	28 390	37 810	53 757	81 488	118 223	147 499	Produits industriels

31

Producers' prices or wholesale prices
Index numbers: 1990 = 100 *[cont.]*

Prix à la production ou prix de gros
Indices : 1990 = 100 *[suite]*

Country or area	1996	1997	1998	1999	2000	2001	2002	Pays ou zone
Serbia and Montenegro								**Serbie-et-Monténégro**
Domestic supply [6]	64	75	100	135	...	...	...	Offre intérieure [6]
Agricultural products [15]	44	52	69	100	258	439	...	Produits agricoles [15]
Industrial products [15]	47	55	69	100	207	382	...	Produits industriels [15]
Consumers' goods [15]	46	56	70	100	185	373	...	Biens de consommation [15]
Capital goods [15]	42	47	62	100	225	321	...	Biens d'équipement [15]
Singapore								**Singapour**
Domestic supply [8]	85	81	79	80	88	87	86	Offre intérieure [8]
Domestic production [2,3,35]	77	70	67	67	72	70	72	Production intérieure [2,3,35]
Imported goods [35]	87	84	83	85	92	92	92	Produits importés [35]
Slovenia								**Slovénie**
Agricultural products	1 077	1 149	1 198	1 206	...	...	...	Produits agricoles
Industrial products	1 226	1 300	1 379	1 408	1 515	1 652	1 736	Produits industriels
Intermediate products [10]	...	...	...	...	100	109	114	Produits intermédiaires [10]
Consumers' goods [10]	77	84	90	94	100	110	118	Biens de consommation [10]
Capital goods [10]	88	89	92	96	100	104	107	Biens d'équipement [10]
South Africa								**Afrique du Sud**
Domestic supply [36]	164	175	181	190	209	226	258	Offre intérieure [36]
Domestic production [36]	168	181	188	197	212	229	260	Production intérieure [36]
Agricultural products	174	188	191	194	202	228	283	Produits agricoles
Industrial products [3]	166	180	188	195	210	226	256	Produits industriels [3]
Imported goods	141	148	153	164	189	208	240	Produits importés
Spain								**Espagne**
Domestic supply [22]	120	121	120	121	128	130	131	Offre intérieure [22]
Consumers' goods	126	127	127	129	131	135	138	Biens de consommation
Capital goods	116	117	119	120	121	123	125	Biens d'équipement
Sri Lanka								**Sri Lanka**
Domestic supply	172	188	199	198	212	...	...	Offre intérieure
Domestic production	168	179	188	194	212	...	...	Production intérieure
Imported goods	151	161	161	161	189	...	...	Produits importés
Consumers' goods	173	189	203	203	201	...	...	Biens de consommation
Capital goods	182	192	210	227	219	...	...	Biens d'équipement
Sweden [22,37]								**Suède** [22,37]
Domestic supply [2]	118	119	119	120	127	131	132	Offre intérieure [2]
Domestic production [2]	116	117	117	117	121	124	124	Production intérieure [2]
Imported goods	120	122	121	124	134	140	141	Produits importés
Switzerland								**Suisse**
Domestic supply [2,8]	98	98	97	95	98	98	...	Offre intérieure [2,8]
Domestic production [2,8]	99	99	98	98	98	99	...	Production intérieure [2,8]
Agricultural products [2]	85	84	81	79	83	92	...	Produits agricoles [2]
Industrial products	101	100	99	98	98	96	...	Produits industriels
Imported goods [8]	92	94	92	90	96	95	...	Produits importés [8]
Raw materials	88	89	84	81	88	78	...	Matières premières
Consumers' goods	103	103	103	104	104	106	...	Biens de consommation
Thailand								**Thaïlande**
Domestic supply [2,12]	125	130	147	138	157	145	147	Offre intérieure [2,12]
Agricultural products	145	148	171	147	145	152	167	Produits agricoles
Industrial products [3]	120	125	139	136	141	144	145	Produits industriels [3]
Raw materials	138	144	173	138	139	149	155	Matières premières
Intermediate products	123	128	150	144	142	144	144	Produits intermédiaires
Consumers' goods	130	137	160	148	151	159	166	Biens de consommation
Capital goods [13]	...	...	...	111	115	118	121	Biens d'équipement [13]
TFYR of Macedonia [6]								**L'ex-R.y. Macédoine** [6]
Domestic supply	92	96	100	100	109	...	...	Offre intérieure
Consumers' goods	92	97	100	101	103	...	...	Biens de consommation
Capital goods	92	96	100	102	103	...	...	Biens d'équipement
Trinidad and Tobago								**Trinité-et-Tobago**
Industrial products	119	122	124	126	127		129	Produits industriels
Tunisia								**Tunisie**
Agricultural products	140	147	153	156	160	163	...	Produits agricoles
Industrial products	134	138	142	144	146	149	...	Produits industriels

31

Producers' prices or wholesale prices
Index numbers: 1990 = 100 *[cont.]*

Prix à la production ou prix de gros
Indices : 1990 = 100 *[suite]*

Country or area	1996	1997	1998	1999	2000	2001	2002	Pays ou zone
Turkey								**Turquie**
Domestic supply [2,22,38]	2 881	5 238	9 000	13 776	20 861	33 718	50 613	Offre intérieure [2,22,38]
Agricultural products	3 054	5 707	10 659	15 117	20 860	29 678	46 418	Produits agricoles
Industrial products	2 746	4 959	8 265	12 991	20 282	33 807	50 141	Produits industriels
United Kingdom								**Royaume-Uni**
Domestic supply	124	125	125	127	130	130	131	Offre intérieure
Domestic production	124	125	126	127	130	130	131	Production intérieure
Agricultural products	114	99	90	76	75	80	75	Produits agricoles
Industrial products [3]	123	123	123	122	123	124	124	Produits industriels [3]
Imported goods [13]	99	91	83	83	92	91	87	Produits importés [13]
Raw materials	102	94	85	87	97	96	93	Matières premières
Intermediate products [13]	99	99	98	99	103	103	100	Produits intermédiaires [13]
Consumers' goods [13]	104	105	106	108	109	111	112	Biens de consommation [13]
Capital goods [13]	101	101	100	100	99	98	98	Biens d'équipement [13]
United States								**Etats-Unis**
Domestic supply [2]	110	110	107	108	114	115	113	Offre intérieure [2]
Agricultural products [2]	109	101	93	88	89	93	88	Produits agricoles [2]
Industrial products [2,39]	110	111	108	109	116	117	114	Produits industriels [2,39]
Raw materials	104	102	89	90	110	110	99	Matières premières
Intermediate products	110	110	107	108	113	113	112	Produits intermédiaires
Consumers' goods	110	110	109	111	202	120	118	Biens de consommation
Capital goods	113	113	112	112	113	114	113	Biens d'équipement
Uruguay [40]								**Uruguay [40]**
Domestic supply [2,8]	887	1 032	1 128	1 118	1 194	...	...	Offre intérieure [2,8]
Domestic production	919	1 069	1 168	1 158	1 237	1 319	...	Production intérieure
Agricultural products	918	1 067	1 170	1 062	1 146	1 256	...	Produits agricoles
Industrial products [8]	934	1 086	1 184	1 208	1 285	1 356	...	Produits industriels [8]
Venezuela [8]								**Venezuela [8]**
Domestic supply	1 164	1 511	1 846	2 145	2 427	2 801	...	Offre intérieure
Domestic production	1 191	1 580	1 966	2 313	2 703	3 109	...	Production intérieure
Agricultural products	793	1 089	1 635	2 265	3 682	5 186	...	Produits agricoles
Industrial products	1 194	1 545	1 863	2 136	2 438	2 722	...	Produits industriels
Imported goods	1 098	1 339	1 548	1 727	1 894	2 043	...	Produits importés
Zimbabwe								**Zimbabwe**
Domestic supply	445	503	662	1 048	...	...	...	Offre intérieure
Domestic production	446	503	661	1 048	...	...	...	Production intérieure

Source:
United Nations Statistics Division, New York, price statistics database.

Source:
Organisation des Nations Unies, Division de statistique, New York, la base de données pour les statistiques des prix.

1	Domestic agricultural products only.	1	Produits agricoles intériéurs seulement.
2	Including exported products.	2	Y compris les produits exportés.
3	Manufacturing industry only.	3	Industries manufacturières seulement.
4	Including service industries.	4	Y compris industries de service.
5	Annual average refers to average of 12 months ending June.	5	Le moyen annuel est le moyen de douze mois finissant juin.
6	Base: 1998=100.	6	Base: 1998=100.
7	Prices relate only to products for sale or transfer to other sectors or for use as capital equipment.	7	Uniquement les prix des produits destinés à être vendus ou transférés à d'autres secteurs ou à être utilisés comme biens d'équipement.
8	Excluding mining and quarrying.	8	Non compris les industries extractives.
9	Including imported products.	9	Y compris les produits importés.
10	Base: 2000=100.	10	Base: 2000=100.
11	Base: 1994=100.	11	Base: 1994=100.
12	Agricultural products and products of the manufacturing industry.	12	Produits agricoles et produits des industries manufacturières.
13	Base: 1995=100.	13	Base: 1995=100.
14	Valued at purchasers' values.	14	A la valeur d'acquisition.
15	Base: 1999=100.	15	Base: 1999=100.
16	Beginning 1999, annual average refers to average of 12 months ending May.	16	A partir de 1999, la moyenne annuelle est la moyenne de 12 mois finissant mai.
17	Base: 2001=100.	17	Base: 2001=100.
18	San Salvador.	18	San Salvador.

31

Producers' prices or wholesale prices
Index numbers: 1990 = 100 *[cont.]*

Prix à la production ou prix de gros
Indices : 1990 = 100 *[suite]*

19	Durable goods only (Finland: beginning 1994; Luxembourg: beginning 1995).	19	Biens durables seulement (Finlande: à partir de 1995; Luxembourg: à partir de 1994).
20	Base: 1991=100.	20	Base: 1991=100.
21	Finished products only.	21	Produits finis uniquement.
22	Excluding electricity, gas and water.	22	Non compris l'électricité, le gaz et l'eau.
23	Including mining and quarrying.	23	Y compris les industries extractives.
24	Annual average refers to average of 12 months ending March.	24	Le moyen annuel est le moyen de douze mois finissant mars.
25	Primary articles include food, non-food articles and minerals.	25	Les articles primaires comprennent des articles des produits alimentaires, non- alimentaires et des minéraux.
26	Excluding Value Added Tax.	26	Non compris taxe sur la valeur ajoutée.
27	Including marine foods.	27	Y compris l'alimentation marine.
28	Base: 1992=100.	28	Base: 1992=100.
29	Mexico City.	29	Mexico.
30	Base: 1997=100.	30	Base: 1997=100.
31	Including all outputs of manufacturing.	31	Y compris toute la production du secteur manufacturière.
32	Including all industrial inputs.	32	Tous les intrants industriels.
33	Excluding fishing.	33	Non compris la pêche.
34	Metro Manila.	34	L'agglomération de Manille.
35	Not a sub-division of the domestic supply index.	35	N'est pas un élément de l'indice de l'offre intérieure.
36	Excluding gold mining.	36	Non compris l'extraction de l'or.
37	Excluding agriculture.	37	Non compris l'agriculture.
38	Excluding industrial finished goods.	38	Non compris les produits finis industriels.
39	Excluding foods and feeds production.	39	Non compris les produits alimentaires et d'affouragement.
40	Montevideo.	40	Montevideo.

32
Consumer price index numbers
All items and food: 1990 = 100

Indices des prix à la consommation
Ensemble des prix et alimentation : 1990 = 100

Country or area Pays ou zone	1995	1996	1997	1998	1999	2000	2001	2002
Albania Albanie								
All items [1] Ensemble des prix [1]	244	275	367	442	444	444	458[4]	482
Food [2] Alimentation [2]	229[1]	263[1]	358[1]	433[1]	432[1]	91[3]	95[3]	100[3]
Algeria Algérie								
All items Ensemble des prix	338	407	431	458	468	465	481	492
Food Alimentation	343	417	437	467	472	462	482	490
American Samoa Samoa américaines								
All items Ensemble des prix	113	118	120[5]	...	123[6]	126	127	...
Food Alimentation	109	112	113[5]	...	112[6]	112	113	...
Angola [7,8] Angola [7,8]								
All items Ensemble des prix	0	1	3	7	24	100	253	528[4]
Food Alimentation	0	1	3	7	26	100	251	509[4]
Anguilla Anguilla								
All items Ensemble des prix	117	121	122	125	126	136	139[4]	140
Food Alimentation	116	119	120	119	122	123	125[4]	126
Antigua and Barbuda [9] Antigua-et-Barbuda [9]								
All items Ensemble des prix	108[10]	112	112	116	117	118	120	...
Food Alimentation	115[10]	119	118	119	123	125	130	...
Argentina [8,11] Argentine [8,11]								
All items Ensemble des prix	404	405	407	411	406	402[4]	398	501
Food Alimentation	391	389	387	393	379	369[4]	362	487
Armenia [12] Arménie [12]								
All items Ensemble des prix	276	328	373	406	408	405	418	422
Food Alimentation	291	334	362	384	362	341	357	365
Aruba Aruba								
All items Ensemble des prix	127[4]	131	135	137	140	146	150[4]	155
Food Alimentation	125[4]	130	134	136	139	142	147[4]	...
Australia Australie								
All items Ensemble des prix	113	116	116	117	119	124	130	134
Food Alimentation	113	116	119	122	126	129	138	143
Austria Autriche								
All items Ensemble des prix	117	119[4]	121	122	123	126[4]	129	131
Food Alimentation	113	114[4]	116	118	118	119[4]	123	125
Azerbaijan [9] Azerbaïdjan [9]								
All items Ensemble des prix	9 025	10 817	11 218	11 131	10 182	10 366	10 526	10 818
Food [2] Alimentation [2]	9 369	11 016	10 964	10 817	9 630	9 853	10 117	10 490

32

Consumer price index numbers
All items and food: 1990 = 100 *[cont.]*

Indices des prix à la consommation
Ensemble des prix et alimentation : 1990 = 100 *[suite]*

Country or area Pays ou zone	1995	1996	1997	1998	1999	2000	2001	2002
Bahamas Bahamas								
All items								
Ensemble des prix	121[4]	122	123	125	126	128	131	134
Food								
Alimentation	113[4]	116	118	121	121	123	126	128
Bahrain Bahreïn								
All items								
Ensemble des prix	107	107	100[13]	100[14]	98[14]	98[14]	96[14]	96[14]
Food								
Alimentation	107	108	100[13]	101[14]	100[14]	99[14]	97[14]	97[14]
Bangladesh [12,15] Bangladesh [12,15]								
All items								
Ensemble des prix	110	113	119	129	137	140	142	147
Food								
Alimentation	111	113	118	130	141	143	145	148
Barbados Barbade								
All items								
Ensemble des prix	117[4]	120	129	127	129	132	136[4]	136
Food								
Alimentation	110[4]	115	130	124	128	131	138[4]	140
Belarus Bélarus								
All items								
Ensemble des prix	242 349	370 042	606 280	1 049 046	4 130 517	11 094 570	17 877 790	25 490 153
Food								
Alimentation	285 492	427 010	725 423	1 275 656	5 264 124	13 945 717	21 871 069	30 381 102
Belgium Belgique								
All items								
Ensemble des prix	113	115[4]	117	118	119	123	126	128
Food								
Alimentation	104	105[4]	107	109	109	110	115	117
Belize Belize								
All items								
Ensemble des prix	116	123	124	123	122	123	124	127
Food [2]								
Alimentation [2]	115	123	125	123	121	122	123	124
Benin [1,8] Bénin [1,8]								
All items								
Ensemble des prix	160	166[4]	172	182	182	190	197	202
Food [16]								
Alimentation [16]	161	183[4]	189	203	202	205	210	221
Bermuda Bermudes								
All items								
Ensemble des prix	115	118	121	123	126	129	133	136
Food								
Alimentation	110	113	116	119	121	124	126	128
Bhutan Bhoutan								
All items								
Ensemble des prix	170	185	197	217	232	241	250	256
Food [2]								
Alimentation [2]	165	180	187	208	220	222	225	230
Bolivia [17] Bolivie [17]								
All items								
Ensemble des prix	176	197	207	223	227	238	242	244
Food								
Alimentation	180	205	212	224	220	225	227	224
Botswana Botswana								
All items								
Ensemble des prix	181	200[4]	217	231	250	271	289	312
Food								
Alimentation	183	207[4]	228	242	259	271	278	304

32

Consumer price index numbers
All items and food: 1990 = 100 *[cont.]*

Indices des prix à la consommation
Ensemble des prix et alimentation : 1990 = 100 *[suite]*

Country or area Pays ou zone	1995	1996	1997	1998	1999	2000	2001	2002
Brazil [12] Brésil [12]								
All items								
Ensemble des prix	166	192	205	212	222	238	254	276
Food								
Alimentation	158	168	169	174	180	189	202	221
British Virgin Islands Iles Vierges britanniques								
All items								
Ensemble des prix	123	129[4]	137	143	146	150	155	...
Food								
Alimentation	120	132[4]	136	140	141	141	147	...
Brunei Darussalam Brunéi Darussalam								
All items								
Ensemble des prix	184	188	191	190	190	192	193	189[4]
Food								
Alimentation	177	183	189	190	190	190	191	191[4]
Bulgaria Bulgarie								
All items								
Ensemble des prix	3 722	222[18]	2 567[19]	3 046[19]	3 125[19]	3 447[19]	3 701[19]	3 916[19]
Food								
Alimentation	3 968	223[18]	2 666[19]	2 962[19]	2 724[19]	3 003[19]	3 199[19]	3 198[19]
Burkina Faso [8] Burkina Faso [8]								
All items								
Ensemble des prix	136	144	148	156[4]	154	154	161	165
Food								
Alimentation	126	145	149	166[4]	156	147	160	165
Burundi [8] Burundi [8]								
All items								
Ensemble des prix	166	210	276	310	321	403	436	...
Food								
Alimentation	171	212	287	323	326	422	425	...
Cambodia [8,19] Cambodge [8,19]								
All items								
Ensemble des prix	100	107	116	133	138	137	136[4]	141
Food [20]								
Alimentation [20]	100	108	115	131	141	136	133[4]	136
Cameroon [12] Cameroun [12]								
All items								
Ensemble des prix	109	113	119	123	125	126	132	141
Food								
Alimentation	108	112	120	123	125	128	137	...
Canada Canada								
All items								
Ensemble des prix	112	113	115	116	118	122	125	128
Food								
Alimentation	109	111	112	114	116	117	122	126
Cape Verde Cap-Vert								
All items								
Ensemble des prix	133	141	153	160	166	162	162	171
Food								
Alimentation	140	148	162	170	176	173	182	...
Cayman Islands Iles Caïmanes								
All items								
Ensemble des prix	120[4]	124	127	131	140	143	145	149
Food								
Alimentation	110[4]	114	116	118	120	122	127	129
Central African Rep. [8] Rép. centrafricaine [8]								
All items [21]								
Ensemble des prix [21]	139	144	146	145	142	146	151	155
Food								
Alimentation	139	147	148	144	140	145	...	...

32

Consumer price index numbers
All items and food: 1990 = 100 *[cont.]*

Indices des prix à la consommation
Ensemble des prix et alimentation : 1990 = 100 *[suite]*

Country or area Pays ou zone	1995	1996	1997	1998	1999	2000	2001	2002
Chad[8] Tchad[8]								
All items								
Ensemble des prix	143	161	170	193	162	168	189	197
Food								
Alimentation	143	164	178	184	161	173	207	218
Chile[8] Chili[8]								
All items								
Ensemble des prix	191	205	218	229[4]	236	246	254	261
Food								
Alimentation	196	207	222	231[4]	231	234	236	241
China Chine								
All items								
Ensemble des prix	193	210	215	214	211	211	212	209
Food								
Alimentation	214	230	230	223	213	208	208	207
China, Hong Kong SAR Chine, Hong Kong RAS								
All items								
Ensemble des prix	157	167	177	182	175	168[22]	166	161
Food								
Alimentation	149	155	161	164	161	158[22]	156	153
China, Macao SAR Chine, Macao RAS								
All items								
Ensemble des prix	145[21]	152[21]	158[4]	158[21]	99[23]	98[4,23]	96[23]	93[23]
Food								
Alimentation	146	152	158[4]	159	152	149[4]	147	144
Colombia[24] Colombie[24]								
All items								
Ensemble des prix	302	364	432	520[4]	578	634	688	738
Food								
Alimentation	280	326	379	465[4]	491	535	582	634
Congo[8] Congo[8]								
All items								
Ensemble des prix	154	170	198	194	202	200	200	209
Food								
Alimentation	149	159	199	198	207	197	193	202
Cook Islands[8] Îles Cook[8]								
All items								
Ensemble des prix	122	121	120	121[4]	123	127	138	143
Food [25]								
Alimentation [25]	115	114	114	116[4]	116	120	131	140
Costa Rica[26] Costa Rica[26]								
All items								
Ensemble des prix	241	283	320	358	394	437	486	530
Food [16]								
Alimentation [16]	100[18]	119[19]	136[19]	156[19]	171[19]	188[19]	208[19]	229[19]
Côte d'Ivoire[8] Côte d'Ivoire[8]								
All items								
Ensemble des prix	...	100[27]	104[28]	109[28]	110[28]	113[28]	117[28]	121[28]
Food [16,27]								
Alimentation [16,27]	...	...	...	...	...	...	...	126
Croatia Croatie								
All items								
Ensemble des prix	56 251	58 670	61 074	65 032	67 259	70 519[22]	73 714	75 169
Food								
Alimentation	54 112	55 844	58 305	62 270	62 294	62 507[22]	63 813	64 320
Cyprus Chypre								
All items								
Ensemble des prix	126	130	134	137[4]	140	145	148	153
Food								
Alimentation	128[16]	132[16]	139[16]	145[16]	101[29]	106[23]	111[23]	116[23]

32

Consumer price index numbers
All items and food: 1990 = 100 *[cont.]*

Indices des prix à la consommation
Ensemble des prix et alimentation : 1990 = 100 *[suite]*

Country or area Pays ou zone	1995	1996	1997	1998	1999	2000	2001	2002
Czech Republic République tchèque								
All items Ensemble des prix	252	275	298	330	337	350[4]	367	373
Food [12,30] Alimentation [12,30]	111	119	125	133	130	132[4]	138	138
Denmark Danemark								
All items Ensemble des prix	110	113	115	117	120	124[4]	127	130
Food Alimentation	108	110	114	116	117	120[4]	124	127
Dominica Dominique								
All items Ensemble des prix	115	116	119	121	122	123	100[31]	100[32]
Food Alimentation	114	116	120	120	121	120	100[31]	102[32]
Dominican Republic [33] Rép. dominicaine [33]								
All items Ensemble des prix	197	207	224	235[4]	251	270	294	309
Food [16] Alimentation [16]	188	197	212[4]	225	238	239	...	...
Ecuador Equateur								
All items Ensemble des prix	522[22]	649	847	1 153	1 756	3 443	4 740	5 332
Food [34] Alimentation [34]	489[22]	598	814	1 146	1 580	3 487	4 575	4 942
Egypt Egypte								
All items Ensemble des prix	179	192	200	207	218[4]	224	229	236
Food [2] Alimentation [2]	164	176	184	191	203[4]	209	211	220
El Salvador [17] El Salvador [17]								
All items Ensemble des prix	183	201	210	216	217	222	230	235
Food [2] Alimentation [2]	206	232	244	248	246	247	256	258
Equatorial Guinea [8] Guinée équatoriale [8]								
Food Alimentation	142	151	162	177	178	...	...	...
Estonia Estonie								
All items Ensemble des prix	4 252	5 232	5 817	108[13]	112[14]	116[14]	123[4,14]	127[14]
Food [35] Alimentation [35]	2 838	3 355	3 540	105[13]	101[14]	103[14]	112[4,14]	115[14]
Ethiopia incl. Eritrea [8] Ethiopie y comp. Erythrée [8]								
All items Ensemble des prix	184[14,21]	178[6]	100[37]	101[39]	105[39]	107[39]	101[4,39]	...
Food Alimentation	199[14]	189[14,36]	100[38]	102[25,39]	111[25,39]	110[25,39]	96[4,25,39]	...
Faeroe Islands Iles Féroé								
All items Ensemble des prix	118	121	124	130	137	142	149	149[4]
Food Alimentation	133	138	142	155	169	173	184	188[4]
Falkland Is. (Malvinas) [8] Iles Falkland (Malvinas) [8]								
All items Ensemble des prix	117	123	125	128	133[4]	139	141	142
Food Alimentation	124	128	124	...	...	...	...	...

32

Consumer price index numbers
All items and food: 1990 = 100 *[cont.]*

Indices des prix à la consommation
Ensemble des prix et alimentation : 1990 = 100 *[suite]*

Country or area Pays ou zone	1995	1996	1997	1998	1999	2000	2001	2002
Fiji Fidji								
All items								
Ensemble des prix	121	125	129	136	139	141	147	148
Food [40]								
Alimentation [40]	109	112	117	126	128	124	129	130
Finland Finlande								
All items								
Ensemble des prix	112[4]	113	114	116	117	121[4]	124	126
Food								
Alimentation	95[4]	93	94	96	96	97[4]	101	104
France France								
All items								
Ensemble des prix	112	114	115	116[4]	117	119	121	123
Food								
Alimentation	106	107	109	111[4]	111	114	119	123
French Guiana Guyane française								
All items								
Ensemble des prix	111	112	113	114[4]	114	115	117	119
Food								
Alimentation	107	108	109	111[4]	110	111	114	117
French Polynesia Polynésie française								
All items								
Ensemble des prix	107	108	109	111	112	113	114	117
Food								
Alimentation	107	108	111	112	112	113	115	121
Gabon [8,41] Gabon [8,41]								
All items								
Ensemble des prix	133	138	144	147	146	147	150	150
Food								
Alimentation	120	121	129	133	132	133	139	...
Gambia [8] Gambie [8]								
All items								
Ensemble des prix	138	139	143	145	150	152	158	...
Food								
Alimentation	137	139	141	146	151	152	151	...
Georgia [19,42] Géorgie [19,42]								
All items								
Ensemble des prix	100	139	149	155	184	192	201	212
Food [2]								
Alimentation [2]	100	133	139	145	171	174	185	199
Germany [41] Allemagne [41]								
All items								
Ensemble des prix	115	117	119	120[4]	120	123	126	127[4]
Food [16]								
Alimentation [16]	108	109	111	109	107	107	111	112[4]
Ghana Ghana								
All items								
Ensemble des prix	323	474	606	720[4]	810	1 014	1 347	...
Food								
Alimentation	307	417	504	610[4]	663	741	914	...
Gibraltar Gibraltar								
All items								
Ensemble des prix	124	126	128	130	131[4]	132	135	136
Food								
Alimentation	114	117	120	122	124[4]	125	130	134
Greece Grèce								
All items								
Ensemble des prix	191	207	218	229	235[4]	242	251	260
Food								
Alimentation	178	190	198	207	212[4]	216	227	239

32

Consumer price index numbers
All items and food: 1990 = 100 *[cont.]*

Indices des prix à la consommation
Ensemble des prix et alimentation : 1990 = 100 *[suite]*

Country or area Pays ou zone	1995	1996	1997	1998	1999	2000	2001	2002
Greenland Groenland								
All items								
Ensemble des prix	109	111	112	113	114[4]	115	119	124
Food								
Alimentation	113[2]	118	120	122	101[43]	104[23]	107[23]	112[23]
Grenada Grenade								
All items								
Ensemble des prix	115	118	120	121	122	125	129	130
Food[2]								
Alimentation[2]	118	123	123	125	125	126	131	134
Guadeloupe Guadeloupe								
All items								
Ensemble des prix	112	114	115	117[4]	118	118	121	123
Food								
Alimentation	111	113	114	117[4]	117	115	121	124
Guam Guam								
All items								
Ensemble des prix	162	170[4]	173	172	171	...	...	...
Food								
Alimentation	226	...	100[13]	101[14]	101[14]	...	...	...
Guatemala[8] Guatemala[8]								
All items								
Ensemble des prix	206	229	250	266	280	297	319[4]	345
Food								
Alimentation	205	229	244	256	261	273	300[4]	331
Guinea[8] Guinée[8]								
All items								
Ensemble des prix	165	170[4]	173	182	190	203	214	220
Food								
Alimentation	167	169[4]	168	185	195	203	...	...
Guinea-Bissau[8,16] Guinée-Bissau[8,16]								
Food								
Alimentation	663	999	1 490	1 609	1 575	1 690	...	...
Guyana[8,41] Guyana[8,41]								
All items								
Ensemble des prix	174	186	193	202	217	230	237	249
Food[2]								
Alimentation[2]	174	187	189	196	213	221	223	231
Haiti[11] Haïti[11]								
All items								
Ensemble des prix	228	...	100[13]	111[14]	120[14]	137[14]	156[14]	171[14]
Food								
Alimentation	216	...	100[13]	110[14]	112[14]	123[14]	142[14]	156[14]
Honduras Honduras								
All items								
Ensemble des prix	254	315	378	430	480	509[4]	558	601
Food								
Alimentation	281	350	420	469	506	531[4]	577	599
Hungary Hongrie								
All items								
Ensemble des prix	310	383	453	518	570	625	683	719
Food								
Alimentation	304	357	419	480	494	539	614	647
Iceland[44] Islande[44]								
All items								
Ensemble des prix	119	122	124	126	130	137	146	153
Food								
Alimentation	107	111	114	117	121	126	135	140

32

Consumer price index numbers
All items and food: 1990 = 100 *[cont.]*

Indices des prix à la consommation
Ensemble des prix et alimentation : 1990 = 100 *[suite]*

Country or area Pays ou zone	1995	1996	1997	1998	1999	2000	2001	2002
India[45] Inde[45]								
All items								
Ensemble des prix	165	180	192	218	228	237	246	256
Food								
Alimentation	173	188	199	229	232	237	242	248
Indonesia Indonésie								
All items								
Ensemble des prix	153	165	176	278[4]	335[46]	348	387	433
Food								
Alimentation	156	171	186	358[4]	448[46]	426	462	512
Iran (Islamic Rep. of) Iran (Rép. islamique d')								
All items								
Ensemble des prix	353	455	534	637	771[4]	868	967	1 075
Food [2]								
Alimentation [2]	405	506	557	688	856[4]	931	1 000	1 138
Iraq Iraq								
All items								
Ensemble des prix	43 295	36 317	...	...	...	...	...	...
Ireland Irlande								
All items								
Ensemble des prix	113	115	117[4]	120	122	128	135	141[4]
Food								
Alimentation	110	112	114[4]	119	123	128	136	141[4]
Isle of Man Ile de Man								
All items								
Ensemble des prix	121	124	127	131	133	137[4]	139	143
Food								
Alimentation	126	133	135	143	148	153[4]	160	173
Israel Israël								
All items								
Ensemble des prix	183	203	222	234[4]	246	249	251	266[4]
Food								
Alimentation	161	177	193	204[4]	218	223	229	235[4]
Italy Italie								
All items [47]								
Ensemble des prix [47]	128[4]	133	135	138	140	144	148	152
Food								
Alimentation	126[4,34]	131[34]	131[34]	132[34]	133	135	141	146
Jamaica Jamaïque								
All items								
Ensemble des prix	530	669	734	797	845	914	978	1 047
Food								
Alimentation	554	688	742	794	812	869	899	954
Japan Japon								
All items								
Ensemble des prix	107[4]	107	109	110	109	109[4]	108	107
Food								
Alimentation	106[4]	106	108	109	109	107[4]	106	105
Jordan Jordanie								
All items								
Ensemble des prix	123	131	135[4]	139	140	141	144	146
Food								
Alimentation	126	135	144[4]	150	149	148	148	148
Kazakhstan[1] Kazakhstan[1]								
All items								
Ensemble des prix	38 389	53 476	62 776	67 246	72 834	82 419	89 309	94 533
Food								
Alimentation	35 521	47 882	50 946	53 208	57 162	66 302	73 894	78 926

32

Consumer price index numbers
All items and food: 1990 = 100 *[cont.]*

Indices des prix à la consommation
Ensemble des prix et alimentation : 1990 = 100 *[suite]*

Country or area Pays ou zone	1995	1996	1997	1998	1999	2000	2001	2002
Kenya[8,24] Kenya[8,24]								
All items Ensemble des prix	297	319	357	378	388	410[4]	425	432
Food Alimentation	310	335	388	402	408	422[4]	432	438
Kiribati[8] Kiribati[8]								
All items Ensemble des prix	127	127	127[5]	...	...	...	...	...
Food Alimentation	123	121	120[5]	...	...	...	...	...
Korea, Republic of Corée, République de								
All items Ensemble des prix	135[4]	142	148	159	160	164[4]	171	176
Food Alimentation	140[4]	145	151	164	169	170[4]	176	183
Kuwait[50] Koweït[50]								
All items Ensemble des prix	126	130	131	131	135	138	140	141[4]
Food Alimentation	120	127	127	128	134	135	135	136[4]
Kyrgyzstan[1] Kirghizistan[1]								
All items Ensemble des prix	4 776[4]	6 303	7 780	8 593	11 678	13 862	14 822	15 139
Food Alimentation	3 898[4]	5 504	6 874	7 593	10 605	12 679	13 407	13 446
Lao People's Dem. Rep.[28] Rép. dém. pop. lao[28]								
All items Ensemble des prix	...	100	120	227	519	...	...	...
Food Alimentation	...	100	125	242	529	...	...	...
Latvia[41] Lettonie[41]								
All items Ensemble des prix	3 735[4]	4 393	4 766	4 986	5 102	5 240	5 371	5 476[4]
Food Alimentation	1 708[4]	1 919	1 969	1 995	1 974	1 986	2 082	2 153[4]
Lebanon[8] Liban[8]								
All items Ensemble des prix	413	438	447	...	...	...	...	...
Food Alimentation	350	379	377	...	...	...	...	...
Lesotho Lesotho								
All items[21] Ensemble des prix[21]	185	202	219[4]	236	257	272	291	325
Food Alimentation	100[51]	110[52]	120[52]	131[52]	140[52]	147[52]	157[52]	198[52]
Lithuania[41] Lituanie[41]								
All items Ensemble des prix	13 749	17 135	18 656	19 602	19 751	19 937	20 196	20 256[4]
Food Alimentation	13 846	17 687	18 760	18 732	17 997	17 563	18 193	18 054[4]
Luxembourg Luxembourg								
All items Ensemble des prix	115	116	118	119	120	124	127	130
Food[35] Alimentation[35]	108	109[4]	110	113	114	116	122	127
Madagascar Madagascar								
All items Ensemble des prix	283[8,21]	339[8,21]	355[8,21]	377[8,21]	414[8,21]	463[8,21]	107[39]	125[39]
Food Alimentation	291[8]	346[8]	360[8]	382[8]	428[8]	489[8]	102[39]	117[39]

32

Consumer price index numbers
All items and food: 1990 = 100 *[cont.]*

Indices des prix à la consommation
Ensemble des prix et alimentation : 1990 = 100 *[suite]*

Country or area Pays ou zone	1995	1996	1997	1998	1999	2000	2001	2002
Malawi Malawi								
All items								
Ensemble des prix	404	556	607	788	1 141	1 478	1 814[4]	2 081
Food								
Alimentation	469	681	737	941	1 346	1 612	1 895[4]	2 198
Malaysia Malaisie								
All items								
Ensemble des prix	121	126	129	136	140	142[4]	144	146
Food								
Alimentation	126	133	139	151	158	161[4]	162	164
Maldives[8] Maldives[8]								
All items								
Ensemble des prix	176	189	226	215	224	213	218	205
Food[16]								
Alimentation[16]	177	191	198	206	216	193	213	231
Mali[8] Mali[8]								
All items								
Ensemble des prix	133	142	141	146[4]	145	144	151	159
Food								
Alimentation	135	147	144	104[53]	100[28]	96[28]	103[28]	111[28]
Malta Malte								
All items								
Ensemble des prix	118[4]	120	124	127	129	132	136	139
Food								
Alimentation	115[4]	119	120	123	124	126	133	135
Marshall Islands[1,8] Iles Marshall[1,8]								
All items								
Ensemble des prix	119	...	...	...	...	...	...	...
Martinique Martinique								
All items								
Ensemble des prix	116	117	119	120[4]	120	122	124	127
Food[2]								
Alimentation[2]	113	114	116	119[4]	119	118	123	130
Mauritania Mauritanie								
All items								
Ensemble des prix	141	148	154	167	173	179	188	195
Food								
Alimentation	135	145	151	165	171	177	189	...
Mauritius Maurice								
All items								
Ensemble des prix	141	150	160[4]	171	183	190	201	216[4]
Food								
Alimentation	142	149	157[4]	169	180	183	190	205[4]
Mexico Mexique								
All items								
Ensemble des prix	225	302	364	422	492	539	573	602[4]
Food[16]								
Alimentation[16]	209	296	352	409	474	503	530	552[4]
Mongolia[28] Mongolie[28]								
All items								
Ensemble des prix	...	100	137	149	161	179	191[4]	192
Food								
Alimentation	...	100	125	128	133[4]	152	155	150
Morocco Maroc								
All items								
Ensemble des prix	134	138	139	143	144	147	148	152
Food[2]								
Alimentation[2]	143	144	142	146	145	147	146	152

32

Consumer price index numbers
All items and food: 1990 = 100 *[cont.]*

Indices des prix à la consommation
Ensemble des prix et alimentation : 1990 = 100 *[suite]*

Country or area Pays ou zone	1995	1996	1997	1998	1999	2000	2001	2002
Mozambique[8,23] Mozambique[8,23]								
All items								
Ensemble des prix	62	92	99	100	103	116	126	148
Food								
Alimentation	68	98	101	100	94	106	114	134
Myanmar Myanmar								
All items								
Ensemble des prix	330[8]	384[8]	100[14]	125[14]	152[14]	152[14]	184[14]	289[14]
Food								
Alimentation	354[8]	421[8]	100[14]	125[14]	152[14]	148[14]	177[14]	299[14]
Namibia[8] Namibie[8]								
All items								
Ensemble des prix	174	188	205	218	236	258	282	314
Food								
Alimentation	170	182	196	201	212	227	253	302
Nepal Népal								
All items								
Ensemble des prix	170	185[22]	198	221	236	241	248	...
Food								
Alimentation	171	189[22]	199	229	247	240	244	...
Netherlands Pays-Bas								
All items								
Ensemble des prix	114[4]	117	119	122	124	127	133	137[4]
Food								
Alimentation	109[2]	100[54]	102[19]	104[19]	105[19]	106[19]	113[19]	117[4,19]
Netherlands Antilles[8] Antilles néerlandaises[8]								
All items								
Ensemble des prix	113	117[4]	120	122	122	129	132	132
Food								
Alimentation	122	129[4]	132	133	136	145	149	155
New Caledonia[8] Nouvelle-Calédonie[8]								
All items								
Ensemble des prix	114	116	118	119	120	122	124	127
Food								
Alimentation	115	118	123	124	125	126	129	132
New Zealand Nouvelle-Zélande								
All items								
Ensemble des prix	111	113	115	116[4]	116	119	122	125
Food								
Alimentation	103	104	107	110[4]	111	113	120	123
Nicaragua[8] Nicaragua[8]								
All items								
Ensemble des prix	5 421	6 050	6 608	7 470	8 308	9 267	9 949[4]	10 346
Food								
Alimentation	4 711	5 248	5 724	6 541	6 898	7 243	7 869[4]	8 096
Niger[8] Niger[8]								
All items [21]								
Ensemble des prix [21]	142	150	154	162[4]	159	163	170	174
Food [2]								
Alimentation [2]	145	162	171	184[55]	174	179	192	201
Nigeria Nigéria								
All items								
Ensemble des prix	688	901	975	1 076	1 147	1 226	1 458	1 602
Food								
Alimentation	654	851	924	985	994	1 018	1 304	1 445
Niue Nioué								
All items								
Ensemble des prix	114	114	117	119	120	124	132	136
Food								
Alimentation	113	111	114	114	114	120	134	138

32

Consumer price index numbers
All items and food: 1990 = 100 *[cont.]*

Indices des prix à la consommation
Ensemble des prix et alimentation : 1990 = 100 *[suite]*

Country or area Pays ou zone	1995	1996	1997	1998	1999	2000	2001	2002
Norfolk Island [41] Ile Norfolk [41]								
All items								
Ensemble des prix	113	117	119	123	127	132	136	...
Food								
Alimentation	112	117	118	120	122	126	131	...
Northern Mariana Islands [8] Iles Mariannes du Nord [8]								
All items								
Ensemble des prix	128	131	133	133	134	137	136	136
Food								
Alimentation	119	121	121	120	119	118	114	110
Norway Norvège								
All items								
Ensemble des prix	112	114	117	119[4]	122	126	130	132
Food								
Alimentation	105[56]	107[56]	110[56]	116[57]	120	122	119	117
Occupied Palestinian Terr. [28] Terr. palestinien occupé [28]								
All items								
Ensemble des prix	...	100	108	114	120	123	125	132
Food								
Alimentation	...	100	106	114	119	121	121	124
Oman [8] Oman [8]								
All items								
Ensemble des prix	105[22]	105	105	104	105	104	103	102
Food [2]								
Alimentation [2]	102[22]	104	105	104	104	103	102	101
Pakistan Pakistan								
All items								
Ensemble des prix	170	188	209	222	231	241	249	259[4]
Food								
Alimentation	177	193	217	229	238	246	250	260[4]
Panama [8] Panama [8]								
All items								
Ensemble des prix	106	107	109	109	111	112	113	114
Food								
Alimentation	108	109	110	110	110	111	111	110
Papua New Guinea Papouasie-Nvl-Guinée								
All items								
Ensemble des prix	141	158	164	186	214	247	270	302
Food								
Alimentation	137	156	166	188	220	250	274	321
Paraguay [8] Paraguay [8]								
All items								
Ensemble des prix	231	254	272	303	324	353	378	418
Food								
Alimentation	224	237	247	275	284	307	319	352
Peru [8,11] Pérou [8,11]								
All items								
Ensemble des prix	1 806	2 015	2 187	2 346	2 427	2 518	2 568	2 573
Food								
Alimentation	1 479	1 659	1 776	1 923	1 918	1 933	1 942	1 937
Philippines Philippines								
All items								
Ensemble des prix	161	176	186	204	217	227	241	248
Food [16]								
Alimentation [16]	154	170	175	191	201	205	213	217
Poland [34] Pologne [34]								
All items								
Ensemble des prix	557	668	767	858	107[43]	118[23]	125[23]	127[23]
Food								
Alimentation	462	550	620	671	102[43]	112[23]	118[23]	117[23]

32

Consumer price index numbers
All items and food: 1990 = 100 *[cont.]*

Indices des prix à la consommation
Ensemble des prix et alimentation : 1990 = 100 *[suite]*

Country or area Pays ou zone	1995	1996	1997	1998	1999	2000	2001	2002
Portugal Portugal								
All items [21]								
Ensemble des prix [21]	142	146	149[4]	153	157	161	168	174
Food [58]								
Alimentation [58]	132	135	136[4]	141	143	147	156	158
Puerto Rico Porto Rico								
All items								
Ensemble des prix	118	124	131	138	146	155	166	177
Food								
Alimentation	142	156	174	195	215	235	268	300
Qatar Qatar								
All items								
Ensemble des prix	111	119	122	126	129	131	...	...
Food [2]								
Alimentation [2]	104	108	108	112	112	113	...	...
Republic of Moldova [1] République de Moldova [1]								
All items								
Ensemble des prix	13 064	16 135	18 034	19 422	27 046	35 512	38 979	41 046
Food								
Alimentation	10 168	12 148	13 004	13 525	17 954	24 487	27 108	28 275
Réunion Réunion								
All items								
Ensemble des prix	116	118	119	121[4]	122	124	127	130
Food								
Alimentation	113	115	117	120[4]	119	119	121	129
Romania [41] Roumanie [41]								
All items								
Ensemble des prix	3 461	4 805	12 241	19 474	28 394	41 361	55 617	68 152
Food								
Alimentation	3 657	4 987	12 536	18 607	23 789	34 188	46 391	54 880
Russian Federation [41] Fédération de Russie [41]								
All items								
Ensemble des prix	192 520	284 428[4]	326 483	416 813[4]	773 813	934 450	1 135 162[4]	...
Food								
Alimentation	210 975	287 151[4]	323 748	412 043[4]	810 254	952 103	1 148 071	...
Rwanda [8] Rwanda [8]								
All items								
Ensemble des prix	293[59]	315	352[60]	374	365	380	392	400
Food								
Alimentation	279[59]	291	361	393	335	338	358	354
Saint Helena Sainte-Hélène								
All items								
Ensemble des prix	128	134	137	139	142	144	149	100[7]
Food								
Alimentation	121	126	126	124	126	126	130	100[7]
Saint Kitts and Nevis [8] Saint-Kitts-et-Nevis [8]								
All items								
Ensemble des prix	114	116	127	131	135	138	...	...
Food								
Alimentation	119	123	134	141	141	145	...	...
Saint Lucia Sainte-Lucie								
All items								
Ensemble des prix	123	124	124	128	133	137	140	140
Food								
Alimentation	128	128	124	130	133	135	139	138
Saint Pierre and Miquelon Saint-Pierre-et-Miquelon								
All items								
Ensemble des prix	...	...	100[13]	101[14]	102[14]	111[14]	113[14]	...
Food								
Alimentation	...	...	100[13]	102[14]	104[14]	110[14]	113[14]	...

32

Consumer price index numbers
All items and food: 1990 = 100 *[cont.]*

Indices des prix à la consommation
Ensemble des prix et alimentation : 1990 = 100 *[suite]*

Country or area Pays ou zone	1995	1996	1997	1998	1999	2000	2001	2002
St. Vincent-Grenadines[8] St. Vincent-Grenadines[8]								
All items								
Ensemble des prix	118	123	124	126	128	128	129	131[4]
Food								
Alimentation	120	128	127	124	125	123	125	126[4]
Samoa Samoa								
All items[21]								
Ensemble des prix[21]	130	139	155	137	...	...	...	...
Food								
Alimentation	128	144	160	123	...	...	...	...
San Marino Saint-Marin								
All items								
Ensemble des prix	132[4]	137	140	143	148	152	...	...
Food								
Alimentation	128[4]	132	136	139	142	144	...	...
Saudi Arabia[61] Arabie saoudite[61]								
All items								
Ensemble des prix	111	112	112	111	110	109	108	108
Food[2]								
Alimentation[2]	112	114	116	117	114	113	114	113
Senegal[8] Sénégal[8]								
All items								
Ensemble des prix	139	143	146	147[4]	148	149	154	157
Food								
Alimentation	143[47]	145[47]	146[47]	152[55]	152	150	158	166
Serbia and Montenegro[14] Serbie-et-Monténégro[14]								
All items								
Ensemble des prix	43	82	100	130	188	349	661	770
Food								
Alimentation	46	84	100	133	193	397	746	795
Seychelles Seychelles								
All items								
Ensemble des prix	108	107	108	111	118	125	132[4]	133
Food								
Alimentation	99	96	98	101	100	101	106[4]	107
Sierra Leone[8] Sierra Leone[8]								
All items								
Ensemble des prix	517	637	731	992	1 330	1 318	1 347	...
Food								
Alimentation	310	379	405	534	716	714	751	...
Singapore Singapour								
All items								
Ensemble des prix	113	115	117	117[22]	117	119	120	119
Food								
Alimentation	110	112	114	115[22]	116	116	117	117
Slovakia Slovaquie								
All items								
Ensemble des prix	272	288	305	326	360	403	432[4]	446
Food								
Alimentation	260	270	286	303	311	327	346[4]	351
Slovenia[17] Slovénie[17]								
All items								
Ensemble des prix	1 208	1 327	1 438	1 552	1 647	1 793	1 944	2 089
Food								
Alimentation	1 162	1 271	1 378	1 495	1 555	1 640	1 788	1 926
Solomon Islands[8] Iles Salomon[8]								
All items								
Ensemble des prix	166	186	201	226	244	262	279	300
Food[34]								
Alimentation[34]	162	184	205	231	256	272	296	323

32

Consumer price index numbers
All items and food: 1990 = 100 *[cont.]*

Indices des prix à la consommation
Ensemble des prix et alimentation : 1990 = 100 *[suite]*

Country or area Pays ou zone	1995	1996	1997	1998	1999	2000	2001	2002
South Africa Afrique du Sud								
All items Ensemble des prix	171	183	199	213	224	236	249[4]	274
Food Alimentation	198	210	230	244	256	276	291[4]	337
Spain Espagne								
All items Ensemble des prix	129	133	136	138	142	146	152	104[31]
Food Alimentation	111[9]	114[9]	113[9]	115[9]	116[9]	119[9]	126[9]	105[31]
Sri Lanka[8] Sri Lanka[8]								
All items Ensemble des prix	163	189	207	227	237	252	287	315
Food Alimentation	162	193	214	238	247	258	297	329
Sudan[24] Soudan[24]								
All items Ensemble des prix	3 482	8 192	...	...	...	...	...	...
Suriname[8] Suriname[8]								
All items Ensemble des prix	6 934	6 879	7 371	8 773	17 446	27 797[62]	38 541[4]	...
Food Alimentation	7 842	7 267	7 209	8 244	15 708	24 273	32 354[4]	...
Swaziland[24] Swaziland[24]								
All items Ensemble des prix	171	183[4]	198	213	225	247	266	297
Food Alimentation	207	229[4]	256	267	280	299	318	387
Sweden Suède								
All items Ensemble des prix	123	123	124	124	125	126	129	131
Food Alimentation	103	96	96	97	99	99	102	105
Switzerland Suisse								
All items Ensemble des prix	117	118	118	118	119	121[4]	122	123
Food Alimentation	105	105	106	106	106	108[4]	110	113
Syrian Arab Republic Rép. arabe syrienne								
All items Ensemble des prix	170	185	189	188	184	183	184	186
Food Alimentation	155	169	173	169	162	159	159	158
Tajikistan Tadjikistan								
All items Ensemble des prix	804 300	2 977 530	5 112 430	73 106 500	92 114 190	114 221 600	...	...
Food Alimentation	1 066 000	4 065 760	7 172 000	...	...	...	...	...
Thailand Thaïlande								
All items Ensemble des prix	126	134	141	153	153	156	158[4]	...
Food Alimentation	132	144	154	168	167	165	166[4]	...
TFYR of Macedonia L'ex-R.y. Macédoine								
All items Ensemble des prix	41 444	42 401	43 499	43 468	43 154	45 665	48 176	49 039
Food Alimentation	37 382	37 336	38 910	38 833	38 216	38 061	40 685	41 411

32

Consumer price index numbers
All items and food: 1990 = 100 *[cont.]*

Indices des prix à la consommation
Ensemble des prix et alimentation : 1990 = 100 *[suite]*

Country or area Pays ou zone	1995	1996	1997	1998	1999	2000	2001	2002
Togo[8] **Togo**[8]								
All items								
Ensemble des prix	165	173	187	184[4]	184	187	206	201
Food[16]								
Alimentation[16]	100[18]	106[19]	121[19]	109[28]	104[28]	100[28]	...	109[28]
Tonga **Tonga**								
All items[21]								
Ensemble des prix[21]	122	126	129	133	138	147	160	176[4]
Food								
Alimentation	117	126	130	138	145	146	163	191[4]
Trinidad and Tobago **Trinité-et-Tobago**								
All items								
Ensemble des prix	140	145	150	159	164	170	179	187
Food								
Alimentation	188	208	228	262	285	309	352	...
Tunisia **Tunisie**								
All items								
Ensemble des prix	132	137	142	147	151	155	158	163[4]
Food								
Alimentation	132	137	143	147	150	157	159	166[4]
Turkey **Turquie**								
All items								
Ensemble des prix	1 872	339[12]	630[12]	1 163[12]	1 917[12]	2 970[12]	4 586[12]	6 649[12]
Food[2]								
Alimentation[2]	1 938	331[12]	637[12]	1 162[12]	1 727[12]	2 587[12]	3 887[12]	5 828[12]
Tuvalu[8] **Tuvalu**[8]								
All items								
Ensemble des prix	109	110	112	112	...	...	...	...
Food								
Alimentation	109	110	110	110	...	...	...	...
Uganda **Ouganda**								
All items								
Ensemble des prix	243	260	281	283	300	310	315	315
Food								
Alimentation	238	254	300	294	314	317	306	293
Ukraine[1] **Ukraine**[1]								
All items								
Ensemble des prix	228 471[16]	411 775[16]	477 190[16]	527 663[16]	647 356	829 931	929 180	936 218[16]
Food								
Alimentation	226 059[16]	357 921[16]	399 575[16]	446 690[16]	570 891	767 855	878 102	878 110[16]
United Arab Emirates **Emirats arabes unis**								
All items								
Ensemble des prix	129[4]	132	135	138	141	143[4]	147	151
Food[63]								
Alimentation[63]	115[4]	120	125	127	130	131[4]	132	134
United Kingdom **Royaume-Uni**								
All items								
Ensemble des prix	118	121	125	129	131	135	137	140
Food								
Alimentation	115	118	119	120	120	120	124	125
United Rep. of Tanzania **Rép.-Unie de Tanzanie**								
All items								
Ensemble des prix	336	406	471	532	574	608	639	668
Food								
Alimentation	347	417	490	562	612	653	693	722
United States[64] **Etats-Unis**[64]								
All items								
Ensemble des prix	117	120	123	125	127	132	136	138
Food								
Alimentation	112	116	119	121	124	127	131	133

32

Consumer price index numbers
All items and food: 1990 = 100 *[cont.]*

Indices des prix à la consommation
Ensemble des prix et alimentation : 1990 = 100 *[suite]*

Country or area Pays ou zone	1995	1996	1997	1998	1999	2000	2001	2002
Uruguay[8] **Uruguay**[8]								
All items Ensemble des prix	1 079	1 385	1 661[4]	1 839	1 943	2 036	2 125	2 422
Food Alimentation	894	1 105	1 308[4]	1 444	1 498	1 582	1 631	1 855
Vanuatu **Vanuatu**								
All items Ensemble des prix	120	121	124	129	131[4]	134	139	142
Food Alimentation	113	112	113	117	118[4]	121	123	124
Venezuela[8] **Venezuela**[8]								
All items Ensemble des prix	627	1 252	1 879	2 551	3 153	3 664[4]	4 122	5 048
Food Alimentation	606	1 140	1 666	2 312	2 704	2 898[4]	3 366	4 317
Viet Nam **Viet Nam**								
All items[63] Ensemble des prix[63]	347	367	379	408	426	419	418	434
Food Alimentation	380	406	408	449	467	450	443	...
Yemen **Yémen**								
All items Ensemble des prix	563	736	752	797	866	906	1 013	...
Food Alimentation	630	825	849	896	989	1 041	1 205	...
Zambia **Zambie**								
All items Ensemble des prix	3 137	4 488	5 581	6 951	8 814	11 109	13 486	16 484
Food[16] Alimentation[16]	3 380	4 818	5 850	7 288	8 933	10 950	13 018	16 540
Zimbabwe **Zimbabwe**								
All items Ensemble des prix	335[4]	407	484	637	1 010	1 574	2 706	6 310
Food Alimentation	429[4]	545	641	893	1 500	2 234	3 579	8 412

Source:
International Labour Office (ILO), Geneva, the ILO labour statistics database and the "Yearbook of Labour Statistics 2003".

Source:
Bureau international du Travail (BIT), Genève, la base de données du BIT et "l'Annuaire des statistiques du travail 2003".

1 Index base: 1992=100.	1 Indice base : 1992=100.
2 Including tobacco.	2 Y compris le tabac.
3 Series (base 2000=100) replacing former series; prior to 2000: including alcoholic beverages and tobacco.	3 Série (base 2000=100) remplaçant la précédente; avant 2000: y compris les boissons alcoolisées et le tabac.
4 Series linked to former series.	4 Série enchaînée à la précédente.
5 Average of the first three quarters.	5 Moyenne des trois premiers trimestres.
6 Series linked to former series; average of the last three quarters.	6 Série enchaînée à la précédente; moyenne des trois derniers trimestres.
7 Series (base 2000=100) replacing former series.	7 Série (base 2000=100) remplaçant la précédente.
8 Data refer to the index of the capital city.	8 Les données se réfèrent à l'indice de la ville principale.
9 Index base: 1993=100.	9 Indice base : 1993=100.
10 January-November.	10 Janvier-novembre.
11 Metropolitan area.	11 Région métropolitaine.
12 Index base: 1994=100.	12 Indice base : 1994=100.
13 Series (base 1997 = 100) replacing former series.	13 Série (base 1997 = 100) remplaçant la précédente.
14 Index base: 1997=100.	14 Indice base : 1997=100.
15 Government officials.	15 Fonctionnaires.
16 Including alcoholic beverages and tobacco.	16 Y compris les boissons alcoolisées et le tabac.
17 Urban areas.	17 Régions urbaines.

32

Consumer price index numbers
All items and food: 1990 = 100 *[cont.]*

Indices des prix à la consommation
Ensemble des prix et alimentation : 1990 = 100 *[suite]*

18	Series (base 1995 = 100) replacing former series.		18	Série (base 1995 = 100) remplaçant la précédente.
19	Index base: 1995=100.		19	Indice base : 1995=100.
20	Beginning 1997, including tobacco.		20	A partir 1997, y compris le tabac.
21	Excluding rent.		21	Non compris le groupe "Loyer".
22	Series replacing former series.		22	Série remplaçant la précédente.
23	Index base: 1998=100.		23	Indice base : 1998=100.
24	Low-income group.		24	Familles à revenu modique.
25	Excluding beverages.		25	Non compris les boissons.
26	Central area.		26	Région centrale.
27	Prior to 1996: low income group; series (base 1996=100) replacing former series.		27	Avant 1996: familles à revenu modique; série (base 1996=100) remplaçant la précédente.
28	Index base: 1996=100.		28	Indices base: 1996=100.
29	Series (base 1998 = 100) replacing former series. Prior to 1999 including alcoholic beverages and tobacco.		29	Série (base 1998=100) remplaçant la précédente; avant 1999 y compris les boissons alcoolisées et le tabac.
30	Including tobacco, beverages and public catering.		30	Y compris le tabac, les boissons et la restauration.
31	Series (base 2001 = 100) replacing former series.		31	Série (base 2001 = 100) remplaçant la précédente.
32	Index base: 2001=100.		32	Indice base : 2001=100.
33	Including direct taxes.		33	Y compris les impôts directs.
34	Including alcoholic beverages.		34	Y compris les boissons alcoolisées.
35	Excluding alcoholic beverages and tobacco.		35	Non compris les boissons alcoolisées et le tabac.
36	January-August.		36	Janvier-août.
37	Prior to sept. 1996: excl. 'Rent'; series (2000 = 100) replacing former series.		37	Avant sept.1996: non compris le groupe 'Loyer'; série (base 2000 = 100) remplaçant la précédente.
38	Beginning Sept. 1996: excluding. beverages; series (base 2000 = 100) replacing former series.		38	A partir de sept. 1996: non compris les boissons; série (base 2000 = 100) remplaçant la précédente.
39	Index base: 2000 = 100.		39	Indices base : 2000 = 100.
40	Excluding beverages and tobacco.		40	Non compris les boissons et le tabac.
41	Index base: 1991=100.		41	Indice base : 1991=100.
42	5 cities.		42	5 villes.
43	Series (base 1998 = 100) replacing former series.		43	Série (base 1998 = 100) remplaçant la précédente.
44	Annual averages are based on the months Feb.-Dec. and the mean of January both years.		44	Les moyennes annuelles sont basées sur les mois de fév.-déc. et la moyenne de janvier des deux années.
45	Industrial workers.		45	Travailleurs de l'industrie.
46	Since November 1999: excluding Dili.		46	A partir de novembre 1999: non compris Dili.
47	Excluding tobacco.		47	Non compris le tabac.
48	Index base: June 2000=100.		48	Indice base : juin 2000=100.
49	June of each year.		49	Juin de chaque année.
50	Index base: 1989=100.		50	Indice base : 1989=100.
51	Series (base 1995=100) replacing former series; prior to 1995 incl. alcoholic beverages and tobacco.		51	Série (base 1995=100) remplaçant la précédente; avant 1995 y compris les boissons alcoolisées et le tabac.
52	March-December; Series linked to fomer series.		52	Mars-décembre; série enchaînée à la précédente.
53	Series (base 1996 = 100) replacing former series.		53	Série (base 1996 = 100) remplaçant la précédente.
54	Series (base 2000 = 100) replacing former series; prior to 1995: incl. tobacco.		54	Série (base 2000 = 100) remplaçant la précédente; avant 1995 y compris le tabac.
55	Series linked to former series; prior 1998: excluding tobacco.		55	Série enchaînée à la précédente; avant 1998: non compris le tabac.
56	Food only.		56	Alimentation seulement.
57	Series replacing former series; prior to 1998: Food only.		57	Série remplaçant la précédente; avant 1998: alimentation seulement.
58	Excluding alcoholic beverages.		58	Non compris les boissons alcooliques.
59	April-December.		59	Avril-décembre.
60	10 months' average.		60	Moyenne de 10 mois.
61	All cities.		61	Ensemble des villes.
62	Official estimate.		62	Estimation officielle.
63	Including beverages and tobacco.		63	Y compris les boissons et le tabac.
64	All urban consumers.		64	Tous les consommateurs urbains.

Technical notes, tables 30-32

Table 30: The series generally relate to the average earnings per worker in manufacturing industries, according to the *International Standard Industrial Classification of All Economic Activities* (ISIC) Revision 2 or Revision 3 [50]. The data are published in the ILO *Yearbook of Labour Statistics* [13] and on the ILO Web site <http://laborsta.ilo.org> and generally cover all employees (i.e. wage earners and salaried employees) of both sexes, irrespective of age. Data which refer exclusively to wage earners (i.e. manual or production workers), salaried employees (i.e. non-manual workers), or to total employment are also shown when available. Earnings generally include bonuses, cost of living allowances, taxes, social insurance contributions payable by the employed person and, in some cases, payments in kind, and normally exclude social insurance contributions payable by the employers, family allowances and other social security benefits. The time of year to which the figures refer is not the same for all countries. In some cases, the series may show wage rates instead of earnings; this is indicated in footnotes.

Table 31: Producer prices are prices at which producers sell their output on the domestic market or for export. Wholesale prices, in the strict sense, are prices at which wholesalers sell their goods on the domestic market or for export. In practice, many national wholesale price indexes are a mixture of producer and wholesale prices for domestic goods representing prices for purchases in large quantities from either source. In addition, these indexes may cover the prices of goods imported in quantity for the domestic market either by producers or by retail or wholesale distributors.

Producer or wholesale price indexes normally cover the prices of the characteristic products of agriculture, forestry and fishing, mining and quarrying, manufacturing, and electricity, gas and water supply. Prices are normally measured in terms of transaction prices, including non-deductible indirect taxes less subsidies, in the case of domestically-produced goods and import duties and other non-deductible indirect taxes less subsidies in the case of imported goods.

The Laspeyres index number formula is generally used and, for the purpose of the presentation, the national index numbers have been recalculated, where necessary, on the reference base 1990=100.

The price index numbers for each country are arranged according to the following scheme:
(a) Components of supply
     Domestic supply
     Domestic production for domestic market

Notes techniques, tableaux 30 à 32

Tableau 30: Les séries se rapportent généralement aux gains moyens des salariés des industries manufacturières (activités de fabrication), suivant la *Classification internationale type, par industrie, de toutes les branches d'activité économique* (CITI, Rev. 2 ou Rev.3) [50]. Les données sont publiées dans *l'Annuaire des statistiques du travail* du BIT [13] et sur le site Web du BIT <http://laborsta.ilo.org> et généralement portent sur l'ensemble des salariés (qu'ils perçoivent un salaire ou un traitement au mois) des deux sexes, indépendamment de leur âge. Les données que portent exclusivement sur les salariés horaires (ouvriers, travailleurs manuels), sur les employés percevant un traitement (travailleurs autres que manuels, cadres), ou sur l'emploi total sont aussi présentées si elles sont disponibles. Les gains comprennent en général les primes, les indemnités pour coût de la vie, les impôts, les cotisations de sécurité sociale à la charge de l'employé, et dans certains cas des paiements en nature, mais ne comprennent pas en règle générale la part patronale des cotisations d'assurance sociale, les allocations familiales et les autres prestations de sécurité sociale. La période de l'année visée par les données n'est pas la même pour tous les pays. Dans certains cas, les séries visent les taux horaires et non pas les gains, ce qui est alors signalé en note.

Tableau 31: Les prix à la production sont les prix auxquels les producteurs vendent leur production sur le marché intérieur ou à l'exportation. Les prix de gros, au sens strict du terme, sont les prix auxquels les grossistes vendent sur le marché intérieur ou à l'exportation. En pratique, les indices nationaux des prix de gros combinent souvent les prix à la production et les prix de gros de biens nationaux représentant les prix d'achat par grandes quantités au producteur ou au grossiste. En outre, ces indices peuvent s'appliquer aux prix de biens importés en quantités pour être vendus sur le marché intérieur par les producteurs, les détaillants ou les grossistes.

Les indices de prix de gros ou de prix à la production comprennent aussi en général les prix des produits provenant de l'agriculture, de la sylviculture et de la pêche, des industries extractives (mines et carrières), de l'industrie manufacturière ainsi que les prix de l'électricité, de gaz et de l'eau. Les prix sont normalement ceux auxquels s'effectue la transaction, y compris les impôts indirects non déductibles, mais non compris les subventions dans le cas des biens produits dans le pays et y compris les taxes à l'importation et autres impôts indirects non déductibles, mais non compris les subventions dans le cas des biens importés.

On utilise généralement la formule de Laspeyres

        Agricultural products
        Industrial products
        Imported goods
(b)   Stage of processing
        Raw materials
        Intermediate products
(c)   End-use
        Consumers' goods
        Capital goods

A description of the general methods used in compiling the related national indexes is given in the United Nations *1977 Supplement to the Statistical Yearbook and the Monthly Bulletin of Statistics* [57].

Table 32: Unless otherwise stated, the consumer price index covers all the main classes of expenditure on all items and on food. Monthly data for many of these series and descriptions of them may be found in the United Nations *Monthly Bulletin of Statistics* [26] and the United Nations *1977 Supplement to the Statistical Yearbook and the Monthly Bulletin of Statistics* [57].

et, pour la présentation, on a recalculé les indices nationaux, le cas échéant, en prenant comme base de référence 1990=100.

Les indices des prix pour chaque pays sont présentés suivant la classification ci-après:

(a)   Eléments de l'offre
        Offre intérieure
        Production nationale pour le marché intérieur
        Produits agricoles
        Produits industriels
        Produits importés
(b)   Stade de la transformation
        Matières premières
        Produits intermédiaires
(c)   Utilisation finale
        Biens de consommation
        Biens d'équipement

Les méthodes générales utilisées pour calculer les indices nationaux correspondants sont exposées dans: *1977 Supplément à l'Annuaire statistique et au Bulletin mensuel de statistique* des Nations Unies [57].

Tableau 32: Sauf indication contraire, les indices des prix à la consommation donnés englobent tous les groupes principaux de dépenses pour l'ensemble des prix et alimentation. Les données mensuelles pour plusieurs de ces séries et définitions figurent dans le *Bulletin mensuel de statistique* [26] et dans le *1977 Supplément à l'Annuaire statistique et au Bulletin mensuel de statistique* des Nations Unies [57].

33
Agricultural production
Index numbers: 1989-91 = 100
Production agricole
Indices: 1989-91 = 100

Country or area Pays ou zone	Agriculture Agriculture					Food Produits alimentaires				
	1998	1999	2000	2001	2002	1998	1999	2000	2001	2002
Africa · Afrique										
Algeria Algérie	129.9	132.4	126.3	139.4	136.7	131.4	134.7	128.2	141.7	138.7
Angola Angola	147.3	140.7	158.5	175.1	173.6	149.6	143.0	161.3	178.8	177.4
Benin Bénin	166.1	168.2	182.5	179.7	189.8	151.6	161.7	170.1	170.0	181.6
Botswana Botswana	90.4	79.1	84.0	92.8	92.6	90.5	79.2	83.9	92.8	92.7
Burkina Faso Burkina Faso	154.7	156.3	134.4	171.1	176.8	149.4	154.4	131.5	172.4	169.9
Burundi Burundi	89.2	91.7	85.8	94.0	93.6	91.3	91.9	87.3	96.1	96.1
Cameroon Cameroun	126.4	135.9	138.5	137.4	134.9	126.3	137.2	139.6	137.9	137.4
Cape Verde Cap-Vert	128.4	162.2	143.8	142.3	144.6	128.8	162.7	144.2	142.8	145.0
Central African Rep. Rép. centrafricaine	128.0	130.4	141.8	138.3	143.1	130.4	132.7	147.8	143.9	147.8
Chad Tchad	151.8	140.5	131.6	154.9	148.4	158.8	143.5	137.0	160.9	155.7
Comoros Comores	123.2	126.4	129.6	132.2	132.5	125.3	128.8	132.3	135.2	135.5
Congo Congo	116.2	125.1	127.3	128.8	132.2	117.3	126.0	128.2	129.6	133.1
Côte d'Ivoire Côte d'Ivoire	134.2	140.6	146.0	132.5	124.5	133.2	140.4	145.9	137.0	126.7
Dem. Rep. of the Congo Rép. dém. du Congo	90.7	88.2	86.4	84.8	82.9	91.8	89.6	87.9	86.4	84.6
Djibouti Djibouti	88.4	89.7	89.1	89.2	89.2	88.4	89.7	89.1	89.2	89.2
Egypt Egypte	139.0	147.5	154.5	154.0	155.2	142.7	151.6	159.1	157.1	158.4
Equatorial Guinea Guinée équatoriale	93.6	101.1	100.0	98.0	98.0	107.9	117.0	115.5	112.8	112.8
Eritrea Erythrée	148.5	133.8	116.6	124.0	107.4	149.5	134.5	117.0	124.4	107.5
Ethiopia Ethiopie	126.3	134.1	142.1	155.3	148.7	128.1	137.1	145.5	159.8	152.4
Gabon Gabon	116.1	117.1	119.6	119.8	119.8	113.1	114.0	116.6	116.8	116.7
Gambia Gambie	85.1	123.8	137.2	149.5	89.7	86.1	125.6	139.2	151.7	90.8
Ghana Ghana	158.7	167.3	171.8	175.9	198.3	157.4	166.5	171.0	175.0	197.6
Guinea Guinée	145.8	152.9	154.9	163.3	170.5	147.2	153.4	153.3	162.2	169.9
Guinea-Bissau Guinée-Bissau	128.2	135.9	141.3	143.6	141.0	128.6	136.1	141.5	143.9	141.2
Kenya Kenya	113.6	117.3	116.6	121.0	123.8	112.6	118.4	117.2	125.2	124.2
Lesotho Lesotho	94.4	96.2	107.5	95.4	126.0	95.5	97.4	109.2	95.9	129.7

33

Agricultural production
Index numbers: 1989-91=100 *[cont.]*

Production agricole
Indices: 1989-91 = 100 *[suite]*

Country or area Pays ou zone	Agriculture Agriculture					Food Produits alimentaires				
	1998	1999	2000	2001	2002	1998	1999	2000	2001	2002
Libyan Arab Jamah. Jamah. arabe libyenne	136.5	136.3	133.3	132.1	133.8	138.5	137.5	134.3	133.0	134.9
Madagascar Madagascar	109.1	111.6	110.4	114.7	114.5	111.3	113.7	113.1	117.3	117.0
Malawi Malawi	134.1	142.3	161.6	162.4	128.1	141.1	160.2	184.1	190.9	146.9
Mali Mali	130.8	134.9	119.4	137.3	147.6	120.5	128.1	123.6	126.3	136.0
Mauritania Mauritanie	107.1	106.7	110.2	107.9	106.9	107.1	106.7	110.2	107.9	106.9
Mauritius Maurice	105.8	82.6	101.0	111.8	98.1	111.2	86.2	106.4	117.7	103.0
Morocco Maroc	112.3	104.8	96.9	103.6	110.3	112.6	105.2	96.7	103.6	110.6
Mozambique Mozambique	140.9	142.5	126.6	132.4	132.7	139.2	140.9	124.9	128.7	128.9
Namibia Namibie	95.5	101.0	105.9	93.1	93.2	95.2	100.4	105.4	92.4	92.5
Niger Niger	153.1	140.5	129.7	151.1	141.5	153.0	138.7	128.1	150.4	141.9
Nigeria Nigéria	148.4	153.8	155.0	152.8	158.3	148.9	154.3	155.5	153.2	158.8
Réunion Réunion	118.2	124.9	125.1	127.4	130.9	118.9	125.6	125.8	128.1	131.8
Rwanda Rwanda	84.1	89.4	108.3	109.5	127.4	84.7	90.2	110.6	110.8	130.6
Sao Tome and Principe Sao Tomé-et-Principe	179.5	187.1	191.0	198.1	198.0	179.5	186.9	191.2	198.3	198.2
Senegal Sénégal	98.8	135.1	133.7	129.4	101.2	100.7	137.8	135.7	130.2	101.4
Seychelles Seychelles	127.9	133.8	133.8	130.2	132.9	128.2	134.9	134.5	131.2	134.0
Sierra Leone Sierra Leone	95.0	82.8	76.9	84.0	85.3	94.7	85.3	78.7	86.0	87.4
South Africa Afrique du Sud	98.0	104.3	109.8	105.3	109.1	100.3	106.8	113.2	107.9	112.1
Sudan Soudan	157.8	154.8	157.3	169.7	160.8	162.8	159.7	162.3	174.7	165.6
Swaziland Swaziland	84.9	90.2	97.1	97.4	94.5	88.5	93.1	100.7	101.1	97.9
Togo Togo	137.7	137.6	129.4	134.7	139.6	129.4	139.6	130.6	131.2	132.4
Tunisia Tunisie	123.1	134.3	131.0	113.9	96.6	124.6	136.3	132.7	115.2	97.2
Uganda Ouganda	120.7	132.6	132.9	141.3	141.6	117.4	127.7	132.0	139.0	139.2
United Rep. of Tanzania Rép.-Unie de Tanzanie	107.2	107.9	112.1	114.0	113.5	107.3	108.4	113.0	113.0	112.4
Zambia Zambie	100.1	121.4	110.7	104.5	110.9	98.9	112.3	109.5	102.7	109.4
Zimbabwe Zimbabwe	110.4	110.8	127.9	119.8	98.8	94.1	103.7	118.0	111.9	95.8

33

Agricultural production
Index numbers: 1989-91=100 *[cont.]*

Production agricole
Indices: 1989-91 = 100 *[suite]*

Country or area Pays ou zone	Agriculture Agriculture					Food Produits alimentaires				
	1998	1999	2000	2001	2002	1998	1999	2000	2001	2002
America, North · Amérique du Nord										
Antigua and Barbuda Antigua-et-Barbuda	97.9	97.1	98.3	101.4	103.2	98.2	97.4	98.6	101.7	103.4
Bahamas Bahamas	167.0	174.9	127.1	133.9	159.5	167.0	174.9	127.1	133.9	159.5
Barbados Barbade	97.2	100.0	106.9	103.2	98.3	97.2	100.0	106.9	103.2	98.3
Belize Belize	157.3	170.2	186.5	195.4	178.5	157.2	170.1	186.4	195.0	178.1
Bermuda Bermudes	78.4	78.4	78.4	78.4	78.4	78.4	78.4	78.4	78.4	78.4
British Virgin Islands Iles Vierges britanniques	104.0	104.0	104.0	104.0	104.0	104.0	104.0	104.0	104.0	104.0
Canada Canada	125.7	131.4	132.8	120.4	115.5	125.4	131.6	133.7	120.9	115.9
Cayman Islands Iles Caïmanes	84.9	84.9	84.9	84.9	84.9	84.9	84.9	84.9	84.9	84.9
Costa Rica Costa Rica	133.3	139.4	141.7	141.8	142.6	139.5	147.4	148.6	149.8	151.6
Cuba Cuba	59.5	67.1	72.5	70.6	70.6	58.5	66.4	72.2	70.2	70.3
Dominica Dominique	83.2	83.1	83.0	79.3	79.6	82.4	82.3	82.2	78.5	78.7
Dominican Republic Rép. dominicaine	104.3	96.3	99.7	105.5	109.1	102.5	99.6	102.1	109.3	112.0
El Salvador El Salvador	102.8	113.5	105.0	104.2	99.1	109.1	115.0	112.9	112.5	109.8
Greenland Groenland	105.7	105.7	105.8	106.0	106.0	106.1	106.1	106.2	106.4	106.4
Grenada Grenade	90.4	101.8	98.4	87.3	94.2	90.4	101.8	98.4	87.2	94.1
Guadeloupe Guadeloupe	95.8	114.3	114.3	114.3	114.3	95.8	114.3	114.3	114.3	114.3
Guatemala Guatemala	125.6	127.3	131.2	132.2	128.4	131.8	129.7	132.6	136.5	139.6
Haiti Haïti	93.4	95.9	101.9	98.2	100.0	94.9	97.5	103.6	100.0	101.6
Honduras Honduras	125.9	114.1	125.1	126.6	133.9	121.3	109.8	117.5	117.5	128.2
Jamaica Jamaïque	119.3	127.3	120.2	128.2	127.8	120.0	128.0	120.6	128.8	128.3
Martinique Martinique	114.2	122.2	123.4	123.4	123.0	114.2	122.2	123.4	123.4	123.0
Mexico Mexique	122.7	128.6	129.1	135.6	133.5	123.8	130.7	131.5	138.6	136.9
Montserrat Montserrat	110.2	110.2	110.2	110.2	110.2	110.2	110.2	110.2	110.2	110.2
Netherlands Antilles Antilles néerlandaises	167.0	153.3	166.1	170.6	162.7	167.0	153.3	166.1	170.6	162.7
Nicaragua Nicaragua	124.2	127.8	143.7	143.6	145.8	130.2	128.8	149.7	153.3	159.8
Panama Panama	102.4	104.0	103.3	105.6	108.5	102.4	104.1	103.7	105.6	108.2

33

Agricultural production
Index numbers: 1989-91=100 *[cont.]*

Production agricole
Indices: 1989-91 = 100 *[suite]*

Country or area Pays ou zone	Agriculture Agriculture					Food Produits alimentaires				
	1998	1999	2000	2001	2002	1998	1999	2000	2001	2002
Puerto Rico Porto Rico	83.2	83.9	84.4	84.4	84.4	82.6	83.5	84.0	84.0	84.0
Saint Kitts and Nevis Saint-Kitts-et-Nevis	113.9	98.0	97.2	97.3	97.3	114.2	98.2	97.5	97.6	97.6
Saint Lucia Sainte-Lucie	67.3	76.8	69.4	55.3	55.6	67.3	76.8	69.4	55.3	55.6
St. Vincent-Grenadines St. Vincent-Grenadines	77.4	76.1	78.1	78.6	78.6	76.9	75.5	77.6	78.0	78.0
Trinidad and Tobago Trinité-et-Tobago	91.9	106.8	126.6	123.0	129.0	93.1	108.3	128.1	124.6	130.8
United States Etats-Unis	119.1	120.7	123.4	121.6	120.9	120.3	121.3	124.3	121.6	121.7
United States Virgin Is. Iles Vierges américaines	104.0	104.0	104.0	104.0	104.0	104.0	104.0	104.0	104.0	104.0
America, South · Amérique du Sud										
Argentina Argentine	131.5	138.1	136.4	136.9	138.5	134.7	142.6	141.4	141.9	144.1
Bolivia Bolivie	136.4	137.2	150.3	148.1	156.6	136.1	137.3	151.1	147.4	156.3
Brazil Brésil	129.0	139.6	143.8	149.4	160.3	131.6	142.6	146.0	151.5	162.2
Chile Chili	132.8	129.7	132.9	142.0	141.9	133.9	130.6	133.9	143.4	143.4
Colombia Colombie	110.2	109.6	111.3	112.5	115.6	115.0	117.8	118.4	119.4	123.2
Ecuador Equateur	125.4	144.1	146.9	151.9	151.5	132.2	148.2	151.1	155.1	155.2
Falkland Is. (Malvinas) Iles Falkland (Malvinas)	90.2	89.6	90.2	88.8	88.8	85.9	83.9	85.9	80.6	80.6
French Guiana Guyane française	135.6	127.2	127.4	117.0	117.0	135.6	127.2	127.4	117.0	117.0
Guyana Guyana	172.3	186.2	194.6	187.0	180.1	172.9	186.9	195.4	187.6	180.7
Paraguay Paraguay	113.7	117.3	116.6	130.6	123.8	128.7	133.9	132.5	147.3	143.3
Peru Pérou	142.1	161.2	166.0	168.5	176.7	146.6	165.7	170.1	172.7	182.1
Suriname Suriname	77.5	77.9	75.3	80.5	83.3	77.5	77.9	75.3	80.5	83.4
Uruguay Uruguay	129.8	129.9	121.9	105.8	117.5	138.0	141.0	132.3	113.3	128.7
Venezuela Venezuela	116.7	119.2	128.4	133.8	135.0	118.6	121.2	131.1	136.4	137.6
Asia · Asie										
Armenia Arménie	80.5	79.7	75.6	80.0	82.8	81.3	79.9	74.9	80.0	83.0
Azerbaijan Azerbaïdjan	57.5	61.2	68.4	72.7	77.4	63.7	69.3	77.1	83.7	90.3
Bahrain Bahreïn	104.6	131.9	121.8	73.9	73.9	104.6	131.9	121.8	73.9	73.9
Bangladesh Bangladesh	114.4	129.2	136.9	134.2	138.2	115.2	131.2	139.0	135.8	140.1

33

Agricultural production
Index numbers: 1989-91=100 *[cont.]*

Production agricole
Indices: 1989-91 = 100 *[suite]*

Country or area Pays ou zone	Agriculture Agriculture					Food Produits alimentaires				
	1998	1999	2000	2001	2002	1998	1999	2000	2001	2002
Bhutan Bhoutan	120.0	117.0	116.2	116.1	96.1	120.0	117.0	116.2	116.1	96.1
Brunei Darussalam Brunéi Darussalam	183.5	229.0	256.0	295.0	346.2	184.4	230.4	257.6	297.1	348.8
Cambodia Cambodge	133.0	148.2	151.6	157.1	142.4	133.0	149.2	152.6	159.1	144.2
China [1] Chine [1]	160.2	167.2	173.5	179.4	184.6	165.9	174.0	180.1	185.8	191.7
Cyprus Chypre	110.6	116.7	120.2	118.6	121.2	110.6	116.6	120.2	118.4	121.1
Georgia Géorgie	72.6	77.5	64.1	66.0	64.1	80.5	84.8	73.8	76.3	74.5
India Inde	124.9	130.2	130.6	132.6	128.9	125.3	130.8	132.0	133.6	129.8
Indonesia Indonésie	117.9	120.0	123.8	122.6	123.1	117.8	119.8	124.0	122.8	123.9
Iran (Islamic Rep. of) Iran (Rép. islamique d')	157.5	153.2	153.0	151.1	159.8	158.3	153.4	152.7	150.7	161.0
Iraq Iraq	97.7	83.6	73.6	78.1	79.3	99.0	84.2	74.0	78.6	79.9
Israel Israël	115.2	110.4	112.6	112.6	112.2	114.8	112.5	115.8	115.0	115.2
Japan Japon	91.1	92.4	92.0	90.0	91.1	91.7	92.9	92.6	90.6	91.6
Jordan Jordanie	137.0	106.3	142.0	127.6	163.1	139.6	108.1	144.9	130.9	166.5
Kazakhstan Kazakhstan	49.8	67.5	63.9	74.0	77.2	50.8	70.0	65.2	75.7	79.6
Korea, Republic of Corée, République de	124.3	131.1	131.2	131.5	130.2	125.6	132.2	132.3	132.9	131.6
Kuwait Koweït	178.5	196.0	194.9	243.8	242.3	180.7	198.2	196.4	246.3	244.4
Kyrgyzstan Kirghizistan	102.1	108.2	114.5	120.1	121.0	113.3	120.2	126.7	134.4	136.5
Lao People's Dem. Rep. Rép. dém. pop. lao	128.6	149.7	174.0	181.2	184.2	130.4	156.2	178.9	188.2	192.2
Lebanon Liban	113.4	111.8	117.7	110.7	107.9	111.3	109.6	115.1	107.3	104.4
Malaysia Malaisie	118.0	120.1	120.6	125.5	129.8	128.7	133.0	136.0	142.9	147.3
Maldives Maldives	127.1	131.5	147.3	148.8	148.8	127.1	131.5	147.3	148.8	148.8
Mongolia Mongolie	91.1	105.8	103.2	81.6	92.6	90.8	106.3	103.0	80.2	92.6
Myanmar Myanmar	138.9	154.4	166.6	180.2	180.6	138.2	154.8	167.0	181.1	181.5
Nepal Népal	120.8	127.3	132.0	136.1	138.2	121.2	127.7	132.4	136.4	138.5
Occupied Palestinian Terr. [2] Terr. palestinien occupé [2]	102.0	102.0	102.0	102.0	102.0	102.0	102.0	102.0	102.0	102.0
Oman Oman	151.4	164.6	159.0	162.6	163.8	152.4	165.9	160.2	163.9	165.1
Pakistan Pakistan	136.5	142.7	145.6	142.8	143.6	146.5	149.6	154.0	151.0	153.2

33

Agricultural production
Index numbers: 1989-91=100 *[cont.]*

Production agricole
Indices: 1989-91 = 100 *[suite]*

Country or area Pays ou zone	Agriculture Agriculture					Food Produits alimentaires				
	1998	1999	2000	2001	2002	1998	1999	2000	2001	2002
Philippines Philippines	114.0	124.1	128.8	133.9	141.4	115.4	126.1	131.0	136.3	144.1
Qatar Qatar	147.5	161.0	173.0	127.3	160.5	147.5	161.0	173.0	127.3	160.5
Saudi Arabia Arabie saoudite	108.3	85.0	84.2	106.6	106.9	107.8	84.1	83.3	105.9	106.2
Singapore Singapour	41.4	27.7	33.4	34.9	27.4	41.4	27.7	33.4	34.9	27.4
Sri Lanka Sri Lanka	113.3	117.2	120.8	117.0	118.1	111.9	117.0	119.7	116.1	115.7
Syrian Arab Republic Rép. arabe syrienne	164.0	135.4	154.3	162.0	170.0	164.7	133.1	151.6	162.2	177.0
Tajikistan Tadjikistan	47.3	46.6	52.0	57.2	56.5	47.9	50.5	59.5	58.6	63.3
Thailand Thaïlande	114.4	117.2	123.4	127.7	125.8	112.5	115.5	121.3	125.7	123.6
Turkey Turquie	117.8	112.5	117.4	109.7	115.1	117.6	112.3	117.9	109.8	116.0
Turkmenistan Turkménistan	84.8	98.3	96.5	91.4	87.3	125.2	133.9	131.8	131.1	131.9
United Arab Emirates Emirats arabes unis	236.9	392.1	597.4	515.8	525.4	238.2	394.5	601.5	519.2	528.9
Uzbekistan Ouzbékistan	98.7	95.1	98.4	100.1	102.8	113.2	112.8	119.3	121.4	126.3
Viet Nam Viet Nam	152.3	164.7	175.0	178.4	189.0	148.0	158.2	165.5	168.1	180.5
Yemen Yémen	133.1	131.9	139.0	148.3	147.8	131.3	130.1	137.0	145.7	145.2
Europe · Europe										
Austria Autriche	109.6	113.1	102.8	105.1	106.0	109.6	113.2	102.8	105.1	106.1
Belarus Bélarus	65.7	59.3	58.9	62.7	63.9	65.9	59.8	59.0	63.0	64.2
Belgium-Luxembourg Belgique-Luxembourg	113.5	114.5	113.7	113.5	114.7	113.6	114.4	113.6	113.4	114.6
Bulgaria Bulgarie	67.9	68.6	65.9	64.3	70.0	69.5	70.4	67.7	65.7	71.1
Croatia Croatie	70.6	73.1	70.2	69.2	66.9	70.1	72.9	70.0	68.9	66.5
Czech Republic République tchèque	80.4	80.9	76.5	80.3	77.2	80.6	80.9	76.6	80.3	77.2
Denmark Danemark	106.0	104.3	104.6	106.5	106.9	106.0	104.3	104.6	106.5	106.9
Estonia Estonie	40.6	41.5	39.8	38.2	41.4	40.7	41.6	39.8	38.2	41.4
Faeroe Islands Iles Féroé	105.7	96.7	56.0	43.4	43.4	105.7	96.7	56.0	43.4	43.4
Finland Finlande	84.6	87.2	94.2	91.8	95.0	84.6	87.2	94.2	91.8	95.0
France France	107.8	108.2	105.9	101.5	105.4	107.9	108.2	105.9	101.5	105.4
Germany Allemagne	94.5	99.1	98.5	98.1	94.6	94.3	98.8	98.5	98.1	94.6

33

Agricultural production
Index numbers: 1989-91=100 *[cont.]*

Production agricole
Indices: 1989-91 = 100 *[suite]*

Country or area Pays ou zone	Agriculture Agriculture					Food Produits alimentaires				
	1998	1999	2000	2001	2002	1998	1999	2000	2001	2002
Greece Grèce	101.6	106.4	109.0	106.4	101.4	97.9	103.1	104.4	101.2	98.3
Hungary Hongrie	77.9	74.4	72.3	90.6	75.1	78.0	74.4	72.4	90.9	75.3
Iceland Islande	94.9	100.3	105.4	104.8	105.6	96.0	101.9	105.5	104.8	106.5
Ireland Irlande	107.2	112.2	107.9	106.4	104.3	107.8	112.8	108.4	107.0	104.8
Italy Italie	101.5	106.3	102.8	102.8	99.6	102.1	106.9	103.4	103.4	100.2
Latvia Lettonie	46.0	40.9	40.6	41.0	45.1	46.1	40.8	40.7	41.2	45.2
Liechtenstein Liechtenstein	91.1	91.1	91.1	91.1	91.1	91.1	91.1	91.1	91.1	91.1
Lithuania Lituanie	65.2	57.2	63.6	63.8	66.2	65.3	57.3	63.6	64.1	66.3
Malta Malte	135.1	128.5	123.4	122.6	114.8	135.3	128.7	123.6	122.8	114.9
Netherlands Pays-Bas	98.6	104.6	101.2	96.2	97.3	98.8	104.7	101.3	96.4	97.4
Norway Norvège	94.6	94.0	92.0	90.4	91.1	94.4	93.9	91.9	90.2	90.9
Poland Pologne	90.8	86.6	84.2	88.5	83.7	91.3	86.9	84.7	89.1	84.2
Portugal Portugal	94.0	106.7	102.6	102.1	101.8	93.8	106.8	102.6	102.2	101.8
Republic of Moldova République de Moldova	46.4	45.4	47.5	49.6	53.6	46.6	45.6	47.7	50.5	55.1
Romania Roumanie	89.3	94.1	78.6	94.1	84.9	90.2	95.3	79.6	95.5	86.1
Russian Federation Fédération de Russie	58.4	61.0	63.7	65.5	68.2	59.1	61.8	64.5	66.3	69.1
Serbia and Montenegro Serbie-et-Monténégro	100.1	87.7	87.3	86.4	77.4	100.3	87.6	87.4	86.3	77.2
Slovakia Slovaquie	78.3	73.2	60.8	66.8	68.1	78.9	73.8	61.2	67.2	68.6
Slovenia Slovénie	102.7	98.7	99.3	102.0	101.5	102.6	98.6	99.2	101.9	101.5
Spain Espagne	112.7	113.1	119.8	121.0	120.2	112.1	112.4	119.9	120.6	119.9
Sweden Suède	100.0	96.0	97.4	95.1	95.4	100.0	95.8	97.3	95.2	95.4
Switzerland Suisse	99.8	93.5	96.9	94.7	95.2	99.8	93.5	96.9	94.8	95.2
TFYR of Macedonia L'ex-R.y. Macédoine	97.5	95.4	95.8	89.0	84.4	95.2	93.5	96.2	88.5	83.8
Ukraine Ukraine	47.5	46.2	50.3	52.2	53.5	47.8	46.5	50.7	52.6	54.0
United Kingdom Royaume-Uni	100.1	99.7	96.6	87.1	93.2	100.0	99.2	96.7	87.2	93.4
Oceania · Océanie										
American Samoa Samoa américaines	96.2	96.2	96.2	96.2	96.2	96.2	96.2	96.2	96.2	96.2

33

Agricultural production
Index numbers: 1989-91=100 *[cont.]*

Production agricole
Indices: 1989-91 = 100 *[suite]*

Country or area Pays ou zone	Agriculture Agriculture					Food Produits alimentaires				
	1998	1999	2000	2001	2002	1998	1999	2000	2001	2002
Australia Australie	125.5	133.5	128.8	132.6	110.9	138.2	148.4	141.6	148.8	126.1
Cocos (Keeling) Islands Iles des Cocos (Keeling)	127.1	127.1	127.1	127.1	127.1	127.1	127.1	127.1	127.1	127.1
Cook Islands Iles Cook	103.0	96.9	96.9	96.9	96.9	102.7	96.8	96.8	96.8	96.8
Fiji Fidji	84.7	98.4	99.3	94.0	96.8	84.9	98.6	99.4	94.0	96.9
French Polynesia Polynésie française	79.5	87.8	96.9	94.6	101.2	79.5	87.8	96.9	94.6	101.2
Guam Guam	129.0	129.0	129.0	129.1	129.1	129.0	129.0	129.0	129.1	129.1
Kiribati Kiribati	133.1	134.6	126.5	128.4	130.5	133.1	134.6	126.5	128.4	130.5
Marshall Islands Iles Marshall	85.4	67.3	54.5	54.5	54.5	85.4	67.3	54.5	54.5	54.5
Nauru Nauru	105.6	105.6	105.6	105.6	105.6	105.6	105.6	105.6	105.6	105.6
New Caledonia Nouvelle-Calédonie	129.4	129.7	128.4	130.7	130.6	131.1	131.4	130.1	132.0	132.3
New Zealand Nouvelle-Zélande	120.7	114.2	121.8	125.6	127.8	128.4	121.4	130.3	136.2	139.1
Niue Nioué	106.8	106.8	106.8	106.8	106.8	106.8	106.8	106.8	106.8	106.8
Papua New Guinea Papouasie-Nvl-Guinée	117.7	124.8	128.9	122.6	120.3	115.8	122.9	127.6	124.0	121.3
Samoa Samoa	97.4	96.6	101.5	102.9	104.3	97.0	96.2	101.2	102.7	104.2
Solomon Islands Iles Salomon	134.6	138.2	148.3	151.3	152.1	134.8	138.3	148.4	151.4	152.3
Tokelau Tokélaou	108.5	108.5	108.5	108.5	108.5	108.5	108.5	108.5	108.5	108.5
Tonga Tonga	91.5	98.3	97.5	97.5	97.5	91.6	98.4	97.6	97.5	97.5
Tuvalu Tuvalu	107.0	110.3	110.6	100.4	100.4	107.0	110.3	110.6	100.4	100.4
Vanuatu Vanuatu	126.0	106.2	100.7	83.7	87.6	125.9	106.1	100.6	83.6	87.6
Wallis and Futuna Islands Iles Wallis et Futuna	101.5	101.5	101.5	101.5	101.5	101.5	101.5	101.5	101.5	101.5

Source:
Food and Agriculture Organization of the United Nations (FAO), Rome, "FAO Production Yearbook 2002" and the FAOSTAT database.

1   Data generally include those for Taiwan Province of China.

2   Data refer to the Gaza Strip.

Source:
Organisation des Nations Unies pour l'alimentation et l'agriculture (FAO), Rome, "Annuaire FAO de la production 2002" et la base de données FAOSTAT.

1   Les données comprennent en général les chiffres pour la province de Taiwan.

2   Les données se rapportent à la Bande de Gaza.

34
Cereals
Production: thousand metric tons
Céréales
Production: milliers de tonnes

Region, country or area Région, pays ou zone	1993	1994	1995	1996	1997	1998	1999	2000	2001	2002
World **Monde**	**1 902 944**	**1 956 480**	**1 896 734**	**2 071 839**	**2 094 226**	**2 083 866**	**2 085 549**	**2 064 263**	**2 106 900**	**2 029 386**
Africa **Afrique**	**99 543**	**110 466**	**97 458**	**125 225**	**110 089**	**115 724**	**113 885**	**112 296**	**116 570**	**115 757**
Algeria Algérie	1 454	965	2 140	4 902	870	3 026	2 021	935	2 659	2 099
Angola Angola	322	285	296	525	457	621	550	520	597	550
Benin Bénin	625	645	734	714	877	867	974	993	943	*926
Botswana Botswana	43	52	42	111	31	12	20	22	27	27
Burkina Faso Burkina Faso	2 527	2 232	2 308	2 482	2 014	2 657	2 700	2 286	3 109	3 119
Burundi Burundi	300	*225	*269	*273	*305	261	265	245	273	274
Cameroon Cameroun	986	961	1 180	1 296	1 268	1 418	1 196	1 294	1 333[1]	1 333[1]
Cape Verde Cap-Vert	12	8[1]	8	10	5	5	36	24	20	20[1]
Central African Rep. Rép. centrafricaine	94	101	113	126	138	148	173	184	195	205
Chad Tchad	617	1 175	907	878	986	1 312	1 231	930	1 321	1 166
Comoros Comores	21	21	21	21	21	21	21	21	21	21[1]
Congo Congo	7	7	9	*10	10	11	7	8	8	8
Côte d'Ivoire Côte d'Ivoire	1 286	1 331	1 409	1 793	1 961	1 873	2 121	2 033	1 898	1 558
Dem. Rep. of the Congo Rép. dém. du Congo	1 655	1 708	1 475	1 557	1 584	1 675	1 648	1 623	1 600	1 574
Egypt Egypte	14 961	15 012	16 097	16 542	18 071	17 964	19 401	20 106	19 310	19 464
Eritrea Erythrée	87	259	*123	*83	*95	450	315	159	186	57
Ethiopia Ethiopie	5 295	5 245	6 740	9 379	9 473	7 197	8 379	8 005	9 637	8 699[1]
Gabon Gabon	27	29	24	24	25	26	26	27	27[1]	27[1]
Gambia Gambie	97	95	98	103	100	106	151	176	200	139
Ghana Ghana	1 645	1 594	1 797	1 770	1 669	1 788	1 686	1 711	1 627	2 162
Guinea Guinée	711	718	825	876	927	982	1 042	973	1 031	1 088
Guinea-Bissau Guinée-Bissau	181	190	201	175	140	139	145	178	164	145
Kenya Kenya	2 530	3 663	3 275	2 714	2 711	2 962	2 802	2 591	3 285	3 351
Lesotho Lesotho	153	223	81	256	206	171	174	255	160	398[1]
Liberia Libéria	*65	*50	*56	*94	168	209	196	183	*145	*190

34

Cereals
Production: thousand metric tons *[cont.]*

Céréales
Production: milliers de tonnes *[suite]*

Region, country or area Région, pays ou zone	1993	1994	1995	1996	1997	1998	1999	2000	2001	2002
Libyan Arab Jamah. Jamah. arabe libyenne	180[1]	165[1]	146	160	206	213[1]	213[1]	213	218[1]	218[1]
Madagascar Madagascar	2 724	2 517	2 642	2 685	2 742	2 610	2 756	2 660	2 853	2 862
Malawi Malawi	2 137	1 109	1 778	1 943	1 349	1 904	2 636	2 631	1 742	1 759
Mali Mali	2 228	2 457	2 189	2 219	2 138	2 548	2 894	2 310	2 572	3 257
Mauritania Mauritanie	169	207	222	234	154	189	146	185	163	100
Mauritius Maurice	2	1	0	0	0	0	0	1	1	0
Morocco Maroc	2 818	9 639	1 783	10 104	4 098	6 632	3 860	2 011	4 604	5 283
Mozambique Mozambique	765	791	1 127	1 379	1 531	1 688	1 822	1 473	1 674	1 681[1]
Namibia Namibie	75	116	66	89	185	70	74	121	107	107[1]
Niger Niger	2 024	2 430	2 096	2 232	1 719	2 973	2 853	2 127	3 161	2 747[1]
Nigeria Nigéria	20 091	20 373	22 513	21 665	21 853	22 040	22 405	21 370	20 114	22 089
Réunion Réunion	14	17	17	16	17[1]	17[1]	17[1]	17[1]	17[1]	17[1]
Rwanda Rwanda	234	131	143	183	223	194	179	240	284	318
Sao Tome and Principe Sao Tomé-et-Principe	4	4	4	5	4	*1	1	2	3[1]	3[1]
Senegal Sénégal	1 086	943	1 059	976	781	717	1 131	1 026	962	835
Sierra Leone Sierra Leone	542	466	408	444	467	373	280	222	256	276
Somalia Somalie	165	405	285	290	284[1]	232	276	373	305	305[1]
South Africa Afrique du Sud	12 792	15 967	7 491	13 648	13 230	10 191	10 035	14 457	10 976	11 955
Sudan Soudan	3 102	5 146	3 305	5 202	4 209	5 583	3 066	3 436	5 411	3 734
Swaziland Swaziland	75	101	79	152	110	126	114	86	86[1]	86[1]
Togo Togo	633	572	591	687	748	624	759	737	715	715[1]
Tunisia Tunisie	1 931	675	637	2 885	1 072	1 684	1 836	1 106	1 374	533
Uganda Ouganda	1 880	1 936	2 030	1 588	1 625	2 085	2 178	2 112	2 309	2 322[1]
United Rep. of Tanzania Rép.-Unie de Tanzanie	3 917	3 534	4 759	5 001	3 309	4 450	4 073	4 312	4 249	4 147
Zambia Zambie	1 756	1 188	870	1 573	1 137	798	1 003	1 050	745	1 044[1]
Zimbabwe Zimbabwe	2 498	2 780	987	3 146	2 784	1 878	1 996	2 537	1 896	761
America, North **Amérique du Nord**	**341 101**	**434 279**	**359 092**	**429 069**	**419 446**	**434 541**	**422 353**	**427 289**	**404 789**	**367 612**

34

Cereals
Production: thousand metric tons *[cont.]*

Céréales
Production: milliers de tonnes *[suite]*

Region, country or area Région, pays ou zone	1993	1994	1995	1996	1997	1998	1999	2000	2001	2002
Barbados [1] Barbade [1]	2	2	2	2	2	2	2	2	2	2
Belize Belize	44	34	43	56	60	52	62	48	57	57
Canada Canada	51 452	46 576	49 304	58 459	49 526	50 907	53 951	50 932	43 298	35 440
Costa Rica Costa Rica	209	240	210	266	282	263	322	315	224	262
Cuba Cuba	227	301	305	474	546	392	555	509	560	560 [1]
Dominican Republic Rép. dominicaine	498	417	548	535	564	530	605	610	771	766
El Salvador El Salvador	909	727	899	867	773	783	857	779	760	805
Guatemala Guatemala	1 446	1 296	1 164	1 140	954	1 164	1 134	1 161	1 199	1 155
Haiti Haïti	420 [1]	425 [1]	410 [1]	412	490 [1]	403	475 [1]	431	363	374 [1]
Honduras Honduras	691	674	770	784	757	590	562	607	599	443
Jamaica Jamaïque	4	4	4	4	3	2	2	2	2	2 [1]
Mexico Mexique	25 200	26 810	26 883	29 311	28 062	29 123	27 419	27 991	30 390	27 734
Nicaragua Nicaragua	588	521	622	674	608	618	559	765	755	837
Panama Panama	329	348	310	316	269	249	280	315	317	418
Puerto Rico Porto Rico	0	1	1 [1]	1 [1]	1	1	1 [1]	1 [1]	1 [1]	1 [1]
St. Vincent-Grenadines St. Vincent-Grenadines	2	2	2	1	1	2	2	2	2	2
Trinidad and Tobago Trinité-et-Tobago	21	23	15	23	12	12	11	12	9	9
United States Etats-Unis	259 057	355 877	277 600	335 744	336 536	349 445	335 553	342 809	325 480	298 745
America, South **Amérique du Sud**	**84 577**	**88 047**	**91 836**	**93 296**	**99 126**	**96 095**	**100 798**	**104 179**	**112 995**	**104 341**
Argentina Argentine	25 175	25 371	24 307	30 700	35 907	37 808	35 036	38 751	35 876	32 023
Bolivia Bolivie	1 114	960	1 092	1 139	920	1 146	1 128	1 256	1 279	1 373
Brazil Brésil	43 073	45 849	49 642	44 962	44 876	40 743	47 431	45 897	56 478	50 436
Chile Chili	2 643	2 619	2 766	2 578	3 077	3 098	2 168	2 590	3 116	3 378
Colombia Colombie	3 522	3 631	3 435	3 177	3 207	2 893	3 396	3 740	3 799	3 954
Ecuador Equateur	1 902	2 061	1 900	1 947	1 815	1 485	1 847	1 909	1 646	1 721
French Guiana Guyane française	28	25	25	31	31	25	20	20 [1]	20 [1]	20 [1]
Guyana Guyana	349	395	532	547	576	526	565	453	498	452 [1]

34

Cereals
Production: thousand metric tons *[cont.]*

Céréales
Production: milliers de tonnes *[suite]*

Region, country or area Région, pays ou zone	1993	1994	1995	1996	1997	1998	1999	2000	2001	2002
Paraguay Paraguay	950	815	1 522	1 210	1 450	1 156	1 156	1 003	1 455	1 284
Peru Pérou	2 013	2 408	2 135	2 338	2 583	2 830	3 398	3 557	3 751	4 660
Suriname Suriname	217	218	242	220	213	189	180	164	191	192[1]
Uruguay Uruguay	1 491	1 515	1 811	2 222	2 057	2 046	2 219	1 880	1 744	1 700
Venezuela Venezuela	2 100	2 181	2 428	2 225	2 413	2 149	2 254	2 961	3 141	3 148[1]
Asia **Asie**	**937 178**	**923 622**	**944 306**	**996 944**	**992 553**	**1 016 896**	**1 036 201**	**999 649**	**1 001 365**	**985 858**
Afghanistan Afghanistan	2 980	3 144	3 142	3 242	3 683	3 876	3 257	1 960	2 160	3 739
Armenia Arménie	312	233	257	323	259	328	302	225	368	413
Azerbaijan Azerbaïdjan	1 137	1 024	869	1 010	1 119	940	1 089	1 496	1 956	2 133
Bangladesh Bangladesh	28 297	26 513	27 702	29 622	29 674	31 725	36 574	39 539	38 014	39 811
Bhutan Bhoutan	118[1]	133[1]	151[1]	165[1]	174	174	159	159	159	107
Brunei Darussalam Brunéi Darussalam	1	*1	*1	*0	*0	*0	0[1]	1[1]	*0	0[1]
Cambodia Cambodge	2 429	2 269	3 503	3 469	3 457	3 558	4 136	4 183	4 285	3 908
China Chine	407 931	396 460	418 665	453 665	445 931	458 396	455 192	407 336	398 395	402 001
Cyprus Chypre	205	162	145	141	48	66	127	48	127	138
Georgia Géorgie	403	471	501	630	892	589	771	418	704	*706
India Inde	208 627	211 941	210 013	218 750	223 232	226 877	236 206	239 080	243 375	213 590
Indonesia Indonésie	54 641	53 510	57 990	60 409	58 148	59 406	60 070	61 575	59 808	60 881
Iran (Islamic Rep. of) Iran (Rép. islamique d')	16 287	16 691	17 032	16 083	15 823	18 979	14 186	12 874	14 945	17 323
Iraq Iraq	3 239	2 829	2 538	3 001	2 212	2 428	1 600	902	1 295	1 455
Israel Israël	297	184	309	264	187	249	122	187	246	255
Japan Japon	10 737	15 787	14 122	13 668	13 320	11 934	12 283	12 796	12 255	12 184
Jordan Jordanie	114	111	125	97	96	76	27	57	45	74
Kazakhstan Kazakhstan	21 533	16 375	9 476	11 210	12 359	6 380	14 248	11 547	15 914	15 952
Korea, Dem. P. R. Corée, R. p. dém. de	9 137	7 215	3 787	2 596	2 866	4 422	3 845	2 951	3 878	4 181
Korea, Republic of Corée, République de	7 042	7 305	6 877	7 617	7 676	7 132	7 458	7 429	7 906	7 106
Kuwait Koweït	2[1]	2	2	3	2	3	3	3	4	4

34

Cereals
Production: thousand metric tons *[cont.]*

Céréales
Production: milliers de tonnes *[suite]*

Region, country or area Région, pays ou zone	1993	1994	1995	1996	1997	1998	1999	2000	2001	2002
Kyrgyzstan Kirghizistan	1 597	1 061	945	1 325	1 610	1 608	1 617	1 550	1 794	1 923
Lao People's Dem. Rep. Rép. dém. pop. lao	1 298	1 633	1 466	1 490	1 738	1 784	2 199	2 319	2 446	2 523
Lebanon Liban	81	79	100	94	90	103	93	123	154	154[1]
Malaysia Malaisie	2 142	2 179	2 170	2 273	2 168	1 994	2 094	2 206	2 161	2 161
Mongolia Mongolie	474	328	261	219	240	194	170	140	141	151
Myanmar Myanmar	17 263	18 727	18 483	18 238	17 196	17 643	20 776	21 966	22 713	22 849
Nepal Népal	5 773	5 375	6 078	6 378	6 350	6 390	6 930	7 116	7 120	7 212
Occupied Palestinian Terr.[2] Terr. palestinien occupé[2]	1	1	1	1	1	1	1	1	1	1
Oman Oman	5[1]	6[1]	6[1]	6[1]	6[1]	5	5	6	6	6
Pakistan Pakistan	23 870	22 338	25 036	25 395	25 260	27 985	27 755	30 461	27 048	26 768
Philippines Philippines	14 232	14 669	14 702	15 629	15 600	12 377	16 371	16 901	17 480	17 590
Qatar Qatar	5	4	4	5	6	6	6	6	5	*6
Saudi Arabia Arabie saoudite	5 043	4 860	2 669	1 932	2 339	2 202	2 454	2 131	2 310	2 111
Sri Lanka Sri Lanka	2 609	2 722	2 850	2 099	2 269	2 731	2 894	2 896	2 728	2 827
Syrian Arab Republic Rép. arabe syrienne	5 386	5 392	6 093	5 989	4 321	5 270	3 300	3 510	6 919	5 930
Tajikistan Tadjikistan	258	250	249	548	559	500	474	545	487	*440
Thailand Thaïlande	22 013	25 339	26 399	27 124	27 366	28 253	28 648	30 276	31 634	30 484
Turkey Turquie	31 749	27 014	28 134	29 344	29 761	33 187	28 886	32 249	29 571	31 940
Turkmenistan Turkménistan	1 009	1 120	1 102	545	759	1 278	1 567	1 208	1 832	2 106
United Arab Emirates Emirats arabes unis	1	1	1	1	0	0	0	0	0	0[1]
Uzbekistan Ouzbékistan	2 165	2 502	3 223	3 558	3 768	4 132	4 304	3 916	4 033	5 510
Viet Nam Viet Nam	23 719	24 672	26 141	27 933	29 175	30 758	33 147	34 535	34 093	36 378
Yemen Yémen	834	802	810	660	646	833	694	673	701	675
Europe **Europe**	**413 002**	**383 823**	**375 991**	**390 710**	**440 896**	**386 380**	**376 032**	**385 514**	**431 003**	**437 171**
Albania Albanie	686	666	662	519	616	621	512	581	517	534
Austria Autriche	4 206	4 436	4 455	4 493	5 009	4 776	4 806	4 490	4 827	4 963
Belarus Bélarus	7 315	5 938	5 314	5 478	5 920	4 495	3 412	*4 548	*4 926	*5 524

34

Cereals
Production: thousand metric tons *[cont.]*

Céréales
Production: milliers de tonnes *[suite]*

Region, country or area Région, pays ou zone	1993	1994	1995	1996	1997	1998	1999	2000	2001	2002
Belgium-Luxembourg Belgique-Luxembourg	2 311	2 174	2 144	2 571	2 393	2 601	2 449	2 571	2 516	2 737
Bosnia and Herzegovina Bosnie-Herzégovine	962[1]	847[1]	*671	*841	*1 242	*1 327	*1 369	*935	904	1 339
Bulgaria Bulgarie	5 666	6 409	6 514	3 380	6 152	5 345	5 209	4 966	6 045	7 400
Croatia Croatie	2 733	2 596	2 760	2 762	3 179	3 210	2 883	2 770	3 396	3 722
Czech Republic République tchèque	6 486	6 790	6 611	6 654	6 995	6 676	6 935	6 460	7 343	6 777
Denmark Danemark	8 203	7 800	9 043	9 218	9 529	9 344	8 782	9 421	9 763	8 922
Estonia Estonie	811	510	513	629	651	576	402	697	558	543
Finland Finlande	3 340	3 400	3 333	3 697	3 807	2 773	2 879	4 095	3 670	3 948
France France	55 626	53 407	53 545	62 599	63 432	68 664	64 342	65 698	60 264	69 158
Germany Allemagne	35 549	36 336	39 863	42 136	45 486	44 575	44 461	45 271	49 710	43 391
Greece Grèce	4 856	5 272	4 903	4 683	4 705	4 359	4 620	4 793	4 662	4 591
Hungary Hongrie	8 545	11 749	11 297	11 344	14 139	13 038	11 392	10 035	15 046	11 682
Ireland Irlande	1 627	1 610	1 796	2 142	1 944	1 865	2 011	2 173	2 166	1 964
Italy Italie	19 772	19 187	19 693	20 900	19 917	20 731	21 068	20 661	19 993	21 887
Latvia Lettonie	1 234	899	692	961	1 036	964	784	941	939	1 044
Lithuania Lituanie	2 673	2 098	1 907	2 615	2 945	2 717	2 049	2 658	2 345	*2 539
Malta Malte	7	7	7	7	11	11	11	12	12	12
Netherlands Pays-Bas	1 466	1 355	1 505	1 659	1 449	1 497	1 387	1 671	1 580	1 584
Norway Norvège	1 402	1 271	1 227	1 345	1 288	1 358	1 218	1 282	1 203	1 191
Poland Pologne	23 417	21 763	25 905	25 298	25 399	27 159	25 750	22 341	26 960	26 833
Portugal Portugal	1 449	1 645	1 446	1 673	1 559	1 622	1 678	1 622	1 291	1 567
Republic of Moldova République de Moldova	3 219	1 628	2 611	1 976	3 487	2 385	2 138	1 904	2 549	2 543
Romania Roumanie	15 493	18 184	19 883	14 200	22 107	15 453	17 038	10 478	18 871	14 007
Russian Federation Fédération de Russie	96 225	78 650	61 902	67 589	86 801	46 937	53 845	64 342	83 263	84 729
Serbia and Montenegro Serbie-et-Monténégro	7 411	8 409	9 245	7 294	10 355	8 667	8 615	5 391	9 032	8 326
Slovakia Slovaquie	3 157	3 700	3 489	3 322	3 740	3 485	2 829	2 201	3 209	3 193
Slovenia Slovénie	457	571	453	487	544	557	469	494	494	486

34

Cereals
Production: thousand metric tons *[cont.]*
Céréales
Production: milliers de tonnes *[suite]*

Region, country or area / Région, pays ou zone	1993	1994	1995	1996	1997	1998	1999	2000	2001	2002
Spain / Espagne	17 479	15 231	11 574	22 366	19 324	22 557	17 988	24 620	17 941	21 567
Sweden / Suède	5 242	4 472	4 791	5 954	5 986	5 618	4 931	5 670	5 391	5 471
Switzerland / Suisse	1 292	1 249	1 281	1 348	1 223	1 263	1 055	1 206	1 108	1 192
TFYR of Macedonia / L'ex-R.y. Macédoine	479	648	725	546	610	660	638	565	476	556
Ukraine / Ukraine	42 725	32 960	32 360	23 448	34 395	25 728	23 953	23 810	38 900	37 973
United Kingdom / Royaume-Uni	19 482	19 955	21 870	24 576	23 523	22 768	22 125	23 989	18 991	23 115
Oceania / Océanie	**27 542**	**16 244**	**28 051**	**36 596**	**32 115**	**34 230**	**36 279**	**35 336**	**40 177**	**18 648**
Australia / Australie	26 709	15 373	27 269	35 661	31 104	33 340	35 370	34 448	39 258	17 656
Fiji / Fidji	23	20	20	19	19	6	19	15	16	16[1]
New Caledonia / Nouvelle-Calédonie	1	1	1	2	2	2	2	3[1]	3[1]	3[1]
New Zealand / Nouvelle-Zélande	803	843	752	904	980	869	873	854	883	955
Papua New Guinea / Papouasie-Nvl-Guinée	6	7	8	9	10	10	11	11	13[1]	13[1]
Solomon Islands / Iles Salomon	0[1]	0[1]	0[1]	0[1]	0[1]	*1	*5	5[1]	5[1]	5[1]
Vanuatu / Vanuatu	1[1]	1[1]	1[1]	1[1]	1	1	1[1]	1[1]	1[1]	1[1]

Source:
Food and Agriculture Organization of the United Nations (FAO), Rome, "FAO Production Yearbook 2002" and the FAOSTAT Database.

1   FAO estimate.
2   Data refer to the Gaza Strip.

Source:
Organisation de Nations Unies pour l'alimentation at l'agriculture (FAO), Rome, "Annuaire FAO de la production 2002" et la base de données FAOSTAT.

1   Estimation de la FAO.
2   Les données se rapportent à la Bande de Gaza.

35

Oil crops
Production in oil equivalent: thousand metric tons

Cultures oléagineuses
Production en équivalent d'huile : milliers de tonnes

Region, country or area Région, pays ou zone	1993	1994	1995	1996	1997	1998	1999	2000	2001	2002
World **Monde**	**79 887**	**88 282**	**91 816**	**93 412**	**98 037**	**102 623**	**108 939**	**110 541**	**112 231**	**112 500**
Africa **Afrique**	**5 723**	**5 813**	**6 079**	**7 085**	**6 602**	**6 782**	**7 578**	**7 211**	**7 277**	**7 204**
Algeria Algérie	84	76	67	108	109	67	119	87	83	83[1]
Angola Angola	70	73	72	74	73	75	72	75	79	81
Benin Bénin	74	70	92	100	94	97	101	103	110	125
Botswana Botswana	1	1[1]	1	2	2[1]	3[1]	3[1]	3	3[1]	3[1]
Burkina Faso Burkina Faso	94	96	90	106	98	118	130	88	156	157
Burundi Burundi	8	6	7	6	6	6	6	5	5	5[1]
Cameroon Cameroun	207	219	217	273	220	226	249	260	270	263
Cape Verde Cap-Vert	1	1	1	1	1	1	1	1	1	1
Central African Rep. Rép. centrafricaine	53	57	61	64	64	68	67	67	67	73
Chad Tchad	78	87	113	122	146	174	143	144	177	175[1]
Comoros Comores	8	7	9	10	10	10	10	10	10	10[1]
Congo Congo	26	27	27	27	25	25	27	27	27	27
Côte d'Ivoire Côte d'Ivoire	394	395	390	416	374	400	399	421	336	405
Dem. Rep. of the Congo Rép. dém. du Congo	417	407	372	356	337	341	335	331	329	325
Egypt Egypte	215	183	206	224	211	189	223	218	231	235
Equatorial Guinea Guinée équatoriale	7[1]	7[1]	7[1]	7[1]	6[1]	6[1]	6	6[1]	6[1]	6[1]
Eritrea Erythrée	7	8	11	7	6	8	7	7	6	5
Ethiopia Ethiopie	72	75[1]	80	117	82	83	79	86	104	102[1]
Gabon Gabon	13	13	13	12	13	12	13	13	13[1]	13[1]
Gambia Gambie	27	28	26	18	27	26	41	46	50	26
Ghana Ghana	198	219	216	202	210	249	239	247	264	343
Guinea Guinée	114	114	118	126	130	131	137	143	149	155
Guinea-Bissau Guinée-Bissau	18	19	19	19	20	20	20	21	20	20
Kenya Kenya	30	33	32	34	34	35	42	40	40[1]	40[1]
Liberia Libéria	41	42	41	53	50	50	50	50	50	50

35

Oil crops
Production in oil equivalent: thousand metric tons *[cont.]*

Cultures oléagineuses
Production en équivalent d'huile : milliers de tonnes *[suite]*

Region, country or area Région, pays ou zone	1993	1994	1995	1996	1997	1998	1999	2000	2001	2002
Libyan Arab Jamah. Jamah. arabe libyenne	31	35	41	45	46	48	49	47	45	45
Madagascar Madagascar	30	27	28	30	31	30	31	30	30	30
Malawi Malawi	25	14	21	29	28	34	44	40	50	53
Mali Mali	89	113	103	101	104	105	112	98	120	142
Mauritania Mauritanie	1	1	2	2	2	2	2[1]	2[1]	2[1]	2[1]
Mauritius Maurice	1	1	1	0	1	0	0	0	0	0
Morocco Maroc	122	141	104	229	158	196	139	108	121	114
Mozambique Mozambique	106	102	112	118	124	132	132	87	86	86[1]
Namibia Namibie	0	1	0	0	0	0	1	1	1[1]	1[1]
Niger Niger	9	22	33	61	28	36	35	41	49	49[1]
Nigeria Nigéria	1 694	1 765	1 887	2 033	2 159	2 202	2 378	2 399	2 352	2 341
Réunion Réunion	0	0	0	0	0	0	0	0	0[1]	0[1]
Rwanda Rwanda	5	6	4	3	3	3	3	5	6	6
Sao Tome and Principe Sao Tomé-et-Principe	5	5	4	5	5	5	5	7	7[1]	7[1]
Senegal Sénégal	197	214	250	207	177	184	316	330	302	164
Sierra Leone Sierra Leone	69	79	71	74	78	64	55	51	52	52[1]
Somalia Somalie	12	12	13	13	13	11[1]	12[1]	13[1]	14[1]	14[1]
South Africa Afrique du Sud	209	227	278	417	273	324	598	314	404	449
Sudan Soudan	251	339	414	476	488	394	478	432	447	435
Swaziland Swaziland	3	2	2	4	5	6	5	4	4[1]	4[1]
Togo Togo	37	42	41	47	44	43	41	43	48	50[1]
Tunisia Tunisie	236	83	72	347	116	215	255	255	128	40
Uganda Ouganda	103	99	101	99	100	106	116	122	131	137
United Rep. of Tanzania Rép.-Unie de Tanzanie	129	122	139	141	134	118	125	131	142	142
Zambia Zambie	26	22	22	32	29	28	36	35	23	23[1]
Zimbabwe Zimbabwe	77	77	49	89	105	76	92	122	128	88
America, North Amérique du Nord	**14 644**	**19 485**	**17 158**	**17 556**	**19 781**	**20 900**	**20 149**	**20 420**	**20 299**	**18 610**

35

Oil crops
Production in oil equivalent: thousand metric tons *[cont.]*

Cultures oléagineuses
Production en équivalent d'huile : milliers de tonnes *[suite]*

Region, country or area Région, pays ou zone	1993	1994	1995	1996	1997	1998	1999	2000	2001	2002
Antigua and Barbuda [1] Antigua-et-Barbuda [1]	0	0	0	0	0	0	0	0	0	0
Barbados Barbade	0	0	0	0	0	0[1]	0[1]	0[1]	0[1]	0[1]
Belize Belize	1	1	1	1	0	0	0	0	0	0
British Virgin Islands [1] Iles Vierges britanniques [1]	0	0	0	0	0	0	0	0	0	0
Canada Canada	2 745	3 653	3 360	2 718	3 350	3 907	3 656	3 589	2 497	2 137
Cayman Islands [1] Iles Caïmanes [1]	0	0	0	0	0	0	0	0	0	0
Costa Rica Costa Rica	96	101	106	110	115	122	122	151	165	171
Cuba Cuba	8	8	8	8	8	8	8	8	8	8
Dominica Dominique	2	2[1]	2[1]	2[1]	2[1]	1[1]	1[1]	1[1]	1[1]	1[1]
Dominican Republic Rép. dominicaine	44	50	49	50	48	50	52	48	51	53
El Salvador El Salvador	17	13	15	15	15	15	16	14	16	16
Grenada [1] Grenade [1]	1	1	1	1	1	1	1	1	1	1
Guadeloupe Guadeloupe	0	0	0	0	0	0	0	0	0	0
Guatemala Guatemala	46	53	59	73	82	79	83	77	83	83
Haiti Haïti	13[1]	13[1]	13[1]	13	14[1]	12	13[1]	12	12	12[1]
Honduras Honduras	92	92	91	94	92	108	105	107	109	111
Jamaica Jamaïque	22	23	23	25	24	23	23	23	23	23[1]
Martinique Martinique	0	0	0	0	0	0	0	0[1]	0[1]	0[1]
Mexico Mexique	313	335	331	347	365	383	364	295	305	267
Montserrat [1] Montserrat [1]	0	0	0	0	0	0	0	0	0	0
Nicaragua Nicaragua	20	35	28	32	31	27	35	34	37	28
Panama Panama	3[1]	2	2	2	2	2	2	2	2[1]	2[1]
Puerto Rico Porto Rico	1	1	1	1	1	0	0[1]	0[1]	0[1]	0[1]
Saint Kitts and Nevis Saint-Kitts-et-Nevis	0	0	0	0	0	0	0	0	0[1]	0[1]
Saint Lucia [1] Sainte-Lucie [1]	3	2	2	2	3	2	3	2	2	2
St. Vincent-Grenadines St. Vincent-Grenadines	3	3	3	3	3	3	3	3	3	3
Trinidad and Tobago [1] Trinité-et-Tobago [1]	7	4	3	3	3	3	3	3	3	3

35

Oil crops
Production in oil equivalent: thousand metric tons *[cont.]*

Cultures oléagineuses
Production en équivalent d'huile : milliers de tonnes *[suite]*

Region, country or area Région, pays ou zone	1993	1994	1995	1996	1997	1998	1999	2000	2001	2002
United States Etats-Unis	11 207	15 093	13 062	14 057	15 622	16 153	15 658	16 050	16 979	15 686
America, South Amérique du Sud	**9 192**	**10 356**	**11 498**	**11 155**	**11 568**	**14 133**	**14 926**	**15 060**	**16 185**	**17 740**
Argentina Argentine	3 438	4 009	4 854	4 921	4 483	6 083	6 780	6 400	6 405	7 191
Bolivia Bolivie	103	146	183	180	231	249	223	275	223	301
Brazil Brésil	4 463	4 918	5 057	4 573	5 270	6 198	6 229	6 676	7 688	8 432
Chile Chili	16	14	15	16	16	23	32	24	28	7
Colombia Colombie	394	435	469	492	523	498	583	608	640	621
Ecuador Equateur	221	255	221	226	275	299	208	259	274	287
French Guiana Guyane française	0	0	0	0	0	0	0	0	0	0
Guyana Guyana	7	8	10	15	16	8	10	11	6	6
Paraguay Paraguay	404	413	490	520	542	599	625	623	714	658
Peru Pérou	48	54	64	69	61	53	61	56	61	58
Suriname Suriname	4	3	3	2	1	1	1	1	1	1[1]
Uruguay Uruguay	27	30	54	51	51	37	71	17	31	71
Venezuela Venezuela	66	71	78	91	99	84	101	109	115	106[1]
Asia Asie	**39 618**	**41 813**	**44 179**	**45 652**	**46 814**	**46 961**	**50 024**	**53 251**	**54 587**	**55 362**
Afghanistan Afghanistan	29	29	27	27	27	28	28	27	27	27
Armenia Arménie	0	0	0	0	0	0	0	0	0	0
Azerbaijan Azerbaïdjan	28	29	26	23	14	13	12	11	11	11
Bangladesh Bangladesh	163	157	161	159	162	163	162	158	154	153
Bhutan [1] Bhoutan [1]	1	1	1	1	1	1	1	1	1	1
Brunei Darussalam Brunéi Darussalam	0[1]	0[1]	0[1]	*0	*0	*0	*0	*0	0[1]	0[1]
Cambodia Cambodge	19	16	15	20	25	20	24	23	22	21
China Chine	10 909	11 884	12 510	12 160	12 460	12 888	13 587	15 223	15 156	15 399
Cyprus Chypre	3	3	3	3	2	3	4	5	4	4[1]
Georgia Géorgie	1	3	3	2	13	10	17	2	18	7
India Inde	8 094	8 528	8 708	9 313	8 975	8 772	7 819	7 926	7 621	7 161

35

Oil crops
Production in oil equivalent: thousand metric tons *[cont.]*

Cultures oléagineuses
Production en équivalent d'huile : milliers de tonnes *[suite]*

Region, country or area Région, pays ou zone	1993	1994	1995	1996	1997	1998	1999	2000	2001	2002
Indonesia Indonésie	6 268	6 902	7 472	7 928	8 384	8 986	9 815	10 559	11 394	12 109
Iran (Islamic Rep. of) Iran (Rép. islamique d')	79	116	91	105	101	105	93	109	97	91
Iraq Iraq	44	37	39	41	40	41	39	38	38	39[1]
Israel Israël	31	27	36	39	34	33	23	32	28	37[1]
Japan Japon	30	36	38	45	36	36	42	51	59	56
Jordan Jordanie	7	21	14	20	13	30	8	30	14	40
Kazakhstan Kazakhstan	81	86	82	57	56	67	91	93	122	141
Korea, Dem. P. R. Corée, R. p. dém. de	72	76	73	76	68	65	65	67	67	69
Korea, Republic of Corée, République de	52	53	57	53	54	50	43	45	45	45
Kuwait Koweït	0[1]	0[1]	0[1]	0[1]	0	0	0	0	0[1]	0
Kyrgyzstan Kirghizistan	5	5	7	8	8	10	11	12	14	14
Lao People's Dem. Rep. Rép. dém. pop. lao	7	7	9	9	9	10	8	8	9	9[1]
Lebanon Liban	14[1]	20	15[1]	24	23	25	17	44	22	22[1]
Malaysia Malaisie	8 615	8 397	9 080	9 691	10 438	9 573	12 080	12 430	13 483	13 541
Maldives Maldives	*2	*2	*2	*2	*2	*2	*1	*2	*3	3[1]
Myanmar Myanmar	311	299	376	433	416	392	406	456	595	499
Nepal Népal	39	44	48	47	49	45	49	49	53	54
Occupied Palestinian Terr. [2] Terr. palestinien occupé [2]	1	1	1	1	1	1	1	1	1	1
Pakistan Pakistan	593	628	763	717	735	715	867	818	781	732
Philippines Philippines	1 551	1 535	1 660	1 626	1 851	1 731	1 646	1 763	1 793	1 855
Saudi Arabia Arabie saoudite	2	2	2	2	2	2	2	2	2[1]	2[1]
Singapore Singapour	0[1]	0[1]	0[1]	0[1]	0	0	0	0[1]	0[1]	0[1]
Sri Lanka Sri Lanka	218	263	277	255	264	254	284	310	280	251[1]
Syrian Arab Republic Rép. arabe syrienne	164	187	171	237	207	290	202	317	232	320
Tajikistan Tadjikistan	51	51	39	29	33	34	29	28	31	34
Thailand Thaïlande	678	722	779	805	838	863	968	922	1 016	989
Turkey Turquie	646	815	745	959	721	994	763	978	665	936

35

Oil crops
Production in oil equivalent: thousand metric tons *[cont.]*
Cultures oléagineuses
Production en équivalent d'huile : milliers de tonnes *[suite]*

Region, country or area Région, pays ou zone	1993	1994	1995	1996	1997	1998	1999	2000	2001	2002
Turkmenistan Turkménistan	115	133	125	42	61	68	125	99	106	58[1]
Uzbekistan Ouzbékistan	418	395	398	343	373	327	376	309	311	314
Viet Nam Viet Nam	265	266	291	315	280	276	276	260	270	276
Yemen Yémen	6	6	7	8	9	10	10	11	11	11[1]
Europe **Europe**	**9 887**	**10 025**	**12 007**	**10 945**	**12 100**	**12 336**	**14 382**	**12 927**	**12 333**	**12 556**
Albania Albanie	6	7	9	7	8	12	11	9	10	7
Austria Autriche	113	142	134	71	76	90	112	79	86	80
Belarus Bélarus	17	16	22	20	20	30	34	*36	*37	40[1]
Belgium-Luxembourg Belgique-Luxembourg	10	12	14	14	14	15	19	14	13	14
Bosnia and Herzegovina Bosnie-Herzégovine	3[1]	2[1]	2	2	*2	*2	*2	2	2	2[1]
Bulgaria Bulgarie	183	252	323	222	186	221	255	251	178	227
Croatia Croatie	39	33	38	26	28	52	71	49	47	66
Czech Republic République tchèque	161	195	280	221	237	298	412	362	410	313
Denmark Danemark	159	141	119	96	112	137	158	112	81	84
Estonia Estonie	1[1]	1	3	4	4	7	11	15	16	25
Finland Finlande	48	41	49	34	35	27	34	27	38	39
France France	1 317	1 590	1 946	1 986	2 221	2 195	2 530	2 134	1 816	1 907
Germany Allemagne	1 185	1 241	1 245	821	1 169	1 394	1 784	1 423	1 620	1 495
Greece Grèce	457	547	616	571	571	581	625	633	619	547
Hungary Hongrie	300	304	368	420	289	342	474	277	352	412
Ireland Irlande	3	6	5	4	5	6	2	3	3	3
Italy Italie	911	976	1 139	888	1 241	1 018	1 222	1 020	1 018	885
Latvia Lettonie	2	1	1	1	1	1	4	4	5	13
Lithuania Lituanie	2	6	10	10	15	28	45	32	25	42
Malta Malte	0[1]	0[1]	0	0	0[1]	0	0	0	0	0[1]
Netherlands Pays-Bas	6	6	5	3	3	3	4	3	3	3
Norway Norvège	6	5	*5	*5	*5	5	4	4	4	7

35

Oil crops
Production in oil equivalent: thousand metric tons *[cont.]*

Cultures oléagineuses
Production en équivalent d'huile : milliers de tonnes *[suite]*

Region, country or area Région, pays ou zone	1993	1994	1995	1996	1997	1998	1999	2000	2001	2002
Poland Pologne	230	295	531	177	231	425	438	368	410	386
Portugal Portugal	85	73	87	84	78	84	86	75	81	94
Republic of Moldova République de Moldova	81	62	96	130	83	83	120	112	106	134
Romania Roumanie	315	335	407	473	382	493	613	338	392	464
Russian Federation Fédération de Russie	1 837	1 674	2 351	1 667	1 667	1 784	2 340	2 292	1 664	2 114
Serbia and Montenegro Serbie-et-Monténégro	174	138	146	196	138	146	166	166	170	162
Slovakia Slovaquie	52	62	94	100	105	91	146	102	143	151
Slovenia Slovénie	2	2	1	1	0	0	0	0	0	1[1]
Spain Espagne	1 170	1 050	645	1 544	1 890	1 494	1 086	1 484	1 892	1 286
Sweden Suède	137	81	76	54	50	49	73	49	41	63
Switzerland Suisse	20	14	18	18	21	21	18	20	21	29
TFYR of Macedonia L'ex-R.y. Macédoine	8	8	10	10	7	6	6	4	3	4
Ukraine Ukraine	891	666	1 203	888	971	966	1 214	1 484	993	1 396
United Kingdom Royaume-Uni	479	505	497	568	617	646	764	455	453	552
Oceania **Océanie**	**823**	**790**	**894**	**1 020**	**1 172**	**1 511**	**1 880**	**1 672**	**1 549**	**1 028**
American Samoa [1] Samoa américaines [1]	1	1	1	1	1	1	1	1	1	1
Australia Australie	260	248	363	393	565	878	1 223	959	891	359
Cocos (Keeling) Islands Iles des Cocos (Keeling)	1[1]	1[1]	1[1]	*1	*1	*1	*1	*1	1[1]	1[1]
Cook Islands Iles Cook	1	0	1[1]	1[1]	1	1	1[1]	1[1]	1[1]	1[1]
Fiji Fidji	26	25	25[1]	28[1]	28	27	22	24	22[1]	22[1]
French Polynesia [1] Polynésie française [1]	11	11	12	12	11	8	9	11	10	11
Guam Guam	5[1]	5[1]	5[1]	*7	*7	*7	*7	*7	7[1]	7[1]
Kiribati Kiribati	*11	*11	*11	*13	*13	*14	*14	*12	12[1]	12[1]
Marshall Islands [1] Iles Marshall [1]	3	3	5	5	4	3	2	2	2	2
Nauru [1] Nauru [1]	0	0	0	0	0	0	0	0	0	0
New Caledonia [1] Nouvelle-Calédonie [1]	2	2	2	2	2	2	2	2	2	2
New Zealand Nouvelle-Zélande	1	2	2	2	2	2	2	2	2	2

35

Oil crops
Production in oil equivalent: thousand metric tons *[cont.]*

Cultures oléagineuses
Production en équivalent d'huile : milliers de tonnes *[suite]*

Region, country or area Région, pays ou zone	1993	1994	1995	1996	1997	1998	1999	2000	2001	2002
Niue Nioué	0[1]	0[1]	0[1]	*0	*0	*0	*0	*0	0[1]	0[1]
Papua New Guinea Papouasie-Nvl-Guinée	363	344	337	426	394	420	464	509	465	473
Samoa Samoa	17[1]	17[1]	17[1]	17[1]	17[1]	17[1]	16	18	18[1]	18[1]
Solomon Islands Iles Salomon	62	61	69	69	71	72	72	82	83	82
Tokelau[1] Tokélaou[1]	0	0	0	0	0	0	0	0	0	0
Tonga Tonga	6[1]	6[1]	5	5[1]	6[1]	7[1]	8	8	8[1]	8[1]
Tuvalu[1] Tuvalu[1]	0	0	0	0	0	0	0	0	0	0
Vanuatu Vanuatu	34	34	36	38	48	51	37	33	24	27[1]
Wallis and Futuna Islands[1] Iles Wallis et Futuna[1]	0	0	0	0	0	0	0	0	0	0

Source:
Food and Agriculture Organization of the United Nations (FAO), Rome, "FAO Production Yearbook 2002" and the FAOSTAT Database.

Source:
Organisation de Nations Unies pour l'alimentation et l'agriculture (FAO), Rome, "Annuaire FAO de la production 2002" et la base de données FAOSTAT.

1   FAO estimate.
2   Data refer to the Gaza Strip.

1   Estimation de la FAO.
2   Les données se rapportent à la Bande de Gaza.

36
Livestock
Stocks: thousand head
Cheptel
Effectifs : milliers de têtes

Region, country or area	1995	1996	1997	1998	1999	2000	2001	2002	Région, pays ou zone
World									**Monde**
Asses	42 083	41 320	40 337	40 013	40 967	40 923	40 835	40 447	**Anes**
Buffaloes	159 319	161 280	160 978	160 761	162 192	164 340	165 413	167 126	**Buffles**
Cattle	1 331 973	1 332 889	1 327 928	1 330 350	1 334 843	1 345 237	1 359 668	1 366 664	**Bovins**
Goats	660 469	691 374	676 325	690 585	705 257	722 023	735 240	743 374	**Caprins**
Horses	58 956	58 542	57 119	56 822	56 871	56 864	56 882	56 324	**Chevaux**
Mules	14 998	14 173	13 601	13 594	13 633	13 625	13 470	13 325	**Mulets**
Pigs	898 830	859 511	834 430	873 854	902 893	908 281	924 839	941 022	**Porcins**
Sheep	1 072 781	1 057 803	1 041 298	1 043 098	1 044 224	1 047 828	1 036 933	1 034 008	**Ovins**
Africa									**Afrique**
Asses	13 058	13 035	13 246	13 401	13 538	13 689	13 642	13 678	**Anes**
Buffaloes	3 018	2 907	3 096	3 149	3 330	3 379	3 532	3 550	**Buffles**
Cattle	201 414	208 354	215 975	222 296	229 653	230 435	236 545	237 398	**Bovins**
Goats	191 090	198 068	201 318	202 739	206 587	213 211	215 592	217 227	**Caprins**
Horses	3 151	3 184	3 239	3 260	3 307	3 355	3 377	3 383	**Chevaux**
Mules	1 379	1 358	1 345	1 331	1 333	1 320	1 322	1 322	**Mulets**
Pigs	17 871	17 914	18 404	18 732	18 614	19 521	20 383	20 765	**Porcins**
Sheep	208 870	213 480	225 052	230 365	236 559	238 782	239 035	239 557	**Ovins**
Algeria									**Algérie**
Asses	224	210	199	183	171	178	170	170[1]	Anes
Cattle	1 267	1 228	1 255	1 317	1 580	1 595	1 613	1 600[1]	Bovins
Goats	2 780	2 895	3 122	3 257	3 062	3 027	3 129	3 200[1]	Caprins
Horses	62	60	52	46	46	44	43	44[1]	Chevaux
Mules	80	76	69	50	49	43	43	43[1]	Mulets
Pigs [1]	6	6	6	6	6	6	6	6	Porcins [1]
Sheep	17 302	17 565	17 387	17 949	17 988	17 616	17 299	17 300[1]	Ovins
Angola									**Angola**
Asses [1]	5	5	5	5	5	5	5	5	Anes [1]
Cattle	3 000	3 309	* 3 556	* 3 898	* 3 900	* 4 042	4 100[1]	4 150[1]	Bovins
Goats	* 1 460	1 590[1]	* 1 720	* 1 861	* 2 000	* 2 150	2 150[1]	2 050[1]	Caprins
Horses [1]	1	1	1	1	1	1	1	1	Chevaux [1]
Pigs	800	810[1]	820[1]	810[1]	800[1]	800[1]	800[1]	780[1]	Porcins
Sheep	* 240	260[1]	* 280	* 305	* 336	* 350	350[1]	340[1]	Ovins
Benin									**Bénin**
Asses	1[1]	1[1]	1[1]	1[1]	1[1]	1	1[1]	1[1]	Anes
Cattle	1 087	1 300	1 345	1 371	1 438	1 487	1 520[1]	1 550[1]	Bovins
Goats	1 013	1 078	1 087	1 114	1 176	1 234	1 250[1]	1 270[1]	Caprins
Horses	0	1	1[1]	1[1]	0	1	1[1]	1[1]	Chevaux
Pigs	554	582	470	264	195	297	454[1]	550[1]	Porcins
Sheep	601	616	634	620	654	672	655[1]	670[1]	Ovins
Botswana									**Botswana**
Asses	303	336	330[1]	320[1]	325[1]	330[1]	330[1]	330[1]	Anes
Cattle [1]	2 200	1 990	1 790	1 620	1 450	1 500	1 600	1 700	Bovins [1]
Goats	2 624	2 205	2 220[1]	2 100[1]	2 150[1]	2 200[1]	2 250[1]	2 250[1]	Caprins
Horses	35	30[1]	33[1]	32[1]	33[1]	33[1]	33[1]	33[1]	Chevaux
Mules [1]	3	3	3	3	3	3	3	3	Mulets [1]
Pigs	1	3	5[1]	2[1]	5[1]	6[1]	8[1]	8[1]	Porcins
Sheep	337	349	360[1]	300[1]	320[1]	350[1]	370[1]	370[1]	Ovins
Burkina Faso									**Burkina Faso**
Asses	454	463	472	482	491	501	502[1]	502[1]	Anes
Cattle	4 346	4 433	4 522	4 612	4 704	4 798	4 800[1]	4 800[1]	Bovins
Goats	7 459	7 683	7 914	8 151	8 395	8 647	8 700[1]	8 700[1]	Caprins
Horses	23	23	24	24	24	26	27[1]	27[1]	Chevaux
Pigs	563	575	587	598	610	622	630[1]	630[1]	Porcins
Sheep	5 851	6 027	6 207	6 393	6 585	6 782	6 800[1]	6 800[1]	Ovins
Burundi									**Burundi**
Cattle	350[1]	330[1]	* 311	346	329	320[1]	315[1]	315[1]	Bovins
Goats	850[1]	750[1]	650[1]	659	850[1]	750[1]	750[1]	750[1]	Caprins
Pigs	80[1]	75[1]	70[1]	73	61	70[1]	70[1]	70[1]	Porcins
Sheep [1]	300	250	210	200	200	215	230	230	Ovins [1]

36

Livestock
Stocks: thousand head [*cont.*]
Cheptel
Effectifs : milliers de têtes [*suite*]

Region, country or area	1995	1996	1997	1998	1999	2000	2001	2002	Région, pays ou zone
Cameroon									**Cameroun**
Asses [1]	36	37	37	37	37	38	38	38	Anes [1]
Cattle	4 650[1]	4 623	4 737	4 846	5 500	5 882	5 900[1]	5 900[1]	Bovins
Goats	3 620[1]	3 650[1]	3 700[1]	3 750[1]	3 800	4 410	4 400[1]	4 400[1]	Caprins
Horses [1]	16	16	16	16	17	17	17	17	Chevaux [1]
Pigs	1 000[1]	1 000[1]	1 000	1 200	1 000	1 346	1 350[1]	1 350[1]	Porcins
Sheep	3 400[1]	3 450[1]	3 500[1]	3 550[1]	3 650[1]	3 753	3 800[1]	3 800[1]	Ovins
Cape Verde									**Cap-Vert**
Asses	13	14[1]	14[1]	14[1]	14[1]	14[1]	14[1]	14[1]	Anes
Cattle	19	21	21[1]	22[1]	22	22	22[1]	22[1]	Bovins
Goats	112	109	110[1]	115[1]	112	110	110[1]	112[1]	Caprins
Mules [1]	2	2	2	2	2	2	2	2	Mulets [1]
Pigs [1]	239	100	143	185	200	186	200	200	Porcins [1]
Sheep	9	9	9[1]	10[1]	9	8	8[1]	9[1]	Ovins
Central African Rep.									**Rép. centrafricaine**
Cattle	2 797	2 861	2 926	2 992	3 060	3 129	3 200	3 273	Bovins
Goats	1 980	2 093	2 213	2 339	2 472	2 614	2 763	2 921	Caprins
Pigs	547	571	596	622	649	678	707	738	Porcins
Sheep	172	181	191	201	211	222	234	246	Ovins
Chad									**Tchad**
Asses	258	258	342	352	350	357	364	370[1]	Anes
Cattle	4 746	4 860	5 451	5 582	5 712	5 852	5 992	5 900[1]	Bovins
Goats	3 804	3 918	4 824	4 939	5 058	5 179	5 304	5 500[1]	Caprins
Horses	224	200	190	208	198	202	205[1]	205	Chevaux
Pigs	18	* 18	* 19	* 20	* 21	* 22	22[1]	24[1]	Porcins
Sheep	2 221	2 313	2 211	2 264	2 318	2 374	2 431	2 450[1]	Ovins
Comoros									**Comores**
Asses [1]	5	5	5	5	5	5	5	5	Anes [1]
Cattle	* 46	* 47	* 48	* 50	50	51[1]	52[1]	52[1]	Bovins
Goats	117	118	119	* 141	170	113	113	115[1]	Caprins
Sheep	* 18	* 19	* 19	* 19	20	21[1]	21[1]	21[1]	Ovins
Congo									**Congo**
Cattle	70[1]	72[1]	75	72	83	87	90	93[1]	Bovins
Goats	296[1]	295[1]	286	280[1]	280[1]	280[1]	280[1]	294[1]	Caprins
Pigs	46[1]	46[1]	45	44[1]	45[1]	46[1]	46[1]	46	Porcins
Sheep	113[1]	114[1]	115	114	115[1]	96	96[1]	96[1]	Ovins
Côte d'Ivoire									**Côte d'Ivoire**
Cattle	1 258	1 286	1 316	1 346	1 377	1 409	1 442	1 476	Bovins
Goats	1 002	1 027	1 053	1 079	1 111	1 134	1 162	1 191	Caprins
Pigs	414	264	271	278	327	336	346	356	Porcins
Sheep	1 282	1 314	1 347	1 381	1 416	1 451	1 487	1 522	Ovins
Dem. Rep. of the Congo									**Rép. dém. du Congo**
Cattle	1 113	1 060	1 102	881	853	822	793	761	Bovins
Goats	4 310	4 317	4 613	4 675	4 197	4 131	4 067	4 004	Caprins
Pigs	1 084	1 117	1 120	1 154	1 100	1 049	1 000	953	Porcins
Sheep	1 019	969	964	954	939	925	911	897	Ovins
Djibouti									**Djibouti**
Asses	* 8	* 8	8[1]	9[1]	9[1]	9[1]	9[1]	9[1]	Anes
Cattle	* 247	* 266	267[1]	268[1]	269[1]	269[1]	269[1]	270[1]	Bovins
Goats	* 508	* 509	510[1]	510	511	511	512[1]	512[1]	Caprins
Sheep	* 457	* 463	465[1]	462	466	473	475[1]	475[1]	Ovins
Egypt									**Egypte**
Asses [1]	3 112	2 980	2 990	2 995	3 000	3 050	3 050	3 050	Anes [1]
Buffaloes	3 018	* 2 907	3 096	3 149	3 330	3 379	3 532[1]	3 550[1]	Buffles
Cattle	2 996	* 3 107	3 117	3 217	3 418	3 530	3 801	3 810[1]	Bovins
Goats	3 131	* 3 131	3 187	3 261	3 308	3 425	3 467	3 470[1]	Caprins
Horses	* 42	* 41	43[1]	45[1]	46[1]	46[1]	46[1]	46[1]	Chevaux
Mules [1]	1	1	1	1	1	1	1	1	Mulets [1]
Pigs	27[1]	27[1]	28[1]	29[1]	29	30	30	30[1]	Porcins
Sheep	4 220	* 4 220	4 260	4 352	4 391	4 469	4 671	4 672[1]	Ovins

36

Livestock
Stocks: thousand head [*cont.*]
Cheptel
Effectifs : milliers de têtes [*suite*]

Region, country or area	1995	1996	1997	1998	1999	2000	2001	2002	Région, pays ou zone
Equatorial Guinea [1]									**Guinée équatoriale** [1]
Cattle	5	5	5	5	5	5	5	5	Bovins
Goats	8	8	9	9	9	9	9	9	Caprins
Pigs	6	6	6	6	6	6	6	6	Porcins
Sheep	36	37	37	37	37	37	38	38	Ovins
Eritrea									**Erythrée**
Cattle	* 1 312	* 1 600	* 1 928	* 2 026	2 100[1]	2 150[1]	2 200[1]	2 200[1]	Bovins
Goats [1]	1 500	1 550	1 600	1 650	1 700	1 700	1 700	1 700	Caprins [1]
Sheep [1]	1 530	1 540	1 550	1 560	1 570	1 570	1 570	1 575	Ovins [1]
Ethiopia									**Ethiopie**
Asses	3 250[1]	3 300[1]	3 300[1]	3 350[1]	3 400[1]	3 400[1]	3 414	3 414[1]	Anes
Cattle	29 825	31 207	32 612	35 372	35 095	33 075	35 383	35 500[1]	Bovins
Goats	8 300[1]	8 400[1]	8 400[1]	8 400[1]	8 400[1]	8 592	9 622	9 622[1]	Caprins
Horses	1 150[1]	1 200[1]	1 220[1]	1 230[1]	1 245[1]	1 250[1]	1 254	1 254[1]	Chevaux
Mules [1]	630	630	630	630	630	630	630	630	Mulets [1]
Pigs [1]	21	22	23	24	25	25	26	26	Porcins [1]
Sheep	10 900[1]	10 930[1]	10 940[1]	10 945[1]	10 950[1]	10 951	11 438	11 438[1]	Ovins
Gabon									**Gabon**
Cattle	* 38	36	33	34[1]	35[1]	36[1]	36[1]	35[1]	Bovins
Goats [1]	86	87	88	89	90	91	90	90	Caprins [1]
Pigs [1]	208	209	210	211	212	213	213	212	Porcins [1]
Sheep [1]	179	183	187	191	195	198	198	195	Ovins [1]
Gambia									**Gambie**
Asses	34	25	33	38	33	35[1]	35[1]	35[1]	Anes
Cattle	351	353	356	359	361	364	323	327	Bovins
Goats	169	164	159	154	150	145	228	262	Caprins
Horses	17	13	16	17	22	17[1]	17[1]	17[1]	Chevaux
Pigs	14	14	14	14[1]	14[1]	14[1]	8	17	Porcins
Sheep	136	130	123	117	111	106	129	146	Ovins
Ghana									**Ghana**
Asses	12[1]	13	14[1]	14[1]	14[1]	14[1]	14[1]	13	Anes
Cattle	1 217	1 248	1 260	1 273	1 288	1 302	1 360[1]	1 430	Bovins
Goats	2 204	2 340	2 634	2 739	2 931	3 077	3 200[1]	3 410	Caprins
Horses	2[1]	3	3[1]	3[1]	3[1]	3[1]	3[1]	3	Chevaux
Pigs	351	318	353	352	332	324	325[1]	350[1]	Porcins
Sheep	2 010	2 419	2 467	2 516	2 658	2 743	2 850[1]	2 970	Ovins
Guinea									**Guinée**
Asses	* 2	2[1]	2[1]	2[1]	2[1]	2[1]	2[1]	2[1]	Anes
Cattle	2 202	2 317	2 437	2 563	2 697	2 837	2 973	3 128[1]	Bovins
Goats	729	776	826	879	935	995	1 052	1 119[1]	Caprins
Horses [1]	3	3	3	3	3	3	3	3	Chevaux [1]
Pigs	46	48	50	52	54	56	58	60[1]	Porcins
Sheep	612	651	693	737	785	835	885	949[1]	Ovins
Guinea-Bissau									**Guinée-Bissau**
Asses [1]	5	5	5	5	5	5	5	5	Anes [1]
Cattle	453	464	475	487	500	512	515[1]	515[1]	Bovins
Goats [1]	285	295	305	315	325	325	325	325	Caprins [1]
Horses [1]	2	2	2	2	2	2	2	2	Chevaux [1]
Pigs [1]	325	330	335	340	345	345	350	350	Porcins [1]
Sheep [1]	265	270	275	280	285	280	285	285	Ovins [1]
Kenya									**Kenya**
Cattle	12 779	12 820	13 235	13 492	13 690	13 931	13 500[1]	13 500[1]	Bovins
Goats	10 396	12 989	10 500	8 945	9 208	9 647	9 000[1]	9 000[1]	Caprins
Horses [1]	2	2	2	2	2	2	2	2	Chevaux [1]
Pigs	231	285	313	291	304	294	371	380[1]	Porcins
Sheep	8 208	8 087	7 617	8 126	8 535	8 462	8 000[1]	8 000[1]	Ovins
Lesotho									**Lesotho**
Asses	146	153	155[1]	150[1]	152[1]	154[1]	154[1]	154[1]	Anes
Cattle	580	539	500[1]	496	571	560[1]	540[1]	540[1]	Bovins
Goats	749	732	811	546	730	650[1]	650[1]	650[1]	Caprins
Horses	100	98	100[1]	95[1]	98[1]	100[1]	100[1]	100[1]	Chevaux

36

Livestock

Stocks: thousand head [*cont.*]

Cheptel

Effectifs : milliers de têtes [*suite*]

Region, country or area	1995	1996	1997	1998	1999	2000	2001	2002	Région, pays ou zone
Mules [1]	1	1	1	1	1	1	1	1	Mulets [1]
Pigs	66	64	58	60[1]	63[1]	65[1]	65[1]	65[1]	Porcins
Sheep	1 131	951	938	696	936	850[1]	850[1]	850[1]	Ovins
Liberia [1]									**Libéria** [1]
Cattle	36	36	36	36	36	36	36	36	Bovins
Goats	220	220	220	220	220	220	220	220	Caprins
Pigs	120	120	120	120	120	130	130	130	Porcins
Sheep	210	210	210	210	210	210	210	210	Ovins
Libyan Arab Jamah.									**Jamah. arabe libyenne**
Asses	* 21	* 25	27[1]	28[1]	29[1]	30[1]	30[1]	30[1]	Anes
Cattle	* 145	* 145	142[1]	180[1]	190[1]	210[1]	220[1]	220[1]	Bovins
Goats	1 250[1]	1 250[1]	1 250[1]	1 250	1 250	* 1 263	1 265[1]	1 265[1]	Caprins
Horses	* 35	* 40	43[1]	44[1]	45[1]	46[1]	46[1]	46[1]	Chevaux
Sheep	* 5 100	* 5 500	5 200[1]	6 000	5 150	4 124	4 125[1]	4 130[1]	Ovins
Madagascar									**Madagascar**
Cattle	10 309	10 320	10 331	10 342	10 353	10 364	11 000[1]	11 000[1]	Bovins
Goats	* 1 399	1 329	1 340[1]	1 350[1]	1 360[1]	1 370[1]	1 350[1]	1 350[1]	Caprins
Pigs	1 592	1 629	1 662	1 650[1]	1 500[1]	1 450[1]	1 600[1]	1 600[1]	Porcins
Sheep	* 821	756	770[1]	780[1]	790[1]	800[1]	790[1]	790[1]	Ovins
Malawi									**Malawi**
Asses	2	2[1]	2[1]	2[1]	2[1]	2[1]	2[1]	2[1]	Anes
Cattle	746	700	598	715	712	764	749	750[1]	Bovins
Goats	843	1 257	1 567	1 598	1 427	1 689	1 670	1 700[1]	Caprins
Pigs	340	313	421	427	444	468	436	456	Porcins
Sheep	87	93	98	103	103	112	115	115[1]	Ovins
Mali									**Mali**
Asses	625	638	652	666	680	680[1]	680[1]	700[1]	Anes
Cattle	5 780	5 882	6 058	6 240	6 428	6 620	6 735	6 819	Bovins
Goats	7 748	8 102	8 507	8 932	9 379	9 849	* 8 691	8 850[1]	Caprins
Horses	112	123	136	150	165	165[1]	165[1]	170[1]	Chevaux
Pigs	63	64	65	65	66	66	83	85[1]	Porcins
Sheep	5 431	5 707	5 993	6 292	6 607	6 200[1]	* 6 039	6 150[1]	Ovins
Mauritania									**Mauritanie**
Asses [1]	155	155	156	156	157	157	158	158	Anes [1]
Cattle	1 111	1 122	1 353	1 394	1 433	1 476	1 500[1]	1 500[1]	Bovins
Goats	* 3 526	4 133	4 200[1]	* 4 555	* 4 784	* 5 023	5 100[1]	5 100[1]	Caprins
Horses	* 19	* 19	20[1]	20[1]	20[1]	20[1]	20[1]	20[1]	Chevaux
Sheep	* 5 288	6 199	6 300[1]	* 6 835	* 7 176	* 7 535	7 600[1]	7 600[1]	Ovins
Mauritius [1]									**Maurice** [1]
Cattle	23	23	21	22	25	27	28	28	Bovins
Goats	91	90	91	92	93	94	95	* 93	Caprins
Pigs	15	16	14	11	10	12	12	14	Porcins
Sheep	12	13	10	13	14	10	12	12	Ovins
Morocco									**Maroc**
Asses	954	919	949	980	1 001	1 099	1 000[1]	1 000[1]	Anes
Cattle	2 371	2 408	2 547	2 569	2 566	2 675	2 647	2 670	Bovins
Goats	4 014	4 595	4 790	4 959	4 704	4 931	5 133	5 090	Caprins
Horses	162	156	145	147	149	154	155[1]	155[1]	Chevaux
Mules	540	523	516	524	527	518	520[1]	520[1]	Mulets
Pigs	10[1]	10[1]	10	8	8[1]	8[1]	8[1]	8[1]	Porcins
Sheep	13 389	14 536	15 287	14 784	16 576	17 300	17 172	16 336	Ovins
Mozambique [1]									**Mozambique** [1]
Asses	19	20	21	22	23	23	23	23	Anes
Cattle	1 250	1 270	1 290	1 300	1 310	1 320	1 320	1 320	Bovins
Goats	382	384	386	388	390	392	392	392	Caprins
Pigs	170	172	174	176	178	180	180	180	Porcins
Sheep	119	120	122	123	124	125	125	125	Ovins
Namibia									**Namibie**
Asses	110[1]	130[1]	140[1]	150[1]	175	168	169	169[1]	Anes
Cattle	2 031	1 990	2 055	2 192	2 294	2 505	2 509	2 509[1]	Bovins
Goats	1 616	1 786	1 821	1 710	1 690	1 850	1 769	1 769[1]	Caprins

36

Livestock

Stocks: thousand head [*cont.*]

Cheptel

Effectifs : milliers de têtes [*suite*]

Region, country or area	1995	1996	1997	1998	1999	2000	2001	2002	Région, pays ou zone
Horses	58	57	57	53	66	62	53	53[1]	Chevaux
Mules [1]	7	7	7	7	7	7	7	7	Mulets [1]
Pigs	20	19	17	15	19	23	22	22[1]	Porcins
Sheep	2 410	2 198	2 429	2 086	2 174	2 446	2 370	2 370[1]	Ovins
Niger									**Niger**
Asses	481	506	516	562	570[1]	570[1]	580[1]	580[1]	Anes
Cattle	2 008	2 048	2 089	2 131	2 174	2 217	2 260[1]	2 260[1]	Bovins
Goats	5 716	5 869	* 6 025	* 6 307	6 560	6 724	6 900[1]	6 900[1]	Caprins
Horses	* 93	* 96	* 99	* 102	103[1]	104[1]	105[1]	105[1]	Chevaux
Pigs [1]	39	39	39	39	39	39	39	39	Porcins [1]
Sheep	3 789	3 849	* 4 151	* 4 140	4 266	4 392	4 500[1]	4 500[1]	Ovins
Nigeria									**Nigéria**
Asses [1]	1 000	1 000	1 000	1 000	1 000	1 000	1 000	1 000	Anes [1]
Cattle	15 405	18 680	19 610	19 700[1]	19 830	19 500[1]	19 700[1]	20 000[1]	Bovins
Goats [1]	24 500	25 000	25 500	25 500	26 000	26 500	26 500	27 000	Caprins [1]
Horses [1]	204	204	204	204	204	204	205	205	Chevaux [1]
Pigs	4 149	4 315	4 487	4 667	4 853	5 048	5 250[1]	5 500[1]	Porcins
Sheep [1]	14 000	14 000	19 500	20 000	20 500	21 000	21 500	22 000	Ovins [1]
Réunion									**Réunion**
Cattle	26	26	* 27	27[1]	27	28	30	30[1]	Bovins
Goats	31	31	* 38	38[1]	37	38	37	37[1]	Caprins
Pigs	86	86	* 89	82[1]	77	77	78	78[1]	Porcins
Sheep	2	2	* 2	2[1]	2	2	2	2[1]	Ovins
Rwanda									**Rwanda**
Cattle	465	500[1]	570[1]	657	749	732	816	815[1]	Bovins
Goats	494	621	526	629	704	757	757	760[1]	Caprins
Pigs	* 120	* 134	* 142	121	160	177	180[1]	180[1]	Porcins
Sheep	* 220	* 248	* 263	192	278	254	260[1]	260[1]	Ovins
Sao Tome and Principe [1]									**Sao Tomé-et-Principe** [1]
Cattle	4	4	4	4	4	4	4	4	Bovins
Goats	5	5	5	5	5	5	5	5	Caprins
Pigs	2	2	2	2	2	2	2	2	Porcins
Sheep	2	2	2	3	3	3	3	3	Ovins
Senegal									**Sénégal**
Asses	366	367	393	375	377	399	410[1]	420[1]	Anes
Cattle	2 800	2 870	2 898	2 912	2 927	3 073	3 227	3 230[1]	Bovins
Goats	3 293	3 440	3 572	3 703	3 833	3 879	3 995	4 000[1]	Caprins
Horses	434	436	465	445	446	471	492	492[1]	Chevaux
Pigs	163	171	191	213	240	269	280	300[1]	Porcins
Sheep	3 890	4 045	4 239	4 344	4 497	4 542	4 818	4 900[1]	Ovins
Seychelles [1]									**Seychelles** [1]
Cattle	2	2	2	2	2	2	1	1	Bovins
Goats	5	5	5	5	5	5	5	5	Caprins
Pigs	18	18	18	18	18	18	18	19	Porcins
Sierra Leone									**Sierra Leone**
Cattle [1]	380	390	400	410	420	420	400	400	Bovins [1]
Goats [1]	180	185	190	195	200	220	220	220	Caprins [1]
Pigs	50[1]	50[1]	50[1]	50[1]	52	52[1]	55[1]	55[1]	Porcins
Sheep [1]	330	340	350	358	365	365	370	370	Ovins [1]
Somalia [1]									**Somalie** [1]
Asses	20	20	21	19	19	20	21	21	Anes
Cattle	5 200	5 400	5 600	5 300	5 000	5 100	5 300	5 300	Bovins
Goats	12 500	12 800	13 000	12 500	12 000	12 300	12 700	12 700	Caprins
Horses	1	1	1	1	1	1	1	1	Chevaux
Mules	19	20	20	18	18	19	19	19	Mulets
Pigs	4	4	5	4	4	4	4	4	Porcins
Sheep	13 500	13 800	15 500	15 000	15 000	15 000	13 100	13 100	Ovins
South Africa									**Afrique du Sud**
Asses	210[1]	210[1]	210[1]	210[1]	210[1]	* 150	150[1]	150[1]	Anes
Cattle	13 015	13 389	13 667	13 772	13 580	13 461	* 13 740	13 722[1]	Bovins
Goats	6 457	6 674	6 644	6 558	6 457	6 706	6 550[1]	6 849[1]	Caprins

36

Livestock
Stocks: thousand head [*cont.*]
Cheptel
Effectifs : milliers de têtes [*suite*]

Region, country or area	1995	1996	1997	1998	1999	2000	2001	2002	Région, pays ou zone
Horses	245[1]	250[1]	255[1]	260[1]	258[1]	* 270	270[1]	270[1]	Chevaux
Mules [1]	14	14	14	14	14	14	14	14	Mulets [1]
Pigs	1 628	1 603	1 617	1 641	1 531	1 556	1 540[1]	1 600[1]	Porcins
Sheep	28 784	28 934	29 187	29 345	28 680	28 551	28 800[1]	29 090[1]	Ovins
Sudan									**Soudan**
Asses [1]	678	680	700	720	730	740	750	750	Anes [1]
Cattle	30 077	31 669	33 103	34 584	35 825	37 093	38 325	38 325[1]	Bovins
Goats	35 215	35 216	36 037	36 498	37 346	38 548	39 952	40 000[1]	Caprins
Horses [1]	24	24	25	25	26	26	26	26	Chevaux [1]
Mules [1]	1	1	1	1	1	1	1	1	Mulets [1]
Sheep	37 180[1]	37 202	39 835	42 363	44 802	46 095	47 042	47 043	Ovins
Swaziland									**Swaziland**
Asses [1]	15	15	15	15	15	15	15	15	Anes [1]
Cattle	642	656	658	623	614	611	615[1]	615[1]	Bovins
Goats	435	438	368	354	333	422	422[1]	422[1]	Caprins
Horses [1]	1	1	1	1	1	1	1	1	Chevaux [1]
Pigs	30	31	32[1]	30[1]	31[1]	30	30[1]	30[1]	Porcins
Sheep	24	27	23	23	22	27	27[1]	27[1]	Ovins
Togo									**Togo**
Asses [1]	3	3	3	3	3	3	3	3	Anes [1]
Cattle	202	217	271	273	275	277	278[1]	279[1]	Bovins
Goats	814	1 091	1 229	1 292	1 357	1 425	1 450[1]	1 460[1]	Caprins
Horses [1]	2	2	2	2	2	2	2	2	Chevaux [1]
Pigs	331	288	312	278	284	289	295[1]	300[1]	Porcins
Sheep	501	841	1 150	1 274	1 415	1 570	1 600[1]	1 700[1]	Ovins
Tunisia									**Tunisie**
Asses [1]	230	230	230	230	230	230	230	230	Anes [1]
Cattle	654	680[1]	701	720[1]	750[1]	767	763	760[1]	Bovins
Goats	1 205	1 250[1]	1 261	1 300[1]	1 350[1]	1 448	1 450	1 450[1]	Caprins
Horses [1]	56	56	56	56	56	56	56	56	Chevaux [1]
Mules [1]	81	81	81	81	81	81	81	81	Mulets [1]
Pigs [1]	6	6	6	6	6	6	6	6	Porcins [1]
Sheep	6 222	6 400[1]	6 293	6 600[1]	6 800[1]	6 926	6 861	6 850[1]	Ovins
Uganda									**Ouganda**
Asses [1]	17	18	18	18	18	18	18	18	Anes [1]
Cattle	5 233	5 301	5 460	5 651	5 820	5 966	6 144	5 900[1]	Bovins
Goats	5 545	5 684	5 825	5 999	6 180	6 396	6 620	6 600[1]	Caprins
Pigs	1 343	1 383	1 425	1 475	1 520	1 573	1 644	1 550[1]	Porcins
Sheep	924	951	980	1 014	1 044	1 081	1 180	1 200[1]	Ovins
United Rep. of Tanzania									**Rép.-Unie de Tanzanie**
Asses [1]	178	176	177	178	179	180	182	182	Anes [1]
Cattle	15 645	13 605	13 700	13 796	17 251	17 300[1]	17 500[1]	17 700[1]	Bovins
Goats	10 682	10 362	10 694	11 035	11 643	11 640[1]	11 650[1]	11 650[1]	Caprins
Pigs	350[1]	370[1]	390[1]	410[1]	446	450[1]	455[1]	455[1]	Porcins
Sheep	3 493	3 552	3 551	3 550	3 489	3 500[1]	3 550[1]	3 550[1]	Ovins
Zambia									**Zambie**
Asses [1]	2	2	2	2	2	2	2	2	Anes [1]
Cattle	2 400[1]	2 200[1]	2 701	2 747	2 905	2 621	2 600[1]	2 600[1]	Bovins
Goats	650[1]	670[1]	* 700	* 890	* 1 069	* 1 249	1 270[1]	1 270[1]	Caprins
Pigs	300[1]	320[1]	* 316	* 320	* 324	309	340[1]	340[1]	Porcins
Sheep	74[1]	77[1]	* 80	* 99	* 120	* 140	150[1]	150[1]	Ovins
Zimbabwe									**Zimbabwe**
Asses [1]	105	105	104	105	106	107	108	108	Anes [1]
Cattle	4 500	5 436	5 400[1]	5 450	6 069	5 700[1]	5 752	5 753[1]	Bovins
Goats	2 615	2 705	2 700[1]	2 750	2 910	2 950[1]	2 968	2 970[1]	Caprins
Horses [1]	25	25	25	25	26	26	27	27	Chevaux [1]
Mules [1]	1	1	1	1	1	1	1	1	Mulets [1]
Pigs	277	266	260[1]	270	279	450[1]	604	605[1]	Porcins
Sheep	487	530	510[1]	520	640	630[1]	600	600[1]	Ovins
America, North									**Amérique du Nord**
Asses	3 730	3 750	3 750	3 750	3 751	3 757	3 773	3 773	**Anes**

36

Livestock
Stocks: thousand head [*cont.*]
Cheptel
Effectifs : milliers de têtes [*suite*]

Region, country or area	1995	1996	1997	1998	1999	2000	2001	2002	Région, pays ou zone
Buffaloes	5	5	5	5	5	5	6	6	**Buffles**
Cattle	166 293	166 953	166 578	164 674	162 264	161 850	161 796	161 630	**Bovins**
Goats	14 663	14 289	13 896	13 403	13 292	13 263	13 713	13 963	**Caprins**
Horses	14 055	14 116	14 119	14 078	14 010	14 084	14 150	14 158	**Chevaux**
Mules	3 736	3 755	3 753	3 749	3 763	3 764	3 766	3 767	**Mulets**
Pigs	91 985	90 263	88 725	93 795	95 848	94 185	95 242	96 503	**Porcins**
Sheep	17 158	16 689	15 982	15 537	15 573	15 530	16 050	16 142	**Ovins**
Antigua and Barbuda									**Antigua-et-Barbuda**
Asses [1]	1	1	1	1	1	1	1	2	Anes [1]
Cattle	16[1]	15[1]	15[1]	14[1]	14[1]	13	14[1]	14[1]	Bovins
Goats	22[1]	25[1]	28[1]	30[1]	32[1]	34	35[1]	35[1]	Caprins
Pigs	3[1]	3[1]	4[1]	4[1]	5[1]	5	5[1]	5[1]	Porcins
Sheep	14[1]	15[1]	16[1]	17[1]	17[1]	18	18[1]	19[1]	Ovins
Bahamas									**Bahamas**
Cattle	1	1	1[1]	1[1]	1	1	1	1[1]	Bovins
Goats	14	16	16[1]	16[1]	14	14	14	14[1]	Caprins
Pigs	* 5	5	5[1]	5[1]	6	5	5	5[1]	Porcins
Sheep	7	6	6[1]	6[1]	6	6	6	6[1]	Ovins
Barbados [1]									**Barbade** [1]
Asses	2	2	2	2	2	2	2	2	Anes
Cattle	31	31	21	21	21	21	21	21	Bovins
Goats	5	5	5	5	5	5	5	5	Caprins
Horses	1	1	1	1	1	1	1	1	Chevaux
Mules	2	2	2	2	2	2	2	2	Mulets
Pigs	30	30	31	33	33	34	35	35	Porcins
Sheep	41	41	41	41	41	42	41	41	Ovins
Belize									**Belize**
Cattle	41	43	47[1]	52[1]	58[1]	66	58	57	Bovins
Goats [1]	1	1	1	1	1	1	2	2	Caprins [1]
Horses [1]	5	5	5	5	5	5	5	5	Chevaux [1]
Mules [1]	4	4	4	4	4	4	4	5	Mulets [1]
Pigs	22	25	21[1]	22	24[1]	24[1]	28	23	Porcins
Sheep	3	3	3[1]	3[1]	3[1]	4[1]	4	6	Ovins
Bermuda									**Bermudes**
Cattle [1]	1	1	1	1	1	1	1	1	Bovins [1]
Goats	1[1]	0	0[1]	0[1]	0[1]	0[1]	0[1]	0[1]	Caprins
Horses [1]	1	1	1	1	1	1	1	1	Chevaux [1]
Pigs	1[1]	1	1[1]	1[1]	1[1]	1[1]	1[1]	1[1]	Porcins
British Virgin Islands [1]									**Iles Vierges britanniques** [1]
Cattle	2	2	2	2	2	2	2	2	Bovins
Goats	10	10	10	10	10	10	10	10	Caprins
Pigs	2	2	2	2	2	2	2	2	Porcins
Sheep	6	6	6	6	6	6	6	6	Ovins
Canada									**Canada**
Cattle	12 709	13 402	13 412	13 360	13 211	13 201	13 608	13 700	Bovins
Goats [1]	28	29	29	29	30	30	30	30	Caprins [1]
Horses [1]	380	376	400	380	380	385	385	385	Chevaux [1]
Mules [1]	4	4	4	4	4	4	4	4	Mulets [1]
Pigs	11 291	11 588	11 480	11 985	12 429	12 904	13 576	14 367	Porcins
Sheep	617	643	628	662	717	793	948	994	Ovins
Cayman Islands [1]									**Iles Caïmanes** [1]
Cattle	1	1	1	1	1	1	1	1	Bovins
Costa Rica									**Costa Rica**
Asses [1]	8	8	8	8	8	8	8	8	Anes [1]
Cattle	* 1 645	* 1 585	* 1 529	* 1 527	1 428	1 358	1 289	1 220	Bovins
Goats [1]	2	2	2	2	2	2	2	2	Caprins [1]
Horses [1]	115	115	115	115	115	115	115	115	Chevaux [1]
Mules [1]	5	5	5	5	5	5	5	5	Mulets [1]
Pigs	300	300	315[1]	360[1]	390[1]	440[1]	485[1]	475[1]	Porcins
Sheep [1]	3	3	3	3	3	3	3	3	Ovins [1]

36

Livestock

Stocks: thousand head [cont.]

Cheptel

Effectifs : milliers de têtes [suite]

Region, country or area	1995	1996	1997	1998	1999	2000	2001	2002	Région, pays ou zone
Cuba									**Cuba**
Asses	6	6	6	6	6	7	7[1]	7[1]	Anes
Cattle	4 632	4 601	4 606	4 644	4 406	4 110	4 038	4 038[1]	Bovins
Goats	105	119	139	162	208	249	291	291[1]	Caprins
Horses	583	568	525	434	430	415	400[1]	400[1]	Chevaux
Mules	32	30	28	24	24	23	23[1]	23[1]	Mulets
Pigs	1 063	994	982	1 020	1 144	1 257	1 307	1 307[1]	Porcins
Sheep	310[1]	310[1]	310[1]	310[1]	861	897	969	970[1]	Ovins
Dominica [1]									**Dominique** [1]
Cattle	13	13	13	13	13	13	13	13	Bovins
Goats	10	10	10	10	10	10	10	10	Caprins
Pigs	5	5	5	5	5	5	5	5	Porcins
Sheep	8	8	8	8	8	8	8	8	Ovins
Dominican Republic									**Rép. dominicaine**
Asses [1]	145	145	145	145	145	145	150	150	Anes [1]
Cattle	2 302	2 435	2 481	2 528	1 954	2 018	2 107	2 160	Bovins
Goats	570[1]	570[1]	570	300[1]	163	178	187	188	Caprins
Horses [1]	329	329	329	330	330	330	340	342	Chevaux [1]
Mules [1]	135	135	135	135	138	138	140	140	Mulets [1]
Pigs	950[1]	950[1]	960	960	540	539	566	577[1]	Porcins
Sheep	135[1]	135[1]	135	135	105	105	106	121	Ovins
El Salvador									**El Salvador**
Asses [1]	3	3	3	3	3	3	3	3	Anes [1]
Cattle	1 125	1 287	1 162	1 038	1 141	1 050	1 216	* 1 392	Bovins
Goats	15[1]	15[1]	15[1]	15[1]	15[1]	15[1]	15[1]	11	Caprins
Horses [1]	96	96	96	96	96	96	96	96	Chevaux [1]
Mules [1]	24	24	24	24	24	24	24	24	Mulets [1]
Pigs	190	194	182	175	248	186	150	153	Porcins
Sheep [1]	5	5	5	5	5	5	5	5	Ovins [1]
Greenland [1]									**Groenland** [1]
Sheep	22	22	22	22	22	22	22	22	Ovins
Grenada									**Grenade**
Asses [1]	1	1	1	1	1	1	1	1	Anes [1]
Cattle	4	4[1]	4[1]	4[1]	4[1]	4[1]	4[1]	4[1]	Bovins
Goats	7	7[1]	7[1]	7[1]	7[1]	7[1]	7[1]	7[1]	Caprins
Pigs	5	5[1]	5[1]	5[1]	6[1]	6[1]	6[1]	6[1]	Porcins
Sheep	13	13[1]	13[1]	13[1]	13[1]	13[1]	13[1]	13[1]	Ovins
Guadeloupe									**Guadeloupe**
Cattle	61	80	85	85	85[1]	85[1]	85[1]	85[1]	Bovins
Goats	40	40	30	29	28[1]	28[1]	28[1]	28[1]	Caprins
Horses [1]	1	1	1	1	1	1	1	1	Chevaux [1]
Pigs	37	31	26	20	19[1]	19[1]	19[1]	19[1]	Porcins
Sheep	3	3	3	3	3[1]	3[1]	3[1]	3[1]	Ovins
Guatemala									**Guatemala**
Asses [1]	9	10	10	10	10	10	10	10	Anes [1]
Cattle	2 293	2 291	* 2 337	* 2 330	2 500[1]	2 500[1]	2 500[1]	2 540[1]	Bovins
Goats	103	109	110	110	111	111	112[1]	112[1]	Caprins
Horses [1]	117	118	118	118	119	120	120	122	Chevaux [1]
Mules [1]	38	38	38	38	39	39	39	39	Mulets [1]
Pigs	462	522	704	760	683[1]	750[1]	763[1]	778[1]	Porcins
Sheep	525	551	475[1]	400[1]	325[1]	240	245	250[1]	Ovins
Haiti									**Haïti**
Asses [1]	210	210	210	210	210	215	215	215	Anes [1]
Cattle	1 250	1 246	1 270	1 300	1 300[1]	1 430	1 440[1]	1 450[1]	Bovins
Goats	* 1 118	* 1 242	* 1 445	* 1 618	1 619[1]	1 942	1 942[1]	1 943[1]	Caprins
Horses [1]	480	490	490	490	490	500	501	501	Chevaux [1]
Mules [1]	80	80	80	80	80	82	82	82	Mulets [1]
Pigs	390	485	600	800	800[1]	1 000	1 001[1]	1 001[1]	Porcins
Sheep	* 124	* 138	* 161	138	138[1]	152	152[1]	153[1]	Ovins
Honduras									**Honduras**
Asses [1]	23	23	23	23	23	23	23	23	Anes [1]

36

Livestock

Stocks: thousand head [*cont.*]

Cheptel

Effectifs : milliers de têtes [*suite*]

Region, country or area	1995	1996	1997	1998	1999	2000	2001	2002	Région, pays ou zone
Cattle	2 111	2 127	2 061	* 1 945	1 715	1 780	1 800[1]	1 860	Bovins
Goats [1]	28	28	29	29	30	31	32	32	Caprins [1]
Horses [1]	174	175	176	177	178	179	180	180	Chevaux [1]
Mules [1]	69	69	69	69	70	70	70	70	Mulets [1]
Pigs	415[1]	445[1]	455[1]	455[1]	473	470	500[1]	538	Porcins
Sheep [1]	13	13	14	14	14	14	14	14	Ovins [1]
Jamaica [1]									**Jamaïque** [1]
Asses	23	23	23	23	23	23	23	23	Anes
Cattle	450	420	400	400	400	400	400	400	Bovins
Goats	440	440	440	440	440	440	440	440	Caprins
Horses	4	4	4	4	4	4	4	4	Chevaux
Mules	10	10	10	10	10	10	10	10	Mulets
Pigs	200	180	180	180	180	180	180	180	Porcins
Sheep	1	1	2	2	1	1	1	1	Ovins
Martinique									**Martinique**
Cattle	30[1]	28	26	25	25[1]	25[1]	25[1]	25[1]	Bovins
Goats [1]	22	22	17	17	17	17	17	17	Caprins [1]
Horses [1]	2	2	2	2	2	2	2	2	Chevaux [1]
Pigs [1]	33	33	32	34	35	35	35	35	Porcins [1]
Sheep [1]	42	42	38	36	34	34	34	34	Ovins [1]
Mexico									**Mexique**
Asses [1]	3 230	3 250	3 250	3 250	3 250	3 250	3 260	3 260	Anes [1]
Cattle	* 30 191	29 301	30 772	31 060	30 193	30 492	30 600[1]	30 600[1]	Bovins
Goats	10 133	9 567	* 9 208	9 040	9 068	8 704	9 000[1]	9 400[1]	Caprins
Horses [1]	6 200	6 250	6 250	6 250	6 250	6 250	6 255	6 255	Chevaux [1]
Mules [1]	3 250	3 270	3 270	3 270	3 280	3 280	3 280	3 280	Mulets [1]
Pigs	15 923	15 405	15 735	14 972	15 748	16 088	16 500[1]	17 000[1]	Porcins
Sheep	6 195	6 183	5 987	5 804	5 949	6 046	6 400[1]	6 700[1]	Ovins
Montserrat [1]									**Montserrat** [1]
Cattle	10	10	10	10	10	10	10	10	Bovins
Goats	7	7	7	7	7	7	7	7	Caprins
Pigs	1	1	1	1	1	1	1	1	Porcins
Sheep	5	5	5	5	5	5	5	5	Ovins
Netherlands Antilles [1]									**Antilles néerlandaises** [1]
Asses	3	3	3	3	3	3	3	3	Anes
Cattle	0	0	1	1	1	1	1	1	Bovins
Goats	12	13	12	13	11	13	13	13	Caprins
Pigs	2	2	2	2	2	2	2	2	Porcins
Sheep	8	7	7	7	7	8	8	8	Ovins
Nicaragua									**Nicaragua**
Asses [1]	8	8	9	9	9	9	9	9	Anes [1]
Cattle	2 700[1]	2 600[1]	2 850[1]	2 735[1]	2 850[1]	3 275	3 300	3 350	Bovins
Goats [1]	6	6	6	6	6	7	7	7	Caprins [1]
Horses [1]	246	245	245	245	245	246	248	250	Chevaux [1]
Mules [1]	46	46	46	46	46	46	46	47	Mulets [1]
Pigs [1]	392	366	385	400	400	402	410	420	Porcins [1]
Sheep [1]	4	4	4	4	4	4	4	4	Ovins [1]
Panama									**Panama**
Cattle	1 456	1 442	1 362	1 382	1 360	1 343	1 533	1 533	Bovins
Goats	5[1]	5[1]	5[1]	5[1]	5[1]	5	5	6	Caprins
Horses [1]	165	165	165	165	166	166	168	170	Chevaux [1]
Mules [1]	4	4	4	4	4	4	4	4	Mulets [1]
Pigs	261	244	240	252	278	278	312	280[1]	Porcins
Puerto Rico									**Porto Rico**
Asses [1]	2	2	2	2	2	2	2	2	Anes [1]
Cattle	368	371	388	387	390[1]	390[1]	390	390[1]	Bovins
Goats	18	8	13[1]	9	9[1]	9[1]	9[1]	9[1]	Caprins
Horses [1]	24	24	24	25	25	26	26	26	Chevaux [1]
Mules [1]	3	3	3	3	3	3	3	3	Mulets [1]
Pigs	205	182	175	115	118[1]	118[1]	118[1]	118[1]	Porcins
Sheep	15[1]	16[1]	16[1]	16	16[1]	16[1]	16[1]	16[1]	Ovins

36

Livestock
Stocks: thousand head [*cont.*]
Cheptel
Effectifs : milliers de têtes [*suite*]

Region, country or area	1995	1996	1997	1998	1999	2000	2001	2002	Région, pays ou zone
Saint Kitts and Nevis									**Saint-Kitts-et-Nevis**
Cattle	4[1]	4[1]	4	4[1]	4[1]	4	4[1]	4[1]	Bovins
Goats	14	15	14[1]	14[1]	14[1]	14	14[1]	14[1]	Caprins
Pigs	2	3	3[1]	3[1]	3	5	4[1]	4[1]	Porcins
Sheep	10	11	11[1]	12[1]	13[1]	14	14[1]	14[1]	Ovins
Saint Lucia									**Sainte-Lucie**
Asses [1]	1	1	1	1	1	1	1	1	Anes [1]
Cattle [1]	12	12	12	12	12	12	12	12	Bovins [1]
Goats	10[1]	10	10[1]	10[1]	10[1]	10[1]	10[1]	10	Caprins
Horses [1]	1	1	1	1	1	1	1	1	Chevaux [1]
Mules [1]	1	1	1	1	1	1	1	1	Mulets [1]
Pigs	14[1]	15	15[1]	15[1]	15[1]	15[1]	15[1]	15	Porcins
Sheep	13[1]	12	13[1]	13[1]	13[1]	13[1]	13[1]	13	Ovins
St. Vincent-Grenadines [1]									**St. Vincent-Grenadines** [1]
Asses	1	1	1	1	1	1	1	1	Anes
Cattle	6	6	6	6	6	6	6	6	Bovins
Goats	6	6	6	6	6	6	6	6	Caprins
Pigs	9	9	9	9	9	10	10	10	Porcins
Sheep	13	13	13	13	13	13	13	13	Ovins
Trinidad and Tobago									**Trinité-et-Tobago**
Asses [1]	2	2	2	2	2	2	2	2	Anes [1]
Buffaloes	5	5[1]	5[1]	5[1]	5[1]	5[1]	6[1]	6[1]	Buffles
Cattle	36	36[1]	35[1]	34[1]	35[1]	30[1]	30[1]	32[1]	Bovins
Goats [1]	59	59	59	59	59	59	60	61	Caprins [1]
Horses [1]	1	1	1	1	1	1	1	1	Chevaux [1]
Mules [1]	2	2	2	2	2	2	2	2	Mulets [1]
Pigs	32	34	45[1]	41[1]	43[1]	62	63	64[1]	Porcins
Sheep	12	12[1]	12[1]	12[1]	12[1]	12[1]	13[1]	13[1]	Ovins
United States									**Etats-Unis**
Asses [1]	52	52	52	52	52	52	52	52	Anes [1]
Cattle	102 785	103 548	101 656	99 744	99 115	98 198	97 277	96 700	Bovins
Goats	1 850	1 900	1 650	1 400	1 350	1 300	1 400	1 250	Caprins
Horses	5 130[1]	5 150[1]	* 5 170	* 5 237	5 170	5 240	5 300[1]	5 300[1]	Chevaux
Mules [1]	28	28	28	28	28	28	28	28	Mulets [1]
Pigs	59 738	58 201	56 124	61 158	62 206	59 342	59 138	59 074	Porcins
Sheep	8 989	8 465	8 024	7 825	7 215	7 032	6 965	6 685	Ovins
United States Virgin Is. [1]									**Iles Vierges américaines** [1]
Cattle	8	8	8	8	8	8	8	8	Bovins
Goats	4	4	4	4	4	4	4	4	Caprins
Pigs	3	3	3	3	3	3	3	3	Porcins
Sheep	3	3	3	3	3	3	3	3	Ovins
America, South									**Amérique du Sud**
Asses	**4 062**	**3 951**	**3 969**	**3 954**	**3 984**	**4 009**	**4 028**	**4 059**	**Anes**
Buffaloes	**1 643**	**1 047**	**978**	**1 018**	**1 069**	**1 103**	**1 119**	**1 200**	**Buffles**
Cattle	**294 060**	**290 743**	**293 162**	**291 080**	**292 797**	**299 016**	**307 629**	**310 656**	**Bovins**
Goats	**23 401**	**19 615**	**21 220**	**20 126**	**21 341**	**22 809**	**22 863**	**23 386**	**Caprins**
Horses	**15 587**	**15 004**	**15 093**	**15 128**	**15 464**	**15 542**	**15 650**	**15 673**	**Chevaux**
Mules	**3 311**	**2 611**	**2 621**	**2 620**	**2 684**	**2 717**	**2 731**	**2 752**	**Mulets**
Pigs	**57 598**	**50 857**	**52 103**	**53 530**	**56 573**	**57 901**	**59 117**	**56 410**	**Porcins**
Sheep	**85 162**	**80 306**	**77 263**	**76 006**	**75 917**	**75 677**	**74 144**	**74 249**	**Ovins**
Argentina									**Argentine**
Asses [1]	90	90	90	90	95	95	95	95	Anes [1]
Cattle	52 649	50 830	50 059	48 049	49 057	48 674	48 851	* 50 669	Bovins
Goats	3 547	3 375	3 428	3 400[1]	3 403	3 490	3 387	3 550[1]	Caprins
Horses [1]	3 300	3 300	3 300	3 300	3 600	3 600	3 600	3 650	Chevaux [1]
Mules [1]	175	175	175	175	180	180	180	180	Mulets [1]
Pigs	3 100	3 100	3 200	3 500[1]	4 200[1]	4 200[1]	4 200[1]	4 250[1]	Porcins
Sheep	15 245	14 308	13 198	13 500[1]	13 703	13 562	13 500[1]	14 000[1]	Ovins
Bolivia									**Bolivie**
Asses [1]	631	631	631	631	631	631	631	632	Anes [1]
Cattle	6 000	6 118	6 238	6 387	6 556	6 725	6 457	6 576	Bovins

36

Livestock
Stocks: thousand head [*cont.*]
Cheptel
Effectifs : milliers de têtes [*suite*]

Region, country or area	1995	1996	1997	1998	1999	2000	2001	2002	Région, pays ou zone
Goats	1 496	1 500[1]	1 496	1 496	1 500	1 500[1]	1 500[1]	1 501[1]	Caprins
Horses [1]	322	322	322	322	322	322	322	323	Chevaux [1]
Mules [1]	81	81	81	81	81	81	81	82	Mulets [1]
Pigs	2 405	2 482	2 569	2 637	2 715	2 793	2 851	2 851	Porcins
Sheep	7 884	8 039	8 232	8 409	8 575	8 752	8 902	8 902	Ovins
Brazil									**Brésil**
Asses	1 344	1 232	1 249	1 233	1 236	1 242	1 239	1 250[1]	Anes
Buffaloes	1 642	1 046	978	1 017	1 068	1 103	1 119	1 200[1]	Buffles
Cattle	161 228	158 289	161 416	163 154	164 621	169 876	176 389	176 000[1]	Bovins
Goats	11 272	7 436	7 968	8 164	8 623	9 347	9 537	9 800[1]	Caprins
Horses	6 394	5 705	5 832	5 867	5 831	5 832	5 801	5 900[1]	Chevaux
Mules	1 990	1 286	1 295	1 292	1 336	1 348	1 346	1 350[1]	Mulets
Pigs	36 062	29 202	29 637	30 007	30 839	31 562	32 605	30 000[1]	Porcins
Sheep	18 336	14 726	14 534	14 268	14 400	14 785	14 639	15 000[1]	Ovins
Chile									**Chili**
Asses [1]	28	28	28	28	28	29	29	29	Anes [1]
Cattle	3 814	3 858	4 142	4 160	4 134	4 068	3 876[1]	3 566[1]	Bovins
Goats	600[1]	600[1]	738	740[1]	740[1]	745[1]	800[1]	900[1]	Caprins
Horses [1]	550	580	600	600	610	620	650	660	Chevaux [1]
Mules [1]	10	10	10	10	10	10	11	11	Mulets [1]
Pigs	1 490	1 486	1 655	1 962	2 221	2 465	2 500[1]	2 750[1]	Porcins
Sheep	4 625	4 516	3 835	3 754	4 116	4 144	4 200[1]	4 100[1]	Ovins
Colombia									**Colombie**
Asses [1]	710	710	710	710	715	718	720	723	Anes [1]
Cattle	25 551	* 26 088	25 673	25 764	24 363	25 206	26 252	27 000[1]	Bovins
Goats	* 965	* 963	1 006	1 050	1 115	1 185	1 136	1 120[1]	Caprins
Horses	2 450	2 450[1]	2 450[1]	2 450[1]	2 500[1]	2 550[1]	2 600[1]	2 650[1]	Chevaux
Mules	586	590[1]	590[1]	590[1]	595[1]	600[1]	605[1]	610[1]	Mulets
Pigs	2 500	2 431	2 480	2 452	2 765	2 193	2 197	2 150[1]	Porcins
Sheep	* 2 540	* 2 540	2 325	1 994	2 196	2 288	2 256	2 260[1]	Ovins
Ecuador									**Equateur**
Asses [1]	265	266	267	268	269	270	270	275	Anes [1]
Cattle	4 995	5 105	5 150	5 076	5 106	5 104	5 574	5 578	Bovins
Goats	295	309	309	280	277	280	273	278	Caprins
Horses [1]	520	520	520	520	521	523	525	528	Chevaux [1]
Mules [1]	154	155	156	157	157	158	158	160	Mulets [1]
Pigs	2 618	2 621	2 708	2 708	2 786	2 721	2 788	2 806	Porcins
Sheep	1 692	1 709	1 802	2 081	2 196	2 196	2 249	2 381	Ovins
Falkland Is. (Malvinas)									**Iles Falkland (Malvinas)**
Cattle	5	4	5	4	4[1]	4[1]	4[1]	4[1]	Bovins
Horses	1	1	1	1	1[1]	1[1]	1[1]	1[1]	Chevaux
Sheep	717	686	707	708	700[1]	710[1]	690[1]	690[1]	Ovins
French Guiana									**Guyane française**
Cattle	8	9	10	9	9[1]	9[1]	9[1]	9[1]	Bovins
Goats	1	1[1]	1[1]	1[1]	1[1]	1[1]	1[1]	1[1]	Caprins
Pigs	9	10	10	10	10[1]	11[1]	11[1]	11[1]	Porcins
Sheep	3	3[1]	3[1]	3[1]	3[1]	3[1]	3[1]	3[1]	Ovins
Guyana [1]									**Guyana** [1]
Asses	1	1	1	1	1	1	1	1	Anes
Cattle	220	180	130	120	110	120	120	100	Bovins
Goats	79	79	79	79	79	79	79	79	Caprins
Horses	2	2	2	2	2	2	2	2	Chevaux
Pigs	15	15	15	15	15	15	15	20	Porcins
Sheep	130	130	130	130	130	130	130	130	Ovins
Paraguay									**Paraguay**
Asses [1]	32	32	32	32	32	32	33	33	Anes [1]
Cattle	9 788	9 765	9 794	* 9 833	9 647	9 737	9 889	9 900[1]	Bovins
Goats	123	124	123	* 131	122	123	124	125[1]	Caprins
Horses	411[1]	478[1]	400[1]	400[1]	400[1]	400[1]	358	358[1]	Chevaux
Mules [1]	14	14	14	14	14	14	15	15	Mulets [1]

36
Livestock
Stocks: thousand head [cont.]
Cheptel
Effectifs : milliers de têtes [suite]

Region, country or area	1995	1996	1997	1998	1999	2000	2001	2002	Région, pays ou zone
Pigs[1]	2 525	2 268	2 300	2 300	2 500	3 100	3 150	2 750	Porcins[1]
Sheep	386[1]	387[1]	387	395	398	402	406	407[1]	Ovins
Peru									**Pérou**
Asses[1]	520	520	520	520	535	550	570	580	Anes[1]
Cattle	4 513	4 646	4 560	4 657	4 903	4 927	4 978	4 950	Bovins
Goats	2 044	2 023	2 048	2 019	2 068	2 023	2 004	2 010	Caprins
Horses[1]	665	665	665	665	675	690	700	710	Chevaux[1]
Mules[1]	224	224	224	224	235	250	260	270	Mulets[1]
Pigs	2 401	2 533	2 481	2 531	2 788	2 819	2 780	2 800	Porcins
Sheep	12 570	12 713	13 108	13 566	14 297	14 686	14 259	14 300	Ovins
Suriname									**Suriname**
Buffaloes	1	1	1	1	1	0	0	0[1]	Buffles
Cattle	102	98	97	111	120	130	135	136[1]	Bovins
Goats	6	8	8	7	8	7	7	7[1]	Caprins
Pigs	20	17[1]	21	20	20	22	22	24[1]	Porcins
Sheep	7	8	9	7	8	7	8	8[1]	Ovins
Uruguay									**Uruguay**
Asses[1]	1	1	1	1	1	1	1	1	Anes[1]
Cattle	10 450	10 651	10 553	10 297	10 389	10 353	10 595	* 11 667	Bovins
Goats[1]	15	15	15	15	15	15	15	15	Caprins[1]
Horses[1]	470	480	500	500	500	501	590	390	Chevaux[1]
Mules[1]	4	4	4	4	4	4	4	4	Mulets[1]
Pigs	270[1]	270	270[1]	330[1]	360[1]	346[1]	343[1]	344[1]	Porcins
Sheep	20 205	19 747	18 280	16 495	14 491	13 198	12 083	11 250	Ovins
Venezuela									**Venezuela**
Asses[1]	440	440	440	440	440	440	440	440	Anes[1]
Cattle	14 737	15 103	15 337	13 459	13 778	14 084	14 500[1]	14 500[1]	Bovins
Goats	2 959	3 182	4 000[1]	2 744	3 392	4 015	4 000[1]	4 000[1]	Caprins
Horses[1]	500	500	500	500	500	500	500	500	Chevaux[1]
Mules[1]	72	72	72	72	72	72	72	72	Mulets[1]
Pigs	4 182	4 422	4 756	5 056	5 355	5 655	5 655[1]	5 655[1]	Porcins
Sheep	822	796	714	696	705	815	820[1]	820[1]	Ovins
Asia									**Asie**
Asses	20 292	19 659	18 453	18 067	18 869	18 663	18 590	18 153	**Anes**
Buffaloes	154 482	157 110	156 693	156 376	157 546	159 587	160 499	162 126	**Buffles**
Cattle	455 997	458 262	450 939	459 968	463 377	469 734	471 930	474 742	**Bovins**
Goats	410 863	439 668	420 097	434 627	444 704	453 826	464 077	469 851	**Caprins**
Horses	17 898	18 036	16 559	16 600	16 651	16 619	16 495	15 921	**Chevaux**
Mules	6 271	6 163	5 598	5 622	5 583	5 560	5 391	5 221	**Mulets**
Pigs	511 654	486 957	464 888	501 329	521 948	531 393	552 569	565 775	**Porcins**
Sheep	411 113	410 580	392 379	398 078	400 449	405 370	403 311	406 807	**Ovins**
Afghanistan									**Afghanistan**
Asses	* 704	* 753	* 805	* 860	920	920[1]	920[1]	920[1]	Anes
Cattle	2 095	* 2 641	* 2 895	3 008	2 600[1]	2 200[1]	* 2 000	2 000[1]	Bovins
Goats	5 389	* 4 609	* 5 531	6 599	6 000[1]	5 500[1]	* 5 000	5 000[1]	Caprins
Horses	100[1]	100[1]	100[1]	100[1]	104	104[1]	104[1]	104[1]	Chevaux
Mules[1]	23	24	26	28	30	30	30	30	Mulets[1]
Sheep	12 568	* 13 965	* 15 110	16 252	14 000[1]	12 000[1]	* 11 000	11 000[1]	Ovins
Armenia									**Arménie**
Asses[1]	3	3	3	3	3	2	3	3	Anes[1]
Cattle	504	508	510	466	469	479	485	520	Bovins
Goats	* 16	14	* 13	* 13	12	11	10	* 11	Caprins
Horses	12	12	13	13	12	12	11	12	Chevaux
Pigs	82	80	54	57	86	71	69	105	Porcins
Sheep	* 620	590	* 566	* 531	508	497	540	555	Ovins
Azerbaijan									**Azerbaïdjan**
Asses	22	25	28	31	33	36	38	38[1]	Anes
Buffaloes	295[1]	298	303	303	292	297	299	304	Buffles
Cattle	1 633	1 682	1 780	1 844	1 913	1 961	2 022	2 098	Bovins
Goats	* 182	210	274	371	381	494	533	556	Caprins
Horses	38	43	49	53	56	61	64	63[1]	Chevaux

36

Livestock
Stocks: thousand head [*cont.*]
Cheptel
Effectifs : milliers de têtes [*suite*]

Region, country or area	1995	1996	1997	1998	1999	2000	2001	2002	Région, pays ou zone
Pigs	33	30	23	21	26	20	19	17	Porcins
Sheep	4 376	4 434	4 648	4 896	5 131	5 280	5 553	6 003	Ovins
Bahrain									**Bahreïn**
Cattle	11	12	12	13	13[1]	11	11[1]	11[1]	Bovins
Goats	16	16	17	16	16[1]	16[1]	16[1]	16[1]	Caprins
Sheep	17	18	18	17	17[1]	18[1]	18[1]	18[1]	Ovins
Bangladesh									**Bangladesh**
Buffaloes	* 882	* 860	* 854	820	828[1]	830[1]	830[1]	830[1]	Buffles
Cattle	23 977	23 573	23 962	23 400	23 652[1]	23 900[1]	24 000[1]	24 000[1]	Bovins
Goats	* 30 330	33 312	34 478	33 500	33 800[1]	34 100[1]	34 400[1]	34 400[1]	Caprins
Sheep	1 070[1]	1 124	1 158	1 110	1 121[1]	1 132[1]	1 143[1]	1 143[1]	Ovins
Bhutan									**Bhoutan**
Asses [1]	18	18	18	18	18	18	18	18	Anes [1]
Buffaloes	1	3	3	3[1]	2[1]	2[1]	2[1]	2	Buffles
Cattle	372	354	354	354[1]	354[1]	355[1]	355[1]	355	Bovins
Goats	35	66	66	59[1]	52[1]	45[1]	38[1]	31	Caprins
Horses [1]	30	30	30	30	30	30	30	30	Chevaux [1]
Mules [1]	10	10	10	10	10	10	10	10	Mulets [1]
Pigs	48	61	61	58[1]	53[1]	48[1]	45[1]	41	Porcins
Sheep	34	34	34	32[1]	30[1]	28[1]	26[1]	23	Ovins
Brunei Darussalam									**Brunéi Darussalam**
Buffaloes	4	4	6	6	6	5	6	7[1]	Buffles
Cattle	2	2	2	2	2	2	2	2[1]	Bovins
Goats	4	3	3	4	4	4	2	3[1]	Caprins
Pigs [1]	4	5	5	5	6	6	6	7	Porcins [1]
Sheep [1]	1	0	0	3	2	2	3	4	Ovins [1]
Cambodia									**Cambodge**
Buffaloes	765	744	694	694	654	694	626	626	Buffles
Cattle	2 786	2 762	2 821	2 680	2 826	2 993	2 869	2 924	Bovins
Horses [1]	21	22	22	23	25	26	27	27	Chevaux [1]
Pigs	2 044	2 151	2 438	2 339	2 189	1 934	2 115	2 105	Porcins
China									**Chine**
Asses	10 923	10 745	9 444	9 528	9 558	9 348	9 227	8 815	Anes
Buffaloes	22 928	23 597	21 733	22 555	22 674	22 596	22 766	* 22 249	Buffles
Cattle	100 556	99 458	* 90 854	99 409	101 878	104 582	106 087	* 106 175	Bovins
Goats	123 394	149 912	123 467	135 116	141 956	148 400	157 362	161 492	Caprins
Horses	10 040	10 074	8 717	8 914	8 983	8 916	8 768	8 262	Chevaux
Mules	5 552	5 389	4 780	4 806	4 739	4 673	4 530	4 362	Mulets
Pigs	424 787	* 398 617	373 644	408 425	429 202	437 541	454 410	464 695	Porcins
Sheep	117 446	127 630	114 125	120 956	127 352	131 095	133 160	136 972	Ovins
Cyprus									**Chypre**
Asses [1]	5	5	5	5	5	5	5	5	Anes [1]
Cattle	64	68	70	62	56	54	54	54	Bovins
Goats	210	220	240	302	322	346	379	447	Caprins
Horses [1]	1	1	1	1	1	1	1	1	Chevaux [1]
Mules [1]	2	2	2	2	2	2	2	2	Mulets [1]
Pigs	356	374	400	415	431	419	414	451	Porcins
Sheep	255	250	252	250	240	233	246	297	Ovins
Georgia									**Géorgie**
Asses	6	8	9	10	11	11	10	10[1]	Anes
Buffaloes	26	29	33	33	33	35	33	33[1]	Buffles
Cattle	944	974	1 008	1 027	1 051	1 122	1 177	1 180	Bovins
Goats	39	51	54	59	65	80	81	92	Caprins
Horses	24	26	28	30	34	35	39	39	Chevaux
Pigs	367	353	333	330	366	411	443	445	Porcins
Sheep	754	674	600	525	522	553	547	568	Ovins
India									**Inde**
Asses	800[1]	800[1]	778	750[1]	750[1]	750[1]	750[1]	750[1]	Anes
Buffaloes	88 375	90 063	91 784	* 90 909	* 92 090	* 93 772	* 94 132	* 95 100	Buffles
Cattle	207 492	208 488	209 489	* 212 121	* 214 877	* 218 800	* 219 642	* 221 900	Bovins
Goats	118 419	119 484	120 560	* 121 362	* 122 530	* 123 000	123 500[1]	124 000[1]	Caprins

36

Livestock
Stocks: thousand head [*cont.*]

Cheptel
Effectifs : milliers de têtes [*suite*]

Region, country or area	1995	1996	1997	1998	1999	2000	2001	2002	Région, pays ou zone
Horses [1]	800	800	800	800	800	800	800	800	Chevaux [1]
Mules	250[1]	250[1]	286	300[1]	300[1]	300[1]	300[1]	300[1]	Mulets
Pigs	14 306	14 848	15 411	* 16 005	16 500[1]	17 000[1]	17 500[1]	18 000[1]	Porcins
Sheep	54 131	55 289	56 472	* 57 100	* 57 600	* 57 900	58 200[1]	58 800[1]	Ovins
Indonesia									**Indonésie**
Buffaloes	3 136	3 171	3 065	2 829	2 504	2 405	2 287	2 300[1]	Buffles
Cattle	11 534	11 816	11 939	11 634	11 276	11 008	11 191	11 200[1]	Bovins
Goats	13 167	13 840	14 163	13 560	12 701	12 585	12 456	12 400[1]	Caprins
Horses	609	579	582	566	484	412	430	450[1]	Chevaux
Pigs	7 720	7 597	8 233	7 798	7 042	5 357	5 867	6 000[1]	Porcins
Sheep	7 169	7 724	7 698	7 144	7 226	7 427	7 294	7 350[1]	Ovins
Iran (Islamic Rep. of)									**Iran (Rép. islamique d')**
Asses	* 1 400	* 1 400	* 1 490	* 1 400	* 1 554	1 600[1]	1 600[1]	1 600[1]	Anes
Buffaloes	447	456	465	474	474	491	507	524	Buffles
Cattle	8 347	8 492	8 638	8 785	8 047	8 270	8 500	8 738	Bovins
Goats	25 757	25 757	26 000	25 757	25 757	25 757	25 757	25 757	Caprins
Horses [1]	150	150	150	130	120	150	150	150	Chevaux [1]
Mules	* 137	* 137	* 147	* 137	* 173	175[1]	175[1]	175[1]	Mulets
Sheep	50 889	51 499	52 117	53 245	53 900	53 900	53 900	53 900	Ovins
Iraq									**Iraq**
Asses	* 396	368[1]	380[1]	385[1]	375[1]	380[1]	380[1]	380[1]	Anes
Buffaloes	* 70	50[1]	* 62	64[1]	64[1]	65[1]	66[1]	67[1]	Buffles
Cattle	1 190[1]	1 050[1]	* 1 300	* 1 320	* 1 325	* 1 350	1 375[1]	1 400[1]	Bovins
Goats	1 450[1]	1 105[1]	* 1 466	1 500[1]	1 550[1]	1 600[1]	1 650[1]	1 650[1]	Caprins
Horses	* 47	46[1]	47[1]	48[1]	46[1]	47[1]	47[1]	47[1]	Chevaux
Mules [1]	12	12	12	13	11	11	11	11	Mulets [1]
Sheep	7 400[1]	* 5 850	* 6 584	* 6 900	* 6 000	* 6 100	6 100[1]	6 200[1]	Ovins
Israel									**Israël**
Asses [1]	5	5	5	5	5	5	5	5	Anes [1]
Cattle	391	391	380	388	395	395	390	390[1]	Bovins
Goats	94	80	75	74	75	62	63	65[1]	Caprins
Horses [1]	4	4	4	4	4	4	4	4	Chevaux [1]
Mules [1]	2	2	2	2	2	2	2	2	Mulets [1]
Pigs [1]	143	145	165	163	122	141	155	155	Porcins [1]
Sheep	327	340	360	350	350	380	389	392[1]	Ovins
Japan									**Japon**
Cattle	4 916	4 828	4 750	4 708	4 658	4 588	4 531	4 564	Bovins
Goats	30	29	29	29[1]	33[1]	35[1]	35[1]	35[1]	Caprins
Horses	29[1]	26[1]	27	26[1]	25[1]	25[1]	21[1]	20[1]	Chevaux
Pigs	10 250	9 900	9 823	9 904	9 879	9 806	9 788	9 612	Porcins
Sheep	20	18	16	13[1]	12[1]	10[1]	10[1]	11[1]	Ovins
Jordan									**Jordanie**
Asses [1]	18	18	18	18	18	18	18	18	Anes [1]
Cattle	58	62	62	61	65	65	67	68	Bovins
Goats	852	807	782	650	631	461	426	557	Caprins
Horses [1]	4	4	4	4	4	4	4	4	Chevaux [1]
Mules [1]	3	3	3	3	3	3	3	3	Mulets [1]
Sheep	2 182	2 375	2 144	1 935	1 581	1 934	1 484	1 458	Ovins
Kazakhstan									**Kazakhstan**
Asses [1]	40	40	35	29	29	30	30	30	Anes [1]
Buffaloes [1]	11	10	10	9	9	9	9	9	Buffles [1]
Cattle	8 073	6 860	5 425	4 307	3 958	3 998	4 107	4 282	Bovins
Goats	859	799	679	691	835	931	1 042	1 271	Caprins
Horses	1 636	1 557	1 310	1 083	986	970	976	986	Chevaux
Pigs	1 983	1 623	1 036	879	892	984	1 076	1 124	Porcins
Sheep	24 273	18 786	13 000	9 693	8 691	8 725	8 939	9 208	Ovins
Korea, Dem. P. R.									**Corée, R. p. dém. de**
Cattle	886	615	545	565	577	579	570	575	Bovins
Goats	712	712	1 077	1 508	1 900	2 276	2 566	2 693	Caprins
Horses [1]	45	40	40	44	45	46	47	48	Chevaux [1]

36

Livestock
Stocks: thousand head [*cont.*]
Cheptel
Effectifs : milliers de têtes [*suite*]

Region, country or area	1995	1996	1997	1998	1999	2000	2001	2002	Région, pays ou zone
Pigs	2 674	2 674	1 859	2 475	2 970	3 120	3 137	3 152	Porcins
Sheep	260[1]	248	160	165	185	185	189	170	Ovins
Korea, Republic of									**Corée, République de**
Cattle	3 147	3 395	3 280	2 922	2 486	2 134	1 954	* 1 951	Bovins
Goats	681	675	604	539	462	445	440	435[1]	Caprins
Horses	6	7	8	8	8	11	11[1]	11[1]	Chevaux
Pigs	6 461	6 517	7 096	7 544	7 864	8 214	8 720	* 8 811	Porcins
Sheep	2	2	1	1	1	1	1[1]	1[1]	Ovins
Kuwait									**Koweït**
Cattle	20	19	21	18	20	21	22[1]	18[1]	Bovins
Goats	68	96	117	130	159	153	130	130[1]	Caprins
Horses [1]	1	1	1	1	1	1	1	1	Chevaux [1]
Sheep	308	395	417	421	476	616	630	800	Ovins
Kyrgyzstan									**Kirghizistan**
Asses [1]	10	10	9	8	8	8	7	7	Anes [1]
Cattle	920	869	848	885	911	947	970	988	Bovins
Goats	152	200	171	* 340	* 500	601	640	661	Caprins
Horses	299	308	314	330[1]	336[1]	350	346[1]	350[1]	Chevaux
Pigs	118	114	88	93	105	101	87	87	Porcins
Sheep	4 924	4 075	3 545	* 3 000	* 3 000	3 198	3 104	3 104	Ovins
Lao People's Dem. Rep.									**Rép. dém. pop. lao**
Buffaloes	1 191	1 212	1 224	1 093	1 008	1 028	1 051	1 060[1]	Buffles
Cattle	1 146	1 186	1 228	1 127	1 000	1 100	1 217	1 150[1]	Bovins
Goats	153	159	172	186	200	217	240[1]	260[1]	Caprins
Horses [1]	29	26	26	27	28	29	29	30	Chevaux [1]
Pigs	1 724	1 772	1 813	1 432	1 320	1 425	1 426	1 426[1]	Porcins
Lebanon									**Liban**
Asses [1]	24	24	25	25	25	25	25	25	Anes [1]
Cattle	* 60	70	69	72	76	77	78	79[1]	Bovins
Goats	* 438	482	497	466	436	417	399	385[1]	Caprins
Horses	* 5	5	5[1]	6[1]	6[1]	6[1]	6[1]	6[1]	Chevaux
Mules	6[1]	5	6[1]	6[1]	6[1]	6[1]	6[1]	6[1]	Mulets
Pigs	45[1]	40[1]	35	34	28	26	23	20[1]	Porcins
Sheep	250[1]	313	322	350	378	354	329	350[1]	Ovins
Malaysia									**Malaisie**
Buffaloes	165	157	151	160	150	142	148	154	Buffles
Cattle	716	694	691	714	715	724	742	748	Bovins
Goats	282	255	242	236	238	233	247	248	Caprins
Horses [1]	4	4	4	5	5	5	5	5	Chevaux [1]
Pigs	3 150	3 103	3 171	2 934	1 955	1 808	1 973	1 824	Porcins
Sheep	222	187	167	166	152	157	129	118	Ovins
Mongolia									**Mongolie**
Cattle	3 005	3 317	3 476	3 613	3 726	3 825	3 098	2 054	Bovins
Goats	7 241	8 521	9 135	10 265	11 062	11 034	10 270	8 858	Caprins
Horses	2 409	2 648	2 771	2 893	3 059	3 163	3 200[1]	3 100[1]	Chevaux
Pigs	23	24	19	21	22	15	15	15[1]	Porcins
Sheep	13 787	13 719	13 561	14 166	14 694	15 191	13 876	11 937	Ovins
Myanmar									**Myanmar**
Buffaloes	2 203	2 266	2 297	2 337	2 391	2 441	2 500	2 552	Buffles
Cattle	9 857	10 121	10 303	10 493	10 740	10 964	11 218	11 551	Bovins
Goats	1 164	1 217	1 275	1 319	1 353	1 392	1 439	1 542	Caprins
Horses [1]	120	120	120	120	120	120	120	120	Chevaux [1]
Mules [1]	8	8	8	8	8	8	8	8	Mulets [1]
Pigs	2 944	3 229	3 358	3 501	3 715	3 914	4 139	4 499	Porcins
Sheep	328	341	357	369	379	390	403	432	Ovins
Nepal									**Népal**
Buffaloes	3 278	3 302	3 362	3 419	3 471	3 526	3 624	3 701	Buffles
Cattle	6 838	7 008	7 025	7 049	7 031	7 023	6 983	6 979	Bovins
Goats	5 649	5 783	5 922	6 080	6 205	6 325	6 478	6 607	Caprins
Pigs	636	670	724	766	825	878	913	934	Porcins
Sheep	919	859	870	869	855	852	850	840	Ovins

36

Livestock
Stocks: thousand head [*cont.*]
Cheptel
Effectifs : milliers de têtes [*suite*]

Region, country or area	1995	1996	1997	1998	1999	2000	2001	2002	Région, pays ou zone
Occ. Palestinian Terr. [1,2]									**Terr. palestinien occ.** [1,2]
Cattle	3	3	3	3	3	3	3	3	Bovins
Goats	16	16	16	16	16	16	16	16	Caprins
Sheep	24	24	24	24	24	24	24	24	Ovins
Oman									**Oman**
Asses [1]	26	27	27	28	28	29	29	29	Anes [1]
Cattle	* 234	* 245	258	271	285	299	314	314	Bovins
Goats	* 886	* 902	925[1]	940	959	979	998	998	Caprins
Sheep	* 267	* 281	295[1]	312	327	344	354	354	Ovins
Pakistan									**Pakistan**
Asses	4 000	3 600	3 600	3 200	3 800	3 800	3 900	3 900[1]	Anes
Buffaloes	19 711	20 273	20 838	21 422	22 032	22 669	23 335	24 000	Buffles
Cattle	17 848	20 424	20 802	21 192	21 592	22 004	22 424	22 857	Bovins
Goats	43 764	41 169	42 650	44 183	45 800	47 400	49 100	50 900	Caprins
Horses	346	334	331	327	300	300	300	300[1]	Chevaux
Mules	78	132	142	151	150	200	200	200[1]	Mulets
Sheep	29 065	23 544	23 668	23 800	23 900	24 100	24 200	24 398	Ovins
Philippines									**Philippines**
Buffaloes	2 708	2 841	2 968	3 013	3 006	3 024	3 066	3 122	Buffles
Cattle	2 021	2 128	2 266	2 395	2 426	2 479	2 496	2 548	Bovins
Goats [1]	6 183	6 230	6 300	6 000	6 125	6 245	6 197	6 250	Caprins [1]
Horses [1]	220	220	230	230	230	230	230	230	Chevaux [1]
Pigs	8 941	9 026	9 752	10 210	10 397	10 713	11 063	11 653	Porcins
Sheep [1]	30	30	30	30	30	30	30	30	Ovins [1]
Qatar									**Qatar**
Cattle	14	14	14	14	15	15	15[1]	15[1]	Bovins
Goats	168	172	174	175	177	178	140	179[1]	Caprins
Horses	1	1	4	4[1]	4[1]	4[1]	4[1]	4[1]	Chevaux
Sheep	192	200	203	206	212	215	150	200[1]	Ovins
Saudi Arabia									**Arabie saoudite**
Asses	102	101	101[1]	100[1]	100[1]	100[1]	100[1]	100[1]	Anes
Cattle	253	259	277	294	297	307	* 320	330[1]	Bovins
Goats	4 373	4 390	4 434	4 350	4 305	* 4 529	4 600[1]	4 650[1]	Caprins
Horses	3	3	3[1]	3[1]	3[1]	3[1]	3[1]	3[1]	Chevaux
Sheep	7 588	7 803	7 452	7 422	7 563	7 931	* 8 049	8 000[1]	Ovins
Singapore [1]									**Singapour** [1]
Pigs	190	190	190	190	190	190	190	190	Porcins
Sri Lanka									**Sri Lanka**
Buffaloes	764	761	726	721	728	694	661	661[1]	Buffles
Cattle	1 704	1 644	1 579	1 599	1 617	1 557	1 565	1 565[1]	Bovins
Goats	591	535	521	519	514	495	493	490[1]	Caprins
Horses [1]	2	2	2	2	2	2	2	2	Chevaux [1]
Pigs	87	85	80	76	74	71	68	67[1]	Porcins
Sheep	19	11	11	12	12	11	12	12[1]	Ovins
Syrian Arab Republic									**Rép. arabe syrienne**
Asses	200	191	190	232	219	216	217[1]	217[1]	Anes
Buffaloes	1	1	2	1	3	3	2	3	Buffles
Cattle	775	810	857	932	978	984	837	867	Bovins
Goats	1 063	1 082	1 100	1 101	1 046	1 050	979	932	Caprins
Horses	27	28	27	26	27	27	27[1]	27[1]	Chevaux
Mules	17	18	18	12	14	13	13[1]	13[1]	Mulets
Pigs	1[1]	1[1]	1[1]	1[1]	1[1]	* 0	* 0	* 0	Porcins
Sheep	12 075	13 120	13 829	15 425	13 998	13 505	12 362	13 497	Ovins
Tajikistan									**Tadjikistan**
Asses	76	80	86	90	106	110	117	123	Anes
Cattle	1 199	1 147	1 082	1 050	1 037	1 037	1 062	1 091	Bovins
Goats	* 743	* 689	688	668	701	706	744	779	Caprins
Horses	58	61	64	66	67	72	72	71	Chevaux
Pigs	32	6	2	1	1	1	1	1	Porcins
Sheep	* 1 958	* 1 805	1 650	1 554	1 494	1 472	1 478	1 490	Ovins

36

Livestock
Stocks: thousand head [*cont.*]
Cheptel
Effectifs : milliers de têtes [*suite*]

Region, country or area	1995	1996	1997	1998	1999	2000	2001	2002	Région, pays ou zone
Thailand									**Thaïlande**
Buffaloes	4 182	3 733	2 865	2 286	1 912	1 712	1 524	1 800[1]	Buffles
Cattle	6 822	6 878	6 778	6 328	5 677	4 602	4 640	4 640[1]	Bovins
Goats	132	98	125	131	133	144	188	150[1]	Caprins
Horses	17	12	15	11	7	9	8	8[1]	Chevaux
Pigs	5 369	6 129	6 894	7 082	6 370	6 558	6 689	6 689[1]	Porcins
Sheep	75	42	42	40	39	37	43	43[1]	Ovins
Turkey									**Turquie**
Asses	809	731	689	640	603	555	489	462	Anes
Buffaloes	305	255	235	194	176	165	146	138	Buffles
Cattle	11 901	11 789	11 886	11 185	11 031	11 054	10 761	10 548	Bovins
Goats	9 564	9 111	8 951	8 376	8 057	7 774	7 201	7 022	Caprins
Horses	437	415	391	345	330	309	271	271	Chevaux
Mules	169	169	154	142	133	125	99	97	Mulets
Pigs	8	5	5	5	5	3	3	3	Porcins
Sheep	35 646	33 791	33 072	30 238	29 435	30 256	28 492	26 972	Ovins
Turkmenistan									**Turkménistan**
Asses [1]	25	26	26	25	25	24	25	25	Anes [1]
Cattle	1 181	1 199	* 959	950[1]	880[1]	850[1]	860[1]	860[1]	Bovins
Goats	* 403	* 424	* 375	370[1]	375[1]	368[1]	375[1]	375[1]	Caprins
Horses [1]	18	17	17	16	16	16	17	17	Chevaux [1]
Pigs	128	82	65[1]	55[1]	48[1]	46[1]	45[1]	45[1]	Porcins
Sheep	* 6 100	* 6 150	* 5 400	5 500[1]	5 650[1]	5 600[1]	6 000[1]	6 000[1]	Ovins
United Arab Emirates									**Emirats arabes unis**
Cattle	69	74	79	85	91	96	97[1]	100[1]	Bovins
Goats	921	985	1 054	1 128	1 207	1 279	1 300[1]	1 300[1]	Caprins
Sheep	356	381	408	437	467	495	550[1]	510[1]	Ovins
Uzbekistan									**Ouzbékistan**
Asses [1]	165	168	169	165	165	160	165	160	Anes [1]
Cattle	5 484	5 204	5 100	5 200	5 225	5 268	5 344	5 400[1]	Bovins
Goats	996	970	* 860	* 894	* 884	* 886	* 830	830[1]	Caprins
Horses	145	146	* 146	150[1]	155[1]	155[1]	150[1]	145[1]	Chevaux
Pigs	350	208	100	70	80	80	89	90[1]	Porcins
Sheep	9 053	* 8 352	* 7 340	* 7 706	* 7 840	* 8 000	* 8 100	8 220[1]	Ovins
Viet Nam									**Viet Nam**
Buffaloes	2 963	2 954	2 944	2 951	2 956	2 897	2 808	2 814	Buffles
Cattle	3 639	3 800	3 905	3 987	4 064	4 128	3 900	4 063	Bovins
Goats	551	513	515	514	516	544	561	622	Caprins
Horses	127	126	120	123	150	127	121	124[1]	Chevaux
Pigs	16 306	16 922	17 636	18 132	18 886	20 194	21 741	23 170	Porcins
Yemen									**Yémen**
Asses [1]	500	500	500	500	500	500	500	500	Anes [1]
Cattle	1 174	1 181	1 201	1 263	1 282	1 339	1 401	1 401[1]	Bovins
Goats	3 328	3 558	3 881	4 089	4 204	4 252	4 453	4 453[1]	Caprins
Horses [1]	3	3	3	3	3	3	3	3	Chevaux [1]
Sheep	3 751	3 922	4 267	4 527	4 667	4 804	5 029	5 029[1]	Ovins
Europe									**Europe**
Asses	932	916	910	831	815	796	793	776	**Anes**
Buffaloes	171	211	205	212	242	265	257	244	**Buffles**
Cattle	178 448	172 420	164 588	155 847	150 646	146 843	142 954	141 340	**Bovins**
Goats	19 682	19 014	19 066	18 952	18 635	18 175	18 217	18 154	**Caprins**
Horses	7 880	7 828	7 728	7 384	7 073	6 896	6 836	6 814	**Chevaux**
Mules	303	288	286	272	270	264	260	262	**Mulets**
Pigs	214 576	208 449	205 184	201 135	204 668	200 229	192 026	195 913	**Porcins**
Sheep	180 786	168 225	163 546	159 651	154 300	148 518	142 794	141 097	**Ovins**
Albania									**Albanie**
Asses [1]	113	113	113	113	113	113	113	113	Anes [1]
Cattle	840	806	771	705	720	728	708	690	Bovins
Goats	1 650	1 250	1 148	1 051	1 120	1 106	1 027	929	Caprins
Horses	71	74	70	65	65[1]	65[1]	65[1]	65[1]	Chevaux
Mules [1]	25	25	25	25	25	25	25	25	Mulets [1]

36

Livestock

Stocks: thousand head [*cont.*]

Cheptel

Effectifs : milliers de têtes [*suite*]

Region, country or area	1995	1996	1997	1998	1999	2000	2001	2002	Région, pays ou zone
Pigs	100	98	97	83	81	103	106	114	Porcins
Sheep	2 480	1 982	1 858	1 872	1 941	1 939	1 906	1 844	Ovins
Austria									**Autriche**
Cattle	2 329	2 326	2 272	2 198	* 2 172	2 172	2 155	2 118	Bovins
Goats	50	54	54	58	54	72	70	59[1]	Caprins
Horses	67	72	73	74	75	82	63[1]	60[1]	Chevaux
Pigs	3 729	3 706	3 664	3 680	3 810	3 431	3 427	3 440	Porcins
Sheep	342	365	381	384	361	352	358	321[1]	Ovins
Belarus									**Bélarus**
Asses [1]	8	8	8	9	9	8	9	9	Anes [1]
Cattle	5 403	5 054	4 855	4 801	4 686	4 326	4 221	4 085	Bovins
Goats	54	58	58	59	56	58	* 61	* 62	Caprins
Horses	220	229	232	233	229	221	217	209	Chevaux
Pigs	4 005	3 895	3 715	3 686	3 698	3 566	3 431	3 373	Porcins
Sheep	230	204	155	127	106	92	89	83	Ovins
Belgium-Luxembourg									**Belgique-Luxembourg**
Cattle	3 369	3 363	3 280	3 184	3 395	3 288	3 245	3 106	Bovins
Goats	9	9	12	11	13	14	17	23	Caprins
Horses	66	66	67	62[1]	60[1]	75[1]	70[1]	75[1]	Chevaux
Pigs	7 053	7 225	7 194	7 436	7 632	7 404	7 349	6 851	Porcins
Sheep	161	161	162	* 155	* 158	126	167	160	Ovins
Bosnia and Herzegovina									**Bosnie-Herzégovine**
Buffaloes [1]	6	6	5	5	7	8	13	13	Buffles [1]
Cattle	519[1]	390[1]	412[1]	* 426	* 443	* 462	440[1]	440[1]	Bovins
Horses	18[1]	18	19	19	20[1]	* 18	18[1]	18[1]	Chevaux
Pigs	290[1]	300[1]	300[1]	* 373	350[1]	355[1]	330[1]	300[1]	Porcins
Sheep	520[1]	473[1]	378[1]	* 581	* 633	* 662	640[1]	670[1]	Ovins
Bulgaria									**Bulgarie**
Asses	276	281	287	225	221	208	210	197	Anes
Buffaloes	14	14	11	11	10	9	8	8	Buffles
Cattle	638	632	582	612	671	682	640	635	Bovins
Goats	795	833	849	966	1 048	1 046	970	899	Caprins
Horses	133	151	170	126	133	140	140	151	Chevaux
Mules	16	17	17	17	16	16	13	15[1]	Mulets
Pigs	1 986	2 140	1 500	1 480	1 722	1 512	1 144	1 014	Porcins
Sheep	3 398	3 383	3 020	2 848	2 774	2 549	2 286	2 418	Ovins
Croatia									**Croatie**
Asses [1]	4	4	4	4	4	4	4	4	Anes [1]
Cattle	493	462	451	443	439	427	438	417	Bovins
Goats	107	105	100	84	79	79	93	97	Caprins
Horses	21	21	19	16	13	11	10	8	Chevaux
Pigs	1 175	1 196	1 175	1 166	1 362	1 233	1 234	1 286	Porcins
Sheep	453	427	452	427	489	529	539	580	Ovins
Czech Republic									**République tchèque**
Cattle	2 030	1 989	1 866	1 701	1 657	1 574	1 582	1 520	Bovins
Goats	45	42	38	35	34	32	28	24[1]	Caprins
Horses	19	19	19	20	23	24	26	27	Chevaux
Pigs	3 867	4 016	4 080	4 013	4 001	3 688	3 594	3 441	Porcins
Sheep	165	134	121	94	86	84	90	96	Ovins
Denmark									**Danemark**
Cattle	2 091	2 093	2 004	1 977	1 887	1 868	1 907	1 923	Bovins
Horses	18	20	39	38	40	40	43	40[1]	Chevaux
Pigs	11 084	10 842	11 383	12 095	11 626	11 922	12 608	12 990	Porcins
Sheep	145	170	142	156	143	145	152	154[1]	Ovins
Estonia									**Estonie**
Cattle	420	370	343	326	308	267	253	261	Bovins
Horses	5	5	4	4	4	4	4	* 6	Chevaux
Pigs	460	449	298	306	326	286	300	345	Porcins
Sheep	62	50	39	36	29	28	29	29	Ovins

36

Livestock
Stocks: thousand head [*cont.*]
Cheptel
Effectifs : milliers de têtes [*suite*]

Region, country or area	1995	1996	1997	1998	1999	2000	2001	2002	Région, pays ou zone
Faeroe Islands[1]									**Iles Féroé**[1]
Cattle	2	2	2	2	2	2	2	2	Bovins
Sheep	68	68	68	68	68	68	68	68	Ovins
Finland									**Finlande**
Cattle	1 148	1 146	1 142	1 117	1 087	1 057	1 037	1 025	Bovins
Goats	5	6	7	7	8	9	7	7	Caprins
Horses	50	52	55	56	56	58	59	60[1]	Chevaux
Pigs	1 295	1 395	1 467	1 401	1 351	1 296	1 261	1 315	Porcins
Sheep	80	115	150	128	107	100	96	96	Ovins
France									**France**
Asses[1]	18	18	17	17	16	16	16	16	Anes[1]
Cattle	20 524	20 661	20 664	20 023	20 265	20 310	20 462	20 281	Bovins
Goats	1 069	1 188	1 202	1 200	1 199	1 211	1 231	1 231	Caprins
Horses	338	338	340	347	348	349	343	350[1]	Chevaux
Mules	13	14	14	14	14	15	15[1]	15[1]	Mulets
Pigs	14 593	14 530	14 976	14 501	14 682	14 930	15 382	15 290	Porcins
Sheep	10 320	10 556	10 463	10 316	10 240	9 578	9 443	9 327	Ovins
Germany									**Allemagne**
Cattle	15 962	15 890	15 760	15 227	14 942	14 658	14 568	14 227	Bovins
Goats	95	100	105	115	125	135	140	160	Caprins
Horses	652	652	670	600	524	476	491	506	Chevaux
Pigs	24 698	23 737	24 283	24 795	26 294	26 001	25 767	25 958	Porcins
Sheep	2 990	2 954	2 884	2 870	2 724	2 743	2 771	2 702	Ovins
Greece									**Grèce**
Asses	95	89	83	78	73	72[1]	72[1]	71[1]	Anes
Buffaloes	1	1	1	1	1[1]	1[1]	1[1]	1[1]	Buffles
Cattle	579	581	580	580	583	590	579	585[1]	Bovins
Goats	5 379	5 525	5 570	5 600	5 520	5 293	5 180	5 023	Caprins
Horses	36	35	33	32	31	33[1]	33[1]	33[1]	Chevaux
Mules	44	41	39	37	35	35[1]	35[1]	35[1]	Mulets
Pigs	1 009	994	987	998	933	906	936	938	Porcins
Sheep	8 802	8 869	8 896	8 884	8 930	8 732	9 269	9 205	Ovins
Hungary									**Hongrie**
Asses[1]	4	4	4	4	4	4	4	4	Anes[1]
Cattle	910	928	909	871	873	857	805	783	Bovins
Goats	52	88	108	129	149	189	103	130	Caprins
Horses	78	71	79	72	70	70	74	78	Chevaux
Pigs	4 356	5 032	5 289	4 931	5 479	5 335	4 834	4 822	Porcins
Sheep	947	977	872	858	909	934	1 129	1 136	Ovins
Iceland									**Islande**
Cattle	73	75	75	76	75	72	70	71[1]	Bovins
Goats	0	0	0	0	1	0	0	0[1]	Caprins
Horses	78	81	80	78	77	74	74	73[1]	Chevaux
Pigs[1]	42	43	43	43	44	44	44	44	Porcins[1]
Sheep	458	464	477	490	491	466	474	470[1]	Ovins
Ireland									**Irlande**
Asses	7[1]	* 7	* 6	* 7	* 6	* 6	7[1]	7[1]	Anes
Cattle	6 410	6 451	6 661	6 882	6 952	6 558	6 330	6 408	Bovins
Goats	14[1]	15	15	15	14	8	7[1]	7[1]	Caprins
Horses	60[1]	70	72	73	76	70	70[1]	70[1]	Chevaux
Mules[1]	1	1	1	1	1	1	1	1	Mulets[1]
Pigs	1 498	1 542	1 665	1 717	1 801	1 763	1 732	1 763	Porcins
Sheep	5 775	5 543	5 342	5 577	5 559	5 319	5 056	4 807	Ovins
Italy									**Italie**
Asses	* 30	26	25[1]	23[1]	23[1]	23[1]	23[1]	23[1]	Anes
Buffaloes	108	148	150	162	186	201	190	* 178	Buffles
Cattle	7 164	7 265	7 163	7 166	7 129	7 162	7 211	* 7 068	Bovins
Goats	1 448	1 373	1 419	1 347	1 331	1 397	1 375	1 327	Caprins
Horses	324	315	305[1]	290[1]	288[1]	280[1]	285[1]	285[1]	Chevaux
Mules	16	12	12[1]	11[1]	10[1]	10[1]	10[1]	10[1]	Mulets

36

Livestock
Stocks: thousand head [*cont.*]
Cheptel
Effectifs : milliers de têtes [*suite*]

Region, country or area	1995	1996	1997	1998	1999	2000	2001	2002	Région, pays ou zone
Pigs	8 023	8 061	8 171	8 281	8 323	8 415	8 329	8 410	Porcins
Sheep	10 682	10 668	10 943	10 894	10 894	11 017	11 089	10 952	Ovins
Latvia									**Lettonie**
Cattle	551	537	509	477	434	378	367	388	Bovins
Goats	7	9	8	9	10	8	10	13	Caprins
Horses	27	27	26	23	19	19	20	20	Chevaux
Pigs	501	553	460	430	421	405	394	453	Porcins
Sheep	86	72	41	29	27	27	29	32	Ovins
Liechtenstein [1]									**Liechtenstein** [1]
Cattle	6	6	6	6	6	6	6	6	Bovins
Pigs	3	3	3	3	3	3	3	3	Porcins
Sheep	3	3	3	3	3	3	3	3	Ovins
Lithuania									**Lituanie**
Cattle	1 152	1 065	1 054	1 016	923	898	748	752	Bovins
Goats	12	14	17	19	24	25	23	24	Caprins
Horses	78	78	81	78	74	75	68	65	Chevaux
Pigs	1 260	1 270	1 128	1 200	1 159	936	868	1 011	Porcins
Sheep	40	32	28	24	16	14	12	12	Ovins
Malta									**Malte**
Asses [1]	1	1	1	1	1	1	1	1	Anes [1]
Cattle	19	21	21[1]	19[1]	20[1]	19	19	18[1]	Bovins
Goats	9	9	9[1]	9[1]	9[1]	3[1]	2[1]	2	Caprins
Horses [1]	1	1	1	1	1	1	1	1	Chevaux [1]
Pigs	103	69	70[1]	70[1]	70[1]	80	80	79	Porcins
Sheep	16	16	16[1]	16[1]	16[1]	9[1]	7[1]	7	Ovins
Netherlands									**Pays-Bas**
Cattle	4 654	4 557	4 411	4 283	4 206	4 070	4 047	4 050[1]	Bovins
Goats	76	102	119	132	153	179	221	215[1]	Caprins
Horses	100	107	112	114	115	118	121	122[1]	Chevaux
Pigs	14 397	* 13 958	15 200	13 446	13 567	13 118	13 073	13 000[1]	Porcins
Sheep	1 674	1 627	1 465	1 394	1 401	1 308	1 296	1 300[1]	Ovins
Norway									**Norvège**
Cattle	998	1 006	1 018	1 036	1 047	1 019	987	967	Bovins
Goats	62	62	63	82	54	53	51	48	Caprins
Horses	22	23	24	26	26	27	28	28[1]	Chevaux
Pigs	768	768[1]	692	689	439	412	392	443	Porcins
Sheep	2 524	2 558	2 448	2 399	2 294	2 332	2 408	2 396	Ovins
Poland									**Pologne**
Cattle	7 306	7 136	7 307	7 029	6 555	6 083	5 734	5 501	Bovins
Horses	636	569	558	561	551	550	546	550[1]	Chevaux
Pigs	20 418	17 964	18 135	19 168	18 538	17 122	17 106	18 707	Porcins
Sheep	713	552	491	453	392	362	343	333	Ovins
Portugal									**Portugal**
Asses [1]	160	150	150	140	135	135	130	130	Anes [1]
Cattle	1 363	1 386	1 389	1 386	1 409	1 421	1 414	1 399	Bovins
Goats	819	799	781	785	750	630	623	565	Caprins
Horses [1]	23	25	22	24	19	17	17	17	Chevaux [1]
Mules [1]	70	60	60	50	50	45	45	45	Mulets [1]
Pigs	2 430	2 375	2 394	2 385	2 350	2 338	2 338	2 389	Porcins
Sheep [1]	5 900	5 800	6 300	5 800	5 850	5 584	5 578	5 478	Ovins [1]
Republic of Moldova									**République de Moldova**
Asses [1]	2	2	2	2	2	2	2	2	Anes [1]
Cattle	832	726	646	551	452	423	394	405	Bovins
Goats	96	93	96	94	94	100	109	112	Caprins
Horses	59	57	59	61	64	67	71	70[1]	Chevaux
Pigs	1 061	1 015	950	798	807	683	447	449	Porcins
Sheep	1 411	1 301	1 248	1 115	1 026	930	830	835	Ovins
Romania									**Roumanie**
Asses [1]	32	31	30	31	31	30	31	28	Anes [1]
Cattle	3 481	3 496	3 435	3 235	3 143	3 051	2 870	2 800	Bovins
Goats	745	705	654	610	585	558	538	525	Caprins

36

Livestock
Stocks: thousand head [*cont.*]
Cheptel
Effectifs : milliers de têtes [*suite*]

Region, country or area	1995	1996	1997	1998	1999	2000	2001	2002	Région, pays ou zone
Horses	784	806	816	822	839	858	865	860	Chevaux
Pigs	7 758	7 960	8 235	7 097	7 194	5 848	4 797	4 447	Porcins
Sheep	10 897	10 381	9 663	8 938	8 409	8 121	7 657	7 251	Ovins
Russian Federation									**Fédération de Russie**
Asses [1]	26	27	26	25	25	22	20	20	Anes [1]
Buffaloes	24	24	21	17	16	16[1]	16[1]	16[1]	Buffles
Cattle	43 296	39 696	35 103	31 520	28 481	28 032	27 294	27 107	Bovins
Goats	2 722	2 682	2 445	2 291	2 144	2 148	2 211	2 292	Caprins
Horses	2 431	2 363	2 197	2 013	1 801	1 683	1 619	1 578	Chevaux
Pigs	24 859	22 631	19 115	17 348	17 248	18 271	15 708	16 048	Porcins
Sheep	31 818	25 345	20 327	16 483	13 413	12 603	12 561	13 035	Ovins
Serbia and Montenegro									**Serbie-et-Monténégro**
Buffaloes	18	18	16	16	21	29	29[1]	29[1]	Buffles
Cattle	1 950	1 926	1 899	1 894	1 831	1 452	1 366	1 355	Bovins
Goats	333	310	293	312	326	241	239	226	Caprins
Horses	96	93	90	86	76	49	49[1]	49[1]	Chevaux
Pigs	4 192	4 446	4 216	4 150	4 372	4 087	3 634	3 608	Porcins
Sheep	2 671	2 656	2 566	2 402	2 195	1 917	1 782	1 691	Ovins
Slovakia									**Slovaquie**
Cattle	916	929	892	803	705	664	645	608	Bovins
Goats	25	25	26	27	51	51	51	40	Caprins
Horses	10	10	10	10	10	9	10	8	Chevaux
Pigs	2 037	2 076	1 985	1 810	1 593	1 562	1 488	1 554	Porcins
Sheep	397	428	419	417	326	348	358	316	Ovins
Slovenia									**Slovénie**
Cattle	477	496	486	446	453	471	494	477	Bovins
Goats	11	9	21	15	17	15	22	22[1]	Caprins
Horses	8	8	8	10	12	14	15[1]	15[1]	Chevaux
Pigs	571	592	552	578	592	558	604	600	Porcins
Sheep	39	43	53	72	73	73	96	94	Ovins
Spain									**Espagne**
Asses	140	140	140	140	140	140[1]	140[1]	140[1]	Anes
Cattle	5 248	5 512	5 925	5 884	5 965	6 291	6 164	6 411	Bovins
Goats	3 157	2 605	2 935	3 007	2 779	2 627	2 830	3 114	Caprins
Horses	248	248	248	248	248	248	248[1]	248[1]	Chevaux
Mules	117	117	117	117	117	117	115[1]	115[1]	Mulets
Pigs	19 288	18 731	18 517	19 397	21 668	22 418	22 149	23 858	Porcins
Sheep	23 058	21 323	23 982	24 857	24 190	23 965	24 400	24 301	Ovins
Sweden									**Suède**
Cattle	1 777	1 790	1 781	1 739	1 713	1 684	1 652	1 638	Bovins
Horses	83	85[1]	87	80[1]	80	89	86[1]	85[1]	Chevaux
Pigs	2 313	2 349	2 351	2 286	2 115	1 918	1 891	1 882	Porcins
Sheep	462	469	442	421	437	432	452	427	Ovins
Switzerland									**Suisse**
Asses [1]	2	2	2	2	2	2	2	2	Anes [1]
Cattle	1 756	1 772	1 673	1 641	1 609	1 588	1 611	1 593	Bovins
Goats	52	53	58	60	62	62	63	68	Caprins
Horses	46[1]	43	46	46[1]	46[1]	45[1]	45[1]	45[1]	Chevaux
Pigs	1 611	1 580	1 395	1 487	1 452	1 498	1 548	1 536	Porcins
Sheep	437	442	420	422	424	421	420	441	Ovins
TFYR of Macedonia									**L'ex-R.y. Macédoine**
Buffaloes	1	1	1	1	1	1	1[1]	1[1]	Buffles
Cattle	281	283	295	289	267	270	* 265	259	Bovins
Horses	62	66	66	60	60	57	57[1]	57[1]	Chevaux
Pigs	172	175	192	184	197	226	204	196	Porcins
Sheep	2 466	2 320	1 814	1 631	1 315	1 289	1 251	1 234	Ovins
Ukraine									**Ukraine**
Asses	15[1]	14[1]	13[1]	13[1]	12[1]	* 12	12[1]	11[1]	Anes
Cattle	19 624	17 557	15 313	12 759	11 722	10 627	9 424	9 421	Bovins
Goats	782	889	854	822	828	825	912	912[1]	Caprins
Horses	737	756	754	737	721	698	701	700[1]	Chevaux

36

Livestock
Stocks: thousand head [*cont.*]
Cheptel
Effectifs : milliers de têtes [*suite*]

Region, country or area	1995	1996	1997	1998	1999	2000	2001	2002	Région, pays ou zone
Pigs	13 946	13 144	11 236	9 479	10 083	10 073	7 652	8 370	Porcins
Sheep	4 793	3 209	2 193	1 540	1 198	1 060	963	963[1]	Ovins
United Kingdom									**Royaume-Uni**
Cattle	11 857	12 040	11 633	11 519	11 423	11 133	10 600	10 343	Bovins
Horses [1]	175	176	177	178	180	182	184	184	Chevaux [1]
Pigs	7 627	7 590	8 072	8 146	7 284	6 482	5 845	5 588	Porcins
Sheep	43 304	42 086	42 823	44 471	44 656	42 261	36 697	35 832	Ovins
Oceania									**Océanie**
Asses	9	9	9	9	9	9	9	9	Anes
Cattle	35 761	36 157	36 687	36 485	36 106	37 360	38 814	40 899	Bovins
Goats	769	720	729	737	698	739	779	795	Caprins
Horses	385	374	382	372	366	369	373	375	Chevaux
Pigs	5 146	5 071	5 127	5 333	5 242	5 050	5 503	5 655	Porcins
Sheep	169 691	168 523	167 076	163 461	161 426	163 951	161 599	156 156	Ovins
American Samoa [1]									**Samoa américaines** [1]
Pigs	11	11	11	11	11	11	11	11	Porcins
Australia									**Australie**
Asses [1]	2	2	2	2	2	2	2	2	Anes [1]
Cattle	25 731	26 377	26 780	26 852	26 578	27 588	28 768	30 500	Bovins
Goats	230[1]	230[1]	230[1]	220	220[1]	260[1]	295[1]	310[1]	Caprins
Horses [1]	240	230	230	220	220	220	220	220	Chevaux [1]
Pigs	2 653	2 526	2 555	2 768	2 626	2 433	2 763	* 2 912	Porcins
Sheep	120 862	121 116	120 228	117 491	115 456	118 552	116 200	113 000	Ovins
Cook Islands									**Iles Cook**
Goats	7	3	3[1]	3[1]	3[1]	3[1]	3[1]	3[1]	Caprins
Pigs	32	40	40[1]	40[1]	40[1]	40[1]	40[1]	40[1]	Porcins
Fiji									**Fidji**
Cattle	354	350[1]	350[1]	345	330[1]	335[1]	340[1]	340[1]	Bovins
Goats	211	207	230	235[1]	237	241	246	247[1]	Caprins
Horses [1]	44	44	44	44	44	44	44	44	Chevaux [1]
Pigs	121	120[1]	115[1]	112	146	135	137	138[1]	Porcins
Sheep	7	8	7	7[1]	7[1]	7[1]	7[1]	7[1]	Ovins
French Polynesia [1]									**Polynésie française** [1]
Cattle	7	7	8	9	9	11	11	11	Bovins
Goats	16	16	16	16	17	17	17	17	Caprins
Horses	2	2	2	2	2	2	2	2	Chevaux
Pigs	39	37	35	35	37	37	37	34	Porcins
Guam [1]									**Guam** [1]
Goats	1	1	1	1	1	1	1	1	Caprins
Pigs	4	4	4	4	5	5	5	5	Porcins
Kiribati									**Kiribati**
Pigs	9[1]	10[1]	10[1]	10[1]	10	11[1]	11[1]	12[1]	Porcins
Micronesia (Fed. States) [1]									**Micronésie(Etats féd. de)** [1]
Cattle	14	14	14	14	14	14	14	14	Bovins
Goats	4	4	4	4	4	4	4	4	Caprins
Pigs	32	32	32	32	32	32	32	32	Porcins
Nauru [1]									**Nauru** [1]
Pigs	3	3	3	3	3	3	3	3	Porcins
New Caledonia [1]									**Nouvelle-Calédonie** [1]
Cattle	110	120	120	122	124	122	123	123	Bovins
Goats	14	2	2	2	2	2	2	2	Caprins
Horses	12	12	12	12	12	12	12	12	Chevaux
Pigs	37	38	38	40	38	40	40	40	Porcins
Sheep	2	1	1	1	1	1	1	1	Ovins
New Zealand									**Nouvelle-Zélande**
Cattle	9 272	9 017	9 145	8 873	8 778	9 015	9 281	9 633	Bovins
Goats	256	228	215	228	186	183	183	183	Caprins
Horses	69	68	75[1]	75[1]	70[1]	73[1]	77	78[1]	Chevaux
Pigs	431	424	407	351	369	369	354	358	Porcins
Sheep	48 816	47 394	46 834	45 956	45 956	45 385	45 385	43 142	Ovins

36

Livestock
Stocks: thousand head [*cont.*]
Cheptel
Effectifs : milliers de têtes [*suite*]

Region, country or area	1995	1996	1997	1998	1999	2000	2001	2002	Région, pays ou zone
Niue [1]									**Nioué** [1]
Pigs	2	2	2	2	2	2	2	2	Porcins
Papua New Guinea									**Papouasie-Nvl-Guinée**
Cattle	90[1]	88[1]	87	86[1]	87[1]	87[1]	88[1]	89[1]	Bovins
Goats	2[1]	2[1]	* 2	2[1]	2[1]	2[1]	2[1]	2[1]	Caprins
Horses [1]	2	2	2	2	2	2	2	2	Chevaux [1]
Pigs	1 400[1]	1 450[1]	1 500	1 550[1]	1 550[1]	1 550[1]	1 650[1]	1 650[1]	Porcins
Sheep	4[1]	4[1]	6	6[1]	6[1]	* 6	7[1]	7[1]	Ovins
Samoa									**Samoa**
Asses [1]	7	7	7	7	7	7	7	7	Anes [1]
Cattle	26[1]	26[1]	26[1]	27[1]	28	* 28	28[1]	28[1]	Bovins
Horses	3[1]	2[1]	2[1]	2[1]	2	2[1]	2[1]	2[1]	Chevaux
Pigs	170[1]	170[1]	170[1]	170[1]	167	170[1]	201	201[1]	Porcins
Solomon Islands [1]									**Iles Salomon** [1]
Cattle	10	10	10	10	10	11	13	13	Bovins
Pigs	55	56	57	57	58	64	67	68	Porcins
Tokelau [1]									**Tokélaou** [1]
Pigs	1	1	1	1	1	1	1	1	Porcins
Tonga									**Tonga**
Cattle	9	10[1]	10[1]	10[1]	10	11[1]	11[1]	11[1]	Bovins
Goats	14	13[1]	12[1]	12[1]	* 12	13[1]	13[1]	13[1]	Caprins
Horses [1]	11	11	11	11	11	11	11	11	Chevaux [1]
Pigs	81	81[1]	81[1]	81[1]	81[1]	81[1]	81[1]	81[1]	Porcins
Tuvalu									**Tuvalu**
Pigs [1]	13	13	13	13	13	13	13	13	Porcins [1]
Vanuatu									**Vanuatu**
Cattle	* 151	151[1]	151[1]	151[1]	151[1]	151[1]	151[1]	151[1]	Bovins
Goats	12	12[1]	12[1]	12[1]	12[1]	12[1]	12[1]	12[1]	Caprins
Horses [1]	3	3	3	3	3	3	3	3	Chevaux [1]
Pigs	60	61[1]	61[1]	62[1]	62[1]	62[1]	62[1]	62[1]	Porcins
Wallis and Futuna Is. [1]									**Iles Wallis et Futuna** [1]
Goats	7	7	7	7	7	7	7	7	Caprins
Pigs	25	25	25	25	25	25	25	25	Porcins

Source:
Food and Agriculture Organization of the United Nations (FAO), Rome, "FAO Production Yearbook 2002" and the FAOSTAT database.

Source:
Organisation des Nations Unies pour l'alimentation et l'agriculture (FAO), Rome, "Annuaire FAO de la production 2002" et la base de données FAOSTAT.

1 FAO estimate.
2 Data refer to the Gaza Strip.

1 Estimation de la FAO.
2 Les données se rapportent à la Bande de Gaza.

37
Roundwood
Production (solid volume of roundwood without bark): million cubic metres
Bois rond
Production (volume solide de bois rond sans écorce) : millions de mètres cubes

Region, country or area Région, pays ou zone	1993	1994	1995	1996	1997	1998	1999	2000	2001	2002
World **Monde**	3 187.5	3 192.9	3 244.1	3 237.5	3 307.7	3 223.6	3 327.1	3 400.3	3 345.2	3 380.5
Africa **Afrique**	538.1	551.1	568.3	576.2	582.5	584.9	588.4	595.4	602.6	617.1
Algeria Algérie	6.6	6.7	6.8	7.0	7.2	7.3	7.4	7.2	7.4	7.5
Angola Angola	3.7	3.7	3.8	3.9	4.0	4.1	4.2	4.3	4.4	4.4
Benin Bénin	6.0[1]	6.1[1]	6.1	6.2	6.2	6.2	6.2	6.2[1]	6.3[1]	6.3[1]
Botswana [1] Botswana [1]	0.7	0.7	0.7	0.7	0.7	0.7	0.7	0.7	0.7	0.7
Burkina Faso Burkina Faso	10.3[1]	10.6	10.8	11.0	11.1	11.3	7.8	8.0	11.8[1]	12.0[1]
Burundi Burundi	6.3	6.6	6.8	7.1	7.4[1]	7.7	5.6	5.8	8.3[1]	8.4[1]
Cameroon Cameroun	11.3	11.9	12.3	12.6	12.2	11.1	10.9	11.0	11.0	11.1[1]
Central African Rep. Rép. centrafricaine	3.7	3.6	3.6	3.2	3.4	3.5	2.9	3.0	3.1	3.1[1]
Chad Tchad	5.6	5.8[1]	5.9[1]	6.0[1]	6.2[1]	6.3[1]	6.5[1]	6.6[1]	6.8[1]	6.9[1]
Congo Congo	2.3	2.4	2.5	2.2	2.7	2.7	2.4	2.4	2.4	2.4
Côte d'Ivoire Côte d'Ivoire	11.2	11.9	11.9	11.7	11.6	11.8	11.7	11.9	12.1	12.1[1]
Dem. Rep. of the Congo Rép. dém. du Congo	57.0	60.1	62.1	63.7	64.9	66.0	67.3[1]	68.6[1]	69.7[1]	67.5
Egypt Egypte	15.1[1]	15.4[1]	15.5[1]	15.8	16.0[1]	16.1	16.3	16.4	16.6[1]	16.8[1]
Equatorial Guinea Guinée équatoriale	0.6	0.7	0.8	0.8[1]	0.8[1]	0.8[1]	0.8[1]	0.8[1]	0.8[1]	0.8[1]
Eritrea Erythrée	1.7	1.8	1.9	1.9	2.0	2.1	2.2	2.2[1]	2.3[1]	2.3[1]
Ethiopia Ethiopie	78.5	80.8	82.5	83.7	85.5	86.5	88.2	89.9	91.3	92.7
Gabon Gabon	2.3	2.6	2.8	2.9	3.3	3.3[1]	2.8	3.1	3.1[1]	3.1[1]
Gambia Gambie	0.6	0.6	0.6	0.6	0.6	0.6	0.6	0.7[1]	0.7[1]	0.7[1]
Ghana Ghana	19.9	22.5	22.0	21.9	22.0	21.9	21.9	21.8	22.0	22.0[1]
Guinea Guinée	8.3	8.6	12.6[1]	12.7[1]	8.7	8.7	12.2[1]	12.1[1]	12.1[1]	12.2[1]
Guinea-Bissau [1] Guinée-Bissau [1]	0.6	0.6	0.6	0.6	0.6	0.6	0.6	0.6	0.6	0.6
Kenya Kenya	20.1	20.4	20.8	21.0	21.3	21.3	21.5	21.6	21.8	22.0
Lesotho Lesotho	1.4	1.4	1.5	1.5	1.6	1.6	2.0[1]	2.0[1]	2.0[1]	2.0[1]
Liberia Libéria	3.8	3.4[1]	3.0[1]	3.1	3.5	4.1	4.5[1]	5.1[1]	5.3[1]	5.5[1]
Libyan Arab Jamah. [1] Jamah. arabe libyenne [1]	0.6	0.6	0.6	0.6	0.7	0.7	0.7	0.7	0.7	0.7

37

Roundwood
Production (solid volume of roundwood without bark): million cubic metres *[cont.]*

Bois rond
Production (volume solide de bois rond sans écorce) : millions de mètres cubes *[suite]*

Region, country or area Région, pays ou zone	1993	1994	1995	1996	1997	1998	1999	2000	2001	2002
Madagascar Madagascar	9.1	9.4	9.8	10.1	9.2	9.2	9.5	9.7	10.0	10.3
Malawi Malawi	5.5	5.6[1]	5.4[1]	5.3[1]	5.3[1]	5.4[1]	5.4[1]	5.5[1]	5.5[1]	5.5[1]
Mali Mali	4.6[1]	4.8[1]	4.8	4.9	5.0[1]	5.0[1]	5.1[1]	5.1[1]	5.2[1]	5.3[1]
Mauritania [1] Mauritanie [1]	1.2	1.3	1.3	1.3	1.3	1.4	1.4	1.4	1.5	1.5
Morocco Maroc	7.3	1.6	1.5	1.5	0.8	1.7	1.1	1.1	1.0	7.5
Mozambique Mozambique	16.8[1]	17.3	17.9	17.9[1]	18.0[1]	18.0[1]	18.0[1]	18.0[1]	18.0[1]	18.0[1]
Niger Niger	6.8[1]	7.0[1]	7.2[1]	7.4[1]	7.6[1]	7.8[1]	8.0[1]	8.2[1]	3.3	8.6[1]
Nigeria Nigéria	62.3	63.8	65.0	66.2	67.7	67.8	68.3[1]	68.8[1]	69.1[1]	69.5[1]
Rwanda Rwanda	3.1	2.6	5.4	5.8	7.4	7.5	7.8	7.8[1]	7.8[1]	7.8[1]
Senegal [1] Sénégal [1]	5.6	5.6	5.6	5.7	5.8	5.8	5.9	5.9	5.9	6.0
Sierra Leone Sierra Leone	4.6	4.5[1]	4.7[1]	4.7[1]	5.1[1]	5.2[1]	5.3[1]	5.5[1]	5.5[1]	5.5[1]
Somalia [1] Somalie [1]	7.2	7.4	7.6	8.0	8.3	8.6	9.0	9.3	9.6	9.9
South Africa Afrique du Sud	28.2	30.5	32.0	32.4	33.2	30.6	30.6	30.6	30.6	30.6
Sudan Soudan	18.0	18.1	18.3[1]	18.4[1]	18.4[1]	18.6[1]	18.7[1]	18.9[1]	19.0[1]	19.2[1]
Swaziland Swaziland	1.5	1.5	1.5	1.5	1.5	0.9	0.9	0.9	0.9	0.9
Togo Togo	5.3	5.4	5.5	5.5	5.6	5.7	5.7	5.8	5.8	5.8[1]
Tunisia Tunisie	2.2	2.2	2.2	2.2	2.3	2.3	2.3	2.3	2.3	2.3
Uganda Ouganda	33.4	34.4[1]	34.9	35.4	36.0	36.4	36.9	37.3[1]	37.8[1]	38.3[1]
United Rep. of Tanzania Rép.-Unie de Tanzanie	22.0	22.3	22.6	22.8	22.9	23.0	23.1	23.1	23.3	23.4
Zambia Zambie	7.9	8.3	8.2[1]	8.1[1]	8.0[1]	8.0[1]	8.1[1]	8.1[1]	8.1[1]	8.1[1]
Zimbabwe Zimbabwe	7.0	8.1	8.4	8.6	8.9	9.0	9.3	9.1	9.1	9.1
America, North **Amérique du Nord**	**751.4**	**769.6**	**777.4**	**770.8**	**769.6**	**764.4**	**784.2**	**794.2**	**764.7**	**773.5**
Bahamas Bahamas	0.1	0.1	0.1	0.1	0.1	0.0	0.0	0.0	0.0	0.0
Belize [1] Belize [1]	0.2	0.2	0.2	0.2	0.2	0.2	0.2	0.2	0.2	0.2
Canada Canada	176.2	183.2	188.4	189.8	191.2	176.9	193.7	200.3	200.3	200.3
Costa Rica Costa Rica	4.6	5.1	5.2	5.2	5.2	5.2	5.2	5.2	5.2	5.2
Cuba Cuba	3.5	3.6[1]	3.6[1]	3.5[1]	3.5[1]	3.5[1]	1.6	1.8	1.7	3.6[1]

37
Roundwood
Production (solid volume of roundwood without bark): million cubic metres *[cont.]*
Bois rond
Production (volume solide de bois rond sans écorce) : millions de mètres cubes *[suite]*

Region, country or area Région, pays ou zone	1993	1994	1995	1996	1997	1998	1999	2000	2001	2002
Dominican Republic Rép. dominicaine	0.6	0.6[1]	0.6[1]	0.6[1]	0.6[1]	0.6[1]	0.6[1]	0.6[1]	0.6[1]	0.6[1]
El Salvador El Salvador	3.9[1]	3.9[1]	4.7	4.3	5.2	5.1	5.2	5.2	5.2	4.8[1]
Guatemala Guatemala	13.0	13.4	13.6	13.5	13.8	14.1[1]	14.7	15.0	15.3	15.7[1]
Haiti [1] Haïti [1]	2.0	2.1	2.1	2.2	2.2	2.2	2.2	2.2	2.2	2.2
Honduras Honduras	9.1	9.3	9.1	9.3	9.4	9.5	9.6	9.5	9.6	9.5[1]
Jamaica Jamaïque	0.6	0.7	0.6	0.8	0.8	0.8	0.9	0.9[1]	0.9[1]	0.9[1]
Mexico Mexique	41.3	41.6	42.5	43.3	44.3	45.0	45.4	45.7	45.2	45.3
Nicaragua Nicaragua	5.8	5.8	5.8	5.9	5.8	5.9[1]	5.9[1]	6.0[1]	5.9	5.9[1]
Panama Panama	1.5	1.5	1.5	1.4	1.4	1.3	1.3	1.3	1.3	1.3[1]
Trinidad and Tobago Trinité-et-Tobago	0.1	0.1	0.2	0.1	0.1	0.1	0.1	0.1	0.1	0.1[1]
United States Etats-Unis	488.8	498.4	499.3	490.6	485.9	494.0	497.6	500.2	471.0	477.8
America, South **Amérique du Sud**	**289.6**	**300.4**	**306.5**	**304.8**	**303.8**	**305.1**	**330.8**	**339.0**	**340.1**	**340.3**
Argentina Argentine	9.8	10.1	10.6	11.4	6.9	5.7	10.6	10.0	10.0	10.0
Bolivia Bolivie	2.7	2.9	2.9	2.9	3.0	2.9	2.6	2.6	2.7	2.7
Brazil Brésil	205.7	208.9	211.1	212.3	213.5	213.7	231.6	235.4	236.4	237.5
Chile Chili	29.9	31.1	34.6	29.8	30.0	31.7	34.0	36.6	37.8	38.0
Colombia Colombie	9.6	9.5	9.5	9.5	9.6	10.1	10.6	13.1	12.5	9.6
Ecuador Equateur	4.7	9.4	10.0	10.6	11.5	10.9	10.7	10.8	10.9	11.0
French Guiana Guyane française	0.1	0.1	0.1[1]	0.1[1]	0.1[1]	0.1[1]	0.1[1]	0.1[1]	0.1[1]	0.1[1]
Guyana Guyana	1.2	1.3	1.4	1.4	1.5	1.3	1.3	1.2	1.2	1.2
Paraguay Paraguay	8.8	9.0	9.3	9.3	9.4	9.5	9.6	9.6[1]	9.7[1]	9.8[1]
Peru Pérou	8.2	9.0	8.0	7.9	8.4	9.2	9.2	9.3	8.4	9.9
Suriname Suriname	0.1	0.1	0.1	0.3	0.2	0.2	0.1	0.2	0.2	0.2[1]
Uruguay Uruguay	4.4	4.5	4.6	4.7	5.0	5.2	5.1	5.4	5.6	5.7
Venezuela Venezuela	4.4	4.4	4.3	4.6	4.7	4.6	5.3	4.7	4.6	4.7
Asia **Asie**	**1 058.4**	**1 053.2**	**1 052.1**	**1 066.5**	**1 071.7**	**1 044.4**	**1 037.0**	**1 020.0**	**1 011.5**	**999.5**
Afghanistan [1] Afghanistan [1]	2.4	2.5	2.6	2.7	2.8	2.9	3.0	3.0	3.1	3.1

37

Roundwood
Production (solid volume of roundwood without bark): million cubic metres *[cont.]*

Bois rond
Production (volume solide de bois rond sans écorce) : millions de mètres cubes *[suite]*

Region, country or area Région, pays ou zone	1993	1994	1995	1996	1997	1998	1999	2000	2001	2002
Armenia Arménie	0.0	0.0	0.0	0.0	0.1	0.0	0.0	0.1	0.0	0.1
Bangladesh Bangladesh	28.6	28.6	28.5	28.5	28.5	28.5	28.5	28.5	28.4	28.4
Bhutan Bhoutan	3.9	3.9[1]	3.9[1]	4.0[1]	4.0[1]	4.1[1]	4.3	4.4	4.4[1]	4.5[1]
Brunei Darussalam Brunéi Darussalam	0.2	0.2[1]	0.2[1]	0.2[1]	0.2[1]	0.2[1]	0.2[1]	0.2[1]	0.2[1]	0.2[1]
Cambodia Cambodge	11.8	12.1	12.0	11.9[1]	11.8[1]	11.6[1]	11.2	10.3	10.0	9.9[1]
China Chine	298.8	303.5	305.7	312.8	311.2	298.5	291.4	287.5	284.9	284.9
Cyprus Chypre	0.1	0.0	0.0	0.0	0.0	0.0	0.0	0.0	0.0	0.0
India Inde	311.3	312.8	313.4	296.8	296.5	296.3	296.7	296.2	296.2	319.4
Indonesia Indonésie	154.8	148.2	143.6	143.1	139.1	135.6	130.2	122.5	119.2	116.1
Iran (Islamic Rep. of) Iran (Rép. islamique d')	1.6	1.6	1.5	1.4	1.5	1.3	1.1	1.1	1.3	1.3
Iraq Iraq	0.1[1]	0.1[1]	0.1[1]	0.1[1]	0.2	0.2	0.1[1]	0.1[1]	0.1[1]	0.1[1]
Israel Israël	0.1	0.1	0.1	0.1	0.1	0.1	0.1	0.1	0.0	0.0
Japan Japon	25.7	24.6	23.1	23.2	22.3	19.6	19.0	18.1	16.2	16.2
Jordan[1] Jordanie[1]	0.2	0.2	0.2	0.2	0.1	0.2	0.2	0.2	0.2	0.2
Kazakhstan Kazakhstan	0.3	0.3	0.3	0.3	0.3	0.0[1]	0.0[1]	0.0[1]	0.0[1]	0.0[1]
Korea, Dem. P. R. Corée, R. p. dém. de	5.4	5.5	5.6	6.1[1]	6.5[1]	6.9[1]	6.9[1]	7.0[1]	7.1[1]	7.1[1]
Korea, Republic of Corée, République de	3.7	3.7	3.8	3.6	3.5	3.9	4.1	4.0	4.0	4.0
Lao People's Dem. Rep. Rép. dém. pop. lao	6.3	6.4	6.7	6.5	6.5	6.4[1]	6.7[1]	6.4	6.5	6.5[1]
Lebanon Liban	0.1	0.1[1]	0.1[1]	0.1[1]	0.1[1]	0.1[1]	0.0	0.0	0.1[1]	0.1[1]
Malaysia Malaisie	41.8	40.1	39.3	35.1	36.0	26.4	26.6	18.4	16.3	16.3
Mongolia[1] Mongolie[1]	0.9	0.8	0.6	0.6	0.6	0.6	0.6	0.6	0.6	0.6
Myanmar Myanmar	21.2	20.7	21.1	21.5	34.8	34.3	37.6	38.1	39.4	39.4[1]
Nepal Népal	13.1[1]	13.0[1]	13.1[1]	13.1[1]	13.2[1]	13.9	13.9	14.0	14.0	14.0[1]
Pakistan Pakistan	24.2	24.3	24.2	29.0	30.9	31.8	33.1	33.6	33.2	27.7
Philippines Philippines	17.7	17.5	17.2	40.3	41.0	42.0	43.0	44.0	44.4	16.0
Sri Lanka Sri Lanka	9.9	10.2	10.4	10.4	6.8	6.6	6.6	6.6	6.5	6.5
Syrian Arab Republic Rép. arabe syrienne	0.1	0.1[1]	0.1[1]	0.1[1]	0.1[1]	0.1[1]	0.1[1]	0.1[1]	0.1[1]	0.1[1]

37
Roundwood
Production (solid volume of roundwood without bark): million cubic metres *[cont.]*
Bois rond
Production (volume solide de bois rond sans écorce) : millions de mètres cubes *[suite]*

Region, country or area Région, pays ou zone	1993	1994	1995	1996	1997	1998	1999	2000	2001	2002
Thailand Thaïlande	24.0	23.7	23.5	23.4	23.4	23.4	23.4	26.8	27.5	27.4[1]
Turkey Turquie	18.9	16.8	19.3	19.4	18.1	17.7	17.6	16.8	16.2	18.5
Viet Nam Viet Nam	31.2	31.2	31.6	31.6	31.3	31.0	30.2	30.9	30.8[1]	30.7[1]
Yemen [1] Yémen [1]	0.2	0.2	0.2	0.3	0.3	0.3	0.3	0.3	0.3	0.3
Europe **Europe**	**502.2**	**468.4**	**488.1**	**468.0**	**527.6**	**472.4**	**532.2**	**591.8**	**564.8**	**588.1**
Albania Albanie	0.6	0.4	0.4	0.4	0.4	*0.0	0.2	0.4	0.3	0.3
Austria Autriche	12.9	15.0	14.4	15.6	15.3	14.0	14.1	13.3	13.5	14.8
Belarus Bélarus	10.0	10.0	10.0	15.7	17.6	5.9	6.6	6.1	6.5	6.9
Belgium Belgique	...	...	...	...	...	...	4.8	4.5[1]	4.2	4.5
Belgium-Luxembourg Belgique-Luxembourg	4.2	4.3	4.1	4.0	4.0	4.8	...	...	...	...
Bosnia and Herzegovina Bosnie-Herzégovine	0.0	0.0	0.0	0.0	4.0	*4.1	*4.1	4.3	3.8	4.2
Bulgaria Bulgarie	3.5	2.7	2.8	3.2	3.0	3.2	4.4	4.8	4.0	4.0
Croatia Croatie	2.5	2.8	2.6	2.5	3.1	3.4	3.5	3.7	3.5	3.6
Czech Republic République tchèque	10.4	12.0	12.4	12.6	13.5	14.0	14.2	14.4	14.4	14.5
Denmark Danemark	2.3	2.3	2.3	2.3	2.1	1.6	1.6	3.0	1.4	1.4
Estonia Estonie	2.4	3.6	3.7	3.9	5.4	6.1	6.7	8.9	10.2	10.5
Finland Finlande	42.2	48.7	50.2	46.6	51.3	53.7	53.6	54.3	52.2	53.0
France France	39.4	42.2	43.4	40.4	41.1	35.5	36.0	45.8	39.8	35.9
Germany Allemagne	33.2	39.8	39.3	37.0	38.2	39.1	37.6	53.7	39.5	42.4
Greece Grèce	2.2	2.1	2.0	2.0	1.7	1.7	2.2	2.2	1.9	1.5
Hungary Hongrie	4.5	4.5	4.3	3.7	4.2	4.2	5.8	5.9	5.8	5.8
Ireland Irlande	1.8	2.0	2.2	2.3	2.2	2.3	2.6	2.7	2.5	2.5
Italy Italie	8.8	9.5	9.7	9.1	9.1	9.6	11.1	9.3	8.1	7.8
Latvia Lettonie	4.9	5.7	6.9	8.1	8.7	10.0	14.0	14.3	12.8	13.5
Lithuania Lituanie	4.5	4.0	6.0	5.5	5.1	4.9	4.9	5.5	5.7	6.3
Luxembourg Luxembourg	...	...	...	...	...	...	0.3	0.3[1]	0.1	0.1
Netherlands Pays-Bas	1.1	1.0	1.1	1.0	1.1	1.0	1.0	1.0	0.9	0.8

37

Roundwood
Production (solid volume of roundwood without bark): million cubic metres *[cont.]*

Bois rond
Production (volume solide de bois rond sans écorce) : millions de mètres cubes *[suite]*

Region, country or area Région, pays ou zone	1993	1994	1995	1996	1997	1998	1999	2000	2001	2002
Norway Norvège	9.7	8.7	9.0	8.4	8.3	8.2	8.4	8.2	9.0	8.6
Poland Pologne	18.6	18.8	20.4	20.3	21.7	23.1	24.3	26.0	25.0	27.2
Portugal Portugal	10.2	9.8	9.4	9.0	9.0	8.5	9.0	10.8	8.9	8.7
Republic of Moldova République de Moldova	0.0	0.0	0.0	0.4	0.4	0.4	0.0	0.1	0.1	0.1[1]
Romania Roumanie	8.8	11.9	12.2	12.3	13.5	11.6	12.7	13.1	12.4	15.2
Russian Federation Fédération de Russie	174.6	111.8	116.2	96.8	134.7	95.0	143.6	158.1	165.6	176.9
Serbia and Montenegro Serbie-et-Monténégro	2.6	2.8	3.1	3.1	2.8	2.7	2.5	3.4	2.5	2.9
Slovakia Slovaquie	5.2	5.3	5.3	5.5	4.9	5.5	5.8	6.2	5.8	5.8
Slovenia Slovénie	1.1	1.9	1.9	2.0	2.2	2.1	2.1	2.3	2.3	2.3
Spain Espagne	13.8	15.3	16.1	15.6	15.6	14.9	14.8	14.3	15.1	15.8
Sweden Suède	54.0	56.3	63.6	56.3	60.2	60.6	58.7	63.3	63.2	67.5
Switzerland Suisse	4.4	4.7	4.7	4.1	4.5	4.3	4.7	9.2	5.7	4.3
TFYR of Macedonia L'ex-R.y. Macédoine	0.9	0.8	0.8	0.8	0.8	0.7	0.8	1.1	0.7	0.7
Ukraine Ukraine	0.0	0.0	0.0	10.4	10.1	8.5	7.9	9.9	9.9[1]	9.9[1]
United Kingdom Royaume-Uni	6.7	7.5	7.6	7.1	7.5	7.3	7.5	7.5	7.6	7.6
Oceania **Océanie**	**48.0**	**50.3**	**51.7**	**51.2**	**52.7**	**52.3**	**54.5**	**59.9**	**61.5**	**61.9**
Australia Australie	21.9	23.3	24.3	24.4	25.2	26.8	26.6	30.4	30.9	31.3
Fiji Fidji	0.5	0.6	0.6	0.6	0.5	0.5	0.5	0.5	0.5	0.5
New Zealand Nouvelle-Zélande	16.0	16.3	16.9	16.4	17.1	15.3	17.7	19.3	20.5	20.5
Papua New Guinea Papouasie-Nvl-Guinée	8.8	9.3	8.8	8.8	8.8	8.6	8.6	8.6	8.6	8.6
Samoa [1] Samoa [1]	0.1	0.1	0.1	0.1	0.1	0.1	0.1	0.1	0.1	0.1
Solomon Islands Iles Salomon	0.5	0.8	0.9	0.9[1]	0.9[1]	0.9[1]	0.9[1]	0.9[1]	0.7	0.7[1]
Vanuatu Vanuatu	0.1[1]	0.1[1]	0.1[1]	0.1[1]	0.1[1]	0.1	0.1	0.1	0.1	0.1[1]

Source:
Food and Agriculture Organization of the United Nations (FAO),
Rome, the FAOSTAT database and the "FAO Yearbook of Forest
Products".

Source:
Organisation des Nations Unies pour l'alimentation et l'agriculture
(FAO), Rome, la base de données FAOSTAT et "l'Annuaire FAO des
produits forestiers".

1   FAO estimate.

1   Estimation de la FAO.

38

Fish production
Capture and aquaculture: metric tons
Production halieutique
Capture et aquaculture : tonnes

Country or area Pays ou zone	Capture production Captures					Aquaculture production Production de l'aquaculture				
	1997	1998	1999	2000	2001	1997	1998	1999	2000	2001
Afghanistan [1] Afghanistan [1]	1 250	1 200	1 200	1 000	800	...	...	...	...	...
Albania Albanie	1 013	2 683	2 745	3 320	3 310	97	124	310	307	286
Algeria Algérie	91 580	92 346	102 396	100 000	100 000	322	283	250	275	281
American Samoa Samoa américaines	431	586	518	830	3 663	...	...	...	...	...
Angola Angola	146 304	163 149	175 799	238 351	252 518	...	...	...	...	...
Anguilla Anguilla	250	250	250	250	250	...	...	...	...	...
Antigua and Barbuda Antigua-et-Barbuda	1 437	1 415	1 361	1 481	1 583	...	...	...	...	...
Argentina Argentine	1 400 162	1 164 829	1 078 313	913 622	923 322	1 314	1 040	1 218	1 784	1 340
Armenia Arménie	580	698	1 144	1 133	866	670	437	889	893	1 331
Aruba Aruba	205	182	175	163	163	...	...	...	...	...
Australia Australie	196 831	203 334	214 954	194 631	192 682	26 637	28 106	34 295	40 032	43 600
Austria Autriche	465	451	432	439	362	3 021	2 912	3 070	2 847	2 393
Azerbaijan Azerbaïdjan	5 161	4 760	20 866	18 797	10 893	364	211	148	120	170
Bahamas Bahamas	10 439	10 124	10 473	11 070	9 290	1	1	1	2	13
Bahrain Bahreïn	10 050	9 849	10 620	11 718	11 230	4 [1]	4 [1]	5	12	...
Bangladesh Bangladesh	829 426	839 141	959 215	1 004 264	1 000 000	432 135	514 842	620 114	657 121	687 000 [1]
Barbados Barbade	2 809	3 644	3 250	3 100	2 676	...	...	...	...	...
Belarus Bélarus	499	457	514	553	943	4 322	4 727	5 289	6 716	4 666
Belgium Belgique	30 499	30 835	29 876	29 800	30 209	846	846	1 597	1 641	1 630
Belize Belize	24 710	26 309	44 587	60 448	14 370	1 397	1 642	3 163	3 630	4 460
Benin Bénin	43 785	42 139	40 436	32 324	38 415	...	...	...	...	...
Bermuda Bermudes	461	466	453	286	315	...	...	...	...	...
Bhutan [1] Bhoutan [1]	300	300	300	300	300	30	30	30	30	30
Bolivia Bolivie	6 038	6 055	6 052	6 106	5 940	387	385	398	405	320
Bosnia and Herzegovina Bosnie-Herzégovine	2 500	2 500	2 500	2 500	2 500	...	...	...	...	...

38

Fish production
Capture and aquaculture: metric tons *[cont.]*

Production halieutique
Capture et aquaculture : tonnes *[suite]*

Country or area Pays ou zone	Capture production Captures					Aquaculture production Production de l'aquaculture				
	1997	1998	1999	2000	2001	1997	1998	1999	2000	2001
Botswana Botswana	160	191	157	166	118	...	...	...	...	...
Brazil Brésil	744 585	706 789	703 941	766 846	770 000	87 674	103 915	140 657	176 531	210 000 [1]
British Virgin Islands Iles Vierges britanniques	105	116	115	43	50	...	...	...	...	...
Brunei Darussalam Brunéi Darussalam	4 521	5 049	3 186	2 487	1 492	157	172	158	113	99
Bulgaria Bulgarie	11 237	18 946	10 556	6 998	6 530	5 437	4 252	7 780	3 654	1 610
Burkina Faso Burkina Faso	8 000	8 335	7 600	8 500	8 500 [1]	45	40	25	5	5
Burundi Burundi	20 296	13 426	9 199	17 315	8 964	50 [1]	55 [1]	55 [1]	100	100 [1]
Cambodia Cambodge	102 800	107 900	269 156	284 368	397 200	11 800	14 100	15 000	14 430	15 500 [1]
Cameroon Cameroun	102 000	106 800	110 000	112 109	111 031	67	67	67 [1]	50	50
Canada Canada	972 294	1 013 977	1 027 511	1 010 489	1 049 508	81 676	91 046	113 016	127 558	152 447
Cape Verde Cap-Vert	9 705	9 424	10 360	10 586	9 653	...	...	...	...	...
Cayman Islands Iles Caïmanes	125	125	125	125	125	...	...	...	...	...
Central African Rep. Rép. centrafricaine	14 250 [1]	14 500 [1]	15 000	15 000 [1]	15 000 [1]	80	80	117	120	125
Chad Tchad	85 000	84 000	84 000 [1]	84 000 [1]	84 000 [1]	...	...	...	...	...
Channel Islands Iles Anglo-Normandes	4 238	4 117	3 601	3 589	3 927	130	196	249	390	487
Chile Chili	5 810 764	3 265 383	5 050 528	4 300 160	3 797 143	272 346	293 044	274 216	391 587	566 096
China Chine	15722344	17229927	17240032	16987325	16529 389	19315623	20795367	22789887	24580671	26050101
China, Hong Kong SAR Chine, Hong Kong RAS	186 000	180 000	127 780	157 012	173 972	8 310	6 439	6 052	4 988	5 627
China, Macao SAR Chine, Macao RAS	1 500	1 500	1 500	1 500	1 500	...	...	...	...	...
Colombia Colombie	147 918	132 908	117 995	129 644	125 000	43 710	45 933	52 947	61 786	65 000
Comoros Comores	12 500	12 500	12 000	13 200	12 180	...	...	...	...	...
Congo Congo	38 082	42 955	43 696	44 000	42 000	99	140 [1]	190	200	200
Cook Islands Iles Cook	820	770	750	720	700	0	0	0	0	0
Costa Rica Costa Rica	26 669	24 757	28 218	35 398	34 733	7 000	7 937	9 324	9 708	10 520
Côte d'Ivoire Côte d'Ivoire	64 169	69 572	74 365	75 772	73 556	450	862	1 000	1 197	1 025

38

Fish production
Capture and aquaculture: metric tons *[cont.]*
Production halieutique
Capture et aquaculture : tonnes *[suite]*

Country or area Pays ou zone	Capture production Captures					Aquaculture production Production de l'aquaculture				
	1997	1998	1999	2000	2001	1997	1998	1999	2000	2001
Croatia Croatie	17 035	21 938	18 900	20 718	18 090	3 510	5 958	6 228	6 674	10 166
Cuba Cuba	84 911	67 076	67 381	56 146	56 000	44 050	46 712	55 163	52 700	54 330
Cyprus Chypre	24 819	19 295	39 638	67 482	75 803	969	1 178	1 422	1 878	1 883
Czech Republic République tchèque	3 321	3 952	4 190	4 654	4 646	17 560	17 231	18 775	19 475	20 098
Dem. Rep. of the Congo Rép. dém. du Congo	162 211	178 041	208 448	208 448	208 448	550 [1]	500 [1]	414	414	400 [1]
Denmark Danemark	1 826 852	1 557 335	1 405 005	1 534 089	1 510 439	39 697	42 368	42 670	43 609	41 573
Djibouti Djibouti	350	350	350	350	350	...	...	...	...	...
Dominica Dominique	1 079	1 212	1 200	1 200	1 150	5 [1]	5 [1]	5 [1]	7	7 [1]
Dominican Republic Rép. dominicaine	14 860	10 283	8 433	11 029	13 217	677	810	748	2 125	2 647
Ecuador Equateur	548 988	310 022	497 872	592 547	586 570	135 297	146 590	127 375	62 111	67 969
Egypt Egypte	342 759	362 741	380 504	384 314	428 651	73 454	139 389	226 276	340 093	342 864
El Salvador El Salvador	11 897	12 657	16 524	9 590	17 747	384	399	279	261	395
Equatorial Guinea Guinée équatoriale	6 090	6 005	7 001	3 634	3 500 [1]	...	...	...	...	...
Eritrea Erythrée	1 038	1 629	6 891	12 612	8 820	...	...	...	...	...
Estonia Estonie	123 613	118 714	111 793	113 146	105 167	260	260	200	225	467
Ethiopia Ethiopie	10 370	14 000	15 858	15 681	15 390	24 [1]	14 [1]	0	0	0
Faeroe Islands Iles Féroé	329 145	363 816	358 133	454 530	524 837	22 538	20 558	39 507	29 297	46 418
Falkland Is. (Malvinas) Iles Falkland (Malvinas)	17 113	43 616	39 164	62 928	59 824	...	...	...	...	...
Fiji Fidji	27 755	28 158	36 713	40 000	42 972	345	298	1 758	1 779	1 717
Finland Finlande	180 185	171 681	160 560	156 501	150 096	16 426	16 024	15 449	15 400	15 739
France France	567 422	542 560	586 487	623 755	606 194	287 181	267 790	264 825	266 770	252 052
French Guiana Guyane française	6 602	6 709	6 271	5 237	5 194	7	18	31	31	37
French Polynesia Polynésie française	11 670	12 473	12 336	13 899	15 404	56	53	48	53	66
Gabon Gabon	43 584	53 609	51 143	47 470	40 457	57	158	558	558	102
Gambia Gambie	32 254	29 002	30 000	29 016	34 527	4	4	4	...	...

38

Fish production
Capture and aquaculture: metric tons *[cont.]*
Production halieutique
Capture et aquaculture : tonnes *[suite]*

Country or area Pays ou zone	Capture production Captures					Aquaculture production Production de l'aquaculture				
	1997	1998	1999	2000	2001	1997	1998	1999	2000	2001
Georgia Géorgie	2 583	3 001	1 413	2 200	1 830	61	96	83	86	80
Germany Allemagne	259 352	266 622	238 925	205 689	211 282	65 433	73 020	79 567	65 891	53 409
Ghana Ghana	447 088	442 641	492 776	452 070	445 287	400	1 800	2 900	5 000	6 000
Greece Grèce	157 088	108 580	118 771	99 280	94 388	48 838	59 926	84 274	95 418	97 802
Greenland Groenland	120 596	128 542	160 253	159 711	158 485	...	...	...	...	...
Grenada Grenade	1 530	1 837	1 658	1 701	2 247	0	0	1	4	0
Guadeloupe Guadeloupe	10 480	9 084	9 114	10 100	10 100	20	14	20	14	14
Guam Guam	158	253	223	275	278	220	220	230	232	232
Guatemala Guatemala	6 896	10 847	21 018	37 978	10 100	4 407	3 124	4 850	3 963	4 200
Guinea Guinée	62 441	69 764	87 314	91 513	90 000	0	0	0	0	0
Guinea-Bissau Guinée-Bissau	7 250	6 000	5 000	5 000	5 000	...	...	...	...	...
Guyana Guyana	53 998	52 840	53 844	48 887	53 405	270	300	606	606	608
Haiti Haïti	5 301	5 259	5 000 [1]	5 000 [1]	5 000 [1]	...	...	...	...	...
Honduras Honduras	18 357	7 393	12 754	11 684	7 451	9 274	8 305	6 552	9 080	9 000
Hungary Hongrie	7 406	7 265	7 514	7 101	6 638	9 334	10 222	11 947	12 886	13 056
Iceland Islande	2 205 944	1 681 951	1 736 267	1 982 522	1 980 715	3 663	3 868	3 897	3 623	4 371
India Inde	3 523 448	3 373 492	3 472 150	3 742 296	3 762 600	1 864 322	1 908 485	2 134 814	1 942 204	2 202 630
Indonesia Indonésie	3 791 240	3 964 897	3 986 919	4 069 691	4 203 830	662 547	629 797	749 269	788 500	864 276
Iran (Islamic Rep. of) Iran (Rép. islamique d')	342 287	367 212	387 200	384 000	336 450	30 279	33 237	31 800	40 550	62 550
Iraq Iraq	31 302	22 574	22 423	20 767	20 800	3 400	7 500	2 183	1 745	2 000 [1]
Ireland Irlande	292 673	324 274	280 957	281 806	356 309	36 854	42 375	43 856	51 247	60 935
Isle of Man Ile de Man	4 289	2 214	2 609	3 552	3 112	...	...	...	...	...
Israel Israël	5 204	6 300	5 884	5 818	5 000	18 264	18 556	18 777	20 098	20 100
Italy Italie	343 693	306 096	282 790	302 149	310 397	190 719	205 625	207 368	213 525	218 269
Jamaica Jamaïque	8 198	6 560	8 508	5 676	5 700	3 450 [1]	3 410	4 150	4 512	4 512

38

Fish production
Capture and aquaculture: metric tons *[cont.]*
Production halieutique
Capture et aquaculture : tonnes *[suite]*

Country or area Pays ou zone	Capture production Captures					Aquaculture production Production de l'aquaculture				
	1997	1998	1999	2000	2001	1997	1998	1999	2000	2001
Japan Japon	5 926 113	5 299 399	5 194 186	4 971 412	4 719 152	806 534	766 812	759 262	762 824	801 948
Jordan Jordanie	450	470	510	550	520	200	293	515	569	540
Kazakhstan Kazakhstan	31 826	25 000	36 170	36 620	30 654	1 921	1 106	1 193	813	417
Kenya Kenya	161 054	172 592	205 287	215 106	164 151	199	153	300	512	1 009
Kiribati Kiribati	30 052	35 304	52 741	25 563	32 375	7	4	13	14	18
Korea, Dem. P. R. Corée, R. p. dém. de	236 462	220 000	210 000	200 850	200 000	70 174	68 500 [1]	68 500 [1]	66 700 [1]	63 700 [1]
Korea, Republic of Corée, République de	2 204 047	2 026 934	2 119 668	1 823 175	1 988 002	392 367	327 462	304 036	293 420	294 484
Kuwait Koweït	7 826	7 799	6 271	6 000	5 846	204	220	264	376	195
Kyrgyzstan Kirghizistan	120	80	48	52	57	168	162	71	58	144
Lao People's Dem. Rep. Rép. dém. pop. lao	18 857	19 642	30 041	29 250	30 000 [1]	21 143	21 216	30 362	42 066	50 000 [1]
Latvia Lettonie	105 682	102 331	125 389	136 403	125 433	345	425	468	325	463
Lebanon Liban	3 655	3 520	3 560	3 666	3 670	300	400	300	400	300
Lesotho Lesotho	30 [1]	30 [1]	30 [1]	32 [1]	24	14 [1]	8	4	8	8
Liberia Libéria	8 580	10 830	15 472	11 726	11 286	0	...	...	22	14
Libyan Arab Jamah. Jamah. arabe libyenne	31 877	32 911	32 850	33 387	33 239	100 [1]	100 [1]	100 [1]	100 [1]	100 [1]
Lithuania Lituanie	44 002	66 578	72 962	78 987	151 931	1 516	1 516	1 650	1 996	2 001
Madagascar Madagascar	116 391	126 395	129 630	132 093	135 583	8 582	4 503	5 811	7 280	7 749
Malawi Malawi	56 340	41 111	45 392	43 000 [1]	40 619	231	229	590	530	568
Malaysia Malaisie	1 172 922	1 153 719	1 251 768	1 289 245	1 234 733	107 984	133 635	155 127	151 773	158 158
Maldives Maldives	122 387	132 566	134 962	136 420	125 814	...	...	...	...	...
Mali Mali	99 550	98 000	98 536	109 870	100 000 [1]	60	60	80	30	35
Malta Malte	1 019	1 143	1 224	1 059	882	1 800	1 950	2 002	1 746	1 235
Marshall Islands Iles Marshall	400	500	500	8 155	37 098	...	...	...	...	...
Martinique Martinique	5 500	5 500	6 000	6 310	6 200	66	55	60	51	51
Mauritania Mauritanie	57 756	61 660	76 026	80 849	83 596	...	...	...	...	...

38

Fish production
Capture and aquaculture: metric tons *[cont.]*

Production halieutique
Capture et aquaculture : tonnes *[suite]*

Country or area Pays ou zone	Capture production Captures					Aquaculture production Production de l'aquaculture				
	1997	1998	1999	2000	2001	1997	1998	1999	2000	2001
Mauritius Maurice	14 025	12 093	12 205	9 615	10 694	118	83	85	87	59
Mayotte Mayotte	1 300 [1]	2 000 [1]	2 000	5 500	5 500	2 [1]	2 [1]	2 [1]	3 [1]	3
Mexico Mexique	1 489 112	1 179 860	1 205 603	1 315 581	1 398 592	39 500	41 068	48 443	53 918	76 075
Micronesia (Fed. States) Micronésie (Etats féd. de)	10 127	16 581	12 838	23 715	18 062	0	0	0	0	0
Monaco [1] Monaco [1]	3	3	3	3	3	...	...	...	...	...
Mongolia Mongolie	180	311	524	425	117	...	...	...	...	...
Montserrat Montserrat	45	46	50	50	50	...	...	...	...	...
Morocco Maroc	791 906	710 436	745 431	896 620	1 083 276	2 329	2 161	2 781	1 875	1 362
Mozambique Mozambique	39 703	36 677	33 989	39 065	32 512	0	0	0	0	0
Myanmar Myanmar	780 295	830 117	919 410	1 069 726	1 166 868	82 740	81 968	91 114	98 912	121 266
Namibia Namibie	513 216	612 343	580 084	589 905	547 492	45 [1]	45 [1]	45 [1]	50 [1]	50
Nauru [1] Nauru [1]	400	400	400	400	400	...	...	...	...	...
Nepal Népal	11 230	12 000	12 752	16 700	16 700	11 977	12 866	13 028	15 023	16 570
Netherlands Pays-Bas	451 799	536 626	514 611	495 804	518 162	98 210	120 094	108 785	75 339	52 064
Netherlands Antilles Antilles néerlandaises	950	950	950	20 494	950	5 [1]	5 [1]	5 [1]	5 [1]	5 [1]
New Caledonia Nouvelle-Calédonie	2 438	3 105	3 152	3 386	3 337	1 152	1 596	1 936	1 754	1 860
New Zealand Nouvelle-Zélande	610 254	639 238	598 475	548 559	561 110	76 850	93 807	91 650	85 640	76 024
Nicaragua Nicaragua	16 176	19 892	23 909	28 008	22 799	3 452	4 788	4 198	5 429	5 721
Niger Niger	6 328	7 013	11 000	16 250	20 800	13	12	14	15	21
Nigeria Nigéria	387 923	463 024	455 628	441 377	452 146	24 297	20 458	21 737	25 718	24 398
Niue Nioué	200	200	200	200	200	...	...	...	...	...
Northern Mariana Islands Iles Mariannes du Nord	250	235	193	189	197	...	...	...	...	...
Norway Norvège	2 863 059	2 861 223	2 627 534	2 703 415	2 687 303	367 617	411 113	475 949	491 284	512 101
Occupied Palestinian Terr. [2] Terr. palestinien occupé [2]	3 791	3 625	3 600	3 600	3 000	...	...	...	...	...
Oman Oman	118 995	106 171	108 809	120 421	126 531	...	1 513	1 870	1 913	2 013

38

Fish production
Capture and aquaculture: metric tons [cont.]
Production halieutique
Capture et aquaculture : tonnes [suite]

Country or area Pays ou zone	Capture production Captures					Aquaculture production Production de l'aquaculture				
	1997	1998	1999	2000	2001	1997	1998	1999	2000	2001
Pakistan Pakistan	589 795	596 980	654 530	614 069	607 020	15 464	17 369	23 076	12 485	16 405
Palau Palaos	1 751	1 777	1 800	2 000	2 000	2	1	1	2	2 [1]
Panama Panama	162 349	202 687	120 848	222 631	235 000	7 217	10 161	3 236	2 802	2 394
Papua New Guinea Papouasie-Nvl-Guinée	46 185	78 029	65 431	96 069	122 419	16	14	16	12	15
Paraguay Paraguay	28 000	25 000 [1]	25 000 [1]	25 000 [1]	25 000 [1]	350	95	95 [1]	103 [1]	110 [1]
Peru Pérou	7 869 871	4 338 437	8 428 601	10 658620	7 986 103	7 381	7 732	8 275	6 801	9 404
Philippines Philippines	1 805 806	1 833 380	1 872 818	1 893 017	1 945 217	330 441	312 505	352 566	393 861	434 657
Pitcairn Pitcairn	8	8	8	8	8	...	...	...	...	...
Poland Pologne	353 661	238 336	235 111	218 354	225 916	28 680	29 791	33 711	35 795	35 460
Portugal Portugal	221 879	224 234	208 459	187 570	191 214	7 185	7 536	6 268	7 538	7 824
Puerto Rico Porto Rico	3 187	3 006	3 020	4 154	3 794	13	164	138	154	158
Qatar Qatar	5 032	5 279	4 207	7 142	8 606	2	0	0	0	1
Republic of Moldova République de Moldova	569	491	309	344	387	1 202	1 129	815	990	1 189
Réunion Réunion	4 288	4 579	4 043	4 079	3 635	134	124	138	142	130
Romania Roumanie	8 446	9 061	7 843	7 372	7 637	11 168	9 614	8 998	9 727	10 818
Russian Federation Fédération de Russie	4 661 853	4 454 759	4 141 158	3 973 535	3 628 323	53 171	63 195	68 615	74 124	89 945
Rwanda Rwanda	4 428	6 641	6 433	6 726	6 828	118 [1]	128	300	270	435
Saint Helena Sainte-Hélène	897	1 060	632	718	866	...	...	...	...	...
Saint Kitts and Nevis Saint-Kitts-et-Nevis	272	533	555	492	591	4 [1]	4 [1]	5 [1]	5 [1]	5
Saint Lucia Sainte-Lucie	1 308	1 589	1 718	1 855	1 983	3	2	1	1	1
Saint Pierre and Miquelon Saint-Pierre-et-Miquelon	3 571	6 108	5 892	6 485	3 802	...	...	...	...	...
St. Vincent-Grenadines St. Vincent-Grenadines	6 093	33 973	17 759	27 694	45 778	...	...	...	...	...
Samoa Samoa	7 041	7 547	10 204	13 004	12 966	1	0	0	0	0
Sao Tome and Principe Sao Tomé-et-Principe	3 338	3 477	3 756	3 500	3 500	...	...	...	...	...
Saudi Arabia Arabie saoudite	49 314	51 206	46 618	49 650	49 167	4 690	5 101	5 620	6 004	8 218

38

Fish production
Capture and aquaculture: metric tons *[cont.]*

Production halieutique
Capture et aquaculture : tonnes *[suite]*

Country or area Pays ou zone	Capture production Captures					Aquaculture production Production de l'aquaculture				
	1997	1998	1999	2000	2001	1997	1998	1999	2000	2001
Senegal Sénégal	457 366	403 872	412 125	402 047	405 409	74	23	155	155	151
Serbia and Montenegro Serbie-et-Monténégro	3 873	2 610	1 251	1 096	1 088	3 493	6 560	3 435	2 843	2 469
Seychelles Seychelles	14 043	23 886	34 297	32 359	47 550	584	649	227	425	282
Sierra Leone Sierra Leone	72 628	63 065	59 407	74 730	75 210	30 [1]	30 [1]	30 [1]	30 [1]	30
Singapore Singapour	9 250	7 733	6 489	5 371	3 342	4 088	3 706	4 029	5 112	5 362
Slovakia Slovaquie	1 364	1 361	1 396	1 368	1 531	1 254	648	872	887	999
Slovenia Slovénie	2 367	2 228	2 027	1 856	1 827	917	909	1 206	1 181	1 262
Solomon Islands Iles Salomon	64 005	61 332	58 428	24 788	30 075	13	13	13	15	15
Somalia [1] Somalie [1]	24 150	22 250	20 250	20 200	20 000	...	...	...	...	...
South Africa Afrique du Sud	515 095	559 049	588 144	643 238	755 345	4 186	5 072	4 143	3 951	4 177
Spain Espagne	1 204 913	1 263 275	1 169 462	1 045 488	1 084 820	239 136	315 477	321 145	312 171	312 647
Sri Lanka Sri Lanka	235 099	263 330	276 080	297 410	279 640	6 440	10 020	8 305	10 660	8 370
Sudan Soudan	47 000	49 500	49 500	53 000	58 000	1 000	1 000	1 000	1 000	1 000
Suriname Suriname	14 000	16 195	16 200	17 500	18 915	1	106	200	345	422
Swaziland Swaziland	65 [1]	70 [1]	70 [1]	70 [1]	70 [1]	66	81	61	69	72
Sweden Suède	357 406	410 886	351 254	338 534	311 816	6 709	5 504	6 035	4 834	6 773
Switzerland Suisse	1 859	1 809	1 840	1 659	1 715	1 150	1 150	1 135	1 100	1 135
Syrian Arab Republic Rép. arabe syrienne	6 131	7 097	7 938	6 572	8 291	5 596	7 233	6 079	6 797	5 880
Tajikistan Tadjikistan	75	100	80	78	137	71	81	74	86	99
Thailand Thaïlande	2 902 898	2 930 354	2 952 008	2 911 173	2 881 316	539 855	594 607	693 771	731 955	724 228
TFYR of Macedonia L'ex-R.y. Macédoine	130	131	135	208	128	879	1 257	1 669	1 626	1 053
Timor-Leste Timor-Leste	...	...	408	362	356	...	...	...	...	...
Togo Togo	14 290	16 655	22 924	22 277	23 163	20	25	150	102	120
Tokelau Tokélaou	200	200	200	200	200	...	...	...	...	...
Tonga Tonga	2 871	4 076	4 221	3 760	4 673	...	...	...	...	...

38

Fish production
Capture and aquaculture: metric tons *[cont.]*
Production halieutique
Capture et aquaculture : tonnes *[suite]*

Country or area Pays ou zone	Capture production Captures					Aquaculture production Production de l'aquaculture				
	1997	1998	1999	2000	2001	1997	1998	1999	2000	2001
Trinidad and Tobago Trinité-et-Tobago	11 283	9 175	8 826	9 786	11 408	13	13	13	22	7
Tunisia Tunisie	87 012	88 075	93 186	95 550	98 482	1 875	1 842	1 095	1 553	1 868
Turkey Turquie	459 153	487 200	573 824	503 348	527 730	45 450	56 700	63 000	79 031	67 241
Turkmenistan Turkménistan	8 179	7 014	9 058	12 228	12 749	605	559	73	68	43
Turks and Caicos Islands Iles Turques et Caïques	1 250	1 318	1 300	1 300	1 300	4	4	4	5	5
Tuvalu Tuvalu	500	500	500	500	500	...	...	...	...	...
Uganda Ouganda	218 026	220 628	226 097	219 356	220 726	360	320	475	820	2 360
Ukraine Ukraine	373 005	462 308	407 853	392 724	351 260	30 000	28 332	33 816	30 969	31 037
United Arab Emirates Emirats arabes unis	114 358	114 739	117 607	110 056	110 000	0	0	0	0	0
United Kingdom Royaume-Uni	886 261	923 085	840 898	747 358	741 106	129 715	137 421	154 800	152 485	170 516
United Rep. of Tanzania Rép.-Unie de Tanzanie	356 960	348 000	310 509	332 779	335 900	200 [1]	200 [1]	200 [1]	210	300
United States Etats-Unis	4 983 440	4 708 980	4 749 646	4 745 321	4 944 406	438 331	445 123	478 679	428 262	460 998
United States Virgin Is. Iles Vierges américaines	350	300	263	300	300	0	0	0	0	0
Uruguay Uruguay	136 954	140 707	103 012	116 588	105 034	19	19	31	85	17
Uzbekistan Ouzbékistan	3 075	2 799	2 871	3 387	4 070	7 490	6 966	5 665	5 142	4 082
Vanuatu Vanuatu	70 862	74 908	93 041	69 260	26 690	...	...	...	...	...
Venezuela Venezuela	470 255	503 504	399 799	357 115	417 947	8 914	9 670	10 860	13 410	16 622
Viet Nam Viet Nam	1 276 325	1 293 954	1 386 300	1 450 590	1 491 123	404 593	413 031	467 267	510 555	518 500 [1]
Wallis and Futuna Islands Iles Wallis et Futuna	176	300	300	300	300	...	...	...	...	...
Yemen Yémen	115 600	127 620	124 385	114 751	142 198	...	...	...	...	...
Zambia Zambie	65 923	69 938	67 327	66 671	65 000 [1]	4 718	4 159	4 180	4 240	4 200
Zimbabwe Zimbabwe	18 156	16 371	12 410	13 114	13 000 [1]	170	170	185	185	200

Source:
Food and Agriculture Organization of the United Nations (FAO), Rome,
FAOSTAT Fisheries database.

1   FAO estimate.
2   Data refer to the Gaza Strip.

Source:
Organisation des Nations Unies pour l'alimentation et l'agriculture (FAO),
Rome, les données des pêches de FAOSTAT.

1   Estimation de la FAO.
2   Les données se rapportent à la Bande de Gaza.

39
Fertilizers
Nitrogenous, phosphate and potash: thousand metric tons
Engrais
Azotés, phosphatés et potassiques : milliers de tonnes

Country or area and traffic	Production					Consumption Consommation				
	1997/98	1998/99	1999/00	2000/01	2001/02	1997/98	1998/99	1999/00	2000/01	2001/02
World Monde										
Nitrogenous fertilizers										
Engrais azotés	87 566.0	88 392.2	89 161.9	86 019.1	86 359.0	81 317.0	82 814.0	84 916.6	80 948.9	81 969.6
Phosphate fertilizers										
Engrais phosphatés	33 080.5	33 328.1	33 093.0	32 200.9	33 544.8	33 293.3	33 311.7	33 288.5	32 471.9	33 049.5
Potash fertilizers										
Engrais potassiques	25 508.5	25 600.8	25 360.6	26 157.2	25 875.5	22 577.5	22 041.3	22 096.4	21 777.6	22 710.6
Africa Afrique										
Nitrogenous fertilizers										
Engrais azotés	2 451.2	2 680.4	2 840.8	2 756.6	2 820.8	2 257.0	2 338.7	2 411.8	2 464.6	2 505.7
Phosphate fertilizers										
Engrais phosphatés	2 264.2	2 430.6	2 478.6	2 530.6	2 675.6	944.0	943.0	1 005.2	927.6	924.8
Potash fertilizers										
Engrais potassiques	...	...	...	...	...	473.3	500.3	480.2	469.6	505.5
Algeria * Algérie *										
Nitrogenous fertilizers										
Engrais azotés	28.4	40.7	54.4	90.7	118.2	36.0	44.0	47.0	44.3	45.3
Phosphate fertilizers										
Engrais phosphatés	...	23.4	8.7	20.3	35.8	35.0	30.8	25.0	25.0	35.0
Potash fertilizers										
Engrais potassiques	...	...	...	...	...	26.0	33.2	21.0	23.0	25.0
Angola Angola										
Nitrogenous fertilizers										
Engrais azotés	...	...	...	...	...	*2.0	*2.3	*2.3	*1.4	0.0
Potash fertilizers *										
Engrais potassiques *	...	...	...	...	...	...	1.1	1.1	...	...
Benin Bénin										
Nitrogenous fertilizers										
Engrais azotés	...	...	...	...	...	18.8	*15.3	*34.6	*14.3	*15.1
Phosphate fertilizers										
Engrais phosphatés	...	...	...	...	...	12.6	*14.6	*10.4	*11.4	*7.5
Potash fertilizers										
Engrais potassiques	...	...	...	...	...	*7.6	*7.8	*11.7	9.5	*8.5
Botswana Botswana										
Nitrogenous fertilizers										
Engrais azotés	...	...	...	...	...	*3.5	3.7	*4.1	*4.1	*4.1
Phosphate fertilizers *										
Engrais phosphatés *	...	...	...	...	...	0.2	0.3	0.3	0.3	0.3
Potash fertilizers *										
Engrais potassiques *	...	...	...	...	...	0.1	0.2	0.2	0.2	0.2
Burkina Faso Burkina Faso										
Nitrogenous fertilizers										
Engrais azotés	...	...	...	...	...	24.4	*16.4	*16.9	*9.9	*9.5
Phosphate fertilizers										
Engrais phosphatés	*0.3	*0.3	0.9	0.4	0.0	9.9	*17.8	18.5	15.1	*14.0
Potash fertilizers										
Engrais potassiques	...	...	...	...	...	8.3	*16.0	*8.0	9.0	*9.0
Burundi Burundi										
Nitrogenous fertilizers *										
Engrais azotés *	...	...	...	...	...	1.0	1.4	1.8	1.5	1.5
Phosphate fertilizers										
Engrais phosphatés	...	...	...	...	...	...	1.2	*1.4	*1.0	*1.0
Potash fertilizers										
Engrais potassiques	...	...	...	...	...	0.0	1.0	0.8	*1.0	*1.0
Cameroon Cameroun										
Nitrogenous fertilizers										
Engrais azotés	...	...	...	...	...	*18.9	16.5	*26.0	21.9	25.6
Phosphate fertilizers										
Engrais phosphatés	...	...	...	...	...	7.0	7.6	*10.0	7.7	9.9

39

Fertilizers

Nitrogenous, phosphate and potash: thousand metric tons [*cont.*]

Engrais

Azotés, phosphatés et potassiques: milliers de tonnes [*suite*]

Country or area and traffic	Production Production					Consumption Consommation				
	1997/98	1998/99	1999/00	2000/01	2001/02	1997/98	1998/99	1999/00	2000/01	2001/02
Potash fertilizers										
Engrais potassiques	...	...	...	...	...	13.3	15.4	*13.5	16.6	17.0
Cape Verde Cap-Vert										
Nitrogenous fertilizers										
Engrais azotés	...	...	...	...	...	0.0	0.1	0.2	0.1	*0.1
Central African Rep. * Rép. centrafricaine *										
Nitrogenous fertilizers										
Engrais azotés	...	...	...	...	...	0.1	0.2	0.2	0.2	0.2
Phosphate fertilizers										
Engrais phosphatés	...	...	...	...	...	0.1	0.2	0.2	0.2	0.2
Potash fertilizers										
Engrais potassiques	...	...	...	...	...	0.1	0.2	0.2	0.2	0.2
Chad Tchad										
Nitrogenous fertilizers *										
Engrais azotés *	...	...	...	...	...	3.5	10.7	11.0	11.0	11.0
Phosphate fertilizers										
Engrais phosphatés	...	...	...	...	...	*2.4	1.7	*2.0	*2.0	*2.0
Potash fertilizers										
Engrais potassiques	...	...	...	...	...	*2.0	4.4	*4.5	*4.5	*4.5
Comoros * Comores *										
Nitrogenous fertilizers										
Engrais azotés	...	...	...	...	...	0.1	0.1	0.1	0.1	0.1
Phosphate fertilizers										
Engrais phosphatés	...	...	...	...	...	0.1	0.1	0.1	0.1	0.1
Potash fertilizers										
Engrais potassiques	...	...	...	...	...	0.1	0.1	0.1	0.1	0.1
Congo * Congo *										
Nitrogenous fertilizers										
Engrais azotés	...	...	...	...	...	2.0	2.0	2.0	2.0	2.0
Phosphate fertilizers										
Engrais phosphatés	...	...	...	...	...	1.0	1.0	1.0	1.0	1.0
Potash fertilizers										
Engrais potassiques	...	...	...	...	...	1.0	2.0	2.0	2.0	2.0
Côte d'Ivoire Côte d'Ivoire										
Nitrogenous fertilizers *										
Engrais azotés *	...	...	...	...	...	60.0	50.0	41.2	40.0	30.0
Phosphate fertilizers *										
Engrais phosphatés *	...	...	...	...	...	25.0	25.0	14.4	11.1	16.5
Potash fertilizers										
Engrais potassiques	...	...	...	...	...	*25.0	*15.0	*15.0	*16.0	16.0
Dem. Rep. of the Congo Rép. dém. du Congo										
Nitrogenous fertilizers										
Engrais azotés	...	...	...	...	...	...	1.7	0.3	*0.3	*1.0
Phosphate fertilizers										
Engrais phosphatés	...	...	...	...	...	...	0.3	0.3	*0.3	*0.3
Potash fertilizers										
Engrais potassiques	...	...	...	...	...	...	1.0	0.2	0.2	*0.2
Egypt Egypte										
Nitrogenous fertilizers										
Engrais azotés	*943.8	*1 111.0	*1 268.5	1 287.5	1 321.0	*915.0	*1 014.0	*984.4	1 073.4	1 097.9
Phosphate fertilizers										
Engrais phosphatés	*195.3	*174.0	*168.6	173.0	193.8	*134.5	*128.6	*150.1	153.8	156.2
Potash fertilizers										
Engrais potassiques	...	...	...	...	...	29.2	28.5	45.0	32.5	53.1
Eritrea Erythrée										
Nitrogenous fertilizers										
Engrais azotés	...	...	...	...	...	*5.0	*5.0	5.4	*5.4	*5.0
Phosphate fertilizers										
Engrais phosphatés	...	...	...	...	...	*1.0	*1.5	5.5	*5.5	*5.0

39

Fertilizers

Nitrogenous, phosphate and potash: thousand metric tons [*cont.*]

Engrais

Azotés, phosphatés et potassiques: milliers de tonnes [*suite*]

Country or area and traffic	Production					Consumption Consommation				
	1997/98	1998/99	1999/00	2000/01	2001/02	1997/98	1998/99	1999/00	2000/01	2001/02
Ethiopia Ethiopie										
Nitrogenous fertilizers						54.1	*75.1	79.8	76.5	63.2
Engrais azotés	...	...	...	...	...					
Phosphate fertilizers						77.6	89.0	88.1	81.0	71.7
Engrais phosphatés	...	...	...	...	...					
Gabon Gabon										
Nitrogenous fertilizers *						0.1	0.1	0.1	0.1	0.1
Engrais azotés *	...	...	...	...	...					
Phosphate fertilizers *						0.1	0.2	0.1	0.1	0.1
Engrais phosphatés *	...	...	...	...	...					
Potash fertilizers						0.0	*0.1	*0.1	*0.1	*0.1
Engrais potassiques	...	...	...	...	...					
Gambia Gambie										
Nitrogenous fertilizers *						0.3	2.3	1.0	0.6	0.6
Engrais azotés *	...	...	...	...	...					
Phosphate fertilizers *						0.5	0.1	0.1	0.1	0.1
Engrais phosphatés *	...	...	...	...	...					
Potash fertilizers						*0.3	*0.1	*0.1	*0.1	0.1
Engrais potassiques	...	...	...	...	...					
Ghana Ghana										
Nitrogenous fertilizers						8.7	7.3	8.0	7.0	*5.9
Engrais azotés	...	...	...	...	...					
Phosphate fertilizers						6.0	3.7	4.2	2.7	*2.1
Engrais phosphatés	...	...	...	...	...					
Potash fertilizers						6.7	4.3	3.2	2.1	*2.2
Engrais potassiques	...	...	...	...	...					
Guinea Guinée										
Nitrogenous fertilizers						0.7	1.1	*1.0	*1.0	*1.0
Engrais azotés	...	...	...	...	...					
Phosphate fertilizers						0.6	1.4	*1.4	*1.4	*1.4
Engrais phosphatés	...	...	...	...	...					
Potash fertilizers						0.5	0.7	*0.8	*0.8	*0.8
Engrais potassiques	...	...	...	...	...					
Guinea-Bissau * Guinée-Bissau *										
Nitrogenous fertilizers						0.1	0.2	0.2	1.0	1.0
Engrais azotés	...	...	...	...	...					
Phosphate fertilizers						0.1	0.2	0.2	0.7	0.7
Engrais phosphatés	...	...	...	...	...					
Potash fertilizers						0.1	0.2	0.2	0.7	0.7
Engrais potassiques	...	...	...	...	...					
Kenya Kenya										
Nitrogenous fertilizers						*51.0	*53.0	*54.2	69.9	75.3
Engrais azotés	...	...	...	...	...					
Phosphate fertilizers						*69.4	*57.1	*84.9	71.2	61.6
Engrais phosphatés	...	...	...	...	...					
Potash fertilizers						*14.0	*17.0	*9.0	4.5	7.8
Engrais potassiques	...	...	...	...	...					
Lesotho Lesotho										
Nitrogenous fertilizers						1.6	*1.8	1.9	3.4	4.9
Engrais azotés	...	...	...	...	...					
Phosphate fertilizers						*2.0	*2.1	1.9	2.4	3.4
Engrais phosphatés	...	...	...	...	...					
Potash fertilizers						*2.0	*2.1	1.3	2.1	3.0
Engrais potassiques	...	...	...	...	...					
Libyan Arab Jamah. Jamah. arabe libyenne										
Nitrogenous fertilizers	*383.4	408.2	386.9	*407.1	*365.2	*17.5	*20.0	*43.6	*31.7	*31.9
Engrais azotés										
Phosphate fertilizers *						40.9	27.0	34.7	18.0	18.6
Engrais phosphatés *	...	...	...	...	...					

39

Fertilizers

Nitrogenous, phosphate and potash: thousand metric tons [cont.]

Engrais

Azotés, phosphatés et potassiques: milliers de tonnes [suite]

Country or area and traffic	Production					Consumption				
	1997/98	1998/99	1999/00	2000/01	2001/02	1997/98	1998/99	1999/00	2000/01	2001/02
Potash fertilizers										
Engrais potassiques	...	...	...	...	...	*3.3	*3.5	*8.2	*5.3	5.5
Madagascar Madagascar										
Nitrogenous fertilizers										
Engrais azotés	...	...	...	...	...	3.6	3.6	4.3	3.8	2.7
Phosphate fertilizers										
Engrais phosphatés	...	...	...	...	...	3.0	2.7	2.3	3.0	2.0
Potash fertilizers										
Engrais potassiques	...	...	...	...	...	2.9	2.4	1.3	2.4	2.0
Malawi Malawi										
Nitrogenous fertilizers										
Engrais azotés	...	...	...	...	...	*41.2	*34.8	*30.0	34.6	12.2
Phosphate fertilizers										
Engrais phosphatés	...	...	...	...	...	*12.6	*11.9	*16.6	*11.4	5.3
Potash fertilizers										
Engrais potassiques	...	...	...	...	...	*3.0	*3.5	*3.5	3.8	5.2
Mali Mali										
Nitrogenous fertilizers										
Engrais azotés	...	...	...	...	...	*25.6	*17.4	*18.1	12.7	*14.0
Phosphate fertilizers										
Engrais phosphatés	...	...	...	...	...	*12.0	*15.8	16.1	13.6	*14.0
Potash fertilizers										
Engrais potassiques	...	...	...	...	...	*10.2	*12.7	15.6	13.6	*14.0
Mauritania Mauritanie										
Nitrogenous fertilizers										
Engrais azotés	...	...	...	...	...	1.5	*1.8	*2.4	...	2.0
Phosphate fertilizers *										
Engrais phosphatés *	...	...	...	...	...	0.2	...	...	...	
Mauritius Maurice										
Nitrogenous fertilizers										
Engrais azotés	14.3	*14.4	*12.4	*16.8	*13.1	11.8	*12.4	*13.4	*13.3	*12.6
Phosphate fertilizers										
Engrais phosphatés	...	...	...	...	...	*7.0	*6.0	*5.7	*6.1	5.4
Potash fertilizers										
Engrais potassiques	...	...	...	...	...	14.7	*14.7	*16.2	*18.1	*19.2
Morocco Maroc										
Nitrogenous fertilizers										
Engrais azotés	*261.9	*271.0	*279.2	*300.0	*356.4	174.1	*176.0	202.9	207.6	*198.0
Phosphate fertilizers										
Engrais phosphatés	923.9	*958.6	*955.6	*1 122.0	*1 230.6	*98.0	*98.0	104.0	108.8	*110.0
Potash fertilizers *										
Engrais potassiques *	...	...	...	...	...	55.2	51.0	57.6	51.0	52.2
Mozambique Mozambique										
Nitrogenous fertilizers *										
Engrais azotés *	...	...	...	...	...	1.5	3.8	8.0	9.7	16.0
Phosphate fertilizers *										
Engrais phosphatés *	...	...	...	...	...	2.6	1.6	...	3.4	2.0
Potash fertilizers										
Engrais potassiques	...	...	...	...	...	*2.4	*2.6	...	*1.2	6.9
Namibia * Namibie *										
Nitrogenous fertilizers										
Engrais azotés	...	...	...	...	...	...	0.1	0.1	0.1	0.1
Phosphate fertilizers										
Engrais phosphatés	...	...	...	...	...	...	...	0.2	0.2	0.2
Niger Niger										
Nitrogenous fertilizers										
Engrais azotés	...	...	...	...	...	*0.5	*0.5	1.7	2.5	3.4
Phosphate fertilizers										
Engrais phosphatés	...	...	...	...	...	...	...	1.4	1.2	1.0

39

Fertilizers
Nitrogenous, phosphate and potash: thousand metric tons [*cont.*]
Engrais
Azotés, phosphatés et potassiques: milliers de tonnes [*suite*]

Country or area and traffic	Production Production					Consumption Consommation				
	1997/98	1998/99	1999/00	2000/01	2001/02	1997/98	1998/99	1999/00	2000/01	2001/02
Potash fertilizers Engrais potassiques	...	...	...	...	...	*0.2	...	1.1	0.8	0.6
Nigeria * Nigéria *										
Nitrogenous fertilizers Engrais azotés	41.2	71.0	70.0	...	...	77.3	100.0	107.0	105.6	146.8
Phosphate fertilizers Engrais phosphatés	5.0	10.5	...	...	...	21.4	39.2	34.7	44.0	40.2
Potash fertilizers Engrais potassiques	...	...	...	...	...	39.0	24.0	26.0	37.9	34.0
Réunion * Réunion *										
Nitrogenous fertilizers Engrais azotés	...	...	...	...	...	2.0	2.1	2.1	2.0	2.3
Phosphate fertilizers Engrais phosphatés	...	...	...	...	...	2.0	1.5	1.5	1.5	1.5
Potash fertilizers Engrais potassiques	...	...	...	...	...	3.0	2.0	2.0	1.3	1.2
Rwanda * Rwanda *										
Nitrogenous fertilizers Engrais azotés	...	...	...	...	...	0.1	0.1	0.1	0.1	0.1
Phosphate fertilizers Engrais phosphatés	...	...	...	...	...	0.2	0.1	0.1	0.1	0.1
Potash fertilizers Engrais potassiques	...	...	...	...	...	0.1	0.1	0.1	0.1	0.1
Senegal * Sénégal *										
Nitrogenous fertilizers Engrais azotés	30.4	38.8	24.5	19.4	25.2	7.1	7.6	14.4	16.2	15.9
Phosphate fertilizers Engrais phosphatés	55.0	67.5	45.0	32.4	32.7	10.8	11.0	15.4	11.0	12.0
Potash fertilizers Engrais potassiques	...	...	...	...	...	5.0	7.0	8.0	11.0	12.0
Sierra Leone Sierra Leone										
Nitrogenous fertilizers Engrais azotés	...	...	...	...	...	*1.0	*0.1	0.0	0.1	*0.1
Phosphate fertilizers Engrais phosphatés	...	...	...	...	...	*1.0	*0.1	0.0	0.1	*0.1
Potash fertilizers Engrais potassiques	...	...	...	...	...	*1.0	*0.1	0.0	0.1	*0.1
Somalia * Somalie *										
Nitrogenous fertilizers Engrais azotés	...	...	...	...	...	0.5	0.5	0.5	0.5	0.5
South Africa Afrique du Sud										
Nitrogenous fertilizers Engrais azotés	*465.0	*423.0	*406.8	*308.9	*296.3	405.0	406.0	*413.0	*415.9	*393.0
Phosphate fertilizers Engrais phosphatés	*378.4	378.8	391.2	*267.9	*264.2	225.0	218.0	*227.3	*187.0	*208.0
Potash fertilizers Engrais potassiques	...	...	...	...	...	131.0	*158.8	*136.4	*137.4	*138.0
Sudan Soudan										
Nitrogenous fertilizers * Engrais azotés *	...	...	...	...	...	69.0	26.2	26.1	32.8	70.0
Phosphate fertilizers Engrais phosphatés	...	...	...	...	...	*8.4	*11.5	*12.1	7.3	*8.0
Potash fertilizers Engrais potassiques	...	...	...	...	...	...	...	0.6	0.6	*1.0
Swaziland * Swaziland *										
Nitrogenous fertilizers Engrais azotés	...	...	...	...	...	1.6	2.0	1.7	2.0	2.0
Phosphate fertilizers Engrais phosphatés	...	...	...	...	...	1.8	1.9	1.9	1.9	2.5

39

Fertilizers
Nitrogenous, phosphate and potash: thousand metric tons [*cont.*]
Engrais
Azotés, phosphatés et potassiques: milliers de tonnes [*suite*]

Country or area and traffic	Production Production					Consumption Consommation				
	1997/98	1998/99	1999/00	2000/01	2001/02	1997/98	1998/99	1999/00	2000/01	2001/02
Potash fertilizers										
Engrais potassiques	...	...	...	...	...	1.8	1.9	1.9	1.9	2.5
Togo Togo										
Nitrogenous fertilizers										
Engrais azotés	...	...	...	...	...	*6.0	*6.6	*8.5	9.0	*9.2
Phosphate fertilizers										
Engrais phosphatés	...	...	...	...	...	*5.4	*5.3	*4.2	5.4	*5.0
Potash fertilizers										
Engrais potassiques	...	...	...	...	...	*5.4	*5.3	*4.2	5.4	*5.0
Tunisia Tunisie										
Nitrogenous fertilizers										
Engrais azotés	*190.4	*225.9	*250.4	*253.9	*265.9	*51.5	63.3	*65.0	*62.1	*59.5
Phosphate fertilizers										
Engrais phosphatés	*673.3	782.0	870.6	*884.6	*892.4	40.0	44.5	*43.0	*45.0	*45.0
Potash fertilizers										
Engrais potassiques	...	...	...	...	...	*5.0	*6.0	*4.2	4.2	*4.2
Uganda Ouganda										
Nitrogenous fertilizers										
Engrais azotés	...	...	...	...	...	*0.2	1.8	2.1	3.4	*3.8
Phosphate fertilizers										
Engrais phosphatés	...	...	...	...	...	*0.2	0.9	1.3	1.7	*1.0
Potash fertilizers										
Engrais potassiques	...	...	...	...	...	*0.2	0.8	1.1	1.5	*1.0
United Rep. of Tanzania Rép.-Unie de Tanzanie										
Nitrogenous fertilizers										
Engrais azotés	...	...	...	...	...	24.9	19.3	12.5	14.1	*14.2
Phosphate fertilizers										
Engrais phosphatés	...	...	...	...	...	*8.3	5.9	6.2	6.0	*6.0
Potash fertilizers										
Engrais potassiques	...	...	...	...	...	6.7	5.6	2.2	2.3	*2.3
Zambia Zambie										
Nitrogenous fertilizers										
Engrais azotés	*4.0	*2.3	1.7	*0.9	...	*32.6	*13.2	10.6	8.0	*13.0
Phosphate fertilizers										
Engrais phosphatés	...	...	...	...	...	*14.1	*13.5	*13.4	13.4	*11.7
Potash fertilizers *										
Engrais potassiques *	...	...	...	...	...	10.0	10.0	10.0	10.0	11.7
Zimbabwe Zimbabwe										
Nitrogenous fertilizers *										
Engrais azotés *	88.4	74.1	86.0	71.4	59.5	94.0	95.0	100.0	87.4	82.0
Phosphate fertilizers *										
Engrais phosphatés *	33.0	35.5	38.0	30.0	26.1	44.0	42.0	43.0	43.4	35.0
Potash fertilizers										
Engrais potassiques	...	...	...	...	...	*37.0	*38.0	42.0	*34.5	*35.2
America, North Amérique du Nord										
Nitrogenous fertilizers										
Engrais azotés	19 111.8	18 749.2	16 698.8	14 776.3	15 119.3	14 668.6	14 842.9	14 719.4	13 948.8	14 347.7
Phosphate fertilizers										
Engrais phosphatés	9 840.5	9 838.1	9 259.2	7 926.9	8 317.9	5 372.0	5 096.4	5 066.2	4 937.5	5 255.2
Potash fertilizers										
Engrais potassiques	10 464.5	10 097.8	9 096.0	9 984.1	8 994.1	5 644.3	5 328.0	5 277.7	5 205.6	5 250.5
Bahamas Bahamas										
Nitrogenous fertilizers *										
Engrais azotés *	...	...	...	...	...	0.1	0.1	0.1	0.1	0.4
Phosphate fertilizers *										
Engrais phosphatés *	...	...	...	...	...	0.1	0.1	0.1	0.1	0.2
Potash fertilizers										
Engrais potassiques	...	...	...	...	...	0.1	*0.1	*0.1	*0.1	*0.2

39

Fertilizers
Nitrogenous, phosphate and potash: thousand metric tons [*cont.*]
Engrais
Azotés, phosphatés et potassiques: milliers de tonnes [*suite*]

Country or area and traffic	Production Production					Consumption Consommation				
	1997/98	1998/99	1999/00	2000/01	2001/02	1997/98	1998/99	1999/00	2000/01	2001/02
Barbados Barbade										
Nitrogenous fertilizers *						2.0	1.8	1.8	1.8	1.8
Engrais azotés *	...	...	...	...	...					
Phosphate fertilizers						*0.2	0.2	*0.2	*0.2	*0.2
Engrais phosphatés	...	...	...	...	...					
Potash fertilizers *						1.0	1.0	1.0	1.0	1.0
Engrais potassiques *	...	...	...	...	...					
Belize Belize										
Nitrogenous fertilizers						*1.3	1.9	*2.3	2.8	*1.9
Engrais azotés	...	...	...	...	...					
Phosphate fertilizers						2.5	*2.7	*2.8	*1.9	*2.3
Engrais phosphatés	...	...	...	...	...					
Potash fertilizers *						1.0	1.0	1.0	1.4	0.5
Engrais potassiques *	...	...	...	...	...					
Bermuda * Bermudes *										
Nitrogenous fertilizers						0.1	0.1	0.1	0.1	0.1
Engrais azotés	...	...	...	...	...					
Canada Canada										
Nitrogenous fertilizers										
Engrais azotés	*3 654.3	*3 737.1	*4 141.4	*3 831.0	*3 524.4	*1 652.7	*1 625.8	1 682.1	1 564.3	*1 517.4
Phosphate fertilizers										
Engrais phosphatés	*372.6	*357.8	*273.0	*239.7	*317.7	*717.0	*666.6	667.9	570.5	*559.2
Potash fertilizers										
Engrais potassiques	*9 029.2	*9 195.1	*8 230.5	*9 174.0	*8 152.2	*356.3	*356.6	339.3	310.5	*310.0
Costa Rica Costa Rica										
Nitrogenous fertilizers										
Engrais azotés	*41.0	*32.0	*52.6	13.4	*0.5	*100.0	*104.0	*80.0	68.0	64.0
Phosphate fertilizers *						31.0	33.0	32.0	29.0	18.2
Engrais phosphatés *	...	...	...	...	...					
Potash fertilizers *						60.0	62.0	72.0	70.0	45.8
Engrais potassiques *	...	...	...	...	...					
Cuba * Cuba *										
Nitrogenous fertilizers										
Engrais azotés	62.0	50.0	50.0	50.0	50.0	133.0	107.0	72.3	78.0	116.6
Phosphate fertilizers						35.0	14.8	23.4	24.3	27.4
Engrais phosphatés	...	...	...	...	...					
Potash fertilizers						71.4	47.5	59.8	28.1	56.8
Engrais potassiques	...	...	...	...	...					
Dominica * Dominique *										
Nitrogenous fertilizers						1.0	1.0	1.0	1.0	1.0
Engrais azotés	...	...	...	...	...					
Phosphate fertilizers						1.0	1.0	1.0	1.0	1.0
Engrais phosphatés	...	...	...	...	...					
Potash fertilizers						1.0	1.0	1.0	1.0	1.0
Engrais potassiques	...	...	...	...	...					
Dominican Republic Rép. dominicaine										
Nitrogenous fertilizers *						55.4	51.3	52.9	48.5	56.9
Engrais azotés *	...	...	...	...	...					
Phosphate fertilizers *						22.0	20.3	18.3	15.4	18.4
Engrais phosphatés *	...	...	...	...	...					
Potash fertilizers						*31.5	*26.2	*22.5	*27.8	22.8
Engrais potassiques	...	...	...	...	...					
El Salvador El Salvador										
Nitrogenous fertilizers						*72.1	*57.0	56.8	48.5	48.3
Engrais azotés	...	...	...	...	...					
Phosphate fertilizers						*13.1	*16.0	11.7	*13.3	8.9
Engrais phosphatés	...	...	...	...	...					
Potash fertilizers *						9.2	9.8	10.0	16.0	16.0
Engrais potassiques *	...	...	...	...	...					

39

Fertilizers

Nitrogenous, phosphate and potash: thousand metric tons [*cont.*]

Engrais

Azotés, phosphatés et potassiques: milliers de tonnes [*suite*]

Country or area and traffic	Production Production					Consumption Consommation				
	1997/98	1998/99	1999/00	2000/01	2001/02	1997/98	1998/99	1999/00	2000/01	2001/02
Guadeloupe Guadeloupe										
Nitrogenous fertilizers *										
Engrais azotés *	...	...	...	...	...	1.5	6.1	6.8	7.0	7.0
Phosphate fertilizers										
Engrais phosphatés	...	...	...	...	...	*1.0	4.8	*7.0	*6.5	*6.5
Potash fertilizers										
Engrais potassiques	...	...	...	...	...	*1.0	*6.7	*5.8	*5.8	5.8
Guatemala Guatemala										
Nitrogenous fertilizers										
Engrais azotés	...	...	...	...	...	118.4	*101.0	*124.0	*124.5	90.0
Phosphate fertilizers *										
Engrais phosphatés *	...	...	...	...	...	48.9	44.3	36.2	46.1	51.7
Potash fertilizers										
Engrais potassiques	...	...	...	...	...	*42.0	*27.3	*36.3	41.0	41.2
Haiti Haïti										
Nitrogenous fertilizers										
Engrais azotés	...	...	...	...	...	8.5	6.3	5.0	8.9	7.7
Phosphate fertilizers										
Engrais phosphatés	...	...	...	...	...	2.0	2.2	1.7	2.7	2.6
Potash fertilizers										
Engrais potassiques	...	...	...	...	...	2.0	2.5	2.0	2.9	3.7
Honduras Honduras										
Nitrogenous fertilizers *										
Engrais azotés *	...	...	...	...	...	82.9	93.9	109.5	135.9	110.0
Phosphate fertilizers *										
Engrais phosphatés *	...	...	...	...	...	24.2	23.0	30.3	21.6	18.0
Potash fertilizers										
Engrais potassiques	...	...	...	...	...	*36.6	*23.0	*24.0	23.0	*23.5
Jamaica Jamaïque										
Nitrogenous fertilizers										
Engrais azotés	...	...	...	...	...	9.0	8.9	9.2	9.9	*6.7
Phosphate fertilizers										
Engrais phosphatés	...	...	...	...	...	6.0	5.2	5.0	*5.2	*1.5
Potash fertilizers										
Engrais potassiques	...	...	...	...	...	8.4	9.3	8.8	*7.3	*3.5
Martinique Martinique										
Nitrogenous fertilizers *										
Engrais azotés *	...	...	...	...	...	3.9	6.4	3.0	2.3	4.6
Phosphate fertilizers										
Engrais phosphatés	...	...	...	...	...	*1.0	*4.4	*0.6	*1.1	2.9
Potash fertilizers *										
Engrais potassiques *	...	...	...	...	...	4.7	10.3	7.6	7.7	10.2
Mexico Mexique										
Nitrogenous fertilizers *										
Engrais azotés *	1 290.9	1 190.2	948.3	702.9	673.4	1 197.0	1 336.0	1 300.0	1 342.0	1 374.1
Phosphate fertilizers *										
Engrais phosphatés *	462.8	479.4	515.9	434.9	357.4	257.0	295.0	306.0	315.0	321.3
Potash fertilizers										
Engrais potassiques	...	...	...	...	...	*190.1	*173.3	*170.0	175.0	174.3
Nicaragua Nicaragua										
Nitrogenous fertilizers										
Engrais azotés	...	...	...	...	...	20.0	*21.9	*20.2	*14.2	*15.3
Phosphate fertilizers										
Engrais phosphatés	...	...	...	...	...	*8.9	*9.0	9.4	*10.7	2.2
Potash fertilizers										
Engrais potassiques	...	...	...	...	...	6.8	*7.7	*6.3	*4.0	5.2
Panama Panama										
Nitrogenous fertilizers										
Engrais azotés	...	...	...	...	...	21.4	21.3	*17.7	15.3	*16.0

39

Fertilizers

Nitrogenous, phosphate and potash: thousand metric tons [*cont.*]

Engrais

Azotés, phosphatés et potassiques: milliers de tonnes [*suite*]

Country or area and traffic	Production Production					Consumption Consommation				
	1997/98	1998/99	1999/00	2000/01	2001/02	1997/98	1998/99	1999/00	2000/01	2001/02
Phosphate fertilizers										
Engrais phosphatés	...	...	...	...	...	9.5	9.2	*9.0	5.5	*7.1
Potash fertilizers										
Engrais potassiques	...	...	...	...	...	5.5	9.4	*7.3	10.4	*6.1
Saint Kitts and Nevis * Saint-Kitts-et-Nevis *										
Nitrogenous fertilizers										
Engrais azotés	...	...	...	...	...	0.8	0.8	0.8	0.8	0.8
Phosphate fertilizers										
Engrais phosphatés	...	...	...	...	...	0.5	0.5	0.5	0.5	0.5
Potash fertilizers										
Engrais potassiques	...	...	...	...	...	0.4	0.4	0.4	0.4	0.4
Saint Lucia Sainte-Lucie										
Nitrogenous fertilizers										
Engrais azotés	...	...	...	...	...	9.6	*2.2	*2.0	2.0	*2.0
Phosphate fertilizers *										
Engrais phosphatés *	...	...	...	...	...	2.0	...	2.5	2.5	2.5
Potash fertilizers *										
Engrais potassiques *	...	...	...	...	...	2.0	...	0.8	0.8	0.8
St. Vincent-Grenadines St. Vincent-Grenadines										
Nitrogenous fertilizers *										
Engrais azotés *	...	...	...	...	...	1.0	1.3	1.3	1.3	1.3
Phosphate fertilizers										
Engrais phosphatés	...	...	...	...	...	*1.0	*1.3	*1.3	1.3	*1.3
Potash fertilizers										
Engrais potassiques	...	...	...	...	...	*1.0	*1.3	*1.3	1.3	1.3
Trinidad and Tobago Trinité-et-Tobago										
Nitrogenous fertilizers										
Engrais azotés	*277.5	*240.7	*276.0	275.3	*267.7	*6.0	*5.0	*4.9	7.3	8.9
Phosphate fertilizers										
Engrais phosphatés	...	...	...	...	...	*1.0	*0.4	*0.3	0.7	0.7
Potash fertilizers										
Engrais potassiques	...	...	...	...	...	*3.6	*1.4	*0.9	1.2	1.2
United States Etats-Unis										
Nitrogenous fertilizers										
Engrais azotés	13 786.1	13 499.2	11 230.5	9 903.7	10 603.4	11 169.7	11 281.5	11 165.3	10 464.1	10 894.6
Phosphate fertilizers										
Engrais phosphatés	9 005.2	9 000.9	8 470.3	7 252.3	7 642.8	4 186.8	3 942.1	3 898.6	3 862.0	4 200.3
Potash fertilizers										
Engrais potassiques	1 435.3	902.7	865.5	810.1	841.9	4 808.7	4 550.3	4 499.5	4 468.9	4 519.2
United States Virgin Is. * Iles Vierges américaines *										
Nitrogenous fertilizers										
Engrais azotés	...	...	...	...	...	1.0	0.3	0.3	0.3	0.3
Phosphate fertilizers										
Engrais phosphatés	...	...	...	...	...	0.3	0.3	0.3	0.3	0.3
America, South Amérique du Sud										
Nitrogenous fertilizers										
Engrais azotés	1 575.9	1 421.1	1 521.3	1 400.8	1 650.8	2 896.9	2 962.1	3 080.9	3 246.4	3 260.4
Phosphate fertilizers										
Engrais phosphatés	1 418.7	1 463.4	1 446.8	1 572.8	1 530.7	2 839.9	2 871.2	2 791.4	3 196.4	3 398.8
Potash fertilizers										
Engrais potassiques	516.4	641.5	709.8	992.2	825.2	2 797.8	2 711.3	2 700.7	3 025.4	3 144.5
Argentina Argentine										
Nitrogenous fertilizers										
Engrais azotés	*97.1	*98.6	*119.6	*147.0	*358.0	*476.4	*422.7	457.3	498.2	*489.6
Phosphate fertilizers										
Engrais phosphatés	...	...	...	...	...	*302.6	*320.7	*340.2	333.8	*334.5
Potash fertilizers										
Engrais potassiques	...	...	...	...	...	*30.6	32.1	*26.0	*31.0	*35.6

39

Fertilizers

Nitrogenous, phosphate and potash: thousand metric tons [*cont.*]

Engrais

Azotés, phosphatés et potassiques: milliers de tonnes [*suite*]

Country or area and traffic	Production Production					Consumption Consommation				
	1997/98	1998/99	1999/00	2000/01	2001/02	1997/98	1998/99	1999/00	2000/01	2001/02
Bolivia Bolivie										
Nitrogenous fertilizers										
Engrais azotés	...	...	...	...	...	4.9	1.3	0.9	3.2	*4.1
Phosphate fertilizers										
Engrais phosphatés	...	...	...	...	...	7.1	2.9	0.7	3.6	*7.0
Potash fertilizers										
Engrais potassiques	...	...	...	...	...	0.6	0.8	0.4	0.7	1.0
Brazil Brésil										
Nitrogenous fertilizers										
Engrais azotés	808.4	728.0	847.6	772.2	657.8	1 438.1	1 545.5	1 660.8	1 668.0	1 640.0
Phosphate fertilizers										
Engrais phosphatés	1 354.1	1 369.0	1 357.8	1 496.1	1 444.9	2 004.4	2 022.4	1 953.7	2 338.0	2 483.0
Potash fertilizers										
Engrais potassiques	281.4	326.5	347.8	353.2	357.2	2 397.4	2 283.2	2 255.3	2 562.0	2 650.0
Chile Chili										
Nitrogenous fertilizers										
Engrais azotés	*115.0	*97.0	*95.0	*112.5	*101.0	*220.0	*215.0	*236.0	*235.0	226.0
Phosphate fertilizers										
Engrais phosphatés	...	...	...	...	...	*160.0	*173.0	*164.7	*172.0	179.0
Potash fertilizers *										
Engrais potassiques *	235.0	315.0	362.0	408.0	468.0	55.0	82.0	74.5	75.0	76.0
Colombia Colombie										
Nitrogenous fertilizers										
Engrais azotés	*92.3	*93.0	*75.5	*76.7	69.3	*265.2	*296.8	*299.8	*334.3	*324.4
Phosphate fertilizers *										
Engrais phosphatés *	9.2	9.3	9.3	7.8	7.8	123.1	127.0	116.7	131.8	129.5
Potash fertilizers *										
Engrais potassiques *	...	...	...	...	...	168.4	172.1	169.4	192.1	186.5
Ecuador * Equateur *										
Nitrogenous fertilizers										
Engrais azotés	...	...	...	...	...	90.6	88.1	69.8	71.6	100.6
Phosphate fertilizers										
Engrais phosphatés	...	...	...	...	...	32.1	29.5	37.1	35.4	53.1
Potash fertilizers										
Engrais potassiques	...	...	...	...	...	39.9	44.1	68.6	57.4	76.9
French Guiana * Guyane française *										
Nitrogenous fertilizers										
Engrais azotés	...	...	...	...	...	1.0	0.4	0.4	0.4	0.4
Phosphate fertilizers										
Engrais phosphatés	...	...	...	...	...	0.3	0.4	0.4	0.4	0.4
Potash fertilizers										
Engrais potassiques	...	...	...	...	...	0.1	0.4	0.4	0.4	0.4
Guyana Guyana										
Nitrogenous fertilizers										
Engrais azotés	...	...	...	...	...	14.0	*13.8	*15.5	10.7	*11.2
Phosphate fertilizers										
Engrais phosphatés	...	...	...	...	...	*0.7	*0.9	*2.8	1.2	*1.2
Potash fertilizers *										
Engrais potassiques *	...	...	...	...	...	1.0	0.2	0.6	0.6	0.6
Paraguay * Paraguay *										
Nitrogenous fertilizers										
Engrais azotés	...	...	...	...	...	15.0	20.5	18.5	18.3	22.1
Phosphate fertilizers										
Engrais phosphatés	...	...	...	...	...	22.0	29.4	25.9	25.9	23.7
Potash fertilizers										
Engrais potassiques	...	...	...	...	...	22.0	22.0	21.0	21.0	21.0
Peru Pérou										
Nitrogenous fertilizers										
Engrais azotés	*11.5	*3.0	...	...	...	*149.7	*170.2	168.1	190.1	*205.7

39

Fertilizers
Nitrogenous, phosphate and potash: thousand metric tons [*cont.*]
Engrais
Azotés, phosphatés et potassiques: milliers de tonnes [*suite*]

	Production					Consumption Consommation				
Country or area and traffic	1997/98	1998/99	1999/00	2000/01	2001/02	1997/98	1998/99	1999/00	2000/01	2001/02
Phosphate fertilizers Engrais phosphatés	*2.5	*3.0	3.7	3.3	*3.0	*45.8	*47.4	43.7	45.0	*70.0
Potash fertilizers Engrais potassiques	...	...	...	...	...	*19.4	*20.5	27.0	19.1	*25.0
Suriname Suriname										
Nitrogenous fertilizers * Engrais azotés *	...	...	...	...	...	6.8	5.7	4.8	5.3	5.1
Phosphate fertilizers Engrais phosphatés	...	...	...	...	...	*0.1	0.8	...	...	...
Potash fertilizers * Engrais potassiques *	...	...	...	...	...	0.2	1.1	0.5	0.5	0.5
Uruguay Uruguay										
Nitrogenous fertilizers Engrais azotés	...	...	...	...	...	*47.0	53.5	*43.0	*36.2	50.2
Phosphate fertilizers Engrais phosphatés	*9.3	*9.3	*9.5	*15.0	*15.0	*80.4	*65.5	*53.5	*56.3	62.4
Potash fertilizers Engrais potassiques	...	...	...	...	...	*1.8	*11.0	9.0	*11.6	7.0
Venezuela * Venezuela *										
Nitrogenous fertilizers Engrais azotés	451.6	401.5	383.6	292.4	464.7	168.3	128.6	106.0	175.0	181.0
Phosphate fertilizers Engrais phosphatés	43.6	72.8	66.5	50.5	60.0	61.3	51.4	52.0	53.0	55.0
Potash fertilizers Engrais potassiques	...	...	...	...	...	61.4	41.7	48.0	54.0	64.0
Asia Asie										
Nitrogenous fertilizers Engrais azotés	43 599.6	45 759.2	47 564.5	46 162.8	46 032.1	46 433.8	47 613.0	49 455.0	46 723.5	46 904.4
Phosphate fertilizers Engrais phosphatés	12 800.1	13 291.6	13 500.7	13 567.6	14 506.6	17 825.7	18 268.0	18 556.4	17 703.1	17 713.1
Potash fertilizers Engrais potassiques	2 532.0	2 812.9	3 017.7	3 191.9	3 358.0	7 420.1	7 571.9	8 031.8	7 864.5	8 579.1
Afghanistan * Afghanistan *										
Nitrogenous fertilizers Engrais azotés	5.0	5.0	5.0	5.0	18.4	5.0	6.0	5.0	5.0	18.4
Phosphate fertilizers Engrais phosphatés	...	...	...	...	...	...	1.0	...	...	...
Armenia Arménie										
Nitrogenous fertilizers Engrais azotés	...	...	...	...	...	*8.0	9.6	6.2	7.0	*5.0
Azerbaijan Azerbaïdjan										
Nitrogenous fertilizers * Engrais azotés *	...	...	...	...	...	20.0	13.0	13.8	2.1	9.9
Phosphate fertilizers * Engrais phosphatés *	...	...	...	...	...	2.7	2.8	...	...	...
Potash fertilizers Engrais potassiques	*5.0	...	...	...	...	1.0	...	...	2.0	2.0
Bahrain Bahreïn										
Nitrogenous fertilizers Engrais azotés	...	214.3	223.4	247.0	*281.8	*0.2	0.7	0.1	0.1	0.1
Phosphate fertilizers Engrais phosphatés	...	0.3	...	...	...	*0.2	*0.3	0.1	0.1	*0.1
Potash fertilizers Engrais potassiques	...	...	...	...	...	*0.2	0.1	0.1	0.1	*0.1
Bangladesh Bangladesh										
Nitrogenous fertilizers Engrais azotés	868.2	*1 010.1	*1 048.8	*1 099.8	*1 117.2	876.6	*882.5	1 014.7	995.9	1 010.8
Phosphate fertilizers Engrais phosphatés	38.9	*41.1	52.8	50.5	52.0	116.8	*161.4	207.4	250.3	221.0

39

Fertilizers
Nitrogenous, phosphate and potash: thousand metric tons [*cont.*]
Engrais
Azotés, phosphatés et potassiques: milliers de tonnes [*suite*]

Country or area and traffic	Production Production					Consumption Consommation				
	1997/98	1998/99	1999/00	2000/01	2001/02	1997/98	1998/99	1999/00	2000/01	2001/02
Potash fertilizers										
Engrais potassiques	...	...	...	...	...	115.8	*126.6	143.6	*74.0	123.0
Bhutan * Bhoutan *										
Nitrogenous fertilizers										
Engrais azotés	...	...	...	...	...	0.1	...	...	...	...
Cambodia Cambodge										
Nitrogenous fertilizers										
Engrais azotés	...	...	...	...	...	*18.9	3.2	...	...	...
Phosphate fertilizers *										
Engrais phosphatés *	...	...	...	...	...	3.0	4.4	...	...	...
China [1] Chine [1]										
Nitrogenous fertilizers *										
Engrais azotés *	20 232.1	21 530.0	22 833.1	21 559.1	22 087.3	22 949.7	22 887.0	24 142.0	22 139.2	22 444.7
Phosphate fertilizers										
Engrais phosphatés	*6 419.0	*6 713.0	6 430.0	*6 687.0	*7 445.0	*9 277.0	*9 457.0	*8 907.0	*8 609.7	*8 884.4
Potash fertilizers										
Engrais potassiques	*170.0	*213.0	*218.0	*275.0	*395.0	3 420.0	*3 486.0	*3 390.0	*3 469.0	*4 046.1
Cyprus Chypre										
Nitrogenous fertilizers										
Engrais azotés	...	...	...	...	...	10.8	10.8	10.9	7.8	11.7
Phosphate fertilizers										
Engrais phosphatés	...	...	...	...	...	7.8	7.5	7.4	4.9	6.8
Potash fertilizers										
Engrais potassiques	...	...	...	...	...	1.8	2.0	1.9	1.7	4.1
Georgia Géorgie										
Nitrogenous fertilizers *										
Engrais azotés *	76.3	55.3	93.9	100.0	39.1	31.5	30.0	40.0	40.0	40.0
Phosphate fertilizers *										
Engrais phosphatés *	...	...	...	...	...	5.0	4.0	...	...	...
Potash fertilizers										
Engrais potassiques	...	...	...	...	...	...	...	...	2.0	2.0
India Inde										
Nitrogenous fertilizers										
Engrais azotés	10 083.1	10 477.3	10 872.8	10 942.8	10 689.5	10 901.9	11 353.8	11 586.3	10 920.2	11 310.2
Phosphate fertilizers										
Engrais phosphatés	3 079.5	3 194.1	3 447.7	3 748.6	3 851.6	3 913.6	*4 112.2	4 796.3	4 214.6	4 382.4
Potash fertilizers										
Engrais potassiques	...	...	...	...	...	1 372.5	1 331.5	1 674.2	1 567.5	1 667.1
Indonesia Indonésie										
Nitrogenous fertilizers *										
Engrais azotés *	2 992.6	2 899.1	2 842.4	2 853.0	2 396.4	1 706.6	2 120.9	1 925.5	1 964.4	1 960.0
Phosphate fertilizers										
Engrais phosphatés	*282.9	*235.2	299.8	*193.3	*243.8	*280.0	*361.8	*324.0	*263.1	*277.6
Potash fertilizers *										
Engrais potassiques *	...	...	...	...	...	241.0	245.0	275.0	266.0	286.0
Iran (Islamic Rep. of) Iran (Rép. islamique d')										
Nitrogenous fertilizers										
Engrais azotés	*727.8	*863.7	*713.2	725.5	735.9	*830.0	*878.0	*847.8	862.6	865.2
Phosphate fertilizers										
Engrais phosphatés	*93.3	*113.6	100.3	136.2	145.9	340.0	*330.0	*361.2	412.7	307.7
Potash fertilizers										
Engrais potassiques	...	...	...	7.5	11.1	37.1	60.0	*121.4	118.3	147.2
Iraq Iraq										
Nitrogenous fertilizers										
Engrais azotés	*235.0	*235.0	*238.0	*238.0	275.0	*242.7	*251.2	*254.7	*250.5	*239.0
Phosphate fertilizers *										
Engrais phosphatés *	90.0	90.0	90.0	90.0	90.0	111.6	132.1	132.7	117.2	91.0
Potash fertilizers										
Engrais potassiques	...	...	...	...	...	*2.5	...	0.7	*3.5	*1.4

39

Fertilizers

Nitrogenous, phosphate and potash: thousand metric tons [*cont.*]

Engrais

Azotés, phosphatés et potassiques: milliers de tonnes [*suite*]

Country or area and traffic	Production Production					Consumption Consommation				
	1997/98	1998/99	1999/00	2000/01	2001/02	1997/98	1998/99	1999/00	2000/01	2001/02
Israel Israël										
Nitrogenous fertilizers * Engrais azotés *	88.0	87.0	83.5	89.4	87.7	61.0	61.0	44.0	49.0	44.0
Phosphate fertilizers Engrais phosphatés	*244.0	*250.0	*272.3	*300.0	*273.1	*23.0	23.0	*15.0	*15.0	*15.0
Potash fertilizers Engrais potassiques	*1 488.0	*1 668.0	*1 701.6	*1 747.8	*1 774.4	*36.0	37.0	*30.0	*30.0	*30.0
Japan Japon										
Nitrogenous fertilizers Engrais azotés	829.7	798.6	802.4	769.2	680.0	495.2	476.0	479.5	487.4	484.0
Phosphate fertilizers Engrais phosphatés	263.0	248.9	234.1	215.7	376.0	592.5	561.3	570.4	583.0	511.0
Potash fertilizers Engrais potassiques	*19.6	*15.7	*18.0	...	...	*422.0	381.3	388.8	381.9	359.0
Jordan Jordanie										
Nitrogenous fertilizers Engrais azotés	127.9	*149.6	*145.0	113.6	*121.0	10.9	14.8	13.0	9.4	*10.3
Phosphate fertilizers Engrais phosphatés	279.4	338.9	*336.0	*234.0	*277.2	9.1	4.6	*5.0	4.5	*4.8
Potash fertilizers Engrais potassiques	849.4	916.2	1 080.1	1 161.6	1 177.5	*4.0	*4.0	*5.0	6.8	*7.2
Kazakhstan Kazakhstan										
Nitrogenous fertilizers Engrais azotés	*17.0	*5.1	*7.7	*2.7	7.6	*15.1	*12.6	*30.0	*30.0	*42.0
Phosphate fertilizers Engrais phosphatés	*74.0	*10.0	*27.2	*5.2	16.3	*35.0	*0.2	2.1	4.9	*5.5
Potash fertilizers Engrais potassiques	...	...	...	...	...	*6.0	*0.2	*2.1	2.1	*2.9
Korea, Dem. P. R. * Corée, R. p. dém. de *										
Nitrogenous fertilizers Engrais azotés	72.0	72.0	72.0	30.0	30.0	149.3	128.3	152.0	165.0	192.0
Phosphate fertilizers Engrais phosphatés	20.0	10.0	32.0	20.0	20.0	21.0	26.0	61.0	52.0	54.0
Potash fertilizers Engrais potassiques	...	...	...	...	...	0.8	2.9	40.0	39.0	41.0
Korea, Republic of Corée, République de										
Nitrogenous fertilizers Engrais azotés	*695.0	*525.0	*557.8	*519.7	*535.0	*507.0	*451.0	428.3	*411.5	*374.6
Phosphate fertilizers Engrais phosphatés	*438.0	*421.0	421.5	421.8	*327.2	*223.0	*188.0	178.5	161.7	*153.4
Potash fertilizers Engrais potassiques	...	...	...	...	...	*262.0	*228.0	214.3	210.1	*188.7
Kuwait Koweït										
Nitrogenous fertilizers Engrais azotés	*348.5	361.3	330.7	287.6	337.9	*1.2	*1.0	*1.1	0.6	1.0
Kyrgyzstan Kirghizistan										
Nitrogenous fertilizers Engrais azotés	...	...	...	...	...	*25.0	*27.7	26.8	27.8	*7.0
Phosphate fertilizers Engrais phosphatés	...	...	...	...	...	*1.0	1.1	1.2	1.4	...
Potash fertilizers Engrais potassiques	...	...	...	...	...	*5.0	*0.3	0.0	0.1	...
Lao People's Dem. Rep. Rép. dém. pop. lao										
Nitrogenous fertilizers Engrais azotés	...	...	...	...	...	*5.0	2.9	4.5	3.2	6.2
Phosphate fertilizers Engrais phosphatés	...	...	...	...	...	*2.6	1.5	3.4	2.4	5.1
Potash fertilizers Engrais potassiques	...	...	...	...	...	*0.2	*0.3	*2.0	0.4	0.9

39

Fertilizers

Nitrogenous, phosphate and potash: thousand metric tons [*cont.*]

Engrais

Azotés, phosphatés et potassiques: milliers de tonnes [*suite*]

Country or area and traffic	Production Production					Consumption Consommation				
	1997/98	1998/99	1999/00	2000/01	2001/02	1997/98	1998/99	1999/00	2000/01	2001/02
Lebanon Liban										
Nitrogenous fertilizers										
Engrais azotés	...	...	...	...	...	21.9	*23.4	*22.0	24.3	28.1
Phosphate fertilizers *										
Engrais phosphatés *	115.0	134.0	85.0	73.4	77.5	32.0	32.0	32.0	18.4	17.6
Potash fertilizers										
Engrais potassiques	...	...	...	...	...	*8.3	*8.3	*9.7	9.6	*8.9
Malaysia Malaisie										
Nitrogenous fertilizers										
Engrais azotés	*231.7	*316.6	*399.2	*586.7	*582.0	*344.0	*417.0	*362.4	348.6	331.9
Phosphate fertilizers										
Engrais phosphatés	...	...	...	...	...	*238.0	*233.0	*230.8	199.7	158.8
Potash fertilizers *										
Engrais potassiques *	...	...	...	...	...	670.0	756.0	730.6	640.0	640.0
Mongolia Mongolie										
Nitrogenous fertilizers										
Engrais azotés	...	...	...	...	...	5.0	*4.2	*2.8	*3.4	*3.2
Phosphate fertilizers										
Engrais phosphatés	...	...	...	...	...	1.0	...	...	...	...
Myanmar Myanmar										
Nitrogenous fertilizers										
Engrais azotés	56.1	51.6	*65.5	77.1	*27.6	135.5	*135.0	*125.0	*165.0	*142.5
Phosphate fertilizers										
Engrais phosphatés	...	...	...	...	...	35.2	34.5	29.1	34.7	*15.7
Potash fertilizers *										
Engrais potassiques *	...	...	...	...	...	7.2	2.3	9.0	6.0	6.0
Nepal Népal										
Nitrogenous fertilizers										
Engrais azotés	...	...	...	...	...	*77.4	*87.4	*62.0	51.8	44.7
Phosphate fertilizers										
Engrais phosphatés	...	...	...	...	...	*28.5	*32.3	*30.4	18.2	22.5
Potash fertilizers										
Engrais potassiques	...	...	...	...	...	*1.6	*1.8	*2.0	3.1	3.1
Oman Oman										
Nitrogenous fertilizers										
Engrais azotés	...	...	...	...	...	3.5	6.7	5.7	4.0	4.3
Phosphate fertilizers										
Engrais phosphatés	...	...	...	...	...	1.0	0.7	0.8	*1.0	*1.0
Potash fertilizers										
Engrais potassiques	...	...	...	...	...	1.0	0.7	*0.8	*0.8	0.7
Pakistan Pakistan										
Nitrogenous fertilizers										
Engrais azotés	1 660.5	1 795.2	2 039.3	2 053.8	2 133.7	2 087.6	2 091.9	2 218.1	2 264.6	2 285.2
Phosphate fertilizers										
Engrais phosphatés	67.5	90.8	223.4	243.8	142.7	551.3	465.0	596.8	675.1	622.1
Potash fertilizers										
Engrais potassiques	...	...	...	...	...	20.4	*21.2	18.1	22.8	16.0
Philippines Philippines										
Nitrogenous fertilizers										
Engrais azotés	213.0	184.6	190.1	168.3	189.9	548.2	409.4	480.4	488.2	507.3
Phosphate fertilizers										
Engrais phosphatés	217.1	192.7	184.7	150.1	172.4	148.6	118.6	142.6	124.1	148.7
Potash fertilizers										
Engrais potassiques	...	...	...	...	...	112.3	*100.5	120.7	122.3	125.4
Qatar Qatar										
Nitrogenous fertilizers										
Engrais azotés	*672.3	*767.0	757.2	748.4	*771.6	1.2	*1.0	*0.8	*0.5	*0.9
Saudi Arabia Arabie saoudite										
Nitrogenous fertilizers										
Engrais azotés	*981.1	*1 079.8	1 071.7	1 278.2	*1 328.5	*181.0	*200.0	*210.0	228.0	*223.1

39

Fertilizers

Nitrogenous, phosphate and potash: thousand metric tons [*cont.*]

Engrais

Azotés, phosphatés et potassiques: milliers de tonnes [*suite*]

Country or area and traffic	Production Production					Consumption Consommation				
	1997/98	1998/99	1999/00	2000/01	2001/02	1997/98	1998/99	1999/00	2000/01	2001/02
Phosphate fertilizers										
Engrais phosphatés	*119.8	*136.9	156.3	159.4	*168.1	*131.0	*121.0	128.0	137.2	*141.7
Potash fertilizers *										
Engrais potassiques *	...	...	...	...	...	9.0	9.0	9.0	21.0	19.0
Singapore Singapour										
Nitrogenous fertilizers										
Engrais azotés	...	...	...	...	...	1.9	2.5	2.3	1.6	1.4
Phosphate fertilizers										
Engrais phosphatés	...	...	...	...	...	0.1	*0.9	0.7	*0.7	*0.5
Potash fertilizers										
Engrais potassiques	...	...	...	...	...	*0.1	*0.7	0.7	*0.7	*0.5
Sri Lanka Sri Lanka										
Nitrogenous fertilizers										
Engrais azotés	...	...	...	...	...	122.5	142.2	163.8	157.5	158.4
Phosphate fertilizers										
Engrais phosphatés	8.3	10.2	8.5	9.8	10.0	30.1	29.1	33.7	30.4	31.2
Potash fertilizers										
Engrais potassiques	...	...	...	...	...	56.1	61.6	61.6	59.1	44.8
Syrian Arab Republic Rép. arabe syrienne										
Nitrogenous fertilizers										
Engrais azotés	*68.7	*113.2	103.9	*82.0	*126.1	236.8	218.4	250.5	236.0	194.5
Phosphate fertilizers										
Engrais phosphatés	*84.2	*96.5	66.1	*112.7	*69.1	124.6	105.1	111.9	*121.4	*75.5
Potash fertilizers										
Engrais potassiques	...	...	...	...	...	7.0	7.4	8.5	8.1	8.1
Tajikistan Tadjikistan										
Nitrogenous fertilizers										
Engrais azotés	*4.0	*4.0	*4.0	*4.0	*4.0	41.2	28.3	*10.6	*8.9	12.1
Phosphate fertilizers *										
Engrais phosphatés *	...	...	...	...	...	6.5	8.5	...	...	...
Potash fertilizers *										
Engrais potassiques *	...	...	...	...	...	3.4	0.1	...	...	...
Thailand Thaïlande										
Nitrogenous fertilizers *										
Engrais azotés *	56.0	79.0	70.4	83.0	83.0	784.0	905.0	1 070.0	924.0	1 000.4
Phosphate fertilizers										
Engrais phosphatés	43.0	85.0	*70.0	*75.0	*80.0	*423.0	*455.0	*415.0	*383.8	*445.4
Potash fertilizers *										
Engrais potassiques *	...	...	...	...	...	274.0	277.0	278.0	253.1	271.2
Turkey Turquie										
Nitrogenous fertilizers										
Engrais azotés	*921.6	*922.4	730.9	*479.0	390.0	*1 167.0	*1 392.0	1 484.1	1 378.2	1 130.6
Phosphate fertilizers										
Engrais phosphatés	*501.8	*491.1	*396.6	327.3	316.1	*592.4	*700.2	*628.6	628.6	470.3
Potash fertilizers										
Engrais potassiques	...	...	...	...	...	*66.3	*88.5	80.7	82.0	67.8
Turkmenistan * Turkménistan *										
Nitrogenous fertilizers										
Engrais azotés	110.0	57.0	60.0	60.0	60.0	159.0	57.0	72.2	86.6	98.0
Phosphate fertilizers										
Engrais phosphatés	5.0	5.0	5.0	5.0	5.0	5.0	5.0	5.0	5.0	5.0
Potash fertilizers										
Engrais potassiques	...	...	...	...	...	14.0	14.0	14.0	14.0	14.0
United Arab Emirates Emirats arabes unis										
Nitrogenous fertilizers										
Engrais azotés	*299.6	*258.9	271.9	*243.4	*276.9	*24.2	*24.7	*25.1	*23.8	*23.5
Phosphate fertilizers *										
Engrais phosphatés *	...	...	...	...	...	3.7	5.0	5.0	5.0	5.0
Potash fertilizers *										
Engrais potassiques *	...	...	...	...	...	4.4	5.7	6.1	6.3	6.5

39

Fertilizers

Nitrogenous, phosphate and potash: thousand metric tons [*cont.*]

Engrais

Azotés, phosphatés et potassiques: milliers de tonnes [*suite*]

Country or area and traffic	Production Production					Consumption Consommation				
	1997/98	1998/99	1999/00	2000/01	2001/02	1997/98	1998/99	1999/00	2000/01	2001/02
Uzbekistan Ouzbékistan										
Nitrogenous fertilizers										
Engrais azotés	*809.3	*731.8	*699.8	*681.5	*573.0	*678.0	*643.0	622.0	*607.0	*559.0
Phosphate fertilizers *										
Engrais phosphatés *	122.1	141.4	170.9	116.7	132.6	122.1	141.4	137.0	116.2	126.3
Potash fertilizers										
Engrais potassiques	...	...	...	...	...	*75.0	*40.0	15.8	*8.0	*8.0
Viet Nam * Viet Nam *										
Nitrogenous fertilizers										
Engrais azotés	117.4	109.8	231.0	35.0	46.0	922.9	1 186.1	1 224.2	1 328.0	1 063.2
Phosphate fertilizers										
Engrais phosphatés	194.2	241.9	390.5	192.0	215.0	386.8	399.8	456.4	506.0	506.0
Potash fertilizers										
Engrais potassiques	...	...	...	...	...	162.0	271.0	377.0	433.0	430.0
Yemen Yémen										
Nitrogenous fertilizers										
Engrais azotés	...	...	...	...	...	*19.3	*15.9	14.8	14.9	16.0
Phosphate fertilizers *										
Engrais phosphatés *	...	...	...	...	...	...	0.8	...	...	...
Potash fertilizers										
Engrais potassiques	...	...	...	...	...	...	*0.9	0.3	*0.3	*0.3
Europe Europe										
Nitrogenous fertilizers										
Engrais azotés	20 495.7	19 390.7	20 112.5	20 429.2	20 237.0	14 063.3	13 912.0	13 976.7	13 372.7	13 634.7
Phosphate fertilizers										
Engrais phosphatés	6 103.5	5 687.4	5 664.1	5 632.5	5 384.9	4 834.1	4 711.7	4 404.7	4 136.2	4 083.1
Potash fertilizers										
Engrais potassiques	11 995.6	12 048.7	12 537.1	11 989.0	12 698.1	5 850.1	5 556.6	5 247.2	4 862.5	4 841.3
Albania Albanie										
Nitrogenous fertilizers *										
Engrais azotés *	...	...	...	...	...	4.2	18.0	5.8	12.1	10.7
Phosphate fertilizers *										
Engrais phosphatés *	3.0	2.0	2.0	...	...	1.0	6.9	4.7	4.9	6.5
Potash fertilizers										
Engrais potassiques	...	...	...	...	...	...	0.1	0.1	*1.7	1.5
Austria Autriche										
Nitrogenous fertilizers										
Engrais azotés	*227.0	*254.0	*236.0	*186.0	*216.0	*128.0	*128.0	122.0	*118.0	*126.0
Phosphate fertilizers *										
Engrais phosphatés *	64.0	62.0	57.0	51.0	67.0	57.0	57.0	48.0	47.0	47.0
Potash fertilizers										
Engrais potassiques	...	...	...	...	...	*63.0	62.0	*55.0	51.2	53.8
Belarus Bélarus										
Nitrogenous fertilizers										
Engrais azotés	*378.9	*442.5	*534.4	*574.3	586.5	*280.0	*280.0	*286.0	*280.0	*290.0
Phosphate fertilizers										
Engrais phosphatés	*128.2	*127.0	*48.8	87.0	*54.0	*100.0	*100.0	*30.0	*75.0	*50.0
Potash fertilizers *										
Engrais potassiques *	3 247.0	3 451.0	3 613.0	3 372.0	3 687.0	475.0	545.0	475.0	450.0	440.0
Belgium-Luxembourg * Belgique-Luxembourg *										
Nitrogenous fertilizers										
Engrais azotés	835.0	899.0	930.0	890.0	842.0	171.0	171.0	171.0	162.0	165.0
Phosphate fertilizers										
Engrais phosphatés	120.0	149.0	170.0	305.0	245.0	44.0	47.0	45.0	45.0	44.0
Potash fertilizers										
Engrais potassiques	...	...	...	...	...	92.0	91.0	88.0	84.0	80.0
Bosnia and Herzegovina * Bosnie-Herzégovine *										
Nitrogenous fertilizers										
Engrais azotés	...	...	...	...	...	3.0	23.0	28.0	27.8	18.6

39

Fertilizers

Nitrogenous, phosphate and potash: thousand metric tons [*cont.*]

Engrais

Azotés, phosphatés et potassiques: milliers de tonnes [*suite*]

Country or area and traffic	Production Production					Consumption Consommation				
	1997/98	1998/99	1999/00	2000/01	2001/02	1997/98	1998/99	1999/00	2000/01	2001/02
Phosphate fertilizers										
Engrais phosphatés	...	...	...	...	...	3.0	12.0	7.0	7.0	7.0
Potash fertilizers										
Engrais potassiques	...	...	...	...	...	3.0	12.0	7.0	7.0	7.0
Bulgaria Bulgarie										
Nitrogenous fertilizers										
Engrais azotés	*694.9	*362.9	*277.5	*403.6	336.3	*157.8	*135.0	110.6	*144.9	150.1
Phosphate fertilizers										
Engrais phosphatés	109.8	*83.1	52.0	*94.2	*93.2	11.0	*9.0	6.0	*4.0	3.9
Potash fertilizers *										
Engrais potassiques *	...	...	...	...	...	31.0	25.0	6.0	2.6	2.6
Croatia Croatie										
Nitrogenous fertilizers										
Engrais azotés	324.1	248.0	309.8	328.1	*285.3	*152.0	95.0	99.4	116.0	*120.0
Phosphate fertilizers										
Engrais phosphatés	*90.0	*96.0	*118.0	99.1	*99.0	*56.0	*38.0	43.8	49.0	*45.6
Potash fertilizers										
Engrais potassiques	...	...	...	...	...	67.9	43.4	51.0	58.0	*49.6
Czech Republic République tchèque										
Nitrogenous fertilizers										
Engrais azotés	264.4	284.4	269.9	306.1	296.4	*225.8	218.8	209.5	262.8	310.8
Phosphate fertilizers										
Engrais phosphatés	24.6	25.6	18.3	22.1	17.0	46.9	51.2	35.4	43.3	52.5
Potash fertilizers										
Engrais potassiques	...	...	...	...	...	41.4	29.9	24.0	24.5	31.4
Denmark Danemark										
Nitrogenous fertilizers *										
Engrais azotés *	156.0	150.0	184.0	131.0	148.0	283.0	263.0	248.0	234.0	207.0
Phosphate fertilizers										
Engrais phosphatés	*47.0	*47.0	*38.0	*24.0	*23.0	*50.0	47.0	*41.0	*36.0	*35.0
Potash fertilizers *										
Engrais potassiques *	...	...	...	...	...	104.0	102.0	86.0	79.0	75.0
Estonia Estonie										
Nitrogenous fertilizers										
Engrais azotés	*41.8	*29.3	*40.4	37.9	39.0	20.5	24.9	19.6	22.4	28.3
Phosphate fertilizers										
Engrais phosphatés	...	...	...	...	...	4.3	4.4	*4.0	6.4	6.9
Potash fertilizers										
Engrais potassiques	...	...	...	...	...	*3.0	3.1	3.7	6.2	7.0
Finland Finlande										
Nitrogenous fertilizers										
Engrais azotés	*238.0	*227.0	*236.0	*253.0	271.0	177.0	*175.0	*176.0	167.0	165.0
Phosphate fertilizers										
Engrais phosphatés	*95.0	96.0	*85.0	*86.0	98.0	56.0	*53.0	*52.0	52.0	52.0
Potash fertilizers										
Engrais potassiques	...	...	...	...	...	*81.0	*81.0	*82.0	80.0	80.0
France France										
Nitrogenous fertilizers *										
Engrais azotés *	1 484.0	1 436.0	1 422.8	983.0	1 078.0	2 513.1	2 488.1	2 571.4	2 316.3	2 397.0
Phosphate fertilizers *										
Engrais phosphatés *	527.6	489.7	450.3	318.0	277.0	1 038.8	1 011.2	965.6	795.0	759.0
Potash fertilizers										
Engrais potassiques	*665.3	*417.1	*311.3	*321.0	*244.2	*1 436.9	*1 337.7	*1 216.4	*1 033.5	1 022.0
Germany Allemagne										
Nitrogenous fertilizers										
Engrais azotés	*1 125.0	*1 175.0	*1 250.0	*1 039.5	*1 068.0	1 788.4	1 903.0	2 014.0	1 847.5	1 791.9
Phosphate fertilizers										
Engrais phosphatés	194.0	*184.0	*185.0	*50.0	*54.0	409.5	406.7	420.0	351.3	314.6
Potash fertilizers										
Engrais potassiques	*3 423.1	*3 582.0	*3 545.0	*3 409.0	*3 550.5	658.9	628.7	599.2	544.0	505.9

39

Fertilizers

Nitrogenous, phosphate and potash: thousand metric tons [*cont.*]

Engrais

Azotés, phosphatés et potassiques: milliers de tonnes [*suite*]

Country or area and traffic	Production Production					Consumption Consommation				
	1997/98	1998/99	1999/00	2000/01	2001/02	1997/98	1998/99	1999/00	2000/01	2001/02
Greece * Grèce *										
Nitrogenous fertilizers										
Engrais azotés	240.0	231.0	214.0	249.9	240.0	307.0	292.0	291.0	285.0	260.0
Phosphate fertilizers										
Engrais phosphatés	125.0	115.0	114.0	98.0	93.0	132.0	120.0	119.0	113.0	103.0
Potash fertilizers										
Engrais potassiques	...	...	...	...	...	65.0	60.0	59.0	58.0	57.0
Hungary Hongrie										
Nitrogenous fertilizers										
Engrais azotés	251.4	*213.5	*278.7	*289.6	*272.8	*285.8	*282.0	*320.6	*320.0	222.9
Phosphate fertilizers										
Engrais phosphatés	*26.5	*20.0	*25.0	25.0	*25.0	*73.5	*37.6	*48.6	45.0	45.6
Potash fertilizers										
Engrais potassiques	...	...	...	...	...	67.8	*51.0	*63.4	52.0	54.8
Iceland * Islande *										
Nitrogenous fertilizers										
Engrais azotés	12.0	11.5	12.0	12.0	12.0	11.8	12.5	13.5	13.0	13.0
Phosphate fertilizers										
Engrais phosphatés	...	...	...	...	...	4.1	4.2	4.2	4.0	4.0
Potash fertilizers										
Engrais potassiques	...	...	...	...	...	3.4	2.0	4.2	4.2	4.2
Ireland Irlande										
Nitrogenous fertilizers										
Engrais azotés	*326.0	*311.0	*277.0	*188.4	180.0	*397.0	*444.0	*429.0	368.4	353.0
Phosphate fertilizers *										
Engrais phosphatés *	...	...	...	...	...	113.0	116.0	115.0	96.0	90.0
Potash fertilizers *										
Engrais potassiques *	...	...	...	...	...	150.0	152.0	148.0	135.0	130.0
Italy * Italie *										
Nitrogenous fertilizers										
Engrais azotés	537.0	463.0	397.0	428.0	412.0	855.0	845.0	868.0	828.0	826.0
Phosphate fertilizers										
Engrais phosphatés	170.0	153.0	158.0	116.0	49.0	501.0	508.0	514.0	504.0	475.0
Potash fertilizers										
Engrais potassiques	...	...	...	...	...	402.0	395.0	402.0	400.0	380.0
Latvia Lettonie										
Nitrogenous fertilizers										
Engrais azotés	...	...	...	...	...	*19.0	*31.5	*33.6	28.5	36.8
Phosphate fertilizers										
Engrais phosphatés	...	...	...	...	...	*8.1	*10.7	*10.6	10.2	15.4
Potash fertilizers										
Engrais potassiques	...	...	...	...	...	*8.0	*7.0	10.3	11.6	11.8
Lithuania Lituanie										
Nitrogenous fertilizers										
Engrais azotés	*322.9	*447.3	*454.7	526.0	524.0	*81.1	*83.4	*94.0	98.0	102.0
Phosphate fertilizers										
Engrais phosphatés	*192.8	*230.5	299.6	298.0	174.8	*18.2	*18.4	20.0	*20.0	*20.0
Potash fertilizers										
Engrais potassiques	...	...	...	...	...	*38.0	*38.0	*40.0	*35.0	40.0
Malta Malte										
Nitrogenous fertilizers										
Engrais azotés	...	...	...	...	...	*1.0	1.2	0.5	*0.5	*0.3
Phosphate fertilizers										
Engrais phosphatés	...	...	...	...	...	0.0	0.2	0.1	*0.2	*0.2
Potash fertilizers										
Engrais potassiques	...	...	...	...	...	0.0	0.2	0.1	*0.2	*0.2
Netherlands Pays-Bas										
Nitrogenous fertilizers *										
Engrais azotés *	1 586.0	1 548.0	1 304.0	1 137.0	1 013.0	375.0	350.0	345.0	300.0	290.0

39

Fertilizers
Nitrogenous, phosphate and potash: thousand metric tons [*cont.*]
Engrais
Azotés, phosphatés et potassiques: milliers de tonnes [*suite*]

Country or area and traffic	Production Production					Consumption Consommation				
	1997/98	1998/99	1999/00	2000/01	2001/02	1997/98	1998/99	1999/00	2000/01	2001/02
Phosphate fertilizers Engrais phosphatés	*402.0	*343.0	*182.0	*188.0	*174.0	60.0	*62.0	*58.0	*54.0	*53.0
Potash fertilizers Engrais potassiques	...	...	...	...	...	*73.0	*73.0	*68.0	*64.0	66.0
Norway * Norvège *										
Nitrogenous fertilizers Engrais azotés	570.0	470.0	510.0	618.0	579.0	112.0	106.0	106.0	102.0	101.0
Phosphate fertilizers Engrais phosphatés	236.0	194.0	245.0	248.0	237.0	30.0	31.0	29.0	30.0	30.0
Potash fertilizers Engrais potassiques	...	...	...	...	...	63.0	64.0	63.0	61.0	60.0
Poland Pologne										
Nitrogenous fertilizers Engrais azotés	*1 557.4	*1 575.6	*1 359.5	*1 496.5	1 569.7	*1 009.7	862.0	861.3	*896.2	*864.3
Phosphate fertilizers Engrais phosphatés	*473.6	*480.2	*473.0	*432.1	467.9	*289.6	308.4	296.3	*317.9	*317.7
Potash fertilizers Engrais potassiques	...	...	...	...	...	*400.9	386.7	368.7	370.0	*375.0
Portugal * Portugal *										
Nitrogenous fertilizers Engrais azotés	143.0	134.0	121.0	125.0	120.0	121.0	131.0	120.0	113.0	117.0
Phosphate fertilizers Engrais phosphatés	56.0	62.0	57.0	54.0	56.0	67.0	71.0	69.0	63.0	68.0
Potash fertilizers Engrais potassiques	...	...	...	...	...	48.0	50.0	48.0	43.0	43.0
Republic of Moldova * République de Moldova *										
Nitrogenous fertilizers Engrais azotés	...	...	...	...	...	9.5	6.8	3.1	5.0	5.0
Phosphate fertilizers Engrais phosphatés	...	...	...	...	...	0.5	0.1	0.1	0.1	0.1
Potash fertilizers Engrais potassiques	...	...	...	...	...	0.2	0.1	...	...	...
Romania Roumanie										
Nitrogenous fertilizers Engrais azotés	663.7	*314.1	517.7	869.0	767.9	*220.0	*268.0	*182.0	*239.3	*268.5
Phosphate fertilizers Engrais phosphatés	*135.8	*96.2	*111.2	99.2	82.2	*85.0	*80.0	*46.0	*56.0	*50.0
Potash fertilizers * Engrais potassiques *	...	...	...	...	...	10.0	12.0	9.0	9.0	9.0
Russian Federation Fédération de Russie										
Nitrogenous fertilizers Engrais azotés	*4 094.7	*4 135.0	*4 966.1	*5 451.9	*5 490.8	*950.0	*831.0	959.0	960.0	1 090.5
Phosphate fertilizers Engrais phosphatés	*1 853.0	*1 688.0	*2 017.0	*2 319.8	*2 402.2	*320.0	*280.0	220.0	280.0	312.8
Potash fertilizers Engrais potassiques	*3 403.0	*3 461.0	*4 050.0	*3 716.0	*4 257.6	*280.0	*153.0	182.0	180.0	199.4
Serbia and Montenegro * Serbie-et-Monténégro *										
Nitrogenous fertilizers Engrais azotés	171.0	185.1	72.0	72.0	82.1	185.0	154.0	138.1	144.9	207.4
Phosphate fertilizers Engrais phosphatés	16.0	24.0	12.0	12.0	12.0	35.0	24.0	26.0	17.0	23.1
Potash fertilizers Engrais potassiques	...	...	...	...	...	24.0	25.0	29.0	29.0	35.4
Slovakia Slovaquie										
Nitrogenous fertilizers Engrais azotés	*283.8	*245.9	*223.0	*286.3	*280.8	*72.5	82.8	65.4	*82.1	*82.0
Phosphate fertilizers Engrais phosphatés	*16.0	*15.0	*15.0	*15.0	*15.0	*17.8	*20.5	13.1	19.2	*20.4
Potash fertilizers Engrais potassiques	...	...	...	...	...	*17.1	*17.1	10.6	*16.8	*17.4

39

Fertilizers

Nitrogenous, phosphate and potash: thousand metric tons [*cont.*]

Engrais

Azotés, phosphatés et potassiques: milliers de tonnes [*suite*]

Country or area and traffic	Production Production					Consumption Consommation				
	1997/98	1998/99	1999/00	2000/01	2001/02	1997/98	1998/99	1999/00	2000/01	2001/02
Slovenia Slovénie										
Nitrogenous fertilizers										
Engrais azotés	...	...	...	...	...	34.1	34.8	34.4	34.8	34.8
Phosphate fertilizers										
Engrais phosphatés	...	...	...	...	...	17.5	18.8	19.8	18.4	16.7
Potash fertilizers										
Engrais potassiques	...	...	...	...	...	22.3	23.0	24.5	22.3	21.0
Spain Espagne										
Nitrogenous fertilizers										
Engrais azotés	918.5	*898.0	*921.0	813.6	832.6	1 041.9	*1 199.0	1 181.0	1 113.7	1 108.5
Phosphate fertilizers										
Engrais phosphatés	*486.0	*530.0	*459.0	439.9	432.5	*589.0	*655.0	*643.0	568.1	603.6
Potash fertilizers										
Engrais potassiques	640.0	*496.0	*549.0	550.7	411.8	*477.0	*513.0	*496.0	467.6	471.1
Sweden Suède										
Nitrogenous fertilizers										
Engrais azotés	*103.0	*94.0	*99.0	*103.0	*87.0	207.0	*196.0	*197.0	*196.7	*200.0
Phosphate fertilizers										
Engrais phosphatés	*15.0	*18.0	*9.0	*24.0	*24.0	49.0	47.0	*43.0	*39.0	*39.0
Potash fertilizers										
Engrais potassiques	...	...	...	...	...	*54.0	*51.0	50.0	*46.7	*48.0
Switzerland Suisse										
Nitrogenous fertilizers										
Engrais azotés	*19.0	*18.0	*18.0	*15.0	*16.0	*60.0	*59.0	*53.0	*48.4	48.5
Phosphate fertilizers										
Engrais phosphatés	...	...	...	...	...	*25.0	*25.0	*18.0	*12.2	14.7
Potash fertilizers										
Engrais potassiques	...	...	...	...	...	*36.0	*36.0	*31.0	28.3	28.3
TFYR of Macedonia L'ex-R.y. Macédoine										
Nitrogenous fertilizers *										
Engrais azotés *	6.5	6.5	7.0	3.0	2.0	28.1	25.2	25.0	19.2	14.6
Phosphate fertilizers										
Engrais phosphatés	*7.0	*7.0	7.5	*7.0	*6.0	*9.2	*9.5	10.5	*11.7	*10.7
Potash fertilizers										
Engrais potassiques	...	...	...	...	...	*9.4	*4.5	8.0	*9.0	5.0
Ukraine Ukraine										
Nitrogenous fertilizers *										
Engrais azotés *	2 001.7	1 687.1	1 910.0	2 129.6	2 068.8	413.0	406.0	327.0	350.0	380.0
Phosphate fertilizers										
Engrais phosphatés	*299.6	*231.1	*211.4	*77.1	*57.1	*104.0	76.0	*62.0	*62.0	*61.0
Potash fertilizers										
Engrais potassiques	*52.2	*33.6	*11.8	*19.3	15.0	*45.0	32.0	*28.0	*28.0	*33.0
United Kingdom * Royaume-Uni *										
Nitrogenous fertilizers										
Engrais azotés	919.0	894.0	760.0	483.0	520.0	1 363.0	1 286.0	1 268.0	1 115.0	1 228.0
Phosphate fertilizers										
Engrais phosphatés	190.0	119.0	44.0	43.0	50.0	408.0	345.0	317.0	279.0	285.0
Potash fertilizers										
Engrais potassiques	565.0	608.0	457.0	601.0	532.0	499.0	450.0	411.0	370.0	396.0
Oceania Océanie										
Nitrogenous fertilizers										
Engrais azotés	331.8	391.5	424.0	493.4	499.1	997.3	1 145.3	1 272.8	1 192.9	1 316.7
Phosphate fertilizers										
Engrais phosphatés	653.4	617.0	743.6	970.5	1 129.2	1 477.6	1 421.4	1 464.6	1 571.0	1 674.6
Potash fertilizers										
Engrais potassiques	...	...	...	...	...	391.8	373.2	358.8	350.1	389.7
Australia Australie										
Nitrogenous fertilizers *										
Engrais azotés *	250.8	299.0	316.0	383.0	379.5	839.4	979.0	1 082.0	951.0	1 034.0

39

Fertilizers
Nitrogenous, phosphate and potash: thousand metric tons [*cont.*]
Engrais
Azotés, phosphatés et potassiques: milliers de tonnes [*suite*]

Country or area and traffic	Production Production					Consumption Consommation				
	1997/98	1998/99	1999/00	2000/01	2001/02	1997/98	1998/99	1999/00	2000/01	2001/02
Phosphate fertilizers										
Engrais phosphatés	*383.4	*357.0	*428.6	588.0	*723.0	*1 090.1	*1 039.0	*1 055.0	*1 107.0	*1 187.0
Potash fertilizers *										
Engrais potassiques *	...	...	...	...	...	254.6	231.9	216.0	217.0	242.0
Fiji * Fidji *										
Nitrogenous fertilizers										
Engrais azotés	...	...	...	...	...	10.2	8.9	6.4	2.5	5.0
Phosphate fertilizers										
Engrais phosphatés	...	...	...	...	...	4.0	3.2	2.0	2.0	2.0
Potash fertilizers										
Engrais potassiques	...	...	...	...	...	5.0	6.3	6.0	3.0	3.0
French Polynesia Polynésie française										
Nitrogenous fertilizers										
Engrais azotés	...	...	...	...	...	*0.4	*0.4	0.5	*0.5	*0.5
Phosphate fertilizers										
Engrais phosphatés	...	...	...	...	...	*0.4	*0.4	0.3	*0.3	*0.3
Potash fertilizers										
Engrais potassiques	...	...	...	...	...	*0.2	*0.2	0.4	*0.4	*0.4
New Caledonia * Nouvelle-Calédonie *										
Nitrogenous fertilizers										
Engrais azotés	...	...	...	...	...	0.3	0.3	0.3	0.3	0.3
Phosphate fertilizers										
Engrais phosphatés	...	...	...	...	...	1.0	0.3	0.3	0.3	0.3
Potash fertilizers										
Engrais potassiques	...	...	...	...	...	0.3	0.3	0.3	0.3	0.3
New Zealand Nouvelle-Zélande										
Nitrogenous fertilizers										
Engrais azotés	*81.0	*92.5	*108.0	110.4	119.6	*138.9	*153.5	*180.0	230.7	269.0
Phosphate fertilizers										
Engrais phosphatés	*270.0	*260.0	*315.0	382.5	406.2	*379.1	*376.0	*403.0	456.6	480.2
Potash fertilizers										
Engrais potassiques	...	...	...	...	...	*129.7	*132.0	*133.0	125.4	140.0
Papua New Guinea * Papouasie-Nvl-Guinée *										
Nitrogenous fertilizers										
Engrais azotés	...	...	...	...	...	8.1	3.2	2.7	4.7	4.8
Phosphate fertilizers										
Engrais phosphatés	...	...	...	...	...	3.0	2.5	3.8	4.0	4.0
Potash fertilizers										
Engrais potassiques	...	...	...	...	...	2.0	2.5	2.8	3.0	3.0
Samoa Samoa										
Nitrogenous fertilizers										
Engrais azotés	...	...	...	...	...	...	...	0.9	3.1	*3.1
Phosphate fertilizers										
Engrais phosphatés	...	...	...	...	...	...	...	0.2	0.8	*0.8
Potash fertilizers										
Engrais potassiques	...	...	...	...	...	...	...	0.2	1.0	*1.0

Source:
Food and Agriculture Organization of the United Nations (FAO), Rome, FAOSTAT Agriculture Database and the Fertilizer Yearbook 2002.

Source:
Organisation des Nations Unies pour l'alimentation et l'agriculture (FAO), Rome, les données de l'agriculture de FAOSTAT et l'Annuaire des Engrais 2002.

1   Data generally include those for Taiwan Province of China.

1   Les données comprennent en général les chiffres pour la province de Taiwan.

Technical notes, tables 33-39

The series shown on agriculture and fishing have been furnished by the Food and Agriculture Organization of the United Nations (FAO). They refer mainly to the long-term trends in the growth of agricultural output and the food supply, and to the output of principal agricultural commodities.

Agricultural production is defined to include all crops and livestock products except those used for seed and fodder and other intermediate uses in agriculture; for example deductions are made for eggs used for hatching. Intermediate input of seeds and fodder and similar items refer to both domestically produced and imported commodities. For further details, reference may be made to FAO Yearbooks [4, 6, 7, 8, 9, 10]. FAO data are also available through the Internet (http://faostat.fao.org).

Table 33: "Agriculture" relates to the production of all crops and livestock products. The "Food Index" includes those commodities which are considered edible and contain nutrients.

The index numbers of agricultural output and food production are calculated by the Laspeyres formula with the base year period 1989-1991. The latter is provided in order to diminish the impact of annual fluctuations in agricultural output during base years on the indices for the period. Production quantities of each commodity are weighted by 1989-1991 average national producer prices and summed for each year. The index numbers are based on production data for a calendar year. These may differ in some instances from those actually produced and published by the individual countries themselves due to variations in concepts, coverage, weights and methods of calculation. Efforts have been made to estimate these methodological differences to achieve a better international comparability of data. The series include a large amount of estimates made by FAO in cases where no official or semi-official figures are available from the countries.

Detailed data on agricultural production are published by FAO in its *Production Yearbook* [6].

Table 34: The data on the production of cereals relate to crops harvested for dry grain only. Cereals harvested for hay, green feed or used for grazing are excluded.

Table 35: Oil crops, or oil-bearing crops, are those crops yielding seeds, nuts or fruits which are used mainly for the extraction of culinary or industrial oils, excluding essential oils. In this table, data for oil crops represent the total production of oil seeds, oil nuts and oil fruits harvested in the year indicated and expressed in terms of oil equivalent. That is to say, these figures do not relate to the actual production of vegetable oils, but

Notes techniques, tableaux 33 à 39

Les séries présentées sur l'agriculture et la pêche ont été fournies par l'Organisation des Nations Unies pour l'alimentation et l'agriculture (FAO) et portent principalement sur les tendances à long terme de la croissance de la production agricole et des approvisionnements alimentaires, et son la production des principales denrées agricoles.

La production agricole se définit comme comprenant l'ensemble des produits agricoles et des produits de l'élevage à l'exception de ceux utilisés comme semences et comme aliments pour les animaux, et pour les autres utilisations intermédiaires en agriculture; par exemple, on déduit les œufs utilisés pour la reproduction. L'apport intermédiaire de semences et d'aliments pour les animaux et d'autres éléments similaires se rapportent à la fois à des produits locaux et importés. Pour tous détails complémentaires, on se reportera aux annuaires de la FAO [4, 6, 7, 8, 9, 10]. Des statistiques peuvent également être consultées sur le site Web de la FAO (http://faostat.fao.org).

Tableau 33: L'"Agriculture" se rapporte à la production de tous les produits de l'agriculture et de l'élevage. L'"Indice des produits alimentaires" comprend les produits considérés comme comestibles et qui contiennent des éléments nutritifs.

Les indices de la production agricole et de la production alimentaire sont calculés selon la formule de Laspeyres avec les années 1989-1991 pour période de base. Le choix d'une période de plusieurs années permet de diminuer l'incidence des fluctuations annuelles de la production agricole pendant les années de base sur les indices pour cette période. Les quantités produites de chaque denrée sont pondérées par les prix nationaux moyens à la production de 1989-1991, et additionnées pour chaque année. Les indices sont fondés sur les données de production d'une année civile. Ils peuvent différer dans certains cas des indices effectivement établis et publiés par les pays eux-mêmes par suite de différences dans les concepts, la couverture, les pondérations et les méthodes de calcul. On s'est efforcé d'estimer ces différences méthodologiques afin de rendre les données plus facilement comparables à l'échelle internationale. Les séries comprennent une grande quantité d'estimations faites par la FAO dans les cas où les pays n'avaient pas fourni de chiffres officiels ou semi-officiels.

Des chiffres détaillés de production sont publiés dans l'*Annuaire FAO de la production* [6].

Tableau 34: Les données sur la production de céréales se rapportent uniquement aux céréales récoltées pour le grain sec; celles cultivées pour le foin, le fourrage vert ou le pâturage en sont exclues.

to the potential production if the total amounts produced from all oil crops were processed into oil in producing countries in the same year in which they were harvested. Naturally, the total production of oil crops is never processed into oil in its entirety, since depending on the crop, important quantities are also used for seed, feed and food. However, although oil extraction rates vary from country to country, in this table the same extraction rate for each crop has been applied for all countries. Moreover, it should be borne in mind that the crops harvested during the latter months of the year are generally processed into oil during the following year.

In spite of these deficiencies in coverage, extraction rates and time reference, the data reported here are useful as they provide a valid indication of year-to-year changes in the size of total oil-crop production. The actual production of vegetable oils in the world is about 80 percent of the production reported here. In addition, about two million tonnes of vegetable oils are produced every year from crops which are not included among those defined above. The most important of these oils are maize-germ oil and rice-bran oil. The actual world production of cake/meal derived from oil crops is also about 80 percent of the production.

Table 36: The data refer to livestock numbers grouped into twelve-month periods ending 30 September of the year stated and cover all domestic animals irrespective of their age and place or purpose of their breeding.

Table 37: The data on roundwood refer to wood in the rough, wood in its natural state as felled or otherwise harvested, with or without bark, round, split, roughly squared or in other form (i.e. roots, stumps, burls, etc.). It may also be impregnated (e.g. telegraph poles) or roughly shaped or pointed. It comprises all wood obtained from removals, i.e. the quantities removed from forests and from trees outside the forest, including wood recovered from natural, felling and logging losses during the period—calendar year or forest year.

Table 38: The data cover (i) capture production from marine and inland fisheries and (ii) aquaculture, and are expressed in terms of live weight. They include fish, crustaceans and molluscs but exclude sponges, corals, pearls, seaweed, crocodiles, and aquatic mammals (such as whales and dolphins).

The flag of the vessel is considered as the paramount indication of the nationality of the catch. Marine fisheries data include landings by domestic craft in foreign ports and exclude landings by foreign craft in domestic ports.

To separate aquaculture from capture fisheries production, at least two criteria must apply i.e., the human intervention in one or more of the phases of the

Tableau 35: On désigne sous le nom de cultures oléagineuses l'ensemble des cultures produisant des graines, des noix ou des fruits, essentiellement destinées à l'extraction d'huiles alimentaires ou industrielles, à l'exclusion des huiles essentielles. Dans ce tableau, les chiffres se rapportent à la production totale de graines, noix et fruits oléagineux récoltés au cours de l'année de référence et sont exprimés en équivalent d'huile. En d'autres termes, ces chiffres ne se rapportent pas à la production effective mais à la production potentielle d'huiles végétales dans l'hypothèse où les volumes totaux de produits provenant de toutes les cultures d'oléagineux seraient transformés en huile dans les pays producteurs l'année même où ils ont été récoltés. Bien entendu, la production totale d'oléagineux n'est jamais transformée intégralement en huile, car des quantités importantes qui varient suivant les cultures sont également utilisées pour les semailles, l'alimentation animale et l'alimentation humaine. Toutefois, bien que les taux d'extraction d'huile varient selon les pays, on a appliqué dans ce tableau le même taux à tous les pays pour chaque oléagineux. En outre, il ne faut pas oublier que les produits récoltés au cours des derniers mois de l'année sont généralement transformés en huile dans le courant de l'année suivante.

En dépit de ces imperfections qui concernent le champ d'application, les taux d'extraction et les périodes de référence, les chiffres présentés ici sont utiles, car ils donnent une indication valable des variations de volume que la production totale d'oléagineux enregistre d'une année à l'autre. La production mondiale effective d'huiles végétales atteint 80 pour cent environ de la production indiquée ici. En outre, environ 2 millions de tonnes d'huiles végétales sont produites chaque année à partir de cultures non comprises dans les catégories définies ci-dessus. Les principales sont l'huile de germes de maïs et l'huile de son de riz. La production mondiale effective tourteau/farine d'oléagineux représente environ 80 pour cent de production indiquée.

Tableau 36: Les statistiques sur les effectifs du cheptel sont groupées en périodes de 12 mois se terminant le 30 septembre de l'année indiquée et s'entendent de tous les animaux domestiques, quel que soit leur âge, leur emplacement ou le but de leur élevage.

Tableau 37: Les données sur le bois rond se réfèrent au bois brut, bois à l'état naturel, tel qu'il a été abattu ou récolté autrement, avec ou sans écorce, fendu, grossièrement équarri ou sous une autre forme (par exemple, racines, souches, loupes, etc.). Il peut être également imprégné (par exemple, dans le cas des poteaux télégraphiques) et dégrossi ou taillé en pointe. Cette catégorie comprend tous les bois provenant des quantités enlevées en forêt ou provenant des arbres poussant hors

growth cycle, and individual, corporate or state ownership of the organism reared and harvested.

Data on aquaculture production are published in the *FAO Yearbook of Fishery Statistics, Aquaculture Production* [7]; capture production statistics are published in the *FAO Yearbook of Fishery Statistics, Capture Production* [8].

Table 39: The data generally refer to the fertilizer year 1 July-30 June.

Nitrogenous fertilizers: data refer to the nitrogen content of commercial inorganic fertilizers.

Phosphate fertilizers: data refer to commercial phosphoric acid (P_2O_5) and cover the P_2O_5 of superphosphates, ammonium phosphate and basic slag.

Potash fertilizers: data refer to K_2O content of commercial potash, muriate, nitrate and sulphate of potash, manure salts, kainit and nitrate of soda potash.

Data on fertilizer production, consumption and trade are available in FAO's *Fertilizer Yearbook* [4].

forêt, y compris le volume récupéré sur les déchets naturels et les déchets d'abattage et de transport pendant la période envisagée (année civile ou forestière).

Tableau 38: Les données ont trait (i) à la pêche maritime et intérieure et (ii) à l'aquaculture, et sont exprimées en poids vif. Elles comprennent poissons, crustacés et mollusques, mais excluent éponges, coraux, perles, algues, crocodiles et les mammifères aquatiques (baleines, dauphins, etc.).

Le pavillon du navire est considéré comme la principale indication de la nationalité de la prise. Les données de pêche maritime comprennent les quantités débarquées par des bateaux nationaux dans des ports étrangers et excluent les quantités débarquées par des bateaux étrangers dans des ports nationaux.

Pour séparer la production d'aquaculture de la pêche de capture, au moins deux critères doivent se vérifier, c'est-à-dire l'intervention humaine dans une ou plusieurs des phases du cycle de croissance, et l'appartenance de l'organisme élevé et récolté à une personne physique, à une personne morale ou à l'état.

Les données sur la production de l'aquaculture sont publiées dans *l'Annuaire statistique des pêches, production de l'aquaculture* [7]; celles sur les captures sont publiées dans *l'Annuaire statistique des pêches, captures* [8].

Tableau 39: Les données sur les engrais se rapportent en général à une période d'un an comptée du 1er juillet au 30 juin.

Engrais azotés: les données se rapportent à la teneur en azote des engrais commerciaux inorganiques.

Engrais phosphatés: les données se rapportent à l'acide phosphorique (P_2O_5) et englobent la teneur en (P_2O_5) des superphosphates, du phosphate d'ammonium et des scories de déphosphoration.

Engrais potassiques: les données se rapportent à la teneur en K_2O des produits potassiques commerciaux, muriate, nitrate et sulfate de potasse, sels d'engrais, kainite et nitrate de soude potassique.

On trouvera des chiffres relatifs à la production, à la consommation et aux échanges d'engrais dans *l'Annuaire FAO des engrais* [4].

40

Sugar

Production and consumption: thousand metric tons; consumption per capita: kilograms

Sucre

Production et consommation : milliers de tonnes ; consommation per habitant : kilogrammes

Country or area	1996	1997	1998	1999	2000	2001	2002	Pays ou zone
World								**Monde**
Production	125 014	125 037	125 893	135 005	130 007	130 562	142 205	Production
Consumption	119 898	122 995	122 637	126 304	127 374	130 939	136 804	Consommation
Consumption per cap. (kg.)	21	21	20	21	21	21	22	Consom. par hab.(kg.)
Afghanistan								**Afghanistan**
Consumption *	45	50	55	60	60	60	65	Consommation *
Consumption per cap. (kg.)	2	3	3	3	3	3	2	Consom. par hab.(kg.)
Albania								**Albanie**
Production	9	*3	*3	*3	*3	*3	*3	Production
Consumption *	80	65	65	65	68	68	63	Consommation *
Consumption per cap. (kg.)	24	20	20	20	22	22	20	Consom. par hab.(kg.)
Algeria								**Algérie**
Consumption *	750	650	800	900	935	965	1 040	Consommation *
Consumption per cap. (kg.)	26	22	27	29	31	32	29	Consom. par hab.(kg.)
Angola								**Angola**
Production	*25	*28	*32	*32	*30[1]	*31[1]	31[1,2]	Production
Consumption *	110	110	85	120	130	155	185	Consommation *
Consumption per cap. (kg.)	9	9	7	10	10	11	13	Consom. par hab.(kg.)
Argentina								**Argentine**
Production	1 393	1 649	1 749	*1 882	*1 580	*1 630	*1 680	Production
Consumption	1 347	*1 350	*1 350	*1 450	*1 485	*1 520	*1 515	Consommation
Consumption per cap. (kg.)	39	38	38	40	41	41	40	Consom. par hab.(kg.)
Armenia								**Arménie**
Consumption *	60	60	65	70	72	73	74	Consommation *
Consumption per cap. (kg.)	16	16	17	18	19	19	23	Consom. par hab.(kg.)
Australia								**Australie**
Production	5 618	5 883	5 085	5 514	4 417	4 768	5 614	Production
Consumption	976	1 003	1 003	*1 005	1 048	1 068	1 100	Consommation
Consumption per cap. (kg.)	53	54	54	53	55	55	56	Consom. par hab.(kg.)
Austria *[1]								**Autriche *[1]**
Production	535	529	533	545	447	460	496	Production
Azerbaijan								**Azerbaïdjan**
Consumption	*170	123	157	*160	*160	*160	*160	Consommation
Consumption per cap. (kg.)	22	16	20	20	20	20	19	Consom. par hab.(kg.)
Bahamas								**Bahamas**
Consumption	12	10	10	10	11	8	9	Consommation
Consumption per cap. (kg.)	44	36	36	35	35	28	32	Consom. par hab.(kg.)
Bangladesh								**Bangladesh**
Production	*194	*138	*159	*162	*110	109	229	Production
Consumption *	290	300	270	300	325	335	375	Consommation *
Consumption per cap. (kg.)	2	2	2	3	3	3	3	Consom. par hab.(kg.)
Barbados								**Barbade**
Production	59	62	46	53	58	*50	*45	Production
Consumption	16	16	15	*15	*16	*15	*15	Consommation
Consumption per cap. (kg.)	60	62	55	56	57	56	50	Consom. par hab.(kg.)
Belarus								**Bélarus**
Production	144	179	180	151	186	196	162	Production
Consumption	358	380	405[3]	*357	380	422	410	Consommation
Consumption per cap. (kg.)	35	37	39	35	38	42	41	Consom. par hab.(kg.)
Belgium-Luxembourg[1]								**Belgique-Luxembourg[1]**
Production	1 036	1 106	863	1 187	*1 023	*913	*1 184	Production
Belize								**Belize**
Production	113	131	123	124	128	114	119	Production
Consumption	15	16	15	15	15	12[4]	12	Consommation
Consumption per cap. (kg.)	69	68	64	61	58	45	43	Consom. par hab.(kg.)
Benin								**Bénin**
Production *	5	4	4	4	5	5	5	Production *
Consumption	*45	*40	*40	*45	*46	22	*28	Consommation
Consumption per cap. (kg.)	8	7	7	8	8	3	4	Consom. par hab.(kg.)
Bermuda								**Bermudes**
Consumption	2	1	2	1	2	2	2	Consommation
Consumption per cap. (kg.)	25	17	25	17	25	25	14	Consom. par hab.(kg.)

40

Sugar
Production and consumption: thousand metric tons; consumption per capita: kilograms *[cont.]*

Sucre
Production et consommation : milliers de tonnes ; consommation par habitant : kilogrammes *[suite]*

Country or area	1996	1997	1998	1999	2000	2001	2002	Pays ou zone
Bolivia								**Bolivie**
Production	*270	*277	282	293	311	*288	*300	Production
Consumption	*225	*235	287	290	*293	*295	*300	Consommation
Consumption per cap. (kg.)	30	30	36	36	35	35	34	Consom. par hab.(kg.)
Bosnia and Herzegovina								**Bosnie-Herzégovine**
Production *	15	0	0	0	0	0	0	Production *
Consumption *	30	30	75	80	90	110	115	Consommation *
Consumption per cap. (kg.)	7	9	21	21	23	27	25	Consom. par hab.(kg.)
Botswana								**Botswana**
Consumption	40	30	45	45	46	46	47	Consommation
Consumption per cap. (kg.)	27	20	29	28	28	27	27	Consom. par hab.(kg.)
Brazil								**Brésil**
Production	14 718	16 371	19 168	20 646	16 464	20 336	23 567	Production
Consumption	*8 490	*8 900	*9 150	*9 500	*9 725	*9 800	10 520	Consommation
Consumption per cap. (kg.)	54	56	57	57	58	58	60	Consom. par hab.(kg.)
Brunei Darussalam								**Brunéi Darussalam**
Consumption	6	4	7	5	6	10	10	Consommation
Consumption per cap. (kg.)	19	11	20	15	18	29	36	Consom. par hab.(kg.)
Bulgaria								**Bulgarie**
Production *	7	6	5	2	2	3	3	Production *
Consumption *	260	260	260	225	230	235	250	Consommation *
Consumption per cap. (kg.)	30	31	32	27	29	30	31	Consom. par hab.(kg.)
Burkina Faso								**Burkina Faso**
Production	*33	*34	*30	30	*30	*35	*40	Production
Consumption *	35	42	50	45	46	50	60	Consommation *
Consumption per cap. (kg.)	3	4	5	4	4	5	6	Consom. par hab.(kg.)
Burundi								**Burundi**
Production	8	8	24	23	24	20	20	Production
Consumption	20	12	22	23	24	23	25	Consommation
Consumption per cap. (kg.)	3	2	4	4	4	4	3	Consom. par hab.(kg.)
Cambodia								**Cambodge**
Consumption *	40	55	65	75	85	90	115	Consommation *
Consumption per cap. (kg.)	4	5	5	6	7	7	10	Consom. par hab.(kg.)
Cameroon								**Cameroun**
Production	*52	*44	*46	*52	41	94	104	Production
Consumption	*85	*80	*95	*95	*95	112	145	Consommation
Consumption per cap. (kg.)	6	6	6	7	6	8	9	Consom. par hab.(kg.)
Canada								**Canada**
Production *	158	115	104	118	123	95	64	Production *
Consumption *	1 225	1 225	1 200	1 200	1 235	1 240	1 255	Consommation *
Consumption per cap. (kg.)	41	41	40	39	40	40	39	Consom. par hab.(kg.)
Cape Verde								**Cap-Vert**
Consumption *	17	18	12	12	13	20	20	Consommation *
Consumption per cap. (kg.)	40	42	33	31	31	46	43	Consom. par hab.(kg.)
Central African Rep.								**Rép. centrafricaine**
Consumption *	5	5	5	4	4	4	5	Consommation *
Consumption per cap. (kg.)	1	2	1	1	1	1	1	Consom. par hab.(kg.)
Chad								**Tchad**
Production *	30	34	31	32	32	32	32	Production *
Consumption *	50	46	55	55	57	57	60	Consommation *
Consumption per cap. (kg.)	7	6	7	7	7	7	14	Consom. par hab.(kg.)
Chile								**Chili**
Production	459	390	511	487	457	*430	576	Production
Consumption	*700	*720	728	729	683	*685	*690	Consommation
Consumption per cap. (kg.)	49	49	49	49	45	44	46	Consom. par hab.(kg.)
China								**Chine**
Production	*7 091	7 415	8 904	8 527	7 616	7 160	9 805	Production
Consumption *	8 250	8 250	8 300	8 300	8 500	8 900	9 975	Consommation *
Consumption per cap. (kg.)	7	7	7	7	7	7	8	Consom. par hab.(kg.)
China, Hong Kong SAR								**Chine, Hong Kong RAS**
Consumption *	180	180	180	180	181	185	185	Consommation *
Consumption per cap. (kg.)	28	28	28	27	27	28	26	Consom. par hab.(kg.)

40

Sugar
Production and consumption: thousand metric tons; consumption per capita: kilograms *[cont.]*

Sucre
Production et consommation : milliers de tonnes ; consommation par habitant : kilogrammes *[suite]*

Country or area	1996	1997	1998	1999	2000	2001	2002	Pays ou zone
China, Macao SAR								**Chine, Macao RAS**
Consumption	6	7	7	7	7	7	8	Consommation
Consumption per cap. (kg.)	13	17	17	16	17	16	16	Consom. par hab.(kg.)
Colombia								**Colombie**
Production	2 149	2 136	2 126	2 241	2 391	2 260	2 523	Production
Consumption [5]	1 206	1 192	1 240	1 281	1 343	1 309	1 356	Consommation [5]
Consumption per cap. (kg.)	31	30	30	31	32	30	32	Consom. par hab.(kg.)
Comoros								**Comores**
Consumption	3	2	5	5	6	8	9	Consommation
Consumption per cap. (kg.)	4	3	8	7	8	11	11	Consom. par hab.(kg.)
Congo								**Congo**
Production	42	*45	*45	*35	*40	*45	33	Production
Consumption	*28	*30	*30	*30	*35	*35	32	Consommation
Consumption per cap. (kg.)	11	11	11	10	13	15	10	Consom. par hab.(kg.)
Costa Rica								**Costa Rica**
Production	*332	*319	*381	*378	338	358	*360	Production
Consumption	*225	*220	*210	*210	208	*210	*225	Consommation
Consumption per cap. (kg.)	70	67	62	61	59	58	61	Consom. par hab.(kg.)
Côte d'Ivoire								**Côte d'Ivoire**
Production	*134	*132	126	152	189	*155	*170	Production
Consumption	*170	*170	137	*170	*180	*190	*200	Consommation
Consumption per cap. (kg.)	12	11	9	11	11	11	11	Consom. par hab.(kg.)
Croatia								**Croatie**
Production	212	154	151	114	57	131	172	Production
Consumption *	190	190	195	180	180	180	180	Consommation *
Consumption per cap. (kg.)	42	42	43	40	41	41	41	Consom. par hab.(kg.)
Cuba								**Cuba**
Production	4 529	4 318	3 291	3 875	4 057	3 748	3 522	Production
Consumption	*670	733	713	711	705	698	698	Consommation
Consumption per cap. (kg.)	61	66	64	64	63	62	61	Consom. par hab.(kg.)
Cyprus								**Chypre**
Consumption	*30	*30	*30	*30	*31	32	*33	Consommation
Consumption per cap. (kg.)	41	41	40	40	41	42	46	Consom. par hab.(kg.)
Czech Republic								**République tchèque**
Production	654	648	535	420	434	484	507	Production
Consumption	412	*425	438	*450	440	*450	*475	Consommation
Consumption per cap. (kg.)	40	41	43	44	43	44	47	Consom. par hab.(kg.)
Dem. Rep. of the Congo								**Rép. dém. du Congo**
Production *	50	86	51	65	75	60	65	Production *
Consumption *	110	90	80	75	75	75	70	Consommation *
Consumption per cap. (kg.)	2	2	2	2	2	1	1	Consom. par hab.(kg.)
Denmark [1]								**Danemark [1]**
Production	536	603	585	600	580	520	*561	Production
Djibouti								**Djibouti**
Consumption	11	10	10	12	13	13	13	Consommation
Consumption per cap. (kg.)	19	17	16	19	20	20	20	Consom. par hab.(kg.)
Dominican Republic								**Rép. dominicaine**
Production	*670	687	409	421	438	491	516	Production
Consumption	*350	274	337	*350	298	352	366	Consommation
Consumption per cap. (kg.)	44	34	42	42	35	41	45	Consom. par hab.(kg.)
Ecuador								**Equateur**
Production	419	190	*354	*420	*500	*495	*495	Production
Consumption	*375	396	*410	*425	*440	*465	*480	Consommation
Consumption per cap. (kg.)	32	33	34	34	35	36	36	Consom. par hab.(kg.)
Egypt								**Egypte**
Production *	1 222	1 228	1 152	1 269	1 450	1 585	1 555	Production *
Consumption *	1 850	2 000	2 075	2 150	2 250	2 325	2 125	Consommation *
Consumption per cap. (kg.)	31	33	34	34	35	36	31	Consom. par hab.(kg.)
El Salvador								**El Salvador**
Production	*352	414	487	585	562	527	476	Production
Consumption	*210	232	237	234	236	244	217	Consommation
Consumption per cap. (kg.)	36	39	39	38	38	39	32	Consom. par hab.(kg.)

40

Sugar
Production and consumption: thousand metric tons; consumption per capita: kilograms *[cont.]*

Sucre
Production et consommation : milliers de tonnes ; consommation par habitant : kilogrammes *[suite]*

Country or area	1996	1997	1998	1999	2000	2001	2002	Pays ou zone
Eritrea								**Erythrée**
Consumption	0	10	10	8	8	8	9	Consommation
Consumption per cap. (kg.)	...	...	...	...	...	...	2	Consom. par hab.(kg.)
Estonia								**Estonie**
Consumption	37	*50	*55	*65	*70	*73	*73	Consommation
Consumption per cap. (kg.)	25	34	38	46	51	51	49	Consom. par hab.(kg.)
Ethiopia								**Ethiopie**
Production	180	126	219	235	251	*305	287	Production
Consumption	206	145	185	199	246	*240	211	Consommation
Consumption per cap. (kg.)	4	3	3	3	4	4	3	Consom. par hab.(kg.)
Fiji								**Fidji**
Production	474	369	278	377	353	327	334	Production
Consumption [6]	48	51	44	38	41	45	53	Consommation [6]
Consumption per cap. (kg.)	62	64	55	47	51	56	64	Consom. par hab.(kg.)
Finland [1]								**Finlande [1]**
Production	135	175	125	180	144	141	161	Production
France [1]								**France [1]**
Production	4 543	5 134	4 637	4 915	4 590	3 962	5 094	Production
Gabon								**Gabon**
Production *	15	16	17	16	17	18	18	Production *
Consumption *	16	16	17	18	19	19	20	Consommation *
Consumption per cap. (kg.)	14	14	15	15	15	15	2	Consom. par hab.(kg.)
Gambia								**Gambie**
Consumption *	30	40	45	50	58	60	60	Consommation *
Consumption per cap. (kg.)	26	34	37	36	41	43	38	Consom. par hab.(kg.)
Georgia								**Géorgie**
Production	0	0	0	0	0	0	0	Production
Consumption *	90	95	100	105	108	110	120	Consommation *
Consumption per cap. (kg.)	17	18	19	21	21	22	22	Consom. par hab.(kg.)
Germany [1]								**Allemagne [1]**
Production	4 569	4 397	4 388	4 784	4 765	4 066	4 380	Production
Ghana								**Ghana**
Consumption *	120	130	140	145	150	155	160	Consommation *
Consumption per cap. (kg.)	7	7	8	8	8	8	8	Consom. par hab.(kg.)
Gibraltar								**Gibraltar**
Consumption	4	4	3	3	3	2	2	Consommation
Consumption per cap. (kg.)	133	133	100	83	83	73	55	Consom. par hab.(kg.)
Greece * [1]								**Grèce * [1]**
Production	288	396	218	252	400	342	326	Production
Guadeloupe [1]								**Guadeloupe [1]**
Production	49	57	38	65	*66	*60	*68	Production
Guatemala								**Guatemala**
Production	1 318	1 390	1 682	1 687	1 675	1 661	*1 900	Production
Consumption	372	392	408	460	468	496	*510	Consommation
Consumption per cap. (kg.)	36	37	38	42	41	42	44	Consom. par hab.(kg.)
Guinea								**Guinée**
Production *	21	22	22	25	25	25	25	Production *
Consumption *	75	80	80	85	90	95	100	Consommation *
Consumption per cap. (kg.)	10	10	10	11	11	12	12	Consom. par hab.(kg.)
Guinea-Bissau								**Guinée-Bissau**
Consumption	4	7	4	5	7	7	7	Consommation
Consumption per cap. (kg.)	4	6	4	4	6	6	6	Consom. par hab.(kg.)
Guyana								**Guyana**
Production	287	283	263	336	273	284	331	Production
Consumption	24	25	25	25	24	24	24	Consommation
Consumption per cap. (kg.)	31	32	32	32	31	35	29	Consom. par hab.(kg.)
Haiti								**Haïti**
Production *	8	9	5	5	5	5	5	Production *
Consumption *	115	120	130	160	165	165	165	Consommation *
Consumption per cap. (kg.)	16	16	17	21	21	20	20	Consom. par hab.(kg.)

40

Sugar
Production and consumption: thousand metric tons; consumption per capita: kilograms *[cont.]*
Sucre
Production et consommation : milliers de tonnes ; consommation par habitant : kilogrammes *[suite]*

Country or area	1996	1997	1998	1999	2000	2001	2002	Pays ou zone
Honduras								**Honduras**
Production	*240	*251	*277	190	*320	316	*320	Production
Consumption	*235	*235	*230	235	236	237	*240	Consommation
Consumption per cap. (kg.)	41	39	37	37	37	37	33	Consom. par hab.(kg.)
Hungary								**Hongrie**
Production	554	460	461	446	309	434	347	Production
Consumption	462	448	386	399	367	317	313	Consommation
Consumption per cap. (kg.)	45	44	38	40	37	32	31	Consom. par hab.(kg.)
Iceland								**Islande**
Consumption *	15	13	13	12	13	12	12	Consommation *
Consumption per cap. (kg.)	50	43	46	43	46	41	43	Consom. par hab.(kg.)
India								**Inde**
Production	16 892	14 440	14 281	17 406	20 247	19 906	19 525	Production
Consumption	15 254	14 971	15 272	16 278	16 546	17 274	17 857	Consommation
Consumption per cap. (kg.)	16	16	16	17	17	17	18	Consom. par hab.(kg.)
Indonesia								**Indonésie**
Production	2 100	2 189	1 493	*1 490	*1 685	*1 850	*2 150	Production
Consumption	3 074	*3 350	2 736	*3 000	*3 375	*3 500	*3 650	Consommation
Consumption per cap. (kg.)	16	17	14	15	16	16	17	Consom. par hab.(kg.)
Iran (Islamic Rep. of)								**Iran (Rép. islamique d')**
Production	692	848	863	*940	*920	*900	*995	Production
Consumption *	1 750	1 800	1 800	1 900	1 960	1 965	1 975	Consommation *
Consumption per cap. (kg.)	29	30	29	30	31	30	31	Consom. par hab.(kg.)
Iraq								**Iraq**
Consumption *	250	350	350	400	405	425	500	Consommation *
Consumption per cap. (kg.)	12	17	16	18	18	18	21	Consom. par hab.(kg.)
Ireland *[1]								**Irlande *[1]**
Production	247	223	238	235	238	226	215	Production
Israel								**Israël**
Production	0	0	0	0	0	0	0	Production
Consumption *	340	350	360	370	380	400	410	Consommation *
Consumption per cap. (kg.)	60	60	60	61	62	66	61	Consom. par hab.(kg.)
Italy[1]								**Italie[1]**
Production	1 561	1 891	*1 735	*1 705	*1 552	*1 430	*1 475	Production
Jamaica								**Jamaïque**
Production	236	233	183	212	210	205	175	Production
Consumption	115	113	120	98	129	136	126	Consommation
Consumption per cap. (kg.)	46	44	47	38	49	52	46	Consom. par hab.(kg.)
Japan								**Japon**
Production	882	783	870	913	842	823	901	Production
Consumption	2 579	2 471	2 427	2 541	2 413	2 339	2 433	Consommation
Consumption per cap. (kg.)	21	20	19	20	19	18	19	Consom. par hab.(kg.)
Jordan								**Jordanie**
Consumption	170	*170	*150	*180	*185	*190	*200	Consommation
Consumption per cap. (kg.)	39	37	32	38	38	38	26	Consom. par hab.(kg.)
Kazakhstan								**Kazakhstan**
Production	*50	*45	*40	*25	*30	*25	46	Production
Consumption *	360	325	300	310	375	390	390	Consommation *
Consumption per cap. (kg.)	22	21	20	21	25	26	27	Consom. par hab.(kg.)
Kenya								**Kenya**
Production	423	436	488	512	437	377	537	Production
Consumption	*500	*525	*600	662	663	*625	652	Consommation
Consumption per cap. (kg.)	16	19	20	22	22	21	21	Consom. par hab.(kg.)
Korea, Dem. P. R.								**Corée, R. p. dém. de**
Consumption *	55	48	30	60	65	70	70	Consommation *
Consumption per cap. (kg.)	3	2	1	3	3	3	3	Consom. par hab.(kg.)
Korea, Republic of								**Corée, République de**
Consumption[7]	1 107	1 113	986	966	1 012	1 086	1 114	Consommation[7]
Consumption per cap. (kg.)	25	24	21	21	21	23	23	Consom. par hab.(kg.)
Kuwait								**Koweït**
Consumption *	65	65	70	70	73	75	75	Consommation *
Consumption per cap. (kg.)	34	33	35	33	33	33	33	Consom. par hab.(kg.)

40

Sugar
Production and consumption: thousand metric tons; consumption per capita: kilograms *[cont.]*

Sucre
Production et consommation : milliers de tonnes ; consommation par habitant : kilogrammes *[suite]*

Country or area	1996	1997	1998	1999	2000	2001	2002	Pays ou zone
Kyrgyzstan								**Kirghizistan**
Production	*35	26	36	45	57	29	41	Production
Consumption	*125	110	*110	*100	*110	*110	*110	Consommation
Consumption per cap. (kg.)	27	23	23	21	22	22	21	Consom. par hab.(kg.)
Lao People's Dem. Rep.								**Rép. dém. pop. lao**
Consumption *	15	15	16	20	21	25	30	Consommation *
Consumption per cap. (kg.)	3	3	3	4	4	5	5	Consom. par hab.(kg.)
Latvia								**Lettonie**
Production	*40	*49	71	72	68	56	77	Production
Consumption	*90	*90	*85	82	78	78	78	Consommation
Consumption per cap. (kg.)	36	37	35	34	32	33	33	Consom. par hab.(kg.)
Lebanon								**Liban**
Production	30	32	37	40	34	0	0	Production
Consumption	*125	*125	*125	*130	122	*135	*135	Consommation
Consumption per cap. (kg.)	40	39	37	38	35	38	35	Consom. par hab.(kg.)
Liberia								**Libéria**
Production	0	0	0	0	0	...	...	Production
Consumption	7	6	10	8	10	9	10	Consommation
Consumption per cap. (kg.)	3	2	4	3	3	3	3	Consom. par hab.(kg.)
Libyan Arab Jamah.								**Jamah. arabe libyenne**
Consumption *	180	220	220	220	225	225	228	Consommation *
Consumption per cap. (kg.)	37	44	44	43	43	42	33	Consom. par hab.(kg.)
Lithuania								**Lituanie**
Production	*75	117	137	121	137	118	150	Production
Consumption	*105	98	119	*110	95	111	89	Consommation
Consumption per cap. (kg.)	28	27	32	30	26	32	26	Consom. par hab.(kg.)
Madagascar								**Madagascar**
Production	*95	*96	95	*85	*70	*50	32	Production
Consumption	*90	*93	*93	*95	*98	*98	104	Consommation
Consumption per cap. (kg.)	6	6	6	6	6	6	6	Consom. par hab.(kg.)
Malawi								**Malawi**
Production	234	210	210	187	209	*205	261	Production
Consumption	173	178	158	137	127	*140	*145	Consommation
Consumption per cap. (kg.)	17	17	15	12	11	12	13	Consom. par hab.(kg.)
Malaysia								**Malaisie**
Production *	107	108	100	107	108	105	110	Production *
Consumption *	1 025	1 030	1 035	1 040	1 045	1 050	1 055	Consommation *
Consumption per cap. (kg.)	49	48	47	46	45	44	42	Consom. par hab.(kg.)
Maldives								**Maldives**
Consumption	8	7	8	5	6	5	5	Consommation
Consumption per cap. (kg.)	31	26	30	18	22	17	14	Consom. par hab.(kg.)
Mali								**Mali**
Production *	26	26	33	31	32	32	32	Production *
Consumption *	65	60	80	75	80	80	90	Consommation *
Consumption per cap. (kg.)	6	6	7	7	7	7	7	Consom. par hab.(kg.)
Malta								**Malte**
Consumption *	20	20	20	22	23	23	23	Consommation *
Consumption per cap. (kg.)	54	53	53	56	58	59	59	Consom. par hab.(kg.)
Martinique [1]								**Martinique** [1]
Production	8	7	7	6	*6	*6	*8	Production
Mauritania								**Mauritanie**
Consumption *	85	90	120	125	130	135	145	Consommation *
Consumption per cap. (kg.)	37	37	48	48	49	49	55	Consom. par hab.(kg.)
Mauritius								**Maurice**
Production	624	658	667	396	604	685	553	Production
Consumption	40	42	43	42	42	44	43	Consommation
Consumption per cap. (kg.)	36	37	37	36	35	36	35	Consom. par hab.(kg.)
Mexico								**Mexique**
Production	4 784	5 048	5 287	5 030	4 816	5 614	5 073	Production
Consumption	4 229	4 231	4 293	4 400	4 619	4 857	5 069	Consommation
Consumption per cap. (kg.)	45	45	44	45	46	48	50	Consom. par hab.(kg.)

40

Sugar
Production and consumption: thousand metric tons; consumption per capita: kilograms *[cont.]*

Sucre
Production et consommation : milliers de tonnes ; consommation par habitant : kilogrammes *[suite]*

Country or area	1996	1997	1998	1999	2000	2001	2002	Pays ou zone
Mongolia								**Mongolie**
Consumption	40	40	19	10	20	20	21	Consommation
Consumption per cap. (kg.)	18	17	8	4	8	8	8	Consom. par hab.(kg.)
Morocco								**Maroc**
Production	434	442	499	522	556	*530	*505	Production
Consumption	967	996	1 002	1 018	1 034	*1 050	*1 100	Consommation
Consumption per cap. (kg.)	36	37	36	36	36	36	42	Consom. par hab.(kg.)
Mozambique								**Mozambique**
Production	*30	*42	39	46	*45	*60	*170	Production
Consumption *	55	50	60	70	90	95	110	Consommation *
Consumption per cap. (kg.)	3	3	4	4	5	5	5	Consom. par hab.(kg.)
Myanmar								**Myanmar**
Production	46	55	51	43	75	*125	*100	Production
Consumption	*55	*50	31	69	*85	*90	*100	Consommation
Consumption per cap. (kg.)	1	1	1	2	2	2	2	Consom. par hab.(kg.)
Namibia								**Namibie**
Consumption *	25	35	40	45	46	46	46	Consommation *
Consumption per cap. (kg.)	...	...	...	...	...	...	26	Consom. par hab.(kg.)
Nepal								**Népal**
Production *	80	90	120	150	110	65	110	Production *
Consumption *	80	95	105	110	115	120	125	Consommation *
Consumption per cap. (kg.)	4	5	5	5	5	5	5	Consom. par hab.(kg.)
Netherlands *[1]								**Pays-Bas *[1]**
Production	1 125	1 109	897	1 217	1 153	1 036	1 112	Production
Netherlands Antilles								**Antilles néerlandaises**
Consumption *	8	12	15	20	21	22	25	Consommation *
Consumption per cap. (kg.)	38	57	71	95	96	96	114	Consom. par hab.(kg.)
New Zealand								**Nouvelle-Zélande**
Consumption	*200	*220	158	198	212	*215	*220	Consommation
Consumption per cap. (kg.)	56	59	42	52	56	56	56	Consom. par hab.(kg.)
Nicaragua								**Nicaragua**
Production	*314	354	330	351	398	*390	*370	Production
Consumption	*180	*180	217	179	157	*160	*175	Consommation
Consumption per cap. (kg.)	40	39	45	36	31	31	31	Consom. par hab.(kg.)
Niger								**Niger**
Production	15	15	*5	*10	*10	*10	*10	Production
Consumption *	35	40	45	50	55	55	60	Consommation *
Consumption per cap. (kg.)	4	4	5	5	5	5	4	Consom. par hab.(kg.)
Nigeria								**Nigéria**
Production	*27	*15	*15	*17	36	7	*6	Production
Consumption	*600	*650	*700	*700	*760	975	1 317	Consommation
Consumption per cap. (kg.)	6	6	7	6	7	8	11	Consom. par hab.(kg.)
Norway								**Norvège**
Consumption	*180	*185	*185	*185	*186	*186	186	Consommation
Consumption per cap. (kg.)	41	42	42	42	41	41	40	Consom. par hab.(kg.)
Pakistan								**Pakistan**
Production	2 662	2 635	3 503	3 709	2 053	2 720	3 334	Production
Consumption	3 033	*3 023	*3 085	*3 196	*3 330	*3 440	*3 490	Consommation
Consumption per cap. (kg.)	23	22	24	24	24	24	25	Consom. par hab.(kg.)
Panama								**Panama**
Production	142	166	181	177	161	146	*150	Production
Consumption	69	73	*75	*85	*95	*105	*110	Consommation
Consumption per cap. (kg.)	26	27	27	30	33	36	37	Consom. par hab.(kg.)
Papua New Guinea								**Papouasie-Nvl-Guinée**
Production	*35	39	41	47	41	45	53	Production
Consumption	*30	37	36	38	35	35	37	Consommation
Consumption per cap. (kg.)	7	9	8	8	7	7	8	Consom. par hab.(kg.)
Paraguay								**Paraguay**
Production *	116	108	114	112	90	95	115	Production *
Consumption *	105	105	105	108	108	110	110	Consommation *
Consumption per cap. (kg.)	21	21	20	20	20	20	19	Consom. par hab.(kg.)

40

Sugar
Production and consumption: thousand metric tons; consumption per capita: kilograms *[cont.]*

Sucre
Production et consommation : milliers de tonnes ; consommation par habitant : kilogrammes *[suite]*

Country or area	1996	1997	1998	1999	2000	2001	2002	Pays ou zone
Peru								**Pérou**
Production	612	693	570	*655	*725	*755	*850	Production
Consumption	745	826	*850	*900	*925	*950	*975	Consommation
Consumption per cap. (kg.)	31	34	34	36	36	36	36	Consom. par hab.(kg.)
Philippines								**Philippines**
Production	1 895	1 954	1 549	1 913	1 826	1 895	1 988	Production
Consumption	1 956	1 959	1 958	1 854	2 052	1 974	2 059	Consommation
Consumption per cap. (kg.)	28	28	27	25	28	26	26	Consom. par hab.(kg.)
Poland								**Pologne**
Production	2 380	2 112	2 242	1 968	2 104	1 626	2 038	Production
Consumption	*1 700	*1 750	1 708	*1 720	*1 730	*1 740	*1 745	Consommation
Consumption per cap. (kg.)	44	45	44	45	45	45	45	Consom. par hab.(kg.)
Portugal [1]								**Portugal** [1]
Production	*3	18 [2]	23 [2]	*76	*60	*60	*79	Production
Republic of Moldova								**République de Moldova**
Production	231	203	186	108	102	130	125	Production
Consumption *	175	160	150	125	105	105	110	Consommation *
Consumption per cap. (kg.)	40	37	41	34	29	29	26	Consom. par hab.(kg.)
Réunion [1]								**Réunion** [1]
Production	205	207	*195	*234	*222	*218	*210	Production
Romania								**Roumanie**
Production	226	204	189	86	54	71	75	Production
Consumption *	500	510	520	530	550	565	570	Consommation *
Consumption per cap. (kg.)	22	23	23	24	25	25	26	Consom. par hab.(kg.)
Russian Federation								**Fédération de Russie**
Production	1 851	1 337	1 370	1 651	1 705	1 757	1 757	Production
Consumption	5 235	5 308	*5 450	5 565	5 707	5 848	*6 500	Consommation
Consumption per cap. (kg.)	35	36	37	38	39	40	44	Consom. par hab.(kg.)
Rwanda								**Rwanda**
Production	0	0	0	0	0	0	0	Production
Consumption *	4	4	3	3	3	10	11	Consommation *
Consumption per cap. (kg.)	1	1	0	0	0	1	1	Consom. par hab.(kg.)
Saint Kitts and Nevis								**Saint-Kitts-et-Nevis**
Production	20	30	24	*20	*20	*20	*20	Production
Consumption *	2	2	2	2	3	3	3	Consommation *
Consumption per cap. (kg.)	50	50	50	50	63	63	75	Consom. par hab.(kg.)
Samoa								**Samoa**
Production	2	2	2	2	2	2	2	Production
Consumption	3	3	3	2	2	2	2	Consommation
Consumption per cap. (kg.)	10	10	10	8	8	8	8	Consom. par hab.(kg.)
Saudi Arabia								**Arabie saoudite**
Consumption *	550	550	550	520	560	600	635	Consommation *
Consumption per cap. (kg.)	30	30	29	26	27	28	31	Consom. par hab.(kg.)
Senegal								**Sénégal**
Production	*85	*91	90	*95	*90	*95	*95	Production
Consumption *	165	170	170	170	165	170	175	Consommation *
Consumption per cap. (kg.)	19	19	18	18	17	17	23	Consom. par hab.(kg.)
Serbia and Montenegro								**Serbie-et-Monténégro**
Production	*285	239	213	248	*170	209	*230	Production
Consumption	*300	299	*300	*300	*275	*300	*300	Consommation
Consumption per cap. (kg.)	28	28	28	28	26	28	28	Consom. par hab.(kg.)
Sierra Leone								**Sierra Leone**
Production *	5	6	6	7	7	7	7	Production *
Consumption *	19	14	15	15	20	20	21	Consommation *
Consumption per cap. (kg.)	5	3	4	4	5	4	4	Consom. par hab.(kg.)
Singapore								**Singapour**
Consumption *	280	290	270	280	285	300	305	Consommation *
Consumption per cap. (kg.)	76	77	69	71	69	69	88	Consom. par hab.(kg.)
Slovakia								**Slovaquie**
Production	*140	237	170	213	140	173	*195	Production
Consumption *	200	220	220	225	230	235	240	Consommation *
Consumption per cap. (kg.)	37	41	41	42	43	43	44	Consom. par hab.(kg.)

40

Sugar
Production and consumption: thousand metric tons; consumption per capita: kilograms *[cont.]*

Sucre
Production et consommation : milliers de tonnes ; consommation par habitant : kilogrammes *[suite]*

Country or area	1996	1997	1998	1999	2000	2001	2002	Pays ou zone
Slovenia								**Slovénie**
Production	71	67	51	*60	44	*50	44	Production
Consumption *	103	103	105	105	105	108	108	Consommation *
Consumption per cap. (kg.)	52	52	53	53	53	54	47	Consom. par hab.(kg.)
Somalia								**Somalie**
Production *	20	19	19	20	15	20	200	Production *
Consumption *	110	135	150	170	180	185	190	Consommation *
Consumption per cap. (kg.)	15	17	19	20	21	20	19	Consom. par hab.(kg.)
South Africa								**Afrique du Sud**
Production	2 471	2 419	2 985	2 547	2 691	2 311	2 767	Production
Consumption	1 330	1 743	1 508	1 386	1 453	1 341	1 478	Consommation
Consumption per cap. (kg.)	33	42	36	32	33	30	33	Consom. par hab.(kg.)
Spain [1]								**Espagne** [1]
Production	1 228	1 260	1 327	1 073	1 260	*1 032	*1 273	Production
Sri Lanka								**Sri Lanka**
Production	73	63	20	*19	*15	*20	*20	Production
Consumption *	525	535	550	550	560	565	585	Consommation *
Consumption per cap. (kg.)	29	29	30	29	29	29	29	Consom. par hab.(kg.)
Sudan								**Soudan**
Production	543	538	610	635	680	719	744	Production
Consumption	*480	*480	391	396	430	523	568	Consommation
Consumption per cap. (kg.)	17	16	13	13	14	16	18	Consom. par hab.(kg.)
Suriname								**Suriname**
Production *	7	10	5	7	10	10	10	Production *
Consumption *	17	17	18	18	19	19	20	Consommation *
Consumption per cap. (kg.)	42	41	44	42	45	46	39	Consom. par hab.(kg.)
Swaziland								**Swaziland**
Production	458	457	537	571	553	567	675	Production
Consumption	108	99	101	103	105	107	107	Consommation
Consumption per cap. (kg.)	115	114	113	113	113	107	112	Consom. par hab.(kg.)
Sweden [1]								**Suède** [1]
Production	398	396	400	448	448	436	470	Production
Switzerland								**Suisse**
Production	*194	*200	191	177	*231	*187	*230	Production
Consumption	*310	*315	206	328	*338	*360	*390	Consommation
Consumption per cap. (kg.)	44	44	29	46	47	50	53	Consom. par hab.(kg.)
Syrian Arab Republic								**Rép. arabe syrienne**
Production	197	191	107	*102	*100	121	*120	Production
Consumption *	675	695	715	720	730	745	750	Consommation *
Consumption per cap. (kg.)	46	46	46	45	45	45	42	Consom. par hab.(kg.)
Tajikistan								**Tadjikistan**
Consumption *	80	70	65	60	60	60	65	Consommation *
Consumption per cap. (kg.)	14	12	11	10	9	10	10	Consom. par hab.(kg.)
Thailand								**Thaïlande**
Production	6 154	6 243	4 143	5 456	6 157	5 370	6 438	Production
Consumption	1 706	1 829	1 834	1 776	1 816	1 955	1 978	Consommation
Consumption per cap. (kg.)	28	30	30	29	29	31	31	Consom. par hab.(kg.)
TFYR of Macedonia								**L'ex-R.y. Macédoine**
Production	18	*15	40	43	32	20	*20	Production
Consumption *	50	50	60	80	80	80	80	Consommation *
Consumption per cap. (kg.)	25	25	30	40	39	40	35	Consom. par hab.(kg.)
Togo								**Togo**
Production *	5	3	3	3	3	5	5	Production *
Consumption *	35	40	45	48	48	50	50	Consommation *
Consumption per cap. (kg.)	8	9	10	11	11	11	12	Consom. par hab.(kg.)
Trinidad and Tobago								**Trinité-et-Tobago**
Production	117	120	79	92	115	89	104	Production
Consumption	73	87	72	70	78	79	70	Consommation
Consumption per cap. (kg.)	57	67	56	55	60	61	56	Consom. par hab.(kg.)

40

Sugar

Production and consumption: thousand metric tons; consumption per capita: kilograms *[cont.]*

Sucre

Production et consommation : milliers de tonnes ; consommation par habitant : kilogrammes *[suite]*

Country or area	1996	1997	1998	1999	2000	2001	2002	Pays ou zone
Tunisia								**Tunisie**
Production	29	28	15	9	2	0	0	Production
Consumption	272	283	287	292	294	309	319	Consommation
Consumption per cap. (kg.)	30	31	31	31	31	30	45	Consom. par hab.(kg.)
Turkey								**Turquie**
Production	2 002	2 187	2 784	2 491	2 273	2 360	2 128	Production
Consumption	*1 900	2 107	2 074	1 836	*1 925	1 973	1 782	Consommation
Consumption per cap. (kg.)	31	34	33	29	29	28	26	Consom. par hab.(kg.)
Turkmenistan								**Turkménistan**
Consumption *	75	70	70	70	70	70	70	Consommation *
Consumption per cap. (kg.)	18	16	16	15	15	15	15	Consom. par hab.(kg.)
Uganda								**Ouganda**
Production	*109	*145	*111	*137	*130	*140	160	Production
Consumption *	100	150	150	150	155	160	180	Consommation *
Consumption per cap. (kg.)	5	7	7	7	7	7	7	Consom. par hab.(kg.)
Ukraine								**Ukraine**
Production	*2 935	*2 170	2 041	1 640	1 686	1 802	*1 545	Production
Consumption	*2 100	*1 800	1 739	*1 800	*1 875	*2 005	*2 100	Consommation
Consumption per cap. (kg.)	41	35	34	36	38	41	42	Consom. par hab.(kg.)
United Kingdom [1]								**Royaume-Uni** [1]
Production	1 605	1 592	1 565	1 683	1 440	1 222	1 390	Production
United Rep. of Tanzania								**Rép.-Unie de Tanzanie**
Production	*100	84	*110	114	*130	*115	187	Production
Consumption	*160	*175	*200	*200	*208	*200	165	Consommation
Consumption per cap. (kg.)	6	6	6	6	6	6	5	Consom. par hab.(kg.)
United States								**Etats-Unis**
Production	6 593	6 731	7 159	*8 243	8 080	7 774	6 805	Production
Consumption	8 701	8 800	9 049	9 067	9 051	9 139[8]	9 079	Consommation
Consumption per cap. (kg.)	33	33	34	33	32	32	32	Consom. par hab.(kg.)
Uruguay								**Uruguay**
Production *	15	19	14	9	8	7	7	Production *
Consumption	*105	*110	*115	101	*102	*105	*105	Consommation
Consumption per cap. (kg.)	33	34	35	31	30	31	32	Consom. par hab.(kg.)
Uzbekistan								**Ouzbékistan**
Production	...	...	11	*20	11	*7	0	Production
Consumption *	370	390	410	435	450	475	490	Consommation *
Consumption per cap. (kg.)	16	17	17	18	18	19	18	Consom. par hab.(kg.)
Venezuela								**Venezuela**
Production *	559	594	590	535	645	585	595	Production *
Consumption *	820	840	855	870	893	910	925	Consommation *
Consumption per cap. (kg.)	37	37	37	37	37	37	39	Consom. par hab.(kg.)
Viet Nam								**Viet Nam**
Production	*550	*559	657	878	1 155	*850	*890	Production
Consumption *	640	675	700	750	810	825	850	Consommation *
Consumption per cap. (kg.)	9	9	9	10	10	11	10	Consom. par hab.(kg.)
Yemen								**Yémen**
Consumption *	350	375	375	390	410	420	420	Consommation *
Consumption per cap. (kg.)	22	23	22	22	22	22	26	Consom. par hab.(kg.)
Zambia								**Zambie**
Production	166	174	173	*210	*190	199	233	Production
Consumption	154	74	*85	*115	*145	102	116	Consommation
Consumption per cap. (kg.)	16	8	8	11	14	11	11	Consom. par hab.(kg.)
Zimbabwe								**Zimbabwe**
Production	337	574	572	583	571	548	565	Production
Consumption	287	335	305	376	374	305	335	Consommation
Consumption per cap. (kg.)	24	27	24	29	30	24	27	Consom. par hab.(kg.)

Source:
International Sugar Organization (ISO), London, "Sugar Yearbook 2002" and the ISO database.

Source:
Organisation internationale du sucre (OIS), Londres, "Annuaire du sucre 2002" et la base de données de l'OIS.

429 Manufacturing Industries manufacturières

40

Sugar
Production and consumption: thousand metric tons; consumption per capita: kilograms *[cont.]*

Sucre
Production et consommation : milliers de tonnes ; consommation par habitant : kilogrammes *[suite]*

1	Source: Food and Agriculture Organization of the United Nations (FAO), (Rome).
2	FAO estimate.
3	Including non-human consumption: 1998 - 15,652 tons.
4	Including store losses of 1,159 tons and accidental losses of 129 tons.
5	Including non-human consumption: 1983 - 6,710 tons; 1984 - 19,797 tons; 1985-79,908 tons; 1986- 98,608 tons; 1987- 147,262 tons; 1988- 122,058 tons; 1989- 52,230 tons; 1991- 13,541 tons; 1994- 12,178 tons; 1995- 10,211 tons; 1996- 14,648 tons; 2000- 31,836 tons.
6	Including 11,572 tons sold to other Pacific Island nations in 1994; 12,520 tons in 1995; 14,154 tons in 1996; 13,109 tons in 1997; 5,305 tons in 1998; and 6,444 tons in 2001.
7	Including consumption of mono-sodium glutamate, lysine and other products: 1987- 44,600 tons; 1988- 92,200 tons; 1989- 94,500 tons; 1990- 89,400 tons; 1991- 77,300 tons; 1992- 75,800 tons; 1993- 89,800 tons; 1994- 170,384 tons; 1995- 200,863 tons; 1996- 257,763 tons; 1997- 257,310 tons; 1998- 258,247 tons; 2000- 159,027 tons.
8	Including 19,780 tons used for livestock feed.

1	Source: Organisation des Nations Unies pour l'alimentation et l'agriculture (FAO), (Rome).
2	Estimation de la FAO.
3	Dont la consommation non humaine: 1998 - 15 652 tonnes.
4	Y compris des pertes de 1 159 tonnes au cours du stockage et des pertes accidentelles de 129 tonnes.
5	Dont consommation non humaine : 1983 - 6 710 tonnes; 1984 - 19 797 tonnes; 1985-79 908 tonnes; 1986- 98 608 tonnes; 1987- 147 262 tonnes; 1988- 122 058 tonnes; 1989- 52 230 tonnes; 1991- 13 541 tonnes; 1994- 12 178 tonnes; 1995- 10 211 tonnes; 1996- 14 648 tonnes; 2000- 31 836 tonnes.
6	Y compris 11 572 tonnes vendues à autres îles pacifiques en 1994; 12 520 tonnes en 1995; 14 154 tonnes en 1996; 13 109 tonnes en 1997; 5,305 tonnes in 1998; et 6,444 tonnes en 2001.
7	Y compris la consommation des produits du glutamate monosodium, lysine et autres: 1987- 44 600 tonnes ; 1988- 92 200 tonnes; 1989- 94 500 tonnes; 1990- 89 400 tonnes; 1991- 77 300 tonnes ; 1992- 75 800 tonnes; 1993- 89 800 tonnes; 1994- 170 384 tonnes; 1995- 200 863 tonnes; 1996-257 763 tonnes; 1997- 257 310 tonnes; 1998- 258 247 tonnes; 2000- 159 027 tonnes; 2001-210,498 tonnes.
8	Y compris 19 780 tonnes utilisées pour les aliments du bétail.

41

Meat
Production: thousand metric tons

Viande
Production: milliers de tonnes

Country or area	1995	1996	1997	1998	1999	2000	2001	2002	Pays ou zone
World									**Monde**
Total	146 081	146 201	151 078	156 751	160 160	160 748	162 026	166 712	Totale
Beef and veal	54 167	54 725	55 399	55 282	56 330	56 869	56 210	57 883	Bœuf et veau
Buffalo	2 825	2 738	2 893	2 891	2 990	3 005	3 068	3 094	Buffle
Goat	3 254	3 116	3 309	3 511	3 593	3 786	3 888	3 963	Chèvre
Mutton and lamb	7 200	7 050	7 170	7 298	7 345	7 554	7 570	7 585	Mouton et agneau
Pork	78 635	78 571	82 306	87 768	89 902	89 533	91 290	94 186	Porc
Africa									**Afrique**
Total	5 932	6 026	6 265	6 453	6 603	6 888	7 040	7 045	Totale
Beef and veal	3 433	3 459	3 576	3 703	3 805	4 014	4 114	4 107	Bœuf et veau
Buffalo	179	208	256	266	277	288	303	303	Buffle
Goat	713	736	761	766	774	800	805	808	Chèvre
Mutton and lamb	954	966	1 003	1 036	1 067	1 087	1 089	1 088	Mouton et agneau
Pork	653	657	670	681	681	699	729	739	Porc
Algeria									**Algérie**
Total	279	289	281	282	293	309	310	310	Totale
Beef and veal	101	99	102	103	117	133	133[1]	133[1]	Bœuf et veau
Goat [1]	8	11	12	12	12	12	12	12	Chèvre [1]
Mutton and lamb	170	179	167	167	163	164	165[1]	165[1]	Mouton et agneau
Angola									**Angola**
Total	97	107	115	123	124	125	125	123	Totale
Beef and veal [1]	65	71	77	85	85	85	85	85	Bœuf et veau [1]
Goat [1]	6	7	8	8	9	10	10	9	Chèvre [1]
Mutton and lamb [1]	1	1	1	1	1	1	1	1	Mouton et agneau [1]
Pork [1]	26	28	29	29	29	29	29	28	Porc [1]
Benin									**Bénin**
Total	28	29	28	29	28	28	31	33	Totale
Beef and veal [1]	15	16	16	20	19	18	18	19	Bœuf et veau [1]
Goat [1]	4	4	4	4	4	4	4	4	Chèvre [1]
Mutton and lamb [1]	2	2	2	2	2	2	2	2	Mouton et agneau [1]
Pork [1]	7	8	6	3	2	4	6	7	Porc [1]
Botswana									**Botswana**
Total	55	52	47	45	35	38	40	40	Totale
Beef and veal [1]	46	44	38	37	27	29	32	32	Bœuf et veau [1]
Goat [1]	8	6	7	6	6	6	6	6	Chèvre [1]
Mutton and lamb [1]	2	2	2	1	2	2	2	2	Mouton et agneau [1]
Pork [1]	0	1	0	1	0	1	0	0	Porc [1]
Burkina Faso									**Burkina Faso**
Total	78	88	91	94	96	100	101	101	Totale
Beef and veal [1]	40	47	50	51	52	55	55	55	Bœuf et veau [1]
Goat [1]	20	21	22	22	22	23	23	23	Chèvre [1]
Mutton and lamb [1]	11	12	13	13	13	14	14	14	Mouton et agneau [1]
Pork [1]	6	7	8	8	8	9	9	9	Porc [1]
Burundi									**Burundi**
Total	20	18	17	18	17	17	17	17	Totale
Beef and veal	10[1]	9[1]	9[1]	10[1]	9	9	9[1]	9[1]	Bœuf et veau
Goat	4[1]	3[1]	3[1]	3[1]	3	3	3[1]	3[1]	Chèvre
Mutton and lamb [1]	1	1	1	1	1	1	1	1	Mouton et agneau [1]
Pork [1]	5	4	4	4	4	4	4	4	Porc [1]
Cameroon									**Cameroun**
Total	113	113	116	120	133	141	143	143	Totale
Beef and veal	73[1]	73[1]	76[1]	77[1]	*91	*93	*95	95[1]	Bœuf et veau
Goat [1]	13	13	13	14	14	15	15	15	Chèvre [1]
Mutton and lamb	15	15	15	15	16	16	16	16	Mouton et agneau [1]
Pork [1]	12	12	12	14	12	16	16	16	Porc [1]
Cape Verde									**Cap-Vert**
Total	9	4	6	8	8	7	8	8	Totale
Beef and veal	0[1]	1	1[1]	1	0	0	1[1]	0[1]	Bœuf et veau
Pork	8	3	5[1]	6	7[1]	7	7[1]	7[1]	Porc
Central African Rep.									**Rép. centrafricaine**
Total	66	81	70	72	72	90	84	84	Totale
Beef and veal	48	*61	*50	*51	*51	67	*60	58	Bœuf et veau

41

Meat
Production: thousand metric tons *[cont.]*
Viande
Production: milliers de tonnes *[suite]*

Country or area	1995	1996	1997	1998	1999	2000	2001	2002	Pays ou zone
Goat	7[1]	7	8	8[1]	8[1]	*10	10[1]	11	Chèvre
Mutton and lamb	1[1]	1	1	1[1]	1[1]	1[1]	1[1]	1[1]	Mouton et agneau
Pork	10[1]	11	12	12[1]	12[1]	*12	13[1]	13	Porc
Chad									**Tchad**
Total	87	91	102	110	108	105	109	108	Totale
Beef and veal [1]	63	66	73	80	78	74	77	73	Bœuf et veau [1]
Goat [1]	13	13	18	18	18	19	20	22	Chèvre [1]
Mutton and lamb [1]	11	11	11	11	11	12	12	12	Mouton et agneau [1]
Comoros									**Comores**
Total	1	1	1	1	2	1	1	1	Totale
Beef and veal [1]	1	1	1	1	1	1	1	1	Bœuf et veau [1]
Goat [1]	0	0	0	0	1	0	0	0	Chèvre [1]
Congo									**Congo**
Total	5	5	5	4	5	5	5	6	Totale
Beef and veal [1]	1	1	1	1	2	2	2	3	Bœuf et veau [1]
Goat [1]	1	1	1	1	1	1	1	1	Chèvre [1]
Pork [1]	2	2	2	2	2	2	2	2	Porc [1]
Côte d'Ivoire									**Côte d'Ivoire**
Total	67	61	72	75	70	71	69	66	Totale
Beef and veal	39[1]	40[1]	50	52	47	48	49[1]	45[1]	Bœuf et veau
Goat	4[1]	4[1]	*5	*5	*5	*5	5[1]	4[1]	Chèvre
Mutton and lamb	5[1]	5[1]	*6	*7	*6	5	5	5	Mouton et agneau
Pork	19[1]	11[1]	11[1]	11[1]	13[1]	*13	11[1]	11[1]	Porc
Dem. Rep. of the Congo									**Rép. dém. du Congo**
Total	67	66	68	68	64	61	59	57	Totale
Beef and veal	16	15	16	14	14	14	13	12	Bœuf et veau
Goat	20[1]	20	21	22	19	19	19	18	Chèvre
Mutton and lamb	3	3	3	3	3	3	3	3	Mouton et agneau
Pork	28	29	29	29	27	26	25	24	Porc
Djibouti									**Djibouti**
Total	8	8	8	8	8	10	10	10	Totale
Beef and veal [1]	3	3	4	4	4	6	6	6	Bœuf et veau [1]
Goat [1]	2	2	2	2	2	2	2	2	Chèvre [1]
Mutton and lamb [1]	2	2	2	2	2	2	2	2	Mouton et agneau [1]
Egypt									**Egypte**
Total	488	546	600	616	612	652	661	661	Totale
Beef and veal	215	244	248[1]	252	233	*256	*247	247[1]	Bœuf et veau
Buffalo	179	208	256	266	277	288	303[1]	303[1]	Buffle
Goat	29[1]	30[1]	30	30	30	32[1]	33[1]	33[1]	Chèvre
Mutton and lamb	62[1]	61	64	65	69[1]	73	75[1]	75[1]	Mouton et agneau
Pork	3[1]	3[1]	3[1]	3[1]	3	*3	*3	3[1]	Porc
Eritrea									**Erythrée**
Total	20	22	25	27	28	28	28	28	Totale
Beef and veal [1]	10	12	14	16	16	16	17	17	Bœuf et veau [1]
Goat [1]	5	5	5	5	6	6	6	6	Chèvre [1]
Mutton and lamb [1]	5	5	5	6	6	6	6	6	Mouton et agneau [1]
Ethiopia									**Ethiopie**
Total	297	329	332	337	353	357	371	372	Totale
Beef and veal	235[1]	267	270	274	290	294[1]	304[1]	304[1]	Bœuf et veau
Goat [1]	25	25	25	25	25	26	29	29	Chèvre [1]
Mutton and lamb [1]	36	36	36	36	36	36	38	38	Mouton et agneau [1]
Pork [1]	1	1	1	1	1	1	1	1	Porc [1]
Gabon									**Gabon**
Total	5	5	5	5	5	5	5	5	Totale
Beef and veal [1]	1	1	1	1	1	1	1	1	Bœuf et veau [1]
Mutton and lamb [1]	1	1	1	1	1	1	1	1	Mouton et agneau [1]
Pork [1]	3	3	3	3	3	3	3	3	Porc [1]
Gambia									**Gambie**
Total	5	5	5	5	5	5	4	5	Totale
Beef and veal [1]	3	3	3	3	3	3	3	3	Bœuf et veau [1]
Goat [1]	0	0	0	0	0	0	1	1	Chèvre [1]

41

Meat
Production: thousand metric tons *[cont.]*

Viande
Production: milliers de tonnes *[suite]*

Country or area	1995	1996	1997	1998	1999	2000	2001	2002	Pays ou zone
Ghana									**Ghana**
Total	43	43	44	45	45	55	57	60	Totale
Beef and veal [1]	21	21	21	21	21	24	26	27	Bœuf et veau [1]
Goat [1]	5	6	6	7	7	10	11	11	Chèvre [1]
Mutton and lamb [1]	6	6	6	7	7	9	10	10	Mouton et agneau [1]
Pork [1]	11	10	11	11	10	11	11	12	Porc [1]
Guinea									**Guinée**
Total	32	34	35	37	39	41	43	44	Totale
Beef and veal [1]	25	26	27	29	30	32	33	34	Bœuf et veau [1]
Goat [1]	3	3	4	4	4	4	5	5	Chèvre [1]
Mutton and lamb [1]	3	3	3	3	3	3	4	4	Mouton et agneau [1]
Pork [1]	1	1	1	2	2	2	2	2	Porc [1]
Guinea-Bissau									**Guinée-Bissau**
Total	15	16	16	16	17	17	17	17	Totale
Beef and veal [1]	4	4	4	4	4	5	5	5	Bœuf et veau [1]
Goat [1]	1	1	1	1	1	1	1	1	Chèvre [1]
Mutton and lamb [1]	1	1	1	1	1	1	1	1	Mouton et agneau [1]
Pork [1]	10	10	10	10	11	11	11	11	Porc [1]
Kenya									**Kenya**
Total	306	328	331	335	346	356	362	361	Totale
Beef and veal	239	252	261	270	279	287	295	295[1]	Bœuf et veau
Goat [1]	32	40	32	28	29	30	28	28	Chèvre [1]
Mutton and lamb [1]	26	26	26	26	28	28	26	26	Mouton et agneau [1]
Pork	8	10	12	11	11	11	14[1]	13[1]	Porc
Lesotho									**Lesotho**
Total	20	18	18	17	17	16	17	17	Totale
Beef and veal [1]	11	10	10	10	9	8	9	9	Bœuf et veau [1]
Goat [1]	2	2	2	1	2	2	2	2	Chèvre [1]
Mutton and lamb [1]	4	3	4	3	3	3	3	3	Mouton et agneau [1]
Pork [1]	3	3	2	3	3	3	3	3	Porc [1]
Liberia									**Libéria**
Total	6	6	6	6	6	7	7	7	Totale
Beef and veal [1]	1	1	1	1	1	1	1	1	Bœuf et veau [1]
Goat [1]	1	1	1	1	1	1	1	1	Chèvre [1]
Mutton and lamb [1]	1	1	1	1	1	1	1	1	Mouton et agneau [1]
Pork [1]	4	4	4	4	4	4	4	4	Porc [1]
Libyan Arab Jamah.									**Jamah. arabe libyenne**
Total	57	63	78	88	55	41	40	40	Totale
Beef and veal [1]	22	15	39	43	15	8	7	7	Bœuf et veau [1]
Goat [1]	6	6	6	6	6	6	6	6	Chèvre [1]
Mutton and lamb [1]	30	43	33	39	34	27	27	27	Mouton et agneau [1]
Madagascar									**Madagascar**
Total	224	226	229	230	223	221	233	233	Totale
Beef and veal [1]	146	147	147	148	148	148	153	153	Bœuf et veau [1]
Goat [1]	7	7	7	7	7	7	7	7	Chèvre [1]
Mutton and lamb [1]	3	3	3	3	3	3	3	3	Mouton et agneau [1]
Pork [1]	68	70	72	72	65	63	70	70	Porc [1]
Malawi									**Malawi**
Total	34	41	37	40	40	44	42	42	Totale
Beef and veal [1]	15	23	12	14	15	16	16	16	Bœuf et veau [1]
Goat [1]	3	5	6	6	5	6	6	6	Chèvre [1]
Pork [1]	16	14	19	19	20	22	20	20	Porc [1]
Mali									**Mali**
Total	135	138	146	152	151	156	159	161	Totale
Beef and veal [1]	85	86	88	91	89	91	98	98	Bœuf et veau [1]
Goat [1]	29	31	32	32	35	36	34	34	Chèvre [1]
Mutton and lamb [1]	19	19	23	26	25	26	26	26	Mouton et agneau [1]
Pork [1]	2	2	2	2	2	2	3	3	Porc [1]
Mauritania									**Mauritanie**
Total	31	35	35	37	39	40	41	41	Totale
Beef and veal	10	10	10	*10	*10	*10	*11	11[1]	Bœuf et veau
Goat [1]	8	10	10	11	11	12	12	12	Chèvre [1]

41

Meat
Production: thousand metric tons *[cont.]*

Viande
Production: milliers de tonnes *[suite]*

Country or area	1995	1996	1997	1998	1999	2000	2001	2002	Pays ou zone
Mutton and lamb [1]	13	15	15	16	17	18	18	18	Mouton et agneau [1]
Mauritius									**Maurice**
Total	4	4	3	4	4	4	4	4	Totale
Beef and veal	2	2	2	3	3	3	2	3[1]	Bœuf et veau
Pork	1	1	1	1	1	1	1	1[1]	Porc
Morocco									**Maroc**
Total	255	216	268	256	278	288	298	292	Totale
Beef and veal	122	103	125	120	130	140	150	150[1]	Bœuf et veau
Goat	20	22	22	20	21	22	22	21[1]	Chèvre
Mutton and lamb	112	90	120	115	126	125	125	120[1]	Mouton et agneau
Pork	1[1]	1[1]	1	1	1	*1	1[1]	1[1]	Porc
Mozambique									**Mozambique**
Total	52	52	53	53	54	54	54	54	Totale
Beef and veal [1]	37	37	38	38	38	38	38	38	Bœuf et veau [1]
Goat [1]	2	2	2	2	2	2	2	2	Chèvre [1]
Mutton and lamb [1]	1	1	1	1	1	1	1	1	Mouton et agneau [1]
Pork [1]	12	12	13	13	13	13	13	13	Porc [1]
Namibia									**Namibie**
Total	57	56	41	45	54	74	70	70	Totale
Beef and veal [1]	48	46	30	38	45	64	58	58	Bœuf et veau [1]
Goat [1]	4	5	5	4	5	5	4	4	Chèvre [1]
Mutton and lamb [1]	3	4	5	2	4	5	7	7	Mouton et agneau [1]
Pork [1]	2	2	1	1	1	1	1	1	Porc [1]
Niger									**Niger**
Total	61	74	76	78	80	81	84	83	Totale
Beef and veal	25[1]	36[1]	38[1]	39[1]	40[1]	*41	*42	42[1]	Bœuf et veau
Goat [1]	22	23	23	23	24	24	25	25	Chèvre [1]
Mutton and lamb [1]	13	14	14	14	15	15	15	15	Mouton et agneau [1]
Pork [1]	1	1	1	1	1	1	1	1	Porc [1]
Nigeria									**Nigéria**
Total	578	604	654	664	680	744	765	788	Totale
Beef and veal [1]	267	280	294	297	298	352[1]	371[1]	376[1]	Bœuf et veau [1]
Goat [1]	130	127	133	133	137	139	140	142	Chèvre [1]
Mutton and lamb [1]	51	62	87	89	91	95	89	97	Mouton et agneau [1]
Pork [1]	131	135	140	144	153	158	165	173	Porc [1]
Réunion									**Réunion**
Total	12	12	14	13	14	14	14	14	Totale
Beef and veal	1	1	2	2	2	2	2	2[1]	Bœuf et veau
Pork	10	10	13	11	12	12	12	12[1]	Porc
Rwanda									**Rwanda**
Total	15	17	19	21	24	24	26	26	Totale
Beef and veal [1]	10	11	14	16	18	17	19	19	Bœuf et veau [1]
Goat [1]	2	2	2	2	2	3	3	3	Chèvre [1]
Mutton and lamb [1]	1	1	1	1	1	1	1	1	Mouton et agneau [1]
Pork [1]	2	3	3	3	3	3	3	3	Porc [1]
Senegal									**Sénégal**
Total	77	79	81	83	85	88	93	93	Totale
Beef and veal [1]	46	47	47	47	48	50	53	53	Bœuf et veau [1]
Goat [1]	14	14	15	16	16	16	17	17	Chèvre [1]
Mutton and lamb [1]	13	14	14	15	15	15	16	16	Mouton et agneau [1]
Pork [1]	4	4	5	5	6	7	7	8	Porc [1]
Seychelles									**Seychelles**
Total	1	1	1	1	1	1	1	1	Totale
Pork [1]	1	1	1	1	1	1	1	1	Porc [1]
Sierra Leone									**Sierra Leone**
Total	10	10	10	10	10	9	9	9	Totale
Beef and veal [1]	6	6	6	6	7	5	5	5	Bœuf et veau [1]
Mutton and lamb [1]	1	1	1	1	1	1	1	1	Mouton et agneau [1]
Pork [1]	2	2	2	2	2	2	2	2	Porc [1]
Somalia									**Somalie**
Total	107	114	118	137	126	132	146	145	Totale
Beef and veal [1]	50	54	61	62	58	59	63	62	Bœuf et veau [1]

41

Meat
Production: thousand metric tons [cont.]

Viande
Production: milliers de tonnes [suite]

Country or area	1995	1996	1997	1998	1999	2000	2001	2002	Pays ou zone
Goat [1]	30	31	31	36	38	37	38	38	Chèvre [1]
Mutton and lamb [1]	27	29	26	39	30	35	46	46	Mouton et agneau [1]
South Africa									**Afrique du Sud**
Total	794	744	732	770	818	835	835	837	Totale
Beef and veal	521	481	484	518	553	568	577	579	Bœuf et veau
Goat [1]	36	37	37	37	36	36	36	36	Chèvre [1]
Mutton and lamb	110	98	91	91	112	118	104	104 [1]	Mouton et agneau
Pork	127	128	120	124	117	113	118	118	Porc
Sudan									**Soudan**
Total	462	469	505	529	532	557	582	587	Totale
Beef and veal	225	226	250 [1]	265 [1]	276 [1]	296 [1]	320 [1]	325 [1]	Bœuf et veau
Goat	110	113	122	123	114	118	118 [1]	118 [1]	Chèvre
Mutton and lamb	127	130	133 [1]	141 [1]	142 [1]	143 [1]	144 [1]	144 [1]	Mouton et agneau
Swaziland									**Swaziland**
Total	18	18	18	18	18	22	18	18	Totale
Beef and veal	14	13	*14	14 [1]	14 [1]	18	14 [1]	14 [1]	Bœuf et veau
Goat [1]	3	3	2	2	2	3	3	3	Chèvre [1]
Mutton and lamb [1]	0	0	0	0	1	0	0	0	Mouton et agneau [1]
Pork [1]	1	1	1	1	1	1	1	1	Porc [1]
Togo									**Togo**
Total	12	13	16	15	16	17	17	18	Totale
Beef and veal [1]	4	4	5	5	5	5	6	6	Bœuf et veau [1]
Goat [1]	2	3	3	3	3	4	4	4	Chèvre [1]
Mutton and lamb [1]	1	2	3	3	3	3	4	4	Mouton et agneau [1]
Pork [1]	5	4	5	4	4	4	5	5	Porc [1]
Tunisia									**Tunisie**
Total	105	108	106	112	120	124	129	113	Totale
Beef and veal	50	52	50	53	58	60	62	55	Bœuf et veau
Goat	8	8	8	9	9	10	10	8	Chèvre
Mutton and lamb	46	47	47	50	53	54	56	50	Mouton et agneau
Uganda									**Ouganda**
Total	178	183	186	194	200	204	214	209	Totale
Beef and veal	86 [1]	88 [1]	89	93 [1]	96 [1]	97 [1]	101 [1]	97 [1]	Bœuf et veau
Goat	21 [1]	22 [1]	22	23 [1]	24 [1]	25 [1]	25 [1]	25 [1]	Chèvre
Mutton and lamb [1]	5	5	5	5	5	5	6	6	Mouton et agneau [1]
Pork [1]	66	69	71	73	75	77	81	81	Porc [1]
United Rep. of Tanzania									**Rép.-Unie de Tanzanie**
Total	293	242	241	247	267	277	283	283	Totale
Beef and veal [1]	246	194	193	198	215	225	230	230	Bœuf et veau [1]
Goat [1]	27	27	27	27	29	29	29	29	Chèvre [1]
Mutton and lamb [1]	10	11	11	11	11	10	10	10	Mouton et agneau [1]
Pork [1]	10	10	11	11	12	13	13	13	Porc [1]
Zambia									**Zambie**
Total	50	53	55	55	61	56	57	57	Totale
Beef and veal [1]	38	40	42	41	47	41	41	41	Bœuf et veau [1]
Goat [1]	2	2	3	3	4	5	5	5	Chèvre [1]
Mutton and lamb [1]	0	0	0	0	0	1	1	1	Mouton et agneau [1]
Pork [1]	10	10	10	10	11	10	11	11	Porc [1]
Zimbabwe									**Zimbabwe**
Total	98	92	98	99	122	135	141	141	Totale
Beef and veal	73 [1]	67 [1]	74 [1]	74 [1]	95	101	101 [1]	101 [1]	Bœuf et veau
Goat [1]	11	12	12	12	13	13	13	13	Chèvre [1]
Mutton and lamb [1]	0	0	0	0	1	1	1	1	Mouton et agneau [1]
Pork	13 [1]	13 [1]	12 [1]	13 [1]	13	20 [1]	26 [1]	26 [1]	Porc
America, North									**Amérique du Nord**
Total	**25 268**	**25 061**	**25 242**	**26 419**	**27 232**	**27 378**	**27 291**	**28 177**	**Totale**
Beef and veal	**14 490**	**14 675**	**14 712**	**14 920**	**15 340**	**15 539**	**15 252**	**15 760**	**Bœuf et veau**
Goat	**48**	**46**	**46**	**49**	**48**	**51**	**51**	**54**	**Chèvre**
Mutton and lamb	**176**	**168**	**164**	**160**	**159**	**156**	**157**	**156**	**Mouton et agneau**
Pork	**10 554**	**10 172**	**10 319**	**11 290**	**11 685**	**11 633**	**11 831**	**12 208**	**Porc**

41

Meat
Production: thousand metric tons *[cont.]*

Viande
Production: milliers de tonnes *[suite]*

Country or area	1995	1996	1997	1998	1999	2000	2001	2002	Pays ou zone
Antigua and Barbuda									**Antigua-et-Barbuda**
Total	1	1	1	1	1	1	1	1	Totale
Beef and veal [1]	1	1	0	0	0	0	1	1	Bœuf et veau [1]
Barbados									**Barbade**
Total	5	5	5	5	5	5	5	5	Totale
Beef and veal	1	1	1	1	1[1]	1[1]	1[1]	1[1]	Bœuf et veau
Pork [1]	4	4	4	4	4	4	4	5	Porc [1]
Belize									**Belize**
Total	2	2	2	2	2	2	3	3	Totale
Beef and veal	1	1	2	1	1	1	1	2	Bœuf et veau
Pork	1	1	1	1	1	1	1	1	Porc
Canada									**Canada**
Total	2 214	2 255	2 356	2 584	2 841	2 916	2 992	3 138	Totale
Beef and veal	928	1 017	1 089	1 182	1 264	1 264	1 250	*1 290	Bœuf et veau
Mutton and lamb	10	11	10	10	11	11	13	13[1]	Mouton et agneau
Pork	1 276	1 228	1 257	1 392	1 566	1 641	1 729	*1 835	Porc
Costa Rica									**Costa Rica**
Total	117	117	107	107	113	113	110	105	Totale
Beef and veal	94	96	86	82	84	82	74	69	Bœuf et veau
Pork	24	20	21	25	29	31	36	36	Porc
Cuba									**Cuba**
Total	137	144	147	169	225	217	194	195	Totale
Beef and veal	64	68	68	69	73	73	*77	*77	Bœuf et veau
Goat [1]	0	0	0	1	1	1	1	1	Chèvre [1]
Mutton and lamb [1]	1	1	1	1	1	1	1	1	Mouton et agneau [1]
Pork	72	74	78	98	151	143	115	*116	Porc
Dominica									**Dominique**
Total	1	1	1	1	1	1	1	1	Totale
Beef and veal [1]	0	1	1	1	1	1	1	1	Bœuf et veau [1]
Dominican Republic									**Rép. dominicaine**
Total	144	146	146	146	124	131	135	137	Totale
Beef and veal	80	80	79	80	66	69	71	72	Bœuf et veau
Goat [1]	2	2	2	1	1	1	1	1	Chèvre [1]
Pork	62[1]	63[1]	64	64	58	61	63	64	Porc
El Salvador									**El Salvador**
Total	36	34	42	41	43	41	44	47	Totale
Beef and veal	29	27	35	34	34	35	*35	*38	Bœuf et veau
Pork [1]	6	6	7	6	9	7	9	9	Porc [1]
Guadeloupe									**Guadeloupe**
Total	5	4	5	5	5	5	5	5	Totale
Beef and veal	3	3	3	3	3	3[1]	3[1]	3[1]	Bœuf et veau
Pork	1	1	1[1]	1[1]	1[1]	1[1]	1[1]	1[1]	Porc
Guatemala									**Guatemala**
Total	66	73	85	85	88	88	89	90	Totale
Beef and veal	54	54	54	54	62	62[1]	62[1]	63[1]	Bœuf et veau
Mutton and lamb [1]	2	3	2	2	2	1	1	1	Mouton et agneau [1]
Pork	9	16	28	28	24	25[1]	25[1]	26[1]	Porc
Haiti									**Haïti**
Total	51	57	59	64	64	76	79	78	Totale
Beef and veal	24	28	28	31	31[1]	40	41[1]	42[1]	Bœuf et veau
Goat	3[1]	*4	*5	*5	5[1]	6	7[1]	7[1]	Chèvre
Mutton and lamb	*0	*0	*1	*1	1[1]	1	1[1]	1[1]	Mouton et agneau
Pork	23	24	25	27	27[1]	28	31[1]	29[1]	Porc
Honduras									**Honduras**
Total	73	77	73	66	64	65	65	70	Totale
Beef and veal	64	68	63	57	55	55	55	*62	Bœuf et veau
Pork	8	9	9	9	9	10	10	*8	Porc
Jamaica									**Jamaïque**
Total	25	24	23	19	23	22	22	21	Totale
Beef and veal	17	16	15	12	15	14	13	*13	Bœuf et veau
Goat [1]	2	2	2	2	2	2	2	2	Chèvre [1]
Pork	7	7	7	6	7	7	6	6[1]	Porc

41

Meat
Production: thousand metric tons *[cont.]*

Viande
Production: milliers de tonnes *[suite]*

Country or area	1995	1996	1997	1998	1999	2000	2001	2002	Pays ou zone
Martinique									**Martinique**
Total	4	4	4	4	4	4	4	4	Totale
Beef and veal	2	3	2	2	2	2[1]	2[1]	2[1]	Bœuf et veau
Pork	2	2	1	2	2	2[1]	2[1]	2[1]	Porc
Mexico									**Mexique**
Total	2 401	2 306	2 345	2 409	2 462	2 511	2 578	2 616	Totale
Beef and veal	1 412	1 330	1 340	1 380	1 400	1 409	1 445	1 451	Bœuf et veau
Goat	38	36	35	38	37	39	39	42	Chèvre
Mutton and lamb	30	29	30	30	31	33	36	37	Mouton et agneau
Pork	922	910	939	961	994	1 030	1 058	1 086	Porc
Montserrat									**Montserrat**
Total	1	1	1	1	1	1	1	1	Totale
Beef and veal [1]	1	1	1	1	1	1	1	1	Bœuf et veau [1]
Nicaragua									**Nicaragua**
Total	54	55	57	52	54	59	60	66	Totale
Beef and veal	49	50	52	46	48	53	54	60	Bœuf et veau
Pork	5	5	5	6	6	6	6	6	Porc
Panama									**Panama**
Total	78	84	79	83	81	81	89	79	Totale
Beef and veal	61	66	60	64	60	59	65[1]	58	Bœuf et veau
Pork	17	19	19	19	21	22	24[1]	21[1]	Porc
Puerto Rico									**Porto Rico**
Total	32	29	29	28	29	30	30	30	Totale
Beef and veal	16	14	16	14[1]	15[1]	15[1]	15[1]	15[1]	Bœuf et veau
Pork	15	15	13	14[1]	14[1]	15[1]	15[1]	15[1]	Porc
Saint Kitts and Nevis									**Saint-Kitts-et-Nevis**
Total	0	0	0	0	0	1	1	1	Totale
Saint Lucia									**Sainte-Lucie**
Total	1	1	1	1	1	1	1	1	Totale
Beef and veal [1]	1	1	1	1	1	1	1	1	Bœuf et veau [1]
Pork [1]	1	1	1	1	1	1	1	1	Porc [1]
St. Vincent-Grenadines									**St. Vincent-Grenadines**
Total	1	1	1	1	1	1	1	1	Totale
Pork [1]	1	1	1	1	1	1	1	1	Porc [1]
Trinidad and Tobago									**Trinité-et-Tobago**
Total	3	3	4	3	3	4	4	4	Totale
Beef and veal	1	1	1	1	1	1	1	1	Bœuf et veau
Pork	2	2	2	2	2	3	3	3[1]	Porc
United States									**Etats-Unis**
Total	19 812	19 635	19 667	20 540	20 994	21 001	20 777	21 475	Totale
Beef and veal	11 585	11 749	11 714	11 803	12 123	12 298	11 983	12 438	Bœuf et veau
Mutton and lamb	130	122	118	114	113	106	103	100	Mouton et agneau
Pork	8 097	7 764	7 835	8 623	8 758	8 597	8 691	8 937	Porc
United States Virgin Is.									**Iles Vierges américaines**
Total	1	1	1	1	1	1	1	1	Totale
Beef and veal [1]	1	1	1	1	1	1	1	1	Bœuf et veau [1]
America, South									**Amérique du Sud**
Total	**13 442**	**14 187**	**14 015**	**13 797**	**14 741**	**15 166**	**15 031**	**16 083**	**Totale**
Beef and veal	**10 639**	**11 264**	**11 180**	**10 816**	**11 628**	**11 825**	**11 583**	**12 432**	**Bœuf et veau**
Goat	**74**	**62**	**71**	**76**	**79**	**82**	**82**	**84**	**Chèvre**
Mutton and lamb	**284**	**265**	**258**	**234**	**244**	**250**	**251**	**253**	**Mouton et agneau**
Pork	**2 445**	**2 596**	**2 506**	**2 670**	**2 790**	**3 009**	**3 115**	**3 314**	**Porc**
Argentina									**Argentine**
Total	2 988	2 945	2 938	2 710	2 988	2 991	2 707	2 975	Totale
Beef and veal	2 688	2 694	2 712	2 469	2 720	2 718	2 452	*2 700	Bœuf et veau
Goat [1]	7	7	7	9	9	9	9	9	Chèvre [1]
Mutton and lamb	81	64	*58	*48	*45	50[1]	50[1]	50[1]	Mouton et agneau
Pork	211	180	161	184	215	214	196	215[1]	Porc
Bolivia									**Bolivie**
Total	221	229	236	248	250	258	259	263	Totale
Beef and veal	140	143	147	155	155	160	161	165	Bœuf et veau
Goat [1]	6	6	6	6	6	6	6	6	Chèvre [1]

41
Meat
Production: thousand metric tons *[cont.]*
Viande
Production: milliers de tonnes *[suite]*

Country or area	1995	1996	1997	1998	1999	2000	2001	2002	Pays ou zone
Mutton and lamb	14	14	15	15	15	16	16[1]	16[1]	Mouton et agneau
Pork [1]	62	66	69	72	74	76	76	76	Porc [1]
Brazil									**Brésil**
Total	7 265	7 884	7 541	7 549	8 207	8 538	8 749	9 353	Totale
Beef and veal	5 710	6 187	5 922	5 794	6 413	6 540	6 671	*7 136	Bœuf et veau
Goat [1]	39	27	31	34	38	39	39	40	Chèvre [1]
Mutton and lamb [1]	86	70	70	68	71	72	72	77	Mouton et agneau [1]
Pork	1 430	1 600	1 518	1 652	1 684	1 888	1 968	2 100[1]	Porc
Chile									**Chili**
Total	445	458	486	508	488	504	537	567	Totale
Beef and veal	258	259	262	256	226	226	218	200	Bœuf et veau
Goat [1]	4	5	5	5	5	5	6	6	Chèvre [1]
Mutton and lamb	10	9	10	11	13	11	11	10	Mouton et agneau
Pork	172	185	209	235	244	261	303	351	Porc
Colombia									**Colombie**
Total	849	875	884	851	835	831	839	863	Totale
Beef and veal	702	730	763	766	716	745	*746	*775	Bœuf et veau
Goat	4[1]	4[1]	6	6	6	7[1]	6[1]	6[1]	Chèvre
Mutton and lamb	10[1]	12[1]	12	3	6	*7	7[1]	7[1]	Mouton et agneau
Pork	133[1]	129[1]	103	75	107	73	80	75[1]	Porc
Ecuador									**Equateur**
Total	245	264	270	265	282	290	305	313	Totale
Beef and veal	149	153	156	158	164	174	189	190[1]	Bœuf et veau
Goat	1[1]	1[1]	1[1]	1[1]	1[1]	2	1[1]	1[1]	Chèvre
Mutton and lamb	6[1]	6[1]	6[1]	6[1]	6[1]	6	6[1]	7[1]	Mouton et agneau
Pork	89[1]	103[1]	107[1]	100	110	108	108[1]	115[1]	Porc
Falkland Is. (Malvinas)									**Iles Falkland (Malvinas)**
Total	1	1	1	1	1	1	1	1	Totale
Mutton and lamb [1]	1	1	1	1	1	1	1	1	Mouton et agneau [1]
French Guiana									**Guyane française**
Total	1	2	2	2	2	2	2	2	Totale
Pork	1	1	1	1	1	1[1]	1[1]	1[1]	Porc
Guyana									**Guyana**
Total	5	4	3	3	3	3	3	2	Totale
Beef and veal	4	3	2	2	2	2	*2	*1	Bœuf et veau
Mutton and lamb [1]	1	1	1	1	1	1	1	1	Mouton et agneau [1]
Pork	1	1[1]	1[1]	1[1]	1[1]	1[1]	1[1]	1[1]	Porc
Paraguay									**Paraguay**
Total	359	345	347	353	369	390	404	406	Totale
Beef and veal	*226	226[1]	226	*231	*246	239	250[1]	250[1]	Bœuf et veau
Goat [1]	1	1	1	1	1	1	1	1	Chèvre [1]
Mutton and lamb [1]	3	3	3	3	3	2	3	3	Mouton et agneau [1]
Pork [1]	130	116	117	119	120	148	151	153	Porc [1]
Peru									**Pérou**
Total	213	220	233	243	263	269	261	264	Totale
Beef and veal	107	110	118	124	134	136	138	142	Bœuf et veau
Goat	7	6	6	6	7	7	6	6	Chèvre
Mutton and lamb	19	20	22	23	30	31	32	32	Mouton et agneau
Pork	80	83	87	91	93	95	85	85	Porc
Suriname									**Suriname**
Total	3	2	3	3	3	3	3	4	Totale
Beef and veal	2	2	2	2	2	2	2	3[1]	Bœuf et veau
Pork	1	1	1	1	1	1	1	1[1]	Porc
Uruguay									**Uruguay**
Total	412	491	536	531	536	530	395	496	Totale
Beef and veal	338	407	454	450	458	453	*317	*421	Bœuf et veau
Mutton and lamb	52	*64	*60	*55	*51	*51	51[1]	48[1]	Mouton et agneau
Pork	22	21	22	26	27	26	27[1]	27[1]	Porc
Venezuela									**Venezuela**
Total	435	469	535	529	513	555	565	574	Totale
Beef and veal	316	350	415	408	391	429	*437	450[1]	Bœuf et veau
Goat	5	5	7	7	5	7	8[1]	8[1]	Chèvre

41

Meat
Production: thousand metric tons [cont.]

Viande
Production: milliers de tonnes [suite]

Country or area	1995	1996	1997	1998	1999	2000	2001	2002	Pays ou zone
Mutton and lamb	2	2	2	2	2	2	3[1]	3[1]	Mouton et agneau
Pork	112	113	111	113	114	117	*118	*114	Porc
Asia									**Asie**
Total	56 959	56 581	62 411	65 893	67 489	68 402	70 294	73 095	**Totale**
Beef and veal	9 195	9 286	10 283	10 662	10 842	11 136	11 054	11 359	Bœuf et veau
Buffalo	2 644	2 526	2 634	2 622	2 711	2 714	2 761	2 787	Buffle
Goat	2 276	2 125	2 289	2 478	2 559	2 712	2 807	2 873	Chèvre
Mutton and lamb	3 018	3 004	3 191	3 263	3 331	3 455	3 519	3 645	Mouton et agneau
Pork	39 827	39 640	44 014	46 869	48 046	48 385	50 153	52 431	Porc
Afghanistan									**Afghanistan**
Total	267	283	312	338	297	255	226	226	Totale
Beef and veal [1]	130	143	156	171	149	126	108	108	Bœuf et veau [1]
Goat [1]	31	27	33	39	35	33	30	30	Chèvre [1]
Mutton and lamb [1]	106	114	123	128	112	96	88	88	Mouton et agneau [1]
Armenia									**Arménie**
Total	42	44	45	47	45	45	45	48	Totale
Beef and veal	30	33	35	35	32	33	32	32	Bœuf et veau
Mutton and lamb	7	6	5	5	5	6	7	7	Mouton et agneau
Pork	5	6	5	7	8	6	6	9	Porc
Azerbaijan									**Azerbaïdjan**
Total	66	71	76	83	88	92	95	105	Totale
Beef and veal	41	44	48	50	52	56	57	63	Bœuf et veau
Mutton and lamb	23	26	26	32	35	35	37	41	Mouton et agneau
Pork	2	2	2	1	2	1	1	1	Porc
Bahrain									**Bahreïn**
Total	9	9	9	8	8	8	8	8	Totale
Beef and veal	1[1]	1[1]	1[1]	1[1]	1	1[1]	1[1]	1[1]	Bœuf et veau
Goat	2[1]	2[1]	2[1]	2[1]	2	2[1]	2[1]	2[1]	Chèvre
Mutton and lamb [1]	7	7	7	5	5	5	5	5	Mouton et agneau [1]
Bangladesh									**Bangladesh**
Total	258	273	294	293	303	307	309	309	Totale
Beef and veal	148	152[1]	165[1]	161	170[1]	172[1]	173[1]	173[1]	Bœuf et veau [1]
Buffalo	3[1]	4	4[1]	4	4[1]	4[1]	4[1]	4[1]	Buffle
Goat	105[1]	115	123[1]	126	127[1]	129[1]	130[1]	130[1]	Chèvre
Mutton and lamb	2[1]	3	3[1]	3	3[1]	3[1]	3[1]	3[1]	Mouton et agneau
Bhutan									**Bhoutan**
Total	8	8	8	7	7	7	7	6	Totale
Beef and veal [1]	6	6	6	5	5	5	5	5	Bœuf et veau [1]
Pork [1]	1	2	2	2	2	1	1	1	Porc [1]
Brunei Darussalam									**Brunéi Darussalam**
Total	1	2	1	2	5	3	4	4	Totale
Beef and veal [1]	1	2	1	1	5	3	3	4	Bœuf et veau [1]
Cambodia									**Cambodge**
Total	134	139	151	155	158	175	179	154	Totale
Beef and veal [1]	40	41	41	42	42	57	58	53	Bœuf et veau [1]
Buffalo [1]	13	12	13	13	13	13	13	13	Buffle [1]
Pork [1]	82	86	97	100	103	105	108	88	Porc [1]
China [2]									**Chine [2]**
Total	38 748	38 414	43 718	47 075	48 645	49 501	51 416	53 349	Totale
Beef and veal *	3 296	3 333	4 105	4 485	4 711	4 991	5 130	5 320	Bœuf et veau *
Buffalo	*302	*252	*326	*339	*367	*361	*379	386[1]	Buffle
Goat *	849	815	942	1 111	1 182	1 304	1 390	1 444	Chèvre *
Mutton and lamb *	900	1 000	1 190	1 239	1 335	1 440	1 540	1 600	Mouton et agneau *
Pork	*33 401	33 015	37 155	39 900	41 050	41 406	42 976	*44 599	Porc
Cyprus									**Chypre**
Total	56	58	60	61	64	67	66	68	Totale
Beef and veal	5	5	5	4	4	4	4	4[1]	Bœuf et veau
Goat	4	4	4	5	6	6	7	8[1]	Chèvre
Mutton and lamb	4	4	4	5	4	4	4	5[1]	Mouton et agneau
Pork	43	46	46	47	49	52	51	52[1]	Porc
Georgia									**Géorgie**
Total	105	109	109	93	89	94	89	88	Totale

41

Meat
Production: thousand metric tons [cont.]
    Viande
    Production: milliers de tonnes [suite]

Country or area	1995	1996	1997	1998	1999	2000	2001	2002	Pays ou zone
Beef and veal	53	54	56	43	41	48	47	48[1]	Bœuf et veau
Mutton and lamb	8	9	7	8	7	9	8	8[1]	Mouton et agneau
Pork	44	46	47	42	41	37	35	32[1]	Porc
India									**Inde**
Total	3 875	3 937	3 995	4 011	4 086	4 137	4 184	4 202	Totale
Beef and veal [1]	1 365	1 370	1 378	1 401	1 421	1 442	1 463	1 463	Bœuf et veau [1]
Buffalo [1]	1 351	1 382	1 403	1 380	1 410	1 421	1 427	1 427	Buffle [1]
Goat [1]	450	454	458	462	466	467	469	470	Chèvre [1]
Mutton and lamb [1]	213	218	222	226	228	229	230	230	Mouton et agneau [1]
Pork [1]	495	514	533	543	560	578	595	613	Porc [1]
Indonesia									**Indonésie**
Total	1 026	1 094	1 141	1 092	984	890	920	930	Totale
Beef and veal	312	347	354	343	309	351	339	339[1]	Bœuf et veau
Buffalo	47	49	47	46	48	46	42	42[1]	Buffle
Goat	56	60	65	48	45	45	43	44[1]	Chèvre
Mutton and lamb	38	39	42	34	32	36*	33	33[1]	Mouton et agneau
Pork [1]	572	600	633	622	550	413	463	471	Porc [1]
Iran (Islamic Rep. of)									**Iran (Rép. islamique d')**
Total	642	699	734	753	694	716	729	746	Totale
Beef and veal	*255	308	317	324	286	269	274	284	Bœuf et veau
Buffalo [1]	10	10	11	11	11	11	11	12	Buffle [1]
Goat	101[1]	100	105	109	104	110	111	105	Chèvre
Mutton and lamb	*276	280	301	309	293	326	333	345	Mouton et agneau
Iraq									**Iraq**
Total	74	59	73	75	76	76	77	77	Totale
Beef and veal [1]	40	36	44	45	45	45	46	47	Bœuf et veau [1]
Buffalo [1]	3	2	2	2	2	2	2	2	Buffle [1]
Goat [1]	8	6	8	8	8	8	8	8	Chèvre [1]
Mutton and lamb [1]	22	16	19	20	20	20	20	20	Mouton et agneau [1]
Israel									**Israël**
Total	58	61	65	62	61	69	74	71	Totale
Beef and veal	41	44	46	44	46	52	57	53[1]	Bœuf et veau
Goat	*1	*1	*1	*1	*1	*1	1[1]	1[1]	Chèvre
Mutton and lamb	*6	*6	*6	*5	*5	*5	*5	5[1]	Mouton et agneau
Pork	11	11	12	12	9	11	12	12[1]	Porc
Japan									**Japon**
Total	1 901	1 818	1 819	1 820	1 818	1 801	1 700	1 771	Totale
Beef and veal	601	555	530	529	540	530	458	535	Bœuf et veau
Pork	1 300	1 263	1 288	1 291	1 277	1 271	1 242	1 236	Porc
Jordan									**Jordanie**
Total	16	16	15	14	11	10	10	8	Totale
Beef and veal	4[1]	3	4	3	4	3	4	3	Bœuf et veau
Goat	3	3	3	4	3	2	2	1	Chèvre
Mutton and lamb	9	10	9	*7	4	5	5	4	Mouton et agneau
Kazakhstan									**Kazakhstan**
Total	867	740	627	546	540	535	566	585	Totale
Beef and veal	548	463	398	348	344	306	288	297	Bœuf et veau
Goat	*6	*5	*5	5	*4	*4	*5	7	Chèvre
Mutton and lamb	*200	*162	143	114	*95	91	92	94	Mouton et agneau
Pork	113	110	82	79	98	133	181	187	Porc
Korea, Dem. P. R.									**Corée, R. p. dém. de**
Total	164	131	108	139	163	171	178	179	Totale
Beef and veal [1]	45	22	19	20	20	20	21	22	Bœuf et veau [1]
Goat [1]	3	3	5	7	9	10	11	11	Chèvre [1]
Mutton and lamb [1]	1	1	1	1	1	1	1	1	Mouton et agneau [1]
Pork [1]	115	105	84	112	134	140	145	146	Porc [1]
Korea, Republic of									**Corée, République de**
Total	1 023	1 138	1 237	1 318	1 342	1 225	1 156	1 213	Totale
Beef and veal	221	248	338	376	342	306	226	*180	Bœuf et veau
Goat [1]	3	3	4	3	3	3	3	3	Chèvre [1]
Pork	799	887	896	939	996	916	928	*1 030	Porc

41

Meat
Production: thousand metric tons [cont.]

Viande
Production: milliers de tonnes [suite]

Country or area	1995	1996	1997	1998	1999	2000	2001	2002	Pays ou zone
Kuwait									**Koweït**
Total	40	41	41	41	40	38	34	36	Totale
Beef and veal	*2	2[1]	2[1]	2[1]	2[1]	2[1]	2[1]	2[1]	Bœuf et veau
Goat [1]	0	0	1	0	1	1	0	0	Chèvre [1]
Mutton and lamb	*38	*39	39[1]	38[1]	38[1]	36[1]	32[1]	34[1]	Mouton et agneau
Kyrgyzstan									**Kirghizistan**
Total	167	169	165	168	170	168	170	169	Totale
Beef and veal	85	86	95	95	95	101	100	98	Bœuf et veau
Goat	*1	*1	1	3	3	4	4	4	Chèvre
Mutton and lamb	*53	*53	44	40	43	39	40	42	Mouton et agneau
Pork	28	29	26	30	29	24	26	26	Porc
Lao People's Dem. Rep.									**Rép. dém. pop. lao**
Total	58	58	61	63	70	67	77	75	Totale
Beef and veal	13	12	14	15	19	16	24[1]	25[1]	Bœuf et veau
Buffalo	15	16	16	16	19	17	17[1]	17[1]	Buffle
Goat [1]	0	0	0	0	0	0	1	1	Chèvre [1]
Pork	29	30	31	31	32	33	*35	32[1]	Porc
Lebanon									**Liban**
Total	33	35	71	52	55	52	60	50	Totale
Beef and veal [1]	18	22	58	38	43	42	38	37	Bœuf et veau [1]
Goat [1]	3	3	4	3	3	3	3	3	Chèvre [1]
Mutton and lamb	7[1]	6	7[1]	7[1]	7[1]	6[1]	17[1]	9[1]	Mouton et agneau
Pork [1]	4	4	3	3	2	2	2	2	Porc [1]
Malaysia									**Malaisie**
Total	305	301	306	282	180	182	191	232	Totale
Beef and veal [1]	16	17	18	18	18	18	19	21	Bœuf et veau [1]
Buffalo [1]	4	5	4	4	3	3	3	4	Buffle [1]
Pork	283	278	282	260	159	160	168	207	Porc
Mongolia									**Mongolie**
Total	182	212	191	199	234	234	174	244	Totale
Beef and veal	69	90	87	86	105	113	67	84	Bœuf et veau
Goat	18	28	26	28	32	30	30	30[1]	Chèvre
Mutton and lamb	94	93	79	84	97	90	77	130	Mouton et agneau
Pork	1	0	0	1	0	1	1	1[1]	Porc
Myanmar									**Myanmar**
Total	190	196	216	220	237	244	256	262	Totale
Beef and veal [1]	95	97	99	101	101	102	104	108	Bœuf et veau [1]
Buffalo [1]	19	19	20	20	20	20	21	21	Buffle [1]
Goat	6	6	6	7	7	7	7	8	Chèvre
Mutton and lamb	2	2	2	2	2	2	2	2	Mouton et agneau
Pork [1]	69	72	89	91	107	113	121	123	Porc [1]
Nepal									**Népal**
Total	195	199	211	217	220	224	228	232	Totale
Beef and veal [1]	46	47	48	48	48	48	47	47	Bœuf et veau [1]
Buffalo	104	105	113	117	120	122	125	128	Buffle
Goat	31	32	35	36	36	37	38	39	Chèvre
Mutton and lamb	3	3	3	3	3	3	3	3	Mouton et agneau
Pork	11	12	12	13	14	15	15	16	Porc
Occupied Palestinian Terr. [3]									**Terr. palestinien occupé [3]**
Total	3	3	3	3	3	3	3	3	Totale
Beef and veal [1]	1	1	1	1	1	1	1	1	Bœuf et veau [1]
Goat [1]	1	1	1	1	1	1	1	1	Chèvre [1]
Mutton and lamb [1]	1	1	1	1	1	1	1	1	Mouton et agneau [1]
Oman									**Oman**
Total	20	22	23	24	25	28	25	25	Totale
Beef and veal [1]	3	4	4	4	5	5	5	5	Bœuf et veau [1]
Goat [1]	5	6	6	7	7	10	7	7	Chèvre [1]
Mutton and lamb [1]	12	12	13	13	13	13	13	13	Mouton et agneau [1]
Pakistan									**Pakistan**
Total	1 530	1 267	1 297	1 327	1 362	1 392	1 428	1 463	Totale
Beef and veal	342	*380	*389	*398	*407	*420	*428	*437	Bœuf et veau
Buffalo	505	*428	*438	*448	*460	*466	*480	*494	Buffle

41

Meat
Production: thousand metric tons *[cont.]*
   Viande
   Production: milliers de tonnes *[suite]*

Country or area	1995	1996	1997	1998	1999	2000	2001	2002	Pays ou zone
Goat	430	*289	*296	*303	*312	*336	*348	*360	Chèvre
Mutton and lamb	253	*170	*174	*178	*183	*170	*172	*172	Mouton et agneau
Philippines									**Philippines**
Total	983	1 051	1 121	1 175	1 265	1 304	1 353	1 625	Totale
Beef and veal	97	113	137	156	190	190	183	183	Bœuf et veau
Buffalo	50	48	52	56	69	72	72	76	Buffle
Goat	*31	*30	*31	*31	33	34	33	34	Chèvre
Pork	805	860	901	933	973	1 008	1 064	1 332	Porc
Qatar									**Qatar**
Total	10	6	8	8	6	7	9	9	Totale
Beef and veal [1]	0	0	0	0	0	0	0	1	Bœuf et veau [1]
Goat [1]	1	1	1	1	1	1	1	1	Chèvre [1]
Mutton and lamb [1]	10	5	7	7	5	6	8	8	Mouton et agneau [1]
Saudi Arabia									**Arabie saoudite**
Total	114	106	101	104	106	110	115	116	Totale
Beef and veal	*26	*18	*16	19	19	*22	23[1]	23[1]	Bœuf et veau
Goat	24[1]	22[1]	21[1]	20	21	*22	22[1]	23[1]	Chèvre
Mutton and lamb	64	66	*64	*65	*66	*67	70[1]	70[1]	Mouton et agneau
Singapore									**Singapour**
Total	87	84	84	84	50	50	50	50	Totale
Pork	86	84	84	84	50	50[1]	50[1]	50[1]	Porc
Sri Lanka									**Sri Lanka**
Total	41	38	38	35	35	39	37	37	Totale
Beef and veal	27	24	25	25	24	29	27	28[1]	Bœuf et veau
Buffalo [1]	9	9	8	7	8	7	6	6	Buffle [1]
Goat	2	2	2	2	2	2	2	2[1]	Chèvre
Pork	2	2	2	2	2	2	2	2[1]	Porc
Syrian Arab Republic									**Rép. arabe syrienne**
Total	170	190	196	204	229	236	216	236	Totale
Beef and veal	34	40	42	43	47	47	42	47	Bœuf et veau
Goat	6	7	5	6	5	5	5	5	Chèvre
Mutton and lamb	131	143	148	154	177	184	169	184[1]	Mouton et agneau
Tajikistan									**Tadjikistan**
Total	51	45	29	28	28	28	28	28	Totale
Beef and veal	*31	34	26	15	*15	*12	*15	15[1]	Bœuf et veau
Mutton and lamb	*19	11	3	13	*13	*16	*13	13[1]	Mouton et agneau
Pork	*1	0	*0	*0	*0	*0	*0	0[1]	Porc
Thailand									**Thaïlande**
Total	827	841	839	749	703	701	717	712	Totale
Beef and veal [1]	232	238	226	210	188	174	172	172	Bœuf et veau [1]
Buffalo [1]	105	91	79	69	60	52	58	53	Buffle [1]
Goat [1]	1	0	1	1	1	1	1	1	Chèvre [1]
Pork [1]	489	511	533	469	454	475	486	486	Porc [1]
Turkey									**Turquie**
Total	671	672	763	738	723	733	685	685	Totale
Beef and veal	292	302	380	359	350	355	332	350[1]	Bœuf et veau
Buffalo	6	3	6	5	5	4	2	2[1]	Buffle
Goat	*57	*55	*54	*57	*55	53[1]	48[1]	47[1]	Chèvre
Mutton and lamb	*315	*311	*324	*317	*313	321[1]	303[1]	286[1]	Mouton et agneau
Pork	0	1	0	0	0	0	0	0[1]	Porc
Turkmenistan									**Turkménistan**
Total	104	107	107	123	127	127	128	128	Totale
Beef and veal	51	52	55	61	63	65[1]	67[1]	67[1]	Bœuf et veau
Goat	*3	*3	*3	*3	*3	3[1]	3[1]	3[1]	Chèvre
Mutton and lamb	*47	*50	*48	*58	*60	59[1]	57[1]	57[1]	Mouton et agneau
Pork	3	1	1	1	1	1[1]	1[1]	1[1]	Porc
United Arab Emirates									**Emirats arabes unis**
Total	48	45	46	40	47	40	31	31	Totale
Beef and veal [1]	11	7	7	8	21	15	8	8	Bœuf et veau [1]
Goat [1]	6	6	7	7	8	8	8	8	Chèvre [1]
Mutton and lamb [1]	32	32	32	24	18	16	14	14	Mouton et agneau [1]

41

Meat
Production: thousand metric tons *[cont.]*

Viande
Production: milliers de tonnes *[suite]*

Country or area	1995	1996	1997	1998	1999	2000	2001	2002	Pays ou zone
Uzbekistan									**Ouzbékistan**
Total	491	447	457	497	465	484	494	501	Totale
Beef and veal	392	362	387	400	*372	*390	*398	404[1]	Bœuf et veau
Mutton and lamb	83	76	*66	82	*73	*79	*81	82[1]	Mouton et agneau
Pork	16	9	4	15	*20	*15	*15	15[1]	Porc
Viet Nam									**Viet Nam**
Total	1 191	1 232	1 323	1 396	1 502	1 599	1 614	1 860	Totale
Beef and veal	83	83[1]	72	79	89	92	97[1]	102	Bœuf et veau
Buffalo [1]	97	92	92	84	90	92	97	99	Buffle [1]
Goat [1]	4	5	5	5	5	5	5	5	Chèvre [1]
Pork	1 007	1 052	1 154	1 228	1 318	1 409	1 416	1 654	Porc
Yemen									**Yémen**
Total	79	81	86	90	93	99	105	105	Totale
Beef and veal	41	42	43	45	47	52	56	56[1]	Bœuf et veau
Goat [1]	18	19	21	22	22	23	24	24	Chèvre [1]
Mutton and lamb [1]	20	20	22	23	24	24	25	25	Mouton et agneau [1]
Europe									**Europe**
Total	**40 407**	**40 409**	**39 101**	**39 929**	**39 864**	**38 635**	**37 911**	**38 008**	**Totale**
Beef and veal	**13 963**	**13 642**	**13 170**	**12 569**	**12 123**	**11 774**	**11 516**	**11 594**	**Bœuf et veau**
Buffalo	**2**	**3**	**3**	**3**	**2**	**3**	**4**	**4**	**Buffle**
Goat	**130**	**135**	**130**	**131**	**122**	**128**	**130**	**130**	**Chèvre**
Mutton and lamb	**1 614**	**1 563**	**1 445**	**1 444**	**1 399**	**1 394**	**1 276**	**1 292**	**Mouton et agneau**
Pork	**24 698**	**25 065**	**24 353**	**25 781**	**26 219**	**25 335**	**24 984**	**24 987**	**Porc**
Albania									**Albanie**
Total	63	56	55	55	58	70	70	73	Totale
Beef and veal *	31	33	33	32	34	36	35	38	Bœuf et veau *
Goat	*4	*5	*4	*6	*6	12	12	12	Chèvre
Mutton and lamb	*15	*12	*11	*11	*12	*12	12[1]	12	Mouton et agneau
Pork	*14	*6	*7	*7	*6	10	10	11	Porc
Austria									**Autriche**
Total	768	821	823	865	894	717	712	733	Totale
Beef and veal	196	221	206	197	203	203	215	215[1]	Bœuf et veau
Goat	1	1	1	1	1	1	1	1[1]	Chèvre
Mutton and lamb	6	6	7	7	6	7	7	7[1]	Mouton et agneau
Pork	*566	*593	*610	*661	*684	*505	489	510[1]	Porc
Belarus									**Bélarus**
Total	582	554	556	594	576	528	556	558	Totale
Beef and veal	316	277	256	271	262	*269	*283	*285	Bœuf et veau
Mutton and lamb	4	4	*3	3	*3	*3	*3	*3	Mouton et agneau
Pork	263	273	298	320	311	*256	*270	*270	Porc
Belgium-Luxembourg									**Belgique-Luxembourg**
Total	1 405	1 436	1 377	1 393	1 290	1 353	1 382	1 405	Totale
Beef and veal	357	362	340	303	281	284	296	315	Bœuf et veau
Mutton and lamb	5	5	4	4	5	4	4	5[1]	Mouton et agneau
Pork	1 043	1 070	1 033	1 085	1 005	1 065	1 082	1 086	Porc
Bosnia and Herzegovina									**Bosnie-Herzégovine**
Total	35	27	24	27	27	26	27	21	Totale
Beef and veal	16	*13	10	12	12[1]	*13	*13	13[1]	Bœuf et veau
Mutton and lamb	3[1]	3	3[1]	3[1]	3[1]	3	3[1]	3[1]	Mouton et agneau
Pork [1]	17	11	11	12	12	11	11	6	Porc [1]
Bulgaria									**Bulgarie**
Total	366	388	334	356	389	353	363	373	Totale
Beef and veal	*63	*78	*56	*54	*63	*49	*62	62[1]	Bœuf et veau
Buffalo [1]	2	2	2	1	1	2	3	3	Buffle [1]
Goat	*5	*7	*6	*7	*8	*7	7[1]	7[1]	Chèvre
Mutton and lamb	*40	*49	*44	*46	*50	*52	*54	54[1]	Mouton et agneau
Pork	256	252	227	248	267	243	237	248[1]	Porc
Croatia									**Croatie**
Total	83	80	83	88	148	145	143	54	Totale
Beef and veal	26	22	26	26	28	28	26	18	Bœuf et veau
Mutton and lamb	*2	*2	*2	*2	4	2	2	0	Mouton et agneau
Pork	*56	*56	*55	*60	*116	115	115	36	Porc

41

Meat
Production: thousand metric tons *[cont.]*

Viande
Production: milliers de tonnes *[suite]*

Country or area	1995	1996	1997	1998	1999	2000	2001	2002	Pays ou zone
Czech Republic									**République tchèque**
Total	676	669	623	613	576	525	525	523	Totale
Beef and veal	170	164	156	134	121	107	109	106	Bœuf et veau
Mutton and lamb	*4	*3	*3	3	3	1	1	1	Mouton et agneau
Pork	502	502	464	476	452	417	415	416	Porc
Denmark									**Danemark**
Total	1 677	1 673	1 697	1 793	1 800	1 780	1 871	1 914	Totale
Beef and veal	182	178	175	162	157	154	153	154	Bœuf et veau
Mutton and lamb	2	2	2	2	1	1	2	1	Mouton et agneau
Pork	1 494	1 494	1 521	1 629	1 642	1 625	1 716	1 759	Porc
Estonia									**Estonie**
Total	62	54	49	52	53	46	48	47	Totale
Beef and veal	26	22	19	19	22	15	14	13	Bœuf et veau
Mutton and lamb	1	1	0	0	0	0	0	0	Mouton et agneau
Pork	35	32	30	32	31	30	34	34	Porc
Faeroe Islands									**Iles Féroé**
Total	1	1	1	1	1	1	1	1	Totale
Mutton and lamb [1]	1	1	1	1	1	1	1	1	Mouton et agneau [1]
Finland									**Finlande**
Total	265	270	281	279	273	265	266	276	Totale
Beef and veal	96	97	100	94	90	91	90	91	Bœuf et veau
Mutton and lamb	2	1	1	1	1	1	1	1	Mouton et agneau
Pork	168	172	180	185	182	173	176	184	Porc
France									**France**
Total	3 975	4 053	4 089	4 104	4 100	3 980	4 022	4 129	Totale
Beef and veal	1 683	1 737	1 720	1 632	1 609	1 528	1 566	1 640	Bœuf et veau
Goat	8	9	9	9	6	7	7	9[1]	Chèvre
Mutton and lamb	140	146	141	135	132	133	134	*130	Mouton et agneau
Pork	2 144	2 161	2 219	2 328	2 353	2 312	2 315	2 350	Porc
Germany									**Allemagne**
Total	5 052	5 160	5 056	5 246	5 521	5 334	5 482	5 483	Totale
Beef and veal	1 408	1 482	1 448	1 367	1 374	1 304	1 362	1 316	Bœuf et veau
Mutton and lamb	41	43	44	44	44	48	46	44	Mouton et agneau
Pork	3 602	3 635	3 564	3 834	4 103	3 982	4 074	4 123	Porc
Greece									**Grèce**
Total	353	352	349	348	330	332	319	317	Totale
Beef and veal	72	71	72	69	67	66	60	60[1]	Bœuf et veau
Goat	53	54	54	55	*46	*48	*44	44[1]	Chèvre
Mutton and lamb	90	91	89	90	*80	*78	*78	77[1]	Mouton et agneau
Pork	137	136	133	134	138	141	137	136[1]	Porc
Hungary									**Hongrie**
Total	638	723	638	619	680	689	633	632	Totale
Beef and veal	*58	*50	55	47	51	67	56	48[1]	Bœuf et veau
Mutton and lamb	*2	*2	2	3	4	8	9	9[1]	Mouton et agneau
Pork	*578	*671	581	570	626	*615	*568	575[1]	Porc
Iceland									**Islande**
Total	15	15	15	16	17	18	18	18	Totale
Beef and veal	3	3	3	3	4	4	4	4[1]	Bœuf et veau
Mutton and lamb	9	8	8	8	9	10	9	9[1]	Mouton et agneau
Pork	3	4	4	4	5	5	5	5[1]	Porc
Ireland									**Irlande**
Total	779	836	866	921	984	886	896	913	Totale
Beef and veal	477	535	568	594	644	577	579	595	Bœuf et veau
Mutton and lamb	89	90	79	86	90	83	78	*73	Mouton et agneau
Pork	212	211	220	242	250	226	238	245	Porc
Italy									**Italie**
Total	2 603	2 670	2 633	2 598	2 711	2 703	2 710	2 634	Totale
Beef and veal	1 180	1 181	1 159	1 111	1 164	1 154	1 133	1 060[1]	Bœuf et veau
Buffalo	0	1	2	1	1	1	1[1]	1[1]	Buffle
Goat	4	4	4	3	4	4	*6	6[1]	Chèvre
Mutton and lamb	73	74	72	70	70	65	60	*57	Mouton et agneau
Pork	1 346	1 410	1 396	1 412	1 472	1 479	1 510	1 510[1]	Porc

41

Meat
Production: thousand metric tons [cont.]

Viande
Production: milliers de tonnes [suite]

Country or area	1995	1996	1997	1998	1999	2000	2001	2002	Pays ou zone
Latvia									**Lettonie**
Total	112	67	63	63	55	54	51	52	Totale
Beef and veal	48	27	26	26	21	22	19	16	Bœuf et veau
Mutton and lamb	1	1	0	0	0	0	0	0	Mouton et agneau
Pork	63	40	37	36	35	32	32	36	Porc
Lithuania									**Lituanie**
Total	182	173	178	178	170	161	156	155	Totale
Beef and veal	87	83	90	81	77	75	64	65[1]	Bœuf et veau
Mutton and lamb	2	1	1	1	1	1	1	1[1]	Mouton et agneau
Pork	93	89	87	96	91	85	92	90[1]	Porc
Malta									**Malte**
Total	10	10	12	12	12	11	12	12	Totale
Beef and veal	2	2	2	2	2	2	2	2	Bœuf et veau
Pork	9	9	10	10	10	9	10	10	Porc
Netherlands									**Pays-Bas**
Total	2 218	2 222	1 956	2 277	2 237	2 112	1 840	1 906	Totale
Beef and veal	*580	580	565	535	508	471	364	*464	Bœuf et veau
Goat	0	0	0	0	*1	*0	0[1]	0[1]	Chèvre
Mutton and lamb	16	18	15	17	18	18	18	22[1]	Mouton et agneau
Pork	1 622	1 624	1 376	1 725	1 711	1 623	1 458	1 420	Porc
Norway									**Norvège**
Total	208	217	221	221	228	218	219	215	Totale
Beef and veal	85	86	89	91	96	91	86	88	Bœuf et veau
Mutton and lamb	27	27	26	23	23	23	24	24	Mouton et agneau
Pork	96	103	105	106	109	103	109	103	Porc
Poland									**Pologne**
Total	2 354	2 483	2 323	2 457	2 429	2 253	2 167	2 026	Totale
Beef and veal	386	415	429	430	385	329	316	*315	Bœuf et veau
Mutton and lamb	6	5	3	1	2	1	1	1[1]	Mouton et agneau
Pork	1 962	2 064	1 891	2 026	2 043	1 923	1 849	*1 710	Porc
Portugal									**Portugal**
Total	435	450	442	454	468	481	462	460	Totale
Beef and veal	104	99	109	96	97	100	95	95[1]	Bœuf et veau
Goat	3	3	3	3	3	2	2	3[1]	Chèvre
Mutton and lamb	24	23	24	23	22	24	22	22[1]	Mouton et agneau
Pork	305	325	306	332	346	*355	*343	340[1]	Porc
Republic of Moldova									**République de Moldova**
Total	110	106	104	86	88	70	61	62	Totale
Beef and veal	47	39	35	24	24	18	16	16	Bœuf et veau
Mutton and lamb	3	3	3	4	4	2	2	2	Mouton et agneau
Pork	60	64	66	58	61	50	44	44	Porc
Romania									**Roumanie**
Total	950	880	916	824	806	717	657	613	Totale
Beef and veal	202	177	185	150	153	162	145	145[1]	Bœuf et veau
Goat	*6	5	5	3	4	4	4	4[1]	Chèvre
Mutton and lamb	69	66	59	53	54	49	49	44[1]	Mouton et agneau
Pork	673	631	667	617	595	502	460	420[1]	Porc
Russian Federation									**Fédération de Russie**
Total	4 859	4 565	4 140	3 931	3 497	3 604	3 503	3 580	Totale
Beef and veal	2 733	2 630	2 394	2 247	1 868	1 895	1 872	*1 858	Bœuf et veau
Goat	*21	22	21	22	20	*17	*20	15[1]	Chèvre
Mutton and lamb	240	208	178	156	124	*123	*113	112[1]	Mouton et agneau
Pork	1 865	1 705	1 546	1 505	1 485	1 569	1 498	*1 595	Porc
Serbia and Montenegro									**Serbie-et-Monténégro**
Total	899	986	883	870	848	873	785	702	Totale
Beef and veal	227	*242	*209	*216	*185	*194	*172	94	Bœuf et veau
Goat [1]	1	1	1	1	1	1	1	1	Chèvre [1]
Mutton and lamb	28	30	30	29	22	23	22	17	Mouton et agneau
Pork	644	*713	*644	*625	*640	655[1]	590[1]	590[1]	Porc
Slovakia									**Slovaquie**
Total	304	314	322	288	272	213	193	194	Totale
Beef and veal	59	61	66	59	50	48	38	38	Bœuf et veau

41

Meat
Production: thousand metric tons *[cont.]*
   Viande
   Production: milliers de tonnes *[suite]*

Country or area	1995	1996	1997	1998	1999	2000	2001	2002	Pays ou zone
Mutton and lamb	2	2	2	2	1	2	2	2	Mouton et agneau
Pork	243	251	255	227	220	164	153	154	Porc
Slovenia									**Slovénie**
Total	112	117	114	106	111	102	116	103	Totale
Beef and veal	51	54	54	45	43	42	48	42[1]	Bœuf et veau
Mutton and lamb	0[1]	0[1]	1	1	1	1	1	1[1]	Mouton et agneau
Pork	61	63	59	61	67	59	66	60[1]	Porc
Spain									**Espagne**
Total	2 925	3 159	3 238	3 645	3 792	3 793	3 889	3 896	Totale
Beef and veal	508	565	592	651	661	632	642	*660	Bœuf et veau
Goat	15	14	16	16	17	16	17	*18	Chèvre
Mutton and lamb	227	223	229	233	221	232	236	233	Mouton et agneau
Pork	2 175	2 356	2 401	2 744	2 893	2 912	2 993	2 985	Porc
Sweden									**Suède**
Total	456	460	482	477	474	431	423	434	Totale
Beef and veal	143	138	149	143	145	150	143	146	Bœuf et veau
Mutton and lamb	3	4	4	3	4	4	4	4	Mouton et agneau
Pork	309	319	329	330	325	277	276	284	Porc
Switzerland									**Suisse**
Total	404	385	373	385	380	359	379	382	Totale
Beef and veal	147	159	152	147	146	128	138	140	Bœuf et veau
Goat	0	0	0	1	1	1	1	1[1]	Chèvre
Mutton and lamb	5	6	6	6	6	6	6	6[1]	Mouton et agneau
Pork	251	220	214	232	226	225	234	236	Porc
TFYR of Macedonia									**L'ex-R.y. Macédoine**
Total	26	26	23	22	21	21	23	24	Totale
Beef and veal	7	7	8	7	8	*7	*9	9[1]	Bœuf et veau
Mutton and lamb	10	10	7	6	4	5[1]	6[1]	6[1]	Mouton et agneau
Pork	9	9	9	9	9	9	8	9[1]	Porc
Ukraine									**Ukraine**
Total	2 032	1 869	1 664	1 482	1 467	1 447	1 253	1 323	Totale
Beef and veal	1 186	1 048	930	793	791	754	646	*680	Bœuf et veau
Goat	9	9	4	4	4	8	8	*10	Chèvre
Mutton and lamb	31	23	20	17	15	9	8	*10	Mouton et agneau
Pork	807	789	710	668	656	676	591	*623	Porc
United Kingdom									**Royaume-Uni**
Total	2 413	2 087	2 100	2 185	2 082	1 964	1 680	1 765	Totale
Beef and veal	1 002	710	688	699	679	706	645	692	Bœuf et veau
Mutton and lamb	394	373	321	351	361	359	258	299	Mouton et agneau
Pork	1 017	1 004	1 091	1 135	1 042	899	777	774	Porc
Oceania									**Océanie**
Total	**4 072**	**3 936**	**4 044**	**4 260**	**4 230**	**4 279**	**4 460**	**4 305**	**Totale**
Beef and veal	**2 447**	**2 399**	**2 478**	**2 611**	**2 593**	**2 581**	**2 692**	**2 632**	**Bœuf et veau**
Goat	**12**	**11**	**11**	**11**	**11**	**13**	**13**	**13**	**Chèvre**
Mutton and lamb	**1 155**	**1 084**	**1 109**	**1 161**	**1 145**	**1 213**	**1 277**	**1 152**	**Mouton et agneau**
Pork	**459**	**441**	**445**	**477**	**481**	**472**	**478**	**507**	**Porc**
Australia									**Australie**
Total	2 786	2 662	2 721	2 946	3 017	3 041	3 171	3 071	Totale
Beef and veal	1 803	1 745	1 810	1 955	2 011	1 988	2 080	2 034	Bœuf et veau
Goat [1]	10	9	9	8	8	11	11	11	Chèvre [1]
Mutton and lamb	622	574	566	616	628	680	715	631	Mouton et agneau
Pork	351	334	336	366	370	363	365	395	Porc
Cook Islands									**Iles Cook**
Total	0	1	1	1	1	1	1	1	Totale
Pork [1]	0	1	1	1	1	1	1	1	Porc [1]
Fiji									**Fidji**
Total	13	13	14	14	14	14	14	14	Totale
Beef and veal [1]	9	9	9	9	9	9	9	9	Bœuf et veau [1]
Goat	1	1	1	1[1]	1[1]	1[1]	1[1]	1[1]	Chèvre
Pork [1]	3	3	4	3	4	4	4	4	Porc [1]

41

Meat
Production: thousand metric tons *[cont.]*

Viande
Production: milliers de tonnes *[suite]*

Country or area	1995	1996	1997	1998	1999	2000	2001	2002	Pays ou zone
French Polynesia									**Polynésie française**
Total	2	1	1	1	2	2	2	1	Totale
Pork	1	1	1	1	1	1	1[1]	*1	Porc
Kiribati									**Kiribati**
Total	1	1	1	1	1	1	1	1	Totale
Pork[1]	1	1	1	1	1	1	1	1	Porc[1]
Micronesia (Fed. States)									**Micronésie (Etats féd. de)**
Total	1	1	1	1	1	1	1	1	Totale
Pork[1]	1	1	1	1	1	1	1	1	Porc[1]
New Caledonia									**Nouvelle-Calédonie**
Total	5	6	5	6	6	5	5	5	Totale
Beef and veal	4	4	4	4	4	4	4[1]	4[1]	Bœuf et veau
Pork	1	1	1	1	1	1	1[1]	1[1]	Porc
New Zealand									**Nouvelle-Zélande**
Total	1 209	1 194	1 240	1 231	1 129	1 153	1 201	1 145	Totale
Beef and veal	623	633	646	634	561	572	590	576	Bœuf et veau
Goat	2	1	2	2	2	1	2	2	Chèvre
Mutton and lamb	533	510	543	545	517	533	562	521	Mouton et agneau
Pork	51	50	49	50	49	47	47	47	Porc
Papua New Guinea									**Papouasie-Nvl-Guinée**
Total	41	42	45	46	46	46	50	50	Totale
Beef and veal[1]	2	3	2	3	3	3	3	3	Bœuf et veau[1]
Pork[1]	39	40	42	44	44	44	47	47	Porc[1]
Samoa									**Samoa**
Total	4	4	4	4	4	5	5	5	Totale
Beef and veal[1]	1	1	1	1	1	1	1	1	Bœuf et veau[1]
Pork	3[1]	3[1]	3[1]	3[1]	3[1]	4[1]	4	4[1]	Porc
Solomon Islands									**Iles Salomon**
Total	2	2	3	2	2	3	3	3	Totale
Beef and veal[1]	0	0	1	0	0	1	1	1	Bœuf et veau[1]
Pork[1]	2	2	2	2	2	2	2	2	Porc[1]
Tonga									**Tonga**
Total	2	2	2	2	2	2	2	2	Totale
Pork[1]	1	1	1	1	1	1	1	1	Porc[1]
Vanuatu									**Vanuatu**
Total	6	6	7	6	7	7	6	6	Totale
Beef and veal	4	4	4	4	4	4	3	3[1]	Bœuf et veau
Pork[1]	3	3	3	3	3	3	3	3	Porc[1]

Source:
Food and Agriculture Organization of the United Nations (FAO), Rome, "FAO Production Yearbook 2002" and the FAOSTAT Database.

Source:
Organisation de Nations Unies pour l'alimentation at l'agriculture (FAO), Rome, "Annuaire FAO de la production 2002" et la base de données FAOSTAT.

1 FAO estimate.
2 Data generally include those for Taiwan Province of China.

3 Data refer to the Gaza Strip.

1 Estimation de la FAO.
2 Les données comprennent en général les chiffres pour la province de Taiwan.
3 Les données se rapportent à la Bande de Gaza.

42
Beer
Production: thousand hectolitres
Bière
Production: milliers d'hectolitres

Country or area Pays ou zone	1992	1993	1994	1995	1996	1997	1998	1999	2000	2001
Albania Albanie	18	5	72	89	9	151	93	87	86	117
Algeria Algérie	337	421	398	402	377	370	382	383	453	435
Angola Angola	345	...	...	280[1]	797[1]	1 150[1]	1 288[1]	1 609[1]	...	...
Argentina Argentine	9 518	10 305	11 272	10 913	11 615	12 687	12 395	12 133	12 090	...
Armenia Arménie	149	70	70	53	29	50	133	84	79	100
Australia[2] Australie[2]	18 040	17 760	17 840	17 700	17 424	17 349	17 570	17 378	17 679	17 449
Austria Autriche	10 176	11 465	10 070	9 767	9 445	9 303	8 837	8 884	8 725	8 528
Azerbaijan Azerbaïdjan	1 855	148	114	22	13	16	12	69	71	116
Barbados Barbade	58	67	73	74	76	75	87	76	69	67
Belarus Bélarus	2 736	2 146	1 489	1 518	2 013	2 413	2 604	2 728	2 371	...
Belgium Belgique	14 259	...	15 055	15 110	14 648	14 758	14 763	15 166	...	...
Belize Belize	38	68	56	49	41	37	42	66	92	...
Benin[3] Bénin[3]	322	338	277	330	349	364	329	347	...	...
Bolivia Bolivie	1 333	1 121	1 262	*1 429	...	1 870	1 862	1 657	...	...
Botswana Botswana	1 289	1 374	1 305	1 366	1 351	1 005	1 019	1 591	1 976	...
Brazil Brésil	43 509	45 336	52 556	67 284	63 559	66 582	66 453	62 491	66 954	67 905
Bulgaria Bulgarie	4 695	4 247	4 792	4 331	4 402	3 031	3 796	4 045	4 048	4 093
Burkina Faso Burkina Faso	71	258	...	372[3]	435[3]	460[3]	501[3]	516[3]	...	...
Burundi Burundi	1 007	1 044	...	1 000[1]	980[1]	820[1]	780[1]	720[1]	...	...
Cameroon Cameroun	3 834	4 373	2 073	2 933	...	3 124	3 370	3 493	5 894	3 740
Central African Rep. Rép. centrafricaine	285	124	450	269	175[3]	209[3]	219[3]	243[3]	...	...
Chad Tchad	129	117	110	95	134[3]	123[3]	...	...	...	...
Chile Chili	3 349	3 623	3 303	3 551	3 459	3 640	3 666	3 343	3 221	3 374
China[4] Chine[4]	83 536	97 565	115 752	128 406	137 664	154 610	162 693	...	...	...
Colombia Colombie	14 574	...	15 739	20 525	...	18 290	16 461	14 213	...	...
Congo Congo	708	759	...	...	...	...	...	...	...	...
Croatia Croatie	2 720	2 481	3 122	3 166	3 292	3 607	3 759	3 663	3 847	3 799

42

Beer
Production: thousand hectolitres *[cont.]*

Bière
Production: milliers d'hectolitres *[suite]*

Country or area Pays ou zone	1992	1993	1994	1995	1996	1997	1998	1999	2000	2001
Cyprus Chypre	370	341	359	352	331	333	365	405	409	...
Czech Republic République tchèque	18 982	17 366	17 876	17 687	18 057	18 558	18 290	17 945	17 796	17 734
Denmark [5] Danemark [5]	9 775	9 435	9 410	9 903	9 591	9 181	8 044	8 205	7 455	7 233
Dominica Dominique	...	...	...	3	14	11	11	8	11	9
Dominican Republic Rép. dominicaine	1 956	1 992	2 190	2 082	447	2 593	2 993	3 484	3 666	3 176
Ecuador Equateur	1 826	1 525	1 131	3 201	2 163	238	633	555	353	...
Egypt Egypte	420	350	360	360	380	...	...	...	...	...
Estonia Estonie	426	419	477	492	459	543	744	957	950	1 015
Ethiopia [6] Ethiopie [6]	428	522	634	724	876	843	831	921	1 111	1 605
Fiji Fidji	173	167	160	150	170	170	170	185	179	184
Finland Finlande	4 685	4 579	4 524	4 702	4 980	4 840	4 341	4 733	4 559	4 798
France France	18 512	18 291	17 688	18 311	17 140	17 010	16 551	16 623	15 993	15 716
French Polynesia Polynésie française	129	...	...	...	...	...	...	...	...	...
Gabon Gabon	785	905	801	816	...	801	847	778	812	867
Georgia Géorgie	235	120	63	65	48	79	97	126	234	257
Germany Allemagne	114 089	111 075	113 428	111 875	108 938	108 729	106 993	107 479	106 877	106 372
Greece Grèce	4 025	4 088	4 376	4 024	3 766	3 950	3 886	4 129	4 223	4 502
Grenada Grenade	26	18	24	...	...	...	...	...	...	...
Guatemala Guatemala	1 172	1 327	805	1 471	1 655	1 303	1 363	1 443	1 406	...
Guyana Guyana	143	145	97	97[7]	112[7]	129[7]	131[7]	129[7]	118[7]	81[7]
Hungary Hongrie	9 162	7 877	8 082	7 697	7 270	6 973	7 163	6 996	5 984	7 142
Iceland Islande	32	41	54	52	63	64	71	77	88	123
India Inde	2 233[8]	3 053[8]	2 778[8]	3 700[8]	4 255[8]	4 331[8]	4 332[8]	3 632[8]	3 025[8]	2 352[9]
Indonesia Indonésie	1 145	871	779	1 136	...	531	502	401	...	...
Iran (Islamic Rep. of) [10] Iran (Rép. islamique d') [10]	...	...	...	...	...	130	155	127	145	...
Ireland Irlande	...	...	...	8 132	10 765	12 095	12 580[11]	...	...	...
Israel Israël	511	587	508	...	...	...	...	...	...	...

42

Beer
Production: thousand hectolitres [cont.]
Bière
Production: milliers d'hectolitres [suite]

Country or area Pays ou zone	1992	1993	1994	1995	1996	1997	1998	1999	2000	2001
Italy Italie	10 489	9 873	10 258	10 616	9 559	10 379	11 073	11 123	11 173	11 375
Jamaica Jamaïque	828	786	760	662	690	674	670	656	...	...
Japan [12] Japon [12]	70 106	69 642	71 007	67 971	69 082	66 370	61 759	58 901	54 638	48 131
Kazakhstan Kazakhstan	23 011	1 692	129	812	636	693	850	824	1 357	1 732
Kenya Kenya	3 686	3 589	3 250	3 474	2 759	#270 396	263 015	188 455	202 932	184 273
Korea, Republic of Corée, République de	15 673	15 252	17 176	17 554	17 210	16 907	14 080	14 866	16 544	17 765
Kyrgyzstan Kirghizistan	31	19	12	12	14	14	13	12	12	...
Lao People's Dem. Rep. Rép. dém. pop. lao	...	...	102	151	...	...	...	...	...	...
Latvia Lettonie	859	546	638	653	645	715	721	953	945	997
Lithuania Lituanie	1 426	1 164	1 353	1 093	1 139	1 413	1 559	1 848	2 105	2 192
Luxembourg Luxembourg	569	558	531	518	484	481	469	450	438	397
Madagascar Madagascar	226	228	219	246	347	234	297	...	...	...
Malawi Malawi	774	763	811	289	277	780	678	684	739	1 033
Mali Mali	41	40	43	52	60	...	...	...	...	...
Mauritius Maurice	295	292	283	309	312	340	376	358	375	*328
Mexico Mexique	42 262	43 630	45 060	44 205	48 111	51 315	54 569	57 905	59 851	61 632
Mozambique Mozambique	211	204	118	244	374	631	75	95	989	982
Myanmar [13] Myanmar [13]	19	24	13	...	...	...	...	...	...	...
Nepal [14] Népal [14]	123	144	149	168	183	215	139	188	217	233
Netherlands [5] Pays-Bas [5]	20 419[15]	19 720[15]	21 200[15]	22 380[15]	22 670[15]	23 780[15]	23 040[15]	23 799[15]	24 956[15]	24 606
New Zealand Nouvelle-Zélande	3 637[5]	3 519[5]	3 568[5]	3 488[5]	3 435[5]	3 214	3 206	3 148	2 980	3 070
Nigeria Nigéria	11 438	16 860	1 561	1 461	...	...	...	...	...	...
Norway Norvège	2 273	...	...	2 255	...	2 396	1 833	2 651	...	2 462
Panama Panama	1 163	1 204	1 291	1 274	1 229	1 335	1 448	1 461	1 399	...
Paraguay Paraguay	1 140	1 710	...	...	...	...	...	...	...	...
Peru Pérou	6 764	7 060	6 957	7 817	7 435	7 431	6 557	6 168	5 706	*5 296
Poland Pologne	14 139	12 585	14 099	15 205	16 667	19 281	21 017	23 360	25 231	25 163

42

Beer
Production: thousand hectolitres *[cont.]*

Bière
Production: milliers d'hectolitres *[suite]*

Country or area Pays ou zone	1992	1993	1994	1995	1996	1997	1998	1999	2000	2001
Portugal Portugal	6 923	6 662	6 902	7 220	6 958	6 766	7 072	6 945	7 090	6 830
Puerto Rico Porto Rico	654	477	438	397	360	317	263	259	...	...
Republic of Moldova République de Moldova	410	297[16]	233[16]	276[16]	226[16]	238[16]	278[16]	202[16]	249[16]	315[16]
Romania Roumanie	10 014	9 929	9 047	8 768	8 118	7 651	9 989	11 133	12 664	12 087
Russian Federation Fédération de Russie	27 900	24 700	21 800	21 400	20 800	26 100	33 600	44 500	51 600	63 700
Saint Kitts and Nevis Saint-Kitts-et-Nevis	16	17	17	17	20	19	...	...	...	...
Serbia and Montenegro Serbie-et-Monténégro	4 413	3 019	5 043	5 611	5 987	6 106	6 630	6 786[17]	6 735	6 063
Seychelles Seychelles	70	65	58	58	63	71	72	68	70	...
Slovakia Slovaquie	3 686	3 967	4 974	4 369	4 666	5 577	4 478	4 473	4 491	4 520
Slovenia Slovénie	1 783	1 978	2 075	2 087	2 223	2 138	2 000	2 022	2 571	...
South Africa Afrique du Sud	18 290	...	...	...	...	...	...	...	...	...
Spain Espagne	24 279	21 353	25 587	25 396	24 520	24 786	22 428	26 007	26 388	26 802
Suriname Suriname	71	107	69	65	72	...	...	...	...	...
Sweden Suède	4 969	5 087	5 379	5 471	5 318	5 078	4 763	4 718	4 686	4 522
Switzerland[5] Suisse[5]	4 020	3 804	3 828	3 672	...	...	...	...	...	...
Syrian Arab Republic Rép. arabe syrienne	102	104	102	102	102	97	97	121	91	...
Tajikistan Tadjikistan	135	82	67	47	6	6	9	7	4	8
Thailand Thaïlande	3 252	4 153	5 230	6 473	7 591	8 742	9 770	10 422	11 650	12 380
TFYR of Macedonia L'ex-R.y. Macédoine	861	952	725	620	622	600	578	652	661	618
Trinidad and Tobago Trinité-et-Tobago	395	424	482	428	419	407	517	522	625	...
Tunisia Tunisie	494	601	689	659	662	780	813	912	1 066	...
Turkey Turquie	4 843	5 524	6 019	6 946	7 381	7 656	7 130	7 188	7 649	7 441
Turkmenistan Turkménistan	372	287	218	113	17	44	29	37	52	79
Uganda Ouganda	187	239	308	512	642	896	1 105	1 178	...	...
Ukraine Ukraine	10 997	9 086	9 087	7 102	6 025	6 125	6 842	8 407	10 765	13 059
United Kingdom Royaume-Uni	...	...	66 161	59 337	61 262	64 816	60 915	62 510	58 913	...
United Rep. of Tanzania Rép.-Unie de Tanzanie	493	570	568	893	125	148	...	...	...	...

42

Beer
Production: thousand hectolitres *[cont.]*
Bière
Production: milliers d'hectolitres *[suite]*

Country or area Pays ou zone	1992	1993	1994	1995	1996	1997	1998	1999	2000	2001
United States [18] Etats-Unis [18]	237 029	237 345	237 987	...	233 485	...	...	...	...	...
Uruguay Uruguay	...	817	...	998	913	939	860	741	706	629
Uzbekistan Ouzbékistan	1 434	1 363	1 291	724	677	619	569[19]	422[19]	609[19]	...
Viet Nam Viet Nam	1 685	...	...	4 650	5 330	5 810	6 700	*6 480	7 791	8 170
Yemen Yémen	40	...	...	...	...	...	...	...	...	...

Source:
United Nations Statistics Division, New York, "Industrial Commodity Statistics Yearbook 2001" and the industrial statistics database.

Source:
Organisation des Nations Unies, Division de statistique, New York, "Annuaire de statistiques industrielles par produit 2001" et la base de données pour les statistiques industrielles.

1   Source: Economist Intelligence Unit (London).
2   Twelve months ending 30 June of the year stated.
3   Source: Afristat: Sub-Saharan African Observatory of Economics and Statistics (Bamako, Mali).
4   Original data in metric tons.
5   Sales.
6   Twelve months ending 7 July of the year stated.
7   Source: Bank of Guyana, Statistical Bulletin.
8   Production by large and medium scale establishments only.
9   Production by establishments employing 50 or more persons.
10 Production by establishments employing 10 or more persons.
11 Beginning 1999, data are confidential.
12 Twelve months beginning 1 April of the year stated.
13 Government production only.
14 Twelve months beginning 16 July of the year stated.
15 Production by establishments employing 20 or more persons.
16 Excluding the Transnistria region.
17 Beginning 1999, data for Kosovo are not included.
18 Twelve months ending 30 September of the year stated.
19 Source: Statistical Yearbook for Asia and the Pacific, United Nations Economic and Social Council for Asia and the Pacific (Bangkok).

1   Source: "Economist Intelligence Unit", (London).
2   Période de 12 mois finissant le 30 juin de l'année indiquée.
3   Source: Afristat: Sub-Saharan African Observatory of Economics and Statistics (Bamako, Mali).
4   Données d'origine exprimées en tonnes.
5   Ventes.
6   Période de 12 mois finissant le 7 juillet de l'année indiquée.
7   Source: Bank of Guyana, "Statistical Bulletin".
8   Production des grandes et moyennes entreprises seulement.
9   Production des établissements occupant 50 personnes ou plus.
10 Production des établissements occupant 10 personnes ou plus.
11 A partir de 1999, les données sont confidentielles.
12 Période de 12 mois commençant le 1er avril de l'année indiquée.
13 Production de l'Etat seulement.
14 Période de 12 mois commençant le 16 juillet de l'année indiquée.
15 Production des établissements occupant 20 personnes ou plus.
16 Non compris la région de Transnistria.
17 A partir de 1999, non compris les données de Kosovo.
18 Période de 12 mois finissant le 30 septembre de l'année indiquée.
19 Source: "Statistical Yearbook for Asia and the Pacific, United Nations Economic and Social Council for Asia and the Pacific" (Bangkok).

43

Cigarettes
Production: millions

Cigarettes
Production: millions

Country or area Pays ou zone	1992	1993	1994	1995	1996	1997	1998	1999	2000	2001
Albania [1] Albanie [1]	1 393	1 395	929	685	4 830	414	764	647	372	126
Algeria [1] Algérie [1]	16 426	16 260	16 345	...	...	...	...	...	...	...
Angola [2] Angola [2]	2 400	...	...	...	...	...	...	...	...	...
Argentina Argentine	1 845	1 929	1 975	1 963	1 971	1 940	1 967	1 996	1 843	...
Armenia Arménie	3 927	1 878	2 014	1 043	152	815	2 489	3 132	2 109	1 623
Australia * [3] Australie * [3]	34 000	...	...	...	...	...	...	...	...	...
Austria Autriche	15 836	16 247	16 429	16 297	...	...	...	...	...	...
Azerbaijan Azerbaïdjan	4 855	5 277	3 179	1 926	766	827	241	416	2 362	6 808
Bangladesh [4] Bangladesh [4]	12 535	11 516	12 655	17 379	16 222	18 601	19 889	19 558	19 732	20 050
Barbados Barbade	115[1]	133[1]	150[1]	65	...	...	...	...	...	...
Belarus Bélarus	8 847	8 670	7 378	6 228	6 267	6 787	7 296	9 259	10 356	
Belgium Belgique	29 576[5]	27 173[5]	21 366	18 826	17 471	18 061	17 519	14 712	...	...
Belize Belize	104	105	101	95	79	88	94	91	84	...
Bolivia Bolivie	116	119	1 490	*170	...	148 409	153 771	140 434		
Brazil [2] Brésil [2]	169 000	...	...	...	...	...	...	...	...	...
Bulgaria Bulgarie	48 558	32 098	53 664	74 603	57 238	43 315	33 181	25 715	26 681	26 659
Burkina Faso Burkina Faso	979	943		...	...	...	...	...	...	...
Burundi Burundi	453	517	...	...	450[6]	377[6]	317[6]	353[6]	286[6]	...
Cambodia [2] Cambodge [2]	4 200	...	...	...	...	...	...	...	...	...
Cameroon Cameroun	5 000[2]	...	...	...	...	2 704	3 084	3 296	5 297	2 814
Canada Canada	45 500[2]	...	...	50 775	49 362	47 263	24 022	46 908	46 078	44 407
Central African Rep. Rép. centrafricaine	21	12	21	30	...	...	...	...	...	...
Chad Tchad	415	499	508	569						
Chile Chili	11 167	10 793	10 801	10 891	11 569	12 522	12 904	13 271	13 796	13 305
China Chine	1 642 340	1 655 630	...	...	...	...	...	...	...	...
China, Hong Kong SAR [5,7] Chine, Hong Kong RAS [5,7]	36 513	25 759	24 747	22 767	21 386	20 929	13 470	...	...	...
China, Macao SAR [1,8,9] Chine, Macao RAS [1,8,9]	500	500	450	450	450	...	...	...	...	...

43

Cigarettes
Production: millions *[cont.]*

Cigarettes
Production: millions *[suite]*

Country or area Pays ou zone	1992	1993	1994	1995	1996	1997	1998	1999	2000	2001
Colombia Colombie	14 877	...	11 566	10 491	...	11 662	12 472	15 182		...
Congo [1] Congo [1]	431	...	...	...		...	...	...		...
Costa Rica Costa Rica	2 000[2]	16[1,9]	16[1,9]	16[1,9]	16[1,9]	...	...	...		...
Côte d'Ivoire [2] Côte d'Ivoire [2]	4 500	...	...	...		...	...	...	...	...
Croatia Croatie	12 833	11 585	12 672	12 110	11 548	11 416	11 987	12 785	13 692	14 738
Cyprus Chypre	6 177	3 530	2 493	2 528	2 728	3 662	4 362	4 783	4 980	...
Dem. Rep. of the Congo [2] Rép. dém. du Congo [2]	5 200	...	...	...		...	...	...		...
Denmark [10] Danemark [10]	11 439	10 980	11 448	11 902	11 804	12 262	12 392	11 749	11 413	11 089
Dominican Republic Rép. dominicaine	4 432	4 356	4 696	4 092	4 192	3 972	4 098	4 005		
Ecuador Equateur	3 000	3 079	2 515	1 734	1 745	1 678	1 997	2 178	2 773	...
Egypt Egypte	42 516	38 844	39 145	42 469	46 000	50 000	52 000	51 000	53 000	...
El Salvador El Salvador	1 620[2]	...	...	1 701	1 756	...	...	...	...	...
Estonia Estonie	1 780	2 630	2 287	1 864	954	...		...	...	...
Ethiopia [11] Ethiopie [11]	1 879	1 932	1 468	1 583	1 862	2 024	2 029	1 829	1 931	1 904
Fiji Fidji	484	506	483	437	439	450	410	446	396	389
Finland Finlande	8 106	7 237	7 232	6 542	5 910	...	...	4 877	3 981	3 999
France France	*53 312	47 912	48 188	46 361	46 931	44 646	43 304	42 405	42 398	41 787
Gabon Gabon	399	334	288	297	...	331	463	670	859	880
Georgia Géorgie	4 953	3 593	3 256	1 840	1 183	917	601	1 327	296	1 615
Germany Allemagne	...	204 730	222 791	...	...	...	...	...	...	...
Ghana Ghana	*2 100	...	...	...	...	1 747	1 399	1 158	1 166	1 481
Greece Grèce	*29 250	30 427	32 843	39 291	38 268	36 909	21 427	34 322	34 381	33 256
Grenada Grenade	20	19	15	...		...	...	...		...
Guatemala Guatemala	2 001[2]	2 010	1 390	2 616	1 725	2 198	4 184	4 376	4 262	...
Guyana Guyana	318	302	314	318[12]	400[12]	221[12]	...	...		...
Haiti Haïti	970	1 110	722	...	...	...	...	...		
Honduras [2] Honduras [2]	2 200	...	...	...	...	...	...	...		...

43

Cigarettes
Production: millions [cont.]

Cigarettes
Production: millions [suite]

Country or area Pays ou zone	1992	1993	1994	1995	1996	1997	1998	1999	2000	2001
Hungary Hongrie	26 835	28 728	29 518	25 709	27 594	26 057	26 849	22 985	21 608	20 787
India Inde	61 413[13]	71 842[13]	71 038[13]	69 589[13]	73 841[13]	83 162[13]	79 313[13]	82 504[13]	75 085[13]	60 577[14]
Indonesia Indonésie	34 382	34 757	36 421	38 768	...	220 157	271 177	254 276		...
Iran (Islamic Rep. of) Iran (Rép. islamique d')	10 171[14]	7 835[14]	7 939[14]	9 787[15]	11 860[15]	10 304[15]	14 335[15]	20 143[15]	13 811[15]	
Iraq[2] Iraq[2]	5 794	...	...	...	...	...	...	...	...	...
Ireland Irlande	*7 850	7 300[1,9]	7 000[1,9]	7 500[1,9]	7 500[1,9]	4 605	6 452	6 176	6 461	6 807
Israel[1] Israël[1]	5 742	5 525	5 638	4 933	4 793	...	...	...	...	...
Italy Italie	53 799[1]	54 943[1]	55 175[1]	50 247[1]	51 489[1]	51 894[1]	50 785	45 159	43 694[1]	45 368[1]
Jamaica Jamaïque	1 299	1 224	1 273	1 216	1 219	1 175	1 160	1 078	991	...
Japan[16] Japon[16]	279 000	...	...	...	...	...	...	...	...	...
Jordan Jordanie	3 091	3 465	4 191	3 675	4 738	1 853[17]	1 144[17]	*1 602[17]	*1 300[17]	...
Kazakhstan Kazakhstan	8 997	10 664	9 393	12 080	19 121	24 109	21 747	18 773	19 293	21 395
Kenya Kenya	7 193	7 267	7 319	7 932	8 436	...	...	8 896	6 009	5 850
Korea, Republic of Corée, République de	96 648	96 887	90 774	87 959	94 709	96 725	101 011	95 995	94 531	94 116
Kyrgyzstan Kirghizistan	3 120	3 428	1 943	1 332	975	716	862	2 103	3 169	...
Lao People's Dem. Rep. Rép. dém. pop. lao	1 200[2]	...	936	1 062	...	856[18]	1 104[18]	...	...	...
Latvia Lettonie	3 435	2 589	2 093	2 101	1 876	1 775	2 018	1 916	...	...
Lebanon Liban	4 000[2]	...	...	535[1,19]	539[1]	793[1]	672[1]	945[1]	1 009[1]	...
Liberia[2] Libéria[2]	22	...	...	...	...	...	...	...	...	...
Libyan Arab Jamah.[2] Jamah. arabe libyenne[2]	3 500	...	...	...	...	...	...	...	...	...
Lithuania Lituanie	5 269	3 435	3 860	4 876	4 538	5 755	7 427	8 217	7 207	8 075
Madagascar[1] Madagascar[1]	2 223	2 304	2 003	2 354	2 957	2 826	3 303	...	...	...
Malawi Malawi	1 000	1 020	1 127	1 160	975	731	501	0	0	0
Malaysia Malaisie	16 574[1]	15 568[1]	15 762[1]	15 918[1]	16 896[1]	20 236[1]	18 410[1]	15 504[1]	27 271[1]	25 618
Mali Mali	24	23	20	22	21	...	...	...	...	...
Malta[2] Malte[2]	1 475	...	...	...	...	...	...	...	...	...
Mauritius Maurice	1 060	1 269	1 300	1 215	1 193	1 144	1 034	979	1 049	*861

43

Cigarettes
Production: millions *[cont.]*

Cigarettes
Production: millions *[suite]*

Country or area Pays ou zone	1992	1993	1994	1995	1996	1997	1998	1999	2000	2001
Mexico Mexique	55 988	53 435	53 402	56 821	59 907	57 618	60 407	59 492	56 383	56 057
Morocco Maroc	515	...	...	...	...	...	...	...	...	...
Mozambique Mozambique	124	377	343	106	250	250	950	1 084	1 417	1 359
Myanmar [20] Myanmar [20]	396	426	440	752	1 727	1 991	2 040	2 270	2 559	2 650
Nepal [21] Népal [21]	6 963	7 846	6 894	7 430	8 067	7 944	8 127	7 315	6 584	6 979
Netherlands [10,22] Pays-Bas [10,22]	78 479	71 254	88 069	97 727	...	...	...	...	...	...
New Zealand Nouvelle-Zélande	3 466	3 381	3 396[10]	3 338[10]	3 660[10]	3 449	3 263	3 010	3 277	2 502
Nicaragua Nicaragua	2 400[2]	...	...	...	...	1 580	1 789	780[23]	...	...
Nigeria Nigéria	8 608	9 384	338	256	...	...	...	...	...	...
Norway [2] Norvège [2]	1 825	...	...	...	...	...	...	...	...	...
Pakistan [4] Pakistan [4]	29 673	29 947	35 895	32 747	45 506	46 101	48 215	51 579	46 976	58 259
Panama Panama	806	903	1 204	1 136	663	752	320	...	...	...
Paraguay Paraguay	777	...	...	...	...	...	...	...	...	...
Peru Pérou	2 501	2 511	2 752	3 041	3 358	3 028	3 115	3 580	3 605	*3 310
Philippines [1,9] Philippines [1,9]	6 771	7 135	7 300	7 440	7 440	...	...	...	...	...
Poland Pologne	86 571	90 713	98 394	100 627	95 293	95 798	96 741	95 056	83 800	81 697
Portugal Portugal	15 619	15 335	13 610	13 215	12 780	13 234	15 781	17 742	21 377	23 479
Republic of Moldova République de Moldova	8 582	8 790[24]	8 001[24]	7 108[24]	9 657[24]	9 539[24]	7 512[24]	8 731[24]	9 262[24]	9 421[24]
Romania [3] Roumanie [3]	17 781	15 222	14 532	14 747	16 536	25 943	...	...	...	...
Russian Federation Fédération de Russie	107 763	100 162	91 601	99 545	112 319	140 077	195 806	266 031	333 953	355 632
Senegal [2] Sénégal [2]	3 350	...	...	...	...	...	...	...	...	...
Serbia and Montenegro Serbie-et-Monténégro	15 654	16 053	12 972	12 686	13 176	10 988	14 597	13 126[25]	14 451	13 968
Seychelles Seychelles	62	65	49	56	62	70	61	60	40	...
Sierra Leone [2] Sierra Leone [2]	1 200	...	...	...	...	...	...	...	...	...
Singapore [2] Singapour [2]	11 760	...	...	...	...	...	...	...	...	...
Slovenia Slovénie	5 278	4 851	4 722	4 543	4 909	5 767	7 555	8 032	7 855	...
South Africa Afrique du Sud	35 563	34 499	...	...	...	...	...	...	...	...

43

Cigarettes
Production: millions *[cont.]*

Cigarettes
Production: millions *[suite]*

Country or area Pays ou zone	1992	1993	1994	1995	1996	1997	1998	1999	2000	2001
Spain Espagne	76 696	80 103	81 886	78 676	77 675	77 315	81 940	74 873	74 799	...
Sri Lanka Sri Lanka	5 359	5 649	5 656	5 822	6 160	5 712	5 797	5 333	4 889	*4 973
Sudan [2] Soudan [2]	750	...	...	...	...	...	...	...	...	...
Suriname Suriname	419	454	443	472	483	...	...	...	...	...
Sweden Suède	9 841	7 420	8 032	7 193	7 251	6 237	5 692	6 060	5 958	5 979
Switzerland Suisse	33 740	34 713	39 906	41 976	42 955	37 638	34 453	32 139	34 299	33 565
Syrian Arab Republic [1] Rép. arabe syrienne [1]	8 093	7 185	7 773	9 699	8 528	10 137	10 398	10 991	11 097	12 007
Tajikistan Tadjikistan	2 607	1 901	1 644	964	604	153	191	209	667	1 155
Thailand Thaïlande	40 691	42 043	45 359	43 020	48 173	43 387	34 585	31 146	30 732	29 807
TFYR of Macedonia L'ex-R.y. Macédoine	...	...	...	...	...	...	...	...		7 766
Trinidad and Tobago Trinité-et-Tobago	656[1]	638	593	920	1 102	1 386	1 680	1 945	2 050	
Tunisia Tunisie	7 797	6 965	7 128	7 421	7 159	7 735	9 813	11 066	12 231	...
Turkey Turquie	67 549[1]	74 845[1]	85 093[1]	80 700[1]	73 787[1]	74 984[1]	81 616[1]	75 135[1]	76 613[1]	77 160
Uganda Ouganda	1 575	1 412	1 459	1 576	1 702	1 864	1 866	1 688	...	...
Ukraine Ukraine	60 990	40 571	47 083	48 033	44 900	54 488	59 275	54 052	58 774	69 731
United Kingdom Royaume-Uni	*126 538	146 138	165 479	155 103	166 496	167 670	152 998	143 794	139 125	
United Rep. of Tanzania Rép.-Unie de Tanzanie	3 789	3 893	3 383	3 699	3 733	4 710	...	...		
United States Etats-Unis	718 500	661 000	725 500	746 500	754 500	719 600	679 700	611 929		
Uruguay Uruguay	3 900[2]	3 736	...	3 561	6 018	6 872	10 187	11 161	10 894	9 616
Uzbekistan Ouzbékistan	4 150	4 151	3 379	2 742	5 172	8 521	7 582[18]	10 668[18]	7 766[18]	...
Venezuela [2] Venezuela [2]	24 400	...	...	...	...	...	...	...	...	...
Viet Nam * Viet Nam *	24 600	...	...	...	...	...	...	...	...	...
Yemen Yémen	6 294[1,9]	8 844[1,9]	5 423[1,9]	6 540	6 740	6 800	5 980	5 760	4 780	4 900
Zambia [2] Zambie [2]	1 500	...	...	...	...	...	...	...	...	...
Zimbabwe [2] Zimbabwe [2]	3 025	...	...	...	...	...	...	...	...	...

Source:
United Nations Statistics Division, New York, "Industrial Commodity Statistics Yearbook 2001" and the industrial statistics database.

Source:
Organisation des Nations Unies, Division de statistique, New York, "Annuaire de statistiques industrielles par produit 2001" et la base de données pour les statistiques industrielles.

43

Cigarettes
Production: millions *[cont.]*

Cigarettes
Production: millions *[suite]*

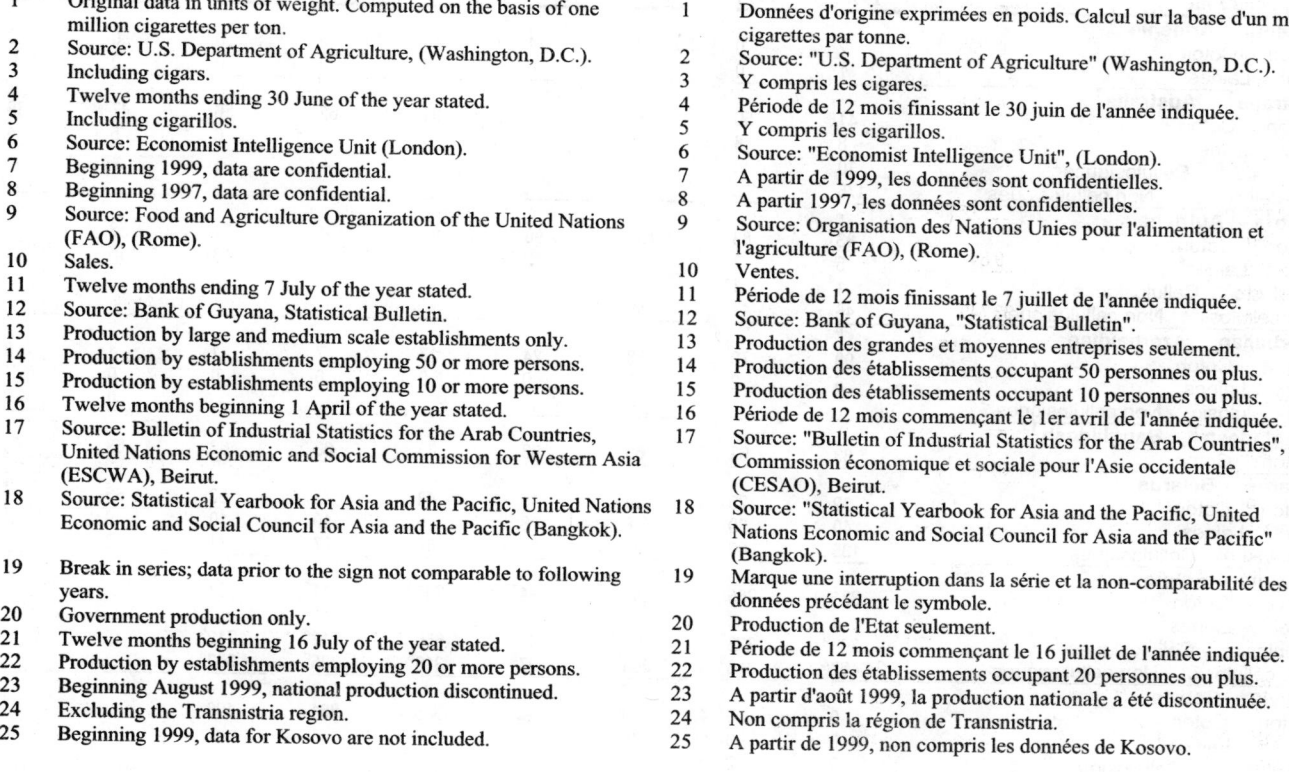

1	Original data in units of weight. Computed on the basis of one million cigarettes per ton.
2	Source: U.S. Department of Agriculture, (Washington, D.C.).
3	Including cigars.
4	Twelve months ending 30 June of the year stated.
5	Including cigarillos.
6	Source: Economist Intelligence Unit (London).
7	Beginning 1999, data are confidential.
8	Beginning 1997, data are confidential.
9	Source: Food and Agriculture Organization of the United Nations (FAO), (Rome).
10	Sales.
11	Twelve months ending 7 July of the year stated.
12	Source: Bank of Guyana, Statistical Bulletin.
13	Production by large and medium scale establishments only.
14	Production by establishments employing 50 or more persons.
15	Production by establishments employing 10 or more persons.
16	Twelve months beginning 1 April of the year stated.
17	Source: Bulletin of Industrial Statistics for the Arab Countries, United Nations Economic and Social Commission for Western Asia (ESCWA), Beirut.
18	Source: Statistical Yearbook for Asia and the Pacific, United Nations Economic and Social Council for Asia and the Pacific (Bangkok).
19	Break in series; data prior to the sign not comparable to following years.
20	Government production only.
21	Twelve months beginning 16 July of the year stated.
22	Production by establishments employing 20 or more persons.
23	Beginning August 1999, national production discontinued.
24	Excluding the Transnistria region.
25	Beginning 1999, data for Kosovo are not included.

1	Données d'origine exprimées en poids. Calcul sur la base d'un million cigarettes par tonne.
2	Source: "U.S. Department of Agriculture" (Washington, D.C.).
3	Y compris les cigares.
4	Période de 12 mois finissant le 30 juin de l'année indiquée.
5	Y compris les cigarillos.
6	Source: "Economist Intelligence Unit", (London).
7	A partir de 1999, les données sont confidentielles.
8	A partir 1997, les données sont confidentielles.
9	Source: Organisation des Nations Unies pour l'alimentation et l'agriculture (FAO), (Rome).
10	Ventes.
11	Période de 12 mois finissant le 7 juillet de l'année indiquée.
12	Source: Bank of Guyana, "Statistical Bulletin".
13	Production des grandes et moyennes entreprises seulement.
14	Production des établissements occupant 50 personnes ou plus.
15	Production des établissements occupant 10 personnes ou plus.
16	Période de 12 mois commençant le 1er avril de l'année indiquée.
17	Source: "Bulletin of Industrial Statistics for the Arab Countries", Commission économique et sociale pour l'Asie occidentale (CESAO), Beirut.
18	Source: "Statistical Yearbook for Asia and the Pacific, United Nations Economic and Social Council for Asia and the Pacific" (Bangkok).
19	Marque une interruption dans la série et la non-comparabilité des données précédant le symbole.
20	Production de l'Etat seulement.
21	Période de 12 mois commençant le 16 juillet de l'année indiquée.
22	Production des établissements occupant 20 personnes ou plus.
23	A partir d'août 1999, la production nationale a été discontinuée.
24	Non compris la région de Transnistria.
25	A partir de 1999, non compris les données de Kosovo.

44

Fabrics
Woven cotton, wool, cellulosic and non-cellulosic fibres: million square metres

Tissus
Tissus de coton, laines, fibres cellulosiques et non cellulosiques : miillions de mètres carrés

Country or area Pays ou zone	1993	1994	1995	1996	1997	1998	1999	2000	2001
Armenia Arménie									
Cotton Coton	2	0	0	1	0	0	0	0	0
Wool Laines	1	0	0	0	0	0	0	0	0
Australia[1] Australie[1]									
Cotton Coton	41	50	52	64	61	62	56	47	39
Wool Laines	8	8	8	7	6	7	6	5	4
Cellulosic [2] Cellulosiques [2]	10	...	...	...	...	...	...	...	...
Non-cellulosic [3] Non cellulosiques [3]	175	...	...	...	...	...	...	...	...
Austria Autriche									
Cotton Coton	83	83	101	96	95	101	74	58	62
Wool Laines	5	3	2	12	13	17	13	15	...
Cellulosic Cellulosiques	1[4]	1[4]	...	...	...	...	...	...	...
Non-cellulosic Non cellulosiques	46	41	59	...	...	...	...	...	...
Azerbaijan Azerbaïdjan									
Cotton Coton	98	78	58	24	17	7	1	1	3
Wool Laines	5	2	1	0	0	0	0	0	...
Non-cellulosic Non cellulosiques	...	...	...	...	...	...	...	0	0
Bangladesh[1] Bangladesh[1]									
Cotton Coton	63	63	63	63	63	63	63	63	63
Belarus Bélarus									
Cotton Coton	92	25	34	45	48	72	50	65	...
Wool Laines	40	20	8	8	9	10	10	9	...
Cellulosic Cellulosiques	135	80	35	39	67	77	71	62	
Belgium Belgique									
Cotton Coton	331	255	256[8]	294[8]	298[8]	311[8]	301[8]	...	
Wool[5] Laines[5]	4	...	...	...	...	...	...	...	
Cellulosic Cellulosiques	309[6]	328[8]	590[8]	602[8]	656[8]	712[8]	712[8]	...	
Non-cellulosic Non cellulosiques	4 467[7]	316[8]	288[8]	297[8]	316[8]	305[8]	302[8]	...	
Bolivia Bolivie									
Cotton Coton	0[9]	0[9]	*0[9]	...	985	881	108	...	
Wool[9] Laines[9]	0	0	*0	...	...	...	...	...	
Cellulosic [9] Cellulosiques [9]	2	2	*2	...	...	...	...	...	
Brazil[9] Brésil[9]									
Cotton Coton	1 568[10,11]	1 566[10]	1 354	1 318	1 278	1 209	1 270	1 339	
Bulgaria Bulgarie									
Cotton Coton	83[12]	86[12]	93[12]	85[12]	98[12]	96[9]	62[9]	59[9]	...
Wool [12] Laines [12]	23	21	20	18	17	10[9]	8[9]	8[9]	
Cameroon[9] Cameroun[9]									
Cotton Coton	18	35	24	...	...	...	...	...	
Chile[9] Chili[9]									
Cotton Coton	32	28	29	34	31	27	21	25	...
China[9] Chine[9]									
Cotton Coton	24 263	25 243	31 091	24 987	29 730	28 800	29 875	33 102	...
Wool Laines	388	413	1 079	758	640	442	451	459	...
China, Hong Kong SAR Chine, Hong Kong RAS									
Cotton Coton	755	692	658	540	506	341[14]	366[14]	306[14]	378[14]
Cellulosic [13] Cellulosiques [13]	3	3	1	...	21	...	...	...	...
Non-cellulosic Non cellulosiques	0	0	0	...	...	...	...	...	...
China, Macao SAR Chine, Macao RAS									
Cotton Coton	15	10	8	9	9	10	11	7	0
Colombia Colombie									
Cotton[9] Coton[9]	238	210	90	...	88	76	54	...	...
Wool[9] Laines[9]	1	1	1	...	1	1	1	...	...
Cellulosic [9] Cellulosiques [9]	...	...	...	...	78	69	...	...	...
Non-cellulosic Non cellulosiques	24[8]	20[8]	22[8]	...	20[9]	21[9]	16[9]	...	...
Congo[9] Congo[9]									
Cotton Coton	2	...	...	...	...	...	...	...	...

44

Fabrics
Woven cotton, wool, cellulosic and non-cellulosic fibres: million square metres *[cont.]*
Tissus
Tissus de coton, laines, fibres cellulosiques et non cellulosiques : millions de mètres carrés *[suite]*

Country or area Pays ou zone	1993	1994	1995	1996	1997	1998	1999	2000	2001
Croatia Croatie									
Cotton Coton	29	23	22	19	34	39	34	34	37
Wool Laines	7	7	7	5	3	2	2	2	2
Cellulosic Cellulosiques	10	10	8	5	6	7	7	6	1
Non-cellulosic Non cellulosiques	4	1	1	3	5	5	2	2	2
Czech Republic République tchèque									
Cotton Coton	337	340	358	330	346	331	265	313	341
Wool Laines	43	34	32	30	28	28	17	14	14
Cellulosic Cellulosiques	...	...	...	...	...	...	...	32	34
Non-cellulosic Non cellulosiques	29	...	...	...	...	...	...	265	290
Denmark [15] Danemark [15]									
Cotton Coton	...	...	...	5	19	6	2	1	0
Wool Laines	1	1	1	1	1	0	0	1	2
Ecuador [9] Equateur [9]									
Wool Laines	2	2	3	2	0	2	2	...	...
Cellulosic Cellulosiques	39	36	36	21	0	21	20	...	...
Egypt Egypte									
Cotton Coton	329	494	414	1 561	1 474	1 559	1 524	1 559	...
Wool Laines	9	14	14	8	8	8	7	6	...
Estonia Estonie									
Cotton Coton	55	74	90	120	130	127	95	124	117
Wool Laines	1	0	0	0	0	0	0	0	0
Ethiopia Ethiopie									
Cotton [16] Coton [16]	36	61	50	48	35	38	43	38	45
Wool Laines	...	0	0	0	0	0	0	0	0
Non-cellulosic [16] Non cellulosiques [16]	4	4	5	5	4	5	4	3	1
Finland Finlande									
Cotton [12] Coton [12]	20	19	8	9	...	...	...	...	...
Wool * [12] Laines * [12]	0	...	...	...	...	...	...	...	...
Cellulosic * [12] Cellulosiques * [12]	1	1	0	0	...	...	...	...	...
Non-cellulosic Non cellulosiques	13	11	8	8	...	...	...	...	...
France France									
Cotton Coton	761[8]	691[8]	682[8]	672[8]	689[8]	658[8]	702[8]	579	548
Wool Laines	9	37	...	...	...	...	...	...	...
Cellulosic Cellulosiques	2 716	2 758	...	...	...	...	...	...	...
Non-cellulosic Non cellulosiques	175	126	...	...	...	...	...	...	...
Georgia Géorgie									
Cotton Coton	7	2	1	1	0	0	0	0	...
Wool Laines	2	1	0	0	0	0	0	0	...
Germany Allemagne									
Cotton Coton	687	635	444	466	489	506	432	452	544
Wool Laines	97	...	87	87	87	79	63	57	56
Cellulosic Cellulosiques	341	324	387	325	311	335	294	290	163
Non-cellulosic Non cellulosiques	813	792	942	851	914	934	938	945	866
Greece Grèce									
Cotton Coton	119[10]	94[10]	72[10]	...	...	29	...	...	27
Wool Laines	3	2	2	2	3	3	...	...	2
Cellulosic Cellulosiques	0	0	...	...	...	...	...	...	...
Non-cellulosic [17,18] Non cellulosiques [17,18]	19	29	15	...	...	...	...	...	...
Hungary Hongrie									
Cotton [12] Coton [12]	78	76	66	...	79	44	48	47	...
Wool [12] Laines [12]	3	1	1	...	0	...	...	...	...
Cellulosic Cellulosiques	14[12]	12[12]	12[12]	...	...	2[12]	0[12]	0[12]	1
Non-cellulosic Non cellulosiques	6[12]	6[12]	6[12]	...	...	95[12,19]	231[12]	255[12]	291
Iceland Islande									
Wool Laines	0	0	...	...	...	...	...	...	...
India Inde									
Cotton Coton	19 648	...	...	...	...	...	...	...	...
Indonesia [9] Indonésie [9]									
Wool Laines	1	...	...	...	...	...	...	...	...

44

Fabrics
Woven cotton, wool, cellulosic and non-cellulosic fibres: million square metres [cont.]

Tissus
Tissus de coton, laines, fibres cellulosiques et non cellulosiques : millions de mètres carrés [suite]

Country or area / Pays ou zone	1993	1994	1995	1996	1997	1998	1999	2000	2001
Italy[8] Italie[8]									
Cotton Coton	1 422	1 521	1 585	1 555	1 609	1 657	1 570	...	...
Wool Laines	426	443	433	431	445	396	...	...	...
Japan Japon									
Cotton Coton	1 205	1 180	1 029	916	917	842	774	664	603
Wool Laines	287[20]	286[20]	249[20]	247[20]	247[20]	213[20]	199[20]	98[20]	95
Cellulosic Cellulosiques	493	435	409	441	456	390	352	273	241
Non-cellulosic Non cellulosiques	2 265[20]	2 143[20]	2 050[20]	1 997[20]	2 041[20]	1 743[20]	1 581[20]	1 573[20]	1 484
Kazakhstan Kazakhstan									
Cotton Coton	136	85	21	21	14	10	9	5	8
Wool Laines	20	10	3	2	2	1	0	0	0
Kenya Kenya									
Cotton Coton	28	27	22	28	...	...	...	...	
Wool Laines	0	9	1	1	...	...	...	...	
Korea, Republic of Corée, République de									
Cotton[12] Coton[12]	480	447	379	...	...	...	...	...	...
Wool Laines	19[12]	20	18	17	14	7	6	9	9
Non-cellulosic Non cellulosiques	2 459	2 540	2 594	...	...	...	...	...	
Kyrgyzstan Kirghizistan									
Cotton Coton	65	49	21	25	20	13	12	6	...
Wool Laines	9	4	2	3	3	2	1	1	
Latvia Lettonie									
Cotton Coton	0	0	2	6	9	12	12	13	15
Wool Laines	2	0[12]	0[12]	0[12]	0[12]	0[12]	...	...	...
Lithuania Lituanie									
Cotton Coton	48	42	35	35	62	64	57	55	44
Wool Laines	12	9	10	13	12	14	11	15	19
Cellulosic Cellulosiques	18	...	...	...	38	40	35	14	5
Non-cellulosic Non cellulosiques	...	...	8	6	5	7	5	5	5
Madagascar[9] Madagascar[9]									
Cotton Coton	42	44	34	27	32	23	...	...	
Mexico[8] Mexique[8]									
Cotton Coton	454	320	304	282	271	300	285	311	...
Wool Laines	12	9	12	16	20	19	19	18	...
Cellulosic Cellulosiques	6	5	...	...	...	...	...	...	
Non-cellulosic Non cellulosiques	552	522	489	624	638	623	626	622	
Mongolia[9] Mongolie[9]									
Wool Laines	0	0	0	0	0	0	0	0	...
Myanmar[9,21] Myanmar[9,21]									
Cotton Coton	16	13	16	12	11	13	21	26	
Nepal[9] Népal[9]									
Non-cellulosic Non cellulosiques	18	23	20	25	25	26	24	33	
Nigeria Nigéria									
Cotton Coton	393	124	113	...	...	...	...	...	
Norway[8] Norvège[8]									
Cotton Coton	7	8	6	7	...	...	*8	6[14]	...
Wool Laines	1	2	2	2	2	2	...	...	
Pakistan[22] Pakistan[22]									
Cotton Coton	325[20]	315	322	327	333	340	385	437	490
Paraguay[9] Paraguay[9]									
Cotton Coton	24	...	...	...	...	...	...	...	...
Poland Pologne									
Cotton[12,23] Coton[12,23]	284	321	263	295	303	275	234	298	285
Wool Laines	48[12,24]	51[12,24]	50[12,24]	50[12,24]	49[12,24]	45[12,24]	35[12,24]	9	10
Cellulosic[12] Cellulosiques[12]	23	22	25	26	28	27	18	...	...
Non-cellulosic[12] Non cellulosiques[12]	63	84	79	69	67	60	40	...	...

44

Fabrics
Woven cotton, wool, cellulosic and non-cellulosic fibres: million square metres *[cont.]*
Tissus
Tissus de coton, laines, fibres cellulosiques et non cellulosiques : millions de mètres carrés *[suite]*

Country or area Pays ou zone	1993	1994	1995	1996	1997	1998	1999	2000	2001
Portugal　Portugal									
Cotton　Coton	388	421	418	401	412	444	399	399	399
Wool　Laines	10	9	8	6	6	8	9	12	12
Cellulosic　Cellulosiques	25	30	24	10	11	9	8	10	12
Non-cellulosic　Non cellulosiques	109	99	103	121	127	142	165	170	152
Republic of Moldova[25]　République de Moldova[25]									
Cotton　Coton	1	0	0	0	0	0	0	0	0
Wool　Laines	0	0	0	0	0	0	0	0	0
Romania[12]　Roumanie[12]									
Cotton　Coton	271	294	275	212	173	170	143	145	154
Wool　Laines	68	65	68	50	34	22	18	13	17
Russian Federation　Fédération de Russie									
Cotton　Coton	2 822	1 631	1 401	1 120	1 374	1 241	1 455	2 026	2 209
Wool　Laines	270	114	107	67	63	52	61	67	67
Cellulosic[9]　Cellulosiques[9]	135	44	29	14	11	8	7	...	
Non-cellulosic[9]　Non cellulosiques[9]	256	122	85	51	45	42	71		
Serbia and Montenegro　Serbie-et-Monténégro									
Cotton[11,26]　Coton[11,26]	27	24	19	22	18	23	21[28]	20	19
Wool[26,27]　Laines[26,27]	13	13	11	11	10	9	7[28]	6	7
Cellulosic　Cellulosiques	4	2	2	1	1	1	0[28]	0	0
Slovakia　Slovaquie									
Cotton　Coton	78	76	90	57	61[9]	125[8]	32[8]	49[8]	5
Wool　Laines	10[12]	10[12]	10[9]	11[9]	11[9]	10[8]	7[8]	9[8]	
Non-cellulosic　Non cellulosiques	...	13	...	...	...	79[8,19]	68[8]	73[8]	...
Slovenia　Slovénie									
Cotton　Coton	81	81	71	53	...	...	...	30	30
Wool　Laines	13	10	7	3	...	...	1	2	...
Cellulosic　Cellulosiques	5	10	24	10	...	...	4	3	...
Non-cellulosic　Non cellulosiques	...	...	...	32	...	...	30	47	
South Africa　Afrique du Sud									
Cotton　Coton	166	195	228	246	269	223	224	219	216
Wool[29]　Laines[29]	10	11	10	9	9	8	7	7	8
Spain　Espagne									
Cotton　Coton	523	622	689	...	...	...	...	...	...
Wool[8]　Laines[8]	17	14	15	...	...	...	...	...	...
Non-cellulosic[8,30]　Non cellulosiques[8,30]	626	785	1 003	...	...	...	...	...	...
Sweden[8]　Suède[8]									
Cellulosic[31]　Cellulosiques[31]	...	2	2	...	...	...	...	...	
Non-cellulosic　Non cellulosiques	18	21	23	38	28	28	21	18	...
Switzerland　Suisse									
Cotton[9]　Coton[9]	74	82	70	...	...	...	...	...	...
Wool[29]　Laines[29]	7	7	5	...	...	...	...	...	...
Syrian Arab Republic[8]　Rép. arabe syrienne[8]									
Cotton　Coton	222	213	184	186	198	199	186	175	...
Wool　Laines	2	2	4	5	8	14	19	18	...
Tajikistan　Tadjikistan									
Cotton　Coton	57	34	28	17	8	13	11	11	14
Wool　Laines	3	1	0	0	0	0	0	0	0
TFYR of Macedonia　L'ex-R.y. Macédoine									
Cotton　Coton	19	23	15	16	8	12	6	6	3
Wool　Laines	7	5	6	4	4	4	3	2	3
Cellulosic　Cellulosiques	2	1	1	1	1	1	0	0	0
Turkey[9]　Turquie[9]									
Cotton　Coton	532	432	414	395	580	479	471	567	...
Wool　Laines	38	38	50	59	78	77	78	91	...
Cellulosic　Cellulosiques	178	254	225	246	224	240	215	228	...
Turkmenistan　Turkménistan									
Cotton　Coton	29	20	17	18	14	15	21	34	61
Wool　Laines	3	3	3	3	3	3	...	...	...
Uganda[12]　Ouganda[12]									
Cotton　Coton	7[26]	4	...	...	...	...	...	...	...

44

Fabrics
Woven cotton, wool, cellulosic and non-cellulosic fibres: million square metres *[cont.]*

Tissus
Tissus de coton, laines, fibres cellulosiques et non cellulosiques : millions de mètres carrés *[suite]*

Country or area Pays ou zone	1993	1994	1995	1996	1997	1998	1999	2000	2001
Ukraine Ukraine									
Cotton Coton	262	145	87	54	28	57	27	37	41
Wool Laines	60	26	19	12	14	8	6	8	7
Cellulosic [9] Cellulosiques [9]	92	29	9	3	3	3	2	1	...
Non-cellulosic [9] Non cellulosiques [9]	40	14	6	3	2	3	2	4	...
United Kingdom Royaume-Uni									
Cotton [9] Coton [9]	130	103	96	99	93	88	...	...	...
Wool * Laines *	33	38	...	...	...	...	...	...	...
Cellulosic [8] Cellulosiques [8]	26	19	...	...	...	...	...	...	...
United Rep. of Tanzania Rép.-Unie de Tanzanie									
Cotton Coton	40	24	10	13	27	...	...	...	...
United States Etats-Unis									
Cotton Coton	3 682	3 740	3 753	4 010	4 246	3 974	3 721	3 718	3 101
Wool Laines	154	149	136	127	138	111	65	57	44
Uzbekistan Ouzbékistan									
Cotton Coton	482	433	456	445	425	314[32]	333[32]	360[32]	...
Wool Laines	1	1	1	1	0	...	...	...	...

Source:
United Nations Statistics Division, New York, "Industrial Commodity Statistics Yearbook 2001" and the industrial statistics database.

Source:
Organisation des Nations Unies, Division de statistique, New York, "Annuaire de statistiques industrielles par produit 2001" et la base de données pour les statistiques industrielles.

1	Twelve months ending 30 June of the year stated.	1	Période de 12 mois finissant le 30 juin de l'année indiquée.
2	Including pile and chenille fabrics of non-cellulosic fibres.	2	Y compris les tissus bouclés et tissus chenille de fibres non-cellulosiques.
3	Excluding pile and chenille fabrics.	3	Non compris les tissus bouclés et tissus chemille.
4	Beginning 1995, data are confidential.	4	A partir de 1995, les données sont confidentielles.
5	Including woollen blankets and carpets.	5	Y compris les couvertures et tapis en laine.
6	Including blankets and carpets of cellulosic fibres.	6	Y compris les couvertures et les tapis en fibres cellulosiques.
7	Including blankets and carpets of non-cellulosic fibres.	7	Y compris les couvertures et les tapis en fibres non cellulosiques.
8	Original data in metric tons.	8	Données d'origine exprimées en tonnes.
9	Original data in metres.	9	Données d'origine exprimées en mètres.
10	Including cotton fabrics after undergoing finishing processes.	10	Y compris les tissus de cotton, après opérations de finition.
11	Including mixed cotton fabrics.	11	Y compris les tissus de cotton mélangé.
12	After undergoing finishing processes.	12	Après opérations de finition.
13	1998 data are confidential.	13	Pour 1998, les données sont confidentielles.
14	Incomplete coverage.	14	Couverture incomplète.
15	Sales.	15	Ventes.
16	Twelve months ending 7 July of the year stated.	16	Période de 12 mois finissant le 7 juillet de l'année indiquée.
17	Including fabrics after undergoing finishing processes.	17	Y compris les tissus, après opérations de finition.
18	Including mixed fabrics.	18	Y compris les tissus mélangés.
19	Break in series; data prior to the sign not comparable to following years.	19	Marque une interruption dans la série et la non-comparabilité des données précédant le symbole.
20	Including finished fabrics and blanketing made of synthetic fibers.	20	Y compris les tissus finis et les couvertures en fibres synthétiques.
21	Production by government-owned enterprises only.	21	Production des établissements d'Etat seulement.
22	Factory production only.	22	Production des fabriques seulement.
23	Including fabrics of cotton substitutes.	23	Y compris les tissus de succédanés de coton.
24	Including fabrics of wool substitutes.	24	Y compris les tissus de succédanés de laine.
25	Excluding the Transnistria region.	25	Non compris la région de Transnistria.
26	Including cellulosic fabrics.	26	Y compris les tissus en fibres cellulosiques.
27	Including mixed wool fabrics.	27	Y compris les tissus de laine mélangée.
28	Beginning 1999, data for Kosovo are not included.	28	A partir de 1999, non compris les données de Kosovo.
29	Pure woollen fabrics only.	29	Tissus de laine pure seulement.
30	Including woven cellulosic fabrics.	30	Y compris les tissus en fibres cellulosiques.
31	Including woven non-cellulosic fabrics.	31	Y compris les tissus en fibres non cellulosiques.
32	Source: Statistical Yearbook for Asia and the Pacific, United Nations Economic and Social Council for Asia and the Pacific (Bangkok).	32	Source: "Statistical Yearbook for Asia and the Pacific, United Nations Economic and Social Council for Asia and the Pacific" (Bangkok).

45

Leather footwear
Production: thousand pairs

Chaussures de cuir
Production : milliers de paires

Country or area Pays ou zone	1992	1993	1994	1995	1996	1997	1998	1999	2000	2001
Albania Albanie	1 214	1 818	266	267	...	...	...	...	...	...
Algeria Algérie	9 040	7 171	6 467	3 986	2 320	2 542	2 149	1 529	1 222	1 214
Angola Angola	48	...	...	...					...	...
Armenia Arménie	5 661	3 517	1 612	656	305	87	65	31	63	51
Australia [1,2] Australie [1,2]	383	283	315	278	...	...	...	...	...	...
Austria Autriche	14 842[3]	13 229[3]	12 767[3]	12 743	10 120	10 615	10 919	...	...	...
Azerbaijan Azerbaïdjan	5 221	4 329	3 057	799	495	313	315	54	122	220
Belarus Bélarus	37 207	33 412	26 358	13 004	11 381	15 587	16 223	16 538	15 388	...
Belgium Belgique	3 190	2 267	...	...	...	...	...	...	...	...
Bolivia Bolivie	1 152	1 308	1 381	*1 222	...	615	180	251	...	...
Brazil Brésil	156 540	190 026	146 540	124 272	163 042	159 861	142 734	145 393	146 938	151 042
Bulgaria Bulgarie	13 421	10 785	10 244	11 980	8 915	6 838	6 401	4 591	4 790	4 054
Burkina Faso [4] Burkina Faso [4]	1 200	...	...	...	...	...	...	...	...	...
Cameroon [4] Cameroun [4]	1 900	...	...	...	...	...	...	...	...	...
Canada [4] Canada [4]	16 000	...	...	...	...	...	...	...	...	...
Cape Verde Cap-Vert	...	...	...	192	...	...	...	...	...	...
Central African Rep. [4] Rép. centrafricaine [4]	200	...	...	...	...	...	...	...	...	...
Chile Chili	9 311	9 270	8 317	7 410	7 134	7 008	6 777	6 237	5 735	5 251
China Chine	1613 647	...							...	...
China, Hong Kong SAR Chine, Hong Kong RAS	8 433	...		...	1 499	752[5]	178[5]	200[5]	437[5]	602[5]
Colombia Colombie	20 651	19 471	20 933	18 277	...	18 736[6]	16 635[6]	12 541[6]	...	...
Congo [4] Congo [4]	300	...	...	...	...	...	...	...	...	...
Côte d'Ivoire [4] Côte d'Ivoire [4]	1 800	...	...	...	...	...	...	...	...	...
Croatia Croatie	11 240	13 449	12 459	9 521	9 271	9 598	9 350	8 367	8 402	9 722
Cuba [4] Cuba [4]	13 400	...	...	...	...	...	...	...	...	...
Cyprus Chypre	6 199	3 835	3 820[7]	3 444[7]	2 507[7]	2 192[7]	2 100[7]	1 208[7]	1 416[7]	...
Czech Republic République tchèque	36 948	32 293	23 323	22 115	21 572	13 455	10 099	7 146	6 109	5 202

45

Leather footwear
Production: thousand pairs *[cont.]*

Chaussures de cuir
Production : milliers de paires *[suite]*

Country or area Pays ou zone	1992	1993	1994	1995	1996	1997	1998	1999	2000	2001
Dem. Rep. of the Congo[4] Rép. dém. du Congo[4]	900	...	...	...	...	...	...	...	...	...
Denmark Danemark	4 600[4]	...	...	...	8 387[8]	10 118[8]	10 444[8]	10 141[8]	10 057[8]	8 052[8]
Dominican Republic[4] Rép. dominicaine[4]	2 200	...	...	...	...	...	...	...	...	...
Ecuador Equateur	1 936	1 691	1 672	1 744	1 507	2	1	1	2	...
Egypt Egypte	48 390	48 385	48 394	48 444	48 300	48 131	48 171	...	49 077	...
El Salvador[4] El Salvador[4]	3 800	...	...	...	...	...	...	...	...	...
Estonia Estonie	3 208	1 035	827	682	711	793	803	840	909	912
Ethiopia Ethiopie	2 419[9]	3 083[9]	2 871[9]	3 751[9]	3 773[9]	6 925[9]	6 252[9]	7 477[9,10]	5 022[9]	6 358
Finland Finlande	3 606	3 291	3 421	3 186	3 220	2 928	3 499	2 650	2 612	2 024
France France	160 320[10]	151 124[10]	154 898[10]	151 704[10]	139 442[10]	135 447[10]	125 524[10]	114 540[10]	98 496	85 620
Georgia Géorgie	2 614	1 046	224	50	48	101	95	101	90	45
Germany Allemagne	63 672	55 485	47 193	45 491	40 675	36 948	38 441	36 581	32 898	20 211
Greece Grèce	9 264	8 166	6 922	7 032	6 769	6 202	5 716	...	...	...
Haiti[4] Haïti[4]	600	...	...	...	...	...	...	...	...	...
Hungary Hongrie	14 752	12 783	12 499	12 178	...	...	...	14 386	15 045	15 536
Iceland Islande	18	...	...	...	9	8	...	...	...	...
India Inde	207 181[11]	188 746[11]	158 263[11]	181 462[11]	157 095[11]	137 837[11]	180 490[11]	134 524[11]	141 941[11]	157 923
Indonesia[12] Indonésie[12]	...	250 053[13]	272 529	249 509	...	238 335	258 780	332 478	...	...
Iran (Islamic Rep. of) Iran (Rép. islamique d')	25 129[14]	21 756[14]	17 598[14]	29 807[15]	28 310[15]	8 721[16]	7 156[15]	5 257[15]	4 833[15]	...
Iraq Iraq	4 087	...	...	...	...	...	...	...	...	...
Ireland[4] Irlande[4]	3 200	...	...	...	...	...	...	...	...	...
Italy[4] Italie[4]	295 000	...	...	...	...	...	...	...	...	...
Jamaica[4] Jamaïque[4]	800	...	...	...	...	...	...	...	...	...
Japan Japon	52 455[17]	47 703[17]	51 503[17]	49 525[17]	48 819[17]	47 573[17]	42 573[17]	37 546[17]	35 961[17]	34 667
Jordan Jordanie	...	...	...	...	...	...	565	277	354	268
Kenya Kenya	1 480	1 571	1 774	2 018	2 089	...	...	...	...	...
Korea, Republic of Corée, République de	27 617	19 085	16 806	15 309	...	...	...	...	...	...

45

Leather footwear
Production: thousand pairs *[cont.]*

Chaussures de cuir
Production : milliers de paires *[suite]*

Country or area Pays ou zone	1992	1993	1994	1995	1996	1997	1998	1999	2000	2001
Kyrgyzstan Kirghizistan	5 757	3 528	1 512	755	605	332	135	85	137	...
Lao People's Dem. Rep. Rép. dém. pop. lao	...	...	240	150	...	...	...	...	...	...
Latvia Lettonie	5 764	2 687	1 633	1 032	939	753	753	451	371	294
Lithuania Lituanie	7 702	3 657	1 565	1 961	2 004	1 663	1 654	1 783	747	898
Madagascar Madagascar	702[12]	306[12]	180	136	158	126	115	...	...	...
Malawi Malawi	...	...	...	...	...	1 591	2 023	1 727	1 467	1 340
Mali Mali	104	86	106	99	98	...	...	...	...	...
Mexico Mexique	33 141	62 315	56 948	44 006	50 340	52 586	47 072	43 916	42 434	38 526
Mongolia Mongolie	2 245	1 031	407	325	146	41	33	7	6	...
Mozambique Mozambique	148	153	87	29	...	12	10	7	7	2
Nepal[18] Népal[18]	800	823	700	685	649	550	550	*605	650	709
Netherlands[8,10,19] Pays-Bas[8,10,19]	5 289	6 315	5 455	5 492	...	...	...	...	...	...
New Zealand[1,20] Nouvelle-Zélande[1,20]	3 765	3 525	3 590	3 119	2 676	2 222	1 484	1 650		
Nicaragua[4] Nicaragua[4]	1 300	...	...	...	...	...	...	...	...	...
Nigeria Nigéria	4 538	4 554	1 182	1 255	...	...	...	...	...	...
Norway[4] Norvège[4]	1 000	...	...	...	...	...	...	...	...	...
Panama Panama	1 377	1 483	1 294	1 287	1 058	1 104	753	799	...	...
Paraguay[4] Paraguay[4]	5 600	...	...	...	...	...	...	...	...	...
Peru[4] Pérou[4]	20 000	...	...	...	...	...	...	...	...	...
Philippines[4] Philippines[4]	15 000	...	...	...	...	...	...	...	...	...
Poland Pologne	55 181	47 905	53 236	59 783	66 620	68 513	54 491	48 538	...	...
Portugal Portugal	60 463	75 422	71 648	68 070	69 439	71 949	68 176	76 632	75 719	75 809
Republic of Moldova République de Moldova	14 504	4 897[21]	2 267[21]	1 506[21]	1 429[21]	1 032[21]	739[21]	705[21]	998[21]	1 090[21]
Romania Roumanie	41 237	41 893	45 666	48 239	44 838	34 365	30 341	30 491	36 863	38 289
Russian Federation Fédération de Russie	231 005	153 343	80 776	54 254	36 764	33 030	23 816	29 864	32 939	36 898
Senegal Sénégal	644	508	...	...	...	...	...	...	...	...
Serbia and Montenegro Serbie-et-Monténégro	16 169	10 590	8 824	5 982	6 461	6 848	6 976	3 892[22]	4 248	4 351

45

Leather footwear
Production: thousand pairs *[cont.]*

Chaussures de cuir
Production : milliers de paires *[suite]*

Country or area Pays ou zone	1992	1993	1994	1995	1996	1997	1998	1999	2000	2001
Singapore [4] Singapour [4]	3 100	...	...	...	...	...	...	...	...	...
Slovakia Slovaquie	22 875	18 332	13 577	46 438	13 188	10 300	9 772	7 643	8 503	8 994
Slovenia Slovénie	9 492	8 923	8 683	6 951	5 739	5 976	5 641	4 779	3 404	...
South Africa [10] Afrique du Sud [10]	42 251	44 492	41 078	39 071[23]	38 858[23]	35 486[23]	29 581[23]	24 257[23]	20 195[23]	19 465[23]
Spain Espagne	106 959	74 883	104 788	140 141	155 218	165 417	177 464		...	165 244
Sri Lanka Sri Lanka	272	274		...		...	...	...	...	...
Sudan [4] Soudan [4]	3 000	...	...	...	...	...	...	...	...	...
Sweden Suède	3 000[4]	1 013	676	372	1 104	1 202	430	956	944	912
Switzerland Suisse	3 065	3 291	3 232	2 490	...	...	...	...	...	
Tajikistan Tadjikistan	5 476	4 044	929	612	394	107	123	72	110	100
TFYR of Macedonia L'ex-R.y. Macédoine	3 786	2 031	1 760	1 121	*1 230	*1 509	*1 722	*2 172	*2 059	
Togo [4] Togo [4]	100	...	...	...	...	...	...	...	...	...
Tunisia Tunisie	13 220	12 870	14 100	16 580	18 380	20 300	...	...	...	...
Turkmenistan Turkménistan	3 231	3 358	1 938	1 910	1 546	1 108	561	416	478	375
Ukraine Ukraine	147 703	105 814	40 309	20 757	13 175	10 408	11 350	11 863	13 468	14 593
United Kingdom Royaume-Uni	43 000[4]	70 837	69 637	61 141	62 157	55 418	44 862	37 148	28 313	...
United Rep. of Tanzania Rép.-Unie de Tanzanie	168	55	89	339	121	152	...	...	...	
United States Etats-Unis	164 904	171 733	156 712	146 979	127 315	127 876	115 808	85 332	58 870	54 757
Uzbekistan Ouzbékistan	40 491	40 466	28 202	5 654	5 591	5 547	...	...	...	...
Viet Nam Viet Nam	5 672	...	...	46 440	61 785	79 289	77 037	*81 780	32 391	...

Source:
United Nations Statistics Division, New York, the industrial statistics database and the "Industrial Commodity Statistics Yearbook 2001".

Source:
Organisation des Nations Unies, Division de statistique, New York, la base de données pour les statistiques industrielles et "Annuaire de statistiques industrielles par produit 2001".

1	Twelve months ending 30 June of the year stated.
2	Excluding sporting footwear.
3	Beginning 1995, data are confidential.
4	Source: Food and Agriculture Organization of the United Nations (FAO), (Rome).
5	Excluding other footwear for confidentiality purposes.
6	Including rubber and plastic footwear.
7	Including other footwear, house footwear, sandals and other light footwear. Also including rubber footwear.

1	Période de 12 mois finissant le 30 juin de l'année indiquée.
2	Y compris les chaussures sportif.
3	A partir de 1995, les données sont confidentielles.
4	Source: Organisation des Nations Unies pour l'alimentation et l'agriculture (FAO), (Rome).
5	A l'exclusion d'autres chaussures, pour raisons de confidentialité.
6	Y compris les chaussures en caoutchouc et en matière plastique.
7	Y compris les autres chaussures, chaussures de maison, sandales et autres chaussures légères. Y compris également les chaussures en caoutchouc.

45

Leather footwear
Production: thousand pairs *[cont.]*

Chaussures de cuir
Production : milliers de paires *[suite]*

8	Sales.
9	Twelve months ending 7 July of the year stated.
10	Including rubber footwear.
11	Production by large and medium scale establishments only.
12	Including plastic footwear.
13	Break in series; data prior to the sign not comparable to following years.
14	Production by establishments employing 50 or more persons.
15	Production by establishments employing 10 or more persons.
16	Production by establishments employing 10 or more persons. Break in series; data prior to the sign not comparable to following years.
17	Shipments. Production by establishments employing 10 or more persons.
18	Twelve months beginning 16 July of the year stated.
19	Production by establishments employing 20 or more persons.
20	Including non-leather footwear.
21	Excluding the Transnistria region.
22	Beginning 1999, data for Kosovo are not included.
23	Excluding children's footwear.

8	Ventes.
9	Période de 12 mois finissant le 7 juillet de l'année indiquée.
10	Y compris les chaussures en caoutchouc.
11	Production des grandes et moyennes entreprises seulement.
12	Y compris les chaussures en matière plastique.
13	Marque une interruption dans la série et la non-comparabilité des données précédant le symbole.
14	Production des établissements occupant 50 personnes ou plus.
15	Production des établissements occupant 10 personnes ou plus.
16	Production des établissements occupant 10 personnes ou plus. Marque une interruption dans la série et la non-comparabilité des données précédant le symbole.
17	Expéditions. Production des établissements occupant 10 personnes ou plus.
18	Période de 12 mois commençant le 16 juillet de l'année indiquée.
19	Production des établissements occupant 20 personnes ou plus.
20	Y compris les chaussures en matières autres que le cuir.
21	Non compris la région de Transnistria.
22	A partir de 1999, non compris les données de Kosovo.
23	Non compris les chaussures pour enfants.

46
Sawnwood
Production (sawn): thousand cubic metres
Sciages
Production (sciés): milliers de mètres cubes

Region, country or area / Région, pays ou zone	1993	1994	1995	1996	1997	1998	1999	2000	2001	2002
World / Monde	**431 143**	**433 911**	**425 238**	**424 190**	**430 934**	**375 307**	**383 898**	**388 135**	**376 880**	**388 907**
Africa / Afrique	**7 850**	**8 490**	**8 243**	**7 867**	**7 505**	**7 423**	**7 415**	**8 096**	**8 414**	**8 414**
Algeria [1] / Algérie [1]	13	13	13	13	13	13	13	13	13	13
Angola [1] / Angola [1]	5	5	5	5	5	5	5	5	5	5
Benin / Bénin	24[1]	24[1]	15	11	12	13	13	13[1]	13[1]	13[1]
Burkina Faso / Burkina Faso	2[1]	1	1	1	2	1	1	1[1]	1[1]	1[1]
Burundi / Burundi	20	21	43	33	33[1]	33[1]	80[1]	83[1]	83[1]	83[1]
Cameroon / Cameroun	579[1]	647[1]	676[1]	685[1]	560	588	600	900	1 150	1 150[1]
Central African Rep. / Rép. centrafricaine	60[1]	73	70	61	72	91	79	102	150	150[1]
Chad / Tchad	2	2[1]	2	2	2[1]	2[1]	2[1]	2[1]	2[1]	2[1]
Congo / Congo	52[1]	57	62	59	64	73	74	93	95	95[1]
Côte d'Ivoire / Côte d'Ivoire	587	708	706	596	613	623	611	603	630	630[1]
Dem. Rep. of the Congo / Rép. dém. du Congo	105[1]	75	65	85	90	80	70	70	70	70[1]
Egypt / Egypte	0	0	0	0	0	3	4	4	4[1]	4[1]
Equatorial Guinea / Guinée équatoriale	7	4	4	4[1]	4[1]	4[1]	4[1]	4[1]	4[1]	4[1]
Ethiopia / Ethiopie	33	45	40	33	60	60[1]	60[1]	60[1]	60[1]	60[1]
Gabon / Gabon	*153	*173	100[1]	50[1]	30[1]	60	98	88	142	142[1]
Gambia [1] / Gambie [1]	1	1	1	1	1	1	1	1	1	1
Ghana / Ghana	504	801	612	604	575	590	454	475	480	480[1]
Guinea / Guinée	65	72	85	85[1]	25	26	26[1]	26[1]	26[1]	26[1]
Guinea-Bissau [1] / Guinée-Bissau [1]	16	16	16	16	16	16	16	16	16	16
Kenya [1] / Kenya [1]	185	185	185	185	185	185	185	185	185	185
Liberia / Libéria	*90	90[1]	90[1]	90[1]	90[1]	6	4	10	20	20[1]
Libyan Arab Jamah. [1] / Jamah. arabe libyenne [1]	31	31	31	31	31	31	31	31	31	31
Madagascar / Madagascar	144	74	84[1]	84[1]	84[1]	84[1]	102	485	400	400[1]
Malawi / Malawi	45	45[1]	45[1]	45[1]	45[1]	45[1]	45[1]	45[1]	45[1]	45[1]
Mali [1] / Mali [1]	13	13	13	13	13	13	13	13	13	13
Mauritius / Maurice	5	4	2	3	3[1]	5	5	3	3	3[1]

46

Sawnwood
Production (sawn): thousand cubic metres *[cont.]*

Sciages
Production (sciés): milliers de mètres cubes *[suite]*

Region, country or area Région, pays ou zone	1993	1994	1995	1996	1997	1998	1999	2000	2001	2002
Morocco[1] Maroc[1]	83	83	83	83	83	83	83	83	83	83
Mozambique Mozambique	30[1]	30	42	42[1]	33	28	28[1]	28[1]	28[1]	28[1]
Niger[1] Niger[1]	4	4	4	4	4	4	4	4	4	4
Nigeria Nigéria	2 711	2 533	2 356	2 178	2 000	2 000[1]	2 000[1]	2 000[1]	2 000[1]	2 000[1]
Réunion[1] Réunion[1]	2	2	2	2	2	2	2	2	2	2
Rwanda Rwanda	36	26	54	59	74	76	79	79[1]	79[1]	79[1]
Sao Tome and Principe[1] Sao Tomé-et-Principe[1]	5	5	5	5	5	5	5	5	5	5
Senegal[1] Sénégal[1]	23	23	23	23	23	23	23	23	23	23
Sierra Leone Sierra Leone	5	5[1]	5[1]	5[1]	5[1]	5[1]	5[1]	5[1]	5[1]	5[1]
Somalia[1] Somalie[1]	14	14	14	14	14	14	14	14	14	14
South Africa Afrique du Sud	1 383	1 499	1 574	1 574[1]	1 574[1]	1 498	1 498[1]	1 498[1]	1 498[1]	1 498[1]
Sudan Soudan	3	45	45	45[1]	45[1]	51[1]	51[1]	51[1]	51[1]	51[1]
Swaziland Swaziland	75	80[1]	90[1]	100[1]	102	102[1]	102[1]	102[1]	102[1]	102[1]
Togo Togo	3[1]	8	14	15	17	18	21	19	15	15[1]
Tunisia Tunisie	19	20	20[1]	20[1]	20[1]	20[1]	20[1]	20[1]	20[1]	20[1]
Uganda Ouganda	107	140[1]	200	215	229	245	264	264[1]	264[1]	264[1]
United Rep. of Tanzania[1] Rép.-Unie de Tanzanie[1]	39	24	24	24	24	24	24	24	24	24
Zambia Zambie	318	367	320[1]	245[1]	157[1]	157[1]	157[1]	157[1]	157[1]	157[1]
Zimbabwe Zimbabwe	250[1]	401	401	418	465	416	438	386	397	397[1]
America, North **Amérique du Nord**	**169 803**	**175 837**	**169 948**	**177 007**	**181 173**	**141 383**	**148 105**	**146 710**	**139 062**	**147 397**
Bahamas[1] Bahamas[1]	1	1	1	1	1	1	1	1	1	1
Belize[1] Belize[1]	14	20	35	35	35	35	35	35	35	35
Canada Canada	59 774	61 650	60 436	62 828	64 764	47 185	50 412	50 465	47 696	52 896
Costa Rica Costa Rica	798	746[1]	780[1]	780[1]	780[1]	780[1]	780[1]	812	812[1]	812[1]
Cuba Cuba	130[1]	130[1]	130[1]	130[1]	130[1]	130[1]	146[1]	179	190	190[1]
El Salvador El Salvador	70[1]	70[1]	70[1]	70[1]	58	58[1]	58[1]	58[1]	58[1]	58[1]
Guadeloupe[1] Guadeloupe[1]	1	1	1	1	1	1	1	1	1	1
Guatemala Guatemala	398	417	355	355[1]	355[1]	308	235	220	220	220[1]

46

Sawnwood
Production (sawn): thousand cubic metres *[cont.]*

Sciages
Production (sciés): milliers de mètres cubes *[suite]*

Region, country or area Région, pays ou zone	1993	1994	1995	1996	1997	1998	1999	2000	2001	2002
Haiti [1] Haïti [1]	14	14	14	14	14	14	14	14	14	14
Honduras Honduras	364	361	231	322	379	369	419	444	417	417[1]
Jamaica Jamaïque	24	63	63	64	65	66	66[1]	66[1]	66[1]	66[1]
Martinique [1] Martinique [1]	1	1	1	1	1	1	1	1	1	1
Mexico Mexique	2 560	2 693	2 329	2 543	2 961	3 260	3 110[1]	3 110[1]	3 387	3 387[1]
Nicaragua Nicaragua	65	27	74	160	148	148[1]	148[1]	148[1]	65	65[1]
Panama Panama	37	37	37	19	17	8	46	48	42	42[1]
Trinidad and Tobago Trinité-et-Tobago	35	58	64	29	38	27	18	32	41	41[1]
United States Etats-Unis	105 516	109 547	105 326	109 654	111 425	88 991	92 615	91 076	86 015	89 151
America, South **Amérique du Sud**	**25 474**	**27 190**	**28 390**	**29 990**	**29 926**	**29 799**	**28 307**	**33 593**	**33 655**	**33 655**
Argentina Argentine	998	1 080	1 329	1 711	1 170	1 377	1 408	821	821[1]	821[1]
Bolivia Bolivie	268	185	162	181	180	515	259	239	308	308[1]
Brazil Brésil	18 628[1]	18 691	19 091	19 091[1]	19 091[1]	18 591	17 280	23 100	23 100[1]	23 100[1]
Chile Chili	3 113	3 364	3 802	4 140	4 661	4 551	5 254	5 698	5 872	5 872[1]
Colombia Colombie	694	644	644	1 134	1 085	910	730	587	539	539[1]
Ecuador Equateur	196	1 600	1 696	1 886	2 075	2 079	1 455	1 455[1]	1 455[1]	1 455[1]
French Guiana Guyane française	18	15	15[1]	15[1]	15[1]	15[1]	15[1]	15[1]	15[1]	15[1]
Guyana Guyana	50[1]	77	101	97	57	50	50	50	30	30[1]
Paraguay [1] Paraguay [1]	357	357	400	500	550	550	550	550	550	550
Peru Pérou	592	649	630	693	482	590	835	646	494	494[1]
Suriname Suriname	33	29	29[1]	40	41	41[1]	28	54	57	57[1]
Uruguay Uruguay	269[1]	269[1]	269[1]	269[1]	269[1]	269[1]	269[1]	203	203	203[1]
Venezuela Venezuela	258	230	222	233	250	261	174	175	211	211[1]
Asia **Asie**	**101 601**	**98 045**	**96 652**	**92 089**	**90 246**	**71 952**	**71 725**	**62 153**	**60 227**	**60 916**
Afghanistan [1] Afghanistan [1]	400	400	400	400	400	400	400	400	400	400
Armenia Arménie	0	0	0	0	0	0	0	4	4	4
Azerbaijan Azerbaïdjan	0	0	0	0	0	0	0	1	0	0[1]

46

Sawnwood
Production (sawn): thousand cubic metres *[cont.]*
Sciages
Production (sciés): milliers de mètres cubes *[suite]*

Region, country or area Région, pays ou zone	1993	1994	1995	1996	1997	1998	1999	2000	2001	2002
Bangladesh [1] Bangladesh [1]	79	79	70	70	70	70	70	70	70	70
Bhutan Bhoutan	18	18[1]	18[1]	18[1]	18[1]	18[1]	22[1]	31[1]	31[1]	31[1]
Brunei Darussalam Brunéi Darussalam	90	90[1]	90[1]	90[1]	90[1]	90[1]	90[1]	90[1]	90[1]	90[1]
Cambodia Cambodge	155[1]	195	140	100	71	40	26	20	5	5[1]
China Chine	25 709[1]	25 603[1]	25 603[1]	27 410[1]	20 982	18 716[1]	16 700[1]	7 345[1]	8 549[1]	8 549[1]
Cyprus Chypre	17	15	15	16	14	11	12	9	9	7
India Inde	17 460[1]	17 460[1]	17 460[1]	10 624[1]	18 520[1]	8 400	8 400	7 900	7 900	7 900[1]
Indonesia Indonésie	8 338	6 838	6 638	7 338	7 238	7 125	6 625	6 500	6 400	6 400[1]
Iran (Islamic Rep. of) Iran (Rép. islamique d')	170	178	159	144	141	129	96	106	106[1]	106[1]
Iraq Iraq	8[1]	8[1]	8[1]	8[1]	8[1]	12	12[1]	12[1]	12[1]	12[1]
Japan Japon	26 260[1]	25 906[1]	24 493[1]	23 844[1]	21 709	18 625	17 952	17 094	15 485	15 485[1]
Kazakhstan Kazakhstan	0	0	0	0	0	*182	*337	*460	230	224
Korea, Dem. P. R. [1] Corée, R. p. dém. de [1]	280	280	280	280	280	280	280	280	280	280
Korea, Republic of Corée, République de	3 249	3 862	3 440	4 291	4 759	2 240	4 300	4 544	4 420	4 420[1]
Kyrgyzstan Kirghizistan	0	0	0	0	2	*23	*23	*6	*6	6[1]
Lao People's Dem. Rep. Rép. dém. pop. lao	262	331	465	320	560	250[1]	350[1]	208	227	227[1]
Lebanon Liban	9	9[1]	9[1]	9[1]	9[1]	9[1]	9[1]	9[1]	9[1]	9[1]
Malaysia Malaisie	9 395	8 858	8 382[1]	8 382[1]	7 326	5 091	5 237	5 590	4 700	4 700[1]
Mongolia Mongolie	84	50	61	170[1]	200[1]	300[1]	300[1]	300[1]	300[1]	300[1]
Myanmar Myanmar	339	347[1]	347[1]	351	372	299	298	545	671	671[1]
Nepal Népal	620[1]	620[1]	620[1]	620[1]	620[1]	630	630	630	630	630[1]
Pakistan Pakistan	1 503	1 127	1 266	1 280	1 024	1 051	1 075	1 087	1 180	1 180[1]
Philippines Philippines	440	407	286	313	351	222	288	151	199	199[1]
Singapore [1] Singapour [1]	25	25	25	25	25	25	25	25	25	25
Sri Lanka Sri Lanka	5	5	6	5	5	5	5	29	61	61[1]
Syrian Arab Republic [1] Rép. arabe syrienne [1]	9	9	9	9	9	9	9	9	9	9
Thailand Thaïlande	715	568	426	307	426	103	178	220	233	233[1]
Turkey Turquie	5 241	4 037	4 331	4 268	3 833	4 891	5 039	5 528	5 036	5 732

46

Sawnwood
Production (sawn): thousand cubic metres *[cont.]*

Sciages
Production (sciés): milliers de mètres cubes *[suite]*

Region, country or area Région, pays ou zone	1993	1994	1995	1996	1997	1998	1999	2000	2001	2002
Viet Nam Viet Nam	721	721[1]	1 606	1 398	1 184	2 705	2 937	2 950	2 950	2 950[1]
Europe **Europe**	**120 148**	**117 683**	**115 000**	**110 310**	**115 072**	**117 460**	**120 681**	**129 343**	**127 827**	**130 830**
Albania Albanie	4	5	5[1]	5[1]	5	28	35	90	197	97
Austria Autriche	6 786	7 572	7 804	8 200	8 450	8 737	9 628	10 390	10 227	10 415
Belarus Bélarus	1 545	1 545[1]	1 545[1]	1 545[1]	1 545[1]	*2 131	2 175	1 808	2 058	2 182
Belgium Belgique	...	...	...	...	...	...	1 056	*1 150	1 275	1 175
Belgium-Luxembourg Belgique-Luxembourg	1 184[1]	1 209	1 150	1 100	1 150	1 267	...	...	...	...
Bosnia and Herzegovina Bosnie-Herzégovine	20	20	20	20	320	*330	*330	*320	*310	310[1]
Bulgaria Bulgarie	253	253[1]	253[1]	253[1]	253[1]	253[1]	325	312	312[1]	312[1]
Croatia Croatie	699	601	578	598	644	676	685	642	574	640
Czech Republic République tchèque	3 025	3 155	3 490	3 405	3 393	3 427	3 584	4 106	3 889	3 800
Denmark Danemark	583	583[1]	583[1]	583[1]	583[1]	238	344	364	281	281[1]
Estonia Estonie	300[1]	341	350	400	729[1]	850	1 200	1 436	1 623	*1 900
Finland Finlande	8 570	10 290	9 940	9 780	11 430	12 300	12 768	13 420	12 770	13 390
France France	9 132	9 649	9 848	9 600	9 607	10 220	10 236	10 536	10 518	10 540
Germany Allemagne	11 522	13 567	14 105	14 267	14 730	14 972	16 096	16 340	16 131	16 879
Greece Grèce	337[1]	337[1]	337[1]	337[1]	130	137	140	123	123[1]	123[1]
Hungary Hongrie	480	417	230	285	317	298	308	291	219	221
Ireland Irlande	637	709	678	687	642	675	811	888	925	969
Italy Italie	1 700	1 808	1 850	1 650	1 751	1 600	1 630	1 630	1 600	1 605
Latvia Lettonie	446	950	1 300	1 614	2 700	3 200	3 640	3 900	3 840	3 947
Lithuania Lituanie	699	760	940	1 450	1 250	1 150	1 150	1 300	1 200	1 200[1]
Luxembourg Luxembourg	...	...	...	...	...	...	133	133[1]	133[1]	133[1]
Netherlands Pays-Bas	389	383	426	359	401	349	362	390	268	253
Norway Norvège	2 315	2 415	2 210	2 420	2 520	2 525	2 336	2 280	2 253	2 225
Poland Pologne	4 260	5 300	3 842	3 747	4 214	4 320	4 137	4 262	3 083	2 910
Portugal Portugal	1 494	1 670	1 731	1 731[1]	1 731[1]	1 490	1 430	1 427	1 492	1 298
Republic of Moldova République de Moldova	0	31	25	29	30	30	6	5	5[1]	5[1]

46

Sawnwood
Production (sawn): thousand cubic metres *[cont.]*
Sciages
Production (sciés): milliers de mètres cubes *[suite]*

Region, country or area Région, pays ou zone	1993	1994	1995	1996	1997	1998	1999	2000	2001	2002
Romania Roumanie	2 460[1]	1 727	1 777	1 693	1 861	2 200	2 818	3 396	3 059	3 696
Russian Federation Fédération de Russie	40 890	30 720	26 500	21 913	20 600	19 580	19 100	20 000	21 000	22 000
Serbia and Montenegro Serbie-et-Monténégro	315	280	304	378	391	438	364	504	391	432
Slovakia Slovaquie	550	700	646	629	767	1 265	1 265[1]	1 265[1]	1 265[1]	1 265[1]
Slovenia Slovénie	513	513	511	496	510	664	455	439	460	446
Spain Espagne	2 717	2 755	3 262	3 080	3 080	3 178	3 178[1]	3 760	4 275	3 524
Sweden Suède	12 738	13 816	14 944	14 370	15 669	15 124	14 858	16 176	15 988	16 560
Switzerland Suisse	1 410	1 320	1 479	1 355	1 280	1 400[1]	1 525	1 625	1 400	1 420
TFYR of Macedonia L'ex-R.y. Macédoine	63	57	42	40	34	27	37	36	23	20
Ukraine Ukraine	0	0	0	0	0	0	0	*2 117	2 117[1]	2 117[1]
United Kingdom Royaume-Uni	2 112	2 225	2 295	2 291	2 356	2 382	2 537	2 482	2 543	2 539
Oceania Océanie	**6 268**	**6 667**	**7 006**	**6 927**	**7 013**	**7 291**	**7 664**	**8 239**	**7 695**	**7 695**
Australia Australie	3 187	3 431	3 691	3 530	3 481	3 711	3 673	3 983	3 525	3 525[1]
Fiji Fidji	111	112	102	102[1]	133	131	64	72	79	79[1]
New Caledonia Nouvelle-Calédonie	2	3	3[1]	3[1]	3[1]	3[1]	3[1]	3[1]	3[1]	3[1]
New Zealand Nouvelle-Zélande	2 805	2 861	2 950	3 032	3 136	3 178	3 653	3 910	3 807	3 807[1]
Papua New Guinea Papouasie-Nvl-Guinée	118	218	218	218[1]	218[1]	218[1]	218[1]	218[1]	218[1]	218[1]
Samoa Samoa	21	21[1]	21[1]	21[1]	21[1]	21[1]	21[1]	21[1]	21[1]	21[1]
Solomon Islands Iles Salomon	16[1]	12	12[1]	12[1]	12[1]	12[1]	12[1]	12[1]	12[1]	12[1]
Tonga Tonga	1[1]	1[1]	1[1]	1[1]	1[1]	2	2[1]	2[1]	2[1]	2[1]
Vanuatu Vanuatu	7	7[1]	7[1]	7[1]	7[1]	15	18	18	28	28[1]

Source:
Food and Agriculture Organization of the United Nations (FAO), Rome, the FAOSTAT database and the "FAO Yearbook of Forest Products".

Source:
Organisation des Nations Unies pour l'alimentation et l'agriculture (FAO), Rome, la base de données FAOSTAT et "l'Annuaire FAO des produits forestiers".

1   FAO estimate.

1   Estimation de la FAO.

47

Paper and paperboard
Production: thousand metric tons

Papiers et cartons
Production: milliers de tonnes

Region, country or area Région, pays ou zone	1993	1994	1995	1996	1997	1998	1999	2000	2001	2002
World **Monde**	**252 250**	**268 515**	**282 286**	**284 297**	**301 413**	**301 736**	**315 687**	**323 808**	**319 948**	**323 475**
Africa **Afrique**	**2 519**	**2 437**	**2 624**	**2 634**	**2 885**	**2 980**	**2 897**	**3 012**	**3 278**	**3 275**
Algeria Algérie	93	87	*78	*56	*65	*55	26	41[1]	41[1]	41[1]
Angola Angola	0	0[1]	0[1]	0[1]	0[1]	0[1]	0[1]	0[1]	0[1]	0[1]
Cameroon Cameroun	5[1]	5[1]	5[1]	5[1]	0	0	0[1]	0[1]	0[1]	0[1]
Dem. Rep. of the Congo Rép. dém. du Congo	3[1]	3[1]	3[1]	3[1]	3[1]	3[1]	3[1]	3[1]	3[1]	0
Egypt Egypte	*220	*219	*221	221[1]	*282	343	343[1]	440[1]	460[1]	460[1]
Ethiopia Ethiopie	7	7	6	8	10	6	10	12	12[1]	12[1]
Kenya Kenya	176[1]	*108	*113	129	129[1]	129[1]	129[1]	129[1]	129[1]	129[1]
Libyan Arab Jamah. [1] Jamah. arabe libyenne [1]	6	6	6	6	6	6	6	6	6	6
Madagascar Madagascar	6	5	4	3	4	5	2	4[1]	4[1]	4[1]
Morocco Maroc	99	103	106	106	107	110	109	109	129	129[1]
Mozambique Mozambique	1[1]	1[1]	1[1]	1[1]	0	0	0[1]	0[1]	0[1]	0[1]
Nigeria Nigéria	5	3	6	21	19	19	19	19	19	19
South Africa Afrique du Sud	*1 710	*1 684	1 871	1 871[1]	2 047	2 105	2 041	2 041[1]	2 267	2 267[1]
Sudan [1] Soudan [1]	3	3	3	3	3	3	3	3	3	3
Tunisia Tunisie	*80	*92	*90	90[1]	97	88	*94	94[1]	94[1]	94[1]
Uganda [1] Ouganda [1]	3	3	3	3	3	3	3	3	3	3
United Rep. of Tanzania [1] Rép.-Unie de Tanzanie [1]	25	25	25	25	25	25	25	25	25	25
Zambia Zambie	4	2	2[1]	2[1]	4[1]	4[1]	4[1]	4[1]	4[1]	4[1]
Zimbabwe Zimbabwe	73	81	81	81	81	76	80	80[1]	80[1]	80[1]
America, North **Amérique du Nord**	**97 399**	**101 968**	**107 536**	**105 823**	**111 272**	**109 388**	**113 229**	**111 720**	**105 717**	**106 463**
Canada Canada	17 557	18 348	18 713	18 414	18 969	18 875	20 280	20 921	19 834	20 226
Costa Rica Costa Rica	19[1]	*20	20[1]	20[1]	20[1]	20[1]	20[1]	20[1]	20[1]	20[1]
Cuba Cuba	*57	57[1]	57[1]	57[1]	57[1]	57[1]	57[1]	57[1]	57[1]	57[1]
Dominican Republic Rép. dominicaine	7	7	7	21	21[1]	130	130[1]	130[1]	130[1]	130[1]
El Salvador El Salvador	17	17	17	56	56[1]	56[1]	56[1]	56[1]	56[1]	56[1]

47

Paper and paperboard
Production: thousand metric tons *[cont.]*

Papiers et cartons
Production: milliers de tonnes *[suite]*

Region, country or area Région, pays ou zone	1993	1994	1995	1996	1997	1998	1999	2000	2001	2002
Guatemala Guatemala	14	25	31	31[1]	31[1]	31[1]	31[1]	31[1]	31[1]	31[1]
Honduras Honduras	0	0	90	103	88	95	95[1]	95[1]	95[1]	95[1]
Jamaica Jamaïque	3	3[1]	0	0[1]	0[1]	0[1]	0[1]	0[1]	0[1]	0[1]
Mexico Mexique	2 447	2 518	*3 047	3 047[1]	3 491	3 673	3 784	3 865	4 056	4 056[1]
Panama Panama	28	28[1]	28[1]	28[1]	28[1]	0	0	0[1]	0[1]	0[1]
United States Etats-Unis	77 250	80 945	85 526	84 046	88 511	86 451	88 776	86 545	81 438	81 792
America, South **Amérique du Sud**	**8 208**	**8 812**	**9 204**	**9 247**	**9 970**	**9 606**	**9 664**	**10 223**	**11 222**	**11 222**
Argentina Argentine	850	*961	1 025	991	1 133	978	1 012	1 270	1 374	1 374[1]
Bolivia Bolivie	0	0[1]	2	2	2[1]	2[1]	0[1]	0[1]	0[1]	0[1]
Brazil Brésil	5 352	5 730	5 856	5 885	6 475	6 524	6 255	6 473	7 354	7 354[1]
Chile Chili	526	553	573	680	614	642	824	861	879	879[1]
Colombia Colombie	595	672	690	693	704	712	733	771[1]	771[1]	771[1]
Ecuador Equateur	103	78	83	86	91	91[1]	91[1]	91[1]	91[1]	91[1]
Paraguay Paraguay	13	13[1]	13[1]	13[1]	13[1]	13[1]	13[1]	13[1]	13[1]	13[1]
Peru Pérou	79	94	140	140[1]	140[1]	63	63[1]	63[1]	63[1]	63[1]
Uruguay Uruguay	83[1]	83[1]	86	86[1]	*90	*88	*92	87[1]	88[1]	88[1]
Venezuela Venezuela	607	628	736	671	708	493	581	594[1]	589[1]	589[1]
Asia **Asie**	**65 822**	**71 791**	**77 457**	**81 636**	**85 208**	**85 584**	**91 731**	**94 739**	**97 223**	**97 377**
Armenia Arménie	0	0	0	0	0	0	0	20[1]	1[1]	2[1]
Azerbaijan Azerbaïdjan	0	0	0	0	0	0	0	28	146	143
Bangladesh Bangladesh	*150	*160	120[1]	90[1]	70	46	46[1]	46[1]	46[1]	46[1]
Cambodia Cambodge	0	0[1]	0[1]	0[1]	0[1]	0[1]	0[1]	0[1]	0[1]	0[1]
China Chine	22 077	25 627	28 517	30 913	31 763	*32 303	34 137	35 439	37 929	37 929[1]
India Inde	2 626	*2 859	*3 025	3 025[1]	2 922	3 320	3 845	3 673	3 973	3 973[1]
Indonesia Indonésie	2 600[1]	*3 054	*3 425	*4 121	*4 822	*5 487	6 978	6 977	6 995	6 995[1]
Iran (Islamic Rep. of) Iran (Rép. islamique d')	260	205	205	205	205	20	25	46	46[1]	46[1]
Iraq Iraq	13[1]	*18	18[1]	18[1]	18[1]	20	20[1]	20[1]	20[1]	20[1]

47

Paper and paperboard
Production: thousand metric tons *[cont.]*

Papiers et cartons
Production: milliers de tonnes *[suite]*

Region, country or area Région, pays ou zone	1993	1994	1995	1996	1997	1998	1999	2000	2001	2002
Israel Israël	213	229	275	275[1]	275[1]	242	275[1]	275[1]	275	275[1]
Japan Japon	27 764	28 527	29 664	30 014	31 014	29 886	30 631	31 828	30 717	30 717[1]
Jordan Jordanie	29	31	31	31	32	32	32	19[1]	27[1]	27[1]
Kazakhstan Kazakhstan	0	0	0	0	0	0	0	19[1]	6[1]	23
Korea, Dem. P. R.[1] Corée, R. p. dém. de[1]	80	80	80	80	80	80	80	80	80	80
Korea, Republic of Corée, République de	5 804	6 435	*6 878	7 681	8 334	7 750	8 875	9 308	9 332	9 332[1]
Kyrgyzstan Kirghizistan	0	0	0	0	0	0	0	2[1]	7[1]	16[1]
Lebanon[1] Liban[1]	42	42	42	42	42	42	42	42	42	42
Malaysia Malaisie	663	574	665	674	711	761	859	791	851	851[1]
Myanmar Myanmar	15	15	15	15	39	41	37	39	42	42[1]
Nepal[1] Népal[1]	13	13	13	13	13	13	13	13	13	13
Pakistan Pakistan	362	403	420	447	500	527	574	592	1 165	1 165[1]
Philippines Philippines	*518	*518	*613	613[1]	613[1]	987	1 010	1 107	1 056	1 056[1]
Singapore Singapour	*96	*97	*87	87[1]	87[1]	87[1]	87[1]	87[1]	87[1]	87[1]
Sri Lanka Sri Lanka	29	31	28	25	25[1]	25[1]	25[1]	24[1]	25[1]	25[1]
Syrian Arab Republic[1] Rép. arabe syrienne[1]	1	1	1	1	1	1	1	1	1	1
Thailand Thaïlande	1 306	1 664	1 970	2 036	2 271	2 367	2 434	2 312	2 445	2 445[1]
Turkey Turquie	1 032	1 102	1 240	1 105	1 246	1 357	1 349	1 567	1 513	1 643
Viet Nam Viet Nam	129	*106	*125	125[1]	125[1]	190	356	384	384[1]	384[1]
Europe **Europe**	**75 427**	**80 446**	**82 310**	**81 773**	**88 771**	**90 794**	**94 785**	**100 400**	**99 017**	**101 646**
Albania Albanie	44[1]	44[1]	44[1]	44[1]	44[1]	44[1]	1	3	3[1]	3[1]
Austria Autriche	3 301	3 603	3 599	3 653	3 816	4 009	4 142	4 386	4 250	4 419
Belarus Bélarus	175	131	131	131	131	195	208	236	224	216
Belgium Belgique	...	...	...	...	...	...	1 727	1 727	1 662	1 662[1]
Belgium-Luxembourg Belgique-Luxembourg	1 147[1]	1 088	1 088[1]	1 432	1 432[1]	1 831	...	...	...	...
Bulgaria Bulgarie	139	148	150	150	150	153	126	136	136[1]	136[1]
Croatia Croatie	114	248	325	304	393	403	417	406[1]	451	467

47

Paper and paperboard
Production: thousand metric tons *[cont.]*

Papiers et cartons
Production: milliers de tonnes *[suite]*

Region, country or area Région, pays ou zone	1993	1994	1995	1996	1997	1998	1999	2000	2001	2002
Czech Republic République tchèque	643	700	738	714	772	768	770	804	864	870
Denmark Danemark	339	345	345[1]	345[1]	391	393	397	263[1]	253[1]	253[1]
Estonia Estonie	42	42	42	53	35	43	48	54[1]	70[1]	81[1]
Finland Finlande	9 990	10 909	10 942	10 442	12 149	12 703	12 947	13 509	12 502	12 776
France France	7 975	8 701	8 619	8 556	9 143	9 161	9 603	10 006	9 625	9 798
Germany Allemagne	13 034	14 457	14 827	14 733	15 930	16 311	16 742	18 182	17 879	18 526
Greece Grèce	750	750[1]	750[1]	750[1]	478	622	545	496	495	495
Hungary Hongrie	292	328	321	363	820	434	456	506	495[1]	517
Ireland Irlande	0	0	0	0[1]	0[1]	42	42	43	43[1]	44[1]
Italy Italie	6 019	6 705	6 810	6 954	8 032	8 254	8 568	9 129	8 926	9 273
Latvia Lettonie	10	4	6	8	16	18	19	16[1]	24[1]	24[1]
Lithuania Lituanie	31	23	29	31	25	37	37	53	68[1]	78
Netherlands Pays-Bas	2 855	3 011	2 967	2 987	3 159	3 180	3 256	3 332	3 174	3 346
Norway Norvège	1 958	2 148	2 261	2 096	2 129	2 260	2 241	2 300	2 220	2 114
Poland Pologne	1 183	1 326	1 477	1 528	1 660	1 718	1 839	1 934	2 086[1]	2 230
Portugal Portugal	878	949	977	1 026	1 080	1 136	1 163	1 290[1]	1 419[1]	1 537
Romania Roumanie	359[1]	288	364	332	324	301	289	340	395	370
Russian Federation Fédération de Russie	4 459	3 412	4 073	3 224	3 339	3 595	4 535	5 310	5 625	5 904
Serbia and Montenegro Serbie-et-Monténégro	222	238	245	249	300	326	230	180	241	254
Slovakia Slovaquie	303	299	327	467	526	597	803	925	988	994
Slovenia Slovénie	401	460	449	456	430	491	417	411	633	494
Spain Espagne	3 348	3 503	3 684	3 768	3 968	3 545	4 435	4 765	5 131	5 365
Sweden Suède	8 781	9 284	9 159	9 018	9 756	9 879	10 071	10 786	10 534	10 724
Switzerland Suisse	1 332	1 450	1 435	1 461	1 583	1 592	1 748	1 616	1 745	1 804
TFYR of Macedonia L'ex-R.y. Macédoine	22	24	34	21	21	15	14	17	15	18
Ukraine Ukraine	0	0	0	288	261	261[1]	373	373	373[1]	373[1]
United Kingdom Royaume-Uni	5 282	5 829	6 093	6 189	6 479	6 477	6 576	6 868	6 467	6 481

47

Paper and paperboard
Production: thousand metric tons *[cont.]*

Papiers et cartons
Production: milliers de tonnes *[suite]*

Region, country or area Région, pays ou zone	1993	1994	1995	1996	1997	1998	1999	2000	2001	2002
Oceania **Océanie**	**2 875**	**3 061**	**3 155**	**3 185**	**3 308**	**3 385**	**3 381**	**3 713**	**3 491**	**3 491**
Australia Australie	2 039	2 197	2 252	2 320	2 418	2 541	2 564	2 836	2 652	2 652[1]
New Zealand Nouvelle-Zélande	836	864	903	865	890	844	817	877	839	839[1]

Source:
Food and Agriculture Organization of the United Nations (FAO),
Rome, the FAOSTAT database and the "FAO Yearbook of Forest
Products".

Source:
Organisation des Nations Unies pour l'alimentation et l'agriculture
(FAO), Rome, la base de données FAOSTAT et "l'Annuaire FAO des
produits forestiers".

1   FAO estimate.

1   Estimation de la FAO.

48
Cement
Production: thousand metric tons
Ciment
Production: milliers de tonnes

Country or area Pays ou zone	1992	1993	1994	1995	1996	1997	1998	1999	2000	2001
Afghanistan *[1] Afghanistan *[1]	115	115	115	115	116	116	116	120	120	...
Albania Albanie	197	198	240	240	204	100	84	108	180	30
Algeria Algérie	7 093	6 951	6 093	6 783	7 470	7 146	7 836	7 685	8 703	8 710
Angola Angola	370	*250[1]	*240[1]	*200[1]	*270[1]	301[1]	*350[1]	*350[1]	*350[1]	...
Argentina Argentine	5 051	5 647	6 306	5 477	5 117	6 769	7 092	7 187	6 119	...
Armenia Arménie	368	198	122	228	281	293	314	287	219	276
Australia Australie	5 897	6 628	7 017	6 606	6 397[2]	6 701	7 235[2]	7 705[2]	7 937[2]	6 786[2]
Austria Autriche	5 029	4 941	4 828	3 843[1]	3 900	3 852[1]	3 789[1]	3 817[1]	3 799[1]	3 863[1]
Azerbaijan Azerbaïdjan	827	643	467	196	223	303	201	171	251	523
Bahrain Bahreïn	...	...	...	...	192[1]	172	230	153[1]	89[1]	89[1]
Bangladesh [2] Bangladesh [2]	272	207	324	316	426	610	543	1 514	1 868	2 340
Barbados Barbade	71	64	76	76	108	176	257	257	268	250
Belarus Bélarus	2 263	1 908	1 488	1 235	1 467	1 876	2 035	1 998	1 847	1 800[3]
Belgium Belgique	8 073	7 569	7 542	7 501	6 996	6 996	6 852	9 252	8 000[1]	...
Benin Bénin	370[1]	506[1]	465[1]	579[1]	*360[1]	*450[1]	*520[1]	*520[1]	759	...
Bhutan [1] Bhoutan [1]	116	108	*120	*140	*160	*160	*150	*150	*150	160
Bolivia Bolivie	650	718	776	877	897	1 048	1 167	1 201	1 072	983
Bosnia and Herzegovina [1] Bosnie-Herzégovine [1]	...	...	...	...	150	200	300	300	300	...
Brazil Brésil	23 902	24 845	25 229	28 256	34 559	37 995	39 942	40 248	39 559	38 735
Brunei Darussalam Brunéi Darussalam	...	...	...	...	...	...	...	222	241	234
Bulgaria Bulgarie	2 132	2 007	1 910	2 070	2 137	1 654	1 742	2 060	2 209	2 088
Burkina Faso [1] Burkina Faso [1]	...	...	...	...	...	40 000	40 000	50 000	50 000	50 000
Cameroon Cameroun	620[1]	*620[1]	*479[1]	522	305[1]	633	740	852	1 570	980
Canada Canada	8 592	9 394	10 584	10 440	11 587	11 736[4]	12 124[4]	12 625[4]	12 612[4]	12 986[4]
Chile Chili	2 660	3 024	3 001	3 304	3 627	3 718	3 890	2 508	2 686	3 145
China Chine	308217	367878	421180	475606	491189	511738	536000	573000	597000	661040
China, Hong Kong SAR Chine, Hong Kong RAS	1 644	1 712	1 927	1 913	2 027	1 925	1 539	1 387	1 284	1 279
Colombia Colombie	9 163	18 205	9 273	9 908	...	10 878	8 673	6 677	7 131	6 776

48

Cement
Production: thousand metric tons [cont.]

Ciment
Production: milliers de tonnes [suite]

Country or area Pays ou zone	1992	1993	1994	1995	1996	1997	1998	1999	2000	2001
Congo Congo	124	95	87	98	43	20	0	0	0	...
Costa Rica[1] Costa Rica[1]	*700	860	940	865	830	940	1 085	1 100	1 150	*1 100
Côte d'Ivoire[1] Côte d'Ivoire[1]	*510	*500	*1 100	*1 000	*1 000	1 100	650	650	650	650
Croatia Croatie	1 771	1 683	2 055	1 708	1 842	2 134	3 873	2 712	2 852	3 246
Cuba Cuba	1 134[5]	1 049[5]	1 085[5]	1 456[5]	1 438	1 701	1 713	1 785	1 633	...
Cyprus Chypre	1 132	1 089	1 053	1 024	1 021	910	1 207	1 157	1 398	...
Czech Republic République tchèque	6 145	5 393	5 252	4 831	5 016	4 874	4 599	4 241	4 093	3 591
Dem. Rep. of the Congo[1] Rép. dém. du Congo[1]	174	149	166	235	241	125	*100	*100	...	...
Denmark[6] Danemark[6]	2 072	2 270	2 427	2 584	2 629	2 683	2 667	2 534	2 639	2 678
Dominican Republic Rép. dominicaine	1 365	1 271	1 276	1 450	1 642	1 822	1 872	2 295	2 521	2 758
Ecuador Equateur	2 072	2 155	2 452	2 549	2 601	2 900[1]	2 539	2 262	2 800[1]	2 947
Egypt Egypte	15 454	12 576	13 544	14 237	15 569	15 569	15 480	11 933	25 101	26 811
El Salvador El Salvador	760[5]	659[5]	915[5]	914[5]	948[1]	1 020[1]	1 065[1]	24 250[1]	25 036[1]	*25 000[1]
Eritrea[1] Erythrée[1]	...	...	...	...	...	60	50	57	45	47
Estonia Estonie	483	354	403	418	388	422	321	358	329	405
Ethiopia Ethiopie	237[7]	377[7]	464[7]	609[7]	672[7]	775[7]	783[7]	767[7]	816[7]	819
Fiji Fidji	85	80	94	91	84	96	89	99	87	99
Finland Finlande	1 133	835	864	907	975	*960[1]	*1 104	*1 164	1 422	1 325
France France	21 584	19 222	20 020	19 724	18 337	18 309	19 434	20 302	20 000[1]	20 652
French Guiana[1] Guyane française[1]	...	...	...	...	...	51	50	50	50	50
Gabon Gabon	116[1]	132[1]	126[1]	154[1]	185	200	198	162	166	240
Georgia Géorgie	426	278	89	59	85	94	199	341	348	335
Germany Allemagne	37 331	36 649	40 217	38 858	37 006	37 210	38 464	39 970	38 088	33 689
Ghana Ghana	1 020[1]	1 200[1]	1 350[1]	*1 300[1]	*1 500[1]	1 446	1 573	1 851	1 673	1 490
Greece Grèce	12 761	12 492	12 633	10 914	13 391	13 660	14 207	13 624	14 147	15 563
Guadeloupe Guadeloupe	292	276	283	*230	*230[1]	*230[1]	*230[1]	*230[1]	*230[1]	...
Guatemala Guatemala	658[5]	1 018[5]	1 163[5]	1 257	1 173	1 480	1 496	2 120	2 039	*1 600[1]
Guinea[1] Guinée[1]	...	...	...	...	...	260	277	297	300	300

48

Cement
Production: thousand metric tons *[cont.]*
   Ciment
   Production: milliers de tonnes *[suite]*

Country or area Pays ou zone	1992	1993	1994	1995	1996	1997	1998	1999	2000	2001
Haiti [5] Haïti [5]	216	228	228	...	...	...	...	...	...	...
Honduras Honduras	760[5]	933[5]	1 000[5]	995[5]	952[1]	*1 041[1]	896[1]	980[1]	1 100[1]	1 100[1]
Hungary Hongrie	2 236	2 533	2 793	2 875	2 747	2 811	2 999	2 980	3 326	3 452
Iceland Islande	100	86	81	82	90	110	118	131	144	125
India Inde	53 936	57 326	63 461	67 722	73 261	82 873	87 646	100230	99 227	106491[8]
Indonesia Indonésie	14 048	19 610	24 564	23 136	*24 648	20 702	*22 344	22 806	22 789[1]	...
Iran (Islamic Rep. of) Iran (Rép. islamique d')	15 094[8]	16 321[8]	16 250[8]	16 904[8]	17 703[8]	16 994[9]	20 049[8]	22 219[9]	23 276[9]	24 000[1]
Iraq Iraq	2 453	*2 000[1]	*2 000[1]	2 108[1]	*1 600[1]	*1 700[1]	*2 000[1]	*2 000[1]	*2 000[1]	2 000[1]
Ireland [1] Irlande [1]	*1 600	1 450	1 623	1 730	1 933	2 100	2 256	2 466	2 620	2 500
Israel Israël	3 960	4 536	4 800	6 204	6 723	5 916	6 476[1]	6 354[1]	6 600[1]	6 900[1]
Italy Italie	41 034	33 771	32 698	33 716	33 327	33 718	35 512	36 827	38 302	38 965
Jamaica Jamaïque	480	441	445	518	559	588	558	504[5]	521[5]	...
Japan Japon	88 252	88 046	91 624	90 474	94 492	91 938	81 328	80 120	81 097	76 550
Jordan Jordanie	2 651	3 437	3 392	3 415	3 512	3 250	2 650	2 688	2 640	3 149
Kazakhstan Kazakhstan	6 436	3 963	2 033	1 772	1 115	657	622	838	1 175	2 029
Kenya Kenya	1 507	1 417	1 470	1 670	1 575	1 580	1 453	1 389	1 367	1 319
Korea, Dem. P. R. [1] Corée, R. p. dém. de [1]	*17 000	*17 000	*17 000	*17 000	*17 000	7 000	7 000	6 000	6 000	5 160
Korea, Republic of Corée, République de	44 444	47 313	52 088	56 101	58 434	60 317	46 791	48 579	51 417	53 062
Kuwait Koweït	534	956	1 232	*1 363	1 113[10]	1 370	2 310	947	1 187	1 600
Kyrgyzstan Kirghizistan	1 096	692	426	310	546	658	709	386	453	500[3]
Lao People's Dem. Rep. Rép. dém. pop. lao	...	...	7	59	78[1]	84[1]	80[1]	80[1]	92[1]	90[1]
Latvia Lettonie	340	114	244	204	325	246	366	301	...	500[1]
Lebanon Liban	2 163	2 591	2 948	3 470	3 430	3 126	3 316	2 714	2 808	2 890
Liberia [1] Libéria [1]	*8	*8	*3	*5	*15	*7	*10	*15	15	15
Libyan Arab Jamah. Jamah. arabe libyenne	4	4	4	3	3	3	3	3	3[1]	...
Lithuania Lituanie	1 485	727	736	649	656	714	788	666	573	529
Luxembourg Luxembourg	695	719	711	714	667	683	699	742	749	725
Madagascar Madagascar	30	36	8	38	44	36	44	46[1]	48[1]	...

48

Cement
Production: thousand metric tons *[cont.]*

Ciment
Production: milliers de tonnes *[suite]*

Country or area Pays ou zone	1992	1993	1994	1995	1996	1997	1998	1999	2000	2001
Malawi Malawi	108	117	122	124	88	70	83	104	198[1]	111
Malaysia Malaisie	8 366	8 797	9 928	10 713	12 349	12 668	10 397	10 104	11 445	13 820
Mali Mali	16	14	14	13	21	10[1]	10[1]	10[1]	10[1]	...
Martinique Martinique	262	234	231	*225	*220[1]	*220[1]	*220[1]	*220[1]	*220[1]	*220[1]
Mauritania[1] Mauritanie[1]	122	111	374	120	*100	*80	*50	*50	*50	...
Mexico Mexique	27 114	28 725	31 594	25 295	28 174	29 685	30 915	31 958	33 429	32 239
Mongolia Mongolie	133	82	86	109	106	*112[1]	109	104	92	...
Morocco Maroc	6 223	6 175	6 284	6 399	6 585	7 236	7 155	7 194	7 497	8 058
Mozambique Mozambique	73	60	62	146	179	217	264	266	348	421
Myanmar[11] Myanmar[11]	472	400	477	525	513	524	371	343	400	384
Nepal[12] Népal[12]	237	248	315	327	309	227	139	191	206	215
Netherlands Pays-Bas	3 296[6,13]	3 142[6,13]	3 180[1]	3 180[1]	3 140[1]	3 220[1]	3 235[1]	3 480[1]	3 450[1]	*3 400[1]
New Caledonia Nouvelle-Calédonie	90	101	97	99	89	100	89	93	91	100
New Zealand Nouvelle-Zélande	599	684	*900[1]	*950[1]	974[1]	976[1]	950[1]	960[1]	950[1]	950[1]
Nicaragua Nicaragua	277[1]	255[1]	309[1]	324[1]	360[1]	361	412	536	568	*588
Niger Niger	29	31	26	31	29[1]	*30[1]	*30[1]	*30[1]	*30[1]	...
Nigeria Nigéria	3 367	3 247	1 275	1 573	2 545[1]	2 520[1]	2 700[1]	2 500[1]	2 500[1]	3 000[1]
Norway Norvège	1 242	1 368	1 464	1 613	1 690	1 724[1]	1 676[1]	1 827[1]	1 851[1]	*1 870[1]
Oman Oman	1 103[14]	1 130[14]	1 191[14]	1 280[14]	1 206[14]	1 233[14]	1 217[14]	1 990[14]	1 815[14]	1 370[1]
Pakistan[2] Pakistan[2]	8 321	8 558	8 100	7 913	9 567	9 536	9 364	9 635	9 314	9 674
Panama Panama	473	620[5]	678[5]	658[5]	651	752	814	976	849[5]	760[1]
Paraguay Paraguay	476	476	529	624	627	603	586	556	516	...
Peru Pérou	2 080	2 327	3 177	3 645	3 678	4 092	4 069	3 327	3 265	*3 172
Philippines Philippines	6 540	7 932	9 576	10 566	12 429[1]	14 681	12 888	12 557	11 959	11 378
Poland Pologne	11 908	12 200	13 834	13 914	13 959	15 003	14 970	15 555	15 046	12 074
Portugal Portugal	7 728	7 662	7 756	8 030	8 444	9 395	9 784	10 079	10 079	10 079
Puerto Rico Porto Rico	1 266	1 303	1 356	1 398	1 508	1 586	1 646	1 757	...	...
Qatar Qatar	354	400	470	475	486	584	857	959	1 029	1 209

48

Cement
Production: thousand metric tons *[cont.]*

Ciment
Production: milliers de tonnes *[suite]*

Country or area Pays ou zone	1992	1993	1994	1995	1996	1997	1998	1999	2000	2001
Republic of Moldova République de Moldova	705	110[15]	39[15]	49[15]	40[15]	122[15]	74[15]	50[15]	222[15]	158[15]
Réunion Réunion	344	325	321	313	229	200	342	263	258	...
Romania Roumanie	6 271	6 158	5 998	6 842	6 956	6 553	7 300	6 252	8 411	5 668
Russian Federation Fédération de Russie	61 699	49 903	37 220	36 466	27 791	26 688	26 018	28 529	32 389	35 271
Rwanda Rwanda	60	60	10	36	42	61	60	66	70[1]	83[1]
Saudi Arabia Arabie saoudite	15 301[10]	16 584	17 013	15 772	16 391	15 448	15 776	16 381	18 296	20 963
Senegal Sénégal	602	591	697	694	810	854	847	1 030	1 000[1]	1 000[1]
Serbia and Montenegro Serbie-et-Monténégro	2 036	1 088	1 612	1 696	2 212	2 011	2 253	1 575[16]	2 117	2 418
Singapore *[1] Singapour *[1]	1 900	2 980	3 100	3 200	3 300	3 300	3 300	3 250	3 250	...
Slovakia Slovaquie	3 374	2 656	2 879	2 981	4 234	5 856	3 066	3 084	3 045	3 123
Slovenia Slovénie	1 568	1 291	1 667	1 807	1 064	1 113	1 149	1 222	1 252	...
South Africa Afrique du Sud	5 850	6 135	7 068	7 437	7 664	7 891	7 676	8 211	8 715	...
Spain Espagne	24 612	21 658	25 884	27 220	26 339	27 860	27 943[1]	35 830[1]	38 154[1]	*40 512[1]
Sri Lanka Sri Lanka	553	466	*925[1]	956	670	966	2 151	2 354	2 432	2 123
Sudan[1] Soudan[1]	*250	*250	*160	391	*380	276	*198	*231	*146	146
Suriname Suriname	11	17	18	*60[1]	*60[1]	*65[1]	*65[1]	*60[1]	60[1]	60[1]
Sweden Suède	2 289	2 152	2 138	2 550	2 503	2 272	2 372	2 293	2 613	2 644
Switzerland Suisse	4 260	*4 000[1]	*4 370[1]	4 024[1]	3 638[1]	3 568[1]	*3 600[1]	*3 600[1]	3 600[1]	3 600[1]
Syrian Arab Republic Rép. arabe syrienne	3 515	3 906	4 344	4 804	4 817	4 838	5 016	5 134	4 631	5 428
Tajikistan Tadjikistan	447	262	178	78	49	36	18	33	55	69
Thailand Thaïlande	21 711	26 300	29 929	34 051	38 749	37 136	22 722	25 354	25 499	27 913
TFYR of Macedonia L'ex-R.y. Macédoine	516	499	486	523	490	610	461	563	801	585
Togo[1] Togo[1]	350	350	286	350	413	421	500	600	700	800
Trinidad and Tobago Trinité-et-Tobago	482	527	583	559	617	677	700	740	743	697
Tunisia Tunisie	4 184	4 508	4 605	4 998	4 566	4 378	4 588	4 864	5 647	...
Turkey Turquie	28 455	31 134	29 356	33 153	35 214	36 035	38 175	34 215	36 238	30 124
Turkmenistan Turkménistan	1 050	1 118	690	437	438	601	750	780	420	448
Uganda Ouganda	38	52	45	84	195	290	321	347	367[1]	416[1]

48

Cement
Production: thousand metric tons [cont.]

Ciment
Production: milliers de tonnes [suite]

Country or area Pays ou zone	1992	1993	1994	1995	1996	1997	1998	1999	2000	2001
Ukraine Ukraine	20 121	15 012	11 435	7 627	5 021	5 101	5 591	5 828	5 311	5 786
United Arab Emirates Emirats arabes unis	4 328[10]	4 734[10]	4 968[10]	5 071[10]	6 000[1]	6 330[1]	7 066[1]	7 069[1]	6 100[1]	6 100[1]
United Kingdom Royaume-Uni	11 006	11 039	12 307	11 805	12 214	12 638[1]	12 409[1]	12 697[1]	12 800[1]	...
United Rep. of Tanzania Rép.-Unie de Tanzanie	677	749	686	739	726	621	178[1]	833[1]	833[1]	875[1]
United States Etats-Unis	69 585	73 807	77 948	76 906	79 266	82 582	83 931	85 952	87 846	88 900
Uruguay Uruguay	552	610	701	593	631	818	940	839	688	674
Uzbekistan Ouzbékistan	5 934	5 277	4 780	3 419	3 277	3 286	3 358[17]	3 331[17]	3 284[17]	3 722[17]
Venezuela Venezuela	6 585	6 876	4 562	*6 900	7 556[1]	8 145[1]	8 202[1]	8 500[1]	8 600[1]	8 700[1]
Viet Nam Viet Nam	3 926	*4 200[1]	*4 700[1]	5 828	6 585	8 019	9 738	*10 381	13 298	...
Yemen Yémen	820	1 000	898	1 100	1 028	1 038	1 195	1 454	1 406	1 493
Zambia Zambie	347[1]	*350[1]	280[1]	312[1]	348[1]	384[1]	351[1]	300[1]	380[1]	303
Zimbabwe Zimbabwe	829	816	624	948	996	954	1 115	1 105	1 000	549

Source:
United Nations Statistics Division, New York, "Industrial Commodity Statistics Yearbook 2001" and the industrial statistics database.

Source:
Organisation des Nations Unies, Division de statistique, New York, "Annuaire de statistiques industrielles par produit 2001" et la base de données pour les statistiques industrielles.

1	Source: U.S. Geological Survey (Washington, D. C.).
2	Twelve months ending 30 June of the year stated.
3	Source: Statistical Yearbook, Commonwealth of Independent States (Moscow).
4	Shipments.
5	Source: United Nations Economic Commission for Latin America and the Caribbean (ECLAC), (Santiago).
6	Sales.
7	Twelve months ending 7 July of the year stated.
8	Production by establishments employing 50 or more persons.
9	Production by establishments employing 10 or more persons.
10	Source: Arab Gulf Cooperation Council (GCC).
11	Government production only.
12	Twelve months beginning 16 July of the year stated.
13	Production by establishments employing 20 or more persons.
14	Source: Bulletin of Industrial Statistics for the Arab Countries, United Nations Economic and Social Commission for Western Asia (ESCWA), Beirut.
15	Excluding the Transnistria region.
16	Beginning 1999, data for Kosovo are not included.
17	Source: Country Economic Review, Asian Development Bank (Manila).

1	Source : U.S. Geological Survey (Washington, D. C.).
2	Période de 12 mois finissant le 30 juin de l'année indiquée.
3	Source: "Statistical Yearbook", Commonwealth of Independent States (Moscow).
4	Expéditions.
5	Source: Commission économique des Nations Unies pour l'Amérique Latine et des Caraïbes (CEPAL), (Santiago).
6	Ventes.
7	Période de 12 mois finissant le 7 juillet de l'année indiquée.
8	Production des établissements occupant 50 personnes ou plus.
9	Production des établissements occupant 10 personnes ou plus.
10	Source: "Arab Gulf Cooperation Council", (GCC).
11	Production de l'Etat seulement.
12	Période de 12 mois commençant le 16 juillet de l'année indiquée.
13	Production des établissements occupant 20 personnes ou plus.
14	Source: "Bulletin of Industrial Statistics for the Arab Countries", Commission économique et sociale pour l'Asie occidentale (CESAO), Beirut.
15	Non compris la région de Transnistria.
16	A partir de 1999, non compris les données de Kosovo.
17	Source: "Country Economic Review, Asian Development Bank" (Manila).

49

Sulphuric acid
Production: thousand metric tons

Acide sulfurique
Production: milliers de tonnes

Country or area Pays ou zone	1992	1993	1994	1995	1996	1997	1998	1999	2000	2001
Albania Albanie	11	6	4	...	0	0	0	0	0	...
Algeria Algérie	52	55	40	45	42	55	45	48	36	22
Argentina Argentine	219	206	204	226	220	...	...	...	...	...
Australia [1] Australie [1]	816	868	833	...	...	...	...	...	...	...
Azerbaijan Azerbaïdjan	269	141	56	24	31	53	24	26	52	10
Bangladesh [1] Bangladesh [1]	4	7	6	5	9	4	4	4	5	4
Belarus Bélarus	616	399	291	437	549	698	640	614	584	...
Belgium Belgique	1 906[2]	1 593[2]	717[3]	673[3]	678[3]	668[3]	596[3]	709[3]	...	...
Bolivia Bolivie	0	1	3	*1	...	831	754	620	...	...
Brazil Brésil	3 257	3 724	4 112	4 043	4 308	4 638	4 624	4 882	5 221	5 211
Bulgaria Bulgarie	404	409	428	454	525	556	506	456	644	620
Canada Canada	3 776	3 713	4 059	3 844	4 278	*4 100	4 333	4 194	3 804	3 846
Chile Chili	887	920	1 174	1 427	1 518	1 864	1 983	2 436	2 363	2 736
China Chine	14 087	13 365	15 365	18 110	18 836	20 369	21 710	23 560	24 270	26 963
Colombia Colombie	91	77	103	86	...	95	93	92	...	...
Croatia Croatie	278	178	206	233	223	202	164	193	200	126
Czech Republic République tchèque	522	383	337	340	345	333	327	318	274	241
Denmark Danemark	38[4,5]	...	5[5]	25[5]	19[5]	2[5]	...	0[6]	...	...
Egypt Egypte	111	122	112	133	299	84	82	83	75	...
Estonia Estonie	46	...	0	...	...	...	...	...	...	...
Finland Finlande	1 087	1 179	1 084	1 159	1 288	2 182	2 496	2 857	1 211	914
France France	2 871	2 357	2 227	2 382[6]	2 263[6]	2 250[6]	2 214[6]	2 177[6]	2 181	2 051
Germany Allemagne	...	...	2 781[6]	1 387	1 225	1 370	1 601	1 618	1 474	1 504
Greece Grèce	617	550	623	753	1 544	1 655	814	911	966	515
Hungary [7] Hongrie [7]	99	77	80	114	94	89	62	53	80	...
India Inde	4 183	3 730	3 745	4 402	4 988	4 830	5 366	5 686	5 540	5 178[8]
Indonesia Indonésie	52	42	35	35	...	224	314	981	...	...

49

Sulphuric acid
Production: thousand metric tons [cont.]

Acide sulfurique
Production: milliers de tonnes [suite]

Country or area Pays ou zone	1992	1993	1994	1995	1996	1997	1998	1999	2000	2001
Iran (Islamic Rep. of) [9] Iran (Rép. islamique d') [9]	...	...	...	...	...	141	170	144	182	...
Italy Italie	1 733	1 430	1 975	2 161	2 214	2 214	2 013	1 017	1 048	988
Japan Japon	7 100	6 937	6 594	6 888	6 851	6 828	6 739	6 943	7 059	6 727
Jordan [10] Jordanie [10]	...	...	...	...	...	1	2	2	2	1
Kazakhstan Kazakhstan	2 349	1 179	681	695	653	635	605	685	635	695
Kenya [10] Kenya [10]	...			...	...	20	20	20	20	20
Kuwait [10] Koweït [10]	...	...	...	...	...	...	...	10	100	150
Lebanon [10] Liban [10]	...	...	...	...	...	174	262	249	357	357
Lithuania Lituanie	141	129	212	344	425	504	619	800	809	465
Mexico Mexique	195	178	375	...	...	...	...	...	...	...
Netherlands Pays-Bas	...	...	...	500[6]	418[6]	356[6]	429[6]	485	1 000[10,11]	*1 000[10]
Norway Norvège	615	...	...	...	...	...	...	...	...	...
Pakistan [1] Pakistan [1]	98	100	102	80	69	31	28	27	58	57
Peru Pérou	143	229	215	216	429	411	541	592	594	*623
Poland Pologne	1 244	1 145	1 452	1 861	1 761	1 741	1 707	1 505	1 948	1 945
Portugal [6] Portugal [6]	...	...	2	3	10	11	15	16	...	...
Romania Roumanie	572	527	491	477	422	329	229	234	181	58
Russian Federation Fédération de Russie	9 704	8 243	6 334	6 946	5 764	6 247	5 840	7 148	8 258	8 209
Serbia and Montenegro Serbie-et-Monténégro	302	80	24	87	231	177	211	30[12]	98	68
Slovakia Slovaquie	...		...	...	62[6]	73	68	16	15	36
Slovenia Slovénie	121	114	123	116	103	109	128	126	133	...
Spain Espagne	1 724	1 199	1 375	2 847	2 265	2 817	3 896[6]	3 334[6]	...	...
Sweden Suède	...	...	487	507	572[6]	566	383	415	359	363
Syrian Arab Republic Rép. arabe syrienne	10	10	...	...	...	214[10,13]	256[10,13]	193[10,13]	318[10,13]	320[10,13]
TFYR of Macedonia L'ex-R.y. Macédoine	95	89	72	82	99	105	101	88	109	101
Tunisia Tunisie	3 644	3 547	4 161	4 239	4 423	4 256	4 657	4 858	...	...
Turkey Turquie	642	757	730	765	798[6]	947	913	828	678	234

49

Sulphuric acid
Production: thousand metric tons *[cont.]*

Acide sulfurique
Production: milliers de tonnes *[suite]*

Country or area Pays ou zone	1992	1993	1994	1995	1996	1997	1998	1999	2000	2001
Turkmenistan Turkménistan	353	206	70	76	120	31	47	104	93	64
Ukraine Ukraine	3 000	1 843	1 646	1 593	1 577	1 438	1 354	1 393	1 036	1 040
United Kingdom Royaume-Uni	1 568	1 268	1 266	1 293	643[6]	698	716	908	581	946
United States [14] Etats-Unis [14]	12 340	11 900	11 300	11 500	10 900	10 700	10 600	10 400	9 620	9 530
Uzbekistan Ouzbékistan	1 476	1 361	805	1 016	984	870	856[15]	897[15]	823[15]	...
Venezuela Venezuela	253	...	...	...	...	...	...	...	...	...
Viet Nam Viet Nam	7	...	...	10	18	15	23	*24	35	...

<table>
<tr><td>

Source:
United Nations Statistics Division, New York, "Industrial Commodity Statistics Yearbook 2001" and the industrial statistics database.

1	Twelve months ending 30 June of the year stated.
2	Production by establishments employing 5 or more persons.
3	Incomplete coverage.
4	Excluding quantities consumed by superphosphate industry.
5	Sales.
6	Source: United Nations Economic Commission for Europe (ECE), (Geneva).
7	Including regenerated sulphuric acid.
8	Production by establishments employing 50 or more persons.
9	Production by establishments employing 10 or more persons.
10	Source: U.S. Geological Survey (Washington, D. C).
11	Break in series; data prior to the sign not comparable to following years.
12	Beginning 1999, data for Kosovo are not included.
13	Gross weight.
14	Sold or used by producers.
15	Source: Statistical Yearbook for Asia and the Pacific, United Nations Economic and Social Council for Asia and the Pacific (Bangkok).

</td><td>

Source:
Organisation des Nations Unies, Division de statistique, New York, "Annuaire de statistiques industrielles par produit 2001" et la base de données pour les statistiques industrielles.

1	Les chiffres se rapportent à 12 mois finissant le 30 juin de l'année indiquée.
2	Production des établissements occupant 5 personnes ou plus.
3	Couverture incomplète.
4	Non compris les quantités utilisées par l'industrie des superphosphates.
5	Ventes.
6	Source: Commission économique des Nations Unies pour l'Europe (CEE), (Genève).
7	Y compris l'acide sulfurique régénéré.
8	Production des établissements occupant 50 personnes ou plus.
9	Production des établissements occupant 10 personnes ou plus.
10	Source : U.S. Geological Survey (Washington, D. C.).
11	Marque une interruption dans la série et la non-comparabilité des données précédant le symbole.
12	A partir de 1999, non compris les données de Kosovo.
13	Poids brut.
14	Vendu ou utilisé par les producteurs.
15	Source: "Statistical Yearbook for Asia and the Pacific, United Nations Economic and Social Council for Asia and the Pacific" (Bangkok).

</td></tr>
</table>

50
Pig iron and crude steel
Production: thousand metric tons
Fonte et acier brut
Production : milliers de tonnes

Country or area	1994	1995	1996	1997	1998	1999	2000	2001	Pays ou zone
Albania									**Albanie**
Crude steel, ingots	19[2]	22[2]	22[2]	22[2]	22[2]	16[2]	65[2]	*0[1]	Acier brut (lingots)
Pig iron, steel-making * [1]	10	10	10	10	10	10	10	10	Fonte d'affinage * [1]
Algeria									**Algérie**
Crude steel, ingots [2]	772	780	590	361	581	675	762	895	Acier brut (lingots) [2]
Pig iron, steel-making [3]	919	962	850	526	757	807	762	895	Fonte d'affinage [3]
Angola * [1]									**Angola * [1]**
Crude steel, ingots	9	9	9	9	9	9	9	9	Acier brut (lingots)
Argentina									**Argentine**
Crude steel, ingots [2]	3 274	3 575	4 069	4 157	4 210	3 797	4 472	4 107[1]	Acier brut (lingots) [2]
Pig iron, steel-making [3]	1 392	1 524	1 966[1]	2 080[1]	*2 122[1]	*1 985[1]	*2 188[1]	*1 910[1]	Fonte d'affinage [3]
Australia									**Australie**
Crude steel, ingots [2]	7 807[4]	8 052[4]	7 944[4]	8 088[4]	8 356[4]	7 678[4]	6 742[4]	7 600[1]	Acier brut (lingots) [2]
Pig iron, steel-making [3]	7 449[4]	7 449[4]	7 554[4]	7 545[4]	7 928[4]	7 513[4]	6 489[4]	*7 200[1]	Fonte d'affinage [3]
Austria									**Autriche**
Crude steel, castings [5]	4 246[6]	*3 719	*3 359	*3 831	*3 858	...	...	...	Acier brut pour moulages [5]
Crude steel, ingots	152[6]	#1 271	1 083	1 350	1 425	1 406	1 417	1 539	Acier brut (lingots)
Pig iron, foundry [6]	0	0	0	0	0	...	...	...	Fonte de moulage [6]
Pig iron, steel-making	3 320[6]	3 878[6]	3 416[1]	3 965[1]	4 022[1]	3 913[1]	4 318[1]	*4 375[1]	Fonte d'affinage
Azerbaijan									**Azerbaïdjan**
Crude steel, castings	40	20	3	25	8	0	0	0	Acier brut pour moulages
Crude steel, ingots	37	19	0	0	0	0	0[1]	2	Acier brut (lingots)
Pig iron, foundry	...	...	...	...	...	...	0	...	Fonte de moulage
Bahrain [7]									**Bahreïn [7]**
Pig iron, foundry	...	...	...	4 000	4 000				Fonte de moulage
Bangladesh									**Bangladesh**
Crude steel, ingots	34[1,4]	36[1,4]	27[4]	23[4]	35[1]	36[1]	*35[1]	35[1]	Acier brut (lingots)
Belarus									**Bélarus**
Crude steel, castings	164	108	91	110	111	114	121	...	Acier brut pour moulages
Crude steel, ingots	716	636	795	1 110	1 300	1 335	1 502	1 500[1]	Acier brut (lingots)
Belgium									**Belgique**
Crude steel, ingots	11 268[2]	11 544[2]	10 752[2]	10 716[2]	11 400[2]	10 908[2]	11 637[1]	12 000[1]	Acier brut (lingots)
Pig iron, steel-making	8 976	9 204	8 628	8 076	8 616	8 436	8 472[1]	8 500[1]	Fonte d'affinage
Bosnia and Herzegovina									**Bosnie-Herzégovine**
Crude steel, ingots	...	...	52[6]	72[6]	75[6]	60[6]	*77[1]	*100[1]	Acier brut (lingots)
Pig iron, steel-making * [1]	100	100	100	100	100	100	100	100	Fonte d'affinage * [1]
Brazil									**Brésil**
Crude steel, castings	38	17	11	15	16	21	22	26	Acier brut pour moulages
Crude steel, ingots	25 709	25 076	25 226	26 138	25 744	24 975	27 843	26 691	Acier brut (lingots)
Pig iron, steel-making [3]	25 092	25 021	23 978	25 013	25 111	24 549	27 723	27 391	Fonte d'affinage [3]
Bulgaria									**Bulgarie**
Crude steel, ingots	2 491[2]	2 724[2]	2 457[2]	2 628[2]	2 240[1]	1 890[1]	2 020[1]	2 000[1]	Acier brut (lingots)
Pig iron, foundry	29	26	23	30	...	...	...	...	Fonte de moulage
Pig iron, steel-making	1 441	1 581	1 481	1 613	1 389[1,3]	1 130[1,3]	1 220[1,3]	1 200[1,3]	Fonte d'affinage
Canada									**Canada**
Crude steel, ingots [1,2]	13 897	14 415	14 735	15 554	15 930	16 300	15 900	16 300	Acier brut (lingots) [1,2]
Pig iron, steel-making [3]	8 112	8 460	8 638[1]	8 679[1]	8 937[1]	8 783[1]	8 904	8 302	Fonte d'affinage [3]
Chile									**Chili**
Crude steel, ingots	996	948	1 178[1]	1 167[1]	1 171[1]	1 291[1]	1 352[1]	1 247[1]	Acier brut (lingots)
Pig iron, steel-making [1]	886	855	996	941	993	1 030	1 024	927	Fonte d'affinage [1]
China									**Chine**
Crude steel, ingots	92 617[2]	95 360[2]	100 056[2]	108 942[2]	115 590[2]	124 260	128 500	151 634	Acier brut (lingots)
Pig iron, steel-making	97 410	105 293	107 225	115 114	118 629	125 392	131 015	155 543	Fonte d'affinage
China, Hong Kong SAR * [1,8]									**Chine, Hong Kong RAS * [1,8]**
Crude steel, castings	350	350	350	350	350	450	500	...	Acier brut pour moulages
Colombia									**Colombie**
Crude steel, ingots [2]	702	714[1]	695[1]	734[1]	636[1]	534[1]	660[1]	637[1]	Acier brut (lingots) [2]
Pig iron, steel-making [1,3]	245	282	286	324	256	264	272	318	Fonte d'affinage [1,3]

50

Pig iron and crude steel
Production: thousand metric tons [cont.]

Fonte et acier brut
Production : milliers de tonnes [suite]

Country or area	1994	1995	1996	1997	1998	1999	2000	2001	Pays ou zone
Croatia									**Croatie**
Crude steel, castings	...	1[6]	1[6]	1	1	1	1	2	Acier brut pour moulages
Crude steel, ingots	63	45	46	69	100	75	68	54	Acier brut (lingots)
Pig iron, steel-making * [1]	40	0	0	0	...	...	...	...	Fonte d'affinage * [1]
Cuba									**Cuba**
Crude steel, ingots	131[1]	207[1]	229	335	283	303	327	282[1]	Acier brut (lingots)
Czech Republic									**République tchèque**
Crude steel, ingots	7 075[2]	7 003[2]	6 519[2]	6 593[2]	6 059[2]	5 453[2]	#2 613	2 430	Acier brut (lingots)
Pig iron, foundry	234[6]	271[6]	...	0	0	...	...	...	Fonte de moulage
Pig iron, steel-making	5 040	5 274	4 898[3]	5 276[3]	5 165[3]	4 137[3]	4 603[3]	4 651	Fonte d'affinage
Denmark [9]									**Danemark** [9]
Crude steel, ingots	2	6	4	3	4	4	5	5	Acier brut (lingots)
Dominican Republic [1,8]									**Rép. dominicaine** [1,8]
Crude steel, castings	0	0	42	82	36	43	*36	...	Acier brut pour moulages
Ecuador [1]									**Equateur** [1]
Crude steel, ingots	32	35	20	44	46	53	58	61	Acier brut (lingots)
Egypt [1]									**Egypte** [1]
Crude steel, ingots [2]	2 622	2 642	2 618	2 717	2 870	2 619	2 820	2 800	Acier brut (lingots) [2]
Pig iron, foundry [10]	1 148	1 062	1 050	1 000	1 334	700	700	700	Fonte de moulage [10]
El Salvador [1,8]									**El Salvador** [1,8]
Crude steel, castings	*40	28	41	45	43	34	41	...	Acier brut pour moulages
Finland									**Finlande**
Crude steel, castings	21	25	20	23	23[6]	19[6]	...	...	Acier brut pour moulages
Crude steel, ingots	3 399	3 151	3 281	3 711	3 928[2,11]	3 934[2,11]	4 091[2,11]	4 100[1,2]	Acier brut (lingots)
Pig iron, steel-making	2 597	2 242	2 457	2 784	2 916	2 954[1]	2 983[1]	31 455	Fonte d'affinage
France									**France**
Crude steel, castings	218	228	220	224	225	223	...	...	Acier brut pour moulages
Crude steel, ingots	18 024	17 872	17 413	19 543	19 901	19 977	21 001[2,11]	20 000[1]	Acier brut (lingots)
Pig iron, foundry	564	588	561	646	710	896[6]	672	600	Fonte de moulage
Pig iron, steel-making	12 444	12 272	11 547	12 778	12 892	12 956	13 621[1]	12 270	Fonte d'affinage
Georgia									**Géorgie**
Crude steel, castings	1	87	82	1	0	0	0	0	Acier brut pour moulages
Crude steel, ingots	121	88	83	103	56	7	50[1]	50[1]	Acier brut (lingots)
Pig iron, foundry	1	2	2	3	1	1	...	...	Fonte de moulage
Pig iron, steel-making	0	2	2	1	0	...	...	...	Fonte d'affinage
Germany									**Allemagne**
Crude steel, castings	430	319[6]	296[6]	295[6]	323[6]	296[6]	...	...	Acier brut pour moulages
Crude steel, ingots	40 533	41 732[6]	39 496[6]	10 296	9 895	9 585	9 880	10 289	Acier brut (lingots)
Pig iron, foundry [6]	430	320	168	183	190	580	...	...	Fonte de moulage [6]
Pig iron, steel-making	29 202[6]	29 279[6]	27 172[6]	30 279[6]	29 515[6]	27 354[6]	30 846[1]	30 000[1]	Fonte d'affinage
Greece									**Grèce**
Crude steel, ingots	852[2]	936[2]	852[2]	1 020[2]	1 104[2]	960[2]	1 056[1]	1 000[1]	Acier brut (lingots)
Hungary									**Hongrie**
Crude steel, castings	0[6]	0[6]	7	0[6]	0[6]	0[6]	...	...	Acier brut pour moulages
Crude steel, ingots	1 932	1 860	2 060[11]	1 819[11]	1 940	1 920	1 970	2 065	Acier brut (lingots)
Pig iron, foundry [6]	0	0	0	0	0	0	...	...	Fonte de moulage [6]
Pig iron, steel-making	1 595[6]	1 515[6]	1 548[1]	1 190[1]	1 258[1]	1 309[1]	1 340[1]	1 300[1]	Fonte d'affinage
India									**Inde**
Crude steel, castings	384	406	467	438	419	435	398	454	Acier brut pour moulages
Crude steel, ingots	12 972	12 972	12 972	12 978	23 480[1]	24 269[1]	26 924[1]	27 300[1]	Acier brut (lingots)
Pig iron, foundry	2 705	2 873	3 304	3 427	2 976	3 201	3 105	3 886	Fonte de moulage
Pig iron, steel-making [1]	17 808	18 626	19 864	19 898	20 194	20 139	21 321	21 900	Fonte d'affinage [1]
Indonesia [1,8]									**Indonésie** [1,8]
Crude steel, castings	3 220	3 500	4 100	3 800	*2 700	*2 890	*3 010	...	Acier brut pour moulages
Iran (Islamic Rep. of) [1]									**Iran (Rép. islamique d')** [1]
Crude steel, castings	4 498[8]	4 696[8]	5 415[8]	6 322[8]	5 608[8]	6 277[8]	6 600[8]	6 890	Acier brut pour moulages
Pig iron, steel-making	1 883	1 532	1 867	2 053[3]	*2 087[3]	*2 147[3]	2 200[3]	2 300	Fonte d'affinage
Iraq [1]									**Iraq** [1]
Crude steel, ingots	*300	*300	*300	*200	*200	*200	50	50	Acier brut (lingots)
Ireland									**Irlande**
Crude steel, ingots	288[2]	312[2]	336[2]	336[2,6]	355[2,6]	337[2,6]	375[1]	100[1]	Acier brut (lingots)

50

Pig iron and crude steel
Production: thousand metric tons *[cont.]*

Fonte et acier brut
Production : milliers de tonnes *[suite]*

Country or area	1994	1995	1996	1997	1998	1999	2000	2001	Pays ou zone
Israel [1]									**Israël** [1]
Crude steel, ingots	180	200	200	270	280	280	270	220	Acier brut (lingots)
Italy									**Italie**
Crude steel, castings	139	136	106	101	137	139	137	137	Acier brut pour moulages
Crude steel, ingots	26 073	27 771	24 285	25 769	25 645	24 641	26 623	26 526	Acier brut (lingots)
Pig iron, foundry	109	74	214	245	275	165	168	298	Fonte de moulage
Pig iron, steel-making	11 052	11 603	10 107	11 232	10 516	10 664	11 007	10 263	Fonte d'affinage
Japan									**Japon**
Crude steel, castings	580	594	594	580	461	415	426	419	Acier brut pour moulages
Crude steel, ingots	97 715	101 046	98 207	103 965	93 087	93 777	106 018	102 447	Acier brut (lingots)
Pig iron, foundry	918	807	900	849	702	603	514	523	Fonte de moulage
Pig iron, steel-making	72 858	74 098	73 697	77 671	74 279	73 917	80 557	78 313	Fonte d'affinage
Jordan [1]									**Jordanie** [1]
Crude steel, castings	...	...	...	30	30	30	30	30	Acier brut pour moulages
Crude steel, ingots	...	...	...	350	325	300	270	331	Acier brut (lingots)
Kazakhstan									**Kazakhstan**
Crude steel, castings	119	67	81	#3 880	3 116	4 105	4 799	4 691	Acier brut pour moulages
Crude steel, ingots	2 849	2 959	3 135	3 816	3 116	4 105	4 770[1]	4 694[1]	Acier brut (lingots)
Pig iron, foundry	2 435	2 530	2 536	3 089	2 594	3 438	4 010	3 907	Fonte de moulage
Korea, Dem. P. R. [1]									**Corée, R. p. dém. de** [1]
Crude steel, ingots	*8 100[2]	*1 500[2]	*1 500[2]	*1 000[2]	*1 000[2]	*1 000[2]	*1 000[2]	1 000	Acier brut (lingots)
Pig iron, steel-making	...	*500[3]	*500[3]	450[3]	*250[3]	*250[3]	*250[3]	250	Fonte d'affinage
Korea, Republic of									**Corée, République de**
Crude steel, castings	142	139	...	...	...	...	...	...	Acier brut pour moulages
Crude steel, ingots	33 745	37 500	39 643[2]	43 405[2]	40 299[2]	41 502[2]	43 423[2]	44 199[2]	Acier brut (lingots)
Pig iron, steel-making [3]	21 169	22 344	23 010	22 712	23 093	23 328	24 943	26 182	Fonte d'affinage [3]
Latvia									**Lettonie**
Crude steel, castings	4	4	3	3	2	2[6]	...	...	Acier brut pour moulages
Crude steel, ingots	328	276	290	462	469	482[6]	500[1]	510[1]	Acier brut (lingots)
Libyan Arab Jamah. [1,8]									**Jamah. arabe libyenne** [1,8]
Crude steel, castings	874	909	*863	897	874	925	1 055	...	Acier brut pour moulages
Lithuania									**Lituanie**
Crude steel, castings	1	1	0	1	1	1	0	0	Acier brut pour moulages
Crude steel, ingots [2]	...	...	1[11]	1[11]	1[11]	0[12]	0[12]	...	Acier brut (lingots) [2]
Luxembourg									**Luxembourg**
Crude steel, ingots	3 073	2 613	2 501	2 580	2 477	2 600	2 571	2 725	Acier brut (lingots)
Pig iron, steel-making	1 927	1 028	829	438	0	0	0	0	Fonte d'affinage
Malaysia [1]									**Malaisie** [1]
Crude steel, castings	2 046	2 450	3 216	2 962	1 903	2 770	3 650	4 100	Acier brut pour moulages
Mexico									**Mexique**
Crude steel, ingots	8 690[2]	9 948[2]	9 852[2]	10 560[2]	10 812	...	...	13 292[1,2]	Acier brut (lingots)
Pig iron, steel-making [3]	3 359	3 660	4 230	4 450	4 532	4 808[1]	4 856[1]	*4 500[1]	Fonte d'affinage [3]
Morocco [1]									**Maroc** [1]
Crude steel, castings	7	7	5	5	5	5	5	5	Acier brut pour moulages
Pig iron, steel-making	*15	*15	*15	*15	*15	*15	*15	15	Fonte d'affinage
Myanmar [1]									**Myanmar** [1]
Crude steel, castings [8]	17	20	40	0	25	25	25	25	Acier brut pour moulages [8]
Pig iron, steel-making	1	1	1	0	2	2	2	2	Fonte d'affinage
Netherlands									**Pays-Bas**
Crude steel, castings	0	0	0	0	...	...	...	...	Acier brut pour moulages
Crude steel, ingots	6 172	6 409	6 326	6 641	6 377	6 075	5 667[1]	6 000[1]	Acier brut (lingots)
Pig iron, steel-making	5 443[9,13]	5 530[9,13]	5 544[9,13]	5 805[9,13]	5 562[9,13]	5 307[1]	4 969[1]	*5 305[1]	Fonte d'affinage
New Zealand [1]									**Nouvelle-Zélande** [1]
Crude steel, ingots	766	842	680	680	*756	*744	*765	770	Acier brut (lingots)
Pig iron, steel-making	563	631	619	534	609	620	600	600	Fonte d'affinage
Nigeria [1]									**Nigéria** [1]
Crude steel, ingots	*58	*36	*0	*0	*2	*0	*0	0	Acier brut (lingots)
Norway									**Norvège**
Crude steel, castings [6]	5	6	6	0	0	0	...	...	Acier brut pour moulages [6]
Crude steel, ingots [6]	451	497	505	564	639	595	...	...	Acier brut (lingots) [6]
Pig iron, steel-making * [1]	70	70	70	70	70	60	60	60	Fonte d'affinage * [1]

50

Pig iron and crude steel
Production: thousand metric tons *[cont.]*

Fonte et acier brut
Production : milliers de tonnes *[suite]*

Country or area	1994	1995	1996	1997	1998	1999	2000	2001	Pays ou zone
Pakistan									**Pakistan**
Crude steel, castings [1,8]	344	409	416	479	494	*500	*500	...	Acier brut pour moulages [1,8]
Pig iron, steel-making	1 253[14]	1 045[14]	1 002[14]	1 069[14]	1 016	989	1 107	1 071	Fonte d'affinage
Paraguay [1]									**Paraguay** [1]
Crude steel, castings [8]	87	95	96	66	56	56	*77	...	Acier brut pour moulages [8]
Pig iron, steel-making	90	103	104	79	66	61	82	72	Fonte d'affinage
Peru [1]									**Pérou** [1]
Crude steel, ingots [2]	506	512	678	607	631	559	749	750	Acier brut (lingots) [2]
Pig iron, steel-making [3]	*150	*247	*273	264	283	197	363	*333	Fonte d'affinage [3]
Philippines [1]									**Philippines** [1]
Crude steel, ingots	473[2]	*923[2]	*920[2]	*950[2]	*880[2]	*530[2]	*530[2]	0	Acier brut (lingots)
Poland									**Pologne**
Crude steel, castings [6]	98	52	235	382	311	30	...	...	Acier brut pour moulages [6]
Crude steel, ingots	11 014	11 840	10 433[6]	11 210	9 605[6]	8 729[6]	10 498[1]	11 000[1]	Acier brut (lingots)
Pig iron, foundry	204	227	219	263	288	197	246	97	Fonte de moulage
Pig iron, steel-making	6 662	7 146	6 321	7 032	5 841	5 036	6 245	5 343	Fonte d'affinage
Portugal									**Portugal**
Crude steel, ingots [2]	744	828	840[6]	879[6]	907[6]	1 013[6]	...	...	Acier brut (lingots) [2]
Pig iron, foundry	0	...	...	...	...	...	...	...	Fonte de moulage
Pig iron, steel-making	420	408	420	431[1]	365[1]	*389[1]	*382[1]	*82[1]	Fonte d'affinage
Qatar									**Qatar**
Crude steel, castings	572[1,8]	614[1,8]	626[1,8]	616[1,8]	646[1,8]	629[1,8]	744[1,8]	714	Acier brut pour moulages
Pig iron, steel-making [7]	...	...	...	593	597	...	...	...	Fonte d'affinage [7]
Republic of Moldova [15]									**République de Moldova** [15]
Crude steel, castings	1	0	0	0	0	0	0	0	Acier brut pour moulages
Romania									**Roumanie**
Crude steel, castings	143	140	133	115	69	39	70	...	Acier brut pour moulages
Crude steel, ingots	5 800	6 557	6 083	6 675	6 336	4 392	4 672	4 936	Acier brut (lingots)
Pig iron, foundry	122	145	187	167	145	69	47	31	Fonte de moulage
Pig iron, steel-making	3 374	4 058	3 838	4 390	4 396	2 900	3 019	3 212	Fonte d'affinage
Russian Federation									**Fédération de Russie**
Crude steel, castings	2 946	2 834	2 625	2 758	2 459	3 125	3 633	3 718	Acier brut pour moulages
Crude steel, ingots	45 866	48 756	46 628	45 744	41 214	48 392	55 517	55 312	Acier brut (lingots)
Pig iron, foundry	1 026	1 182	793	890	1 061	1 032	1 140	1 306	Fonte de moulage
Pig iron, steel-making	35 454	38 494	36 286	36 387	33 521	39 663	43 352	43 634	Fonte d'affinage
Saudi Arabia [1]									**Arabie saoudite** [1]
Crude steel, ingots	2 411	2 451	2 683	2 539	2 356	*2 610	*2 973	3 400	Acier brut (lingots)
Serbia and Montenegro									**Serbie-et-Monténégro**
Crude steel, castings	4	3	8	7	7	4[16]	5	4	Acier brut pour moulages
Crude steel, ingots	40	25	37	39	38	25[16]	21	22	Acier brut (lingots)
Pig iron, steel-making	17	109	565	907[6]	792	128[16]	560	461	Fonte d'affinage
Singapore *[1,8]									**Singapour** *[1,8]
Crude steel, castings	500	500	500	500	500	500	500	...	Acier brut pour moulages
Slovakia									**Slovaquie**
Crude steel, ingots	3 974	3 958	253	255	36	16	17	17	Acier brut (lingots)
Pig iron, steel-making	3 330	3 207	2 928	3 072[6]	2 756[6]	2 897[6]	3 166	3 000[1]	Fonte d'affinage
Slovenia									**Slovénie**
Crude steel, castings	9	9	4	2	3	3	3	...	Acier brut pour moulages
Crude steel, ingots	415	399	90	97	95	76	92	...	Acier brut (lingots)
South Africa [1]									**Afrique du Sud** [1]
Crude steel, ingots [2]	8 525	8 741	7 999	8 311	7 506	6 830	8 481	8 821	Acier brut (lingots) [2]
Pig iron, steel-making [3]	6 982	7 137	6 876	6 192	5 650	4 587	6 300	5 800	Fonte d'affinage [3]
Spain									**Espagne**
Crude steel, castings [6]	100	120	128	118	121	121	...	...	Acier brut pour moulages [6]
Crude steel, ingots	13 340	13 812	12 038[6]	13 559[6]	14 698[6]	14 754[6]	16[1]	15[1]	Acier brut (lingots)
Pig iron, foundry [6]	0	0	0	0	0	...	...	...	Fonte de moulage [6]
Pig iron, steel-making	5 447[6]	5 106[6]	4 128[1]	3 926[1]	4 235[1]	4 146[1]	4 059[1]	*4 094[1]	Fonte d'affinage
Sri Lanka *[1,8]									**Sri Lanka** *[1,8]
Crude steel, castings	30	30	30	30	30	30	30	...	Acier brut pour moulages

50

Pig iron and crude steel
Production: thousand metric tons *[cont.]*

Fonte et acier brut
Production : milliers de tonnes *[suite]*

Country or area	1994	1995	1996	1997	1998	1999	2000	2001	Pays ou zone
Sweden									**Suède**
Crude steel, castings [6]	22	29	28	31	29	28	...	...	Acier brut pour moulages [6]
Crude steel, ingots	4 934	4 891	4 880	5 117	5 143	5 038[6]	3 566	5 450[1]	Acier brut (lingots)
Pig iron, steel-making [3]	3 036	3 020	1 223	1 317	1 272	1 281	1 411	1 433	Fonte d'affinage [3]
Switzerland									**Suisse**
Crude steel, ingots	1 100[6]	850[6]	750[6]	1 047[1]	1 018[1]	1 037[1]	1 140[1]	1 100[1]	Acier brut (lingots)
Pig iron, foundry	88[10]	97[10]	100[1,10]	*100[1,10]	*100[1,10]	*100[1,10]	100[1,10]	100[1]	Fonte de moulage
Syrian Arab Republic									**Rép. arabe syrienne**
Crude steel, castings	*70[1,8]	*70[1,8]	*70[1,8]	*70[1,8]	*70[1,8]	*70[1,8]	*70[1,8]	70	Acier brut pour moulages
Thailand									**Thaïlande**
Crude steel, ingots	1 391[1]	2 134[1]	2 143[1]	2 101	1 619	1 474	1 650	1 710	Acier brut (lingots)
TFYR of Macedonia									**L'ex-R.y. Macédoine**
Crude steel, castings	...	...	...	...	...	...		228	Acier brut pour moulages
Crude steel, ingots	67	31	21	27	45	47	*161	218	Acier brut (lingots)
Pig iron, steel-making	20	*20[1]	*20[1]	*0[1]	*0[1]	*0[1]	*0[1]	...	Fonte d'affinage
Trinidad and Tobago									**Trinité-et-Tobago**
Crude steel, castings	631[1,8]	738[1,8]	695[1,8]	736[1,8]	777[1,8]	*729[1,8]	*741[1,8]	668	Acier brut pour moulages
Tunisia									**Tunisie**
Crude steel, castings	183	201	186	195	171	231	237	...	Acier brut pour moulages
Pig iron, foundry	145	152	145	152	123	180	195	...	Fonte de moulage
Turkey									**Turquie**
Crude steel, castings	4 604	3 743	4 505	4 717	4 431	4 449	4 374	4 561	Acier brut pour moulages
Crude steel, ingots	11 257	10 695	12 684	13 078	12 571	12 372	12 677	12 258	Acier brut (lingots)
Pig iron, foundry	296	246	363	337	171	192	250	234	Fonte de moulage
Pig iron, steel-making	30	...	...	577[1]	456[1]	315[1]	300[1]	*300[1]	Fonte d'affinage
Uganda [1]									**Ouganda** [1]
Crude steel, castings	*10[8]	*12[8]	*12[8]	*7[8]	*7[8]	*8[8]	*7[8]	7	Acier brut pour moulages
Crude steel, ingots	*10[2]	*12[2]	*12[2]	*7[2]	*7[2]	*8[2]	*7[2]	7	Acier brut (lingots)
Ukraine									**Ukraine**
Crude steel, castings	554	452	385	343	342	320	482	500	Acier brut pour moulages
Crude steel, ingots	24 081	22 309	22 333	25 629	24 447	27 393	31 782	33 523	Acier brut (lingots)
Pig iron, foundry	657	316	278	444	302	305	353	157	Fonte de moulage
Pig iron, steel-making	20 180	17 998	17 832	20 616	20 937	23 010	25 699	26 379	Fonte d'affinage
United Kingdom									**Royaume-Uni**
Crude steel, castings	174	180	188	186	185	128	...	...	Acier brut pour moulages
Crude steel, ingots	17 112	17 424	17 804	18 313	17 130	16 156	15 022[1]	15 000[1]	Acier brut (lingots)
Pig iron, foundry	0[6]	0[6]	0[6]	0[6]	0	...	...	...	Fonte de moulage
Pig iron, steel-making	11 943	12 236	12 830	13 056	12 746	12 139	10 891[1]	9 900[1]	Fonte d'affinage
United States									**Etats-Unis**
Crude steel, ingots	91 200[2]	95 200[2]	95 500[2]	98 500[2]	98 600[2]	97 400[2]	102 000[2]	90 100	Acier brut (lingots)
Pig iron, steel-making [3]	49 400	50 900	49 400	49 600	48 200	46 300	47 900	42 100	Fonte d'affinage [3]
Uruguay [1]									**Uruguay** [1]
Crude steel, ingots	36	40	34	39	52	45	38	*31	Acier brut (lingots)
Uzbekistan [8,14]									**Ouzbékistan** [8,14]
Crude steel, castings	364	367	466	379	357	355	415	446	Acier brut pour moulages
Venezuela									**Venezuela**
Crude steel, ingots [1]	3 524[2]	3 568[2]	3 956[2]	3 987[2]	3 553[2]	3 261[2]	*3 835[2]	3 814	Acier brut (lingots) [1]
Pig iron, steel-making [3,17]	0	0	...	...	...	...	...	...	Fonte d'affinage [3,17]
Viet Nam									**Viet Nam**
Crude steel, ingots	*301[1]	*271[1]	*311[1]	*330	*306[1]	*308[1]	109	*310[1]	Acier brut (lingots)
Zimbabwe [1]									**Zimbabwe** [1]
Crude steel, ingots	187	210	212	214	212	255	258	156	Acier brut (lingots)
Pig iron, steel-making	*100	*209	*210	*216	*217	*228	*240	240	Fonte d'affinage

Source:
United Nations Statistics Division, New York, "Industrial Commodity Statistics Yearbook 2001" and the industrial statistics database.

Source:
Organisation des Nations Unies, Division de statistique, New York, "Annuaire de statistiques industrielles par produit 2001" et la base de données pour les statistiques industrielles.

50

Pig iron and crude steel
Production: thousand metric tons *[cont.]*

Fonte et acier brut
Production : milliers de tonnes *[suite]*

1	Source: U.S. Geological Survey (Washington, D. C).
2	Including crude steel for casting.
3	Including foundry pig iron.
4	Twelve months ending 30 June of the year stated.
5	1999 data are confidential.
6	Source: Annual Bulletin of Steel Statistics for Europe, America and Asia, United Nations Economic Commission of Europe (Geneva).
7	Source: Organisation of the Islamic Conference (Jeddah, Saudi Arabia).
8	Including ingots.
9	Sales.
10	Including pig-iron for steel making.
11	Source: Eurostat (Luxembourg).
12	Source: Statistical Yearbook for Asia and the Pacific, United Nations Economic and Social Council for Asia and the Pacific (Bangkok).
13	Production by establishments employing 20 or more persons.
14	Source: Country Economic Review, Asian Development Bank (Manila).
15	Excluding the Transnistria region.
16	Beginning 1999, data for Kosovo are not included.
17	Source: United Nations Economic Commission for Latin America and the Caribbean (ECLAC), (Santiago).

1	Source : U.S. Geological Survey (Washington, D. C.).
2	Y compris l'acier pour les moulage.
3	Y compris la fonte de moulage.
4	Période de 12 mois finissant le 30 juin de l'année indiquée.
5	Pour 1999, les données sont confidentielles.
6	Source: Bulletin annuel de statistiques de l'acier pour l'Europe, l'Amérique et l'Asie, Commission économique des Nations Unies pour l'Europe (Genève).
7	Source: "Organisation of the Islamic Conference," (Jeddah, Saudi Arabia).
8	Y compris l'acier brut (lingots).
9	Ventes.
10	Y compris la fonte d'affinage.
11	Source: "Eurostat," (Luxembourg).
12	Source: "Statistical Yearbook for Asia and the Pacific, United Nations Economic and Social Council for Asia and the Pacific" (Bangkok).
13	Production des établissements occupant 20 personnes ou plus.
14	Source: "Country Economic Review, Asian Development Bank" (Manila).
15	Non compris la région de Transnistria.
16	A partir de 1999, non compris les données de Kosovo.
17	Source: Commission économique des Nations Unies pour l'Amérique Latine et des Caraïbes (CEPAL), (Santiago).

51
Aluminium
Production: thousand metric tons
Aluminium
Production : milliers de tonnes

Country or area / Pays ou zone	1992	1993	1994	1995	1996	1997	1998	1999	2000	2001
Argentina Argentine										
Primary Neuf	153	171	173	183	185	187	187	206	261	252[2]
Secondary[1] Récupéré[1]	19	14	14	10	16	13	17	14	23	23
Australia[3] Australie[3]										
Primary Neuf	1 194	1 306	1 384	1 285	1 331	1 395	1 589	1 686	1 742	1 788
Secondary[1] Récupéré[1]	40	35	55	...	...	...	...	...	...	...
Austria Autriche										
Primary Neuf	33	0[1]	0[1]	0[1]	0[1]	0[1]	0[1]	0[1]	0[1]	...
Secondary Récupéré	45[1]	43[1]	53[1]	94[1]	98[1]	119[1]	126	143[1]	158[1]	158[1]
Azerbaijan[2] Azerbaïdjan[2]										
Primary Neuf	*25	*20	*5	4	1	5	0	0	0	0
Bahrain Bahreïn										
Primary Neuf	293	448	451	449	456	490[2]	501[2]	502	512	510[2]
Belgium[1] Belgique[1]										
Secondary Récupéré	0	0	0	0	0	0	0	0	0	...
Bosnia and Herzegovina *[2] Bosnie-Herzégovine *[2]										
Primary Neuf	30	15	10	10	10	15	28	70	90	110
Brazil[1] Brésil[1]										
Primary Neuf	1 193	1 172	1 185	1 188	1 197	1 189	1 208	1 250	1 271	1 132
Secondary Récupéré	67	77	91	117	146	163	180	186	229	229
Bulgaria[2] Bulgarie[2]										
Secondary Récupéré	...	...	...	...	4	3	4	4	4	...
Cameroon Cameroun										
Primary Neuf	83[1]	87[1]	81[1]	71	82[1]	98	89	93	172	181
Canada Canada										
Primary Neuf	1 972[1]	2 309[1]	2 255[1]	2 172[1]	2 283[1]	2 327	2 374	2 390	2 373	2 583
Secondary[1] Récupéré[1]	86	90	97	97	101	106	111	112	112	112
China Chine										
Primary Neuf	1 096	1 255	1 498	1 870	1 896	2 180	2 362	2 809	2 989	3 576
Colombia Colombie										
Total Totale	0	1	...	0	...	...	...	...	...	...
Croatia Croatie										
Primary Neuf	29	26	26	31	33	35[2]	16	14	14	15
Czech Republic[2] République tchèque[2]										
Secondary Récupéré	...	...	...	...	45	45	45	40	40	...
Denmark[4] Danemark[4]										
Secondary Récupéré	16	21	22	28	27	35	34	34	32	33
Egypt[5] Egypte[5]										
Primary Neuf	139	139	149	136	150	119	187[1]	193[2]	193[2]	193[2]
Finland Finlande										
Secondary Récupéré	*5	*4	*4	*5	*5	38[2,6]	41[2]	44[2]	45[2]	34[2]
France France										
Primary Neuf	414	425	481	364	380	399	424	455	441	460
Secondary Récupéré	222[7]	203[7]	227[7]	...	236[2]	236	239	239	260	253
Germany Allemagne										
Primary Neuf	603	552	503	576	577	572[2]	612[2]	634[2]	644[2]	*652[2]
Secondary Récupéré	52	58	56	531[2]	417[2]	432[2]	453[2]	483[2]	572[2]	*620[2]
Ghana[1] Ghana[1]										
Primary Neuf	180	175	141	135	137	152	56	114	156	162
Greece Grèce										
Primary Neuf	174	148	142	132	141	132	146	161	168[2]	163[2]
Hungary Hongrie										
Primary Neuf	27	29	31	35	94	98	92	89	35[2]	*35[2]
Secondary[2] Récupéré[2]	...	...	...	...	64	63	64	54	55	...
Iceland Islande										
Primary Neuf	89	94	99	100	102	123	160	161	167	169
India Inde										
Primary Neuf	499	478	479	518	516	539	542[2]	614[2]	644[2]	624[2]
Indonesia Indonésie										
Primary Neuf	213	202	222[1]	228[1]	223[1]	219[1]	133[1]	112[1]	191[1]	209[1]

51

Aluminum
Production: thousand metric tons *[cont.]*
Aluminium
Production : milliers de tonnes *[suite]*

Country or area Pays ou zone	1992	1993	1994	1995	1996	1997	1998	1999	2000	2001
Iran (Islamic Rep. of)[1] **Iran (Rép. islamique d')**[1]										
Primary Neuf	79	92	116	115	78	91	111	138	140	145
Secondary Récupéré	39	15	26	26	26	26	26	26	10	10
Italy Italie										
Primary Neuf	161	156	175	178	184	188	187	187	190	188
Secondary Récupéré	353	346	376	412	377	443	503	502	568	578
Japan Japon										
Primary Neuf	38	39	41	46	46	53	51	46[2]	48[2]	34[2]
Secondary Récupéré	1 074[7]	1 006[7]	1 175[7]	1 181[7]	1 191[7]	1 277[7]	1 155[7]	1 158[7]	1 214[7]	1 171
Kenya[2] **Kenya**[2]										
Secondary Récupéré	...	...	...	...	...	2	1	1	1	1
Mexico Mexique										
Primary Neuf	17	25	29	33	69	71	68	70	63	56
Secondary[2] Récupéré[2]	62	74	46	59	98	123	218	363	350	350
Netherlands Pays-Bas										
Primary Neuf	227	228	230	216	227[2]	232[2]	264[2]	286[2]	300[2]	294[2]
Secondary Récupéré	150	139	175	192	150[2]	150[2]	102[2]	88[2]	119[2]	120[2]
New Zealand Nouvelle-Zélande										
Primary[1] Neuf[1]	243	277	269	273	285	310	318	327	328	322
Secondary Récupéré	7[1]	7[1]	8[1]	8[1]	8[1]	8[1]	8[1]	21[2]	22[2]	22[2]
Norway Norvège										
Primary Neuf	838	887	857	847	863	919[1]	996[1]	1 020[1]	1 026[1]	1 068[1]
Secondary[1] Récupéré[1]	40	56	49	72	60	59	62	178	255	224
Poland Pologne										
Primary Neuf	44	47	50	56	52	54	54	51	47	45
Portugal Portugal										
Secondary Récupéré	12	12	12	14[1]	16[1]	16[1]	18[1]	18[1]	18[1]	18[1]
Romania Roumanie										
Primary Neuf	112[7,8]	112[7,8]	120[7,8]	141[7,8]	141[7,8]	162[7,8]	174[7,8]	174[7,8]	179	182
Secondary[7] Récupéré[7]	8	4	3	3	4	2	1[8]	0[8]	2[8]	1[8]
Russian Federation[2] **Fédération de Russie**[2]										
Primary Neuf	2 700	2 820	2 670	2 724	2 874	2 906	3 005	3 146	3 245	3 300
Serbia and Montenegro Serbie-et-Monténégro										
Primary Neuf	67	26	4	17	37	66	61	73[9]	88	100
Secondary Récupéré	0	0	0	0	0	1	0[9]	...	...	...
Slovakia Slovaquie										
Primary Neuf	...	18	4	25	311	110[1]	115	109[1]	110[1]	110
Secondary Récupéré	...	1	...	...	...		6	...	...	...
Slovenia Slovénie										
Primary Neuf	85	83	77	58	27	9	10	9	9	...
South Africa[2] **Afrique du Sud**[2]										
Primary Neuf	173	175	172	229	570	673	677	679	674	663
Spain[1] **Espagne**[1]										
Primary Neuf	359	356	338	362	362	360	360	364	366	376
Secondary Récupéré	97	100	104	107	154	173	210	224	240	240
Suriname Suriname										
Primary Neuf	32	30	27	28	29	32[2]	29[2]	10[2]	0[2]	0[2]
Sweden[1] **Suède**[1]										
Primary Neuf	77	82	84	95	98	98	96	99	100	102
Secondary Récupéré	19	19	22	23	25	25	27	28	30	30
Switzerland Suisse										
Primary Neuf	52	36	24	21	27[1]	27[1]	32[1]	34[1]	36[1]	36[1]
Secondary[1] Récupéré[1]	11	4	6	5	6	8	15	6	6	6
Tajikistan Tadjikistan										
Primary Neuf	345[10]	252	237	237	198	189	196	229	269[10]	289[10]
TFYR of Macedonia L'ex-R.y. Macédoine										
Total Totale	6	6	7	5	5	5	7	6	4	...
Turkey Turquie										
Primary Neuf	61	59	60	62	62	62	62	62	62	62

51

Aluminum
Production: thousand metric tons *[cont.]*

Aluminium
Production : milliers de tonnes *[suite]*

Country or area Pays ou zone	1992	1993	1994	1995	1996	1997	1998	1999	2000	2001
Ukraine[2] Ukraine[2]										
Primary * Neuf *	100	100	100	98	90	101	107	115	119	122
Secondary Récupéré	72	50	40	40	40	40	71	111	129	...
United Kingdom Royaume-Uni										
Primary Neuf	244[7]	239[7]	231[7]	238[7]	240[7]	248[2]	258[2]	272[2]	305[2]	341[2]
Secondary Récupéré	197	236	224	230	261	258[2]	236[2]	275[2]	285[2]	238[2]
United States Etats-Unis										
Primary Neuf	4 042	3 695	3 299	3 375	3 577	3 603	3 713	3 779	3 668	2 637
Secondary[7] Récupéré[7]	2 760	2 940	3 090	3 190	3 310	3 550	3 440	3 690	3 450	2 980
Uzbekistan[2] Ouzbékistan[2]										
Secondary Récupéré	...	...	...	...	3	3	3	3	3	...
Venezuela Venezuela										
Primary Neuf	508	568	585[1]	627[1]	635[1]	641[1]	584[1]	567[1]	569[1]	572[1]
Secondary[1] Récupéré[1]	35	35	32	28	21	27	33	27	24	24

Source:
United Nations Statistics Division, New York, "Industrial Commodity Statistics Yearbook 2001" and the industrial statistics database.

Source:
Organisation des Nations Unies, Division de statistique, New York, "Annuaire de statistiques industrielles par produit 2001" et la base de données pour les statistiques industrielles.

1	Source: World Metal Statistics, (London).	1	Source: "World Metal Statistics," (Londres).
2	Source: U.S. Geological Survey (Washington, D. C).	2	Source : U.S. Geological Survey (Washington, D. C.).
3	Twelve months ending 30 June of the year stated.	3	Période de 12 mois finissant le 30 juin de l'année indiquée.
4	Sales.	4	Ventes.
5	Including aluminium plates, shapes and bars.	5	Aluminum de deuxième fusion produit de débris de metal.
6	Break in series; data prior to the sign not comparable to following years.	6	Marque une interruption dans la série et la non-comparabilité des données précédant le symbole.
7	Including alloys.	7	Y compris les alliages.
8	Including pure content of virgin alloys.	8	Y compris la teneur pure des alliages de première fusion.
9	Beginning 1999, data for Kosovo are not included.	9	A partir de 1999, non compris les données de Kosovo.
10	Source: Country Economic Review, Asian Development Bank (Manila).	10	Source: "Country Economic Review, Asian Development Bank" (Manila).

52

Radio and television receivers
Production: thousands

Récepteurs de radio et de télévision
Production : milliers

Country or area Pays ou zone	Radio receivers Récepteurs de radio					Television receivers Récepteurs de télévision				
	1997	1998	1999	2000	2001	1997	1998	1999	2000	2001
Albania Albanie	0	0	0	0	0	0	0	0	0	0
Algeria Algérie	...	...	...	...	...	172	251	173	194	245
Argentina Argentine	...	...	...	...	...	1 630	1 592	1 335	1 556	...
Azerbaijan Azerbaïdjan	0	0	0	...	...	1	3	0	0	...
Bangladesh Bangladesh	20	10	13	6	3	93	152	107	127	133
Belarus Bélarus	170	114	195	101	...	454	468	516	532	727[1]
Brazil Brésil	4 211	2 753	2 039	1 629	1 184	7 976	5 711	4 328	6 078	5 463
Bulgaria Bulgarie	...	0	0	0	0	6	3	2	...	...
China Chine	...	...	...	...	...	36 372	42 809	49 113	45 012	46 110
Colombia Colombie	...	...	...	...	...	58	50	19	...	...
Czech Republic République tchèque	...	...	...	...	...	180	567	707	1 141	...
Denmark [2] Danemark [2]	...	...	...	...	...	93	95	85	95	89
Egypt Egypte	...	...	...	...	...	114	43	30	27	...
Finland Finlande	...	...	...	...	...	...	...	...	92	130
France France	3 853	4 586	2 961	...	...	...	...	...	...	...
Georgia Géorgie	...	...	...	...	...	2	1	1	2	...
Germany Allemagne	3 632	3 884	4 021	4 025	4 746	...	1 269	1 335	1 533	...
Hungary Hongrie	528	2 328	2 412	2 320	3 459	...	...	...	...	...
India Inde	33	2	0	0	0[3]	2 370	2 461	2 561	2 399	1 979[3]
Indonesia [4] Indonésie [4]	4 177	#80	4 937	...	...	...	...	...	...	...
Iran (Islamic Rep. of) Iran (Rép. islamique d')	76[5]	127[5]	114	139	...	751[5]	769[5]	904[5]	855[5]	...
Italy Italie	...	...	...	...	...	1 920	1 659	1 627	1 350	1 208
Japan Japon	2 434	2 623	2 678	2 384	1 972	7 559	6 567	4 386	3 382	2 862
Jordan Jordanie	...	...	...	...	...	...	16	15	14	18
Kazakhstan Kazakhstan	3	3	0	0	0	61	103	112	338	347
Korea, Republic of Corée, République de	...	...	...	...	...	16 428	12 763	15 556	10 054	9 321
Kyrgyzstan Kirghizistan	...	...	...	...	...	0	4	1	3	6[1]

52

Radio and television receivers
Production: thousands *[cont.]*

Récepteurs de radio et de télévision
Production : milliers *[suite]*

Country or area Pays ou zone	Radio receivers Récepteurs de radio					Television receivers Récepteurs de télévision				
	1997	1998	1999	2000	2001	1997	1998	1999	2000	2001
Latvia Lettonie	10	2	2	...	...	...	...	...	...	...
Lithuania Lituanie	...	...	...	...	...	52	84	187	207	143
Malaysia Malaisie	33 491	30 265	32 957	36 348	28 839	7 774	8 035	7 611	10 551	9 501
Pakistan Pakistan	...	...	...	...	...	186	107	128	122	97
Poland Pologne	143	154	132	109	13	3 020	4 436	5 121	6 287	7 502
Portugal Portugal	4 552	5 076	5 939	6 848	7 158	...	...	...	...	...
Republic of Moldova [6] République de Moldova [6]	94	51	10	18	3	19	10	3	2	2
Romania Roumanie	28[4]	10[4]	0[4]	0	0	89	134	56	32	29
Russian Federation Fédération de Russie	342	235	332	390	281	327	329	281	1 116	1 024
Serbia and Montenegro Serbie-et-Monténégro	0	0	0[7]	1	0	25	30	13[7]	6	5
Slovakia Slovaquie	...	...	...	...	...	...	304	311	431	594
Slovenia Slovénie	0	0	0	0	...	0	231	244	349	...
South Africa Afrique du Sud	...	...	...	...	...	...	273	273	290	260
Spain Espagne	313	508	357	57	85	...	...	...	...	...
Syrian Arab Republic Rép. arabe syrienne	...					128	151	150	169	139
Tunisia Tunisie	...	...	...	...	...	108	90	104	99	...
Turkey Turquie	...	...	...	...	...	4 657	5 795	6 941	8 789	8 025
Ukraine Ukraine	25	10	27	36	26	50	93	81	62	53
United Kingdom Royaume-Uni	2 062	...	...	545		...	...	...	...	...
United Rep. of Tanzania Rép.-Unie de Tanzanie	56	...	...	...	...	...	...	...	...	...
United States [8] Etats-Unis [8]	...	...	...	...	...	11 476	10 715	10 914	9 272	8 264
Uzbekistan Ouzbékistan	...	...	...	...	...	269	192[9]	50[9]	26[9]	...

Source:
United Nations Statistics Division, New York, "Industrial Commodity Statistics Yearbook 2001" and the industrial statistics database.

Source:
Organisation des Nations Unies, Division de statistique, New York, "Annuaire de statistiques industrielles par produit 2001" et la base de données pour les statistiques industrielles.

1   Source: Statistical Yearbook, Commonwealth of Independent States (Moscow).
2   Sales.
3   Production by establishments employing 50 or more persons.

1   Source: "Statistical Yearbook", Commonwealth of Independent States (Moscow).
2   Ventes.
3   Production des établissements occupant 50 personnes ou plus.

52

Radio and television receivers
Production: thousands *[cont.]*

Récepteurs de radio et de télévision
Production : milliers *[suite]*

4	Including radios with tape recording units.
5	Production by establishments employing 10 or more persons.
6	Excluding the Transnistria region.
7	Beginning 1999, data for Kosovo are not included.
8	Shipments.
9	Source: Statistical Yearbook for Asia and the Pacific, United Nations Economic and Social Council for Asia and the Pacific (Bangkok).

4	Y compris les récepteurs de radio avec appareil enregistreur à bande magnétique incorporés.
5	Production des établissements occupant 10 personnes ou plus.
6	Non compris la région de Transnistria.
7	A partir de 1999, non compris les données de Kosovo.
8	Expéditions.
9	Source: "Statistical Yearbook for Asia and the Pacific, United Nations Economic and Social Council for Asia and the Pacific" (Bangkok).

53

Passenger cars
Production: thousands

Voitures de tourisme
Production: milliers

Country or area Pays ou zone	1992	1993	1994	1995	1996	1997	1998	1999	2000	2001
Argentina [1] Argentine [1]	221	287	338	227	269	366	353	225	239	...
Australia Australie	270	285	310	294	305	301	336	323	330	328
Belarus [2] Bélarus [2]	...	...	...	...	...	1	1	0	0	...
Brazil [3] Brésil [3]	338	392	367	271	245	253	242	221	260	296
Canada Canada	901	838	...	...	...	...	...	...	...	...
Colombia [4] Colombie [4]	...	63	65	66	63	69	50	25	38	...
Ecuador Equateur	...	...	...	...	...	...	27	...	...	...
Egypt Egypte	7	4	7	8	14	13	13	12	11	...
Finland Finlande	13[1]	7[1]	...	...	0[1]	...	...	34	38	41
France France	3 326	2 837	3 176	3 052	...	3 352	3 932	4 265	4 652	3 182[5]
Germany Allemagne	4 895	3 875	4 222	...	4 713[1]	...	...	...	...	...
Hungary Hongrie	...	...	...	...	...	...	90	125	...	...
India Inde	162[6]	210[6]	262[6]	331[6]	400[6]	384[6]	393[6]	577[6]	506	573[7]
Indonesia Indonésie	28	20	85	19	...	11	56	39	...	...
Italy Italie	1 475[6]	1 116[6]	1 340[6]	1 422[6]	1 244[6]	1 563[6]	1 379[6]	1 384[6]	1 423[6]	1 272
Japan Japon	9 379	8 494	7 801	7 611	7 864	8 491	8 056	8 100	8 363	8 118
Korea, Republic of [1] Corée, République de [1]	1 259	1 528	1 755	1 999	2 256	2 313	1 577	2 158	2 626	2 477
Mexico Mexique	799[1]	861	887	705	802	858	947	988	1 294	1 273
Netherlands [1,8,9] Pays-Bas [1,8,9]	95	80	92	98	...	...	...	...	...	...
Poland Pologne	219	334	338	366	441	520	592	647	532	364
Romania Roumanie	74	93	56	70	97	109	104	89	64	57
Russian Federation Fédération de Russie	963	956	798	835	868	986	840	954	969	1 022
Serbia and Montenegro Serbie-et-Monténégro	22	8	8	8	9	10	12	8[10]	12	8
Slovakia Slovaquie	...	5	8	22	32	42	125	127	181	277
Slovenia Slovénie	84	58	74	88	89	96	127	119	123	119
Spain Espagne	1 817	1 774[1,8]	2 146[1,8]	2 254[1,8]	2 334[1,8]	2 278[1,8]	2 468[1,8]	2 473[1,8]	2 619[1,8]	2 406[1,8]
Sweden Suède	205	173	193	...	207	219	214	235	278	272

53

Passenger cars
Production: thousands *[cont.]*

Voitures de tourisme
Production: milliers *[suite]*

Country or area Pays ou zone	1992	1993	1994	1995	1996	1997	1998	1999	2000	2001
Ukraine Ukraine	135	140	94	59	7	2	26	10	17	26
United Kingdom Royaume-Uni	1 291	1 504	1 654	1 735	1 707	1 818	1 709	...	...	...
United States [11] Etats-Unis [11]	5 684	5 956	*6 614	...	...	...	...	...	...	...
Uzbekistan Ouzbékistan	...	...	...	...	25[2]	65[2]	54[2]	58[2]	32[5]	32[5]

Source:
United Nations Statistics Division, New York, "Industrial Commodity Statistics Yearbook 2001" and the industrial statistics database.

Source:
Organisation des Nations Unies, Division de statistique, New York, "Annuaire de statistiques industrielles par produit 2001" et la base de données pour les statistiques industrielles.

1   Including assembly.
2   Source: Statistical Yearbook, Commonwealth of Independent States (Moscow).
3   Excluding station wagons.
4   Source: United Nations Economic Commission for Latin America and the Caribbean (ECLAC), (Santiago).
5   Source: International Organization of Motor Vehicle Manufacturers (Paris).
6   Excluding production for armed forces.
7   Production by establishments employing 50 or more persons.
8   Sales.
9   Production by establishments employing 20 or more persons.
10   Beginning 1999, data for Kosovo are not included.
11   Factory sales.

1   Y compris le montage.
2   Source: "Statistical Yearbook", Commonwealth of Independent States (Moscow).
3   Non compris les stations-wagons.
4   Source: Commission économique des Nations Unies pour l'Amérique Latine et des Caraïbes (CEPAL), (Santiago).
5   Source : "International Organization of Motor Vehicle Manufacturers," (Paris).
6   Non compris la production destinée aux forces armées.
7   Production des établissements occupant 50 personnes ou plus.
8   Ventes.
9   Production des établissements occupant 20 personnes ou plus.
10   A partir de 1999, non compris les données de Kosovo.
11   Ventes des fabriques.

54

Refrigerators for household use
Production: thousands

Réfrigérateurs à usage domestique
Production: en milliers

Country or area Pays ou zone	1992	1993	1994	1995	1996	1997	1998	1999	2000	2001
Algeria Algérie	317	183	119	131	137	175	215	181	117	64
Angola Angola	2	...	...	...	...	...	...	...	...	...
Antigua and Barbuda [1] Antigua-et-Barbuda [1]	...	3	3	...	...	...	...	...	...	...
Argentina Argentine	554	688	494	49	45	401	424	354	325	...
Australia Australie	363	421	444	423	403	398	441	427	...	...
Azerbaijan Azerbaïdjan	223	228	97	25	7	0	3	1	1	2
Belarus Bélarus	740	738	742	746	754	795	802	802	812	...
Brazil Brésil	1 704	2 098	2 721	3 242	3 776	3 592	3 034	2 796	2 921	3 371
Bulgaria Bulgarie	106	81	69	49	36	21	56	45	18	145
Chile Chili	136	192	221	272	213	268	229	242	271	280
China Chine	4 858	5 967	7 681	9 185	9 797	10 444	10 600	12 100	12 790	13 513
Colombia Colombie	306	396	465	465	...	...	...	...	...	...
Denmark [2] Danemark [2]	294	261	808	1 502	1 276	1 523	1 589	1 560	1 475	1 225
Ecuador Equateur	66	72	111	156	17	133	88	38	55	...
Egypt Egypte	232	204	236	236	250	2	5	3	...	...
Finland Finlande	144	128	134	104	68	102	107	...	...	...
France France	566	487	554	...	...	490	640	509	555	...
Germany Allemagne	4 298	3 838	3 794	...	2 747	...	...	...	...	...
Greece Grèce	80	...	...	...	...	...	...	...	...	...
Guyana Guyana	6	5	5	...	...	...	...	...	...	...
Hungary Hongrie	483	520	603	714	736	835	708	849	995	1 058
India Inde	997	1 382	1 668	1 913	1 705	1 600	1 902	2 012	2 009	2 469[3]
Indonesia Indonésie	...	172	469	291	...	573	417	240	...	...
Iran (Islamic Rep. of) Iran (Rép. islamique d')	896[3]	789[3]	629[3]	575[4]	756[4]	786[4]	860[4]	798[4]	791[4]	...
Iraq Iraq	35	...	...	...	...	...	...	...	...	...
Italy Italie	4 285	4 753	5 033	5 908	5 402	5 562	6 280	6 582	6 987	6 936
Japan Japon	4 425	4 351	4 952	5 013	5 163	5 369	4 851	4 543	4 224	3 875

54

Refrigerators for household use
Production: thousands *[cont.]*

Réfrigérateurs à usage domestique
Production: en milliers *[suite]*

Country or area Pays ou zone	1992	1993	1994	1995	1996	1997	1998	1999	2000	2001
Kazakhstan Kazakhstan	...	13	...	...	...	...	...	...	...	...
Korea, Republic of Corée, République de	3 296	3 585	3 943	3 975	4 292	4 257	3 790	4 235	5 224	5 128
Kyrgyzstan Kirghizistan	1	0	3	1	0	0	...	...	...	...
Lithuania Lituanie	137	207	183	187	138	172	154	153	154	260
Malaysia Malaisie	288	250	266	295	257	249	206	194	215	186
Mexico Mexique	541	1 065	1 356	1 256	1 447	1 942	1 986	2 083	2 049	2 071
Nigeria Nigéria	52	53	20	19	...	...	...	...	...	...
Peru Pérou	54	57	86	161	81	101	118	42	51	*68
Poland Pologne	500	588	605	585	584	705	714	726	693	589
Portugal Portugal	251	224	244	...	173	211	257	304	308	257
Republic of Moldova République de Moldova	55	58[5]	53[5]	24[5]	1[5]	2[5]	0[5]	...	...	...
Romania [6] Roumanie [6]	402	435	383	435	446	429	366	323	341	292
Russian Federation Fédération de Russie	2 972	3 049	2 283	1 531	966	1 108	956	1 041	1 151	1 542
Serbia and Montenegro Serbie-et-Monténégro	85	39	41	50	51	81	48	5[7]	20	0
Slovakia Slovaquie	552	482	371	330	393	258	228	206	177	27
Slovenia Slovénie	661	665	797	863	592	692	756	780	841	...
South Africa [8] Afrique du Sud [8]	318	318	321	365	411	388	399	440	508	662
Spain Espagne	1 322	1 240	1 461	1 269	1 260	1 960	2 415	2 107	2 153	...
Sweden Suède	562	549	582	610	478	523	545	604	620	538
Syrian Arab Republic Rép. arabe syrienne	129	150	148	156	155	138	137	120	96	...
Tajikistan Tadjikistan	61	18	3	0	1	2	1	2	2	2
Thailand [9] Thaïlande [9]	...	...	...	...	2 246	2 384	1 631	...	...	...
TFYR of Macedonia L'ex-R.y. Macédoine	139	98	95	51	20	12	*4	0	0	0
Trinidad and Tobago Trinité-et-Tobago	10	3	3	1	0	...	...	...	...	...
Tunisia Tunisie	123	141	129	...	...	...	...	...	...	...
Turkey Turquie	1 040	1 254	1 258	1 680	1 612	1 945	1 993	2 083	2 405	2 245
Ukraine Ukraine	838	757	653	562	431	382	390	409	451	509

54

Refrigerators for household use
Production: thousands *[cont.]*

Réfrigérateurs à usage domestique
Production: en milliers *[suite]*

Country or area Pays ou zone	1992	1993	1994	1995	1996	1997	1998	1999	2000	2001
United Kingdom Royaume-Uni	...	1 033	1 094	1 256	1 225	1 251	1 095	912	...	...
United States [10,11] Etats-Unis [10,11]	9 676	10 306	11 276	11 005	11 132	12 092	11 279	11 716	12 355	11 776
Uzbekistan Ouzbékistan	85	82	20	19	13	13	16[12]	2[12]	1[12]	...

Source:
United Nations Statistics Division, New York, the industrial statistics database and the "Industrial Commodity Statistics Yearbook 2001".

Source:
Organisation des Nations Unies, Division de statistique, New York, la base de données pour les statistiques industrielles et "l'Annuaire de statistiques industrielles par produit 2001".

1	Twelve months beginning 21 March of the year stated.
2	Sales.
3	Production by establishments employing 50 or more persons.
4	Production by establishments employing 10 or more persons.
5	Excluding the Transnistria region.
6	Including freezers.
7	Beginning 1999, data for Kosovo are not included.
8	Including deep freezers and deep freeze-refrigerator combinations.
9	Beginning 1999, series discontinued.
10	Electric domestic refrigerators only.
11	Shipments.
12	Source: Statistical Yearbook for Asia and the Pacific, United Nations Economic and Social Council for Asia and the Pacific (Bangkok).

1   Période de 12 mois commençant le 21 mars de l'année indiquée.
2   Ventes.
3   Production des établissements occupant 50 personnes ou plus.
4   Production des établissements occupant 10 personnes ou plus.
5   Non compris la région de Transnistria.
6   Y compris les congélateurs.
7   A partir de 1999, non compris les données de Kosovo.
8   Y compris congélateurs-conservateurs et congélateurs combinés avec un réfrigérateur.
9   A partir de 1999, les séries ont été discontinuées.
10   Réfrigérateurs électriques de ménage seulement.
11   Expéditions.
12   Source: "Statistical Yearbook for Asia and the Pacific, United Nations Economic and Social Council for Asia and the Pacific" (Bangkok).

55

Washing machines for household use
Production: thousands

Machines à laver à usage domestique
Production: en milliers

Country or area Pays ou zone	1992	1993	1994	1995	1996	1997	1998	1999	2000	2001
Argentina Argentine	756	801	702	458	524	603	...	...	...	...
Armenia Arménie	9	0	0	1	0	...	...	...	...	...
Australia Australie	295	328	314	310	266	268	321	354	...	...
Belarus Bélarus	62	71	77	37	61	88	91	92	88	...
Belgium [1,2] Belgique [1,2]	138	49	...	...	...	...	...	...	...	...
Brazil Brésil	849	1 167	1 461	1 681	2 160	2 095	1 851	1 940	2 302	2 257
Bulgaria Bulgarie	69	42	41	26	24	5	...	2	1	0
Chile Chili	301	386	447	434	310	...	...	...	...	...
China Chine	7 079	8 959	10 941	9 484	10 747	12 545	12 073	13 422	14 430	13 416
Colombia Colombie	41	41	50	45	...	...	...	...	...	...
Croatia Croatie	1	0	0	0	0	0	...	...	...	...
Ecuador Equateur	...	...	...	11	12	...	...	...	...	...
Egypt Egypte	198	200	209	198	200	201	201	252	...	...
France France	1 713[1]	1 943[1]	2 244[1]	2 200[1]	1 868[1]	1 933[1]	1 941[1]	2 229[1]	2 751	...
Germany Allemagne	...	...	...	2 703	2 816	3 035	3 370	4 768	4 611	4 542
Greece Grèce	...	31	20	15	10	...	...	...	...	...
Hungary Hongrie	219	...	...	...	...	...	...	...	...	...
Indonesia Indonésie	27	32	44	13	...	86	33	48	...	...
Iran (Islamic Rep. of) Iran (Rép. islamique d')	63[4]	59[4]	79[4]	98[5]	159[5]	194[5]	190[5]	183[5]	189[5]	...
Italy Italie	5 140	5 693	6 251	6 996	7 135	7 967	8 119	7 367	8 186	8 507
Japan Japon	5 225	5 163	5 042	4 876	5 006	4 818	4 468	4 287	4 179	4 059
Kazakhstan Kazakhstan	370	255	88	46	23	11	3	2	5	11
Korea, Republic of Corée, République de	1 896	2 199	2 443	2 827	2 878	2 967	2 643	2 822	3 271	3 529
Kyrgyzstan Kirghizistan	94	77	17	4	3	2	0	...	...	...
Latvia Lettonie	18	18	10	8	3	3	2	...	...	...
Mexico Mexique	646	1 085	1 185	882	1 091	1 448	1 512	1 593	1 720	1 636
Peru Pérou	5	3	5	6	3	1	0	0	0	*0

55

Washing machines for household use
Production: thousands *[cont.]*

Machines à laver à usage domestique
Production: en milliers *[suite]*

Country or area Pays ou zone	1992	1993	1994	1995	1996	1997	1998	1999	2000	2001
Poland Pologne	363	402	449	419	445	412	416	448	564	759
Republic of Moldova République de Moldova	102	123[6]	81[6]	49[6]	54[6]	46[6]	43[6]	18[6]	25[6]	25[6]
Romania Roumanie	159	161	109	125	138	82	36	28	25	24
Russian Federation Fédération de Russie	4 289	3 901	2 122	1 294	762	800	862	999	954	1 039
Serbia and Montenegro Serbie-et-Monténégro	68	39	63	36	33	33	30	12[7]	10	5
Slovakia Slovaquie	122	100	...	...	...	...	...	...	...	...
Slovenia Slovénie	188	189	200	220	291	405	474	447	488	...
South Africa Afrique du Sud	44	52	55	57	55	44	44	45	35	34
Spain Espagne	1 540	1 334	1 632	1 655	1 945	2 270	2 281	...	...	...
Sweden Suède	91	94	113	106	103	120	119	122	117	121
Syrian Arab Republic Rép. arabe syrienne	41	47	50	78	80	72	68	65	66	...
Thailand [8] Thaïlande [8]	...	...	...	...	541	794	800	...	...	...
Turkey Turquie	802	980	780	873	1 015	1 485	1 408	1 249	1 346	1 035
Ukraine Ukraine	805	643	422	213	149	147	138	127	125	166
United Kingdom Royaume-Uni	...	...	...	...	...	1 148	1 111	...	...	...
United States Etats-Unis	6 566[1]	6 739[1]	7 081[1]	6 605[1]	6 873[1]	6 942[1]	7 504[1]	7 991[1]	8 043	7 979[1]
Uzbekistan Ouzbékistan	9	10	9	14	4	4	5[9]	0[9]	0[9]	...

Source:
United Nations Statistics Division, New York, the industrial statistics database and the "Industrial Commodity Statistics Yearbook 2001".

Source:
Organisation des Nations Unies, Division de statistique, New York, la base de données pour les statistiques industrielles et "l'Annuaire de statistiques industrielles par produit 2001".

1 Shipments.
2 Production by establishments employing 5 or more persons.
3 Sales.
4 Production by establishments employing 50 or more persons.
5 Production by establishments employing 10 or more persons.
6 Excluding the Transnistria region.
7 Beginning 1999, data for Kosovo are not included.
8 Beginning 1999, series discontinued.
9 Source: Statistical Yearbook, Commonwealth of Independent States (Moscow).

1 Expéditions.
2 Production des établissements occupant 5 personnes ou plus.
3 Ventes.
4 Production des établissements occupant 50 personnes ou plus.
5 Production des établissements occupant 10 personnes ou plus.
6 Non compris la région de Transnistria.
7 A partir de 1999, non compris les données de Kosovo.
8 A partir de 1999, les séries ont été discontinuées.
9 Source: "Statistical Yearbook", Commonwealth of Independent States (Moscow).

56
Machine tools
Production: number
Machines-outils
Production : nombre

Country or area Pays ou zone	1992	1993	1994	1995	1996	1997	1998	1999	2000	2001
Algeria Algérie										
Drilling and boring machines										
Perceuses	122	30	...	...	...	...	...	...	...	...
Lathes										
Tours	310	194	118	196	189	110	14	177	38	27
Milling machines										
Fraiseuses	103	81	124	119	124	75	80	72	69	44
Armenia Arménie										
Lathes										
Tours	1 079	486	395	190	141	81	71	33	40	47
Milling machines										
Fraiseuses	410	0	63	73	47	188	82	27	19	40
Metal-working presses										
Presses pour de travail de métaux	45	100	29	43	34	31	18	11	11	3
Austria[1] Autriche[1]										
Lathes										
Tours	1 421	915	709	1 482	1 452	801	1 914	...	...	1 091
Milling machines										
Fraiseuses	844	223	209	625	362	284	279	...	...	
Azerbaijan Azerbaïdjan										
Drilling and boring machines										
Perceuses	428	86	102	112	49	24	29	1	...	...
Bangladesh[2] Bangladesh[2]										
Lathes										
Tours	3	1	1	...	...	...	...	...		
Belarus Bélarus										
Lathes										
Tours	162	332	57	70	93	117	131	96	122	...
Milling machines										
Fraiseuses	56	13	0	1	3	5	3	2	16	...
Brazil Brésil										
Metal-working presses										
Presses pour de travail de métaux	1 194	1 763	1 836	1 858	1 657	1 678	1 531	1 102	1 386	1 285
Bulgaria Bulgarie										
Drilling and boring machines										
Perceuses	996	759	850	864	953	906	*1 025	*940	1 436	1 212
Lathes										
Tours	3 587	2 197	1 979	2 496	2 513	2 315	1 761	1 611	1 563	1 916
Milling machines										
Fraiseuses	432	324	200	227	295	412	104	139	218	306
Colombia Colombie										
Lathes										
Tours	97	103	155	112	...	...	...	...	...	...
Metal-working presses										
Presses pour de travail de métaux	16 992	13 366	22 661	26 344	...	...	...	...	...	...
Croatia Croatie										
Drilling and boring machines										
Perceuses	346	255	...	4 369	3 212	# 66	31	28	16	4
Lathes										
Tours	463	358	...	52	68	98	144	186	122	74
Milling machines										
Fraiseuses	168	192	...	77	90	165	224	196	162	206
Czech Republic République tchèque										
Drilling and boring machines										
Perceuses	...	...	...	...	1 235	1 263	1 352	986	982	840
Lathes										
Tours	1 017	709	685	735	943	932	994	989	1 046	1 254
Milling machines										
Fraiseuses	1 358	...	...	...	1 109	1 039	1 117	821	860	906
Metal-working presses										
Presses pour de travail de métaux	106	47	60	114	231	239	...	...	...	...

56

Machine tools
Production: number *[cont.]*

Machines-outils
Production : nombre *[suite]*

Country or area Pays ou zone	1992	1993	1994	1995	1996	1997	1998	1999	2000	2001
Denmark [3] Danemark [3]										
Drilling and boring machines										
Perceuses	223	197	...	...	...	...	...	...	...	...
Lathes										
Tours	279	374	...	...	...	...	...	...	...	...
Milling machines										
Fraiseuses	200	0	0	0	...	...	...	...	...	...
Finland Finlande										
Drilling and boring machines										
Perceuses	54	78	88	106	109	...	67	13	89	56
Lathes										
Tours	1	1	2	3	2	...	...	...	...	...
Metal-working presses										
Presses pour de travail de métaux	17	6	180	1 764	2 159	2 101	2 285	2 315	2 735	2 400
France France										
Drilling and boring machines [4]										
Perceuses [4]	1 212	...	...	...	...	...	...	...	...	...
Lathes [5]										
Tours [5]	942	11	546	...	...	...	...	...	...	...
Milling machines [5]										
Fraiseuses [5]	401	7	394	...	...	...	...	...	...	...
Metal-working presses [5]										
Presses pour de travail de métaux [5]	1 385	970	605	...	...	...	...	...	...	...
Georgia Géorgie										
Lathes										
Tours	1 001	348	109	57	18	28	21	2	...	...
Germany Allemagne										
Drilling and boring machines										
Perceuses	15 085	21 222	15 955	13 049	11 730	...	11 396	14 440	...	...
Lathes										
Tours	7 689	4 755	5 322	8 232	6 375	5 542	6 070	5 754	6 027	20 845
Milling machines										
Fraiseuses	...	6 680	6 327	...	5 213	5 335	5 348	5 755	6 806	21 355
Metal-working presses										
Presses pour de travail de métaux	55 997	18 939	23 284	16 399	...	21 531	...	...	21 170	...
Greece Grèce										
Milling machines										
Fraiseuses	...	...	...	...	...	...	4	...	...	...
Metal-working presses										
Presses pour de travail de métaux	355	...	...	...	...	...	...	...	...	...
Hungary Hongrie										
Drilling and boring machines										
Perceuses	75	78	15	4	...	...	...	...	167	...
Lathes										
Tours	63	135	33	7	...	...	...	...	100	...
Milling machines										
Fraiseuses	256	50	3	...	...	...	...	...	...	...
India Inde										
Lathes										
Tours	...	...	6 747 000	6 279 000	4 685 000	4 881 000	6 902 000	12436000	21579000	20469000
Indonesia Indonésie										
Drilling and boring machines										
Perceuses	1 000	52	...	12 155	...	...	5 153	14	...	...
Lathes										
Tours	42	46	96	166	...	23	4	4	...	...
Milling machines										
Fraiseuses	...	50	...	...	...	...	...	...	...	...
Metal-working presses										
Presses pour de travail de métaux	...	54	...	...	...	...	...	...	...	...

56

Machine tools
Production: number *[cont.]*

Machines-outils
Production : nombre *[suite]*

Country or area Pays ou zone	1992	1993	1994	1995	1996	1997	1998	1999	2000	2001
Iran (Islamic Rep. of)[6] Iran (Rép. islamique d')[6]										
Drilling and boring machines										
Perceuses	...	...	...	...	...	500	2	20	...	...
Lathes										
Tours	...	...	...	...	...	1 720	2 836	1 529	1 474	...
Metal-working presses										
Presses pour de travail de métaux	...	...	...	...	...	230	199	1 518	171	...
Japan Japon										
Drilling and boring machines										
Perceuses	22 973	14 496	11 936	14 678	16 414	17 097	12 531	9 377	12 784	10 225
Lathes										
Tours	16 155	12 343	14 961	20 339	21 443	23 357	22 652	16 924	22 027	19 813
Milling machines										
Fraiseuses	3 913	2 007	1 791	1 832	2 198	2 368	2 019	1 022	1 260	1 042
Metal-working presses										
Presses pour de travail de métaux	12 458	9 516	9 531	10 512	10 068	11 575	8 546	7 285	8 884	6 992
Korea, Republic of Corée, République de										
Drilling and boring machines[7]										
Perceuses[7]	7 336	7 416	11 107	10 861	8 025	8 741	1 491	2 805	...	...
Lathes										
Tours	6 643	6 931	10 265	12 526	11 094	8 357	4 809	6 542	8 439	7 530
Milling machines										
Fraiseuses	2 509	2 824	4 667	5 293	3 952	2 900	825	2 242	3 664	2 434
Latvia Lettonie										
Lathes										
Tours	...	28	87	36	26	20	29	...	...	...
Milling machines										
Fraiseuses	...	12	44	44	9	26	78	...	...	...
Lithuania Lituanie										
Drilling and boring machines										
Perceuses	...	...	...	749	437	333	192	171	109	84
Lathes										
Tours	110	93	27	64	4	1	6	6	6	5
Milling machines										
Fraiseuses	1 035	450	341	255	213	161	130	58	55	48
Mexico Mexique										
Drilling and boring machines										
Perceuses	855	487	...	...	...	...	...	...	...	...
Poland Pologne										
Drilling and boring machines										
Perceuses	1 858	1 348	998	771	840	1 253	917	624	...	...
Lathes										
Tours	1 105	910	900	1 012	1 037	900	963	732	748	1 055
Milling machines										
Fraiseuses	500	248	260	274	281	354	257	222	180	141
Metal-working presses										
Presses pour de travail de métaux	13	11	8	2	2	15	...	...	...	1
Portugal Portugal										
Drilling and boring machines										
Perceuses	75	52	...	...	...	...	...	...	...	...
Metal-working presses										
Presses pour de travail de métaux	742	670	649	...	...	...	...	...	...	...
Romania Roumanie										
Lathes										
Tours	1 583	489	312	471	587	681	573	330	307	388
Milling machines										
Fraiseuses	764	436	162	341	458	403	321	333	242	236
Russian Federation Fédération de Russie										
Drilling and boring machines										
Perceuses	12 835	10 607	5 291	5 021	3 088	2 522	1 877	1 898	1 669	1 333

56

Machine tools
Production: number *[cont.]*

Machines-outils
Production : nombre *[suite]*

Country or area Pays ou zone	1992	1993	1994	1995	1996	1997	1998	1999	2000	2001
Lathes
Tours	7 079	6 506	3 807	3 269	2 095	2 135	1 798	1 681	2 067	2 444
Milling machines
Fraiseuses	4 144	3 424	1 560	897	622	591	641	724	1 163	1 128
Serbia and Montenegro   Serbie-et-Monténégro
Drilling and boring machines
Perceuses	607	276	206	328	100	106	133	111[8]	97	...
Lathes
Tours	338	67	135	206	110	256	213	231[8]	181	...
Milling machines
Fraiseuses	...	...	...	...	...	...	...	3[8]	...	...
Metal-working presses
Presses pour de travail de métaux	1 046	167	54	114	53	47	66	29[8]	28	...
Slovakia   Slovaquie
Drilling and boring machines
Perceuses	...	0	...	...	...	...	...	...	...	...
Lathes
Tours	...	1 637	1 566	1 549	3 121	3 084	1 660	1 786	1 769	1 699
Metal-working presses
Presses pour de travail de métaux	261	184	301	282	199	73	276	195	147	151
Slovenia   Slovénie
Drilling and boring machines
Perceuses	60	0	...	...	...	4	0	...	...	...
Milling machines
Fraiseuses	12	15	26	27	...	...	...	...	...	...
Metal-working presses
Presses pour de travail de métaux	92	145	153	215	719	...	...	...	91	...
Spain   Espagne
Drilling and boring machines
Perceuses	2 060	886	1 738	2 313	2 185	2 689	3 317	4 732	4 976	4 548
Lathes
Tours	925	1 237	1 713	2 475	2 887	3 080	3 509	3 559	3 492	4 240
Milling machines
Fraiseuses	4 553	788	1 458	1 600	1 852	1 605	2 986	3 075	3 964	4 404
Metal-working presses
Presses pour de travail de métaux	1 687	2 436	723	5 452	...	...	...	...	...	...
Sweden   Suède
Drilling and boring machines
Perceuses	...	...	...	...	...	3 158	3 661	3 003	2 232	1 933
Lathes
Tours	...	...	...	...	259	40	22	25	17	18
Milling machines
Fraiseuses	48	22	27	25	...	...	...	...	...	...
Turkey   Turquie
Drilling and boring machines
Perceuses	239	41	185	12	57	22	21	7	85	67
Lathes
Tours	2	10	59	12	16	0	0	0	0	0
Milling machines
Fraiseuses	39	85	107	84	169	75	1	0	50	11
Ukraine   Ukraine
Drilling and boring machines
Perceuses	11 113	12 996	3 745	1 337	563	750	418	306	225	306
Lathes
Tours	2 420	1 619	867	808	338	352	234	213	260	293
Milling machines
Fraiseuses	1 040	752	195	90	48	161	168	45	77	36
Metal-working presses
Presses pour de travail de métaux	268	277	117	146	35	42	38	29	34	25

56

Machine tools
Production: number *[cont.]*
Machines-outils
Production : nombre *[suite]*

Country or area Pays ou zone	1992	1993	1994	1995	1996	1997	1998	1999	2000	2001
United Kingdom Royaume-Uni										
Drilling and boring machines										
Perceuses	...	901	1 061	...	...	...	...	...	...	...
Lathes										
Tours	...	2 429	2 941	3 568	3 845	3 102	3 478	2 047	...	...
Milling machines										
Fraiseuses	...	824	856	493	268	529	...	...	132	...
Metal-working presses										
Presses pour de travail de métaux	...	667	615	...	...	827	...	...	...	...
United States [5] Etats-Unis [5]										
Drilling and boring machines										
Perceuses	7 542	7 182	...	10 465	7 927	6 234	5 812	5 096	4 277	2 803
Lathes										
Tours	2 409	3 042	3 662	4 643	4 190	5 058	5 089	3 807	3 278	2 949
Milling machines										
Fraiseuses	2 581	3 386	4 087	4 747	4 102	4 240	3 416	2 749	3 545	1 990
Metal-working presses										
Presses pour de travail de métaux	5 822	6 236	10 947	5 045	11 023	12 084	12 559	12 301	11 079	10 059

Source:
United Nations Statistics Division, New York, "Industrial Commodity Statistics Yearbook 2001" and the industrial statistics database.

Source:
Organisation des Nations Unies, Division de statistique, New York, "Annuaire de statistiques industrielles par produit 2001" et la base de données pour les statistiques industrielles.

1	Beginning 1999, data are confidential.
2	Twelve months ending 30 June of the year stated.
3	Sales.
4	Limited coverage.
5	Shipments.
6	Production by establishments employing 10 or more persons.
7	Drilling machines only.
8	Beginning 1999, data for Kosovo are not included.

1	A partir de 1999, les données sont confidentielles.
2	Période de 12 mois finissant le 30 juin de l'année indiquée.
3	Ventes.
4	Couverture limitée.
5	Expéditions.
6	Production des établissements occupant 10 personnes ou plus.
7	Perceuses seulement.
8	A partir de 1999, non compris les données de Kosovo.

57

Lorries (trucks)
Production or assembly from imported parts: number

Camions
Production ou montage avec des pièces importées : nombre

Country or area Pays ou zone	1992	1993	1994	1995	1996	1997	1998	1999	2000	2001
Algeria Algérie										
Assembled Assemblés	2 434	2 304	1 230	2 570	2 136	1 293	1 798	1 583	1 719	2 811
Argentina[1] Argentine[1]										
Produced Fabriqués	36 999	50 805	64 022	...	...	...	...	...	...	...
Armenia Arménie										
Produced Fabriqués	3 171	1 247	446	232	114	27	51	2	...	...
Australia[2,3] Australie[2,3]										
Produced Fabriqués	14 550	15 459	...	...	...	...	...	...	...	...
Austria Autriche										
Produced Fabriqués	4 089	3 565	3 098	2 903[4]	...	...	...	...	...	...
Azerbaijan Azerbaïdjan										
Produced Fabriqués	402	93	8	2	1	0	0	0	0	...
Bangladesh Bangladesh										
Assembled Assemblés	549	236	430	830	797	887	788	793	629	714
Belarus Bélarus										
Produced Fabriqués	32 951	30 771	21 264	12 902	10 671	13 002	12 799	13 370	14 656	...
Belgium[5,6] Belgique[5,6]										
Assembled Assemblés	70 532	56 244	...	...	...	...	...	...	...	...
Brazil[7] Brésil[7]										
Produced Fabriqués	32 025	47 876	64 137	70 495	48 712	63 744	63 773	55 277	71 686	77 342
Bulgaria Bulgarie										
Produced Fabriqués	945[1]	406[1]	321	259	66	43	...	...	...	...
Canada[8] Canada[8]										
Produced Fabriqués	901 000	838 000	...	...	...	...	...	...	...	...
Chile[9] Chili[9]										
Assembled Assemblés	14 352	16 584	15 960	...	...	...	...	...	...	...
China Chine										
Produced Fabriqués	476 700	597 897	662 600	595 997	625 100	573 600	...	...	...	...
Colombia Colombie										
Assembled Assemblés	10 116[9]	13 992[9]	15 660[9]	...	...	736	903	219	...	...
Croatia Croatie										
Produced Fabriqués	4	7	...	5	8	10	96	10	0	0
Czech Republic République tchèque										
Produced Fabriqués	14 030	33 873	30 103	22 052	27 036	39 537	39 098	23 113	23 641	4 701
Egypt Egypte										
Produced Fabriqués	1 529	1 208	1 379	1 241	738	328	467	444	180	...
Finland[1] Finlande[1]										
Produced Fabriqués	578	435	546	540	492	493	687	721	655	646
France France										
Produced Fabriqués	494 124	373 200	453 344	381 360	...	440 244	608 369	627 588	741 780	...

57

Lorries (trucks)
Production or assembly from imported parts: number *[cont.]*
Camions
Production ou montage avec des pièces importées : nombre *[suite]*

Country or area Pays ou zone	1992	1993	1994	1995	1996	1997	1998	1999	2000	2001
Georgia Géorgie										
Produced Fabriqués	650	384	137	209	95	82	39	38	50[7]	...
Germany Allemagne										
Produced Fabriqués	325 901	240 014	259 575	...	240 604[1]	272 916[1]	292 581[1]	291 817	299 151	282 758
Greece Grèce										
Assembled Assemblés	1 920	62	...	57	128	...	219	...	...	...
Hungary[9] Hongrie[9]										
Produced Fabriqués	360	...	...	...	...	...	...	...	...	...
India[8,9] Inde[8,9]										
Produced Fabriqués	141 600	148 800	163 200	...	...	...	...	...	...	...
Indonesia Indonésie										
Produced Fabriqués	174	...	2 890	4 755	...	575	# 465464[10]	...	...	...
Iran (Islamic Rep. of) Iran (Rép. islamique d')										
Assembled Assemblés	34 842[11]	21 234[11]	15 785[11]	8 836[12]	19 777[12]	16 689[12]	42 005[12]	54 492[12]	51 336[12]	...
Israel Israël										
Assembled Assemblés	852	836	1 260	1 217	1 199	...	...	...	...	...
Italy Italie										
Produced Fabriqués	194 616	155 476	191 288	234 354	188 852	256 062	278 322	288 038	283 094	280 731
Japan Japon										
Produced Fabriqués	3 053477	2 674941	2 689340	2 519319	2 417370	2 410124	1 930965	1 742111	1 719584	1 596080
Kazakhstan[7] Kazakhstan[7]										
Produced Fabriqués	600	...	...	200	20	30	100	300	200	100
Kenya Kenya										
Assembled Assemblés	315	310	428	1 103	1 430	...	...	...	...	...
Korea, Republic of[1] Corée, République de[1]										
Produced Fabriqués	293 260	310 639	332 263	331 328	340 179	297 565	182 218	264 212	265 448	254 233
Kyrgyzstan Kirghizistan										
Produced Fabriqués	14 818	5 026	206	8	1	12	...	...	...	...
Latvia Lettonie										
Assembled Assemblés	...	...	...	...	...	...	...	5	...	...
Malaysia Malaisie										
Assembled Assemblés	34 711[13]	34 711[13]	42 618[13]	55 961[13]	78 571[13]	94 977[13]	19 693[13]	44 951[13]	55 721[13]	62 722
Mexico Mexique										
Produced Fabriqués	269 591[1]	222 807	217 359	210 072	396 377	468 931	445 125	451 880	542 809	521 357
Morocco[9] Maroc[9]										
Assembled Assemblés	11 976	9 734	...	...	...	...	...	...	...	...
Myanmar[14] Myanmar[14]										
Assembled Assemblés	85	172	846	500	550	255	31	102	135	204
Netherlands[15,16] Pays-Bas[15,16]										
Produced Fabriqués	10 034	9 538	13 938	15 818	...	...	...	...	...	...

57

Lorries (trucks)
Production or assembly from imported parts: number *[cont.]*
Camions
Production ou montage avec des pièces importées : nombre *[suite]*

Country or area Pays ou zone	1992	1993	1994	1995	1996	1997	1998	1999	2000	2001
New Zealand *[13] Nouvelle-Zélande *[13]										
Assembled										
Assemblés	10 210	...	...	...	...	...	...	...	...	...
Nigeria Nigéria										
Assembled										
Assemblés	2 683	1 097	696	715	...	...	...	...	...	...
Pakistan Pakistan										
Assembled										
Assemblés	13 270[3]	13 700[3]	6 522[3]	5 857[3]	9 864[3]	12 733[3]	11 736[3]	9 210[3]	7 633	7 917
Peru[9] Pérou[9]										
Assembled										
Assemblés	600	768	...	...	...	...	...	...	...	...
Poland[17] Pologne[17]										
Produced										
Fabriqués	17 657	18 811	21 356	30 662	44 159	57 254	56 080	62 719	58 104	24 670
Romania Roumanie										
Produced										
Fabriqués	4 456	4 433	3 044	3 098	3 142	1 956	1 263	900	762	352
Russian Federation Fédération de Russie										
Produced										
Fabriqués	582 963	466 925	185 018	142 483	134 130	145 850[7]	141 484[7]	176 207[7]	184 489[7]	172 597[7]
Serbia and Montenegro Serbie-et-Monténégro										
Produced										
Fabriqués	4 169	287	685	708	824	1 278	1 139	407[18]	710	590
Slovakia Slovaquie										
Assembled										
Assemblés	...	...	...	...	1 421	709	312	72	37	70
Produced										
Fabriqués	...	744	369	663	1 421	709	312	72	37	70
Slovenia Slovénie										
Assembled										
Assemblés	...	1	...	...	...	...	...	...	...	...
Produced										
Fabriqués	377	424	397	277	195	...	...	16	16	...
South Africa Afrique du Sud										
Assembled										
Assemblés	93 599	96 772	118 221	147 792	132 383	132 338	117 092	113 310	130 589	125 873
Spain Espagne										
Produced										
Fabriqués	256 070	17 923[1,15]	32 217[1,15]	50 255[1,15]	73 319[1,15]	280 708[1,15]	343 699[1,15]	366 702[1,15]	404 249[1,15]	402 518[1,15]
Sweden Suède										
Produced										
Fabriqués	...	...	...	...	...	51 378	30 582	30 399	32 546	29 455
Thailand[9] Thaïlande[9]										
Assembled										
Assemblés	223 680	323 508	324 780	...	...	...	...	...	...	...
Trinidad and Tobago[9] Trinité-et-Tobago[9]										
Assembled										
Assemblés	1 698	1 083	621	0	0	...	...	...	...	...
Tunisia Tunisie										
Assembled										
Assemblés	768	922	1 084	616	954	1 003	1 016	770	1 130	...
Turkey Turquie										
Assembled										
Assemblés	37 195	49 827	21 591	35 930	50 471	73 946	67 985	44 457	77 514	30 112
Ukraine Ukraine										
Produced										
Fabriqués	33 386	23 052	11 741	6 492	4 164	3 386	4 768	7 769	11 185	6 747

57

Lorries (trucks)
Production or assembly from imported parts: number *[cont.]*

Camions
Production ou montage avec des pièces importées : nombre *[suite]*

Country or area Pays ou zone	1992	1993	1994	1995	1996	1997	1998	1999	2000	2001
United Kingdom Royaume-Uni										
Produced										
Fabriqués	239 936	320 456	372 633	247 022	188 215	189 464	185 152	...	...	...
United Rep. of Tanzania [19] Rép.-Unie de Tanzanie [19]										
Assembled										
Assemblés	171	40	115	0	0	0	...	...	...	...
United States Etats-Unis										
Produced										
Fabriqués	4118578	...	...	...	...	...	...	...	...	...
Uzbekistan [7] Ouzbékistan [7]										
Produced										
Fabriqués	...	...	...	300	30	20	60	300	...	...
Venezuela Venezuela										
Assembled										
Assemblés	30 000	...	...	...	...	...	...	...	...	...

Source:
United Nations Statistics Division, New York, "Industrial Commodity Statistics Yearbook 2001" and the industrial statistics database.

Source:
Organisation des Nations Unies, Division de statistique, New York, "Annuaire de statistiques industrielles par produit 2001" et la base de données pour les statistiques industrielles.

1	Including assembly.	1	Y compris le montage.
2	Finished and partly finished.	2	Finis et semi-finis.
3	Twelve months ending 30 June of the year stated.	3	Période de 12 mois finissant le 30 juin de l'année indiquée.
4	Beginning 1995, data are confidential.	4	A partir de 1995, les données sont confidentielles.
5	Production by establishments employing 5 or more persons.	5	Production des établissements occupant 5 personnes ou plus.
6	Shipments.	6	Expéditions.
7	Trucks only.	7	Camions seulement.
8	Excluding production for armed forces.	8	Non compris la production destinée aux forces armées.
9	Including motor coaches and buses.	9	Y compris les autocars et autobus.
10	Break in series; data prior to the sign not comparable to following years.	10	Marque une interruption dans la série et la non-comparabilité des données précédant le symbole.
11	Production by establishments employing 50 or more persons.	11	Production des établissements occupant 50 personnes ou plus.
12	Production by establishments employing 10 or more persons.	12	Production des établissements occupant 10 personnes ou plus.
13	Including vans and buses.	13	Y compris les autobus et les camionnettes.
14	Government production only.	14	Production de l'Etat seulement.
15	Sales.	15	Ventes.
16	Production by establishments employing 20 or more persons.	16	Production des établissements occupant 20 personnes ou plus.
17	Including special-purpose vehicles.	17	Y compris véhicules à usages spéciaux.
18	Beginning 1999, data for Kosovo are not included.	18	A partir de 1999, non compris les données de Kosovo.
19	Including buses.	19	Y compris les autobus.

Technical notes, tables 40-57

Industrial activity includes mining and quarrying, manufacturing and the production of electricity, gas and water. These activities correspond to the major divisions 2, 3 and 4 respectively of the *International Standard Industrial Classification of All Economic Activities* [50].

Many of the tables are based primarily on data compiled for the United Nations *Industrial Commodity Statistics Yearbook* [24]. Data taken from alternate sources are footnoted.

The methods used by countries for the computation of industrial output are, as a rule, consistent with those described in the United Nations *International Recommendations for Industrial Statistics* [49] and provide a satisfactory basis for comparative analysis. In some cases, however, the definitions and procedures underlying computations of output differ from approved guidelines. The differences, where known, are indicated in the footnotes to each table.

Table 40: The statistics on sugar were obtained from the database and the *Sugar Yearbook* [16] of the International Sugar Organization. The data shown cover the production and consumption of centrifugal sugar from both beet and cane, and refer to calendar years.

The consumption data relate to the apparent consumption of centrifugal sugar in the country concerned, including sugar used for the manufacture of sugar-containing products whether exported or not and sugar used for purposes other than human consumption as food. Unless otherwise specified, the statistics are expressed in terms of raw value (i.e. sugar polarizing at 96 degrees). The world and regional totals also include data for countries not shown separately whose sugar consumption was less than 10,000 metric tons.

Table 41: The data refer to meat from animals slaughtered within the national boundaries irrespective of the origin of the animals. Production figures of beef, veal, buffalo meat, pork (including bacon and ham), mutton, lamb and goat meat are in terms of carcass weight, excluding edible offals, tallow and lard. All data refer to total meat production, i.e from both commercial and farm slaughter.

Table 42: The data refer to beer made from malt, including ale, stout, porter.

Table 43 presents data on cigarettes only, unless otherwise indicated.

Table 44: The data on cotton fabrics refer to woven fabrics of cotton at the loom stage before undergoing finishing processes such as bleaching, dyeing, printing, mercerizing, lazing, etc.; those on wool refer to woollen and worsted fabrics before undergoing finishing processes. Fabrics of fine hair are excluded.

Notes techniques, tableaux 40 à 57

L'activité industrielle comprend les industries extractives (mines et carrières), les industries manufacturières et la production d'électricité, de gaz et d'eau. Ces activités correspondent aux grandes divisions 2, 3 et 4, respectivement, de la *Classification internationale type par industrie de toutes les branches d'activité économique* [50].

Un grand nombre de ces tableaux sont établis principalement sur la base de données compilées pour l'*Annuaire de statistiques industrielles par produit* des Nations Unies [24]. Les données tirées des autres sources sont signalées par une note.

En règle générale, les méthodes employées par les pays pour le calcul de leur production industrielle sont conformes à celles dans *Recommandations internationales concernant les statistiques industrielles* des Nations Unies [49] et offrent une base satisfaisante pour une analyse comparative. Toutefois, dans certains cas, les définitions des méthodes sur lesquelles reposent les calculs de la production diffèrent des directives approuvées. Lorsqu'elles sont connues, les différences sont indiquées par une note.

Tableau 40: Les données sur le sucre proviennent de la base de données et de l'*Annuaire du sucre* [16] de l'Organisation internationale du sucre. Les données présentées portent sur la production et la consommation de sucre centrifugé à partir de la betterave et de la canne à sucre, et se rapportent à des années civiles.

Les données de la consommation se rapportent à la consommation apparente de sucre centrifugé dans le pays en question, y compris le sucre utilisé pour la fabrication de produits à base de sucre, exportés ou non, et le sucre utilisé à d'autres fins que pour la consommation alimentaire humaine. Sauf indication contraire, les statistiques sont exprimés en valeur brute (sucre polarisant à 96°). Les totaux mondiaux et régionaux comprennent également les données relatives aux pays où la consommation de sucre est inférieure à 10.000 tonnes.

Le *tableau 41* indique la production de viande provenant des animaux abattus à l'intérieur des frontières nationales, quelle que soit leur origine. Les chiffres de production de viande de bœuf, de veau, de la viande de buffle, de porc (y compris le bacon et le jambon), de mouton et d'agneau (y compris la viande de chèvre) se rapportent à la production en poids de carcasses et ne comprennent pas le saindoux, le suif et les abats comestibles. Toutes les données se rapportent à la production totale de viande, c'est-à-dire à la fois aux animaux abattus à des fins commerciales et des animaux sacrifiés à la ferme.

Tableau 42: Les données se rapportent à la bière produite à partir du malte, y compris ale, stout et porter (bière anglaise, blonde et brune).

The data on woven fabrics of cellulosic and non-cellulosic fibres include fabrics of continuous and discontinuous rayon and acetate fibres, and non-cellulosic fibres other than textile glass fibres. Pile and chenille fabrics at the loom stage are also included.

Table 45: The data refer to the total production of leather footwear for children, men and women and all other footwear such as footwear with outer soles of wood or cork, sports footwear and orthopedic leather footwear. House slippers and sandals of various types are included, but rubber footwear is excluded.

Table 46: The data refer to the aggregate of sawn-wood and sleepers, coniferous or non-coniferous. The data cover wood planed, unplaned, grooved, tongued and the like, sawn lengthwise or produced by a profile-chipping process, and planed wood which may also be finger-jointed, tongued or grooved, chamfered, rabbeted, V-jointed, beaded and so on. Wood flooring is excluded. Sleepers may be sawn or hewn.

Table 47 presents statistics on the production of all paper and paper board. The data cover newsprint, printing and writing paper, construction paper and paperboard, household and sanitary paper, special thin paper, wrapping and packaging paper and paperboard.

Table 48: Statistics on all hydraulic cements used for construction (portland, metallurgic, aluminous, natural, and so on) are shown.

Table 49: The data refer to H_2SO_4 in terms of pure monohydrate sulphuric acid, including the sulphuric acid equivalent of oleum or fuming sulphuric acid.

Table 50: The data on pig iron include foundry and steel making pig-iron. Figures on crude steel include both ingots and steel for castings. The series are based on data compiled for the United Nations *Industrial Commodity Statistics Yearbook* [24]. In selected cases, data are obtained from the United States Bureau of Mines (Washington, D.C.), the Latin American Iron and Steel Institute (Santiago) and the United Nations Economic Commission for Europe (Geneva).

Pig iron is iron in liquid or solid form, containing at least 3 per cent of carbon and possibly one or more of the following elements within the weight limits specified: less than 6 per cent of silicon, less than 6 per cent of manganese, and less than 3 per cent of phosphorus. It may also contain small proportions of other elements, for example, chromium and nickel. Foundry pig iron is pig iron for use in making cast iron, including forge pig iron and pig iron for direct casting. Steel-making pig-iron is distinguished from foundry pig iron on the basis of the uses to which it is put. Steel-making pig iron is pig iron for use in making crude steel.

Crude steel is steel (including alloy steel) in the

Le *Tableau 43* se rapporte seulement aux cigarettes, sauf indication contraire.

Tableau 44: Les données sur les tissus de coton et de laine se rapportent aux tissus de coton, avant les opérations de finition, c'est-à-dire avant d'être blanchis teints, imprimés, mercerisés, glacés, etc., et aux tissus de laine cardée ou peignée, avant les opérations de finition. A l'exclusion des tissus de poils fins.

Les données sur les tissus de fibres cellulosiques et non-cellulosiques comprennent les tissus sortant du métier à tisser de fibres de rayonne et d'acétate et tissus composés de fibres non cellulosiques, autres que les fibres de verre, continues ou discontinues. Cette rubrique comprend les velours, peluches, tissus boucles et tissus chenille.

Tableau 45: Les données se rapportent à la production totale de chaussures de cuir pour enfants, hommes et dames et toutes les autres chaussures telles que chaussures à semelles en bois ou en liège, chaussures pour sports et orthopédiques en cuir. Chaussures en caoutchouc ne sont pas compris.

Tableau 46: Les données sont un agrégat des sciages de bois de conifères et de non-conifères et des traverses de chemins de fer. Elles comprennent les bois rabotés, non rabotés, rainés, languetés, etc. sciés en long ou obtenus à l'aide d'un procédé de profilage par enlèvement de copeaux et les bois rabotés qui peuvent être également à joints digitiformes languetés ou rainés, chanfreinés, à feuillures, à joints en V, à rebords, etc. Cette rubrique ne comprend pas les éléments de parquet en bois. Les traverses de chemin de fer comprennent les traverses sciées ou équaries à la hache.

Le *tableau 47* présente les statistiques sur la production de tout papier et carton. Les données comprennent le papier journal, les papiers d'impression et d'écriture, les papiers et cartons de construction, les papiers de ménage et les papiers hygiéniques, les papiers minces spéciaux, les papiers d'empaquetage et d'emballage et carton.

Tableau 48: Les données sur tous les ciments hydrauliques utilisés dans la construction (portland métallurgique, alumineux, naturel, etc.) sont présentées.

Tableau 49: Les données se rapportent au H_2SO_4 sur la base de l'acide sulfurique monohydraté, y compris l'équivalent en acide sulfurique de l'oléum ou acide sulfurique fumant.

Tableau 50: Les données se rapportent à la production de fonte et d'acier. Les données sur l'acier brut comprennent les lingots et l'acier pour moulage. Les séries sont basées sur l'*Annuaire des statistiques industrielles* par produit des Nations Unies [24]. Dans certains cas, les données proviennent du United States Bureau of Mines (Washington, D.C.), de l'Institut latino-américain du fer et de l'acier (Santiago) et de la Commission économique

form in which it emerges from the Bassemer, Thomas, open-hearth or electric process or from one of the various oxygen-blowing processes. Puddled iron is excluded. Steel ingots are primary products for rolling or forging obtained by casting the molten steel into moulds which are usually square, rectangular or octagonal in cross-section with one end thicker than the other, to facilitate removal from the mould. Continuously-cast blooms, billets and slabs are included as ingots.

Table 51: The data refer to aluminium obtained by electrolytic reduction of alumina (primary) and re-melting metal waste or scrap (secondary).

Table 52: The data on radio receivers include complete receiving sets, irrespective of frequencies covered, made for home, automobile and general use, including battery sets. Radio-gramophone combinations are also included.

The data on television receivers include household television receivers, colour, of all kinds (table models, consoles, television sets incorporating a radio receiver or a gramophone).

Table 53: Passenger cars include three-and four-wheeled road motor vehicles other than motorcycle combinations, intended for the transport of passengers and seating not more than nine persons (including the driver), which are manufactured wholly or mainly from domestically-produced parts and passenger cars shipped in "knocked-down" form for assembly abroad.

Table 54: The data refer to refrigerators of the compression type or of the absorption type, of the sizes commonly used in private households. Insulated cabinets to contain an active refrigerating element (block ice) but no machine are excluded.

Table 55: These washing machines usually include electrically-driven paddles or rotating cylinders (for keeping the cleaning solution circulating through the fabrics) or alternative devices. Washing machines with attached wringers or centrifugal spin driers, and centrifugal spin driers designed as independent units, are included.

Table 56: The data on machine tools presented in this table include drilling and boring machines, lathes, milling machines, and metal-working presses. Drilling and boring machines refer to metal-working machines fitted with a baseplate, stand or other device for mounting on the floor, or on a bench, wall or another machine. Lathes refer to metal-working lathes of all kinds, whether or not automatic, including slide lathes, vertical lathes, capstan and turret lathes, production (or copying) lathes. Milling machines refer to metal-working machines designed to work a plane or profile surface by means of rotating tools, known as milling cutters. Metal-

pour l'Europe (Genève).

La fonte est du fer à l'état liquide ou solide contenant au moins 3 p. 100 de carbone et pouvant contenir un ou plusieurs des éléments suivants dans les limites de poids indiquées: moins de 6 p. 100 de silicium, moins de 6 p. 100 de manganèse et moins de 3 p. 100 de phosphore. Elle peut aussi contenir de faibles proportions d'autres éléments, tels que le chrome et le nickel. La fonte de moulage est de la fonte servant à la fabrication de pièces moulées en fonte et comprend notamment la fonte pour forge et la fonte pour moulages de première coulé. La fonte d'affinage ne se distingue de la fonte de moulage que par sa destination. La fonte d'affinage est de la fonte servant à la fabrication d'acier brut.

On entend par acier brut l'acier (y compris l'acier allié) produit par les procédés Bessemer, Thomas, Martin ou électrique ou par les procédés à l'oxygène. Cette rubrique ne comprend pas le fer puddlé. Les lingots d'acier sont des produits de base destinés à être transformés par laminage ou forgeage et obtenus en coulant l'acier liquide dans des lingotières qui sont ordinairement de section carrée, rectangulaire ou octogonale et dont l'une des extrémités est plus épaisse que l'autre pour faciliter le démoulage. Les blooms, les billettes et les brames obtenus par coulée continue sont classés parmi les lingots.

Tableau 51: Les données se rapportent à la production d'aluminium obtenue par réduction électrolytique de l'alumine (production primaire) et par refusion de déchets métalliques (production secondaire).

Tableau 52: Les données sur les récepteurs de radio comprennent les récepteurs complets, quelles que soient les longueurs d'ondes captées, d'appartement, d'automobiles et d'usage général, y compris les postes à piles. Cette rubrique comprend les récepteurs avec phonographes ou tourne-disques incorporés.

Les données sur les récepteurs de télévision comprennent de tous genres pour usage privé en noir et couleurs (récepteurs de table, récepteurs-meubles, etc., même avec appareils récepteur de radio diffusion, phonographe ou tourne-disques incorporés).

Tableau 53: Les voitures de tourisme comprennent les véhicules automobiles routiers à trois ou quatre roues, autres que les motocycles, destinés au transport de passagers, dont le nombre de places assises (y compris celle du conducteur) n'est pas supérieur à neuf et qui sont construits entièrement ou principalement avec des pièces fabriqués dans le pays, et les voitures destinées au transport de passagers exportées en pièces détachées pour être montées à l'étranger.

Tableau 54: Les données se rapportent aux appareils frigorifiques du type à compression ou à absorption de la taille des appareils communément utilisés dans les ména-

working presses are mechanical, hydraulic and pneumatic presses used for forging, stamping, cutting out, etc. Forge hammers are excluded. Detailed product definitions are given in the United Nations *Industrial Commodity Statistics Yearbook* [24].

Table 57 presents data on lorries, distinguishing between lorries assembled from imported parts and those manufactured wholly or mainly from domestically-produced parts. Both include road motor vehicles designed for the conveyance of goods, including vehicles specially equipped for the transport of certain goods, and articulated vehicles (that is, units made up of a road motor vehicle and a semi-trailer). Ambulances, prison vans and special purpose lorries and vans, such as fire-engines are excluded.

ges. Cette rubrique ne comprend pas les glacières conçues pour contenir un élément frigorifique actif (glace en bloc) mais non un équipement frigorifique.

Tableau 55: Ces machines à laver comprennent généralement des pales ou des cylindres rotatifs (destinés à assurer le brassage continu du liquide et du linge) ou des dispositifs à mouvements alternés, mus électriquement. Cette rubrique comprend les machines à laver avec essoreuses à rouleau ou essoreuses centrifuges et les essoreuses centrifuges conçues comme des appareils indépendants.

Tableau 56: Les données sur les machines-outils présentés dans ce tableau comprennent les perceuses, tours, fraiseuses, et presses pour le travail des métaux. Perceuses se rapportent aux machines-outils pour le travail des métaux, munies d'un socle, d'un pied ou d'un autre dispositif permettant de les fixer au sol, à un établi, à une paroi ou à une autre machine. Tours se rapportent aux tours à métaux, de tous types, automatiques ou non, y compris les tours parallèles, les tours verticaux, les tours à revolver, les tours à reproduire. Fraiseuses se rapportent aux machines-outils pour le travail des métaux conçues pour usiner une surface plane ou un profil au moyen d'outils tournants appelés fraises. Presses pour le travail des métaux se rapportent aux presses à commande mécanique, hydraulique et pneumatique servant à forger, à estamper, à matricer etc. Cette rubrique ne comprend pas les outils agissant par chocs. Pour plus de détails sur les description des produits se reporter à l'*Annuaire des statistiques industrielles par produit* [24] des Nations Unies.

Tableau 57 présente les données sur les camions et fait la distinction entre les camions assemblés à partir de pièces importées et les camions qui sont montés entièrement ou principalement avec des pièces importées. Les deux comprennent les véhicules automobiles routiers conçus pour le transport des marchandises, y compris les véhicules spécialement équipés pour le transport de certaines marchandises, et les véhicules articulés (c'est-à-dire les ensembles composés d'un véhicule automobile routier et d'une semi-remorque). Cette rubrique ne comprend pas les ambulances, les voitures cellulaires et les camions à usages spéciaux, tels que les voitures-pompes à incendie.

58
Railways: traffic
Passenger and net ton-kilometres: millions
Chemins de fer : trafic
Voyageurs et tonnes-kilomètres nettes : millions

Country or area Pays ou zone	1993	1994	1995	1996	1997	1998	1999	2000	2001	2002
Albania Albanie										
Passenger-kilometres										
Voyageurs-kilometres	223	215	197	168	95	116	121	183	138	123
Net ton-kilometres										
Tonnes-kilomètres nettes	54	53	53	42	23	25	26	28	19	20
Algeria Algérie										
Passenger-kilometres										
Voyageurs-kilomètres	3 009	2 234	1 574	1 826	1 360	1 163	1 069	1 142	981	...
Net ton-kilometres										
Tonnes-kilomètres nettes	2 296	2 261	1 946	2 194	2 892	2 174	2 033	1 980	1 990	...
Argentina Argentine										
Passenger-kilometres [1]										
Voyageurs-kilomètres [1]	4 171	4 905	7 017	8 524	9 324	9 652	9 102	8 939	7 934	...
Net ton-kilometres										
Tonnes-kilomètres nettes	4 477	6 613	7 613	8 505	9 835	9 852	9 101	8 696	8 989	...
Armenia Arménie										
Passenger-kilometres										
Voyageurs-kilomètres	435	353	166	84	84	52	46	47	48	48
Net ton-kilometres										
Tonnes-kilomètres nettes	451	378	403	351	381	419	323	354	344	452
Australia [2] Australie [2]										
Net ton-kilometres										
Tonnes-kilomètres nettes	92 123	97 779	99 727	104 311	114 500	125 200	127 400	134 200	139 700	134 109
Austria Autriche										
Passenger-kilometres										
Voyageurs-kilomètres	9 342	9 629	9 625	9 689	8 140	7 971	7 997	8 206	...	...
Net ton-kilometres										
Tonnes-kilomètres nettes	11 798	13 050	13 715	13 909	14 791	15 348	15 556	17 110	17 387	17 627
Azerbaijan Azerbaïdjan										
Passenger-kilometres										
Voyageurs-kilomètres	1 330	1 081	791	558	489	533	422	493	537	584
Net ton-kilometres										
Tonnes-kilomètres nettes	7 300	3 312	2 409	2 778	3 515	4 702	5 052	5 770	6 141	6 980
Bangladesh [3] Bangladesh [3]										
Passenger-kilometres										
Voyageurs-kilomètres	5 112	4 570	4 037	3 333	3 754	3 855	...	...	...	...
Net ton-kilometres										
Tonnes-kilomètres nettes	641	641	760	689	782	804	...	...	...	...
Belarus Bélarus										
Passenger-kilometres [4]										
Voyageurs-kilomètres [4]	19 500	16 063	12 505	11 657	12 909	13 268	16 874	17 722	15 264	14 349
Net ton-kilometres										
Tonnes-kilomètres nettes	42 919	27 963	25 510	26 018	30 636	30 370	30 529	31 425	29 727	34 169
Belgium Belgique										
Passenger-kilometres										
Voyageurs-kilomètres	6 694	6 638	6 757	6 788	6 984	7 097	7 354	7 755	8 036	...
Net ton-kilometres										
Tonnes-kilomètres nettes	7 581	8 081	7 287	7 244	7 465	7 600	7 392	7 674	7 080	...
Benin Bénin										
Passenger-kilometres										
Voyageurs-kilomètres	75	107	116	117	121	111	108	100	...	...
Net ton-kilometres										
Tonnes-kilomètres nettes	225	253	207	178	218	219	204	89	...	...
Bolivia Bolivie										
Passenger-kilometres										
Voyageurs-kilomètres	279	277	240	197	225	270	271	259	267	...
Net ton-kilometres										
Tonnes-kilomètres nettes	695	782	758	780	839	908	832	856	750	...
Botswana Botswana										
Passenger-kilometres										
Voyageurs-kilomètres	95	119	110	81	82	71	75	...	...	...

58

Railways: traffic
Passenger and net ton-kilometres: millions *[cont.]*

Chemins de fer : trafic
Voyageurs et tonnes-kilomètres nettes : millions *[suite]*

Country or area Pays ou zone	1993	1994	1995	1996	1997	1998	1999	2000	2001	2002
Net ton-kilometres Tonnes-kilomètres nettes	585	569	687	668	1 049	1 278	1 037	...	...	...
Brazil Brésil										
Passenger-kilometres [5] Voyageurs-kilomètres [5]	14 040	15 758	9 936	9 048	7 876	7 224	6 528	5 852	...	...
Net ton-kilometres [6] Tonnes-kilomètres nettes [6]	124 677	133 735	136 460	128 976	138 724	142 446	140 957	154 870	...	...
Bulgaria Bulgarie										
Passenger-kilometres Voyageurs-kilomètres	5 837	5 059	4 693	5 065	5 886	4 740	3 819	3 472	2 990	2 598
Net ton-kilometres [7] Tonnes-kilomètres nettes [7]	7 702	7 774	8 595	7 549	7 444	6 152	5 297	5 538	4 904	4 627
Cambodia Cambodge										
Passenger-kilometres Voyageurs-kilomètres	97	39	38	22	51	44	50	15	...	...
Net ton-kilometres Tonnes-kilomètres nettes	28	16	6	4	37	76	76	91	...	...
Cameroon Cameroun										
Passenger-kilometres Voyageurs-kilomètres	352	317	301	306[8]	283[8]	292[8]	311[8]	711[8]	303[8]	...
Net ton-kilometres Tonnes-kilomètres nettes	653	812	607	869[8]	850[8]	888[8]	916[8]	1 063[8]	1 159[8]	...
Canada Canada										
Passenger-kilometres Voyageurs-kilomètres	1 413	1 440	1 473	1 519	1 515	1 458	1 593	...	...	...
Net ton-kilometres Tonnes-kilomètres nettes	257 805[7]	288 864[7]	280 474	282 489	306 943	299 508	298 836		...	...
Chile Chili										
Passenger-kilometres Voyageurs-kilomètres	938	816	691	644	552	519	638	737	871	781
Net ton-kilometres Tonnes-kilomètres nettes	2 496	2 371	2 262	2 366	2 330	2 650	2 896	3 135	3 318	3 356
China [9] Chine [9]										
Passenger-kilometres Voyageurs-kilomètres	348 330	363 605	354 570	332 537	358 486	377 342	413 593	453 300	476 700	...
Net ton-kilometres Tonnes-kilomètres nettes	1195464	1245750	1287025	1297046	1325330	1251707	1283840	1390200	1457500	...
China, Hong Kong SAR [10] Chine, Hong Kong RAS [10]										
Passenger-kilometres Voyageurs-kilomètres	3 269	3 497	3 662	3 914	4 172	4 252	4 321	4 533	4 559	4 618
Net ton-kilometres Tonnes-kilomètres nettes	51	47	41	30	24	15	15	15	12	13
Colombia [7] Colombie [7]										
Net ton-kilometres Tonnes-kilomètres nettes	459	666	753	747	736	658	373	...	...	...
Congo Congo										
Passenger-kilometres Voyageurs-kilomètres	312	227	302	360	235	242	8	84	171	76
Net ton-kilometres Tonnes-kilomètres nettes	257	222	267	289	139	135	16	85	228	307
Croatia Croatie										
Passenger-kilometres [11] Voyageurs-kilomètres [11]	1 094	1 182	1 139	1 205	1 158	1 092	1 137	1 252	1 241	1 195
Net ton-kilometres Tonnes-kilomètres nettes	1 592	1 563	1 974	1 717	1 876	2 001	1 849	1 928	2 249	2 206[12]
Cuba Cuba										
Passenger-kilometres Voyageurs-kilomètres	2 512	2 353	2 188	2 156	1 962	1 750	1 499	1 737	1 758	1 682
Net ton-kilometres Tonnes-kilomètres nettes	764	653	745	871	859	822	806	808	842	814

58

Railways: traffic
Passenger and net ton-kilometres: millions *[cont.]*

Chemins de fer : trafic
Voyageurs et tonnes-kilomètres nettes : millions *[suite]*

Country or area Pays ou zone	1993	1994	1995	1996	1997	1998	1999	2000	2001	2002
Czech Republic République tchèque										
Passenger-kilometres										
Voyageurs-kilomètres	8 548	8 481	8 005	8 111	7 721	7 018	6 954	7 300	7 299	6 595
Net ton-kilometres [13]										
Tonnes-kilomètres nettes [13]	25 579	24 393	22 623	22 338	21 010	18 709	16 713	17 496	16 882	15 772
Denmark Danemark										
Passenger-kilometres										
Voyageurs-kilomètres	4 737	4 847	4 684	4 621	4 978	5 163	5 113	5 327	5 548	...
Net ton-kilometres [14]										
Tonnes-kilomètres nettes [14]	1 751	2 008	1 985	1 757	1 983	2 058	1 938	2 025	1 961	...
Ecuador Equateur										
Passenger-kilometres										
Voyageurs-kilomètres	39	27	47	51	47	44	5	5	32	33
Net ton-kilometres										
Tonnes-kilomètres nettes	3	9	3	1	0	14	0	0	0	0
Egypt [2] Egypte [2]										
Passenger-kilometres										
Voyageurs-kilomètres	49 025	51 098	52 839	55 888	60 617	64 077	68 423	57 859	55 807	...
Net ton-kilometres										
Tonnes-kilomètres nettes	3 142	3 621	4 073	4 117	3 969	4 012	3 464	4 184	4 198	...
El Salvador El Salvador										
Passenger-kilometres										
Voyageurs-kilomètres	6	6	5	7	7	6	8	...	...	...
Net ton-kilometres										
Tonnes-kilomètres nettes	35	30	13	17	17	24	19	...	...	...
Estonia Estonie										
Passenger-kilometres										
Voyageurs-kilomètres	722	537	421	309	261	236	238	263	183	177
Net ton-kilometres										
Tonnes-kilomètres nettes	4 152	3 612	3 846	4 198	5 141	6 079	7 295	8 102	8 557	9 697
Ethiopia [15,16] Ethiopie [15,16]										
Passenger-kilometres										
Voyageurs-kilomètres	230	280	293	218	206	151	...	...	...	...
Net ton-kilometres										
Tonnes-kilomètres nettes	112	102	93	104	106	90	...	...	...	...
Finland Finlande										
Passenger-kilometres										
Voyageurs-kilomètres	3 007	3 037	3 184	3 254	3 376	3 377	3 415	3 405	3 282	3 305
Net ton-kilometres [17]										
Tonnes-kilomètres nettes [17]	9 259	9 949	9 293	8 806	9 856	9 885	9 753	10 107	9 857	9 664
France France										
Passenger-kilometres										
Voyageurs-kilomètres	58 610	58 930	55 560	59 770	61 830	64 460	66 590	69 870	71 550	...
Net ton-kilometres [18]										
Tonnes-kilomètres nettes [18]	45 830	49 720	49 170	50 500	54 820	55 090	54 350	554 505	50 400	...
Georgia Géorgie										
Passenger-kilometres										
Voyageurs-kilomètres	917	1 165	371	380	294	397	355	453	401	392
Net ton-kilometres										
Tonnes-kilomètres nettes	1 554	955	1 246	1 141	2 006	2 574	3 160	3 912	4 481	5 058
Germany Allemagne										
Passenger-kilometres										
Voyageurs-kilomètres	58 003	61 962	74 970	75 975	73 917	72 389	73 587	75 111	75 314	70 814
Net ton-kilometres										
Tonnes-kilomètres nettes	64 902	70 203	68 046	67 227	72 703	73 560	71 356	76 032	74 260	72 014
Ghana Ghana										
Passenger-kilometres										
Voyageurs-kilomètres	118	196	213	209	215	230	240	235	238	242
Net ton-kilometres										
Tonnes-kilomètres nettes	137	149	157	160	163	165	169	164	168	170

58

Railways: traffic
Passenger and net ton-kilometres: millions *[cont.]*

Chemins de fer : trafic
Voyageurs et tonnes-kilomètres nettes : millions *[suite]*

Country or area Pays ou zone	1993	1994	1995	1996	1997	1998	1999	2000	2001	2002
Greece Grèce										
Passenger-kilometres Voyageurs-kilomètres	1 726	1 399	1 569	1 752	1 783	1 552	1 453	1 629	...	...
Net ton-kilometres [19] Tonnes-kilomètres nettes [19]	523	325	306	350	330	322	347	427	...	...
Guatemala Guatemala										
Passenger-kilometres Voyageurs-kilomètres	3 427	991	...	...	...	...	...	...	...	...
Net ton-kilometres Tonnes-kilomètres nettes	29 186	25 295	14 242	836	...	...	...	...	...	...
Hungary Hongrie										
Passenger-kilometres Voyageurs-kilomètres	8 432	8 508	8 441	8 582	8 669	8 884	9 514	9 693	10 005	10 531
Net ton-kilometres Tonnes-kilomètres nettes	7 708	7 707	8 422	7 634	8 149	8 150	7 734	8 095	7 731	7 752
India [20] Inde [20]										
Passenger-kilometres Voyageurs-kilomètres	296 245	319 365	341 999	357 013	379 897	403 884	430 666	457 022	493 488	...
Net ton-kilometres Tonnes-kilomètres nettes	252 411	249 564	270 489	277 567	284 249	281 513	305 201	312 371	333 228	...
Indonesia Indonésie										
Passenger-kilometres Voyageurs-kilomètres	12 337	13 728	15 500	15 223	15 518	16 970	17 820	19 228	18 270	16 829
Net ton-kilometres Tonnes-kilomètres nettes	3 955	3 854	4 172	4 700	5 030	4 963	5 035	4 997	4 859	4 450
Iran (Islamic Rep. of) Iran (Rép. islamique d')										
Passenger-kilometres Voyageurs-kilomètres	6 422	6 479	7 294	7 044	6 103	5 637	6 451	7 128	8 043	...
Net ton-kilometres Tonnes-kilomètres nettes	9 124	10 700	11 865	13 638	14 400	12 638	14 082	14 179	14 613	...
Iraq Iraq										
Passenger-kilometres Voyageurs-kilomètres	1 566	2 334	2 198	...	...	...	...	...	...	...
Net ton-kilometres [21] Tonnes-kilomètres nettes [21]	1 587	1 901	1 120	...	...	...	...	...	...	...
Ireland Irlande										
Passenger-kilometres Voyageurs-kilomètres	1 274	1 260	1 291	1 295	1 388	1 421	1 458	1 389	1 515	1 628
Net ton-kilometres Tonnes-kilomètres nettes	575	569	602	570	522	466	526	491	516	426
Israel Israël										
Passenger-kilometres Voyageurs-kilomètres	214	231	269	294	346	383	529	781	961	...
Net ton-kilometres Tonnes-kilomètres nettes	1 072	1 089	1 176	1 152	992	1 049	1 128	1 173	1 098	...
Italy Italie										
Passenger-kilometres Voyageurs-kilomètres	47 101	48 900	49 700	50 300	49 500	47 285	49 424	#47 133	46 675	...
Net ton-kilometres [21] Tonnes-kilomètres nettes [21]	20 226	22 564	24 050	23 314	25 285	24 704	23 781	#24 995	24 352	...
Japan Japon										
Passenger-kilometres Voyageurs-kilomètres	401 864	402 513	393 907	400 712	301 510	391 073	384 943	384 906	385 403	...
Net ton-kilometres Tonnes-kilomètres nettes	25 619	25 946	23 695	24 991	18 661	23 136	22 676	22 131	22 363	...
Jordan Jordanie										
Passenger-kilometres Voyageurs-kilomètres	2	2	1	1	2	2	2	2	4	3
Net ton-kilometres Tonnes-kilomètres nettes	711	676	698	735	625	596	585	671	371	531

58

Railways: traffic
Passenger and net ton-kilometres: millions *[cont.]*
Chemins de fer : trafic
Voyageurs et tonnes-kilomètres nettes : millions *[suite]*

Country or area Pays ou zone	1993	1994	1995	1996	1997	1998	1999	2000	2001	2002
Kazakhstan　Kazakhstan										
Passenger-kilometres										
Voyageurs-kilomètres	20 507	17 362	13 159	14 188	12 802	10 668	8 859	10 215	10 384	10 449
Net ton-kilometres										
Tonnes-kilomètres nettes	192 258	146 778	124 502	112 688	106 425	103 045	91 700	124 983	135 653	133 088
Kenya　Kenya										
Passenger-kilometres										
Voyageurs-kilomètres	395	408	363	385	393	432	306	302	166	...
Net ton-kilometres										
Tonnes-kilomètres nettes	1 479	1 282	1 371	1 338	1 068	1 111	1 492	1 557	1 603	...
Korea, Republic of　Corée, République de										
Passenger-kilometres										
Voyageurs-kilomètres	31 048	28 859	29 292	29 580	30 073	28 576	28 606	27 787	29 172	28 743
Net ton-kilometres										
Tonnes-kilomètres nettes	14 658	14 070	13 838	12 947	12 710	10 372	10 072	10 803	10 492	10 784
Kyrgyzstan　Kirghizistan										
Passenger-kilometres										
Voyageurs-kilomètres	296	172	87	92	93	59	31	44	50	43
Net ton-kilometres										
Tonnes-kilomètres nettes	923	629	403	481	472	466	354	338	332	395
Latvia　Lettonie										
Passenger-kilometres										
Voyageurs-kilomètres	2 359	1 794	1 256	1 149	1 154	1 059	984	715	706	744
Net ton-kilometres [14]										
Tonnes-kilomètres nettes [14]	9 852	9 520	9 757	12 412	13 970	12 995	12 210	13 310	14 179	15 020
Lithuania　Lituanie										
Passenger-kilometres										
Voyageurs-kilomètres	2 700	1 574	1 130	954	842	800	745	611	533	498
Net ton-kilometres [23]										
Tonnes-kilomètres nettes [23]	11 030	7 996	7 220	8 103	8 622	8 265	7 849	8 918	7 741	9 767
Luxembourg　Luxembourg										
Passenger-kilometres										
Voyageurs-kilomètres	262	289	286	284	295	300	310	332	346	...
Net ton-kilometres										
Tonnes-kilomètres nettes	647	686	566	574	613	624	660	683	634	...
Madagascar　Madagascar										
Passenger-kilometres										
Voyageurs-kilomètres	...	...	...	...	81	35	28	19	...	...
Net ton-kilometres [7,24]										
Tonnes-kilomètres nettes [7,24]	...	...	...	...	81	71	44	26		
Malawi [20]　Malawi [20]										
Passenger-kilometres										
Voyageurs-kilomètres	46	20	22	26	17	21	19	...	...	...
Net ton-kilometres										
Tonnes-kilomètres nettes	43	58	74	57	46	55	62	...	...	...
Malaysia [25]　Malaisie [25]										
Passenger-kilometres										
Voyageurs-kilomètres	1 543	1 348	1 270	1 370	1 492	1 397	1 313	1 220	1 181	...
Net ton-kilometres										
Tonnes-kilomètres nettes	1 157	1 463	1 416	1 397	1 336	992	908	917	1 094	...
Mali　Mali										
Net ton-kilometres										
Tonnes-kilomètres nettes	191	220	254	405	...	...	...	...	...	...
Mexico　Mexique										
Passenger-kilometres										
Voyageurs-kilomètres	3 219	1 855	1 899	1 799	1 508	460	254	82	67	66
Net ton-kilometres										
Tonnes-kilomètres nettes	35 672	37 315	37 613	41 723	42 442	46 873	47 273	48 333	47 353	47 809
Mongolia　Mongolie										
Passenger-kilometres										
Voyageurs-kilomètres	583	790	680	733	951	981	1 010	1 067	...	...

58

Railways: traffic
Passenger and net ton-kilometres: millions *[cont.]*

Chemins de fer : trafic
Voyageurs et tonnes-kilomètres nettes : millions *[suite]*

Country or area / Pays ou zone	1993	1994	1995	1996	1997	1998	1999	2000	2001	2002
Net ton-kilometres / Tonnes-kilomètres nettes	2 531	2 132	2 280	2 529	2 254	2 815	3 492	4 283	...	...
Morocco Maroc										
Passenger-kilometres / Voyageurs-kilomètres	1 904	1 881	1 564	1 776	1 856	1 875	1 880	1 956	2 019	2 145
Net ton-kilometres / Tonnes-kilomètres nettes	4 415	4 679	4 621	4 757	4 835	4 827	4 795	4 650	4 699	4 974
Myanmar Myanmar										
Passenger-kilometres / Voyageurs-kilomètres	4 706	4 390	4 178	4 294	3 784	3 948	4 112	4 451	...	...
Net ton-kilometres [7] / Tonnes-kilomètres nettes [7]	663	726	659	748	674	988	1 043	1 222	...	...
Netherlands Pays-Bas										
Passenger-kilometres / Voyageurs-kilomètres	14 788	14 439	13 977	14 131	14 485	14 879	...	...	...	...
Net ton-kilometres / Tonnes-kilomètres nettes	2 681	2 830	3 097	3 123	3 406	3 778	...	...	...	...
New Zealand [2] Nouvelle-Zélande [2]										
Net ton-kilometres / Tonnes-kilomètres nettes	2 468	2 835	3 202	3 260	3 505	3 547	3 636	4 040	...	...
Nigeria Nigéria										
Passenger-kilometres / Voyageurs-kilomètres	55	220	161	170	179	...	...	...	...	...
Net ton-kilometres / Tonnes-kilomètres nettes	162	141	108	114	120	...	...	...	...	...
Norway Norvège										
Passenger-kilometres / Voyageurs-kilomètres	2 341	2 398	2 381	2 449	2 561	2 652	2 866	2 857	2 850	2 477
Net ton-kilometres / Tonnes-kilomètres nettes	2 873	2 681	2 684	2 804	2 975	2 948	2 894	2 955	2 887	3 019
Pakistan [3] Pakistan [3]										
Passenger-kilometres / Voyageurs-kilomètres	16 274	18 044	18 905	19 114	18 771	18 979	18 761	19 292	20 004	19 793
Net ton-kilometres / Tonnes-kilomètres nettes	5 940	5 660	5 078	4 538	4 444	3 939	3 612	3 799	4 681	4 594
Panama Panama										
Passenger-kilometres / Voyageurs-kilomètres	2 315[27]	2 619[29]	1 069[29]	122[29]	9[28,29]	...	...	...	24 576[28]	35 693
Net ton-kilometres [26] / Tonnes-kilomètres nettes [26]	1 669	1 199	1 728	710	306[28]	...	...	...	4 896[28]	20 665
Paraguay Paraguay										
Passenger-kilometres / Voyageurs-kilomètres	1	...	...	...	...	...	...	...	...	...
Net ton-kilometres / Tonnes-kilomètres nettes	3	6	4	3	2	1	...	1	...	...
Peru [7] Pérou [7]										
Passenger-kilometres / Voyageurs-kilomètres	165	240	231	222	206	177	69	107	122	98
Net ton-kilometres / Tonnes-kilomètres nettes	850	864	843	878	839	890	512	877	1 148	1 008
Philippines Philippines										
Passenger-kilometres / Voyageurs-kilomètres	102	106	163	69	175	181	171	123	110	93
Net ton-kilometres / Tonnes-kilomètres nettes	5	3	4	0[30]	0	0	...	49	67	63
Poland Pologne										
Passenger-kilometres / Voyageurs-kilomètres	30 865	27 610	26 635	26 569	25 806	25 664	26 198	24 093	22 469	20 809
Net ton-kilometres / Tonnes-kilomètres nettes	64 359	65 788	69 116	68 332	68 651	61 760	55 471	54 448	47 913	47 756

58

Railways: traffic
Passenger and net ton-kilometres: millions *[cont.]*

Chemins de fer : trafic
Voyageurs et tonnes-kilomètres nettes : millions *[suite]*

Country or area Pays ou zone	1993	1994	1995	1996	1997	1998	1999	2000	2001	2002
Portugal Portugal										
Passenger-kilometres										
Voyageurs-kilomètres	5 397	5 149	4 840	4 503[31]	4 563[31]	4 602[31]	4 380	3 834	3 898	...
Net ton-kilometres										
Tonnes-kilomètres nettes	1 786	1 826	2 342	2 178	2 632	2 340	2 562	2 569	2 498	...
Republic of Moldova République de Moldova[4]										
Passenger-kilometres[4]										
Voyageurs-kilomètres[4]	1 661	1 204	1 019	882	789	656	343	315	325	355
Net ton-kilometres										
Tonnes-kilomètres nettes	4 965	3 533	3 134	2 897	2 937	2 575	1 191	1 513	1 980	2 748
Romania Roumanie										
Passenger-kilometres[32]										
Voyageurs-kilomètres[32]	19 402	18 313	18 879	18 356	15 795	13 422	12 304	11 632	10 966	8 502
Net ton-kilometres										
Tonnes-kilomètres nettes	22 046	21 746	17 907	24 254	22 111	16 619	14 679	16 354	16 102	15 218
Russian Federation Fédération de Russie										
Passenger-kilometres										
Voyageurs-kilomètres	272 200	227 100	192 200	181 200	170 300	152 900	141 000	167 100	157 900	152 900
Net ton-kilometres										
Tonnes-kilomètres nettes	1608000	1195000	1214000	1131000	1100000	1020000	1205000	1373000	1434000	1510000
Saudi Arabia Arabie saoudite										
Passenger-kilometres										
Voyageurs-kilomètres	136	153	159	170	192	222	224	...	...	...
Net ton-kilometres										
Tonnes-kilomètres nettes	868	927	728	691	726	856	938	...	...	...
Senegal Sénégal										
Passenger-kilometres										
Voyageurs-kilomètres	140	179	194	103	78	63	71	74	88	105
Net ton-kilometres										
Tonnes-kilomètres nettes	393	386	475	474	446	435	401	361	321	345
Serbia and Montenegro Serbie-et-Monténégro										
Passenger-kilometres										
Voyageurs-kilomètres	3 379	2 525	2 611	1 830	1 744	1 622	860	1 436	1 263	1 198
Net ton-kilometres[7]										
Tonnes-kilomètres nettes[7]	1 699	1 387	1 855	2 062	2 432	2 793	1 267	1 969	2 042	2 306
Slovakia Slovaquie										
Passenger-kilometres										
Voyageurs-kilomètres	4 569	4 548	4 202	3 769	3 057	3 092	2 968	2 870	2 805	26 821
Net ton-kilometres										
Tonnes-kilomètres nettes	14 201	12 236	13 674	12 017	12 373	11 753	9 859	11 234	10 929	10 983
Slovenia Slovénie										
Passenger-kilometres										
Voyageurs-kilomètres	566	590	595	613	616	645	623	705	746	749
Net ton-kilometres										
Tonnes-kilomètres nettes	2 262	2 448	3 076	2 550	2 852	2 859	2 784	2 857	2 837	3 018
South Africa[33,34] Afrique du Sud[33,34]										
Passenger-kilometres										
Voyageurs-kilomètres	895	686	1 007	1 198	1 393	1 775	1 794	3 930	...	...
Net ton-kilometres										
Tonnes-kilomètres nettes	91 472	92 538	98 798	99 818	99 773	103 866	102 777	106 786	...	...
Spain Espagne										
Passenger-kilometres										
Voyageurs-kilomètres	16 490	16 142	16 582	16 637	17 883	18 875	19 659	18 547	19 190	...
Net ton-kilometres[7]										
Tonnes-kilomètres nettes[7]	8 132	9 048	10 419	10 219	11 488	11 801	12 029	11 620	11 748	...
Sri Lanka[35] Sri Lanka[35]										
Passenger-kilometres										
Voyageurs-kilomètres	2 822	3 202	3 321	3 103	3 146	3 073	3 104	3 208	3 979	4 079
Net ton-kilometres										
Tonnes-kilomètres nettes	159	154	136	107	98	105	103	88	109	131

58

Railways: traffic
Passenger and net ton-kilometres: millions *[cont.]*

Chemins de fer : trafic
Voyageurs et tonnes-kilomètres nettes : millions *[suite]*

Country or area Pays ou zone	1993	1994	1995	1996	1997	1998	1999	2000	2001	2002
Sudan Soudan										
Passenger-kilometres										
Voyageurs-kilomètres	1 183	...	...	...	...	...	...	...	...	...
Net ton-kilometres										
Tonnes-kilomètres nettes	2 240	...	...	...	...	...	...	...	...	...
Swaziland Swaziland										
Net ton-kilometres										
Tonnes-kilomètres nettes	...	675	743	684	670	653	677	753	746	...
Sweden Suède										
Passenger-kilometres										
Voyageurs-kilomètres	6 922	6 507	6 839	6 970[36]	7 039[36]	7 230[36]	7 720[36]	8 301	8 792	...
Net ton-kilometres										
Tonnes-kilomètres nettes	18 578	19 069	19 391	18 846[36]	19 181[36]	19 163[36]	19 090[36]	20 088[36]	79 547[36]	...
Switzerland Suisse										
Passenger-kilometres										
Voyageurs-kilomètres	13 384	13 836	13 408	13 326	14 104	...	...	...	...	...
Net ton-kilometres										
Tonnes-kilomètres nettes	7 821	8 586	8 626	7 847	8 629	...	...	...	...	...
Syrian Arab Republic Rép. arabe syrienne										
Passenger-kilometres										
Voyageurs-kilomètres	855	769	498	454	294	182	187	197	307	...
Net ton-kilometres										
Tonnes-kilomètres nettes	1 097	1 190	1 285	1 864	1 472	1 430	1 577	1 568	1 492	...
Tajikistan [37] Tadjikistan [37]										
Passenger-kilometres										
Voyageurs-kilomètres	117	366	134	95	129	121	61	73	32	42
Net ton-kilometres										
Tonnes-kilomètres nettes	329	2 169	2 115	1 719	1 384	1 458	1 282	1 326	1 248	1 086
Thailand [35] Thaïlande [35]										
Passenger-kilometres										
Voyageurs-kilomètres	13 702	13 814	12 975	12 205	11 804	10 947	9 894	9 935	10 321	10 378
Net ton-kilometres										
Tonnes-kilomètres nettes	3 059	3 072	3 242	3 286	3 410	2 874	2 929	3 384	3 724	3 898
TFYR of Macedonia L'ex-R.y. Macédoine										
Passenger-kilometres										
Voyageurs-kilomètres	66	67	65	120	141	150	150	176	133	98
Net ton-kilometres										
Tonnes-kilomètres nettes	493	151	169	271	279	408	380	527	462	334
Tunisia Tunisie [19]										
Passenger-kilometres [19]										
Voyageurs-kilomètres [19]	1 057	1 038	996	988	1 094	1 133	1 196	1 258	1 285	1 265
Net ton-kilometres [7,38]										
Tonnes-kilomètres nettes [7,38]	2 012	2 225	2 317	2 329	2 338	2 349	2 365	2 274	2 279	2 250
Turkey Turquie										
Passenger-kilometres										
Voyageurs-kilomètres	7 147	6 335	5 797	5 229	5 840	6 161	6 146	5 833	5 568	5 204
Net ton-kilometres										
Tonnes-kilomètres nettes	8 517	8 339	8 632	9 018	9 717	8 466	8 446	9 895	7 562	7 224
Uganda Ouganda										
Passenger-kilometres										
Voyageurs-kilomètres	60	35	30	25	5	0[39]	0[39]	0[39]	0[39]	...
Net ton-kilometres										
Tonnes-kilomètres nettes	130	208	245	184	144	148	200	219	217	...
Ukraine Ukraine										
Passenger-kilometres										
Voyageurs-kilomètres	75 896	70 882	63 759	59 080	54 540	49 938	47 600	51 767	52 661	...
Net ton-kilometres										
Tonnes-kilomètres nettes	246 356	200 422	195 762	160 384	160 433	158 693	156 336	172 840	177 465	...
United Kingdom [20,40] Royaume-Uni [20,40]										
Passenger-kilometres										
Voyageurs-kilomètres	30 363	28 650	30 039	32 135	34 950	36 517	38 738	38 421	39 327	...

58

Railways: traffic
Passenger and net ton-kilometres: millions *[cont.]*

Chemins de fer : trafic
Voyageurs et tonnes-kilomètres nettes : millions *[suite]*

Country or area Pays ou zone	1993	1994	1995	1996	1997	1998	1999	2000	2001	2002
Net ton-kilometres										
Tonnes-kilomètres nettes	13 765	12 979	13 136	15 144	16 949	17 369	18 200	18 100	19 700	...
United States Etats-Unis										
Passenger-kilometres [41]										
Voyageurs-kilomètres [41]	9 976	9 529	8 924	8 127	8 317	8 573	8 515	8 974	8 969	...
Net ton-kilometres [42]										
Tonnes-kilomètres nettes [42]	1619588	1753020	1906300	1984654	1974337	2015138	2098066	2145632	2188827	...
Uruguay Uruguay										
Passenger-kilometres										
Voyageurs-kilomètres	221	467	...	...	17	14	10	9	...	...
Net ton-kilometres										
Tonnes-kilomètres nettes	178	188	184	182	204	244	272	239	...	...
Uzbekistan Ouzbékistan										
Passenger-kilometres										
Voyageurs-kilomètres	5	5	3	2	2	2	2	2	2	...
Net ton-kilometres										
Tonnes-kilomètres nettes	36	19	17	20	17	16	14	15	16	...
Venezuela Venezuela										
Passenger-kilometres										
Voyageurs-kilomètres	44	31	12	...	...	...	...	...	...	...
Net ton-kilometres										
Tonnes-kilomètres nettes	26	47	53	...	...	...	...	...	...	...
Viet Nam Viet Nam										
Passenger-kilometres										
Voyageurs-kilomètres	1 921	1 796	2 133	2 261	2 476	2 542	2 722	3 200	3 426	...
Net ton-kilometres										
Tonnes-kilomètres nettes	978	1 370	1 751	1 684	1 533	1 369	1 446	1 955	2 044	...
Yemen Yémen										
Passenger-kilometres										
Voyageurs-kilomètres	...	1 714	2 051	2 260	2 492	...	...	...	...	
Zambia Zambie										
Passenger-kilometres										
Voyageurs-kilomètres	690	702	778	749	755	586	...	...	...	
Net ton-kilometres										
Tonnes-kilomètres nettes	123	151	90	666	758	702	...	...	...	
Zimbabwe [2,44] Zimbabwe [2,44]										
Net ton-kilometres										
Tonnes-kilomètres nettes	4 581	4 489	7 180	4 990	5 115	9 122	4 375	3 326	...	2 504

Source:
United Nations Statistics Division, New York, transport statistics database.

Source:
Organisation des Nations Unies, Division de statistique, New York, la base de données pour les statistiques des transports.

1	Including urban transport only.
2	Data refer to fiscal years ending 30 June.
3	Data refer to fiscal years beginning 1 July.
4	Including passengers carried without revenues.
5	Including urban railways traffic.
6	Including service traffic, animals, baggage and parcels.
7	Including service traffic.
8	Beginning 1996, annual data cover 12 months ending June.
9	May include service traffic.
10	Kowloon - Canton Railway only.
11	Beginning 1993, railway transport of passengers includes urban transport of passengers organized by ZET City Rail and HZ State Rail.
12	Excluding privately-owned wagons.
13	Including only state-owned railways.

1	Les chemins de fer urbains seulement.
2	Les données se réfèrent aux exercices budgétaires finissant le 30 juin.
3	Les données se réfèrent aux exercices budgétaires commençant le 1er juillet.
4	Y compris passagers transportés gratuitement.
5	Y compris le trafic de chemins-de-fer urbains.
6	Y compris le trafic de service, les animaux, les baggages et les colis.
7	Y compris le trafic de service.
8	A partir de 1996, les données de l'année se réfèrent aux 12 mois finissant juin.
9	Le trafic de service peut être compris.
10	Chemin de fer de Kowloon-Canton seulement.
11	A compter de l'annee 1993 y compris le transport urbain de passagers organisés par ZET City Rail et HZ State Rail.
12	Non compris wagons privés.
13	Y compris chemins-de-fer de l'état seulement.

58

Railways: traffic
Passenger and net ton-kilometres: millions *[cont.]*

Chemins de fer : trafic
Voyageurs et tonnes-kilomètres nettes : millions *[suite]*

14	Including passengers' baggage and parcel post (Latvia: also mail).	14	Y compris les bagages des voyageurs et les colis postaux (Lettonie : courrier aussi).
15	Including traffic of the Djibouti portion of the Djibouti-Addis Ababa line.	15	Y compris le trafic de la ligne Djibouti-Addis Abeba en Djibouti.
16	Data refer to fiscal years beginning 7 July.	16	Les données se réfèrent aux exercices budgétaires commençant le 7 juillet.
17	Beginning 1995, wagon loads traffic only.	17	A compter de 1995, y compris trafic de charge de waggon seulement.
18	Including passengers' baggage.	18	Y compris les bagages des voyageurs.
19	Including military traffic (Greece: also government traffic).	19	Y compris le trafic militaire (Grèce: et de l'Etat aussi).
20	Data refer to fiscal years beginning 1 April.	20	Les données se réfèrent aux exercices budgétaires commençant le 1er avril.
21	Excluding livestock.	21	Non compris le bétail.
22	Beginning 2000, break in series.	22	A partir de 2000, discontinuité dans la série.
23	Prior to 1994, data refer to operated ton-kilometres which is the weight in tons of freight carried multiplied by the distance in kilometres actually run; beginning 1994, data refer to net ton-kilometres which is the weight in tons of freight carried multiplied by distance in kilometres for which payments were made.	23	Avant de 1994, les données se réfèrent aux tonnes-kilomètres transportées, c'est-à-dire le produit du poids et de la distance effectivement parcourue. A partir de l'année 1994, l'unité utilisée est la tonne-kilomètre nette, c'est-à-dire le produit du poids et de la distance pour lequel un paiement a été effectué.
24	Including baggage and service traffic.	24	Y compris bagages et les transports pour les besoins du service.
25	Data refer to Peninsular Malaysia only.	25	Les données se rapportent à Malasie péninsulaire seulement.
26	Panama Railway only.	26	Chemin de fer de Panama seulement.
27	National Railway of Chiriqui only.	27	Chemin de fer national de Chiriqui seulement.
28	Beginning August 1997, railway operations closed. Beginning July 2001, Panama Railway resumed operations.	28	A cessé de fonctionner en août 1997. A compter de juillet 2001, le Chemin de fer de Panama a recommencé des opérations.
29	Panama Railway and National Railway of Chiriqui.	29	Chemin de fer de Panama et chemin de fer national de Chiriqui.
30	Freight train operations suspended from November 1995 to August 1996 due to typhoon damages.	30	Les opérations de train de marchandises interrompues pendant la période de novembre 1995 à août 1996 à cause des dommages de typhon.
31	Excluding river traffic of the railway company.	31	Non compris le trafic fluvial de la compagnie des chemins de fer.
32	Including military and government personnel.	32	Y compris les militaires et les fonctionnaires.
33	Beginning 1988, excluding Namibia.	33	A partir de 1988, non compris la Namibie.
34	Data refer to fiscal years ending 31 March.	34	Les données se réfèrent aux exercices budgétaires finissant le 31 mars.
35	Data refer to fiscal years ending 30 September.	35	Les données se réfèrent aux exercices budgétaires finissant le 30 septembre.
36	Including Swedish State Railways and MTAB.	36	Y compris chemins-de-fer de l'état y MTAB.
37	Beginning 1992, decline due to border changes affecting the Dushanbe branch of the Csredniya Niyatskaya (Central Asia) Railway Co.	37	A compter de 1992, réduction imputable à des changements de frontière affectant la ligne de Douchanbé de la Compagnie Csredniya Niyatskaya (Asie centrale).
38	Ordinary goods only.	38	Petite vitesse seulement.
39	Beginning late 1997, passenger services suspended.	39	A compter de l'année de 1997, transport passager interrompu.
40	Excluding Northern Ireland.	40	Non compris l'Irlande du Nord.
41	Beginning 1986, excluding commuter railroads.	41	A partir de 1986, non compris les chemins de fer de banlieue.
42	Class I railways only.	42	Réseaux de catégorie 1 seulement.
43	Passenger transport suspended from 1988 to 1992.	43	Transport passager interrompu pendant la période 1988 à 1992.
44	Including traffic in Botswana.	44	Y compris le trafic en Botswana.

59

Motor vehicles in use
Passenger cars and commercial vehicles: thousands

Véhicules automobiles en circulation
Voitures de tourisme et véhicules utilitaires : milliers de véhicules

Country or area Pays ou zone	1993	1994	1995	1996	1997	1998	1999	2000	2001	2002
Afghanistan Afghanistan										
Passenger cars										
Voitures de tourisme	1.6	1.6	1.6	4.1	4.6	4.9	5.4	6.2	8.6[1]	...
Commercial vehicles										
Véhicules utilitaires	0.6	0.6	0.6	4.5	5.3	5.4	6.2	7.0	4.5[1]	...
Albania Albanie										
Passenger cars										
Voitures de tourisme	56.7	67.9	58.6	67.2	76.8	90.7	99.0	114.5	133.5	148.5
Commercial vehicles										
Véhicules utilitaires	39.3	51.1	29.1	30.6	33.2	37.1	40.9	43.0	73.0	73.0
Algeria Algérie										
Passenger cars										
Voitures de tourisme	1 547.8	1 555.8	1 562.1	1 588.0	1 615.1	1 634.4	1 676.8	1 692.1	1 708.4	...
Commercial vehicles										
Véhicules utilitaires	926.0	930.8	933.1	958.1	952.7	963.9	986.7	995.7	1 002.3	...
American Samoa Samoa américaines										
Passenger cars										
Voitures de tourisme	4.6	4.6	4.7	5.4	5.3	5.7	6.2	...	...	...
Commercial vehicles										
Véhicules utilitaires	0.5	0.4	0.4	0.5	0.5	0.7	0.7	...	...	...
Angola[1] Angola[1]										
Passenger cars										
Voitures de tourisme	...	...	...	...	...	103.4	107.1	117.2	117.2	...
Commercial vehicles										
Véhicules utilitaires	...	...	...	...	...	107.6	110.5	118.3	118.3	...
Antigua and Barbuda Antigua-et-Barbuda										
Passenger cars										
Voitures de tourisme	14.8	15.0	15.1	21.6[2]	23.7[2]	24.0[2]	...	...	...	...
Commercial vehicles										
Véhicules utilitaires	4.6	4.8	4.8	...	...	...	...	...	...	...
Argentina Argentine										
Passenger cars										
Voitures de tourisme	4 856.0	4 427.0	4 665.0	4 783.9	4 904.3	5 047.8	5 056.7	5 386.7	...	...
Commercial vehicles										
Véhicules utilitaires	1 664.0	1 342.0	1 233.0	4 254.0	1 172.0	1 094.0	1 029.0	1 004.0	...	...
Australia[3] Australie[3]										
Passenger cars										
Voitures de tourisme	8 050.0	8 209.0	8 660.6	9 021.5	9 239.5	9 526.7	9 686.2	...	9 835.9	...
Commercial vehicles										
Véhicules utilitaires	2 043.0	2 151.0	1 990.3	2 075.6	2 111.7	2 177.5	2 214.9	...	2 236.4	...
Austria[4] Autriche[4]										
Passenger cars										
Voitures de tourisme	3 367.6	3 479.6	3 593.6	3 690.7	3 782.5	3 887.2	4 009.6	4 097.1	4 182.0	3 987.1
Commercial vehicles [5]										
Véhicules utilitaires [5]	685.7	698.2	710.1	721.1	736.2	752.1	767.8	779.7	787.9	765.6
Azerbaijan Azerbaïdjan										
Passenger cars										
Voitures de tourisme	263.3	276.4	278.3	273.7	271.3	281.3	311.6	332.1	343.0	350.6
Commercial vehicles										
Véhicules utilitaires	132.3	127.5	125.5	122.9	115.6	117.6	122.8	133.4	127.6	120.4
Bahamas Bahamas										
Passenger cars										
Voitures de tourisme	46.1[1]	54.4	67.1	86.6[6]	89.7[6]	86.6[1]	97.5[1]	80.0[1]	80.0[1]	...
Commercial vehicles										
Véhicules utilitaires	11.9[1]	9.3	13.7	16.9[6]	17.6[6]	15.9[1]	18.6[1]	24.3[1]	25.0[1]	...
Bahrain Bahreïn										
Passenger cars										
Voitures de tourisme	122.9	130.7	135.4	140.0	147.9	160.2	169.6	175.7	187.0	...
Commercial vehicles										
Véhicules utilitaires	28.2	29.4	30.5	31.5	32.8	34.5	35.7	36.8	38.4	...

59

Motor vehicles in use
Passenger cars and commercial vehicles: thousands *[cont.]*

Véhicules automobiles en circulation
Voitures de tourisme et véhicules utilitaires : milliers de véhicules *[suite]*

Country or area Pays ou zone	1993	1994	1995	1996	1997	1998	1999	2000	2001	2002
Bangladesh Bangladesh										
Passenger cars Voitures de tourisme	46.6	48.1	51.1	55.8	61.2	65.0	...	...	...	...
Commercial vehicles Véhicules utilitaires	92.4	99.4	111.7	126.8	138.1	145.9	...	...	...	...
Barbados Barbade										
Passenger cars [7] Voitures de tourisme [7]	46.4	43.5	47.2	49.8	53.6	57.5	62.1	...	...	
Commercial vehicles [8] Véhicules utilitaires [8]	5.8	5.8	7.1	6.9	7.9	8.6	9.4	...	...	
Belarus Bélarus										
Passenger cars Voitures de tourisme	773.6	875.6	939.6	1 035.8	1 132.8	1 279.2	1 351.1	1 421.9	1 467.6	1 548.5
Belgium Belgique										
Passenger cars Voitures de tourisme	4 079.5	4 208.1	4 270.3	4 336.1	4 412.1	4 488.5	4 580.0	4 675.1	4 736.6	4 784.1
Commercial vehicles Véhicules utilitaires	427.7	444.4	457.1	471.8	491.3	510.1	539.0	563.2	587.3	602.1
Belize [6,9] Belize [6,9]										
Passenger cars Voitures de tourisme	...	...	16.1	17.0	19.1	19.3	24.2	26.1	28.8	32.6
Commercial vehicles Véhicules utilitaires	...	...	3.0	3.1	3.6	3.7	6.5	6.4	7.6	7.8
Benin [1] Bénin [1]										
Passenger cars Voitures de tourisme	7.1	7.3	7.3	7.3	7.3	7.3	...	...	...	...
Commercial vehicles Véhicules utilitaires	5.3	5.5	5.7	5.8	6.0	6.2		...	...	
Bermuda Bermudes										
Passenger cars Voitures de tourisme	20.1	20.7	21.1	21.2	21.6	22.0	22.6	21.3[1]	22.2[1]	...
Commercial vehicles Véhicules utilitaires	4.0	4.2	4.4	4.1	4.2	5.0	4.2	5.1[1]	5.8[1]	
Bolivia Bolivie										
Passenger cars Voitures de tourisme	164.7	183.7	201.9	220.3	234.1	274.1	295.1	310.5	316.3	...
Commercial vehicles Véhicules utilitaires	95.3	103.4	112.2	119.8	124.8	138.0	147.2	153.2	155.5	
Botswana Botswana										
Passenger cars Voitures de tourisme	26.3	27.1	30.5	26.7	28.2	37.0	44.5	...	...	
Commercial vehicles Véhicules utilitaires	55.0	60.9	63.7	48.1	52.3	58.7	67.9	...	...	
Brazil [1] Brésil [1]										
Passenger cars Voitures de tourisme	8 098.4	9 524.0	10 320.5	12 666.0	9 385.8	10 828.8	11 630.7	14 820.0	15 210.0	...
Commercial vehicles Véhicules utilitaires	1 839.0	2 378.7	2 520.4	2 896.0	2 087.5	2 429.5	2 630.1	3 300.0	4 256.7	
British Virgin Islands [2] Iles Vierges britanniques [2]										
Passenger cars Voitures de tourisme	6.7	7.0	...	...	...	...	...		...	...
Brunei Darussalam Brunéi Darussalam										
Passenger cars Voitures de tourisme	130.0	135.9	141.7	150.0	163.0	170.6	176.3	182.7	189.1	200.1
Commercial vehicles Véhicules utilitaires	14.5	15.4	16.3	17.3	18.3	18.7	19.1	19.3	19.7	20.3
Bulgaria Bulgarie										
Passenger cars Voitures de tourisme	1 505.5	1 587.9	1 647.6	1 707.0	1 730.5	1 809.4	1 908.4	1 992.8	2 085.7	2 174.1
Commercial vehicles Véhicules utilitaires	243.2	255.4	264.2	270.7	273.2	283.8	293.5	301.7	312.5	323.0

59

Motor vehicles in use
Passenger cars and commercial vehicles: thousands *[cont.]*
Véhicules automobiles en circulation
Voitures de tourisme et véhicules utilitaires : milliers de véhicules *[suite]*

Country or area Pays ou zone	1993	1994	1995	1996	1997	1998	1999	2000	2001	2002
Burkina Faso Burkina Faso										
Passenger cars										
Voitures de tourisme	29.9	32.0	35.5[1]	35.5[1]	35.5[1]	25.3[1]	26.3	26.5[1]	26.5[1]	...
Commercial vehicles										
Véhicules utilitaires	23.4	24.0	19.5[1]	19.5[1]	19.5[1]	14.9[1]	19.6	22.6[1]	22.6[1]	
Burundi Burundi										
Passenger cars										
Voitures de tourisme	18.5	17.5	8.2[1]	8.2[1]	8.2[1]	6.6[1]	6.9[1]	7.0[1]	7.0[1]	...
Commercial vehicles										
Véhicules utilitaires	12.3	10.2	11.8[1]	11.8[1]	11.8[1]	9.3[1]	9.3[1]	9.3[1]	9.3[1]	...
Cambodia Cambodge										
Passenger cars										
Voitures de tourisme	6.8	7.4	8.0	6.3	8.4	8.0	8.5	8.3	...	...
Commercial vehicles										
Véhicules utilitaires	0.7	1.7	2.1	1.4	1.8	1.6	1.5	3.1	...	...
Cameroon Cameroun										
Passenger cars										
Voitures de tourisme	92.8	88.3	94.7	100.9	102.2	105.8	110.7	115.9	...	...
Commercial vehicles										
Véhicules utilitaires	39.0	37.6	39.6	40.6	41.6	43.2	45.3	47.4	...	...
Canada[4] Canada[4]										
Passenger cars										
Voitures de tourisme	12 926.8	13 122.5	13 182.9	13 251.1	13 486.9	13 887.3	16 538.0	16 860.5	17 054.8	17 543.6
Commercial vehicles										
Véhicules utilitaires	3 346.1	3 401.8	3 420.3	3 476.2	3 526.9	3 625.8	649.1[10]	668.0[10]	654.5[11]	644.3[11]
Cape Verde Cap-Vert										
Passenger cars										
Voitures de tourisme	6.5	7.7	8.0	9.3	10.3	11.4	13.5	...	...	...
Commercial vehicles										
Véhicules utilitaires	1.3	2.0	2.0	2.2	2.5	2.8	3.1	...	...	...
Cayman Islands Iles Caïmanes										
Passenger cars										
Voitures de tourisme	11.6	12.3	13.5	14.9	16.0	15.8	17.9	19.8	...	...
Commercial vehicles										
Véhicules utilitaires	2.7	2.8	9.1	3.4	3.7	3.6	4.1	4.4	...	...
Central African Rep. Rép. centrafricaine										
Passenger cars										
Voitures de tourisme	10.4	11.9	8.9	...	...	4.5[1]	4.9[1]	5.3[1]	5.3[1]	...
Commercial vehicles										
Véhicules utilitaires	2.4	2.8	3.5	...	...	5.4[1]	5.8[1]	6.3[1]	6.3[1]	...
Chad[12] Tchad[12]										
Passenger cars										
Voitures de tourisme	9.5	9.5	8.7	...	...	...	...	...	...	...
Commercial vehicles										
Véhicules utilitaires	7.2	7.2	12.4	...	...	...	...	...	...	...
Chile Chili										
Passenger cars										
Voitures de tourisme	896.5	914.3	1 026.0	1 121.2	1 175.8	1 236.9	1 323.8	1 320.5	1 351.9	1 373.1
Commercial vehicles [13]										
Véhicules utilitaires [13]	211.0[14]	492.7[15]	540.0[15]	585.7[15]	635.2[15]	672.2[15]	708.5[15]	701.3	712.9	734.0
China Chine										
Passenger cars										
Voitures de tourisme	2 859.8	3 497.4	4 179.0	4 880.2	5 805.6	6 548.3	...	...	...	...
Commercial vehicles										
Véhicules utilitaires	5 010.0	5 603.3	5 854.3	5 750.3	6 012.3	6 278.9	...	...	...	...
China, Hong Kong SAR Chine, Hong Kong RAS										
Passenger cars										
Voitures de tourisme	277.5	297.3	303.3	311.2	332.8	336.2	339.6	350.4	358.6	358.9
Commercial vehicles										
Véhicules utilitaires	135.6	137.0	134.2	133.7	135.9	133.4	132.3	133.2	132.0	130.8

59

Motor vehicles in use
Passenger cars and commercial vehicles: thousands *[cont.]*

Véhicules automobiles en circulation
Voitures de tourisme et véhicules utilitaires : milliers de véhicules *[suite]*

Country or area Pays ou zone	1993	1994	1995	1996	1997	1998	1999	2000	2001	2002
China, Macao SAR [13] **Chine, Macao RAS** [13]										
Passenger cars Voitures de tourisme	32.6	34.0	34.5	38.9	42.9	46.3	47.8	48.9	49.9	53.3
Commercial vehicles Véhicules utilitaires	6.6	6.3	6.2	6.3	6.6	6.6	7.4	7.1	6.6	6.9
Colombia [1] **Colombie** [1]										
Passenger cars Voitures de tourisme	761.7	688.1	718.9	800.0	584.1	714.3	762.0	812.1	812.1	...
Commercial vehicles Véhicules utilitaires	672.6	385.1	405.6	530.0	339.1	495.7	542.0	402.9	402.9	...
Congo [1] **Congo** [1]										
Passenger cars Voitures de tourisme	29.0	29.0	29.0	29.0	29.0	24.9	26.2	29.7	29.7	...
Commercial vehicles Véhicules utilitaires	16.6	16.6	16.6	16.6	16.6	19.2	20.4	23.1	23.1	...
Costa Rica **Costa Rica**										
Passenger cars Voitures de tourisme	220.1[4]	238.5[4]	254.8[4]	272.9[4]	294.1	316.8	326.5	342.0	354.4	367.8
Commercial vehicles Véhicules utilitaires	114.9[4]	127.1[4]	141.4[4]	151.1[4]	153.1	164.8	169.8	177.9	184.3	191.3
Côte d'Ivoire [1] **Côte d'Ivoire** [1]										
Passenger cars Voitures de tourisme	109.9	109.9	111.9	74.2	76.2	98.4	109.6	113.9	113.9	...
Commercial vehicles Véhicules utilitaires	46.1	47.1	50.3	35.3	35.3	45.4	54.1	54.9	54.9	...
Croatia **Croatie**										
Passenger cars Voitures de tourisme	646.2	698.4	710.9	835.7	932.3	1 000.0	1 063.5	1 124.8	1 195.5	1 244.3
Commercial vehicles Véhicules utilitaires	55.0	68.5	77.4	99.5	114.5	120.6	123.4	127.2	134.3	143.5
Cuba **Cuba**										
Commercial vehicles Véhicules utilitaires	...	10.0	10.0	9.9	10.3	10.5	11.0	10.1	...	...
Cyprus **Chypre**										
Passenger cars Voitures de tourisme	203.6	210.4	219.7	226.8	235.0	249.2	257.0	267.6	280.1	287.6
Commercial vehicles Véhicules utilitaires	93.5	98.0	104.9	108.0	109.7	113.6	115.8	119.6	123.2	123.3
Czech Republic [16] **République tchèque** [16]										
Passenger cars Voitures de tourisme	2 693.9	2 967.3[18]	3 113.5[18]	3 192.5[18]	3 391.5[18]	3 493.0[18]	3 439.7[18]	3 438.9[18]	3 529.8	3 647.1
Commercial vehicles [17] Véhicules utilitaires [17]	515.2	469.5[19]	490.0[19]	381.1[19]	305.1[19]	320.6[19]	329.9[19]	339.3[19]	364.1	397.6
Dem. Rep. of the Congo [1] **Rép. dém. du Congo** [1]										
Passenger cars Voitures de tourisme	...	...	...	...	...	172.6	172.6	...	...	...
Commercial vehicles Véhicules utilitaires	...	...	...	...	...	28.2	34.6	...	...	...
Denmark [4,20] **Danemark** [4,20]										
Passenger cars Voitures de tourisme	1 617.7	1 611.2	1 679.0	1 738.9	1 783.1	1 817.1	1 843.8	1 854.1	1 872.6	1 888.3
Commercial vehicles Véhicules utilitaires	325.3	335.6	347.4	353.7	359.8	371.5	387.2	398.8	406.2	415.7
Djibouti [12] **Djibouti** [12]										
Passenger cars Voitures de tourisme	13.5	13.5	...	...	...	...	...	...	...	...
Commercial vehicles Véhicules utilitaires	3.0	3.0	...	...	...	...	...	...	...	...
Dominica **Dominique**										
Passenger cars Voitures de tourisme	5.8	7.0	7.4	7.9	8.3	8.7	...	...	...	...

59

Motor vehicles in use
Passenger cars and commercial vehicles: thousands *[cont.]*
Véhicules automobiles en circulation
Voitures de tourisme et véhicules utilitaires : milliers de véhicules *[suite]*

Country or area Pays ou zone	1993	1994	1995	1996	1997	1998	1999	2000	2001	2002
Commercial vehicles [21] Véhicules utilitaires [21]	2.7	2.8	2.9	3.3	3.3	3.4	...	...	...	...
Dominican Republic Rép. dominicaine										
Passenger cars Voitures de tourisme	174.4	...	183.8	271.0	331.0	384.7	445.9	455.6	561.3	...
Commercial vehicles Véhicules utilitaires	118.5[22]	...	117.5	164.8	202.3	236.7	247.2	283.0	284.7	...
Ecuador Equateur										
Passenger cars Voitures de tourisme	202.4	219.8	253.5	268.2	276.5	301.4	322.3	335.5	326.2	...
Commercial vehicles Véhicules utilitaires	231.4	243.4	244.0	248.4	256.3	257.6	272.0	280.7	268.2	...
Egypt Egypte										
Passenger cars Voitures de tourisme	1 143.0	1 225.0	1 313.0	1 372.0	1 439.0	1 525.0	1 616.0	1 700.0	1 766.0	1 847.0
Commercial vehicles Véhicules utilitaires	423.0	445.0	466.0	484.0	508.0	539.0	577.0	600.0	624.0	650.0
El Salvador El Salvador										
Passenger cars Voitures de tourisme	88.4	86.9	113.8	121.8	129.8	136.6	142.2	148.0	...	...
Commercial vehicles Véhicules utilitaires	165.9	195.5	209.9	218.6	227.3	235.4	243.0	250.8	...	...
Estonia Estonie										
Passenger cars Voitures de tourisme	317.4	337.8	383.4	406.6	427.7	451.0	458.7	463.9	407.3	400.7
Commercial vehicles Véhicules utilitaires	82.8	60.0	72.6	78.0	83.1	86.9	87.2	88.2	80.5	80.2
Ethiopia [23] Ethiopie [23]										
Passenger cars Voitures de tourisme	47.0	52.7	60.0	62.4	66.2	68.9	71.0	...	...	...
Commercial vehicles Véhicules utilitaires	16.0	17.0	23.3	29.0	30.3	34.0	34.6	...	...	...
Fiji Fidji										
Passenger cars [24] Voitures de tourisme [24]	45.3	47.7	49.7	51.7	50.4	51.7	...	...	...	...
Commercial vehicles [25] Véhicules utilitaires [25]	44.8	46.4	47.5	48.5	48.0	48.6	...	...	...	...
Finland Finlande										
Passenger cars Voitures de tourisme	1 872.9	1 872.6	1 900.9	1 942.8	1 948.1	2 021.1	2 082.6	2 134.7	2 160.6	2 194.7
Commercial vehicles [26] Véhicules utilitaires [26]	261.4	257.5	260.1	266.9	275.4	289.7	303.2	314.2	322.3	329.7
France France										
Passenger cars Voitures de tourisme	24 385.0	24 900.0	25 100.0	25 500.0	26 090.0	26 810.0	27 480.0	28 060.0	28 700.0	29 160.0
Commercial vehicles [27] Véhicules utilitaires [27]	5 238.0	5 314.0	5 374.0	5 437.0	5 561.0	5 680.0	5 790.0	5 933.0	6 083.0	6 178.0
French Guiana [1] Guyane française [1]										
Passenger cars Voitures de tourisme	29.1	24.4	26.5	28.2	28.2	32.9	32.9	32.9	32.9	...
Commercial vehicles Véhicules utilitaires	10.6	7.6	8.1	8.9	9.4	11.9	11.9	11.9	11.9	...
Gabon [12] Gabon [12]										
Passenger cars Voitures de tourisme	24.0	24.0	23.0	...	...	...	...	...	...	...
Commercial vehicles Véhicules utilitaires	17.5	18.0	10.0	...	...	...	...	...	...	...
Gambia Gambie										
Passenger cars Voitures de tourisme	6.1	6.2	6.4	...	...	...	...	...	...	...

59

Motor vehicles in use
Passenger cars and commercial vehicles: thousands *[cont.]*

Véhicules automobiles en circulation
Voitures de tourisme et véhicules utilitaires : milliers de véhicules *[suite]*

Country or area Pays ou zone	1993	1994	1995	1996	1997	1998	1999	2000	2001	2002
Commercial vehicles Véhicules utilitaires	3.4	3.5	3.5	...	...	...	...	...	...	...
Georgia Géorgie										
Passenger cars Voitures de tourisme	485.9	452.3	360.6	323.6	265.6	260.4	247.9	244.9	247.8	252.0
Commercial vehicles Véhicules utilitaires	147.7	101.2	104.3	90.7	79.6	71.0	68.9	66.8	69.6	69.6
Germany[28] Allemagne[28]										
Passenger cars Voitures de tourisme	38 772.5	39 765.4	40 404.3	40 987.5	41 372.0	41 673.8	42 323.7	42 839.9	43 772.2	44 383.3
Commercial vehicles Véhicules utilitaires	...	2 619.3	2 754.9	2 851.4	2 931.3	3 023.9	3 166.4	...	3 378.7	3 455.3
Ghana Ghana										
Passenger cars Voitures de tourisme	30.4[1]	30.7[1]	30.8[1]	31.2[1]	31.9[1]	63.5[1]	90.4[1]	92.0	90.8	91.2
Commercial vehicles Véhicules utilitaires	31.5[1]	33.1[1]	35.7[1]	38.4[1]	38.4[1]	109.0[1]	119.9[1]	120.2	121.1	123.5
Gibraltar Gibraltar										
Passenger cars Voitures de tourisme	18.0	18.5	18.4	19.0[1]	20.5[1]	21.8[1]	22.4[1]	25.5[1]	27.2[1]	...
Commercial vehicles Véhicules utilitaires	1.1	1.2	1.0	12.2[1]	12.3[1]	1.1[1]	1.8[1]	3.2[1]	3.6[1]	...
Greece Grèce										
Passenger cars Voitures de tourisme	1 958.5	2 074.1	2 204.8	2 339.4	2 500.1	2 675.7	2 928.9	3 195.1	3 423.7	...
Commercial vehicles Véhicules utilitaires	848.9	872.6	908.4	939.9	977.5	1 013.7	1 050.8	1 084.5	1 112.9	...
Greenland[4] Groenland[4]										
Passenger cars Voitures de tourisme	2.1	1.9	1.9	2.6	1.8	2.0	2.4	1.9	2.5	2.5
Commercial vehicles Véhicules utilitaires	1.4	1.6	1.4	1.2	1.5	1.4	1.5	0.9	1.7	1.8
Grenada Grenade										
Passenger cars[29] Voitures de tourisme[29]	...	...	9.0	9.7	10.7	12.0	13.3	14.6	15.8	...
Commercial vehicles Véhicules utilitaires	...	...	2.2	2.4	2.7	3.1	3.6	3.9	4.2	...
Guadeloupe[1] Guadeloupe[1]										
Passenger cars Voitures de tourisme	101.6	90.5	97.0	106.5	107.6	117.7	117.7	117.7	117.7	...
Commercial vehicles Véhicules utilitaires	37.5	26.6	28.9	32.5	34.1	31.4	31.4	31.4	31.4	...
Guam Guam										
Passenger cars Voitures de tourisme	74.7	65.1	79.8	79.1	67.8	69.0	66.4	64.5	45.5	52.7
Commercial vehicles Véhicules utilitaires	30.6	27.5	34.7	33.8	28.9	28.9	27.4	26.6	19.3	21.9
Guatemala Guatemala										
Passenger cars Voitures de tourisme	...	...	...	...	...	646.5	...	...	...	...
Commercial vehicles Véhicules utilitaires	...	...	...	...	...	21.2	...	...	...	...
Guinea[12] Guinée[12]										
Passenger cars Voitures de tourisme	24.0	24.0	23.2	...	...	...	...	...	...	...
Commercial vehicles Véhicules utilitaires	13.5	14.0	13.0	...	...	...	...	...	...	...
Guyana[1] Guyana[1]										
Passenger cars Voitures de tourisme	...	...	...	...	...	61.3	61.3	61.3	61.3	...

59

Motor vehicles in use
Passenger cars and commercial vehicles: thousands *[cont.]*

Véhicules automobiles en circulation
Voitures de tourisme et véhicules utilitaires : milliers de véhicules *[suite]*

Country or area Pays ou zone	1993	1994	1995	1996	1997	1998	1999	2000	2001	2002
Commercial vehicles Véhicules utilitaires	...	...	...	...	...	15.5	15.5	15.5	15.5	...
Haiti Haïti										
Passenger cars Voitures de tourisme	32.0	30.0	49.0	59.0	...	...	93.0		...	...
Commercial vehicles Véhicules utilitaires	21.0	30.0	29.0	35.0	...	...	61.6	...	...	...
Honduras Honduras										
Passenger cars Voitures de tourisme	38.0	41.9	44.2	46.3	50.3	73.1	46.0		...	...
Commercial vehicles Véhicules utilitaires	130.1	45.3	48.0	48.6	49.1	53.9	39.3	...	...	...
Hungary Hongrie										
Passenger cars Voitures de tourisme	2 091.6	2 176.9	2 245.4	2 264.2	2 297.1	2 218.0	2 255.5	2 364.7	2 482.8	2 629.5
Commercial vehicles Véhicules utilitaires	296.2	318.5	345.0	351.3	360.9	355.4	363.0	384.3	398.3	399.3
Iceland Islande										
Passenger cars Voitures de tourisme	116.2	116.2	119.2	124.9	132.5	140.4	151.4	158.9	159.8	161.7
Commercial vehicles [30] Véhicules utilitaires [30]	15.6	15.6	16.0	16.6	17.5	18.1	19.4	21.1	21.7	21.9
India Inde										
Passenger cars Voitures de tourisme [31]	3 361.0	3 569.0	3 841.0	4 204.0	4 672.0	5 138.0	5 556.0	6 042.0	...	...
Commercial vehicles [31] Véhicules utilitaires [31]	4 961.0	5 192.0	5 623.0	6 327.0	6 931.0	7 588.0	7 991.0	8 438.0	...	...
Indonesia Indonésie										
Passenger cars Voitures de tourisme	1 700.5	1 890.3	2 107.3	2 409.1	2 639.5	2 772.5	2 897.8	3 038.9	3 244.7	3 403.4
Commercial vehicles Véhicules utilitaires	1 729.0	1 903.6	2 024.7	2 030.2	2 160.0	2 220.5	2 273.2	2 373.4	2 482.4	2 579.6
Iran (Islamic Rep. of) [1,32] Iran (Rép. islamique d') [1,32]										
Passenger cars Voitures de tourisme	779.8	819.6	819.6	454.2	572.9	684.5	847.9	1 139.5	1 351.8	...
Commercial vehicles Véhicules utilitaires	589.2	589.2	589.2	346.4	346.4	355.1	378.8	384.9	384.9	...
Iraq Iraq										
Passenger cars Voitures de tourisme	672.4	678.5	680.1	728.7[33]	721.6[33]	735.5[33]	753.4[33]	744.7[33]	754.1[33]	...
Commercial vehicles Véhicules utilitaires	309.3	317.2	319.9	346.7[33]	323.9[33]	349.2[33]	342.4[33]	357.0[33]	372.2[33]	...
Ireland [34] Irlande [34]										
Passenger cars [35,36] Voitures de tourisme [35,36]	898.3	947.2	999.7	1 067.8	1 145.9	1 209.2	1 283.4	1 333.9	1 402.3	...
Commercial vehicles [21] Véhicules utilitaires [21]	142.9	143.9	150.5	155.9	168.2	181.0	199.0	217.3	231.7	...
Israel Israël										
Passenger cars Voitures de tourisme	992.9	1 064.9	1 131.0	1 195.1	1 252.0	1 298.0	1 341.3	1 422.0	1 474.0	...
Commercial vehicles Véhicules utilitaires	217.0	250.0	263.0	279.0	292.0	297.9	308.8	328.0	350.2	...
Italy Italie										
Passenger cars Voitures de tourisme	29 652.0	29 665.3	30 149.6	30 467.1	30 741.9	31 370.8	31 953.2	32 583.8	33 129.3[1]	...
Commercial vehicles Véhicules utilitaires	2 663.0	2 745.5	2 863.5	3 177.7	3 253.7	3 336.4	3 409.5	3 377.6	3 749.2[1]	...
Jamaica Jamaïque										
Passenger cars Voitures de tourisme	81.1	86.8	104.0	120.7	156.8	140.4[1]	140.4[1]	129.4[1]	129.4[1]	...

59

Motor vehicles in use
Passenger cars and commercial vehicles: thousands *[cont.]*

Véhicules automobiles en circulation
Voitures de tourisme et véhicules utilitaires : milliers de véhicules *[suite]*

Country or area Pays ou zone	1993	1994	1995	1996	1997	1998	1999	2000	2001	2002
Commercial vehicles Véhicules utilitaires	36.2	41.3	49.1	52.8	56.1	54.7[1]	56.6[1]	57.6[1]	65.2[1]	...
Japan[37] Japon[37]										
Passenger cars[38] Voitures de tourisme[38]	40 772.0	42 679.0	44 680.0	46 869.0	48 611.0	49 896.0	51 165.0	52 738.0	53 541.2	54 540.5
Commercial vehicles Véhicules utilitaires	21 132.0	20 916.0	20 676.0	20 334.0	19 859.0	19 821.0	18 869.0	18 463.6	18 103.6	17 716.3
Jordan[4] Jordanie[4]										
Passenger cars Voitures de tourisme	175.3	164.0	188.0	212.2	202.1	200.0	213.0	255.8	322.4	346.0
Commercial vehicles Véhicules utilitaires	63.8	75.3	76.7	80.6	85.1	106.9	109.0	104.5	138.6	176.7
Kazakhstan Kazakhstan										
Passenger cars Voitures de tourisme	955.9	991.7	1 034.1	997.5	973.3	971.2	987.7	1 000.3	1 057.8	1 062.6
Commercial vehicles Véhicules utilitaires	456.4	428.1	390.9	360.4	315.3	277.1	257.4	256.6	268.5	280.3
Kenya Kenya										
Passenger cars Voitures de tourisme	171.5	171.6	172.8	202.7	211.9	225.1	238.9	244.8	255.4	...
Commercial vehicles Véhicules utilitaires	162.2	162.3	163.3	187.7	196.1	239.4	249.8	256.2	263.7	...
Korea, Republic of[39] Corée, République de[39]										
Passenger cars Voitures de tourisme	4 271.3	5 148.7	6 006.3	6 893.6	7 586.5	7 580.9	7 837.2	8 083.9	8 889.3	9 737.4
Commercial vehicles Véhicules utilitaires	1 976.6	2 226.7	2 429.2	2 625.6	2 791.2	2 854.0	3 291.3	3 938.2	3 985.4	4 169.7
Kuwait Koweït										
Passenger cars Voitures de tourisme	600.0	629.7	662.9	701.2	540.0	585.0	624.0	667.0	715.0	...
Commercial vehicles Véhicules utilitaires	147.0	148.7	153.5	160.0	115.0	124.0	130.0	134.0	226.0	...
Kyrgyzstan Kirghizistan										
Passenger cars Voitures de tourisme	188.3	140.0	197.5	172.4	176.1	187.7	187.3	189.8	189.8	188.7
Latvia Lettonie										
Passenger cars Voitures de tourisme	367.5	251.6	331.8	379.9	431.8	482.7	525.6	556.8	586.2	619.1
Commercial vehicles Véhicules utilitaires	72.1	73.5	85.1	90.2	95.4	96.5	101.8	108.6	111.0	113.9
Lebanon Liban										
Passenger cars Voitures de tourisme	943.1	1 141.7	1 197.5	1 250.5	1 299.4[33]	1 335.7[33]	1 370.6[33]	1 370.8[33]	1 370.9[33]	...
Commercial vehicles Véhicules utilitaires	77.3	82.9	84.7	87.4	92.1[33]	95.4[33]	98.2[33]	100.2[33]	102.4[33]	...
Liberia[1] Libéria[1]										
Passenger cars Voitures de tourisme	17.4	17.4	17.4	17.4	17.4	17.4	15.3	17.1	17.1	...
Commercial vehicles Véhicules utilitaires	10.7	10.7	10.7	10.7	10.7	10.7	11.9	12.8	12.8	...
Libyan Arab Jamah. Jamah. arabe libyenne										
Passenger cars Voitures de tourisme	448.0[12]	740.1[12]	763.2[12]	796.3	859.0	...	...	549.6[40]	552.7[40]	...
Commercial vehicles Véhicules utilitaires	322.0[12]	341.4[12]	353.0[12]	357.5	362.4	...	...	177.4[40]	195.5[40]	...
Lithuania Lituanie										
Passenger cars Voitures de tourisme	597.7	652.8	718.5	785.1	882.1	980.9	1 089.3	1 172.4	1 133.5	1 180.9
Commercial vehicles Véhicules utilitaires	115.1	118.2	125.9	104.8	108.6	114.6	112.2	113.7	115.6	120.9

59

Motor vehicles in use
Passenger cars and commercial vehicles: thousands *[cont.]*

Véhicules automobiles en circulation
Voitures de tourisme et véhicules utilitaires : milliers de véhicules *[suite]*

Country or area Pays ou zone	1993	1994	1995	1996	1997	1998	1999	2000	2001	2002
Luxembourg Luxembourg										
Passenger cars										
Voitures de tourisme	208.8	217.8	229.0	231.7	236.8	244.1	253.4	272.1	280.7	...
Commercial vehicles										
Véhicules utilitaires	22.4	25.0	26.1	25.5	26.2	27.3	28.8	48.6	48.7	...
Madagascar Madagascar										
Passenger cars										
Voitures de tourisme	11.1[1]	11.1[1]	11.1[1]	11.1[1]	11.3[1]	64.0	...	...	...	...
Commercial vehicles										
Véhicules utilitaires	13.3[1]	13.3[1]	13.3[1]	13.9[1]	15.5[1]	9.1	...	...	...	...
Malawi Malawi										
Passenger cars										
Voitures de tourisme	1.8[4]	2.3[4]	1.5[4]	1.6[4]	...	6.3[1]	12.6[1]	22.5[1]	22.5[1]	...
Commercial vehicles										
Véhicules utilitaires	1.4[4]	1.8[4]	2.2[4]	1.9[4]	...	19.6[1]	22.7[1]	57.6[1]	57.6[1]	
Malaysia Malaisie										
Passenger cars										
Voitures de tourisme	132.8	186.6	256.4	325.7	379.5	163.8	300.4	350.4	400.4	...
Commercial vehicles [26]										
Véhicules utilitaires [26]	33.5	49.9	74.9	102.7	96.5	19.0	28.6	36.8	40.1	
Maldives Maldives										
Passenger cars										
Voitures de tourisme	0.1	0.2	0.1	0.2	0.2	0.2	0.2	0.3	0.1	
Commercial vehicles										
Véhicules utilitaires	0.2	0.2	0.1	0.1	0.2	0.2	0.2	0.4	0.1	...
Mali Mali										
Passenger cars										
Voitures de tourisme	6.3	6.3	6.3	6.3[1]	6.3[1]	15.8[1]	17.6[1]	18.9[1]	18.9[1]	...
Commercial vehicles										
Véhicules utilitaires	6.6	6.8	7.2	7.6[1]	7.6[1]	21.5[1]	28.1[1]	31.7[1]	31.7[1]	...
Malta Malte										
Passenger cars										
Voitures de tourisme	152.6	170.6	199.3	166.2	183.8	191.8	201.8	210.9	219.0	227.0
Commercial vehicles										
Véhicules utilitaires	50.9	55.7	40.8	39.4	47.4	49.5	51.2	51.4	52.6	53.3
Martinique[1] Martinique[1]										
Passenger cars										
Voitures de tourisme	80.8	86.7	95.0	...	...	...	...	...	...	...
Commercial vehicles										
Véhicules utilitaires	19.3	20.0	21.5	...	...	...	...	...	...	
Mauritania[1] Mauritanie[1]										
Passenger cars										
Voitures de tourisme	5.0	5.1	5.1	5.2	5.3	8.6	9.9	12.2	12.2	...
Commercial vehicles										
Véhicules utilitaires	5.0	5.3	5.6	6.0	6.3	16.7	17.3	18.2	18.2	...
Mauritius Maurice										
Passenger cars										
Voitures de tourisme	55.8	59.6	63.6	68.1	73.4	78.5	83.0	87.5	92.7	98.9
Commercial vehicles										
Véhicules utilitaires	22.1	23.3	24.4	25.3	26.6	29.1	31.7	34.2	36.5	38.0
Mexico[4] Mexique[4]										
Passenger cars										
Voitures de tourisme	8 112.0	7 772.0	8 074.0	8 437.0	9 023.0	9 761.0	10 281.0	10 985.0	12 270.0	12 965.0
Commercial vehicles										
Véhicules utilitaires	3 695.0	3 759.0	3 751.0	3 773.0	4 034.0	4 282.0	4 569.0	5 255.0	5 772.0	5 919.0
Morocco[13] Maroc[13]										
Passenger cars										
Voitures de tourisme	849.3	944.0	992.0	1 018.1	1 060.3	1 108.7	1 161.9	1 211.1	1 253.0	...
Commercial vehicles										
Véhicules utilitaires	316.7	332.1	343.2	351.6	365.7	382.0	400.3	415.7	431.0	...

59

Motor vehicles in use
Passenger cars and commercial vehicles: thousands *[cont.]*

Véhicules automobiles en circulation
Voitures de tourisme et véhicules utilitaires : milliers de véhicules *[suite]*

Country or area Pays ou zone	1993	1994	1995	1996	1997	1998	1999	2000	2001	2002
Mozambique[1] **Mozambique**[1]										
Passenger cars										
Voitures de tourisme	84.0	27.2	27.2	27.2	27.2	52.2	78.6	81.6	81.6	...
Commercial vehicles										
Véhicules utilitaires	26.8	14.3	14.4	14.5	14.5	26.5	46.9	76.0	76.0	...
Myanmar[4] **Myanmar**[4]										
Passenger cars										
Voitures de tourisme	115.9	125.4	145.4	171.3	177.9	177.6	171.1	173.9	175.4	...
Commercial vehicles										
Véhicules utilitaires	66.6	58.2	63.1	68.3	74.8	75.9	83.4	90.4	98.9	...
Nepal **Népal**										
Passenger cars										
Voitures de tourisme	28.4	31.5	34.5	39.8	42.8	46.9	49.4	47.5	59.1	63.5
Commercial vehicles										
Véhicules utilitaires	103.7	99.5	113.8	131.8	147.9	164.2	185.8	51.6	66.0	72.7
Netherlands[4,41] **Pays-Bas**[4,41]										
Passenger cars										
Voitures de tourisme	5 341.0	5 456.0	5 581.0	5 664.0	5 810.0	5 931.0	6 120.0	...	...	...
Commercial vehicles										
Véhicules utilitaires	631.0	652.0	654.0	666.0	695.0	738.0	806.0	...	...	...
New Caledonia **Nouvelle-Calédonie**										
Passenger cars										
Voitures de tourisme	58.5[1]	50.4[1]	52.8[1]	55.1[1]	57.9[1]	76.4[2]	80.3[2]	83.5[2]	85.5[2]	92.6[2]
Commercial vehicles [1]										
Véhicules utilitaires [1]	22.6	17.2	18.4	20.8	23.0	...	...	...	...	...
New Zealand[42] **Nouvelle-Zélande**[42]										
Passenger cars										
Voitures de tourisme	1 575.6	1 615.9	1 665.0	1 655.8	1 697.2	1 768.2	1 855.8	1 905.6	1 936.8	1 988.9
Commercial vehicles										
Véhicules utilitaires	344.9	396.2	411.9	403.1	407.8	422.6	433.6	438.1	436.3	443.0
Nicaragua **Nicaragua**										
Passenger cars										
Voitures de tourisme	68.4	72.4	44.9	50.7	57.6	62.9	67.9	73.0	82.2	...
Commercial vehicles										
Véhicules utilitaires	66.3	69.5	56.7	63.8	72.8	81.7	91.1	98.1	107.7	...
Niger **Niger**										
Passenger cars										
Voitures de tourisme	16.0[12]	16.0[12]	16.0[12]	...	...	12.1[1]	26.0[1]	57.8[1]	57.8[1]	...
Commercial vehicles										
Véhicules utilitaires	18.0[12]	18.0[12]	18.0[12]	...	...	30.6[1]	35.6[1]	41.0[1]	41.0[1]	...
Nigeria[43] **Nigéria**[43]										
Passenger cars										
Voitures de tourisme	63.6	45.4	46.1	40.7	52.3	...	...	...	...	...
Commercial vehicles										
Véhicules utilitaires	1.4	6.8	8.6	10.5	13.5	...	...	...	...	...
Norway[4] **Norvège**[4]										
Passenger cars										
Voitures de tourisme	1 633.0	1 653.7	1 684.7	1 661.2	1 758.0	1 786.0	1 813.6	1 851.9	1 872.9	1 899.7
Commercial vehicles [44]										
Véhicules utilitaires [44]	352.5	366.3	382.0	392.1	412.2	427.0	440.0	451.0	462.2	464.8
Oman **Oman**										
Passenger cars [45]										
Voitures de tourisme [45]	183.0	193.0	202.3	216.2	245.1	279.1	310.4	344.0	359.2	390.0
Commercial vehicles [11]										
Véhicules utilitaires [11]	86.6	88.2	89.3	92.0	101.2	110.7	117.6	124.6	132.9	140.2
Pakistan[3,4] **Pakistan**[3,4]										
Passenger cars										
Voitures de tourisme	670.0	690.9	772.6	816.1	863.0	930.1	1 004.3	1 066.1	1 130.6	1 170.8
Commercial vehicles										
Véhicules utilitaires	269.6	285.8	305.8	333.6	351.7	379.0	406.4	434.5	463.0	488.6

59

Motor vehicles in use
Passenger cars and commercial vehicles: thousands *[cont.]*
Véhicules automobiles en circulation
Voitures de tourisme et véhicules utilitaires : milliers de véhicules *[suite]*

Country or area Pays ou zone	1993	1994	1995	1996	1997	1998	1999	2000	2001	2002
Panama Panama										
Passenger cars										
Voitures de tourisme	161.2	169.8	178.3	188.3	198.7	212.6	222.4	223.1	219.4	...
Commercial vehicles										
Véhicules utilitaires	55.0	56.5	60.4	60.5	64.2	68.4	71.9	74.4	70.3	...
Papua New Guinea Papouasie-Nvl-Guinée										
Passenger cars										
Voitures de tourisme	13.0[12]	11.5[12]	20.0[12]	21.7[1]	21.7[1]	21.7[1]	18.8[1]	24.9[1]	24.9[1]	...
Commercial vehicles										
Véhicules utilitaires	32.0[12]	30.8[12]	35.0[12]	81.1[1]	85.5[1]	89.7[1]	87.0[1]	87.8[1]	87.8[1]	...
Paraguay Paraguay										
Passenger cars										
Voitures de tourisme	250.7	275.8	294.1	305.5	272.1	357.7	401.7	415.8	...	...
Commercial vehicles										
Véhicules utilitaires	37.7	39.9	41.1	42.0	36.9	48.0	53.6	56.4	...	...
Peru Pérou										
Passenger cars										
Voitures de tourisme	418.6	444.2	505.8	557.0	595.8	645.9	684.5	716.9	750.6	834.2
Commercial vehicles										
Véhicules utilitaires	288.8	316.6	356.8	379.5	389.9	409.8	429.7	445.9	458.4	508.0
Philippines Philippines										
Passenger cars										
Voitures de tourisme	1 365.4	1 485.4	1 624.9	1 803.7	1 934.7	1 993.2	2 084.7	2 156.1	2 218.6	2 401.9
Commercial vehicles										
Véhicules utilitaires	189.9	207.4	221.0	249.7	274.8	263.1	276.6	282.3	285.3	291.7
Poland Pologne										
Passenger cars										
Voitures de tourisme	6 770.6	7 153.1	7 517.3	8 054.4	8 533.5	8 890.8	9 282.8	9 991.3	10 503.1	...
Commercial vehicles [46]										
Véhicules utilitaires [46]	1 321.9	1 394.3	1 440.1	1 517.6	1 569.9	1 644.4	1 762.9	1 962.7	2 062.9	...
Portugal [47] Portugal [47]										
Passenger cars [48]										
Voitures de tourisme [48]	3 295.1	3 532.0	3 751.0	4 002.6[49]	4 272.5[49]	4 587.3[49]	4 931.7[49]	5 260.3	5 537.1	...
Commercial vehicles										
Véhicules utilitaires	1 050.1	1 158.6	1 218.8	1 292.2[49]	1 383.9[49]	1 492.4[49]	1 600.1[49]	1 727.9	1 828.1	...
Puerto Rico [3] Porto Rico [3]										
Passenger cars										
Voitures de tourisme	1 393.3	1 484.7	1 597.0	1 726.4	1 840.6	1 962.4	2 038.9	2 035.3	2 064.1	2 201.6
Commercial vehicles										
Véhicules utilitaires	239.6	257.7	270.6	290.2	288.9	298.9	306.6	...	...	...
Qatar Qatar										
Passenger cars										
Voitures de tourisme	132.1	137.6	143.4	151.9	164.7	178.0	188.0	199.6	...	...
Commercial vehicles										
Véhicules utilitaires	61.5	65.8	69.5	73.8	79.1	85.0	88.9	92.9	...	...
Republic of Moldova [50] République de Moldova [50]										
Passenger cars										
Voitures de tourisme	166.4	169.4	165.9	173.6	206.0	222.8	232.3	238.4	256.5	268.9
Commercial vehicles [51]										
Véhicules utilitaires [51]	8.9	7.8	12.9	11.5	10.4	9.2	8.1	6.9	6.3	5.7
Réunion Réunion										
Passenger cars										
Voitures de tourisme	127.8	133.1	142.1	150.6	159.3	167.9	180.6	247.8[2]	...	...
Commercial vehicles										
Véhicules utilitaires	39.2	40.9	43.6	46.2	49.0	51.6	54.0	...	...	...
Romania Roumanie										
Passenger cars										
Voitures de tourisme	1 793.0	2 020.0	2 197.0	2 392.0	2 605.0	2 822.0	2 980.0	3 129.0	3 226.0	...
Commercial vehicles										
Véhicules utilitaires	336.0	362.0	385.0	409.0	428.0	456.0	489.0	497.0	504.0	...

59

Motor vehicles in use
Passenger cars and commercial vehicles: thousands *[cont.]*

Véhicules automobiles en circulation
Voitures de tourisme et véhicules utilitaires : milliers de véhicules *[suite]*

Country or area Pays ou zone	1993	1994	1995	1996	1997	1998	1999	2000	2001	2002
Russian Federation Fédération de Russie										
Passenger cars [52]										
Voitures de tourisme [52]	11 518.3	12 863.5	14 195.3	15 740.7	17 548.8	18 731.1	19 624.4	20 246.9	21 152.1	22 342.3
Commercial vehicles										
Véhicules utilitaires	2 924.0	3 006.0	3 078.1	3 902.3	3 980.3	3 964.0	4 082.7	4 122.0	4 217.7	4 331.1
Rwanda Rwanda										
Passenger cars										
Voitures de tourisme	...	...	1.2	3.2	5.8	7.7	9.2	10.7	...	...
Commercial vehicles										
Véhicules utilitaires	...	...	1.7	4.6	9.0	11.3	13.6	16.3	...	...
Saint Kitts and Nevis Saint-Kitts-et-Nevis										
Passenger cars										
Voitures de tourisme	4.5	4.8	5.2	5.5	6.3	6.3	7.7	...	...	...
Commercial vehicles										
Véhicules utilitaires	2.4	2.4	2.3	2.5	2.4	2.9	3.9	...	...	...
Saint Lucia Sainte-Lucie										
Passenger cars										
Voitures de tourisme	10.1	11.4	12.5	13.5	...	...	...	...	...	...
Commercial vehicles										
Véhicules utilitaires	10.5	9.5	...	10.8	...	...	...	...	...	...
St. Vincent-Grenadines St. Vincent-Grenadines										
Passenger cars										
Voitures de tourisme	5.4	5.7	5.3	6.1	7.4	8.0	8.7	9.1	9.9	...
Commercial vehicles										
Véhicules utilitaires	3.1	3.2	3.7	3.2	3.8	4.1	3.9	4.0	4.0	...
Saudi Arabia [2,53] Arabie saoudite [2,53]										
Passenger cars										
Voitures de tourisme	5 588.0	5 861.6	6 111.1	6 333.9	6 580.0	7 046.0	...	...	...	...
Senegal Sénégal										
Passenger cars										
Voitures de tourisme	102.0	105.0	106.0	112.0	118.0	132.0	150.0	169.0	193.0	...
Commercial vehicles										
Véhicules utilitaires	46.0	45.0	48.0	51.0	54.0	59.0	65.0	71.0	79.0	...
Serbia and Montenegro Serbie-et-Monténégro										
Passenger cars										
Voitures de tourisme	1 090.3	1 346.2	1 360.3	1 397.0	1 583.8	1 749.1	1 690.7	1 392.6	1 481.4	...
Commercial vehicles										
Véhicules utilitaires	464.5	563.5	569.5	576.6	594.0	609.8	620.1	322.6	330.5	...
Seychelles Seychelles										
Passenger cars										
Voitures de tourisme	6.1	5.6	5.5	6.2	6.7	6.5	6.4	...	...	...
Commercial vehicles										
Véhicules utilitaires	1.8	1.8	1.9	2.0	2.1	2.2	2.2	...	...	...
Sierra Leone [1] Sierra Leone [1]										
Passenger cars										
Voitures de tourisme	32.4	32.4	32.4	32.4	32.4	18.5	19.2	20.1	20.1	...
Commercial vehicles										
Véhicules utilitaires	11.9	11.9	11.9	11.9	11.9	14.8	14.8	15.8	15.8	...
Singapore Singapour										
Passenger cars										
Voitures de tourisme	321.9	340.6	363.9	384.5	396.4	395.2	403.2	413.5	426.4	425.7
Commercial vehicles										
Véhicules utilitaires	135.2	136.8	140.0	142.7	144.8	142.6	141.3	137.2	139.9	138.6
Slovakia Slovaquie										
Passenger cars										
Voitures de tourisme	994.9	994.0	1 015.8	1 058.4	1 135.9	1 196.1	1 236.4	1 274.2	1 292.8	1 326.9
Commercial vehicles										
Véhicules utilitaires	130.6	131.2	131.5	127.2	135.0	144.4	149.4	153.2	161.5	174.3
Slovenia Slovénie										
Passenger cars										
Voitures de tourisme	641.7	667.2	709.6	740.9	778.3	813.4	848.3	868.3	884.2	896.7

59

Motor vehicles in use
Passenger cars and commercial vehicles: thousands *[cont.]*
Véhicules automobiles en circulation
Voitures de tourisme et véhicules utilitaires : milliers de véhicules *[suite]*

Country or area Pays ou zone	1993	1994	1995	1996	1997	1998	1999	2000	2001	2002
Commercial vehicles Véhicules utilitaires	34.7	36.6	40.2	42.6	44.9	46.4	48.5	50.8	52.6	54.3
Somalia [12] **Somalie** [12]										
Passenger cars Voitures de tourisme	10.7	11.8	12.0	...	...	...	...	...	...	...
Commercial vehicles Véhicules utilitaires	12.0	12.2	12.0	...	...	...	...	...	...	...
South Africa **Afrique du Sud**										
Passenger cars Voitures de tourisme	3 488.6[1]	3 814.9[1]	3 830.8[1]	3 846.8[1]	3 664.0[1]	3 540.6[1]	3 966.3[54]	...	...	...
Commercial vehicles Véhicules utilitaires	1 784.9[1]	1 596.8[1]	1 625.5[1]	1 653.5[1]	1 868.0[1]	1 736.0[1]	2 248.1[55]	...	...	...
Spain **Espagne**										
Passenger cars Voitures de tourisme	13 440.7	13 733.8	14 212.3	14 753.8	15 297.4	16 050.1	16 847.4	17 449.2	18 150.8	...
Commercial vehicles Véhicules utilitaires	2 859.6	2 952.8	3 071.6	3 200.3	3 360.1	3 561.5	3 788.7	3 977.9	4 161.1	...
Sri Lanka [4] **Sri Lanka** [4]										
Passenger cars Voitures de tourisme	197.3	210.1	228.9	246.5	261.6	284.3	309.5	335.0[56]	353.7[56]	386.6
Commercial vehicles Véhicules utilitaires	166.3	175.3	184.3	191.5	199.2	211.2	227.1	238.3	245.7	255.3
Sudan **Soudan**										
Passenger cars Voitures de tourisme	30.8[12]	30.8[12]	30.8[12]	...	...	38.0[1]	40.6[1]	46.0[1]	46.0[1]	...
Commercial vehicles Véhicules utilitaires	35.9[12]	35.9[12]	35.9[12]	...	...	50.4[1]	53.9[1]	60.5[1]	60.5[1]	...
Suriname **Suriname**										
Passenger cars Voitures de tourisme	46.6	42.2	49.3	46.4	50.2	55.4	59.9	61.4	...	...
Commercial vehicles Véhicules utilitaires	18.2	17.9	17.3	19.5	20.5	21.1	22.5	23.5	...	...
Swaziland [6] **Swaziland** [6]										
Passenger cars Voitures de tourisme	25.4	26.6	28.1	29.0	39.9	33.9	35.8	37.9	39.9	41.5
Commercial vehicles Véhicules utilitaires	33.4	34.2	35.9	37.3	40.2	42.5	45.1	47.6	49.9	51.8
Sweden **Suède**										
Passenger cars Voitures de tourisme	3 566.0	3 594.2	3 630.8	3 654.9	3 702.8	3 790.7	3 890.2	3 998.6	4 018.5	4 042.8
Commercial vehicles Véhicules utilitaires	652.6	653.7	659.3	664.1	674.8	693.0	711.0	731.8	753.0	769.6
Switzerland [34] **Suisse** [34]										
Passenger cars Voitures de tourisme	3 109.5	3 165.0	3 229.2	3 268.1	3 323.4	3 383.2	3 467.3	3 545.2	3 629.7	3 701.1
Commercial vehicles Véhicules utilitaires	288.8	292.4	299.3	300.7	302.7	306.4	313.6	318.8	326.6	332.5
Syrian Arab Republic **Rép. arabe syrienne**										
Passenger cars Voitures de tourisme	149.8	159.1	166.5	173.6	175.9	179.0	180.7	181.7	193.5	...
Commercial vehicles Véhicules utilitaires	162.3	188.4	224.0	251.4	269.1	282.6	313.5	345.6	348.7	...
Tajikistan **Tadjikistan**										
Passenger cars Voitures de tourisme	...	175.0	166.4	151.5	154.1	146.6	141.7	117.1	...	...
Commercial vehicles Véhicules utilitaires	...	10.9	9.8	9.6	10.2	13.3	16.4	16.8	...	...
Thailand **Thaïlande**										
Passenger cars [57] Voitures de tourisme [57]	1 598.2	1 798.8	1 913.2	2 098.6	2 350.4	2 529.2	2 650.5	2 665.4	2 864.0	3 259.5

59

Motor vehicles in use
Passenger cars and commercial vehicles: thousands *[cont.]*

Véhicules automobiles en circulation
Voitures de tourisme et véhicules utilitaires : milliers de véhicules *[suite]*

Country or area Pays ou zone	1993	1994	1995	1996	1997	1998	1999	2000	2001	2002
Commercial vehicles [58]										
Véhicules utilitaires [58]	2 091.1	2 384.1	2 735.6	3 149.3	3 534.9	3 746.7	4 065.3	4 220.1	4 373.4	4 580.0
TFYR of Macedonia L'ex-R.y. Macédoine										
Passenger cars										
Voitures de tourisme	290.0	263.0	286.0	284.0	289.0	289.0	290.0	300.0	309.6	307.6
Commercial vehicles										
Véhicules utilitaires	29.6	25.9	29.2	29.0	29.6	29.9	30.1	31.8	33.9	33.0
Togo [1] Togo [1]										
Passenger cars										
Voitures de tourisme	18.2	74.6	74.7	74.7	74.7	27.2	36.0	51.4	51.4	...
Commercial vehicles										
Véhicules utilitaires	11.6	34.6	34.6	34.6	34.6	11.0	17.6	24.5	24.5	...
Tonga Tonga										
Passenger cars										
Voitures de tourisme	4.7	5.3	7.7	8.6	9.0	9.7	10.8	4.8	...	...
Commercial vehicles										
Véhicules utilitaires	5.0	5.9	8.1	9.7	8.9	9.4	10.4	4.4	...	...
Trinidad and Tobago Trinité-et-Tobago										
Passenger cars										
Voitures de tourisme	159.0	162.1	166.8	180.2	194.3	213.4	229.4	...	...	...
Commercial vehicles										
Véhicules utilitaires	39.2	40.2	42.2	44.9	47.7	51.1	53.9	...	...	...
Tunisia Tunisie										
Passenger cars										
Voitures de tourisme	299.1	327.0	356.3	379.2	415.2	445.6	482.2	516.5	552.9	...
Commercial vehicles [59]										
Véhicules utilitaires [59]	165.3	177.7	189.3	201.5	217.1	233.0	250.3	265.7	281.5	...
Turkey Turquie										
Passenger cars [60]										
Voitures de tourisme [60]	2 619.9	2 861.6	3 058.5	3 274.1	3 570.1	3 838.3	4 072.3	4 422.2	4 534.8	4 600.1
Commercial vehicles [30]										
Véhicules utilitaires [30]	929.6	968.5	1 010.2	1 083.9	1 215.7	1 353.6	1 443.2	1 583.7	1 629.9	1 679.1
Uganda Ouganda										
Passenger cars										
Voitures de tourisme	20.5	24.2	28.9	35.4	42.0	46.9	48.4	49.0	53.1	54.2
Commercial vehicles										
Véhicules utilitaires	29.4	36.5	44.1	52.5	59.1	66.8	72.6	74.3	79.9	82.3
Ukraine Ukraine										
Passenger cars										
Voitures de tourisme	4 206.5	4 384.1	4 603.1	4 872.3	5 024.0	5 127.3	5 210.8	5 250.1	5 312.6	...
United Arab Emirates Emirats arabes unis										
Passenger cars										
Voitures de tourisme	297.1	332.5	321.6	346.3	695.7[1]	693.5[1]	717.3[1]	745.3[1]	794.1[1]	...
Commercial vehicles										
Véhicules utilitaires	78.8	87.2	84.2	89.3	385.7[1]	420.2[1]	440.6[1]	453.1[1]	477.9[1]	...
United Kingdom [61] Royaume-Uni [61]										
Passenger cars										
Voitures de tourisme	21 291.0	21 740.0	21 949.9	22 819.0	23 450.0	23 922.0	24 628.0	25 067.0	25 822.0	...
Commercial vehicles										
Véhicules utilitaires	2 990.0	2 994.0	2 987.3	3 035.0	3 104.0	3 167.0	3 333.0	3 388.0	3 497.0	...
United Rep. of Tanzania [1] Rép.-Unie de Tanzanie [1]										
Passenger cars										
Voitures de tourisme	13.6	13.6	13.8	13.8	13.8	31.2	33.9	35.6	35.6	...
Commercial vehicles										
Véhicules utilitaires	33.7	35.4	37.5	42.5	42.5	87.3	98.8	98.8	98.8	...
United States Etats-Unis										
Passenger cars [62]										
Voitures de tourisme [62]	187 291.5	191 071.6	193 963.4	198 662.0	199 973.0	203 168.7	207 788.4	212 706.4	221 821.1	...
Commercial vehicles										
Véhicules utilitaires	7 959.6	7 258.3	7 404.9	7 707.4	7 780.8	8 447.8	8 520.2	8 768.8	8 607.2	...

59

Motor vehicles in use
Passenger cars and commercial vehicles: thousands *[cont.]*

Véhicules automobiles en circulation
Voitures de tourisme et véhicules utilitaires : milliers de véhicules *[suite]*

Country or area Pays ou zone	1993	1994	1995	1996	1997	1998	1999	2000	2001	2002
Uruguay Uruguay										
Passenger cars										
Voitures de tourisme	425.6	444.8	464.5	485.1	516.9	578.3	662.3	652.3	...	...
Commercial vehicles										
Véhicules utilitaires	44.3	46.2	45.8	48.4	50.3	53.9	57.8	56.1	...	...
Vanuatu[1] Vanuatu[1]										
Passenger cars										
Voitures de tourisme	2.7	7.1	7.4	2.7	2.7	2.5	2.6	2.6	2.6	...
Commercial vehicles										
Véhicules utilitaires	2.7	1.7	1.8	3.2	3.5	3.8	4.1	4.4	4.4	
Venezuela Venezuela										
Passenger cars										
Voitures de tourisme	1 805.0	1 813.0	1 823.0	1 393.5[1]	1 313.9[1]	1 402.9[1]	1 420.0[1]	1 326.2[1]	1 372.0[1]	...
Commercial vehicles										
Véhicules utilitaires	576.0	578.0	581.0	664.6[1]	352.1[1]	786.2[1]	846.0[1]	1 078.6[1]	1 107.9[1]	
Viet Nam Viet Nam										
Commercial vehicles										
Véhicules utilitaires	41.5	33.8	39.1	41.5	41.5	49.4	57.8	69.9	...	...
Yemen Yémen										
Passenger cars										
Voitures de tourisme	176.1	196.5	224.1	259.4	327.1	380.6	301.2[33]	323.1[33]	346.6[33]	...
Commercial vehicles										
Véhicules utilitaires	251.8	266.4	291.7	345.3	413.1	422.1	534.0[33]	560.3[33]	587.9[33]	...
Zambia Zambie										
Passenger cars										
Voitures de tourisme	3.0	3.9	5.7	3.7	...	...	...	...	...	...
Commercial vehicles										
Véhicules utilitaires	2.7	4.2	7.3	3.9	...	...	...	...	...	...
Zimbabwe Zimbabwe										
Passenger cars										
Voitures de tourisme	328.3	349.1	384.0	422.4	464.7	521.0	534.6	544.5	562.3	567.3
Commercial vehicles										
Véhicules utilitaires	32.5	34.5	37.9	42.2	46.4	54.3	58.5	67.7	80.9	83.5

Source:
United Nations Statistics Division, New York, transport statistics database.

Source:
Organisation des Nations Unies, Division de statistique, New York, la base de données pour les statistiques des transports.

1	Source: World Automotive Market Report, Auto and Truck International (Illinois).	1	Source : "World Automotive Market Report, Auto and Truck International" (Illinois).
2	Including commercial vehicles.	2	Y compris véhicules utilitaires.
3	Data refer to fiscal years beginning 1 July.	3	Les données se réfèrent aux exercices budgétaires commençant le 1er juillet.
4	Including vehicles operated by police or other governmental security organizations.	4	Y compris véhicules de la police ou d'autres services gouvernementales d'ordre public.
5	Including farm tractors.	5	Y compris tracteurs agricoles.
6	Excluding government vehicles.	6	Non compris les véhicules des administrations publiques.
7	Including buses and coaches.	7	Y compris autobus et autocars.
8	Including pick-ups.	8	Y compris fourgonnettes.
9	Number of licensed vehicles.	9	Nombre de véhicules automobiles licensés.
10	Including only vehicles (trucks) weighing 4,500 kilograms to 14,999 kilograms and vehicles (tractor-trailers and Class A trucks) weighing 15,000 kilograms or more.	10	Y compris seulement véhicules (camions) pesant de 4,500 kilogrammes à 14,999 kilogrammes et véhicules (semi-remorques et camions de Classe A) pesant 15,000 kilogrammes ou plus.
11	Trucks only.	11	Camions seulement.
12	Source: AAMA Motor Vehicle Facts and Figures, American Automobile Manufacturers Association (Michigan).	12	Source: AAMA Motor Vehicle Facts and Figures, American Automobile Manufacturers Association (Michigan).
13	Including special-purpose vehicles.	13	Y compris véhicules à usages spéciaux.
14	Excluding pick-ups.	14	Non compris fourgonnettes.
15	Including mini-buses.	15	Y compris minibuses.
16	Beginning 1996, methodological change in calculation.	16	Changement de méthode de calcul introduit en 1996.

59

Motor vehicles in use
Passenger cars and commercial vehicles: thousands *[cont.]*
Véhicules automobiles en circulation
Voitures de tourisme et véhicules utilitaires : milliers de véhicules *[suite]*

17	Including special-purpose commercial vehicles and farm tractors.	17	Y compris véhicules utilitaires à usages spéciaux et tracteurs agricoles.
18	Including vans.	18	Y compris fourgons.
19	Excluding vans.	19	Non compris fourgons.
20	Excluding Faeroe Islands.	20	Non compris les Iles Féroés.
21	Including large public service excavators and trench diggers.	21	Y compris les grosses excavatrices et machines d'excavation de tranchées de travaux publics.
22	Including dump trucks and motor scooters.	22	Y compris camions-bennes et scooters.
23	Data refer to fiscal years ending 7 July.	23	Les données se réfèrent aux exercices budgétaires finissant le 7 juillet.
24	Including private and government cars, rental and hired cars.	24	Y compris les voitures particulières et celles des administrations publiques, les voitures de location et de louage.
25	Including pick-ups, ambulances, light and heavy fire engines and all other vehicles such as trailers, cranes, loaders, forklifts, etc.	25	Y compris les fourgonnettes, les ambulances, les voitures de pompiers légères pompiers légères et lourdes, et tous autres véhicules tels que remoques, grues, chargeuses, chariots élévateurs à fourches, etc.
26	Excluding tractors.	26	Non compris tracteurs.
27	Including only trailers and semi-trailer combinations less than 10 years old.	27	Y compris les légères remorques et semi-remorques de moins de 10 ans seulement.
28	Beginning 2001, data refer to fiscal years ending 1 January. For all previous years data refer to fiscal years ending 1 July.	28	A compter de l'année 2001, les données se réfèrent aux exercices budgétaires finissant le 1er janvier. Pour toutes les années antérieures, les données se réfèrent aux exercices budgétaires finissant le 1er juillet.
29	Including "other, not specified", registered motor vehicles.	29	Y compris "autres, non-spécifiés", véhicules automobiles enregistrés.
30	Excluding tractors and semi-trailer combinations.	30	Non compris ensembles tracteur-remorque et semi-remorque.
31	Including goods vehicles, tractors, trailers, three-wheeled passengers and goods vehicles and other miscellaneous vehicles which are not separately classified.	31	Y compris véhicules de transport de marchandises, camions-remorques, remorques, véhicules à trois roues (passagers et marchandises) et autres véhicules divers qui ne font pas l'objet d'une catégories separée.
32	Data refer to fiscal years ending 20 March.	32	Les données se réfèrent aux exercices budgétaires finissant le 20 mars.
33	Source: United Nations Economic and Social Commission for Western Asia (ESCWA).	33	Source : Commission économique et sociale pour l'Asie occidentale (CESAO).
34	Data refer to fiscal years ending 30 September.	34	Les données se réfèrent aux exercices budgétaires finissant le 30 septembre.
35	Including mini-buses equipped for transport of nine to fifteen passengers.	35	Y compris mini-buses ayant une capacité de neuf à quinze passagers.
36	Including school buses.	36	Y compris l'autobus de l'école.
37	Excluding small vehicles.	37	Non compris véhicules petites.
38	Including cars with a seating capacity of up to 10 persons.	38	Y compris véhicules comptant jusqu'à 10 places.
39	Number of registered motor vehicles.	39	Nombre de véhicules automobiles enregistrès.
40	Beginning 2000, excluding government passenger-cars.	40	A partir de 2000, non compris les voitures de tourisme du gouvernement.
41	Excluding diplomatic corps vehicles.	41	Non compris véhicules des diplomates.
42	Data refer to fiscal years ending 31 March.	42	Les données se réfèrent aux exercices budgétaires finissant le 31 mars.
43	Newly registered.	43	Enregistrés récemment.
44	Including hearses (Norway: registered before 1981).	44	Y compris corbillards (Norvège : enregistrés avant 1981).
45	Excluding taxis.	45	Non compris taxis.
46	Excluding buses and tractors, but including special lorries.	46	Non compris autobus et tracteurs, mais y compris camions spéciaux.
47	Excluding Madeira and Azores.	47	Non compris Madère et Azores.
48	Including light miscellaneous vehicles.	48	Y compris les véhicules légers divers.
49	Including vehicles no longer in circulation.	49	Y compris véhicules retirés de la circulation.
50	Excluding the Transnistria region.	50	Non compris la région de Transnistria.
51	For the period 1980-1994, including motor vehicles for general use owned by Ministry of Transport. For the period 1995-2000, including motor vehicles owned by enterprises with main activity as road transport enterprises.	51	Pour la période 1980 - 1994, y compris les véhicules à moteur d'usage général appartenant au Ministère des transports. Pour la période 1995 - 2000, y compris les véhicules pour les entreprises de transport.
52	Beginning 1996, data provided by State Inspection for security of road traffic of the Russian Federation Ministry of Internal Affairs.	52	A partir de 1996, données fournies par l'Inspecteurat d'Etat pour la sécurité routière du Ministère de l'Intérieur de la Fédération de Russie.
53	Including motorcycles.	53	Y compris motocyclettes.
54	Including all mini-buses and passenger vehicles which transport fewer than 12 persons.	54	Y compris tous les minibus et véhicules qui transportant moins de 12 passagers.

59

Motor vehicles in use
Passenger cars and commercial vehicles: thousands *[cont.]*
Véhicules automobiles en circulation
Voitures de tourisme et véhicules utilitaires : milliers de véhicules *[suite]*

55 Including vehicles which transport 12 persons or more and all light and heavy load vehicles, whether self-propelled or semi-trailer.

56 Including three-wheelers.
57 Including micro-buses and passenger pick-ups.
58 Including pick-ups, taxis, cars for hire, small rural buses.

59 Beginning 1987, including trailers.
60 Including vehicles seating not more than eight persons, including the driver.
61 Figures prior to 1992 were derived from vehicle taxation class; beginning 1992, figures derived from vehicle body type.

62 Including motorcycles (prior to 1993 only), mini-vans, sport-utility vehicles and pick-up trucks.

55 Y compris véhicules transportant 12 personnes ou plus et tous véhicules poids légèrs ou poids lourds, auto-propulsés ou semi-remorque.

56 Y compris véhicules à trois roues.
57 Y compris les microbus et les camionnettes de transport de passagers.
58 Y compris les camionnettes, les taxis, les voitures de louage, les petits autobus ruraux.

59 A compter de l'année 1987, y compris remorques.
60 Y compris véhicules dont le nombre de places assises (y compris celle du conducteur) n'est pas supérieur à huit.
61 Les chiffres antérieurs à 1992 ont été calculés selon les catégories fiscales de véhicules; à partir de 1992, ils ont été calculés selan les types de carrosserie.

62 Y compris motocyclettes (antérieur à 1993 seulement), fourgonnettes, véhicules de la classe quatre-x-quatre et camionettes légères.

60
Merchant shipping: fleets
All ships, oil tankers, and ore and bulk carrier fleets: thousand gross registered tons
Transports maritimes : flotte marchande
Tous les navires, pétroliers, et minéraliers et transporteurs de vracs : milliers de tonneaux de jauge brute

Country or area	1995	1996	1997	1998	1999	2000	2001	2002	Pays ou zone
World									**Monde**
All ships	490 662	507 873	522 197	531 893	543 610	558 054	574 551	585 583	Tous les navires
Oil tankers	143 521	146 366	147 108	151 036	154 092	155 429	156 068	154 559	Pétroliers
Ore and bulk carriers	151 694	157 382	162 169	158 565	158 957	161 186	168 000	169 954	Minéral. et transp. de vracs
Albania									**Albanie**
All ships	63	43	30	29	21	24	25	49	Tous les navires
Algeria									**Algérie**
All ships	980	983	983	1 005	1 005	961	964	936	Tous les navires
Oil tankers	35	34	34	33	33	19	19	19	Pétroliers
Ore and bulk carriers	172	172	172	172	172	173	173	173	Minéral. et transp. de vracs
Angola									**Angola**
All ships	90	82	68	74	66	66	63	55	Tous les navires
Oil tankers	2	2	3	3	3	3	3	3	Pétroliers
Anguilla									**Anguilla**
All ships	2	2	2	1	1	1	1	1	Tous les navires
Antigua and Barbuda									**Antigua-et-Barbuda**
All ships	1 842	2 176	2 214	2 788	3 622	4 224	4 688	5 066	Tous les navires
Oil tankers	4	4	4	7	5	5	5	3	Pétroliers
Ore and bulk carriers	102	174	174	294	196	194	251	206	Minéral. et transp. de vracs
Argentina									**Argentine**
All ships	595	586	579	499	477	464	422	423	Tous les navires
Oil tankers	107	114	105	102	100	83	49	51	Pétroliers
Ore and bulk carriers	62	34	34	34	34	34	34	34	Minéral. et transp. de vracs
Australia									**Australie**
All ships	2 853	2 718	2 607	2 188	2 084	1 912	1 888	1 861	Tous les navires
Oil tankers	579	467	380	226	226	226	226	264	Pétroliers
Ore and bulk carriers	1 011	1 039	1 036	893	801	624	624	573	Minéral. et transp. de vracs
Austria									**Autriche**
All ships	92	95	83	68	71	90	35	30	Tous les navires
Azerbaijan									**Azerbaïdjan**
All ships	655	636	633	651	654	647	641	633	Tous les navires
Oil tankers	188	181	180	176	176	176	175	175	Pétroliers
Bahamas									**Bahamas**
All ships	23 603	24 409	25 523	27 716	29 483	31 445	33 386	35 798	Tous les navires
Oil tankers	10 326	10 863	10 810	11 982	13 158	13 504	14 469	14 574	Pétroliers
Ore and bulk carriers	4 501	4 425	4 728	4 990	4 943	4 833	5 339	5 249	Minéral. et transp. de vracs
Bahrain									**Bahreïn**
All ships	166	164	194	284	292	256	338	288	Tous les navires
Oil tankers	54	54	55	54	54	1	81	81	Pétroliers
Ore and bulk carriers	8	8	33	33	33	43	43	43	Minéral. et transp. de vracs
Bangladesh									**Bangladesh**
All ships	379	436	419	414	378	370	388	432	Tous les navires
Oil tankers	51	59	59	59	61	62	63	63	Pétroliers
Ore and bulk carriers	7	7	7	6	6	6	6	6	Minéral. et transp. de vracs
Barbados									**Barbade**
All ships	292	497	888	688	725	733	687	328	Tous les navires
Oil tankers	44	22	350	350	350	350	350	8	Pétroliers
Ore and bulk carriers	74	226	268	174	174	174	174	174	Minéral. et transp. de vracs
Belgium									**Belgique**
All ships	240	278	169	127	132	144	151	187	Tous les navires
Oil tankers	2	2	2	4	4	4	4	4	Pétroliers
Ore and bulk carriers	...	56	...	...	...	...	...	...	Minéral. et transp. de vracs
Belize									**Belize**
All ships	517	1 016	1 761	2 382	2 368	2 251	1 828	1 473	Tous les navires
Oil tankers	22	67	338	360	321	348	311	236	Pétroliers
Ore and bulk carriers	20	160	195	190	210	178	145	159	Minéral. et transp. de vracs
Benin									**Bénin**
All ships	1	1	1	1	1	1	1	1	Tous les navires
Bermuda									**Bermudes**
All ships	3 048	3 462	4 610	4 811	6 187	5 752	5 313	4 798	Tous les navires
Oil tankers	1 586	1 586	2 069	2 144	2 652	2 152	1 661	898	Pétroliers
Ore and bulk carriers	248	301	1 018	1 089	1 910	1 911	1 885	1 863	Minéral. et transp. de vracs

60

Merchant shipping: fleets
All ships, oil tankers, and ore and bulk carrier fleets: thousand gross registered tons *[cont.]*
Transports maritimes : flotte marchande
Tous les navires, pétroliers, et minéraliers et transporteurs de vracs : milliers de tonneaux de jauge brute *[suite]*

Country or area	1995	1996	1997	1998	1999	2000	2001	2002	Pays ou zone
Bolivia									**Bolivie**
All ships	...	...	2	16	179	178	174	358	Tous les navires
Oil tankers	...	...	...	...	18	25	65	242	Pétroliers
Ore and bulk carriers	...	...	...	7	49	28	25	14	Minéral. et transp. de vracs
Brazil									**Brésil**
All ships	5 077	4 530	4 372	4 171	3 933	3 809	3 687	3 449	Tous les navires
Oil tankers	2 090	1 803	1 854	1 825	1 770	1 642	1 564	1 397	Pétroliers
Ore and bulk carriers	2 077	1 890	1 706	1 501	1 453	1 437	1 418	1 334	Minéral. et transp. de vracs
British Virgin Islands									**Iles Vierges britanniques**
All ships	5	5	5	4	4	74	3	23	Tous les navires
Brunei Darussalam									**Brunéi Darussalam**
All ships	366	369	369	362	362	362	363	483	Tous les navires
Bulgaria									**Bulgarie**
All ships	1 166	1 150	1 128	1 091	1 036	990	955	889	Tous les navires
Oil tankers	216	194	163	145	145	143	114	114	Pétroliers
Ore and bulk carriers	502	532	542	532	518	518	517	517	Minéral. et transp. de vracs
Cambodia									**Cambodge**
All ships	60	206	439	616	999	1 447	1 997	2 426	Tous les navires
Oil tankers	...	...	...	...	7	31	111	141	Pétroliers
Ore and bulk carriers	...	95	146	169	305	405	511	626	Minéral. et transp. de vracs
Cameroon									**Cameroun**
All ships	37	37	11	13	14	14	14	17	Tous les navires
Canada									**Canada**
All ships	2 401	2 406	2 527	2 501	2 496	2 658	2 727	2 798	Tous les navires
Oil tankers	118	110	254	255	250	329	338	400	Pétroliers
Ore and bulk carriers	1 335	1 347	1 352	1 352	1 338	1 307	1 321	1 295	Minéral. et transp. de vracs
Cape Verde									**Cap-Vert**
All ships	16	15	21	20	21	21	17	16	Tous les navires
Oil tankers	0	0	1	1	1	1	1	1	Pétroliers
Cayman Islands									**Iles Caïmanes**
All ships	368	827	844	1 282	1 165	1 796	2 054	2 377	Tous les navires
Oil tankers	6	87	114	318	123	304	519	704	Pétroliers
Ore and bulk carriers	104	282	282	455	526	634	602	632	Minéral. et transp. de vracs
Channel Islands									**Iles Anglo-Normandes**
All ships	2	3	3	2	2	2	1	1	Tous les navires
Chile									**Chili**
All ships	761	691	722	753	820	842	880	880	Tous les navires
Oil tankers	71	93	93	100	100	100	100	139	Pétroliers
Ore and bulk carriers	294	191	213	188	203	217	224	170	Minéral. et transp. de vracs
China									**Chine**
All ships	16 943	16 993	16 339	16 503	16 315	16 499	16 646	17 316	Tous les navires
Oil tankers	2 295	2 190	2 014	2 029	2 084	2 250	2 352	2 480	Pétroliers
Ore and bulk carriers	6 677	6 781	6 464	6 832	6 648	6 618	6 634	6 876	Minéral. et transp. de vracs
China, Hong Kong SAR									**Chine, Hong Kong RAS**
All ships	8 795	7 863	5 771	6 171	7 973	10 242	13 710	16 164	Tous les navires
Oil tankers	669	396	22	340	515	734	1 537	2 450	Pétroliers
Ore and bulk carriers	6 405	5 749	4 211	4 208	5 233	6 947	8 740	9 862	Minéral. et transp. de vracs
China, Macao SAR									**Chine, Macao RAS**
All ships	2	2	2	2	4	4	4	4	Tous les navires
Colombia									**Colombie**
All ships	144	122	118	112	97	81	66	68	Tous les navires
Oil tankers	6	6	6	6	6	6	6	6	Pétroliers
Comoros									**Comores**
All ships	2	2	2	1	1	20	54	407	Tous les navires
Oil tankers	...	...	...	...	...	...	37	273	Pétroliers
Ore and bulk carriers	...	...	...	...	...	...	...	59	Minéral. et transp. de vracs
Congo									**Congo**
All ships	12	6	7	4	4	3	3	3	Tous les navires
Cook Islands									**Iles Cook**
All ships	4	5	6	7	7	6	5	8	Tous les navires

60

Merchant shipping: fleets
All ships, oil tankers, and ore and bulk carrier fleets: thousand gross registered tons *[cont.]*

Transports maritimes : flotte marchande
Tous les navires, pétroliers, et minéraliers et transporteurs de vracs : milliers de tonneaux de jauge brute *[suite]*

Country or area	1995	1996	1997	1998	1999	2000	2001	2002	Pays ou zone
Costa Rica									**Costa Rica**
All ships	7	6	6	6	6	6	3	4	Tous les navires
Côte d'Ivoire									**Côte d'Ivoire**
All ships	40	13	11	10	10	9	9	9	Tous les navires
Oil tankers	1	1	1	1	1	1	1	1	Pétroliers
Croatia									**Croatie**
All ships	333	580	871	896	869	734	775	835	Tous les navires
Oil tankers	6	8	13	11	11	9	9	8	Pétroliers
Ore and bulk carriers	19	186	469	517	504	438	527	499	Minéral. et transp. de vracs
Cuba									**Cuba**
All ships	410	291	203	158	130	120	101	103	Tous les navires
Oil tankers	64	27	8	8	3	3	3	20	Pétroliers
Ore and bulk carriers	1	1	2	2	2	2	5	5	Minéral. et transp. de vracs
Cyprus									**Chypre**
All ships	24 653	23 799	23 653	23 302	23 641	23 206	22 762	22 997	Tous les navires
Oil tankers	4 341	3 733	3 779	3 848	3 987	4 165	3 803	3 602	Pétroliers
Ore and bulk carriers	13 084	12 653	11 819	11 090	11 511	11 437	11 776	12 374	Minéral. et transp. de vracs
Czech Republic									**République tchèque**
All ships	140	78	16	...	...	...	...	...	Tous les navires
Ore and bulk carriers	98	78	16	...	...	...	...	...	Minéral. et transp. de vracs
Dem. Rep. of the Congo									**Rép. dém. du Congo**
All ships	15	15	15	13	13	13	13	13	Tous les navires
Denmark									**Danemark**
All ships	5 747	5 885	5 754	5 687	5 809	6 823	6 913	7 403	Tous les navires
Oil tankers	1 053	1 024	741	379	494	1 171	1 230	1 522	Pétroliers
Ore and bulk carriers	493	521	522	522	464	356	204	124	Minéral. et transp. de vracs
Djibouti									**Djibouti**
All ships	4	4	4	4	4	4	2	3	Tous les navires
Dominica									**Dominique**
All ships	2	2	3	3	2	2	2	4	Tous les navires
Dominican Republic									**Rép. dominicaine**
All ships	12	12	11	9	10	10	9	9	Tous les navires
Oil tankers	1	1	1	...	...	...	...	...	Pétroliers
Ecuador									**Equateur**
All ships	168	178	145	171	309	301	306	313	Tous les navires
Oil tankers	77	81	80	93	223	219	219	219	Pétroliers
Egypt									**Egypte**
All ships	1 269	1 230	1 288	1 368	1 368	1 346	1 350	1 275	Tous les navires
Oil tankers	222	222	223	210	209	208	207	223	Pétroliers
Ore and bulk carriers	510	487	575	613	601	546	586	512	Minéral. et transp. de vracs
El Salvador									**El Salvador**
All ships	1	1	1	1	2	2	1	6	Tous les navires
Equatorial Guinea									**Guinée équatoriale**
All ships	3	21	35	59	44	46	37	29	Tous les navires
Oil tankers	...	...	...	5	...	...	...	...	Pétroliers
Eritrea									**Erythrée**
All ships	12	1	7	7	16	16	21	21	Tous les navires
Oil tankers	...	...	...	2	2	2	2	2	Pétroliers
Estonia									**Estonie**
All ships	598	545	602	522	453	379	347	357	Tous les navires
Oil tankers	10	6	6	7	8	6	9	9	Pétroliers
Ore and bulk carriers	160	160	160	96	65	33	33	33	Minéral. et transp. de vracs
Ethiopia									**Ethiopie**
All ships	80	86	86	83	96	92	82	82	Tous les navires
Oil tankers	4	4	...	2	2	2	2	2	Pétroliers
Faeroe Islands									**Iles Féroé**
All ships	104	109	105	103	104	103	195	200	Tous les navires
Oil tankers	1	3	2	2	2	2	80	80	Pétroliers
Falkland Is. (Malvinas)									**Iles Falkland (Malvinas)**
All ships	20	30	38	39	45	53	55	54	Tous les navires

60

Merchant shipping: fleets
All ships, oil tankers, and ore and bulk carrier fleets: thousand gross registered tons *[cont.]*
Transports maritimes : flotte marchande
Tous les navires, pétroliers, et minéraliers et transporteurs de vracs : milliers de tonneaux de jauge brute *[suite]*

Country or area	1995	1996	1997	1998	1999	2000	2001	2002	Pays ou zone
Fiji									**Fidji**
All ships	32	36	36	29	29	29	29	27	Tous les navires
Oil tankers	3	3	3	3	3	3	3	1	Pétroliers
Finland									**Finlande**
All ships	1 519	1 511	1 559	1 629	1 658	1 620	1 595	1 545	Tous les navires
Oil tankers	303	303	303	303	303	304	304	275	Pétroliers
Ore and bulk carriers	80	80	80	90	90	90	105	60	Minéral. et transp. de vracs
France [1]									**France** [1]
All ships	4 086	4 291	4 570	4 738	4 766	4 681	4 495	4 574	Tous les navires
Oil tankers	1 943	1 797	2 049	2 248	2 198	2 108	1 900	1 709	Pétroliers
Ore and bulk carriers	291	448	355	354	539	538	355	354	Minéral. et transp. de vracs
Gabon									**Gabon**
All ships	32	33	35	27	16	13	13	13	Tous les navires
Oil tankers	1	1	1	1	1	1	1	1	Pétroliers
Ore and bulk carriers	24	24	24	12	...	...	...	...	Minéral. et transp. de vracs
Gambia									**Gambie**
All ships	1	1	2	2	2	2	2	2	Tous les navires
Georgia									**Géorgie**
All ships	282	206	128	118	132	119	277	569	Tous les navires
Oil tankers	136	115	73	73	76	8	21	41	Pétroliers
Ore and bulk carriers	104	48	0	0	0	0	5	126	Minéral. et transp. de vracs
Germany									**Allemagne**
All ships	5 626	5 842	6 950	8 084	6 514	6 552	6 300	6 546	Tous les navires
Oil tankers	14	11	17	9	8	29	51	49	Pétroliers
Ore and bulk carriers	238	48	2	2	2	2	2	1	Minéral. et transp. de vracs
Ghana									**Ghana**
All ships	114	135	130	115	118	119	123	126	Tous les navires
Oil tankers	1	1	2	6	6	6	7	8	Pétroliers
Gibraltar									**Gibraltar**
All ships	307	306	297	314	451	604	816	961	Tous les navires
Oil tankers	272	272	263	233	288	342	342	341	Pétroliers
Ore and bulk carriers	...	...	...	...	16	16	85	19	Minéral. et transp. de vracs
Greece									**Grèce**
All ships	29 435	27 507	25 288	25 225	24 833	26 402	28 678	28 783	Tous les navires
Oil tankers	12 836	13 066	11 894	12 587	13 158	13 681	14 889	14 562	Pétroliers
Ore and bulk carriers	12 795	10 705	9 472	8 771	7 709	8 077	9 026	9 255	Minéral. et transp. de vracs
Grenada									**Grenade**
All ships	5	1	1	1	1	1	1	1	Tous les navires
Guatemala									**Guatemala**
All ships	1	1	1	1	5	5	5	9	Tous les navires
Guinea									**Guinée**
All ships	7	7	9	11	11	11	11	12	Tous les navires
Guinea-Bissau									**Guinée-Bissau**
All ships	5	6	6	6	6	7	6	6	Tous les navires
Guyana									**Guyana**
All ships	15	16	17	16	14	16	15	15	Tous les navires
Haiti									**Haïti**
All ships	0	1	2	1	1	1	1	1	Tous les navires
Honduras									**Honduras**
All ships	1 206	1 198	1 053	1 083	1 220	1 111	967	933	Tous les navires
Oil tankers	97	103	107	108	131	143	184	214	Pétroliers
Ore and bulk carriers	138	115	114	77	133	101	74	73	Minéral. et transp. de vracs
Hungary									**Hongrie**
All ships	45	50	27	15	12	...	...	4	Tous les navires
Iceland									**Islande**
All ships	209	218	215	198	192	187	193	187	Tous les navires
Oil tankers	2	2	2	2	2	2	1	1	Pétroliers
Ore and bulk carriers	0	0	0	0	0	0	0	0	Minéral. et transp. de vracs

60

Merchant shipping: fleets
All ships, oil tankers, and ore and bulk carrier fleets: thousand gross registered tons *[cont.]*

Transports maritimes : flotte marchande
Tous les navires, pétroliers, et minéraliers et transporteurs de vracs : milliers de tonneaux de jauge brute *[suite]*

Country or area	1995	1996	1997	1998	1999	2000	2001	2002	Pays ou zone
India									**Inde**
All ships	7 127	7 127	6 934	6 777	6 915	6 662	6 688	6 142	Tous les navires
Oil tankers	2 553	2 622	2 515	2 530	2 698	2 526	2 522	2 564	Pétroliers
Ore and bulk carriers	3 183	3 081	3 013	2 832	2 748	2 663	2 706	2 249	Minéral. et transp. de vracs
Indonesia									**Indonésie**
All ships	2 771	2 973	3 195	3 252	3 241	3 384	3 613	3 723	Tous les navires
Oil tankers	738	849	844	841	830	805	831	827	Pétroliers
Ore and bulk carriers	205	222	335	358	380	335	344	324	Minéral. et transp. de vracs
Iran (Islamic Rep. of)									**Iran (Rép. islamique d')**
All ships	2 902	3 567	3 553	3 347	3 546	4 234	3 944	4 128	Tous les navires
Oil tankers	1 234	1 860	1 844	1 592	1 754	2 101	1 846	2 145	Pétroliers
Ore and bulk carriers	1 015	1 015	1 015	990	957	1 148	1 142	1 073	Minéral. et transp. de vracs
Iraq									**Iraq**
All ships	858	857	572	511	511	511	241	188	Tous les navires
Oil tankers	698	698	422	361	361	361	102	59	Pétroliers
Ireland									**Irlande**
All ships	213	219	235	184	219	248	300	280	Tous les navires
Oil tankers	9	3	3	0	0	0	...	...	Pétroliers
Ore and bulk carriers	...	...	...	...	8	26	26	26	Minéral. et transp. de vracs
Isle of Man									**Ile de Man**
All ships	2 300	3 140	4 759	4 203	4 729	5 431	6 057	5 672	Tous les navires
Oil tankers	872	1 023	2 401	1 893	2 409	2 877	3 154	2 761	Pétroliers
Ore and bulk carriers	414	756	831	783	732	795	911	923	Minéral. et transp. de vracs
Israel									**Israël**
All ships	599	679	794	752	728	612	611	765	Tous les navires
Oil tankers	1	1	1	1	1	1	1	1	Pétroliers
Ore and bulk carriers	12	12	12	...	...	...	...	...	Minéral. et transp. de vracs
Italy									**Italie**
All ships	6 699	6 594	6 194	6 819	8 048	9 049	9 655	9 596	Tous les navires
Oil tankers	1 956	1 781	1 608	1 547	1 660	1 639	1 426	1 104	Pétroliers
Ore and bulk carriers	1 535	1 553	1 303	1 525	1 851	2 049	1 829	1 518	Minéral. et transp. de vracs
Jamaica									**Jamaïque**
All ships	9	9	10	4	4	4	23	75	Tous les navires
Oil tankers	2	2	2	2	2	2	2	2	Pétroliers
Ore and bulk carriers	...	...	...	...	...	...	...	44	Minéral. et transp. de vracs
Japan									**Japon**
All ships	19 913	19 201	18 516	17 780	17 063	15 257	14 565	13 918	Tous les navires
Oil tankers	6 033	5 819	5 510	5 434	5 006	3 742	3 341	3 160	Pétroliers
Ore and bulk carriers	5 445	4 956	4 558	3 869	3 556	3 243	3 093	2 776	Minéral. et transp. de vracs
Jordan									**Jordanie**
All ships	21	41	43	42	42	42	42	69	Tous les navires
Ore and bulk carriers	21	40	40	21	21	11	...	...	Minéral. et transp. de vracs
Kazakhstan									**Kazakhstan**
All ships	12	9	10	9	9	11	13	12	Tous les navires
Kenya									**Kenya**
All ships	18	20	21	21	21	21	19	19	Tous les navires
Oil tankers	4	5	5	5	5	5	5	5	Pétroliers
Kiribati									**Kiribati**
All ships	6	6	6	4	4	4	4	4	Tous les navires
Oil tankers	2	2	2	...	...	...	...	...	Pétroliers
Korea, Dem. P. R.									**Corée, R. p. dém. de**
All ships	715	693	667	631	658	653	698	870	Tous les navires
Oil tankers	116	4	5	6	6	6	12	16	Pétroliers
Ore and bulk carriers	107	107	96	50	53	63	63	153	Minéral. et transp. de vracs
Korea, Republic of									**Corée, République de**
All ships	6 972	7 558	7 430	5 694	5 735	6 200	6 395	7 050	Tous les navires
Oil tankers	399	380	385	328	404	607	843	841	Pétroliers
Ore and bulk carriers	3 706	3 650	3 542	2 809	2 708	2 915	2 874	3 431	Minéral. et transp. de vracs
Kuwait									**Koweït**
All ships	2 057	2 028	1 984	2 459	2 456	2 415	2 292	2 256	Tous les navires
Oil tankers	1 343	1 343	1 313	1 662	1 644	1 628	1 628	1 628	Pétroliers
Ore and bulk carriers	...	...	...	17	17	17	17	17	Minéral. et transp. de vracs

60

Merchant shipping: fleets
All ships, oil tankers, and ore and bulk carrier fleets: thousand gross registered tons *[cont.]*
Transports maritimes : flotte marchande
Tous les navires, pétroliers, et minéraliers et transporteurs de vracs : milliers de tonneaux de jauge brute *[suite]*

Country or area	1995	1996	1997	1998	1999	2000	2001	2002	Pays ou zone
Lao People's Dem. Rep.									**Rép. dém. pop. lao**
All ships	3	3	3	2	2	2	2	2	Tous les navires
Latvia									**Lettonie**
All ships	798	723	319	118	118	98	68	89	Tous les navires
Oil tankers	323	279	137	9	9	7	4	4	Pétroliers
Lebanon									**Liban**
All ships	285	275	297	263	322	363	302	229	Tous les navires
Oil tankers	1	2	2	1	1	1	1	1	Pétroliers
Ore and bulk carriers	81	73	124	108	152	191	126	83	Minéral. et transp. de vracs
Liberia									**Libéria**
All ships	59 801	59 989	60 058	60 492	54 107	51 451	51 784	50 400	Tous les navires
Oil tankers	29 002	28 044	26 699	26 361	21 298	19 759	18 733	18 638	Pétroliers
Ore and bulk carriers	16 373	16 744	17 711	16 739	14 426	10 533	11 747	10 947	Minéral. et transp. de vracs
Libyan Arab Jamah.									**Jamah. arabe libyenne**
All ships	733	681	686	567	439	434	251	165	Tous les navires
Oil tankers	572	505	511	395	267	267	81	7	Pétroliers
Lithuania									**Lituanie**
All ships	610	572	510	481	424	434	393	435	Tous les navires
Oil tankers	8	5	5	4	4	4	5	5	Pétroliers
Ore and bulk carriers	111	110	110	110	110	100	80	80	Minéral. et transp. de vracs
Luxembourg									**Luxembourg**
All ships	881	878	820	932	1 343	1 079	1 469	1 494	Tous les navires
Oil tankers	3	165	165	244	543	311	630	495	Pétroliers
Ore and bulk carriers	365	86	86	86	93	6	14	14	Minéral. et transp. de vracs
Madagascar									**Madagascar**
All ships	38	39	40	42	43	44	43	35	Tous les navires
Oil tankers	11	11	11	11	11	11	11	5	Pétroliers
Malaysia									**Malaisie**
All ships	3 283	4 175	4 842	5 209	5 245	5 328	5 207	5 394	Tous les navires
Oil tankers	412	589	689	854	918	868	871	767	Pétroliers
Ore and bulk carriers	982	1 272	1 305	1 448	1 513	1 568	1 447	1 509	Minéral. et transp. de vracs
Maldives									**Maldives**
All ships	85	96	98	101	90	78	67	58	Tous les navires
Oil tankers	6	6	6	6	4	3	4	5	Pétroliers
Ore and bulk carriers	11	11	...	...	...	...	...	...	Minéral. et transp. de vracs
Malta									**Malte**
All ships	17 678	19 479	22 984	24 075	28 205	28 170	27 053	26 331	Tous les navires
Oil tankers	6 793	7 370	9 043	9 848	12 151	11 595	10 546	9 398	Pétroliers
Ore and bulk carriers	6 857	7 478	8 623	8 616	9 984	10 533	10 661	11 574	Minéral. et transp. de vracs
Marshall Islands									**Iles Marshall**
All ships	3 099	4 897	6 314	6 442	6 762	9 745	11 719	14 673	Tous les navires
Oil tankers	1 502	2 721	3 388	3 561	4 313	5 462	5 955	7 177	Pétroliers
Ore and bulk carriers	701	1 095	1 666	1 602	1 255	2 067	2 747	3 310	Minéral. et transp. de vracs
Mauritania									**Mauritanie**
All ships	39	43	43	48	49	49	47	48	Tous les navires
Mauritius									**Maurice**
All ships	238	244	275	206	150	91	97	63	Tous les navires
Oil tankers	53	53	53	...	...	...	...	...	Pétroliers
Ore and bulk carriers	2	2	4	4	4	4	4	10	Minéral. et transp. de vracs
Mexico									**Mexique**
All ships	1 129	1 128	1 145	1 085	918	883	908	937	Tous les navires
Oil tankers	425	425	435	409	464	460	454	455	Pétroliers
Micronesia (Fed. States)									**Micronésie (Etats féd. de)**
All ships	8	9	9	10	10	10	9	13	Tous les navires
Morocco									**Maroc**
All ships	383	403	417	444	448	467	461	502	Tous les navires
Oil tankers	14	12	12	12	12	12	9	4	Pétroliers
Mozambique									**Mozambique**
All ships	38	45	39	35	36	37	38	37	Tous les navires
Oil tankers	0	0	...	...	...	...	...	...	Pétroliers

60

Merchant shipping: fleets
All ships, oil tankers, and ore and bulk carrier fleets: thousand gross registered tons *[cont.]*

Transports maritimes : flotte marchande
Tous les navires, pétroliers, et minéraliers et transporteurs de vracs : milliers de tonneaux de jauge brute *[suite]*

Country or area	1995	1996	1997	1998	1999	2000	2001	2002	Pays ou zone
Myanmar									**Myanmar**
All ships	523	687	568	492	540	446	380	402	Tous les navires
Oil tankers	3	45	3	3	3	3	3	3	Pétroliers
Ore and bulk carriers	215	310	298	283	301	231	162	185	Minéral. et transp. de vracs
Namibia									**Namibie**
All ships	52	59	55	55	55	63	66	69	Tous les navires
Netherlands									**Pays-Bas**
All ships	3 409	3 995	3 880	4 263	4 814	5 168	5 605	5 664	Tous les navires
Oil tankers	405	412	18	16	25	29	37	46	Pétroliers
Ore and bulk carriers	99	68	68	77	77	10	9	10	Minéral. et transp. de vracs
Netherlands Antilles									**Antilles néerlandaises**
All ships	1 197	1 168	1 067	971	1 110	1 235	1 250	1 391	Tous les navires
Oil tankers	139	215	158	135	135	135	0	0	Pétroliers
Ore and bulk carriers	71	108	108	...	...	2	72	42	Minéral. et transp. de vracs
New Zealand									**Nouvelle-Zélande**
All ships	307	386	367	336	265	180	175	180	Tous les navires
Oil tankers	76	61	61	73	73	20	50	50	Pétroliers
Ore and bulk carriers	25	25	12	12	12	12	12	12	Minéral. et transp. de vracs
Nicaragua									**Nicaragua**
All ships	4	4	4	4	4	4	4	4	Tous les navires
Nigeria									**Nigéria**
All ships	479	447	452	452	432	438	404	411	Tous les navires
Oil tankers	251	252	250	252	265	265	287	285	Pétroliers
Norway									**Norvège**
All ships	21 551	21 806	22 839	23 136	23 446	22 604	22 591	22 195	Tous les navires
Oil tankers	8 779	8 895	9 244	8 993	9 195	7 949	7 575	6 936	Pétroliers
Ore and bulk carriers	4 010	3 858	3 908	4 041	3 913	3 863	4 048	4 216	Minéral. et transp. de vracs
Oman									**Oman**
All ships	16	16	15	15	17	19	20	19	Tous les navires
Oil tankers	0	0	0	0	0	0	0	...	Pétroliers
Pakistan									**Pakistan**
All ships	398	444	435	401	308	260	247	247	Tous les navires
Oil tankers	49	49	50	50	50	50	50	50	Pétroliers
Ore and bulk carriers	115	159	158	125	30	...	...	...	Minéral. et transp. de vracs
Panama									**Panama**
All ships	71 922	82 131	91 128	98 222	105 248	114 382	122 352	124 729	Tous les navires
Oil tankers	19 513	20 910	21 272	22 680	23 856	27 588	28 528	28 758	Pétroliers
Ore and bulk carriers	26 726	33 019	38 617	40 319	42 726	45 734	49 947	50 189	Minéral. et transp. de vracs
Papua New Guinea									**Papouasie-Nvl-Guinée**
All ships	49	57	60	61	65	73	77	72	Tous les navires
Oil tankers	3	7	4	3	3	2	2	2	Pétroliers
Paraguay									**Paraguay**
All ships	39	44	44	45	43	45	47	47	Tous les navires
Oil tankers	2	4	4	4	4	4	4	4	Pétroliers
Peru									**Pérou**
All ships	341	346	337	270	285	257	240	240	Tous les navires
Oil tankers	80	76	76	31	31	19	14	15	Pétroliers
Ore and bulk carriers	31	15	...	...	15	...	...	...	Minéral. et transp. de vracs
Philippines									**Philippines**
All ships	8 744	9 034	8 849	8 508	7 650	7 002	6 030	5 320	Tous les navires
Oil tankers	147	158	163	162	159	154	142	146	Pétroliers
Ore and bulk carriers	6 138	6 334	5 951	5 597	4 822	4 366	3 751	3 065	Minéral. et transp. de vracs
Poland									**Pologne**
All ships	2 358	2 293	1 878	1 424	1 319	1 119	618	586	Tous les navires
Oil tankers	7	6	5	5	5	6	5	5	Pétroliers
Ore and bulk carriers	1 455	1 455	1 360	1 082	993	851	391	391	Minéral. et transp. de vracs
Portugal									**Portugal**
All ships	897	676	952	1 130	1 165	1 191	1 199	1 100	Tous les navires
Oil tankers	490	217	349	416	416	354	424	424	Pétroliers
Ore and bulk carriers	127	128	128	188	160	261	214	156	Minéral. et transp. de vracs

60

Merchant shipping: fleets
All ships, oil tankers, and ore and bulk carrier fleets: thousand gross registered tons *[cont.]*
Transports maritimes : flotte marchande
Tous les navires, pétroliers, et minéraliers et transporteurs de vracs : milliers de tonneaux de jauge brute *[suite]*

Country or area	1995	1996	1997	1998	1999	2000	2001	2002	Pays ou zone
Qatar									**Qatar**
All ships	482	562	648	744	749	715	691	623	Tous les navires
Oil tankers	105	183	263	263	263	214	214	210	Pétroliers
Ore and bulk carriers	142	142	142	142	142	142	142	142	Minéral. et transp. de vracs
Romania									**Roumanie**
All ships	2 536	2 568	2 345	2 088	1 221	767	638	622	Tous les navires
Oil tankers	429	429	249	204	68	67	64	64	Pétroliers
Ore and bulk carriers	850	865	865	788	320	138	143	139	Minéral. et transp. de vracs
Russian Federation									**Fédération de Russie**
All ships	15 202	13 755	12 282	11 090	10 649	10 486	10 248	10 380	Tous les navires
Oil tankers	2 294	1 917	1 646	1 608	1 429	1 402	1 430	1 504	Pétroliers
Ore and bulk carriers	1 768	1 767	1 568	1 031	889	864	783	782	Minéral. et transp. de vracs
Saint Helena									**Sainte-Hélène**
All ships	...	0	1	1	1	1	1	1	Tous les navires
Saint Kitts and Nevis									**Saint-Kitts-et-Nevis**
All ships	0	0	0	0	0	0	0	0	Tous les navires
Saint Lucia									**Sainte-Lucie**
All ships	1	1	...	...	...	...	...	...	Tous les navires
St. Vincent-Grenadines									**St. Vincent-Grenadines**
All ships	6 165	7 134	8 374	7 875	7 105	7 026	7 073	6 584	Tous les navires
Oil tankers	1 101	1 228	1 061	913	569	450	459	313	Pétroliers
Ore and bulk carriers	2 328	2 627	3 202	2 858	2 656	2 672	3 019	2 716	Minéral. et transp. de vracs
Samoa									**Samoa**
All ships	6	...	1	3	3	2	10	10	Tous les navires
Sao Tome and Principe									**Sao Tomé-et-Principe**
All ships	3	3	3	10	42	173	190	86	Tous les navires
Oil tankers	...	...	...	...	1	7	11	7	Pétroliers
Ore and bulk carriers	...	...	...	...	...	10	62	17	Minéral. et transp. de vracs
Saudi Arabia									**Arabie saoudite**
All ships	1 187	1 208	1 164	1 278	1 208	1 260	1 133	1 472	Tous les navires
Oil tankers	238	258	203	220	218	219	224	664	Pétroliers
Ore and bulk carriers	12	12	12	12	...	...	...	...	Minéral. et transp. de vracs
Senegal									**Sénégal**
All ships	48	50	51	51	48	50	48	47	Tous les navires
Serbia and Montenegro									**Serbie-et-Monténégro**
All ships	2	2	2	5	4	4	3	1	Tous les navires
Seychelles									**Seychelles**
All ships	5	4	5	18	24	22	34	65	Tous les navires
Sierra Leone									**Sierra Leone**
All ships	23	19	19	19	17	17	13	23	Tous les navires
Oil tankers	1	1	1	1	3	...	...	9	Pétroliers
Singapore									**Singapour**
All ships	13 611	16 448	18 875	20 370	21 780	21 491	21 023	21 148	Tous les navires
Oil tankers	5 102	6 614	7 787	8 781	9 619	9 118	8 647	8 528	Pétroliers
Ore and bulk carriers	3 766	4 344	4 358	4 585	4 695	4 753	4 800	4 958	Minéral. et transp. de vracs
Slovakia									**Slovaquie**
All ships	19	19	15	15	15	15	15	7	Tous les navires
Ore and bulk carriers	...	...	...	...	...	...	...	7	Minéral. et transp. de vracs
Slovenia									**Slovénie**
All ships	2	2	2	2	2	2	2	2	Tous les navires
Solomon Islands									**Iles Salomon**
All ships	8	10	10	10	10	9	8	8	Tous les navires
Somalia									**Somalie**
All ships	16	14	11	11	6	7	6	6	Tous les navires
Oil tankers	...	...	...	...	1	1	1	1	Pétroliers
South Africa									**Afrique du Sud**
All ships	340	371	383	384	379	380	382	144	Tous les navires
Oil tankers	1	4	3	3	3	3	3	3	Pétroliers

60

Merchant shipping: fleets
All ships, oil tankers, and ore and bulk carrier fleets: thousand gross registered tons *[cont.]*

Transports maritimes : flotte marchande
Tous les navires, pétroliers, et minéraliers et transporteurs de vracs : milliers de tonneaux de jauge brute *[suite]*

Country or area	1995	1996	1997	1998	1999	2000	2001	2002	Pays ou zone
Spain									**Espagne**
All ships	1 619	1 675	1 688	1 838	1 903	2 030	2 148	2 371	Tous les navires
Oil tankers	437	515	510	585	583	600	598	603	Pétroliers
Ore and bulk carriers	68	23	39	42	42	42	42	42	Minéral. et transp. de vracs
Sri Lanka									**Sri Lanka**
All ships	227	242	217	189	195	150	154	81	Tous les navires
Oil tankers	3	5	5	5	5	2	6	6	Pétroliers
Ore and bulk carriers	93	93	95	77	77	77	77	...	Minéral. et transp. de vracs
Sudan									**Soudan**
All ships	48	42	42	43	43	43	43	33	Tous les navires
Oil tankers	1	1	1	1	1	1	1	1	Pétroliers
Suriname									**Suriname**
All ships	8	8	8	6	6	5	5	5	Tous les navires
Oil tankers	2	2	2	2	2	2	2	2	Pétroliers
Sweden									**Suède**
All ships	2 955	3 002	2 754	2 552	2 947	2 887	2 958	3 178	Tous les navires
Oil tankers	385	392	307	105	102	103	101	81	Pétroliers
Ore and bulk carriers	52	44	38	32	32	29	29	29	Minéral. et transp. de vracs
Switzerland									**Suisse**
All ships	381	400	434	383	439	429	502	559	Tous les navires
Ore and bulk carriers	351	370	389	349	393	393	463	503	Minéral. et transp. de vracs
Syrian Arab Republic									**Rép. arabe syrienne**
All ships	352	420	415	428	440	465	498	472	Tous les navires
Oil tankers	...	...	...	...	...	1	1	1	Pétroliers
Ore and bulk carriers	48	45	14	22	30	26	54	61	Minéral. et transp. de vracs
Thailand									**Thaïlande**
All ships	1 743	2 042	2 158	1 999	1 956	1 945	1 771	1 880	Tous les navires
Oil tankers	196	385	411	364	361	364	231	209	Pétroliers
Ore and bulk carriers	387	480	567	491	476	443	392	457	Minéral. et transp. de vracs
Togo									**Togo**
All ships	1	1	2	2	43	5	8	13	Tous les navires
Tonga									**Tonga**
All ships	12	11	12	22	25	25	338	291	Tous les navires
Oil tankers	...	...	...	...	...	...	31	41	Pétroliers
Ore and bulk carriers	...	...	...	...	...	...	49	39	Minéral. et transp. de vracs
Trinidad and Tobago									**Trinité-et-Tobago**
All ships	28	19	19	19	22	22	27	27	Tous les navires
Oil tankers	...	...	...	...	1	1	1	1	Pétroliers
Tunisia									**Tunisie**
All ships	160	158	180	193	200	208	203	186	Tous les navires
Oil tankers	9	7	7	22	20	20	20	20	Pétroliers
Ore and bulk carriers	38	38	38	27	17	17	17	17	Minéral. et transp. de vracs
Turkey									**Turquie**
All ships	6 268	6 426	6 567	6 251	6 325	5 833	5 897	5 659	Tous les navires
Oil tankers	821	709	514	503	584	625	772	625	Pétroliers
Ore and bulk carriers	4 007	4 168	4 444	4 023	3 939	3 303	3 178	2 904	Minéral. et transp. de vracs
Turkmenistan									**Turkménistan**
All ships	32	40	39	38	44	42	46	46	Tous les navires
Oil tankers	3	3	3	2	2	2	6	6	Pétroliers
Ore and bulk carriers	...	...	...	...	5	3	3	3	Minéral. et transp. de vracs
Turks and Caicos Islands									**Iles Turques et Caïques**
All ships	2	2	2	1	1	1	1	1	Tous les navires
Tuvalu									**Tuvalu**
All ships	64	57	55	49	43	59	36	38	Tous les navires
Ukraine									**Ukraine**
All ships	4 613	3 825	2 690	2 033	1 775	1 546	1 408	1 350	Tous les navires
Oil tankers	81	79	89	62	56	56	45	39	Pétroliers
Ore and bulk carriers	729	452	254	207	161	100	100	100	Minéral. et transp. de vracs
United Arab Emirates									**Emirats arabes unis**
All ships	961	890	924	933	786	979	746	703	Tous les navires
Oil tankers	519	410	426	369	248	240	233	221	Pétroliers
Ore and bulk carriers	35	37	20	20	20	0	0	0	Minéral. et transp. de vracs

60

Merchant shipping: fleets
All ships, oil tankers, and ore and bulk carrier fleets: thousand gross registered tons *[cont.]*

Transports maritimes : flotte marchande
Tous les navires, pétroliers, et minéraliers et transporteurs de vracs : milliers de tonneaux de jauge brute *[suite]*

Country or area	1995	1996	1997	1998	1999	2000	2001	2002	Pays ou zone
United Kingdom									**Royaume-Uni**
All ships	4 413	3 872	3 486	4 085	4 331	5 532	6 029	8 045	Tous les navires
Oil tankers	1 115	876	476	625	544	538	562	515	Pétroliers
Ore and bulk carriers	74	67	64	48	33	52	78	665	Minéral. et transp. de vracs
United Rep. of Tanzania									**Rép.-Unie de Tanzanie**
All ships	46	45	46	36	36	38	38	47	Tous les navires
Oil tankers	5	5	5	4	4	4	4	8	Pétroliers
United States									**Etats-Unis**
All ships	12 761	12 025	11 789	11 852	12 026	11 111	10 907	10 371	Tous les navires
Oil tankers	3 987	3 630	3 372	3 436	3 491	3 176	2 965	2 296	Pétroliers
Ore and bulk carriers	1 513	1 301	1 275	1 268	1 268	1 271	1 339	1 291	Minéral. et transp. de vracs
Uruguay									**Uruguay**
All ships	124	100	121	107	62	67	73	75	Tous les navires
Oil tankers	46	48	48	48	6	6	6	6	Pétroliers
Vanuatu									**Vanuatu**
All ships	1 874	1 711	1 578	1 602	1 444	1 379	1 496	1 381	Tous les navires
Oil tankers	38	40	14	11	11	11	4	55	Pétroliers
Ore and bulk carriers	841	706	620	708	518	506	529	518	Minéral. et transp. de vracs
Venezuela									**Venezuela**
All ships	787	697	705	665	657	667	872	865	Tous les navires
Oil tankers	361	275	275	222	222	212	374	376	Pétroliers
Ore and bulk carriers	111	111	111	126	116	126	121	121	Minéral. et transp. de vracs
Viet Nam									**Viet Nam**
All ships	700	808	766	784	865	1 002	1 074	1 131	Tous les navires
Oil tankers	19	20	22	63	105	136	158	162	Pétroliers
Ore and bulk carriers	21	63	94	94	94	122	122	150	Minéral. et transp. de vracs
Wallis and Futuna Islands									**Iles Wallis et Futuna**
All ships	108	92	111	111	159	135	183	158	Tous les navires
Oil tankers	75	75	75	75	75	50	50	25	Pétroliers
Yemen									**Yémen**
All ships	27	25	26	25	25	28	74	78	Tous les navires
Oil tankers	2	2	2	2	2	5	51	51	Pétroliers

Source:
Lloyd's Register of Shipping, London, "World Fleet Statistics 2002" and previous issues.

Source:
"Lloyd's Register of Shipping", Londres, "World Fleet Statistics 2002" et éditions précédentes.

1   Including the French Antarctic Territory.

1   Y compris le territoire antarctique français.

61
International maritime transport
Vessels entered and cleared: thousand net registered tons
Transports maritimes internationaux
Navires entrés et sortis : milliers de tonneaux de jauge nette

Country or area Pays ou zone	1993	1994	1995	1996	1997	1998	1999	2000	2001	2002
Albania Albanie										
Vessels entered										
Navires entrés	288	576	1 002	1 218	1 053	1 419	1 115	2 212	2 558	1 675
Vessels cleared										
Navires sortis	121	198	309	213	123	61	29	72	69	57
Algeria[1] Algérie[1]										
Vessels entered										
Navires entrés	84 744	86 500	88 502	93 913	103 201	106 256	113 681	117 918	118 994	...
Vessels cleared										
Navires sortis	84 659	86 767	88 865	93 676	103 187	106 036	113 627	117 937	119 074	...
American Samoa[2] Samoa américaines[2]										
Vessels entered										
Navires entrés	440	581	526	452	725	589	884	...	...	...
Vessels cleared										
Navires sortis	440	581	526	452	725	589	884	...	...	...
Antigua and Barbuda Antigua-et-Barbuda										
Vessels entered										
Navires entrés	...	...	...	57 386	94 907	...	...	...	...	...
Vessels cleared										
Navires sortis	...	...	...	544 328	667 126	...	...	...	...	...
Argentina[3] Argentine[3]										
Vessels entered										
Navires entrés	20 092[4]	12 345[5]	...	...	...	...	...	...	...	...
Australia[1,2] Australie[1,2]										
Vessels entered										
Navires entrés	...	...	2 299	2 268	2 231	...	1 864	1 730	...	...
Azerbaijan Azerbaïdjan										
Vessels entered										
Navires entrés	142	127	925	1 022	2 007	3 967	4 015	5 118	...	...
Vessels cleared										
Navires sortis	1 568	2 289	1 751	1 702	1 737	1 483	624	703	...	...
Bahrain Bahreïn										
Vessels entered										
Navires entrés	1	1	1	2	2	...	...	...	...	...
Bangladesh[6] Bangladesh[6]										
Vessels entered										
Navires entrés	4 835	4 832	6 013	5 928	5 488	5 794	6 509	...	...	...
Vessels cleared										
Navires sortis	3 103	2 556	3 094	3 136	2 866	2 556	2 949	...	...	...
Barbados Barbade										
Vessels entered										
Navires entrés	12 195	13 703	12 780	14 002	15 146	16 893	14 470	15 875	...	...
Belgium Belgique										
Vessels entered										
Navires entrés	229 915	239 678	253 427	297 664	337 862	367 684	386 211	415 640	436 927	...
Vessels cleared										
Navires sortis	190 795	201 448	210 144	297 610	333 694	360 987	375 519	404 159	422 703	...
Benin Bénin										
Vessels entered										
Navires entrés	1 134	1 163	1 192	1 321	1 296	1 289	1 095	1 184	...	...
Brazil Brésil										
Vessels entered										
Navires entrés	74 314	78 757	79 732	82 593	86 720	92 822	78 774	84 423	88 562	...
Vessels cleared										
Navires sortis	173 624	185 291	197 955	192 889	209 331	216 273	217 810	237 170	258 962	...
Brunei Darussalam Brunéi Darussalam										
Vessels entered										
Navires entrés	...	...	...	...	...	...	...	...	...	1 735
Vessels cleared										
Navires sortis	...	...	...	...	...	...	...	...	...	1 732

61

International maritime transport
Vessels entered and cleared: thousand net registered tons *[cont.]*

Transports maritimes internationaux
Navires entrés et sortis : milliers de tonneaux de jauge nette *[suite]*

Country or area Pays ou zone	1993	1994	1995	1996	1997	1998	1999	2000	2001	2002
Cambodia Cambodge										
Vessels entered [7]										
Navires entrés [7]	463	608	647	726	715	781	1 056	1 313	...	...
Vessels cleared										
Navires sortis	193	182	214	145	293	319	191	179		
Cameroon [3,8] Cameroun [3,8]										
Vessels entered										
Navires entrés	5 279	964	1 543	1 157	1 159	1 154	1 234	1 215	1 243	...
Canada [9] Canada [9]										
Vessels entered										
Navires entrés	56 769	60 417	62 415	66 166	74 422	81 539	82 976	90 925	92 790	...
Vessels cleared										
Navires sortis	108 587	116 279	114 040	117 452	124 999	120 349	122 282	128 549	121 712	...
Cape Verde Cap-Vert										
Vessels entered										
Navires entrés	...	3 409	3 628	3 601	3 590	4 296	...	...	...	...
China, Hong Kong SAR Chine, Hong Kong RAS										
Vessels entered										
Navires entrés	184 166	201 919	216 437	229 444	250 303	261 694	267 255	300 606	340 027	372 415
Vessels cleared										
Navires sortis	184 023	201 607	217 539	229 474	250 399	261 552	267 419	300 522	340 163	372 574
China, Macao SAR [3] Chine, Macao RAS [3]										
Vessels cleared										
Navires sortis	...	...	...	...	...	...	...	10 736[10]	1 975	2 820
Colombia Colombie										
Vessels entered [3]										
Navires entrés [3]	24 874	28 138	32 191	35 787	40 863	50 712	68 649	52 442	...	...
Vessels cleared										
Navires sortis	24 967	27 919	31 813	34 585	39 562	48 530	65 790	50 787	...	...
Congo Congo										
Vessels entered										
Navires entrés	6 176	5 665	6 449	7 645	...	8 045	8 507	8 529	8 522	9 432
Vessels cleared										
Navires sortis	1 108	997	1 342	1 878	...	1 732	1 706	1 781	1 921	2 015
Costa Rica Costa Rica										
Vessels entered										
Navires entrés	3 684	4 004	4 202	4 135	3 555	4 024	2 168	2 019	1 923	2 101
Vessels cleared										
Navires sortis	2 760	2 983	3 070	2 992	2 941	3 405	2 168	2 019	1 923	2 101
Croatia Croatie										
Vessels entered										
Navires entrés	4 686	5 028	6 023	13 587[1]	16 131[1]	16 410[1]	14 685[1]	13 925	22 425	24 436
Vessels cleared										
Navires sortis	3 251	4 161	4 297	10 393[1]	11 502[1]	11 912[1]	11 374[1]	12 686	20 560	20 577
Cyprus Chypre										
Vessels entered										
Navires entrés	14 918	15 350	15 700	19 033	16 478	15 955	18 001	20 571	20 310	20 154
Dominica Dominique										
Vessels entered										
Navires entrés	...	2 214	2 252	2 289	2 145	2 218	...	...	...	...
Dominican Republic Rép. dominicaine										
Vessels entered										
Navires entrés	7 563	8 421	8 751	9 238	10 113	10 719	13 603	14 245	13 892	...
Vessels cleared										
Navires sortis	788	770	1 162	1 341	1 822	1 673	1 609	2 170	2 507	...
Ecuador Equateur										
Vessels entered										
Navires entrés	2 719	3 006	3 665	3 283	3 263	3 158	2 019	4 711	3 064	...
Vessels cleared										
Navires sortis	15 459	16 958	18 010	17 450	18 277	16 937	18 051	16 779	18 761	...

61

International maritime transport
Vessels entered and cleared: thousand net registered tons *[cont.]*

Transports maritimes internationaux
Navires entrés et sortis : milliers de tonneaux de jauge nette *[suite]*

Country or area Pays ou zone	1993	1994	1995	1996	1997	1998	1999	2000	2001	2002
Egypt Egypte										
Vessels entered Navires entrés	41 253	44 726	48 008	47 824	48 866	40 834	36 333	69 801	...	...
Vessels cleared Navires sortis	34 307	37 377	41 257	43 386	40 924	33 711	32 186	54 142	...	...
El Salvador El Salvador										
Vessels entered Navires entrés	3 012	3 393	3 185	3 345	5 633	7 969	3 374	...	...	
Vessels cleared Navires sortis	938	861	625	822	550	490	566	...	...	
Estonia Estonie										
Vessels entered Navires entrés	3 419	2 376[1]	...	...	...	...	...	...	...	
Vessels cleared Navires sortis	3 087	3 813[1]	...	...	...	...	...	...	...	
Fiji Fidji										
Vessels entered Navires entrés	2 876	2 843	4 065	4 070	...	...	...	...	...	...
Finland[3] Finlande[3]										
Vessels entered Navires entrés	117 003	111 934	127 711	131 338	144 923	148 690	153 149	155 556	157 730	166 143
Vessels cleared Navires sortis	121 946	117 143	132 879	135 650	148 366	150 969	154 700	152 143	157 639	166 291
France[11,12] France[11,12]										
Vessels entered Navires entrés	1896742	1941433	1921826	2202359	2235239	2164285	2080509	2120282	2225279	...
Gambia[2] Gambie[2]										
Vessels entered Navires entrés	1 153	...	...	...	...	...	...	...	...	...
Germany Allemagne										
Vessels entered Navires entrés	221 741	223 363	221 226	251 500	260 553	263 470	271 978	959 448[13]	953 366	958 945
Vessels cleared Navires sortis	196 456	201 316	197 339	229 959	235 110	237 071	249 225	938 028[13]	953 287	958 503
Gibraltar Gibraltar										
Vessels entered Navires entrés	307	276	256	...	...	...	...	...	...	...
Greece Grèce										
Vessels entered Navires entrés	32 429	33 048	38 573	38 549	38 704	43 786	44 662	45 072	45 973	...
Vessels cleared Navires sortis	18 467	21 087	21 940	21 356	19 359	21 865	22 302	22 526	23 970	
Guatemala Guatemala										
Vessels entered Navires entrés	3 367	4 008	3 976	3 680	4 505	...	...	...	...	...
Vessels cleared Navires sortis	2 266	2 280	2 854	3 275	3 815	...	...	...	...	...
Haiti[14] Haïti[14]										
Vessels entered Navires entrés	897	529	1 285	1 680	1 304	...	...	...	...	
India[15,16] Inde[15,16]										
Vessels entered Navires entrés	27 825	39 619	47 857	48 358	47 055	48 512	60 850	55 466	55 982	...
Vessels cleared Navires sortis	36 325	42 885	48 497	44 494	45 819	39 031	41 187	38 043	41 716	
Indonesia Indonésie										
Vessels entered Navires entrés	140 861	155 869	163 597	259 096	286 314	246 838	252 893	303 587	331 164	361 246
Vessels cleared Navires sortis	41 993	48 857	48 753	75 055	97 885	82 711	73 938	79 813	83 115	86 554

61

International maritime transport
Vessels entered and cleared: thousand net registered tons *[cont.]*

Transports maritimes internationaux
Navires entrés et sortis : milliers de tonneaux de jauge nette *[suite]*

Country or area Pays ou zone	1993	1994	1995	1996	1997	1998	1999	2000	2001	2002
Iran (Islamic Rep. of) Iran (Rép. islamique d')										
Vessels entered										
Navires entrés	11 218	13 795	14 686	17 155	27 756	46 937	62 828	65 008	67 267	...
Ireland Irlande										
Vessels entered [3]										
Navires entrés [3]	36 408	37 896	45 968	54 602	165 925[1]	176 228[1]	190 818[1]	196 713	210 882	...
Vessels cleared										
Navires sortis	13 199	15 113	15 890	16 787	16 463	16 669	17 645	17 954	17 234	...
Italy Italie										
Vessels entered										
Navires entrés	168 545	180 175	181 733	190 910	226 977	250 830	277 384	211 242	...	...
Vessels cleared										
Navires sortis	84 044	91 288	96 505	160 757	132 532	152 655	167 550	137 864		
Jamaica Jamaïque										
Vessels entered										
Navires entrés	...	9 892	10 531	12 339	12 815	...	...	...	...	...
Vessels cleared										
Navires sortis	5 576	5 599	5 730	6 043	6 457	6 553	...	...	...	...
Japan [3] Japon [3]										
Vessels entered										
Navires entrés	397 582	410 164	412 163	422 256	438 111	425 193	446 482	461 903	459 840	461 420
Jordan Jordanie										
Vessels entered										
Navires entrés	2 143	1 910	2 382	2 735	2 997	2 608	2 551	2 505	2 673	2 789
Vessels cleared										
Navires sortis	347	576	...	...	...	...	...	...		
Kenya [3,8] Kenya [3,8]										
Vessels entered										
Navires entrés	7 102	7 108	7 973	8 694	8 442	8 561	8 188	9 126	10 600	...
Korea, Republic of Corée, République de										
Vessels entered										
Navires entrés	383 311	430 872	487 834	537 163	578 373	586 629	691 166	755 225	770 284	...
Vessels cleared										
Navires sortis	381 545	429 538	485 374	542 600	584 164	595 072	695 598	737 999	776 250	...
Kuwait Koweït										
Vessels entered										
Navires entrés	6 248	9 775	10 723	9 676	9 171	9 357	10 711	10 842	2 189	2 052
Vessels cleared										
Navires sortis	944	1 184	1 222	1 223	1 285	1 178	1 201	1 071	1 071	1 178
Libyan Arab Jamah. Jamah. arabe libyenne										
Vessels entered										
Navires entrés	6 492	5 277	5 142	5 638	5 980	6 245	5 304	2 721	2 538	...
Vessels cleared										
Navires sortis	556	572	751	624	647	739	815	1 009	949	...
Lithuania [1,3] Lituanie [1,3]										
Vessels entered										
Navires entrés	...	...	25 642	32 187	34 259	35 680	32 438	37 138	34 310	38 532
Vessels cleared										
Navires sortis	...	...	25 477	31 383	34 161	35 658	32 419	37 044	33 932	38 269
Madagascar [3] Madagascar [3]										
Vessels entered										
Navires entrés	...	...	...	...	4 169	3 920	2 629	4 842	...	...
Malaysia [17] Malaisie [17]										
Vessels entered										
Navires entrés	109 300	110 330	...	...	...	...	...	...	...	...
Vessels cleared										
Navires sortis	109 000	110 650	...	...	...	...	...	...	...	...
Malta Malte										
Vessels entered										
Navires entrés	6 802	7 657	9 404	9 830	11 597	13 738	16 725	17 299	18 279	24 278

61

International maritime transport
Vessels entered and cleared: thousand net registered tons *[cont.]*

Transports maritimes internationaux
Navires entrés et sortis : milliers de tonneaux de jauge nette *[suite]*

Country or area Pays ou zone	1993	1994	1995	1996	1997	1998	1999	2000	2001	2002
Vessels cleared Navires sortis	3 534	2 471	2 887	3 779	4 976	2 493	5 084	7 528	7 795	4 186
Mauritius Maurice										
Vessels entered [3] Navires entrés [3]	5 271	5 500	5 356	4 999	5 485	5 925	6 725	6 387	7 026	8 595
Vessels cleared Navires sortis	5 219	5 550	5 313	5 140	5 263	5 924	6 129	6 087	6 482	7 871
Mexico Mexique										
Vessels entered Navires entrés	20 241	21 919	19 697	27 533	33 317	43 185	44 184	51 814	50 380	51 718
Vessels cleared Navires sortis	101 688	100 757	103 355	117 598	125 571	125 682	119 284	124 880	129 020	130 536
Morocco [18] Maroc [18]										
Vessels entered Navires entrés	22 436	22 633	24 034	26 271	27 088	27 478	29 918	30 170	30 664	32 240
Myanmar Myanmar										
Vessels entered Navires entrés	1 278	1 587	2 388	2 286	2 230	2 955	2 729	4 545	...	...
Vessels cleared Navires sortis	1 408	1 612	1 624	1 108	794	1 235	1 656	2 252	...	...
Netherlands [1] Pays-Bas [1]										
Vessels entered Navires entrés	375 906	403 355	431 997	441 281	456 522	472 977	...	...	...	...
Vessels cleared Navires sortis	237 817	258 152	280 667	291 089	290 813	301 559	...	...	...	...
New Zealand [1] Nouvelle-Zélande [1]										
Vessels entered Navires entrés	37 603	39 700	48 827	...	...	...	...	...	...	...
Vessels cleared Navires sortis	35 128	37 421	42 985	...	...	...	...	...	...	...
Nigeria Nigéria										
Vessels entered Navires entrés	2 776	1 908	1 846[19]	2 043	2 464	...	...	...	...	...
Vessels cleared Navires sortis	2 830	1 879	1 852[19]	2 104	2 510	...	...	...	...	...
Norway Norvège										
Vessels entered Navires entrés	82 369[20]	112 247[20]	139 252[20]	147 192[20]	148 060[20]	148 764[20]	155 805[20]	...	...	45 651[21]
Oman Oman										
Vessels entered Navires entrés	2 190	2 119	2 099	2 155	2 226	2 102	2 087	2 142	2 457	2 688
Vessels cleared Navires sortis	1 146	1 192	1 309	5 529	6 781	7 147	7 008	...	...	...
Pakistan [6] Pakistan [6]										
Vessels entered Navires entrés	18 785	20 195	21 268	22 632	26 915	26 502	26 702	27 005	26 453	27 262
Vessels cleared Navires sortis	7 284	8 287	7 411	7 728	5 748	6 983	7 296	7 500	9 173	11 861
Panama Panama										
Vessels entered Navires entrés	2 178	2 404	2 766	3 263	4 431	9 879	12 008	13 301	13 742	11 341
Vessels cleared Navires sortis	1 560	1 643	1 972	2 367	2 927	6 453	7 298	7 369	9 693	10 200
Peru Pérou										
Vessels entered Navires entrés	6 066	7 145	7 454	7 515	6 701	7 675	6 948	6 901	7 150	8 260
Vessels cleared Navires sortis	9 186	4 930	4 640	4 731	6 082	4 668	5 696	6 499	6 637	6 112
Philippines Philippines										
Vessels entered Navires entrés	32 388	38 222	40 876	...	...	...	...	...	...	...

61

International maritime transport
Vessels entered and cleared: thousand net registered tons *[cont.]*

Transports maritimes internationaux
Navires entrés et sortis : milliers de tonneaux de jauge nette *[suite]*

Country or area Pays ou zone	1993	1994	1995	1996	1997	1998	1999	2000	2001	2002
Vessels cleared Navires sortis	22 431	25 582	27 829	...	...	...	...	...	...	...
Poland Pologne										
Vessels entered Navires entrés	15 544	14 816	18 316	20 997	24 280	25 549	24 161	26 176	26 568	...
Vessels cleared Navires sortis	23 222	25 552	25 269	25 566	28 877	30 065	30 062	32 225	31 730	
Portugal Portugal										
Vessels entered Navires entrés	32 654	34 544	36 095	...	...	...	...	...	...	...
Réunion [18] Réunion [18]										
Vessels entered Navires entrés	2 421	2 349	2 715	2 595	2 755	3 065	3 059	3 266	...	...
Russian Federation [3] Fédération de Russie [3]										
Vessels entered Navires entrés	...	...	...	...	...	67 110	82 544	76 376	83 581	117 306
Vessels cleared Navires sortis	...	...	...	...	...	68 830	82 939	76 369	81 830	100 620
Saint Helena Sainte-Hélène										
Vessels entered Navires entrés	319	254	55	...	...	...	...	...	...	...
Saint Lucia Sainte-Lucie										
Vessels entered Navires entrés	...	...	4 755	5 317	6 803	...	...	...	...	...
St. Vincent-Grenadines St. Vincent-Grenadines										
Vessels entered Navires entrés	1 336	1 037	932	1 204	1 253	1 274	1 478	1 674	1 790	...
Vessels cleared Navires sortis	1 336	1 037	932	1 204	1 253	1 274	1 478	1 674	1 790	...
Samoa Samoa										
Vessels entered Navires entrés	530	563	579	544	662	685	827	...	...	...
Senegal Sénégal										
Vessels entered Navires entrés	3 123	2 429	2 395	2 542	2 460	2 467	2 511	2 205	2 235	2 360
Vessels cleared Navires sortis	3 123	2 429	2 395	2 542	2 460	2 467	2 511	2 213	2 235	2 360
Serbia and Montenegro Serbie-et-Monténégro										
Vessels entered Navires entrés	...	...	805	1 960	1 828	1 589	1 859	2 057	2 165	1 780
Vessels cleared Navires sortis	...	...	769	1 155	1 360	1 091	1 091	1 368	1 148	1 373
Seychelles Seychelles										
Vessels entered Navires entrés	871	764	879	872	1 059	1 099	1 139	...	...	...
Singapore [22] Singapour [22]										
Vessels entered Navires entrés	92 655	101 107	104 014	117 723	130 333	140 922	141 523	145 383	146 265	142 745
Vessels cleared Navires sortis	92 477	101 017	104 123	117 662	130 237	140 838	141 745	145 415	146 322	142 765
Slovakia [23] Slovaquie [23]										
Vessels entered Navires entrés	387	379	374	401	367	381	336	...	...	...
Slovenia Slovénie										
Vessels entered Navires entrés	3 963	4 049	4 280	5 067	5 960	6 686	7 762	6 605	6 444	6 825
Vessels cleared Navires sortis	2 362	2 095	2 388	2 251	3 254	3 652	4 394	3 969	3 986	4 430
South Africa [1] Afrique du Sud [1]										
Vessels entered Navires entrés	13 437	13 037	13 285	14 075	14 383	13 559	12 695	12 041	12 763	13 593

61

International maritime transport
Vessels entered and cleared: thousand net registered tons *[cont.]*

Transports maritimes internationaux
Navires entrés et sortis : milliers de tonneaux de jauge nette *[suite]*

Country or area Pays ou zone	1993	1994	1995	1996	1997	1998	1999	2000	2001	2002
Vessels cleared Navires sortis	441 053	472 025	515 278	586 492	629 033	631 059	606 231	577 520	634 997	688 975
Spain Espagne										
Vessels entered Navires entrés	130 171	137 951	154 134	149 874	152 951	170 817	184 362	194 911	198 696	...
Vessels cleared Navires sortis	46 942	47 813	48 176	51 657	54 243	56 449	56 817	59 247	59 297	...
Sri Lanka Sri Lanka										
Vessels entered Navires entrés	24 955	25 120	25 368	29 882	33 188	36 011	37 399	37 418	34 690	39 336
Suriname Suriname										
Vessels entered Navires entrés	1 265	1 301	1 167	1 270	1 307	1 411	1 344	1 120	...	...
Vessels cleared Navires sortis	1 595	1 714	1 926	2 018	2 135	2 206	2 391	2 186	...	...
Sweden Suède										
Vessels entered Navires entrés	62 159[1]	74 334[1]	82 386[1]	88 828[1]	95 655[1]	101 977[1]	158 718[24]	935 481[25]	925 202	...
Vessels cleared Navires sortis	55 058[1]	63 026[1]	73 139[1]	79 888[1]	82 877[1]	84 722[1]	143 200[24]	917 926[25]	910 735	...
Syrian Arab Republic[3] Rép. arabe syrienne[3]										
Vessels entered[8] Navires entrés[8]	3 525	3 433	2 884	2 901	2 640	2 622	2 928	2 798	2 827	...
Vessels cleared Navires sortis	3 459	3 537	2 701	2 792	2 573	2 562	2 845	2 696	2 794	...
Thailand Thaïlande										
Vessels entered Navires entrés	79 647	84 929	98 759	93 033	84 052	62 339	71 094	68 079	...	...
Vessels cleared Navires sortis	22 205	24 692	28 689	22 231	23 757	24 920	31 125	33 154	...	...
Tunisia[1] Tunisie[1]										
Vessels entered Navires entrés	28 746	32 498	36 205	38 513	42 749	43 546	52 441	56 632	58 610	...
Vessels cleared Navires sortis	28 753	32 462	36 232	38 541	42 561	43 513	52 464	56 551	58 595	...
Turkey Turquie										
Vessels entered Navires entrés	56 687	52 925	57 170	59 861	78 474	142 303[1]	136 456[1]	152 191[1]	125 997[1]	...
Vessels cleared Navires sortis	55 329	51 303	56 221	58 766	77 952	89 712[1]	88 761[1]	92 406[1]	96 867[1]	...
Ukraine Ukraine										
Vessels entered Navires entrés	5 072	3 381	4 270	3 287	3 108	4 843	5 085	6 840	7 404	...
Vessels cleared Navires sortis	29 120	25 189	21 916	21 550	28 765	36 027	44 030	42 704	49 310	...
United States[9,26] Etats-Unis[9,26]										
Vessels entered Navires entrés	340 507	363 896	352 411	371 107	410 157	431 565	440 341	464 358	451 929	...
Vessels cleared Navires sortis	277 520	281 709	303 707	305 250	318 435	327 092	302 344	332 445	310 973	...
Uruguay Uruguay										
Vessels entered Navires entrés	4 036	5 297	5 414	5 505	5 844	5 262	4 386	5 257	...	...
Vessels cleared Navires sortis	16 059	20 266	24 608	24 975	26 844	24 499	21 596	19 587	...	...
Venezuela Venezuela										
Vessels entered Navires entrés	22 087	21 657	21 009	...	...	...	...	...	...	...
Vessels cleared Navires sortis	17 211	12 045	8 461	...	...	...	...	...	...	...

61

International maritime transport
Vessels entered and cleared: thousand net registered tons *[cont.]*

Transports maritimes internationaux
Navires entrés et sortis : milliers de tonneaux de jauge nette *[suite]*

Country or area Pays ou zone	1993	1994	1995	1996	1997	1998	1999	2000	2001	2002
Yemen Yémen										
Vessels entered Navires entrés	12 459	9 323	10 353	10 477	10 268	11 210	...	...	...	...
Vessels cleared Navires sortis	12 243	10 386	10 524	4 562	5 958	9 851	...	...	...	...

Source:
United Nations Statistics Division, New York, transport statistics database.

Source:
Organisation des Nations Unies, Division de statistique, New York, la base de données pour les statistiques des transports.

1	Gross registered tons.	1	Tonneaux de jauge brute.
2	Data refer to fiscal years ending 30 June.	2	Les données se réfèrent aux exercices budgétaires finissant le 30 juin.
3	Including vessels in ballast.	3	Y compris navires sur lest.
4	Comprising Buenos Aires, Rosario, Lib. Gral. San Martin, Quequén and La Plata.	4	Buenos Aires, Rosario, Lib. Gral, San Martín, Quequén et La Plata.
5	Buenos Aires only.	5	Buenos Aires seulement.
6	Data refer to fiscal years beginning 1 July.	6	Les données se réfèrent aux exercices budgétaires commençant le 1er juillet.
7	Sihanoukville Port and Phnom Penh Port.	7	Port de Sihanoukville et Port de Phnom Penh.
8	All entrances counted.	8	Toutes entrées comprises.
9	Including Great Lakes international traffic (Canada: also St. Lawrence).	9	Y compris trafic international des Grands Lacs (Canada: et du St. Laurent).
10	Including passenger vessels entered from and departed for Mainland China and Hong Kong SAR; gross registered tons.	10	Y compris les navires à passagers en provenance de Chine continentale et de la RAS de Hong Kong, ou en partance pour ces deux destinations; tonneaux de jauge brute.
11	Taxable volume in thousands of cubic metres.	11	Volume taxable en milliers de mètres cubes.
12	Including national maritime transport.	12	Y compris transports maritimes nationaux.
13	Beginning this year, gross registered tons.	13	De compter à cette année, tonneaux de jauge brute.
14	Port-au-Prince.	14	Port-au-Prince.
15	Data refer to fiscal years beginning 1 April.	15	Les données se réfèrent aux exercices budgétaires commençant le 1er avril.
16	Excluding minor and intermediate ports.	16	Non compris les ports petits et moyens.
17	Data for Sarawak include vessels in ballast and all entrances counted.	17	Les données pour Sarawak comprennent navires sur lest et toutes entrées comprises.
18	Including vessels cleared.	18	Y compris navires sortis.
19	Data cover only the first three quarters of the year.	19	Les données se réfèrent aux premières trois trimestres de l'année.
20	Gross tonnage for a sample of Norwegian ports.	20	Tonnage brute pour un échantillon de ports norvègiens.
21	Vessels entering more than once a day are counted as one port call.	21	Un navire entrant au port plus d'une fois par jour compte pour une seule relâche.
22	Vessels exceeding 75 gross registered tons.	22	Navires dépassant 75 tonneaux de jauge brute.
23	Inland waterway system.	23	Transport fluvial.
24	Break in series. Beginning this year, data are based on a survey of all ports in Sweden.	24	Discontinuité dans la série. A compter de cette année, les données sont basées sur une enquête menée auprès de tous les ports de Suède.
25	Beginning this year, including all passenger vessels and ferries.	25	De compter à cette année, y compris tous les navires à passagers et les transbordeurs.
26	Excluding traffic with United States Virgin Islands.	26	Non compris le trafic avec les Iles Vierges américaines.

62

Civil aviation
Passengers on scheduled services (thousands); Kilometers (millions)

Aviation civile
Passagers sur les services réguliers (milliers) ; Kilomètres (millions)

Country or area and traffic	Total Totale				International Internationaux				Région, pays ou zone et trafic
	1998	1999	2000	2001	1998	1999	2000	2001	
World									**Monde**
Kilometers flown	22 430	23 672	25 155	25 277	10 589	11 231	12 043	12 097	Kilomètres parcourus
Passengers carried	1 470 730	1 558 628	1 655 164	1 623 491	457 151	491 126	538 200	531 749	Passagers transportés
Passengers-km	2 627 056	2 793 003	3 014 211	2 929 426	1 511 533	1 619 369	1 778 860	1 715 562	Passagers-km
Total ton-km	348 480	369 881	400 740	385 385	231 389	247 284	271 482	259 477	Total tonnes-km
Africa [1]									**Afrique [1]**
Kilometers flown	532	574	595	595	408	445	456	451	Kilomètres parcourus
Passengers carried	29 076	31 195	32 057	30 933	16 062	17 617	18 420	18 108	Passagers transportés
Passengers-km	55 736	62 223	66 637	66 548	47 448	53 226	57 204	57 741	Passagers-km
Total ton-km	6 830	7 598	8 278	8 236	6 031	6 719	7 331	7 337	Total tonnes-km
Algeria									**Algérie**
Kilometers flown	31	32	34	42	16	21	19	25	Kilomètres parcourus
Passengers carried	3 382	2 937	2 997	3 419	1 436	1 663	1 863	2 076	Passagers transportés
Passengers-km	3 012	2 991	3 051	3 501	1 785	2 226	2 389	2 722	Passagers-km
Total ton-km	292	286	287	338	177	214	225	264	Total tonnes-km
Angola									**Angola**
Kilometers flown	8	7	6	5	5	4	5	3	Kilomètres parcourus
Passengers carried	553	531	235	193	125	120	142	101	Passagers transportés
Passengers-km	622	597	619	465	369	355	565	413	Passagers-km
Total ton-km	95	92	116	92	71	68	111	87	Total tonnes-km
Benin [2]									**Bénin [2]**
Kilometers flown	3	3	3	1	3	3	3	1	Kilomètres parcourus
Passengers carried	91	84	77	46	91	84	77	46	Passagers transportés
Passengers-km	258	235	216	130	258	235	216	130	Passagers-km
Total ton-km	38	36	32	19	38	36	32	19	Total tonnes-km
Botswana									**Botswana**
Kilometers flown	3	3	3	3	2	2	2	2	Kilomètres parcourus
Passengers carried	124	144	164	170	92	108	121	123	Passagers transportés
Passengers-km	57	67	74	77	42	50	53	55	Passagers-km
Total ton-km	5	6	7	7	4	5	5	5	Total tonnes-km
Burkina Faso [2]									**Burkina Faso [2]**
Kilometers flown	3	4	4	2	3	4	4	2	Kilomètres parcourus
Passengers carried	102	147	144	100	99	132	128	83	Passagers transportés
Passengers-km	264	269	253	158	263	264	247	154	Passagers-km
Total ton-km	39	39	35	22	39	39	35	21	Total tonnes-km
Burundi									**Burundi**
Kilometers flown	1	...	...	...	1	...	...	...	Kilomètres parcourus
Passengers carried	12	...	...	...	12	...	...	...	Passagers transportés
Passengers-km	8	...	...	...	8	...	...	...	Passagers-km
Total ton-km	1	...	...	...	1	...	...	...	Total tonnes-km
Cameroon									**Cameroun**
Kilometers flown	6	6	6	5	5	5	5	4	Kilomètres parcourus
Passengers carried	290	293	312	247	189	204	221	157	Passagers transportés
Passengers-km	568	597	646	489	492	533	580	423	Passagers-km
Total ton-km	108	106	115	91	100	99	108	84	Total tonnes-km
Cape Verde									**Cap-Vert**
Kilometers flown	5	5	6	4	3	4	4	3	Kilomètres parcourus
Passengers carried	236	252	264	243	87	114	120	87	Passagers transportés
Passengers-km	269	334	356	276	219	287	307	240	Passagers-km
Total ton-km	26	32	34	27	21	27	29	23	Total tonnes-km
Central African Rep. [2]									**Rép. centrafricaine [2]**
Kilometers flown	3	3	3	1	3	3	3	1	Kilomètres parcourus
Passengers carried	91	84	77	46	91	84	77	46	Passagers transportés
Passengers-km	258	235	216	130	258	235	216	130	Passagers-km
Total ton-km	38	36	32	19	38	36	32	19	Total tonnes-km
Chad [2]									**Tchad [2]**
Kilometers flown	3	3	3	1	3	3	3	1	Kilomètres parcourus
Passengers carried	98	84	77	46	91	84	77	46	Passagers transportés
Passengers-km	263	235	216	130	258	235	216	130	Passagers-km
Total ton-km	38	36	32	19	38	36	32	19	Total tonnes-km

62

Civil aviation

Passengers on scheduled services (thousands); Kilometers (millions)

Aviation civile

Passagers sur les services réguliers (milliers) ; Kilomètres (millions)

Country or area and traffic	Total Totale				International Internationaux				Région, pays ou zone et trafic
	1998	1999	2000	2001	1998	1999	2000	2001	
Congo [2]									**Congo** [2]
Kilometers flown	5	4	4	3	3	3	3	2	Kilomètres parcourus
Passengers carried	241	132	128	95	93	87	81	49	Passagers transportés
Passengers-km	321	263	245	157	261	240	222	134	Passagers-km
Total ton-km	44	39	34	22	38	36	32	19	Total tonnes-km
Côte d'Ivoire [2]									**Côte d'Ivoire** [2]
Kilometers flown	4	6	3	1	4	6	3	1	Kilomètres parcourus
Passengers carried	162	260	108	46	153	233	103	46	Passagers transportés
Passengers-km	318	381	242	130	313	366	240	130	Passagers-km
Total ton-km	44	50	34	19	43	48	34	19	Total tonnes-km
Egypt									**Egypte**
Kilometers flown	63	68	64	64	58	62	58	59	Kilomètres parcourus
Passengers carried	4 022	4 620	4 522	4 389	2 793	3 065	2 860	2 981	Passagers transportés
Passengers-km	8 036	9 074	8 828	8 893	7 470	8 355	8 065	8 241	Passagers-km
Total ton-km	989	1 097	1 085	1 051	938	1 032	1 015	991	Total tonnes-km
Équatorial Guinea									**Guinée équatoriale**
Kilometers flown	0	...	...	...	0	...	...	...	Kilomètres parcourus
Passengers carried	21	...	...	...	7	...	...	...	Passagers transportés
Passengers-km	4	...	...	...	1	...	...	...	Passagers-km
Total ton-km	0	...	...	...	0	...	...	...	Total tonnes-km
Ethiopia									**Ethiopie**
Kilometers flown	27	29	29	32	22	25	26	28	Kilomètres parcourus
Passengers carried	790	861	945	1 028	460	617	683	754	Passagers transportés
Passengers-km	1 881	2 458	2 753	2 953	1 743	2 358	2 641	2 835	Passagers-km
Total ton-km	318	371	383	402	304	362	373	392	Total tonnes-km
Gabon									**Gabon**
Kilometers flown	8	8	8	7	6	6	7	5	Kilomètres parcourus
Passengers carried	467	423	447	374	194	226	244	173	Passagers transportés
Passengers-km	829	782	847	637	748	712	774	565	Passagers-km
Total ton-km	111	124	135	107	103	117	128	100	Total tonnes-km
Ghana									**Ghana**
Kilometers flown	6	9	9	18	6	9	9	18	Kilomètres parcourus
Passengers carried	210	304	314	301	210	304	314	301	Passagers transportés
Passengers-km	705	1 097	1 204	1 233	705	1 097	1 204	1 233	Passagers-km
Total ton-km	97	151	162	157	97	151	162	157	Total tonnes-km
Guinea									**Guinée**
Kilometers flown	1	1	...	...	1	1	...	...	Kilomètres parcourus
Passengers carried	36	59	...	...	31	59	...	...	Passagers transportés
Passengers-km	55	94	...	...	50	94	...	...	Passagers-km
Total ton-km	6	10	...	...	5	10	...	...	Total tonnes-km
Guinea-Bissau									**Guinée-Bissau**
Kilometers flown	0	...	...	...	0	...	...	...	Kilomètres parcourus
Passengers carried	20	...	...	...	8	...	...	...	Passagers transportés
Passengers-km	10	...	...	...	6	...	...	...	Passagers-km
Total ton-km	1	...	...	...	1	...	...	...	Total tonnes-km
Kenya									**Kenya**
Kilometers flown	21	24	34	32	17	19	27	27	Kilomètres parcourus
Passengers carried	1 138	1 358	1 555	1 418	658	808	973	990	Passagers transportés
Passengers-km	2 091	2 513	3 271	3 706	1 883	2 286	3 040	3 522	Passagers-km
Total ton-km	243	292	377	427	223	271	355	410	Total tonnes-km
Lesotho									**Lesotho**
Kilometers flown	1	0	...	...	1	0	...	...	Kilomètres parcourus
Passengers carried	28	1	...	...	23	1	...	...	Passagers transportés
Passengers-km	9	0	...	...	8	0	...	...	Passagers-km
Total ton-km	1	0	...	...	1	0	...	...	Total tonnes-km
Libyan Arab Jamah.									**Jamah. arabe libyenne**
Kilometers flown	4	4	4	4	...	...	...	...	Kilomètres parcourus
Passengers carried	571	571	601	583	...	...	...	...	Passagers transportés
Passengers-km	377	377	409	409	...	...	...	...	Passagers-km
Total ton-km	27	27	33	33	...	...	...	...	Total tonnes-km

62

Civil aviation

Passengers on scheduled services (thousands); Kilometers (millions)

Aviation civile

Passagers sur les services réguliers (milliers) ; Kilomètres (millions)

Country or area and traffic	Total Totale 1998	1999	2000	2001	International Internationaux 1998	1999	2000	2001	Région, pays ou zone et trafic
Madagascar									**Madagascar**
Kilometers flown	9	12	14	12	7	7	9	7	Kilomètres parcourus
Passengers carried	318	635	667	566	145	168	183	146	Passagers transportés
Passengers-km	718	1 037	1 146	835	646	841	907	654	Passagers-km
Total ton-km	94	126	137	103	86	107	114	86	Total tonnes-km
Malawi									**Malawi**
Kilometers flown	3	2	3	3	2	1	2	2	Kilomètres parcourus
Passengers carried	158	112	116	113	79	63	64	66	Passagers transportés
Passengers-km	337	224	210	221	300	150	136	148	Passagers-km
Total ton-km	33	21	22	23	31	14	15	16	Total tonnes-km
Mali [2]									**Mali** [2]
Kilometers flown	3	3	3	1	3	3	3	1	Kilomètres parcourus
Passengers carried	91	84	77	46	91	84	77	46	Passagers transportés
Passengers-km	258	235	216	130	258	235	216	130	Passagers-km
Total ton-km	38	36	32	19	38	36	32	19	Total tonnes-km
Mauritania [2]									**Mauritanie** [2]
Kilometers flown	4	4	4	2	3	3	3	2	Kilomètres parcourus
Passengers carried	250	187	185	156	115	103	98	61	Passagers transportés
Passengers-km	340	290	275	174	283	255	238	147	Passagers-km
Total ton-km	46	41	37	23	40	38	34	21	Total tonnes-km
Mauritius									**Maurice**
Kilometers flown	24	29	29	30	23	28	27	29	Kilomètres parcourus
Passengers carried	810	831	949	1 002	743	756	865	913	Passagers transportés
Passengers-km	3 826	4 073	4 888	5 194	3 788	4 027	4 837	5 140	Passagers-km
Total ton-km	526	539	647	669	523	535	643	664	Total tonnes-km
Morocco									**Maroc**
Kilometers flown	56	63	64	63	51	59	60	59	Kilomètres parcourus
Passengers carried	3 012	3 392	3 671	3 681	2 265	2 587	2 800	2 766	Passagers transportés
Passengers-km	5 868	6 614	7 185	7 112	5 625	6 355	6 904	6 820	Passagers-km
Total ton-km	573	667	722	715	549	641	693	687	Total tonnes-km
Mozambique									**Mozambique**
Kilometers flown	4	5	6	7	2	2	3	3	Kilomètres parcourus
Passengers carried	201	235	260	264	73	87	93	85	Passagers transportés
Passengers-km	295	326	376	353	163	171	207	169	Passagers-km
Total ton-km	33	36	41	39	19	20	24	20	Total tonnes-km
Namibia									**Namibie**
Kilometers flown	9	7	8	9	7	5	6	6	Kilomètres parcourus
Passengers carried	229	201	247	215	200	165	212	179	Passagers transportés
Passengers-km	630	548	740	754	614	528	720	734	Passagers-km
Total ton-km	59	49	151	151	57	47	149	149	Total tonnes-km
Niger [2]									**Niger** [2]
Kilometers flown	3	3	3	1	3	3	3	1	Kilomètres parcourus
Passengers carried	91	84	77	46	91	84	77	46	Passagers transportés
Passengers-km	258	235	216	130	258	235	216	130	Passagers-km
Total ton-km	38	36	32	19	38	36	32	19	Total tonnes-km
Nigeria									**Nigéria**
Kilometers flown	5	7	7	4	2	4	2	1	Kilomètres parcourus
Passengers carried	313	668	507	529	49	162	48	33	Passagers transportés
Passengers-km	245	560	565	402	122	370	63	25	Passagers-km
Total ton-km	32	82	57	37	18	61	8	3	Total tonnes-km
Sao Tome and Principe									**Sao Tomé-et-Principe**
Kilometers flown	0	0	0	0	0	0	0	0	Kilomètres parcourus
Passengers carried	24	34	35	35	15	20	21	21	Passagers transportés
Passengers-km	9	13	14	14	5	6	7	7	Passagers-km
Total ton-km	1	1	1	1	0	1	1	1	Total tonnes-km
Senegal [2]									**Sénégal** [2]
Kilometers flown	3	3	3	4	3	3	3	4	Kilomètres parcourus
Passengers carried	121	103	98	176	91	84	77	145	Passagers transportés
Passengers-km	267	241	222	319	258	235	216	304	Passagers-km
Total ton-km	39	37	32	116	38	36	32	109	Total tonnes-km

62

Civil aviation

Passengers on scheduled services (thousands); Kilometers (millions)

Aviation civile

Passagers sur les services réguliers (milliers) ; Kilomètres (millions)

Country or area and traffic	Total Totale				International Internationaux				Région, pays ou zone et trafic
	1998	1999	2000	2001	1998	1999	2000	2001	
Seychelles									**Seychelles**
Kilometers flown	9	9	9	9	8	8	8	9	Kilomètres parcourus
Passengers carried	369	347	394	420	113	110	127	153	Passagers transportés
Passengers-km	755	735	807	925	743	725	795	917	Passagers-km
Total ton-km	84	85	94	101	83	84	93	100	Total tonnes-km
Sierra Leone									**Sierra Leone**
Kilometers flown	...	0	1	1	...	0	1	1	Kilomètres parcourus
Passengers carried	...	19	19	14	...	19	19	14	Passagers transportés
Passengers-km	...	30	93	73	...	30	93	73	Passagers-km
Total ton-km	...	3	18	13	...	3	18	13	Total tonnes-km
South Africa									**Afrique du Sud**
Kilometers flown	128	144	151	167	75	84	87	92	Kilomètres parcourus
Passengers carried	6 480	7 374	8 001	7 948	1 913	2 189	2 483	2 693	Passagers transportés
Passengers-km	16 997	19 021	21 015	22 061	12 869	14 247	15 857	17 192	Passagers-km
Total ton-km	2 046	2 381	2 579	2 746	1 636	1 904	2 041	2 225	Total tonnes-km
Sudan									**Soudan**
Kilometers flown	6	7	6	6	4	4	5	5	Kilomètres parcourus
Passengers carried	499	390	414	415	311	245	265	270	Passagers transportés
Passengers-km	148	693	748	761	126	588	639	652	Passagers-km
Total ton-km	19	94	101	98	16	80	87	85	Total tonnes-km
Swaziland									**Swaziland**
Kilometers flown	1	1	2	...	1	1	2	...	Kilomètres parcourus
Passengers carried	41	12	90	...	41	12	90	...	Passagers transportés
Passengers-km	43	13	68	...	43	13	68	...	Passagers-km
Total ton-km	4	1	6	...	4	1	6	...	Total tonnes-km
Togo [2]									**Togo [2]**
Kilometers flown	3	3	3	1	3	3	3	1	Kilomètres parcourus
Passengers carried	91	84	77	46	91	84	77	46	Passagers transportés
Passengers-km	258	235	216	130	258	235	216	130	Passagers-km
Total ton-km	38	36	32	19	38	36	32	19	Total tonnes-km
Tunisia									**Tunisie**
Kilometers flown	27	27	27	26	27	27	27	26	Kilomètres parcourus
Passengers carried	1 888	1 923	1 908	1 926	1 888	1 923	1 908	1 926	Passagers transportés
Passengers-km	2 683	2 762	2 690	2 696	2 683	2 762	2 690	2 696	Passagers-km
Total ton-km	266	282	284	283	266	282	284	283	Total tonnes-km
Uganda									**Ouganda**
Kilometers flown	2	5	2	2	2	2	2	2	Kilomètres parcourus
Passengers carried	100	179	39	41	100	36	39	41	Passagers transportés
Passengers-km	110	356	215	235	110	198	215	235	Passagers-km
Total ton-km	11	54	40	42	11	37	40	42	Total tonnes-km
United Rep. of Tanzania									**Rép.-Unie de Tanzanie**
Kilometers flown	5	3	4	4	3	2	3	3	Kilomètres parcourus
Passengers carried	220	190	193	175	89	75	90	77	Passagers transportés
Passengers-km	236	176	198	181	171	115	146	134	Passagers-km
Total ton-km	25	18	21	21	18	12	15	15	Total tonnes-km
Zambia									**Zambie**
Kilometers flown	1	1	2	2	1	1	1	0	Kilomètres parcourus
Passengers carried	49	42	90	49	42	36	45	12	Passagers transportés
Passengers-km	44	34	51	16	42	32	38	5	Passagers-km
Total ton-km	4	3	5	1	4	3	4	0	Total tonnes-km
Zimbabwe									**Zimbabwe**
Kilometers flown	19	13	17	15	16	10	14	14	Kilomètres parcourus
Passengers carried	706	567	605	308	310	248	288	188	Passagers transportés
Passengers-km	955	918	771	723	791	788	653	674	Passagers-km
Total ton-km	234	114	228	224	221	102	217	219	Total tonnes-km
America, North [1]									**Amérique du Nord [1]**
Kilometers flown	**10 224**	**10 908**	**11 553**	**11 414**	**2 473**	**2 601**	**2 754**	**2 779**	**Kilomètres parcourus**
Passengers carried	**640 789**	**688 567**	**721 303**	**674 391**	**85 779**	**91 296**	**98 240**	**91 893**	**Passagers transportés**
Passengers-km	**1 086 197**	**1 154 217**	**1 226 291**	**1 158 788**	**339 436**	**361 495**	**387 991**	**364 771**	**Passagers-km**
Total ton-km	**130 124**	**137 802**	**147 429**	**138 072**	**49 173**	**52 481**	**57 021**	**54 267**	**Total tonnes-km**

62

Civil aviation

Passengers on scheduled services (thousands); Kilometers (millions)

Aviation civile

Passagers sur les services réguliers (milliers) ; Kilomètres (millions)

Country or area and traffic	Total Totale 1998	1999	2000	2001	International Internationaux 1998	1999	2000	2001	Région, pays ou zone et trafic
Antigua and Barbuda									**Antigua-et-Barbuda**
Kilometers flown	12	11	10	12	12	11	10	12	Kilomètres parcourus
Passengers carried	1 245	1 371	1 426	1 369	1 245	1 371	1 426	1 369	Passagers transportés
Passengers-km	251	276	298	304	251	276	298	304	Passagers-km
Total ton-km	23	26	28	30	23	26	28	30	Total tonnes-km
Bahamas									**Bahamas**
Kilometers flown	2	7	7	7	1	3	3	4	Kilomètres parcourus
Passengers carried	701	1 719	1 861	1 626	294	944	1 016	975	Passagers transportés
Passengers-km	140	366	415	391	76	244	280	286	Passagers-km
Total ton-km	13	42	47	48	7	28	32	35	Total tonnes-km
Canada									**Canada**
Kilometers flown	547	570	598	567	317	337	370	357	Kilomètres parcourus
Passengers carried	24 653	24 039	25 281	24 204	11 382	11 875	12 775	12 135	Passagers transportés
Passengers-km	63 801	65 323	69 985	68 804	42 071	43 728	47 408	46 436	Passagers-km
Total ton-km	7 751	7 929	8 293	7 979	5 402	5 599	5 882	5 624	Total tonnes-km
Costa Rica									**Costa Rica**
Kilometers flown	28	27	20	24	25	24	18	22	Kilomètres parcourus
Passengers carried	1 070	1 055	878	738	933	923	742	631	Passagers transportés
Passengers-km	2 004	2 145	2 358	2 152	1 983	2 112	2 334	2 143	Passagers-km
Total ton-km	289	245	252	179	287	242	250	178	Total tonnes-km
Cuba									**Cuba**
Kilometers flown	34	26	20	19	28	22	16	17	Kilomètres parcourus
Passengers carried	1 138	1 259	1 007	882	647	684	598	567	Passagers transportés
Passengers-km	4 791	3 712	2 964	3 171	4 470	3 463	2 769	3 019	Passagers-km
Total ton-km	524	421	335	361	497	392	312	340	Total tonnes-km
Dominican Republic									**Rép. dominicaine**
Kilometers flown	1	0	...	...	1	0	...	...	Kilomètres parcourus
Passengers carried	34	10	...	...	34	10	...	...	Passagers transportés
Passengers-km	16	5	...	...	16	5	...	...	Passagers-km
Total ton-km	1	0	...	...	1	0	...	...	Total tonnes-km
El Salvador									**El Salvador**
Kilometers flown	22	28	34	26	22	26	30	26	Kilomètres parcourus
Passengers carried	1 585	1 624	2 476	1 692	1 525	1 467	1 960	1 692	Passagers transportés
Passengers-km	2 292	5 091	3 020	2 907	2 284	5 025	2 829	2 907	Passagers-km
Total ton-km	253	502	302	308	252	496	284	308	Total tonnes-km
Guatemala									**Guatemala**
Kilometers flown	7	5	...	...	7	5	...	...	Kilomètres parcourus
Passengers carried	794	506	...	...	760	472	...	...	Passagers transportés
Passengers-km	480	342	...	...	469	331	...	...	Passagers-km
Total ton-km	50	33	...	...	49	32	...	...	Total tonnes-km
Jamaica									**Jamaïque**
Kilometers flown	23	35	32	46	23	35	32	46	Kilomètres parcourus
Passengers carried	1 454	1 670	1 922	1 946	1 454	1 670	1 922	1 946	Passagers transportés
Passengers-km	2 961	3 495	4 087	4 412	2 961	3 495	4 087	4 412	Passagers-km
Total ton-km	293	377	400	471	293	377	400	471	Total tonnes-km
Mexico									**Mexique**
Kilometers flown	360	368	359	363	176	179	160	157	Kilomètres parcourus
Passengers carried	18 685	19 263	20 894	20 173	4 728	5 049	6 137	5 743	Passagers transportés
Passengers-km	25 976	27 847	30 299	29 621	11 703	12 939	15 059	14 511	Passagers-km
Total ton-km	2 566	2 742	3 061	3 029	1 241	1 377	1 635	1 606	Total tonnes-km
Nicaragua									**Nicaragua**
Kilometers flown	1	1	1	...	1	1	1	...	Kilomètres parcourus
Passengers carried	52	59	61	...	52	59	61	...	Passagers transportés
Passengers-km	93	67	72	...	93	67	72	...	Passagers-km
Total ton-km	10	7	7	...	10	7	7	...	Total tonnes-km
Panama									**Panama**
Kilometers flown	21	24	34	40	21	24	34	40	Kilomètres parcourus
Passengers carried	856	933	1 117	1 115	856	933	1 117	1 115	Passagers transportés
Passengers-km	1 373	1 697	2 604	3 004	1 373	1 697	2 604	3 004	Passagers-km
Total ton-km	174	215	312	317	174	215	312	317	Total tonnes-km

62

Civil aviation

Passengers on scheduled services (thousands); Kilometers (millions)

Aviation civile

Passagers sur les services réguliers (milliers) ; Kilomètres (millions)

Country or area and traffic	Total Totale				International Internationaux				Région, pays ou zone et trafic
	1998	1999	2000	2001	1998	1999	2000	2001	
Trinidad and Tobago									**Trinité-et-Tobago**
Kilometers flown	21	25	28	29	21	24	28	29	Kilomètres parcourus
Passengers carried	880	1 112	1 254	1 388	880	1 046	1 126	1 079	Passagers transportés
Passengers-km	2 567	2 720	2 765	2 723	2 567	2 715	2 754	2 697	Passagers-km
Total ton-km	315	309	300	288	315	309	299	285	Total tonnes-km
United States									**Etats-Unis**
Kilometers flown	9 134	9 759	10 386	10 268	1 809	1 888	2 030	2 057	Kilomètres parcourus
Passengers carried	586 402	632 440	661 461	618 149	60 126	63 644	68 037	63 793	Passagers transportés
Passengers-km	978 498	1 039 643	1 105 728	1 040 472	268 253	284 008	305 895	284 299	Passagers-km
Total ton-km	117 773	124 817	133 937	124 982	40 540	43 254	47 431	44 999	Total tonnes-km
America, South									**Amérique du Sud**
Kilometers flown	**1 099**	**1 088**	**1 049**	**1 050**	**445**	**426**	**412**	**401**	**Kilomètres parcourus**
Passengers carried	**63 745**	**62 391**	**64 647**	**67 124**	**13 731**	**13 523**	**12 992**	**12 821**	**Passagers transportés**
Passengers-km	**91 204**	**86 711**	**91 229**	**85 648**	**53 043**	**49 626**	**51 849**	**45 190**	**Passagers-km**
Total ton-km	**12 559**	**11 599**	**12 245**	**11 486**	**8 568**	**7 735**	**8 174**	**7 307**	**Total tonnes-km**
Argentina									**Argentine**
Kilometers flown	157	170	160	107	54	53	58	28	Kilomètres parcourus
Passengers carried	8 623	9 192	8 904	5 809	2 108	1 980	2 305	1 032	Passagers transportés
Passengers-km	14 379	14 024	15 535	8 330	8 447	7 621	9 287	3 580	Passagers-km
Total ton-km	1 597	1 559	1 751	883	1 055	970	1 171	445	Total tonnes-km
Bolivia									**Bolivie**
Kilometers flown	28	21	20	18	19	15	15	13	Kilomètres parcourus
Passengers carried	2 115	1 873	1 757	1 557	773	659	657	550	Passagers transportés
Passengers-km	2 179	1 851	1 809	1 567	1 629	1 398	1 403	1 201	Passagers-km
Total ton-km	273	186	181	159	218	147	143	124	Total tonnes-km
Brazil									**Brésil**
Kilometers flown	535	530	519	547	173	156	151	155	Kilomètres parcourus
Passengers carried	29 137	28 273	31 819	34 286	4 648	3 980	3 903	3 819	Passagers transportés
Passengers-km	46 978	42 224	45 812	46 603	25 479	21 504	22 812	21 502	Passagers-km
Total ton-km	5 980	5 333	5 712	5 726	3 627	3 088	3 246	3 050	Total tonnes-km
Chile									**Chili**
Kilometers flown	117	107	108	110	63	65	67	73	Kilomètres parcourus
Passengers carried	5 095	5 188	5 175	5 316	1 768	2 056	2 059	2 200	Passagers transportés
Passengers-km	9 679	10 650	10 859	11 520	6 300	7 438	7 678	8 308	Passagers-km
Total ton-km	2 124	2 107	2 296	2 329	1 768	1 766	1 955	1 981	Total tonnes-km
Colombia									**Colombie**
Kilometers flown	125	120	120	122	57	60	65	65	Kilomètres parcourus
Passengers carried	9 051	8 665	8 570	9 604	1 320	1 553	1 773	2 090	Passagers transportés
Passengers-km	7 350	7 848	8 662	8 657	3 835	4 659	5 366	5 082	Passagers-km
Total ton-km	1 436	1 348	1 384	1 386	1 061	985	1 046	1 031	Total tonnes-km
Ecuador									**Equateur**
Kilometers flown	23	16	12	8	18	11	6	3	Kilomètres parcourus
Passengers carried	2 048	1 387	1 319	1 285	674	351	163	87	Passagers transportés
Passengers-km	2 282	1 388	1 042	715	1 788	976	544	188	Passagers-km
Total ton-km	286	157	108	70	239	118	62	21	Total tonnes-km
Guyana									**Guyana**
Kilometers flown	3	2	2	1	2	2	2	1	Kilomètres parcourus
Passengers carried	126	70	73	48	59	70	73	48	Passagers transportés
Passengers-km	249	277	299	175	231	277	299	175	Passagers-km
Total ton-km	26	28	30	17	24	28	30	17	Total tonnes-km
Paraguay									**Paraguay**
Kilometers flown	5	5	5	6	5	4	4	5	Kilomètres parcourus
Passengers carried	222	232	266	281	222	217	249	266	Passagers transportés
Passengers-km	247	244	270	294	247	239	266	290	Passagers-km
Total ton-km	22	22	24	26	22	21	24	26	Total tonnes-km
Peru									**Pérou**
Kilometers flown	41	27	24	38	18	6	8	21	Kilomètres parcourus
Passengers carried	2 774	1 900	1 595	1 844	508	150	145	442	Passagers transportés
Passengers-km	3 014	1 590	1 555	2 627	1 526	450	548	1 605	Passagers-km
Total ton-km	286	149	196	357	144	42	95	254	Total tonnes-km

62

Civil aviation

Passengers on scheduled services (thousands); Kilometers (millions)

Aviation civile

Passagers sur les services réguliers (milliers) ; Kilomètres (millions)

Country or area and traffic	Total Totale 1998	1999	2000	2001	International Internationaux 1998	1999	2000	2001	Région, pays ou zone et trafic
Suriname									**Suriname**
Kilometers flown	7	6	6	5	7	6	5	5	Kilomètres parcourus
Passengers carried	278	194	233	203	274	190	227	198	Passagers transportés
Passengers-km	1 072	726	1 151	898	1 071	725	1 149	896	Passagers-km
Total ton-km	127	91	130	103	127	91	129	103	Total tonnes-km
Uruguay									**Uruguay**
Kilometers flown	7	8	8	7	7	8	8	7	Kilomètres parcourus
Passengers carried	557	728	642	559	557	728	642	559	Passagers transportés
Passengers-km	642	839	747	582	642	839	747	582	Passagers-km
Total ton-km	70	94	82	65	70	94	82	65	Total tonnes-km
Venezuela									**Venezuela**
Kilometers flown	52	75	66	80	22	39	23	24	Kilomètres parcourus
Passengers carried	3 720	4 690	4 295	6 334	820	1 590	795	1 534	Passagers transportés
Passengers-km	3 133	5 050	3 487	3 681	1 848	3 500	1 750	1 781	Passagers-km
Total ton-km	332	526	350	364	213	383	190	190	Total tonnes-km
Asia[1]									**Asie**[1]
Kilometers flown	**4 189**	**4 321**	**4 627**	**4 862**	**2 593**	**2 729**	**2 959**	**2 998**	**Kilomètres parcourus**
Passengers carried	**336 963**	**351 455**	**379 120**	**392 265**	**116 720**	**127 479**	**143 253**	**143 124**	**Passagers transportés**
Passengers-km	**621 807**	**665 643**	**737 948**	**744 611**	**439 870**	**480 286**	**544 206**	**533 154**	**Passagers-km**
Total ton-km	**91 631**	**100 049**	**109 528**	**108 917**	**74 427**	**82 323**	**90 964**	**87 626**	**Total tonnes-km**
Afghanistan									**Afghanistan**
Kilometers flown	3	3	3	...	2	2	2	...	Kilomètres parcourus
Passengers carried	53	140	150	...	27	36	40	...	Passagers transportés
Passengers-km	88	129	143	...	72	90	101	...	Passagers-km
Total ton-km	24	19	21	...	22	15	17	...	Total tonnes-km
Armenia									**Arménie**
Kilometers flown	9	8	7	9	9	8	7	9	Kilomètres parcourus
Passengers carried	365	343	298	369	365	343	298	369	Passagers transportés
Passengers-km	765	639	572	706	765	639	572	706	Passagers-km
Total ton-km	80	70	61	81	80	70	61	81	Total tonnes-km
Azerbaijan									**Azerbaïdjan**
Kilometers flown	9	10	10	10	7	8	7	8	Kilomètres parcourus
Passengers carried	669	572	546	544	311	188	146	147	Passagers transportés
Passengers-km	843	614	503	511	632	390	272	282	Passagers-km
Total ton-km	169	113	93	112	145	90	70	89	Total tonnes-km
Bahrain[3]									**Bahreïn**[3]
Kilometers flown	19	21	28	28	19	21	28	28	Kilomètres parcourus
Passengers carried	1 207	1 307	1 382	1 250	1 207	1 307	1 382	1 250	Passagers transportés
Passengers-km	2 653	2 836	3 185	3 076	2 653	2 836	3 185	3 076	Passagers-km
Total ton-km	357	387	510	525	357	387	510	525	Total tonnes-km
Bangladesh									**Bangladesh**
Kilometers flown	20	21	25	27	19	20	23	26	Kilomètres parcourus
Passengers carried	1 162	1 215	1 331	1 450	855	892	969	1 110	Passagers transportés
Passengers-km	3 422	3 515	3 988	4 395	3 358	3 448	3 910	4 323	Passagers-km
Total ton-km	524	545	632	599	519	538	626	593	Total tonnes-km
Bhutan									**Bhoutan**
Kilometers flown	1	1	1	1	1	1	1	1	Kilomètres parcourus
Passengers carried	36	31	34	35	36	31	34	35	Passagers transportés
Passengers-km	49	41	47	47	49	41	47	47	Passagers-km
Total ton-km	4	4	4	4	4	4	4	4	Total tonnes-km
Brunei Darussalam									**Brunéi Darussalam**
Kilometers flown	35	25	25	26	35	25	25	26	Kilomètres parcourus
Passengers carried	877	808	864	1 008	877	808	864	1 008	Passagers transportés
Passengers-km	2 972	2 563	3 001	3 624	2 972	2 563	3 001	3 624	Passagers-km
Total ton-km	386	380	410	458	386	380	410	458	Total tonnes-km
China									**Chine**
Kilometers flown	730	784	854	1 017	127	138	153	165	Kilomètres parcourus
Passengers carried	53 481	55 853	61 892	72 661	5 086	6 005	6 417	6 604	Passagers transportés
Passengers-km	75 823	80 575	90 960	105 870	17 181	19 877	22 232	23 699	Passagers-km
Total ton-km	8 893	10 115	11 603	13 802	3 047	3 845	4 465	4 529	Total tonnes-km

62

Civil aviation

Passengers on scheduled services (thousands); Kilometers (millions)

Aviation civile

Passagers sur les services réguliers (milliers) ; Kilomètres (millions)

Country or area and traffic	Total Totale				International Internationaux				Région, pays ou zone et trafic
	1998	1999	2000	2001	1998	1999	2000	2001	
China, Hong Kong SAR									**Chine, Hong Kong RAS**
Kilometers flown	228	228	251	251	228	228	251	251	Kilomètres parcourus
Passengers carried	12 203	12 593	14 378	14 064	12 203	12 593	14 378	14 064	Passagers transportés
Passengers-km	42 964	43 907	50 248	48 268	42 964	43 907	50 248	48 268	Passagers-km
Total ton-km	8 274	8 759	9 933	9 693	8 274	8 759	9 933	9 693	Total tonnes-km
China, Macao SAR									**Chine, Macao RAS**
Kilometers flown	...	...	14	16	...	...	14	16	Kilomètres parcourus
Passengers carried	...	...	1 532	1 706	...	...	1 532	1 706	Passagers transportés
Passengers-km	...	...	1 730	1 908	...	...	1 730	1 908	Passagers-km
Total ton-km	...	...	195	213	...	...	195	213	Total tonnes-km
Cyprus									**Chypre**
Kilometers flown	20	20	21	22	20	20	21	22	Kilomètres parcourus
Passengers carried	1 346	1 337	1 396	1 503	1 346	1 337	1 396	1 503	Passagers transportés
Passengers-km	2 711	2 687	2 785	3 012	2 711	2 687	2 785	3 012	Passagers-km
Total ton-km	284	285	297	314	284	285	297	314	Total tonnes-km
Georgia									**Géorgie**
Kilometers flown	7	5	4	4	5	5	4	4	Kilomètres parcourus
Passengers carried	205	159	118	111	175	159	118	111	Passagers transportés
Passengers-km	409	307	230	235	340	307	230	235	Passagers-km
Total ton-km	45	30	23	23	34	30	23	23	Total tonnes-km
India									**Inde**
Kilometers flown	200	190	202	221	68	66	65	78	Kilomètres parcourus
Passengers carried	16 547	16 005	17 303	17 419	3 478	3 640	3 748	4 291	Passagers transportés
Passengers-km	24 722	24 215	25 905	25 708	12 947	13 100	13 798	13 888	Passagers-km
Total ton-km	2 776	2 734	2 903	2 854	1 607	1 624	1 693	1 682	Total tonnes-km
Indonesia									**Indonésie**
Kilometers flown	155	122	138	150	56	47	48	50	Kilomètres parcourus
Passengers carried	9 603	8 047	9 916	10 397	2 017	1 927	2 192	2 217	Passagers transportés
Passengers-km	15 974	14 544	16 764	16 169	9 770	9 329	10 706	9 793	Passagers-km
Total ton-km	1 826	1 560	1 865	1 978	1 173	1 022	1 252	1 269	Total tonnes-km
Iran (Islamic Rep. of)									**Iran (Rép. islamique d')**
Kilometers flown	68	63	66	73	22	23	25	30	Kilomètres parcourus
Passengers carried	9 303	8 277	8 722	9 533	1 404	1 388	1 775	1 916	Passagers transportés
Passengers-km	8 539	7 852	8 202	8 793	2 632	2 704	3 220	3 439	Passagers-km
Total ton-km	856	799	801	854	322	339	350	370	Total tonnes-km
Israel									**Israël**
Kilometers flown	79	86	92	83	72	80	82	74	Kilomètres parcourus
Passengers carried	3 699	4 033	4 443	3 989	2 741	2 984	3 102	2 695	Passagers transportés
Passengers-km	12 418	13 515	14 507	13 514	12 152	13 225	14 127	13 146	Passagers-km
Total ton-km	2 241	2 259	2 200	2 083	2 217	2 233	2 166	2 050	Total tonnes-km
Japan									**Japon**
Kilometers flown	828	841	878	853	426	440	471	447	Kilomètres parcourus
Passengers carried	101 701	105 960	109 123	107 823	16 388	18 057	20 571	18 487	Passagers transportés
Passengers-km	154 402	162 798	174 149	162 290	85 608	91 463	102 683	90 194	Passagers-km
Total ton-km	20 896	22 348	23 868	21 717	14 905	16 144	17 572	15 426	Total tonnes-km
Jordan									**Jordanie**
Kilometers flown	35	36	37	36	35	36	37	36	Kilomètres parcourus
Passengers carried	1 187	1 252	1 282	1 178	1 187	1 252	1 282	1 178	Passagers transportés
Passengers-km	4 065	4 195	4 207	3 848	4 065	4 195	4 207	3 848	Passagers-km
Total ton-km	596	579	591	530	596	579	591	530	Total tonnes-km
Kazakhstan									**Kazakhstan**
Kilometers flown	35	33	15	16	25	25	10	10	Kilomètres parcourus
Passengers carried	726	667	461	501	318	318	234	247	Passagers transportés
Passengers-km	1 533	1 477	1 208	1 268	1 149	1 149	916	945	Passagers-km
Total ton-km	162	156	133	137	123	123	104	105	Total tonnes-km
Korea, Dem. P. R.									**Corée, R. p. dém. de**
Kilometers flown	3	2	1	1	3	2	1	1	Kilomètres parcourus
Passengers carried	64	59	83	79	64	59	83	79	Passagers transportés
Passengers-km	192	178	37	33	192	178	37	33	Passagers-km
Total ton-km	19	18	5	5	19	18	5	5	Total tonnes-km

62

Civil aviation

Passengers on scheduled services (thousands); Kilometers (millions)

Aviation civile

Passagers sur les services réguliers (milliers) ; Kilomètres (millions)

Country or area and traffic	Total Totale				International Internationaux				Région, pays ou zone et trafic
	1998	1999	2000	2001	1998	1999	2000	2001	
Korea, Republic of									**Corée, République de**
Kilometers flown	319	336	367	361	266	285	309	304	Kilomètres parcourus
Passengers carried	27 109	31 319	34 331	33 710	8 973	10 646	12 137	12 215	Passagers transportés
Passengers-km	47 711	56 116	62 837	60 143	40 982	48 806	54 926	52 403	Passagers-km
Total ton-km	11 605	13 424	13 302	12 265	10 929	12 692	12 526	11 503	Total tonnes-km
Kuwait									**Koweït**
Kilometers flown	45	36	37	37	45	36	37	37	Kilomètres parcourus
Passengers carried	2 190	2 130	2 113	2 085	2 190	2 130	2 113	2 085	Passagers transportés
Passengers-km	6 207	6 158	6 134	6 010	6 207	6 158	6 134	6 010	Passagers-km
Total ton-km	932	829	805	777	932	829	805	777	Total tonnes-km
Kyrgyzstan									**Kirghizistan**
Kilometers flown	9	9	6	6	6	6	5	5	Kilomètres parcourus
Passengers carried	427	312	241	192	143	136	114	102	Passagers transportés
Passengers-km	519	532	423	363	407	463	373	326	Passagers-km
Total ton-km	60	56	44	39	50	50	39	35	Total tonnes-km
Lao People's Dem. Rep.									**Rép. dém. pop. lao**
Kilometers flown	1	2	2	2	1	1	1	1	Kilomètres parcourus
Passengers carried	124	197	211	211	31	54	61	61	Passagers transportés
Passengers-km	48	78	85	86	20	34	38	38	Passagers-km
Total ton-km	5	8	9	9	2	4	4	4	Total tonnes-km
Lebanon									**Liban**
Kilometers flown	20	20	20	20	20	20	20	20	Kilomètres parcourus
Passengers carried	716	719	806	816	716	719	806	816	Passagers transportés
Passengers-km	1 504	1 288	1 484	1 658	1 504	1 288	1 484	1 658	Passagers-km
Total ton-km	247	222	223	229	247	222	223	229	Total tonnes-km
Malaysia									**Malaisie**
Kilometers flown	189	207	220	217	140	158	171	169	Kilomètres parcourus
Passengers carried	13 654	14 985	16 561	16 107	6 105	6 770	7 390	7 197	Passagers transportés
Passengers-km	29 372	33 708	37 939	35 658	25 392	29 253	32 905	31 011	Passagers-km
Total ton-km	3 777	4 431	5 346	5 233	3 407	4 014	4 875	4 807	Total tonnes-km
Maldives									**Maldives**
Kilometers flown	4	5	6	7	3	4	4	4	Kilomètres parcourus
Passengers carried	247	344	315	367	192	273	222	226	Passagers transportés
Passengers-km	355	501	425	447	331	470	385	385	Passagers-km
Total ton-km	42	62	54	56	40	59	50	49	Total tonnes-km
Mongolia									**Mongolie**
Kilometers flown	8	6	6	6	4	3	3	4	Kilomètres parcourus
Passengers carried	255	225	254	255	95	98	118	136	Passagers transportés
Passengers-km	469	436	520	574	331	325	401	470	Passagers-km
Total ton-km	50	46	51	52	35	35	41	43	Total tonnes-km
Myanmar									**Myanmar**
Kilometers flown	8	9	...	...	5	5	...	...	Kilomètres parcourus
Passengers carried	522	537	...	...	148	145	...	...	Passagers transportés
Passengers-km	345	355	...	...	156	152	...	...	Passagers-km
Total ton-km	40	40	...	...	25	24	...	...	Total tonnes-km
Nepal									**Népal**
Kilometers flown	11	9	10	9	7	8	9	8	Kilomètres parcourus
Passengers carried	754	583	643	641	385	452	506	517	Passagers transportés
Passengers-km	908	1 023	1 155	1 153	855	1 004	1 135	1 135	Passagers-km
Total ton-km	99	108	121	119	94	106	119	117	Total tonnes-km
Oman [3]									**Oman** [3]
Kilometers flown	27	30	32	33	26	29	31	31	Kilomètres parcourus
Passengers carried	1 768	1 933	2 118	1 980	1 590	1 768	1 942	1 817	Passagers transportés
Passengers-km	3 405	3 435	4 148	4 026	3 257	3 295	4 002	3 889	Passagers-km
Total ton-km	415	437	549	518	404	427	533	502	Total tonnes-km
Pakistan									**Pakistan**
Kilometers flown	75	73	76	71	53	52	57	54	Kilomètres parcourus
Passengers carried	5 414	4 972	5 294	6 012	2 568	2 443	2 785	2 690	Passagers transportés
Passengers-km	10 972	10 466	12 054	11 649	8 922	8 550	10 103	9 854	Passagers-km
Total ton-km	1 408	1 293	1 452	1 438	1 186	1 085	1 243	1 241	Total tonnes-km

62

Civil aviation

Passengers on scheduled services (thousands); Kilometers (millions)

Aviation civile

Passagers sur les services réguliers (milliers) ; Kilomètres (millions)

Country or area and traffic	Total Totale				International Internationaux				Région, pays ou zone et trafic
	1998	1999	2000	2001	1998	1999	2000	2001	
Philippines									**Philippines**
Kilometers flown	40	53	67	69	28	37	50	52	Kilomètres parcourus
Passengers carried	3 944	5 004	5 756	5 652	1 306	1 922	2 343	2 501	Passagers transportés
Passengers-km	7 503	10 292	13 063	13 454	5 918	8 405	10 958	11 483	Passagers-km
Total ton-km	925	1 303	1 661	1 666	785	1 112	1 438	1 457	Total tonnes-km
Qatar[3]									**Qatar[3]**
Kilometers flown	19	21	48	50	19	21	48	50	Kilomètres parcourus
Passengers carried	1 207	1 307	2 673	2 778	1 207	1 307	2 673	2 778	Passagers transportés
Passengers-km	2 653	2 836	6 042	6 510	2 653	2 836	6 042	6 510	Passagers-km
Total ton-km	357	387	823	876	357	387	823	876	Total tonnes-km
Saudi Arabia									**Arabie saoudite**
Kilometers flown	120	128	133	126	71	76	79	73	Kilomètres parcourus
Passengers carried	11 816	12 328	12 566	12 836	3 895	4 074	4 246	4 218	Passagers transportés
Passengers-km	18 820	19 618	20 229	20 217	12 875	13 357	13 807	13 495	Passagers-km
Total ton-km	2 645	2 783	2 836	2 633	2 030	2 138	2 173	1 945	Total tonnes-km
Singapore									**Singapour**
Kilometers flown	293	326	346	350	293	326	346	350	Kilomètres parcourus
Passengers carried	13 316	15 283	16 704	16 374	13 316	15 283	16 704	16 374	Passagers transportés
Passengers-km	58 174	65 471	71 786	70 232	58 174	65 471	71 786	70 232	Passagers-km
Total ton-km	10 381	11 824	12 986	12 595	10 381	11 824	12 986	12 595	Total tonnes-km
Sri Lanka									**Sri Lanka**
Kilometers flown	23	28	47	34	23	28	47	34	Kilomètres parcourus
Passengers carried	1 213	1 422	1 756	1 719	1 213	1 422	1 756	1 719	Passagers transportés
Passengers-km	4 136	5 156	6 840	6 641	4 136	5 156	6 840	6 641	Passagers-km
Total ton-km	553	669	1 125	822	553	669	1 125	822	Total tonnes-km
Syrian Arab Republic									**Rép. arabe syrienne**
Kilometers flown	13	12	15	15	13	12	14	14	Kilomètres parcourus
Passengers carried	665	668	750	761	643	581	640	647	Passagers transportés
Passengers-km	1 410	1 287	1 422	1 465	1 398	1 259	1 381	1 422	Passagers-km
Total ton-km	140	134	149	153	139	131	145	149	Total tonnes-km
Tajikistan									**Tadjikistan**
Kilometers flown	5	4	4	6	3	3	4	5	Kilomètres parcourus
Passengers carried	217	156	168	274	105	79	99	202	Passagers transportés
Passengers-km	322	229	286	573	275	197	257	542	Passagers-km
Total ton-km	32	23	29	54	28	20	26	51	Total tonnes-km
Thailand									**Thaïlande**
Kilometers flown	158	163	172	182	136	142	147	158	Kilomètres parcourus
Passengers carried	15 015	15 950	17 392	17 662	9 147	10 100	11 054	11 343	Passagers transportés
Passengers-km	34 340	38 345	42 236	44 142	31 049	35 057	38 676	40 584	Passagers-km
Total ton-km	4 682	5 184	5 571	5 702	4 355	4 854	5 215	5 345	Total tonnes-km
Turkey									**Turquie**
Kilometers flown	123	134	142	143	90	98	106	108	Kilomètres parcourus
Passengers carried	10 132	10 097	11 513	10 604	3 988	4 065	5 075	4 990	Passagers transportés
Passengers-km	13 037	13 350	16 492	16 058	9 792	10 002	12 938	12 907	Passagers-km
Total ton-km	1 371	1 514	1 865	1 996	1 092	1 223	1 555	1 679	Total tonnes-km
Turkmenistan									**Turkménistan**
Kilometers flown	11	9	20	22	6	9	10	11	Kilomètres parcourus
Passengers carried	890	220	1 284	1 407	250	220	315	345	Passagers transportés
Passengers-km	832	640	1 466	1 608	511	640	1 007	1 104	Passagers-km
Total ton-km	79	74	144	156	49	74	102	110	Total tonnes-km
United Arab Emirates[3]									**Emirats arabes unis[3]**
Kilometers flown	94	106	123	136	94	106	123	136	Kilomètres parcourus
Passengers carried	5 264	5 848	6 893	7 676	5 264	5 848	6 893	7 676	Passagers transportés
Passengers-km	15 633	18 154	22 691	26 202	15 633	18 154	22 691	26 202	Passagers-km
Total ton-km	2 403	2 950	3 649	4 148	2 403	2 950	3 649	4 148	Total tonnes-km
Uzbekistan									**Ouzbékistan**
Kilometers flown	33	37	39	57	23	27	30	45	Kilomètres parcourus
Passengers carried	1 401	1 658	1 745	2 256	673	878	950	1 379	Passagers transportés
Passengers-km	2 609	3 328	3 732	5 268	2 258	2 952	3 332	4 806	Passagers-km
Total ton-km	284	370	417	580	252	335	380	538	Total tonnes-km

62

Civil aviation

Passengers on scheduled services (thousands); Kilometers (millions)

Aviation civile

Passagers sur les services réguliers (milliers) ; Kilomètres (millions)

Country or area and traffic	Total Totale 1998	1999	2000	2001	International Internationaux 1998	1999	2000	2001	Région, pays ou zone et trafic
Viet Nam									**Viet Nam**
Kilometers flown	33	31	34	40	20	18	21	27	Kilomètres parcourus
Passengers carried	2 373	2 600	2 878	3 427	899	994	1 165	1 472	Passagers transportés
Passengers-km	3 644	3 831	4 499	5 621	2 371	2 523	3 099	4 083	Passagers-km
Total ton-km	426	445	524	645	285	303	375	479	Total tonnes-km
Yemen									**Yémen**
Kilometers flown	12	15	16	18	11	13	15	17	Kilomètres parcourus
Passengers carried	765	731	842	841	462	480	585	601	Passagers transportés
Passengers-km	1 104	1 031	1 588	1 580	1 017	960	1 498	1 497	Passagers-km
Total ton-km	120	114	179	174	111	107	170	166	Total tonnes-km
Europe [1]									**Europe [1]**
Kilometers flown	**5 629**	**6 045**	**6 482**	**6 512**	**4 310**	**4 679**	**5 033**	**5 069**	**Kilomètres parcourus**
Passengers carried	**356 166**	**381 397**	**409 735**	**408 675**	**212 517**	**229 568**	**251 520**	**251 317**	**Passagers transportés**
Passengers-km	**669 007**	**720 219**	**777 230**	**756 247**	**560 344**	**603 478**	**656 321**	**633 100**	**Passagers-km**
Total ton-km	**94 522**	**99 950**	**109 339**	**104 713**	**83 633**	**88 458**	**97 401**	**92 635**	**Total tonnes-km**
Albania									**Albanie**
Kilometers flown	0	0	3	2	0	0	3	2	Kilomètres parcourus
Passengers carried	21	20	137	146	21	20	137	146	Passagers transportés
Passengers-km	7	7	101	93	7	7	101	93	Passagers-km
Total ton-km	1	1	9	8	1	1	9	8	Total tonnes-km
Austria									**Autriche**
Kilometers flown	126	131	139	134	121	127	135	130	Kilomètres parcourus
Passengers carried	5 880	6 057	6 642	6 550	5 510	5 694	6 261	6 188	Passagers transportés
Passengers-km	11 923	13 380	14 232	13 875	11 814	13 271	14 121	13 770	Passagers-km
Total ton-km	1 411	1 694	1 885	1 786	1 400	1 683	1 874	1 776	Total tonnes-km
Belarus									**Bélarus**
Kilometers flown	9	8	7	7	9	8	7	7	Kilomètres parcourus
Passengers carried	226	212	211	222	226	212	211	222	Passagers transportés
Passengers-km	397	338	317	339	397	338	317	339	Passagers-km
Total ton-km	40	33	31	33	40	33	31	33	Total tonnes-km
Belgium									**Belgique**
Kilometers flown	197	219	216	186	197	219	216	186	Kilomètres parcourus
Passengers carried	8 748	9 965	10 738	8 489	8 748	9 965	10 738	8 489	Passagers transportés
Passengers-km	15 338	17 692	19 379	15 320	15 338	17 692	19 379	15 320	Passagers-km
Total ton-km	1 853	2 128	2 921	2 356	1 853	2 128	2 921	2 356	Total tonnes-km
Bosnia and Herzegovina									**Bosnie-Herzégovine**
Kilometers flown	1	1	2	1	1	1	2	1	Kilomètres parcourus
Passengers carried	50	60	69	65	50	60	69	65	Passagers transportés
Passengers-km	40	42	48	44	40	42	48	44	Passagers-km
Total ton-km	5	5	6	6	5	5	6	6	Total tonnes-km
Bulgaria									**Bulgarie**
Kilometers flown	22	20	14	6	21	18	12	5	Kilomètres parcourus
Passengers carried	828	735	535	234	750	650	466	185	Passagers transportés
Passengers-km	2 026	1 512	834	362	1 992	1 478	804	342	Passagers-km
Total ton-km	214	149	70	31	211	146	68	29	Total tonnes-km
Croatia									**Croatie**
Kilometers flown	10	10	10	11	8	8	9	9	Kilomètres parcourus
Passengers carried	828	833	929	1 063	465	503	583	688	Passagers transportés
Passengers-km	544	560	644	736	436	460	538	622	Passagers-km
Total ton-km	52	53	61	70	42	44	51	59	Total tonnes-km
Czech Republic									**République tchèque**
Kilometers flown	32	36	39	42	32	36	39	41	Kilomètres parcourus
Passengers carried	1 606	1 853	2 229	2 566	1 606	1 853	2 204	2 523	Passagers transportés
Passengers-km	2 637	2 870	3 313	3 576	2 637	2 870	3 306	3 564	Passagers-km
Total ton-km	264	286	333	351	264	286	332	350	Total tonnes-km
Denmark [4]									**Danemark [4]**
Kilometers flown	81	82	85	92	69	72	76	83	Kilomètres parcourus
Passengers carried	5 947	5 971	5 923	6 382	3 976	4 249	4 305	4 845	Passagers transportés
Passengers-km	5 658	5 883	6 128	6 952	4 990	5 300	5 543	6 380	Passagers-km
Total ton-km	725	769	810	876	657	708	747	814	Total tonnes-km

62

Civil aviation

Passengers on scheduled services (thousands); Kilometers (millions)

Aviation civile

Passagers sur les services réguliers (milliers) ; Kilomètres (millions)

Country or area and traffic	Total Totale 1998	1999	2000	2001	International Internationaux 1998	1999	2000	2001	Région, pays ou zone et trafic
Estonia									**Estonie**
Kilometers flown	6	7	6	6	6	7	6	6	Kilomètres parcourus
Passengers carried	297	302	278	277	294	300	275	275	Passagers transportés
Passengers-km	177	228	235	246	177	228	235	246	Passagers-km
Total ton-km	17	22	23	24	17	22	23	24	Total tonnes-km
Finland									**Finlande**
Kilometers flown	95	81	92	95	73	60	70	74	Kilomètres parcourus
Passengers carried	6 771	6 050	6 427	6 698	3 986	3 391	3 622	3 960	Passagers transportés
Passengers-km	10 714	7 802	7 556	8 195	9 467	6 592	6 270	6 923	Passagers-km
Total ton-km	1 250	967	984	920	1 140	861	871	808	Total tonnes-km
France [5]									**France** [5]
Kilometers flown	726	819	961	888	486	564	643	630	Kilomètres parcourus
Passengers carried	43 826	48 693	52 581	49 008	18 494	21 437	24 103	23 549	Passagers transportés
Passengers-km	90 225	101 449	113 438	112 308	59 584	67 462	75 250	75 804	Passagers-km
Total ton-km	14 033	14 279	15 639	15 126	10 784	10 909	11 871	11 593	Total tonnes-km
Germany									**Allemagne**
Kilometers flown	736	788	850	861	625	680	736	738	Kilomètres parcourus
Passengers carried	49 417	54 247	58 679	56 389	31 281	34 963	38 568	37 251	Passagers transportés
Passengers-km	90 393	104 602	114 124	111 303	82 922	96 402	105 552	103 102	Passagers-km
Total ton-km	15 301	16 950	18 495	18 004	14 522	16 108	17 619	17 161	Total tonnes-km
Greece									**Grèce**
Kilometers flown	68	75	90	95	53	54	70	68	Kilomètres parcourus
Passengers carried	6 403	6 267	7 937	8 430	2 621	2 630	3 384	3 320	Passagers transportés
Passengers-km	8 561	8 306	9 841	9 801	7 455	7 234	8 504	8 212	Passagers-km
Total ton-km	936	899	1 067	1 029	829	796	939	879	Total tonnes-km
Hungary									**Hongrie**
Kilometers flown	35	39	42	39	35	39	42	39	Kilomètres parcourus
Passengers carried	1 749	1 944	2 198	2 075	1 749	1 944	2 198	2 075	Passagers transportés
Passengers-km	2 510	2 861	3 573	3 146	2 510	2 861	3 573	3 146	Passagers-km
Total ton-km	267	301	377	324	267	301	377	324	Total tonnes-km
Iceland									**Islande**
Kilometers flown	33	35	34	32	31	35	34	32	Kilomètres parcourus
Passengers carried	1 593	1 350	1 432	1 358	1 298	1 350	1 432	1 358	Passagers transportés
Passengers-km	3 774	4 096	3 937	3 714	3 712	4 096	3 937	3 714	Passagers-km
Total ton-km	426	458	491	475	420	458	491	475	Total tonnes-km
Ireland									**Irlande**
Kilometers flown	78	90	106	119	77	88	104	118	Kilomètres parcourus
Passengers carried	10 401	11 949	13 983	15 451	9 917	11 398	13 431	15 093	Passagers transportés
Passengers-km	8 510	11 026	13 664	13 917	8 442	10 953	13 584	13 871	Passagers-km
Total ton-km	889	1 121	1 396	1 458	883	1 115	1 389	1 454	Total tonnes-km
Italy									**Italie**
Kilometers flown	344	368	392	393	239	254	274	270	Kilomètres parcourus
Passengers carried	28 037	28 049	30 418	31 031	11 113	11 092	12 246	12 153	Passagers transportés
Passengers-km	38 122	39 519	44 389	40 950	28 889	29 951	34 271	30 706	Passagers-km
Total ton-km	5 261	5 526	6 136	5 568	4 338	4 586	5 147	4 574	Total tonnes-km
Latvia									**Lettonie**
Kilometers flown	6	5	7	6	6	5	7	6	Kilomètres parcourus
Passengers carried	222	199	278	255	222	199	278	255	Passagers transportés
Passengers-km	174	132	236	180	174	132	236	180	Passagers-km
Total ton-km	16	12	22	17	16	12	22	17	Total tonnes-km
Lithuania									**Lituanie**
Kilometers flown	10	11	10	10	10	11	10	10	Kilomètres parcourus
Passengers carried	259	250	284	304	259	249	284	304	Passagers transportés
Passengers-km	307	272	322	347	307	272	322	347	Passagers-km
Total ton-km	31	27	31	33	31	27	31	33	Total tonnes-km
Luxembourg									**Luxembourg**
Kilometers flown	43	57	61	66	43	57	61	66	Kilomètres parcourus
Passengers carried	701	843	871	886	701	843	871	886	Passagers transportés
Passengers-km	454	738	557	586	454	738	557	586	Passagers-km
Total ton-km	2 287	2 573	3 573	3 821	2 287	2 573	3 573	3 821	Total tonnes-km

62

Civil aviation

Passengers on scheduled services (thousands); Kilometers (millions)

Aviation civile

Passagers sur les services réguliers (milliers) ; Kilomètres (millions)

Country or area and traffic	Total Totale				International Internationaux				Région, pays ou zone et trafic
	1998	1999	2000	2001	1998	1999	2000	2001	
Malta									**Malte**
Kilometers flown	20	24	26	25	20	24	26	25	Kilomètres parcourus
Passengers carried	1 143	1 421	1 365	1 340	1 143	1 421	1 365	1 340	Passagers transportés
Passengers-km	1 888	2 320	2 384	2 359	1 888	2 320	2 384	2 359	Passagers-km
Total ton-km	177	214	229	227	177	214	229	227	Total tonnes-km
Monaco									**Monaco**
Kilometers flown	0	1	1	1	0	1	1	1	Kilomètres parcourus
Passengers carried	44	75	83	78	44	75	83	78	Passagers transportés
Passengers-km	1	2	2	2	1	2	2	2	Passagers-km
Total ton-km	0	0	0	0	0	0	0	0	Total tonnes-km
Netherlands[6]									**Pays-Bas**[6]
Kilometers flown	390	422	445	425	390	421	444	424	Kilomètres parcourus
Passengers carried	17 950	18 540	19 556	19 261	17 879	18 409	19 393	19 128	Passagers transportés
Passengers-km	68 597	70 117	73 030	68 793	68 590	70 099	73 008	68 775	Passagers-km
Total ton-km	10 864	11 204	11 811	11 154	10 864	11 202	11 809	11 152	Total tonnes-km
Norway[4]									**Norvège**[4]
Kilometers flown	134	151	149	149	62	70	71	74	Kilomètres parcourus
Passengers carried	14 279	15 020	15 182	14 556	4 068	4 367	4 646	4 659	Passagers transportés
Passengers-km	9 480	9 874	10 367	10 461	5 171	5 432	5 870	6 140	Passagers-km
Total ton-km	1 082	1 154	1 218	1 224	673	722	777	793	Total tonnes-km
Poland									**Pologne**
Kilometers flown	46	49	55	70	42	45	51	64	Kilomètres parcourus
Passengers carried	2 061	2 141	2 341	2 670	1 724	1 791	1 928	2 078	Passagers transportés
Passengers-km	4 255	4 632	4 757	4 915	4 155	4 528	4 635	4 739	Passagers-km
Total ton-km	483	498	547	562	475	489	537	547	Total tonnes-km
Portugal[7]									**Portugal**[7]
Kilometers flown	98	102	105	112	78	83	87	94	Kilomètres parcourus
Passengers carried	5 832	6 054	6 721	6 650	3 462	3 604	4 019	4 003	Passagers transportés
Passengers-km	10 107	10 070	11 217	11 182	8 475	8 595	9 594	9 540	Passagers-km
Total ton-km	1 157	1 128	1 252	1 236	981	976	1 088	1 071	Total tonnes-km
Republic of Moldova									**République de Moldova**
Kilometers flown	4	2	4	5	4	2	4	5	Kilomètres parcourus
Passengers carried	118	43	118	120	118	43	118	120	Passagers transportés
Passengers-km	146	97	125	146	146	97	125	146	Passagers-km
Total ton-km	14	9	13	14	14	9	13	14	Total tonnes-km
Romania									**Roumanie**
Kilometers flown	22	24	30	26	20	22	29	24	Kilomètres parcourus
Passengers carried	921	980	1 218	1 139	758	844	1 105	1 036	Passagers transportés
Passengers-km	1 712	1 757	2 098	1 856	1 647	1 704	2 053	1 816	Passagers-km
Total ton-km	167	171	202	178	161	166	198	175	Total tonnes-km
Russian Federation									**Fédération de Russie**
Kilometers flown	581	550	534	568	212	196	189	198	Kilomètres parcourus
Passengers carried	18 685	18 600	17 688	20 301	5 960	5 190	5 480	6 688	Passagers transportés
Passengers-km	46 158	45 863	42 950	48 321	18 811	16 862	17 584	19 638	Passagers-km
Total ton-km	4 931	5 036	4 948	5 292	2 179	2 088	2 285	2 305	Total tonnes-km
Serbia and Montenegro									**Serbie-et-Monténégro**
Kilometers flown	...	...	...	13	...	...	...	11	Kilomètres parcourus
Passengers carried	...	...	...	1 117	...	...	...	615	Passagers transportés
Passengers-km	...	...	...	897	...	...	...	750	Passagers-km
Total ton-km	...	...	...	85	...	...	...	72	Total tonnes-km
Slovakia									**Slovaquie**
Kilometers flown	3	3	2	2	3	2	2	1	Kilomètres parcourus
Passengers carried	107	111	57	43	82	75	44	34	Passagers transportés
Passengers-km	128	117	108	85	119	105	103	82	Passagers-km
Total ton-km	11	10	10	11	10	9	10	11	Total tonnes-km
Slovenia									**Slovénie**
Kilometers flown	8	9	10	11	8	9	10	11	Kilomètres parcourus
Passengers carried	460	555	628	690	460	555	628	690	Passagers transportés
Passengers-km	411	515	563	657	411	515	563	657	Passagers-km
Total ton-km	41	50	55	63	41	50	55	63	Total tonnes-km

62

Civil aviation

Passengers on scheduled services (thousands); Kilometers (millions)

Aviation civile

Passagers sur les services réguliers (milliers) ; Kilomètres (millions)

Country or area and traffic	Total Totale				International Internationaux				Région, pays ou zone et trafic
	1998	1999	2000	2001	1998	1999	2000	2001	
Spain									**Espagne**
Kilometers flown	331	365	418	460	179	200	235	268	Kilomètres parcourus
Passengers carried	31 594	33 559	39 712	41 470	8 971	9 581	11 911	12 807	Passagers transportés
Passengers-km	40 042	44 172	52 427	55 324	26 027	29 035	35 003	37 295	Passagers-km
Total ton-km	4 378	4 828	5 635	5 897	3 038	3 360	3 966	4 173	Total tonnes-km
Sweden [4]									**Suède** [4]
Kilometers flown	143	150	167	167	89	94	92	96	Kilomètres parcourus
Passengers carried	11 878	12 933	13 354	13 123	5 571	5 785	5 901	5 811	Passagers transportés
Passengers-km	10 249	10 607	11 192	11 277	7 198	7 312	7 765	7 879	Passagers-km
Total ton-km	1 234	1 309	1 387	1 384	959	1 001	1 064	1 059	Total tonnes-km
Switzerland									**Suisse**
Kilometers flown	263	295	317	304	258	289	311	299	Kilomètres parcourus
Passengers carried	14 299	16 209	17 268	16 915	12 868	14 735	15 800	15 567	Passagers transportés
Passengers-km	29 415	33 309	36 625	33 470	29 147	33 030	36 339	33 211	Passagers-km
Total ton-km	4 897	5 195	5 616	4 970	4 870	5 167	5 588	4 945	Total tonnes-km
TFYR of Macedonia									**L'ex-R.y. Macédoine**
Kilometers flown	5	7	10	5	5	7	10	5	Kilomètres parcourus
Passengers carried	295	488	599	315	295	488	599	315	Passagers transportés
Passengers-km	328	599	740	377	328	599	740	377	Passagers-km
Total ton-km	31	57	70	36	31	57	70	36	Total tonnes-km
Ukraine									**Ukraine**
Kilometers flown	37	31	32	30	30	24	25	26	Kilomètres parcourus
Passengers carried	1 064	891	951	986	807	661	704	816	Passagers transportés
Passengers-km	1 720	1 312	1 387	1 418	1 556	1 165	1 240	1 322	Passagers-km
Total ton-km	188	138	145	149	173	125	132	140	Total tonnes-km
United Kingdom [8]									**Royaume-Uni** [8]
Kilometers flown	885	977	1 013	1 049	768	845	893	921	Kilomètres parcourus
Passengers carried	61 625	67 928	70 115	70 021	45 017	48 941	52 131	51 703	Passagers transportés
Passengers-km	151 880	161 541	170 388	158 717	144 933	153 697	162 865	151 059	Passagers-km
Total ton-km	19 589	20 692	21 839	19 914	18 984	20 021	21 191	19 257	Total tonnes-km
Oceania [1]									**Océanie** [1]
Kilometers flown	**757**	**735**	**850**	**843**	**360**	**351**	**429**	**399**	**Kilomètres parcourus**
Passengers carried	**43 990**	**43 622**	**48 303**	**50 103**	**12 343**	**11 643**	**13 776**	**14 485**	**Passagers transportés**
Passengers-km	**103 104**	**103 991**	**114 876**	**117 585**	**71 392**	**71 257**	**81 288**	**81 605**	**Passagers-km**
Total ton-km	**12 813**	**12 883**	**13 921**	**13 961**	**9 558**	**9 568**	**10 590**	**10 304**	**Total tonnes-km**
Australia									**Australie**
Kilometers flown	479	474	558	556	193	194	248	238	Kilomètres parcourus
Passengers carried	30 180	30 007	32 578	33 477	6 894	6 579	7 508	8 530	Passagers transportés
Passengers-km	73 647	75 575	81 689	84 931	46 525	47 436	53 007	54 549	Passagers-km
Total ton-km	8 929	9 107	9 806	10 050	6 116	6 236	6 936	7 008	Total tonnes-km
Fiji									**Fidji**
Kilometers flown	20	20	23	23	13	13	16	14	Kilomètres parcourus
Passengers carried	516	525	586	613	334	361	399	407	Passagers transportés
Passengers-km	2 000	2 159	2 385	2 391	1 956	2 120	2 355	2 355	Passagers-km
Total ton-km	200	218	309	306	196	214	307	302	Total tonnes-km
Kiribati									**Kiribati**
Kilometers flown	1	...	...	...	0	...	...	...	Kilomètres parcourus
Passengers carried	28	...	...	...	3	...	...	...	Passagers transportés
Passengers-km	11	...	...	...	7	...	...	...	Passagers-km
Total ton-km	2	...	...	...	1	...	...	...	Total tonnes-km
Marshall Islands									**Iles Marshall**
Kilometers flown	1	1	1	1	1	0	0	0	Kilomètres parcourus
Passengers carried	32	19	16	19	9	5	1	1	Passagers transportés
Passengers-km	20	12	22	25	12	7	2	2	Passagers-km
Total ton-km	2	1	2	2	1	1	0	0	Total tonnes-km
Nauru									**Nauru**
Kilometers flown	2	3	3	3	2	3	3	3	Kilomètres parcourus
Passengers carried	137	143	161	164	137	143	161	164	Passagers transportés
Passengers-km	243	254	287	287	243	254	287	287	Passagers-km
Total ton-km	24	25	28	29	24	25	28	29	Total tonnes-km

62

Civil aviation

Passengers on scheduled services (thousands); Kilometers (millions)

Aviation civile

Passagers sur les services réguliers (milliers) ; Kilomètres (millions)

Country or area and traffic	Total Totale				International Internationaux				Région, pays ou zone et trafic
	1998	1999	2000	2001	1998	1999	2000	2001	
New Zealand									**Nouvelle-Zélande**
Kilometers flown	174	172	198	190	98	100	121	101	Kilomètres parcourus
Passengers carried	8 655	8 892	10 781	11 467	2 773	2 829	3 673	3 443	Passagers transportés
Passengers-km	19 014	19 322	23 374	23 069	16 352	16 679	20 338	19 414	Passagers-km
Total ton-km	2 700	2 746	3 006	2 846	2 479	2 529	2 762	2 453	Total tonnes-km
Papua New Guinea									**Papouasie-Nvl-Guinée**
Kilometers flown	15	12	17	17	5	3	7	6	Kilomètres parcourus
Passengers carried	1 110	1 102	1 100	1 188	159	110	271	276	Passagers transportés
Passengers-km	736	641	1 036	1 110	361	250	628	628	Passagers-km
Total ton-km	87	80	118	124	49	39	77	77	Total tonnes-km
Samoa									**Samoa**
Kilometers flown	4	3	2	2	3	3	1	1	Kilomètres parcourus
Passengers carried	149	92	164	173	77	77	88	90	Passagers transportés
Passengers-km	250	244	290	291	242	242	281	281	Passagers-km
Total ton-km	24	23	28	29	23	23	28	28	Total tonnes-km
Solomon Islands									**Iles Salomon**
Kilometers flown	3	4	3	4	1	1	1	1	Kilomètres parcourus
Passengers carried	94	98	75	81	28	23	18	18	Passagers transportés
Passengers-km	74	80	50	52	58	47	37	37	Passagers-km
Total ton-km	9	9	6	6	7	6	4	4	Total tonnes-km
Tonga									**Tonga**
Kilometers flown	1	1	1	1	...	...	...	...	Kilomètres parcourus
Passengers carried	49	91	52	57	...	...	...	...	Passagers transportés
Passengers-km	10	19	11	13	...	...	...	...	Passagers-km
Total ton-km	1	2	1	1	...	...	...	...	Total tonnes-km
Vanuatu									**Vanuatu**
Kilometers flown	3	3	3	3	3	3	3	3	Kilomètres parcourus
Passengers carried	89	86	102	97	89	86	102	97	Passagers transportés
Passengers-km	179	178	221	212	179	178	221	212	Passagers-km
Total ton-km	19	18	22	21	19	18	22	21	Total tonnes-km

Source:
International Civil Aviation Organization (ICAO), Montreal, the ICAO database.

Source:
Organisation de l'aviation civile international (OACI), Montréal, la base de données de l'OACI.

1   The statistics of France, the Netherlands, Portugal, United Kingdom and United States have been distributed between two or more regions - France (Europe, Africa, North America and Oceania), Netherlands (Europe and North America), Portugal (1997-1999 only; Europe and Asia), United Kingdom (Europe, Asia and North America) and United States (North America and Oceania).

2   Includes apportionment (1/10) of the traffic of Air Afrique, a multi-national airline with headquarters in Cote d'Ivoire and operated by 10 African states unitl 1991. From 1992 includes apportionment (1/11) of the traffic of Air Afrique and operated by 11 African states.

3   Includes apportionment (1/4) of the traffic of Gulf Air, a multinational airline with headquarters in Bahrain and operated by four Gulf States.

4   Includes the apportionment of international operations performed by Scandinavian Airlines System (SAS): Denmark (2/7), Norway (2/7), Sweden (3/7).

5   Includes data for airlines based in the territories and dependancies of France.

6   Includes data for airlines based in the territories and dependancies of Netherlands.

7   From 1997 to 1999, data include those for Macao (SAR) of China.

8   Includes data for airlines based in the territories and dependancies of United Kingdom.

1   Les statistiques de la France, des Pays-Bas, du Portugal, du Royaume-Uni et des Etats-Unis concernent deux régions ou plus; France (Europe, Afrique, Amérique du Nord et Océanie), Pays-Bas (Europe et Amérique du Nord), Portugal (1997 à 1999 seulement; Europe et Asie), Royaume-Uni (Europe, Asie et Amérqiue du Nord) et Etats-Unis (Amérique du Nord et Océanie).

2   Ces chiffres comprennent une partie du trafic (1/10) assurée par Air Afrique, compagnie aérienne multinationale dont le siège est situé en Côte d'Ivoire et est exploitée conjointement par 10 Etats Africains jusqu'à 1991. A partir de 1992 ces chiffres comprennent une partie du trafic (1/11) assurée par Air Afrique et exploitée conjointement par11 Etats Africains.

3   Ces chiffres comprennent une partie du trafic (1/4) assurée par Gulf Air, compagnie aérienne multinationale dont le siège est situé en Bahreïn et est exploitée conjointement par 4 Etats Gulf.

4   Y compris une partie des vols internationaux effectués par le SAS; Danemark (2/7), Norvège (2/7) et Suède (3/7).

5   Y compris les données relatives aux compagnies aériennes ayant des bases d'opérations dans les territoires et dépendances de France.

6   Y compris les données relatives aux compagnies aériennes ayant des bases d'opérations dans les territoires et dépendances des Pays-Bas.

7   1997 à 1999, y compris Macao.

8   Y compris les données relatives aux compagnies aériennes ayant des bases d'opération dans les territoires et dépendances du Royaume-Uni.

Technical notes, tables 58-62

Table 58: Data refer to domestic and international traffic on all railway lines within each country shown, except railways entirely within an urban unit, and plantation, industrial mining, funicular and cable railways. The figures relating to passenger-kilometres include all passengers except military, government and railway personnel when carried without revenue. Those relating to ton-kilometres are freight net ton-kilometres and include both fast and ordinary goods services but exclude service traffic, mail, baggage and non-revenue governmental stores.

Table 59: For years in which a census or registration took place, the census or registration figure is shown; for other years, unless otherwise indicated, the officially estimated number of vehicles in use is shown. The time of year to which the figures refer is variable. Special purpose vehicles such as two- or three-wheeled cycles and motorcycles, trams, trolley-buses, ambulances, hearses, military vehicles operated by police or other governmental security organizations are excluded. Passenger cars include vehicles seating not more than nine persons (including the driver), such as taxis, jeeps and station wagons. Commercial vehicles include: vans, lorries (trucks), buses, tractor and semi-trailer combinations but excludes trailers and farm tractors.

Table 60: Data refer to merchant fleets registered in each country as at 31 December, except for data prior to 1992 which refer to 30 June of the year stated. They are given in gross registered tons (100 cubic feet or 2.83 cubic metres) and represent the total volume of all the permanently enclosed spaces of the vessels to which the figures refer. Vessels without mechanical means of propulsion are excluded, but sailing vessels with auxiliary power are included.

Data are shown for all ships (cargo carrying ships and ships of miscellaneous activities), oil tanker fleets, and for ore and bulk carrier fleets. The data are published by Lloyd's Register of Shipping in "World Fleet Statistics". (See also www.lrfairplay.com).

Table 61: The figures for vessels entered and cleared, unless otherwise stated, represent the sum of the net registered tonnage of sea-going foreign and domestic merchant vessels (power and sailing) entered with cargo from or cleared with cargo to a foreign port and refer to only one entrance or clearance for each foreign voyage. Where possible, the data exclude vessels "in ballast", i.e. entering without unloading or clearing without loading goods.

Table 62: Data for total services cover both domestic and international scheduled services operated by airlines registered in each country. Scheduled services in-

Notes techniques, tableaux 58 à 62

Tableau 58: Les données se rapportent au trafic intérieur et international de toutes les lignes de chemins de fer du pays indiqué, à l'exception des lignes situées entièrement à l'intérieur d'une agglomération urbaine ou desservant une plantation ou un complexe industriel minier, des funiculaires et des téléfériques. Les chiffres relatifs aux voyageurs-kilomètres se rapportent à tous les voyageurs sauf les militaires, les fonctionnaires et le personnel des chemins de fer, qui sont transportés gratuitement. Les chiffres relatifs aux tonnes-kilomètres se rapportent aux tonnes-kilomètres nettes de fret et comprennent les services rapides et ordinaires de transport de marchandises, à l'exception des transports pour les besoins du service, du courrier, des bagages et des marchandises transportées gratuitement pour les besoins de l'Etat.

Tableau 59: Pour les années où a eu lieu un recensement ou un enregistrement des véhicules, le chiffre indiqué est le résultat de cette opération; pour les autres années, sauf indication contraire, le chiffre indiqué correspond à l'estimation officielle du nombre de véhicules en circulation. L'époque de l'année à laquelle se rapportent les chiffres varie. Les véhicules à usage spécial, tels que les cycles à deux ou trois roues et motocyclettes, les tramways, les trolley-bus, les ambulances, les corbillards, les véhicules militaires utilisés par la police ou par d'autres services publics de sécurité ne sont pas compris dans ces chiffres. Les voitures de tourisme comprennent les véhicules automobiles dont le nombre de places assises (y compris celle du conducteur) n'est pas supérieur à neuf, tels que les taxis, jeeps et breaks. Les véhicules utilitaires comprennent les fourgons, camions, autobus et autocars, les ensembles tracteurs-remorques et semi-remorques, mais ne comprennent pas les remorques et les tracteurs agricoles.

Tableau 60: Les données se rapportent à la flotte marchande enregistrée dans chaque pays au 31 décembre de l'année indiquée à l'exception des données qui se rapportent aux années avant 1992, qui se réfèrent à la flotte marchande au 30 juin. Elles sont exprimées en tonneaux de jauge brute (100 pieds cubes ou 2,83 mètres cubes) et représentent le volume total de tous les espaces clos en permanence dans les navires auxquels elle s'appliquent. Elles excluent les navires sans moteur, mais pas les voiliers avec moteurs auxiliaires.

Les données sont présentées pour tous les navires, pour la flotte des pétroliers, et pour la flotte des minéraliers et des transporteurs de vrac et d'huile. Les données sont publiées par Lloyd's Register of Shipping dans *World Fleet Statistics* [19]. (Voir aussi <www.lrfairplay.com>).

clude supplementary services occasioned by overflow traffic on regularly scheduled trips and preparatory flights for newly scheduled services. Freight means all goods, except mail and excess baggage, carried for remuneration. The data are prepared by the International Civil Aviation Organization and published in the *Digest of Statistics-Traffic* [12]. (See also <www.icao.int>).

Tableau 61: Sauf indication contraire, les données relatives aux navires entrés et sortis représentent la jauge nette totale des navires marchands de haute mer (à moteur ou à voile) nationaux ou étrangers, qui entrent ou sortent chargés, en provenance ou à destination d'un port étranger. On ne compte qu'une seule entrée et une seule sortie pour chaque voyage international. Dans la mesure du possible, le tableau exclut les navires sur lest (c'est-à-dire les navires entrant sans décharger ou sortant sans avoir chargé).

Tableau 62: Les données relatives au total des services se rapportent aux services réguliers, intérieurs ou internationaux des compagnies de transport aérien enregistrées dans chaque pays. Les services réguliers comprennent aussi les vols supplémentaires nécessités par un surcroît d'activité des services réguliers et les vols préparatoires en vue de nouveaux services réguliers. Par fret, on entend toutes les marchandises transportées contre paiement, mais non le courrier et les excédents de bagage. Les données sont préparées par l'Organisation de l'aviation civile internationale et publiées dans le *Recueil de statistiques-trafic* [12]. (Voir aussi <www.icao.int>).

63

Production, trade and consumption of commercial energy
Thousand metric tons of oil equivalent and kilograms per capita

Production, commerce et consommation d'énergie commerciale
Milliers de tonnes d'équivalent pétrole et kilogrammes par habitant

Region, country or area	Year Année	Primary energy production – Production d'énergie primaire					Changes in stocks		Export
		Total Totale	Solids Solides	Liquids Liquides	Gas Gaz	Electricity Electricité	Variations des stocks	Imports Importations	Export Exportation
World	1998	9 053 195	2 309 588	3 639 961	2 203 359	900 286	53 352	3 387 879	3 395 94
	1999	8 912 519	2 185 005	3 571 702	2 226 337	929 475	-87 150	3 418 572	3 385 36
	2000	9 118 671	2 173 001	3 714 154	2 282 656	948 860	-49 947	3 647 430	3 598 83
	2001	9 397 483	2 328 232	3 715 066	2 365 660	988 525	46 498	3 706 945	3 650 73
Africa	1998	654 906	160 372	381 032	103 797	9 704	16 837	71 337	395 75
	1999	659 624	160 920	374 979	113 358	10 367	8 452	78 095	409 90
	2000	680 840	161 392	387 501	121 704	10 242	976	76 356	432 27
	2001	686 784	162 260	393 725	120 688	10 111	4 133	76 250	429 11
Algeria	1998	144 348	*6	68 911	75 423	*9	-48	772	102 12
	1999	146 618	*4	66 544	80 062	*9	343	*709	109 65
	2000	147 453	...	69 172	78 276	5	*-513	591	114 07
	2001	140 984	...	67 642	73 336	6	*-404	592	107 08
Angola	1998	37 036	...	36 418	*527	91	153	92	35 07
	1999	37 475	...	36 890	*509	77	354	203	35 0
	2000	37 347	...	36 742	*527	78	490	326	34 82
	2001	37 073	...	36 505	*481	87	124	564	34 97
Benin	1998	62	...	62	...	...	2	*434	6
	1999	44	...	44	...	...	3	*452	5
	2000	38	...	38	...	...	*-34	533	8
	2001	40	...	40	...	...	*-9	596	6
Burkina Faso	1998	*10	...	...	...	*10	...	*334	
	1999	*10	...	...	...	*10	...	*334	
	2000	*11	...	...	...	*11	...	*338	
	2001	*11	...	...	...	*11	...	*347	
Burundi	1998	14	*4	...	...	9	...	*77	
	1999	13	*4	...	...	8	...	*82	
	2000	13	*4	...	...	9	...	*90	
	2001	14	*4	...	...	10	2	*84	
Cameroon	1998	6 180	*1	5 911	...	268	*91	1 637	5 59
	1999	7 144	*1	6 857	...	287	*7	1 633	6 77
	2000	*6 839	*1	*6 552	...	287	*103	1 530	6 44
	2001	*7 298	...	*7 002	...	296	1	66	5 93
Cape Verde	1998	...	...	...	...	...	...	*41	
	1999	...	...	...	...	...	...	*46	
	2000	...	...	...	...	...	...	*46	
	2001	...	...	...	...	...	...	*50	
Central African Rep.	1998	*7	...	...	...	*7	*1	*99	
	1999	*7	...	...	...	*7	*1	*105	
	2000	*7	...	...	...	*7	*1	*107	
	2001	*7	...	...	...	*7	*2	*111	
Chad	1998	...	...	...	...	...	...	*58	
	1999	...	...	...	...	...	...	*62	
	2000	...	...	...	...	...	...	*63	
	2001	...	...	...	...	...	...	*65	
Comoros	1998	*0	...	...	...	*0	...	*24	
	1999	*0	...	...	...	*0	...	*27	
	2000	*0	...	...	...	*0	...	*28	
	2001	*0	...	...	...	*0	...	*28	
Congo	1998	12 884	...	12 723	*123	39	*3	85	12 16
	1999	13 541	...	13 378	133	30	285	68	12 51
	2000	13 377	...	13 235	117	26	-365	*71	13 36
	2001	12 286	...	12 137	117	32	*-250	*65	12 03
Côte d'Ivoire	1998	2 858	...	1 900	841	117	*572	*3 812	*2 91
	1999	3 045	...	1 485	1 409	151	*232	4 365	2 91
	2000	2 356	...	*796	1 409	152	*184	3 623	2 23
	2001	2 010	...	435	1 419	155	-170	3 403	2 77
Dem. Rep. of the Congo	1998	*1 689	*67	*1 156	...	*465	...	*705	*1 03
	1999	1 625	*67	1 069	...	489	*-101	*719	1 05
	2000	*1 841	67	*1 306	...	467	*-100	799	1 30
	2001	*1 805	62	*1 249	...	494	*-107	718	1 19

Bunkers - Soutes			Consumption - Consommation							
Air Avion	Sea Maritime	Unallocated Nondistribué	Per capita Par habitant	Total Totale	Solids Solides	Liquids Liquides	Gas Gaz	Electricity Electricité	Year Année	Région, pays ou zone
92 026	140 496	382 456	1 364	8 376 802	2 331 373	2 967 130	2 178 012	900 286	1998	**Monde**
96 605	143 405	401 391	1 348	8 391 478	2 237 034	2 985 115	2 239 855	929 475	1999	
97 593	148 977	449 512	1 351	8 521 133	2 256 353	3 014 846	2 301 074	948 860	2000	
99 117	140 144	442 398	1 362	8 725 535	2 338 627	3 048 231	2 350 152	988 525	2001	
2 583	7 290	23 192	348	280 590	113 475	102 601	54 810	9 704	1998	**Afrique**
3 023	8 399	14 695	354	293 245	117 627	108 543	56 709	10 367	1999	
2 853	7 683	23 772	341	289 639	116 396	105 210	57 790	10 242	2000	
3 325	7 545	23 044	340	295 875	116 725	108 893	60 147	10 111	2001	
*279	239	5 445	1 257	37 085	445	10 085	26 547	*9	1998	Algérie
*279	238	132	1 225	36 678	*446	11 484	24 740	*9	1999	
...	246	5 490	946	28 742	281	9 163	19 293	5	2000	
...	138	5 275	959	29 484	383	9 161	19 934	6	2001	
220	...	225	118	1 459	...	841	*527	91	1998	Angola
386	...	177	135	1 727	...	1 141	*509	77	1999	
463	...	201	129	1 690	...	1 085	*527	78	2000	
502	...	186	145	1 847	...	1 279	*481	87	2001	
33	...	...	67	*392	...	*392	...	...	1998	Bénin
24	...	...	69	*416	...	*416	...	...	1999	
24	...	...	80	497	...	497	...	...	2000	
25	...	0	86	555	...	555	...	...	2001	
...	...	...	32	*344	...	*334	...	*10	1998	Burkina Faso
...	...	...	31	*344	...	*334	...	*10	1999	
...	...	...	30	*349	...	*338	...	*11	2000	
...	...	...	29	*357	...	*347	...	*11	2001	
*6	...	...	13	*85	*4	*71	...	9	1998	Burundi
*6	...	...	14	*89	*4	*76	...	8	1999	
*7	...	...	15	95	*4	*82	...	9	2000	
*9	...	...	14	*87	*4	*73	...	10	2001	
*7	5	564	108	*1 554	*1	*1 285	...	268	1998	Cameroun
*8	8	422	107	*1 556	*1	*1 268	...	287	1999	
59	19	541	81	1 203	*1	916	...	287	2000	
63	...	70	84	1 291	...	995	...	296	2001	
...	...	...	99	*41	...	*41	...	...	1998	Cap-Vert
...	...	...	108	*46	...	*46	...	...	1999	
...	...	...	109	*46	...	*46	...	...	2000	
...	...	...	112	*50	...	*50	...	...	2001	
*14	...	...	25	*90	...	*83	...	*7	1998	Rép. centrafricaine
*14	...	...	27	*97	...	*89	...	*7	1999	
*15	...	...	26	*98	...	*90	...	*7	2000	
*19	...	...	26	*98	...	*90	...	*7	2001	
*20	...	...	5	*38	...	*38	...	...	1998	Tchad
*21	...	...	5	*41	...	*41	...	...	1999	
*21	...	...	5	*42	...	*42	...	...	2000	
*21	...	...	5	*44	...	*44	...	...	2001	
...	...	...	36	*24	...	*24	...	*0	1998	Comores
...	...	...	39	*27	...	*27	...	*0	1999	
...	...	...	40	*28	...	*28	...	*0	2000	
...	...	...	38	*28	...	*28	...	*0	2001	
...	*10	142	229	*652	...	*490	*123	39	1998	Congo
...	*10	163	217	*635	...	*472	133	30	1999	
...	*10	30	135	407	...	265	117	26	2000	
...	*12	31	148	525	...	376	117	32	2001	
*169	82	176	179	2 755	...	1 796	841	117	1998	Côte d'Ivoire
*176	83	425	228	3 575	...	2 016	1 409	151	1999	
142	93	269	186	3 053	...	1 492	1 409	152	2000	
132	93	125	153	2 461	...	887	1 419	155	2001	
*117	*2	21	25	*1 218	*228	*525	...	*465	1998	Rép. dém. du Congo
*117	*2	-11	26	*1 285	*233	*564	...	489	1999	
120	2	-1	26	1 318	221	630	...	467	2000	
108	2	57	25	1 269	221	554	...	494	2001	

63

Production, trade and consumption of commercial energy
Thousand metric tons of oil equivalent and kilograms per capita *[cont.]*

Production, commerce et consommation d'énergie commerciale
Milliers de tonnes d'équivalent pétrole et kilogrammes par habitant *[suite]*

Region, country or area	Year Année	Primary energy production – Production d'énergie primaire					Changes in stocks Variations des stocks	Imports Importations	Export Exportation
		Total Totale	Solids Solides	Liquids Liquides	Gas Gaz	Electricity Electricité			
Djibouti	1998	...	...	...	...	...	...	*550	
	1999	...	...	...	...	...	...	*560	
	2000	...	...	...	...	...	...	*562	
	2001	...	...	...	...	...	...	*563	
Egypt	1998	55 771	...	43 200	11 523	1 048	8 424	2 752	6 90
	1999	57 709	...	40 797	15 601	1 311	7 066	8 090	7 63
	2000	57 966	...	37 148	19 592	1 227	694	3 967	7 90
	2001	56 904	...	35 760	19 968	1 176	723	4 053	8 13
Equatorial Guinea	1998	4 172	...	4 172	...	*0	*2	*49	4 17
	1999	4 826	...	4 826	...	*0	*2	*53	4 82
	2000	5 911	...	5 911	...	*0	*2	*54	5 90
	2001	9 810	...	9 810	...	*0	...	*54	9 81
Eritrea	1998	...	...	...	...	...	...	182	
	1999	...	...	...	...	...	...	201	
	2000	...	...	...	...	...	...	203	
	2001	...	...	...	...	...	...	232	
Ethiopia	1998	142	...	...	...	142	*23	*1 660	*11
	1999	144	...	...	...	144	*-22	*1 806	*9
	2000	148	...	...	...	148	*-51	1 835	*9
	2001	160	...	...	...	160	*-28	1 859	*9
Gabon	1998	18 984	...	18 223	698	63	-87	*377	17 64
	1999	17 377	...	16 557	761	60	-11	*368	15 80
	2000	16 302	...	15 485	756	61	*-21	334	14 71
	2001	15 848	...	15 010	765	*73	*-31	298	14 22
Gambia	1998	...	...	...	...	...	...	*80	*
	1999	...	...	...	...	...	...	*88	*
	2000	...	...	...	...	...	...	93	*
	2001	...	...	...	...	...	...	*96	*
Ghana	1998	329	...	...	...	329	...	*2 129	*15
	1999	511	...	9	...	502	...	1 821	17
	2000	580	...	12	...	568	...	*2 095	29
	2001	614	...	*12	...	602	...	*2 117	*29
Guinea	1998	*27	...	...	...	*27	...	*383	
	1999	*34	...	...	...	*34	...	*392	
	2000	*35	...	...	...	*35	...	*395	
	2001	*37	...	...	...	*37	...	*398	
Guinea-Bissau	1998	...	...	...	...	...	...	*85	
	1999	...	...	...	...	...	...	*93	
	2000	...	...	...	...	...	...	*94	
	2001	...	...	...	...	...	...	*97	
Kenya	1998	622	...	...	...	622	...	3 646	65
	1999	579	...	...	...	579	...	3 547	63
	2000	450	...	...	...	450	...	3 504	45
	2001	548	...	...	...	548	...	3 266	44
Liberia	1998	*16	...	...	...	*16	...	*142	*
	1999	*17	...	...	...	*17	...	*147	
	2000	*17	...	...	...	*17	...	*148	*
	2001	*17	...	...	...	*17	...	*154	*
Libyan Arab Jamah.	1998	75 656	...	69 725	5 931	...	...	*7	60 50
	1999	70 808	...	65 959	4 850	...	...	*7	58 61
	2000	72 922	...	67 222	5 700	...	...	*7	54 50
	2001	73 972	...	68 360	5 613	...	...	*2	55 27
Madagascar	1998	44	...	...	...	44	...	*611	*2
	1999	44	...	...	...	44	...	681	*3
	2000	45	...	...	...	45	...	785	*2
	2001	46	...	...	...	46	...	800	*2
Malawi	1998	*74	...	...	...	*74	...	*238	
	1999	*74	...	...	...	*74	...	*243	
	2000	*74	...	...	...	*74	...	*246	
	2001	*75	...	...	...	*75	...	*250	

Bunkers - Soutes			Consumption - Consommation							
Air Avion	Sea Maritime	Unallocated Nondistribué	Per capita Par habitant	Total Totale	Solids Solides	Liquids Liquides	Gas Gaz	Electricity Electricité	Year Année	Région, pays ou zone
*69	*360	...	203	*121	...	*121	...	...	1998	Djibouti
*70	*363		206	*127		*127	...	...	1999	
*70	*363	...	203	*128	...	*128	...	...	2000	
*70	*363	...	190	*129	...	*129	...	...	2001	
...	2 228	1 746	639	39 225	743	25 911	11 523	1 048	1998	Egypte
...	2 708	5 394	686	42 994	609	25 472	15 601	1 311	1999	
...	2 760	4 911	714	45 660	55	24 787	19 592	1 227	2000	
...	2 734	2 607	689	46 756	87	25 525	19 968	1 176	2001	
...	...	0	114	*49	...	*49	...	*0	1998	Guinée équatoriale
...	...	0	120	*53	...	*53	...	*0	1999	
...	...	0	119	*54	...	*54	...	*0	2000	
...	...	...	116	*54	...	*54	...	*0	2001	
...	...	...	53	182	...	182	...	...	1998	Erythrée
...	...	...	57	201	...	201	...	...	1999	
...	...	...	56	203	...	203	...	...	2000	
...	...	...	60	232	...	232	...	...	2001	
*137	*14	103	25	*1 405	...	*1 263		142	1998	Ethiopie
*130	*15	0	30	*1 737	...	*1 593		144	1999	
79	*15	134	29	1 713	...	1 565		148	2000	
89	*15	133	28	1 716	...	1 556		160	2001	
*66	*275	86	1 195	1 372	...	611	698	63	1998	Gabon
*60	308	59	1 299	1 529	...	708	761	60	1999	
*38	*318	134	1 201	1 449	...	632	756	61	2000	
73	*274	115	1 201	1 486	...	648	765	*73	2001	
...	...	...	64	*78	...	*78	...	...	1998	Gambie
...	...	...	62	*85	...	*85	...	...	1999	
...	...	...	65	91	...	91	...	...	2000	
...	...	...	66	94	...	94	...	...	2001	
*30	*16	50	119	*2 205	*2	*1 874	...	329	1998	Ghana
*30	*18	66	108	2 038	*2	1 534	...	502	1999	
102	*18	45	120	2 211	*2	1 640	...	568	2000	
*100	*18	39	114	2 280	*2	1 677	...	602	2001	
*15	...	...	50	*395	...	*369	...	*27	1998	Guinée
*15	...	...	51	*411	...	*377	...	*34	1999	
*17	...	...	51	*413	...	*378	...	*35	2000	
*17	...	...	51	*418	...	*381	...	*37	2001	
*6	...	...	68	*78	...	*78	...	...	1998	Guinée-Bissau
*6	...	...	74	*87	...	*87	...	...	1999	
*6	...	...	73	*88	...	*88	...	...	2000	
*6	...	...	64	*91	...	*91	...	...	2001	
...	72	328	109	3 216	66	2 528	...	622	1998	Kenya
...	110	479	97	2 904	69	2 256	...	579	1999	
...	67	469	97	2 965	69	2 446	...	450	2000	
...	62	377	94	2 931	69	2 314	...	548	2001	
*2	*12	...	57	*143	...	*127	...	*16	1998	Libéria
*3	*12	...	54	*147	...	*131	...	*17	1999	
*3	*13	...	51	*148	...	*131	...	*17	2000	
*3	*2	...	53	*165	...	*148	...	*17	2001	
305	89	1 617	2 597	13 151	*4	8 042	5 105	...	1998	Jamah. arabe libyenne
458	89	-789	2 404	12 440	*4	8 459	3 978	...	1999	
554	89	4 549	2 502	13 236	*4	8 259	4 973	...	2000	
727	89	4 542	2 499	13 346	*2	8 430	4 913	...	2001	
*2	*15	51	38	*565	*8	*513	...	44	1998	Madagascar
2	*15	82	38	595	6	*545	...	44	1999	
2	*17	142	41	648	*7	*597	...	45	2000	
2	*17	146	40	661	*7	*608	...	46	2001	
*19	...	...	27	*293	*12	*207	...	*74	1998	Malawi
*19	...	...	27	*298	*12	*212	...	*74	1999	
*19	...	...	27	*302	*12	*215	...	*74	2000	
*20	...	...	26	*305	*13	*217	...	*75	2001	

63

Production, trade and consumption of commercial energy
Thousand metric tons of oil equivalent and kilograms per capita *[cont.]*

Production, commerce et consommation d'énergie commerciale
Milliers de tonnes d'équivalent pétrole et kilogrammes par habitant *[suite]*

Region, country or area	Year Année	Total Totale	Solids Solides	Liquids Liquides	Gas Gaz	Electricity Electricité	Variations des stocks	Imports Importations	Export Exportation
		Primary energy production – Production d'énergie primaire					Changes in stocks		
Mali	1998	*20	...	...	...	*20	...	*191	
	1999	*20	...	...	...	*20	...	*199	
	2000	*20	...	...	...	*20	...	*200	
	2001	*20	...	...	...	*20	...	*201	
Mauritania	1998	*2	...	...	...	*2		*1 068	
	1999	*3	...	...	...	*3		*1 106	
	2000	*3	...	...	...	*3		*1 107	
	2001	*3	...	...	...	*3	...	*1 116	
Mauritius	1998	9	...	...	...	9	36	972	
	1999	3	...	...	...	3	*-27	1 019	
	2000	8	...	...	...	8	*-140	1 087	
	2001	6	...	...	...	6	13	1 219	
Morocco	1998	386	188	12	35	151	*-163	9 224	
	1999	213	90	11	41	70	*-69	10 361	
	2000	142	22	13	47	61	*-293	10 734	
	2001	131	1	10	46	74	574	12 475	
Mozambique	1998	397	*13	...	1	383	*-3	368	*
	1999	793	15	...	1	778	*-2	399	
	2000	709	17	...	1	692	3	433	
	2001	857	20	...	1	836	10	500	
Niger	1998	*122	*122	...	...	...	...	*242	
	1999	*123	*123	...	...	...	...	*252	
	2000	*123	*123	...	...	...	...	*255	
	2001	*123	*123	...	...	...	...	*257	
Nigeria	1998	112 952	41	106 855	5 559	497	*-269	1 634	95 0
	1999	112 241	41	105 122	6 549	529	*-76	2 757	93 5
	2000	124 600	43	112 333	11 740	484	95	6 298	108 7
	2001	132 503	44	117 090	14 774	595	699	4 682	109 7
Réunion	1998	48	...	...	...	48	...	717	
	1999	48	...	...	...	48	...	743	
	2000	*48	...	...	...	*48	...	777	
	2001	48	...	...	...	48	...	769	
Rwanda	1998	*14	...	...	*0	*14	...	*177	
	1999	*14	...	...	*0	*14	...	*186	
	2000	*14	...	...	*0	*14	...	*188	
	2001	*15	...	...	*0	*14	...	*189	
Saint Helena	1998	...	...	...	...	...	...	*6	
	1999	...	...	...	...	...	...	7	
	2000	...	...	...	...	...	...	4	
	2001	...	...	...	...	...	...	4	
Sao Tome and Principe	1998	*1	...	...	...	*1	...	*27	
	1999	*1	...	...	...	*1	...	*30	
	2000	*1	...	...	...	*1	...	30	
	2001	*1	...	...	...	*1	...	*31	
Senegal	1998	19	...	...	19	...	*-8	*1 454	*
	1999	6	...	...	6	...	*-1	1 619	*
	2000	1	...	...	1	...	*-1	1 658	
	2001	1	...	...	1	...	*-13	1 706	1
Seychelles	1998	...	...	...	...	...	...	255	
	1999	...	...	...	...	...	...	281	
	2000	...	...	...	...	...	...	306	
	2001	...	...	...	...	...	...	373	
Sierra Leone	1998	...	...	...	...	...	...	*297	
	1999	...	...	...	...	...	...	*306	
	2000	...	...	...	...	...	...	*315	
	2001	...	...	...	...	...	...	*327	
South Africa[1]	1998	169 659	156 871	7 499	1 290	3 999	8 553	23 771	46 8
	1999	170 609	157 173	7 995	1 688	3 754	1 173	22 133	52 8
	2000	171 812	157 865	8 524	1 554	3 869	184	20 552	54 8
	2001	173 037	159 011	8 868	1 912	3 246	2 302	21 485	54 3

Bunkers - Soutes			Consumption - Consommation							
Air Avion	Sea Maritime	Unallocated Nondistribué	Per capita Par habitant	Total Totale	Solids Solides	Liquids Liquides	Gas Gaz	Electricity Electricité	Year Année	Région, pays ou zone
*18	...	...	18	*194	...	*174	...	*20	1998	Mali
*18	...	...	18	*201	...	*181	...	*20	1999	
*18	...	...	18	*202	...	*182	...	*20	2000	
*18	...	...	17	*203	...	*183	...	*20	2001	
*12	*10	85	385	*963	*4	*956	...	*2	1998	Mauritanie
*12	*10	102	381	*985	*4	*978	...	*3	1999	
*12	*10	100	371	*988	*4	*981	...	*3	2000	
*13	*10	99	365	*995	*4	*988	...	*3	2001	
55	164		627	727	50	668	...	9	1998	Maurice
80	170	...	680	798	95	700	...	3	1999	
91	220	...	780	925	178	739	...	8	2000	
78	203	...	775	930	209	714	...	6	2001	
*88	...	926	315	8 759	2 587	5 987	35	151	1998	Maroc
*88	...	1 167	332	9 388	2 455	6 822	41	70	1999	
*88	...	1 316	340	9 766	2 865	6 793	47	61	2000	
*93	...	957	376	10 982	3 518	7 344	46	74	2001	
28	1	...	43	724	...	340	1	383	1998	Mozambique
33	*1	...	66	1 143	...	365	1	778	1999	
40	1	...	61	1 081	0	388	1	692	2000	
35	3	...	73	1 289	0	452	1	836	2001	
*22	...	...	34	*342	*122	*220	...	...	1998	Niger
*23	...	...	34	*352	*123	*229	...	...	1999	
*23	...	...	33	*355	*123	*232	...	...	2000	
*23	...	...	32	*357	*123	*234	...	...	2001	
285	482	4 627	133	14 366	46	8 265	5 559	497	1998	Nigéria
346	761	4 875	140	15 517	44	9 092	5 851	529	1999	
190	473	4 011	151	17 398	46	10 225	6 643	484	2000	
432	567	5 301	174	20 485	47	12 446	7 397	595	2001	
...	14	...	1 074	751	...	703	...	48	1998	Réunion
...	15	...	1 093	776	...	728	...	48	1999	
...	15	...	1 123	809	...	761	...	*48	2000	
...	10	...	1 098	807	...	759	...	48	2001	
*9	...	...	28	*182	...	*167	*0	*14	1998	Rwanda
*9	...	...	27	*191	...	*177	*0	*14	1999	
*10	...	...	25	*192	...	*178	*0	*14	2000	
*10	...	...	24	*193	...	*179	*0	*14	2001	
...	...	...	1 242	*6	...	*6	...	...	1998	Sainte-Hélène
...	...	...	1 452	7	...	7	...	...	1999	
...	...	...	822	4	...	4	...	...	2000	
...	...	...	822	4	...	4	...	...	2001	
...	...	...	206	*27	...	*27	...	*1	1998	Sao Tomé-et-Principe
...	...	...	226	*30	...	*30	...	*1	1999	
...	...	...	222	31	...	30	...	*1	2000	
...	...	...	206	*32	...	*31	...	*1	2001	
*189	71	108	116	*1 052	...	*1 033	19	...	1998	Sénégal
*236	77	14	132	1 228	...	1 222	6	...	1999	
265	77	0	129	1 224	...	1 224	1	...	2000	
238	77	104	120	1 178	...	1 177	1	...	2001	
29	*80	...	1 843	146	...	146	...	...	1998	Seychelles
32	*80	...	2 113	169	...	169	...	...	1999	
32	*81	...	2 381	193	...	193	...	...	2000	
31	*81	...	3 221	261	...	261	...	...	2001	
*19	*85	53	33	*137	...	*137	...	...	1998	Sierra Leone
*19	*86	53	34	*145	...	*145	...	...	1999	
*19	*86	59	33	*147	...	*147	...	...	2000	
*19	*87	63	34	*154	...	*154	...	...	2001	
...	2 858	6 829	2 660	128 365	106 252	16 825	1 290	3 999	1998	Afrique du Sud [1]
...	3 176	749	2 729	134 807	110 261	19 104	1 688	3 754	1999	
...	2 645	1 408	2 654	133 274	109 538	18 312	1 554	3 869	2000	
...	2 645	2 288	2 613	132 916	109 232	18 527	1 912	3 246	2001	

63

Production, trade and consumption of commercial energy
Thousand metric tons of oil equivalent and kilograms per capita *[cont.]*

Production, commerce et consommation d'énergie commerciale
Milliers de tonnes d'équivalent pétrole et kilogrammes par habitant *[suite]*

Region, country or area	Year Année	Primary energy production – Production d'énergie primaire					Changes in stocks Variations des stocks	Imports Importations	Expo Exportatio
		Total Totale	Solids Solides	Liquids Liquides	Gas Gaz	Electricity Electricité			
Sudan	1998	421	...	330	...	*90	*-46	1 188	
	1999	3 548	...	3 453	...	95	*-1 161	1 254	2
	2000	9 411	...	9 309	...	102	209	576	7
	2001	10 511	...	10 404	...	106	99	558	8
Togo	1998	*0	...	...	...	*0	*-884	*338	
	1999	0	...	...	...	0	32	430	
	2000	0	...	...	...	0	1	507	
	2001	0	...	...	...	0	...	400	
Tunisia	1998	5 769	...	3 935	1 829	6	194	4 867	4
	1999	5 741	...	3 983	1 751	8	200	4 832	4
	2000	5 697	...	3 703	*1 986	7	163	5 467	4
	2001	5 652	...	3 390	*2 255	7	202	5 538	3
Uganda	1998	109	...	...	...	109	...	397	
	1999	109	...	...	...	109	...	412	
	2000	135	...	...	...	135	...	452	
	2001	143	...	...	...	143	...	471	
United Rep. of Tanzania	1998	210	32	...	...	179	...	869	
	1999	239	53	...	...	186	...	837	
	2000	240	55	...	...	184	...	1 305	
	2001	276	55	...	...	221	...	1 435	
Western Sahara	1998	...	...	...	...	...	...	*79	
	1999	...	...	...	...	...	...	*84	
	2000	...	...	...	...	...	...	*85	
	2001	...	...	...	...	...	...	*85	
Zambia	1998	763	114	...	...	648	55	668	
	1999	775	112	...	...	663	48	515	
	2000	781	114	...	...	666	38	494	
	2001	819	120	...	...	699	44	569	
Zimbabwe	1998	3 080	2 914	...	...	166	26	1 470	
	1999	3 492	3 238	...	...	254	*-166	1 434	
	2000	3 360	3 080	...	...	280	*-98	1 062	
	2001	3 078	2 820	...	...	258	*-102	982	
America, North	**1998**	**2 326 111**	**613 242**	**713 673**	**720 392**	**278 804**	**18 079**	**774 038**	**390**
	1999	**2 296 152**	**600 079**	**689 404**	**708 452**	**298 217**	**-28 172**	**794 937**	**377**
	2000	**2 279 173**	**586 670**	**700 459**	**691 933**	**300 112**	**-54 318**	**844 027**	**395**
	2001	**2 381 064**	**617 134**	**699 291**	**739 927**	**324 712**	**52 281**	**879 445**	**399**
Antigua and Barbuda	1998	...	...	...	...	...	...	*164	
	1999	...	...	...	...	...	...	*170	
	2000	...	...	...	...	...	...	*171	
	2001	...	...	...	...	...	...	*171	
Aruba	1998	...	...	...	...	...	...	*619	
	1999	...	...	...	...	...	...	*626	
	2000	...	...	...	...	...	...	*633	
	2001	...	...	...	...	...	...	*637	
Bahamas	1998	...	...	...	...	...	*2	*2 912	*2
	1999	...	...	...	...	...	*2	*2 913	*2
	2000	...	...	...	...	...	*2	*2 915	*2
	2001	...	...	...	...	...	*2	*2 915	*2
Barbados	1998	115	...	80	35	...	6	498	
	1999	141	...	97	44	...	*-10	510	
	2000	112	...	77	35	...	*-12	519	
	2001	93	...	63	30	...	*-16	531	
Belize	1998	6	...	...	...	6	...	148	
	1999	7	...	...	...	7	...	226	
	2000	8	...	...	...	8	...	288	
	2001	8	...	...	...	8	...	270	
Bermuda	1998	...	...	...	...	...	...	*171	
	1999	...	...	...	...	...	...	*171	
	2000	...	...	...	...	...	...	*171	
	2001	...	...	...	...	...	...	*171	

Bunkers - Soutes			Consumption - Consommation							
Air Avion	Sea Maritime	Unallocated Nondistribué	Per capita Par habitant	Total Totale	Solids Solides	Liquids Liquides	Gas Gaz	Electricity Electricité	Year Année	Région, pays ou zone
*111	*8	-101	55	1 626	...	1 536	...	*90	1998	Soudan
*116	*8	1 105	61	1 848	*1	1 752	...	95	1999	
123	8	-127	65	2 014	...	1 912	...	102	2000	
125	8	340	68	2 160	*1	2 053	...	106	2001	
19	...	...	283	1 203	...	1 202	...	*0	1998	Togo
*19	...	...	87	380	...	379	...	0	1999	
25	...	...	106	480	...	480	...	0	2000	
18	...	...	81	381	...	381	...	0	2001	
4	74	46	640	5 974	55	3 369	2 543	6	1998	Tunisie
*8	10	15	617	5 833	79	3 754	1 992	8	1999	
*10	11	65	696	6 656	74	3 695	*2 880	7	2000	
*13	11	56	727	6 998	68	3 731	*3 193	7	2001	
...	...	...	24	503	...	394	...	109	1998	Ouganda
...	...	...	24	517	...	408	...	109	1999	
...	...	...	26	584	...	449	...	135	2000	
...	...	...	27	614	...	471	...	143	2001	
*31	*24	1	30	*991	32	*781	...	179	1998	Rép.-Unie de Tanzanie
*34	*25	-1	29	985	53	746	...	186	1999	
33	25	25	41	1 431	55	1 191	...	184	2000	
67	23	25	44	1 564	55	1 288	...	221	2001	
*4	...	...	317	*75	...	*75	...	...	1998	Sahara occidental
*5	...	...	324	*79	...	*79	...	...	1999	
*5	...	...	317	*80	...	*80	...	...	2000	
*5	...	...	273	*80	...	*80	...	...	2001	
28	...	62	127	1 285	122	515	...	648	1998	Zambie
32	...	19	114	1 187	74	450	...	663	1999	
40	...	3	111	1 190	76	448	...	666	2000	
42	...	36	119	1 257	79	479	...	699	2001	
117	...	...	330	4 188	2 695	1 328	...	166	1998	Zimbabwe
89	...	...	372	4 859	3 054	1 551	...	254	1999	
87	...	...	340	4 289	2 907	1 102	...	280	2000	
79	...	...	309	3 938	2 664	1 016	...	258	2001	
21 513	**27 908**	**102 826**	**5 426**	**2 539 406**	**575 254**	**983 227**	**702 121**	**278 804**	**1998**	**Amérique du Nord**
22 984	**31 143**	**95 082**	**5 468**	**2 592 499**	**574 772**	**999 337**	**720 173**	**298 217**	**1999**	
22 318	**38 286**	**97 713**	**5 408**	**2 623 310**	**581 934**	**1 017 203**	**724 062**	**300 112**	**2000**	
21 250	**24 608**	**101 671**	**5 400**	**2 661 015**	**588 938**	**1 031 532**	**715 833**	**324 712**	**2001**	
*44	...	...	1 763	*113	...	*113	...	...	1998	Antigua-et-Barbuda
*45	...	...	1 799	*117	...	*117	...	...	1999	
*45	...	...	1 815	*118	...	*118	...	...	2000	
*45	...	...	1 638	*118	...	*118	...	...	2001	
...	...	322	3 228	*297	...	*297	...	...	1998	Aruba
...	...	325	3 203	*301	...	*301	...	...	1999	
...	...	325	3 042	*307	...	*307	...	...	2000	
...	...	325	3 243	*311	...	*311	...	...	2001	
*36	*184	...	2 026	*593	1	*593	...	...	1998	Bahamas
*36	*184	...	1 994	*594	*1	*593	...	...	1999	
*37	*184	...	1 964	*595	*1	*594	...	...	2000	
*37	*184	...	1 939	*595	*1	*594	...	...	2001	
162	...	0	1 311	349	...	314	35	...	1998	Barbade
166	...	0	1 406	375	...	332	44	...	1999	
205	...	...	1 352	361	...	326	35	...	2000	
205	...	...	1 387	372	...	342	30	...	2001	
*5	*8	...	590	140	...	135	...	6	1998	Belize
8	*7	...	978	217	...	211	...	7	1999	
12	*12	...	1 087	272	...	264	...	8	2000	
4	*7	...	1 040	267	...	259	...	8	2001	
*17	...	...	2 495	*155	...	*155	...	...	1998	Bermudes
*17	...	...	2 456	*155	...	*155	...	...	1999	
*17	...	...	2 456	*155	...	*155	...	...	2000	
*17	...	...	1 934	*155	...	*155	...	...	2001	

63

Production, trade and consumption of commercial energy
Thousand metric tons of oil equivalent and kilograms per capita *[cont.]*

Production, commerce et consommation d'énergie commerciale
Milliers de tonnes d'équivalent pétrole et kilogrammes par habitant *[suite]*

Region, country or area	Year Année	Primary energy production – Production d'énergie primaire					Changes in stocks Variations des stocks	Imports Importations	Export Exportations
		Total Totale	Solids Solides	Liquids Liquides	Gas Gaz	Electricity Electricité			
British Virgin Islands	1998	...	...	...	...	...	...	*20	.
	1999	...	...	...	...	...	...	*20	
	2000	...	...	...	...	...	...	*20	
	2001	...	...	...	...	...	...	*20	.
Canada	1998	386 875	38 947	136 409	164 250	47 269	2 000	56 975	180 86
	1999	384 299	37 336	134 799	163 322	48 843	*-3 511	58 569	181 81
	2000	379 332	35 276	139 896	154 315	49 845	*-9 906	65 223	192 81
	2001	391 537	35 759	137 562	167 193	51 023	*-2 393	71 375	200 87
Cayman Islands	1998	...	...	...	...	...	...	*113	
	1999	...	...	...	...	...	...	*112	
	2000	...	...	...	...	...	...	*113	
	2001	...	...	...	...	...	...	*113	
Costa Rica	1998	925	...	...	...	925	*-3	1 659	15
	1999	1 141	...	...	...	1 141	27	1 943	18
	2000	1 344	...	...	...	1 344	57	1 848	15
	2001	1 351	...	...	...	1 351	6	1 937	14
Cuba	1998	1 804	...	1 680	116	8	184	7 709	
	1999	2 576	...	2 138	429	9	172	7 625	
	2000	3 241	...	2 698	535	8	481	7 799	
	2001	3 435	...	2 889	540	6	361	7 550	
Dominica	1998	3	...	...	...	3	...	26	.
	1999	3	...	...	...	3	...	27	
	2000	3	...	...	...	3	...	34	
	2001	2	...	...	...	2	...	37	
Dominican Republic	1998	*208	...	...	...	*208		7 121	
	1999	119	...	...	...	119	9	7 282	
	2000	48	...	...	...	48	...	6 319	
	2001	66	...	...	...	66	...	6 376	
El Salvador	1998	547	...	...	...	547	*-8	2 079	21
	1999	666	...	...	...	666	*-7	2 030	23
	2000	777	...	...	...	777	*-5	2 121	26
	2001	931	...	...	...	931	*-21	2 143	28
Greenland	1998	...	...	...	...	...	...	*182	*
	1999	...	...	...	...	...	...	*186	*
	2000	...	...	...	...	...	...	*192	*
	2001	...	...	...	...	...	...	*194	*
Grenada	1998	...	...	...	...	...	1	71	.
	1999	...	...	...	...	...	...	74	
	2000	...	...	...	...	...	...	74	
	2001	...	...	...	...	...	1	80	
Guadeloupe	1998	...	...	...	...	...	...	*556	.
	1999	...	...	...	...	...	...	*581	.
	2000	...	...	...	...	...	...	*590	
	2001	...	...	...	...	...	...	*601	.
Guatemala	1998	1 462	...	1 273	10	179	113	2 833	1 10
	1999	1 403	...	1 164	*10	229	*-5	2 675	96
	2000	1 276	...	1 036	*10	229	*-89	2 828	94
	2001	1 326	...	1 150	*10	166	40	3 019	1 06
Haiti	1998	*24	...	...	...	*24	...	425	
	1999	23	...	...	...	23	7	484	.
	2000	23	...	...	...	23	...	489	
	2001	19	...	...	...	19	...	525	
Honduras	1998	165	...	...	...	165	*-30	1 427	1
	1999	183	...	...	...	183	*-17	1 456	1
	2000	243	...	...	...	243	5	1 411	1
	2001	251	...	...	...	251	150	1 753	1
Jamaica	1998	12	...	...	...	12	*-133	3 679	3
	1999	10	...	...	...	10	*-133	3 248	6
	2000	12	...	...	...	12	131	3 833	22
	2001	13	...	...	...	13	30	3 658	8

Air Avion	Sea Maritime	Unallocated Nondistribué	Per capita Par habitant	Total Totale	Solids Solides	Liquids Liquides	Gas Gaz	Electricity Electricité	Year Année	Région, pays ou zone
...	...	...	890	*20	...	*20	...	...	1998	Iles Vierges britanniques
...	...	...	851	*20	...	*20	...	...	1999	
...	...	...	816	*20	...	*20	...	...	2000	
...	...	...	979	*20	...	*20	...	...	2001	
932	1 163	14 639	8 075	244 255	26 903	88 124	81 959	47 269	1998	Canada
1 010	1 108	16 173	8 076	246 273	25 885	90 966	80 579	48 843	1999	
1 008	1 076	17 792	7 862	241 768	28 233	91 326	72 364	49 845	2000	
1 054	1 060	13 781	8 012	248 538	28 440	91 657	77 418	51 023	2001	
*17	...	...	2 681	*97	...	*97	...	...	1998	Iles Caïmanes
*18	...	...	2 553	*94	...	*94	...	...	1999	
*18	...	...	2 512	*95	...	*95	...	...	2000	
*18	...	...	2 329	*95	...	*95	...	...	2001	
...	...	-114	722	2 546	...	1 621	...	925	1998	Costa Rica
...	...	-1	802	2 878	...	1 737	...	1 141	1999	
...	...	5	778	2 977	...	1 633	...	1 344	2000	
...	...	48	796	3 085	...	1 734	...	1 351	2001	
286	114	1 249	691	7 680	10	7 546	116	8	1998	Cuba
273	143	1 853	695	7 760	10	7 312	429	9	1999	
217	103	2 147	723	8 091	11	7 538	535	8	2000	
189	103	2 379	708	7 953	9	7 397	540	6	2001	
...	...	...	379	29	...	26	...	3	1998	Dominique
...	...	...	419	30	...	27	...	3	1999	
...	...	...	514	37	...	34	...	3	2000	
...	...	...	509	40	...	37	...	2	2001	
...	...	911	792	6 418	57	6 153	...	*208	1998	Rép. dominicaine
...	...	489	829	6 903	55	6 730	...	119	1999	
...	...	365	705	6 002	65	5 889	...	48	2000	
...	...	606	684	5 835	142	5 627	...	66	2001	
...	...	89	386	2 326	...	1 780	...	547	1998	El Salvador
...	...	63	392	2 411	...	1 744	...	666	1999	
...	...	104	403	2 531	...	1 754	...	777	2000	
...	...	98	425	2 716	...	1 786	...	931	2001	
...	...	...	3 127	*175	...	*175	...	...	1998	Groenland
...	...	...	3 201	*179	...	*179	...	...	1999	
...	...	...	3 292	*184	...	*184	...	...	2000	
...	...	...	3 329	*186	...	*186	...	...	2001	
*2	...	...	734	68	...	68	...	...	1998	Grenade
*2	...	...	707	71	...	71	...	...	1999	
*2	...	...	707	71	...	71	...	...	2000	
*2	...	...	758	77	...	77	...	...	2001	
*80	...	...	1 135	*477	...	*477	...	...	1998	Guadeloupe
*81	...	...	1 181	*501	...	*501	...	...	1999	
*83	...	...	1 186	*508	...	*508	...	...	2000	
*83	...	...	1 199	*518	...	*518	...	...	2001	
...	...	75	278	3 003	...	2 814	10	179	1998	Guatemala
...	...	140	269	2 983	...	2 744	*10	229	1999	
...	...	41	282	3 207	...	2 967	*10	229	2000	
...	...	165	264	3 080	...	2 904	*10	166	2001	
...	...	...	59	449	...	425	...	*24	1998	Haïti
...	...	...	64	499	...	476	...	23	1999	
...	...	...	64	512	...	489	...	23	2000	
...	...	...	67	544	...	525	...	19	2001	
...	...	...	261	1 610	...	1 445	...	165	1998	Honduras
...	...	...	257	1 640	...	1 457	...	183	1999	
...	...	...	255	1 637	...	1 394	...	243	2000	
...	...	...	278	1 842	...	1 591	...	251	2001	
...	...	521	1 272	3 271	50	3 209	...	12	1998	Jamaïque
...	...	-35	1 296	3 357	50	3 296	...	10	1999	
...	...	96	1 290	3 398	50	3 335	...	12	2000	
...	...	217	1 274	3 339	37	3 289	...	13	2001	

63

Production, trade and consumption of commercial energy
Thousand metric tons of oil equivalent and kilograms per capita *[cont.]*

Production, commerce et consommation d'énergie commerciale
Milliers de tonnes d'équivalent pétrole et kilogrammes par habitant *[suite]*

Region, country or area	Year Année	Primary energy production – Production d'énergie primaire					Changes in stocks Variations des stocks	Imports Importations	Exports Exportations
		Total Totale	Solids Solides	Liquids Liquides	Gas Gaz	Electricity Electricité			
Martinique	1998	...	...	...	...	...	...	*870	*202
	1999	...	...	...	...	...	...	*880	*209
	2000	...	...	...	...	...	...	*885	*208
	2001	...	...	...	...	...	...	*899	*213
Mexico	1998	234 574	3 501	187 734	33 927	9 412	*-474	18 005	95 775
	1999	228 320	3 515	182 084	32 563	10 158	*-170	18 772	88 341
	2000	235 519	3 548	188 368	33 529	10 074	1 524	23 940	96 554
	2001	237 299	3 604	191 291	32 885	9 519	*-205	21 835	96 943
Montserrat	1998	...	...	...	...	...	...	*16	..
	1999	...	...	...	...	...	...	*18	
	2000	...	...	...	...	...	...	*18	
	2001	...	...	...	...	...	...	*18	
Netherlands Antilles	1998	...	...	...	...	...	...	*16 037	*9 621
	1999	...	...	...	...	...	...	*16 557	*10 066
	2000	...	...	...	...	...	...	*16 704	*8 835
	2001	...	...	...	...	...	...	*16 714	*8 857
Nicaragua	1998	*600	...	...	...	*600	53	1 136	..
	1999	459	...	...	...	459	*-64	1 132	11
	2000	495	...	...	...	495	*-40	1 177	30
	2001	548	...	...	...	548	24	1 330	19
Panama	1998	184	...	...	...	184	45	3 221	*1 183
	1999	269	...	...	...	269	*-64	3 233	*1 348
	2000	292	...	...	...	292	68	3 095	*1 116
	2001	331	...	...	...	331	142	3 678	993
Puerto Rico	1998	10	...	...	...	10	-28	5 471	*437
	1999	*10	...	...	...	*10	-100	5 340	*394
	2000	*10	...	...	...	*10	-100	5 204	*420
	2001	*10	...	...	...	*10	*20	*5 418	*416
Saint Kitts and Nevis	1998	...	...	...	...	...	...	*34	..
	1999	...	...	...	...	...	...	*34	
	2000	...	...	...	...	...	...	*34	
	2001	...	...	...	...	...	...	*34	
Saint Lucia	1998	...	...	...	...	...	...	98	..
	1999	...	...	...	...	...	...	108	
	2000	...	...	...	...	...	...	*113	
	2001	...	...	...	...	...	...	*115	
Saint Pierre and Miquelon	1998	...	...	...	...	...	...	*22	..
	1999	...	...	...	...	...	...	*22	
	2000	...	...	...	...	...	...	*22	
	2001	...	...	...	...	...	...	*22	
St. Vincent-Grenadines	1998	2	...	...	...	2	...	55	..
	1999	*2	...	...	...	*2	...	*55	
	2000	*2	...	...	...	*2	...	*57	
	2001	*2	...	...	...	*2	...	*60	
Trinidad and Tobago	1998	14 294	...	6 391	7 903	...	102	3 759	8 961
	1999	16 171	...	6 509	9 662	...	*-156	4 053	9 545
	2000	*15 948	...	6 225	*9 723	...	128	5 004	9 546
	2001	*15 948	...	6 225	*9 723	...	128	5 004	9 540
United States	1998	1 684 301	570 794	380 107	514 151	219 250	16 060	618 096	75 649
	1999	1 660 350	559 228	362 613	502 422	236 087	*-24 269	635 543	68 098
	2000	1 640 489	547 846	362 159	493 785	236 699	*-46 721	671 792	68 505
	2001	1 727 893	577 771	360 110	529 546	260 465	53 851	701 850	63 993
United States Virgin Is.	1998	...	...	...	...	...	*189	*17 830	*14 000
	1999	...	...	...	...	...	*118	*18 261	*14 046
	2000	...	...	...	...	...	*160	18 394	*14 078
	2001	...	...	...	...	...	*160	18 394	*14 078
America, South	**1998**	**503 439**	**30 206**	**345 493**	**81 150**	**46 590**	**1 231**	**84 742**	**249 84**
	1999	**500 202**	**29 239**	**342 760**	**81 750**	**46 454**	**-4 010**	**76 738**	**238 44**
	2000	**519 954**	**33 753**	**349 886**	**86 882**	**49 434**	**1 811**	**76 628**	**245 979**
	2001	**514 691**	**36 584**	**343 948**	**84 904**	**49 255**	**4 696**	**77 265**	**247 61**

Bunkers - Soutes			Consumption - Consommation							
Air Avion	Sea Maritime	Unallocated Nondistribué	Per capita Par habitant	Total Totale	Solids Solides	Liquids Liquides	Gas Gaz	Electricity Electricité	Year Année	Région, pays ou zone
...	*39	50	1 525	*578	...	*578	...	...	1998	Martinique
...	*40	46	1 535	*585	...	*585	...	...	1999	
...	*40	51	1 530	*586	...	*586	...	...	2000	
...	*40	52	1 532	*594	...	*594	...	...	2001	
2 503	785	19 272	1 406	134 718	4 958	85 364	34 984	9 412	1998	Mexique
2 604	835	23 552	1 344	131 931	4 719	84 419	32 635	10 158	1999	
2 425	1 334	20 239	1 416	137 382	5 331	86 481	35 496	10 074	2000	
2 602	1 107	23 303	1 331	135 385	5 482	84 300	36 084	9 519	2001	
...	*1	...	2 575	*15	...	*15	...	...	1998	Montserrat
...	*1	...	3 307	*17	...	*17	...	...	1999	
...	*1	...	3 307	*17	...	*17	...	...	2000	
...	*1	...	5 512	*17	...	*17	...	...	2001	
*68	*1 726	3 650	4 677	*973	...	*973			1998	Antilles néerlandaises
*70	*1 759	4 064	2 916	598	...	598	...	...	1999	
*70	*1 708	4 036	9 558	2 055	...	2 055	...	...	2000	
*70	*1 725	4 029	9 367	2 033	...	2 033	...	...	2001	
...	...	18	347	1 665	...	1 065	...	*600	1998	Nicaragua
...	...	15	330	1 629	...	1 169	...	459	1999	
...	...	36	324	1 645	...	1 151	...	495	2000	
...	...	67	340	1 768	...	1 220	...	548	2001	
...	...	54	768	2 122	39	1 842	*57	184	1998	Panama
...	...	145	738	2 073	49	1 698	*57	269	1999	
...	...	76	745	2 127	42	1 736	*57	292	2000	
...	...	894	684	1 981	44	1 548	*57	331	2001	
...	*175	53	1 264	*4 845	*123	*4 712	...	10	1998	Porto Rico
...	*160	-67	1 276	4 963	*112	4 841	...	*10	1999	
...	*155	-180	1 268	4 920	*112	4 798	...	*10	2000	
...	*150	-12	1 264	*4 855	*109	*4 736	...	*10	2001	
...	...	...	869	*34	...	*34	...	...	1998	Saint-Kitts-et-Nevis
...	...	...	807	*34	...	*34	...	...	1999	
...	...	...	847	*34	...	*34	...	...	2000	
...	...	...	847	*34	...	*34	...	...	2001	
...	...	...	645	98	...	98	...	...	1998	Sainte-Lucie
...	...	...	741	108	...	108	...	...	1999	
...	...	...	765	*113	...	*113	...	...	2000	
...	...	...	731	*115	...	*115	...	...	2001	
...	4	...	2 625	*18	...	*18	...	...	1998	Saint-Pierre-et-Miquelon
...	4	...	2 625	*18	...	*18	...	...	1999	
...	4	...	2 625	*18	...	*18	...	...	2000	
...	4	...	3 063	*18	...	*18	...	...	2001	
...	...	...	510	57	...	55	...	2	1998	St. Vincent-Grenadines
...	...	...	505	*57	...	*55	...	*2	1999	
...	...	...	519	*59	...	*57	...	*2	2000	
...	...	...	567	*62	...	*60	...	*2	2001	
63	185	223	6 665	8 518	...	615	7 903	...	1998	Trinité-et-Tobago
71	176	63	8 166	10 525	...	863	9 662	...	1999	
11	202	214	8 416	*10 857	...	1 134	*9 723	...	2000	
11	202	214	8 390	*10 857	...	1 134	*9 723	...	2001	
17 299	23 325	61 007	7 795	2 109 057	542 936	769 813	577 057	219 250	1998	Etats-Unis
18 583	26 523	47 026	7 921	2 159 932	543 713	783 376	596 757	236 087	1999	
18 167	33 260	51 142	7 725	2 187 929	547 909	797 481	605 840	236 699	2000	
16 913	19 818	54 280	7 798	2 220 887	554 494	813 958	591 970	260 465	2001	
...	*198	806	22 355	*2 638	*178	*2 460	...	...	1998	Iles Vierges américaines
...	*203	1 230	22 255	*2 671	*179	*2 492	...	...	1999	
...	*207	1 227	22 507	*2 723	*180	*2 543	...	...	2000	
...	*207	1 227	24 758	*2 723	*180	*2 543	...	...	2001	
2 356	3 394	30 382	908	300 978	21 188	152 051	81 149	46 590	1998	Amérique du Sud
2 225	4 384	37 554	882	298 343	21 166	150 006	80 718	46 454	1999	
1 984	4 988	38 085	885	303 736	20 101	147 314	86 887	49 434	2000	
2 173	5 262	29 344	863	302 870	19 531	149 402	84 683	49 255	2001	

63
Production, trade and consumption of commercial energy
Thousand metric tons of oil equivalent and kilograms per capita *[cont.]*

Production, commerce et consommation d'énergie commerciale
Milliers de tonnes d'équivalent pétrole et kilogrammes par habitant *[suite]*

Region, country or area	Year Année	Primary energy production – Production d'énergie primaire					Changes in stocks Variations des stocks	Imports Importations	Export Exportations
		Total Totale	Solids Solides	Liquids Liquides	Gas Gaz	Electricity Electricité			
Argentina	1998	78 331	171	43 813	30 132	4 215	409	5 024	21 80
	1999	82 191	198	42 697	35 611	3 684	*-350	3 379	21 46
	2000	83 169	153	41 256	37 664	4 096	*-733	3 325	22 88
	2001	84 834	110	42 082	37 193	5 449	*-17	2 295	26 48
Bolivia	1998	5 618	...	2 085	3 394	139	11	303	1 82
	1999	*4 667	...	1 839	*2 681	147	*-25	359	1 23
	2000	*5 440	...	1 845	*3 446	149	*-9	291	2 15
	2001	6 638	...	2 082	4 406	150	1	243	3 52
Brazil	1998	85 746	2 451	51 364	6 012	25 918	632	47 746	3 96
	1999	92 935	2 515	57 795	6 389	26 236	*-550	42 945	3 52
	2000	103 225	3 024	65 700	6 744	27 757	991	42 058	6 27
	2001	104 944	2 512	68 807	6 859	26 766	*-1 070	45 169	12 20
Chile	1998	4 438	658	789	1 620	1 371	92	16 601	14
	1999	4 055	340	704	1 843	1 168	*-584	17 914	18
	2000	4 326	256	480	1 949	1 641	530	19 287	55
	2001	4 730	403	508	1 954	1 864	304	18 394	68
Colombia	1998	68 540	21 694	37 872	6 327	2 647	170	1 315	44 02
	1999	69 619	21 290	39 984	5 442	2 902	*-580	255	46 87
	2000	69 601	24 792	35 983	6 067	2 758	136	258	46 78
	2001	69 188	28 237	31 774	6 442	2 735	653	200	44 72
Ecuador	1998	20 479	...	19 634	224	622	*-135	1 499	14 42
	1999	20 352	...	19 522	210	620	*-50	1 539	14 61
	2000	21 926	...	20 967	229	730	479	1 022	15 14
	2001	22 112	...	21 270	233	608	457	1 355	14 91
Falkland Is. (Malvinas)	1998	3	3	...	...	...	...	9	
	1999	*3	*3	...	...	...	...	*9	
	2000	*3	*3	...	...	...	...	*9	
	2001	*3	*3	...	...	...	...	*10	
French Guiana	1998	...	...	...	...	...	...	*309	
	1999	...	...	...	...	...	...	*313	
	2000	...	...	...	...	...	...	*313	
	2001	...	...	...	...	...	...	*322	
Guyana	1998	*0	...	...	...	*0	...	559	
	1999	*0	...	...	...	*0	...	569	
	2000	*0	...	...	...	*0	*-4	537	
	2001	*0	...	...	...	*0	...	558	
Paraguay	1998	4 371	...	...	...	4 371	5	1 301	
	1999	4 465	...	...	...	4 465	*-63	1 278	
	2000	4 599	...	...	...	4 599	38	1 143	
	2001	3 901	...	...	...	3 901	19	1 047	
Peru	1998	7 640	14	5 724	530	1 372	285	6 297	3 82
	1999	8 193	11	6 025	719	1 438	*-1 131	4 954	2 67
	2000	7 892	8	5 623	679	1 581	79	5 703	2 24
	2001	7 289	13	4 858	710	1 708	*-96	5 365	2 94
Suriname	1998	360	...	248		111	1	493	4
	1999	361	...	248		113	...	496	4
	2000	716	...	603		113	...	278	19
	2001	776	...	644		132	...	228	13
Uruguay	1998	787	...	...	...	787	*-23	2 141	
	1999	473	...	...	...	473	42	2 646	
	2000	606	...	...	...	606	*-80	2 333	1
	2001	743	...	...	...	743	*-29	2 014	4
Venezuela	1998	227 127	5 216	183 964	32 911	5 036	*-215	1 145	159 78
	1999	212 888	4 883	173 945	28 853	5 208	*-718	*81	147 81
	2000	218 453	5 516	177 429	30 105	5 403	384	*69	149 72
	2001	209 534	5 306	171 924	27 106	5 199	4 472	*66	141 94
Asia	1998	3 126 018	970 276	1 519 991	443 245	192 507	13 345	1 097 763	1 297 79
	1999	3 006 366	862 563	1 484 060	466 553	193 190	-46 640	1 125 669	1 287 03
	2000	3 144 211	856 323	1 566 199	522 333	199 356	-5 573	1 241 972	1 388 75
	2001	3 264 306	955 968	1 548 664	556 650	203 024	-11 990	1 235 121	1 406 2'

| Bunkers - Soutes | | | Consumption - Consommation | | | | | | | |
Air Avion	Sea Maritime	Unallocated Nondistribué	Per capita Par habitant	Total Totale	Solids Solides	Liquids Liquides	Gas Gaz	Electricity Electricité	Year Année	Région, pays ou zone
...	550	5 741	1 518	54 847	750	19 856	30 027	4 215	1998	Argentine
...	600	5 823	1 587	58 034	569	20 929	32 852	3 684	1999	
...	507	4 595	1 600	59 243	437	20 810	33 900	4 096	2000	
...	570	4 669	1 479	55 423	430	17 982	31 562	5 449	2001	
...	...	271	480	3 816	...	1 767	1 910	139	1998	Bolivie
...	...	166	449	*3 653	...	1 795	*1 711	147	1999	
...	...	254	400	*3 331	...	1 710	*1 472	149	2000	
...	...	483	339	2 873	...	1 598	1 125	150	2001	
963	1 703	10 373	716	115 854	12 289	71 634	6 012	25 918	1998	Brésil
815	2 624	12 462	708	117 009	12 713	71 300	6 759	26 236	1999	
667	2 961	14 051	717	120 334	13 513	70 316	8 749	27 757	2000	
818	2 865	12 667	711	122 623	13 353	71 380	11 124	26 766	2001	
25	...	712	1 354	20 066	4 671	10 818	3 207	1 371	1998	Chili
1	56	1 146	1 409	21 163	4 892	10 955	4 148	1 168	1999	
...	219	751	1 417	21 557	3 759	10 504	5 652	1 641	2000	
57	243	641	1 376	21 199	2 860	10 126	6 349	1 864	2001	
*690	203	3 354	525	21 414	2 060	10 380	6 327	2 647	1998	Colombie
681	174	3 776	456	18 952	2 567	8 041	5 442	2 902	1999	
625	231	3 114	448	18 971	1 719	8 426	6 067	2 758	2000	
625	231	2 359	483	20 795	2 289	9 329	6 442	2 735	2001	
...	*148	576	572	6 967	...	6 122	224	622	1998	Equateur
...	*136	1 329	472	5 859	...	5 029	210	620	1999	
...	157	1 065	482	6 100	...	5 140	229	730	2000	
...	257	759	549	7 076	...	6 234	233	608	2001	
...	...	...	5 959	12	3	9	...	...	1998	Iles Falkland (Malvinas)
...	...	...	5 959	*12	*3	*9	...	...	1999	
...	...	...	5 959	*12	*3	*9	...	...	2000	
...	...	...	4 387	*13	*3	*10	...	...	2001	
*17	...	...	1 901	*293	...	*293	...	...	1998	Guyane française
*18	...	...	1 861	*296	...	*296	...	...	1999	
*18	...	...	1 793	*296	...	*296	...	...	2000	
*18	...	...	1 800	*304	...	*304	...	...	2001	
12	*2	...	723	545	...	545	...	*0	1998	Guyana
12	...	...	723	557	...	557	...	*0	1999	
12	...	...	686	529	...	529	...	*0	2000	
13	...	...	715	545	...	544	...	*0	2001	
...	...	3	1 085	5 664	...	1 293	...	4 371	1998	Paraguay
...	...	5	1 082	5 796	...	1 331	...	4 465	1999	
...	...	3	1 037	5 701	...	1 103	...	4 599	2000	
...	...	1	879	4 927	...	1 026	...	3 901	2001	
*342	...	-682	410	10 167	412	7 853	530	1 372	1998	Pérou
*362	...	452	427	10 785	307	8 320	719	1 438	1999	
*311	...	444	410	10 514	476	7 778	679	1 581	2000	
*326	56	-514	377	9 935	543	6 974	710	1 708	2001	
...	...	191	1 443	613	...	502	...	111	1998	Suriname
...	...	191	1 437	618	...	505	...	113	1999	
...	...	196	1 390	606	...	493	...	113	2000	
...	...	198	1 557	668	...	536	...	132	2001	
56	281	102	764	2 512	1	1 721	2	787	1998	Uruguay
73	293	161	768	2 544	1	2 049	22	473	1999	
72	297	305	698	2 330	1	1 688	34	606	2000	
54	387	104	654	2 198	1	1 422	31	743	2001	
252	507	9 740	2 504	58 207	1 002	19 259	32 911	5 036	1998	Venezuela
262	500	12 043	2 238	53 064	*114	18 890	28 853	5 208	1999	
279	617	13 306	2 243	54 213	193	18 512	30 105	5 403	2000	
262	653	7 977	2 204	54 292	*52	21 935	27 106	5 199	2001	
20 272	54 574	160 305	744	2 677 494	1 085 976	944 005	455 006	192 507	1998	Asie
19 250	53 763	180 519	723	2 638 104	1 003 689	956 878	484 347	193 190	1999	
20 046	49 861	220 341	734	2 712 758	1 009 880	987 032	516 491	199 356	2000	
20 499	53 085	217 262	749	2 814 363	1 073 692	986 469	551 177	203 024	2001	

63

Production, trade and consumption of commercial energy
Thousand metric tons of oil equivalent and kilograms per capita *[cont.]*

Production, commerce et consommation d'énergie commerciale
Milliers de tonnes d'équivalent pétrole et kilogrammes par habitant *[suite]*

Region, country or area	Year Année	Primary energy production – Production d'énergie primaire					Changes in stocks Variations des stocks	Imports Importations	Expor Exportatio
		Total Totale	Solids Solides	Liquids Liquides	Gas Gaz	Electricity Electricité			
Afghanistan	1998	*156	*1	...	*128	*27	*10	*247	
	1999	*146	*1	...	*118	*27	*10	*229	
	2000	*137	*1	...	*109	*27	*10	*227	
	2001	*129	*1	...	*102	*27	*10	*221	
Armenia	1998	547	...	...	...	547	...	1 514	
	1999	646	...	...	...	646	...	1 321	
	2000	632	...	...	...	632	...	1 576	
	2001	602	...	...	...	602	...	1 592	
Azerbaijan	1998	16 828	...	11 449	5 211	168	289	301	4 4
	1999	19 555	...	13 833	5 593	130	*-205	270	6 7
	2000	19 436	...	14 043	5 262	132	*-82	340	7 5
	2001	20 033	...	14 934	4 987	112	113	3 025	10 5
Bahrain	1998	9 714	...	2 293	7 421	...	*-711	10 540	10 2
	1999	9 970	...	2 280	7 690	...	*-237	11 259	10 7
	2000	*10 116	...	2 273	*7 843	...	*-85	10 959	10 :
	2001	*10 559	...	2 260	*8 300	...	*-602	10 123	9 7
Bangladesh	1998	7 075	...	37	6 964	74	206	3 252	
	1999	7 737	...	*36	7 630	72	76	3 397	
	2000	8 204	...	*36	8 087	82	*-134	3 395	
	2001	*9 805	...	215	*9 507	84	*-125	4 229	
Bhutan	1998	190	*35	...	...	155	...	*79	
	1999	*190	*35	...	...	*155	...	*80	
	2000	*191	*35	...	...	*156	...	*83	
	2001	*198	*35	...	...	*163	...	*85	
Brunei Darussalam	1998	*18 116	...	*8 472	*9 644	...	-50	14	*16
	1999	18 185	...	9 231	*8 954	...	*89	4	16 :
	2000	20 833	...	10 307	10 526	...	*-102	...	18
	2001	21 036	...	10 395	10 642	...	15	1	18
Cambodia	1998	*7	...	...	...	*7	...	*170	
	1999	*7	...	...	...	*7	...	*174	
	2000	*7	...	...	...	*7	...	*177	
	2001	*7	...	...	...	*7	...	*178	
China	1998	833 878	624 375	161 161	26 774	21 568	*-6 479	56 667	45
	1999	732 548	521 978	160 160	28 981	21 430	*-14 309	63 827	39
	2000	716 442	498 501	163 163	31 282	23 496	*-4 541	100 982	57
	2001	807 232	579 810	164 123	34 880	28 419	189	90 908	72
China, Hong Kong SAR	1998	...	...	...	...	...	75	25 472	8
	1999	...	...	...	...	...	281	23 007	3
	2000	...	...	...	...	...	1 170	18 879	1
	2001	...	...	...	...	...	677	19 540	1
China, Macao SAR	1998	...	...	...	...	...	10	522	
	1999	...	...	...	...	...	4	502	
	2000	...	...	...	...	...	*-13	525	
	2001	...	...	...	...	...	23	581	
Cyprus	1998	...	...	...	...	...	*-12	2 125	
	1999	...	...	...	...	...	68	2 299	
	2000	...	...	...	...	...	18	2 384	
	2001	...	...	...	...	...	*-30	2 413	
Georgia	1998	675	8	119	...	548	25	1 954	
	1999	670	9	107	...	554	61	1 992	
	2000	673	4	110	55	504	*-31	2 106	
	2001	613	1	99	37	477	22	1 300	
India	1998	249 163	178 145	36 860	23 811	10 347	985	68 670	1
	1999	245 512	177 209	36 841	20 921	10 541	*-7 918	67 089	1
	2000	257 781	188 433	36 502	21 886	10 960	*-2 549	92 308	1
	2001	262 677	192 641	36 381	22 096	11 558	*-1 798	91 716	6
Indonesia	1998	199 109	42 225	95 211	58 216	3 457	6 671	18 271	115
	1999	191 450	49 492	90 587	47 828	3 543	-17 224	18 764	124
	2000	195 863	53 774	88 087	50 545	3 458	*-2 512	22 024	114
	2001	206 699	64 782	85 851	52 565	3 500	*-6 770	20 634	121

Energy   Energie

kers - Soutes			Consumption - Consommation							
Air vion	Sea Maritime	Unallocated Nondistribué	Per capita Par habitant	Total Totale	Solids Solides	Liquids Liquides	Gas Gaz	Electricity Electricité	Year Année	Région, pays ou zone
*5	...	...	19	*388	*1	*232	*128	*27	1998	Afghanistan
*5	...	...	17	*360	*1	*214	*118	*27	1999	
*5	...	...	16	*348	*1	*212	*109	*27	2000	
*5	...	...	15	*335	*1	*206	*102	*27	2001	
22	...	...	537	2 040	4	133	1 356	547	1998	Arménie
22	...	...	512	1 944	2	192	1 105	646	1999	
63	...	...	564	2 145	...	267	1 246	632	2000	
60	...	...	561	2 134	...	263	1 269	602	2001	
187	...	1 577	1 359	10 653	1	5 335	5 149	168	1998	Azerbaïdjan
171	...	2 408	1 355	10 718	...	4 910	5 678	130	1999	
121	...	1 020	1 395	11 136	...	5 457	5 548	132	2000	
222	...	731	1 405	11 397	...	3 233	8 053	112	2001	
357	...	2 043	12 936	8 318	...	897	7 421	...	1998	Bahreïn
342	...	1 832	12 758	8 497	...	806	7 690	...	1999	
365	...	1 739	12 581	*8 694	...	850	*7 843	...	2000	
390	...	2 021	13 973	*9 152	...	853	*8 300	...	2001	
...	*43	156	75	9 922	87	2 798	6 964	74	1998	Bangladesh
...	*36	421	79	10 601	46	2 854	7 630	72	1999	
...	*36	557	81	11 140	330	2 642	8 087	82	2000	
...	*36	908	94	*13 215	400	3 224	*9 507	84	2001	
...	...	...	125	247	*48	*44	...	155	1998	Bhoutan
...	...	...	121	*246	*46	*45	...	*155	1999	
...	...	...	120	*250	*46	*48	...	*156	2000	
...	...	...	122	*259	*46	*50	...	*163	2001	
...	...	-272	7 582	*2 388	...	906	*1 482	...	1998	Brunéi Darussalam
...	...	-163	5 248	*1 737	...	*928	*809	...	1999	
...	...	399	7 128	2 409	...	942	1 468	...	2000	
...	...	364	6 858	2 359	...	957	1 402	...	2001	
...	...	...	16	*177	...	*170	...	*7	1998	Cambodge
...	...	...	14	*182	...	*174	...	*7	1999	
...	...	...	14	*184	...	*177	...	*7	2000	
...	...	...	14	*185	...	*178	...	*7	2001	
...	2 267	45 292	641	804 101	605 525	150 234	26 774	21 568	1998	Chine
...	3 977	44 503	571	722 219	509 873	161 936	28 981	21 430	1999	
...	4 161	51 387	556	709 344	481 624	172 942	31 282	23 496	2000	
...	4 285	51 186	599	770 467	530 424	176 743	34 880	28 419	2001	
2 708	2 858	...	1 698	11 284	3 800	5 245	2 240	...	1998	Chine, Hong Kong RAS
2 268	3 582	...	1 991	13 379	3 420	7 489	2 470	...	1999	
2 100	3 407	...	1 570	10 673	3 240	5 200	2 232	...	2000	
2 461	3 777	...	1 680	11 300	4 297	4 749	2 253	...	2001	
...	...	...	1 202	512	...	512	...	...	1998	Chine, Macao RAS
...	...	...	1 149	499	...	499	...	...	1999	
...	...	...	1 229	538	...	538	...	...	2000	
...	...	...	1 285	558	...	558	...	...	2001	
266	98	26	2 332	1 747	20	1 726	...	...	1998	Chypre
272	154	22	2 369	1 784	24	1 760	...	...	1999	
277	192	16	2 484	1 880	37	1 844	...	...	2000	
337	191	35	2 476	1 879	40	1 839	...	...	2001	
106	...	19	451	2 391	11	1 067	765	548	1998	Géorgie
109	...	11	448	2 420	16	1 083	767	554	1999	
26	...	-8	515	2 708	16	1 254	935	504	2000	
10	...	-1	341	1 779	2	397	903	477	2001	
681	...	21 493	302	293 450	186 392	72 899	23 811	10 347	1998	Inde
681	...	20 349	302	298 271	197 082	69 727	20 921	10 541	1999	
702	...	31 865	318	318 490	203 840	81 804	21 886	10 960	2000	
*707	...	30 118	309	319 161	206 686	78 820	22 096	11 558	2001	
722	339	27 808	327	66 811	8 782	42 541	12 031	3 457	1998	Indonésie
*464	317	28 372	355	73 544	11 272	45 733	*12 996	3 543	1999	
*464	327	23 775	385	81 074	13 852	49 809	13 955	3 458	2000	
464	321	25 392	417	86 892	18 464	48 073	16 854	3 500	2001	

63

Production, trade and consumption of commercial energy
Thousand metric tons of oil equivalent and kilograms per capita *[cont.]*
Production, commerce et consommation d'énergie commerciale
Milliers de tonnes d'équivalent pétrole et kilogrammes par habitant *[suite]*

Region, country or area	Year Année	Primary energy production – Production d'énergie primaire					Changes in stocks Variations des stocks	Imports Importations	Exp Exportati
		Total Totale	Solids Solides	Liquids Liquides	Gas Gaz	Electricity Electricité			
Iran (Islamic Rep. of)	1998	237 213	882	189 099	46 629	603	11 547	3 231	117
	1999	236 904	883	182 666	52 930	425	...	3 964	118
	2000	249 429	900	192 012	56 093	424	...	5 470	132
	2001	255 150	793	192 700	61 220	437	...	7 456	130
Iraq	1998	107 480	...	104 679	2 751	50	3 439	...	78
	1999	127 863	...	124 848	2 966	50	...	...	103
	2000	130 654	...	127 116	3 485	53	...	207	104
	2001	121 174	...	116 940	4 181	53	...	131	92
Israel	1998	116	98	5	11	2	787	21 506	2
	1999	113	99	4	9	1	113	20 268	2
	2000	99	86	4	8	1	*-778	21 982	2
	2001	101	91	4	5	1	82	22 340	2
Japan	1998	103 639	2 125	655	2 256	98 602	*-4 606	387 818	7
	1999	98 930	2 265	602	2 235	93 828	*-3 166	395 139	6
	2000	100 051	1 719	620	2 443	95 270	3 655	415 503	5
	2001	99 293	1 750	602	2 412	94 529	*-3 100	406 376	4
Jordan	1998	231	...	2	228	1	175	4 729	
	1999	229	...	2	226	1	64	4 611	
	2000	221	...	2	216	3	*-106	4 774	
	2001	234	...	2	229	*3	101	4 859	
Kazakhstan	1998	64 630	30 804	26 137	7 161	528	...	6 397	31
	1999	65 656	25 743	30 425	8 962	527	*-680	5 244	35
	2000	79 399	31 840	35 716	11 195	648	*-305	6 457	46
	2001	84 941	32 971	40 446	10 829	695	43	7 584	51
Korea, Dem. P. R.	1998	54 828	53 115	...	...	1 713	...	5 418	
	*1999	50 352	48 636	...	...	1 716	...	5 500	
	2000	46 150	44 317	...	...	1 834	...	5 494	
	2001	*46 146	*44 254	...	...	*1 892	...	*5 541	
Korea, Republic of	1998	25 895	1 962	...	...	23 933	1 209	167 413	33
	1999	29 310	1 888	...	...	27 421	1 499	179 997	33
	2000	30 789	1 867	...	...	28 922	3 588	192 500	34
	2001	31 341	1 717	...	...	29 624	2 222	191 280	32
Kuwait [2]	1998	115 522	...	106 671	8 851	...	...	1	88
	1999	105 883	...	97 782	8 101	...	...	1	76
	2000	128 209	...	119 651	8 559	...	...	78	93
	2001	126 734	...	117 991	8 742	...	...	349	94
Kyrgyzstan	1998	1 087	137	78	17	855	...	1 830	
	1999	1 274	129	77	23	1 044	*-41	1 277	
	2000	1 416	133	77	30	1 177	*-42	1 262	
	2001	1 323	147	76	31	1 069	*-56	1 046	
Lao People's Dem. Rep.	1998	211	109	...	...	*102	...	*123	
	1999	229	127	...	...	*102	...	*123	
	2000	*260	*158	...	...	*102	...	*123	
	2001	*300	*196	...	...	*104	...	*128	
Lebanon	1998	68	...	...	...	68	...	4 931	
	1999	28	...	...	...	28	...	5 191	
	2000	39	...	...	...	39	...	4 673	
	2001	*45	...	...	...	*45	*-21	5 020	
Malaysia	1998	72 621	246	36 170	35 788	418	565	13 547	41
	1999	72 810	193	33 219	38 752	647	*-960	12 755	39
	2000	*77 096	*269	*31 259	*44 970	*598	-1 003	*16 770	*40
	2001	*77 696	344	35 329	*41 417	*607	108	19 150	42
Maldives	1998	...	...	...	...	...	...	179	
	1999	...	...	...	...	...	...	227	
	2000	...	...	...	...	...	...	227	
	2001	...	...	...	...	...	...	374	
Mongolia	1998	1 632	1 632	...	...	...	...	435	
	1999	1 562	1 562	...	...	...	...	463	
	2000	1 548	1 548	...	...	...	...	474	
	2001	1 626	1 626	...	...	...	...	508	

Air Avion	Sea Maritime	Unallocated Nondistribué	Per capita Par habitant	Total Totale	Solids Solides	Liquids Liquides	Gas Gaz	Electricity Electricité	Year Année	Région, pays ou zone
809	694	-3 707	1 829	113 122	1 140	62 998	48 381	603	1998	Iran (Rép. islamique d')
833	811 -	5 759	1 829	114 741	1 785	57 611	54 921	425	1999	
887	730	-1 302	1 919	122 142	1 659	60 874	59 185	424	2000	
905	731	6 183	1 949	123 789	1 436	56 786	65 130	437	2001	
445	...	2 350	1 036	22 542	...	19 741	2 751	50	1998	Iraq
429	...	1 267	998	22 284	...	19 269	2 966	50	1999	
470	...	1 689	1 065	24 439	...	20 901	3 485	53	2000	
498	...	1 789	1 075	26 676	...	22 442	4 181	53	2001	
*4	870	431	2 803	16 735	6 756	9 966	11	2	1998	Israël
4	766	-321	2 837	17 377	6 452	10 915	9	1	1999	
4	964	376	3 068	18 532	7 500	11 022	8	1	2000	
4	856	-558	3 058	19 688	8 132	11 550	5	1	2001	
6 344	5 648	14 779	3 653	461 795	90 740	206 208	66 246	98 602	1998	Japon
6 166	5 352	15 438	3 665	464 144	94 346	206 894	69 075	93 828	1999	
6 413	4 938	17 496	3 766	477 743	105 530	203 685	73 258	95 270	2000	
6 117	4 170	19 034	3 732	474 486	109 641	198 252	72 064	94 529	2001	
226	1	90	958	4 467	...	4 238	228	1	1998	Jordanie
226	4	69	935	4 476	...	4 249	226	1	1999	
251	11	77	969	4 762	...	4 543	216	3	2000	
221	2	115	898	4 654	...	4 422	229	*3	2001	
326	...	1 898	2 448	36 903	21 244	7 298	7 833	528	1998	Kazakhstan
256	...	2 057	2 261	33 749	20 125	5 451	7 644	527	1999	
209	...	1 688	2 535	37 767	21 161	5 698	10 260	648	2000	
163	...	1 882	2 614	38 775	20 936	7 489	9 655	695	2001	
...	...	*-16	2 734	60 016	54 437	3 866	...	1 713	1998	Corée, R. p. dém. de
...	...	30	2 513	55 573	49 966	3 891	...	1 716	*1999	
...	...	*-218	2 317	51 603	45 603	4 166	...	1 834	2000	
...	...	-85	*2 299	*51 509	*45 564	*4 052	...	*1 892	2001	
516	6 230	20 113	2 830	131 376	35 995	57 810	13 637	23 933	1998	Corée, République de
476	6 732	21 459	3 098	145 187	37 644	63 495	16 627	27 421	1999	
568	6 264	22 994	3 284	155 262	42 934	64 909	18 497	28 922	2000	
654	6 146	21 379	3 367	159 407	45 592	64 214	19 977	29 624	2001	
495	621	3 926	10 797	21 885	...	13 034	8 851	...	1998	Koweït [2]
391	644	7 762	9 712	20 463	...	12 362	8 101	...	1999	
356	458	15 862	8 256	18 081	...	9 522	8 559	...	2000	
410	514	10 660	9 040	20 567	...	11 824	8 742	...	2001	
...	...	7	608	2 892	473	615	949	855	1998	Kirghizistan
...	...	5	533	2 578	472	503	559	1 044	1999	
...	...	4	553	2 707	460	435	636	1 177	2000	
...	...	-2	486	2 396	289	386	652	1 069	2001	
...	...	...	66	*334	109	*123	...	*102	1998	Rép. dém. pop. lao
...	...	...	68	*352	127	*123	...	*102	1999	
...	...	...	73	*383	*158	*123	...	*102	2000	
...	...	...	79	*428	*196	*128	...	*104	2001	
*186	...	...	1 424	4 813	86	4 659	...	68	1998	Liban
120	...	...	1 483	5 100	*82	4 990	...	28	1999	
119	...	...	1 314	4 593	83	4 471	...	39	2000	
132	...	...	1 401	4 954	*85	4 824	...	*45	2001	
...	445	3 619	1 817	40 297	1 852	20 191	17 837	418	1998	Malaisie
...	390	816	2 005	45 532	1 526	20 257	23 102	647	1999	
...	*176	1 900	2 226	*51 799	*2 633	*21 098	*27 469	*598	2000	
...	153	5 079	2 066	*48 531	2 909	22 005	*23 010	*607	2001	
...	...	...	415	111	...	111	...	...	1998	Maldives
...	...	...	557	155	...	155	...	...	1999	
...	...	...	613	166	...	166	...	...	2000	
...	...	...	1 111	307	...	307	...	...	2001	
...	...	...	859	2 066	1 658	408	...	...	1998	Mongolie
...	...	...	859	2 025	1 622	403	...	...	1999	
...	...	...	846	2 022	1 578	444	...	...	2000	
...	...	...	874	2 134	1 633	501	...	...	2001	

63

Production, trade and consumption of commercial energy
Thousand metric tons of oil equivalent and kilograms per capita *[cont.]*

Production, commerce et consommation d'énergie commerciale
Milliers de tonnes d'équivalent pétrole et kilogrammes par habitant *[suite]*

Region, country or area	Year Année	Primary energy production – Production d'énergie primaire					Changes in stocks Variations des stocks	Imports Importations	Exp Exportati
		Total Totale	Solids Solides	Liquids Liquides	Gas Gaz	Electricity Electricité			
Myanmar	1998	3 076	13	390	2 591	82	19	1 230	1
	1999	4 969	98	444	4 338	89	43	1 437	2
	2000	6 582	244	420	5 755	163	*-67	1 425	4
	2001	6 465	46	430	5 832	157	*-13	1 148	4
Nepal	1998	101	11	...	...	90	...	898	
	1999	119	13	...	...	106	...	972	
	2000	*120	13	...	...	*108	...	995	
	2001	*115	7	...	...	*108	...	1 048	
Oman	1998	50 308	...	44 659	5 649	...	*-83	108	43
	1999	51 155	...	44 990	6 165	...	*-739	254	43
	2000	57 538	...	47 750	9 788	...	*-592	192	49
	2001	61 604	...	46 769	14 835	...	*-1 052	308	53
Pakistan	1998	22 112	1 494	2 889	15 733	1 995	...	15 759	
	1999	23 224	1 637	2 833	16 750	2 005	...	16 002	
	2000	24 302	1 498	2 893	18 148	1 763	...	17 022	
	2001	25 562	1 464	2 969	19 130	2 000	...	17 752	
Philippines	1998	8 627	473	41	8	8 105	*-1	21 923	
	1999	10 397	557	47	6	9 787	379	21 554	
	2000	11 374	640	55	10	10 669	116	22 674	
	2001	10 251	581	65	13	9 593	*-455	21 950	
Qatar	1998	50 060	...	31 800	18 260	...	*-1 769	...	34
	1999	58 558	...	31 708	26 850	...	*-2 432	...	38
	2000	64 698	...	37 133	27 566	...	*-2 381	...	48
	2001	67 252	...	37 969	29 283	...	*-574	...	50
Saudi Arabia [2]	1998	500 512	...	456 942	43 570	...	...	...	386
	1999	464 370	...	421 285	43 085	...	...	...	350
	2000	492 629	...	446 178	46 452	...	...	...	366
	2001	484 588	...	432 498	52 090	...	...	...	350
Singapore	1998	...	...	...	...	...	*1	85 533	42
	1999	...	...	...	...	...	*1	84 217	40
	2000	...	...	...	...	...	...	80 560	35
	2001	...	...	...	...	...	...	86 851	35
Sri Lanka	1998	337	...	...	...	337	15	3 061	
	1999	359	...	...	...	359	33	3 252	
	2000	275	...	...	...	275	103	3 837	
	2001	268	...	...	...	268	*-45	3 567	
Syrian Arab Republic	1998	34 280	...	29 059	*4 989	*232	-1 075	773	18
	1999	34 490	...	29 149	*5 108	*234	-1 789	715	18
	2000	36 810	...	31 374	*5 158	*278	-826	906	19
	2001	35 540	...	30 308	4 938	*293	-1 538	910	19
Tajikistan	1998	1 268	5	19	27	1 217	...	1 903	
	1999	1 383	5	19	32	1 327	...	1 894	
	2000	1 252	5	18	36	1 192	...	1 501	
	2001	1 268	5	18	36	1 209	...	1 570	
Thailand	1998	28 479	8 870	5 266	13 896	447	*-79	36 366	4
	1999	29 062	8 035	5 721	15 000	306	*-688	39 209	5
	2000	30 899	7 790	7 287	15 302	520	*-6	40 245	5
	2001	34 168	8 630	7 927	*17 067	544	*-216	43 203	7
Turkey	1998	21 916	14 490	3 226	493	3 706	*-132	45 550	1
	1999	21 001	14 358	2 944	643	3 055	179	46 267	1
	2000	19 715	13 665	2 765	561	2 725	*-400	53 280	
	2001	19 209	14 249	2 523	288	2 149	*-175	49 597	1
Turkmenistan	1998	19 332	...	7 387	11 945	0	...	1 344	8
	1999	28 429	...	7 756	20 672	0	...	688	14
	2000	50 266	...	7 779	42 486	0	...	688	35
	2001	55 143	...	8 688	46 455	0	...	688	39
United Arab Emirates	1998	152 550	...	119 538	33 012	...	178	445	117
	1999	143 607	...	109 732	33 876	...	383	401	107
	2000	151 276	...	115 798	35 479	...	57	...	106
	2001	153 530	...	113 510	40 020	...	*-90	...	102

Air Avion	Sea Maritime	Unallocated Nondistribué	Per capita Par habitant	Total Totale	Solids Solides	Liquids Liquides	Gas Gaz	Electricity Electricité	Year Année	Région, pays ou zone
13	2	142	66	3 069	14	1 443	1 531	82	1998	Myanmar
13	1	172	69	3 240	52	1 652	1 447	89	1999	
18	2	203	69	3 277	94	1 690	1 331	163	2000	
18	2	174	56	2 680	46	1 397	1 081	157	2001	
...	...	...	46	999	237	672	...	90	1998	Népal
...	...	...	49	1 091	293	691	...	106	1999	
...	...	...	49	1 115	305	703	...	*108	2000	
...	...	...	48	1 163	344	711	...	*108	2001	
187	39	-393	3 302	7 553	...	2 309	5 244	...	1998	Oman
187	54	-522	3 699	8 601	...	2 841	5 759	...	1999	
212	56	-573	3 859	9 268	...	3 058	6 210	...	2000	
261	50	-1 943	4 429	10 974	...	3 938	7 036	...	2001	
138	15	713	280	36 777	2 159	16 890	15 733	1 995	1998	Pakistan
121	15	782	282	37 874	2 267	16 852	16 750	2 005	1999	
126	16	747	291	40 079	2 161	18 007	18 148	1 763	2000	
120	24	1 302	291	41 435	2 122	18 184	19 130	2 000	2001	
448	218	1 396	377	28 319	2 616	17 589	8	8 105	1998	Philippines
513	241	1 175	389	29 113	3 131	16 189	6	9 787	1999	
536	210	2 053	395	30 158	4 182	15 298	10	10 669	2000	
591	219	2 154	377	29 103	4 123	15 375	13	9 593	2001	
185	...	805	29 627	16 117	...	2 173	13 944	...	1998	Qatar
174	...	899	38 852	21 563	...	2 012	19 551	...	1999	
180	...	1 090	30 399	17 175	...	2 260	14 915	...	2000	
334	...	-438	29 766	17 592	...	3 175	14 416	...	2001	
*2 270	1 971	1 160	5 400	108 978	...	65 408	43 570	...	1998	Arabie saoudite [2]
2 320	2 118	4 435	5 015	104 799	...	61 713	43 085	...	1999	
2 425	2 118	12 994	5 077	108 641	...	62 189	46 452	...	2000	
2 358	2 118	11 986	5 132	117 161	...	65 071	52 090	...	2001	
1 191	17 750	10 932	3 474	13 624	...	12 042	1 582	...	1998	Singapour
1 233	17 601	10 959	3 559	14 060	...	12 771	1 289	...	1999	
1 282	16 743	13 638	3 290	13 592	...	12 276	1 316	...	2000	
*1 282	18 761	13 982	4 180	17 268	...	12 812	4 456	...	2001	
90	257	138	153	2 878	1	2 540	...	337	1998	Sri Lanka
101	231	137	162	3 088	1	2 728	...	359	1999	
105	159	195	183	3 551	1	3 274	...	275	2000	
68	154	137	188	3 521	1	3 253	...	268	2001	
95	...	964	1 066	16 621	...	11 399	*4 989	*232	1998	Rép. arabe syrienne
97	...	1 390	1 042	16 785	3	11 441	*5 108	*234	1999	
137	...	1 827	1 021	16 663	3	11 224	*5 158	*278	2000	
97	...	1 300	1 025	17 131	1	11 898	4 938	*293	2001	
5	...	14	516	3 148	53	1 162	716	1 217	1998	Tadjikistan
5	...	13	521	3 252	51	1 162	712	1 327	1999	
5	...	13	442	2 730	51	788	698	1 192	2000	
5	...	13	447	2 815	51	1 005	549	1 209	2001	
...	...	3 991	915	55 975	10 158	31 454	13 915	447	1998	Thaïlande
...	...	4 804	950	58 503	10 702	32 468	15 027	306	1999	
...	...	5 448	970	60 422	11 090	31 592	17 220	520	2000	
...	787	3 665	1 067	65 694	11 580	30 848	*22 722	544	2001	
498	161	4 400	960	60 869	22 539	24 702	9 923	3 706	1998	Turquie
495	284	3 584	946	60 835	20 844	25 186	11 750	3 055	1999	
523	406	4 113	1 038	67 755	24 230	26 772	14 028	2 725	2000	
521	237	4 052	915	62 759	20 839	24 901	14 870	2 149	2001	
...	...	663	2 441	11 861	...	2 126	9 735	0	1998	Turkménistan
...	...	695	3 080	14 279	...	2 367	11 912	0	1999	
...	...	697	3 063	14 511	...	2 389	12 122	0	2000	
...	...	780	3 386	15 982	...	3 214	12 768	0	2001	
682	10 957	-9 066	12 090	32 933	...	5 861	27 072	...	1998	Emirats arabes unis
690	6 612	-4 690	11 476	33 717	...	5 789	27 928	...	1999	
1 006	4 982	3 787	13 492	35 159	...	5 977	29 183	...	2000	
988	6 974	4 250	13 456	38 740	...	6 137	32 602	...	2001	

63
Production, trade and consumption of commercial energy
Thousand metric tons of oil equivalent and kilograms per capita *[cont.]*

Production, commerce et consommation d'énergie commerciale
Milliers de tonnes d'équivalent pétrole et kilogrammes par habitant *[suite]*

Region, country or area	Year Année	Total Totale	Solids Solides	Liquids Liquides	Gas Gaz	Electricity Electricité	Changes in stocks Variations des stocks	Imports Importations	Exp Exportati
Uzbekistan	1998	59 090	801	8 179	49 615	495	...	35	4
	1999	60 033	814	8 399	50 331	489	19	8	6
	2000	60 099	706	7 814	51 074	505	16	6	5
	2001	60 744	754	7 482	51 991	517	17	7	5
Viet Nam	1998	22 906	8 170	12 412	819	1 504	1 698	7 076	14
	1999	24 908	6 740	15 402	1 023	1 744	50	7 475	17
	2000	27 687	8 126	16 473	1 264	1 823	*266	9 083	18
	2001	29 987	9 073	17 047	1 738	2 129	223	9 038	19
Yemen	1998	19 032	...	19 032	...	...	-691	1	15
	1999	20 887	...	20 887	...	...	-691	*1	*15
	2000	21 450	...	21 450	...	...	*751	1	17
	2001	22 074	...	22 074	...	...	*425	1	18
Europe	**1998**	**2 209 673**	**379 650**	**642 504**	**820 614**	**366 905**	**3 455**	**1 327 258**	**928**
	1999	**2 219 509**	**374 244**	**649 307**	**820 786**	**375 172**	**-12 655**	**1 303 506**	**934**
	2000	**2 242 745**	**367 049**	**669 631**	**822 503**	**383 562**	**6 304**	**1 373 025**	**987**
	2001	**2 281 291**	**373 167**	**687 770**	**825 212**	**395 141**	**-2 270**	**1 402 298**	**1 006**
Albania	1998	821	14	368	15	423	...	184	
	1999	806	14	323	15	454	...	524	
	2000	732	9	317	10	395	...	529	
	2001	632	7	311	8	306	...	622	
Austria	1998	6 223	297	1 055	1 408	3 463	*-209	21 605	1
	1999	6 772	297	1 029	1 564	3 882	*-543	20 982	1
	2000	6 948	325	1 074	1 634	3 914	*-228	20 866	1
	2001	6 782	314	1 017	1 554	3 896	*-1 073	22 012	1
Belarus	1998	2 531	464	1 832	233	2	*-121	25 606	3
	1999	2 784	705	1 842	236	2	131	26 266	4
	2000	2 554	462	1 853	237	2	94	29 072	7
	2001	2 546	454	1 854	235	3	*-17	28 359	6
Belgium	1998	12 368	188	...	*0	12 180	746	72 191	20
	1999	13 143	219	...	0	12 924	*-617	70 058	21
	2000	12 946	226	...	2	12 717	*-547	72 352	22
	2001	12 378	131	...	4	12 243	788	72 511	21
Bosnia and Herzegovina	1998	4 006	3 614	...	...	392	...	864	
	1999	3 867	3 391	...	...	476	...	856	
	2000	4 587	4 148	...	...	438	...	1 118	
	2001	4 587	4 148	...	...	438	...	1 118	
Bulgaria	1998	9 725	4 970	33	26	4 697	65	11 771	1
	1999	8 647	4 199	40	24	4 384	*-354	10 768	1
	2000	9 436	4 382	42	14	4 998	*-135	11 173	2
	2001	9 752	4 407	34	20	5 290	*-206	11 694	2
Croatia	1998	3 920	36	1 989	1 426	470	*-61	5 539	1
	1999	3 647	11	1 661	1 408	567	*-21	6 127	1
	2000	3 475	...	1 462	1 506	507	*-36	5 623	1
	2001	3 743	...	1 351	1 826	566	*-68	5 752	1
Czech Republic	1998	28 779	24 809	179	188	3 602	222	18 899	6
	1999	25 846	21 792	183	195	3 677	*-973	17 761	6
	2000	27 899	23 741	175	188	3 794	*-1 089	17 508	5
	2001	28 485	24 105	183	136	4 062	*-365	18 567	5
Denmark	1998	18 331	...	11 454	6 625	252	*-442	14 575	14
	1999	21 503	...	14 492	6 741	270	*-1 019	13 204	18
	2000	25 583	...	17 813	7 378	392	*-415	12 339	21
	2001	25 733	...	16 915	8 438	380	66	11 827	19
Estonia	1998	2 846	2 845	...	...	0	*-56	2 276	
	1999	2 540	2 540	...	...	0	*-179	2 075	
	2000	2 724	2 724	...	...	0	*-13	2 004	
	2001	2 748	2 748	...	...	1	*-125	1 999	
Faeroe Islands	1998	*7	...	...	...	*7	...	*213	
	1999	*7	...	...	...	*7	...	*215	
	2000	*7	...	...	...	*7	...	*215	
	2001	*7	...	...	...	*7	...	*215	

Bunkers - Soutes		Unallocated	Consumption - Consommation						Year	
Air Avion	Sea Maritime	Nondistribué	Per capita Par habitant	Total Totale	Solids Solides	Liquids Liquides	Gas Gaz	Electricity Electricité	Année	Région, pays ou zone
...	...	1 377	2 205	53 040	800	6 226	45 519	495	1998	Ouzbékistan
...	...	1 739	2 177	52 160	794	6 071	44 806	489	1999	
...	...	1 708	2 140	52 957	689	5 805	45 958	505	2000	
...	...	1 562	2 150	53 671	736	5 630	46 788	517	2001	
...	...	0	179	13 658	4 313	7 021	819	1 504	1998	Viet Nam
...	...	-1	192	14 820	4 409	7 646	1 023	1 744	1999	
...	...	-1	231	17 923	5 585	9 251	1 264	1 823	2000	
...	...	-2	241	19 053	5 860	9 325	1 738	2 129	2001	
*63	100	546	226	3 855	...	3 855		...	1998	Yémen
*63	*100	2 149	201	*3 557	...	*3 557	...	...	1999	
93	99	338	142	2 602	...	2 602	...	...	2000	
94	100	675	139	2 627	...	2 627	...	...	2001	
41 903	**46 044**	**63 150**	**2 869**	**2 454 340**	**482 536**	**744 288**	**860 612**	**366 905**	**1998**	**Europe**
45 635	**44 357**	**70 145**	**2 854**	**2 441 065**	**465 663**	**727 910**	**872 321**	**375 172**	**1999**	
47 236	**46 740**	**66 709**	**2 883**	**2 460 994**	**473 829**	**714 829**	**888 774**	**383 562**	**2000**	
48 124	**48 317**	**69 874**	**2 943**	**2 513 426**	**477 972**	**730 489**	**909 824**	**395 141**	**2001**	
...	...	87	242	918	14	466	15	423	1998	Albanie
37	...	166	360	1 128	30	628	15	454	1999	
41	...	150	341	1 070	19	645	10	395	2000	
44	...	142	342	1 067	22	731	8	306	2001	
279	...	717	3 168	25 634	3 643	11 121	7 407	3 463	1998	Autriche
505	...	355	3 211	25 987	3 455	11 135	7 515	3 882	1999	
554	...	696	3 149	25 542	3 591	10 597	7 441	3 914	2000	
540	...	876	3 283	26 691	3 738	11 409	7 647	3 896	2001	
...	...	1 092	2 300	23 442	1 050	7 364	15 026	2	1998	Bélarus
...	...	1 152	2 274	22 821	833	6 454	15 532	2	1999	
...	...	2 071	2 238	22 387	901	5 630	15 854	2	2000	
...	...	2 341	2 222	22 161	755	5 334	16 070	3	2001	
1 512	5 563	3 712	5 167	52 771	8 667	18 056	13 869	12 180	1998	Belgique
1 482	4 494	3 675	5 163	52 801	7 575	17 471	14 832	12 924	1999	
1 483	5 508	3 921	5 099	52 259	8 391	16 288	14 864	12 717	2000	
1 122	5 384	2 933	5 171	53 196	7 929	18 367	14 657	12 243	2001	
...	...	...	1 333	4 869	3 614	707	157	392	1998	Bosnie-Herzégovine
...	...	...	1 228	4 722	3 391	695	160	476	1999	
...	...	...	1 434	5 705	4 148	860	258	438	2000	
...	...	...	1 403	5 705	4 148	860	258	438	2001	
21	71	929	2 315	19 119	7 187	3 756	3 479	4 697	1998	Bulgarie
51	8	743	2 109	17 314	6 295	3 649	2 987	4 384	1999	
80	65	794	2 229	17 720	6 332	3 129	3 260	4 998	2000	
104	97	532	2 382	18 847	7 078	3 434	3 045	5 290	2001	
63	26	931	1 563	7 035	277	3 887	2 401	470	1998	Croatie
37	22	759	1 609	7 326	208	4 116	2 435	567	1999	
33	18	572	1 605	7 033	475	3 595	2 456	507	2000	
21	29	518	1 668	7 401	529	3 732	2 574	566	2001	
118	...	1 299	3 794	39 056	20 413	6 496	8 545	3 602	1998	République tchèque
115	...	1 333	3 573	36 741	18 131	6 340	8 594	3 677	1999	
160	...	1 284	3 821	39 249	21 113	6 004	8 339	3 794	2000	
135	...	1 368	3 906	39 939	20 570	6 377	8 930	4 062	2001	
712	1 400	-18	3 180	16 855	5 500	7 302	3 801	252	1998	Danemark
763	1 316	-422	3 016	16 040	4 539	7 287	3 944	270	1999	
779	1 353	-356	2 859	15 256	3 954	6 826	4 084	392	2000	
798	1 120	-114	3 045	16 317	4 131	6 657	5 149	380	2001	
13	108	...	3 434	4 979	3 209	1 112	659	0	1998	Estonie
18	167	...	3 150	4 542	2 933	969	640	0	1999	
20	107	...	3 321	4 547	3 055	756	736	0	2000	
17	102	...	3 439	4 680	3 073	817	790	1	2001	
...	...	...	4 879	*220	...	*213	...	*7	1998	Iles Féroé
...	...	...	4 822	*222	...	*215	...	*7	1999	
...	...	...	4 822	*222	...	*215	...	*7	2000	
...	...	...	4 827	*222	...	*215	...	*7	2001	

63
Production, trade and consumption of commercial energy
Thousand metric tons of oil equivalent and kilograms per capita *[cont.]*

Production, commerce et consommation d'énergie commerciale
Milliers de tonnes d'équivalent pétrole et kilogrammes par habitant *[suite]*

Region, country or area	Year Année	Primary energy production – Production d'énergie primaire					Changes in stocks Variations des stocks	Imports Importations	Expo Exportati
		Total Totale	Solids Solides	Liquids Liquides	Gas Gaz	Electricity Electricité			
Finland	1998	7 424	424	...	...	7 000	*-1 257	20 922	4
	1999	9 142	2 043	...	...	7 100	*-1 285	20 270	4
	2000	8 365	1 231	...	...	7 134	126	21 275	4
	2001	8 531	1 446	...	...	7 085	*-87	21 360	4
France [3]	1998	118 008	3 790	4 761	2 102	107 355	*-1 206	159 212	19
	1999	119 959	3 559	4 487	1 920	109 994	1 156	154 545	17
	2000	124 021	2 176	4 838	1 964	115 043	3 631	162 155	19
	2001	125 659	1 412	4 832	2 345	117 070	*-1 654	160 498	17
Germany	1998	128 887	64 146	2 937	16 863	44 941	*-705	229 207	18
	1999	130 204	62 058	2 749	18 050	47 346	*-2 155	221 594	20
	2000	127 674	59 236	3 169	17 087	48 182	*-4 434	223 182	24
	2001	126 539	57 630	3 281	17 268	48 359	*-2 519	236 965	23
Gibraltar	1998	...	...	...	...	...	...	*2 167	
	1999	...	...	...	...	...	...	*2 191	
	2000	...	...	...	...	...	...	*2 206	
	2001	...	...	...	...	...	...	*2 212	
Greece	1998	8 691	7 976	317	44	355	941	24 170	2
	1999	8 806	8 129	222	3	453	*-610	23 588	2
	2000	9 090	8 369	279	46	396	182	25 898	3
	2001	9 285	8 691	193	44	357	*-79	25 888	3
Hungary	1998	12 531	3 021	2 559	3 297	3 654	761	16 413	1
	1999	11 885	3 000	2 274	2 918	3 695	*-8	16 084	1
	2000	11 486	2 894	2 122	2 754	3 716	145	15 595	1
	2001	11 336	2 869	2 010	2 754	3 703	*-790	16 204	1
Iceland	1998	1 048	...	...	...	1 048	4	831	
	1999	1 151	...	...	...	1 151	32	853	
	2000	1 205	...	...	...	1 205	38	910	
	2001	1 099	...	...	...	1 099	*-3	812	
Ireland	1998	2 530	813	...	1 564	152	7	11 997	1
	1999	2 670	1 252	...	1 275	143	308	12 994	1
	2000	2 289	1 065	...	1 065	158	*-110	13 502	
	2001	1 848	966	...	732	150	358	15 071	1
Italy [4]	1998	30 701	44	5 629	17 309	7 719	*-379	160 227	21
	1999	29 519	27	5 005	16 213	8 275	*-972	161 647	18
	2000	28 818	26	4 597	15 146	9 049	4 561	171 994	19
	2001	27 485	...	4 104	14 162	9 220	*-2 047	166 625	19
Latvia	1998	385	14	...	...	371	57	3 029	
	1999	305	67	...	...	237	*-191	2 433	
	2000	258	16	...	...	243	*-100	2 292	
	2001	260	16	...	...	244	*-226	2 598	
Lithuania	1998	3 906	14	277	...	3 615	*-154	9 678	4
	1999	2 899	19	232	...	2 648	*-185	7 191	2
	2000	2 579	10	316	...	2 253	160	7 666	3
	2001	3 505	8	471	...	3 026	*-149	9 277	4
Luxembourg	1998	92	...	...	...	92	36	2 964	
	1999	71	...	...	...	71	*-47	3 046	
	2000	79	...	...	...	79	49	3 235	
	2001	80	...	...	...	80	*-29	3 307	
Malta	1998	...	...	...	...	...	...	1 120	
	1999	...	...	...	...	...	...	1 264	
	2000	...	...	...	...	...	6	1 068	
	2001	...	...	...	...	...	...	952	
Netherlands	1998	67 747	...	2 738	63 950	1 060	*-442	107 578	85
	1999	63 746	...	2 611	60 071	1 064	*-1 627	107 309	82
	2000	61 622	...	2 464	58 049	1 109	2 384	121 485	89
	2001	65 800	...	2 335	62 345	1 120	166	131 368	103
Norway [5]	1998	212 860	220	154 839	47 733	10 069	151	5 528	183
	1999	214 481	328	154 542	49 094	10 516	*-15	5 313	185
	2000	227 181	424	163 604	50 916	12 237	304	4 692	199
	2001	236 463	1 200	169 841	54 432	10 990	*-2 002	4 595	204

Bunkers - Soutes			Consumption - Consommation							
Air Avion	Sea Maritime	Unallocated Nondistribué	Per capita Par habitant	Total Totale	Solids Solides	Liquids Liquides	Gas Gaz	Electricity Electricité	Year Année	Région, pays ou zone
334	528	-1 229	4 951	25 512	4 765	10 039	3 709	7 000	1998	Finlande
356	566	-1 479	5 131	26 502	5 467	10 225	3 711	7 100	1999	
346	680	-1 694	4 913	25 428	5 094	9 395	3 805	7 134	2000	
355	582	-1 909	5 076	26 332	6 226	8 899	4 121	7 085	2001	
4 528	2 894	10 620	4 097	241 255	17 693	76 130	40 077	107 355	1998	France [3]
5 160	2 926	8 552	4 051	239 551	15 686	75 471	38 400	109 994	1999	
5 160	3 028	11 131	4 131	243 419	15 098	73 722	39 555	115 043	2000	
4 644	2 720	12 801	4 223	249 939	12 638	78 776	41 456	117 070	2001	
6 241	2 051	8 427	3 949	323 950	83 976	114 731	80 302	44 941	1998	Allemagne
6 699	2 089	8 809	3 848	315 782	79 414	109 501	79 521	47 346	1999	
7 023	2 198	6 803	3 841	315 038	80 764	106 684	79 408	48 182	2000	
6 927	2 239	7 219	3 966	326 573	84 785	109 830	83 598	48 359	2001	
*3	*2 128	...	1 306	*35	...	*35	...	...	1998	Gibraltar
*3	*2 129	...	2 156	*58	...	*58	...	...	1999	
*3	*2 130	...	2 670	*72	...	*72	...	...	2000	
*4	*2 139	...	2 435	*68	...	*68	...	...	2001	
831	3 542	-1 058	2 508	26 378	8 769	16 449	805	355	1998	Grèce
933	3 147	-1 276	2 597	27 360	8 647	16 906	1 354	453	1999	
818	3 633	-1 129	2 843	28 448	9 181	16 977	1 894	396	2000	
761	3 528	-996	2 879	28 845	9 604	17 013	1 871	357	2001	
193	...	1 875	2 437	24 652	3 745	6 384	10 870	3 654	1998	Hongrie
207	...	1 394	2 458	24 747	3 822	6 217	11 013	3 695	1999	
220	...	1 496	2 357	23 629	3 464	5 747	10 702	3 716	2000	
219	...	1 422	2 428	24 740	3 516	5 613	11 908	3 703	2001	
110	57	...	6 232	1 708	66	594	...	1 048	1998	Islande
119	52	...	6 506	1 802	57	593	...	1 151	1999	
133	69	...	6 673	1 875	98	572	...	1 205	2000	
115	47	...	6 149	1 753	92	562	...	1 099	2001	
427	159	-32	3 460	12 821	3 095	6 457	3 116	152	1998	Irlande
505	173	43	3 637	13 621	2 762	7 336	3 380	143	1999	
547	151	109	3 732	14 132	2 912	7 242	3 820	158	2000	
703	163	-42	3 743	14 425	3 033	7 257	3 985	150	2001	
2 889	2 634	599	2 845	163 897	11 225	88 109	56 844	7 719	1998	Italie [4]
3 289	2 425	605	2 903	167 404	11 807	85 241	62 082	8 275	1999	
3 508	2 721	972	2 933	169 485	12 713	83 303	64 420	9 049	2000	
3 410	2 834	-1 250	2 956	171 290	13 536	83 655	64 879	9 220	2001	
30	...	...	1 307	3 202	134	1 548	1 148	371	1998	Lettonie
30	...	...	1 114	2 708	96	1 274	1 100	237	1999	
27	...	...	1 066	2 591	113	1 021	1 215	243	2000	
27	198	...	1 214	2 859	102	1 101	1 412	244	2001	
29	31	-292	2 603	9 638	177	3 897	1 950	3 615	1998	Lituanie
27	74	-87	2 062	7 629	149	2 802	2 030	2 648	1999	
27	94	-65	1 862	6 882	109	2 196	2 324	2 253	2000	
10	102	-33	2 276	7 922	98	2 384	2 414	3 026	2001	
284	...	...	6 383	2 719	205	1 719	703	92	1998	Luxembourg
333	...	...	6 507	2 811	210	1 802	729	71	1999	
322	...	...	6 709	2 925	144	1 957	745	79	2000	
348	...	...	6 871	3 037	110	2 074	772	80	2001	
54	*12	...	2 797	1 054	*191	863	...	...	1998	Malte
*54	12	...	3 162	1 199	*192	1 006	...	...	1999	
123	23	...	2 343	916	*194	722	...	...	2000	
59	23	...	2 203	870	*195	675	...	...	2001	
3 191	12 446	-7 429	5 243	82 347	8 879	33 660	38 748	1 060	1998	Pays-Bas
3 314	12 867	-7 103	5 124	81 025	7 747	33 865	38 350	1 064	1999	
3 273	13 564	-8 733	5 243	83 174	7 809	35 323	38 932	1 109	2000	
3 205	14 886	-9 046	5 267	84 521	7 756	35 721	39 924	1 120	2001	
129	901	3 981	6 672	29 566	1 048	11 908	6 541	10 069	1998	Norvège [5]
570	861	4 513	6 405	28 579	1 059	11 694	5 309	10 516	1999	
480	832	2 076	6 483	29 126	1 075	11 800	4 013	12 237	2000	
362	816	6 498	6 839	30 872	944	12 833	6 104	10 990	2001	

63

Production, trade and consumption of commercial energy
Thousand metric tons of oil equivalent and kilograms per capita *[cont.]*

Production, commerce et consommation d'énergie commerciale
Milliers de tonnes d'équivalent pétrole et kilogrammes par habitant *[suite]*

Region, country or area	Year Année	Primary energy production – Production d'énergie primaire					Changes in stocks Variations des stocks	Imports Importations	Ex Exporta
		Total Totale	Solids Solides	Liquids Liquides	Gas Gaz	Electricity Electricité			
Poland	1998	83 191	78 845	360	3 612	374	*-296	30 181	1
	1999	79 558	75 303	434	3 449	371	*-336	29 128	1
	2000	75 804	71 109	654	3 684	357	*-606	29 648	1
	2001	76 502	71 488	768	3 883	364	*-589	30 700	1
Portugal	1998	1 187	...	...	...	1 187	*-154	20 438	
	1999	744	...	...	...	744	469	22 725	
	2000	1 091	...	...	...	1 091	*-323	22 039	
	2001	1 349	...	...	...	1 349	193	21 928	
Republic of Moldova	1998	7	...	...	...	7	*-112	4 015	
	1999	8	...	...	...	8	*-118	2 715	
	2000	5	...	...	...	5	*-7	2 881	
	2001	6	...	...	...	6	16	3 163	
Romania	1998	26 828	4 844	6 579	12 396	3 009	*-433	15 288	
	1999	25 977	4 199	6 404	12 444	2 930	*-704	10 230	
	2000	26 332	5 129	6 313	12 195	2 695	*-157	10 959	
	2001	26 741	5 788	6 262	11 986	2 705	311	12 500	
Russian Federation	1998	964 284	90 835	301 707	530 514	41 228	2 541	21 845	38
	1999	977 950	98 095	303 542	530 601	45 712	*-2 583	16 346	38
	2000	993 408	99 624	322 014	523 381	48 389	5 436	29 322	39
	2001	1 021 936	103 615	346 187	521 193	50 942	6 683	21 555	40
Serbia and Montenegro	1998	12 454	9 398	1 234	713	1 109	...	4 561	
	1999	9 932	7 093	1 031	658	1 150	...	3 267	
	2000	9 931	7 325	816	754	1 037	...	3 515	
	2001	9 920	7 384	881	658	998	...	4 611	
Slovakia	1998	4 806	1 157	60	222	3 367	*-223	15 342	
	1999	5 180	1 097	66	182	3 834	*-573	15 179	
	2000	6 020	1 068	59	148	4 745	109	15 456	
	2001	6 120	1 003	46	168	4 904	*-429	15 327	
Slovenia	1998	2 544	923	1	8	1 613	*-51	3 789	
	1999	2 422	868	1	5	1 547	121	4 123	
	2000	2 554	974	1	6	1 572	54	3 919	
	2001	2 604	899	1	6	1 699	*-204	3 831	
Spain	1998	28 584	8 743	873	375	18 594	1 984	93 090	
	1999	27 097	8 267	*652	392	17 785	1 429	99 044	
	2000	28 367	7 967	610	410	19 379	1 237	102 831	
	2001	29 800	7 539	*736	524	21 001	*-446	101 836	
Sweden	1998	25 967	331	...	...	25 636	702	29 131	
	1999	25 548	255	...	...	25 294	*-1 089	27 950	
	2000	22 016	228	...	...	21 788	*-143	29 073	1
	2001	25 952	275	...	...	25 677	*-222	28 805	
Switzerland[6]	1998	9 820	...	...	...	9 820	19	16 178	
	1999	10 356	...	...	...	10 356	*-597	15 300	
	2000	10 309	...	...	...	10 309	*-393	15 123	
	2001	10 669	...	...	...	10 669	*-178	16 496	
TFYR of Macedonia	1998	2 301	2 208	...	...	93	81	1 285	
	1999	2 111	1 991	...	...	119	*-112	1 108	
	2000	2 130	2 029	...	...	101	*-97	1 261	
	2001	2 242	2 189	...	...	54	*-56	1 110	
Ukraine	1998	82 680	39 715	5 203	16 756	21 007	...	69 445	
	1999	82 802	41 089	5 021	16 872	19 820	...	71 972	
	2000	84 491	41 693	4 949	16 678	21 171	...	68 222	
	2001	85 021	43 198	3 791	17 101	20 931	...	71 249	
United Kingdom	1998	280 654	24 956	135 519	93 236	26 944	1 438	73 905	10
	1999	285 423	22 339	140 462	96 456	26 166	611	75 259	11
	2000	278 731	18 437	130 090	107 251	22 954	*-3 379	88 820	12
	2001	267 147	19 238	120 367	103 393	24 149	2 713	96 779	11
Oceania	**1998**	**233 048**	**155 842**	**37 269**	**34 161**	**5 776**	**405**	**32 740**	**13**
	1999	**230 666**	**157 961**	**31 192**	**35 438**	**6 075**	**-4 125**	**39 626**	**13**
	2000	**251 747**	**167 815**	**40 477**	**37 300**	**6 155**	**853**	**35 422**	**14**
	2001	**269 346**	**183 118**	**41 667**	**38 279**	**6 282**	**-351**	**36 565**	**16**

Bunkers - Soutes			Consumption - Consommation							
Air Avion	Sea Maritime	Unallocated Nondistribué	Per capita Par habitant	Total Totale	Solids Solides	Liquids Liquides	Gas Gaz	Electricity Electricité	Year Année	Région, pays ou zone
258	268	864	2 391	92 458	64 383	17 123	10 578	374	1998	Pologne
257	549	332	2 342	90 515	61 591	18 255	10 299	371	1999	
370	290	1 354	2 234	86 328	57 769	17 128	11 073	357	2000	
349	265	1 441	2 260	87 315	57 751	17 664	11 537	364	2001	
485	388	1 452	1 778	17 723	3 139	12 622	775	1 187	1998	Portugal
536	598	1 299	1 944	19 415	3 820	12 694	2 157	744	1999	
572	675	1 269	1 973	19 748	3 933	12 462	2 261	1 091	2000	
591	482	1 378	1 907	19 644	3 175	12 613	2 507	1 349	2001	
22	...	...	1 126	4 112	259	700	3 145	7	1998	République de Moldova
12	...	...	776	2 828	118	447	2 255	8	1999	
21	...	...	789	2 872	97	421	2 350	5	2000	
18	...	...	864	3 136	69	474	2 587	6	2001	
105	...	1 792	1 666	37 495	7 411	10 416	16 660	3 009	1998	Roumanie
131	...	1 959	1 458	32 740	6 156	8 388	15 267	2 930	1999	
127	...	1 586	1 477	33 136	6 875	8 357	15 210	2 695	2000	
114	...	1 399	1 540	34 500	7 487	9 655	14 654	2 705	2001	
8 279	...	17 058	3 924	574 991	89 890	98 136	345 737	41 228	1998	Fédération de Russie
8 557	...	21 119	4 009	585 016	92 821	96 744	349 739	45 712	1999	
8 997	...	20 230	4 107	597 470	94 530	99 870	354 681	48 389	2000	
9 253	...	22 140	4 194	603 785	90 620	100 528	361 695	50 942	2001	
68	...	1 032	1 478	15 696	9 767	2 491	2 330	1 109	1998	Serbie-et-Monténégro
186	...	679	1 158	12 312	7 259	2 288	1 614	1 150	1999	
32	...	393	1 222	13 000	7 598	2 592	1 774	1 037	2000	
62	...	370	1 318	14 035	7 888	3 021	2 127	998	2001	
...	...	1 453	3 063	16 510	4 463	2 377	6 304	3 367	1998	Slovaquie
...	...	1 545	3 065	16 537	4 233	2 089	6 380	3 834	1999	
...	...	1 569	3 135	16 928	3 940	1 821	6 422	4 745	2000	
...	...	252	3 421	18 404	4 036	2 606	6 858	4 904	2001	
19	...	53	3 127	6 201	1 287	2 390	911	1 613	1998	Slovénie
21	...	45	3 083	6 123	1 226	2 401	949	1 547	1999	
24	...	24	3 100	6 164	1 345	2 280	966	1 572	2000	
27	...	...	3 241	6 456	1 417	2 345	995	1 699	2001	
2 450	6 138	6 515	2 496	98 265	17 264	49 238	13 168	18 594	1998	Espagne
2 535	5 990	6 734	2 663	104 965	20 539	51 619	15 022	17 785	1999	
2 723	6 118	6 513	2 773	109 437	21 319	51 572	17 166	19 379	2000	
2 774	6 846	7 372	2 747	110 593	19 351	52 007	18 234	21 001	2001	
451	1 601	1 546	4 759	42 124	2 534	13 163	792	25 636	1998	Suède
481	1 543	1 508	4 707	41 707	2 520	13 100	794	25 294	1999	
476	1 384	1 284	4 242	37 633	2 545	12 524	777	21 788	2000	
713	1 417	1 389	4 721	41 996	2 724	12 743	853	25 677	2001	
1 440	11	-17	3 320	24 072	92	11 535	2 626	9 820	1998	Suisse [6]
1 466	12	-13	3 342	24 229	97	11 056	2 720	10 356	1999	
1 528	11	36	3 258	23 619	123	10 482	2 705	10 309	2000	
1 489	12	-108	3 514	25 419	148	11 786	2 816	10 669	2001	
17	...	23	1 708	3 430	2 445	872	20	93	1998	L'ex-R.y. Macédoine
*37	...	0	1 593	3 214	2 212	845	37	119	1999	
29	...	21	1 600	3 254	2 243	849	60	101	2000	
23	...	7	1 546	3 146	2 340	672	80	54	2001	
684	...	2 172	2 911	145 673	43 711	14 811	66 145	21 007	1998	Ukraine
679	...	3 837	2 887	144 681	42 746	10 361	71 754	19 820	1999	
681	...	1 659	2 893	143 379	43 860	9 115	69 232	21 171	2000	
317	...	1 735	2 976	145 912	44 755	10 975	69 251	20 931	2001	
5 637	3 086	4 995	3 916	231 957	38 351	75 415	91 247	26 944	1998	Royaume-Uni
6 133	2 337	9 369	3 804	226 360	35 819	74 675	89 700	26 166	1999	
6 496	2 088	10 675	3 864	229 894	36 903	74 076	95 961	22 954	2000	
8 468	2 288	9 237	3 829	228 813	41 601	69 008	94 055	24 149	2001	
3 398	**1 286**	**2 601**	**4 194**	**123 948**	**52 944**	**40 959**	**24 315**	**5 776**	**1998**	**Océanie**
3 488	**1 359**	**3 395**	**4 284**	**128 221**	**54 117**	**42 442**	**25 587**	**6 075**	**1999**	
3 157	**1 418**	**2 893**	**4 310**	**130 696**	**54 213**	**43 259**	**27 070**	**6 155**	**2000**	
3 746	**1 327**	**1 204**	**4 415**	**137 987**	**61 769**	**41 447**	**28 489**	**6 282**	**2001**	

63

Production, trade and consumption of commercial energy
Thousand metric tons of oil equivalent and kilograms per capita [cont.]

Production, commerce et consommation d'énergie commerciale
Milliers de tonnes d'équivalent pétrole et kilogrammes par habitant [suite]

Region, country or area	Year Année	Primary energy production – Production d'énergie primaire					Changes in stocks Variations des stocks	Imports Importations	Exp Exportat
		Total Totale	Solids Solides	Liquids Liquides	Gas Gaz	Electricity Electricité			
American Samoa	1998	...	...	...	...	...	...	*186	
	1999	...	...	...	...	...	...	*182	
	2000	...	...	...	...	...	...	*182	
	2001	...	...	...	...	...	...	*185	
Australia	1998	215 800	153 998	30 862	29 552	1 389	428	22 676	127
	1999	212 431	155 880	24 984	30 099	1 467	*-4 576	29 020	131
	2000	233 436	165 805	34 463	31 688	1 479	931	25 147	141
	2001	250 414	180 906	35 673	32 374	1 461	*-81	26 119	155
Cook Islands	1998	...	...	...	...	...	...	*15	
	1999	...	...	...	...	...	...	*19	
	2000	...	...	...	...	...	...	*19	
	2001	...	...	...	...	...	...	*19	
Fiji	1998	*37	...	...	...	*37	...	*439	
	1999	*37	...	...	...	*37	...	*458	
	2000	*37	...	...	...	*37	...	528	
	2001	*36	...	...	...	*36	...	603	
French Polynesia	1998	13	...	...	...	13	...	*226	
	1999	8	...	...	...	8	...	*222	
	2000	10	...	...	...	10	...	251	
	2001	9	...	...	...	9	...	226	
Guam	1998	...	...	...	...	...	...	*1 476	
	1999	...	...	...	...	...	...	*1 463	
	2000	...	...	...	...	...	...	*1 463	
	2001	...	...	...	...	...	...	*1 476	
Kiribati	1998	...	...	...	...	...	...	11	
	1999	...	...	...	...	...	...	10	
	2000	...	...	...	...	...	...	11	
	2001	...	...	...	...	...	...	10	
Nauru	1998	...	...	...	...	...	...	*50	
	1999	...	...	...	...	...	...	*50	
	2000	...	...	...	...	...	...	*50	
	2001	...	...	...	...	...	...	*52	
New Caledonia	1998	34	...	...	...	34	...	605	
	1999	41	...	...	...	41	...	682	
	2000	39	...	...	...	39	...	*596	
	2001	32	...	...	...	32	...	*602	
New Zealand	1998	13 105	1 845	2 503	4 531	4 226	*-23	5 660	2
	1999	14 056	2 081	2 274	5 261	4 441	450	6 106	2
	2000	14 131	2 010	2 080	5 534	4 507	*-79	5 766	2
	2001	14 697	2 212	2 000	5 827	4 658	*-270	5 862	2
Niue	1998	...	...	...	...	...	...	*1	
	1999	...	...	...	...	...	...	*1	
	2000	...	...	...	...	...	...	*1	
	2001	...	...	...	...	...	...	*1	
Palau	1998	*3	...	...	...	*3	...	*97	
	1999	*2	...	...	...	*2	...	*96	
	2000	*2	...	...	...	*2	...	*96	
	2001	*2	...	...	...	*2	...	*91	
Papua New Guinea	1998	*4 054	...	*3 904	*78	72	...	*709	*3
	1999	*4 090	...	*3 934	*78	78	...	*716	*3
	2000	*4 090	...	*3 934	*78	78	...	*716	*3
	2001	*4 152	...	*3 994	*79	79	...	*713	*3
Samoa	1998	*3	...	...	...	*3	...	*44	
	1999	*3	...	...	...	*3	...	*46	
	2000	*3	...	...	...	*3	...	*46	
	2001	*3	...	...	...	*3	...	*48	
Solomon Islands	1998	...	...	...	...	...	...	*55	
	1999	...	...	...	...	...	...	*57	
	2000	...	...	...	...	...	...	*57	
	2001	...	...	...	...	...	...	*59	

Bunkers - Soutes			Consumption - Consommation							
Air Avion	Sea Maritime	Unallocated Nondistribué	Per capita Par habitant	Total Totale	Solids Solides	Liquids Liquides	Gas Gaz	Electricity Electricité	Year Année	Région, pays ou zone
...	*91	...	1 503	*95	...	*95	...	...	1998	Samoa américaines
...	*86	...	1 473	*96	...	*96	...	...	1999	
...	*86	...	1 408	*96	...	*96	...	...	2000	
...	*89	...	1 623	*96	...	*96	...	...	2001	
2 325	708	2 308	5 602	104 928	51 571	32 261	19 706	1 389	1998	Australie
2 336	810	2 921	5 720	108 322	52 857	33 749	20 249	1 467	1999	
2 067	909	2 656	5 748	110 112	53 023	34 154	21 457	1 479	2000	
2 605	788	1 164	6 008	116 486	60 330	32 112	22 583	1 461	2001	
*8	...	...	422	*7	...	*7	...	...	1998	Iles Cook
*9	...	...	578	*9	...	*9	...	...	1999	
*9	...	...	513	*9	...	*9	...	...	2000	
*9	...	...	513	*9	...	*9	...	...	2001	
*21	*27	...	407	*324	*14	*273	...	*37	1998	Fidji
*19	*27	...	449	*362	*13	*313	...	*37	1999	
*19	*41	...	515	419	*13	370	...	*37	2000	
*18	*41	...	573	471	*11	424	...	*36	2001	
*5	*38	...	876	196	...	183	...	13	1998	Polynésie française
*4	*32	...	849	194	...	186	...	8	1999	
*4	*32	...	964	225	...	214	...	10	2000	
*5	*38	...	809	192	...	183	...	9	2001	
*11	*90	...	9 225	*1 374	...	*1 374	...	...	1998	Guam
*11	*90	...	8 955	*1 361	...	*1 361	...	...	1999	
*11	*90	...	8 782	*1 361	...	*1 361	...	...	2000	
*13	*95	...	8 654	*1 367	...	*1 367	...	...	2001	
...	...	...	140	11	...	11	...	...	1998	Kiribati
...	...	...	125	10	...	10	...	...	1999	
...	...	...	136	11	...	11	...	...	2000	
...	...	...	121	10	...	10	...	...	2001	
*5	...	...	3 752	*45	...	*45	...	...	1998	Nauru
*6	...	...	3 666	*44	...	*44	...	...	1999	
*6	...	...	3 666	*44	...	*44	...	...	2000	
*7	...	...	3 749	*45	...	*45	...	...	2001	
18	*9	...	2 945	601	84	483	...	34	1998	Nouvelle-Calédonie
*18	*10	...	3 316	683	78	565	...	41	1999	
*18	*10	...	2 817	*594	*81	*475	...	39	2000	
*19	*10	...	2 771	*593	*81	*480	...	32	2001	
561	306	292	4 032	15 289	1 274	5 258	4 531	4 226	1998	Nouvelle-Zélande
641	285	455	4 197	15 993	1 169	5 123	5 260	4 441	1999	
580	232	216	4 354	16 680	1 096	5 541	5 535	4 507	2000	
620	247	0	4 565	17 576	1 348	5 744	5 827	4 658	2001	
...	...	...	508	*1	...	*1	...	...	1998	Nioué
...	...	...	508	*1	...	*1	...	...	1999	
...	...	...	508	*1	...	*1	...	...	2000	
...	...	...	508	*1	...	*1	...	...	2001	
*15	...	...	4 402	*84	...	*81	...	*3	1998	Palaos
*14	...	...	4 381	*83	...	*81	...	*2	1999	
*14	...	...	4 381	*83	...	*81	...	*2	2000	
*13	...	...	4 008	*80	...	*78	...	*2	2001	
*21	*3	1	189	*869	*1	*719	*78	72	1998	Papouasie-Nvl-Guinée
*21	*3	20	188	*882	*1	*726	*78	78	1999	
*21	*3	20	184	*883	*1	*726	*78	78	2000	
*23	*3	40	161	*881	*1	*722	*79	79	2001	
...	...	...	279	*47	...	*44	...	*3	1998	Samoa
...	...	...	290	*49	...	*46	...	*3	1999	
...	...	...	289	*49	...	*46	...	*3	2000	
...	...	...	294	*51	...	*48	...	*3	2001	
*2	...	...	127	*53	...	*53	...	...	1998	Iles Salomon
*2	...	...	128	*55	...	*55	...	...	1999	
*2	...	...	124	*55	...	*55	...	...	2000	
*2	...	...	127	*57	...	*57	...	...	2001	

63

Production, trade and consumption of commercial energy
Thousand metric tons of oil equivalent and kilograms per capita *[cont.]*

Production, commerce et consommation d'énergie commerciale
Milliers de tonnes d'équivalent pétrole et kilogrammes par habitant *[suite]*

Region, country or area	Year Année	Primary energy production – Production d'énergie primaire					Changes in stocks Variations des stocks	Imports Importations	Expo Exportatio
		Total Totale	Solids Solides	Liquids Liquides	Gas Gaz	Electricity Electricité			
Tonga	1998	...	...	...	...	...	...	40	
	1999	...	...	...	...	...	...	45	
	2000	...	...	...	...	...	...	41	
	2001	...	...	...	...	...	...	37	
Vanuatu	1998	...	...	...	...	...	...	27	
	1999	...	...	...	...	...	...	*27	
	2000	...	...	...	...	...	...	*27	
	2001	...	...	...	...	...	...	*29	
Wake Island	1998	...	...	...	...	...	...	*421	
	1999	...	...	...	...	...	...	*424	
	2000	...	...	...	...	...	...	*424	
	2001	...	...	...	...	...	...	*432	

Source:
United Nations Statistics Division, New York, "Energy Statistics Yearbook 2001" and the energy statistics database.

Source:
Organisation des Nations Unies, Division de statistique, New York, "Annuaire des statistiques de l'énergie 2001" et la base de données pour les statistiques énergétiques.

1 Refers to the Southern African Customs Union.	1 Se réfèrent à l'Union douanière d'afrique australe.
2 Including part of the Neutral Zone.	2 Y compris une partie de la Zone Neutrale.
3 Including Monaco.	3 Y compris Monaco.
4 Including San Marino.	4 Y compris Saint-Marin.
5 Including Svalbard and Jan Mayen Islands.	5 Y compris îles Svalbard et Jan Mayen.
6 Including Liechtenstein.	6 Y compris Liechtenstein.

Bunkers - Soutes			Consumption - Consommation							
Air Avion	Sea Maritime	Unallocated Nondistribué	Per capita Par habitant	Total Totale	Solids Solides	Liquids Liquides	Gas Gaz	Electricity Electricité	Year Année	Région, pays ou zone
3	...	...	378	37	...	37	...	...	1998	Tonga
2	...	...	438	43	...	43	...	...	1999	
1	...	...	407	40	...	40	...	...	2000	
1	...	...	357	36	...	36	...	...	2001	
...	...	...	142	27	...	27	...	...	1998	Vanuatu
...	...	...	138	*27	...	*27	...	...	1999	
...	...	...	135	*27	...	*27	...	...	2000	
...	...	...	142	*29	...	*29	...	...	2001	
*402	*13	...	6 125	*6	...	*6	...	...	1998	Ile de Wake
*404	*14	...	6 125	*6	...	*6	...	...	1999	
*404	*14	...	6 125	*6	...	*6	...	...	2000	
*410	*15	...	6 125	*6	...	*6	...	...	2001	

64

Production of selected energy commodities
Thousand metric tons of oil equivalent

Production des principaux biens de l'énergie
Milliers de tonnes d'équivalent pétrole

Region, country or area Région, pays ou zone	Year Année	Hard coal, lignite and peat Houille, lignite et tourbe	Briquettes and cokes Agglom-érés et cokes	Crude petroleum and NGL Pétrole Brut et GNL	Light petroleum products Produits pétroliers légers	Heavy petroleum products Produits pétroliers lourds	Other petroleum products Autres produits pétroliers	LPG and refinery gas GLP et gas de raffinerie	Natural gas Gaz naturel	Electricity Electricité
World	**1998**	**2 309 588**	**236 951**	**3 639 961**	**1 381 222**	**1 646 600**	**261 638**	**197 469**	**2 203 359**	**1 702 375**
Monde	**1999**	**2 185 005**	**227 784**	**3 571 702**	**1 386 818**	**1 631 535**	**278 059**	**199 268**	**2 226 337**	**1 765 752**
	2000	**2 173 001**	**231 825**	**3 714 154**	**1 411 358**	**1 657 164**	**286 483**	**216 202**	**2 282 656**	**1 831 878**
	2001	**2 328 232**	**233 815**	**3 715 066**	**1 407 394**	**1 671 526**	**292 571**	**219 977**	**2 365 660**	**1 904 827**
Africa	**1998**	**160 372**	**2 952**	**381 032**	**45 511**	**65 279**	**3 615**	**4 836**	**103 797**	**37 933**
Afrique	**1999**	**160 920**	**2 638**	**374 979**	**45 981**	**72 334**	**3 741**	**5 033**	**113 358**	**39 120**
	2000	**161 392**	**2 678**	**387 501**	**44 919**	**67 236**	**3 940**	**4 994**	**121 704**	**40 262**
	2001	**162 260**	**2 732**	**393 725**	**48 259**	**71 745**	**4 438**	**5 357**	**120 688**	**41 941**
Algeria	1998	*6	...	68 911	7 212	11 306	275	507	75 423	*2 031
Algérie	1999	*4	...	66 544	7 846	12 181	297	631	80 062	2 120
	2000	...	...	69 172	7 961	11 574	360	593	78 276	2 185
	2001	...	...	67 642	8 075	12 241	405	619	73 336	2 290
Angola	1998	...	...	36 418	575	1 119	5	71	*527	113
Angola	1999	...	...	36 890	660	1 250	6	76	*509	115
	2000	...	...	36 742	591	1 156	9	73	*527	124
	2001	...	...	36 505	605	1 207	8	76	*481	137
Benin	1998	...	...	62	...	...	...	...	...	5
Bénin	1999	...	...	44	...	...	...	...	...	5
	2000	...	...	38	...	...	...	...	...	5
	2001	...	...	40	...	...	...	...	...	8
Burkina Faso *	1998	...	...	...	...	...	...	...	...	24
Burkina Faso *	1999	...	...	...	...	...	...	...	...	24
	2000	...	...	...	...	...	...	...	...	24
	2001	...	...	...	...	...	...	...	...	25
Burundi	1998	*4	...	...	...	...	...	...	...	10
Burundi	1999	*4	...	...	...	...	...	...	...	9
	2000	*4	...	...	...	...	...	...	...	9
	2001	*4	...	...	...	...	...	...	...	10
Cameroon	1998	*1	...	5 911	*595	*785	21	*30	...	276
Cameroun	1999	*1	...	6 857	*608	*709	21	36	...	295
	2000	*1	...	*6 552	665	859	21	28	...	296
	2001	...	...	*7 002	728	784	21	35	...	300
Cape Verde *	1998	...	...	...	...	...	...	...	...	4
Cap-Vert *	1999	...	...	...	...	...	...	...	...	4
	2000	...	...	...	...	...	...	...	...	4
	2001	...	...	...	...	...	...	...	...	4
Central African Rep. *	1998	...	...	...	...	...	...	...	...	9
Rép. centrafricaine *	1999	...	...	...	...	...	...	...	...	9
	2000	...	...	...	...	...	...	...	...	9
	2001	...	...	...	...	...	...	...	...	9
Chad *	1998	...	...	...	...	...	...	...	...	8
Tchad *	1999	...	...	...	...	...	...	...	...	8
	2000	...	...	...	...	...	...	...	...	8
	2001	...	...	...	...	...	...	...	...	8
Comoros *	1998	...	...	...	...	...	...	...	...	1
Comores *	1999	...	...	...	...	...	...	...	...	1
	2000	...	...	...	...	...	...	...	...	2
	2001	...	...	...	...	...	...	...	...	2
Congo	1998	...	...	12 723	*70	*367	*12	4	*123	39
Congo	1999	...	...	13 378	*76	*359	*13	5	133	30
	2000	...	...	13 235	121	284	10	2	117	26
	2001	...	...	12 137	158	373	10	3	117	33
Côte d'Ivoire	1998	...	...	1 900	1 725	2 175	249	77	841	344
Côte d'Ivoire	1999	...	...	1 485	1 781	2 238	221	82	1 409	415
	2000	...	...	*796	1 234	1 559	227	71	1 409	414
	2001	...	...	435	1 178	1 782	181	100	1 419	421

64

Production of selected energy commodities
Thousand metric tons of oil equivalent [cont.]

Production des principaux biens de l'énergie
Milliers de tonnes d'équivalent pétrole [suite]

Region, country or area / Région, pays ou zone	Year / Année	Hard coal, lignite and peat / Houille, lignite et tourbe	Briquettes and cokes / Agglom- érés et cokes	Crude petroleum and NGL / Pétrole Brut et GNL	Light petroleum products / Produits pétroliers légers	Heavy petroleum products / Produits pétroliers lourds	Other petroleum products / Autres produits pétroliers	LPG and refinery gas / GLP et gas de raffinerie	Natural gas / Gaz naturel	Electricity / Electricité
Dem. Rep. of the Congo	*1998	67	...	1 156	129	27	13	1	...	467
Rép. dém. du Congo	1999	*67	...	1 069	158	*30	*15	*2	...	490
	2000	67	...	*1 306	152	27	15	2	...	469
	2001	62	...	*1 249	150	28	15	2	...	496
Djibouti *	1998	...	...	...	...	...	...	...	...	16
Djibouti *	1999	...	...	...	...	...	...	...	...	16
	2000	...	...	...	...	...	...	...	...	17
	2001	...	...	...	...	...	...	...	...	17
Egypt	1998	...	1 227	43 200	10 872	19 168	1 496	882	11 523	5 125
Egypte	1999	...	1 070	40 797	10 420	18 442	1 564	907	15 601	5 605
	2000	...	1 070	37 148	10 057	16 916	1 469	818	19 592	*6 042
	2001	...	1 123	35 760	10 309	17 194	1 530	820	19 968	6 590
Equatorial Guinea	1998	...	...	4 172	...	...	...	...	...	*2
Guinée équatoriale	1999	...	...	4 826	...	...	...	...	...	*2
	2000	...	...	5 911	...	...	...	...	...	*2
	2001	...	...	9 810	...	...	...	...	...	*2
Eritrea	1998	...	...	...	...	...	...	...	...	17
Erythrée	1999	...	...	...	...	...	...	...	...	18
	2000	...	...	...	...	...	...	...	...	19
	2001	...	...	...	...	...	...	...	...	20
Ethiopia	1998	...	...	...	*19	*474	*2	*3	...	146
Ethiopie	1999	...	...	...	*20	*613	*2	*3	...	148
	2000	...	...	...	*24	*589	*2	3	...	152
	2001	...	...	...	*26	*593	*2	3	...	164
Gabon	1998	...	...	18 223	228	456	36	44	698	111
Gabon	1999	...	...	16 557	245	513	36	52	761	115
	2000	...	...	15 485	249	468	41	43	756	116
	2001	...	...	15 010	281	472	43	40	765	*129
Gambia	*1998	...	...	...	...	...	...	...	...	7
Gambie	1999	...	...	...	...	...	...	...	...	8
	2000	...	...	...	...	...	...	...	...	11
	2001	...	...	...	...	...	...	...	...	12
Ghana	1998	...	...	...	*381	*561	*60	*35	...	431
Ghana	1999	...	...	9	253	624	*60	47	...	567
	2000	...	...	12	415	624	*60	44	...	649
	2001	...	...	*12	423	630	*62	44	...	683
Guinea *	1998	...	...	...	...	...	...	...	...	57
Guinée *	1999	...	...	...	...	...	...	...	...	65
	2000	...	...	...	...	...	...	...	...	66
	2001	...	...	...	...	...	...	...	...	68
Guinea-Bissau *	1998	...	...	...	...	...	...	...	...	5
Guinée-Bissau *	1999	...	...	...	...	...	...	...	...	5
	2000	...	...	...	...	...	...	...	...	5
	2001	...	...	...	...	...	...	...	...	5
Kenya	1998	...	...	...	892	908	117	32	...	680
Kenya	1999	...	...	...	*718	915	111	29	...	676
	2000	...	...	...	*849	1 100	119	37	...	623
	2001	...	...	...	617	943	119	30	...	717
Liberia *	1998	...	...	...	...	...	...	...	...	43
Libéria *	1999	...	...	...	...	...	...	...	...	45
	2000	...	...	...	...	...	...	...	...	45
	2001	...	...	...	...	...	...	...	...	46
Libyan Arab Jamah.	1998	...	...	69 725	4 890	8 436	112	800	5 931	1 677
Jamah. arabe libyenne	1999	...	...	65 959	5 138	9 395	100	901	4 850	1 724
	2000	...	...	67 222	5 144	9 023	111	860	5 700	*1 724
	2001	...	...	68 360	5 206	9 142	124	856	5 613	1 846

64

Production of selected energy commodities
Thousand metric tons of oil equivalent [cont.]

Production des principaux biens de l'énergie
Milliers de tonnes d'équivalent pétrole [suite]

Region, country or area Région, pays ou zone	Year Année	Hard coal, lignite and peat Houille, lignite et tourbe	Briquettes and cokes Agglomérés et cokes	Crude petroleum and NGL Pétrole Brut et GNL	Light petroleum products Produits pétroliers légers	Heavy petroleum products Produits pétroliers lourds	Other petroleum products Autres produits pétroliers	LPG and refinery gas GLP et gas de raffinerie	Natural gas Gaz naturel	Electricity Electricité
Madagascar Madagascar	1998	...	...	...	131	*126	*10	*7	...	68
	1999	...	...	...	*172	*130	*10	*7	...	68
	2000	...	...	...	*181	*132	*10	*7	...	69
	2001	...	...	...	*186	*132	*10	*7		72
Malawi * Malawi *	1998	...	...	...	...	...	...	...	...	75
	1999	...	...	...	...	...	...	...	...	76
	2000	...	...	...	...	...	...	...	...	76
	2001	...	...	...	...	...	...	...	...	77
Mali * Mali *	1998	...	...	...	...	...	...	...	...	34
	1999	...	...	...	...	...	...	...	...	35
	2000	...	...	...	...	...	...	...	...	35
	2001	...	...	...	...	...	...	...	...	36
Mauritania * Mauritanie *	1998	...	...	...	313	510	99	41	...	13
	1999	...	...	...	317	514	101	44	...	13
	2000	...	...	...	317	516	101	44	...	14
	2001	...	...	...	317	518	101	45		14
Mauritius Maurice	1998	...	...	...	...	...	...	...	...	132
	1999	...	...	...	...	...	...	...	...	136
	2000	...	...	...	...	...	...	...	...	153
	2001	...	...	...	...	...	...	...	...	164
Morocco Maroc	1998	188	...	12	1 140	4 170	260	274	35	1 156
	1999	90	...	11	1 332	5 063	266	290	41	1 132
	2000	22	...	13	1 313	4 701	270	260	47	1 145
	2001	1	...	10	1 317	4 829	245	254	46	1 294
Mozambique Mozambique	1998	*13	...	...	...	...	...	...	1	422
	1999	15	...	...	...	...	...	...	1	843
	2000	17	...	...	...	...	...	...	1	749
	2001	20	...	...	...	...	...	...	1	918
Niger * Niger *	1998	122	...	...	...	...	...	...	...	20
	1999	123	...	...	...	...	...	...	...	20
	2000	123	...	...	...	...	...	...	...	20
	2001	123	...	...	...	...	...	...	...	21
Nigeria Nigéria	1998	41	...	106 855	3 991	3 248	111	152	5 559	1 299
	1999	41	...	105 122	3 750	3 892	219	169	6 549	1 384
	2000	43	...	112 333	1 962	2 489	330	132	11 740	1 267
	2001	44	...	117 090	4 405	5 251	729	311	14 774	1 557
Réunion Réunion	1998	...	...	...	...	...	...	...	...	135
	1999	...	...	...	...	...	...	...	...	135
	*2000	...	...	...	...	...	...	...	...	135
	*2001	...	...	...	...	...	...	...	...	136
Rwanda * Rwanda *	1998	...	...	...	...	...	...	...	0	14
	1999	...	...	...	...	...	...	...	0	15
	2000	...	...	...	...	...	...	...	0	15
	2001	...	...	...	...	...	...	...	0	15
Saint Helena Sainte-Hélène	1998	...	...	...	...	...	...	...	...	1
	1999	...	...	...	...	...	...	...	...	1
	2000	...	...	...	...	...	...	...	...	1
	2001	...	...	...	...	...	...	...	...	1
Sao Tome and Principe * Sao Tomé-et-Principe *	1998	...	...	...	...	...	...	...	...	1
	1999	...	...	...	...	...	...	...	...	1
	2000	...	...	...	...	...	...	...	...	2
	2001	...	...	...	...	...	...	...	...	2
Senegal Sénégal	1998	...	...	...	*221	534	*12	15	19	107
	1999	...	...	...	*241	619	*13	17	6	118
	2000	...	...	...	267	631	*15	18	1	127
	2001	...	...	...	222	627	*15	16	1	127

64

Production of selected energy commodities
Thousand metric tons of oil equivalent *[cont.]*
Production des principaux biens de l'énergie
Milliers de tonnes d'équivalent pétrole *[suite]*

Region, country or area Région, pays ou zone	Year Année	Hard coal, lignite and peat Houille, lignite et tourbe	Briquettes and cokes Agglom- érés et cokes	Crude petroleum and NGL Pétrole Brut et GNL	Light petroleum products Produits pétroliers légers	Heavy petroleum products Produits pétroliers lourds	Other petroleum products Autres produits pétroliers	LPG and refinery gas GLP et gas de raffinerie	Natural gas Gaz naturel	Electricity Electricité
Seychelles	1998	...	...	...	...	...	...	...	...	14
Seychelles	1999	...	...	...	...	...	...	...	...	15
	2000	...	...	...	...	...	...	...	...	16
	2001	...	...	...	...	...	...	...	...	17
Sierra Leone *	1998	...	...	...	65	125	27	...	...	21
Sierra Leone *	1999	...	...	...	66	128	31	...	...	21
	2000	...	...	...	67	128	31	...	...	21
	2001	...	...	...	68	130	32	...	...	22
Somalia *	1998	...	...	...	...	...	...	...	...	24
Somalie *	1999	...	...	...	...	...	...	...	...	24
	2000	...	...	...	...	...	...	...	...	24
	2001	...	...	...	...	...	...	...	...	24
South Africa [1]	1998	156 871	1 349	7 499	10 953	8 489	557	1 686	1 290	*20 260
Afrique du Sud [1]	1999	157 173	1 123	7 995	11 072	12 534	532	1 590	1 688	19 941
	2000	157 865	1 188	8 524	11 792	11 833	625	1 653	1 554	20 626
	2001	159 011	1 225	8 868	11 625	12 052	649	1 722	1 912	20 466
Sudan	1998	...	...	330	*223	*485	*104	*8	...	*150
Soudan	1999	...	...	3 453	*212	658	*104	*6	...	181
	2000	...	...	9 309	818	1 150	*106	179	...	211
	2001	...	...	10 404	1 441	1 226	*108	237	...	220
Togo	1998	...	...	...	...	...	...	...	...	11
Togo	1999	...	...	...	...	...	...	...	...	7
	2000	...	...	...	...	...	...	...	...	7
	2001	...	...	...	...	...	...	...	...	7
Tunisia	1998	...	...	3 935	507	1 198	...	138	1 829	770
Tunisie	1999	...	...	3 983	622	1 138	...	122	1 751	819
	2000	...	...	3 703	526	1 192	...	120	*1 986	868
	2001	...	...	3 390	567	1 066	...	120	*2 255	917
Uganda	1998	...	...	...	...	...	...	...	...	109
Ouganda	1999	...	...	...	...	...	...	...	...	110
	2000	...	...	...	...	...	...	...	...	135
	2001	...	...	...	...	...	...	...	...	144
United Rep. of Tanzania	1998	32	...	...	*196	*312	*4	*7	...	212
Rép.-Unie de Tanzanie	1999	53	...	...	201	281	*5	*8	...	220
	2000	55	...	...	*206	*271	*5	8	...	219
	2001	55	...	...	*209	*274	*5	*8	...	256
Western Sahara *	1998	...	...	...	...	...	...	...	...	7
Sahara occidental *	1999	...	...	...	...	...	...	...	...	8
	2000	...	...	...	...	...	...	...	...	8
	2001	...	...	...	...	...	...	...	...	8
Zambia	1998	114	*16	...	184	297	30	21	...	654
Zambie	1999	112	*13	...	71	109	11	9	...	668
	2000	114	*9	...	8	13	1	1	...	671
	2001	120	*8	...	147	249	22	12	...	703
Zimbabwe	1998	2 914	360	...	...	...	...	...	...	574
Zimbabwe	1999	3 238	432	...	...	...	...	...	...	*610
	2000	3 080	411	...	...	...	...	...	...	*602
	2001	2 820	376	...	...	...	...	...	...	*682
America, North	**1998**	**613 242**	**15 453**	**713 673**	**531 148**	**320 384**	**108 690**	**65 139**	**720 392**	**549 491**
Amérique du Nord	**1999**	**600 079**	**15 563**	**689 404**	**534 479**	**314 985**	**120 578**	**65 144**	**708 452**	**577 266**
	2000	**586 670**	**15 906**	**700 459**	**538 916**	**326 611**	**122 287**	**66 391**	**691 933**	**600 237**
	2001	**617 134**	**14 736**	**699 291**	**533 715**	**333 518**	**120 323**	**65 628**	**739 927**	**641 760**
Antigua and Barbuda *	1998	...	...	...	...	...	...	...	...	9
Antigua-et-Barbuda *	1999	...	...	...	...	...	...	...	...	9
	2000	...	...	...	...	...	...	...	...	9
	2001	...	...	...	...	...	...	...	...	9

64

Production of selected energy commodities
Thousand metric tons of oil equivalent *[cont.]*

Production des principaux biens de l'énergie
Milliers de tonnes d'équivalent pétrole *[suite]*

Region, country or area Région, pays ou zone	Year Année	Hard coal, lignite and peat Houille, lignite et tourbe	Briquettes and cokes Agglom-érés et cokes	Crude petroleum and NGL Pétrole Brut et GNL	Light petroleum products Produits pétroliers légers	Heavy petroleum products Produits pétroliers lourds	Other petroleum products Autres produits pétroliers	LPG and refinery gas GLP et gas de raffinerie	Natural gas Gaz naturel	Electricity Electricité
Aruba	1998	...	...	...	...	...	...	...	...	63
Aruba	1999	...	...	...	...	...	...	...	...	63
	2000	...	...	...	...	...	...	...	...	67
	2001	...	...	...	...	...	...	...	...	69
Bahamas	1998	...	...	...	...	...	...	...	...	132
Bahamas	*1999	...	...	...	...	...	...	...	...	143
	*2000	...	...	...	...	...	...	...	...	143
	*2001	...	...	...	...	...	...	...	...	143
Barbados	1998	...	...	80	...	...	...	...	35	64
Barbade	1999	...	...	97	...	...	...	...	44	69
	2000	...	...	77	...	...	...	...	35	68
	2001	...	...	63	...	...	...	...	30	71
Belize	1998	...	...	...	...	...	...	...	...	16
Belize	1999	...	...	...	...	...	...	...	...	11
	2000	...	...	...	...	...	...	...	...	12
	2001	...	...	...	...	...	...	...	...	13
Bermuda	*1998	...	...	...	...	...	...	...	...	46
Bermudes	1999	...	...	...	...	...	...	...	...	47
	2000	...	...	...	...	...	...	...	...	52
	2001	...	...	...	...	...	...	...	...	53
British Virgin Islands *	1998	...	...	...	...	...	...	...	...	4
Iles Vierges britanniques *	1999	...	...	...	...	...	...	...	...	4
	2000	...	...	...	...	...	...	...	...	4
	2001	...	...	...	...	...	...	...	...	4
Canada	1998	38 947	2 055	136 409	40 417	32 939	12 561	6 370	164 250	60 871
Canada	1999	37 336	2 163	134 799	42 319	33 430	11 944	6 293	163 322	62 527
	2000	35 276	2 121	139 896	42 465	35 126	12 127	5 695	154 315	63 488
	2001	35 759	2 080	137 562	43 666	36 406	12 339	6 020	167 193	64 861
Cayman Islands	*1998	...	...	...	...	...	...	...	...	26
Iles Caïmanes	1999	...	...	...	...	...	...	...	...	28
	*2000	...	...	...	...	...	...	...	...	28
	*2001	...	...	...	...	...	...	...	...	28
Costa Rica	1998	...	...	...	6	165	12	...	...	956
Costa Rica	1999	...	...	...	2	...	*12	...	...	1 153
	2000	...	...	...	3	3	*12	...	...	1 349
	2001	...	...	...	...	237	...	...	...	1 360
Cuba	1998	...	...	1 680	413	756	169	*135	116	1 217
Cuba	1999	...	...	2 138	447	471	164	*139	429	1 247
	2000	...	...	2 698	840	1 204	163	184	535	1 292
	2001	...	...	2 889	778	1 366	192	179	540	1 316
Dominica	1998	...	...	...	...	...	...	...	...	6
Dominique	1999	...	...	...	...	...	...	...	...	6
	2000	...	...	...	...	...	...	...	...	7
	2001	...	...	...	...	...	...	...	...	7
Dominican Republic	1998	...	...	...	494	1 081	...	45	...	*662
Rép. dominicaine	1999	...	...	...	666	1 064	...	75	...	799
	2000	...	...	...	672	940	...	42	...	801
	2001	...	...	...	501	778	...	41	...	904
El Salvador	1998	...	...	...	202	641	...	17	...	704
El Salvador	1999	...	...	...	204	716	...	20	...	787
	2000	...	...	...	193	698	...	15	...	913
	2001	...	...	...	183	745	...	16	...	1 085
Greenland *	1998	...	...	...	...	...	...	...	...	22
Groenland *	1999	...	...	...	...	...	...	...	...	22
	2000	...	...	...	...	...	...	...	...	23
	2001	...	...	...	...	...	...	...	...	23

64

Production of selected energy commodities
Thousand metric tons of oil equivalent [cont.]

Production des principaux biens de l'énergie
Milliers de tonnes d'équivalent pétrole [suite]

Region, country or area Région, pays ou zone	Year Année	Hard coal, lignite and peat Houille, lignite et tourbe	Briquettes and cokes Agglom- érés et cokes	Crude petroleum and NGL Pétrole Brut et GNL	Light petroleum products Produits pétroliers légers	Heavy petroleum products Produits pétroliers lourds	Other petroleum products Autres produits pétroliers	LPG and refinery gas GLP et gas de raffinerie	Natural gas Gaz naturel	Electricity Electricité
Grenada	1998	...	...	...	...	...	...	...	...	10
Grenade	1999	...	...	...	...	...	...	...	...	10
	2000	...	...	...	...	...	...	...	...	10
	2001	...	...	...	...	...	...	...	...	10
Guadeloupe	1998	...	...	...	...	...	...	...	...	104
Guadeloupe	1999	...	...	...	...	...	...	...	...	105
	*2000	...	...	...	...	...	...	...	...	105
	*2001	...	...	...	...	...	...	...	...	105
Guatemala	1998	...	...	1 273	168	591	...	5	10	386
Guatemala	1999	...	...	1 164	197	620	...	13	*10	450
	2000	...	...	1 036	206	616	...	10	*10	520
	2001	...	...	1 150	218	559	...	9	*10	504
Haiti	*1998	...	...	...	...	...	...	...	...	59
Haïti	1999	...	...	...	...	...	...	...	...	55
	2000	...	...	...	...	...	...	...	...	55
	2001	...	...	...	...	...	...	...	...	47
Honduras	1998	...	...	...	...	...	...	...	...	305
Honduras	1999	...	...	...	...	...	...	...	...	295
	2000	...	...	...	...	...	...	...	...	316
	2001	...	...	...	...	...	...	...	...	343
Jamaica	1998	...	...	...	155	519	12	11	...	557
Jamaïque	1999	...	...	...	100	372	7	3	...	568
	2000	...	...	...	232	724	17	9	...	570
	2001	...	...	...	225	607	17	11	...	572
Martinique	*1998	...	...	...	298	435	...	23	...	93
Martinique	1999	...	...	...	*301	*440	...	*24	...	96
	*2000	...	...	...	301	440	...	24	...	96
	*2001	...	...	...	305	443	...	26	...	96
Mexico	1998	3 501	1 469	187 734	21 727	40 177	3 744	2 445	33 927	21 797
Mexique	1999	3 515	1 486	182 084	20 749	38 404	3 680	2 438	32 563	25 715
	2000	3 548	1 400	188 368	20 071	38 426	3 604	2 946	33 529	25 689
	2001	3 604	1 377	191 291	19 600	38 690	3 505	2 948	32 885	25 328
Montserrat	*1998	...	...	...	...	...	...	...	...	2
Montserrat	*1999	...	...	...	...	...	...	...	...	1
	2000	...	...	...	...	...	...	...	...	1
	2001	...	...	...	...	...	...	...	...	1
Netherlands Antilles	1998	...	...	...	*2 766	*7 523	*2 661	*100	...	96
Antilles néerlandaises	1999	...	...	...	*2 680	7 612	*2 949	106	...	96
	2000	...	...	...	*2 842	7 629	*2 980	108	...	96
	2001	...	...	...	*2 844	7 635	*2 989	109	...	97
Nicaragua	1998	...	...	...	145	662	21	*27	...	*694
Nicaragua	1999	...	...	...	135	650	21	*31	...	566
	2000	...	...	...	146	615	21	31	...	621
	2001	...	...	...	145	715	18	35	...	678
Panama	1998	...	...	...	362	1 916	...	*70	...	373
Panama	1999	...	...	...	392	1 902	...	*72	...	424
	2000	...	...	...	362	1 707	...	75	...	416
	2001	...	...	...	391	1 458	...	79	...	447
Puerto Rico	1998	...	...	...	*2 014	*1 248	*1 635	*125	...	1 751
Porto Rico	1999	...	...	...	*1 691	976	1 560	*120	...	*1 752
	2000	...	...	...	1 670	971	1 905	*109	...	*1 753
	*2001	...	...	...	1 639	953	1 895	103	...	1 753
Saint Kitts and Nevis	1998	...	...	...	...	...	...	...	...	8
Saint-Kitts-et-Nevis	1999	...	...	...	...	...	...	...	...	8
	*2000	...	...	...	...	...	...	...	...	9
	*2001	...	...	...	...	...	...	...	...	9

64

Production of selected energy commodities
Thousand metric tons of oil equivalent [cont.]

Production des principaux biens de l'énergie
Milliers de tonnes d'équivalent pétrole [suite]

Region, country or area Région, pays ou zone	Year Année	Hard coal, lignite and peat Houille, lignite et tourbe	Briquettes and cokes Agglom- érés et cokes	Crude petroleum and NGL Pétrole Brut et GNL	Light petroleum products Produits pétroliers légers	Heavy petroleum products Produits pétroliers lourds	Other petroleum products Autres produits pétroliers	LPG and refinery gas GLP et gas de raffinerie	Natural gas Gaz naturel	Electricity Electricité
Saint Lucia	1998	...	...	...	...	...	...	...	...	20
Sainte-Lucie	1999	...	...	...	...	...	...	...	...	22
	2000	...	...	...	...	...	...	...	...	24
	2001	...	...	...	...	...	...	...	...	25
Saint Pierre and Miquelon	1998	...	...	...	...	...	...	...	...	4
Saint-Pierre-et-Miquelon	*1999	...	...	...	...	...	...	...	...	4
	*2000	...	...	...	...	...	...	...	...	4
	*2001	...	...	...	...	...	...	...	...	4
St. Vincent-Grenadines	1998	...	...	...	...	...	...	...	...	7
St. Vincent-Grenadines	*1999	...	...	...	...	...	...	...	...	7
	*2000	...	...	...	...	...	...	...	...	7
	*2001	...	...	...	...	...	...	...	...	7
Trinidad and Tobago	1998	...	...	6 391	2 085	4 532	*42	509	7 903	446
Trinité-et-Tobago	1999	...	...	6 509	2 120	4 909	50	785	9 662	451
	2000	...	...	6 225	2 288	4 987	49	902	*9 723	470
	2001	...	...	6 225	2 288	4 987	49	902	*9 723	470
Turks and Caicos Islands *	1998	...	...	...	...	...	...	...	...	0
Iles Turques et Caïques *	1999	...	...	...	...	...	...	...	...	0
	2000	...	...	...	...	...	...	...	...	0
	2001	...	...	...	...	...	...	...	...	0
United States	1998	570 794	11 929	380 107	455 742	220 478	83 292	54 999	514 151	457 889
Etats-Unis	1999	559 228	11 913	362 613	458 284	216 690	95 644	54 767	502 422	479 632
	2000	547 846	12 385	362 159	462 391	225 783	96 842	55 981	493 785	501 127
	2001	577 771	11 278	360 110	456 699	231 195	94 751	54 890	529 546	541 225
United States Virgin Is. *	1998	...	...	...	4 154	6 722	4 541	258	...	93
Iles Vierges américaines *	1999	...	...	...	4 191	6 730	4 547	259	...	93
	2000	...	...	...	4 233	6 744	4 568	261	...	94
	2001	...	...	...	4 233	6 744	4 568	261	...	94
America, South	**1998**	**30 206**	**7 007**	**345 493**	**72 198**	**104 075**	**13 866**	**13 834**	**81 150**	**58 291**
Amérique du Sud	**1999**	**29 239**	**6 608**	**342 760**	**74 113**	**104 113**	**14 484**	**13 804**	**81 750**	**59 904**
	2000	**33 753**	**6 993**	**349 886**	**71 144**	**108 184**	**16 487**	**13 940**	**86 882**	**62 936**
	2001	**36 584**	**6 766**	**343 948**	**72 533**	**112 016**	**15 971**	**15 063**	**84 904**	**63 130**
Argentina	1998	171	673	43 813	7 909	13 544	2 198	1 584	30 132	7 688
Argentine	1999	198	692	42 697	9 646	13 603	2 065	1 635	35 611	8 188
	2000	153	740	41 256	9 832	12 837	2 216	2 018	37 664	8 736
	2001	110	721	42 082	9 448	12 989	2 142	2 045	37 193	9 091
Bolivia	1998	...	...	2 085	651	420	385	56	3 394	317
Bolivie	1999	...	...	1 839	626	395	425	57	*2 681	335
	2000	...	...	1 845	621	393	439	57	*3 446	340
	2001	...	...	2 082	567	354	435	55	4 406	342
Brazil	1998	2 451	5 770	51 364	24 371	42 905	4 727	6 914	6 012	28 242
Brésil	1999	2 515	5 318	57 795	25 513	44 218	4 976	7 155	6 389	29 482
	2000	3 024	5 604	65 700	26 037	43 787	5 948	7 697	6 744	31 064
	2001	2 512	5 395	68 807	26 352	45 178	5 717	8 334	6 859	30 696
Chile	1998	658	328	789	3 277	5 028	126	762	1 620	3 053
Chili	1999	340	415	704	3 371	4 900	761	785	1 843	3 301
	2000	256	442	480	3 253	5 349	662	621	1 949	3 549
	2001	403	454	508	3 550	5 414	754	698	1 954	3 777
Colombia	1998	21 694	236	37 872	6 020	5 949	1 719	1 093	6 327	3 953
Colombie	1999	21 290	182	39 984	6 420	5 330	1 768	1 071	5 442	3 796
	2000	24 792	207	35 983	6 434	5 535	1 804	1 101	6 067	3 779
	2001	28 237	197	31 774	6 898	6 321	1 804	1 195	6 442	3 757
Ecuador	1998	...	...	19 634	1 754	5 079	150	113	224	937
Equateur	1999	...	...	19 522	1 670	4 751	198	83	210	886
	2000	...	...	20 967	1 622	5 656	242	148	229	912
	2001	...	...	21 270	1 876	5 582	295	131	233	950

64

Production of selected energy commodities
Thousand metric tons of oil equivalent *[cont.]*

Production des principaux biens de l'énergie
Milliers de tonnes d'équivalent pétrole *[suite]*

Region, country or area Région, pays ou zone	Year Année	Hard coal, lignite and peat Houille, lignite et tourbe	Briquettes and cokes Agglom-érés et cokes	Crude petroleum and NGL Pétrole Brut et GNL	Light petroleum products Produits pétroliers légers	Heavy petroleum products Produits pétroliers lourds	Other petroleum products Autres produits pétroliers	LPG and refinery gas GLP et gas de raffinerie	Natural gas Gaz naturel	Electricity Electricité
Falkland Is. (Malvinas)	1998	3	...	...	...	...	...	...	...	1
Iles Falkland (Malvinas)	*1999	3	...	...	...	...	...	...	...	1
	*2000	3	...	...	...	...	...	...	...	1
	*2001	3	...	...	...	...	...	...	...	1
French Guiana *	1998	...	...	...	...	...	...	...	...	39
Guyane française *	1999	...	...	...	...	...	...	...	...	39
	2000	...	...	...	...	...	...	...	...	39
	2001	...	...	...	...	...	...	...	...	39
Guyana	1998	...	...	...	...	...	...	...	...	73
Guyana	1999	...	...	...	...	...	...	...	...	77
	2000	...	...	...	...	...	...	...	...	77
	2001	...	...	...	...	...	...	...	...	78
Paraguay	1998	...	...	...	26	103	...	...	...	4 375
Paraguay	1999	...	...	...	18	96	...	...	...	4 469
	2000	...	...	...	15	88	...	...	...	4 603
	2001	...	...	...	13	84	...	...	...	3 905
Peru	1998	14	...	5 724	3 331	5 394	*279	356	530	1 598
Pérou	1999	11	...	6 025	3 315	4 588	404	313	719	1 638
	2000	8	...	5 623	3 279	4 614	255	335	679	1 712
	2001	13	...	4 858	3 048	5 085	216	300	710	1 787
Suriname	1998	...	...	248	...	...	...	...	...	139
Suriname	1999	...	...	248	...	...	...	...	...	141
	2000	...	...	603	...	282	...	...	...	142
	2001	...	...	644	...	351	...	...	...	161
Uruguay	1998	...	...	...	461	1 161	222	121	...	823
Uruguay	1999	...	...	...	467	913	268	108	...	619
	2000	...	...	...	495	1 249	177	131	...	653
	2001	...	...	...	421	1 083	224	122	...	796
Venezuela	1998	5 216	...	183 964	24 398	24 492	4 060	2 836	32 911	7 052
Venezuela	1999	4 883	...	173 945	23 066	25 318	3 619	2 598	28 853	6 931
	2000	5 516	...	177 429	19 557	28 393	4 742	1 833	30 105	7 328
	2001	5 306	...	171 924	20 360	29 575	4 383	2 183	27 106	7 750
Asia	**1998**	**970 276**	**137 572**	**1 519 991**	**396 097**	**617 346**	**58 551**	**52 668**	**443 245**	**467 644**
Asie	**1999**	**862 563**	**130 026**	**1 484 060**	**407 220**	**626 888**	**58 677**	**54 831**	**466 553**	**487 395**
	2000	**856 323**	**131 901**	**1 566 199**	**430 965**	**632 275**	**63 326**	**60 784**	**522 333**	**512 216**
	2001	**955 968**	**136 771**	**1 548 664**	**431 030**	**624 414**	**68 290**	**63 962**	**556 650**	**528 203**
Afghanistan *	1998	1	...	...	...	...	...	...	128	42
Afghanistan *	1999	1	...	...	...	...	...	...	118	42
	2000	1	...	...	...	...	...	...	109	41
	2001	1	...	...	...	...	...	...	102	40
Armenia	1998	...	...	...	...	...	...	...	...	811
Arménie	1999	...	...	...	...	...	...	...	...	855
	2000	...	...	...	...	...	...	...	...	863
	2001	...	...	...	...	...	...	...	...	842
Azerbaijan	1998	...	...	11 449	1 780	6 079	134	292	5 211	1 548
Azerbaïdjan	1999	...	...	13 833	1 495	5 760	117	278	5 593	1 563
	2000	...	...	14 043	1 884	6 022	278	259	5 262	1 608
	2001	...	...	14 934	1 621	4 210	85	244	4 987	1 631
Bahrain	1998	...	...	2 293	4 700	7 387	315	347	7 421	496
Bahreïn	1999	...	...	2 280	4 953	7 930	269	285	7 690	512
	2000	...	...	2 273	4 884	7 732	209	295	*7 843	*542
	2001	...	...	2 260	4 763	6 731	336	290	*8 300	*583
Bangladesh	1998	...	...	37	295	280	...	15	6 964	1 192
Bangladesh	1999	...	...	*36	350	260	11	11	7 630	1 327
	2000	...	...	*36	464	345	15	14	8 087	*1 361
	2001	...	...	215	443	318	15	22	*9 507	*1 398

64

Production of selected energy commodities
Thousand metric tons of oil equivalent *[cont.]*

Production des principaux biens de l'énergie
Milliers de tonnes d'équivalent pétrole *[suite]*

Region, country or area / Région, pays ou zone	Year / Année	Hard coal, lignite and peat / Houille, lignite et tourbe	Briquettes and cokes / Agglomérés et cokes	Crude petroleum and NGL / Pétrole Brut et GNL	Light petroleum products / Produits pétroliers légers	Heavy petroleum products / Produits pétroliers lourds	Other petroleum products / Autres produits pétroliers	LPG and refinery gas / GLP et gas de raffinerie	Natural gas / Gaz naturel	Electricity / Electricité
Bhutan	1998	*35	...	...	...	...	...	...	...	155
Bhoutan	*1999	35	...	...	...	...	...	...	...	155
	*2000	35	...	...	...	...	...	...	...	156
	*2001	35	...	...	...	...	...	...	...	163
Brunei Darussalam	1998	...	...	*8 472	377	209	...	1	*9 644	241
Brunéi Darussalam	1999	...	...	9 231	383	216	...	...	*8 954	235
	2000	...	...	10 307	393	221	...	...	10 526	244
	2001	...	...	10 395	405	231	...	...	10 642	250
Cambodia *	1998	...	...	...	...	...	...	...	...	18
Cambodge *	1999	...	...	...	...	...	...	...	...	19
	2000	...	...	...	...	...	...	...	...	20
	2001	...	...	...	...	...	...	...	...	20
China	1998	624 375	87 585	161 161	65 923	70 527	12 286	13 581	26 774	102 761
Chine	1999	521 978	81 980	160 160	67 864	82 070	11 231	15 066	28 981	109 196
	2000	498 501	81 212	163 163	75 105	92 210	12 197	16 908	31 282	119 511
	2001	579 810	87 532	164 123	74 649	94 455	12 291	17 091	34 880	129 620
China, Hong Kong SAR	1998	...	...	...	...	...	...	...	...	2 702
Chine, Hong Kong RAS	1999	...	...	...	...	...	...	...	...	2 537
	2000	...	...	...	...	...	...	...	...	2 694
	2001	...	...	...	...	...	...	...	...	2 789
China, Macao SAR	1998	...	...	...	...	...	...	...	...	132
Chine, Macao RAS	1999	...	...	...	...	...	...	...	...	132
	2000	...	...	...	...	...	...	...	...	135
	2001	...	...	...	...	...	...	...	...	138
Cyprus	1998	...	...	...	177	826	37	55	...	254
Chypre	1999	...	...	...	187	908	37	65	...	270
	2000	...	...	...	197	900	36	62	...	290
	2001	...	...	...	196	874	42	53	...	305
Georgia	1998	8	...	119	5	31	...	1	...	694
Géorgie	1999	9	...	107	7	45	...	1	...	692
	2000	4	...	110	4	41	4	1	...	636
	2001	1	...	99	...	10	6	...	37	597
India	1998	178 145	7 484	36 860	20 330	36 213	5 717	1 823	23 811	44 822
Inde	1999	177 209	7 215	36 841	21 572	43 827	6 976	2 225	20 921	48 453
	2000	188 433	7 419	36 502	29 922	51 183	11 685	4 344	21 886	51 190
	2001	192 641	7 296	36 381	31 973	52 352	11 676	4 929	22 096	*53 128
Indonesia	1998	42 225	...	95 211	16 632	25 080	1 526	2 444	58 216	9 749
Indonésie	1999	49 492	...	90 587	18 046	25 511	1 622	2 463	47 828	10 363
	2000	53 774	...	88 087	20 428	26 004	1 788	2 242	50 545	10 608
	2001	64 782	...	85 851	19 226	25 757	1 871	2 175	52 565	10 485
Iran (Islamic Rep. of)	1998	882	11	189 099	22 028	47 224	3 600	1 739	46 629	8 893
Iran (Rép. islamique d')	1999	883	217	182 666	22 639	50 491	2 859	1 802	52 930	9 683
	2000	900	74	192 012	22 035	50 065	3 763	1 767	56 093	10 435
	2001	793	*95	192 700	23 123	39 546	4 118	1 786	61 220	10 843
Iraq	1998	...	...	104 679	5 392	14 804	796	*1 587	2 751	*2 610
Iraq	1999	...	...	124 848	5 201	14 280	768	1 531	2 966	*2 622
	2000	...	...	127 116	5 296	14 543	782	1 559	3 485	*2 625
	2001	...	...	116 940	5 721	15 708	844	1 684	4 181	3 090
Israel	1998	98	...	5	4 551	7 010	370	542	11	3 266
Israël	1999	99	...	4	4 037	6 732	344	509	9	3 374
	2000	86	...	4	3 974	6 820	330	508	8	3 694
	2001	91	...	4	4 085	6 727	344	567	5	3 770
Japan	1998	2 125	24 946	655	88 558	102 471	11 338	14 407	2 256	150 874
Japon	1999	2 265	23 007	602	88 399	98 913	11 223	14 431	2 235	149 766
	2000	1 719	24 367	620	89 819	97 219	8 742	15 112	2 443	150 667
	2001	1 750	24 356	602	90 111	91 818	8 727	14 525	2 412	148 320

64

Production of selected energy commodities
Thousand metric tons of oil equivalent [cont.]

Production des principaux biens de l'énergie
Milliers de tonnes d'équivalent pétrole [suite]

Region, country or area Région, pays ou zone	Year Année	Hard coal, lignite and peat Houille, lignite et tourbe	Briquettes and cokes Agglom- érés et cokes	Crude petroleum and NGL Pétrole Brut et GNL	Light petroleum products Produits pétroliers légers	Heavy petroleum products Produits pétroliers lourds	Other petroleum products Autres produits pétroliers	LPG and refinery gas GLP et gas de raffinerie	Natural gas Gaz naturel	Electricity Electricité
Jordan	1998	...	...	2	1 013	2 184	162	212	228	580
Jordanie	1999	...	...	2	1 021	2 193	156	202	226	609
	2000	...	...	2	1 167	2 391	130	222	216	634
	2001	...	...	2	1 115	2 387	129	202	229	*649
Kazakhstan	1998	30 804	1 742	26 137	2 346	5 557	893	141	7 161	4 226
Kazakhstan	1999	25 743	2 258	30 425	1 618	3 971	727	96	8 962	*4 085
	2000	31 840	2 657	35 716	1 532	4 279	757	96	11 195	*4 441
	2001	32 971	2 655	40 446	1 730	4 991	1 083	1 669	10 829	*4 760
Korea, Dem. P. R.	1998	53 115	1 924	...	1 066	1 457	...	...	...	2 665
Corée, R. p. dém. de	*1999	48 636	1 952	...	1 064	1 473	...	...	...	2 705
	2000	44 317	*1 952	...	1 138	1 577	...	...	...	2 822
	*2001	44 254	1 931	...	1 104	1 534	...	...	...	2 881
Korea, Republic of	1998	1 962	8 529	...	44 785	64 092	2 845	2 569	...	36 386
Corée, République de	1999	1 888	8 517	...	48 266	66 713	3 040	2 823	...	40 983
	2000	1 867	9 118	...	49 210	66 508	3 155	3 261	...	44 452
	2001	1 717	8 065	...	47 779	64 507	3 249	3 676	...	46 624
Kuwait [2]	1998	...	...	106 671	19 284	23 608	1 576	341	8 851	2 624
Koweït [2]	1999	...	...	97 782	18 572	24 653	1 854	420	8 101	2 761
	2000	...	...	119 651	15 631	20 365	1 455	328	8 559	2 825
	2001	...	...	117 991	14 262	20 020	1 331	348	8 742	2 995
Kyrgyzstan	1998	137	...	78	56	77	...	...	17	999
Kirghizistan	1999	129	...	77	76	102	...	...	23	1 132
	2000	133	...	77	65	71	...	...	30	1 283
	2001	147	...	76	50	83	...	...	31	1 175
Lao People's Dem. Rep.	1998	109	...	...	...	...	...	...	...	*105
Rép. dém. pop. lao	1999	127	...	...	...	...	...	...	...	*105
	*2000	158	...	...	...	...	...	...	...	105
	*2001	196	...	...	...	...	...	...	...	108
Lebanon	1998	...	...	...	...	...	...	...	...	775
Liban	1999	...	...	...	...	...	...	...	...	777
	2000	...	...	...	...	...	...	...	...	794
	*2001	...	...	...	...	...	...	...	...	812
Malaysia	1998	246	...	36 170	6 137	9 151	*148	641	35 788	5 219
Malaisie	1999	193	...	33 219	7 027	9 308	261	847	38 752	5 606
	*2000	269	...	31 259	7 889	10 557	218	1 079	44 970	5 958
	2001	344	...	35 329	8 888	10 723	*213	1 163	*41 417	*6 139
Maldives	1998	...	...	...	...	...	...	...	...	7
Maldives	1999	...	...	...	...	...	...	...	...	8
	2000	...	...	...	...	...	...	...	...	9
	2001	...	...	...	...	...	...	...	...	10
Mongolia	1998	1 632	...	...	...	...	...	...	...	238
Mongolie	1999	1 562	...	...	...	...	...	...	...	252
	2000	1 548	...	...	...	...	...	...	...	252
	2001	1 626	...	...	...	...	...	...	...	259
Myanmar	1998	13	...	390	331	557	47	7	2 591	356
Myanmar	1999	98	...	444	340	512	50	9	4 338	399
	2000	244	...	420	342	482	51	10	5 755	440
	2001	46	...	430	312	485	51	9	5 832	488
Nepal	1998	11	...	...	...	...	...	...	...	103
Népal	1999	13	...	...	...	...	...	...	...	120
	2000	13	...	...	...	...	...	...	...	*122
	2001	7	...	...	...	...	...	...	...	*122
Oman	1998	...	...	44 659	1 052	3 055	...	39	5 649	918
Oman	1999	...	...	44 990	978	3 035	...	41	6 165	966
	2000	...	...	47 750	1 035	3 034	...	35	9 788	1 037
	2001	...	...	46 769	1 086	3 170	...	53	14 835	1 091

64

Production of selected energy commodities
Thousand metric tons of oil equivalent *[cont.]*

Production des principaux biens de l'énergie
Milliers de tonnes d'équivalent pétrole *[suite]*

Region, country or area Région, pays ou zone	Year Année	Hard coal, lignite and peat Houille, lignite et tourbe	Briquettes and cokes Agglom-érés et cokes	Crude petroleum and NGL Pétrole Brut et GNL	Light petroleum products Produits pétroliers légers	Heavy petroleum products Produits pétroliers lourds	Other petroleum products Autres produits pétroliers	LPG and refinery gas GLP et gas de raffinerie	Natural gas Gaz naturel	Electricity Electricité
Pakistan	1998	1 494	...	2 889	2 278	3 622	401	60	15 733	5 407
Pakistan	1999	1 637	...	2 833	2 303	3 650	420	74	16 750	5 674
	2000	1 498	...	2 893	2 415	3 743	422	69	18 148	5 724
	2001	1 464	...	2 969	2 754	5 491	414	202	19 130	6 208
Philippines	1998	473	...	41	4 155	10 750	129	996	8	10 475
Philippines	1999	557	...	47	4 355	10 581	287	906	6	11 753
	2000	640	...	55	4 213	9 926	239	791	10	12 893
	2001	581	...	65	4 076	9 406	*134	852	13	12 058
Qatar	1998	...	...	31 800	1 106	1 652	...	137	18 260	703
Qatar	1999	...	...	31 708	1 057	1 687	...	119	26 850	702
	2000	...	...	37 133	956	1 552	...	113	27 566	788
	2001	...	...	37 969	1 119	1 194	...	*118	29 283	848
Saudi Arabia [2]	1998	...	...	456 942	25 509	49 964	*2 551	3 196	43 570	9 691
Arabie saoudite [2]	1999	...	...	421 285	26 598	47 561	*2 623	2 999	43 085	10 459
	2000	...	...	446 178	27 807	48 693	*2 685	3 322	46 452	10 874
	2001	...	...	432 498	26 578	53 245	*2 747	3 327	52 090	*11 815
Singapore	1998	...	...	...	17 832	26 909	2 895	1 093	...	2 432
Singapour	1999	...	...	...	15 833	20 881	3 138	1 058	...	2 539
	2000	...	...	...	15 482	16 249	2 950	961	...	2 723
	2001	...	...	...	14 149	16 069	2 591	932	...	2 846
Sri Lanka	1998	...	...	...	595	1 441	156	70	...	489
Sri Lanka	1999	...	...	...	506	1 255	120	55	...	532
	2000	...	...	...	633	1 507	167	69	...	589
	2001	...	...	...	584	1 344	128	59	...	570
Syrian Arab Republic	1998	...	...	29 059	2 242	9 691	1 024	208	*4 989	*1 706
Rép. arabe syrienne	1999	...	...	29 149	2 083	9 631	1 074	210	*5 108	*1 855
	2000	...	...	31 374	2 265	9 233	1 055	212	*5 158	*2 059
	2001	...	...	30 308	2 493	9 609	1 034	326	4 938	*2 197
Tajikistan	1998	5	...	19	13	...	...	...	27	1 240
Tadjikistan	1999	5	...	19	13	...	...	...	32	1 359
	2000	5	...	18	13	...	...	...	36	1 221
	2001	5	...	18	13	...	...	...	36	1 238
Thailand	1998	8 870	...	5 266	9 246	21 447	697	1 402	13 896	8 150
Thaïlande	1999	8 035	...	5 721	9 839	21 104	847	1 611	15 000	8 184
	2000	7 790	...	7 287	9 695	20 399	1 005	1 814	15 302	8 737
	2001	8 630	...	7 927	10 148	20 499	1 145	1 977	*17 067	9 326
Turkey	1998	14 490	2 140	3 226	7 568	16 228	2 488	1 521	493	9 614
Turquie	1999	14 358	1 962	2 944	6 630	16 130	1 925	1 381	643	10 077
	2000	13 665	2 048	2 765	5 920	14 695	2 176	1 323	561	10 801
	2001	14 249	1 812	2 523	6 523	15 830	2 030	1 395	288	10 623
Turkmenistan	1998	...	...	7 387	1 158	4 505	...	360	11 945	810
Turkménistan	1999	...	...	7 756	1 184	4 608	...	368	20 672	762
	2000	...	...	7 779	1 189	4 624	...	369	42 486	847
	2001	...	...	8 688	1 347	5 242	...	418	46 455	931
United Arab Emirates	1998	...	...	119 538	5 663	16 092	...	515	33 012	2 700
Emirats arabes unis	1999	...	...	109 732	5 688	12 313	...	495	33 876	*2 743
	2000	...	...	115 798	7 962	10 931	...	1 047	35 479	*2 743
	2001	...	...	113 510	7 854	12 840	...	1 050	40 020	*3 453
Uzbekistan	1998	801	11	8 179	2 083	4 220	823	230	49 615	3 947
Ouzbékistan	1999	814	11	8 399	2 155	3 988	802	248	50 331	3 896
	2000	706	11	7 814	2 226	3 613	855	247	51 074	4 028
	2001	754	*7	7 482	2 197	3 467	819	237	51 991	4 122
Viet Nam	1998	8 170	...	12 412	...	...	...	...	819	*2 359
Viet Nam	1999	6 740	...	15 402	...	...	...	...	1 023	*2 529
	2000	8 126	...	16 473	...	...	...	...	1 264	*2 802
	2001	9 073	...	17 047	...	...	...	...	1 738	3 155

64

Production of selected energy commodities
Thousand metric tons of oil equivalent [cont.]

Production des principaux biens de l'énergie
Milliers de tonnes d'équivalent pétrole [suite]

Region, country or area Région, pays ou zone	Year Année	Hard coal, lignite and peat Houille, lignite et tourbe	Briquettes and cokes Agglomérés et cokes	Crude petroleum and NGL Pétrole Brut et GNL	Light petroleum products Produits pétroliers légers	Heavy petroleum products Produits pétroliers lourds	Other petroleum products Autres produits pétroliers	LPG and refinery gas GLP et gas de raffinerie	Natural gas Gaz naturel	Electricity Electricité
Yemen	1998	...	...	19 032	2 560	2 966	59	22	...	216
Yémen	1999	...	...	20 887	*2 365	*2 994	*59	18	...	235
	2000	...	...	21 450	2 057	2 389	62	24	...	255
	2001	...	...	22 074	2 079	2 418	65	24	...	266
Europe	**1998**	**379 650**	**71 026**	**642 504**	**314 326**	**523 894**	**73 371**	**58 664**	**820 614**	**566 490**
Europe	**1999**	**374 244**	**70 189**	**649 307**	**302 999**	**498 256**	**77 486**	**58 054**	**820 786**	**578 625**
	2000	**367 049**	**71 870**	**669 631**	**303 223**	**507 194**	**77 777**	**67 647**	**822 503**	**592 283**
	2001	**373 167**	**70 499**	**687 770**	**300 812**	**514 382**	**80 992**	**67 502**	**825 212**	**604 602**
Albania	1998	14	...	368	103	154	66	30	15	436
Albanie	1999	14	...	323	39	109	146	10	15	464
	2000	9	...	317	42	116	139	10	10	407
	2001	7	...	311	53	107	138	9	8	318
Austria	1998	297	1 137	1 055	2 824	5 285	809	381	1 408	5 073
Autriche	1999	297	1 136	1 029	2 772	5 068	1 408	362	1 564	5 978
	2000	325	953	1 074	2 472	4 773	1 375	349	1 634	5 966
	2001	314	952	1 017	2 549	5 056	1 598	328	1 554	5 652
Belarus	1998	464	604	1 832	2 106	7 582	768	687	233	2 020
Bélarus	1999	705	589	1 842	1 875	7 715	602	708	236	2 280
	2000	462	588	1 853	2 223	8 492	541	684	237	2 244
	2001	454	517	1 854	2 052	8 306	657	629	235	2 154
Belgium	1998	188	2 114	...	10 788	20 603	5 951	1 352	*0	15 242
Belgique	1999	219	2 201	...	10 436	18 758	6 039	1 206	0	15 846
	2000	226	2 176	...	10 305	20 607	6 389	1 473	2	15 652
	2001	131	2 262	...	10 224	19 921	9 089	1 356	4	15 128
Bosnia and Herzegovina	1998	3 614	...	...	...	...	...	...	...	828
Bosnie-Herzégovine	1999	3 391	...	...	...	...	...	...	...	907
	2000	4 148	...	...	...	...	...	...	...	897
	2001	4 148	...	...	...	...	...	...	...	897
Bulgaria	1998	4 970	1 087	33	1 810	3 301	357	211	26	6 544
Bulgarie	1999	4 199	1 063	40	1 826	3 343	422	300	24	6 057
	2000	4 382	940	42	1 683	3 080	253	274	14	6 701
	2001	4 407	873	34	1 872	3 093	328	314	20	7 203
Croatia	1998	36	...	1 989	1 493	2 927	341	451	1 426	937
Croatie	1999	11	...	1 661	1 483	3 275	322	490	1 408	1 053
	2000	...	...	1 462	1 597	2 792	355	571	1 506	920
	2001	...	...	1 351	1 523	2 687	303	506	1 826	1 047
Czech Republic	1998	24 809	2 692	179	1 715	4 017	1 233	254	188	7 906
République tchèque	1999	21 792	2 246	183	1 588	3 322	1 209	246	195	7 901
	2000	23 741	2 279	175	1 637	3 060	1 285	272	188	8 696
	2001	24 105	2 362	183	1 946	3 050	1 125	326	136	9 001
Denmark	1998	...	...	11 454	2 688	4 839	...	442	6 625	3 969
Danemark	1999	...	...	14 492	2 923	4 907	...	474	6 741	3 835
	2000	...	...	17 813	2 910	5 010	...	489	7 378	3 744
	2001	...	...	16 915	2 917	4 821	...	386	8 438	3 809
Estonia	1998	2 845	64	...	...	...	...	...	...	733
Estonie	1999	2 540	59	...	...	...	...	...	...	711
	2000	2 724	54	...	...	...	...	...	...	732
	2001	2 748	69	...	...	...	...	...	...	730
Faeroe Islands *	1998	...	...	...	...	...	...	...	...	16
Iles Féroé *	1999	...	...	...	...	...	...	...	...	16
	2000	...	...	...	...	...	...	...	...	16
	2001	...	...	...	...	...	...	...	...	16
Finland	1998	424	575	...	5 571	6 627	377	945	...	10 103
Finlande	1999	2 043	567	...	5 770	6 320	346	796	...	10 214
	2000	1 231	573	...	5 223	6 721	351	804	...	10 296
	2001	1 446	573	...	4 708	6 428	341	630	...	10 389

64

Production of selected energy commodities
Thousand metric tons of oil equivalent *[cont.]*

Production des principaux biens de l'énergie
Milliers de tonnes d'équivalent pétrole *[suite]*

Region, country or area Région, pays ou zone	Year Année	Hard coal, lignite and peat Houille, lignite et tourbe	Briquettes and cokes Agglom-érés et cokes	Crude petroleum and NGL Pétrole Brut et GNL	Light petroleum products Produits pétroliers légers	Heavy petroleum products Produits pétroliers lourds	Other petroleum products Autres produits pétroliers	LPG and refinery gas GLP et gas de raffinerie	Natural gas Gaz naturel	Electricity Electricité
France [3]	1998	3 790	3 911	4 761	33 212	48 568	9 905	5 727	2 102	111 524
France [3]	1999	3 559	3 832	4 487	30 294	43 813	11 197	4 920	1 920	114 970
	2000	2 176	3 677	4 838	30 465	46 017	11 159	5 472	1 964	120 037
	2001	1 412	3 551	4 832	29 706	46 848	9 694	5 675	2 345	122 034
Germany	1998	64 146	9 904	2 937	41 556	62 007	9 361	6 884	16 863	77 083
Allemagne	1999	62 058	8 514	2 749	42 798	58 566	9 484	6 856	18 050	79 123
	2000	59 236	8 872	3 169	42 351	60 144	8 733	7 428	17 087	80 140
	2001	57 630	7 554	3 281	40 659	60 720	8 296	7 174	17 268	80 897
Gibraltar	1998	...	...	...	...	...	...	...	...	10
Gibraltar	1999	...	...	...	...	...	...	...	...	8
	2000	...	...	...	...	...	...	...	...	11
	2001	...	...	...	...	...	...	...	...	11
Greece	1998	7 976	28	317	6 896	12 524	761	1 200	44	4 003
Grèce	1999	8 129	27	222	6 267	11 208	727	1 015	3	4 287
	2000	8 369	51	279	7 201	13 174	891	1 321	46	4 239
	2001	8 691	50	193	6 727	12 981	919	1 345	44	4 164
Hungary	1998	3 021	756	2 559	2 887	3 867	918	282	3 297	5 639
Hongrie	1999	3 000	713	2 274	2 682	4 082	600	462	2 918	5 720
	2000	2 894	705	2 122	2 508	3 932	738	466	2 754	5 508
	2001	2 869	519	2 010	2 663	3 865	617	474	2 754	5 604
Iceland	1998	...	...	...	...	...	...	...	...	1 048
Islande	1999	...	...	...	...	...	...	...	...	1 152
	2000	...	...	...	...	...	...	...	...	1 207
	2001	...	...	...	...	...	...	...	...	1 100
Ireland	1998	813	139	...	837	2 228	31	115	1 564	1 887
Irlande	1999	1 252	168	...	801	1 976	*25	98	1 275	2 039
	2000	1 065	154	...	941	2 298	27	114	1 065	2 075
	2001	966	157	...	964	2 312	5	143	732	2 156
Italy [4]	1998	44	3 634	5 629	33 269	57 118	5 894	5 340	17 309	26 298
Italie [4]	1999	27	3 493	5 005	29 726	54 279	6 317	5 493	16 213	26 367
	2000	26	3 153	4 597	27 942	56 314	6 596	5 563	15 146	28 008
	2001	...	3 380	4 104	28 553	56 753	7 152	5 672	14 162	28 084
Latvia	1998	14	5	...	...	...	...	...	...	499
Lettonie	1999	67	3	...	...	...	...	...	...	353
	2000	16	1	...	...	...	...	...	...	356
	2001	16	0	...	...	...	...	...	...	368
Lithuania	1998	14	7	277	2 603	3 587	239	473	...	3 888
Lituanie	1999	19	7	232	1 751	2 357	177	341	...	2 890
	2000	10	5	316	2 118	2 263	209	433	...	2 456
	2001	8	4	471	2 674	3 202	216	710	...	3 256
Luxembourg	1998	...	...	...	...	...	...	...	...	110
Luxembourg	1999	...	...	...	...	...	...	...	...	97
	2000	...	...	...	...	...	...	...	...	106
	2001	...	...	...	...	...	...	...	...	107
Malta	1998	...	...	...	...	...	...	...	...	148
Malte	1999	...	...	...	...	...	...	...	...	158
	2000	...	...	...	...	...	...	...	...	167
	2001	...	...	...	...	...	...	...	...	168
Netherlands	1998	...	1 931	2 738	32 960	35 888	5 780	7 512	63 950	8 485
Pays-Bas	1999	...	1 584	2 611	31 249	33 052	6 151	7 848	60 071	8 517
	2000	...	1 448	2 464	35 026	33 438	6 287	7 691	58 049	8 614
	2001	...	1 507	2 335	35 663	33 182	6 562	8 184	62 345	8 737
Norway [5]	1998	220	...	154 839	5 068	8 778	168	1 104	47 733	10 135
Norvège [5]	1999	328	...	154 542	5 200	9 242	165	1 059	49 094	10 590
	2000	424	...	163 604	5 616	8 707	169	1 053	50 916	12 305
	2001	1 200	...	169 841	5 107	8 207	183	801	54 432	11 064

64

Production of selected energy commodities
Thousand metric tons of oil equivalent *[cont.]*
Production des principaux biens de l'énergie
Milliers de tonnes d'équivalent pétrole *[suite]*

Region, country or area Région, pays ou zone	Year Année	Hard coal, lignite and peat Houille, lignite et tourbe	Briquettes and cokes Agglom-érés et cokes	Crude petroleum and NGL Pétrole Brut et GNL	Light petroleum products Produits pétroliers légers	Heavy petroleum products Produits pétroliers lourds	Other petroleum products Autres produits pétroliers	LPG and refinery gas GLP et gas de raffinerie	Natural gas Gaz naturel	Electricity Electricité
Poland Pologne	1998	78 845	6 613	360	4 672	10 339	1 078	758	3 612	12 280
	1999	75 303	5 676	434	5 438	10 691	1 296	853	3 449	12 223
	2000	71 109	6 071	654	5 835	10 853	1 106	981	3 684	12 486
	2001	71 488	6 045	768	5 954	10 641	1 254	942	3 883	12 523
Portugal Portugal	1998	...	236	...	5 028	7 590	1 263	446	...	3 404
	1999	...	243	...	4 916	7 456	1 065	371	...	3 793
	2000	...	248	...	4 331	6 824	1 113	301	...	4 143
	2001	...	45	...	4 451	7 280	1 218	404	...	4 081
Republic of Moldova * République de Moldova *	1998	...	...	...	...	...	...	...	...	394
	1999	...	...	...	...	...	...	...	...	356
	2000	...	...	...	...	...	...	...	...	285
	2001	...	...	...	...	...	...	...	...	308
Romania Roumanie	1998	4 844	1 973	6 579	3 997	6 019	1 981	1 212	12 396	5 529
	1999	4 199	1 081	6 404	3 382	4 993	1 285	960	12 444	5 271
	2000	5 129	1 016	6 313	3 658	5 317	1 088	1 095	12 195	5 421
	2001	5 788	890	6 262	3 896	6 043	1 191	1 196	11 986	5 586
Russian Federation Fédération de Russie	1998	90 835	13 940	301 707	35 583	103 042	10 259	12 925	530 514	89 590
	1999	98 095	16 809	303 542	36 227	102 549	13 453	13 528	530 601	94 125
	2000	99 624	18 454	322 014	37 627	102 855	14 476	21 344	523 381	98 408
	2001	103 615	18 880	346 187	38 345	105 988	15 752	20 613	521 193	100 684
Serbia and Montenegro Serbie-et-Monténégro	1998	9 398	345	1 234	897	1 331	368	96	713	*3 251
	1999	7 093	295	1 031	350	724	214	39	658	*2 870
	2000	7 325	299	816	216	714	233	23	754	*2 743
	2001	7 384	305	881	836	1 338	193	77	658	*2 736
Slovakia Slovaquie	1998	1 157	977	60	1 914	3 133	630	126	222	4 184
	1999	1 097	1 042	66	1 870	3 077	702	103	182	4 681
	2000	1 068	1 101	59	2 286	2 695	883	89	148	5 585
	2001	1 003	1 095	46	2 164	3 154	448	518	168	5 749
Slovenia Slovénie	1998	923	...	1	74	174	9	...	8	2 062
	1999	868	...	1	124	165	1	...	5	1 962
	2000	974	...	1	83	98	7	...	6	2 005
	2001	899	...	1	6	...	...	...	6	2 164
Spain Espagne	1998	8 743	1 903	873	18 320	35 191	6 399	3 282	375	27 342
	1999	8 267	1 686	*652	17 824	34 672	6 093	3 287	392	28 579
	2000	7 967	1 787	610	17 900	33 329	6 195	3 279	410	30 255
	2001	7 539	1 915	*736	17 173	32 158	6 140	3 255	524	31 579
Sweden Suède	1998	331	769	...	6 357	13 528	1 188	320	...	26 509
	1999	255	767	...	6 539	13 186	1 545	292	...	26 216
	2000	228	768	...	6 331	14 227	1 064	338	...	22 713
	2001	275	769	...	5 661	13 658	1 148	304	...	26 526
Switzerland [6] Suisse [6]	1998	...	...	...	1 723	2 845	144	471	...	10 026
	1999	...	...	...	1 839	2 828	133	441	...	10 500
	2000	...	...	...	1 607	2 622	149	376	...	10 537
	2001	...	...	...	1 632	2 823	179	384	...	10 876
TFYR of Macedonia L'ex-R.y. Macédoine	1998	2 208	...	...	359	566	...	10	...	606
	1999	1 991	...	...	284	451	...	8	...	590
	2000	2 029	...	...	307	636	...	9	...	586
	2001	2 189	...	...	250	507	...	12	...	547
Ukraine Ukraine	1998	39 715	11 370	5 203	3 792	8 529	1 332	531	16 756	28 030
	1999	41 089	12 192	5 021	3 365	7 186	1 060	458	16 872	27 414
	2000	41 693	12 093	4 949	2 878	5 854	853	370	16 678	28 279
	2001	43 198	12 400	3 791	4 221	10 251	1 549	667	17 101	28 205
United Kingdom Royaume-Uni	1998	24 956	4 312	135 519	43 226	41 708	5 759	5 101	93 236	48 719
	1999	22 339	4 196	140 462	41 362	38 887	5 302	5 034	96 456	48 510
	2000	18 437	4 403	130 090	37 905	40 233	5 112	4 974	107 251	47 335
	2001	19 238	3 825	120 367	35 664	39 003	4 699	4 470	103 393	48 948

64

Production of selected energy commodities
Thousand metric tons of oil equivalent [cont.]

Production des principaux biens de l'énergie
Milliers de tonnes d'équivalent pétrole [suite]

Region, country or area Région, pays ou zone	Year Année	Hard coal, lignite and peat Houille, lignite et tourbe	Briquettes and cokes Agglomérés et cokes	Crude petroleum and NGL Pétrole Brut et GNL	Light petroleum products Produits pétroliers légers	Heavy petroleum products Produits pétroliers lourds	Other petroleum products Autres produits pétroliers	LPG and refinery gas GLP et gas de raffinerie	Natural gas Gaz naturel	Electricity Electricité
Oceania	1998	155 842	2 941	37 269	21 941	15 621	3 546	2 328	34 161	22 525
Océanie	1999	157 961	2 761	31 192	22 026	14 959	3 094	2 402	35 438	23 441
	2000	167 815	2 477	40 477	22 190	15 664	2 666	2 446	37 300	23 945
	2001	183 118	2 311	41 667	21 046	15 452	2 557	2 465	38 279	25 192
American Samoa *	1998	...	...	...	...	...	...	...	...	11
Samoa américaines *	1999	...	...	...	...	...	...	...	...	11
	2000	...	...	...	...	...	...	...	...	11
	2001	...	...	...	...	...	...	...	...	12
Australia	1998	153 998	2 941	30 862	19 414	13 453	3 314	2 086	29 552	16 854
Australie	1999	155 880	2 761	24 984	19 702	12 684	2 838	2 193	30 099	17 492
	2000	165 805	2 477	34 463	19 804	13 260	2 449	2 217	31 688	17 869
	2001	180 906	2 311	35 673	18 607	13 156	2 359	2 239	32 374	18 682
Cook Islands	1998	...	...	...	...	...	...	...	...	2
Iles Cook	1999	...	...	...	...	...	...	...	...	2
	2000	...	...	...	...	...	...	...	...	2
	2001	...	...	...	...	...	...	...	...	2
Fiji *	1998	...	...	...	...	...	...	...	...	45
Fidji *	1999	...	...	...	...	...	...	...	...	45
	2000	...	...	...	...	...	...	...	...	45
	2001	...	...	...	...	...	...	...	...	45
French Polynesia	1998	...	...	...	...	...	...	...	...	30
Polynésie française	1999	...	...	...	...	...	...	...	...	31
	2000	...	...	...	...	...	...	...	...	35
	2001	...	...	...	...	...	...	...	...	43
Guam	1998	...	...	...	...	...	...	...	...	138
Guam	1999	...	...	...	...	...	...	...	...	147
	*2000	...	...	...	...	...	...	...	...	147
	*2001	...	...	...	...	...	...	...	...	150
Kiribati	1998	...	...	...	...	...	...	...	...	1
Kiribati	1999	...	...	...	...	...	...	...	...	1
	2000	...	...	...	...	...	...	...	...	1
	2001	...	...	...	...	...	...	...	...	1
Nauru *	1998	...	...	...	...	...	...	...	...	3
Nauru *	1999	...	...	...	...	...	...	...	...	3
	2000	...	...	...	...	...	...	...	...	3
	2001	...	...	...	...	...	...	...	...	3
New Caledonia	1998	...	...	...	...	...	...	...	...	137
Nouvelle-Calédonie	1999	...	...	...	...	...	...	...	...	139
	2000	...	...	...	...	...	...	...	...	141
	2001	...	...	...	...	...	...	...	...	149
New Zealand	1998	1 845	...	2 503	2 509	2 137	232	243	4 531	5 161
Nouvelle-Zélande	1999	2 081	...	2 274	2 305	2 244	256	210	5 261	5 419
	2000	2 010	...	2 080	2 367	2 372	217	229	5 534	5 536
	2001	2 212	...	2 000	2 419	2 266	198	226	5 827	5 953
Niue *	1998	...	...	...	...	...	...	...	...	0
Nioué *	1999	...	...	...	...	...	...	...	...	0
	2000	...	...	...	...	...	...	...	...	0
	2001	...	...	...	...	...	...	...	...	0
Palau *	1998	...	...	...	...	...	...	...	...	16
Palaos *	1999	...	...	...	...	...	...	...	...	15
	2000	...	...	...	...	...	...	...	...	15
	2001	...	...	...	...	...	...	...	...	14
Papua New Guinea	1998	...	...	*3 904	*19	*30	...	...	*78	111
Papouasie-Nvl-Guinée	1999	...	...	*3 934	*19	*31	...	...	*78	118
	2000	...	...	*3 934	*19	*31	...	...	*78	121
	2001	...	...	*3 994	*20	*30	...	...	*79	120

64

Production of selected energy commodities
Thousand metric tons of oil equivalent *[cont.]*

Production des principaux biens de l'énergie
Milliers de tonnes d'équivalent pétrole *[suite]*

Region, country or area Région, pays ou zone	Year Année	Hard coal, lignite and peat Houille, lignite et tourbe	Briquettes and cokes Agglom-érés et cokes	Crude petroleum and NGL Pétrole Brut et GNL	Light petroleum products Produits pétroliers légers	Heavy petroleum products Produits pétroliers lourds	Other petroleum products Autres produits pétroliers	LPG and refinery gas GLP et gas de raffinerie	Natural gas Gaz naturel	Electricity Electricité
Samoa * Samoa *	1998	...	...	...	...	...	...	...	...	7
	1999	...	...	...	...	...	...	...	...	7
	2000	...	...	...	...	...	...	...	...	8
	2001	...	...	...	...	...	...	...	...	9
Solomon Islands * Iles Salomon *	1998	...	...	...	...	...	...	...	...	3
	1999	...	...	...	...	...	...	...	...	3
	2000	...	...	...	...	...	...	...	...	3
	2001	...	...	...	...	...	...	...	...	3
Tonga Tonga	1998	...	...	...	...	...	...	...	...	3
	*1999	...	...	...	...	...	...	...	...	3
	*2000	...	...	...	...	...	...	...	...	3
	*2001	...	...	...	...	...	...	...	...	3
Vanuatu * Vanuatu *	1998	...	...	...	...	...	...	...	...	3
	1999	...	...	...	...	...	...	...	...	3
	2000	...	...	...	...	...	...	...	...	4
	2001	...	...	...	...	...	...	...	...	4

Source:
United Nations Statistics Division, New York, "Energy Statistics Yearbook 2001" and the energy statistics database.

Source:
Organisation des Nations Unies, Division de statistique, New York, "Annuaire des statistiques de l'énergie 2001" et la base de données pour les statistiques énergétiques.

1	Refers to the Southern African Customs Union.
2	Including part of the Neutral Zone.
3	Including Monaco.
4	Including San Marino.
5	Including Svalbard and Jan Mayen Islands.
6	Including Liechtenstein.

1	Se réfèrent à l'Union douanière d'afrique australe.
2	Y compris une partie de la Zone Neutrale.
3	Y compris Monaco.
4	Y compris Saint-Marin.
5	Y compris îles Svalbard et Jan Mayen.
6	Y compris Liechtenstein.

Technical notes, tables 63 and 64

Tables 63 and 64: Data are presented in metric tons of oil equivalent (TOE), to which the individual energy commodities are converted in the interests of international uniformity and comparability.

To convert from original units to TOE, the data in original units (metric tons, terajoules, kilowatt hours, cubic metres) are multiplied by conversion factors. For a list of the relevant conversion factors and a detailed description of methods, see the United Nations *Energy Statistics Yearbook* and related methodological publications [23, 45, 46].

Table 63: Included in the production of commercial primary energy for *solids* are hard coal, lignite, peat and oil shale; *liquids* are comprised of crude petroleum and natural gas liquids; *gas* comprises natural gas; and *electricity* is comprised of primary electricity generation from hydro, nuclear, geothermal, wind, tide, wave and solar sources.

In general, data on stocks refer to changes in stocks of producers, importers and/or industrial consumers at the beginning and end of each year.

International trade of energy commodities is based on the "general trade" system, that is, all goods entering and leaving the national boundary of a country are recorded as imports and exports.

Sea/air bunkers refer to the amounts of fuels delivered to ocean-going ships or aircraft of all flags engaged in international traffic. Consumption by ships engaged in transport in inland and coastal waters, or by aircraft engaged in domestic flights, is not included.

Data on consumption refer to "apparent consumption" and are derived from the formula "production + imports − exports − bunkers +/− stock changes". Accordingly, the series on apparent consumption may in some cases represent only an indication of the magnitude of actual gross inland availability.

Included in the consumption of commercial energy for *solids* are consumption of primary forms of solid fuels, net imports and changes in stocks of secondary fuels; *liquids* are comprised of consumption of energy petroleum products including feedstocks, natural gasolene, condensate, refinery gas and input of crude petroleum to thermal power plants; *gases* include the consumption of natural gas, net imports and changes in stocks of gasworks and coke-oven gas; and *electricity* is comprised of production of primary electricity and net imports of electricity.

Table 64: The definitions of the energy commodities are as follows:

− Hard coal: Coal that has a high degree of coalification with a gross calorific value above 23,865 KJ/kg (5,700 kcal/kg) on an ash-free but moist basis, and a mean random reflectance of vitrinite of at least 0.6. Slurries, middlings and

Notes techniques, tableaux 63 et 64

Tableaux 63 et 64: Les données relatives aux divers produits énergétiques ont été converties en tonnes d'équivalent pétrole (TEP), dans un souci d'uniformité et pour permettre les comparaisons entre la production de différents pays.

Pour passer des unités de mesure d'origine à l'unité commune, les données en unités d'origine (tonnes, terajoules, kilowatt-heures, mètres cubes) sont multipliées pour les facteurs de conversion. Pour une liste des facteurs de conversion appropriée et pour des descriptions détaillées des méthodes appliquées, se reporter à *l'Annuaire des* statistiques *de l'énergie* des Nations Unies et aux publications méthodologiques connexes [23, 45, 46].

Tableau 63: Sont compris dans la production d'énergie primaire commerciale: pour *les solides*, la houille, le lignite, la tourbe et le schiste bitumineux; pour *les* liquides, le pétrole brut et les liquides de gaz naturel; pour *les gaz*, le gaz naturel; pour *l'électricité*, l'électricité primaire de source hydraulique, nucléaire, géothermique, éolienne, marémotrice, des vagues et solaire.

En général, les variations des stocks se rapportent aux différences entre les stocks des producteurs, des importateurs ou des consommateurs industriels au début et à la fin de chaque année.

Le commerce international des produits énergétiques est fondé sur le système du "commerce général", c'est-à-dire que tous les biens entrant sur le territoire national d'un pays ou en sortant sont respectivement enregistrés comme importations et exportations.

Les soutages maritimes/aériens se rapportent aux quantités de combustibles livrées aux navires de mer et aéronefs assurant des liaisons commerciales internationales, quel que soit leur pavillon. La consommation des navires effectuant des opérations de transport sur les voies navigables intérieures ou dans les eaux côtières n'est pas incluse, non plus que celle des aéronefs effectuant des vols intérieurs.

Les données sur la consommation se rapportent à la "consommation apparente" et sont obtenues par la formule "production + importations - exportations - soutage +/- variations des stocks". En conséquence, les séries relatives à la consommation apparente peuvent occasionnellement ne donner qu'une indication de l'ordre de grandeur des disponibilités intérieures brutes réelles.

Sont compris dans la consommation d'énergie commerciale: pour *les solides*, la consommation de combustibles solides primaires, les importations nettes et les variations de stocks de combustibles solides secondaires; pour *les liquides*, la consommation de produits pétroliers énergétiques y compris les charges d'alimentation des usines de traitement, l'essence natu-

other low-grade coal products, which cannot be classified according to the type of coal from which they are obtained, are included under hard coal.

    – Lignite: Non-agglomerating coal with a low degree of coalification which retained the anatomical structure of the vegetable matter from which it was formed. Its gross calorific value is less than 17,435 KJ/kg (4,165 kcal/kg), and it contains greater than 31 per cent volatile matter on a dry mineral matter free basis.

    – Peat: A solid fuel formed from the partial decomposition of dead vegetation under conditions of high humidity and limited air access (initial stage of coalification). Only peat used as fuel is included.

    – Patent fuel (hard coal briquettes): A composition fuel manufactured from coal fines by shaping with the addition of a binding agent (pitch).

    – Lignite briquettes: A composition fuel manufactured from lignite. The lignite is crushed, dried and molded under high pressure into an even-shaped briquette without the addition of binders.

    – Peat briquettes: A composition fuel manufactured from peat. Raw peat, after crushing and drying, is molded under high pressure into an even-shaped briquette without the addition of binders.

    – Coke: The solid residue obtained from coal or lignite by heating it to a high temperature in the absence or near absence of air. It is high in carbon and low in moisture and volatile matter. Several categories are distinguished: coke-oven coke; gas coke; and brown coal coke.

    – Crude oil: A mineral oil consisting of a mixture of hydrocarbons of natural origin, yellow to black in color, of variable density and viscosity. Data in this category also includes lease or field condensate (separator liquids) which is recovered from gaseous hydrocarbons in lease separation facilities, as well as synthetic crude oil, mineral oils extracted from bituminous minerals such as shales and bituminous sand, and oils from coal liquefaction.

    – Natural gas liquids (NGL): Liquid or liquefied hydrocarbons produced in the manufacture, purification and stabilization of natural gas. NGLs include, but are not limited to, ethane, propane, butane, pentane, natural gasolene, and plant condensate.

    – Light petroleum products: Light products are defined in the table as liquid products obtained by distillation of crude petroleum at temperatures between 30°C and 350°C, and/or which have a specific gravity between 0.625 and 0.830. They comprise: aviation gasolene; motor gasolene; natural gasolene; jet fuel; kerosene; naphtha; and white spirit/industrial spirit.

    – Heavy petroleum products: are defined in the table as products obtained by the distillation of crude petroleum at temperatures above 350°C, and which have a specific gravity higher than 0.83. Products which are not

relle, le condensat et le gaz de raffinerie ainsi que le pétrole brut consommé dans les centrales thermiques pour la production d'électricité; pour *les gaz*, la consommation de gaz naturel, les importations nettes et les variations de stocks de gaz d'usines à gaz et de gaz de cokerie; pour *l'électricité*, la production d'électricité primaire et les importations nettes d'électricité.

Tableau 64: Les définitions des produits énergétiques sont données ci-après :

    – Houille: Charbon à haut degré de houillification et de pouvoir calorifique brut supérieur à 23 865 kJ/kg (5 700 kcal/kg), valeur mesurée pour un combustible exempt de cendres, mais humide et ayant un indice moyen de réflectance de la vitrinite au moins égal à 0,6. Les schlamms, les mixtes et autres produits du charbon de faible qualité qui ne peuvent être classés en fonction du type de charbon dont ils sont dérivés, sont inclus dans cette rubrique.

    – Lignite: Le charbon non agglutinant d'un faible degré de houillification qui a gardé la structure anatomique des végétaux dont il est issu. Son pouvoir calorifique supérieur est inférieur à 17 435 kJ/kg (4 165 kcal/kg) et il contient plus de 31% de matières volatiles sur produit sec exempt de matières minérales.

    – Tourbe: Combustible solide issu de la décomposition partielle de végétaux morts dans des conditions de forte humidité et de faible circulation d'air (phase initiale de la houillification). N'est prise en considération ici que la tourbe utilisée comme combustible.

    – Agglomérés (briquettes de houille): Combustibles composites fabriqués par moulage au moyen de fines de charbon avec l'addition d'un liant (brai).

    – Briquettes de lignite: Combustibles composites fabriqués au moyen de lignite. Le lignite est broyé, séché et moulé sous pression élevée pour donner une briquette de forme régulière sans l'addition d'un élément liant.

    – Briquettes de tourbe: Combustibles composites fabriqués au moyen de tourbe. La tourbe brute, après broyage et séchage, est moulée sous pression élevée pour donner une briquette de forme régulière sans l'addition d'un élément liant.

    – Coke: Résidu solide obtenu lors de la distillation de houille ou de lignite en l'absence totale ou presque total d'air. Il a un haut contenu de carbone, et a peu d'humidité et matières volatiles. On distingue plusieurs catégories de coke: coke de four; coke de gaz; et coke de lignite.

    – Pétrole brut: Huile minérale constituée d'un mélange d'hydrocarbures d'origine naturelle, de couleur variant du jaune au noir, d'une densité et d'une viscosité variable. Figurent également dans cette rubrique les condensats directement récupérés sur les sites d'exploitation des hydrocarbures gazeux (dans les installations prévues pour la séparation des phases liquide et gazeuse), le pétrole brut synthétique, les huiles minérales brutes extraites des roches bitumineuses telles que schistes, sables asphaltiques et les huiles issues de la liquéfaction du charbon.

used for energy purposes, such as insulating oils, lubricants, paraffin wax, bitumen and petroleum coke, are excluded. Heavy products comprise residual fuel oil and gas-diesel oil (distillate fuel oil).

– Liquefied petroleum gas (LPG): Hydrocarbons which are gaseous under conditions of normal temperature and pressure but are liquefied by compression or cooling to facilitate storage, handling and transportation. It comprises propane, butane, or a combination of the two. Also included is ethane from petroleum refineries or natural gas producers' separation and stabilization plants.

– Refinery gas: Non-condensable gas obtained during distillation of crude oil or treatment of oil products (e.g. cracking) in refineries. It consists mainly of hydrogen, methane, ethane and olefins.

– Natural gas: Gases consisting mainly of methane occurring naturally in underground deposits. It includes both non-associated gas (originating from fields producing only hydrocarbons in gaseous form) and associated gas (originating from fields producing both liquid and gaseous hydrocarbons), as well as methane recovered from coal mines and sewage gas. Production of natural gas refers to dry marketable production, measured after purification and extraction of natural gas liquids and sulphur. Extraction losses and the amounts that have been reinjected, flared, and vented are excluded from the data on production.

– Electricity production refers to gross production, which includes the consumption by station auxiliaries and any losses in the transformers that are considered integral parts of the station. Included also is total electric energy produced by pumping installations without deduction of electric energy absorbed by pumping.

– Liquides de gaz naturel (LGN): Hydrocarbures liquides ou liquéfiés produits lors de la fabrication, de la purification et de la stabilisation du gaz naturel. Les liquides de gaz naturel comprennent l'éthane, le propane, le butane, le pentane, l'essence naturelle et les condensats d'usine, sans que la liste soit limitative.

– Produits pétroliers légers: Les produits légers sont définis ici comme des produits liquides obtenus par distillation du pétrole brut à des températures comprises entre 30°C et 350°C et/ou ayant une densité comprise entre 0,625 et 0,830. Ces produits sont les suivants: l'essence aviation; l'essence auto; l'essence naturelle; les carburéacteurs du type essence et du type kérosène; le pétrole lampant; les naphtas; et le white spirit/essences spéciales.

– Produits pétroliers lourds sont définis ici comme des produits obtenus par distillation du pétrole brut à des températures supérieures à 350°C et ayant une densité supérieure à 0,83. En sont exclus les produits qui ne sont pas utilisés à des fins énergétiques, tels que les huiles isolantes, les lubrifiants, les paraffines, le bitume et le coke de pétrole. Les produits lourds comprennent le mazout résiduel et le gazole/carburant diesel (mazout distillé).

– Gaz de pétrole liquéfiés (GPL): Hydrocarbures qui sont à l'état gazeux dans des conditions de température et de pression normales mais sont liquéfiés par compression ou refroidissement pour en faciliter l'entreposage, la manipulation et le transport. Dans cette rubrique figurent le propane et le butane ou un mélange de ces deux hydrocarbures. Est également inclus l'éthane produit dans les raffineries ou dans les installations de séparation et de stabilisation des producteurs de gaz naturel.

– Gaz de raffinerie: Comprend les gaz non condensables obtenus dans les raffineries lors de la distillation du pétrole brut ou du traitement des produits pétroliers (par craquage par exemple). Il s'agit principalement d'hydrogène, de méthane, d'éthane et d'oléfines.

– Gaz naturel: Est constitué de gaz, méthane essentiellement, extraits de gisements naturels souterrains. Il peut s'agir aussi bien de gaz non associé (provenant de gisements qui produisent uniquement des hydrocarbures gazeux) que de gaz associé (provenant de gisements qui produisent à la fois des hydrocarbures liquides et gazeux) ou de méthane récupéré dans les mines de charbon et le gaz de gadoues. La production de gaz naturel se rapporte à la production de gaz commercialisable sec, mesurée après purification et extraction des condensats de gaz naturel et du soufre. Les quantités réinjectées, brûlées à la torchère ou éventées et les pertes d'extraction sont exclus des données sur la production.

– Production d'électricité se rapporte à la production brute, qui comprend la consommation des équipements auxiliaires des centrales et les pertes au niveau des transformateurs considérés comme faisant partie intégrante de ces centrales, ainsi que la quantité totale d'énergie électrique produits par les installations de pompage sans déductions de l'énergie électrique absorbée par ces dernières.

65
Land
Terres

Country or area Pays ou zone	2001 Land area Superficie des terres	2001 Arable land Terres arables	2001 Permanent crops Cultures permanentes	2000 Forest cover Superficie forestière	Net change – Variation nette 1990–2001 Arable land Terres arables	Net change – Variation nette 1990–2001 Permanent crops Cultures permanentes	Net change – Variation nette 1990-2000 Forest cover Superficie forestière	2003 Protected areas Aires protégées	2003 Protected areas Aires protégées %[1]
	Area in thousand hectares – Superficie en milliers de hectares								
Africa · Afrique									
Algeria Algérie	238 174	7 665[1]	587	2 145	584	33	27	11 951.7	5.0
Angola Angola	124 670	3 000[1]	300[1]	69 756	100	-200	-124	8 181.2	6.6
Benin Bénin	11 062	2 000[1]	265[1]	2 650	385	160	-70	2 642.8	23.5
Botswana Botswana	56 673	370[1]	3[1]	12 427	-48	0	-118	10 956.6	18.8
Burkina Faso Burkina Faso	27 360	3 948[1]	52[1]	7 089	428	-3	-15	4 110.5	15.0
Burundi Burundi	2 568	900[1]	360[1]	94	-30	0	-15	146.2	5.3
Cameroon Cameroun	46 540	5 960[1]	1 200[1]	23 858	20	-30	-222	3 786.9	8.0
Cape Verde Cap-Vert	403	39[1]	2[1]	85	-2	0	5	1.4	0.4
Central African Rep. Rép. centrafricaine	62 298	1 930[1]	90[1]	22 907	10	4	-30	9 131.9	14.7
Chad Tchad	125 920	3 600[1]	30[1]	12 692	327	3	-82	11 636.7	9.1
Comoros Comores	223	80	52[1]	8	2	17	...	40.4	18.1
Congo Congo	34 150	175[1]	45[1]	22 060	21	3	-17	5 474.8	16.0
Côte d'Ivoire Côte d'Ivoire	31 800	3 100[1]	4 400[1]	7 117	670	900	-265	2 186.4	6.8
Dem. Rep. of the Congo Rép. dém. du Congo	226 705	6 700[1]	1 180[1]	135 207	30	-10	-532	15 708.2	6.7
Djibouti Djibouti	2 318	1[1]	...	6	0	...	0	10.0	0.4
Egypt Egypte	99 545	2 858[1]	480[1]	72	574	116	2	10 956.2	10.4
Equatorial Guinea Guinée équatoriale	2 805	130[1]	100[1]	1 752	0	0	-11	586.0	20.9
Eritrea Erythrée	10 100	500[1]	3[1]	1 585	...	...	-5	500.6	4.3
Ethiopia Ethiopie	100 000	10 712[1]	750[1]	4 593	...	...	-40	18 609.8	16.9
Gabon Gabon	25 767	325[1]	170[1]	21 826	30	8	-10	4 119.3	15.4
Gambia Gambie	1 000	250[1]	5[1]	481	68	0	4	56.5	5.0
Ghana Ghana	22 754	3 700[1]	2 200[1]	6 335	1 000	700	-120	3 640.4	15.3
Guinea Guinée	24 572	890[1]	635[1]	6 929	162	135	-35	1 012.0	4.1
Guinea-Bissau Guinée-Bissau	2 812	300[1]	248[1]	2 187	0	131	-22	0.0	0.0
Kenya Kenya	56 914	4 600[1]	560[1]	17 096	400	60	-93	6 382.4	11.0

65

Land *[cont.]*

Terres *[suite]*

Country or area Pays ou zone	2001 Land area Superficie des terres	2001 Arable land Terres arables	2001 Permanent crops Cultures permanentes	2000 Forest cover Superficie forestière	Net change – Variation nette 1990 – 2001 Arable land Terres arables	Net change – Variation nette 1990 – 2001 Permanent crops Cultures permanentes	Net change – Variation nette 1990-2000 Forest cover Superficie forestière	2003 Protected areas Aires protégées	Protected areas Aires protégées % [1]
	Area in thousand hectares – Superficie en milliers de hectares								
Lesotho Lesotho	3 035	330[1]	4[1]	14	13	0	...	6.8	0.2
Liberia Libéria	9 632	380[1]	220[1]	3 481	-20	5	-76	2 084.8	18.7
Libyan Arab Jamah. Jamah. arabe libyenne	175 954	1 815[1]	335[1]	358	10	-15	5	220.9	0.1
Madagascar Madagascar	58 154	2 950[1]	600[1]	11 727	230	-5	-117	1 792.0	3.1
Malawi Malawi	9 408	2 200[1]	140[1]	2 562	385	25	-71	1 802.4	15.2
Mali Mali	122 019	4 660[1]	40[1]	13 186	2 607	0	-99	5 207.5	4.2
Mauritania Mauritanie	102 522	488[1]	12[1]	317	88	6	-10	1 746.0	1.7
Mauritius Maurice	203	100[1]	6[1]	16	0	0	0	16.2	7.9
Mayotte Mayotte	...	...	...	...	...	...	...	6.4	17.2
Morocco Maroc	44 630	8 750[1]	970[1]	3 025	43	234	-1	558.7	1.2
Mozambique Mozambique	78 409	4 000[1]	235[1]	30 601	550	5	-64	7 484.2	9.3
Namibia Namibie	82 329	816[1]	4[1]	8 040	156	2	-73	11 251.0	13.7
Niger Niger	126 670	4 489[1]	11[1]	1 328	894	1	-62	9 694.1	7.7
Nigeria Nigéria	91 077	28 500	2 700[1]	13 517	-1 039	165	-398	4 911.9	5.3
Réunion Réunion	250	34	3	71	-13	-2	-1	31.1	12.4
Rwanda Rwanda	2 467	1 000[1]	300[1]	307	120	-5	-15	194.1	7.4
Saint Helena Sainte-Hélène	31	4[1]	...	2	2	...	0	9.1	29.3
Sao Tome and Principe Sao Tomé-et-Principe	96	6[1]	47[1]	27	4	8	0	...	...
Senegal Sénégal	19 253	2 460[1]	40[1]	6 205	135	15	-45	2 135.7	10.9
Seychelles Seychelles	45	1[1]	6[1]	30	0	1	...	45.2	100.5
Sierra Leone Sierra Leone	7 162	500[1]	64[1]	1 055	14	10	-36	217.5	3.0
Somalia Somalie	62 734	1 045[1]	26[1]	7 515	23	6	-77	344.6	0.5
South Africa Afrique du Sud	122 104	14 753[1]	959[1]	8 917	1 313	99	-8	5 320.1	4.4
Sudan Soudan	237 600	16 233[1]	420[1]	61 627	3 233	185	-959	12 224.0	4.9
Swaziland Swaziland	1 720	178	12[1]	522	-2	0	6	60.1	3.5

65

Land *[cont.]*

Terres *[suite]*

Country or area Pays ou zone	2001 Land area Superficie des terres	2001 Arable land Terres arables	2001 Permanent crops Cultures permanentes	2000 Forest cover Superficie forestière	Net change – Variation nette 1990 – 2001 Arable land Terres arables	Net change – Variation nette 1990 – 2001 Permanent crops Cultures permanentes	Net change – Variation nette 1990-2000 Forest cover Superficie forestière	2003 Protected areas Aires protégées	2003 Protected areas Aires protégées %[1]
	Area in thousand hectares – Superficie en milliers de hectares								
Togo Togo	5 439	2 510[1]	120[1]	510	410	30	-21	632.2	11.1
Tunisia Tunisie	15 536	2 774	2 135	510	-135	193	1	289.7	1.5
Uganda Ouganda	19 710	5 100[1]	2 100[1]	4 190	100	250	-91	5 498.2	22.8
United Rep. of Tanzania Rép.-Unie de Tanzanie	88 359	4 000[1]	950[1]	38 811	500	50	-91	26 512.2	28.1
Zambia Zambie	74 339	5 260[1]	20[1]	31 246	11	1	-851	31 225.1	41.5
Zimbabwe Zimbabwe	38 685	3 220[1]	130[1]	19 040	330	10	-320	5 600.4	14.3
America, North · Amérique du Nord									
Antigua and Barbuda Antigua-et-Barbuda	44	8[1]	2[1]	9	0	0	...	6.6	15.1
Aruba Aruba	19	2[1]	...	...	0	...	...	0.1	0.4
Bahamas Bahamas	1 001	8[1]	4[1]	842	0	2	...	283.2	20.4
Barbados Barbade	43	16[1]	1[1]	2	0	0	...	0.2	0.6
Belize Belize	2 280	65[1]	39[1]	1 348	13	14	-36	1 226.6	53.4
Bermuda Bermudes	5	1[1]	...	0	0	...	0	13.5	269.9
British Virgin Islands Iles Vierges britanniques	15	3[1]	1[1]	3	0	0	...	5.2	34.6
Canada Canada	922 097	45 740[1]	140[1]	244 571	-80	10	...	100 961.5	10.1
Cayman Islands Iles Caïmanes	26	1[1]	...	13	0	...	...	24.1	92.7
Costa Rica Costa Rica	5 106	225[1]	300[1]	1 968	-35	50	-16	1 630.3	31.9
Cuba Cuba	10 982	3 630[1]	835[1]	2 348	380	25	28	754.5	6.8
Dominica Dominique	75	5[1]	15[1]	46	0	4	0	20.7	27.6
Dominican Republic Rép. dominicaine	4 838	1 096[1]	500[1]	1 376	46	50	...	2 043.7	41.9
El Salvador El Salvador	2 072	660[1]	250[1]	121	110	-10	-7	5.2	0.3
Greenland Groenland	41 045[2]	...	...	...	...	...	...	98 250.0	287.5
Grenada Grenade	34	2[1]	10[1]	5	0	0	...	0.7	2.1
Guadeloupe Guadeloupe	169	19	6	82	-2	-2	2	81.7	47.8
Guatemala Guatemala	10 843	1 360[1]	545[1]	2 850	60	60	-54	2 397.9	22.0

65

Land *[cont.]*

Terres *[suite]*

Country or area Pays ou zone	2001			2000	Net change – Variation nette			2003	
					1990 – 2001		1990-2000		
	Land area Superficie des terres	Arable land Terres arables	Permanent crops Cultures permanentes	Forest cover Superficie forestière	Arable land Terres arables	Permanent crops Cultures permanentes	Forest cover Superficie forestière	Protected areas Aires protégées	Protected areas Aires protégées %[1]
	Area in thousand hectares – Superficie en milliers de hectares								
Haiti Haïti	2 756	780[1]	320[1]	88	0	0	-7	7.4	0.3
Honduras Honduras	11 189	1 068[1]	360[1]	5 383	-394	2	-59	2 302.2	20.5
Jamaica Jamaïque	1 083	174[1]	110[1]	325	55	10	-5	994.8	90.5
Martinique Martinique	106	11	10	47	1	0	...	78.3	71.2
Mexico Mexique	190 869	24 800[1]	2 500[1]	55 205	800	600	-631	17 677.2	9.0
Montserrat Montserrat	10	2[1]	...	3	0	...	...	1.1	10.7
Netherlands Antilles Antilles néerlandaises	80	8[1]	...	1	0	...	...	12.3	15.3
Nicaragua Nicaragua	12 140	1 935[1]	236[1]	3 278	635	41	-117	2 159.4	16.6
Panama Panama	7 443	548	147	2 876	49	-8	-52	3 250.3	43.0
Puerto Rico Porto Rico	887	35[1]	49[1]	229	-30	-1	-1	50.6	5.7
Saint Kitts and Nevis Saint-Kitts-et-Nevis	36	7[1]	1[1]	4	-1	-1	...	0.0	0.1
Saint Lucia Sainte-Lucie	61	4[1]	14[1]	9	-1	1	-1	5.3	8.6
Saint Pierre and Miquelon Saint-Pierre-et-Miquelon	23	3[1]	...	...	0	...	...	12.7	52.8
St. Vincent-Grenadines St. Vincent-Grenadines	39	7[1]	7[1]	6	2	0	...	8.3	21.2
Trinidad and Tobago Trinité-et-Tobago	513	75[1]	47[1]	259	1	1	-2	32.2	6.3
Turks and Caicos Islands Iles Turques et Caïques	43	1[1]	...	...	0	...	...	71.7	166.8
United States Etats-Unis	915 896	175 209[1]	2 050[1]	225 993	-10 533	16	388	163 318.3	17.0
United States Virgin Is. Iles Vierges américaines	34	4[1]	1[1]	14	0	0	...	17.3	50.8

America, South · Amérique du Sud

Country or area Pays ou zone									
Argentina Argentine	273 669	33 700[1]	1 300[1]	34 648	4 800	100	-285	18 186.8	6.5
Bolivia Bolivie	108 438	2 900[1]	201[1]	53 068	800	46	-161	13 296.7	12.1
Brazil Brésil	845 651	58 865[1]	7 600[1]	543 905	8 184	873	-2 309	109 350.7	12.8
Chile Chili	74 880	1 982[1]	318[1]	15 536	-820	71	-20	14 202.8	18.8
Colombia Colombie	103 870	2 516	1 733	49 601	-789	38	-190	56 690.1	49.8
Ecuador Equateur	27 684	1 620[1]	1 365[1]	10 557	16	44	-137	20 641.9	72.8

65
Land *[cont.]*

Terres *[suite]*

Country or area Pays ou zone	2001 Land area Superficie des terres	2001 Arable land Terres arables	2001 Permanent crops Cultures permanentes	2000 Forest cover Superficie forestière	Net change – Variation nette 1990 – 2001 Arable land Terres arables	Net change – Variation nette 1990 – 2001 Permanent crops Cultures permanentes	Net change – Variation nette 1990-2000 Forest cover Superficie forestière	2003 Protected areas Aires protégées	2003 Protected areas Aires protégées % [1]
	Area in thousand hectares – Superficie en milliers de hectares								
Falkland Is. (Malvinas) Iles Falkland (Malvinas)	1 217	...	...	...	...	...	...	11.1	0.9
French Guiana Guyane française	8 815	12	4	7 926	2	2	...	1 488.7	16.5
Guyana Guyana	19 685	480[1]	30[1]	16 879	0	8	-49	486.0	2.3
Paraguay Paraguay	39 730	3 020[1]	90[1]	23 372	910	1	-123	1 702.9	4.2
Peru Pérou	128 000	3 700[1]	510[1]	65 215	200	90	-269	15 853.3	12.3
Suriname Suriname	15 600	57[1]	10[1]	14 113	0	-1	...	2 034.2	12.5
Uruguay Uruguay	17 502	1 300[1]	40[1]	1 292	40	-5	50	72.5	0.4
Venezuela Venezuela	88 205	2 598[1]	810[1]	49 506	-234	32	-218	66 573.3	73.0
Asia · Asie									
Afghanistan Afghanistan	65 209	7 910[1]	144[1]	1 351	0	0	...	218.6	0.3
Armenia Arménie	2 820	495[1]	65[1]	351	...	...	4	299.1	10.0
Azerbaijan Azerbaïdjan	8 660	1 700[1]	235[1]	1 094	...	...	13	515.1	6.0
Bahrain Bahreïn	71	2[1]	4[1]	...	0	2	...	6.0	8.7
Bangladesh Bangladesh	13 017	8 085[1]	400[1]	1 334	-1 052	100	17	111.5	0.6
Bhutan Bhoutan	4 700	145[1]	20[1]	3 016	32	1	...	1 295.6	27.6
Brunei Darussalam Brunéi Darussalam	527	3[1]	4[1]	442	0	0	-1	340.9	59.1
Cambodia Cambodge	17 652	3 700[1]	107[1]	9 335	5	7	-56	4 346.5	21.6
China Chine	932 742[3]	143 625[1,3]	11 650[1,3]	163 480[3]	19 947[3]	3 931[3]	1 806[3]	71 657.9	7.2
China, Hong Kong SAR Chine, Hong Kong RAS	...	...	...	...	...	...	...	54.7	51.5
Cyprus Chypre	924	72	41	172	-34	-10	5	78.2	8.5
Georgia Géorgie	6 949	795	268	2 988	...	...	...	341.1	4.9
India Inde	297 319	161 750[1]	8 150[1]	64 113	-1 388	1 850	38	16 963.8	4.9
Indonesia Indonésie	181 157	20 500[1]	13 100[1]	104 986	247	1 380	-1 312	32 477.9	6.4
Iran (Islamic Rep. of) Iran (Rép. islamique d')	163 620	14 268[1]	2 280	7 299	-922	970	...	11 273.9	6.6
Iraq Iraq	43 737	*5 750	340[1]	799	450	50	...	0.5	0.0

65
Land *[cont.]*
Terres *[suite]*

Country or area Pays ou zone	2001 Land area Superficie des terres	2001 Arable land Terres arables	2001 Permanent crops Cultures permanentes	2000 Forest cover Superficie forestière	Net change – Variation nette 1990 – 2001 Arable land Terres arables	Net change – Variation nette 1990 – 2001 Permanent crops Cultures permanentes	Net change – Variation nette 1990-2000 Forest cover Superficie forestière	2003 Protected areas Aires protégées	2003 Protected areas Aires protégées %
	Area in thousand hectares – Superficie en milliers de hectares								
Israel Israël	2 062	338[1]	86[1]	132	-5	-2	5	391.3	15.6
Japan Japon	36 450[1]	4 445	349	24 081	-323	-126	3	6 443.8	8.6
Jordan Jordanie	8 893	237	163	86	-53	73	...	975.0	10.9
Kazakhstan Kazakhstan	269 970	21 535[1]	136[1]	12 148	...	...	239	7 791.9	2.9
Korea, Dem. P. R. Corée, R. p. dém. de	12 041	2 500[1]	300[1]	8 210	212	0	...	315.9	2.4
Korea, Republic of Corée, République de	9 873	1 696	193	6 248	-257	37	-5	701.2	3.9
Kuwait Koweït	1 782	13	2	5	9	1	...	28.1	1.2
Kyrgyzstan Kirghizistan	19 180	1 400[1]	67[1]	1 003	...	...	23	715.2	3.6
Lao People's Dem. Rep. Rép. dém. pop. lao	23 080	877[1]	81[1]	12 561	78	20	-53	3 522.8	14.9
Lebanon Liban	1 023	170[1]	143	36	-13	21	...	7.0	0.5
Malaysia Malaisie	32 855	1 800[1]	5 785	19 292	100	537	-237	9 253.2	19.2
Maldives Maldives	30	4[1]	5[1]	1	0	1	...	0.0	0.0
Mongolia Mongolie	156 650	1 199[1]	1[1]	10 645	-171	0	-60	21 791.2	13.9
Myanmar Myanmar	65 755	9 990	635	34 419	423	133	-517	3 657.2	4.4
Nepal Népal	14 300	3 100[1]	92[1]	3 900	814	26	-78	2 697.1	18.3
Occupied Palestinian Terr.[4] Terr. palestinien occupé[4]	38	11[1]	8	...	2	-2	...	...	...
Oman Oman	30 950	38[1]	*43	1	3	-2	0	2 982.8	11.3
Pakistan Pakistan	77 088	21 488	672	2 361	1 004	216	-39	11 383.2	13.8
Philippines Philippines	29 817	5 650[1]	5 000[1]	5 789	170	600	-89	4 076.4	4.2
Qatar Qatar	1 100	18[1]	*3	1	8	2	...	13.7	1.2
Saudi Arabia Arabie saoudite	214 969	3 600[1]	194	1 504	210	103	...	82 582.9	37.0
Singapore Singapour	61	1[1]	0	2	0	0	...	4.0	3.1
Sri Lanka Sri Lanka	6 463	896[1]	1 015[1]	1 940	21	-10	-35	1 337.0	13.9
Syrian Arab Republic Rép. arabe syrienne	18 378	4 635	815	461	-250	74	...	276.4	1.5
Tajikistan Tadjikistan	14 060	930[1]	130[1]	400	...	...	2	2 575.3	18.0

65

Land [cont.]

Terres [suite]

	2001			2000	Net change – Variation nette			2003	
					1990 – 2001		1990-2000		
Country or area Pays ou zone	Land area Superficie des terres	Arable land Terres arables	Permanent crops Cultures permanentes	Forest cover Superficie forestière	Arable land Terres arables	Permanent crops Cultures permanentes	Forest cover Superficie forestière	Protected areas Aires protégées	Protected areas Aires protégées
	Area in thousand hectares – Superficie en milliers de hectares								%[1]
Thailand Thaïlande	51 089	15 000[1]	3 300[1]	14 762	-2 494	191	-112	8 722.2	14.8
Timor-Leste Timor-Leste	1 487	70[1]	10[1]	507	0	0	-3	187.6	1.2
Turkey Turquie	76 963	23 805	2 550	10 225	-842	-480	22	2 612.2	3.1
Turkmenistan Turkménistan	46 993	1 750[1]	65[1]	3 755	...	...	...	1 978.2	4.1
United Arab Emirates Emirats arabes unis	8 360	50[1]	188[1]	321	15	168	8	0.3	0.0
Uzbekistan Ouzbékistan	41 424	4 485[1]	345[1]	1 969	...	...	5	2 120.3	4.7
Viet Nam Viet Nam	32 549	6 500[1]	1 938[1]	9 819	1 161	893	52	1 405.7	2.9
Yemen Yémen	52 797	*1 466	129[1]	449	-57	26	-9	...	...
Europe · Europe									
Albania Albanie	2 740	578	121	991	-1	-4	-8	102.9	2.9
Andorra Andorre	45	1[1]	...	0	0	...	0	3.3	7.2
Austria Autriche	8 273	1 399[1]	71[1]	3 886	-27	-8	8	2 347.5	28.0
Belarus Bélarus	20 748	6 131[1]	124[1]	9 402	...	...	256	886.6	4.3
Belgium Belgique	...	...	...	...	...	...	...	87.9	2.8
Belgium-Luxembourg Belgique-Luxembourg	3 282	842	24	728	76	9	-1	...	...
Bosnia and Herzegovina Bosnie-Herzégovine	5 073	690[1]	150[1]	2 273	...	...	...	27.4	0.5
Bulgaria Bulgarie	11 055	4 424[1]	212[1]	3 690	568	-88	20	594.9	5.1
Croatia Croatie	5 592	1 459	127	1 783	...	...	2	609.2	6.9
Czech Republic République tchèque	7 728	3 076	236	2 632	...	...	1	1 251.4	15.9
Denmark Danemark	4 243	2 292	8	455	-269	-2	1	441.1	6.5
Estonia Estonie	4 227	678	19	2 060	...	...	13	568.3	8.2
Faeroe Islands Iles Féroé	140	3[1]	...	...	0	...	...	...	...
Finland Finlande	30 459	2 191[1]	8[1]	21 935	-78	2	8	3 044.2	7.7
France France	55 010	18 447	1 138	15 341	448	-53	62	1 675.8	2.7
Germany Allemagne	34 895	11 813	207	10 740	-158	-236	...	11 397.0	30.4

65
Land *[cont.]*
Terres *[suite]*

Country or area Pays ou zone	2001 Land area Superficie des terres	2001 Arable land Terres arables	2001 Permanent crops Cultures permanentes	2000 Forest cover Superficie forestière	Net change – Variation nette 1990 – 2001 Arable land Terres arables	Net change – Variation nette 1990 – 2001 Permanent crops Cultures permanentes	Net change – Variation nette 1990-2000 Forest cover Superficie forestière	2003 Protected areas Aires protégées	2003 Protected areas Aires protégées %[1]
	Area in thousand hectares – Superficie en milliers de hectares								
Gibraltar Gibraltar	1	...	...	...	...	...	...	0.0	3.5
Greece Grèce	12 890	2 720	1 132	3 599	-179	64	30	688.4	2.8
Hungary Hongrie	9 211	4 614	190	1 840	-440	-44	7	830.0	8.9
Iceland Islande	10 025	7	...	31	0	...	1	980.7	5.6
Ireland Irlande	6 889	1 047[1]	*2	659	6	-1	17	81.4	0.7
Italy Italie	29 411	8 172	2 804[1]	10 003	-840	-156	30	3 539.0	7.8
Latvia Lettonie	6 205	1 841	29	2 923	...	...	13	984.7	12.8
Liechtenstein Liechtenstein	16	4[1]	...	7	0	...	...	6.2	38.5
Lithuania Lituanie	6 480	2 930	59	1 994	...	...	5	646.5	9.6
Luxembourg Luxembourg	...	...	...	...	...	...	...	57.7	22.3
Malta Malte	32	9[1]	1[1]	...	-3	...	...	6.3	19.8
Netherlands Pays-Bas	3 388	905	33	375	26	3	1	462.3	8.5
Norway Norvège	30 683	880	...	8 868	16	...	31	2 080.2	4.8
Poland Pologne	30 435	13 974	340	9 047	-414	-5	18	6 633.8	19.9
Portugal Portugal	9 150	1 990[1]	715[1]	3 666	-354	-66	57	603.6	3.9
Republic of Moldova République de Moldova	3 291	1 820[1]	355[1]	325	...	...	1	47.1	1.4
Romania Roumanie	23 034	9 402	519	6 448	-48	-72	15	1 206.3	5.0
Russian Federation Fédération de Russie	1 688 850	123 860	1 858	851 392	...	...	135	51 820.4	2.8
San Marino Saint-Marin	6	1[1]	...	...	0	...	...	...	...
Serbia and Montenegro Serbie-et-Monténégro	10 200	3 402	326	2 887	...	...	-1	384.8	3.8
Slovakia Slovaquie	4 808	1 450	126	2 177	...	...	18	1 095.5	22.4
Slovenia Slovénie	2 012	173	30	1 107	...	...	2	149.8	7.3
Spain Espagne	49 944	*13 019	*4 929	14 370	-2 316	92	86	4 650.0	7.5
Svalbard and Jan Mayen Is Svalbard et îles Jan Mayen	...	...	...	...	...	...	...	6 651.1	107.3
Sweden Suède	41 162	2 694	*3	27 134	-151	-1	1	4 912.0	9.2

65
Land *[cont.]*
Terres *[suite]*

	2001			2000	Net change – Variation nette			2003	
					1990 – 2001		1990-2000		
Country or area Pays ou zone	Land area Superficie des terres	Arable land Terres arables	Permanent crops Cultures permanentes	Forest cover Superficie forestière	Arable land Terres arables	Permanent crops Cultures permanentes	Forest cover Superficie forestière	Protected areas Aires protégées	Protected areas Aires protégées
	Area in thousand hectares – Superficie en milliers de hectares								%[1]
Switzerland Suisse	3 955	412	24	1 199	21	3	4	1 072.1	26.0
TFYR of Macedonia L'ex-R.y. Macédoine	2 543	566[1]	46[1]	906	...		0	179.8	7.0
Ukraine Ukraine	57 935	32 564[1]	930[1]	9 584	...	...	31	2 188.0	3.3
United Kingdom Royaume-Uni	24 088	5 652	51	2 794	-968	-15	17	8 706.7	21.2
Oceania · Océanie									
American Samoa Samoa américaines	20	2[1]	3[1]	12	0	1	...	5.1	25.6
Australia Australie	768 230[5]	50 304[1]	296[1]	154 539	2 404	115	-282	141 857.4	18.3
Christmas Is. Ile Christmas	13	...	...	...	...	...	...	8.7	62.3
Cocos (Keeling) Islands Iles des Cocos (Keeling)	1	...	...	...	...	...	...	...	...
Cook Islands Iles Cook	23	4[1]	3[1]	...	2	-1	...	0.2	0.7
Fiji Fidji	1 827	200[1]	85[1]	815	40	5	-2	6.6	0.4
French Polynesia Polynésie française	366	3[1]	20[1]	105	1	-1	...	19.0	4.8
Guam Guam	55	5[1]	9[1]	21	0	1	...	16.9	30.8
Kiribati Kiribati	73	2[1]	37[1]	28	...	0	...	58.9	80.6
Marshall Islands Iles Marshall	18	3[1]	7[1]	...	...	...	...	...	...
Micronesia (Fed. States) Micronésie (Etats féd. de)	70	4[1]	32[1]	15	...	...	-1	...	...
Nauru Nauru	2	...	...	...	...	...	...	...	...
New Caledonia Nouvelle-Calédonie	1 828	7[1]	6[1]	372	0	0	...	718.9	38.7
New Zealand Nouvelle-Zélande	26 799	1 500[1]	1 872	7 946	-1 011	518	39	5 580.0	20.6
Niue Nioué	26	4[1]	3[1]	6	0	0	...	5.5	21.0
Norfolk Island Ile Norfolk	4	...	...	...	...	...	...	0.7	23.2
Northern Mariana Islands Iles Mariannes du Nord	46	6[1]	2[1]	14	...	...	0	2.3	4.9
Palau Palaos	46	4[1]	2[1]	35	...	...	...	1.5	3.2
Papua New Guinea Papouasie-Nvl-Guinée	45 286	210[1]	650[1]	30 601	18	70	-113	1 078.9	2.3
Samoa Samoa	283	60[1]	69[1]	105	5	2	-3	25.5	9.0

65

Land *[cont.]*

Terres *[suite]*

Country or area Pays ou zone	2001			2000	Net change – Variation nette			2003	
					1990 – 2001		1990-2000		
	Land area Superficie des terres	Arable land Terres arables	Permanent crops Cultures permanentes	Forest cover Superficie forestière	Arable land Terres arables	Permanent crops Cultures permanentes	Forest cover Superficie forestière	Protected areas Aires protégées	Protected areas Aires protégées %[1]
	Area in thousand hectares – Superficie en milliers de hectares								
Solomon Islands Iles Salomon	2 799	18[1]	56[1]	2 536	1	4	-4	1.1	0.0
Tokelau Tokélaou	1	...	...	...	...	...	...	...	...
Tonga Tonga	72	17[1]	31[1]	4	0	0	...	3.7	5.0
Tuvalu Tuvalu	3	...	...	...	...	...	...	...	...
Vanuatu Vanuatu	1 219	30[1]	90[1]	447	0	0	1	8.8	0.7
Wallis and Futuna Islands Iles Wallis et Futuna	20	1[1]	5[1]	...	0	0	...	...	...

Source:
Food and Agriculture Organization of the United Nations (FAO), Rome, "FAO Production Yearbook 2002", the FAOSTAT database and the "Global Forest Resources Assessment 2000;" and the United Nations Environment Programme (UNEP), World Conservation Monitoring Centre, "United Nations List of Protected Areas".

Source :
Organisation des Nations Unies pour l'alimentation et l'agriculture (FAO), Rome, ''Annuaire FAO de la production 2002'' et la base de données de FAOSTAT et ''Global Forest Resources Assessment 2000 ;'' et le Programme des Nations Unies pour l'environnement (PNUE), Centre mondial de surveillance pour laconservation, ''United Nations List of Protected Areas''.

1   FAO estimate.
2   Area free from ice.
3   Data generally include those for Taiwan Province of China.

4   Data refer to the Gaza Strip.
5   Includes about 27 million hectares of cultivated grassland.

1   Estimation de la FAO.
2   Superficie non couverte de glace.
3   Les données comprennent en général les chiffres pour la province de Taiwan.
4   Les données se rapportent à la Bande de Gaza.
5   Y compris 27 million d'hectares d'herbages cultivés.

66

CO$_2$ emission estimates
From fossil fuel combustion, cement production and gas flared (thousand metric tons of carbon dioxide)

Estimation des émissions de CO$_2$
Dues à la combustion de combustibles fossiles, à la production de ciment et au gaz brûlés à la torchère

Country or area Pays ou zone	1990	1993	1994	1995	1996	1997	1998	1999	2000	Change : 1990 - 2000 Variation : 1990 à 2000 (%)
Afghanistan Afghanistan	2 614	1 342	1 291	1 239	1 177	1 096	1 038	964	906	-65
Albania Albanie	7 275	2 339	1 925	1 874	1 815	1 467	1 577	2 754	2 860	-61
Algeria Algérie	80 498	82 570	86 189	94 530	96 404	99 510	106 502	90 827	89 481	11
Angola Angola	4 649	5 878	4 198	11 304	9 933	6 255	5 830	6 527	6 406	38
Antigua and Barbuda Antigua-et-Barbuda	301	304	312	323	323	337	337	348	352	17
Argentina Argentine	109 809	114 609	120 652	119 365	126 042	130 706	132 396	141 812	138 288	26
Armenia Arménie	...	2 783	2 853	3 410	2 563	3 238	3 362	3 014	3 513	...
Aruba Aruba	1 841	1 767	1 782	1 800	1 833	1 874	1 885	1 907	1 925	5
Australia [1] Australie [1]	277 867	285 480	291 431	301 101	310 586	318 222	334 904	339 385	347 006	25
Austria [1] Autriche [1]	62 297	60 717	61 995	64 015	65 386	67 012	65 464	66 025	66 102	6
Azerbaijan Azerbaïdjan	...	44 766	41 679	32 674	30 389	28 857	30 034	32 743	29 062	...
Bahamas Bahamas	1 951	1 716	1 720	1 731	1 731	1 742	1 793	1 797	1 797	-8
Bahrain Bahreïn	11 719	14 883	15 015	15 851	16 551	17 200	18 726	19 026	19 514	67
Bangladesh Bangladesh	15 371	17 123	18 414	22 502	23 815	24 834	24 171	26 756	29 275	90
Barbados Barbade	1 078	1 115	748	825	876	898	1 137	1 217	1 177	9
Belarus Bélarus	...	78 448	69 956	63 261	64 240	62 487	59 704	57 856	59 195	...
Belgium [1] Belgique [1]	117 966	120 887	124 072	127 647	130 367	125 579	128 607	125 639	127 040	8
Belize Belize	312	378	374	378	308	389	400	620	781	151
Benin Bénin	719	1 140	1 269	1 327	1 265	1 214	1 269	1 342	1 621	126
Bermuda Bermudes	590	462	458	455	462	462	462	462	462	-22
Bhutan Bhoutan	128	187	216	253	301	392	389	385	396	209
Bolivia Bolivie	5 504	7 968	8 811	9 335	9 896	12 177	13 020	11 568	11 073	101
Bosnia and Herzegovina Bosnie-Herzégovine	...	3 744	4 044	4 044	5 273	12 654	16 533	15 649	19 265	...
Botswana Botswana	2 171	3 483	3 480	3 513	3 113	3 377	3 780	3 505	3 854	78
Brazil Brésil	202 759	225 031	234 850	249 795	276 661	288 849	301 327	303 120	307 743	52
British Virgin Islands Iles Vierges britanniques	48	51	51	51	59	59	59	59	59	23

66

CO₂ emission estimates
From fossil fuel combustion, cement production and gas flared (thousand metric tons of carbon dioxide) *[cont.]*

Estimation des émissions de CO₂
Dues à la combustion de combustibles fossiles, à la production de ciment et au gaz brûlès à la torchère *[suite]*

Country or area Pays ou zone	1990	1993	1994	1995	1996	1997	1998	1999	2000	Change : 1990 - 2000 Variation : 1990 à 2000 (%)
Brunei Darussalam Brunéi Darussalam	5 823	5 284	5 100	5 210	5 148	5 496	5 401	4 954	6 299	8
Bulgaria [1] Bulgarie [1]	103 856	61 859	59 178	62 332	66 825	58 742	52 277	48 440	...	...
Burkina Faso Burkina Faso	994	920	950	972	983	994	1 012	1 016	1 030	4
Burundi Burundi	194	205	213	216	224	227	231	242	242	25
Cambodia Cambodge	451	477	539	550	601	587	587	524	532	18
Cameroon Cameroun	3 711	4 085	4 246	4 235	4 572	5 676	6 087	8 818	6 545	76
Canada [1] Canada [1]	471 563	473 976	488 138	500 627	513 343	524 505	534 224	550 073	571 427	21
Cape Verde Cap-Vert	84	106	117	117	121	121	121	139	139	65
Cayman Islands Iles Caïmanes	249	286	286	286	282	282	290	282	286	15
Central African Rep. Rép. centrafricaine	198	224	235	235	235	246	249	268	271	37
Chad Tchad	143	92	95	95	103	114	114	121	125	-13
Chile Chili	35 358	35 710	41 206	44 235	50 461	58 117	60 243	62 561	59 543	68
China Chine	2 400 603	2 788 361	2 960 225	3 199 977	3 345 166	3 295 673	3 119 215	2 827 081	2 792 482	16
China, Hong Kong SAR Chine, Hong Kong RAS	26 202	34 892	29 854	29 891	27 463	27 775	35 508	41 221	33 092	26
China, Macao SAR Chine, Macao RAS	1 027	1 181	1 272	1 232	1 408	1 511	1 558	1 518	1 635	59
Colombia Colombie	55 983	63 122	66 282	59 077	59 462	63 334	66 367	55 924	58 502	4
Comoros Comores	66	66	66	66	66	66	70	81	81	22
Congo Congo	2 006	2 207	2 405	2 145	2 908	2 376	2 299	2 361	1 811	-10
Cook Islands Iles Cook	22	22	22	22	22	22	22	29	29	33
Costa Rica Costa Rica	2 919	3 945	5 236	4 862	4 734	4 968	4 998	5 694	5 427	86
Côte d'Ivoire Côte d'Ivoire	5 397	5 632	5 005	6 871	8 118	7 905	7 168	9 544	10 483	94
Croatia Croatie	...	17 013	16 944	17 761	18 506	19 602	20 211	20 607	19 595	...
Cuba Cuba	32 072	29 011	31 871	25 377	26 653	27 155	27 478	29 315	30 936	-4
Cyprus Chypre	4 649	5 108	5 262	5 133	5 276	5 423	5 936	6 013	6 428	38
Czech Republic [1] République tchèque [1]	163 990	134 851	127 745	128 817	132 780	137 357	128 268	121 093	127 902	-22
Dem. Rep. of the Congo Rép. dém. du Congo	3 975	3 168	2 596	2 552	2 570	2 497	2 534	2 578	2 732	-31

66

CO$_2$ emission estimates
From fossil fuel combustion, cement production and gas flared (thousand metric tons of carbon dioxide) *[cont.]*
Estimation des émissions de CO$_2$
Dues à la combustion de combustibles fossiles, à la production de ciment et au gaz brûlès à la torchère *[suite]*

Country or area Pays ou zone	1990	1993	1994	1995	1996	1997	1998	1999	2000	Change : 1990 - 2000 Variation : 1990 à 2000 (%)
Denmark [1] Danemark [1]	52 635	59 884	63 855	61 001	74 514	65 161	60 006	57 245	52 852	0
Djibouti Djibouti	352	378	367	370	367	367	367	385	385	9
Dominica Dominique	59	62	70	81	73	81	81	81	103	75
Dominican Republic Rép. dominicaine	9 570	11 939	12 672	16 086	17 556	18 429	22 378	22 865	25 150	163
Ecuador Equateur	16 581	25 153	14 458	23 258	24 732	20 500	24 354	23 313	25 469	54
Egypt Egypte	75 489	92 283	84 799	95 095	103 503	107 613	108 944	123 677	142 329	89
El Salvador El Salvador	2 618	3 894	4 426	5 287	4 704	5 570	6 017	6 593	6 670	155
Equatorial Guinea Guinée équatoriale	117	125	128	132	143	796	257	649	205	75
Estonia [1] Estonie [1]	38 107	20 553	21 378	19 315	20 264	20 225	18 318	16 771	16 849	-56
Ethiopia Ethiopie	2 966	5 097	2 919	2 134	3 725	4 275	4 506	5 133	5 581	88
Faeroe Islands Iles Féroé	616	576	513	620	631	634	642	649	649	5
Falkland Is. (Malvinas) Iles Falkland (Malvinas)	37	37	37	40	44	48	37	37	**37**	0
Fiji Fidji	814	711	722	755	774	759	730	726	726	-11
Finland [1] Finlande [1]	62 466	59 172	65 468	62 684	68 130	66 842	64 601	64 073	62 305	0
France [1,2] France [1,2]	394 067	388 491	384 050	390 492	404 177	398 310	419 453	407 004	401 923	2
Gabon Gabon	5 995	3 843	3 428	3 725	3 619	3 696	3 505	3 824	3 502	-42
Gambia Gambie	191	209	209	216	216	216	235	253	271	42
Georgia Géorgie	...	9 816	6 021	2 284	4 008	4 283	4 957	5 075	6 175	...
Germany [1] Allemagne [1]	1 014 501	918 268	904 111	903 665	923 085	892 649	885 963	859 246	857 908	-15
Ghana Ghana	3 729	4 495	4 976	5 254	5 691	5 988	6 490	5 599	5 900	58
Gibraltar Gibraltar	62	293	356	301	180	84	103	176	216	247
Greece [1] Grèce [1]	84 336	85 847	87 479	87 644	90 163	94 668	99 419	98 626	103 727	23
Greenland Groenland	554	499	502	502	517	521	528	539	557	1
Grenada Grenade	121	143	165	172	176	194	202	213	213	76
Guatemala Guatemala	5 089	5 658	6 838	7 165	6 666	7 612	9 508	9 530	9 893	94
Guinea Guinée	1 012	1 063	1 188	1 206	1 228	1 236	1 254	1 291	1 294	28

66

CO$_2$ emission estimates
From fossil fuel combustion, cement production and gas flared (thousand metric tons of carbon dioxide) *[cont.]*

Estimation des émissions de CO$_2$
Dues à la combustion de combustibles fossiles, à la production de ciment et au gaz brûlès à la torchère *[suite]*

Country or area Pays ou zone	1990	1993	1994	1995	1996	1997	1998	1999	2000	Change: 1990 - 2000 Variation: 1990 à 2000 (%)
Guinea-Bissau Guinée-Bissau	209	227	227	231	231	235	235	260	264	26
Guyana Guyana	1 133	1 049	1 327	1 474	1 518	1 595	1 650	1 687	1 599	41
Haiti Haïti	994	664	301	942	1 078	1 393	1 261	1 415	1 423	43
Honduras Honduras	2 592	2 849	3 337	3 879	3 975	4 169	4 844	4 921	4 792	85
Hungary [1] Hongrie [1]	83 676	60 826	59 196	59 758	60 475	58 893	57 601	60 117	59 445	-29
Iceland [1] Islande [1]	2 065	2 228	2 193	2 228	2 313	2 388	2 411	2 494	2 444	18
India Inde	675 752	807 935	860 853	908 193	1 003 501	1 026 201	1 060 653	1 077 773	1 071 638	59
Indonesia Indonésie	165 821	197 556	201 142	186 490	252 179	252 802	196 130	204 996	269 764	63
Iran (Islamic Rep. of) Iran (Rép. islamique d')	216 880	227 656	292 079	272 294	275 403	290 459	286 843	302 691	310 526	43
Iraq Iraq	49 298	64 123	72 769	74 008	73 612	76 696	79 050	74 294	76 391	55
Ireland [1] Irlande [1]	31 599	32 458	33 893	34 529	35 729	38 102	40 062	41 932	43 925	39
Israel Israël	34 976	46 237	48 257	54 454	53 889	56 984	59 536	61 171	63 144	81
Italy [1] Italie [1]	439 478	425 929	419 673	445 009	439 066	442 116	454 352	457 202	463 381	5
Jamaica Jamaïque	7 964	8 419	8 631	9 702	10 164	10 732	11 711	10 223	10 787	35
Japan [1] Japon [1]	1 119 319	1 136 428	1 194 757	1 207 994	1 219 442	1 219 422	1 191 671	1 232 770	1 237 107	11
Jordan Jordanie	10 190	12 100	13 633	13 592	14 212	14 417	14 575	14 582	15 561	53
Kazakhstan Kazakhstan	...	214 218	196 959	165 675	138 706	128 003	122 349	112 761	121 363	...
Kenya Kenya	5 826	6 241	6 527	7 491	9 005	6 970	9 288	8 844	9 361	61
Kiribati Kiribati	22	22	22	22	22	22	22	26	26	17
Korea, Dem. P. R. Corée, R. p. dém. de	244 812	262 115	259 618	259 325	256 659	234 667	223 168	205 810	188 995	-23
Korea, Republic of Corée, République de	241 355	317 574	343 083	373 872	408 225	424 116	363 601	393 796	427 324	77
Kuwait [3] Koweït [3]	43 435	30 290	35 849	43 663	44 209	41 463	48 763	46 739	47 923	10
Kyrgyzstan Kirghizistan	...	8 356	6 087	4 627	5 797	5 621	5 988	4 675	4 642	...
Lao People's Dem. Rep. Rép. dém. pop. lao	231	275	301	315	370	389	407	407	414	79
Latvia [1] Lettonie [1]	23 527	12 861	11 911	10 145	9 550	8 619	8 287	7 545	6 847	-71
Lebanon Liban	9 101	11 656	12 742	13 622	13 798	15 184	16 016	16 683	15 173	67

66

CO$_2$ emission estimates
From fossil fuel combustion, cement production and gas flared (thousand metric tons of carbon dioxide) *[cont.]*
Estimation des émissions de CO$_2$
Dues à la combustion de combustibles fossiles, à la production de ciment et au gaz brûlès à la torchère *[suite]*

Country or area Pays ou zone	1990	1993	1994	1995	1996	1997	1998	1999	2000	Change : 1990 - 2000 Variation : 1990 à 2000 (%)
Lesotho [1] Lesotho [1]	...	...	636	...	...	...	...	...	...	...
Liberia Libéria	466	315	312	323	337	348	385	400	400	-14
Libyan Arab Jamah. Jamah. arabe libyenne	37 800	39 776	39 248	44 286	40 810	48 741	36 472	42 801	57 167	51
Liechtenstein [1] Liechtenstein [1]	195	...	...	...	...	...	...	196	...	...
Lithuania [1] Lituanie [1]	39 535	...	...	15 200	16 200	16 200	16 694			...
Luxembourg [1] Luxembourg [1]	12 750	...	11 998	9 545	...		...	5 432	5 399	-58
Madagascar Madagascar	942	1 027	1 269	1 261	1 360	1 646	1 734	1 921	2 270	141
Malawi Malawi	601	682	700	711	697	744	730	770	766	27
Malaysia Malaisie	55 319	90 475	92 715	119 079	122 335	130 632	123 944	123 743	144 518	161
Maldives Maldives	154	216	220	275	319	367	334	466	499	224
Mali Mali	422	455	462	466	488	524	539	554	557	32
Malta Malte	2 079	2 493	2 629	2 695	2 845	2 911	3 293	3 608	2 816	35
Mauritania Mauritanie	2 636	2 908	3 065	2 944	2 941	2 933	2 955	3 065	3 073	17
Mauritius Maurice	1 463	1 775	1 624	1 830	1 951	1 998	2 200	2 471	2 897	98
Mexico Mexique	375 595	369 695	388 307	367 528	366 879	384 982	406 754	413 083	424 281	13
Micronesia (Fed. States) [1] Micronésie (Etats féd. de) [1]	...	...	236	...	141	...	...	...	...	...
Monaco [1] Monaco [1]	98	121	123	120	126	125	121	129		...
Mongolia Mongolie	9 988	9 284	7 942	7 920	8 041	7 711	7 704	7 553	7 502	-25
Montserrat Montserrat	33	37	37	44	40	48	48	48	48	44
Morocco Maroc	23 503	28 219	29 649	30 353	31 189	30 543	32 637	36 029	36 575	56
Mozambique Mozambique	997	1 067	1 063	1 162	1 056	1 159	1 228	1 236	1 181	18
Myanmar Myanmar	4 151	5 394	6 299	6 985	7 267	7 487	8 147	9 207	9 156	121
Namibia Namibie	7	18	29	1 690	1 830	1 852	1 925	1 815	1 822	24 750
Nauru Nauru	132	136	136	139	139	139	139	136	136	3
Nepal Népal	631	1 467	1 698	2 039	2 486	2 783	3 047	3 322	3 403	440
Netherlands [1] Pays-Bas [1]	159 630	167 935	168 764	172 659	179 706	168 973	175 057	172 061	173 527	9

66

CO₂ emission estimates
From fossil fuel combustion, cement production and gas flared (thousand metric tons of carbon dioxide) *[cont.]*

Estimation des émissions de CO₂
Dues à la combustion de combustibles fossiles, à la production de ciment et au gaz brûlès à la torchère *[suite]*

Country or area Pays ou zone	1990	1993	1994	1995	1996	1997	1998	1999	2000	Change : 1990 - 2000 Variation : 1990 à 2000 (%)
Netherlands Antilles Antilles néerlandaises	895	7 216	6 970	6 849	6 486	5 845	6 369	5 610	9 937	1 011
New Zealand [1] Nouvelle-Zélande [1]	25 267	27 136	27 199	27 206	28 223	30 210	28 684	30 331	30 852	22
Nicaragua Nicaragua	2 647	2 299	2 548	2 838	2 926	3 135	3 425	3 722	3 740	41
Niger Niger	1 049	1 096	1 089	1 133	1 137	1 140	1 137	1 166	1 184	13
Nigeria Nigéria	45 371	60 056	46 655	22 572	27 232	28 391	30 569	35 189	36 175	-20
Niue Nioué	4	4	4	4	4	4	4	4	4	0
Norway [1] Norvège [1]	35 163	35 822	37 659	37 756	40 940	41 193	41 314	41 743	41 273	17
Oman Oman	11 546	13 310	15 352	17 237	16 258	17 886	20 427	19 903	19 789	71
Pakistan Pakistan	68 075	77 785	84 553	84 542	93 401	93 276	96 338	99 092	104 881	54
Palau Palaos	235	231	231	238	246	238	242	242	242	3
Panama Panama	3 131	4 121	4 781	3 472	4 836	7 704	6 406	6 424	6 340	102
Papua New Guinea Papouasie-Nvl-Guinée	2 431	2 530	2 504	2 409	2 409	2 453	2 347	2 427	2 427	0
Paraguay Paraguay	2 262	2 948	3 498	4 011	3 960	4 154	4 191	4 327	3 663	62
Peru Pérou	21 674	24 277	23 907	24 581	25 249	27 647	26 481	30 540	29 564	36
Philippines Philippines	43 941	51 157	56 034	62 839	65 817	77 209	75 819	73 278	77 587	77
Poland [1] Pologne [1]	476 625	363 133	371 588	348 172	372 530	361 626	337 448	329 697	314 812	-34
Portugal [1] Portugal [1]	44 109	48 620	48 713	52 688	50 986	53 102	56 894	64 062	63 150	43
Qatar Qatar	11 858	31 053	30 598	31 332	32 366	36 905	37 913	49 760	40 715	243
Republic of Moldova République de Moldova	...	15 558	12 067	11 187	11 521	10 791	9 603	6 464	6 574	...
Romania [1] Roumanie [1]	194 826	127 086	125 597	...	...	...	...	...	...	
Russian Federation [1] Fédération de Russie [1]	2 372 300	1 855 302	1 660 000	1 590 420	1 495 920	...	...	...	...	...
Rwanda Rwanda	528	502	484	491	510	532	535	565	572	8
Saint Helena Sainte-Hélène	7	7	7	11	15	15	18	22	11	50
Saint Kitts and Nevis Saint-Kitts-et-Nevis	66	84	88	95	103	103	103	103	103	56
Saint Lucia Sainte-Lucie	161	172	260	308	323	301	293	323	337	109
St. Vincent-Grenadines St. Vincent-Grenadines	81	103	121	128	132	132	161	161	169	109

66

CO$_2$ emission estimates
From fossil fuel combustion, cement production and gas flared (thousand metric tons of carbon dioxide) *[cont.]*
Estimation des émissions de CO$_2$
Dues à la combustion de combustibles fossiles, à la production de ciment et au gaz brûlès à la torchère *[suite]*

Country or area Pays ou zone	1990	1993	1994	1995	1996	1997	1998	1999	2000	Change : 1990 - 2000 Variation : 1990 à 2000 (%)
Samoa Samoa	125	128	121	132	132	132	132	139	139	12
Sao Tome and Principe Sao Tomé-et-Principe	66	73	73	77	77	77	81	88	88	33
Saudi Arabia [3] Arabie saoudite [3]	123 512	200 068	264 268	321 050	344 025	330 788	319 095	332 270	374 616	203
Senegal Sénégal	3 131	3 546	3 850	3 469	3 707	3 747	3 824	4 052	4 180	33
Serbia and Montenegro Serbie-et-Monténégro	...	38 988	37 968	40 051	45 247	49 100	51 975	40 451	41 796	...
Seychelles Seychelles	114	161	183	187	191	198	198	216	227	100
Sierra Leone Sierra Leone	334	436	502	506	543	554	502	543	565	69
Singapore Singapour	45 100	53 306	64 266	46 845	53 724	63 976	54 747	56 954	59 088	31
Slovakia [1] Slovaquie [1]	59 746	46 232	43 365	44 898	45 156	45 556	44 811	43 600	41 472	-31
Slovenia [1] Slovénie [1]	13 935	...	...	...	...	...	...	...	...	...
Solomon Islands Iles Salomon	161	158	154	161	161	161	161	165	165	2
Somalia Somalie	18	11	11	11	0	0	0	0	0	...
South Africa Afrique du Sud	285 688	297 004	312 734	325 450	324 933	333 773	336 054	332 981	327 518	15
Spain [1] Espagne [1]	227 233	229 942	242 657	254 411	242 215	261 369	270 130	295 233	306 632	35
Sri Lanka Sri Lanka	3 762	4 895	5 401	5 797	6 974	7 561	7 740	8 521	10 190	171
Sudan Soudan	3 018	1 291	2 314	2 812	2 944	3 707	2 530	2 955	5 225	73
Suriname Suriname	1 811	2 127	2 138	2 156	2 101	2 116	2 138	2 149	2 119	17
Swaziland Swaziland	425	132	484	455	341	400	400	385	381	-10
Sweden [1] Suède [1]	56 065	54 879	59 233	58 574	62 062	57 056	58 142	56 458	55 855	0
Switzerland [1] Suisse [1]	44 420	43 570	42 946	43 825	44 227	43 561	44 833	44 843	43 853	-1
Syrian Arab Republic Rép. arabe syrienne	35 871	45 896	43 949	45 716	45 368	46 853	50 743	52 862	54 226	51
Tajikistan Tadjikistan	...	13 563	5 082	5 170	5 782	5 089	5 100	5 089	3 975	...
Thailand Thaïlande	95 810	142 538	158 257	181 438	202 543	209 810	186 058	195 492	198 792	107
TFYR of Macedonia L'ex-R.y. Macédoine	...	10 208	10 344	10 692	11 741	10 633	11 821	10 985	11 194	...
Togo Togo	752	818	792	895	1 001	1 063	3 788	1 445	1 797	139
Tonga Tonga	77	103	106	110	110	114	110	128	121	57

66

CO$_2$ emission estimates
From fossil fuel combustion, cement production and gas flared (thousand metric tons of carbon dioxide) *[cont.]*
Estimation des émissions de CO$_2$
Dues à la combustion de combustibles fossiles, à la production de ciment et au gaz brûlès à la torchère *[suite]*

Country or area Pays ou zone	1990	1993	1994	1995	1996	1997	1998	1999	2000	Change : 1990 - 2000 Variation : 1990 à 2000 (%)
Trinidad and Tobago Trinité-et-Tobago	16 936	16 801	19 298	20 251	20 926	20 629	21 366	24 875	26 382	56
Tunisia Tunisie	13 270	16 485	15 939	15 723	16 383	16 647	22 378	17 468	18 407	39
Turkey Turquie	143 924	159 881	155 760	171 028	188 305	198 154	202 184	198 638	221 716	54
Turkmenistan Turkménistan	...	27 661	33 473	34 617	31 361	29 927	28 809	34 115	34 617	...
Tuvalu [1] Tuvalu [1]	...		5	...	...	...	...	...	...	...
Uganda Ouganda	814	818	744	953	1 052	1 137	1 335	1 390	1 525	87
Ukraine [1] Ukraine [1]	703 792	504 222	406 838	380 928	346 768	322 907	314 445	...	...	...
USSR - former URSS (anc.)	3 708 734	...	...	...	...	...	...	...	...	...
United Arab Emirates Emirats arabes unis	55 183	58 443	76 443	76 285	79 816	85 250	88 264	88 092	58 956	7
United Kingdom [1] Royaume-Uni [1]	583 705	558 945	555 933	547 374	566 961	542 718	545 116	536 490	542 743	-7
United Rep. of Tanzania Rép.-Unie de Tanzanie	2 332	2 592	2 398	3 538	3 447	3 194	2 867	2 860	4 308	85
United States [1,2] Etats-Unis [1,2]	4 998 516	5 157 298	5 260 956	5 305 896	5 483 671	5 567 981	5 575 083	5 665 472	5 840 039	17
Uruguay Uruguay	3 912	4 407	4 019	4 525	5 511	5 544	5 562	6 611	5 412	38
Uzbekistan [1] Ouzbékistan [1]	114 559	...	102 157	...	...	...	...	...	...	...
Vanuatu Vanuatu	66	62	62	66	84	84	81	81	81	22
Venezuela Venezuela	117 810	118 782	151 969	148 449	153 762	153 578	160 351	154 341	157 865	34
Viet Nam Viet Nam	21 443	24 299	26 275	31 086	36 175	40 517	44 044	46 618	57 504	168
Western Sahara Sahara occidental	198	202	202	209	213	220	227	238	242	22
former Yemen Arab Rep. l'ex-Yémen rép. arabe	3 766	...	...	...	...	...	...	...	...	...
Dem. Yemen - former Yémen dém. (anc.)	5 830	...	...	...	...	...	...	...	...	...
Yemen Yémen	...	8 595	10 644	10 644	12 166	12 958	12 896	17 032	8 444	...
Yugoslavia, SFR Yougoslavie, Rfs	130 548	...	...	...	...	...	...	...	...	...
Zambia Zambie	2 446	2 497	2 420	2 171	1 870	2 391	2 314	1 819	1 826	-25
Zimbabwe Zimbabwe	16 658	17 336	18 546	16 067	15 756	14 953	14 733	16 720	14 813	-11

Source:
Carbon Dioxide Information Analysis Center (CDIAC) of the Oak
Ridge National Laboratory, Oak Ridge, Tennessee, U.S.A., database
on national CO$_2$ emission estimates from fossil fuel burning, cement

Source:
"Carbon Dioxide Information Analysis Center (CDIAC) of the Oak
Ridge National Laboratory, Oak Ridge, Tennessee, U.S.A., database
on national CO$_2$ emission estimates from fossil fuel burning, cement

66

CO$_2$ emission estimates

From fossil fuel combustion, cement production and gas flared (thousand metric tons of carbon dioxide) *[cont.]*

Estimation des émissions de CO$_2$

Dues à la combustion de combustibles fossiles, à la production de ciment et au gaz brûlès à la torchère *[suite]*

production and gas flaring: 1751- 2000 and the Secretariat of the United Nations Framework Convention on Climate Change (UNFCCC), Bonn, Secretariat of the UNFCCC database.

The majority of the data have been taken from the CDIAC database; all other data have been taken from the UNFCCC database and are footnoted accordingly.

1   Source: Secretariat of the UNFCCC.
2   Including territories.
3   Including part of the Neutral Zone.

production and gas flaring: 1751- 2000" et la Secrétariat de la convention-cadre concernant les changements climatiques (CCCC) des Nations Unies, Bonn, la base de données du Secrétariat de la CCCC.

La majorité des données proviennent de la base de données du CDIAC ; les autres, qui proviennent de la base de données du Secrétariat de la CCCC, sont signalées par une note.

1   Source : Secrétariat de la CCC des Nations Unies.
2   Y compris les territoires.
3   Y compris une partie de la Zone Neutrale.

67

Ozone-depleting chlorofluorocarbons (CFCs)
Consumption: ozone-depleting potential (ODP) metric tons

Chlorofluorocarbones (CFC) qui appauvrissent la couche d'ozone
Consommation : tonnes de potentiel de destruction de l'ozone (PDO)

Region, country or area Région, pays ou zone	1992	1993	1994	1995	1996	1997	1998	1999	2000	2001
Albania Albanie	...	...	...	40	40	42	47	53	62	69
Algeria Algérie	...	2 146	2 226	2 292	2 292	1 774	1 549	1 502	1 475	1 022
Angola Angola	...	...	...	116	...	116	116	...	...	9
Antigua and Barbuda Antigua-et-Barbuda	429	426	12	12	10	10	26	-2	5	3
Argentina Argentine	4 306	1 806	4 569	6 366	4 202	3 524	3 546	4 316	2 397	3 293
Armenia Arménie	...	...	...	...	...	...	...	9	25	163
Australia Australie	5 556	3 409	3 895	2 585	234	184	195	274	6	6
Azerbaijan Azerbaïdjan	...	...	...	...	456	201	152	100	88	52
Bahamas Bahamas	1	66	68	70	72	53	55	54	66	...
Bahrain Bahreïn	119	111	118	122	137	147	150	129	113	106
Bangladesh Bangladesh	213	227	181	281	628	832	830	801	805	...
Barbados Barbade	21	30	35	25	22	17	22	17	8	12
Belarus Bélarus	914	914	900	579	524	372	256	194	0	0
Belize Belize	...	...	...	16	11	20	25	25	16	28
Benin Bénin	44	37	37	62	58	60	54	57	55	54
Bolivia Bolivie	...	...	76	82	87	58	74	72	79	77
Bosnia and Herzegovina Bosnie-Herzégovine	...	...	...	3	21	49	45	151	176	200
Botswana Botswana	12	15	8	8	5	7	3	3	2	...
Brazil Brésil	8 934	9 818	10 778	10 896	10 872	9 810	9 543	11 612	9 275	6 231
Brunei Darussalam Brunéi Darussalam	59	81	63	65	80	90	63	37	47	31
Bulgaria Bulgarie	1 279	690	684	322	4	0	0	0	0	0
Burkina Faso Burkina Faso	29	31	34	34	38	38	37	31	25	20
Burundi Burundi	48	...	...	56	59	62	64	60	54	46
Cameroon Cameroun	64	157	157	231	280	260	312	362	369	364
Canada Canada	10 747	4 521	4 853	4 816	129	136	42	-5	10	0
Central African Rep. Rép. centrafricaine	45	31	31	27	6	0	7	1	4	...
Chad Tchad	30	31	32	33	35	36	38	37	37	32

67

Ozone-depleting chlorofluorocarbons (CFCs) *[cont]*
Consumption: ozone-depleting potential (ODP) metric tons *[cont]*
Chlorofluorocarbones (CFC) qui appauvrissent la couche d'ozone *[suite]*
Consommation : tonnes de potentiel de destruction de l'ozone (PDO) *[suite]*

Region, country or area / Région, pays ou zone	1992	1993	1994	1995	1996	1997	1998	1999	2000	2001
Chile / Chili	573	892	853	933	878	674	738	658	576	470
China / Chine	57 045	66 283	70 779	75 291	47 089	51 076	55 414	42 983	39 124	33 923
Colombia / Colombie	...	...	2 115	2 156	2 302	2 166	1 224	986	1 149	1 165
Comoros / Comores	...	...	...	2	2	3	4	2	3	2
Congo / Congo	...	...	27	14	13	9	7	9	11	2
Costa Rica / Costa Rica	216	222	184	159	497	95	-204	152	106	145
Côte d'Ivoire / Côte d'Ivoire	...	204	342	354	384	144	268	166	206	148
Croatia / Croatie	434	253	314	194	184	280	86	142	171	114
Cuba / Cuba	122	122	150	546	664	665	531	571	534	504
Cyprus / Chypre	265	429	196	165	141	143	81	115	165	138
Czech Republic / République tchèque	...	1 039	403	369	50	12	8	11	5	3
Dem. Rep. of the Congo / Rép. dém. du Congo	...	...	...	793	735	469	...	371	387	639
Dominica / Dominique	...	1	1	1	2	2	2	1	...	...
Dominican Republic / Rép. dominicaine	274	330	433	634	559	427	311	752	399	486
Ecuador / Equateur	403	261	78	315	269	320	272	153	230	207
Egypt / Egypte	2 015	1 746	1 870	1 640	1 732	1 632	1 540	1 374	1 267	1 335
El Salvador / El Salvador	645	398	256	330	312	278	195	110	99	117
Estonia / Estonie	...	...	...	765	-442	45	70	56	16	0
Ethiopia / Ethiopie	...	...	...	33	34	35	38	39	39	...
Fiji / Fidji	8	7	0	60	27	14	13	9	0	0
Gabon / Gabon	...	13	12	7	11	12	12	8	14	6
Gambia / Gambie	12	21	23	23	21	28	11	7	6	6
Georgia / Géorgie	...	...	53	13	23	31	26	22	22	19
Ghana / Ghana	72	24	39	44	14	49	50	47	47	36
Grenada / Grenade	...	4	4	7	5	7	4	...	...	...
Guatemala / Guatemala	357	357	269	231	236	207	189	191	188	265
Guinea / Guinée	30	30	32	37	44	46	42	40	38	35

67

Ozone-depleting chlorofluorocarbons (CFCs) *[cont]*

Consumption: ozone-depleting potential (ODP) metric tons *[cont]*

Chlorofluorocarbones (CFC) qui appauvrissent la couche d'ozone *[suite]*

Consommation : tonnes de potentiel de destruction de l'ozone (PDO) *[suite]*

Region, country or area Région, pays ou zone	1992	1993	1994	1995	1996	1997	1998	1999	2000	2001
Guyana Guyana	23	59	42	91	41	28	29	40	24	20
Haiti Haïti	...	...	...	...	...	...	...	...	...	169
Honduras Honduras	...	...	115	118	523	354	157	335	172	122
Hungary Hongrie	1 675	1 381	844	566	0	4	1	1	0	0
Iceland Islande	65	62	31	0	0	0	0	0	0	0
India Inde	4 501	5 277	6 387	6 402	6 937	6 703	5 265	4 143	5 614	...
Indonesia Indonésie	5 249	4 363	6 910	8 351	9 012	7 635	6 183	5 866	5 411	5 003
Iran (Islamic Rep. of) Iran (Rép. islamique d')	4 750	4 495	4 328	4 140	3 692	5 883	5 571	4 399	4 157	4 205
Israel Israël	4 063	3 524	897	1 095	7	0	0	0	0	0
Jamaica Jamaïque	464	66	49	82	91	107	199	210	60	49
Japan Japon	58 477	47 452	19 713	23 064	-614	-113	-208	23	-24	-6
Jordan Jordanie	531	580	520	535	627	857	647	398	354	321
Kazakhstan Kazakhstan	...	2 218	...	...	826	669	1 025	730	524	...
Kenya Kenya	47	47	273	301	167	251	245	241	203	169
Kiribati Kiribati	...	1	1	1	1	1	0	...	...	...
Korea, Dem. P. R. Corée, R. p. dém. de	...	...	...	825	267	233	112	106	77	...
Korea, Republic of Corée, République de	19 605	8 728	10 070	10 039	8 220	9 220	5 299	7 403	410	6 724
Kuwait Koweït	...	546	600	485	472	485	399	450	420	354
Kyrgyzstan Kirghizistan	106	93	85	82	67	70	57	52	53	53
Lao People's Dem. Rep. Rép. dém. pop. lao	4	...	...	43	43	43	43	44	45	41
Latvia Lettonie	...	...	...	665	307	23	25	22	35	...
Lebanon Liban	...	908	726	820	735	621	475	463	528	533
Lesotho Lesotho	...	...	5	6	6	4	3	3	2	...
Libyan Arab Jamah. Jamah. arabe libyenne	...	...	...	773	730	647	660	894	985	985
Liechtenstein Liechtenstein	10	6	4	1	0	0	0	0	0	...
Lithuania Lituanie	2 450	...	596	361	289	100	104	85	37	0
Madagascar Madagascar	...	...	...	19	21	104	24	26	14	...

67

Ozone-depleting chlorofluorocarbons (CFCs) *[cont]*
Consumption: ozone-depleting potential (ODP) metric tons *[cont]*
Chlorofluorocarbones (CFC) qui appauvrissent la couche d'ozone *[suite]*
Consommation : tonnes de potentiel de destruction de l'ozone (PDO) *[suite]*

Region, country or area Région, pays ou zone	1992	1993	1994	1995	1996	1997	1998	1999	2000	2001
Malawi Malawi	46	88	30	62	56	56	57	51	...	...
Malaysia Malaisie	3 421	3 624	4 730	3 427	3 038	3 348	2 334	2 010	1 980	1 947
Maldives Maldives	6	6	7	6	0	8	1	1	5	14
Mali Mali	...	...	...	104	109	111	113	37	29	...
Malta Malte	65	62	61	63	70	60	107	97	68	63
Marshall Islands Iles Marshall	1	1	1	1	1	1	1	1	1	...
Mauritania Mauritanie	...	...	17	23	8	16	15	13	...	...
Mauritius Maurice	67	64	42	24	36	27	39	19	19	14
Mexico Mexique	8 513	9 198	9 652	4 859	4 859	4 157	3 483	2 838	3 060	2 224
Monaco Monaco	6	9	5	0	0	0	0	0	0	0
Mongolia Mongolie	...	...	...	7	12	13	13	12	11	9
Morocco Maroc	1 070	630	757	707	814	886	924	871	564	435
Mozambique Mozambique	...	...	18	20	22	13	3	14	...	...
Myanmar Myanmar	16	...	2	49	59	55	52	31	26	39
Namibia Namibie	...	34	35	27	19	19	14	21	22	24
Nepal Népal	20	20	20	25	27	29	33	25	94	...
New Zealand Nouvelle-Zélande	651	805	338	189	2	0	0	0	-3	0
Nicaragua Nicaragua	95	100	106	110	83	56	37	53	44	35
Niger Niger	18	18	17	19	18	59	61	58	40	29
Nigeria Nigéria	1 071	1 996	1 795	1 536	4 548	4 866	4 762	4 286	4 095	3 666
Norway Norvège	255	222	173	3	3	3	-16	-60	-40	-48
Oman Oman	305	244	309	230	265	250	261	260	282	207
Pakistan Pakistan	945	1 781	1 823	2 104	1 671	1 264	1 196	1 422	1 945	1 666
Palau Palaos	...	...	...	2	1	2	2	0	1	1
Panama Panama	168	359	254	440	355	358	346	301	250	180
Papua New Guinea Papouasie-Nvl-Guinée	39	39	53	10	63	36	45	35	48	15
Paraguay Paraguay	240	191	221	211	159	102	113	345	153	116

67

Ozone-depleting chlorofluorocarbons (CFCs) *[cont]*
Consumption: ozone-depleting potential (ODP) metric tons *[cont]*
Chlorofluorocarbones (CFC) qui appauvrissent la couche d'ozone *[suite]*
Consommation : tonnes de potentiel de destruction de l'ozone (PDO) *[suite]*

Region, country or area Région, pays ou zone	1992	1993	1994	1995	1996	1997	1998	1999	2000	2001
Peru Pérou	243	279	249	367	243	259	327	296	347	189
Philippines Philippines	3 520	3 779	3 959	3 382	3 039	2 747	2 130	2 088	2 905	2 049
Poland Pologne	2 537	2 589	1 678	1 756	549	308	314	187	175	179
Qatar Qatar	...	...	...	91	102	111	121	89	86	85
Republic of Moldova République de Moldova	...	...	...	85	51	83	40	11	32	23
Romania Roumanie	...	1 649	960	544	763	720	582	338	361	186
Russian Federation Fédération de Russie	36 607	30 130	23 413	20 990	12 345	10 986	11 821	14 824	23 821	0
Saint Kitts and Nevis Saint-Kitts-et-Nevis	6	5	5	4	3	4	2	3	...	...
Saint Lucia Sainte-Lucie	...	11	8	8	8	8	6	3	4	3
St. Vincent-Grenadines St. Vincent-Grenadines	...	...		2	1	2	2	...	6	7
Samoa Samoa	4	4	4	4	5	5	3	6	1	2
Saudi Arabia Arabie saoudite	833	645	2 082	1 828	1 668	1 899	1 922	1 710	1 594	...
Senegal Sénégal	102	156	118	151	178	138	128	121	117	98
Serbia and Montenegro Serbie-et-Monténégro	1 079	999	868	820	896	832	519	549	...	...
Seychelles Seychelles	5	10	4	4	2	2	2	1	1	1
Singapore Singapour	1 372	1 482	792	774	37	-179	17	24	22	22
Slovakia Slovaquie	609	986	229	381	0	1	1	1	2	3
Slovenia Slovénie	1 098	594	564	354	1	0	0	0	0	3
Solomon Islands Iles Salomon	3	5	0	2	2	2	1	6	0	1
South Africa Afrique du Sud	3 951	4 127	2 417	1 680	0	98	155	117	81	16
Sri Lanka Sri Lanka	216	294	347	520	498	183	250	216	220	190
Sudan Soudan	...	320	338	635	430	306	295	295	292	266
Swaziland Swaziland	...	83	83	35	22	16	2	2	0	1
Switzerland Suisse	1 562	1 206	741	275	-43	-41	-28	-5	-6	...
Syrian Arab Republic Rép. arabe syrienne	1 365	1 406	2 380	2 370	2 260	2 044	1 246	1 281	1 175	1 392
Tajikistan Tadjikistan	...	...	...	32	35	48	56	51	28	28
Thailand Thaïlande	9 057	8 053	6 865	8 248	5 550	4 448	3 783	3 611	3 568	3 375

67

Ozone-depleting chlorofluorocarbons (CFCs) *[cont]*
Consumption: ozone-depleting potential (ODP) metric tons *[cont]*
Chlorofluorocarbones (CFC) qui appauvrissent la couche d'ozone *[suite]*
Consommation : tonnes de potentiel de destruction de l'ozone (PDO) *[suite]*

Region, country or area Région, pays ou zone	1992	1993	1994	1995	1996	1997	1998	1999	2000	2001
TFYR of Macedonia L'ex-R.y. Macédoine	...	...	206	558	514	487	63	192	49	47
Togo Togo	45	46	48	50	34	35	37	42	37	35
Tonga Tonga	...	...	...	2	1	1	0	83	0	1
Trinidad and Tobago Trinité-et-Tobago	104	97	109	111	114	135	156	82	101	79
Tunisia Tunisie	568	581	508	758	882	970	791	566	555	570
Turkey Turquie	4 118	4 451	2 661	3 789	3 759	3 870	3 985	1 791	820	731
Turkmenistan Turkménistan	67	61	57	56	30	26	25	19	...	...
Tuvalu Tuvalu	...	0	0	0	0	0	0	0	0	0
Uganda Ouganda	15	16	9	12	13	14	11	12	13	13
Ukraine Ukraine	3 432	1 703	2 421	746	1 401	1 405	1 101	951	839	1 077
United Arab Emirates Emirats arabes unis	498	478	425	514	511	563	737	529	476	423
United Rep. of Tanzania Rép.-Unie de Tanzanie	...	185	263	280	294	188	132	89	215	131
United States Etats-Unis	144 856	111 459	72 534	35 530	1 897	743	2 706	2 904	2 613	2 805
Uruguay Uruguay	305	223	312	232	172	193	194	111	107	102
Uzbekistan Ouzbékistan	...	585	250	294	260	53	120	53	...	...
Venezuela Venezuela	4 071	3 624	3 093	3 220	3 041	3 704	3 214	1 922	2 706	2 546
Viet Nam Viet Nam	...	...	380	480	520	500	392	294	220	243
Yemen Yémen	...	...	...	306	329	412	453	1 041	1 045	1 023
Zambia Zambie	24	25	38	23	30	29	27	24	23	...
Zimbabwe Zimbabwe	...	218	476	462	457	435	390	229	145	259

Source:
United Nations Environment Programme (UNEP) Ozone Secretariat, Nairobi, "Production and Consumption of Ozone Depleting Substances, 1986 – 1998" and the Ozone Secretariat database.

Source:
Sécretariat de l'ozone du programme des Nations Unies pour l'environnement (PNUE), Nairobi, "Production et consommation des substances qui appauvrissent la couche d'ozone, 1986 – 1998" et la base de données du Sécretariat de l'ozone.

68
Water supply and sanitation coverage
Accès à l'eau et à l'assainissement

Country or area Pays ou zone	Year Année	Percent of population with access to: - Pourcentage de la population ayant accès à :					
		Improved water supply Un système amélioré de distribution d'eau			Improved sanitation facilities Un système amélioré d'assainissement		
		Urban (%) Urbaine (%)	Rural (%) Rurale (%)	Total (%) Totale (%)	Urban (%) Urbaine (%)	Rural (%) Rurale (%)	Total (%) Totale (%)
Afghanistan Afghanistan	2000	19	11	13	25	8	12
Albania Albanie	2000	99	95	97	99	85	91
Algeria Algérie	2000	94	82	89	99	81	92
Andorra Andorre	2000	100	100	100	100	100	100
Angola Angola	2000	34	40	38	70	30	44
Antigua and Barbuda Antigua-et-Barbuda	2000	95	89	91	98	94	95
Argentina Argentine	1990	97	73	94	87	47	82
Australia Australie	1990	100	100	100	100	100	100
	2000	100	100	100	100	100	100
Austria Autriche	1990	100	100	100	100	100	100
	2000	100	100	100	100	100	100
Azerbaijan Azerbaïdjan	2000	93	58	78	90	70	81
Bahamas Bahamas	2000	98	86	97	100	100	100
Bangladesh Bangladesh	1990	99	93	94	81	31	41
	2000	99	97	97	71	41	48
Barbados Barbade	2000	100	100	100	100	100	100
Belarus Bélarus	2000	100	100	100	...	...	...
Belize Belize	2000	100	82	92	71	25	50
Benin Bénin	1990	...	...	...	46	6	20
	2000	74	55	63	46	6	23
Bhutan Bhoutan	2000	86	60	62	65	70	70
Bolivia Bolivie	1990	91	47	71	73	26	52
	2000	95	64	83	86	42	70
Botswana Botswana	1990	100	88	93	87	41	60
	2000	100	90	95	88	43	66
Brazil Brésil	1990	93	54	83	82	38	71
	2000	95	53	87	84	43	76
Bulgaria Bulgarie	2000	100	100	100	100	100	100
Burkina Faso Burkina Faso	2000	66	37	42	39	27	29
Burundi Burundi	1990	96	67	69	65	89	87
	2000	91	77	78	68	90	88
Cambodia Cambodge	2000	54	26	30	56	10	17
Cameroon Cameroun	1990	78	32	51	97	64	77
	2000	78	39	58	92	66	79
Canada Canada	1990	100	99	100	100	99	100
	2000	100	99	100	100	99	100
Cape Verde Cap-Vert	2000	64	89	74	95	32	71
Central African Rep. Rép. centrafricaine	1990	71	35	48	38	16	24
	2000	89	57	70	38	16	25
Chad Tchad	1990	...	...	...	70	4	18
	2000	31	26	27	81	13	29

68
Water supply and sanitation coverage *[cont.]*
Accès à l'eau et à l'assainissement *[suite]*

Country or area Pays ou zone	Year Année	Percent of population with access to: - Pourcentage de la population ayant accès à :					
		Improved water supply Un système amélioré de distribution d'eau			Improved sanitation facilities Un système amélioré d'assainissement		
		Urban (%) Urbaine (%)	Rural (%) Rurale (%)	Total (%) Totale (%)	Urban (%) Urbaine (%)	Rural (%) Rurale (%)	Total (%) Totale (%)
Chile Chili	1990 2000	98 99	49 58	90 93	98 96	92 97	97 96
China Chine	1990 2000	99 94	60 66	71 75	56 69	2 27	17 40
Colombia Colombie	1990 2000	98 99	84 70	94 91	96 96	55 56	83 86
Comoros Comores	1990 2000	97 98	84 95	88 96	98 98	98 98	98 98
Congo Congo	2000	71	17	51	14	...	...
Costa Rica Costa Rica	2000	99	92	95	89	97	93
Côte d'Ivoire Côte d'Ivoire	1990 2000	97 92	69 72	80 81	70 71	29 35	46 52
Cuba Cuba	2000	95	77	91	99	95	98
Cyprus Chypre	1990 2000	100 100	100 100	100 100	100 100	100 100	100 100
Dem. Rep. of the Congo Rép. dém. du Congo	2000	89	26	45	54	6	21
Denmark Danemark	2000	100	100	100	...	...	...
Djibouti Djibouti	2000	100	100	100	99	50	91
Dominica Dominique	2000	100	90	97	86	75	83
Dominican Republic Rép. dominicaine	1990 2000	92 90	71 78	83 86	70 70	60 60	66 67
Ecuador Equateur	1990 2000	82 90	58 75	71 85	88 92	49 74	70 86
Egypt Egypte	1990 2000	97 99	92 96	94 97	96 100	79 96	87 98
El Salvador El Salvador	1990 2000	88 91	48 64	66 77	87 89	62 76	73 82
Equatorial Guinea Guinée équatoriale	2000	45	42	44	60	46	53
Eritrea Erythrée	2000	63	42	46	66	1	13
Estonia Estonie	2000	...	...	...	93	...	...
Ethiopia Ethiopie	1990 2000	80 81	17 12	25 24	24 33	6 7	8 12
Fiji Fidji	2000	43	51	47	75	12	43
Finland Finlande	1990 2000	100 100	100 100	100 100	100 100	100 100	100 100
Gabon Gabon	2000	95	47	86	55	43	53
Gambia Gambie	2000	80	53	62	41	35	37
Georgia Géorgie	2000	90	61	79	100	99	100
Ghana Ghana	1990 2000	85 91	36 62	53 73	56 74	64 70	61 72
Grenada Grenade	2000	97	93	95	96	97	97
Guatemala Guatemala	1990 2000	88 98	69 88	76 92	82 83	62 79	70 81

68

Water supply and sanitation coverage *[cont.]*
Accès à l'eau et à l'assainissement *[suite]*

Country or area Pays ou zone	Year Année	Percent of population with access to: - Pourcentage de la population ayant accès à :					
		Improved water supply Un système amélioré de distribution d'eau			Improved sanitation facilities Un système amélioré d'assainissement		
		Urban (%) Urbaine (%)	Rural (%) Rurale (%)	Total (%) Totale (%)	Urban (%) Urbaine (%)	Rural (%) Rurale (%)	Total (%) Totale (%)
Guinea Guinée	1990	72	36	45	94	41	55
	2000	72	36	48	94	41	58
Guinea-Bissau Guinée-Bissau	1990	...	...	...	87	33	44
	2000	79	49	56	95	44	56
Guyana Guyana	2000	98	91	94	97	81	87
Haiti Haïti	1990	59	50	53	33	19	23
	2000	49	45	46	50	16	28
Honduras Honduras	1990	89	78	83	88	41	61
	2000	95	81	88	93	55	75
Hungary Hongrie	1990	100	98	99	100	98	99
	2000	100	98	99	100	98	99
India Inde	1990	88	61	68	44	6	16
	2000	95	79	84	61	15	28
Indonesia Indonésie	1990	92	62	71	66	38	47
	2000	90	69	78	69	46	55
Iran (Islamic Rep. of) Iran (Rép. islamique d')	2000	98	83	92	86	79	83
Iraq Iraq	2000	96	48	85	93	31	79
Jamaica Jamaïque	1990	98	87	93	99	99	99
	2000	98	85	92	99	99	99
Jordan Jordanie	1990	99	92	97	100	95	98
	2000	100	84	96	100	98	99
Kazakhstan Kazakhstan	2000	98	82	91	100	98	99
Kenya Kenya	1990	91	31	45	91	77	80
	2000	88	42	57	96	82	87
Kiribati Kiribati	2000	82	25	48	54	44	48
Korea, Dem. P. R. Corée, R. p. dém. de	2000	100	100	100	99	100	99
Korea, Republic of Corée, République de	2000	97	71	92	76	4	63
Kyrgyzstan Kirghizistan	2000	98	66	77	100	100	100
Lao People's Dem. Rep. Rép. dém. pop. lao	2000	61	29	37	67	19	30
Lebanon Liban	2000	100	100	100	100	87	99
Lesotho Lesotho	2000	88	74	78	72	40	49
Libyan Arab Jamah. Jamah. arabe libyenne	1990	72	68	71	97	96	97
	2000	72	68	72	97	96	97
Madagascar Madagascar	1990	85	31	44	70	25	36
	2000	85	31	47	70	30	42
Malawi Malawi	1990	90	43	49	96	70	73
	2000	95	44	57	96	70	76
Malaysia Malaisie	2000	...	94	...	...	98	...
Maldives Maldives	2000	100	100	100	100	41	56
Mali Mali	1990	65	52	55	95	62	70
	2000	74	61	65	93	58	69
Malta Malte	1990	100	100	100	100	100	100
	2000	100	100	100	100	100	100
Mauritania Mauritanie	1990	34	40	37	44	19	30
	2000	34	40	37	44	19	33

68

Water supply and sanitation coverage *[cont.]*
Accès à l'eau et à l'assainissement *[suite]*

| Country or area
Pays ou zone | Year
Année | Percent of population with access to: - Pourcentage de la population ayant accès à : ||||||
| | | Improved water supply
Un système amélioré de distribution d'eau ||| Improved sanitation facilities
Un système amélioré d'assainissement |||
		Urban (%) Urbaine (%)	Rural (%) Rurale (%)	Total (%) Totale (%)	Urban (%) Urbaine (%)	Rural (%) Rurale (%)	Total (%) Totale (%)
Mauritius	1990	100	100	100	100	100	100
Maurice	2000	100	100	100	100	99	99
Mexico	1990	90	52	80	87	26	70
Mexique	2000	95	69	88	88	34	74
Monaco							
Monaco	2000	100	100	100	100	100	100
Mongolia							
Mongolie	2000	77	30	60	46	2	30
Morocco	1990	94	58	75	88	31	58
Maroc	2000	98	56	80	86	44	68
Mozambique							
Mozambique	2000	81	41	57	68	26	43
Myanmar							
Myanmar	2000	89	66	72	84	57	64
Namibia	1990	98	63	72	84	14	33
Namibie	2000	100	67	77	96	17	41
Nepal	1990	93	64	67	69	15	20
Népal	2000	94	87	88	73	22	28
Netherlands	1990	100	100	100	100	100	100
Pays-Bas	2000	100	100	100	100	100	100
New Zealand	1990	100	...	...	...	...	...
Nouvelle-Zélande	2000	100	...	...	...	...	...
Nicaragua	1990	93	44	70	97	53	76
Nicaragua	2000	91	59	77	95	72	85
Niger	1990	65	51	53	71	4	15
Niger	2000	70	56	59	79	5	20
Nigeria	1990	83	37	53	69	44	53
Nigéria	2000	78	49	62	66	45	54
Norway	1990	100	100	100	100	...	...
Norvège	2000	100	100	100	...	...	...
Occupied Palestinian Terr.							
Terr. palestinien occupé	2000	97	86	86	100	100	100
Oman	1990	41	30	37	98	61	84
Oman	2000	41	30	39	98	61	92
Pakistan	1990	96	77	83	77	17	36
Pakistan	2000	95	87	90	95	43	62
Palau							
Palaos	2000	100	20	79	100	100	100
Panama							
Panama	2000	99	79	90	99	83	92
Papua New Guinea	1990	88	32	40	92	80	82
Papouasie-Nvl-Guinée	2000	88	32	42	92	80	82
Paraguay	1990	80	46	63	96	91	93
Paraguay	2000	93	59	78	94	93	94
Peru	1990	88	42	74	77	21	60
Pérou	2000	87	62	80	79	49	71
Philippines	1990	93	82	87	85	63	74
Philippines	2000	91	79	86	93	69	83
Republic of Moldova							
République de Moldova	2000	97	88	92	100	98	99
Romania							
Roumanie	2000	91	16	58	86	10	53
Russian Federation							
Fédération de Russie	2000	100	96	99	...	...	...
Rwanda							
Rwanda	2000	60	40	41	12	8	8
Saint Kitts and Nevis							
Saint-Kitts-et-Nevis	2000	...	...	98	...	...	96

68

Water supply and sanitation coverage *[cont.]*

Accès à l'eau et à l'assainissement *[suite]*

		Percent of population with access to: - Pourcentage de la population ayant accès à :					
		Improved water supply Un système amélioré de distribution d'eau			Improved sanitation facilities Un système amélioré d'assainissement		
Country or area Pays ou zone	Year Année	Urban (%) Urbaine (%)	Rural (%) Rurale (%)	Total (%) Totale (%)	Urban (%) Urbaine (%)	Rural (%) Rurale (%)	Total (%) Totale (%)
Saint Lucia Sainte-Lucie	2000	...	...	98	...	...	89
St. Vincent-Grenadines St. Vincent-Grenadines	2000	...	...	93	...	...	96
Samoa Samoa	2000	95	100	99	95	100	99
Saudi Arabia Arabie saoudite	2000	100	64	95	100	100	100
Senegal Sénégal	1990 2000	90 92	60 65	72 78	86 94	38 48	57 70
Serbia and Montenegro Serbie-et-Monténégro	2000	99	97	98	100	99	100
Sierra Leone Sierra Leone	2000	75	46	57	88	53	66
Singapore Singapour	1990 2000	100 100	... ...	100 100	100 100	... ...	100 100
Slovakia Slovaquie	2000	100	100	100	100	100	100
Slovenia Slovénie	1990 2000	100 100	100 100	100 100	100 ...	... ...	... ...
Solomon Islands Iles Salomon	2000	94	65	71	98	18	34
South Africa Afrique du Sud	1990 2000	99 99	73 73	86 86	93 93	80 80	86 87
Sri Lanka Sri Lanka	1990 2000	91 98	62 70	68 77	94 97	82 93	85 94
Sudan Soudan	1990 2000	86 86	60 69	67 75	87 87	48 48	58 62
Suriname Suriname	2000	93	50	82	99	75	93
Sweden Suède	1990 2000	100 100	100 100	100 100	100 100	100 100	100 100
Switzerland Suisse	1990 2000	100 100	100 100	100 100	100 100	100 100	100 100
Syrian Arab Republic Rép. arabe syrienne	2000	94	64	80	98	81	90
Tajikistan Tadjikistan	2000	93	47	60	97	88	90
Thailand Thaïlande	1990 2000	87 95	78 81	80 84	95 96	75 96	79 96
Togo Togo	1990 2000	82 85	38 38	51 54	71 69	24 17	37 34
Tonga Tonga	2000	100	100	100	...	...	...
Trinidad and Tobago Trinité-et-Tobago	1990 2000	... ...	... ...	91 90	... ...	... ...	99 99
Tunisia Tunisie	1990 2000	91 92	54 58	75 80	96 96	48 62	76 84
Turkey Turquie	1990 2000	83 81	72 86	79 82	97 97	70 70	87 90
Uganda Ouganda	1990 2000	81 80	40 47	45 52	... 93	... 77	... 79
Ukraine Ukraine	2000	100	94	98	100	98	99
United Kingdom Royaume-Uni	1990 2000	100 100	100 100	100 100	100 100	100 100	100 100
United Rep. of Tanzania Rép.-Unie de Tanzanie	1990 2000	76 90	28 57	38 68	84 99	84 86	84 90

68

Water supply and sanitation coverage *[cont.]*

Accès à l'eau et à l'assainissement *[suite]*

| | | Percent of population with access to: - Pourcentage de la population ayant accès à : | | | | | |
| | | Improved water supply Un système amélioré de distribution d'eau | | | Improved sanitation facilities Un système amélioré d'assainissement | | |
Country or area Pays ou zone	Year Année	Urban (%) Urbaine (%)	Rural (%) Rurale (%)	Total (%) Totale (%)	Urban (%) Urbaine (%)	Rural (%) Rurale (%)	Total (%) Totale (%)
United States Etats-Unis	1990 2000	100 100	100 100	100 100	100 100	100 100	100 100
Uruguay Uruguay	2000	98	93	98	95	85	94
Uzbekistan Ouzbékistan	2000	94	79	85	97	85	89
Vanuatu Vanuatu	2000	63	94	88	100	100	100
Venezuela Venezuela	2000	85	70	83	71	48	68
Viet Nam Viet Nam	1990 2000	86 95	48 72	55 77	52 82	23 38	29 47
Yemen Yémen	1990 2000	... 74	... 68	... 69	69 89	21 21	32 38
Zambia Zambie	1990 2000	88 88	28 48	52 64	86 99	48 64	63 78
Zimbabwe Zimbabwe	1990 2000	99 100	69 73	78 83	70 71	50 57	56 62

Source:
World Health Organization and United Nations Children's Fund, Geneva and New York, Water Supply and Sanitation Collaborative Council, "Global Water Supply and Sanitation Assessment, 2000 Report".

Source :
Organisation mondial de la santé et Fonds des Nations Unies pour l'enfance, Genève et New York, Conseil de concertation pour l'approvisionnement en eau et l'assainissement, "Evaluation mondiale 2000 des condition d'alimentation en eau et d'assainissement".

69

Threatened species
Number by taxonomic group, 2002

Espèces menacées
Nombre par groupe taxonomique, 2002

Country or area Pays ou zone	Mammals Mammifères	Birds Oiseaux	Reptiles Reptiles	Amphibians Amphibiens	Fishes Poissons	Molluscs Mollusques	Invertebrates Inverterrés	Plants Plantes	Total
Africa · Afrique									
Algeria Algérie	13	6	2	0	1	0	11	2	35
Angola Angola	19	15	4	0	0	5	1	19	63
Benin Bénin	8	2	1	0	0	0	0	11	22
Botswana Botswana	6	7	0	0	0	0	0	0	13
British Indian Ocean Terr. Territoire britannique de	0	0	2	0	0	0	0	1	3
Burkina Faso Burkina Faso	7	2	1	0	0	0	0	2	12
Burundi Burundi	6	7	0	0	0	0	3	2	18
Cameroon Cameroun	40	15	1	1	27	1	3	155	243
Cape Verde Cap-Vert	3	2	0	0	1	0	0	2	8
Central African Rep. Rép. centrafricaine	14	3	1	0	0	0	0	10	28
Chad Tchad	17	5	1	0	0	1	0	2	26
Comoros Comores	2	9	2	0	1	0	4	5	23
Congo Congo	15	3	1	0	1	1	0	33	54
Côte d'Ivoire Côte d'Ivoire	19	12	2	1	0	1	0	101	136
Dem. Rep. of the Congo Rép. dém. du Congo	40	28	2	0	1	41	4	55	171
Djibouti Djibouti	4	5	0	0	1	0	0	2	12
Egypt Egypte	13	7	6	0	0	0	1	2	29
Equatorial Guinea Guinée équatoriale	16	5	2	1	0	0	2	23	49
Eritrea Erythrée	12	7	6	0	0	0	0	3	28
Ethiopia Ethiopie	35	16	1	0	0	3	1	22	78
Gabon Gabon	15	5	1	0	1	0	1	71	94
Gambia Gambie	3	2	1	0	1	0	0	3	10
Ghana Ghana	14	8	2	0	0	0	0	115	139
Guinea Guinée	12	10	1	1	0	0	3	21	48
Guinea-Bissau Guinée-Bissau	3	0	1	0	1	0	1	4	10
Kenya Kenya	51	24	5	0	18	12	3	98	211

69
Threatened species
Number by taxonomic group, 2002 *[cont.]*
Espèces menacées
Nombre par groupe taxonomique, 2002) *[suite]*

Country or area Pays ou zone	Mammals Mammifères	Birds Oiseaux	Reptiles Reptiles	Amphibians Amphibiens	Fishes Poissons	Molluscs Mollusques	Invertebrates Inverterrés	Plants Plantes	Total
Lesotho Lesotho	3	7	0	0	1	0	1	1	13
Liberia Libéria	17	11	2	0	0	1	1	46	78
Libyan Arab Jamah. Jamah. arabe libyenne	8	1	3	0	0	0	0	1	13
Madagascar Madagascar	50	27	18	2	14	24	8	162	305
Malawi Malawi	8	11	0	0	0	8	0	13	40
Mali Mali	13	4	1	0	1	0	0	6	25
Mauritania Mauritanie	10	2	2	0	0	0	0	0	14
Mauritius Maurice	3	9	4	0	1	27	5	87	136
Mayotte Mayotte	0	3	2	0	0	0	1	0	6
Morocco Maroc	16	9	2	0	1	0	7	2	37
Mozambique Mozambique	14	16	5	0	4	6	1	36	82
Namibia Namibie	15	11	3	1	3	1	0	5	39
Niger Niger	11	3	0	0	0	0	1	2	17
Nigeria Nigéria	27	9	2	0	2	0	1	119	160
Réunion Réunion	3	5	2	0	1	14	2	14	41
Rwanda Rwanda	9	9	0	0	0	0	2	3	23
Saint Helena Sainte-Hélène	1	13	1	0	7	0	2	9	33
Sao Tome and Principe Sao Tomé-et-Principe	3	9	1	0	0	1	1	27	42
Senegal Sénégal	12	4	6	0	1	0	0	7	30
Seychelles Seychelles	4	10	4	4	0	1	2	43	68
Sierra Leone Sierra Leone	12	10	3	0	0	0	4	43	72
Somalia Somalie	19	10	2	0	3	1	0	17	52
South Africa Afrique du Sud	42	28	19	9	29	10	102	45	284
Sudan Soudan	23	6	2	0	0	0	1	17	49
Swaziland Swaziland	4	5	0	0	0	0	0	3	12
Togo Togo	9	0	2	0	0	0	0	9	20
Tunisia Tunisie	11	5	3	0	0	0	5	0	24

69

Threatened species
Number by taxonomic group, 2002 *[cont.]*
Espèces menacées
Nombre par groupe taxonomique, 2002) *[suite]*

Country or area Pays ou zone	Mammals Mammifères	Birds Oiseaux	Reptiles Reptiles	Amphibians Amphibiens	Fishes Poissons	Molluscs Mollusques	Invertebrates Inverterrés	Plants Plantes	Total
Uganda Ouganda	20	13	0	0	27	7	3	33	103
United Rep. of Tanzania Rép.-Unie de Tanzanie	42	33	5	0	17	41	6	235	379
Western Sahara Sahara occidental	3	0	0	0	0	0	0	0	3
Zambia Zambie	11	11	0	0	0	4	2	8	36
Zimbabwe Zimbabwe	11	10	0	0	0	0	2	14	37
America, North · Amérique du Nord									
Anguilla Anguilla	0	0	4	0	0	0	0	3	7
Antigua and Barbuda Antigua-et-Barbuda	0	1	5	0	0	0	0	4	10
Aruba Aruba	1	0	3	0	0	0	1	0	5
Bahamas Bahamas	5	4	6	0	4	0	1	4	24
Barbados Barbade	0	1	3	0	1	0	0	2	7
Belize Belize	4	2	4	0	6	0	1	28	45
Bermuda Bermudes	2	2	2	0	2	0	25	4	37
British Virgin Islands Iles Vierges britanniques	0	2	6	1	0	0	0	4	13
Canada Canada	14	8	2	1	16	0	10	1	52
Cayman Islands Iles Caïmanes	0	1	2	0	0	1	0	2	6
Costa Rica Costa Rica	14	13	7	1	1	0	9	110	155
Cuba Cuba	11	18	7	0	6	0	3	160	205
Dominica Dominique	1	3	4	0	0	0	0	11	19
Dominican Republic Rép. dominicaine	5	15	10	1	0	0	2	29	62
El Salvador El Salvador	2	0	4	0	2	0	1	23	32
Greenland Groenland	7	0	0	0	0	0	0	1	8
Grenada Grenade	0	1	4	0	1	0	0	3	9
Guadeloupe Guadeloupe	5	1	5	0	0	1	0	7	19
Guatemala Guatemala	6	6	8	0	3	2	6	77	108
Haiti Haïti	4	14	8	1	2	0	2	27	58
Honduras Honduras	10	5	6	0	1	0	2	108	132

69

Threatened species
Number by taxonomic group, 2002 *[cont.]*
Espèces menacées
Nombre par groupe taxonomique, 2002) *[suite]*

Country or area / Pays ou zone	Mammals Mammifères	Birds Oiseaux	Reptiles Reptiles	Amphibians Amphibiens	Fishes Poissons	Molluscs Mollusques	Invertebrates Inverterrés	Plants Plantes	Total
Jamaica / Jamaïque	5	12	8	4	1	0	5	206	241
Martinique / Martinique	0	2	5	0	0	1	0	8	16
Mexico / Mexique	70	39	18	4	88	4	36	221	480
Montserrat / Montserrat	1	2	3	0	0	0	0	3	9
Netherlands Antilles / Antilles néerlandaises	3	1	6	0	0	0	0	2	12
Nicaragua / Nicaragua	6	5	7	0	1	2	0	39	60
Panama / Panama	20	16	7	0	5	0	2	192	242
Puerto Rico / Porto Rico	2	8	8	3	0	0	1	48	70
Saint Kitts and Nevis / Saint-Kitts-et-Nevis	0	1	3	0	1	0	0	2	7
Saint Lucia / Sainte-Lucie	1	5	6	0	0	0	0	6	18
Saint Pierre and Miquelon / Saint-Pierre-et-Miquelon	0	1	0	0	0	0	0	0	1
St. Vincent-Grenadines / St. Vincent-Grenadines	2	2	4	0	0	0	0	4	12
Trinidad and Tobago / Trinité-et-Tobago	1	1	5	0	0	0	0	1	8
Turks and Caicos Islands / Iles Turques et Caïques	0	3	5	0	0	0	0	2	10
United States / Etats-Unis	37	55	27	25	130	256	301	169	1 000
United States Virgin Is. / Iles Vierges américaines	1	2	5	0	0	0	0	7	15
America, South · Amérique du Sud									
Argentina / Argentine	34	39	5	5	2	0	11	42	138
Bolivia / Bolivie	24	28	2	1	0	0	1	70	126
Brazil / Brésil	81	114	22	6	17	21	13	381	655
Chile / Chili	21	22	0	3	4	0	0	40	90
Colombia / Colombie	41	78	14	0	8	0	0	213	354
Ecuador / Equateur	33	62	10	0	3	23	0	197	328
Falkland Is. (Malvinas) / Iles Falkland (Malvinas)	4	6	0	0	0	0	0	0	10
French Guiana / Guyane française	10	0	7	0	0	0	0	16	33
Guyana / Guyana	11	2	6	0	0	0	1	23	43
Paraguay / Paraguay	10	26	2	0	0	0	0	10	48

69
Threatened species
Number by taxonomic group, 2002 *[cont.]*
Espèces menacées
Nombre par groupe taxonomique, 2002) *[suite]*

Country or area Pays ou zone	Mammals Mammifères	Birds Oiseaux	Reptiles Reptiles	Amphibians Amphibiens	Fishes Poissons	Molluscs Mollusques	Invertebrates Inverterrés	Plants Plantes	Total
Peru Pérou	49	76	6	1	1	0	2	269	404
Suriname Suriname	12	1	6	0	0	0	0	27	46
Uruguay Uruguay	6	11	3	0	2	0	1	1	24
Venezuela Venezuela	26	24	13	0	7	0	1	67	138
Asia · Asie									
Afghanistan Afghanistan	13	11	1	1	0	0	1	1	28
Armenia Arménie	11	4	5	0	1	0	7	1	29
Azerbaijan Azerbaïdjan	13	8	5	0	5	0	6	0	37
Bahrain Bahreïn	1	6	0	0	1	0	0	0	8
Bangladesh Bangladesh	23	23	20	0	0	0	0	12	78
Bhutan Bhoutan	22	12	0	0	0	0	1	7	42
Brunei Darussalam Brunéi Darussalam	11	14	3	0	2	0	0	99	129
Cambodia Cambodge	24	19	10	0	7	0	0	29	89
China Chine	79	74	31	1	32	1	3	168	389
China, Hong Kong SAR Chine, Hong Kong RAS	1	11	1	0	2	1	0	4	20
China, Macao SAR Chine, Macao RAS	0	1	0	0	0	0	0	0	1
Cyprus Chypre	3	3	3	0	1	0	0	1	11
Georgia Géorgie	13	3	7	1	6	0	10	0	40
India Inde	88	72	25	3	9	2	21	244	464
Indonesia Indonésie	147	114	28	0	68	3	28	384	772
Iran (Islamic Rep. of) Iran (Rép. islamique d')	22	13	8	2	7	0	3	1	56
Iraq Iraq	11	11	2	0	2	0	2	0	28
Israel Israël	14	12	4	0	1	5	5	0	41
Japan Japon	37	34	11	10	13	25	20	11	161
Jordan Jordanie	10	8	1	0	0	0	3	0	22
Kazakhstan Kazakhstan	16	15	2	1	7	0	4	1	46
Korea, Dem. P. R. Corée, R. p. dém. de	13	19	0	0	0	0	1	3	36

69
Threatened species
Number by taxonomic group, 2002 *[cont.]*
Espèces menacées
Nombre par groupe taxonomique, 2002) *[suite]*

Country or area Pays ou zone	Mammals Mammifères	Birds Oiseaux	Reptiles Reptiles	Amphibians Amphibiens	Fishes Poissons	Molluscs Mollusques	Invertebrates Inverterrés	Plants Plantes	Total
Korea, Republic of Corée, République de	13	25	0	0	0	0	1	0	39
Kuwait Koweït	1	7	1	0	0	0	0	0	9
Kyrgyzstan Kirghizistan	7	4	2	0	0	0	3	1	17
Lao People's Dem. Rep. Rép. dém. pop. lao	31	20	12	0	6	0	0	18	87
Lebanon Liban	5	7	1	0	0	0	1	0	14
Malaysia Malaisie	50	37	21	0	20	1	2	681	812
Maldives Maldives	0	1	2	0	0	0	0	0	3
Mongolia Mongolie	14	16	0	0	1	0	3	0	34
Myanmar Myanmar	39	35	20	0	1	1	1	37	134
Nepal Népal	31	25	5	0	0	0	1	6	68
Occupied Palestinian Terr. Terr. palestinien occupé	1	1	0	0	0	0	0	0	2
Oman Oman	9	10	4	0	4	0	1	6	34
Pakistan Pakistan	19	17	9	0	3	0	0	2	50
Philippines Philippines	50	67	8	23	31	3	16	193	391
Qatar Qatar	0	6	1	0	0	0	0	0	7
Saudi Arabia Arabie saoudite	8	15	2	0	1	0	1	3	30
Singapore Singapour	3	7	3	0	5	0	1	54	73
Sri Lanka Sri Lanka	22	14	8	0	11	0	2	280	337
Syrian Arab Republic Rép. arabe syrienne	4	8	3	0	0	0	3	0	18
Tajikistan Tadjikistan	9	7	1	0	3	0	2	2	24
Thailand Thaïlande	37	37	18	0	22	1	0	78	193
Timor-Leste Timor-Leste	0	6	0	0	0	0	0	0	6
Turkey Turquie	17	11	12	3	22	0	13	3	81
Turkmenistan Turkménistan	13	6	2	0	7	0	5	0	33
United Arab Emirates Emirats arabes unis	3	8	1	0	1	0	0	0	13
Uzbekistan Ouzbékistan	9	9	2	0	4	0	1	1	26
Viet Nam Viet Nam	40	37	24	1	9	0	0	126	237

69
Threatened species
Number by taxonomic group, 2002 *[cont.]*
Espèces menacées
Nombre par groupe taxonomique, 2002) *[suite]*

Country or area Pays ou zone	Mammals Mammifères	Birds Oiseaux	Reptiles Reptiles	Amphibians Amphibiens	Fishes Poissons	Molluscs Mollusques	Invertebrates Inverterrés	Plants Plantes	Total
Yemen Yémen	5	12	2	0	0	2	0	52	73
Europe · Europe									
Albania Albanie	3	3	4	0	7	0	4	0	21
Andorra Andorre	3	0	0	0	0	1	3	0	7
Austria Autriche	7	3	0	0	7	22	22	3	64
Belarus Bélarus	7	3	0	0	0	0	5	0	15
Belgium Belgique	11	2	0	0	0	4	7	0	24
Bosnia and Herzegovina Bosnie-Herzégovine	10	3	1	1	6	0	10	1	32
Bulgaria Bulgarie	14	10	2	0	10	0	7	0	43
Croatia Croatie	9	4	1	1	22	0	11	0	48
Czech Republic République tchèque	8	2	0	0	7	2	17	4	40
Denmark Danemark	5	1	0	0	0	1	10	3	20
Estonia Estonie	4	3	0	0	0	0	4	0	11
Faeroe Islands Iles Féroé	3	0	0	0	0	0	0	0	3
Finland Finlande	5	3	0	0	0	1	9	1	19
France France	18	5	3	2	5	34	31	2	100
Germany Allemagne	11	5	0	0	6	9	22	12	65
Gibraltar Gibraltar	0	1	0	0	0	2	0	0	3
Greece Grèce	13	7	6	1	20	1	10	2	60
Hungary Hongrie	9	8	1	0	8	1	24	1	52
Iceland Islande	6	0	0	0	0	0	0	0	6
Ireland Irlande	5	1	0	0	0	1	1	1	9
Italy Italie	14	5	4	4	9	16	41	3	96
Latvia Lettonie	4	3	0	0	1	0	8	0	16
Liechtenstein Liechtenstein	2	1	0	0	0	0	5	0	8
Lithuania Lituanie	5	4	0	0	1	0	5	0	15
Luxembourg Luxembourg	3	1	0	0	0	2	2	0	8

69
Threatened species
Number by taxonomic group, 2002 *[cont.]*
Espèces menacées
Nombre par groupe taxonomique, 2002) *[suite]*

Country or area Pays ou zone	Mammals Mammifères	Birds Oiseaux	Reptiles Reptiles	Amphibians Amphibiens	Fishes Poissons	Molluscs Mollusques	Invertebrates Inverterrés	Plants Plantes	Total
Malta Malte	2	1	0	0	2	3	0	0	8
Netherlands Pays-Bas	10	4	0	0	2	1	6	0	23
Norway Norvège	10	2	0	0	0	1	8	2	23
Poland Pologne	15	4	0	0	1	1	14	4	39
Portugal Portugal	17	7	0	1	9	67	15	15	131
Republic of Moldova République de Moldova	6	5	1	0	9	0	5	0	26
Romania Roumanie	17	8	2	0	10	0	22	1	60
Russian Federation Fédération de Russie	45	38	6	0	13	1	29	7	139
San Marino Saint-Marin	2	0	0	0	0	0	0	0	2
Serbia and Montenegro Serbie-et-Monténégro	12	5	1	0	10	0	19	1	48
Slovakia Slovaquie	9	4	1	0	8	6	13	2	43
Slovenia Slovénie	9	1	0	1	8	0	42	0	61
Spain Espagne	24	7	7	3	11	27	35	14	128
Svalbard and Jan Mayen Is Svalbard et îles Jan Mayen	5	0	0	0	0	0	0	0	5
Sweden Suède	7	2	0	0	0	1	12	3	25
Switzerland Suisse	5	2	0	0	4	0	30	2	43
TFYR of Macedonia L'ex-R.y. Macédoine	11	3	2	0	4	0	5	0	25
Ukraine Ukraine	16	8	2	0	11	0	14	1	52
United Kingdom Royaume-Uni	12	2	0	0	3	2	9	13	41
Oceania · Océanie									
American Samoa Samoa américaines	3	2	2	0	0	5	0	1	13
Australia Australie	63	37	38	35	44	175	107	38	537
Christmas Is. Ile Christmas	0	5	2	0	0	0	0	1	8
Cook Islands Iles Cook	1	7	2	0	0	0	0	1	11
Fiji Fidji	5	12	6	1	1	2	0	65	92
French Polynesia Polynésie française	3	23	1	0	5	29	0	47	108
Guam Guam	2	2	2	0	1	5	0	3	15

69

Threatened species
Number by taxonomic group, 2002 *[cont.]*
Espèces menacées
Nombre par groupe taxonomique, 2002) *[suite]*

Country or area Pays ou zone	Mammals Mammifères	Birds Oiseaux	Reptiles Reptiles	Amphibians Amphibiens	Fishes Poissons	Molluscs Mollusques	Invertebrates Inverterrés	Plants Plantes	Total
Kiribati Kiribati	0	4	1	0	0	1	0	0	6
Marshall Islands Iles Marshall	1	1	2	0	0	1	0	0	5
Micronesia (Fed. States) Micronésie (Etats féd. de)	6	5	2	0	1	4	0	4	22
Nauru Nauru	0	2	0	0	0	0	0	0	2
New Caledonia Nouvelle-Calédonie	6	10	2	0	1	10	1	214	244
New Zealand Nouvelle-Zélande	8	63	11	1	8	5	8	21	125
Niue Nioué	0	1	1	0	0	0	0	0	2
Norfolk Island Ile Norfolk	0	7	2	0	0	12	0	1	22
Northern Mariana Islands Iles Mariannes du Nord	2	8	2	0	0	2	0	4	18
Palau Palaos	3	2	2	0	0	5	0	3	15
Papua New Guinea Papouasie-Nvl-Guinée	58	32	9	0	13	2	10	142	266
Pitcairn Pitcairn	0	8	0	0	0	5	0	7	20
Samoa Samoa	3	7	1	0	0	1	0	2	14
Solomon Islands Iles Salomon	20	23	4	0	2	2	4	16	71
Tokelau Tokélaou	0	1	2	0	0	0	0	0	3
Tonga Tonga	2	3	2	0	1	2	0	2	12
Tuvalu Tuvalu	0	1	1	0	0	1	0	0	3
Vanuatu Vanuatu	5	7	2	0	0	0	0	9	23
Wallis and Futuna Islands Iles Wallis et Futuna	0	1	0	0	0	0	0	1	2

Source:
The World Conservation Union (IUCN) / Species Survival Commission (SSC), Gland, Switzerland and Cambridge, United Kingdom, "2002 IUCN Red List of Threatened Species".

Source:
Union mondiale pour la nature (UICN) / Commission de la sauvegarde des espèces, Gland, Suisse, et Cambridge, Royaume-Uni, " La liste rouge des espèces menacées 2002 de l'UICN ".

Technical notes, tables 65-69

Table 65: The data on land and forest cover are compiled by the Food and Agriculture Organization of the United Nations (FAO). The protected areas data are taken from the United Nations Environment Programme (UNEP) World Conservation Monitoring Centre.

FAO's definitions of the land categories and forest cover are as follows:

Land area: Total area excluding area under inland water bodies. The definition of inland water bodies generally includes major rivers and lakes.

Arable land: Land under temporary crops (double-cropped areas are counted only once); temporary meadows for mowing or pasture; land under market and kitchen gardens; and land temporarily fallow (less than five years). Abandoned land resulting from shifting cultivation is not included in this category. Data for "arable land" are not meant to indicate the amount of land that is potentially cultivable.

Permanent crops: Land cultivated with crops that occupy the land for long periods and need not be replanted after each harvest, such as cocoa, coffee and rubber. This category includes land under flowering shrubs, fruit trees, nut trees and vines, but excludes land under trees grown for wood or timber.

Forest: In the *Global Forest Resources Assessment 2000* [10] the following definition is used for forest. Forest includes natural forests and forest plantations and is used to refer to land with a tree crown cover (or equivalent stocking level) of more than 10 per cent and area of more than 0.5 ha. The trees should be able to reach a minimum height of 5 m at maturity *in situ*. Forest may consist either of closed forest formations where trees of various storeys and undergrowth cover a high proportion of the ground; or open forest formations with a continuous vegetation cover in which the tree crown cover exceeds 10 per cent. Young natural stands and all plantations established for forestry purposes that have yet to reach a crown density of 10 per cent or tree height of 5 m are included under forest, as are areas normally forming part of the forest area that are temporarily unstocked as a result of human intervention or natural causes but that are expected to revert to forest.

The *United Nations List of Protected Areas* [33] is the definitive list of the world's national parks and reserves. It is compiled by the UNEP World Conservation Monitoring Centre working in close collaboration with the World Conservation Union (IUCN) World Commission on Protected Areas. Information is provided by national protected areas authorities and the secretariats of international conventions and programmes.

Countries vary considerably in their mechanisms

Notes techniques, tableaux 65 à 69

Tableau 65: Les données relatives aux terres et à la superficie forestière sont compilées par l'Organisation des Nations Unies pour l'alimentation et l'agriculture (FAO). Les données relatives aux aires protégées viennent du Centre mondial de surveillance pour la conservation du Programme des Nations Unies pour l'environnement (PNUE).

Les définitions de la FAO en ce qui concerne les terres et la superficie forestière sont les suivantes:

Superficie totale des terres: Superficie totale, à l'exception des eaux intérieures. Les eaux intérieures désignent généralement les principaux fleuves et lacs.

Terres arables: Terres affectées aux cultures temporaires (les terres sur lesquelles est pratiquée la double culture ne sont comptabilisées qu'une fois), prairies temporaires à faucher ou à pâturer, jardins maraîchers ou potagers et terres en jachère temporaire (moins de cinq ans). Cette définition ne comprend pas les terres abandonnées du fait de la culture itinérante. Les données relatives aux terres arables ne peuvent être utilisées pour calculer la superficie des terres aptes à l'agriculture.

Cultures permanentes: Superficie des terres avec des cultures qui occupent la terre pour de longues périodes et qui ne nécessitent pas d'être replantées après chaque récolte, comme le cacao, le café et le caoutchouc. Cette catégorie comprend les terres plantées d'arbustes à fleurs, d'arbres fruitiers, d'arbres à noix et de vignes, mais ne comprend pas les terres plantées d'arbres destinés à la coupe.

Superficie forestière: Dans *l'Évaluation des ressources forestières mondiales 2000* [10], la FAO a défini les forêts comme suit : les forêts, qui comprennent les forêts naturelles et les plantations forestières, sont des terres où le couvert arboré (ou la densité de peuplement équivalente) est supérieur à 10 % et représente une superficie de plus de 0,5 ha. Les arbres doivent être susceptibles d'atteindre sur place, à leur maturité, une hauteur de 5 m minimum. Il peut s'agir de forêts denses, où les arbres de différente hauteur et le sous-bois couvrent une proportion importante du sol, ou de forêts claires, avec un couvert végétal continu, où le couvert arboré est supérieur à 10 %. Les jeunes peuplements naturels et toutes les plantations d'exploitation forestière n'ayant pas encore atteint une densité de couvert arboré de 10 % ou une hauteur de 5 m sont inclus dans les forêts, de même que les aires formant naturellement partie de la superficie forestière mais temporairement déboisées du fait d'une intervention de l'homme ou de causes naturelles, mais devant redevenir boisées.

La *Liste des Nations Unies des zones protégées* [33] est la liste la plus fiable des parcs et réserves natu-

for creating and maintaining systems of protected areas. In order to facilitate international comparisons for protected areas, IUCN has adopted a definition of a protected area which is, an area of land and/or sea especially dedicated to the protection and maintenance of biological diversity, and of natural and associated cultural resources, and managed through legal or other effective means.

IUCN has defined a series of six protected area management categories, based on primary management objectives. These categories are as follows:

Category Ia: Strict Nature Reserve;
Category Ib: Wilderness Area;
Category II: National Park;
Category III: Natural Monument;
Category IV: Habitat/Species Management Area;
Category V: Protected Landscape/Seascape;
Category VI: Managed Resource Protected Area.

Table 66: The sources of the data presented on the emissions of carbon dioxide (CO_2) are the Carbon Dioxide Information Analysis Center (CDIAC) of the Oak Ridge National Laboratory in the USA and the Secretariat of the United Nations Framework Convention on Climate Change (UNFCCC). The majority of the data have been taken from the CDIAC database. The data taken from the UNFCCC database are footnoted accordingly.

The CDIAC estimates of CO_2 emissions are derived primarily from United Nations energy statistics on the consumption of liquid and solid fuels and gas consumption and flaring, and from cement production estimates from the Bureau of Mines of the U.S. Department of Interior. The emissions presented in the table are in units of 1,000 metric tons of carbon dioxide (CO_2); to convert CO_2 into carbon, multiply the data by 0.272756. Full details of the procedures for calculating emissions are given in *Global, Regional, and National Annual CO_2 Emissions Estimates from Fossil Fuel Burning, Hydraulic Cement Production, and Gas Flaring* [3] and in the CDIAC Web site (see <http://cdiac.esd.ornl.gov>. Relative to other industrial sources for which CO_2 emissions are estimated, statistics on gas flaring activities are sparse and sporadic. In countries where gas flaring activities account for a considerable proportion of the total CO_2 emissions, the sporadic nature of gas flaring statistics may produce spurious or misleading trends in national CO_2 emissions over the period covered by the table.

The UNFCCC data in the table are indicated by a footnote, and cover the countries that joined the convention and those which voluntarily reported time-series data on their emissions to the UNFCCC. The CO_2 data from national reports to the Secretariat of the UNFCCC are based on the methodology of the Intergovernmental

rels du monde. Elle est établie par le Centre mondial de surveillance pour la conservation du PNUE, en collaboration étroite avec la Commission mondiale des aires protégées de l'Union mondiale pour la nature (UICN). Les renseignements sont communiqués par les services nationaux responsables des aires protégées et les secrétariats des conventions et programmes internationaux.

Les mécanismes nationaux de création et d'entretien des systèmes de zones protégées sont très différents d'un pays à l'autre. Pour faciliter les comparaisons internationales, l'UICN a adopté une définition des aires protégées, zone terrestre ou marine (ou les deux) spécialement consacrée à la protection et à la sauvegarde de la diversité biologique et des ressources naturelles, ainsi que des ressources culturelles qui y sont associées, dont la gestion est assurée par des moyens juridiques ou autres moyens efficaces.

L'UICN a défini une série de six catégories de gestion des aires protégées, en fonction des objectifs principaux:

Catégorie Ia:: Réserve naturelle intégrale;
Catégorie Ib: Zone vierge;
Catégorie II: Parc national;
Catégorie III: Monument naturel;
Catégorie IV: Aire de gestion des habitats/des espèces;
Catégorie V: Paysage terrestre/marin protégé;
Catégorie VI: Aire protégée de ressources naturelles.

Tableau 66: Les données sur les émissions de dioxyde de carbone (CO_2) proviennent du Carbon Dioxide Information Analysis Center (CDIAC) du Oak Ridge National Laboratory (États-Unis) et du Secrétariat de la convention-cadre concernant les changements climatiques (CCCC) des Nations Unies. La majorité des données proviennent de la base de données du CDIAC. Les données qui proviennent du Secrétariat de la CCCC sont signalées par une note.

Les estimations du Carbon Dioxide Information Analysis Center sont obtenues essentiellement à partir des statistiques de l'énergie des Nations Unies relatives à la consommation de combustibles liquides et solides, à la production et à la consommation de gaz de torche, et des chiffres de production de ciment du Bureau of Mines du Department of Interior des États-Unis. Les émissions sont indiquées en milliers de tonnes de dioxyde de carbone (à multiplier par 0,272756 pour avoir les chiffres de carbone). On peut voir dans le détail les méthodes utilisées pour calculer les émissions dans *Global, Regional, and National Annual CO_2 Emissions Estimates from Fossil Fuel Burning, Hydraulic Cement Production, and Gas Flaring* [3] et sur le site Web du Carbon Dioxide Information Analysis Center (voir <http://cdiac.esd.ornl.gov>. Par rapport à d'autres

Panel for Climate Change (IPCC) 1996 Guidebook.

Table 67: Chlorofluorocarbons (CFCs) are synthetic compounds formerly used as refrigerants and aerosol propellants and known to be harmful to the ozone layer of the atmosphere. In the Montreal Protocol on Substances that Deplete the Ozone Layer, CFCs to be measured are found in vehicle air conditioning units, domestic and commercial refrigeration and air conditioning/heat pump equipment, aerosol products, portable fire extinguishers, insulation boards, panels and pipe covers, and pre-polymers.

The Parties to the Montreal Protocol on Substances that Deplete the Ozone Layer report data on CFCs to the Ozone Secretariat of the United Nations Environment Programme. The data on CFCs are shown in ozone depleting potential (ODP) tons that are calculated by multiplying the quantities in metric tons reported by the Parties, by the ODP of that substance, and added together.

Consumption is defined as production plus imports, minus exports of controlled substances. Feedstocks are exempt and are therefore subtracted from the imports and/or production. Similarly, the destroyed amounts are also subtracted. Negative numbers can occur when destruction and/or exports exceed production plus imports, implying that the destruction and/or exports are from stockpiles.

Table 68: Data were extracted from the *Global water supply and sanitation assessment, 2000 Report*, [35] published by the WHO/UNICEF Joint Monitoring Programme for Water Supply and Sanitation. A review of water and sanitation coverage data from the 1980s and the first part of the 1990s showed that the definition of safe, or improved, water supply and sanitation facilities sometimes differed not only from one country to another, but also for a given country over time. Coverage data were based on estimates by service *providers*, rather than on the responses of *consumers* to household surveys, and these estimates can differ substantially. The Assessment 2000 marks a shift from gathering provider-based information only to include also consumer-based information.

Data were collected from two main sources: assessment questionnaires and household surveys. Assessment questionnaires were sent to all WHO country representatives, to be completed in liaison with local UNICEF staff and relevant national agencies involved in the sector. Household survey results and data obtained from Demographic Health Surveys (DHS) and Multiple Indicator Cluster Surveys (MICS) were collected and reviewed. The DHS and MICS are national cluster sample surveys, covering several thousand households in each country. They collect information on the main source of drinking water used, as well as the sanitation

sources industrielles pour lesquelles on calcule les émissions de CO_2, les statistiques sur la production de gaz de torche sont rares et sporadiques. Dans les pays où cette production représente une proportion considérable de l'ensemble des émissions de dioxyde de carbone, on peut voir apparaître de ce fait des chiffres parasites ou trompeurs pour ce qui est des tendances des émissions nationales de dioxyde de carbone durant la période visée par le tableau.

Les données provenant du secrétariat de la Convention-cadre, qui sont signalées par une note, couvrent les pays qui ont adhéré à la Convention et les pays qui ont bénévolement communiqué des séries chronologiques sur leurs émissions au secrétariat. Les données sur le CO_2 tirées des rapports de pays au secrétariat de la Convention-cadre ont été obtenues par les méthodes recommandées dans le Manuel de 1996 du Groupe intergouvernemental d'experts pour l'étude du changement climatique.

Tableau 67: Les chlorofluorocarbones (CFC) sont des substances de synthèse utilisées comme réfrigérants et propulseurs d'aérosols, dont on sait qu'elles appauvrissent la couche d'ozone. Aux termes du Protocole de Montréal relatif à des substances qui appauvrissent la couche d'ozone, la production de certains CFC doit être mesurée : ils sont utilisés dans les climatiseurs de véhicules, le matériel domestique et commercial de réfrigération et de climatisation (pompes à chaleur), les produits sous forme d'aérosols, les extincteurs d'incendie portables, les planches, panneaux et gaines isolants, et les prépolymères.

Les Parties au Protocole de Montréal communiquent leurs données concernant les CFC au secrétariat de l'ozone du Programme des Nations Unies pour l'environnement. Les données sur les CFC, indiquées en tonnes de potentiel d'appauvrissement de la couche d'ozone (PAO), sont calculées en multipliant le nombre de tonnes signalé par les Parties par le potentiel d'appauvrissement (coefficient) de la substance considérée, et en faisant la somme de ces PAO.

La consommation est définie comme production de substances contrôlées, plus les importations, moins les exportations. Les produits intermédiaires de l'industrie sont exemptés, et on les soustrait donc des importations et/ou de la production. De même, on soustrait aussi les quantités détruites. On peut obtenir des quantités négatives, lorsque les quantités détruites et/ou exportées sont supérieures à la somme production + importations, ce qui signifie que les quantités détruites ou exportées ont été prélevées sur les stocks accumulés.

Tableau 68: Les données proviennent du *Bilan mondial de l'approvisionnement en eau et de l'assainissement à l'horizon 2002*, [35] publié par

facility.

While the type of water source and the type of excreta disposal facility can be associated with the quality of water and the adequacy of disposal, respectively, they cannot adequately measure population coverage of *safe* water or of *sanitary* excreta disposal. Access to water and sanitation does not imply that the level of service or quality of water is "adequate" or "safe". The assessment questionnaire did not include any methodology for discounting coverage figures to allow for intermittence or poor quality of the water supplies. Hence, the coverage estimates presented represent the population covered by *improved* water sources and *improved* sanitary facilities.

Access to water supply and sanitation is defined in terms of the types of technology and levels of service afforded. For water, this included house connections, public standpipes, boreholes with handpumps, protected dug wells, protected springs and rainwater collection; allowance was also made for other locally-defined technologies. "Reasonable access" was broadly defined as the availability of at least 20 litres per person per day from a source within one kilometre of the user's dwelling. Sanitation was defined to include connection to a sewer or septic tank system, pour-flush latrine, simple pit or ventilated improved pit latrine, again with allowance for acceptable local technologies.

The Assessment 2000 did not provide a standard definition of urban or rural areas. The countries' own working definition of urban and rural was used. Similarly, when using household survey data, definitions predetermined by those responsible for the survey were accepted.

Estimates of percentage coverage for a region are based upon available data from the reporting countries in the region. When no data were available for countries in a region, estimates were extrapolated from countries in the region for which data were available. Such extrapolation, however, is used only to compute regional statistics: any country data reported in this assessment are based on reports for the country concerned.

Table 69: Data on the numbers of threatened species in each group of animals and plants are compiled by the World Conservation Union (IUCN)/Species Survival Commission (SSC) and published in the 2002 IUCN *Red List of Threatened Species*.

This list provides a catalogue of those species that are considered globally threatened. The categories used in the Red List are as follows: Extinct, Extinct in the Wild, Critically Endangered, Endangered, Vulnerable, Near Threatened and Data Deficient.

l'OMS et l'UNICEF (Programme commun de surveillance de l'eau et de l'assainissement). Lorsqu'on a examiné ce que couvraient les données sur l'eau et l'assainissement des années 80 et de la première moitié des années 90, on a constaté que la définition de l'approvisionnement en eau potable (ou améliorée) et des installations d'assainissement n'étaient pas la même non seulement d'un pays à un autre, mais dans un même pays, d'une période à une autre. Les données sur la couverture proviennent de chiffres communiqués par les *prestataires* de services, et non pas des réponses d'usagers à des enquêtes sur les ménages, qui peuvent donner des chiffres assez différents des premiers. Le Bilan à l'horizon 2000, pour la première fois, présente non seulement des chiffres provenant des prestataires, mais aussi des usagers.

Les données ont été collectées à deux sources principales : les réponses aux questionnaires envoyés pour le bilan, et les enquêtes sur les ménages. Les questionnaires ont été adressés à tous les représentants de pays de l'OMS, remplis en liaison avec les agents locaux de l'UNICEF et les organismes nationaux compétents et actifs dans ce secteur. On a réuni et utilisé les résultats d'enquêtes sur les ménages et les données tirées d'enquêtes sur la démographie et la santé et d'enquêtes en grappe à indicateurs multiples. Ces deux derniers types d'enquête sont des enquêtes réalisées par les pays sur un échantillon en grappe de plusieurs milliers de ménages dans chaque pays participant. Elles permettent de réunir des renseignements sur la principale provenance de l'eau utilisée pour l'alimentation, ainsi que sur les installations d'assainissement.

Si la provenance de l'eau utilisée de même que le type d'installation d'évacuation des excréments peuvent renseigner sur la qualité de l'eau et celle de l'évacuation, ils ne suffisent pas à mesurer la proportion de la population qui dispose d'eau *potable* ou d'un système d'évacuation *hygiénique*. L'accès à l'eau ou à l'assainissement ne signifie pas que le service ou la qualité de l'eau soient "suffisants" ou "salubres". On n'avait pas prévu pour le questionnaire du bilan de moyens permettant d'ajuster les chiffres de couverture si le service était intermittent ou l'eau de mauvaise qualité. Les chiffres de population couverte visent donc la population ayant accès à un approvisionnement en eau et à des installations d'assainissement *de qualité améliorée*.

L'accès à la distribution d'eau et à l'assainissement est défini par les types de technologie et le niveau de service accessibles. Pour l'eau, il s'agissait d'eau courante dans le logement, de bornes-fontaines, de points d'eau équipés de pompe à bras, de puits protégés, de sources protégées et de systèmes de captage des eaux pluviales; on a tenu compte aussi

d'autres méthodes de définition locale. Un "accès raisonnable" était défini en gros comme la possibilité de se procurer 20 litres d'eau par personne et par jour à moins d'un kilomètre du logement. L'assainissement était défini comme branchement à un égout ou à une fosse septique, à des latrines à chasse d'eau, à une fosse d'aisance ou à des latrines améliorées à fosse autoventilée, compte tenu là aussi de méthodes locales acceptables.

Le Bilan à l'horizon 2000 ne comportait pas de définition normalisée des zones urbaines ou rurales. On a utilisé la définition opérationnelle en usage dans le pays considéré. De même, on a accepté pour les données issues d'enquêtes sur les ménages les définitions choisies par les responsables de l'enquête.

Les chiffres de couverture (en pourcentage) pour une région donnée sont basés sur les données disponibles communiquées par les pays de la région. Lorsqu'il n'y avait pas de données pour des pays d'une région, on a extrapolé les chiffres disponibles des pays de la même région. Mais l'extrapolation n'a servi qu'à calculer des statistiques régionales: les données de pays figurant dans le bilan sont tirés de chiffres effectivement communiqués pour le pays en cause.

Tableau 69: Les données relatives aux espèces menacées pour chaque groupe d'animaux et de plantes, réunies par la Commission de la sauvegarde des espèces de l'Union mondiale pour la nature (UICN), sont publiées dans la *Liste rouge des espèces menacées 2002* de l'UICN.

Cette liste répertorie les espèces animales considérées comme menacées à l'échelle mondiale, réparties entre les catégories ci-après: éteintes, éteintes à l'état sauvage, gravement menacées d'extinction, menacées d'extinction, vulnérables, quasi menacées, et catégorie à données insuffisantes.

70

Researchers, technicians and equivalent staff, and other supporting staff engaged in research and development
Full-time equivalent (FTE)

Chercheurs, techniciens et personnel assimilé, et autre personnel de soutien employés à des travaux de recherche et de développement
Equivalent plein temps (EPT)

Country or area Pays ou zone	Year Année	Total	Researchers Chercheurs Total M & W Total H & F	Women Femmes	Technicians Techniciens Total M & W Total H & F	Women Femmes	Other supporting staff Autre personnel de soutien Total M & W Total H & F	Women Femmes
Argentina	1996	...	22 927	...	...	...	...	...
Argentine	1997	35 974	24 804	10 539	5 702	...	5 468	...
	1998	36 852	25 419	11 117	6 157	...	5 276	...
	1999	36 939	26 004	12 297	5 707	...	5 228	...
	2000	37 515	26 420	12 820	5 836	...	5 259	...
	2001	37 444	25 656	12 674	6 211	...	5 577	...
Armenia	1997[1]	7 716	5 492	2 509	653	321	1 571	...
Arménie	1999	6 523	4 856	...	903	...	764	...
	2000	...	4 971	...	846	...	529	...
Australia	1996	90 692	61 041	...	...	...	29 671[2]	...
Australie	1998	91 784	63 043	...	...	...	28 700[2]	...
	2000	95 254	65 805	...	...	...	...	...
Austria[3]								
Autriche[3]	1998	31 308	18 715	...	7 919	...	4 674	
Azerbaijan	1996	25 556	21 234	8 889	1 428	...	2 894	
Azerbaïdjan	1997	25 322	21 387	...	1 226	...	2 709	
Belarus	1996	38 030	23 324	...	2 758	...	8 816	...
Bélarus	1997	33 200	19 598	...	2 830	...	10 772	...
	1998	32 477	19 153	...	2 637	...	10 687	...
	1999	31 791	18 817	...	2 452	...	10 522	...
	2000	32 926	19 707	...	2 574	...	10 645	...
	2001	32 119	19 133	...	2 332	...	10 654	...
	2002	30 711	18 557	...	2 050	...	10 104	...
Belgium	1996	45 548	25 579	...	9 931	...	8 139	...
Belgique	1997	44 220	25 579	...	10 259	...	8 382	...
	1998	46 428	28 149	...	11 142	...	7 136	...
	1999	49 477	30 219	...	11 843	...	7 415	...
Bolivia	1998	820	590	...	200	...	30	...
Bolivie	1999	830	600	237	200	130	30	...
	2000	820	600	231	170	111	50	...
	2001	1 200	1 050	415	50	30	100	...
Brazil[4]								
Brésil[4]	2000	78 565	55 103	21 252[5]	21 914	...	1 548	...
Bulgaria	1996	26 158	14 751	6 114	8 169	5 462	3 238	...
Bulgarie	1997	18 625	11 980	5 431	4 550	3 166	2 095	...
	1998	19 116	11 972	5 321	4 862	3 295	2 282	...
	1999	16 087	10 580	4 656	3 829	2 578	1 678	...
	2000	15 259	9 479	4 354	3 833	2 441	1 947	...
Burkina Faso	1996	738	162	32	158	13	418	...
Burkina Faso	1997	780	176	34	165	16	439	...
Cameroon	1996	208	44	...	58	...	106	...
Cameroun	1997	204	44	...	56	...	104	...
	1998	198	43	...	55	...	100	...
	1999	196	43	...	53	...	100	...
Canada	1996	145 300	91 600	...	34 140	...	19 560	...
Canada	1997	146 190	93 440	...	33 660	...	19 090	...
	1998[6]	139 570	90 200	...	31 380	...	17 990	...
	1999	*140 440[6]	*90 810	...	31 570[6]	...	18 060[6]	...
Central African Rep.								
Rép. centrafricaine	1996	19 500	...	...	...	2 555	...	...

70

Researchers, technicians and equivalent staff, and other supporting staff engaged in research and development
Full-time equivalent (FTE) *[cont.]*

Chercheurs, techniciens et personnel assimilé, et autre personnel de soutien employés à des travaux de recherche et de développement

Equivalent plein temps (EPT) *[suite]*

Country or area Pays ou zone	Year Année	Total	Researchers Chercheurs		Technicians Techniciens		Other supporting staff Autre personnel de soutien	
			Total M & W Total H & F	Women Femmes	Total M & W Total H & F	Women Femmes	Total M & W Total H & F	Women Femmes
Chile	1996	12 976	5 158	...	5 478	...	...	...
Chili	*1997	13 409	5 278	...	...	...	...	...
	*1998	14 040	5 439	...	...	...	...	...
	*1999	14 957	5 549	...	...	...	...	...
	*2000	15 415	5 629	...	...	...	...	...
	2001	11 173	6 447	...	4 727	...	...	...
China	1996	787 000	559 000[8]	...	...	...	...	...
Chine	1997[3,7]	831 200	588 700	...	...	...	...	...
	1998[3,7]	755 200	485 500	...	...	...	...	...
	1999[3,7]	821 700	531 100	...	...	...	...	...
	2000[3,7]	922 131	695 062	...	...	...	...	...
	2001	956 500	742 700	...	...	...	...	...
China, Hong Kong SAR								
Chine, Hong Kong RAS	1998	5 809	...	...	...	...	...	...
China, Macao SAR [9]	1999	18	12	2	6	...	...	...
Chine, Macao RAS [9]	2000	28	18	2	10	2	...	...
Colombia	1996	4 436	3 277	1 151	1 159	1 268	...	...
Colombie	1997	4 978	3 534	1 246	1 444	1 404	...	...
	1998	5 504	3 816	1 369	1 688	1 485	...	...
	1999	5 925	4 065	1 507	1 860	1 536	...	...
	2000	6 262	4 240	1 599	2 022	1 602	...	...
Congo	1996	268	142	18	122	22	4	...
Congo	1997	265	142	18	119	21	3	...
	1998	242	120	15	118	22	3	...
	1999	227	110	15	114	22	2	...
	2000[10]	217	101	13	111	22	3	...
Costa Rica [4]								
Costa Rica [4]	1996	1 866	...	...	...	...	...	...
Croatia	1996	15 787	8 597	3 364	3 204	2 033	3 986	...
Croatie	1998	7 642	4 736	2 007	1 493	906	1 413	...
	1999	8 827	5 523	2 426	1 615	954	1 689	...
Cuba [4]	1996	62 684	5 151	...	18 806	...	38 727	...
Cuba [4]	1997	61 052	5 163	...	18 317	...	37 572	...
	1998	62 935	5 525	...	18 878	...	38 532	...
	1999	62 512	5 468	...	23 595	...	33 449	...
	2000	64 074	5 378	...	24 190	...	34 506	...
	2001	69 778	5 496	...	26 872	...	37 410	...
Cyprus	1998	564	237	69	168	60	159	...
Chypre	1999	681	278	81	198	71	205	...
	2000	680	303	91	195	68	181	...
Czech Republic	1996	23 501	12 963	...	7 026	...	3 512	...
République tchèque	1997	23 230	12 580	...	7 298	...	3 352	...
	1998	22 740	12 566	...	7 015	...	3 159	...
	1999	24 106	13 535	...	7 403	...	3 168	...
	2000	24 198	13 852	7 055	7 319	...	3 027	...
	2001	26 107	14 987	7 133[11]	...	...	...	...
Denmark	1996[6]	32 148	16 699	...	...	...	...	...
Danemark	1997	34 187	17 511	...	13 344	...	3 330	...
	1999	35 650	18 438	...	13 758	...	3 454	...
Ecuador	1996	3 695	983	238	1 322	...	1 390	...
Equateur	1997	2 735	932	245	885	...	918	...
	1998	2 907	1 014	319	874	...	1 019	...
El Salvador	1996	...	85	...	...	...	...	...
El Salvador	1997	...	85	...	...	...	...	...
	1998	...	193	...	...	...	...	...
	1999	...	199	...	...	...	...	...
	2000	...	293	...	...	...	...	...

70

Researchers, technicians and equivalent staff, and other supporting staff engaged in research and development
Full-time equivalent (FTE) *[cont.]*
Chercheurs, techniciens et personnel assimilé, et autre personnel de soutien employés à des travaux de recherche et de développement
Equivalent plein temps (EPT) *[suite]*

Country or area Pays ou zone	Year Année	Total	Researchers Chercheurs Total M & W Total H & F	Women Femmes	Technicians Techniciens Total M & W Total H & F	Women Femmes	Other supporting staff Autre personnel de soutien Total M & W Total H & F	Women Femmes
Estonia Estonie	1996	4 689[12]	3 047	1 252[12]	545[12]	390[12]	1 097[12]	...
	1997	4 605[12]	2 956	1 155[12]	573[12]	398[12]	1 076[12]	...
	1998[12]	4 713	3 045	1 239	782	547	886	...
	1999	4 545[13]	3 001[13]	1 251[12]	749[12]	538[12]	795[12]	...
	2000	3 710[13]	2 666[13]	1 109[12]	530[12]	368[12]	514[12]	...
Finland Finlande	1997	41 256	21 149	...	...	...	...	...
	1998	46 517	23 745	...	...	...	...	...
	1999	50 604	25 398	...	...	...	...	...
	2000	52 604	34 847	12 904[11]	...	...	...	...
	2001	53 424	36 889	...	...	...	...	...
France France	1996	320 805	154 827	...	...	...	...	...
	#1997	306 178	154 742	...	...	...	...	...
	1998	309 161	155 727	...	...	...	...	...
	1999	314 452	160 424	...	...	...	...	...
Georgia Géorgie	1996[14]	19 504	16 523	7 488	3 936[15]	...	2 981	...
	1997	17 762[14]	16 364[14]	7 565[14]	495	...	1 398[14]	...
	1998[14]	17 009	13 692	...	...	...	3 317	...
	1999[14]	15 138	12 786	...	...	...	2 353	...
Germany Allemagne	1996[6]	453 679	230 189	...	110 154	...	113 336	...
	1997	460 411	235 793	...	111 749	...	112 869	...
	1998[6]	461 539	237 712	...	111 065	...	112 763	...
	1999	480 415	255 260	...	110 364	...	114 415	...
	2000[6]	484 526	257 774	...	...	...	...	...
	2001[6]	487 378	259 597	...	...	...	...	...
Greece Grèce	1997	20 173	10 972	...	4 265	...	4 935	...
	1999	26 495	14 828	...	5 867	...	5 800	...
Honduras[4] Honduras[4]	2000	2 167	479	...	1 688	...	...	...
Hungary Hongrie	1996[16]	19 776	10 408	...	5 114	...	4 254	...
	1997[16]	20 758	11 154	...	5 205	...	4 399	...
	1998[16]	20 315	11 731	...	4 907	...	3 677	...
	1999[16]	21 329	12 579	...	5 037	...	3 713	...
	2000	23 534[16]	14 406[16]	9 537[11]	5 166[16]	...	3 962[16]	...
	2001	22 942[16]	14 666[16]	9 363[11]	...	...	...	...
Iceland Islande	1997	2 150	1 341	...	...	...	...	...
	1998[6]	2 273	1 414	...	...	...	...	...
	1999	2 390	1 578	...	...	...	...	...
	2001	2 901	1 859	1 122[11]	...	...	...	...
	2002[6]	2 797	...	...	...	...	...	...
India Inde	1996	357 172	149 326	11 078	108 817	9 121	99 029	...
Ireland[6] Irlande[6]	1996	10 838	6 801	...	2 106	...	1 931	...
	1997	12 030	7 825	...	2 157	...	2 048	...
	1998	11 613	7 720	...	...	...	...	...
	1999	12 289	8 217	...	...	...	...	...
Israel[4] Israël[4]	1996	12 267	7 620	...	3 558	...	789	...
	1997	13 110	9 161	...	3 023	...	926	...
Italy Italie	1996	142 288	76 441	...	46 794	...	19 053	...
	1997	141 737	76 056	...	46 379	...	19 302	...
	1998	145 969	65 354	...	...	...	...	...
	1999	142 506	64 886	...	...	...	...	...
Japan Japon	#1996	891 783	617 365	...	83 906	...	190 512	...
	1997	894 003	625 442	...	83 539	...	185 022	...
	1998	925 569	652 845	...	86 822	...	185 902	...
	1999	919 132	658 910	...	84 527	...	175 695	...
	2000	896 847	647 572	...	...	...	...	...
	2001	892 057	675 898	85 207[11]	...	...	...	...

70

Researchers, technicians and equivalent staff, and other supporting staff engaged in research and development
Full-time equivalent (FTE) *[cont.]*

Chercheurs, techniciens et personnel assimilé, et autre personnel de soutien employés à des travaux de recherche et de développement

Equivalent plein temps (EPT) *[suite]*

Country or area Pays ou zone	Year Année	Total	Researchers Chercheurs Total M & W Total H & F	Women Femmes	Technicians Techniciens Total M & W Total H & F	Women Femmes	Other supporting staff Autre personnel de soutien Total M & W Total H & F	Women Femmes
Jordan								
Jordanie	1998	23 946	9 090	1 629	3 345	737	11 511	...
Kazakhstan	1996	20 620	14 600	...	5 140	...	880	...
Kazakhstan	1997	18 980	11 720	...	4 800	...	2 500	...
Korea, Republic of [12]	1996	135 703	99 433	...	28 600	...	7 670	...
Corée, République de [12]	1997	136 559	102 660	...	26 385	...	7 514	...
	1998	128 669	92 541	...	24 444	...	11 684	...
	1999	137 874	100 210	...	26 160	...	11 504	...
	2000	138 077	108 370	16 385	...	...	...	...
	2001	165 715	136 337	19 930	...	...	...	...
Kuwait	1996	763	397	...	122	...	244	...
Koweït	1997	742	387	107	100	39	254	...
	1998	743	393	111	99	40	251	...
	1999	750	397	115	96	38	257	...
	2000	746	406	120	102	46	256	...
Kyrgyzstan	1996	4 126	2 629	...	256	...	1 241	...
Kirghizistan	1997	4 161	2 685	1 249	226	...	1 250	...
Latvia	1996	4 744	2 839	1 324	850	512	1 055	...
Lettonie	1997	4 437	2 610	1 197	872	470	955	...
	1998	4 437	2 557	1 201	777	422	1 103	...
	1999	4 301	2 626	1 277	726	419	949	...
Lithuania	1996	12 569	7 532	...	2 344	1 546	2 693	...
Lituanie	1997	12 171	7 800	...	2 204	...	2 167	...
	1998	12 847	8 436	...	2 104	...	2 307	...
	1999	12 794	8 539	...	1 983	...	2 272	...
	2000	11 791	7 777	3 388	1 774	1 156	2 240	...
	2001	11 949	8 075	3 766	1 725	1 215	2 149	...
Madagascar	1998	1 166	213	...	928	...	25	...
Madagascar	1999	1 114	227	...	862	...	25	...
	2000	985	240	...	730	...	15	...
Malaysia	1996	4 437	1 894	509	655	146	1 889	...
Malaisie	1998	6 656	3 415	935	966	201	2 274	...
	2000	10 060	6 422	...	...	...	...	...
Mexico	1996	33 920	19 895	...	14 025	...	...	...
Mexique	1997	36 880	21 418	...	15 462	...	...	...
	1998	40 520	22 190	...	18 330	...	...	...
	1999	39 736	21 879	...	17 857	...	...	...
Monaco [17]								
Monaco [17]	1998	48	22	...	15	...	11	...
Mongolia	1996	2 880	1 442	753	325	142	1 113	...
Mongolie	1997	2 496	1 380	743	198	76	918	...
	1998	2 623	1 518	823	204	77	907	...
	1999	2 141	1 114	557	219	96	808	...
	2000	2 531	1 344	746	294	150	893	...
Netherlands	#1996	80 789	34 482	...	...	...	...	...
Pays-Bas	1997	83 967	38 055	...	...	...	...	...
	1998	85 486	39 081	...	...	...	...	...
	1999	87 006	40 623	...	...	...	...	...
New Zealand								
Nouvelle-Zélande	1997	12 908	8 264	...	...	...	...	...
Nicaragua								
Nicaragua	1997	620	340	...	153	...	127	...
Norway	1997	24 877	17 490	...	...	...	...	...
Norvège	1999	25 400	18 295	...	...	...	...	...
	*2001	26 705	19 752	9 808[11]	...	...	...	...
Oman [18]	1999	9	8	...	1	...	...	...
Oman [18]	2000	10	9	...	1	...	...	...

70

Researchers, technicians and equivalent staff, and other supporting staff engaged in research and development
Full-time equivalent (FTE) *[cont.]*
Chercheurs, techniciens et personnel assimilé, et autre personnel de soutien employés à des travaux de recherche et de développement
Equivalent plein temps (EPT) *[suite]*

Country or area Pays ou zone	Year Année	Total	Researchers Chercheurs Total M & W Total H & F	Women Femmes	Technicians Techniciens Total M & W Total H & F	Women Femmes	Other supporting staff Autre personnel de soutien Total M & W Total H & F	Women Femmes
Pakistan Pakistan	1997	36 706	9 977	859	1 749	27	24 980	...
Panama Panama	1996	1 104	313	84	535	193	256	
	1997	1 214	327	68	595	161	292	...
	1998	1 614	461	144	733	269	420	...
	1999	1 750	350	...	687	...	713	...
	2000	1 400	286	113	678	...	436	...
	2001	1 332	276	97	618	260	438	...
Paraguay Paraguay	2001	2 026	481	241	669	408	877	
Peru Pérou	1996	5 785	5 522		220	...	...	
	1997	5 610	5 576	...	34	...	...	
Poland Pologne	1996	83 348	52 474	...	18 836	...	...	
	1997	83 803	55 602	...	17 895	...	12 038	
	1998	84 510	56 179	...	16 939	...	10 306	
	1999	82 368	56 433	...	15 362	...	11 392	
	2000	78 925	55 174	33 572[11]	13 648	...	10 573	
	2001	78 027	56 919	...	...	...	10 103	
Portugal Portugal	1997	18 035	13 642	...	4 393	...	...	
	1999	20 806	15 752	...	5 054	...	...	...
	2000[6]	21 767	16 667	...	...	...	...	...
	*2001	22 732	17 584	...	...	...	...	...
	*2002[6]	24 213	...	...	...	...	...	...
Republic of Moldova République de Moldova	1996	10 697	1 096	...	7 142	3 118	2 459	
	1997	10 667	1 442	...	7 181	325	2 044	...
	1998	9 978	...	...	...	...	...	...
	1999	8 957	...	...	...	...	...	...
	2000	8 173	...	...	...	...	...	...
Romania Roumanie	1996	59 907	30 303	...	13 857	...	15 747	
	1997	54 436	28 431	13 579	12 114	...	13 891	...
	1998	52 454	27 494	10 335	8 843	5 155	11 775	...
	1999	44 091	23 473	10 335	8 843	5 155	11 775	...
	2000	33 892	20 476	8 785	6 482	3 853	6 934	...
	2001	32 639	19 726	10 107	...	...	...	...
Russian Federation Fédération de Russie	1996	1 132 440	562 070	229 959	96 922	...	454 252	...
	1997	1 053 013	532 469	210 662	89 003	...	431 541	...
	1998	967 499	492 494	188 464	83 499	...	391 506	...
	1999	989 291	497 030	186 264	80 498	...	411 763	...
	2000	1 007 257	506 420	187 792	...	...	...	...
	2001	1 008 091	505 778	185 609	...	...	...	...
Saint Helena[19] Sainte-Hélène[19]	1998	29	3	1	26	11	...	...
	1999	40	4	1	38	13	...	...
	2000	33	2	...	8	4	23	...
Senegal[20] Sénégal[20]	1996	78	19	5	29	7	30	...
	1997	66	16	...	23	...	27	...
Serbia and Montenegro Serbie-et-Monténégro	1996	22 195	...	...	4 274	...	6 438	...
Singapore Singapour	1996	11 125	9 108	...	1 131	...	885	...
	1997	12 064	9 704	...	...	...	...	...
	1998	13 804	11 396	...	...	...	...	...
	1999	15 098	12 598	...	...	...	...	...
	2000	19 365	16 633	...	...	...	...	...
	2001	19 453	16 740	...	...	...	...	...

70

Researchers, technicians and equivalent staff, and other supporting staff engaged in research and development
Full-time equivalent (FTE) *[cont.]*

Chercheurs, techniciens et personnel assimilé, et autre personnel de soutien employés à des travaux de recherche et de développement

Equivalent plein temps (EPT) *[suite]*

Country or area Pays ou zone	Year Année	Total	Researchers Chercheurs Total M & W Total H & F	Women Femmes	Technicians Techniciens Total M & W Total H & F	Women Femmes	Other supporting staff Autre personnel de soutien Total M & W Total H & F	Women Femmes
Slovakia	1996[16]	16 613	10 010	7 164	4 244	3 601	2 359	...
Slovaquie	1997[16]	16 365	9 993	3 618	4 318	2 343	2 054	...
	1998[16]	16 461	10 145	3 778	4 331	2 478	1 985	...
	1999[16]	14 849	9 204	3 517	3 858	2 198	1 787	...
	2000[16]	15 221	9 955	3 867	3 597	1 979	1 669	...
	2001	14 422	9 585	...	...	...	...	...
Slovenia	1996[16]	8 882	4 489	1 486	2 048	961	2 345	...
Slovénie	1997[16]	7 985	4 022	1 331	1 723	730	2 240	...
	1998[16]	8 290	4 285	1 430	1 739	751	2 266	...
	1999	8 495[16]	4 427[16]	1 487[16]	1 783	758	2 285	...
	2000	9 568[16]	4 336[16]	1 525[16]	1 776	773	2 456	...
	2001[16]	8 608	4 498	2 383	...	...	...	...
South Africa * Afrique du Sud *	2001	33 897	8 661	...	...	...	...	...
Spain	1996[6]	87 263	51 633	...	35 631	...	...	...
Espagne	1997[6]	87 150	53 883	...	33 267	...	...	...
	1998[6]	97 098	60 269	...	36 828	...	...	...
	1999	102 237	61 568	...	40 670[6]	...	...	...
	2000[6]	120 618	76 670	...	...	...	...	...
	2001	125 750	80 081	49 664[11]	...	...	...	...
Sri Lanka Sri Lanka	1996	4 281	3 448	1 103	833	...	...	...
Sweden	1997	65 495	36 878	...	...	...	...	...
Suède	1999	66 674	39 921	...	...	...	...	...
	2001	72 190	45 995	...	...	...	...	...
Switzerland	1996	50 265	21 635	...	...	...	...	...
Suisse	2000	52 225	25 755	...	...	...	...	...
Syrian Arab Republic Rép. arabe syrienne	1997	804	440	...	364	...	...	...
Thailand	1996	10 209	6 038	5 846	2 303	2 129	1 868	...
Thaïlande	1997	14 022	4 409	5 455	4 446	7 318	5 167	...
Trinidad and Tobago	1997	515	185	80	330	129	515	...
Trinité-et-Tobago	2000[4]	1 732	590	228	1 142[15]	445[15]	...	...
Tunisia	1996	3 589	1 085	...	524	...	1 980	...
Tunisie	1997	3 680	1 145	...	524	...	2 011	...
	1998	5 105	2 848[21]	...	301	...	1 956	...
	1999	5 363	3 149[21]	...	292	...	1 922	...
	2000	5 708	...	...	303	...	1 943	...
Turkey[3]	1996	21 995	18 092	...	...	...	...	...
Turquie[3]	1997	23 432	18 908	...	...	...	...	...
	1998	22 892	18 925	...	...	...	...	...
	1999	24 267	20 065	...	...	...	...	...
Uganda	1996	890	386	149	285	27	219	...
Ouganda	1997	950	422	162	272	34	256	...
	1998	1 023	461	173	290	24	272	...
	1999	1 102	503	189	309	25	290	...
	2000	1 187	549	206	330	27	308	...
Ukraine	1996	240 709	147 732	...	36 524	...	56 453	...
Ukraine	1997	193 397	112 327	...	29 725	...	51 345	...
	1998	183 872	108 438	...	30 012	...	45 422	...
	1999	170 599	102 196	...	27 851	...	40 552	...
	2000	170 079	104 970	...	29 465	...	35 664	...
United Kingdom	1996	...	144 735	...	...	...	...	...
Royaume-Uni	1997	...	145 946	...	...	...	...	...
	1998	...	157 662	...	...	...	...	...
United States	1996	...	1 040 900	...	...	...	...	...
Etats-Unis	1997	...	1 114 100	...	...	...	...	...

70

Researchers, technicians and equivalent staff, and other supporting staff engaged in research and development
Full-time equivalent (FTE) *[cont.]*

Chercheurs, techniciens et personnel assimilé, et autre personnel de soutien employés à des travaux de recherche et de développement

Equivalent plein temps (EPT) [suite]

Country or area Pays ou zone	Year Année	Total	Researchers Chercheurs		Technicians Techniciens		Other supporting staff Autre personnel de soutien	
			Total M & W Total H & F	Women Femmes	Total M & W Total H & F	Women Femmes	Total M & W Total H & F	Women Femmes
Uruguay	1999	949	724	...	68	...	157	...
Uruguay	2000	1 166	922	401	175	64	69	...
Venezuela	1999	...	4 435	...	...	...	...	...
Venezuela	2000	...	4 688[22]	1 969	...	...	...	...
	2001	...	4 756	...	...	...	...	...

Source:
United Nations Educational, Scientific and Cultural Organization (UNESCO) Institute for Statistics, Montreal, the UNESCO Institute of Statistics database and the 1999 Statistical Yearbook.

Source:
L'Institut de statistique de l'Organisation des Nations Unies pour l'éducation, la science et la culture (UNESCO), Montréal, la base de données de l'Institut de statistique del'UNESCO et l'Annuaire Statistique 1999.

Countries covered by OECD: Australia, Austria, Belgium, Canada, Czech Republic, Denmark, Finland, France, Germany, Greece, Hungary, Iceland, Ireland, Italy, Japan, Korea, Mexico, Netherlands, New Zealand, Norway, Poland, Portugal, Slovakia, Spain, Sweden, Switzerland, Turkey, United Kingdom, United States. Non members: China, Israel, Romania, Russian Federation, Singapore, Slovenia.

Pays dont la source est OCDE: Allemagne, Australie, Autriche, Belgique, Canada, Corée, Danemark, Espagne, Etats-Unis, Fédération de Russie, Finlande, France, Grèce, Hongrie, Islande, Irlande, Italie, Japon, Mexique, Norvège, Nouvelle-Zélande, Pays-Bas, Pologne, Portugal, République tchèque, Royaume-Uni, Slovaquie, Suède, Suisse, Turquie. Non-membres: Chine, Israël, Roumanie, Singapour, Slovénie.

Countries covered by Red Ibero Americana de Indicadores de Ciencia y Tecnologia (RICYT): Argentina, Bermuda, Bolivia, Brazil, Chile, Colombia, Costa Rica, Cuba, Ecuador, El Salvador, Honduras, Nicaragua, Panama, Paraguay, Peru, Trinidad & Tobago, Uruguay, Venezuela.

Pays dont la source est Red IberoAmericana de Indicadores de Ciencia y Tecnologia (RICYT): Argentine, Bermudes, Bolivie, Brésil, Chili, Colombie, Costa Rica, Cuba, Ecuador, El Salvador, Honduras, Nicaragua, Panama, Paraguay, Pérou, Trinité-et-Tobago, Uruguay, Venezuela.

Countries covered by EUROSTAT: Bulgaria, Cyprus, Estonia, Lithuania.

Pays dont la source est EUROSTAT: Bulgarie, Chypre, Estonie, Lithuanie.

1	Excludes international organizations located in the country, military, and defence R&D.	1	A l'exclusion des organisations internationales présentes dans le pays, ainsi que de la recherche- développement dans les domaines militaire et de la defénse.
2	Includes other classes.	2	Comprend d'autres catégories.
3	Under-estimated or based on under-estimated data.	3	Sous-estimation ou chiffre établi sur la base de données sous-estimées.
4	Employed persons engaged in R&D (not full time equivalent).	4	Personnel affecté à la recherche-développement (ne correspond pas à un équivalent plein temps).
5	The number of female researchers is not available for the business enterprise sector.	5	Le nombre de femmes chercheurs n'est pas disponible pour le secteur des entreprises industrielles.
6	National estimate or projection adjusted by OECD.	6	Estimation nationale ou projection corrigée par l'OCDE.
7	The sum of the breakdown does not add to the total.	7	La somme de toutes les valeurs diffère du total.
8	Scientists and engineers.	8	Scientists et ingénieurs.
9	Includes only three faculties' R&D projects from the University of Macao: Faculty of Science and Technology (FST), Faculty of Business Administration (GFBA), Faculty of Social Science and Humanity (FSH).	9	Ne comprend que les projets de recherche-développement de trois facultés de l'Université de Macao, à savoir la faculté de sciences et technologies, la faculté de hautes études commerciales et la faculté de sciences sociales et humanités.
10	Data relate to persons employed in government institutions only.	10	Les données se réfèrent exclusivement au personnel des institutions gouvernementales.
11	Head count.	11	Comptage.
12	Excluding R&D in the social sciences and humanities.	12	À l'exclusion de la recherche-développement en sciences sociales et humanités.
13	Excluding the business enterprise sector.	13	Non compris les secteurs des entreprises.
14	Includes part-time.	14	Y compris à temps partiel.
15	Auxiliary personnel and technicians are counted together.	15	Le personnel de soutien y les techniciens sont compté ensembles.
16	Defence excluded (all or mostly).	16	A l'exclusion de la défense (en totalité ou en grande partie).
17	Personnel in public or parapublic sector only.	17	Personnel du secteur public ou parapublic seulement.
18	Data refer only to the animal production center (Ministry of Agriculture and Fisheries).	18	Les données concernent uniquement le centre de la production animale (Ministère de l'agriculture et de la pêche).

70
Researchers, technicians and equivalent staff, and other supporting staff engaged in research and development
Full-time equivalent (FTE) *[cont.]*
Chercheurs, techniciens et personnel assimilé, et autre personnel de soutien employés à des travaux de recherche et de développement
Equivalent plein temps (EPT) *[suite]*

19 Includes only private research into class teacher attrition, and these sectors: tourism, electricity, gas and water supply, agriculture.

20 Data relate to one research institute only.
21 Secondary or higher education teachers who reserve 35% of their time for research and development activities.

22 Number of researchers who applied to the research program (expressed in number of persons).

19 Données provenant exclusivement d'études privées portant sur la réduction naturelle des effectifs du corps enseignant et sur les secteurs suivants : tourisme, électricité, alimentation en gaz et en eau, agriculture.

20 Les données ne concernent qu'un institut de recherche seulement.
21 Sont comptabilisés comme chercheurs, les enseignants de l'enseignement supérieur qui réservent 35% de leur activités pour les recherche et développement.

22 Nombre de chercheurs ayant demandé à suivre le programme de recherche (en nombre de personnes).

71

Gross domestic expenditure on R & D by source of funds
National currency

Dépenses intérieures brutes de recherche et développement par source de fonds
Monnaie nationale

Country or area (Monetary unit) Pays ou zone Unité monétaire) γ	Year Année	Gross domestic expenditure on R&D Dépenses int. brutes de R-D (thousands)	Source of funds (%) / Source de fonds (%)					
			Business enterprises Enterprises	Gov't Etat	Higher education Enseigne-ment supérieur	Private non-profit Institut. privées sans but lucratif	Funds from abroad Fonds de l'étranger	Not dis-tributed Non répartis
Argentina (Argentine peso)	2000	1 247 200	23.4	41.9	30.8	1.9	1.8	...
Argentine (peso argentin)	2001	1 140 900	21.9	46.4	28.8	1.7	1.2	...
Australia (Australian dollar)	1998	8 936 400	45.7	47.1	4.7	...	2.5	...
Australie (dollar australien)	2000	10 251 400	45.9	46.1	4.7	...	3.3	...
Austria (euro)	2001	*4 030 900[1]	39.4	41.3	0.3	...	18.9	...
Autriche (euro)	2002	*4 217 300[1]	39.0	42.1	0.3	...	18.6	...
Belarus (Belarussian rouble)	2001	121 700 000	...	...	...	...	...	...
Bélarus (rouble bélarussien)	2002	162 300 000	...	...	...	...	...	...
Belgium (euro)	1998	4 276 800	65.7	23.5	3.2	...	7.7	...
Belgique (euro)	1999	4 618 100	66.2	23.2	3.3	...	7.3	...
Bermuda (Bermuda dollar) Bermudes (dollar des Bermudes)	1997	1 726						
Bolivia (boliviano)	2000	149 000	21.9	21.9	31.9	15.0	9.0	...
Bolivie (boliviano)	2001	180 000	11.0	19.0	48.0	15.0	7.0	...
Brazil (real)	1999	8 395 900	...	...	...	...	...	...
Brésil (real)	2000	11 455 200	38.2	60.2	1.6	...	...	...
Bulgaria (lev)	1999	134 449[2]	22.8	69.7	3.2	0.2	4.1	...
Bulgarie (lev)	2000	139 927	24.4	69.2	0.9	0.3	5.3	...
Burkina Faso (CFA franc)	1996	2 095 056	...	...	...	...	...	...
Burkina Faso (franc CFA)	1997	2 586 462	...	...	...	...	...	...
Burundi (Burundi franc) [3,4] Burundi (franc burundais) [3,4]	1989	536 187	...	39.4	...	...	60.6	...
Canada (Canadian dollar)	2001	*20 828 000[1]	41.9	31.3	9.0	...	17.8	...
Canada (dollar canadien)	2002	*20 745 000[1]	40.0	33.2	9.9	...	16.9	...
Chile (Chilean peso)	2000	213 076 965	23.0	70.3	...	1.9	4.7	...
Chili (peso chilien)	2001	228 800 000	24.9	68.8	...	2.1	4.1	...
China (yuan)	2000	#89 566 500	57.6	33.4	...	...	2.7	6.3
Chine (yuan)	2001	104 248 000	...	...	...	...	...	...
China, Hong Kong SAR (HK dollar) Chine, Hong Kong RAS (dollar HK)	1995	2 742 000[5]	2.8	91.0	5.7	...	0.5	...
Colombia (Colombian peso)	2000	306 385 210	48.4	16.6	33.6	1.4	...	...
Colombie (peso colombien)	2001	313 720 990	46.9	13.2	38.3	1.7	...	...
Congo (CFA franc) Congo (franc CFA)	1984	25 530	25.5	68.8	...	...	5.7	...
Costa Rica (Costa Rican colón)	1997	6 395 015	...	...	...	...	...	...
Costa Rica (colón costa-ricien)	1998	7 252 308	...	...	...	...	...	...
Croatia (kuna)	1997[6]	484 897	...	...	...	...	...	...
Croatie (kuna)	1999	1 397 761	53.3	42.6	...	...	0.8	3.3
Cuba (Cuban peso)	2000	146 300	40.1	53.1	...	...	6.8	...
Cuba (peso cubain)	2001	179 100	36.2	57.6	...	...	6.2	...
Cyprus (Cyprus pound)	1999	12 417	17.4	68.5	1.8	4.6	7.7	...
Chypre (livre chypriote)	2000	14 070	17.5	66.5	1.9	4.6	9.4	...
Czech Republic (Czech koruna)	2000	26 487 200	51.2	44.5	0.5	0.7	3.1	...
République tchèque (couronne tchèque)	2001	28 337 000	52.5	43.6	1.7	...	2.2	...
Denmark (Danish krone)	1998[1]	23 793 100	...	...	...	...	...	...
Danemark (couronne danoise)	1999	26 415 100	59.0	31.2	3.3	...	5.4	1.1
Ecuador (U.S. dollar)	1997	15 840	...	...	...	...	...	...
Equateur (dollar E.-U.)	1998	15 000	...	...	...	...	...	...
Egypt (Egyptian pound)	1999[7]	573 700	...	...	...	...	...	...
Egypte (livre égyptienne)	2000	654 600	...	...	...	...	...	...
El Salvador (El Salvadoran colón)	1992[8]	1 083 559	...	47.4	...	...	52.6	...
El Salvador (cólon salvadorien)	2001	9 650	1.2	51.9	13.2	10.4	23.4	...

71

Gross domestic expenditure on R & D by source of funds
National currency [cont.]

Dépenses intérieures brutes de recherche et développement par source de fonds
Monnaie nationale [suite]

Country or area (Monetary unit) Pays ou zone Unité monétaire)	Year Année	Gross domestic expenditure on R&D Dépenses int. brutes de R-D (thousands)	Source of funds (%) / Source de fonds (%)					
			Business enterprises Enterprises	Gov't Etat	Higher education Enseigne- ment supérieur	Private non-profit Institut. privées sans but lucratif	Funds from abroad Fonds de l'étranger	Not dis- tributed Non répartis
Estonia (Estonian kroon)	1999	573 000	24.3	64.6	0.7	1.6	8.9	...
Estonie (couronne estonienne)	2000	579 400	24.2	59.2	1.8	2.2	12.7	...
Fiji (Fiji dollar) [9]								
Fidji (dollar des Fidji) [9]	1986	3 800	...	73.7	...	...	26.3	...
Finland (euro)	2000	4 422 600	70.3	26.2	0.9	...	2.7	...
Finlande (euro)	2001	4 619 000	70.8	25.5	1.2	...	2.5	...
France (euro)	2000	#30 953 600	52.5	38.7	1.6	...	7.2	...
France (euro)	*2001	32 227 400	...	...	...	...	...	...
Georgia (lari) [7]	1998	16 200	...	...	...	...	...	...
Géorgie (lari) [7]	1999	18 600	...	...	...	...	...	...
Germany (euro)	2001	51 538 900 [1]	66.0	31.5	0.4	...	2.1	...
Allemagne (euro)	2002 [1]	52 762 500	...	...	...	...	...	...
Greece (euro) [10]	1997	492 200	21.6	54.2	1.6	...	22.6	...
Grèce (euro) [10]	1999	760 400	24.2	48.7	2.5	...	24.7	...
Guam (US dollar) [5,11]	*1989	1 926	...	88.6	11.4	...	...	...
Guam (dollar des Etats-Unis) [5,11]	1991	2 215	...	87.7	12.3	...	...	...
Guatemala (quetzal)								
Guatemala (quetzal)	1988	31 859 [12]	0.5	36.7	45.7	...	17.0 [13]	...
Honduras (lempira)								
Honduras (lempira)	2000	47 485	...	...	...	...	...	...
Hungary (forint)	2000	105 387 600 [14]	37.8	49.5	0.3	...	10.6	1.8
Hongrie (forint)	2001	140 605 200 [14]	34.8	53.6	0.4	...	9.2	1.9
Iceland (Icelandic króna)	2001	22 783 800 [1]	46.2	34.0	1.6	...	18.3	...
Islande (couronne islandaise)	2002 [1]	24 097 000	...	...	...	...	...	...
India (Indian rupee)	2000	150 902 200	...	...	...	...	...	...
Inde (roupie indienne)	2001	176 602 100	...	...	...	...	...	...
Indonesia (Indonesian rupiah)	1986 [15,16]	241 750 000	...	100.0	...	...	...	...
Indonésie (roupie indonésien)	1994	244 843 000 [17]	76.4	15.8	0.5	...	7.2	...
Iran (Islamic Rep. of) (Iranian rial)	1985 [16]	22 010 713	...	100.0	...	...	...	...
Iran (Rép. islamique d') (rial iranien)	1994	620 849 320	...	86.8	13.2	...	...	...
Ireland (euro)	2000	1 183 300	66.0	22.6	2.6	...	8.9	...
Irlande (euro)	2001 [1]	1 338 700	...	...	...	...	...	...
Israel (new sheqel) [14]	2000	21 990 100	...	...	...	...	...	...
Israël (nouveau sheqel) [14]	2001	22 611 100	...	...	...	...	...	...
Italy (euro)	1999	11 524 100	...	...	...	...	...	...
Italie (euro)	2000	12 460 400	...	...	...	...	...	...
Jamaica (Jamaican dollar)								
Jamaïque (dollar jamaïcain)	1986	4 016 [18]	...	100.0	...	...	...	...
Japan (yen)	2000	15 304 423 000	72.4	19.6	7.6	...	0.4	...
Japon (yen)	2001	15 542 822 000	73.0	18.5	8.1	...	0.4	...
Kazakhstan (tenge)								
Kazakhstan (tenge)	1997	4 905 638	1.1	44.1	...	6.2	0.7	54.2
Korea, Republic of (Korean won)	2000	13 848 501 000 [19]	72.4	23.9	3.6	...	0.1	...
Corée, République de (won coréen)	2001	16 110 522 000 [19]	72.5	25.0	2.1	...	0.5	...
Kuwait (Kuwaiti dinar)								
Koweït (dinar koweïtien)	1984	71 163 [20]	64.3	34.3	1.4	...	...	...
Kyrgyzstan (Kyrgyz som)	1995	46 309	29.4	67.3	1.8	...	1.5 [13]	...
Kirghizistan (som kirghize)	1997	59 466	24.8	63.3	3.5	...	8.5	...
Latvia (lats)	1997	13 893	14.1	59.0	...	...	26.9	...
Lettonie (lats)	1999	15 512	15.7	55.6	...	7.1	21.6	...
Lithuania (litas)	1999	220 340 000	...	...	...	...	...	...
Lituanie (litas)	2000	269 930 000	...	...	...	...	...	...
Madagascar (Malagasy franc)	1999	22 425 000	...	...	...	...	...	...
Madagascar (franc malgache)	2000	31 428 000	...	...	...	...	...	...

71

Gross domestic expenditure on R & D by source of funds
National currency [cont.]
Dépenses intérieures brutes de recherche et développement par source de fonds
Monnaie nationale [suite]

Country or area (Monetary unit) Pays ou zone Unité monétaire)	Year Année	Gross domestic expenditure on R&D Dépenses int. brutes de R-D (thousands)	Source of funds (%) / Source de fonds (%)					
			Business enterprises Enterprises	Gov't Etat	Higher education Enseigne-ment supérieur	Private non-profit Institut. privées sans but lucratif	Funds from abroad Fonds de l'étranger	Not dis-tributed Non répartis
Malaysia (ringgit)	1998	1 127 010	...	...	...	...	...	...
Malaisie (ringgit)	2000	1 671 500	...	...	...	...	...	...
Mauritius (Mauritian rupee)	1989[11]	54 300	2.4	35.0	62.6			...
Maurice (roupie mauricienne)	1997	246 000	...	94.7	...	...	5.3	...
Mexico (Mexican peso)	1998	14 524 600	23.6	60.8	8.1	...	7.5	...
Mexique (peso mexicain)	1999	19 746 100	23.6	61.3	9.8	...	5.3	...
Monaco (French franc) Monaco (franc français)	1998	132 671[21]	85.8	14.2				
Netherlands (euro)	1999	7 563 609	49.7	35.8	3.4	...	11.2	...
Pays-Bas (euro)	2000	*7 812 800	50.1	35.9	2.6	...	11.4	
New Zealand (New Zealand dollar)	1997	1 107 355	30.5	52.3	12.0	...	5.2	
Nouvelle-Zélande (dollar néo-zélandais)	1999	1 091 400	34.1	50.6	11.0	...	4.3	
Nicaragua (córdoba)	*1987	988 970[11]	...	80.8	...	...	19.2	
Nicaragua (córdoba)	1997	27 000	...	...	...	...	...	
Nigeria (naira)[16] Nigéria (naira)[16]	1987	86 270	...	100.0				
Norway (Norwegian krone)	1999	20 318 700	49.5	42.6	1.6	...	6.4	
Norvège (couronne norvégienne)	2001	*24 443 700	51.7	39.8	1.4	...	7.1	
Pakistan (Pakistan rupee)	1984	3 834 287[16,22]	...	100.0		...		
Pakistan (roupie pakistanaise)	1987	5 582 081[16,22]	...	100.0	...	...	...	
Panama (balboa)	2000	44 647	0.5	34.3	0.4	0.6	64.1	
Panama (balboa)	2001	45 100	10.2	32.8	0.6	1.2	55.1	
Paraguay (guaraní) Paraguay (guaraní)	2001	23 367 270	3.9	51.1	4.0	0.8	40.1	
Peru (new sol)	2000	203 450	...	...	...	...	...	...
Pérou (nouveau sol)	2001	202 540	...	...	...	...	...	
Philippines (Philippine peso)	1984	614 080	23.6	60.8	2.4	...	13.0	0.1
Philippines (peso philippin)	*1992	2 940 549	1.9	3.2	70.2	...	24.7[13]	...
Poland (new zloty)	2000	4 796 100	32.6	63.4	2.1	0.4	1.8	...
Pologne (nouveau zloty)	2001	4 858 100	30.8	64.8	2.0	...	2.4	
Portugal (euro)	2001	1 014 700	32.4	61.2	2.1	...	4.4	
Portugal (euro)	2002	993 100	...	...	...	...	...	
Qatar (Qatar riyal) Qatar (riyal qatarien)	1986	6 650	...	100.0				
Republic of Moldova (Moldovan leu)	1999	78 900	...	...	...	...	...	...
République de Moldova (leu moldove)	2000	99 400	...	...	...	...	...	
Romania (Romanian leu)	2000	2 962 046 000	49.0	40.8	5.4	0.1	4.9	
Roumanie (leu roumain)	2001	4 593 429 000	47.6	43.0	1.2		8.2	...
Russian Federation (ruble)	2000	76 697 100	32.9	54.8	0.4	...	12.0	
Fédération de Russie (ruble)	2001	105 260 700	33.6	57.2	0.5	...	8.6	...
Rwanda (Rwanda franc) Rwanda (franc rwandais)	1984	260 750	...	72.5			17.8	9.7
Saint Helena (pound sterling)	1999	40 390	...	...	...	...	...	...
Sainte-Hélène (livre sterling)	2000	151 774	...	42.6	...	...	...	57.4
Senegal (CFA franc)	1996	410 160	...	...	...	...	...	
Sénégal (franc CFA)	1997	314 000	...	...	...	...	...	
Serbia and Montenegro (dinar) Serbie-et-Monténégro (dinar)	1995	424 831[11]	28.2	54.1	16.8	...	0.8	
Seychelles (Seychelles rupee)	1983	12 854	...	48.8	...	...	51.2	
Seychelles (roupie seychelloises)	1991[16]	4 593	...	100.0	...			...
Singapore (Singapore dollar)	2000	3 009 500	55.0	40.3	0.7	...	4.0	...
Singapour (dollar singapourien)	2001	3 232 700	54.2	38.1	1.0	...	6.6	
Slovakia (Slovak koruna)	2000	6 086 000[23]	54.4	42.6	0.7	...	2.3	...
Slovaquie (couronne slovaque)	2001	6 467 000[23]	56.1	41.3	0.8	...	1.9	...

71
Gross domestic expenditure on R & D by source of funds
National currency [cont.]
Dépenses intérieures brutes de recherche et développement par source de fonds
Monnaie nationale [suite]

Country or area (Monetary unit) Pays ou zone Unité monétaire)	Year Année	Gross domestic expenditure on R&D Dépenses int. brutes de R-D (thousands)	Source of funds (%) / Source de fonds (%)					
			Business enterprises Enterprises	Gov't Etat	Higher education Enseignement supérieur	Private non-profit Institut. privées sans but lucratif	Funds from abroad Fonds de l'étranger	Not distributed Non répartis
Slovenia (tolar)	2000	61 436 000	53.3	40.0	0.4	...	6.2	...
Slovénie (tolar)	2001	74 379 300	54.7	37.1	1.1	...	7.2	...
South Africa (rand)	1993	2 594 107	54.4	42.7	1.8	...	1.0[13]	...
Afrique du Sud (rand)	2001	7 499 600	...	...	...	...	...	...
Spain (euro)	2000	5 719 000[1]	49.7	38.6	6.8	...	4.9	...
Espagne (euro)	2001	6 227 200[1]	47.2	39.9	5.3	...	7.7	...
Sri Lanka (Sri Lanka rupee)	1984	256 799	...	83.7	...	...	16.3	...
Sri Lanka (roupie sri-lankaise)	1996	1 410 000	...	...	...	...	...	...
Sweden (Swedish krona)	1999	75 813 500[23]	67.8	24.5	4.2	...	3.5	...
Suède (couronne suédoise)	2001	96 794 600[23]	71.9	21.0	3.8	...	3.4	...
Switzerland (Swiss franc)	1996	9 990 000	67.5	26.9	2.5	...	3.1	...
Suisse (franc suisse)	2000	10 675 000	69.1	23.2	3.4	...	4.3	...
Syrian Arab Republic (Syrian pound) Rép. arabe syrienne (livre syrienne)	1997	1 368 000	...	...	100.0	...	...	...
Thailand (baht)	1996	5 528 134	18.4	61.1	6.8	8.7	5.0	...
Thaïlande (baht)	1997	4 811 234	...	...	...	...	...	...
TFYR of Macedonia (denar) L'ex-R.y. Macédoine (denar)	1995	876 244[11]	48.4	41.9	7.5	...	2.2[13]	...
Togo (CFA franc)[24] Togo (franc CFA)[24]	1995	52 737 405	...	...	...	...	100.0	...
Trinidad and Tobago (dollar)	1996	45 600	34.0	50.2	15.8	...	...	...
Trinité-et-Tobago (dollar)	1997	49 200	34.5	48.2	17.3	...	...	...
Tunisia (Tunisian dinar)	1999	108 249	...	...	...	...	...	...
Tunisie (dinar tunisien)	2000	120 402	7.0	45.1	44.9	...	3.0	...
Turkey (Turkish lira)	1999	489 163 000 000	43.3	47.7	4.2	...	4.8	...
Turquie (livre turque)	2000	798 438 000 000	42.9	50.6	5.3	...	1.2	...
Uganda (Uganda shilling)	1996	34 866 530	2.2	6.6	0.6	0.3	90.3	...
Ouganda (shilling ougandais)	1999	65 740 280	2.2	6.6	0.6	0.3	90.3	...
Ukraine (hryvnia)	1997	1 113 188	...	...	...	...	...	...
Ukraine (hryvnia)	2000	1 636 362	31.4	39.3	0.1	...	29.2	...
United Kingdom (pound sterling)	2000	17 543 800	49.3	28.9	5.5	...	16.3	...
Royaume-Uni (livre sterling)	2001	18 815 300	46.2	30.1	5.7	...	18.0	...
United States (US dollar)	2001	282 292 700	68.3	26.9	4.8	...	...	...
Etats-Unis (dollar des Etats-Unis)	2002	*292 170 300[25]	66.2	28.7	5.1	...	...	...
Uruguay (Uruguayan peso)	1999	609 655	35.6	9.4	47.1	...	7.9	...
Uruguay (peso uruguayen)	2000	577 860	39.3	20.2	35.7	...	4.8	...
Venezuela (bolívar)	2000	275 279 510	...	...	...	...	...	...
Venezuela (bolívar)	2001	399 900 000	...	...	...	...	...	...
Viet Nam (dong)[16]	1984	516 000	...	100.0	...	...	...	...
Viet Nam (dong)[16]	1985	498 000	...	100.0	...	...	...	...
Zambia (Zambia kwacha)	1996	479 570	...	100.0	...	...	...	...
Zambie (kwacha zambie)	1997	417 000	...	...	...	...	...	...

Source:
United Nations Educational, Scientific and Cultural Organization (UNESCO) Institute for Statistics, Montreal, the UNESCO Institute of Statistics database and the 1999 Statistical Yearbook.

Countries covered by OECD: Australia, Austria, Belgium, Canada, Czech Republic, Denmark, Finland, France, Germany, Greece, Hungary, Iceland, Ireland, Italy, Japan, Korea, Mexico, Netherlands,

Source:
L'Institut de statistique de l'Organisation des Nations Unies pour l'éducation, la science et la culture (UNESCO), Montréal, la base de données de l'Institut de statistique de l'UNESCO et l'Annuaire statistique 1999.

Pays dont la source est OCDE: Allemagne, Australie, Autriche, Belgique, Canada, Corée, Danemark, Espagne, Etats-Unis, Fédération de Russie, Finlande, France, Grèce, Hongrie, Islande,

71

Gross domestic expenditure on R & D by source of funds
National currency *[cont.]*
Dépenses intérieures brutes de recherche et développement par source de fonds
Monnaie nationale *[suite]*

New Zealand, Norway, Poland, Portugal, Slovakia, Spain, Sweden, Switzerland, Turkey, United Kingdom, United States. Non members: China, Israel, Romania, Russian Federation, Singapore, Slovenia.

Irlande, Italie, Japon, Mexique, Norvège, Nouvelle-Zélande, Pays-Bas, Pologne, Portugal, République tchèque, Royaume-Uni, Slovaquie, Suède, Suisse, Turquie. Non-membres: Chine, Israël, Roumanie, Singapour, Slovénie.

Countries covered by Red Ibero Americana de Indicadores de Ciencia y Tecnologia (RICYT): Argentina, Bermuda, Bolivia, Brazil, Chile, Colombia, Costa Rica, Cuba, Ecuador, El Salvador, Honduras, Nicaragua, Panama, Paraguay, Peru, Trinidad & Tobago, Uruguay, Venezuela.

Pays dont la source est Red IberoAmericana de Indicadores de Ciencia y Tecnologia (RICYT): Argentine, Bermudes, Bolivie, Brésil, Chili, Colombie, Costa Rica, Cuba, Ecuador, El Salvador, Honduras, Nicaragua, Panama, Paraguay, Pérou, Trinité-et-Tobago, Uruguay, Venezuela.

Countries covered by EUROSTAT: Bulgaria, Cyprus, Estonia, Lithuania.

Pays dont la source est EUROSTAT: Bulgarie, Chypre, Estonie, Lithuanie.

1	National estimate or projection adjusted by OECD.	1
2	Denomination change in 1999.	2
3	Excluding data for the productive sector.	3
4	Excluding labour costs at the Ministry of Public Health.	4
5	Data refer to the higher education sector only.	5

1   National estimate or projection adjusted by OECD.
2   Denomination change in 1999.
3   Excluding data for the productive sector.
4   Excluding labour costs at the Ministry of Public Health.
5   Data refer to the higher education sector only.

6   Part of the total revenue data which could be defined as "revenue for R&D purposes"; detailed specifications of sources are not available.
7   General budget (government only)
8   Data refer to R&D activites performed in public enterprises.

9   Data relate to one research institute only.
10   National currency data are expressed in euros. Data have been converted from the former national currency using the appropriate irrevocable conversion rate (Greece: 1 EUR = 340.750 GRD). Please note, however, that the pre-EMU euro is a notional unit and should not be used to form area aggregates or to carry out cross-country comparisons.

11   Data refer to current expenditure only.
12   Excluding data for the productive sector (non-integrated R&D) and the general service sector.
13   Including private non-profit funds.
14   Defence excluded (all or mostly).
15   Data refer to the general service sector only.
16   Data refer to government funds only.
17   Data refer to the productive sector only.
18   Data relate to the Scientific Research Council only.
19   Excluding R&D in the social sciences and humanities.

20   Data refer to scientific and technological activities (STA).

21   Partial estimate.
22   Data refer to R&D activities which are concentrated mainly in government-financed research establishments. Social sciences and humanities in the higher education and general service sectors are not included.
23   Under-estimated or based on under-estimated data.

24   Data refer to funds from abroad only.
25   Excludes most or all capital expenditure.

1   Estimation nationale ou projection corrigée par l'OCDE.
2   Changement de dénomination en 1999.
3   Non compris les données du secteur de la production.
4   Non compris les coûts salariaux du Ministère de la Santé Publique.
5   Les données se réfèrent au secteur de l'enseignement supérieur seulement.

6   Partie des recettes totales considérées comme étant destinées à la recherche-développement; les sources précises ne sont pas connues.
7   Budget général (état seulement).
8   Les données se réfèrent aux activités de R-D dans les entreprises publiques.
9   Les données ne concernent qu'un institut de recherche seulement.
10   Les données en monnaie nationale sont exprimées en euros. Les données ont été converties à partir de l'ancienne monnaie nationale et du taux de conversion irrévocable approprié (Grèce 1 EUR = 340.750 GRD). L'euro avant l'entrée dans l'UEM est une unité fictive qui ne se prête ni à des agrégats de pays ni à des comparaisons internationales.

11   Les données se réfèrent aux dépenses courantes seulement.
12   Non compris les données du secteur de la production (activités de R-D non intégrées) et du secteur de service général.
13   Y compris les fonds non-profits privés.
14   A l'exclusion de la défense (en totalité ou en grande partie).
15   Les données se réfèrent au secteur de service général seulement.
16   Les données se réfèrent aux fonds publics seulement.
17   Les données se réfèrent au secteur de la production seulement.
18   Les données se réfèrent au 'Scientific Research Council' seulement.
19   À l'exclusion de la recherche-développement en sciences sociales et humanités.
20   Les données se réfèrent aux activités scientifiques ettechnologiques (AST).

21   Estimation partielle.
22   Les données se réfèrent aux activités de R-D concentrées pour la plupart dans les établissements de recherche financés par le gouvernement. Non compris les sciences sociales et humaines dans le secteur de service général.
23   Sous-estimation ou chiffre établi sur la base de données sous-estimées.
24   Les données se réfèrent aux fonds étrangers seulement.
25   A l'exclusion des dépenses d'équipement (en totalité ou en grande partie).

72

Patents
Applications, grants, patents in force: number

Brevets
Demandes, délivrances, brevets en vigueur: nombre

Country or area Pays ou zone	Applications for patents Demandes de brevets			Grants of patents Brevets délivrés			Patents in force Brevets en vigueur		
	1999	2000	2001	1999	2000	2001	1999	2000	2001
Albania Albanie	89 519	111 610	129 865	52	203	502	...	...	...
Algeria Algérie	282	33 650	72 309	...	...	...	1 501	1 484	...
Antigua and Barbuda Antigua-et-Barbuda	3	32 394	72 069	...	...	...	...	...	...
Argentina Argentine	6 457	6 634	...	1 241	1 587	...	...	...	...
Armenia Arménie	40 272	58 277	75 657	205	168	185	279	285	...
Australia Australie	63 355	80 721	95 173	13 528	13 916	13 983	88 361	93 211	...
Austria Autriche	162 121	201 030	233 181	14 347	11 266	14 326	12 845	12 132	...
Azerbaijan Azerbaïdjan	40 042	58 076	75 462	...	...	...	...	...	...
Barbados Barbade	41 272	58 943	76 051	3	...	...	9	...	...
Belarus Bélarus	41 792	59 430	76 695	550	537	529	...	...	...
Belgium Belgique	120 981	141 766	156 629	15 802	12 122	15 081	85 370	...	...
Belize Belize	...	21 308	71 685	...	...	...	...	...	...
Bosnia and Herzegovina Bosnie-Herzégovine	41 224	59 188	76 414	5	1	...	79	79	...
Botswana Botswana	54	15	58	26	43	33	...	...	...
Brazil Brésil	52 295	64 686	94 007	3 219	...	3 589	22 375	...	...
Bulgaria Bulgarie	42 952	60 480	77 622	533	481	425	2 136	1 460	...
Canada Canada	69 777	85 926	98 489	13 778	12 125	12 019	209 333	196 519	...
Chile Chili	2 812	3 120	...	418	601	...	...	...	...
China Chine	89 042	122 306	149 294	7 637	13 356	16 296	49 402	34 848	...
China, Hong Kong SAR Chine, Hong Kong RAS	6 040	8 295	8 914	2 502	2 737	1 146	...	...	...
China, Macao SAR Chine, Macao RAS	...	...	7	9	1	...	...	...	...
Colombia Colombie	1 683	1 799	44 945	590	595	363	...	...	...
Costa Rica Costa Rica	9 105	52 437	74 360	...	...	...	...	...	...
Croatia Croatie	40 279	58 936	76 491	275	379	289	...	...	...
Cuba Cuba	41 039	58 418	75 691	70	...	...	1 427	...	...

72

Patents
Applications, grants, patents in force: number *[cont.]*
Brevets
Demandes, délivrances, brevets en vigueur: nombre *[suite]*

Country or area Pays ou zone	Applications for patents Demandes de brevets			Grants of patents Brevets délivrés			Patents in force Brevets en vigueur		
	1999	2000	2001	1999	2000	2001	1999	2000	2001
Cyprus Chypre	118 767	139 700	154 362	3	23	660	...	...	...
Czech Republic République tchèque	45 309	62 645	79 253	1 482	1 611	1 719	7 249	7 789	...
Denmark Danemark	161 564	200 652	232 921	10 754	8 484	10 618	...	...	...
Dominica Dominique	8 500	52 176	74 307	...	...	...	...	...	...
Ecuador Equateur	490	11	28 909	142	...	...	...	...	...
Egypt Egypte	1 682	1 615	1 387	410	453	430	...	...	...
Estonia Estonie	41 756	60 237	77 167	103	84	257	320	390	...
Ethiopia Ethiopie	12	7	...	1	1	...	1	4	...
European Patent Office [1] Office européen de brevets [1]	121 816	143 074	158 290	35 358	27 523	34 704	...	...	...
Finland Finlande	159 033	198 293	230 441	1 618	2 557	5 362	...	...	...
France France	138 455	160 178	175 122	44 287	36 404	42 963	345 808	371 428	...
Gambia Gambie	79 703	115 420	150 082	26	51	53	...	...	...
Georgia Géorgie	41 960	59 368	76 464	398	451	268	728	1 163	...
Germany Allemagne	220 761	262 550	292 398	49 548	41 585	48 207	371 816	377 001	...
Ghana Ghana	80 028	115 543	150 196	17	64	65			
Greece Grèce	119 774	140 540	155 346	7 598	6 059	7 870	...	...	...
Grenada Grenade	34 698	57 014	75 423	...	...	...	...	...	...
Guatemala Guatemala	231	226	265	36	23	6	...	...	...
Guinea-Bissau Guinée-Bissau	1	...	...	...	...	...	...	...	...
Haiti Haïti	6	...	...	7	...	...	...	...	...
Honduras Honduras	156	139	162	77	63	238	198	375	...
Hungary Hongrie	44 974	62 438	79 200	1 881	1 605	1 445	11 438	11 441	...
Iceland Islande	41 570	59 656	76 698	27	16	42	248	237	...
India Inde	41 496	60 942	78 522	2 160	...	...	8 639	...	...
Indonesia Indonésie	42 503	60 363	77 407	...	...	...	...	...	...

72

Patents
Applications, grants, patents in force: number *[cont.]*
Brevets
Demandes, délivrances, brevets en vigueur: nombre *[suite]*

Country or area Pays ou zone	Applications for patents Demandes de brevets			Grants of patents Brevets délivrés			Patents in force Brevets en vigueur		
	1999	2000	2001	1999	2000	2001	1999	2000	2001
Iran (Islamic Rep. of) Iran (Rép. islamique d')	543	616	993	322	448	881	...	...	...
Ireland Irlande	120 795	140 519	156 489	7 288	5 916	8 472	23 209	...	...
Israel Israël	49 414	67 858	84 405	2 024	2 033	1 833	12 040	...	...
Italy Italie	128 260	151 188	156 858	32 476	24 937	25 130	...	...	...
Jamaica Jamaïque	...	101	69	17	20	69	...	...	...
Japan Japon	442 245	486 204	496 621	150 059	125 880	121 742	1 005 304	1 040 607	...
Kazakhstan Kazakhstan	41 828	59 587	77 170	1 553	1 417	1 280	6 658	3 717	...
Kenya Kenya	80 544	115 936	150 445	94	117	100	...	...	...
Kiribati Kiribati	2	...	...	2	...	...	17	...	...
Korea, Dem. P. R. Corée, R. p. dém. de	40 391	57 805	74 672	...	...	...	...	...	...
Korea, Republic of Corée, République de	133 127	172 184	190 022	62 635	34 956	34 675	...	215 882	...
Kyrgyzstan Kirghizistan	40 191	58 196	75 573	93	104	60	501	446	...
Latvia Lettonie	90 276	112 228	130 439	353	644	1 103	1 883	1 903	...
Lebanon Liban	...	104	...	...	...	...	...	...	...
Lesotho Lesotho	80 315	115 822	150 362	43	80	70	...	...	...
Liberia Libéria	41 120	58 896	76 005	...	...	...	...	...	...
Lithuania Lituanie	90 417	112 240	130 357	440	798	1 209	1 137	1 047	...
Luxembourg Luxembourg	159 601	198 631	230 724	7 490	5 901	7 492	30 503	29 575	...
Madagascar Madagascar	41 246	59 029	76 048	35	...	51	81	187	...
Malawi Malawi	80 431	115 894	150 689	84	110	151	...	817	...
Malta Malte	83	116	133	35	89	97	237	332	...
Mexico Mexique	50 000	66 916	82 470	3 899	5 527	5 476	38 965	20 414	...
Monaco Monaco	119 539	140 333	155 065	4 137	3 502	4 588	6 287	6 519	...
Mongolia Mongolie	41 240	58 983	76 239	161	...	176	...	...	...
Morocco Maroc	3 649	52 011	74 468	...	...	...	...	...	...

72

Patents
Applications, grants, patents in force: number *[cont.]*
Brevets
Demandes, délivrances, brevets en vigueur: nombre *[suite]*

Country or area Pays ou zone	Applications for patents Demandes de brevets			Grants of patents Brevets délivrés			Patents in force Brevets en vigueur		
	1999	2000	2001	1999	2000	2001	1999	2000	2001
Mozambique Mozambique	...	56 555	146 279	...	...	...	...	...	...
Netherlands Pays-Bas	123 513	144 341	158 932	21 403	17 052	20 624	120 748	120 181	...
New Zealand Nouvelle-Zélande	47 640	67 938	83 282	2 463	4 587	3 539	...	...	...
Nicaragua Nicaragua	145	143	...	12	136	...	205	343	...
Norway Norvège	50 662	68 055	84 373	2 362	2 412	2 448	...	...	...
OAPI [2] OAPI [2]	41 098	58 146	75 081	380	364	...	1 494	1 684	...
Oman Oman	...	...	2 174	...	...	...	...	...	...
Pakistan Pakistan	...	1 195	1 226	...	381	350	...	...	...
Panama Panama	...	160	...	...	15	...	...	414	...
Peru Pérou	992	1 078	...	271	308	...	1 007	1 183	...
Philippines Philippines	3 361	3 636	13 598	648	566	...	...	...	...
Poland Pologne	47 480	64 873	81 074	2 236	2 463	2 022	13 614	13 851	...
Portugal Portugal	159 666	198 700	230 908	8 493	6 354	8 567	22 219	22 573	...
Republic of Moldova République de Moldova	40 455	58 418	75 986	231	234	226	1 006	1 216	...
Romania Roumanie	91 304	113 379	131 750	1 083	1 320	1 509	18 425	15 574	...
Russian Federation Fédération de Russie	67 876	89 429	107 678	19 508	17 592	16 292	191 129	144 325	...
Rwanda Rwanda	4	...	...	4	...	...	47	...	...
Saint Lucia Sainte-Lucie	40 901	58 724	75 932	...	...	7	...	...	...
St. Vincent-Grenadines St. Vincent-Grenadines	...	2	...	...	2	...	...	...	...
Saudi Arabia Arabie saoudite	1 216	873	729	16	8	10	22	28	...
Serbia and Montenegro Serbie-et-Monténégro	42 084	59 669	77 513	175	8	154	2 238	2 242	...
Sierra Leone Sierra Leone	72 449	116 129	150 466	1	...	4	...	...	...
Singapore Singapour	51 495	70 191	79 026	4 410	5 090	...	...	...	...
Slovakia Slovaquie	43 079	60 511	77 391	773	894	1 043	...	...	...
Slovenia Slovénie	90 972	112 864	130 943	871	1 276	1 855	3 218	3 407	...

72

Patents
Applications, grants, patents in force: number *[cont.]*
Brevets
Demandes, délivrances, brevets en vigueur: nombre *[suite]*

Country or area Pays ou zone	Applications for patents Demandes de brevets			Grants of patents Brevets délivrés			Patents in force Brevets en vigueur		
	1999	2000	2001	1999	2000	2001	1999	2000	2001
South Africa Afrique du Sud	26 470	58 166	76 746	...	...	...	...	...	...
Spain Espagne	163 090	202 439	234 543	20 066	15 809	19 709	178 782	142 188	...
Sri Lanka Sri Lanka	41 263	58 929	76 095	...	...	...	...	...	...
Sudan Soudan	80 426	115 860	150 393	59	97	79	...	...	...
Swaziland Swaziland	40 673	58 033	75 092	57	85	70	...	...	...
Sweden Suède	165 051	204 173	231 483	17 649	13 812	14 873	97 980	97 345	...
Switzerland Suisse	162 403	201 571	233 652	15 434	12 258	15 639	87 033	87 008	...
Syrian Arab Republic Rép. arabe syrienne	...	296	...	...	50	62	...	...	...
Tajikistan Tadjikistan	40 141	58 133	75 462	42	43	...	222	281	...
Thailand Thaïlande	...	5 665	...	...	541	...	...	352	...
TFYR of Macedonia L'ex-R.y. Macédoine	89 425	111 683	130 061	55	86	240	378	434	...
Trinidad and Tobago Trinité-et-Tobago	41 238	58 974	76 046	...	...	...	...	...	...
Tunisia Tunisie	...	...	195	...	...	...	...	...	...
Turkey Turquie	43 833	77 274	229 339	1 122	1 157	2 137	21 183	22 040	...
Turkmenistan Turkménistan	40 114	58 061	75 440	95	...	...	...	...	...
Uganda Ouganda	80 421	115 875	150 408	74	112	92	...	...	...
Ukraine Ukraine	48 273	65 917	84 430	1 294	5 772	11 670	16 270	15 005	...
United Arab Emirates Emirats arabes unis	24 218	56 158	75 414	...	...	...	...	...	...
United Kingdom Royaume-Uni	192 875	233 223	264 706	40 683	33 756	39 649	...	312 802	...
United Rep. of Tanzania Rép.-Unie de Tanzanie	14 467	108 930	148 740	8	...	...	...	...	...
United States Etats-Unis	294 706	331 773	375 657	153 487	157 496	166 038	1 242 853	1 295 176	...
Uruguay Uruguay	552	616	...	113	140	...	356	396	...
Uzbekistan Ouzbékistan	42 365	59 859	77 235	512	476	485	727	2 586	...
Venezuela Venezuela	...	2 348	...	...	756	...	...	...	...
Viet Nam Viet Nam	42 212	59 776	76 542	490	727	...	...	...	...

72

Patents
Applications, grants, patents in force: number *[cont.]*
Brevets
Demandes, délivrances, brevets en vigueur: nombre *[suite]*

Country or area Pays ou zone	Applications for patents Demandes de brevets			Grants of patents Brevets délivrés			Patents in force Brevets en vigueur		
	1999	2000	2001	1999	2000	2001	1999	2000	2001
Zambia Zambie	92	10	3 186	67	46	63	1 346	...	...
Zimbabwe Zimbabwe	80 168	115 750	150 408	34	86	78	...	...	...

Source:
World Intellectual Property Organization (WIPO), Geneva, "Industrial Property Statistics 2001, Publication A" and previous issues.

Source :
Organisation mondiale de la propriété intellectuelle (OMPI), Genève, '' Statistiques de propriété industrielle 2001, Publication A'' et éditions précédentes.

1 In 1992, the European Patent Office (EPO) was constituted by the following member countries: Austria, Belgium, Denmark, France, Germany, Greece, Ireland, Italy, Liechtenstein, Luxembourg, Monaco, Netherlands, Portugal, Spain, Sweden, Switzerland, United Kingdom.

2 Members of the African Intellectual Property Organization (OAPI), which includes Benin, Burkina Faso, Cameroon, Central African Republic, Chad, Congo, Côte d'Ivoire, Gabon, Guinea, Mali, Mauritania, Niger, Senegal, Togo.

1 En 1992, l'Office européen de brevets (OEB) comprenait les pays membres suivants: Allemagne, Autriche, Belgique, Danemark, Espagne, France, Grèce, Irlande, Italie, Liechtenstein, Luxembourg, Monaco, Pays-Bas, Portugal, Royaume-Uni, Suède, Suisse.

2 Les membres de l'Organisation africaine de la propriété intellectuelle (OAPI): Bénin, Burkina Faso, Cameroun, Congo, Côte d'Ivoire, Gabon, Guinée, Mali, Mauritanie, Niger, République centrafricaine, Sénégal, Tchad, Togo.

Technical notes, tables 70-72

Table 70: The data presented on personnel engaged in research and experimental development (R&D) are compiled by the UNESCO Institute for Statistics. The definitions and classifications applied by UNESCO in the table are based on those set out in the *Recommendation concerning the International Standardization of Statistics on Science and Technology* (for data covering the years prior to 1998) and in the *Frascati Manual* (for data referring to 1998 and on).

The three categories of personnel shown are defined as follows:

Researchers are professionals engaged in the conception or creation of new knowledge, products, processes, methods and systems, and in the planning and management of R&D projects. Post-graduate students engaged in R&D are considered as researchers. The data shown for researchers for the years prior to 1998 refer to "R&D scientists and engineers".

Technicians (and equivalent staff) comprise persons whose main tasks require technical knowledge and experience in one or more fields of engineering, physical and life sciences, or social sciences and humanities.

Other supporting staff includes skilled and unskilled craftsmen, secretarial and clerical staff participating in or directly associated with R&D projects.

More information can be found on the UNESCO Institute for Statistics Web site <www.uis.unesco.org>.

Table 71: The data presented on gross domestic expenditure on research and development are compiled by the UNESCO Institute for Statistics. Data for certain countries are provided to UNESCO by OECD, EUROSTAT and the Science and Technology Ibero-American Indicators Network.

Gross domestic expenditure on R&D (GERD) is total intramural expenditure on R&D performed on the national territory during a given period. It includes R&D performed within a country and funded from abroad but excludes payments made abroad for R&D.

The sources of funds for GERD are classified according to the following five categories:

Business enterprise funds include funds allocated to R&D by all firms, organizations and institutions whose primary activity is the market production of goods and services (other than the higher education sector) for sale to the general public at an economically significant price, and those private non-profit institutes mainly serving these firms, organizations and institutions.

Government funds refer to funds allocated to R&D by the central (federal), state or local government autho-

Notes techniques, tableaux 70 à 72

Tableau 70: Les données présentées sur le personnel employé à des travaux de recherche scientifique et le développement expérimental (R-D) sont compilées par l'Institut de statistique de l'UNESCO. Les définitions et classifications appliquées par l'UNESCO sont basées sur la *Recommandation concernant la normalisation internationale des statistiques relatives à la science et à la technologie* (pour les chiffres des années antérieures à 1998) et sur le *Manuel de Frascati* (à compter de 1998).

Les trois catégories du personnel présentées sont définies comme suivant:

Les chercheurs sont des spécialistes travaillant à la conception ou à la création de connaissances, de produits, de procédés, de méthodes et de systèmes, et dans la planification et la gestion de projets de R-D. Les étudiants diplômés ayant des activités de R-D sont également considérés comme des chercheurs. Les données relatives aux chercheurs pour les années antérieures à 1998 se rapportent aux « scientifiques et ingénieurs employés à des travaux de R-D ».

Techniciens (et personnel assimilé) comprend des personnes dont les tâches principales requièrent des connaissances et une expérience technique dans un ou plusieurs domaines de l'ingénierie, des sciences physiques et de la vie ou des sciences sociales et humaines.

Autre personnel de soutien comprend les travailleurs, qualifiés ou non, et le personnel de secrétariat et de bureau qui participent à l'exécution des projets de R-D ou qui sont directement associés à l'exécution de tels projets.

Pour tout renseignement complémentaire, voir le site Web de l'Institut de statistique de l'UNESCO <www.uis.unesco.org>.

Tableau 71: Les données présentées sur les dépenses intérieures brutes de recherche et développement sont compilées par l'Institut de statistique de l'UNESCO. Les données de certains pays ont été fournies à l'UNESCO par l'OCDE, EUROSTAT et la Red Ibero-Americana de Indicadores de Ciencia y Technología.

Dépense intérieure brute de R-D (DIRD) est la dépense totale intra-muros afférente aux travaux de R-D exécutés sur le territoire national pendant une période donnée. Elle comprend la R-D exécutée sur le territoire national et financée par l'étranger mais ne tient pas compte des paiements effectués à l'étranger pour des travaux de R-D.

Les sources de financement pour la DIRD sont classées selon les cinq catégories suivantes:

Fonds des entreprises inclut les fonds alloués à la R-D par toutes les firmes, organismes et institutions dont

rities. Public enterprises funds are included in the business enterprise funds sector. These authorities also include private non-profit institutes controlled and mainly financed by government.

Higher education funds include funds allocated to R&D by institutions of higher education comprising all universities, colleges of technology, other institutes of post-secondary education, and all research institutes, experimental stations and clinics operating under the direct control of or administered by or associated with higher educational establishments.

Private non-profit funds are funds allocated to R&D by non-market, private non-profit institutions serving the general public, as well as by private individuals and households.

Funds from abroad refer to funds allocated to R&D by institutions and individuals located outside the political frontiers of a country except for vehicles, ships, aircraft and space satellites operated by domestic organizations and testing grounds acquired by such organizations, and by all international organizations (except business enterprises) including their facilities and operations within the frontiers of a country.

The absolute figures for R&D expenditure should not be compared country by country. Such comparisons would require the conversion of national currencies into a common currency by means of special R&D exchange rates. Official exchange rates do not always reflect the real costs of R&D activities and comparisons are based on such rates can result in misleading conclusions, although they can be used to indicate a gross order of magnitude.

Beginning 1996, national currency data are expressed in euros for the Euro-area countries. Data for the years from 1996 to 1998 for Austria, Belgium, Finland, France, Germany, Ireland, Italy, Netherlands, Portugal and Spain, and for Greece from 1997 to 2000, have been converted from the former national currency using the appropriate irrevocable conversion rate. Please note, however, that the pre-EMU euro is a notional unit and should not be used to form area aggregates or to carry out cross-country comparisons.

The Euro-area countries, their irrevocable EUR/national currency exchange rate and year of EMU accession are as follows:

    Austria 1 EUR = 13.7603 ATS (1999)
    Belgium 1 EUR = 40.3399 BEF (1999)
    Finland 1 EUR = 5.94573 FIM (1999)
    France 1 EUR = 6.55957 FRF (1999)
    Germany 1 EUR = 1.95583 DEM (1999)
    Greece 1 EUR = 340.750 GRD (2001)
    Ireland 1 EUR = 0.787564 IEP (1999)
    Italy 1 EUR = 1936.27 ITL (1999)

l'activité première est la production marchande de biens ou de services (autres que dans le secteur d'enseignement supérieur) en vue de leur vente au public, à un prix qui correspond à la réalité économique, et les institutions privées sans but lucratif principalement au service de ces entreprises, organismes et institutions.

Fonds de l'Etat sont les fonds fournis à la R-D par le gouvernement central (fédéral), d'état ou par les autorités locales. Les fonds des entreprises publiques sont comprises dans ceux du secteur des entreprises. Les fonds de l'Etat incluent également les institutions privées sans but lucratif contrôlées et principalement financées par l'Etat.

Fonds de l'enseignement supérieur inclut les fonds fournis à la R-D par les établissements d'enseignement supérieur tels que toutes les universités, grandes écoles, instituts de technologie et autres établissements post-secondaires, ainsi que tous les instituts de recherche, les stations d'essais et les cliniques qui travaillent sous le contrôle direct des établissements d'enseignement supérieur ou qui sont administrés par ces derniers ou leur sont associés.

Fonds d'institutions privées à but non lucratif sont les fonds destinés à la R-D par les institutions privées sans but lucratif non marchandes au service du public, ainsi que par les simples particuliers ou les ménages.

Fonds étrangers concernent les fonds destinés à la R-D par les institutions et les individus se trouvant en dehors des frontières politiques d'un pays, à l'exception des véhicules, navires, avions et satellites utilisés par des institutions nationales, ainsi que des terrains d'essai acquis par ces institutions, et par toutes les organisations internationales (à l'exception des entreprises), y compris leurs installations et leurs activités à l'intérieur des frontières d'un pays.

Il faut éviter de comparer les chiffres absolus concernant les dépenses de R-D d'un pays à l'autre. On ne pourrait procéder à des comparaisons détaillées qu'en convertissant en une même monnaie les sommes libellées en monnaie nationale au moyen de taux de change spécialement applicables aux activités de R-D. Les taux de change officiels ne reflètent pas toujours le coût réel des activités de R-D, et les comparaisons établies sur la base de ces taux peuvent conduire à des conclusions trompeuses; toutefois, elles peuvent être utilisées pour donner une idée de l'ordre de grandeur.

A partir de 1996, les données en monnaie nationale sont exprimées en euros pour les pays de la zone Euro. Les données pour les années 1996 à 1998 pour Allemagne, Autriche, Belgique, Espagne, Finlande, France, Irlande, Italie, Pays-Bas, et Portugal, et pour Grèce pour les années 1997 à 2000, ont été converties à partir de l'ancienne monnaie nationale et du taux de conversion

Netherlands 1 EUR = 2.20371 NLG (1999)
Portugal 1 EUR = 200.482 PTE (1999)
Spain 1 EUR = 166.386 ESP (1999).

More information can be found on the UNESCO Institute for Statistics Web site (www.uis.unesco.org).

Table 72: Data on patents include patent applications filed directly with the office concerned and grants made on the basis of such applications; inventors' certificates; patents of importation, including patents of introduction, revalidation patents and "patentes precaucionales"; petty patents; patents applied and granted under the Patent Cooperation Treaty (PCT), the European Patent Convention, the Havana Agreement, the Harare Protocol of the African Regional Industrial Property Organization (ARIPO) and the African Intellectual Property Organization (OAPI). The data are compiled and published by the World Intellectual Property Organization (see [37] and <www.wipo.int>).

irrévocable approprié. Noter, cependant, que l'euro avant l'entrée dans l'UEM est une unité fictive qui ne se prête ni à des agrégats de pays ni à des comparaisons internationales.

Les pays de la zone Euro, leur taux de change irrévocable EUR/monnaie nationale et leur année d'accession à l'UEM sont présentés ci-dessous :

Allemagne 1 EUR = 1.95583 DEM (1999)
Autriche 1 EUR = 13.7603 ATS (1999)
Belgique 1 EUR = 40.3399 BEF (1999)
Espagne 1 EUR = 166.386 ESP (1999)
Finlande 1 EUR = 5.94573 FIM (1999)
France 1 EUR = 6.55957 FRF (1999)
Grèce 1 EUR = 340.750 GRD (2001)
Irlande 1 EUR = 0.787564 IEP (1999)
Italie 1 EUR = 1936.27 ITL (1999)
Pays-Bas 1 EUR = 2.20371 NLG (1999)
Portugal 1 EUR = 200.482 PTE (1999).

Pour tout renseignement complémentaire, voir le site Web de l'Institut de statistique de l'UNESCO <www.uis.unesco.org>.

Tableau 72: Les données relatives aux brevets comprennent les demandes de brevet déposées directement auprès de l'office intéressé et brevets délivrés sur la base de telles demandes; les brevets d'invention; les brevets d'importation; y compris les brevets d'introduction, les brevets de revalidation et les brevets "precaucionales"; les petits brevets, les brevets demandés et délivrés en vertu du traité de coopération sur les brevets, de la Convention européenne relative aux brevets, de l'Accord de la Havane, du Protocole d'Hararé de l'Organisation régionale africaine de la propriété industrielle (ARIPO) et de l'Organisation africaine de la propriété intellectuelle (OAPI). Les données sont compilées et publiées par l'Organisation mondiale de la propriété intellectuelle (voir [37] et <www.wipo.int>).

Part Four
International Economic Relations

Chapter XVI   **International merchandise trade (tables 73-75)**

Chapter XVII   **International tourism (tables 76-78)**

Chapter XVIII   **Balance of payments (table 79)**

Chapter XIX   **International finance (tables 80 and 81)**

Chapter XX   **Development assistance (tables 82-84)**

Part Four of the *Yearbook* presents statistics on international economic relations in areas of international merchandise trade, international tourism, balance of payments and assistance to developing countries. The series cover all countries or areas of the world for which data are available.

Quatrième partie
Relations économiques internationales

Chapitre XVI   **Commerce international des marchandises (tableaux 73 à 75)**

Chapitre XVII   **Tourisme international (tableaux 76 à 78)**

Chapitre XVIII   **Balance des paiements (tableau 79)**

Chapitre XIX   **Finances internationales (tableaux 80 et 81)**

Chapitre XX   **Aide au développement (tableaux 82 à 84)**

La quatrième partie de l'*Annuaire* présente des statistiques sur les relations économiques internationales dans les domaines du commerce international des marchandises, du tourisme international, de la balance des paiements et de l'assistance aux pays en développement. Les séries couvrent tous les pays ou les zones du monde pour lesquels des données sont disponibles.

73
Total imports and exports
Imports c.i.f., exports f.o.b. and balance, value in million US dollars
Importations et exportations totales
Importations c.a.f., exportations f.o.b. et balance, valeur en millions de dollare E.-U.

Country or area	Sys.&	1996	1997	1998	1999	2000	2001	2002	Pays ou zone
World									**Monde**
Imports		5 178 436	5 351 251	5 293 113	5 506 955	6 234 282	5 990 065	6 192 522	Importations
Exports		5 110 378	5 298 054	5 230 596	5 412 607	6 062 739	5 816 189	6 070 693	Exportations
Balance		-68 059	-53 196	-62 518	-94 347	-171 543	-173 876	-121 829	Balance
Developed economies[1,2]									**Economies développées**[1,2]
Imports		3 543 988	3 627 163	3 714 991	3 894 188	4 292 827	4 110 645	4 206 125	Importations
Exports		3 545 561	3 631 086	3 653 486	3 703 492	3 950 715	3 823 947	3 933 464	Exportations
Balance		1 573	3 922	-61 505	-190 696	-342 112	-286 698	-272 660	Balance
Developing economies[2]									**Econ. en dévelop.**[2]
Imports		1 439 281	1 512 802	1 364 123	1 421 141	1 724 140	1 638 323	1 718 355	Importations
Exports		1 366 328	1 461 478	1 376 654	1 510 368	1 861 690	1 728 605	1 844 626	Exportations
Balance		-72 954	-51 324	12 531	89 227	137 550	90 283	126 271	Balance
Other[3]									**Autres**[3]
Imports		195 167	211 285	213 999	191 626	217 315	241 098	268 042	Importations
Exports		198 489	205 490	200 456	198 747	250 333	263 636	292 602	Exportations
Balance		3 322	-5 795	-13 543	7 121	33 019	22 539	24 560	Balance

Americas · Amériques

Country or area	Sys.&	1996	1997	1998	1999	2000	2001	2002	Pays ou zone
Developed economies[2]									**Economies développées**[2]
Imports		939 950	1 037 793	1 085 185	1 208 522	1 414 250	1 321 315	1 345 511	Importations
Exports		773 940	845 918	836 244	874 811	973 908	911 039	867 388	Exportations
Balance		-166 010	-191 875	-248 941	-333 711	-440 342	-410 277	-478 123	Balance
Canada[4]	G								**Canada**[4]
Imports		170 694	195 980	201 061	214 791	238 812	221 757	221 961	Importations
Exports		201 636	214 428	214 335	238 422	276 645	259 857	252 408	Exportations
Balance		30 942	18 448	13 274	23 631	37 833	38 100	30 447	Balance
United States[5]	G								**Etats-Unis**[5]
Imports		822 025	899 019	944 353	1 059 440	1 259 300	1 179 180	1 202 430	Importations
Exports		625 073	688 696	682 138	702 098	781 125	730 803	693 860	Exportations
Balance		-196 952	-210 323	-262 215	-357 342	-478 175	-448 377	-508 570	Balance
Developing economies[2]									**Econ. en dévelop.**[2]
Imports		274 639	320 421	335 337	323 378	373 316	366 417	343 049	Importations
Exports		252 147	279 052	276 766	294 962	353 172	338 031	343 816	Exportations
Balance		-22 492	-41 368	-58 571	-28 416	-20 144	-28 387	767	Balance
LAIA +									**ALAI +**
Imports		235 615	281 439	292 164	279 504	326 208	318 368	293 537	Importations
Exports		234 240	259 458	256 389	273 344	329 605	315 975	322 369	Exportations
Balance		-1 375	-21 980	-35 775	-6 161	3 397	-2 393	28 833	Balance
Argentina	S								**Argentine**
Imports		23 762	30 450	31 404	25 508	25 280	20 320	8 990	Importations
Exports		23 811	26 370	26 441	23 333	26 341	26 543	25 709	Exportations
Balance		49	-4 080	-4 963	-2 175	1 061	6 223	16 720	Balance
Bolivia	G								**Bolivie**
Imports		1 635	1 851	1 983	1 755	1 830	1 708	1 770	Importations
Exports		1 137	1 167	1 104	1 051	1 230	1 285	1 299	Exportations
Balance		-498	-684	-879	-704	-600	-423	-471	Balance
Brazil	G								**Brésil**
Imports		56 947	64 996	60 652	51 759	58 631	58 351	49 577	Importations
Exports		47 747	52 994	51 140	48 011	55 086	58 223	60 362	Exportations
Balance		-9 200	-12 001	-9 512	-3 748	-3 545	-128	10 785	Balance
Chile	S								**Chili**
Imports		19 123	20 825	19 880	15 988	18 507	17 814	17 093	Importations
Exports		15 657	17 902	16 323	17 162	19 210	18 466	18 340	Exportations
Balance		-3 466	-2 923	-3 557	1 174	703	652	1 247	Balance
Colombia	G								**Colombie**
Imports		13 684	15 378	14 635	10 659	11 539	12 834	12 738	Importations
Exports		10 587	11 522	10 852	11 576	13 040	12 257	12 001	Exportations
Balance		-3 097	-3 855	-3 782	918	1 502	-577	-737	Balance
Cuba	S								**Cuba**
Imports		3 205	...	...	...	...	...	...	Importations
Exports		2 015	...	...	...	...	...	...	Exportations
Balance		-1 190	...	...	...	...	...	...	Balance

73
Total imports and exports
Imports c.i.f., exports f.o.b., and balance, value in million US dollars
Importations et exportations totales
Importations c.a.f., exportations f.o.b. et balance, valeur en millions de dollare E.-U.

Country or area	Sys.&	1996	1997	1998	1999	2000	2001	2002	Pays ou zone
Ecuador	G								**Equateur**
Imports		3 935	4 955	5 576	3 017	3 721	5 363	6 431	Importations
Exports		4 900	5 264	4 203	4 451	4 927	4 678	5 030	Exportations
Balance		965	310	-1 373	1 434	1 205	-685	-1 401	Balance
Mexico [4,6]	G								**Mexique** [4,6]
Imports		89 469	109 808	125 373	141 975	174 500	168 276	168 679	Importations
Exports		96 000	110 431	117 460	136 391	166 367	158 547	160 682	Exportations
Balance		6 531	623	-7 913	-5 584	-8 133	-9 729	-7 997	Balance
Paraguay	S								**Paraguay**
Imports		2 850	3 099	2 471	1 725	2 050	1 989	...	Importations
Exports		1 044	1 089	1 014	741	869	990	...	Exportations
Balance		-1 807	-2 011	-1 457	-984	-1 181	-999	...	Balance
Peru [4]	S								**Pérou** [4]
Imports		7 894	8 554	8 222	6 729	7 331	7 164	7 423	Importations
Exports		5 897	6 841	5 757	6 113	7 028	7 100	7 669	Exportations
Balance		-1 997	-1 712	-2 466	-616	-303	-65	247	Balance
Uruguay	G								**Uruguay**
Imports		3 323	3 727	3 811	3 357	3 466	3 061	...	Importations
Exports		2 397	2 726	2 771	2 237	2 295	2 060	...	Exportations
Balance		-926	-1 001	-1 040	-1 120	-1 171	-1 000	...	Balance
Venezuela	G								**Venezuela**
Imports		9 794	14 577	15 750	13 835	16 142	18 263	...	Importations
Exports		23 053	21 073	17 175	20 880	31 737	24 345	26 881	Exportations
Balance		13 260	6 496	1 425	7 045	15 596	6 082	...	Balance
CACM +									**MCAC +**
Imports		13 110	15 355	18 029	18 380	19 618	20 734	21 947	Importations
Exports		8 568	10 005	11 455	11 861	11 907	10 600	10 599	Exportations
Balance		-4 543	-5 349	-6 574	-6 519	-7 710	-10 134	-11 349	Balance
Costa Rica	S								**Costa Rica**
Imports		4 300	4 924	6 230	6 320	6 372	6 564	7 188	Importations
Exports		3 730	4 268	5 511	6 577	5 865	5 010	5 253	Exportations
Balance		-569	-656	-719	257	-508	-1 555	-1 935	Balance
El Salvador	S								**El Salvador**
Imports		2 671	2 981	3 121	3 140	3 795	3 866	3 907	Importations
Exports		1 024	1 371	1 256	1 177	1 332	1 214	1 234	Exportations
Balance		-1 647	-1 609	-1 865	-1 963	-2 462	-2 653	-2 674	Balance
Guatemala	S								**Guatemala**
Imports		3 146	3 852	4 651	4 382	4 791	5 607	6 078	Importations
Exports		2 031	2 344	2 582	2 398	2 696	2 466	2 232	Exportations
Balance		-1 115	-1 508	-2 070	-1 984	-2 095	-3 141	-3 846	Balance
Honduras	S								**Honduras**
Imports		1 840	2 149	2 535	2 676	2 855	2 918	2 979	Importations
Exports		1 316	1 446	1 533	1 164	1 370	1 318	1 284	Exportations
Balance		-524	-703	-1 002	-1 512	-1 485	-1 600	-1 694	Balance
Nicaragua	G								**Nicaragua**
Imports		1 154	1 450	1 492	1 862	1 805	1 779	1 795	Importations
Exports		466	577	573	545	645	592	596	Exportations
Balance		-687	-873	-918	-1 317	-1 160	-1 187	-1 199	Balance
Other America									**Autres pays d'Amérique**
Imports		25 913	23 627	25 144	25 494	27 490	27 315	27 565	Importations
Exports		9 339	9 589	8 922	9 757	11 659	11 456	10 848	Exportations
Balance		-16 574	-14 039	-16 222	-15 737	-15 831	-15 860	-16 717	Balance
Anguilla	S								**Anguilla**
Imports		...	54	58	...	...	...	...	Importations
Exports		...	2	5	...	...	...	...	Exportations
Balance		...	-53	-53	...	...	...	...	Balance
Antigua and Barbuda	G								**Antigua-et-Barbuda**
Imports		365	370	385	414			...	Importations
Exports		38	38	36	38	...	...	...	Exportations
Balance		-328	-333	-349	-376	...	...	...	Balance

73

Total imports and exports

Imports c.i.f., exports f.o.b., and balance, value in million US dollars

Importations et exportations totales

Importations c.a.f., exportations f.o.b. et balance, valeur en millions de dollare E.-U.

Country or area	Sys.&	1996	1997	1998	1999	2000	2001	2002	Pays ou zone
Aruba	S								**Aruba**
Imports		578	614	815	782	835	841	841	Importations
Exports		12	24	29	29	173	149	128	Exportations
Balance		-566	-590	-786	-753	-662	-693	-713	Balance
Bahamas [7]	G								**Bahamas** [7]
Imports		1 366	1 666	1 873	1 772	1 764	1 742	1 614	Importations
Exports		180	181	300	532	805	649	617	Exportations
Balance		-1 186	-1 484	-1 573	-1 240	-959	-1 093	-997	Balance
Barbados	G								**Barbade**
Imports		834	996	1 010	1 108	1 156	1 087	1 039	Importations
Exports		281	283	252	264	272	259	206	Exportations
Balance		-553	-713	-758	-844	-884	-827	-833	Balance
Belize	G								**Belize**
Imports		255	286	295	370	452	500	521	Importations
Exports		168	176	172	186	185	174	180	Exportations
Balance		-88	-110	-123	-184	-268	-327	-340	Balance
Bermuda	G								**Bermudes**
Imports		569	619	629	712	720	721	...	Importations
Exports		68	57	45	...	...	...	...	Exportations
Balance		-501	-562	-584	...	...	...	...	Balance
Cayman Islands	G								**Iles Caïmanes**
Imports		379	...	...	...	...	...	...	Importations
Exports		3	...	...	...	...	...	...	Exportations
Balance		-377	...	...	...	...	...	...	Balance
Dominica	S								**Dominique**
Imports		130	125	132	138	148	131	115	Importations
Exports		51	53	62	56	54	43	42	Exportations
Balance		-79	-72	-70	-83	-95	-88	-73	Balance
Dominican Republic [4,8]	G								**Rép. dominicaine** [4,8]
Imports		3 581	4 192	4 897	5 207	6 416	5 937	6 037	Importations
Exports		945	1 017	880	805	966	805	834	Exportations
Balance		-2 635	-3 175	-4 016	-4 402	-5 450	-5 132	-5 204	Balance
Greenland	G								**Groenland**
Imports		469	397	409	408	351	...	...	Importations
Exports		369	293	254	276	262	...	...	Exportations
Balance		-100	-104	-155	-132	-88	...	...	Balance
Grenada	S								**Grenade**
Imports		152	173	200	...	...	...	...	Importations
Exports		20	23	27	...	...	...	...	Exportations
Balance		-132	-151	-173	...	...	...	...	Balance
Guyana	S								**Guyana**
Imports		598	629	...	...	...	584	563	Importations
Exports		517	643	485	523	498	478	493	Exportations
Balance		-81	14	...	...	...	-106	-70	Balance
Haiti	G								**Haïti**
Imports		666	648	800	1 035	1 041	1 017	1 122	Importations
Exports		90	212	320	338	313	275	279	Exportations
Balance		-576	-436	-480	-697	-728	-742	-842	Balance
Jamaica	G								**Jamaïque**
Imports		2 965	3 128	3 033	2 899	3 326	3 361	3 533	Importations
Exports		1 382	1 382	1 312	1 241	1 304	1 220	1 114	Exportations
Balance		-1 583	-1 746	-1 721	-1 658	-2 022	-2 140	-2 419	Balance
Netherlands Antilles [9]	S								**Antilles néerlandaises** [9]
Imports		2 519	2 083	...	...	...	...	...	Importations
Exports		1 269	1 488	...	...	...	...	...	Exportations
Balance		-1 249	-594	...	...	...	...	...	Balance
Panama [10]	S								**Panama** [10]
Imports		2 780	3 002	3 398	3 516	3 379	2 964	2 982	Importations
Exports		723	723	784	822	859	911	846	Exportations
Balance		-2 057	-2 279	-2 614	-2 694	-2 519	-2 053	-2 136	Balance

73

Total imports and exports

Imports c.i.f., exports f.o.b., and balance, value in million US dollars

Importations et exportations totales

Importations c.a.f., exportations f.o.b. et balance, valeur en millions de dollare E.-U.

Country or area	Sys.&	1996	1997	1998	1999	2000	2001	2002	Pays ou zone
Saint Kitts and Nevis	S								**Saint-Kitts-et-Nevis**
Imports		149	148	148	...	...	...	...	Importations
Exports		22	36	...	...	...	...	...	Exportations
Balance		-127	-112	...	...	...	...	...	Balance
Saint Lucia	S								**Sainte-Lucie**
Imports		313	332	335	355	355	355	...	Importations
Exports		80	61	62	56	43	44	...	Exportations
Balance		-234	-271	-273	-299	-312	-311	...	Balance
St. Vincent-Grenadines	S								**St. Vincent-Grenadines**
Imports		132	182	193	201	163	186	174	Importations
Exports		46	46	50	49	47	41	38	Exportations
Balance		-85	-136	-143	-152	-116	-144	-136	Balance
Suriname	G								**Suriname**
Imports		501	657	551	...	...	...	...	Importations
Exports		433	700	435	...	...	...	...	Exportations
Balance		-68	43	-116	...	...	...	...	Balance
Trinidad and Tobago	S								**Trinité-et-Tobago**
Imports		2 144	2 990	2 999	2 740	3 308	3 569	3 643	Importations
Exports		2 500	2 542	2 258	2 803	4 274	4 280	3 881	Exportations
Balance		356	-448	-741	63	965	711	237	Balance

Europe · Europe

Country or area	Sys.&	1996	1997	1998	1999	2000	2001	2002	Pays ou zone
Developed economies [2]									**Economies développées [2]**
Imports		2 126 490	2 122 056	2 229 678	2 250 805	2 364 950	2 320 365	2 397 286	Importations
Exports		2 249 782	2 249 173	2 328 003	2 308 484	2 377 732	2 395 023	2 537 302	Exportations
Balance		123 292	127 117	98 325	57 678	12 782	74 658	140 017	Balance
EU+									**UE+**
Imports		2 010 317	2 009 359	2 111 690	2 134 351	2 246 976	2 203 519	2 276 116	Importations
Exports		2 120 170	2 124 285	2 207 818	2 182 473	2 238 027	2 253 221	2 388 918	Exportations
Balance		109 854	114 925	96 129	48 122	-8 949	49 702	112 802	Balance
Austria	S								**Autriche**
Imports		67 336	64 786	68 187	69 557	68 986	70 461	71 863	Importations
Exports		57 822	58 599	62 747	64 126	64 167	66 671	72 746	Exportations
Balance		-9 514	-6 187	-5 441	-5 431	-4 819	-3 789	884	Balance
Belgium [11]	S								**Belgique [11]**
Imports		163 615	157 283	162 212	164 620	177 001	178 715	195 984	Importations
Exports		175 367	171 906	177 666	178 965	187 885	190 352	213 525	Exportations
Balance		11 752	14 623	15 454	14 345	10 884	11 637	17 541	Balance
Denmark	S								**Danemark**
Imports		44 434	44 044	45 427	44 067	43 713	43 430	47 707	Importations
Exports		50 099	47 720	47 481	48 698	49 756	50 738	55 762	Exportations
Balance		5 665	3 676	2 054	4 632	6 043	7 309	8 055	Balance
Finland	G								**Finlande**
Imports		29 265	29 786	32 301	31 617	33 900	32 114	33 642	Importations
Exports		38 435	39 318	42 963	41 841	45 482	42 802	44 671	Exportations
Balance		9 171	9 533	10 662	10 224	11 582	10 688	11 029	Balance
France [12]	S								**France [12]**
Imports		281 776	272 721	288 412	294 916	310 942	300 744	308 389	Importations
Exports		287 643	290 972	305 664	302 472	300 022	296 233	309 952	Exportations
Balance		5 867	18 252	17 252	7 556	-10 920	-4 512	1 563	Balance
Germany [13]	S								**Allemagne [13]**
Imports		458 808	445 683	471 448	473 551	495 480	486 053	492 112	Importations
Exports		524 226	512 503	543 431	542 884	550 260	571 460	612 857	Exportations
Balance		65 418	66 820	71 983	69 334	54 780	85 407	120 745	Balance
Greece	S								**Grèce**
Imports		29 672	27 899	29 388	28 720	29 221	29 928	31 164	Importations
Exports		11 948	11 128	10 732	10 475	10 747	9 483	10 315	Exportations
Balance		-17 724	-16 771	-18 656	-18 244	-18 474	-20 444	-20 849	Balance
Ireland	G								**Irlande**
Imports		45 577	49 814	56 684	47 195	51 444	51 304	51 508	Importations
Exports		61 798	67 951	81 576	71 221	77 097	83 020	87 498	Exportations
Balance		16 221	18 137	24 893	24 026	25 653	31 715	35 989	Balance

73
Total imports and exports
Imports c.i.f., exports f.o.b., and balance, value in million US dollars
Importations et exportations totales
Importations c.a.f., exportations f.o.b. et balance, valeur en millions de dollare E.-U.

Country or area	Sys.&	1996	1997	1998	1999	2000	2001	2002	Pays ou zone
Italy	S								**Italie**
Imports		208 097	210 297	218 459	220 327	238 071	236 128	244 292	Importations
Exports		252 045	240 438	245 716	235 180	239 934	244 253	253 349	Exportations
Balance		43 948	30 141	27 257	14 852	1 863	8 125	9 057	Balance
Luxembourg[14]	S								**Luxembourg[14]**
Imports		...	9 380	7 409	11 045	10 718	11 154	11 617	Importations
Exports		...	7 000	7 912	7 895	7 950	8 240	8 574	Exportations
Balance		...	-2 380	503	-3 150	-2 768	-2 914	-3 043	Balance
Netherlands	S								**Pays-Bas**
Imports		180 642	178 133	187 754	187 530	198 331	194 925	193 665	Importations
Exports		197 420	194 909	201 382	200 290	208 889	216 117	222 410	Exportations
Balance		16 778	16 776	13 628	12 760	10 558	21 193	28 745	Balance
Portugal	S								**Portugal**
Imports		35 179	35 066	38 539	39 826	38 192	39 422	38 326	Importations
Exports		24 606	23 974	24 816	25 228	23 279	24 449	25 536	Exportations
Balance		-10 572	-11 092	-13 723	-14 599	-14 913	-14 973	-12 791	Balance
Spain	S								**Espagne**
Imports		121 792	122 721	133 164	144 438	152 901	153 634	163 575	Importations
Exports		102 003	104 368	109 240	109 966	113 348	115 175	123 563	Exportations
Balance		-19 788	-18 353	-23 923	-34 473	-39 553	-38 459	-40 012	Balance
Sweden	G								**Suède**
Imports		66 931	65 697	68 633	68 721	72 981	63 471	66 108	Importations
Exports		84 904	82 956	85 003	84 772	86 963	75 791	81 141	Exportations
Balance		17 973	17 258	16 370	16 050	13 982	12 320	15 033	Balance
United Kingdom	G								**Royaume-Uni**
Imports		287 472	306 592	314 036	317 963	334 371	320 956	335 458	Importations
Exports		262 130	281 083	271 851	268 203	281 525	267 357	276 315	Exportations
Balance		-25 342	-25 509	-42 185	-49 760	-52 846	-53 599	-59 143	Balance
EFTA+									**AELE+**
Imports		112 118	108 781	113 852	112 114	113 024	112 293	116 293	Importations
Exports		127 489	122 905	117 894	123 602	136 831	139 340	145 725	Exportations
Balance		15 371	14 124	4 042	11 488	23 807	27 048	29 432	Balance
Iceland	G								**Islande**
Imports		2 031	1 992	2 489	2 503	2 591	2 253	2 274	Importations
Exports		1 638	1 852	2 050	2 005	1 891	2 021	2 227	Exportations
Balance		-393	-140	-438	-498	-700	-232	-47	Balance
Norway	G								**Norvège**
Imports		35 616	35 713	37 478	34 172	34 351	32 954	34 890	Importations
Exports		49 646	48 547	40 405	45 474	60 063	59 193	59 575	Exportations
Balance		14 030	12 834	2 926	11 302	25 712	26 239	24 686	Balance
Switzerland	S								**Suisse**
Imports		74 471	71 075	73 885	75 440	76 082	77 086	79 129	Importations
Exports		76 205	72 506	75 439	76 124	74 876	78 126	83 922	Exportations
Balance		1 735	1 431	1 554	684	-1 206	1 041	4 793	Balance
Other developed Europe[2]									**Autres pays dév. d'Eur.[2]**
Imports		4 056	3 916	4 136	4 340	4 950	4 553	4 877	Importations
Exports		2 123	1 983	2 291	2 409	2 874	2 461	2 660	Exportations
Balance		-1 933	-1 933	-1 846	-1 931	-2 076	-2 092	-2 217	Balance
Andorra	S								**Andorre**
Imports		816	946	972	...	...	...	...	Importations
Exports		35	42	52	...	...	...	...	Exportations
Balance		-781	-904	-920	...	...	...	...	Balance
Faeroe Islands	G								**Iles Féroé**
Imports		370	358	387	470	532	504	...	Importations
Exports		417	389	435	468	472	520	...	Exportations
Balance		47	31	48	-2	-60	16	...	Balance
Malta	G								**Malte**
Imports		2 796	2 552	2 666	2 841	3 401	2 726	2 840	Importations
Exports		1 731	1 630	1 833	1 980	2 447	1 958	2 131	Exportations
Balance		-1 064	-922	-834	-861	-953	-768	-709	Balance

73

Total imports and exports

Imports c.i.f., exports f.o.b., and balance, value in million US dollars

Importations et exportations totales

Importations c.a.f., exportations f.o.b. et balance, valeur en millions de dollare E.-U.

Country or area	Sys.&	1996	1997	1998	1999	2000	2001	2002	Pays ou zone
Developing economies[2]									Econ. en dévelop.[2]
Imports		23 029	27 989	27 951	25 560	26 519	28 655	32 337	Importations
Exports		15 892	16 598	18 097	17 029	17 407	17 966	18 368	Exportations
Balance		-7 137	-11 391	-9 854	-8 531	-9 112	-10 689	-13 969	Balance
Bosnia and Herzegovina	S								Bosnie-Herzégovine
Imports		...	...	2 921	3 276	3 085	3 219	4 066	Importations
Exports		...	...	594	748	1 067	1 083	1 020	Exportations
Balance		...	...	-2 327	-2 528	-2 017	-2 136	-3 047	Balance
Croatia	G								Croatie
Imports		7 788	9 104	8 383	7 799	7 887	9 147	10 714	Importations
Exports		4 512	4 171	4 541	4 303	4 432	4 666	4 899	Exportations
Balance		-3 276	-4 933	-3 842	-3 496	-3 455	-4 481	-5 815	Balance
Serbia and Montenegro	S								Serbie-et-Monténégro
Imports		4 102	4 799	4 622	...	...	...	...	Importations
Exports		1 842	2 368	2 604	...	...	...	...	Exportations
Balance		-2 260	-2 431	-2 018	...	...	...	...	Balance
Slovenia	S								Slovénie
Imports		9 423	9 357	10 110	9 952	10 107	10 144	10 937	Importations
Exports		8 312	8 372	9 048	8 604	8 733	9 251	9 471	Exportations
Balance		-1 111	-985	-1 062	-1 348	-1 374	-892	-1 466	Balance
TFYR of Macedonia	S								L'ex-R.y. Macédoine
Imports		1 627	1 779	1 915	1 796	2 085	1 676	1 928	Importations
Exports		1 148	1 237	1 311	1 192	1 319	1 154	1 112	Exportations
Balance		-479	-542	-604	-604	-766	-522	-816	Balance
Eastern Europe									Europe orientale
Imports		113 395	118 464	132 624	130 461	147 167	160 231	178 495	Importations
Exports		85 649	89 592	100 201	101 311	116 084	129 539	148 319	Exportations
Balance		-27 746	-28 872	-32 422	-29 150	-31 084	-30 692	-30 176	Balance
Albania	G								Albanie
Imports		841	649	829	1 140	1 091	1 331	1 504	Importations
Exports		208	139	205	264	261	305	330	Exportations
Balance		-633	-510	-624	-876	-829	-1 026	-1 173	Balance
Bulgaria	S								Bulgarie
Imports		6 861	5 223	4 954	5 454	6 505	7 263	7 987	Importations
Exports		6 602	5 322	4 197	3 964	4 809	5 115	5 749	Exportations
Balance		-259	99	-757	-1 490	-1 696	-2 148	-2 238	Balance
Czech Republic[4]	S								République tchèque[4]
Imports		27 724	27 189	28 814	28 087	32 180	36 473	40 756	Importations
Exports		21 917	22 751	26 417	26 245	29 057	33 399	38 361	Exportations
Balance		-5 807	-4 438	-2 396	-1 842	-3 123	-3 075	-2 395	Balance
Hungary[15,16]	S								Hongrie[15,16]
Imports		18 058	21 116	25 679	27 923	31 955	33 725	37 787	Importations
Exports		15 631	18 989	22 992	24 950	28 016	30 530	34 512	Exportations
Balance		-2 426	-2 126	-2 687	-2 973	-3 939	-3 195	-3 276	Balance
Poland	S								Pologne
Imports		37 045	42 237	46 803	45 778	48 970	50 378	55 141	Importations
Exports		24 389	25 708	27 370	27 323	31 684	36 159	41 032	Exportations
Balance		-12 656	-16 529	-19 433	-18 455	-17 285	-14 219	-14 108	Balance
Romania	S								Roumanie
Imports		11 435	11 280	11 821	10 392	13 055	15 561	17 862	Importations
Exports		8 085	8 431	8 300	8 505	10 367	11 391	13 876	Exportations
Balance		-3 351	-2 849	-3 521	-1 887	-2 688	-4 170	-3 986	Balance
Slovakia	S								Slovaquie
Imports		11 431	10 770	13 725	11 688	13 413	15 501	17 458	Importations
Exports		8 818	8 251	10 721	10 062	11 889	12 641	14 459	Exportations
Balance		-2 613	-2 519	-3 004	-1 625	-1 524	-2 860	-2 999	Balance
Former USSR - Europe									anc. URSS - Europe
Imports		81 772	92 821	81 375	61 165	70 148	80 867	89 547	Importations
Exports		112 840	115 898	100 254	97 436	134 250	134 097	144 283	Exportations
Balance		31 068	23 077	18 879	36 271	64 102	53 230	54 736	Balance

73

Total imports and exports

Imports c.i.f., exports f.o.b., and balance, value in million US dollars

Importations et exportations totales

Importations c.a.f., exportations f.o.b. et balance, valeur en millions de dollare E.-U.

Country or area	Sys.&	1996	1997	1998	1999	2000	2001	2002	Pays ou zone
Belarus	G								**Bélarus**
Imports		6 939	8 689	8 549	6 674	8 646	8 178	8 980	Importations
Exports		5 652	7 301	7 070	5 909	7 326	7 448	8 098	Exportations
Balance		-1 288	-1 388	-1 480	-765	-1 320	-730	-882	Balance
Estonia[16]	G								**Estonie**[16]
Imports		3 245	4 429	4 611	4 094	4 242	4 280	4 810	Importations
Exports		2 087	2 924	3 130	2 937	3 132	3 275	3 444	Exportations
Balance		-1 157	-1 506	-1 482	-1 157	-1 109	-1 005	-1 367	Balance
Latvia	S								**Lettonie**
Imports		2 320	2 721	3 191	2 945	3 187	3 504	4 053	Importations
Exports		1 443	1 672	1 811	1 723	1 867	2 001	2 284	Exportations
Balance		-876	-1 049	-1 380	-1 222	-1 320	-1 504	-1 769	Balance
Lithuania	G								**Lituanie**
Imports		4 559	5 644	5 794	4 835	5 457	6 353	7 825	Importations
Exports		3 355	3 860	3 711	3 004	3 810	4 583	5 553	Exportations
Balance		-1 204	-1 784	-2 083	-1 831	-1 647	-1 770	-2 271	Balance
Republic of Moldova	G								**République de Moldova**
Imports		1 072	1 171	1 024	586	776	897	...	Importations
Exports		795	874	632	463	471	570	...	Exportations
Balance		-277	-297	-392	-123	-305	-327	...	Balance
Russian Federation	G								**Fédération de Russie**
Imports		46 034	53 039	43 530	30 185	33 884	41 879	46 161	Importations
Exports		85 107	85 036	71 265	71 817	103 070	99 955	106 435	Exportations
Balance		39 073	31 997	27 735	41 632	69 186	58 076	60 274	Balance
Ukraine	G								**Ukraine**
Imports		17 603	17 128	14 676	11 846	13 956	15 775	16 977	Importations
Exports		14 401	14 232	12 637	11 582	14 573	16 265	17 957	Exportations
Balance		-3 203	-2 896	-2 039	-264	617	490	980	Balance

Africa · Afrique

Country or area	Sys.&	1996	1997	1998	1999	2000	2001	2002	Pays ou zone
South Africa[17,18]									**Afrique du Sud**[17,18]
Imports		29 105	31 939	28 277	25 890	28 980	27 421	28 261	Importations
Exports		28 145	29 964	25 396	25 901	29 267	28 439	28 713	Exportations
Balance		-960	-1 975	-2 881	11	287	1 019	452	Balance
Developing economies[2]									**Economies en dévelop.**[2]
Imports		88 692	89 167	101 239	99 492	98 306	104 055	108 190	Importations
Exports		85 557	84 230	75 888	88 870	110 447	98 545	101 123	Exportations
Balance		-3 135	-4 937	-25 351	-10 622	12 140	-5 510	-7 067	Balance
Northern Africa									**Afrique du Nord**
Imports		45 257	45 367	50 609	48 965	48 351	50 169	54 869	Importations
Exports		38 031	38 097	31 671	37 808	51 325	43 273	44 704	Exportations
Balance		-7 226	-7 271	-18 938	-11 157	2 974	-6 896	-10 165	Balance
Algeria	S								**Algérie**
Imports		9 112	8 691	9 404	9 190	...	...	...	Importations
Exports		13 521	13 728	10 215	...	...	...	...	Exportations
Balance		4 409	5 037	811	...	...	...	...	Balance
Egypt[19]	S								**Egypte**[19]
Imports		13 038	13 211	16 166	16 022	14 010	12 756	12 552	Importations
Exports		3 539	3 921	3 130	3 559	4 691	4 128	4 708	Exportations
Balance		-9 499	-9 290	-13 036	-12 463	-9 319	-8 628	-7 844	Balance
Libyan Arab Jamah.	G								**Jamah. arabe libyenne**
Imports		4 383	4 640	4 708	4 158	3 732	4 388	6 986	Importations
Exports		8 190	7 497	5 072	7 933	10 195	8 899	9 173	Exportations
Balance		3 807	2 857	364	3 775	6 463	4 510	2 188	Balance
Morocco	S								**Maroc**
Imports		9 704	9 526	10 290	9 925	11 534	11 037	11 647	Importations
Exports		6 881	7 033	7 153	7 367	6 956	7 144	7 772	Exportations
Balance		-2 823	-2 493	-3 137	-2 558	-4 577	-3 893	-3 874	Balance
Sudan[20]	G								**Soudan**[20]
Imports		1 548	1 580	1 915	1 415	1 553	1 586	...	Importations
Exports		620	594	596	780	1 807	1 699	...	Exportations
Balance		-927	-985	-1 319	-635	254	113	...	Balance

73

Total imports and exports

Imports c.i.f., exports f.o.b., and balance, value in million US dollars

Importations et exportations totales

Importations c.a.f., exportations f.o.b. et balance, valeur en millions de dollare E.-U.

Country or area	Sys.&	1996	1997	1998	1999	2000	2001	2002	Pays ou zone
Tunisia	G								**Tunisie**
Imports		7 701	7 948	8 350	8 475	8 567	9 529	9 526	Importations
Exports		5 517	5 560	5 738	5 872	5 850	6 609	6 874	Exportations
Balance		-2 185	-2 388	-2 613	-2 603	-2 717	-2 920	-2 652	Balance
Other Africa									**Autre Afrique**
Imports		43 435	43 799	50 630	50 527	49 956	53 886	53 321	Importations
Exports		47 526	46 133	44 217	51 062	59 122	55 272	56 419	Exportations
Balance		4 090	2 334	-6 413	535	9 166	1 386	3 097	Balance
EMCCA +									**CEMAC +**
Imports		4 498	4 192	4 108	3 850	3 835	4 748	5 511	Importations
Exports		6 855	7 443	5 816	6 608	8 217	7 418	8 135	Exportations
Balance		2 357	3 251	1 709	2 758	4 383	2 670	2 624	Balance
Cameroon	S								**Cameroun**
Imports		1 226	1 359	1 503	1 314	...	...	...	Importations
Exports		1 768	1 860	1 675	1 595	...	...	...	Exportations
Balance		542	501	172	281	...	...	...	Balance
Central African Rep.	S								**Rép. centrafricaine**
Imports		141	141	146	131	118	107	...	Importations
Exports		147	163	151	147	161	143	...	Exportations
Balance		5	22	5	15	44	35	...	Balance
Chad	S								**Tchad**
Imports		332	335	356	317	318	621	995	Importations
Exports		238	238	262	202	184	189	189	Exportations
Balance		-94	-97	-94	-115	-135	-432	-806	Balance
Congo	S								**Congo**
Imports		1 550	925	682	820	464	...	...	Importations
Exports		1 343	1 666	1 373	1 555	2 477	...	...	Exportations
Balance		-207	741	691	735	2 013	...	...	Balance
Equatorial Guinea	G								**Guinée équatoriale**
Imports		292	330	317	425	451	...	...	Importations
Exports		175	495	438	708	1 097	...	...	Exportations
Balance		-117	165	122	284	646	...	...	Balance
Gabon	S								**Gabon**
Imports		956	1 103	1 103	844	996	858	...	Importations
Exports		3 183	3 021	1 916	2 401	2 465	2 646	...	Exportations
Balance		2 227	1 918	813	1 557	1 470	1 788	...	Balance
ECOWAS +									**CEDEAO +**
Imports		17 719	20 354	21 117	21 357	20 335	23 115	21 214	Importations
Exports		26 368	25 114	20 512	24 745	30 515	27 233	26 546	Exportations
Balance		8 650	4 760	-605	3 389	10 180	4 117	5 332	Balance
Benin	S								**Bénin**
Imports		654	681	736	749	613	603	664	Importations
Exports		653	417	407	422	392	372	377	Exportations
Balance		-1	-264	-328	-327	-221	-231	-286	Balance
Burkina Faso	G								**Burkina Faso**
Imports		647	588	732	678	611	656	740	Importations
Exports		234	232	319	255	209	234	237	Exportations
Balance		-413	-355	-412	-423	-401	-422	-502	Balance
Cape Verde	G								**Cap-Vert**
Imports		234	237	229	248	237	233	...	Importations
Exports		13	14	10	12	11	10	...	Exportations
Balance		-222	-223	-218	-237	-227	-223	...	Balance
Côte d'Ivoire	S								**Côte d'Ivoire**
Imports		2 900	2 782	3 358	3 217	2 782	2 636	3 799	Importations
Exports		4 444	4 460	4 610	4 675	3 905	3 956	5 157	Exportations
Balance		1 543	1 679	1 252	1 458	1 123	1 320	1 358	Balance
Gambia	G								**Gambie**
Imports		258	174	245	192	...	...	...	Importations
Exports		21	15	27	7	...	...	...	Exportations
Balance		-237	-159	-218	-185	...	...	...	Balance

73
Total imports and exports
Imports c.i.f., exports f.o.b., and balance, value in million US dollars
Importations et exportations totales
Importations c.a.f., exportations f.o.b. et balance, valeur en millions de dollare E.-U.

Country or area	Sys.&	1996	1997	1998	1999	2000	2001	2002	Pays ou zone
Ghana	G								**Ghana**
Imports		2 101	2 310	2 561	3 505	2 973	...	...	Importations
Exports		1 670	1 636	1 792	...	...	...	...	Exportations
Balance		-431	-674	-769	...	...	...	...	Balance
Guinea-Bissau	G								**Guinée-Bissau**
Imports		85	89	63	51	59	74	105	Importations
Exports		28	49	26	51	62	62	55	Exportations
Balance		-57	-40	-37	0	3	-12	-50	Balance
Mali	S								**Mali**
Imports		772	738	761	824	807	708	752	Importations
Exports		433	561	561	566	547	725	918	Exportations
Balance		-340	-177	-199	-258	-261	16	167	Balance
Niger	S								**Niger**
Imports		448	374	470	395	395	370	399	Importations
Exports		325	272	334	288	285	273	279	Exportations
Balance		-123	-102	-136	-107	-111	-97	-120	Balance
Nigeria	G								**Nigéria**
Imports		6 438	9 501	9 211	8 588	8 721	11 586	7 547	Importations
Exports		16 154	15 207	9 855	13 856	20 975	17 261	15 107	Exportations
Balance		9 715	5 706	644	5 268	12 254	5 675	7 560	Balance
Senegal	G								**Sénégal**
Imports		1 435	1 333	1 455	1 561	1 519	1 478	...	Importations
Exports		987	904	968	1 025	920	1 005	1 106	Exportations
Balance		-448	-429	-487	-535	-599	-473	...	Balance
Sierra Leone	S								**Sierra Leone**
Imports		211	92	95	80	149	182	264	Importations
Exports		47	17	7	6	13	29	49	Exportations
Balance		-164	-75	-88	-74	-136	-153	-216	Balance
Togo	S								**Togo**
Imports		664	645	589	572	562	553	592	Importations
Exports		441	424	969	389	361	357	251	Exportations
Balance		-224	-221	381	-183	-201	-196	-341	Balance
Rest of Africa									**Reste de l'Afrique**
Imports		21 219	19 253	25 405	25 320	25 786	26 023	26 596	Importations
Exports		14 302	13 577	17 888	19 708	20 389	20 621	21 738	Exportations
Balance		-6 916	-5 676	-7 516	-5 612	-5 397	-5 402	-4 858	Balance
Botswana	G								**Botswana**
Imports		...	...	2 320	2 197	2 469	1 816	...	Importations
Exports		...	...	2 075	2 645	2 681	2 480	...	Exportations
Balance		...	...	-245	447	213	664	...	Balance
Burundi	S								**Burundi**
Imports		127	121	158	118	148	139	129	Importations
Exports		40	87	65	54	50	39	30	Exportations
Balance		-87	-35	-93	-64	-98	-101	-99	Balance
Dem. Rep. of the Congo	S								**Rép. dém. du Congo**
Imports		424	...	...	...	...	...	...	Importations
Exports		592	...	...	...	...	...	...	Exportations
Balance		167	...	...	...	...	...	...	Balance
Djibouti	G								**Djibouti**
Imports		179	148	158	153	...	...	...	Importations
Exports		14	11	12	12	...	...	...	Exportations
Balance		-165	-137	-146	-140	...	...	...	Balance
Eritrea	G								**Erythrée**
Imports		450	425	356	382	...	...	...	Importations
Exports		76	52	26	20	...	...	...	Exportations
Balance		-374	-373	-330	-362	...	...	...	Balance
Ethiopia	G								**Ethiopie**
Imports		1 401	...	...	1 317	...	...	...	Importations
Exports		417	587	560	...	...	...	...	Exportations
Balance		-984	...	...	...	...	...	...	Balance

73

Total imports and exports
Imports c.i.f., exports f.o.b., and balance, value in million US dollars
Importations et exportations totales
Importations c.a.f., exportations f.o.b. et balance, valeur en millions de dollare E.-U.

Country or area	Sys.&	1996	1997	1998	1999	2000	2001	2002	Pays ou zone
Kenya	G								**Kenya**
Imports		2 949	3 296	3 195	2 833	3 105	3 189	3 245	Importations
Exports		2 068	2 054	2 007	1 747	1 734	1 943	2 116	Exportations
Balance		-881	-1 243	-1 188	-1 086	-1 372	-1 246	-1 129	Balance
Lesotho	G								**Lesotho**
Imports		...	...	863	781	728	681	776	Importations
Exports		...	...	194	172	221	280	369	Exportations
Balance		...	...	-670	-609	-507	-401	-407	Balance
Madagascar	S								**Madagascar**
Imports		507	467	514	377	...	...	...	Importations
Exports		299	222	243	221	...	...	...	Exportations
Balance		-208	-245	-271	-156	...	...	...	Balance
Malawi	G								**Malawi**
Imports		623	791	515	673	533	563	669	Importations
Exports		481	537	430	453	379	449	447	Exportations
Balance		-143	-255	-85	-221	-153	-113	-222	Balance
Mauritius	G								**Maurice**
Imports		2 289	2 181	2 073	2 248	2 091	1 993	...	Importations
Exports		1 802	1 592	1 645	1 554	1 551	1 615	...	Exportations
Balance		-487	-588	-428	-694	-540	-377	...	Balance
Mozambique	S								**Mozambique**
Imports		759	739	790	1 139	1 158	...	...	Importations
Exports		217	222	230	263	364	...	...	Exportations
Balance		-542	-517	-560	-876	-794	...	...	Balance
Namibia	G								**Namibie**
Imports		...	...	1 636	1 609	1 539	1 542	...	Importations
Exports		...	...	1 224	1 233	1 317	1 180	...	Exportations
Balance		...	...	-412	-376	-222	-362	...	Balance
Rwanda	G								**Rwanda**
Imports		257	297	284	250	211	250	203	Importations
Exports		61	87	60	60	52	85	56	Exportations
Balance		-197	-210	-224	-190	-159	-165	-148	Balance
Sao Tome and Principe	S								**Sao Tomé-et-Principe**
Imports		22	16	...	...	...	...	...	Importations
Exports		5	5	...	...	...	...	...	Exportations
Balance		-18	-11	...	...	...	...	...	Balance
Seychelles	G								**Seychelles**
Imports		379	340	384	434	342	523	...	Importations
Exports		139	113	122	145	194	216	...	Exportations
Balance		-239	-227	-261	-289	-149	-307	...	Balance
Swaziland	G								**Swaziland**
Imports		...	...	1 071	1 068	1 031	1 097	983	Importations
Exports		...	...	963	937	896	1 031	939	Exportations
Balance		...	...	-108	-131	-135	-66	-44	Balance
Uganda	G								**Ouganda**
Imports		1 190	1 317	1 414	1 342	1 512	1 594	1 112	Importations
Exports		587	555	501	517	469	457	442	Exportations
Balance		-603	-762	-913	-825	-1 043	-1 137	-670	Balance
United Rep. of Tanzania	G								**Rép.-Unie de Tanzanie**
Imports		1 386	1 336	1 453	1 550	1 523	1 713	1 687	Importations
Exports		783	752	589	543	663	777	875	Exportations
Balance		-603	-584	-864	-1 007	-860	-935	-812	Balance
Zambia	S								**Zambie**
Imports		836	819	...	...	...	...	...	Importations
Exports		1 049	914	...	...	...	...	...	Exportations
Balance		213	96	...	...	...	...	...	Balance
Zimbabwe	G								**Zimbabwe**
Imports		2 817	3 058	2 700	2 178	1 863	...	...	Importations
Exports		2 419	2 456	2 044	2 140	2 109	...	...	Exportations
Balance		-399	-601	-656	-38	246	...	...	Balance

73
Total imports and exports
Imports c.i.f., exports f.o.b., and balance, value in million US dollars
Importations et exportations totales
Importations c.a.f., exportations f.o.b. et balance, valeur en millions de dollare E.-U.

Country or area	Sys.&	1996	1997	1998	1999	2000	2001	2002	Pays ou zone
Asia · Asie									
Developed economies [2]									**Economies développées [2]**
Imports		371 510	358 277	298 083	328 931	402 984	368 352	352 302	Importations
Exports		422 252	432 218	399 238	429 180	496 439	416 378	425 652	Exportations
Balance		50 742	73 941	101 154	100 249	93 455	48 026	73 350	Balance
Israel [21]	S								**Israël [21]**
Imports		31 620	30 782	29 342	33 166	37 686	35 449	35 517	Importations
Exports		20 610	22 503	22 993	25 794	31 404	29 048	29 347	Exportations
Balance		-11 010	-8 279	-6 349	-7 371	-6 281	-6 401	-6 170	Balance
Japan	G								**Japon**
Imports		349 174	338 830	280 632	310 039	379 491	349 189	337 209	Importations
Exports		410 926	421 050	388 135	417 659	479 227	403 616	416 730	Exportations
Balance		61 752	82 220	107 503	107 620	99 736	54 427	79 520	Balance
Developing economies [2,22]									**Econ. en dévelop. [2,22]**
Imports		1 045 542	1 067 802	892 374	965 220	1 218 543	1 131 604	1 226 715	Importations
Exports		1 007 080	1 076 361	1 001 233	1 104 339	1 375 305	1 269 272	1 376 723	Exportations
Balance		-38 462	8 559	108 859	139 119	156 762	137 668	150 007	Balance
Asia Middle East									**Moyen-Orient d'Asie**
Imports		151 878	161 667	156 072	151 902	191 201	171 550	189 832	Importations
Exports		174 238	186 138	157 478	195 905	274 424	243 003	246 395	Exportations
Balance		22 359	24 471	1 405	44 003	83 223	71 453	56 563	Balance
Bahrain	G								**Bahreïn**
Imports		4 273	4 026	3 566	3 698	4 634	4 306	4 985	Importations
Exports		4 702	4 384	3 270	4 363	6 195	5 577	5 369	Exportations
Balance		429	358	-296	665	1 561	1 271	384	Balance
Cyprus	G								**Chypre**
Imports		3 983	3 655	3 687	3 618	3 846	3 938	4 084	Importations
Exports		1 391	1 250	1 062	997	954	976	843	Exportations
Balance		-2 591	-2 405	-2 625	-2 621	-2 893	-2 962	-3 240	Balance
Iran (Islamic Rep. of) [23,24]	S								**Iran (Rép. islamique d') [23,24]**
Imports		16 274	14 196	14 323	12 683	14 296	17 938	22 190	Importations
Exports		22 391	18 381	13 118	21 030	28 345	23 716	24 440	Exportations
Balance		6 117	4 185	-1 205	8 347	14 049	5 778	2 250	Balance
Jordan	G								**Jordanie**
Imports		4 293	4 102	3 828	3 717	4 597	4 844	...	Importations
Exports		1 817	1 836	1 802	1 832	1 899	2 293	...	Exportations
Balance		-2 476	-2 266	-2 026	-1 885	-2 698	-2 551	...	Balance
Kuwait	S								**Koweït**
Imports		8 373	8 246	8 617	7 617	7 157	7 869	9 010	Importations
Exports		14 889	14 225	9 553	12 164	19 436	16 203	15 369	Exportations
Balance		6 515	5 979	936	4 547	12 279	8 334	6 359	Balance
Lebanon	G								**Liban**
Imports		7 540	7 467	7 070	6 207	6 228	...	...	Importations
Exports		736	643	662	677	714	...	...	Exportations
Balance		-6 804	-6 824	-6 408	-5 530	-5 514	...	...	Balance
Oman	G								**Oman**
Imports		4 578	5 026	5 682	4 674	5 040	5 798	6 005	Importations
Exports		7 346	7 630	5 508	7 238	11 319	11 074	11 172	Exportations
Balance		2 768	2 604	-173	2 564	6 279	5 276	5 167	Balance
Qatar	S								**Qatar**
Imports		2 868	3 322	3 409	2 499	...	...	...	Importations
Exports		3 752	3 791	4 880	7 059	...	...	...	Exportations
Balance		884	470	1 471	4 560	...	...	...	Balance
Saudi Arabia	S								**Arabie saoudite**
Imports		27 744	28 732	30 013	28 010	30 237	31 223	32 312	Importations
Exports		60 729	60 732	38 822	50 760	77 583	68 064	...	Exportations
Balance		32 985	32 000	8 809	22 750	47 345	36 841	...	Balance
Syrian Arab Republic	S								**Rép. arabe syrienne**
Imports		5 380	4 028	3 895	3 832	16 706	5 846	5 097	Importations
Exports		3 999	3 916	2 890	3 464	19 260	6 451	6 831	Exportations
Balance		-1 381	-111	-1 005	-368	2 553	605	1 734	Balance

73

Total imports and exports

Imports c.i.f., exports f.o.b., and balance, value in million US dollars

Importations et exportations totales

Importations c.a.f., exportations f.o.b. et balance, valeur en millions de dollare E.-U.

Country or area	Sys.&	1996	1997	1998	1999	2000	2001	2002	Pays ou zone
Turkey	S								**Turquie**
Imports		43 627	48 559	45 921	40 671	54 503	41 399	49 663	Importations
Exports		23 225	26 261	26 974	26 587	27 775	31 334	34 561	Exportations
Balance		-20 402	-22 298	-18 947	-14 084	-26 728	-10 065	-15 101	Balance
United Arab Emirates	G								**Emirats arabes unis**
Imports		22 638	29 952	24 728	33 231	38 139	...	...	Importations
Exports		28 085	39 613	42 666	43 307	...	...	...	Exportations
Balance		5 447	9 661	17 938	10 076	...	...	...	Balance
Yemen	S								**Yémen**
Imports		2 442	2 017	2 172	2 006	2 326	2 309	...	Importations
Exports		3 206	2 509	1 501	2 438	4 078	3 214	...	Exportations
Balance		763	491	-671	432	1 751	905	...	Balance
Non Petrol. Exports[25]									**Pétrole non Compris**[25]
Exports		111 242	62 312	60 768	73 025	102 397	100 182	92 853	Exportations
Other Asia									**Autre Asie**
Imports		879 944	892 407	723 341	801 399	1 013 386	943 789	1 020 738	Importations
Exports		817 965	874 701	832 230	895 704	1 082 853	1 007 789	1 110 837	Exportations
Balance		-61 979	-17 707	108 889	94 306	69 467	64 000	90 099	Balance
ASEAN+									**ANASE+**
Imports		374 911	370 119	280 236	299 142	367 558	337 567	345 796	Importations
Exports		340 008	350 776	327 666	357 424	424 563	382 885	403 307	Exportations
Balance		-34 903	-19 343	47 429	58 282	57 005	45 318	57 511	Balance
Brunei Darussalam	S								**Brunéi Darussalam**
Imports		2 494	2 203	1 552	...	...	...	...	Importations
Exports		2 481	2 467	2 058	...	...	...	...	Exportations
Balance		-13	264	506	...	...	...	...	Balance
Cambodia	S								**Cambodge**
Imports		...	1 116	1 129	1 243	1 424	1 456	...	Importations
Exports		...	626	933	1 040	1 123	1 296	...	Exportations
Balance		...	-491	-195	-203	-302	-160	...	Balance
Indonesia	S								**Indonésie**
Imports		42 929	41 694	27 337	24 003	33 515	31 010	25 388	Importations
Exports		49 814	53 443	48 848	48 666	62 124	56 447	58 120	Exportations
Balance		6 885	11 749	21 511	24 662	28 609	25 437	32 732	Balance
Lao People's Dem. Rep.	S								**Rép. dém. pop. lao**
Imports		690	706	553	525	535	528	431	Importations
Exports		323	359	370	311	330	331	298	Exportations
Balance		-367	-347	-183	-214	-205	-197	-133	Balance
Malaysia	G								**Malaisie**
Imports		78 408	79 030	58 278	65 385	81 963	73 867	79 868	Importations
Exports		78 318	78 742	73 255	84 617	98 230	88 006	93 264	Exportations
Balance		-90	-288	14 977	19 231	16 266	14 139	13 396	Balance
Myanmar	G								**Myanmar**
Imports		1 371	2 056	2 695	2 323	2 401	2 877	...	Importations
Exports		754	874	1 077	1 136	1 647	2 382	...	Exportations
Balance		-618	-1 182	-1 617	-1 187	-755	-496	...	Balance
Philippines	G								**Philippines**
Imports		34 127	38 604	31 542	32 569	36 887	34 944	37 202	Importations
Exports		20 408	24 895	29 449	36 577	39 794	32 664	36 510	Exportations
Balance		-13 719	-13 709	-2 093	4 008	2 907	-2 280	-692	Balance
Singapore	G								**Singapour**
Imports		131 340	132 443	104 728	111 062	134 546	116 004	116 448	Importations
Exports		125 016	124 990	109 905	114 682	137 806	121 755	125 177	Exportations
Balance		-6 324	-7 453	5 177	3 620	3 259	5 752	8 730	Balance
Thailand	S								**Thaïlande**
Imports		72 336	62 880	42 971	50 343	61 924	62 058	64 658	Importations
Exports		55 721	57 402	54 458	58 440	69 057	65 114	68 768	Exportations
Balance		-16 616	-5 479	11 487	8 098	7 133	3 055	4 110	Balance
Viet Nam	G								**Viet Nam**
Imports		11 144	11 592	11 500	11 742	15 638	15 999	19 000	Importations
Exports		7 256	9 185	9 361	11 540	14 449	15 100	16 530	Exportations
Balance		-3 888	-2 407	-2 139	-202	-1 189	-899	-2 470	Balance

73

Total imports and exports
Imports c.i.f., exports f.o.b., and balance, value in million US dollars
Importations et exportations totales
Importations c.a.f., exportations f.o.b. et balance, valeur en millions de dollare E.-U.

Country or area	Sys.&	1996	1997	1998	1999	2000	2001	2002	Pays ou zone
Rest of Asia									**Reste de l'Asie**
Imports		505 032	522 289	443 105	502 256	645 828	606 222	674 942	Importations
Exports		477 957	523 925	504 565	538 280	658 291	624 904	707 530	Exportations
Balance		-27 075	1 636	61 460	36 024	12 462	18 682	32 588	Balance
Bangladesh	G								**Bangladesh**
Imports		6 621	6 896	6 978	7 685	8 358	8 349	7 913	Importations
Exports		3 297	3 778	3 831	3 919	4 787	4 826	4 566	Exportations
Balance		-3 324	-3 117	-3 147	-3 766	-3 572	-3 523	-3 348	Balance
Bhutan	G								**Bhoutan**
Imports		128	137	135	182	203	...	...	Importations
Exports		100	118	108	116	121	...	...	Exportations
Balance		-27	-19	-26	-66	-81	...	...	Balance
China	S								**Chine**
Imports		138 833	142 370	140 237	165 699	225 094	243 553	295 171	Importations
Exports		151 048	182 792	183 712	194 931	249 203	266 098	325 591	Exportations
Balance		12 215	40 422	43 475	29 232	24 109	22 545	30 420	Balance
China, Hong Kong SAR	G								**Chine, Hong Kong RAS**
Imports		198 550	208 614	184 518	179 520	212 805	201 076	207 644	Importations
Exports		180 750	188 059	174 002	173 885	201 860	189 894	200 092	Exportations
Balance		-17 800	-20 555	-10 516	-5 635	-10 945	-11 182	-7 552	Balance
China, Macao SAR	G								**Chine, Macao RAS**
Imports		2 000	2 082	1 955	2 040	2 255	2 386	2 530	Importations
Exports		1 996	2 148	2 141	2 200	2 539	2 300	2 356	Exportations
Balance		-4	66	186	160	284	-87	-174	Balance
India	G								**Inde**
Imports		37 944	41 430	42 999	46 971	51 563	50 390	56 496	Importations
Exports		33 107	35 006	33 463	35 666	42 378	43 338	49 293	Exportations
Balance		-4 837	-6 425	-9 536	-11 305	-9 185	-7 052	-7 202	Balance
Korea, Republic of	G								**Corée, République de**
Imports		150 339	144 616	93 282	119 725	160 481	141 098	152 126	Importations
Exports		129 715	136 164	132 313	143 685	172 267	150 439	162 470	Exportations
Balance		-20 624	-8 452	39 031	23 960	11 786	9 341	10 344	Balance
Maldives	G								**Maldives**
Imports		302	349	354	402	389	393	392	Importations
Exports		59	73	74	64	76	76	90	Exportations
Balance		-243	-276	-280	-338	-313	-317	-301	Balance
Mongolia	G								**Mongolie**
Imports		451	468	503	513	615	630	...	Importations
Exports		424	452	345	358	466	448	...	Exportations
Balance		-27	-17	-158	-154	-148	-182	...	Balance
Nepal	G								**Népal**
Imports		1 398	1 693	1 245	1 418	1 573	1 475	1 419	Importations
Exports		385	406	474	600	804	738	567	Exportations
Balance		-1 013	-1 287	-772	-818	-768	-737	-851	Balance
Pakistan	G								**Pakistan**
Imports		12 191	11 652	9 331	10 154	10 864	10 192	11 227	Importations
Exports		9 367	8 760	8 515	8 380	9 028	9 238	9 908	Exportations
Balance		-2 824	-2 893	-816	-1 775	-1 836	-953	-1 319	Balance
Sri Lanka	G								**Sri Lanka**
Imports		5 442	5 864	5 877	5 960	7 210	5 973	6 105	Importations
Exports		4 095	4 639	4 787	4 594	5 433	4 815	4 699	Exportations
Balance		-1 347	-1 225	-1 091	-1 367	-1 776	-1 158	-1 406	Balance
Timor-Leste	S								**Timor-Leste**
Imports		132	142	135	82	...	...	...	Importations
Exports		41	48	56	45	...	...	...	Exportations
Balance		-91	-94	-79	-37	...	...	...	Balance
Former USSR - Asia									**anc URSS - Asie**
Imports		13 720	13 728	12 961	11 920	13 956	16 265	16 145	Importations
Exports		14 877	15 523	11 525	12 730	18 028	18 480	19 491	Exportations
Balance		1 157	1 795	-1 436	810	4 072	2 216	3 346	Balance

73

Total imports and exports

Imports c.i.f., exports f.o.b., and balance, value in million US dollars

Importations et exportations totales

Importations c.a.f., exportations f.o.b. et balance, valeur en millions de dollare E.-U.

Country or area	Sys.&	1996	1997	1998	1999	2000	2001	2002	Pays ou zone
Armenia	S								**Arménie**
Imports		856	892	902	800	882	874	991	Importations
Exports		290	233	221	232	294	343	507	Exportations
Balance		-566	-660	-682	-568	-588	-532	-484	Balance
Azerbaijan	G								**Azerbaïdjan**
Imports		961	794	1 077	1 036	1 172	1 431	1 666	Importations
Exports		631	781	606	929	1 745	2 314	2 164	Exportations
Balance		-329	-13	-471	-107	573	883	499	Balance
Georgia	G								**Géorgie**
Imports		687	944	878	...	...	...	...	Importations
Exports		199	240	192	...	...	...	...	Exportations
Balance		-489	-704	-686	...	...	...	...	Balance
Kazakhstan	G								**Kazakhstan**
Imports		4 241	4 301	4 314	3 655	5 040	6 446	6 584	Importations
Exports		5 911	6 497	5 334	5 872	8 812	8 639	9 670	Exportations
Balance		1 670	2 196	1 020	2 217	3 772	2 193	3 086	Balance
Kyrgyzstan	S								**Kirghizistan**
Imports		838	709	842	615	559	472	592	Importations
Exports		505	604	514	463	511	480	488	Exportations
Balance		-332	-105	-328	-152	-48	9	-104	Balance
Tajikistan	G								**Tadjikistan**
Imports		668	750	711	664	675	688	721	Importations
Exports		770	746	597	689	784	652	737	Exportations
Balance		102	-5	-114	25	109	-36	16	Balance
Uzbekistan	G								**Ouzbékistan**
Imports		4 721	4 523	3 289	3 111	2 947	3 137	2 712	Importations
Exports		4 590	4 388	3 528	3 236	3 265	3 265	2 988	Exportations
Balance		-131	-136	240	125	317	128	276	Balance
Oceania · Océanie									
Developed economies [2]									**Economies développées [2]**
Imports		76 932	77 098	73 768	80 039	81 663	73 192	82 764	Importations
Exports		71 441	73 814	64 605	65 116	73 370	73 068	74 409	Exportations
Balance		-5 490	-3 285	-9 163	-14 923	-8 293	-124	-8 355	Balance
Australia	G								**Australie**
Imports		65 428	65 892	64 630	69 158	71 537	63 890	72 679	Importations
Exports		60 300	62 910	55 893	56 080	63 878	63 389	65 037	Exportations
Balance		-5 128	-2 982	-8 737	-13 078	-7 659	-501	-7 643	Balance
New Zealand	G								**Nouvelle-Zélande**
Imports		14 724	14 519	12 496	14 299	13 906	13 347	15 077	Importations
Exports		14 362	14 216	12 069	12 454	13 272	13 724	14 364	Exportations
Balance		-362	-303	-427	-1 844	-634	377	-713	Balance
Developing economies [2]									**Economies en dévelop. [2]**
Imports		7 380	7 424	7 222	7 491	7 455	7 590	8 064	Importations
Exports		5 652	5 237	4 669	5 169	5 359	4 790	4 597	Exportations
Balance		-1 727	-2 186	-2 553	-2 322	-2 097	-2 800	-3 467	Balance
Cook Islands	G								**Iles Cook**
Imports		43	48	38	41	50	47	46	Importations
Exports		3	3	3	4	9	7	5	Exportations
Balance		-40	-45	-35	-38	-41	-40	-41	Balance
Fiji	G								**Fidji**
Imports		987	965	721	903	830	794	898	Importations
Exports		749	619	510	609	585	537	550	Exportations
Balance		-239	-346	-211	-294	-246	-257	-348	Balance
French Polynesia	S								**Polynésie française**
Imports		1 016	936	1 096	927	974	1 108	...	Importations
Exports		251	222	248	253	222	204	...	Exportations
Balance		-765	-714	-847	-674	-753	-904	...	Balance
Kiribati [4]	G								**Kiribati [4]**
Imports		38	39	33	41	40	...	...	Importations
Exports		5	6	6	9	6	...	...	Exportations
Balance		-33	-33	-27	-32	-33	...	...	Balance

73
Total imports and exports

Imports c.i.f., exports f.o.b., and balance, value in million US dollars

Importations et exportations totales

Importations c.a.f., exportations f.o.b. et balance, valeur en millions de dollare E.-U.

Country or area	Sys.&	1996	1997	1998	1999	2000	2001	2002	Pays ou zone
Marshall Islands	G								**Iles Marshall**
Imports		72	58	67	...	68	...	...	Importations
Exports		18	28	6	8	7	...	...	Exportations
Balance		-54	-30	-62	...	-61	...	...	Balance
Micronesia (Fed. States)	S								**Micronésie (Etats féd. de)**
Imports		84	...	49	12	...	...	...	Importations
Exports		14	...	...	...	...	...	...	Exportations
Balance		-70	...	...	...	...	...	...	Balance
New Caledonia	S								**Nouvelle-Calédonie**
Imports		1 001	928	938	1 009	925	977	...	Importations
Exports		554	542	382	468	606	465	...	Exportations
Balance		-447	-386	-555	-541	-319	-512	...	Balance
Northern Mariana Islands	G								**Iles Mariannes du Nord**
Exports		...	...	1 000				...	Exportations
Palau	S								**Palaos**
Imports		72	69	66	78	123	...	...	Importations
Exports		14	12	11	11	...	...	...	Exportations
Balance		-58	-57	-55	-67	...	...	...	Balance
Papua New Guinea	G								**Papouasie-Nvl-Guinée**
Imports		1 741	1 709	1 240	1 236	1 151	1 073	1 103	Importations
Exports		2 531	2 160	1 772	1 927	2 096	1 813	1 549	Exportations
Balance		789	451	532	691	945	740	446	Balance
Samoa	S								**Samoa**
Imports		100	97	97	115	106	130	113	Importations
Exports		10	15	15	20	14	16	14	Exportations
Balance		-90	-82	-82	-95	-92	-115	-99	Balance
Solomon Islands	S								**Iles Salomon**
Imports		151	183	150	...	...	...	...	Importations
Exports		162	174	126	...	...	...	...	Exportations
Balance		11	-10	-24	...	...	...	...	Balance
Tonga	G								**Tonga**
Imports		75	73	69	73	69	73	...	Importations
Exports		13	10	8	12	9	7	...	Exportations
Balance		-61	-63	-61	-60	-61	-66	...	Balance
Vanuatu	G								**Vanuatu**
Imports		97	94	88	96	89	...	...	Importations
Exports		30	35	34	26	26	...	...	Exportations
Balance		-67	-59	-54	-70	-63	...	...	Balance
ANCOM+									**ANCOM+**
Imports		36 936	45 310	46 162	35 992	40 559	45 329	42 185	Importations
Exports		45 570	45 864	39 087	44 068	57 959	49 662	52 878	Exportations
Balance		8 634	553	-7 075	8 076	17 399	4 333	10 693	Balance
APEC+									**CEAP+**
Imports		2 329 501	2 451 731	2 275 662	2 500 086	3 020 207	2 819 943	2 912 322	Importations
Exports		2 215 152	2 368 475	2 266 380	2 414 351	2 824 772	2 595 750	2 667 605	Exportations
Balance		-114 348	-83 255	-9 282	-85 735	-195 435	-224 192	-244 716	Balance
CARICOM+									**CARICOM+**
Imports		10 294	12 060	12 267	12 171	13 059	13 478	13 431	Importations
Exports		5 478	6 054	5 418	6 231	7 801	7 484	6 875	Exportations
Balance		-4 816	-6 006	-6 848	-5 941	-5 258	-5 993	-6 556	Balance
CIS+									**CEI+**
Imports		85 369	93 755	80 704	61 211	71 219	82 994	89 005	Importations
Exports		120 832	122 966	103 128	102 501	143 469	142 719	152 493	Exportations
Balance		35 462	29 211	22 389	41 290	72 250	59 725	63 489	Balance
COMESA+									**COMESA+**
Imports		30 664	31 458	36 963	36 261	34 625	34 013	33 942	Importations
Exports		16 649	16 651	17 748	19 794	22 321	21 896	23 279	Exportations
Balance		-14 015	-14 807	-19 215	-16 467	-12 303	-12 117	-10 662	Balance
LDC+									**PMA+**
Imports		33 187	34 604	37 236	38 356	40 278	41 418	42 514	Importations
Exports		21 581	21 869	22 356	25 043	30 072	30 587	31 761	Exportations
Balance		-11 606	-12 735	-14 880	-13 313	-10 206	-10 831	-10 753	Balance

73

Total imports and exports

Imports c.i.f., exports f.o.b., and balance, value in million US dollars

Importations et exportations totales

Importations c.a.f., exportations f.o.b. et balance, valeur en millions de dollare E.-U.

Country or area	Sys.&	1996	1997	1998	1999	2000	2001	2002	Pays ou zone
MERCOSUR+									**MERCOSUR+**
Imports		86 882	102 272	98 336	82 349	89 427	83 720	62 337	Importations
Exports		74 998	83 179	81 366	74 322	84 590	87 816	88 979	Exportations
Balance		-11 884	-19 093	-16 971	-8 027	-4 836	4 096	26 642	Balance
NAFTA+									**ALENA+**
Imports		1 029 419	1 147 601	1 210 558	1 350 497	1 588 750	1 489 591	1 514 190	Importations
Exports		869 940	956 349	953 704	1 011 202	1 140 275	1 069 586	1 028 070	Exportations
Balance		-159 479	-191 252	-256 854	-339 295	-448 475	-420 006	-486 120	Balance
OECD+									**OCDE+**
Imports		3 856 899	3 964 983	4 033 014	4 246 851	4 737 432	4 530 283	4 659 241	Importations
Exports		3 814 377	3 925 354	3 967 235	4 044 843	4 354 445	4 217 259	4 358 983	Exportations
Balance		-42 521	-39 630	-65 779	-202 008	-382 987	-313 024	-300 257	Balance
OPEC+									**OPEP+**
Imports		151 025	164 673	149 291	145 849	167 383	175 738	173 195	Importations
Exports		241 153	251 439	207 604	254 764	352 094	306 092	306 215	Exportations
Balance		90 128	86 767	58 312	108 915	184 711	130 355	133 021	Balance
EU - 15 [26]									**UE - 15 [26]**
Imports		...	...	...	829 780	950 433	920 531	931 745	Importations
Exports		...	...	...	808 092	866 124	881 834	939 448	Exportations
Balance		...	...	...	-21 688	-84 309	-38 697	7 703	Balance

Source:
United Nations Statistics Division, New York, trade statistics database.

Source:
Organisation des Nations Unies, Division de statistique, New York, la base de données pour les statistiques du commerce extérieur.

+ For member states of this grouping, see Annex I – Other groupings. The totals have been re-calculated for all periods shown according to the current composition.

+ Pour les Etats membres de ce groupements, voir annexe I – Autres groupements. Les totals ont été récalculés pour toutes les périodes données suivant la composition présente.

& System of trade : Two systems of recording trade, the General trade system (G) and the Special trade system (S), are in common use. They differ mainly in the way warehoused and re-exported goods are recorded. See the Technical notes for an explanation of the trade system.

& Systèmes de commerce : Deux systèmes d'enregistrement du commerce sont couramment utilisés, le Commerce général (G) et le Commerce spécial (S). Ils ne diffèrent que par la façon don't sont enregistées les merchandises entreposées et les merchandises réexportées. Voir les Notes techniques pour une explication des Systèmes de commerce.

1	United States, Canada, Developed Economies of Europe, Israel, Japan, Australia, New Zealand and South Africa.	1	Etats-Unis, Canada, pays a économie développés d'Europe, Israël, Japon, Australie, Nouvelle-Zélande et l'Afrique du Sud.
2	This classification is intended for statistical convenience and does not, necessarily, express a judgement about the stage reached by a particular country in the development process.	2	Cette classification est utilisée pour plus de commodité dans la presentation des statistique et n'implique pas nécessairement un jugement quant au stage de développement auquel est parvenu un pays donné.
3	Comprises Eastern Europe and the European countries of the former USSR.	3	Compris de l'Europe l'Est et les pays européennes de l'ancienne URSS.
4	Imports FOB.	4	Importations FOB.
5	Including the trade of the U.S. Virgin Islands and Puerto Rico but excluding shipments of merchandise between the United States and its other possessions (Guam, American Samoa, etc.). Data include imports and exports of non-monetary gold.	5	Y compris le commerce des Iles Vierges américaines et de Porto Rico mais non compris les échanges de marchandise, entre les Etats-Unis et leurs autres possessions (Guam, Samoa americaines, etc.). Les données comprennent les importations et exportations d'or non-monétaire.
6	Trade data include maquiladoras and exclude goods from customs-bonded warehouses. Total exports include revaluation and exports of silver.	6	Les statistiques du commerce extérieur comprennent maquiladoras et ne comprennent pas les marchandises provenant des entrepôts en douane. Les exportations comprennent la réevaluation et les données sur les exportations d'argent.
7	Beginning 1990, trade statistics exclude certain oil and chemical products.	7	A compter de 1990, les statistiques commerciales font exclusion de certains produits pétroliers et chimiques.
8	Export and import values exclude trade in the processing zone.	8	Les valeurs à l'exportation et à l'importation excluent le commerce de la zone de transformation.
9	Prior to 1986, includes Aruba.	9	Avant 1986, comprend Aruba.
10	Exports include re-exports and petroleum products.	10	Exportations comprennent re-exportations et produits pétroliers.
11	Economic Union of Belgium and Luxembourg. Intertrade between	11	L'Union économique belgo-luxembourgeoise. Non compris le

73

Total imports and exports

Imports c.i.f., exports f.o.b., and balance, value in million US dollars

Importations et exportations totales

Importations c.a.f., exportations f.o.b. et balance, valeur en millions de dollare E.-U.

the two countries is excluded. Beginning January 1997, data refer to Belgium only and include trade between Belgium and Luxembourg.	commerce entre ces pays. A partir de janvier 1997, les données se rapportent à Belgique seulement et recouvrent les échanges entre la Belgique et le Luxembourg
12 Beginning 1997, trade data for France include the import and export values of French Guiana, Guadeloupe, Martinique, and Reunion.	12 A compter de 1997, les valeurs de commerce pour la France comprennent les valeurs des importations et des exportations de la Guyane française, la Guadeloupe, la Martinique, et la Réunion.
13 Prior to January 1991, excludes trade conducted in accordance with the supplementary protocol to the treaty on the basis of relations between the Federal Republic of Germany and the former German Democratic Republic.	13 Avant janvier 1991, non compris le commerce effectué en accord avec le protocole additionnel au traité définissant la base des relations entre la République Fédérale d'Allemagne et l'ancienne République Démocratique Allemande.
14 Prior to 1997, included under Belgium. See also footnote for Belgium.	14 Avant 1997, inclus sous la Belgique. Voir également l'apostille pour la Belgique.
15 Prior to 1996 data exclude customs free zones, repairs on goods, and operational leasing.	15 Avant 1996 les données excluent des zones franches, des réparations sur des marchandises, et le crédit-bail opérationnel.
16 Data exclude re-exports; Hungary beginning 1989; Estonia beginning January 1994.	16 Les données non compris les réexportations. Hongrie à compter de 1989; Estonie à compter de 1994.
17 Exports include gold.	17 Les exportations comprennent l'or.
18 Beginning in January 1998, foreign trade data refer to South Africa only, excluding intra-trade of the Southern African Common Customs Area. Prior to January 1998, trade data refer to the Southern African Common Customs Area, which includes Botswana, Lesotho, Namibia, South Africa and Swaziland.	18 A compter de janvier 1998, les données sur le commerce extérieur ne se rapportent qu'à l'Afrique du Sud. et ne tiennent pas compte des échanges commerciaux entre les pays de l'Union douanière de l'Afrique du Sud. qui incluait l'Afrique du Sud, Botswana, Lesotho, Namibie, et Swaziland.
19 Imports exclude petroleum imported without stated value. Exports cover domestic exports.	19 Non compris le petrole brute dont la valeur des importations ne sont pas stipulée. Les exportations sont les exportations d'intérieur.
20 Year ending June 30 through 1994. Year ending December 31 thereafter.	20 Année finissant juin 30 à 1994. Année finissant décembre 31 ensuite.
21 Imports and exports net of returned goods. The figures also exclude Judea and Samaria and the Gaza area.	21 Importations et exportations nets, ne comprennant pas les marchandises retournées. Sont également exclues les données de la Judée et de Samaria et ainsi que la zone de Gaza.
22 Data include Armenia, Azerbaijan, Georgia, Kazakhstan, Kyrgyzstan, Tajikistan, Turkmenistan, and Uzbekistan.	22 Données compris Arménie, Azerbaïdjan, Géorgie, Kazakhstan, Kirghizistan, Ouzbékistan, Tadjikistan et Turkménistan.
23 Data include oil and gas. Data on the value and volume of oil exports and on the value of total exports are rough estimates based on information published in various petroleum industry journals.	23 Les données comprennent le pétrole et le gaz. La valeur des exportations de pétrole et des exportations totales sont des évaluations grossières basées sur l'information pubilée à divers journaux d'industrie de pétrole.
24 Year ending 20 March of the years stated.	24 Année finissant le 20 mars de l'année indiquée.
25 Data refer to total exports less petroleum exports of Asia Middle East countries where petroleum, in this case, is the sum of SITC groups 333, 334 and 335.	25 Les données se rapportent aux exportations totales moins les exportations pétrolières de moyen-orient d'Asie. Dans ce cas, le pétrole est la somme des groupes CTCI 333, 334 et 335.
26 Excluding intra-EU trade.	26 Non compris le commerce de l'intra-UE.

74
Total imports and exports : index numbers
Importations et exportations : indices

1990 = 100

Country or area	1994	1995	1996	1997	1998	1999	2000	2001	2002	Pays ou zone
Argentina										**Argentine**
Imports : volume	459	503	601	789	856	738	732	605	275	Imp. : volume
Imports : unit value	100	98	97	95	90	85	85	82	80	Imp. : valeur unitaire
Exports : volume	179	152	162	186	207	206	212	221	221	Exp. : volume
Exports: unit value	115	111	119	115	103	92	101	97	93	Exp. : valeur unitaire
Terms of trade	115	113	122	121	115	108	119	118	116	Termes de l'echange
Purchasing power	206	173	198	225	237	222	251	261	256	Pouvoir d'achat
Australia										**Australie**
Imports : volume	133	148	161	180	195	215	233	223	252	Imp. : volume
Imports : unit value [1]	105	109	109	103	95	95	94	88	89	Imp. : valeur unitaire [1]
Exports : volume	139	141	157	179	178	187	205	211	213	Exp. : volume
Exports: unit value [1]	86	94	95	91	81	77	80	79	81	Exp. : valeur unitaire [1]
Terms of trade	82	85	87	88	85	81	86	89	91	Termes de l'echange
Purchasing power	114	120	136	158	152	151	176	188	194	Pouvoir d'achat
Austria										**Autriche**
Imports : volume	140	125	129	164	188	206	223	237	243	Imp. : volume
Imports : unit value	94	108	98	80	74	69	60	58	60	Imp. : valeur unitaire
Exports : volume	152	140	147	192	220	269	268	292	308	Exp. : volume
Exports: unit value	84	97	89	72	67	56	54	51	54	Exp. : valeur unitaire
Terms of trade	90	90	91	90	91	81	89	88	90	Termes de l'echange
Purchasing power	138	126	134	173	200	218	240	256	279	Pouvoir d'achat
Belgium										**Belgique**
Imports : volume	115	121	126	131	141	141	155	161	175	Imp. : volume
Imports : unit value	91	106	105	96	93	90	88	87	90	Imp. : valeur unitaire
Exports : volume	123	131	134	144	151	156	171	175	190	Exp. : volume
Exports: unit value	94	110	107	98	96	92	87	86	90	Exp. : valeur unitaire
Terms of trade	103	103	102	102	104	102	99	99	101	Termes de l'echange
Purchasing power	127	135	137	146	156	159	170	174	191	Pouvoir d'achat
Bolivia										**Bolivie**
Exports : volume	95	91	93	98	93	85	97	103	124	Exp. : volume
Exports: unit value	66	73	72	55	49	48	61	58	50	Exp. : valeur unitaire
Brazil										**Brésil**
Imports : volume	142	176	178	174	181	170	185	185	180	Imp. : volume
Imports : unit value	113	136	141	178	150	137	143	142	124	Imp. : valeur unitaire
Exports : volume	116	120	119	125	138	137	146	163	177	Exp. : volume
Exports: unit value	119	124	128	136	119	112	120	114	109	Exp. : valeur unitaire
Terms of trade	106	91	91	76	79	82	84	80	88	Termes de l'echange
Purchasing power	123	109	108	95	109	112	123	131	155	Pouvoir d'achat
Canada										**Canada**
Imports : volume	133	143	151	179	190	207	226	226	216	Imp. : volume
Imports : unit value	98	102	102	101	98	97	100	96	98	Imp. : valeur unitaire
Exports : volume	138	152	161	175	189	210	229	229	220	Exp. : volume
Exports: unit value	94	102	103	101	94	94	102	98	98	Exp. : valeur unitaire
Terms of trade	96	100	101	100	96	97	103	103	100	Termes de l'echange
Purchasing power	133	152	163	174	182	204	234	235	219	Pouvoir d'achat
China, Hong Kong SAR										**Chine, Hong Kong RAS**
Imports : volume	187	213	222	238	221	221	261	256	276	Imp. : volume
Imports : unit value	105	110	109	106	101	99	99	96	92	Imp. : valeur unitaire
Exports : volume	176	197	207	219	210	218	255	247	267	Exp. : volume
Exports: unit value	105	109	108	107	103	100	99	97	94	Exp. : valeur unitaire
Terms of trade	100	99	100	100	102	101	100	101	102	Termes de l'echange
Purchasing power	177	195	206	220	213	220	255	248	273	Pouvoir d'achat
Colombia										**Colombie**
Imports : unit value	94	100	101	99	91	85	82	81	78	Imp. : valeur unitaire
Exports: unit value	104	112	104	116	103	96	100	89	85	Exp. : valeur unitaire
Terms of trade	111	112	104	117	113	114	122	111	109	Termes de l'echange
Denmark										**Danemark**
Imports : volume	118	126	128	139	145	148	156	158	168	Imp. : volume
Imports : unit value	93	107	104	94	93	88	82	82	85	Imp. : valeur unitaire
Exports : volume	122	116	119	127	128	135	144	157	166	Exp. : volume
Exports: unit value	94	107	105	94	92	89	83	80	84	Exp. : valeur unitaire
Terms of trade	102	100	101	100	99	100	102	98	98	Termes de l'echange
Purchasing power	124	116	120	126	127	136	146	154	163	Pouvoir d'achat

74

Total imports and exports : index numbers

Importations et exportations : indices

1990 = 100

Country or area	1994	1995	1996	1997	1998	1999	2000	2001	2002	Pays ou zone
Dominica										**Dominique**
Exports : volume	107	68	90	87	80	79	86	67	62	Exp. : volume
Exports: unit value	97	100	93	119	100	101	89	90	90	Exp. : valeur unitaire
Dominican Republic										**Rép. dominicaine**
Exports : volume	92	96	101	104	99	...	...	...	...	Exp. : volume
Exports: unit value	90	101	102	106	83	...	...	...	...	Exp. : valeur unitaire
Ecuador										**Equateur**
Imports : volume	103	138	133	182	228	132	137	171	216	Imp. : volume
Exports : volume	138	154	157	157	149	143	154	156	153	Exp. : volume
Exports: unit value	83	84	96	94	70	85	110	95	102	Exp. : valeur unitaire
Ethiopia										**Ethiopie**
Exports : volume	94	80	...	...	...	...	...	...	...	Exp. : volume
Exports: unit value	94	118	...	...	...	...	...	...	...	Exp. : valeur unitaire
Finland										**Finlande**
Imports : volume	95	102	110	119	129	129	135	132	140	Imp. : volume
Imports : unit value	91	108	104	95	92	92	90	89	87	Imp. : valeur unitaire
Exports : volume	133	143	151	169	178	185	200	199	209	Exp. : volume
Exports: unit value	83	106	100	90	90	87	85	82	80	Exp. : valeur unitaire
Terms of trade	92	98	96	95	97	95	94	92	91	Termes de l'echange
Purchasing power	122	141	146	161	173	176	189	183	191	Pouvoir d'achat
France										**France**
Imports : volume	117	123	126	135	146	152	168	180	189	Imp. : volume
Imports : unit value	92	104	103	92	90	86	70	67	66	Imp. : valeur unitaire
Exports : volume	120	129	134	147	157	166	185	191	242	Exp. : volume
Exports: unit value	99	111	109	98	96	91	70	68	69	Exp. : valeur unitaire
Terms of trade	107	107	105	106	106	106	100	102	104	Termes de l'echange
Purchasing power	127	137	141	155	166	175	185	195	251	Pouvoir d'achat
Germany										**Allemagne**
Imports : volume	114	115	122	133	146	153	172	173	172	Imp. : volume
Imports : unit value	94	110	102	91	88	82	79	77	77	Imp. : valeur unitaire
Exports : volume	112	116	125	140	152	159	182	188	190	Exp. : volume
Exports: unit value	93	107	100	87	85	80	72	72	74	Exp. : valeur unitaire
Terms of trade	98	98	98	96	97	98	91	93	95	Termes de l'echange
Purchasing power	110	114	123	134	148	155	166	174	181	Pouvoir d'achat
Greece										**Grèce**
Imports : volume	150	163	178	180	219	231	257	...	...	Imp. : volume
Imports : unit value	72	77	69	65	66	64	58	56	62	Imp. : valeur unitaire
Exports : volume	149	164	175	194	221	235	244	...	...	Exp. : volume
Exports: unit value	79	84	69	58	61	72	68	65	73	Exp. : valeur unitaire
Terms of trade	110	109	100	90	93	112	118	117	118	Termes de l'echange
Purchasing power	164	179	175	174	205	263	289	...	...	Pouvoir d'achat
Guatemala										**Guatemala**
Imports : volume	148	...	...	...	...	...	...	...	...	Imp. : volume
Imports : unit value	109	...	...	...	...	...	...	...	...	Imp. : valeur unitaire
Exports : volume	147	...	...	...	...	...	...	...	...	Exp. : volume
Exports: unit value	88	98	89	...	...	...	...	...	...	Exp. : valeur unitaire
Terms of trade	81	...	...	...	...	...	...	...	...	Termes de l'echange
Purchasing power	119	...	...	...	...	...	...	...	...	Pouvoir d'achat
Honduras										**Honduras**
Exports : volume	79	83	95	72	91	83	118	122	139	Exp. : volume
Exports: unit value	89	123	115	130	117	99	98	111	107	Exp. : valeur unitaire
Hungary										**Hongrie**
Imports : volume	136	131	138	174	218	249	300	313	328	Imp. : volume
Imports : unit value	121	134	133	123	120	114	108	109	115	Imp. : valeur unitaire
Exports : volume	97	106	110	143	176	204	248	267	283	Exp. : volume
Exports: unit value	113	126	123	115	114	106	98	99	105	Exp. : valeur unitaire
Terms of trade	93	94	93	93	95	93	91	90	91	Termes de l'echange
Purchasing power	91	99	102	134	167	190	225	242	257	Pouvoir d'achat
Iceland										**Islande**
Imports : volume	90	96	111	118	147	154	160	145	...	Imp. : volume
Imports : unit value	99	111	111	104	103	99	98	96	...	Imp. : valeur unitaire
Exports : volume	108	105	115	117	113	122	122	131	...	Exp. : volume
Exports: unit value	94	108	104	100	107	104	98	97	...	Exp. : valeur unitaire
Terms of trade	96	97	93	96	105	104	100	101	...	Termes de l'echange

74

Total imports and exports : index numbers

Importations et exportations : indices

1990 = 100

Country or area	1994	1995	1996	1997	1998	1999	2000	2001	2002	Pays ou zone
Purchasing power	103	102	107	113	119	127	122	133	...	Pouvoir d'achat
India										**Inde**
Imports : volume	168	261	186	199	292	309	346	370	303	Imp. : volume
Imports : unit value	68	59	83	102	59	58	62	57	77	Imp. : valeur unitaire
Exports : volume	154	189	236	205	206	213	287	324	336	Exp. : volume
Exports: unit value	94	90	78	91	85	93	84	74	77	Exp. : valeur unitaire
Terms of trade	137	152	93	89	143	161	134	130	100	Termes de l'echange
Purchasing power	211	286	220	182	294	343	384	421	336	Pouvoir d'achat
Indonesia										**Indonésie**
Exports : volume	163	171	179	230	214	176	209	253	209	Exp. : volume
Exports: unit value	97	111	117	111	87	70	108	97	67	Exp. : valeur unitaire
Ireland										**Irlande**
Imports : volume	128	146	161	185	218	236	275	274	268	Imp. : volume
Imports : unit value	98	109	107	102	99	96	90	90	93	Imp. : valeur unitaire
Exports : volume	153	184	202	232	289	336	401	422	419	Exp. : volume
Exports: unit value	94	102	102	97	94	94	85	84	88	Exp. : valeur unitaire
Terms of trade	96	94	94	95	95	97	94	93	95	Termes de l'echange
Purchasing power	147	173	191	221	275	328	379	391	399	Pouvoir d'achat
Israel										**Israël**
Imports : volume	166	182	194	197	197	226	257	238	240	Imp. : volume
Imports : unit value	94	102	101	96	91	88	91	90	90	Imp. : valeur unitaire
Exports : volume	140	150	161	177	188	206	260	246	249	Exp. : volume
Exports: unit value	100	105	105	104	101	101	101	98	98	Exp. : valeur unitaire
Terms of trade	107	103	104	108	111	114	110	110	110	Termes de l'echange
Purchasing power	150	155	167	191	208	236	287	269	273	Pouvoir d'achat
Italy										**Italie**
Imports : volume	108	119	113	124	135	145	158	158	161	Imp. : volume
Imports : unit value	85	73	78	71	68	64	63	63	64	Imp. : valeur unitaire
Exports : volume	125	141	138	145	149	149	167	168	167	Exp. : volume
Exports: unit value	116	96	106	96	95	91	83	84	87	Exp. : valeur unitaire
Terms of trade	136	131	136	135	140	141	130	133	136	Termes de l'echange
Purchasing power	169	184	188	195	209	211	218	224	227	Pouvoir d'achat
Japan										**Japon**
Imports : volume	121	136	143	145	138	151	167	165	168	Imp. : volume
Imports : unit value	97	105	104	99	87	87	96	90	85	Imp. : valeur unitaire
Exports : volume	103	107	107	120	119	121	132	119	129	Exp. : volume
Exports: unit value	134	145	133	122	114	120	126	118	113	Exp. : valeur unitaire
Terms of trade	138	138	128	123	132	138	131	131	132	Termes de l'echange
Purchasing power	143	147	138	148	156	167	173	156	170	Pouvoir d'achat
Jordan										**Jordanie**
Imports : volume	219	152	164	160	151	149	178	186	...	Imp. : volume
Imports : unit value	83	94	101	99	98	96	98	100	...	Imp. : valeur unitaire
Exports : volume	153	137	134	143	147	151	163	200	...	Exp. : volume
Exports: unit value	96	111	117	113	107	104	100	101	...	Exp. : valeur unitaire
Terms of trade	115	118	115	114	109	109	101	101	...	Termes de l'echange
Purchasing power	176	162	154	163	160	164	165	202	...	Pouvoir d'achat
Kenya										**Kenya**
Imports : volume	121	141	140	149	150	136	157	...	...	Imp. : volume
Imports : unit value	78	96	95	100	98	92	94	...	...	Imp. : valeur unitaire
Exports : volume	153	183	...	...	...	...	...	...	...	Exp. : volume
Exports: unit value	111	129	123	141	138	112	110	...	...	Exp. : valeur unitaire
Terms of trade	143	134	130	142	141	122	118	...	...	Termes de l'echange
Purchasing power	219	246	...	...	...	...	...	...	...	Pouvoir d'achat
Korea, Republic of										**Corée, République de**
Imports : volume	287	187	216	220	165	213	253	247	278	Imp. : volume
Imports : unit value	95	104	99	95	78	77	89	81	78	Imp. : valeur unitaire
Exports : volume	264	181	213	244	291	326	393	396	448	Exp. : volume
Exports: unit value	117	106	92	86	67	65	66	57	55	Exp. : valeur unitaire
Terms of trade	123	102	93	90	86	84	74	71	70	Termes de l'echange
Purchasing power	324	185	197	220	251	275	290	279	315	Pouvoir d'achat
Malaysia										**Malaisie**
Exports : volume	84	84	...	...	...	...	...	...	...	Exp. : volume
Mauritius										**Maurice**
Imports : unit value	105	115	119	103	96	98	97	94	...	Imp. : valeur unitaire

74

Total imports and exports : index numbers

Importations et exportations : indices

1990 = 100

Country or area	1994	1995	1996	1997	1998	1999	2000	2001	2002	Pays ou zone
Exports: unit value	107	117	126	110	111	105	99	91	...	Exp. : valeur unitaire
Terms of trade	102	102	106	107	115	108	102	97	...	Termes de l'echange
Mexico										**Mexique**
Imports : unit value	...	...	111	111	111	110	113	...	...	Imp. : valeur unitaire
Morocco										**Maroc**
Imports : volume	96	110	106	111	136	141	...	...	...	Imp. : volume
Imports : unit value	102	110	110	101	87	89	...	...	...	Imp. : valeur unitaire
Exports : volume	115	113	110	118	121	127	...	...	...	Exp. : volume
Exports: unit value	84	140	...	...	...	...	...	...	...	Exp. : valeur unitaire
Terms of trade	82	127	...	...	...	...	...	...	...	Termes de l'echange
Purchasing power	95	144	...	...	...	...	...	...	...	Pouvoir d'achat
Myanmar										**Myanmar**
Exports : volume	145	151	104	110	...	...	...	...	...	Exp. : volume
Exports : unit value	91	150	139	133	...	...	...	...	...	Exp. : valeur unitaire
Netherlands										**Pays-Bas**
Imports : volume	121	136	143	152	166	179	187	188	176	Imp. : volume
Imports : unit value	92	104	100	92	88	84	81	81	84	Imp. : valeur unitaire
Exports : volume	129	140	146	159	171	179	195	195	198	Exp. : volume
Exports: unit value	92	106	101	93	89	83	82	82	81	Exp. : valeur unitaire
Terms of trade	100	102	101	102	101	98	100	101	97	Termes de l'echange
Purchasing power	129	143	148	162	173	176	195	197	191	Pouvoir d'achat
New Zealand										**Nouvelle-Zélande**
Imports : volume	122	129	134	139	142	161	157	160	173	Imp. : volume
Imports : unit value	104	113	115	110	92	93	93	87	91	Imp. : valeur unitaire
Exports : volume	130	134	140	147	146	149	157	165	174	Exp. : volume
Exports: unit value	102	110	111	104	89	89	89	90	89	Exp. : valeur unitaire
Terms of trade	98	97	97	95	96	96	96	103	98	Termes de l'echange
Purchasing power	127	130	135	140	141	142	152	170	169	Pouvoir d'achat
Norway										**Norvège**
Imports : volume [2]	122	134	147	160	181	182	194	196	201	Imp. : volume [2]
Imports : unit value [2]	86	97	94	84	78	73	67	65	68	Imp. : valeur unitaire [2]
Exports : volume [2]	136	145	163	172	172	176	185	194	197	Exp. : volume [2]
Exports: unit value [2]	75	86	91	84	70	77	98	92	94	Exp. : valeur unitaire [2]
Terms of trade	87	89	97	100	89	105	147	140	137	Termes de l'echange
Purchasing power	119	128	158	172	154	186	273	271	269	Pouvoir d'achat
Pakistan										**Pakistan**
Imports : volume	120	129	127	130	130	140	138	155	170	Imp. : volume
Imports : unit value	98	107	103	47	41	44	48	45	46	Imp. : valeur unitaire
Exports : volume	139	110	130	123	119	134	150	153	164	Exp. : volume
Exports: unit value	96	117	114	114	117	108	99	93	89	Exp. : valeur unitaire
Terms of trade	99	110	111	245	282	244	206	206	196	Termes de l'echange
Purchasing power	137	121	144	300	336	326	309	315	321	Pouvoir d'achat
Panama										**Panama**
Exports : volume	...	...	...	...	113	84	79	...	...	Exp. : volume
Papua New Guinea										**Papouasie-Nvl-Guinée**
Exports : volume	154	149	139	125	...	...	...	...	...	Exp. : volume
Exports: unit value	124	137	132	135	105	95	...	...	...	Exp. : valeur unitaire
Peru										**Pérou**
Exports : volume	132	133	141	153	132	148	168	191	216	Exp. : volume
Exports: unit value	86	106	112	109	84	90	120	100	106	Exp. : valeur unitaire
Philippines										**Philippines**
Imports : volume	70	41	48	52	41	46	49	48	...	Imp. : volume
Imports : unit value [1]	101	101	104	94	70	68	58	49	...	Imp. : valeur unitaire [1]
Exports : volume	93	60	67	79	85	93	107	95	...	Exp. : volume
Exports: unit value [1]	...	...	...	...	69	79	65	54	...	Exp. : valeur unitaire [1]
Terms of trade	...	...	...	...	98	116	113	112	...	Termes de l'echange
Purchasing power	...	...	...	...	84	108	121	107	...	Pouvoir d'achat
Poland										**Pologne**
Imports : volume	211	254	325	397	473	492	526	543	582	Imp. : volume
Imports : unit value [1]	94	100	105	98	97	90	85	85	87	Imp. : valeur unitaire [1]
Exports : volume	111	130	142	162	173	183	226	253	274	Exp. : volume
Exports: unit value [1]	102	116	113	105	107	100	92	94	99	Exp. : valeur unitaire [1]
Terms of trade	109	117	108	107	109	110	108	111	114	Termes de l'echange
Purchasing power	121	152	154	174	189	202	245	281	312	Pouvoir d'achat

74

Total imports and exports : index numbers

Importations et exportations : indices

1990 = 100

Country or area	1994	1995	1996	1997	1998	1999	2000	2001	2002	Pays ou zone
Portugal										**Portugal**
Imports : volume	115	117	125	138	158	174	...	...	...	Imp. : volume
Imports : unit value	90	104	104	94	91	85	80	78	...	Imp. : valeur unitaire
Exports : volume	111	116	127	138	146	151	...	...	...	Exp. : volume
Exports: unit value	97	113	110	99	96	92	84	83	...	Exp. : valeur unitaire
Terms of trade	107	108	105	105	107	108	105	106	...	Termes de l'echange
Purchasing power	119	126	134	144	155	164	...	...	...	Pouvoir d'achat
Rwanda										**Rwanda**
Exports : volume	30	51	49	121	129	...	...	...	...	Exp. : volume
Exports: unit value	61	127	124	140	67	...	...	...	...	Exp. : valeur unitaire
Seychelles										**Seychelles**
Imports : volume	124	135	227	200	243	310	294	...	...	Imp. : volume
Imports : unit value	89	92	89	91	85	75	62	...	...	Imp. : valeur unitaire
Exports : volume	172	139	256	343	343	521	672	...	...	Exp. : volume
Exports: unit value	95	125	116	147	190	151	133	...	...	Exp. : valeur unitaire
Terms of trade	106	135	130	161	225	202	214	...	...	Termes de l'echange
Purchasing power	183	187	333	552	771	1 052	1 435	...	...	Pouvoir d'achat
Singapore										**Singapour**
Imports : volume	157	177	188	203	184	194	220	196	198	Imp. : volume
Imports : unit value [1]	108	116	115	107	94	94	100	97	96	Imp. : valeur unitaire [1]
Exports : volume	187	216	229	245	248	261	302	288	303	Exp. : volume
Exports: unit value [1]	98	104	103	97	84	83	86	80	78	Exp. : valeur unitaire [1]
Terms of trade	91	90	90	90	90	89	86	83	81	Termes de l'echange
Purchasing power	171	194	207	221	223	232	260	238	246	Pouvoir d'achat
South Africa										**Afrique du Sud**
Imports : volume	125	136	147	155	157	146	156	156	...	Imp. : volume
Imports : unit value	100	112	103	102	95	94	96	91	...	Imp. : valeur unitaire
Exports : volume	115	119	130	137	140	142	156	157	...	Exp. : volume
Exports: unit value	100	114	106	105	97	93	93	89	...	Exp. : valeur unitaire
Terms of trade	99	102	103	102	102	98	97	98	...	Termes de l'echange
Purchasing power	114	122	134	140	143	140	151	154	...	Pouvoir d'achat
Spain										**Espagne**
Imports : volume	131	...	...	...	...	...	...	...	...	Imp. : volume
Imports : unit value [1]	81	91	90	81	77	74	72	70	71	Imp. : valeur unitaire [1]
Exports : volume	160	...	...	...	...	...	...	...	...	Exp. : volume
Exports: unit value [1]	83	95	94	84	83	78	72	72	76	Exp. : valeur unitaire [1]
Terms of trade	102	104	105	105	107	106	100	103	106	Termes de l'echange
Purchasing power	164	...	...	...	...	...	...	...	...	Pouvoir d'achat
Sri Lanka										**Sri Lanka**
Imports : volume	153	178	179	201	218	219	244	221	245	Imp. : volume
Imports : unit value	98	109	112	109	...	...	...	...	...	Imp. : valeur unitaire
Exports : volume	118	145	151	167	165	171	205	188	190	Exp. : volume
Exports: unit value	98	132	136	140	146	135	133	129	124	Exp. : valeur unitaire
Terms of trade	100	120	122	128	...	...	...	...	...	Termes de l'echange
Purchasing power	117	175	184	214	...	...	...	...	...	Pouvoir d'achat
Sweden										**Suède**
Imports : volume	108	109	112	124	136	140	158	149	147	Imp. : volume
Imports : unit value [1]	90	103	106	95	90	89	86	80	85	Imp. : valeur unitaire [1]
Exports : volume	114	112	118	131	143	151	168	163	167	Exp. : volume
Exports: unit value [1]	85	97	98	87	83	79	74	67	70	Exp. : valeur unitaire [1]
Terms of trade	94	94	93	92	92	89	86	83	82	Termes de l'echange
Purchasing power	108	105	110	120	132	135	144	136	136	Pouvoir d'achat
Switzerland										**Suisse**
Imports : volume	102	109	110	117	126	137	146	146	142	Imp. : volume
Imports : unit value	97	109	104	94	90	85	80	82	85	Imp. : valeur unitaire
Exports : volume	109	114	115	124	130	135	144	147	148	Exp. : volume
Exports: unit value	104	117	113	100	99	97	89	91	96	Exp. : valeur unitaire
Terms of trade	107	107	108	107	110	114	111	111	113	Termes de l'echange
Purchasing power	117	122	125	132	143	153	160	164	167	Pouvoir d'achat
Syrian Arab Republic										**Rép. arabe syrienne**
Imports : volume	276	248	250	218	...	...	...	...	...	Imp. : volume
Imports : unit value	105	118	125	107	...	...	...	...	...	Imp. : valeur unitaire
Exports : volume	171	167	164	183	...	...	...	...	...	Exp. : volume
Exports: unit value	72	90	95	75	...	...	...	...	...	Exp. : valeur unitaire

74

Total imports and exports : index numbers

Importations et exportations : indices

1990 = 100

Country or area	1994	1995	1996	1997	1998	1999	2000	2001	2002	Pays ou zone
Terms of trade	69	76	76	70	...	...	...	...	...	Termes de l'echange
Purchasing power	117	127	125	128	...	...	...	...	...	Pouvoir d'achat
Thailand										**Thaïlande**
Imports : volume	151	170	154	137	100	124	150	134	149	Imp. : volume
Imports : unit value	111	125	139	136	122	119	125	136	128	Imp. : valeur unitaire
Exports : volume	177	243	219	235	254	284	346	327	371	Exp. : volume
Exports: unit value	111	121	132	126	110	106	104	102	95	Exp. : valeur unitaire
Terms of trade	100	97	95	93	90	89	83	75	74	Termes de l'echange
Purchasing power	177	235	207	218	229	253	287	246	275	Pouvoir d'achat
Tunisia										**Tunisie**
Imports : volume	120	...	...	...	...	...	...	...	...	Imp. : volume
Exports : volume	137	...	...	...	...	...	...	...	...	Exp. : volume
Exports: unit value	87	...	...	...	...	...	...	...	...	Exp. : valeur unitaire
Turkey										**Turquie**
Imports : volume	99	128	166	205	200	198	262	197	238	Imp. : volume
Imports : unit value	95	111	105	96	92	87	91	90	89	Imp. : valeur unitaire
Exports : volume	134	143	157	178	195	201	224	274	317	Exp. : volume
Exports: unit value	95	107	102	97	93	87	83	81	80	Exp. : valeur unitaire
Terms of trade	99	96	97	102	102	100	92	90	89	Termes de l'echange
Purchasing power	133	137	153	181	199	202	206	246	283	Pouvoir d'achat
United Kingdom										**Royaume-Uni**
Imports : volume	108	112	123	135	148	159	178	183	186	Imp. : volume
Imports : unit value [1]	99	112	111	109	103	99	97	92	103	Imp. : valeur unitaire [1]
Exports : volume	116	125	136	146	148	155	173	174	172	Exp. : volume
Exports: unit value [1]	101	111	111	110	105	102	99	94	104	Exp. : valeur unitaire [1]
Terms of trade	102	99	100	101	102	102	102	102	101	Termes de l'echange
Purchasing power	118	124	135	147	151	159	176	178	174	Pouvoir d'achat
United States										**Etats-Unis**
Imports : volume	131	140	148	166	186	206	230	224	234	Imp. : volume
Imports : unit value [1]	102	106	107	105	98	99	106	102	100	Imp. : valeur unitaire [1]
Exports : volume [3]	126	137	145	162	166	173	190	179	171	Exp. : volume [3]
Exports: unit value [1,3]	104	109	109	108	104	103	105	104	103	Exp. : valeur unitaire [1,3]
Terms of trade	102	102	102	103	106	104	99	102	103	Termes de l'echange
Purchasing power	128	140	148	167	176	179	188	182	177	Pouvoir d'achat
Uruguay										**Uruguay**
Exports: unit value	95	105	102	100	99	85	84	82	78	Exp. : valeur unitaire
Venezuela [1]										**Venezuela [1]**
Imports : unit value	108	139	122	129	134	135	131	133	130	Imp. : valeur unitaire

Source:
United Nations Statistics Division, New York, trade statistics database.

Source:
Organisation des Nations Unies, Division de statistique, New York, la base de données pour les statistiques du commerce extérieur.

1   Price index numbers. For United Kingdom beginning 1999, for Philippines 1998 and for United States 1989.
2   Excluding ships.
3   Excludes military goods.

1   Indices de prix. Pour le Royaume-Uni, à partir de 1999; pour Philippines, à partir de 1998; pour les Etats-Unis, à partir de 1989.
2   Non compris les navires.
3   Non compris les exportations militaires.

75
Manufactured goods exports
Unit value and volume indices: 1990 = 100; value: thousand million US dollars
Exportations des produits manufacturés
Indices de valeur unitaire et de volume: 1990 = 100; valeur: milliards de dollars des E.-U.

Country or area / Pays ou zone	1993	1994	1995	1996	1997	1998	1999	2000	2001	2002
Total Total										
Unit value indices, US $ [1]										
Ind. de valeur unitaire, $ des E.-U. [1]	99	101	110	106	99	97	92	90	87	...
Unit value indices, SDR										
Ind. de valeur unitaire, DTS	96	95	99	99	97	97	91	92	94	...
Volume indices [1]										
Indices de volume [1]	115	130	141	152	171	176	191	215	217	...
Value, thousand million US $ [1]										
Valeur, milliards de $ des E.-U. [1]	2 729.60	3 141.80	3 744.20	3 872.70	4 068.50	4 104.40	4 225.50	4 641.40	4 563.70	...
Developed economies Economies développées										
Unit value indices, US $										
Ind. de valeur unitaire, $ des E.-U.	97	99	110	106	99	98	93	89	86	86
Unit value indices, SDR										
Ind. de valeur unitaire, DTS	95	94	99	99	97	98	93	91	92	90
Volume indices										
Indices de volume	108	121	129	137	153	157	166	185	191	192
Value, thousand million US $										
Valeur, milliards de $ des E.-U.	2 064.30	2 346.20	2 774.60	2 847.20	2 959.80	2 993.30	3 031.70	3 211.60	3 208.30	3 221.90
Americas Amériques										
Unit value indices, US $										
Ind. de valeur unitaire, $ des E.-U.	99	99	102	102	103	102	101	102	101	101
Volume indices										
Indices de volume	121	137	152	162	179	183	193	207	214	187
Value, thousand million US $										
Valeur, milliards de $ des E.-U.	435.09	490.11	557.03	593.68	667.70	675.62	703.74	763.59	781.36	685.24
Canada Canada										
Unit value indices, US $										
Ind. de valeur unitaire, $ des E.-U.	88	84	87	88	89	85	83	84	81	80
Unit value indices, national currency										
Ind. de val. unitaire, monnaie nat.	98	99	102	103	105	108	106	106	108	108
Volume indices										
Indices de volume	135	164	187	193	204	223	253	254	263	262
Value, thousand million US $										
Valeur, milliards de $ des E.-U.	93.80	109.17	128.22	134.01	142.90	148.67	165.60	167.30	168.78	166.49
United States Etats-Unis										
Unit value indices, US $ [2]										
Ind. de valeur unitaire, $ des E.-U. [2]	103	104	107	106	108	108	108	109	108	111
Unit value indices, national currency [2]										
Ind. de val. unitaire, monnaie nat. [2]	103	104	107	106	108	108	108	109	108	111
Volume indices										
Indices de volume	117	130	142	153	172	172	176	194	200	166
Value, thousand million US $										
Valeur, milliards de $ des E.-U.	341.29	380.94	428.81	459.67	524.79	526.96	538.14	596.29	612.57	518.75
Europe Europe										
Unit value indices, US $										
Ind. de valeur unitaire, $ des E.-U.	91	93	107	104	93	93	87	79	78	79
Volume indices										
Indices de volume	106	119	126	135	153	158	166	188	198	205
Value, thousand million US $										
Valeur, milliards de $ des E.-U.	1 244.10	1 432.40	1 741.30	1 803.10	1 830.80	1 894.10	1 866.90	1 922.40	1 979.60	2 076.90
EU+ UE+										
Unit value indices, US $										
Ind. de valeur unitaire, $ des E.-U.	92	93	107	103	92	92	87	79	77	78
Volume indices										
Indices de volume	105	120	127	137	155	160	168	191	202	210
Value, thousand million US $										
Valeur, milliards de $ des E.-U.	1 170.60	1 352.80	1 646.90	1 709.30	1 739.00	1 798.60	1 767.80	1 824.90	1 883.60	1 983.80

75

Manufactured goods exports
Unit value and volume indices: 1990 = 100; value: thousand million US dollars *[cont.]*
Exportations des produits manufacturés
Indices de valeur unitaire et de volume: 1990 = 100; valeur: milliards de dollars des E.-U. *[suite]*

Country or area / Pays ou zone	1993	1994	1995	1996	1997	1998	1999	2000	2001	2002
Austria Autriche										
Unit value indices, US $ [3]										
Ind. de valeur unitaire, $ des E.-U. [3]	91	90	104	94	77	72	60	51	48	51
Unit value indices, national currency [3]										
Ind. de val. unitaire, monnaie nat. [3]	93	91	92	88	83	78	68	67	65	65
Volume indices										
Indices de volume	107	119	130	147	181	190	223	259	321	297
Value, thousand million US $										
Valeur, milliards de $ des E.-U.	36.70	40.88	51.38	52.28	53.05	51.65	50.44	49.82	58.30	57.09
Belgium-Luxembourg Belgique-Luxembourg										
Unit value indices, US $ [4]										
Ind. de valeur unitaire, $ des E.-U. [4]	90	94	109	106	97	96	91	86	85	90
Volume indices										
Indices de volume	112	123	128	132	142	157	164	185	194	261
Value, thousand million US $										
Valeur, milliards de $ des E.-U.	95.90	110.73	133.05	133.30	131.23	143.26	142.52	151.41	156.72	222.80
Denmark Danemark										
Unit value indices, US $										
Ind. de valeur unitaire, $ des E.-U.	92	97	112	108	98	97	94	84	84	86
Unit value indices, national currency										
Ind. de val. unitaire, monnaie nat.	97	100	102	102	105	105	106	110	112	109
Volume indices										
Indices de volume	111	118	125	128	145	152	170	180	189	205
Value, thousand million US $										
Valeur, milliards de $ des E.-U.	21.65	24.30	29.43	29.22	30.17	31.22	33.76	31.83	33.45	37.16
Finland Finlande										
Unit value indices, US $										
Ind. de valeur unitaire, $ des E.-U.	74	83	105	99	89	88	85	82	78	82
Unit value indices, national currency										
Ind. de val. unitaire, monnaie nat.	112	112	120	119	121	123	124	138	135	135
Volume indices										
Indices de volume	117	132	144	153	172	188	188	211	217	207
Value, thousand million US $										
Valeur, milliards de $ des E.-U.	20.05	25.11	34.68	34.77	35.12	38.00	36.70	39.71	38.85	38.87
France France										
Unit value indices, US $										
Ind. de valeur unitaire, $ des E.-U.	94	98	111	107	96	96	90	80	78	67
Unit value indices, national currency										
Ind. de val. unitaire, monnaie nat.	98	100	101	101	103	104	102	104	105	86
Volume indices										
Indices de volume	104	116	122	129	143	154	163	189	225	226
Value, thousand million US $										
Valeur, milliards de $ des E.-U.	162.83	187.22	222.89	229.44	225.78	244.30	242.53	249.20	290.20	251.88
Germany Allemagne										
Unit value indices, US $										
Ind. de valeur unitaire, $ des E.-U.	93	94	108	101	87	89	80	72	71	74
Unit value indices, national currency										
Ind. de val. unitaire, monnaie nat.	95	94	96	94	94	97	92	95	97	98
Volume indices										
Indices de volume	100	112	117	126	145	148	158	184	193	200
Value, thousand million US $										
Valeur, milliards de $ des E.-U.	334.59	380.38	455.79	459.69	455.26	477.85	461.09	481.03	499.18	534.76
Greece Grèce										
Unit value indices, US $										
Ind. de valeur unitaire, $ des E.-U.	78	83	88	84	72	66	63	59	...	...
Unit value indices, national currency										
Ind. de val. unitaire, monnaie nat.	112	127	128	128	123	123	122	136	...	...
Volume indices										
Indices de volume	139	133	153	168	195	215	199	232	...	...
Value, thousand million US $										
Valeur, milliards de $ des E.-U.	4.83	4.88	5.99	6.29	6.21	6.34	5.58	6.06	5.99	...

75

Manufactured goods exports
Unit value and volume indices: 1990 = 100; value: thousand million US dollars *[cont.]*

Exportations des produits manufacturés
Indices de valeur unitaire et de volume: 1990 = 100; valeur: milliards de dollars des E.-U. *[suite]*

Country or area Pays ou zone	1993	1994	1995	1996	1997	1998	1999	2000	2001	2002
Ireland Irlande										
Unit value indices, US $ [4]										
Ind. de valeur unitaire, $ des E.-U. [4]	96	89	98	97	81	75	...	...	...	...
Volume indices										
Indices de volume	124	166	193	232	320	434	...	...	...	...
Value, thousand million US $										
Valeur, millards de $ des E.-U.	19.58	24.29	31.21	36.99	42.82	53.58	59.55	65.59	75.13	77.65
Italy Italie										
Unit value indices, US $ [4]										
Ind. de valeur unitaire, $ des E.-U. [4]	89	86	96	98	90	95	91	80	80	...
Volume indices										
Indices de volume	112	132	144	153	159	153	151	176	184	...
Value, thousand million US $										
Valeur, millards de $ des E.-U.	150.13	170.55	208.98	226.89	215.04	219.73	206.69	212.62	223.24	223.29
Netherlands Pays-Bas										
Unit value indices, US $ [5]										
Ind. de valeur unitaire, $ des E.-U. [5]	92	92	109	102	91	89	85	77	...	...
Unit value indices, national currency [5]										
Ind. de val. unitaire, monnaie nat. [5]	94	92	96	95	97	97	97	102	...	...
Volume indices										
Indices de volume	107	121	130	139	184	170	180	205	...	...
Value, thousand million US $										
Valeur, millards de $ des E.-U.	79.18	89.86	113.91	114.03	133.46	121.70	122.17	127.52	120.92	...
Portugal Portugal										
Unit value indices, US $ [4]										
Ind. de valeur unitaire, $ des E.-U. [4]	98	94	111	105	94	92	88	81	80	...
Volume indices										
Indices de volume	100	120	132	143	157	173	183	195	202	...
Value, thousand million US $										
Valeur, millards de $ des E.-U.	12.88	14.86	19.45	19.85	19.48	21.10	21.33	20.96	21.35	...
Spain Espagne										
Unit value indices, US $ [4]										
Ind. de valeur unitaire, $ des E.-U. [4]	85	86	99	99	88	86	...	...	...	...
Volume indices										
Indices de volume	132	157	169	191	220	231	...	...	...	...
Value, thousand million US $										
Valeur, millards de $ des E.-U.	47.54	57.74	71.35	80.45	82.32	84.75	88.72	89.43	91.38	...
Sweden Suède										
Unit value indices, US $										
Ind. de valeur unitaire, $ des E.-U.	82	85	105	106	94	90	85	80	...	...
Unit value indices, national currency										
Ind. de val. unitaire, monnaie nat.	108	111	126	120	121	120	119	124	...	...
Volume indices										
Indices de volume	108	128	131	131	156	157	171	171	...	...
Value, thousand million US $										
Valeur, millards de $ des E.-U.	43.13	53.35	67.44	67.70	71.39	68.70	71.11	67.16	58.69	66.86
United Kingdom Royaume-Uni										
Unit value indices, US $										
Ind. de valeur unitaire, $ des E.-U.	98	103	114	113	113	112	106	98	92	95
Unit value indices, national currency										
Ind. de val. unitaire, monnaie nat.	117	120	129	129	123	121	117	116	114	114
Volume indices										
Indices de volume	95	108	116	128	139	139	140	156	151	161
Value, thousand million US $										
Valeur, millards de $ des E.-U.	141.64	168.65	201.32	218.42	237.73	236.39	225.63	232.53	210.23	232.60

75

Manufactured goods exports
Unit value and volume indices: 1990 = 100; value: thousand million US dollars *[cont.]*

Exportations des produits manufacturés
Indices de valeur unitaire et de volume: 1990 = 100; valeur: milliards de dollars des E.-U. *[suite]*

Country or area Pays ou zone	1993	1994	1995	1996	1997	1998	1999	2000	2001	2002
EFTA+ AELE+										
Unit value indices, US $										
Ind. de valeur unitaire, $ des E.-U.	87	96	116	114	101	99	97	90	92	96
Volume indices										
Indices de volume	111	108	106	108	119	125	134	141	136	126
Value, thousand million US $										
Valeur, millards de $ des E.-U.	72.26	78.21	92.70	92.26	90.34	93.84	97.39	95.38	94.31	91.13
Iceland Islande										
Unit value indices, US $ [4]										
Ind. de valeur unitaire, $ des E.-U. [4]	76	80	114	106	101	89	...	...	...	...
Volume indices										
Indices de volume	102	131	120	130	149	168	...	...	...	...
Value, thousand million US $										
Valeur, millards de $ des E.-U.	0.23	0.31	0.40	0.40	0.44	0.44	0.56	0.61	0.67	0.73
Norway Norvège										
Unit value indices, US $										
Ind. de valeur unitaire, $ des E.-U.	80	82	102	96	88	85	80	75	73	75
Unit value indices, national currency										
Ind. de val. unitaire, monnaie nat.	92	93	104	99	100	103	100	107	106	97
Volume indices										
Indices de volume	105	96	100	106	136	147	149	155	142	152
Value, thousand million US $										
Valeur, millards de $ des E.-U.	12.05	11.20	14.46	14.39	17.01	17.67	16.84	16.60	14.82	16.26
Switzerland Suisse										
Unit value indices, US $ [4]										
Ind. de valeur unitaire, $ des E.-U. [4]	88	99	120	118	105	104	101	93	97	102
Volume indices										
Indices de volume	112	111	107	108	114	120	130	138	134	119
Value, thousand million US $										
Valeur, millards de $ des E.-U.	59.98	66.70	77.84	77.47	72.88	75.73	79.99	78.18	78.82	74.13
Other developed economies Autres economies développées										
Unit value indices, US $										
Ind. de valeur unitaire, $ des E.-U.	120	129	138	128	121	115	113	116	110	104
Volume indices										
Indices de volume	104	107	112	115	124	120	133	148	132	144
Value, thousand million US $										
Valeur, millards de $ des E.-U.	385.08	423.70	476.20	450.37	461.27	423.65	461.04	525.60	447.35	459.77
Australia Australie										
Unit value indices, US $										
Ind. de valeur unitaire, $ des E.-U.	81	88	96	94	89	78	78	80	72	73
Unit value indices, national currency										
Ind. de val. unitaire, monnaie nat.	94	94	102	94	94	97	94	108	112	105
Volume indices										
Indices de volume	161	180	196	254	277	267	291	320	323	333
Value, thousand million US $										
Valeur, millards de $ des E.-U.	10.85	13.07	15.63	19.75	20.43	17.29	18.73	21.21	19.32	20.23
Israel Israël										
Unit value indices, US $										
Ind. de valeur unitaire, $ des E.-U.	102	101	105	105	102	105	114	137	...	...
Volume indices										
Indices de volume	126	146	155	170	194	197	203	207	...	...
Value, thousand million US $										
Valeur, millards de $ des E.-U.	13.48	15.50	17.09	18.79	20.84	21.67	24.22	29.71	27.59	27.53

75

Manufactured goods exports
Unit value and volume indices: 1990 = 100; value: thousand million US dollars *[cont.]*

Exportations des produits manufacturés
Indices de valeur unitaire et de volume: 1990 = 100; valeur: milliards de dollars des E.-U. *[suite]*

Country or area Pays ou zone	1993	1994	1995	1996	1997	1998	1999	2000	2001	2002
Japan Japon										
Unit value indices, US $										
Ind. de valeur unitaire, $ des E.-U.	124	134	144	133	126	121	119	121	118	111
Unit value indices, national currency										
Ind. de val. unitaire, monnaie nat.	95	95	93	101	106	109	94	91	99	96
Volume indices										
Indices de volume	101	103	107	107	115	110	121	135	116	127
Value, thousand million US $										
Valeur, millards de $ des E.-U.	348.56	381.06	425.75	393.58	402.10	369.56	397.48	454.78	378.01	391.77
New Zealand Nouvelle-Zélande										
Unit value indices, US $										
Ind. de valeur unitaire, $ des E.-U.	89	98	112	109	102	84	80	83	81	83
Unit value indices, national currency										
Ind. de val. unitaire, monnaie nat.	98	99	101	94	92	93	90	109	115	106
Volume indices										
Indices de volume	132	152	155	162	178	203	221	222	240	234
Value, thousand million US $										
Valeur, millards de $ des E.-U.	2.98	3.78	4.38	4.46	4.60	4.32	4.50	4.69	4.95	4.91
South Africa Afrique du Sud										
Unit value indices, US $										
Ind. de valeur unitaire, $ des E.-U.	100	101	123	107	...	...	...	...	...	...
Unit value indices, national currency										
Ind. de val. unitaire, monnaie nat.	127	139	173	178	...	...	...	...	...	...
Volume indices										
Indices de volume	114	126	134	159	...	...	...	...	...	...
Value, thousand million US $										
Valeur, millards de $ des E.-U.	9.22	10.28	13.36	13.79	13.31	10.81	16.12	15.21	17.49	15.33
Developing economies Econ. en dévelop.										
Unit value indices, US $										
Ind. de valeur unitaire, $ des E.-U.	102	104	111	105	99	96	89	92	90	...
Unit value indices, SDR										
Ind. de valeur unitaire, DTS	99	99	99	98	97	96	88	95	97	...
Volume indices										
Indices de volume	146	171	196	218	250	260	300	348	335	...
Value, thousand million US $										
Valeur, millards de $ des E.-U.	665.29	795.55	969.59	1 025.50	1 108.70	1 111.00	1 193.80	1 429.70	1 355.30	...
China, Hong Kong SAR Chine, Hong Kong RAS										
Unit value indices, US $										
Ind. de valeur unitaire, $ des E.-U.	104	105	108	108	104	101	99	97	93	90
Unit value indices, national currency										
Ind. de val. unitaire, monnaie nat.	103	105	107	107	103	100	98	97	93	91
Volume indices										
Indices de volume	95	93	95	87	90	84	78	84	74	78
Value, thousand million US $										
Valeur, millards de $ des E.-U.	27.12	27.11	28.22	25.83	25.69	23.26	21.16	22.43	18.94	19.42
India Inde										
Unit value indices, US $										
Ind. de valeur unitaire, $ des E.-U.	89	88	86	69	84	79	90	74	...	...
Unit value indices, national currency										
Ind. de val. unitaire, monnaie nat.	154	158	160	141	174	187	221	190	...	...
Volume indices										
Indices de volume	147	181	215	278	246	253	259	375	...	...
Value, thousand million US $										
Valeur, millards de $ des E.-U.	16.42	20.15	23.34	24.32	25.97	25.28	29.27	35.01	33.55	...

75

Manufactured goods exports
Unit value and volume indices: 1990 = 100; value: thousand million US dollars *[cont.]*

Exportations des produits manufacturés
Indices de valeur unitaire et de volume: 1990 = 100; valeur: milliards de dollars des E.-U. *[suite]*

Country or area Pays ou zone	1993	1994	1995	1996	1997	1998	1999	2000	2001	2002
Korea, Republic of Corée, République de										
Unit value indices, US $ [5]										
Ind. de valeur unitaire, $ des E.-U. [5]	95	98	103	94	85	76	62	75	70	62
Unit value indices, national currency [5]										
Ind. de val. unitaire, monnaie nat. [5]	108	111	112	107	114	150	122	120	126	109
Volume indices										
Indices de volume	132	151	184	202	232	252	346	341	321	321
Value, thousand million US $										
Valeur, millards de $ des E.-U.	76.79	89.86	115.54	115.97	119.96	116.33	130.55	156.87	137.26	121.43
Pakistan Pakistan										
Unit value indices, US $										
Ind. de valeur unitaire, $ des E.-U.	98	107	125	123	129	127	117	110	110	...
Unit value indices, national currency										
Ind. de val. unitaire, monnaie nat.	127	151	182	203	245	265	270	269	314	...
Volume indices										
Indices de volume	136	137	124	146	132	128	146	162	164	...
Value, thousand million US $										
Valeur, millards de $ des E.-U.	5.79	6.38	6.74	7.76	7.40	7.08	7.41	7.73	7.79	8.42
Singapore Singapour										
Unit value indices, US $										
Ind. de valeur unitaire, $ des E.-U.	99	108	112	109	102	92	90	88	86	88
Volume indices										
Indices de volume	155	195	236	255	274	267	292	354	315	318
Value, thousand million US $										
Valeur, millards de $ des E.-U.	58.74	80.54	100.99	105.95	106.55	94.15	99.68	119.26	103.68	106.67
Turkey Turquie										
Unit value indices, US $ [6]										
Ind. de valeur unitaire, $ des E.-U. [6]	95	90	106	97	89	84	80	85	84	82
Volume indices										
Indices de volume	130	164	170	197	250	279	294	297	343	412
Value, thousand million US $										
Valeur, millards de $ des E.-U.	11.17	13.30	16.32	17.32	20.02	21.04	21.19	22.70	25.98	30.33

Source:
United Nations Statistics Division, New York, trade statistics database.

Source:
Organisation des Nations Unies, Division de statistique, New York, la base de données pour les statistiques du commerce extérieur.

+ For member states of this grouping, see Annex I – Other groupings.

+ Pour les Etats members de ce groupement, voir annexe I – Autres groupements.

1   Excludes trade of the countries of Eastern Europe and the former USSR.

1   Non compris le commerce des pays de l'Europe de l'Est et l'ex-URSS.

2   Beginning 1989, derived from price indices; national unit value index is discontinued.

2   A partir de 1989, calculés à partir des indices des prix; l'indice de la valeur unitaire nationale est discontinué.

3   Series linked at 1988 and 1995 by a factor calculated by the United Nations Statistics Division.

3   Les series sont enchaînées à 1988 et 1995 par un facteur calculé par la Division de Statistique des Nations Unies.

4   Beginning 1981, indices are calculated by the United Nations Statistics Division; for Belgium 1988 to 1994 and for Switzerland 1987 to 1995.

4   A partir de 1981, les indices sont calculés par la Division de statistique des Nations Unies; pour la Belgique 1988-1994 et pour la Suisse 1987 to 1995.

5   Derived from sub-indices using current weights; for Netherlands 1988 to 1996.

5   Calculés à partir de sous-indices à coéfficients de pondération correspondant à la période en cours; pour les Pays-Bas de 1988 à 1996.

6   Industrial product.

6   Produit industriel.

Technical notes, tables 73-75

Tables 73-75: Current data (annual, monthly and/or quarterly) for most of the series are published regularly by the Statistics Division in the United Nations *Monthly Bulletin of Statistics* [26]. More detailed descriptions of the tables and notes on methodology appear in the United Nations *1977 Supplement to the Statistical Yearbook and Monthly Bulletin of Statistics* [57], *International Trade Statistics: Concepts and Definitions* [51] and the *International Trade Statistics Yearbook* [25]. More detailed data including series for individual countries showing the value in national currencies for imports and exports and notes on these series can be found in the *International Trade Statistics Yearbook* [25] and in the *Monthly Bulletin of Statistics* [26].

Data are obtained from national published sources; from data supplied by the governments for publication in United Nations publications and from publications of other United Nations agencies.

Territory

The statistics reported by a country refer to the customs area of the country. In most cases, this coincides with the geographical area of the country.

Systems of trade

Two systems of recording trade are in common use, differing mainly in the way warehoused and re-exported goods are recorded:

(a)   Special trade (S): special imports are the combined total of imports for direct domestic consumption (including transformation and repair) and withdrawals from bonded warehouses or free zones for domestic consumption. Special exports comprise exports of national merchandise, namely, goods wholly or partly produced or manufactured in the country, together with exports of nationalized goods. (Nationalized goods are goods which, having been included in special imports, are then exported without transformation);

(b)   General trade (G): general imports are the combined total of imports for direct domestic consumption and imports into bonded warehouses or free zones. General exports are the combined total of national exports and re-exports. Re-exports, in the general trade system, consist of the outward movement of nationalized goods plus goods which, after importation, move outward from bonded warehouses or free zones without having been transformed.

Valuation

Goods are, in general, valued according to the transaction value. In the case of imports, the transaction value is the value at which the goods were purchased by

Notes techniques, tableaux 73 à 75

Tableaux 73-75: La Division de statistique des Nations Unies publie régulièrement dans le *Bulletin mensuel de statistique* [26] des données courantes (annuelles, mensuelles et/ou trimestrielles) pour la plupart des séries de ces tableaux. Des descriptions plus détaillées des tableaux et des notes méthodologiques figurent dans *1977 Supplément à l'Annuaire statistique et au Bulletin mensuel de statistique* des Nations Unies [57], dans la publication *Statistiques du commerce international, Concepts et définitions* [51] et dans l'*Annuaire statistique du Commerce international* [25]. Des données plus détaillées, comprenant des séries indiquant la valeur en monnaie nationale des importations et des exportations des divers pays et les notes accompagnant ces séries figurent dans l'*Annuaire statistique du Commerce international* [25] et dans le *Bulletin mensuel de statistique* [26].

Les données proviennent de publications nationales et des informations fournies par les gouvernements pour les publications des Nations Unies ainsi que de publications d'autres institutions des Nations Unies.

Territoire

Les statistiques fournies par pays se rapportent au territoire douanier de ce pays. Le plus souvent, ce territoire coïncide avec l'étendue géographique du pays.

Systèmes de commerce

Deux systèmes d'enregistrement du commerce sont couramment utilisés, qui ne diffèrent que par la façon dont sont enregistrées les marchandises entreposées et les marchandises réexportées:

(a)   Commerce spécial (S): les importations spéciales représentent le total combiné des importations destinées directement à la consommation intérieure (transformations et réparations comprises) et les marchandises retirées des entrepôts douaniers ou des zones franches pour la consommation intérieure. Les exportations spéciales comprennent les exportations de marchandises nationales, c'est-à-dire des biens produits ou fabriqués en totalité ou en partie dans le pays, ainsi que les exportations de biens nationalisés. (Les biens nationalisés sont des biens qui, ayant été inclus dans les importations spéciales, sont ensuite réexportés tels quels.)

(b)   Commerce général (G): les importations générales sont le total combiné des importations destinées directement à la consommation intérieure et des importations placées en entrepôt douanier ou destinées aux zones franches. Les exportations générales sont le total combiné des exportations de biens nationaux et des ré-exportations. Ces dernières, dans le système du com-

the importer plus the cost of transportation and insurance to the frontier of the importing country (c.i.f. valuation). In the case of exports, the transaction value is the value at which the goods were sold by the exporter, including the cost of transportation and insurance to bring the goods onto the transporting vehicle at the frontier of the exporting country (f.o.b. valuation).

Currency conversion

Conversion of values from national currencies into United States dollars is done by means of external trade conversion factors which are generally weighted averages of exchange rates, the weight being the corresponding monthly or quarterly value of imports or exports.

Coverage

The statistics relate to merchandise trade. Merchandise trade is defined to include, as far as possible, all goods which add to or subtract from the material resources of a country as a result of their movement into or out of the country. Thus, ordinary commercial transactions, government trade (including foreign aid, war reparations and trade in military goods), postal trade and all kinds of silver (except silver coins after their issue), are included in the statistics. Since their movement affects monetary rather than material resources, monetary gold, together with currency and titles of ownership after their issue into circulation, are excluded.

Commodity classification

The commodity classification of trade is in accordance with the United Nations *Standard International Trade Classification* (SITC) [56].

World and regional totals

The regional, economic and world totals have been adjusted: (a) to include estimates for countries or areas for which full data are not available; (b) to include insurance and freight for imports valued f.o.b.; (c) to include countries or areas not listed separately; (d) to approximate special trade; (e) to approximate calendar years; and (f) where possible, to eliminate incomparabilities owing to geographical changes, by adjusting the figures for periods before the change to be comparable to those for periods after the change.

Volume and unit value index numbers

These index numbers show the changes in the volume of imports or exports (quantum index) and the average price of imports or exports (unit value index).

Description of tables

Table 73: World imports and exports are the sum of imports and exports of Developed economies, Developing economies and other. The regional totals for im-

merce général, comprennent les exportations de biens nationalisés et de biens qui, après avoir été importés, sortent des entrepôts de douane ou des zones franches sans avoir été transformés.

Evaluation

En général, les marchandises sont évaluées à la valeur de la transaction. Dans le cas des importations, cette valeur est celle à laquelle les marchandises ont été achetées par l'importateur plus le coût de leur transport et de leur assurance jusqu'à la frontière du pays importateur (valeur c.a.f.). Dans le cas des exportations, la valeur de la transaction est celle à laquelle les marchandises ont été vendues par l'exportateur, y compris le coût de transport et d'assurance des marchandises jusqu'à leur chargement sur le véhicule de transport à la frontière du pays exportateur (valeur f.à.b.).

Conversion des monnaies

Le conversion en dollars des Etats-Unis de valeurs exprimées en monnaie nationale se fait par application de coefficients de conversion du commerce extérieur, qui sont généralement les moyennes pondérées des taux de change, le poids étant la valeur mensuelle ou trimestrielle correspondante des importations ou des exportations.

Couverture

Les statistiques se rapportent au commerce des marchandises. Le commerce des marchandises se définit comme comprenant, dans toute la mesure du possible, toutes les marchandises qui ajoutent ou retranchent aux ressources matérielles d'un pays par suite de leur importation ou de leur exportation par ce pays. Ainsi, les transactions commerciales ordinaires, le commerce pour le compte de l'Etat (y compris l'aide extérieure, les réparations pour dommages de guerre et le commerce des fournitures militaires), le commerce par voie postale et les transactions de toutes sortes sur l'argent (à l'exception des transactions sur les pièces d'argent après leur émission) sont inclus dans ces statistiques. La monnaie or ainsi que la monnaie et les titres de propriété après leur mise en circulation sont exclus, car leurs mouvements influent sur les ressources monétaires plutôt que sur les ressources matérielles.

Classification par marchandise

La classification par marchandise du commerce extérieur est celle adoptée dans la *Classification type pour le commerce international* des Nations Unies (CTCI) [56].

Totaux mondiaux et régionaux

Les totaux économiques, régionaux et mondiaux

ports and exports and have been adjusted to exclude the re-exports of countries or areas comprising each region. Estimates for certain countries or areas not shown separately as well as for those shown separately but for which no data are yet available are included in the regional and world totals. Export and import values in terms of U.S. dollars are derived by the United Nations Statistics Division from data published in national publications, from data in the replies to the *Monthly Bulletin of Statistics* questionnaires and from data published by the International Monetary Fund (IMF) in the publication *International Financial Statistics* [15].

Table 74: These index numbers show the changes in the volume (quantum index) and the average price (unit value index) of total imports and exports. The terms of trade figures are calculated by dividing export unit value indices by the corresponding import unit value indices. The product of the net terms of trade and the volume index of exports is called the index of the purchasing power of exports. The footnotes to countries appearing in table 73 also apply to the index numbers in this table.

Table 75: Manufactured goods are defined here to comprise sections 5 through 8 of the Standard International Trade Classification (SITC). These sections are: chemicals and related products, manufactured goods classified chiefly by material, machinery and transport equipment and miscellaneous manufactured articles. The economic and geographic groupings in this table are in accordance with those of table 73, although table 73 includes more detailed geographical sub-groups which make up the groupings "other developed market economies" and "developing market economies" of this table.

The unit value indices are obtained from national sources, except those of a few countries which the United Nations Statistics Division compiles using their quantity and value figures. For countries that do not compile indices for manufactured goods exports conforming to the above definition, sub-indices are aggregated to approximate an index of SITC sections 5-8. Unit value indices obtained from national indices are rebased, where necessary, so that 1990=100. Indices in national currency are converted into US dollars using conversion factors obtained by dividing the weighted average exchange rate of a given currency in the current period by the weighted average exchange rate in the base period. All aggregate unit value indices are current period weighted.

The indices in Special Drawing Rights (SDRs) are calculated by multiplying the equivalent aggregate indices in United States dollars by conversion factors obtained by dividing the SDR/US $ exchange rate in the

ont été ajustés de manière: (a) à inclure les estimations pour les pays ou régions pour lesquels on ne disposait pas de données complètes; (b) à inclure l'assurance et le fret dans la valeur f.o.b. des importations; (c) à inclure les pays ou régions non indiqués séparément; (d) à donner une approximation du commerce spécial; (e) à les ramener à des années civiles; et (f) à éliminer, dans la mesure du possible, les données non comparables par suite de changements géographiques, en ajustant les chiffres correspondant aux périodes avant le changement de manière à les rendre comparables à ceux des périodes après le changement.

Indices de volume et de valeur unitaire

Ces indices indiquent les variations du volume des importations ou des exportations (indice de quantum) et du prix moyen des importations ou des exportations (indice de valeur unitaire).

Description des tableaux

Tableau 73: Les importations et les exportations totales pour le monde se composent des importations et exportations des Economies développées, des Economies en développement et des autres. Les totaux régionaux pour importations et exportations ont été ajustés pour exclure les re-exportations des pays ou zones qui comprennent la région. Les totaux régionaux et mondiaux comprennent des estimations pour certains pays ou zones ne figurant pas séparément mais pour lesquels les données ne sont pas encore disponibles. Les valeurs en dollars des E.U. des exportations et des importations ont été obtenues par la Division de statistique des Nations Unies à partir des réponses aux questionnaires du *Bulletin Mensuel de Statistique*, des données publiées par le Fonds Monétaire International dans la publication *Statistiques financières internationales* [15].

Tableau 74: Ces indices indiquent les variations du volume (indice de quantum) et du prix moyen (indice de valeur unitaire) des importations et des exportations totales. Les chiffres relatifs aux termes de l'échange se calculent en divisant les indices de valeur unitaire des exportations par les indices correspondants de valeur unitaire des importations. Le produit de la valeur nette des termes de l'échange et de l'indice du volume des exportations est appelé indice du pouvoir d'achat des exportations. Les notes figurant au bas du tableau 73 concernant certains pays s'appliquent également aux indices du présent tableau.

Tableau 75: Les produits manufacturés se définissent comme correspondant aux sections 5 à 8 de la Classification type pour le commerce international (CTCI). Ces sections sont: produits chimiques et produits connexes, biens manufacturés classés principalement par

current period by the rate in the base period.

The volume indices are derived from the value data and the unit value indices. All aggregate volume indices are base period weighted.

matière première, machines et équipements de transport et articles divers manufacturés. Les groupements économiques et géographiques de ce tableau sont conformes à ceux du tableau 73; toutefois, le tableau 73 comprend des subdivisions géographiques plus détaillées qui composent les groupements "autres pays développés à économie de marché" et "pays en développement à économie de marché" du présent tableau.

Les indices de valeur unitaire sont obtenus de sources nationales, à l'exception de ceux de certains pays que la Division de statistique des Nations Unies compile en utilisant les chiffres de ces pays relatifs aux quantités et aux valeurs. Pour les pays qui n'établissent pas d'indices conformes à la définition ci-dessus pour leurs exportations de produits manufacturés, on fait la synthèse de sous-indices de manière à établir un indice proche de celui des sections 5 à 8 de la CTCI. Le cas échéant, les indices de valeur unitaire obtenus à partir des indices nationaux sont ajustés sur la base 1990=100. On convertit les indices en monnaie nationale en indices en dollars des Etats-Unis en utilisant des facteurs de conversion obtenus en divisant la moyenne pondérée des taux de change d'une monnaie donnée pendant la période courante par la moyenne pondérée des taux de change de la période de base. Tous les indices globaux de valeur unitaire sont pondérés pour la période courante.

On calcule les indices en droits de tirages spécial (DTS) en multipliant les indices globaux équivalents en dollars des Etats-Unis par les facteurs de conversion obtenus en divisant le taux de change DTS/dollars E.U. de la période courante par le taux correspondant de la période de base.

On détermine les indices de volume à partir des données de valeur et des indices de valeur unitaire. Tous les indices globaux de volume sont pondérés par rapport à la période de base.

76
Tourist/visitor arrivals by region of origin
Arrivées de touristes/visiteurs par région de provenance

Country or area of destination and region of origin +	Series Série	1997	1998	1999	2000	2001	Pays ou zone de destination et région de provenance +
Albania	VF						**Albanie**
Total		...	...	358 481	317 149	342 908	Totale
Africa		...	...	243	244	66	Afrique
Americas		...	...	10 964	13 977	13 596	Amériques
Europe		...	...	322 183	295 149	320 477	Europe
Asia, East/S.East/Oceania		...	...	1 423	1 932	2 035	Asie, Est/S.-Est/Océanie
Southern Asia		...	...	185	355	309	Asie du Sud
Western Asia		...	...	1 427	1 439	1 074	Asie occidentale
Region not specified		...	...	22 056	4 053	5 351	Région non spécifiée
Algeria	VF						**Algérie**
Total [1]		634 761	678 436	748 536	865 984	901 446	Totale [1]
Africa		34 027	37 373	51 303	55 508	62 661	Afrique
Americas		1 838	2 297	2 563	3 207	3 220	Amériques
Europe		48 440	56 509	72 573	98 563	107 162	Europe
Asia, East/S.East/Oceania		1 342	2 609	4 414	5 080	5 373	Asie, Est/S.-Est/Océanie
Western Asia		9 194	8 414	10 008	13 180	17 843	Asie occidentale
Region not specified		539 920	571 234	607 675	690 446	705 187	Région non spécifiée
American Samoa	TF						**Samoa américaines**
Total [2]		15 809	35 672	41 287	44 158	...	Totale [2]
Africa		10	14	9	14	...	Afrique
Americas		8 646	6 803	14 799	7 763	...	Amériques
Europe		1 396	435	486	887	...	Europe
Asia, East/S.East/Oceania		5 631	28 354	25 934	35 326	...	Asie, Est/S.-Est/Océanie
Southern Asia		61	45	46	53	...	Asie du Sud
Western Asia		20	5	8	24	...	Asie occidentale
Region not specified		45	16	5	91	...	Région non spécifiée
Andorra	TF						**Andorre**
Total		...	...	2 347 001	2 949 087	3 516 261	Totale
Europe		...	...	2 207 081	2 744 581	3 338 906	Europe
Region not specified		...	...	139 920	204 506	177 355	Région non spécifiée
Angola	TF						**Angola**
Total		45 139	52 011	45 477	50 765	67 379	Totale
Africa		13 863	7 332	7 887	8 343	14 580	Afrique
Americas		3 154	7 509	6 074	7 666	9 192	Amériques
Europe		27 422	34 444	29 113	30 868	38 176	Europe
Asia, East/S.East/Oceania		674	2 125	2 009	3 028	4 391	Asie, Est/S.-Est/Océanie
Southern Asia		26	359	328	661	661	Asie du Sud
Western Asia		...	242	66	199	379	Asie occidentale
Anguilla	TF						**Anguilla**
Total [3]		43 181	43 874	46 782	43 789	47 965	Totale [3]
Americas		36 642	34 658	33 449	33 127	38 726	Amériques
Europe		5 455	7 986	11 720	9 422	8 027	Europe
Region not specified		1 084	1 230	1 613	1 240	1 212	Région non spécifiée
Antigua and Barbuda	TF						**Antigua-et-Barbuda**
Total [1,4]		240 402	234 254	239 572	236 669	...	Totale [1,4]
Americas		138 028	133 607	...	...	...	Amériques
Europe		89 884	88 082	...	...	...	Europe
Region not specified		12 490	12 565	239 572	236 669	...	Région non spécifiée
Argentina	TF						**Argentine**
Total [3]		2 764 226	3 012 472	2 898 241	2 909 468	2 620 464	Totale [3]
Americas		2 378 327	2 595 379	2 490 667	2 480 150	2 157 191	Amériques
Europe		319 787	344 323	336 676	354 050	370 933	Europe
Region not specified		66 112	72 770	70 898	75 268	92 340	Région non spécifiée
Armenia	TCE						**Arménie**
Total		23 430	31 837	40 745	45 222	123 262	Totale
Africa		10	32	43	48	62	Afrique
Americas		3 282	5 028	6 156	8 117	41 408	Amériques
Europe		16 109	23 099	26 880	25 487	47 896	Europe
Asia, East/S.East/Oceania		602	906	923	787	2 762	Asie, Est/S.-Est/Océanie
Southern Asia		2 203	1 300	4 845	8 704	18 350	Asie du Sud
Western Asia		1 224	1 472	1 898	2 079	12 784	Asie occidentale

76

Tourist/visitor arrivals by region of origin *[cont.]*

Arrivées de touristes/visiteurs par région de provenance *[suite]*

Country or area of destination and region of origin +	Series Série	1997	1998	1999	2000	2001	Pays ou zone de destination et région de provenance +
Aruba	TF						**Aruba**
Total		649 893	647 437	683 320	721 224	691 419	Totale
Americas		587 776	595 186	629 597	670 271	642 995	Amériques
Europe		57 335	49 042	49 370	47 063	44 961	Europe
Asia, East/S.East/Oceania		346	320	273	215	169	Asie, Est/S.-Est/Océanie
Region not specified		4 436	2 889	4 080	3 675	3 294	Région non spécifiée
Australia	VF						**Australie**
Total [3,5]		4 317 847	4 167 164	4 459 408	4 931 336	...	Totale [3,5]
Africa		57 569	71 543	71 623	78 629	...	Afrique
Americas		420 100	473 603	527 616	620 927	...	Amériques
Europe		887 823	964 882	1 088 042	1 212 422	...	Europe
Asia, East/S.East/Oceania		2 892 640	2 583 848	2 683 340	2 911 569	...	Asie, Est/S.-Est/Océanie
Southern Asia		39 520	43 942	50 159	60 011	...	Asie du Sud
Western Asia		19 410	26 857	34 591	35 166	...	Asie occidentale
Region not specified		785	2 489	4 037	12 612	...	Région non spécifiée
Austria	TCE						**Autriche**
Total [6]		16 647 281	17 352 477	17 466 714	17 982 204	18 180 079	Totale [6]
Africa		23 080	32 818	32 575	35 511	35 737	Afrique
Americas		718 578	827 764	767 196	933 841	787 930	Amériques
Europe		15 063 175	15 680 020	15 843 176	16 084 063	16 474 203	Europe
Asia, East/S.East/Oceania		530 304	499 515	534 948	623 939	576 226	Asie, Est/S.-Est/Océanie
Southern Asia		24 174	21 533	30 685	35 357	32 159	Asie du Sud
Western Asia		25 703	25 583	25 030	28 858	33 320	Asie occidentale
Region not specified		262 267	265 244	233 104	240 635	240 504	Région non spécifiée
Azerbaijan	TF						**Azerbaïdjan**
Total		305 830	483 163	602 047	681 000	766 992	Totale
Americas		4 895	3 350	1 815	...	...	Amériques
Europe		182 506	331 377	446 415	367 443	328 722	Europe
Southern Asia		106 183	140 459	122 231	242 354	321 882	Asie du Sud
Western Asia		405	208	94	...	...	Asie occidentale
Region not specified		11 841	7 769	31 492	71 203	116 388	Région non spécifiée
Bahamas	TF						**Bahamas**
Total		1 617 595	1 527 707	1 576 888	1 543 962	1 537 777	Totale
Africa		...	...	...	1 627	469	Afrique
Americas		1 413 485	1 333 112	1 381 208	1 406 515	1 417 575	Amériques
Europe		130 365	117 954	125 484	105 433	94 897	Europe
Asia, East/S.East/Oceania		...	...	...	15 524	11 350	Asie, Est/S.-Est/Océanie
Southern Asia		...	...	...	360	291	Asie du Sud
Western Asia		...	...	...	648	548	Asie occidentale
Region not specified		73 745	76 641	70 196	13 855	12 647	Région non spécifiée
Bahrain	VF						**Bahreïn**
Total [3]		2 600 320	2 897 562	3 280 452	3 868 738	4 387 930	Totale [3]
Africa		18 389	21 910	26 396	32 442	38 907	Afrique
Americas		86 358	96 881	101 859	120 801	139 550	Amériques
Europe		173 258	179 472	191 040	215 951	235 484	Europe
Asia, East/S.East/Oceania		82 767	96 886	100 646	107 445	135 121	Asie, Est/S.-Est/Océanie
Southern Asia		221 615	260 817	299 168	331 893	391 812	Asie du Sud
Western Asia		2 017 933	2 241 596	2 561 343	3 060 206	3 447 056	Asie occidentale
Bangladesh	TF						**Bangladesh**
Total		182 420	171 961	172 781	199 211	207 199	Totale
Africa		1 150	1 609	1 511	1 787	1 561	Afrique
Americas		15 435	15 653	12 444	15 110	19 230	Amériques
Europe		47 934	36 920	39 599	46 036	50 184	Europe
Asia, East/S.East/Oceania		33 609	35 757	34 865	38 429	37 937	Asie, Est/S.-Est/Océanie
Southern Asia		81 728	77 692	78 878	93 709	94 382	Asie du Sud
Western Asia		2 548	4 291	5 333	3 893	3 811	Asie occidentale
Region not specified		16	39	151	247	94	Région non spécifiée
Barbados	TF						**Barbade**
Total		472 290	512 397	514 614	544 696	507 078	Totale
Africa		...	...	563	646	852	Afrique
Americas		245 004	254 982	264 129	278 391	256 125	Amériques

76

Tourist/visitor arrivals by region of origin *[cont.]*

Arrivées de touristes/visiteurs par région de provenance *[suite]*

Country or area of destination and region of origin +	Series Série	1997	1998	1999	2000	2001	Pays ou zone de destination et région de provenance +
Europe		220 618	251 735	245 143	262 331	247 165	Europe
Asia, East/S.East/Oceania		1 490	1 515	4 242	2 334	2 021	Asie, Est/S.-Est/Océanie
Southern Asia		...	...	363	460	454	Asie du Sud
Western Asia		...	...	174	170	160	Asie occidentale
Region not specified		5 178	4 165	...	364	301	Région non spécifiée
Belarus	TF						**Bélarus**
Total		254 023	355 342	75 440	59 676	61 033	Totale
Africa		235	703	133	100	67	Afrique
Americas		9 214	9 607	2 452	2 972	4 883	Amériques
Europe		241 549	339 587	72 060	55 655	55 007	Europe
Asia, East/S.East/Oceania		2 311	4 388	427	566	550	Asie, Est/S.-Est/Océanie
Southern Asia		508	676	83	177	278	Asie du Sud
Western Asia		206	381	285	206	248	Asie occidentale
Belgium	TCE						**Belgique**
Total		6 037 031	6 179 254	6 369 030	6 457 325	6 451 513	Totale
Africa		63 003	61 028	57 058	64 094	64 293	Afrique
Americas		410 712	420 335	434 012	448 770	427 918	Amériques
Europe		5 197 330	5 363 775	5 522 422	5 549 692	5 592 062	Europe
Asia, East/S.East/Oceania		286 455	266 801	287 214	297 402	267 755	Asie, Est/S.-Est/Océanie
Southern Asia		27 946	17 149	19 211	23 448	26 644	Asie du Sud
Western Asia		18 083	19 275	17 898	20 363	19 140	Asie occidentale
Region not specified		33 502	30 891	31 215	53 556	53 701	Région non spécifiée
Belize	VF						**Belize**
Total [7]		328 143	299 725	339 581	373 995	384 572	Totale [7]
Americas		275 704	248 188	288 212	320 283	330 805	Amériques
Europe		47 489	45 130	44 364	47 993	47 171	Europe
Asia, East/S.East/Oceania		3 780	3 972	3 917	2 654	3 102	Asie, Est/S.-Est/Océanie
Region not specified		1 170	2 435	3 088	3 065	3 494	Région non spécifiée
Benin	TF						**Bénin**
Total		...	...	80 228	96 146	...	Totale
Africa		...	...	55 369	50 140	...	Afrique
Americas		...	...	2 006	4 651	...	Amériques
Europe		...	...	21 557	39 881	...	Europe
Asia, East/S.East/Oceania		...	...	701	518	...	Asie, Est/S.-Est/Océanie
Southern Asia		...	...	301	322	...	Asie du Sud
Western Asia		...	...	294	634	...	Asie occidentale
Bermuda	TF						**Bermudes**
Total [8]		380 058	369 971	354 815	332 191	278 153	Totale [8]
Americas		338 725	323 609	311 065	287 341	241 268	Amériques
Europe		31 646	37 254	35 669	35 918	28 508	Europe
Asia, East/S.East/Oceania		1 010	985	853	1 126	868	Asie, Est/S.-Est/Océanie
Region not specified		8 677	8 123	7 228	7 806	7 509	Région non spécifiée
Bhutan	TF						**Bhoutan**
Total		5 362	6 203	7 158	7 559	6 374	Totale
Africa		5	8	12	7	26	Afrique
Americas		1 046	1 622	2 346	3 024	2 457	Amériques
Europe		2 576	3 145	3 140	3 029	2 435	Europe
Asia, East/S.East/Oceania		1 679	1 403	1 576	1 425	1 334	Asie, Est/S.-Est/Océanie
Southern Asia		33	24	23	50	108	Asie du Sud
Western Asia		...	...	...	...	14	Asie occidentale
Region not specified		23	1	61	24	...	Région non spécifiée
Bolivia	THS						**Bolivie**
Total [9]		397 517	420 491	409 142	381 077	378 551	Totale [9]
Africa		641	1 016	943	1 117	862	Afrique
Americas		257 203	269 344	242 075	219 636	215 131	Amériques
Europe		124 895	135 759	146 138	142 170	145 969	Europe
Asia, East/S.East/Oceania		14 778	14 372	19 986	18 154	16 589	Asie, Est/S.-Est/Océanie
Bonaire	TF						**Bonaire**
Total		62 776	61 737	61 495	51 269	50 395	Totale
Americas		40 495	39 976	40 883	33 067	33 816	Amériques
Europe		22 090	21 605	20 393	17 950	16 326	Europe

76

Tourist/visitor arrivals by region of origin *[cont.]*

Arrivées de touristes/visiteurs par région de provenance *[suite]*

Country or area of destination and region of origin +	Série	1997	1998	1999	2000	2001	Pays ou zone de destination et région de provenance +
Asia, East/S.East/Oceania		38	25	19	16	31	Asie, Est/S.-Est/Océanie
Region not specified		153	131	200	236	222	Région non spécifiée
Bosnia and Herzegovina	TF						**Bosnie-Herzégovine**
Total		76 000	90 000	89 000	108 000	90 000	Totale
Americas		9 000	9 000	8 000	9 000	8 000	Amériques
Europe		66 000	80 000	79 000	92 000	78 000	Europe
Asia, East/S.East/Oceania		1 000	1 000	1 000	1 000	1 000	Asie, Est/S.-Est/Océanie
Region not specified		...	...	1 000	6 000	3 000	Région non spécifiée
Botswana	TF						**Botswana**
Total		606 781	749 535	843 314	...	...	Totale
Africa		516 328	629 033	720 310	...	...	Afrique
Americas		8 614	10 714	12 070	...	...	Amériques
Europe		38 311	38 755	44 024	...	...	Europe
Asia, East/S.East/Oceania		9 281	9 127	9 841	...	...	Asie, Est/S.-Est/Océanie
Southern Asia		1 174	1 063	1 384	...	...	Asie du Sud
Western Asia		...	...	20	...	...	Asie occidentale
Region not specified		33 073	60 843	55 665	...	...	Région non spécifiée
Brazil	TF						**Brésil**
Total		2 849 750	4 818 084[10]	5 107 169	5 313 463	4 772 575	Totale
Africa		23 747	40 959	41 294	34 503	36 352	Afrique
Americas		1 998 967	3 449 456	3 643 223	3 803 069	3 131 693	Amériques
Europe		713 059	1 160 673	1 246 155	1 320 325	1 445 576	Europe
Asia, East/S.East/Oceania		95 228	121 692	130 070	121 791	127 394	Asie, Est/S.-Est/Océanie
Western Asia		7 674	13 661	15 254	11 174	11 326	Asie occidentale
Region not specified		11 075	31 643	31 173	22 601	20 234	Région non spécifiée
British Virgin Islands	TF						**Iles Vierges britanniques**
Total		244 318	279 097	285 858	281 119	295 625	Totale
Americas		209 840	220 111	234 974	235 161	257 321	Amériques
Europe		22 137	31 457	32 614	38 619	33 616	Europe
Region not specified		12 341	27 529	18 270	7 339	4 688	Région non spécifiée
Brunei Darussalam	VF						**Brunéi Darussalam**
Total		...	964 080	966 684	984 093	...	Totale
Americas		...	10 184	8 751	9 469	...	Amériques
Europe		...	48 152	44 865	41 728	...	Europe
Asia, East/S.East/Oceania		...	892 624	896 925	912 667	...	Asie, Est/S.-Est/Océanie
Southern Asia		...	13 100	12 501	16 168	...	Asie du Sud
Western Asia		...	...	886	781	...	Asie occidentale
Region not specified		...	20	2 756	3 280	...	Région non spécifiée
Bulgaria	VF						**Bulgarie**
Total		7 543 185	5 239 691[11]	5 056 240[11]	4 922 118[11]	5 103 797[11]	Totale
Africa		6 838	6 675	4 418	3 523	2 984	Afrique
Americas		21 515	39 788	39 241	42 435	52 124	Amériques
Europe		7 247 812	4 821 516	4 911 853	4 780 489	4 950 963	Europe
Asia, East/S.East/Oceania		19 054	20 715	21 275	23 674	23 873	Asie, Est/S.-Est/Océanie
Southern Asia		15 963	14 778	14 570	15 917	12 916	Asie du Sud
Western Asia		21 438	19 840	17 964	17 403	14 811	Asie occidentale
Region not specified		210 565	316 379	46 919	38 677	46 126	Région non spécifiée
Burkina Faso	THS						**Burkina Faso**
Total		138 364	160 284	116 955	125 719	128 761	Totale
Africa		57 459	62 673	42 241	47 208	50 241	Afrique
Americas		8 209	10 062	6 798	7 539	8 041	Amériques
Europe		57 997	77 785	59 687	62 998	63 182	Europe
Asia, East/S.East/Oceania		2 153	3 199	3 754	3 540	2 834	Asie, Est/S.-Est/Océanie
Western Asia		677	1 016	855	652	454	Asie occidentale
Region not specified		11 869	5 549	3 620	3 782	4 009	Région non spécifiée
Burundi	TF						**Burundi**
Total[1]		10 553	15 404	26 000	29 000	36 000	Totale[1]
Africa		5 011	7 394	12 000	14 000	17 000	Afrique
Americas		639	1 092	2 000	2 000	2 000	Amériques
Europe		4 051	5 700	10 000	12 000	14 000	Europe
Asia, East/S.East/Oceania		852	1 218	2 000	1 000	3 000	Asie, Est/S.-Est/Océanie

76
Tourist/visitor arrivals by region of origin *[cont.]*
Arrivées de touristes/visiteurs par région de provenance *[suite]*

Country or area of destination and region of origin +	Series Série	1997	1998	1999	2000	2001	Pays ou zone de destination et région de provenance +
Cambodia	TF						**Cambodge**
Total [12]		218 843	186 333	262 907	351 661	408 377	Totale [12]
Americas		24 561	21 773	36 233	42 156	43 905	Amériques
Europe		43 331	46 165	60 031	65 657	66 088	Europe
Asia, East/S.East/Oceania		147 470	105 422	134 609	152 383	158 407	Asie, Est/S.-Est/Océanie
Southern Asia		2 735	1 999	2 445	2 967	4 691	Asie du Sud
Region not specified		746	10 974	29 589	88 498	135 286	Région non spécifiée
Cameroon	THS						**Cameroun**
Total		231 904	246 884	261 923	277 070	220 578	Totale
Africa		97 335	76 114	80 750	88 618	100 282	Afrique
Americas		19 301	20 689	21 949	23 124	12 611	Amériques
Europe		104 425	137 891	146 291	150 096	99 624	Europe
Asia, East/S.East/Oceania		5 973	6 941	7 364	8 308	4 168	Asie, Est/S.-Est/Océanie
Western Asia		2 993	3 983	4 226	5 539	1 087	Asie occidentale
Region not specified		1 877	1 266	1 343	1 385	2 806	Région non spécifiée
Canada	TF						**Canada**
Total [13]		17 669 000	18 870 000	19 411 000	19 627 415	19 679 392	Totale [13]
Africa		58 700	59 200	66 300	64 588	61 264	Afrique
Americas		13 741 900	15 256 000	15 564 300	15 604 782	15 973 802	Amériques
Europe		2 329 900	2 273 800	2 381 800	2 498 863	2 323 626	Europe
Asia, East/S.East/Oceania		1 392 600	1 145 400	1 251 000	1 340 222	1 195 365	Asie, Est/S.-Est/Océanie
Southern Asia		77 700	55 700	62 500	73 998	78 435	Asie du Sud
Western Asia		34 900	38 000	40 700	73 998	78 435	Asie occidentale
Region not specified		33 300	41 900	44 400	44 962	46 900	Région non spécifiée
Cape Verde	TF						**Cap-Vert**
Total [8]		45 000	52 000	67 042	83 259	115 282	Totale [8]
Africa		...	...	...	...	2 651	Afrique
Americas		...	...	...	3 039	2 190	Amériques
Europe		37 834	44 408	...	70 600	86 922	Europe
Region not specified		7 166	7 592	67 042	9 620	23 519	Région non spécifiée
Cayman Islands	TF						**Iles Caïmanes**
Total [8]		334 000 [14]	354 000 [14]	345 000 [14]	354 087	334 071	Totale [8]
Africa		...	...	...	310	279	Afrique
Americas		...	...	...	328 069	310 698	Amériques
Europe		...	...	...	23 817	21 655	Europe
Asia, East/S.East/Oceania		...	...	...	1 891	1 439	Asie, Est/S.-Est/Océanie
Central African Rep.	TF						**Rép. centrafricaine**
Total		...	7 478	...	...	...	Totale
Africa		...	3 439	...	...	...	Afrique
Americas		...	455	...	...	...	Amériques
Europe		...	3 054	...	...	...	Europe
Asia, East/S.East/Oceania		...	313	...	...	...	Asie, Est/S.-Est/Océanie
Western Asia		...	89	...	...	...	Asie occidentale
Region not specified		...	128	...	...	...	Région non spécifiée
Chad	THS						**Tchad**
Total		26 980	41 244	46 603	43 034	56 850	Totale
Africa		3 700	12 160	13 649	12 542	16 911	Afrique
Americas		615	3 963	4 546	8 216	5 122	Amériques
Europe		4 764	21 206	24 134	21 306	31 889	Europe
Asia, East/S.East/Oceania		180	216	420	436	1 623	Asie, Est/S.-Est/Océanie
Western Asia		116	139	591	534	924	Asie occidentale
Region not specified		17 605	3 560	3 263	...	381	Région non spécifiée
Chile	TF						**Chili**
Total		1 643 640	1 759 279	1 622 252	1 742 407	1 723 107	Totale
Africa		1 794	2 092	2 470	2 392	2 495	Afrique
Americas		1 402 868	1 492 699	1 356 414	1 456 648	1 429 293	Amériques
Europe		203 373	226 653	223 731	240 144	249 985	Europe
Asia, East/S.East/Oceania		32 023	34 281	35 511	36 996	37 155	Asie, Est/S.-Est/Océanie
Southern Asia		1 818	2 442	2 232	2 746	1 807	Asie du Sud
Western Asia		519	455	646	912	721	Asie occidentale
Region not specified		1 245	657	1 248	2 569	1 651	Région non spécifiée

76

Tourist/visitor arrivals by region of origin *[cont.]*

Arrivées de touristes/visiteurs par région de provenance *[suite]*

Country or area of destination and region of origin +	Series Série	1997	1998	1999	2000	2001	Pays ou zone de destination et région de provenance +
China	TF						**Chine**
Total [15]		7 427 934	7 107 529	8 432 050	10 160 432	11 226 384	Totale [15]
Africa		38 027	39 167	42 851	54 015	62 827	Afrique
Americas		867 166	947 927	1 025 996	1 217 091	1 278 383	Amériques
Europe		2 039 424	1 896 160	2 148 520	2 537 222	2 732 112	Europe
Asia, East/S.East/Oceania		4 312 645	4 057 595	5 022 581	6 103 863	6 823 674	Asie, Est/S.-Est/Océanie
Southern Asia		130 716	132 853	160 990	210 347	277 288	Asie du Sud
Western Asia		21 644	20 993	26 051	34 658	37 202	Asie occidentale
Region not specified		18 312	12 834	5 061	3 236	14 898	Région non spécifiée
China, Hong Kong SAR	VF						**Chine, Hong Kong RAS**
Total [16]		11 273 377	10 159 646	11 328 272	13 059 477	13 725 332	Totale [16]
Africa		73 559	63 939	65 027	73 093	77 079	Afrique
Americas		1 125 138	1 104 888	1 155 313	1 295 908	1 258 567	Amériques
Europe		1 195 345	1 042 231	1 059 155	1 117 435	1 063 767	Europe
Asia, East/S.East/Oceania		8 695 439	7 761 524	8 852 807	10 335 534	11 046 891	Asie, Est/S.-Est/Océanie
Southern Asia		167 690	167 766	171 615	205 899	249 204	Asie du Sud
Western Asia		16 206	19 298	24 355	31 608	29 824	Asie occidentale
China, Macao SAR	VF						**Chine, Macao RAS**
Total [17]		7 000 370	6 948 535	7 443 924	9 162 212	10 278 973	Totale [17]
Africa		5 579	4 786	4 114	4 334	4 092	Afrique
Americas		121 286	110 619	105 715	117 989	118 817	Amériques
Europe		239 364	262 783	163 427	148 361	130 265	Europe
Asia, East/S.East/Oceania		6 434 682	6 498 013	7 154 937	8 871 880	10 005 009	Asie, Est/S.-Est/Océanie
Southern Asia		16 221	12 532	14 010	17 008	17 731	Asie du Sud
Western Asia		586	719	682	773	938	Asie occidentale
Region not specified		182 652	59 083	1 039	1 867	2 121	Région non spécifiée
Colombia	TF						**Colombie**
Total [18]		639 250	674 425	546 035	557 281	615 719	Totale [18]
Americas		408 947	463 987	395 443	413 172	467 802	Amériques
Europe		153 220	156 710	130 085	123 370	124 322	Europe
Region not specified		77 083	53 728	20 507	20 739	23 595	Région non spécifiée
Comoros	TF						**Comores**
Total [8]		26 219	27 474	24 479	23 893	...	Totale [8]
Africa		14 202	11 155	14 420	15 812	...	Afrique
Americas		337	783	144	230	...	Amériques
Europe		11 143	12 799	9 083	7 240	...	Europe
Asia, East/S.East/Oceania		537	460	210	153	...	Asie, Est/S.-Est/Océanie
Region not specified		...	2 277	622	458	...	Région non spécifiée
Congo	THS						**Congo**
Total		26 738	20 315	13 964	18 798	...	Totale
Africa		10 351	7 425	5 540	9 301	...	Afrique
Americas		1 812	1 110	627	785	...	Amériques
Europe		13 891	11 063	7 293	8 294	...	Europe
Region not specified		684	717	504	418	...	Région non spécifiée
Cook Islands	TF						**Iles Cook**
Total [4]		49 866	48 630	55 599	72 994	74 575	Totale [4]
Americas		9 491	8 987	11 083	12 726	13 413	Amériques
Europe		19 896	19 291	18 382	23 683	22 816	Europe
Asia, East/S.East/Oceania		20 293	20 239	25 974	36 359	38 061	Asie, Est/S.-Est/Océanie
Region not specified		186	113	160	226	285	Région non spécifiée
Costa Rica	TF						**Costa Rica**
Total		811 490	942 853	1 031 585	1 088 075	1 131 406	Totale
Africa		689	748	897	789	837	Afrique
Americas		661 574	791 219	863 324	907 381	952 087	Amériques
Europe		130 713	131 657	145 586	156 562	156 571	Europe
Asia, East/S.East/Oceania		14 484	14 447	15 885	15 993	14 648	Asie, Est/S.-Est/Océanie
Region not specified		4 030	4 782	5 893	7 350	7 263	Région non spécifiée
Côte d'Ivoire	TF						**Côte d'Ivoire**
Total [19]		274 094	301 039	...	...	...	Totale [19]
Africa		137 886	158 808	...	...	...	Afrique
Americas		20 703	23 328	...	...	...	Amériques

76

Tourist/visitor arrivals by region of origin *[cont.]*

Arrivées de touristes/visiteurs par région de provenance *[suite]*

Country or area of destination and region of origin +	Series Série	1997	1998	1999	2000	2001	Pays ou zone de destination et région de provenance +
Europe		107 304	109 176	...	...	...	Europe
Asia, East/S.East/Oceania		5 649	6 172	...	...	...	Asie, Est/S.-Est/Océanie
Southern Asia		...	1 000	...	...	...	Asie du Sud
Western Asia		2 552	2 555	...	...	...	Asie occidentale
Croatia	TCE						**Croatie**
Total [20]		4 177 764	4 499 138	3 805 343	5 831 180	6 544 217	Totale [20]
Americas		60 353	52 764	46 672	66 869	67 316	Amériques
Europe		4 072 325	4 411 729	3 730 199	5 719 995	6 428 582	Europe
Asia, East/S.East/Oceania		10 938	16 072	15 013	23 305	26 675	Asie, Est/S.-Est/Océanie
Region not specified		34 148	18 573	13 459	21 011	21 644	Région non spécifiée
Cuba	VF						**Cuba**
Total		1 170 083	1 415 832	1 602 781	1 773 986	1 774 541	Totale
Africa		5 178	5 919	6 269	7 262	6 565	Afrique
Americas		496 913	594 354	696 521	783 425	834 660	Amériques
Europe		648 265	793 246	874 444	949 328	898 110	Europe
Asia, East/S.East/Oceania		13 775	16 368	20 060	27 103	28 586	Asie, Est/S.-Est/Océanie
Southern Asia		4 083	4 278	3 366	4 442	4 273	Asie du Sud
Western Asia		1 554	1 319	1 782	2 168	1 866	Asie occidentale
Region not specified		315	348	339	258	481	Région non spécifiée
Curaçao	TF						**Curaçao**
Total [1,8]		205 045	198 570	198 271	191 246	204 603	Totale [1,8]
Americas		125 078	125 419	120 121	99 366	99 189	Amériques
Europe		76 926	69 462	68 001	61 105	66 082	Europe
Region not specified		3 041	3 689	10 149	30 775	39 332	Région non spécifiée
Cyprus	TF						**Chypre**
Total		2 088 000	2 222 706	2 434 285	2 686 205	2 696 732	Totale
Africa		...	5 769	8 509	10 247	7 424	Afrique
Americas		...	26 030	30 747	38 737	30 185	Amériques
Europe		1 978 509	2 111 879	2 312 058	2 553 842	2 591 547	Europe
Asia, East/S.East/Oceania		...	9 921	11 358	14 031	9 821	Asie, Est/S.-Est/Océanie
Southern Asia		...	11 304	13 053	15 820	11 755	Asie du Sud
Western Asia		52 825	51 133	55 674	51 388	45 043	Asie occidentale
Region not specified		56 666	6 670	2 886	2 140	957	Région non spécifiée
Czech Republic	TCE						**République tchèque**
Total		4 975 658	5 482 080	5 609 700	*4 666 305	*5 193 973	Totale
Africa		15 538	22 089	26 317	14 122	15 482	Afrique
Americas		257 313	317 618	313 151	284 537	279 410	Amériques
Europe		4 507 425	4 925 570	5 037 345	4 167 620	4 649 830	Europe
Asia, East/S.East/Oceania		195 382	216 803	232 887	200 026	249 251	Asie, Est/S.-Est/Océanie
Dem. Rep. of the Congo	TF						**Rép. dém. du Congo**
Total		30 000	53 139	79 922	102 770	...	Totale
Africa		...	22 223	73 428	96 594	...	Afrique
Americas		...	1 231	799	495	...	Amériques
Europe		...	7 975	4 295	5 681	...	Europe
Asia, East/S.East/Oceania		...	1 333	1 400	...	...	Asie, Est/S.-Est/Océanie
Region not specified		30 000	20 377	...	...	...	Région non spécifiée
Denmark	TCE						**Danemark**
Total [21]		2 157 665	2 072 800	2 023 056	2 087 681	2 028 367	Totale [21]
Americas		95 437	100 781	101 039	112 706	119 758	Amériques
Europe		1 850 525	1 792 981	1 748 024	1 795 286	1 730 584	Europe
Asia, East/S.East/Oceania		51 230	55 921	60 947	62 474	61 785	Asie, Est/S.-Est/Océanie
Region not specified		160 473	123 117	113 046	117 215	116 240	Région non spécifiée
Dominica	TF						**Dominique**
Total		65 446	65 501	73 506	69 598	68 372	Totale
Americas		52 295	52 776	60 670	58 071	56 263	Amériques
Europe		12 215	11 710	12 264	11 394	12 109	Europe
Asia, East/S.East/Oceania		806	339	145	133	...	Asie, Est/S.-Est/Océanie
Region not specified		130	676	427	...	...	Région non spécifiée
Dominican Republic	TF						**Rép. dominicaine**
Total [1]		2 184 688[22]	2 334 493[22]	2 651 249[22]	2 972 552[8]	2 881 999[8]	Totale [1]
Americas		732 535	804 941	924 553	1 131 479	1 179 512	Amériques

76

Tourist/visitor arrivals by region of origin *[cont.]*

Arrivées de touristes/visiteurs par région de provenance *[suite]*

Country or area of destination and region of origin +	Series Série	1997	1998	1999	2000	2001	Pays ou zone de destination et région de provenance +
Europe		1 013 863	1 063 766	1 206 007	1 301 563	1 108 472	Europe
Asia, East/S.East/Oceania		2 553	2 455	1 841	3 132	2 123	Asie, Est/S.-Est/Océanie
Region not specified		435 737	463 331	518 848	536 378	591 892	Région non spécifiée
Ecuador	VF						**Equateur**
Total [3]		529 492	510 626	517 670	627 090	640 561	Totale [3]
Africa		1 033	980	1 054	1 507	1 588	Afrique
Americas		406 379	387 560	395 808	503 056	510 714	Amériques
Europe		108 473	107 845	107 124	103 893	112 390	Europe
Asia, East/S.East/Oceania		13 595	14 195	13 681	18 633	15 863	Asie, Est/S.-Est/Océanie
Region not specified		12	46	3	1	6	Région non spécifiée
Egypt	VF						**Egypte**
Total		3 961 416	3 453 866	4 796 520	5 506 179	4 648 485	Totale
Africa		120 145	130 671	150 552	147 425	145 554	Afrique
Americas		256 668	217 403	276 769	340 770	251 462	Amériques
Europe		2 394 414	1 956 833	3 224 097	3 805 389	3 132 459	Europe
Asia, East/S.East/Oceania		230 769	130 835	211 107	280 831	209 888	Asie, Est/S.-Est/Océanie
Southern Asia		29 549	30 193	34 682	39 304	39 536	Asie du Sud
Western Asia		893 351	985 947	897 108	889 886	867 911	Asie occidentale
Region not specified		36 520	1 984	2 205	2 574	1 675	Région non spécifiée
El Salvador	TF						**El Salvador**
Total [3]		387 052	541 863	658 191	794 678	734 627	Totale [3]
Americas		343 209	498 160	596 044	719 615	659 611	Amériques
Europe		27 401	27 107	26 469	27 012	21 731	Europe
Asia, East/S.East/Oceania		3 719	3 965	3 406	3 075	3 239	Asie, Est/S.-Est/Océanie
Region not specified		12 723	12 631	32 272	44 976	50 046	Région non spécifiée
Eritrea	VF						**Erythrée**
Total [1]		409 544	187 647	56 699	70 355	113 024	Totale [1]
Africa		279 666	119 357	3 729	4 023	7 092	Afrique
Americas		2 960	2 088	783	2 093	2 829	Amériques
Europe		11 948	7 757	3 605	6 276	9 734	Europe
Asia, East/S.East/Oceania		1 614	1 406	2 126	2 960	2 568	Asie, Est/S.-Est/Océanie
Southern Asia		475	408	345	562	2 231	Asie du Sud
Western Asia		1 403	1 543	1 501	1 512	4 021	Asie occidentale
Region not specified		111 478	55 088	44 610	52 929	84 549	Région non spécifiée
Estonia	VF						**Estonie**
Total		2 618 484	2 908 819	3 180 530	3 310 300	3 230 323	Totale
Americas		44 519	78 590	65 448	99 652	106 769	Amériques
Europe		2 547 620	2 783 501	3 090 765	3 186 491	3 076 463	Europe
Asia, East/S.East/Oceania		24 338	28 156	14 142	13 521	14 886	Asie, Est/S.-Est/Océanie
Region not specified		2 007	18 572	10 175	10 636	32 205	Région non spécifiée
Ethiopia	TF						**Ethiopie**
Total [23]		114 732	90 847	91 859	135 954	148 438	Totale [23]
Africa		29 255	25 368	28 496	48 796	61 234	Afrique
Americas		15 957	15 126	16 162	14 279	14 514	Amériques
Europe		40 905	29 536	25 704	34 941	32 540	Europe
Asia, East/S.East/Oceania		4 705	4 297	4 462	6 951	7 478	Asie, Est/S.-Est/Océanie
Southern Asia		2 066	1 642	1 755	3 480	3 244	Asie du Sud
Western Asia		13 538	14 814	15 221	8 605	9 908	Asie occidentale
Region not specified		8 306	64	59	18 902	19 520	Région non spécifiée
Fiji	TF						**Fidji**
Total [3]		359 441	371 342	409 955	294 070	348 014	Totale [3]
Americas		57 735	61 227	75 683	63 066	68 263	Amériques
Europe		67 825	68 675	67 394	51 721	51 425	Europe
Asia, East/S.East/Oceania		232 157	239 600	263 734	177 697	226 190	Asie, Est/S.-Est/Océanie
Region not specified		1 724	1 840	3 144	1 586	2 136	Région non spécifiée
Finland	TCE						**Finlande**
Total		1 831 500	1 866 842	1 830 560	1 970 817	1 999 298	Totale
Africa		4 032	3 583	3 495	4 051	4 603	Afrique
Americas		114 740	113 959	113 986	123 479	119 946	Amériques
Europe		1 511 328	1 539 863	1 502 238	1 589 433	1 615 004	Europe
Asia, East/S.East/Oceania		123 961	110 937	119 036	133 492	142 081	Asie, Est/S.-Est/Océanie

76

Tourist/visitor arrivals by region of origin *[cont.]*

Arrivées de touristes/visiteurs par région de provenance *[suite]*

Country or area of destination and region of origin +	Series Série	1997	1998	1999	2000	2001	Pays ou zone de destination et région de provenance +
Southern Asia		4 682	4 756	3 995	5 610	5 849	Asie du Sud
Western Asia		1 669	1 729	1 358	2 023	3 408	Asie occidentale
Region not specified		71 088	92 015	86 452	112 729	108 407	Région non spécifiée
France [24]	TF						**France**
Total [24]		66 591 000	70 109 000	73 147 000	77 190 000	75 202 000	Totale [24]
Africa		1 030 000	1 065 000	981 000	1 074 000	921 000	Afrique
Americas		4 556 000	4 849 000	5 028 000	5 699 000	5 291 000	Amériques
Europe		58 515 000	61 643 000	64 453 000	67 580 000	66 491 000	Europe
Asia, East/S.East/Oceania		2 036 000	2 140 000	2 261 000	2 353 000	2 114 000	Asie, Est/S.-Est/Océanie
Western Asia		273 000	234 000	233 000	399 000	325 000	Asie occidentale
Region not specified		181 000	178 000	191 000	85 000	60 000	Région non spécifiée
French Polynesia	TF						**Polynésie française**
Total [3,8]		180 440	188 933	210 800	252 000[25]	227 547	Totale [3,8]
Africa		207	161	212	...	280	Afrique
Americas		53 811	62 225	80 148	...	106 875	Amériques
Europe		83 697	87 454	91 785	...	83 556	Europe
Asia, East/S.East/Oceania		42 020	38 381	37 780	...	36 386	Asie, Est/S.-Est/Océanie
Southern Asia		32	33	44	...	43	Asie du Sud
Western Asia		186	213	283	...	191	Asie occidentale
Region not specified		487	466	548	...	216	Région non spécifiée
Gabon	TF						**Gabon**
Total [26]		*167 197	*195 323	177 834	155 432	169 191	Totale [26]
Africa		33 341	47 819	37 995	37 712	42 399	Afrique
Americas		24 094	26 562	6 000	2 000	2 700	Amériques
Europe		93 699	103 294	103 839	112 000	118 631	Europe
Asia, East/S.East/Oceania		1 285	1 416	5 000	1 000	1 330	Asie, Est/S.-Est/Océanie
Western Asia		3 212	3 541	5 000	2 000	2 987	Asie occidentale
Region not specified		11 566	12 691	20 000	720	1 144	Région non spécifiée
Gambia	TF						**Gambie**
Total [27]		84 751	91 106	96 122	78 710	*75 209	Totale [27]
Africa		1 388	1 541	1 156	804	...	Afrique
Americas		575	779	935	910	...	Amériques
Europe		80 694	85 994	91 056	74 643	...	Europe
Region not specified		2 094	2 792	2 975	2 353	...	Région non spécifiée
Georgia	TF						**Géorgie**
Total		313 290	317 063	383 817	387 258	302 215	Totale
Africa		139	140	340	326	730	Afrique
Americas		4 248	5 278	8 919	10 958	7 719	Amériques
Europe		304 547	303 572	362 548	357 798	281 691	Europe
Asia, East/S.East/Oceania		1 091	1 513	4 784	7 327	5 265	Asie, Est/S.-Est/Océanie
Southern Asia		2 522	4 832	4 872	6 058	5 289	Asie du Sud
Western Asia		685	774	1 877	2 167	1 261	Asie occidentale
Region not specified		58	954	477	2 624	260	Région non spécifiée
Germany	TCE						**Allemagne**
Total		15 836 797	16 511 486	17 115 685	18 983 264	17 861 293	Totale
Africa		133 811	136 740	141 843	159 991	147 387	Afrique
Americas		2 127 253	2 351 112	2 399 923	2 865 485	2 334 247	Amériques
Europe		11 490 712	11 979 093	12 497 088	13 515 662	13 093 176	Europe
Asia, East/S.East/Oceania		1 589 968	1 514 879	1 567 293	1 799 132	1 651 279	Asie, Est/S.-Est/Océanie
Western Asia		83 888	96 820	93 341	106 459	116 740	Asie occidentale
Region not specified		411 165	432 842	416 197	536 535	518 464	Région non spécifiée
Ghana	TF						**Ghana**
Total		325 433	347 949	372 651	398 998	438 828	Totale
Africa		110 725	118 384	126 788	135 754	149 305	Afrique
Americas		27 331	29 222	31 297	33 509	36 855	Amériques
Europe		80 672	86 255	92 378	98 909	108 782	Europe
Asia, East/S.East/Oceania		15 652	16 736	17 924	19 191	21 106	Asie, Est/S.-Est/Océanie
Western Asia		2 468	2 639	2 827	3 026	3 329	Asie occidentale
Region not specified		88 585	94 713	101 437	108 609	119 451	Région non spécifiée

76

Tourist/visitor arrivals by region of origin *[cont.]*

Arrivées de touristes/visiteurs par région de provenance *[suite]*

Country or area of destination and region of origin +	Series Série	1997	1998	1999	2000	2001	Pays ou zone de destination et région de provenance +
Greece	TF						**Grèce**
Total [28]		10 070 325	*10 916 046	*12 164 088	*13 095 545	*14 033 378	Totale [28]
Africa		23 072	21 134	23 995	24 244	...	Afrique
Americas		314 057	291 507	305 261	300 213	...	Amériques
Europe		9 404 889	10 333 580	11 555 502	12 464 615	...	Europe
Asia, East/S.East/Oceania		280 749	224 193	225 275	231 255	...	Asie, Est/S.-Est/Océanie
Southern Asia		3 730	3 848	3 809	3 330	...	Asie du Sud
Western Asia		43 828	41 784	50 246	71 888	...	Asie occidentale
Grenada	TF						**Grenade**
Total		110 749	115 794	125 289	128 864	123 351	Totale
Africa		238	337	481	612	632	Afrique
Americas		51 727	54 578	64 000	62 214	66 036	Amériques
Europe		37 796	38 081	40 549	46 325	40 170	Europe
Asia, East/S.East/Oceania		977	1 279	1 802	1 394	1 279	Asie, Est/S.-Est/Océanie
Western Asia		75	104	118	122	166	Asie occidentale
Region not specified		19 936	21 415	18 339	18 197	15 068	Région non spécifiée
Guadeloupe	THS						**Guadeloupe**
Total [29]		147 010	133 030	146 201	623 134	379 000	Totale [29]
Americas		16 740	7 097	8 435	125 871	13 000	Amériques
Europe		129 436	125 231	137 030	495 385	361 000	Europe
Region not specified		834	702	736	1 878	5 000	Région non spécifiée
Guam	TF						**Guam**
Total [4]		1 381 513	1 137 026	1 161 849	1 286 807	1 159 895	Totale [4]
Americas		44 087	42 415	41 798	42 284	42 545	Amériques
Europe		1 786	1 890	1 628	1 618	1 312	Europe
Asia, East/S.East/Oceania		1 323 597	1 079 175	1 105 110	1 231 413	1 077 140	Asie, Est/S.-Est/Océanie
Region not specified		12 043	13 546	13 313	11 492	38 898	Région non spécifiée
Guatemala	TF						**Guatemala**
Total		576 361	636 278	822 695	826 240	835 492	Totale
Americas		457 156	504 757	692 626	688 121	676 176	Amériques
Europe		104 475	115 406	113 698	119 202	134 869	Europe
Asia, East/S.East/Oceania		13 746	14 739	15 084	16 852	22 490	Asie, Est/S.-Est/Océanie
Western Asia		261	296	345	382	418	Asie occidentale
Region not specified		723	1 080	942	1 683	1 539	Région non spécifiée
Guinea	TF						**Guinée**
Total [30]		17 000	23 000	27 345	32 598	37 677	Totale [30]
Africa		2 886	4 400	9 098	12 308	14 858	Afrique
Americas		2 300	2 434	3 638	3 636	3 557	Amériques
Europe		8 966	11 562	11 173	14 315	12 928	Europe
Asia, East/S.East/Oceania		353	489	2 408	1 160	1 703	Asie, Est/S.-Est/Océanie
Southern Asia		...	...	229	373	552	Asie du Sud
Western Asia		2 495	4 115	409	290	726	Asie occidentale
Region not specified		...	...	390	516	3 353	Région non spécifiée
Guinea-Bissau	TF						**Guinée-Bissau**
Total [8]		...	...	...	...	7 754	Totale [8]
Africa		...	...	...	...	2 052	Afrique
Americas		...	...	...	...	433	Amériques
Europe		...	...	...	...	3 824	Europe
Asia, East/S.East/Oceania		...	...	...	...	159	Asie, Est/S.-Est/Océanie
Southern Asia		...	...	...	...	103	Asie du Sud
Western Asia		...	...	...	...	169	Asie occidentale
Region not specified		...	...	...	...	1 014	Région non spécifiée
Guyana	TF						**Guyana**
Total		75 794	68 403	...	...	...	Totale
Africa		128	63	...	...	...	Afrique
Americas		69 419	62 930	...	...	...	Amériques
Europe		5 425	4 927	...	...	...	Europe
Asia, East/S.East/Oceania		543	265	...	...	...	Asie, Est/S.-Est/Océanie
Southern Asia		268	207	...	...	...	Asie du Sud
Western Asia		11	11	...	...	...	Asie occidentale

76

Tourist/visitor arrivals by region of origin *[cont.]*

Arrivées de touristes/visiteurs par région de provenance *[suite]*

Country or area of destination and region of origin +	Series Série	1997	1998	1999	2000	2001	Pays ou zone de destination et région de provenance +
Haiti	TF						**Haïti**
Total		148 735	146 837	143 362	140 492	141 632	Totale
Americas		132 706	131 385	129 854	128 048	129 041	Amériques
Europe		14 112	13 607	11 783	10 960	11 132	Europe
Region not specified		1 917	1 845	1 725	1 484	1 459	Région non spécifiée
Honduras	TF						**Honduras**
Total		306 646	321 149	370 847	470 727	517 914	Totale
Africa		231	168	222	204	242	Afrique
Americas		265 600	280 437	330 821	420 112	460 223	Amériques
Europe		32 954	32 892	33 670	43 022	50 242	Europe
Asia, East/S.East/Oceania		7 823	7 618	5 767	6 914	6 662	Asie, Est/S.-Est/Océanie
Southern Asia		...	...	156	168	173	Asie du Sud
Western Asia		...	...	150	132	136	Asie occidentale
Region not specified		38	34	61	175	236	Région non spécifiée
Hungary	VF						**Hongrie**
Total [31]		37 314 892 [32]	33 624 091	28 802 636	31 141 271	30 679 480	Totale [31]
Africa		11 669	11 762	13 680	15 630	12 972	Afrique
Americas		404 487	451 965	405 275	448 433	451 043	Amériques
Europe		36 652 051	32 967 543	28 147 860	30 407 612	29 978 851	Europe
Asia, East/S.East/Oceania		171 908	124 281	166 156	197 898	194 379	Asie, Est/S.-Est/Océanie
Southern Asia		13 431	14 593	17 831	21 546	16 553	Asie du Sud
Western Asia		33 926	30 743	23 901	22 667	12 364	Asie occidentale
Region not specified		27 420	23 204	27 933	27 485	13 318	Région non spécifiée
Iceland	TF						**Islande**
Total		201 666	232 219	262 604	302 913	...	Totale
Africa		407	487	706	945	...	Afrique
Americas		35 757	44 414	48 568	58 679	...	Amériques
Europe		158 767	179 783	204 837	232 697	...	Europe
Asia, East/S.East/Oceania		6 187	7 001	7 701	9 754	...	Asie, Est/S.-Est/Océanie
Southern Asia		205	421	615	551	...	Asie du Sud
Western Asia		314	82	133	243	...	Asie occidentale
Region not specified		29	31	44	44	...	Région non spécifiée
India	TF						**Inde**
Total [3]		2 374 094	2 358 629	2 481 928	2 649 378	2 537 282	Totale [3]
Africa		98 910	106 045	129 520	93 079	89 197	Afrique
Americas		339 875	348 621	372 857	455 436	439 672	Amériques
Europe		898 929	924 753	895 300	954 911	890 359	Europe
Asia, East/S.East/Oceania		358 472	343 102	368 703	363 754	336 543	Asie, Est/S.-Est/Océanie
Southern Asia		583 706	558 772	624 945	673 917	672 133	Asie du Sud
Western Asia		93 555	77 153	90 359	68 506	67 380	Asie occidentale
Region not specified		647	183	244	39 775	41 998	Région non spécifiée
Indonesia	TF						**Indonésie**
Total		5 185 243	4 606 416	4 727 520	5 064 217	5 153 620	Totale
Africa		24 253	52 312	37 551	37 573	40 282	Afrique
Americas		208 726	201 488	186 727	232 117	243 097	Amériques
Europe		820 340	641 374	688 234	799 769	861 970	Europe
Asia, East/S.East/Oceania		4 061 865	3 608 283	3 747 388	3 909 094	3 920 183	Asie, Est/S.-Est/Océanie
Southern Asia		39 580	58 707	35 484	50 260	51 223	Asie du Sud
Western Asia		30 479	44 252	32 136	35 404	36 865	Asie occidentale
Iran (Islamic Rep. of)	TF						**Iran (Rép. islamique d')**
Total		764 092	1 007 597	1 320 905	1 341 762	1 402 160	Totale
Africa		2 596	2 914	3 410	...	...	Afrique
Americas		2 640	2 986	1 825	...	...	Amériques
Europe		449 115	631 020	735 202	...	...	Europe
Asia, East/S.East/Oceania		10 847	17 800	20 805	...	...	Asie, Est/S.-Est/Océanie
Southern Asia		194 409	255 776	298 954	...	...	Asie du Sud
Western Asia		80 104	97 101	113 494	...	...	Asie occidentale
Region not specified		24 381	...	147 215	...	...	Région non spécifiée
Iraq	VF						**Iraq**
Total		14 906	44 885	30 328	78 457	126 654	Totale
Africa		264	250	207	256	127	Afrique

76

Tourist/visitor arrivals by region of origin *[cont.]*

Arrivées de touristes/visiteurs par région de provenance *[suite]*

Country or area of destination and region of origin +	Series Série	1997	1998	1999	2000	2001	Pays ou zone de destination et région de provenance +
Americas		143	88	145	183	32	Amériques
Europe		1 287	1 088	685	1 461	501	Europe
Asia, East/S.East/Oceania		229	65	42	134	110	Asie, Est/S.-Est/Océanie
Southern Asia		9 704	40 018	28 139	76 367	124 434	Asie du Sud
Western Asia		3 279	3 376	1 110	56	20	Asie occidentale
Region not specified		...	...	...	...	1 430	Région non spécifiée
Ireland	TF						**Irlande**
Total		5 587 000	6 064 000	6 403 000	6 736 000	6 450 000	Totale
Americas		787 000	871 000	961 000	1 069 000	920 000	Amériques
Europe		4 598 000	4 984 000	5 211 000	5 416 000	5 280 000	Europe
Asia, East/S.East/Oceania		180 000	184 000	205 000	223 000	213 000	Asie, Est/S.-Est/Océanie
Region not specified		22 000	25 000	26 000	28 000	37 000	Région non spécifiée
Israel	TF						**Israël**
Total [3]		2 010 242	1 941 620	2 312 411	2 416 756	1 195 689	Totale [3]
Africa		42 837	37 085	36 173	45 381	35 597	Afrique
Americas		548 385	571 409	645 040	683 917	350 484	Amériques
Europe		1 178 934	1 117 249	1 340 682	1 442 158	703 607	Europe
Asia, East/S.East/Oceania		107 478	66 303	98 734	111 238	53 231	Asie, Est/S.-Est/Océanie
Southern Asia		14 480	12 715	17 152	19 052	14 262	Asie du Sud
Western Asia		94 094	100 507	111 684	107 882	30 842	Asie occidentale
Region not specified		24 034	36 352	62 946	7 128	7 666	Région non spécifiée
Italy	VF						**Italie**
Total [33]		57 998 188	58 499 261	59 521 444	62 702 228	60 433 226	Totale [33]
Africa		241 635	181 150	155 103	212 873	198 922	Afrique
Americas		2 645 989	2 474 646	2 004 432	2 292 254	2 164 151	Amériques
Europe		52 920 478	54 049 369	55 840 818	58 643 827	56 679 391	Europe
Asia, East/S.East/Oceania		2 018 245	1 626 810	1 346 538	1 362 568	1 214 619	Asie, Est/S.-Est/Océanie
Southern Asia		72 052	73 450	74 396	93 151	76 895	Asie du Sud
Western Asia		99 789	93 751	100 157	97 555	99 248	Asie occidentale
Region not specified		...	85	...	...	...	Région non spécifiée
Jamaica	TF						**Jamaïque**
Total [1,8]		1 192 194	1 225 287	1 248 397	1 322 690	1 276 516	Totale [1,8]
Africa		1 023	1 026	1 361	1 388	1 271	Afrique
Americas		959 027	995 137	1 024 015	1 108 727	1 083 499	Amériques
Europe		211 551	213 893	209 576	200 269	181 891	Europe
Asia, East/S.East/Oceania		19 621	14 144	12 248	11 194	8 725	Asie, Est/S.-Est/Océanie
Southern Asia		700	595	751	670	731	Asie du Sud
Western Asia		63	423	367	361	334	Asie occidentale
Region not specified		209	69	79	81	65	Région non spécifiée
Japan	TF						**Japon**
Total [3]		4 218 208	4 106 057	4 437 863	4 757 146	4 771 555	Totale [3]
Africa		11 928	12 556	12 939	14 512	14 640	Afrique
Americas		780 711	828 240	852 751	899 277	866 137	Amériques
Europe		545 783	577 278	580 135	624 850	630 128	Europe
Asia, East/S.East/Oceania		2 817 089	2 622 286	2 925 323	3 148 918	3 189 259	Asie, Est/S.-Est/Océanie
Southern Asia		55 525	57 662	60 114	63 725	66 120	Asie du Sud
Western Asia		2 841	3 095	3 317	3 154	3 062	Asie occidentale
Region not specified		4 331	4 940	3 284	2 710	2 209	Région non spécifiée
Jordan	TF						**Jordanie**
Total		1 127 028	1 256 428	1 357 822	1 426 879	1 477 697	Totale
Africa		2 338	2 750	2 811	31 940	33 580	Afrique
Americas		107 676	108 612	123 525	126 411	74 568	Amériques
Europe		365 036	338 706	418 285	463 311	393 607	Europe
Asia, East/S.East/Oceania		47 877	33 933	51 603	59 990	41 955	Asie, Est/S.-Est/Océanie
Western Asia		604 101	772 427	761 598	745 227	933 987	Asie occidentale
Kazakhstan	VF						**Kazakhstan**
Total		284 000	257 000	394 000	1 682 604	2 692 590	Totale
Africa		...	...	...	441	1 687	Afrique
Americas		...	...	...	18 017	19 134	Amériques
Europe		...	...	...	1 583 711	2 585 032	Europe
Asia, East/S.East/Oceania		...	...	...	68 835	68 649	Asie, Est/S.-Est/Océanie

76

Tourist/visitor arrivals by region of origin *[cont.]*

Arrivées de touristes/visiteurs par région de provenance *[suite]*

Country or area of destination and region of origin +	Series Série	1997	1998	1999	2000	2001	Pays ou zone de destination et région de provenance +
Southern Asia		...	...	...	9 177	10 049	Asie du Sud
Western Asia		...	...	...	2 423	2 234	Asie occidentale
Region not specified		...	...	...	...	5 805	Région non spécifiée
Kenya	VF						**Kenya**
Total [34]		1 000 600	894 300	969 419	1 036 628	993 600	Totale [34]
Africa		272 674	251 243	264 145	282 458	270 734	Afrique
Americas		85 161	79 864	82 496	88 216	84 555	Amériques
Europe		573 672	504 204	556 577	595 162	570 149	Europe
Asia, East/S.East/Oceania		44 313	38 145	42 927	45 903	44 003	Asie, Est/S.-Est/Océanie
Southern Asia		24 026	20 844	23 274	24 889	23 858	Asie du Sud
Region not specified		754	...	...	...	301	Région non spécifiée
Kiribati	VF						**Kiribati**
Total [8]		5 054	5 679	4 854	4 035	4 555	Totale [8]
Americas		1 039	1 460	1 452	1 202	1 303	Amériques
Europe		289	144	254	152	213	Europe
Asia, East/S.East/Oceania		2 819	3 200	2 756	2 229	2 474	Asie, Est/S.-Est/Océanie
Region not specified		907	875	392	452	565	Région non spécifiée
Korea, Republic of	VF						**Corée, République de**
Total [35]		3 908 140	4 250 176	4 659 785	5 321 792	5 147 204	Totale [35]
Africa		10 681	11 368	13 986	14 085	15 511	Afrique
Americas		493 942	471 317	463 937	534 519	506 787	Amériques
Europe		436 078	401 309	408 481	479 238	454 777	Europe
Asia, East/S.East/Oceania		2 582 236	2 977 078	3 380 795	3 916 518	3 787 356	Asie, Est/S.-Est/Océanie
Southern Asia		71 251	65 727	81 044	95 677	88 338	Asie du Sud
Western Asia		6 907	9 382	10 515	4 232	7 850	Asie occidentale
Region not specified		307 045	313 995	301 027	277 523	286 585	Région non spécifiée
Kuwait	VF						**Koweït**
Total		1 637 805	1 762 641	1 883 633	1 944 233	2 069 051	Totale
Africa		13 885	18 648	17 679	17 093	18 495	Afrique
Americas		31 807	33 428	39 191	39 389	39 261	Amériques
Europe		66 155	65 998	73 638	71 409	72 689	Europe
Asia, East/S.East/Oceania		54 516	65 908	81 737	95 263	98 798	Asie, Est/S.-Est/Océanie
Southern Asia		471 276	513 475	537 496	518 160	572 066	Asie du Sud
Western Asia		983 464	1 045 852	1 117 588	1 191 168	1 264 107	Asie occidentale
Region not specified		16 702	19 332	16 304	11 751	3 635	Région non spécifiée
Kyrgyzstan	TF						**Kirghizistan**
Total		87 386	59 363	68 863	...	...	Totale
Americas		...	1 386	3 224	...	...	Amériques
Europe		72 202	46 287	50 352	...	...	Europe
Asia, East/S.East/Oceania		...	6 791	8 786	...	...	Asie, Est/S.-Est/Océanie
Southern Asia		...	2 656	2 930	...	...	Asie du Sud
Western Asia		...	90	160	...	...	Asie occidentale
Region not specified		15 184	2 153	3 411	...	...	Région non spécifiée
Lao People's Dem. Rep.	VF						**Rép. dém. pop. lao**
Total		463 200	500 200	614 278	737 208	673 823	Totale
Americas		18 213	25 326	31 780	42 111	34 370	Amériques
Europe		39 096	52 749	70 755	89 703	84 153	Europe
Asia, East/S.East/Oceania		397 253	410 888	503 324	599 908	549 112	Asie, Est/S.-Est/Océanie
Southern Asia		6 528	10 308	7 379	4 346	4 137	Asie du Sud
Region not specified		2 110	929	1 040	1 140	2 051	Région non spécifiée
Latvia	TCE						**Lettonie**
Total		219 939	238 835	240 799	268 083	322 916	Totale
Africa		68	144	77	136	86	Afrique
Americas		9 312	10 762	10 991	11 574	13 427	Amériques
Europe		199 147	214 066	217 050	240 686	297 865	Europe
Asia, East/S.East/Oceania		4 010	4 097	5 928	6 816	7 782	Asie, Est/S.-Est/Océanie
Southern Asia		214	286	793	285	278	Asie du Sud
Western Asia		79	106	157	257	94	Asie occidentale
Region not specified		7 109	9 374	5 803	8 329	3 384	Région non spécifiée

76

Tourist/visitor arrivals by region of origin *[cont.]*

Arrivées de touristes/visiteurs par région de provenance *[suite]*

Country or area of destination and region of origin +	Series Série	1997	1998	1999	2000	2001	Pays ou zone de destination et région de provenance +
Lebanon	TF						**Liban**
Total [36]		557 568	630 781	673 261	741 648	837 072	Totale [36]
Africa		19 380	23 497	27 887	24 183	29 995	Afrique
Americas		59 404	68 321	84 516	89 962	101 199	Amériques
Europe		173 887	195 950	223 945	228 960	237 411	Europe
Asia, East/S.East/Oceania		40 683	40 962	46 986	55 638	54 266	Asie, Est/S.-Est/Océanie
Southern Asia		26 598	35 273	36 004	51 313	82 183	Asie du Sud
Western Asia		207 866	235 992	253 423	288 083	329 945	Asie occidentale
Region not specified		29 750	30 786	500	3 509	2 073	Région non spécifiée
Lesotho	VF						**Lesotho**
Total		323 868	289 819	...	...	...	Totale
Africa		313 323	285 734	...	...	...	Afrique
Americas		2 861	794	...	...	...	Amériques
Europe		5 682	2 311	...	...	...	Europe
Asia, East/S.East/Oceania		2 002	980	...	...	...	Asie, Est/S.-Est/Océanie
Libyan Arab Jamah.	VF						**Jamah. arabe libyenne**
Total [37]		913 251	850 292	965 307	962 559	...	Totale [37]
Africa		571 868	461 533	531 123	533 223	...	Afrique
Americas		861	456	463	647	...	Amériques
Europe		28 140	22 649	33 409	34 296	...	Europe
Asia, East/S.East/Oceania		3 177	3 088	2 841	1 669	...	Asie, Est/S.-Est/Océanie
Southern Asia		2 100	1 271	867	977	...	Asie du Sud
Western Asia		307 105	361 295	396 604	391 747	...	Asie occidentale
Liechtenstein	THS						**Liechtenstein**
Total		57 077	59 228	59 502	61 550	56 475	Totale
Africa		155	173	176	224	193	Afrique
Americas		5 252	4 879	4 861	4 728	3 667	Amériques
Europe		49 237	52 319	52 554	54 759	51 018	Europe
Asia, East/S.East/Oceania		2 433	1 857	1 911	1 839	1 597	Asie, Est/S.-Est/Océanie
Lithuania	TCE						**Lituanie**
Total		288 028	306 228	293 120	299 976	353 669	Totale
Africa		234	208	166	220	290	Afrique
Americas		12 407	14 918	15 194	15 120	15 252	Amériques
Europe		267 822	284 489	270 082	275 503	327 478	Europe
Asia, East/S.East/Oceania		7 565	6 613	7 678	9 133	10 649	Asie, Est/S.-Est/Océanie
Luxembourg	TCE						**Luxembourg**
Total		778 304	789 176	862 822	835 256	811 615	Totale
Americas		35 911	40 172	41 657	40 238	34 180	Amériques
Europe		718 864	721 519	792 900	766 382	751 335	Europe
Region not specified		23 529	27 485	28 265	28 636	26 100	Région non spécifiée
Madagascar	TF						**Madagascar**
Total		100 762	121 207	138 253	160 071	170 208	Totale
Africa		5 844	15 515	20 461	24 534	31 488	Afrique
Americas		2 015	2 424	6 913	6 402	6 808	Amériques
Europe		64 488	82 421	95 395	110 449	119 144	Europe
Asia, East/S.East/Oceania		1 008	1 454	2 489	2 055	3 404	Asie, Est/S.-Est/Océanie
Region not specified		27 407	19 393	12 995	16 631	9 364	Région non spécifiée
Malawi	TF						**Malawi**
Total		207 259	219 570	254 352	*228 106	*266 300	Totale
Africa		152 876	161 955	187 610	179 000	184 900	Afrique
Americas		10 362	10 979	12 718	10 000	23 000	Amériques
Europe		33 161	35 131	40 696	26 106	51 100	Europe
Asia, East/S.East/Oceania		8 290	8 783	10 174	10 000	7 300	Asie, Est/S.-Est/Océanie
Southern Asia		2 342	2 481	2 874	3 000	...	Asie du Sud
Western Asia		228	241	280	...	...	Asie occidentale
Malaysia	TF						**Malaisie**
Total [38]		6 210 921	5 550 748	7 931 149	10 221 582	12 775 073	Totale [38]
Africa		23 502	25 519	29 863	74 314	161 926	Afrique
Americas		137 164	121 569	122 079	307 692	321 841	Amériques
Europe		386 790	367 660	308 713	590 304	703 724	Europe
Asia, East/S.East/Oceania		5 449 937	4 696 660	6 826 835	8 716 429	10 832 535	Asie, Est/S.-Est/Océanie

76

Tourist/visitor arrivals by region of origin *[cont.]*

Arrivées de touristes/visiteurs par région de provenance *[suite]*

Country or area of destination and region of origin +	Series Série	1997	1998	1999	2000	2001	Pays ou zone de destination et région de provenance +
Southern Asia		53 644	56 117	68 992	180 016	212 083	Asie du Sud
Western Asia		16 460	19 571	19 128	44 665	108 384	Asie occidentale
Region not specified		143 424	263 652	555 539	308 162	434 580	Région non spécifiée
Maldives	TF						**Maldives**
Total [8]		365 563	395 725	429 666	467 154	460 984	Totale [8]
Africa		7 962	7 168	1 846	2 311	2 060	Afrique
Americas		6 101	6 119	6 082	7 108	6 814	Amériques
Europe		273 066	304 905	340 469	362 196	364 105	Europe
Asia, East/S.East/Oceania		60 644	56 983	60 598	73 411	68 967	Asie, Est/S.-Est/Océanie
Southern Asia		16 443	19 284	19 393	20 648	17 007	Asie du Sud
Western Asia		1 347	1 266	1 278	1 480	2 031	Asie occidentale
Mali	THS						**Mali**
Total		65 649	83 000	82 159	86 469	88 639	Totale
Africa		14 321	18 000	15 852	18 962	19 241	Afrique
Americas		6 841	8 000	8 671	9 306	8 393	Amériques
Europe		38 278	49 000	49 733	48 304	50 694	Europe
Asia, East/S.East/Oceania		1 621	2 000	782	1 020	1 081	Asie, Est/S.-Est/Océanie
Western Asia		321	400	1 369	2 206	2 445	Asie occidentale
Region not specified		4 267	5 600	5 752	6 671	6 785	Région non spécifiée
Malta	TF						**Malte**
Total		1 111 161	1 182 240	1 214 230	1 215 713	1 180 145	Totale
Africa		5 730	6 342	7 387	9 691	8 694	Afrique
Americas		21 197	25 258	25 951	26 932	27 945	Amériques
Europe		1 023 222	1 087 709	1 107 725	1 103 937	1 079 646	Europe
Asia, East/S.East/Oceania		13 930	15 706	17 620	21 162	22 246	Asie, Est/S.-Est/Océanie
Southern Asia		1 250	1 987	2 054	1 944	1 613	Asie du Sud
Western Asia		42 117	41 067	48 480	46 384	33 771	Asie occidentale
Region not specified		3 715	4 171	5 013	5 663	6 230	Région non spécifiée
Marshall Islands	TF						**Iles Marshall**
Total [8]		6 354	6 374	4 622	5 246	5 444	Totale [8]
Americas		2 471	2 388	2 064	2 022	2 107	Amériques
Europe		354	229	220	129	221	Europe
Asia, East/S.East/Oceania		3 411	3 497	2 234	2 673	3 076	Asie, Est/S.-Est/Océanie
Region not specified		118	260	104	422	40	Région non spécifiée
Martinique	TF						**Martinique**
Total		513 229	548 767	564 304	526 291	460 382	Totale
Americas		77 759	77 270	85 291	80 168	54 744	Amériques
Europe		431 096	467 263	474 475	443 046	403 316	Europe
Region not specified		4 374	4 234	4 538	3 077	2 322	Région non spécifiée
Mauritius	TF						**Maurice**
Total		536 125	558 195	578 085	656 453	660 318	Totale
Africa		164 082	163 024	156 228	163 763	168 319	Afrique
Americas		5 509	5 842	5 820	7 643	8 055	Amériques
Europe		326 522	352 688	379 051	440 279	437 615	Europe
Asia, East/S.East/Oceania		25 283	22 677	21 531	24 083	24 534	Asie, Est/S.-Est/Océanie
Southern Asia		13 998	13 395	14 694	19 598	20 946	Asie du Sud
Western Asia		682	509	527	591	729	Asie occidentale
Region not specified		49	60	234	496	120	Région non spécifiée
Mexico	TF						**Mexique**
Total [1]		19 351 028	19 392 005	19 042 726	20 641 358	19 810 459	Totale [1]
Americas		18 940 987	18 550 480	18 182 563	19 949 917	19 172 090	Amériques
Europe		346 530	476 654	562 790	400 566	362 480	Europe
Region not specified		63 511	364 871	297 373	290 875	275 889	Région non spécifiée
Micronesia (Fed. States)	TF						**Micronésie (Etats féd. de)**
Total [39]		17 249	12 899	16 140	20 501	15 265	Totale [39]
Americas		7 340	5 634	7 449	8 991	7 074	Amériques
Europe		1 039	1 012	1 379	1 461	1 188	Europe
Asia, East/S.East/Oceania		8 784	6 201	7 242	9 925	6 936	Asie, Est/S.-Est/Océanie
Region not specified		86	52	70	124	67	Région non spécifiée

76

Tourist/visitor arrivals by region of origin *[cont.]*

Arrivées de touristes/visiteurs par région de provenance *[suite]*

Country or area of destination and region of origin +	Series Série	1997	1998	1999	2000	2001	Pays ou zone de destination et région de provenance +
Monaco	THS						**Monaco**
Total		258 604	278 474	278 448	300 185	269 925	Totale
Africa		576	555	2 326	2 459	2 372	Afrique
Americas		45 817	42 929	41 660	43 622	35 991	Amériques
Europe		172 201	194 000	202 394	210 506	195 531	Europe
Asia, East/S.East/Oceania		14 202	12 061	11 689	19 311	13 473	Asie, Est/S.-Est/Océanie
Western Asia		3 660	4 816	3 717	4 173	3 325	Asie occidentale
Region not specified		22 148	24 113	16 662	20 114	19 233	Région non spécifiée
Mongolia	TF						**Mongolie**
Total		82 084	197 424	158 734	158 205	165 890	Totale
Africa		81	72	115	183	180	Afrique
Americas		5 129	5 442	6 059	7 217	6 296	Amériques
Europe		25 956	79 818	72 430	69 354	79 368	Europe
Asia, East/S.East/Oceania		50 328	111 493	79 421	80 720	79 491	Asie, Est/S.-Est/Océanie
Southern Asia		526	490	584	625	462	Asie du Sud
Western Asia		64	109	115	106	93	Asie occidentale
Region not specified		...	...	10	...	...	Région non spécifiée
Montserrat	TF						**Montserrat**
Total [1,8]		5 132	7 467	9 885	10 337	...	Totale [1,8]
Americas		3 770	5 560	6 278	7 212	...	Amériques
Europe		1 085	1 496	2 300	2 653	...	Europe
Region not specified		277	411	1 307	472	...	Région non spécifiée
Morocco	TF						**Maroc**
Total [1]		3 071 668	3 094 705	3 816 641	4 113 037	4 223 315	Totale [1]
Africa		78 327	80 686	87 888	88 689	96 694	Afrique
Americas		129 543	141 693	178 642	178 625	149 103	Amériques
Europe		1 362 996	1 466 933	1 753 652	1 918 545	1 864 450	Europe
Asia, East/S.East/Oceania		36 046	38 998	45 397	49 486	43 459	Asie, Est/S.-Est/Océanie
Southern Asia		3 490	4 015	5 256	5 107	5 548	Asie du Sud
Western Asia		66 055	76 797	78 271	78 514	85 391	Asie occidentale
Region not specified		1 395 211	1 285 583	1 667 535	1 794 071	1 978 670	Région non spécifiée
Myanmar	TF						**Myanmar**
Total [40]		189 000	201 000	198 210	207 665	204 862	Totale [40]
Africa		...	...	316	304	312	Afrique
Americas		14 747	13 304	12 748	15 312	16 671	Amériques
Europe		54 859	51 659	51 627	54 905	57 490	Europe
Asia, East/S.East/Oceania		113 927	119 721	126 136	129 347	122 327	Asie, Est/S.-Est/Océanie
Southern Asia		1 948	10 816	5 967	6 534	6 646	Asie du Sud
Western Asia		...	...	1 416	1 263	1 416	Asie occidentale
Region not specified		3 519	5 500	...	...	...	Région non spécifiée
Namibia	TF						**Namibie**
Total		502 012	614 368	...	...	670 497	Totale
Africa		383 515	469 130	...	...	536 203	Afrique
Americas		9 181	12 054	...	...	9 056	Amériques
Europe		101 162	120 595	...	...	112 182	Europe
Region not specified		8 154	12 589	...	...	13 056	Région non spécifiée
Nepal	TF						**Népal**
Total		421 857	463 684	491 504	463 646	361 237	Totale
Africa		1 734	1 803	1 891	2 038	2 038	Afrique
Americas		38 797	47 348	51 422	52 964	42 751	Amériques
Europe		146 889	160 539	173 976	169 367	142 483	Europe
Asia, East/S.East/Oceania		84 765	87 514	95 565	111 667	88 005	Asie, Est/S.-Est/Océanie
Southern Asia		149 662	166 475	168 649	127 602	85 960	Asie du Sud
Region not specified		10	5	1	8	...	Région non spécifiée
Netherlands	TCE						**Pays-Bas**
Total		7 841 000	9 312 000	9 874 000	10 003 000	9 499 900	Totale
Africa		72 000	80 000	107 000	108 000	140 500	Afrique
Americas		900 000	1 144 000	1 162 000	1 216 000	1 202 900	Amériques
Europe		6 149 000	7 371 000	7 905 000	7 956 000	7 478 900	Europe
Asia, East/S.East/Oceania		720 000	717 000	700 000	723 000	677 600	Asie, Est/S.-Est/Océanie

76
Tourist/visitor arrivals by region of origin *[cont.]*
Arrivées de touristes/visiteurs par région de provenance *[suite]*

Country or area of destination and region of origin +	Series Série	1997	1998	1999	2000	2001	Pays ou zone de destination et région de provenance +
New Caledonia	TF						**Nouvelle-Calédonie**
Total [1]		105 137	103 835	99 735	109 587	100 515	Totale [1]
Africa		480	511	597	583	592	Afrique
Americas		1 311	1 529	1 738	2 523	1 870	Amériques
Europe		32 608	31 421	32 111	33 651	27 652	Europe
Asia, East/S.East/Oceania		70 475	70 005	64 749	72 129	69 980	Asie, Est/S.-Est/Océanie
Region not specified		263	369	540	701	421	Région non spécifiée
New Zealand	VF						**Nouvelle-Zélande**
Total [41]		1 497 183	1 484 512	1 607 241	1 789 078	1 909 809	Totale [41]
Africa		15 529	17 499	17 135	18 882	20 849	Afrique
Americas		185 257	205 738	228 654	244 546	240 037	Amériques
Europe		280 766	294 904	317 810	371 652	387 164	Europe
Asia, East/S.East/Oceania		941 659	887 317	958 485	1 087 770	1 181 365	Asie, Est/S.-Est/Océanie
Southern Asia		6 255	6 751	8 307	10 345	14 707	Asie du Sud
Western Asia		3 535	3 691	4 558	4 516	5 247	Asie occidentale
Region not specified		64 182	68 612	72 292	51 367	60 440	Région non spécifiée
Nicaragua	TF						**Nicaragua**
Total		358 439	405 702	468 159	485 909	482 869	Totale
Africa		121	155	192	563	560	Afrique
Americas		322 241	365 011	424 072	437 062	432 474	Amériques
Europe		30 315	33 639	35 521	38 357	40 153	Europe
Asia, East/S.East/Oceania		5 318	6 170	7 763	9 189	8 940	Asie, Est/S.-Est/Océanie
Southern Asia		359	647	461	531	590	Asie du Sud
Western Asia		85	80	97	128	131	Asie occidentale
Region not specified		...	...	53	79	21	Région non spécifiée
Niger	TF						**Niger**
Total [42]		44 018	41 961	42 826	50 263	...	Totale [42]
Africa		7 500	8 000	26 618	28 181	...	Afrique
Americas		2 030	3 000	1 383	2 500	...	Amériques
Europe		8 000	7 902	9 380	14 083	...	Europe
Asia, East/S.East/Oceania		500	1 000	706	...	...	Asie, Est/S.-Est/Océanie
Western Asia		500	...	...	...	...	Asie occidentale
Region not specified		25 488	22 059	4 739	5 499	...	Région non spécifiée
Nigeria	VF						**Nigéria**
Total		1 292 247	1 356 958	1 424 840	1 491 767	1 752 948	Totale
Africa		909 867	955 362	1 003 133	1 050 993	1 234 733	Afrique
Americas		50 421	52 944	55 593	58 242	68 435	Amériques
Europe		200 178	210 301	220 817	230 316	270 056	Europe
Asia, East/S.East/Oceania		79 650	83 606	87 815	91 997	108 097	Asie, Est/S.-Est/Océanie
Southern Asia		29 418	30 892	32 435	33 978	36 335	Asie du Sud
Western Asia		21 668	22 756	23 895	25 034	29 414	Asie occidentale
Region not specified		1 045	1 097	1 152	1 207	5 878	Région non spécifiée
Niue	TF						**Nioué**
Total [8,43]		1 820	1 736	2 252	2 010	2 069	Totale [8,43]
Africa		...	...	15	4	...	Afrique
Americas		98	86	247	163	193	Amériques
Europe		81	78	226	111	180	Europe
Asia, East/S.East/Oceania		1 623	1 552	1 617	1 416	1 679	Asie, Est/S.-Est/Océanie
Western Asia		...	...	1	10	...	Asie occidentale
Region not specified		18	20	146	306	17	Région non spécifiée
Northern Mariana Islands	VF						**Iles Mariannes du Nord**
Total		694 888	490 165	501 788	528 608	444 284	Totale
Africa		39	34	15	36	...	Afrique
Americas		76 217	61 491	49 892	52 331	35 460	Amériques
Europe		2 860	2 852	2 374	2 166	566	Europe
Asia, East/S.East/Oceania		614 558	425 178	449 339	473 883	407 104	Asie, Est/S.-Est/Océanie
Southern Asia		187	141	66	93	...	Asie du Sud
Western Asia		63	100	74	49	...	Asie occidentale
Region not specified		964	369	28	50	1 154	Région non spécifiée

76

Tourist/visitor arrivals by region of origin *[cont.]*

Arrivées de touristes/visiteurs par région de provenance *[suite]*

Country or area of destination and region of origin +	Series Série	1997	1998	1999	2000	2001	Pays ou zone de destination et région de provenance +
Norway	TCE						**Norvège**
Total		...	4 538 221	4 481 400	4 348 039	4 244 261	Totale
Africa		...	9 316	7 763	7 964	7 130	Afrique
Americas		...	277 624	302 965	296 410	277 167	Amériques
Europe		...	3 960 482	3 846 408	3 697 345	3 609 561	Europe
Asia, East/S.East/Oceania		...	187 482	209 961	243 073	227 848	Asie, Est/S.-Est/Océanie
Region not specified		...	103 317	114 303	103 247	122 555	Région non spécifiée
Occupied Palestinian Terr.	VF						**Terr. palestinien occupé**
Total		685 000	767 000	907 000	1 055 000	81 472	Totale
Africa		21 000	15 000	18 000	21 000	1 682	Afrique
Americas		143 000	176 000	181 000	211 000	23 377	Amériques
Europe		418 000	499 000	608 000	717 000	24 571	Europe
Asia, East/S.East/Oceania		41 000	33 000	38 000	43 000	7 286	Asie, Est/S.-Est/Océanie
Southern Asia		14 000	13 000	17 000	21 000	1 742	Asie du Sud
Western Asia		48 000	31 000	45 000	42 000	58	Asie occidentale
Region not specified		...	...	...	...	22 756	Région non spécifiée
Oman	THS						**Oman**
Total		375 753	423 953	502 788	571 110	562 119	Totale
Africa		21 747	26 752	37 345	20 033	22 815	Afrique
Americas		12 355	49 617	58 626	34 089	48 574	Amériques
Europe		159 675	176 123	172 022	227 143	197 279	Europe
Asia, East/S.East/Oceania		69 837	54 977	84 692	98 295	36 913	Asie, Est/S.-Est/Océanie
Southern Asia		31 200	39 466	53 887	65 555	77 033	Asie du Sud
Western Asia		80 939	77 018	96 216	125 995	151 930	Asie occidentale
Region not specified		...	...	...	...	27 575	Région non spécifiée
Pakistan	TF						**Pakistan**
Total		374 800	428 781	432 217	556 805	499 719	Totale
Africa		8 261	8 330	9 694	16 499	14 877	Afrique
Americas		54 169	61 073	60 676	89 783	82 159	Amériques
Europe		153 788	183 855	189 979	257 504	205 140	Europe
Asia, East/S.East/Oceania		41 935	48 798	44 484	49 654	42 711	Asie, Est/S.-Est/Océanie
Southern Asia		97 000	107 302	107 214	108 960	123 957	Asie du Sud
Western Asia		19 587	19 375	19 792	33 107	30 466	Asie occidentale
Region not specified		60	48	378	1 298	409	Région non spécifiée
Palau	TF						**Palaos**
Total [44]		73 719	64 194	55 493	57 732	54 111	Totale [44]
Africa		...	6	16	...	...	Afrique
Americas		10 481	6 347	5 818	6 704	5 375	Amériques
Europe		1 767	1 257	1 779	974	930	Europe
Asia, East/S.East/Oceania		59 909	54 926	46 886	48 630	46 197	Asie, Est/S.-Est/Océanie
Southern Asia		...	141	105	...	...	Asie du Sud
Western Asia		...	10	19	...	...	Asie occidentale
Region not specified		1 562	1 507	870	1 424	1 609	Région non spécifiée
Panama	VF						**Panama**
Total [45]		418 846	422 228	445 957	467 228	482 040	Totale [45]
Africa		276	216	228	324	425	Afrique
Americas		370 752	377 594	398 852	419 348	433 103	Amériques
Europe		32 415	30 934	33 729	35 350	36 425	Europe
Asia, East/S.East/Oceania		15 338	13 426	13 098	12 151	11 988	Asie, Est/S.-Est/Océanie
Western Asia		65	58	50	55	99	Asie occidentale
Papua New Guinea	TF						**Papouasie-Nvl-Guinée**
Total		66 143	67 465	67 357	58 448	54 235	Totale
Africa		...	310	320	212	244	Afrique
Americas		6 878	7 013	6 542	7 191	6 142	Amériques
Europe		5 984	6 646	7 282	5 198	5 161	Europe
Asia, East/S.East/Oceania		53 019	53 316	53 055	44 828	41 675	Asie, Est/S.-Est/Océanie
Southern Asia		...	...	...	1 019	1 013	Asie du Sud
Western Asia		...	162	142	...	...	Asie occidentale
Region not specified		262	18	16	...	...	Région non spécifiée

76

Tourist/visitor arrivals by region of origin *[cont.]*

Arrivées de touristes/visiteurs par région de provenance *[suite]*

Country or area of destination and region of origin +	Series Série	1997	1998	1999	2000	2001	Pays ou zone de destination et région de provenance +
Paraguay	TF						**Paraguay**
Total [3,5]		395 058	349 592	269 021	323 041	294 576	Totale [3,5]
Africa		1 541	723	289	388	147	Afrique
Americas		316 244	282 668	213 662	264 603	274 957	Amériques
Europe		41 995	33 280	32 200	36 536	16 288	Europe
Asia, East/S.East/Oceania		11 219	3 852	4 260	4 522	3 184	Asie, Est/S.-Est/Océanie
Region not specified		24 059	29 069	18 610	16 992	...	Région non spécifiée
Peru	THS						**Pérou**
Total		1 061 987	1 120 427	1 356 971	1 412 686	1 446 188	Totale
Americas		540 087	590 224	655 531	671 442	676 236	Amériques
Europe		237 929	261 715	314 440	331 028	329 028	Europe
Asia, East/S.East/Oceania		42 630	33 358	59 072	67 617	41 951	Asie, Est/S.-Est/Océanie
Region not specified		241 341	235 130	327 928	342 599	398 973	Région non spécifiée
Philippines	TF						**Philippines**
Total [1]		2 222 523	2 149 357	2 170 514	1 992 169	1 796 893	Totale [1]
Africa		1 888	2 054	1 824	1 192	1 685	Afrique
Americas		496 213	540 596	534 480	510 862	451 008	Amériques
Europe		294 679	310 762	293 722	252 195	201 815	Europe
Asia, East/S.East/Oceania		1 232 487	1 050 917	1 076 862	1 021 967	985 941	Asie, Est/S.-Est/Océanie
Southern Asia		27 384	30 954	25 920	24 092	22 193	Asie du Sud
Western Asia		15 104	16 123	15 868	14 711	16 073	Asie occidentale
Region not specified		154 768	197 951	221 838	167 150	118 178	Région non spécifiée
Poland	VF						**Pologne**
Total		87 817 369	88 592 355	89 117 875	84 514 858	61 431 266	Totale
Africa		5 558	7 988	8 387	9 496	9 497	Afrique
Americas		276 272	307 205	297 944	329 591	306 743	Amériques
Europe		87 369 361	88 145 239	88 677 996	84 043 060	60 981 868	Europe
Asia, East/S.East/Oceania		74 777	71 173	77 679	87 690	83 495	Asie, Est/S.-Est/Océanie
Southern Asia		10 558	9 234	9 198	8 990	8 554	Asie du Sud
Western Asia		8 121	7 123	6 430	6 763	6 414	Asie occidentale
Region not specified		72 722	44 393	40 241	29 268	34 695	Région non spécifiée
Portugal	TF						**Portugal**
Total [3,46]		10 172 423	11 294 973	11 631 996	12 096 680	12 167 200	Totale [3,46]
Americas		373 915	408 580	417 122	479 501	454 425	Amériques
Europe		9 550 552	10 588 648	10 869 577	11 191 804	11 365 683	Europe
Asia, East/S.East/Oceania		37 769	44 209	40 570	46 135	43 570	Asie, Est/S.-Est/Océanie
Region not specified		210 187	253 536	304 727	379 240	303 522	Région non spécifiée
Puerto Rico	TF						**Porto Rico**
Total [47]		3 241 774	3 396 115	3 024 088	3 341 400	3 551 200	Totale [47]
Americas		2 474 433	2 569 596	2 284 058	2 500 800	2 635 000	Amériques
Region not specified		767 341	826 519	740 030	840 600	916 200	Région non spécifiée
Qatar	TF						**Qatar**
Total		...	46 110	51 491	66 821	75 760	Totale
Africa		...	2 694	2 843	4 156	4 261	Afrique
Americas		...	3 022	3 176	3 216	3 535	Amériques
Europe		...	15 474	16 420	17 428	18 765	Europe
Asia, East/S.East/Oceania		...	4 080	4 437	4 911	6 531	Asie, Est/S.-Est/Océanie
Southern Asia		...	15 216	16 899	23 218	28 049	Asie du Sud
Western Asia		...	5 624	7 716	13 892	14 619	Asie occidentale
Republic of Moldova	VF						**République de Moldova**
Total [48]		21 169	19 896	14 088	18 964	15 690	Totale [48]
Africa		13	42	10	20	27	Afrique
Americas		1 050	894	910	1 109	1 148	Amériques
Europe		19 692	18 634	12 832	17 230	14 028	Europe
Asia, East/S.East/Oceania		277	187	224	398	377	Asie, Est/S.-Est/Océanie
Southern Asia		48	75	23	48	30	Asie du Sud
Western Asia		89	64	89	159	80	Asie occidentale
Réunion	TF						**Réunion**
Total		370 255 [8]	400 000	394 000	429 999	424 000	Totale
Africa		40 626	48 197	52 769	44 240	45 805	Afrique
Americas		1 269	...	...	...	...	Amériques

76

Tourist/visitor arrivals by region of origin *[cont.]*

Arrivées de touristes/visiteurs par région de provenance *[suite]*

Country or area of destination and region of origin +	Series Série	1997	1998	1999	2000	2001	Pays ou zone de destination et région de provenance +
Europe		325 045	328 978	316 642	359 689	342 663	Europe
Asia, East/S.East/Oceania		1 351	...	...	...	...	Asie, Est/S.-Est/Océanie
Southern Asia		285	...	...	...	...	Asie du Sud
Region not specified		1 679	22 825	24 589	26 070	35 532	Région non spécifiée
Romania	VF						**Roumanie**
Total		5 149 151	4 830 838	5 223 896	5 263 715	4 938 375	Totale
Africa		5 031	4 529	4 667	5 131	4 735	Afrique
Americas		80 907	89 889	84 184	94 642	96 012	Amériques
Europe		4 970 543	4 649 726	5 048 614	5 074 204	4 757 141	Europe
Asia, East/S.East/Oceania		40 839	40 504	36 020	37 260	36 393	Asie, Est/S.-Est/Océanie
Southern Asia		13 511	14 534	16 174	16 909	13 971	Asie du Sud
Western Asia		35 927	30 156	32 140	33 647	28 181	Asie occidentale
Region not specified		2 393	1 500	2 097	1 922	1 942	Région non spécifiée
Russian Federation	VF						**Fédération de Russie**
Total		17 462 627	15 805 242	18 493 012	21 169 100	...	Totale
Africa		33 593	31 321	28 616	...	...	Afrique
Americas		293 230	291 751	255 017	198 800	...	Amériques
Europe		16 034 061	14 286 682	16 780 247	18 964 000	...	Europe
Asia, East/S.East/Oceania		757 046	754 049	747 677	752 600	...	Asie, Est/S.-Est/Océanie
Southern Asia		51 155	51 851	43 137	...	...	Asie du Sud
Western Asia		39 429	64 264	28 290	...	...	Asie occidentale
Region not specified		254 113	325 324	610 028	1 253 700	...	Région non spécifiée
Rwanda	TF						**Rwanda**
Total		...	...	...	104 216	113 185[49]	Totale
Africa		...	...	...	93 058	99 928	Afrique
Americas		...	...	...	2 250	2 785	Amériques
Europe		...	...	...	6 412	8 395	Europe
Asia, East/S.East/Oceania		...	...	...	751	699	Asie, Est/S.-Est/Océanie
Southern Asia		...	...	...	1 241	1 045	Asie du Sud
Western Asia		...	...	...	504	333	Asie occidentale
Saba	TF						**Saba**
Total[50]		10 556	10 565	9 252	9 120	9 005	Totale[50]
Americas		8 295	8 172	7 022	6 695	7 036	Amériques
Europe		994	1 110	850	848	1 354	Europe
Region not specified		1 267	1 283	1 380	1 577	615	Région non spécifiée
Saint Eustatius	TF						**Saint-Eustache**
Total[51]		8 533	8 636	9 176	9 072	9 597	Totale[51]
Americas		2 854	2 967	2 888	3 393	3 447	Amériques
Europe		4 125	4 309	4 293	3 988	4 499	Europe
Region not specified		1 554	1 360	1 995	1 691	1 651	Région non spécifiée
Saint Kitts and Nevis	TF						**Saint-Kitts-et-Nevis**
Total[8]		88 297	93 190	84 002	73 149	74 543	Totale[8]
Americas		74 662	77 056	67 684	45 407	59 353	Amériques
Europe		13 068	15 166	15 759	15 155	10 593	Europe
Asia, East/S.East/Oceania		62	91	114	...	58	Asie, Est/S.-Est/Océanie
Region not specified		505	877	445	12 587	4 539	Région non spécifiée
Saint Lucia	TF						**Sainte-Lucie**
Total[3]		248 406	252 237	263 793	269 850	250 132	Totale[3]
Americas		149 334	161 000	162 010	168 150	165 239	Amériques
Europe		96 398	88 642	98 555	98 869	82 672	Europe
Asia, East/S.East/Oceania		207	179	237	503	205	Asie, Est/S.-Est/Océanie
Region not specified		2 467	2 416	2 991	2 328	2 016	Région non spécifiée
Saint Maarten	TF						**Saint-Martin**
Total[52]		418 340	458 486	444 812	432 292	402 649	Totale[52]
Americas		271 923	289 670	281 213	271 753	269 613	Amériques
Europe		110 030	132 881	125 828	121 819	97 449	Europe
Region not specified		36 387	35 935	37 771	38 720	35 587	Région non spécifiée
St. Vincent-Grenadines	TF						**St. Vincent-Grenadines**
Total		65 143	67 228	68 293	72 895	70 686	Totale
Americas		45 722	46 186	46 980	...	50 572	Amériques

76

Tourist/visitor arrivals by region of origin *[cont.]*

Arrivées de touristes/visiteurs par région de provenance *[suite]*

Country or area of destination and region of origin +	Series Série	1997	1998	1999	2000	2001	Pays ou zone de destination et région de provenance +
Europe		18 625	20 301	20 264	...	18 850	Europe
Region not specified		796	741	1 049	...	1 264	Région non spécifiée
Samoa	TF						**Samoa**
Total		67 960	77 926	85 124	87 688	88 263	Totale
Americas		6 956	8 037	8 252	9 422	8 837	Amériques
Europe		4 494	4 917	5 460	6 396	5 797	Europe
Asia, East/S.East/Oceania		55 370	64 695	70 603	71 314	73 403	Asie, Est/S.-Est/Océanie
Region not specified		1 140	277	809	556	226	Région non spécifiée
San Marino [53]	VF						**Saint-Marin** [53]
Total		3 307 983	3 264 385	3 148 477	3 071 005	3 035 650	Totale
Sao Tome and Principe	TF						**Sao Tomé-et-Principe**
Total		4 924	5 584	5 800	7 137	7 569	Totale
Africa		1 109	1 417	1 159	1 141	2 615	Afrique
Americas		236	...	...	...	456	Amériques
Europe		3 395	3 491	4 333	3 818	4 380	Europe
Asia, East/S.East/Oceania		146	...	...	...	62	Asie, Est/S.-Est/Océanie
Southern Asia		17	...	...	...	23	Asie du Sud
Western Asia		21	...	...	...	33	Asie occidentale
Region not specified		...	676	308	2 178	...	Région non spécifiée
Senegal	THS						**Sénégal**
Total		313 642	352 389	369 116	389 433	...	Totale
Africa		70 224	84 244	81 101	96 834	...	Afrique
Americas		11 597	11 632	10 057	13 192	...	Amériques
Europe		224 971	247 533	269 692	274 035	...	Europe
Asia, East/S.East/Oceania		3 583	2 588	2 680	2 669	...	Asie, Est/S.-Est/Océanie
Western Asia		1 335	1 611	955	988	...	Asie occidentale
Region not specified		1 932	4 781	4 631	1 715	...	Région non spécifiée
Serbia and Montenegro	TCE						**Serbie-et-Monténégro**
Total		298 415	282 639	151 650	238 957	351 333	Totale
Americas		6 288	9 952	2 595	3 631	10 555	Amériques
Europe		280 363	258 992	140 806	222 074	327 263	Europe
Asia, East/S.East/Oceania		1 942	2 156	1 525	2 360	3 089	Asie, Est/S.-Est/Océanie
Region not specified		9 822	11 539	6 724	10 892	10 426	Région non spécifiée
Seychelles	TF						**Seychelles**
Total		130 070	128 258	124 865	130 046	129 762	Totale
Africa		13 966	12 675	14 188	13 746	13 821	Afrique
Americas		6 726	6 787	4 144	6 239	6 854	Amériques
Europe		102 510	102 736	101 320	104 545	103 270	Europe
Asia, East/S.East/Oceania		3 523	2 916	2 543	2 716	2 624	Asie, Est/S.-Est/Océanie
Southern Asia		1 875	1 782	1 251	1 288	1 690	Asie du Sud
Western Asia		1 470	1 362	1 419	1 512	1 503	Asie occidentale
Sierra Leone	TF						**Sierra Leone**
Total [8]		...	12 895 [54]	10 615	15 713	24 067	Totale [8]
Africa		...	5 294	4 265	4 810	11 427	Afrique
Americas		...	1 410	139	2 454	3 211	Amériques
Europe		...	3 967	4 205	5 658	6 250	Europe
Asia, East/S.East/Oceania		...	1 119	600	1 923	1 812	Asie, Est/S.-Est/Océanie
Western Asia		...	1 055	1 406	868	1 367	Asie occidentale
Region not specified		...	50	...	...	...	Région non spécifiée
Singapore	VF						**Singapour**
Total [55]		7 197 871	6 242 152	6 958 201	7 691 399	7 522 163	Totale [55]
Africa		64 978	72 197	83 808	92 003	81 150	Afrique
Americas		460 435	425 424	444 252	482 984	433 552	Amériques
Europe		996 814	990 805	1 058 433	1 138 518	1 124 435	Europe
Asia, East/S.East/Oceania		5 216 166	4 287 819	4 849 620	5 347 318	5 297 821	Asie, Est/S.-Est/Océanie
Southern Asia		396 147	394 617	444 088	516 293	508 302	Asie du Sud
Western Asia		48 106	59 976	66 045	70 628	71 516	Asie occidentale
Region not specified		15 225	11 314	11 955	43 655	5 387	Région non spécifiée
Slovakia	TCE						**Slovaquie**
Total		814 138	896 100	975 105	1 045 614 [56]	1 219 099	Totale
Africa		2 305	3 039	2 664	2 670	3 131	Afrique

76

Tourist/visitor arrivals by region of origin *[cont.]*

Arrivées de touristes/visiteurs par région de provenance *[suite]*

Country or area of destination and region of origin +	Series Série	1997	1998	1999	2000	2001	Pays ou zone de destination et région de provenance +
Americas		25 982	30 206	30 683	35 821	35 922	Amériques
Europe		762 025	839 445	917 862	980 250	1 147 970	Europe
Asia, East/S.East/Oceania		21 143	22 901	23 204	25 417	30 089	Asie, Est/S.-Est/Océanie
Southern Asia		...	...	425	1 117	1 515	Asie du Sud
Western Asia		...	...	180	238	334	Asie occidentale
Region not specified		2 683	509	87	101	138	Région non spécifiée
Slovenia	TCE						**Slovénie**
Total		974 350	976 514	884 048	1 089 549	1 218 721	Totale
Americas		17 193	20 510	22 290	30 221	33 344	Amériques
Europe		942 022	940 365	844 728	1 037 797	1 159 864	Europe
Asia, East/S.East/Oceania		5 820	7 775	8 286	11 725	15 065	Asie, Est/S.-Est/Océanie
Region not specified		9 315	7 864	8 744	9 806	10 448	Région non spécifiée
Solomon Islands	TF						**Iles Salomon**
Total		15 894	13 229	21 318	...	...	Totale
Americas		1 145	789	1 824	...	...	Amériques
Europe		1 356	1 073	2 193	...	...	Europe
Asia, East/S.East/Oceania		13 318	11 278	16 247	...	...	Asie, Est/S.-Est/Océanie
Region not specified		75	89	1 054	...	...	Région non spécifiée
South Africa	VF						**Afrique du Sud**
Total [3,57]		5 170 096	5 898 236	6 026 086	6 000 538	5 908 024	Totale [3,57]
Africa		3 676 810	4 304 878	4 362 677	4 309 893	4 204 904	Afrique
Americas		207 891	254 840	245 297	257 697	250 042	Amériques
Europe		924 497	1 015 942	1 048 633	1 070 284	1 052 916	Europe
Asia, East/S.East/Oceania		190 022	199 248	187 576	189 717	189 909	Asie, Est/S.-Est/Océanie
Southern Asia		29 918	33 666	38 656	38 839	42 594	Asie du Sud
Western Asia		7 095	10 614	10 582	10 210	11 865	Asie occidentale
Region not specified		133 863	79 048	132 665	123 898	155 794	Région non spécifiée
Spain	TF						**Espagne**
Total		39 552 719	43 396 083	46 775 869	47 897 915	50 093 554	Totale
Americas		1 904 078	2 165 477	2 238 148	2 518 590	2 174 428	Amériques
Europe		36 743 065	40 261 677	43 587 460	44 499 469	46 827 293	Europe
Asia, East/S.East/Oceania		299 337	387 815	359 113	300 828	265 059	Asie, Est/S.-Est/Océanie
Western Asia		...	...	...	...	826 774	Asie occidentale
Region not specified		606 239	581 114	591 148	579 028	...	Région non spécifiée
Sri Lanka	TF						**Sri Lanka**
Total [3]		366 165	381 063	436 440	400 414	336 794	Totale [3]
Africa		1 533	1 035	1 236	894	952	Afrique
Americas		16 455	17 937	18 849	17 766	16 412	Amériques
Europe		218 481	246 198	282 000	267 664	211 049	Europe
Asia, East/S.East/Oceania		58 632	54 474	66 528	58 197	49 079	Asie, Est/S.-Est/Océanie
Southern Asia		66 645	57 387	63 006	51 552	53 758	Asie du Sud
Western Asia		4 419	4 032	4 821	4 341	5 544	Asie occidentale
Sudan	TF						**Soudan**
Total [58]		29 749	36 064	38 661	37 609	50 000	Totale [58]
Africa		...	4 624	7 035	5 111	...	Afrique
Europe		...	5 531	6 720	8 988	...	Europe
Asia, East/S.East/Oceania		...	4 787	4 332	7 230	...	Asie, Est/S.-Est/Océanie
Region not specified		...	21 122	20 574	16 280	...	Région non spécifiée
Suriname	TF						**Suriname**
Total [59]		61 361	54 585	...	...	...	Totale [59]
Africa		70	62	...	...	...	Afrique
Americas		9 553	5 501	...	...	...	Amériques
Europe		49 929	46 061	...	...	...	Europe
Asia, East/S.East/Oceania		1 744	1 714	...	...	...	Asie, Est/S.-Est/Océanie
Southern Asia		59	45	...	...	...	Asie du Sud
Region not specified		6	1 202	...	...	...	Région non spécifiée
Swaziland	THS						**Swaziland**
Total [60]		269 113	284 116	289 383	280 870	283 177	Totale [60]
Africa		131 440	201 288	198 921	177 216	145 169	Afrique
Americas		17 616	5 121	9 733	10 823	20 217	Amériques
Europe		104 338	76 288	72 916	84 514	84 988	Europe

76

Tourist/visitor arrivals by region of origin [cont.]

Arrivées de touristes/visiteurs par région de provenance [suite]

Country or area of destination and region of origin +	Series Série	1997	1998	1999	2000	2001	Pays ou zone de destination et région de provenance +
Asia, East/S.East/Oceania		13 550	1 298	6 313	7 053	5 676	Asie, Est/S.-Est/Océanie
Region not specified		2 169	121	1 500	1 264	27 127	Région non spécifiée
Switzerland	THS						**Suisse**
Total		7 039 225	7 185 379	7 153 967	7 821 158	7 454 855	Totale
Africa		81 015	82 431	73 139	77 345	79 164	Afrique
Americas		990 354	1 074 217	1 019 743	1 198 553	1 026 667	Amériques
Europe		4 846 684	5 050 341	5 029 798	5 343 044	5 277 161	Europe
Asia, East/S.East/Oceania		1 026 559	879 624	923 645	1 079 068	937 554	Asie, Est/S.-Est/Océanie
Southern Asia		42 190	55 102	64 543	71 912	72 291	Asie du Sud
Western Asia		52 423	43 664	43 099	51 236	62 018	Asie occidentale
Syrian Arab Republic	VF						**Rép. arabe syrienne**
Total [3]		2 331 628	2 463 724	2 681 534	3 014 758	3 389 091	Totale [3]
Africa		76 116	70 906	64 920	66 131	71 383	Afrique
Americas		26 265	27 766	30 591	38 209	43 415	Amériques
Europe		342 767	342 615	369 479	397 871	471 541	Europe
Asia, East/S.East/Oceania		18 215	16 319	22 287	26 115	24 762	Asie, Est/S.-Est/Océanie
Southern Asia		139 693	170 143	220 741	242 529	237 188	Asie du Sud
Western Asia		1 696 803	1 799 683	1 928 846	2 196 287	2 425 119	Asie occidentale
Region not specified		31 769	36 292	44 670	47 616	115 683	Région non spécifiée
Tajikistan	VF						**Tadjikistan**
Total		2 100	3 190	4 500	7 673	5 200	Totale
Africa		...	...	15	72	...	Afrique
Americas		263	398	401	796	887	Amériques
Europe		1 615	2 110	3 069	4 921	3 300	Europe
Asia, East/S.East/Oceania		32	656	416	1 093	467	Asie, Est/S.-Est/Océanie
Southern Asia		187	21	494	668	512	Asie du Sud
Western Asia		3	5	105	123	34	Asie occidentale
Thailand	TF						**Thaïlande**
Total [61]		7 293 957	7 842 760	8 651 260	9 578 826	10 132 509	Totale [61]
Africa		50 963	72 097	73 233	80 389	90 963	Afrique
Americas		388 190	448 761	514 595	584 967	604 041	Amériques
Europe		1 635 581	1 946 154	2 055 430	2 242 466	2 395 806	Europe
Asia, East/S.East/Oceania		4 840 429	4 931 506	5 546 527	6 134 335	6 491 790	Asie, Est/S.-Est/Océanie
Southern Asia		235 623	258 815	280 422	339 413	333 248	Asie du Sud
Western Asia		70 559	107 597	110 125	127 053	146 102	Asie occidentale
Region not specified		72 612	77 830	70 928	70 203	70 559	Région non spécifiée
TFYR of Macedonia	TCE						**L'ex-R.y. Macédoine**
Total		121 337	156 670	180 788	224 016	98 946	Totale
Americas		5 424	8 788	15 526	17 023	7 846	Amériques
Europe		112 752	143 830	158 754	198 298	87 396	Europe
Asia, East/S.East/Oceania		1 644	2 280	2 440	2 803	1 082	Asie, Est/S.-Est/Océanie
Region not specified		1 517	1 772	4 068	5 892	2 622	Région non spécifiée
Togo	THS						**Togo**
Total		92 081	69 461	69 818	59 541	56 629	Totale
Africa		52 275	39 026	41 268	29 546	33 554	Afrique
Americas		4 263	4 853	3 339	2 050	2 343	Amériques
Europe		30 488	21 857	21 336	25 376	17 680	Europe
Asia, East/S.East/Oceania		1 739	1 091	1 453	1 271	1 311	Asie, Est/S.-Est/Océanie
Western Asia		3 163	2 588	2 344	1 203	1 619	Asie occidentale
Region not specified		153	46	78	95	122	Région non spécifiée
Tonga	TF						**Tonga**
Total [8]		26 162	27 132	30 949	34 694	32 386	Totale [8]
Africa		8	15	67	53	55	Afrique
Americas		5 166	6 093	6 153	8 005	6 706	Amériques
Europe		4 225	4 031	4 855	5 977	4 601	Europe
Asia, East/S.East/Oceania		16 712	16 921	19 790	20 557	20 920	Asie, Est/S.-Est/Océanie
Southern Asia		51	72	84	102	104	Asie du Sud
Trinidad and Tobago	TF						**Trinité-et-Tobago**
Total [8]		324 293	334 037	358 220	398 559	383 101	Totale [8]
Africa		613	736	904	996	935	Afrique
Americas		249 552	254 963	277 819	309 122	285 882	Amériques

76

Tourist/visitor arrivals by region of origin *[cont.]*

Arrivées de touristes/visiteurs par région de provenance *[suite]*

Country or area of destination and region of origin +	Series Série	1997	1998	1999	2000	2001	Pays ou zone de destination et région de provenance +
Europe		69 887	73 970	74 260	82 661	89 002	Europe
Asia, East/S.East/Oceania		1 758	2 098	3 141	3 507	3 874	Asie, Est/S.-Est/Océanie
Southern Asia		937	876	1 093	1 196	1 492	Asie du Sud
Western Asia		233	110	267	279	262	Asie occidentale
Region not specified		1 313	1 284	736	798	1 654	Région non spécifiée
Tunisia	TF						**Tunisie**
Total [3]		4 263 107	4 717 705	4 831 658	5 057 513	5 387 300	Totale [3]
Africa		671 432	750 322	671 501	665 812	675 838	Afrique
Americas		26 689	27 831	27 050	31 275	28 486	Amériques
Europe		2 845 952	3 011 383	3 460 857	3 615 793	3 609 526	Europe
Asia, East/S.East/Oceania		5 506	8 354	9 314	8 343	7 804	Asie, Est/S.-Est/Océanie
Western Asia		675 264	879 931	634 898	712 932	1 046 582	Asie occidentale
Region not specified		38 264	39 884	28 038	23 358	19 064	Région non spécifiée
Turkey	TF						**Turquie**
Total		9 039 671	8 959 712	6 892 636	9 585 695	10 782 673	Totale
Africa		95 596	95 504	82 332	106 289	118 870	Afrique
Americas		267 575	317 451	282 616	360 920	326 732	Amériques
Europe		7 874 694	7 786 373	5 786 258	8 234 233	9 473 313	Europe
Asia, East/S.East/Oceania		204 989	195 477	167 166	233 669	249 116	Asie, Est/S.-Est/Océanie
Southern Asia		348 318	320 779	366 621	397 348	342 218	Asie du Sud
Western Asia		232 704	230 797	198 723	242 352	260 980	Asie occidentale
Region not specified		15 795	13 331	8 920	10 884	11 444	Région non spécifiée
Turkmenistan	VF						**Turkménistan**
Total		332 425	...	...	...	...	Totale
Africa		109	...	...	...	...	Afrique
Americas		2 647	...	...	...	...	Amériques
Europe		150 705	...	...	...	...	Europe
Asia, East/S.East/Oceania		2 189	...	...	...	...	Asie, Est/S.-Est/Océanie
Southern Asia		175 542	...	...	...	...	Asie du Sud
Western Asia		1 233	...	...	...	...	Asie occidentale
Turks and Caicos Islands	TF						**Iles Turques et Caïques**
Total		93 011	110 855	120 898	152 291	165 341	Totale
Americas		78 736	90 321	98 316	136 211	148 025	Amériques
Europe		9 121	11 887	11 498	11 829	11 086	Europe
Asia, East/S.East/Oceania		...	...	...	113	57	Asie, Est/S.-Est/Océanie
Region not specified		5 154	8 647	11 084	4 138	6 173	Région non spécifiée
Tuvalu	TF						**Tuvalu**
Total		1 029	1 077	...	...	...	Totale
Americas		76	118	...	...	...	Amériques
Europe		127	123	...	...	...	Europe
Asia, East/S.East/Oceania		822	804	...	...	...	Asie, Est/S.-Est/Océanie
Region not specified		4	32	...	...	...	Région non spécifiée
Uganda	TF						**Ouganda**
Total		175 073	194 790	189 347	192 755	205 287	Totale
Africa		99 609	115 847	116 207	131 687	149 907	Afrique
Americas		13 857	14 550	12 898	11 947	12 922	Amériques
Europe		43 656	45 720	43 133	36 050	30 395	Europe
Asia, East/S.East/Oceania		6 107	6 738	6 123	4 899	4 757	Asie, Est/S.-Est/Océanie
Southern Asia		6 926	7 950	7 048	5 538	5 514	Asie du Sud
Western Asia		4 251	3 614	3 183	2 032	1 792	Asie occidentale
Region not specified		667	371	755	602	...	Région non spécifiée
Ukraine	TF						**Ukraine**
Total		6 183 602	6 207 640	4 232 358	4 405 746	5 791 250	Totale
Africa		10 559	3 843	6 928	15 296	5 227	Afrique
Americas		79 638	63 941	70 158	70 542	64 096	Amériques
Europe		5 991 007	6 091 006	4 098 338	4 258 221	5 678 136	Europe
Asia, East/S.East/Oceania		28 129	22 473	23 979	26 625	17 107	Asie, Est/S.-Est/Océanie
Southern Asia		36 381	12 675	10 774	11 363	7 453	Asie du Sud
Western Asia		28 585	8 940	14 195	18 436	13 399	Asie occidentale
Region not specified		9 303	4 762	7 986	5 263	5 832	Région non spécifiée

76

Tourist/visitor arrivals by region of origin [cont.]

Arrivées de touristes/visiteurs par région de provenance [suite]

Country or area of destination and region of origin +	Series Série	1997	1998	1999	2000	2001	Pays ou zone de destination et région de provenance +
United Arab Emirates	THS						**Emirats arabes unis**
Total [62]		2 475 868	2 990 539	3 392 614	3 906 545	4 133 531	Totale [62]
Africa		118 629	145 851	153 899	173 601	218 162	Afrique
Americas		80 290	110 618	130 280	139 474	149 802	Amériques
Europe		787 395	947 183	1 016 869	1 076 813	1 115 373	Europe
Asia, East/S.East/Oceania		199 633	235 811	247 673	263 609	284 878	Asie, Est/S.-Est/Océanie
Southern Asia		372 242	425 982	500 985	568 453	590 378	Asie du Sud
Western Asia		641 607	797 285	923 248	1 088 753	1 220 738	Asie occidentale
Region not specified [63]		276 072	327 809	419 660	595 842	554 200	Région non spécifiée [63]
United Kingdom	VF						**Royaume-Uni**
Total [31]		25 515 000	25 744 000	25 396 000	25 211 000	22 835 000	Totale [31]
Africa		525 000	570 000	588 000	618 000	630 000	Afrique
Americas		4 509 000	5 053 000	5 000 000	5 287 000	4 582 000	Amériques
Europe		17 644 000	17 581 000	17 046 000	16 307 000	15 060 000	Europe
Asia, East/S.East/Oceania		2 155 000	1 872 000	2 062 000	2 256 000	1 834 000	Asie, Est/S.-Est/Océanie
Southern Asia		269 000	264 000	291 000	314 000	326 000	Asie du Sud
Western Asia		413 000	404 000	409 000	429 000	403 000	Asie occidentale
United Rep. of Tanzania	VF						**Rép.-Unie de Tanzanie**
Total		360 500	482 331	627 417	501 669	525 122	Totale
Africa		150 861	201 845	262 559	201 934	213 013	Afrique
Americas		35 570	47 594	61 908	49 001	45 544	Amériques
Europe		107 051	143 229	186 311	157 470	162 225	Europe
Asia, East/S.East/Oceania		27 520	36 824	47 898	38 299	46 605	Asie, Est/S.-Est/Océanie
Southern Asia		17 696	23 677	30 797	24 626	28 060	Asie du Sud
Western Asia		21 802	29 162	37 944	30 339	29 675	Asie occidentale
United States	TF						**Etats-Unis**
Total		47 752 476	46 395 587	48 491 187	50 944 701	45 490 497	Totale
Africa		233 972	258 228	273 762	295 090	290 052	Afrique
Americas		28 141 272	27 512 761	28 746 665	30 064 382	27 733 279	Amériques
Europe		10 734 881	11 040 602	11 634 166	12 052 331	10 233 106	Europe
Asia, East/S.East/Oceania		8 201 299	7 081 823	7 301 839	7 921 004	6 631 806	Asie, Est/S.-Est/Océanie
Southern Asia		235 416	282 112	300 673	362 634	364 071	Asie du Sud
Western Asia		205 636	220 061	234 082	249 260	238 183	Asie occidentale
United States Virgin Is.	THS						**Iles Vierges américaines**
Total		386 740	480 064	484 156	496 349	608 684	Totale
Africa		248	539	322	140	177	Afrique
Americas		360 897	453 047	451 618	435 544	546 545	Amériques
Europe		14 875	14 570	19 435	10 285	8 827	Europe
Asia, East/S.East/Oceania		1 063	764	783	653	396	Asie, Est/S.-Est/Océanie
Region not specified		9 657	11 144	11 998	49 727	52 739	Région non spécifiée
Uruguay	VF						**Uruguay**
Total [1]		2 462 532	2 323 993	2 273 164	2 235 887	2 136 446	Totale [1]
Americas		1 888 852	1 809 579	1 759 517	1 758 399	1 708 380	Amériques
Europe		83 626	96 190	86 167	85 039	70 009	Europe
Asia, East/S.East/Oceania		...	...	...	6 515	5 531	Asie, Est/S.-Est/Océanie
Western Asia		...	...	...	201	2 627	Asie occidentale
Region not specified		490 054	418 224	427 480	385 733	349 899	Région non spécifiée
Uzbekistan	TF						**Ouzbékistan**
Total		959 800	810 500	486 800	301 900	344 900	Totale
Africa		...	...	...	...	1 000	Afrique
Americas		3 800	3 700	8 500	6 000	10 000	Amériques
Europe		642 000	468 000	145 000	72 000	109 000	Europe
Asia, East/S.East/Oceania		259 000	295 000	301 800	195 900	192 900	Asie, Est/S.-Est/Océanie
Southern Asia		7 000	7 000	8 000	7 000	8 000	Asie du Sud
Western Asia		48 000	36 800	23 500	21 000	24 000	Asie occidentale
Vanuatu	TF						**Vanuatu**
Total		49 605	52 085	50 746	57 591	53 300	Totale
Americas		1 248	1 297	1 343	1 547	1 413	Amériques
Europe		2 788	2 337	3 063	3 401	2 683	Europe
Asia, East/S.East/Oceania		44 623	47 547	45 525	51 803	48 234	Asie, Est/S.-Est/Océanie
Region not specified		946	904	815	840	970	Région non spécifiée

76

Tourist/visitor arrivals by region of origin *[cont.]*

Arrivées de touristes/visiteurs par région de provenance *[suite]*

Country or area of destination and region of origin +	Series Série	1997	1998	1999	2000	2001	Pays ou zone de destination et région de provenance +
Venezuela	TF						**Venezuela**
Total		813 862	685 429	586 900	469 047	584 399	Totale
Africa		929	3 364	860	380	819	Afrique
Americas		454 427	366 315	296 212	172 071	280 101	Amériques
Europe		346 182	301 795	277 014	288 037	290 914	Europe
Asia, East/S.East/Oceania		7 065	9 179	5 069	3 286	6 835	Asie, Est/S.-Est/Océanie
Southern Asia		966	462	686	256	468	Asie du Sud
Western Asia		1 716	1 051	519	462	643	Asie occidentale
Region not specified		2 577	3 263	6 540	4 555	4 619	Région non spécifiée
Viet Nam	VF						**Viet Nam**
Total [1]		1 715 637	1 520 128	1 781 754	2 140 000	2 330 050	Totale [1]
Africa		626	...	4 599	1 707	...	Afrique
Americas		176 159	176 578	243 549	241 708	266 433	Amériques
Europe		218 502	123 002	241 537	271 183	307 722	Europe
Asia, East/S.East/Oceania		1 033 527	679 577	1 059 357	1 398 885	1 432 694	Asie, Est/S.-Est/Océanie
Southern Asia		6 151	...	6 428	6 639	8 086	Asie du Sud
Region not specified		280 672	540 971	226 284	219 878	315 115	Région non spécifiée
Yemen	THS						**Yémen**
Total		80 451	87 627	58 370	72 836	75 579	Totale
Africa		2 156	2 696	4 312	5 658	4 867	Afrique
Americas		4 676	5 585	6 732	8 161	2 879	Amériques
Europe		50 560	54 163	22 201	24 825	26 920	Europe
Asia, East/S.East/Oceania		8 447	7 437	4 862	8 788	6 209	Asie, Est/S.-Est/Océanie
Western Asia		14 612	17 746	20 263	25 404	34 704	Asie occidentale
Zambia	TF						**Zambie**
Total		340 897	362 025	404 247	457 419	491 991	Totale
Africa		203 777	260 162	301 942	294 479	316 736	Afrique
Americas		27 819	14 893	15 121	27 469	29 546	Amériques
Europe		71 427	67 055	67 253	105 409	113 375	Europe
Asia, East/S.East/Oceania		34 419	17 494	17 451	27 709	29 803	Asie, Est/S.-Est/Océanie
Southern Asia		3 455	2 421	2 480	2 353	2 531	Asie du Sud
Zimbabwe	TF						**Zimbabwe**
Total [64]		1 281 205	1 986 474	2 100 520	1 868 412	2 067 864	Totale [64]
Africa		935 089	1 485 774	1 508 326	1 403 774	1 593 558	Afrique
Americas		62 224	119 521	114 865	116 128	110 106	Amériques
Europe		227 606	301 884	377 377	268 980	262 071	Europe
Asia, East/S.East/Oceania		56 286	79 295	99 952	79 530	102 129	Asie, Est/S.-Est/Océanie

Source:
World Tourism Organization (WTO), Madrid, WTO statistics database and the "Yearbook of Tourism Statistics", 2003 edition.

+   For a listing of the Member States of the regions of origin, see Annex I, with the following exceptions:

   Africa includes the countries and territories listed under Africa in Annex I but excludes Egypt, Guinea-Bissau, Liberia, Libyan Arab Jamahiriya, Mozambique and Western Sahara.

   Americas is as shown In Annex I, but excludes Falkland Islands (Malvinas), French Guyana, Greenland and Saint Pierre and Miquelon.

   Europe is as shown in Annex I, but excludes Andorra, Channel Islands, Faeroe Islands, Holy See, Isle of Man and Svalbard and Jan Mayen Islands. The Europe group also includes Armenia, Azerbaijan, Cyprus, Israel, Kyrgyzstan, Turkey and Turkmenistan.

   Asia, East and South East/Oceania includes the countries and territories listed under Eastern Asia and South-eastern Asia in Annex I (except for Timor-Leste), and under Oceania except for Christmas Island, Cocos Island, Norfolk Island, Nauru, Wake Island, Johnston Island, Midway Islands, Pitcairn, Tokelau and Wallis and Futuna Islands. The Asia, East and South East/Oceania group also includes Taiwan Province of China.

   Southern Asia is as shown in Annex I under South-central Asia, but excludes Kazakhstan, Kyrgyzstan, Tajikistan, Turkmenistan and Uzbekistan.

Source:
Organisation mondiale du tourisme (OMT), Madrid, la base de données de l'OMT, et "l'Annuaire des statistiques du tourisme", 2003 édition.

+   On se reportera à l'Annexe I pour les États Membres classés dans les différentes régions de provenance, avec les exceptions ci-après ;

   Afrique – Comprend les États et territoires énumérés à l'Annexe I, sauf l'Égypte, la Guinée-Bissau, le Libéria, la Jamahiriya arabe libyenne, le Mozambique et le Sahara occidental.

   Amériques – Comprend les États et territoires énumérés à l'Annexe I, sauf les îles Falkland (Malvinas), le Groënland, la Guyane française et Saint-Pierre-et-Miquelon.

   Europe – Comprend les États et territoires énumérés à l'Annexe I, sauf l'Andorre, les îles Anglo-normandes, les îles Féroé, l'île de Man, le Saint-Siège et les îles Svalbard et Jan Mayen. Le Groupe comprend en revanche l'Arménie, l'Azerbaïdjan, Chypre, Israël, l'Kirghizistan, la Turquie et le Turkménistan.

   L'Asie de l'Est et du Sud-Est/Océanie – Comprend les États et territoires énumérés à l'Annexe I dans les Groupes Asie de l'Est et Asie de Sud-Est sauf le Timor-Leste, et les États et territoires énumérés dans le Groupe Océanie sauf les îles Christmas, les îles Cocos, l'île Johnston, les îles Midway, Nauru, l'îles Norfolk, Pitcairn, Tokélou, l'île Wake et Wallis-et-Futuna. Le Groupe Asie de l'Est et du Sud-Est/Océanie comprend en

76

Tourist/visitor arrivals by region of origin *[cont.]*

Arrivées de touristes/visiteurs par région de provenance *[suite]*

Western Asia is as shown in Annex I but excludes Armenia, Azerbaijan, Cyprus, Georgia, Israel, Occupied Palestinian Territory, and Turkey. The Western Asia group also includes Egypt and the Libyan Arab Jamahiriya.

revanche la Province chinoise de Taiwan.

Asie du Sud – Comprend les États et territoires énumérés à l'Annexe I, sauf le Kazakhstan, le Kirghizistan, l'Ouzbékistan, le Tadjikistan et le Turkménistan.

Asie occidentale – Comprend les États et territoires énumérés à l'Annexe I, sauf l'Arménie, l'Azerbaïdjan, Chypre, la Géorgie, Israël, le territoire Palestinien Occupé et la Turquie. Le Groupe comprend en revanche l'Égypte et la Jamahiriya arabe libyenne.

TCE: Arrivals of non-resident tourists in all types of tourism accommodation.

TF: Arrivals of non-resident tourists at national borders (excluding same-day visitors).

THS: Arrivals of non-resident tourists in hotels and similar establishments.

VF: Arrivals of non-resident visitors at national borders (including tourists and same-day visitors).

TCE : Arrivées de touristes non résidents dans tous les types d'établissements.

TF : Arrivées de touristes non résidents aux frontières nationales (à l'exclusion de visiteurs de la journée).

THS : Arrivées de touristes non résidents dans les hôtels et établissements assimilés.

VF : Arrivées de visiteurs non résidents aux frontières nationales (y compris touristes et visiteurs de la journée).

NOTE: Footnotes apply to all of the regions.

NOTE : Les notes de pied se réfèrent aux toutes les régions.

1   Including nationals of the country residing abroad.
2   Including arrivals from Western Samoa. 1990-1997, excluding arrivals from Western Samoa.
3   Excluding nationals of the country residing abroad.
4   Air and sea arrivals.
5   Excluding crew members.
6   Including private accommodation.
7   Including transit passengers, border permits and returning residents.

8   Air arrivals.
9   International tourist arrivals in hotels of regional capitals.

10 Change in methodology.
11 Excluding children without own passports. (Bulgaria: 1998-2000). Including transit visitors.
12 Air arrivals at Pochentong and Siem Reap Airports. Region Not Specified 1998 to 2001: Including arrivals at Siem Reap Airport by direct-flights; 1998: 10,423; 1999: 28,525; 2000: 87,012; 2001: 133,688.
13 Different types of methodological changes that affect the estimates for 2000 and 2001 for expenditures and characteristics of International Tourists to Canada, have been introduced in 2002. Therefore, Statistics Canada advises not to compare the estimates for 2000 and 2001 with the years prior because of these methodological changes for the non-count estimates (one of the reasons ALS numbers are not provided).

14 1997-1999: Revised estimates.
15 Excluding ethnic Chinese arriving from China, Hong Kong SAR, Macao SAR and Taiwan: 1987: 25,174,446; 1988: 29,852,598; 1989: 28,040,424; 1990: 25,714,506; 1991: 30,639,658; 1992: 34,108,578; 1993: 36,871,088; 1994: 38,502,396; 1995: 40,499,795; 1996: 44,383,182; 1997: 50,159,917; 1998: 56,370,654; 1999: 64,363,298; 2000: 73,283,449; 2001: 77,786,540. Also including stateless persons and employees of the United Nations Organizations.

16 From 1996 and onwards, figures adjusted to include non-Macanese arrivals via Macao,China.
17 Including arrivals by sea, land and by air (helicopter). 1995, Nov.: Arrivals by air began (Macao SAR International Airport). Including stateless and Chinese people whodo not have permanent residency in Hong Kong SAR, China: 1992: 93,965; 1993: 92,679; 1994: 147,304; 1995: 167,361; 1996: 189,364.

1   Y compris les nationaux du pays résidant à l'étranger.
2   Y compris des arrivées en provenance de Samoa occidentale. 1990-1997, à l'exclusion des arrivées en provenance de Samoa occidentale.
3   A l'exclusion des nationaux du pays résidant à l'étranger.
4   Arrivées par voie aérienne et maritime.
5   A l'exclusion des membres des équipages.
6   Y compris hébergement privé.
7   Y compris passagers en transit, passages à la frontière et résidents de retour de voyage.
8   Arrivées par voie aérienne.
9   Arrivées de touristes internationaux dans les hôtels des capitales de département.
10 Changement de méthode.
11 A l'exclusion d'enfants sans passeports personnels (Bulgarie : 1998-2000). Y compris les visiteurs en transit.
12 Arrivées par voie aérienne aux aéroports de Pochentong et de Siem Reap. Région non spécifiée 1998 à 2001: Y compris les arrivées à l'aéroport de Siem Reap en vols directs; 1998: 10,423; 1999: 28,525; 2000: 87,012; 2001: 133,688.
13 En 2002, il a été adopté différents types de changements méthodologiques qui ont eu des effets sur les estimations des dépenses et des caractéristiques des touristes internationaux ayant visité le Canada en 2000 et 2001. Pour 2000 et 2001, Statistique Canada conseille par conséquent de ne pas comparer les estimations ne reposant pas sur des comptages aux données des années précédentes (c'est une des raisons pour lesquelles les données DMS ne sont pas fournies).
14 1997-1999: Estimations revues.
15 A l'exclusion des arrivées de personnes d'ethnie chinoise en provenance de Chine, Hong Kong RAS, Macao et Taiwan: 1987: 25.174.446; 1988: 29.852.598; 1989: 28,040,424;1990: 25,714,506; 1991: 30,639,658; 1992: 34,108.578; 1993: 36,871,088; 1994: 38,502,396; 1994: 38,502,396; 1995: 40,499,795; 1996: 44,383,182;1997: 50,159,917; 1998: 56,370,654; 1999: 64,363,298; 2000: 73,283,449; 2001: 77,786,540. Y compris également les apatrides et les employés des organisations des Nations Unis.
16 A partir de 1996, les chiffres ont été ajustés pour inclure les arrivées de non-macanais arrivant via Macao, Chine.
17 Y compris les arrivées par mer, terre et air (hélicoptère). 1995, Nov.: Début de l'inclusion des arrivées par air (Aéroport international de Macao SAR). Y compris les aptrides et les chinois qui ne résident pas de manière permanente à Hong Kong SAR, Chine: 1992: 93 .965; 1993: 92.679; 1994: 147.304; 1995: 167.361; 1996:

76
Tourist/visitor arrivals by region of origin *[cont.]*

Arrivées de touristes/visiteurs par région de provenance *[suite]*

18	Beginning 1996, change in national source.	
19	Prior to 1997. air arrivals at the International FHB Airport at Port Bouet. Arrivals at land frontiers, Bouake Airport and Air Ivoire Airport at Abidjan are not taken into consideration. 1997-1998: Air arrivals at the International FHB Airport at Port Bouet and arrivals at land frontiers.	
20	Including arrivals in ports of nautical tourism.	
21	Beginning 1996, including camp sites with more than 74 units only.	
22	Departures by air.	
23	Including nationals of the country residing abroad. 1996-1999: Arrivals at Bole airport only. 1998-1999: Arrivals compiled by country of residence. 2000: Arrivals through all ports of entry.	
24	Estimates based on the 1996 survey at national borders. Data revised from 1996.	
25	Figure estimated by the "Institut de la Statistique (ISPF)". Due to problems of E/D card distributions, the breakdown by country of origin could not be elaborated.	
26	Arrivals at Libreville Airport.	
27	Charter tourists only.	
28	Data based on surveys.	
29	1996-1999: Arrivals at 21 traditional hotel establishments.2000: Arrivals at 175 traditional hotel establishments.2001: Estimates for continental Guadeloupe (without Saint-Martin and Saint-Barthelemy).	
30	Air arrivals at Conakry airport.	
31	Departures.	
32	Arrivals correspond to a new series and source of data from 1990 to 1999.	
33	Prior to 1996: travellers. From 1996 new methodology, excluding seasonal and border workers.	
34	Excluding nationals of the country residing abroad. All data are estimates, projected using 1989 market shares. Source: Economic survey various years.	
35	Including nationals residing abroad and from June 1988, also crew members.	
36	Excluding Syrian nationals, Palestinians and students.	
37	Travellers.	
38	Foreign tourist departures; includes Singapore residents crossing the frontier by road through Johore Causeway.	
39	Arrivals in the States of Kosrae, Chuuk, Pohnpei and Yap. Excluding FSM citizens.	
40	Including tourist arrivals through border entry points to Yangon.	
41	Data regarding to short term movements are compiled from a random sample of passenger declarations. Including nationals of the country residing abroad. Source: Statistics New Zealand, External Migration.	
42	Air arrivals (Niamey Airport).	
43	Including Niuans residing usually in New Zealand.	
44	Air arrivals (Palau International Airport). 1996-1997: arrivals by nationality. 1998-2001: arrivals by country of residence.	
45	Total number of visitors broken down by permanent residence who arrived in Panama at Tocumen International Airport and Paso Canoa border post.	
46	Including arrivals from abroad to insular possessions of Madeira and the Azores.	
47	Arrivals by air. Fiscal year July to June. 2001: Preliminary data. Source: "Junta de Planificación de Puerto Rico".	

189.364.

18   A partir de 1996, changement de la source national des données.

19   Avant 1997, arrivées par voie aérienne à l'aéroport international FHB de Port-Bouet. Les arrivées aux frontières terrestres, à l'aéroport de Bouaké, ainsi qu'à l'aéroport Air Ivoire d'Abidjan ne sont pas prises en compte. 1997-1998 : Arrivées par voie aérienne à l'aéroport international FHB de Port-Bouet et arrivées aux frontières terrestres.

20   Y compris les arrivées dans des ports à tourisme nautique.

21   A partir de 1996, y compris terrains de camping de plus de 74 unités seulement.

22   Départs par voie aérienne.

23   Y compris les nationaux du pays résidant à l'étranger. 1996-1999: Arrivées à l'aéroport de Bole seulement. 1998-1999: Arrivées compilées par pays de residence. 2000: Arrivées à travers tous les ports d'entrée.

24   Estimation à partir de l'enquête aux frontières 1996. Données révisées depuis 1996.

25   Estimation réalisée par l'Institut de la Statistique (ISPF). En raison de problèmes de distribution de formulaires, la ventilation par pays d'origine n'a pas pu être réalisée.

26   Arrivées à l'aéroport de Libreville.

27   Arrivées en vols à la demande seulement.

28   Données obtenues au moyen d'enquêtes.

29   1996-1999: Arrivées dans 21 établissements hôteliers.2000: Arrivées dans 175 établissements hôteliers.2001: Estimations pour la Guadeloupe continentale (sans Saint-Martin et Saint-Barthélemy).

30   Arrivées par voie aérienne à l'aéroport de Conakry.

31   Départs.

32   Les arrivées constituent une nouvelle série et sourçe de données de 1990 à 1999.

33   Avant 1996: voyageurs. A partir de 1996 Nouvelle méthodologie, à l'exclusion des travailleurs saisoniers et frontaliers.

34   A l'exclusion des nationaux du pays résidant à l'étranger. Toutes les données représentent des estimations, dont la projection a été faite sur la base des taux de marché de l'année 1989. Source: Enquête économique de diverses années.

35   Y compris les nationaux résidant à l'étranger, à partir de juin 1988, également membres des équipages.

36   A l'exclusion des ressortissants syriens, palestiniens et sous-études.

37   Voyageurs.

38   Départs de touristes étrangers; y compris les résidents de Singapour traversant la frontière par voie terrestre à travers le Johore Causeway.

39   Arrivées dans les États de Kosrae, Chuuk, Pohnpei et Yap. Excluyant citoyens de EFM.

40   Comprenant les arrivées de touristes aux postes-frontières de Yangon.

41   Les données relatives aux mouvements de courte durée sont obtenues à partir d'un échantillon aléatoire de déclarations des passagers. Y compris les nationaux du pays résidant à l'étranger. Source : Statistiques de la Nouvelle Zélande, Immigration.

42   Arrivées par voie aérienne (Aéroport de Niamey).

43   Y compris les nationaux de Niue résidant habituellement en Nouvelle-Zélande.

44   Arrivées par voie aérienne (Aéroport international de Palau). 1996-1997 : arrivées par nationalité. 1998-2001 : arrivées par pays de résidence.

45   Nombre total de visiteurs arrivées au Panama par l'aéroport international de Tocúmen et le poste frontière de Paso Canoa, classes selon leur résidence permanente.

46   Y compris les arrivées en provenance de l'étranger aux possessions insulaires de Madère et des Açores.

47   Arrivées par voie aérienne. Année fiscale de juillet à juin. 2001: Données préliminaires. Source: "Junta de Planificación de Puerto

76

Tourist/visitor arrivals by region of origin *[cont.]*

Arrivées de touristes/visiteurs par région de provenance *[suite]*

		Rico".
48	Persons who enjoyed the services of the economic agents which carry out the tourist's activity in the republic (except left-bank Dniester river regions and municipality of Bender).	48 Personnes qui ont bénéficié des services des agents économiques chargés de l'activité touristique dans le pays (à l'exception des régions de la rive gauche du Dniester et la municipalité de Bender).
49	January-November.	49 Janvier-novembre.
50	Prior to 1994, air arrivals. Beginning 1994, air and sea arrivals.	50 Avant 1996, arrivées par voie aérienne. A partir de 1994, arrivées par voie aérienne et maritime.
51	Excluding Netherlands Antillean residents.	51 A l'exclusion des résidents des Antilles Néerlandaises.
52	Arrivals at Princess Juliana International airport. Including visitors to St. Maarten (the French side of the island).	52 Arrivées à l'aéroport international "Princess Juliana". Y compris les visiteurs à Saint-Martin (partie française de l'île).
53	Including Italian visitors.	53 Y compris les visiteurs italiens.
54	Statistics available only after March 10th.	54 Statistiques disponibles uniquement à compter du 10 mars.
55	Excluding Malaysian citizens arriving by land.	55 Non compris les arrivées de malaysiens par voie terrestre.
56	Excluding arrivals in private accommodation = 7,086.	56 A l'exclusion des arrivées dans l'hébergement privé = 7.086.
57	Beginning January 1992, contract and border traffic concession workers are excluded.	57 A partir de janvier 1992, les données excluent les travailleurs contractuels et ceux de la zone frontière.
58	Arrivals at Khartoum airport.	58 Arrivées à l'aéroport de Khartoum.
59	Arrivals at Zanderij Airport.	59 Arrivées à l'aéroport de Zanderij.
60	Arrivals in hotels only.	60 Arrivées dans les hôtels uniquement.
61	Prior to 1996, excluding nationals of the country residing abroad. Beginning 1996, including nationals of the country residing abroad.	61 Avant 1996, à l'exclusion des nationaux du pays résidant à l'étranger. A partir de 1996, y compris les nationaux du pays résidant à l'étranger.
62	Data refer to Dubai only.	62 Les données se réfèrent au Dubai seulement.
63	Region not specified: Including domestic tourism and nationals of the country residing abroad.	63 Région non spécifiée: Y compris le tourisme interne et les nationaux résidant à l'étranger.
64	Excluding transit passengers.	64 A l'exclusion des passagers en transit.

77

Tourist/visitor arrivals and tourism expenditure
Arrivées de touristes/visiteurs et dépenses touristiques

Region, country or area / Region, pays ou zone	Number of tourist/visitor arrivals (thousands) Nombre d'arrivées de touristes/visiteurs (milliers)					Tourism expenditure (million US dollars) Dépenses touristiques (millions de dollars E.–U.)				
	1998	1999	2000	2001	2002	1998	1999	2000	2001	2002
Albania / Albanie	28	26	32	34	...	54	211	389	446	487
Algeria / Algérie	678	749	866	901	988	74	80	96	100	133
American Samoa [1] / Samoa américaines [1]	36	41	44	...	...	...	...	...	...	...
Andorra / Andorre	...	2 347	2 949	3 516	3 387	...	...	...	...	...
Angola / Angola	52	45	51	67	91	8	13	18	22	...
Anguilla / Anguilla	44	47	44	48	44	58	56	55	61	55
Antigua and Barbuda / Antigua-et-Barbuda	234	240	237	...	...	256	290	290	272	...
Argentina / Argentine	3 012	2 898	2 909	2 620	2 820	2 936	2 813	2 817	2 547	...
Armenia / Arménie	32	41	45	123	...	24	31	38	65	63
Aruba / Aruba	647	683	721	691	643	732	778	638	890	898
Australia / Australie	4 167	4 459	4 931	4 856	4 841	7 335	8 028	8 451	7 624	8 087
Austria / Autriche	17 352	17 467	17 982	18 180	18 611	11 276	11 035	9 931	10 118	11 237
Azerbaijan / Azerbaïdjan	483	602	681	767	834	125	81	63	43	51
Bahamas / Bahamas	1 528	1 577	1 544	1 538	...	1 354	1 583	1 719	1 636	...
Bahrain / Bahreïn	1 640	2 019	2 420	2 789	3 167	366	518	573	630	741
Bangladesh / Bangladesh	172	173	199	207	207	52	50	50	48	57
Barbados / Barbade	512	515	545	507	498	703	677	711	687	...
Belarus / Bélarus	355	75	60	61	...	22	12	93	171	193
Belgium / Belgique	6 179	6 369	6 457	6 452	6 724	4 623	6 472	6 592	6 903	6 892
Belize / Belize	176	181	196	196	200	108	111	120	121	133
Benin / Bénin	*152	80	96	88	72	64	94	77	73	60
Bermuda / Bermudes	370[2]	355[2]	332[2]	278[2]	284[2]	487	479	431	351	...
Bhutan / Bhoutan	6	7	8	6	6	8	9	10	...	...
Bolivia / Bolivie	387	342	306	308	...	200	174	160	156	...
Bosnia and Herzegovina / Bosnie-Herzégovine	148	...	171	139	160	131	114	97	101	112
Botswana / Botswana	750	843	1 104	1 049	1 037	175	234	313	300	309
Brazil / Brésil	4 818[3]	5 107	5 313	4 773	3 783	3 678[3,4]	3 994[4]	4 228[4]	3 701[4]	3 120[4]

77

Tourist/visitor arrivals and tourism expenditure
[cont.]

Arrivées de touristes/visiteurs et dépenses touristiques
[suite]

Region, country or area Region, pays ou zone	Number of tourist/visitor arrivals (thousands) Nombre d'arrivées de touristes/visiteurs (milliers)					Tourism expenditure (million US dollars) Dépenses touristiques (millions de dollars E. –U.)				
	1998	1999	2000	2001	2002	1998	1999	2000	2001	2002
British Virgin Islands Iles Vierges britanniques	279	286	281	296	285	255	300	315	337	...
Brunei Darussalam Brunéi Darussalam	964	967	984	...	...	...	...	...	...	...
Bulgaria Bulgarie	2 667	2 472	2 785	3 186	3 433	966[5]	932	1 074	1 201	1 344
Burkina Faso Burkina Faso	160	117	126	128	149	42	...	...	34	...
Burundi Burundi	15	26	29	36	...	0	1	1	1	1
Cambodia Cambodge	286[6]	368[6]	466[6]	605[6]	787[6]	166	190	228	304	379
Cameroon Cameroun	247	262	277	221	...	...	...	39	...	...
Canada Canada	18 870	19 411	19 627	19 679	20 057	8 452[7]	10 190[7]	10 839[7]	10 774[7]	9 700[7]
Cape Verde Cap-Vert	52[2]	67[2]	83[2]	115[2]	126[2]	20	28	41	54	66
Cayman Islands Iles Caïmanes	404[2]	395[2]	354[2]	334[2]	303[2]	534[8]	525[8]	559[8]	585[8]	...
Central African Rep. [2] Rép. centrafricaine [2]	7	10	...	...	...	...	...	...	...	...
Chad Tchad	41	47	43	57	32	...	...	...	...	...
Chile Chili	1 759	1 622	1 742	1 723	1 412	1 105	911	819	799	845
China Chine	25 073	27 047	31 229	33 167	36 803	12 602	14 099	16 224	17 792	20 385
China, Hong Kong SAR Chine, Hong Kong RAS	10 160	11 328	13 059	13 725	16 566	7 496[9]	7 210[9]	7 886[9]	8 282[9]	10 117[9]
China, Macao SAR Chine, Macao RAS	4 517	5 050	5 197	5 842	6 565	2 648[10]	2 598[10]	3 205[10]	3 745[10]	4 415[10]
Colombia Colombie	674	546	557	616	541	928	927	1 026	1 209	962
Comoros Comores	27[2]	24[2]	24[2]	...	...	16	19	15	...	...
Congo Congo	20	14	19	...	...	9	12	12	22	25
Cook Islands Iles Cook	49	56	73	75	73	34	39	36	38	46
Costa Rica Costa Rica	943	1 032	1 088	1 131	1 113	884	1 036	1 229	1 096	1 078
Côte d'Ivoire Côte d'Ivoire	301	...	...	...	...	98	100	49	53	50
Croatia Croatie	4 499	3 805	5 831	6 544	6 944	2 733	2 493	2 758	3 335	3 811
Cuba Cuba	1 390[2]	1 561[2]	1 741[2]	1 736[2]	1 656[2]	1 556	1 695	1 737	1 692	1 633
Cyprus Chypre	2 223	2 434	2 686	2 697	2 418	1 696	1 878	1 894	1 981	1 863
Czech Republic République tchèque	*5 482	*5 610	*4 666	*5 194	*4 579	3 871	3 154	2 982	3 106	2 941
Dem. Rep. of the Congo Rép. dém. du Congo	*53	80	103	...	...	...	...	...	...	...

77

Tourist/visitor arrivals and tourism expenditure
[cont.]

Arrivées de touristes/visiteurs et dépenses touristiques
[suite]

Region, country or area	Number of tourist/visitor arrivals (thousands) Nombre d'arrivées de touristes/visiteurs (milliers)					Tourism expenditure (million US dollars) Dépenses touristiques (millions de dollars E. –U.)				
Region, pays ou zone	1998	1999	2000	2001	2002	1998	1999	2000	2001	2002
Denmark Danemark	2 073	2 023	2 088	2 028	2 010	3 313	3 836	4 038	4 600	5 785
Djibouti Djibouti	21	...	...	...	...	...	...	...	...	...
Dominica Dominique	66	74	70	66	67	47	51	48	39	36
Dominican Republic Rép. dominicaine	2 309[2]	2 649[2]	2 972[2]	2 882[2]	2 811[2]	2 153	2 483	2 860	2 798	2 736
Ecuador Equateur	511	518	627	641	654	291	343	402	430	447
Egypt Egypte	3 213	4 490	5 116	4 357	4 906	2 565	3 903	4 345	3 800	3 764
El Salvador El Salvador	542	658	795	735	951	125	211	254	235	342
Eritrea Erythrée	188	57	70	113	101	34	28	36	74	73
Estonia Estonie	825	950	1 220	1 320	1 360	534	560	506	507	555
Ethiopia Ethiopie	112[11]	115[11]	136[11]	148[11]	...	16	16	68[12]	75[12]	...
Fiji Fidji	371	410	294	348	398	244	282	181	217	261
Finland Finlande	2 644	2 454	2 714	2 826	2 875	1 643[13]	1 528[13]	1 412[13]	1 441[13]	1 573[13]
France France	70 109	73 147	77 190	75 202	77 012	29 931	31 507[14]	30 754[14]	29 979[14]	32 329[14]
French Guiana Guyane française	68	70	...	65	65	51	50	...	42	45
French Polynesia Polynésie française	189	211	252	228	189	354	394	...	...	...
Gabon Gabon	*195[2]	177[2]	155[2]	169[2]	212[2]	8	11	7	7	...
Gambia Gambie	91[15]	96[15]	79[15]	*75[15]	...	49	...	...	...	...
Georgia Géorgie	317	384	387	302	298	423	400	413	442	472
Germany Allemagne	16 511	17 116	18 983	17 861	17 969	17 911[16]	17 225[16]	18 479[16]	18 422[16]	19 158[16]
Ghana Ghana	348	373	399	439	483	284	304	335	351	358
Greece * Grèce *	10 916	12 164	13 096	14 057	14 180	6 188[17]	8 783[17]	9 221[17]	9 447[17]	9 741[17]
Grenada Grenade	116	125	129	123	132	83	88	93	83	84
Guadeloupe Guadeloupe	580[2,18]	561[2,18]	603[2,18]	521[2,18]	...	466	375	418	...	...
Guam Guam	1 137	1 162	1 287	1 160	1 059	2 361	1 908	...	...	...
Guatemala Guatemala	636	823	826	835	884	323	399	535	493	612
Guinea Guinée	23	27	33	38	43	1	7	12	14	31
Guinea-Bissau[2] Guinée-Bissau[2]	...	...	...	8	...	...	...	...	...	...

77

Tourist/visitor arrivals and tourism expenditure
[cont.]

Arrivées de touristes/visiteurs et dépenses touristiques
[suite]

Region, country or area Region, pays ou zone	Number of tourist/visitor arrivals (thousands) Nombre d'arrivées de touristes/visiteurs (milliers)					Tourism expenditure (million US dollars) Dépenses touristiques (millions de dollars E. –U.)				
	1998	1999	2000	2001	2002	1998	1999	2000	2001	2002
Guyana Guyana	68	75	105	95	104	108	106	75	61	49
Haiti Haïti	147	143	140	142	...	56	55	54	54	...
Honduras Honduras	321	371	471	518	550	168	195	260	275	342
Hungary Hongrie	2 871	2 789	2 992	3 070	3 013	3 644	3 563	3 445	3 770	3 273
Iceland Islande	232	263	303	...	278	206	223	228	235	250
India Inde	2 359	2 482	2 649	2 537	2 384	2 948	3 009	3 168	3 042	2 923
Indonesia Indonésie	4 606	4 728	5 064	5 154	5 033	4 331	4 710	5 749	5 396	4 306
Iran (Islamic Rep. of) Iran (Rép. islamique d')	1 008	1 321	1 342	1 402	...	465	586	671	1 122	...
Iraq Iraq	45	30	78	127	...	...	...	...	...	...
Ireland Irlande	6 064	6 403	6 646	6 353	6 476	2 601	2 637	2 608	2 790	3 089
Israel Israël	1 942	2 312	2 417	1 196	862	2 808	3 659	3 338	1 570	1 197
Italy Italie	34 933	36 516	41 181	39 563	39 799	29 866	28 359	27 500	25 796	26 915
Jamaica Jamaïque	1 225[2]	1 248[2]	1 323[2]	1 277[2]	1 266[2]	1 197	1 280	1 333	1 233	1 209
Japan Japon	4 106	4 438	4 757	4 772	5 239	3 742	3 428	3 373	3 301	3 499
Jordan Jordanie	1 256	1 358	1 427	1 478	1 622	773	795	722	700	786
Kazakhstan Kazakhstan	...	...	1 471	1 845	2 832	407	363	356	396	621
Kenya Kenya	792	862	899	841	838	290	304	276	308	297
Kiribati Kiribati	6[19]	5[19]	5[19]	5[19]	5[19]	3	3	3	3	...
Korea, Republic of Corée, République de	4 250	4 660	5 322	5 147	5 347	6 865[20]	6 802[20]	6 811[20]	6 373[20]	5 277[20]
Kuwait Koweït	77	84	78	73	...	207	92	98	104	119
Kyrgyzstan Kirghizistan	59	69	...	...	...	8	14	15	24	36
Lao People's Dem. Rep. Rép. dém. pop. lao	200	259	191	173	215	80	97	114	104	113
Latvia Lettonie	576	544	509	591	848	182	117	131	120	161
Lebanon Liban	631	673	742	837	956	1 221	673[21]	742[21]	837[21]	956[21]
Lesotho Lesotho	150	186	...	...	...	24	23	24	23	20
Libyan Arab Jamah. Jamah. arabe libyenne	32	178	174	...	...	18	28	...	...	...
Liechtenstein Liechtenstein	59	60	62	56	49	...	...	...	...	...

77

Tourist/visitor arrivals and tourism expenditure
[cont.]

Arrivées de touristes/visiteurs et dépenses touristiques
[suite]

Region, country or area Region, pays ou zone	Number of tourist/visitor arrivals (thousands) Nombre d'arrivées de touristes/visiteurs (milliers)					Tourism expenditure (million US dollars) Dépenses touristiques (millions de dollars E. –U.)				
	1998	1999	2000	2001	2002	1998	1999	2000	2001	2002
Lithuania Lituanie	1 416	1 422	1 083	1 271	...	460	550	391	383	513
Luxembourg Luxembourg	789	863	852	829	876	1 763	1 820	1 807	1 915	2 186
Madagascar Madagascar	121[2]	138[2]	160[2]	170[2]	...	92	100	121	115	...
Malawi Malawi	220	254	*228	*266	*285	15	20	*27	*28	*125
Malaysia Malaisie	5 551	7 931	10 222	12 775	13 292	2 189	3 242	4 562	6 374	6 785
Maldives Maldives	396[2]	430[2]	467[2]	461[2]	485[2]	303	314	321	327	318
Mali Mali	83[2]	82[2]	86[2]	89[2]	96[2]	89	77	71	...	...
Malta Malte	1 182	1 214	1 216	1 180	1 134	656	679	614	579	568
Marshall Islands Iles Marshall	6[2]	5[2]	5[2]	5[2]	6[2]	3	4	4	...	4
Martinique Martinique	549	564	526	460	447	415	404	302	245	237
Mauritania Mauritanie	...	24	30	...	...	20	28	...	...	...
Mauritius Maurice	558	578	656	660	682	503	543	542	624	612
Mexico Mexique	19 392	19 043	20 641	19 810	19 667	7 493[22]	7 223[22]	8 295[22]	8 401[22]	8 858[22]
Micronesia (Fed. States) Micronésie (Etats féd. de)	13[23]	16[23]	21[23]	15[23]	19[23]	11	12	15	13	...
Monaco Monaco	278	278	300	270	263	...	...	...	...	...
Mongolia Mongolie	165	138	137	166	198	35	36	36	39	130
Montserrat Montserrat	7	10	10	10	10	6	8	9	8	8
Morocco Maroc	3 095	3 817	4 113	4 223	4 193	1 712	1 880	2 040	2 526	2 152
Mozambique Mozambique	...	...	...	...	...	146	156	186	134	144
Myanmar Myanmar	201	198	208	205	217	35	35	42	45	...
Namibia Namibie	614	...	...	670	...	288	...	...	404	...
Nepal Népal	464	492	464	361	275	153	168	167	140	107
Netherlands Pays-Bas	9 312	9 874	10 003	9 500	9 595	6 850	6 996	7 217	6 723	7 706
Netherlands Antilles [24] Antilles néerlandaises [24]	*734	*766	*812	*821	273	739	722	692	677	672
New Caledonia Nouvelle-Calédonie	104	100	110	101	104	110	112	110	93	...
New Zealand Nouvelle-Zélande	1 485	1 607	1 787	1 909	2 045	1 835	2 232	2 240	2 334	2 918
Nicaragua Nicaragua	406	468	486	483	472	90	107	111	109	116

77

Tourist/visitor arrivals and tourism expenditure
[cont.]

Arrivées de touristes/visiteurs et dépenses touristiques
[suite]

Region, country or area Region, pays ou zone	Number of tourist/visitor arrivals (thousands) Nombre d'arrivées de touristes/visiteurs (milliers)					Tourism expenditure (million US dollars) Dépenses touristiques (millions de dollars E. –U.)				
	1998	1999	2000	2001	2002	1998	1999	2000	2001	2002
Niger Niger	42^2	43^2	50^2	52^2	...	18	24	...	...	...
Nigeria Nigéria	739	776	813	831	...	142	145	148	156	...
Niue Nioué	2^{25}	2^{25}	2^{25}	2^{25}	2^{25}	1	...	...	...	...
Northern Mariana Islands[2] Iles Mariannes du Nord[2]	481	493	517	438	466	...	...	...	...	...
Norway Norvège	$3\ 256^{26}$	$3\ 223^{26}$	$3\ 104^{26}$	$3\ 073^{26}$	$3\ 107^{26}$	2 230	2 335	1 992	2 037	2 738
Occupied Palestinian Terr. Terr. palestinien occupé	201	271	330	7	...	114	132	155	9	0
Oman Oman	424	503	571	562	602	114^{27}	106^{27}	120^{27}	118^{27}	116^{27}
Pakistan Pakistan	429	432	557	500	498	98	76	84	92	105
Palau Palaos	64^2	55^2	58^2	54^2	59^2	58	54	53	59	59
Panama Panama	431	457	484	519	534	494	538	576	626	679
Papua New Guinea Papouasie-Nvl-Guinée	67	67	58	54	...	75	76	92	101	...
Paraguay Paraguay	350	269	289	279	250	111	81	73	69	62
Peru Pérou	723	691	796	797	862	845	890	911	788	801
Philippines Philippines	2 149	2 171	1 992	1 797	1 933	2 413	2 531	2 134	1 723	1 741
Poland Pologne	18 780	17 950	17 400	15 000	13 980	$7\ 946^{28}$	$6\ 100^{28}$	$6\ 100^{28}$	$4\ 815^{28}$	$4\ 500^{28}$
Portugal Portugal	11 295	11 632	12 097	12 167	11 666	5 302	5 261	5 282	5 505	5 919
Puerto Rico Porto Rico	$3\ 396^2$	$3\ 024^2$	$3\ 341^2$	$3\ 551^2$	$3\ 087^2$	$2\ 233^{29}$	$2\ 139^{29}$	$2\ 388^{29}$	$2\ 728^{29}$	$2\ 486^{29}$
Qatar[30] Qatar[30]	46	51	67	76	...	...	...	...	...	...
Republic of Moldova République de Moldova	19	14	18	16	18	40	34	39	37	47
Réunion Réunion	400	394	430	424	426	271	259	255	244	284
Romania Roumanie	2 966	*3 209	*3 274	*3 300	*3 204	260	254	359	500	612
Russian Federation Fédération de Russie	16 188	18 820	7 030	7 400	7 943	6 508	3 723	3 429	3 560	4 188
Rwanda Rwanda	...	...	104	113	...	19	17	23	25	31
Saint Kitts and Nevis Saint-Kitts-et-Nevis	93	84	73	71	68	76	68	58	60	57
Saint Lucia Sainte-Lucie	252	264	270	250	253	278	279	297	258	256
St. Vincent-Grenadines St. Vincent-Grenadines	67	68	73	71	78	73	76	75	80	81
Samoa Samoa	78	85	88	88	89	39	42	41	40	45

77

Tourist/visitor arrivals and tourism expenditure
[cont.]

Arrivées de touristes/visiteurs et dépenses touristiques
[suite]

Region, country or area Region, pays ou zone	Number of tourist/visitor arrivals (thousands) Nombre d'arrivées de touristes/visiteurs (milliers)					Tourism expenditure (million US dollars) Dépenses touristiques (millions de dollars E. –U.)				
	1998	1999	2000	2001	2002	1998	1999	2000	2001	2002
San Marino [31] Saint-Marin [31]	36	35	43	49	45	...	...	...	...	...
Sao Tome and Principe Sao Tomé-et-Principe	6	6	7	8	...	4	9	10	10	10
Saudi Arabia Arabie saoudite	...	...	6 585	6 727	7 511	...	...	...	3 420	...
Senegal Sénégal	352	369	389	396	427	178	166	140	...	...
Serbia and Montenegro Serbie-et-Monténégro	283	152	239	351	448	40	18	28	43	77
Seychelles Seychelles	128	125	130	130	132	111	112	115	113	130
Sierra Leone Sierra Leone	13[2]	11[2]	16[2]	24[2]	28[2]	8	8	...	...	...
Singapore Singapour	5 631	6 258	6 917	6 726	6 996	5 402	5 859	6 018	5 081	4 932
Slovakia Slovaquie	896	975	1 053	1 219	1 399	*489	*461	*432	*639	*724
Slovenia Slovénie	977	884	1 090	1 219	1 302	1 088[32]	958[32]	961[32]	1 001[32]	1 083[32]
Solomon Islands Iles Salomon	13	21	...	...	...	7	6	...	...	...
South Africa Afrique du Sud	5 898	6 026	6 001	5 908	6 550	2 717	2 637	2 513	2 428	2 728
Spain Espagne	43 396	46 776	47 898	50 094	51 748	29 839	32 497	31 454	32 873	33 609
Sri Lanka Sri Lanka	381	436	400	337	...	231	275	253	211	253
Sudan Soudan	36[2]	39[2]	38[2]	50[2]	52[2]	21	22	30	56	...
Suriname Suriname	55[33]	63[33]	58[33]	...	...	2	9	16	14	3
Swaziland Swaziland	284	289	281	283	256	47	34	37	29	26
Sweden Suède	2 573	2 595	2 746	7 154	7 458	4 124	4 151	4 079	4 275	4 496
Switzerland Suisse	*10 900	*10 700	*11 000	*10 800	*10 000	7 973	7 769	7 581	7 310	7 628
Syrian Arab Republic Rép. arabe syrienne	1 267[3]	1 386	1 416	1 318	1 658	1 017	1 031	1 082	...	1 366
Tajikistan Tadjikistan	...	2	4	4	...	...	...	...	...	2
Thailand Thaïlande	7 843	8 651	9 579	10 133	10 873	6 202	7 040	7 489	7 077	7 902
TFYR of Macedonia L'ex-R.y. Macédoine	157	181	224	99	123	15	37	37	25	39
Togo Togo	69	70	60	57	...	13[34]	9[34]	5[34]	11[34]	...
Tonga Tonga	27[2]	31[2]	35[2]	32[2]	37[2]	8	9	7	7	9
Trinidad and Tobago Trinité-et-Tobago	334[2]	358[2]	399[2]	383[2]	379[2]	201	210	213	*201	224
Tunisia Tunisie	4 718	4 832	5 058	5 387	5 064	1 557	1 560	1 496	1 605	1 422

77

Tourist/visitor arrivals and tourism expenditure
[cont.]

Arrivées de touristes/visiteurs et dépenses touristiques
[suite]

Region, country or area Region, pays ou zone	Number of tourist/visitor arrivals (thousands) Nombre d'arrivées de touristes/visiteurs (milliers)					Tourism expenditure (million US dollars) Dépenses touristiques (millions de dollars E. –U.)				
	1998	1999	2000	2001	2002	1998	1999	2000	2001	2002
Turkey Turquie	8 960	6 893	9 586	10 784	12 782	7 809	5 203	7 636	7 386	9 010
Turkmenistan Turkménistan	300	...	...	...	...	192	...	...	...	...
Turks and Caicos Islands Iles Turques et Caïques	111	121	152	165	155	157	238	285	311	292
Tuvalu Tuvalu	1	1	1	1	1	...	...	...	...	...
Uganda Ouganda	195	189	193	205	254	95	102	113	163	185
Ukraine Ukraine	6 208	4 232	4 406	5 791	6 326	3 317	2 124	2 207	2 725	2 992
United Arab Emirates [35] Emirats arabes unis [35]	2 991	3 393	3 907	4 134	5 445	859[36]	893[36]	1 012[36]	1 064[36]	1 328[36]
United Kingdom Royaume-Uni	25 745	25 394	25 209	22 835	24 180	20 985	20 221	19 374	16 276	17 591
United Rep. of Tanzania Rép.-Unie de Tanzanie	450	564	459	501	550	570	733	739	725	730
United States Etats-Unis	46 396	48 492	50 945	44 898	41 892	71 325	74 801	82 400	*71 893	66 547
United States Virgin Is. Iles Vierges américaines	422	484	607	592	553	940	955	1 292	1 323	1 240
Uruguay Uruguay	2 163	2 073	1 968	1 892	1 258	695	653	652	561	318
Uzbekistan Ouzbékistan	811	487	302	345	332	167	102	63	72	68
Vanuatu Vanuatu	52	51	58	53	49	52	56	58	46	...
Venezuela Venezuela	685	587	469	584	432	961	673	634	682	468
Viet Nam Viet Nam	978	1 211	1 383	1 599	...	...	...	...	...	...
Yemen Yémen	88	58	73	76	...	84	61	73	38	38
Zambia Zambie	362	404	457	492	565	75	85	111	117	...
Zimbabwe Zimbabwe	1 986	2 101	1 868	2 068	...	158	202	125	81	76

Source:
World Tourism Organization (WTO), Madrid, "Yearbook of Tourism Statistics", 54th edition, 2003 and the WTO Statistics Database.

Source:
Organisation mondiale du tourisme (OMT), Madrid, "Annuaire des statistiques du tourisme", 54e édition, 2003 et la base de données de l'OMT.

1	Including arrivals from Western Samoa.
2	Air arrivals.
3	Change in methodology.
4	Data based on the sample survey conducted by EMBRATUR.
5	New methodology of the Bulgarian Central Bank and Ministry of Economy.
6	Including tourist arrivals by all means of transport.
7	Including medical, education and crew spending. Excluding international fares.
8	Including expenditure by cruise passengers.

1	Y compris des arrivées en provenance de Samoa occidentale.
2	Arrivées par voie aérienne.
3	Changement de méthode.
4	Données basées sur une enquête sur échantillon réalisée par EMBRATUR.
5	Nouvelle méthodologie élaborée par la Banque Centrale de la Bulgarie et le Ministère de l'Economie.
6	Arrivées de touristes internationaux par tous moyens de transport.
7	Incluyant frais médicaux, d'éducation et des membres des équipage. Excluyant transport international.
8	Y compris les recettes provenant des passagers de navires de

77

Tourist/visitor arrivals and tourism expenditure
[cont.]

Arrivées de touristes/visiteurs et dépenses touristiques
[suite]

			croisière.
9	Including receipts from servicemen, air crew members and transit passengers.	9	Y compris les recettes provenant des militaires, des équipages d'avions et des passagers en transit.
10	Including gambling receipts.	10	Y compris les recettes tirées des jeux de hasard.
11	Arrivals through all ports of entry.	11	Arrivées à travers tous les ports d'entrée.
12	Incorporates all revenues obtained from the sector based on estimation.	12	Comporte une estimation de toutes les recettes du secteur.
13	Data collected by travel surveys.	13	Données collectées au moyen d'enquêtes sur les voyages.
14	New series since 1999 excluding frontier workers paid in foreign currency.	14	A partir de 1999, non compris les travailleurs frontaliers rémunérés en devises.
15	Charter tourists only.	15	Arrivées en vols à la demande seulement.
16	Including border merchandise transactions and purchases of inward-bound and outward-bound commuters.	16	Y compris les transactions frontalières en marchandises, et les achats des migrants quotidiens entrant et sortant.
17	Including registrations through new methodology.	17	Y compris les mouvements enregistrés selon la nouvelle méthode.
18	Excluding the north islands (Saint Maarten and Saint Bartholemy).	18	Excluant les îles du Nord (Saint Martin et Saint Barthélemy).
19	Arrivals at Tarawa and Christmas Islands.	19	Arrivées aux Iles Tarawa et Christmas.
20	Excluding expenses of students studying overseas.	20	Non compris les dépenses des étudiants poursuivant leurs études à l'étranger.
21	Due to the lack of data on international tourism receipts concerning statistics on inbound tourism, the Department of "Internet and Statistics Service of the Ministry of Tourism" considers that a tourist spends an average of US$ 1,000.	21	Du fait d'un manque de données sur les recettes du tourisme international concernant les statistiques sur le tourisme récepteur, le Département « Internet et Service Statistique du Ministère du Tourisme » considère qu'un touriste dépense en moyenne 1.000$EU.
22	Including receipts from cruise passengers and frontier visitors.	22	Y compris les recettes provenant des passagers de navires de croisière et des visiteurs frontaliers.
23	Arrivals in the States of Kosrae, Chuuk, Pohnpei and Yap. Excluding FSM citizen.	23	Arrivées dans les États de Kosrae, Chuuk, Pohnpei et Yap. Excluant citoyens de EFM.
24	Data refer to Bonaire, Curaçao, Saba, St. Eustatius and Saint Maarten; in 2002, data refer to Curaçao only.	24	Les données se rapportent à Bonaire, Curaçao, Saba, Saint-Eustache et la partie néederlandaise de Saint-Martin; les données pour 2002 se réfèrent à Curaçao seulement.
25	Arrivals by air, including Niueans residing usually in New Zealand.	25	Arrivées par voie aérienne et y compris les nationaux de Niue résidant habituellement en Nouvelle-Zélande.
26	Arrivals correspond to new series.	26	Les arrivées constituent une nouvelle série.
27	Hotel sales.	27	Chiffre d'affaires des hôtels.
28	Based on surveys and estimations by the Institute of Tourism.	28	Chiffres basés sur des enquêtes et des estimations de l'Institut du tourisme.
29	Source: "Junta de Planificacion de Puerto Rico".	29	Source : "Junta de Planificacion de Puerto Rico".
30	Arrivals in hotels only.	30	Arrivées dans les hôtels uniquement.
31	Including Italian visitors.	31	Y compris les visiteurs italiens.
32	Data refer to the item "travel" of the Balance of Payments.	32	Données relatives à la rubrique "Voyages" de la balance des paiements.
33	Arrivals at Zanderij Airport.	33	Arrivées à l'aéroport de Zanderij.
34	Hotel receipts.	34	Recettes des hôtels.
35	Data refer to Dubai only.	35	Les données se réfèrent au Dubai seulement.
36	Hotel revenues. Including domestic tourism and nationals of the country residing abroad.	36	Recettes des hôtels. Y compris le tourisme interne et les nationaux du pays résidant à l'étranger.

78

Tourism expenditure in other countries
Million US dollars

Dépenses touristiques dans d'autres pays
Millions de dollars E.-U.

Region, country or area Région, pays ou zone	1993	1994	1995	1996	1997	1998	1999	2000	2001	2002
Afghanistan Afghanistan	1	1	1	1	1	...	...	...	...	...
Albania Albanie	7	6	7	12	5	5	12	272	257	366
Algeria Algérie	163	24	186	188	144	269	250	193	...	...
Angola Angola	66	88	75	73	98	75	127	136	66	...
Anguilla Anguilla	5	6	6	6	6	8	8	9	9	9
Antigua and Barbuda Antigua-et-Barbuda	23	24	23	26	26	29	30	31	32	...
Argentina Argentine	3 117	3 306	3 190	3 497	3 874	3 993	4 107	4 338	3 800	...
Armenia Arménie	...	1	3	22	41	41	37	40	40	54
Aruba Aruba	58	65	73	96	131	135	148	158	133	154
Australia Australie	3 451	3 969	4 587	5 445	6 150	5 388	6 046	6 131	5 764	6 116
Austria Autriche	7 776	8 788	11 663[1]	11 782[1]	10 712[1]	9 592[1]	9 190[1]	8 512[1]	8 886	9 391
Azerbaijan Azerbaïdjan	...	...	146	100	186	170	139	132	109	106
Bahamas Bahamas	171	193	213	235	250	256	309	293	297	...
Bahrain Bahreïn	130	146	122	109	122	142	212	224	250	378
Bangladesh Bangladesh	153	210	229	200	170	151	211	290	165	202
Barbados Barbade	53	59	71	74	79	82	87	94	101	...
Belarus Bélarus	56	74	87	119	114	124	116	243	501	559
Belgium Belgique	...	...	...	...	...	8 311	9 775	9 429	9 782	10 435
Belgium-Luxembourg Belgique-Luxembourg	6 338	7 773	9 003	8 562	8 281	...	...	...	...	...
Belize Belize	20	19	25	26	34	21	26	30	41	43
Benin Bénin	12	6	5	6	7	20	26	12	10	7
Bermuda Bermudes	140	143	145	148	148	...	...	...	...	...
Bolivia Bolivie	137	140	112	140	142[2]	150[2]	130[2]	101[2]	118[2]	...
Bosnia and Herzegovina Bosnie-Herzégovine	...	...	...	...	...	27	30	35	39	49
Botswana Botswana	79	76	145	78	92	126	143	...	...	...
Brazil Brésil	1 892	2 931	3 412	5 825	5 446	5 731	3 085	3 893	3 199	2 380
British Virgin Islands Iles Vierges britanniques	33	36	40	42	42	...	...	...	...	...

78
Tourism expenditure in other countries
Million US dollars [cont.]

Dépenses touristiques dans d'autres pays
Millions de dollars E.-U. [suite]

Region, country or area Région, pays ou zone	1993	1994	1995	1996	1997	1998	1999	2000	2001	2002
Bulgaria Bulgarie	257	244	195	199	222	519[3]	526	538	569	616
Burkina Faso Burkina Faso	21	23	30	32	32	...	...	...	...	...
Burundi Burundi	20	18	25	12	12	11	8	14	12	14
Cambodia Cambodge	4	8	8	15	13	25	28	33	37	38
Cameroon Cameroun	225	58	105	107	107	...	...	...	...	...
Canada Canada	11 133	10 014	10 267	11 253	11 464	9 271	9 649	10 638	10 250	9 929
Cape Verde Cap-Vert	9	12	16	18	17	24	41	36	47	56
Central African Rep. Rép. centrafricaine	50	43	37	39	39	...	...	...	...	...
Chad Tchad	86	26	23	24	24	...	...	...	...	...
Chile Chili	560	535	774	806	945	888	752	620	708	793
China Chine	2 797	3 036	3 688	4 474	8 130	9 205	10 864	13 114	13 909	15 398
China, Hong Kong SAR Chine, Hong Kong RAS	...	...	...	...	...	13 474	13 135	12 477	12 316	12 417
Colombia Colombie	694	841	878	1 116	1 209	1 120	1 013	1 057	1 160	1 072
Comoros Comores	6	6	7	8	8	3	...	...	...	...
Congo Congo	70	34	52	77	64	54	63	50	65	70
Costa Rica Costa Rica	267	300	321	335	358	409	446	482	361	367
Côte d'Ivoire Côte d'Ivoire	169	157	190	221	200	213	222	189	187	290
Croatia Croatie	375	396	422	510	530	600	751	568	606	781
Cyprus Chypre	133	176	241	263	278	276	289	285	283	424
Czech Republic République tchèque	527	1 585	1 633	2 953	2 380	1 894	1 496	1 279	1 388	1 575
Dem. Rep. of the Congo Rép. dém. du Congo	16	12	10	7	7	...	...	...	...	...
Denmark[4] Danemark[4]	3 214	3 583	4 280	4 142	4 137	4 643	5 044	5 047	5 464	6 856
Djibouti Djibouti	5	3	4	5	5	...	...	...	...	...
Dominica Dominique	5	6	6	7	7	8	9	9	9	...
Dominican Republic Rép. dominicaine	128	145	173	198	221	254	264	309	291	295
Ecuador Equateur	190	203	235	219	227	241	271	299	340	364
Egypt Egypte	1 048	1 067	1 278	1 317	1 347	1 148	1 078	1 073	1 132	1 278

78

Tourism expenditure in other countries
Million US dollars *[cont.]*

Dépenses touristiques dans d'autres pays
Millions de dollars E.-U. *[suite]*

Region, country or area Région, pays ou zone	1993	1994	1995	1996	1997	1998	1999	2000	2001	2002
El Salvador El Salvador	61	70	72	73	153	179	169	165	195	229
Equatorial Guinea Guinée équatoriale	9	8	7	8	8	...	...	...	...	...
Estonia Estonie	25	48	90	98	118	133	217	204	192	231
Ethiopia Ethiopie	11	15	25	25	40	46	51	74	44	45
Fiji Fidji	47	62	64	70	69	52	66	78	...	...
Finland [5] Finlande [5]	1 617	1 608	2 272	2 287	2 082	2 078	2 035	1 856	1 854	1 966
France [6] France [6]	12 836	13 773	16 328	17 746	16 576	17 791	18 631	17 758	17 718	19 460
Gabon Gabon	154	143	173	176	178	180	183	174	170	...
Gambia Gambie	14	14	14	15	16	...	...	...	...	...
Georgia Géorgie	...	...	...	...	156	226	130	110	158	174
Germany [7] Allemagne [7]	40 878	45 198	54 007	52 938	47 920	54 863	56 042	53 040	51 933	53 196
Ghana Ghana	20	20	21	22	23	85	91	100	105	120
Greece Grèce	1 003[8]	1 125[8]	1 323[8]	1 210[8]	1 327	1 756	3 989	4 558	4 181	2 450
Grenada Grenade	4	4	5	5	5	6	7	8	8	...
Guatemala Guatemala	117	151	141	135	119	157	183	182	226	267
Guinea Guinée	28	24	21	27	23	27	24	9	15	21
Guyana Guyana	18	23	21	22	22	63	75	69	55	38
Haiti Haïti	10	14	35	37	35	37	...	...	...	...
Honduras Honduras	55	57	57	60	62	81	94	107	157	185
Hungary Hongrie	739	925	1 071	957	925	1 475	1 542	1 388	1 456	1 722
Iceland Islande	270	247	282	308	324	396	436	471	373	365
India Inde	474	769	996	913	1 341	1 713	2 010	2 918	2 306	3 449
Indonesia Indonésie	1 539	1 900	2 172	2 399	2 411	2 102	2 353	3 197	3 406	3 368
Iran (Islamic Rep. of) Iran (Rép. islamique d')	862	149	241	529	677	382	153	631	238	...
Ireland [9] Irlande [9]	1 220	1 615	2 034	2 198	2 210	2 374	2 627	2 590	2 876	3 741
Israel Israël	2 052	2 135	2 120	2 278	2 283	2 376	2 566	2 804	2 896	2 547
Italy Italie	15 903	13 941	14 827	15 805	16 631	17 653	16 913	15 693	14 802	16 935

78
Tourism expenditure in other countries
Million US dollars *[cont.]*

Dépenses touristiques dans d'autres pays
Millions de dollars E.-U. *[suite]*

Region, country or area Région, pays ou zone	1993	1994	1995	1996	1997	1998	1999	2000	2001	2002
Jamaica Jamaïque	82	81	148	157	181	198	227	209	206	258
Japan Japon	26 860	30 715	36 792	37 040	33 041	28 815	32 808	31 886	26 530	26 681
Jordan Jordanie	344[10]	394[10]	420[10]	381[10]	398[11]	353[11]	355[11]	387[11]	420[11]	416[11]
Kazakhstan Kazakhstan	...	...	283	319	445	498	394	408	474	756
Kenya Kenya	48	114	145	167	194	190	115	132	143	...
Kiribati Kiribati	3	3	3	4	4	2	2	...	...	...
Korea, Republic of [12] Corée, République de [12]	3 259	4 088	5 903	6 963	6 262	2 640	3 975	6 174	6 547	7 642
Kuwait Koweït	1 819	2 146	2 248	2 492	2 377	2 517	2 270	2 494	2 843	3 021
Kyrgyzstan Kirghizistan	...	2	7	6	4	3	11	16	12	10
Lao People's Dem. Rep. Rép. dém. pop. lao	11	18	30	22	21	23	12	8		...
Latvia Lettonie	29	31	24	373	326	305	268	248	224	230
Lesotho Lesotho	6	7	13	12	14	13	14	9	9	14
Libyan Arab Jamah. Jamah. arabe libyenne	206	210	212	215	*154	*143	*150	...	...	...
Lithuania Lituanie	12	50	106	266	277	292	341	253	218	341
Luxembourg Luxembourg	...	...	...	...	...	1 348	1 324	1 318	1 466	1 896
Madagascar Madagascar	34	47	59	72	80	119	111	115	115	...
Malawi Malawi	11	15	16	17	17	39	47	50	40	78
Malaysia Malaisie	1 838	1 994	2 314	2 569	2 590	1 785	1 973	2 075	2 614	2 618
Maldives Maldives	29	28	31	38	39	42	45	46	45	46
Mali Mali	58	42	49	46	42	52	44	41	...	...
Malta Malte	154	177	214	219	191	193	201	200	180	153
Mauritania Mauritanie	20	18	23	36	48	42	55	...	...	...
Mauritius Maurice	128	143	159	179	173	185	187	182	198	204
Mexico [13] Mexique [13]	5 562	5 338	3 171	3 387	3 891[10]	4 209[10]	4 541[10]	5 499[10]	5 702[10]	6 060[10]
Mongolia Mongolie	3	3	20	19	14	45	41	51	55	119
Montserrat Montserrat	3	3	2	3	3	1	1	2	2	2
Morocco Maroc	245	303	304	300	316	424	440	430	380	444

78

Tourism expenditure in other countries
Million US dollars *[cont.]*

Dépenses touristiques dans d'autres pays
Millions de dollars E.-U. *[suite]*

Region, country or area Région, pays ou zone	1993	1994	1995	1996	1997	1998	1999	2000	2001	2002
Mozambique Mozambique	...	...	...	...	...	226	343	257	283	296
Myanmar Myanmar	10	12	18	28	33	27	21	25	27	...
Namibia Namibie	71	77	90	89	99	88	...	...	...	...
Nepal Népal	93	112	136	125	103	78	71	73	80	...
Netherlands Pays-Bas	8 920	9 371	11 661	11 528	11 285	12 099	12 070	12 229	12 016	12 919
Netherlands Antilles [14] Antilles néerlandaises [14]	125	147	209	236	243	109	179	218	194	...
New Zealand Nouvelle-Zélande	1 002	1 194	824	923	965	...	...	...	...	...
Nicaragua Nicaragua	31	30	40	60	65	70	78	78	76	69
Niger Niger	29	21	21	23	24	25	26	28	...	...
Nigeria Nigéria	298	858	906	1 304	1 816	1 567	620	730	700	...
Norway Norvège	3 364	3 712	4 247	4 536	4 306	4 729	4 749	4 334	4 305	5 814
Oman Oman	47	47	47	255	252	294	328	351	367	...
Pakistan Pakistan	633	397	449	900	364	352	180	252	255	179
Palau Palaos	...	...	...	...	...	2	2	2	2	2
Panama Panama	123	123	128	136	164	176	184	187	176	178
Papua New Guinea Papouasie-Nvl-Guinée	69	71	58	72	78	52	53	50	38	...
Paraguay [15] Paraguay [15]	138	177	133	139	139	142	109	81	72	65
Peru Pérou	269	266	296	350	434	452	443	530	592	616
Philippines Philippines	130	196	422	1 266	1 935	1 950	1 308	1 005	1 229	871
Poland [10] Pologne [10]	181	316	5 500	6 240	5 750	4 430	3 600	3 600	3 500	3 200
Portugal Portugal	1 893	1 698	2 141	2 283	2 161	2 319	2 261	2 237	2 153	2 274
Puerto Rico Porto Rico	776	797	833	821	869[16]	874[16]	815[16]	931[16]	1 004[16]	928[16]
Republic of Moldova République de Moldova	...	...	56	52	65	59	57	72	74	86
Romania Roumanie	195	449	697	666	783	451	395	420	449	396
Russian Federation Fédération de Russie	...	7 092	11 599	10 270	9 363	8 677	7 097	8 848	9 960	12 005
Rwanda Rwanda	18	18	10	12	13	16	18	22	20	24
Saint Kitts and Nevis Saint-Kitts-et-Nevis	5	6	5	6	6	6	7	9	8	...

78

Tourism expenditure in other countries
Million US dollars *[cont.]*

Dépenses touristiques dans d'autres pays
Millions de dollars E.-U. *[suite]*

Region, country or area Région, pays ou zone	1993	1994	1995	1996	1997	1998	1999	2000	2001	2002
Saint Lucia Sainte-Lucie	20	23	25	29	29	31	33	33	32	...
St. Vincent-Grenadines St. Vincent-Grenadines	5	6	7	8	7	8	9	10	10	...
Samoa Samoa	2	4	3	4	5	4	4	...	...	...
Sao Tome and Principe Sao Tomé-et-Principe	2	1	1	1	1	1	1	1	1	1
Saudi Arabia Arabie saoudite	...	...	...	...	...	...	...	...	...	7 356
Senegal Sénégal	50	48	72	53	53	54	54	...	...	...
Seychelles Seychelles	35	31	39	30	30	26	21	25	30	32
Sierra Leone Sierra Leone	4	4	2	2	...	4	4	...	...	...
Singapore Singapour	3 412	3 368	4 631	5 797	4 605	4 707	4 666	4 970	4 647	5 213
Slovakia * Slovaquie *	262	284	330	483	439	475	339	295	287	442
Slovenia [17] Slovénie [17]	305	369	573	602	518	561	541	511	528	614
Solomon Islands Iles Salomon	12	13	13	15	9	6	7	...	...	...
South Africa Afrique du Sud	1 868	1 861	1 849	1 754	1 961	1 908	2 028	2 085	1 878	1 804
Spain Espagne	4 735	4 129	4 461	4 919	4 467	5 001	5 523	5 572	5 974	6 638
Sri Lanka Sri Lanka	121	170	186	176	180	202	219	244	245	253
Sudan Soudan	15	47	43	28	33	29	35	55	74	91
Suriname Suriname	3	3	3	8	11	11	13	23	23	10
Swaziland Swaziland	43	38	43	42	38	58	59	64	46	33
Sweden Suède	4 483	4 864	5 624	6 448	6 898	7 632	8 011	8 049	6 926	7 241
Switzerland Suisse	5 954	6 370	7 346	7 570	6 960	6 798	6 718	6 187	6 088	6 427
Syrian Arab Republic Rép. arabe syrienne	300	512	498	513	545	580	630	640	610	...
Tajikistan Tadjikistan	...	...	...	...	...	...	...	...	...	2
Thailand Thaïlande	2 092	2 906	3 373	4 171	1 888	1 970	2 476	2 775	2 923	3 303
TFYR of Macedonia L'ex-R.y. Macédoine	...	22	27	26	27	30	32	34	38	45
Togo Togo	20	18	18	3	5	3	3	2	5	...
Tonga Tonga	1	3	3	3	3	...	...	...	3	...
Trinidad and Tobago Trinité-et-Tobago	106	90	69	76	72	67	83	147	151	...

78

Tourism expenditure in other countries
Million US dollars [cont.]

Dépenses touristiques dans d'autres pays
Millions de dollars E.-U. [suite]

Region, country or area Région, pays ou zone	1993	1994	1995	1996	1997	1998	1999	2000	2001	2002
Tunisia Tunisie	203	216	251	251	235	235	239	263	273	260
Turkey Turquie	934	886	912	1 265	1 716	1 754	1 471	1 711	1 738	1 881
Turkmenistan Turkménistan	...	...	...	73	125	...	...	...	...	...
Turks and Caicos Islands Iles Turques et Caïques	...	134	153	174	235	194	244	...	...	...
Uganda Ouganda	40	78	80	135	113	...	...	...	...	...
Ukraine Ukraine	...	2 650	3 041	2 596	2 564	2 021	1 774	2 017	2 179	2 087
United Kingdom Royaume-Uni	19 477	21 998	24 268	25 309	27 710	32 276	35 628	36 692	36 467	40 409
United Rep. of Tanzania Rép.-Unie de Tanzanie	180	206	360	412	407	493	370	337	327	337
United States Etats-Unis	40 713	43 782	44 916	48 078	52 051	56 483	58 963	64 705	60 200	58 044
Uruguay Uruguay	129	234	236	192	264	265	280	281	252	178
Vanuatu Vanuatu	4	4	5	5	5	8	9	9	8	...
Venezuela Venezuela	2 083	1 973	1 865	2 251	2 381	2 451	1 646	1 705	1 799	1 418
Yemen Yémen	80	78	76	78	124	130	136	70	79	78
Zambia Zambie	56	58	57	59	59	24	43	44	...	...
Zimbabwe Zimbabwe	44	96	106	118	120	131	...	...	...	...

Source:
World Tourism Organisation (WTO), Madrid, "Yearbook of Tourism Statistics – 2003 edition", and the WTO Statistics Database.

Source:
Organisation mondiale du tourisme (OMT), Madrid, "Annuaire des statistiques du tourisme – 2003 édition", et la base de données de l'OMT.

1	Including international transport.
2	Data based on surveys.
3	Beginning 1998, new methodology of the Bulgarian Central Bank and Ministry of Economy was applied.
4	Including international fare expenditure.
5	Data collected by travel surveys.
6	New series since 1999 excluding frontier workers paid in foreign currency.
7	Including border merchandise transactions and purchases of inward-bound and outward-bound commuters.
8	Including registrations through new methodology.
9	Excluding fare paid to national carriers.
10	Based on surveys and estimations by the Institute of Tourism.
11	Including education payments.
12	Excluding expenses of students studying overseas.
13	Including expenditure from frontier visitors.
14	Prior to 1995, data refer to Curaçao only; between 1995 and 1997, to Curaçao and Saint Maarten; from 1998 to 2000, to Bonaire and Saint

1	Y compris les transports internationaux.
2	Données obtenues au moyen d'enquêtes.
3	A partir de l'année 1998, une nouvelle méthodologie élaborée par la Banque Centrale de la Bulgarie et le Ministère de l'Economie a été appliquée.
4	Y compris les dépenses de billets internationaux.
5	Données collectées au moyen d'enquêtes sur les voyages.
6	A partir de 1999, non compris les travailleurs frontaliers rémunérés en devises.
7	Y compris les transactions frontalières en marchandises, et les achats des migrants quotidiens entrant et sortant.
8	Y compris les mouvements enregistrés selon la nouvelle méthode.
9	Non compris les billets achetés à des transporteurs nationaux.
10	Chiffres basés sur des enquêtes et des estimations de l'Institut du tourisme.
11	Y compris les paiements pour l'éducation.
12	Non compris les dépenses des étudiants poursuivant leurs études à l'étranger.
13	Y compris les dépenses des visiteurs frontaliers.
14	Avant 1995, les données ne se rapportent qu'à Curaçao; de 1995 à 1997, les données se rapportent à Curaçao et Saint-Martin; de 1998 à

78

Tourism expenditure in other countries
Million US dollars *[cont.]*

Dépenses touristiques dans d'autres pays
Millions de dollars E.-U. *[suite]*

Maarten; in 2001, to Saint Maarten only.

15   Beginning 1995, change in methodology. The data reported relate only to expenditure by tourists; expenditure by same-day visitors are not included.

16   Source: "Junta de Planificacion de Puerto Rico".

17   Data refer to the item "travel" of the Balance of Payments.

2000, à Bonaire et Saint-Martin; 2001, à Saint-Martin seulement.

15   Avant 1995, changement de méthode. Les données communiquées ne se rapportent qu'aux dépenses des touristes, à l'exclusion de celles des visiteurs ne restant pas au-delà d'une journée.

16   Source : "Junta de Planificacion de Puerto Rico".

17   Données relatives à la rubrique "Voyages" de la balance des paiements.

Technical notes, tables 76-78

The data on international tourism have been supplied by the World Tourism Organization (WTO), which publishes detailed tourism information in the *Compendium of Tourism Statistics* [38]. Additional information on data collection methods and definitions can be found in the *Methodological Supplement to World Travel and Tourism Statistics* [63] also published by the WTO. (See also [54] and [55]).

For statistical purposes, the term "international visitor" describes "any person who travels to a country other than that in which he/she has his/her usual residence but outside his/her usual environment for a period not exceeding 12 months and whose main purpose of visit is other than the exercise of an activity remunerated from within the country visited".

International visitors include:

(a) *Tourists* (overnight visitors): "visitors who stay at least one night in a collective or private accommodation in the country visited"; and

(b) *Same-day visitors*: "visitors who do not spend the night in a collective or private accommodation in the country visited".

The figures do not include immigrants, residents in a frontier zone, persons domiciled in one country or area and working in an adjoining country or area, members of the armed forces and diplomats and consular representatives when they travel from their country of origin to the country in which they are stationed and vice-versa.

The figures also exclude persons in transit who do not formally enter the country through passport control, such as air transit passengers who remain for a short period in a designated area of the air terminal or ship passengers who are not permitted to disembark. This category includes passengers transferred directly between airports or other terminals. Other passengers in transit through a country are classified as visitors.

Tables 76 and 77: Data on arrivals of international (or non-resident) visitors may be obtained from different sources. In some cases data are obtained from border statistics derived from administrative records (police, immigration, traffic and other type of controls applied at national borders), and eventually, completed by means of border statistical surveys. In other cases, data are obtained from different types of tourism accommodation establishments (hotels and similar establishments and/or all types of tourism accommodation establishments).

Unless otherwise stated, table 76 shows the number of tourist/visitor arrivals at frontiers classified by their region of origin. Totals correspond to the total number of arrivals from the regions indicated in the table. However, these totals may not correspond to the

Notes techniques, tableaux 76 à 78

Les données sur le tourisme international ont été fournies par l'Organisation mondiale du tourisme (l'OMT) qui publie des renseignements détaillés sur le tourisme dans *le Compendium des statistiques du tourisme* [38]. On trouvera plus de renseignements sur les méthodes de collecte et sur les définitions dans « *Methodological Supplement to World Travel and Tourism Statistics* » [63] publié par l'OMT. (Voir aussi [54] et [55]). A des fins statistiques, l'expression "*visiteur international*" désigne "toute personne qui se rend dans un pays autre que celui où elle a son lieu de résidence habituelle, mais différent de son environnement habituel, pour une période de 12 mois au maximum, dans un but principal autre que celui d'y exercer une profession rémunérée".

Entrent dans cette catégorie:

(a) Les *touristes* (visiteurs passant la nuit), c'est à dire "les visiteurs qui passent une nuit au moins en logement collectif ou privé dans le pays visité";

(b) Les *visiteurs ne restant que la journée*, c'est à dire "les visiteurs qui ne passent pas la nuit en logement collectif ou privé dans le pays visité".

Ces chiffres ne comprennent pas les immigrants, les résidents frontaliers, les personnes domiciliées dans une zone ou un pays donné et travaillant dans une zone ou pays limitrophe, les membres des forces armées et les membres des corps diplomatique et consulaire lorsqu'ils se rendent de leur pays d'origine au pays où ils sont en poste, et vice versa.

Ne sont pas non plus inclus les voyageurs en transit, qui ne pénètrent pas officiellement dans le pays en faisant contrôler leurs passeports, tels que les passagers d'un vol en escale, qui demeurent pendant un court laps de temps dans une aire distincte de l'aérogare, ou les passagers d'un navire qui ne sont pas autorisés à débarquer. Cette catégorie comprend également les passagers transportés directement d'une aérogare à l'autre ou à un autre terminal. Les autres passagers en transit dans un pays sont classés parmi les visiteurs.

Tableaux 76 et 77: Les données relatives aux arrivées des visiteurs internationaux (ou non résidents) peuvent être obtenues de différentes sources. Dans certains cas, elles proviennent des statistiques des frontières tirées des registres administratifs (contrôles de police, de l'immigration, de la circulation et autres effectués aux frontières nationales) et, éventuellement, complétées à l'aide d'enquêtes statistiques aux frontières. Dans d'autres cas, elles proviennent de différents types d'établissements d'hébergement touristique (hôtels et établissements assimilés et/ou tous types d'établissements d'hébergement touristique).

number of tourist arrivals shown in table 77. The latter excludes same-day visitors whereas they may be included in table 76. More detailed information can be found in the *Compendium of Tourism Statistics* [38].

When a person visits the same country several times a year, an equal number of arrivals is recorded. Likewise, if a person visits several countries during the course of a single trip, his/her arrival in each country is recorded separately. Consequently, *arrivals* cannot be assumed to be equal to the number of persons traveling.

Tourism expenditure (in the country of reference) corresponds to the "expenditure of non-resident visitors (tourists and same-day visitors)" within the economic territory of the country of reference. International transport is excluded. The data are obtained by the WTO from the item "Travel receipts" of the Balance of Payments of each country shown in the *Balance of Payments Statistics Yearbook* published by the International Monetary Fund [14].

Table 78: The data on tourism expenditure in other countries are obtained from the item "Travel expenditure" of the Balance of Payments of each country and corresponds to the "expenditure of resident visitors (tourists and same-day visitors)" outside the economic territory of the country of reference.

For more information, see the *Compendium of Tourism Statistics* published by the World Tourism Organization [38] and the *Balance of Payments Statistics Yearbook* published by the International Monetary Fund [14].

Sauf indication contraire, le tableau 77 indique le nombre d'arrivées de touristes/visiteurs par région de provenance. Les totaux correspondent au nombre total d'arrivées de touristes des régions indiquées sur le tableau. Les chiffres totaux peuvent néanmoins, ne pas coïncider avec le nombre des arrivées de touristes indiqué dans le tableau 77, qui ne comprend pas les visiteurs ne restant que la journée, lesquels peuvent au contraire être inclus dans les chiffres du tableau 76. Pour plus de renseignements, consulter *le Compendium des statistiques du tourisme* [38].

Lorsqu'une personne visite le même pays plusieurs fois dans l'année, il est enregistré un nombre égal d'arrivées. En outre, si une personne visite plusieurs pays au cours d'un seul et même voyage, son arrivée dans chaque pays est enregistrée séparément. Par conséquent, on ne peut pas partir du postulat que les *arrivées* sont égales au nombre de personnes qui voyagent.

Dépenses touristiques (dans le pays de référence) correspondent aux «dépenses des visiteurs (touristes et visiteurs de la journée) non résidents» dans le territoire économique du pays dont il s'agit. Les données excluent les dépenses du transport international. Ils sont tirées par l'OMT du poste «recettes au titre des voyages» de la balance des paiements de chaque pays présentée dans le "*Balance of Payments Statistics Yearbook*" publié par le Fonds monétaire international [14].

Tableau 77: Les dépenses touristiques dans d'autres pays sont tirées du poste «dépenses au titre des voyages» de la balance des paiements de chaque pays et correspondent aux «dépenses des visiteurs (touristes et visiteurs de la journée) résidents» en dehors du territoire économique du pays de référence.

On trouvera plus de renseignements dans le *Compendium des statistiques du tourisme* publié par l'Organisation mondiale du tourisme [38] et dans "*Balance of Payments Statistics Yearbook*" publié par le Fonds monétaire international [14].

79

Summary of balance of payments
Millions of US dollars

Résumé des balances des paiements
Millions de dollars des E.-U.

Country or area	1996	1997	1998	1999	2000	2001	2002	Pays ou zone
Albania								**Albanie**
Goods: Exports fob	243.7	158.6	208.0	275.0	255.7	304.5	330.2	Biens : exportations, fab
Goods: Imports fob	-922.0	-693.6	-811.7	-938.0	-1 070.0	-1 331.6	-1 485.4	Biens : importations, fab
Serv. & Income: Credit	212.9	125.2	172.6	354.9	563.7	696.8	733.3	Serv. & revenu : crédit
Serv. & Income: Debit	-201.3	-127.0	-138.0	-173.3	-438.6	-457.6	-610.8	Serv & revenu : débit
Current Trans.,nie: Credit	595.9	299.8	560.8	508.9	629.0	647.5	683.7	Transf. cour.,nia : crédit
Current Transfers: Debit	-36.5	-35.2	-56.9	-182.9	-96.1	-76.9	-58.6	Transf. courants : débit
Capital Acct.,nie: Credit	4.8	2.0	31.0	22.6	78.0	117.7	121.2	Compte de cap.,nia : crédit
Capital Account: Debit	0.0	0.0	0.0	0.0	0.0	0.0	0.0	Compte de capital : débit
Financial Account, nie	61.5	151.4	15.4	33.7	188.4	110.0	213.4	Compte d'op. fin., nia
Net Errors and Omissions	96.9	158.4	71.1	206.2	9.8	136.3	108.5	Erreurs et omissions nettes
Reserves & Related Items	-55.9	-39.5	-52.4	-107.1	-119.9	-146.7	-35.6	Rés. et postes appareutés
Angola								**Angola**
Goods: Exports fob	5 095.0	5 006.8	3 542.9	5 156.5	7 920.7	6 534.3	...	Biens : exportations, fab
Goods: Imports fob	-2 040.5	-2 597.0	-2 079.4	-3 109.1	-3 039.5	-3 179.2	...	Biens : importations, fab
Serv. & Income: Credit	311.0	250.7	156.3	177.1	301.7	225.5	...	Serv. & revenu : crédit
Serv. & Income: Debit	-3 940.0	-3 638.6	-3 638.4	-3 990.7	-4 414.7	-5 102.1	...	Serv & revenu : débit
Current Trans.,nie: Credit	3 949.4	176.4	238.2	154.5	123.5	208.3	...	Transf. cour.,nia : crédit
Current Transfers: Debit	-108.6	-81.8	-86.7	-98.7	-96.0	-117.8	...	Transf. courants : débit
Capital Acct.,nie: Credit	0.0	11.2	8.4	6.8	18.3	3.9	...	Compte de cap.,nia : crédit
Capital Account: Debit	0.0	0.0	0.0	0.0	0.0	0.0	...	Compte de capital : débit
Financial Account, nie	-654.5	449.9	368.3	1 739.6	-445.6	950.0	...	Compte d'op. fin., nia
Net Errors and Omissions	149.2	-181.8	378.5	-78.9	-50.6	-308.6	...	Erreurs et omissions nettes
Reserves & Related Items	-2 761.0	604.3	1 112.0	42.9	-317.8	785.6	...	Rés. et postes appareutés
Anguilla								**Anguilla**
Goods: Exports fob	1.8	1.6	3.5	2.9	4.4	3.6	4.8	Biens : exportations, fab
Goods: Imports fob	-52.9	-54.3	-63.0	-80.9	-83.3	-68.5	-61.5	Biens : importations, fab
Serv. & Income: Credit	59.5	69.3	81.0	72.5	68.7	72.5	68.2	Serv. & revenu : crédit
Serv. & Income: Debit	-36.1	-36.0	-43.6	-45.2	-47.3	-43.4	-40.9	Serv & revenu : débit
Current Trans.,nie: Credit	12.6	7.2	8.8	6.8	8.9	7.8	8.0	Transf. cour.,nia : crédit
Current Transfers: Debit	-5.2	-6.5	-6.4	-7.2	-7.3	-7.6	-7.7	Transf. courants : débit
Capital Acct.,nie: Credit	6.5	3.9	3.4	4.0	6.2	5.0	4.6	Compte de cap.,nia : crédit
Capital Account: Debit	-1.3	-1.4	-1.3	-1.3	-1.3	-1.3	-1.3	Compte de capital : débit
Financial Account, nie	35.7	19.2	11.6	58.8	41.3	18.3	13.9	Compte d'op. fin., nia
Net Errors and Omissions	-19.3	-1.1	7.9	-8.7	10.3	17.7	13.9	Erreurs et omissions nettes
Reserves & Related Items	-1.4	-1.9	-1.8	-1.8	-0.4	-3.9	-2.0	Rés. et postes appareutés
Antigua and Barbuda								**Antigua-et-Barbuda**
Goods: Exports fob	38.9	38.8	37.4	36.8	42.3	38.6	...	Biens : exportations, fab
Goods: Imports fob	-309.9	-313.9	-320.8	-352.7	-342.4	-321.2	...	Biens : importations, fab
Serv. & Income: Credit	369.4	408.2	441.2	450.9	431.9	421.3	...	Serv. & revenu : crédit
Serv. & Income: Debit	-189.4	-190.3	-202.7	-217.5	-202.7	-192.2	...	Serv & revenu : débit
Current Trans.,nie: Credit	35.2	19.9	12.4	23.6	17.9	15.4	...	Transf. cour.,nia : crédit
Current Transfers: Debit	-3.6	-10.1	-14.3	-3.9	-8.9	-9.4	...	Transf. courants : débit
Capital Acct.,nie: Credit	4.4	9.2	13.5	10.3	17.8	18.4	...	Compte de cap.,nia : crédit
Capital Account: Debit	0.0	0.0	0.0	0.0	0.0	0.0	...	Compte de capital : débit
Financial Account, nie	55.0	50.5	49.1	55.2	65.0	23.6	...	Compte d'op. fin., nia
Net Errors and Omissions	-11.2	-9.4	-6.9	7.7	-27.1	21.6	...	Erreurs et omissions nettes
Reserves & Related Items	11.3	-3.0	-8.7	-10.4	6.2	-16.2	...	Rés. et postes appareutés
Argentina								**Argentine**
Goods: Exports fob	24 042.7	26 430.8	26 433.7	23 308.6	26 341.0	26 542.7	25 709.4	Biens : exportations, fab
Goods: Imports fob	-22 283.2	-28 553.5	-29 530.9	-24 103.2	-23 889.1	-19 157.8	-8 470.1	Biens : importations, fab
Serv. & Income: Credit	8 778.9	9 984.0	10 828.8	10 648.6	12 254.0	9 771.5	6 124.9	Serv. & revenu : crédit
Serv. & Income: Debit	-17 808.2	-20 565.0	-22 667.9	-22 217.2	-23 997.8	-21 415.5	-14 185.6	Serv & revenu : débit
Current Trans.,nie: Credit	704.2	760.0	719.6	704.2	723.5	680.5	576.8	Transf. cour.,nia : crédit
Current Transfers: Debit	-256.7	-296.7	-313.5	-306.8	-368.5	-399.4	-163.8	Transf. courants : débit
Capital Acct.,nie: Credit	71.5	111.8	91.5	97.6	120.8	108.7	42.7	Compte de cap.,nia : crédit
Capital Account: Debit	-20.7	-17.4	-18.6	-11.5	-14.9	-8.2	-4.1	Compte de capital : débit
Financial Account, nie	11 713.2	16 755.4	18 936.2	14 407.6	7 717.7	-14 953.6	-23 464.4	Compte d'op. fin., nia
Net Errors and Omissions	-1 684.0	-1 278.8	-388.7	-515.3	-62.7	-2 574.6	-1 547.8	Erreurs et omissions nettes
Reserves & Related Items	-3 257.7	-3 330.6	-4 090.3	-2 012.6	1 176.1	21 405.7	15 381.9	Rés. et postes appareutés
Armenia								**Arménie**
Goods: Exports fob	290.4	233.6	228.9	247.3	309.9	353.1	513.8	Biens : exportations, fab

79

Summary of balance of payments
Millions of US dollars [cont.]

Résumé des balances des paiements
Millions de dollars des E.-U. [suite]

Country or area	1996	1997	1998	1999	2000	2001	2002	Pays ou zone
Goods: Imports fob	-759.6	-793.1	-806.3	-721.4	-773.4	-773.3	-882.5	Biens : importations, fab
Serv. & Income: Credit	155.8	235.6	234.3	229.4	240.7	289.6	320.4	Serv. & revenu : crédit
Serv. & Income: Debit	-161.8	-199.8	-252.2	-236.5	-243.6	-243.9	-273.0	Serv & revenu : débit
Current Trans.,nie: Credit	199.0	252.4	203.0	200.6	208.5	200.8	199.7	Transf. cour.,nia : crédit
Current Transfers: Debit	-14.4	-35.2	-25.6	-26.5	-20.5	-26.8	-26.3	Transf. courants : débit
Capital Acct.,nie: Credit	13.4	10.9	9.7	16.9	29.5	32.6	70.2	Compte de cap.,nia : crédit
Capital Account: Debit	0.0	0.0	0.0	-4.3	-1.2	-2.5	-2.1	Compte de capital : débit
Financial Account, nie	216.8	334.8	390.4	286.2	249.9	176.9	155.5	Compte d'op. fin., nia
Net Errors and Omissions	15.1	10.8	18.4	13.1	17.0	12.1	-11.7	Erreurs et omissions nettes
Reserves & Related Items	45.5	-50.0	-0.6	-4.8	-16.9	-18.6	-63.9	Rés. et postes appareutés
Aruba								**Aruba**
Goods: Exports fob	1 735.7	1 728.7	1 164.8	1 413.5	2 582.1	1 515.8	...	Biens : exportations, fab
Goods: Imports fob	-2 043.4	-2 115.9	-1 518.2	-2 005.2	-2 610.4	-2 049.6	...	Biens : importations, fab
Serv. & Income: Credit	789.1	836.5	932.6	1 027.0	1 078.7	1 106.5	...	Serv. & revenu : crédit
Serv. & Income: Debit	-546.9	-634.0	-593.2	-781.9	-732.2	-750.7	...	Serv & revenu : débit
Current Trans.,nie: Credit	18.4	18.4	29.3	59.3	46.2	36.2	...	Transf. cour.,nia : crédit
Current Transfers: Debit	-22.0	-29.5	-34.1	-45.9	-82.2	-102.6	...	Transf. courants : débit
Capital Acct.,nie: Credit	28.7	21.6	10.2	0.9	10.5	21.5	...	Compte de cap.,nia : crédit
Capital Account: Debit	-0.7	-0.6	-5.0	-0.9	-0.6	-2.2	...	Compte de capital : débit
Financial Account, nie	10.7	158.9	64.2	336.4	-314.6	263.2	...	Compte d'op. fin., nia
Net Errors and Omissions	4.3	-2.5	0.6	-0.7	6.5	-5.3	...	Erreurs et omissions nettes
Reserves & Related Items	26.1	18.4	-51.3	-2.5	15.9	-32.7	...	Rés. et postes appareutés
Australia								**Australie**
Goods: Exports fob	60 396.9	64 892.7	55 883.6	56 096.0	64 052.5	63 675.8	65 098.9	Biens : exportations, fab
Goods: Imports fob	-61 031.7	-63 043.6	-61 215.2	-65 826.0	-68 751.8	-61 801.6	-70 502.6	Biens : importations, fab
Serv. & Income: Credit	24 558.0	25 650.3	22 713.8	24 731.0	27 520.1	24 418.7	25 160.5	Serv. & revenu : crédit
Serv. & Income: Debit	-39 826.3	-39 844.2	-35 114.2	-37 177.9	-37 993.2	-35 054.1	-37 574.7	Serv & revenu : débit
Current Trans.,nie: Credit	2 698.9	2 765.1	2 650.6	3 002.7	2 621.8	2 242.4	2 309.9	Transf. cour.,nia : crédit
Current Transfers: Debit	-2 606.2	-2 804.7	-2 932.7	-3 031.7	-2 669.1	-2 221.4	-2 374.0	Transf. courants : débit
Capital Acct.,nie: Credit	1 674.1	1 606.1	1 315.3	1 534.7	1 405.9	1 319.8	1 393.5	Compte de cap.,nia : crédit
Capital Account: Debit	-709.8	-703.3	-645.6	-715.5	-790.9	-728.9	-853.2	Compte de capital : débit
Financial Account, nie	16 069.5	16 820.4	15 116.5	27 283.8	12 771.2	8 600.9	17 240.7	Compte d'op. fin., nia
Net Errors and Omissions	1 248.0	-2 465.6	187.8	808.2	468.7	644.1	222.5	Erreurs et omissions nettes
Reserves & Related Items	-2 471.5	-2 873.3	2 040.0	-6 705.5	1 364.7	-1 095.7	-121.6	Rés. et postes appareutés
Austria								**Autriche**
Goods: Exports fob	57 937.3	58 662.3	63 299.1	64 421.7	64 684.0	66 900.2	73 667.5	Biens : exportations, fab
Goods: Imports fob	-65 251.9	-62 936.3	-66 983.3	-68 050.8	-67 420.7	-68 169.3	-70 095.6	Biens : importations, fab
Serv. & Income: Credit	43 828.9	39 998.0	39 715.8	43 978.5	43 333.2	45 382.1	48 370.7	Serv. & revenu : crédit
Serv. & Income: Debit	-39 621.5	-39 251.5	-39 356.2	-44 973.7	-44 108.5	-46 547.6	-49 752.5	Serv & revenu : débit
Current Trans.,nie: Credit	3 144.8	2 911.6	2 940.4	2 924.8	2 914.2	3 266.8	4 003.9	Transf. cour.,nia : crédit
Current Transfers: Debit	-4 928.0	-4 605.2	-4 874.0	-4 956.1	-4 266.6	-4 468.4	-5 618.6	Transf. courants : débit
Capital Acct.,nie: Credit	591.3	590.0	483.5	554.6	530.2	483.3	814.8	Compte de cap.,nia : crédit
Capital Account: Debit	-513.0	-563.7	-830.6	-820.0	-962.1	-1 012.5	-1 386.0	Compte de capital : débit
Financial Account, nie	5 324.9	1 665.9	9 534.8	4 788.7	3 407.2	1 794.9	-4 949.8	Compte d'op. fin., nia
Net Errors and Omissions	562.1	475.5	-447.2	-39.7	1 143.2	482.3	3 222.9	Erreurs et omissions nettes
Reserves & Related Items	-1 075.0	3 053.3	-3 481.9	2 171.9	745.8	1 888.4	1 722.6	Rés. et postes appareutés
Azerbaijan								**Azerbaïdjan**
Goods: Exports fob	643.7	808.3	677.8	1 025.2	1 858.3	2 078.9	2 304.9	Biens : exportations, fab
Goods: Imports fob	-1 337.6	-1 375.2	-1 723.9	-1 433.4	-1 539.0	-1 465.1	-1 823.3	Biens : importations, fab
Serv. & Income: Credit	164.3	364.6	370.0	267.8	315.7	331.3	399.3	Serv. & revenu : crédit
Serv. & Income: Debit	-468.1	-758.2	-752.3	-541.1	-875.9	-1 073.5	-1 719.6	Serv & revenu : débit
Current Trans.,nie: Credit	107.2	95.7	145.0	134.5	135.0	176.5	228.2	Transf. cour.,nia : crédit
Current Transfers: Debit	-40.7	-50.9	-80.9	-52.8	-62.0	-99.9	-157.9	Transf. courants : débit
Capital Acct.,nie: Credit	0.0	0.0	0.0	0.0	0.0	0.0	18.4	Compte de cap.,nia : crédit
Capital Account: Debit	0.0	-10.2	-0.7	0.0	0.0	0.0	-47.1	Compte de capital : débit
Financial Account, nie	822.5	1 092.1	1 326.0	690.2	493.4	126.0	918.7	Compte d'op. fin., nia
Net Errors and Omissions	23.6	-27.0	-20.1	42.4	0.0	-0.9	-87.4	Erreurs et omissions nettes
Reserves & Related Items	85.0	-139.2	59.2	-132.9	-325.6	-73.4	-34.2	Rés. et postes appareutés
Bahamas								**Bahamas**
Goods: Exports fob	273.3	295.0	362.9	379.9	805.3	614.1	...	Biens : exportations, fab
Goods: Imports fob	-1 287.4	-1 410.7	-1 737.1	-1 808.1	-2 176.4	-1 764.7	...	Biens : importations, fab
Serv. & Income: Credit	1 662.8	1 698.6	1 680.9	2 040.8	2 248.6	1 983.7	...	Serv. & revenu : crédit

79

Summary of balance of payments
Millions of US dollars *[cont.]*

Résumé des balances des paiements
Millions de dollars des E.-U. *[suite]*

Country or area	1996	1997	1998	1999	2000	2001	2002	Pays ou zone
Serv. & Income: Debit	-949.2	-1 094.3	-1 336.3	-1 321.0	-1 392.2	-1 222.9	...	Serv & revenu : débit
Current Trans.,nie: Credit	45.9	50.0	45.0	49.0	53.8	52.7	...	Transf. cour.,nia : crédit
Current Transfers: Debit	-8.7	-10.7	-10.8	-12.5	-10.5	-10.9	...	Transf. courants : débit
Capital Acct.,nie: Credit	0.0	0.0	0.0	0.0	0.0	0.0	...	Compte de cap.,nia : crédit
Capital Account: Debit	-24.4	-12.9	-11.7	-14.5	-16.4	-20.3	...	Compte de capital : débit
Financial Account, nie	181.1	412.0	817.7	611.4	429.3	279.8	...	Compte d'op. fin., nia
Net Errors and Omissions	99.0	129.5	308.6	140.2	-2.6	58.6	...	Erreurs et omissions nettes
Reserves & Related Items	7.6	-56.5	-119.2	-65.2	61.0	29.9	...	Rés. et postes appareutés
Bahrain								**Bahreïn**
Goods: Exports fob	4 702.1	4 383.0	3 270.2	4 362.8	6 195.0	5 576.9	5 785.6	Biens : exportations, fab
Goods: Imports fob	-4 037.0	-3 778.2	-3 298.7	-3 468.4	-4 393.6	-4 047.3	-4 672.9	Biens : importations, fab
Serv. & Income: Credit	4 481.4	4 908.0	5 488.6	5 977.4	7 261.4	4 744.8	2 733.3	Serv. & revenu : crédit
Serv. & Income: Debit	-4 452.9	-5 141.8	-5 577.9	-6 089.1	-7 289.9	-4 863.5	-3 042.6	Serv & revenu : débit
Current Trans.,nie: Credit	126.3	232.7	65.2	36.7	22.3	22.9	14.7	Transf. cour.,nia : crédit
Current Transfers: Debit	-559.3	-634.8	-725.0	-856.1	-1 012.8	-1 286.9	-1 334.2	Transf. courants : débit
Capital Acct.,nie: Credit	50.0	125.0	100.0	100.0	50.0	100.0	26.6	Compte de cap.,nia : crédit
Capital Account: Debit	0.0	0.0	0.0	0.0	0.0	0.0	0.0	Compte de capital : débit
Financial Account, nie	-510.4	15.4	22.3	230.1	-29.8	-418.9	-872.6	Compte d'op. fin., nia
Net Errors and Omissions	193.3	-6.5	638.7	-268.1	-602.6	295.6	1 396.9	Erreurs et omissions nettes
Reserves & Related Items	6.4	-102.8	16.6	-25.3	-200.1	-123.5	-34.8	Rés. et postes appareutés
Bangladesh								**Bangladesh**
Goods: Exports fob	4 009.3	4 839.9	5 141.5	5 458.3	6 399.2	6 084.7	6 078.4	Biens : exportations, fab
Goods: Imports fob	-6 284.6	-6 550.7	-6 715.7	-7 535.5	-8 052.9	-8 133.4	-7 714.0	Biens : importations, fab
Serv. & Income: Credit	734.2	773.9	815.4	872.0	893.4	828.8	949.6	Serv. & revenu : crédit
Serv. & Income: Debit	-1 359.1	-1 481.7	-1 443.2	-1 655.2	-1 965.0	-1 883.4	-1 814.9	Serv & revenu : débit
Current Trans.,nie: Credit	1 912.8	2 136.5	2 172.9	2 501.4	2 426.5	2 572.8	3 248.4	Transf. cour.,nia : crédit
Current Transfers: Debit	-4.0	-4.3	-5.9	-5.3	-7.0	-4.9	-6.0	Transf. courants : débit
Capital Acct.,nie: Credit	371.2	366.8	238.7	364.1	248.7	235.4	363.7	Compte de cap.,nia : crédit
Capital Account: Debit	0.0	0.0	0.0	0.0	0.0	0.0	0.0	Compte de capital : débit
Financial Account, nie	92.4	-140.2	-116.0	-446.9	-256.0	262.1	-258.2	Compte d'op. fin., nia
Net Errors and Omissions	113.5	-75.5	201.0	258.0	282.4	-106.0	-347.1	Erreurs et omissions nettes
Reserves & Related Items	414.3	135.1	-288.5	189.2	30.7	143.9	-499.8	Rés. et postes appareutés
Barbados								**Barbade**
Goods: Exports fob	286.7	289.0	270.1	275.3	286.4	271.2	...	Biens : exportations, fab
Goods: Imports fob	-743.0	-887.7	-920.7	-989.4	-1 030.3	-952.3	...	Biens : importations, fab
Serv. & Income: Credit	981.0	1 019.7	1 087.1	1 096.1	1 160.4	1 158.2	...	Serv. & revenu : crédit
Serv. & Income: Debit	-493.4	-517.6	-551.7	-596.4	-639.8	-664.9	...	Serv & revenu : débit
Current Trans.,nie: Credit	64.8	71.7	78.4	94.0	108.9	125.6	...	Transf. cour.,nia : crédit
Current Transfers: Debit	-26.6	-25.1	-26.2	-27.7	-31.0	-32.3	...	Transf. courants : débit
Capital Acct.,nie: Credit	0.4	0.0	0.7	0.7	1.8	1.3	...	Compte de cap.,nia : crédit
Capital Account: Debit	0.0	0.0	0.0	0.0	0.0	0.0	...	Compte de capital : débit
Financial Account, nie	-22.2	20.0	55.5	119.3	286.3	283.0	...	Compte d'op. fin., nia
Net Errors and Omissions	38.5	47.4	0.7	64.6	35.0	32.6	...	Erreurs et omissions nettes
Reserves & Related Items	-86.4	-17.4	6.1	-36.4	-177.6	-222.4	...	Rés. et postes appareutés
Belarus								**Bélarus**
Goods: Exports fob	5 790.1	6 918.7	6 172.3	5 646.4	6 640.5	7 334.1	7 964.7	Biens : exportations, fab
Goods: Imports fob	-6 938.6	-8 325.7	-7 673.4	-6 216.4	-7 524.6	-8 140.8	-8 879.0	Biens : importations, fab
Serv. & Income: Credit	982.1	950.0	951.9	774.1	1 041.3	1 128.8	1 344.3	Serv. & revenu : crédit
Serv. & Income: Debit	-440.8	-480.6	-562.9	-501.6	-635.0	-911.1	-981.1	Serv & revenu : débit
Current Trans.,nie: Credit	135.5	106.1	120.9	137.0	177.1	202.6	235.1	Transf. cour.,nia : crédit
Current Transfers: Debit	-44.2	-27.7	-25.3	-33.2	-22.4	-48.5	-61.5	Transf. courants : débit
Capital Acct.,nie: Credit	257.2	248.0	261.3	131.1	125.6	132.3	119.8	Compte de cap.,nia : crédit
Capital Account: Debit	-156.1	-114.8	-91.2	-70.7	-56.2	-76.0	-67.1	Compte de capital : débit
Financial Account, nie	378.7	738.1	354.8	399.5	140.1	265.0	482.5	Compte d'op. fin., nia
Net Errors and Omissions	-178.1	53.0	172.3	-246.3	238.9	35.1	-60.6	Erreurs et omissions nettes
Reserves & Related Items	214.2	-65.1	319.3	-19.9	-125.3	78.5	-97.1	Rés. et postes appareutés
Belgium								**Belgique**
Goods: Exports fob	...	...	...	...	...	...	168 126.0	Biens : exportations, fab
Goods: Imports fob	...	...	...	...	...	...	-160 731.0	Biens : importations, fab
Serv. & Income: Credit	...	...	...	...	...	...	73 270.7	Serv. & revenu : crédit
Serv. & Income: Debit	...	...	...	...	...	...	-65 092.3	Serv & revenu : débit
Current Trans.,nie: Credit	...	...	...	...	...	...	5 336.1	Transf. cour.,nia : crédit

79

Summary of balance of payments
Millions of US dollars *[cont.]*

Résumé des balances des paiements
Millions de dollars des E.-U. *[suite]*

Country or area	1996	1997	1998	1999	2000	2001	2002	Pays ou zone
Current Transfers: Debit	...	...	...	...	...	...	-9 705.3	Transf. courants : débit
Capital Acct.,nie: Credit	...	...	...	...	...	...	196.6	Compte de cap.,nia : crédit
Capital Account: Debit	...	...	...	...	...	...	-811.7	Compte de capital : débit
Financial Account, nie	...	...	...	...	...	...	-19 140.5	Compte d'op. fin., nia
Net Errors and Omissions	...	...	...	...	...	...	8 519.0	Erreurs et omissions nettes
Reserves & Related Items	...	...	...	...	...	...	32.2	Rés. et postes appareutés
Belgium-Luxembourg [1]								**Belgique-Luxembourg** [1]
Goods: Exports fob	154 695.0	149 497.0	153 558.0	161 263.0	164 677.0	163 498.0	...	Biens : exportations, fab
Goods: Imports fob	-146 004.0	-141 794.0	-146 577.0	-154 237.0	-162 086.0	-159 790.0	...	Biens : importations, fab
Serv. & Income: Credit	97 585.7	93 739.2	103 332.2	117 183.2	125 461.8	129 219.4	...	Serv. & revenu : crédit
Serv. & Income: Debit	-87 907.4	-83 546.1	-93 725.8	-105 292.2	-112 493.2	-119 314.9	...	Serv & revenu : débit
Current Trans.,nie: Credit	7 473.8	7 142.1	7 005.7	7 040.6	7 013.9	7 315.7	...	Transf. cour.,nia : crédit
Current Transfers: Debit	-12 080.6	-11 124.3	-11 425.5	-11 871.8	-11 192.8	-11 535.3	...	Transf. courants : débit
Capital Acct.,nie: Credit	673.5	782.5	323.1	449.2	222.5	479.7	...	Compte de cap.,nia : crédit
Capital Account: Debit	-494.3	-379.2	-436.3	-502.7	-435.8	-454.1	...	Compte de capital : débit
Financial Account, nie	-12 257.2	-12 090.7	-16 042.8	-13 470.1	-9 232.8	-7 978.4	...	Compte d'op. fin., nia
Net Errors and Omissions	-1 090.9	-1 171.0	1 893.0	-2 430.2	-2 893.9	2.5	...	Erreurs et omissions nettes
Reserves & Related Items	-592.6	-1 056.0	2 095.0	1 867.4	959.0	-1 442.1	...	Rés. et postes appareutés
Belize								**Belize**
Goods: Exports fob	171.3	193.4	186.2	213.2	212.3	275.0	310.4	Biens : exportations, fab
Goods: Imports fob	-229.5	-282.9	-290.9	-337.5	-403.7	-488.7	-500.3	Biens : importations, fab
Serv. & Income: Credit	144.2	145.3	147.7	164.3	177.2	185.6	191.2	Serv. & revenu : crédit
Serv. & Income: Debit	-123.7	-122.5	-138.3	-154.7	-178.6	-205.0	-210.0	Serv & revenu : débit
Current Trans.,nie: Credit	34.2	38.2	38.4	40.6	56.6	50.0	48.0	Transf. cour.,nia : crédit
Current Transfers: Debit	-3.1	-3.4	-2.8	-3.5	-3.2	-1.8	-2.1	Transf. courants : débit
Capital Acct.,nie: Credit	0.0	0.0	0.0	0.5	0.9	2.1	9.6	Compte de cap.,nia : crédit
Capital Account: Debit	-2.2	-3.4	-1.9	-2.4	-0.5	-1.7	-2.1	Compte de capital : débit
Financial Account, nie	11.0	27.6	23.5	91.5	88.4	171.5	143.7	Compte d'op. fin., nia
Net Errors and Omissions	18.4	9.1	24.5	0.9	7.3	9.4	3.8	Erreurs et omissions nettes
Reserves & Related Items	-20.6	-1.4	13.7	-12.9	43.3	3.5	7.7	Rés. et postes appareutés
Benin								**Bénin**
Goods: Exports fob	527.7	424.0	414.3	421.5	392.4	373.5	...	Biens : exportations, fab
Goods: Imports fob	-559.7	-576.9	-572.6	-635.2	-516.1	-553.0	...	Biens : importations, fab
Serv. & Income: Credit	155.8	140.4	170.1	204.5	164.1	176.6	...	Serv. & revenu : crédit
Serv. & Income: Debit	-239.4	-216.7	-232.7	-254.4	-232.0	-234.8	...	Serv & revenu : débit
Current Trans.,nie: Credit	92.4	77.8	102.0	87.1	91.3	87.3	...	Transf. cour.,nia : crédit
Current Transfers: Debit	-34.2	-18.5	-32.7	-14.9	-10.7	-10.0	...	Transf. courants : débit
Capital Acct.,nie: Credit	6.4	84.5	66.6	69.9	73.4	70.0	...	Compte de cap.,nia : crédit
Capital Account: Debit	0.0	0.0	0.0	0.0	-0.1	0.0	...	Compte de capital : débit
Financial Account, nie	-104.2	-21.3	-8.9	25.4	10.8	40.5	...	Compte d'op. fin., nia
Net Errors and Omissions	6.3	6.7	7.1	7.3	6.7	3.6	...	Erreurs et omissions nettes
Reserves & Related Items	149.0	100.0	86.7	88.7	20.3	46.4	...	Rés. et postes appareutés
Bolivia								**Bolivie**
Goods: Exports fob	1 132.0	1 166.6	1 104.0	1 051.2	1 246.1	1 284.8	1 298.7	Biens : exportations, fab
Goods: Imports fob	-1 368.0	-1 643.6	-1 759.5	-1 539.0	-1 610.2	-1 477.4	-1 532.1	Biens : importations, fab
Serv. & Income: Credit	209.5	345.4	378.6	416.7	363.7	357.1	338.0	Serv. & revenu : crédit
Serv. & Income: Debit	-600.2	-713.4	-729.8	-803.0	-832.7	-834.8	-820.7	Serv & revenu : débit
Current Trans.,nie: Credit	226.2	300.3	352.3	414.7	420.0	431.6	404.8	Transf. cour.,nia : crédit
Current Transfers: Debit	-3.8	-8.8	-11.7	-28.6	-33.2	-35.5	-35.4	Transf. courants : débit
Capital Acct.,nie: Credit	2.8	25.3	9.9	0.0	0.0	0.0	0.0	Compte de cap.,nia : crédit
Capital Account: Debit	0.0	0.0	0.0	0.0	0.0	0.0	0.0	Compte de capital : débit
Financial Account, nie	701.0	889.9	1 181.6	868.2	461.8	447.2	726.9	Compte d'op. fin., nia
Net Errors and Omissions	-31.6	-260.7	-400.7	-353.2	-54.8	-209.0	-697.9	Erreurs et omissions nettes
Reserves & Related Items	-268.0	-101.0	-124.7	-27.0	39.4	36.0	317.7	Rés. et postes appareutés
Bosnia and Herzegovina								**Bosnie-Herzégovine**
Goods: Exports fob	...	...	663.8	831.8	1 173.6	1 131.2	1 115.1	Biens : exportations, fab
Goods: Imports fob	...	...	-3 779.5	-4 128.7	-3 795.9	-4 091.4	-4 518.8	Biens : importations, fab
Serv. & Income: Credit	...	...	822.3	775.0	683.8	699.0	641.4	Serv. & revenu : crédit
Serv. & Income: Debit	...	...	-249.7	-281.2	-264.4	-270.0	-315.5	Serv & revenu : débit
Current Trans.,nie: Credit	...	...	1 384.5	1 347.4	1 013.8	972.0	967.6	Transf. cour.,nia : crédit
Current Transfers: Debit	...	...	-2.8	-2.9	-3.2	-3.9	-28.4	Transf. courants : débit
Capital Acct.,nie: Credit	...	...	435.2	515.1	406.3	367.4	344.1	Compte de cap.,nia : crédit

79

Summary of balance of payments
Millions of US dollars *[cont.]*

Résumé des balances des paiements
Millions de dollars des E.-U. *[suite]*

Country or area	1996	1997	1998	1999	2000	2001	2002	Pays ou zone
Capital Account: Debit	...	...	0.0	0.0	0.0	0.0	0.0	Compte de capital : débit
Financial Account, nie	...	...	-15.8	345.9	491.2	1 384.6	1 206.8	Compte d'op. fin., nia
Net Errors and Omissions	...	...	-17.9	15.2	16.0	229.3	69.5	Erreurs et omissions nettes
Reserves & Related Items	...	...	759.8	582.4	278.8	-418.2	518.2	Rés. et postes appareutés
Botswana								**Botswana**
Goods: Exports fob	2 217.5	2 819.8	2 060.6	2 671.0	...	...	...	Biens : exportations, fab
Goods: Imports fob	-1 467.7	-1 924.5	-1 983.1	-1 996.5	...	...	...	Biens : importations, fab
Serv. & Income: Credit	664.7	832.3	878.0	802.4	...	...	...	Serv. & revenu : crédit
Serv. & Income: Debit	-1 098.4	-1 207.5	-1 025.5	-1 211.9	...	...	...	Serv & revenu : débit
Current Trans.,nie: Credit	355.4	456.8	460.9	474.4	...	...	...	Transf. cour.,nia : crédit
Current Transfers: Debit	-176.6	-255.5	-220.8	-222.6	...	...	...	Transf. courants : débit
Capital Acct.,nie: Credit	18.0	29.4	44.2	33.5	...	...	...	Compte de cap.,nie : crédit
Capital Account: Debit	-11.9	-12.5	-12.4	-12.9	...	...	...	Compte de capital : débit
Financial Account, nie	42.4	5.6	-202.4	-175.2	...	...	...	Compte d'op. fin., nia
Net Errors and Omissions	-32.9	-108.9	44.6	8.7	...	...	...	Erreurs et omissions nettes
Reserves & Related Items	-510.7	-635.1	-44.2	-371.0	...	...	...	Rés. et postes appareutés
Brazil								**Brésil**
Goods: Exports fob	47 851.0	53 189.0	51 136.0	48 011.0	55 085.6	58 222.6	60 361.8	Biens : exportations, fab
Goods: Imports fob	-53 304.0	-59 841.0	-57 739.0	-49 272.0	-55 783.3	-55 572.2	-47 218.8	Biens : importations, fab
Serv. & Income: Credit	10 005.0	11 333.0	12 545.0	11 125.0	13 119.1	12 601.5	12 900.9	Serv. & revenu : crédit
Serv. & Income: Debit	-30 241.0	-36 986.0	-41 207.0	-36 952.0	-38 167.0	-40 104.0	-36 129.7	Serv & revenu : débit
Current Trans.,nie: Credit	2 699.0	2 130.0	1 795.0	1 969.0	1 827.7	1 933.7	2 626.9	Transf. cour.,nia : crédit
Current Transfers: Debit	-258.0	-316.0	-359.0	-281.0	-306.6	-296.2	-237.0	Transf. courants : débit
Capital Acct.,nie: Credit	507.0	519.0	488.0	361.0	300.2	328.2	464.4	Compte de cap.,nie : crédit
Capital Account: Debit	-13.0	-37.0	-113.0	-22.0	-27.7	-364.2	-31.5	Compte de capital : débit
Financial Account, nie	33 428.0	24 918.0	20 063.0	8 056.0	29 376.2	20 331.3	-3 102.4	Compte d'op. fin., nia
Net Errors and Omissions	-1 991.6	-3 160.2	-2 910.7	239.6	2 557.1	-498.3	-901.0	Erreurs et omissions nettes
Reserves & Related Items	-8 682.4	8 251.2	16 301.7	16 765.4	-7 981.3	3 417.5	11 266.4	Rés. et postes appareutés
Bulgaria								**Bulgarie**
Goods: Exports fob	4 890.2	4 939.6	4 193.5	4 006.4	4 824.6	5 113.0	5 692.1	Biens : exportations, fab
Goods: Imports fob	-4 702.6	-4 559.3	-4 574.2	-5 087.4	-6 000.1	-6 693.3	-7 286.6	Biens : importations, fab
Serv. & Income: Credit	1 547.0	1 548.2	2 094.5	2 051.8	2 498.2	2 777.7	2 913.7	Serv. & revenu : crédit
Serv. & Income: Debit	-1 823.1	-1 738.4	-2 005.4	-1 955.3	-2 313.6	-2 538.0	-2 547.9	Serv & revenu : débit
Current Trans.,nie: Credit	231.8	275.5	261.4	328.7	354.1	598.5	655.6	Transf. cour.,nia : crédit
Current Transfers: Debit	-127.6	-38.7	-31.6	-28.9	-64.4	-100.1	-106.2	Transf. courants : débit
Capital Acct.,nie: Credit	65.9	0.0	0.0	0.0	25.0	0.0	0.0	Compte de cap.,nia : crédit
Capital Account: Debit	0.0	0.0	0.0	-2.4	0.0	-0.1	-0.1	Compte de capital : débit
Financial Account, nie	-715.0	462.0	266.7	777.4	883.3	1 126.0	1 420.8	Compte d'op. fin., nia
Net Errors and Omissions	-105.3	256.4	-299.2	6.1	-70.1	89.6	-26.3	Erreurs et omissions nettes
Reserves & Related Items	738.7	-1 145.4	94.3	-96.4	-137.0	-373.3	-715.2	Rés. et postes appareutés
Burkina Faso								**Burkina Faso**
Goods: Exports fob	223.5	...	...	...	...	...	...	Biens : exportations, fab
Goods: Imports fob	-509.3	...	...	...	...	...	...	Biens : importations, fab
Serv. & Income: Credit	51.7	...	...	...	...	...	...	Serv. & revenu : crédit
Serv. & Income: Debit	-180.9	...	...	...	...	...	...	Serv & revenu : débit
Current Trans.,nie: Credit	72.0	...	...	...	...	...	...	Transf. cour.,nia : crédit
Current Transfers: Debit	-37.9	...	...	...	...	...	...	Transf. courants : débit
Capital Acct.,nie: Credit	0.0	...	...	...	175.9	165.2	...	Compte de cap.,nie : crédit
Capital Account: Debit	0.0	...	...	...	0.0	0.0	...	Compte de capital : débit
Financial Account, nie	25.2	...	...	...	...	...	...	Compte d'op. fin., nia
Net Errors and Omissions	3.4	...	...	...	...	...	...	Erreurs et omissions nettes
Reserves & Related Items	187.0	...	...	...	...	...	...	Rés. et postes appareutés
Burundi								**Burundi**
Goods: Exports fob	40.4	87.5	64.0	55.0	49.1	39.2	31.0	Biens : exportations, fab
Goods: Imports fob	-100.0	-96.1	-123.5	-97.3	-107.9	-108.3	-104.0	Biens : importations, fab
Serv. & Income: Credit	16.9	13.0	11.2	8.2	8.5	8.7	8.5	Serv. & revenu : crédit
Serv. & Income: Debit	-58.7	-62.2	-61.4	-43.9	-57.3	-53.8	-55.9	Serv & revenu : débit
Current Trans.,nie: Credit	62.5	61.3	59.3	52.9	61.1	82.1	120.8	Transf. cour.,nia : crédit
Current Transfers: Debit	-1.1	-4.5	-3.3	-1.8	-1.8	-2.9	-3.3	Transf. courants : débit
Capital Acct.,nie: Credit	0.0	0.0	0.0	0.0	0.0	0.0	0.0	Compte de cap.,nia : crédit
Capital Account: Debit	-0.3	-0.1	0.0	0.0	0.0	0.0	-0.5	Compte de capital : débit
Financial Account, nie	14.1	13.7	28.8	17.0	58.9	16.1	18.0	Compte d'op. fin., nia

79

Summary of balance of payments
Millions of US dollars [cont.]

Résumé des balances des paiements
Millions de dollars des E.-U. [suite]

Country or area	1996	1997	1998	1999	2000	2001	2002	Pays ou zone
Net Errors and Omissions	-9.2	-21.4	-14.1	-13.5	-34.6	-32.8	-3.8	Erreurs et omissions nettes
Reserves & Related Items	35.3	8.8	39.0	23.5	23.9	51.6	-10.9	Rés. et postes appareutés
Cambodia								**Cambodge**
Goods: Exports fob	643.6	736.0	800.5	1 129.3	1 401.1	1 571.2	1 750.1	Biens : exportations, fab
Goods: Imports fob	-1 071.8	-1 064.0	-1 165.8	-1 591.0	-1 939.3	-2 094.0	-2 313.5	Biens : importations, fab
Serv. & Income: Credit	175.4	176.4	225.2	345.2	495.5	582.1	651.0	Serv. & revenu : crédit
Serv. & Income: Debit	-313.1	-246.5	-328.5	-441.7	-517.5	-540.6	-598.7	Serv & revenu : débit
Current Trans.,nie: Credit	383.4	188.5	299.0	378.0	432.0	403.8	456.5	Transf. cour.,nia : crédit
Current Transfers: Debit	-2.4	-0.3	-5.6	-7.6	-7.3	-8.3	-9.3	Transf. courants : débit
Capital Acct.,nie: Credit	75.8	65.2	89.5	78.7	79.8	102.8	76.7	Compte de cap.,nia : crédit
Capital Account: Debit	0.0	0.0	-94.3	-67.7	-44.2	-58.0	-63.4	Compte de capital : débit
Financial Account, nie	259.1	219.8	230.0	191.8	175.2	133.3	266.5	Compte d'op. fin., nia
Net Errors and Omissions	-78.0	-41.2	-31.3	29.9	16.6	-24.2	-50.2	Erreurs et omissions nettes
Reserves & Related Items	-72.0	-33.9	-18.7	-44.8	-92.0	-68.1	-165.7	Rés. et postes appareutés
Canada								**Canada**
Goods: Exports fob	205 443.0	219 063.0	220 539.0	248 494.0	289 468.0	272 359.0	264 078.0	Biens : exportations, fab
Goods: Imports fob	-174 352.0	-200 498.0	-204 617.0	-220 203.0	-243 889.0	-226 495.0	-227 240.0	Biens : importations, fab
Serv. & Income: Credit	48 446.4	55 594.1	55 665.9	58 275.0	64 638.3	55 333.8	57 369.3	Serv. & revenu : crédit
Serv. & Income: Debit	-76 660.9	-82 890.6	-79 971.6	-85 350.3	-90 465.8	-84 859.1	-80 169.3	Serv & revenu : débit
Current Trans.,nie: Credit	3 593.5	3 634.0	3 406.8	3 796.0	4 108.5	4 513.6	4 458.2	Transf. cour.,nia : crédit
Current Transfers: Debit	-3 091.8	-3 135.5	-2 862.9	-3 247.1	-3 264.7	-3 431.0	-3 587.6	Transf. courants : débit
Capital Acct.,nie: Credit	6 262.1	5 862.3	3 793.7	3 861.6	4 045.3	4 191.4	3 599.0	Compte de cap.,nia : crédit
Capital Account: Debit	-428.7	-433.0	-457.5	-461.5	-493.4	-518.6	-530.7	Compte de capital : débit
Financial Account, nie	-9 276.8	3 393.6	4 944.4	-5 968.2	-16 752.2	-13 013.1	-11 690.8	Compte d'op. fin., nia
Net Errors and Omissions	5 562.8	-2 983.0	4 555.1	6 736.1	-3 674.3	-5 909.2	-6 471.4	Erreurs et omissions nettes
Reserves & Related Items	-5 497.7	2 393.1	-4 996.3	-5 933.1	-3 720.0	-2 172.2	185.2	Rés. et postes appareutés
Cape Verde								**Cap-Vert**
Goods: Exports fob	23.9	43.2	32.7	26.0	38.3	37.2	41.8	Biens : exportations, fab
Goods: Imports fob	-207.5	-215.1	-218.8	-239.0	-225.7	-231.5	-278.0	Biens : importations, fab
Serv. & Income: Credit	80.5	96.2	89.0	107.0	112.6	137.2	159.2	Serv. & revenu : crédit
Serv. & Income: Debit	-77.4	-80.4	-98.7	-126.2	-117.9	-131.7	-160.3	Serv & revenu : débit
Current Trans.,nie: Credit	148.4	129.9	142.5	167.1	146.3	155.5	181.6	Transf. cour.,nia : crédit
Current Transfers: Debit	-2.9	-3.6	-5.1	-9.0	-11.7	-22.5	-15.7	Transf. courants : débit
Capital Acct.,nie: Credit	12.8	6.3	19.0	4.5	10.8	24.4	8.6	Compte de cap.,nia : crédit
Capital Account: Debit	0.0	0.0	0.0	0.0	0.0	0.0	0.0	Compte de capital : débit
Financial Account, nie	46.0	44.1	37.0	127.8	31.5	38.5	80.7	Compte d'op. fin., nia
Net Errors and Omissions	-1.3	-20.4	13.3	-8.7	-12.0	-23.9	-7.7	Erreurs et omissions nettes
Reserves & Related Items	-22.5	-0.2	-10.8	-49.3	27.8	16.7	-10.1	Rés. et postes appareutés
Chile								**Chili**
Goods: Exports fob	16 626.8	17 870.2	16 322.8	17 162.3	19 210.2	18 465.8	18 340.1	Biens : exportations, fab
Goods: Imports fob	-17 698.8	-19 297.8	-18 363.1	-14 735.1	-17 091.4	-16 411.4	-15 826.7	Biens : importations, fab
Serv. & Income: Credit	4 594.4	5 065.5	5 326.1	5 008.9	5 662.2	5 373.7	5 259.1	Serv. & revenu : crédit
Serv. & Income: Debit	-7 112.6	-7 818.4	-7 666.6	-7 979.2	-9 105.3	-9 048.3	-8 751.7	Serv & revenu : débit
Current Trans.,nie: Credit	665.2	835.0	809.9	840.9	765.3	678.4	698.1	Transf. cour.,nia : crédit
Current Transfers: Debit	-157.6	-314.7	-347.5	-198.4	-207.3	-250.4	-271.7	Transf. courants : débit
Capital Acct.,nie: Credit	0.0	0.0	0.0	0.0	0.0	0.0	0.0	Compte de cap.,nia : crédit
Capital Account: Debit	0.0	0.0	0.0	0.0	0.0	0.0	0.0	Compte de capital : débit
Financial Account, nie	5 660.4	6 742.1	1 966.5	237.5	827.7	1 760.4	998.7	Compte d'op. fin., nia
Net Errors and Omissions	16.1	236.6	-239.3	-1 083.4	255.2	-1 167.1	-260.8	Erreurs et omissions nettes
Reserves & Related Items	-2 593.9	-3 318.5	2 191.3	746.5	-316.5	599.0	-185.0	Rés. et postes appareutés
China								**Chine**
Goods: Exports fob	151 077.0	182 670.0	183 529.0	194 716.0	249 131.0	266 075.0	325 651.0	Biens : exportations, fab
Goods: Imports fob	-131 542.0	-136 448.0	-136 915.0	-158 734.0	-214 657.0	-232 058.0	-281 484.0	Biens : importations, fab
Serv. & Income: Credit	27 919.0	30 279.0	29 479.0	34 578.0	42 980.4	42 722.0	48 088.5	Serv. & revenu : crédit
Serv. & Income: Debit	-42 340.0	-44 682.0	-48 900.0	-54 389.0	-63 246.9	-67 830.0	-69 817.5	Serv & revenu : débit
Current Trans.,nie: Credit	2 368.0	5 477.0	4 661.0	5 368.0	6 860.8	9 125.0	13 795.4	Transf. cour.,nia : crédit
Current Transfers: Debit	-239.0	-333.0	-382.0	-424.0	-549.5	-633.0	-810.9	Transf. courants : débit
Capital Acct.,nie: Credit	0.0	0.0	0.0	0.0	0.0	0.0	0.0	Compte de cap.,nia : crédit
Capital Account: Debit	0.0	-21.0	-47.0	-26.0	-35.3	-54.0	-49.6	Compte de capital : débit
Financial Account, nie	39 966.0	21 037.0	-6 275.0	5 204.0	1 957.9	34 832.0	32 341.0	Compte d'op. fin., nia
Net Errors and Omissions	-15 504.0	-22 121.8	-18 901.8	-17 640.5	-11 747.9	-4 732.5	7 503.5	Erreurs et omissions nettes
Reserves & Related Items	-31 705.0	-35 857.2	-6 248.2	-8 652.5	-10 693.1	-47 446.5	-75 216.9	Rés. et postes appareutés

79

Summary of balance of payments
Millions of US dollars *[cont.]*

Résumé des balances des paiements
Millions de dollars des E.-U. *[suite]*

Country or area	1996	1997	1998	1999	2000	2001	2002	Pays ou zone
China, Hong Kong SAR								**Chine, Hong Kong RAS**
Goods: Exports fob	...	...	175 833.0	174 719.0	202 698.0	190 926.0	200 220.0	Biens : exportations, fab
Goods: Imports fob	...	...	-183 666.0	-177 878.0	-210 891.0	-199 257.0	-205 352.0	Biens : importations, fab
Serv. & Income: Credit	...	...	81 963.3	83 013.6	94 253.0	90 743.3	86 715.4	Serv. & revenu : crédit
Serv. & Income: Debit	...	...	-68 107.8	-66 273.4	-75 282.9	-68 349.6	-62 245.2	Serv & revenu : débit
Current Trans.,nie: Credit	...	...	668.7	569.5	538.2	605.1	686.9	Transf. cour.,nia : crédit
Current Transfers: Debit	...	...	-2 265.0	-2 109.3	-2 208.3	-2 384.6	-2 542.7	Transf. courants : débit
Capital Acct.,nie: Credit	...	...	377.4	103.3	56.5	41.3	27.3	Compte de cap.,nia : crédit
Capital Account: Debit	...	...	-2 759.0	-1 883.3	-1 602.2	-1 215.3	-2 043.6	Compte de capital : débit
Financial Account, nie	...	...	-8 475.8	1 060.9	4 165.4	-6 626.3	-24 906.1	Compte d'op. fin., nia
Net Errors and Omissions	...	...	-358.1	-1 294.6	-1 682.5	201.3	7 061.9	Erreurs et omissions nettes
Reserves & Related Items	...	...	6 789.1	-10 027.7	-10 043.7	-4 684.0	2 377.4	Rés. et postes appareutés
Colombia								**Colombie**
Goods: Exports fob	10 966.2	12 064.9	11 480.1	12 037.3	13 620.2	12 772.0	12 302.5	Biens : exportations, fab
Goods: Imports fob	-13 057.8	-14 702.7	-13 930.0	-10 262.1	-11 089.6	-12 268.9	-12 077.5	Biens : importations, fab
Serv. & Income: Credit	2 907.7	3 075.1	2 904.0	2 863.2	3 087.0	3 084.0	2 563.2	Serv. & revenu : crédit
Serv. & Income: Debit	-6 163.6	-6 901.5	-6 062.4	-5 422.2	-6 661.1	-7 101.2	-6 833.2	Serv & revenu : débit
Current Trans.,nie: Credit	923.6	930.7	912.3	1 703.0	1 907.5	2 564.8	2 710.7	Transf. cour.,nia : crédit
Current Transfers: Debit	-217.7	-217.4	-161.9	-248.4	-238.2	-301.5	-304.3	Transf. courants : débit
Capital Acct.,nie: Credit	0.0	0.0	0.0	0.0	0.0	0.0	0.0	Compte de cap.,nia : crédit
Capital Account: Debit	0.0	0.0	0.0	0.0	0.0	0.0	0.0	Compte de capital : débit
Financial Account, nie	6 683.0	6 587.5	3 306.9	-551.0	-23.6	2 397.1	1 295.3	Compte d'op. fin., nia
Net Errors and Omissions	-311.9	-558.7	153.4	-431.8	259.6	79.0	482.1	Erreurs et omissions nettes
Reserves & Related Items	-1 729.5	-277.9	1 397.6	311.9	-861.7	-1 225.4	-138.8	Rés. et postes appareutés
Congo								**Congo**
Goods: Exports fob	1 654.9	1 661.5	1 367.8	1 560.1	2 491.8	2 055.3	2 288.8	Biens : exportations, fab
Goods: Imports fob	-587.2	-648.8	-558.4	-522.7	-455.3	-681.3	-691.1	Biens : importations, fab
Serv. & Income: Credit	101.2	105.6	121.6	175.6	150.5	159.1	171.0	Serv. & revenu : crédit
Serv. & Income: Debit	-1 850.8	-1 276.1	-1 168.5	-1 438.4	-1 557.7	-1 546.2	-1 793.3	Serv & revenu : débit
Current Trans.,nie: Credit	54.5	9.0	10.0	14.9	38.9	18.3	12.9	Transf. cour.,nia : crédit
Current Transfers: Debit	-23.5	-6.9	-13.0	-20.2	-20.1	-33.5	-22.7	Transf. courants : débit
Capital Acct.,nie: Credit	11.6	17.5	0.0	10.3	8.9	13.3	5.3	Compte de cap.,nia : crédit
Capital Account: Debit	-0.7	0.0	-0.2	-0.1	-0.6	-0.7	0.0	Compte de capital : débit
Financial Account, nie	-663.4	-604.5	-715.9	-336.2	-821.8	-653.1	-464.3	Compte d'op. fin., nia
Net Errors and Omissions	-12.8	60.5	-72.0	-99.0	-77.6	-11.8	-219.7	Erreurs et omissions nettes
Reserves & Related Items	1 316.1	682.4	1 028.6	655.6	242.8	680.6	713.1	Rés. et postes appareutés
Costa Rica								**Costa Rica**
Goods: Exports fob	3 774.1	4 220.6	5 538.3	6 576.8	5 813.4	4 923.2	5 259.3	Biens : exportations, fab
Goods: Imports fob	-4 023.3	-4 718.2	-5 937.4	-5 996.3	-6 024.7	-5 744.5	-6 522.7	Biens : importations, fab
Serv. & Income: Credit	1 196.0	1 314.0	1 526.1	1 858.8	2 193.1	2 095.0	2 025.6	Serv. & revenu : crédit
Serv. & Income: Debit	-1 360.0	-1 422.8	-1 761.0	-3 221.8	-2 780.5	-2 157.9	-1 877.6	Serv & revenu : débit
Current Trans.,nie: Credit	192.7	191.9	190.5	190.8	192.3	248.8	274.5	Transf. cour.,nia : crédit
Current Transfers: Debit	-43.2	-65.7	-77.3	-88.4	-100.1	-100.9	-105.5	Transf. courants : débit
Capital Acct.,nie: Credit	28.2	0.0	0.0	0.0	8.9	12.4	5.7	Compte de cap.,nia : crédit
Capital Account: Debit	0.0	0.0	0.0	0.0	0.0	0.0	0.0	Compte de capital : débit
Financial Account, nie	47.5	129.7	199.0	568.0	-81.3	484.6	758.5	Compte d'op. fin., nia
Net Errors and Omissions	118.7	157.8	-182.5	213.4	154.8	103.4	144.8	Erreurs et omissions nettes
Reserves & Related Items	69.3	193.3	504.3	-101.3	624.2	136.0	37.4	Rés. et postes appareutés
Côte d'Ivoire								**Côte d'Ivoire**
Goods: Exports fob	4 446.1	4 451.2	4 606.5	4 661.4	3 888.0	3 945.9	5 166.6	Biens : exportations, fab
Goods: Imports fob	-2 622.4	-2 658.4	-2 886.5	-2 766.0	-2 401.8	-2 417.8	-2 432.0	Biens : importations, fab
Serv. & Income: Credit	736.4	740.8	783.5	748.6	623.9	715.2	725.5	Serv. & revenu : crédit
Serv. & Income: Debit	-2 379.8	-2 307.8	-2 400.0	-2 378.4	-2 021.4	-1 993.3	-2 211.0	Serv & revenu : débit
Current Trans.,nie: Credit	204.1	137.7	148.1	136.8	79.4	88.5	77.0	Transf. cour.,nia : crédit
Current Transfers: Debit	-546.6	-518.3	-541.7	-522.7	-409.4	-398.7	-558.9	Transf. courants : débit
Capital Acct.,nie: Credit	49.8	50.5	35.9	17.4	9.9	11.5	10.0	Compte de cap.,nia : crédit
Capital Account: Debit	-2.7	-9.9	-10.3	-3.6	-1.4	-1.4	-1.5	Compte de capital : débit
Financial Account, nie	-717.8	-323.0	-417.0	-577.2	-362.5	-63.8	-1 101.1	Compte d'op. fin., nia
Net Errors and Omissions	-15.4	-39.6	32.0	-24.0	-13.0	27.8	-30.3	Erreurs et omissions nettes
Reserves & Related Items	848.4	476.6	649.6	707.8	608.3	86.1	355.7	Rés. et postes appareutés
Croatia								**Croatie**
Goods: Exports fob	4 677.5	4 021.1	4 580.6	4 394.7	4 567.2	4 758.7	4 994.6	Biens : exportations, fab

79
Summary of balance of payments
Millions of US dollars *[cont.]*

Résumé des balances des paiements
Millions de dollars des E.-U. *[suite]*

Country or area	1996	1997	1998	1999	2000	2001	2002	Pays ou zone
Goods: Imports fob	-8 165.5	-9 404.1	-8 652.1	-7 693.3	-7 770.9	-8 860.0	-10 273.9	Biens : importations, fab
Serv. & Income: Credit	3 463.1	4 348.3	4 343.9	3 977.9	4 441.7	5 293.5	5 975.4	Serv. & revenu : crédit
Serv. & Income: Debit	-2 046.7	-2 660.0	-2 446.2	-2 708.9	-2 580.5	-2 883.5	-3 378.1	Serv & revenu : débit
Current Trans.,nie: Credit	1 173.3	963.8	919.1	967.4	1 101.0	1 174.5	1 358.5	Transf. cour.,nia : crédit
Current Transfers: Debit	-150.8	-94.5	-213.3	-335.0	-217.8	-208.8	-282.3	Transf. courants : débit
Capital Acct.,nie: Credit	18.0	23.5	24.1	28.2	24.4	137.6	450.1	Compte de cap.,nia : crédit
Capital Account: Debit	-1.8	-2.2	-5.0	-3.4	-3.6	-4.6	-6.7	Compte de capital : débit
Financial Account, nie	2 996.3	3 020.8	1 610.3	2 331.1	1 929.4	2 528.4	3 037.8	Compte d'op. fin., nia
Net Errors and Omissions	-946.1	173.7	-0.9	-548.7	-880.1	-593.7	-1 049.5	Erreurs et omissions nettes
Reserves & Related Items	-1 017.3	-390.4	-160.5	-410.0	-610.7	-1 342.1	-825.9	Rés. et postes appareutés
Cyprus								**Chypre**
Goods: Exports fob	1 392.4	1 245.8	1 064.6	1 000.3	951.0	976.5	843.6	Biens : exportations, fab
Goods: Imports fob	-3 575.7	-3 317.2	-3 490.4	-3 309.5	-3 556.5	-3 526.9	-3 702.7	Biens : importations, fab
Serv. & Income: Credit	3 231.5	3 209.8	3 371.4	3 608.4	3 714.9	3 916.8	4 993.7	Serv. & revenu : crédit
Serv. & Income: Debit	-1 547.0	-1 502.4	-1 577.9	-1 603.8	-1 690.9	-1 782.7	-2 717.6	Serv & revenu : débit
Current Trans.,nie: Credit	43.1	40.9	49.6	113.6	153.3	49.3	226.6	Transf. cour.,nia : crédit
Current Transfers: Debit	-9.9	-15.0	-20.3	-26.3	-27.5	-27.7	-160.6	Transf. courants : débit
Capital Acct.,nie: Credit	0.0	0.0	0.0	0.0	0.0	0.0	0.0	Compte de cap.,nia : crédit
Capital Account: Debit	0.0	0.0	0.0	0.0	0.0	0.0	0.0	Compte de capital : débit
Financial Account, nie	419.0	383.7	657.9	1 006.4	263.5	845.7	850.7	Compte d'op. fin., nia
Net Errors and Omissions	-13.3	-92.5	-137.6	-150.0	184.0	161.4	60.8	Erreurs et omissions nettes
Reserves & Related Items	59.8	47.0	82.5	-639.0	8.2	-612.3	-389.0	Rés. et postes appareutés
Czech Republic								**République tchèque**
Goods: Exports fob	21 950.3	22 318.6	25 885.5	26 258.9	29 019.3	33 403.6	38 479.7	Biens : exportations, fab
Goods: Imports fob	-27 656.2	-27 257.1	-28 532.5	-28 161.3	-32 114.5	-36 481.6	-40 719.7	Biens : importations, fab
Serv. & Income: Credit	9 350.6	8 536.6	9 377.8	8 907.7	8 791.3	9 324.8	9 276.7	Serv. & revenu : crédit
Serv. & Income: Debit	-8 156.2	-7 585.4	-8 556.0	-9 058.8	-8 758.8	-9 989.3	-12 433.6	Serv & revenu : débit
Current Trans.,nie: Credit	616.6	866.0	1 066.5	1 309.7	948.0	958.9	1 464.7	Transf. cour.,nia : crédit
Current Transfers: Debit	-232.6	-500.6	-549.7	-722.0	-575.1	-488.9	-552.6	Transf. courants : débit
Capital Acct.,nie: Credit	1.0	16.7	13.8	18.4	5.8	2.4	6.7	Compte de cap.,nia : crédit
Capital Account: Debit	-0.5	-5.5	-11.6	-20.5	-10.9	-11.3	-10.7	Compte de capital : débit
Financial Account, nie	4 202.5	1 122.2	2 908.2	3 079.8	3 834.9	4 569.3	11 235.3	Compte d'op. fin., nia
Net Errors and Omissions	-900.7	730.0	288.3	27.4	-296.4	499.3	-128.2	Erreurs et omissions nettes
Reserves & Related Items	825.2	1 758.4	-1 890.4	-1 639.3	-843.6	-1 787.1	-6 618.2	Rés. et postes appareutés
Denmark								**Danemark**
Goods: Exports fob	50 734.7	48 102.9	47 907.8	49 932.0	50 183.3	50 502.2	55 586.1	Biens : exportations, fab
Goods: Imports fob	-43 202.5	-42 734.2	-44 021.5	-43 533.0	-43 442.8	-43 050.8	-47 278.6	Biens : importations, fab
Serv. & Income: Credit	54 128.5	32 817.7	25 612.8	29 189.9	35 922.5	36 258.4	39 451.5	Serv. & revenu : crédit
Serv. & Income: Debit	-57 005.8	-35 929.8	-30 026.4	-29 942.6	-37 236.7	-36 372.4	-40 155.9	Serv & revenu : débit
Current Trans.,nie: Credit	2 398.3	3 632.9	3 442.8	4 156.2	3 395.1	3 876.7	4 119.5	Transf. cour.,nia : crédit
Current Transfers: Debit	-3 963.4	-4 968.0	-4 923.7	-6 887.6	-6 409.6	-6 293.6	-6 731.5	Transf. courants : débit
Capital Acct.,nie: Credit	0.0	127.8	81.3	1 330.8	320.1	253.1	351.3	Compte de cap.,nia : crédit
Capital Account: Debit	0.0	0.0	-31.3	-247.7	-334.0	-278.2	-250.7	Compte de capital : débit
Financial Account, nie	1 882.0	8 495.6	-1 489.1	6 247.2	-3 830.0	-5 145.9	2 525.0	Compte d'op. fin., nia
Net Errors and Omissions	-1 408.3	-3 012.5	-792.3	-807.8	-4 217.1	3 520.1	-2 001.2	Erreurs et omissions nettes
Reserves & Related Items	-3 563.3	-6 532.1	4 239.4	-9 437.3	5 649.3	-3 269.7	-5 615.5	Rés. et postes appareutés
Dominica								**Dominique**
Goods: Exports fob	52.9	53.8	63.2	56.0	54.7	44.4	...	Biens : exportations, fab
Goods: Imports fob	-117.2	-118.7	-116.4	-121.6	-130.4	-115.3	...	Biens : importations, fab
Serv. & Income: Credit	71.8	87.0	93.1	105.4	94.4	79.4	...	Serv. & revenu : crédit
Serv. & Income: Debit	-68.8	-74.7	-75.7	-89.3	-90.4	-74.8	...	Serv & revenu : débit
Current Trans.,nie: Credit	17.8	17.4	19.9	20.5	25.1	24.8	...	Transf. cour.,nia : crédit
Current Transfers: Debit	-7.7	-7.1	-7.2	-6.9	-7.0	-7.3	...	Transf. courants : débit
Capital Acct.,nie: Credit	25.4	22.6	14.9	12.1	9.7	18.1	...	Compte de cap.,nia : crédit
Capital Account: Debit	-0.1	-0.1	-0.1	-0.3	-1.5	-0.1	...	Compte de capital : débit
Financial Account, nie	6.1	25.8	-1.7	37.3	46.4	27.5	...	Compte d'op. fin., nia
Net Errors and Omissions	22.0	-5.5	13.3	-2.1	-0.6	7.9	...	Erreurs et omissions nettes
Reserves & Related Items	-2.2	-0.6	-3.5	-11.0	-0.5	-4.5	...	Rés. et postes appareutés
Dominican Republic								**Rép. dominicaine**
Goods: Exports fob	4 052.8	4 613.7	4 980.5	5 136.7	5 736.7	5 276.3	5 183.4	Biens : exportations, fab
Goods: Imports fob	-5 727.0	-6 608.7	-7 597.3	-8 041.1	-9 478.5	-8 779.3	-8 882.5	Biens : importations, fab
Serv. & Income: Credit	2 270.3	2 587.0	2 669.7	3 068.6	3 527.3	3 381.5	3 355.5	Serv. & revenu : crédit

79

Summary of balance of payments
Millions of US dollars *[cont.]*

Résumé des balances des paiements
Millions de dollars des E.-U. *[suite]*

Country or area	1996	1997	1998	1999	2000	2001	2002	Pays ou zone
Serv. & Income: Debit	-1 976.5	-2 107.1	-2 377.8	-2 441.2	-2 714.3	-2 646.8	-2 719.9	Serv & revenu : débit
Current Trans.,nie: Credit	1 187.6	1 373.1	2 016.9	1 997.1	2 095.6	2 232.0	2 424.7	Transf. cour.,nia : crédit
Current Transfers: Debit	-19.9	-21.0	-30.4	-149.3	-193.3	-204.5	-236.3	Transf. courants : débit
Capital Acct.,nie: Credit	0.0	0.0	0.0	0.0	0.0	0.0	0.0	Compte de cap.,nia : crédit
Capital Account: Debit	0.0	0.0	0.0	0.0	0.0	0.0	0.0	Compte de capital : débit
Financial Account, nie	64.1	447.6	688.1	1 061.0	1 596.6	1 707.4	1 289.2	Compte d'op. fin., nia
Net Errors and Omissions	108.8	-193.7	-338.6	-480.4	-618.5	-451.9	-966.3	Erreurs et omissions nettes
Reserves & Related Items	39.8	-90.9	-11.1	-151.4	48.4	-514.7	552.2	Rés. et postes appareutés
Ecuador								**Equateur**
Goods: Exports fob	4 929.4	5 360.5	4 326.2	4 615.5	5 137.2	4 862.3	5 192.0	Biens : exportations, fab
Goods: Imports fob	-4 008.1	-4 869.1	-5 457.9	-3 027.9	-3 742.6	-5 324.7	-6 196.0	Biens : importations, fab
Serv. & Income: Credit	763.3	814.5	797.7	804.7	919.8	959.0	1 010.5	Serv. & revenu : crédit
Serv. & Income: Debit	-2 231.2	-2 383.6	-2 531.4	-2 563.7	-2 745.2	-2 840.8	-2 882.0	Serv & revenu : débit
Current Trans.,nie: Credit	615.9	738.2	933.0	1 188.2	1 436.8	1 550.1	1 659.1	Transf. cour.,nia : crédit
Current Transfers: Debit	-124.2	-117.3	-166.1	-98.7	-85.0	-5.6	-5.3	Transf. courants : débit
Capital Acct.,nie: Credit	18.1	17.0	22.7	11.3	8.1	16.7	23.8	Compte de cap.,nia : crédit
Capital Account: Debit	-3.7	-6.0	-8.6	-9.2	-9.5	-84.1	-4.0	Compte de capital : débit
Financial Account, nie	103.4	-14.1	1 447.6	-1 343.5	-6 602.3	1 007.2	984.7	Compte d'op. fin., nia
Net Errors and Omissions	-189.1	-61.6	-147.3	-521.0	-14.5	-399.5	-3.4	Erreurs et omissions nettes
Reserves & Related Items	126.2	521.4	784.1	944.3	5 697.3	259.3	220.6	Rés. et postes appareutés
Egypt								**Egypte**
Goods: Exports fob	4 779.0	5 525.3	4 403.0	5 236.5	7 061.0	7 024.9	7 117.7	Biens : exportations, fab
Goods: Imports fob	-13 169.0	-14 156.8	-14 617.0	-15 164.8	-15 382.0	-13 959.6	-12 879.4	Biens : importations, fab
Serv. & Income: Credit	11 172.0	11 501.4	10 171.0	11 281.5	11 674.0	10 510.7	10 018.4	Serv. & revenu : crédit
Serv. & Income: Debit	-6 640.0	-7 955.0	-7 567.0	-7 496.4	-8 496.0	-7 921.6	-7 594.2	Serv & revenu : débit
Current Trans.,nie: Credit	3 888.0	4 737.7	5 166.0	4 563.8	4 224.0	4 055.6	4 001.6	Transf. cour.,nia : crédit
Current Transfers: Debit	-222.0	-363.1	-122.0	-55.4	-52.0	-98.4	-41.7	Transf. courants : débit
Capital Acct.,nie: Credit	0.0	0.0	0.0	0.0	0.0	0.0	0.0	Compte de cap.,nia : crédit
Capital Account: Debit	0.0	0.0	0.0	0.0	0.0	0.0	0.0	Compte de capital : débit
Financial Account, nie	-1 459.0	1 957.8	1 901.0	-1 421.4	-1 646.0	189.8	-3 332.7	Compte d'op. fin., nia
Net Errors and Omissions	-73.6	-1 882.3	-721.9	-1 557.6	586.8	-1 146.1	1 906.5	Erreurs et omissions nettes
Reserves & Related Items	1 724.6	635.1	1 386.9	4 613.8	2 030.2	1 344.7	803.8	Rés. et postes appareutés
El Salvador								**El Salvador**
Goods: Exports fob	1 787.4	2 437.1	2 459.5	2 534.3	2 963.2	2 890.8	3 016.8	Biens : exportations, fab
Goods: Imports fob	-3 029.7	-3 580.3	-3 765.2	-3 890.4	-4 702.8	-4 796.0	-4 922.3	Biens : importations, fab
Serv. & Income: Credit	458.5	550.9	699.8	753.3	839.7	865.1	915.5	Serv. & revenu : crédit
Serv. & Income: Debit	-639.1	-866.4	-1 011.7	-1 218.0	-1 327.7	-1 434.0	-1 396.8	Serv & revenu : débit
Current Trans.,nie: Credit	1 258.6	1 363.6	1 534.1	1 590.5	1 830.3	2 359.2	2 079.5	Transf. cour.,nia : crédit
Current Transfers: Debit	-4.8	-2.7	-7.3	-9.0	-33.2	-75.2	-76.5	Transf. courants : débit
Capital Acct.,nie: Credit	0.0	11.6	28.9	78.8	109.4	197.8	72.2	Compte de cap.,nia : crédit
Capital Account: Debit	0.0	0.0	-0.3	-0.2	-0.4	-0.1	-0.5	Compte de capital : débit
Financial Account, nie	358.1	653.2	1 034.3	574.5	287.4	127.3	364.6	Compte d'op. fin., nia
Net Errors and Omissions	-24.2	-204.4	-668.9	-206.0	-11.4	-312.6	-176.0	Erreurs et omissions nettes
Reserves & Related Items	-164.8	-362.7	-303.3	-207.8	45.5	177.7	123.5	Rés. et postes appareutés
Equatorial Guinea								**Guinée équatoriale**
Goods: Exports fob	175.3	...	...	...	...	...	...	Biens : exportations, fab
Goods: Imports fob	-292.0	...	...	...	...	...	...	Biens : importations, fab
Serv. & Income: Credit	5.0	...	...	...	...	...	...	Serv. & revenu : crédit
Serv. & Income: Debit	-229.8	...	...	...	...	...	...	Serv & revenu : débit
Current Trans.,nie: Credit	4.0	...	...	...	...	...	...	Transf. cour.,nia : crédit
Current Transfers: Debit	-6.6	...	...	...	...	...	...	Transf. courants : débit
Capital Acct.,nie: Credit	0.0	...	...	...	...	...	...	Compte de cap.,nia : crédit
Capital Account: Debit	0.0	...	...	...	...	...	...	Compte de capital : débit
Financial Account, nie	313.8	...	...	...	...	...	...	Compte d'op. fin., nia
Net Errors and Omissions	24.8	...	...	...	...	...	...	Erreurs et omissions nettes
Reserves & Related Items	5.5	...	...	...	...	...	...	Rés. et postes appareutés
Eritrea								**Erythrée**
Goods: Exports fob	98.0	56.8	28.1	20.7	36.8	...	...	Biens : exportations, fab
Goods: Imports fob	-552.8	-525.3	-508.3	-510.2	-471.4	...	...	Biens : importations, fab
Serv. & Income: Credit	113.2	170.0	93.3	56.0	70.1	...	...	Serv. & revenu : crédit
Serv. & Income: Debit	-69.3	-114.7	-194.3	-106.7	-38.9	...	...	Serv & revenu : débit
Current Trans.,nie: Credit	354.6	423.5	293.3	346.5	306.1	...	...	Transf. cour.,nia : crédit

79

Summary of balance of payments
Millions of US dollars *[cont.]*

Résumé des balances des paiements
Millions de dollars des E.-U. *[suite]*

Country or area	1996	1997	1998	1999	2000	2001	2002	Pays ou zone
Current Transfers: Debit	-3.5	-5.3	-4.9	-15.1	-7.3	...	...	Transf. courants : débit
Capital Acct.,nie: Credit	0.0	0.0	2.7	0.6	0.0	...	...	Compte de cap.,nia : crédit
Capital Account: Debit	0.0	0.0	0.0	0.0	0.0	...	...	Compte de capital : débit
Financial Account, nie	181.4	255.4	197.0	196.3	63.2	...	...	Compte d'op. fin., nia
Net Errors and Omissions	-64.5	-140.4	-66.5	12.8	-22.9	...	...	Erreurs et omissions nettes
Reserves & Related Items	-57.1	-120.1	159.5	-0.9	64.3	...	...	Rés. et postes appareutés
Estonia								**Estonie**
Goods: Exports fob	1 812.4	2 289.6	2 690.1	2 453.1	3 311.4	3 359.7	3 517.5	Biens : exportations, fab
Goods: Imports fob	-2 831.5	-3 413.7	-3 805.4	-3 330.6	-4 079.5	-4 148.4	-4 621.0	Biens : importations, fab
Serv. & Income: Credit	1 220.5	1 433.1	1 613.2	1 623.5	1 616.5	1 820.6	2 185.6	Serv. & revenu : crédit
Serv. & Income: Debit	-700.2	-987.4	-1 124.7	-1 153.1	-1 258.1	-1 522.7	-2 027.8	Serv & revenu : débit
Current Trans.,nie: Credit	116.8	135.3	172.9	153.7	144.7	181.4	205.5	Transf. cour.,nia : crédit
Current Transfers: Debit	-16.3	-18.6	-24.6	-41.3	-29.1	-29.4	-61.3	Transf. courants : débit
Capital Acct.,nie: Credit	0.2	0.7	2.1	1.4	16.8	5.5	20.1	Compte de cap.,nia : crédit
Capital Account: Debit	-0.8	-0.9	-0.3	-0.2	-0.2	-0.4	-1.0	Compte de capital : débit
Financial Account, nie	540.9	802.8	508.1	418.2	392.9	269.4	805.0	Compte d'op. fin., nia
Net Errors and Omissions	-35.6	-25.1	5.9	-5.5	12.2	22.3	46.8	Erreurs et omissions nettes
Reserves & Related Items	-106.3	-215.9	-37.3	-119.3	-127.6	41.9	-69.3	Rés. et postes appareutés
Ethiopia								**Ethiopie**
Goods: Exports fob	417.5	588.3	560.3	467.4	486.0	455.6	480.2	Biens : exportations, fab
Goods: Imports fob	-1 002.8	-1 001.6	-1 359.8	-1 387.2	-1 131.4	-1 625.8	-1 455.0	Biens : importations, fab
Serv. & Income: Credit	418.4	415.0	412.5	490.3	522.4	539.2	599.7	Serv. & revenu : crédit
Serv. & Income: Debit	-424.9	-459.8	-519.8	-516.8	-542.7	-573.9	-619.5	Serv & revenu : débit
Current Trans.,nie: Credit	679.0	425.5	589.8	500.7	697.9	774.6	865.5	Transf. cour.,nia : crédit
Current Transfers: Debit	-7.5	-7.6	-15.7	-19.7	-17.6	-24.0	-20.5	Transf. courants : débit
Capital Acct.,nie: Credit	0.9	0.0	1.4	1.8	0.0	0.0	0.0	Compte de cap.,nia : crédit
Capital Account: Debit	0.0	0.0	0.0	0.0	0.0	0.0	0.0	Compte de capital : débit
Financial Account, nie	-499.6	241.2	-21.3	-180.1	22.8	-175.2	-79.0	Compte d'op. fin., nia
Net Errors and Omissions	-45.8	-629.5	-7.9	407.2	-233.0	-141.7	-858.4	Erreurs et omissions nettes
Reserves & Related Items	464.8	428.6	360.4	236.3	195.6	771.3	1 087.0	Rés. et postes appareutés
Euro Area								**Zone euro**
Goods: Exports fob	...	...	878 676.0	870 875.0	911 010.0	925 452.0	1 000 940.0	Biens : exportations, fab
Goods: Imports fob	...	...	-756 382.0	-790 353.0	-882 204.0	-859 848.0	-876 927.0	Biens : importations, fab
Serv. & Income: Credit	...	...	481 900.0	483 245.0	511 027.0	538 313.0	551 616.0	Serv. & revenu : crédit
Serv. & Income: Debit	...	...	-521 121.0	-540 223.0	-552 061.0	-571 358.0	-566 653.0	Serv & revenu : débit
Current Trans.,nie: Credit	...	...	70 062.7	69 683.3	62 258.4	70 930.8	80 230.4	Transf. cour.,nia : crédit
Current Transfers: Debit	...	...	-123 105.0	-118 399.0	-111 989.0	-116 417.0	-124 818.0	Transf. courants : débit
Capital Acct.,nie: Credit	...	...	19 851.5	20 309.7	16 811.8	15 561.4	17 861.1	Compte de cap.,nia : crédit
Capital Account: Debit	...	...	-5 934.8	-6 725.8	-7 763.8	-9 572.2	-7 661.0	Compte de capital : débit
Financial Account, nie	...	...	-86 053.5	3 337.3	49 866.2	-37 118.0	-94 557.4	Compte d'op. fin., nia
Net Errors and Omissions	...	...	32 470.0	-3 326.5	-13 108.2	27 165.2	22 547.9	Erreurs et omissions nettes
Reserves & Related Items	...	...	9 640.0	11 576.6	16 152.4	16 890.2	-2 579.5	Rés. et postes appareutés
Fiji								**Fidji**
Goods: Exports fob	672.2	535.6	428.9	537.7	...	...	...	Biens : exportations, fab
Goods: Imports fob	-839.9	-818.9	-614.6	-653.3	...	...	...	Biens : importations, fab
Serv. & Income: Credit	676.2	729.7	557.8	572.4	...	...	...	Serv. & revenu : crédit
Serv. & Income: Debit	-504.5	-504.8	-462.6	-472.6	...	...	...	Serv & revenu : débit
Current Trans.,nie: Credit	44.1	54.6	45.3	42.7	...	...	...	Transf. cour.,nia : crédit
Current Transfers: Debit	-34.6	-30.3	-14.7	-14.2	...	...	...	Transf. courants : débit
Capital Acct.,nie: Credit	114.5	88.9	100.6	59.3	...	...	...	Compte de cap.,nia : crédit
Capital Account: Debit	-43.8	-40.5	-40.0	-45.3	...	...	...	Compte de capital : débit
Financial Account, nie	3.6	-15.1	28.7	-104.0	...	...	...	Compte d'op. fin., nia
Net Errors and Omissions	-9.7	-24.3	-24.6	32.5	...	...	...	Erreurs et omissions nettes
Reserves & Related Items	-78.1	25.1	-4.9	44.9	...	...	...	Rés. et postes appareutés
Finland								**Finlande**
Goods: Exports fob	40 725.0	41 148.2	43 393.4	41 983.0	45 703.2	42 979.6	44 856.0	Biens : exportations, fab
Goods: Imports fob	-29 410.6	-29 604.4	-30 902.9	-29 815.1	-32 018.9	-30 320.8	-31 713.0	Biens : importations, fab
Serv. & Income: Credit	9 996.7	10 776.1	10 934.6	12 185.7	13 442.2	14 399.7	15 208.7	Serv. & revenu : crédit
Serv. & Income: Debit	-15 319.5	-14 834.7	-15 087.1	-15 327.2	-17 428.7	-17 677.5	-17 498.4	Serv & revenu : débit
Current Trans.,nie: Credit	1 253.0	1 209.8	1 522.7	1 658.0	1 611.4	1 562.0	1 706.4	Transf. cour.,nia : crédit
Current Transfers: Debit	-2 242.0	-2 062.2	-2 521.1	-2 639.7	-2 334.0	-2 238.7	-2 354.2	Transf. courants : débit
Capital Acct.,nie: Credit	129.9	247.5	90.7	85.3	110.8	93.1	90.6	Compte de cap.,nia : crédit

79

Summary of balance of payments
Millions of US dollars *[cont.]*

Résumé des balances des paiements
Millions de dollars des E.-U. *[suite]*

Country or area	1996	1997	1998	1999	2000	2001	2002	Pays ou zone
Capital Account: Debit	-74.3	0.0	0.0	-36.3	-7.4	-9.8	-3.8	Compte de capital : débit
Financial Account, nie	-7 718.4	-2 975.8	-1 722.3	-6 414.4	-8 841.0	-10 942.2	-8 603.5	Compte d'op. fin., nia
Net Errors and Omissions	-375.5	-1 600.3	-5 412.2	-1 666.6	113.7	2 564.8	-1 802.0	Erreurs et omissions nettes
Reserves & Related Items	3 035.7	-2 304.2	-295.8	-12.8	-351.3	-410.1	113.1	Rés. et postes appareutés
France								**France**
Goods: Exports fob	281 846.0	286 071.0	303 025.0	300 052.0	298 198.0	294 621.0	305 617.0	Biens : exportations, fab
Goods: Imports fob	-266 911.0	-259 172.0	-278 084.0	-282 064.0	-301 817.0	-291 785.0	-296 626.0	Biens : importations, fab
Serv. & Income: Credit	131 078.2	137 920.2	151 623.2	147 348.3	153 308.6	160 837.9	167 495.5	Serv. & revenu : crédit
Serv. & Income: Debit	-117 529.5	-114 201.3	-125 732.6	-120 642.4	-117 853.3	-126 466.4	-136 878.4	Serv & revenu : débit
Current Trans.,nie: Credit	22 759.8	19 614.0	19 653.9	18 880.0	17 871.6	17 772.9	20 386.1	Transf. cour.,nia : crédit
Current Transfers: Debit	-30 683.5	-32 430.6	-32 786.3	-31 703.6	-31 127.1	-31 857.4	-34 251.2	Transf. courants : débit
Capital Acct.,nie: Credit	1 883.4	2 412.6	2 098.5	1 885.7	1 923.2	1 102.3	906.6	Compte de cap.,nia : crédit
Capital Account: Debit	-648.9	-933.9	-632.4	-313.5	-531.1	-1 410.4	-1 086.1	Compte de capital : débit
Financial Account, nie	-22 642.6	-37 598.8	-29 288.9	-36 133.7	-32 549.0	-35 232.7	-33 355.5	Compte d'op. fin., nia
Net Errors and Omissions	1 086.8	4 258.9	9 939.3	1 299.2	10 142.9	6 850.6	3 826.3	Erreurs et omissions nettes
Reserves & Related Items	-239.3	-5 940.0	-19 815.1	1 392.3	2 432.6	5 566.6	3 965.1	Rés. et postes appareutés
Gabon								**Gabon**
Goods: Exports fob	3 334.2	3 032.7	1 907.6	2 498.8	...	...	...	Biens : exportations, fab
Goods: Imports fob	-961.6	-1 030.6	-1 163.2	-910.5	...	...	...	Biens : importations, fab
Serv. & Income: Credit	276.7	271.9	277.1	365.1	...	...	...	Serv. & revenu : crédit
Serv. & Income: Debit	-1 723.6	-1 708.2	-1 563.5	-1 520.1	...	...	...	Serv & revenu : débit
Current Trans.,nie: Credit	65.2	62.7	36.6	42.6	...	...	...	Transf. cour.,nia : crédit
Current Transfers: Debit	-102.1	-97.1	-90.0	-85.6	...	...	...	Transf. courants : débit
Capital Acct.,nie: Credit	9.6	7.5	3.6	5.7	...	...	...	Compte de cap.,nia : crédit
Capital Account: Debit	-4.5	-1.7	-1.8	-0.3	...	...	...	Compte de capital : débit
Financial Account, nie	-1 047.6	-626.2	-165.8	-686.8	...	...	...	Compte d'op. fin., nia
Net Errors and Omissions	-97.4	-108.4	92.5	-106.7	...	...	...	Erreurs et omissions nettes
Reserves & Related Items	251.2	197.4	667.0	397.8	...	...	...	Rés. et postes appareutés
Gambia								**Gambie**
Goods: Exports fob	118.7	119.6	...	...	...	...	...	Biens : exportations, fab
Goods: Imports fob	-217.1	-207.1	...	...	...	...	...	Biens : importations, fab
Serv. & Income: Credit	107.2	113.1	...	...	...	...	...	Serv. & revenu : crédit
Serv. & Income: Debit	-86.3	-86.0	...	...	...	...	...	Serv & revenu : débit
Current Trans.,nie: Credit	35.1	45.0	...	...	...	...	...	Transf. cour.,nia : crédit
Current Transfers: Debit	-5.4	-8.2	...	...	...	...	...	Transf. courants : débit
Capital Acct.,nie: Credit	8.5	5.7	...	...	...	...	...	Compte de cap.,nia : crédit
Capital Account: Debit	0.0	0.0	...	...	...	...	...	Compte de capital : débit
Financial Account, nie	58.6	39.4	...	...	...	...	...	Compte d'op. fin., nia
Net Errors and Omissions	-4.9	-14.2	...	...	...	...	...	Erreurs et omissions nettes
Reserves & Related Items	-14.5	-7.4	...	...	...	...	...	Rés. et postes appareutés
Georgia								**Géorgie**
Goods: Exports fob	...	376.5	299.9	329.5	459.0	496.1	583.4	Biens : exportations, fab
Goods: Imports fob	...	-1 162.9	-994.5	-863.4	-970.5	-1 045.6	-1 041.6	Biens : importations, fab
Serv. & Income: Credit	...	384.6	608.7	428.3	385.0	411.8	537.8	Serv. & revenu : crédit
Serv. & Income: Debit	...	-308.9	-397.9	-288.5	-277.4	-302.3	-483.4	Serv & revenu : débit
Current Trans.,nie: Credit	...	205.5	219.9	228.7	163.2	246.4	183.3	Transf. cour.,nia : crédit
Current Transfers: Debit	...	-9.0	-11.8	-33.0	-28.3	-18.1	-30.0	Transf. courants : débit
Capital Acct.,nie: Credit	...	0.0	0.0	0.0	0.0	0.0	26.2	Compte de cap.,nia : crédit
Capital Account: Debit	...	-6.5	-6.1	-7.1	-4.8	-5.2	-8.6	Compte de capital : débit
Financial Account, nie	...	322.7	348.8	135.5	92.8	209.7	34.3	Compte d'op. fin., nia
Net Errors and Omissions	...	136.0	-170.5	55.7	187.4	34.9	12.3	Erreurs et omissions nettes
Reserves & Related Items	...	62.0	103.5	14.3	-6.4	-27.7	186.4	Rés. et postes appareutés
Germany								**Allemagne**
Goods: Exports fob	522 579.0	510 022.0	542 620.0	542 719.0	549 781.0	570 518.0	615 018.0	Biens : exportations, fab
Goods: Imports fob	-453 199.0	-439 903.0	-465 707.0	-472 692.0	-492 416.0	-481 321.0	-492 836.0	Biens : importations, fab
Serv. & Income: Credit	166 987.5	164 241.0	168 766.2	173 092.8	186 816.9	198 183.4	209 259.0	Serv. & revenu : crédit
Serv. & Income: Debit	-216 338.2	-213 125.7	-227 556.0	-240 241.6	-243 980.0	-261 875.0	-259 748.0	Serv & revenu : débit
Current Trans.,nie: Credit	17 495.3	15 954.6	15 964.1	17 071.6	14 973.5	14 826.9	15 828.9	Transf. cour.,nia : crédit
Current Transfers: Debit	-51 316.9	-46 331.0	-46 302.6	-43 656.9	-41 011.6	-39 323.3	-40 936.7	Transf. courants : débit
Capital Acct.,nie: Credit	2 760.6	2 826.0	3 310.8	3 004.8	9 407.2	1 869.0	2 091.3	Compte de cap.,nia : crédit
Capital Account: Debit	-4 938.9	-2 824.5	-2 591.8	-3 161.2	-3 218.8	-2 195.9	-2 317.8	Compte de capital : débit
Financial Account, nie	16 122.3	1 192.0	17 843.7	-28 119.7	37 308.6	-16 604.3	-77 079.0	Compte d'op. fin., nia

79

Summary of balance of payments
Millions of US dollars *[cont.]*

Résumé des balances des paiements
Millions de dollars des E.-U. *[suite]*

Country or area	1996	1997	1998	1999	2000	2001	2002	Pays ou zone
Net Errors and Omissions	-1 346.2	4 197.9	-2 332.4	37 868.4	-22 883.3	10 455.4	28 741.1	Erreurs et omissions nettes
Reserves & Related Items	1 195.0	3 751.2	-4 015.4	14 114.8	5 222.2	5 466.1	1 978.8	Rés. et postes appareutés
Ghana								**Ghana**
Goods: Exports fob	1 570.1	1 489.9	2 090.8	2 005.5	1 936.3	1 867.1	2 015.2	Biens : exportations, fab
Goods: Imports fob	-1 937.0	-2 128.2	-2 991.6	-3 279.9	-2 766.6	-2 968.5	-2 705.1	Biens : importations, fab
Serv. & Income: Credit	180.3	191.6	467.6	482.8	519.9	548.0	569.6	Serv. & revenu : crédit
Serv. & Income: Debit	-619.8	-663.1	-822.4	-792.8	-706.9	-730.2	-810.5	Serv & revenu : débit
Current Trans.,nie: Credit	497.9	576.5	751.0	637.8	649.3	978.4	912.4	Transf. cour.,nia : crédit
Current Transfers: Debit	-16.2	-16.4	-17.1	-17.8	-18.4	-19.4	-12.2	Transf. courants : débit
Capital Acct.,nie: Credit	0.0	0.0	0.0	0.0	0.0	0.0	0.0	Compte de cap.,nia : crédit
Capital Account: Debit	-1.0	-1.0	-1.0	-1.0	0.0	0.0	0.0	Compte de capital : débit
Financial Account, nie	285.1	493.8	561.6	746.0	369.5	392.4	-47.6	Compte d'op. fin., nia
Net Errors and Omissions	20.1	83.6	89.0	159.0	-207.4	-54.6	64.6	Erreurs et omissions nettes
Reserves & Related Items	20.4	-26.8	-127.9	60.3	224.4	-13.2	13.6	Rés. et postes appareutés
Greece								**Grèce**
Goods: Exports fob	5 890.0	5 576.0	...	8 544.7	10 201.5	10 615.0	9 867.8	Biens : exportations, fab
Goods: Imports fob	-21 395.0	-20 951.0	...	-26 495.6	-30 440.4	-29 702.0	-31 320.0	Biens : importations, fab
Serv. & Income: Credit	10 504.0	10 495.0	...	19 082.3	22 046.1	21 340.7	21 753.0	Serv. & revenu : crédit
Serv. & Income: Debit	-7 575.0	-7 490.0	...	-12 498.8	-14 978.5	-15 240.6	-14 163.7	Serv & revenu : débit
Current Trans.,nie: Credit	8 053.0	7 538.0	...	4 956.5	4 115.8	4 592.0	4 900.6	Transf. cour.,nia : crédit
Current Transfers: Debit	-31.0	-28.0	...	-884.0	-764.2	-1 005.0	-1 442.9	Transf. courants : débit
Capital Acct.,nie: Credit	0.0	0.0	...	2 318.2	2 243.5	2 320.0	1 692.0	Compte de cap.,nia : crédit
Capital Account: Debit	0.0	0.0	...	-107.0	-131.2	-167.0	-169.6	Compte de capital : débit
Financial Account, nie	8 658.0	119.0	...	7 477.5	10 830.0	536.7	11 573.7	Compte d'op. fin., nia
Net Errors and Omissions	110.6	225.8	...	41.6	-549.8	1 010.9	-827.7	Erreurs et omissions nettes
Reserves & Related Items	-4 214.6	4 515.2	...	-2 435.5	-2 572.8	5 699.4	-1 863.0	Rés. et postes appareutés
Grenada								**Grenade**
Goods: Exports fob	25.0	32.8	45.9	74.3	83.0	63.6	...	Biens : exportations, fab
Goods: Imports fob	-147.4	-154.9	-183.0	-184.6	-220.9	-196.8	...	Biens : importations, fab
Serv. & Income: Credit	111.4	110.8	123.9	148.1	158.6	137.3	...	Serv. & revenu : crédit
Serv. & Income: Debit	-65.9	-78.1	-96.3	-109.4	-122.6	-110.8	...	Serv & revenu : débit
Current Trans.,nie: Credit	25.5	25.5	34.2	26.8	30.4	31.0	...	Transf. cour.,nia : crédit
Current Transfers: Debit	-4.1	-4.0	-5.0	-7.6	-10.2	-9.4	...	Transf. courants : débit
Capital Acct.,nie: Credit	31.4	33.4	30.4	33.1	31.7	44.0	...	Compte de cap.,nia : crédit
Capital Account: Debit	0.0	-1.6	-1.8	-1.9	-2.1	-2.0	...	Compte de capital : débit
Financial Account, nie	27.4	59.2	55.6	26.3	66.8	36.9	...	Compte d'op. fin., nia
Net Errors and Omissions	-2.8	-16.1	0.2	-0.4	-4.6	12.0	...	Erreurs et omissions nettes
Reserves & Related Items	-0.4	-6.9	-4.2	-4.7	-10.0	-5.8	...	Rés. et postes appareutés
Guatemala								**Guatemala**
Goods: Exports fob	2 236.9	2 602.9	2 846.9	2 780.6	3 085.1	2 859.8	2 628.4	Biens : exportations, fab
Goods: Imports fob	-2 880.3	-3 542.7	-4 255.7	-4 225.7	-4 742.0	-5 142.0	-5 578.4	Biens : importations, fab
Serv. & Income: Credit	599.2	661.2	731.3	775.7	991.4	1 362.3	1 291.2	Serv. & revenu : crédit
Serv. & Income: Debit	-929.8	-961.6	-1 066.9	-1 071.4	-1 249.4	-1 329.8	-1 492.7	Serv & revenu : débit
Current Trans.,nie: Credit	537.1	628.8	742.9	754.4	908.2	1 024.3	2 059.9	Transf. cour.,nia : crédit
Current Transfers: Debit	-14.6	-22.1	-37.6	-39.5	-42.9	-27.5	-101.5	Transf. courants : débit
Capital Acct.,nie: Credit	65.0	85.0	71.0	68.4	85.5	93.4	129.8	Compte de cap.,nia : crédit
Capital Account: Debit	0.0	0.0	0.0	0.0	0.0	0.0	0.0	Compte de capital : débit
Financial Account, nie	672.3	737.4	1 136.7	637.5	1 520.7	1 546.7	1 172.7	Compte d'op. fin., nia
Net Errors and Omissions	-71.7	40.7	66.8	195.0	86.1	87.2	-88.3	Erreurs et omissions nettes
Reserves & Related Items	-214.1	-229.6	-235.4	125.0	-642.7	-474.4	-21.2	Rés. et postes appareutés
Guinea								**Guinée**
Goods: Exports fob	636.5	630.1	693.0	635.7	666.3	731.0	886.0	Biens : exportations, fab
Goods: Imports fob	-525.3	-512.5	-572.0	-581.7	-587.1	-561.9	-668.4	Biens : importations, fab
Serv. & Income: Credit	136.9	118.4	119.7	137.8	91.5	114.1	96.5	Serv. & revenu : crédit
Serv. & Income: Debit	-527.9	-442.9	-516.3	-471.4	-385.9	-432.6	-406.0	Serv & revenu : débit
Current Trans.,nie: Credit	137.8	131.4	116.2	80.0	88.6	91.5	70.6	Transf. cour.,nia : crédit
Current Transfers: Debit	-35.3	-15.6	-24.3	-15.1	-28.5	-44.5	-24.8	Transf. courants : débit
Capital Acct.,nie: Credit	0.0	0.0	0.0	0.0	0.0	0.0	0.0	Compte de cap.,nia : crédit
Capital Account: Debit	0.0	0.0	0.0	0.0	0.0	0.0	0.0	Compte de capital : débit
Financial Account, nie	47.5	-89.3	8.0	116.5	8.2	-12.1	13.8	Compte d'op. fin., nia
Net Errors and Omissions	69.9	49.8	17.8	22.3	84.0	-2.1	8.5	Erreurs et omissions nettes
Reserves & Related Items	59.9	130.6	157.8	75.9	62.9	116.5	23.7	Rés. et postes appareutés

79

Summary of balance of payments
Millions of US dollars *[cont.]*

Résumé des balances des paiements
Millions de dollars des E.-U. *[suite]*

Country or area	1996	1997	1998	1999	2000	2001	2002	Pays ou zone
Guinea-Bissau								**Guinée-Bissau**
Goods: Exports fob	21.6	48.9	...	...	...	...	...	Biens : exportations, fab
Goods: Imports fob	-56.8	-62.5	...	...	...	...	...	Biens : importations, fab
Serv. & Income: Credit [2]	7.0	8.0	...	...	...	...	...	Serv. & revenu : crédit [2]
Serv. & Income: Debit	-47.9	-40.5	...	...	...	...	...	Serv & revenu : débit
Current Trans.,nie: Credit	15.7	15.8	...	...	...	...	...	Transf. cour.,nia : crédit
Current Transfers: Debit	0.0	0.0	...	...	...	...	...	Transf. courants : débit
Capital Acct.,nie: Credit	40.7	32.2	...	...	...	...	...	Compte de cap.,nia : crédit
Capital Account: Debit	0.0	0.0	...	...	...	...	...	Compte de capital : débit
Financial Account, nie	-12.3	2.0	...	...	...	...	...	Compte d'op. fin., nia
Net Errors and Omissions	-11.5	-19.2	...	...	...	...	...	Erreurs et omissions nettes
Reserves & Related Items	43.5	15.2	...	...	...	...	...	Rés. et postes appareutés
Guyana								**Guyana**
Goods: Exports fob	574.8	593.4	547.0	525.0	505.2	490.3	494.9	Biens : exportations, fab
Goods: Imports fob	-595.0	-641.6	-601.2	-550.2	-585.4	-584.1	-563.1	Biens : importations, fab
Serv. & Income: Credit	157.7	160.6	153.7	158.3	180.9	182.1	180.1	Serv. & revenu : crédit
Serv. & Income: Debit	-247.6	-263.8	-245.5	-250.3	-263.0	-266.1	-262.5	Serv & revenu : débit
Current Trans.,nie: Credit	69.1	67.1	74.3	76.1	100.8	98.1	128.7	Transf. cour.,nia : crédit
Current Transfers: Debit	-28.1	-27.1	-30.3	-37.1	-53.8	-54.1	-88.7	Transf. courants : débit
Capital Acct.,nie: Credit	0.0	23.7	13.1	15.5	16.3	31.9	33.7	Compte de cap.,nia : crédit
Capital Account: Debit	0.0	0.0	0.0	0.0	0.0	0.0	0.0	Compte de capital : débit
Financial Account, nie	69.5	96.9	64.0	87.3	114.6	101.9	89.5	Compte d'op. fin., nia
Net Errors and Omissions	11.5	-10.8	11.9	-3.0	24.6	26.2	2.1	Erreurs et omissions nettes
Reserves & Related Items	-11.9	1.6	13.0	-21.6	-40.2	-26.2	-14.7	Rés. et postes appareutés
Haiti								**Haïti**
Goods: Exports fob	82.5	205.4	299.3	...	...	...	...	Biens : exportations, fab
Goods: Imports fob	-498.6	-559.6	-640.7	...	...	...	...	Biens : importations, fab
Serv. & Income: Credit [2]	109.1	173.7	180.0	...	...	...	...	Serv. & revenu : crédit [2]
Serv. & Income: Debit	-293.2	-345.1	-392.3	...	...	...	...	Serv & revenu : débit
Current Trans.,nie: Credit	462.5	477.9	515.6	...	...	...	...	Transf. cour.,nia : crédit
Current Transfers: Debit	0.0	0.0	0.0	...	...	...	...	Transf. courants : débit
Capital Acct.,nie: Credit	0.0	0.0	0.0	...	...	...	...	Compte de cap.,nia : crédit
Capital Account: Debit	0.0	0.0	0.0	...	...	...	...	Compte de capital : débit
Financial Account, nie	67.9	61.5	193.1	...	...	...	...	Compte d'op. fin., nia
Net Errors and Omissions	19.5	16.1	-120.6	...	...	...	...	Erreurs et omissions nettes
Reserves & Related Items	50.4	-29.9	-34.4	...	...	...	...	Rés. et postes appareutés
Honduras								**Honduras**
Goods: Exports fob	1 638.4	1 856.5	2 047.9	1 756.3	2 011.6	1 942.7	1 930.4	Biens : exportations, fab
Goods: Imports fob	-1 925.8	-2 150.4	-2 370.5	-2 509.6	-2 669.6	-2 807.4	-2 804.4	Biens : importations, fab
Serv. & Income: Credit	344.5	404.9	436.6	554.6	589.1	574.9	587.3	Serv. & revenu : crédit
Serv. & Income: Debit	-619.8	-642.7	-710.4	-738.1	-854.2	-861.0	-841.0	Serv & revenu : débit
Current Trans.,nie: Credit	271.7	306.8	241.7	354.6	717.9	894.0	935.5	Transf. cour.,nia : crédit
Current Transfers: Debit	-44.4	-47.3	-40.1	-42.4	-70.4	-73.1	-74.0	Transf. courants : débit
Capital Acct.,nie: Credit	29.2	15.3	29.4	110.9	30.1	36.7	23.1	Compte de cap.,nia : crédit
Capital Account: Debit	-0.7	-0.7	0.0	0.0	0.0	0.0	0.0	Compte de capital : débit
Financial Account, nie	70.2	243.3	113.9	203.4	-29.5	165.5	104.4	Compte d'op. fin., nia
Net Errors and Omissions	157.9	196.5	96.1	122.0	118.4	53.8	120.0	Erreurs et omissions nettes
Reserves & Related Items	78.8	-182.2	155.4	188.3	156.6	74.0	18.7	Rés. et postes appareutés
Hungary								**Hongrie**
Goods: Exports fob	15 966.3	19 283.9	23 698.2	25 607.7	28 761.7	31 080.5	34 792.1	Biens : exportations, fab
Goods: Imports fob	-17 639.5	-20 611.4	-25 583.2	-27 777.8	-31 674.5	-33 317.7	-36 911.0	Biens : importations, fab
Serv. & Income: Credit	7 188.5	7 331.7	6 981.2	6 537.0	7 169.0	8 786.1	9 022.2	Serv. & revenu : crédit
Serv. & Income: Debit	-6 662.3	-6 891.5	-7 567.2	-7 208.5	-7 474.6	-8 660.6	-9 994.8	Serv & revenu : débit
Current Trans.,nie: Credit	269.6	463.0	509.7	672.5	634.1	733.8	1 000.6	Transf. cour.,nia : crédit
Current Transfers: Debit	-272.1	-260.0	-266.4	-277.3	-316.0	-375.7	-553.6	Transf. courants : débit
Capital Acct.,nie: Credit	266.2	266.5	408.0	509.0	458.3	417.5	224.8	Compte de cap.,nia : crédit
Capital Account: Debit	-110.3	-149.4	-219.3	-479.5	-188.0	-100.6	-46.2	Compte de capital : débit
Financial Account, nie	-1 357.0	196.3	2 980.4	5 140.1	3 861.9	1 577.0	127.5	Compte d'op. fin., nia
Net Errors and Omissions	1 113.3	196.1	9.4	-388.1	-179.6	-224.1	545.9	Erreurs et omissions nettes
Reserves & Related Items	1 237.4	174.9	-950.8	-2 335.0	-1 052.2	83.9	1 792.4	Rés. et postes appareutés
Iceland								**Islande**
Goods: Exports fob	1 889.8	1 854.6	1 927.4	2 009.0	1 901.9	2 015.8	2 239.9	Biens : exportations, fab

79
Summary of balance of payments
Millions of US dollars *[cont.]*
Résumé des balances des paiements
Millions de dollars des E.-U. *[suite]*

Country or area	1996	1997	1998	1999	2000	2001	2002	Pays ou zone
Goods: Imports fob	-1 871.2	-1 849.6	-2 278.6	-2 316.2	-2 376.0	-2 090.6	-2 095.2	Biens : importations, fab
Serv. & Income: Credit	871.9	943.9	1 073.6	1 059.0	1 190.9	1 256.6	1 337.1	Serv. & revenu : crédit
Serv. & Income: Debit	-1 015.0	-1 074.1	-1 263.3	-1 330.4	-1 554.3	-1 510.7	-1 496.4	Serv & revenu : débit
Current Trans.,nie: Credit	9.8	17.1	4.3	4.8	6.1	8.0	36.4	Transf. cour.,nia : crédit
Current Transfers: Debit	-16.8	-20.5	-18.3	-14.9	-15.6	-17.3	-22.0	Transf. courants : débit
Capital Acct.,nie: Credit	9.8	11.4	8.9	17.4	17.5	15.3	13.7	Compte de cap.,nia : crédit
Capital Account: Debit	-10.3	-11.1	-13.5	-18.2	-20.6	-11.5	-15.1	Compte de capital : débit
Financial Account, nie	317.9	203.1	682.7	863.8	846.4	192.7	180.0	Compte d'op. fin., nia
Net Errors and Omissions	-33.1	-118.8	-91.1	-188.8	-70.4	93.5	-116.9	Erreurs et omissions nettes
Reserves & Related Items	-152.9	44.0	-32.0	-85.6	74.1	48.3	-61.4	Rés. et postes appareutés
India								**Inde**
Goods: Exports fob	33 737.3	35 702.1	34 075.7	36 877.3	45 635.9	45 398.8	52 742.9	Biens : exportations, fab
Goods: Imports fob	-43 789.0	-45 730.1	-44 828.0	-45 556.2	-60 268.0	-58 231.7	-65 158.7	Biens : importations, fab
Serv. & Income: Credit	8 649.4	10 594.3	13 497.2	16 428.5	21 580.0	23 663.7	27 156.8	Serv. & revenu : crédit
Serv. & Income: Debit	-15 837.6	-17 444.4	-19 982.5	-22 900.6	-22 944.0	-21 714.3	-24 874.8	Serv & revenu : débit
Current Trans.,nie: Credit	11 349.5	13 975.4	10 401.8	11 957.9	13 434.2	12 711.6	15 155.6	Transf. cour.,nia : crédit
Current Transfers: Debit	-65.8	-62.4	-67.4	-34.9	-78.0	-67.6	-365.8	Transf. courants : débit
Capital Acct.,nie: Credit	0.0	0.0	0.0	0.0	4 058.6	3 661.9	6 368.9	Compte de cap.,nia : crédit
Capital Account: Debit	0.0	0.0	0.0	0.0	-4 354.7	-3 500.1	-2 889.0	Compte de capital : débit
Financial Account, nie	11 847.8	9 634.7	8 583.9	9 578.6	9 390.7	9 378.4	8 065.4	Compte d'op. fin., nia
Net Errors and Omissions	-1 934.1	-1 348.4	1 389.9	313.2	-475.4	596.5	666.5	Erreurs et omissions nettes
Reserves & Related Items	-3 957.6	-5 321.1	-3 070.7	-6 663.7	-5 979.2	-11 897.3	-16 867.9	Rés. et postes appareutés
Indonesia								**Indonésie**
Goods: Exports fob	50 188.0	56 298.0	50 371.0	51 242.0	65 406.0	57 364.0	58 773.4	Biens : exportations, fab
Goods: Imports fob	-44 240.0	-46 223.0	-31 942.0	-30 598.0	-40 366.0	-34 669.0	-35 652.2	Biens : importations, fab
Serv. & Income: Credit	7 809.0	8 796.0	6 389.0	6 490.0	7 669.0	7 504.0	7 891.8	Serv. & revenu : crédit
Serv. & Income: Debit	-22 357.0	-24 794.0	-22 060.0	-23 263.0	-26 540.0	-24 820.0	-25 313.3	Serv & revenu : débit
Current Trans.,nie: Credit	937.0	1 034.0	1 338.0	1 914.0	1 816.0	1 520.0	2 254.5	Transf. cour.,nia : crédit
Current Transfers: Debit	0.0	0.0	0.0	0.0	0.0	0.0	-503.7	Transf. courants : débit
Capital Acct.,nie: Credit	0.0	0.0	0.0	0.0	0.0	0.0	0.0	Compte de cap.,nia : crédit
Capital Account: Debit	0.0	0.0	0.0	0.0	0.0	0.0	0.0	Compte de capital : débit
Financial Account, nie	10 847.0	-603.0	-9 638.0	-5 941.0	-7 896.0	-7 614.0	-1 684.7	Compte d'op. fin., nia
Net Errors and Omissions	1 318.7	-2 645.4	1 849.5	2 127.5	3 637.1	700.2	-807.9	Erreurs et omissions nettes
Reserves & Related Items	-4 502.7	8 137.4	3 692.5	-1 971.5	-3 726.1	14.8	-4 957.9	Rés. et postes appareutés
Iran (Islamic Rep. of)								**Iran (Rép. islamique d')**
Goods: Exports fob	22 391.0	18 381.0	13 118.0	21 030.0	28 345.0	...	...	Biens : exportations, fab
Goods: Imports fob	-14 989.0	-14 123.0	-14 286.0	-13 433.0	-15 207.0	...	...	Biens : importations, fab
Serv. & Income: Credit	1 348.0	1 658.0	2 023.0	1 397.0	1 786.0	...	...	Serv. & revenu : crédit
Serv. & Income: Debit	-3 981.0	-4 096.0	-3 491.0	-2 930.0	-2 900.0	...	...	Serv & revenu : débit
Current Trans.,nie: Credit	471.0	400.0	500.0	508.0	539.0	...	...	Transf. cour.,nia : crédit
Current Transfers: Debit	-8.0	-7.0	-3.0	17.0	82.0	...	...	Transf. courants : débit
Capital Acct.,nie: Credit	0.0	0.0	0.0	0.0	0.0	...	...	Compte de cap.,nia : crédit
Capital Account: Debit	0.0	0.0	0.0	0.0	0.0	...	...	Compte de capital : débit
Financial Account, nie	-5 508.0	-4 822.0	2 270.0	-5 894.0	-10 189.0	...	...	Compte d'op. fin., nia
Net Errors and Omissions	2 717.3	-1 088.2	-1 121.7	-243.5	-1 372.5	...	...	Erreurs et omissions nettes
Reserves & Related Items	-2 441.3	3 697.2	990.7	-451.5	-1 083.5	...	...	Rés. et postes appareutés
Ireland								**Irlande**
Goods: Exports fob	49 183.9	55 292.7	78 562.0	68 539.8	73 432.9	77 622.9	85 829.8	Biens : exportations, fab
Goods: Imports fob	-33 429.7	-36 667.7	-53 172.1	-44 283.6	-48 016.9	-50 360.0	-50 931.4	Biens : importations, fab
Serv. & Income: Credit	11 325.4	13 538.9	42 165.6	39 964.6	46 760.8	52 315.6	54 644.6	Serv. & revenu : crédit
Serv. & Income: Debit	-27 220.2	-32 254.0	-68 425.3	-65 120.1	-73 719.3	-80 540.4	-91 272.8	Serv & revenu : débit
Current Trans.,nie: Credit	3 538.2	3 083.4	7 428.5	5 308.1	4 303.7	7 399.6	7 189.1	Transf. cour.,nia : crédit
Current Transfers: Debit	-1 349.0	-1 127.7	-5 542.6	-4 054.9	-3 354.6	-7 127.8	-6 384.0	Transf. courants : débit
Capital Acct.,nie: Credit	880.8	961.7	1 326.7	674.4	1 167.1	719.2	656.1	Compte de cap.,nia : crédit
Capital Account: Debit	-96.0	-91.0	-108.3	-81.0	-70.2	-84.1	-81.1	Compte de capital : débit
Financial Account, nie	-2 779.7	-7 484.3	4 686.1	-3 892.6	8 901.2	16.4	-181.5	Compte d'op. fin., nia
Net Errors and Omissions	-106.0	3 639.4	-3 708.0	971.8	-9 283.6	433.8	239.7	Erreurs et omissions nettes
Reserves & Related Items	52.3	1 108.7	-3 212.4	1 973.5	-121.2	-395.2	291.6	Rés. et postes appareutés
Israel								**Israël**
Goods: Exports fob	21 514.7	22 867.4	23 190.4	25 826.8	31 152.9	27 974.1	27 652.6	Biens : exportations, fab
Goods: Imports fob	-28 468.7	-27 875.4	-26 241.0	-30 040.8	-34 035.8	-30 978.5	-31 212.2	Biens : importations, fab
Serv. & Income: Credit	9 859.3	10 802.0	11 998.2	14 447.5	18 920.1	14 830.9	13 704.6	Serv. & revenu : crédit

79

Summary of balance of payments
Millions of US dollars *[cont.]*

Résumé des balances des paiements
Millions de dollars des E.-U. *[suite]*

Country or area	1996	1997	1998	1999	2000	2001	2002	Pays ou zone
Serv. & Income: Debit	-14 165.0	-15 132.6	-16 173.3	-18 058.4	-23 191.0	-20 011.8	-17 920.6	Serv & revenu : débit
Current Trans.,nie: Credit	6 440.2	6 377.4	6 682.7	7 122.0	7 467.7	7 516.0	7 891.1	Transf. cour.,nia : crédit
Current Transfers: Debit	-304.3	-327.5	-606.4	-809.4	-984.5	-1 106.8	-1 341.9	Transf. courants : débit
Capital Acct.,nie: Credit	773.4	727.7	577.0	568.7	455.2	681.2	150.5	Compte de cap.,nia : crédit
Capital Account: Debit	0.0	0.0	0.0	0.0	0.0	0.0	0.0	Compte de capital : débit
Financial Account, nie	4 536.6	7 206.8	-171.7	3 463.8	3 427.8	630.9	-2 059.6	Compte d'op. fin., nia
Net Errors and Omissions	1 019.9	2 430.7	588.6	-2 637.4	-3 044.5	836.3	2 255.4	Erreurs et omissions nettes
Reserves & Related Items	-1 206.1	-7 076.5	155.5	117.2	-168.0	-372.3	880.1	Rés. et postes appareutés
Italy								**Italie**
Goods: Exports fob	252 039.0	240 404.0	242 572.0	235 856.0	240 473.0	244 931.0	253 680.0	Biens : exportations, fab
Goods: Imports fob	-197 921.0	-200 527.0	-206 941.0	-212 420.0	-230 925.0	-229 392.0	-237 147.0	Biens : importations, fab
Serv. & Income: Credit	105 801.3	112 725.1	118 867.5	105 148.5	95 226.8	96 250.6	103 554.9	Serv. & revenu : crédit
Serv. & Income: Debit	-112 706.0	-116 163.1	-127 015.2	-115 118.3	-106 281.1	-106 663.3	-121 395.4	Serv & revenu : débit
Current Trans.,nie: Credit	14 320.3	15 551.5	14 402.3	16 776.2	15 797.4	16 136.5	20 871.9	Transf. cour.,nia : crédit
Current Transfers: Debit	-21 534.8	-19 587.9	-21 887.4	-22 132.3	-20 073.0	-21 915.3	-26 305.4	Transf. courants : débit
Capital Acct.,nie: Credit	1 414.0	4 582.4	3 359.4	4 571.9	4 172.1	2 098.0	2 059.5	Compte de cap.,nia : crédit
Capital Account: Debit	-1 348.0	-1 147.9	-1 001.5	-1 608.0	-1 293.0	-1 251.8	-1 323.2	Compte de capital : débit
Financial Account, nie	-7 982.2	-6 878.3	-18 074.0	-17 414.7	7 504.3	-3 569.7	11 191.6	Compte d'op. fin., nia
Net Errors and Omissions	-20 176.2	-15 809.8	-25 753.7	-1 710.8	-1 355.2	2 787.5	-2 018.1	Erreurs et omissions nettes
Reserves & Related Items	-11 906.7	-13 149.7	21 471.9	8 051.1	-3 247.0	587.9	-3 169.1	Rés. et postes appareutés
Jamaica								**Jamaïque**
Goods: Exports fob	1 721.0	1 700.3	1 613.4	1 499.1	1 562.8	1 454.4	1 309.1	Biens : exportations, fab
Goods: Imports fob	-2 715.2	-2 832.6	-2 743.9	-2 685.6	-3 004.3	-3 072.6	-3 179.6	Biens : importations, fab
Serv. & Income: Credit	1 743.7	1 846.2	1 926.7	2 144.2	2 218.8	2 115.2	2 140.4	Serv. & revenu : crédit
Serv. & Income: Debit	-1 515.7	-1 670.9	-1 758.0	-1 821.3	-1 965.5	-2 169.9	-2 475.1	Serv & revenu : débit
Current Trans.,nie: Credit	709.3	705.7	727.6	757.9	969.4	1 090.7	1 336.9	Transf. cour.,nia : crédit
Current Transfers: Debit	-85.7	-80.9	-99.6	-110.6	-148.6	-176.6	-251.0	Transf. courants : débit
Capital Acct.,nie: Credit	42.5	21.7	20.3	19.1	29.6	15.2	18.9	Compte de cap.,nia : crédit
Capital Account: Debit	-25.9	-33.3	-29.0	-30.0	-27.4	-37.5	-35.8	Compte de capital : débit
Financial Account, nie	388.6	163.5	337.3	94.8	853.9	1 660.5	867.1	Compte d'op. fin., nia
Net Errors and Omissions	8.8	9.9	49.1	-4.0	29.7	-14.4	32.9	Erreurs et omissions nettes
Reserves & Related Items	-271.4	170.4	-43.9	136.4	-518.4	-865.0	236.2	Rés. et postes appareutés
Japan								**Japon**
Goods: Exports fob	400 287.0	409 240.0	374 044.0	403 694.0	459 513.0	383 592.0	395 581.0	Biens : exportations, fab
Goods: Imports fob	-316 702.0	-307 640.0	-251 655.0	-280 369.0	-342 794.0	-313 378.0	-301 751.0	Biens : importations, fab
Serv. & Income: Credit	180 150.2	181 128.5	162 747.0	153 046.8	166 437.3	167 611.2	157 189.9	Serv. & revenu : crédit
Serv. & Income: Debit	-188 936.3	-177 081.0	-157 544.9	-149 628.7	-153 662.7	-142 122.7	-133 649.2	Serv & revenu : débit
Current Trans.,nie: Credit	6 023.4	6 010.6	5 531.1	6 211.5	7 380.4	6 151.7	10 037.9	Transf. cour.,nia : crédit
Current Transfers: Debit	-15 030.2	-14 844.7	-14 373.3	-18 350.3	-17 211.1	-14 056.0	-14 960.4	Transf. courants : débit
Capital Acct.,nie: Credit	1 224.8	1 516.7	1 568.7	745.9	780.9	994.7	914.6	Compte de cap.,nia : crédit
Capital Account: Debit	-4 512.4	-5 566.0	-16 022.9	-17 213.4	-10 039.5	-3 863.5	-4 236.0	Compte de capital : débit
Financial Account, nie	-28 016.8	-120 509.0	-114 816.0	-38 845.4	-78 312.7	-48 160.3	-63 380.5	Compte d'op. fin., nia
Net Errors and Omissions	652.7	34 311.3	4 357.0	16 965.2	16 865.9	3 718.4	388.2	Erreurs et omissions nettes
Reserves & Related Items	-35 140.5	-6 567.2	6 164.4	-76 256.3	-48 955.0	-40 487.0	-46 133.7	Rés. et postes appareutés
Jordan								**Jordanie**
Goods: Exports fob	1 816.9	1 835.5	1 802.4	1 831.9	1 899.3	2 294.4	2 770.0	Biens : exportations, fab
Goods: Imports fob	-3 818.1	-3 648.5	-3 404.0	-3 292.0	-4 073.6	-4 301.4	-4 450.4	Biens : importations, fab
Serv. & Income: Credit	1 958.0	1 985.0	2 132.0	2 169.3	2 306.8	2 130.2	1 996.6	Serv. & revenu : crédit
Serv. & Income: Debit	-2 010.4	-1 994.2	-2 228.8	-2 177.7	-2 258.0	-2 186.5	-2 108.4	Serv & revenu : débit
Current Trans.,nie: Credit	1 970.2	2 096.1	1 984.3	2 154.9	2 461.5	2 365.9	2 524.3	Transf. cour.,nia : crédit
Current Transfers: Debit	-138.5	-244.6	-271.9	-281.4	-277.4	-306.9	-264.3	Transf. courants : débit
Capital Acct.,nie: Credit	157.7	163.8	81.1	90.3	64.9	21.6	68.8	Compte de cap.,nia : crédit
Capital Account: Debit	0.0	0.0	0.0	0.0	0.0	0.0	0.0	Compte de capital : débit
Financial Account, nie	233.9	242.3	-177.3	725.1	1 387.6	522.6	674.6	Compte d'op. fin., nia
Net Errors and Omissions	-357.9	-160.8	-454.0	28.7	315.6	85.3	-48.6	Erreurs et omissions nettes
Reserves & Related Items	188.2	-274.6	536.1	-1 249.0	-1 826.6	-625.3	-1 162.6	Rés. et postes appareutés
Kazakhstan								**Kazakhstan**
Goods: Exports fob	6 291.6	6 899.3	5 870.5	5 988.7	9 288.1	8 927.8	10 027.6	Biens : exportations, fab
Goods: Imports fob	-6 626.7	-7 175.7	-6 671.7	-5 645.0	-6 848.2	-7 607.3	-7 726.3	Biens : importations, fab
Serv. & Income: Credit	731.1	915.7	999.8	1 041.1	1 272.1	1 531.5	1 821.3	Serv. & revenu : crédit
Serv. & Income: Debit	-1 205.4	-1 513.2	-1 545.9	-1 712.5	-3 285.5	-4 192.9	-4 931.8	Serv & revenu : débit
Current Trans.,nie: Credit	83.4	104.7	141.4	174.7	352.2	394.4	425.6	Transf. cour.,nia : crédit

79

Summary of balance of payments
Millions of US dollars *[cont.]*

Résumé des balances des paiements
Millions de dollars des E.-U. *[suite]*

Country or area	1996	1997	1998	1999	2000	2001	2002	Pays ou zone
Current Transfers: Debit	-25.0	-30.1	-19.0	-18.0	-103.2	-162.4	-312.2	Transf. courants : débit
Capital Acct.,nie: Credit	87.9	58.3	65.9	61.1	66.3	92.4	109.7	Compte de cap.,nia : crédit
Capital Account: Debit	-403.4	-498.1	-435.0	-295.1	-356.9	-286.5	-229.6	Compte de capital : débit
Financial Account, nie	2 005.1	2 901.6	2 229.1	1 299.2	1 308.1	2 613.7	1 357.3	Compte d'op. fin., nia
Net Errors and Omissions	-780.0	-1 114.1	-1 078.4	-641.6	-1 122.7	-926.1	-6.5	Erreurs et omissions nettes
Reserves & Related Items	-158.6	-548.4	443.3	-252.6	-570.3	-384.7	-535.1	Rés. et postes appareutés
Kenya								**Kenya**
Goods: Exports fob	2 083.3	2 062.6	2 017.0	1 756.7	1 782.2	1 894.0	...	Biens : exportations, fab
Goods: Imports fob	-2 598.2	-2 948.4	-3 028.7	-2 731.8	-3 044.0	-3 176.1	...	Biens : importations, fab
Serv. & Income: Credit	957.6	937.4	871.7	966.2	1 038.3	1 130.0	...	Serv. & revenu : crédit
Serv. & Income: Debit	-1 096.2	-1 080.9	-909.4	-761.3	-902.6	-1 015.7	...	Serv & revenu : débit
Current Trans.,nie: Credit	585.4	572.5	578.6	685.3	926.6	850.0	...	Transf. cour.,nia : crédit
Current Transfers: Debit	-5.4	0.0	-4.5	-4.7	-4.2	0.0	...	Transf. courants : débit
Capital Acct.,nie: Credit	0.0	76.8	84.3	55.4	49.6	69.0	...	Compte de cap.,nia : crédit
Capital Account: Debit	-0.4	0.0	0.0	0.0	0.0	0.0	...	Compte de capital : débit
Financial Account, nie	589.1	362.6	562.1	165.7	157.4	84.3	...	Compte d'op. fin., nia
Net Errors and Omissions	-128.2	32.8	-88.6	-165.5	-10.0	117.0	...	Erreurs et omissions nettes
Reserves & Related Items	-387.0	-15.5	-82.6	34.0	6.8	47.5	...	Rés. et postes appareutés
Korea, Republic of								**Corée, République de**
Goods: Exports fob	129 968.0	138 619.0	132 122.0	145 164.0	175 948.0	151 262.0	162 554.0	Biens : exportations, fab
Goods: Imports fob	-144 933.0	-141 798.0	-90 494.8	-116 793.0	-159 076.0	-137 770.0	-148 374.0	Biens : importations, fab
Serv. & Income: Credit	27 078.5	30 179.5	28 239.5	29 773.4	36 909.0	35 704.5	34 949.5	Serv. & revenu : crédit
Serv. & Income: Debit	-35 073.4	-35 834.6	-32 853.7	-35 583.4	-42 219.5	-40 730.2	-41 958.7	Serv & revenu : débit
Current Trans.,nie: Credit	4 279.0	5 287.9	6 736.6	6 421.3	6 500.1	6 686.7	7 293.2	Transf. cour.,nia : crédit
Current Transfers: Debit	-4 325.1	-4 620.9	-3 384.3	-4 505.5	-5 820.0	-6 914.0	-8 371.7	Transf. courants : débit
Capital Acct.,nie: Credit	18.9	16.6	463.6	95.1	97.8	42.4	44.1	Compte de cap.,nia : crédit
Capital Account: Debit	-616.5	-624.2	-292.5	-484.4	-713.0	-773.4	-1 135.1	Compte de capital : débit
Financial Account, nie	23 924.4	-9 195.0	-8 381.0	12 708.8	12 725.2	3 140.5	2 614.0	Compte d'op. fin., nia
Net Errors and Omissions	1 094.6	-5 009.6	-6 224.9	-3 536.0	-561.2	2 629.2	4 155.1	Erreurs et omissions nettes
Reserves & Related Items	-1 415.7	22 979.4	-25 930.1	-33 260.2	-23 790.0	-13 277.6	-11 770.2	Rés. et postes appareutés
Kuwait								**Koweït**
Goods: Exports fob	14 946.1	14 280.6	9 617.5	12 223.5	19 478.3	16 238.3	15 366.2	Biens : exportations, fab
Goods: Imports fob	-7 949.0	-7 746.9	-7 714.4	-6 708.0	-6 451.5	-7 046.4	-8 117.4	Biens : importations, fab
Serv. & Income: Credit	7 929.0	9 503.9	8 925.2	7 654.0	9 137.7	7 088.8	5 373.2	Serv. & revenu : crédit
Serv. & Income: Debit	-6 329.1	-6 596.4	-6 838.3	-6 156.1	-5 536.4	-5 879.4	-6 284.7	Serv & revenu : débit
Current Trans.,nie: Credit	53.4	79.1	98.4	98.5	84.8	52.2	49.4	Transf. cour.,nia : crédit
Current Transfers: Debit	-1 543.0	-1 585.6	-1 873.6	-2 102.4	-2 040.7	-2 129.2	-2 194.7	Transf. courants : débit
Capital Acct.,nie: Credit	3.3	115.4	288.8	716.1	2 236.3	2 950.9	1 704.4	Compte de cap.,nia : crédit
Capital Account: Debit	-207.1	-211.0	-210.0	-13.1	-19.6	-19.6	-36.2	Compte de capital : débit
Financial Account, nie	-7 708.5	-6 184.3	-2 920.4	-5 706.0	-13 773.4	-6 312.7	-5 156.1	Compte d'op. fin., nia
Net Errors and Omissions	780.4	-1 648.9	884.6	911.5	-847.4	-2 038.1	-1 677.3	Erreurs et omissions nettes
Reserves & Related Items	24.5	-5.9	-257.9	-918.1	-2 268.2	-2 904.8	973.1	Rés. et postes appareutés
Kyrgyzstan								**Kirghizistan**
Goods: Exports fob	531.2	630.8	535.1	462.6	510.9	480.3	498.1	Biens : exportations, fab
Goods: Imports fob	-782.9	-646.1	-755.7	-551.1	-506.4	-440.3	-552.0	Biens : importations, fab
Serv. & Income: Credit	35.9	51.8	75.4	75.9	78.8	92.1	144.4	Serv. & revenu : crédit
Serv. & Income: Debit	-292.9	-242.6	-267.4	-239.8	-249.7	-202.1	-211.1	Serv & revenu : débit
Current Trans.,nie: Credit	85.9	69.8	2.2	1.2	43.0	21.6	39.9	Transf. cour.,nia : crédit
Current Transfers: Debit	-1.9	-2.2	-2.0	-1.2	-2.4	-3.2	-4.3	Transf. courants : débit
Capital Acct.,nie: Credit	9.0	6.2	3.9	14.6	22.8	9.2	15.1	Compte de cap.,nia : crédit
Capital Account: Debit	-25.0	-14.6	-12.0	-29.8	-34.2	-41.2	-43.0	Compte de capital : débit
Financial Account, nie	362.5	250.4	284.6	220.8	56.9	31.6	94.1	Compte d'op. fin., nia
Net Errors and Omissions	58.4	-57.4	63.4	-3.0	9.8	19.9	7.9	Erreurs et omissions nettes
Reserves & Related Items	19.8	-46.2	72.7	49.7	70.4	32.0	11.0	Rés. et postes appareutés
Lao People's Dem. Rep.								**Rép. dém. pop. lao**
Goods: Exports fob	322.8	318.3	342.1	338.2	330.3	311.1	...	Biens : exportations, fab
Goods: Imports fob	-643.7	-601.3	-506.8	-527.7	-535.3	-527.9	...	Biens : importations, fab
Serv. & Income: Credit	113.6	116.9	151.9	140.5	183.0	171.9	...	Serv. & revenu : crédit
Serv. & Income: Debit	-139.5	-139.4	-137.3	-101.7	-102.7	-71.3	...	Serv & revenu : débit
Current Trans.,nie: Credit	0.0	0.0	0.0	80.2	116.3	33.7	...	Transf. cour.,nia : crédit
Current Transfers: Debit	0.0	0.0	0.0	-50.6	0.0	0.0	...	Transf. courants : débit
Capital Acct.,nie: Credit	44.9	40.3	49.4	0.0	0.0	0.0	...	Compte de cap.,nia : crédit

79

Summary of balance of payments
Millions of US dollars *[cont.]*

Résumé des balances des paiements
Millions de dollars des E.-U. *[suite]*

Country or area	1996	1997	1998	1999	2000	2001	2002	Pays ou zone
Capital Account: Debit	-9.9	-6.9	-6.3	0.0	0.0	0.0	...	Compte de capital : débit
Financial Account, nie	135.7	3.5	-43.4	-46.9	126.1	135.7	...	Compte d'op. fin., nia
Net Errors and Omissions	17.7	-100.5	-103.8	-165.1	-74.2	-57.2	...	Erreurs et omissions nettes
Reserves & Related Items	158.4	369.1	254.2	333.1	-43.4	3.9	...	Rés. et postes appareutés
Latvia								**Lettonie**
Goods: Exports fob	1 487.6	1 838.1	2 011.2	1 889.1	2 058.1	2 215.9	2 575.7	Biens : exportations, fab
Goods: Imports fob	-2 285.9	-2 686.0	-3 141.4	-2 916.1	-3 116.3	-3 566.4	-4 020.0	Biens : importations, fab
Serv. & Income: Credit	1 266.0	1 210.0	1 315.8	1 182.0	1 427.3	1 467.0	1 541.0	Serv. & revenu : crédit
Serv. & Income: Debit	-841.0	-784.5	-959.6	-902.1	-961.0	-926.6	-1 003.8	Serv & revenu : débit
Current Trans.,nie: Credit	98.1	90.9	137.3	113.8	202.8	221.4	537.4	Transf. cour.,nia : crédit
Current Transfers: Debit	-4.6	-13.6	-12.8	-21.0	-105.4	-142.9	-277.7	Transf. courants : débit
Capital Acct.,nie: Credit	0.0	13.7	14.1	12.6	38.5	55.9	24.6	Compte de cap.,nia : crédit
Capital Account: Debit	0.0	0.0	0.0	0.0	-8.9	-11.3	-6.9	Compte de capital : débit
Financial Account, nie	537.1	346.9	601.1	768.4	494.0	953.9	698.6	Compte d'op. fin., nia
Net Errors and Omissions	-46.3	86.5	96.9	38.3	-26.2	47.5	-57.0	Erreurs et omissions nettes
Reserves & Related Items	-211.1	-102.2	-62.6	-165.0	-2.9	-314.3	-12.1	Rés. et postes appareutés
Lesotho								**Lesotho**
Goods: Exports fob	186.9	196.1	193.4	172.5	211.1	278.6	354.8	Biens : exportations, fab
Goods: Imports fob	-998.6	-1 024.4	-866.0	-779.2	-727.6	-678.6	-736.0	Biens : importations, fab
Serv. & Income: Credit	495.6	534.3	411.2	368.7	331.4	275.8	213.2	Serv. & revenu : crédit
Serv. & Income: Debit	-175.4	-177.6	-175.8	-130.7	-105.2	-105.7	-72.0	Serv & revenu : débit
Current Trans.,nie: Credit	190.2	202.9	158.0	149.4	139.8	137.2	123.0	Transf. cour.,nia : crédit
Current Transfers: Debit	-1.1	-0.5	-1.2	-1.6	-1.0	-2.5	-1.7	Transf. courants : débit
Capital Acct.,nie: Credit	45.5	44.5	22.9	15.2	22.0	16.8	23.4	Compte de cap.,nia : crédit
Capital Account: Debit	0.0	0.0	0.0	0.0	0.0	0.0	0.0	Compte de capital : débit
Financial Account, nie	350.6	323.7	316.1	135.8	85.2	88.6	85.7	Compte d'op. fin., nia
Net Errors and Omissions	23.3	42.1	56.8	29.0	62.1	155.4	-115.7	Erreurs et omissions nettes
Reserves & Related Items	-116.9	-141.0	-115.6	40.8	-17.8	-165.7	125.3	Rés. et postes appareutés
Libyan Arab Jamah.								**Jamah. arabe libyenne**
Goods: Exports fob	7 930.2	8 176.6	5 326.2	7 275.8	...	...	...	Biens : exportations, fab
Goods: Imports fob	-5 844.8	-5 927.8	-4 929.9	-4 302.0	...	...	...	Biens : importations, fab
Serv. & Income: Credit	500.0	557.4	572.3	605.0	...	...	...	Serv. & revenu : crédit
Serv. & Income: Debit	-1 085.1	-1 057.9	-1 095.3	-1 223.8	...	...	...	Serv & revenu : débit
Current Trans.,nie: Credit	2.5	3.3	4.3	6.9	...	...	...	Transf. cour.,nia : crédit
Current Transfers: Debit	-283.2	-202.0	-228.8	-226.0	...	...	...	Transf. courants : débit
Capital Acct.,nie: Credit	0.0	0.0	0.0	0.0	...	...	...	Compte de cap.,nia : crédit
Capital Account: Debit	0.0	0.0	0.0	0.0	...	...	...	Compte de capital : débit
Financial Account, nie	185.7	-731.9	-466.9	-1 045.3	...	...	...	Compte d'op. fin., nia
Net Errors and Omissions	-184.7	735.4	392.0	-402.8	...	...	...	Erreurs et omissions nettes
Reserves & Related Items	-1 220.7	-1 553.1	426.1	-688.0	...	...	...	Rés. et postes appareutés
Lithuania								**Lituanie**
Goods: Exports fob	3 413.2	4 192.4	3 961.6	3 146.7	4 050.4	4 889.0	6 028.4	Biens : exportations, fab
Goods: Imports fob	-4 309.3	-5 339.9	-5 479.9	-4 551.3	-5 154.1	-5 997.0	-7 343.3	Biens : importations, fab
Serv. & Income: Credit	849.5	1 112.3	1 233.5	1 206.4	1 244.3	1 362.7	1 655.3	Serv. & revenu : crédit
Serv. & Income: Debit	-819.7	-1 176.1	-1 248.4	-1 158.6	-1 058.0	-1 085.8	-1 289.9	Serv & revenu : débit
Current Trans.,nie: Credit	149.4	237.0	240.4	167.4	246.8	262.0	231.7	Transf. cour.,nia : crédit
Current Transfers: Debit	-5.6	-7.0	-5.4	-4.6	-4.3	-4.5	-2.9	Transf. courants : débit
Capital Acct.,nie: Credit	5.5	4.5	0.9	2.7	2.6	1.5	56.8	Compte de cap.,nia : crédit
Capital Account: Debit	0.0	-0.4	-2.6	-6.0	-0.4	-0.1	-0.4	Compte de capital : débit
Financial Account, nie	645.6	1 005.6	1 443.9	1 060.7	702.4	777.6	1 048.4	Compte d'op. fin., nia
Net Errors and Omissions	66.7	195.8	282.9	-42.2	128.3	153.6	78.5	Erreurs et omissions nettes
Reserves & Related Items	4.8	-224.2	-426.8	178.7	-158.0	-359.0	-462.7	Rés. et postes appareutés
Luxembourg								**Luxembourg**
Goods: Exports fob	7 944.4	7 744.7	8 557.1	8 565.1	8 635.4	8 995.7	9 668.0	Biens : exportations, fab
Goods: Imports fob	-9 871.9	-9 769.6	-10 881.4	-11 151.3	-11 055.6	-11 394.8	-11 741.0	Biens : importations, fab
Serv. & Income: Credit	52 405.1	51 021.8	60 897.8	65 065.6	70 701.0	72 246.9	70 256.3	Serv. & revenu : crédit
Serv. & Income: Debit	-47 703.2	-46 654.8	-56 524.5	-60 252.7	-65 258.4	-67 649.0	-65 846.2	Serv & revenu : débit
Current Trans.,nie: Credit	2 186.5	1 984.9	2 185.2	2 281.7	2 750.0	2 268.5	2 679.8	Transf. cour.,nia : crédit
Current Transfers: Debit	-2 741.3	-2 493.3	-2 608.3	-2 858.7	-3 210.8	-2 793.5	-3 381.4	Transf. courants : débit
Capital Acct.,nie: Credit	0.0	0.0	0.0	0.0	0.0	0.0	60.2	Compte de cap.,nia : crédit
Capital Account: Debit	0.0	0.0	0.0	0.0	0.0	0.0	-226.1	Compte de capital : débit
Financial Account, nie	0.0	0.0	0.0	0.0	0.0	0.0	-274.8	Compte d'op. fin., nia

79

Summary of balance of payments
Millions of US dollars *[cont.]*

Résumé des balances des paiements
Millions de dollars des E.-U. *[suite]*

Country or area	1996	1997	1998	1999	2000	2001	2002	Pays ou zone
Net Errors and Omissions	0.0	0.0	0.0	0.0	0.0	0.0	-1 159.6	Erreurs et omissions nettes
Reserves & Related Items	0.0	0.0	0.0	0.0	0.0	0.0	-35.3	Rés. et postes appareutés
Madagascar								**Madagascar**
Goods: Exports fob	509.3	516.1	538.2	584.0	823.7	928.2	485.6	Biens : exportations, fab
Goods: Imports fob	-629.0	-694.1	-692.7	-742.5	-997.5	-955.0	-602.7	Biens : importations, fab
Serv. & Income: Credit	299.5	292.0	315.6	346.7	386.5	374.5	250.2	Serv. & revenu : crédit
Serv. & Income: Debit	-542.4	-500.9	-538.6	-519.3	-586.2	-617.2	-498.7	Serv & revenu : débit
Current Trans.,nie: Credit	94.4	156.3	109.5	110.9	121.9	114.2	88.0	Transf. cour.,nia : crédit
Current Transfers: Debit	-22.6	-35.3	-32.7	-31.8	-31.3	-14.9	-20.6	Transf. courants : débit
Capital Acct.,nie: Credit	5.1	115.4	102.7	128.8	115.0	112.8	57.7	Compte de cap.,nia : crédit
Capital Account: Debit	0.0	0.0	0.0	0.0	0.0	0.0	0.0	Compte de capital : débit
Financial Account, nie	133.3	109.7	-76.3	-13.6	-30.7	-138.6	-54.0	Compte d'op. fin., nia
Net Errors and Omissions	58.8	24.6	-25.0	32.4	38.6	-56.9	11.1	Erreurs et omissions nettes
Reserves & Related Items	93.7	16.1	299.2	104.3	160.0	252.9	283.5	Rés. et postes appareutés
Malawi								**Malawi**
Goods: Exports fob	509.6	540.2	539.6	448.4	403.1	427.9	422.4	Biens : exportations, fab
Goods: Imports fob	-587.5	-698.7	-500.6	-575.0	-462.0	-472.2	-573.2	Biens : importations, fab
Serv. & Income: Credit	46.2	51.0	43.0	74.8	67.5	55.8	55.4	Serv. & revenu : crédit
Serv. & Income: Debit	-230.6	-260.1	-209.7	-235.3	-217.7	-214.0	-266.4	Serv & revenu : débit
Current Trans.,nie: Credit	138.0	116.2	134.1	137.7	143.1	148.8	170.0	Transf. cour.,nia : crédit
Current Transfers: Debit	-23.0	-24.9	-10.8	-8.2	-7.6	-6.2	-8.9	Transf. courants : débit
Capital Acct.,nie: Credit	0.0	0.0	0.0	0.0	0.0	0.0	0.0	Compte de cap.,nia : crédit
Capital Account: Debit	0.0	0.0	0.0	0.0	0.0	0.0	0.0	Compte de capital : débit
Financial Account, nie	170.5	146.5	237.8	219.6	188.8	213.4	134.0	Compte d'op. fin., nia
Net Errors and Omissions	-144.6	145.2	-407.6	-28.8	-23.9	-221.5	156.7	Erreurs et omissions nettes
Reserves & Related Items	121.6	-15.5	174.1	-33.3	-91.4	68.0	-90.0	Rés. et postes appareutés
Malaysia								**Malaisie**
Goods: Exports fob	76 985.1	77 538.3	71 882.8	84 096.8	98 429.1	87 980.5	93 382.8	Biens : exportations, fab
Goods: Imports fob	-73 136.8	-74 028.7	-54 377.8	-61 452.6	-77 602.4	-69 597.4	-75 247.7	Biens : importations, fab
Serv. & Income: Credit	17 828.3	18 212.0	13 058.9	13 922.5	15 926.6	16 301.8	17 017.2	Serv. & revenu : crédit
Serv. & Income: Debit	-24 956.0	-26 147.6	-18 572.7	-22 234.8	-26 341.1	-25 246.3	-25 182.0	Serv & revenu : débit
Current Trans.,nie: Credit	765.9	944.1	727.8	800.8	756.2	536.8	661.3	Transf. cour.,nia : crédit
Current Transfers: Debit	-1 948.4	-2 453.4	-3 190.3	-2 529.1	-2 680.5	-2 688.7	-3 441.8	Transf. courants : débit
Capital Acct.,nie: Credit	0.0	0.0	0.0	0.0	0.0	0.0	0.0	Compte de cap.,nia : crédit
Capital Account: Debit	0.0	0.0	0.0	0.0	0.0	0.0	0.0	Compte de capital : débit
Financial Account, nie	9 476.8	2 197.5	-2 549.7	-6 619.4	-6 275.5	-3 893.6	-3 142.4	Compte d'op. fin., nia
Net Errors and Omissions	-2 501.6	-136.9	3 038.8	-1 272.8	-3 220.9	-2 394.2	-390.5	Erreurs et omissions nettes
Reserves & Related Items	-2 513.3	3 874.7	-10 017.7	-4 711.9	1 008.8	-1 000.3	-3 656.8	Rés. et postes appareutés
Maldives								**Maldives**
Goods: Exports fob	79.9	89.7	95.6	91.5	108.7	110.2	133.6	Biens : exportations, fab
Goods: Imports fob	-265.5	-307.0	-311.5	-353.9	-342.0	-346.3	-344.7	Biens : importations, fab
Serv. & Income: Credit	295.0	319.7	339.9	351.8	358.8	360.9	359.6	Serv. & revenu : crédit
Serv. & Income: Debit	-115.7	-129.1	-135.6	-148.2	-150.0	-154.6	-151.9	Serv & revenu : débit
Current Trans.,nie: Credit	26.2	20.0	20.3	20.4	19.3	22.0	9.6	Transf. cour.,nia : crédit
Current Transfers: Debit	-27.3	-27.9	-30.4	-40.5	-46.2	-49.6	-50.2	Transf. courants : débit
Capital Acct.,nie: Credit	0.0	0.0	0.0	0.0	0.0	0.0	0.0	Compte de cap.,nia : crédit
Capital Account: Debit	0.0	0.0	0.0	0.0	0.0	0.0	0.0	Compte de capital : débit
Financial Account, nie	52.2	71.0	60.2	76.2	40.2	35.5	78.9	Compte d'op. fin., nia
Net Errors and Omissions	-16.4	-14.0	-18.2	11.4	6.9	-7.9	-27.1	Erreurs et omissions nettes
Reserves & Related Items	-28.3	-22.2	-20.2	-8.6	4.3	29.7	-7.8	Rés. et postes appareutés
Mali								**Mali**
Goods: Exports fob	432.8	561.5	556.2	571.0	545.1	725.2	...	Biens : exportations, fab
Goods: Imports fob	-551.5	-545.7	-558.2	-605.5	-592.1	-734.7	...	Biens : importations, fab
Serv. & Income: Credit	118.5	100.2	112.7	143.4	136.9	177.4	...	Serv. & revenu : crédit
Serv. & Income: Debit	-453.0	-420.7	-433.4	-474.9	-470.9	-613.6	...	Serv & revenu : débit
Current Trans.,nie: Credit	218.3	151.9	151.6	145.8	157.2	160.7	...	Transf. cour.,nia : crédit
Current Transfers: Debit	-25.9	-25.5	-37.1	-32.2	-30.8	-25.0	...	Transf. courants : débit
Capital Acct.,nie: Credit	138.1	112.5	124.0	113.4	101.6	107.5	...	Compte de cap.,nia : crédit
Capital Account: Debit	0.0	-1.1	0.0	-0.1	0.0	-0.1	...	Compte de capital : débit
Financial Account, nie	257.1	119.9	-50.3	1.1	141.4	32.9	...	Compte d'op. fin., nia
Net Errors and Omissions	14.1	4.1	-9.7	8.9	-4.8	9.4	...	Erreurs et omissions nettes
Reserves & Related Items	-148.5	-56.9	144.2	129.2	16.3	160.3	...	Rés. et postes appareutés

79

Summary of balance of payments
Millions of US dollars *[cont.]*

Résumé des balances des paiements
Millions de dollars des E.-U. *[suite]*

Country or area	1996	1997	1998	1999	2000	2001	2002	Pays ou zone
Malta								**Malte**
Goods: Exports fob	1 772.8	1 663.4	1 824.5	2 017.3	2 478.5	2 002.2	2 243.8	Biens : exportations, fab
Goods: Imports fob	-2 611.2	-2 384.6	-2 497.5	-2 680.2	-3 232.0	-2 568.2	-2 653.0	Biens : importations, fab
Serv. & Income: Credit	1 379.5	1 472.0	1 692.2	2 454.7	2 000.2	1 929.9	1 950.2	Serv. & revenu : crédit
Serv. & Income: Debit	-977.9	-1 008.0	-1 298.4	-1 956.2	-1 741.8	-1 537.2	-1 584.0	Serv & revenu : débit
Current Trans.,nie: Credit	86.7	122.4	115.0	120.4	101.8	190.5	238.1	Transf. cour.,nia : crédit
Current Transfers: Debit	-56.0	-67.2	-57.2	-77.9	-76.4	-182.3	-251.8	Transf. courants : débit
Capital Acct.,nie: Credit	64.4	32.9	33.3	31.1	24.1	4.4	8.0	Compte de cap.,nia : crédit
Capital Account: Debit	-6.0	-24.4	-4.7	-5.4	-5.5	-2.9	-1.7	Compte de capital : débit
Financial Account, nie	206.1	106.6	293.5	402.6	156.2	267.4	219.5	Compte d'op. fin., nia
Net Errors and Omissions	56.3	93.7	90.2	-68.2	73.0	151.3	118.7	Erreurs et omissions nettes
Reserves & Related Items	85.4	-6.7	-190.9	-238.3	221.8	-255.0	-287.9	Rés. et postes appareutés
Mauritania								**Mauritanie**
Goods: Exports fob	480.0	423.6	358.6	...	...	...	...	Biens : exportations, fab
Goods: Imports fob	-346.1	-316.5	-318.7	...	...	...	...	Biens : importations, fab
Serv. & Income: Credit	32.5	36.3	36.4	...	...	...	...	Serv. & revenu : crédit
Serv. & Income: Debit	-277.2	-240.2	-186.6	...	...	...	...	Serv & revenu : débit
Current Trans.,nie: Credit	217.5	157.9	198.3	...	...	...	...	Transf. cour.,nia : crédit
Current Transfers: Debit	-15.5	-13.3	-10.8	...	...	...	...	Transf. courants : débit
Capital Acct.,nie: Credit	0.0	0.0	0.0	...	...	...	...	Compte de cap.,nia : crédit
Capital Account: Debit	0.0	0.0	0.0	...	...	...	...	Compte de capital : débit
Financial Account, nie	-86.1	-17.3	-25.9	...	...	...	...	Compte d'op. fin., nia
Net Errors and Omissions	-1.0	-3.0	-8.1	...	...	...	...	Erreurs et omissions nettes
Reserves & Related Items	-4.2	-27.6	-43.2	...	...	...	...	Rés. et postes appareutés
Mauritius								**Maurice**
Goods: Exports fob	1 810.6	1 600.1	1 669.3	1 589.2	1 552.2	1 628.2	1 830.2	Biens : exportations, fab
Goods: Imports fob	-2 136.3	-2 036.1	-1 933.3	-2 107.9	-1 944.4	-1 846.0	-2 018.3	Biens : importations, fab
Serv. & Income: Credit	991.9	940.6	964.8	1 078.6	1 118.8	1 297.2	1 209.6	Serv. & revenu : crédit
Serv. & Income: Debit	-748.0	-720.9	-792.4	-787.7	-827.4	-871.0	-851.6	Serv & revenu : débit
Current Trans.,nie: Credit	182.8	206.4	186.8	196.4	167.6	193.1	188.3	Transf. cour.,nia : crédit
Current Transfers: Debit	-67.0	-79.0	-91.8	-92.8	-103.8	-125.5	-98.9	Transf. courants : débit
Capital Acct.,nie: Credit	0.0	0.0	0.0	0.0	0.0	0.4	0.0	Compte de cap.,nia : crédit
Capital Account: Debit	-0.8	-0.5	-0.8	-0.5	-0.6	-1.8	-1.9	Compte de capital : débit
Financial Account, nie	91.9	-18.6	-26.0	180.5	258.0	-247.8	123.4	Compte d'op. fin., nia
Net Errors and Omissions	-76.8	73.4	-41.9	133.9	10.1	-78.6	-39.6	Erreurs et omissions nettes
Reserves & Related Items	-48.3	34.6	65.4	-189.7	-230.6	51.8	-341.1	Rés. et postes appareutés
Mexico								**Mexique**
Goods: Exports fob	96 002.0	110 431.0	117 459.0	136 391.0	166 455.0	158 443.0	160 763.0	Biens : exportations, fab
Goods: Imports fob	-89 469.0	-109 808.0	-125 374.0	-141 975.0	-174 458.0	-168 396.0	-168 679.0	Biens : importations, fab
Serv. & Income: Credit	14 756.0	15 613.0	16 573.0	16 208.9	19 803.3	17 799.0	16 790.2	Serv. & revenu : crédit
Serv. & Income: Debit	-28 323.0	-29 152.0	-30 743.0	-30 937.9	-36 956.2	-35 251.4	-33 146.2	Serv & revenu : débit
Current Trans.,nie: Credit	4 535.0	5 245.0	6 016.0	6 313.3	6 999.4	9 336.4	10 287.3	Transf. cour.,nia : crédit
Current Transfers: Debit	-30.0	-25.0	-28.0	-26.9	-29.5	-21.9	-35.2	Transf. courants : débit
Capital Acct.,nie: Credit	0.0	0.0	0.0	0.0	0.0	0.0	0.0	Compte de cap.,nia : crédit
Capital Account: Debit	0.0	0.0	0.0	0.0	0.0	0.0	0.0	Compte de capital : débit
Financial Account, nie	4 248.0	25 745.0	12 194.0	17 452.0	22 237.3	25 276.9	22 206.9	Compte d'op. fin., nia
Net Errors and Omissions	229.4	2 411.4	401.6	823.9	3 075.0	129.0	-827.6	Erreurs et omissions nettes
Reserves & Related Items	-1 948.4	-20 460.4	3 501.4	-4 249.5	-7 126.2	-7 314.5	-7 359.1	Rés. et postes appareutés
Mongolia								**Mongolie**
Goods: Exports fob	423.4	568.5	462.4	454.3	535.8	523.2	524.0	Biens : exportations, fab
Goods: Imports fob	-459.7	-453.1	-524.2	-510.7	-608.4	-623.8	-680.2	Biens : importations, fab
Serv. & Income: Credit	69.1	58.8	87.9	82.5	90.7	128.3	198.0	Serv. & revenu : crédit
Serv. & Income: Debit	-139.5	-123.2	-156.5	-152.3	-182.3	-222.2	-284.5	Serv & revenu : débit
Current Trans.,nie: Credit	6.2	4.2	5.5	17.6	25.0	40.3	126.9	Transf. cour.,nia : crédit
Current Transfers: Debit	0.0	0.0	-3.6	-3.6	-16.9	0.0	-42.3	Transf. courants : débit
Capital Acct.,nie: Credit	0.0	0.0	0.0	0.0	0.0	0.0	0.0	Compte de cap.,nia : crédit
Capital Account: Debit	0.0	0.0	0.0	0.0	0.0	0.0	0.0	Compte de capital : débit
Financial Account, nie	41.3	27.0	126.2	69.6	89.9	107.0	157.4	Compte d'op. fin., nia
Net Errors and Omissions	-28.1	-75.6	-50.2	23.6	-19.3	-32.2	14.1	Erreurs et omissions nettes
Reserves & Related Items	87.3	-6.6	52.5	19.0	85.5	79.4	-13.4	Rés. et postes appareutés
Montserrat								**Montserrat**
Goods: Exports fob	41.3	8.2	1.2	1.3	1.1	0.7	1.5	Biens : exportations, fab

79

Summary of balance of payments
Millions of US dollars *[cont.]*

Résumé des balances des paiements
Millions de dollars des E.-U. *[suite]*

Country or area	1996	1997	1998	1999	2000	2001	2002	Pays ou zone
Goods: Imports fob	-36.0	-28.1	-19.4	-19.3	-21.6	-17.1	-25.4	Biens : importations, fab
Serv. & Income: Credit	16.1	14.8	13.8	21.5	17.3	15.5	15.4	Serv. & revenu : crédit
Serv. & Income: Debit	-19.4	-16.2	-24.8	-28.7	-23.0	-26.0	-27.6	Serv & revenu : débit
Current Trans.,nie: Credit	14.9	20.4	33.2	26.5	18.9	23.7	28.5	Transf. cour.,nia : crédit
Current Transfers: Debit	-1.3	-1.1	-2.2	-2.7	-1.9	-2.5	-2.6	Transf. courants : débit
Capital Acct.,nie: Credit	2.3	7.2	7.2	5.0	7.2	11.8	18.5	Compte de cap.,nia : crédit
Capital Account: Debit	-14.8	-3.6	-3.6	-3.6	-2.9	-2.0	-2.1	Compte de capital : débit
Financial Account, nie	-6.0	-9.1	3.7	-5.9	3.6	-5.8	-6.0	Compte d'op. fin., nia
Net Errors and Omissions	2.6	10.1	4.3	-4.6	-2.3	3.6	1.9	Erreurs et omissions nettes
Reserves & Related Items	0.1	-2.6	-13.5	10.6	3.6	-2.1	-2.0	Rés. et postes appareutés
Morocco								**Maroc**
Goods: Exports fob	6 886.2	7 039.1	7 143.7	7 509.0	7 418.6	7 141.8	7 838.9	Biens : exportations, fab
Goods: Imports fob	-9 079.6	-8 903.0	-9 462.6	-9 956.6	-10 653.6	-10 163.7	-10 900.3	Biens : importations, fab
Serv. & Income: Credit	2 932.0	2 643.4	3 020.3	3 301.7	3 310.2	4 355.0	4 736.6	Serv. & revenu : crédit
Serv. & Income: Debit	-3 279.9	-3 071.8	-3 189.9	-3 174.9	-3 032.7	-3 277.2	-3 528.4	Serv & revenu : débit
Current Trans.,nie: Credit	2 565.4	2 204.2	2 437.7	2 246.1	2 574.2	3 670.3	3 441.0	Transf. cour.,nia : crédit
Current Transfers: Debit	-82.5	-80.6	-95.0	-96.0	-117.7	-120.1	-115.4	Transf. courants : débit
Capital Acct.,nie: Credit	78.1	0.5	0.1	0.2	0.1	0.0	0.0	Compte de cap.,nia : crédit
Capital Account: Debit	-4.8	-5.0	-10.2	-8.8	-6.0	-8.9	-6.1	Compte de capital : débit
Financial Account, nie	-896.6	-989.8	-644.1	-13.0	-773.5	-966.2	-1 336.3	Compte d'op. fin., nia
Net Errors and Omissions	208.7	174.8	160.4	123.5	114.0	229.6	-181.9	Erreurs et omissions nettes
Reserves & Related Items	673.1	988.2	639.5	68.8	1 166.4	-860.5	52.0	Rés. et postes appareutés
Mozambique								**Mozambique**
Goods: Exports fob	226.1	230.0	244.6	283.8	364.0	726.0	...	Biens : exportations, fab
Goods: Imports fob	-704.4	-684.0	-735.6	-1 090.0	-1 046.0	-997.3	...	Biens : importations, fab
Serv. & Income: Credit	314.2	342.3	332.5	353.0	404.7	305.7	...	Serv. & revenu : crédit
Serv. & Income: Debit	-481.1	-496.8	-584.0	-620.5	-717.2	-909.0	...	Serv & revenu : débit
Current Trans.,nie: Credit	224.7	312.9	313.2	256.3	337.3	254.6	...	Transf. cour.,nia : crédit
Current Transfers: Debit	0.0	0.0	0.0	-94.6	-106.4	-37.1	...	Transf. courants : débit
Capital Acct.,nie: Credit	0.0	0.0	0.0	180.3	226.8	256.7	...	Compte de cap.,nia : crédit
Capital Account: Debit	0.0	0.0	0.0	0.0	0.0	0.0	...	Compte de capital : débit
Financial Account, nie	235.0	182.2	300.4	403.9	83.2	-24.8	...	Compte d'op. fin., nia
Net Errors and Omissions	-238.3	-364.8	-263.8	1.5	37.5	-59.6	...	Erreurs et omissions nettes
Reserves & Related Items	423.8	478.2	392.7	326.3	416.1	484.9	...	Rés. et postes appareutés
Myanmar								**Myanmar**
Goods: Exports fob	946.9	983.7	1 077.3	1 293.9	1 661.6	2 316.9	...	Biens : exportations, fab
Goods: Imports fob	-1 887.2	-2 126.4	-2 478.2	-2 181.3	-2 165.4	-2 587.9	...	Biens : importations, fab
Serv. & Income: Credit	441.0	533.2	644.1	563.8	513.3	459.6	...	Serv. & revenu : crédit
Serv. & Income: Debit	-358.4	-468.0	-380.2	-345.7	-496.9	-782.8	...	Serv & revenu : débit
Current Trans.,nie: Credit	604.1	691.6	638.1	384.8	289.8	298.5	...	Transf. cour.,nia : crédit
Current Transfers: Debit	-29.1	-30.0	-0.3	-0.3	-14.1	-12.8	...	Transf. courants : débit
Capital Acct.,nie: Credit	0.0	0.0	0.0	0.0	0.0	0.0	...	Compte de cap.,nia : crédit
Capital Account: Debit	0.0	0.0	0.0	0.0	0.0	0.0	...	Compte de capital : débit
Financial Account, nie	269.4	473.5	540.9	251.2	212.8	399.1	...	Compte d'op. fin., nia
Net Errors and Omissions	-11.8	-26.3	18.7	-12.4	-24.5	89.3	...	Erreurs et omissions nettes
Reserves & Related Items	25.0	-31.3	-60.4	45.9	23.4	-179.8	...	Rés. et postes appareutés
Namibia								**Namibie**
Goods: Exports fob	1 403.7	1 343.3	1 278.3	1 196.8	1 312.8	1 147.0	1 071.6	Biens : exportations, fab
Goods: Imports fob	-1 530.9	-1 615.0	-1 450.9	-1 396.9	-1 430.0	-1 325.5	-1 250.5	Biens : importations, fab
Serv. & Income: Credit	656.5	632.1	553.8	595.1	478.2	413.5	413.4	Serv. & revenu : crédit
Serv. & Income: Debit	-829.9	-714.3	-622.8	-553.9	-578.5	-551.5	-382.9	Serv & revenu : débit
Current Trans.,nie: Credit	437.3	462.2	418.2	380.4	419.2	347.4	276.1	Transf. cour.,nia : crédit
Current Transfers: Debit	-21.0	-18.0	-14.7	-59.5	-37.9	-36.4	-31.2	Transf. courants : débit
Capital Acct.,nie: Credit	42.5	33.9	24.2	23.2	112.9	96.0	107.7	Compte de cap.,nia : crédit
Capital Account: Debit	-0.5	-0.4	-0.4	-0.3	-0.3	-0.2	-0.2	Compte de capital : débit
Financial Account, nie	-174.0	-71.4	-145.6	-173.6	-223.2	-414.2	-335.0	Compte d'op. fin., nia
Net Errors and Omissions	39.1	15.3	15.7	-46.2	-156.4	-12.9	80.8	Erreurs et omissions nettes
Reserves & Related Items	-22.9	-67.8	-55.8	34.8	103.3	336.9	50.2	Rés. et postes appareutés
Nepal								**Népal**
Goods: Exports fob	388.7	413.8	482.0	612.3	776.1	720.5	...	Biens : exportations, fab
Goods: Imports fob	-1 494.7	-1 691.9	-1 239.1	-1 494.2	-1 590.1	-1 485.7	...	Biens : importations, fab
Serv. & Income: Credit	790.6	897.6	610.6	710.9	578.1	483.6	...	Serv. & revenu : crédit

79

Summary of balance of payments
Millions of US dollars *[cont.]*

Résumé des balances des paiements
Millions de dollars des E.-U. *[suite]*

Country or area	1996	1997	1998	1999	2000	2001	2002	Pays ou zone
Serv. & Income: Debit	-274.8	-253.1	-222.7	-240.9	-235.1	-273.5	...	Serv & revenu : débit
Current Trans.,nie: Credit	281.6	267.4	326.0	182.3	189.0	240.2	...	Transf. cour.,nia : crédit
Current Transfers: Debit	-18.0	-21.8	-24.1	-26.9	-16.7	-24.3	...	Transf. courants : débit
Capital Acct.,nie: Credit	0.0	0.0	0.0	0.0	0.0	0.0	...	Compte de cap.,nia : crédit
Capital Account: Debit	0.0	0.0	0.0	0.0	0.0	0.0	...	Compte de capital : débit
Financial Account, nie	275.2	340.3	212.9	-24.5	76.1	-216.9	...	Compte d'op. fin., nia
Net Errors and Omissions	82.3	216.6	134.0	58.3	145.7	256.5	...	Erreurs et omissions nettes
Reserves & Related Items	-30.9	-168.8	-279.7	222.7	77.0	299.6	...	Rés. et postes appareutés
Netherlands								**Pays-Bas**
Goods: Exports fob	195 079.0	188 988.0	196 041.0	195 691.0	204 410.0	204 507.0	206 887.0	Biens : exportations, fab
Goods: Imports fob	-172 312.0	-168 051.0	-175 611.0	-179 657.0	-186 983.0	-183 667.0	-186 943.0	Biens : importations, fab
Serv. & Income: Credit	83 533.8	88 151.3	85 047.4	92 793.5	94 814.4	91 112.0	96 065.1	Serv. & revenu : crédit
Serv. & Income: Debit	-78 028.2	-77 891.6	-85 264.8	-89 479.1	-99 206.4	-97 383.2	-99 684.6	Serv & revenu : débit
Current Trans.,nie: Credit	4 319.3	4 345.5	3 798.7	4 565.8	4 399.1	4 475.2	5 540.4	Transf. cour.,nia : crédit
Current Transfers: Debit	-11 089.3	-10 465.2	-10 980.6	-10 917.8	-10 617.6	-11 214.3	-11 748.8	Transf. courants : débit
Capital Acct.,nie: Credit	1 266.7	1 099.2	1 037.4	1 688.0	2 216.3	1 117.8	856.9	Compte de cap.,nia : crédit
Capital Account: Debit	-3 290.7	-2 396.3	-1 457.2	-1 902.1	-2 313.8	-4 317.3	-1 402.3	Compte de capital : débit
Financial Account, nie	-5 473.7	-14 304.0	-14 397.6	-9 905.3	-7 483.9	504.1	-12 550.2	Compte d'op. fin., nia
Net Errors and Omissions	-19 699.6	-12 184.5	-553.0	-7 488.1	984.2	-5 485.0	2 847.8	Erreurs et omissions nettes
Reserves & Related Items	5 694.9	2 709.0	2 339.4	4 611.0	-219.5	350.7	132.0	Rés. et postes appareutés
Netherlands Antilles								**Antilles néerlandaises**
Goods: Exports fob	614.6	501.4	465.6	467.0	676.1	657.3	589.3	Biens : exportations, fab
Goods: Imports fob	-1 743.7	-1 476.7	-1 513.2	-1 584.3	-1 661.7	-1 752.5	-1 602.7	Biens : importations, fab
Serv. & Income: Credit	1 541.3	1 525.8	1 655.1	1 565.9	1 739.8	1 753.2	1 817.7	Serv. & revenu : crédit
Serv. & Income: Debit	-695.7	-628.8	-720.6	-783.4	-836.8	-850.7	-859.9	Serv & revenu : débit
Current Trans.,nie: Credit	174.7	165.3	137.2	179.6	246.6	222.5	368.8	Transf. cour.,nia : crédit
Current Transfers: Debit	-145.0	-152.1	-161.0	-175.8	-214.3	-216.2	-256.8	Transf. courants : débit
Capital Acct.,nie: Credit	71.9	76.9	91.3	109.8	31.3	37.9	29.3	Compte de cap.,nia : crédit
Capital Account: Debit	-0.6	-1.7	-4.4	-1.5	-1.4	-0.6	-1.6	Compte de capital : débit
Financial Account, nie	95.8	-31.2	58.0	123.2	-126.3	344.1	-11.5	Compte d'op. fin., nia
Net Errors and Omissions	14.8	14.9	17.4	24.6	17.1	22.8	-13.0	Erreurs et omissions nettes
Reserves & Related Items	71.9	6.3	-25.5	74.7	129.6	-217.7	-59.5	Rés. et postes appareutés
New Zealand								**Nouvelle-Zélande**
Goods: Exports fob	14 337.5	14 282.4	12 245.6	12 656.8	13 530.5	13 919.7	14 516.8	Biens : exportations, fab
Goods: Imports fob	-13 814.5	-13 379.6	-11 333.5	-13 028.0	-12 849.4	-12 448.5	-14 014.6	Biens : importations, fab
Serv. & Income: Credit	5 024.8	4 647.5	4 642.9	5 304.5	5 145.7	4 981.3	6 167.3	Serv. & revenu : crédit
Serv. & Income: Debit	-9 981.4	-10 151.6	-7 991.7	-8 617.8	-8 487.4	-7 850.6	-8 995.2	Serv & revenu : débit
Current Trans.,nie: Credit	896.7	680.5	680.9	609.5	633.6	577.3	614.2	Transf. cour.,nia : crédit
Current Transfers: Debit	-354.0	-383.0	-400.9	-440.5	-432.5	-486.4	-557.1	Transf. courants : débit
Capital Acct.,nie: Credit	1 838.2	782.9	263.1	260.2	238.3	821.5	1 122.3	Compte de cap.,nia : crédit
Capital Account: Debit	-502.4	-541.1	-443.7	-476.8	-418.0	-378.3	-357.2	Compte de capital : débit
Financial Account, nie	3 571.4	4 045.4	1 580.3	1 973.6	2 502.5	3 185.0	1 268.5	Compte d'op. fin., nia
Net Errors and Omissions	755.8	-1 425.7	271.1	1 946.9	-6.0	-2 508.2	1 321.4	Erreurs et omissions nettes
Reserves & Related Items	-1 772.2	1 442.3	486.0	-188.4	142.8	187.2	-1 086.5	Rés. et postes appareutés
Nicaragua								**Nicaragua**
Goods: Exports fob	470.2	581.6	580.1	552.4	649.9	614.6	605.1	Biens : exportations, fab
Goods: Imports fob	-1 044.3	-1 371.2	-1 397.1	-1 698.2	-1 653.1	-1 620.4	-1 636.4	Biens : importations, fab
Serv. & Income: Credit	183.7	230.4	276.9	317.6	334.5	332.3	312.2	Serv. & revenu : crédit
Serv. & Income: Debit	-587.6	-518.8	-479.0	-562.2	-575.9	-608.1	-545.2	Serv & revenu : débit
Current Trans.,nie: Credit	95.0	150.0	200.0	300.0	320.0	335.7	376.5	Transf. cour.,nia : crédit
Current Transfers: Debit	0.0	0.0	0.0	0.0	0.0	0.0	0.0	Transf. courants : débit
Capital Acct.,nie: Credit	317.1	278.9	325.7	461.6	441.8	404.7	367.8	Compte de cap.,nia : crédit
Capital Account: Debit	0.0	0.0	0.0	0.0	0.0	0.0	0.0	Compte de capital : débit
Financial Account, nie	-332.0	33.5	231.6	525.5	62.7	58.3	1.0	Compte d'op. fin., nia
Net Errors and Omissions	149.7	322.5	-140.1	-291.9	-35.7	-41.9	90.5	Erreurs et omissions nettes
Reserves & Related Items	748.2	293.1	401.9	395.2	455.8	524.8	428.5	Rés. et postes appareutés
Nigeria								**Nigéria**
Goods: Exports fob	16 117.0	15 207.3	8 971.2	12 875.7	...	...	...	Biens : exportations, fab
Goods: Imports fob	-6 438.4	-9 501.4	-9 211.3	-8 587.6	...	...	...	Biens : importations, fab
Serv. & Income: Credit	847.5	1 044.9	1 216.6	1 219.3	...	...	...	Serv. & revenu : crédit
Serv. & Income: Debit	-7 964.1	-8 115.7	-6 789.5	-6 293.3	...	...	...	Serv & revenu : débit
Current Trans.,nie: Credit	946.6	1 920.3	1 574.2	1 301.1	...	...	...	Transf. cour.,nia : crédit

79
Summary of balance of payments
Millions of US dollars *[cont.]*
Résumé des balances des paiements
Millions de dollars des E.-U. *[suite]*

Country or area	1996	1997	1998	1999	2000	2001	2002	Pays ou zone
Current Transfers: Debit	-1.7	-3.8	-4.7	-9.4	...	...	...	Transf. courants : débit
Capital Acct.,nie: Credit	0.0	0.0	0.0	0.0	...	...	...	Compte de cap.,nia : crédit
Capital Account: Debit	-68.1	-49.4	-54.3	-47.7	...	...	...	Compte de capital : débit
Financial Account, nie	-4 155.0	-424.9	1 502.5	-4 002.4	...	...	...	Compte d'op. fin., nia
Net Errors and Omissions	-44.8	-62.1	-77.5	6.8	...	...	...	Erreurs et omissions nettes
Reserves & Related Items	761.0	-15.1	2 872.8	3 537.6	...	...	...	Rés. et postes appareutés
Norway								**Norvège**
Goods: Exports fob	50 080.6	49 375.4	40 887.8	46 224.3	60 463.3	59 650.1	60 064.0	Biens : exportations, fab
Goods: Imports fob	-37 108.8	-37 727.0	-38 826.6	-35 501.5	-34 488.0	-33 203.8	-35 692.7	Biens : importations, fab
Serv. & Income: Credit	19 983.4	21 297.4	22 350.9	21 978.4	23 904.2	25 478.8	28 562.9	Serv. & revenu : crédit
Serv. & Income: Debit	-20 480.4	-21 516.8	-22 872.7	-22 879.9	-22 743.8	-23 716.8	-25 401.4	Serv & revenu : débit
Current Trans.,nie: Credit	1 329.2	1 468.1	1 500.5	1 680.7	1 604.8	1 474.5	1 649.4	Transf. cour.,nia : crédit
Current Transfers: Debit	-2 835.2	-2 861.2	-3 033.7	-3 124.3	-2 889.5	-3 153.2	-4 034.0	Transf. courants : débit
Capital Acct.,nie: Credit	64.5	30.2	43.7	40.5	134.7	113.3	43.4	Compte de cap.,nia : crédit
Capital Account: Debit	-191.9	-214.1	-159.9	-156.4	-225.4	-203.3	-119.1	Compte de capital : débit
Financial Account, nie	-1 461.6	-6 607.3	60.7	431.4	-13 394.7	-25 164.6	-7 522.5	Compte d'op. fin., nia
Net Errors and Omissions	-2 910.0	-4 442.6	-6 334.6	-2 709.5	-8 679.7	-4 087.6	-13 525.2	Erreurs et omissions nettes
Reserves & Related Items	-6 469.9	1 197.9	6 384.0	-5 983.7	-3 685.8	2 812.5	-4 024.9	Rés. et postes appareutés
Occupied Palestinian Terr. [3]								**Terr. palestinien occupé** [3]
Goods: Exports fob	529.9	611.7	610.6	602.8	697.4	544.1	...	Biens : exportations, fab
Goods: Imports fob	-2 893.4	-3 054.9	-3 021.7	-3 220.7	-3 000.0	-2 010.6	...	Biens : importations, fab
Serv. & Income: Credit	891.3	964.9	1 325.8	1 435.1	1 260.5	612.0	...	Serv. & revenu : crédit
Serv. & Income: Debit	-460.4	-538.9	-537.5	-542.9	-566.6	-758.2	...	Serv & revenu : débit
Current Trans.,nie: Credit	598.5	591.7	545.1	572.9	709.6	1 070.8	...	Transf. cour.,nia : crédit
Current Transfers: Debit	-90.3	-122.0	-134.9	-174.1	-123.8	-99.4	...	Transf. courants : débit
Capital Acct.,nie: Credit	264.1	278.4	264.4	281.5	198.1	229.8	...	Compte de cap.,nia : crédit
Capital Account: Debit	0.0	0.0	0.0	0.0	0.0	0.0	...	Compte de capital : débit
Financial Account, nie	206.0	936.5	643.7	829.4	1 067.4	320.9	...	Compte d'op. fin., nia
Net Errors and Omissions	1 175.7	490.6	251.6	180.9	-158.5	52.0	...	Erreurs et omissions nettes
Reserves & Related Items	-221.4	-158.0	52.9	35.1	-84.1	38.6	...	Rés. et postes appareutés
Oman								**Oman**
Goods: Exports fob	7 373.2	7 656.7	5 521.5	7 238.8	11 318.6	11 074.1	...	Biens : exportations, fab
Goods: Imports fob	-4 231.5	-4 645.0	-5 214.6	-4 299.6	-4 593.0	-5 310.8	...	Biens : importations, fab
Serv. & Income: Credit	494.1	652.8	707.4	587.8	715.2	658.0	...	Serv. & revenu : crédit
Serv. & Income: Debit	-1 927.2	-2 241.6	-2 497.0	-2 380.0	-2 567.0	-2 574.8	...	Serv & revenu : débit
Current Trans.,nie: Credit	0.0	0.0	0.0	0.0	0.0	0.0	...	Transf. cour.,nia : crédit
Current Transfers: Debit	-1 370.6	-1 500.7	-1 466.8	-1 438.4	-1 451.2	-1 531.9	...	Transf. courants : débit
Capital Acct.,nie: Credit	28.6	54.6	20.8	15.6	33.8	7.8	...	Compte de cap.,nia : crédit
Capital Account: Debit	-18.2	-23.4	-26.0	-18.2	-26.0	-18.2	...	Compte de capital : débit
Financial Account, nie	260.1	52.0	1 487.7	109.2	-494.1	-886.9	...	Compte d'op. fin., nia
Net Errors and Omissions	-420.1	525.5	701.7	399.3	-673.9	-383.8	...	Erreurs et omissions nettes
Reserves & Related Items	-188.5	-531.0	765.4	-214.6	-2 262.4	-1 033.6	...	Rés. et postes appareutés
Pakistan								**Pakistan**
Goods: Exports fob	8 507.3	8 350.7	7 850.0	7 673.0	8 739.0	9 131.0	9 792.0	Biens : exportations, fab
Goods: Imports fob	-12 163.7	-10 750.2	-9 834.0	-9 520.0	-9 896.0	-9 741.0	-10 406.0	Biens : importations, fab
Serv. & Income: Credit	2 191.7	1 771.8	1 487.0	1 492.0	1 498.0	1 572.0	2 597.0	Serv. & revenu : crédit
Serv. & Income: Debit	-5 656.6	-5 024.6	-4 524.0	-4 105.0	-4 588.0	-4 519.0	-4 557.0	Serv & revenu : débit
Current Trans.,nie: Credit	2 739.5	3 980.6	2 801.0	3 582.0	4 200.0	5 496.0	6 490.0	Transf. cour.,nia : crédit
Current Transfers: Debit	-54.1	-39.9	-28.0	-42.0	-38.0	-61.0	-45.0	Transf. courants : débit
Capital Acct.,nie: Credit	0.0	0.0	0.0	0.0	0.0	0.0	0.0	Compte de cap.,nia : crédit
Capital Account: Debit	0.0	0.0	0.0	0.0	0.0	0.0	0.0	Compte de capital : débit
Financial Account, nie	3 496.2	2 321.1	-1 873.0	-2 364.0	-3 099.0	-389.0	-362.0	Compte d'op. fin., nia
Net Errors and Omissions	159.6	-71.8	1 011.2	768.1	556.9	707.7	632.0	Erreurs et omissions nettes
Reserves & Related Items	780.3	-537.7	3 109.8	2 515.9	2 627.1	-2 196.7	-4 141.0	Rés. et postes appareutés
Panama								**Panama**
Goods: Exports fob	5 822.9	6 669.7	6 350.1	5 303.3	5 838.5	5 996.4	5 283.8	Biens : exportations, fab
Goods: Imports fob	-6 467.0	-7 354.9	-7 714.6	-6 689.4	-6 981.4	-6 671.7	-6 460.2	Biens : importations, fab
Serv. & Income: Credit	3 014.1	3 156.7	3 516.5	3 296.5	3 560.7	3 409.0	3 210.1	Serv. & revenu : crédit
Serv. & Income: Debit	-2 705.3	-3 128.8	-3 492.9	-3 401.7	-3 310.3	-3 085.7	-2 399.9	Serv & revenu : débit
Current Trans.,nie: Credit	167.7	185.2	195.2	202.7	208.7	226.0	242.0	Transf. cour.,nia : crédit
Current Transfers: Debit	-33.0	-34.6	-36.6	-31.6	-31.7	-28.1	-29.5	Transf. courants : débit
Capital Acct.,nie: Credit	2.5	72.7	50.9	3.0	1.7	1.6	0.0	Compte de cap.,nia : crédit

79

Summary of balance of payments
Millions of US dollars *[cont.]*

Résumé des balances des paiements
Millions de dollars des E.-U. *[suite]*

Country or area	1996	1997	1998	1999	2000	2001	2002	Pays ou zone
Capital Account: Debit	0.0	0.0	0.0	0.0	0.0	0.0	0.0	Compte de capital : débit
Financial Account, nie	561.2	972.3	1 076.8	1 398.2	-11.4	547.8	266.4	Compte d'op. fin., nia
Net Errors and Omissions	-96.3	-195.0	-325.1	-228.7	398.2	-693.8	729.8	Erreurs et omissions nettes
Reserves & Related Items	-266.8	-343.3	379.7	147.7	327.0	298.5	-842.5	Rés. et postes appareutés
Papua New Guinea								**Papouasie-Nvl-Guinée**
Goods: Exports fob	2 529.8	2 160.1	1 773.3	1 927.4	2 094.1	1 812.9	...	Biens : exportations, fab
Goods: Imports fob	-1 513.3	-1 483.3	-1 078.3	-1 071.4	-998.8	-932.4	...	Biens : importations, fab
Serv. & Income: Credit	464.3	432.1	339.0	266.1	274.7	305.1	...	Serv. & revenu : crédit
Serv. & Income: Debit	-1 239.7	-1 268.4	-1 073.6	-1 019.0	-1 014.4	-912.2	...	Serv & revenu : débit
Current Trans.,nie: Credit	252.1	69.9	82.4	60.3	62.4	75.9	...	Transf. cour.,nia : crédit
Current Transfers: Debit	-304.2	-102.6	-71.6	-68.7	-72.7	-67.3	...	Transf. courants : débit
Capital Acct.,nie: Credit	15.2	13.9	9.7	7.8	7.2	5.9	...	Compte de cap.,nia : crédit
Capital Account: Debit	-15.2	-13.9	-9.7	-7.8	-7.2	-5.9	...	Compte de capital : débit
Financial Account, nie	46.6	8.0	-179.7	16.0	-254.1	-151.9	...	Compte d'op. fin., nia
Net Errors and Omissions	-33.1	7.3	-12.5	14.3	13.1	-1.6	...	Erreurs et omissions nettes
Reserves & Related Items	-202.5	177.0	221.0	-125.0	-104.5	-128.6	...	Rés. et postes appareutés
Paraguay								**Paraguay**
Goods: Exports fob	3 796.9	3 327.5	3 548.6	2 312.4	2 225.8	1 951.8	2 319.3	Biens : exportations, fab
Goods: Imports fob	-4 383.4	-4 192.4	-3 941.5	-2 752.9	-2 904.0	-2 507.0	-2 390.9	Biens : importations, fab
Serv. & Income: Credit	881.4	933.1	891.8	787.9	866.4	777.9	705.8	Serv. & revenu : crédit
Serv. & Income: Debit	-830.0	-899.5	-836.2	-688.0	-655.5	-634.1	-456.5	Serv & revenu : débit
Current Trans.,nie: Credit	183.0	182.2	178.3	176.7	178.3	168.0	117.6	Transf. cour.,nia : crédit
Current Transfers: Debit	-0.8	-1.3	-1.0	-1.0	-1.5	-1.6	-1.6	Transf. courants : débit
Capital Acct.,nie: Credit	14.2	7.5	5.4	19.6	3.0	15.2	4.0	Compte de cap.,nia : crédit
Capital Account: Debit	0.0	0.0	0.0	0.0	0.0	0.0	0.0	Compte de capital : débit
Financial Account, nie	152.4	421.3	312.9	89.2	27.4	265.4	-168.3	Compte d'op. fin., nia
Net Errors and Omissions	139.8	5.8	-141.6	-244.3	-79.3	-85.8	-227.1	Erreurs et omissions nettes
Reserves & Related Items	46.5	215.8	-16.7	300.9	339.4	50.2	97.7	Rés. et postes appareutés
Peru								**Pérou**
Goods: Exports fob	5 877.4	6 824.4	5 756.8	6 088.0	6 951.2	7 006.8	7 647.0	Biens : exportations, fab
Goods: Imports fob	-7 868.5	-8 567.2	-8 262.2	-6 793.3	-7 406.6	-7 273.4	-7 439.9	Biens : importations, fab
Serv. & Income: Credit	2 023.8	2 272.5	2 560.6	2 248.4	2 340.3	2 157.4	1 881.7	Serv. & revenu : crédit
Serv. & Income: Debit	-4 594.6	-4 878.0	-4 422.5	-4 026.6	-4 441.0	-4 116.1	-4 338.3	Serv & revenu : débit
Current Trans.,nie: Credit	921.8	928.5	988.9	992.4	1 007.9	1 050.1	1 051.6	Transf. cour.,nia : crédit
Current Transfers: Debit	-8.0	-8.2	-11.7	-26.8	-8.6	-8.5	-8.3	Transf. courants : débit
Capital Acct.,nie: Credit	50.7	24.4	20.8	25.0	24.2	32.0	14.4	Compte de cap.,nia : crédit
Capital Account: Debit	-29.2	-74.3	-78.1	-79.4	-91.3	-100.2	-109.8	Compte de capital : débit
Financial Account, nie	3 805.7	5 697.1	1 832.5	527.9	992.8	1 523.8	2 130.4	Compte d'op. fin., nia
Net Errors and Omissions	700.6	-164.6	373.9	176.5	501.5	127.4	143.3	Erreurs et omissions nettes
Reserves & Related Items	-879.8	-2 054.6	1 241.1	867.9	129.7	-399.2	-972.2	Rés. et postes appareutés
Philippines								**Philippines**
Goods: Exports fob	20 543.0	25 228.0	29 496.0	34 211.0	37 295.0	31 243.0	34 383.0	Biens : exportations, fab
Goods: Imports fob	-31 885.0	-36 355.0	-29 524.0	-29 252.0	-33 481.0	-31 986.0	-33 975.0	Biens : importations, fab
Serv. & Income: Credit	19 006.0	22 835.0	13 917.0	12 885.0	11 776.0	10 300.0	10 987.0	Serv. & revenu : crédit
Serv. & Income: Debit	-12 206.0	-17 139.0	-12 778.0	-11 137.0	-9 769.0	-8 681.0	-7 701.0	Serv & revenu : débit
Current Trans.,nie: Credit	1 185.0	1 670.0	758.0	607.0	552.0	517.0	594.0	Transf. cour.,nia : crédit
Current Transfers: Debit	-596.0	-590.0	-323.0	-95.0	-115.0	-70.0	-91.0	Transf. courants : débit
Capital Acct.,nie: Credit	0.0	0.0	0.0	44.0	74.0	12.0	2.0	Compte de cap.,nia : crédit
Capital Account: Debit	0.0	0.0	0.0	-52.0	-36.0	-24.0	-21.0	Compte de capital : débit
Financial Account, nie	11 277.0	6 498.0	483.0	-2 250.0	-4 042.0	-394.0	-2 740.0	Compte d'op. fin., nia
Net Errors and Omissions	-2 986.0	-5 241.4	-749.9	-1 310.9	-2 629.6	-433.5	-1 431.7	Erreurs et omissions nettes
Reserves & Related Items	-4 338.0	3 094.4	-1 279.1	-3 650.1	375.5	-483.5	-6.3	Rés. et postes appareutés
Poland								**Pologne**
Goods: Exports fob	27 557.0	30 731.0	32 467.0	30 060.0	35 902.0	41 664.0	46 742.0	Biens : exportations, fab
Goods: Imports fob	-34 844.0	-40 553.0	-45 303.0	-45 132.0	-48 210.0	-49 324.0	-53 991.0	Biens : importations, fab
Serv. & Income: Credit	11 274.0	10 382.0	13 066.0	10 200.0	12 637.0	12 380.0	11 985.0	Serv. & revenu : crédit
Serv. & Income: Debit	-8 945.0	-8 339.0	-10 008.0	-9 829.0	-12 707.0	-12 966.0	-13 023.0	Serv & revenu : débit
Current Trans.,nie: Credit	2 825.0	2 700.0	3 520.0	2 898.0	3 008.0	3 737.0	4 182.0	Transf. cour.,nia : crédit
Current Transfers: Debit	-1 131.0	-665.0	-623.0	-684.0	-628.0	-848.0	-902.0	Transf. courants : débit
Capital Acct.,nie: Credit	5 833.0	91.0	117.0	95.0	109.0	112.0	46.0	Compte de cap.,nia : crédit
Capital Account: Debit	-5 739.0	-25.0	-54.0	-40.0	-77.0	-37.0	-53.0	Compte de capital : débit
Financial Account, nie	6 673.0	7 410.0	13 282.0	10 462.0	10 202.0	3 173.0	6 955.0	Compte d'op. fin., nia

79

Summary of balance of payments
Millions of US dollars *[cont.]*

Résumé des balances des paiements
Millions de dollars des E.-U. *[suite]*

Country or area	1996	1997	1998	1999	2000	2001	2002	Pays ou zone
Net Errors and Omissions	321.3	1 309.3	-519.6	2 125.6	389.2	1 680.7	-1 292.8	Erreurs et omissions nettes
Reserves & Related Items	-3 824.3	-3 041.3	-5 924.4	-155.6	-625.2	428.3	-648.2	Rés. et postes appareutés
Portugal								**Portugal**
Goods: Exports fob	25 623.0	25 379.2	25 617.9	25 473.6	25 225.2	25 251.2	27 009.0	Biens : exportations, fab
Goods: Imports fob	-35 344.8	-35 721.2	-37 828.9	-39 187.5	-39 077.9	-38 551.9	-39 124.0	Biens : importations, fab
Serv. & Income: Credit	12 289.6	12 239.9	13 325.4	12 940.9	13 060.5	14 161.0	15 289.1	Serv. & revenu : crédit
Serv. & Income: Debit	-12 055.4	-12 316.3	-13 037.9	-12 843.5	-13 706.1	-14 646.3	-15 302.5	Serv & revenu : débit
Current Trans.,nie: Credit	6 514.8	5 985.1	6 169.6	6 047.6	5 386.0	5 555.7	6 048.5	Transf. cour.,nia : crédit
Current Transfers: Debit	-2 243.2	-2 031.3	-2 079.5	-2 164.5	-2 001.3	-2 173.1	-2 733.6	Transf. courants : débit
Capital Acct.,nie: Credit	2 836.4	2 892.7	2 724.2	2 641.9	1 680.6	1 277.7	2 083.2	Compte de cap.,nia : crédit
Capital Account: Debit	-141.4	-188.9	-178.7	-183.1	-168.7	-210.3	-196.0	Compte de capital : débit
Financial Account, nie	3 835.2	6 662.3	5 980.3	9 106.5	10 728.3	10 329.5	9 176.9	Compte d'op. fin., nia
Net Errors and Omissions	-766.7	-1 927.7	-184.5	-1 616.4	-755.8	-141.0	-1 233.2	Erreurs et omissions nettes
Reserves & Related Items	-547.5	-973.7	-507.9	-215.6	-370.7	-852.5	-1 017.5	Rés. et postes appareutés
Republic of Moldova								**République de Moldova**
Goods: Exports fob	822.9	889.6	643.6	474.3	476.8	567.3	659.8	Biens : exportations, fab
Goods: Imports fob	-1 082.5	-1 237.6	-1 031.7	-611.4	-770.5	-878.6	-1 038.1	Biens : importations, fab
Serv. & Income: Credit	205.3	300.5	288.8	256.0	337.9	403.0	486.5	Serv. & revenu : crédit
Serv. & Income: Debit	-210.6	-281.4	-300.9	-274.0	-302.9	-344.8	-366.0	Serv & revenu : débit
Current Trans.,nie: Credit	72.9	104.1	110.9	111.5	160.9	159.5	163.9	Transf. cour.,nia : crédit
Current Transfers: Debit	-2.8	-50.0	-45.5	-35.4	-9.1	-11.7	-14.8	Transf. courants : débit
Capital Acct.,nie: Credit	0.1	0.1	2.1	1.5	2.8	1.1	0.8	Compte de cap.,nia : crédit
Capital Account: Debit	-0.1	-0.3	-2.5	-0.4	-0.9	-3.1	-0.5	Compte de capital : débit
Financial Account, nie	76.6	95.2	5.2	-31.9	140.1	59.5	24.8	Compte d'op. fin., nia
Net Errors and Omissions	15.5	-7.9	-22.8	-3.9	-10.6	12.2	21.9	Erreurs et omissions nettes
Reserves & Related Items	102.7	187.8	352.8	113.8	-24.5	35.5	61.6	Rés. et postes appareutés
Romania								**Roumanie**
Goods: Exports fob	8 085.0	8 431.0	8 302.0	8 503.0	10 366.0	11 385.0	13 876.0	Biens : exportations, fab
Goods: Imports fob	-10 555.0	-10 411.0	-10 927.0	-9 595.0	-12 050.0	-14 354.0	-16 487.0	Biens : importations, fab
Serv. & Income: Credit	1 641.0	1 727.0	1 489.0	1 517.0	2 072.0	2 487.0	2 760.0	Serv. & revenu : crédit
Serv. & Income: Debit	-2 335.0	-2 430.0	-2 534.0	-2 348.0	-2 603.0	-2 890.0	-3 210.0	Serv & revenu : débit
Current Trans.,nie: Credit	667.0	731.0	886.0	804.0	1 079.0	1 417.0	1 808.0	Transf. cour.,nia : crédit
Current Transfers: Debit	-82.0	-152.0	-133.0	-178.0	-219.0	-274.0	-272.0	Transf. courants : débit
Capital Acct.,nie: Credit	152.0	43.0	39.0	46.0	37.0	108.0	100.0	Compte de cap.,nia : crédit
Capital Account: Debit	0.0	0.0	0.0	-1.0	-1.0	-13.0	-7.0	Compte de capital : débit
Financial Account, nie	1 486.0	2 458.0	2 042.0	697.0	2 102.0	2 938.0	4 079.0	Compte d'op. fin., nia
Net Errors and Omissions	358.6	1 061.9	193.4	794.5	125.0	730.6	-856.0	Erreurs et omissions nettes
Reserves & Related Items	582.4	-1 458.9	642.6	-239.5	-908.0	-1 534.6	-1 791.0	Rés. et postes appareutés
Russian Federation								**Fédération de Russie**
Goods: Exports fob	89 684.0	86 895.0	74 443.0	75 549.0	105 034.0	101 884.0	107 601.0	Biens : exportations, fab
Goods: Imports fob	-68 093.0	-71 982.0	-58 014.0	-39 537.0	-44 862.0	-53 763.7	-60 965.8	Biens : importations, fab
Serv. & Income: Credit	17 619.0	18 446.0	16 674.0	12 949.0	14 317.0	18 217.2	19 268.1	Serv. & revenu : crédit
Serv. & Income: Debit	-28 433.0	-33 083.0	-32 550.0	-24 951.0	-27 720.0	-32 006.7	-35 993.6	Serv & revenu : débit
Current Trans.,nie: Credit	771.0	410.0	308.0	1 183.0	808.0	381.4	1 600.1	Transf. cour.,nia : crédit
Current Transfers: Debit	-701.0	-766.0	-645.0	-582.0	-737.0	-1 139.9	-1 604.6	Transf. courants : débit
Capital Acct.,nie: Credit	3 066.0	2 138.0	1 705.0	887.0	11 543.0	2 124.9	7 528.2	Compte de cap.,nia : crédit
Capital Account: Debit	-3 529.0	-2 934.0	-2 087.0	-1 213.0	-868.0	-11 502.8	-19 924.2	Compte de capital : débit
Financial Account, nie	-19 890.0	3 164.0	-11 404.0	-17 434.0	-34 435.0	-4 080.8	169.5	Compte d'op. fin., nia
Net Errors and Omissions	-7 711.9	-8 807.6	-9 808.4	-8 555.4	-9 157.8	-8 848.0	-6 115.7	Erreurs et omissions nettes
Reserves & Related Items	17 217.9	6 519.6	21 378.4	1 704.4	-13 922.2	-11 265.8	-11 563.4	Rés. et postes appareutés
Rwanda								**Rwanda**
Goods: Exports fob	61.8	93.2	64.2	61.5	68.4	93.3	67.2	Biens : exportations, fab
Goods: Imports fob	-219.0	-278.4	-233.0	-246.9	-223.2	-245.2	-233.3	Biens : importations, fab
Serv. & Income: Credit	27.0	59.2	57.0	58.5	73.1	80.0	73.7	Serv. & revenu : crédit
Serv. & Income: Debit	-168.9	-223.2	-205.6	-211.7	-228.5	-223.2	-228.7	Serv & revenu : débit
Current Trans.,nie: Credit	294.6	311.9	251.4	209.9	232.9	210.5	215.3	Transf. cour.,nia : crédit
Current Transfers: Debit	-4.1	-25.0	-16.8	-12.7	-17.0	-17.9	-20.4	Transf. courants : débit
Capital Acct.,nie: Credit	0.0	0.0	0.0	70.2	62.1	50.2	66.2	Compte de cap.,nia : crédit
Capital Account: Debit	0.0	0.0	0.0	0.0	0.0	0.0	-0.3	Compte de capital : débit
Financial Account, nie	24.8	46.8	-16.7	-33.2	10.7	-44.1	75.5	Compte d'op. fin., nia
Net Errors and Omissions	4.1	46.0	92.3	32.3	-109.6	26.0	-36.0	Erreurs et omissions nettes
Reserves & Related Items	-20.4	-30.6	7.1	72.1	131.1	70.3	20.8	Rés. et postes appareutés

79

Summary of balance of payments
Millions of US dollars *[cont.]*

Résumé des balances des paiements
Millions de dollars des E.-U. *[suite]*

Country or area	1996	1997	1998	1999	2000	2001	2002	Pays ou zone
Saint Kitts and Nevis								**Saint-Kitts-et-Nevis**
Goods: Exports fob	39.1	45.5	44.4	45.0	51.5	55.0	...	Biens : exportations, fab
Goods: Imports fob	-131.9	-131.0	-131.0	-135.2	-172.7	-166.7	...	Biens : importations, fab
Serv. & Income: Credit	91.7	97.6	110.1	106.0	104.0	109.7	...	Serv. & revenu : crédit
Serv. & Income: Debit	-80.1	-88.9	-92.1	-120.2	-109.4	-112.9	...	Serv & revenu : débit
Current Trans.,nie: Credit	20.8	21.8	33.7	24.1	69.9	26.9	...	Transf. cour.,nia : crédit
Current Transfers: Debit	-4.6	-6.7	-6.6	-3.6	-7.3	-8.6	...	Transf. courants : débit
Capital Acct.,nie: Credit	5.6	4.4	8.4	6.0	6.2	10.5	...	Compte de cap.,nia : crédit
Capital Account: Debit	-0.2	-0.2	-0.2	-0.2	-0.2	-0.2	...	Compte de capital : débit
Financial Account, nie	49.1	48.2	44.0	111.3	65.8	98.5	...	Compte d'op. fin., nia
Net Errors and Omissions	9.6	13.0	0.2	-30.4	-12.2	-1.0	...	Erreurs et omissions nettes
Reserves & Related Items	0.9	-3.7	-11.0	-2.7	4.3	-11.2	...	Rés. et postes appareutés
Saint Lucia								**Sainte-Lucie**
Goods: Exports fob	86.3	70.3	70.4	60.9	63.0	51.8	...	Biens : exportations, fab
Goods: Imports fob	-267.4	-292.4	-295.1	-312.0	-312.5	-258.7	...	Biens : importations, fab
Serv. & Income: Credit	270.2	291.7	317.2	323.5	343.7	308.1	...	Serv. & revenu : crédit
Serv. & Income: Debit	-160.1	-160.9	-178.4	-176.2	-174.0	-152.6	...	Serv & revenu : débit
Current Trans.,nie: Credit	28.5	24.6	29.6	31.6	28.5	27.0	...	Transf. cour.,nia : crédit
Current Transfers: Debit	-15.4	-11.6	-10.1	-9.6	-11.4	-13.4	...	Transf. courants : débit
Capital Acct.,nie: Credit	11.1	10.3	23.3	26.8	16.5	27.5	...	Compte de cap.,nia : crédit
Capital Account: Debit	-0.7	-0.8	-0.8	-0.7	-2.3	-1.1	...	Compte de capital : débit
Financial Account, nie	49.2	85.1	57.2	61.9	68.6	34.4	...	Compte d'op. fin., nia
Net Errors and Omissions	-8.0	-11.4	1.7	1.7	-12.1	-11.2	...	Erreurs et omissions nettes
Reserves & Related Items	6.3	-5.0	-15.1	-7.8	-8.1	-11.9	...	Rés. et postes appareutés
St. Vincent-Grenadines								**St. Vincent-Grenadines**
Goods: Exports fob	52.6	47.3	50.1	49.6	51.7	45.7	...	Biens : exportations, fab
Goods: Imports fob	-128.1	-152.6	-170.0	-177.0	-144.3	-152.0	...	Biens : importations, fab
Serv. & Income: Credit	100.7	102.1	110.2	128.9	129.4	133.6	...	Serv. & revenu : crédit
Serv. & Income: Debit	-71.2	-91.7	-95.9	-89.0	-83.7	-80.1	...	Serv & revenu : débit
Current Trans.,nie: Credit	19.7	20.8	21.6	23.4	25.4	24.2	...	Transf. cour.,nia : crédit
Current Transfers: Debit	-9.3	-10.1	-10.6	-8.0	-6.7	-8.9	...	Transf. courants : débit
Capital Acct.,nie: Credit	4.9	7.0	14.6	9.1	13.4	9.7	...	Compte de cap.,nia : crédit
Capital Account: Debit	-1.1	-1.1	-1.3	-1.3	-1.3	-1.4	...	Compte de capital : débit
Financial Account, nie	41.8	81.5	92.5	54.9	16.1	51.7	...	Compte d'op. fin., nia
Net Errors and Omissions	-9.8	-2.1	-4.9	13.3	14.1	-13.5	...	Erreurs et omissions nettes
Reserves & Related Items	-0.4	-1.1	-6.4	-3.9	-14.0	-9.1	...	Rés. et postes appareutés
Samoa								**Samoa**
Goods: Exports fob	10.1	14.6	20.4	18.2	...	...	...	Biens : exportations, fab
Goods: Imports fob	-90.8	-100.1	-96.9	-115.7	...	...	...	Biens : importations, fab
Serv. & Income: Credit	70.6	70.8	68.5	64.1	...	...	...	Serv. & revenu : crédit
Serv. & Income: Debit	-36.8	-44.2	-31.5	-26.9	...	...	...	Serv & revenu : débit
Current Trans.,nie: Credit	66.9	73.7	64.1	44.7	...	...	...	Transf. cour.,nia : crédit
Current Transfers: Debit	-7.8	-5.6	-4.6	-3.1	...	...	...	Transf. courants : débit
Capital Acct.,nie: Credit	0.0	0.0	0.0	27.1	...	...	...	Compte de cap.,nia : crédit
Capital Account: Debit	0.0	0.0	0.0	-2.7	...	...	...	Compte de capital : débit
Financial Account, nie	-3.6	-5.9	-5.0	-0.7	...	...	...	Compte d'op. fin., nia
Net Errors and Omissions	-1.3	7.9	-9.6	2.1	...	...	...	Erreurs et omissions nettes
Reserves & Related Items	-7.4	-11.1	-5.5	-7.0	...	...	...	Rés. et postes appareutés
Sao Tome and Principe								**Sao Tomé-et-Principe**
Goods: Exports fob	...	0.0	4.7	3.9	2.7	3.3	5.1	Biens : exportations, fab
Goods: Imports fob	...	0.0	-16.9	-21.9	-25.1	-24.4	-28.0	Biens : importations, fab
Serv. & Income: Credit	...	0.0	6.6[2]	12.5[2]	13.6[2]	12.8[2]	13.4[2]	Serv. & revenu : crédit
Serv. & Income: Debit	...	0.0	-15.6	-17.1	-14.6	-16.7	-18.2	Serv & revenu : débit
Current Trans.,nie: Credit	...	0.0	10.7	6.4	4.4	4.0	4.9	Transf. cour.,nia : crédit
Current Transfers: Debit	...	0.0	0.0	0.0	0.0	0.0	0.0	Transf. courants : débit
Capital Acct.,nie: Credit	...	0.0	3.9	9.3	12.0	15.2	12.1	Compte de cap.,nia : crédit
Capital Account: Debit	...	0.0	0.0	0.0	0.0	0.0	0.0	Compte de capital : débit
Financial Account, nie	...	0.3	0.0	4.4	3.3	1.7	3.7	Compte d'op. fin., nia
Net Errors and Omissions	...	0.3	0.0	0.1	-1.7	2.7	0.0	Erreurs et omissions nettes
Reserves & Related Items	...	6.0	0.0	2.6	5.5	1.5	7.0	Rés. et postes appareutés
Saudi Arabia								**Arabie saoudite**
Goods: Exports fob	60 728.7	60 732.4	38 821.9	50 756.6	77 584.0	68 063.6	71 678.5	Biens : exportations, fab

79

Summary of balance of payments
Millions of US dollars [cont.]

Résumé des balances des paiements
Millions de dollars des E.-U. [suite]

Country or area	1996	1997	1998	1999	2000	2001	2002	Pays ou zone
Goods: Imports fob	-25 358.3	-26 370.1	-27 534.6	-25 717.5	-27 741.0	-28 645.2	-29 642.0	Biens : importations, fab
Serv. & Income: Credit	7 899.1	10 012.3	10 539.1	11 191.1	8 134.6	9 144.5	8 956.2	Serv. & revenu : crédit
Serv. & Income: Debit	-26 975.8	-28 934.8	-19 921.9	-21 741.7	-28 130.9	-23 956.9	-23 321.9	Serv & revenu : débit
Current Transfers: Debit	-15 613.2	-15 134.4	-15 054.1	-14 076.9	-15 510.8	-15 240.1	-15 974.9	Transf. courants : débit
Capital Acct.,nie: Credit	0.0	0.0	0.0	0.0	0.0	0.0	0.0	Compte de cap.,nia : crédit
Capital Account: Debit	0.0	0.0	0.0	0.0	0.0	0.0	0.0	Compte de capital : débit
Financial Account, nie	5 068.7	342.5	12 430.7	2 402.8	-11 671.0	-11 274.7	-8 960.0	Compte d'op. fin., nia
Net Errors and Omissions	0.0	0.1	0.0	0.2	-0.1	-0.1	0.1	Erreurs et omissions nettes
Reserves & Related Items	-5 749.0	-648.1	718.9	-2 814.6	-2 664.8	1 908.8	-2 736.1	Rés. et postes appareutés
Senegal								**Sénégal**
Goods: Exports fob	988.0	904.6	967.7	1 027.1	...	...	...	Biens : exportations, fab
Goods: Imports fob	-1 264.0	-1 176.0	-1 280.6	-1 372.8	...	...	...	Biens : importations, fab
Serv. & Income: Credit	459.9	439.6	501.8	499.4	...	...	...	Serv. & revenu : crédit
Serv. & Income: Debit	-550.0	-531.5	-607.5	-632.9	...	...	...	Serv & revenu : débit
Current Trans.,nie: Credit	244.3	258.8	254.7	225.4	...	...	...	Transf. cour.,nia : crédit
Current Transfers: Debit	-77.8	-80.3	-83.6	-66.3	...	...	...	Transf. courants : débit
Capital Acct.,nie: Credit	169.3	96.3	98.8	99.0	...	...	...	Compte de cap.,nia : crédit
Capital Account: Debit	-0.1	-0.3	-0.4	-0.5	...	...	...	Compte de capital : débit
Financial Account, nie	-179.1	3.5	-109.7	-54.8	...	...	...	Compte d'op. fin., nia
Net Errors and Omissions	7.6	-9.3	10.7	8.2	...	...	...	Erreurs et omissions nettes
Reserves & Related Items	201.9	94.7	248.1	268.2	...	...	...	Rés. et postes appareutés
Seychelles								**Seychelles**
Goods: Exports fob	96.7	113.6	122.8	145.7	194.8	216.4	236.7	Biens : exportations, fab
Goods: Imports fob	-267.0	-303.5	-334.6	-369.7	-311.6	-421.9	-376.3	Biens : importations, fab
Serv. & Income: Credit	247.5	265.5	252.9	285.8	303.5	304.6	314.0	Serv. & revenu : crédit
Serv. & Income: Debit	-139.6	-149.5	-157.5	-188.3	-232.3	-221.4	-301.3	Serv & revenu : débit
Current Trans.,nie: Credit	15.2	14.2	9.8	10.1	4.3	7.9	7.8	Transf. cour.,nia : crédit
Current Transfers: Debit	-12.1	-13.1	-11.4	-10.8	-10.0	-8.9	-11.6	Transf. courants : débit
Capital Acct.,nie: Credit	5.7	6.8	21.7	16.5	0.9	9.4	5.0	Compte de cap.,nia : crédit
Capital Account: Debit	0.0	0.0	0.0	0.0	0.0	0.0	0.0	Compte de capital : débit
Financial Account, nie	-15.9	9.5	27.1	13.9	-32.1	52.3	-64.0	Compte d'op. fin., nia
Net Errors and Omissions	7.0	11.7	-4.3	-2.1	-20.8	14.4	0.5	Erreurs et omissions nettes
Reserves & Related Items	62.5	44.8	73.6	99.1	103.3	47.1	189.1	Rés. et postes appareutés
Singapore								**Singapour**
Goods: Exports fob	129 547.0	129 780.0	110 264.0	116 546.0	139 861.0	124 443.0	128 374.0	Biens : exportations, fab
Goods: Imports fob	-123 894.0	-125 099.0	-95 916.7	-104 570.0	-127 563.0	-109 675.0	-109 825.0	Biens : importations, fab
Serv. & Income: Credit	42 519.2	42 912.8	34 495.3	42 626.3	45 389.5	44 421.7	44 068.6	Serv. & revenu : crédit
Serv. & Income: Debit	-33 137.1	-31 526.2	-29 198.0	-38 406.8	-43 286.9	-41 906.9	-42 809.5	Serv & revenu : débit
Current Trans.,nie: Credit	160.9	152.5	130.6	134.8	127.5	122.4	122.5	Transf. cour.,nia : crédit
Current Transfers: Debit	-1 219.7	-1 311.7	-1 230.9	-1 145.8	-1 248.1	-1 267.9	-1 227.0	Transf. courants : débit
Capital Acct.,nie: Credit	0.0	0.0	0.0	0.0	0.0	0.0	0.0	Compte de cap.,nia : crédit
Capital Account: Debit	-138.7	-189.8	-225.7	-191.2	-162.7	-161.2	-160.1	Compte de capital : débit
Financial Account, nie	-9 343.3	-12 535.4	-18 663.5	-12 746.8	-1 925.5	-15 388.8	-15 655.3	Compte d'op. fin., nia
Net Errors and Omissions	2 901.0	5 756.7	3 310.2	1 947.5	-4 385.9	-1 448.2	-1 546.3	Erreurs et omissions nettes
Reserves & Related Items	-7 395.6	-7 939.8	-2 965.4	-4 193.9	-6 806.0	860.9	-1 342.0	Rés. et postes appareutés
Slovakia								**Slovaquie**
Goods: Exports fob	8 823.8	9 640.7	10 720.2	10 201.3	11 896.1	...	...	Biens : exportations, fab
Goods: Imports fob	-11 106.5	-11 725.2	-13 070.9	-11 310.3	-12 790.6	...	...	Biens : importations, fab
Serv. & Income: Credit	2 289.1	2 482.5	2 729.4	2 167.7	2 508.9	...	...	Serv. & revenu : crédit
Serv. & Income: Debit	-2 297.8	-2 532.7	-2 870.8	-2 411.8	-2 428.5	...	...	Serv & revenu : débit
Current Trans.,nie: Credit	482.9	540.4	645.0	466.0	343.8	...	...	Transf. cour.,nia : crédit
Current Transfers: Debit	-282.0	-367.1	-279.3	-268.1	-224.0	...	...	Transf. courants : débit
Capital Acct.,nie: Credit	30.3	0.0	82.8	171.0	105.7	...	...	Compte de cap.,nia : crédit
Capital Account: Debit	0.0	0.0	-12.4	-13.4	-14.8	...	...	Compte de capital : débit
Financial Account, nie	2 267.9	1 780.1	1 911.5	1 788.8	1 472.4	...	...	Compte d'op. fin., nia
Net Errors and Omissions	162.2	280.1	-333.1	-14.3	50.7	...	...	Erreurs et omissions nettes
Reserves & Related Items	-370.0	-98.9	477.6	-777.0	-919.7	...	...	Rés. et postes appareutés
Slovenia								**Slovénie**
Goods: Exports fob	8 352.6	8 405.9	9 090.9	8 623.2	8 807.9	9 342.8	10 472.6	Biens : exportations, fab
Goods: Imports fob	-9 178.7	-9 180.7	-9 882.9	-9 858.3	-9 946.9	-9 962.3	-10 715.7	Biens : importations, fab
Serv. & Income: Credit	2 547.8	2 432.2	2 437.5	2 302.3	2 321.7	2 422.2	2 779.3	Serv. & revenu : crédit
Serv. & Income: Debit	-1 754.1	-1 721.2	-1 880.9	-1 885.0	-1 845.8	-1 901.0	-2 295.2	Serv & revenu : débit

79

Summary of balance of payments
Millions of US dollars *[cont.]*

Résumé des balances des paiements
Millions de dollars des E.-U. *[suite]*

Country or area	1996	1997	1998	1999	2000	2001	2002	Pays ou zone
Current Trans.,nie: Credit	250.9	259.5	299.8	334.9	340.8	390.0	451.4	Transf. cour.,nia : crédit
Current Transfers: Debit	-163.1	-145.3	-182.4	-215.3	-225.4	-260.8	-317.7	Transf. courants : débit
Capital Acct.,nie: Credit	5.5	5.0	3.5	3.3	6.8	3.3	4.9	Compte de cap.,nia : crédit
Capital Account: Debit	-7.4	-3.9	-5.0	-4.0	-3.3	-6.9	-3.3	Compte de capital : débit
Financial Account, nie	534.5	1 162.9	215.8	576.1	680.4	1 204.3	1 456.8	Compte d'op. fin., nia
Net Errors and Omissions	2.0	74.0	61.4	41.5	42.1	53.0	33.6	Erreurs et omissions nettes
Reserves & Related Items	-590.0	-1 288.4	-157.8	81.4	-178.3	-1 284.6	-1 866.9	Rés. et postes appareutés
Solomon Islands								**Iles Salomon**
Goods: Exports fob	161.5	156.4	141.8	164.6	...	...	...	Biens : exportations, fab
Goods: Imports fob	-150.5	-184.5	-159.9	-110.0	...	...	...	Biens : importations, fab
Serv. & Income: Credit	55.5	73.0	57.2	61.8	...	...	...	Serv. & revenu : crédit
Serv. & Income: Debit	-94.9	-118.4	-64.5	-109.9	...	...	...	Serv & revenu : débit
Current Trans.,nie: Credit	57.5	52.6	56.4	41.5	...	...	...	Transf. cour.,nia : crédit
Current Transfers: Debit	-14.5	-17.1	-22.9	-26.5	...	...	...	Transf. courants : débit
Capital Acct.,nie: Credit	0.5	0.3	6.9	9.2	...	...	...	Compte de cap.,nia : crédit
Capital Account: Debit	-2.7	-1.3	-0.3	0.0	...	...	...	Compte de capital : débit
Financial Account, nie	-1.4	45.7	16.9	-33.8	...	...	...	Compte d'op. fin., nia
Net Errors and Omissions	7.0	2.3	-14.4	-1.6	...	...	...	Erreurs et omissions nettes
Reserves & Related Items	-18.0	-9.1	-17.2	4.7	...	...	...	Rés. et postes appareutés
South Africa								**Afrique du Sud**
Goods: Exports fob	30 262.8	31 171.3	29 263.7	28 626.6	31 636.1	30 715.8	31 084.8	Biens : exportations, fab
Goods: Imports fob	-27 567.7	-28 847.5	-27 207.6	-24 553.7	-27 320.2	-25 855.6	-26 712.9	Biens : importations, fab
Serv. & Income: Credit	6 104.4	6 631.4	6 588.0	6 641.8	7 155.5	6 780.1	6 302.2	Serv. & revenu : crédit
Serv. & Income: Debit	-9 926.7	-10 504.4	-10 057.8	-10 427.9	-11 120.0	-11 197.6	-9 827.9	Serv & revenu : débit
Current Trans.,nie: Credit	54.3	138.4	60.3	66.2	106.4	126.1	139.1	Transf. cour.,nia : crédit
Current Transfers: Debit	-807.5	-862.5	-803.8	-992.7	-1 032.9	-864.6	-695.5	Transf. courants : débit
Capital Acct.,nie: Credit	25.0	29.5	24.4	20.5	19.0	15.8	20.2	Compte de cap.,nia : crédit
Capital Account: Debit	-72.0	-222.1	-80.4	-82.2	-71.0	-47.0	-35.1	Compte de capital : débit
Financial Account, nie	3 018.0	8 131.1	4 851.9	5 305.4	98.6	1 172.1	-116.9	Compte d'op. fin., nia
Net Errors and Omissions	-2 362.7	-1 069.8	-1 718.5	-388.7	928.2	1 703.2	1 451.0	Erreurs et omissions nettes
Reserves & Related Items	1 272.0	-4 595.4	-920.2	-4 215.2	-399.8	-2 548.4	-1 609.0	Rés. et postes appareutés
Spain								**Espagne**
Goods: Exports fob	102 735.0	106 926.0	111 986.0	112 664.0	116 205.0	117 935.0	125 795.0	Biens : exportations, fab
Goods: Imports fob	-119 017.0	-120 333.0	-132 744.0	-143 002.0	-151 025.0	-150 474.0	-158 893.0	Biens : importations, fab
Serv. & Income: Credit	58 482.4	57 322.2	63 928.4	66 053.9	68 556.1	78 030.3	82 946.7	Serv. & revenu : crédit
Serv. & Income: Debit	-44 185.9	-44 225.9	-49 555.1	-52 618.8	-54 551.2	-63 564.0	-67 966.3	Serv & revenu : débit
Current Trans.,nie: Credit	11 111.8	11 738.0	12 690.5	13 434.6	11 628.7	12 568.7	14 073.7	Transf. cour.,nia : crédit
Current Transfers: Debit	-8 718.4	-8 915.9	-9 441.2	-10 291.7	-10 050.3	-10 900.4	-11 898.1	Transf. courants : débit
Capital Acct.,nie: Credit	7 713.0	7 274.6	7 159.8	8 060.4	5 806.0	5 864.2	8 191.4	Compte de cap.,nia : crédit
Capital Account: Debit	-1 123.8	-837.2	-829.5	-1 093.8	-1 013.6	-894.7	-1 119.5	Compte de capital : débit
Financial Account, nie	20 138.2	8 547.4	-14 155.7	-10 997.2	16 942.2	16 601.9	18 842.3	Compte d'op. fin., nia
Net Errors and Omissions	-2 856.1	-5 740.9	-3 394.6	-5 059.2	-5 378.7	-6 507.3	-6 281.7	Erreurs et omissions nettes
Reserves & Related Items	-24 278.8	-11 755.7	14 355.5	22 850.3	2 880.9	1 340.3	-3 690.1	Rés. et postes appareutés
Sri Lanka								**Sri Lanka**
Goods: Exports fob	4 095.2	4 638.7	4 808.0	4 596.2	5 439.6	4 816.9	4 699.2	Biens : exportations, fab
Goods: Imports fob	-4 895.0	-5 278.3	-5 313.4	-5 365.5	-6 483.6	-5 974.0	-6 105.6	Biens : importations, fab
Serv. & Income: Credit	940.6	1 108.6	1 130.8	1 131.1	1 087.7	1 463.3	1 343.6	Serv. & revenu : crédit
Serv. & Income: Debit	-1 582.5	-1 695.5	-1 756.2	-1 833.0	-2 070.3	-1 554.7	-1 323.7	Serv & revenu : débit
Current Trans.,nie: Credit	881.4	966.5	1 054.5	1 078.1	1 165.7	1 155.4	1 287.1	Transf. cour.,nia : crédit
Current Transfers: Debit	-122.4	-134.7	-151.3	-168.2	-182.7	-171.7	-190.2	Transf. courants : débit
Capital Acct.,nie: Credit	99.7	91.3	84.6	85.2	55.0	55.2	61.3	Compte de cap.,nia : crédit
Capital Account: Debit	-3.8	-4.2	-4.7	-5.2	-5.7	-5.3	-5.9	Compte de capital : débit
Financial Account, nie	452.2	466.7	345.1	413.4	447.2	-136.3	-200.2	Compte d'op. fin., nia
Net Errors and Omissions	143.6	148.0	26.3	-27.3	186.2	92.6	103.0	Erreurs et omissions nettes
Reserves & Related Items	-9.0	-307.2	-223.6	95.2	360.8	258.5	331.5	Rés. et postes appareutés
Sudan								**Soudan**
Goods: Exports fob	620.3	594.2	595.7	780.1	1 806.7	1 698.7	1 949.1	Biens : exportations, fab
Goods: Imports fob	-1 339.5	-1 421.9	-1 732.2	-1 256.0	-1 366.3	-1 395.1	-2 152.8	Biens : importations, fab
Serv. & Income: Credit	57.0	48.4	29.5	100.7	32.0	32.4	66.5	Serv. & revenu : crédit
Serv. & Income: Debit	-201.5	-178.1	-214.6	-398.1	-1 227.2	-1 232.2	-1 454.6	Serv & revenu : débit
Current Trans.,nie: Credit	236.3	439.1	731.8	702.2	651.3	730.4	1 085.9	Transf. cour.,nia : crédit
Current Transfers: Debit	-199.4	-309.8	-366.7	-393.7	-453.3	-452.5	-454.5	Transf. courants : débit

79

Summary of balance of payments
Millions of US dollars *[cont.]*

Résumé des balances des paiements
Millions de dollars des E.-U. *[suite]*

Country or area	1996	1997	1998	1999	2000	2001	2002	Pays ou zone
Capital Acct.,nie: Credit	0.0	0.0	13.0	45.8	16.5	11.9	44.8	Compte de cap.,nia : crédit
Capital Account: Debit	0.0	0.0	-67.2	-68.7	-135.8	-105.2	-87.8	Compte de capital : débit
Financial Account, nie	136.8	195.0	333.4	435.3	431.6	561.2	763.6	Compte d'op. fin., nia
Net Errors and Omissions	727.5	651.2	750.5	167.2	368.4	-0.5	529.8	Erreurs et omissions nettes
Reserves & Related Items	-37.5	-18.1	-73.2	-114.8	-123.9	150.9	-290.1	Rés. et postes appareutés
Suriname								**Suriname**
Goods: Exports fob	397.2	401.6	349.7	342.0	399.1	437.0	369.3	Biens : exportations, fab
Goods: Imports fob	-398.8	-365.5	-376.9	-297.9	-246.1	-297.2	-321.9	Biens : importations, fab
Serv. & Income: Credit	110.8	99.0	78.5	87.0	104.1	64.8	46.9	Serv. & revenu : crédit
Serv. & Income: Debit	-173.8	-203.8	-203.9	-158.7	-222.7	-287.3	-216.8	Serv & revenu : débit
Current Trans.,nie: Credit	3.6	4.0	1.3	1.8	1.2	2.1	12.9	Transf. cour.,nia : crédit
Current Transfers: Debit	-2.5	-3.0	-3.6	-3.3	-3.3	-3.0	-21.4	Transf. courants : débit
Capital Acct.,nie: Credit	41.6	14.6	6.6	3.5	2.3	1.5	5.9	Compte de cap.,nia : crédit
Capital Account: Debit	0.0	0.0	0.0	0.0	0.0	0.0	0.0	Compte de capital : débit
Financial Account, nie	27.7	26.9	30.5	-21.6	-139.1	104.1	-38.1	Compte d'op. fin., nia
Net Errors and Omissions	-7.5	45.3	125.9	42.8	114.3	56.1	144.1	Erreurs et omissions nettes
Reserves & Related Items	1.7	-19.1	-8.1	4.4	-9.8	-78.1	19.1	Rés. et postes appareutés
Swaziland								**Swaziland**
Goods: Exports fob	850.5	961.3	967.8	936.7	905.0	1 039.8	955.2	Biens : exportations, fab
Goods: Imports fob	-1 054.4	-1 065.5	-1 073.8	-1 068.1	-1 041.1	-1 116.4	-1 034.6	Biens : importations, fab
Serv. & Income: Credit	301.5	274.6	259.3	233.5	367.2	280.8	258.0	Serv. & revenu : crédit
Serv. & Income: Debit	-309.4	-289.5	-379.1	-268.3	-403.3	-291.5	-235.3	Serv & revenu : débit
Current Trans.,nie: Credit	268.7	226.8	242.7	241.4	234.1	229.7	218.9	Transf. cour.,nia : crédit
Current Transfers: Debit	-108.9	-110.5	-110.3	-110.2	-127.0	-195.3	-208.6	Transf. courants : débit
Capital Acct.,nie: Credit	0.1	0.1	0.0	0.0	0.1	0.2	0.5	Compte de cap.,nia : crédit
Capital Account: Debit	0.0	0.0	0.0	0.0	0.0	-0.4	-0.1	Compte de capital : débit
Financial Account, nie	6.8	47.0	130.5	25.1	-9.6	-31.5	26.8	Compte d'op. fin., nia
Net Errors and Omissions	37.0	-16.8	4.1	13.4	46.7	41.6	18.9	Erreurs et omissions nettes
Reserves & Related Items	8.1	-27.5	-41.3	-3.3	28.0	43.0	0.2	Rés. et postes appareutés
Sweden								**Suède**
Goods: Exports fob	84 689.6	83 193.7	85 179.0	87 568.0	87 431.0	76 200.0	81 537.8	Biens : exportations, fab
Goods: Imports fob	-66 053.4	-65 194.8	-67 547.3	-71 854.2	-72 215.7	-62 368.4	-66 068.9	Biens : importations, fab
Serv. & Income: Credit	31 268.4	32 173.3	34 515.3	39 774.8	40 325.8	39 931.0	40 870.5	Serv. & revenu : crédit
Serv. & Income: Debit	-41 396.3	-40 037.1	-44 069.9	-45 907.3	-45 577.0	-43 805.3	-42 852.1	Serv & revenu : débit
Current Trans.,nie: Credit	2 524.0	2 318.6	2 266.0	2 340.6	2 602.5	2 577.6	3 320.8	Transf. cour.,nia : crédit
Current Transfers: Debit	-5 140.0	-5 048.1	-5 703.7	-5 939.6	-5 950.1	-5 838.8	-6 184.3	Transf. courants : débit
Capital Acct.,nie: Credit	31.3	210.9	1 502.2	1 288.6	1 225.7	1 110.7	529.4	Compte de cap.,nia : crédit
Capital Account: Debit	-22.4	-438.6	-634.0	-3 431.9	-841.2	-601.2	-608.5	Compte de capital : débit
Financial Account, nie	-10 046.2	-10 121.2	5 960.7	-1 412.9	-3 296.6	1 824.2	-9 546.6	Compte d'op. fin., nia
Net Errors and Omissions	-2 240.6	-3 768.9	-8 214.5	-544.6	-3 533.9	-10 077.8	-337.3	Erreurs et omissions nettes
Reserves & Related Items	6 385.6	6 712.1	-3 253.8	-1 881.4	-170.5	1 048.2	-660.7	Rés. et postes appareutés
Switzerland								**Suisse**
Goods: Exports fob	95 543.6	95 039.5	93 781.7	91 823.3	94 842.0	95 825.8	100 475.0	Biens : exportations, fab
Goods: Imports fob	-93 676.0	-92 301.8	-92 848.9	-90 980.2	-92 738.0	-94 262.5	-94 042.9	Biens : importations, fab
Serv. & Income: Credit	59 246.5	60 366.4	72 657.2	78 569.6	90 493.4	80 844.0	70 807.6	Serv. & revenu : crédit
Serv. & Income: Debit	-36 074.3	-33 022.9	-43 134.4	-45 687.3	-55 254.9	-54 526.8	-47 049.9	Serv & revenu : débit
Current Trans.,nie: Credit	2 960.7	2 625.3	2 786.0	7 637.6	6 854.3	9 731.4	10 695.7	Transf. cour.,nia : crédit
Current Transfers: Debit	-6 949.0	-6 027.3	-6 466.8	-11 751.9	-9 780.3	-13 714.4	-14 874.7	Transf. courants : débit
Capital Acct.,nie: Credit	18.5	35.6	754.9	52.4	489.2	2 312.7	271.9	Compte de cap.,nia : crédit
Capital Account: Debit	-233.0	-202.5	-616.1	-567.1	-427.9	-790.6	-1 404.9	Compte de capital : débit
Financial Account, nie	-27 316.9	-24 712.5	-31 161.5	-34 076.8	-30 228.9	-37 037.8	-33 692.2	Compte d'op. fin., nia
Net Errors and Omissions	9 001.5	354.2	5 427.2	2 496.0	-4 653.7	12 256.5	11 215.9	Erreurs et omissions nettes
Reserves & Related Items	-2 521.5	-2 153.9	-1 179.2	2 484.5	4 004.6	-638.3	-2 401.9	Rés. et postes appareutés
Syrian Arab Republic								**Rép. arabe syrienne**
Goods: Exports fob	4 178.0	4 057.0	3 142.0	3 806.0	5 146.0	...	...	Biens : exportations, fab
Goods: Imports fob	-4 516.0	-3 603.0	-3 320.0	-3 590.0	-3 723.0	...	...	Biens : importations, fab
Serv. & Income: Credit	2 326.0	2 003.0	2 035.0	2 007.0	2 045.0	...	...	Serv. & revenu : crédit
Serv. & Income: Debit	-2 572.0	-2 495.0	-2 330.0	-2 511.0	-2 891.0	...	...	Serv & revenu : débit
Current Trans.,nie: Credit	630.0	504.0	533.0	491.0	495.0	...	...	Transf. cour.,nia : crédit
Current Transfers: Debit	-6.0	-5.0	-2.0	-2.0	-10.0	...	...	Transf. courants : débit
Capital Acct.,nie: Credit	26.0	18.0	27.0	80.0	63.0	...	...	Compte de cap.,nia : crédit
Capital Account: Debit	0.0	0.0	0.0	0.0	0.0	...	...	Compte de capital : débit

79

Summary of balance of payments
Millions of US dollars *[cont.]*

Résumé des balances des paiements
Millions de dollars des E.-U. *[suite]*

Country or area	1996	1997	1998	1999	2000	2001	2002	Pays ou zone
Financial Account, nie	782.0	65.0	196.0	173.0	-392.0	...	...	Compte d'op. fin., nia
Net Errors and Omissions	139.0	-95.0	153.1	-195.0	-192.0	...	...	Erreurs et omissions nettes
Reserves & Related Items	-987.0	-449.0	-434.1	-259.0	-541.0	...	...	Rés. et postes appareutés
Tajikistan								**Tadjikistan**
Goods: Exports fob	...	...	...	...	...	...	699.1	Biens : exportations, fab
Goods: Imports fob	...	...	...	...	...	...	-822.9	Biens : importations, fab
Serv. & Income: Credit	...	...	...	...	...	...	70.2	Serv. & revenu : crédit
Serv. & Income: Debit	...	...	...	...	...	...	-147.2	Serv & revenu : débit
Current Trans.,nie: Credit	...	...	...	...	...	...	201.7	Transf. cour.,nia : crédit
Current Transfers: Debit	...	...	...	...	...	...	-16.1	Transf. courants : débit
Capital Acct.,nie: Credit	...	...	...	...	...	...	0.0	Compte de cap.,nia : crédit
Capital Account: Debit	...	...	...	...	...	...	0.0	Compte de capital : débit
Financial Account, nie	...	...	...	...	...	...	72.4	Compte d'op. fin., nia
Net Errors and Omissions	...	...	...	...	...	...	-55.6	Erreurs et omissions nettes
Reserves & Related Items	...	...	...	...	...	...	-1.7	Rés. et postes appareutés
Thailand								**Thaïlande**
Goods: Exports fob	54 408.4	56 655.9	52 752.9	56 775.1	67 893.6	63 201.8	66 795.0	Biens : exportations, fab
Goods: Imports fob	-63 896.6	-55 084.3	-36 514.9	-42 761.8	-56 193.0	-54 619.7	-57 019.7	Biens : importations, fab
Serv. & Income: Credit	20 976.3	19 505.6	16 479.3	17 726.9	18 103.1	16 857.7	18 675.2	Serv. & revenu : crédit
Serv. & Income: Debit	-26 939.3	-24 577.0	-18 889.1	-19 665.6	-21 076.5	-19 819.1	-21 417.9	Serv & revenu : débit
Current Trans.,nie: Credit	1 651.0	1 392.1	819.8	805.6	951.6	990.0	992.6	Transf. cour.,nia : crédit
Current Transfers: Debit	-891.3	-913.3	-405.4	-452.5	-365.7	-389.2	-375.0	Transf. courants : débit
Capital Acct.,nie: Credit	0.0	0.0	0.0	0.0	0.0	0.0	0.0	Compte de cap.,nia : crédit
Capital Account: Debit	0.0	0.0	0.0	0.0	0.0	0.0	0.0	Compte de capital : débit
Financial Account, nie	19 486.0	-12 055.7	-14 110.3	-11 073.0	-10 434.3	-3 678.2	-2 685.2	Compte d'op. fin., nia
Net Errors and Omissions	-2 627.3	-3 173.0	-2 828.2	33.4	-685.3	-68.6	570.5	Erreurs et omissions nettes
Reserves & Related Items	-2 167.3	18 249.8	2 696.0	-1 388.3	1 806.4	-2 474.6	-5 535.4	Rés. et postes appareutés
TFYR of Macedonia								**L'ex-R.y. Macédoine**
Goods: Exports fob	1 147.4	1 201.4	1 291.5	1 190.0	1 320.7	1 155.4	1 110.5	Biens : exportations, fab
Goods: Imports fob	-1 464.0	-1 589.1	-1 806.6	-1 685.8	-2 011.1	-1 681.8	-1 878.1	Biens : importations, fab
Serv. & Income: Credit	199.6	167.3	172.8	297.0	358.3	297.2	304.1	Serv. & revenu : crédit
Serv. & Income: Debit	-384.3	-345.4	-277.6	-297.4	-355.2	-357.1	-360.1	Serv & revenu : débit
Current Trans.,nie: Credit	475.4	535.0	542.7	618.5	788.2	725.7	655.3	Transf. cour.,nia : crédit
Current Transfers: Debit	-262.3	-244.8	-192.5	-154.8	-173.3	-383.0	-157.0	Transf. courants : débit
Capital Acct.,nie: Credit	0.0	0.0	0.0	0.0	0.3	3.6	9.9	Compte de cap.,nia : crédit
Capital Account: Debit	0.0	0.0	-1.8	0.0	0.0	-2.3	-1.7	Compte de capital : débit
Financial Account, nie	174.3	186.8	329.9	14.2	290.3	325.7	207.2	Compte d'op. fin., nia
Net Errors and Omissions	18.8	-29.9	-15.1	159.9	61.0	2.3	-12.2	Erreurs et omissions nettes
Reserves & Related Items	95.1	118.6	-43.3	-141.7	-279.2	-85.6	122.1	Rés. et postes appareutés
Togo								**Togo**
Goods: Exports fob	440.6	422.5	420.3	391.5	361.8	357.2	...	Biens : exportations, fab
Goods: Imports fob	-567.8	-530.6	-553.5	-489.4	-484.6	-516.1	...	Biens : importations, fab
Serv. & Income: Credit	161.8	123.5	120.4	108.6	94.7	97.7	...	Serv. & revenu : crédit
Serv. & Income: Debit	-273.4	-231.7	-217.0	-209.1	-179.5	-185.1	...	Serv & revenu : débit
Current Trans.,nie: Credit	106.8	120.2	101.8	73.6	73.3	88.3	...	Transf. cour.,nia : crédit
Current Transfers: Debit	-21.9	-20.8	-12.2	-2.2	-5.4	-11.1	...	Transf. courants : débit
Capital Acct.,nie: Credit	5.6	5.8	6.1	6.9	8.7	21.4	...	Compte de cap.,nia : crédit
Capital Account: Debit	0.0	0.0	0.0	0.0	0.0	0.0	...	Compte de capital : débit
Financial Account, nie	151.3	126.9	114.1	155.5	162.8	151.2	...	Compte d'op. fin., nia
Net Errors and Omissions	-27.9	-2.7	2.7	-3.7	5.0	-5.4	...	Erreurs et omissions nettes
Reserves & Related Items	24.9	-13.1	17.2	-31.6	-36.8	2.0	...	Rés. et postes appareutés
Tonga								**Tonga**
Goods: Exports fob	...	...	...	...	...	6.7	...	Biens : exportations, fab
Goods: Imports fob	...	...	...	...	...	-63.7	...	Biens : importations, fab
Serv. & Income: Credit	...	...	...	...	...	22.8	...	Serv. & revenu : crédit
Serv. & Income: Debit	...	...	...	...	...	-29.4	...	Serv & revenu : débit
Current Trans.,nie: Credit	...	...	...	...	...	62.5	...	Transf. cour.,nia : crédit
Current Transfers: Debit	...	...	...	...	...	-11.7	...	Transf. courants : débit
Capital Acct.,nie: Credit	...	...	...	...	...	11.7	...	Compte de cap.,nia : crédit
Capital Account: Debit	...	...	...	...	...	-2.6	...	Compte de capital : débit
Financial Account, nie	...	...	...	...	...	1.0	...	Compte d'op. fin., nia
Net Errors and Omissions	...	...	...	...	...	4.3	...	Erreurs et omissions nettes

79

Summary of balance of payments
Millions of US dollars *[cont.]*

Résumé des balances des paiements
Millions de dollars des E.-U. *[suite]*

Country or area	1996	1997	1998	1999	2000	2001	2002	Pays ou zone
Reserves & Related Items	...	...	...	...	...	-1.6	...	Rés. et postes appareutés
Trinidad and Tobago								**Trinité-et-Tobago**
Goods: Exports fob	2 354.1	2 448.0	2 258.0	2 815.8	4 290.3	4 304.2	...	Biens : exportations, fab
Goods: Imports fob	-1 971.6	-2 976.6	-2 998.9	-2 752.2	-3 321.5	-3 586.1	...	Biens : importations, fab
Serv. & Income: Credit	500.3	610.3	735.8	671.5	634.7	682.5	...	Serv. & revenu : crédit
Serv. & Income: Debit	-770.6	-699.0	-660.7	-742.2	-1 097.1	-1 018.0	...	Serv & revenu : débit
Current Trans.,nie: Credit	34.2	37.0	58.4	68.9	63.9	64.0	...	Transf. cour.,nia : crédit
Current Transfers: Debit	-41.3	-33.2	-36.2	-31.2	-26.0	-30.6	...	Transf. courants : débit
Capital Acct.,nie: Credit	0.0	0.0	0.0	0.0	0.0	0.0	...	Compte de cap.,nia : crédit
Capital Account: Debit	0.0	0.0	0.0	0.0	0.0	0.0	...	Compte de capital : débit
Financial Account, nie	43.0	697.2	471.5	38.3	173.7	321.5	...	Compte d'op. fin., nia
Net Errors and Omissions	90.0	110.1	252.2	93.2	-276.9	-235.3	...	Erreurs et omissions nettes
Reserves & Related Items	-238.1	-193.6	-80.2	-162.1	-441.1	-502.2	...	Rés. et postes appareutés
Tunisia								**Tunisie**
Goods: Exports fob	5 518.8	5 559.2	5 724.0	5 873.3	5 840.2	6 605.9	6 857.1	Biens : exportations, fab
Goods: Imports fob	-7 279.6	-7 514.2	-7 875.5	-8 014.5	-8 093.0	-8 996.9	-8 980.6	Biens : importations, fab
Serv. & Income: Credit	2 697.7	2 690.1	2 847.9	3 009.5	2 860.6	3 006.9	2 753.0	Serv. & revenu : crédit
Serv. & Income: Debit	-2 274.5	-2 121.3	-2 203.3	-2 212.1	-2 254.4	-2 460.5	-2 506.1	Serv & revenu : débit
Current Trans.,nie: Credit	879.4	821.0	851.8	919.7	854.3	1 016.2	1 155.6	Transf. cour.,nia : crédit
Current Transfers: Debit	-19.5	-29.8	-20.2	-17.7	-29.2	-34.1	-24.6	Transf. courants : débit
Capital Acct.,nie: Credit	46.2	94.9	82.5	72.5	8.8	55.6	83.0	Compte de cap.,nia : crédit
Capital Account: Debit	-9.2	-18.1	-22.0	-13.5	-5.8	-2.8	-7.7	Compte de capital : débit
Financial Account, nie	815.7	699.0	489.1	1 083.3	646.4	1 085.7	856.7	Compte d'op. fin., nia
Net Errors and Omissions	67.0	205.6	-12.0	37.6	-32.8	12.4	-47.1	Erreurs et omissions nettes
Reserves & Related Items	-442.0	-386.5	137.6	-738.1	205.0	-288.4	-139.3	Rés. et postes appareutés
Turkey								**Turquie**
Goods: Exports fob	32 067.0	32 110.0	30 662.0	28 842.0	30 721.0	34 373.0	39 818.0	Biens : exportations, fab
Goods: Imports fob	-42 681.0	-47 513.0	-44 926.0	-39 311.0	-53 131.0	-38 916.0	-48 130.0	Biens : importations, fab
Serv. & Income: Credit	15 007.0	21 810.0	26 360.0	19 231.0	23 265.0	18 812.0	17 288.0	Serv. & revenu : crédit
Serv. & Income: Debit	-11 277.0	-13 911.0	-15 839.0	-15 281.0	-15 899.0	-14 682.0	-13 954.0	Serv & revenu : débit
Current Trans.,nie: Credit	4 466.0	4 909.0	5 861.0	5 295.0	5 317.0	3 861.0	3 542.0	Transf. cour.,nia : crédit
Current Transfers: Debit	-19.0	-43.0	-134.0	-120.0	-92.0	-58.0	-46.0	Transf. courants : débit
Capital Acct.,nie: Credit	0.0	0.0	0.0	0.0	0.0	0.0	0.0	Compte de cap.,nia : crédit
Capital Account: Debit	0.0	0.0	0.0	0.0	0.0	0.0	0.0	Compte de capital : débit
Financial Account, nie	5 483.0	6 969.0	-840.0	4 979.0	8 584.0	-14 644.0	1 352.4	Compte d'op. fin., nia
Net Errors and Omissions	1 497.5	-987.8	-703.1	1 719.5	-2 698.5	-1 633.5	-83.9	Erreurs et omissions nettes
Reserves & Related Items	-4 543.5	-3 343.2	-440.9	-5 354.5	3 933.5	12 887.5	213.6	Rés. et postes appareutés
Turkmenistan								**Turkménistan**
Goods: Exports fob	1 692.0	774.2	...	...	...	...	...	Biens : exportations, fab
Goods: Imports fob	-1 388.3	-1 005.1	...	...	...	...	...	Biens : importations, fab
Serv. & Income: Credit	209.6	428.7	...	...	...	...	...	Serv. & revenu : crédit
Serv. & Income: Debit	-518.4	-746.6	...	...	...	...	...	Serv & revenu : débit
Current Trans.,nie: Credit	4.8	49.9	...	...	...	...	...	Transf. cour.,nia : crédit
Current Transfers: Debit	0.0	-81.2	...	...	...	...	...	Transf. courants : débit
Capital Acct.,nie: Credit	2.8	14.0	...	...	...	...	...	Compte de cap.,nia : crédit
Capital Account: Debit	-159.7	-22.9	...	...	...	...	...	Compte de capital : débit
Financial Account, nie	113.4	1 060.0	...	...	...	...	...	Compte d'op. fin., nia
Net Errors and Omissions	51.6	-72.9	...	...	...	...	...	Erreurs et omissions nettes
Reserves & Related Items	-7.9	-398.0	...	...	...	...	...	Rés. et postes appareutés
Uganda								**Ouganda**
Goods: Exports fob	639.3	592.6	510.2	483.5	449.9	451.6	480.7	Biens : exportations, fab
Goods: Imports fob	-986.9	-1 042.6	-1 166.3	-989.1	-949.7	-1 026.6	-1 113.5	Biens : importations, fab
Serv. & Income: Credit	174.4	205.1	227.0	231.1	266.3	258.3	263.4	Serv. & revenu : crédit
Serv. & Income: Debit	-753.8	-724.6	-788.0	-581.7	-624.3	-700.8	-689.9	Serv & revenu : débit
Current Trans.,nie: Credit	674.7	602.6	714.6	329.7	340.0	583.0	899.8	Transf. cour.,nia : crédit
Current Transfers: Debit	0.0	0.0	0.0	-184.2	-307.6	-367.9	-261.9	Transf. courants : débit
Capital Acct.,nie: Credit	61.4	31.9	49.5	0.0	0.0	0.0	0.0	Compte de cap.,nia : crédit
Capital Account: Debit	0.0	0.0	0.0	0.0	0.0	0.0	0.0	Compte de capital : débit
Financial Account, nie	140.5	298.8	372.8	253.3	320.5	499.7	266.2	Compte d'op. fin., nia
Net Errors and Omissions	41.3	-4.8	39.7	2.0	40.6	63.8	8.0	Erreurs et omissions nettes
Reserves & Related Items	9.1	40.9	40.6	455.4	464.3	238.9	147.3	Rés. et postes appareutés

79

Summary of balance of payments
Millions of US dollars *[cont.]*

Résumé des balances des paiements
Millions de dollars des E.-U. *[suite]*

Country or area	1996	1997	1998	1999	2000	2001	2002	Pays ou zone
Ukraine								**Ukraine**
Goods: Exports fob	15 547.0	15 418.0	13 699.0	13 189.0	15 722.0	17 091.0	18 669.0	Biens : exportations, fab
Goods: Imports fob	-19 843.0	-19 623.0	-16 283.0	-12 945.0	-14 943.0	-16 893.0	-17 959.0	Biens : importations, fab
Serv. & Income: Credit	4 901.0	5 095.0	4 044.0	3 967.0	3 943.0	4 162.0	4 847.0	Serv. & revenu : crédit
Serv. & Income: Debit	-2 298.0	-3 070.0	-3 538.0	-3 259.0	-4 089.0	-4 414.0	-4 304.0	Serv & revenu : débit
Current Trans.,nie: Credit	619.0	942.0	868.0	754.0	967.0	1 516.0	1 967.0	Transf. cour.,nia : crédit
Current Transfers: Debit	-110.0	-97.0	-86.0	-48.0	-119.0	-60.0	-46.0	Transf. courants : débit
Capital Acct.,nie: Credit	5.0	0.0	0.0	0.0	0.0	8.0	28.0	Compte de cap.,nia : crédit
Capital Account: Debit	0.0	0.0	-3.0	-10.0	-8.0	-5.0	-11.0	Compte de capital : débit
Financial Account, nie	317.0	1 413.0	-1 340.0	-879.0	-752.0	-191.0	-1 065.0	Compte d'op. fin., nia
Net Errors and Omissions	259.3	-780.7	-817.9	-953.1	-148.2	-220.8	-895.5	Erreurs et omissions nettes
Reserves & Related Items	602.8	702.7	3 456.9	184.1	-572.8	-993.2	-1 230.5	Rés. et postes appareutés
United Kingdom								**Royaume-Uni**
Goods: Exports fob	261 247.0	281 537.0	271 723.0	268 884.0	284 378.0	273 654.0	279 330.0	Biens : exportations, fab
Goods: Imports fob	-282 475.0	-301 739.0	-307 851.0	-313 179.0	-330 269.0	-321 858.0	-332 380.0	Biens : importations, fab
Serv. & Income: Credit	231 834.2	255 456.7	279 154.0	277 147.0	321 286.0	317 253.0	311 015.0	Serv. & revenu : crédit
Serv. & Income: Debit	-214 997.0	-228 595.7	-237 348.0	-253 864.8	-288 938.1	-277 324.9	-258 550.0	Serv & revenu : débit
Current Trans.,nie: Credit	29 456.4	21 443.0	20 589.5	22 699.1	18 656.7	20 136.7	16 849.6	Transf. cour.,nia : crédit
Current Transfers: Debit	-38 506.2	-30 952.4	-34 233.0	-33 512.3	-33 796.0	-29 750.6	-30 678.0	Transf. courants : débit
Capital Acct.,nie: Credit	2 182.8	2 771.4	2 435.5	2 906.5	4 361.8	3 917.0	3 438.6	Compte de cap.,nia : crédit
Capital Account: Debit	-1 039.8	-1 452.0	-1 647.2	-1 385.0	-1 604.2	-1 749.3	-1 763.4	Compte de capital : débit
Financial Account, nie	7 983.0	-12 157.5	234.8	29 337.3	25 091.9	17 406.1	11 711.7	Compte d'op. fin., nia
Net Errors and Omissions	3 663.2	9 786.8	6 684.3	-69.0	6 131.6	-6 140.5	392.2	Erreurs et omissions nettes
Reserves & Related Items	651.0	3 902.5	257.0	1 035.9	-5 298.4	4 456.5	634.7	Rés. et postes appareutés
United Rep. of Tanzania								**Rép.-Unie de Tanzanie**
Goods: Exports fob	764.1	715.3	589.5	543.3	663.3	776.4	902.5	Biens : exportations, fab
Goods: Imports fob	-1 213.1	-1 164.5	-1 365.3	-1 415.4	-1 367.6	-1 560.3	-1 511.3	Biens : importations, fab
Serv. & Income: Credit	658.4	539.0	590.0	643.4	677.7	734.7	740.3	Serv. & revenu : crédit
Serv. & Income: Debit	-1 058.7	-965.5	-1 124.9	-943.2	-862.8	-829.9	-803.3	Serv & revenu : débit
Current Trans.,nie: Credit	370.9	313.6	426.6	445.6	463.7	469.5	472.9	Transf. cour.,nia : crédit
Current Transfers: Debit	-32.3	-67.7	-35.5	-109.0	-72.9	-70.0	-52.4	Transf. courants : débit
Capital Acct.,nie: Credit	191.0	360.6	422.9	347.8	420.4	1 078.6	1 168.0	Compte de cap.,nia : crédit
Capital Account: Debit	0.0	0.0	0.0	0.0	0.0	0.0	0.0	Compte de capital : débit
Financial Account, nie	-92.8	3.6	77.6	565.2	492.6	-483.7	-507.0	Compte d'op. fin., nia
Net Errors and Omissions	158.6	-31.9	-90.3	-156.7	-415.7	16.1	-83.8	Erreurs et omissions nettes
Reserves & Related Items	254.0	297.5	509.4	79.0	1.3	-131.4	-325.9	Rés. et postes appareutés
United States								**Etats-Unis**
Goods: Exports fob	614 013.0	680 325.0	672 377.0	686 271.0	774 632.0	721 842.0	685 384.0	Biens : exportations, fab
Goods: Imports fob	-803 112.0	-876 505.0	-917 122.0	-1 029 990.0	-1 224 430.0	-1 145 950.0	-1 164 760.0	Biens : importations, fab
Serv. & Income: Credit	463 174.0	514 602.0	518 845.0	569 397.0	642 281.0	563 099.0	544 264.0	Serv. & revenu : crédit
Serv. & Income: Debit	-352 370.0	-404 806.0	-430 330.0	-469 789.0	-548 266.0	-486 117.0	-486 890.0	Serv & revenu : débit
Current Trans.,nie: Credit	10 392.6	9 864.7	9 636.8	8 848.2	10 779.7	8 560.2	11 497.6	Transf. cour.,nia : crédit
Current Transfers: Debit	-49 254.1	-51 157.2	-58 072.2	-55 603.6	-66 458.3	-55 175.2	-70 349.8	Transf. courants : débit
Capital Acct.,nie: Credit	893.8	825.2	932.6	1 079.1	1 075.7	1 051.9	1 106.0	Compte de cap.,nia : crédit
Capital Account: Debit	-1 547.2	-1 869.3	-1 673.3	-5 920.9	-1 874.8	-2 113.8	-2 391.3	Compte de capital : débit
Financial Account, nie	130 537.0	220 181.0	82 511.7	227 821.0	456 631.0	420 503.0	531 679.0	Compte d'op. fin., nia
Net Errors and Omissions	-19 393.4	-90 448.0	129 625.0	59 164.1	-44 080.0	-20 771.4	-45 842.6	Erreurs et omissions nettes
Reserves & Related Items	6 666.8	-1 012.0	-6 731.3	8 727.0	-294.9	-4 926.7	-3 692.5	Rés. et postes appareutés
Uruguay								**Uruguay**
Goods: Exports fob	2 448.5	2 793.1	2 829.3	2 290.6	2 383.8	2 139.4	1 933.1	Biens : exportations, fab
Goods: Imports fob	-3 135.4	-3 497.5	-3 601.4	-3 187.2	-3 311.1	-2 914.7	-1 872.9	Biens : importations, fab
Serv. & Income: Credit	1 859.2	1 971.4	1 927.1	1 997.1	2 057.2	1 954.5	1 230.6	Serv. & revenu : crédit
Serv. & Income: Debit	-1 488.2	-1 628.6	-1 689.5	-1 681.6	-1 723.6	-1 696.6	-1 098.5	Serv & revenu : débit
Current Trans.,nie: Credit	90.7	83.0	75.0	78.4	48.0	48.0	83.7	Transf. cour.,nia : crédit
Current Transfers: Debit	-8.2	-8.8	-16.0	-4.9	-20.5	-18.3	-14.3	Transf. courants : débit
Capital Acct.,nie: Credit	0.0	0.0	0.0	0.0	0.0	0.0	0.0	Compte de cap.,nia : crédit
Capital Account: Debit	0.0	0.0	0.0	0.0	0.0	0.0	0.0	Compte de capital : débit
Financial Account, nie	233.6	608.7	545.1	147.1	779.3	506.6	-2 032.2	Compte d'op. fin., nia
Net Errors and Omissions	152.2	78.8	285.5	250.9	-46.6	285.1	-2 121.1	Erreurs et omissions nettes
Reserves & Related Items	-152.4	-400.1	-355.1	109.6	-166.5	-304.0	3 891.6	Rés. et postes appareutés
Vanuatu								**Vanuatu**
Goods: Exports fob	30.2	35.3	33.8	25.7	27.2	19.9	...	Biens : exportations, fab

79

Summary of balance of payments
Millions of US dollars *[cont.]*

Résumé des balances des paiements
Millions de dollars des E.-U. *[suite]*

Country or area	1996	1997	1998	1999	2000	2001	2002	Pays ou zone
Goods: Imports fob	-81.1	-79.0	-76.2	-84.5	-76.9	-78.0	...	Biens : importations, fab
Serv. & Income: Credit	108.6	103.2	134.9	135.8	148.5	136.5	...	Serv. & revenu : crédit
Serv. & Income: Debit	-84.0	-81.6	-86.2	-98.2	-101.9	-94.2	...	Serv & revenu : débit
Current Trans.,nie: Credit	22.4	21.8	15.6	18.7	27.4	39.5	...	Transf. cour.,nia : crédit
Current Transfers: Debit	-22.9	-19.0	-31.2	-30.8	-38.0	-38.3	...	Transf. courants : débit
Capital Acct.,nie: Credit	43.4	23.8	25.4	23.9	31.9	46.1	...	Compte de cap.,nia : crédit
Capital Account: Debit	-38.5	-29.2	-46.3	-73.7	-55.5	-62.1	...	Compte de capital : débit
Financial Account, nie	20.9	-16.7	17.4	56.2	19.3	12.8	...	Compte d'op. fin., nia
Net Errors and Omissions	-4.1	39.4	6.0	3.6	-0.9	7.5	...	Erreurs et omissions nettes
Reserves & Related Items	5.3	2.2	6.9	23.2	18.8	10.3	...	Rés. et postes appareutés
Venezuela								**Venezuela**
Goods: Exports fob	23 707.0	23 871.0	17 707.0	20 963.0	33 194.0	26 252.0	26 656.0	Biens : exportations, fab
Goods: Imports fob	-9 937.0	-14 917.0	-16 755.0	-14 492.0	-16 592.0	-18 660.0	-13 732.0	Biens : importations, fab
Serv. & Income: Credit	3 152.0	3 735.0	3 902.0	3 349.0	4 466.0	3 923.0	2 634.0	Serv. & revenu : crédit
Serv. & Income: Debit	-8 146.0	-8 860.0	-9 085.0	-7 916.0	-8 846.0	-9 309.0	-7 824.0	Serv & revenu : débit
Current Trans.,nie: Credit	526.0	233.0	169.0	203.0	261.0	356.0	284.0	Transf. cour.,nia : crédit
Current Transfers: Debit	-388.0	-330.0	-370.0	-270.0	-431.0	-504.0	-479.0	Transf. courants : débit
Capital Acct.,nie: Credit	0.0	0.0	0.0	0.0	0.0	0.0	0.0	Compte de cap.,nia : crédit
Capital Account: Debit	0.0	0.0	0.0	0.0	0.0	0.0	0.0	Compte de capital : débit
Financial Account, nie	-1 784.0	879.0	2 689.0	-241.0	-3 239.0	-186.0	-9 486.0	Compte d'op. fin., nia
Net Errors and Omissions	-891.8	-1 516.6	-1 662.3	-538.0	-2 855.2	-3 701.4	-2 481.3	Erreurs et omissions nettes
Reserves & Related Items	-6 238.2	-3 094.4	3 405.3	-1 058.0	-5 957.8	1 829.4	4 428.3	Rés. et postes appareutés
Viet Nam								**Viet Nam**
Goods: Exports fob	7 255.0	9 185.0	9 361.0	11 540.0	14 448.0	15 027.0	16 706.0	Biens : exportations, fab
Goods: Imports fob	-10 030.0	-10 432.0	-10 350.0	-10 568.0	-14 073.0	-14 546.0	-17 760.0	Biens : importations, fab
Serv. & Income: Credit	2 383.0	2 666.0	2 743.0	2 635.0	3 033.0	3 128.0	3 115.0	Serv. & revenu : crédit
Serv. & Income: Debit	-2 828.0	-3 832.0	-3 950.0	-3 611.0	-4 034.0	-4 177.0	-4 586.0	Serv & revenu : débit
Current Trans.,nie: Credit	1 200.0	885.0	1 122.0	1 181.0	1 732.0	1 250.0	1 921.0	Transf. cour.,nia : crédit
Current Transfers: Debit	0.0	0.0	0.0	0.0	0.0	0.0	0.0	Transf. courants : débit
Capital Acct.,nie: Credit	0.0	0.0	0.0	0.0	0.0	0.0	0.0	Compte de cap.,nia : crédit
Capital Account: Debit	0.0	0.0	0.0	0.0	0.0	0.0	0.0	Compte de capital : débit
Financial Account, nie	2 909.0	2 125.0	1 646.0	1 058.0	-316.0	371.0	2 090.0	Compte d'op. fin., nia
Net Errors and Omissions	-611.3	-269.2	-534.9	-925.0	-680.1	-846.7	-1 037.7	Erreurs et omissions nettes
Reserves & Related Items	-277.7	-327.8	-37.1	-1 310.0	-109.9	-206.3	-448.3	Rés. et postes appareutés
Yemen								**Yémen**
Goods: Exports fob	2 262.7	2 274.0	1 503.7	2 478.3	3 797.2	3 366.9	3 620.7	Biens : exportations, fab
Goods: Imports fob	-2 293.5	-2 406.5	-2 288.8	-2 120.5	-2 484.4	-2 600.4	-2 932.0	Biens : importations, fab
Serv. & Income: Credit	232.5	277.2	243.4	239.9	360.5	344.9	301.1	Serv. & revenu : crédit
Serv. & Income: Debit	-1 236.1	-1 348.0	-1 106.3	-1 471.0	-1 736.2	-1 717.2	-1 835.4	Serv & revenu : débit
Current Trans.,nie: Credit	1 140.1	1 177.6	1 223.5	1 262.1	1 471.9	1 344.4	1 456.9	Transf. cour.,nia : crédit
Current Transfers: Debit	-66.9	-43.1	-47.7	-30.7	-72.4	-71.4	-73.1	Transf. courants : débit
Capital Acct.,nie: Credit	0.0	4 236.2	2.2	1.5	338.9	49.5	0.0	Compte de cap.,nia : crédit
Capital Account: Debit	0.0	0.0	0.0	0.0	0.0	0.0	0.0	Compte de capital : débit
Financial Account, nie	-367.8	-197.6	-418.0	-415.1	-376.2	-53.5	-156.8	Compte d'op. fin., nia
Net Errors and Omissions	-107.0	48.4	307.0	129.4	295.1	-110.0	43.3	Erreurs et omissions nettes
Reserves & Related Items	436.0	-4 018.2	580.9	-74.0	-1 594.4	-553.2	-424.7	Rés. et postes appareutés
Zambia								**Zambie**
Goods: Exports fob	...	1 110.4	818.0	772.0	757.0	...	...	Biens : exportations, fab
Goods: Imports fob	...	-1 056.0	-971.0	-870.0	-978.0	...	...	Biens : importations, fab
Serv. & Income: Credit	...	188.6	146.3	150.5	160.6	...	...	Serv. & revenu : crédit
Serv. & Income: Debit	...	-577.2	-539.7	-483.4	-505.9	...	...	Serv & revenu : débit
Current Trans.,nie: Credit	...	0.0	0.0	0.0	0.0	...	...	Transf. cour.,nia : crédit
Current Transfers: Debit	...	-19.0	-27.0	-16.0	-18.0	...	...	Transf. courants : débit
Capital Acct.,nie: Credit	...	0.0	203.0	196.0	153.0	...	...	Compte de cap.,nia : crédit
Capital Account: Debit	...	0.0	0.0	0.0	0.0	...	...	Compte de capital : débit
Financial Account, nie	...	-323.8	-263.7	-173.9	-273.6	...	...	Compte d'op. fin., nia
Net Errors and Omissions	...	-255.4	-37.4	-229.4	184.8	...	...	Erreurs et omissions nettes
Reserves & Related Items	...	932.4	671.4	654.2	520.2	...	...	Rés. et postes appareutés

79

Summary of balance of payments
Millions of US dollars *[cont.]*

Résumé des balances des paiements
Millions de dollars des E.-U. *[suite]*

Source:
International Monetary Fund (IMF), Washington, D.C., "International Financial Statistics," January 2004 and the IMF database.

Source:
Fonds monétaire international (FMI), Washington, D.C.,"Statistiques Financières Internationales," janvier 2004 et la base de données du FMI.

1   BLEU trade data refer to the Belgium-Luxembourg Economic Union and exclude transactions between the two countries. Beginning in 1997, trade data are for Belgium only, which includes trade between Belgium and Luxembourg.

2   Services only.

3   Data refer to the Gaza Strip.

1   Les données sur le commerce extérieur se rapportent à l'Union économique belgo-luxembourgeoise (UEBL) et ne couvrent pas les transactions entre les deux pays. A compter de 1997, les données sur le commerce extérieur ne se rapportent qu'à la Belgique, et recouvrent les échanges entre la Belgique et le Luxembourg.

2   Service seulement.

3   Les données se rapportent à la Bande de Gaza.

Technical notes, table 79

A balance of payments can be broadly described as the record of an economy's international economic transactions. It shows (a) transactions in goods, services and income between an economy and the rest of the world, (b) changes of ownership and other changes in that economy's monetary gold, special drawing rights (SDRs) and claims on and liabilities to the rest of the world, and (c) unrequited transfers and counterpart entries needed to balance in the accounting sense any entries for the foregoing transactions and changes which are not mutually offsetting.

The balance of payments are presented on the basis of the methodology and presentation of the fifth edition of the *Balance of Payments Manual* (BPM5) [41], published by the International Monetary Fund in September 1993. The BPM5 incorporates several major changes to take account of developments in international trade and finance over the past decade, and to better harmonize the Fund's balance of payments methodology with the methodology of the 1993 *System of National Accounts* (SNA) [59]. The Fund's balance of payments has been converted for all periods from the BPM4 basis to the BPM5 basis; thus the time series conform to the BPM5 methodology with no methodological breaks.

The detailed definitions concerning the content of the basic categories of the balance of payments are given in the *Balance of Payments Manual (fifth edition)* [41]. Brief explanatory notes are given below to clarify the scope of the major items.

Goods: Exports f.o.b. and *Goods: Imports f.o.b.* are both measured on the "free-on-board" (f.o.b.) basis—that is, by the value of the goods at the border of the exporting country; in the case of imports, this excludes the cost of freight and insurance incurred beyond the border of the exporting country.

Services and income covers transactions in real resources between residents and non-residents other than those classified as merchandise, including (a) shipment and other transportation services, including freight, insurance and other distributive services in connection with the movement of commodities, (b) travel, i.e. goods and services acquired by non-resident travellers in a given country and similar acquisitions by resident travellers abroad, and (c) investment income which covers income of non-residents from their financial assets invested in the compiling economy (debit) and similar income of residents from their financial assets invested abroad (credit).

Current Transfers, n.i.e.: *Credit* comprises all current transfers received by the reporting country, except those made to the country to finance its "overall bal-

Notes techniques, tableau 79

La balance des paiements peut se définir d'une façon générale comme le relevé des transactions économiques internationales d'une économie. Elle indique (a) les transactions sur biens, services et revenus entre une économie et le reste du monde, (b) les transferts de propriété et autres variations intervenues dans les avoirs en or monétaire de cette économie, dans ses avoirs en droits de tirages spéciaux (DTS) ainsi que dans ses créances financières sur le reste du monde ou dans ses engagements financiers envers lui et (c) les "inscriptions de transferts sans contrepartie" et de "contrepartie" destinées à équilibrer, d'un point de vue comptable, les transactions et changements précités qui ne se compensent pas réciproquement.

Les données de balance des paiements sont présentées conformément à la méthodologie et à la classification recommandées dans la cinquième édition du *Manuel de la balance des paiements* [41], publiée en septembre 1993 par le Fonds monétaire international. La cinquième édition fait état de plusieurs changements importants qui ont été opérés de manière à rendre compte de l'évolution des finances et des changes internationaux pendant la décennie écoulée et à harmoniser davantage la méthodologie de la balance des paiements du FMI avec celle du *Système de comptabilité nationale* (SCN) [59] de 1993. Les statistiques incluses dans la balance des paiements du FMI ont été converties et sont désormais établies, pour toutes les périodes, sur la base de la cinquième et non plus de la quatrième édition; en conséquence, les séries chronologiques sont conformes aux principes de la cinquième édition, sans rupture due à des différences d'ordre méthodologique.

Les définitions détaillées relatives au contenu des postes fondamentaux de la balance des paiements figurent dans le *Manuel de la balance des paiements (cinquième édition)* [41]. De brèves notes explicatives sont présentées ci-après pour clarifier la portée de ces principales rubriques.

Les Biens: exportations, f.à.b. et *Biens: importations, f.à.b.* sont évalués sur la base f.à.b. (franco à bord)—c'est-à-dire à la frontière du pays exportateur; dans le cas des importations, cette valeur exclut le coût du fret et de l'assurance au-delà de la frontière du pays exportateur.

Services et revenus: transactions en ressources effectuées entre résidents et non résidents, autres que celles qui sont considérées comme des marchandises, notamment: (a) expéditions et autres services de transport, y compris le fret, l'assurance et les autres services de distribution liés aux mouvements de marchandises; (b) voyages, à savoir les biens et services acquis par des

ance", hence, the label "n.i.e." (not included elsewhere). (Note: some of the capital and financial accounts labeled "n.i.e." denote that *Exceptional Financing items* and *Liabilities Constituting Foreign Authorities' Reserves* (LCFARs) have been excluded.)

Capital Account, n.i.e.: *Credit* refers mainly to capital transfers linked to the acquisition of a fixed asset other than transactions relating to debt forgiveness plus the disposal of nonproduced, nonfinancial assets. *Capital Account*: *Debit* refers mainly to capital transfers linked to the disposal of fixed assets by the donor or to the financing of capital formation by the recipient, plus the acquisition of nonproduced, nonfinancial assets.

Financial Account, n.i.e. is the net sum of the balance of direct investment, portfolio investment, and other investment transactions.

Net Errors and Omissions is a residual category needed to ensure that all debit and credit entries in the balance of payments statement sum to zero and reflects statistical inconsistencies in the recording of the credit and debit entries.

Reserves and Related Items is the sum of transactions in reserve assets, LCFARs, exceptional financing, and use of Fund credit and loans.

For further information see *International Financial Statistics* [15] and <www.imf.org>.

voyageurs non résidents dans un pays donné et achats similaires faits par des résidents voyageant à l'étranger; et (c) revenus des investissements, qui correspondent aux revenus que les non résidents tirent de leurs avoirs financiers placés dans l'économie déclarante (débit) et les revenus similaires que les résidents tirent de leurs avoirs financiers placés à l'étranger (crédit).

Les transferts courants, n.i.a: *Crédit* englobent tous les transferts courants reçus par l'économie qui établit sa balance des paiements, à l'exception de ceux qui sont destinés à financer sa "balance globale"—c'est ce qui explique la mention "n.i.a." (non inclus ailleurs). (Note: comptes de capital et d'opérations financières portent la mention "n.i.a.", ce qui signifie que les postes de *Financement exceptionnel* et les *Engagements constituant des réserves pour les autorités étrangères* ont été exclus de ces composantes du compte de capital et d'opérations financières.

Le Compte de capital, n.i.a.: *crédit* retrace principalement les transferts de capital liés à l'acquisition d'un actif fixe autres que les transactions ayant trait à des remises de dettes plus les cessions d'actifs non financiers non produits. Le *Compte de capital*: *débit* retrace principalement les transferts de capital liés à la cession d'actifs fixes par le donateur ou au financement de la formation de capital par le bénéficiaire, plus les acquisitions d'actifs non financiers non produits.

Le solde du *Compte d'op. Fin., n.i.a.* (compte d'opérations financières, n.i.a.) est la somme des soldes des investissements directs, des investissements de portefeuille et des autres investissements.

Le poste des *Erreurs et omissions* nettes est une catégorie résiduelle qui est nécessaire pour assurer que la somme de toutes les inscriptions effectuées au débit et au crédit est égal à zéro et qui laisse apparaître les écarts entre les montants portés au débit et ceux qui sont inscrits au crédit.

Le montant de *Réserves et postes apparentés* est égal à la somme de transactions afférentes aux avoirs de réserve, aux engagements constituant des réserves pour les autorités étrangères, au financement exceptionnel et à l'utilisation des crédits et des prêts du FMI.

Pour plus de renseignements, voir *Statistiques financières internationales* [15] et <www.imf.org>.

80

Exchange rates
National currency per US dollar

Cours des changes
Valeur du dollar des États-Unis en monnaie nationale

Country or area Pays ou zone	1993	1994	1995	1996	1997	1998	1999	2000	2001	2002
Afghanistan [1] (afghani) Afghanistan [1] (afghani)										
End of period										
Fin de période	50.600	500.000	1 000.000	3 000.000	3 000.000	3 000.000	3 000.000	3 000.000	3 000.000	3 000.000
Period average										
Moyenne sur période	50.600	425.100	833.333	2 333.330	3 000.000	3 000.000	3 000.000	3 000.000	3 000.000	3 000.000
Albania (lek) Albanie (lek)										
End of period										
Fin de période	98.700	95.590	94.240	103.070	149.140	140.580	135.120	142.640	136.550	133.740
Period average										
Moyenne sur période	102.062	94.623	92.698	104.499	148.933	150.633	137.691	143.709	143.485	140.155
Algeria (Algerian dinar) Algérie (dinar algérien)										
End of period										
Fin de période	24.123	42.893	52.175	56.186	58.414	60.353	69.314	75.343	77.820	79.723
Period average										
Moyenne sur période	23.345	35.059	47.663	54.749	57.707	58.739	66.574	75.260	77.215	79.682
Angola (readjusted kwanza) Angola (réajusté kwanza)										
End of period										
Fin de période	0.000	0.001	0.006	0.202	0.262	0.697	5.580	16.818	31.949	58.666
Period average										
Moyenne sur période	0.000	0.000	0.003	0.128	0.229	0.393	2.791	10.041	22.058	43.530
Anguilla (EC dollar) Anguilla (dollar des Caraïbes orientales)										
End of period										
Fin de période	2.700	2.700	2.700	2.700	2.700	2.700	2.700	2.700	2.700	2.700
Antigua and Barbuda (EC dollar) Antigua-et-Barbuda (dollar des Caraïbes orientales)										
End of period										
Fin de période	2.700	2.700	2.700	2.700	2.700	2.700	2.700	2.700	2.700	2.700
Argentina [2] (Argentine peso) Argentine [2] (peso argentin)										
End of period										
Fin de période	0.999	1.000	1.000	1.000	1.000	1.000	1.000	1.000	1.000	3.320
Period average										
Moyenne sur période	0.999	0.999	1.000	1.000	1.000	1.000	1.000	1.000	1.000	3.063
Armenia (dram) Arménie (dram)										
End of period										
Fin de période	75.000	405.510	402.000	435.070	494.980	522.030	523.770	552.180	561.810	584.890
Period average										
Moyenne sur période	9.105	288.651	405.908	414.041	490.847	504.915	535.062	539.526	555.078	573.353
Aruba (Aruban florin) Aruba (florin de Aruba)										
End of period										
Fin de période	1.790	1.790	1.790	1.790	1.790	1.790	1.790	1.790	1.790	1.790
Australia (Australian dollar) Australie (dollar australien)										
End of period										
Fin de période	1.477	1.287	1.342	1.256	1.532	1.629	1.530	1.805	1.959	1.766
Period average										
Moyenne sur période	1.471	1.368	1.349	1.278	1.347	1.592	1.550	1.725	1.933	1.841
Austria [3] (Austrian schilling) Autriche [3] (schilling autrichien)										
End of period										
Fin de période	12.143	10.969	10.088	10.954	12.633	11.747	...	...	...	...
Period average										
Moyenne sur période	11.632	11.422	10.082	10.587	12.204	12.379	...	...	...	...
Azerbaijan (manat) Azerbaïdjan (manat)										
End of period										
Fin de période	118.000	4 182.000	4 440.000	4 098.000	3 888.000	3 890.000	4 378.000	4 565.000	4 775.000	4 893.000
Period average										
Moyenne sur période	99.975	1 570.220	4 413.540	4 301.260	3 985.370	3 869.000	4 120.170	4 474.150	4 656.580	4 860.820
Bahamas [1] (Bahamian dollar) Bahamas [1] (dollar des Bahamas)										
End of period										
Fin de période	1.000	1.000	1.000	1.000	1.000	1.000	1.000	1.000	1.000	1.000
Bahrain (Bahrain dinar) Bahreïn (dinar de Bahreïn)										
End of period										
Fin de période	0.376	0.376	0.376	0.376	0.376	0.376	0.376	0.376	0.376	0.376

80

Exchange rates
National currency per US dollar [cont.]

Cours des changes
Valeur du dollar des Etats-Unis en monnaie nationale [suite]

Country or area Pays ou zone	1993	1994	1995	1996	1997	1998	1999	2000	2001	2002
Bangladesh[1] (taka) Bangladesh[1] (taka)										
End of period										
Fin de période	39.850	40.250	40.750	42.450	45.450	48.500	51.000	54.000	57.000	57.900
Period average										
Moyenne sur période	39.567	40.212	40.278	41.794	43.892	46.906	49.085	52.142	55.807	57.888
Barbados (Barbados dollar) Barbade (dollar de la Barbade)										
End of period										
Fin de période	2.000	2.000	2.000	2.000	2.000	2.000	2.000	2.000	2.000	2.000
Belarus (Belarussian rouble) Bélarus (rouble bélarussien)										
End of period										
Fin de période	0.699	10.600	11.500	15.500	30.740	106.000	320.000	1 180.000	1 580.000	1 920.000
Period average										
Moyenne sur période	...	...	11.521	13.230	26.020	46.127	248.795	876.750	1 390.000	1 790.920
Belgium[3] (Belgian franc) Belgique[3] (franc belge)										
End of period										
Fin de période	36.110	31.838	29.415	32.005	36.920	34.575	...	...	...	...
Period average										
Moyenne sur période	34.597	33.457	29.480	30.962	35.774	36.299	...	...	...	...
Belize (Belize dollar) Belize (dollar du Belize)										
End of period										
Fin de période	2.000	2.000	2.000	2.000	2.000	2.000	2.000	2.000	2.000	2.000
Benin[4] (CFA franc) Bénin[4] (franc CFA)										
End of period										
Fin de période	294.775	534.600	490.000	523.700	598.810	562.210	652.953	704.951	744.306	625.495
Period average										
Moyenne sur période	283.163	555.205	499.148	511.552	583.669	589.952	615.699	711.976	733.039	696.988
Bhutan (ngultrum) Bhoutan (ngultrum)										
End of period										
Fin de période	31.380	31.380	35.180	35.930	39.280	42.480	43.490	46.750	48.180	48.030
Period average										
Moyenne sur période	30.493	31.374	32.427	35.433	36.313	41.259	43.055	44.942	47.186	48.610
Bolivia[5] (boliviano) Bolivie[5] (boliviano)										
End of period										
Fin de période	4.475	4.695	4.935	5.185	5.365	5.645	5.990	6.390	6.820	7.490
Period average										
Moyenne sur période	4.265	4.621	4.800	5.075	5.254	5.510	5.812	6.184	6.607	7.170
Bosnia and Herzegovina (convertible mark) Bosnie-Herzégovine (mark convertible)										
End of period										
Fin de période	...	...	...	...	1.792	1.673	1.947	2.102	2.219	1.865
Period average										
Moyenne sur période	...	...	...	...	1.734	1.760	1.836	2.123	2.186	2.078
Botswana (pula) Botswana (pula)										
End of period										
Fin de période	2.565	2.717	2.822	3.644	3.810	4.458	4.632	5.362	6.983	5.468
Period average										
Moyenne sur période	2.423	2.685	2.772	3.324	3.651	4.226	4.624	5.102	5.841	6.328
Brazil[6] (real) Brésil[6] (real)										
End of period										
Fin de période	#0.119	0.846	0.973	1.039	1.116	1.209	1.789	1.955	2.320	3.533
Period average										
Moyenne sur période	#0.032	0.639	0.918	1.005	1.078	1.161	1.815	1.830	2.358	2.921
Brunei Darussalam (Brunei dollar) Brunéi Darussalam (dollar du Brunéi)										
End of period										
Fin de période	1.608	1.461	1.414	1.400	1.676	1.661	1.666	1.732	1.851	1.737
Period average										
Moyenne sur période	1.616	1.527	1.417	1.410	1.485	1.674	1.695	1.724	1.792	1.791
Bulgaria (lev) Bulgarie (lev)										
End of period										
Fin de période	0.033	0.066	0.071	0.487	1.777	1.675	1.947	2.102	2.219	1.885
Period average										
Moyenne sur période	0.028	0.054	0.067	0.178	1.682	1.760	1.836	2.123	2.185	2.077

80

Exchange rates
National currency per US dollar [cont.]

Cours des changes
Valeur du dollar des Etats-Unis en monnaie nationale [suite]

Country or area Pays ou zone	1993	1994	1995	1996	1997	1998	1999	2000	2001	2002
Burkina Faso [4] (CFA franc) Burkina Faso [4] (franc CFA)										
End of period										
Fin de période	294.775	534.600	490.000	523.700	598.810	562.210	652.953	704.951	744.306	625.495
Period average										
Moyenne sur période	283.163	555.205	499.148	511.552	583.669	589.952	615.699	711.976	733.039	696.988
Burundi (Burundi franc) Burundi (franc burundais)										
End of period										
Fin de période	264.380	246.940	277.920	322.350	408.380	505.160	628.580	778.200	864.200	1 071.230
Period average										
Moyenne sur période	242.780	252.662	249.757	302.747	352.351	447.766	563.562	720.673	830.353	930.749
Cambodia (riel) Cambodge (riel)										
End of period										
Fin de période	2 305.000	2 575.000	2 526.000	2 713.000	3 452.000	3 770.000	3 770.000	3 905.000	3 895.000	3 930.000
Period average										
Moyenne sur période	2 689.000	2 545.250	2 450.830	2 624.080	2 946.250	3 744.420	3 807.830	3 840.750	3 916.330	3 912.080
Cameroon [4] (CFA franc) Cameroun [4] (franc CFA)										
End of period										
Fin de période	294.775	534.600	490.000	523.700	598.810	562.210	652.953	704.951	744.306	625.495
Period average										
Moyenne sur période	283.163	555.205	499.148	511.552	583.669	589.952	615.699	711.976	733.039	696.988
Canada (Canadian dollar) Canada (dollar canadien)										
End of period										
Fin de période	1.324	1.403	1.365	1.370	1.429	1.531	1.443	1.500	1.593	1.580
Period average										
Moyenne sur période	1.290	1.366	1.372	1.364	1.385	1.484	1.486	1.485	1.549	1.569
Cape Verde (Cape Verde escudo) Cap-Vert (escudo du Cap-Vert)										
End of period										
Fin de période	85.992	81.140	77.455	85.165	96.235	94.255	109.765	118.506	125.122	105.149
Period average										
Moyenne sur période	80.427	81.891	76.853	82.592	93.177	98.158	103.502	119.687	123.228	117.168
Central African Rep. [4] (CFA franc) Rép. centrafricaine [4] (franc CFA)										
End of period										
Fin de période	294.775	534.600	490.000	523.700	598.810	562.210	652.953	704.951	744.306	625.495
Period average										
Moyenne sur période	283.163	555.205	499.148	511.552	583.669	589.952	615.699	711.976	733.039	696.988
Chad [4] (CFA franc) Tchad [4] (franc CFA)										
End of period										
Fin de période	294.775	534.600	490.000	523.700	598.810	562.210	652.953	704.951	744.306	625.495
Period average										
Moyenne sur période	283.163	555.205	499.148	511.552	583.669	589.952	615.699	711.976	733.039	696.988
Chile [1] (Chilean peso) Chili [1] (peso chilien)										
End of period										
Fin de période	431.040	404.090	407.130	424.970	439.810	473.770	530.070	572.680	656.200	712.380
Period average										
Moyenne sur période	404.166	420.177	396.773	412.267	419.295	460.287	508.777	539.587	634.938	688.936
China [1] (yuan) Chine [1] (yuan)										
End of period										
Fin de période	5.800	8.446	8.317	8.298	8.280	8.279	8.280	8.277	8.277	8.277
Period average										
Moyenne sur période	5.762	8.619	8.351	8.314	8.290	8.279	8.278	8.279	8.277	8.277
China, Hong Kong SAR (Hong Kong dollar) Chine, Hong Kong RAS (dollar de Hong Kong)										
End of period										
Fin de période	7.726	7.738	7.732	7.736	7.746	7.746	7.771	7.796	7.797	7.798
Period average										
Moyenne sur période	7.736	7.728	7.736	7.734	7.742	7.745	7.758	7.791	7.799	7.799
China, Macao SAR (Macao pataca) Chine, Macao RAS (pataca de Macao)										
End of period										
Fin de période	7.956	7.970	7.965	7.968	7.982	7.980	8.005	8.034	8.031	8.033
Period average										
Moyenne sur période	7.968	7.960	7.968	7.966	7.975	7.979	7.992	8.026	8.034	8.033

80

Exchange rates
National currency per US dollar [cont.]

Cours des changes
Valeur du dollar des Etats-Unis en monnaie nationale [suite]

Country or area Pays ou zone	1993	1994	1995	1996	1997	1998	1999	2000	2001	2002
Colombia (Colombian peso) Colombie (peso colombien)										
End of period										
Fin de période	917.330	831.270	987.650	1 005.330	1 293.580	1 507.520	1 873.770	2 187.020	2 301.330	2 864.790
Period average										
Moyenne sur période	863.065	844.836	912.826	1 036.690	1 140.960	1 426.040	1 756.230	2 087.900	2 299.630	2 504.240
Comoros[7] (Comorian franc) Comores[7] (franc comorien)										
End of period										
Fin de période	294.772	400.948	367.498	392.773	449.105	421.655	489.715	528.714	558.230	469.122
Period average										
Moyenne sur période	283.160	416.399	374.357	383.660	437.747	442.459	461.775	533.982	549.779	522.741
Congo[4] (CFA franc) Congo[4] (franc CFA)										
End of period										
Fin de période	294.775	534.600	490.000	523.700	598.810	562.210	652.953	704.951	744.306	625.495
Period average										
Moyenne sur période	283.163	555.205	499.148	511.552	583.669	589.952	615.699	711.976	733.039	696.988
Costa Rica (Costa Rican colón) Costa Rica (colón costa-ricien)										
End of period										
Fin de période	151.440	165.070	194.900	220.110	244.290	271.420	298.190	318.020	341.670	378.720
Period average										
Moyenne sur période	142.172	157.067	179.729	207.689	232.597	257.229	285.685	308.187	328.871	359.817
Côte d'Ivoire[4] (CFA franc) Côte d'Ivoire[4] (franc CFA)										
End of period										
Fin de période	294.775	534.600	490.000	523.700	598.810	562.210	652.953	704.951	744.306	625.495
Period average										
Moyenne sur période	283.163	555.205	499.148	511.552	583.669	589.952	615.699	711.976	733.039	696.988
Croatia (kuna) Croatie (kuna)										
End of period										
Fin de période	6.562	5.629	5.316	5.540	6.303	6.248	7.648	8.155	8.356	7.146
Period average										
Moyenne sur période	3.577	5.996	5.230	5.434	6.101	6.362	7.112	8.277	8.340	7.869
Cyprus (Cyprus pound) Chypre (livre chypriote)										
End of period										
Fin de période	0.520	0.476	0.457	0.470	0.526	0.498	0.575	0.617	0.650	0.547
Period average										
Moyenne sur période	0.497	0.492	0.452	0.466	0.514	0.518	0.543	0.622	0.643	0.611
Czech Republic (Czech koruna) République tchèque (couronne tchèque)										
End of period										
Fin de période	29.955	28.049	26.602	27.332	34.636	29.855	35.979	37.813	36.259	30.141
Period average[1]										
Moyenne sur période[1]	29.153	28.785	26.541	27.145	31.698	32.281	34.569	38.598	38.035	32.739
Dem. Rep. of the Congo[8] (Congo franc) Rép. dém. du Congo[8] (franc congolais)										
End of period										
Fin de période	350.000	#32.500	148.310	1 156.000	1 060.000	#2.450	4.500	50.000	313.600	382.140
Period average										
Moyenne sur période	25.144	#11.941	70.245	501.849	1 313.450	#1.607	4.018	21.818	206.617	346.485
Denmark (Danish krone) Danemark (couronne danoise)										
End of period										
Fin de période	6.773	6.083	5.546	5.945	6.826	6.387	7.399	8.021	8.410	7.082
Period average										
Moyenne sur période	6.484	6.361	5.602	5.799	6.605	6.701	6.976	8.083	8.323	7.895
Djibouti (Djibouti franc) Djibouti (franc djiboutien)										
End of period										
Fin de période	177.721	177.721	177.721	177.721	177.721	177.721	177.721	177.721	177.721	177.721
Dominica (EC dollar) Dominique (dollar des Caraïbes orientales)										
End of period										
Fin de période	2.700	2.700	2.700	2.700	2.700	2.700	2.700	2.700	2.700	2.700
Dominican Republic[1] (Dominican peso) Rép. dominicaine[1] (peso dominicain)										
End of period										
Fin de période	12.767	13.064	13.465	14.062	14.366	15.788	16.039	16.674	17.149	21.194
Period average										
Moyenne sur période	12.676	13.160	13.597	13.775	14.266	15.267	16.033	16.415	16.952	18.610

80

Exchange rates
National currency per US dollar [cont.]

Cours des changes
Valeur du dollar des Etats-Unis en monnaie nationale [suite]

Country or area Pays ou zone	1993	1994	1995	1996	1997	1998	1999	2000	2001	2002
Ecuador [1] (sucre) Equateur [1] (sucre)										
End of period										
Fin de période	2 043.780	2 269.000	2 923.500	3 635.000	4 428.000	6 825.000	20 243.000	25 000.000	25 000.000	25 000.000
Period average										
Moyenne sur période	1 919.100	2 196.730	2 564.490	3 189.470	3 998.270	5 446.570	11 786.800	24 988.400	25 000.000	25 000.000
Egypt [1] (Egyptian pound) Egypte [1] (livre égyptienne)										
End of period										
Fin de période	3.372	3.391	3.390	3.388	3.388	3.388	3.405	3.690	4.490	4.500
Period average										
Moyenne sur période	3.353	3.385	3.392	3.392	3.389	3.388	3.395	3.472	3.973	4.500
El Salvador [1] (El Salvadoran colón) El Salvador [1] (cólon salvadorien)										
End of period										
Fin de période	8.670	8.750	8.755	8.755	8.755	8.755	8.755	8.755	8.750	8.750
Period average										
Moyenne sur période	8.703	8.729	8.755	8.755	8.756	8.755	8.755	8.755	8.750	8.750
Equatorial Guinea [4] (CFA franc) Guinée équatoriale [4] (franc CFA)										
End of period										
Fin de période	294.775	534.600	490.000	523.700	598.810	562.210	652.953	704.951	744.306	625.495
Period average										
Moyenne sur période	283.163	555.205	499.148	511.552	583.669	589.952	615.699	711.976	733.039	696.988
Eritrea (Nakfa) Erythrée (Nakfa)										
End of period										
Fin de période	5.000	5.950	6.320	6.426	7.125	7.597	9.600	10.200	13.798	14.131
Period average										
Moyenne sur période	5.008	5.473	6.168	6.362	6.837	7.362	8.153	9.625	11.310	13.958
Estonia (Estonian kroon) Estonie (couronne estonienne)										
End of period										
Fin de période	13.878	12.390	11.462	12.440	14.336	13.410	15.562	16.820	17.692	14.936
Period average										
Moyenne sur période	13.223	12.991	11.465	12.034	13.882	14.075	14.678	16.969	17.478	16.612
Ethiopia (Ethiopian birr) Ethiopie (birr éthiopien)										
End of period										
Fin de période	5.000	5.950	6.320	6.426	6.864	7.503	8.134	8.314	8.558	8.581
Period average										
Moyenne sur période	5.000	5.465	6.158	6.352	6.709	7.116	7.942	8.217	8.458	8.568
Euro Area [9] (euro) Zone euro [9] (euro)										
End of period										
Fin de période	...	...	...	...	...	...	0.995	1.075	1.135	0.954
Period average										
Moyenne sur période	...	...	...	...	...	...	0.939	1.085	1.118	1.063
Fiji (Fiji dollar) Fidji (dollar des Fidji)										
End of period										
Fin de période	1.541	1.409	1.429	1.384	1.549	1.986	1.966	2.186	2.309	2.065
Period average										
Moyenne sur période	1.542	1.464	1.406	1.403	1.444	1.987	1.970	2.129	2.277	2.187
Finland [3] (Finnish markka) Finlande [3] (markka finlandais)										
End of period										
Fin de période	5.785	4.743	4.359	4.644	5.421	5.096	...	...	...	...
Period average										
Moyenne sur période	5.712	5.224	4.367	4.594	5.191	5.344	...	...	...	...
France [3] (French franc) France [3] (franc français)										
End of period										
Fin de période	5.896	5.346	4.900	5.237	5.988	5.622	...	...	...	...
Period average										
Moyenne sur période	5.663	5.552	4.992	5.116	5.837	5.900	...	...	...	...
Gabon [4] (CFA franc) Gabon [4] (franc CFA)										
End of period										
Fin de période	294.775	534.600	490.000	523.700	598.810	562.210	652.953	704.951	744.306	625.495
Period average										
Moyenne sur période	283.163	555.205	499.148	511.552	583.669	589.952	615.699	711.976	733.039	696.988

80

Exchange rates
National currency per US dollar [cont.]

Cours des changes
Valeur du dollar des Etats-Unis en monnaie nationale [suite]

Country or area Pays ou zone	1993	1994	1995	1996	1997	1998	1999	2000	2001	2002
Gambia (dalasi) Gambie (dalasi)										
End of period										
Fin de période	9.535	9.579	9.640	9.892	10.530	10.991	11.547	14.888	16.932	23.392
Period average										
Moyenne sur période	9.129	9.576	9.546	9.789	10.200	10.643	11.395	12.788	15.687	19.918
Georgia (lari) Géorgie (lari)										
End of period										
Fin de période	...	...	1.230	1.276	1.304	1.800	1.930	1.975	2.060	2.090
Period average										
Moyenne sur période	...	...	...	1.263	1.298	1.390	2.025	1.976	2.073	2.196
Germany[3] (deutsche mark) Allemagne[3] (deutsche mark)										
End of period										
Fin de période	1.726	1.549	1.434	1.555	1.792	1.673	...	...	...	...
Period average										
Moyenne sur période	1.653	1.623	1.433	1.505	1.734	1.760	...	...	...	...
Ghana[1] (cedi) Ghana[1] (cedi)										
End of period										
Fin de période	819.672	1 052.630	1 449.280	1 754.390	2 272.730	2 325.580	3 535.140	7 047.650	7 321.940	8 438.820
Period average										
Moyenne sur période	649.061	956.711	1 200.430	1 637.230	2 050.170	2 314.150	2 669.300	5 455.060	7 170.760	7 932.700
Greece[3] (drachma) Grèce[3] (drachme)										
End of period										
Fin de période	249.220	240.100	237.040	247.020	282.610	282.570	328.440	365.620	...	...
Period average										
Moyenne sur période	229.250	242.603	231.663	240.712	273.058	295.529	305.647	365.399	...	...
Grenada (EC dollar) Grenade (dollar des Caraïbes orientales)										
End of period										
Fin de période	2.700	2.700	2.700	2.700	2.700	2.700	2.700	2.700	2.700	2.700
Guatemala (quetzal) Guatemala (quetzal)										
End of period										
Fin de période	5.815	5.649	6.042	5.966	6.177	6.848	7.821	7.731	8.001	7.807
Period average										
Moyenne sur période	5.635	5.751	5.810	6.050	6.065	6.395	7.386	7.763	7.859	7.822
Guinea (Guinean franc) Guinée (franc guinéen)										
End of period										
Fin de période	972.414	981.024	997.984	1 039.130	1 144.950	1 298.030	1 736.000	1 882.270	1 988.330	1 976.000
Period average										
Moyenne sur période	955.490	976.636	991.411	1 004.020	1 095.330	1 236.830	1 387.400	1 746.870	1 950.560	1 975.840
Guinea-Bissau[10] (CFA franc) Guinée-Bissau[10] (franc CFA)										
End of period										
Fin de période	176.366	236.451	337.366	537.482	598.810	562.210	652.953	704.951	744.306	625.495
Period average										
Moyenne sur période	155.106	198.341	278.039	405.745	583.669	589.952	615.699	711.976	733.039	696.988
Guyana[1] (Guyana dollar) Guyana[1] (dollar guyanais)										
End of period										
Fin de période	130.750	142.500	140.500	141.250	144.000	162.250	180.500	184.750	189.500	191.750
Period average										
Moyenne sur période	126.730	138.290	141.989	140.375	142.401	150.519	177.995	182.430	187.321	190.665
Haïti[1] (gourde) Haïti[1] (gourde)										
End of period										
Fin de période	12.805	12.947	16.160	15.093	17.311	16.505	17.965	22.524	26.339	37.609
Period average										
Moyenne sur période	12.823	15.040	15.110	15.701	16.655	16.766	16.938	21.171	24.429	29.251
Honduras[1] (lempira) Honduras[1] (lempira)										
End of period										
Fin de période	7.260	9.400	10.343	12.869	13.094	13.808	14.504	15.141	15.920	16.923
Period average										
Moyenne sur période	6.472	8.409	9.471	11.705	13.004	13.385	14.213	14.839	15.474	16.433

80

Exchange rates
National currency per US dollar [cont.]
Cours des changes
Valeur du dollar des Etats-Unis en monnaie nationale [suite]

Country or area Pays ou zone	1993	1994	1995	1996	1997	1998	1999	2000	2001	2002
Hungary (forint) Hongrie (forint)										
End of period										
Fin de période	100.700	110.690	139.470	164.930	203.500	219.030	252.520	284.730	279.030	225.160
Period average										
Moyenne sur période	91.933	105.160	125.681	152.647	186.789	214.402	237.146	282.179	286.490	257.887
Iceland (Icelandic króna) Islande (couronne islandaise)										
End of period										
Fin de période	72.730	68.300	65.230	66.890	72.180	69.320	72.550	84.700	102.950	80.580
Period average										
Moyenne sur période	67.603	69.944	64.692	66.500	70.904	70.958	72.335	78.616	97.425	91.662
India (Indian rupee) Inde (roupie indienne)										
End of period										
Fin de période	31.380	31.380	35.180	35.930	39.280	42.480	43.490	46.750	48.180	48.030
Period average										
Moyenne sur période	30.493	31.374	32.427	35.433	36.313	41.259	43.055	44.942	47.186	48.610
Indonesia (Indonesian rupiah) Indonésie (roupie indonésien)										
End of period										
Fin de période	2 110.000	2 200.000	2 308.000	2 383.000	4 650.000	8 025.000	7 085.000	9 595.000	10 400.000	8 940.000
Period average										
Moyenne sur période	2 087.100	2 160.750	2 248.610	2 342.300	2 909.380	10 013.600	7 855.150	8 421.770	10 260.800	9 311.190
Iran (Islamic Rep. of) [1] (Iranian rial) Iran (Rép. islamique d') [1] (rial iranien)										
End of period										
Fin de période	1 758.560	1 735.970	1 747.500	1 749.140	1 754.260	1 750.930	1 752.290	2 262.930	1 750.950	7 951.980
Period average										
Moyenne sur période	1 267.770	1 748.750	1 747.930	1 750.760	1 752.920	1 751.860	1 752.930	1 764.430	1 753.560	6 906.960
Iraq [1] (Iraqi dinar) Iraq [1] (dinar iraquien)										
End of period										
Fin de période	0.311	0.311	0.311	0.311	0.311	0.311	0.311	0.311	0.311	0.311
Ireland [3] (Irish pound) Irlande [3] (livre irlandaise)										
End of period										
Fin de période	0.709	0.646	0.623	0.595	0.699	0.672	...	...	...	...
Period average										
Moyenne sur période	0.677	0.669	0.624	0.625	0.660	0.702	...	...	...	...
Israel (new sheqel) Israël (nouveau sheqel)										
End of period										
Fin de période	2.986	3.018	3.135	3.251	3.536	4.161	4.153	4.041	4.416	4.737
Period average										
Moyenne sur période	2.830	3.011	3.011	3.192	3.449	3.800	4.140	4.077	4.206	4.738
Italy [3] (Italian lira) Italie [3] (lire italienne)										
End of period										
Fin de période	1 703.970	1 629.740	1 584.720	1 530.570	1 759.190	1 653.100	...	...	...	...
Period average										
Moyenne sur période	1 573.670	1 612.440	1 628.930	1 542.950	1 703.100	1 736.210	...	...	...	...
Jamaica (Jamaican dollar) Jamaïque (dollar jamaïcain)										
End of period										
Fin de période	32.475	33.202	39.616	34.865	36.341	37.055	41.291	45.415	47.286	50.762
Period average										
Moyenne sur période	24.949	33.086	35.142	37.120	35.405	36.550	39.044	42.701	45.996	48.416
Japan (yen) Japon (yen)										
End of period										
Fin de période	111.850	99.740	102.830	116.000	129.950	115.600	102.200	114.900	131.800	119.900
Period average										
Moyenne sur période	111.198	102.208	94.060	108.779	120.991	130.905	113.907	107.765	121.529	125.388
Jordan (Jordan dinar) Jordanie (dinar jordanien)										
End of period										
Fin de période	0.704	0.701	0.709	0.709	0.709	0.709	0.709	0.709	0.709	0.709
Period average										
Moyenne sur période	0.693	0.699	0.700	0.709	0.709	0.709	0.709	0.709	0.709	0.709

80

Exchange rates
National currency per US dollar [cont.]

Cours des changes
Valeur du dollar des Etats-Unis en monnaie nationale [suite]

Country or area Pays ou zone	1993	1994	1995	1996	1997	1998	1999	2000	2001	2002
Kazakhstan (tenge) Kazakhstan (tenge)										
End of period										
Fin de période	6.310	54.260	63.950	73.300	75.550	83.800	138.200	144.500	150.200	154.600
Period average										
Moyenne sur période	...	35.538	60.950	67.303	75.438	78.303	119.523	142.133	146.736	153.279
Kenya (Kenya shilling) Kenya (shilling du Kenya)										
End of period										
Fin de période	68.163	44.839	55.939	55.021	62.678	61.906	72.931	78.036	78.600	77.072
Period average										
Moyenne sur période	58.001	56.051	51.430	57.115	58.732	60.367	70.326	76.176	78.563	78.749
Kiribati (Australian dollar) Kiribati (dollar australien)										
End of period										
Fin de période	1.477	1.287	1.342	1.256	1.532	1.629	1.530	1.805	1.959	1.766
Period average										
Moyenne sur période	1.471	1.368	1.349	1.278	1.347	1.592	1.550	1.725	1.933	1.841
Korea, Republic of (Korean won) Corée, République de (won coréen)										
End of period										
Fin de période	808.100	788.700	774.700	844.200	1 695.000	1 204.000	1 138.000	1 264.500	1 313.500	1 186.200
Period average										
Moyenne sur période	802.671	803.446	771.273	804.453	951.289	1 401.440	1 188.820	1 130.960	1 290.990	1 251.090
Kuwait (Kuwaiti dinar) Koweït (dinar koweïtien)										
End of period										
Fin de période	0.298	0.300	0.299	0.300	0.305	0.302	0.304	0.305	0.308	0.300
Period average										
Moyenne sur période	0.302	0.297	0.298	0.299	0.303	0.305	0.304	0.307	0.307	0.304
Kyrgyzstan (Kyrgyz som) Kirghizistan (som kirghize)										
End of period										
Fin de période	8.030	10.650	11.200	16.700	17.375	29.376	45.429	48.304	47.719	46.095
Period average										
Moyenne sur période	...	10.842	10.822	12.810	17.363	20.838	39.008	47.704	48.378	46.937
Lao People's Dem. Rep. (kip) Rép. dém. pop. lao (kip)										
End of period										
Fin de période	718.000	719.000	#923.000	935.000	2 634.500	4 274.000	7 600.000	8 218.000	9 490.000	10 680.000
Period average										
Moyenne sur période	716.250	717.667	#804.691	921.022	1 259.980	3 298.330	7 102.020	7 887.640	8 954.580	10 056.300
Latvia (lats) Lettonie (lats)										
End of period										
Fin de période	0.595	0.548	0.537	0.556	0.590	0.569	0.583	0.613	0.638	0.594
Period average										
Moyenne sur période	0.675	0.560	0.528	0.551	0.581	0.590	0.585	0.607	0.628	0.618
Lebanon (Lebanese pound) Liban (livre libanaise)										
End of period										
Fin de période	1 711.000	1 647.000	1 596.000	1 552.000	1 527.000	1 508.000	1 507.500	1 507.500	1 507.500	1 507.500
Period average										
Moyenne sur période	1 741.360	1 680.070	1 621.410	1 571.440	1 539.450	1 516.130	1 507.840	1 507.500	1 507.500	1 507.500
Lesotho [1] (loti) Lesotho [1] (loti)										
End of period										
Fin de période	3.398	3.544	3.648	4.683	4.868	5.860	6.155	7.569	12.127	8.640
Period average										
Moyenne sur période	3.268	3.551	3.627	4.299	4.608	5.528	6.110	6.940	8.609	10.541
Liberia [1] (Liberian dollar) Libéria [1] (dollar libérien)										
End of period										
Fin de période	1.000	1.000	1.000	1.000	1.000	43.250	39.500	42.750	49.500	65.000
Period average										
Moyenne sur période	1.000	1.000	1.000	1.000	1.000	41.508	41.903	40.953	48.583	61.754
Libyan Arab Jamah. (Libyan dinar) Jamah. arabe libyenne (dinar libyen)										
End of period										
Fin de période	0.325	0.434	0.427	0.441	0.470	0.450	0.462	0.540	0.650	1.210
Period average										
Moyenne sur période	0.304	0.348	0.418	0.437	0.461	0.468	0.464	0.512	0.605	1.271

80

Exchange rates
National currency per US dollar [cont.]

Cours des changes
Valeur du dollar des Etats-Unis en monnaie nationale [suite]

Country or area Pays ou zone	1993	1994	1995	1996	1997	1998	1999	2000	2001	2002
Lithuania (litas) Lituanie (litas)										
End of period										
Fin de période	3.900	4.000	4.000	4.000	4.000	4.000	4.000	4.000	4.000	3.311
Period average										
Moyenne sur période	4.344	3.978	4.000	4.000	4.000	4.000	4.000	4.000	4.000	3.677
Luxembourg [3] (Luxembourg franc) Luxembourg [3] (franc luxembourgeois)										
End of period										
Fin de période	36.110	31.838	29.415	32.005	36.920	34.575	...	...	...	...
Period average										
Moyenne sur période	34.597	33.457	29.480	30.962	35.774	36.299	...	...	...	...
Madagascar (Malagasy franc) Madagascar (franc malgache)										
End of period										
Fin de période	1 962.670	3 871.080	3 422.970	4 328.470	5 284.670	5 402.210	6 543.200	6 550.440	6 631.190	6 434.770
Period average										
Moyenne sur période	1 913.780	3 067.340	4 265.630	4 061.250	5 090.890	5 441.400	6 283.770	6 767.480	6 588.490	6 831.960
Malawi (Malawi kwacha) Malawi (kwacha malawien)										
End of period										
Fin de période	4.494	15.299	15.303	15.323	21.228	43.884	46.438	80.076	67.294	87.139
Period average										
Moyenne sur période	4.403	8.736	15.284	15.309	16.444	31.073	44.088	59.544	72.197	76.687
Malaysia (ringgit) Malaisie (ringgit)										
End of period										
Fin de période	2.702	2.560	2.542	2.529	3.892	3.800	3.800	3.800	3.800	3.800
Period average										
Moyenne sur période	2.574	2.624	2.504	2.516	2.813	3.924	3.800	3.800	3.800	3.800
Maldives (rufiyaa) Maldives (rufiyaa)										
End of period										
Fin de période	11.105	11.770	11.770	11.770	11.770	11.770	11.770	11.770	12.800	12.800
Period average										
Moyenne sur période	10.957	11.586	11.770	11.770	11.770	11.770	11.770	11.770	12.242	12.800
Mali [4] (CFA franc) Mali [4] (franc CFA)										
End of period										
Fin de période	294.775	534.600	490.000	523.700	598.810	562.210	652.953	704.951	744.306	625.495
Period average										
Moyenne sur période	283.163	555.205	499.148	511.552	583.669	589.952	615.699	711.976	733.039	696.988
Malta (Maltese lira) Malte (lire maltaise)										
End of period										
Fin de période	0.395	0.368	0.352	0.360	0.391	0.377	0.412	0.438	0.452	0.399
Period average										
Moyenne sur période	0.382	0.378	0.353	0.361	0.386	0.389	0.399	0.438	0.450	0.434
Mauritania (ouguiya) Mauritanie (ouguiya)										
End of period										
Fin de période	124.160	128.370	137.110	142.450	168.350	205.780	225.000	252.300	264.120	268.710
Period average										
Moyenne sur période	120.806	123.575	129.768	137.222	151.853	188.476	209.514	238.923	255.629	271.739
Mauritius (Mauritian rupee) Maurice (roupie mauricienne)										
End of period										
Fin de période	18.656	17.863	17.664	17.972	22.265	24.784	25.468	27.882	30.394	29.197
Period average										
Moyenne sur période	17.648	17.960	17.386	17.948	21.057	23.993	25.186	26.250	29.129	29.962
Mexico [1] (Mexican peso) Mexique [1] (peso mexicain)										
End of period										
Fin de période	3.106	5.325	7.643	7.851	8.083	9.865	9.514	9.572	9.142	10.313
Period average										
Moyenne sur période	3.116	3.375	6.419	7.600	7.919	9.136	9.560	9.456	9.342	9.656
Micronesia (Fed. States) (US dollar) Micronésie (Etats féd. de) (dollar des Etats-Unis)										
End of period										
Fin de période	1.000	1.000	1.000	1.000	1.000	1.000	1.000	1.000	1.000	1.000

80

Exchange rates
National currency per US dollar [cont.]

Cours des changes
Valeur du dollar des Etats-Unis en monnaie nationale [suite]

Country or area Pays ou zone	1993	1994	1995	1996	1997	1998	1999	2000	2001	2002
Mongolia (togrog) Mongolie (togrog)										
End of period										
Fin de période	#396.510	414.090	473.620	693.510	813.160	902.000	1 072.370	1 097.000	1 102.000	1 125.000
Period average										
Moyenne sur période	303.201	#412.721	448.613	548.403	789.992	840.828	1 021.870	1 076.670	1 097.700	1 110.310
Montserrat (EC dollar) Montserrat (dollar des Caraïbes orientales)										
End of period										
Fin de période	2.700	2.700	2.700	2.700	2.700	2.700	2.700	2.700	2.700	2.700
Morocco (Moroccan dirham) Maroc (dirham marocain)										
End of period										
Fin de période	9.651	8.960	8.469	8.800	9.714	9.255	10.087	10.619	11.560	10.167
Period average										
Moyenne sur période	9.299	9.203	8.540	8.716	9.527	9.604	9.804	10.626	11.303	11.021
Mozambique [1] (metical) Mozambique [1] (metical)										
End of period										
Fin de période	5 324.240	6 627.450	10 851.400	11 336.700	11 502.100	12 322.200	13 252.900	17 140.500	23 320.400	23 854.300
Period average										
Moyenne sur période	3 951.110	6 158.400	9 203.390	11 517.800	11 772.600	12 110.200	13 028.600	15 447.100	20 703.600	23 678.000
Myanmar (kyat) Myanmar (kyat)										
End of period										
Fin de période	6.195	5.828	5.724	5.917	6.306	6.043	6.199	6.530	6.770	6.258
Period average										
Moyenne sur période	6.094	5.945	5.611	5.861	6.184	6.274	6.223	6.426	6.684	6.573
Namibia (Namibia dollar) Namibie (Dollar namibia)										
End of period										
Fin de période	3.398	3.544	3.648	4.683	4.868	5.860	6.155	7.569	12.127	8.640
Period average										
Moyenne sur période	3.268	3.551	3.627	4.299	4.608	5.528	6.110	6.940	8.609	10.541
Nepal (Nepalese rupee) Népal (roupie népalaise)										
End of period										
Fin de période	49.240	49.880	56.000	57.030	63.300	67.675	68.725	74.300	76.475	78.300
Period average										
Moyenne sur période	48.607	49.398	51.890	56.692	58.010	65.976	68.239	71.094	74.949	77.877
Netherlands [3] (Netherlands guilder) Pays-Bas [3] (florin néerlandais)										
End of period										
Fin de période	1.941	1.735	1.604	1.744	2.017	1.889	...	...	...	...
Period average										
Moyenne sur période	1.857	1.820	1.606	1.686	1.951	1.984	...	...	...	...
Netherlands Antilles (Netherlands Antillean guilder) Antilles néerlandaises (florin des Antilles néerlandaises)										
End of period										
Fin de période	1.790	1.790	1.790	1.790	1.790	1.790	1.790	1.790	1.790	1.790
New Zealand (New Zealand dollar) Nouvelle-Zélande (dollar néo-zélandais)										
End of period										
Fin de période	1.790	1.556	1.531	1.416	1.719	1.898	1.921	2.272	2.407	1.899
Period average										
Moyenne sur période	1.851	1.687	1.524	1.455	1.512	1.868	1.890	2.201	2.379	2.162
Nicaragua [1,11] (córdoba) Nicaragua [1,11] (córdoba)										
End of period										
Fin de période	6.350	7.112	7.965	8.924	9.995	11.194	12.318	13.057	13.841	14.671
Period average										
Moyenne sur période	5.620	6.723	7.546	8.436	9.448	10.582	11.809	12.684	13.372	14.251
Niger [4] (CFA franc) Niger [4] (franc CFA)										
End of period										
Fin de période	294.775	534.600	490.000	523.700	598.810	562.210	652.953	704.951	744.306	625.495
Period average										
Moyenne sur période	283.163	555.205	499.148	511.552	583.669	589.952	615.699	711.976	733.039	696.988
Nigeria [1] (naira) Nigéria [1] (naira)										
End of period										
Fin de période	21.882	21.997	21.887	21.886	21.886	21.886	97.950	109.550	112.950	126.400
Period average										
Moyenne sur période	22.065	21.996	21.895	21.884	21.886	21.886	92.338	101.697	111.231	120.578

80

Exchange rates
National currency per US dollar [cont.]

Cours des changes
Valeur du dollar des Etats-Unis en monnaie nationale [suite]

Country or area Pays ou zone	1993	1994	1995	1996	1997	1998	1999	2000	2001	2002
Norway (Norwegian krone) Norvège (couronne norvégienne)										
End of period										
Fin de période	7.518	6.762	6.319	6.443	7.316	7.600	8.040	8.849	9.012	6.966
Period average										
Moyenne sur période	7.094	7.058	6.335	6.450	7.073	7.545	7.799	8.802	8.992	7.984
Oman (rial Omani) Oman (rial omani)										
End of period										
Fin de période	0.385	0.385	0.385	0.385	0.385	0.385	0.385	0.385	0.385	0.385
Pakistan (Pakistan rupee) Pakistan (roupie pakistanaise)										
End of period										
Fin de période	30.120	30.800	34.250	40.120	44.050	45.885	#51.785	58.029	60.864	58.534
Period average										
Moyenne sur période	28.107	30.567	31.643	36.079	41.112	45.047	49.501	53.648	61.927	59.724
Panama (balboa) Panama (balboa)										
End of period										
Fin de période	1.000	1.000	1.000	1.000	1.000	1.000	1.000	1.000	1.000	1.000
Papua New Guinea (kina) Papouasie-Nvl-Guinée (kina)										
End of period										
Fin de période	0.981	1.179	1.335	1.347	1.751	2.096	2.695	3.072	3.762	4.019
Period average										
Moyenne sur période	0.978	1.011	1.280	1.319	1.438	2.074	2.571	2.782	3.389	3.895
Paraguay (guaraní) Paraguay (guaraní)										
End of period										
Fin de période	1 880.000	1 924.700	1 979.660	2 109.670	2 360.000	2 840.190	3 328.860	3 526.900	4 682.000	7 103.590
Period average										
Moyenne sur période	1 744.350	1 904.760	1 963.020	2 056.810	2 177.860	2 726.490	3 119.070	3 486.350	4 105.920	5 716.260
Peru [12] (new sol) Pérou [12] (nouveau sol)										
End of period										
Fin de période	2.160	2.180	2.310	2.600	2.730	3.160	3.510	3.527	3.444	3.514
Period average										
Moyenne sur période	1.988	2.195	2.253	2.453	2.664	2.930	3.383	3.490	3.507	3.517
Philippines (Philippine peso) Philippines (peso philippin)										
End of period										
Fin de période	27.699	24.418	26.214	26.288	39.975	39.059	40.313	49.998	51.404	53.096
Period average										
Moyenne sur période	27.120	26.417	25.715	26.216	29.471	40.893	39.089	44.192	50.993	51.604
Poland (new zloty) Pologne (nouveau zloty)										
End of period										
Fin de période	2.134	2.437	2.468	2.876	3.518	3.504	4.148	4.143	3.986	3.839
Period average										
Moyenne sur période	1.812	2.272	2.425	2.696	3.279	3.475	3.967	4.346	4.094	4.080
Portugal [3] (Portuguese escudo) Portugal [3] (escudo portugais)										
End of period										
Fin de période	176.812	159.093	149.413	156.385	183.326	171.829	...	...	...	...
Period average										
Moyenne sur période	160.800	165.993	151.106	154.244	175.312	180.104	...	...	...	...
Qatar (Qatar riyal) Qatar (riyal qatarien)										
End of period										
Fin de période	3.640	3.640	3.640	3.640	3.640	3.640	3.640	3.640	3.640	3.640
Republic of Moldova (Moldovan leu) République de Moldova (leu moldove)										
End of period										
Fin de période	#3.640	4.270	4.499	4.674	4.661	8.323	11.590	12.383	13.091	13.822
Period average										
Moyenne sur période	...	...	4.496	4.605	4.624	5.371	10.516	12.434	12.865	13.571
Romania [1] (Romanian leu) Roumanie [1] (leu roumain)										
End of period										
Fin de période	1 276.000	1 767.000	2 578.000	4 035.000	8 023.000	10 951.000	18 255.000	25 926.000	31 597.000	33 500.000
Period average										
Moyenne sur période	760.051	1 655.090	2 033.280	3 084.220	7 167.940	8 875.580	15 332.800	21 708.700	29 060.800	33 055.400

80

Exchange rates
National currency per US dollar [cont.]

Cours des changes
Valeur du dollar des Etats-Unis en monnaie nationale [suite]

Country or area Pays ou zone	1993	1994	1995	1996	1997	1998	1999	2000	2001	2002
Russian Federation [13] (ruble) Fédération de Russie [13] (ruble)										
End of period										
Fin de période	1.247	3.550	4.640	5.560	5.960	20.650	27.000	28.160	30.140	31.784
Period average										
Moyenne sur période	0.992	2.191	4.559	5.121	5.785	9.705	24.620	28.129	29.169	31.349
Rwanda (Rwanda franc) Rwanda (franc rwandais)										
End of period										
Fin de période	146.619	137.953	299.811	304.161	304.843	320.128	349.170	430.316	455.820	511.854
Period average										
Moyenne sur période	144.237	140.704	262.182	306.098	301.321	313.717	337.831	393.435	442.801	476.327
Saint Kitts and Nevis (EC dollar) Saint-Kitts-et-Nevis (dollar des Caraïbes orientales)										
End of period										
Fin de période	2.700	2.700	2.700	2.700	2.700	2.700	2.700	2.700	2.700	2.700
Saint Lucia (EC dollar) Sainte-Lucie (dollar des Caraïbes orientales)										
End of period										
Fin de période	2.700	2.700	2.700	2.700	2.700	2.700	2.700	2.700	2.700	2.700
St. Vincent-Grenadines (EC dollar) St. Vincent-Grenadines (dollar des Caraïbes orientales)										
End of period										
Fin de période	2.700	2.700	2.700	2.700	2.700	2.700	2.700	2.700	2.700	2.700
Samoa (tala) Samoa (tala)										
End of period										
Fin de période	2.608	2.452	2.527	2.434	2.766	3.010	3.018	3.341	3.551	3.217
Period average										
Moyenne sur période	2.569	2.535	2.473	2.462	2.559	2.948	3.013	3.286	3.478	3.376
San Marino [3] (Italian lira) Saint-Marin [3] (lire italienne)										
End of period										
Fin de période	1 703.970	1 629.740	1 584.720	1 530.570	1 759.190	1 653.100	...	...	...	...
Period average										
Moyenne sur période	1 573.670	1 612.440	1 628.930	1 542.950	1 703.100	1 736.210	...	...	...	...
Sao Tome and Principe (dobra) Sao Tomé-et-Principe (dobra)										
End of period										
Fin de période	516.700	1 185.310	1 756.870	2 833.210	6 969.730	6 885.000	7 300.000	8 610.650	9 019.710	9 191.840
Period average										
Moyenne sur période	429.854	732.628	1 420.340	2 203.160	4 552.510	6 883.240	7 118.960	7 978.170	8 842.110	9 088.320
Saudi Arabia (Saudi Arabian riyal) Arabie saoudite (riyal saoudien)										
End of period										
Fin de période	3.745	3.745	3.745	3.745	3.745	3.745	3.745	3.745	3.745	3.745
Senegal [4] (CFA franc) Sénégal [4] (franc CFA)										
End of period										
Fin de période	294.775	534.600	490.000	523.700	598.810	562.210	652.953	704.951	744.306	625.495
Period average										
Moyenne sur période	283.163	555.205	499.148	511.552	583.669	589.952	615.699	711.976	733.039	696.988
Seychelles (Seychelles rupee) Seychelles (roupie seychelloises)										
End of period										
Fin de période	5.258	4.970	4.864	4.995	5.125	5.452	5.368	6.269	5.752	5.055
Period average										
Moyenne sur période	5.182	5.056	4.762	4.970	5.026	5.262	5.343	5.714	5.858	5.480
Sierra Leone (leone) Sierra Leone (leone)										
End of period										
Fin de période	577.634	613.008	943.396	909.091	1 333.330	1 590.760	2 276.050	1 666.670	2 161.270	2 191.730
Period average										
Moyenne sur période	567.459	586.740	755.216	920.732	981.482	1 563.620	1 804.190	2 092.120	1 986.150	2 099.030
Singapore (Singapore dollar) Singapour (dollar singapourien)										
End of period										
Fin de période	1.608	1.461	1.414	1.400	1.676	1.661	1.666	1.732	1.851	1.737
Period average										
Moyenne sur période	1.616	1.527	1.417	1.410	1.485	1.674	1.695	1.724	1.792	1.791

80

Exchange rates
National currency per US dollar [cont.]
Cours des changes
Valeur du dollar des Etats-Unis en monnaie nationale [suite]

Country or area Pays ou zone	1993	1994	1995	1996	1997	1998	1999	2000	2001	2002
Slovakia (Slovak koruna) Slovaquie (couronne slovaque)										
End of period										
Fin de période	33.202	31.277	29.569	31.895	34.782	36.913	42.266	47.389	48.467	40.036
Period average [1]										
Moyenne sur période [1]	30.770	32.045	29.713	30.654	33.616	35.233	41.363	46.035	48.355	45.327
Slovenia (tolar) Slovénie (tolar)										
End of period										
Fin de période	131.842	126.458	125.990	141.480	169.180	161.200	196.770	227.377	250.946	221.071
Period average										
Moyenne sur période	113.242	128.809	118.518	135.364	159.688	166.134	181.769	222.656	242.749	240.248
Solomon Islands (Solomon Islands dollar) Iles Salomon (dollar des Iles Salomon)										
End of period										
Fin de période	3.248	3.329	3.476	3.622	4.748	4.859	5.076	5.099	5.565	7.457
Period average										
Moyenne sur période	3.188	3.291	3.406	3.566	3.717	4.816	4.838	5.089	5.278	6.749
South Africa [1] (rand) Afrique du Sud [1] (rand)										
End of period										
Fin de période	3.398	3.544	3.648	4.683	4.868	5.860	6.155	7.569	12.127	8.640
Period average										
Moyenne sur période	3.268	3.551	3.627	4.299	4.608	5.528	6.110	6.940	8.609	10.541
Spain [3] (peseta) Espagne [3] (peseta)										
End of period										
Fin de période	142.214	131.739	121.409	131.275	151.702	142.607	...	...	...	...
Period average										
Moyenne sur période	127.260	133.958	124.689	126.662	146.414	149.395	...	...	...	...
Sri Lanka (Sri Lanka rupee) Sri Lanka (roupie sri-lankaise)										
End of period										
Fin de période	49.562	49.980	54.048	56.705	61.285	68.297	72.170	82.580	93.159	96.725
Period average										
Moyenne sur période	48.322	49.415	51.252	55.271	58.995	64.450	70.635	77.005	89.383	95.662
Sudan [1] (Sudanese pound) Soudan [1] (livre soudanaise)										
End of period										
Fin de période	21.739	40.000	52.632	144.928	172.206	237.801	257.700	257.350	261.430	261.680
Period average										
Moyenne sur période	15.931	28.961	58.087	125.079	157.574	200.802	252.550	257.122	258.702	263.306
Suriname (Suriname guilder) Suriname (florin surinamais)										
End of period										
Fin de période	1.785	#409.500	407.000	401.000	401.000	401.000	987.500	2 178.500	2 178.500	2 515.000
Period average										
Moyenne sur période	1.785	#134.117	442.228	401.258	401.000	401.000	859.437	1 322.470	2 178.500	2 346.750
Swaziland (lilangeni) Swaziland (lilangeni)										
End of period										
Fin de période	3.398	3.544	3.648	4.683	4.868	5.860	6.155	7.569	12.127	8.640
Period average										
Moyenne sur période	3.268	3.551	3.627	4.299	4.608	5.528	6.110	6.940	8.609	10.541
Sweden (Swedish krona) Suède (couronne suédoise)										
End of period										
Fin de période	8.304	7.462	6.658	6.871	7.877	8.061	8.525	9.535	10.668	8.825
Period average										
Moyenne sur période	7.783	7.716	7.133	6.706	7.635	7.950	8.262	9.162	10.329	9.737
Switzerland (Swiss franc) Suisse (franc suisse)										
End of period										
Fin de période	1.480	1.312	1.151	1.346	1.455	1.377	1.600	1.637	1.677	1.387
Period average										
Moyenne sur période	1.478	1.368	1.183	1.236	1.451	1.450	1.502	1.689	1.688	1.559
Syrian Arab Republic [1] (Syrian pound) Rép. arabe syrienne [1] (livre syrienne)										
End of period										
Fin de période	11.225	11.225	11.225	11.225	11.225	11.225	11.225	11.225	11.225	11.225

80

Exchange rates
National currency per US dollar [cont.]

Cours des changes
Valeur du dollar des Etats-Unis en monnaie nationale [suite]

Country or area Pays ou zone	1993	1994	1995	1996	1997	1998	1999	2000	2001	2002
Tajikistan (somoni) Tadjikistan (somoni)										
End of period										
Fin de période	0.014	0.039	0.294	0.328	0.747	0.978	1.436	2.200	2.550	3.000
Period average										
Moyenne sur période	0.010	0.025	0.123	0.296	0.562	0.777	1.238	2.076	2.372	2.764
Thailand (baht) Thaïlande (baht)										
End of period										
Fin de période	25.540	25.090	25.190	25.610	#47.247	36.691	37.470	43.268	44.222	43.152
Period average										
Moyenne sur période	25.320	25.150	24.915	25.343	31.364	41.359	37.814	40.112	44.432	42.960
TFYR of Macedonia (TFYR Macedonian denar) L'ex-R.y. Macédoine (denar de l'ex-R.Y. Macédoine)										
End of period										
Fin de période	44.456	40.596	37.980	41.411	55.421	51.836	60.339	66.328	69.172	58.598
Period average										
Moyenne sur période	...	43.263	37.882	39.981	50.004	54.462	56.902	65.904	68.037	64.350
Togo[4] (CFA franc) Togo[4] (franc CFA)										
End of period										
Fin de période	294.775	534.600	490.000	523.700	598.810	562.210	652.953	704.951	744.306	625.495
Period average										
Moyenne sur période	283.163	555.205	499.148	511.552	583.669	589.952	615.699	711.976	733.039	696.988
Tonga (pa'anga) Tonga (pa'anga)										
End of period										
Fin de période	1.379	1.259	1.270	1.213	1.362	1.616	1.608	1.977	2.207	2.229
Period average										
Moyenne sur période	1.384	1.320	1.271	1.232	1.264	1.492	1.599	1.759	2.124	2.195
Trinidad and Tobago (Trinidad and Tobago dollar) Trinité-et-Tobago (dollar de la Trinité-et-Tobago)										
End of period										
Fin de période	5.814	5.933	5.997	6.195	6.300	6.597	6.300	6.300	6.290	6.300
Period average										
Moyenne sur période	5.351	5.925	5.948	6.005	6.252	6.298	6.299	6.300	6.233	6.249
Tunisia (Tunisian dinar) Tunisie (dinar tunisien)										
End of period										
Fin de période	1.047	0.991	0.951	0.999	1.148	1.101	1.253	1.385	1.468	1.334
Period average										
Moyenne sur période	1.004	1.012	0.946	0.973	1.106	1.139	1.186	1.371	1.439	1.422
Turkey (Turkish lira) Turquie (livre turque)										
End of period				107	205	314	541	673	1 450	1 643
Fin de période	14 472.500	38 726.000	59 650.000	775.000	605.000	464.000	400.000	385.000	130.000	700.000
Period average					151	260	418	625	1 225	1 507
Moyenne sur période	10 984.600	29 608.700	45 845.100	81 404.900	865.000	724.000	783.000	218.000	590.000	230.000
Turkmenistan (Turkmen manat) Turkménistan (manat turkmene)										
End of period										
Fin de période	1.990	75.000	200.000	4 070.000	4 165.000	5 200.000	5 200.000	5 200.000	5 200.000	...
Period average										
Moyenne sur période	...	19.198	110.917	3 257.670	4 143.420	4 890.170	5 200.000	5 200.000	5 200.000	...
Uganda[1] (Uganda shilling) Ouganda[1] (shilling ougandais)										
End of period										
Fin de période	1 130.150	926.770	1 009.450	1 029.590	1 140.110	1 362.690	1 506.040	1 766.680	1 727.400	1 852.570
Period average										
Moyenne sur période	1 195.020	979.445	968.917	1 046.080	1 083.010	1 240.310	1 454.830	1 644.480	1 755.660	1 797.550
Ukraine (hryvnia) Ukraine (hryvnia)										
End of period										
Fin de période	0.126	1.042	1.794	#1.889	1.899	3.427	5.216	5.435	5.299	5.332
Period average										
Moyenne sur période	0.045	0.328	1.473	1.830	1.862	2.450	4.130	5.440	5.372	5.327
United Arab Emirates (UAE dirham) Emirats arabes unis (dirham des EAU)										
End of period										
Fin de période	3.671	3.671	3.671	3.671	3.671	3.673	3.673	3.673	3.673	3.673

80

Exchange rates
National currency per US dollar [cont.]

Cours des changes
Valeur du dollar des Etats-Unis en monnaie nationale [suite]

Country or area Pays ou zone	1993	1994	1995	1996	1997	1998	1999	2000	2001	2002
United Kingdom (pound sterling) Royaume-Uni (livre sterling)										
End of period										
Fin de période	0.675	0.640	0.645	0.589	0.605	0.601	0.619	0.670	0.690	0.620
Period average										
Moyenne sur période	0.667	0.653	0.634	0.641	0.611	0.604	0.618	0.661	0.695	0.667
United Rep. of Tanzania (Tanzania shilling) Rép.-Unie de Tanzanie (shilling tanzanien)										
End of period										
Fin de période	479.871	523.453	550.360	595.640	624.570	681.000	797.330	803.260	916.300	976.300
Period average										
Moyenne sur période	405.274	509.631	574.762	579.977	612.122	664.671	744.759	800.409	876.412	966.583
Uruguay (Uruguayan peso) Uruguay (peso uruguayen)										
End of period										
Fin de période	#4.416	5.601	7.111	8.713	10.040	10.817	11.615	12.515	14.768	27.200
Period average										
Moyenne sur période	#3.941	5.044	6.349	7.972	9.442	10.472	11.339	12.100	13.319	21.257
Uzbekistan (Uzbek som) Ouzbékistan (som ouzbek)										
End of period										
Fin de période	...	...	...	...	...	...	140.000	...	...	...
Period average										
Moyenne sur période	...	...	29.775	40.067	62.917	94.492	124.625	236.608	...	...
Vanuatu (vatu) Vanuatu (vatu)										
End of period										
Fin de période	120.800	112.080	113.740	110.770	124.310	129.780	128.890	142.810	146.740	133.170
Period average										
Moyenne sur période	121.581	116.405	112.112	111.719	115.873	127.517	129.075	137.643	145.312	139.198
Venezuela (bolívar) Venezuela (bolívar)										
End of period										
Fin de période	105.640	#170.000	290.000	476.500	504.250	564.500	648.250	699.750	763.000	1 401.250
Period average										
Moyenne sur période	90.826	148.503	#176.842	417.332	488.635	547.556	605.717	679.960	723.666	1 160.950
Viet Nam (dong) Viet Nam (dong)										
End of period										
Fin de période	10 842.500	11 051.000	11 015.000	11 149.000	12 292.000	13 890.000	14 028.000	14 514.000	15 084.000	15 403.000
Period average										
Moyenne sur période	10 641.000	10 965.700	11 038.200	11 032.600	11 683.300	13 268.000	13 943.200	14 167.700	14 725.200	15 279.500
Yemen (Yemeni rial) Yémen (rial yéménite)										
End of period										
Fin de période	12.010	12.010	#50.040	#126.910	130.460	141.650	159.100	165.590	173.270	179.010
Period average										
Moyenne sur période	12.010	12.010	#40.839	#94.160	129.281	135.882	155.718	161.718	168.672	175.625
Zambia (Zambia kwacha) Zambie (kwacha zambie)										
End of period										
Fin de période	500.000	680.272	956.130	1 282.690	1 414.840	2 298.920	2 632.190	4 157.830	3 830.400	4 334.400
Period average										
Moyenne sur période	452.763	669.371	864.119	1 207.900	1 314.500	1 862.070	2 388.020	3 110.840	3 610.930	4 398.590
Zimbabwe (Zimbabwe dollar) Zimbabwe (dollar zimbabwéen)										
End of period										
Fin de période	6.935	8.387	9.311	10.839	18.608	37.369	38.139	55.066	55.036	55.036
Period average										
Moyenne sur période	6.483	8.152	8.665	10.002	12.111	23.679	38.301	44.418	55.052	55.036

Source:
International Monetary Fund (IMF), Washington, D.C., "International Financial Statistics," January 2004 and the IMF database.

Source:
Fonds monétaire international (FMI), Washington, D.C.,"Statistiques Financières Internationales," janvier 2004 et la base de données du FMI.

1   Principal rate.
2   Pesos per million US dollars through 1983, per thousand US dollars through 1988 and per US dollar thereafter.

1   Taux principal.
2   Pesos par million de dollars des États-Unis jusqu'en 1983, par millier de dollars des États-Unis jusqu'en 1988 et par dollar des États-Unis après cette date.

80

Exchange rates
National currency per US dollar [cont.]

Cours des changes
Valeur du dollar des Etats-Unis en monnaie nationale [suite]

3   Beginning 1999, see Euro Area. Greece, beginning 2001.

4   Prior to January 1999, the official rate was pegged to the French franc. On 12 January 1994, the CFA franc was devalued to CFAF 100 per French franc from CFAF 50 at which it had been fixed since 1948. From 1 January 1 1999, the CFAF is pegged to the euro at a rate of CFA francs 655.957 per euro.

5   Bolivianos per million US dollars through 1983, per thousand US dollars for 1984, and per US dollar thereafter.

6   Reals per trillion US dollars through 1983, per billion US dollars 1984-1988, per million US dollars 1989-1992, and per US dollar thereafter.

7   The official rate is pegged to the French franc. Beginning January 12, 1994, the CFA franc was devalued to CFAF 75 per French franc from CFAF 50 at which it had been fixed since 1948.

8   New Zaires per million US dollars through 1990, per thousand US dollars for 1991-1995, and per US dollar thereafter.

9   "Euro Area" is an official descriptor for the European Economic and Monetary Union (EMU). The participating member states of the EMU are Austria, Belgium, Finland, France, Germany, Greece (beginning 2001), Ireland, Italy, Luxembourg, Netherlands, Portugal, and Spain.

10   Prior to January 1999, the official rate was pegged to the French franc at CFAF 100 per French franc. The CFA franc was adopted as national currency as of May 2, 1997. The Guinean peso and the CFA franc were set at PG65 per CFA franc. From January 1, 1999, the CFAF is pegged to the euro at a rate of CFA franc 655.957 per euro.

11   Gold córdoba per billion US dollars through 1987, per million US dollars for 1988, per thousand US dollars for 1989-1990 and per US dollar thereafter.

12   New soles per billion US dollars through 1987, per million US dollars for 1988-1989, and per US dollar thereafter.

13   The post-1 January 1998 ruble is equal to 1,000 of the pre-January 1998 rubles.

3   A partir de 1999, voir la Zone euro. Grèce, à partir de 2001.

4   Avant janvier 1999, le taux officiel était établi par référence au franc français. Le 12 janvier 1994, le franc CFA a été dévalué; son taux par rapport au franc français, auquel il est rattaché depuis 1948, est passé de 50 à 100 francs CFA pour 1 franc français. A compter du 1er janvier 1999, le taux officiel est établi par référence à l'euro à un taux de 655 957 francs CFA pour un euro.

5   Bolivianos par million de dollars des États-Unis jusqu'en 1983, par millier de dollars des États-Unis en 1984, et par dollar des États-Unis après cette date.

6   Reals par trillion de dollars des États-Unis jusqu'en 1983, par milliard de dollars des États-Unis 1984-1988, par million de dollars des États-Unis 1989-1992, et par dollar des État-Unis après cette date.

7   Le taux de change officiel est raccroché au taux de change du franc français. Le 12 janvier 1994, le CFA a été dévalué de 50 par franc français, valeur qu'il avait conservée depuis 1948, à 75 par franc français.

8   Nouveaux zaïres par million de dollars des États-Unis jusqu'en 1990, par millier de dollars des États-Unis en 1991 et 1995, et par dollar des États-Unis après cette date.

9   L'expression "zone euro" est un intitulé officiel pour l'Union économique et monétaire (UEM) européenne. L'UEM est composée des pays membres suivants : Allemagne, Autriche, Belgique, Espagne, Finlande, France, Grèce (à partir de 2001), Irlande, Italie, Luxembourg, Pays-Bas et Portugal.

10   Le taux de change officiel est raccroché au taux de change du franc français à CFA 100 pour franc français. Le franc CFA été adopté comme monnaie nationale au 2 mai 1997. Le peso guinéen et le franc CFA été établi à 65 pesos guinéen pour 1 franc CFA. A compter du 1er janvier 1999, le taux officiel est établi par référence à l'euro à un taux de 655 957 francs CFA pour un euro.

11   Cordobas or par milliard de dollars des États-Unis jusqu'en 1987, par million de dollars en 1988, par millier de dollars des États-Unis en 1989-1990 et par dollar des États Unis après cette date.

12   Nouveaux soles par milliard de dollars des États-Unis jusqu'en 1987, par million de dollars des États-Unis en 1988-1989 et par dollar des États-Unis après cette date.

13   Le rouble ayant cours après le 1er janvier 1998 vaut 1 000 roubles de la période antérieure à cette date.

81

Total external and public/publicly guaranteed long-term debt of developing countries
Millions of US dollars

Total de la dette extérieure et dette publique extérieure à long terme garantie par l'Etat des pays en développement
Millions de dollars des E.-U.

A. Total external debt [+] • Total de la dette extérieure [+]

Country or area	1995	1996	1997	1998	1999	2000	2001	Pays ou zone
Total long-term debt (LDOD)	1 627 611	1 667 756	1 722 621	1 946 810	1 999 331	1 968 315	1 907 814	Total de la dette à long) terme (LDOD
Public and publicly guaranteed	1 408 121	1 392 473	1 373 866	1 452 496	1 469 585	1 433 739	1 394 373	Dette publique ou garantie par l'Etat
Official creditors	858 200	825 194	783 159	829 190	849 454	821 819	791 387	Créanciers publics
Mulitilateral	287 220	283 660	282 829	317 421	333 875	332 620	338 741	Multilatéraux
IBRD	111 706	105 320	101 531	108 462	111 335	112 149	112 532	BIRD
IDA	71 549	75 140	77 398	84 088	86 604	86 844	89 222	IDA
Bilateral	570 980	541 534	500 330	511 768	515 579	489 199	452 647	Bilatéraux
Private creditors	549 921	567 280	590 707	623 306	620 140	611 920	602 986	Créanciers privés
Bonds	246 312	279 301	288 760	323 090	340 990	372 200	373 399	Obligations
Commercial banks	167 755	164 633	200 294	211 473	192 284	167 656	164 067	Banques commerciales
Other private	135 855	123 346	101 654	88 743	86 865	72 065	65 519	Autres institutions privées
Private non-guaranteed	219 490	275 283	348 755	494 314	529 745	534 576	513 441	Dette privée non garantie
Undisbursed debt	262 595	252 716	249 691	276 090	300 328	229 058	195 694	Dette (montants non versés)
Official creditors	207 156	194 478	188 259	212 722	241 224	177 379	159 669	Créanciers publics
Private creditors	55 439	58 239	61 432	63 368	59 104	51 678	36 026	Créanciers privés
Commitments	149 746	167 959	180 898	186 937	147 932	151 834	138 266	Engagements
Official creditors	80 662	61 957	68 535	84 049	66 488	48 330	60 621	Créanciers publics
Private creditors	69 084	106 002	112 362	102 888	81 444	103 504	77 645	Créanciers privés
Disbursements	198 403	245 888	279 001	287 229	261 974	257 186	248 640	Versements
Public and publicly guaranteed	139 356	155 550	164 663	165 485	145 778	147 832	126 753	Dette publique ou garantie par l'Etat
Official creditors	66 200	55 780	60 815	63 530	60 234	53 657	52 322	Créanciers publics
Multilateral	32 207	33 479	35 870	41 727	36 905	34 697	35 122	Mutilatéraux
IBRD	13 094	13 148	14 499	14 376	14 082	13 430	12 305	BIRD
IDA	5 476	6 315	5 937	5 556	5 397	5 221	6 095	IDA
Bilateral	33 994	22 300	24 945	21 803	23 329	18 960	17 200	Bilatéraux
Private creditors	73 156	99 771	103 848	101 955	85 544	94 175	74 431	Créanciers privés
Bonds	25 448	52 236	53 262	52 371	50 723	55 882	47 325	Obligations
Commercial banks	26 382	28 023	31 981	35 709	21 739	29 993	20 201	Banques commerciales
Other private	21 325	19 512	18 604	13 875	13 082	8 300	6 905	Autres institutions privés
Private non-guaranteed	59 047	90 337	114 338	121 744	116 196	109 355	120 852	Dette privé non garantie
Principal repayments	122 324	161 221	185 289	179 798	224 443	238 197	247 730	Remboursements du principal
Public and publicly guaranteed	94 238	118 262	126 375	107 946	113 536	126 068	126 860	Dette publique ou garantie par l'ETat
Official creditors	44 248	53 021	51 152	43 542	44 556	49 169	43 799	Créanciers publics
Multilateral	20 795	20 487	19 340	18 392	18 968	23 154	18 861	Multilatéraux
IBRD	11 674	11 612	10 583	10 446	9 836	9 829	9 807	BIRD
IDA	542	589	646	732	869	949	1 080	IDA
Bilateral	23 453	32 534	31 812	25 150	25 588	26 015	24 938	Bilatéraux
Private creditors	49 990	65 241	75 223	64 404	68 980	76 899	83 061	Créanciers privés
Bonds	12 094	20 776	33 945	22 848	23 201	35 275	37 024	Obligations
Commercial banks	18 623	26 885	25 200	24 042	30 907	27 852	32 165	Banques commerciales
Other private	19 273	17 579	16 077	17 515	14 873	13 772	13 872	Autres institutions privées
Private non-guaranteed	28 086	42 958	58 914	71 852	110 907	112 129	120 870	Dette privée non garantie

81

Total external and public/publicly guaranteed long-term debt of developing countries
Millions of US dollars *[cont.]*

Total de la dette extérieure et dette publique extérieure à long terme garantie par l'Etat des pays en développement
Millions de dollars des E.-U. *[suite]*

A. Total external debt [+] • Total de la dette extérieure [+]

Country or area	1995	1996	1997	1998	1999	2000	2001	Pays ou zone
Net flows	**76 079**	**84 667**	**93 712**	**107 431**	**37 531**	**18 989**	**-124**	**Apports nets**
Public and publicly guaranteed	**45 118**	**37 288**	**38 289**	**57 538**	**32 242**	**21 764**	**-107**	**Dette publique ou garantie par l'Etat**
Official creditors	21 952	2 758	9 664	19 988	15 678	4 488	8 524	Créanciers publics
Multilateral	11 412	12 992	16 530	23 335	17 937	11 543	16 261	Multilatéraux
IBRD	1 420	1 535	3 916	3 930	4 246	3 601	2 499	BIRD
IDA	4 934	5 726	5 291	4 824	4 528	4 272	5 015	IDA
Bilateral	10 541	-10 234	-6 867	-3 347	-2 259	-7 055	-7 737	Bilatéraux
Private creditors	23 166	34 530	28 625	37 551	16 563	17 276	-8 630	Créanciers privés
Bonds	13 354	31 460	19 317	29 523	27 522	20 607	10 301	Obligations
Commercial banks	7 759	1 138	6 781	11 667	-9 169	2 141	-11 964	Banques commerciales
Other private	2 052	1 932	2 527	-3 640	-1 790	-5 472	-6 967	Autres institutions privées
Private non-guaranteed	**30 961**	**47 379**	**55 424**	**49 892**	**5 289**	**-2 775**	**-18**	**Dette privée non garantie**
Interest payments (LINT)	**73 865**	**77 738**	**83 102**	**92 413**	**97 105**	**101 853**	**102 504**	**Paiements d'intérêts (LINT)**
Public and publicly guaranteed	**62 390**	**63 496**	**63 540**	**63 779**	**65 242**	**68 991**	**72 370**	**Dette publique ou granatie par l'Etat**
Official creditors	29 886	30 440	28 010	27 265	27 994	28 409	29 328	Créanciers publics
Multilateral	13 758	13 592	12 656	12 677	14 895	15 569	15 280	Multilatéraux
IBRD	7 969	7 667	6 721	6 612	7 268	7 683	7 469	BIRD
IDA	504	512	531	550	588	578	576	IDA
Bilateral	16 128	16 848	15 355	14 588	13 099	12 841	14 049	Bilatéraux
Private creditors	32 504	33 056	35 530	36 514	37 248	40 582	43 041	Créanciers privés
Bonds	16 431	16 147	18 462	19 684	23 184	26 703	29 245	Obligations
Commercial banks	8 993	10 404	11 206	11 395	9 372	9 987	10 155	Banques commerciales
Other private	7 080	6 504	5 862	5 436	4 691	3 891	3 641	Autres institutions privées
Private non-guaranteed	**11 475**	**14 242**	**19 562**	**28 634**	**31 986**	**32 862**	**30 134**	**Dette privée non garantie**
Net transfers	**2 214**	**6 929**	**10 610**	**15 017**	**-59 697**	**-82 864**	**-102 628**	**Transferts nets**
Public and publicly guaranteed	**-17 272**	**-26 208**	**-25 252**	**-6 241**	**-33 000**	**-47 228**	**-72 476**	**Dette publique ou garantie par l'Etat**
Official creditors	-7 934	-27 682	-18 346	-7 277	-12 316	-23 922	-20 805	Créanciers publics
Multilateral	-2 346	-600	3 875	10 658	3 042	-4 026	982	Multilatéraux
IBRD	-6 549	-6 131	-2 805	-2 683	-3 021	-4 081	-4 970	BIRD
IDA	4 430	5 214	4 759	4 274	3 940	3 694	4 439	IDA
Bilateral	-5 588	-27 082	-22 221	-17 935	-15 357	-19 896	-21 786	Bilatéraux
Private creditors	-9 338	1 474	-6 906	1 036	-20 685	-23 306	-51 672	Créanciers privés
Bonds	-3 077	15 312	855	9 840	4 338	-6 097	-18 944	Obligations
Commercial banks	-1 234	-9 266	-4 425	272	-18 541	-7 846	-22 119	Banques commerciales
Other private	-5 028	-4 572	-3 335	-9 076	-6 482	-9 363	-10 608	Autres institutions privées
Private non-guaranteed	**19 486**	**33 137**	**35 862**	**21 258**	**-26 697**	**-35 636**	**-30 152**	**Dette privée non garantie**
Total debt service (LTDS)	**196 190**	**238 959**	**268 391**	**272 211**	**321 548**	**340 050**	**350 233**	**Total du service de la dette) (LTDS**
Public and publicly guaranteed	**156 628**	**181 759**	**189 915**	**171 725**	**178 778**	**195 059**	**199 229**	**Dette publique ou garantie par l'Etat**
Official creditors	74 134	83 462	79 162	70 807	72 550	77 578	73 127	Créanciers publics
Multilateral	34 553	34 080	31 996	31 068	33 863	38 723	34 141	Multilatéraux
IBRD	19 643	19 279	17 304	17 059	17 103	17 511	17 276	BIRD
IDA	1 046	1 101	1 177	1 282	1 457	1 526	1 656	IDA
Bilateral	39 581	49 382	47 166	39 738	38 687	38 856	38 986	Bilatéraux
Private creditors	82 494	98 297	110 753	100 919	106 228	117 481	126 102	Créanciers publics
Bonds	28 525	36 924	52 408	42 532	46 385	61 979	66 269	Obligations
Commercial banks	27 616	37 289	36 406	35 437	40 279	37 839	42 320	Banques commerciales
Other private	26 353	24 084	21 939	22 950	19 564	17 663	17 513	Autres institutions privées
Private non-guaranteed	**39 561**	**57 200**	**78 476**	**100 486**	**142 893**	**144 991**	**151 004**	**Dette privée non garantie**

81
Total external and public/publicly guaranteed long-term debt of developing countries
Million US dollars *[cont.]*
Total de la dette extérieure et dette publique extérieure à long terme garantie par l'Etat des pays en développement
Millions de dollars E.-U. *[suite]*

B. Public and publicly guaranteed long-term debt • Dette publique extérieure à long terme garantie par l'Etat

Country or area Pays ou zone	1992	1993	1994	1995	1996	1997	1998	1999	2000	2001
Albania Albanie	126.9	179.0	247.6	329.6	405.1	412.1	506.1	585.5	923.3	969.6
Algeria Algérie	25 753.6	25 094.1	28 437.5	31 303.0	31 285.5	28 712.0	28 481.6	25 895.6	23 333.3	20 785.7
Angola Angola	8 139.6	8 704.1	9 123.8	9 544.2	9 379.0	8 683.0	9 067.4	8 647.3	7 985.5	7 443.1
Argentina Argentine	47 611.0	46 176.4	50 634.0	55 250.0	62 519.3	67 143.9	77 285.4	84 081.5	86 598.9	85 336.8
Armenia Arménie	...	133.9	188.6	298.3	402.7	484.4	568.6	651.4	728.1	766.2
Azerbaijan Azerbaïdjan	...	35.5	103.2	206.1	247.9	235.9	313.1	493.3	682.9	726.0
Bangladesh Bangladesh	12 595.4	13 420.7	14 758.0	15 103.0	14 657.9	13 874.0	15 094.2	15 996.4	15 168.9	14 772.8
Barbados Barbade	400.3	348.3	373.4	371.5	383.0	366.9	387.8	443.9	548.2	700.7
Belarus Bélarus	...	865.1	1 123.8	1 301.1	728.9	681.4	796.4	708.2	688.9	640.9
Belize Belize	170.0	175.6	182.4	219.4	250.4	268.1	282.9	341.0	556.8	657.6
Benin Bénin	1 324.1	1 371.4	1 487.3	1 483.0	1 446.4	1 395.8	1 471.4	1 472.3	1 444.8	1 503.2
Bhutan Bhoutan	88.3	94.9	103.8	105.2	112.9	117.6	171.0	181.8	202.2	265.2
Bolivia Bolivie	3 669.4	3 694.8	4 122.4	4 461.5	4 259.4	4 133.0	4 295.8	4 245.7	4 147.9	3 116.1
Bosnia and Herzegovina Bosnie-Herzégovine	...	...	...	...	...	...	...	2 524.7	2 225.9	2 045.2
Botswana Botswana	606.8	653.0	682.9	698.5	612.2	525.8	512.2	466.9	408.0	349.2
Brazil Brésil	90 991.5	91 560.9	95 367.5	98 295.4	96 351.8	87 305.0	98 174.7	92 117.8	93 370.1	93 467.4
Bulgaria Bulgarie	9 654.7	9 693.3	8 371.1	8 720.3	8 145.3	7 680.5	7 874.0	7 688.9	7 634.3	7 377.7
Burkina Faso Burkina Faso	978.9	1 068.2	1 042.3	1 138.5	1 161.9	1 140.6	1 282.5	1 350.8	1 209.9	1 309.6
Burundi Burundi	947.0	998.0	1 061.9	1 095.1	1 081.0	1 022.1	1 078.9	1 049.6	1 028.0	973.7
Cambodia Cambodge	1 675.0	1 681.0	1 743.7	2 109.9	2 177.3	2 192.7	2 261.4	2 294.1	2 336.0	2 400.7
Cameroon Cameroun	6 279.5	6 166.3	7 247.6	8 009.7	7 950.7	7 729.5	8 183.5	7 611.6	7 389.6	6 913.0
Cape Verde Cap-Vert	136.1	140.8	166.5	185.0	196.1	199.6	240.9	308.0	314.6	340.2
Central African Rep. Rép. centrafricaine	729.6	773.2	802.4	853.9	850.4	801.5	841.0	826.1	795.7	756.9
Chad Tchad	671.1	713.4	758.5	831.6	910.8	935.2	1 004.0	1 044.2	1 008.4	991.6
Chile Chili	9 577.5	8 867.3	8 995.0	7 178.3	4 883.3	4 367.3	5 005.0	5 654.7	5 204.2	5 543.7
China Chine	58 462.6	70 076.2	82 391.2	94 674.5	102260.2	112821.4	99 424.1	99 217.3	94 836.9	91 705.7
Colombia Colombie	13 476.1	13 242.9	14 357.6	13 949.6	14 854.1	15 436.5	16 749.4	20 220.1	20 803.2	21 776.5

81

Total external and public/publicly guaranteed long-term debt of developing countries
Million US dollars *[cont.]*

Total de la dette extérieure et dette publique extérieure à long terme garantie par l'Etat de pays en développement
Millions de dollars E.-U. *[suite]*

B.   Public and publicly guaranteed long term debt ● Dette publique extérieure à long terme garantie par l'Etat

Country or area Pays ou zone	1992	1993	1994	1995	1996	1997	1998	1999	2000	2001
Comoros Comores	177.3	174.0	188.4	200.1	205.0	202.7	211.6	206.2	201.9	220.8
Congo Congo	3 875.6	4 114.2	4 774.0	4 955.4	4 665.7	4 283.8	4 250.5	3 933.7	3 757.5	3 631.1
Costa Rica Costa Rica	3 175.7	3 130.8	3 218.4	3 133.4	2 923.2	2 766.8	3 026.1	3 186.3	3 250.8	3 208.3
Côte d'Ivoire Côte d'Ivoire	11 243.9	11 110.6	11 241.0	11 902.1	11 366.7	10 427.1	10 799.7	9 699.1	9 063.4	8 590.4
Croatia Croatie	...	601.2	643.4	1 860.4	3 337.1	4 273.8	4 922.9	5 519.3	6 106.9	6 399.7
Czech Republic République tchèque	4 539.8	5 869.8	7 023.6	9 688.1	12 218.4	12 837.5	11 557.6	7 676.1	6 563.6	5 915.3
Dem. Rep. of the Congo Rép. dém. du Congo	8 960.7	8 780.9	9 293.9	9 635.8	9 275.2	8 628.3	9 214.3	8 262.3	7 880.2	7 584.0
Djibouti Djibouti	219.3	230.9	254.9	268.9	279.3	253.0	263.8	248.4	237.9	234.9
Dominica Dominique	88.6	92.4	88.7	98.6	102.1	94.6	98.1	97.6	143.7	184.5
Dominican Republic Rép. dominicaine	3 736.4	3 791.5	3 619.3	3 652.6	3 523.4	3 461.1	3 482.4	3 583.5	3 310.3	3 748.7
Ecuador Equateur	9 826.7	9 966.8	10 544.5	12 067.7	12 443.8	12 876.2	13 089.0	13 555.8	11 337.3	11 148.6
Egypt Egypte	27 809.3	27 860.6	29 878.1	30 548.3	28 875.0	26 804.3	27 622.1	26 101.7	24 350.2	25 242.9
El Salvador El Salvador	2 148.0	1 916.1	2 014.2	2 079.8	2 316.6	2 397.1	2 443.2	2 649.2	2 774.9	3 257.4
Equatorial Guinea Guinée équatoriale	214.4	214.8	219.3	229.6	222.2	208.6	216.5	207.9	198.9	192.1
Eritrea Erythrée	...	...	29.1	36.7	44.3	75.5	146.1	252.6	298.0	397.6
Estonia Estonie	33.8	84.9	108.6	159.3	216.5	197.5	234.4	205.5	210.5	186.5
Ethiopia Ethiopie	9 003.2	9 286.6	9 567.0	9 773.6	9 483.8	9 424.8	9 613.8	5 361.9	5 326.9	5 532.1
Fiji Fidji	226.9	199.4	180.7	168.3	147.2	129.9	140.1	193.5	174.0	159.2
Gabon Gabon	3 048.8	2 933.3	3 694.4	3 976.4	3 971.6	3 664.8	3 832.8	3 290.2	3 446.6	3 030.2
Gambia Gambie	346.2	350.2	368.1	385.5	411.9	401.2	433.6	431.1	437.9	437.5
Georgia Géorgie	79.3	558.8	924.1	1 039.4	1 106.3	1 189.5	1 301.0	1 309.1	1 273.9	1 313.5
Ghana Ghana	3 319.2	3 637.8	4 156.9	4 639.1	4 975.7	5 056.2	5 651.0	5 729.2	5 519.8	5 666.0
Grenada Grenade	104.1	104.7	113.6	112.7	120.0	115.2	114.4	119.3	158.5	160.7
Guatemala Guatemala	2 376.4	2 493.7	2 739.2	2 823.6	2 755.4	2 871.9	2 992.1	3 134.0	3 179.2	3 456.1
Guinea Guinée	2 450.2	2 659.2	2 886.4	2 987.1	2 980.6	3 008.7	3 126.4	3 061.0	2 940.4	2 843.9
Guinea-Bissau Guinée-Bissau	692.3	712.5	761.6	797.7	856.2	838.4	874.3	834.2	715.5	627.2
Guyana Guyana	1 697.1	1 755.5	1 811.0	1 805.8	1 394.2	1 370.3	1 229.1	1 186.4	1 180.1	1 176.1

81

Total external and public/publicly guaranteed long-term debt of developing countries
Million US dollars *[cont.]*

Total de la dette extérieure et dette publique extérieure à long terme garantie par l'Etat de pays en développement
Millions de dollars E.-U. *[suite]*

B.   Public and publicly guaranteed long term debt • Dette publique extérieure à long terme garantie par l'Etat

Country or area Pays ou zone	1992	1993	1994	1995	1996	1997	1998	1999	2000	2001
Haiti Haïti	655.0	662.2	646.8	760.8	843.2	902.1	982.4	1 041.2	1 039.4	1 028.1
Honduras Honduras	3 510.0	3 929.3	4 156.1	4 187.4	4 020.9	4 058.5	4 042.9	4 311.6	4 421.0	3 995.4
Hungary Hongrie	17 896.2	19 949.6	22 378.5	23 973.1	18 710.8	15 116.7	15 885.8	16 858.4	14 345.3	12 680.8
India Inde	77 920.8	83 905.9	87 480.2	80 422.0	78 045.2	79 398.1	84 611.3	86 410.3	83 156.2	82 694.5
Indonesia Indonésie	53 664.1	57 155.9	63 925.9	65 308.8	60 011.9	55 856.7	67 304.7	73 448.3	69 414.7	68 377.9
Iran (Islamic Rep. of) Iran (Rép. islamique d')	1 780.1	5 898.7	15 529.7	15 115.6	11 710.6	8 285.1	7 712.0	5 731.9	4 710.5	5 294.8
Jamaica Jamaïque	3 554.8	3 440.7	3 426.0	3 396.9	3 122.7	2 919.0	3 099.6	2 899.1	3 356.2	3 946.7
Jordan Jordanie	7 075.1	6 796.4	6 732.4	6 622.4	6 446.3	6 175.6	6 555.2	6 736.6	6 199.2	6 599.5
Kazakhstan Kazakhstan	25.7	1 621.1	2 227.0	2 833.8	1 946.5	2 621.6	3 037.8	3 353.4	3 617.1	3 445.7
Kenya Kenya	5 149.0	5 245.6	5 588.5	5 959.9	5 684.6	5 224.5	5 560.7	5 323.2	5 180.3	4 930.3
Korea, Republic of Corée, République de	24 049.9	24 565.6	19 252.6	22 123.4	25 423.1	34 006.3	58 129.0	57 955.5	43 174.7	33 742.1
Kyrgyzstan Kirghizistan	5.5	231.7	356.1	472.2	626.3	750.6	933.9	1 134.4	1 220.2	1 256.1
Lao People's Dem. Rep. Rép. dém. pop. lao	1 886.7	1 948.2	2 022.0	2 091.2	2 185.8	2 246.8	2 373.1	2 471.3	2 452.6	2 455.9
Latvia Lettonie	30.0	123.6	207.5	271.1	300.4	313.7	404.2	864.8	827.1	978.2
Lebanon Liban	300.5	368.0	778.2	1 550.5	1 933.4	2 349.1	4 047.8	5 332.4	6 579.4	8 956.5
Lesotho Lesotho	464.7	503.2	577.4	642.0	663.5	641.9	660.5	661.0	656.3	573.3
Liberia Libéria	1 081.2	1 101.9	1 137.0	1 161.4	1 110.0	1 061.3	1 092.3	1 062.2	1 040.1	1 011.8
Lithuania Lituanie	27.4	205.2	277.3	429.9	736.2	1 053.4	1 220.6	2 122.6	2 188.2	2 358.8
Madagascar Madagascar	3 469.0	3 316.2	3 536.6	3 705.7	3 552.0	3 875.0	4 106.4	4 368.9	4 295.3	3 793.5
Malawi Malawi	1 568.0	1 729.5	1 900.4	2 083.0	2 095.6	2 099.2	2 309.9	2 595.7	2 555.2	2 483.3
Malaysia Malaisie	12 370.5	13 460.3	14 692.9	16 022.7	15 702.0	16 807.5	18 154.5	18 930.1	19 089.6	24 068.1
Maldives Maldives	90.5	109.3	122.5	151.9	163.5	164.3	183.4	194.1	184.7	180.7
Mali Mali	2 778.4	2 786.2	2 545.4	2 739.3	2 762.7	2 692.3	2 826.4	2 800.3	2 654.8	2 616.0
Malta Malte	129.4	127.9	161.5	160.1	145.1	125.8	1 111.3	784.7	641.7	616.0
Mauritania Mauritanie	1 825.3	1 903.4	1 989.5	2 080.8	2 125.0	2 039.8	2 009.9	2 137.7	2 150.1	1 864.9
Mauritius Maurice	747.9	733.0	852.2	1 147.9	1 152.5	1 152.4	1 126.0	1 138.1	834.4	765.3
Mexico Mexique	71 155.2	75 143.2	79 521.8	95 159.5	94 040.8	84 373.3	87 974.1	88 697.7	89 653.2	86 199.4

81

Total external and public/publicly guaranteed long-term debt of developing countries
Million US dollars *[cont.]*
Total de la dette extérieure et dette publique extérieure à long terme garantie par l'Etat de pays en développement
Millions de dollars E.-U. *[suite]*

B.   Public and publicly guaranteed long term debt • Dette publique extérieure à long terme garantie par l'Etat

Country or area Pays ou zone	1992	1993	1994	1995	1996	1997	1998	1999	2000	2001
Mongolia Mongolie	276.7	343.2	405.7	472.1	485.8	533.3	650.0	841.1	833.4	823.8
Morocco Maroc	21 030.1	20 680.2	21 529.5	22 084.5	21 172.2	19 011.9	19 164.1	17 313.9	15 792.9	14 325.4
Mozambique Mozambique	4 701.1	4 841.1	5 219.0	5 208.7	5 357.8	5 211.0	5 972.6	4 644.9	4 550.2	2 221.9
Myanmar Myanmar	5 003.0	5 389.8	6 153.8	5 377.7	4 803.5	5 068.7	5 052.7	5 337.1	5 241.6	5 006.5
Nepal Népal	1 757.6	1 939.6	2 209.9	2 346.5	2 345.7	2 332.3	2 590.6	2 909.9	2 784.3	2 642.6
Nicaragua Nicaragua	9 346.6	9 339.3	9 703.6	8 565.7	5 148.3	5 364.4	5 635.6	5 778.8	5 492.3	5 437.2
Niger Niger	1 166.0	1 209.9	1 268.2	1 330.0	1 331.0	1 323.7	1 443.8	1 424.5	1 412.9	1 370.6
Nigeria Nigéria	26 477.8	26 420.6	27 954.5	28 140.0	25 430.5	22 631.2	23 445.0	22 357.7	30 019.9	29 215.1
Oman Oman	2 340.3	2 314.7	2 607.5	2 637.3	2 645.8	2 567.1	2 235.0	2 595.8	2 970.0	2 691.0
Pakistan Pakistan	18 562.7	20 421.6	22 709.4	23 787.5	23 627.8	23 979.4	26 150.3	28 144.0	27 183.2	26 800.9
Panama Panama	3 619.5	3 647.6	3 799.0	3 790.8	5 144.6	5 082.9	5 427.6	5 687.3	5 711.8	6 331.9
Papua New Guinea Papouasie-Nvl-Guinée	1 592.1	1 616.1	1 732.1	1 667.7	1 544.9	1 338.4	1 430.0	1 523.0	1 494.7	1 413.0
Paraguay Paraguay	1 367.2	1 285.5	1 416.2	1 571.0	1 548.2	1 704.8	1 792.6	2 297.5	2 227.0	2 119.5
Peru Pérou	15 579.9	16 384.8	17 680.6	18 927.4	20 219.3	19 221.1	19 316.0	19 499.1	19 250.4	18 831.1
Philippines Philippines	25 618.1	27 481.9	29 687.0	28 294.0	26 869.2	26 200.3	28 637.5	34 560.9	33 748.0	34 189.9
Poland Pologne	42 740.8	41 296.5	39 503.4	41 073.4	39 208.4	34 177.5	35 136.2	33 150.6	30 784.5	24 827.9
Republic of Moldova République de Moldova	38.5	190.2	326.4	449.5	554.5	801.4	801.4	722.5	867.7	779.1
Romania Roumanie	1 294.6	2 091.4	2 925.3	3 908.9	5 523.0	6 212.5	6 428.1	5 750.5	6 369.8	6 682.3
Russian Federation Fédération de Russie	64 551.3	101681.1	108281.7	102077.0	102371.9	106937.6	121796.2	121312.1	111095.5	101918.1
Rwanda Rwanda	789.9	837.6	905.3	970.1	984.5	993.5	1 119.8	1 161.7	1 146.6	1 162.9
Saint Kitts and Nevis Saint-Kitts-et-Nevis	47.4	49.7	55.2	54.1	62.6	112.0	124.3	133.7	150.2	186.0
Saint Lucia Sainte-Lucie	89.8	96.5	103.6	111.3	121.4	119.9	133.6	143.2	169.3	168.2
St. Vincent-Grenadines St. Vincent-Grenadines	74.4	78.4	92.3	92.3	93.9	92.8	108.1	162.6	164.2	163.0
Samoa Samoa	117.8	140.4	156.7	168.1	162.8	148.3	154.3	156.6	147.3	143.3
Sao Tome and Principe Sao Tomé-et-Principe	169.1	181.9	201.2	231.0	225.7	226.0	242.8	290.2	293.6	293.2
Senegal Sénégal	2 992.3	3 046.5	3 048.5	3 190.5	3 115.7	3 102.6	3 270.5	3 114.8	2 958.0	2 961.0
Serbia and Montenegro Serbie-et-Monténégro	11 116.9	8 231.4	6 613.4	6 827.4	6 565.6	6 147.9	6 500.1	6 233.6	6 090.9	6 001.7

81

Total external and public/publicly guaranteed long-term debt of developing countries
Million US dollars *[cont.]*

Total de la dette extérieure et dette publique extérieure à long terme garantie par l'Etat de pays en développement
Millions de dollars E.-U. *[suite]*

B.   Public and publicly guaranteed long term debt • Dette publique extérieure à long terme garantie par l'Etat

Country or area Pays ou zone	1992	1993	1994	1995	1996	1997	1998	1999	2000	2001
Seychelles Seychelles	130.5	132.1	147.8	145.8	138.1	131.3	145.0	132.2	124.4	117.1
Sierra Leone Sierra Leone	1 163.1	1 320.1	1 395.6	1 057.8	1 046.7	1 023.5	1 093.4	1 066.0	1 005.8	1 014.0
Slovakia Slovaquie	1 709.7	2 120.3	2 866.2	3 487.5	3 962.8	4 488.9	5 437.8	5 925.7	6 272.3	5 498.2
Solomon Islands Iles Salomon	92.5	94.3	98.4	100.3	100.5	96.5	113.7	125.3	120.7	130.9
Somalia Somalie	1 897.8	1 897.0	1 934.8	1 960.8	1 918.2	1 852.5	1 886.4	1 859.4	1 825.1	1 795.1
South Africa Afrique du Sud	...	...	7 789.0	9 836.7	10 347.5	11 516.9	10 667.8	8 173.3	9 087.7	7 941.0
Sri Lanka Sri Lanka	5 661.5	6 029.6	6 721.9	7 149.0	7 065.3	6 985.6	7 948.2	8 317.3	7 794.0	7 472.4
Sudan Soudan	8 983.6	8 993.8	9 399.9	9 779.4	9 369.2	8 998.2	9 225.9	8 852.0	8 646.5	8 489.3
Swaziland Swaziland	204.1	188.9	197.5	208.7	205.8	227.0	246.5	248.5	231.4	235.5
Syrian Arab Republic Rép. arabe syrienne	16 111.8	16 437.1	16 628.9	16 853.3	16 762.2	16 326.4	16 352.6	16 142.4	15 929.8	15 811.3
Tajikistan Tadjikistan	9.7	384.9	562.0	590.4	656.8	669.0	709.1	748.5	762.1	788.7
Thailand Thaïlande	13 282.5	14 696.7	16 202.7	16 826.4	16 887.1	22 292.0	28 086.4	31 304.7	29 437.9	26 411.3
TFYR of Macedonia L'ex-R.y. Macédoine	...	703.9	708.9	788.4	856.3	941.7	1 053.8	1 138.3	1 191.0	1 135.5
Togo Togo	1 135.3	1 127.8	1 229.2	1 286.2	1 310.2	1 214.1	1 325.3	1 284.8	1 229.9	1 203.0
Tonga Tonga	42.6	43.7	57.6	62.8	62.5	57.7	64.2	68.7	65.1	62.7
Trinidad and Tobago Trinité-et-Tobago	1 802.7	1 820.3	1 972.2	1 949.8	1 876.2	1 532.8	1 477.9	1 485.4	1 489.0	1 451.8
Tunisia Tunisie	7 201.9	7 417.0	8 007.2	9 023.7	9 377.8	9 334.3	9 499.5	9 494.6	8 869.3	9 084.5
Turkey Turquie	40 462.7	44 063.7	48 436.8	50 317.0	48 203.8	47 513.5	50 197.2	50 755.3	57 368.2	56 003.9
Turkmenistan Turkménistan	...	276.4	346.3	384.9	464.2	1 242.4	1 731.2	...	...	...
Uganda Ouganda	2 432.9	2 599.2	2 869.1	3 065.0	3 154.0	3 370.3	3 379.4	2 988.5	3 048.2	3 305.9
Ukraine Ukraine	453.6	3 682.1	4 809.6	6 580.5	6 647.5	7 015.2	8 971.9	9 590.4	8 141.8	8 197.2
United Rep. of Tanzania Rép.-Unie de Tanzanie	5 849.1	5 809.6	6 131.1	6 208.9	6 088.3	6 049.9	6 432.8	6 686.9	6 245.2	5 757.7
Uruguay Uruguay	3 140.2	3 369.0	3 749.9	3 833.2	4 096.9	4 585.7	5 142.0	5 109.7	5 596.9	6 109.8
Uzbekistan Ouzbékistan	59.7	939.5	952.8	1 417.6	1 995.8	2 032.6	2 579.0	3 476.2	3 601.7	3 759.3
Vanuatu Vanuatu	39.6	39.4	41.5	43.2	42.2	38.9	54.2	63.4	67.2	64.5
Venezuela Venezuela	25 829.5	26 855.3	28 040.0	28 222.5	27 745.9	27 053.7	28 035.2	27 654.2	27 432.8	24 915.9
Viet Nam Viet Nam	21 648.5	21 599.0	21 854.5	21 777.3	21 963.6	18 984.9	19 918.0	20 528.7	11 593.9	11 427.5

81

Total external and public/publicly guaranteed long-term debt of developing countries
Million US dollars *[cont.]*

Total de la dette extérieure et dette publique extérieure à long terme garantie par l'Etat de pays en développement
Millions de dollars E.-U. *[suite]*

B.   Public and publicly guaranteed long term debt • Dette publique extérieure à long terme garantie par l'Etat

Country or area Pays ou zone	1992	1993	1994	1995	1996	1997	1998	1999	2000	2001
Yemen Yémen	5 253.4	5 341.3	5 459.6	5 527.9	5 622.0	3 433.8	4 357.7	4 521.5	4 524.2	4 062.3
Zambia Zambie	4 513.5	4 397.4	5 186.6	5 297.5	5 375.2	5 257.2	5 332.2	4 510.8	4 449.0	4 394.2
Zimbabwe Zimbabwe	2 841.5	3 097.4	3 407.8	3 479.5	3 309.3	3 103.4	3 331.8	3 221.9	2 967.6	2 847.4

Source:
World Bank, Washington, D.C., "Global Development
Finance 2003", volumes 1 and 2.

+ The following abbreviations have been used in the table:
   LDOD: Long-term debt outstanding and disbursed
   IBRD: International Bank for Reconstruction and Development
   IDA: International Development Association
   LINT: Loan interest
   LTDS: Long-term debt service

Source:
Banque mondiale, Washington, D.C., "Global Development
Finance 2003 ", volumes 1 et 2.

+ Les abbréviations ci-après ont été utilisées dans le tableau :
   LDOD : Dette à long terme
   BIRD : Banque internationale pour la réconstruction et la
   développement
   IDA : Association internationale de développement
   LINT : Paiement d'intérêts
   LTDS : Service de la dette à long terme

Technical notes, tables 80 and 81

Table 80: Foreign exchange rates are shown in units of national currency per US dollar. The exchange rates are classified into three broad categories, reflecting both the role of the authorities in the determination of the exchange and/or the multiplicity of exchange rates in a country. The *market rate* is used to describe exchange rates determined largely by market forces; the *official rate* is an exchange rate determined by the authorities, sometimes in a flexible manner. For countries maintaining multiple exchange arrangements, the rates are labeled *principal rate, secondary rate,* and *tertiary rate.* Unless otherwise stated, the table refers to end of period and period averages of market exchange rates or official exchange rates. For further information see *International Financial Statistics* [15] and <www.imf.org>.

Table 81: Data were extracted from *Global Development Finance 2003* [34], published by the World Bank.

Long term external debt is defined as debt that has an original or extended maturity of more than one year and is owed to non-residents and repayable in foreign currency, goods, or services. A distinction is made between:

– Public debt which is an external obligation of a public debtor, which could be a national government, a political sub-division, an agency of either of the above or, in fact, any autonomous public body;

– Publicly guaranteed debt, which is an external obligation of a private debtor that is guaranteed for repayment by a public entity;

– Private non-guaranteed external debt, which is an external obligation of a private debtor that is not guaranteed for repayment by a public entity.

The data referring to public and publicly guaranteed debt do not include data for (a) transactions with the International Monetary Fund, (b) debt repayable in local currency, (c) direct investment and (d) short-term debt (that is, debt with an original maturity of less than a year).

The data referring to private non-guaranteed debt also exclude the above items but include contractual obligations on loans to direct-investment enterprises by foreign parent companies or their affiliates.

Data are aggregated by type of creditor. The breakdown is as follows:

Official creditors:

(a) Loans from international organizations (multilateral loans), excluding loans from funds administered by an international organization on behalf of a single donor government. The latter are classified as loans from governments;

(b) Loans from governments (bilateral loans) and

Notes techniques, tableaux 80 et 81

Tableau 80: Les taux des changes sont exprimés par nombre d'unités de monnaie nationale pour un dollar des Etats-Unis. Les taux de change sont classés en trois catégories, qui dénotent le rôle des autorités dans l'établissement des taux de change et/ou la multiplicité des taux de change dans un pays. Par *taux du marché*, on entend les taux de change déterminés essentiellement par les forces du marché; le *taux officiel* est un taux de change établi par les autorités, parfois selon des dispositions souples. Pour les pays qui continuent de mettre en œuvre des régimes de taux de change multiples, les taux sont désignés par les appellations suivantes: "taux principal", "taux secondaire" et "taux tertiaire". Sauf indication contraire, le tableau indique des taux de fin de période et les moyennes sur la période, des taux de change du marché ou des taux de change officiels. Pour plus de renseignements, voir *Statistiques financières internationales* [15] et <www.imf.org>.

Tableau 81: Les données sont extraites de *Global Development Finance 2003* [34] publié par la Banque mondiale.

La dette extérieure à long terme désigne la dette dont l'échéance initiale ou reportée est de plus d'un an, due à des non résidents et remboursable en devises, biens ou services. On établit les distinctions suivantes:

– La dette publique, qui est une obligation extérieure d'un débiteur public, pouvant être un gouvernement, un organe politique, une institution de l'un ou l'autre ou, en fait, tout organisme public autonome.

– La dette garantie par l'Etat, qui est une obligation extérieure d'un débiteur privé, dont le remboursement est garanti par un organisme public.

– La dette extérieure privée non garantie, qui est une obligation extérieure d'un débiteur privé, dont le remboursement n'est pas garanti par un organisme public.

Les statistiques relatives à la dette publique ou à la dette garantie par l'Etat ne comprennent pas les données concernant: (a) les transactions avec le Fonds monétaire international; (b) la dette remboursable en monnaie nationale; (c) les investissements directs; et (d) la dette à court terme (c'est-à-dire la dette dont l'échéance initiale est inférieure à un an).

Les statistiques relatives à la dette privée non garantie ne comprennent pas non plus les éléments précités, mais comprennent les obligations contractuelles au titre des prêts consentis par des sociétés mères étrangères ou leurs filiales à des entreprises créées dans le cadre d'investissements directs.

Les données sont groupées par type de créancier, comme suit:

Créanciers publics:

(a) Les prêts obtenus auprès d'organisations interna-

from autonomous public bodies;

Private creditors:

(a) Suppliers: Credits from manufacturers, exporters, or other suppliers of goods;

(b) Financial markets: Loans from private banks and other private financial institutions as well as publicly issued and privately placed bonds;

(c) Other: External liabilities on account of nationalized properties and unclassified debts to private creditors.

A distinction is made between the following categories of external public debt:

– Debt outstanding (including undisbursed) is the sum of disbursed and undisbursed debt and represents the total outstanding external obligations of the borrower at year-end;

– Debt outstanding (disbursed only) is total outstanding debt drawn by the borrower at year end;

– Commitments are the total of loans for which contracts are signed in the year specified;

– Disbursements are drawings on outstanding loan commitments during the year specified;

– Service payments are actual repayments of principal amortization and interest payments made in foreign currencies, goods or services in the year specified;

– Net flows (or net lending) are disbursements minus principal repayments;

– Net transfers are net flows minus interest payments or disbursements minus total debt-service payments.

The countries included in the table are those for which data are sufficiently reliable to provide a meaningful presentation of debt outstanding and future service payments.

tionales (prêts multilatéraux), à l'exclusion des prêts au titre de fonds administrés par une organisation internationale pour le compte d'un gouvernement donateur précis, qui sont classés comme prêts consentis par des gouvernements;

(b) Les prêts consentis par des gouvernements (prêts bilatéraux) et par des organisations publiques autonomes.

Créanciers privés:

(a) Fournisseurs: Crédits consentis par des fabricants exportateurs et autre fournisseurs de biens;

(b) Marchés financiers: prêts consentis par des banques privées et autres institutions financières privées, et émissions publiques d'obligations placées auprès d'investisseurs privés;

(c) Autres créanciers: engagements vis-à-vis de l'extérieur au titre des biens nationalisés et dettes diverses à l'égard de créanciers privés.

On fait une distinction entre les catégories suivantes de dette publique extérieure:

– L'encours de la dette (y compris les fonds non décaissés) est la somme des fonds décaissés et non décaissés et représente le total des obligations extérieures en cours de l'emprunteur à la fin de l'année;

– L'encours de la dette (fonds décaissés seulement) est le montant total des tirages effectués par l'emprunteur sur sa dette en cours à la fin de l'année;

– Les engagements représentent le total des prêts dont les contrats ont été signés au cours de l'année considérée;

– Les décaissements sont les sommes tirées sur l'encours des prêts pendant l'année considérée;

– Les paiements au titre du service de la dette sont les remboursements effectifs du principal et les paiements d'intérêts effectués en devises, biens ou services pendant l'année considérée;

– Les flux nets (ou prêts nets) sont les décaissements moins les remboursements de principal;

– Les transferts nets désignent les flux nets moins les paiements d'intérêts, ou les décaissements moins le total des paiements au titre du service de la dette.

Les pays figurant sur ce tableau sont ceux pour lesquels les données sont suffisamment fiables pour permettre une présentation significative de l'encours de la dette et des paiements futurs au titre du service de la dette.

82
Disbursements of bilateral and multilateral official development assistance and official aid to individual recipients
Versements d'aide publique au développement et d'aide publique bilatérales et multilatérales aux bénéficiares

Region, country or area Région, pays ou zone	Year Année	Net disbursements (US $) - Versements nets ($E. –U.)			
		Bilateral Bilatérale (millions)	Multilateral[1] Multilatérale[1] (millions)	Total (millions)	Per capita[2] Par habitant[2]
World **Monde**	**1999**	**42 716.8**	**17 244.6**	**59 961.4**	...
	2000	**40 929.6**	**16 393.2**	**57 322.8**	...
	2001	**38 653.4**	**18 538.2**	**57 191.5**	...
Africa **Afrique**	**1999**	**10 291.1**	**5 484.6**	**78 878.6**	...
	2000	**10 354.8**	**5 047.7**	**77 012.4**	...
	2001	**10 041.7**	**6 043.3**	**80 425.1**	...
Algeria Algérie	1999	37.1	21.0	58.1	2.0
	2000	27.1	64.1	91.1	3.0
	2001	24.8	103.6	128.4	4.2
Angola Angola	1999	251.8	135.7	387.5	32.2
	2000	189.1	111.5	300.6	24.3
	2001	179.4	89.9	269.3	21.1
Benin Bénin	1999	119.3	93.2	212.5	35.0
	2000	190.5	49.2	239.7	38.5
	2001	144.5	127.3	271.8	42.6
Botswana Botswana	1999	41.1	20.7	61.8	36.4
	2000	23.5	8.1	31.6	18.3
	2001	24.2	3.5	27.7	15.8
Burkina Faso Burkina Faso	1999	232.0	156.8	388.8	33.6
	2000	227.8	104.5	332.2	27.9
	2001	220.9	154.3	375.2	30.6
Burundi Burundi	1999	52.0	22.2	74.3	12.0
	2000	40.9	51.7	92.6	14.8
	2001	54.7	76.0	130.7	20.4
Cameroon Cameroun	1999	254.3	183.4	437.7	29.6
	2000	213.5	169.1	382.6	25.3
	2001	274.6	125.7	400.3	25.9
Cape Verde Cap-Vert	1999	88.7	48.3	137.0	321.1
	2000	69.7	24.7	94.4	216.8
	2001	49.0	27.8	76.8	172.7
Central African Rep. Rép. centrafricaine	1999	59.1	59.0	118.1	32.3
	2000	53.1	22.5	75.5	20.3
	2001	47.9	28.1	76.0	20.2
Chad Tchad	1999	64.5	116.4	180.8	23.7
	2000	53.3	76.7	130.0	16.5
	2001	72.8	105.9	178.7	22.1
Comoros Comores	1999	13.2	8.3	21.4	31.3
	2000	10.8	7.8	18.6	26.3
	2001	9.6	16.5	26.1	35.9
Congo Congo	1999	121.4	20.2	141.6	42.3
	2000	23.0	10.2	33.2	9.6
	2001	29.6	45.1	74.7	21.1
Côte d'Ivoire Côte d'Ivoire	1999	365.6	81.0	446.6	28.7
	2000	250.1	101.2	351.2	22.2
	2001	158.5	28.2	186.8	11.6
Dem. Rep. of the Congo Rép. dém. du Congo	1999	87.0	45.3	132.3	2.8
	2000	102.7	80.7	183.4	3.8
	2001	143.4	107.4	250.7	5.0
Djibouti Djibouti	1999	55.4	18.7	74.1	114.5
	2000	42.1	19.7	61.8	92.8
	2001	28.1	27.1	55.2	81.1

82
Disbursements of bilateral and multilateral official development assistance and official aid to individual recipients *[cont.]*
Versements d'aide publique au développement et d'aide publique bilatérales et multilatérales aux bénéficiares *[suite]*

Region, country or area Région, pays ou zone	Year Année	Net disbursements (US $) - Versements nets ($E. –U.)			
		Bilateral Bilatérale (millions)	Multilateral[1] Multilatérale[1] (millions)	Total (millions)	Per capita[2] Par habitant[2]
Egypt Egypte	1999 2000 2001	1 298.1 1 138.9 1 090.3	210.8 135.6 103.5	1 508.9 1 274.5 1 193.8	22.7 18.8 17.3
Equatorial Guinea Guinée équatoriale	1999 2000 2001	14.6 18.2 13.1	5.5 3.3 1.3	20.2 21.5 14.4	45.3 47.1 30.8
Eritrea Erythrée	1999 2000 2001	80.5 111.9 151.4	49.7 54.9 126.1	130.2 166.8 277.4	36.3 44.9 72.1
Ethiopia Ethiopie	1999 2000 2001	325.0 379.5 367.1	303.3 298.4 684.8	628.3 677.9 1 051.9	9.8 10.3 15.6
Gabon Gabon	1999 2000 2001	34.5 -11.7 -8.0	13.1 23.4 16.5	47.6 11.7 8.5	38.7 9.3 6.6
Gambia Gambie	1999 2000 2001	13.2 14.6 13.4	19.1 32.0 35.1	32.3 46.6 48.5	25.4 35.5 35.9
Ghana Ghana	1999 2000 2001	355.6 385.0 396.0	250.0 222.1 252.9	605.5 607.1 648.9	31.6 31.0 32.4
Guinea Guinée	1999 2000 2001	111.1 92.8 120.3	108.6 57.6 152.8	219.7 150.4 273.2	27.5 18.5 33.1
Guinea-Bissau Guinée-Bissau	1999 2000 2001	32.1 41.6 30.4	20.3 38.8 28.2	52.4 80.4 58.6	39.5 58.8 41.6
Kenya Kenya	1999 2000 2001	253.7 293.0 270.5	53.4 214.3 176.7	307.1 507.3 447.2	10.2 16.6 14.4
Lesotho Lesotho	1999 2000 2001	25.7 21.8 29.5	6.6 16.1 25.7	32.3 37.9 55.2	18.2 21.2 30.7
Liberia Libéria	1999 2000 2001	44.6 23.8 15.6	49.4 44.0 21.3	94.0 67.8 36.9	34.0 23.0 11.9
Libyan Arab Jamah. Jamah. arabe libyenne	1999 2000 2001	3.3 11.9 4.3	3.9 3.1 5.2	7.3 15.0 9.4	1.4 2.9 1.8
Madagascar Madagascar	1999 2000 2001	192.5 138.7 137.9	166.1 184.6 217.3	358.6 323.2 355.2	23.1 20.2 21.6
Malawi Malawi	1999 2000 2001	227.7 269.2 195.8	214.3 170.9 195.1	442.0 440.1 391.0	39.9 38.7 33.6
Mali Mali	1999 2000 2001	237.3 299.8 208.5	117.4 61.3 128.2	354.7 361.0 336.8	30.7 30.3 27.5
Mauritania Mauritanie	1999 2000 2001	88.7 82.5 81.3	124.8 129.3 182.0	213.5 211.8 263.3	83.1 80.1 96.7
Mauritius Maurice	1999 2000 2001	5.1 12.4 8.1	36.7 7.5 6.5	41.8 19.9 14.6	35.6 16.7 12.2
Mayotte Mayotte	1999 2000 2001	109.3 103.0 119.3	2.5 0.2 0.9	111.8 103.2 120.2	... ...

82

Disbursements of bilateral and multilateral official development assistance and official aid to individual recipients *[cont.]*
Versements d'aide publique au développement et d'aide publique bilatérales et multilatérales aux bénéficiares *[suite]*

| Region, country or area
Région, pays ou zone | Year
Année | Net disbursements (US $)   -   Versements nets ($E. –U.) | | | |
		Bilateral Bilatérale (millions)	Multilateral[1] Multilatérale[1] (millions)	Total (millions)	Per capita[2] Par habitant[2]
Morocco Maroc	1999	333.5	316.0	649.5	22.7
	2000	293.1	130.4	423.4	14.6
	2001	342.1	139.9	482.0	16.3
Mozambique Mozambique	1999	593.2	213.2	806.4	46.0
	2000	623.5	253.5	877.0	49.1
	2001	720.2	210.3	930.5	51.1
Namibia Namibie	1999	117.2	60.4	177.6	96.0
	2000	96.8	54.8	151.6	80.1
	2001	77.5	30.3	107.7	55.8
Niger Niger	1999	120.2	66.3	186.4	18.0
	2000	105.8	105.1	210.9	19.6
	2001	113.6	133.8	247.4	22.2
Nigeria Nigéria	1999	52.9	96.3	149.2	1.3
	2000	84.3	100.2	184.5	1.6
	2001	107.5	78.6	186.1	1.6
Rwanda Rwanda	1999	180.5	192.5	373.0	51.7
	2000	175.4	146.5	321.9	41.7
	2001	148.9	141.5	290.4	36.0
Saint Helena Sainte-Hélène	1999	13.5	0.3	13.8	2 713.7
	2000	18.4	0.3	18.7	3 697.8
	2001	14.7	0.4	15.2	3 013.5
Sao Tome and Principe Sao Tomé-et-Principe	1999	19.1	8.5	27.5	189.6
	2000	17.7	17.3	35.0	234.7
	2001	21.9	16.0	37.9	248.1
Senegal Sénégal	1999	416.2	115.2	531.5	57.9
	2000	288.4	139.7	428.2	45.6
	2001	223.7	195.7	419.4	43.6
Seychelles Seychelles	1999	4.8	6.2	11.0	140.9
	2000	3.3	8.4	11.7	148.2
	2001	8.2	5.2	13.5	169.0
Sierra Leone Sierra Leone	1999	59.9	13.4	73.3	17.1
	2000	115.6	66.8	182.4	41.3
	2001	166.8	164.7	331.6	72.5
Somalia Somalie	1999	75.9	38.7	114.6	13.7
	2000	56.4	47.3	103.7	11.9
	2001	88.5	45.9	134.3	14.8
South Africa Afrique du Sud	1999	386.2	153.4	539.6	12.4
	2000	353.6	132.0	485.5	11.0
	2001	313.3	114.1	427.4	9.6
Sudan Soudan	1999	158.5	58.2	216.7	7.1
	2000	90.3	35.7	125.9	4.0
	2001	107.6	54.4	162.1	5.0
Swaziland Swaziland	1999	14.9	14.1	28.9	28.2
	2000	2.8	10.3	13.0	12.5
	2001	4.2	21.9	26.1	24.6
Togo Togo	1999	47.1	21.2	68.3	15.4
	2000	51.9	16.4	68.3	15.0
	2001	28.5	14.5	43.0	9.2
Tunisia Tunisie	1999	102.0	161.2	263.2	28.0
	2000	150.3	71.9	222.1	23.3
	2001	183.7	193.4	377.1	39.2
Uganda Ouganda	1999	357.5	232.3	589.8	25.9
	2000	578.2	235.6	813.8	34.7
	2001	386.3	394.3	780.6	32.2
United Rep. of Tanzania Rép.-Unie de Tanzanie	1999	613.4	375.7	989.1	29.0
	2000	778.7	246.0	1 024.7	29.4
	2001	943.8	295.1	1 238.9	34.8

82

Disbursements of bilateral and multilateral official development assistance and official aid to individual recipients *[cont.]*
Versements d'aide publique au développement et d'aide publique bilatérales et multilatérales aux bénéficiares *[suite]*

Region, country or area Région, pays ou zone	Year Année	Net disbursements (US $) - Versements nets ($E. –U.)			
		Bilateral Bilatérale (millions)	Multilateral[1] Multilatérale[1] (millions)	Total (millions)	Per capita[2] Par habitant[2]
Zambia Zambie	1999	340.0	283.4	623.4	60.9
	2000	486.2	308.6	794.8	76.3
	2001	274.1	98.5	372.6	35.3
Zimbabwe Zimbabwe	1999	219.2	25.5	244.8	19.6
	2000	192.6	-13.9	178.7	14.1
	2001	148.6	14.2	162.7	12.8
Africa unspecified **Afrique non specifiée**	**1999**	**770.6**	**247.1**	**1 017.7**	...
	2000	**847.7**	**336.4**	**1 184.1**	...
	2001	**911.4**	**254.3**	**1 165.7**	...
Americas **Amériques**	**1999**	**4 239.9**	**1 788.9**	**6 028.8**	...
	2000	**4 034.1**	**1 075.6**	**5 109.7**	...
	2001	**4 512.1**	**1 487.2**	**5 999.3**	...
Anguilla Anguilla	1999	2.7	-0.3	2.4	217.1
	2000	3.8	-0.3	3.5	312.9
	2001	3.0	0.5	3.5	309.3
Antigua and Barbuda Antigua-et-Barbuda	1999	8.2	0.8	9.0	126.9
	2000	3.7	1.1	4.8	67.4
	2001	6.0	1.8	7.8	108.2
Argentina Argentine	1999	31.3	64.1	95.5	2.6
	2000	43.5	25.3	68.8	1.9
	2001	10.1	137.9	148.0	3.9
Aruba Aruba	1999	-7.1	-0.3	-7.4	-81.4
	2000	10.7	0.8	11.5	123.3
	2001	-1.5	-0.2	-1.7	-17.8
Bahamas Bahamas	1999	0.9	10.7	11.6	38.6
	2000	5.2	0.3	5.5	18.2
	2001	7.3	1.2	8.5	27.6
Barbados Barbade	1999	1.4	-3.5	-2.1	-7.9
	2000	1.0	-0.8	0.2	0.9
	2001	2.8	-4.0	-1.2	-4.4
Belize Belize	1999	37.5	8.8	46.3	197.0
	2000	2.9	11.2	14.0	58.4
	2001	10.2	10.7	20.9	85.2
Bermuda Bermudes	1999	0.1	0.0	0.1	1.0
	2000	0.1	0.0	0.1	0.8
	2001	0.0	0.0	0.0	0.3
Bolivia Bolivie	1999	397.3	171.5	568.8	69.8
	2000	336.1	138.3	474.4	57.1
	2001	530.2	197.6	727.8	85.8
Brazil Brésil	1999	98.4	87.6	185.9	1.1
	2000	222.5	98.4	320.9	1.9
	2001	156.8	191.1	347.9	2.0
British Virgin Islands Iles Vierges britanniques	1999	2.8	-0.2	2.6	23.7
	2000	1.2	3.6	4.8	44.6
	2001	0.2	1.9	2.1	18.8
Cayman Islands Iles Caïmanes	1999	0.5	2.6	3.0	84.6
	2000	-3.2	-0.5	-3.6	-97.9
	2001	0.0	-0.8	-0.8	-20.6
Chile Chili	1999	63.5	6.0	69.5	4.6
	2000	41.0	7.7	48.7	3.2
	2001	39.6	17.4	57.0	3.7
Colombia Colombie	1999	292.3	9.3	301.7	7.3
	2000	178.5	7.8	186.3	4.4
	2001	372.3	6.8	379.1	8.9
Costa Rica Costa Rica	1999	-4.3	-4.9	-9.1	-2.4
	2000	17.2	-6.2	11.0	2.8
	2001	6.1	-4.6	1.5	0.4

82

Disbursements of bilateral and multilateral official development assistance and official aid to individual recipients *[cont.]*
Versements d'aide publique au développement et d'aide publique bilatérales et multilatérales aux bénéficiares *[suite]*

Region, country or area Région, pays ou zone	Year Année	Net disbursements (US $) - Versements nets ($E. –U.)			
		Bilateral Bilatérale (millions)	Multilateral[1] Multilatérale[1] (millions)	Total (millions)	Per capita[2] Par habitant[2]
Cuba Cuba	1999	35.5	22.7	58.1	5.2
	2000	30.8	12.9	43.7	3.9
	2001	33.7	16.6	50.3	4.5
Dominica Dominique	1999	6.9	2.9	9.8	126.8
	2000	5.9	6.5	12.4	159.4
	2001	5.0	13.9	18.9	241.6
Dominican Republic Rép. dominicaine	1999	151.9	42.8	194.7	23.7
	2000	44.6	17.8	62.4	7.5
	2001	101.9	3.3	105.2	12.4
Ecuador Equateur	1999	128.9	17.1	146.0	12.0
	2000	137.4	8.6	146.0	11.8
	2001	147.6	22.8	170.4	13.5
El Salvador El Salvador	1999	173.7	9.3	183.1	30.0
	2000	172.3	7.1	179.4	28.9
	2001	231.1	2.6	233.7	37.0
Falkland Is. (Malvinas) Iles Falkland (Malvinas)	1999	0.0	-0.2	-0.2	-82.3
	2000	0.0	-0.2	-0.2	-80.3
	2001	0.0	-0.2	-0.2	-75.8
Grenada Grenade	1999	2.4	3.0	5.4	65.9
	2000	9.9	3.2	13.1	162.0
	2001	3.3	4.1	7.5	92.4
Guatemala Guatemala	1999	230.7	62.3	293.0	26.3
	2000	230.3	32.8	263.1	23.0
	2001	201.2	23.5	224.7	19.2
Guyana Guyana	1999	39.6	39.9	79.5	105.2
	2000	51.9	55.4	107.3	141.3
	2001	46.0	55.7	101.7	133.6
Haiti Haïti	1999	157.2	105.7	262.8	33.3
	2000	153.9	54.4	208.3	26.0
	2001	136.0	29.7	165.7	20.4
Honduras Honduras	1999	355.1	460.2	815.3	129.6
	2000	310.6	133.9	444.6	68.9
	2001	422.3	253.8	676.2	102.2
Jamaica Jamaïque	1999	-22.7	0.0	-22.7	-8.9
	2000	-26.4	30.0	3.5	1.4
	2001	-1.0	44.2	43.2	16.6
Mexico Mexique	1999	21.9	14.8	36.7	0.4
	2000	-68.4	13.7	-54.7	-0.6
	2001	40.7	33.5	74.2	0.7
Montserrat Montserrat	1999	40.5	0.4	40.9	8 391.1
	2000	30.9	0.1	30.9	7 933.3
	2001	32.7	0.3	33.0	9 691.8
Netherlands Antilles Antilles néerlandaises	1999	126.2	0.8	127.0	594.8
	2000	173.8	3.1	177.0	822.0
	2001	55.6	3.3	58.9	271.2
Nicaragua Nicaragua	1999	323.4	349.0	672.3	136.0
	2000	325.9	235.3	561.1	110.6
	2001	714.7	213.3	927.9	178.3
Panama Panama	1999	15.2	-0.8	14.3	5.0
	2000	11.7	-3.3	8.4	2.8
	2001	17.1	0.3	17.4	5.8
Paraguay Paraguay	1999	65.5	12.1	77.6	14.5
	2000	72.9	8.5	81.3	14.9
	2001	58.3	2.5	60.8	10.9
Peru Pérou	1999	405.0	45.0	450.0	17.6
	2000	372.7	26.0	398.7	15.4
	2001	425.4	24.5	449.9	17.1

82

Disbursements of bilateral and multilateral official development assistance and official aid to individual recipients *[cont.]*
Versements d'aide publique au développement et d'aide publique bilatérales et multilatérales aux bénéficiares *[suite]*

Region, country or area Région, pays ou zone	Year Année	Net disbursements (US $) - Versements nets ($E. –U.)			
		Bilateral Bilatérale (millions)	Multilateral[1] Multilatérale[1] (millions)	Total (millions)	Per capita[2] Par habitant[2]
Saint Kitts and Nevis Saint-Kitts-et-Nevis	1999	0.3	4.3	4.6	107.7
	2000	0.1	4.1	4.2	98.8
	2001	1.3	7.7	8.9	213.0
Saint Lucia Sainte-Lucie	1999	9.9	14.1	24.0	165.8
	2000	7.1	4.4	11.5	79.1
	2001	0.8	15.8	16.5	112.6
St. Vincent-Grenadines St. Vincent-Grenadines	1999	6.0	8.6	14.5	124.1
	2000	3.8	1.1	5.0	42.1
	2001	0.7	7.8	8.5	71.6
Suriname Suriname	1999	30.1	5.8	36.0	85.3
	2000	29.1	5.2	34.3	80.7
	2001	20.0	3.2	23.2	54.1
Trinidad and Tobago Trinité-et-Tobago	1999	0.2	26.1	26.2	20.4
	2000	4.4	-5.9	-1.5	-1.2
	2001	4.3	-6.1	-1.8	-1.4
Turks and Caicos Islands Iles Turques et Caïques	1999	5.4	2.0	7.4	414.2
	2000	5.6	1.1	6.7	359.4
	2001	5.1	1.6	6.7	347.5
Uruguay Uruguay	1999	19.0	2.7	21.7	6.6
	2000	15.3	1.4	16.7	5.0
	2001	10.7	3.9	14.7	4.4
Venezuela Venezuela	1999	34.2	9.8	43.9	1.9
	2000	61.3	14.6	75.9	3.1
	2001	33.5	10.9	44.4	1.8
Americas unspecified Amériques non specifiées	**1999**	**952.9**	**176.6**	**1 129.4**	...
	2000	**1 002.7**	**117.4**	**1 120.1**	...
	2001	**621.1**	**137.3**	**758.5**	...
Asia Asie	**1999**	**13 578.7**	**4 739.5**	**18 318.2**	...
	2000	**11 625.7**	**4 599.3**	**16 225.0**	...
	2001	**10 747.0**	**5 335.5**	**16 082.5**	...
Afghanistan Afghanistan	1999	104.1	38.3	142.4	6.8
	2000	87.5	52.7	140.2	6.6
	2001	322.9	73.2	396.1	17.9
Armenia Arménie	1999	75.3	133.2	208.5	66.3
	2000	139.3	75.6	214.9	69.1
	2001	124.2	87.0	211.2	68.4
Azerbaijan Azerbaïdjan	1999	52.4	109.3	161.7	20.0
	2000	70.7	60.5	131.1	16.1
	2001	148.4	67.3	215.7	26.2
Bahrain Bahreïn	1999	1.7	0.6	2.3	3.4
	2000	1.6	0.0	1.6	2.4
	2001	1.2	-0.1	1.0	1.5
Bangladesh Bangladesh	1999	607.3	588.2	1 195.5	8.9
	2000	616.5	519.5	1 136.0	8.2
	2001	578.4	431.5	1 009.9	7.2
Bhutan Bhoutan	1999	53.0	14.7	67.8	33.8
	2000	33.7	20.0	53.7	26.0
	2001	42.5	18.0	60.5	28.5
Brunei Darussalam Brunéi Darussalam	1999	1.4	0.0	1.4	4.3
	2000	0.6	0.0	0.6	1.7
	2001	0.3	0.1	0.3	1.0
Cambodia Cambodge	1999	167.1	109.8	276.9	21.6
	2000	248.0	149.7	397.7	30.3
	2001	264.8	142.6	407.5	30.2
China Chine	1999	1 821.6	548.3	2 369.8	1.9
	2000	1 257.5	460.4	1 717.9	1.4
	2001	1 075.1	334.9	1 409.9	1.1

82

Disbursements of bilateral and multilateral official development assistance and official aid to individual recipients *[cont.]*
Versements d'aide publique au développement et d'aide publique bilatérales et multilatérales aux bénéficiares *[suite]*

Region, country or area Région, pays ou zone	Year Année	Net disbursements (US $) - Versements nets ($E. –U.)			
		Bilateral Bilatérale (millions)	Multilateral[1] Multilatérale[1] (millions)	Total (millions)	Per capita[2] Par habitant[2]
China, Hong Kong SAR Chine, Hong Kong RAS	1999	3.8	-0.1	3.7	0.6
	2000	4.2	0.1	4.3	0.6
	2001	3.6	0.0	3.6	0.5
China, Macao SAR Chine, Macao RAS	1999	0.3	0.0	0.3	0.8
	2000	0.2	0.5	0.7	1.5
	2001	0.4	0.1	0.5	1.2
Georgia Géorgie	1999	77.7	161.2	238.9	45.2
	2000	120.3	43.1	163.4	31.1
	2001	151.6	131.7	283.2	54.2
India Inde	1999	838.3	664.6	1 502.8	1.5
	2000	650.3	846.5	1 496.9	1.5
	2001	904.5	805.4	1 710.0	1.7
Indonesia Indonésie	1999	2 169.4	40.2	2 209.6	10.6
	2000	1 617.2	109.5	1 726.7	8.2
	2001	1 375.4	100.5	1 475.9	6.9
Iran (Islamic Rep. of) Iran (Rép. islamique d')	1999	138.4	23.0	161.4	2.5
	2000	112.8	17.2	129.9	2.0
	2001	90.8	23.3	114.1	1.7
Iraq Iraq	1999	79.0	-3.2	75.8	3.4
	2000	84.1	16.6	100.7	4.3
	2001	100.8	20.8	121.6	5.1
Israel Israël	1999	901.6	4.1	905.7	153.2
	2000	800.4	-0.4	800.0	132.4
	2001	148.5	23.9	172.3	27.9
Jordan Jordanie	1999	325.3	105.8	431.1	88.2
	2000	385.3	168.0	553.3	109.9
	2001	302.1	132.1	434.1	83.8
Kazakhstan Kazakhstan	1999	133.6	27.1	160.7	10.2
	2000	159.3	14.8	174.1	11.1
	2001	122.7	16.2	138.9	8.9
Korea, Dem. P. R. Corée, R. p. dém. de	1999	165.1	35.6	200.7	9.1
	2000	26.9	48.3	75.2	3.4
	2001	52.3	66.6	118.9	5.3
Korea, Republic of Corée, République de	1999	-53.8	-1.4	-55.2	-1.2
	2000	-196.6	-1.5	-198.0	-4.2
	2001	-108.6	-2.9	-111.4	-2.4
Kuwait Koweït	1999	5.6	1.7	7.2	3.4
	2000	2.0	0.9	2.9	1.3
	2001	2.9	0.8	3.6	1.5
Kyrgyzstan Kirghizistan	1999	115.6	151.2	266.7	55.1
	2000	91.3	111.7	203.0	41.2
	2001	71.3	112.0	183.3	36.7
Lao People's Dem. Rep. Rép. dém. pop. lao	1999	210.5	84.6	295.0	57.2
	2000	194.9	86.1	281.0	53.2
	2001	149.9	92.7	242.5	44.9
Lebanon Liban	1999	80.3	67.6	147.9	43.3
	2000	90.5	91.3	181.8	52.3
	2001	101.7	60.3	162.0	45.8
Malaysia Malaisie	1999	140.1	6.8	146.9	6.5
	2000	43.3	3.3	46.6	2.0
	2001	24.9	3.3	28.1	1.2
Maldives Maldives	1999	25.5	6.6	32.0	113.5
	2000	13.3	7.2	20.5	70.4
	2001	15.2	10.0	25.2	83.9
Mongolia Mongolie	1999	138.2	79.5	217.7	87.9
	2000	150.8	60.6	211.3	84.5
	2001	141.1	64.8	205.8	81.4

82
Disbursements of bilateral and multilateral official development assistance and official aid to individual recipients *[cont.]*
Versements d'aide publique au développement et d'aide publique bilatérales et multilatérales aux bénéficiares *[suite]*

| Region, country or area Région, pays ou zone | Year Année | Net disbursements (US $) - Versements nets ($E. –U.) | | | |
		Bilateral Bilatérale (millions)	Multilateral[1] Multilatérale[1] (millions)	Total (millions)	Per capita[2] Par habitant[2]
Myanmar Myanmar	1999	44.7	28.6	73.2	1.6
	2000	68.1	37.8	105.9	2.2
	2001	89.2	37.1	126.3	2.6
Nepal Népal	1999	204.8	138.8	343.6	15.0
	2000	231.2	154.9	386.1	16.4
	2001	270.2	112.0	382.2	15.9
Occupied Palestinian Terr. Terr. palestinien occupé	1999	326.6	168.6	495.2	161.1
	2000	306.4	226.1	532.6	166.9
	2001	280.2	337.9	618.0	186.7
Oman Oman	1999	8.8	2.3	11.1	4.4
	2000	9.2	2.3	11.5	4.4
	2001	8.1	0.1	8.2	3.1
Pakistan Pakistan	1999	435.2	297.2	732.4	5.3
	2000	475.1	226.7	701.7	4.9
	2001	1 110.1	813.5	1 923.6	13.2
Philippines Philippines	1999	616.0	79.1	695.1	9.4
	2000	502.3	72.2	574.4	7.6
	2001	505.0	68.5	573.5	7.4
Qatar Qatar	1999	4.7	0.2	4.9	8.6
	2000	1.1	-0.6	0.5	0.8
	2001	0.8	0.2	1.0	1.7
Saudi Arabia Arabie saoudite	1999	19.1	9.7	28.8	1.3
	2000	18.0	11.2	29.2	1.3
	2001	10.5	16.5	27.1	1.2
Singapore Singapour	1999	-1.5	0.4	-1.1	-0.3
	2000	0.7	0.4	1.1	0.3
	2001	0.7	0.2	1.0	0.2
Sri Lanka Sri Lanka	1999	207.7	43.6	251.4	13.6
	2000	240.2	25.2	265.4	14.3
	2001	279.9	37.6	317.5	16.9
Syrian Arab Republic Rép. arabe syrienne	1999	172.3	34.6	206.9	12.8
	2000	97.3	38.7	136.0	8.2
	2001	92.3	34.3	126.6	7.5
Tajikistan Tadjikistan	1999	35.1	86.9	122.0	20.2
	2000	38.1	103.5	141.7	23.3
	2001	63.5	93.6	157.1	25.6
Thailand Thaïlande	1999	994.8	16.4	1 011.2	16.8
	2000	625.2	17.7	642.9	10.6
	2001	270.9	15.0	285.9	4.6
Timor-Leste Timor-Leste	1999	147.2	5.6	152.8	213.6
	2000	212.3	20.6	232.9	331.6
	2001	153.9	40.7	194.6	273.6
Turkmenistan Turkménistan	1999	11.5	9.0	20.5	4.5
	2000	9.9	5.7	15.6	3.4
	2001	33.1	7.2	40.4	8.6
United Arab Emirates Emirats arabes unis	1999	2.9	1.2	4.2	1.5
	2000	2.7	1.3	4.0	1.4
	2001	2.5	0.5	3.0	1.0
Uzbekistan Ouzbékistan	1999	112.8	20.9	133.7	5.5
	2000	133.8	17.0	150.8	6.1
	2001	106.7	16.8	123.5	4.9
Viet Nam Viet Nam	1999	1 017.7	407.1	1 424.8	18.5
	2000	1 247.6	419.5	1 667.2	21.3
	2001	822.1	575.7	1 397.8	17.7
Yemen Yémen	1999	177.3	278.9	456.2	26.2
	2000	159.6	104.0	263.6	14.6
	2001	99.8	208.3	308.1	16.5

82
Disbursements of bilateral and multilateral official development assistance and official aid to individual recipients *[cont.]*
Versements d'aide publique au développement et d'aide publique bilatérales et multilatérales aux bénéficiares *[suite]*

Region, country or area / Région, pays ou zone	Year / Année	Net disbursements (US $) - Versements nets ($E. –U.) Bilateral / Bilatérale (millions)	Multilateral[1] / Multilatérale[1] (millions)	Total (millions)	Per capita[2] / Par habitant[2]
Asia unspecified **Asie non specifiée**	**1999**	**650.0**	**113.1**	**763.1**	...
	2000	**431.4**	**153.2**	**584.5**	...
	2001	**329.3**	**103.9**	**433.3**	...
Europe **Europe**	**1999**	**6 395.5**	**4 029.6**	**10 425.1**	...
	2000	**5 337.6**	**4 458.3**	**9 795.9**	...
	2001	**4 270.9**	**4 223.5**	**8 494.4**	...
Albania Albanie	1999	254.1	224.8	478.9	153.8
	2000	141.9	176.5	318.4	102.3
	2001	149.8	116.7	266.5	85.3
Belarus Bélarus	1999	15.5	9.6	25.1	2.5
	2000	14.9	8.6	23.5	2.3
	2001	22.1	5.9	28.0	2.8
Bosnia and Herzegovina Bosnie-Herzégovine	1999	699.2	325.2	1 024.5	266.4
	2000	452.2	266.4	718.6	180.7
	2001	376.7	242.1	618.9	152.2
Bulgaria Bulgarie	1999	137.1	131.0	268.1	32.9
	2000	207.0	101.8	308.8	38.1
	2001	173.4	169.6	343.0	42.7
Croatia Croatie	1999	27.8	20.3	48.2	10.9
	2000	42.5	22.8	65.3	14.7
	2001	74.4	24.5	98.9	22.3
Cyprus Chypre	1999	4.9	50.3	55.3	71.2
	2000	11.9	45.8	57.6	73.6
	2001	21.5	31.6	53.1	67.2
Czech Republic République tchèque	1999	29.8	293.7	323.6	31.5
	2000	25.3	411.9	437.2	42.6
	2001	29.7	283.4	313.1	30.5
Estonia Estonie	1999	28.6	54.1	82.7	59.9
	2000	23.7	39.4	63.2	46.2
	2001	25.6	42.4	68.0	50.3
Gibraltar Gibraltar	1999	0.0	0.0	0.0	1.1
	2000	0.0	0.0	0.0	1.5
	2001	0.7	0.0	0.7	26.8
Hungary Hongrie	1999	29.2	219.0	248.2	24.7
	2000	53.5	197.1	250.5	25.0
	2001	54.5	362.1	416.6	41.8
Latvia Lettonie	1999	44.2	52.9	97.1	40.6
	2000	34.3	53.7	88.0	37.1
	2001	49.6	54.9	104.5	44.5
Lithuania Lituanie	1999	61.3	68.8	130.1	37.1
	2000	46.2	48.0	94.2	26.9
	2001	48.4	78.1	126.5	36.3
Malta Malte	1999	23.8	3.2	27.0	69.7
	2000	21.2	0.9	22.2	56.9
	2001	0.0	3.1	3.1	8.0
Poland Pologne	1999	580.1	605.3	1 185.4	30.7
	2000	552.5	843.0	1 395.5	36.1
	2001	486.9	477.8	964.7	25.0
Republic of Moldova République de Moldova	1999	51.2	51.0	102.2	23.8
	2000	61.5	51.2	112.7	26.3
	2001	78.8	34.4	113.2	26.5
Romania Roumanie	1999	122.5	251.3	373.9	16.6
	2000	158.0	271.5	429.5	19.1
	2001	142.1	504.7	646.8	28.8
Russian Federation Fédération de Russie	1999	1 599.9	224.9	1 824.9	12.5
	2000	1 344.5	121.4	1 465.9	10.1
	2001	906.6	151.6	1 058.2	7.3

82

Disbursements of bilateral and multilateral official development assistance and official aid to individual recipients *[cont.]*
Versements d'aide publique au développement et d'aide publique bilatérales et multilatérales aux bénéficiares *[suite]*

| Region, country or area
Région, pays ou zone | Year
Année | Net disbursements (US $) - Versements nets ($E. –U.) | | | |
		Bilateral Bilatérale (millions)	Multilateral[1] Multilatérale[1] (millions)	Total (millions)	Per capita[2] Par habitant[2]
Serbia and Montenegro Serbie-et-Monténégro	1999 2000 2001	670.4 592.9 631.1	3.1 541.3 669.8	673.5 1 134.3 1 300.9	63.7 107.5 123.4
Slovakia Slovaquie	1999 2000 2001	35.0 25.3 33.8	283.6 87.2 130.1	318.6 112.5 163.9	59.1 20.9 30.4
Slovenia Slovénie	1999 2000 2001	1.3 0.6 0.0	29.7 60.2 125.5	31.0 60.8 125.5	15.5 30.6 63.2
TFYR of Macedonia L'ex-R.y. Macédoine	1999 2000 2001	136.5 110.9 164.2	134.3 139.5 82.1	270.8 250.4 246.4	134.6 123.7 121.1
Turkey Turquie	1999 2000 2001	-66.4 97.5 -31.4	27.3 190.7 143.3	-39.1 288.2 111.8	-0.6 4.2 1.6
Ukraine Ukraine	1999 2000 2001	401.7 352.3 342.5	78.3 79.4 116.4	480.0 431.7 458.9	9.6 8.7 9.3
Yugoslavia, SFR[3] Yougoslavie, Rfs[3]	1999 2000 2001	161.6 223.4 91.3	272.6 81.3 47.0	434.2 304.7 138.3	... ...
Europe unspecified **Europe non specifiée**	**1999** **2000** **2001**	**1 346.2** **743.7** **398.6**	**615.1** **618.5** **326.3**	**1 961.3** **1 362.2** **724.9**	... ...
Oceania **Océanie**	**1999** **2000** **2001**	**1 371.8** **1 459.2** **1 376.7**	**51.5** **107.0** **82.2**	**1 423.3** **1 566.1** **1 458.9**	... ...
Cook Islands Iles Cook	1999 2000 2001	4.5 3.4 3.9	1.4 0.9 0.9	6.0 4.3 4.8	322.8 235.2 261.9
Fiji Fidji	1999 2000 2001	38.0 28.7 24.0	-3.6 0.2 1.8	34.5 28.8 25.7	42.8 35.5 31.3
French Polynesia Polynésie française	1999 2000 2001	353.2 400.2 383.7	-1.7 2.4 4.6	351.5 402.6 388.3	1 530.8 1 725.5 1 638.3
Kiribati Kiribati	1999 2000 2001	19.6 14.8 10.4	1.3 3.1 2.0	20.9 17.9 12.4	251.9 212.4 145.2
Marshall Islands Iles Marshall	1999 2000 2001	58.7 47.1 67.4	4.2 10.1 6.6	62.9 57.2 74.0	1 247.6 1 120.4 1 430.9
Micronesia (Fed. States) Micronésie (Etats féd. de)	1999 2000 2001	102.3 96.6 134.6	5.6 5.0 2.9	107.9 101.6 137.6	1 007.8 949.3 1 279.8
Nauru Nauru	1999 2000 2001	6.5 3.9 7.1	0.1 0.1 0.1	6.6 4.0 7.2	550.7 328.3 579.6
New Caledonia Nouvelle-Calédonie	1999 2000 2001	314.9 348.7 295.0	-0.4 1.4 -0.8	314.5 350.2 294.2	1 491.4 1 626.5 1 338.9
Niue Nioué	1999 2000 2001	3.9 3.0 3.2	0.2 0.2 0.1	4.1 3.2 3.3	2 023.5 1 586.5 1 665.8
Northern Mariana Islands Iles Mariannes du Nord	1999 2000	0.0 0.0	0.1 0.2	0.1 0.2	1.8 2.6

82

Disbursements of bilateral and multilateral official development assistance and official aid to individual recipients *[cont.]*
Versements d'aide publique au développement et d'aide publique bilatérales et multilatérales aux bénéficiares *[suite]*

Region, country or area Région, pays ou zone	Year Année	Net disbursements (US $) - Versements nets ($E. –U.)			
		Bilateral Bilatérale (millions)	Multilateral[1] Multilatérale[1] (millions)	Total (millions)	Per capita[2] Par habitant[2]
Palau Palaos	1999	28.7	0.1	28.8	1 530.4
	2000	38.9	0.2	39.0	2 031.2
	2001	33.9	0.2	34.1	1 734.5
Papua New Guinea Papouasie-Nvl-Guinée	1999	212.3	3.9	216.3	41.5
	2000	268.6	5.2	273.8	51.3
	2001	198.0	1.7	199.8	36.6
Samoa Samoa	1999	22.4	0.5	22.9	133.8
	2000	18.1	9.2	27.3	157.8
	2001	27.3	15.7	43.0	246.2
Solomon Islands Iles Salomon	1999	20.5	16.5	37.0	87.3
	2000	20.8	46.3	67.1	153.6
	2001	24.6	34.2	58.8	130.5
Tokelau Tokélaou	1999	4.6	0.1	4.7	3 051.7
	2000	3.4	0.1	3.5	2 302.2
	2001	3.8	0.1	3.9	2 537.6
Tonga Tonga	1999	15.2	5.9	21.2	211.2
	2000	14.8	4.0	18.8	186.6
	2001	20.6	-0.4	20.2	199.2
Tuvalu Tuvalu	1999	3.6	3.2	6.8	672.2
	2000	3.8	0.2	4.0	394.9
	2001	6.9	2.6	9.5	918.2
Vanuatu Vanuatu	1999	28.9	8.3	37.2	193.9
	2000	28.3	17.5	45.8	232.7
	2001	24.1	7.4	31.5	156.3
Wallis and Futuna Islands Iles Wallis et Futuna	1999	50.1	0.3	50.4	3 503.4
	2000	52.1	0.0	52.1	3 603.3
	2001	50.3	...	50.3	3 458.2
Oceania unspecified **Océanie non specifiée**	**1999**	**83.8**	**5.5**	**89.3**	...
	2000	**64.0**	**0.7**	**64.7**	...
	2001	**57.9**	**2.5**	**60.4**	...
Areas not specified **Zones non spécifiées**	**1999**	**6 839.8**	**1 150.5**	**7 990.2**	...
	2000	**8 118.3**	**1 105.4**	**9 223.7**	...
	2001	**7 705.0**	**1 366.4**	**9 071.4**	...

Source:

Organization for Economic Co-operation and Development (OECD), Paris, the OECD Development Assistance Committee database and "Geographical Distribution of Financial Flows to Aid Recipients, 1997 – 2001". Per capita calculated by the United Nations Statistics Division.

Source:

Organisation de coopération et de développement économiques (OCDE), Paris, la base de données du comité d'aide au développement de l'OCDE et "Répartition géographique des ressources financières allouées aux pays bénéficiaires de l'aide, 1997 – 2001". Les données par habitant ont été calculées par la Division de statistiques de l'ONU.

1 As reported by OECD/DAC, covers agencies of the United Nations family, the European Union, IDA and the concessional lending facilities of regional development banks. Excludes non-concessional flows (i.e., less than 25% grant elements).

2 Population based on estimates of mid-year population.

3 Data refer to Yugoslavia SFR, unspecified.

1 Communiqué par le Comité d'aide au développement de l'OCDE. Comprend les institutions et organismes du système des Nations Unies, l'Union européene, l'Association internationale de développement, et les mécanismes de prêt à des conditions privilégiées des banques régionales de développement. Les apports aux conditions du marché (élément de libéralité inférieur à 25) en sont exclus.

2 Population d'après des estimations de la population au milieu de l'année.

3 Les données concernent Yougoslavie, Rfs non spécifié.

83

Net official development assistance from DAC countries to developing countries and multilateral organizations
Net disbursements: millions of US dollars and as a percentage of gross national income (GNI)

Aide publique au développement nette de pays du CAD aux pays en développement et aux organisations multilatérales
Versements nets: millions de dollars E.-U. et en pourcentage du revenu national brut (RNB)

Country or area Pays ou zone	1997 US $ $ E.-U. (millions)	1997 As % of GNI En % du RNB	1998 US $ $ E.-U. (millions)	1998 As % of GNI En % du RNB	1999 US $ $ E.-U. (millions)	1999 As % of GNI En % du RNB	2000 US $ $ E.-U. (millions)	2000 As % of GNI En % du RNB	2001 US $ $ E.-U. (millions)	2001 As % of GNI En % du RNB	2002 US $ $ E.-U. (millions)	2002 As % of GNI En % du RNB
Total Total	48 497	0.22	52 084	0.23	53 268	0.22	53 733	0.22	52 337	0.22	*56 854	*0.23
Australia Australie	1 061	0.27	960	0.27	982	0.26	987	0.27	873	0.25	*962	*0.25
Austria Autriche	527	0.26	456	0.22	527	0.26	423	0.23	533	0.29	*475	*0.23
Belgium Belgique	764	0.31	883	0.35	760	0.30	820	0.36	867	0.37	*1 061	*0.42
Canada Canada	2 045	0.34	1 707	0.30	1 706	0.28	1 744	0.25	1 533	0.22	*2 013	*0.28
Denmark Danemark	1 637	0.97	1 704	0.99	1 733	1.01	1 664	1.06	1 634	1.03	*1 632	*0.96
Finland Finlande	379	0.32	396	0.31	416	0.33	371	0.31	389	0.32	*466	*0.35
France France	6 307	0.45	5 742	0.40	5 639	0.39	4 105	0.32	4 198	0.32	*5 182	*0.36
Germany Allemagne	5 857	0.28	5 581	0.26	5 515	0.26	5 030	0.27	4 990	0.27	*5 359	*0.27
Greece Grèce	173	0.14	179	0.15	194	0.15	226	0.20	202	0.17	*295	*0.22
Ireland Irlande	187	0.31	199	0.30	245	0.31	234	0.29	287	0.33	*398	*0.40
Italy Italie	1 266	0.11	2 278	0.20	1 806	0.15	1 376	0.13	1 627	0.15	*2 313	*0.20
Japan Japon	9 358	0.21	10 640	0.27	12 163	0.27	13 508	0.28	9 847	0.23	*9 041	*0.22
Luxembourg Luxembourg	95	0.55	112	0.65	119	0.66	123	0.71	141	0.82	*143	*0.78
Netherlands Pays-Bas	2 947	0.81	3 042	0.80	3 134	0.79	3 135	0.84	3 172	0.82	*3 377	*0.82
New Zealand Nouvelle-Zélande	154	0.26	130	0.27	134	0.27	113	0.25	112	0.25	*124	*0.23
Norway Norvège	1 306	0.84	1 321	0.89	1 370	0.88	1 264	0.76	1 346	0.80	*1 746	*0.91
Portugal Portugal	250	0.25	259	0.24	276	0.26	271	0.26	268	0.25	*323	*0.27
Spain Espagne	1 234	0.24	1 376	0.24	1 363	0.23	1 195	0.22	1 737	0.30	*1 608	*0.25
Sweden Suède	1 731	0.79	1 573	0.72	1 630	0.70	1 799	0.80	1 666	0.77	*1 754	*0.74
Switzerland Suisse	911	0.34	898	0.32	984	0.35	890	0.34	908	0.34	*933	*0.32
United Kingdom Royaume-Uni	3 433	0.26	3 864	0.27	3 426	0.24	4 501	0.32	4 579	0.32	*4 749	*0.30
United States Etats-Unis	6 878	0.09	8 786	0.10	9 145	0.10	9 955	0.10	11 429	0.11	*12 900	*0.12

Source:
Organisation for Economic Co-operation and Development (OECD), Paris, the OECD Development Assistance Committee database and the "Development Co-operation Report".

Source :
Organisation de Coopération et de Développement Economiques (OCDE), Paris, la base de données du Comité d'aide au développement de l'OCDE et "Coopération pour le développement".

84

Socio-economic development assistance through the United Nations system
Thousand US dollars

Assistance en matière de développement socioéconomique fournie par le système des Nations Unies
Milliers de dollars E.-U.

Development grant expenditures [1]   •   Aide au développement [1]

Region, country or area Région, pays ou zone	Year Année	UNDP PNUD Central resources Ressources centrales	Special funds Fonds gérés	UNFPA FNUAP	UNICEF	WFP PAM	Other UN system Autres organis. - ONU Regular budget Budget ordinaire	Extra-budgetary Extra-budgétaire	Total	Gov't self-supporting Auto-assistance gouverne-mentalle
Total	**2001**	**1 526 176**	**500 432**	**313 625**	**1 011 923**	**1 744 073**	**423 991**	**1 612 681**	**7 132 902**	**570 871**
Total	**2002**	**1 492 934**	**645 103**	**312 497**	**1 043 912**	**1 592 160**	**479 353**	**1 772 373**	**7 338 331**	**632 979**
Regional programmes	**2001**	**79 966**	**95 201**	**124 522**	**46 059**	**59 475**	**187 601**	**894 020**	**1 486 843**	**232 468**
Totaux régionaux	**2002**	**85 093**	**120 954**	**74 761**	**56 651**	**108 194**	**209 323**	**1 010 067**	**1 665 043**	**265 797**
Africa	2001	24 147	13 233	2 787	7 745	12 653	32 275	165 917	258 758	134 735
Afrique	2002	17 341	20 084	5 249	9 284	19 286	46 898	134 079	252 221	81 342
Asia and the Pacific	2001	12 692	13 615	8 900	4 211	41 376	26 560	47 978	155 332	20 291
Asie et le Pacifique	2002	11 852	13 944	8 172	5 170	85 410	25 881	60 082	210 510	25 427
Europe	2001	3 142	6 853	810	1 915	4 929	21 612	22 166	61 427	12 866
Europe	2002	3 013	11 089	1 536	3 138	3 149	20 957	41 199	84 081	22 084
Latin America	2001	10 291	7 509	1 503	1 665	517	21 108	24 580	67 173	4 942
Amérique latine	2002	11 501	10 128	2 484	1 575	309	28 344	26 417	80 758	3 906
Western Asia	2001	4 318	3 401	694	1 421	0	21 655	365 808	397 297	8 770
Asie occidentale	2002	5 306	5 917	928	1 627	40	28 394	404 512	446 724	21 141
Interregional	2001	15 954	34 982	0	29 102	0	8 979	145 290	234 307	50 730
Interrégional	2002	8 910	15 234	56 392	0	0	45 227	115 123	240 887	153
Global	2001	9 422	15 608	109 828	0	0	55 411	122 280	312 550	133
Global	2002	27 170	44 559	0	35 857	0	13 621	228 655	349 861	111 745
Country programmes	**2001**	**1 414 879**	**365 092**	**183 451**	**890 646**	**1 587 026**	**221 354**	**692 272**	**5 354 720**	**329 055**
Programmes, pays	**2002**	**1 371 916**	**474 705**	**233 435**	**842 446**	**1 406 968**	**255 027**	**727 951**	**5 312 446**	**352 531**
Afghanistan	2001	7 746	1 364	771	29 870	119 050	3 600	6 255	168 656	3 600
Afghanistan	2002	24 988	66 691	9 030	94 200	135 141	4 176	20 553	354 779	4 777
Albania	2001	3 196	730	449	5 866	1 663	416	1 353	13 673	508
Albanie	2002	3 775	1 591	369	3 068	2 378	374	2 148	13 702	1 201
Algeria	2001	1 193	68	1 168	1 252	6 738	1 318	973	12 709	96
Algérie	2002	1 964	308	1 257	1 283	7 499	1 912	697	14 920	159
Andorra	2001	0	0	0	0	0	92	0	92	0
Andorre	2002	0	0	0	0	0	27	0	27	0
Angola	2001	2 519	793	1 726	15 884	94 033	1 451	8 100	124 506	5 871
Angola	2002	3 363	3 927	2 439	25 410	108 557	2 712	12 362	158 770	7 338
Anguilla	2001	14	0	0	0	0	0	0	14	0
Anguilla	2002	29	0	0	0	0	0	0	29	0
Antigua and Barbuda	2001	49	66	0	0	0	419	0	534	0
Antigua-et-Barbuda	2002	2	52	0	0	0	123	0	177	0
Argentina	2001	135 634	1 289	6	3 367	0	1 927	8 798	151 022	5 450
Argentine	2002	57 519	1 355	301	1 906	0	877	4 494	66 452	1 140
Aruba	2001	175	0	0	0	0	90	0	265	0
Aruba	2002	77	0	0	0	0	100	0	177	0
Azerbaijan	2001	3 610	468	778	1 548	5 653	388	152	12 597	165
Azerbaïdjan	2002	4 089	1 261	749	1 544	3 794	422	55	11 914	54
Bahamas	2001	-15	-20	0	0	0	430	56	451	56
Bahamas	2002	24	77	0	0	0	508	0	609	0
Bahrain	2001	1 190	46	9	0	0	390	61	1 695	55
Bahreïn	2002	1 309	0	0	0	0	173	288	1 770	232
Bangladesh	2001	13 738	500	13 718	31 155	45 922	6 619	10 408	122 060	5 198
Bangladesh	2002	15 862	807	10 329	25 911	36 966	7 084	8 477	105 437	3 870
Barbados	2001	4	341	0	0	0	690	1	1 036	1
Barbade	2002	0	84	0	0	0	378	118	580	118
Belize	2001	4	2 247	0	996	204	643	23	4 116	3
Belize	2002	176	1 967	66	711	3	713	-34	3 601	0

84

Socio-economic development assistance through the United Nations system
Thousand US dollars [*cont.*]

Assistance en matière de développement socioéconomique fournie par le système des Nations Unies
Milliers de dollars E.-U. *[suite]*

Region, country or area Région, pays ou zone	Year Année	Development grant expenditures [1] • Aide au développement [1]					Other UN system Autres organis. - ONU			Gov't self-supporting Auto-assistance gouverne-mentalle
		UNDP PNUD								
		Central resources Ressources centrales	Special funds Fonds gérés	UNFPA FNUAP	UNICEF	WFP PAM	Regular budget Budget ordinaire	Extra-budgetary Extra-budgétaire	Total	
Benin	2001	1 262	577	1 867	3 613	1 287	1 044	1 888	11 538	1 549
Bénin	2002	3 535	876	3 579	5 684	1 666	2 315	833	18 488	383
Bermuda	2001	0	0	0	0	0	0	0	0	0
Bermudes	2002	0	0	0	0	0	0	0	0	0
Bhutan	2001	1 987	1 459	626	2 203	1 990	949	109	9 322	44
Bhoutan	2002	1 395	1 260	529	1 947	2 800	1 705	279	9 914	152
Bolivia	2001	23 929	1 711	2 722	7 532	6 001	2 315	5 330	49 539	1 269
Bolivie	2002	21 116	2 935	3 204	5 746	5 304	2 019	8 102	48 427	1 188
Botswana	2001	3 864	443	1 006	1 341	0	487	380	7 521	303
Botswana	2002	3 701	1 757	1 276	2 052	0	1 213	387	10 385	374
Brazil	2001	209 477	10 329	1 222	7 401	4 714	3 816	125 743	362 703	120 119
Brésil	2002	189 239	7 028	854	7 656	0	3 786	135 114	343 677	127 227
British Virgin Islands	2001	0	0	0	0	0	113	0	113	0
Iles Vierges britanniques	2002	0	0	0	0	0	0	0	0	0
Brunei Darussalam	2001	0	0	0	0	0	55	0	55	0
Brunéi Darussalam	2002	0	0	0	0	0	11	76	87	76
Bulgaria	2001	18 235	452	133	0	0	794	328	19 943	26
Bulgarie	2002	14 061	838	159	0	0	878	576	16 512	273
Burkina Faso	2001	4 434	1 108	1 415	7 996	1 805	1 575	3 289	21 621	2 653
Burkina Faso	2002	5 324	2 599	1 945	7 627	3 316	2 479	2 789	26 080	1 814
Burundi	2001	5 795	5 551	784	11 262	24 222	518	313	48 444	222
Burundi	2002	7 229	2 904	1 515	11 641	14 041	2 064	3 601	42 995	576
Cambodia	2001	6 973	13 231	3 054	13 206	25 206	2 134	8 738	72 541	2 036
Cambodge	2002	10 928	12 413	3 595	16 471	19 242	1 661	8 016	72 325	2 637
Cameroon	2001	2 438	150	1 336	4 357	1 086	1 668	1 283	12 318	906
Cameroun	2002	1 749	664	2 294	6 470	1 776	2 139	722	15 814	629
Cape Verde	2001	338	997	846	868	649	1 107	698	5 503	35
Cap-Vert	2002	420	453	710	1 025	2 311	1 385	654	6 958	440
Cayman Islands	2001	0	0	0	0	0	0	0	0	0
Iles Caïmanes	2002	31	0	0	0	0	0	0	31	0
Central African Rep.	2001	1 315	1 308	746	2 714	710	1 113	605	8 510	587
Rép. centrafricaine	2002	3 300	2 864	1 043	2 659	2 797	2 085	263	15 011	36
Chad	2001	3 478	34	933	4 107	10 339	1 800	2 063	22 755	1 990
Tchad	2002	4 193	392	2 690	5 022	4 212	2 933	1 182	20 624	854
Chile	2001	20 083	756	61	891	0	1 362	1 050	24 203	232
Chili	2002	18 334	1 106	173	811	0	1 237	991	22 651	353
China	2001	28 728	22 415	3 630	16 242	12 495	7 042	21 588	112 140	2 477
Chine	2002	35 028	15 372	4 570	16 104	14 493	5 704	21 074	112 346	3 922
China, Hong Kong SAR	2001	32	0	0	0	0	10	0	42	0
Chine, Hong Kong RAS	2002	-5	0	0	1 986	0	0	0	1 981	0
China, Macao SAR	2001	0	0	0	0	0	41	9	50	9
Chine, Macao RAS	2002	0	0	0	0	0	0	39	39	39
Colombia	2001	130 466	844	703	3 863	0	1 668	1 316	138 859	386
Colombie	2002	135 200	976	923	4 703	1 860	1 950	2 768	148 380	1 272
Comoros	2001	1 101	1 311	490	740	0	631	125	4 398	93
Comores	2002	775	1 681	626	758	0	1 731	87	5 658	61
Congo	2001	3 879	1 158	271	3 110	2 608	960	1 976	13 963	1 015
Congo	2002	2 947	1 839	708	3 885	2 390	1 514	1 215	14 498	520
Cook Islands	2001	83	90	50	0	0	332	0	555	0
Iles Cook	2002	42	6	93	0	0	248	0	389	0
Costa Rica	2001	4 172	1 818	237	1 070	0	1 017	1 834	10 148	446
Costa Rica	2002	4 097	851	352	573	0	829	887	7 588	171
Côte d'Ivoire	2001	2 820	845	991	4 605	3 988	1 191	3 252	17 692	988
Côte d'Ivoire	2002	2 729	712	2 043	5 070	4 066	1 594	2 461	18 676	860

84

Socio-economic development assistance through the United Nations system
Thousand US dollars [*cont.*]
Assistance en matière de développement socioéconomique fournie par le système des Nations Unies
Milliers de dollars E.-U. *[suite]*

Development grant expenditures [1] • Aide au développement [1]

Region, country or area / Région, pays ou zone	Year / Année	UNDP PNUD Central resources / Ressources centrales	Special funds / Fonds gérés	UNFPA FNUAP	UNICEF	WFP PAM	Other UN system / Autres organis. - ONU Regular budget / Budget ordinaire	Extra-budgetary / Extra-budgétaire	Total	Gov't self-supporting / Auto-assistance gouverne-mentalle
Cuba	2001	2 207	3 541	567	1 804	2 961	1 708	993	13 781	94
Cuba	2002	1 602	4 755	1 000	1 084	2 243	1 601	1 256	13 540	127
Cyprus	2001	12 019	41	0	0	0	338	121	12 520	10
Chypre	2002	10 673	621	0	0	0	145	198	11 638	41
Czech Republic	2001	138	294	0	0	0	306	201	939	174
République tchèque	2002	213	359	0	0	0	439	238	1 249	51
Dem. Rep. of the Congo	2001	5 242	242	1 740	35 844	31 571	2 320	23 303	100 262	19 490
Rép. dém. du Congo	2002	7 147	267	1 724	42 924	42 189	3 663	18 351	116 266	12 804
Djibouti	2001	568	201	539	893	7 685	839	43	10 768	2
Djibouti	2002	857	150	507	965	5 515	1 233	188	9 416	117
Dominica	2001	48	197	0	0	0	380	42	667	42
Dominique	2002	66	58	0	0	0	342	25	491	0
Dominican Republic	2001	8 309	765	979	4 886	2 924	1 078	1 213	20 154	797
Rép. dominicaine	2002	8 568	834	1 081	5 676	897	1 069	956	19 080	535
Ecuador	2001	30 235	1 004	953	3 011	2 275	1 073	2 215	40 767	314
Equateur	2002	36 848	2 250	1 463	4 330	2 130	2 387	1 582	50 990	266
Egypt	2001	19 374	3 679	3 169	6 963	1 548	3 371	2 973	41 078	1 031
Egypte	2002	13 265	1 884	1 099	4 065	4 218	2 687	3 683	30 901	1 814
El Salvador	2001	17 106	3 796	952	4 992	8 233	1 375	1 639	38 093	174
El Salvador	2002	21 357	2 821	1 048	4 961	2 555	1 038	1 530	35 310	53
Equatorial Guinea	2001	1 138	-85	522	646	0	454	12	2 686	12
Guinée équatoriale	2002	417	6	500	3 119	0	1 120	166	5 328	65
Eritrea	2001	6 374	6 775	2 705	10 841	46 046	550	1 894	75 184	325
Erythrée	2002	4 445	7 762	1 955	673	22 205	1 703	2 005	40 749	378
Ethiopia	2001	18 833	2 173	3 328	42 614	168 377	2 271	18 342	255 938	12 067
Ethiopie	2002	15 200	1 890	3 802	0	128 016	3 799	14 226	166 933	9 293
Fiji	2001	629	125	115	0	0	900	52	1 821	33
Fidji	2002	230	149	214	36 914	0	1 161	36	38 704	25
French Guiana	2001	0	0	0	0	0	106	0	106	0
Guyane française	2002	0	0	0	0	0	15	0	15	0
French Polynesia	2001	0	0	0	0	0	27	0	27	0
Polynésie française	2002	0	0	0	0	0	10	0	10	0
Gabon	2001	448	216	181	1 370	259	588	753	3 816	237
Gabon	2002	30	126	254	0	311	1 172	576	2 469	222
Gambia	2001	2 311	571	409	1 739	1 967	1 119	789	8 905	95
Gambie	2002	3 000	333	545	845	1 170	1 937	1 762	9 591	94
Ghana	2001	4 293	2 416	2 795	8 936	1 109	1 509	4 348	25 406	2 687
Ghana	2002	3 586	1 402	3 380	0	1 092	1 954	3 035	14 449	1 173
Greece	2001	0	0	0	0	0	133	619	753	619
Grèce	2002	0	0	0	0	0	141	591	732	591
Grenada	2001	60	93	0	0	0	204	0	357	0
Grenade	2002	51	330	0	0	0	171	4	556	4
Guadeloupe										
Guadeloupe	2002	0	0	0	0	0	0	0	0	0
Guam	2001	0	0	0	0	0	110	873	983	0
Guam	2002	0	0	0	0	0	10	0	10	0
Guatemala	2001	36 897	3 106	612	5 234	2 265	637	3 837	52 588	130
Guatemala	2002	46 890	5 621	13 455	0	5 702	1 329	4 943	77 940	433
Guinea	2001	1 492	837	799	7 278	8 995	1 433	949	21 783	734
Guinée	2002	1 604	890	486	3 747	10 986	2 118	1 748	21 579	1 102
Guinea-Bissau	2001	1 174	1 330	501	1 444	1 251	1 468	1 806	8 974	204
Guinée-Bissau	2002	3 349	2 405	696	6 224	2 252	1 838	578	17 342	30
Guyana	2001	1 906	874	66	859	0	563	2	4 270	0
Guyana	2002	1 298	373	193	2 510	0	453	225	5 052	166

84

Socio-economic development assistance through the United Nations system
Thousand US dollars [*cont.*]
Assistance en matière de développement socioéconomique fournie par le système des Nations Unies
Milliers de dollars E.-U. [*suite*]

Development grant expenditures [1] • Aide au développement [1]

Region, country or area / Région, pays ou zone	Year / Année	UNDP PNUD Central resources Ressources centrales	UNDP PNUD Special funds Fonds gérés	UNFPA FNUAP	UNICEF	WFP PAM	Other UN system Autres organis. - ONU Regular budget Budget ordinaire	Other UN system Autres organis. - ONU Extra-budgetary Extra-budgétaire	Total	Gov't self-supporting Auto-assistance gouverne-mentalle
Haiti	2001	3 016	2 476	2 872	3 806	5 165	1 322	1 677	20 333	57
Haïti	2002	3 833	2 447	3 286	961	5 208	1 332	782	17 848	93
Honduras	2001	38 530	8 897	1 345	2 300	7 296	454	3 555	62 376	575
Honduras	2002	48 484	5 137	2 026	0	4 164	742	2 896	63 449	832
Hungary	2001	389	19	0	0	0	548	137	1 093	0
Hongrie	2002	331	289	0	0	0	231	302	1 153	0
India	2001	20 568	17 002	11 090	103 221	21 546	7 744	27 011	208 181	22 468
Inde	2002	25 163	15 088	13 214	0	10 253	10 512	28 855	103 085	22 553
Indonesia	2001	9 542	8 641	6 777	10 284	15 830	6 412	6 189	63 676	3 792
Indonésie	2002	9 787	16 288	6 145	83 163	11 060	7 107	11 175	144 724	7 445
Iran (Islamic Rep. of)	2001	1 502	6 304	2 132	4 440	3 373	3 186	6 577	27 513	2 749
Iran (Rép. islamique d')	2002	1 370	2 346	2 378	18 767	2 722	2 593	4 039	34 214	926
Iraq	2001	1 121	95 368	255	7 499	26 587	1 881	158 964	291 674	1 278
Iraq	2002	1 094	147 725	364	4 039	31 753	1 132	153 531	339 638	9 522
Jamaica	2001	297	202	-11	1 235	0	1 338	37	3 099	0
Jamaïque	2002	358	270	281	0	0	1 477	232	2 618	70
Jordan	2001	2 984	937	846	1 454	1 579	1 783	2 214	11 796	45
Jordanie	2002	2 324	923	765	0	2 302	1 617	3 081	11 012	266
Kazakhstan	2001	1 639	4 190	676	14 309	0	821	723	22 358	322
Kazakhstan	2002	1 251	1 567	609	1 810	0	774	434	6 444	7
Kenya	2001	7 219	1 652	2 108	12 254	122 255	1 490	3 233	150 212	1 907
Kenya	2002	5 676	3 009	4 893	8 152	58 308	2 692	3 851	86 582	2 474
Kiribati	2001	18	129	11	0	0	285	0	443	0
Kiribati	2002	72	-86	65	14 718	0	393	4	15 166	0
Korea, Dem. P. R.	2001	1 051	464	722	6 663	230 859	2 600	4 200	246 558	2 242
Corée, R. p. dém. de	2002	854	976	1 053	8 760	102 735	2 470	4 554	121 400	1 622
Korea, Republic of	2001	370	27	0	0	0	781	187	1 365	187
Corée, République de	2002	545	24	0	0	0	1 072	440	2 081	211
Kuwait	2001	2 998	0	0	0	0	181	45	3 223	45
Koweït	2002	4 062	0	0	0	0	282	15	4 359	15
Kyrgyzstan	2001	1 429	1 105	455	2 453	0	362	577	6 380	490
Kirghizistan	2002	1 772	1 301	626	597	0	461	435	5 192	341
Lao People's Dem. Rep.	2001	3 930	1 815	1 869	4 571	2 623	1 651	1 361	17 820	648
Rép. dém. pop. lao	2002	3 458	4 400	1 792	1 212	3 490	1 733	2 392	18 476	270
Lebanon	2001	6 531	1 046	1 071	1 355	0	1 191	1 561	12 755	355
Liban	2002	5 948	1 353	594	0	0	1 675	2 224	11 794	537
Lesotho	2001	748	435	245	1 219	872	811	39	4 370	7
Lesotho	2002	1 164	1 043	449	1 172	10 362	756	235	15 180	117
Liberia	2001	3 233	12	823	5 303	12 721	1 341	926	24 359	814
Libéria	2002	983	-637	527	1 956	10 350	2 603	722	16 504	714
Libyan Arab Jamah.	2001	3 219	326	0	0	0	1 102	3 318	7 966	3 111
Jamah. arabe libyenne	2002	3 850	1 722	0	3 545	0	461	3 714	13 291	3 480
Madagascar	2001	6 519	3 358	1 769	6 290	5 058	1 749	2 915	27 658	298
Madagascar	2002	6 176	1 868	1 740	0	4 757	1 550	4 913	21 005	3 147
Malawi	2001	3 943	3 753	2 482	11 207	7 050	1 727	570	30 732	309
Malawi	2002	4 278	2 649	2 943	7 773	50 948	2 137	1 408	72 135	811
Malaysia	2001	1 098	3 327	143	678	0	1 187	202	6 636	59
Malaisie	2002	807	3 107	149	16 677	0	995	182	21 917	4
Maldives	2001	1 046	575	733	654	0	828	177	4 013	177
Maldives	2002	941	281	503	381	0	1 483	-5	3 584	-5
Mali	2001	5 016	3 326	2 074	9 305	4 135	1 397	3 359	28 611	2 176
Mali	2002	6 456	4 162	2 227	688	5 556	2 436	1 875	23 401	726
Malta	2001	0	10	0	0	0	213	26	249	15
Malte	2002	0	117	0	11 135	0	263	151	11 666	134

84

Socio-economic development assistance through the United Nations system
Thousand US dollars [*cont.*]
Assistance en matière de développement socioéconomique fournie par le système des Nations Unies
Milliers de dollars E.-U. [*suite*]

Development grant expenditures [1]   •   Aide au développement [1]

Region, country or area Région, pays ou zone	Year Année	UNDP PNUD Central resources Ressources centrales	Special funds Fonds gérés	UNFPA FNUAP	UNICEF	WFP PAM	Other UN system Autres organis. - ONU Regular budget Budget ordinaire	Extra- budgetary Extra- budgétaire	Total	Gov't self- supporting Auto- assistance gouverne- mentalle
Marshall Islands	2001	93	0	50	0	0	201	-7	338	0
Iles Marshall	2002	67	30	52	0	0	91	4	244	0
Martinique Martinique	2002	0	0	0	0	0	0	0	0	0
Mauritania	2001	1 682	1 993	1 292	2 437	3 472	911	786	12 572	225
Mauritanie	2002	1 270	109	2 031	0	5 806	2 209	1 207	12 632	934
Mauritius	2001	202	246	193	561	0	659	493	2 354	351
Maurice	2002	292	279	157	2 856	0	886	138	4 607	134
Mexico	2001	3 189	2 373	1 560	2 513	0	2 520	2 353	14 508	1 607
Mexique	2002	6 305	2 651	4 672	463	0	1 905	3 210	19 207	2 670
Micronesia (Fed. States)	2001	55	387	66	0	0	304	43	854	39
Micronésie (Etats féd. de)	2002	113	326	86	2 137	0	118	14	2 794	0
Mongolia	2001	3 256	1 165	2 166	2 443	0	3 093	1 992	14 114	318
Mongolie	2002	2 478	1 647	1 986	0	0	3 019	876	10 006	312
Montserrat	2001	128	6	0	0	0	0	15	148	15
Montserrat	2002	120	87	0	1 649	0	0	0	1 856	0
Morocco	2001	2 908	686	827	2 295	2 045	2 927	3 533	15 221	428
Maroc	2002	3 712	2 093	931	0	1 338	2 042	4 256	14 372	519
Mozambique	2001	23 891	7 864	5 784	23 070	17 889	1 315	12 642	92 454	1 605
Mozambique	2002	20 343	3 817	5 867	2 086	25 491	2 768	8 747	69 120	2 015
Myanmar	2001	15 949	0	1 464	14 534	1 337	3 335	2 733	39 353	1 534
Myanmar	2002	6 959	0	1 448	0	1 484	4 255	2 129	16 274	1 466
Namibia	2001	515	87	550	1 941	1 094	1 666	881	6 734	612
Namibie	2002	694	317	1 183	14 219	1 271	2 013	1 048	20 746	828
Nauru	2001	0	0	0	0	0	126	0	126	0
Nauru	2002	0	0	0	0	0	0	0	0	0
Nepal	2001	9 365	1 501	4 888	13 140	16 543	3 260	5 166	53 864	3 442
Népal	2002	9 042	2 523	3 303	0	12 851	4 618	5 504	37 841	4 408
Netherlands Antilles	2001	163	0	0	0	0	152	0	315	0
Antilles néerlandaises	2002	59	0	0	0	0	31	0	90	0
New Caledonia	2001	0	0	0	0	0	20	0	20	0
Nouvelle-Calédonie	2002	0	0	0	0	0	0	0	0	0
Nicaragua	2001	5 148	4 271	2 433	3 175	11 736	1 115	2 636	30 514	702
Nicaragua	2002	7 002	4 132	2 031	0	5 125	998	2 320	21 609	379
Niger	2001	5 439	1 321	2 341	8 184	6 468	2 148	2 989	28 891	1 613
Niger	2002	3 852	2 176	2 866	3 245	4 168	2 928	2 769	22 005	1 270
Nigeria	2001	9 799	3 841	5 628	46 319	0	3 280	18 691	87 557	16 995
Nigéria	2002	15 976	3 107	6 402	8 929	0	3 392	21 763	59 569	19 786
Niue	2001	37	51	0	0	0	59	11	158	0
Nioué	2002	147	22	0	32 725	0	134	0	33 028	0
Oman	2001	0	0	27	521	0	687	547	1 782	517
Oman	2002	0	7	36	0	0	766	1 187	1 995	699
Pakistan	2001	10 229	5 173	3 277	33 070	10 390	3 769	8 320	74 228	6 182
Pakistan	2002	13 854	2 158	4 148	2 645	9 674	3 676	12 745	48 900	10 118
Palau	2001	0	0	0	0	0	175	0	175	0
Palaos	2002	0	0	0	35 241	0	121	0	35 362	0
Panama	2001	117 768	553	399	1 533	0	628	529	121 410	529
Panama	2002	130 332	598	484	0	0	952	584	132 950	510
Papua New Guinea	2001	2 317	377	543	1 112	0	1 282	330	5 961	263
Papouasie-Nvl-Guinée	2002	3 056	229	775	953	0	1 517	219	6 749	208
Paraguay	2001	28 320	939	649	1 047	0	539	148	31 642	4
Paraguay	2002	19 209	2 021	617	1 169	0	909	49	23 974	1
Peru	2001	43 761	3 250	1 590	4 360	3 153	2 090	4 873	63 077	3 510
Pérou	2002	65 330	3 454	6 393	1 255	4 754	2 191	9 059	92 436	7 437

84

Socio-economic development assistance through the United Nations system
Thousand US dollars [*cont.*]

Assistance en matière de développement socioéconomique fournie par le système des Nations Unies
Milliers de dollars E.-U. [*suite*]

Development grant expenditures [1] • Aide au développement [1]

Region, country or area / Région, pays ou zone	Year / Année	UNDP PNUD Central resources Ressources centrales	Special funds Fonds gérés	UNFPA FNUAP	UNICEF	WFP PAM	Other UN system Autres organis. - ONU Regular budget Budget ordinaire	Extra-budgetary Extra-budgétaire	Total	Gov't self-supporting Auto-assistance gouverne-mentalle
Philippines	2001	4 681	1 683	2 915	8 995	0	4 084	4 615	26 973	1 437
Philippines	2002	5 528	2 239	3 334	5 407	0	1 547	4 160	22 215	1 761
Poland	2001	1 371	740	109	0	0	565	23	2 807	20
Pologne	2002	1 206	950	77	6 363	0	805	333	9 733	35
Portugal	2001	0	0	0	0	0	118	26	143	24
Portugal	2002	0	0	0	0	0	30	62	92	56
Qatar	2001	0	72	0	0	0	216	353	640	1
Qatar	2002	0	71	0	0	0	32	381	484	78
Réunion	2001	0	0	0	0	0	80	0	80	0
Réunion	2002	0	0	0	2 239	0	37	0	2 276	0
Romania	2001	1 451	129	483	1 824	0	1 143	684	5 714	-10
Roumanie	2002	1 426	217	406	0	0	768	1 157	3 975	287
Rwanda	2001	3 173	8 649	1 556	5 792	20 806	1 487	1 037	42 501	-428
Rwanda	2002	2 660	3 817	1 723	-1	15 028	2 132	1 927	27 284	1 111
Saint Helena	2001	385	0	0	0	0	46	0	431	0
Sainte-Hélène	2002	459	0	0	0	0	15	0	474	0
Saint Kitts and Nevis	2001	0	78	0	0	0	311	0	389	0
Saint-Kitts-et-Nevis	2002	0	66	0	0	0	117	4	187	4
Saint Lucia	2001	0	52	0	0	0	289	26	367	25
Sainte-Lucie	2002	54	14	51	0	0	132	0	251	0
St. Vincent-Grenadines	2001	13	4	0	0	0	260	0	277	0
St. Vincent-Grenadines	2002	16	0	0	0	0	156	0	172	0
Samoa	2001	382	88	50	0	0	771	6	1 297	0
Samoa	2002	273	129	31	0	0	1 067	108	1 609	0
Sao Tome and Principe	2001	427	56	581	946	499	484	99	3 092	58
Sao Tomé-et-Principe	2002	295	520	282	0	457	1 092	46	2 692	27
Saudi Arabia	2001	3 591	0	4	0	0	565	14 071	18 231	14 040
Arabie saoudite	2002	5 513	5	25	644	0	577	10 440	17 205	10 313
Senegal	2001	2 593	1 918	2 191	4 768	2 470	1 553	3 912	19 405	131
Sénégal	2002	3 712	2 199	2 180	0	3 869	2 241	5 073	19 273	558
Serbia and Montenegro	2001	15 902	4 095	1 563	11 883	68 126	132	8 950	110 651	1 953
Serbie-et-Monténégro	2002	11 648	5 616	2 009	8 763	13 779	168	10 261	52 242	1 443
Seychelles	2001	27	18	59	0	0	715	42	861	42
Seychelles	2002	16	23	50	0	0	1 079	27	1 195	-1
Sierra Leone	2001	3 542	190	500	11 198	16 714	1 462	5 170	38 776	1 685
Sierra Leone	2002	3 030	1 976	1 061	12 958	21 598	2 163	5 134	47 918	849
Singapore	2001	0	0	0	0	0	75	123	198	123
Singapour	2002	0	0	0	0	0	91	207	298	207
Solomon Islands	2001	1 092	153	77	0	0	820	65	2 208	72
Iles Salomon	2002	462	62	77	0	0	515	134	1 249	130
Somalia	2001	11 920	1 684	147	18 572	6 202	2 388	7 010	47 924	1 983
Somalie	2002	9 875	2 258	618	22 778	8 441	3 255	8 212	55 438	2 808
South Africa	2001	1 978	186	1 576	4 390	0	2 631	1 451	12 212	622
Afrique du Sud	2002	1 938	-121	1 493	4 272	0	3 179	1 848	12 609	858
Sri Lanka	2001	3 534	590	1 385	5 086	3 548	3 586	1 813	19 542	201
Sri Lanka	2002	3 481	1 565	1 233	7 567	7 764	4 388	2 959	28 958	403
Sudan	2001	2 652	1 392	2 467	22 401	118 808	5 945	9 634	163 299	4 858
Soudan	2002	2 983	3 080	2 048	19 835	100 045	4 810	12 286	145 088	7 586
Suriname	2001	106	6 334	39	0	0	371	265	7 114	1
Suriname	2002	209	403	159	-14	0	391	250	1 398	33
Swaziland	2001	540	183	201	778	0	1 080	110	2 892	110
Swaziland	2002	340	500	629	2 647	2 999	1 682	384	9 181	384
Syrian Arab Republic	2001	1 135	1 608	2 491	940	2 416	2 787	4 361	15 738	2 367
Rép. arabe syrienne	2002	2 390	1 199	3 969	928	2 068	1 810	5 928	18 292	4 446

84

Socio-economic development assistance through the United Nations system
Thousand US dollars [*cont.*]
Assistance en matière de développement socioéconomique fournie par le système des Nations Unies
Milliers de dollars E.-U. [*suite*]

Development grant expenditures [1] • Aide au développement [1]

Region, country or area / Région, pays ou zone	Year / Année	UNDP PNUD Central resources / Ressources centrales	Special funds / Fonds gérés	UNFPA FNUAP	UNICEF	WFP PAM	Other UN system / Autres organis. - ONU Regular budget / Budget ordinaire	Extra-budgetary / Extra-budgétaire	Total	Gov't self-supporting / Auto-assistance gouvernementalle
Tajikistan	2001	4 737	614	631	1 773	37 869	427	1 335	47 386	553
Tadjikistan	2002	5 958	848	720	3 701	40 107	248	469	52 052	64
Thailand	2001	1 271	389	707	4 109	0	2 692	1 391	10 558	-10
Thaïlande	2002	794	643	292	3 920	0	4 449	1 687	11 785	535
TFYR of Macedonia	2001	1 132	409	0	6 352	829	500	3 069	12 290	799
L'ex-R.y. Macédoine	2002	2 405	319	0	2 753	43	704	3 079	9 303	631
Timor-Leste	2001	3 794	586	281	5 763	6 488	571	2 339	19 822	781
Timor-Leste	2002	6 280	1 469	1 422	2 330	954	770	1 903	15 128	723
Togo	2001	2 424	97	1 239	3 533	0	1 276	2 361	10 929	593
Togo	2002	1 983	804	1 102	0	0	1 655	387	5 931	24
Tokelau	2001	98	0	0	0	0	2	0	100	0
Tokélaou	2002	94	2	0	0	0	62	0	159	0
Tonga	2001	11	31	24	0	0	741	0	807	0
Tonga	2002	117	117	83	0	0	708	15	1 040	0
Trinidad and Tobago	2001	113	407	0	0	0	473	94	1 087	0
Trinité-et-Tobago	2002	316	417	33	0	0	613	1 455	2 834	1 363
Tunisia	2001	493	465	765	1 058	0	1 377	2 696	6 855	736
Tunisie	2002	499	1 167	389	3 227	0	1 116	4 968	11 365	196
Turkey	2001	2 981	859	724	3 631	0	759	1 830	10 784	608
Turquie	2002	3 967	766	891	1 297	0	918	965	8 804	214
Turkmenistan	2001	1 056	202	693	1 262	1 973	141	67	5 395	67
Turkménistan	2002	554	241	636	0	0	77	13	1 521	13
Turks and Caicos Islands	2001	380	0	0	0	0	12	0	392	0
Iles Turques et Caïques	2002	335	0	0	0	0	44	0	379	0
Tuvalu	2001	157	0	0	0	0	58	0	215	0
Tuvalu	2002	93	5	101	11 023	0	50	0	11 270	0
Uganda	2001	4 436	4 746	4 831	14 858	27 344	2 200	5 669	64 084	2 954
Ouganda	2002	4 313	4 858	5 374	0	25 432	3 278	5 100	48 355	2 183
United Arab Emirates	2001	3 879	0	0	0	0	256	611	4 746	611
Emirats arabes unis	2002	2 509	1	4	0	0	134	375	3 023	375
United Rep. of Tanzania	2001	6 667	3 785	4 095	15 085	55 201	2 173	5 282	92 290	2 723
Rép.-Unie de Tanzanie	2002	7 319	3 457	7 484	0	31 687	3 363	6 268	59 579	2 915
Uruguay	2001	21 172	748	134	942	0	767	475	24 238	219
Uruguay	2002	14 437	390	90	5 187	0	1 149	435	21 689	128
Uzbekistan	2001	13 370	342	719	1 899	0	522	353	17 205	77
Ouzbékistan	2002	6 349	429	571	0	0	352	781	8 481	159
Vanuatu	2001	136	14	71	0	0	502	13	736	4
Vanuatu	2002	68	3	86	1 052	0	847	122	2 178	28
Venezuela	2001	32 677	1 735	640	1 842	10	1 131	1 610	39 644	399
Venezuela	2002	19 687	709	647	9 069	0	1 544	1 455	33 110	560
Viet Nam	2001	12 208	6 564	3 903	10 653	193	6 000	4 196	43 718	973
Viet Nam	2002	8 224	4 172	2 873	4 504	0	4 086	5 434	29 292	2 352
Yemen	2001	7 760	1 731	4 002	6 714	4 597	3 000	4 482	32 286	2 944
Yémen	2002	10 776	1 778	2 786	6 716	6 005	2 548	2 634	33 243	1 228
Zambia	2001	4 030	1 316	1 078	9 747	12 788	2 077	1 843	32 878	437
Zambie	2002	3 700	-20	2 434	12 011	45 375	2 422	5 512	71 434	1 521
Zimbabwe	2001	2 485	2 001	1 623	4 694	1 240	2 012	4 110	18 164	2 002
Zimbabwe	2002	3 136	3 255	1 045	6 238	89 291	2 503	4 131	109 599	1 815
Other countries	2001	25 788	8 713	2 224	8 345	92 418	12 301	37 692	187 481	22 332
Autres pays	2002	30 215	17 221	347	60 516	63 127	11 155	28 539	211 120	10 610
Not elsewhere classified	**2001**	**5 543**	**31 426**	**3 428**	**66 873**	**5 154**	**2 736**	**-11 302**	**103 858**	**-12 983**
Non-classé ailleurs	**2002**	**5 710**	**32 222**	**3 954**	**84 299**	**13 871**	**3 849**	**5 817**	**149 721**	**4 040**

84

Socio-economic development assistance through the United Nations system
Thousand US dollars [*cont.*]

Assistance en matière de développement socioéconomique fournie par le système des Nations Unies

Milliers de dollars E.-U. [*suite*]

Source:
United Nations, "Operational activities of the United Nations for international development cooperation, Report of the Secretary-General, Addendum, Comprehensive statistical data on operational activities for development for the year 2001" (E/2003/57) and "Operational activities of the United Nations for international development cooperation, Report of the Secretary-General, Addendum, Comprehensive statistical data on operational activities for development for the year 2002" (Advance version).

1   The following abbreviations have been used in the table:
UNDP: United Nations Development Programme
UNFPA: United Nations Population Fund
UNICEF: United Nations Children's Fund
WFP: World Food Programme.

Source:
Nations Unies, "Activités opérationnelles du système des Nations Unies au service de la coopération internationale pour le développement, Rapport du Secrétaire général, Additif, Données statistiques globales sur les activités opérationnelles au service du développement pour 2001" (E/2003/57) et "Activités opérationnelles du système des Nations Unies au service de la coopération internationale pour le développement, Rapport du Secrétaire général, Additif, Données statistiques globales sur les activités opérationnelles au service du développement pour 2002" (version préliminaire).

1   Les abbréviations ci-après ont été utilisées dans le tableau :
PNUD : Programme des Nations Unies pour le développement
FNUAP : Fonds des Nations Unies pour la population
UNICEF : Fonds des Nations Unies pour l'enfance
PAM : Programme alimentaire mondial.

Technical notes, tables 82-84

Table 82 presents estimates of flows of financial resources to individual recipients either directly (bilaterally) or through multilateral institutions (multilaterally).

The multilateral institutions include the World Bank Group, regional banks, financial institutions of the European Union and a number of United Nations institutions, programmes and trust funds.

The main source of data is the Development Assistance Committee of OECD to which member countries reported data on their flow of resources to developing countries and territories and countries and territories in transition, and multilateral institutions.

Additional information on definitions, methods and sources can be found in OECD's *Geographical Distribution of Financial Flows to Aid Recipients* [21] and <www.oecd.org>.

Table 83 presents the development assistance expenditures of donor countries. This table includes donors' contributions to multilateral agencies, so the overall totals differ from those in table 82, which include disbursements by multilateral agencies.

Table 84 includes data on expenditures on operational activities for development undertaken by the organizations of the United Nations system. Operational activities encompass, in general, those activities of a development cooperation character that seek to mobilize or increase the potential and capacity of countries to promote economic and social development and welfare, including the transfer of resources to developing countries or regions in a tangible or intangible form. The table also covers, as a memo item, expenditures on activities of an emergency character, the purpose of which is immediate relief in crisis situations, such as assistance to refugees, humanitarian work and activities in respect of disasters.

Expenditures on operational activities for development are financed from contributions from governments and other official and non-official sources to a variety of funding channels in the United Nations system. These include United Nations funds and programmes such as contributions to the United Nations Development Programme, contributions to funds administered by the United Nations Development Programme, and regular (assessed) and other extrabudgetary contributions to specialized agencies.

Data are taken from the 2001 and 2002 reports of the Secretary-General to the General Assembly on operational activities for development [28].

Notes techniques, tableaux 82 à 84

Le *Tableau 82* présente les estimations des flux de ressources financières mises à la disposition des pays soit directement (aide bilatérale) soit par l'intermédiaire d'institutions multilatérales (aide multilatérale).

Les institutions multilatérales comprennent le Groupe de la Banque mondiale, les banques régionales, les institutions financières de l'Union européenne et un certain nombre d'institutions, de programmes et de fonds d'affectation spéciale des Nations Unies.

La principale source de données est le Comité d'aide au développement de l'OCDE, auquel les pays membres ont communiqué des données sur les flux de ressources qu'ils mettent à la disposition des pays et territoires en développement et en transition et des institutions multilatérales.

Pour plus de renseignements sur les définitions, méthodes et sources, se reporter à la publication de l'OCDE, la *Répartition géographique des ressources financières de aux pays bénéficiaires de l'Aide* [21] et <www.oecd.org>.

Le *Tableau 83* présente les dépenses que les pays donateurs consacrent à l'aide publique au développement (APD). Ces chiffres incluent les contributions des donateurs à des agences multilatérales, de sorte que les totaux diffèrent de ceux du tableau 82, qui incluent les dépenses des agences multilatérales.

Le *Tableau 84* présente des données sur les dépenses consacrées à des activités opérationnelles pour le développement par les organisations du système des Nations Unies. Par "activités opérationnelles", on entend en général les activités ayant trait à la coopération au développement, qui visent à mobiliser ou à accroître les potentialités et aptitudes que présentent les pays pour promouvoir le développement et le bien-être économiques et sociaux, y compris les transferts de ressources vers les pays ou régions en développement sous forme tangible ou non. Ce tableau indique également, pour mémoire, les dépenses liées à des activités revêtant un caractère d'urgence, qui ont pour but d'apporter un secours immédiat dans les situations de crise, telles que l'aide aux réfugiés, l'assistance humanitaire et les secours en cas de catastrophe.

Les dépenses consacrées aux activités opérationnelles pour le développement sont financées au moyen de contributions que les gouvernements et d'autres sources officielles et non officielles apportent à divers organes de financement, tels que fonds et programmes du système des Nations Unies. On peut citer notamment les contributions au Programme des Nations Unies pour le développement, les contributions aux fonds gérés par le Programme des Nations Unies pour le développement, les contributions régulières (budgétaires) et les contributions extrabudgétaires aux institutions spécialisées.

Les données sont extraites des rapports annuels de 2001 et de 2002 du Secrétaire général à la session de l'Assemblée générale sur les activités opérationnelles pour le développement [28].

Annex I

Country and area nomenclature, regional and other groupings

A. *Changes in country or area names*
In the periods covered by the statistics in the *Statistical Yearbook*, the following changes in designation have taken place:

Brunei Darussalam was formerly listed as Brunei;
Burkina Faso was formerly listed as Upper Volta;
Cambodia was formerly listed as Democratic Kampuchea;
Cameroon was formerly listed as United Republic of Cameroon;
Côte d'Ivoire was formerly listed as Ivory Coast;
Czech Republic, Slovakia: Since 1 January 1993, data for the Czech Republic and Slovakia, where available, are shown separately under the appropriate country name. For periods prior to 1 January 1993, where no separate data are available for the Czech Republic and Slovakia, unless otherwise indicated, data for the former Czechoslovakia are shown under the country name "former Czechoslovakia";
Democratic Republic of the Congo was formerly listed as Zaire;
Germany: Through the accession of the German Democratic Republic to the Federal Republic of Germany with effect from 3 October 1990, the two German States have united to form one sovereign State. As from the date of unification, the Federal Republic of Germany acts in the United Nations under the designation "Germany". All data shown which pertain to Germany prior to 3 October 1990 are indicated separately for the Federal Republic of Germany and the former German Democratic Republic based on their respective territories at the time indicated;
Hong Kong Special Administrative Region of China: Pursuant to a Joint Declaration signed on 19 December 1984, the United Kingdom restored Hong Kong to the People's Republic of China with effect from 1 July 1997; the People's Republic of China resumed the exercise of sovereignty over the territory with effect from that date;
Macao Special Administrative Region of China: Pursuant to the joint declaration signed on 13 April 1987, Portugal restored Macao to the People's Republic of China with effect from 20 December 1999; the People's Republic of China resumed the exercise of sovereignty over the territory with effect from that date;
Myanmar was formerly listed as Burma;
Palau was formerly listed as Pacific Islands and includes data for Federated States of Micronesia, Marshall Islands and Northern Mariana Islands;
Saint Kitts and Nevis was formerly listed as Saint Christopher and Nevis;
~~Serbia~~ and Montenegro: As of 4 February 2003, ~~the name~~ of the "Federal Republic of Yugoslavia" ~~was~~ changed to "Serbia and Montenegro". ~~Unless otherw~~ise indicated, data provided for Yugosla~~via prior to~~ January 1992 refer to the Socialist Federal

Annexe I

Nomenclature des pays ou zones, groupements régionaux et autres groupements

A. *Changements dans le nom des pays ou zones*
Au cours des périodes sur lesquelles portent les statistiques, dans l'*Annuaire Statistique* les changements de désignation suivants ont eu lieu:

Le *Brunéi Darussalam* apparaissait antérieurement sous le nom de Brunéi;
Le *Burkina Faso* apparaissait antérieurement sous le nom de la Haute-Volta;
Le *Cambodge* apparaissait antérieurement sous le nom de la Kampuchea démocratique;
Le *Cameroun* apparaissait antérieurement sous le nom de République-Unie du Cameroun;
République tchèque, Slovaquie: Depuis le 1er janvier 1993, les données relatives à la République tchèque, et à la Slovaquie, lorsqu'elles sont disponibles, sont présentées séparément sous le nom de chacun des pays. En ce qui concerne la période précédant le 1er janvier 1993, pour laquelle on ne possède pas de données séparées pour les deux Républiques, les données relatives à l'ex-Tchécoslovaquie sont, sauf indication contraire, présentées sous le titre "l'ex-Tchécoslovaquie";
La *République démocratique du Congo* apparaissait antérieurement sous le nom de Zaïre;
Allemagne: En vertu de l'adhésion de la République démocratique allemande à la République fédérale d'Allemagne, prenant effet le 3 octobre 1990, les deux Etats allemands se sont unis pour former un seul Etat souverain. A compter de la date de l'unification, la République fédérale d'Allemagne est désigné à l'ONU sous le nom d'"Allemagne". Toutes les données se rapportant à l'Allemagne avant le 3 octobre figurent dans deux rubriques séparées basées sur les territoires respectifs de la République fédérale d'Allemagne et l'ex-République démocratique allemande selon la période indiquée;
Hong Kong, région administrative spéciale de Chine: Conformément à une Déclaration commune signée le 19 décembre 1984, le Royaume-Uni a rétrocédé Hong Kong à la République populaire de Chine, avec effet au 1er juillet 1997; la souveraineté de la République populaire de Chine s'exerce à nouveau sur le territoire à compter de cette date;
Macao, région administrative spéciale de Chine: Conformément à une Déclaration commune signée le 13 avril 1987, le Portugal a rétrocédé Macao à la République populaire de Chine, avec effet au 20 décembre 1999; la souveraineté de la République populaire de Chine s'exerce à nouveau sur le territoire à compter de cette date;
Le *Myanmar* apparaissait antérieurement sous le nom de Birmanie;
Les *Palaos* apparaissait antérieurement sous le nom de Iles du Pacifique y compris les données pour les Etats fédérés de Micronésie, les îles Marshall et îles Mariannes du Nord;
Saint-Kitts-et-Nevis apparaissait antérieurement sous le nom de Saint-Christophe-et-Nevis;
Serbie-et-Monténégro: A compter de février 2003, la "République fédérale de Yougoslavie" ayant changé de nom officiel, est devenue la "Serbie-et-Monténégro". Sauf indication contraire, les données fournies pour la Yougoslavie avant le 1er janvier 1992 se rapportent à la République fédé-

Republic of Yugoslavia which was composed of six republics. Data provided for Yugoslavia after that date refer to the Federal Republic of Yugoslavia which is composed of two republics (Serbia and Montenegro);

Timor-Leste: Formerly East Timor;

Former *USSR*: In 1991, the Union of Soviet Socialist Republics formally dissolved into fifteen independent countries (Armenia, Azerbaijan, Belarus, Estonia, Georgia, Kazakhstan, Kyrgyzstan, Latvia, Lithuania, Republic of Moldova, Russian Federation, Tajikistan, Turkmenistan, Ukraine and Uzbekistan). Whenever possible, data are shown for the individual countries. Otherwise, data are shown for the former USSR;

Yemen: On 22 May 1990 Democratic Yemen and Yemen merged to form a single State. Since that date they have been represented as one Member with the name 'Yemen'.

Data relating to the People's Republic of China generally include those for Taiwan Province in the field of statistics relating to population, area, land use, agriculture, natural resources and natural conditions such as climate. In other fields of statistics, they do not include Taiwan Province unless otherwise stated.

B.   *Regional groupings*

The scheme of regional groupings given below presents seven regions based mainly on continents. Five of the seven continental regions are further subdivided into 21 regions that are so drawn as to obtain greater homogeneity in sizes of population, demographic circumstances and accuracy of demographic statistics. This nomenclature is widely used in international statistics and is followed to the greatest extent possible in the present *Yearbook* in order to promote consistency and facilitate comparability and analysis. However, it is by no means universal in international statistical compilation, even at the level of continental regions, and variations in international statistical sources and methods dictate many unavoidable differences in particular fields in the present *Yearbook*. General differences are indicated in the footnotes to the classification presented below. More detailed differences are given in the footnotes and technical notes to individual tables.

Neither is there international standardization in the use of the terms "developed" and "developing" countries, areas or regions. These terms are used in the present publication to refer to regional groupings generally considered as "developed": these are Europe and the former USSR, the United States of America and Canada in Northern America, and Australia, Japan and New Zealand in Asia and Oceania. These designations are intended for statistical convenience and do not necessarily express a judgement about the stage reached by a particular country or area in the development process. Differences from this usage are indicated in the notes to individual tables.

rative socialiste de Yougoslavie, qui était composée de six républiques. Les données fournies pour la Yougoslavie après cette date se rapportent à la République fédérative de Yougoslavie, qui est composée de deux républiques (Serbie et Monténégro);

Timor-Leste: Ex Timor oriental;

L'ex-*URSS*: En 1991, l'Union des républiques socialistes soviétiques s'est séparé en 15 pays distincts (Arménie, Azerbaïdjan, Bélarus, Estonie, Géorgie, Kazakhstan, Kirghizistan, Lettonie, Lituanie, République de Moldova, Fédération de Russie, Tadjikistan, Turkménistan, Ukraine, Ouzbékistan). Les données sont présentées pour ces pays pris séparément quand cela est possible. Autrement, les données sont présentées pour l'ex-URSS;

Yémen: Le Yémen et le Yémen démocratique ont fusionné le 22 mai 1990 pour ne plus former qu'un seul Etat, qui est depuis lors représenté comme tel à l'Organisation, sous le nom 'Yémen'.

Les données relatives à la République populaire de Chine comprennent en général les données relatives à la province de Taïwan lorsqu'il s'agit de statistiques concernant la population, la superficie, l'utilisation des terres, l'agriculture, les ressources naturelles, et les conditions naturelles telles que le climat, etc. Dans les statistiques relatives à d'autres domaines, la province de Taïwan n'est pas comprise, sauf indication contraire.

B.   *Groupements régionaux*

Le système de groupements régionaux présenté ci-dessous comporte sept régions basés principalement sur les continents. Cinq des sept régions continentales sont elles-mêmes subdivisées, formant ainsi 21 régions délimitées de manière à obtenir une homogénéité accrue dans les effectifs de population, les situations démographiques et la précision des statistiques démographiques. Cette nomenclature est couramment utilisée aux fins des statistiques internationales et a été appliquée autant qu'il a été possible dans le présent *Annuaire* en vue de renforcer la cohérence et de faciliter la comparaison et l'analyse. Son utilisation pour l'établissement des statistiques internationales n'est cependant rien moins qu'universelle, même au niveau des régions continentales, et les variations que présentent les sources et méthodes statistiques internationales entraînent inévitablement de nombreuses différences dans certains domaines de cet *Annuaire*. Les différences d'ordre général sont indiquées dans les notes figurant au bas de la classification présentée ci-dessous. Les différences plus spécifiques sont mentionnées dans les notes techniques et notes infrapaginales accompagnant les divers tableaux.

L'application des expressions "développés" et "en développement" aux pays, zones ou régions n'est pas non plus normalisée à l'échelle internationale. Ces expressions sont utilisées dans la présente publication en référence aux groupements régionaux généralement considérés comme "développés", à savoir l'Europe et l'ex-URSS, les Etats-Unis d'Amérique et le Canada en Amérique septentrionale, et l'Australie, le Japon et la Nouvelle-Zélande dans la région de l'Asie et du Pacifique. Ces appellations sont employées pour des raisons de commodité statistique et n'expriment pas nécessairement un jugement sur le stade de développement atteint par tel ou tel pays ou zone. Les cas différant de cet usage sont signalés dans les notes accompagnant les tableaux concernés.

Africa

Eastern Africa

Burundi
Comoros
Djibouti
Eritrea
Ethiopia
Kenya
Madagascar
Malawi
Mauritius
Mozambique

Réunion
Rwanda
Seychelles
Somalia
Uganda
United Republic of
  Tanzania
Zambia
Zimbabwe

Middle Africa

Angola
Cameroon
Central African Republic
Chad
Congo

Democratic Republic of
  the Congo
Equatorial Guinea
Gabon
Sao Tome and Principe

Northern Africa

Algeria
Egypt
Libyan Arab Jamahiriya
Morocco

Sudan
Tunisia
Western Sahara

Southern Africa

Botswana
Lesotho
Namibia

South Africa
Swaziland

Western Africa

Benin
Burkina Faso
Cape Verde
Côte d'Ivoire
Gambia
Ghana
Guinea
Guinea-Bissau
Liberia

Mali
Mauritania
Niger
Nigeria
Saint Helena
Senegal
Sierra Leone
Togo

Americas

Latin America and the Caribbean
Caribbean

Anguilla
Antigua and Barbuda
Aruba
Bahamas
Barbados
British Virgin Islands
Cayman Islands
Cuba
~~inica
~~epublic

Jamaica
Martinique
Montserrat
Netherlands Antilles
Puerto Rico
Saint Kitts and Nevis
Saint Lucia
Saint Vincent and the
  Grenadines
Trinidad and Tobago
Turks and Caicos Islands
United States Virgin Islands

Afrique

Afrique orientale

Burundi
Comores
Djibouti
Erythrée
Ethiopie
Kenya
Madagascar
Malawi
Maurice
Mozambique

Ouganda
République-Unie de
  Tanzanie
Réunion
Rwanda
Seychelles
Somalie
Zambie
Zimbabwe

Afrique centrale

Angola
Cameroun
Congo
Gabon
Guinée équatoriale

République centrafricaine
République démocratique
  du Congo
Sao Tomé-et-Principe
Tchad

Afrique septentrionale

Algérie
Egypte
Jamahiriya arabe libyenne
Maroc

Sahara occidental
Soudan
Tunisie

Afrique australe

Afrique du Sud
Botswana
Lesotho

Namibie
Swaziland

Afrique occidentale

Bénin
Burkina Faso
Cap-Vert
Côte d'Ivoire
Gambie
Ghana
Guinée
Guinée-Bissau
Libéria

Mali
Mauritanie
Niger
Nigéria
Sainte-Hélène
Sénégal
Sierra Leone
Togo

Amériques

Amérique latine et Caraïbes
Caraïbes

Anguilla
Antigua-et-Barbuda
Antilles néerlandaises
Aruba
Bahamas
Barbade
Cuba
Dominique
Grenade
Guadeloupe
Haïti
Iles Caïmanes

Iles Turques et Caïques
Iles Vierges américaines
Iles Vierges britanniques
Jamaïque
Martinique
Montserrat
Porto Rico
République dominicaine
Sainte-Lucie
Saint-Kitts-et-Nevis
Saint-Vincent-et-les Grenadines
Trinité-et-Tobago

Central America

Belize	Honduras
Costa Rica	Mexico
El Salvador	Nicaragua
Guatemala	Panama

South America

Argentina	French Guiana
Bolivia	Guyana
Brazil	Paraguay
Chile	Peru
Colombia	Suriname
Ecuador	Uruguay
Falkland Islands (Malvinas)	Venezuela

Northern America [a]

Bermuda	Saint Pierre and Miquelon
Canada	United States of America
Greenland	

Asia

Eastern Asia

China	Democratic People's
China, Hong Kong Special	Republic of Korea
Administrative Region	Japan
China, Macao Special	Mongolia
Administrative Region	Republic of Korea

South-central Asia

Afghanistan	Maldives
Bangladesh	Nepal
Bhutan	Pakistan
India	Sri Lanka
Iran (Islamic Republic of)	Tajikistan
Kazakhstan	Turkmenistan
Kyrgyzstan	Uzbekistan

South-eastern Asia

Brunei Darussalam	Myanmar
Cambodia	Philippines
Indonesia	Singapore
Lao People's Democratic	Thailand
Republic	Timor-Leste
Malaysia	Viet Nam

Western Asia

Armenia	Occupied Palestinian
Azerbaijan	Territory
Bahrain	Oman
Cyprus	Qatar
Georgia	Saudi Arabia
Iraq	Syrian Arab Republic
Israel	Turkey
Jordan	United Arab Emirates
Kuwait	Yemen
Lebanon	

Amérique centrale

Belize	Honduras
Costa Rica	Mexique
El Salvador	Nicaragua
Guatemala	Panama

Amérique du Sud

Argentine	Guyane française
Bolivie	Iles Falkland (Malvinas)
Brésil	Paraguay
Chili	Pérou
Colombie	Suriname
Equateur	Uruguay
Guyana	Venezuela

Amérique septentrionale [a]

Bermudes	Groenland
Canada	Saint-Pierre-et-Miquelon
Etats-Unis d'Amérique	

Asie

Asie orientale

Chine	Japon
Chine, Hong Kong, région	Mongolie
administrative spéciale	République de Corée
Chine, Macao, région	République populaire
administrative spéciale	démocratique de Corée

Asie centrale et du Sud

Afghanistan	Maldives
Bangladesh	Népal
Bhoutan	Ouzbékistan
Inde	Pakistan
Iran (République	Sri Lanka
islamique d')	Tadjikistan
Kazakhstan	Turkménistan
Kirghizistan	

Asie du Sud-Est

Brunéi Darussalam	République démocratique
Cambodge	populaire lao
Indonésie	Singapour
Malaisie	Thaïlande
Myanmar	Timor-Leste
Philippines	Viet Nam

Asie occidentale

Arabie saoudite	Jordanie
Arménie	Koweït
Azerbaïdjan	Liban
Bahreïn	Oman
Chypre	Qatar
Emirats arabes unis	République arabe syrienne
Géorgie	Territoire palestinien occupé
Iraq	Turquie
Israël	Yémen

Europe

Eastern Europe

Belarus	Republic of Moldova
Bulgaria	Romania
Czech Republic	Russian Federation
Hungary	Slovakia
Poland	Ukraine

Northern Europe

Channel Islands	Latvia
Denmark	Lithuania
Estonia	Norway
Faeroe Islands	Svalbard and Jan Mayen
Finland	Islands
Iceland	Sweden
Ireland	United Kingdom
Isle of Man	

Southern Europe

Albania	Malta
Andorra	Portugal
Bosnia and Herzegovina	San Marino
Croatia	Serbia and Montenegro
Gibraltar	Slovenia
Greece	Spain
Holy See	The former Yugoslav Re-
Italy	public of Macedonia

Western Europe

Austria	Luxembourg
Belgium	Monaco
France	Netherlands
Germany	Switzerland
Liechtenstein	

Oceania

Australia and New Zealand

Australia	Norfolk Island
New Zealand	

Melanesia

Fiji	Solomon Islands
New Caledonia	Vanuatu
Papua New Guinea	

Micronesia-Polynesia
Micronesia

Guam	Nauru
Kiribati	Northern Mariana
Marshall Islands	Islands
Micronesia (Federated States of)	Palau

Polynesia

moa	Samoa
s	Tokelau
ynesia	Tonga

Europe

Europe orientale

Bélarus	République de Moldova
Bulgarie	République tchèque
Fédération de Russie	Roumanie
Hongrie	Slovaquie
Pologne	Ukraine

Europe septentrionale

Danemark	Irlande
Estonie	Islande
Finlande	Lettonie
Ile de Man	Lituanie
Iles Anglo-Normandes	Norvège
Iles Féroé	Royaume-Uni
Iles Svalbard et Jan Mayen	Suède

Europe méridionale

Albanie	Grèce
Andorre	Italie
Bosnie-Herzégovine	Malte
Croatie	Portugal
Espagne	Saint-Marin
Ex-République yougoslave de Macédoine	Saint-Siège
	Serbie-et-Monténégro
Gibraltar	Slovénie

Europe occidentale

Allemagne	Luxembourg
Autriche	Monaco
Belgique	Pays-Bas
France	Suisse
Liechtenstein	

Océanie

Australie et Nouvelle-Zélande

Australie	Nouvelle-Zélande
Ile Norfolk	

Mélanésie

Fidji	Papouasie-Nouvelle-Guinée
Iles Salomon	Vanuatu
Nouvelle-Calédonie	

Micronésie-Polynésie
Micronésie

Guam	Kiribati
Iles Mariannes septentrionales	Micronésie (Etats fédérés de)
	Nauru
Iles Marshall	Palaos

Polynésie

Iles Cook	Samoa
Iles Wallis-et-Futuna	Samoa américaines
Nioué	Tokélaou

Niue	Tuvalu	Pitcairn	Tonga
Pitcairn	Wallis and Futuna Islands	Polynésie française	Tuvalu

<table>
<tr><td>

C. Other groupings

Following is a list of other groupings and their compositions presented in the *Yearbook*. These groupings are organized mainly around economic and trade interests in regional associations.

Andean Common Market (ANCOM)
  Bolivia
  Colombia
  Ecuador
  Peru
  Venezuela

Asia-Pacific Economic Cooperation (APEC)
  Australia
  Brunei Darussalam
  Canada
  Chile
  China
  China, Hong Kong Special Administrative Region
  Indonesia
  Japan
  Malaysia
  Mexico
  New Zealand
  Papua New Guinea
  Peru
  Philippines
  Republic of Korea
  Russian Federation
  Singapore
  Taiwan Province of China
  Thailand
  United States of America
  Viet Nam

Association of Southeast Asian Nations (ASEAN)
  Brunei Darussalam
  Cambodia
  Indonesia
  Lao People's Democratic Republic
  Malaysia
  Myanmar
  Philippines
  Singapore
  Thailand
  Viet Nam

Caribbean Community and Common Market (CARICOM)
  Antigua and Barbuda
  Bahamas (member of the Community only)
  Barbados
  Belize
  Dominica
  Grenada
  Guyana
  Haiti

</td><td>

C. Autres groupements

On trouvera ci-après une liste des autres groupements et de leur composition, présentée dans l'*Annuaire*. Ces groupements correspondent essentiellement à des intérêts économiques et commerciaux d'après les associations régionales.

Marché commun andin (ANCOM)
  Bolivie
  Colombie
  Equateur
  Pérou
  Vénézuela

Coopération économique Asie-Pacifique (CEAP)
  Australie
  Brunéi Darussalam
  Canada
  Chili
  Chine
  Chine, Hong Kong, région administrative spéciale
  Etats-Unis d'Amérique
  Fédération de Russie
  Indonésie
  Japon
  Malaisie
  Mexique
  Nouvelle-Zélande
  Papouasie-Nouvelle-Guinée
  Pérou
  Philippines
  Province chinoise de Taiwan
  République de Corée
  Singapour
  Thaïlande
  Viet Nam

Association des nations de l'Asie du Sud-Est (ANASE)
  Brunéi Darussalam
  Cambodge
  Indonésie
  Malaisie
  Myanmar
  Philippines
  République démocratique populaire lao
  Singapour
  Thaïlande
  Viet Nam

Communauté des Caraïbes et Marché commun des Caraïbes (CARICOM)
  Antigua-et-Barbuda
  Bahamas (membre de la communauté seulement)
  Barbade
  Belize
  Dominique
  Grenade
  Guyana
  Haïti

</td></tr>
</table>

Jamaica	Jamaïque
Montserrat	Montserrat
Saint Kitts and Nevis	Sainte-Lucie
Saint Lucia	Saint-Kitts-et-Nevis
Saint Vincent and the Grenadines	Saint-Vincent-et-les Grenadines
Suriname	Suriname
Trinidad and Tobago	Trinité-et-Tobago

Central American Common Market (CACM)	*Marché commun centraméricain* (MCC)
Costa Rica	Costa Rica
El Salvador	El Salvador
Guatemala	Guatemala
Honduras	Honduras
Nicaragua	Nicaragua

Common Market for Eastern and Southern Africa (COMESA)	*Marché commun de l'Afrique de l'Est et de l'Afrique australe* (COMESA)
Angola	Angola
Burundi	Burundi
Comoros	Comores
Democratic Republic of the Congo	Djibouti
Djibouti	Egypte
Egypt	Erythrée
Eritrea	Ethiopie
Ethiopia	Kenya
Kenya	Madagascar
Madagascar	Malawi
Malawi	Maurice
Mauritius	Namibie
Namibia	Ouganda
Rwanda	République démocratique du Congo
Seychelles	Rwanda
Sudan	Seychelles
Swaziland	Soudan
Uganda	Swaziland
Zambia	Zambie
Zimbabwe	Zimbabwe

Commonwealth of Independent States (CIS)	*Communauté d'Etats indépendants* (CEI)
Armenia	Arménie
Azerbaijan	Azerbaïdjan
Belarus	Bélarus
Georgia	Fédération de Russie
Kazakhstan	Géorgie
Kyrgyzstan	Kazakhstan
Republic of Moldova	Kirghizistan
Russian Federation	Ouzbékistan
Tajikistan	République de Moldova
Turkmenistan	Tadjikistan
Ukraine	Turkménistan
Uzbekistan	Ukraine

Economic and Monetary Community of Central Africa (EMCCA)	*Communauté économique et monétaire de l'Afrique centrale* (CEMAC)
Cameroon	Cameroun
Central African Republic	Congo
Chad	Gabon
Congo	Guinée équatoriale
ial Guinea	République centrafricaine
	Tchad

Economic Community of West African States (ECOWAS)
- Benin
- Burkina Faso
- Cape Verde
- Côte d'Ivoire
- Gambia
- Ghana
- Guinea
- Guinea-Bissau
- Liberia
- Mali
- Niger
- Nigeria
- Senegal
- Sierra Leone
- Togo

European Free Trade Association (EFTA)
- Iceland
- Liechtenstein
- Norway
- Switzerland

European Union (EU)
- Austria
- Belgium
- Denmark
- Finland
- France
- Germany
- Greece
- Ireland
- Italy
- Luxembourg
- Netherlands
- Portugal
- Spain
- Sweden
- United Kingdom

Latin American Integration Association (LAIA)
- Argentina
- Bolivia
- Brazil
- Chile
- Colombia
- Cuba
- Ecuador
- Mexico
- Paraguay
- Peru
- Uruguay
- Venezuela

Least developed countries (LDCs) [b]
- Afghanistan
- Angola
- Bangladesh
- Benin
- Bhutan
- Burkina Faso

Communauté économique des Etats de l'Afrique de l'Ouest (CEDEAO)
- Bénin
- Burkina Faso
- Cap-Vert
- Côte d'Ivoire
- Gambie
- Ghana
- Guinée
- Guinée-Bissau
- Libéria
- Mali
- Niger
- Nigéria
- Sénégal
- Sierra Leone
- Togo

Association européenne de libre-échange (AELE)
- Islande
- Liechtenstein
- Norvège
- Suisse

Union européenne (UE)
- Allemagne
- Autriche
- Belgique
- Danemark
- Espagne
- Finlande
- France
- Grèce
- Irlande
- Italie
- Luxembourg
- Pays-Bas
- Portugal
- Royaume-Uni
- Suède

Association latino-américaine pour l'intégration (ALAI)
- Argentine
- Bolivie
- Brésil
- Chili
- Colombie
- Cuba
- Equateur
- Mexique
- Paraguay
- Pérou
- Uruguay
- Venezuela

Pays les moins avancés (PMA) [b]
- Afghanistan
- Angola
- Bangladesh
- Bénin
- Bhoutan
- Burkina Faso

Burundi	Burundi
Cambodia	Cambodge
Cape Verde	Cap-Vert
Central African Republic	Comores
Chad	Djibouti
Comoros	Erythrée
Democratic Republic of the Congo	Ethiopie
Djibouti	Gambie
Equatorial Guinea	Guinée
Eritrea	Guinée équatoriale
Ethiopia	Guinée-Bissau
Gambia	Haïti
Guinea	Iles Salomon
Guinea-Bissau	Kiribati
Haiti	Lesotho
Kiribati	Libéria
Lao People's Democratic Republic	Madagascar
Lesotho	Malawi
Liberia	Maldives
Madagascar	Mali
Malawi	Mauritanie
Maldives	Mozambique
Mali	Myanmar
Mauritania	Népal
Mozambique	Niger
Myanmar	Ouganda
Nepal	République centrafricaine
Niger	République démocratique du Congo
Rwanda	République démocratique populaire lao
Samoa	République-Unie de Tanzanie
Sao Tome and Principe	Rwanda
Senegal	Samoa
Sierra Leone	Sao Tomé-et-Principe
Solomon Islands	Sénégal
Somalia	Sierra Leone
Sudan	Somalie
Togo	Soudan
Tuvalu	Tchad
Uganda	Togo
United Republic of Tanzania	Tuvalu
Vanuatu	Vanuatu
Yemen	Yémen
Zambia	Zambie

Mercado Común Sudamericano (MERCOSUR)
Argentina
Brazil
Paraguay
Uruguay

North American Free Trade Agreement (NAFTA)
Canada
Mexico
United States of America

Marché commun sud-américain (Mercosur)
Argentine
Brésil
Paraguay
Uruguay

Accord de libre-échange nord-américain (ALENA)
Canada
Etats-Unis d'Amérique
Mexique

*for Economic Cooperation and
)ECD)*

ı

Organisation de coopération et de développement économiques (OCDE)
Allemagne
Australie
Autriche

Canada	Belgique
Czech Republic	Canada
Denmark	Danemark
Finland	Espagne
France	Etats-Unis d'Amérique
Germany	Finlande
Greece	France
Hungary	Grèce
Iceland	Hongrie
Ireland	Irlande
Italy	Islande
Japan	Italie
Luxembourg	Japon
Mexico	Luxembourg
Netherlands	Mexique
New Zealand	Norvège
Norway	Nouvelle-Zélande
Poland	Pays-Bas
Portugal	Pologne
Republic of Korea	Portugal
Slovakia	République de Corée
Spain	République tchèque
Sweden	Royaume-Uni
Switzerland	Slovaquie
Turkey	Suède
United Kingdom	Suisse
United States of America	Turquie

Organization of Petroleum Exporting Countries (OPEC)
Algeria
Indonesia
Iran (Islamic Republic of)
Iraq
Kuwait
Libyan Arab Jamahiriya
Nigeria
Qatar
Saudi Arabia
United Arab Emirates
Venezuela

Organisation des pays exportateurs de pétrole (OPEP)
Algérie
Arabie saoudite
Emirats arabes unis
Indonésie
Iran (République islamique d')
Iraq
Jamahiriya arabe libyenne
Koweït
Nigéria
Qatar
Venezuela

Southern African Customs Union (SACU)
Botswana
Lesotho
Namibia
South Africa
Swaziland

Union douanière d'Afrique australe
Afrique du Sud
Botswana
Lesotho
Namibie
Swaziland

---

a   The continent of North America comprises Northern
     America, Caribbean and Central America.
b   As determined by the General Assembly in its resolution
     49/133.

---

a   Le continent de l'Amérique du Nord comprend l'Amérique
     septentrionale, les Caraïbes et l'Amérique centrale.
b   Comme déterminé par l'Assemblée générale dans sa résolu-
     tion 49/133.

Annex II

Conversion coefficients and factors

The metric system of weights and measures is employed in the *Statistical Yearbook*. In this system, the relationship between units of volume and capacity is: 1 litre = 1 cubic decimetre (dm^3) exactly (as decided by the 12th International Conference of Weights and Measures, New Delhi, November 1964).

Section A shows the equivalents of the basic metric, British imperial and United States units of measurements. According to an agreement between the national standards institutions of English-speaking nations, the British and United States units of length, area and volume are now identical, and based on the yard = 0.9144 metre exactly. The weight measures in both systems are based on the pound = 0.45359237 kilogram exactly (Weights and Measures Act 1963 (London), and *Federal Register* announcement of 1 July 1959: *Refinement of Values for the Yard and Pound* (Washington D.C.)).

Section B shows various derived or conventional conversion coefficients and equivalents.

Section C shows other conversion coefficients or factors which have been utilized in the compilation of certain tables in the *Statistical Yearbook*. Some of these are only of an approximate character and have been employed solely to obtain a reasonable measure of international comparability in the tables.

For a comprehensive survey of international and national systems of weights and measures and of units weights for a large number of commodities in different countries, see *World Weights and Measures* [61].

Annexe II

Coefficients et facteurs de conversion

L'*Annuaire statistique* utilise le système métrique pour les poids et mesures. La relation entre unités métriques de volume et de capacité est: 1 litre = 1 décimètre cube (dm^3) exactement (comme fut décidé à la Conférence internationale des poids et mesures, New Delhi, novembre 1964).

La section A fournit les équivalents principaux des systèmes de mesure métrique, britannique et américain. Suivant un accord entre les institutions de normalisation nationales des pays de langue anglaise, les mesures britanniques et américaines de longueur, superficie et volume sont désormais identiques, et sont basées sur le yard = 0:9144 mètre exactement. Les mesures de poids se rapportent, dans les deux systèmes, à la livre (pound) = 0.45359237 kilogramme exactement ("Weights and Measures Act 1963" (Londres), et "Federal Register Announcement of 1 July 1959: Refinement of Values for the Yard and Pound" (Washington, D.C.)).

La section B fournit divers coefficients et facteurs de conversion conventionnels ou dérivés.

La section C fournit d'autres coefficients ou facteurs de conversion utilisés dans l'élaboration de certains tableaux de l'*Annuaire statistique*. D'aucuns ne sont que des approximations et n'ont été utilisés que pour obtenir un degré raisonnable de comparabilité sur le plan international.

Pour une étude d'ensemble des systèmes internationaux et nationaux de poids et mesures, et d'unités de poids pour un grand nombre de produits dans différents pays, voir "*World Weights and Measures*" [61].

A. Equivalents of metric, British imperial and United States units of measure

A. Equivalents des unités métriques, britanniques et des Etats-Unis

Metric units Unités métriques	British imperial and US equivalents Equivalents en mesures britanniques et des Etats-Unis	British imperial and US units Unités britanniques et des Etats-Unis	Metric equivalents Equivalents en mesures métriques	
Length — Longeur				
1 centimetre – centimètre (cm)	0.3937008 inch	1 inch	2.540	cm
1 metre – mètre (m)	3.280840 feet	1 foot	30.480	cm
	1.093613 yard	1 yard	0.9144	m
1 kilometre – kilomètre (km)	0.6213712 mile	1 mile	1609.344	m
	0.5399568 int. naut. mile	1 international nautical mile	1852.000	m
Area — Superficie				
1 square centimetre – (cm²)	0.1550003 square inch	1 square inch	6.45160	cm²
1 square metre – (m²)	10.763910 square feet	1 square foot	9.290304	dm²
	1.195990 square yards	1 square yard	0.83612736	m²
1 hectare – (ha)	2.471054 acres	1 acre	0.4046856	ha
1 square kilometre – (km²)	0.3861022 square mile	1 square mile	2.589988	km²
Volume				
cubic centimetre – (cm³)	0.06102374 cubic inch	1 cubic inch	16.38706	cm³
1 cubic metre – (m³)	35.31467 cubic feet	1 cubic foot	28.316847	dm³
	1.307951 cubic yards	1 cubic yard	0.76455486	m³
Capacity — Capacité				
1 litre (l)	0.8798766 imp. quart	1 British imperial quart	1.136523	l
	1.056688 U.S. liq. quart	1 U.S. liquid quart	0.9463529	l
	0.908083 U.S. dry quart	1 U.S. dry quart	1.1012208	l
1 hectolitre (hl)	21.99692 imp. gallons	1 imperial gallon	4.546092	l
	26.417200 U.S. gallons	1 U.S. gallon	3.785412	l
	2.749614 imp. bushels	1 imperial bushel	36.368735	l
	2.837760 U.S. bushels	1 U.S. bushel	35.239067	l
Weight or mass — Poids				
1 kilogram (kg)	35.27396 av. ounces	1 av. ounce	28.349523	g
	32.15075 troy ounces	1 troy ounce	31.10348	g
	2.204623 av. pounds	1 av. pound	453.59237	g
		1 cental (100 lb.)	45.359237	kg
		1 hundredweight (112 lb.)	50.802345	kg
1 ton – tonne (t)	1.1023113 short tons	1 short ton (2 000 lb.)	0.9071847	t
	0.9842065 long tons	1 long ton (2 240 lb.)	1.0160469	t

B. Various conventional or derived coefficients

Railway and air transport
1 passenger-mile = 1.609344 passenger kilometre

1 short ton-mile = 1.459972 ton-kilometre
1 long ton-mile = 1.635169 ton-kilometre

Ship tonnage
1 registered ton (100 cubic feet) = 2.83m3

1 British shipping ton (42 cubic feet) = 1.19m^3
1 U.S. shipping ton (40 cubic feet) = 1.13m^3
1 deadweight ton (dwt ton = long ton) = 1.016047 metric ton

Electric energy
1 Kilowatt (kW) = 1.34102 British horsepower (hp)
1Kilowatt(kW)=1.35962 metric horsepower

C. Other coefficients or conversion factors employed in *Statistical Yearbook* tables

Roundwood
Equivalent in solid volume without bark.

Sugar
1 metric ton raw sugar = 0.9 metric ton refined sugar.
For the United States and its possessions:
1 metric ton refined sugar = 1.07 metric tons raw sugar.

B. Divers coefficients conventionnels ou dérivés

Transport ferroviaire et aérien
1 passager-kilomètre = 0.621371 passager-mile

1 tonne-kilomètre = 0.684945 tonne courte-mile
1tonne-kilomètre=0.611558 tonne forte-mile

Tonnage de navire
1 mètre cube (m^3) = 0.353 tonne de jauge

1 mètre cube   = 0.841 British shipping ton
                   =0.885 US shipping ton
1 tonne métrique   = 0.984 dwt ton

Energie électrique
1 cheval vapeur britannique (hp) = 0.7457 kW
1 cheval vapeur métrique (cv) = 0.735499 kW

C. Autres coefficients ou facteurs de conversion utilisés dans les tableaux de l'*Annuaire statistique*

Bois rond
Equivalences en volume solide sans écorce.

Sucre
1 tonne métrique de sucre brut = 0.9 tonne métrique de sucre raffiné.
Pour les Etats-Unis et leurs possessions:
1 tonne métrique de sucre raffiné = 1.07 t.m. de sucre brut.

Annex III

Tables added and omitted

A.   Tables added

The present issue of the *Statistical Yearbook* (2001) includes the following three tables which were not presented in the previous issue:

Table 11: Selected indicators of life expectancy, childbearing and mortality;

Table 68: Water supply and sanitation coverage;

Table 69: Threatened species.

B.   The following five tables which were presented in previous issues are not presented in the present issue. They will be updated in future issues of the *Yearbook* when new data become available:

Table 9: Population in urban and rural areas, rates of growth and largest urban agglomeration population (46th issue);

Table 10: Public expenditure on education: total and current (45th issue);

Table 10: Illiterate population by sex (47th issue);

Table 11: HIV/AIDS epidemic (47th issue);

Table 17: Television and radio receivers (46th issue).

Annexe III

Tableaux ajoutés et supprimés

A.   Tableaux ajoutés

Dans ce numéro de l'*Annuaire statistique* (2001), les trois tableaux suivants qui n'ont pas été présentés dans le numéro antérieur, ont été ajoutés:

Tableau 11: Choix d'indicateurs de l'espérance de vie, de maternité et de la mortalité;

Tableau 68: Accès à l'eau et à l'assainissement;

Tableau 69: Espèces menacées.

B.   Les cinq tableaux suivants qui ont été repris dans les éditions antérieures n'ont pas été repris dans la présente édition. Ils seront actualisés dans les futures livraisons de l'*Annuaire* à mesure que des données nouvelles deviendront disponibles:

Tableau 9: Population urbaine, population rurale, taux d'accroissement et population de l'agglomération urbaine la plus peuplée (46ème édition);

Tableau 10: Dépenses publiques afférentes à l'éducation: totales et ordinaires (45ème édition);

Tableau 10: Population analphabète, selon le sexe (47ème édition);

Tableau 11: L'épidémie de VIH/SIDA (47ème édition);

Tableau 17: Récepteurs de télévision et de radiodiffusion sonore (46ème édition).

Statistical sources and references

A.   Statistical sources

1. American Automobile Manufacturers Association, *Motor Vehicle Facts and Figures 1997* (Detroit, USA).

2. Auto and Truck International, *2001-2002 World Automotive Market Report* (Illinois, USA).

3. Carbon Dioxide Information Analysis Center, *Global, Regional, and National CO_2 Emissions Estimates from Fossil-Fuel Burning, Hydraulic Cement Production, and Gas Flaring* (Oak Ridge, Tennessee, USA).

4. Food and Agriculture Organization of the United Nations, *FAO Fertilizer Yearbook 2002* (Rome).

5. _____, *FAO Food balance sheets, 1999-2001 average,* (Rome).

6. _____, *FAO Production Yearbook 2002* (Rome).

7. _____, *FAO Yearbook of Fishery Statistics 2001, Aquaculture production* (Rome).

8. _____, *FAO Yearbook of Fishery Statistics 2001, Capture production* (Rome).

9. _____, *FAO Yearbook of Forest Products 2001* (Rome).

10. _____, *Global Forest Resources Assessment 2000* (Rome).

11. International Civil Aviation Organization, *Civil Aviation Statistics of the World 1998* (Montreal).

12. _____, *Digest of statistics — Traffic 1997-2001* (Montreal).

13. International Labour Office, *Yearbook of Labour Statistics 2003* (Geneva).

14. International Monetary Fund, *Balance of Payments Statistics Yearbook 2002* (Washington, D.C.).

15. _____, *International Financial Statistics,* January 2004 (Washington, D.C.).

16. International Sugar Organization, *Sugar Yearbook 2002* (London).

17. International Telecommunication Union, *World Telecommunication Development Report 2003* (Geneva).

18. _____, *Yearbook of Statistics, Telecommunication Services, Chronological Time Series 1993-2002* (Geneva).

19. Lloyd's Register of Shipping, *World Fleet Statistics 2002* (London).

20. Organisation for Economic Cooperation and Development, *Development Cooperation, 2002 Report* (Paris).

21. _____, *Geographical Distribution of Financial Flows to Aid Recipients, 1997-2001* (Paris).

22. United Nations, *Demographic Yearbook 2001* (United Nations publication).

Sources statistiques et références

A.   Sources statistiques

1. "American Automobile Manufacturers Association, *Motor Vehicle Facts and Figures 1997*" (Detroit, USA).

2. "Auto and Truck International, *2001-2002 World Automotive Market Report*" (Illinois, USA).

3. "Carbon Dioxide Information Analysis Center, *"Global, Regional, and National CO_2 Emissions Estimates from Fossil-Fuel Burning, Hydraulic Cement Production, and Gas Flaring*" (Oak Ridge, Tennessee, USA).

4. Organisation des Nations Unies pour l'alimentation et l'agriculture, *Annuaire FAO des engrais 2002* (Rome).

5. _____, *Bilans alimentaires de la FAO, moyenne 1999-2001* (Rome).

6. _____, *Annuaire FAO de la production 2002* (Rome).

7. _____, *Annuaire statistique des pêches 2001, production de l'aquaculture* (Rome).

8. _____, *Annuaire statistique des pêches 2001, captures* (Rome).

9. _____, *Annuaire FAO des produits forestiers 2001* (Rome).

10. _____, *Evaluation des ressources forestières mondiales 2000* (Rome).

11. Organisation de l'aviation civile internationale, *Statistiques de l'aviation civile dans le monde 1998* (Montréal).

12. _____, *Recueil de statistiques — trafic 1997-2001* (Montréal).

13. Bureau international du Travail, *Annuaire des statistiques du Travail 2003* (Genève).

14. Fonds monétaire international, *"Balance of Payments Statistics Yearbook 2002"*, (Washington, D.C.).

15. _____, *Statistiques financières internationales,* janvier 2004 (Washington, D.C.).

16. Organisation internationale du sucre, *Annuaire du sucre 2002* (Londres).

17. Union internationale des télécommunications, *"World Telecommunication Development Report 2003"* (Genève).

18. _____, *"Yearbook of Statistics, Telecommunication Services, Chronological Time Series 1993-2002"* (Genève).

19. "Lloyd's Register of Shipping, *World Fleet Statistics 2002*" (Londres).

20. Organisation de Coopération et de Développement Economiques, *Coopération pour le développement, Rapport 2002* (Paris).

21. _____, *Répartition géographique des ressources financières allouées aux pays bénéficiaires de l'aide, 1997-2001* (Paris).

23. _____, *Energy Statistics Yearbook 2000* (United Nations publication, Sales No. E/F.02.XVII.12).

24. _____, *Industrial Commodity Statistics Yearbook 2001* (United Nations publications, Sales No. E/F.03.XVII.10).

25. _____, *International Trade Statistics Yearbook 2001*, vols. I and II (United Nations publication, Sales No. E/F.03.XVII.2).

26. _____, *Monthly Bulletin of Statistics*, various issues up to January 2004 (United Nations publication, Series Q).

27. _____, *National Accounts Statistics: Main Aggregates and Detailed Tables, 2001* (United Nations publication, Sales No. E.03.XVII.14).

28. _____, *Operational activities of the United Nations for international development cooperation , Report of the Secretary-General, Addendum, Comprehensive statistical data on operational activities for development for the year 2001* (E/2003/57) and *Operational activities ... for the year 2002* (advance version).

29. _____, *World Population Prospects: The 2002 Revision*, vols. I and II (United Nations publication, Sales No. E.03.XIII.6 and E.03.XIII.7).

30. _____, *World Urbanization Prospects: The 2001 Revision, Data Tables and Highlights* (ESA/P/WP.173, 20 March 2002).

31. United Nations Educational, Scientific and Cultural Organization Institute for Statistics, *Statistical Yearbook 1999* (Paris).

32. United Nations Environment Programme, Ozone Secretariat, *Production and Consumption of Ozone-Depleting Substances, 1986-1998* (Nairobi).

33. _____, World Conservation Monitoring Centre, *United Nations List of Protected Areas* (Nairobi).

34. World Bank, *Global Development Finance*, vols. I and II, 2003 (Washington, D.C.).

35. World Health Organization and United Nations Children's Fund, Water Supply and Sanitation Collaborative Council, *Global Water Supply and Sanitation Assessment, 2000 Report* (Geneva and New York).

36. World Health Organization, United Nations Children's Fund and United Nations Population Fund, *Maternal Mortality in 1995: Estimates developed by WHO, UNICEF, UNFPA* (Geneva).

37. World Intellectual Property Organization, *Industrial Property Statistics 2001, Publication A* (Geneva).

38. World Tourism Organization, *Compendium of Tourism Statistics, 2004 edition* (Madrid).

B.   References

39. Food and Agriculture Organization of the United Nations, *The Fifth World Food Survey 1985*

22. Nations Unies, *Annuaire démographique 2001* (publication des Nations Unies).

23. _____, *Annuaire des statistiques de l'énergie 2000* (publication des Nations Unies, No de vente E/F.02.XVII.12).

24. _____, *Annuaire des statistiques industrielles par produit 2001* (publications des Nations Unies, No de vente E/F.03.XVII.10).

25. _____, *Annuaire statistique du commerce international 2001*, Vols. I et II (publication des Nations Unies, No de vente E/F.03.XVII.2).

26. _____, *Bulletin mensuel de statistique*, différentes éditions, jusqu'à janvier 2004 (publication des Nations Unies, Série Q).

27. _____, "*National Accounts Statistics: Main Aggregates and Detailed Tables 2001*" (publication des Nations Unies, No de vente E.03.XVII.14).

28. _____, *Activités opérationnelles du système des Nations Unies au service de la coopération internationale pour le développement, Rapport du Secrétaire général, Additif, Données statistiques globales sur les activités opérationnelles au service du développement pour 2001* (E/2003/57) et *Activités ... pour 2002* (version préliminaire).

29. _____, "*World Population Prospects: The 2002 Revision*", Vols. I et II (publication des Nations Unies, No de vente E.03.XIII.6 et E.03.XIII.7).

30. _____, *World Urbanization Prospects: The 2001 Revision, Data Tables and Highlights* (ESA/P/WP.173, 20 mars 2002).

31. Institut de statististique de l'Organisation des Nations Unies pour l'éducation, la science et la culture, *Annuaire statistique 1999* (Paris).

32. Programme des Nations Unies pour l'environnement, Secrétariat de l'ozone, "Production et consommation des substances qui appauvrissent la couche d'ozone, 1986-1998" (Nairobi).

33. _____,, Centre mondial de surveillance pour la conservation, "United Nations List of Protected Areas" (Nairobi).

34. Banque mondiale, "*Global Development Finance*, Vols. I et II, 2003" (Washington, D.C.).

35. Organisation mondial de la santé et Fonds des Nations Unies pour l'enfance, Conseil de concertation pour l'approvisionnement en eau et l'assainissement, *Evaluation mondiale 2000 des conditions d'alimentation en eau et d'assainissement* (Genève et New York).

36. Organisation mondiale de la santé, Fonds des Nations Unies pour l'enfance et Fonds des Nations Unies pour la population, "*Maternal Mortality in 1995: Estimates developed by WHO, UNICEF, UNFPA*" (Genève).

37. Organisation mondiale de la propriété intellectuelle, *Statistiques de propriété industrielle 2001, Publication A* (Genève).

(Rome 1985).

40.   International Labour Office, *International Standard Classification of Occupations, Revised Edition 1968* (Geneva, 1969); revised edition, 1988, *ISCO-88* (Geneva, 1990).

41.   International Monetary Fund, *Balance of Payments Manual, Fifth Edition* (Washington, D.C., 1993).

42.   Stanton, C. et al, *Modelling maternal mortality in the developing world*, mimeo, November 1995 (Geneva and New York, WHO, UNICEF).

43.   United Nations, *Basic Methodological Principles Governing the Compilation of the System of Statistical Balances of the National Economy*, Studies in Methods, Series F, No. 17, Rev. 1, vols. 1 and 2 (United Nations publications, Sales No. E.89.XVII.5 and E.89.XVII.3).

44.   _____, *Classifications of Expenditure According to Purpose: Classification of the Functions of Government (COFOG), Classification of Individual Consumption According to Purpose (COICOP), Classification of the Purposes of Non-Profit Institutions Serving Households (COPNI), Classification of the Outlays of Producers According to Purpose (COPP)*, Series M, No. 84 (United Nations publication, Sales No. E.00.XVII.6).

45.   _____, *Energy Statistics: Definitions, Units of Measure and Conversion Factors*, Series F, No. 44 (United Nations publication, Sales No. E.86.XVII.21).

46.   _____, *Energy Statistics: Manual for Developing Countries*, Series F, No. 56 (United Nations publication, Sales No. E.91.XVII.10).

47.   _____, *Handbook of Vital Statistics Systems and Methods*, vol. I, *Legal, Organization and Technical Aspects*, Series F, No. 35, vol. I (United Nations publication, Sales No. E.91.XVII.5).

48.   _____, *Handbook on Social Indicators*, Studies in Methods, Series F, No. 49 (United Nations publication, Sales No. E.89.XVII.6).

49.   _____, *International Recommendations for Industrial Statistics*, Series M, No. 48, Rev. 1 (United Nations publication, Sales No. E.83.XVII.8).

50.   _____, *International Standard Industrial Classification of All Economic Activities*, Statistical Papers, Series M, No. 4, Rev. 2 (United Nations publication, Sales No. E.68.XVII.8); Rev. 3 (United Nations publication, Sales No. E.90.XVII.11).

51.   _____, *International Trade Statistics: Concepts and Definitions*, Series M, No. 52, Rev. 1 (United Nations publication, Sales No. E.82.XVII.14).

52.   _____, *Methods Used in Compiling the United Nations Price Indexes for External Trade*, volume 1, Statistical Papers, Series M, No. 82 (United Nations Publication, Sales No. E.87.XVII.4).

53.   _____, *Principles and Recommendations for Population and Housing Censuses*, Statistical Papers, Series M, No. 67 (United Nations publication, Sales No.

38.   Organisation mondiale du tourisme, *Compendium des statistiques du tourisme, édition 2004* (Madrid).

B.   *Références*

39.   Organisation des Nations Unies pour l'alimentation et l'agriculture, *Cinquième enquête mondiale sur l'alimentation 1985* (Rome, 1985).

40.   Organisation internationale du Travail, *Classification internationale type des professions, édition révisée* 1968 (Genève, 1969); édition révisée 1988, *CITP-88* (Genève, 1990).

41.   Fonds monétaire international, *Manuel de la balance des paiements, cinquième édition* (Washington, D.C., 1993).

42.   Stanton, C, et al, "*Modelling maternal mortality in the developing world*", novembre 1995 (Genève et New York, WHO, UNICEF).

43.   Organisation des Nations Unies, *Principes méthodologiques de base régissant l'établissement des balances statistiques de l'économie nationale*, Série F, No 17, Rev.1 Vol. 1 et Vol. 2 (publication des Nations Unies, No de vente F.89.XVII.5 et F.89.XVII.3).

44.   _____, "*Classifications of Expenditure According to Purpose: Classification of the Functions of Government (COFOG), Classification of Individual Consumption According to Purpose (COICOP), Classification of the Purposes of Non-Profit Institutions Serving Households (COPNI), Classification of the Outlays of Producers According to Purpose (COPP)*", Série M, No 84 (publication des Nations Unies, No de vente E. 00.XVII.6).

45.   _____, *Statistiques de l'énergie: définitions, unités de mesures et facteurs de conversion*, Série F, No 44 (publication des Nations Unies, No de vente F.86.XVII.21).

46.   _____, *Statistiques de l'énergie: Manuel pour les pays en développement*, Série F, No 56 (publication des Nations Unies, No de vente F.91.XVII.10).

47.   _____, "*Handbook of Vital Statistics System and Methods*, Vol. 1, *Legal, Organization and Technical Aspects*", Série F, No 35, Vol. 1 (publication des Nations Unies, No de vente E.91.XVII.5).

48.   _____, *Manuel des indicateurs sociaux*, Série F, No 49 (publication des Nations Unies, No de vente F.89.XVII.6).

49.   _____, *Recommandations internationales concernant les statistiques industrielles*, Série M, No 48, Rev. 1 (publication des Nations Unies, No de vente F.83.XVII.8).

50.   _____, *Classification internationale type, par industrie, de toutes les branches d'activité économique*, Série M, No 4, Rev. 2 (publication des Nations Unies, No de vente F.68.XVII.8); Rev. 3 (publication des Nations Unies, No de vente F.90.XVII.11).

51.   _____, *Statistiques du commerce international:*

E.80.XVII.8).

54. _____, *Provisional Guidelines on Statistics of International Tourism*, Statistical Papers, Series M, No. 62 (United Nations publication, Sales No. E.78.XVII.6).

55. _____ and World Tourism Organization, *Recommendations on Tourism Statistics*, Statistical Papers, Series M, No. 83 (United Nations publication, Sales No. E.94.XVII.6).

56. _____, *Standard International Trade Classification, Revision 3*, Statistical Papers, Series M, No. 34, Rev. 3 (United Nations publication, Sales No. E.86.XVII.12), *Revision 2*, Series M, No. 34, Rev. 2 (United Nations publication), *Revision*, Series M, No. 34, Revision (United Nations publication, Sales No. E.61.XVII.6).

57. _____, *Supplement to the Statistical Yearbook and the Monthly Bulletin of Statistics, 1977*, Series S and Series Q, Supplement 2 (United Nations publication, Sales No. E.78.XVII.10).

58. _____, *System of National Accounts, Studies in Methods*, Series F, No. 2, Rev. 3 (United Nations publication, Sales No. E.69.XVII.3).

59. _____, *System of National Accounts 1993*, Studies in Methods, Series F, No. 2, Rev. 4 (United Nations publication, Sales No. E.94.XVII.4).

60. _____, *Towards a System of Social and Demographic Statistics, Studies in Methods*, Series F, No. 18 (United Nations publication, Sales No. E.74.XVII.8).

61. _____, World Weights and Measures (United Nations publication, Sales No. E.66.XVII.3).

62. World Health Organization, *Manual of the International Statistical Classification of Diseases, Injuries and Causes of Death*, vol. 1 (Geneva, 1977).

63. World Tourism Organization, *Methodological Supplement to World Travel and Tourism Statistics* (Madrid, 1985).

Concepts et définitions, Série M, No 52, Rev. 1 (publication des Nations Unies, No de vente F.82.XVII.14).

52. _____, *Méthodes utilisées par les Nations Unies pour établir les indices des prix des produits de base entrant dans le commerce international*, Série M, No 82, Vol. 1 (publication des Nations Unies, No de vente F.87.XVII.4).

53. _____, *Principes et recommandations concernant les recensements de la population et de l'habitation*, Série M, No 67 (publication des Nations Unies, No de vente F.80.XVII.8).

54. _____, *Directives provisoires pour l'établissement des statistiques du tourisme international*, Série M, No 62 (publication des Nations Unies, No de vente 78.XVII.6).

55. _____ et l'Organisation mondiale du tourisme, *"Recommendations on Tourism Statistics*, Statistical Papers"*, Série M, No. 83 (publication des Nations Unies, No. de vente E.94.XVII.6).

56. _____, *Classification type pour le commerce international (troisième version révisée)*, Série M, No 34, Rev. 3 (publication des Nations Unies, No de vente F.86.XVII.12), *Révision 2*, Série M, No 34, Rev. 2 (publication des Nations Unies), *Révision*, Série M, No. 34, Révision (publication des Nations Unies, No de vente F.61.XVII.6).

57. _____, *Supplément à l'Annuaire statistique et au bulletin mensuel de statistique, 1977*, Série S et Série Q, supplément 2 (publication des Nations Unies, No de vente F.78.XVII.10).

58. _____, *Système de comptabilité nationale*, Série F, No 2, Rev. 3 (publication des Nations Unies, No de vente F.69.XVII.3).

59. _____, *Système de comptabilité nationale 1993*, Série F, No 2, Rev. 4 (publication des Nations Unies, No de vente F.94.XVII.4).

60. _____, *Vers un système de statistiques démographiques et sociales, Etudes méthodologiques*, Série F, No 18 (publication des Nations Unies, No. de vente F.74.XVII.8).

61. _____, *"World Weights and Measures"* (publication des Nations Unies, No. de vente E.66.XVII.3).

62. Organisation mondiale de la santé, *Manuel de la classification statistique internationale des maladies, traumatismes et causes de décès*, Vol. 1 (Genève, 1977).

63. Organisation mondiale du tourisme, *Supplément méthodologique aux statistiques des voyages et du tourisme mondiaux* (Madrid, 1985).

Index

Note: References to tables are indicated by **boldface** type. For citations of organizations, see the Index of Organizations.

aggregates, national account (e.g., GDP), relationships between, **176–187**, 230

agricultural production, **14, 333–340**
  method of calculating series, 28–29, 415
  per capita, 15
  sources of information, 415

agricultural products (nonfood):
  defined, 415
  external trade in, **10**
  price indexes, **10**
  prices, **305–311**
  production, **333–340**
  See also food

agriculture, hunting, forestry, fishing:
  employment, **248–253, 254–270**
  production, **9, 333–418**
  value added by, **163–175**

aid. See development assistance

airline traffic. See civil aviation

aluminium:
  defined, 518
  production, **10, 494–496**

animals, threatened. See threatened species

apparel industry. See textile, apparel, leather industry

arable lands, as percentage of total land area, **633–642**

asses, number raised, **356–378**

automobiles. See motor vehicles, passenger

aviation. See civil aviation

balance of payments:
  by category of payment, **785–819**
  definition of terms, 818–819

Balance of Payments Manual (IMF), 818

Balance of Payments Statistics Yearbook (IMF), 784

beef, veal, and buffalo, production, **430–446**

beer:
  defined, 516
  production, **447–451**

beverage industry. See food, beverages, tobacco industries

beverages, alcoholic. See beer

births, rate of, **12–13**

book production:
  method of calculating series, 129
  by UDC class, **81–86**

boring machines. See drilling and boring machines

briquettes:
  defined, 631
  production, **614–629**

brown coal. See lignite and brown coal

buffalo. See beef, veal, and buffalo

business enterprises, research and development expenditures, **687–691**

business services industry. See finance, insurance, real estate, business service industries

call money rates. See money market rate

capital account:
  in balance of payments, **785–819**
  defined, 819

capital goods, prices, **305–311**

carbon dioxide emissions, **643–651**
  method of calculating series, 674

cars. See motor vehicles, passenger

cattle and buffaloes, number raised, **356–378**

cellular mobile telephones:
  defined, 129
  subscribers, **101–109**

cellulosic and non-cellulosic fibre:
  defined, 517
  production, **9**

cellulosic and non-cellulosic fibre fabrics, production, **458–462**

cement:
  defined, 517
  production, **10, 479–484**

central banks, discount rates, **233–237**

cereals (grain):
  defined, 415
  production, **9, 341–347**

chemical industry, production, **16–22, 199–227, 479–493**

child mortality, **70–77**
  defined, 79

chlorofluorocarbon (CFC) consumption, **652–657**
  method of calculating series, 675

cigarettes, production, **452–457**

cinemas:
  definition of terms, 129
  method of calculating series, 129
  number, attendance, and receipts, **96–100**

civil aviation:
  definition of terms, 581–582
  passengers and freight carried, **566–580**

clothing and footwear:
  expenditures, as percentage of household consumption, **194–198**

See also fabrics
coal:
   defined, 630
   production, **9, 16–22, 614–629**
coke:
   defined, 631
   production, **614–629**
commodities:
   classification of, 733
   conversion tables for, **878–879**
   external trade in, **10**
commodities, primary. *See* primary commodities
communication industry. *See* transportation, storage and
   communication industries
communications, **81–130**. *See also* transportation and
   communications
community, social and personal service industries,
   employment, **248–253**
Compendium of Tourism Statistics (WTO), 783, 784
compensation of employees to and from the rest of the
   world, as percentage of GDP, **176–187**
construction industry:
   employment, **248–253, 254–270**
   value added by, **163–175**
consumer prices, **305–311**
   indexes of, **312–329**
consumption. *See* government final consumption;
   household final consumption
consumption of fixed capital, as percentage of GDP, **176–
187**
conversion factors, currency, 150, 229
conversion tables:
   for selected commodities, **878–879**
   for units of measure and weight, **878–879**
cotton, production, **9**
cotton fabrics:
   defined, 516–517
   production, **458–462**
countries and areas:
   boundaries and legal status of, not implied by this
     publication, iv
   economic and regional associations, **873–877**
   recent name changes, xi, **868–869**
   regional groupings for statistical purposes, 3, 869
   statistics reported for, 732, 733
   surface area, **33–45**
   See also developed countries or areas; developing
     countries or areas
croplands, permanent, as percentage of total land area,
   633–642
crops:
   production, **9**

See also agricultural production
crude oil. *See* petroleum, crude
cultural indicators, **81–130**
   sources of information, 129
currency:
   conversion factors, 150, 229
   euro conversion, 699–700
   exchange rates, **821–836**
   method of calculating series, 4, 150, 229, 733, 734
current transfers:
   in balance of payments, **785–819**
   defined, 818–819
customs areas, 732

death, rate of, **12–13, 70–77**
defence, national:
   employment, **254–270**
   expenditures, as percentage of government final
     consumption, **188–193**
Demographic Yearbook (UN), 28, 46, 79
developed countries or areas:
   defined, iv, 3, 869
   development assistance from, **858**
developing countries or areas:
   defined, iv, 3, 869
   development assistance to, **858**
   external debt of, **837–844**
development assistance, **847–867**
   bilateral and multilateral, to individuals, **847–857**
   to developing countries and multilateral organizations,
     858
   United Nations system, **859–866**, 867
Development Assistance Committee (DAC) countries,
   development assistance from, **858**
Digest of Statistics—Traffic (ICAO), 582
discount rates, **233–237**
   defined, 247
domestic production, prices, **305–311**
domestic service, employment, **254–270**
domestic supply, prices, **305–311**
drilling and boring machines:
   defined, 518
   production, **10, 507–511**

earnings. *See* wages
economic activity (industry):
   employment by, **248–270**
   value added by kind of, **163–175**
economic associations, country lists, **873–877**
economic relations, international. *See* international
   economic relations
economic statistics, **131–700**

education:
    definition of terms, 60
    expenditures on, as percentage of government final
        consumption, **188–193**
    levels of, primary, secondary and tertiary levels, number
        of students, **47–59**
    method of calculating series, 60
    sources of information, 60
    See also recreation, education and entertainment
education sector:
    employment in, **254–270**
    research and development expenditures by, **687–691**
electrical products. *See* office and related electrical
        products
electricity:
    consumption, **24–25, 584–613**
    defined, 632
    production, **10, 24–25, 584–613, 614–629**
electricity, gas, water utilities:
    employment, **248–253, 254–270**
    production, **16–22, 199–227**
    value added by, **163–175**
employment:
    defined, 292
    by industry, **248–270**
    method of calculating series, 293
    See also unemployment
endangered species. *See* threatened species
energy, **584–632**
energy commodities (solid, liquid, gas, and electrical):
    consumption, **24–25, 584–613**
    definition of terms, 630–632
    method of calculating series, 630
    production, **24–25, 584–613, 614–629**
    stocks, **584–613**
    trade, **24–25, 584–613**
*Energy Statistics: Definitions, Units of Measure and
        Conversion Factors* (UN), 630
Energy Statistics: Manual for Developing Countries (UN),
        630
Energy Statistics Yearbook (UN), 28, 630
entertainment. *See* recreation, education and entertainment
environment, **633–677**
environment protection, expenditures, as percentage of
        government final consumption, **188–193**
European Patent Convention, 700
exchange rates, 150, **821–836**
    definition of terms, 845
expectation of life. *See* life expectancy
exports:
    in balance of payments, **785–819**
    defined, 818

index numbers, **720–725, 726–731**
    as percentage of GDP, **151–162**
    prices, **305–311**
    purchasing power of, **720–725**
    value of, **10, 26–27, 703–719, 720–725, 726–731**
    volume of, **26–27, 720–725, 726–731**
    See also external trade
external debt:
    definition of terms, 845–846
    of developing countries or areas, **837–844**
external trade (international trade), **703–735**
    by commodity classes, **10**
    method of calculating series, 732–733
    as percentage of GDP, **151–162**
    sources of information, 28, 732
    systems for recording of, 732
    value of, **10, 26–27, 703–719**
    volume of, **10, 26–27**
    See also exports; imports
extraterritorial organizations, employment by, **254–270**

fabrics:
    defined, 516–517
    production, **9, 16–22, 458–462**
    See also fibres
factor income, 230
FAO Fertilizer Yearbook, 415, 417
FAO Food Balance Sheets, 78
FAO Production Yearbook, 28, 29, 415
*FAO Yearbook of Fishery Statistics, Aquaculture
        Production*, 28, 415, 417
FAO Yearbook of Fishery Statistics, Capture Production,
        28, 415, 417
FAO Yearbook of Forest Products, 28, 415
ferro-alloys, production, **9**
fertility rate, **70–77**
    total, defined, 79
fertilizer:
    consumption, **394–414**
    production, **10, 394–414**
    types of, defined, 417
fibres:
    production, **9**
    See also cellulosic and non-cellulosic fibre; fabrics
finance, insurance, real estate, business service industries,
        employment, **248–253, 254–270**
finance, international. *See* international finance
financial account:
    in balance of payments, **785–819**
    defined, 819
financial intermediation, employment, **254–270**
financial statistics, **233–247**

sources of information, 247

finished goods, prices, **305–311**

fish:
  aquaculture, **385–393**
  captures, **385–393**
  production, **9**, **385–393**

fishing:
  method of calculating series, 416–417
  sources of information, 415
  See also agriculture, hunting, forestry, fishing

fixed capital. *See* gross fixed capital formation

food:
  defined, 415
  external trade in, **10**
  price indexes, **10**
  prices, **312–329**
  production, **9**, **14**, **333–340**
  production per capita, **15**
  supply, method of calculating series, 78
  supply and composition of, in terms of calories, protein, and fats, **63–69**

food, beverages, tobacco, expenditures, as percentage of household consumption, **194–198**

food, beverages, tobacco industries, production, **16–22**, **199–227**, **419–457**

footwear, leather:
  defined, 517
  production, **9**, **463–467**

foreign exchange reserves, **11**

forestry. *See* agriculture, hunting, forestry, fishing

forests, as percentage of total land area, **633–642**

Frascati Manual, 698

free-on-board (f.o.b.), defined, 818

freight traffic:
  air, **566–580**
  rail, **521–530**

fuel. *See* rents and utilities

furniture, household equipment, maintenance, expenditures, as percentage of household consumption, **194–198**

furniture industry. *See* wood and wood products

gas. *See* liquefied petroleum gas; natural gas; natural gas liquids; refinery gas

gas utilities. *See* electricity, gas, water utilities

Geographical Distribution of Financial Flows to Aid Recipients (OECD), 867

Global, Regional, and National Annual CO$_2$ Emissions ... (Carbon Dioxide Information Analysis Center), 674

Global Development Finance (World Bank), 845

Global Forest Resources Assessment (FAO), 415, 673

Global water supply and sanitation assessment, 675

government:

research and development expenditures by, **687–691**
  See also public administration

government final consumption:
  expenditure by function, **188–193**
  method of calculating series, 230
  as percentage of GDP, **151–162**

government finance, **11**
  sources of information, 28

grain. *See* cereals

gross domestic product:
  distribution by expenditure (government final consumption, household consumption, changes in inventories, gross fixed capital formation, exports, imports), **151–162**, 229
  method of calculating series, 228
  related to other national accounting aggregates, **176–187**
  total and per capita, **133–150**

gross fixed capital formation, as percentage of GDP, **151–162**

gross national disposable income, as percentage of GDP, **176–187**

gross national income, as percentage of GDP, **176–187**

gross savings, as percentage of GDP, **176–187**

Harare Protocol, 700

Havana Agreement, 700

health and nutrition, **63–79**

health and social work, employment, **254–270**

health expenditures:
  as percentage of government final consumption, **188–193**
  See also medical expenditures, private

heavy petroleum products:
  defined, 631
  production, **614–629**

horses, number raised, **356–378**

hotel industry. *See* trade (wholesale/retail), restaurants, hotel industries

household equipment. *See* furniture, household equipment, maintenance

household final consumption:
  expenditure as percentage of GDP, **151–162**, **176–187**
  expenditure by type and purpose, **194–198**
  method of calculating series, 230

housing. *See* rents and utilities

hunting. *See* agriculture, hunting, forestry, fishing

imports:
  in balance of payments, **785–819**
  defined, 818
  index numbers, **720–725**
  as percentage of GDP, **151–162**
  prices, **305–311**

value of, **10**, **26–27**, **703–719**, **720–725**

volume of, **26–27**, **720–725**

See also external trade

income. *See* property income to and from the rest of the world

individuals, development assistance, bilateral and multilateral, to, **847–857**

Industrial Commodity Statistics Yearbook (UN), 28, 516, 517, 519

industrial production, **9–10**, **133–231**

indexes of, **199–227**

method of calculating series, 29

prices, **305–311**

by region, **16–22**

sources of information, 516

industry. *See* economic activity

infant mortality, **70–77**

defined, 79

insurance industry. *See* finance, insurance, real estate, business service industries

intellectual property, **679–700**

Intellectual Property Statistics, 700

interest rates. *See* rates

intermediate products, prices, **305–311**

international economic relations, **701–867**

international finance, **821–846**

sources of information, 845

International Financial Statistics (IMF), 28, 228, 247, 734, 819, 845

International Recommendations for Industrial Statistics (UN), 516

international reserves minus gold, **11**

International Standard Industrial Classification of All Economic Activities (ISIC) (UN), 29, 229, 230, 293, 330, 516

Rev. 2, **248–253**, 250

Rev. 3, **254–270**, 268

International Standardization of Education Statistics (ISCED), 60

international trade. *See* external trade

International Trade Statistics: Concepts and Definitions (UN), 732

International Trade Statistics Yearbook (UN), 28, 732

Internet, statistics available on the, vi

Internet users, **120–128**

method of calculating series, 130

inventories (stocks), changes in, as percentage of GDP, **151–162**

investment income. *See* property income to and from the rest of the world

iron. *See* pig iron

IUCN Red List of Threatened Species (WCU), 676

labour force, **248–293**

sources of information, 292–293

wages, **295–304**

lands:

categories of, arable, croplands, forested, and protected, area of, **633–642**

definition of terms, 673–674

lathes:

defined, 518

production, **10**, **507–511**

leather footwear. *See* footwear, leather

leather industry. *See* textile, apparel, leather industry

life expectancy, **70–77**

defined, 78

light petroleum products:

defined, 631

production, **614–629**

lignite and brown coal:

defined, 631

production, **9**, **614–629**

liquefied petroleum gas (LPG):

defined, 632

production, **614–629**

livestock:

defined, 416

production, **9**, **356–378**

lorries (trucks):

assembly, **10**

defined, 519

production, **10**

production or assembly, **512–515**

machinery and equipment, production, **497–519**

machine tools:

defined, 518

production, **10**, **507–511**

manufactured goods:

defined, 734

external trade in, **10**, **726–731**

value of, **10**

manufacturing industries:

employment, **248–253**, **254–270**

production, **9**, **16–22**, **199–227**, **419–519**

value added by, **163–175**

wages, **295–304**

maritime transport, international:

definition of terms, 581

vessels entered and cleared, **558–565**

market exchange rates (MERs), 150, 228

maternal mortality, **70–77**

method of calculating series, 79

Maternal Mortality in 1995, 79

MBS On-Line, vi
meat:
   defined, 516
   production, **9, 430–446**
medical expenditures, government. *See* health expenditures
medical expenditures, private, as percentage of household consumption, **194–198**
merchant vessels:
   defined, 581
   in international transport, **558–565**
   tonnage registered, **548–557**
metal ores, production, **16–22**
metal products industries, production, **16–22, 497–519**
metals, basic:
   production, **16–22, 199–227, 488–496**
   sources of information, 517
metal-working presses:
   defined, 518
   production, **507–511**
Methodological Supplement to World Travel and Tourism Statistics (WTO), 783
milling machines:
   defined, 518
   production, **507–511**
mineral products, non-metallic, production, **16–22**
minerals:
   external trade in, **10**
   price indexes, **10**
mining and quarrying:
   employment, **248–253, 254–270**
   production, **9, 16–22, 199–227**
   value added by, **163–175**
monetary gold and silver, 733
money market rate, **238–246**
   defined, 247
Monthly Bulletin of Statistics (UN), vi, 247, 331, 732, 734
mortality, **12–13, 70–77**
Motor Vehicle Facts and Figures (AAMA), 28
motor vehicles, commercial:
   defined, 581
   number in use, **10, 531–547**
   production, **10**
motor vehicles, passenger:
   defined, 518, 581
   number in use, **10, 531–547**
   production, **10, 500–501**
mules, number raised, **356–378**
multilateral institutions:
   defined, 867
   development assistance by, **847–857**
   development contributions to, **858**
mutton, lamb, and goat, production, **430–446**

national accounts, **133–231**
   definition of terms, 230
   relationships between principal aggregates of, **176–187**, 230
   sources of information, 228–231
National Accounts Statistics: Main Aggregates and Detailed Tables (UN), 228
national income, as percentage of GDP, **176–187**
natural gas:
   defined, 632
   production, **9, 16–22, 614–629**
natural gas liquids (NGL):
   defined, 631
   production, **614–629**
net current transfers to and from the rest of the world, as percentage of GDP, **176–187**
net errors and omissions in balance of payments, **785–819**
   defined, 819
newspapers:
   daily, numbers and circulation, **87–89**
   non-daily, numbers and circulation, **90–95**
   types of, defined, 129
nitrogenous fertilizers, production and consumption, **394–414**
nutrition. *See* food; health and nutrition

office and related electrical products, **16–22**
oil crops:
   defined, 415–416
   production, **9, 348–355**
oil tankers, tonnage registered, **548–557**
Operational activities of the United Nations for international development cooperation … (UN), 867
ore and bulk carriers, tonnage registered, **548–557**
"other" economic activities, value added by, **163–175**
"other functions," governmental, expenditures, as percentage of government final consumption, **188–193**
ozone-depleting chlorofluorocarbons (CFC), consumption, **652–657**

paper, printing, publishing, recorded media industries, production, **16–22**
paper and paperboard:
   defined, 517
   production, **474–478**
passenger traffic:
   air, **566–580**
   rail, **521–530**
Patent Cooperation Treaty (PCT), 700
patents:
   applied for, granted, and in force, **692–697**

sources of information, 700
peat:
    defined, 631
    production, **614–629**
periodicals:
    numbers and circulation, **90–95**
    types of, defined, 129
personal service industry. *See* community, social and
        personal service industries
petroleum, crude:
    defined, 631
    production, **9, 16–22, 614–629**
petroleum products:
    defined, 631
    production, **614–629**
phosphate fertilizers, production and consumption, **394–
    414**
pig iron:
    defined, 517
    production, **9, 488–493**
pigs, number raised, **356–378**
plants, threatened. *See* threatened species
population, **33–46**
    definition of terms, 28
    density, **12–13, 33–45**
    method of calculating series, 28
    numbers, **9, 12–13, 33–45**
    rate of increase, **12–13, 33–45**
    by sex, **33–45**
    sources of information, 28
pork, production, **430–446**
potash fertilizers, production and consumption, **394–414**
power. *See* rents and utilities
prices:
    consumer, **305–311, 312–329**
    indexes of, **10, 312–329,** 330
    method of calculating series, 330
    producer and wholesale, **305–311**
    types of, defined, 330
primary commodities (raw materials):
    price indexes, **10**
    prices, **305–311**
primary income, 230
printing industry. *See* paper, printing, publishing, recorded
        media industries
private consumption. *See* household final consumption
producer prices, **305–311**
    defined, 330
    indexes of, **199–227**
production, sources of information, 28
property income to and from the rest of the world:
    in balance of payments, **785–819**

defined, 818
    as percentage of GDP, **176–187**
protected lands:
    categories of, 674
    as percentage of land area, **633–642**
*Provisional Guidelines on Statistics of International
        Tourism* (UN), 783
public administration:
    employment, **254–270**
    expenditures, as percentage of government final
        consumption, **188–193**
public order and safety, expenditures, as percentage of
        government final consumption, **188–193**
publishing industry. *See* paper, printing, publishing,
        recorded media industries
purchasing power of exports, **720–725**

quarrying. *See* mining and quarrying

radio receivers, production, **497–499**
railway traffic:
    definition of terms, 581
    passengers and freight carried, **521–530**
rates:
    discount, **233–237**
    money market, **238–246**
    treasury bills, **238–246**
raw materials. *See* primary commodities
real estate, renting, and business activities. *See* finance,
        insurance, real estate, business service industries
receivers, radio and television:
    defined, 518
    production, **497–499**
*Recommendation concerning the International
        Standardization of Statistics on Science and
        Technology,* 698
Recommendations on Tourism Statistics (UN, WTO), 783
recreation, education and entertainment, expenditures, as
        percentage of household consumption, **194–198**
refinery gas:
    defined, 632
    production, **614–629**
refrigerators, household:
    defined, 518
    production, **9, 502–504**
regional associations, countries included, **873–877**
regions, statistical:
    countries included, 3, **870–873**
    purpose of, 28
    surface area, **12–13**
renting activities. *See* finance, insurance, real estate,
        business service industries

rents and utilities, expenditures, as percentage of household consumption, **194–198**

repair services, employment, **254–270**

research and development:
    expenditures on, business and governmental, **687–691**
    expenditures on, method of calculating series, 698–699
    sources of information, 698
    staff engaged in, **679–686**

researchers:
    defined, 698
    number of, **679–686**

reserve positions in IMF, **11**

reserves and related items in balance of payments, **785–819**
    defined, 819

restaurant industry. *See* trade (wholesale/retail), restaurants, hotel industries

rest of the world, compensation of employees, property income, and transfers to and from, **176–187**

retail trade. *See* trade (wholesale/retail), restaurants, hotel industries

roundwood:
    defined, 416
    production, **9, 379–384**

sanitation facilities:
    access to, **658–663**
    defined, 676

savings, as percentage of GDP, **176–187**

sawnwood:
    defined, 517
    production, **10, 468–473**

science and technology, **679–700**

scientists. *See* researchers

service activities, other, employment, **254–270**

services to and from rest of world:
    in balance of payments, **785–819**
    defined, 818

sex, population by, **33–45**

sheep and goats, number raised, **356–378**

shipping. *See* maritime transport, international; merchant vessels

short term rates, **238–246**
    defined, 247

social security and welfare services, expenditures, as percentage of government final consumption, **188–193**

social security sector, employment, **254–270**

social service industry. *See* community, social and personal service industries

social statistics, **31–130**

social work. *See* health and social work

special drawing rights (SDRs), **11**
    method of calculating series, **734–735**

species, endangered. *See* threatened species

Standard International Trade Classification (SITC) (UN), 733

Statistical Yearbook (UN), 1–6
    CD-ROM version, v
    contents and coverage of, v
    how to order, vi
    organization of, 2–3
    sources and references, v, 881–884
    tables added and omitted in present edition, 880

Statistical Yearbook (UNESCO), 60

statistics:
    comparability of, vi, 4–5
    on the Internet, vi
    machine-readable, v
    reliability of, 5
    sources of, v, 4, 881–884
    timeliness of, 5
    units and symbols used, xi

steel, crude:
    defined, 517–518
    production, **488–493**

stocks. *See* inventories

storage industry. *See* transportation, storage and communication industries

sugar:
    consumption, **419–429**
    defined, 516
    production, **10, 419–429**

Sugar Yearbook (ISO), 516

sulphuric acid:
    defined, 517
    production, **9, 485–487**

Supplement to the Statistical Yearbook and the Monthly Bulletin of Statistics, 1977 (UN), 331, 732

System of National Accounts, Rev. 3 (1968, UN), 228

System of National Accounts, Rev. 4 (1993, UN), 228, 818

systems of trade, 732

technicians:
    defined, 698
    number of, **679–686**

telephones:
    method of calculating series, 130
    number in use and per capita, **110–119**
    See also cellular mobile telephones

television receivers, production, **497–499**

terms of trade, **26–27, 720–725**

textile, apparel, leather industry, production, **16–22, 199–227, 458–467**

textiles. *See* fabrics; fibres

threatened species, **664–672**

tobacco industry. *See* food, beverages, tobacco industries

tobacco products. *See* cigarettes

ton-km. *See* freight traffic

ton of oil equivalent (TOE), defined, 630

tourism, international, **737–784**
  definition of terms, 783
  method of calculating series, 783–784
  sources of information, 783

tourists:
  arrivals, **737–765, 766–774**
  inbound, receipts from, **766–774**
  origin and destination of, **737–765**
  outbound, expenditures of, **775–782**

trade, international. *See* external trade

trade (wholesale/retail), restaurants, hotel industries:
  employment, **248–253, 254–270**
  value added by, **163–175**

transfer income, **176–187**

transportation, **521–584**

transportation, storage and communication industries:
  employment, **248–253, 254–270**
  value added by, **163–175**

transportation and communications, expenditures, as
    percentage of household consumption, **194–198**

transportation equipment:
  number of vehicles in use, **10**
  production, **16–22**
  sources of information, 28
  See also motor vehicles, commercial; motor vehicles,
    passenger

treasury bill rate, **238–246**
  defined, 247

trees, threatened. *See* threatened species

trucks. *See* lorries; motor vehicles, commercial

unemployment:
  defined, 292
  numbers and percentages, **271–291**

United Nations List of Protected Areas (UNEP), 673

units of measure and weight, conversion tables, **878–879**

university (tertiary) education, **47–59**

value added, by industry (kind of economic activity), **163–175**

veal. *See* beef, veal, and buffalo

vessels. *See* merchant vessels

visitors, international, defined, 783

wages:
  in manufacturing, **295–304**
  method of calculating series, 330

washing machines, household:
  defined, 518

production, **9, 505–506**

water supply:
  access to, **658–663**
  defined, 676

water utilities. *See* electricity, gas, water utilities

welfare services. *See* social security and welfare services

wholesale prices, **305–311**
  defined, 330

wholesale trade. *See* trade (wholesale/retail), restaurants,
    hotel industries

wildlife species, threatened, **664–672**

wood and wood products:
  production, **16–22, 468–478**
  See also roundwood; sawnwood

woodpulp, production, **10**

wool, production, **9**

wool fabrics:
  defined, 516
  production, **458–462**

World Debt Tables. See Global Development Finance

World Fleet Statistics, 581

World Population Prospects (UN), 28, 78

world statistics:
  selected, **9–11**
  summary, **7–30**

World Weights and Measures, 878

Yearbook of Labour Statistics (ILO), 292, 330

Yearbook of Statistics, Telecommunication Services ...
    (ITU), 129

Index of Organizations

African Intellectual Property Organization (OAPI), 700
African Regional Industrial Property Organization
(ARIPO), 700

Carbon Dioxide Information Analysis Center (CDIAC)
(Oak Ridge National Laboratory, USA), 650, 674

Development Assistance Committee (DAC) (OECD), 867

Food and Agriculture Organization of the United Nations
(FAO), 11, 14, 15, 69, 78, 340, 347, 355, 378, 384,
393, 414, 415, 446, 473, 478, 642, 673

International Civil Aviation Organization (ICAO), 580, 582
International Labour Office (ILO), 250, 268, 289, 302, 328
International Monetary Fund (IMF), 11, 150, 228, 237, 246,
734, 784, 817, 818, 835, 845
International Sugar Organization (ISO), 428
International Telecommunications Union (ITU), 108, 118,
128

Latin American Iron and Steel Institute, 517
Lloyd's Register of Shipping, 557, 581

Organisation for Economic Co-operation and Development
(OECD), 857, 858, 867

Statistics Division, UN. *See* United Nations Statistics
Division

United Nations:
    development assistance programs, **859–866**, 867
    document symbols, iv
United Nations Children's Fund (UNICEF), 663, 675
United Nations Development Programme (UNDP), 867
United Nations Economic Commission for Europe (ECE),
517
United Nations Educational, Scientific, and Cultural
Organization (UNESCO), Institute for Statistics, 59,
60, 86, 89, 94, 100, 129, 685, 690, 698
United Nations Environment Programme (UNEP), 642, 673
Ozone Secretariat, 657, 675
United Nations Framework Convention on Climate Change
(UNFCCC), 650, 674
United Nations Population Division, 28, 78
United Nations Secretary-General, 866, 867
United Nations Statistical Commission, 4
United Nations Statistics Division, v, 1, 11, 228, 732, 734,
857

demographic statistics database, 13, 42
energy statistics database, 24, 612, 629
how to contact, vi
industrial statistics database, 22, 227, 451, 456, 462, 466,
484, 487, 492, 498, 501, 504, 506, 511, 515
Internet address, vi
national accounts database, 150, 162, 174, 187, 192, 197
price statistics database, 310
staff, 5
trade statistics database, 27, 718, 725, 731
transport statistics database, 529, 545, 565
United States of America, Bureau of Mines, 517, 674

World Bank, 844, 845
World Conservation Monitoring Center (WCMC), 642, 673
World Conservation Union (IUCN), 672, 673–674, 676
World Health Organization (WHO), 663, 675
World Intellectual Property Organization (WIPO), 697, 700
World Tourism Organization (WTO), 762, 773, 781, 783,
784

Litho in United Nations, New York
03-67823—May 2004—4,925
ISBN 92-1-061208-6
ISSN 0082-8459

United Nations publication
Sales No. E/F.04.XVII.1
ST/ESA/STAT/SER.S/24